HEALTH LAW

CASES, MATERIALS AND PROBLEMS

Fourth Edition

By

Barry R. Furrow
Professor of Law and Director, Health Law Institute
Widener University

Thomas L. Greaney
Professor of Law
Co-Director, Center for Health Law Studies
St. Louis University

Sandra H. Johnson
Tenet Chair in Health Care Law and Ethics,
Provost, Professor of Law in Health Care Administration and
Professor of Law in Internal Medicine
Saint Louis University

Timothy Stoltzfus Jost
Robert L. Willett Family Professor of Law
Washington and Lee University School of Law

Robert L. Schwartz
Professor of Law and Professor of Pediatrics
University of New Mexico

AMERICAN CASEBOOK SERIES®

WEST GROUP
A THOMSON COMPANY

ST. PAUL, MINN., 2001

COPYRIGHT © 1987, 1991 WEST PUBLISHING CO.

COPYRIGHT © 1997 WEST GROUP

COPYRIGHT © 2001 By WEST GROUP
          610 Opperman Drive
          P.O. Box 64526
          St. Paul, MN 55164–0526
          1–800–328–9352

ISBN 0–314–25192–8

 TEXT IS PRINTED ON 10% POST CONSUMER RECYCLED PAPER

To Donna Jo, Elena, Michael, Nicholas, Eva and Robert
B.R.F.

To Nancy, T.J., and Katie
T.L.G.

To Bob, Emily and Kathleen
S.H.J.

To Ruth, Jacob, Micah and David
T.S.J.

To Jane, Mirra and Elana
R.L.S.

This book is also dedicated to the memory of Nancy Rhoden and Jay Healey, great teachers, wonderful colleagues and warm friends.

*

iii

Preface

Over the past almost fifteen years since the first edition of this book was published in 1987, no part of the American landscape has changed more than the American health care system. The system has been stressed by demographic changes, buffeted by the health care system winds of political change, and utterly transformed by economic developments. The formal structure of the business of health care was a small part of the subject of health law when we published our first edition; it is now the subject of entire graduate programs. The for-profit commercial sector of the health care economy sounded like a lamb ten years ago; now it roars like a lion. Until a few years ago virtually no one attained elective office because of his position on issues related to health care; now it is an important part of every politician's platform. Over the last few years both economic and political fortunes have been made (and lost) predicting the American reaction to changes in the system we have adopted for delivering health care.

While the perspective that we must bring to the legal analysis of health care is far broader now than it was fifteen years ago, the questions on which that analysis is brought to bear are surprisingly unchanged. As was the case in 1987, we want to know what the role of the law might be in promoting the quality of health care, in organizing the delivery of health care, in assuring adequate control of the cost of health care, in promoting access to necessary health care, and in protecting the human rights of those who are provided care within the health care system.

This edition of this casebook continues to use the broad organization that health law teachers and students found so helpful in the last three editions. As was the case in previous editions, we employ materials from a variety of sources. This book continues to contain the most significant and useful judicial opinions dealing with issues in health law, drawn from the federal and state courts. The book also contains statutes, legislative history, administrative regulations, excerpts from contracts, and a host of other kinds of materials designed to bring the subject of health law to life in the classroom. It also contains many classroom-tested problems that should be helpful in encouraging reflection on the other materials. While many of the problems and other materials have been brought forward from earlier editions of this book, every section of this casebook has been rewritten and the organization of the text reflects new developments in American health care. The cases, statutes, regulations and other materials that have been carried forward have been edited to maintain their teaching value while assuring that they reflect problems faced by health lawyers coping with a health system of the twenty-first century. The notes are written to expose students to a range of the most subtle health law inquiries under discussion at the time of publication.

This casebook is divided into an introduction and four major sections. Chapter 1, the introduction, provides some benchmarks against which we can measure other developments in health care. It addresses how we define illness and health, how we assess quality within the health care system, and how we might fairly distribute health care within our society. New materials on medical error are provided, in recognition of the new focus on medical error and its control in health care institutions.

The next five chapters (chapters 2 through 6) address ways in which the law can contribute to the promotion of the quality of health care. This part of the casebook includes thorough materials on licensing, certification and accreditation, and new materials on medical malpractice law.

The second part of the text (chapters 7 through 11) addresses the issues of access to health care and control of health care cost. These chapters address both private and public financing mechanisms in the many varieties that have bloomed over the past few years, including the Medicare and Medicaid systems and their alternatives. State and federal regulations of managed care has been expanded including important new ERISA decisions addressing the liability of MCO.'s. The expansion of managed care liability is treated here against the backdrop of ERISA.

The third part of the book (chapters 12 through 15) describes the role of the law in organizing the health care enterprise. This section of the casebook includes the latest materials on different ways in which the business of health care delivery can be organized as well as materials describing the legal relationships among different players in the health care enterprise, a chapter on government regulation of financial relationships of providers, and a clear, simple chapter on one facet of health law that is sure to become even more significant over the next few years-the application of the antitrust laws to health the care enterprise.

Finally, the fourth major section of the text, chapters (chapters 16 through 20) provides students with background on the role law plays in protecting the human rights of those who confront the health care system described in the previous fourteen chapters. This section of the casebook addresses the current status of laws regulating abortion, assisted conception, and human reproduction generally, with attention to new issues in the law of human genetics. It also contains the newest Supreme Court decisions, extensive discussions of the controversy over the definition of death, the law relating to making life and death decisions (including physician assisted death), legal regulation of research involving human subjects, and the legal position of health care ethics committees. Updated and expanded materials on HIV have been included throughout this text, and the materials have been reviewed to assure that a wide range of perspectives, including those of feminist and law and economics scholars, leaven the authors' analysis of health law.

This casebook is designed to be a teachable book. We are grateful for the many comments and helpful suggestions that health law teachers across the United States (and from elsewhere, too) have made to help us improve the fourth edition. We continue to present all sides of policy issues, not to evangelize for any political, economic or social agenda of our own. This task is made easier, undoubtedly, by the diverse views on virtually all policy issues that the several different authors of this casebook bring to this endeavor. A large number of very well respected health law teachers have contributed a great deal to this and previous editions by making suggestions, reviewing problems, or encouraging our more thorough investigation of a wide range of health law subjects. We are especially grateful to Charles Baron, Eugene Basanta, David Bennahum, Kathleen Boozang, Arnold Celnicker, Ellen Wright Clayton, Dena Davis, Ileana Dominguez-Urban, Stewart Duban, Margaret Farrell, David Frankford, Michael Gerhart, Joan McIver Gibson, Susan Goldberg, Jesse Goldner, Andrew Grubb, Art LaFrance, Diane Hoffman, Thomasine Kushner, Pam Lambert, Theodore LaBlang, Antoinette Sedillo Lopez, Lawrence Singer, Joan Krause, Thomas Mayo, Maxwell Mehlman, Alan Meisel, Vicki Michel, Frances Miller, John Munich, David Orentlicher, Vernellia Randall, Ben Rich, Arnold Rosoff, Karen Rothenberg, Mark Rothstein, Loane Skene, Giles Scofield, Jeff Sconyers, George Smith, Sheila Taub, Michael Vitiello, Sidney Watson, Ellen Wertheimer, William Winslade and Susan M. Wolf for the benefit of their wisdom and experience.

We wish to thank those who assisted us in our research and in the preparation of the manuscript: Heather Bearden, Michael Bokerman, Matt Berkle, Joseph Blecha, Reva Chapman, Claire Conrad, Ivan Dale, Peggy Garves, Carl Geraci, Karla Harris, Mandy Hobson, Timothy Hoerman, Mary Ann Jauer, Stephanie Kane, Rhonda Krulik, Ed McDonald, Leslie Mansfield, Kari Morrissey, Alan Naidoff, Jennifer Pennell, Carol Pierano, Roberts Remington, Carol Reynols, Kate Rogers, Barbara Ruane, Laura Schauer, Matt Shorey, Michele Whetzel-Newton and Chris White.

Finally, we wish to thank our deans for their support: Dean Douglas Ray, Dean Jeffrey E. Lewis, Dean Robert Desiderio, Dean Gregory Williams, and President Lawrence Biondi, S.J.

A note on editorial style: Elipses in the text of the quoted material indicate an omission of material within the quoted paragraph. Centered elipses indicate the omission of a paragraph or more; this, the first line following centered elipses may not be the first line of the next paragraph, and the last line preceding centered elipses may not be the last line of the preceding paragraph. Brackets indicate the omission of a citation without the omission of other materials. There is no acknowledgment of omitted footnotes. To the extent it is possible, the style of this casebook is consistent with the principle that legal writing form should follow function, and the function of this text is to help students understand health law.

BARRY R. FURROW
THOMAS L. GREANEY
SANDRA H. JOHNSON
TIMOTHY S. JOST
ROBERT L. SCHWARTZ

May, 2001

*

Acknowledgements

Abraham, K., Medical Liability Reform: A Conceptual Framework, 260 Journal of the American Medical Association 68-72 (1988). Copyright 1988, American Medican Association. Reprinted with permission of the American Medical Association.

Annas, George J., A National Bill of Patients' Rights, 338 New England Journal fo Medicine 695 (1998). Copyright 1998 George Annas. Used with permission.

Austin, C.R., Human Embryos: The Debate on Assisted Reproduction (1989). Copyright 1989, Oxford University Press. Reprinted by permission of Oxford University Press.

Battin, Margaret, A Dozen Caveats Concerning the Discussion of Euthanasia in the Netherlands, in the Least Worst Death (1994). Copyright 1994, Oxford University Press. Reprinted by permission of Oxford University Press.

Battin, Margaret, The Least Worst Death, 13 Hastings Center Report (2) 13 (April 1983). Copyright 1983, the Hastings Center. Reprinted with permission of the Hastings Center and the author.

Bernat, James, Charles Culver and Bernard Gert, Defining Death in Theory and Practice, 12 Hastings Center Report (1) 5 (February 1982). Copyright 1982, the Hastings Center. Reprinted with permission of the Hastings Center and the authors.

Callahan, Daniel, Morality and Contemporary Culture: The President's Commission and Beyond, 6 Cardozo L. Rev. 347 (1984). Copyright 1984, Cardozo Law Review. Reprinted with permission of the Cardozo Law Review.

Callahan, Daniel, Special Supplement, 19 Hastings Center Report 4 (Jan./Feb. 1989). Copyright 1989, the Hastings Center. Reprinted with permission of the Hastings Center and the author.

Capron, Alexander Morgan and Leon Kass, A Statutory Definition of the Standards for Determining Human Death: An Appraisal and a Proposal, 121 U. Pa. L. Rev. 87 (1972). Copyright 1972, the University of Pennsylvania Law Review. Reprinted with permission of the University of ennsylvania Law Review and Fred B. Rothman & Company.

Cassel, Christine. and Diane Meier, Morals and Moralism in the Debate Over Euthanasia and Assisted Suicide, 323 N. Eng. J. Med. 750 (1990). Copyright 1990, Massachusetts Medical Society. All rights reserved. Reprinted with permission of the Massachusetts Medical Society.

Council on Ethical and Judicial Affairs, Current Ethical Opinions 2.035: Futile Care and 9.11: Ethics Committees in Health Care Institutions, in Code of Medical Ethics: Current Opinions with Annotations (1996). Copyright 1996, American Medical Association. Reprinted with permission of American Medical Association.

Council on Ethical and Judicial Affairs, The Use of Anencephalic Neonates as Organ Donors, 273 JAMA 1614 (1995). Copyright 1995, American Medical Association. Reprinted with permission of American Medical Association.

Daniels, Norman et al., Benchmarks of Fairness for Health Care Reform: A Policy Tool for Developing Countries, 78 Bull. World Health Org. 740. Copyright 2000. The World Health Organization (2000). Reprinted with permission of The World Health Organization.

Donabedian, Avedis, The Definition of Quality and Approaches to its Assessment, 1st ed., 4-6, 7, 13, 14, 27, 79-84, 102, 119 (Health Administration Press, Ann Arbor, MI, 1980). Reprinted from Avedis Donabedian, The Definition of Quality and Approaches to its Assessment, in Explorations in Quality Assessment and Monitoring, volume 1. Copyright 1980. Reprinted with permission.

Enthoven, Alain, Health Plan: The Only Practical Solution to the Soaring Costs of Health Care 1-12 (1980). Copyright 1980 Alain Enthoven. Reprinted with permission of Alain Enthoven.

European Parliament, Directorate General Research, Working Paper: Health Care Systems in the European Union (1998). Copyright 1998, European Parliament. Reprinted with permission.

Fletcher, Joseph, Drawing Moral Lines in Fetal Therapy, 29 Clin. Obstetrics & Gynecology 595 (1986). Copyright 1986. Reprinted with permission of Lippincott-Raven Publishers.

Fletcher, Joseph, Indicators of Humanhood, 2 Hastings Center Report (5) 1 (November 1972). Copyright 1972, the Hastings Center. Reprinted with permission of the Hastings Center.

Hacker, Jacob S., and Theodore R. Marmor, How Not to Think About "Managed Care," 32 University of Michigan Journal of Law Reform 661 (1999). Copyright University of Michigan Journal of Law Reform. Used with permission.

Hyman, David A., Regulating Managed Care: What's Wrong with a Patient Bill of Rights, 73 Southern California Law Review 221 (2000). Copyright 2000, Southern California Law Review. Reprinted with permission.

Leape, Lucian L., Error in Medicine, 272 JAMA 1851 (1994). Copyright 1994, American Medical Association. Reprinted with permission of the American Medical Association.

Morreim, E Haavi, "Redefining Quality by Reassigning Responsibility," 20 American Journal of Law and Medicine 79-104 (1994). Reprinted with permission of the American Society of Law, Medicine, and Ethics and Boston University School of Law.

National Conference of Commissioners on Uniform State Laws, Uniform Anatomical Gift Act. Copyright 1977, National Conference of Commissioners on Uniform State Laws. Reprinted with permission of National Conference of Commissioners on Uniform State Laws.

National Conference of Commissioners on Uniform State Laws, Uniform Determination of Death Act. Copyright 1980, National Conference of Commissioners on Uniform State Laws. Reprinted with permission of National Conference of Commissioners on Uniform State Laws.

National Conference of Commissioners of Uniform State Laws, Uniform Health Care Decisions Act. Copyright, National Conference of Commissioners on Uniform State Laws. Reprinted with permission of National Conference of Commissioners on Uniform State Laws.

National Conference of Commissioners on Uniform State Laws, Uniform Parentage Act. Copyright 1973, 2000 National Conference of Commissioners on Uniform State Laws. Reprinted with permission of National Conference of Commissioners on Uniform State Laws.

National Conference of Commissioners on Uniform State Laws, Uniform Probate Code. Copyright, National Conference of Commissioners on Uniform State Laws. Reprinted with permission of National Conference of Commissioners on Uniform State Laws.

Oberlander, Jonathan, Jacob Hacker, Mark Goldberg, Theodore Marmor, The Breaux Plan: Why It's Wrong Medicine for Medicare. Copyright 1999. Used by permission.

Report of the Ad Hoc Committee of the Harvard Medical School to Examine the Definition of Brain Death: A Definition of Irreversible Coma, 205 J.A.M.A. 85 (August 1968). Copyright 1968, American Medical Association. Reprinted with permission of American Medical Association.

Report of the Committee of Inquiry into Human Fertilisation and Embryology (Cmnd 9314) (1984). Copyright 1984, Her Majesty's Stationery Office. Crown copyright is reproduced with the permission of the Controller of Her Majesty's Stationery Office.

Ross, Judith, Case Consultation: The Committee or the Clinical Consultant, 2 Hospital Ethics Committee Forum 289 (1990). Copyright 1990. Reprinted with permission of Hospital Ethics Committee Forum.

Roth, Loren, Alan Meisel and Charles Lidz, Tests of Competency to Consent to Treatment, 134 Am. J. Psychiatry 279 (1977). Copyright 1977, the American Psychiatric Association. Reprinted by permission.

Sage, William M., Physicians as Advocates, 35 Houston L. Rev. 1529 (1999).

Showalter, J. Stuart, Determining Death: The Legal and Theological Aspects of Brain-Related Criteria, 27 Catholic Lawyer 112 (1982). Copyright 1982, Catholic Lawyer. Reprinted with permission of the Catholic Lawyer.

Sinsheimer, Robert L., Whither the Genome Project?, 20 Hastings Center Report (4) 5 (July/August 1990). Copyright 1990, the Hastings Center. Reprinted with permission of the Hastings Center.

Sullivan, Mark and Stuart Youngner, Depression, Competence, and the Right to Refuse Lifesaving Medical Treatment, 151 Am. J. Psychiatry 971 (1994). Copyright 1994, the American Psychiatric Association. Reprinted by permission.

Ulrich, Lawrence P., Reproductive Rights of Genetic Disease, in J. Humber and R. Almeder, eds., Biomedical Ethics and the Law. Copyright 1986, Plenum Press. Reprinted with permission of Plenum Press and the author.

Veatch, Robert, Correspondence—What it Means to be Dead, 12 Hastings Center Report (5) 45 (October 1982). Copyright 1982, the Hastings Center. Reprinted with permission of the Hastings Center and the author.

Wolf, Susan, Ethics Committees and Due Process: Nesting Rights in a Community of Caring, 50 Md. L. Rev. 798 (1991). Copyright 1991, Maryland Law Review. Reprinted with permission of the author.

Wolf, Susan, Gender, Feminism and Death: Physician Assisted Suicide and Euthanasia, in Feminism and Bioethics: Beyond Reproduction (1996). Copyright 1996, Oxford University Press. Reprinted by permission of Oxford University Press.

Summary of Contents

*

Table of Contents

PART II.   ACCESS AND COST CONTROL

PART III. ORGANIZING THE HEALTH CARE ENTERPRIZE

*

Table of Cases

The principal cases are in bold type. Cases cited or discussed in the text are roman type. References are to pages. Cases cited in principal cases and within other quoted materials are not included.

*

HEALTH LAW

CASES, MATERIALS AND PROBLEMS

Fourth Edition

*

Chapter 1

DEFINING, EVALUATING AND DISTRIBUTING HEALTH CARE: AN INTRODUCTION

Part I of this chapter will consider the definition of illness and the nature of health care. Part II will examine the definition of quality and its measurement. Part III will analyze the problem of medical error, including its definition and origins and strategies for reducing its incidence. Part IV of this chapter will present issues and controversies in the distribution and supply of human organs for transplantation, using this as a paradigmatic case for an introductory analysis of values in the health care system.

I. DEFINING SICKNESS

Before examining the meaning of quality in health care, consider the meaning of health and of sickness. We all have an operational definition of health and sickness. I know when I am depressed, have a broken leg, a headache or a hangover. In these circumstances I consider myself to be in ill health because I am not functioning as well as I usually do, even though I may lack a scientific medical explanation of my malaise. But am I in poor health because my arteries are gradually becoming clogged, a process that probably began when I was a teenager? Am I sick or in poor health if I am obese, or addicted to alcohol or drugs, or if I am very old and enfeebled?

We need some definition of health in order to assess the quality of care needed to promote or restore it. A malpractice suit or medical quality audit depends on an ability to distinguish a bad from a good medical care outcome. An understanding of the nature of sickness and health is required to determine what health care society should provide the poor and how much society ought to spend on health care. Should Medicaid (a federal/state health care program for the poor) or a commercial insurer, for example, cover in vitro fertilization or abortions? Does the possibility of organ transplantation mean that replacement hearts should become the normal treatment for a condition that formerly inevitably ended in death? Should organ transplantation be available to all, without regard to the ability to pay? If the state of being old becomes a state of sickness (and particularly if that sickness must be "cured" at public expense), what will be the cost? Is this cost justified? Finally, the definition of health raises questions of autonomy, responsibility and personhood. Should health be defined by the doctor as scientist or the patient as person, or both? Is the drunkard or serial killer diseased or sinning or both or neither?

The Constitution of the World Health Organization defines health as "[A] State of complete physical, mental and social well-being and not merely the absence of disease or infirmity." When did you last feel that way? Can health ever be achieved under this definition, or is everyone always in a state of ill health? How much can physicians and hospitals contribute to health under this definition? A further provision of the WHO Constitution provides that "Governments have a responsibility for the health of their peoples which can be fulfilled only by the provision of adequate health and social measures." What are the political ramifications of these principles?

Health can be viewed in a more limited sense as the performance by each part of the body of its "natural" function. Definitions in terms of biological functioning tend to be more descriptive and less value-laden. As Englehardt writes, "The notion required for an analysis of health is not that of a good man or a good shark, but that of a good specimen of a human being or shark." H. Tristam Englehardt, "The Concepts of Health and Disease," in Concepts of Health and Disease 552 (Arthur Caplan, H. Tristam Engelhardt, and James McCartney, eds. 1981) (hereafter Concepts). Boorse compares health to the mechanical condition of a car, which can be described as good because it conforms to the designers' specifications, even though the design is flawed. Disease is then a biological malfunction, a deviation from the biological norm of natural function. C. Boorse, "On the Distinction Between Disease and Illness," in Concepts, supra at 553.

Illness can be defined as a subset of disease. Boorse writes:

An illness must be, first, a reasonably *serious* disease with incapacitating effects that make it undesirable. A shaving cut or mild athlete's foot cannot be called an illness, nor could one call in sick on the basis of a single dental cavity, though all these conditions are diseases. Secondly, to call a disease an illness is to view its owner as deserving special treatment and diminished moral accountability * * *. Where we do not make the appropriate normative judgments or activate the social institutions, no amount of disease will lead us to use the term "ill." Even if the laboratory fruit flies fly in listless circles and expire at our feet, we do not say they succumbed to an illness, and for roughly the same reasons as we decline to give them a proper funeral.

There are, then, two senses of "health". In one sense it is a theoretical notion, the opposite of "disease." In another sense it is a practical or mixed ethical notion, the opposite of "illness."

Illness is thus a socially constructed deviance. Something more than a mere biological abnormality is needed. To be ill is to have deviant characteristics for which the sick role is appropriate. The sick role, as Parsons has described it, exempts one from normal social responsibilities and removes individual responsibility. See Talcott Parsons, The Social System (1951). Our choice of words reflects this: an alcoholic is sick; a drunkard is not.

A sick person can be assisted by treatment defined by the medical model. He becomes a patient, an object of medical attention by a doctor. The doctor has the right and the ability to label someone ill, to determine whether the lump on a patient's skin is a blister, a wart or a cancer. The doctor can thus decide whether a patient is culpable or not, disabled or malingering. Illness also enjoins the physician to action to restore the patient to health.

Illness thus has many ramifications. First, it affects the individual. It relieves responsibility. The sick person need not report for work at 8:00; the posttraumatic stress syndrome or premenstrual syndrome victim may be declared not guilty for an assault. It means loss of control. The mild pain may have disproportionate effects on the individual who sees it as the harbinger of cancer or a brain tumor. The physician can restore control by providing a rational explanation for the experience of impairment. Illness costs the patient money, in lost time and in medical expenses. And someone receives that money for trying to treat that patient's illness.

Our understanding of illness also affects society. Defining a condition as an illness to be aggressively treated, rather than as a natural condition of life to be accepted and tolerated, has significant economic effects. Medical care is an object of economic choice, a good that many perceive to be different from other goods, with greater, sometimes immeasurable value. Some people are willing to pay far more for medical care than they would for other goods, or, more typically, to procure insurance that will deliver them from ever having to face the choice of paying for health care and abandoning all else. Society may also feel a special obligation to pay for the medical expenses of those who need treatment but lack resources to pay for it.

KATSKEE v. BLUE CROSS/BLUE SHIELD OF NEBRASKA

Supreme Court of Nebraska, 1994.
245 Neb. 808, 515 N.W.2d 645.

WHITE, JUSTICE.

This appeal arises from a summary judgment issued by the Douglas County District Court dismissing appellant Sindie Katskee's action for breach of contract. This action concerns the determination of what constitutes an illness within the meaning of a health insurance policy issued by appellee, Blue Cross/Blue Shield of Nebraska. We reverse the decision of the district court and remand the cause for further proceedings.

In January 1990, upon the recommendation of her gynecologist, Dr. Larry E. Roffman, appellant consulted with Dr. Henry T. Lynch regarding her family's history of breast and ovarian cancer, and particularly her health in relation to such a history. After examining appellant and investigating her family's medical history, Dr. Lynch diagnosed her as suffering from a genetic condition known as breast-ovarian carcinoma syndrome. Dr. Lynch then recommended that appellant have a total abdominal hysterectomy and bilateral salpingo-oophorectomy, which involves the removal of the uterus, the ovaries, and the fallopian tubes. Dr. Roffman concurred in Dr. Lynch's diagnosis and agreed that the recommended surgery was the most medically appropriate treatment available.

After considering the diagnosis and recommended treatment, appellant decided to have the surgery. In preparation for the surgery, appellant filed a claim with Blue Cross/Blue Shield. Both Drs. Lynch and Roffman wrote to Blue Cross/Blue Shield and explained the diagnosis and their basis for recommending the surgery. Initially, Blue Cross/Blue Shield sent a letter to appellant and indicated that it might pay for the surgery. Two weeks before the surgery, Dr. Roger Mason, the chief medical officer for Blue Cross/Blue Shield, wrote to appellant and stated that Blue Cross/Blue Shield would not cover the cost of the surgery. Nonetheless, appellant had the surgery in November 1990.

Appellant filed this action for breach of contract, seeking to recover $6,022.57 in costs associated with the surgery. Blue Cross/Blue Shield filed a motion for summary judgment. The district court granted the motion. It found that there was no genuine issue of material fact and that the policy did not cover appellant's surgery. Specifically, the court stated that (1) appellant did not suffer from cancer, and although her high-risk condition warranted the surgery, it was not covered by the policy; (2) appellant did not have a bodily illness or disease which was covered by the policy; and (3) under the terms of the policy, Blue Cross/Blue Shield reserved the right to determine what is medically necessary. Appellant filed a notice of appeal to the Nebraska Court of Appeals, and on our motion, we removed the case to the Nebraska Supreme Court.

Appellant contends that the district court erred in finding that no genuine issue of material fact existed and granting summary judgment in favor of appellee.

* * *

Blue Cross/Blue Shield contends that appellant's costs are not covered by the insurance policy. The policy provides coverage for services which are medically necessary. The policy defines "medically necessary" as follows: The services, procedures, drugs, supplies or Durable Medical Equipment provided by the Physician, Hospital or other health care provider, in the diagnosis or treatment of the Covered Person's Illness, Injury, or Pregnancy, which are: 1. Appropriate for the symptoms and diagnosis of the patient's Illness, Injury or Pregnancy; and 2. Provided in the most appropriate setting and at the most appropriate level of services[;] and 3. Consistent with the standards of good medical practice in the medical community of the State of Nebraska; and 4. Not provided primarily for the convenience of any of the following: a. the Covered Person; b. the Physician; c. the Covered Person's family; d. any other person or health care provider; and 5. Not considered to be unnecessarily repetitive when performed in combination with other diagnoses or treatment procedures. We shall determine whether services provided are Medically Necessary. Services will not automatically be considered Medically Necessary because they have been ordered or provided by a Physician. (Emphasis supplied.) Blue Cross/Blue Shield denied coverage because it concluded that appellant's condition does not constitute an illness, and thus the treatment she received was not medically necessary. Blue Cross/Blue Shield has not raised any other basis for its denial, and we therefore will limit our consideration to whether appellant's condition constituted an illness within the meaning of the policy.

The policy broadly defines "illness" as a "bodily disorder or disease." The policy does not provide definitions for either bodily disorder or disease.

An insurance policy is to be construed as any other contract to give effect to the parties' intentions at the time the contract was made. When the terms of the contract are clear, a court may not resort to rules of construction, and the terms are to be accorded their plain and ordinary meaning as the ordinary or reasonable person would understand them. In such a case, a court shall seek to ascertain the intention of the parties from the plain language of the policy. [ ]

Whether a policy is ambiguous is a matter of law for the court to determine. If a court finds that the policy is ambiguous, then the court may employ rules of construction and look beyond the language of the policy to ascertain the intention of the parties. A general principle of construction, which we have applied to ambiguous insurance policies, holds that an ambiguous policy will be construed in favor of the insured. However, we will not read an ambiguity into policy language which is plain and unambiguous in order to construe it against the insurer. [ ]

When interpreting the plain meaning of the terms of an insurance policy, we have stated that the " ' "natural and obvious meaning of the provisions in a policy is to be adopted in preference to a fanciful, curious, or hidden meaning." ' " [ ] We have further stated that " '[w]hile for the purpose of judicial decision dictionary definitions often are not controlling, they are at least persuasive that meanings which they do not embrace are not common.' " [ ]

Applying these principles, our interpretation of the language of the terms employed in the policy is guided by definitions found in dictionaries, and additionally by judicial opinions rendered by other courts which have considered the meaning of these terms. Webster's Third New International Dictionary, Unabridged 648 (1981), defines disease as an impairment of the normal state of the living animal or plant body or of any of its components that interrupts or modifies the performance of the vital functions, being a response to environmental factors ... to specific infective agents ... to inherent defects of the organism (as various genetic anomalies), or to combinations of these factors: Sickness, Illness. The same dictionary defines disorder as "a derangement of function: an abnormal physical or mental condition: Sickness, Ailment, Malady." Id. at 652. [ ]

These lay definitions are consistent with the general definitions provided in Dorland's Illustrated Medical Dictionary (27th ed. 1988). Dorland's defines disease as any deviation from or interruption of the normal structure or function of any part, organ, or system ... of the body that is manifested by a characteristic set of symptoms and signs and whose etiology [theory of origin or cause], pathology [origin or cause], and prognosis may be known or unknown. Id. at 481. [ ] Dorland's defines disorder as "a derangement or abnormality of function; a morbid physical or mental state." Id. at 495. [ ]

* * *

[The court looked at similar definitional disputes in other jurisdictions, noting that hemophilia, aneurysms, and chronic alcoholism had been held to be diseases or illnesses under insurance policies.]

We find that the language used in the policy at issue in the present case is not reasonably susceptible of differing interpretations and thus not ambiguous. The plain and ordinary meaning of the terms "bodily disorder" and "disease," as they are used in the policy to define illness, encompasses any abnormal condition of the body or its components of such a degree that in its natural progression would be expected to be problematic; a deviation from the healthy or normal state affecting the functions or tissues of the body; an inherent defect of the body; or a morbid physical or mental state which deviates from or interrupts the normal structure or function of any part, organ, or system of the body and which is manifested by a characteristic set of symptoms and signs.

The issue then becomes whether appellant's condition—breast-ovarian carcinoma syndrome—constitutes an illness.

Blue Cross/Blue Shield argues that appellant did not suffer from an illness because she did not have cancer. Blue Cross/Blue Shield characterizes appellant's condition only as a "predisposition to an illness (cancer)" and fails to address whether the condition itself constitutes an illness. Brief for appellee at 13. This failure is traceable to Dr. Mason's denial of appellant's claim. Despite acknowledging his inexperience and lack of knowledge about this specialized area of cancer research, Dr. Mason denied appellant's claim without consulting any medical literature or research regarding breast-ovarian carcinoma syndrome. Moreover, Dr. Mason made the decision without submitting appellant's claim for consideration to a claim review committee. The only basis for the denial was the claim filed by appellant, the letters sent by Drs. Lynch and Roffman, and the insurance policy. Despite his lack of information regarding the nature and severity of appellant's condition, Dr. Mason felt qualified to decide that appellant did not suffer from an illness.

Appellant's condition was diagnosed as breast-ovarian carcinoma syndrome. To adequately determine whether the syndrome constitutes an illness, we must first understand the nature of the syndrome.

The record on summary judgment includes the depositions of Drs. Lynch, Roffman, and Mason. In his deposition, Dr. Lynch provided a thorough discussion of this syndrome. In light of Dr. Lynch's extensive research and clinical experience in this particular area of medicine, we consider his discussion extremely helpful in our understanding of the syndrome.

According to Dr. Lynch, some forms of cancer occur on a hereditary basis. Breast and ovarian cancer are such forms of cancer which may occur on a hereditary basis. It is our understanding that the hereditary occurrence of this form of cancer is related to the genetic makeup of the woman. In this regard, the genetic deviation has conferred changes which are manifest in the individual's body and at some time become capable of being diagnosed.

At the time that he gave his deposition, Dr. Lynch explained that the state of medical research was such that detecting and diagnosing the syndrome was achieved by tracing the occurrences of hereditary cancer throughout the patient's family. Dr. Lynch stated that at the time of appellant's diagnosis, no conclusive physical test existed which would demonstrate the presence of the condition. However, Dr. Lynch stated that this area of research is progressing toward the development of a more determinative method of identifying and tracing a particular gene throughout a particular family, thus providing a physical method of diagnosing the condition.

Women diagnosed with the syndrome have at least a 50–percent chance of developing breast and/or ovarian cancer, whereas unaffected women have only a 1.4–percent risk of developing breast or ovarian cancer. In addition to the genetic deviation, the family history, and the significant risks associated with this condition, the diagnosis also may encompass symptoms of anxiety and stress, which some women experience because of their knowledge of the substantial likelihood of developing cancer.

The procedures for detecting the onset of ovarian cancer are ineffective. Generally, by the time ovarian cancer is capable of being detected, it has already developed to a very advanced stage, making treatment relatively unsuccessful. Drs. Lynch and Roffman agreed that the standard of care for treating women with breast carcinoma syndrome ordinarily involves surveillance methods. However, for women at an inordinately high risk for ovarian cancer, such as appellant, the standard of care may require radical surgery which involves the removal of the uterus, ovaries, and fallopian tubes.

Dr. Lynch explained that the surgery is labeled "prophylactic" and that the surgery is prophylactic as to the prevention of the onset of cancer. Dr. Lynch also stated that appellant's condition itself is the result of a genetic deviation from the normal, healthy state and that the recommended surgery treats that condition by eliminating or significantly reducing the presence of the condition and its likely development.

Blue Cross/Blue Shield has not proffered any evidence disputing the premise that the origin of this condition is in the genetic makeup of the individual and that in its natural development it is likely to produce devastating results. Although handicapped by his limited knowledge of the syndrome, Dr. Mason did not dispute the nature of the syndrome as explained by Dr. Lynch and supported by Dr. Roffman, nor did Dr. Mason dispute the fact that the surgery falls within the standard of care for many women afflicted with this syndrome.

In light of the plain and ordinary meaning of the terms "illness," "bodily disorder," and "disease," we find that appellant's condition constitutes an illness within the meaning of the policy. Appellant's condition is a deviation from what is considered a normal, healthy physical state or structure. The abnormality or deviation from a normal state arises, in part, from the genetic makeup of the woman. The existence of this unhealthy state results in the woman's being at substantial risk of developing cancer. The recommended surgery is intended to correct that morbid state by reducing or eliminating that risk.

Although appellant's condition was not detectable by physical evidence or a physical examination, it does not necessarily follow that appellant does not suffer from an illness. The record establishes that a woman who suffers from breast-ovarian carcinoma syndrome does have a physical state which significantly deviates from the physical state of a normal, healthy woman. Specifically, appellant suffered from a different or abnormal genetic constitution which, when combined with a particular family history of hereditary cancer, significantly increases the risk of a devastating outcome.

We are mindful that not every condition which itself constitutes a predisposition to another illness is necessarily an illness within the meaning of an insurance policy. There exists a fine distinction between such conditions, which was recognized by Chief Justice Cardozo in Silverstein v. Metropolitan Life Ins. Co., 254 N.Y. 81, 171 N.E. 914 (1930). Writing for the court, Chief Justice Cardozo explained that when a condition is such that in its probable and natural progression it may be expected to be a source of mischief, it may reasonably be described as a disease or an illness. On the other hand, he stated that if the condition is abnormal when tested by a standard of perfection, but so remote in its potential mischief that common speech would not label it a disease or infirmity, such a condition is at most a predisposing tendency. The Silverstein court found that a pea-size ulcer, which was located at the site of damage caused by a severe blow to the deceased's stomach, was not a disease or infirmity within the meaning of an exclusionary clause of an accident insurance policy because if left unattended, the ulcer would have been only as harmful as a tiny scratch.

Blue Cross/Blue Shield relies upon our decision in Fuglsang v. Blue Cross, 235 Neb. 552, 456 N.W.2d 281 (1990), and contends that we have already supplied a definition for the terms "disease," "condition," and "illness." Although we find that reliance on Fuglsang is somewhat misplaced, the opinion is relevant to our determination of the meaning of "disease," "illness," and "disorder," and whether the condition from which appellant suffered constitutes an illness.

The issue raised in Fuglsang was whether the disease from which the plaintiff suffered constituted a preexisting condition which was excluded from coverage by the terms of the policy. Blue Cross/Blue Shield relies on the following rule from Fuglsang as a definition of "disease": A disease, condition, or illness exists within the meaning of a health insurance policy excluding preexisting conditions only at such time as the disease, condition, or illness is manifest or active or when there is a distinct symptom or condition from which one learned in medicine can with reasonable accuracy diagnose the disease. [ ]

This statement concerns when an illness exists, not whether the condition itself is an illness. If the condition is not a disease or illness, it would be unnecessary to apply the above rule to determine whether the condition was a preexisting illness. In the present case, Blue Cross/Blue Shield maintains that the condition is not even an illness.

Even assuming arguendo that the rule announced in Fuglsang is a definition of "disease," "illness," and "condition," the inherent problems with the argument put forth by Blue Cross/Blue Shield undermine its reliance on that rule. Blue Cross/Blue Shield emphasizes the fact that appellant was never diagnosed with cancer and therefore, according to Blue Cross/Blue Shield, appellant did not have an illness because cancer was not active or manifest. Appellant concedes that she did not have cancer prior to her surgery. The issue is whether the condition she did have was an illness. Blue Cross/Blue Shield further argues that "[n]o disease or illness is 'manifest or active' and there is no 'distinct symptom or condition' from which Dr. Lynch or Dr. Roffman could diagnose a disease." Brief for appellee at 13. We stated above that lack of a physical test to detect the presence of an illness does not necessarily indicate that the person does not have an illness.

When the condition at issue—breast-ovarian carcinoma syndrome—is inserted into the formula provided by the Fuglsang rule, the condition would constitute an "illness" as Blue Cross/Blue Shield defines the term. The formula is whether the breast-ovarian carcinoma syndrome was manifest or active, or whether there was a distinct symptom or condition from which one learned in medicine could with reasonable accuracy diagnose the disease. The record establishes that the syndrome was manifest, at least in part, from the genetic deviation, and evident from the family medical history. The condition was such that one learned in medicine, Dr. Lynch, could with a reasonable degree of accuracy diagnose it. Blue Cross/Blue Shield does not dispute the nature of the syndrome, the method of diagnosis, or the accuracy of the diagnosis.

In the present case, the medical evidence regarding the nature of breast-ovarian carcinoma syndrome persuades us that appellant suffered from a bodily disorder or disease and, thus, suffered from an illness as defined by the insurance policy. Blue Cross/Blue Shield, therefore, is not entitled to judgment as a matter of law. Moreover, we find that appellant's condition did constitute an illness within the meaning of the policy. We reverse the decision of the district court and remand the cause for further proceedings. [ ]

Notes and Questions

1. Why did the court hold that Katskee was ill when she had no symptoms and no cancer? Can we have a variable definition of illness? For example, could Katskee be "ill" for purposes of payment for the surgery but not ill for purposes of pre-existing condition exclusions or excuse from work?

2. The syndrome in *Katskee*, if it materializes, is a medical problem for which the patient bears no responsibility. A more difficult problem area in defining "disease" involves those conditions or syndromes within the control of the individual. Consider for example alcoholism as a "disease". What difference does such a label make? What characteristics of alcohol consumption justify the label "disease"? See H. Thomas Milhorn, The Diagnosis of Alcoholism, AFP 175 (June 1988) ("... alcoholism can be defined as the continuation of drinking when it would be in the patient's best interest to stop.") See Traynor v. Turnage, 485 U.S. 535, 108 S.Ct. 1372, 99 L.Ed.2d 618 (1988) (considering alcoholism as attributable to "willful misconduct" under Veterans' Administration rules). See also Herbert Fingarette, Heavy Drinking: The Myth of Alcoholism as a Disease (1988); contra, see George Vaillant, The Natural History of Alcoholism (1983).

3. What other emerging clinical "syndromes" or diseases can you think of that raise troubling problems for the medical model of disease? How about anorexia? Obesity? "Battered wife" syndrome? What forces have led to the proliferation of these new syndromes or diseases?

Problem: The Couple's Illness

You represent Thomas and Jill Henderson, a couple embroiled in a dispute with their health insurance plan over coverage of infertility treatments. The Hendersons have been having trouble getting pregnant. Thomas has a low sperm count and motility, while Jill has irregular ovulation. They have undergone infertility treatment successfully in the past and have one child. They again sought further treatment, in order to have a second child. A simple insemination procedure failed. The health and disability group benefit plan of Thomas's employer, Clarion, paid their health benefits for this procedure.

They were then advised to try a more complex and expensive procedure, called Protocol I, which involved treating Thomas' sperm to improve its motility.

Drug therapy was prescribed for Jill to induce ovulation. Semen was then taken from Thomas, and put through an albumin gradient to improve its mobility. The semen was then reduced to a small pellet size and injected directly into the uterine cavity at the time of ovulation.

The Hendersons underwent Protocol I and submitted a bill to Clarion, which refused to pay it. Clarion cited a provision in its plan, Article VI, section 6.7, which provided:

> If a covered individual incurs outpatient expenses relating to injury or illness, those expenses charged, including but not limited to, office calls and for diagnostic services such as laboratory, x-ray, electrocardiography, therapy or injections, are covered expenses under the provisions of [the plan].

Under section 2.24 of the plan, "illness" was defined as "any sickness occurring to a covered individual which does not arise out of or in the course of employment for wage or profit." Clarion denied the Hendersons' claim on the grounds that the medical services were not performed because of any illness of Jill, as required under section 6.7. No provisions in the plan specifically excluded fertilization treatments like Protocol I.

What arguments can you make on behalf of the Hendersons that their situation is an "illness"? What arguments can you make for the insurance company that it is not?

ALAIN ENTHOVEN, PH.D., WHAT MEDICAL CARE IS AND ISN'T

In Alain Enthoven, Health Plan: The Only Practical Solution
to the Soaring Costs of Health Care (1980).

[SOME] MISCONCEPTIONS ABOUT MEDICAL CARE

* * * In order to establish a conceptual framework that fits the realities, we must clear away seven popular misconceptions that underlie the acceptance of these inappropriate models.

1. *"The doctor should be able to know what condition the patient has, be able to answer patient's questions precisely, and prescribe the right treatment. If the doctor doesn't, that is incompetence or even malpractice."*

Of course, in many cases the diagnosis is clear-cut. But in many others there is a great deal of *uncertainty* in each step of medical care. Doctors are confronted with patients who have symptoms and syndromes, not labels with their diseases. A set of symptoms can be associated with any of several diseases. The chest pains produced by a gall bladder attack and by a heart attack can be confused by excellent doctors. Diagnostic tests are not 100 percent reliable. Consider a young woman with a painless lump in her breast. Is it cancer? There is a significant probability that a breast X-ray (mammogram), will produce a false result; that is, it will say that she does have cancer when she does not, or vice versa. There is less chance of error if a piece of the tissue is removed surgically (biopsy) and examined under a microscope by a pathologist. But even pathologists may reach different conclusions in some cases.

There are often no clear links between treatment and outcome. If a woman is found to have breast cancer, will she be better off if the whole breast and supporting tissue are removed (radical mastectomy), only the breast (simple mastectomy), or only the lump (lumpectomy)? There is considerable disagreement among doctors because there is, in fact, a great deal of uncertainty about the answer. Because of these uncertainties, there is wide variation among doctors in the tests ordered for similar cases and in the treatments prescribed. * * *

2. *"For each medical condition, there is a 'best' treatment. It is up to the doctor to know about that treatment and to use it. Anything else is unnecessary surgery, waste, fraud, or underservice."*

Of course, in many cases there is a clearly indicated treatment. But for many other medical conditions there are *several possible treatments*, each of which is legitimate and associated with different benefits, risks, and costs. Consider a few examples.

A forty-year-old laborer's chronic lower-back pain sometimes requires prolonged bed rest and potent pain medication. One doctor may recommend surgery; another, hoping to avoid the need for surgery, may recommend continued bed rest and traction followed by exercises. Whether one treatment is "better" than the other depends in part on the interpretation of the diagnostic tests (how strong the evidence is of a surgically correctable condition), but also in considerable part on the patient's values and the surgeon's judgment (how large a surgical risk the patient is willing to accept for the predicted likelihood of improvement).

As another common example with more than one treatment, consider a young woman with abnormal uterine bleeding, a nuisance but not a serious health hazard. One doctor may recommend a hysterectomy, whereas a second may advise that a dilatation and curettage be done as the first course of therapy, a third may feel that hormonal treatment is indicated, and a fourth may recommend no treatment. Any of the four might make sense, depending on the circumstances. There is no formula for calculating "the best" treatment, no clear dividing line between a "necessary" and an "unnecessary" operation.

A patient's needs, preferences, and lifestyle are important. Consider a woman who likes to ski and ride horseback and who has a partially detached retina in one eye. One ophthalmologist believes in an operation that does a minimum amount of "welding" (photocoagulation) and would minimize her loss of vision. Although that might satisfy the physician's criterion of technical excellence, it does not allow the woman to resume her athletic pursuits safely. Another ophthalmologist might propose to coagulate a complete circle around her retina. In this case the patient would lose some vision, but would have more of a guarantee that the retina will not detach again, and she could ski and ride again.

Patients suffering from severe angina pectoris (chest pain thought to be due to a lack of oxygen supply to the heart) pose another therapeutic dilemma. One doctor may recommend heart surgery; another, treatment with drugs such as nitroglycerine. For most such patients, there is no consensus among physicians today as to which is the better treatment.

What is "best" in a particular case will depend on the values and needs of the patient, the skills of the doctor, and the other resources available. The quality of the outcome depends a great deal on how the patient feels about it.

What is an annoyance for one patient may mean the inability to keep a job for another with the same condition. There is nothing wrong with the fact that doctors disagree. There is plenty of room for honest differences based on these and other factors. There are more and less costly treatments, practice patterns, and styles of medical care that produce substantially equivalent medical outcomes.

Medical care differs in important ways from repair of collision damage to your car. If you have a smashed fender, you can get three bids and make a deal to have it fixed. You can tell when it is fixed. There is one "correct treatment." Ordinarily, it should not be an open-ended task. But caring for a patient can be open-ended, especially when there is a great deal of uncertainty or when the patient has a chronic disease. Walter McClure, an analyst with InterStudy, a leading health policy research institute, put the point effectively when he wrote:

> The medical care system can legitimately absorb every dollar society will give it. If health insurance is expanded without seriously addressing the medical care system itself, cost escalation is likely to be severe and chronic. For example, why provide $50 of tests to be 95% certain of a diagnosis, if $250 of tests will provide 97% certainty. [ ]

Although there are generally accepted treatments for many diseases, and doctors can agree that there has been bad care in some cases, for many others there are no generally agreed standards of what is "the best" care. Physicians reject suggestions of what they refer to as "cookbook medicine"; recognizing the infinite variety of conditions, values, and uncertainties, they are understandably reluctant to impose such standards on one another.

The misconception that best-treatment standards exist for most cases underlies much of the belief in the feasibility of an insurance system like Medicare and the hope that regulatory schemes such as Professional Standards Review Organizations can control costs. If we understand that often there is no clear-cut best course of action in medical care, we will think in terms of alternatives, value judgments, and incentives rather than numerical standards.

3.   *"Medicine is an exact science. Unlike 50 or 100 years ago, there is now a firm scientific base for what the doctor does. Standard treatments are supported by scientific proof of efficacy."*

In fact, medicine remains more of an art than a science. To be sure, it uses and applies scientific knowledge, and to become a physician, one must have command of a great deal of scientific information. But the application of this knowledge is a matter of judgment.

To prove beyond reasonable doubt that a medical treatment is effective often requires what is called a "randomized clinical trial (RCT)." In an RCT a large sample of patients is assigned randomly to two or more treatment groups. Each group is given one of the alternative treatments and then is evaluated by unbiased observers to see which treatment produced the better results. One of the "treatments" may be no treatment. (Of course, RCTs may not be needed in the case of "clear winners" such as penicillin, treatment of fractures, and congenital anomalies.) However, many practical difficulties stand in the way of doing a satisfactory clinical trial. As a result, RCTs are the exception, not the rule.

When medical or surgical innovations have been evaluated in this way, more often than not the innovation has been found to yield no benefit or even to be inferior to previous methods of treatment. Even when a clinical trial has established the value of a given treatment, judgment must be used in deciding whether a particular patient or set of circumstances is enough like those in the trial that the same good results can be expected in this particular case.

There are shifting opinions in medical care. Many operations have been invented and enjoyed popularity, only to be subsequently discarded when systematic testing failed to demonstrate their value. * * * Whether or not the coronary artery bypass graft operation that has recently become a billion-dollar-a-year industry will continue indefinitely at its present scale is uncertain. One good reason for not having national standards of care established by government is to avoid either imposing unsubstantiated treatments or freezing them into current practice.

Scientific and balanced analysis of the costs, risks, and benefits of different treatments is still the exception, not the rule.

4. Medical care consists of standard products that can be described precisely and measured meaningfully in standard units such as "inpatient days", "outpatient visits", or "doctor office visits".

In fact, medical care is usually anything but a standard product. Much of it is a uniquely personal interaction between two people. The elements of personal trust and confidence are an integral part of the process. Much of the process consists of reassurance and support—*caring* rather than *curing*. What doctors do ranges from the technical marvels of the heart surgeon to marriage counseling by the family doctor, each of which may fill a legitimate human need. A "doctor office visit" might last a few minutes or more than an hour. An "inpatient day" might be accompanied by the use of the most costly and complex technology or be merely a quiet day of rest, with an occasional visit by a nurse.

It is important to correct the misconception that medical care consists of standard products, because it underlies much of the thinking about costs and regulation. People will decry the rapid increase in hospital cost per day without giving recognition to the fact that the services provided during a typical hospital day now are much more complex and use much more elaborate technology than they did a decade ago. Proposals to regulate cost per day or cost per case assume that days or cases are more or less standard, so that the costs of a day in two different hospitals can be compared meaningfully. In fact, before one can make a meaningful comparison, one must specify many conditions, such as severity of illness, the length of stay, and the services provided. The belief that controls on physician fees are a feasible method of controlling the cost of physician services rests on the assumption that "doctor office visits" are more or less standard. They aren't.

Quality of medical care has many different dimensions: accessibility, convenience, style, and effectiveness. There are different systems and styles of care. This variability is desirable. It allows the medical care system to accommodate the preferences and needs of different patients and doctors. But it defies the public-utility regulators, who need standard units, such as passenger miles and kilowatt-hours.

5. *"Much of medical care is a matter of life and death or serious pain or disability."*

This view may come from watching television programs that emphasize the dramatic side of medicine. It is a foundation for the assertion that "health care is a right." As a society, we have agreed that all people should have access to life-saving care without regard to income, race, or social status.

Of course some medical care is life-saving, and its benefits are obvious and clear-cut. But most medical care is not a life-or-death matter at all. Even in the case of care for life-threatening diseases, the effectiveness of much care is measured in terms of small changes in life expectancy (for example, changes in the probability of surviving another year), as opposed to complete cures. Most medical care is a matter of "quality of life." Much of it is concerned with the relief of pain or dysfunction, with caring and reassurance.

All this is not to diminish the importance or value of medical care. But it does suggest that we are dealing with matters of darker or lighter shades of grey, conflicting values, and not clear-cut cases of life or death. Recognizing this makes it much less clear what it is that people have a "right" to or what is "necessary" as opposed to "unnecessary."

6. *"More medical care is better than less care."*

There is a tremendous amount of bias in favor of more care versus less. For example, the observation that physicians in group practices hospitalize their patients much less than do their fellow doctors in traditional solo practice is much more likely to cause suspicion that they are denying their patients necessary care than that the solo-practice doctors are providing too much care.

A.L. Cochrane, a British physician, supplied a nice example of this bias. Dr. H.G. Mather and colleagues in the National Health Service in Bristol did a randomized clinical trial comparing home and hospital treatment of uncomplicated heart attack (acute myocardial infarction) victims. They found that patients cared for in the coronary care units (CCUS) of hospitals survived in no greater proportion than did those cared for at home. Cochrane wrote:

> There is a great deal of bias, and a considerable amount of vested interest. The bias is beautifully illustrated by a story of the early days of Mather's trial. The first report after a few months of the trial showed a slightly greater death-rate in those treated in hospital than those treated at home. Someone reversed the figures and showed them to a CCU enthusiast who immediately declared that the trial was unethical and must be stopped at once. When, however, he was shown the table the correct way round he could not be persuaded to declare CCUs unethical!
> [ ]

In fact, more care may not be better than less care. More care may just be useless. Drs. Hill, Hampton, and Mitchell of Nottingham General Hospital recently repeated Dr. Mather's trial and got a similar result. Of 500 patients whose general practitioners called for the mobile coronary care unit (a specially equipped ambulance with a doctor), 70 percent were suspected of having a myocardial infarction. Of these, 24 percent were excluded from the trial and were hospitalized because of their medical condition or lack of suitable home environment. The rest were assigned by random method to home or hospital. The result for these patients was no discernable benefit from costly coronary care units compared with less costly home care. In many cases there may be nothing the medical care can do other than to relieve the patient's discomfort, and this relief may be accomplished as well or better at home as in a costly hospital bed.

Of course, in some cases more care will be better than less. But not in all cases. Above some minimum level that might be provided at a much lower per capita cost, more medical care may yield little, if any, discernible health benefit. This view is supported by two studies of the relationship of health resources to health indicators in different parts of the United States. One study looked at the health status of people living in different places as measured by such things as blood pressure, cholesterol concentration, abnormal electrocardiogram, and abnormal chest X-rays. The other looked at infant mortality and age-adjusted overall mortality. Each attempted to correlate these indicators with such measures of health resources as numbers and variables such as income, education, and occupation. Both found little or no significant relationship between health resources and health status.

More medical care may actually be harmful. There is such a thing as physician-caused (known as "iatrogenic") disease. People do die or are seriously injured on the operating table, and some are injured or die from the complications of anesthesia. * * *

WHY FINANCIAL INCENTIVES MAKE A DIFFERENCE

* * *

If medical diagnoses were always clear-cut, if the best treatment were always obvious, if the element of science were large, if the timing of care were determined by medical necessity, and especially if medical care were mostly a matter of life and death, it would be easier to understand how people could believe that the institutional arrangements for providing medical care, including the financial incentives, would be irrelevant to the amounts and kinds of care provided. This kind of medicine would fit into both the casualty-insurance and public-utility models. Making it free at the time of service would not lead patients to demand more of it. Every medical treatment would be "necessary" or "unnecessary," and medical review boards could audit physician performance if unnecessary care were suspected.

Making the decision to use medical care free or almost free to consumers is bound to lead them to resolve their doubts in favor of more, and more costly, care than if they had to pay for it themselves. And think of the physicians, with their concern for the patient and a humanitarian desire to do everything possible to help alleviate suffering, professional standards that emphasize the most advanced technology, and concern over the threat of malpractice suits in a society that believes that more care is always better than less. If in addition to all that, the financing arrangements make the care free to the patient and also yield more revenue to the doctor for giving more, and more costly, care, it should not be difficult to see how fee-for-service payment contributes to ever more costly care.

Studies show that institutional settings and financial incentives do make a difference in the behavior of patients and doctors. For example, Anne Scitovsky, a leading health services researcher, did a study of visits to the doctor by Stanford University employees and their families cared for under a prepaid plan with the Palo Alto Medical Clinic. In 1966 such visits were fully paid in advance by the monthly premiums. This led to such high use of services and costs that in 1967, the plan was changed to require the families to pay one-quarter of each doctor bill. In 1968 the same people's visits to the doctor's office decreased by 25 percent. (The decline in hospital visits was by only 3 percent.) As far as Mrs. Scitovsky and other investigators could tell, the introduction of this financial disincentive was the only thing that had changed between the two years.

Incentives for the physicians can also be important; indeed, they are much more important than patient incentives from an economic point of view, because physicians make the costly decisions. George Monsma, Jr., an economist at Amherst College, highlighted this by comparing the number of operations per capita in groups of employees and their families, some of whom were cared for under group-practice prepayment plans, and some of whom were cared for under traditional insured fee-for-service plans. In the group-practice prepayment plans the surgery is free to the beneficiary, and the doctors get no more money for doing the surgery, because they are paid on the basis of a monthly per capita payment that is independent of the number of services performed. Under the traditional insured fee-for-service plans, the beneficiary pays 20 to 25 percent of the doctor bill, and the doctor gets more money for doing the operation than for not doing it.

The consumer incentive would be to have less surgery under the insured plan. But Monsma found significantly higher rates of surgery under the insured plan, thus lending support to the view that the physicians' incentives (which are in turn a function of how the physicians are organized and paid) dominate decision making on use of surgery. Numerous other comparative studies have reached similar conclusions.

To observe that financial incentives play an important role in the use of medical services is not to imply that they are the only, or even the most important, factor. Physicians are concerned primarily with curing their sick patients, regardless of the cost. That ethic has been instilled in them through years of arduous training. Many take a failure to cure a sick patient as a personal defeat. When we are sick, we want our doctors to be concerned with curing us and nothing else. Physicians and other health professionals are also motivated by a desire to achieve professional excellence and the esteem of their peers and the public. But their use of resources is inevitably shaped by financial incentives. Physicians who survive and prosper must ultimately do what brings in money and curtail those activities that lose money.

* * *

These insights also help explain why qualitative distinctions such as one finds in legal usage are not very helpful. One simply cannot divide all medical care into the categories "necessary" and "unnecessary." What is "necessary" care? Is "necessary" care limited to treatment of serious pain or life-threatening conditions? If it were, a great deal of care would not be "necessary." Even in life-and-death cases, the concept of "necessary" poorly describes many situations. Suppose that a patient with terminal cancer has 99–to–1 odds of dying within a year. Suppose that treatment costing $20,000 will reduce those odds to 97 to 1. Would that be "necessary" or "unnecessary" care? There are doubtless examples that most observers would judge to be "unnecessary." But the fact that two doctors disagree and that the doctor offering the "second opinion" says that the operation is "unnecessary" does not make it so.

Similarly, forceful assertions that "health care is a right" do not help in this large grey zone. In view of the variety of systems and styles of care and treatments, exactly what is a *right*? A *right* to *anything* health care providers can do to make you feel better? That interpretation would make "health care is a right" mean "money is no object." Our society cannot afford and will not support such a generous definition.

The concepts and language most useful for analyzing the problem of health care costs are concepts that have been developed for decision making under uncertainty and for choices of "a little more or a little less."

We need to think in terms of judgments about probabilities and in terms of the balancing of various costs, risks, and benefits. The issues are not, for example, "complete care vs. no care for a heart-attack patient." Rather, they are more of the character "seven vs. fourteen or twenty-one days in the hospital after a heart attack." What is the medical value of the extra days? How do they affect the probability that the patient will be alive a year later? What do they cost, not only in resources measured in money, but also in other terms? Are the extra benefits worth the extra costs? These are the kinds of questions we must keep asking if we want to make sense out of the problem and to get good value for the money we spend on health care. They are matters of judgment, possibly aided by calculation.

Notes and Questions

1. What are the implications of Enthoven's discussion for the regulation of health care quality? Is such regulation likely to be effective? How about the merits of a market in health care? Does Enthoven's analysis raise problems for the operation of a market in health care? What kind of problems?

2. Enthoven talks about the importance of institutional setting and financial setting. The fee-for-service mode of paying physicians has been blamed for much of the rapid inflation in health care costs over the past two decades. Physicians control up to 70% of the spending for health care, as agents for their patients. As a result, with few external controls on their ability to order health care tests and treatments, health care costs have risen much faster than the general rate of inflation of the Gross Domestic Product over the past two decades. What ideas might you propose to shift physician incentives toward a more cost-sensitive style of practice? Has managed care been successful in doing so? Are other inflationary forces at work? See Chapter 8 infra.

II. QUALITY IN HEALTH CARE

Lawyers become involved with quality of health care issues through a variety of routes. They file, or defend against, malpractice suits when a patient is injured because of a doctor's deviation from a standard of medical practice. They handle medical staff privilege cases that frequently turn on the quality of the staff doctor's performance. They represent the government in administering programs that aim to cut the cost of health care and improve its quality and providers that must adjust to these programs. Quality is a central concern in health care politics and law.

A. DEFINING THE NATURE OF QUALITY IN HEALTH CARE

AVEDIS DONABEDIAN, THE DEFINITION OF QUALITY AND APPROACHES TO ITS ASSESSMENT
(Vol. 1) (1980) 4–6.

The search for a definition of quality can usefully begin with what is perhaps the simplest complete module of care: the management by a physician, or any other primary practitioner, of a clearly definable episode of illness in a given patient. It is possible to divide this management into two domains: the technical and the interpersonal. Technical care is the application of the science and technology of medicine, and of the other health sciences, to the management of a personal health problem. Its accompaniment is the management of the social and psychological interaction between client and practitioner. The first of these has been called the science of medicine and the second its art * * *.

There may also be a third element in care which could be called its "amenities". * * * In a way, the amenities are properties of the more intimate aspects of the settings in which care is provided. But the amenities sometimes seem to be properties of the care itself * * *.

* * * At the very least, the quality of technical care consists in the application of medical science and technology in a manner that maximizes its benefits to health without correspondingly increasing its risks. The degree of quality is, therefore, the extent to which the care provided is expected to achieve the more favorable balance of risks and benefits.

What constitutes goodness in the interpersonal process is more difficult to summarize. The management of the interpersonal relationship must meet socially defined values and norms that govern the interaction of individuals in general and in particular situations. These norms are reinforced in part by the ethical dicta of health professions, and by the expectations and aspirations of individual patients. It follows that the degree of quality in the management of the interpersonal relationship is measured by the extent of conformity to these values, norms, expectations, and aspirations. * * * All these postulates lead us to a unifying concept of the quality of care as that kind of care which is expected to maximize an inclusive measure of patient welfare, after one has taken account of the balance of expected gains and losses that attend the process of care in all its parts.

Notes and Questions

1. Donabedian is a leader in the theory of health care assessment. Does his definition capture most of what you find important in thinking about quality health care?

2. The Institute of Medicine, in assessing the Medicare program, has developed its own definition:

> . . . quality of care is the degree to which health services for individuals and populations increase the likelihood of desired health outcomes and are consistent with current professional knowledge.

Institute of Medicine, Medicare: A Strategy for Quality Assurance, Vol. I, 20 (K. Lohr, Ed.1990).

In order for "health services for individuals and populations to increase the likelihood of desired health outcomes," they must be used appropriately and effectively. Poor quality care can be caused by underuse, overuse, or misuse. Mark R. Chassin, R.W. Galvin, and the National Roundtable on Health Care Quality, The Urgent Need to Improve Health Care Quality, 280 JAMA 1000(1998)

Does this definition differ from Donabedian's? If so, what is the difference? Does the difference matter?

2. Unnecessary care that causes harm, by Donabedian's criteria, is poor in quality, since such care that causes harm unnecessarily is not counterbalanced by any expectation of benefit. How about care that is unnecessary yet harmless, like over-the-counter medicines that contain no therapeutic ingredients? Or medical interventions that have no proven value? Donabedian argues that such care should be judged as poor in quality.

> First, such care is not expected to yield benefits. Second, it can be argued that it causes reductions in individual and social welfare through improper use of resources. By spending time and money on medical care the patient has less to use for other things he values. Similarly, by providing excessive care to some, society has less to offer to others who may need it more. Finally, the use of redundant care, even when it is harmless, indicates carelessness, poor judgment, or ignorance on the part of the practitioner who is responsible for care. (Id. at 6–7).

Courts have generally deferred to a doctor's medical judgment as to the benefit of a particular treatment to a patient. Where the diagnostic or treatment modality is found to have no value, the physician may be negligent if a bad outcome results. In Riser v. American Medical International, Inc., 620 So.2d 372 (La.App. 5th Cir., 1993), the doctor performed a femoral arteriogram on the patient, who suffered a stroke and died. The court found that the physician had breached the standard of care by subjecting the patient to a technology which he should reasonably have known would be of "no practical benefit to the patient".

3. Effectiveness is rapidly becoming the test for a medical treatment or test. The "effectiveness initiative" in modern medicine is based on three premises: (1) many current medical practices either are ineffective or could be replaced with less expensive substitutes; (2) physicians often select more expensive treatments because of bias, fear of litigation, or financial incentives; and (3) patients would often choose different options from those recommended by their physicians if they had better information about treatment risks, benefits and costs.

Much of American medical practice does not improve health. In controlled trials, many cherished practices have been found unhelpful and even harmful. Treatments effective for one indication are frequently extended to other indications where effectiveness data do not exist. Higher quality care may cost more, raising the question of cost-effectiveness. But higher quality care may also be obtained for less money, as by cutting out ineffective services. Medicare reforms designed to contain the system's escalating costs, such as Diagnosis–Related Groups (DRGs), have been based on the assumption that the costs of caring for the elderly can be cut without affecting quality, that the corpus of health care delivery has substantial fat that can be trimmed. Empirical evidence to date supports this hypothesis. See also Volume 264, No. 15 (1990) of the Journal of the American Medical Association (J.A.M.A.)(issue devoted to a study of the prospective payment system and its effects on the quality of medical care); William L. Roper et al., Effectiveness in Health Care: An Initiative to Evaluate and Improve Medical Practice, 319 N.E.J.M. 1197 (1988); Paul M. Ellwood, Outcomes Management: A Technology of Patient Experience, 318 N.E.J.M. 1549 (1988); David M. Eddy, Variations in Physician Practice: The Role of Uncertainty, 3 Health Affairs 74 (1984); John M. Eisenberg, Doctors' Decisions and the Cost of Medical Care (1986); John E. Wennberg, Outcomes Research, Cost Containment, and the Fear of Health Care Rationing, 323 N.E.J.M. 1202 (1990).

4. What is the role of the patient and her values in the delivery of medical care? Donabedian's definition of quality combines the doctor's technical management with the patient's expectations and values, as well as cost considerations. An "absolutist" medical view, on the other hand, might define quality as a doctor's management of a patient's problems in a way that the doctor expects will best balance health benefits and risks. Donabedian characterizes this position as follows: "[i]t is the responsibility of the practitioner to recommend and carry out such care. All other factors, including monetary costs, as well as the patient's expectations and valuations, are thereby regarded as either obstacles or facilitators to the implementation of the standard of quality." (Donabedian, supra at 13).

A second view, also reflected in the judicial discussions of informed consent, is described by Donabedian as an "individualized" definition of quality:

> A long and honorable tradition of the health professions holds that the primary function of medical care is to advance the patient's welfare. If this is so, it is inevitable that the patient must share with the practitioner the responsibility for defining the objectives of care, and for placing a valuation on the benefits and risks that are expected as the results of alternative strategies of management. In fact, it can be argued that the practitioner merely provides expert information, while the task of valuation falls on the patient or on those who can, legitimately, act on his behalf. Donabedian, supra at 13–14.

How do cost considerations fit into this individualized definition of quality? If the patient has no insurance and probably cannot pay for an expensive surgical procedure, or if the patient decides to forego a treatment after making his or her own cost tradeoffs, how should the doctor respond? Must the doctor be satisfied with giving the patient less medical care than would be possible, and than would in fact help the patient?

> [I]n real life, we do not have the option of excluding monetary costs from the individualized definition of quality. Their inclusion means that the practitioner does for each patient what the patient has decided his circumstances allow. In so doing, the practitioner has discharged his responsibility to the patient, provided that he has helped the patient to discover and use every available means of paying for care. Donabedian, supra at 27.

Patients' insurance status significantly affects the procedures they receive to treat various medical problems. A study of in-hospital cardiac procedures found that patients with private health insurance, compared to patients with either Medicaid or no insurance, were 80% more likely to receive angiography, 40% more likely to receive bypass grafting, and 28% more likely to receive angioplasty. See Mark B. Wenneker, et al., The Association of Payer with Utilization of Cardiac Procedures in Massachusetts, 264 J.A.M.A. 1255 (1990).

Even in a society with comprehensive social benefits, such as a national health insurance program, costs must be considered by the practitioner, who is still constrained by the resources available for health care. The doctor as citizen must choose whether to help the patient as much as possible, with the taxpayers absorbing the costs; or to stop short of giving the individual the maximum help.

5. The common law of battery has been applied in cases where a doctor performed a procedure on a patient against the patient's will or without his or her consent. What if the doctor's decision was correct, in the technical sense of achieving a good outcome for the patient? Consider Donabedian:

> Taken by and large, outcomes tend to be inherently valid, in the sense that there is usually no need to argue whether they are, in themselves, good or bad. For example, there is general agreement that life is preferable to death, functional integrity preferable to disability, and comfort preferable to pain. By contrast, the validity of the elements of process is fundamentally derivative, because it depends on the contribution of process to desired outcomes. But there are important exceptions. * * * [T]here are some attributes of the interpersonal process that are valid in themselves, because they represent approved or desirable behaviors in specified social situations. Attributes such as these may be valued and preserved even though they make it more difficult to achieve certain outcomes. Donabedian, supra at 102.

Should the legal system allow an individual to rank a value higher than his or her health, or than life itself?

6. A third definition of quality adds a social dimension, looking at the distribution of benefits within a population. Underuse of health care is a signification social problem in the United States, the result of lack of insurance, poor access to providers, and social attitudes by both patients and providers. As a society, we may value different segments of our population differently, based on our political choice, indifference, or social values. For example, various Federal cutbacks in maternity and child care benefits in the early 1980s disproportionately affected minorities and lower class families, reflecting political choices that seriously reduced the quality of health care received by a significant percentage of the U.S. population. Organ transplantation practices may have unduly disadvantaged African–Americans and other minorities in terms of access to organs. Access is an important measure of the quality of the American health care system.

Edward L. Hannan, The Continuing Quest for Measuring and Improving Access to Necessary Care, 284 JAMA 2374 (2000). See generally Avedis Donabedian, A Primer of Quality Assurance and Monitoring in Medical Care, 20 Toledo L.Rev. 401 (1989); A. Donabedian, The Definition of Quality and Approaches to Its Assessment (1980); A. Donabedian, The Criteria and Standards of Quality (1982); A. Donabedian, The Methods and Findings of Quality Assessment and Monitoring: An Illustrated Analysis (1985).

B. ASSESSING QUALITY

Thus far we have attempted to give some content to a definition of "quality" in health care. The next step is to examine how to evaluate quality. We need to take the definition of quality, and particularize it to describe acceptable medical procedures, and institutional structures and processes.

The elements of such an evaluation have again been provided by Donabedian, whose trichotomy is generally accepted as a starting point for thinking about the evaluation of health care.

AVEDIS DONABEDIAN, THE DEFINITION OF QUALITY AND APPROACHES TO ITS ASSESSMENT

Vol. 1 (1980) 79–84.

[T]he primary object of study is a set of activities that go on within and between practitioners and patients. This set of activities I have called the "process" of care. A judgment concerning the quality of that process may be made either by direct observation or by review of recorded information * * *. But, while "process" is the primary *object* of assessment, the *basis* for the judgment of quality is what is known about the relationship between the characteristics of the medical care process and their consequences to the health and welfare of individuals and of society, in accordance with the value placed upon health and welfare by the individual and by society.

With regard to technical management, the relationship between the characteristics of the process of care and its consequences is determined, in the abstract, by the state of medical science and technology at any given time. More specifically, this relationship is revealed in the work of the leading exponents of that science and technology; through their published research, their teachings, and their own practice these leaders define, explicitly or implicitly, the technical norms of good care.

Another set of norms governs the management of the interpersonal process. These norms arise from the values and the ethical principles and rules that govern the relationships among people, in general, and between health professionals and clients, in particular. * * *

It follows, therefore, that the quality of the "process" of care is defined, in the first place, as normative behavior. * * *

* * *

I have argued, so far, that the most direct route to an assessment of the quality of care is an examination of that care. But there are * * * two other, less direct approaches to assessment: one of these is the assessment of "structure", and the other the assessment of "outcome."

By "structure" I mean the relatively stable characteristics of the providers of care, of the tools and resources they have at their disposal, and of the physical and organizational settings in which they work. The concept of structure includes the human, physical, and financial resources that are needed to provide medical care. The term embraces the number, distribution, and qualifications of professional personnel, and so, too, the number, size, equipment, and geographic disposition of hospitals and other facilities. [Donabedian goes on to include within structure the organization of financing and delivery, how doctors practice and how they are paid, staff organization, and how medical work is reviewed in institutions] * * * The basic characteristics of structure are that it is relatively stable, that it functions to produce care or is a feature of the "environment" of care, and that it influences the kind of care that is provided.

* * * Structure, therefore, is relevant to quality in that it increases or decreases the probability of good performances. * * * But as a means for

assessing the quality of care, structure is a rather blunt instrument; it can only indicate general tendencies.

* * *

I believe that good structure, that is, a sufficiency of resources and proper system design, is probably the most important means of protecting and promoting the quality of care. * * * As a source of accurate current information about quality, the assessment of structure is of a good deal less importance than the assessment of process or outcome.

* * *

The study of "outcomes" is the other of the indirect approaches that I have said could be used to assess the quality of care. [Outcome is] * * * a change in a patient's current and future health status that can be attributed to antecedent health care. * * * I shall include improvements of social and psychological function in addition to the more usual emphasis on the physical and physiological aspects of performance. By still another extension I shall add patient attitudes (including satisfaction), health-related knowledge acquired by the patient, and health-related behavioral change.

* * *

* * * [T]here are three major approaches to quality assessment: "structure," "process," and "outcome." This three-fold approach is possible because there is a fundamental functional relationship among the three elements, which can be shown schematically as follows:

Structure → Process → Outcome

This means that structural characteristics of the settings in which care takes place have a propensity to influence the process of care so that its quality is diminished or enhanced. Similarly, changes in the process of care, including variations in its quality, will influence the effect of care on health status, broadly defined.

Notes and Questions

1. Quality assurance strategies depend on evaluation tools that apply the definition of quality to a health care professional or institution. Structure evaluation is the easiest to do. Personnel, equipment, and buildings can be counted or described; internal regulations and staff organization measured against specific criteria; and budgets critiqued. Structure evaluation is the least useful, however, since the connection between structural components and quality of care is not necessarily direct.

2. Process evaluation of health care has several advantages over structural evaluations. It allows doctors to specify criteria and standards of good care or to establish a range of acceptable practice before all the research evidence is in; it assures documentation in the medical record for preventive and informative purposes; and it permits attribution of responsibility for discrete clinical decisions.

The process perspective has three major drawbacks, however. First, "[t]he major drawback * * * is the weakness of the scientific basis for much of accepted practice. The use of prevalent norms as a basis for judging quality may, therefore, encourage dogmatism and help perpetuate error." Donabedian, supra at 119. Second, the emphasis on the need for technical interventions may lead to high cost care. Third, the interpersonal process is slighted, since process evaluation focuses on the technical proficiency of the doctor.

How should process review take place within a medical practice? Within a hospital? Should surgeons or internists assess each other's work? What if an errant colleague is spotted?

3. Outcome evaluation has substantial advantages over both process and structure measures. It provides a flexible approach that focuses on what works and on integrated care that includes consideration of the patient's own contribution. The goal of all health care is, after all, the best possible outcome for the patient.

Outcome measures also have their problems, however: the duration, timing, or extent of outcomes of optimal care are often hard to specify; it is often hard to credit a good outcome to a specific medical intervention; and the outcome is often known too late to affect practice. See Katherine L. Kahn, et al., Measuring Quality of Care With Explicit Process Criteria Before and After Implementation of the DRG–Based Prospective Payment System, 264 N.Eng.J.Med. 1969 (1990).

Are outcome measures useful for comparing hospitals? Consider the Department of Health and Human Services' release of mortality figures for various medical procedures at hospitals around the country. Hospitals had widely differing mortality and morbidity rates and success rates for different procedures. This seems to be a pure outcome indicator, a kind of Consumer Reports rating of hospitals to be used comparatively for purposes of consumer information. Is release of such statistics desirable? Does it benefit the health care consumer? Does the consumer care? A recent study concluded that provider quality of care can be accurately measured and compared. Short term mortality rates following a heart attack are excellent indicators of quality of care, varying dramatically across hospitals. See Mark McClellan and Douglas Staiger, The Quality of Health Care Providers, NBER Working Paper (August 1999).

It appears that even before such explicit data became available, the relative quality of hospitals played a part in the choices made by admitting physicians and their patients. It is likely that the admitting physicians were aware of hospital differences, and chose selectively for their patients. The proliferation of specific comparative data might accelerate these tendencies to stratify hospitals by their mortality and morbidity records. Harold Luft et al., Does Quality Influence Choice of Hospital? 263 J.A.M.A. 2899 (1990); Donald M. Berwick and David L. Wald, Hospital Leaders' Opinions of the HCFA Mortality Data, 263 J.A.M.A. 247 (1990).

The Joint Commission on the Accreditation of Healthcare Organizations has moved to outcome review for the nation's accredited hospitals. Under this plan, the JCAHO gathers clinical information in order to predict outcomes and provide an ongoing survey of the clinical activities in the hospitals which it accredits. The goal is to develop clinical indicators, using outcomes data produced by hospitals, to spot potential quality control problems. See Outcomes in Action: the JCAHO's Clinical Indicators, Hospital 34 (Oct. 5, 1990).

A concept of outcomes management has been articulated for the health care industry, as a reaction to the increasing volume of outcomes data that is currently being produced. It has been defined by Ellwood as based on a "permanent national medical data base that uses a common set of definitions for measuring quality of life to enable patients, payers, and providers to make informed health choices ..." Paul Ellwood, Shattuck Lecture—Outcomes Management: A Technology of Patient Experience, 318 N.Eng.J.Med. 1549, 1555 (1988). Ellwood writes that outcomes management:

> ... consists of a common patient-understood language of health outcomes; a national data base containing information and analysis on clinical, financial, and health outcomes that estimates as best we can the relation between medical interventions and health outcomes, as well as the relation between health outcomes and money; and an opportunity for each decision-maker to have access to the analyses that are relevant to the choices they must make. Id. at 1551.

Outcomes management systems are being developed to track the effects of medical care on patients over time, measuring patient clinical condition, functional status, and satisfaction with care. See generally David J. Brailer and Lorence H. Kim, From Nicety to Necessity: Outcome Measures Come of Age, Health Systems Review 20 (Sept./Oct. 1996).

Such approaches are currently primitive, given deficiencies in studies and information gathering. One of the risks of such systems is that deceptively objective measures can be easily misapplied. In assessing hospital based care, particularly mortality, the severity of the patient's illness at admission needs to be considerably refined before many such outcome comparisons can be trusted. Jesse Green, et al., The Importance of Severity of Illness in Assessing Hospital Mortality, 263 J.A.M.A. 241 (1990). Patient satisfaction, as measured through a survey, is a central part of the outcome assessment.

4. A study by the Office of Technology Assessment proposed a variety of indicators of good or bad quality health care. Some of these quality-of-care indicators include:

a. hospital mortality rates;

b. adverse events that affect patients, such as nosocomial infections in hospitals;

c. formal disciplinary actions taken by state medical boards against physicians;

d. malpractice awards;

e. process evaluation of physicians' performance in treating a particular condition, such as hypertension screening and management;

f. physician specialization;

g. patient self-assessment of their own care;

h. scope of hospital services, evaluated by external guidelines like those of the JCAHO.

See Office of Technology Assessment, The Quality of Medical Care: Information for Consumers (1988).

Which of these indicators are structure measures? Which are process or outcome based? These indicators could be used in a variety of ways, but one common proposal is to give health care consumers information about comparative performance of providers using several of these measures. This market approach would then allow the consumers to select higher quality providers. Are individual patients likely to be good consumers? How can individuals be helped to process the kind of quantitative comparative information that can be produced? Might the other consumers of health care, such as insurers and employers, be better able to use such information than individual patients? How?

See Timothy S. Jost, The Necessary and Proper Role of Regulation to Assure the Quality of Health Care, 25 Houston L.Rev. 525 (1988); Walter McClure, Buying Right: How to Do It, 2 Bus. & Health 41 (1985); General Accounting Office, Medicare: Improved Patient Outcome Analyses Could Enhance Quality Assessment (1988). For a discussion of the legal and regulatory issues, see Maxwell Mehlman, Assuring the Quality of Medical Care: The Impact of Outcome Measurement and Practice Standards, 18 Law, Medicine & Health Care 368 (1990); Barry R. Furrow, The Changing Role of the Law in Promoting Quality in Health Care: From Sanctioning Outlaws to Managing Outcomes, 26 Houston L.Rev. 147 (1989).

C. IMPROVING QUALITY

The health care industry is rapidly reorganizing in response to market forces. The prevalence of the sole practitioner mode that dominated medical practice until the last two decades continues to decline as group practices and physicians employed by health care institutions or managed care organizations or allied with hospitals in integrated delivery systems become ever more common. The large health care corporation is coming to dominate the delivery of health care services. Both institutions that provide health care, such as hospitals or nursing homes, and entities that pay for health care, including insurers or self-insured employers, have become much more interested in overseeing the work of the professionals who practice within them or whose care they purchase. The emergence of managed care organizations that both pay for and provide care, moreover, gives lay managers even greater control over medical practice.

A revolution in information processing has accompanied the reorganization of the health care industry. Advances in information processing technology have enhanced the ability of the health care industry to collect, process, and analyze data. These advances allow the analysis of the outcomes of health care processes. Data describing large numbers of patients can be studied to determine the efficacy of alternative diagnostic and treatment modalities. This information can be used to construct practice guidelines, which can in some cases be reduced to algorithms used to enable computer review of the quality of the practices of individual practitioners or institutions. Outcome data can also be used to support pattern analysis, comparing the outcome of the care provided by individual practitioners or institutions with average or optimal practice as revealed by outcome analysis.

These new developments in information technology and industry structure have allowed the development of methods of comparing practitioners and institutions, increasingly enabling consumers to evaluate their physicians, hospitals, and managed care organizations. Several attempts have been made in recent years to enable consumers to comparatively evaluate quality in health care markets. From 1986 until 1992 the federal Health Care Financing Administration published annual data comparing the mortality experience of hospitals for certain procedures. Several states, most notably Pennsylvania, New York, and California, have begun to assemble and release comparative outcome data, permitting prospective patients to compare the performance of various health care institutions and professionals. Other information initiatives have also been proposed, such as the Joint Commission's new disclosure policy, which includes hospital report cards.

Second, information processing technology and industry reorganization enables lay managers to monitor physicians. The use of algorithms or profiles allow computes and lay managers to assess physician quality. This has led to new industry-originated practices of continuous quality improvement (CQI) or total quality management (TQM). The application of these principles is described in the following excerpt.

TIMOTHY S. JOST, OVERSIGHT OF THE QUALITY OF MEDICAL CARE: REGULATION, MANAGEMENT, OR THE MARKET?

37 Ariz. L. Rev. 825, 837 (1995).

The continuous quality improvement or total quality management movement is based on quality improvement strategies developed in the industrial setting. The ideas of Deming, Juran, Shewhart and others had a significant impact on Japanese, and then American industrial production. Within the past few years these ideas have begun to be applied widely in health care as well. Lay managers (sometimes in conjunction with physicians) are using their new-found power within reorganized health care institutions and their new and greatly enhanced access to and ability to manipulate data to improve the quality of medical care delivered in institutional settings.

The quality improvement philosophy is based on several principles:

1) Quality is defined in terms of meeting the needs of "customers," defined broadly to include not only patients but also others who consume the services of the institution, including physicians themselves. This orientation is immediately appealing to managers, who are increasingly oriented toward regarding patients as consumers. While this definition short-circuits debates over the true nature of quality, as quality is viewed as what consumers want, it is inherently problematic. If patients as consumers cannot recognize or assess the quality of medical care, as the law has assumed since Dent, how can they define quality?

2) Energy is better directed toward improving the system through which care is delivered than toward looking for "bad apples." Most quality deficiencies are caused by faulty systems, not by incompetents working within those systems. One can accomplish more, therefore, by raising the mean of the performance curve than by chopping off the tail. This emphasis on improving the average performance rather than punishing the bad actor is perhaps the clearest distinction between quality improvement and traditional quality assurance, which has tended to be preoccupied with looking for "bad apples." This orientation gives quality improvement a more positive tone than quality assurance, thus making it more palatable to hospital employees and medical staff. It also results in a heavy emphasis on process and on systems.

3) Data are very important for driving and shaping systems improvement. Outcomes data are particularly useful for identifying areas where improvement is possible or necessary. Not only must systems be monitored continuously, but improvements in systems must also be monitored to assure that they are in fact effective. Much of the arcanity of the quality improvement movement (Ishikawa diagrams, Pareto diagrams, histograms, etc.) re-

sults from attempts to organize, make sense out of, and devise rational responses to patterns revealed by data.

4) Management and staff must be involved at all levels in the process of improvement. This is a particular focus of total quality management. The culture of the organization must be molded to emphasize quality.

5) Quality improvement is never finished. This is the primary insight of continuous quality improvement. There is always room for further progress. This should be reassuring, however, and not lead to discouragement.

This newfound confidence in the market and in internal management has been accompanied by a decline in confidence in external public regulation. The cost of health care quality regulation programs has long been recognized, and criticism of the high cost of regulation has become increasingly shrill. The whole range of federal and state regulatory programs, including the PRO program, CLIA, nursing home regulation, and even professional licensure have been criticized for their direct costs and for the costs they impose on the industry. Increasingly, the benefits of traditional forms of regulation that focus on competence and error have been questioned. The continuous quality improvement/total quality management program poses a serious challenge to traditional regulatory programs that focus on "bad apples." The view of TQM is that such programs depress morale, discourage innovation, and do little to improve the care provided in the vast majority of instances.

Notes and Questions

1. This approach to improving the processes of health care delivery is modelled after Japanese management practices, adopting managerial principles to improve quality:

(1) active visible support from clinical and managerial leadership for the continuous improvement of quality;

(2) focus on processes as the objects of improvement;

(3) elimination of unnecessary variation; and

(4) revised strategies for personnel management.

This ethic of continuous improvement, termed in the parlance of the industry either Continuous Quality Improvement (CQI) or Total Quality Management (TQM), assumes that processes are complex and frequently characterized by unnecessary rework and waste, whose reduction might both improve quality and reduce cost. It combines outcome measures with process technology and emphasis on personnel management, treating staff as resources central to quality improvement. The methodology was developed for use by industrial organizations by W. Edwards Deming, in Quality, Productivity, and Competitive Position (1982) and Joseph M. Juran, Managerial Breakthrough (1964). The techniques have been widely applied in health care as well as American industry. See, e.g., Donald M. Berwick et al., Curing Health Care: New Strategies for Quality Improvement (1991); Ellen J. Gaucher & Richard J. Coffey, Total Quality in Healthcare: From Theory to Practice (1993). Its application in health care was suggested by Donald Berwick, Continuous Improvement as an Ideal in Health Care, 320 N.Eng.J.Med. 53 (1989).

2. A 1994 survey found that more than two thirds of the hospitals surveyed were adopting a TQM/CQI program. Linda Oberman, Quality Quandary: Little Clinical Impact Yet, Am. Med. News, Apr. 25, 1994, at 3. Physicians typically

resist such TQM/CQI programs and the high level of administrative intervention they often appear to threaten. Can you see any reason why physicians might object to the application of these management strategies to their professional services?

III. THE PROBLEM OF MEDICAL ERROR

How prevalent is medical error? How often does such error injure patients? How should a regulatory regime handle medical error that does not result in injury? If we discover that a substantial number of patients are injured by medical error, what should the legal system do about it? Even if we conclude that errors are infrequent, how do we "raise the average" of medical practice?

Medical error is a major source of iatrogenesis—disease or illness induced by medical treatment or diagnosis. Such iatrogenesis has also been characterized as medical misadventure, and we will use the two terms interchangeably. As you read through the chapter, critically evaluate the perspectives presented with an eye toward developing your own position on the problem of medical error and how to handle it through the legal system.

A. MEDICAL IATROGENESIS: DEFINITIONS AND EXTENT

Injury caused by doctors and health care institutions, or iatrogenesis, is the inverse of quality medicine. It is thus helpful to refine our understanding of injury, medical error, and medical fault, as part of our inquiry into the meaning of quality in health care. The literature on iatrogenesis is surprisingly sparse, considering the importance of the subject.

Consider a spectrum of sources of patient injury.

a. *Willful or reckless acts.* Both lawyers and doctors generally view intentional deviation from professional norms of good practice, without good cause, as culpable error. Many quality control mechanisms now in place, such as licensing and medical board disciplinary actions, seem to be aimed at these "bad apples."

b. *Negligent acts.* A negligence standard measures a physician's actions against accepted norms of practice. A doctor may fall short, injuring a patient for a number of reasons:

1. Inattentiveness on a particular occasion, even though the doctor is otherwise skillful and well trained;

2. A systematic failure of training resulting from failure to keep up with the field of practice or to be properly educated generally. In Darling v. Charleston Community Memorial Hospital, 33 Ill.2d 326, 211 N.E.2d 253 (1965), the defendant doctor had not read the latest texts on setting bone fractures;

3. A personal incapacity of the doctor to deal with this particular disease or patient, because of his or her own impairment, or inability to carry out the procedure with technical proficiency.

We feel no unfairness in generally holding doctors accountable for wilful misconduct, or for negligence based on inattentiveness, failures of education, or personal incapacity. They have failed to live up to the level of competence that their professional membership indicates they should have achieved.

Two categories of patient injury are usually viewed as based on nonculpable conduct, since it is argued that the doctor could not have done any better.

a. *Error due to patient variation.* The argument has been made that doctors cannot be held responsible for some errors because their knowledge of particular patients is necessarily limited. Each patient is unique, more than just the sum total of physical and chemical mechanisms. Each patient is a product of his or her own history. Perfect knowledge is thus impossible. If a bad result occurs, therefore, the fault lies not with any scientific ignorance but, rather, with an unavoidable "ignorance of the contingencies of the environmental context." Samuel Gorovitz and Alasdair MacIntyre, Toward a Theory of Medical Fallibility, 1 J.Med.Phil. 51 (1976). Given the uncertain results of therapeutic intervention on a given patient, regardless of the state of general knowledge about interventions of that type, every therapeutic intervention is an experiment that risks hurting the patient.

b. *Injuries of ignorance.* Much of medical treatment is still primitive: the etiologies and optimal treatments for many illnesses are not known; many treatment techniques, such as cancer chemotherapy, create substantial side-effects. Iatrogenic effects often result from the infant nature of the medical specialty. Use of the word "error" is arguably inappropriate, since the concept of error implies that an alternative error-free treatment exists.

The argument of medical ignorance has some justification. Can we in fairness ask a doctor to do more than medical science and his or her specialty have said is possible? But what if a whole profession has lagged behind, failing to discover the benefits of a desirable new practice or the risks of a generally accepted older practice? We might like more research, more efforts to bring specialty consensus on diagnosis and treatment, more systematic efforts at analysis of cost-effective medicine. Iatrogenesis due to ignorance and patient variation is, therefore, reducible with further research. Medicine is not static.

Is a concept of error also important to us as lawyers? Do lawyers have a similar set of problems with the iatrogenic effects of legal practice? Think of the harm that lawyers can do, and how it compares to the harm that doctors can do. Are the two professions comparable? Or is the doctor burdened with a heavier responsibility, and correspondingly heavier costs of error?

In Healing the Wounds: A Physician Looks at His Work (1986), Dr. David Hilfiker explores the stresses experienced by a doctor. He chronicles the stresses in the practice of medicine—the drains on a physician's time and energy, fears of making a wrong decision, lack of time to integrate experiences, and difficulties in keeping up with rapidly changing medical specialties. A busy physician—buffeted by the pressures of uncertainties in decisionmaking, the need to keep up, and the demands of a schedule—makes mistakes. As Hilfiker writes,

> it is not only in the emergency room, the operating room, the intensive care unit, or the delivery room that a doctor can blunder into tragedy. Errors are always possible, even in the midst of the humdrum routine of daily care. * * * A doctor has to confront the possibility of a mistake with every patient visit. Id. at 82.

The well trained physician may simply be inattentive on a particular occasion; he may have failed to keep up with new developments; he may have problems dealing with a particular patient for personal reasons. Some of these causes of error can be addressed by particular correctives—an eased schedule, an expanded collegial support setting, the transfer of a patient to another doctor. How should the law respond to these exigencies in medical malpractice litigation? In disciplinary actions?

As you become familiar with the health care enterprise, and the role of physicians and other professionals within that enterprise, think about the range of regulatory tools that might be valuable in improving the quality of health care. Consider how hospitals monitor physician errors and iatrogenesis. Although the physicians are often the active agent in causing patient harm, the hospital provides an indispensable workplace for their activities. Can a health care institution also be "impaired", i.e., suffering from a systemic problem that impairs its functioning?

The law has historically focused on physician "error". Until recently, malpractice cases were brought against the treating physician and not his institution because of a variety of legal rules that shielded the hospital. State licensing boards brought disciplinary actions against the individual errant doctor. Staff privilege cases involved the individual doctor's qualifications. The narrow focus on individual error facilitated a clear definition of "bad medicine." Bad medicine was what bad doctors did, "bad apples," doctors whose incompetence was obvious and offensive.

Consider the traditional malpractice suit for a moment. Suppose that a doctor followed generally accepted, "customary," community practice in the use of a drug to control heart problems (See Chapter 4 infra), yet his patient died. In most jurisdictions, the doctor would not be liable, since he or she conformed to an accepted community practice. Now suppose that we introduce an outcome measure into our assessment. Can you design a liability rule that would take an outcome approach? Would it be desirable to apply this rule to most of medical practice?

This focus on individual responsibility and error has been the starting point for quality assessment, even though it misses many causes of poor quality health care. Such a concept of error provides a necessary starting point, but bad outcomes at the individual physician level typically occur too infrequently to identify poor or good physicians. The larger problem of quality in medical care must also address systemic failures, poor administrative design for review of health care, inadequacies in training of physicians, and the nature of practice incentives.

B. THE EXTENT OF MEDICAL MISADVENTURES

Medical errors that cause iatrogenic harms to patients also impose costs on society, including the cost of correcting the bad result (when it can be corrected) and the loss to society of that patient's productivity. How extensive are such medical mishaps?

PATIENTS, DOCTORS, AND LAWYERS: MEDICAL INJURY, MALPRACTICE LITIGATION, AND PATIENT COMPENSATION IN NEW YORK

The Report of the Harvard Medical Practice
Study to the State of New York (1990).

[The Harvard Medical Practice Study in New York looked at the incidence of injuries resulting from medical interventions, "adverse events," beginning with a sample of more than 31,000 New York hospital records drawn from the study year 1984. The review was conducted by medical record administrators and nurses in the screening phase, and by board certified physicians for the physician-review phase.]

* * *

We analyzed 30,121 (96%) of the 31,429 records selected for the study sample. After preliminary screening, physicians reviewed 7,743 records, from which a total of 1,133 adverse events were identified that occurred as a result of medical management in the hospital or required hospitalization for treatment. Of this group, 280 were judged to result from negligent care. Weighting these figures according to the sample plan, we estimated the incidence of adverse events for hospitalizations in New York in 1984 to be 3.7%, or a total of 98,609. Of these, 27.6%, 27,179 cases, or 1.0% of all hospital discharges, were due to negligence.

Physician confidence in the judgments of causation of adverse events spanned a broad range, but only 1.3% of all discharges were in the close-call range (defined as a confidence in causation of just under or just over 50–50). An even smaller fraction, 0.7% of discharges were close-call negligent adverse events, but they constituted a larger proportion of total negligent adverse events.

The majority of adverse events (57%) resulted in minimal and transient disability, but 14% of patients died at least in part as a result of their adverse event, and in another 9% the resultant disability lasted longer than 6 months. Based on these figures, we estimated that about 2,500 cases of permanent total disability resulted from medical injury in New York hospitals in 1984. Further, we found evidence that medical injury contributed at least in part to the deaths of more than 13,000 patients in that year. Many of the deaths occurred in patients who had greatly shortened life expectancies from their underlying diseases, however. Negligent adverse events resulted, overall, in greater disability than did non-negligent events and were associated with 51% of all deaths from medical injury.

Risk factors

The risk of sustaining an adverse event increased with age. When rates were standardized for DRG level, persons over 65 years had twice the chance of sustaining an adverse event of those in the 16–44 years group. Newborns had half the adverse event rate of the 16–44 years group. The percent of adverse events resulting from negligence was increased in elderly patients. We found no gender differences in adverse event or negligence rates. Although the rates were higher in the self-pay group than in the insured categories, the differences were not significant. Blacks had higher rates of adverse events and adverse events resulting from negligence, but these differences overall were not significant. However, higher rates of adverse events and negligent events were found in hospitals that served a higher proportion of minority patients. At hospitals that cared for a mix of white and minority patients, blacks and whites had nearly identical rates.

Adverse event rates varied 10–fold between individual hospitals, when standardized for age and DRG level. Although standardized adverse event and negligence rates for small hospitals (fewer than 8,000 discharges/year) were less than for larger hospitals, these differences were not significant. Hospital ownership (private, non-profit, or government) also was not associated with significantly different rates of adverse events. The fraction of adverse events due to negligence in government hospitals was 50% higher than in non-profit institutions, however, and three times that in proprietary hospitals. These differences were significant. The standardized rate of adverse events in upstate, non–MSA hospitals was one-third that of upstate metropolitan hospitals and less than one-fourth that in New York City. These differences were highly significant. The percent of adverse events due to negligence was not significantly different across regions. Non-teaching hospitals had half the adverse event rates of university or affiliated teaching hospitals, but university teaching hospitals had rates of negligence that were less than half those of the non-teaching or affiliated hospitals.

The nature of adverse events

Nearly half (47%) of all adverse events occurred in patients undergoing surgery, but the percent caused by negligence was lower than for non-surgical adverse events (17% vs 37%). Adverse events resulting from errors in diagnosis and in non-invasive treatment were judged to be due to negligence in over three-fourths of patients. Falls were considered due to negligence in 45% of instances.

The high rate of adverse events in patients over 65 years occurred in three categories: non-technical postoperative complications, complications of non-invasive therapy, and falls. A larger proportion of adverse events in younger patients was due to surgical failures. The operating room was the site of management for the highest fraction of adverse events, but relatively few of these were negligent. On the other hand, most (70%) adverse events in the emergency room resulted from negligence.

The most common type of error resulting in an adverse event was that involved in performing a procedure, but diagnostic errors and prevention errors were more likely to be judged negligent, and to result in serious disability.

The more severe the degree of negligence the greater the likelihood of resultant serious disability (moderate impairment with recovery taking more than six months, permanent disability, or death).

2. Litigation data

We estimated that the incidence of malpractice claims filed by patients for the study year was between 2,967 and 3,888. Using these figures, together with the projected statewide number of injuries from medical negligence during the same period, we estimated that eight times as many patients suffered an injury from negligence as filed a malpractice claim in New York State. About 16 times as many patients suffered an injury from negligence as received compensation from the tort liability system.

These aggregate estimates understate the true size of the gap between the frequency of malpractice claims and the incidence of adverse events caused by negligence. When we identified the malpractice claims actually filed by patients in our sample and reviewed the judgments of our physician reviewers, we found that many cases in litigation were brought by patients in whose records we found no evidence of negligence or even of adverse events. Because the legal system has not yet resolved many of these cases, we do not have the information that would permit an assessment of the success of the tort litigation system in screening out claims with no negligence.

* * *

Notes and Questions

1. The Harvard Study was designed to produce empirical data to better inform the debate about reform of the tort system, including no-fault reforms. Do the findings of the study, as to level of patient injury attributable to medical error, surprise you?

A second recent study, the Utah–Colorado Medical Practice Study (UCMPS), found that adverse events connected to surgery accounted for about half (44.9%) of adverse events across both states, with only 16.9% of the surgical adverse events involving negligence. Drug related adverse events comprised the second most prevalent group. The authors concluded that the UCMPS produced results similar to the earlier New York Harvard Study. That is three to four percent of hospitalizations give rise to adverse events. "Together, the two studies provide overwhelming evidence that the burden of iatrogenic injury is large, enduring, and an innate feature of hospital care in the United States." David M. Studdert, Troyen A. Brennan, and Eric J. Thomas, Beyond Dead Reckoning: Measures of Medical Injury Burden, Malpractice Litigation, and Alternative Compensation Models from Utah and Colorado, 33 Ind. L. Rev. 1643, 1662 (2000).

A study based upon insurance company closed malpractice claims files for anesthesia-related patient injuries concluded that payment was made in more than 80% of the claims filed by patients judged to have received substandard anesthetic care. The claims were reviewed by expert anesthesiologists and divided into inappropriate and appropriate care. The authors found that a patient was much more likely to be paid if the care received was substandard. These favorable odds for payment cut across all severities of injury. The authors also concluded that when a patient files suit for anesthesia-related injury, and the care was judged to be appropriate by peers, payment was made to the patient in 42% of the cases. The authors concluded that "... the tort-based system of patient compensation for injury clearly favors payment to the injured patient, but inequities exist for both patient and physician." See Frederick W. Cheney et al., Standard of Care and Anesthesia Liability, 261 J.A.M.A. 1599 (1989).

Do these conclusions support the existing tort system's value as a quality control system in detecting and deterring error? Or do they support the need for reform? For an exploration of the role of the tort system in insuring against inadvertent negligence or accidents not caused by a professional failure, see Mark F. Grady, Why Are People Negligent? Technology, Nondurable Precautions, and the Medical Malpractice Explosion, 82 Nw.Univ.L.Rev. 293 (1988).

2. As you read Chapter 4, try to sort out the various tort doctrines and rules of admissibility to see whether they protect or ferret out medical error. Do liability doctrines adequately attack medical errors? Do the defenses available to doctors adequately protect non-errant doctors?

3. Other studies have also concluded that the hospital setting exposes patients to significant risks of iatrogenic illness. One study found that more than 36% of the patients admitted to a hospital developed iatrogenic illnesses, either a major or minor complication. Nine percent had major complications, and 2% of all patients died for reasons related to the iatrogenic illness. Exposure to drugs was an important factor in patient complications. Knight Steel et al., Iatrogenic Illness on a General Medical Service at a University Hospital, 304 N.Eng.J.Med. 638, 641 (1981). See David C. Classen et al., Adverse Drug Events in Hospitalized Patients: Excess Length of Stay, Extra Costs, and Attributable Mortality, 277 J.A.M.A. 301 (1997) (adverse drug events associated with significantly prolonged lengths of stay, increased economic costs, and an almost 2–fold increased risk of death); David W. Bates et al., The Costs of Adverse Drug Events in Hospitalized Patients, 277 J.A.M.A. 307 (1997) (found that an adverse drug event was associated with about $2,600 of additional costs to the hospital, and for preventable ADEs the figure was almost twice as high); Timothy S. Lesar, Laurie Briceland, and Daniel S. Stein, Factors Related to Errors in Medication Prescribing, 277 J.A.M.A. 312 (1997) (risks of adverse drug events can be reduced by improving focus of organization, technological, and risk management educational and training efforts).

4. Surgery is also risky. One study concluded that patients experiencing care on a surgical ward experienced about a 1% incidence or mishap rate. Diagnostic errors, and delay in performing a procedure, were major contributors to the mishaps. More than half the medical errors surveyed were errors of commission, including unnecessary or contraindicated surgery, defective execution of an indicated operation, and performance of an improper surgical procedure. The authors of the study concluded that " * * * in 31 instances, or 90 per cent of the errors of therapeutic commission, the mistakes were those of unnecessary, contraindicated, or technically defective surgical activity." Nathan P. Couch et al., The High Cost of Low–Frequency Events, 304 N.Eng.J.Med. 634, 635 (1981).

5. These medical mishaps are expensive. The hospital based study found that costs attributable to error were 1.3% of the hospital's patient-service billings for the year. The research confirmed an earlier study, which had concluded that medical misadventure contributed significantly to the costs of health care. Christopher J. Zook and Francis D. Moore, High Cost Users of Medical Care, 302 N.Eng.J.Med. 996 (1980).

**Doing What Counts for
Patient Safety:
Federal Actions to Reduce
Medical Errors and Their Impact**

**Report of the Quality Interagency Coordination Task Force (QuIC)
To the President
February 2000**

CHAPTER 1

Understanding Medical Errors

Growing Concerns About Medical Errors

The IOM's release of *To Err is Human* brought medical errors and patient safety the attention it has long needed but never had. The information presented in the report is not new. Indeed, many studies, some as early as the 1960s, showed that patients were frequently injured by the same medical care that was intended to help them [ ]. While evidence of medical error has existed for some time, the report succeeded in capturing the public's attention by revealing the magnitude of this pervasive problem and presenting it in a uniquely compelling fashion. The IOM estimates that medical errors cause between 44,000 and 98,000 deaths annually in the United States. Using the more conservative figure, medical errors rank as the eighth leading cause of death, killing more Americans than motor vehicle accidents, breast cancer, or AIDS. In addition to this extraordinary human toll, medical errors result in annual costs of $17 to $29 billion in the United States [ ]. Additionally, fear of becoming a victim of medical error may lead patients to delay obtaining potentially beneficial medical care, which may allow their illnesses to worsen.

Experiencing harm as a result of receiving health care is a growing concern for the American public. Front-page articles in newspapers, television exposes, and cover stories in magazine have provided the stark details of the latest and most dramatic examples of medical errors. Until recently, the perception of medical errors among health care providers and the public has been shaped by these anecdotes, and remedies have focused on fixing blame on individual providers, including health plans, hospitals, doctors, pharmacists, nurses, and other caregivers. That approach, however, has proven ineffective in addressing patient safety, as documented by the ongoing problems noted in the IOM report. The IOM's recommended alternative approaches and other ways in which the Federal agencies can work to reduce medical errors are described in this report.medical errors complicates the development of a response to the issues outlined in the IOM report. A number of definitions have been applied to medical errors and patient safety. In *To Err is Human*, the IOM adopted the following definition:

Definitions and Context

The lack of standardized nomenclature and a universal taxonomy for

An error is defined as the failure of a planned action to be completed as intended or the use of a wrong plan to achieve an aim.

In an effort to thoroughly consider all of the relevant issues related to medical errors, the QuIC expanded on the IOM definition, as follows:

An error is defined as the failure of a planned action to be completed as intended or the use of a wrong plan to achieve an aim. Errors can include problems in practice, products, procedures, and systems.

The explicit acknowledgment of the broad scope of errors reflected in this definition respects the responsibilities and capabilities of the Government agencies and departments contributing to this report. The term "patient safety" as used here applies to initiatives designed to prevent adverse outcomes from medical errors. The enhancement of patient safety encompasses three complementary activities: preventing errors, making errors visible, and mitigating the effects of errors.

It is critical to recognize that not all bad outcomes for patients are due to medical errors. Patients may not be cured of their disease or disability despite the fact that they are provided the very best of care. Additionally, not all adverse events that are the result of medical care are, in fact, errors. An adverse event is defined broadly as an injury that was caused by medical management and that resulted in measurable disability [ ]. Some adverse events, termed "unpreventable adverse events," result from a complication that cannot be prevented given the current state of knowledge. Many drugs, even when used appropriately, have a chance of side effects, such as nausea from an antibiotic. The occurrence of nausea would be an adverse event, but it would not be considered a medical error to have given the antibiotic if the patient had an infection that was expected to respond to the chosen antibiotic. Medical errors are adverse events that are preventable with our current state of medical knowledge. Figure 1 shows this set of possible outcomes of medical care.

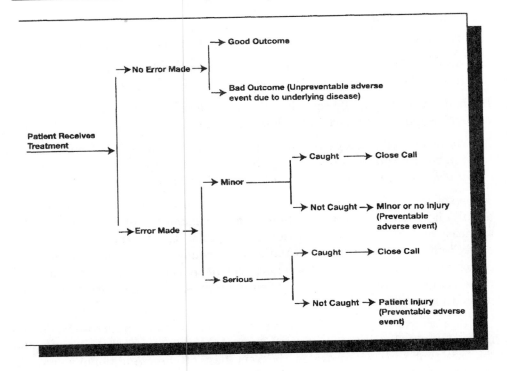

In this report, the consideration of errors is broadened beyond preventable adverse events that lead to actual patient harm to include "near misses," sometimes know as "close calls." A "near miss" is an event or situation that could have resulted in an accident, injury, or illness, but did not, either by chance or through timely intervention. Experience in other industries, including aviation, manufacturing, and nuclear energy, demonstrates that there is as much to learn from close calls as there is from incidents leading to actual harm.

It is also important to situate medical errors within the broader context of problems in health care quality. These can be classified under three categories: overuse (the service is unlikely to have net benefit), underuse (a potentially beneficial service is withheld), and misuse (a service is inappropriately used)[ ]. The majority of medical errors fall into the category of misuse, but some problems with overuse (e.g., when an unnecessary therapy is prescribed, leading to harm) or underuse (e.g., when an error in diagnosis leads to the failure to apply timely treatment) blur these distinctions. These are related quality problems and may be addressed, in part, by using some of the same approaches. In some cases, however, distinct approaches may be required. That is why the IOM has chosen to deal with the issue of errors separately in its report and plans to issue future reports on underuse and overuse quality problems. Our report will also focus exclusively on errors. Nevertheless, the QuIC participants recognize that the improvements made in patient safety will lay the foundation for, and may encourage, other quality improvements.

A Framework for Thinking About Errors

There are many possible ways to categorize medical errors, but no universally accepted taxonomy. Classifications have included:

Type of health care service provided (e.g., classification of medication errors by the National Coordinating Council for Medication Error Reporting and Prevention).

Severity of the resulting injury (e.g., sentinel events, defined as "any unexpected occurrence involving death or serious physical or psychological injury" by the Joint Commission on Accreditation of Healthcare Organizations [JCAHO]).

Legal definition (e.g., errors resulting from negligence [Institute of Medicine, 1999]).

Type of setting (e.g., outpatient clinic, intensive care unit), and

Type of individual involved (e.g., physician, nurse, patient).

Implicit in the current variety of classifications is the understanding that different types of medical errors are likely to require different solutions and preventive measures. A single approach to error reduction will fail because it does not account for important differences in types of errors. For example, for the Food and Drug Administration (FDA), product risk category may be a crucial dimension for shaping regulatory policy, but a health care provider may see this dimension as a minor consideration in shaping its error-control methods.

An "ideal" classification of errors would need to be well suited to the purpose to which it is being applied, but there is no single classification system that could be successfully applied to the full set of IOM recommendations being addressed by the QuIC. A framework for reporting may include considerations of the level of reporting (Federal versus State versus organizational), the reasons for which the reporting is being done (learning versus accountability), or the level of injury (near-miss versus minor versus severe). A framework for developing a research agenda may require more focus on the populations involved, available data, and research tools that can be applied to the problem. The experience with the Aviation Safety Reporting System (ASRS), which relies on narrative reporting without a formal framework, demonstrates that rigorous classification may not be necessary at all for some purposes.

C. REMEDYING QUALITY PROBLEMS OF HEALTH CARE SERVICES

1. Origins of Clinical Standards of Practice

The standard of care applied in a tort suit or a hospital peer review process does not normally derive from an external authority such as a government standard. In the medical profession, as in other professions, standards develop in a complicated way involving the interaction of leaders of the profession, professional journals and meetings, and networks of colleagues. Neither the Food and Drug Administration, the National Institutes of Health, the Department of Health and Human Services, nor state licensing boards have had much to do with shaping medical practice. Most clinical policies derive from a flow of reports in the literature, at meetings, and in peer discussions. Over a period of time, hundreds of separate comments come together to form a clinical policy. If this becomes generally accepted, we can call it "standard practice." See generally David Eddy, Clinical Policies and the Quality of Clinical Practice, 307 N.Eng.J.Med. 343 (1982).

This decentralized process of policy setting has some advantages, as Eddy notes: the individual doctor benefits from collective wisdom; unwarranted bursts of enthusiasm are dampened; the policies are tested by the best minds (through statistical and other tools); and flexibility, allowing adaptation to local skills and values, is promoted. Such a policy making process also has drawbacks: oversimplification may ignore side-effects, costs and risks; over-broad conclusions may be drawn from a few observations; examples may be chosen that tend to support the expected result; incentives may favor overuse rather than underuse; an advocacy system may arise in which proponents push and counterarguments may be ignored; the policy consensus may be based upon little more than repetition by the largest or loudest voices; and the inertia inherent in the status quo may dominate.

The diffusion of new medical technologies of diagnosis and treatment poses special problems for the individual physician. Most doctors will note new ideas as they show up in the literature. But they may not be appropriately skeptical. In spite of insufficient evidence of efficacy, doctors in various specialties have been quick to adopt new technologies such as respirator therapy, gastric freezing of ulcers, and other now-discredited techniques. Other tools, such as the CT scan and magnetic resonance imaging, have proliferated rapidly before the evidence on their efficacy was in. The adoption of what has been termed "slam-bang" technologies often precedes careful evaluation.

Even if a cautious and conscientious doctor is skeptical, the data and opinions available are often inadequate to allow evaluation of research findings. The studies may have defects; they may fail, for example, to explain how to translate limited clinical research into practice or may inadequately evaluate controversy over earlier studies. Or the doctor may not be aware of the unique nature of clinical trials.

The phenomenon of medical practice variation highlights the role of uncertainty in the setting of medical standards. Wennberg, whose studies in this area are often cited, looked at states and at regions within states for variation in surgical and other practices:

> [I]n Maine by the time women reach seventy years of age in one hospital market the likelihood they have undergone a hysterectomy is 20 percent while in another market it is 70 percent. In Iowa, the chances that male residents who reach age eighty-five have undergone prostatectomy range from a low of 15 percent to a high of more than 60 percent in different hospital markets. In Vermont the probability that resident children will undergo a tonsillectomy has ranged from a low of 8 percent in one hospital market to a high of nearly 70 percent in another.

John E. Wennberg, Dealing with Medical Practice Variations: A Proposal for Action, 3 Health Affairs 6, 9 (1984); John E. Wennberg et al., Professional Uncertainty and the Problem of Supplier–Induced Demand , 16 Soc. Sci. Med. 811, 812–17 (1982) (reviewing variations in surgical practices). See also Mark

R. Chassin et al., Variations in the Use of Medical and Surgical Services by the Medicare Population, 314 New Eng. J. Med. 285, 287 (1986); David M. Eddy, Clinical Decision Making: From Theory to Practice (pts. 1–4), 263 JAMA 287, 441, 877, 1265 (1990).

Physician variation in treatment approaches is greatest with aging-related conditions, where the outcomes of conservative treatment are unknown. By contrast, the procedures least subject to variation are those "for which there is a professional consensus on the preferred place or style of treatment." Wennberg, supra. A study of a range of medical and surgical services used by Medicare beneficiaries during 1981 confirm Wennberg's findings. The study documented large variations "linked directly to the degree of medical consensus concerning the indications for use." Mark R. Chassin et al., Variations in the Use of Medical and Surgical Services by the Medicare Population, 314 N.Eng.J.Med. 285, 288 (1986).

The appropriateness of much medical treatment has been questioned. Wide variation has been noted in the use of laboratory tests, prescription drugs, X-rays, return appointments, and telephone consultations among similarly trained doctors in a wide variety of practice settings. Research on appropriateness indicates that from one quarter to one third of medical services may be of no value to patients. Robert Brook and Kathleen Lohr, Will We Need to Ration Effective Medical Care?, Issues in Science and Technology 68 (Fall 1986). The extent of inappropriate hospital use is also significant. One study concluded that 21% of pediatric hospital use is medically inappropriate. Kathi J. Kemper, Medically Inappropriate Hospital Use in a Pediatric Population, 318 N.Eng.J.Med. 1033 (1988). Other studies have found that between 20% and 40% of hospital ancillary services are unnecessary. Robert A. Hughes, The Ancillary Services Review Program in Massachusetts: Experience of the 1982 Pilot Project, 252 N.Eng.J.Med. 1727 (1984). Carotid enterectomies, procedures that remove clots in arteries leading to the brain, were judged as appropriate in only 35% of the cases surveyed. Mark R. Chassin, et al., How Coronary Angiography Is Used, J.A.M.A. 2543 (1988).

In another study, the researchers looked at implantation of permanent cardiac pacemakers in a large population. They found that 44% of the implants were definitely indicated, 36% possibly indicated, and 20% were not indicated. Seventy-three percent of the hospitals had an incidence of 10% or more unwarranted implantations, regardless of type of hospital. Lee Goldman, et al., Costs and Effectiveness of Routine Therapy with Long–Term Beta–Adrenergic Antagonists After Acute Myocardial Infarction, 319 N.Eng.J.Med. 152 (1988). One study found a seventeen-fold variation in lab use among internists dealing with clinical patients. Steven A. Schroeder et al., Use of Laboratory Tests and Pharmaceutical Variation Among Physicians and Effect of Cost Audit on Subsequent Use, 225 J.A.M.A. 969 (1973).

The attitudes of individual doctors influence the range of variation where consensus is lacking; Wennberg has termed this the "practice style factor." This style can exert its influence in the absence of scientific information on outcomes; in other cases it may be unrelated to controversies.

Physicians in some hospital markets practice medicine in ways that have extremely adverse implications for the cost of care, motivated perhaps by reasons of their own or their patients' convenience, or because of individ-

ualist interpretations of the requirements for defensive medicine. Whatever the reason, it certainly is not because of adherence to medical
standards based on clinical outcome criteria or even on statistical norms
based on average performance.

Wennberg, supra at 7. See also John E. Wennberg, The Paradox of Appropriate Care, 258 J.A.M.A. 2568 (1987). See generally John Eisenberg, Doctors'
Decisions and the Cost of Medical Care (1986).

Doctors make mistakes, and some of these errors injure patients. The
frequency of medical misadventures in the nation's hospitals and clinical
settings is substantial. Much health care is of unproven value, but consumes
consumer and governmental resources. The American health care system is
therefore not of optimal quality, and could stand improvement. We have a
definition of quality, we have criteria and standards for its evaluation. How do
we translate the criteria into a strategy to modify behavior and performance
to improve the quality of care delivered?

Several approaches to quality improvement can be pursued. We can rely
on the traditional forces of professional ethics and socialization. We can
expand the role of the marketplace, using dissemination of quality information to consumers and buyers of health, on the theory that prudent buyers
will reject lower quality providers. We can improve the current modes of self-
regulation of the medical profession and the industry, which include accreditation, medical staff privileges, and medical licensing actions. The process by
which a patient sues for malpractice can be improved. And the government, as
a primary source of financing for much health care in the United States, can
intervene, setting standards and demanding better processes and outcomes.
We will examine each of these methods of quality improvement in later
sections and chapters.

The combined problems of variation in medical practice and lack of
evidence of efficacy of many treatment approaches have launched a movement
toward practice parameters. Specialty societies and now the Medicare program have moved to study practices, to articulate consensus on acceptable
practice, and to disseminate information on the consensus. The development
of practice parameters or protocols has intensified in recent years, as the
medical profession attempts to sift through the available research knowledge
and reduce variation in medical practice. A new agency within the Public
Health Service, the Agency for Health Care Policy and Research, was created
to further such research efforts. 42 U.S.C.A., Title ix, section 901. Promotion
of quality work is done within this Agency by the Office of the Forum for
Quality and Effectiveness in Health Care. 42 U.S.C.A. 201, § 911.

Measuring appropriateness and developing parameters has its problems:
it is easier to study overuse than underuse because of difficulties in defining
relevant populations; the scientific evidence is always incomplete, requiring
reliance on expert judgment; and parameters are slow and expensive to
develop in many areas of medical practice. Robert Brook, Practice Guidelines
and Practicing Medicine: Are They Compatible? 262 J.A.M.A. 3027 (1989).

Given the patterns of variation in medical practice, and the unscientific
way in which various medical treatments diffuse into common use, is it likely
that newly developed practice parameters will be adopted by physicians in
practice? One study evaluated the effect of distributing practice guidelines

generated under the auspices of a national specialty association—the 1986 Canadian guidelines advocating a lower rate of cesarean sections. The dissemination of guidelines had little effect on actual physician practice. Physician awareness of them was high, and the attitudes of obstetricians were positive toward the recommendations. One third of the obstetricians and hospitals reported changing their practices because of the guidelines.

* * * [T]his high level of awareness, the apparently positive attitudes, and the reported changes in practice coexisted with a demonstrated poor knowledge of the actual recommendations and very little actual change in practices. These results agree with the findings in other evaluations in this area.

See Jonathan Lomas et al., Do Practice Guidelines Guide Practice? The Effect of a Consensus Statement on the Practice of Physicians, 321 N.Eng.J.Med. 1306 (1989). The authors speculated that many forces besides research evidence affect physician decisions, including financial incentives favoring one approach over another, patient pressure, and fears of malpractice. "In the absence of any accompanying strategies to overcome these other influences, the dissemination of research evidence in the form of practice guidelines issues by a national body is unlikely to have much effect on inappropriate practices that are sustained by powerful nonscientific forces." Id. at 1310.

2. Strategies for Reducing Medical Error

LUCIAN L. LEAPE, ERROR IN MEDICINE
272 JAMA 1851 (1994).

* * *

WHY IS THE ERROR RATE IN THE PRACTICE OF MEDICINE SO HIGH?

Physicians, nurses, and pharmacists are trained to be careful and to function at a high level of proficiency. Indeed, they probably are among the most careful professionals in our society. It is curious, therefore, that high error rates have not stimulated more concern and efforts at error prevention. One reason may be a lack of awareness of the severity of the problem. Hospital-acquired injuries are not reported in the newspapers like jumbo-jet crashes, for the simple reason that they occur one at a time in 5000 different locations across the country. Although error rates are substantial, serious injuries due to errors are not part of the everyday experience of physicians or nurses, but are perceived as isolated and unusual events—"outliers." Second, most errors do no harm. Either they are intercepted or the patient's defenses prevent injury. (Few children die from a single misdiagnosed or mistreated urinary infection, for example.)

But the most important reason physicians and nurses have not developed more effective methods of error prevention is that they have a great deal of difficulty in dealing with human error when it does occur. The reasons are to be found in the culture of medical practice.

Physicians are socialized in medical school and residency to strive for error-free practice. There is a powerful emphasis on perfection, both in diagnosis and treatment. In everyday hospital practice, the message is equally clear: mistakes are unacceptable. Physicians are expected to function without error, an expectation that physicians translate into the need to be infallible. One result is that physicians, not unlike test pilots, come to view an error as a failure of character—you weren't careful enough, you didn't try hard enough. This kind of thinking lies behind a common reaction by physicians: 'How can there be an error without negligence?'

Cultivating a norm of high standards is, of course, highly desirable. It is the counterpart of another fundamental goal of medical education: developing the physician's sense of responsibility for the patient. If you are responsible for everything that happens to the patient, it follows that you are responsible for any errors that occur. While the logic may be sound, the conclusion is absurd, because physicians do not have the power to control all aspects of patient care. Nonetheless, the sense of duty to perform faultlessly is strongly internalized.

Role models in medical education reinforce the concept of infallibility. The young physician's teachers are largely specialists, experts in their fields, and authorities. Authorities are not supposed to err. It has been suggested that this need to be infallible creates a strong pressure to intellectual dishonesty, to cover up mistakes rather than to admit them. The organization of medical practice, particularly in the hospital, perpetuates these norms. Errors are rarely admitted or discussed among physicians in private practice. Physicians typically feel, not without reason, that admission of error will lead to censure or increased surveillance or, worse, that their colleagues will regard them as incompetent or careless. Far better to conceal a mistake or, if that is impossible, to try to shift the blame to another, even the patient.

Yet physicians are emotionally devastated by serious mistakes that harm or kill patients. Almost every physician who cares for patients has had that experience, usually more than once. The emotional impact is often profound, typically a mixture of fear, guilt, anger, embarrassment, and humiliation. However, as Christensen et al. note, physicians are typically isolated by their emotional responses; seldom is there a process to evaluate the circumstances of a mistake and to provide support and emotional healing for the fallible physician. Wu et al. found that only half of house officers discussed their most significant mistakes with attending physicians.

Thus, although the individual may learn from a mistake and change practice patterns accordingly, the adjustment often takes place in a vacuum. Lessons learned are shared privately, if at all, and external objective evaluation of what went wrong often does not occur. As Hilfiker points out, "We see the horror of our own mistakes, yet we are given no permission to deal with their enormous emotional impact.... The medical profession simply has no place for its mistakes."

Finally, the realities of the malpractice threat provide strong incentives against disclosure or investigation of mistakes. Even a minor error can place the physician's entire career in jeopardy if it results in a serious bad outcome. It is hardly surprising that a physician might hesitate to reveal an error to either the patient or hospital authorities or to expose a colleague to similar devastation for a single mistake.

The paradox is that although the standard of medical practice is perfection—error-free patient care—all physicians recognize that mistakes are inevitable. Most would like to examine their mistakes and learn from them. From an emotional standpoint, they need the support and understanding of their colleagues and patients when they make mistakes. Yet, they are denied both insight and support by misguided concepts of infallibility and by fear: fear of embarrassment by colleagues, fear of patient reaction, and fear of litigation. Although the notion of infallibility fails the reality test, the fears are well grounded.

THE MEDICAL APPROACH TO ERROR PREVENTION

Efforts at error prevention in medicine have characteristically followed what might be called the perfectibility model: if physicians and nurses could be properly trained and motivated, then they would make no mistakes. The methods used to achieve this goal are training and punishment. Training is directed toward teaching people to do the right thing. In nursing, rigid adherence to protocols is emphasized. In medicine, the emphasis is less on rules and more on knowledge.

Punishment is through social opprobrium or peer disapproval. The professional cultures of medicine and nursing typically use blame to encourage proper performance. Errors are regarded as someone's fault, caused by a lack of sufficient attention or, worse, lack of caring enough to make sure you are correct. Punishment for egregious (negligent) errors is primarily (and capriciously) meted out through the malpractice tort litigation system.

Students of error and human performance reject this formulation. While the proximal error leading to an accident is, in fact, usually a 'human error,' the causes of that error are often well beyond the individual's control. All humans err frequently. Systems that rely on error-free performance are doomed to fail.

The medical approach to error prevention is also reactive. Errors are usually discovered only when there is an incident—an untoward effect or injury to the patient. Corrective measures are then directed toward preventing a recurrence of a similar error, often by attempting to prevent that individual from making a repeat error. Seldom are underlying causes explored.

For example, if a nurse gives a medication to the wrong patient, a typical response would be exhortation or training in double-checking the identity of both patient and drug before administration. Although it might be noted that the nurse was distracted because of an unusually large case load, it is unlikely that serious attention would be given to evaluating overall work assignments or to determining if large caseloads have contributed to other kinds of errors.

It is even less likely that questions would be raised about the wisdom of a system for dispensing medications in which safety is contingent on inspection by an individual at the end point of use. Reliance on inspection as a mechanism of quality control was discredited long ago in industry. A simple procedure, such as the use of bar coding like that used at supermarket checkout counters, would probably be more effective in this situation. More imaginative solutions could easily be found—if it were recognized that both systems and individuals contribute to the problem.

It seems clear, and it is the thesis of this article, that if physicians, nurses, pharmacists, and administrators are to succeed in reducing errors in hospital care, they will need to fundamentally change the way they think about errors and why they occur. Fortunately, a great deal has been learned about error prevention in other disciplines, information that is relevant to the hospital practice of medicine.

* * *

* * *

Prevention of Accidents

The multiplicity of mechanisms and causes of errors (internal and external, individual and systemic) dictates that there cannot be a simple or universal means of reducing errors. Creating a safe process, whether it be flying an airplane, running a hospital, or performing cardiac surgery, requires attention to methods of error reduction at each stage of system development: design, construction, maintenance, allocation of resources, training, and development of operational procedures. This type of attention to error reduction requires responsible individuals at each stage to think through the consequences of their decisions and to reason back from discovered deficiencies to redesign and reorganize the process. Systemic changes are most likely to be successful because they reduce the likelihood of a variety of types of errors at the end-user stage.

The primary objective of system design for safety is to make it difficult for individuals to err. But it is also important to recognize that errors will inevitably occur and plan for their recovery. Ideally, the system will automatically correct errors when they occur. If that is impossible, mechanisms should be in place to at least detect errors in time for corrective action. Therefore, in addition to designing the work environment to minimize psychological precursors, designers should provide feedback through instruments that provide monitoring functions and build in buffers and redundancy. Buffers are design features that automatically correct for human or mechanical errors. Redundancy is duplication (sometimes triplication or quadruplication) of critical mechanisms and instruments, so that a failure does not result in loss of the function.

Another important system design feature is designing tasks to minimize errors. Norman has recommended a set of principles that have general applicability. Tasks should be simplified to minimize the load on the weakest aspects of cognition: short-term memory, planning, and problem solving. The power of constraints should be exploited. One way to do this is with "forcing functions," which make it impossible to act without meeting a precondition (such as the inability to release the parking gear of a car unless the brake pedal is depressed). Standardization of procedures, displays, and layouts reduces error by reinforcing the pattern recognition that humans do well. Finally, where possible, operations should be easily reversible or difficult to perform when they are not reversible.

Training must include, in addition to the usual emphasis on application of knowledge and following procedures, a consideration of safety issues. These issues include understanding the rationale for procedures as well as how errors can occur at various stages, their possible consequences, and instruction in methods for avoidance of errors. Finally, it must be acknowledged that injuries can result from behavioral problems that may be seen in impaired physicians or incompetent physicians despite well-designed systems; methods for identifying and correcting egregious behaviors are also needed.

THE AVIATION MODEL

The practice of hospital medicine has been compared, usually unfavorably, to the aviation industry, also a highly complicated and risky enterprise but one that seems far safer. Indeed, there seem to be many similarities. As Allnutt observed,

> Both pilots and doctors are carefully selected, highly trained professionals who are usually determined to maintain high standards, both externally and internally imposed, whilst performing difficult tasks in life-threatening environments. Both use high technology equipment and function as key members of a team of specialists ... both exercise high level cognitive skills in a most complex domain about which much is known, but where much remains to be discovered.

While the comparison is apt, there are also important differences between aviation and medicine, not the least of which is a substantial measure of uncertainty due to the number and variety of disease states, as well as the unpredictability of the human organism. Nonetheless, there is much physicians and nurses could learn from aviation.

Aviation—airline travel, at least—is indeed generally safe: more than 10 million takeoffs and landings each year with an average of fewer than four crashes a year. But, it was not always so. The first powered flight was in 1903, the first fatality in 1908, and the first midair collision in 1910. By 1910, there were 2000 pilots in the world and 32 had already died. The US Air Mail Service was founded in 1918. As a result of efforts to meet delivery schedules in all kinds of weather, 31 of the first 40 Air Mail Service pilots were killed. This appalling toll led to unionization of the pilots and their insistence that local field controllers could not order pilots to fly against their judgment unless the field controllers went up for a flight around the field themselves. In 1922, there were no Air Mail Service fatalities. Since that time, a complex system of aircraft design, instrumentation, training, regulation, and air traffic control has developed that is highly effective at preventing fatalities.

There are strong incentives for making flying safe. Pilots, of course, are highly motivated. Unlike physicians, their lives are on the line as well as those of their passengers. But, airlines and airplane manufacturers also have strong incentives to provide safe flight. Business decreases after a large crash, and if a certain model of aircraft crashes repeatedly, the manufacturer will be discredited. The lawsuits that inevitably follow a crash can harm both reputation and profitability.

Designing for safety has led to a number of unique characteristics of aviation that could, with suitable modification, prove useful in improving hospital safety.

First, in terms of system design, aircraft designers assume that errors and failures are inevitable and design systems to "absorb" them, building in multiple buffers, automation, and redundancy. * * *

Second, procedures are standardized to the maximum extent possible. Specific protocols must be followed for trip planning, operations, and maintenance. Pilots go through a checklist before each takeoff. Required maintenance is specified in detail and must be performed on a regular (by flight hours) basis.

Third, the training, examination, and certification process is highly developed and rigidly, as well as frequently, enforced. Airline pilots take proficiency examinations every 6 months. Much of the content of examinations is directly concerned with procedures to enhance safety.

Pilots function well within this rigorously controlled system, although not flawlessly. For example, one study of cockpit crews observed that human errors or instrument malfunctions occurred on the average of one every 4 minutes during an overseas flight. Each event was promptly recognized and corrected with no untoward effects. Pilots also willingly submit to an external authority, the air traffic controller, when within the constrained air and ground space at a busy airport.

Finally, safety in aviation has been institutionalized. Two independent agencies have government-mandated responsibilities: the Federal Aviation Administration (FAA) regulates all aspects of flying and prescribes safety procedures, and the National Transportation Safety Board investigates every accident. The adherence of airlines and pilots to required safety standards is closely monitored. The FAA recognized long ago that pilots seldom reported an error if it led to disciplinary action. Accordingly, in 1975 the FAA established a confidential reporting system for safety infractions, the Air Safety Reporting System (ASRS). If pilots, controllers, or others promptly report a dangerous situation, such as a near-miss midair collision, they will not be penalized. This program dramatically increased reporting, so that unsafe conditions at airports, communication problems, and traffic control inadequacies are now promptly communicated. Analysis of these reports and subsequent investigations appear as a regular feature in several pilots' magazines. The ASRS receives more than 5000 notifications each year.

THE MEDICAL MODEL

By contrast, accident prevention has not been a primary focus of the practice of hospital medicine. It is not that errors are ignored. Mortality and morbidity conferences, incident reports, risk management activities, and quality assurance committees abound. But, as noted previously, these activities focus on incidents and individuals. When errors are examined, a problem-solving approach is usually used: the cause of the error is identified and corrected. Root causes, the underlying systems failures, are rarely sought. System designers do not assume that errors and failures are inevitable and design systems to prevent or absorb them. There are, of course, exceptions. Implementation of unit dosing, for example, markedly reduced medication dosing errors by eliminating the need for the nurse to measure out each dose. Monitoring in intensive care units is sophisticated and extensive (although perhaps not sufficiently redundant). Nonetheless, the basic health care system approach is to rely on individuals not to make errors rather than to assume they will.

Second, standardization and task design vary widely. In the operating room, it has been refined to a high art. In patient care units, much more could be done, particularly to minimize reliance on short-term memory, one of the weakest aspects of cognition. On-time and correct delivery of medications, for example, is often contingent on a busy nurse remembering to do so, a nurse who is responsible for four or five patients at once and is repeatedly interrupted, a classic set up for a "loss-of-activation" error.

On the other hand, education and training in medicine and nursing far exceed that in aviation, both in breadth of content and in duration, and few professions compare with medicine in terms of the extent of continuing education. Although certification is essentially universal, including the recent introduction of periodic recertification, the idea of periodically testing performance has never been accepted. Thus, we place great emphasis on education and training, but shy away from demonstrating that it makes a difference.

Finally, unlike aviation, safety in medicine has never been institutionalized, in the sense of being a major focus of hospital medical activities. Investigation of accidents is often superficial, unless a malpractice action is likely; noninjurious error (a "near miss") is rarely examined at all. Incident reports are frequently perceived as punitive instruments. As a result, they are often not filed, and when they are, they almost invariably focus on the individual's misconduct.

One medical model is an exception and has proved quite successful in reducing accidents due to errors: anesthesia. Perhaps in part because the effects of serious anesthetic errors are potentially so dramatic—death or brain damage—and perhaps in part because the errors are frequently transparently clear and knowable to all, anesthesiologists have greatly emphasized safety. The success of these efforts has been dramatic. Whereas mortality from anesthesia was one in 10,000 to 20,000 just a decade or so ago, it is now estimated at less than one in 200,000. Anesthesiologists have led the medical profession in recognizing system factors as causes of errors, in designing fail-safe systems, and in training to avoid errors.

Systems Changes to Reduce Hospital Injuries

Can the lessons from cognitive psychology and human factors research that have been successful in accident prevention in aviation and other industries be applied to the practice of hospital medicine? There is every reason to think they could be. Hospitals, physicians, nurses, and pharmacists who wish to reduce errors could start by considering how cognition and error mechanisms apply to the practice of hospital medicine. Specifically, they can examine their care delivery systems in terms of the systems' ability to discover, prevent, and absorb errors and for the presence of psychological precursors.

Discovery of Errors

The first step in error prevention is to define the problem. Efficient, routine identification of errors needs to be part of hospital practice, as does routine investigation of all errors that cause injuries. The emphasis is on "routine." Only when errors are accepted as an inevitable, although manageable, part of everyday practice will it be possible for hospital personnel to shift from a punitive to a creative frame of mind that seeks out and identifies the underlying system failures.

Data collecting and investigatory activities are expensive, but so are the consequences of errors. Evidence from industry indicates that the savings from reduction of errors and accidents more than make up for the costs of data collection and investigation. (While these calculations apply to 'rework' and other operational inefficiencies resulting from errors, additional savings from reduced patient care costs and liability costs for hospitals and physicians could also be substantial.)

Prevention of Errors

Many health care delivery systems could be redesigned to significantly reduce the likelihood of error. Some obvious mechanisms that can be used are as follows:

Reduced Reliance on Memory.—Work should be designed to minimize the requirements for human functions that are known to be particularly fallible, such as short-term memory and vigilance (prolonged attention). Clearly, the components of work must be well delineated and understood before system redesign. Checklists, protocols, and computerized decision aids could be used more widely. For example, physicians should not have to rely on their memories to retrieve a laboratory test result, and nurses should not have to remember the time a medication dose is due. These are tasks that computers do much more reliably than humans.

Improved Information Access.—Creative ways need to be developed for making information more readily available: displaying it where it is needed, when it is needed, and in a form that permits easy access. Computerization of the medical record, for example, would greatly facilitate bedside display of patient information, including tests and medications.

Error Proofing.—Where possible, critical tasks should be structured so that errors cannot be made. The use of "forcing functions" is helpful. For example, if a computerized system is used for medication orders, it can be designed so that a physician cannot enter an order for a lethal overdose of a drug or prescribe a medication to which a patient is known to be allergic.

Standardization.—One of the most effective means of reducing error is standardizing processes wherever possible. The advantages, in efficiency as well as in error reduction, of standardizing drug doses and times of administration are obvious. Is it really acceptable to ask nurses to follow six different "K-scales" (directions for how much potassium to give according to patient serum potassium levels) solely to satisfy different physician prescribing patterns? Other candidates for standardization include information displays, methods for common practices (such as surgical dressings), and the geographic location of equipment and supplies in a patient care unit. There is something bizarre, and really quite inexcusable, about "code" situations in hospitals where house staff and other personnel responding to a cardiac arrest waste precious seconds searching for resuscitation equipment simply because it is kept in a different location on each patient care unit.

Training.—Instruction of physicians, nurses, and pharmacists in procedures or problem solving should include greater emphasis on possible errors and how to prevent them. (Well-written surgical atlases do this.) For example, many interns need more rigorous instruction and supervision than is currently provided when they are learning new procedures. Young physicians need to be taught that safe practice is as important as effective practice. Both physicians and nurses need to learn to think of errors primarily as symptoms of systems failures.

Absorption of Errors

Because it is impossible to prevent all error, buffers should be built into each system so that errors are absorbed before they can cause harm to patients. At minimum, systems should be designed so that errors can be identified in time to be intercepted. The drug delivery systems in most hospitals do this to some degree already. Nurses and pharmacists often identify errors in physician drug orders and prevent improper administration to the patient. As hospitals move to computerized records and ordering systems, more of these types of interceptions can be incorporated into the computer programs. Critical systems (such as life-support equipment and monitors) should be provided in duplicate in those situations in which a mechanical failure could lead to patient injury.

Psychological Precursors

Finally, explicit attention should be given to work schedules, division of responsibilities, task descriptions, and other details of working arrangements where improper managerial decisions can produce psychological precursors such as time pressures and fatigue that create an unsafe environment. While the influence of the stresses of everyday life on human behavior cannot be eliminated, stresses caused by a faulty work environment can be. Elimination of fear and the creation of a supportive working environment are other potent means of preventing errors.

Institutionalization of Safety

Although the idea of a national hospital safety board that would investigate every accident is neither practical nor necessary, at the hospital level such activities should occur. Existing hospital risk management activities could be broadened to include all potentially injurious errors and deepened to seek out underlying system failures. Providing immunity, as in the FAA ASRS system, might be a good first step. At the national level, the Joint Commission on Accreditation of Healthcare Organizations should be involved in discussions regarding the institutionalization of safety. Other specialty societies might well follow the lead of the anesthesiologists in developing safety standards and require their instruction to be part of residency training.

Implementing Systems Changes

Many of the principles described herein fit well within the teachings of total quality management. One of the basic tenets of total quality management, statistical quality control, requires data regarding variation in processes. In a generic sense, errors are but variations in processes. Total quality management also requires a culture in which errors and deviations are regarded not as human failures, but as opportunities to improve the system, "gems," as they are sometimes called. Finally, total quality management calls for grassroots participation to identify and develop system modifications to eliminate the underlying failures.

Like total quality management, systems changes to reduce errors require commitment of the organization's leadership. None of the aforementioned changes will be effective or, for that matter, even possible without support at the highest levels (hospital executives and departmental chiefs) for making safety a major goal of medical practice.

But it is apparent that the most fundamental change that will be needed if hospitals are to make meaningful progress in error reduction is a cultural one. Physicians and nurses need to accept the notion that error is an inevitable accompaniment of the human condition, even among conscientious professionals with high standards. Errors must be accepted as evidence of systems flaws not character flaws. Until and unless that happens, it is unlikely that any substantial progress will be made in reducing medical errors.

TO ERR IS HUMAN: BUILDING A SAFER HEALTH SYSTEM

Committee on Quality of Health Care In America
Institute of Medicine, 1999.
www.nap.edu/readingroom

Executive Summary

The knowledgeable health reporter for the Boston Globe, Betsy Lehman, died from an overdose during chemotherapy. Willie King had the wrong leg amputated. Ben Kolb was eight years old when he died during "minor" surgery due to a drug mix-up.

These horrific cases that make the headlines are just the tip of the iceberg. Two large studies, one conducted in Colorado and Utah and the other in New York, found that adverse events occurred in 2.9 and 3.7 percent of hospitalizations, respectively. In Colorado and Utah hospitals, 8.8 percent of adverse events led to death, as compared with 13.6 percent in New York hospitals. In both of these studies, over half of these adverse events resulted from medical errors and could have been prevented.

When extrapolated to the over 33.6 million admissions to U.S. hospitals in 1997, the results of the study in Colorado and Utah imply that at least 44,000 Americans die each year as a result of medical errors. The results of the New York Study suggest the number may be as high as 98,000. Even when using the lower estimate, deaths due to medical errors exceed the number attributable to the 8th leading cause of death. More people die in a given year as result of medical errors than from motor vehicle accidents (43,458), breast cancer (42,297), or AIDS (16,516).

Total national costs (lost income, lost household production, disability and health care costs) of preventable adverse events (medical errors resulting in injury) are estimated to be between $17 billion and $29 billion, of which health care costs represent over one half.

In terms of lives lost, patient safety is as important an issue as worker safety. Every year, over 6,000 Americans die from workplace injuries. Medication errors alone, occurring either in or out of the hospital, are estimated to account for over 7,000 deaths annually.

Medication-related errors occur frequently in hospitals and although not all result in actual harm, those that do, are costly. One recent study conducted at two prestigious teaching hospitals, found that about two out of every 100 admissions experienced a preventable adverse drug event, resulting in average increased hospital costs of $4,700 per admission or about $2.8 million annually for a 700 bed teach hospital. If these findings are generalizable, the increased hospital costs alone of preventable adverse drug events affecting inpatients are about $2 billion for the nation as a whole.

These figures offer only a very modest estimate of the magnitude of the problem since hospital patients represent only a small proportion of the total population at risk, and direct hospital costs are only a fraction of total costs. More care and increasingly complex care is provided in ambulatory settings. Outpatient surgical centers, physical offices and clinics serve thousands of patients daily. Home care requires patients and their families to use complicated equipment and perform follow-up care. Retail pharmacies play a major role in filling prescriptions for patients and educating them about their use. Other institutional settings, such as nursing homes, provide a broad array of services to vulnerable populations. Although many of the available studies have focus on the hospital setting, medical errors present a problem in any setting, not just hospitals.

Errors are also costly in terms of opportunity costs. Dollars spent on having to repeat diagnostic tests or counteract adverse drug events are dollars unavailable for other purposes. Purchasers and patients pay for errors when insurance costs and copayments are inflated by services that would not have been necessary had proper care been provided. It is impossible for the nation to achieve the greatest value possible from the hundreds of millions of dollars pent on medical care if the care contains errors.

But not all the costs can be directly measured. Errors are also costly in terms of loss of trust in the system by patients and diminished satisfaction by both patients and health professionals. Patients who experienced a longer hospital stay or disability as a result of errors pay with physical and psychological discomfort. Health care professionals pay with loss of morale and frustration at not being able to provide the best care possible. Employers and society, in general, pay in terms of lost worker productivity, reduced school attendance by children, and lower levels of population health status.

Yet silence surrounds this issue. For the most part, consumers believe they are protected. Media coverage has been limited to reporting of anecdotal cases. Licensure and accreditation confer, in the eyes of the public, a "Good Housekeeping Seal of Approval." Yet, licensing and accreditation processes have focused only limited attention on the issue, and even these minimal efforts have confronted some resistance from health care organizations and providers. Providers are perceive the medical liability systems as a serious impediment to systematic efforts to uncover and learn from errors.

The decentralized and fragmented nature of the health care delivery system (some would say "nonsystem") also contributes to unsafe conditions for patients, and serves as an impediment to efforts to improve safety. Even within hospitals and large medical groups, there are rigidly-defined areas of specialization and influence. For example, when patients see multiple providers in different settings, none of whom have access to complete information, it is easier for something to go wrong than when care is better coordinated. At the same time, the provision of care to patients by a collection of loosely affiliated organizations and providers makes it difficult to implement improved clinical information systems capable of providing timely access to complete patient information. Unsafe care is one of the prices we pay for not having organized systems of care with clear lines of accountability.

Lastly, the context in which health care is purchased further exacerbates these problems. Group purchasers have made few demands for improvements in safety. Most third party payment systems provide little incentive for a health care organization to improve safety, not do they recognize and reward safety or quality.

The goal of this report is to break this cycle of inaction. The status quo is not acceptable and cannot be tolerated any longer. Despite the cost pressures, liability constraints, resistance to change and other seemingly insurmountable barriers, it is simply not acceptable for patients to be harmed by the same health care system that is supposed to offer healing and comfort. "First do not harm" is an often quoted term from Hippocrates. Everyone working in health care is familiar with the term. At a very minimum, the health system needs to offer that assurance and security to the public.

A comprehensive approach to improving patient safety is needed. This approach cannot focus on a single solution since there is no "magic bullet" that will solve this problem, and indeed, no single recommendation in this report should be considered as *the* answer. Rather, large, complex problems require thoughtful, multifaceted responses, The combined goal of the recommendations is for the external environment to create sufficient pressure to make errors costly to health care organizations and providers, so they are compelled to take action to improve safety. At the same time, there is a need to enhance knowledge and tools to improve safety and break down legal and cultural barriers that impede safety improvement. Given current knowledge about the magnitude of the problem, the committee believes it would be irresponsible to expect anything less than a 50 percent reduction in errors over five years.

In this report, safety is defined as freedom from accidental injury. This definition recognizes that this is the primary safety goal from the patient's perspective. Error is defined as the failure of a planned action to be completed as intended or the use of a wrong plan to achieve an aim. According to noted expert James Reason, errors depend on two kinds of failures: either the correct action does not proceed as intended (an error of execution) or the original intended action is not correct, (an error of planning). Errors can happen in all stages in the process of care, from diagnosis, to treatment, to preventive care.

Not all errors result in harm. Errors that do result in injury are sometimes called preventable adverse events. An adverse event is an injury resulting from a medical intervention, or in other words, it is not due to the underlying condition of the patient. While all adverse events result from medical management, not all are preventable (i.e., not all are attributable to errors). For example, if a patient has surgery and dies from pneumonia he or she got postoperatively, it is an adverse event. If analysis of the case reveals that the patient got pneumonia because of poor hand washing or instrument cleaning techniques by staff, the adverse event was preventable (attributable to an error of execution). But the analysis may conclude that no error occurred and the patient would be presumed to have had a difficult surgery and recovery (not a preventable adverse event).

Much can be learned from the analysis of errors. All adverse events resulting in serious injury or death should be evaluated to assess whether improvements in the delivery system can be made to reduce the likelihood of similar events occurring in the future. Errors that do not result in harm also represent an important opportunity to identify system improvements having the potential to prevent adverse events.

Preventing errors means designing the health care system at all levels to make it safer. Building safety into processes of care is a more effective way to reduce errors than blaming individuals (some experts, such as Deming, believe improving processes is the *only* way to improve quality). The focus must shift from blaming individuals for past errors to a focus on preventing future errors by designing safety into the system. This does not mean that individuals can be careless. People must still be vigilant and held responsible for their actions. But when an error occurs, blaming an individual does little to make the system safer and prevent someone else from committing the same error.

Health care is a decade or more behind other high-risk industries in its attention to ensuring basic safety. Aviation has focused extensively on building safe systems and has been doing so since World War II. Between 1990 and 1994, the U.S. airline fatality rate was less than one-third the rate experienced in mid century. In 1998, there were no deaths in the United States in commercial aviation. In health care, preventable injuries from care have been estimated to affect between three to four percent of hospital patients. Although health care may never achieve aviation's impressive record, there is clearly room for improvement.

To err is human, but errors can be prevented. Safety is a critical first step in improving quality of care. The Harvard Medical Practice Study, a seminal research study on this issue, was published almost ten years ago; other studies have corroborated its findings. Yet few tangible actions to improve patient safety can be found. Must we wait another decade to be safe in our health system?

RECOMMENDATIONS

The IOM Quality of Health Care in America Committee was formed in June 1998 to develop a strategy that will result in a threshold improvement in quality over the next ten years. This report addresses issues related to patient safety, a subset of overall quality-related concerns, and lays out a national agenda for reducing errors in health care and improving patient safety. Although it is a national agenda, many activities are aimed at prompting responses at the state and local levels and within health care organizations and professional groups.

The committee believes that although there is still much to learn about the types of errors committed in health care and why they occur, enough is known today to recognize that a serious concern exists for patients. Whether a person is sick or just trying to stay healthy, they should not have to worry about being harmed by the health system itself. This report is a call to action to make health care safer for patients.

The committee believes that a major force for improving patient safety is the intrinsic motivation of health care providers, shaped by professional ethics, norms and expectations. But the interaction between factors in the external environment and factors inside health care organizations can also prompt the changes needed to improve patient safety. Factors in the external environment include availability of knowledge and tools to improve safety, strong and visible professional leadership, legislative and regulatory initiatives, and actions of purchasers and consumers to demand safety improvements. Factors inside health care organizations include strong leadership for safety, an organizational culture that encourages recognition and learning from errors, and an effective patient safety program.

* * *

The recommendations contained in this report lay out a four-tiered approach:

• establishing a national focus to create leadership, research, tools and protocols to enhance the knowledge based about safety;

• identifying and learning from errors through the immediate and strong mandatory reporting efforts, as well as the encouragement of voluntary efforts, both with the aim of making sure the system continues to be made safer for patients;

• raising standards and expectations for improvements in safety through the actions of oversight organizations, group purchasers, and professional groups; and

• creating safety systems inside health care organizations through the implementation of safe practices at the delivery level. This level is the ultimate target of all the recommendations.

LEADERSHIP AND KNOWLEDGE

Other industries that have been successful in improving safety, such as aviation and occupational health, have had the support of a designated agency that sets and communicates priorities, monitors progress in achieving goals, directs resources toward areas of need, and brings visibility to important issues. Although various agencies and organizations in health care may contribute to certain of these activities, there is no focal point for raising and sustaining attention to patient safety. Without it, health care is unlikely to match the safety improvements achieved in other industries.

* * *

RECOMMENDATION 4.1 Congress should create a Center for Patient Safety within the Agency for Health Care Policy and Research. This center should

• set the national goals for patient safety, track progress in meeting these goals, and issue an annual report to the President and Congress on patient safety; and

• **develop knowledge and understanding of errors in health care by developing a research agenda, funding Centers of Excellence, evaluating methods for identifying and preventing errors, and funding dissemination and communication activities to improve patient safety.**

IDENTIFYING AND LEARNING FROM ERRORS

Another critical component of a comprehensive strategy to improve patient safety is to create an environment that encourages organizations to identify errors, evaluate causes and take appropriate actions to improve performance in the future. External reporting systems represent one mechanism to enhance our understanding of errors and the underlying factors that contribute to them.

Reporting systems can be designed to meet two purposes. They can be designed as part of a public system for holding health care organizations accountable for performance. In this instance, reporting is often mandatory, usually focuses on specific cases that involve serious harm or death, may result in fines or penalties relative to the specific case, and information about the event may become known to the public. Such systems ensure a response to specific reports of serious injury, hold organizations and providers accountable for maintaining safety, respond to the public's right to know, and provide incentives to health care organizations to implement internal safety systems that reduce the likelihood of such events occurring. Currently, at least twenty states have mandatory adverse event reporting systems.

Voluntary, confidential reporting systems can also be part of an overall program for improving patient safety and can be designed to complement the mandatory reporting systems previously described. Voluntary reporting systems, which generally focus on a much broader set of errors and strive to detect system weaknesses before the occurrence of serious harm, can provide rich information to health care organizations in support of their quality improvement efforts.

For either purpose, the goal of reporting systems is to analyze the information they gather and identify ways to prevent future errors from occurring. The goal is *not* data collection. Collecting reports and not doing anything with the information serves no useful purpose. Adequate resources and other support must be provided for analysis and response to critical issues.

RECOMMENDATION 5.1 A nationwide mandatory reporting system should be established that provides for the collection of standardized information by state governments about adverse events that result in death or serious harm. Reporting should initially be required of hospitals and eventually be required of other institutional and ambulatory care delivery settings. Congress should

• **designate the forum for Health Care Quality Measurement and Reporting as the entity responsible for promulgating and maintaining a core set of reporting standards to be used by states, including a nomenclature and taxonomy for reporting;**

● require all health care organizations to report standardized information on a defined list of adverse events;

● provide funds and technical expertise for state governments to establish or adapt their current error reporting systems to collect the standardized information, analyze it and conduct follow-up action as needed with health care organizations. Should a state choose not to implement the mandatory reporting system, the Department of Health and Human Services should be designated as the responsible entity; and

● designate the Center for Patient Safety to:

(1) convene states to share information and expertise, and to evaluate alternative approaches taken for implementing reporting programs, identify best practices for implementation, and assess the impact of state programs; and

(2) receive and analyze aggregate reports from States to identify persistent safety issues that require more intensive analysis and/or a broader-based response (e.g., designing prototype systems or requesting a response by agencies, manufacturers or others).

RECOMMENDATION 5.2 The development of voluntary reporting efforts should be encouraged. The Center for Patient Safety should

● describe and disseminate information on external voluntary reporting programs to encourage greater participation in them and track the development of new reporting systems as they form;

● convene sponsors and users of external reporting systems to evaluate what works and what does not work well in the programs, and ways to make them more effective;

● periodically assess whether additional efforts are needed to address taps in information to improve patient safety and to encourage health care organizations to participate in voluntary reporting programs; and

● fund and evaluate pilot projects for reporting systems, both within individual health care organizations and collaborative efforts among health care organizations.

The committee believes there is a role both for mandatory, public reporting systems and voluntary, confidential reporting systems. However, because of their distinct purposes, such systems should be operated and maintained separately. A nationwide mandatory reporting system should be established by building upon the current patchwork of state systems and by standardizing the types of adverse events and information to be reported. The newly established Forum for Health Care Quality Measurement and Reporting, a public/private partnership, should be charged with the establishment of such standards. Voluntary reporting systems should also be promoted and the participation of health care organizations in them should be encouraged by accrediting bodies.

RECOMMENDATION 6.1 Congress should pass legislation to extend peer review protections to data related to patient safety and quality improvement that are collected and analyzed by health care organizations for internal use or shared with others solely for purposes of improving safety and quality.

The committee believes that information about the most serious adverse events which result in harm to patients and which are subsequently found to result from errors should not be protected from public disclosure. However, the committee also recognizes that for events not falling under this category, fears about the legal discover ability of information may undercut motivations to detect and analyze errors to improve safety. Unless such data are assured protection, information about errors will continue to be hidden and errors will be repeated. A more conducive environment is needed to encourage health care professionals and organizations to identify, analyze, and report errors without threat of litigation and without compromising patients' legal rights.

SETTING PERFORMANCE STANDARDS AND EXPECTATIONS FOR SAFETY

Setting and enforcing explicit standards for safety through regulatory and related mechanisms, such as licensing, certification, and accreditation, can define minimum performance levels for health care organizations and professionals. Additionally, the process of developing and adopting standards helps to form expectations for safety among providers and consumers. However, standards and expectations are not only set through regulations. The actions of purchasers and consumers affect the behaviors of health care organizations, and the values and norms set by health professions influence standards of practice, training and education for providers. Standards for patient safety can be applied to health care professionals, the organizations in which they work, and the tools (drugs and devices) they use to care for patients.

RECOMMENDATION 7.1 Performance standards and expectations for health care organizations should focus greater attention on patient safety.

• Regulators and accreditors should require health care organizations to implement meaningful patient safety programs with defined executive responsibility.

• Public private purchasers should provide incentives to health care organizations to demonstrate continuous improvement in patient safety.

Health care organizations are currently subject to compliance with licensing and accreditation standards. Although both devote some attention to issues related to patient safety, there is opportunity to strengthen such efforts. Regulators and accreditors have a role in encouraging and supporting actions in health care organizations by holding them accountable for ensuring a safe environment for patients. After a reasonable period of time for health care organizations to develop patient safety programs, regulators and accreditors should require them as a minimum standard.

Purchaser and consumer demands also exert influence on health care organizations. Public and private purchasers should consider safety issues in their contracting decisions and reinforce the importance of patient safety by providing relevant information to their employees or beneficiaries. Purchasers should also communicate concerns about patient safety to accrediting bodies to support stronger oversight for patient safety.

RECOMMENDATION 7.2 Performance standards and expectations for health professionals should focus greater attention on patient safety.

- **Health professional licensing bodies should**

(1) implement periodic re-examinations and re-licensing of doctors, nurses, and other key providers, based on both competence and knowledge of safety practices, and

(2) work with certifying and credentialing organizations to develop more effective methods to identify unsafe providers and take action.

- **Professional societies should make a visible commitment to patient safety by establishing a permanent committee dedicated to safety improvement. This committee should**

(1) develop a curriculum on patient safety and encourage its adoption into training and certification requirements;

(2) disseminate information on patient safety to members through special sessions at annual conferences, journal articles and editorials, newsletters, publications and websites on a regular basis;

(3) recognize patient safety considerations in practice guidelines and in standards related to the introduction and diffusion of new technologies, therapies and drugs;

(4) work with the Center for Patient Safety to develop community-based, collaborative initiatives for error reporting and analysis and implementation of patient safety improvements; and

(5) collaborate with other professional societies and disciplines in a national summit on the professional's role in patient safety.

Although unsafe practitioners are believed to be few in number, the rapid identification of such practitioners and corrective action are important to a comprehensive safety program. Responsibilities for documenting continuing skills are dispersed among licensing boards, specialty boards and professional groups, and health care organizations with little communication or coordination. In their ongoing assessments, existing licensing, certification and accreditation processes for health professionals should place greater attention on safety and performance skills.

Additionally, professional societies and groups should become active leaders in encouraging and demanding improvements inpatient safety. Setting standards, convening and communicating with members about safety, incorporating attention to patient safety into training programs and collaborating across disciplines are all mechanisms that will contribute to creating a culture of safety.

RECOMMENDATION 7.3 The Food and Drug Administration (FDA) should increase attention to the safe use of drugs in both pre-and post-marketing processes through the following actions:

● **develop and enforce standards for the design of drug packaging and labeling that will maximize safety I use;**

● **require pharmaceutical companies to test (using FDA-approved methods) proposed drug names to identify and remedy potential sound-alike and look-alike confusion with existing drug names; and**

● **work with physicians, pharmacists, consumers, and others to establish appropriate responses to problems identified through post-marketing surveillance, especially for concerns that are perceived to require immediate response to protect the safety of patients.**

The FDA's role is to regulate manufacturers for the safety and effectiveness of their drugs and devices. However, even approved products can present safety problems in practice. For example, different drugs with similar sounding names can create confusion for both patients and providers. Attention to the safety of products in actual use should be increased during approval processes and in post-marketing monitoring systems. The FDA should also work with drug manufacturers, distributors, pharmacy benefit managers, health plans and other organizations to assist clinicians in identifying and preventing problems in the use of drugs.

IMPLEMENTING SAFETY SYSTEMS IN HEALTH CARE ORGANIZATIONS

Experience in other high-risk industries has provided well-understood illustrations that can be used to improve health care safety. However, health care management and professionals have rarely provided specific, clear, high-level, organization-wide incentives to apply what has been learned in other industries about ways to prevent error and reduce harm within their own organizations. Chief Executive Officers and Boards of Trustees should be held accountable for making a serious, visible and on-going commitment to creating safe systems of care.

RECOMMENDATION 8.1 Health care organizations and the professionals affiliated with them should make continually improved patient safety a declared and serious aim by establishing patient safety programs with defined executive responsibility. Patient safety programs should

● **provide strong, clear and visible attention to safety;**

● **implement non-punitive systems for reporting and analyzing errors within their organizations;**

● **incorporate well-understood safety principles, such as, standardizing and simplifying equipment, supplies and processes; and**

● **establish interdisciplinary team training programs for providers that incorporate proven methods of team training, such as simulation.**

Health care organizations must develop a culture of safety such that an organization's care processes and workforce are focused on improving the reliability and safety of care for patients. Safety should be an explicit organizational goal that is demonstrated by the strong direction and involvement of governance, management and clinical leadership. In addition, a meaningful patient safety program should include defined program objectives, personnel, and budget and should be monitored by regular progress reports to governance.

RECOMMENDATION 8.2 Health care organizations should implement proven medication safety practices.

A number of practices have been shown to reduce errors in the medication process. Several professional and collaborative organizations interested in patient safety have developed and published recommendations for safe medication practices, especially for hospitals. Although some of these recommendations have been implemented, none have been universally adopted and some are not yet implemented in a majority of hospitals. Safe medication practices should be implemented in all hospitals and health care organizations in which they are appropriate.

* * *

Notes and Questions

1.   What are the implications of a focus on system errors? Does the physician as virtuous disappear from the model of the health care system as we move toward a model of organizations that deliver care, rather than physicians that treat patients? Are we better off acknowledging the inevitability of the changes that Leape, Jost, and Enthoven describe? See Barry R. Furrow, Incentivizing Medical Practice: What (If Anything) Happens to Professionalism? 1 Widener Law Symp. J. 1, 9–10 (1996); contra, see David M. Frankford, Managing Medical Clinician's Work Through the Use of Financial Incentives, 29 Wake Forest L. Rev. 71, 96 (1994) An excellent discussion of current issues of health care quality improvement can be found in Volume 76 of The Milbank Quarterly (No.4 1998), entitled Improving the Quality of Health Care. See also Larry I. Palmer, Patient Safety, Risk Reduction, and the Law, 36 Houston L.Rev. 1609(1999).

2.   If we focus on system errors and system excellence, what happens to the traditional tort suit that starts with physician error? If errors are preventable by attention to the overall organization, then physicians should no longer be viewed as at "fault" when a patient is injured. What about medical licensing? The merits of discipline for physician errors should be reconsidered, if most errors are due to failures of an organization to provide resources, support, or other structures. What about differential pay for physicians in different practice areas? As health care is integrated and outcomes used to evaluate the overall benefits to a population of patients, why should we pay differentials that reflect the older model of the physician as craftsperson or artist? Perhaps this new model suggests a salary approach to compensation, with bonuses at best for compliance with institutional norms.

3.   The issue of mandatory versus voluntary reporting has loomed large for health care providers, afraid that disclosure of an error will come to plaintiff lawyers' attention. Recommendation 5.1 of the Institute of Medicine report calls for mandatory reporting by hospitals and other institutions of adverse events that lead to death or serious bodily harm .. Critics worry that

this may drive honest disclosure even further underground, deterring providers from revealing errors. The only study to date of error reporting systems found that there was little difference between systems that provided confidentiality and those that did not. Underreporting occurred in both systems at about the same levels. See National Academy for State Health Policy, Medical Errors and Adverse Events: A Report of a 50–State Survey. *www.nashp.org.*

3.   As described previously, total quality management and continuous quality improvement are important methods for fostering quality in health care institutions. Other more traditional methods of quality control include the quality assurance systems that exist within hospitals and other health care institutions. Most hospitals employ two distinct but closely related systems to oversee the quality of care: risk management and quality assurance. The goals of an effective risk management program are to eliminate the causes of loss experienced by the hospital and its patients, employees, and visitors; lessen the operational and financial effects of unavoidable losses; and cover inevitable losses at the lowest cost. As such, risk management is concerned not only with the quality of patient care delivered by a hospital but also with the safety and security of the hospital's employees, visitors, and property. The risk manager also administers claims against the hospital if injuries occur and oversees the hospital's insurance programs, determining which risks the hospital ought to insure against and which it ought to retain through self-insurance or high deductibles. Finally, the risk manager must be concerned with public and patient relations, as dissatisfied patients are more likely to sue for medical errors.

4.   The most important tool of the risk manager is the incident report. Hospitals require incident reports on occurrences not consistent with routine patient care or hospital operation that have resulted or could have resulted in hospital liability or patient dissatisfaction. Examples include sudden deaths, falls, drug errors or reactions, injuries due to faulty equipment, threats of legal action, and unexplained requests from attorneys for medical records. The filing of incident reports (usually prepared by nurses) is the responsibility of department heads or supervisors. Incident reports are directed to the hospital risk manager, who investigates them as necessary. The risk manager also informs appropriate administrative and medical staff about the incident. By compiling data from incident reports, the risk manager can identify problem areas within the hospital and thus help prevent errors and injuries. Incident reports also assist in claims management, permitting the hospital to avoid costly lawsuits by quickly coming to terms with injured patients where liability seems clear and facilitating early coordination with an attorney to plan a defense where litigation seems unavoidable. Some malpractice insurance contracts include reservation of rights clauses, which permit the insurer to refuse to pay claims based on unreported incidents, underscoring the importance of incident reports.

5.   Hospital quality assurance programs are directly concerned with assessing and improving patient care. Quality assurance focuses more narrowly on patient care than does risk management. It is broader than risk management, however, in that it considers a wide range of quality concerns, not just discrete mishaps. Incident reports play a major role in quality assurance, as they permit the hospital to identify serious quality deficiencies. The most significant tools of hospital quality assurance, however, are the hospital committees that oversee the quality of various hospital functions. These committees carry out functions mandated by JCAHO accreditation standards, and are in some states required by state law or regulation. See West's Ann.Cal.Admin.Code tit. 22, § 70703(e); N.Y.—McKinney's Pub.Health Law § 2805–j. Common hospital committees include a tissue commit-

tee, which oversees the quality and necessity of surgery; an infections committee, which evaluates patients' infections and oversees the disposal of infectious material and the use of antibiotics; a pharmacy and therapeutics committee, which monitors the use and handling of drugs; a medical records committee, which assures the quality and completeness of medical records; a utilization review committee, which assures that patients are not admitted inappropriately or hospitalized too long; and medical audit committees, which review the quality of care provided in the hospital as a whole or in certain departments. Some hospitals also have an overall quality control committee, which coordinates quality assurance efforts throughout the hospital. Two other very important committees are the executive and credentials committees. The former serves as the cabinet of the medical staff, and in this capacity oversees all efforts of the medical staff to ensure quality. The credentials committee passes on applications for medical staff appointments and reappointments, and establishes and reviews physician clinical privileges; i.e., it determines which doctors can practice in the hospital and what procedures they may perform. As such, it has a vital role in assuring the quality of care provided by the hospital.

Some committees, such as the credentials or executive committee, are medical staff committees; i.e., they are composed of and answerable to physicians who practice in the hospital. Others, such as the quality assurance or infections control committees, are likely to be hospital committees, answerable to the hospital administration and including other professionals besides physicians. In many hospitals, committees play an active role in assuring the quality of care; in others, they exist primarily to meet accreditation requirements and do little.

6. Risk management is outcome oriented—it operates primarily by reacting to bad outcomes. Quality assurance is more process oriented. Some quality assurance activities involve concurrent review of the care process, such as the proctoring of doctors with probationary staff privileges. Quality assurance may also include retrospective review of care, another form of process review. Risk management is a managerial function, while quality assurance is predominantly a clinical function.

7. The new JCAHO Sentinel Event Policy has adopted the view of medical errors of the Institute of Medicine report, To Err is Human. It defines a sentinel event as "an unexpected occurrence involving death or severe physical or psychological injury, or the risk thereof", including unanticipated death or major loss of functioning unrelated to the patient's condition; patient suicide; wrong-side surgery; infant abduction/discharge to the wrong family; rape; and hemolytic transfusion reactions. JCAHO , "Sentinel Event Policy and Procedures", online at *www.jcaho.org* (15 January, 2001).

Problem: ManageCare

You are the advisor to the Chief Executive Officer of U.S. ManageCare, a large managed care organization that is expanding through the country. The CEO, a physician, wants to set the standard for other organizations by providing the highest level of quality care for ManageCare subscribers at the lowest cost in the marketplace. He wants you to create a model for care that will reduce errors that occur in ManageCare affiliated hospitals, physician practices, and specialty care groups. What questions will you ask? What additional information do you need? What methods or devices might you use to improve care at all levels? Consider how a reporting system could be designed, the merits of voluntary versus mandatory reporting of adverse events, and how such a reporting system can be enforced. Examine the JCAHO Sentinel Events Policy for ideas that might be applicable to managed care.

IV. DISTRIBUTIVE JUSTICE AND THE ALLOCATION OF HEALTH CARE RESOURCES —THE EXAMPLE OF HUMAN ORGAN TRANSPLANTATION

A. INTRODUCTION

Despite the debate over whether a workable concept of "necessary" health care can be developed and the acknowledged fact that more health care is sometimes worse than less health care, our society still struggles over the basic principles that underlie the uneven distribution of and unequal access to health care services in the U.S. We do not find similar debates over other goods and do not often ask whether the distribution of automobiles or abflexers or lack of access to Caribbean cruises is "just."

Some argue that health care has a special status because it is the sine qua non of life as a human being. Without some measure of health, without "normal species functioning," in the words of philosopher Norman Daniels, meaningful life is simply impossible. We cannot speak of giving people the opportunity to participate in life in our society without, at the least, some minimal level of health. Further, we cannot expect citizens to meet their civic duties unless we assure them of the health to do so. Others argue that the need for health care is different from the need for other goods or services because the need is unfairly distributed throughout the society—essentially, people who take this position argue that those who are sick have been dealt a bad hand in life, and adequate health care levels the playing field for the sick in relation to the healthy. Further, some argue, we all benefit by the general good health of the rest of society, so we should be willing to commit our social resources to attain this end. The rest of us will be less subject to disease if others are healthy, and our economy will generate more for all of us if the work force is healthy. Finally, some argue that we have a moral duty to address the suffering that is caused to our fellow man by ill health. This last argument may be restated: we are offended to see pervasive illness in our society, and our sensibilities are best served by assuring that everyone has adequate health care.

Libertarians accuse those who seek to redistribute health resources of unjustified paternalism. People can make their own choices about whether to spend their money on medical treatment, pharmaceuticals, travel, or fast cars. What we are really trying to do, they may argue, is just redistribute wealth. If that is the goal, we ought to give the poor additional resources and let them spend those resources as they feel will best allow them to fully participate in society. Some may spend it on health care, to be sure, but others may reasonably decide that it ought to be spent on education, clothing, or other goods and services in which there is a tremendous disparity among members of our society. There is a very helpful account of the reasons that health care might be different from other kinds of goods and services, and a response to each of those arguments, in Einer Elhauge, Allocating Health Care Morally, 82 Cal. L. Rev. 1452 (1994). One of the earliest and most oft-cited theories regarding the application of the principle of distributive justice to health care resources is found in Norman Daniels, Just Health Care (1985). See also Normal Daniels et al., Is Equality Bad for Our Health? (2000). For a general introduction to this issue, see Tom Beauchamp and James Childress, Principles of Medical Ethics 326–394 (4th ed. 1994).

There is a wide range of approaches to distributive justice that might be applied to health care (and to anything else of which there is a scarce supply). One approach, the libertarian market approach, would accept the current distribution of resources as a general matter, and allow for a change only if willing participants in the market were to trade for one. Under this approach, anyone who wants more health care or more health insurance than that person has now should be able to buy it from any willing seller, but the government should not redistribute resources from those who now have those resources to those who do not have them. Such a redistribution would constitute an unjust taking of resources from those who have earned them to those who have been unwilling or unable to be productive or have chosen to spend their resources for other purposes.

In contrast, theories of distributive justice, when applied to health care, do permit or require some redistribution of resources. An egalitarian and communitarian theorist, at the other extreme from the libertarian marketeers, might argue that justice requires equality and that all members of society should be provided with the same health care. This theory, whatever merits it might have in providing for the distribution of housing or clothing, for example, does not make much sense when applied to the distribution of health care because individuals' needs vary so substantially from one to another across the society. Those who take the communitarian approach are more likely to distribute health care so that each person has access to the same range of health care resources whenever those resources are required. Many national health care systems outside of the United States are based, at least in part, on this "equal opportunity" theory.

There are a number of approaches to distributive justice that fall in between the pure market theory of the libertarians and the pure equality models of the egalitarians and communitarians. Virtually all of these approaches depend upon the identification of a package of basic services that would be made available to every person within the society. In addition, under most of these theories, individuals could purchase more health care (directly or through insurance) if they wished to do so and could afford it. The health resources included in such a package of basic services could be defined as a "minimum package," that is, the resources required by those in the society with the least health care needs. Alternatively, every person could be provided a "generally adequate package," which would include the resources required by most people in society. Each person could also be provided something greater than that—perhaps a package sufficient to provide for the health care needs of nearly all members of society.

The socially guaranteed package of health care services could also vary from group to group within society. In the United States, children, the elderly, those with end stage renal disease, and pregnant women are entitled, as a general matter, to more socially guaranteed services than are most others. Further, a plan which provides a package of basic services could also provide that some people deemed less worthy by the society—those who put their health at risk through their own conduct, for example, or those who are not employed—would be entitled to fewer services than those deemed worthy by the society.

Of course, it is not so easy to decide what, exactly, ought to be in the package of basic services, or even how that package should be defined. Should it be defined in terms of particular goods and health care services, in terms of prospective patient desires, in terms of needs defined by primary care physicians, or in some other way? Some kinds of services—for example, mental health services or infertility services—are deemed to be necessary by some people and to be inessential luxuries by others. The development of such a package of basic health care services that is available to every person has been fundamental to most efforts at systematic health care reform in the United States over the past several years; the difficulty in defining such a package may be one reason such reform has failed.

Injustice in the distribution of health care resources may manifest itself in many different ways. While some are concerned by any differential access to health resources, many people are especially concerned by what appear to be particularly invidious distinctions based on race and gender in the distribution of those resources. There is little question that African Americans have less access to many kinds of health care than do Whites, even after adjusting for differences in income. Similarly, the poor, people in rural areas, women, and other minorities may be provided with less access to health care—especially high tech and expensive health care—than their richer, urban, male nonminority counterparts. A series of studies showing substantial differences in access to some kinds of health care by race are noted in N. Krieger and S. Sidney, Racial Discrimination and Blood Pressure: The CARDIA Study of Young Black and White Adults, 86 Am. J. Pub. Health 1370 (1996). See also Vernellia Randall, Health Care Reform: Does Clinton Health Care Reform Ensure Equality of Health Care for Ethnic Americans and the Poor?, 60 Brooklyn L. Rev. 167 (1994) and Hilde Lindemann Nelson and James Lindemann Nelson, Justice in the Allocation of Health Care Resources: A Feminist Account, in Susan Wolf, ed., Feminism and Bioethics 351 (1996) and David Barton Smith, Health Care Divided: Race and Healing a Nation (1999).

Do you think that there is some reason to distribute health care through a mechanism other than the market? What theory of distributive justice would you apply to the distribution of health care resources? How would you address the evidence that suggests that the poor, members of racial minorities, women, and people in rural areas have less access to health care than do others? Ultimately, is there any way to determine whether a particular health care distribution is fair, or, for that matter, whether a health care system is a fair or just system? What is the baseline for making such determinations? Is it possible, for example, to apply universal standards of fairness to the many different and diverse communities in the United States, or to the wide range of societies across the globe? Consider this attempt, on behalf of the World Health Organization, to establish benchmarks to determine the fairness of health care systems. Although prepared for use with developing nations' health care systems, it is based on benchmarks applied in evaluating health care reform in the United States. Have Professor Daniels and his colleagues identified the proper benchmarks? Are there others you would add?

NORMAN DANIELS ET AL., BENCHMARKS OF FAIRNESS FOR HEALTH CARE REFORM: A POLICY TOOL FOR DEVELOPING COUNTRIES

78 Bull. World Health Org. 740 (2000).

A new tool for policy analysis

We report here on progress towards developing the benchmarks of fairness into a policy tool that will be useful in developing countries for analyzing the overall fairness of health care reforms. Fairness is a many-sided concept, broader than the concept of equity. Fairness includes equity in health outcomes, in access to all forms of care and in financing. Fairness also includes efficiency in management and allocation, since when resources are constrained their inefficient use means that some needs will not be met that could have been. For the public to have influence over health care, fairness must also include accountability. Finally, fairness also includes appropriate forms of patient and provider autonomy. . . .

When originally developed and presented in the United States, the benchmarks had an ethical rationale that appealed to a theory of justice and health care. The central thought is that disease and disability reduce the opportunities open to individuals, and that the principle of equal opportunity provides a basis for regulating a health care system. The same theory can also be extended to look beyond the point of delivery of health care to the social determinants of health.

* * *

History of the Benchmark approach

The original "benchmarks of fairness" were developed to assess and promote discussion about comprehensive medical insurance reforms proposed in the United States in the first Clinton Administration. These benchmarks focussed heavily on the needs in reforming a technologically advanced but, inefficient and inequitable system that lacked universal coverage. Despite this specific focus, the original benchmarks addressed basic questions that must be asked about *any* reform:

- Does it reduce barriers to public health measures and medical services?
- Does it provide health care services appropriate to the needs of the population?
- Does it distribute the burdens of paying for health protection fairly?
- Does the reform promote clinical and administrative efficiency?
- Does it make institutions publicly accountable for their decisions?
- How does it affect the choices people can exercise?

* * *

Benchmark 1: Intersectorial public health. The rationale for this benchmark [that looks at the way education, housing, public works and other programs affect health care] is that social determinants and other risk factors "upstream" from the point of health care delivery affect population health.

* * *

Benchmark 2: Financial barriers to equitable access. Fairness requires reducing financial and nonfinancial barriers to access to needed services. Benchmark 2 recognizes the large "informal," nontaxable employment sector in many developing countries, often including 60 to 90% of the population. Since workers and their families in the informal sector generally include the poorest part of the population, services must be provided in full or in large part through general tax revenues. The larger the informal sector, the larger the need for public financing, but the smaller the tax base to meet it.

* * *

Benchmark 3: Nonfinancial barriers to access.

* * *

Benchmark 4: Comprehensiveness of benefits and tiering. The underlying rationale is that all people, regardless of class or ethnicity or gender, have comparable health needs and there are similar social obligations to meet these. Inequalities in the coverage and quality of care ("tiering") reduce the fairness of systems. Some kinds of tiering are worse than others. It is less serious if a small, but wealthy group does better than others, provided the others do well (e.g., private-sector insurance in the United Kingdom) than if a poor group is worse off than the rest of society (e.g. failing to insure the working poor in the United States, or failing to deliver a minimal benefit package to the whole informal sector, while the top 5% of the population has excellent private insurance, as in Colombia). Some tiering is also unavoidable in systems with severe resource constraints and a large informal sector.

* * *

Benchmark 5: Equitable financing. This rests on the fundamental idea that financing medical services, as opposed to access, should be according to ability to pay.

* * *

Benchmark 6: Efficacy, efficiency, and quality of care. The rationale for this and the next benchmark is that, other things being equal, a system that gets more value for money in the use of its resources is fairer to those in need. Distributive justice and fairness are issues because resources are always limited.

* * *

Benchmark 7: Administrative efficiency.

* * *

Benchmark 8: Democratic accountability and empowerment.

* * *

Benchmark 9: Patient and provider autonomy. This is the benchmark that most directly addresses a culturally variable issue. How important is autonomy or choice? In some market-based approaches, informed choice is necessary if quality is to be improved and true preferences met. But how much choice, and what kinds of choices? Similarly, provider autonomy is much sought by professionals, but that is often seen by planners as an obstacle to efficient use of services, since professionals and provider institutions are influenced by incentives to utilize what they can supply.

* * *

While the issue of fairness arises in a host of contexts, the rest of this chapter will investigate the issue of the just distribution of health care resources by focusing on the distribution of organs for transplant rather than the reform of the health care system as a whole. Because organs for suitable transplant are scarce, and because there often is no adequate alternative to the transplant, they put the issue of the just and proper distribution of health care in stark relief.

ALLOCATION AND RATIONING

Through allocation, a society determines how much of its resources to devote to a particular purpose: for example, how much money should be allocated to Medicare or Medicaid as compared to education or defense; within Medicare or Medicaid, how much should be allocated to dialysis or transplantation as compared to long-term care; how much federal support should be devoted to medical research and for which diseases or conditions; how many long-term care or hospital facilities should a state approve through its certificate-of-need program?

Through rationing, a society decides which individuals get the particular resources available. In the United States, ability to pay is the dominant means through which we distribute available health care resources. But for some few resources, we have created nearly universal entitlement (as the Medicare program has done with dialysis and kidney transplantation for any person with end-stage renal disease) but experience a shortage of resources (e.g., human kidneys for transplant). For other resources, we maintain intentional shortages in order to contain consumption, as may be the case with state control of the supply of nursing homes or with publicly funded health services. Finally, there may be resources that are price-controlled, where patients are required to pay something for the service, but where they are not allowed to offer more dollars and, in effect, bid against one another. This final situation describes the distribution of solid organs in the U.S. In these cases, non-market means are developed to ration health care resources.

Obviously, allocation decisions affect rationing decisions: if more re-sources are allocated to a particular purpose or legal restrictions on supply are removed, rationing may become less pressing or less frequent. Rationing decisions also affect allocation decisions: uncomfortable public rationing deci-sions may stimulate a greater allocation to increase the supply of the scarce resources.

Allocation and rationing decisions often treat the loss of human life differently, with greater tolerance for "statistical lives" lost and much less tolerance for the loss of "identifiable lives." A classic scenario illustrates the difference: cost-sensitive decisions concerning mine safety that increase the statistical risk of death are accepted even when the predicted loss is quite precise and clear, while at the same time the expense of rescue is of very little concern when an individual miner is trapped in a collapsed mine. Under the concepts discussed earlier, allocation deals mostly with statistical lives, while rationing most often deals with identifiable lives. Whether the individual has a name, a face and a personality, or is just a number, may alter decisions.

Many processes can be used to allocate or ration health care resources. As already noted, the U.S. relies on the market for the rationing of most, but not all, health care resources. A second option is to allocate resources and establish rationing rules through a political process. Allocation decisions are often made through political processes including federal and state budgeting processes. "Responsible" or "black box" committees that are not required to provide reasons for the selection of one recipient over another and that cannot be subject to effective public scrutiny may be used to ration scarce resources. Expert panels may ration scarce resources and may do so under a mantle of scientific or medical or financial expertise. Bureaucratic organizations also shield rationing decision from broad public scrutiny. For a classic and influential analysis of allocation and rationing over several contexts, see Guido Calabresi and Philip Bobbitt, Tragic Choices (1970).

The advent of managed care and certain other cost containment devices has stimulated debate over whether or how extensively and on what principles medical professionals and health care institutions should become involved in rationing care among patients. Rationing health care "at the bedside" is a substantial departure from the physician's traditional role as determined advocate for each individual patient. Are physicians in the best position to ration care among patients? How might their decisions differ, if at all, from black box committees or bureaucracies, for example? Will physician decisions be more or less reviewable than decisions by others? What impact would such a change in role identification have on physician-patient relationships? See, Mark A. Hall, Rationing Health Care at the Bedside, 69 N.Y.U.L. Rev. 693 (1994); David Mechanic, Professional Judgment and the Rationing of Medical Care, 140 Penn. L. Rev. 1713 (1992); Edmund D. Pelligrino, Rationing Health Care; The Ethics of Moral Gatekeeping, 2 J. of Contemp. Health L. & Pol. 23 (1986); E. Haavi Morreim, Balancing Act: The New Medical Ethics of Medicine's New Economics (Boston: Kluwer Acad. Pub. 1991); Susan M. Wolf, Health Care Reform and the Future of Physician Ethics, 24 Hastings Center Rep. 28 (1994); E.J. Emanuel and Nancy N. Dubler, Preserving the Physician–Patient Relationship in the Era of Managed Care, 273 JAMA 323 (1995).

By what criteria should health care services be rationed? During the 1960s, before hemodialysis became widely available, the Seattle Artificial Kidney Center was reported to have selected patients for hemodialysis partially on the basis of "age and sex of patient; marital status and number of dependents; income; net worth; emotional stability, with particular regard to the patient's capacity to accept treatment; educational background; the nature of the occupation; past performance and future potential; the names of people who could serve as references." Shana Alexander, They Decide Who Lives, Who Dies, 53 Life 102–104 (Nov. 9, 1962) as quoted in Maxwell Mehlman, Rationing Expensive Lifesaving Medical Treatments, 1985 Wisc. L.Rev. 239, 256.

Should more "neutral" standards be used to ration scarce health care resources? What standards would be neutral? Are medical indications relating to survivability with and without the treatment neutral standards? Would a lottery or a "first come-first served" system be more acceptable? How should the pool for these latter two methods be defined: should it be geographically defined; should it matter whether the patient is a resident of the state or of the United States; who should decide where the line starts and who is allowed to get in line?

B. RATIONING OF SCARCE HUMAN ORGANS

Problem: Selecting an Organ Transplant Recipient

You are awakened in the middle of the night by an urgent phone call from an administrative staff member of the large urban teaching hospital that you represent. The hospital is a transplant center. The hospital has encountered the following problem.

For the last few weeks two patients have been under treatment at the hospital for acute liver failure. One, James Patterson, is a 65–year-old retired CEO of a major computer software company. He has two children, a 40–year-old daughter with a child of her own and a 24–year-old son. James is an alcoholic and has been in and out of the hospital for the past few years for problems secondary to his alcoholism. Although he has been through detoxification programs several times, he always has returned to his drinking. This time, though, he has abstained from alcohol for more than six months and so meets the minimum criterion for former alcoholics for liver transplant. James is active in his church and is a financial supporter of the local university athletics department. He is still on his employer's health insurance plan, which has a cap on transplant coverage. The second patient is Antonia Friedman, a 30-year-old, attorney with two children, ages 2 and 4. She is an active member of the local city council and has contributed generously in the past year to the hospital's building fund. She recently was exposed to Hepatitis A, which has quickly destroyed most of her liver. Friedman has full coverage health insurance. Within the last week both patients have taken a turn for the worse, and both will die within the next few weeks if they do not receive a liver transplant.

A few hours ago, a patient was admitted to the hospital with massive head trauma caused by an automobile accident. The patient is now brain dead, but is being kept on life support systems to preserve his organs for transplantation. The liver is undamaged, and normal legal procedures have already been followed to assure that it is available for transplantation. Tissue matching shows that it would be an acceptable organ for either Patterson or Friedman.

Because both Patterson and Friedman would be a match, and assuming that both cases are equally medically urgent, current practice would view Patterson as the recipient because his physician, who is relatively new to the hospital, was first to request an organ transplant for his patient, a step he took three days ago.

Who should receive the organ and why? Assume that the hospital is prohibited under federal funding requirements from discrimination on the basis of gender, race, age or disability. How would such a prohibition operate in this situation?

For discussion of the issues, see V.H. Schmidt, Selection of Recipients for Donor Organs in Transplant Medicine 23 J. Med & Philosophy (1998); United Network for Organ Sharing Policy 3.6 (as modified Nov. 19, 1999); M. Benjamin, Transplantation for Alcoholic Liver Disease: The Ethical Issues 3 Liver Transplantation & Surgery 337 (1997); Alvin H. Moss & Mark Siegler, Should Alcoholics Compete Equally for Liver Transplantation? 265 JAMA (March 13, 1991); Carl Cohen, et al., Alcoholics and Liver Transplantation? 265 JAMA (1991).

Suppose instead that Antonia Friedman is a convicted felon serving 25 years for money laundering. Who should receive the liver? See "UNOS Ethics Committee Position Statement Regarding Convicted Criminals and Transplant Evaluation;" L.J. Schneidermein & N.S. Jecker, Should a Criminal Receive a Heart Transplant? Medical Justice v. Social Justice 17 Theoretical Medicine 33 (1996), reprinted in Arthur Kaplan & Daniel Coelho, The Ethics of Organ Transplants: The Current Debate 294 (1998); Jessica Wright, Medically Necessary Organ Transplants for Prisoners: Who is Responsible for Payment? 39 B.C. L. Rev 1251 (1998).

Note: The Organ Procurement Transplant Network

The National Organ Transplant Act (NOTA) requires the Department of Health and Human Services (HHS) to establish an Organ Procurement Transplant Network (OPTN) through which the retrieval, distribution and transplantation of human organs is organized. HHS has contracted with the United Network for Organ Sharing (UNOS), a private nonprofit organization, for the establishment and implementation of the federal OPTN. Prior to 1998, the federal government had not been very actively involved in regulating transplantation policies.

In a 1993 study of the national organ procurement and distribution system, the General Accounting Office found that nearly every Organ Procurement Organization did not comply with UNOS policy on at least one factor for distribution of organs. GAO, Organ Transplants: Increased Effort Needed to Boost Supply and Ensure Equitable Distribution of Organs (April 1993). In 1998, HHS issued for notice and comment a new regulation which ultimately was promulgated in 1999. Through this new regulation, the federal government has taken a more active role in determining how organs should be allocated. UNOS no longer enjoys the deference that had been accorded to its policies, but rather must follow the procedures in the final rule. However, the regulation does allow OPTN, and thus UNOS, to propose alternative policies which must be agreed upon by an HHS oversight committee. From the standpoint of the federal government, the new regulation is intended to insure consistency between OPTN policies as implemented by UNOS, and NOTA. See 64 Fed. Reg. 16296 codified at 42 C.F.R. pt. 121 (1998); Special Section: Organ Transplantation: Shaping Policy and Keeping Public Trust, 8 Cambridge Quarterly (1999).

The regulation establishes standardized criteria for placing patients on transplant waiting lists and allocation of donated organs based on medical status nationally, rather than locally. The new regulation also sets standards for the availability of organ transplant data, and UNOS has made new policy to improve their data collection system. See United Network for Organ Sharing Policy 7.0 (as modified Nov. 19, 1999).

The Institute of Medicine of the National Academy of Sciences has published a report evaluating the new HHS rule. Assessing Current Policies and the

Potential Impact of the DHHS Final Rule (1999). The report is generally favorable toward the Rule and quite supportive of increased federal oversight of OPTN.

This area of law has been extremely controversial and volatile throughout the past decade. Because the shortage of organs leads to some individuals not receiving needed transplants, many battles occur over what the proper allocating policies should be. As a result, litigation in this area is constant and public outcry is often overwhelming. For example, when HHS issued the 1998 regulations, it lead to such controversy and opposition in the transplant community that Congress delayed the regulations for one year so that the IOM could review the current policies and the proposed effects of the new rules. As a result of the constant struggles to find appropriate transplant policies, this area of law is constantly changing. Even as this is being written, the OPTN/UNOS Board is recommending major changes in the policies governing the liver allocation system. These changes are just a taste of what is expected in the future for this area.

1. Geographic Distribution of Organs

The HHS regulation provides that organs no longer be allocated with a priority for local use. Prior to 1998, UNOS policy was to retain organs in the geographic area where they were harvested if a patient in the appropriate medical status was in that area. Under that system, geographic disparities in the amount of wait time occurred. Median waiting times by region varied considerably. The median wait time for a liver, for example, ranged from 20 to 78 days in Region 3, while the wait in Region 9 amounted to 279 to 443 days. 59 Fed. Reg. 46482, 46486 (September 8, 1994). Similar variations exist for other organs as well. The geographic priorities meant that a transplantable organ harvested in Region 3 would stay in Region 3 as long as there was a qualified patient in that region even if patients with a more urgent need or who present marginally better survival waited. The rationale behind the old UNOS policy was to reduce organ preservation, improve organ quality and survival outcomes, reduce the costs incurred by the patient, and increase access to transplantation by increasing interest in donation. The purpose of the new rule is to make the most effective use of organs, by allocating them to the most medically urgent and appropriate patients. With the exception of thoracic organs which are still allocated locally, regionally, and then nationally, all other organs are now allocated based on medical urgency rather than geography. For example, under UNOS policy 3.5.2., cadaveric kidneys are allocated under mandatory sharing of zero antigen mismatched kidneys. If there is any patient on the national UNOS Patient Waiting List for whom there is a zero antigen mismatch with a donor, the donor kidney is to be offered to the appropriate participating transplant center for the patient with the zero antigen mismatch subject to time limitations for survival of the organ. (Currently, the donated organ must be offered within eight hours after procurement.) See UNOS Policy 3.5.2.3.1, November 19, 1999, for a detailed description of the allocation policy regarding kidneys. See also P.A. Ubel & A.L. Caplan, Geographic Favoritism in Liver Transplantation: Unfortunate or Unfair? 338 NEJM 1322 (1998). Because organs are now allocated according to medical urgency rather than strictly geographically, the HHS hopes wait times will become less disparate throughout the country.

2. Listing Patients for Transplantation

Individual private physicians and hospitals control who gets on the UNOS computer registry and when. Individuals and hospitals decide when a patient is placed on the list for an organ. Patients receive priority points for the length of time they have been on the list, among other criteria, so getting on the list earlier rather than later is quite significant. Once a patient is on the waiting list, the patient data is placed on the UNOS national databank and the patient's medical status places them in line for an organ.

There has been "wide variability" in patient listing practices for heart, lung, and liver transplant programs around the country. For this reason, UNOS developed national policies for patient listing for the differing types of transplants including liver, kidney, thoracic organ, intestine, and pancreas, as well as a general policy for those organs not specifically addressed. Under the 1998 HHS regulation, the policies are to be reviewed by the Advisory Committee on Organ Transplantation who advises the Secretary of HHS on the proposed actions.

UNOS Policy 3.6.3, for example, describes the determination of waiting time for liver transplant recipients. The liver wait list is based on a point system which combines both how long a patient has been on the list and the patient's medical status. Thus, liver patients are categorized into four groups depending on their medical urgency when they are added to the UNOS National Waiting List. The order of urgency from least to greatest is Status 3, then 2B, 2A, and Status 1. If a patient is listed as either Status 2A or 1, they will have a life expectancy of less than one week. See Policy 3.6 for a more detailed description of the way in which patients are listed according to medical urgency. Livers are allocated locally, regionally, and nationally on the point system for each status level. See United Network for Organ Sharing Policy 3.6 (as modified Nov. 19, 1999).

Thoracic organs are to be allocated first locally and then within specified geographic zones; i.e. Zone A is within 500 miles of the transplant center, Zone B is between 500 and 1000 miles and Zone C is beyond 1000 miles from the center. In addition, each patient is given a status code representing medical urgency. The statuses range from most urgent 1A to less urgent 1B and 2 to an ineligible patient listed as Status 7. A patient listed as Status 1A has a life expectancy of less than seven days. When wait time is used as an allocation measure, i.e. if two potential recipients have the same medical status, the time spent within the same status category becomes determinative.

In the past, psychosocial factors have played a large role in considering which patients received donated organs. In 1999, UNOS expressed its concern with the concept of non-medical transplant candidate criteria in an UNOS Ethics Committee, General Considerations in Assessment of Transplant Candidacy. The committee justifies the use of certain non-medical criteria based on the shortage of available organs for transplantation. With organs in such short supply, UNOS believes the best potential recipients should be identified based on both medical and non-medical criteria. Examples of non-medical criteria currently used by physicians and other health care providers include life expectancy, organ failure caused by behavior, compliance/ adherence, repeat transplantation, and alternative therapies. Although there is some concern with allowing private physicians great deference by which to evaluate transplant patients, UNOS mandates that to the greatest extent possible, acceptance criteria should be broad and universal.

According to the UNOS Ethics Committee, the non-medical criteria by which transplant candidates are evaluated should be constantly reassessed and modified to reflect changes that occur in technology, medicine, and other related fields. Additionally, the criteria should reflect the most current knowledge of both social and scientific issues in transplantation. See http://www.unos.org/Resources/bioethics_whitepapers_considerations.htm. (visited January 9, 2001).

3. *Zero Antigen Mismatch and Disparate Impact by Race*

Zero antigen mismatch occurs when a recipient patient and a donated kidney have no antigen mismatches, even though all six antigens on which kidneys and recipients would be matched for a "perfect match" may not have shown up on testing a particular kidney. A partial match occurs when a mismatch for one or more of the six antigens has been detected.

UNOS policy requires mandatory distribution of kidneys for which a patient has a zero antigen mismatch. If there is a patient anywhere in the nation with a zero antigen mismatch with the available kidney, that kidney must be given to the patient with the zero antigen mismatch. A zero antigen mismatch with an available kidney is a ticket to override distribution to any local or regional patients with less than zero antigen mismatch. Where there is partial antigen match, UNOS policy favors patients with a higher degree of partial antigen match over others who are otherwise in the same category. Prior to the HHS regulation, kidney allocation was slightly different. Zero antigen mismatch was still favored nationally, but those with less than zero antigen mismatch were under the ordinary geographically-based policy which preferred transplantation in a patient in the same locale or region as the donee. The rationale behind this system of allocation was the same as for other types of organs: to reduce organ preservation, improve organ quality and survival outcomes, reduce the costs incurred by the patient, and to increase access to transplantation.

Data indicate that the priority for zero antigen mismatch has a disparate impact by race on recipient patients. African-Americans may be disadvantaged in the rationing of kidneys by zero antigen mismatch standard and by the partial match standard because antigens are distributed differently among different racial groups.

African–American transplant candidates wait twice as long as whites. Minority registrants constituted 51% of the kidney waiting list in 1998 compared to 44% in 1989 and most of those registrants were African–Americans. Although the majority of registrants are minority, the majority of patients who receive kidneys are white. Whites received 63% of donated kidneys between 1994 and 1998. At the same time, end stage renal disease is much more prevalent among African-Americans, at nearly four times the rate of the white population.

Approximately 25% of cadaveric kidneys go to zero antigen mismatch recipients. Since antigens are distributed differently among different racial groups, white recipients are more likely to have a zero mismatch with kidneys from white donors than are black recipients. In 1995, white donors provided 90% of kidneys available for transplant, but in 1998 whites accounted for only 76% of the transplantable kidneys. This change is attributed to the increased efforts of UNOS and other organizations to increase organ donation awareness. However, to level off the zero antigen mismatch standard the donation rate for African–Americans would have to increase five times over the current rate for African–Americans and four times over the current rate for white donors. The antigen match problem also exists within the preference for higher degree of match where only a partial match is found.

Transplantation is significantly more likely to succeed where there is a perfect six-antigen match. Data on zero antigen mismatch also show significantly better survival rates. In contrast, partial antigen match shows much smaller differences in survival rates across differences in the numbers of antigens matched. Data from 1999 indicate graft one-year survival rates for cadaveric kidney transplants of 86.7% for mismatch of 5 antigens; 87.5% for 4; 88.6% for 3; 88.3% for 2; and 90.1 when there is only 1 mismatch. UNOS 1999 Annual Report (September 1999). Are these differences significant? The advent of more effective immuno-suppressant drugs may overcome these differences in survivability rates, although there will be a greater cost per transplant where the antigen match is not strong.

Kidney-recipient selection policies do not uniformly prefer survivability. For example, "presensitized" patients, who have previously received a kidney that failed within a short time after transplant receive priority. Presensitized patients have priority for transplant even though the presensitization caused by the earlier transplant diminishes the chances for successful transplant significantly.

How would you resolve the policy issues in regard to these standards if you were the Secretary of HHS, a member of Congress, or UNOS? Must the system be consistent in its priorities? For example, if antigen matching is preferred because of increased survivability, should the preferences for type O and presensitized patients be eliminated? How much of a difference in survival rates is significant and how much is tolerable? There is wide variation in transplant survival rates among the hospitals doing transplants. Should these be added to the calculation of who gets priority for transplant with organs shifted away from transplant centers with poorer records?

See Ian Ayres, Laura G. Dooley, Robert S. Gaston, Unequal Racial Access to Kidney Transplantation, 46 Vand. L. Rev. 805 (1993); Benjamin Mintz, Analyzing the OPTN Under the State Action Doctrine—Can UNOS Organ Allocation Criteria Survive Strict Scrutiny? 28 Colum. J.L. & Soc. Probls. 339 (1995).

Problem: State or Federal Control?

The HHS Final Rule attempts to eliminate the disparity in median wait times for various geographic regions. However, currently seven states have enacted laws which directly conflict with the uniform allocation of organs and instead favor geographic distribution by placing restrictions on out-of-state organ transfers. In effect, the state laws are upholding the policy as it was before the promulgation of the Final Rule. See, e.g. La. Rev. Stat. Ann. § 17:2353 (West 1999) which states in part:

* * *

[I]n the event an anatomical gift is made in the state of Louisiana of any vascular organ for transplantation purposes, if the donor does not name a specific donee and the organ is deemed suitable for transplantation to an individual, the vascular organ shall be donated to the Louisiana-designated organ procurement organization. Said organization shall use its best efforts to determine if there is a suitable recipient in the state.

* * *

[T]he Louisiana-designated organ procurement organization may only transfer a vascular organ to an out-of-state organ procurement organization or suitable out-of-state recipient for transplantation if either:

(a) A suitable recipient in the state of Louisiana cannot be found in a reasonable amount of time.

(b) The Louisiana-designated organ procurement organization has a reciprocal agreement with the out-of-state procurement organization ...

Assume you are on the staff of a U.S. Senator from a state that has a statute against the national uniform distribution of organs as mandated by HHS. The Senator has asked you to develop a position paper on whether the HHS regulation should be overturned legislatively. Do you support the federal or state approach for organ allocation policy? How do you support your state's position to keep allocation local and not follow the national guidelines? Is the federal government making allocation political by stepping in and taking more control? Should UNOS, as a private corporation and an expert in the field, be able to establish their own policies without federal governmental oversight? See Roderick T. Chen, Organ Allocation and the States: Can States Restrict Broader Organ Sharing? 49 Duke I.J. 261 (1999); Laura E. McMullen, Equitable Allocation of Human Organs: An Examination of the New Federal Regulation. 20 J. Legal Med. 405 (1999).

C. INCREASING THE SUPPLY OF ORGANS FOR TRANSPLANTATION: THE IMPACT OF LEGAL RESTRAINTS

As with most health care services, the availability of organs for transplantation is determined in part by funding. Partly as a result of discomfort with the activity of the Seattle Artificial Kidney Center (the "God Committee"), Congress elected to provide funds under Medicare for treatment for almost all individuals with end-stage renal disease (ESRD), regardless of whether they otherwise qualified for Medicare. Because kidney transplantation has proven very successful and less expensive and burdensome than life-long dialysis, Medicare now pays for kidney transplants and dialysis for persons with ESRD. Do you think that Congress could now be persuaded to fund care for everyone with any other particular terminal disease for which effective treatment is available? If you believe you can unlatch the federal purse, which disease or which treatment is likely to attract such support? Breast cancer? Prostate cancer? Pediatric liver transplants?

In setting benefits for private insurance or for a government program, should transplants be treated differently than other treatments? In its attempt to redefine its Medicaid benefits through a public process some years ago, the state of Oregon decided to make more dollars available for pre-natal care by eliminating payment for organ transplants. In 1987, a young Oregon boy died when his family's attempts to raise funds for a bone marrow transplant, which would have been covered by Medicaid in other states, failed. Oregon thereafter restored Medicaid funding for organ transplants. Which was irrational: excluding organ transplants as a class of treatment; or undoing a decision founded on statistical improvements in overall health status in the face of a single individual's suffering?

For most health care services and goods scarcity could be resolved if enough funds were provided. In contrast, organ transplantation is limited by the number of human organs made available for transplantation. In 1999, there were 12,517 kidney transplants; 4,700 liver transplants, and 2,185 heart transplants. By comparison in 1995, there were 11,807 kidney transplants; 3,923 liver transplants; and 2,361 heart transplants (UNOS Scientific Data Registry, September 7, 1999). The number of reported deaths on the waiting list in 1998 increased with 2,307 dying on the kidney wait list; 1,317 on the liver list; and 768 on the heart list. Comparative figures for 1995 were 1,520 for kidneys; 804 for livers; and 770 for hearts. Demand continues to outstrip supply. On May 21, 2000, 69,728 organs were needed for patients listed, compared to 43,854 in 1995. More funding may have some impact on supply, especially in the development of nonhuman-organ substitutes. But substantial increases in supply require that many more individuals become organ sources through post-mortem organ donation or otherwise, and this may require radical alteration of legal constraints on organ harvesting, including the elimination of personal choice in the donation of organs or the repeal of legal prohibitions on the sale of human organs.

As you analyze the statutes and case law presented below, consider what values are implied in the law relating to the production of human organs for transplantation. What role does personal autonomy play in the law, for example? Where does it take priority, and where is it less significant? What values are implicated in the treatment of humans after death? How does the law balance the goal of saving lives through increasing the supply of human organs against other goals?

1. Cadaver Organs

UNIFORM ANATOMICAL GIFT ACT

(1987).

§ 2. Making, Amending, Revoking, and Refusing to Make Anatomical Gifts by Individual.

(a) An individual who is at least [18] years of age may (i) make an anatomical gift [defined as a "donation of all or part of a human body to take effect upon or after death"] for any of the purposes stated in Section 6(a), (ii) limit an anatomical gift to one or more of those purposes, or (iii) refuse to make an anatomical gift.

(b) An anatomical gift may be made only by a document of gift [a writing] signed by the donor. If the donor cannot sign, the document of gift must be signed by another individual and by two witnesses, all of whom have signed at the direction and in the presence of the donor and of each other, and state that it has been so signed.

(c) If a document of gift is attached to or imprinted on a donor's motor vehicle operator's or chauffeur's license, the document of gift must comply with subsection (b). Revocation, suspension, expiration, or cancellation of the license does not invalidate the anatomical gift.

. . .

(f) A donor may amend or revoke an anatomical gift . . .

. . .

(h) An anatomical gift that is not revoked by the donor before death is irrevocable and does not require the consent or concurrence of any person after the donor's death.

(i) An individual may refuse to make an anatomical gift of the individual's body or part by (i) a writing signed in the same manner as a document of gift, (ii) a statement attached to or imprinted on a donor's motor vehicle operator's or chauffeur's license, or (iii) any other writing used to identify the individual as refusing to make an anatomical gift. During a terminal illness or injury, the refusal may be an oral statement or other form of communication.

(j) In the absence of contrary indications by the donor, an anatomical gift of a part is neither a refusal to give other parts nor a limitation on an anatomical gift under Section 3 or on a removal or release of other parts under Section 4.

(k) In the absence of contrary indications by the donor, a revocation or amendment of an anatomical gift is not a refusal to make another anatomical gift. If the donor intends a revocation to be a refusal to make an anatomical gift, the donor shall make the refusal pursuant to subsection (i).

§ 3. Making, Revoking, and Objecting to Anatomical Gifts, by Others.

(a) Any member of the following classes of persons, in the order of priority listed, may make an anatomical gift of all or a part of the decedent's body for an authorized purpose, unless the decedent, at the time of death, has made an unrevoked refusal to make that anatomical gift: (1) the spouse of the decedent; (2) an adult son or daughter of the decedent; (3) either parent of the decedent; (4) an adult brother or sister of the decedent; (5) a grandparent of the decedent; and (6) a guardian of the person of the decedent at the time of death.

(b) An anatomical gift may not be made by a person listed in subsection (a) if:

(1) a person in a prior class is available at the time of death to make an anatomical gift;

(2) the person proposing to make an anatomical gift knows of a refusal or contrary indications by the decedent; or

(3) the person proposing to make an anatomical gift knows of an objection to making an anatomical gift by a member of the person's class or a prior class.

. . .

(e) A failure to make an anatomical gift under subsection (a) is not an objection to the making of an anatomical gift.

§ 4. Authorization by [Coroner] [Medical Examiner] or [Local Public Health Official].

(a) The [coroner] [medical examiner] may release and permit the removal of a part from a body within that official's custody, for transplantation or therapy, if:

(1) the official has received a request for the part from a hospital, physician, surgeon, or procurement organization;

(2) the official has made a reasonable effort, taking into account the useful life of the part, to locate and examine the decedent's medical records and inform persons listed in Section 3(a) of their option to make, or object to making, an anatomical gift;

(3) the official does not know of a refusal or contrary indication by the decedent or objection by a person having priority to act as listed in Section 3(a);

(4) the removal will be by a physician, surgeon, or technician; but in the case of eyes, by one of them or by an enucleator;

(5) the removal will not interfere with any autopsy or investigation; .

(6) the removal will be in accordance with accepted medical standards; and

(7) cosmetic restoration will be done, if appropriate.

(b) If the body is not within the custody of the [coroner] [medical examiner], the [local public health officer] may release and permit the removal of any part from a body in the [local public health officer's] custody for transplantation or therapy if the requirements of subsection (a) are met.

§ 5. Routine Inquiry and Required Request; Search and Notification.

(a) On or before admission to a hospital, or as soon as possible thereafter, a person designated by the hospital shall ask each patient who is at least [18] years of age: "Are you an organ or tissue donor?" If the answer is affirmative the person shall request a copy of the document of gift. If the answer is negative or there is no answer and the attending physician consents, the person designated shall discuss with the patient the option to make or refuse to make an anatomical gift. The answer to the question, an available copy of any document of gift or refusal to make an anatomical gift, and any other relevant information, must be placed in the patient's medical record.

(b) If, at or near the time of death of a patient, there is no medical record that the patient has made or refused to make an anatomical gift, the hospital [administrator] or a representative designated by the [administrator] shall discuss the option to make or refuse to make an anatomical gift and request the making of an anatomical gift pursuant to Section 3(a). The request must be made with reasonable discretion and sensitivity to the circumstances of the family. A request is not required if the gift is not suitable, based upon accepted medical standards, for a purpose specified in Section 6. An entry must be made in the medical record of the patient, stating the name and affiliation of the individual making the request, and of the name, response, and relationship to the patient of the person to whom the request was made. The [Commissioner of Health] shall [establish guidelines] [adopt regulations] to implement this subsection.

(c) The following persons shall make a reasonable search for a document of gift or other information identifying the bearer as a donor or as an individual who has refused to make an anatomical gift:

(1) a law enforcement officer, fireman, paramedic, or other emergency rescuer finding an individual who the searcher believes is dead or near death; and

(2) a hospital, upon the admission of an individual at or near the time of death, if there is not immediately available any other source of that information.

(d) If a document of gift or evidence of refusal to make an anatomical gift is located by the search required by subsection (c)(1), and the individual or body to whom it relates is taken to a hospital, the hospital must be notified of the contents and the document or other evidence must be sent to the hospital.

§ 6. Persons Who May Become Donees; Purposes for Which Anatomical Gifts may be Made.

(a) The following persons may become donees of anatomical gifts for the purposes stated:

(1) a hospital, physician, surgeon, or procurement organization, for transplantation, therapy, medical or dental education, research, or advancement of medical or dental science;

(2) an accredited medical or dental school, college, or university for education, research, advancement of medical or dental science; or

(3) a designated individual for transplantation or therapy needed by that individual.

(b) An anatomical gift may be made to a designated donee or without designating a donee. If a donee is not designated or if the donee is not available or rejects the anatomical gift, the anatomical gift may be accepted by any hospital.

(c) If the donee knows of the decedent's refusal or contrary indications to make an anatomical gift or that an anatomical gift by a member of a class having priority to act is opposed by a member of the same class or a prior class under Section 3(a), the donee may not accept the anatomical gift.

§ 8. Rights and Duties at Death.

(a) The time of death must be determined by a physician or surgeon who attends the donor at death or, if none, the physician or surgeon who certifies the death. Neither the physician or surgeon who attends the donor at death nor the physician or surgeon who determines the time of death may participate in the procedures for removing or transplanting a part unless the document of gift designates a particular physician or surgeon pursuant to Section 2(d).

(b) If there has been an anatomical gift, a technician may remove any donated parts and an enucleator may remove any donated eyes or parts of eyes, after determination of death by a physician or surgeon.

§ 10. Sale or Purchase of Parts Prohibited.

(a) A person may not knowingly, for valuable consideration, purchase or sell a part for transplantation or therapy, [defined as "an organ, tissue, eye bone, artery, blood, fluid or other portion of a human body"] if removal of the part is intended to occur after the death of the decedent.

(b) Valuable consideration does not include reasonable payment for the removal, processing, disposal, preservation, quality control, storage, transportation, or implantation of a part.

§ 11. Examination, Autopsy, Liability.

(a) A hospital, physician, surgeon, [coroner], [medical examiner], [local public health officer], enucleator, technician, or other person, who acts in accordance with this [Act] or with the applicable anatomical gift law of another state [or a foreign country] or attempts in good faith to do so is not liable for that act in a civil action or criminal proceeding.

(b) An individual who makes an anatomical gift pursuant to Section 2 or 3 and the individual's estate are not liable for any injury or damage that may result from the making or the use of the anatomical gift.

* * *

Notes and Questions

1. The 1987 UAGA has been adopted by all fifty states. The 1987 Act was developed in recognition that the earlier 1968 version simply was not producing enough donated organs. The major differences in the two Acts are summarized in the Prefatory Note to the 1987 Act:

The proposed amendments simplify the manner of making an anatomical gift and require that the intentions of a donor be followed. For example, no witnesses are required on the document of gift and consent of next of kin after death is not required if the donor has made an anatomical gift. The identification of actual donors is facilitated by a duty to search for a document of gift and of potential donors by the provisions for routine inquiry and required request. A gift of one organ, e.g., eyes, is not a limitation on the gift of other organs after death, in the absence of contrary indication by the decedent. The right to refuse to make an anatomical gift and the manner of expressing the refusal are specified.... Hospitals have been substituted for attending physicians as donees of anatomical gifts, and they are required to establish agreements or affiliations with other hospitals and procurement organizations in the region to coordinate the procurement and utilization of anatomical gifts. If a request for an anatomical gift has been made for transplant or therapy by a person specified in the Act and if there is no contrary indication by the decedent or known objection by the next of kin to an anatomical gift, the [coroner] [medical examiner] or [local public health official] may authorize release and removal of a part subject to specific requirements.

2. In the absence of a written gift, should the physician be required to make a reasonable effort to find the family as under the UAGA, or should consent to organ donation be presumed unless the individual or family has been able to actually inform the physician or hospital of their objection? Should the patient's objection prior to his death govern whether the organs can be removed, or should the need for organs outweigh the individual's interest in the disposition of his body? Should religious objections be treated differently than others? What values are at stake here? If the decedent has properly signed an anatomical gift form, do you think physicians would be likely to remove transplantable organs over the objection of the family? Without the consent of the family? See Aaron Spital, Mandated Choice: A Plan to Increase Public Commitment to Organ Donation, 273 JAMA 504 (Feb. 8, 1995), describing the common practice of deferring to family override.

3. The UAGA requires that the patient or family be informed of the opportunity to donate organs upon admission to the hospital or after the patient's death. It had been hoped that such "routine inquiry" or "required request" mandates would increase the number of organs donated. That has not been the case. Why do people refuse? See Gina Kolata, Families Often Block Organ Donation, Study Finds, Plain Dealer, 9E (July 11, 1995) (1995 WL 7119412). Some facilities have found that who asks the family makes a difference. See e.g., Pulling Together, UNOS Update, July/August 1996, at p. 10, reporting on comparative donation rates for requests made by doctors, nurses or bereavement staff in ascending order in terms of positive response. Should every institution provide special training on asking for organs?

4. A more radical proposal for increasing the supply of cadaver organs is sale by the potential donor while living (for harvesting after death for life-sustaining organs and before death for others) or by the next-of-kin at death. Brush up on your knowledge of future interests—could an individual transfer a vested remainder in his heart while retaining a life estate?

The UAGA prohibits the sale of body parts under some circumstances, and federal law provides that it is illegal for "any person to knowingly acquire, receive, or otherwise transfer any human organ for valuable consideration for use in human transplantation if the transfer affects interstate commerce." The federal statute defines human organ as "human (including fetal) kidney, liver, heart, lung, pancreas, bone marrow, cornea, eye, bone, and skin or any subpart thereof." How does the sale of blood and semen co-exist with these statutes? Is the sale of these items different in kind from the sales prohibited under the UAGA or the federal act? Federal law also provides that "valuable consideration" does not include "the reasonable payments associated with the removal, transportation, implantation, processing, preservation, quality control, and storage of a human organ or the expenses of travel, housing, and lost wages incurred by the donor of a human organ in connection with the donation . . .". 42 U.S.C.A. § 274(e).

Could an unemployed living kidney donor be paid "lost wages" for the time spent on the removal of the organ and recovery? What should the hourly rate for organ transplantation be? If the donor earns minimum wage, is that the amount that should be paid? Should the lawyer-donor and the cook-donor be paid differently for the same labor? Are ova donors, who are paid about $2,000 for the extraction procedure, being paid for their ova or for expenses? If it could be proven that allowing the sale of non-life-sustaining organs (such as a single kidney or a part of the liver) by living persons or the sale of any organs by or on behalf of the estate (or creditors) of cadavers would substantially increase the number of organs available and so save lives, would you support legalization of such sales? If so, under what circumstances? Would the economic needs of the seller affect your opinion?

On the use of market incentives in transplantation, see James F. Blumstein, The Use of Financial Incentives in Medical Care: the Case of Commerce in Transplantable Organs, 3 Health Matrix 1 (1993); Gregory S. Crespi, Overcoming the Legal Obstacles to the Creation of a Futures Market in Bodily Organs, 55 Ohio St. L.J. 1 (1994); Julia D. Mahoney, The Market for Human Tissue 86 Va.L.Rev. 169 (March 2000); Shelby E. Robinson, Organs for Sale? An Analysis of Proposed Systems for Compensatory Organ Providers. 70 U.Colo.L.Rev. 1019 (Summer 1999). While organ sales are prohibited and consent is required prior to harvesting cadaver organs, is the scarcity of human organs any less "artificial" or "intentional" than is the scarcity of other health care services or goods?

5. Life-sustaining organs may be removed only from persons who have died. Chapter 19 presents the current legal standard for determination of death, the whole brain death standard, which was adopted in part to allow for removal of organs while the person is still attached to a ventilator so that the organs remain oxygenated and transplantable. That chapter also describes efforts to expand the legal standard for determination of death to encompass anencephalic infants, who are born with only a brain stem but no upper brain and who can breathe for some amount of time on their own but have no ability to perceive, think or interact. Arguments in favor of the adoption of such an expanded legal standard have focused on the potential for harvesting usable organs from such infants, an opportunity which is lost if one waits until the child can no longer breathe on his or her own.

6. With recent advances in genetic engineering, it appears likely that transplantation of animal organs and tissue into humans will become practical and increase significantly. This possibility raises a significant range of public health and ethical issues including the potential for transmission of infectious diseases. Margaret A. Clark, The Little Piggy Went to Market: The Xenotransplantation and Xenozoonose Debate. 27 J.L. Med. & Ethics 137 (Summer 1999); Frank Morgan, Babe the Magnificent Organ Donor? The Perils and Promises Surrounding Xenotransplantation. 14 J.Contemp. Health L. & Pol'y 127 Fall (1997).

Problem: Organ Donation From an Adolescent

Laurel Singer, aged sixteen, has been brought to General Hospital with extremely serious injuries she suffered while diving from the river bluffs nearby. Efforts by the ambulance emergency medical technicians and the emergency room doctor to resuscitate her have failed. She has died. Laurel's friends have tried to call her parents, but they are on vacation somewhere in Australia. In lookingIn looking for other contacts, they have come across her driver's license. Laurel signed the organ donor card on the back of her driver's license.

May a surgeon remove her organs that may be transplantable? Under the UAGA, what must the doctor do in order to proceed? If the parents arrive after the surgery has been completed and they object to the harvesting of the child's organs, do they have any action against the emergency room doctor, the surgeon or the hospital? What would their damages be if they did have a claim? May a state statute allow for the taking of body parts without the prior consent of the deceased or his family? See, State v. Powell, 497 So.2d 1188 (Fla.1986); Note, "She's Got Bette Davis Eyes: Assessing the Nonconsensual Removal of Cadaver Organs under the Takings and Due Process Clauses," 90 Colum. L. Rev. 528 (1990).

Questions

How far does the good faith immunity provision of the UAGA extend? If hospital personnel knowingly or recklessly mislead family donors and frustrate the donor's actual and expressed wishes, does immunity apply? See Perry v. Saint Francis Hospital, 886 F.Supp. 1551 (D.Kan.1995), holding the hospital liable. See also, Jacobsen v. Marin General Hospital, 192 F.3d 881 (9th Cir.1999), holding that the hospital was not liable for negligence in a failed effort to reach next of kin; Ramirez v. Health Partners of Southern Arizona, 193 Ariz. 325, 972 P.2d 658 (Ariz.Ct.App.1998), where the hospital was held to have immunity. What is the definition of good faith? Does an honest belief, the absence of malice and the absence of design to defraud or to seek an unconscionable advantage constitute good faith? See Lyon v. United States, 843 F.Supp. 531 (D.Minn.1994). If there is ambiguity in the organ consent form is the hospital acting in good faith in removing organs within the ambiguous gift? See Rahman v. Mayo Clinic, 578 N.W.2d 802 (Minn.App.1998). See also, Crocker v. Pleasant, 727 So.2d 1087 (Fla.Dist.Ct.App.1999); Alexander Powhida, Forced Organ Donation: The Presumed Consent to Organ Donation Laws of the Various States and United States Constitution. 9 ALB.L.J.Sci & Tech. 349 (1999).

Note: *Organs from Living Donors*

Living donors who are legally competent may donate (but not sell) non-life-sustaining organs and frequently do so for family members in need. Legal issues arise when the donor is legally incompetent or when the donor refuses consent. The principles discussed in these cases govern many medical treatment decisions for incompetent patients.

In Strunk v. Strunk, 445 S.W.2d 145 (1969), the Court of Appeals of Kentucky decided that a court had the power to permit a kidney to be removed from an incompetent ward of the state upon petition of his committee, who was also his mother, for the purpose of being transplanted into the body of his brother, who was dying of a kidney disease. In its holding, the court concluded that the inherent rule in cases regarding incompetents is that the court has the power to deal with the personal affairs of the incompetent in the same manner as the incompetent would if he had his faculties. In addition, the court stated that the best interests of the incompetent brother were served by allowing the transplant, because in donating a kidney to save his brother's life, the incompetent brother's mental well-being was ensured.

The court in Guardianship of Pescinski, 67 Wis.2d 4, 226 N.W.2d 180 (1975), explicitly rejected the "substituted judgment" rule of *Strunk* in favor of examining whether the organ donation was in the "best interests" of the incompetent. In *Pescinski*, the court concluded that there was "absolutely no evidence here that any interests of the ward will be served by the transplant." The court appeared to base its conclusion on Pescinski's mental illness which was characterized by "marked indifference" and "flight from reality." The court described no relationship between Pescinski and his sister who needed the kidney. Would *Pescinski* have been decided differently if the facts were the same as those in *Strunk?* Would *Strunk* have been decided differently if a "best interests" rather than substituted judgment test were applied? See, discussing these cases, John Robertson, Organ Donations by Incompetents and the Substituted Judgment Doctrine, 76 Colum.L.Rev. 48 (1976).

In *Strunk*, a sibling donor for the needy brother already existed. What if he had not? Could his parents have deliberately conceived another child to be an organ donor for him? In 1989 the parents of Anissa Ayala, who suffered from leukemia and needed a bone marrow transplant, decided to have another child. Although they hoped that the new sibling could donate bone marrow to Anissa, they realized that there was only a one in four chance she would be a match. Anissa's sister, Marissa, was born in 1990, and she qualified as a match. She was physically able to donate marrow at six months. Extracting bone marrow for transplantation is risky and may be painful. Should the hospital require court approval before proceeding, or is this the kind of decision parents should ordinarily make for their children? How should the court rule in the case of an infant donor? The results of a survey of 15 of the 27 bone marrow transplant centers indicated that at least forty children had been conceived for the purpose of bone marrow donation to a sibling (as described in Vicki G. Norton, Unnatural Selection: Nontherapeutic Preimplantation Genetic Screening and Proposed Regulation, 41 U.C.L.A. L. Rev. 1581 (1994)).

HEAD v. COLLOTON

Supreme Court of Iowa, 1983.
331 N.W.2d 870.

McCORMICK, JUSTICE.

This appeal presents a question concerning the right of access of a member of the general public to a hospital's record of the identity of a potential bone marrow donor . . .

* * *

The University of Iowa Hospitals and Clinics include a bone marrow transplant unit. That unit maintains a bone marrow transplant registry, listing persons whose blood has been tissue-typed by the hospital. The tissue typing reveals blood antigen characteristics which must be known for determining whether a donor's bone marrow will be a suitable match-up for the bone marrow of a donee. A bone marrow transplant consists of removing bone marrow from a healthy person and infusing it into the body of a patient in the hope it will generate healthy white blood cells. The procedure is experimental between unrelated persons.

Late in 1982, plaintiff phoned the transplant unit and, through a series of conversations with a staff member, learned that the hospital's registry included the name of a woman who might, upon further testing, prove to be a suitable donor to him. Only one in approximately 6,000 persons would have blood with the necessary antigen characteristics.

The tissue typing of the woman, referred to in the record as "Mrs. X," had not been done for reasons of her own health but to determine her suitability as a blood platelet donor to a member of her family who was ill. The hospital subsequently placed her name in its platelet donor registry. Then, when it later established an experimental program involving bone marrow transplants between unrelated persons, the hospital, without Mrs. X's knowledge or consent, placed her name in the bone marrow transplant registry. When the hospital established the new program, its institutional review board approved a procedure for contacting persons listed on the registry to determine whether they would act as donors. The procedure involved sending a letter informing the person of the program, its nature and goals, and inviting the person's participation in it. If the letter was not answered, a staff member was authorized to telephone the person and ask a series of general questions designed to determine whether the person would volunteer as a donor.

After plaintiff's contact with the bone marrow unit, the unit staff on December 31, 1982, sent Mrs. X the general letter informing her about the program and encouraging her to participate in it. When no response to the letter was received, a staff member telephoned Mrs. X on January 10, 1983, and asked her the series of questions. In responding to those questions, Mrs. X said she was not interested in being a bone marrow donor. When asked if she might ever be interested in being a donor, she said, "Well, if it was for family, yes. Otherwise, no." Despite plaintiff's subsequent request that the hospital make a specific inquiry of Mrs. X in plaintiff's behalf or to disclose her identity to him so he could contact her, the hospital refused to contact her or to disclose her identity to plaintiff. He then brought the present action.

Plaintiff asked for a mandatory injunction to require [the hospital] to disclose the name and identity of the potential donor either to the court or to his attorney. He proposed that the court or counsel then be permitted to write the woman to notify her of plaintiff's need and her possible suitability as a donor, asking her if she would consider being a donor to plaintiff.

* * *

This case involves application of the provisions of chapter 68A, Iowa's public records statute. Under section 68A.1, "public records" include "all records and documents of or belonging to this state...." § 68A.1. Defendants concede that the records of the University of Iowa hospital, a state hospital, are public records within the meaning of this provision. Thus the bone marrow donor registry is a public record. Section 68A.2 provides for public access to all public records "unless some other provision of the Code expressly limits such right or requires such records to be kept confidential."

Defendants contend that the registry is required to be kept confidential pursuant to section 68A.7(2). In material part, section 68A.7 provides:

The following public records shall be kept confidential, unless otherwise ordered by a court, by the lawful custodian of the records, or by another person duly authorized to release information:

* * *

2.   Hospital records and medical records of the condition, diagnosis, care, or treatment of a patient or former patient, including outpatient.

* * *

[Plaintiff]   contends section 68A.7(2) is inapplicable on two bases. One is that a hospital record is not confidential unless it is a patient record. The other basis is that the tissue-typing record of Mrs. X is not a patient record. Defendants also offer a two-pronged argument. One prong is that a hospital record need not be a patient record to be confidential. The other is that the tissue-typing record is a hospital record of a patient within the meaning of the statute. We are thus confronted with a legal issue, requiring interpretation of section 68A.7(2).

* * *

We agree with plaintiff that the only hospital records made confidential by the statute are those "of the condition, diagnosis, care, or treatment of a patient or former patient, including outpatient." . . .

* * *

We must next determine whether the record to which plaintiff seeks access is that kind of hospital record.

* * *

The critical issue is whether Mrs. X was a hospital patient for purposes of section 68A.7(2) when she submitted to tissue typing as a potential platelet donor. The ordinary meaning of the word "patient" is "a person under medical or surgical treatment." [ ] The word "treatment" is broad enough to embrace all steps in applying medical arts to a person . . .

* * *

The evidence shows the hospital believed Mrs. X became a patient when she submitted to tissue typing. Dr. Roger Gingrich, director of the hospital's bone marrow transplant program, testified she was a patient. He said: "I would regard any person who interfaces themselves with the medical profession and out of that interaction there's biologic information obtained about the person, in fact to be a patient, to [have] established a doctor-patient relationship." Although this testimony is not conclusive on the issue, it is consistent with the broad dictionary definition of the treatment concept.

It is also consistent with caselaw that recognizes the same duty between physician and donor as exists between physician and patient generally. [ ] In [one] case the court said the relationship is the same: "Once a [blood] donor is accepted (medical reasons rule out some donors) his person is unquestionably placed under the control of the hospital personnel operating the laboratory, and he must rely on their professional skills as in any other hospital-patient relationship." [ ]

Perhaps even more importantly the doctors' testimony is consistent with the reality of the situation. When a person submits to a hospital procedure, the hospital's duty should not depend on whether the procedure is for that person's benefit or the potential benefit of someone else. The fiduciary relationship is the same, and the standard of care is the same. In addition, just as with patients generally, a potential donor has a valuable right of privacy.

An individual's interest in avoiding disclosure of personal matters is constitutionally based. [ ] This right is also recognized at common law. [ ] A valuable part of the right of privacy is the right to avoid publicity concerning private facts. This right can be as important to a potential donor as to a person in ill health. The Hippocratic Oath makes no distinction based on how medical confidences are acquired. [ ] Nor does the American Medical Record Association make such a distinction in its model policy for maintenance of confidentiality of patient health information [ ].

The conclusion that a potential donor is a patient and should have the privacy rights of a patient is merely reenforced by the testimony in the present record concerning the possible chilling effect of disclosure upon medical research. That evidence is not determinative of the issue.

We conclude that the hospital record of Mrs. X is the hospital record of the "condition, diagnosis, care or treatment of a patient, or former patient" within the meaning of section 68A.7(2). Therefore the record is confidential.

* * *

Notes and Questions

1. Why would the hospital refuse to contact Mrs. X and tell her that she may be a match for a specific individual needing a bone marrow transplant? If we tend to treat "statistical lives" differently than "identifiable lives," shouldn't Mrs. X have been informed of the need? The case turned on the legal issue of confidentiality. How was the confidentiality of Mrs. X's records affected by Mr. Head's request

that the hospital approach her? How does an approach to Mrs. X differ, if at all, from the situation faced by an individual to give an organ for a family member? How does it differ from "required request?" A problem similar to that faced in *Head* also emerges where a transplant candidate who has been adopted is seeking her natural family. Here the interest of the potential donor may conflict with the confidentiality policy of the adoption laws. See In re George, 630 S.W.2d 614 (Mo.App.1982). See also, Curran v. Bosze, 141 Ill.2d 473, 153 Ill.Dec. 213, 566 N.E.2d 1319 (1990), for decision refusing order for blood testing of toddlers for potential transplant to half-sibling.

2. Should the hospital have entered Mrs. X in its bone marrow registry without her consent? Bone marrow transplantation still requires extremely close matching, and very few people have volunteered to be listed in bone marrow registries. Would you support legislation that would pay people to have their blood typed and be listed in a national registry? Legislation that would require potential donors, selected by a random method, to be blood typed and listed on the registry if the ultimate donation were voluntary? If the ultimate donation were also compulsory? See Mark F. Anderson, Encouraging Bone Marrow Transplants From Unrelated Donors: Some Proposed Solutions to a Pressing Social Problem, 54 U. Pitt. L. Rev. 477 (1993).

Part I

PROMOTING QUALITY

Chapter 2

QUALITY CONTROL REGULATION: LICENSING OF HEALTH CARE PROFESSIONALS

State law controls licensure of health care professionals under the state's police power. Licensing statutes govern entry into the licensed professions and disciplinary actions against licensed health care professionals. Licensure also regulates the scope of health care services that licensed professionals may provide and prohibits unlicensed persons from providing services reserved for the licensed professions.

These statutes are implemented by boards that operate as state agencies but which are generally dominated by members of the licensed profession. Licensure in the U.S. is often described as a system of professional self-regulation, even though the boards act as state agencies; usually include lay members; are governed by procedures and standards set in the state's licensing statute and administrative procedures act; and are subject to judicial review in both their adjudicatory and rulemaking decisions.

Professional participation in licensure may further the public interest by bringing expertise to the evaluation of professionals' competency and behavior. Professional domination of licensure has been strongly criticized, however, as serving the interests of the professions at the expense of their competitors; of organizations that seek to curtail medical control of health care decisions; and of the public.

Although this debate is an old one, it has been reenergized by changes in the health care system, including the advent of managed care and its control over physician practices; the momentum of a strong movement for alternative or complementary medicine; the institutionalization of non-physician licensed health care professions; and fundamental changes in medical practice itself, including, for example, the movement to increase access to controlled substances for pain relief and the emergence of cybermedicine, especially in relation to prescribing practices.

In each of these, the traditional forms of regulation of medical practice play a significant role, at times engaging in combat against these changes but always at least molding their structure and their relationship to medical practice. For recent analyses of the debate over professional control of licensure and the role of the market as opposed to restrictive licensure, see

Carl F. Ameringer, State Medical Boards and the Politics of Public Protection (Johns Hopkins University Press 1999); Ezekiel Emmanuel and Linda Emmanuel, Preserving Community in Health Care, 22 J. of Health Policy, Politics and Law 147 (1997); Frances H. Miller, Medical Discipline in the Twenty–First Century; Are Purchasers the Answer? 60 L. and Contemp. Probs. 31 (1997); Timothy S. Jost, Oversight of the Quality of Medical Care: Regulation, Management or the Market, 37 Ariz. L. Rev. 825 (1995); and E. Clarke Ross, Regulating Managed Care: Interest Group Competition for Control and Behavioral Health Care, 24 J. of Health Politics, Policy and Law 599 (1999). For a historical perspective, see Paul Stark, The Social Transformation of American Medicine (1982); and for the classic study of medical licensure and discipline, see Robert C. Derbyshire, Medical Licensure and Discipline in the United States (1969).

I. DISCIPLINE

IN RE WILLIAMS

Supreme Court of Ohio, 1991.
60 Ohio St.3d 85, 573 N.E.2d 638.

SYLLABUS BY THE COURT

* * *

... Between 1983 and 1986, Dr. Williams prescribed Biphetamine or Obetrol for fifty patients as part of a weight control treatment regimen. [Both drugs are controlled substances.]

On November 17, 1986, appellant, the Ohio State Medical Board ("board"), promulgated Ohio Adm.Code 4731–11–03(B), which prohibited the use of [drugs such as Biphetamine and Obetrol] for purposes of weight control. Dr. Williams ceased prescribing Biphetamine and Obetrol for weight control upon becoming aware of the rule.

By letter dated March 12, 1987, the board charged Dr. Williams with violating R.C. 4731.22(B)* by prescribing these stimulants without "reasonable care," and thereby failing to conform to minimal standards of medical practice. The crux of the board's charge was that Dr. Williams had departed from accepted standards of care by using these drugs as a long-term, rather than a short-term, treatment.

A hearing was held before a board examiner. The parties stipulated to the accuracy of the medical records of the patients in question, which detailed the use of Biphetamine and Obetrol for periods ranging from nearly seven months to several years. The board also introduced into evidence the Physician's Desk

---

* R.C. 4731.22(B) provides in pertinent part:

"The board, pursuant to an adjudicatory hearing ... shall, to the extent permitted by law, ... [discipline] the holder of a certificate [to practice medicine] for one or more of the following reasons:

. . .

"(2) Failure to use reasonable care, discrimination in the administration of drugs, or failure to employ acceptable scientific methods in the selection of drugs or other modalities for treatment of disease;

"(3) Selling, prescribing, giving away, or administering drugs for other than legal and legitimate therapeutic purposes ...

. . .

"(6) A departure from, or the failure to conform to, minimal standards of care ... [.]"

Reference entries for Biphetamine and Obetrol, which recommend that these drugs be used for only "a few weeks" in the treatment of obesity. The board presented no testimony or other evidence of the applicable standard of care.

Dr. Williams presented expert testimony from Dr. John P. Morgan, the director of the pharmacology program at the City University of New York Medical School, and Dr. Eljorn Don Nelson, an associate professor of clinical pharmacology at the University of Cincinnati College of Medicine. These experts stated that there are two schools of thought in the medical community concerning the use of stimulants for weight control. The so-called "majority" view holds that stimulants should only be used for short periods, if at all, in weight control programs. The "minority" view holds that the long-term use of stimulants is proper in the context of a supervised physician-patient relationship. Both experts testified that, though they themselves supported the "majority" view, Dr. Williams's application of the "minority" protocol was not substandard medical practice.

The hearing examiner found that Dr. Williams's practices violated R.C. 4731.22(B). The examiner recommended subjecting Dr. Williams to a three-year monitored probation period. The board modified the penalty, imposing a one-year suspension of Dr. Williams's license followed by a five-year probationary period, during which he would be unable to prescribe or dispense controlled substances.

Dr. Williams appealed to the Court of Common Pleas of Franklin County pursuant to R.C. 119.12. The court found that the board's order was ". . . not supported by reliable, probative and substantial evidence and . . . [was] not in accordance with law." The court of appeals affirmed.

HERBERT R. BROWN, JUSTICE.

In an appeal from an administrative agency, a reviewing court is bound to uphold the agency's order if it is ". . . supported by reliable, probative, and substantial evidence and is in accordance with law. . . ." [ ]. In the instant case, we must determine if the common pleas court erred by finding that the board's order was not supported by sufficient evidence. For the reasons, which follow, we conclude that it did not and affirm the judgment of the court below.

In its arguments to this court, the board contends that Arlen v. Ohio State Medical Bd. (1980), 61 Ohio St.2d 168, 15 O.O.3d 190, 399 N.E.2d 1251, is dispositive. In *Arlen*, the physician was disciplined because he had written prescriptions for controlled substances to a person who the physician knew was redistributing the drugs to others, a practice prohibited by R.C. 3719.06(A). The physician appealed on the ground that the board failed to present expert testimony that such prescribing practices fell below a reasonable standard of care.

We held that the board is not required in every case to present expert testimony on the acceptable standard of medical practice before it can find that a physician's conduct falls below this standard. We noted that the usual purpose of expert testimony is to assist the trier of facts in understanding "issues that require scientific or specialized knowledge or experience beyond the scope of common occurrences. . . ." [ ] The board was then made up of ten (now twelve) persons, eight of whom are licensed physicians. [ ] Thus, a majority of board members are themselves experts in the medical field who already possess the specialized knowledge needed to determine the acceptable standard of general medical practice.

While the board need not, in every case, present expert testimony to support a charge against an accused physician, the charge must be supported by some reliable, probative and substantial evidence. It is here that the case against Dr. Williams fails, as it is very different from *Arlen*.

Arlen involved a physician who dispensed controlled substances in a manner that not only fell below the acceptable standard of medical practice, but also violated the applicable statute governing prescription and dispensing of these drugs. In contrast, Dr. Williams dispensed controlled substances in what was, at the time, a legally permitted manner, albeit one which was disfavored by many in the medical community. The only evidence in the record on this issue was the testimony of Dr. Williams's expert witnesses that his use of controlled substances in weight control programs did not fall below the acceptable standard of medical practice. While the board has broad discretion to resolve evidentiary conflicts [ ] and determine the weight to be given expert testimony [ ], it cannot convert its own disagreement with an expert's opinion into affirmative evidence of a contrary proposition where the issue is one on which medical experts are divided and there is no statute or rule governing the situation.

It should be noted, however, that where the General Assembly has prohibited a particular medical practice by statute, or where the board has done so through its rulemaking authority, the existence of a body of expert opinion supporting that practice would not excuse a violation. Thus, if Dr. Williams had continued to prescribe Biphetamine or Obetrol for weight control after the promulgation of Ohio Adm.Code 4731–11–03(B), this would be a violation of R.C. 4731.22(B)(3), and the existence of the "minority" view supporting the use of these substances for weight control would provide him no defense. Under those facts, *Arlen* would be dispositive. Here, however, there is insufficient evidence, expert or otherwise, to support the charges against Dr. Williams. Were the board's decision to be affirmed on the facts in this record, it would mean that a doctor would have no access to meaningful review of the board's decision. The board, though a majority of its members have special knowledge, is not entitled to exercise such unbridled discretion.

MOYER, C.J., and SWEENEY, HOLMES and DOUGLAS, JJ., concur.

WRIGHT, JUSTICE, dissenting.

The message we send to the medical community's regulators with today's decision is one, I daresay, we would never countenance for their counterparts in the legal community. We are telling those charged with policing the medical profession that their expertise as to what constitutes the acceptable standard of medical practice is not enough to overcome the assertion that challenged conduct does not violate a state statute. . . .

HOOVER v. THE AGENCY FOR HEALTH CARE ADMINISTRATION

District Court of Appeal of Florida, 1996.
676 So.2d 1380.

JORGENSON, JUDGE.

Dr. Katherine Anne Hoover, a board-certified physician in internal medicine, appeals a final order of the Board of Medicine penalizing her and restricting her license to practice medicine in the State of Florida. We reverse because the board has once again engaged in the uniformly rejected practice of overzealously supplanting a hearing officer's valid findings of fact regarding a doctor's prescription practices with its own opinion in a case founded on a woefully inadequate quantum of evidence.

In March 1994, the Department of Business and Professional Regulation (predecessor in these proceedings to the Agency for Health Care Administration) filed an administrative complaint alleging that Dr. Hoover (1) inappropriately and excessively prescribed various . . . controlled substances to seven of her patients and (2) provided care of those patients that fell below that level of care, skill, and treatment which is recognized by a reasonably prudent similar physician as being acceptable under similar conditions and circumstances; in violation of sections 458.331(1)(q) and (t), Florida Statutes, respectively. All seven of the patients had been treated by Dr. Hoover for intractable pain arising from various non-cancerous diseases or ailments.

Dr. Hoover disputed the allegations of the administrative complaint and requested a formal hearing. . . .

The agency presented the testimony of two physicians as experts. Neither had examined any of the patients or their medical records. The sole basis for the opinions of the agency physicians was computer printouts from pharmacies in Key West where the doctor's patients had filled their prescriptions. These printouts indicated only the quantity of each drug filled for each patient, occasionally referring to a simplified diagnosis. Both of these physicians practiced internal medicine and neither specialized in the care of chronic pain. In fact, both doctors testified that they did not treat but referred their chronic pain patients to pain management clinics. The hearing officer found that this was a common practice among physicians—perhaps to avoid prosecutions like this case.* Both doctors "candidly testified that without being provided with copies of the medical records for those patients they could not evaluate Respondent's diagnoses of what alternative modalities were attempted or what testing was done to support the use of the medication chosen by Respondent to treat those patients." Despite this paucity of evidence, lack of familiarity, and seeming lack of expertise, the agency's physicians testified at the hearing that the doctor had prescribed excessive, perhaps lethal amounts of narcotics, and had practiced below the standard of care.

Dr. Hoover testified in great detail concerning the condition of each of the patients, her diagnoses and courses of treatment, alternatives attempted, the patients' need for medication, the uniformly improved function of the patients with the amount of medication prescribed, and her frequency of writing prescriptions to allow her close monitoring of the patients. She presented corroborating physician testimony regarding the appropriateness of the particular medications and the amounts prescribed and her office-setting response to the patients' requests for relief from intractable pain.

---

* Referral to a pain management clinic was not an option for Dr. Hoover's indigent Key West resident patients.

Following post-hearing submissions, the hearing officer issued her recommended order finding that the agency had failed to meet its burden of proof on all charges. The hearing officer concluded, for instance, "Petitioner failed to provide its experts with adequate information to show the necessary similar conditions and circumstances upon which they could render opinions that showed clearly and convincingly that Respondent failed to meet the standard of care required of her in her treatment of the patients in question."

The agency filed exceptions to the recommended findings of fact and conclusions of law as to five of the seven patients. The board of medicine accepted all the agency's exceptions, amended the findings of fact in accordance with the agency's suggestions, and found the doctor in violation of sections 458.331(1)(q) and (t), Florida Statutes. The board imposed the penalty recommended by the agency: a reprimand, a $4,000 administrative fine, continuing medical education on prescribing abusable drugs, and two years probation. This appeal follows.

For each of the five patients, the hearing officer found the prescribing practices of Doctor Hoover to be appropriate. This was based upon (1) the doctor's testimony regarding the specific care given, (2) the corroborating testimony of her physician witness, and (3) the fact that the doctor's prescriptions did not exceed the federal guidelines for treatment of intractable pain in cancer patients, though none of the five patients were diagnosed as suffering from cancer.

The board rejected these findings as not based on competent substantial evidence. As particular reasons, the board adopted the arguments of the agency's exceptions to the recommended order that (1) the hearing officer's findings were erroneously based on irrelevant federal guidelines, and (2) the agency's physicians had testified that the doctor's prescription pattern was below the standard of care and outside the practice of medicine. . . .

First, the board mischaracterizes the hearing officer's reference to the federal guidelines. The board reasoned in its final order that "[t]he record reflects that the federal guidelines relied upon by the Hearing Officer for this finding were designed for cancer patients and [the five patients at issue were] not being treated for cancer." It is true, as the hearing officer noted,

> Respondent presented expert evidence that there is a set of guidelines which have been issued for the use of Schedule II controlled substances to treat intractable pain and that although those guidelines were established to guide physicians in treating cancer patients, those are the only guidelines available at this time. Utilizing those guidelines, because they exist, the amount of medication prescribed by Respondent to the patients in question was not excessive or inappropriate.

In so finding, however, the hearing officer did not, as the board suggests, rely solely upon the federal guidelines in its ruling that the doctor's prescribing practices were not excessive. Rather, the federal guidelines merely buttressed fact findings that were independently supported by the hearing officer's determination of the persuasiveness and credibility of the physician witnesses on each side. For example, though he admitted he had not even reviewed the federal guidelines, one of the agency physicians asserted that the amounts prescribed constituted a "tremendous number of pills" and that the doses involved would be lethal. That Dr. Hoover's prescriptions fell within the guidelines for chronic-pained cancer patients may properly be considered to refute this assertion. Such a use of the federal guidelines was relevant and reasonable.

Second, Dr. Hoover testified in great detail concerning her treatment of each patient, the patient's progress under the medication she prescribed, and that the treatment was within the standard of care and practice of medicine. The hearing officer, as arbiter of credibility, was entitled to believe what the doctor and her physician expert opined. [ ] The agency's witnesses' ultimate conclusions do not strip the hearing officer's reliance upon Dr. Hoover of its competence and substantiality. The hearing officer was entitled to give Dr. Hoover's testimony greater weight than that of the agency's witnesses, who did not examine these patients or regularly engage in the treatment of intractable pain.

[T]he hearing officer explicitly recognized that the 1994 [Florida] intractable pain law was not in effect at the time of Dr. Hoover's alleged infractions but cited it for a permissible purpose—to rebut any claim that there is a strong public policy mandate in favor of the board's draconian policy of policing pain prescription practice. [ ] ...

Reversed.

Notes and Questions

1. As you see in the dissent in *Williams*, the rationale for physicians' dominance of the membership of state medical boards is the notion of peer review. This concept holds that practitioners of the regulated profession are in the best position to judge the practices of their peers. What, then, is at the heart of this dispute over expert testimony in *Williams*? On what basis did the Florida court reject the testimony of the agency's experts in *Hoover*?

2. Both *Williams* and *Hoover* involve disputes within the medical profession concerning appropriate medical treatment, during a transition in professional standards. The Ohio State Medical Board promulgated an administrative rule, cited in *Williams*, requiring that physicians meet the "majority" standard of practice regarding the prescription of controlled substances. Should licensure boards establish standards of practice or practice guidelines that prefer one approach over another; or should they simply recognize the full range of medical practices, including minority views? Would your answer depend on whether the board was acting in a rulemaking or in an adjudicatory role? How should the boards respond in the absence of well-the accepted standards of care or a well-established mainstream of practice, as in the *Hoover* case? See the *Guess* case, *infra*, for a discussion of the scope of judicial review of medical board rules and regulations.

3. The court in *Hoover* implies that disciplinary actions by a state medical board against individual physicians have an effect on other physicians' practices. Beyond penalizing the "bad apple," this is the broader intended impact of professional disciplinary actions. In the case of treatment for pain, however, the medical boards were more influenced by the "war against drugs" than they were by neglected pain. Furthermore, significant new research indicated that the traditional medical practice in the use of opioids for pain needed to be changed, as these drugs are safer than has been assumed. The change in practice that this research stimulated caused some problems in the disciplinary system, as evidenced in *Hoover*. The negative impact of medical board practices relating to the prescription of controlled substances for pain management received considerable attention

as a result. See for example, Symposium on Legal and Institutional Constraints on Effective Pain Relief, 24 Journal of Law, Medicine & Ethics (1997) and Symposium on Legal and Regulatory Issues in Pain Management, 26 Journal of Law, Medicine & Ethics (1998). The Federation of State Medical Boards developed a model policy that emphasized improvements in patient functioning and pain relief and practice management techniques (including record keeping and physical examination) over standards based merely on the quantity and chronicity of the prescriptions. See, Model Guidelines for the Use of Controlled Substances for the Treatment of Pain (1998), available at *www.fsmb.org* (visited December 27, 2000). Some states have enacted legislation generally referred to as "intractable pain treatment acts." The Florida statute referenced in *Hoover*, which is an early version of such statutes, provides:

> Notwithstanding any other provision of law, a physician may prescribe or administer any controlled substance to a person for the treatment of intractable pain, provided the physician does so in accordance with that level of care, skill, and treatment recognized by a reasonably prudent physician under similar conditions and circumstances.

Would this statute provide adequate protection to physicians such as Dr. Hoover? Should it be more specific? Is it appropriate for legislatures to enact statutes concerning permissible medical practices, or should they leave that to the licensure boards?

4. The number of disciplinary actions against physicians has increased. In the 1960s, 0.06% of doctors were disciplined, primarily for offenses involving abuse of drugs or inappropriate prescribing; and by 1981, the number disciplined had grown to 0.14% of licensed physicians. Robert C. Derbyshire, How Effective is Medical Self–Regulation? 7 Law & Human Behavior 193 (1983). The Federation's Data Bank lists approximately 4,000 disciplinary actions yearly through the 1990s. See *www.fsmb.org*. A study of California disciplinary actions published in 1998 found that 0.24% of California physicians were disciplined in 1997, with negligence and incompetence constituting about one-third of those actions. The next largest numbers related to abuse of alcohol or drugs (14%), inappropriate prescribing practices (11%), and inappropriate contact with patients (10%). The penalties levied included license revocation (21%), licensed suspension (13%), stayed suspension of license (45%), and reprimand (21%). James Morrison and Peter Wickersham, Physicians Disciplined by the State Medical Boards, 279 JAMA 1889 (1998). An accompanying commentary notes the number of physicians who were disciplined and states that "even 1% is still far too many." The Role of the Medical Profession in Physician Discipline, 279 JAMA 1914 (1998). Is 0.24% too many or too few? How would you measure whether the number of disciplinary actions in your state was too many, too few or just right? If the boards must set priorities due to limited resources, what should those priorities be? Should they focus on the more easily proven cases? Should they respond first to consumer complaints? For a general discussion see, Timothy S. Jost, et al., Consumers, Complaints, and Professional Discipline: A Look at Medical Licensure Boards, 3 Health Matrix 309 (1993).

5. In assessing incompetency, how should the board treat suits for malpractice? Settlements? Judgments? One study has concluded that the filing of a malpractice claim against a physician, even if no payment was made on the claim, was predictive of future malpractice claims. Randall R. Bovbjerg and Kenneth R. Petronis, The Relationship Between Physicians' Malpractice Claims History and Later Claims: Does the Past Predict the Future? 272 JAMA 1421 (1994). What

implication does this have for disciplinary boards, if any? See, Mich. C.L.A. § 333.16231, requiring the medical board to investigate physicians who have experienced "3 or more malpractice settlements, awards, or judgments ... in a period of 5 consecutive years or 1 or more malpractice settlements, awards, or judgments ... totaling more than $200,000.00 in a period of 5 consecutive years."

6. Most states have established programs to provide rehabilitative, non-punitive interventions for impaired nurses, doctors and other health professionals. The rehabilitative approach to impairment naturally emerges from the recent emphasis on chemical dependency as an illness rather than a failure in character, especially in professionals. It also responds to perceived concerns that a punitive disciplinary approach pushes impaired health care providers undercover, risking greater injury to the public. It is hoped that the availability of a program of non-punitive rehabilitation encourages a higher rate of reporting and self-reporting of impaired physicians. See e.g., C. Morrow, Doctors Helping Doctors, 14 Hastings Center Report 32 (1984). A focus on rehabilitation rather than punishment may be meeting more resistance in nurse discipline. H. Lippman and S. Nagle, Addicted Nurses: Tolerated, Tormented or Treated?, 55 RN 36 (1992).

Some studies of physician treatment programs indicate relapse rates of 10% to 20%. M. F. Fleming, Physician Impairment: Options for Intervention, 50 American Family Physician 41 (July 1994); B. Schneidman, Editorial: The Philosophy of Rehabilitation for Impaired Physicians, 82 Federation Bulletin 125 (1995). Other studies indicate relapse rates ranging from 30% to 57%, though the severity and duration of relapse may vary. K. L. Sprinkle, Physician Alcoholism: A Survey of the Literature, 81 Federation Bulletin 113 (1994).

Should voluntary enrollment in an impaired professional program be confidential, or should the program be required to notify the board? Can rehabilitation be coerced? Should boards allow impaired professionals to choose a rehabilitative program with discipline stayed and then expunged upon successful completion? Should physicians who are abusing alcohol or drugs or who are participating in a state-sanctioned rehabilitation program be required to inform their patients? Would this protect the public? See Barry R. Furrow, Doctors' Dirty Little Secrets: The Dark Side of Medical Privacy, 37 Washburn L.J. 283 (1998), arguing that informed consent is inadequate protection in such a case.

7. "Impairment" is a term of art in professional licensure; but it is also a central term in the federal Americans with Disabilities Act, which prohibits discrimination against persons who have a physical or mental impairment or a record of such impairment or are viewed as having such an impairment. 42 U.S.C.A. § 12101 et seq. (1990). Title II of the ADA applies to the licensing functions of the professional licensure boards of the States. 28 C.F.R. § 35.130(b)(6) (1991). See, for example, Alexander v. Margolis, 921 F.Supp. 482 (W.D.Mich.1995); *aff'd* 98 F.3d 1341 (6th Cir.1996).

8. The number of disciplinary actions for sexual misconduct has increased rapidly, nearly tripling between 1990 and 1995. Estimates of the incidence of physician sexual activity with patients vary, ranging between 5% to 10% of practicing physicians, although these estimates are viewed by some as understated. Council on Ethical and Judicial Affairs, Sexual Misconduct in the Practice of Medicine, 266 JAMA 2741 (1991); N. Gartrell, et al., Physician-patient Sexual Contact: Prevalence and Problems, 157 Western Journal of Medicine 139 (1992). The House of Delegates of the AMA formally adopted an Opinion of the Association's Council on Ethical and Judicial Affairs holding that "sexual contact or romantic relationship concurrent with the physician-patient relationship is uneth-

ical." Opinions of the Council on Ethical and Judicial Affairs § 8.14 (1992). State statutes provide for disciplinary action against doctors for sexual misconduct with patients. In some states, such actions are brought under general provisions prohibiting "unprofessional conduct." In a few states, there are specific statutory prohibitions but their scope varies widely. For example, some states proscribe "exercising influence" over a patient for the purpose of engaging in sexual activity. See e.g., Mo.Ann.Stat. § 334.100(2)(4)(i). See also, Levin v. Idaho State Bd. of Medicine, 133 Idaho 413, 987 P.2d 1028 (Idaho 1999). For a review of the case law on disciplinary sanctions against doctors and a comparison with norms for lawyers, see Sandra H. Johnson, Judicial Review for Disciplinary Actions for Sexual Misconduct in the Practice of Medicine, 270 JAMA 1596 (1993). For an analysis of the incidence of actions and the level of sanctions against physicians, see Christine E. Dehlendorf and Sidney M. Wolfe, Physicians Disciplined for Sex–Related Offenses, 279 JAMA 1883 (1998).

9. One area of new and controversial disciplinary activity involves the state medical board's jurisdiction over the practice of utilization review. The first issue is whether utilization review is the practice of medicine so that managed care organizations must hire only licensed physicians to provide that service. See, Managed Care Industry "Under Siege" Over Utilization Review Licensure, External HMO Review Panels, BNA Health Law Reporter (May 7, 1998). See generally, the section on scope of practice regulation, *infra*. The second issue is whether a physician utilization reviewer can be disciplined for charges of incompetency or professional misconduct in the conduct of utilization review. See, State Bd. of Reg. for Healing Arts v. Fallon, ___ S.W.2d ___, 2001 WL 348980 (Mo. 2001). One of the legal issues involved in this particular dispute is whether the state has authority under federal ERISA law to regulate utilization reviewers through licensure statutes. See Chapter ___.

10. Congress established the National Practitioner Data Bank in part to create an effective system for preventing doctors with disciplinary history in one state from moving to another and practicing until detected, if ever. 42 U.S.C.A. §§ 11101–11152. State disciplinary and licensure boards are required to report certain disciplinary actions against physicians. Hospitals and other entities engaging in peer review processes are required to report adverse actions as well. Licensure boards have access to the Data Bank to check on licensees, and hospitals must check the Data Bank for physicians applying for staff privileges and periodically for physicians who hold staff privileges. The general public is not allowed access to the information in the Data Bank though there have been several proposals for allowing increased access. The federal General Accounting Office has issued a report that is quite critical of the accuracy of the information contained in the Data Bank, including the information that is reported by state medical boards. National Practitioner Data Bank: Major Improvements Are Needed to Enhance Data Bank's Reliability. (GAO–01–130, Nov. 30, 2000).

Note: State Medical Boards, Licensing and Online Prescribing

In the previous material on disciplinary actions by state medical boards, you noted the problems that the state medical boards and the disciplinary system experience when there is a change in medical treatment. Medical boards must also react when there is a change in the method of delivery.

Currently, medical boards (and the federal government and professional associations such as the American Medical Association and scholars and lawyers) are struggling with the issues raised by telemedicine generally and Internet prescribing in particular. The term telemedicine encompasses a wide range of activities—including online physician consultations with specialists, review of imaging by offsite radiologists, and continuing contact with a physician's patients through e-mail—many of which do not raise unique legal issues. Online prescribing, however, captures many of the controversial attributes of telemedicine that have generated volumes examining the application of tort theory, the jurisdiction of dozens of regulatory bodies, and the scope of contract and intellectual property issues. See generally, Symposium on Electronic Medical Information: Privacy, Liability and Quality Issues, 25 Am. J. of L. & M. 191 (1999); Christopher Guttman–McCabe, Telemedicine's Imperiled Future? Funding, Reimbursement, Licensing and Privacy Hurdles, 14 Contemporary Health Law and Policy 161 (1997). For a discussion of the broader reaches of telemedicine, see Nicolas P. Terry, Cyber–Malpractice: Legal Exposure for Cybermedicine, 25 Am. J. of L. and Med. 327 (1999).

Internet pharmacy services vary in their operation. For example, patients may purchase prescription medications from an online "drug store" that operates just like a "real" pharmacy in that the entity holds a pharmacy license and requires an offsite doctor's prescription before shipping medication. Although these virtual drug stores raise some legal issues, it is a second kind of online drug purchase that raises more difficult issues for medical licensure and the state medical boards. These latter entities offer one-stop shopping for an individual seeking a prescription. The "patient" typically fills out an online medical questionnaire, which is reviewed by a physician associated with the Internet site. That physician then issues a prescription, and the drug is shipped directly to the patient. There is no other contact between the physician and the patient, and the patient does not know who the doctor is or what training the doctor has. Sites that provide prescriptions for medications for conditions that might be considered by some to be too embarrassing to see a doctor in person and for which prescription drugs have been heavily advertised seem to be the most popular. Online pharmacies also offer prices that are generally lower than other pharmacies as well as the convenience of home delivery. Chester Chuang (Note), Is There a Doctor in the House? Using Failure-to-Warn Liability to Enhance the Safety of Online Prescribing, 75 N.Y.U.L.Rev. 1452 (2000), detailing the scope of Internet pharmacy services and providing an overview of legal issues.

Naturally, these sites have raised issues of quality and access to health care. Personal knowledge of the patient and physical examination have been the traditional hallmarks of quality prescribing, and some argue that patients may be injured by taking inappropriate prescription medications when there has been no physical contact with the physician and when there is no follow-up. Others argue that telemedicine generally will improve access to care by removing the perceived stigma of certain conditions that may lead individuals to forego medical treatment entirely; by lowering cost; and by reaching geographic areas that are underserved by specialists. See, for example, Talley L. Kaleko (Comment), A Bold Step: What Florida Should Do Concerning the Health of Its Rural Communities, Licensure, and Telemedicine, 27 Fla.St.U.L.Rev. 767 (2000).

Telemedicine and online prescribing are oblivious to state boundaries. Medical licensure, however, is controlled by each state individually, and physicians, with few exceptions, must hold a license in each state in which they practice, although they are granted this license "by endorsement" if they hold a current license in another state. Even endorsement, however, involves a time-consuming application process. Should medical licensure remain the province of the states, in this one context, or should there be national licensure? Assuming that the individual states retain control of medical licensure, how should they regulate online prescribing?

Some states have already enacted legislation to govern the licensure of physicians practicing telemedicine. The Federation of State Medical Boards developed a model act in 1996 to govern the issue of electronically mediated medical practices. A Model Act to Regulate the Practice of Medicine Across State Lines (1996). This act requires licensure in the state in which the patient resides but provides for a special limited license to facilitate telemedicine. The model act has been criticized both as too liberal and as too restrictive of the practice of telemedicine.

The state of Indiana, for example, permits physicians outside of Indiana to provide consultation services to Indiana physicians but otherwise requires an Indiana medical license for any physician who is "providing diagnostic or treatment services to a person in Indiana when [those services] are transmitted through electronic communications; and are on a regular, routine and non-episodic basis . . ." Ind. Code Ann. § 25–22.5–1–1.1(a)(4). Most states that have amended their licensure statutes have followed a similar form although some states do not include the exception for consultation.

Why would a state not rely on the licensure of another state? If the only contact between patient and doctor is via the Internet, has the doctor gone to the patient or has the patient come to the doctor? Will the Indiana statute encourage or impede the development of telemedicine? Should online consulting with another physician be treated differently than direct physician-to-patient online prescribing? If your state requires that a doctor using electronic communications to diagnose or treat patients residing in your state have a license issued by your state, what disciplinary standards should the medical board use to govern the practice? Should your board discipline physicians who prescribe medication without examining the patient? Rather than taking a case-by-case adjudicatory approach, should your board instead promulgate regulations for online prescribing?

For an analysis of the FSMB model act and current state legislation, see Center for Telemedicine Law, Telemedicine and Interstate Licensure: Findings and Recommendations of the CTL Licensure Task Force 73 N.D.L.Rev.109 (1997); Alison M. Sulentic, Crossing Borders: The Licensure of Interstate Telemedicine Practitioners, 25 J. Legis. 1 (1998).

II. ALTERNATIVE AND COMPLEMENTARY MEDICINE

IN RE GUESS

Supreme Court of North Carolina, 1990.
327 N.C. 46, 393 S.E.2d 833.

MITCHELL, JUSTICE.

* * *

The facts of this case are essentially uncontested. The record evidence tends to show that Dr. George Albert Guess is a licensed physician practicing family medicine in Asheville. In his practice, Guess regularly administers homeopathic medical treatments to his patients. Homeopathy has been defined as:

A system of therapy developed by Samuel Hahnermann on the theory that large doses of a certain drug given to a healthy person will produce certain conditions which, when occurring spontaneously as symptoms of a disease, are relieved by the same drug in small doses. This [is] ... a sort of "fighting fire with fire" therapy.

Stedman's Medical Dictionary 654 (24th ed. 1982); *see* Schmidt's Attorneys' Dictionary of Medicine H–110 (1962). Homeopathy thus differs from what is referred to as the conventional or allopathic system of medical treatment. Allopathy "employ[s] remedies which affect the body in a way *opposite* from the effect of the disease treated." Schmidt's Attorneys' Dictionary of Medicine A–147 (emphasis added); *see* Stedman's Medical Dictionary 44.

On 25 June 1985, the Board charged Dr. Guess with unprofessional conduct, pursuant to N.C.G.S. § 90–14(a)(6), specifically based upon his practice of homeopathy. In a subsequent Bill of Particulars, the Board alleged that in his practice of medicine, Guess utilized "so-called 'homeopathic medicines' prepared from substances including, but not limited to, moss, the night shade plant and various other animal, vegetable and mineral substances." ...

Following notice, a hearing was held by the Board on the charge against Dr. Guess. The hearing evidence chiefly consisted of testimony by a number of physicians. Several physicians licensed to practice in North Carolina testified that homeopathy was not an acceptable and prevailing system of medical practice in North Carolina. In fact, there was evidence indicating that Guess is the only homeopath openly practicing in the State. Guess presented evidence that homeopathy is a recognized system of practice in at least three other states and many foreign countries. There was no evidence that Guess' homeopathic treatment had ever harmed a patient, and there was anecdotal evidence that Guess' homeopathic remedies had provided relief to several patients who were apparently unable to obtain relief through allopathic medicine.

Following its hearing, the Board revoked Dr. Guess' license to practice medicine in North Carolina, based upon findings and conclusions that Guess' practice of homeopathy "departs from and does not conform to the standards of acceptable and prevailing medical practice in this State," thus constituting unprofessional conduct as defined and prohibited by N.C.G.S. § 90–14(a)(6). The Board, however, stayed the revocation of Guess' license for so long as he refrained from practicing homeopathy.

Guess appealed the Board's decision. ... After review, the Superior Court entered an order on 20 May 1987, which reversed and vacated the Board's decision. The Superior Court found and concluded that Guess' substantial rights had been violated because the Board's findings, conclusions and decision were "not supported by competent, material and substantial evidence and [were] arbitrary and capricious."

... [T]he Court of Appeals rejected the Superior Court's reasoning to the effect that the Board's findings, conclusions and decision were not supported by competent evidence. *In re Guess,* 95 N.C.App. 435, 437, 382 S.E.2d 459, 461 (1989). The Court of Appeals, nonetheless, affirmed the Superior Court's order reversing the Board's decision,

Because the Board neither charged nor found that Dr. Guess' departures from approved and prevailing medical practice either endangered or harmed his patients or the public, and in our opinion the revocation of a physician's license to practice his profession in this state must be based upon conduct that is detrimental to the public; it cannot be based upon conduct that is merely different from that of other practitioners.

Id. at 437, 382 S.E.2d at 461. We granted the Board's Petition for Discretionary Review, and now reverse the Court of Appeals.

I.

The statute central to the resolution of this case provides in relevant part: [The Board shall have the power to deny, annul, suspend or revoke a license where the licensee has engaged in:]

(6) Unprofessional conduct, including, but not limited to, *any departure* from, or the failure to conform to, the *standards of acceptable and prevailing medical practice*, or the ethics of the medical profession, *irrespective of whether or not a patient is injured thereby.*

N.C.G.S. § 90–14 (1985) (emphasis added). The Court of Appeals concluded that in exercising the police power, the legislature may properly act only to protect the public from harm. [ ] Therefore, the Court of Appeals reasoned that, in order to be a valid exercise of the police power, the statute must be construed as giving the Board authority to prohibit or punish the action of a physician only when it can be shown that *the particular action in question* poses a danger of harm to the patient or the public. Specifically, the Court of Appeals held that:

Before a physician's license to practice his profession in this state can be lawfully revoked under G.S. 90–14(a)(6) for practices contrary to acceptable and prevailing medical practice that *it must also appear that the deviation complained of posed some threat of harm to either the physician's patients or the public.* [ ]

Our analysis begins with a basic constitutional principle: the General Assembly, in exercising the state's police power, may legislate to protect the public health, safety and general welfare. [ ]

Turning to the subject of this case, regulation of the medical profession is plainly related to the legitimate public purpose of protecting the public health and safety. [ ] State regulation of the medical profession has long been recognized as a legitimate exercise of the police power. As the Supreme Court of the United States has pointed out:

* * *

Few professions require more careful preparation by one who seeks to enter it than that of medicine. It has to deal with all those subtle and mysterious influences upon which health and life depend. ... The physician must be able to detect readily the presence of disease, and prescribe appropriate remedies for its removal. Everyone may have occasion to consult him, but comparatively few can judge of the qualifications of learning and skill, which he possesses. Reliance must be placed upon the assurance given by his license, issued by an authority competent to judge in that respect, that he possesses the requisite qualifications. ... The same reasons which control in imposing conditions, upon compliance with which the physician is allowed to practice in the first instance, may call for further conditions as new modes of treating disease are discovered, or a more thorough acquaintance is obtained of the remedial properties of vegetable and mineral substances, or a more accurate knowledge is acquired of the human system and of the agencies by which it is affected.

Dent v. West Virginia, 129 U.S. 114, 122–23, 9 S.Ct. 231, 233, 32 L.Ed. 623, 626 (1889).

. . . We conclude that the legislature, in enacting N.C.G.S. § 90–14(a)(6), reasonably believed that a general risk of endangering the public is *inherent* in *any* practices which fail to conform to the standards of "acceptable and prevailing" medical practice in North Carolina. We further conclude that the legislative intent was to prohibit any practice departing from acceptable and prevailing medical standards without regard to whether the particular practice itself could be shown to endanger the public. Our conclusion is buttressed by the plain language of N.C.G.S. § 90–14(a)(6), which allows the Board to act against *any* departure from acceptable medical practice "irrespective of whether or not a patient is injured thereby." By authorizing the Board to prevent or punish *any* medical practice departing from acceptable and prevailing standards, irrespective of whether a patient is injured thereby, the statute works as a regulation which "tend[s] to secure" the public generally "against the consequences of ignorance and incapacity as well as of deception and fraud," even though it may not immediately have that direct effect in a particular case.

* * *

II.

* * *

Dr. Guess strenuously argues that many countries and at least three states recognize the legitimacy of homeopathy. While some physicians may value the homeopathic system of practice, it seems that others consider homeopathy an outmoded and ineffective system of practice. This conflict, however interesting, simply is irrelevant here in light of the uncontroverted evidence and the Board's findings and conclusion that homeopathy is not currently an "acceptable and prevailing" system of medical practice in North Carolina.

While questions as to the efficacy of homeopathy and whether its practice should be allowed in North Carolina may be open to valid debate among members of the medical profession, the courts are not the proper forums for that debate. The legislature may one day choose to recognize the homeopathic system of treatment, or homeopathy may evolve by proper experimentation and research to the point of being recognized by the medical profession as an acceptable and prevailing form of medical practice in our state; such choices, however, are not for the courts to make.

We stress that we do not intend for our opinion in this case to retard the ongoing research and development of the healing arts in any way. The Board argues, and we agree within our admittedly limited scope of medical knowledge, that preventing the practice of homeopathy will not restrict the development and acceptance of new and beneficial medical practices. Instead, the development and acceptance of such new practices simply must be achieved by "acceptable and prevailing" methods of medical research, experimentation, testing, and approval by the appropriate regulatory or professional bodies.

* * *

Reversed and Remanded.

FRYE, JUSTICE, dissenting.

* * *

... All of the evidence tended to show that Dr. Guess is a highly qualified practicing physician who uses homeopathic medicines as a last resort when allopathic medicines are not successful. He takes 150 credits of continuing medical education approved by the American Medical Association every three years and from fifty to eighty hours of homeopathic continuing medical education each year. The homeopathic medications prescribed by him are listed in the Homeopathic Pharmacopoeia of the United States and are regulated by the United States Federal Food, Drug and Cosmetic Act. The homeopathic approach is often preferred, in Dr. Guess' words, "primarily because of its well documented safety." This is not a case of a quack beguiling the public with snake oil and drums, but a dedicated physician seeking to find new ways to relieve human suffering. The legislature could hardly have intended this practice to be considered "unprofessional conduct" so as to revoke a physician's license in the absence of some evidence of harm or potential harm to the patients or to the public. Nothing in the record before the Board or this Court justifies so broad a sweep in order to secure the public "against the consequences of ignorance and incapacity as well as of deception and fraud." [ ]

* * *

... I do not believe that the General Assembly would require a physician to undergo a possibly lengthy wait for legislative action while it is attending to other matters before allowing him to make non-dangerous, beneficial treatments available to members of the public who knowingly consent. Where there is no showing of danger, I do not believe specific legislative approval is a prerequisite to a physician engaging in a practice, which is by all indications helpful when used wisely.

* * *

Notes and Questions

1. In *Williams*, the court set aside disciplinary sanction where the doctor's practice, though generally rejected, was accepted by a minority of practicing physicians. In *Guess*, the defendant produced evidence that homeopathy is a recognized system of practice in some states, but this did not cause the court to overturn disciplinary sanctions. Can you explain the different results in *Williams* and in *Guess*?

2. After the *Guess* decision, the North Carolina legislature amended the grounds for discipline to limit the section under which Guess was penalized:

> The Board shall not revoke the license of or deny a license to a person solely because of that person's practice of a therapy that is experimental, nontraditional, or that departs from acceptable and prevailing medical prac-

tices unless, by competent evidence, the Board can establish that the treatment has a safety risk greater than the prevailing treatment or that the treatment is generally not effective.

How does this amendment alter what is ordinarily required of a professional licensure board in justifying its decisions in specific cases? Does a board usually have to justify its rulemaking with empirical evidence? Does safety risk include an assessment of effectiveness? Many alternative approaches to health care are not founded on empirical scientifically-based research on effectiveness and safety. Under this amendment, does the board have to commission such research if it wants to exclude the practice?

3. The interest in alternative and complementary medicine and nonconforming practices, whether new and innovative or traditional but no longer mainstream, has increased dramatically. See e.g., David M. Eisenberg, Unconventional Medicine in the United States, 328 N.E.J.M. 246 (1993); A.L. Berrey and K.R. White, Search for the New Medicine, 100 American Journal of Nursing 45 (2000). The National Institutes of Health has established an Office of Alternative Medicine to evaluate nonconforming practices using the empirical methodology applied to allopathic medicine. This has been a controversial effort. See e.g., Clinical Practice Guidelines in Complementary and Alternative Medicine: An Analysis of Opportunities and Obstacles, 6 Archives of Family Medicine 149 (1997). For a review of legal and policy issues, see Michael H. Cohen, Complementary and Alternative Medicine: Legal Boundaries and Regulatory Perspectives (1998), suggesting that occupational licensure for practitioners of alternative and complementary medicine would encourage such practices while providing oversight for quality; Julie Stone and Joan Matthews, Complementary Medicine and the Law (1996), arguing that while some alternative or complementary practices have a technological base and are subject to the same type of verification as allopathic medicine, other practices are not amenable to such testing and, therefore, conventional quality-control regulation would be inadequate. See also, Kathleen M. Boozang, Western Medicine Opens the Door to Alternative Medicine, 24 Am.J.Law & Med. 185 (1998).

Some states allow only licensed M.D.s to provide complementary or alternative interventions such as homeopathy or acupuncture. Is this a satisfactory resolution of the interests at stake? Aside from licensure, what other barriers exist in access to nonconventional therapies?

III.   UNLICENSED PROVIDERS

The state medical board generally has the primary responsibility for enforcing the prohibition against the unauthorized practice of medicine by unlicensed providers. This prohibition is enforced by criminal sanctions against the unlicensed practitioner and license revocation against any physician who aids and abets the unlicensed practitioner. The state medical practice acts define the practice of medicine quite broadly and indeterminately and prohibit anyone but licensed physicians and other licensed health care professionals, practicing within the bounds of their own licensure, from practicing medicine. For example, the Indiana statute prohibits an unlicensed person from engaging in:

> the diagnosis, treatment, correction or prevention of any disease, ailment, defect, injury, infirmity, deformity, pain or other condition of human beings, or the suggestion, recommendation or prescription or administration of any form of treatment, without limitation, or the performing of

any kind of surgical operation upon a human being, including tattooing
..., or the penetration of the skin or body orifice by any means, for the
intended palliation, relief, cure or prevention of any physical, mental or
functional ailment or defect of any person.

Would this prohibition extend to services offered by a health club,
including fitness assessment and advice on nutrition and exercise designed to
respond to specific areas needing improvement? Would it extend to the
recommendation of over-the-counter medications for particular aches, pains or
illnesses by a cashier at a pharmacy? What is the impact of a very broadly
drawn statutory definition of the practice of medicine on patient choice? On
access? On cost? On competition? On quality? On the authority of the agency
itself to control services provided by non-physicians? For a case interpreting
this statute, see Stetina v. State ex rel. Medical Licensing Board of Indiana,
513 N.E.2d 1234 (Ind.App.1987).

STATE BOARD OF NURSING AND STATE BOARD OF HEALING ARTS v. RUEBKE

Supreme Court of Kansas, 1996.
259 Kan. 599, 913 P.2d 142.

LARSON, JUSTICE:

The State Board of Healing Arts (Healing Arts) and the State Board of
Nursing (Nursing) appeal the trial court's denial of a temporary injunction by
which the Boards had sought to stop E. Michelle Ruebke, a practicing lay
midwife, from continuing her alleged practice of medicine and nursing.

* * *

FACTUAL BACKGROUND
* * *

The hearing on the temporary injunction revealed that Ruebke acts as a
lay midwife comprehensively assisting pregnant women with prenatal care,
delivery, and post-partum care. She is president of the Kansas Midwives
Association and follows its promulgated standards, which include a risk
screening assessment based upon family medical history; establishing prenatal
care plans, including monthly visitations; examinations and assistance in
birth; and post-partum care. She works with supervising physicians who are
made aware of her mode of practice and who are available for consultation
and perform many of the medical tests incident to pregnancy.

* * *

Dr. Debra L. Messamore, an obstetrician/gynecologist, testified she had
reviewed the Kansas Midwives Association standards of care and opined those
standards were similar to the assessments incident to her practice as an
OB/GYN. Dr. Messamore concluded that in her judgment the prenatal assessments made by Ruebke were obstetrical diagnoses.

Dr. Messamore testified that the prescriptions Ruebke has women obtain
from their physicians are used in obstetrics to produce uterine contractions.
She further testified the Kansas Midwives Association standard of care

relating to post-delivery conditions of the mother and baby involved obstetrical judgments. She reviewed the birth records of [one] birth and testified that obstetrical or medical judgments were reflected. [She admitted] that many procedures at issue could be performed by a nurse rather than a physician.... She also stated her opinion that so defined obstetrics as a branch of medicine or surgery.

Ginger Breedlove, a Kansas certified advanced registered nurse practitioner and nurse-midwife, testified on behalf of Nursing. She reviewed the records [of two births] and testified nursing functions were involved. She admitted she could not tell from the records who had engaged in certain practices and that taking notes, giving enemas, and administering oxygen is often done by people who are not nurses, although education, experience, and minimum competency are required.

... The court held that provisions of both acts were unconstitutionally vague, Ruebke's midwifery practices did not and were not intended to come within the healing arts act or the nursing act, and her activities fell within exceptions to the two acts even if the acts did apply and were constitutional.

The factual findings, highly summarized, were that Ruebke had not been shown to hold herself out as anything other than a lay midwife; has routinely used and consulted with supervising physicians; was not shown to administer any prescription drugs; was not shown to do any suturing or episiotomies, make cervical or vaginal lacerations, or diagnose blood type; and had engaged only in activities routinely and properly done by people who are not physicians.

REGULATORY HISTORY OF MIDWIFERY

One of the specific statutory provisions we deal with, K.S.A. 65–2802(a), defines the healing arts as follows:

> The healing arts include any system, treatment, operation, diagnosis, prescription, or practice for the ascertainment, cure, relief, palliation, adjustment, or correction of any human disease, ailment, deformity, or injury, and includes specifically but not by way of limitation the practice of medicine and surgery; the practice of osteopathic medicine and surgery; and the practice of chiropractic.

K.S.A. 65–2869 specifically provides that for the purpose of the healing arts act, the following persons shall be deemed to be engaged in the practice of medicine and surgery:

> (a) Persons who publicly profess to be physicians or surgeons, or publicly profess to assume the duties incident to the practice of medicine or surgery or any of their branches.

> (b) Persons who prescribe, recommend or furnish medicine or drugs, or perform any surgical operation of whatever nature by the use of any surgical instrument, procedure, equipment or mechanical device for the diagnosis, cure or relief of any wounds, fractures, bodily injury, infirmity, disease, physical or mental illness or psychological disorder, of human beings.

* * *

In describing the history of lay midwifery, a law review comment, Choice in Childbirth: Parents, Lay Midwives, and Statutory Regulation, 30 St. Louis U.L.J. 985, 989–90 (1986), recounts that midwifery belonged to women from Biblical times through the Middle Ages. However, subsequent to the Middle Ages, women healers were often barred from universities and precluded from obtaining medical training or degrees. With the rise of barber-surgeon guilds, women were banned from using surgical instruments.

When midwives immigrated to America, they occupied positions of great prestige. Some communities licensed midwives and others did not. This continued until the end of the 19th century. In the 19th and 20th centuries, medical practice became more standardized. Economically and socially well-placed doctors pressed for more restrictive licensing laws and for penalties against those who violated them. The law review comment suggests that licensure was a market control device; midwives were depriving new obstetricians of the opportunity for training, and elimination of midwifery would allow the science of obstetrics to grow into a mature medical specialty.

There is a notable absence of anything in the history of Kansas healing arts regulation illustrating any attempt to specifically target midwives. In 1870, the Kansas Legislature adopted its first restriction on the practice of medicine ...

[T]here can be little doubt that in 1870 Kansas, particularly in rural areas, there were not enough educated physicians available to deliver all of the children born in the state. In fact, until 1910 approximately 50 percent of births in this country were midwife assisted. [ ]

* * *

Although obstetricians held themselves out as a medical specialty in the United States as early as 1868, midwives were not seen as engaged in the practice of obstetrics, nor was obstetrics universally viewed as being a branch of medicine. In 1901, North Carolina recognized obstetricians as engaged in the practice of medicine but women midwives, as a separate discipline, were exempted from the licensure act. [ ] ...

Although many states in the early 1900's passed laws relating to midwifery, Kansas has never expressly addressed the legality of the practice. In 1915 [ ] this court implied that a woman with considerable midwife experience was qualified to testify as an expert witness in a malpractice case against an osteopath for allegedly negligently delivering the plaintiff's child.

* * *

The 1978 Kansas Legislature created a new classification of nurses, Advanced Registered Nurse Practitioner (ARNP). [ ] One classification of ARNP is certified nurse midwives. Although the regulations permitting the practice of certified nurse midwives might be argued to show additional legislative intent to prohibit the practice of lay midwives, this argument has been rejected elsewhere. [ ]

In 1978, Kansas Attorney General opinion No. 78–164 suggested that the practice of midwifery is a violation of the healing arts act.... Although potentially persuasive, such an opinion is not binding on us.

Most probably in response to the 1978 Attorney General opinion, a 1978 legislative interim committee undertook a study of a proposal to recognize and regulate the practice of lay midwifery. However, the committee reached no conclusion.

* * *

A 1986 review of the laws of every state found that lay midwifery was specifically statutorily permitted, subject to licensing or regulation, in 25 jurisdictions. Twelve states, including Kansas, had no legislation governing or prohibiting lay midwifery directly or by direct implication. Several states recognized both lay and nurse midwives. Some issued new licensing only for nurse midwives, while others regulated and recognized both, often as separate professions, subject to separate standards and restrictions. [ ]

* * *

In April 1993, the Board of Healing Arts released Policy Statement No. 93–02, in which the Board stated it reaffirmed its previous position of August 18, 1984, that

> [m]idwifery is the practice of medicine and surgery and any practice thereof by individuals not regulated by the Kansas State Board of Nursing or under the supervision of or by order of or referral from a licensed medical or osteopathic doctor constitutes the unlicensed practice of medicine and surgery.

* * *

This historical background brings us to the question of whether the healing arts act is unconstitutionally vague. . . .

Scope of Review

* * *

[A] statute "is vague and violates due process if it prohibits conduct in terms so vague that a person of common intelligence cannot understand what conduct is prohibited, and it fails to adequately guard against arbitrary and discriminatory enforcement." [ ] A statute which requires specific intent is more likely to withstand a vagueness challenge than one, like that here, which imposes strict liability. [ ]

* * *

We have held that the interpretation of a statute given by an administrative agency within its area of expertise is entitled to deference, although final construction of a statute always rests with courts. [ ] . . .

We do, of course, attempt wherever possible to construe a statute as constitutional [ ] . . . .

* * *

The definition of healing arts uses terms that have an ordinary, definite, and ascertainable meaning. The trial court's conclusion that "disease, ailment, deformity or injury" are not commonly used words with settled meanings cannot be justified.

* * *

. . . Although we hold the act not to be unconstitutionally vague, we also hold the definitional provisions do not cover midwifery. In their ordinary usage the terms in K.S.A. 65–2802(a) used to define healing arts clearly and unequivocally focus exclusively on pathologies (i.e., diseases) and abnormal human conditions (i.e., ailments, deformities, or injuries). Pregnancy and childbirth are neither pathologies nor abnormalities.

* * *

Healing Arts argues that the "practice of medicine" includes the practice of obstetrics. It reasons, in turn, that obstetrics includes the practices traditionally performed by midwives. From this, it concludes midwifery is the practice of medicine.

However, equating midwifery with obstetrics, and thus with the practice of medicine, ignores the historical reality, discussed above, that midwives and obstetricians coexisted for many years quite separately. From the time of our statehood, the relationship between obstetricians and midwives changed from that of harmonious coexistence, cooperation, and collaboration, to open market competition and hostility. [ ]

* * *

To even the most casual observer of the history of assistance to childbirth, it is clear that over the course of this century the medical profession has extended its reach so deeply into the area of birthing as to almost completely occupy the field. The introduction of medical advances to the childbirth process drew women to physicians to assist during the birth of their children. Yet, this widespread preference for physicians as birth attendants hardly mandates the conclusion that only physicians may assist with births.

. . . The fact that a person with medical training provides services in competition with someone with no medical degree does not transform the latter's practices into the practice of medicine.

* * *

Although we hold the practice of midwifery is not itself the practice of the healing arts under our statutory scheme, our conclusions should not be interpreted to mean that a midwife may engage in any activity whatsoever with regard to a pregnant woman merely by virtue of her pregnancy. . . .

. . . However, we need not decide the precise boundaries of what a midwife may do without engaging in the practice of the healing arts because, in the case before us, Ruebke was found to have worked under the supervision of physicians who were familiar with her practices and authorized her actions. Any of Ruebke's actions that were established at trial, which might otherwise have been the practice of the healing arts, were exempt from the healing arts act because she had worked under the supervision of such physicians.

K.S.A. 65–2872 exempts certain activities from the licensure requirements of the healing arts act. In relevant part it provides:

The practice of the healing arts shall not be construed to include the following persons:

> (g) Persons whose professional services are performed under the supervision or by order of or referral from a practitioner who is licensed under this act.

* * *

In light of the uncontested factual findings of the trial court, which were supported by competent evidence in the record, we agree with the trial court that the exception to the healing arts act recognized by K.S.A. 65–2872(g) applies to any of Ruebke's midwifery activities which might otherwise be considered the practice of the healing arts under K.S.A. 65–2802(a) and K.S.A. 65–2869.

* * *

As we have held, the legislature has never specifically acted with the intent to restrict or regulate the traditional practice of lay midwifery. Nevertheless, Nursing argues such birth assistants must be licensed nurses before they may render aid to pregnant women. In oral argument, Nursing conceded much of its argument would be muted were we to hold, as we do above, that the practice of midwifery is not the practice of the healing arts and thus not part of a medical regimen.

* * *

The practice of nursing is defined [in the Kansas nurse practice act] by reference to the practitioner's substantial specialized knowledge in areas of the biological, physical, and behavioral sciences and educational preparation within the field of the healing arts. Ruebke claims no specialized scientific knowledge, but rather readily admits she has no formal education beyond high school. Her assistance is valued not because it is the application of a firm and rarified grasp of scientific theory, but because, like generations of midwives before, she has practical experience assisting in childbirth.

Moreover, "nursing" deals with "persons who are experiencing changes in the normal health processes." As these words are commonly understood, pregnancy and childbirth do not constitute changes in the normal health process, but the continuation of it.

. . . As we have held, the practice of lay midwifery has, throughout the history of the regulation of nursing, been separate and distinct from the practice of the healing arts, to which nursing is so closely joined. While we have no doubt of the legislature's power to place lay midwifery under the authority of the State Board of Nursing, the legislature has not done so.

We find no legislative intent manifested in the language of the nursing act clearly illustrating the purpose of including the historically separate practice of midwifery within the practice of nursing. [ ] Assistance in childbirth rendered by one whose practical experience with birthing provides comfort to the mother is not nursing under the nursing act, such that licensure is required.

Affirmed in part and reversed in part.

Notes and Questions

1. Courts have adopted many approaches to analyzing whether services provided in assistance at childbirth constitute the unauthorized practice of medicine. Some have examined individual actions that may be performed during childbirth. For example, in Leigh v. Board of Registration in Nursing, 395 Mass. 670, 481 N.E.2d 1347 (Mass. 1985), the court distinguished "ordinary assistance in the normal cases of childbirth" from that in which a lay midwife used "obstetrical instruments" and "printed prescriptions or formulas," and concluded that the former does not constitute the practice of medicine while the latter does. In People v. Jihan, 127 Ill.2d 379, 130 Ill.Dec. 422, 537 N.E.2d 751 (Ill. 1989), the court distinguished "assisting" at birth from "delivering" the child. Does dividing childbirth assistance into discrete activities reflect health and safety concerns?

2. In Hunter v. State, 110 Md.App. 144, 676 A.2d 968 (1996), the court concluded that the legislative history of provisions for certification of nurse midwives (similar to the Kansas provisions cited in *Ruebke*) required the conclusion that the statute permitted only registered nurses certified by the board as nurse midwives to provide midwifery services. In Leggett v. Tennessee Board of Nursing, 612 S.W.2d 476 (Tenn.App.1980), the court considered a case in which a nurse violating the nursing board's prohibition against assistance at home births by nurse midwives claimed to be acting as a lay midwife instead. The court concluded that the exemption for lay midwifery in the medical practice act allowed the nurse to claim that she was acting as a lay midwife rather than as a nurse midwife. See also, Marion OB/GYN v. State Med. Bd., 137 Ohio App.3d 522, 739 N.E.2d 15 (Ohio App. 2000), in which the court held that delivering infants was beyond the scope of practice allowed a physician assistant (who, though not a nurse, apparently had been certified by the American College of Nurse Midwives) although state law allowed licensed nurses to practice midwifery.

3. Should the Kansas Supreme Court have analyzed research on the quality and safety of services provided by nurse midwives as compared to direct-entry or lay midwives? The Kansas provision on certified nurse midwives describes substantial educational requirements for the provision of nurse midwife services. The court concludes, however, that formal education is unnecessary and that practical experience can be valued as highly. Given the opportunity to amend its statute, should the legislature provide for minimal educational requirements for persons assisting in childbirth? Should that education adopt an obstetrical model or a midwifery model for childbirth? Should it require certification as a nurse midwife? See Colo. § 12–37–101, as amended in 1996 for regulation of lay-midwives. See, Michael H. Cohen, A Fixed Star in Health Care Reform: The Emerging Paradigm of Holistic Healing, 27 Ariz. St. L.J. 79 (1995).

4. Part of the issue often arising in the legal status of lay midwives is access to home births. See Leggett v. Tennessee Bd. of Nursing, 612 S.W.2d 476 (Tenn.App.1980); Leigh v. Board of Registration in Nursing, 395 Mass. 670, 481 N.E.2d 1347 (Mass. 1985). See also, Lori B. Andrews, The Shadow Health Care System: Regulation of Alternative Health Care Providers, 32 Hous. L. Rev. 1273 (1996). One researcher has observed:

> Home births evoke strong emotions among health professionals, and attitudes are rarely based on research data. Proponents argue that home deliveries for women who are at low risk of complications during pregnancy and delivery have perinatal outcomes as good as or better than hospital births. Opponents, including the American College of Obstetrics and Gynecology, argue that unexpected complications may arise during any labor, making hospital deliv-

ery a safer option for all women. Studies have compared the safety of home and hospital births in Missouri, Tennessee, North Carolina, Kentucky, and Washington State. Neonatal morbidity and mortality did not differ between planned home deliveries and hospital births when care included continuous risk assessment and a qualified birth attendant. However, studies of home births have had methodological problems, which have weakened their findings.... [T]he safety of home birth is not likely to be established by a randomized controlled trial because most women would probably refuse to be randomly allocated a birth place and a large sample size would be required to detect adverse outcomes. Jeanne Raisler, Evidence from US Suggests That Trials Will Not Alter Obstetric Behavior, 312 British Medical Journal 754 (1996).

Some states have enacted statutes concerning the legality and regulation of home births. See e.g., Alaska § 08.65.140; Mont. Code Annot. § 37–27–311 (both providing for mandatory informed consent). Given this state of evidence, how should the state medical or nursing boards assess whether home births should be regulated or prohibited?

5. Should disclosure and consent of the patient be taken into account in prosecutions for the unauthorized practice of medicine? Consider the following "release" which the lay midwife in *People v. Jihan*, cited above, provided to her clients:

We initiated the relationship with [Jihan] and asked her to be present at the birth of our child as a midwife. We are fully aware that she is not a doctor or a nurse, and has no medical or nursing training, and agree that she is not representing that she can or will perform any tasks, which require such training. We understand that her experiences are limited to having given birth three times herself and having attended a few other births as a lay midwife or as an assistant to a doctor. We further realize that [Jihan] does not have a license as a midwife, and that Illinois does not license midwives. We understand that [Jihan] does not hold herself out to the public as a midwife, but is only agreeing to attend our birth because she feels she could be of help to us.

6. Claims of a constitutional right to choice of provider of health care services consistently fail even when made in the context of the woman's right to privacy in reproductive decision making, the lack of empirical evidence of better outcomes with commonly used obstetrical technology, and the substantial history of conflict between medical and other approaches to childbirth. See, for example, Lange–Kessler v. Department of Educ., 109 F.3d 137 (2d Cir.1997); Hunter v. State, 110 Md.App. 144, 676 A.2d 968 (1996). See also Chris Hafner–Eaton and Laurie K. Pearce, Birth Choices, the Law, and Medicine: Balancing Individual Freedoms and Protection of the Public's Health, 19 J. Health Pol. Pol'y & L. 813 (1994) (including review of state laws on direct-entry midwifery); David M. Smolin, The Jurisprudence of Privacy in a Splintered Supreme Court, 75 Marq. L. Rev. 975 (1992), with a substantial section on choices in childbirth; Lisa C. Ikemoto, The Code of Perfect Pregnancy: At the Intersection of The Ideology of Motherhood, the Practice of Defaulting to Science, and the Interventionist Mindset of Law, 53 Ohio State L. Rev. 1205 (1992).

7. Prosecution for the unauthorized practice of medicine or nursing does not require proof that the defendant actually knew that he or she was violating the statute. That is why the *Ruebke* court refers to the statute as a strict liability statute. *Ruebke* is in the overwhelming majority in refusing to declare the medical

practice act void for vagueness. See, e.g., Weyandt v. State, 35 S.W.3d 144 (Tex.App.2000); State v. Saunders, 542 N.W.2d 67 (Minn.App.1996). But see, Miller v. Medical Assoc. of Georgia, 262 Ga. 605, 423 S.E.2d 664 (Ga. 1992).

8. The court in *Ruebke* ultimately decides that where the actions of the lay midwife fell within the practice of medicine there was no violation of the statute because her actions would then fall within the statutory exception for delegated medical services performed under the supervision of a licensed physician. But see, People v. Bickham, 250 Ill.App.3d 141, 190 Ill.Dec. 217, 621 N.E.2d 86 (Ill.App. 1993), rejecting the argument by an unlicensed person who performed pelvic examinations under the direction of a physician that this activity was not the authorized practice of medicine since the exams could be conducted by physician assistants and nurses. See also, People v. Stults, 291 Ill.App.3d 71, 225 Ill.Dec. 353, 683 N.E.2d 521 (Ill.App.1997), examining practice of medical assistant as unlicensed practice of nursing. As you read the next section of materials, consider what issues the Kansas court's reliance on the authority to delegate might raise.

IV. SCOPE OF PRACTICE REGULATION

Licensed nonphysician health care providers cannot legally practice medicine, but practices that fall within their own licensure (for example, as a nurse or a physician assistant) are not considered the practice of medicine. So, for example, a nurse who is providing services authorized under the nurse practice act would not be practicing medicine while an unlicensed practitioner providing the same services could be guilty of the unauthorized practice of medicine or nursing. If a nurse engages in practices that exceed the services authorized in the nurse practice act, however, that nurse could be guilty of violating the prohibition against the unauthorized practice of medicine. In this way, the medical and nonphysician licensure statutes establish the legal framework for the roles and functions of health care professionals.

Regulation of the authorized scope of practice of the various licensed health care professions faces two inherent difficulties. First, scope of practice regulation focuses on boundary-setting between the professions and attempts to separate medicine from nursing from other health care disciplines. Second, to the extent that scope of practice regulation has depended on the identification of discrete activities that "belong" to each profession, it has applied a notion that reflects neither the overlapping competencies of health care professionals nor the nature of treatment for illness or injury.

At least two studies have advocated an integrated or multidisciplinary approach to primary care in which it would be recognized that different professions perform the same rather than different functions and activities. Linda O. Prager, Licensing Proposals Seek to Overhaul Current System, 38 Am. Med. News 9 (October 2, 1995), reviewing reports by the Pew Health Professions Commission and the Institute of Medicine. See also, Linda H. Aiken and William M. Sage, Staffing National Health Care Reform: A Role for Advanced Practice Nurses, 26 Akron L. Rev. 187 (1992).

How would you change state licensure statutes or licensing board practices to achieve more integrated care and cost-containment while assuring quality of care? How should consumer preferences be accommodated?

SERMCHIEF v. GONZALES

Supreme Court of Missouri, 1983.
660 S.W.2d 683.

WELLIVER, JUDGE.

This is a petition for a declaratory judgment and injunction brought by two nurses and five physicians* employed by the East Missouri Action Agency (Agency) wherein the plaintiff-appellants ask the Court to declare that the practices of the Agency nurses are authorized under the nursing law of this state, § 335.016.8, RSMo 1978 and that such practices do not constitute the unauthorized practice of medicine under Chapter 334 relating to the Missouri State Board of Registration For the Healing Arts (Board). ... The holding below was against appellants who make direct appeal to this Court alleging that the validity of the statutes is involved. Mo. Const. art. V, § 3. ...

I

The facts are simple and for the most part undisputed. The Agency is a federally tax exempt Missouri not-for-profit corporation that maintains offices in Cape Girardeau (main office), Flat River, Ironton, and Fredericktown. The Agency provides medical services to the general public in fields of family planning, obstetrics and gynecology. The services are provided to an area that includes the counties of Bollinger, Cape Girardeau, Perry, St. Francis, Ste. Genevieve, Madison, Iron and Washington. Some thirty-five hundred persons utilized these services during the year prior to trial. The Agency is funded from federal grants, Medicaid reimbursements and patient fees. The programs are directed toward the lower income segment of the population. Similar programs exist both statewide and nationwide.

Appellant nurses Solari and Burgess are duly licensed professional nurses in Missouri pursuant to the provisions of Chapter 335 and are employed by the Agency. Both nurses have had post-graduate special training in the field of obstetrics and gynecology. Appellant physicians are also employees of the Agency and duly licensed to practice medicine (the healing arts) pursuant to Chapter 334. Respondents are the members and the executive secretary of the Missouri State Board of Registration for the Healing Arts (Board) and as such are charged with the enforcement, implementation, and administration of Chapter 334.

The services routinely provided by the nurses and complained of by the Board included, among others, the taking of history; breast and pelvic examinations; laboratory testing of Papanicolaou (PAP) smears, gonorrhea cultures, and blood serology; the providing of and giving of information about oral contraceptives, condoms, and intrauterine devices (IUD); the dispensing of certain designated medications; and counseling services and community education. If the nurses determined the possibility of a condition designated in the standing orders or protocols that would contraindicate the use of contraceptives until further examination and evaluation, they would refer the patients to one of the Agency physicians. No act by either nurse is alleged to

---

* The physicians are joined for the reason that they are charged with aiding and abetting the unauthorized practice of medicine by the nurses.

have caused injury or damage to any person. All acts by the nurses were done pursuant to written standing orders and protocols signed by appellant physicians. The standing orders and protocols were directed to specifically named nurses and were not identical for all nurses.

The Board threatened to order the appellant nurses and physicians to show cause why the nurses should not be found guilty of the unauthorized practice of medicine and the physicians guilty of aiding and abetting such unauthorized practice. Appellants sought Court relief in this proceeding.

... [T]he trial court described in its memorandum opinion as the ultimate issues for determination:

A. Does the conduct of plaintiff nurses Solari and Burgess constitute "Professional Nursing" as that term is defined in § 335.016.8, RSMo?

B. If the Court finds and concludes that any act or acts of plaintiff nurses Solari and Burgess does not or do not constitute(s) "professional nursing" and, constitutes the unauthorized practice of medicine under § 334.010, RSMo the Court must then determine if § 334.010, RSMo is unconstitutionally vague and uncertain on its face and, thus, is in violation of the specificity requirements of the Fifth and Fourteenth Amendments to the United States Constitution and of Article 1, § 10 of the Missouri Constitution.

* * *

In our opinion the trial court correctly defined the issues of the case, both of which we deem to be matters of law to be determined by the Court.

* * *

III

The statutes involved are:

It shall be unlawful for any person not now a registered physician within the meaning of the law to practice medicine or surgery in any of its departments, or to profess to cure and attempt to treat the sick and others afflicted with bodily or mental infirmities, or engage in the practice of midwifery in this state, except as herein provided.

Section 334.010.

This Chapter does not apply ... *to nurses licensed and lawfully practicing their profession within the provisions of chapter 335, RSMo;* ...

Section 334.155, RSMo Supp.1982 (emphasis added).

Definitions.—As used in sections 335.011 to 335.096, unless the context clearly requires otherwise, the following words and terms shall have the meanings indicated:

* * *

(8) "Professional nursing" is the performance for compensation of any act which requires substantial specialized education, judgment and skill based

on knowledge and application of principles derived from the biological, physical, social and nursing sciences, including, but not limited to:

(a) Responsibility for the teaching of health care and the prevention of illness to the patient and his family; or

(b) Assessment, nursing diagnosis, nursing care, and counsel of persons who are ill, injured or experiencing alterations in normal health processes; or

(c) The administration of medications and treatments as prescribed by a person licensed in this state to prescribe such medications and treatments; or

(d) The coordination and assistance in the delivery of a plan of health care with all members of the health team; or

(e) The teaching and supervision of other persons in the performance of any of the foregoing.

Section 335.016.8(a)–(e).

At the time of enactment of the Nursing Practice Act of 1975, the following statutes were repealed:

2. A person practices professional nursing who for compensation or personal profit performs, *under the supervision and direction of a practitioner authorized to sign birth and death certificates,* any professional services requiring the application of principles of the biological, physical or social sciences and nursing skills in the care of the sick, in the prevention of disease or in the conservation of health.

Section 335.010.2, RSMo 1969 (emphasis added).

Nothing contained in this chapter shall be construed as conferring any authority on any person to practice medicine or osteopathy or to undertake the treatment or cure of disease.

Section 335.190, RSMo 1969.

The parties on both sides request that in construing these statutes we define and draw that thin and elusive line that separates the practice of medicine and the practice of professional nursing in modern day delivery of health services. A response to this invitation, in our opinion, would result in an avalanche of both medical and nursing malpractice suits alleging infringement of that line and would hinder rather than help with the delivery of health services to the general public. Our consideration will be limited to the narrow question of whether the acts of these nurses were permissible under § 335.016.8 or were prohibited by Chapter 334.

* * *

The legislature substantially revised the law affecting the nursing profession with enactment of the Nursing Practice Act of 1975.* Perhaps the most

---

* The impetus for the legislation was the ongoing expansion of nursing responsibilities. Several national commissions investigated the causes of and the implications of this phenomenon during the early 1970's. One committee concluded: "Professional nursing * * * is in a period of rapid and progressive change in response to the growth of biomedical knowledge, changes in patterns of demand for health services, and the evolution of professional relationships among nurses, physicians and other health professions." Secretary's Committee to

significant feature of the Act was the redefinition of the term "professional nursing," which appears in § 335.016.8. Even a facile reading of that section reveals a manifest legislative desire to expand the scope of authorized nursing practices. Every witness at trial testified that the new definition of professional nursing is a broader definition than that in the former statute. A comparison with the prior definition vividly demonstrates this fact. Most apparent is the elimination of the requirement that a physician directly supervise nursing functions. Equally significant is the legislature's formulation of an open-ended definition of professional nursing. The earlier statute limited nursing practice to "services . . . in the care of the sick, in the prevention of disease or in the conservation of health." § 335.010.2, RSMo 1969. The 1975 Act not only describes a much broader spectrum of nursing functions, it qualifies this description with the phrase "including, but not limited to." We believe this phrase evidences an intent to avoid statutory constraints on the evolution of new functions for nurses delivering [sic] health services. Under § 335.016.8, a nurse may be permitted to assume responsibilities heretofore not considered to be within the field of professional nursing so long as those responsibilities are consistent with her or his "specialized education, judgment and skill based on knowledge and application of principles derived from the biological, physical, social and nursing sciences." § 335.016.8.

The acts of the nurses herein clearly fall within this legislative standard. All acts were performed pursuant to standing orders and protocols approved by physicians. Physician prepared standing orders and protocols for nurses and other paramedical personnel were so well established and accepted at the time of the adoption of the statute that the legislature could not have been unaware of the use of such practices. We see nothing in the statute purporting to limit or restrict their continued use.

Respondents made no challenge of the nurses' level of training or the degree of their skill. They challenge only the legal right of the nurses to undertake these acts. We believe the acts of the nurses are precisely the types of acts the legislature contemplated when it granted nurses the right to make assessments and nursing diagnoses. There can be no question that a nurse undertakes only a nursing diagnosis, as opposed to a medical diagnosis, when she or he finds or fails to find symptoms described by physicians in standing orders and protocols for the purpose of administering courses of treatment prescribed by the physician in such orders and protocols.

The Court believes that it is significant that while at least forty states have modernized and expanded their nursing practice laws during the past fifteen years neither counsel nor the Court have discovered any case challenging nurses' authority to act as the nurses herein acted.

Study Extended Roles for Nurses, Dep't. of Health, Education and Welfare, Pub. No. (HSM) 73–2037, "Extending the Scope of Nursing Practice: A Report of the Secretary's Committee to Study Extended Roles for Nurses" 8 (1971). *See also* National Comm'n for the Study of Nursing and Nursing Education, An Abstract for Action (1970); National Comm'n for the Study of Nursing and Nursing Education, From Abstract Into Action (1973). The broadening of nursing roles necessitated altering existing nursing practice laws to reflect the changes in a nurse's professional duties. At the time the Missouri legislature acted, thirty states had amended their laws regulating the nursing profession. *See* Comment, "Interpreting Missouri's Nursing Practice Act," 26 St. Louis U.L.J. 931, 931 n. 1 (1982). Forty states currently have broadened nursing practice statutes similar to § 335.016.8.

The broadening of the field of practice of the nursing profession authorized by the legislature and here recognized by the Court carries with it the
profession's responsibility for continuing high educational standards and the
individual nurse's responsibility to conduct herself or himself in a professional
manner. The hallmark of the professional is knowing the limits of one's
professional knowledge. The nurse, either upon reaching the limit of her or
his knowledge or upon reaching the limits prescribed for the nurse by the
physician's standing orders and protocols, should refer the patient to the
physician. There is no evidence that the assessments and diagnoses made by
the nurses in this case exceeded such limits.

* * *

Having found that the nurses' acts were authorized by § 335.016.8, it
follows that such acts do not constitute the unlawful practice of medicine for
the reason that § 334.155 makes the provisions of Chapter 334 inapplicable
"to nurses licensed and lawfully practicing their profession within the provisions of Chapter 335 RSMo."

This cause is reversed and remanded with instructions to enter judgment
consistent with this opinion.

Notes and Questions

1.   The nurse practice act in *Sermchief* contains an open-ended definition of
the practice of nursing. Who has the authority to define the authorized practice of
nursing under this type of definition? Why did plaintiffs file their action against
the Board of Healing Arts (the board of medicine)? If the board of nursing had
issued regulations embracing the plaintiffs' practice within the authorized practice
of nursing, under what standard would the court review such regulations if
challenged? Would the regulation of the board of nursing prevent the board of
medicine from proceeding against the nurses? See e.g., Oklahoma Bd. of Med.
Licensure & Supervision v. Oklahoma Bd. of Examiners in Optometry, 893 P.2d
498 (Okla.1995), allowing medical board to challenge regulations of optometry
board; Washington State Nurses Ass'n v. Board of Medical Examiners, 93 Wash.2d
117, 605 P.2d 1269 (1980), challenging medical board rules expanding practice for
physician assistants; Ohio Nurses Association, Inc. v. State Board of Nursing, 44
Ohio St.3d 73, 540 N.E.2d 1354 (Ohio 1989), concerning board of nursing rules
expanding practice for licensed practical nurses.

2.   Why did the *Sermchief* plaintiffs seek a declaratory judgment action if
they had not been charged with violating the statute? See also, Group Health
Plan, Inc. v. State Bd. of Registration for the Healing Arts, 787 S.W.2d 745
(Mo.App.1990), discussing the appropriateness of a declaratory judgment action in
similar circumstances. See also, Lori B. Andrews, The Shadow Health Care
System: Regulation of Alternative Health Care Providers, 32 Hous. L. Rev. 1273
(1996), on this point and for a comprehensive analysis of the legal issues relating
to nonphysician providers.

3.   The authority to prescribe medication has been a major issue in debates
over the appropriate scope of practice of nurses and physician assistants. See e.g.,
Mary Beck, Improving America's Health Care: Authorizing Independent Prescrip-
tive Privileges for Advanced Practice Nurses, 29 U.S.F.L. Rev. 951 (1995); Phyllis
Coleman and Ronald A. Shellow, Extending Physician's Standard of Care to Non-
Physician Prescribers: The Rx for Protecting Patients, 35 Idaho L. Rev. 37 (1998).

4. Physician assistants and nurses have assumed different professional identities. Physician assistants are educated in a medical model of care and view themselves as practicing medicine through physician delegation of tasks and under the supervision of physicians. In nursing, nurse practitioners or advanced practice nurses (including nurse midwives, nurse anesthetists and specialist nurse practitioners) view themselves as operating from a nursing model of health care and acting as independent practitioners who collaborate with physicians. The relationship described in *Sermchief* illustrates a collaborative practice. Currently, organized medicine asserts that both physician assistants and nurse practitioners must be supervised by physicians, a position accepted by the American Academy of Physician Assistants, but rejected by the American Nurses Association.

What is at issue in the controversy over whether the nurse practitioner is required to practice under a doctor's supervision or in collaboration with a doctor or even more independently? Will it have an impact on the location of the nurse's practice? On control of the practice? On nurses' ability to charge insurers directly for services provided?

Some advanced practice nursing statutes provide that the nurse practitioner practice under the supervision of a physician. See e.g., Cal. Bus & Prof Code § 2746.5 (certificate authorizes nurse-midwife to practice nurse-midwifery "under the supervision of a licensed physician and surgeon who has current practice or training in obstetrics"); Cal. Bus & Prof Code § 2836.1(d) (requiring physician supervision for the furnishing of drugs or devices by nurse practitioner). Others recognize advanced practice nursing in collaboration with licensed physicians. See e.g., Mo. V.A.M.S. § 334.104 (authorizing collaborative practice arrangements in the form of written agreements, protocols or standing orders, but describing the prescriptive authority of the nurse practitioner as delegated). Some describe the advanced nursing practice without reference to the participation of a supervisory or collaborative physician. See e.g., Md. Health Occup. § 8–601 (recognizing nurse midwives).

5. Some state nursing practice statutes specifically recognize advanced practice nurses or nurse practitioners. Which is preferable: explicit statutory recognition of advanced practice nurses or an open-ended nursing practice act as in *Sermchief*? The nurse practitioner statutes typically require that the nurse have completed more advanced education and training than is required for licensure as a registered nurse. In the absence of statutory requirements, how might the legal standard for adequate education and skills be established?

6. Physician assistants first practiced under delegation exceptions traditionally included in medical practice acts. Delegation exceptions in medical practice acts tend to be quite broad as you saw in *Ruebke*. See Jacobs v. United States, 436 A.2d 1286 (D.C.App.1981). *Jacobs* involved the appropriate degree of supervision required for the practice of a physician assistant under the D.C. medical practice act and specifically the use of pre-signed prescription pads by the PA. The D.C. statute exempted "the accepted use of qualified paramedical personnel" from the prohibition against unauthorized medical practice. When is delegation appropriate and when is supervision adequate in the absence of more specific statutory requirements? Two experts testified in *Jacobs* on the issue of the pre-signed prescriptions. One testified that use of pre-signed prescriptions was not an accepted use and that the doctor must be present in the same building while the PA treated patients and must approve any prescription in advance or at least review the prescription and the record within 24 hours. Another expert testified that the use of pre-signed pads was a common practice and that there was no

standard governing the appropriate time for review, though accepted practice required review of PA prescriptions within 48 to 72 hours. Are accepted use and common practice the same thing? Does uncertainty as to questions of appropriate delegation and supervision encourage or discourage the use of physician assistants? Would more specific requirements hinder or foster the growth of the scope of practice of PAs?

7. The states vary in the standards and methods they use to assure that delegation to physician assistants is appropriate and supervision is adequate. Some states take an individualized approach and require the physician assistant or supervising physician to submit particular details about the specific position for review by an agency. See e.g., Md. Health Occup. § 15–302 (requiring submission of specific "job description" for approval by the board). Some limit the number of physician assistants a doctor may supervise. See e.g., Ohio Rev. Code § 4730.21. Other states simply define "supervision," with great variations. See e.g., Mo. V.A.M.S. § 334.735(10), defining supervision as "control exercised over a physician assistant working within the same office facility of the supervising physician except a physician assistant may make follow-up patient examinations in hospitals, nursing homes and correctional facilities, each such examination being reviewed, approved and signed by the supervising physician." Some provide for specific requirements for prescriptive authority. See e.g., Cal. Bus. & Prof. Code § 3502.1 (governing "transmittal" of prescriptions).

8. Should medical boards bear the burden of proving that the practice of the nonphysician-licensed provider presents a greater risk of harm than does the practice of the licensed medical doctor? Should reductions in the cost of health care be considered as well? See Barbara J. Safriet, Health Care Dollars and Regulatory Sense: The Role of Advanced Practice Nursing, 9 Yale J. on Reg. 417 (1992), for reviews of the literature on comparative quality. See also, Jerry Cromwell, Barriers to Achieving a Cost–Effective Workforce Mix: Lessons from Anesthesiology, 24 J. Health Politics, Policy and Law 1331 (1999).

Problem: Physicians, Physician Assistants, and Nurses

Drs. Allison Jones and Emily Johnson have a practice in Jerrold, which is located in south St. Louis County. Both Drs. Jones and Johnson are board-certified internists with a rather broad family practice. They would like to expand their practice to Jackson County, a primarily rural area about seventy miles south of Jerrold. They are especially interested in Tesson, a town of approximately 6,000 that is centrally located among the four or five small towns in the area. They are interested in Tesson because it has a small community hospital and is located close to the interstate highway. They also believe the town is underserved by physicians. There is no pediatrician in Tesson, although there is one thirty miles away. The town has one internist. It has no obstetricians, although Joan Mayo, a certified nurse midwife, has an office in a small town about eighteen miles distant from Tesson.

Ms. Mayo has been providing childbirth, family planning and other women's health services. She has an agreement with an obstetrician in Jerrold through which protocols and standing orders for her practice were established and are maintained. She can consult with this OB by phone at any time, and they make it a practice to meet once a month to discuss Ms. Mayo's patients. Ms. Mayo refers patients who require special services to this OB or to the internist in Tesson. Ms. Mayo has clinical privileges for childbirth services at the community hospital, though her patients must be admitted by the internist. She also has assisted at a few home births, though it is not her custom to do so.

Drs. Jones and Johnson would like to open an office in Tesson and employ a physician assistant and a pediatric nurse practitioner to staff the office full-time. Either Dr. Jones or Dr. Johnson would have office hours at that office once a week. They are also interested in establishing an affiliation with Ms. Mayo because they see room for growth in that area. They hope to serve the needs of Tesson by establishing active obstetrical and pediatric practices.

They have a physician assistant in their office in Jerrold. The PA is not certified, but they have been impressed with her handling of the "routine" patients that come to the office with minor injuries such as cuts and sprains and illnesses such as chicken pox and strep throat. In most cases, the assistant examines the patient, decides on a course of treatment and prescribes medication using pre-signed prescription slips. In more difficult cases, the physician assistant asks for advice from one of the physicians. There is high patient satisfaction with her work. The doctors would like her to provide services in their Tesson office as well.

For their Tesson office, they would like to find a physician assistant with extensive experience in trauma so that the assistant could care for the high incidence of farming and hunting injuries expected in that area. This PA, then, would complement the doctors' own skills as the doctors have had little experience with such injuries.

Drs. Jones and Johnson have come to you for advice concerning their plans. They have many questions, but their first concerns the Board of Healing Arts, which supervises the licensing and discipline of physicians in Allstate, and whether their plans are consistent with the laws regulating practice in Allstate.

Please specify how they might comply with the law while maintaining a "low cost" practice. If for some reason the Board decides to take action against them, what is the likelihood of the physicians' success in challenging the Board's action?

If you were counsel to Ms. Mayo, would you advise her to affiliate with Drs. Jones and Johnson? What advantages and disadvantages might such an affiliation bring? Is her current practice authorized within the Allstate statutes?

In solving this problem, assume that your jurisdiction's: 1) relevant caselaw is identical to *Sermchief* and *Ruebke*; 2) medical practice act includes a delegation exception identical to the Kansas statute quoted in *Ruebke*; 3) has a nurse practice act that provides for a definition of nursing identical to the Missouri statute reproduced in *Sermchief*; and 4) has only the following additional statutory provision:

Allstate Stat. § 2746.5.

As used in this chapter, the practice of nurse-midwifery constitutes the furthering or undertaking by any certified person, under the supervision of a licensed physician and surgeon who has current practice or training in obstetrics, to assist a woman in childbirth so long as progress meets criteria accepted as normal. All complications shall be referred to a physician immediately. The practice of nurse-midwifery does not include the assisting of childbirth by any artificial, forcible, or mechanical means, nor the performance of any version. As used in this article, "supervision" shall not be construed to require the physical presence of the supervising physician. A nurse-midwife is not authorized to practice medicine and surgery by the provisions of this chapter.

Chapter 3

QUALITY CONTROL REGULATION OF HEALTH CARE INSTITUTIONS

I. INTRODUCTION

Although hospitals, nursing homes and other health care facilities do not themselves practice medicine, the quality of the institution itself can have a very significant impact on the quality of care. The range of institutional quality issues is very broad. It extends from building design, maintenance and sanitation, fiscal and managerial soundness, through the selection, training and monitoring of the individuals directly providing care.

A major challenge for quality control regulation in health care is the vast and now rapidly changing structure of health care organizations. To illustrate the range of health care institutions regulated in a typical state, consider the Illinois Public Health and Safety Code, which includes specific regulatory requirements for the following institutional health care providers, as defined by the statute:

Hospitals: any institution . . . devoted primarily to the maintenance and operation of facilities for the diagnosis and treatment or care of . . . persons admitted for overnight stay or longer in order to obtain medical . . . care of illness, disease, injury, infirmity, or deformity.

Long-term care facility: a private home, institution . . . or any other place, . . . which provides . . . personal care, sheltered care or nursing for 3 or more persons . . . not includ[ing] . . . a hospital.

Home health agency: a public agency or private organization that provides skilled nursing services [in a patient's home] and at least one other home health service.

Hospice: a coordinated program of home and inpatient care providing . . . palliative and supportive medical, health and other services to terminally ill patients and their families.

Ambulatory surgical treatment center: any institution [or place located within an institution, subject to some restrictions] . . . devoted primarily to the maintenance and operation of facilities for the performance of surgical procedures.

What health care organizations are missing from this list? Are there freestanding emergicenters, assisted living centers, rehabilitation institutes, birthing centers, mobile mammogram services, infusion centers, chemical dependency care units, sub-acute facilities or other health care facilities in your area? Are these organizations covered by the Illinois statute? Does a home care agency that provides bathing and other personal services but not nursing or other skilled therapy fit within the statutory definition? What is the reach of the statutory definition of "nursing home"? Does it cover a retirement center that provides apartments, dining facilities, supportive household services, transportation, and space for doctors and nurses to see patients? Would such an institution have to meet the statutory standards for nursing homes? If a "hospital" provides services in a person's home after discharge, is it required to get a license as a "home health agency"?

A state agency may regulate only under its statutory authority; and if there is no legislative authorization for the regulation of a specific institution, the state may not reach that entity. Consider the following case.

MAUCERI v. CHASSIN

Supreme Court, Albany County, New York, 1993.
156 Misc.2d 802, 594 N.Y.S.2d 605.

* * *

Since 1979, the plaintiff has operated a business out of her home providing patients and their families with the names of home health aides. It is up to the patient or the family to contact the home health aide and work out the specific pay scale, hours, and duties. The plaintiff receives compensation directly from the patient or the patient's family at a flat rate of 80 cents per hour for each hour the home health aide works for the client. Plaintiff does not conduct any investigation as to the qualifications of the aides, nor does she create a care plan for the patient, or maintain medical records. During 1990, the Department of Health received a complaint that the plaintiff was referring home health aides without being licensed as a home care services agency. Plaintiff took the position that the services that she rendered were not encompassed by the statutory definition of home care services agency. The defendants disagree.

* * *

If the plaintiff, and other small businesses such as hers, are forced to comply with all of the requirements of article 36 of the Public Health Law, and the regulations thereunder, the cost of home health aides to the general public will undoubtedly increase. That is because the overhead expense of the recordkeeping and supervisory duties the plaintiff and others performing similar functions will be required to perform must be passed along in the price she charges. In a time of rising health care costs, that hardly seems a worthy goal of State government. Moreover, to those adherents of free enterprise still operating within this State it is no doubt abhorrent that a patient or his or her family cannot hire an agent to assist in employing a home health aide without that agent being subject to the requirement of having a license from the Department of Health. Be that as it may, the construction given to a statute by the agency charged with implementing it should be upheld if not irrational [ ]. Subdivision 2 of section 3602 of the Public Health Law provides as follows:

"2. 'Home care services agency' means an organization primarily engaged in arranging and/or providing directly or through contract arrangement one or more of the following: Nursing services, home health aide services, and other therapeutic and related services which may include, but shall not be limited to, physical, speech and occupational therapy, nutritional services, medical social services, personal care services, homemaker services, and housekeeper or chore services, which may be of a preventive, therapeutic, rehabilitative, health guidance, and/or supportive nature to persons at home".

Clearly, the plaintiff's business is an organization engaged in arranging for home health aide services. The fact that the plaintiff does not provide or supervise those services does not mean that she is not arranging for them when she provides her clients with a list of home health aides. Since the defendants' interpretation of the statute is not irrational, it will be upheld. That being the case, plaintiff will be enjoined from operating her home health care referral service until such time she has been licensed under article 36. . . .

Notes and Questions

1. If a family simply hired a person to provide home care services, would that person require a license as a "home care agency?" Had plaintiff made any warranties about her own services?

2. What might explain the absence of legislation regulating a particular health care organization or service? Noticeably absent from the list of facilities requiring a license are doctors' offices. Why is that? Why would Illinois define home health agency as it does rather than more broadly? See Steven J. Snyder, Providing Services to Assisted Living Facility Residents Through Home Health Agencies: Meeting the Need in Changing Times, 8 J. Affordable Housing & Community Dev. L. (Winter 1999).

II. REGULATORY SYSTEMS

The materials in this chapter focus primarily on long-term care providers. Long-term care is a critically important and growing portion of our nation's health care sector. Nursing homes are subject to a high degree of public quality control regulation by both federal and state governments, especially as compared to hospitals, home health agencies and other health care organizations. The enforcement of nursing home standards over the past three decades has created an informative case study of the challenges of public quality control regulation.

A. DIFFERENCES AMONG INSTITUTIONS

Nursing homes, home health agencies and hospitals are transforming themselves in response to significant changes in payment systems for health care, to increased competitive pressures and to forces marshaled toward integrating health care providers into seamless systems. Futurists have attempted to predict what the nursing home and the hospital will look like in the next century. See, e.g., Margaret M. Byrne and Carol M. Ashton, Incentives for Vertical Integration in Healthcare: The Effect of Reimbursement Systems, 44 J. Healthcare Management 34 (1999); Jeffrey B. Barber et al., Evolution of an Integrated Health System: A Life Cycle Framework, 43 J.

Healthcare Management 359 (1998); and Robert E. Toomey, Integrated Healthcare Systems Governance: Prevention of Illness and Care for the Sick and Injured, 25 Health Care Management Review 59 (2000). One thing is clear: some traditional notions of what each entity does have already blurred. For example, nursing homes are treating increasingly sicker patients with increased medical as opposed to custodial or supportive needs; hospitals are dedicating portions of their facilities to longer term, lower intensity care; and home health agencies are responding to individuals who are receiving intense and highly sophisticated medical care in their homes as well as to those who need basic support in functions of daily life. Still, there are significant differences among these institutions.

Part of what makes nursing homes unique in the health care system is their responsibility for the complete and total environment of their residents over a very long time. Their involvement with the daily life of residents almost always includes assistance in bathing and often includes assistance in dressing, continence and eating. Nursing homes provide increasingly intensive health care treatment as well, though nurses, rather than physicians, direct day-to-day patient care. Of course, the term "nursing home" in the U.S. also raises the spectre of widely publicized scandals of poor care and abuse. Although the number of facilities involved in these instances is very small, the public and legislative perception of the industry is affected by this image.

Unlike hospital patients, nursing home residents are chronically rather than acutely ill. The majority of residents of a nursing home typically have resided in the facility for eighteen months, but the average length of stay for persons entering nursing homes is only a few months. Only 11 in 1000 persons 65–74 years of age reside in nursing homes compared to 46 out of 1000 persons 75–84 and 192 out of 1000 persons 85 years of age or older. E. Kramarow et al., Health and Aging Chartbook. Health, United States, 1999 (1999). Nursing home residents typically bear multiple serious, chronic and intractable medical conditions. With the increasing utilization of home care, the average nursing home patient is much sicker than the typical nursing home resident of the 1980s. Joseph L. Bianculli, Developments in Long–Term Care and Assisted Living, 700 PLI/Comm 307 (1994).

The characteristics of the nursing home population have limited their ability to bring suit for harms suffered as a result of poor care or abuse. Causation may be difficult to prove. Physical injuries in very frail elderly persons may be caused either by ordinary touching or by poor care or abuse. Mental impairment makes many nursing home residents poor witnesses. Limited remaining life spans and disabilities minimize legally recognizable damages. They do not suffer lost wages and costs of medical care for injuries for the majority of patients will be covered by Medicaid or Medicare. See Terri D. Keville et al., Developments in Long–Term Care Law and Litigation, 20 Whittier L. Rev. 325 (Winter 1998). There are indications that litigation against nursing homes has increased. Marshall B. Kapp, Malpractice Liability in Long–Term Care: A Changing Environment, 24 Creighton L. Rev. 1235 (1991); David F. Bragg, Dealing with Nursing Home Neglect: The Need for Private Litigation, 39 S. Tex. L. Rev. 1 (December 1997); and J. Thomas Rhodes III & Juliette Castillo, Proving Damages in Nursing Home Cases, 36 Trial 41 (August 2000). For a nursing home case with punitive damages awarded, see First Healthcare Corporation v. Hamilton, 740 So.2d 1189 (Fla.Dist.Ct.App.1999).

While hospitals developed in the United States as charitable institutions often under the direction of religious organizations, nursing homes developed originally as "mom-and-pop" enterprises, in which individuals boarded elderly persons in private homes. After the advent of Medicare and Medicaid, nursing homes attracted substantial activity from investors and were viewed primarily as real estate investments. Most nursing homes are for-profit, while most hospitals are not-for-profit. National for-profit chains own a significant segment of the nursing home industry.

Nursing homes have only recently developed quality assurance or continuous quality improvement systems, which have been long established internally in hospitals. Physicians are still largely absent from these facilities, and professional nurses act primarily as administrators rather than direct care providers. Further, while hospitals have long participated in a substantial private accreditation program of the Joint Commission on Accreditation of Healthcare Organizations, nursing homes do not have an equivalent influential, substantial private accreditation system (although JCAHO and others do offer accreditation for nursing homes).

The demand for nursing home spaces exceeds the supply, especially once source of payment and level of care required are considered. See Margaret M. Flint, Nursing Homes, 75 PLI/NY 721 (June 2000). Proximity to family is a common concern due to the length of stay. The choice of nursing home is still most commonly made during the hospitalization of the elderly person with the natural stress of such a decision within the short timeframe before discharge. The future resident, who is the actual consumer of services, is not usually the person who selects the home. Further, the ability of a resident to leave one facility for another is limited by the physical and mental frailty of many residents.

Over 46.3% of nursing home care in the U.S. was paid for by the Medicaid program in 1998, while about 11.9% was paid for by Medicare. HCFA, Nursing Home Care Expenditures Aggregate and Per Capita Amounts and Percent Distribution, By Source of Funds (visited Nov. 10, 2000) http://www.hcfa.glv/stats/nhe-oact/tables/t7.htm. As you will see in later chapters, Medicaid is the need-based federal-state program for health care for certain groups of poor people. Medicaid is viewed as a welfare program, while Medicare, which is not need-based but which is supported in part by general tax revenue, is generally viewed as an insurance program.

Long-term health care increasingly includes health care provided in the home. Home health care has been one of the fastest growing segments of the health care system. The total amount of expenditures on home health care has grown from around $2 billion per year in 1987 to over $18 billion per year in 1996. Brian E. Davis, The Home Health Care Crisis: Medicare's Fastest Growing Program Legalizes Spiraling Costs, 6 Elder L.J. 215 (1998). However, this spending has decreased dramatically over the past few years. See, e.g., J.P. Bender, 20 South Florida Business Journal 1 (May 26, 2000). This decline has been attributed to changes in Medicare reimbursement rates mandated by Congress in the Balanced Budget Act of 1997.

As much as nursing homes bear a negative image, home health care enjoys a positive image of "home and hearth." Yet, home health care can include high tech medical procedures that were formerly performed only in hospitals as well as basic personal care services. Home health care patients may be rehabilitation patients who are recovering from stroke or other injury, or disabled patients living at home. They may be receiving temporary follow-up care after hospital discharge, infused chemotherapy, long-term medical treatment, or palliative care in the case of terminal illness.

Home environments can be conducive to more independence and better recovery, but they can also be inadequate to the task of care. In fact, there is little known about the quality of home health services because home health by definition takes place in private home settings with providers caring for patients in many different locations, usually one patient at a time.

Home care is often "orchestrated" care, involving providers from several different agencies with the individual providers working variably as independent contractors, subcontractors or employees. The director of care formally may be the patient's physician, but in reality may be a case manager for the insurer. Home health care relies upon care provided by professionals, by paraprofessionals and by family members, with family members frequently performing functions that ordinarily are performed by licensed health care professionals.

Litigation against home health agencies for injuries to patients is relatively uncommon due to several problems including issues relating to the cause of injuries when care has been provided by both professional providers and family members; to multiple providers from a variety of agencies; and to the legal structure of the professional-agency relationship. Private accreditation reached few home health agencies in the 1980s, but has begun to extend its reach.

Notes and Questions

1. Governmental quality control regulation is only one source of quality control in health care. What role does private litigation play? The market? Internal quality assurance or quality improvement mechanisms? Professional ethics and licensure? What are some other public and private quality control mechanisms? The debate over whether government "command and control" regulation or the market is most effective in improving the quality of health care institutions has raged for decades. See, for example, William M. Sage, Regulating Through Information Disclosure Laws and American Health Care, 99 Col.L.Rev. 1701 (1999); Troyen A. Brennan and Donald M. Berwick, New Rules: Regulation, Markets and the Quality of American Health Care (1996).

2. How might the differences among hospitals, nursing homes and home health care affect the relative strength of these quality control instruments? As you read the following materials, consider what demands these institutional differences might make on a specific governmental quality control program. How will standards differ among institutions? Will the focus be the same for nursing home regulation as for hospital regulation, for example? How might the survey or inspection process differ? How would you go about inspecting home health agencies, for example? Would the tenor of the regulatory effort differ among these organizations?

3. See, for a comparison among nursing homes, hospitals and home health care: Rosalie A. Kane, et al., Perspectives on Home Care Quality, 16 Health Care

Fin. Rev. 69 (1994); Bruce C. Vladeck and Nancy A. Miller, The Medicare Home Health Initiative, 16 Health Care Financing Review 7 (1994); Robert Morris, The Evolution of the Nursing Home as Intermediary Institution, 19 Generations 57 (1995); Sandra H. Johnson, Quality–Control Regulation of Home Health Care, 26 Hous.L.Rev. 901 (1989). See also John Braithwaite, The Nursing Home Industry, 18 Crime & Justice 11 (1993), for a comparison of nursing home regulation in the U.S. and Australia. See also, Randall Wainoris, Changes in Medicare Resulting from the Balanced Budget Act of 1997 and Their Affect on Home Health Care, 13–WTR NAELA Q 16 (Winter 2000).

B. LICENSURE AND MEDICARE/MEDICAID

In the 1970s, state nursing home licensure laws underwent significant reforms as to standards and sanctions. State licensure programs were central to the public quality control effort through the 1980s. Every state also licenses hospitals, but that system has been less enforcement-oriented and has received less budget support than the nursing home licensure system. In many states, hospital licensure relies extensively on the standards of the Joint Commission on Accreditation of Healthcare Organizations (JCAHO), which is discussed later in this chapter. Most states license some home health agencies, though the licensure system for home health agencies typically is the least developed and receives the least financial support, but this may be changing.

While the states have authority to regulate health care facilities under their police power, the federal government's authority arises primarily from its financing authority—its role as purchaser of health care for Medicare and Medicaid. Only providers who wish to receive payment for services to Medicare or Medicaid beneficiaries must meet federal standards in order to enter into a provider agreement with those programs. The federal government has used its authority to impose requirements that reach beyond Medicare and Medicaid beneficiaries, however. For example, hospitals receiving payment for treatment of Medicare beneficiaries must meet federal requirements in the provision of emergency care services to any person—beneficiary or not—who presents at the facility's emergency department. (See Chapter 11.)

Quality in nursing facilities is regulated at two different levels—state and federal. In order for a nursing home to operate, it must be licensed by the state. A second line of quality assurance comes from the federal government. Certification must be obtained before a nursing facility is allowed to participate and receive federal money from the Medicare and Medicaid programs.

For nursing facilities, Medicare/Medicaid certification is optional while state licensure is mandatory. If a nursing facility cannot or chooses not to participate in Medicare/Medicaid, it will only be subject to state licensure requirements. Realistically, however, most nursing homes cannot survive without Medicare and Medicaid payments. Therefore, most nursing facilities must meet both state licensure and federal Medicare/Medicaid standards.

Until the late 1980s, the federal government largely deferred quality control regulation of nursing homes to the state licensure systems. With federal nursing home reform in 1987 (the Omnibus Budget Reconciliation Act of 1987), however, the federal government undertook a very significant role in that arena. It is still struggling with the appropriate standards and enforcement system for home health care, however; and it still largely defers to private accreditation by JCAHO for Medicare and Medicaid certification of hospitals. See Senator Charles Grassley, The Resurrection of Nursing Home Reform: A Historical Account of the Recent Revival of the Quality of Care Standards for Long–Term Care Facilities Established in the Omnibus Reconciliation Act of 1987, 7 Elder L.J. 267 (1999).

C. THE REGULATORY PROCESS

The regulatory process—whether licensure or Medicare/Medicaid certification—can be divided usefully into three functions: standard setting; survey and inspection; and sanctions.

1. Standard Setting

IN RE THE ESTATE OF MICHAEL PATRICK SMITH v. HECKLER

United States Court of Appeals, Tenth Circuit, 1984.
747 F.2d 583.

McKay, Circuit Judge:

Plaintiffs, seeking relief under 42 U.S.C.A. § 1983, brought this class action on behalf of Medicaid recipients residing in nursing homes in Colorado. They alleged that the Secretary of Health and Human Services (Secretary) has a statutory duty under Title XIX of the Social Security Act, 42 U.S.C.A. §§ 1396–1396n (1982), commonly known as the Medicaid Act, to develop and implement a system of nursing home review and enforcement designed to ensure that Medicaid recipients residing in Medicaid-certified nursing homes actually receive the optimal medical and psychosocial care that they are entitled to under the Act. The plaintiffs contended that the enforcement system developed by the Secretary is "facility-oriented," not "patient-oriented" and thereby fails to meet the statutory mandate. The district court found that although a patient care or "patient-oriented" management system is feasible, the Secretary does not have a duty to introduce and require the use of such a system. In re Estate of Smith v. O'Halloran, 557 F.Supp. 289, 295 (D.Colo.1983).

The primary issue on appeal is whether the trial court erred in finding that the Secretary does not have a statutory duty to develop and implement a system of nursing home review and enforcement, which focuses on and ensures high quality patient care. . . .

Background

The factual background of this complex lawsuit is fully discussed in the district court's opinion. In re Estate of Smith v. O'Halloran, 557 F.Supp. 289 (D.Colo.1983). Briefly, plaintiffs instituted the lawsuit in an effort to improve the deplorable conditions at many nursing homes. They presented evidence of the lack of adequate medical care and of the widespread knowledge that care is inadequate. Indeed, the district court concluded that care and life in some nursing homes is so bad that the homes "could be characterized as orphanages for the aged." Id. at 293.

* * *

THE MEDICAID ACT

An understanding of the Medicaid Act (the Act) is essential to understand plaintiffs' contentions. The purpose of the Act is to enable the federal government to assist states in providing medical assistance to "aged, blind or disabled individuals, whose income and resources are insufficient to meet the costs of necessary medical services, and . . . rehabilitation and other services to help such . . . individuals to attain or retain capabilities for independence or self care." 42 U.S.C.A. § 1396 (1982). To receive funding, a state must submit to the Secretary and have approved by the Secretary, a plan for medical assistance, which meets the requirements of 42 U.S.C.A. § 1396a(a).

. . . A state seeking plan approval must establish or designate a single state agency to administer or supervise administration of the state plan, 42 U.S.C.A. § 1396a(a)(5), and must provide reports and information as the Secretary may require. Id. § 1396a(a)(6). Further, the state agency is responsible for establishing and maintaining health standards for institutions where the recipients of the medical assistance under the plan receive care or services. Id. § 1396a(a)(9)(A). The plan must include descriptions of the standards and methods the state will use to assure that medical or remedial care services provided to the recipients "are of high quality." Id. § 1396a(a)(22)(D).

The state plan must also provide "for a regular program of medical review . . . of each patient's need for skilled nursing facility care . . . , a written plan of care, and, where applicable, a plan of rehabilitation prior to admission to a skilled nursing facility. . . ." Id. § 1396a(a)(26)(A). Further, the plan must provide for periodic inspections by medical review teams of:

(i) the care being provided in such nursing facilities . . . to persons receiving assistance under the State plan; (ii) with respect to each of the patients receiving such care, the adequacy of the services available in particular nursing facilities . . . to meet the current health needs and promote the maximum physical well-being of patients receiving care in such facilities . . .; (iii) the necessity and desirability of continued placement of such patients in such nursing facilities . . .; and (iv) the feasibility of meeting their health care needs through alternative institutional or noninstitutional services. Id. § 1396a(a)(26)(B).

The state plan must provide that any skilled nursing facility receiving payment comply with 42 U.S.C.A. § 1395x(j), which defines "skilled nursing facility" and sets out standards for approval under a state plan. Id. § 1396a(a)(28). The key requirement for purposes of this lawsuit is that a skilled nursing facility must meet "such other conditions relating to the health and safety of individuals who are furnished services in such institution or relating to the physical facilities thereof as the Secretary may find necessary. . . ." Id. § 1395x(j)(15).

The state plan must provide for the appropriate state agency to establish a plan, consistent with regulations prescribed by the Secretary, for professional health personnel to review the appropriateness and quality of care and services furnished to Medicaid recipients. Id. § 1396a(a)(33)(A). The appropriate state agency must determine on an ongoing basis whether participating institutions meet the requirements for continued participation in the Medicaid program. Id. § 1396a(a)(33)(B). While the state has the initial responsibility for determining whether institutions are meeting the conditions of partic-ipation, section 1396a(a)(33)(B) gives the Secretary the authority to "look behind" the state's determination of facility compliance, and make an inde-pendent and binding determination of whether institutions meet the require-ments for participation in the state Medicaid plan. Thus, the state is responsi-ble for conducting the review of facilities to determine whether they comply with the state plan. In conducting the review, however, the states must use federal standards, forms, methods, and procedures. 42 C.F.R. § 431.610(f)(1) (1983). . . .

IMPLEMENTING REGULATIONS

Congress gave the Secretary a general mandate to promulgate rules and regulations necessary to the efficient administration of the functions with which the Secretary is charged by the Act. 42 U.S.C.A. § 1302 (1982). Pursuant to this mandate the Secretary has promulgated standards for the care to be provided by skilled nursing facilities and intermediate care facili-ties. See 42 C.F.R. § 442.200–.516 (1983). . . .

The Secretary has established a procedure for determining whether state plans comply with the standards set out in the regulations. This enforcement mechanism is known as the "survey/certification" inspection system. Under this system, the states conduct reviews of nursing homes pursuant to 42 U.S.C.A. § 1396a(a)(33). The Secretary then determines, on the basis of the survey results, whether the nursing home surveyed is eligible for certification and, thus, eligible for Medicaid funds. The states must use federal standards, forms, methods, and procedures in conducting the survey. 42 C.F.R. § 431.610(f)(1). At issue in this case is the form SSA–1569, [ ], which the Secretary requires the states to use to show that the nursing homes partici-pating in Medicaid under an approved state plan meet the conditions of participation contained in the Act and the regulations. Plaintiffs contend that the form is "facility-oriented," in that it focuses on the theoretical capability of the facility to provide high quality care, rather than "patient-oriented," which would focus on the care actually provided. The district court found, with abundant support in the record, that the "facility-oriented" characteriza-tion is appropriate and that the Secretary has repeatedly admitted that the form is "facility-oriented." [ ]

THE PLAINTIFFS' CLAIMS

* * *

The plaintiffs do not challenge the substantive medical standards, or "conditions of participation," which have been adopted by the Secretary and which states must satisfy to have their plans approved. See 42 C.F.R. § 405.1101–.1137. Rather, plaintiffs challenge the enforcement mechanism the Secretary has established. The plaintiffs contend that the federal forms, form SSA–1569 in particular, which states are required to use, evaluate only the physical facilities and theoretical capability to render quality care. The surveys assess the care provided almost totally on the basis of the records, documentation, and written policies of the facility being reviewed. [ ] Further, out of the 541 questions contained in the Secretary's form SSA–1569 which must be answered by state survey and certification inspection teams, only 30 are "even marginally related to patient care or might require any patient observation. ... " [ ] Plaintiffs contend that the enforcement mechanism's focus on the facility, rather than on the care actually provided in the facility, results only in "paper compliance" with the substantive standards of the Act. Thus, plaintiffs contend, the Secretary has violated her statutory duty to assure that federal Medicaid monies are paid only to facilities, which meet the substantive standards of the Act—facilities which actually provide high quality medical, rehabilitative, and psychosocial care to resident Medicaid recipients.

The District Court's Holding

After hearing the evidence, the district court found the type of patient care management system advocated by plaintiffs clearly feasible and characterized the current enforcement system as "facility-oriented." [ ] However, the court concluded that the failure to implement and require the use of a "patient-oriented" system is not a violation of the Secretary's statutory duty. [ ] The essence of the district court's holding was that the State of Colorado, not the federal government, is responsible for developing and enforcing standards which would assure high quality care in nursing homes and, thus, the State of Colorado, not the federal government, should have been the defendant in this case. [ ]

* * *

The Secretary's Duty

After carefully reviewing the statutory scheme of the Medicaid Act, the legislative history, and the district court's opinion, we conclude that the district court improperly defined the Secretary's duty under the statute. The federal government has more than a passive role in handing out money to the states. The district court erred in finding that the burden of enforcing the substantive provisions of the Medicaid Act is on the states. The Secretary of Health and Human Services has a duty to establish a system to adequately inform herself as to whether the facilities receiving federal money are satisfying the requirements of the Act, including providing high quality patient care. This duty to be adequately informed is not only a duty to be informed at the time a facility is originally certified, but is a duty of continued supervision.

Nothing in the Medicaid Act indicates that Congress intended the physical facilities to be the end product. Rather, the purpose of the Act is to provide medical assistance and rehabilitative services. 42 U.S.C.A. § 1396. The Act repeatedly focuses on the care to be provided, with facilities being only part of that care. For example, the Act provides that health standards are to be developed and maintained, *id.* § 1396a(a)(9)(A), and that states must inform the Secretary what methods they will use to assure high quality care. *Id.* § 1396a(a)(22). In addition to the "adequacy of the services available," the periodic inspections must address "the care being provided" in nursing facilities. *Id.* § 1396a(a)(26)(B). State plans must provide review of the "appropriateness and quality of care and services furnished," *id.* § 1396a(a)(33)(A), and do so on an ongoing basis. *Id.* § 1396a(a)(33)(B).

While the district court correctly noted that it is the state, which develops specific standards and actually conducts the inspection, there is nothing in the Act to indicate that the state function relieves the Secretary of all responsibility to ensure that the purposes of the Act are being accomplished. The Secretary, not the states, determines which facilities are eligible for federal funds. [ ] While participation in the program is voluntary, states who choose to participate must comply with federal statutory requirements. [ ] The inspections may be conducted by the states, but the Secretary approves or disapproves the state's plan for review. Further, the inspections must be made with federal forms, procedures, and methods.

It would be anomalous to hold that the Secretary has a duty to determine whether a state plan meets the standards of the Act while holding that the Secretary can certify facilities without informing herself as to whether the facilities actually perform the functions required by the state plan. The Secretary has a duty to ensure more than paper compliance. The federal responsibility is particularly evident in the "look behind" provision. 42 U.S.C.A. § 1396a(a)(33)(B) (1982). We do not read the Secretary's "look behind" authority as being "nothing more than permitted authority . . . ," 557 F.Supp. 296, as the district court found. Rather, we find that the purpose of that section is to assure that compliance is not merely facial, but substantive.

* * *

By enacting section 1302 Congress gave the Secretary authority to promulgate regulations to achieve the functions with which she is charged. The "look-behind" provision and its legislative history clearly show that Congress intended the Secretary to be responsible for assuring that federal Medicaid money is given only to those institutions that actually comply with Medicaid requirements. The Act's requirements include providing high quality medical care and rehabilitative services. In fact, the quality of the care provided to the aged is the focus of the Act. Being charged with this function, we must conclude that a failure to promulgate regulations that allow the Secretary to remain informed, on a continuing basis, as to whether facilities receiving federal money are meeting the requirements of the Act, is an abdication of the Secretary's duty. While the Medicaid Act is admittedly very complex and the Secretary has "exceptionally broad authority to prescribe standards for applying certain sections of the Act," *Schweiker v. Gray Panthers*, 453 U.S. 34, 43 (1981), the Secretary's authority cannot be interpreted so as to hold that that authority is merely permissive authority. The Secretary must insure that states comply with the congressional mandate to provide high quality medical care and rehabilitative services.

. . . Having determined that the purpose and the focus of the Act is to provide high quality medical care, we conclude that by promulgating a facility-oriented enforcement system the Secretary has failed to follow that focus and such failure is arbitrary and capricious. [ ]

Reversed and Remanded.

Notes and Questions

1. What explains the opposition of the federal government to patient-oriented standards in the *Smith* litigation? Should an administrative agency, as a matter of policy, simply resist all judicial mandates in standard setting? Would nursing homes oppose the implementation of a patient-oriented system?

2. Did the plaintiffs in *Smith* contest the standards as enacted in the statute? As promulgated in regulations? Would a challenge to the statute itself

likely be successful? On what basis would plaintiffs be able to challenge the regulations? Why would the survey forms themselves be of interest to attorneys representing facilities or residents?

3. In 1986, the Secretary issued final regulations to implement a new survey system as ordered by the court in *Smith*. The Secretary refused to include the survey instrument itself in the regulations, however: "[T]he new forms and instructions are not set forth in these regulations, and any future changes will be implemented through general instructions, without further changes in these regulations. This allows flexibility to revise and improve the survey process as experience is gained." 51 Fed.Reg. 21,550 (6/13/86). What else does this allow the agency to do? The federal district court rejected the final rules because they did not include the survey instruments or instructions and held the Secretary in contempt of court. Smith v. Bowen, 675 F.Supp. 586 (D.Colo.1987). What was the judge's concern here?

4. In 1987, Congress enacted comprehensive federal nursing home reform legislation as part of the Omnibus Budget Reconciliation Act (OBRA). The legislation adopted most of the recommendations of a Congressionally commissioned study of nursing homes conducted by the Institute of Medicine (IOM) of the National Academy of Sciences. See, Improving the Quality of Care in Nursing Homes (National Academy of Sciences Press 1986). OBRA 1987 represented a comprehensive change in standards, surveillance methods and enforcement. The new standards, survey process and sanctions adopted in OBRA 1987 were the result of a "partnership" among representatives of state government, the federal government, providers and consumers and shifted the emphasis toward resident-focused outcome standards that promote the quality of life of each resident and that required an individualized plan of care. Bruce C. Vladeck, The Past, Present, and Future of Nursing Home Quality, 275 JAMA 425 (Feb. 14, 1996).

5. Research indicates that standards incorporated in OBRA '87 may have had an effect on several practices although these changes may be coincidental with other factors as well. For example, the use of physical restraints has declined by 50%; inappropriate use of antipsychotic drugs has declined at least 25%; the incidence of dehydration has been reduced by 50%; the use of indwelling catheters by nearly 30%; and hospitalizations by 25%. Bruce C. Vladeck, The Past, Present and Future of Nursing Home Quality, 275 JAMA 425 (Feb. 14, 1996), reviewing the literature. But see, Catherine Hawes et al., The OBRA–87 Nursing Home Regulations and Implementation of the Resident Assessment Instrument: Effects on Process Quality, 45 J. Am. Geriatrics Soc'y 977 (1997), discussing the difficulty of proving that changes in practices and outcomes were caused by the new regulations. Marshall Kapp, in an article that is quite skeptical about research indicating that the standards of OBRA 1987 have had a significant positive effect, observes:

> In terms of OBRA 87's impact on the general quality of care and quality of life within [nursing facilities], the overall verdict to date has been largely, although not unanimously, positive. Not surprisingly, past and current HCFA Administrators have given the law (and, not coincidentally, themselves) a glowing endorsement, by pointing to such post-OBRA quality indicators as reduction in resident dehydration, decreased utilization of indwelling urinary catheters, lowering of the hospitalization rate, and an increase in the number of hearing impaired residents who now have hearing aids. Interviews with nursing home employees, regulators, advocates, and representatives of professional associations have yielded favorable perceptions regarding the law's

impact. Marshall B. Kapp, Quality of Care and Quality of Life in Nursing Facilities: What's Regulation Got To Do With It? 31 McGeorge L. Rev. 707 (2000).

Kapp notes, however, that government studies of the quality of nursing home care observe persistent problems in the quality of care and the effectiveness of the regulatory system. See e.g., General Accounting Office, Nursing Homes: Additional Steps Needed to Strengthen Enforcement of Federal Quality Standards, GAO/ HEHS–99–46 (1999); General Accounting Office, California Nursing Homes: Care Problems Persist Despite Federal and State Oversight, GAO/HEHS–98–202 (1998).

6. Some advocates argue that OBRA 1987 is now outdated, "designed for an industry that no longer exists," and argue that "improvements in staff quality and the experience nursing homes have acquired in recent years have transformed today's regulations into barriers to genuine quality and efficiency." Michael J. Stoil, AAHSA Climbs on the Deregulatory Bandwagon, 44 Nursing Homes 7 (1995), quoting the president of AAHSA, the organization of not-for-profit nursing homes. How could regulations intended to improve quality become a barrier to quality? If the OBRA standards are outdated, will change require Congressional action or would HCFA be able to make needed changes?

7. The court's opinion in *Smith* describes the allocation of authority in the federal-state Medicaid quality control program. Exactly which functions are allocated to the state and which to the federal government? If Congress were to reconsider the role of the federal government in Medicaid regulation of nursing homes, should it continue the involvement of both the state and the federal governments? Should it consider requiring merely that nursing facilities receiving Medicaid or Medicare dollars be licensed by the state?

8. HCFA has initiated another round of major changes in its regulatory process overall, and particularly for nursing facilities and home health care. Barbara J. Gagel, Health Care Quality Improvement Program: A New Approach, 16 Health Care Fin. Rev. 15 (1995). One aspect is a shift in emphasis from identifying poor care providers toward the promotion of improved health status for all beneficiaries. HCFA is also emphasizing direct information to consumers to allow consumers to discriminate between the better and the poorer providers. HCFA has joined the general movement in health care toward an emphasis on outcomes rather than structure and process standards. (Review the material on measuring quality in Chapter 1.) HCFA bases this shift toward outcome standards in part on changes in the health care industry itself, including the movement toward scientifically-based practice guidelines and quality indicators, data systems technology improvements, and the adoption of quality improvement methods by the institutions themselves. Reviewing the comparative information on hospitals, nursing homes and home health provided in the beginning of this chapter, do you foresee any differences among these three providers that might determine the success of this shift in policy? For example, an emphasis on outcomes is not without its problems in nursing facilities as compared to hospitals. See Robert L. Kane, Improving the Quality of Long–Term Care, 273 JAMA 1376 (May 3, 1995). As to outcomes standards for home care, see Rosalie A. Kane, et al., Perspectives on Home Care Quality, 16 Health Care Fin. Rev. 69 (1994). What is unique to home health care that might affect reliance on outcomes as a measure of quality? As to application of quality improvement approaches to home care, see Eleanor D. Kinney, Joy A. Freedman, Cynthia A. Loveland Cook, Quality Improvement in

Community–Based Long–Term Care: Theory and Reality, 20 Am.J.L. & Med. 59 (1994).

9. What legal issues might outcome standards raise? Does an emphasis on outcome standards mean that a negative outcome must be identified in each individual case? Or that standards would be validated by research indicating that they have a direct impact on quality? Is it ever reasonable to assume that a particular process or structure standard has an effect on quality without empirical proof? If the statute specifies certain structural or process standards (e.g., requiring that a nursing home be administered by a licensed nursing home administrator, or requiring minimum staffing ratios or staff training), could a facility contest enforcement of those standards for lack of empirical evidence of an impact on quality? In Beverly California Corporation v. Shalala, 78 F.3d 403 (8th Cir.1996), the administrative law judge reviewing termination of the facility's Medicaid certification determined that termination was inappropriate because HCFA had not proved that any resident had suffered actual harm as a result of the deficiencies. The Appeals Council overturned the ALJ's decision and affirmed the Secretary's sanction stating that "deficiencies which substantially limit a facility's capacity to render adequate care or which adversely affect the health and safety of residents constitute noncompliance.... [A] strong potential for adverse effect on resident health and safety will constitute noncompliance as will an actual adverse effect or 'actual harm'." The District Court and the Eighth Circuit affirmed the Appeals Council decision.

10. OBRA '87 adopted new standards concerning the use of physical and chemical restraints which aimed at reducing their use. This represented not only a regulatory change but a fundamental change in the foundation of a customary practice. Prior to the mid 1980s, physically restraining a nursing home patient was viewed as protective of the patient in that it prevented falls. It was also believed that a nursing home would be liable for injuries due to falls if it did not restrain patients. Research in the field changed that view. See, for example, Julie A. Braun and Elizabeth A. Capezuti, The Legal and Medical Aspects of Physical Restraints and Bed Siderails and Their Relationship to Falls and Fall–Related Injuries in Nursing Homes, 4 DePaul J. of Health Care Law 1 (2000); Sandra H. Johnson, The Fear of Liability and the Use of Restraints in Nursing Homes, 18 Law, Med. & Health Care 263, 264 (1990).

Problem: Residents' Rights

Assume that you are the attorney for Pine Acres Nursing Home, located in an older section of the city. The administrator has approached you regarding problems with certain patients. One patient, Francis Scott, aged 88, has been a resident of the facility for a few months. Scott's mental and physical condition has been deteriorating slowly for several years and much more rapidly in the past six months. His family placed him in the nursing home because they wanted him to be safe. They were concerned because he had often left his apartment and become totally lost on the way back. Mr. Scott's family always promptly pays the monthly fee. Scott is angry about the placement, tends to be rude and insists on walking through the hallways and around the fenced-in grounds of the facility on his own. He has always been an early riser and likes to take his shower at the crack of dawn. He refuses to be assisted in showering by a nurses' aide. In addition, his friends from the neighborhood like to visit. They like to play pinochle when they come, and they usually bring a six-pack.

Another patient, Emma Kaitz, has fallen twice, apparently while trying to get out of bed. The staff is very concerned that she will be hurt. The physician who is medical director of the facility will write an order for restraints "as needed" for any resident upon the request of the director of nursing. Mrs. Kaitz's daughter is willing to try whatever the doctor advises. The staff have begun using "soft restraints" (cloth straps on her wrists) tied to the bedrails, but Mrs. Kaitz becomes agitated and cries. She says she feels like a dog when they tie her up. Other times they just use the bedrails alone. When she becomes agitated, she is given a sedative to help her relax, but it also tends to make her appear confused. To avoid the agitation as much as possible during the day, they have been able to position her wheelchair so that she can't get out by herself. She stops trying after a while and becomes so relaxed she nods off.

The administrator wants to know what he can do. What would you advise this administrator? Can he restrict the visiting hours for Mr. Scott? Can he require Scott to be assisted in the shower? Can Mr. Scott be transferred or discharged? Is the facility dealing with Mrs. Kaitz well? How should an inspector treat Mr. Scott's and Mrs. Kaitz's complaints? What does your nursing home client expect of you here? What role should you play in regard to quality of care standards?

The text that follows includes excerpts from the Residents' Rights section of the Medicaid statute; the regulation on the use of physical restraints; and the interpretive guidelines on physical restraints provided to surveyors for the inspection of Medicaid facilities. Find out where you can find the interpretive guidelines on other provisions of the Medicaid nursing home statutes.

42 U.S.C.A. § 1396r

(b)(1) QUALITY OF LIFE.—

(A) IN GENERAL.—A nursing facility must care for its residents in such a manner and in such an environment as will promote maintenance or enhancement of the quality of life of each resident.

* * *

(c) REQUIREMENTS RELATING TO RESIDENTS' RIGHTS—

(1) GENERAL RIGHTS.—

(A) SPECIFIED RIGHTS.—A nursing facility must protect and promote the rights of each resident, including each of the following rights:

(i) FREE CHOICE.—The right to choose a personal attending physician, to be fully informed in advance about care and treatment, to be fully informed in advance of any changes in care or treatment that may affect the resident's well-being, and (except with respect to a resident adjudged incompetent) to participate in planning care and treatment or changes in care and treatment.

(ii) FREE FROM RESTRAINTS.—The right to be free from physical or mental abuse, corporal punishment, involuntary seclusion, and any physical or chemical restraints imposed for purposes of discipline or convenience and not required to treat the resident's medical symptoms. Restraints may only be imposed—

(I) to ensure the physical safety of the resident or other residents, and

(II) only upon the written order of a physician that specifies the duration and circumstances under which the restraints are to be used (except in emergency circumstances specified by the Secretary until such an order could reasonably be obtained).

(iii) PRIVACY.—The right to privacy with regard to accommodations, medical treatment, written and telephonic communications, visits, and meetings of family and of resident groups. [Does not require private rooms.]

(v) ACCOMMODATION OF NEEDS.—The right—

(I) to reside and receive services with reasonable accommodations of individual needs and preferences, except where the health or safety of the individual or other residents would be endangered, and

(II) to receive notice before the room or roommate of the resident in the facility is changed.

(viii) PARTICIPATION IN OTHER ACTIVITIES.—The right of the resident to participate in social, religious, and community activities that do not interfere with the rights of other residents in the facility.

* * *

(D) USE OF PSYCHOPHARMACOLOGIC DRUGS.

Psychopharmacologic drugs may be administered only on the orders of a physician and only as part of a plan (included in the written plan of care ...) designed to eliminate or modify the symptoms for which the drugs are prescribed and only if, at least annually an independent, external consultant reviews the appropriateness of the drug plan of each resident receiving such drugs.

(2) TRANSFER AND DISCHARGE RIGHTS.—

(A) IN GENERAL.—A nursing facility must permit each resident to remain in the facility and must not transfer or discharge the resident from the facility unless—

(i) the transfer or discharge is necessary to meet the resident's welfare and the resident's welfare cannot be met in the facility;

(ii) the transfer or discharge is appropriate because the resident's health has improved sufficiently so the resident no longer needs the services provided by the facility;

(iii) the safety of individuals in the facility is endangered;

(iv) the health of individuals in the facility would otherwise be endangered;

(v) the resident has failed, after reasonable and appropriate notice, to pay ... for a stay at the facility; or

(vi) the facility ceases to operate.

* * *

(B) PRE–TRANSFER AND PRE–DISCHARGE NOTICE.—

(i) IN GENERAL.—Before effecting a transfer or discharge of a resident, a nursing facility must—

(I) notify the resident (and, if known, an immediate family member of the resident or legal representative) of the transfer or discharge and the reasons therefor,

(II) record the reasons in the resident's clinical record * * * and

(III) include in the notice the items described in clause (iii). [concerning appeal of transfer]

(ii) TIMING OF NOTICE.—The notice under clause (i)(I) must be made at least 30 days in advance of the resident's transfer or discharge except—

(I) in a case described in clause (iii) or (iv) of subparagraph (A);

(II) in a case described in clause (ii) of subparagraph (A), where the resident's health improves sufficiently to allow a more immediate transfer or discharge;

(III) in a case described in clause (i) of subparagraph (A), where a more immediate transfer or discharge is necessitated by the resident's urgent medical needs; or

(IV) in a case where a resident has not resided in the facility for 30 days.

In the case of such exceptions, notice must be given as many days before the date of the transfer or discharge as is practicable. [The statute also requires the state to establish a hearing process for transfers and discharges contested by the resident or surrogate.]

(3) ACCESS AND VISITATION RIGHTS.—A nursing facility must—

(A) permit immediate access to any resident by any representative of the Secretary, by any representative of the State, by an ombudsman . . ., or by the resident's individual physician;

(B) permit immediate access to a resident, subject to the resident's right to deny or withdraw consent at any time, by immediate family or other relatives of the resident;

(C) permit immediate access to a resident, subject to reasonable restrictions and the resident's right to deny or withdraw consent at any time, by others who are visiting with the consent of the resident;

(D) permit reasonable access to a resident by any entity or individual that provides health, social, legal, or other services to the resident, subject to the resident's right to deny or withdraw consent at any time; and

(E) permit representatives of the State ombudsman (. . .), with the permission of the resident (or the resident's legal representative) and consistent with State law, to examine a resident's clinical records.

(4) EQUAL ACCESS TO QUALITY CARE.—

A skilled nursing facility must establish and maintain identical policies and practices regarding transfer, discharge and the provision of services . . . for all individuals regardless of source of payment.

42 C.F.R. § 483.13

Restraints. The resident has the right to be free from any physical or chemical restraints imposed for purposes of discipline or convenience, and not required to treat the resident's medical symptoms.

HCFA "GUIDANCE TO SURVEYORS" June 1995

Guidelines: § 483.13(a)

"Physical restraints" are defined as any manual method or physical or mechanical device, material, or equipment attached or adjacent to the resident's body that the individual cannot remove easily which restricts freedom of movement or normal access to one's body.

Restraint use may constitute an accident hazard and professional standards of practice have eliminated the need for physical restraints except under limited medical circumstances. Therefore, medical symptoms that would warrant the use of restraints should be reflected in the comprehensive assessment and care planning. It is further expected that for those residents whose care plans indicate the need for restraints that the facility engage in a systematic and gradual process toward reducing restraints. . . .

The resident's right to participate in care planning and the right to refuse treatment [ ] include the right to accept or refuse restraints.

For the resident to make an informed choice about the use of restraints, the facility should explain to the resident the negative outcomes of restraint use. Potential negative outcomes include incontinence, decreased range of motion, and decreased ability to ambulate, symptoms of withdrawal or depression, or reduced social contact.

In the case of a resident who is incapable of making a decision, the surrogate or representative may exercise this right based on the same information that would have been provided to the resident. [ ] However, the surrogate or representative cannot give permission to use restraints for the sake of discipline or staff convenience or when the restraint is not necessary to treat the resident's medical symptoms. That is, the facility may not use restraints in violation of the regulation solely because a surrogate or representative has approved or requested them.

"Physical restraints" include, but are not limited to, leg restraints, arm restraints, hand mitts, soft ties or vests, lap cushions and lap trays the resident cannot remove. Also included as restraints are facility practices that meet the definition of a restraint, such as: using bed rails to keep a resident from voluntarily getting out of bed as opposed to enhancing mobility while in bed; tucking in a sheet so tightly that a bed bound resident cannot move; using wheel chair safety bars to prevent a resident from rising out of a chair; placing a resident in a chair that prevents rising; and placing a resident who uses a wheelchair so close to a wall that the wall prevents the resident from rising.

Bed rails may be used to restrain residents or to assist in mobility and transfer of residents. The use of bed rails as restraints is prohibited unless they are necessary to treat a resident's medical symptoms. Bed rails used as restraints add risk to the resident. They potentially increase the risk of more significant injury from a fall from a bed with raised bed rails than from a fall from a bed without bed rails. They also potentially increase the likelihood that the resident will spend more time in bed and fall when attempting to transfer from bed.

2. Survey and Inspection

SOUTHERN HEALTH FACILITIES, INC. v. SOMANI

Court of Appeals of Ohio, 1995.
1995 WL 765161.

DESHLER, J.

The ... complaint alleged that plaintiff, Southern Health Facilities, Inc., dba Greenbriar Convalescent Center ("Greenbriar"), is an Ohio proprietary corporation licensed and authorized to operate a one-hundred fifty-one bed nursing home under the provisions of R.C. Chapter 3721, and that Greenbriar is also certified to participate in Medicare and Medicaid programs. It was averred that defendant ODH is the agency of the state designated as the "State Survey Agency" as that term is used in federal law, and that ODH is a party to an agreement with the Ohio Department of Human Services authorizing ODH to conduct inspections of Medicare and Medicaid certified skilled nursing facilities in Ohio. [Defendants filed a motion to dismiss for failure to state a claim which the trial court granted.]

* * *

The thrust of plaintiffs' complaint is that the manner in which defendants conduct certification compliance surveys is violative of federal and state law. Specifically, plaintiffs assert that defendants failed to conduct a survey in accordance with the State Operations Manual, in violation of R.C. 5111.39(C), R.C. 3721.022, and in accordance with Section 1396r, Title 42, U.S.C.A. It is averred that, while federal standards require that defendants conduct an exit conference at the conclusion of a survey, and the State Operations Manual requires that an exit conference include an opportunity to provide the surveyors with relevant additional information to assist in determining whether a deficiency occurred, defendants failed to communicate the nature of the surveyors' impressions and concerns and did not permit Greenbriar to question or provide additional documentation. The complaint alleged that the failure to follow mandated procedures resulted in defendants inappropriately citing Greenbriar for deficiencies....

The complaint further included allegations that defendants made incorrect survey determinations at the Greenbriar facility, refused to remove these improper statements regarding the care and services provided by Greenbriar, and issued public notices falsely stating that Greenbriar delivered sub-standard care. It was averred that such improper determinations are routinely made at other facilities throughout the state. The complaint also alleged that defendants have failed to properly train and assist the persons performing the surveys, that the surveys are required to be, but are not, uniformly and consistently applied between providers and from one survey to the next, and that the care delivered to residents in facilities such as Greenbriar is not assessed in a systematic manner by defendants.

* * *

Plaintiffs contend that the trial court failed to apply the proper standard in ruling on the motion to dismiss. Specifically, plaintiffs assert that the complaint sets forth sufficient facts describing in detail the deficiencies of the survey conducted at Greenbriar and that the court failed to presume the truth of the facts alleged.

We agree with plaintiffs' contention that, accepting the allegations in the complaint as true, as we must in considering a motion to dismiss, the trial court erred in granting the motion to dismiss. Upon review, we conclude that plaintiffs' complaint sufficiently alleges cognizable procedural and substantive due process claims as well as violations of state and federal provisions.

* * *

We note that the issue whether a provider is entitled to a pre-termination evidentiary hearing has been the subject of litigation in federal courts. It appears that the majority of courts which have addressed the issue have found that such a hearing is not required. [ ] Regardless of whether such an evidentiary hearing would be required, plaintiffs' complaint alleges that other procedural safeguards which are required by law were not complied with by defendants. As noted above, the complaint alleges that, contrary to federal regulations and state law, defendants failed to communicate the nature of the surveyors' impressions during the exit interview and did not permit Greenbriar to question or provide additional documentation. Presumably, compliance with mandated procedural safeguards would obviate the need for an evidentiary hearing; however, the complaint alleges that these procedures were not followed. Assuming the truth of the allegations, the complaint sufficiently sets forth a procedural due process claim.

* * *

. . . We note that the trial court, in addressing the factual allegations regarding the survey, concluded that the allegations merely constituted disagreements with the survey's findings. The issue, however, is whether it appears from the complaint that there can be no set of facts which would entitle plaintiffs to the relief requested. While we make no comment regarding the probable success of plaintiffs' action beyond this stage, we conclude that the allegations are sufficient to withstand dismissal. . . .

* * *

Notes and Questions

1. Plaintiff's claim in *Southern Health Facilities* survived a motion to dismiss. What will plaintiff have to prove to succeed on the merits? How far should the courts go in testing the accuracy of the finding of a violation? Is a decision to cite a facility for a violation of standards entitled to deference? See, EPI Corporation v. Chater, 91 F.3d 143 (6th Cir.1996) and Beverly California Corporation v. Shalala, 78 F.3d 403 (8th Cir.1996), rejecting similar claims on the merits. In *EPI*, the Sixth Circuit found that the survey team had substantially complied with survey procedures; that some of the steps identified by plaintiff were optional; and that the plaintiff facility did not suffer substantial prejudice to its interests by the surveyors' failure to complete a particular form in advance of the exit conference. In *Beverly*, the Eighth Circuit also found that the surveyors had substantially complied with the procedures described in the regulations and rejected plaintiff's claim.

2. In *Beverly*, Beverly argued that the Secretary had exceeded her statutory look-behind authority in conducting a federal survey of the facility without having first articulated some reason for believing that the state survey had been inadequate. (Refer back to *Smith v. Heckler*. What is the look-behind authority?) In this case, the court found that the federal survey team

> observed numerous regulatory violations including the following: restraints left on residents without release for periods exceeding two hours; vest restraints applied improperly creating a risk of strangulation; frail residents lifted and ambulated in a manner that posed a substantial threat of injury; failure to observe basic hygiene conventions creating a serious risk of infection; dirty and unlabeled personal items and equipment scattered throughout the facility; physical therapy administered by an unqualified employee; inadequate physical therapy regimens; and discontinuation or delay of physical therapy without physician consultation.

The court held that the Secretary had not exceeded her authority in conducting a federal inspection. The facility was one of a sample of facilities selected to test the state survey process.

3. Why might the results of a federal inspection differ from one conducted by state surveyors? What role should the courts play in the question of surveyor discretion or inconsistency? Should the survey standards be more rigid? States vary widely as to the average number of deficiencies per facility, ranging from a high of 19.48 in Nevada to a low of 2.34 in Colorado. Richard L. Butler, Jenean M. Erickson, and Vincent Mor, Avoid Survey Surprises by Being Prepared, 8 Brown University Long–Term Care Quality Letter 1 (Mar. 25, 1996). The authors of the article note that even the most frequently cited violations nationally (which are violations of requirements of comprehensive assessment, development of comprehensive care plans, and sanitary storage, preparation and distribution of food) are "rarely named in states with very low deficiency rates" and conclude that OBRA "has not been successful in 'leveling' differences between states in terms of the likelihood of receiving a deficiency." Does this range reflect varying quality of facilities or of inspection processes?

4. An evaluation of the new survey process revealed that surveyors have difficulty with the emphasis on outcomes and with the patient-focused and outcome-oriented survey techniques. In particular, researchers reported that the surveyors hesitated to cite the facility for outcome difficulties because they may be uncomfortable with the sophisticated level of assessment required for a citation on an outcome standard and may instead opt to cite the facility for less serious but more easily documented violations. For a description of this research, see Michael J. Stoil, Surveyors Stymied by Survey Criteria, Researchers Find, 43 Nursing Homes 58 (1994). See Kathy J. Vaca et al., Review of Nursing Home Regulation, 7 MedSurg Nursing 165 (June 1998). What might steer surveyors toward "documentable" citations and away from problems on which there might be more room for disagreement? A study of surveyor practices by the General Accounting Office, conducted in response to industry concerns about overly aggressive surveyors, found that surveyors were not being overzealous in their efforts. Nursing Home Oversight: Industry Examples Do Not Demonstrate That Regulatory Actions Were Reasonable, GAO/HEHS–99–154R (1999).

5. What relationship should the surveyor establish with the facility? Is the surveyor a consultant or advisor? Should the surveyor offer suggestions for improvement? Should the surveyor commend the facility on noted improvements or other indicators of quality identified during the inspection? How might expecta-

tions concerning this relationship have affected the dispute over the exit conference described in *Southern Health Facilities*? See Facility and Surveyors: Cooperation, Not Confrontation, 9 The Brown University Long–Term Care Quality
Advisor 1 (1997). For a critique of the enforcement-oriented survey process, see
John Braithwaite, The Nursing Home Industry, 18 Crime & Justice 11 (1993);
Mary Kathleen Robbins, Nursing Home Reform: Objective Regulation or Subjective Decisions?, 11 Thomas Cooley L. Rev. 185 (1994).

3. *Sanctions*

VENCOR NURSING CENTERS v. SHALALA

United States District Court, District of Columbia, 1999.
63 F.Supp.2d 1.

URBINA, DISTRICT JUDGE.

This matter comes before the court on an application by the plaintiff
Vencor Nursing Centers, L.P. ("Vencor") for an order temporarily restraining
the defendant, Secretary of the United States Department of Health and
Human Services Donna E. Shalala ("HHS") from terminating one of Vencor's
California facilities from the Medicare and Medicaid programs, and seeking
other declaratory and injunctive relief . . .

Vencor owns and operates Village Square Nursing and Rehabilitation
Center, a 120–bed skilled nursing facility in San Marcos, San Diego County,
California ("Village Square"). During the relevant period, Village Square had
between 92 and 104 residents, including about fifty Medicare and Medicaid
beneficiaries . . . The California Department of Human Services ("the survey
agency" or "SA") is the state agency that inspected Village Square on behalf
of HHS. From November 1998 through May 1999, HHS authorized the SA to
carry out three on-site surveys of Village Square. The SA conducted the first
survey on November 25, 1998 and issued a Statement of Deficiencies on
November 28, 1998. Village Square filed a Plan of Correction (POC) on
December 18, 1998 and notified the SA that it had regained substantial
compliance as of January 9, 1999. The SA conducted a follow-up survey on
April 1, 1999 and issued a Statement of Deficiencies, and Village Square
submitted a POC. On May 12, 1999, HCFA notified Village Square that it
concurred with the SA's findings and terminated Village Square effective May
29, 1999 for failure to maintain substantial compliance for six months. In
response to Village Square's representation that it was in substantial compliance, the SA conducted a third survey on May 28, 1999 and issued a
Statement of Deficiencies on June 8, 1999. HCFA exercised its discretion to
continue payments until June 28, 1999, thirty days from the effective date of
termination. Village Square relocated 18 Medicare and Medicaid residents by
July 2, 1999 and it planned to relocate the others by July 5, 1999.

* * *

A preliminary injunction may be granted only when the movant demonstrates:

(1) a substantial likelihood of success on the merits; (2) that irreparable
harm will result in the absence of the relief requested; (3) that no other party

will be harmed if the motion is granted; and (4) that the public interest supports granting the requested relief.

The gravemen of Vencor's dispute with HHS is its contention that a nursing home may be terminated from Medicare and Medicaid participation only where conditions at the facility place residents' health or safety in "immediate jeopardy." Therefore, Vencor argues, by terminating Village Square in the absence of a finding of "immediate jeopardy" HHS violated the Medicare Act, the Medicaid Act and the Due Process Clause. Conversely, HHS relies on 42 C.F.R. §§ 488.412 and 488.456, which provide that HHS may terminate a facility which is not in "substantial compliance," even if there is no immediate jeopardy.

In deciding whether this court is likely to adopt Vencor's interpretation of the remedy provisions, the court accords substantial deference to HHS's regulations. [ ] Broad deference is particularly warranted where the regulation "concerns a complex and highly technical regulatory program", like Medicare, "in which the identification and classification of relevant criteria necessarily require significant expertise and entail the exercise of judgment grounded in policy concerns." [ ].

The Medicare and Medicaid acts authorize HHS to impose a variety of remedies and/or sanctions against noncompliant nursing homes. Prior to 1987 the only available remedies were outright termination or a blanket ban on reimbursement for care of newly admitted residents. [ ]. While the Medicare Act formerly permitted termination without a finding of "immediate jeopardy," 42 U.S.C. § 1395cc(f), that provision is no longer in force. In 1987 Congress enacted the Federal Nursing Home Reform Act, which added a greater variety of remedies to the Medicare and Medicaid Acts. These new remedies include, inter alia, civil money penalties, imposition of independent temporary managers and orders to adopt plans of correction (POC's). The 1987 legislation establishes categories of non-compliance and provides a number of possible remedies for HHS to choose from based on the severity of the alleged noncompliance.

* * *

... There are two provisions in the Medicare Act which tend to support HHS's position. First, Congress explicitly states, "Nothing in this subparagraph shall be construed as restricting the remedies available to HHS to remedy a skilled nursing facility's deficiencies." 42 U.S.C. § 1395i–3(h)(2)(B). Second, the Act authorizes HHS to terminate the Medicare agreement of any provider which "fails to comply substantially with the provisions of the agreement, with the provisions of this subchapter and regulations thereunder . . . ." 42 U.S.C. § 1395cc(b)(2). As the compliance provisions are "provisions of this subchapter" and § 1395cc(b)(2) does not require a finding of immediate jeopardy prior to termination, the court could infer that HHS is entitled to terminate without immediate jeopardy.

Several courts which have addressed the issue have held that HHS does not have the authority to order termination in the absence of immediate jeopardy ...

... In enacting the enforcement provisions to the Medicare and Medicaid Acts, Congress expressly wished to expand the panoply of remedies available to HHS. [ ]. Committee reports noted with concern the "yo-yo" phenomenon in which noncomplying facilities temporarily correct their deficiencies before an on-site survey and then quickly lapse into noncompliance until the next review. [ ]. Presumably, the new version of the statute ameliorates this problem by giving HHS a set of intermediate sanctions to choose from rather than the extreme choices of termination or no sanction. There is no indication in the legislative history that Congress wished to limit HHS's ability to terminate a persistently noncompliant facility. [ ]. In fact, the recurring theme emerging from the legislative history is that the new provisions would grant HHS remedial powers in addition to those already available. [ ].

Against this backdrop, the court could well conclude that the statute should be read as a guidepost for HHS rather than a limitation on its power. The immediate-jeopardy provision mandates that HHS must terminate or appoint temporary management when a facility's deficiencies are found to put residents' health or safety in immediate jeopardy. By contrast, the non-jeopardy provision affords HHS discretion, allowing (but not requiring) HHS to impose intermediate sanctions on facilities whose deficiencies do not immediately jeopardize health or safety. In light of the foregoing, Vencor has not shown that this court is likely to hold that HHS lacked authority to terminate Village Square absent a finding of immediate jeopardy.

Notes and Questions

1.   Was termination the correct remedy in this situation? Would a less severe intermediate sanction have been more appropriate? What happens to the approximately 50 non-Medicare and non-Medicaid residents remaining in the facility? Will their care be compromised? Will the nursing facility survive without the income from Medicare and Medicaid residents?

2.   If a facility is cited for but then corrects a deficiency, should it still be penalized for that violation? What arguments would support an emphasis on correction rather than punishment? What would argue against? One study concludes that the nursing home regulatory system relies extensively on correction and voluntary compliance rather than punishment even though the emphasis in OBRA was to use penalties as a deterrent. The study points out that correction may be cheaper to the facility than contesting the citation (except where there are seriously and automatically increased penalties for repeat violations), especially where agencies lack the capacity to effectively follow up on promised corrections. In addition, the study reports that nursing home chains sometimes simply shift staff from one institution to another and back again to temporarily respond to cited deficiencies in individual facilities within the chain. Still, the director of the study concludes that the emphasis on surveillance in the U.S. system has led to more regimentation and inflexibility in U.S. nursing homes than in other countries with different systems, implying that quality of care and quality of life suffer. John Braithwaite, The Nursing Home Industry, 18 Crime & Justice 11 (1993). See also, Richard L. Peck, Does Europe Have the Answers?, 49 Nursing Homes 54 (June 2000).

3.   Recent reform proposals have examined the idea of federal criminal sanctions as a way of enforcing quality. See, e.g., Angela S. Quin, Imposing Federal Criminal Liability on Nursing Homes: A Way of Deterring Inadequate Health Care and Improving the Quality of Care Delivered?, 43 St. Louis U.L.J. 653 (Spring 1999). Additionally, *qui tam* provisions have also been used to litigate quality issues. See, e.g., John T. Boese, When Angry Patients Become Angry

Prosecutors: Medical Necessity Determinations, Quality of Care and the Qui Tam Law, 43 St. Louis U.L.J. 53 (Spring 1999) and Kathleen A. Peterson, First Nursing Homes, Next Managed Care?: Limiting Liability in Quality of Care Cases Under the False Claims Act, 26 Am.J.L. & Med. 69 (2000).

Problem: Restful Manor

Restful Manor is a skilled nursing facility licensed by the state and operating in its largest city. It has 117 residents, all of whom are elderly. Only twenty percent of the residents are ambulatory. Until eighteen months ago, the home had a good record of compliance with state nursing home standards. The facility has begun to have problems with compliance, although it still consistently has corrected violations or has submitted an acceptable plan of correction. The facility has also experienced some financial difficulties recently.

The most recent inspection of the facility took place four months ago. At that time, the facility was out of compliance with several standards relating to quality of meals, cleanliness of the kitchen and maintenance of patients' medical records. The facility also had some staffing problems. Other problems included the lack of a qualified dietitian and a high, though borderline acceptable, rate of errors in the administration of medications by the nurses. As a result of this inspection report, the facility was required to submit a written plan of correction in which it agreed to remedy the violations. The next on-site inspection was scheduled to take place within six to eight weeks to check on progress in correcting the violations.

Prior to that inspection, however, an investigative news team from a local television station visited the facility with a hidden camera. The news team posed as potential out-of-town buyers interested in the facility. The visit revealed several patients who were soiled and unattended and several others who were restrained in wheelchairs. A recorded conversation with the Director of Nursing indicated that there was one nurses' aide for every ten patients, which the D.O.N. thought was probably "not enough to do a good job for some of these patients." When asked about these incidents, the owner attributed these "temporary" problems to financial constraints and to his inability to hire a good administrator who was willing to work within a reasonable budget.

The news team showed portions of the videotape on the nightly news. Three days later it followed up with a report that one of the ambulatory, mentally-impaired patients at the facility had wandered out of the building. A passerby had found the patient walking aimlessly along the main thoroughfare near the facility and called the police.

The state agency felt pressured to respond. It conducted an unannounced inspection two days after the latest news report. The surveyor conducting this inspection cited the facility for violations of several regulations including the following:

1. Each resident should receive adequate skin care that supports his or her health and well-being and avoids decubitus ulcers (bed sores). (The surveyor found that the facility was not turning or positioning bed-bound patients in the manner that is advised for avoidance of ulcers. The facility also lacked supportive supplies, such as certain kinds of pads, ordinarily used to reduce the incidence of ulcers. At the time of the inspection, however, only two patients had minor incipient pressure sores. The surveyor believes, but could not confirm, that another patient had been transferred to the hospital eight months ago for serious bedsores.)

2. The facility must assure that a resident who did not present mental or psychosocial adjustment difficulties at admission does not display patterns of decreased social interaction or increased withdrawal, angry or depressive behaviors, unless the residents' clinical condition demonstrates that such a pattern was unavoidable. (The surveyor identifies several residents who report boredom, lethargy, loss of appetite and feelings of uselessness and who complain of a lack of interesting things to do. Their medical records do not indicate any clinical diagnosis that would explain their psychosocial states.)

3. The facility shall provide a nursing staff that is appropriately trained and adequate in number to care for the residents of the facility. (The surveyor wrote in his report that the facility provided one nurses' aide for every ten patients and that this was "inadequate in light of the dependency of the residents.")

4. The facility shall employ a certified dietitian. (The surveyor noted that "the facility currently does not employ a certified dietitian, but in the exit conference the owner reported that he has been trying to hire one for the last three months.")

5. The nurses of the facility shall administer ordered medications safely and adequately. An error rate in excess of 5% in the administration of medication is unacceptable and shall constitute a violation of this standard. (The surveyor reported an error rate of 5% in one sample medications pass and an error rate of 4.9% in another.)

Even though the facility is currently in violation of several standards, families of Restful Manor's patients have rallied to the facility's support. They believe the care is good despite the problems cited. The Department disagrees. Assume that the following (an edited version of the federal regulations) is your state statute.

488.404. Factors to be considered in selecting remedies

(b) Determining seriousness of deficiencies. To determine the seriousness of the deficiency, the State must consider at least the following factors:

(1) Whether a facility's deficiencies constitute—

(i) No actual harm with a potential for minimal harm; (ii) No actual harm with a potential for more than minimal harm, but not immediate jeopardy; (iii) Actual harm that is not immediate jeopardy; or (iv) Immediate jeopardy to resident health or safety.

(2) Whether the deficiencies—

(i) Are isolated; (ii) Constitute a pattern; or (iii) Are widespread.

(c) . . . Following the initial assessment, the State may consider other factors, which may include, but are not limited to the following:

(1) The relationship of the one deficiency to other deficiencies resulting in noncompliance.

(2) The facility's prior history of noncompliance in general and specifically with reference to the cited deficiencies.

488.406. Available remedies

(a) General. In addition to the remedy of termination of the provider agreement, the following remedies are available:

(1) Temporary management.

(2) Civil money penalties.

(3) State monitoring.

(4) Transfer of residents.

(5) Closure of the facility and transfer of residents.

(6) Directed plan of correction.

(7) Directed in-service training.

488.408. Selection of remedies

(a) Categories of remedies. In this section, the remedies specified in § 488.406 (a) are grouped into categories and applied to deficiencies according to how serious the noncompliance is.

(c) (1) Category 1 remedies include the following:

(i) Directed plan of correction.

(ii) State monitoring.

(iii) Directed in-service training.

(2) The State must apply one or more of the remedies in Category 1 when there—

(i) Are isolated deficiencies that constitute no actual harm with a potential for more than minimal harm but not immediate jeopardy; or (ii) Is a pattern of deficiencies that constitutes no actual harm with a potential for more than minimal harm but not immediate jeopardy.

(3) Except when the facility is in substantial compliance, HCFA or the State may apply one or more of the remedies in Category 1 to any deficiency.

(d) (1) Category 2 remedies include the following

(iii) Civil money penalties of $50–$3,000 per day.

(iv) Civil money penalty of $1,000–$10,000 per instance of noncompliance.

(2) The State must apply one or more of the remedies in Category 2 when there are—

(i) Widespread deficiencies that constitute no actual harm with a potential for more than minimal harm but not immediate jeopardy; or (ii) One or more deficiencies that constitute actual harm that is not immediate jeopardy.

(3) The State may apply one or more of the remedies in Category 2 to any deficiency except when—

(i) The facility is in substantial compliance; or (ii) the State imposes a civil money penalty for a deficiency that constitutes immediate jeopardy, the penalty must be in the upper range of penalty amounts, as specified in § 488.438(a).

(e) (1) Category 3 remedies include the following:

(i) Temporary management.

(ii) Immediate licensure revocation.

(iii) Civil money penalty of $1,000–$10,000 per instance of noncompliance.

(2) When there are one or more deficiencies that constitute immediate jeopardy to resident health or safety—

(i) The State must do one or both of the following;

(A) Impose temporary management; or

(B) Revoke the facility license;

(ii) The State may impose a civil money penalty of $3,050–$10,000 per day or $1,000–$10,000 per instance of noncompliance, in addition to imposing the remedies specified in paragraph (e) (2) (i) of this section.

(3) When there are widespread deficiencies that constitute actual harm that is not immediate jeopardy, the State may impose temporary management, in addition to Category 2 remedies.

(f) Plan of correction.

(1) Except as specified in paragraph (f) (2) of this section, each facility that has a deficiency with regard to a requirement for long term care facilities must submit a plan of correction for approval by the State, regardless of—

(i) Which remedies are imposed; or (ii) The seriousness of the deficiencies.

(2) When there are only isolated deficiencies that HCFA or the State determines constitute no actual harm with a potential for minimal harm, the facility need not submit a plan of correction.

488.410. Action when there is immediate jeopardy

(a) If there is immediate jeopardy to resident health or safety, the State must either revocate the facility license within 23 calendar days of the last date of the survey or appoint a temporary manager to remove the immediate jeopardy . . .

(b) The State may also impose other remedies, as appropriate.

(d) The State must provide for the safe and orderly transfer of residents when the facility is terminated.

(e) If the immediate jeopardy is also substandard quality of care, the State survey agency must notify attending physicians and the State board responsible for licensing the facility administrator of the finding of substandard quality of care.

488.412. Action when there is no immediate jeopardy

(a) If a facility's deficiencies do not pose immediate jeopardy to residents' health or safety, and the facility is not in substantial compliance, the State may revoke the facility's license agreement or may allow the facility to continue to participate for no longer than 6 months from the last day of the survey if—

(1) The State survey agency finds that it is more appropriate to impose alternative remedies than to terminate the facility's provider agreement;

(2) The facility has submitted an approved plan and timetable for corrective action.

488.415. Temporary management

(a) Temporary management means the temporary appointment by the State of a substitute facility manager or administrator with authority to hire, terminate or reassign staff, obligate facility funds, alter facility procedures, and manage the facility to correct deficiencies identified in the facility's operation.

(e) Duration of temporary management. Temporary management ends when the facility ceases operation or meets standards.

The Department of Health expects litigation as a result of any enforcement action it takes in this case. It has come to the office of the state's Attorney General for advice. The Director of the Department wants to be aggressive in this case in part because the poor condition of the facility has become public knowledge. She believes that the agency's effectiveness has been challenged and that the facility is seriously deficient and heading for more problems.

Several students should serve as the assistant A.G. who has been assigned to this case. Please advise the Department on the course of action they should follow in this instance.

Other students should serve in the role of attorneys representing the facility. Please identify any defenses available to the facility, your strategy and the course the dispute is likely to take.

Having worked through these provisions, what recommendations for change would you make to this state's legislature, both as to enforcement mechanisms and as to the standards?

III. PRIVATE ACCREDITATION OF HEALTH CARE FACILITIES

Private accreditation is a nongovernmental, voluntary activity typically conducted by not-for-profit associations. The Joint Commission on Accreditation of Healthcare Organizations (JCAHO), which offers accreditation programs for hospitals, nursing homes, home health, and other facilities, and the National Committee on Quality Assurance (NCQA), which accredits health maintenance organizations, are two of the leading organizations in the accreditation of health care entities.

Accrediting associations set standards for and engage in some form of surveillance of entities seeking to gain or maintain accreditation. As a voluntary process, accreditation may be viewed as providing the accredited health care entity merely with a seal of approval—a method for communicating in shorthand that it meets standards established by an external organization.

This definitional view of accreditation certainly captures the theory of health care accreditation as a private communicative device. But in practice in the U.S., there is a much closer marriage between some private accreditation programs and government regulation of health care facilities. This is especially true of the hospital accreditation program of the JCAHO. JCAHO's hospital accreditation program is the largest of the JCAHO accreditation programs and is perhaps the most influential of all private health care accreditation programs in the U.S. Virtually all U.S. hospitals with more than 25 beds are JCAHO-accredited.

A number of important economic and professional opportunities are restricted to JCAHO-accredited hospitals. For example, payers for health care services may allow payments only to JCAHO-accredited institutions. In addition, both state and federal governments have to a great extent relied on JCAHO accreditation in their hospital licensure and Medicare/Medicaid certification programs. Most states have incorporated JCAHO accreditation standards, some explicitly, into their hospital licensure standards. Some have accepted JCAHO accreditation in lieu of a state license. See e.g., Tex. Health & Safety Code § 222.024. Under the Medicare statute, JCAHO-accredited hospitals are "deemed" to have met requirements for Medicare certification. 42 U.S.C. §§ 1395x(e), 1395bb. Although the Secretary retains a look-behind authority, JCAHO substitutes for the routine surveillance process.

Originally, the acceptance of JCAHO accreditation by the Medicare program was designed to entice an adequate number of hospitals to participate in the then-new Medicare program. That original rationale has dissipated as hospitals have become much more dependent on Medicare payments. The federal government's reliance on private accreditation as a substitute for routine government surveillance has expanded considerably beyond the original hospital setting, however, and now extends to clinical laboratories and home health care.

In 1981 the Reagan administration proposed extending deemed status to nursing homes accredited by the JCAHO. This proposal was opposed vigorously by consumer advocates and was withdrawn. Should nursing homes be treated differently, and arguably more restrictively, than hospitals on the question of deemed status? What might explain this extensive reliance on private organizations for public regulation? Some would argue that private accreditation more effectively encourages voluntary compliance and avoids some of the "prosecutorial" environment of a government-conducted inspection program. Furthermore, and perhaps more importantly, deemed status allows the government to shift the cost of the inspection process as accredited facilities pay the accrediting organization for the costs of the accreditation program, including the site visit.

How does the private accreditation process compare to public regulation? Private accreditation programs traditionally have engaged in practices that encourage voluntary subscription to the accreditation program. For example, accreditation programs often perform only announced site visits and keep negative evaluations confidential, at least until the accreditation itself is reduced or not renewed. Standards established by accreditation programs, which are often dominated by professionals in the industry rather than consumer groups, may differ from those set by a process that arguably fosters broader public participation. With JCAHO, in particular, governance and policymaking is dominated by physician organization members (e.g., the American Medical Association, the American College of Physicians, the American College of Surgeons) and the American Hospital Association.

For a history of the JCAHO and a broad review of legal issues related to private accreditation, see Timothy S. Jost, The Joint Commission on Accreditation of Hospitals: Private Regulation of Health Care and the Public Interest, 24 B.C.L.Rev.835 (1983). For a discussion of the relation between private accreditation and public regulation, see Jody Freeman, The Private Role in

Public Governance, 75 N.Y.U.L.Rev. 543 (2000); Symposium on Private Accreditation in the Regulatory State, 57 Law and Contemp. Prob.1 (1994).

Review the final rule reproduced below. How does the regulation alter the ordinary private accreditation process? Has the Department adequately preserved its interests and authority while granting deemed status to home health agencies accredited by JCAHO?

DEPARTMENT OF HEALTH AND HUMAN SERVICES

58 Fed.Reg. 35007 (June 30, 1993).

As a result of this notice, HHAs [home health agencies] accredited by JCAHO are deemed to meet the requirements for participation in the Medicare program and, therefore, may participate in the Medicaid program as a provider of home health services. . . .

* * *

[W]e would remove recognition of JCAHO accreditation if either of the following circumstances occur:

— JCAHO revises its standards so that the revised standards fail to provide reasonable assurance that JCAHO-accredited HHAs meet the Medicare conditions of participation. Conversely, we revise the Medicare HHA conditions of participation to such a degree that JCAHO's standards or accreditation policies would no longer provide reasonable assurance that JCAHO-accredited HHAs meet the conditions of participation; or

— Our validation or complaint surveys reveal widespread, systematic, or unresolvable problems with the JCAHO accreditation process, thereby providing evidence that there is not reasonable assurance that JCAHO-accredited HHAs meet the Medicare conditions of participation.

* * *

The proposed notice also made our recognition of JCAHO's accreditation program contingent on JCAHO's continued agreement to:

— Release JCAHO survey reports to us routinely and to the public upon request. If the reports reveal deficiencies which we believe warrant action by us, we may survey the HHAs identified as having deficiencies, withdraw recognition of the accreditation program if appropriate, and apply any other appropriate corrective measures or sanctions. The information to be released includes the accreditation findings, supporting documentation, the official accreditation survey reports of JCAHO surveyors, and other related information.

— Report to either the Office of Inspector General (OIG) (for Medicare) or to the State agency responsible for investigating fraud and abuse (for Medicaid), or to both, complaints received from persons working in the accredited HHA or any substantial complaints from others, anonymous or identified, concerning potential fraud and abuse violations, and any other indication of a Medicare or Medicaid program abuse encountered by JCAHO during a JCAHO inspection.

— Make JCAHO surveyors available to serve as witnesses if adverse action is taken by HCFA after JCAHO accreditation has been withdrawn.

Finally, we proposed to make our approval of JCAHO's accreditation program contingent on the following revisions to JCAHO's survey and accreditation process (JCAHO had already agreed to make these changes):

— Implementation of an annual, unannounced survey of those HHAs requesting JCAHO accreditation for Medicare deeming purposes.

— Adoption of the standardized functional assessment instrument used by HCFA and State agency surveyors and training of the JCAHO surveyors in its use.

— Adoption of a case-mix, stratified random sampling process and sample sizes of clinical records for review and home visits comparable to HCFA's.

— Maintenance of a timeframe and process for following up deficiencies found during an HHA survey comparable to HCFA's.

* * *

As appropriate . . . we will perform announced and unannounced validation and complaint surveys of HHAs to assure that JCAHO-accredited HHAs that participate in Medicare meet the Medicare conditions of participation. As established in the proposed notice of February 3, 1992, we may withdraw recognition of JCAHO accreditation of HHAs at any time if we determine that JCAHO accreditation does not continue to provide reasonable assurance that Medicare conditions of participation are met.

In 1999, the Office of Inspector General of the Department of Health and Human Services issued a report critical of both the JCAHO surveys and the oversight provided by HCFA in relation to hospitals. External Review of Hospital Quality: A Call for Greater Accountability (OEI–01–97–00050). See also, External Quality Review of Psychiatric Hospitals (OEI–01–99–00160).

In its report on hospitals, the OIG concluded that JCAHO provided a significant tool for quality control but that its surveys are "unlikely to detect substandard patterns of care or individual practitioners with questionable skills" because the visits are fast-paced, highly structured and still tend to be consultative. The OIG noted that the states do not survey unaccredited hospitals in a timely fashion, reporting that about 50% of unaccredited hospitals had not been surveyed within the three-year period expected. The OIG also noted that HCFA failed to check on JCAHO surveys adequately. In summary, the OIG concluded that the hospital certification system was more "collegial" than "regulatory" and recommended a greater emphasis on the regulatory nature of the surveys.

JCAHO made some changes subsequent to the OIG report. For example, it issued a plan for conducting unannounced surveys, eliminating its practice of providing 24–hour notice, and for resurveying institutions anywhere between nine and thirty months after a full survey. At the same time, JCAHO surveyed its accredited institutions to see how it might make its processes more acceptable to the providers, indicating that the organization is intent on reducing the costs of the survey process perhaps by reducing the on-site visit to one day and developing more reliance on self-assessment and continuous quality improvement. Hospitals Face Random Unannounced Visits Under

Amended JCAHO Survey Policy, BNA Health Law Reporter August 19, 1999; Hospital Survey Process Under Review as Joint Commission Solicits Opinions, BNA Health Law Reporter, June 22, 2000.

In 2000, HCFA extended approval of JCAHO accreditation for Medicare certification of home health agencies. In its notice of reapproval, HCFA lists several changes JCAHO made in its procedures and standards in response to HCFA concerns. 65 Fed.Reg. 8722–01 (Feb.22,2000).

Chapter 4

LIABILITY OF HEALTH CARE PROFESSIONALS

This chapter will examine the framework for a malpractice suit against health care professionals and the doctrinal and evidentiary dimensions of such litigation. As you read the chapter, think about the cases and materials on three levels. First, how is the plaintiff's case proved and how does the defendant counter it? Second, how does tort doctrine respond to different categories of medical error? And third, how does malpractice litigation affect medical practice and the quality of medical care?

I. THE STANDARD OF CARE

A. ESTABLISHING THE STANDARD OF CARE

HALL v. HILBUN

Supreme Court of Mississippi, 1985.
466 So.2d 856.

ROBERTSON, JUSTICE, for the Court:

I.

This matter is before the Court on Petition for Rehearing presenting primarily the question whether we should, as a necessary incident to a just adjudication of the case at bar, refine and elaborate upon our law regarding (a) the standard of care applicable to physicians in medical malpractice cases and (b) the matter of how expert witnesses may be qualified in such litigation.

* * *

When this matter was before the Court on direct appeal, we determined that the judgment below in favor of the surgeon, Dr. Glyn R. Hilbun, rendered following the granting of a motion for a directed verdict, had been correctly entered. * * *

For the reasons set forth below, we now regard that our original decision was incorrect. * * *

II.

Terry O. Hall was admitted to the Singing River Hospital in Jackson County, Mississippi, in the early morning hours of May 18, 1978, complaining of abdominal discomfort. Because he was of the opinion his patient had a surgical problem, Dr. R.D. Ward, her physician, requested Dr. Glyn R. Hilbun, a general surgeon, to enter the case for consultation. Examination suggested that the discomfort and illness were probably caused by an obstruction of the small bowel. Dr. Hilbun recommended an exploratory laparotomy [sic]. Consent being given, Dr. Hilbun performed the surgery about noon on May 20, 1978, with apparent success.

Following surgery Mrs. Hall was moved to a recovery room at 1:35 p.m., where Dr. Hilbun remained in attendance with her until about 2:50 p.m. At that time Mrs. Hall was alert and communicating with him. All vital signs were stable. Mrs. Hall was then moved to a private room where she expired some 14 hours later.

On May 19, 1980, Glenn Hall commenced this wrongful death action by the filing of his complaint * * *.

* * *

At trial Glenn Hall, plaintiff below and appellant here, described the fact of the surgery. He then testified that he remained with his wife in her hospital room from the time of her arrival from the recovery room at approximately 3:00 p.m. on May 20, 1978, until she ultimately expired at approximately 5:00 a.m. on the morning of May 21. Hall stated that his wife complained of pain at about 9:00 p.m. and was given morphine for relief, after which she fell asleep. Thereafter, Hall observed that his wife had difficulty in breathing which he reported to the nurses. He inquired if something was wrong and was told his wife was all right and that such breathing was not unusual following surgery. The labored breathing then subsided for an hour or more. Later, Mrs. Hall awakened and again complained of pain in her abdomen and requested a sedative, which was administered following which she fell asleep. Mrs. Hall experienced further difficulty in breathing, and her husband reported this, too. Again, a nurse told Hall that such was normal, that patients sometimes make a lot of noise after surgery.

After the nurse left the following occurred, according to Hall.

[A]t this time I followed her [the nurse] into the hall and walked in the hall a minute. Then I walked back into the room, and walked back out in the hall. Then I walked into the room again and I walked over to my wife and put my hand on her arm because she had stopped making that noise. Then I bent over and flipped the light on and got closer to her where I could see her, and it looked like she was having a real hard problem breathing and she was turning pale or a bluish color. And I went to screaming.

Dr. Hilbun was called and came to the hospital immediately only to find his patient had expired. The cause of the death of Terry O. Hall was subsequently determined to be adult respiratory distress syndrome (cardio-respiratory failure).

Dr. Hilbun was called as an adverse witness and gave testimony largely in accord with that above. * * *.

Dr. Hilbun stated the surgery was performed on a Saturday. Following the patient's removal to her room, he "went home and was on call that weekend for anything that might come up." Dr. Hilbun made no follow-up contacts with his patient, nor did he make any inquiry that evening regarding Mrs. Hall's post-operative progress. Moreover, he was *not* contacted by the nursing staff or others concerning Mrs. Hall's condition during the afternoon or evening of May 20 following surgery, or the early morning hours of May 21, although the exhibits introduced at trial disclose fluctuations in the vital signs late in the evening of May 20 and more so, in the early morning hours of May 21. Dr. Hilbun's next contact with his patient came when he was called by Glenn Hall about 4:55 or 5:00 that morning. By then it was too late.

* * *

The autopsy performed upon Mrs. Hall's body revealed the cause of death and, additionally, disclosed that a laparotomy [sic] sponge had been left in the patient's abdominal cavity. The evidence, however, without contradiction establishes that the sponge did not contribute to Mrs. Hall's death. Although the sponge may ultimately have caused illness, this possibility was foreclosed by the patient's untimely death.

Plaintiff's theory of the case centered around the post-operative care provided by Dr. Hilbun. Two areas of fault suggested were Dr. Hilbun's failure to make inquiry regarding his patient's post-operative course prior to his retiring on the night of May 20 and his alleged failure to give appropriate post-operative instructions to the hospital nursing staff.

When questioned at trial, Dr. Hilbun first stated that he had practiced for 16 years in the Singing River Hospital and was familiar with the routine of making surgical notes, i.e., a history of the surgery. He explained that the post-operative orders were noted on the record out of courtesy by Dr. Judy Fabian, the anesthesiologist on the case. He stated such orders were customarily approved by his signature or he would add or subtract from the record to reflect the exact situation.

[Dr. Hilbun testified as to the post-operative orders noted in the medical records as of May 20, 1978. Mrs. Hall had a nasogastric tube, an i.v., a catheter; she was receiving medications for pain, nausea, and infections.] His testimony continued:

Q. Now after this surgery, while Mrs. Hall was in the recovery room did I understand you to say earlier that you checked on her there?

A. When I got through operating on Mrs. Hall, with this major surgical procedure in an emergency situation—and I always do—I went to the recovery room with Mrs. Hall, stayed in the recovery room with Mrs. Hall, listened to her chest, took her vital signs, stayed there with her and discharged her to the floor. The only time I left the recovery room was to go into the waiting room and tell Mr. Hall. Mrs. Hall waked up, I talked to her, she said she was cold. She was completely alert.

* * *

Q. Now, you went to the recovery room to see her because you were still her physician following her post-surgery?

A. I was one of her physicians. I operated on her, and I go to the recovery room with everybody.

Q. Okay. You were the surgeon and you were concerned about the surgical procedures and how she was doing post-operatively, or either you are not concerned with your patients, how they do post-operatively?

A. As I said, I go to the recovery room with every one of my patients.

Q. Then you are still the doctor?

A. I was one of her physicians.

Q. Okay. And you customarily follow your patients following the surgery to see how they are doing as a result of the surgery, because you are the surgeon. Is that correct?

A. Yes.

* * *

Q. How long do you follow a patient like Terry Hall?

A. Until she leaves the hospital.

Q. Okay. So ever how long she is in the hospital, you are going to continue to see her?

A. As long as my services are needed.

Insofar as the record reflects, Dr. Hilbun gave the nursing staff no instructions regarding the post-operative monitoring and care of Mrs. Hall beyond those [summarized above]. Dr. Hilbun had no contact with Mrs. Hall after 3:00 p.m. on May 20. Fourteen hours later she was dead.

The plaintiff called Dr. S.O. Hoerr, a retired surgeon of Cleveland, Ohio, as an expert witness. The record reflects that Dr. Hoerr is a *cum laude* graduate of the Harvard Medical School, enjoys the respect of his peers, and has had many years of surgical practice. Through him the plaintiff sought to establish that there is a national standard of surgical practice and surgical care of patients in the United States to which all surgeons, including Dr. Hilbun, are obligated to adhere. Dr. Hoerr conceded that he did not know for a fact the standard of professional skill, including surgical skills and post-operative care, practiced by general surgeons in Pascagoula, Mississippi, but that he did know what the standard should have been.

* * * [T]he trial court ruled that Dr. Hoerr was not qualified to give an opinion as to whether Dr. Hilbun's post-operative regimen departed from the obligatory standard of care. * * *.

* * *

Parts of Dr. Hoerr's testimony excluded under the trial judge's ruling follow:

A. My opinion is that she [Mrs. Hall] did not receive the type of care that she should have received from the general surgical specialist and that he [Dr. Hilbun] was negligent in not following this patient; contacting, checking on the condition of his patient sometime in the evening of

May 20th. *It is important in the post-operative care of patients to remember that very serious complications can follow abdominal operations, in particular in the first few hours after a surgical procedure.* And this can be inward bleeding; it can be an explosive development in an infection; or *it can be the development of a serious pulmonary complication, as it was in this patient. As a result of her condition, it is my opinion that he lost the opportunity to diagnose a condition, which in all probability could have been diagnosed at the time by an experienced general surgeon, one with expertise in thoracic surgery. And then appropriate treatment could have been undertaken to abort the complications and save her life.*

There are different ways that a surgeon can keep track of his patient—"follow her" as the expression goes—besides a bedside visit, which is the best way and which need not be very long at all, in which the vital signs are checked over. The surgeon gets a general impression of what's going on. He can delegate this responsibility to a competent physician, who need not be a surgeon but could be a knowledgeable family practitioner. He could call in and ask to speak to the registered nurse in charge of the patient and determine through her what the vital signs are, and if she is an experienced Registered Nurse what her evaluation of the patient is. *From my review of the record, none of these things took place, and there is no effort as far as I can see that Dr. Hilbun made any effort to find out what was going on with this patient during that period of time.* I might say or add an additional belief that I felt that the nursing responsibility which should have been exercised was not exercised, particularly at the 4:00 a.m. level when the pulse rate was recorded at 140 per minute without any effort as far as I can see to have any physician see the patient or to get in touch with the operating surgeon and so on.

There is an additional thing that Dr. Hilbun could have done if he felt that the nursing services might be spotty—sometimes good, sometimes bad. This is commonly done in Columbus, Ohio, in Ashtabula, Pascagoula, etcetera. *He could put limits on the degree in which the vital signs can vary, expressing the order that he should be called if they exceeded that.* Examples would be: Call me if the pulse rate goes over 110; call me if the temperature exceeds 101; call me if the blood pressure drops below 100. There is a simple way of spelling out for the nursing services what the limits of discretion belong to them and the point at which the doctor should be called.

* * *

Dr. Hilbun did not place any orders on the chart for the nurses to call him in the event of a change in the vital signs of Mrs. Hall. He normally made afternoon rounds between 4:00 and 5:00 p.m. but didn't recall whether he went by to see her before going home. Dr. Hilbun was on call at the hospital that weekend for anything which might come up. Subsequent to the operation and previous to Mrs. Hall's death, he was called about one other person on the same ward, one door down, twice during the night. He made no inquiry concerning Mrs. Hall, nor did he see or communicate with her.

Dr. Donald Dohn, of expertise unquestioned by plaintiff and with years of practical experience, gave testimony for the defendant. He had practiced on the staff at the Cleveland Clinic Foundation in Cleveland, Ohio, beginning in 1958. Fortuitously, he had moved to Pascagoula, Mississippi, about one month before the trial. Dr. Dohn stated he had practiced in the Singing River Hospital for a short time and there was a great difference in the standard of care in medical procedures in Cleveland, Ohio, and those in Pascagoula, Mississippi. Although he had practiced three weeks in Pascagoula, he was still in the process of acquainting himself with the local conditions. He explained the differences as follows:

> Well, there are personnel differences. There are equipment differences. There are diagnostic differences. There are differences in staff responsibility and so on. For example, at the Cleveland Clinic on our service we had ten residents that we were training. They worked with us as our right hands. Here we have no staff. So it is up to us to do the things that our residents would have done there. There we had a team of five or six nurses and other personnel in the operating room to help us. Here we have nurses in the operating room, but there is no assigned team. You get the luck of the draw that day. I am finding out these things myself. Up there it is a big center; a thousand beds, and it is a regional center. We have tremendous advantages with technical systems, various types of x-ray equipment that is [sic] sophisticated. Also in terms of the intensive care unit, we had a Neurosurgical Intensive Care with people who were specially trained as a team to work there. From my standpoint personally, I seldom had to do much paperwork there as compared to what I have to do now. I have to dictate everything and take all my notes. So, as you can see, there is a difference.

Finally, he again stated the standard of care in Ohio and the standard of care in the Singing River Hospital are very different, although it is obvious to the careful reader of Dr. Dohn's testimony that in so doing he had reference to the differences in equipment, personnel and resources and not differences in the standards of skill, medical knowledge and general medical competence a physician could be expected to bring to bear upon the treatment of a patient.

At the conclusion of the plaintiff's case, defendant moved for a directed verdict on the obvious grounds that, the testimony of Drs. Hoerr and Sachs having been excluded, the Plaintiff had failed to present a legally sufficient quantum of evidence to establish a prima facie case. The Circuit Court granted the motion. * * *

III.

A. *General Considerations*

Medical malpractice is legal fault by a physician or surgeon. It arises from the failure of a physician to provide the quality of care required by law. When a physician undertakes to treat a patient, he takes on an obligation enforceable at law to use minimally sound medical judgment and render minimally competent care in the course of the services he provides. A physician does not guarantee recovery. If a patient sustains injury because of the physician's failure to perform the duty he has assumed under our law, the physician may be liable in damages. A competent physician is not liable *per se* for a mere error of judgment, mistaken diagnosis or the occurrence of an undesirable result.

The twin principles undergirding our stewardship of the law regulating professional liability of physicians have always been reason and fairness. For years in medical malpractice litigation we regarded as reasonable and fair what came to be known as the "locality rule" (but which has always consisted of at least two separate rules, one a rule of substantive law, the other a rule of evidence).

* * *

C.   *The Physician's Duty of Care: A primary rule of substantive law*

1.   *The Backdrop*

* * *

2.   *The Inevitable Ascendency of National Standards*

* * *

We would have to put our heads in the sand to ignore the "nationalization" of medical education and training. Medical school admission standards are similar across the country. Curricula are substantially the same. Internship and residency programs for those entering medical specialties have substantially common components. Nationally uniform standards are enforced in the case of certification of specialists. Differences and changes in these areas occur temporally, not geographically.

Physicians are far more mobile than they once were. They frequently attend medical school in one state, do a residency in another, establish a practice in a third and after a period of time relocate to a fourth. All the while, they have ready access to professional and scientific journals and seminars for continuing medical education from across the country. Common sense and experience inform us that the laws of medicine do not vary from state to state in anything like the manner our public law does.

Medicine is a science, though its practice be an art (as distinguished from a business). Regarding the basic matter of the learning, skill and competence a physician may bring to bear in the treatment of a given patient, state lines are largely irrelevant. That a patient's temperature is 105 degrees means the same in New York as in Mississippi. Bones break and heal in Washington the same as in Florida, in Minnesota the same as in Texas. * * *

* * *

3.   *The Competence–Based National Standard of Care: Herein of the Limited Role of Local Custom*

All of the above informs our understanding and articulation of the competence-based duty of care. Each physician may with reason and fairness be expected to possess or have reasonable access to such medical knowledge as is commonly possessed or reasonably available to minimally competent physicians in the same specialty or general field of practice throughout the United States, to have a realistic understanding of the limitations on his or her knowledge or competence, and, in general, to exercise minimally adequate medical judgment. Beyond that, each physician has a duty to have a practical working knowledge of the facilities, equipment, resources (including personnel in health related fields and their general level of knowledge and competence), and options (including what specialized services or facilities may be available in larger communities, e.g., Memphis, Birmingham, Jackson, New Orleans, etc.) reasonably available to him or her as well as the practical limitations on same.

In the care and treatment of each patient, each physician has a non-delegable duty to render professional services consistent with that objectively ascertained minimally acceptable level of competence he may be expected to apply given the qualifications and level of expertise he holds himself out as possessing and given the circumstances of the particular case. The professional services contemplated within this duty concern the entire caring process, including but not limited to examination, history, testing, diagnosis, course of treatment, medication, surgery, follow-up, after-care and the like.

* * *

Mention should be made in this context of the role of good medical judgment which, because medicine is not an exact science, must be brought to bear in diagnostic and treatment decisions daily. Some physicians are more reluctant to recommend radical surgery than are other equally competent physicians. There exist legitimate differences of opinion regarding medications to be employed in particular contexts. "Waiting periods" and their duration are the subject of bona fide medical controversy. What diagnostic tests should be performed is a matter of particularly heated debate in this era of ever-escalating health care costs. We must be vigilant that liability never be imposed upon a physician for the mere exercise of a bona fide medical judgment which turns out, with the benefit of 20–20 hindsight (a) to have been mistaken, and (b) to be contrary to what a qualified medical expert witness in the exercise of his good medical judgment would have done. We repeat: a physician may incur civil liability only when the quality of care he renders (including his judgment calls) falls below minimally acceptable levels.

Different medical judgments are made by physicians whose offices are across the street from one another. Comparable differences in medical judgment or opinion exist among physicians geographically separated by much greater distances, and in this sense local custom does and must continue to play a role within our law, albeit a limited one.

We recognize that customs vary within given medical communities and from one medical community to another. Conformity with established medical custom practiced by minimally competent physicians in a given area, while evidence of performance of the duty of care, may never be conclusive of such compliance. [ ] The content of the duty of core must be objectively determined by reference to the availability of medical and practical knowledge which would be brought to bear in the treatment of like or similar patients under like or similar circumstances by minimally competent physicians in the same field, given the facilities, resources and options available. The content of the duty of care may be informed by local medical custom but never subsumed by it.

* * *

4. The Resources–Based Caveat to the National Standard of Care

The duty of care, as it thus emerges from considerations of reason and fairness, when applied to the facts of the world of medical science and practice, takes two forms: (a) a duty to render a quality of care consonant with the level of medical and practical knowledge the physician may reasonably be expected to possess and the medical judgment he may be expected to exercise, and (b) a duty based upon the adept use of such medical facilities, services, equipment and options as are reasonably available. With respect to this second form of the duty, we regard that there remains a core of validity to the premises of the old locality rule.

* * *

A physician practicing in Noxubee County, for example, may hardly be faulted for failure to perform a CAT scan when the necessary facilities and equipment are not reasonably available. In contradistinction, objectively reasonable expectations regarding the physician's knowledge, skill, capacity for sound medical judgment and general competence are, consistent with his field of practice and the facts and circumstances in which the patient may be found, *the same everywhere.*

* * *

As a result of its resources-based component, the physician's non-delegable duty of care is this: given the circumstances of each patient, each physician has a duty to use his or her knowledge and therewith treat through maximum reasonable medical recovery, each patient, with such reasonable diligence, skill, competence, and prudence as are practiced by minimally competent physicians in the same specialty or general field of practice throughout the United States, who have available to them the same general facilities, services, equipment and options.

* * *

As we deal with general principles, gray areas necessarily exist. One involves the case where needed specialized facilities and equipment are not available locally but are reasonably accessible in major medical centers—New Orleans, Jackson, Memphis. Here as elsewhere the local physician is held to minimally acceptable standards. In determining whether the physician's actions comport with his duty of care, consideration must always be given to the time factor—is the physician confronted with what reasonably appears to be a medical emergency, or does it appear likely that the patient may be transferred to an appropriate medical center without substantial risk to the health or life of the patient? Consideration must also be given to the economic factors—are the proposed transferee facilities sufficiently superior to justify the trouble and expense of transfer? Further discussion of these factors should await proper cases.

    D.   *Who May Qualify As Expert Medical Witness In Malpractice Case: A rule of evidence*

As a general rule, if scientific, technical or other specialized knowledge will assist the trier of fact to understand the evidence or to determine a fact in issue, a witness qualified as an expert by knowledge, skill, experience, training or education (or a combination thereof), coupled with independence and lack of bias, may testify thereto in the form of an opinion or otherwise. Medical malpractice cases generally require expert witnesses to assist the trier of fact to understand the evidence. [ ]

Generally, where the expert lives or where he or she practices his or her profession has no relevance *per se* with respect to whether a person may be qualified and accepted by the court as an expert witness. There is no reason on principle why these factors should have *per se* relevance in medical malpractice cases.

* * *

In view of the refinements in the physician's duty of care * * * we hold that a qualified medical expert witness may without more express an opinion regarding the meaning and import of the duty of care * * *, given the peculiar circumstances of the case. Based on the information reasonably available to the physician, i.e., symptoms, history, test results, results of the doctor's own physical examination, x-rays, vital signs, etc., a qualified medical expert may express an opinion regarding the conclusions (possible diagnoses or areas for further examination and testing) minimally knowledgeable and competent physicians in the same specialty or general field of practice would draw, or actions (not tied to the availability of specialized facilities or equipment not generally available) they would take.

Before the witness may go further, he must be familiarized with the facilities, resources, services and options available. This may be done in any number of ways. The witness may prior to trial have visited the facilities, etc. He may have sat in the courtroom and listened as other witnesses described the facilities. He may have known and over the years interacted with physicians in the area. There are no doubt many other ways in which this could be done, but, significantly, we should allow the witness to be made familiar with the facilities (and customs) of the medical community in question via a properly predicated and phrased hypothetical question.

Once he has become informed of the facilities, etc. available to the defendant physician, the qualified medical expert witness may express an opinion what the care duty of the defendant physician was and whether the acts or omissions of the defendant physician were in compliance with, or fell substantially short of compliance with, that duty.

* * *

V.   Disposition Of The Case At Bar

[The court reversed and remanded for a new trial, on the grounds that the testimony of Drs. Hoerr and Sachs was improperly excluded, and with their testimony, the plaintiff might have survived the defense motion for a directed verdict.]

Notes and Questions

1.   How did the court in *Hall v. Hilbun* view the customary practice of the defendant's medical specialty? Why did it adopt this position? How much of a burden is it for a defendant to rebut the plaintiff's evidence on customary practice?

2.   The standards by which the delivery of professional medical services is judged are not normally established by either judge or jury. The medical profession itself sets the standards of practice and the courts enforce these standards in tort suits. Defendants trying to prove a standard of care normally present expert

testimony describing the actual pattern of medical practice, without any reference to the effectiveness of that practice. Most jurisdictions give professional medical standards conclusive weight, so that the trier of fact is not allowed to reject the practice as improper. See, e.g., Holt v. Godsil, 447 So.2d 191 (Ala.1984).

3. Why should conformity to customary practice be a conclusive shield for a health care professional? In tort litigation not involving professionals, courts are willing to reject customary practice if they find the practice dangerous or out of date. See Joseph King, In Search of a Standard of Care for the Medical Profession—the "Accepted Practice" Formula, 28 Vand.L.Rev. 1213, 1236 (1975). Critics such as King worry that standard practice may at times be little more than a routine into which physicians have drifted by default.

The customary or accepted practice standard follows the general tort rule that physicians are measured against the standard of their profession, not merely the standard of a reasonable and prudent person. Medical practices are always evolving as new developments and scientific studies alter the customary practice. Such evolution in medical practices often creates tensions for the physician who believes that the customary practice is dangerous but the new standard has not yet been generally accepted. Courts have however been unwilling generally to allow a plaintiff to present evidence to attack a customary practice that the defendant physician complied with, except under rare circumstances.

In Burton v. Brooklyn Doctors Hospital, 88 A.D.2d 217, 452 N.Y.S.2d 875 (1982), the plaintiff was exposed while in the hospital as a newborn to a prolonged liberal application of oxygen. He developed retrolental fibroplasia (RFL) as a result. At the time of his birth, a "significant segment of the medical community continued to believe that the liberal administration of oxygen to prematures was important in preventing death or brain damage. Yet, a respected body of medical opinion believed that oxygen contributed to RLF." He was part of a study at the hospital examining various level of oxygen and the effects of its withdrawal or curtailment; the study found in 1954 that prolonged liberal use led to the development of RLF, and cutting off oxygen to premature infants after 48 hours decreased the incidence of RLF without increasing the risk of either death or brain damage.

> * * * [T]he jury's finding of malpractice should not be disturbed. The issue was submitted to the jury under a proper charge. "If a physician fails to employ his expertise or best judgment, and that omission causes injury, he should not automatically be freed from liability because in fact he adhered to acceptable practice."

See also Toth v. Community Hospital at Glen Cove, 22 N.Y.2d 255, 292 N.Y.S.2d 440, 239 N.E.2d 368 (1968), where the defendant doctor had ordered a reduction in the flow of oxygen to the plaintiff, and the nursing staff had failed to carry out the order.

> * * * evidence that the defendant followed customary practice is not the sole test of professional malpractice. If a physician fails to employ his expertise or best judgment, and that omission causes injury, he should not automatically be freed from liability because in fact he adhered to acceptable practice. There is no policy reason why a physician, who knows or believes there are unnecessary dangers in the community practice, should not be required to take whatever precautionary measures he deems appropriate.

4. Judicial deference to customary practice may be weakening. The Wisconsin Supreme Court observed that:

* * * [S]hould customary medical practice fail to keep pace with developments and advances in medical science, adherence to custom might constitute a failure to exercise ordinary care.

* * *

We agree with the parties and the Medical Society that while evidence of the usual and customary conduct of others under similar circumstances is ordinarily relevant and admissible as an indication of what is reasonably prudent, customary conduct is not dispositive and cannot overcome the requirement that physicians exercise ordinary care.

Nowatske v. Osterloh, 198 Wis.2d 419, 543 N.W.2d 265, 272 (1996).

5. Courts expect the standard of care to be compliance with available technology at the time the diagnosis or treatment was offered to the patient. See, e.g., Klisch v. Meritcare Medical Group, Inc., 134 F.3d 1356 (C.A. 8th Cir. 1998), where the patient sued for negligent performance of surgery. The Court of Appeals held that: (1) a jury instruction that the jury should consider the state of medical technology at time of allegedly negligent surgery was appropriate; (2) under Minnesota law, the jury in a medical malpractice action should weigh information available to physicians at the time of treatment and without benefit of hindsight.

6. Could a plaintiff use the studies cited in Chapter 1 to support a position that the efficacy of a standard practice is not proven? How would a court react to such studies?

1. The Locality Rule

Hall provides an excellent discussion of the locality rule. Most courts have moved from the locality rule to a similar locality or a national standard, in part due to worries about a "conspiracy of silence" that unfairly limits the pool of available experts. Doctors do not like to testify against one another. As the court noted in Mulder v. Parke Davis & Co., 288 Minn. 332, 181 N.W.2d 882 (1970), "All too frequently, and perhaps understandably, practicing physicians are reluctant to testify against one another. Unfortunately, the medical profession has been slow to fashion machinery for making impartial and objective assessments of the performance of their fellow practitioners."

For a first hand account of physician reluctance, by an M.D.–J.D., see Robinson, Why the Conspiracy of Silence Won't Die, Medical Economics 180 (Feb. 20, 1984).

Rural communities face substantial difficulties in getting doctors: salaries are lower, availability of peers is limited, health insurance for doctor and patient may be harder to get. The locality rule has been viewed as a subsidy for rural areas, an additional incentive to attract doctors to areas that they don't otherwise find attractive. Absent the added protection of the locality rule, it is argued, rural areas will suffer even more from little or no medical care. Henry C. Karlson and Roger D. Erwin, Medical Malpractice: Informed Consent to the Locality Rule, 12 Ind.L.Rev. 653, 664–657 (1979). Most courts have proved hostile to this position, since medical practice has become national in scope and rural residents deserve the same level of care as urban residents. See Shilkret v. Annapolis Emergency Hospital Ass'n., 276 Md. 187, 349 A.2d 245 (1975). In any event, rural residents do not sue for malpractice at anywhere near the level of urban residents. Danzon concluded that urbanization was the "single most powerful predictor" of the frequency and severity of claims. Patricia Danzon, Medical Malpractice 82–83 (1985). See also Patricia Danzon, The Frequency and Severity of Medical Malpractice Claims: New Evidence, 49 Law & Contemp.Probs. 57, 69 (1986). Rural practitioners are simply not likely to get sued, perhaps because of more personal relationships with their patients or the attitudes of rural residents generally toward litigation.

The debate over the locality rule has been largely won by the national standard test, as *Hall* evidences. But many courts, like *Hall*, also allow evidence describing the practice limitations under which the defendant labors. *Hall*'s "resource component" allows the trier of fact to consider the facilities, staff and other equipment available to the practitioner in the institution, following the general rule that courts should take into account the locality, proximity of specialists and special facilities for diagnosis and treatment. Blair v. Eblen, 461 S.W.2d 370 (Ky.1970); Restatement (Second) of Torts, sec. 299A, Comment g. ("Allowance must be made also for the type of community in which the actor carries on his practice. A country doctor cannot be expected to have the equipment, facilities, experience, knowledge or opportunity to obtain it, afforded him by a large city.")

A national standard of practice may not exist for many procedures, and the "highest and best" practice may not be the safest or most effective in the long run. Substantial regional variations exist in the use of many procedures, with no apparent differences in outcome (life expectancy, morbidity, days missed from work). Different practice styles exist in different regions, and even within states, based on local concepts of good practice. What do these findings suggest? Does the evidence on variation in medical practice among regions support the locality rule? Might it be better to allow the locality rule in a tort suit as a way of supporting local practices against a monolithic national practice under some circumstances?

Note: Telemedicine and Rural Practices

Access by physicians to computer databases makes information on advances in medical knowledge instantly available whether the doctor is rural or urban. MEDLINE, the largest, has over five million references and articles from 4,000 journals. The level of skill required to access such a database has steadily decreased, with more user friendly command structures and access through commercial services such as MEDLARS and MEDIS. A physician with a phone, a modem and a personal computer can pay a monthly subscription fee and then call up information 24 hours a day. In fact such databases are now freely accessible to a consumer with a computer through such online services such as America Online, and Medline is now accessible on the World Wide Web, with free software available online to access it.

The possibilities of telemedicine go far beyond access to large medical databases. A physician in a rural area could get the assistance of a large medical center in diagnosing a patient's problems; such a physician might also be able to track a patient at home to monitor vital signs and symptoms. As Bradham et al. write,

> Through telemedicine, patients and doctors in rural or economically depressed areas might immediately access specialized services that their communities lack, thereby increasing convenience, diagnostic ability, and the overall quality of local medical care. Further, telemedicine technologies might allow

hospitals to release patients sooner by permitting clinicians to monitor patient progress remotely, which in turn would reduce costly hospital stays.

What exactly is "telemedicine"? Kuszler sums it up as follows:

Telemedicine's "simple, but serviceable" definition is the use of telecommunication to diagnose and treat a patient. Telemedicine encompasses a panoply of technologies and communication modalities that allow health care providers to connect with, examine, counsel and advise patients about treatment options. These include teleradiology and other teleimaging diagnostics, telesurgery and robotics, video and Internet/e-mail conferencing, transmission of electrocardiographic and other physiological data by telephone, telecommunications, or Internet lines and "telehealth" education via the Internet and cable television. Although many of these examples rely on relatively recent communications technologies, telemedicine escaped the bounds of the simple telephone call at least thirty years ago and has already acquired an impressive history.

* * *

Telemedicine is no longer limited to transmission of hazy images and telemetry data from the remote, isolated Alaskan village or orbiting spacecraft. Highly sophisticated communication and computer systems provide high-resolution images, "crunch" complex data, have analytic, even artificial intelligence, capacity, and allow access to real-time, delayed and stored information.

Telemedicine is becoming an integral part of health care delivery in diverse settings. It is breaking down boundaries between different types of health care providers, revolutionizing rural health care delivery, improving and facilitating care for underserved and difficult to manage populations and enhancing discourse between patients and providers. There is also a growing telehealth movement.

Patricia C. Kuszler, Telemedicine and Integrated Health Care Delivery: Compounding Malpractice Liability, 25 Am. J.L. & Med. 297, 299–300 (1999)

What will this do the standard of care? Kuszler writes:

Telemedicine will provide physicians in all geographic areas with the opportunity to obtain consultations from specialists, have diagnostic tests and data reviewed at state-of-the-art tertiary care centers and have the patient "examined" by another provider for a second opinion.Telemedicine potentially can conquer distance in an instant. Differences between services available to providers and patients in different geographic areas should further evaporate, resulting in greater pervasiveness of a single standard of care. Id at 316.

Ease of access to medical databases necessarily raises the standard of knowledge required of the average physician. No court has yet required an individual physician to have access to a database or to telemedicine links, but a requirement of such access seems inevitable as sophistication about the Internet and databases grows. Don't computerized databases reinforce a national standard of care against which to judge medical practice? Not only will such access continue to diminish the importance of the locality rule or its manifestations, but it may also limit the "respectable minority" rule and other judgment rules by narrowing the range of variation in medical opinion as to what is acceptable. A physician relying on a contraindicated drug, an outdated surgical technique, or an inappropriate description of risk factors in getting a patient's informed consent may be attacked by the plaintiff using the results of a computer search. See Warrick v. Giron, 290 N.W.2d 166 (Minn.1980) (the defendants introduced a computerized search they had conducted, revealing no evidence that the surgical and anesthesiological techniques utilized by the defendants were improper.) See generally Patricia C. Kuszler, Telemedicine and Integrated Health Care Delivery: Compounding Medical Liability, 25 Am.J.L. & Med. 297(1999); Jerry V. Glowniak and Marilyn K. Bushway, Computer Networks as a Medical Resource: Accessing and Using the Internet, 271 J.A.M.A. 1934 (1994); Douglas D. Bradham, Sheron Morgan, and Margaret E. Dailey, The Information Superhighway: A Critical Discussion of Its Possibilities and Legal Implications, 30 Wake Forest L. Rev. 145, 147 (1995) (discussing existing telemedicine projects around the United States). See also Daniel McCarthy, The Virtual Health Economy: Telemedicine and the Supply of Primary Care Physicians in Rural America, 21 Am. J.L. & Med. 111 (1995); Robin Elizabeth Margolis, Law and Policy Barriers Hamper Growth of Telemedicine, 11 No. 10 HealthSpan 14 (1994) (noting among other problems complicated conflict-of-law problems that might arise with a out-of-state physician giving a telemedicine consultation). See also Second Invitational Consensus Conference on Telemedicine and the National Information Infrastructure, 1 Telemedicine J. 321 et seq. (1995).

2. *Expert Testimony*

The standard of practice in the defendant doctor's specialty or area of practice is normally established through the testimony of medical experts. The cases above illustrate the burden that the plaintiff bears. In any jurisdiction, plaintiffs, to withstand a motion for a directed verdict, must 1) qualify their medical witnesses as experts; 2) satisfy the court that the expert's testimony will assist the trier of fact; and 3) have the witnesses testify based upon facts that support their expert opinions. The requirement that the expert be of the same specialty as the defendant typically governs the qualifying of the expert for testifying at trial.

A plaintiff must offer proof that the defendant physician breached the legally required standard of care and was thus negligent. Expert testimony is needed to establish both the standard of proper professional skill or care and a failure by the defendant to conform. The expert does not have to testify explicitly that the conduct was "malpractice." "In medical malpractice cases, it is proper for the trier of fact to draw inferences and reach conclusions from facts that are found to be proved." Campbell v. Palmer, 20 Conn.App. 544, 568 A.2d 1064, 1067 (1990) (radiologist testified for plaintiff that the defendant's barium enema procedure was inadequate to exclude pathology and that it should have been repeated and a sigmoidoscopy suggested to the patient; he testified that the defendant's procedure was not the way he would have done it and "not the way most of the people [he knew] would have acted.").

The plaintiff's expert must testify that the standard of care breached by the defendant is a national one. The standard of care may be based upon the expert's own practice and education. Practice guidelines or parameters, particularly statements by medical societies as to good practice, will provide a ready-made particularized standard that an expert can use as a benchmark against which to test a defendant's conduct. Some courts are becoming more demanding, requiring that an expert needs "published medical standards, manuals, or protocols" to support the expert opinion, rather than just the expert's own opinion or casual conversation with a few colleagues. Travers v. District of Columbia, 672 A.2d 566 (D.C.App.1996).

The abolition of the locality rule has been one way to ease the plaintiff's burden of proof, broadening the plaintiff's choices of available experts. Many states still require that the expert at least be familiar with the standard of practice in a similar locality, and some testimony is required as to the similarities between the two localities. See, e.g., First Commercial Trust Company v. Rank, 323 Ark. 390, 915 S.W.2d 262 (1996) (family practitioner was sued for medical negligence and failure to report suspected child abuse; held that Florida emergency room physician should have been allowed to testify on the standard of care for diagnosing child abuse).

Plaintiff's experts normally must be in the same specialty as the defendant. Under some circumstances, however, courts have allowed physicians in other specialties to testify, so long as the alleged negligence involved matters within the knowledge of every physician. A general surgeon can testify as to the standard of care of a plastic surgeon performing elective surgery, as to general surgical issues as to whether nerves in the forehead should have been protected, Hauser v. Bhatnager, 537 A.2d 599 (Me.1988); a cardiologist can testify in a case involving a family practice physician, Fiedler v. Spoelhof, 483 N.W.2d 486 (Minn.App.1992); a psychiatrist has been allowed to testify as to the standard of post-operative care for a breast implant procedure, Miller v. Silver, 181 Cal.App.3d 652, 226 Cal.Rptr. 479 (1986). See also Searle v. Bryant, 713 S.W.2d 62 (Tenn.1986) (expert in infectious diseases could testify as to the standard of care for a surgeon, where the patient developed an abdominal infection following surgery.) Contra, see Melville v. Southward, 791 P.2d 383 (Colo.1990) (orthopedic surgeon could not offer expert testimony on the standard of care applicable to a podiatrist).

An expert need not be board certified in the subject of the suit, so long as he has the appropriate education and experience. Hanson v. Baker, 534 A.2d 665 (Me.1987). The liberal view is that an expert need not possess a medical degree so long as he has the medical knowledge. " * * * [B]efore one may testify as an expert, that person must be shown to know a great deal regarding the subject of his testimony." Thompson v. Carter, 518 So.2d 609 (Miss.1987) (toxicologist allowed to testify as to side effects of a drug prescribed by defendant physician). See also Pratt v. Stein, 298 Pa.Super. 92, 444 A.2d 674 (1982); Cornfeldt v. Tongen, 262 N.W.2d 684 (Minn.1977) (nurse anesthetist competent to testify); Hudgins v. Serrano, 186 N.J.Super. 465, 453 A.2d 218 (1982); Glover v. Ballhagen, 232 Mont. 427, 756 P.2d 1166 (Mont. 1988)(expert does not have to be a board certified family practitioner to testify as to practice).

Some jurisdictions adopt a narrower view, requiring that the expert have practiced in the same area as the defendant. See Lundgren v. Eustermann, 370 N.W.2d 877 (Minn.1985) (licensed psychologist could not testify as to standard of a physician); Bell v. Hart, 516 So.2d 562 (Ala.1987) (pharmacist and toxicologist testimony disallowed).

Expert testimony is often based upon clinical literature, FDA statements, and other evidence of the standard of practice and of side-effects of treatments and drugs. Several sources of reliable and authoritative statements may be used by experts in professional liability cases, or relied upon by the trial judge as definitive.

a. pharmaceutical package insert instructions and warnings. Package inserts may be used to establish the standard of care for use of the particular drug. In Thompson v. Carter, 518 S.2d 609 (Miss.1987), the physician used Bactrim, a sulfonamide antibiotic, to treat the plaintiff's kidney infection. She developed Stevens Johnson Syndrome, a severe allergic reaction associated with use of Bactrim. The court allowed the admission of the package insert, holding that the package insert was prima facie proof of the proper method of use of Bactrim, an "authoritative published compilation by a pharmaceutical manufacturer."

Accord, Garvey v. O'Donoghue, 530 A.2d 1141 (D.C.App.1987) (relevant evidence of the medical standard of care). But see Tarter v. Linn, 396 Pa.Super. 155, 578 A.2d 453 (Pa.Super 1990) (sustaining trial court's refusal to allow plaintiff to establish the standard of care by introducing information on adverse drug reactions to the drug Diamox from the Physician's Desk Reference); Craft v. Peebles, 78 Hawai'i 287, 893 P.2d 138 (1995)("some evidence"); Mozer v. Kerth, 224 Ill.App.3d 525, 166 Ill.Dec. 801, 586 N.E.2d 759 (1992)(while package insert may establish the standard of care, "plaintiff must still show by expert testimony that physician failed to follow explicit instructions of the manufacturer").

The Physicians Desk Reference is allowed by most courts as some evidence of the standard of care, if an expert witness relies on it. See, e.g., Morlino v. Medical Center, 152 N.J. 563, 706 A.2d 721 (N.J.1998), where a pregnant patient whose fetus died after she took an antibiotic brought action against prescribing physician, medical center, and obstetrician. The court held that Physicians' Desk Reference (PDR) entries alone did not establish standard of care, but the trier of fact can consider package inserts and parallel PDR references when they are supported by expert testimony. "When supported by expert testimony, PDR entries and package inserts may provide useful information of the standard of care. Physicians frequently rely on the PDR when making decisions concerning the administration and dosage of drugs."

b. judicial notice. When the defendant physician's clinical decisions violate a clearly articulated practice within the specialty, courts are willing to make a finding of per se negligence. See Deutsch v. Shein, 597 S.W.2d 141 (Ky.1980), where the defendant was negligent per se in ordering radiology and other tests on the pregnant plaintiff, injuring the fetus. In United States v. Zwick, 413 F.Supp. 113, 115 (N.D.Ohio 1976), the court considered an action for injunctive relief brought by the United States against a physician who had prescribed over 3,800,000 doses of anorectic controlled substances in a three year period. The court issued an injunction, declaring that minimum standards of medical practice for physicians in bariatric practice require that such drugs not be used as a routine part of treatment of obesity. " * * * [I]t is not proper for the physician dispensing and prescribing anorectic controlled drugs to adopt a unitary approach to the treatment of obesity in that no standard approach to treatment exists." The court cited, as support for its per se finding, a monograph by the National Institutes of Health; a New

England Journal of Medicine article; two treatises; Food and Drug Administration regulations; and standards set forth by the American Society of Bariatric Physicians, "Standards of Bariatric Practice".

c. substantive use of a learned treatise. At the common law, a treatise could be used only to impeach the opponent's experts during cross-examination. It could only undercut the expert's testimony, not build the plaintiff's case. The concern was hearsay, since the author of the treatise was not available for cross-examination as to statements contained in the treatise. Federal Rule of Evidence (FRE) 803(18) creates an exception to the hearsay rule, so that the learned treatise can be used for substantive purposes, so long as the treatise is accepted as reliable. Jacober v. St. Peter's Med. Ctr., 128 N.J. 475, 608 A.2d 304 (N.J. 1992). An expert must be on the stand to explain and assist in the application of the treatise. Tart v. McGann, 697 F.2d 75 (2d Cir.1982). The treatise must be declared reliable by the trial court, after a motion by the moving lawyer to use the treatise substantively under FRE 803(18) or its state equivalent. Maggipinto v. Reichman, 481 F.Supp. 547 (E.D.Pa.1979).

Experts in malpractice cases base their testimony on their knowledge, education and experience. They may also rely on outside studies in the research literature. On rare occasions, courts have allowed such research material into evidence in a malpractice suit. In Young v. Horton, 259 Mont. 34, 855 P.2d 502 (Mont. 1993), the court allowed into evidence four medical journal articles that had concluded that a majority of patients forget that they gave informed consent to their doctors prior to surgery. The medical expert then testified based both on his experience with informed consent and on the articles' conclusions.

The admissibility of "novel" scientific evidence is often a thorny issue in environmental and toxic tort cases, although rarely in malpractice cases. The standard for evaluating such evidence had long been held to be established by the Court in Frye v. United States, 54 App.D.C. 46, 293 Fed. 1013 (1923), where the Supreme Court considered the polygraph test and its limitations. The Court held that expert opinion based on a scientific technique is inadmissible unless the technique is "generally accepted" as reliable in the relevant scientific community. In Daubert v. Merrell Dow Pharmaceuticals, Inc., 509 U.S. 579, 113 S.Ct. 2786, 125 L.Ed.2d 469 (1993), the Court again considered the admissibility of scientific evidence, in this case epidemiological and other evidence of birth defects caused by mothers' ingestion of Bendectin. The Court rejected the *Frye* test of "general acceptability" as a threshold test of admissibility of novel scientific evidence, holding that the Federal Rules of Evidence, particularly Rule 702, make the trial judge the gatekeeper of such evidence, with the responsibility to assess the reliability of an expert's testimony, its relevance, and the underlying reasoning or methodology. Expert testimony must have a valid scientific connection to the issues in the case, and be based on "scientifically valid principles". The scientific evidence must pertain to scientific knowledge defined as falsifiable scientific theories capable of empirical testing.

The Supreme Court has extended the Daubert factors to all expert testimony, not just scientific testimony. In Kumho v. Carmichael, 526 U.S. 137, 119 S.Ct. 1167, 143 L.Ed.2d 238 (1999), the Court held that Daubert's gatekeeping role for federal courts, requiring an inquiry into both relevance and reliability, applies not only to scientific testimony but to all expert testimony. The Court noted that this was a flexible test, not a checklist, and it is tied to the particular facts of the case. But "some of these factors may be helpful in evaluating the reliability even of experience-based expert testimony ... " Id. At 1176. The use of the Daubert test is "make certain that an expert, whether basing testimony upon professional studies or personal experience employs in the courtroom the same level of intellectual rigor that characterizes the practice of an expert in the relevant field." Id. This would seem to impose a higher level of scrutiny on the typical malpractice expert, particularly in cases involving institutional liability, where the expert may testify about a system design in a hospital or a salary incentive system in a managed care system. It remains to be seen how the Kumho case will affect judicial screening of malpractice experts. In some state courts, so-called "Kumho" motions challenging experts have become common, asking the trial court to evaluate the reliability of the bases of the expert's testimony.

In Reese v. Stroh, 128 Wash.2d 300, 907 P.2d 282 (Wash. 1995), the Washington Supreme Court considered the use of Prolastin, protein replacement therapy, for emphysema. The treatment, while FDA-approved, lacked statistical proof of efficacy. The court held that "[a]n expert opinion regarding application of an accepted theory or methodology to a particular medical condition does not implicate *Frye*." They also declined to accept the *Daubert* test, finding that it was unnecessary to do so. They held that an expert's practical experience and acquired knowledge is sufficient without further proof of statistical efficacy. Since the defendant did not argue that the theory or methodology involved in Prolastin therapy lacked acceptance in the scientific community, an expert opinion regarding application of an accepted theory to a particular medical condition does not implicate Frye. Id. at 286. See generally Katherine M. Atikian, Note and Comment, Nasty Medicine: Daubert v. Merrell Dow Pharmaceuticals, Inc. Applied to a Hypothetical Medical Malpractice Case, 27 Loy. L.A. L. Rev. 1513 (1994).

     d.   evidentiary uses of clinical practice guidelines. Clinical practice guidelines, so long as they are developed by an expert witness as a testamentary anchor, will be allowed in evidence to help establish the standard of care. They can also be used to impeach the opinion of an expert witness. In Roper v. Blumenfeld, 309 N.J.Super. 219, 706 A.2d 1151, 1156 (N.J.Super.A.D.1998), the defendant used 1992 Parameters of Care for Oral and Maxillofacial Surgery: A Guide of Practice, Monitoring and Evaluation in order to cross examine plaintiff's expert and to examine his expert. As used to impeach, it was permissible to counter the doctor's opinion that because plaintiff was injured during defendant's failed attempt at extraction, defendant must have deviated from the standard of care because the injury is not a medically accepted risk of the procedures he performed. "As to this claim, the article is quite relevant for it lists as a known risk and complication of 'erupted' teeth '[o]ralfacial neurologic dysfunction.' "

B.   PRACTICE GUIDELINES AS CODIFIED STANDARDS OF CARE

A national standard of practice does not exist for many procedures and tools, and the "highest and best" practice may not be the safest or most effective in the long run. Substantial regional variations exist in the use of many procedures, with no apparent differences in outcome (life expectancy, morbidity, days missed from work). See generally John Wennberg and A. Gittlesohn, Small Area Variations in Health Care Delivery, 182 Science 1102 (1973); Pamela Paul–Shaheen, Jane Deane Clark, and Daniel Williams, "Small Area Analysis: A Review and Analysis of the North American Literature," 12 J. Health Politics, Policy and Law 741 (1987).

Different practice styles exist in different regions, and even within states, based on a local concept of good practice, as the locality rule litigation demonstrates. Practices may continue to be used by physicians out of sheer inertia, or because reimbursement reinforces their use, or because it makes a physician at least feel like she is doing something for a patient.

American physicians have in recent years put forth substantial efforts toward standard setting, specifying treatments for particular diseases, under pressure from the government, insurers and managed care organizations looking for ways to reduce variation and "trim the fat" out of clinical practice. Clinical practice guidelines (also referred to as practice parameters and clinical pathways) have been developed by specialty societies such as the American Academy of Pediatrics; by the government, through the Agency for Health Care Policy and Research (AHCPR); and by individual hospitals in the clinical setting. Such guidelines are sets of suggestions, described in decision rules, based on current medical consensus on how to treat a certain illness or condition. The Institute of Medicine has defined clinical guidelines as "systematically developed statements to assist practitioner and patient decisions about appropriate health care for specific clinical circumstances." They are standardized specifications for using a procedure or managing a particular clinical problem. In Hall v. Hilbun, the central issue was the value of such guidelines in directing the nursing staff. Such guidelines may be quality-oriented, reducing variations in practice with improving patient care; they may also be cost-reducing, promoting a lower cost approach to care. The Agency for Health Care Policy and Research (AHCPR) within the Public Health Service, a subdivision of the Department of Health and Human Services (DHHS), has the responsibility for the Department's Medical Treatment Effectiveness Program. This program supports research, data development, and other activities to develop and review clinically relevant guidelines, standards of quality, performance measures, and medical review criteria, in order to improve the quality and effectiveness of health care services.

Clinical pathways share many common attributes with practice guidelines. They are interdisciplinary plans of care that outline the ideal sequence and timing of interventions for patients with a particular diagnosis, procedure, or symptom. They are designed to reduce delays and resource use while maintaining quality of care. They guide care of patients with a highly predictable course of illness, and have been developed for high-volume, high-cost or high-risk diagnoses or procedures. Pathways are intended for use in hospitals or for cases as they move from hospital to home. They cover longer periods of treatment, presenting a kind of map of treatment to guide physicians and support staff, while also educating patients as to the sequence of treatment. They also allow a way to track patient outcomes and document whether or not a patient's outcomes were achieved.

Critical pathways are specific: they describe what will happen to a patient every day that the patient is in the hospital. This specificity includes not only traditional nursing functions, but also medication and treatments that can be ordered only by a physician. An example of such a critical pathway is one developed by University Hospitals of Cleveland for patients chronically dependent on a ventilator, to reduce the costs of caring for this population, based on a retrospective chart review of ventilator-dependent patients and projected reimbursement by third-party payers to the hospital for the patients. The pathway is developed with the patient's physician to fit the patient's needs. Other pathways include one developed by Johns Hopkins Hospital for patients undergoing a radical, retropubic prostatectomy (removal of the prostate gland).

See generally Donna D. Ignatavicius and Kathy A. Hausman, Clinical Pathways for Collaborative Practice 10 (1995); Karen Butler, Health Care Quality Revolution: Legal Landmines for Hospitals and the Rise of the Critical Pathway, 58 Alb. L. Rev. 843 (1995).

Clinical guidelines raise difficult legal questions, since they potentially offer an authoritative and settled statement of what the standard of care should be for a given treatment or illness. A court has several choices when such guidelines are offered in evidence. Such a guideline might be evidence of the customary practice in the medical profession. A doctor practicing in conformity with a guideline would be shielded from liability to the same extent as one who can establish that she or he followed professional custom. The guideline acts like an authoritative expert witness or a well-accepted review article. Using guidelines as evidence of professional custom, however, is problematic if they are ahead of prevailing medical practice. A guideline could also serve as evidence of a "respectable" minority practice. See generally Andrew L. Hyams, David W. Shapiro, and Troyen A. Brennan, Medical Practice Guidelines in Malpractice Litigation: An Early Retrospective, 21 J.Health Pol., Pol'cy & Law 289 (1996).

Guidelines have already had an effect on settlement patterns, according to surveys of malpractice lawyers. Id. Plaintiffs have used such guidelines to their advantage in malpractice cases, particularly the guidelines of the American College of Obstetricians and Gynecologists (ACOG). See, e.g., Miles v. Tabor, 387 Mass. 783, 443 N.E.2d 1302 (1982) (obstetrician's failure to initiate resuscitation of infant immediately after delivery violated ACOG guidelines); Green v. Goldberg, 630 So.2d 606 (Fla.Dist.Ct.App.1993)(ACOG bulletin on breast cancer treatment used to support expert testimony); Basten v. United States, 848 F.Supp. 962 (M.D.Ala.1994)(ACOG guidelines requiring that alpha-fetoprotein screening be offered and that acceptance or rejection be documented.) See generally Andrew L. Hyams et al., id. at 296–299.

Such guidelines provide a particularized source of standards against which to judge the conduct of the defendant physician. A widely accepted clinical standard may be presumptive evidence of due care, but expert testimony will still be required to introduce the standard and establish its sources and its relevancy. A guideline could thus be treated as negligence per se or at least a rebuttable presumption that could then be countered with evidence.

Professional societies often attach disclaimers to their guidelines, thereby undercutting their defensive use in litigation. The American Medical Association, for instance, calls its guidelines "parameters" instead of protocols to indicate a large sphere of physician discretion, and further suggests that all guidelines contain disclaimers stating that they are not intended to displace physician discretion. Such guidelines therefore cannot be treated as conclusive.

Might medical societies that develop guidelines expose themselves to liability if poorly crafted guidelines lead to injury, or if they fail to keep the guidelines up-to-date as medical knowledge advances? See Mark R. Chassin, Standards of Care in Medicine, 25 Inquiry 437 (1988).

What effect will this development of standards in many areas of medicine have on the proof of a malpractice case? Will it move all medical practice toward a national standard?

A outpouring of writing on practice guidelines has occurred over the past several years. See generally Arnold J. Rosoff, The Role of Clinical Practice Guidelines in Health Care Reform, 5 Health Matrix 369 (1995); Institute of Medicine, Clinical Practice Guidelines: Directions For A New Program 8 (Marilyn J. Field & Kathleen N. Lohr eds., 1990); John Ayres, The Use and Abuse of Medical Practice Guidelines, 15 J. Legal Med. 421, 436–38 (1994); Office of Technology Assessment, U.S. Congress, OTA–H–608, Identifying Health Technologies That Work: Searching For Evidence 145–47 (1994).

C. OTHER METHODS OF PROVING NEGLIGENCE

The plaintiff will usually use his own experts to establish a standard of care, defendant's deviation from it, and causation, as was done in *Hall*. As discussed above, practice guidelines also provide evidence of the standard of care. A physician's negligence can also be established in several other ways.

1. Examination of defendant's expert witnesses. The plaintiff may establish the standard of care through defense witnesses, leaving the issue of breach within the province of the fact finder, not the trial court on summary disposition. Porter v. Henry Ford Hospital, 181 Mich.App. 706, 450 N.W.2d 37 (1989).

2. An admission by the defendant that he or she was negligent. In Grindstaff v. Tygett, 698 S.W.2d 33 (Mo.App.1985), the defendant described a delivery in the hospital records as a "tight midforceps rotation". In his deposition, when asked what this phrase meant, he described the rotation as "[o]ne in which you would have to apply excessive pressure to effect the maneuver." This was held to be sufficient to submit the case to the jury. See also Bro v. Glaser, 22 Cal.App.4th 1398, 27 Cal.Rptr.2d 894 (1994)(suit for negligent infliction of emotional distress; defendant admitted in a written interrogatory that the baby he delivered sustained a small cut from the scalpel on her left cheek).

An implicit admission of culpability can be found through evidence of intimidation by defendant of plaintiff's expert witnesses, which a jury is allowed to consider as defendant's consciousness of the weakness of his case. "This, in conjunction with the other evidence in the case, may lead to the further inference that appellee considers his case to be weak because he, in fact, is guilty of the negligence which appellant asserts he committed. Such inferences are, of course, merely permissible * * *." Meyer v. McDonnell, 40

Md.App. 524, 392 A.2d 1129 (Md.App. 1978)(defendant surgeon had message relayed through other physicians to plaintiff's medical experts to the effect that their testimony would be transcribed and disseminated to their local medical societies and the American Academy of Orthopedic Surgeons). But see McCool v. Gehret, 657 A.2d 269 (Del.1995), where the plaintiff's expert had felt threatened by the defendant during a telephone conversation and decided not to testify, only to change his mind out of feelings of guilt when plaintiff again asked that he testify; the court held that "even though the doctor's conduct was reprehensible", the plaintiff suffered no injury from Dr. Gehret's efforts to intimidate because the expert did testify.

3.   Testimony by the plaintiff, in the rare case where he or she is a medical expert qualified to evaluate the doctor's conduct. Lamont v. Brookwood Health Services, Inc., 446 So.2d 1018 (Ala.1983).

4.   Common knowledge in situations where a layperson could understand the negligence without the assistance of experts. See Gannon v. Elliot, 19 Cal.App.4th 1, 23 Cal.Rptr.2d 86 (1993)(plastic cap from a surgical instrument left in plaintiff's hip socket after a hip joint replacement); Seippel–Cress v. Lackamp, 23 S.W.3d 660 (Mo.C.A.2000)(evidence showed that patient became unusually fatigued during barium swallow test; average person knows that a provider in such a case must determine the cause of the change in condition, without expert testimony).

A physician's obvious or admitted ignorance of an illness or a procedure may create a duty to investigate and consult another physician. In Largess v. Tatem, 130 Vt. 271, 291 A.2d 398 (1972), the defendant, a general practitioner in Vermont, treated the plaintiff, a 77 year old woman, for a fracture of her left hip. He called in a specialist in orthopedic surgery, who implanted a Jewett nail. This fixation device was not designed to permit full early weight bearing. Dr. Tatem was not familiar with the postoperative instructions for such a device and released the patient without instructions. The device broke and a second surgery was required. The court held that expert testimony was not required, since the violation of the standard of care was obvious to a lay trier of fact.

5.   Use of res ipsa loquitur, as discussed infra.

Note: The Role of the Internet

The Internet enables a doctor to stay current through bulletin boards, physician-directed online services, and both commercial and government-sponsored Websites. Doctors are increasingly expected to seek and use the data. Medical knowledge about evidence-based medicine has accumulated at a staggering rate. Between 1966 and 1995, the number of clinical research articles based on randomized clinical trials jumped from about 100 per year to 10,000 annually. Mark R. Chassin, Is Health Care Ready for Six Sigma Quality? 76 the Milbank Quarterly 565, 574 (1998). Web-based databases have proliferated to sort and promote access by physicians to the newest clinical practice guidelines and other medical developments. The goal has been to help physicians handle the information overload in an efficient and user-friendly way.

The National Guideline Clearinghouse, *http://www.guideline.gov*, offers free access by physicians and others to the current clinical practice guidelines, with instantaneous searches of the database. A search produces all guidelines on a given subject, along with an appropriateness analysis of each guideline. The

Clearinghouse provides a standardized abstract of each guideline, and grades the scientific basis of its recommendations and the development process for each. Full text or links to sites with the guidelines are provided. Readers are given synopses to produce a side-by-side comparison of guidelines, outlining where those agree and disagree, and physicians can access electronic mail groups to discuss development and implementation. These guidelines must pass certain entry criteria to be included: they must be current, contain systematically developed statements to guide physician decisions, have been produced by a medical or other professional group, government agency, health care organization or other private or public organization; and they must show that they were developed through systematic search of peer-reviewed scientific evidence. The benefits: easy search features, database comprehensiveness and Internet location make this the most powerful tool to date. Various appropriateness tests have been developed to evaluate guidelines. See Paul G Shekelle and David L. Schriger, Evaluating the Use of the Appropriateness Method in the Agency for Health Care Policy and Research Clinical Practice Guideline Development Process, 31 Health Services Research (1996)

Other Internet based services are available on a commercial basis. One example is MDConsult, a commercial database available by subscription that makes available hundreds of medical textbooks and treatises, as well as easy access to clinical practice guidelines. Subscribership in such commercial sites, designed to be user-friendly, has grown geometrically over the past few years, as physicians look for easy research access to data about patient problems. A survey by MDConsult of physician subscribers found that physicians were accessing the website for a fast and easy way to check the literature while treating patients, allowing for immediate answers; to keep up and to expand a physician's knowledge base about particular conditions. Physicians felt that the immediacy of access to a comprehensive website improved their informational base and therefore their quality of practice.

Medscape is another commercial site that provides a full range of online resources for physicians. It offers a journal scan on the newest research findings, free access to abstracts on MEDLINE, access to drug searching through First DataBank, the largest Web-based drug and disease database, access to clinical practice guidelines, treatment updates, full text articles in many journals, and a clinical management series n the form of interactive e-med texts. A subscriber can also set up an email account to get specific information sent on a regular basis on specific topics. These commercial services in particular offer a busy physician quick and painless access, to both journals and guidelines, as well as to new literature and comments by experts. The location of current information on the Internet facilitates its ease of access to physicians, and its link to other commercial sites makes it easy to connect to, no matter what portal a physician uses to access medical information databases on the Web. Failure to access such data bases is likely to become an important piece of evidence in a malpractice suit, since it is evidence that a physician has failed to stay current in his or her field of practice.

Computer technologies pose other liability risks for physicians. As patient records are computerized, it becomes easier to gain access to a full patient history. Patient records can be easily stored on CDROM or other media, so that access is virtually instantaneous. Patient drug records and possible interactions can therefore be researched effortlessly. For a physician to fail to make such a search and miss a possible problem or drug interaction leads to liability. Another liability risk created by reliance on computer record keeping is the failure to protect such computerized patient records. Computer storage raises issues of security, privacy and integrity of computer records. Breaches of security and unauthorized access to patient information can lead to a range of tort suits, from invasion of privacy to negligence in record maintenance. A physician or institution also has a duty to detect and cripple viruses. Physicians who fail to properly protect patient and other files from corruption may be as negligent as physicians who fail to keep proper paper records.

Problem: Evidentiary Hurdles

You have been approached by Clinton Scott, whose wife Diane died of toxemia at the end of pregnancy. The facts are as follows. Clinton tells you that Diane had experienced symptoms of blurred vision, headaches, chest pains and swelling in the second half of pregnancy, with worsening symptoms in early February. She had had long-standing severe hypertension, as her medical record indicated. Diane had described these symptoms to her obstetrician, Dr. Fowles, during her January examination. He had told her not to worry, that this was normal in first pregnancies, and that everything would be fine. He did not test her urinary protein excretion or her platelet count. Early in February her symptoms got markedly worse. Dr. Fowles then tested her urinary protein excretion and her platelet count and concluded that she had pre-eclampsia (toxemia). He admitted her to the hospital and drugs were administered to control Diane's condition, but she went into convulsions a few hours later. Later that day the staff failed to detect fetal heart tones and a C-section was promptly performed. A stillborn baby girl was delivered. Six days later, Diane's brain had ceased to function. She was taken off life-support with Clinton's approval, and died.

In your preliminary discovery, you have had trouble finding a local obstetrician to testify against Dr. Fowles, who is the president of the local medical society and is quite well-respected among his peers. Your jurisdiction follows the *Hall* rule, so you could hire an expert from elsewhere in the state or region, but you would prefer to use someone who can claim familiarity with local practices and who would cost you less in discovery costs as well.

Consider the following evidence issues. Will you be successful in getting this evidence admitted? In getting the case to the jury? In winning a jury trial?

1. You took the deposition of Dr. Fowles, who was forthright and candid during the examination. The following questions and answers are particularly interesting.

Q. Is the standard of care when managing a pregnant patient that where you have a condition of persistent headaches, blurred vision, fatigue, significant epigastric pain, and developing edema of the feet, that the physician managing the woman should suspect pre-eclampsia as a cause?

A. Yes, those symptoms should put a doctor on notice of the potential of toxemia. When you suspect this, you should promptly treat the patient, since immediate treatment increases the likelihood of a cure without the development of any adverse complications.

Q. Would earlier diagnosis and treatment of Diane have prevented her brain death and the loss of the infant?

A. That is impossible to say.

2. A review article in the New England Journal of Medicine stated as follows:

Hypertensive disorders are the most common medical complications of pregnancy and are an important cause of maternal and perinatal morbidity and mortality worldwide. * * *

* * *

Pregnant women with chronic hypertension are at increased risk for superimposed preeclampsia and abruptio placentae, and their babies are at increased risk for perinatal morbidity and mortality. * * *

Women with preeclampsia require close observation because the disorder may worsen suddenly. The presence of symptoms (such as headache, epigastric pain, and visual abnormalities) and proteinuria increase the risk of both eclampsia and abruptio placentae; women with these findings require close observation in the hospital. * * * The management should include close monitoring of the mother's blood pressure, weight, urinary protein excretion, and platelet count, as well as of fetal status. In addition, the woman must be informed about the symptoms of worsening preeclampsia. If there is evidence of disease progression, hospitalization is indicated.

Baha M. Sibai, Drug Therapy: Treatment of Hypertension in Pregnant Women, 335 New Eng. J. Med. 257 (1996).

3. You have interviewed a nurse-practitioner in obstetrics in the area, who examined the medical records and talked with Clinton. She is willing to testify that based upon her experience as an obstetric nurse for over 10 years, Dr. Fowles was negligent in failing to immediately treat Diane when her symptoms were first related to him in January.

4. **Williams on Obstetrics**, a leading textbook used in many medical schools, states the following:

Since eclampsia is preceded in most cases by premonitory signs and symptoms, its prophylaxis is in many ways more important than its cure and is identical with the treatment of pre-eclampsia. Indeed, a major aim in treating of pre-eclampsia is to prevent convulsions. The necessity of regular and frequent blood pressure measurements thus becomes clear, as well as the importance of detection of rapid gain of weight and of proteinuria, and the immediate institution of appropriate dietary and medical treatment as soon as the earliest signs and symptoms appear. By the employment of these precautionary measures and by prompt termination of pregnancy in those cases that do not improve or that become progressively worse under treatment, frequency of eclampsia will be greatly diminished and many lives will be saved. Prophylaxis, while valuable, is not invariably successful. * * *

5. You have learned during discovery that two hospital committees, the Morbidity Committee and the Obstetrics Committee, have investigated Dr. Fowles' past performance in dealing with patients with eclampsia. You would like to obtain hospital incident reports and committee minutes to find out whether the medical staff has described his performance as substandard. Consider the note below in analyzing this issue.

6. You have decided to seek an out-of-state expert to testify about toxemia. You are considering hiring Dr. Matthew Berkle, an obstetrician in practice in Pennsylvania. Dr. Berkle has strong opinions on the importance of early and accurate diagnosis of toxemia, formed as the result of his delivery of over a thousand babies in his career and his own study of his patients, over fifty of whom manifested symptoms of toxemia during their pregnancies. He has kept careful

records and has determined that several subtle warning signs can be detected by a properly trained physician who follows his methods. Dr. Berkle is not a trained researcher, but rather a highly intelligent and thoughtful physician who cares about his patients.

The relevant rules of evidence in your jurisdiction are identical to the Federal Rules of Evidence below. These rules were amended to reflect the scientific evidence concerns raised in *Daubert* and *Kumho* by the Supreme Court and were effective December 1, 2000.

Federal Rule of Evidence 701 (Opinion testimony by lay witnesses)

If the witness is not testifying as an expert, the witness' testimony in the form of opinions or inferences is limited to those opinions or inferences which are (a) rationally based on the perception of the witness, (b) helpful to a clear understanding of the witness' testimony or the determination of a fact in issue, and (c) not based on scientific, technical, or other specialized knowledge within the scope of Rule 702.

Federal Rule of Evidence 702 (Testimony by experts)

If scientific, technical, or other specialized knowledge will assist the trier of fact to understand the evidence or to determine a fact in issue, a witness qualified as an expert by knowledge, skill, experience, training, or education, may testify thereto in the form of an opinion or otherwise, if (1) the testimony is based upon sufficient facts or data, (2) the testimony is the product of reliable principles and methods, and (3) the witness has applied the principles and methods reliably to the facts of the case.

Federal Rule of Evidence 703 (Bases of opinion testimony by experts)

The facts or data in the particular case upon which an expert bases an opinion or inference may be those perceived by or made known to the expert at or before the hearing. If of a type reasonably relied upon by experts in the particular field in forming opinions or inferences upon the subject, the facts or data need not be admissible in evidence in order for the opinion or inference to be admitted. Facts or data that are otherwise inadmissible shall not be disclosed to the jury by the proponent of the opinion or inference unless the court determines that their probative value in assisting the jury to evaluate the expert's opinion substantially outweighs their prejudicial effect.

Federal Rule of Evidence 803(6) (Records of Regularly Conducted Activity)

A memorandum, report, record, or data compilation, in any form, of acts, events, conditions, opinions, or diagnoses, made at or near the time by, or from information transmitted by, a person with knowledge, if kept in the course of a regularly conducted business activity, and if it was the regular practice of that business activity to make the memorandum, report, record or data compilation, all as shown by the testimony of the custodian or other qualified witness, or by certification that complies with Rule 902(11), Rule 902(12), or a statute permitting certification, unless the source of information or the method or circumstances of preparation indicate lack of trustworthiness. The term "business" as used in this paragraph includes business, institution, association, profession, occupation, and calling of every kind, whether or not conducted for profit.

Note: Discovery of Hospital Committee Proceedings and Incident Reports

A hospital's risk management and quality assurance functions can figure in a variety of legal problems. The most important of these is whether a hospital is liable in tort for injuries caused by its failure to oversee adequately the quality of care provided by its employees or medical staff. A second issue is when and how a hospital may exclude a high risk, poor quality physician. A third issue is when hospital records can be used against a physician sued for malpractice.

Hospital Committee Proceedings. Plaintiffs in malpractice actions frequently seek discovery of the proceedings of hospital quality assurance committees. They may request production of a committee's minutes or reports, propound interrogatories about the committee process or outcome, or ask to depose committee members concerning committee deliberations. If the plaintiff is suing a health care professional whose work was reviewed by the committee, the discovery may seek to confirm the negligence of the professional or to uncover additional evidence substantiating the plaintiff's claim. If the suit is against the hospital on a theory of corporate liability (i.e., claiming that the hospital itself was negligent in appointing or failing to supervise a professional), evidence of committee proceedings may prove vital to establishing the hospital's liability.

These discovery requests are usually met with a claim that information generated within or by hospital committees is not discoverable. In Coburn v. Seda, 101 Wash.2d 270, 677 P.2d 173 (1984), the court considered the plaintiff's discovery requests for the records of the hospital quality review committees.

* * * The discovery protection granted hospital quality review committee records, like work product immunity, prevents the opposing party from taking advantage of a hospital's careful self-assessment. The opposing party must utilize his or her own experts to evaluate the facts underlying the incident which is the subject of suit and also use them to determine whether the hospital's care comported with proper quality standards.

The discovery prohibition, like an evidentiary privilege, also seeks to protect certain communications and encourage the quality review process. Statutes bearing similarities to RCW 4.24.250 prohibit discovery of records on the theory that external access to committee investigations stifles candor and inhibits constructive criticism thought necessary to effective quality review. Courts determining that hospital quality review records should be subject to a common law privilege have advanced this same rationale. As the court stated in Bredice v. Doctors Hosp., Inc., 50 F.R.D. 249, 250 (D.D.C.1970), aff'd, 479 F.2d 920 (D.C.Cir.1973):

> Confidentiality is essential to effective functioning of these staff meetings; and these meetings are essential to the continued improvement in the care and treatment of patients. Candid and conscientious evaluation of clinical practices is a *sine qua non* of adequate hospital care * * *. Constructive professional criticism cannot occur in an atmosphere of apprehension that one doctor's suggestion will be used as a denunciation of a colleague's conduct in a malpractice suit.

Most states have statutes affording hospital quality assurance proceedings some degree of protection from discovery. Critics of discovery immunity, on the other hand, argue that immunity deprives plaintiffs, particularly those claiming hospital corporate negligence, of necessary evidence. Moreover, they argue, JCA-HO and licensing requirements, plus the threat of tort liability, provide ample incentives for hospital quality assurance efforts so that immunity is unnecessary. See, arguing the immunity question, James F. Flanagan, Rejecting a General Privilege for Self–Critical Analysis, 51 Geo.Wash.L.Rev. 551 (1983); Arthur F. Southwick & Debra A. Slee, Quality Assurance in Health Care: Confidentiality of Information and Immunity for Participants, 5 J.Leg.Med. 343 (1984).

Statutes protecting committee proceedings from discovery are often subject to exceptions, either explicitly or through judicial interpretation. One common exception affords discovery to physicians challenging the results of committee action against them. Thus a physician whose staff privileges were revoked may discover information from the credentialing committee, Schulz v. Superior Court, 66 Cal.App.3d 440, 446, 136 Cal.Rptr. 67, 70 (1977). This seems to be required by notions of fair process. On the other hand, do statutes that grant physicians access to information that is denied to malpractice plaintiffs violate equal protection? See Jenkins v. Wu, 102 Ill.2d 468, 82 Ill.Dec. 382, 386–88, 468 N.E.2d 1162, 1166–68 (1984). If a court in a public proceeding grants a physician access to the transcript of a committee hearing under such an exception, must it subsequently grant a patient access to further information regarding the same proceeding? See Henry Mayo Newhall Memorial Hospital v. Superior Court, 81 Cal.App.3d 626, 146 Cal.Rptr. 542 (1978).

In the absence of a statute providing immunity from discovery, a few courts have refused discovery of peer review committee proceedings under the court's inherent power to control discovery. See Bredice v. Doctors Hospital, Inc., 50 F.R.D. 249, 250 (D.D.C.1970), affirmed, 479 F.2d 920 (D.C.Cir.1973); Dade County Med. Ass'n v. Hlis, 372 So.2d 117 (Fla.App.1979). More courts have rejected common law immunity, holding that the plaintiff's need for evidence outweighs the defendant's claim to protection. See State ex rel. Chandra v. Sprinkle, 678 S.W.2d 804 (Mo.1984); Wesley Medical Center v. Clark, 234 Kan. 13, 669 P.2d 209 (1983).

A number of statutes immunizing committee proceedings from discovery do not explicitly render information from those committees privileged from admission into evidence if the plaintiff can obtain it otherwise. But would such information be otherwise admissible? Would it be hearsay? If so, would it be subject to the business records exception? See Fed.R.Evid. 803(6). Might committee records indicating that a hospital was concerned about the performance of a physician be admissible as an admission in a subsequent corporate negligence action against the hospital? See Fed.R.Evid. 801(d)(2)(D). Might a plaintiff's expert be permitted to testify on the basis of information gleaned from committee records, even though those records were themselves hearsay? See Fed.R.Evid. 703. In a suit brought by one particular patient, would committee records documenting errors made by a physician in the treatment of other patients be relevant? Might opinions concerning a physician's negligence found in committee records or reports invade the province of the jury? See, addressing these questions, Robert F. Holbrook & Lee J. Dunn, Medical Malpractice Litigation: The Discoverability and Use of Hospitals' Quality Assurance Records, 16 Washburn L.J. 54, 68–70 (1976).

Hospital Incident Reports. When a plaintiff seeks discovery of incident reports rather than committee proceedings, policy considerations are somewhat different. Hospitals have greater incentives to investigate untoward events than they have to carry on continuing quality review, and are less dependent on voluntary participation. The incident report would usually be more directly relevant to a single claim for malpractice than would general committee investigations. Possibly for these reasons, immunity statutes that protect committee proceedings less often protect incident reports, and courts have been less willing to immunize incident reports from discovery. On the other hand, since incident reports are more directly related to litigation of specific mishaps, two privileges can be asserted to protect them that would seldom apply to committee proceedings: the work product immunity and attorney client privilege.

The work product immunity protects materials prepared in anticipation of litigation. See Federal Rules of Civil Procedure 56. Courts look to the nature and purpose of incident reports. If they are regularly prepared and distributed for future loss prevention, they are not considered to be documents prepared in anticipation of litigation so as to invoke application of the work product exception to discovery. See St. Louis Little Rock Hospital, Inc. v. Gaertner, 682 S.W.2d 146, 150–51 (Mo.App.1984).

The attorney-client privilege protects communications, even if the attorney is not yet representing a client, provided that the communication was made between the client as an insured to his liability insuror during the course of an existing insured-insuror relationship. To be privileged, a communication between a client and his attorney, or between an insured and his insuror, must be within the context of the attorney-client relationship, with a purpose of securing legal advice from the client's attorney. If an incident report is used for loss prevention, the mere fact that it was later used by an attorney is irrelevant.

See Kay Laboratories, Inc. v. District Court, 653 P.2d 721 (Colo.1982); but see Sierra Vista Hospital v. Superior Ct., 248 Cal.App.2d 359, 56 Cal.Rptr. 387 (1967).

D. ALTERING THE BURDEN OF PROOF

In the typical malpractice case, the plaintiff must introduce expert testimony as to the standard of care or face a nonsuit. The courts have developed several doctrines that ease the plaintiff's burden of proof, shifting either the burden of production of evidence or the burden of persuasion onto the defendant.

1. Res Ipsa Loquitur

The best known of these evidentiary devices is the doctrine of *res ipsa loquitur* (Latin for "The thing speaks for itself"), which eliminates the plaintiff's need to present expert testimony as to negligence of the defendant. *Ybarra* is the classic statement of the justifications for the doctrine in a medical malpractice case.

YBARRA v. SPANGARD

Supreme Court of California, 1944.
25 Cal.2d 486, 154 P.2d 687.

[The plaintiff underwent an appendectomy. His primary physician, the surgeon and a variety of hospital personnel were present during the operation. Afterwards the plaintiff complained of pain in his right arm and shoulder, which he had first felt when he awoke from the surgery. The pain spread down his arm and grew worse until he was unable to rotate or lift his arm. His medical experts testified that the injury was a paralysis of traumatic origin, probably caused by pressure.]

Plaintiff's theory is that the foregoing evidence presents a proper case for the application of the doctrine of res ipsa loquitur, and that the inference of negligence arising therefrom makes the granting of a nonsuit improper. Defendants take the position that, assuming that plaintiff's condition was in fact the result of an injury, there is no showing that the act of any particular defendant, nor any particular instrumentality, was the cause thereof. They attack plaintiff's action as an attempt to fix liability "en masse" on various defendants, some of whom were not responsible for the acts of others; and they further point to the failure to show which defendants had control of the instrumentalities that may have been involved. * * * We are satisfied, however, that these objections are not well taken in the circumstances of this case.

The doctrine of res ipsa loquitur has three conditions: "(1) the accident must be of a kind which ordinarily does not occur in the absence of someone's negligence; (2) it must be caused by an agency or instrumentality within the exclusive control of the defendant; (3) it must not have been due to any voluntary action or contribution on the part of the plaintiff." [ ] It is applied in a wide variety of situtations, including cases of medical or dental treatment and hospitalcare. [ ]

* * *

The present case is of a type which comes within the reason and spirit of the doctrine more fully perhaps than any other. * * * [I]t is difficult to see how the doctrine can, with any justification, be so restricted in its statement as to become inapplicable to a patient who submits himself to the care and custody of doctors and nurses, is rendered unconscious, and receives some injury from instrumentalities used in his treatment. Without the aid of the doctrine a patient who received permanent injuries of a serious character, obviously the result of some one's negligence, would be entirely unable to recover unless the doctors and nurses in attendance voluntarily chose to disclose the identity of the negligent person and the facts establishing liability. [ ]If this were the state of the law of negligence, the courts, to avoid gross injustice, would be forced to invoke the principles of absolute liability, irrespective of negligence, in actions by persons suffering injuries during the course of treatment under anesthesia. But we think this juncture has not yet been reached, and that the doctrine of res ipsa loquitur is properly applicable to the case before us.

The condition that the injury must not have been due to the plaintiff's voluntary action is of course fully satisfied under the evidence produced herein; and the same is true of the condition that the accident must be one which ordinarily does not occur unless some one was negligent. We have here no problem of negligence in treatment, but of distinct injury to a healthy part of the body not the subject of treatment, nor within the area covered by the operation. The decisions in this state make it clear that such circumstances raise the inference of negligence and call upon the defendant to explain the unusual result. [ ]

* * *

We have no doubt that in a modern hospital a patient is quite likely to come under the care of a number of persons in different types of contractual and other relationships with each other. For example, in the present case it appears that Drs. Smith, Spangard and Tilley were physicians or surgeons commonly placed in the legal category of independent contractors; and Dr.

Reser, the anesthetist, and defendant Thompson, the special nurse, were employees of Dr. Swift and not of the other doctors. But we do not believe that either the number or relationship of the defendants alone determines whether the doctrine of res ipsa loquitur applies. * * *

* * *

It may appear at the trial that, consistent with the principles outlined above, one or more defendants will be found liable and others absolved, but this should not preclude the application of the rule of res ipsa loquitur. The control at one time or another, of one or more of the various agencies or instrumentalities which might have harmed the plaintiff was in the hands of every defendant or of his employees or temporary servants. This, we think, places upon them the burden of initial explanation. Plaintiff was rendered unconscious for the purpose of undergoing surgical treatment by the defendants; it is manifestly unreasonable for them to insist that he identify any one of them as the person who did the alleged negligent act.

The other aspect of the case which defendants so strongly emphasize is that plaintiff has not identified the instrumentality any more than he has the particular guilty defendant. Here, again, there is a misconception which, if carried to the extreme for which defendants contend, would unreasonably limit the application of the res ipsa loquitur rule. It should be enough that the plaintiff can show an injury resulting from an external force applied while he lay unconscious in the hospital; this is as clear a case of identification of the instrumentality as the plaintiff may ever be able to make.

An examination of the recent cases, particularly in this state, discloses that the test of actual exclusive control of an instrumentality has not been strictly followed, but exceptions have been recognized where the purpose of the doctrine of res ipsa loquitur would otherwise be defeated. * * *

In the face of these examples of liberalization of the tests for res ipsa loquitur, there can be no justification for the rejection of the doctrine in the instant case. As pointed out above, if we accept the contention of defendants herein, there will rarely be any compensation for patients injured while unconscious. A hospital today conducts a highly integrated system of activities, with many persons contributing their efforts. There may be, e.g., preparation for surgery by nurses and interns who are employees of the hospital, administering of an anesthetic by a doctor who may be an employee of the hospital, an employee of the operating surgeon, or an independent contractor; performance of an operation by a surgeon and assistants who may be his employees, employees of the hospital, or independent contractors; and post surgical care by the surgeon, a hospital physician, and nurses. The number of those in whose care the patient is placed is not a good reason for denying him all reasonable opportunity to recover for negligent harm. It is rather a good reason for re-examination of the statement of legal theories which supposedly compel such a shocking result.

We do not at this time undertake to state the extent to which the reasoning of this case may be applied to other situations in which the doctrine of res ipsa loquitur is invoked. We merely hold that where a plaintiff receives unusual injuries while unconscious and in the course of medical treatment, all those defendants who had any control over his body or the instrumentalities which might have caused the injuries may properly be called upon to meet the inference of negligence by giving an explanation of their conduct.

The judgment is reversed.

Notes and Questions

1. What justifications did the court cite in favor of applying res ipsa loquitur? Does *res ipsa loquitur* operate here purely as a recognition of the probability of negligence, or as something more?

2. In most states, res ipsa loquitur operates as an inference of negligence. That is, the jury may infer that the defendant was in some way negligent, but it is not compelled to conclude negligence. It can reject the inference as well as accepting it. A few states treat res ipsa as a presumption, so that a plaintiff who proves a res ipsa case should win unless the defendant comes forward with some evidence to rebut the presumed negligence. See generally Dan Dobbs, The Law of Torts § 249 (2000).

The doctrine continues to be applied in medical malpractice cases where the injury is to a part of the body outside the scope of an operation. See, e.g., Zumwalt v. Koreckij, 24 S.W.3d 166 (Mo.C.A. 2000)(patient suffered nerve injury to her right hand, arm and shoulder during a knee replacement operation); Adams v. Family Planning Associates Medical Group, Inc., 315 Ill.App.3d 533, 248 Ill.Dec. 91, 733 N.E.2d 766 (Ill.C.A.2000)(patient died during abortion under general anesthesia; res ipsa applied).

The doctrine has become increasingly unpopular, with many jurisdictions reluctant to apply the doctrine in medical malpractice cases out of concern that doctors might be held liable for rare bad outcomes, whether or not they were related to any negligence by the defendant. As Justice Gibson, author of *Ybarra*, wrote in Siverson v. Weber, 57 Cal.2d 834, 22 Cal.Rptr. 337, 372 P.2d 97 (1962), " * * * this would place too great a burden upon the medical profession and might result in an undesirable limitation on the use of operations or new procedures involving an inherent risk of injury even when due care is used."

See also Jackson v. Oklahoma Memorial Hospital, 909 P.2d 765 (Okl.1995); Hoven v. Rice Memorial Hospital, 396 N.W.2d 569 (Minn.1986).

Many states have eliminated the availability of res ipsa loquitur by statute as part of malpractice reform packages.

2. Shifting the Burden of Persuasion

Courts have in special situations used a variety of burden-shifting devices to ease the plaintiff's burden of proof. Res ipsa loquitur, as applied in *Ybarra*, *supra*, obviated the plaintiff's need to prove a specific error by the defendants. In rare cases, courts have gone even further, shifting the burden of persuasion onto the defendants, requiring that they present evidence to exonerate themselves or face liability.

Consider the case of Anderson v. Somberg, 67 N.J. 291, 338 A.2d 1 (N.J. 1975). The plaintiff underwent a laminectomy. During surgery, the tip of a pituitary rongeur, a surgical implement, broke off in the plaintiff's spinal canal. The surgeon, unable to retrieve the metal fragment, terminated the operation. The fragment caused medical complications and necessitated further surgical interventions. The rongeur had been used five times a year, or in about twenty previous surgical procedures. The rongeur had been purchased from the distributor about four years before; the distributor obtained it from the manufacturer.

The plaintiff sued the surgeon for medical malpractice, the hospital for negligently furnishing a defective surgical instrument, the medical supply distributor on a warranty theory, and the manufacturer of the rongeur, on a strict liability in tort claim. The surgeon testified that he had not examined the rongeur prior to the day of surgery but that day had inspected it visually, and had not twisted it while performing the laminectomy. Other testimony stated that the rongeur was a delicate instrument that might break if twisted. A metallurgist found neither structural defects nor faulty workmanship, but only a small crack of unknown origin. He concluded that the instrument had been strained, probably because of "an improper 'twisting'" of the tool.

The court noted that "[t]he plaintiff was left with multiple defendants, a range of hypothetical causes for the rongeur's failure, and an inability to prove either the cause of the defect or the source of it." The court then continued:

> In the ordinary case, the law will not assist an innocent plaintiff at the expense of an innocent defendant. However, in the type of case we consider here, where an unconscious or helpless patient suffers an admitted mishap not reasonably foreseeable and unrelated to the scope of the surgery (such as cases where foreign objects are left in the body of the patient), those who had custody of the patient, and who owed him a duty of care as to medical treatment, or not to furnish a defective instrument for use in such treatment can be called to account for their default. They must prove their nonculpability, or else risk liability for the injuries suffered.

The court noted that their rule was not the application of *res ipsa loquitur*. It was limited only to those cases where the injury fell outside the scope of the surgical procedure, where the burden of proof should shift to multiple defendants to "prove their freedom from liability."

A "missing witness" instruction has been upheld in a few jurisdictions, allowing the jury to presume negligence and causation from the mere absence of a crucial piece of evidence. In Welsh v. United States, 844 F.2d 1239 (6th Cir.1988), the court shifted the burden of persuasion to the defendants, holding that "acts by the hospital surgeons in this case create a rebuttable presumption of negligence and proximate causation against the defendant— the negligent destruction of a skull bone flap after the second [of two] operations, and the consequent failure at that time to undertake a pathological examination of this evidence * * *". Id. at 1239–40. See also C. McCormick, McCormick on Evidence, § 273, at 810 at n. 20 (3rd Ed.1984). Rejecting "missing evidence" as substantive proof that shifts the burden, see Battocchi v. Washington Hospital Center, 581 A.2d 759 (D.C.App.1990) (limiting the effect of a showing of missing evidence to an instruction allowing the jury to draw an adverse inference against the defendants, upon a showing of gross indifference to or reckless disregard for the relevance of the evidence to a possible claim).

3. *Strict Liability*

Courts have generally resisted applying strict liability (or implied warranty) to a health care professional or institution. Medicine is usually distinguished from "commercial" enterprises. As the Wisconsin Supreme Court notes in Hoven v. Kelble, 79 Wis.2d 444, 256 N.W.2d 379 (1977):

> There are differences between the rendition of medical services and transactions in goods (or perhaps other types of services as well). Medical and many other professional services tend often to be experimental in nature, dependent on factors beyond the control of the professional, and devoid of certainty or assurance of results. Medical services are an absolute necessity to society, and they must be readily available to the people. It is said that strict liability will inevitably increase the cost for medical services, which might make them beyond the means of many consumers, and that imposition of strict liability might hamper progress in developing new medicines and medical techniques.

Does this distinction seem as convincing in light of the growth of modern corporate health care and the increased blend of professional judgment and medical tools and devices? A medical intervention often requires the use of medical products: knee joints, bone graft material, pig heart valves. Breast implant prostheses are a common example of such a service-product intervention. Courts apply strict liability to the distributors of such products but are reluctant to extend strict liability to a health care provider using the product in a way incidental to the primary function of providing medical services. See, e.g., Cafazzo v. Central Medical Health Services, 430 Pa.Super. 480, 635 A.2d 151 (Pa.Super.1993)(mandibular prosthesis); Hoff v. Zimmer, 746 F.Supp. 872 (W.D.Wis.1990)(hip prosthesis); Budding v. SSM Healthcare System, 19 S.W.3d 678 (Mo.2000)(mandibular implant).

In Porter v. Rosenberg, 650 So.2d 79, 83 (Fla.App. 4 Dist.1995), the court considered a strict liability claim against the physician for a breast implant. The court rejected strict liability in the case but opened the door slightly to a judicial "essence of the transaction" test for future cases.

> . . . we conclude that whether or not a plaintiff may bring an action against a physician, hospital, or other health care provider for strict liability depends upon the essence of the physician-patient relationship for the particular transaction. If the medical services could not have been rendered without utilizing the product, then strict liability does not apply. If the predominant purpose of the physician-patient relationship for that transaction is the provision of medical services based upon the physician's medical judgment, skill, or expertise, the malpractice statute applies and strict liability is inapplicable.
>
> The fact that the physician or health care provider is not solely or primarily in the business of distributing products is not the determinative factor for application of strict liability as long as distributing products is part of its business. [ ][1] Therefore, if distributing products is part of the

---

1. Such examples might include a nutrition doctor selling diet products or a dentist selling electric toothbrushes. Some manufacturers may rely solely or mainly on utilizing health care professionals for distribution of their products and the health care professional may rely on selling the product as part of its business as additional profit separate from provision of other medical services.

health care provider's business and the sales or distribution aspect in the particular transaction between the health care provider and the patient predominates over the services aspect an action instinct liability may lie against the health care provider.

The court however rejected the action in this case on the grounds that the plaintiff had sued several other defendants from the manufacturers to distributors. "We perceive of no overriding public policy argument which would justify an obvious circumvention of the medical malpractice statute and an extension of strict liability to physicians under the circumstances presented here."

For a detailed analysis that rejects strict liability for both physicians and hospitals, see Tanuz v. Carlberg, 122 N.M. 113, 921 P.2d 309 (App.1996) (surgical insertion of temporomandibular joint implants); Parker v. St. Vincent Hospital, 122 N.M. 39, 919 P.2d 1104 (App.1996)(hospitals not distributors or suppliers of product); Parker v. E.I. DuPont de Nemours & Co., 121 N.M. 120, 909 P.2d 1 (App.1995)(analysis of strict liability principles and medical devices). For a proposal to apply strict liability to a particular medical specialty based on a statistical outcomes analysis, see Barry R. Furrow, Defective Mental Treatment: A Proposal for the Application of Strict Liability to Psychiatric Services, 58 B.U.L.Rev. 391 (1978).

Problem: Breathing Hard

Sam had chronic obstructive pulmonary disease and his doctor, Dr. Donahue, recommended treatment with the Intermittent Positive Pressure Breathing ventilator (IPPB). Sam had severe side-effects from the treatment and died. Dr. Donahue used the IPPB ventilator properly, but an alternative device, the nebulizer, is cheaper and safer than IPPB for all IPPB uses. Despite this, IPPB is still reimbursed by most third party payers and continues to be used by some physicians in the hospital setting for obstructive pulmonary disease.

Your research uncovers the following information about IPPB. Intermittent Positive Pressure Breathing is a technology that diffused into use in spite of evidence that it did not work. Research studies have confirmed that it is no better than the cheaper and less dangerous nebulizer. While its use has declined, it has not disappeared and reimbursement is still available for its use from Medicare and private insurers. Doctors continue to use such a technology in the face of clear evidence and authoritative declarations that it is both ineffective and dangerous. The reasons may include habit; clinical impressions that it gives patients short-term relief; and financial benefits to physicians. The medical director of the respiratory therapy department, the primary source of service orders, often receives a cut of the department's income. As long as third party payors still pay for IPPB, cash will flow for its use.

Sam's family has asked you to consider the merits of a lawsuit against Dr. Donahue. What are your options, and what defenses will the defendant raise if you file suit?

See generally Duffy, S.Q., and Farley, D.E., Intermittent Positive Pressure Breathing: Old Technologies Rarely Die, AHCPR Pub. 94–0001, Div. Provider Studies Research Note 18, Agency for Health Care Policy and Research (1993).

II. JUDICIAL RISK—BENEFIT BALANCING

HELLING v. CAREY

Supreme Court of Washington, 1974.
83 Wash.2d 514, 519 P.2d 981.

HUNTER, ASSOC. JUSTICE.

The plaintiff suffers from primary open angle glaucoma. Primary open angle glaucoma is essentially a condition of the eye in which there is an interference in the ease with which the nourishing fluids can flow out of the eye. Such a condition results in pressure gradually rising above the normal level to such an extent that damage is produced to the optic nerve and its fibers with resultant loss in vision. The first loss usually occurs in the periphery of the field of vision. The disease usually has few symptoms and, in the absence of a pressure test, is often undetected until the damage has become extensive and irreversible.

The defendants (respondents), Dr. Thomas F. Carey and Dr. Robert C. Laughlin, are partners who practice the medical specialty of ophthalmology. Ophthalmology involves the diagnosis and treatment of defects and diseases of the eye.

The plaintiff first consulted the defendants for myopia, nearsightedness, in 1959. At that time she was fitted with contact lenses. She next consulted the defendants in September, 1963, concerning irritation caused by the contact lenses. Additional consultations occurred in October, 1963; February, 1967; September, 1967; October, 1967; May, 1968; July, 1968; August, 1968; September, 1968; and October, 1968. Until the October 1968 consultation, the defendants considered the plaintiff's visual problems to be related solely to complications associated with her contact lenses. On that occasion, the defendant, Dr. Carey, tested the plaintiff's eye pressure and field of vision for the first time. This test indicated that the plaintiff had glaucoma. The plaintiff, who was then 32 years of age, had essentially lost her peripheral vision and her central vision was reduced to approximately 5 degrees vertical by 10 degrees horizontal.

Thereafter, in August of 1969, after consulting other physicians, the plaintiff filed a complaint against the defendants alleging, among other things, that she sustained severe and permanent damage to her eyes as a proximate result of the defendants' negligence. During trial, the testimony of the medical experts for both the plaintiff and the defendants established that the standards of the profession for that specialty in the same or similar circumstances do not require routine pressure tests for glaucoma upon patients under 40 years of age. The reason the pressure test for glaucoma is not given as a regular practice to patients under the age of 40 is that the disease rarely occurs in this age group. Testimony indicated, however, that the standards of the profession do require pressure tests if the patient's complaints and symptoms reveal to the physician that glaucoma should be suspected.

The trial court entered judgment for the defendants following a defense verdict. The plaintiff thereupon appealed to the Court of Appeals, which affirmed the judgment of the trial court. [ ] The plaintiff then petitioned this Court for review, which we granted.

* * * [T]he plaintiff contends * * * that she was unable to argue her theory of the case to the jury that the standard of care for the specialty of ophthalmology was inadequate to protect the plaintiff from the incidence of glaucoma, and that the defendants, by reason of their special ability, knowledge and information, were negligent in failing to give the pressure test to the plaintiff at an earlier point in time which, if given, would have detected her condition and enabled the defendants to have averted the resulting substantial loss in her vision.

We find this to be a unique case. The testimony of the medical experts is undisputed concerning the standards of the profession for the specialty of ophthalmology. It is not a question in this case of the defendants having any greater special ability, knowledge and information than other ophthalmologists which would require the defendants to comply with a higher duty of care than that "degree of care and skill which is expected of the average practitioner in the class to which he belongs, acting in the same or similar circumstances." [ ] The issue is whether the defendants' compliance with the standard of the profession of ophthalmology, which does not require the giving of a routine pressure test to persons under 40 years of age, should insulate them from liability under the facts in this case where the plaintiff has lost a substantial amount of her vision due to the failure of the defendants to timely give the pressure test to the plaintiff.

The defendants argue that the standard of the profession, which does not require the giving of a routine pressure test to persons under the age of 40, is adequate to insulate the defendants from liability for negligence because the risk of glaucoma is so rare in this age group. * * *

The incidence of glaucoma in one out of 25,000 persons under the age of 40 may appear quite minimal. However, that one person, the plaintiff in this instance, is entitled to the same protection, as afforded persons over 40, essential for timely detection of the evidence of glaucoma where it can be arrested to avoid the grave and devastating result of this disease. The test is a simple pressure test, relatively inexpensive. There is no judgment factor involved, and there is no doubt that by giving the test the evidence of glaucoma can be detected. The giving of the test is harmless if the physical condition of the eye permits. The testimony indicates that although the condition of the plaintiff's eyes might have at times prevented the defendants from administering the pressure test, there is an absence of evidence in the record that the test could not have been timely given.

Justice Holmes stated [ ] in Texas & Pac.Ry. v. Behymer,| Œ:

What usually is done may be evidence of what ought to be done, but what ought to be done is fixed by a standard of reasonable prudence, whether it usually is complied with or not.

In The T.J. Hooper, 60 F.2d 737 * * *, Justice Hand stated:

[I]n most cases reasonable prudence is in fact common prudence; but strictly it is never its measure; a whole calling may have unduly lagged in the adoption of new and available devices. It never may set its own tests, however persuasive be its usages. *Courts must in the end say what is required; there are precautions so imperative that even their universal disregard will not excuse their omission.*

(Italics ours.)

Under the facts of this case reasonable prudence required the timely giving of the pressure test to this plaintiff. The precaution of giving this test to detect the incidence of glaucoma to patients under 40 years of age is so imperative that irrespective of its disregard by the standards of the ophthalmology profession, it is the duty of the courts to say what is required to protect patients under 40 from the damaging results of glaucoma.

We therefore hold, as a matter of law, that the reasonable standard that should have been followed under the undisputed facts of this case was the timely giving of this simple, harmless pressure test to this plaintiff and that, in failing to do so, the defendants were negligent, which proximately resulted in the blindness sustained by the plaintiff for which the defendants are liable.

* * *

Notes and Questions

1. Is the court correct in imposing its own risk-benefit result on the specialty of ophthalmology? Certainly its view of the tradeoff between blindness and a low-cost test seems to lead inevitably to the *Helling* conclusion. A survey of Washington ophthalmologists subsequent to the *Helling* decision found that they did test for glaucoma with some regularity before *Helling,* with 20.3% reporting that they tested "quite often", and 30.1% testing "virtually always". Jerry Wiley, "The Impact of Judicial Decisions on Professional Conduct: An Empirical Study", 55 S.Cal.L.Rev. 345, 383 (1981). Yet the expert testimony in the case was that testing was not the practice for patients under forty.

The court assumed that the test was harmless as well as low in cost: "the giving of the test is harmless if the physical condition of the eye permits." This view ignores both the costs of false-positives and the merits of treatment when a true positive result is found. It has been estimated that more than 15 patients per one million population go blind from glaucoma annually. Screening for glaucoma using tonometry (the pressure test in *Helling*) is recommended on the theory that early treatment will stop the progression of glaucoma into blindness.

The value of tonometry is limited by its imprecision. First, it has a high false positive rate. Only one percent of those patients who test abnormally high using tonometry actually have glaucoma. Ninety-nine percent of those who test positive therefore have to undergo further testing and are subjected to considerable worry for a disease they do not have. Second, patients who are correctly diagnosed as having glaucoma or at least elevated intraocular pressure may not gain much from this knowledge, since drug treatments often do not produce significant improvements, nor does current evidence support the theory that early treatment will halt the progression of glaucoma. See generally Eliot Robin, Matters of Life & Death: Risks v. Benefits of Medical Care 147 (1984); Eric E. Fortess and Marshall B. Kapp, Medical Uncertainty, Diagnostic Testing, and Legal Liability, 13 Law, Medicine & Health Care 213 (1985) (because of high false-positive rate, follow-up testing would cost a great deal, and patients who tested positive falsely would also suffer unnecessary anxiety about incipient glaucoma.)

A new screening device, the GDX Access, can now directly test the presence and extent of damage to the nerve fiber layer at the back of the eye: This allows early and accurate diagnosis of glaucoma. See "New Device Helps to Diagnose Glaucoma More Reliably," N.Y. Times (March 5, 2001.)

2. Do these opinions change your view of the rightness of the court's position in *Helling*? Why didn't the defendant ophthalmologists make these arguments to justify the conservative non-testing approach? Why did the defense fail to prove that a significant minority, or even a majority of Washington ophthalmologists, used the pressure test routinely? Should we be reluctant to encourage courts to move beyond the customary practice, given the complexity inherent in medical practice? Or should courts be aggressive in judging the community standard, so long as the parties present full evidence as to the pros and cons of the procedure at issue?

3. *Helling v. Carey* is one of a small number of cases rejecting a customary medical practice. See also Lundahl v. Rockford Memorial Hospital Association, 93 Ill.App.2d 461, 465, 235 N.E.2d 671, 674 (1968) ("what is usual or customary procedure might itself be negligence"); Favalora v. Aetna Casualty & Surety Company, 144 So.2d 544 (La.App.1962); Toth v. Community Hospital at Glen Cove, 22 N.Y.2d 255, 263, 292 N.Y.S.2d 440, 447–48, 239 N.E.2d 368, 373 (1968) ("evidence that the defendant followed customary practice is not the sole test of professional malpractice"). These cases involve a readily understandable therapy or diagnostic procedure, and the courts have allowed the trier of fact to weigh without expert testimony the relative risks of using the procedure or omitting it. Most jurisdictions have been reluctant to follow *Helling* in replacing the established medical standard of care with a case-by-case judicial balancing.

For an interesting judicial discussion of the limits of a customary practice defense, see Nowatske v. Osterloh, 198 Wis.2d 419, 543 N.W.2d 265 (1996). The court considered the standard Wisconsin jury instruction on the standard of care applicable to physicians. Upholding the instruction, they wrote:

> We agree with the parties and the Medical Society that while evidence of the usual and customary conduct of others under similar circumstances is ordinarily relevant and admissible as an indication of what is reasonably prudent, customary conduct is not dispositive and cannot overcome the requirement that physicians exercise ordinary care.

* * *

> We recognize that in most situations there will be no significant difference between customary and reasonable practices. In most situations physicians, like other professionals, will revise their customary practices so that the care they offer reflects a due regard for advances in the profession. An emphasis on reasonable rather than customary practices, however, insures that custom will not shelter physicians who fail to adopt advances in their respective fields and who consequently fail to conform to the standard of care which both the profession and its patients have a right to expect.

It has been argued that the customary practice standard of care, protective of physician behavior, is gradually eroding in favor of a general negligence standard. See Philip G. Peters, Jr., The Quiet Demise of Deference to Custom: Malpractice Law at the Millennium, 57 Wash. & Lee L.Rev. 163 (2000).

Note: The Effects of Tort Suits on Provider Behavior

Are tort suits likely to change potentially dangerous patterns of medical practice? Malpractice litigation in theory operates as a quality control mechanism. From the economist's perspective, tort doctrine should be designed to achieve an optimal prevention policy, reducing the sum total of the costs of medical accidents and the costs of preventing them. In theory, the tort system deters accident producing behavior. How? The existence of a liability rule and the resulting threat of a lawsuit and judgment encourages health care providers to reduce error and patient injury in circumstances where patients themselves lack the information (and ability) to monitor the quality of care they receive. Potential defendants will take precautions to avoid error and will buy insurance to cover any errors that injure patients. By finding fault and assessing damages against a defendant, a court sends a signal to health care providers that if they wish to avoid similar damages in the future they may need to change their behavior. See Michelle J. White, The Value of Liability in Medical Malpractice, 13 Health Affairs 75 (1994); Ann G. Lawthers, et al., Physicians' Perceptions of the Risk of Being Sued, 17 J. Health Pol., Policy & L. 463, 479 (1992); Mark I. Taragin, et al., The Influence of Standard of Care and Severity of Injury on the Resolution of Medical Malpractice Claims, 117 Ann. Int. Med. 780 (1992); and Frederick W. Cheney, et al., Standard of Care and Anesthesia Liability, 261 JAMA 1599 (1989). Other critics have noted the limitations on physician understanding of how the negligence system works and what their liability exposure really is. See, e.g., Bryan A. Liang, Medical Malpractice: Do Physicians Have Knowledge of Legal Standards and Assess Cases as Juries Do? 3 U. Chi. L. Sch. Roundtable 59 (1996).

How does the existence of malpractice insurance alter this analysis? If the insurer does not employ experience rating to distinguish the litigation-prone providers from their colleagues, it is in effect causing an inaccurate signal to be sent, since all physicians in a practice area pay the same premiums regardless of their level of malpractice claims. The existence of insurance therefore dilutes or eliminates the financial incentives for physicians or other providers to change their behavior.

Malpractice insurers, particularly the physician-owned companies in many states, now engage in aggressive review of claims. These companies insure about 40% of physicians in active patient care. They routinely use physicians to review applications for insurance and to review the competence of those sued. Physicians with claims due to negligence, as assessed by the peer reviews, may be terminated, may be surcharged, or have restrictions on practice imposed. William B. Schwartz and Daniel N. Mendelson, The Role of Physician–Owned Insurance Companies in the Detection and Deterrence of Negligence, 262 J.A.M.A. 1342 (1989). If a physician loses his malpractice insurance, he may quit, switch jobs, or go without insurance. He may also go to a surplus-lines insurance company that charges much higher premiums for coverage. Claims exposure thus can lead to a direct financial impact on the physician forced to carry such expensive insurance. See William B. Schwartz and Daniel N. Mendelson, Physicians Who Have Lost Their Malpractice Insurance, 262 J.A.M.A. 1335 (1989).

What is the likely effect on a physician of being named a defendant? How might a provider modify her behavior to avoid or reduce negligent behavior? She may spend more time on exams or patient histories, invest in further training, increase support staff or stop doing procedures that she does not do well. The few available studies have found that physicians who have been malpractice defendants often alter their practice as a reaction, even if they win the litigation. They also suffer chronic stress until the trial is over. See, for example, Charles, Wilbert, and Kennedy, Physicians' Self–Reports of Reactions to Malpractice Litigation, 141 Am.J.Psychiatry 563, 565 (1984) ("A malpractice suit was considered a serious and often a devastating event in the personal and professional lives of the respondent physicians").

Malpractice litigation does affect medical practice, making anxious providers either overestimate the risks of a suit or at least adjust their practice to a new assessment of the risk of suit, regardless of the incentive effects of judgments and premium increases. Physicians perceive a threat from the system, judging their risk of being sued as much higher than it actually is. The Harvard New York Study, surveying New York physicians, found that physicians who had been sued were more likely to explain risks to patients, to restrict their scope of practice, and to order more tests and procedures. Patients, Doctors, and Lawyers: Medical Injury, Malpractice Litigation, and Patient Compensation in New York 9–29 (1990). Physicians surveyed in the New York study felt that the malpractice threat was important in maintaining standards of care. Id. at 9–24. The Report notes that " * * * the perception of incentives largely shapes the behavior that ultimately affects patient care." Id. at 3–19. Perceived risk is thus important to physician conduct. See Peter A. Bell, Legislative Intrusions in the Common Law of Medical Malpractice: Thoughts About the Deterrent Effect of Tort Liability, 35 Syracuse L.Rev. 939, 973–90 (1984). Hospitals have instituted risk management offices and quality assurance programs; informed consent forms have become ubiquitous; medical record-keeping with an eye toward proof at trial has become the rule. One economist has estimated (based upon admittedly limited data) that " * * * the current non-trivial incidence of injury due to negligence would be at least 10 percent higher, were it not for the incentives for injury prevention created by the one in ten incidents of malpractice that result in a claim." Patricia Danzon, An Economic Analysis of the Medical Malpractice System, 1 Behavioral Sciences & the Law 39 (1983). See also Patricia M. Danzon, Medical Malpractice 10 (1984); Guido Calabresi, The Costs of Accidents (1970); William B. Schwartz and Neil K. Komesar, Doctors, Damages and Deterrence: An Economic View of Medical Malpractice, 298 New Eng.J.Med. 1282 (1978); The Economics of Medical Malpractice (S. Rottenberg, ed. 1978). For a skeptical view of the signalling effect of tort litigation generally, see Stephen D. Sugarman, Doing Away with Tort Law, 73 Cal.L.Rev. 555 (1985); critiquing Sugarman's view, see Howard A. Latin, Problem–Solving Behavior and Theories of Tort Liability, 73 Cal.L.Rev. 677, 740 (1985).

It can be argued that courts should be willing to articulate clear standards for practice. Such standards are more likely to be heeded by health care professionals in their practice where the rule is a relatively simple one. Daniel J. Givelber, William J. Bowers, and Carolyn L. Blitch, Tarasoff, Myth and Reality: An Empirical Study of Private Law In Action, 1984 Wisc.L.Rev. 443, 485–486. Givelber et al. concluded, after surveying 2875 psychotherapists nationwide, that therapists now warn third parties when a patient utters a threat. They feel bound by *Tarasoff*, even though the case is binding only on California therapists. Therapists feel capable of assessing dangerousness and were comfortable with warning victims.

The authors argued that

" * * * [I]f an appellate court desires to change behavior, it should use judicially established standards of behavior, not jury determined standards. The judicially determined rule of *Tarasoff I*, protect through warning, appears to have affected therapist attitudes, knowledge and behavior to a far greater degree than *Tarasoff II*. Id. at 487."

What other forces and incentives affect the quality of health care delivery by physicians, other professionals, and institutions? If you were a physician or a nurse who conscientiously wanted to reduce medical errors in your own practice, what steps would you consider? A technological innovation for example may reduce both the level of medical injury for a procedure and the risks of being sued. Consider the pulse oximeter, which monitors a patient's blood oxygen to indicate when his oxygen level drops due to breathing problems or overuse of anesthesia. This can give physicians three or four minutes to correct a problem before brain damage results. In 1984, no hospital operating room had such a device, but by 1990 all operating rooms did. Patients under anesthesia now suffer fewer injuries as a result.

III. OTHER THEORIES

A. NEGLIGENT INFLICTION OF MENTAL DISTRESS

Most medical malpractice suits are negligence suits for physical injury and lost wages suffered by the patient, or in a wrongful death action, for damages that include harm to the deceased's relatives. Recent cases however have allowed plaintiffs to sue a health care provider for the negligent infliction of emotional distress under particularly egregious circumstances.

OSWALD v. LeGRAND

Supreme Court of Iowa, 1990.
453 N.W.2d 634.

NEUMAN, JUSTICE.

This appeal challenges a grant of summary judgment for medical professionals in a case involving the spontaneous abortion of a 19–22 week-old fetus. The trial court barred the plaintiffs from introducing expert testimony due to their failure to timely designate an expert in accordance with Iowa Code section 668.11(2) (1987). Accordingly, the district court determined that plaintiffs could not generate a material issue of fact concerning the defendants' negligence. Because we conclude that expert testimony is crucial to some but not all of plaintiffs' claims, we affirm in part, reverse in part, and remand for further proceedings.

I. * * *

To establish a prima facie case of medical malpractice, a plaintiff must produce evidence that (1) establishes the applicable standard of care, (2) demonstrates a violation of this standard, and (3) develops a causal relationship between the violation and the injury sustained. [ ] from p. 181 3d.

> One is where the physician's lack of care is so obvious as to be within the comprehension of a lay[person] and requires only common knowledge and experience to understand. The other exception is really an example of the first situation. It arises when the physician injures a part of the body not being treated.

[ ] It is the "common knowledge" exception upon which plaintiffs base their argument for reversal in the present case.

II. * * * [W]e accept the following facts as established for purposes of this appeal.

Plaintiffs Susan and Larry Oswald have been married for ten years and are the parents of two healthy sons. During Susan's third pregnancy, she began experiencing bleeding and painful cramping just prior to her five-month checkup. At that time, she was under the care of a family practice physician, defendant Barry Smith. He ordered an ultrasound test and Susan was then examined in his office by one of his colleagues, defendant Larry LeGrand, an obstetrician. Neither the test nor the examination revealed an explanation for the bleeding and Susan was instructed to go home and stay off her feet. Later that day, however, Susan began to bleed heavily. She was taken by ambulance to defendant Mercy Health Center. The bleeding eventually stopped, Dr. Smith's further examination failed to yield a cause of the problem, and Susan was discharged the following day with directions to take it easy.

The following day, Susan's cramping and bleeding worsened. Susan thought she was in labor and feared a miscarriage. She was unable to reach Dr. Smith by telephone and so Larry drove her to the emergency room at Mercy. There Dr. Christopher Clark, another physician in association with Smith and LeGrand, examined her. He advised her there was nothing to be done and she should go home. Larry was angered by this response and insisted Susan be admitted to the hospital. Dr. Clark honored this request and Susan was transferred to the labor and delivery ward.

In considerable pain and anxious about her pregnancy, Susan's first contact on the ward was with a nurse who said, "What are you doing here? The doctor told you to stay home and rest." Susan felt like "a real pest." A short while later, while attached to a fetal monitor, Susan was told by another nurse that if she miscarried it would not be a baby, it would be a "big blob of blood." Susan was scared.

The next morning, an argument apparently ensued over which physician was responsible for Susan's care. Standing outside Susan's room, Dr. Clark yelled, "I don't want to take that patient. She's not my patient and I am sick and tired of Dr. Smith dumping his case load on me." At the urging of Larry and a nurse, Dr. Clark apologized to Susan for this outburst. He assured her that he would care for her until he left for vacation at noon that day when he was scheduled to go "off call" and Dr. LeGrand would take over.

Around 9:00 a.m. Susan began experiencing a great deal of pain that she believed to be labor contractions. Dr. Clark prescribed Tylenol and scheduled her for an ultrasound and amniocentesis at 11:00 a.m. By that time, Susan was screaming in pain and yelling that she was in labor. Dr. Clark arrived in the x-ray department halfway through the ultrasound procedure and determined from viewing the sonogram that there was insufficient fluid in the amniotic sac to perform an amniocentesis. He told the Oswalds that the situation was unusual but did not reveal to them his suspicion that there was an infection in the uterus. He examined Susan abdominally but did not do a pelvic exam. By all accounts, Susan was hysterical and insisting she was about to deliver. Dr. Clark wanted her transferred upstairs for further monitoring. He told Larry to calm her down. Then he left on vacation, approximately one-half hour before the end of his scheduled duty.

Within minutes, Susan began delivering her baby in the hallway outside the x-ray lab. When Larry lifted the sheet covering Susan and "saw [his] daughter hanging from her belly" he kicked open a glass door to get the attention of hospital personnel. Susan was quickly wheeled to the delivery room where two nurses delivered her one-pound baby girl at 11:34 a.m.

After visually observing neither a heartbeat nor any respiratory activity, one of the nurses announced that the baby was stillborn. The nurse wrapped the infant in a towel and placed her on an instrument tray. Ten minutes later, Dr. LeGrand arrived and delivered the placenta. At Susan's request, he checked the fetus for gender. He made no further examination of the infant, assuming it to be a nonviable fetus. After assuring himself that Susan was fine, and offering his condolences to the disappointed parents, he returned to his office.

Meanwhile, Larry called relatives to advise them of the stillbirth. Upon his return to Susan's room, he touched the infant's finger. Much to his surprise, his grasp was returned. Larry told a nurse in attendance that the baby was alive but the nurse retorted that it was only a "reflex motion." The nurses subsequently determined that the baby *was* alive. After having left her on an instrument tray for nearly half an hour, the nurses rushed the infant to the neonatal intensive care unit. The infant, registered on her birth certificate as Natalie Sue, received comfort support measures until she died about twelve hours later. Further facts will be detailed as they become pertinent to the issues on appeal.

III.   In January 1987, the Oswalds sued the hospital and doctors Clark, Smith and LeGrand on theories of negligence, negligent loss of chance of survival, breach of implied contract and breach of implied warranty. As to Dr. LeGrand and the hospital, Oswalds additionally alleged gross negligence. Factually, these causes of action were premised on violation of the standard of prenatal care owed to Susan Oswald and alleged negligence in the examination and treatment of Natalie Sue including failure to recognize signs of an imminent premature birth, failure to properly prepare for such delivery, and delaying timely and vital treatment to the infant upon her birth. The Oswalds claimed damages for Natalie Sue's lost chance to live, their loss of society and companionship flowing from Natalie Sue's death, severe emotional distress and anxiety resulting from the defendants' negligence in the care of both Susan and Natalie Sue, and severe emotional distress and mental anguish caused by witnessing the negligent treatment of their newborn infant.

* * *

IV.   * * *

A.   *Evidence not within common knowledge.* To begin, there is no evidence in this record that more prompt or heroic efforts to sustain Natalie Sue's life would have been successful. * * *

Similarly, the record contains no evidence that the doctors' or hospital's treatment of Susan in any way prompted Susan's premature delivery or could have, in any way, prevented it. * * *

B.   *Evidence within the "common knowledge" exception.* Beyond these fundamental treatment issues, however, lie plaintiffs' claims that the care provided by defendants Clark, LeGrand, and Mercy Hospital fell below the standard of medical professionalism understood by laypersons and expected by them. Into this category fall Nurse Slater's unwelcoming remarks upon Susan's arrival at the birthing area; Nurse Gardner's deprecating description of a fetus as a "big blob of blood"; Dr. Clark's tirade outside Susan's door; Dr. Clark's insensitivity to Susan's insistence that she was in the final stage of labor, leaving her in a hysterical state minutes before her delivery in a hospital corridor while he went "off call"; Nurse Flynn's determination that the fetus was stillborn, only to discover it gasping for breath half-an-hour later; and Dr. LeGrand's admitted failure to make an independent determination of the viability of the fetus, conceding it was his obligation to do so. Larry and Susan contend that they have suffered severe emotional distress as a result of these alleged breaches of professional conduct.

We note preliminarily that because the Oswalds can sustain no claim of physical injury, they would ordinarily be denied recovery in a negligence action for emotional distress. [ ] An exception exists, however, where the nature of the relationship between the parties is such that there arises a duty to exercise ordinary care to avoid causing emotional harm. [ ] Such claims have been recognized in the negligent performance of contractual services that carry with them deeply emotional responses in the event of breach as, for example, in the transmission and delivery of telegrams announcing the death of a close relative, [ ] and services incident to a funeral and burial. [ ] Under the comparable circumstances demonstrated by this record, we think liability for emotional injury should attach to the delivery of medical services. As we observed by way of analogy in *Meyer*, the birth of a child involves a matter of life and death evoking such "mental concern and solicitude" that the breach of a contract incident thereto "will inevitably result in mental anguish, pain and suffering." *Meyer*, 241 N.W.2d at 920 (quoting *Stewart v. Rudner*, 349 Mich. 459, 84 N.W.2d 816). * * * [ ]

Insofar as the sufficiency of damages are concerned, the Oswalds' claim appears undisputed.[2] The question is whether these six incidents, if proven at trial, would demonstrate a breach of professional medical conduct so obvious as to be within the common knowledge of laypersons without the aid of expert testimony; or, in the alternative, whether plaintiffs could prove the standard of care and its breach through defendants' own testimony. In other words, is the evidence presented by plaintiffs' resistance to the motion sufficient to overcome summary judgment on defendants' claim that no material dispute exists with respect to the issues of negligence and causation? We are persuaded that it is.

The first three incidents described above raise commonly understood issues of professional courtesy in communication regarding a patient's care and treatment. No expert testimony is needed to elaborate on whether the statements by the nurses and Dr. Clark were rude and uncaring; a lay fact finder could easily evaluate the statements in light of the surrounding circumstances to determine whether the language used or message conveyed breached the standard of care expected of medical professionals, and deter-

2. Because the trial court determined plaintiffs' proof was insufficient on the elements of negligence and causation, it did not reach the question of damages. The record reveals that both Susan and Larry have undergone psychological counseling in an effort to overcome the stress, anxiety, and depression associated with Susan's fear of becoming pregnant again and Larry's anger and guilt over the extraordinary helplessness he felt as a witness to his wife's painful and humiliating experience at Mercy Hospital. To the extent that the trial court considered, and dismissed, any claim of intentional infliction of emotional distress due to a perceived lack of "outrageousness" in defendants' conduct, we note that plaintiffs' emotional distress claim has not been pleaded as an independent tort but rather as an element of damages flowing from the underlying breach of professional conduct. Under such circumstances, the dismissal was not warranted because proof of outrageous conduct need not be shown.

mine the harm, if any, resulting to the plaintiffs. In reaching this conclusion we hasten to emphasize that our decision in this case is closely limited to its facts. We in no way suggest that a professional person must ordinarily answer in tort for rudeness, even in a professional relationship. In order for liability to attach there must appear a combination of the two factors existing here: extremely rude behavior or crass insensitivity coupled with an unusual vulnerability on the part of the person receiving professional services.

We are similarly convinced that a lay jury is also capable of evaluating the professional propriety of Dr. Clark's early departure from the hospital, knowing that he had left Susan Oswald unattended in a hospital corridor screaming hysterically that she was about to give birth. * * *

* * *

C. *Evidence demonstrable through defendants' admissions.* * * *

* * *

Defendants argue that because Natalie Sue's death was inevitable, the emotional distress suffered by the Oswalds is understandable but not compensable. What defendants overlook is the colorable claim of severe emotional distress proximately caused by the equivocation of these health care professionals on the very question of her life or death. Under this record, we think the plaintiffs have produced evidence minimally sufficient to overcome summary judgment on this claim of malpractice.

* * *

In conclusion, we affirm in part, reverse in part, and remand this case for further proceedings not inconsistent with this opinion.

Affirmed in part, reversed in part, and remanded.

Notes and Questions

1. *Oswald* focuses on the vulnerability of the plaintiffs, coupled with the "crass insensitivity" of the medical staff. Consider, as a companion case, Wargelin v. Sisters of Mercy Health Corporation, 149 Mich.App. 75, 385 N.W.2d 732 (1986). In *Wargelin,* a series of obstetric disasters befell the plaintiffs. The obstetrician made only two visits during labor, even though a Caesarean section was indicated due to the plaintiff's lopsided uterus; the fetal monitor indicated distress, but the staff failed to react; an intern subsequently delivered the plaintiff's child, not breathing and blue in color, and placed it on her stomach as if it were a healthy child; the obstetrician then grabbed the child and began to pound on its chest and administer electrical shocks to revive it; a call for a pediatrician to help went unanswered; and after fifteen minutes the rescue attempt was abandoned.

The Michigan court applied the bystander rule, which allows that a member of the family witnessing an injury to a third person may recover if they are present or suffer shock "fairly contemporaneous" with the accident. The court held that the series of events related above, including negligent acts, were sufficient. " * * * [T]he cumulative effect of all the events surrounding the stillbirth of the child, if proven to be negligent at trial, are sufficient to cause a parent to suffer emotional and mental distress."

Do *Oswald* and *Wargelin,* read together, expand the applicability of the tort of negligent infliction of mental distress? They indicate judicial sensitivity to hospital failures to provide sensitive, well-trained health care, and willingness to extend the bystander doctrine to allow recovery in these highly charged situations.

2. Negligent infliction of mental distress cases typically involve "bystanders" who witness injury to a loved one. Dillon v. Legg, 68 Cal.2d 728, 69 Cal.Rptr. 72, 441 P.2d 912 (1968) was the first case to articulate a general test of foreseeability of harm, a primary guideline being whether the distress resulted from the "sensory and contemporaneous observance of the accident." Parents would thus need to "observe" the accident or trauma in jurisdictions following the *Dillon* approach.

The California Supreme Court limited the *Dillon* "foreseeability" approach in Thing v. La Chusa, 48 Cal.3d 644, 257 Cal.Rptr. 865, 771 P.2d 814 (1989). The court noted that " * * * [t]he emotional distress for which monetary damages may be recovered * * * ought not to be that form of acute emotional distress or the transient emotional reaction to the occasional gruesome or horrible incident to which every person may potentially be exposed in an industrial and sometimes violent society." The court then said that a plaintiff could recover only if he:

(1) is closely related to the injury victim; (2) is present at the scene of the injury producing event at the time it occurs and is then aware that it is causing injury to the victim; and (3) as a result suffers serious emotional distress—a reaction beyond that which would be anticipated in a disinterested witness and which is not an abnormal response to the circumstances.

Observation of the disturbing events is generally required before courts will allow recovery. Johnson v. Ruark Obstetrics and Gynecology Associates, P.A., 327 N.C. 283, 395 S.E.2d 85 (1990) (expectant parents of a stillborn fetus sued the physicians for the negligent infliction of mental distress, alleging that they had observed events surrounding the death of the fetus; the North Carolina Supreme Court allowed negligent infliction of emotional distress based on a test of reasonably foreseeable consequences). "Observation" has been liberally construed by some state courts. See, for example, Frame v. Kothari, 212 N.J.Super. 498, 515 A.2d 810 (1985)(defendant physician's misdiagnosis of a cerebellar hemorrhage and acute hydrocephalus due to blunt trauma to the skull was held to be an event perceived by the parents; first, the parents' discussion with the defendant about their son's deteriorating condition was an "observation;" and second, their distress was foreseeable after the doctor was informed of the condition and failed to properly treat it.) See also Ochoa v. Superior Court of Santa Clara County, 39 Cal.3d 159, 216 Cal.Rptr. 661, 703 P.2d 1 (1985), where a mother suffered distress after visiting her son who was receiving "woefully inadequate" medical care in a juvenile detention home.

In Estate of Davis v. Yale–New Haven Hospital, 2000 WL 157921 (Conn. Super. 2000), the court allowed a bystander emotional distress claim against the doctor and hospital where the decedent underwent cardiac surgery, became paranoid and detached from reality, was discharged without an anti-pyschotic drug prescription or a treatment plan, and killed himself. The court held that in an appropriate case, which would be rare in misdiagnosis cases, an action for bystander emotional disturbance would be allowed.

Most courts require some direct observation of the events causing the bad outcome, not just observation of the bad outcome itself. See, for example, Smelko v. Brinton, 241 Kan. 763, 740 P.2d 591 (1987)(parents waiting outside the operating room for their baby to undergo surgery; he is negligently burned during the surgery and they discover the burn when he is brought out; held that merely seeing the bad result is not sufficient for recovery). Contra, see Martinez v. Long

Island Jewish Hillside Medical Center, 70 N.Y.2d 697, 518 N.Y.S.2d 955, 512 N.E.2d 538 (1987) (physician negligently diagnoses a pregnant woman's condition as requiring an abortion; the woman aborts the fetus and then discovers the abortion was not needed; recovery allowed).

3. If a contractual relationship forms the basis for liability for emotional distress, some jurisdictions have held that the injured party need not have observed the disaster, as foreseeability is not required. In Newton v. Kaiser Hospital, 184 Cal.App.3d 386, 228 Cal.Rptr. 890 (1986) the plaintiffs' baby was born partially paralyzed as the result of the doctor's failure to perform a caesarian section. The father was not present and the mother was unconscious, but both were allowed to sue for their emotional distress. The court held that "[t]he mother had a contract with Kaiser by which it undertook, for consideration, to provide care and treatment for the delivery of a healthy fetus. Kaiser's contract was the source of its duty and a determination of foreseeability is unnecessary to establish a duty of care". (Id. at 894). For a discussion of the tortuous California jurisprudence on the negligent infliction of emotional distress in the health care setting, see Schwarz v. Regents of the University of California, 226 Cal.App.3d 149, 276 Cal.Rptr. 470 (1990).

This "direct victim" concept, developed in Molien v. Kaiser Foundation Hospitals, 27 Cal.3d 916, 167 Cal.Rptr. 831, 616 P.2d 813 (1980), requires a preexisting relationship between defendant and plaintiff and foreseeability of injury. See Mercado v. Leong, 43 Cal.App.4th 317, 50 Cal.Rptr.2d 569 (C.A.3d Dist. 1996).

In Rowe v. Bennett, 514 A.2d 802 (Me.1986), a lesbian psychotherapist continued to treat her lesbian patient even though she had developed an emotional relationship with the patient's lover. The Maine Supreme Court held that the nature of the therapist-patient relationship could provide the basis for a claim of emotional distress. The court wrote:

> Given the fact that a therapist undertakes the treatment of a patient's mental problems and that the patient is encouraged to divulge his innermost thoughts, the patient is extremely vulnerable to mental harm if the therapist fails to adhere to the standards of care recognized by the profession. Any psychological harm that may result from such negligence is neither speculative nor easily feigned. Unlike evidence of mental distress occurring in other situations, objective proof of the existence vel non of a psychological injury in these circumstances should not be difficult to obtain. (Id. at 819–20).

Are the courts in Newton and Rowe expanding notions of fiduciary obligations arising out of professional relationships to justify emotional distress damages? What theme ties these cases together?

4. The AIDS epidemic has given rise to public fears of infection, and the health care setting has not escaped this anxiety. Patients exposed to providers or blood materials in the health care setting have sued for the negligent infliction of emotional distress, based on their fear of contagion of the HIV virus. Courts have resisted such claims. In K.A.C. v. Benson, 527 N.W.2d 553 (Minn.1995), the plaintiff sued a physician who had performed two gynecological examinations of her during a period when he suffered from AIDS and had open sores on his hands and forearms as a result of dermatitis. Shortly after the second examination, the Minnesota Department of Health contacted 336 patients on whom Dr. Benson had performed one or more invasive procedures while gloved, but while suffering from exudative dermatitis. None of the patients tested HIV positive, but over 50 sued him and the Clinic where he worked. The plaintiff argued that she was in

the 'zone of danger' for purposes of a claim of negligent infliction of emotional distress. The court wrote:

> This court has long recognized that a person within the zone of danger of physical impact who reasonably fears for his or her own safety during the time of exposure, and who consequently suffers severe emotional distress with resultant physical injury may recover emotional distress damages whether or not physical impact results. [ ] However, a remote possiblity of personal peril is sufficient to place plaintiff within a zone of danger for purposes of a claim of negligent infliction of emotional distress. Consequently, we hold that a plaintif who fails to allege actual exposure to HIV is not, as a matter of law, in personal physical danger of contracting HIV, and thus not within a zone of danger for purposes of establishing a claim for negligent infliction of emotional distress. Id. at 559.

The majority of jurisdictions considering this issue have agreed that the plaintiff must allege actual exposure to HIV to recover emotional distress damages. See, e.g., Burk v. Sage Products, Inc., 747 F.Supp. 285 (E.D.Pa.1990); Ordway v. County of Suffolk, 154 Misc.2d 269, 583 N.Y.S.2d 1014(1992); Carroll v. Sisters of St. Francis Health Serv., Inc., 868 S.W.2d 585 (Tenn.1993); Johnson v. West Virginia Univ. Hosps., 186 W.Va. 648, 413 S.E.2d 889 (1991). See also John R. Austin, HIV/AIDS and the Health Care Industry Liability: An Annotated Bibliography, 27 J. Marshall L.Rev. 513 (1994).

B.   DUTIES TO CONTEST REIMBURSEMENT LIMITS

Solo practice, once the norm in American medical practice, is rapidly disappearing. By 1996, more than a third of physicians were located in group practices of three or more and another third were employees or contractors. The reorganization of the health care industry has pushed physicians into group practices and employment with health care institutions or managed care organizations or alliances with hospitals in integrated delivery systems. Health care is more constrained by explicit financial limits. Institutions that provide health care—such as hospitals or nursing homes—and entities that pay for health care—including insurers and self-insured employers—now oversee the work of the medical professionals who practice within them or whose care they purchase. The emergence of managed care organizations that both pay for and provide care gives lay managers even greater control over medical practice, in the name of both cost containment and quality of care.

The use of prospective payment systems and the expansion of managed care organizations have imposed substantial constraints on the formerly open ended fee-for-service system of American health care. Physicians in the past could order tests, referrals and hospitalization for patients with little resistance from either insurers or employers who may have footed the premium bill. Cost-constrained systems now create tensions between cost control and quality of care. Heavy pressure is put on physicians to reduce diagnostic tests, control lengths of stay in hospitals, and trim the fat out of medical practice. As physicians experience outside utilization review, limits in drug formularies as to what may be prescribed, and constraints on specialist and hospital referrals, they feel caught between duties to patients and duties to the institutions in which they now operate.

A physician may have an obligation to assist patients in obtaining payment for health care. At a minimum, this means that the doctor must be aware of reimbursement constraints, so that he can promptly advise the patient or direct him to an appropriate institutional office for further information. Must a physician actively assist a patient in obtaining funding for a procedure that the physician feels is necessary? No court would require a physician to pay out of his own pocket for a treatment that a patient needs; there is no "duty to rescue" in the sense of a physician's financial obligation to support his patient. However, the *Wickline* case and others support the argument that a physician operating within a constrained reimbursement structure and an institutional bureaucracy is expected to be familiar with limits on payment.

WICKLINE v. STATE

Court of Appeal, Second District, Division 5, California, 1986.
192 Cal.App.3d 1630, 239 Cal.Rptr. 810.

ROWEN, ASSOCIATE JUSTICE.

This is an appeal from a judgment for plaintiff entered after a trial by jury. For the reasons discussed below, we reverse the judgment.

Principally, this matter concerns itself with the legal responsibility that a third party payor, in this case, the State of California, has for harm caused to a patient when a cost containment program is applied in a manner which is alleged to have affected the implementation of the treating physician's medical judgment.

The plaintiff, respondent herein, Lois J. Wickline (plaintiff or Wickline) sued defendant, appellant herein, State of California (State or Medi–Cal). The essence of the plaintiff's claim is found in paragraph 16 of her second amended complaint which alleges: "Between January 6, 1977, and January 21, 1977, Doe I an employee of the State of California, while acting within the scope of employment, negligently discontinued plaintiff's Medi–Cal eligibility, causing plaintiff to be discharged from Van Nuys Community Hospital prematurely and whil [sic] in need of continuing hospital care. As a result of said negligent act, plaintiff suffered a complete occlusion of the right infra-renoaorta, necessitating an amputation of plaintiff's right leg."

I

Responding to concerns about the escalating cost of health care, public and private payors have in recent years experimented with a variety of cost containment mechanisms. We deal here with one of those programs: The prospective utilization review process.

At the outset, this court recognizes that this case appears to be the first attempt to tie a health care payor into the medical malpractice causation chain and that it, therefore, deals with issues of profound importance to the health care community and to the general public. For those reasons we have permitted the filing of amicus curiae briefs in support of each of the respective parties in the matter to assure that due consideration is given to the broader issues raised before this court by this case.

Traditionally, quality assurance activities, including utilization review programs, were performed primarily within the hospital setting under the general control of the medical staff. * * * The principal focus of such quality assurance review schema was to prevent overutilization due to the recognized financial incentives to both hospitals and physicians to maximize revenue by increasing the amount of service provided and to insure that patients were not unnecessarily exposed to risks as a result of unnecessary surgery and/or hospitalization.

Early cost containment programs utilized the retrospective utilization review process. In that system the third party payor reviewed the patient's chart after the fact to determine whether the treatment provided was medically necessary. If, in the judgment of the utilization reviewer, it was not, the health care provider's claim for payment was denied.

In the cost containment program in issue in this case, prospective utilization review, authority for the rendering of health care services must be obtained before medical care is rendered. Its purpose is to promote the well recognized public interest in controlling health care costs by reducing unnecessary services while still intending to assure that appropriate medical and hospital services are provided to the patient in need. However, such a cost containment strategy creates new and added pressures on the quality assurance portion of the utilization review mechanism. The stakes, the risks at issue, are much higher when a prospective cost containment review process is utilized than when a retrospective review process is used.

A mistaken conclusion about medical necessity following retrospective review will result in the wrongful withholding of payment. An erroneous decision in a prospective review process, on the other hand, in practical consequences, results in the withholding of necessary care, potentially leading to a patient's permanent disability or death.

II

[A summary of the facts follows. Mrs. Wickline, a woman in her 40s, was treated in 1976 by Dr. Daniels, a physician in general family practice. She failed to respond to physical therapy and was admitted to Van Nuys Community Hospital and examined by Dr. Polonsky, a specialist in peripheral vascular surgery. He diagnosed Leriche's Syndrome, a condition caused by obstruction of the terminal aorta due to arteriosclerosis. He recommended surgery. Ms. Wickline was eligible for Medi–Cal, California's medical assistance program. Dr. Daniels submitted a treatment authorization request to Medi–Cal, which authorized the surgery and 10 days of hospitalization. Dr. Polonsky then performed the surgery, which involved removing a part of Ms. Wickline's artery and substituting a synthetic artery. She then developed a clot and a second operation was required. Her recovery after these two procedures was described as "stormy".

Ms. Wickline was to leave the hospital on January 17, 1977. Dr. Polonsky decided on January 16 however that it was "medically necessary" for her to remain in the hospital for another eight days beyond the scheduled discharge date. He was worried about infection, and also about his ability to respond quickly to any emergency that might develop in her legs. He therefore filed a Medi–Cal form 180. The physician puts on this form the patient's diagnosis, significant history, clinical status and treatment plan, in order to permit the Medi–Cal representative—either an "on-site" nurse and/or the Medi–Cal physician consultant—to evaluate the request. The form as filled out by Dr.

Polonsky was complete and accurate, and was signed off by Dr. Daniels and submitted to the nurse responsible for completing such forms. The nurse, Doris Futerman, felt that she should not approve the entire eight-day extension. She therefore telephoned the Medi–Cal consultant, Dr. Glassman, a board certified surgeon. Dr. Glassman rejected Wickline's physician's request and authorized only four days beyond the original discharge date.

Doctors Polonsky and Daniels each then wrote discharge orders based on the limited four day extension. As the court described their actions, "[w]hile all three doctors were aware that they could attempt to obtain a further extension of Wickline's hospital stay by telephoning the Medi–Cal Consultant to request such an extension, none of them did so."

Ms. Wickline was discharged. At the time of her departure from the hospital, her condition appeared stable, with no evidence that her leg was in danger. Dr. Polonsky testified that he felt his hands were tied as to further appeals on his part. In the words of the court,

> Dr. Polonsky testified that at the time in issue he felt that Medi–Cal Consultants had the State's interest more in mind than the patient's welfare and that that belief influenced his decision not to request a second extension of Wickline's hospital stay. In addition, he felt that Medi–Cal had the power to tell him, as a treating doctor, when a patient must be discharged from the hospital. Therefore, while still of the subjective, non-communicated, opinion that Wickline was seriously ill and that the danger to her was not over, Dr. Polonsky discharged her from the hospital on January 21, 1977. He testified that had Wickline's condition, in his medical judgment, been critical or in a deteriorating condition on January 21, he would have made some effort to keep her in the hospital beyond that day even if denied authority by Medi–Cal and even if he had to pay her hospital bill himself.

The medical experts in the case agreed that Dr. Polonsky was within the standard of practice in discharging Wickline on January 21. Within a few days of her arrival home, Ms. Wickline had problems with her right leg. She was ordered back to the hospital on January 30, nine days after her last discharge. Attempts to save the leg were unsuccessful, and on February 8 Dr. Polonsky amputated Wickline's leg below the knee, to save her life. On February 17, because of the failure to heal, her leg was amputated above the knee. Dr. Polonsky testified that if she had remained in the hospital, he would have observed the leg's change in color, realized that a clot had formed, and ordered her back into surgery to reopen the graft to remove the clot. He testified to a reasonable medical certainty that she would not have lost her leg if she had remained in the hospital. He further testified, in the court's words, that the "Medi–Cal Consultant's rejection of the requested eight-day extension of acute care hospitalization and his authorization of a four-day extension in its place did not conform to the usual medical standards as they existed in 1977. He stated that, in accordance with those standards, a physician would not be permitted to make decisions regarding the care of a patient without either first seeing the patient, reviewing the patient's chart or discussing the patient's condition with her treating physician or physicians."]

III

From the facts thus presented, appellant takes the position that it was not negligent as a matter of law. Appellant contends that the decision to discharge was made by each of the plaintiff's three doctors, was based upon the prevailing standards of practice, and was justified by her condition at the time of her discharge. It argues that Medi–Cal had no part in the plaintiff's hospital discharge and therefore was not liable even if the decision to do so was erroneously made by her doctors.

* * *

IV

[In this section the court examined the negligence liability rules in California, and concluded that Medi–Cal is absolved from liability in this case.]

Dr. Kaufman, the chief Medi–Cal Consultant for the Los Angeles field office, was called to testify on behalf of the defendant. He testified that in January 1977, the criteria, or standard, which governed a Medi–Cal Consultant in acting on a request to consider an extension of time was founded on title 22 of the California Administrative Code. That standard was "the medical necessity" for the length and level of care requested. That, Dr. Kaufman contended, was determined by the Medi–Cal Consultant from the information provided him in the 180 form. The Medi–Cal Consultant's decision required the exercise of medical judgment and, in doing so, the Medi–Cal Consultant would utilize the skill, knowledge, training and experience he had acquired in the medical field.

Dr. Kaufman supported Dr. Glassman's decision. He testified, based upon his examination of the MC–180 form in issue in this matter, that Dr. Glassman's four-day hospital stay extension authorization was ample to meet the plaintiff's medically necessary needs at that point in time. Further, in Dr. Kaufman's opinion, there was no need for Dr. Glassman to seek information beyond that which was contained in Wickline's 180 form.

Dr. Kaufman testified that it was the practice in the Los Angeles Medi–Cal office for Medi–Cal Consultants not to review other information that might be available, such as the TAR 160 form (request for authorization for initial hospitalization), unless called by the patient's physician and requested to do so and, instead, to rely only on the information contained in the MC–180 form. Dr. Kaufman also stated that Medi–Cal Consultants did not initiate telephone calls to patient's treating doctors because of the volume of work they already had in meeting their prescribed responsibilities. Dr. Kaufman testified that any facts relating to the patient's care and treatment that was not shown on the 180 form was of no significance.

As to the principal issue before this court, i.e., who bears responsibility for allowing a patient to be discharged from the hospital, her treating physicians or the health care payor, each side's medical expert witnesses agreed that, in accordance with the standards of medical practice as it existed in January 1977, it was for the patient's treating physician to decide the course of treatment that was medically necessary to treat the ailment. It was also that physician's responsibility to determine whether or not acute care hospitalization was required and for how long. Finally, it was agreed that the patient's physician is in a better position than the Medi–Cal Consultant to determine the number of days medically necessary for any required hospital care. The decision to discharge is, therefore, the responsibility of the patient's own treating doctor.

Dr. Kaufman testified that if, on January 21, the date of the plaintiff's discharge from Van Nuys, any one of her three treating doctors had decided that in his medical judgment it was necessary to keep Wickline in the hospital for a longer period of time, they, or any of them, should have filed another request for extension of stay in the hospital, that Medi–Cal would expect those physicians to make such a request if they felt it was indicated, and upon receipt of such a request further consideration of an additional extension of hospital time would have been given.

Title 22 of the California Administrative Code section 51110, provided, in pertinent part, at the relevant time in issue here, that: "The determination of need for acute care shall be made in accordance with the usual standards of medical practice in the community."

The patient who requires treatment and who is harmed when care which should have been provided is not provided should recover for the injuries suffered from all those responsible for the deprivation of such care, including, when appropriate, health care payors. Third party payors of health care services can be held legally accountable when medically inappropriate decisions result from defects in the design or implementation of cost containment mechanisms as, for example, when appeals made on a patient's behalf for medical or hospital care are arbitrarily ignored or unreasonably disregarded or overridden. However, the physician who complies without protest with the limitations imposed by a third party payor, when his medical judgment dictates otherwise, cannot avoid his ultimate responsibility for his patient's care. He cannot point to the health care payor as the liability scapegoat when the consequences of his own determinative medical decisions go sour.

There is little doubt that Dr. Polonsky was intimidated by the Medi–Cal program but he was not paralyzed by Dr. Glassman's response nor rendered powerless to act appropriately if other action was required under the circumstances. If, in his medical judgment, it was in his patient's best interest that she remain in the acute care hospital setting for an additional four days beyond the extended time period originally authorized by Medi–Cal, Dr. Polansky should have made some effort to keep Wickline there. He himself acknowledged that responsibility to his patient. It was his medical judgment, however, that Wickline could be discharged when she was. All the plaintiff's treating physicians concurred and all the doctors who testified at trial, for either plaintiff or defendant, agreed that Dr. Polonsky's medical decision to discharge Wickline met the standard of care applicable at the time. Medi–Cal was not a party to that medical decision and therefore cannot be held to share in the harm resulting if such decision was negligently made.

In addition thereto, while Medi–Cal played a part in the scenario before us in that it was the resource for the funds to pay for the treatment sought, and its input regarding the nature and length of hospital care to be provided was of paramount importance, Medi–Cal did not override the medical judgment of Wickline's treating physicians at the time of her discharge. It was given no opportunity to do so. Therefore, there can be no viable cause of action against it for the consequences of that discharge decision.

* * *

[The court, after discussing relevant California statutory law, concluded that " * * * the Medi–Cal Consultant's decision, vis-a-vis the request to extend Wickline's hospital stay, was in accord with then existing statutory law."]

V

This court appreciates that what is at issue here is the effect of cost containment programs upon the professional judgment of physicians to prescribe hospital treatment for patients requiring the same. While we recognize, realistically, that cost consciousness has become a permanent feature of the health care system, it is essential that cost limitation programs not be permitted to corrupt medical judgment. We have concluded, from the facts in issue here, that in this case it did not.

For the reasons expressed herein, this court finds that appellant is not liable for respondent's injuries as a matter of law. That makes unnecessary any discussion of the other contentions of the parties.

The judgment is reversed.

Notes and Questions

1. What are the limits of the duty? Does it require only that a physician engage in bureaucratic infighting, exhausting her procedural rights, when a utilization review process has rejected her recommendation? The Medi–Cal consultant took a rather casual approach to his review, and the treating physicians acted passively in the face of the initial Medi–Cal rejection. Medi–Cal had argued that the decision to discharge was made by each of the plaintiff's three doctors, and Medi–Cal had no part in the discharge. Both sides agreed that "the decision to discharge is . . . the responsibility of the patient's own treating doctor." The chief Medi–Cal consultant testified that if any of the three doctors had filed another request for an extension based upon their determination of medical necessity, such a request would have been granted. The system, in other words, was designed to generate initial denials, which could be reversed with further appeals.

2. California passed legislation in 1994 to protect physicians who "advocate for medically appropriate health care", following the Wickline decision. See Cal. Bus. & Prof. Code § 2056(a) (West Supp. 1998) (prohibiting termination of or retaliation against physicians as a result of patient advocacy). The law states: "It is the public policy of the State of California that a health care practitioner be encouraged to advocate for appropriate health care for his or her patients," and defines advocacy as "to appeal a payer's decision to deny payment for a service pursuant to the reasonable grievance or appeal procedure established by a [managed care organization] or to protest a decision, policy, or practice that the health care practitioner . . . reasonably believes impairs the . . . ability to provide appropriate health care. . . . " Id. § 2056(b); see also id. § 510(b).

In Khajavi v. Feather River Anesthesia Medical Group, 84 Cal.App.4th 32, 100 Cal.Rptr.2d 627 (Cal.App. 3 Dist.2000), the court held that § 2056 is not limited to the facts and issues of Wickline. It protects physicians broadly from retaliation for advocating medically appropriate health care, whether or not the advocacy protests a cost-containment provision.

3. Later cases have held that external utilization review bodies can be held liable for negligent review if a patient suffers harm through denial of care. In Wilson v. Blue Cross of Southern California, 271 Cal.Rptr. 876, 222 Cal.App.3d 660 (1990), the court limited *Wickline* but expanded potential liability of outside reviewers. Howard Wilson suffered from major depression, drug dependency, and anorexia. On March 3, 1983 he entered a hospital for treatment. His insurer contracted with Western Medical, a third party utilization review organization, to make determinations of medical necessity. On March 11, Western Medical decided that Wilson's hospital stay was "not justified or approved." The treating physician felt that Wilson needed 3–4 weeks of care, but did not appeal the utilization review determination. Wilson was discharged, and on March 31 he killed himself. His physician testified that he would have survived if he could have remained longer in the hospital for treatment. The court, in overturning summary judgment for the insurer, held that the test for joint liability for tortious conduct, Restatement, Torts, 2d 431:

> ... actor's negligent conduct is legal cause of harm to another if (a) his conduct is a substantial factor in bringing about the harm, and (b) there is no rule of law relieving the actor from liability because of the manner in which his negligence has resulted in harm.

While the doctor had no obligation to appeal the negative decision in *Wilson*, the court clearly held that under the right facts, the doctor is jointly liable with the utilization reviewer for a denial that leads to a bad patient outcome.

4. Some courts have allowed plaintiffs to plead a duty of a physician to assist patients in finding other sources of funding for expensive procedures. In Wilson v. Chesapeake Health Plan, Inc., Circuit Court, Baltimore, Maryland 1988 (No. 88019032/CL76201), the plaintiff pleaded a variety of theories against the specialist, the managed care plan, and the hospital. The underlying facts of the suit were as follows.[3] The plaintiff Hugh Wilson, a thirty one year old employee of the city of Baltimore, developed liver disease. He was a member of a prepaid health plan, the Chesapeake Health Plan, Inc.(Chesapeake). Dr. Cooper, a Maryland gastroenterologist to whom Wilson was referred by his primary care physician, diagnosed Wilson as having non-alcoholic cirrhosis of the liver. Mr. Wilson and his wife were informed that this condition would be fatal without a liver transplant. Cooper reassured Wilson that a liver transplant would be covered under his HMO coverage. Chesapeake however decided that such a transplant was not a covered service under the subscriber agreement. Dr. Cooper contacted Dr. Starzl, the head of the transplant service at Presbyterian University Hospital (PUH) in Pittsburgh, Pennsylvania. Despite Mr. Wilson's lack of insurance coverage, Dr. Starzl agreed to admit Mr. Wilson and told Dr. Cooper to have Mr. Wilson come to PUH the following Monday. As Dr. Starzl testified: "My honest assessment at the time was ... that Dr. Cooper was laboring under a dictate, a decision by the governance group of this HMO that they would not allow transplantation coverage. And that Dr. Cooper took it upon himself to say to the system, I am not going to go with this, I am going to try to sneak the patient out. That was my impression. And that, on the other end, I told him, Dr. Cooper, I am going to take the patient, and carry on the battle." The Wilsons arrived in Pittsburgh two days later.

---

3. The facts are taken in part from the court's description in Presbyterian University Hospital v. Wilson, 337 Md. 541, 654 A.2d 1324 (1995), where the Maryland court of appeals held that the trial court was justified in finding that hospital had sufficient contacts with Maryland to justify exercise of specific personal jurisdiction without violating due process.

Upon his arrival, Mr. Wilson was refused admittance to PUH because Mr. Edward Berkowitz, PUH's credit administrator, had informed the admitting office that coverage for Mr. Wilson's liver transplant had not been confirmed. After being refused admittance, the Wilsons were provided accommodations at a hostel connected with PUH. Mr. Berkowitz participated in protracted discussions with Chesapeake and Mr. Wilson's union, the International Brotherhood of Electrical Workers' (IBEW), to discuss the possibility of providing coverage for Mr. Wilson's liver transplant.

Due to deteriorating health, Mr. Wilson was admitted to the emergency room at PUH under his insurance three days later. At Dr. Starzl's urging, Mrs. Wilson returned to Baltimore to work further on the financing problem, and she then learned that the Maryland Medical Assistance Program would pay for the procedure once the Wilsons had spent down their savings. During this period a second liver became available, but it was also thrown away. Mr. Wilson died before Mrs. Wilson could obtain Maryland MA coverage and despite the fact that two suitable livers had become available to PUH for transplant during the time Mr. Wilson was in Pittsburgh.

The plaintiff's complaint, Count 16, Negligence, alleged that Dr. Cooper and the health plan

> knew or should have known that staff and resources existed ... to assist the Wilsons in determining the scope of coverage provided by their HMO, other insurers, and alternative funding sources, but they failed to utilize such resources, alert plaintiffs to the existence of such resources or advise them of the need to identify a funding source. (Complaint, p. 33).

The trial court refused to dismiss this count in the complaint. The plaintiff then settled with Dr. Cooper and the Chesapeake Health Plan, and the case went to trial against Presbyterian Hospital. The plaintiff obtained a multi-million dollar jury verdict in the case.

What are the limits of the duty pleaded by the plaintiff? Dr. Cooper certainly went out of his way to get Mr. Wilson into the hospital for a transplant. The problem was that he simply wasn't an expert on the Maryland Medical Assistance program and eligibility. Can we expect physicians to be reimbursement experts on their patients' behalf? Shouldn't we expect managed care organizations, even if they don't cover a procedure, to offer financial advice to subscribers as to reimbursement options? Why shouldn't we add such duties to the fiduciary relationship between physician and patient, insurer and subscriber? The central office of the managed care organization should be expected to know in the intricacies of its own coverage of subscribers, as well as other sources for funding if the plan's coverage is limited.

5. Insurance benefit denial cases often impose duties on physicians. Few other cases have considered a duty such as that proposed in *Wilson*. But consider *Ferguson v. New Eng. Mutual Life Insurance Co.*, 196 Ill.App.3d 766, 143 Ill.Dec. 941, 554 N.E.2d 1013 (1st Dist.1990), where the patient and her husband sued the physician and the insurer where benefits were denied for medically unnecessary and inappropriate services. The physician had assured the plaintiffs through his staff that the prescribed treatment would be covered by their insurance policy. The court extended implied contract law to include physician knowledge of the insurer's rules. Since HMO contracts often prohibit the physician from charging the beneficiary for denied payments, one can argue for an obligation on the physician to advocate for the patient and to have "full knowledge of the scope of the insured's coverage."

An analogous line of caselaw can also be found in the insurance benefit cases, where a plaintiff is denied insurance coverage because a physician neglected to complete benefit forms. In Murphy v. Godwin, 303 A.2d 668 (Del.Super.1973), the plaintiff's family doctor neglected to complete a medical form they needed to obtain health insurance. As a result, their application was declined by the insurance company. The court held:

> Although it is well known that physicians usually accommodate patients by filling in the forms required by them for various reasons connected with insurance, the question of a doctor's legal duty toward his patients with respect to completing insurance forms is apparently novel. The existence of such a duty may be found, however, by reference to established tort theory and recognized incidents of the doctor-patient relationship.

> In the absence of special circumstances it was Dr. Godwin's duty to recognize his unique position as the treating physician who alone could comply with the insurance requirement without the expense and delay of a further examination. * * *

A physician who simply examines a person for purposes of employment by a third party and not treatment is generally not obligated to complete insurance forms. See, e.g. Ahnert v. Wildman, 176 Ind.App. 630, 376 N.E.2d 1182 (Ind.App. 1978) (" . . . to impose a duty of filling out insurance forms on a doctor who has only consented to examine a patient for a third party, and has not undertaken to treat or advise that patient and is not paid by him, would be inconsistent with the very nature of the limited relationship. No case has gone so far as to saddle an examining physician with such a burden. And neither do we.")

Courts have generally been reluctant to find a hospital or physician negligent for failing to advise patients that they were eligible for government funding. See, e.g., Mraz v. Taft, 85 Ohio App.3d 200, 619 N.E.2d 483 (Ohio App. 8th Dist. 1993)(neither hospital nor nursing home had any duty to advise husband that he qualified for Medicaid). Nor is a physician liable for the financial consequences of a misdiagnosis, for example a patient's cancellation of a life insurance policy upon being erroneously informed that he did not have cancer. See Blacher v. Garlett, 857 P.2d 566, 568 (Colo.C.A., Div.III 1993).

6. A physician may be required to know state law. In Stecker v. First Commercial Trust Company, 331 Ark. 452, 962 S.W.2d 792 (Ark.1998), the administrator of a child's estate sued doctor for medical negligence and failure to report suspected child abuse as required under Arkansas statute. Evidence that the child's life could have been saved if doctor had reported potential abuse presented question for jury on issue of proximate cause for purposes of medical malpractice claim.

Consider the following passage by William Sage, a physician and lawyer, discussing the limits of physicians as advocates.

WILLIAM M. SAGE, PHYSICIANS AS ADVOCATES

35 Houston L. Rev.1529, 1533–34, 1577 (1999)

[P]hysician advocacy should neither be taken for granted nor saddled with expectations which potentially are inconsistent with one another or with normative goals for the health care system. For example, given the undisputed importance of clinical expertise to an efficient health care system, physicians arguably need to direct the provision of care rather than advocate for causes. Nor would patients necessarily accept procedural justice in lieu of substantive entitlements to resources. Moreover, the medical profession's reputation for objective competence might not withstand the adversarial partisanship that accompanies lawyerly advocacy. Because of these and other considerations, I argue that physicians should not aspire to be lawyers when they claim the mantle of "advocate," and the public should not regard them as such.* * *

Should [physicians] accept a new ethic that is population-based? Given the current structure of the health care system, I think not. I believe that intentionally providing minimally acceptable care to some for the benefit of others in an arbitrary group—let alone for the benefit of the bottom line—is wrong. Customizing care on the basis of a patient's insurance coverage is also wrong. When patients are sick and vulnerable, they expect their physicians to be their advocates for optimal care, not for some minimalist standard.... If we capitulate to an ethic of the group rather than the individual, and if we allow market forces to distort our ethical standards, we risk becoming economic agents instead of health care professionals.

* * * [M]anaged care has awakened physicians to the primacy of agency relationships in today's health care system. Health plans claim to represent their shareholders, their customers (usually employers and ERISA plans), and their insurance subscribers as a group. On the other hand, whether health plans have agency obligations to individuals similar to those of physicians remains an open question. Because most physicians are contractually affiliated with or even employed by these organizations, they sometimes struggle to maintain their traditional commitment to serve patient rather than corporate interests.

Managed care has heightened organizational conflicts of interest. As Hall and Berenson note, physicians worry that aggressive advocacy on behalf of patients could jeopardize their relationships with health plans. In addition to financial incentives, the other principal method by which managed care organizations reduce expense is selective contracting. Predictably, most health plans choose to extend network membership to physicians who not only provide high-quality care, but whose style of practice conserves health care resources. Because managed care organizations often control large blocs of patients through their relationships with employers and other group purchasers, physicians increasingly rely on these contracts for their livelihoods. Moreover, many physicians belong to large medical groups, or are affiliated with hospitals or other institutions, all of which have their own economic relationships with health plans to consider.

* * *

Physician advocacy implies a health care system governed more by rules than by incentives. Although financial incentives may taint physician advocacy, managed care organizations that place physicians at financial risk for the overall cost of patient care have less cause to make direct, administrative decisions denying coverage. By contrast, if the use of financial incentives is foreclosed or significantly restricted in the name of advocacy, health plans will be forced to employ more direct mechanisms to review proposed treatments and grant or deny approval. When these decisions are subjected to independent review requirements or other appeal processes, they must be defended—

and in any event an ultimate decision must be rendered—based on explicit rules and standards.

Despite its greater transparency, a rule-based health care system is grossly inefficient, if not wholly unmanageable. Certainly, a significant contribution of managed care has been to demand from physicians objective evidence of clinical benefit and cost-effectiveness, rather than meekly deferring to professional habit. Indeed, expert, evidence-based clinical practice guidelines help disseminate useful information about common medical conditions and reduce unwarranted practice variation. Because medical decisions must be customized to the needs of individual patients, however, no compilation of guidelines can feasibly substitute for the clinical judgment of individual physicians. Moreover, physician participation is needed on both ends, describing "best practices" and applying them to specific situations. This is hard to reconcile with advocacy. Having two sets of physicians, one group to treat patients and serve as their advocates and another to rule dispassionately on disputed claims, seems obviously wasteful in the majority of cases. Nor would most members of the medical profession, notwithstanding their theoretical desire to be patient advocates, prefer an externally micromanaged health care system to one that allows physicians to reach decisions using clinical discretion and established patterns of collegial consultation, even if those decisions were subjected to incentive-based financial constraints.

C. FRAUDULENT CONCEALMENT AND SPOLIATION OF EVIDENCE ACTIONS

In a few jurisdictions, courts have allowed a separate intentional tort theory to be pleaded along with a negligence claim where the physician has deliberately altered records to create misleading entries or has knowingly made a false material representation to a plaintiff. The rules allowing these claims have three purposes: (1) to show fraudulent concealment by the physician of obvious negligence, so that the statute of limitations will be tolled; (2) to void the patient's informed consent to a procedure, so that a battery theory may be used; (3) as a separate theory of recovery. See generally D. Louisell and H. Williams, Medical Malpractice, para. 8.11, p. 8–144 (1984). Fraudulent concealment will toll the statute of limitations.

The party seeking to take advantage of a defendant's fraudulent concealment has the burden of proving that the defendant affirmatively concealed the facts upon which the cause of action is based. As one court noted, however, " * * * the close relationship of trust and confidence between patient and physician gives rise to duties of disclosure which may obviate the need for a patient to prove an affirmative act of concealment." Koppes v. Pearson, 384 N.W.2d 381 (Iowa 1986). But see Simcuski v. Saeli, 44 N.Y.2d 442, 406 N.Y.S.2d 259, 265, 377 N.E.2d 713 (1978)("clear and convincing evidence must be shown as to material misrepresentation and likelihood of cure absent fraud.")

An action for deceit requires proof that a false representation of a material fact was made and was relied upon by the patient in ignorance of the true facts, and that damage resulted. The representation must be made fraudulently, since an intention to deceive by the physician is needed. See Harris v. Penninger, 613 S.W.2d 211 (Mo.App.1981); Hart v. Browne, 103

Cal.App.3d 947, 163 Cal.Rptr. 356 (1980)(physician advised the lawyer for a surgeon's patient that the surgeon's conduct was not negligent; fraud found); Henry v. Deen, 310 N.C. 75, 310 S.E.2d 326 (1984) (civil conspiracy and a punitive damages claim allowed); Krueger v. St. Joseph's Hospital, 305 N.W.2d 18 (N.D.1981) (a claim in fraud allowed based upon the physician's false representations.)

A separate action for spoliation is allowed in some jurisdictions. Spoliation of evidence may consist of altering the medical record or adding to it after an initial entry, deleting, substituting, or destroying x-rays, laboratory reports, or physical evidence. One estimate is that up to fifty percent of medical malpractice cases involve altered records and ten percent involve fraudulently altered records. A spoliation claim may allow the plaintiff to circumvent statutory limitations on damages in some states, allowing punitive damages, for example. See Temple Community Hospital v. Superior Ct. of Los Angeles Cty., 51 Cal.Rptr.2d 57 (2d Dist. 1996). For a general discussion, see Robert C. Mathews, Altering the Medical Record, 10 Am. J. Emerg. Med. 162, 162 (1992); Richard F. Gibbs, The Present and Future Medicolegal Importance of Record Keeping in Anesthesia and Intensive Care: The Case for Automation, 5 J. Clinical Monitoring 251, 253 (1989). See also Anthony C. Casamassima, Comment: Spoliation of Evidence and Medical Malpractice, 14 Pace L. Rev. 235 (1994).

Problem: The Hospital Revolving Door

Donna Natoli is a member of U.S. Wellcare, a large managed care organization known for its frugal subscriber benefits. Ms. Natoli's obstetrician, Dr. Omar Benton, arranged with the Plan hospital, Sacred Fegato Hospital, for labor and delivery. Ms. Natoli entered Fegato in active labor. Dr. Benton noted that the baby's heart rate was consistently low, and as he was examining Ms. Natoli, the placenta suddenly separated from the uterus, posing an immediate threat to the life of the mother and the child. He performed an emergency caesarean section. The child, Elena, exhibited signs of hypoxia and cyanosis (lack of oxygen causing a blue appearance) at birth, but was resuscitated and placed in the neonatal intensive care unit (NICU). Within twelve hours, she was transferred to the regular nursery. Elena weighed in excess of five pounds at birth, within the range of normal birth weights.

Two days later, just prior to her discharge under the minimum stay rule of 48 hours required by state law, Elena's bilirubin level in her blood became elevated to 21.3, causing a jaundiced condition. A level above twenty is considered dangerous. This occurs when antigens in the child's blood cause the immune system to destroy its own red blood cells in a process called hemolysis. Bilirubin is a by-product of this process and high levels of it are toxic. The substance is normally extracted from the blood by the liver. In newborns, the liver is often not yet mature enough to perform this function efficiently. If levels of this substance become too high, it can pass between the blood-brain barrier and cause damage to the nervous system, including brain damage. This condition is known as bilirubin encephalopathy or kernicterus.

Dr. Benton called Wellcare to get an authorization for an additional two days in the hospital for Elena to monitor the bilirubin levels. The Wellcare representative would only allow an additional day. Benton then treated Elena's elevated bilirubin level with phototherapy, which acts to neutralize the toxic effects of the bilirubin, and gave her fluids to flush the bilirubin from her system and glycerin suppositories to eliminate excess bilirubin through the stool. He also gave her albumin, which binds with the bilirubin and helps prevent it from damaging the brain.

These measures reduced the bilirubin level at first to 11, a safe level, but it then rose steadily back to 21. Dr. Benton told Ms. Natoli to get Elena and check out; he explained that Wellcare's policy was quite rigid in his experience and he was tired of fighting with them in cases like this. He suggested that she take Elena home and keep an eye on her for a few days. Elena suffered seizures the next day and now has a permanent hearing loss in both ears.

How will you proceed against Dr. Benton?

IV. DEFENSES TO A MALPRACTICE SUIT

A. THE RESPECTABLE MINORITY RULE

CHUMBLER v. McCLURE

United States Court of Appeals, Sixth Circuit, 1974.
505 F.2d 489.

[The plaintiff was injured in an electrical explosion. Dr. McClure diagnosed his illness as cerebral vascular insufficiency and prescribed a female hormone, estrogen, produced and marketed commercially as Premarin. Premarin's known side effects included enlargement of the breasts and loss of libido. The trial court directed a verdict for the defendant on the grounds that the plaintiff failed to show any deviation from accepted medical practice. The testimony in the case was that Dr. McClure was the only neurosurgeon, out of nine in Nashville, using such therapy for cerebral vascular disease. One expert admitted that there was no specific established treatment for the disease.]

> The most favorable interpretation that may be placed on the testimony adduced at trial below is that there is a division of opinion in the medical profession regarding the use of Premarin in the treatment of cerebral vascular insufficiency, and that Dr. McClure was alone among neurosurgeons in Nashville in using such therapy. The test for malpractice and for community standards is not to be determined solely by a plebiscite. Where two or more schools of thought exist among competent members of the medical profession concerning proper medical treatment for a given ailment, each of which is supported by responsible medical authority, it is not malpractice to be among the minority in a given city who follow one of the accepted schools.

[The court affirmed the directed verdict for the defendant.]

HENDERSON v. HEYER–SCHULTE CORP.

Court of Civil Appeals of Texas, 1980.
600 S.W.2d 844.

[The plaintiff Carol Henderson underwent mammary augmentation operations in which artificial breast implants, consisting of silicone envelopes filled with a soft silicone gel, were inserted. The surgeon then intentionally slit the envelope to allow the gel to escape in to the retro-mammary pockets. The plaintiff experienced pain and inflammation, and developed small lumps under the skin of her chest and abdomen; these were siliconomas caused by accumulations of migrating silicone gel. After twenty operations, the lumps continued to appear and her breasts suffered several deformities in shape and placement. The court, in stating the facts, noted that "[s]he has consulted many other physicians and has undergone subsequent augmentation procedures, some of which were sought to further increase the size of her breasts."

The surgical technique used on the plaintiff had been in common use in Houston at one time but was no longer recognized or accepted. The issue in the case was whether the use of the technique of slitting the silicone implants after implantation was negligent. The jury instructions therefore became critical. The court rejected the trial court's instruction as to recognition by plastic surgeons of more than one method for performing the procedures in question.]

The court continued:

We agree that the instruction should not have been given. The Supreme Court of Texas in *Hood v. Phillips,* [ ] established the proper test for the standard of care in a medical malpractice case where the plaintiff attacks the surgical procedure selected and employed by the doctor. * * * [T]he Court concluded:

> We are of the opinion that the statement of the law most serviceable to this jurisdiction is as follows: A physician who undertakes a mode or form of treatment which a reasonable and prudent member of the medical profession would undertake under the same or similar circumstances shall not be subject to liability for harm caused thereby to the patient. The question which conveys to the jury the standard which should be applicable is as follows: Did the physician undertake a mode or form of treatment which a reasonable and prudent member of the medical profession would not undertake under the same or similar circumstances? [ ]

The court expressly rejected standards which would release doctors from liability when a "respectable minority" or a "considerable number" of physicians adhere to the procedures in question. As Mrs. Henderson points out, the instruction given in this case does not even go that far in establishing a minimal threshold. It simply directs the jury to consider whether "other plastic surgeons" recognized the method used by Dr. Rothenberg. There is no requirement that the "other" surgeons be reasonable or prudent or that they be prepared to employ that method under circumstances similar to those Dr. Rothenberg faced, the two factors most stressed in *Hood.*

[The court concluded that the instruction was harmless error, and that the plaintiff's evidence was insufficient to show that the "rupture method" was no longer in use by reasonable plastic surgeons.]

The judgment is affirmed.

Notes and Questions

1. Can you articulate the difference between the "respectable minority" test and the "reasonable and prudent" physician test? If you were a juror, would you come to a difference conclusion depending on the instruction? In *Chumbler,* the minority of which the defendant was a part seems to have consisted only of himself. Is that sufficiently "respectable"? By what measure should the courts

measure a respectable minority practice? Is this doctrine little more than a judicial acknowledgement of the medical profession's uncertainty over how to treat diseases such as cerebral vascular insufficiency?

Some courts reject the idea that counting the number of physicians who follow a particular practice is helpful in establishing a medical standard of care. See United Blood Services v. Quintana, 827 P.2d 509 (Colo.1992).

2.   States that instruct on "two schools of thought" often impose restrictions on the defense.

a.   Size of the respectable minority. Pennsylvania limits the doctrine to cases involving schools of thought followed by a "considerable number of physicians." Duckworth v. Bennett, 320 Pa. 47, 181 A. 558 (1935), cited with approval by the court in D'Angelis v. Zakuto, 383 Pa.Super. 65, 556 A.2d 431, 433 (1989).

b.   Failures to properly diagnose. Where the critical issue is what the diagnosis is, as for example whether the patient had a localized or a generalized infection, then the "two schools of thought" or "alternative means of treatment" instruction may not be appropriate where there is only one agreed approach to each type of infection. See Hutchinson v. Broadlawns Medical Center, 459 N.W.2d 273 (Iowa 1990). In D'Angelis v. Zakuto, 383 Pa.Super. 65, 556 A.2d 431, 433 (1989), the Superior Court held that the instruction is intended for situations where medical experts may disagree among themselves. It is however not appropriately given where "the symptoms of a disease or the effects of an injury are so well known that a reasonably competent and skillful physician or surgeon ought to be able to diagnose the disease or injury * * *" (quoting Morganstein v. House), 377 Pa.Super. 512, 547 A.2d 1180 (1988).

c.   Weight given to plaintiff experts as to good practice. In Ourada v. Cochran, 234 Neb. 63, 449 N.W.2d 211 (1989), the court rejected a jury instruction that seemed to give the jury too much leeway to reject the plaintiff's experts' testimony. The rejected instruction read in part: "A physician who is a specialist is not bound to use any particular method of procedure; and if, among physicians of ordinary skill and learning in that specialty, more than one method of procedure is recognized as proper, it is not negligence for a physician to adopt any of such methods. . . . "

But see DiFilippo v. Preston, 53 Del. 539, 173 A.2d 333 (1961): choice by defendant surgeon of one of two acceptable techniques is not negligence.

4.   The "respectable minority" rule allows for variation in clinical judgment: " * * * a physician does not incur liability merely by electing to pursue one of several recognized courses of treatment." Downer v. Veilleux, 322 A.2d 82, 87 (Me.1974). In the typical case, the minority approach is followed by at least a few doctors, and is often the "best available" for a certain problem. Leech v. Bralliar, 275 F.Supp. 897 (D.Ariz.1967) (prolotherapy for whiplash; 65 doctors in the country used this treatment, with a claimed 85% success rate; the defendant was held liable because he varied the treatment and therefore became a minority of one within the respectable minority.)

5.   The "honest error in judgment" doctrine is a corollary of the "respectable minority" rule. The respectable minority rule allows for a choice between alternative approaches to diagnosis or treatment; the honest error in judgment doctrine allows for a range of uncertainty in choosing between alternative treatments. A typical jury instruction reads:

a [physician] is not a guarantor of a cure or a good result from his treatment and he is not responsible for an honest error in judgment in choosing between accepted methods of treatment.

This was a standard Minnesota instruction, rejected in Ouellette v. Subak, 391 N.W.2d 810 (Minn.1986), where the court found that the instruction is misleading and subjective. The court proposed an instruction that focused the jury's attention on both the diagnostic work-up and its adequacy, and on the accepted nature of the treatment choice:

A doctor is not negligent simply because his or her efforts prove unsuccessful. The fact a doctor may have chosen a method of treatment that later proves to be unsuccessful is not negligence if the treatment chosen was an accepted treatment on the basis of the information available to the doctor at the time a choice had to be made; a doctor must, however, use reasonable care to obtain the information needed to exercise his or her professional judgment, and an unsuccessful method of treatment chosen because of a failure to use such reasonable care would be negligence.

Is the court's reshaping of the doctrine in its proposed instructions an improvement over the previous "honest error in judgment" instruction? What are the court's concerns? Does their instruction address those concerns? See McKersie v. Barnes Hosp., 912 S.W.2d 562 (Mo.App. E.D.1995) (failure of emergency room intern to diagnose appendicitis was negligence rather than mere honest error of judgment.) Contra, see Haase v. Garfinkel, 418 S.W.2d 108 (Mo.1967)("As long as there is room for an honest difference of opinion among competent physicians, a physician who uses his own best judgment cannot be convicted of negligence, even though it may afterward develop that he was mistaken.)" [ ]

Problem: To Monitor or Not?

You are general counsel for the Columbia Hospital for Women. The head obstetric resident has just walked into your office to get your advice regarding hospital policy. Jane Rudd, pregnant with her second child, has just been admitted to the Obstetrics Ward at term and in labor. The charts reveal that her first delivery of a healthy 7½ pound baby boy had been uncomplicated. Upon admission, she asked not to be given intravenous fluids and stated that she does not want continuous fetal monitoring (EFM). Rather, she wished to be free to walk around with her husband during labor. The nurses told her that hospital policy requires electronic monitoring of all women in labor. The patient responded that she did not need EFM during her first labor, which went well, and expects the same experience again. She has appealed to the resident, who has discussed the request with the staff.

The staff split over the issue. One doctor argued that the policy is a wise measure intended to protect infants. Further, EFM shields staff from accusations that the best care was not provided, if a bad outcome occurs. Another doctor opposed routine EFM, arguing that unmonitored fetuses run an extremely small risk of fetal distress or intrapartum death. Without monitoring the intrapartum death rate was only 1.5 per 1,000 among all labors involving infants who weighed 5½ pounds or more. The mother's risk status is altered, however, since the likelihood of a Caesarean section is increased. This doctor pointed out that a careful British study of low-risk patients revealed that the rate of C-sections doubled, from 4.4 to 9%, when EFM was used. An American study found that the number of Caesareans performed on women hospitalized for delivery between 1980 and 1987 jumped 48%, much of this increase traceable to fetal monitoring.

If Ms. Rudd is allowed to labor with reasonable staff surveillance by auscultation, i.e. use of the stethoscope by staff on a regular basis, and if the obstetric unit can resuscitate her infant if the unexpected occurs, then, this doctor argued, the risks for both mother and child are very low.

You have done some further reading. The conclusions of Karin B. Nelson et al. are striking:

> Electronic fetal monitoring during labor was developed to detect fetal-heart-rate patterns thought to indicate hypoxia. The early recognition of hypoxia would, it was reasoned, alert clinicians to potential problems and enable them to intervene quickly to prevent fetal death or irreversible brain injury....
> More than 20 years and 11 randomized trials later, electronic fetal monitoring appears to have little documented benefit over intermittent auscultation with respect to perinatal mortality or long-term neurologic outcome. Furthermore, probably in part because of the widespread use of fetal monitoring, the rate of cesarean section has increased, with a resulting increase in maternal morbidity and costs but without apparent decrease in the incidence of cerebral palsy.

Karin B. Nelson et al., Uncertain Value of Electronic Fetal Monitoring in Predicting Cerebral Palsy, 334 N.E.J.M. 334, 334 (1996). The authors found that cesarean sections did not prevent cerebral palsy in infants born at term, that monitoring did not correlate with reductions in perinatal mortality, nor were low Apgar scores, acidosis, neotal apnea, or need for intubation less frequent among monitored infants.

A second study analyzed the neurologic development of premature infants. The authors compared the early development of children born prematurely whose heart rates were monitored electronically during delivery, compared to children born prematurely whose heart rates were monitored by auscultation. The authors found that not only had the infants' neurologic development not improved with monitoring, compared with auscultation, but there was a 2.9–fold increase in the odds of having cerebral palsy with the monitored infants. Shy et al., Effects of Electronic Fetal–Heart–Rate Monitoring, As Compared with Periodic Auscultation, on the Neurologic Development of Premature Infants, 322 N.Eng.J.Med. 588 (1990). The authors noted, however, that the trials for the study had dedicated nurses assigned to the auscultation group, "a circumstance that is not always possible in a busy clinical setting."

What policies will minimize the hospital's liability exposure while also respecting the patient's wishes whenever it is safe to do so? How do the tort doctrines we have discussed interact?

B. PRACTICE GUIDELINES AS AN AFFIRMATIVE DEFENSE

Medical practice guidelines or practice protocols might be used as an affirmative defense by physicians in a malpractice suit to show compliance with accepted practice. Maine has passed legislation to immunize physicians from suit if they practice in accordance with such standards. Me.Gen.Laws, Ch. 931 (1990). The law was premised on concerns that physicians practiced too much "defensive medicine" in response to liability fears, ordering tests primarily to protect themselves from subsequent suits. If given some protection in the liability area, they could change their practice patterns without fear of liability. The Maine legislation includes physicians in emergency medicine, anesthesia, and obstetrics and gynecology. Physicians who elect to participate can assert compliance with established practice parameters and risk management protocols as an affirmative defense in any malpractice suit brought against them during the five years of the demonstration project. The practice parameters and risk management protocols will be developed by advisory committees in each of the practice areas.

The Maine statute provides:

* * * in any claims for professional negligence against a physician or the employer of a physician participating in the project in which a violation of standard of care is alleged, only the physician or the physician's employer may introduce into evidence as an affirmative defense the existence of the practice parameters and risk management protocols developed pursuant to the project.

Me. Rev. Stat. Ann., tit. 24, § 2972(1) (West Supp. 1994). Outside experts will not be able to challenge the standard, and the physician is not bound by the standard in a case in which he deviated from the protocol. The project will not take effect until 50% in any specialty elect to participate. See generally General Accounting Office, GAO/HRD–94–8, Medical Malpractice: Maine's Use of Practice Guidelines to Reduce Costs (1993) (describing the Maine demonstration); Professional Liability: Maine's Experiment with Practice Guidelines Produces Little Evidence, 3 Health L. Rep. (BNA) 753, 754 (June 9, 1994).

Minnesota and Kentucky also allow the use of practice parameters by physicians as an affirmative defense. See Ky. Rev. Stat. Ann. § 342.035 (Michie 1995) indicating that "[a]ny provider of medical services under this chapter who has followed the practice parameters or guidelines developed or adopted pursuant to this subsection shall be presumed to have met the appropriate legal standard of care in medical malpractice cases regardless of unanticipated complication that may develop or be discovered after". Id. See Minn. Stat. § 62J.34(3)(a) (1994) (providing an absolute defense for providers). Florida and Vermont also have adopted this approach, and several other states—e.g., Colorado, Pennsylvania, Rhode Island, Virginia, and Hawaii— also have considered or are considering adoption of guidelines legislation. Maryland, by contrast, under Md. Code Ann., [Health–Gen.] § 19–1606 (1995), has mandated that practice parameters are not admissible into evidence in any legal proceeding under the statute.

C. CLINICAL INNOVATION

BROOK v. ST. JOHN'S HICKEY MEMORIAL HOSPITAL

Supreme Court of Indiana, 1978.
269 Ind. 270, 380 N.E.2d 72.

HUNTER, JUSTICE.

This case began as an action by Tracy Lynn Brook and her father (Arthur) against St. John's Hickey Memorial Hospital, Guy E. Ross, M.D., Lawrence Allen, M.D., and Dr. Fischer. The record discloses that Tracy was diagnosed by a specialist as having a possible urological disorder and that X-rays taken with a contrast medium would be necessary to confirm the diagnosis. The Court of Appeals summarized Dr. Fischer's role in Tracy's treatment as follows:

"Dr. Fischer, a radiologist, injected the contrast medium into the calves of both of Tracy's legs, because he was unable to find a vein which he could use. The package insert, which contained the manufacturer's directions for injecting the contrast medium, recommended that the contrast medium be injected into the gluteal muscles (buttocks). * * *

"A short while [four months later] after being discharged from the hospital Tracy began to have trouble with her right leg. Her leg was stiff and her heel began to lift off the ground. Tracy's problem was later diagnosed as a shortening of the achilles tendon, which *may* have been precipitated by some kind of trauma to her ankle or calf muscle. After two operations and other expensive treatment, including the wearing of a leg brace, Tracy's problem was substantially corrected." 368 N.E.2d 264, 266, 267 [emphasis added].

* * *

* * * [T]he Brooks contended that the trial court erred in refusing to give to the jury plaintiffs' tendered instruction No. 4 which reads as follows:

"You are instructed that a Radiologist is not limited to the most generally used of several modes of procedure and the use of another mode known and proved by the profession is proper, but every new method of procedure should pass through an experimental stage in its development and a Radiologist is not authorized in trying untested experiments on patients."

The Brooks alleged that Dr. Fischer was negligent in choosing an injection site which had not been specifically recommended by the medical community and that this choice of an unusual injection site was a medical experiment. The trial court refused to give this instruction on the basis that since no substantial evidence of a medical experiment had been introduced, it would be erroneous to give an instruction covering medical experiments. We agree.

The Court of Appeals found that since there was no evidence presented which showed that any other doctors had used the calf muscles as an injection site, Dr. Fischer's use of them may have been a medical experiment. We disagree. The record clearly shows that Dr. Fischer had several compelling, professional reasons for choosing the calf muscles as an injection site for the contrast medium in this case.

First, the record shows that Dr. Fischer had read medical journals which cautioned against the injection of the contrast medium into the buttocks (gluteal area) and thighs of infants and small children. * * *.

Tracy Brook was only twenty-three months old when the injection was given. Dr. Fischer testified that other articles had also warned against the use of the thighs in young children. Because Dr. Fischer was trying to avoid any damage to the sciatic nerve, he chose the next largest muscle mass "away from the trunk" as the site for the injection.

Second, Dr. Fischer had used this injection site successfully on children on prior occasions. He also testified that he had never read or heard anything that proscribed the selection of the calf muscles as an injection site.

Too often courts have confused judgmental decisions and experimentation. Therapeutic innovation has long been recognized as permissible to avoid serious consequences. The everyday practice of medicine involves constant judgmental decisions by physicians as they move from one patient to another in the conscious institution of procedures, special tests, trials and observations recognized generally by their profession as effective in treating the patient or providing a diagnosis of a diseased condition. Each patient presents a slightly different problem to the doctor. A physician is presumed to have the knowledge and skill necessary to use some innovation to fit the peculiar circumstances of each case.

Thus, the choice of the calf muscles as the site for the injection of a contrast medium in a two-year old child, based upon prior successful uses of this same injection site, is not a medical experiment where the use of more common sites had been warned against and where it was reasonably and prudently calculated by the physician [radiologist] to accomplish the intended purpose of diagnosis of the patient's condition.

* * *

The judgment of the trial court is in all respects affirmed.

Notes and Questions

1. If you disagree with the Supreme Court of Indiana, what do you think Dr. Fischer should have done? Should he have refused to treat Tracy? Should he have explained that his treatment was experimental? How would that have helped Tracy? See Chapter 20 for a discussion of legal limitations on human research.

Doctors tend to admire innovators. See, for example, Edenfield v. Vahid, 621 So.2d 1192, 1196 (La.App.1993), where the defendant surgeon attempted to repair the plaintiff's anal fistula with a Prolene suture, and the plaintiff ended up incontinent. Such a suture was an unconventional choice, and the medical panel considered its use below the standard of care. One of the experts stated, however, that trends change through "mavericks" trying different techniques: "Unless this something different is so dramatic that [sic] would result in loss of life or limb then I would say more power to him, somebody has got to try something different and show us that here are other ways of doing things.... the result wasn't ideal, but to consider that a malpractice, no."

2. Should the law allow a defense such as clinical innovation? Are clinicians likely to be trained scientists, keeping careful records and publishing their results for peer review? Medical researchers have criticized such clinical "experiments," calling instead for randomized scientifically valid trials. See Gordon Guyatt et al., Determining Optimal Therapy—Randomized Trials in Individual Patients, 314 N.Eng.J.Med. 889 (1986).

3. Experiments are acceptable to the courts when conventional treatments are largely ineffective or where the patient is terminally ill and has little to lose by experimentation with potentially useful treatments. Organ transplantation often involves therapeutic innovation. The classic case is Karp v. Cooley, 493 F.2d 408 (5th Cir.1974), where Dr. Denton Cooley was sued for the wrongful death of Haskell Karp. Dr. Cooley had implanted the first totally mechanical heart in Mr. Karp, who died some 32 hours after the transplant surgery. The court directed a verdict for Dr. Cooley on the issue of experimentation. It held:

> The record contains no evidence that Mr. Karp's treatment was other than therapeutic and we agree that in this context an action for experimentation must be measured by traditional malpractice evidentiary standards. Whether there was informed consent is necessarily linked to the charge of experimentation, and Mr. Karp's consent was expressly to all three stages of the

operation actually performed—each an alternative in the event of a preceding failure.

The court excluded testimony by Dr. DeBakey that the heart pump he himself had tested was not ready for use in humans and that he would not have recommended its use. Dr. DeBakey refused however to give his opinion on the pump used by Dr. Cooley, except that it was similar to his pump.

4. New surgical procedures and treatments, other than drugs and medical devices, fall into a regulatory gap. Drugs and medical devices are carefully regulated by the Food and Drug Administration through licensing. See the Federal Food, Drug, and Cosmetic Act, 21 U.S.C.A. § 301 et seq. Human experimentation generally, if the institution is funded by the federal government in whole or part, is governed by regulations of the Department of Health and Human Services. The regulations require the institution sponsoring the research to establish Institutional Review Boards (IRBs). These evaluate the research proposals before any experimentation begins, in order to determine whether human subjects might be "at risk" and if so, how to protect them. See 45 C.F.R. § 46.101(a) and Chapter 20 infra.

It is generally not difficult to determine whether a new drug or device is being used experimentally. It is often very difficult to determine whether a particular surgical procedure is experimental. Surgeons tend to view themselves as artists rather than scientists, custom-tailoring a treatment for a patient's ailment. Such attitudes can produce bad results. In Felice v. Valleylab, 520 So.2d 920 (La.App. 3d Cir.1987), the physician, a third year general surgical resident, used an electrosurgical unit (ESU) to perform a circumcision procedure, although she admitted that she had been taught to perform circumcisions with a scalpel as the standard technique. She testified that the ESU was a new technique that might produce better results. She burned the child's penis so badly that it had to be amputated. The court held that the surgeon's behavior fell below the standard of care in her modification of a familiar technique without knowing the potential risks and by failing to consult with supervising personnel about such risks. In Tramontin v. Glass, 668 So.2d 1252 (La.App.1996), the same surgeon, using the same device, the ESU, burned the breast of a patient on whom she was performing breast augmentation surgery. In this case the use was not experimental, and the jury found for the defendant.

5. Most clinical innovation falls somewhere between standard practice and experimental research. Much of this innovation is unregulated by the government. What kinds of controls, direct or indirect, apply to innovation in medicine? The absence of controls over experimentation has worried some commentators, who have argued that the patient's informed consent is not a sufficient protection against untested procedures. Such experimentation has been termed "nonvalidated practice," since the most salient attribute of a novel practice is the lack of suitable validation of its safety and efficacy. The National Commission for the Protection of Human Subjects of Biomedical and Behavioral Research, discussing innovation, wrote:

> Radically new procedures * * * should * * * be made the object of formal research at an early stage in order to determine whether they are safe and effective. Thus, it is the responsibility of medical practice committees, for example, to insist that a major innovation be incorporated into a formal research project.

For a good discussion of the problem, see Dale H. Cowan and Eva Bertsch, Innovative Therapy: The Responsibility of Hospitals, 5 J.Leg.Med. 219 (1984).

D. GOOD SAMARITAN ACTS

Forty-nine states and the District of Columbia have adopted Good Samaritan legislation to protect health care professionals who render emergency aid from civil liability for damages for any injury they cause or enhance. The statutes take a variety of forms. West's Ann.Cal.Bus. & Prof.Code § 2395, for example, states, in relevant part:

No licensee, who in good faith renders emergency care at the scene of an emergency, shall be liable for any civil damages as a result of any acts or omissions by such person in rendering the emergency care.

"The scene of an emergency" as used in this section shall include, but not be limited to, the emergency rooms of hospitals in the event of a medical disaster. * * *

The following case applies the California statute in a hospital setting.

McKENNA v. CEDARS OF LEBANON HOSPITAL

Court of Appeal of California, 1979.
93 Cal.App.3d 282, 155 Cal.Rptr. 631.

Mrs. Evangeline McKenna underwent a therapeutic abortion and tubal ligation at Cedars of Lebanon Hospital on January 17, 1974. That afternoon, she had a seizure and was treated by a resident of the hospital. She stopped breathing and went into a coma from which she never recovered. She died over a week later. Her husband and children sued Dr. Margolin, her physician; Dr. Gilman, the anesthesiologist; Dr. Warner, the resident who responded to an alert from his beeper; and Cedars of Lebanon Hospital. The jury verdict was 10–2 in favor of the hospital and Dr. Warner and against plaintiffs. Plaintiffs appeal from the judgment. The primary issue here is whether there can be an emergency, as that term is used in the "Good Samaritan" statute within a hospital, so as to invoke that statute's application as a defense to the malpractice action against the doctor and hospital.

FACTS:

Mrs. McKenna entered Cedars of Lebanon Hospital January 16, 1974. Dr. Margolin, her gynecologist, performed a therapeutic abortion and a tubal sterilization on Mrs. McKenna on the morning of January 17, 1974. She was taken to the recovery room at 9:25 a.m. and stated that she had some difficulty breathing. The recovery room records show that later that morning she stated she felt much better and was returned to her room at about 10:45 a.m. She had lunch at 12:30, and the regular diet was "taken well."

At about 2 p.m., Mrs. McKenna started having seizures. The patient sharing the room with Mrs. McKenna called for assistance. The nurse's notes reveal "Unable to get pulse. Dr. Weirner [sic] called stat * * *." The nurse who originally arrived testified that the patient was "moving her arms and her legs in an uncoordinated, rigid manner which appeared to be some type of seizure activity at that time." Dr. Warner was on the floor above when his beeper sounded. He picked up the phone, spoke to the page operator, and "dashed" to Mrs. McKenna's room. About one minute elapsed from the time he heard his beeper to the time a nurse guided him into Mrs. McKenna's room.

Dr. Warner testified that he observed the patient having a grand-mal type seizure. He observed the patient, asked for Valium from a nurse, and slowly gave the patient approximately five milligrams of Valium into the I.V. tubing in order to stop the convulsions. The patient's convulsions stopped; she had a cardiac arrest and complete cessation of breathing. An anesthesiologist inserted an endotracheal tube; Dr. Warner was giving external cardiac massage, and he called for a Code Blue cardiac pulmonary resuscitation team. The patient was eventually transferred to the intensive care unit where she remained in a coma until her death on January 28, 1974. Appellants claim malpractice by Dr. Warner. As is usual in this type of case, appellants produced a doctor who testified that Dr. Warner's response to the patient's seizure fell below the standard of care and the respondents produced evidence that Dr. Warner's conduct was proper.

* * *

The jury in the case at bench was instructed: "No licensed physician, who in good faith renders emergency care at the scene of the emergency, shall be liable for any civil damages as a result of any of his acts or omissions in rendering the emergency care." * * * Appellants contend that the policy behind the Good Samaritan Statute does not apply to hospital emergencies and that the instruction should not have been given. * * *

Business and Professions Code section 2144 applies to "emergency care at the scene of the emergency * * *." There is no limitation as to the situs of the "scene of the emergency." A 1976 amendment to the statute defined "the scene of the emergency" and included, but did not limit, that phrase to "the emergency rooms of hospitals in the event of a medical disaster." Nothing in the statute itself precludes application of the Good Samaritan Statute to emergency situations in hospitals.

* * *

Dr. Warner in the case at bench was on duty as chief resident the afternoon of the emergency; appellants have failed to demonstrate that he had any legal duty to respond to an emergency call. He was, in essence, a medical volunteer, called to the scene of an emergency from the floor above where he was conducting a routine pelvic examination. Mrs. McKenna was another doctor's patient; there is no showing Dr. Warner had a legal duty to render emergency treatment arising from his contract of employment with Cedars. In such a situation, the legislative intent of encouraging emergency medical care by doctors who have no legal duty to treat a patient is carried out by applying Business and Professions Code section 2144 to Dr. Warner.

* * *

* * * [T]he "need to encourage physicians to render emergency medical care when they otherwise might not" prevails over the policy of vindicating the rights of a malpractice victim.

In the instant case, Dr. Warner proved he was not "on call" for emergencies, was not a member of the hospital team whose job it was to respond to emergencies and did not have a previous physician-patient relationship with Mrs. McKenna. In short, at the time he responded to Mrs. McKenna's emergency, Dr. Warner was truly a volunteer. Since there was evidence showing that Dr. Warner rendered emergency care to Mrs. McKenna in good faith at the place where her emergency occurred, the Good Samaritan statute applied on its face.

Notes and Questions

1. What kinds of situations do the Good Samaritan statutes cover? Suppose a physician walking down the street on Sunday morning to buy her New York Times sees a man fall to the pavement, gasping for breath and turning blue. The physician does not have her black bag, never met the victim before, and is aware of a gathering crowd. If she attempts to help the man and is negligent in administering aid, should she be sued for malpractice? Certainly physicians have worried about such situations. Is the setting of *McKenna* distinguishable from the street rescue situation? In McCain v. Batson, 233 Mont. 288, 760 P.2d 725 (1988), a physician on vacation sutured a hiker's wound at his condominium, using limited medical supplies on hand. The court held that this was an "emergency" within the meaning of statute.

2. The majority of state statutes exclude medical services rendered in the hospital from the coverage of the statutes, either by excluding emergency services provided in the ordinary course of work or services that doctors render to those with whom they have a doctor-patient relationship or to whom they owe a pre-existing duty. Guerrero v. Copper Queen Hospital, 112 Ariz. 104, 537 P.2d 1329 (1975) (statute not applicable to services in hospital); Colby v. Schwartz, 78 Cal.App.3d 885, 144 Cal.Rptr. 624 (1978) (normal course of practice not protected); Gragg v. Neurological Associates, 152 Ga.App. 586, 263 S.E.2d 496 (1979) (crisis during operating procedure is not emergency within meaning of statute).

Hospital-based emergency assistance by a physician is often protected, however, where the physician is not on duty at the time of the call for help. See Gordin v. William Beaumont Hospital, 180 Mich.App. 488, 447 N.W.2d 793 (1989), where the plaintiff's decedent was admitted to the emergency room after a car accident. The ER physician called for the on-call surgeon to assist, but the surgeon was unavailable. He then called Dr. Howard, who was not officially on call. The court held that the Good Samaritan Statute applied. The plaintiff argued that the statute should only be applied in the "biblical" Good Samaritan situation, to a doctor who renders care outside his training, not to a trained surgeon summoned to the hospital to render care for which he was trained and compensated. As in *McKenna,* however, the Michigan statute had been amended to include hospital settings and off-duty physicians. In Kearns v. Superior Court, 204 Cal.App.3d 1325, 252 Cal.Rptr. 4 (2 Dist.1988), a physician happened to be in the hospital treating his own patients when another surgeon asked his help during the course of an operation. The assisting physician was held to be rendering assistance in an "emergency" for purposes of California's Good Samaritan law.

3. Some statutes protect health care professionals, while others protect all Good Samaritans, without regard to their profession. Some states grant statutory immunity from suit to emergency medical personnel unless gross negligence is shown. Mallory v. City of Detroit, 181 Mich.App. 121, 449 N.W.2d 115 (1989). Is there any reason, except for the political power of doctors, to limit the application of such statutes to doctors or health care professionals? See generally Anno., Construction of 'Good Samaritan' Statutes Excusing from Civil Liability One Rendering Care in Emergency, 39 A.L.R.3d 222.

4. The malpractice crisis of 1974 undoubtedly played a role in the push by state legislatures to enact such laws. They are an interesting example of a protective response to a low risk of suit. There is no reason to believe that

physicians have any idea as to whether the state in which they practice has a Good Samaritan law, or what its terms might be. Nor can evidence be found to establish that such laws have encouraged emergency treatment. In a study over thirty years ago, the American Medical Association found that the existence of Good Samaritan legislation made no difference to the willingness of physicians to stop and assist. 51.5% said they would stop to furnish emergency aid if the statutes were in effect, and 48.8% if no statute was in effect. Law Dept. of the AMA 1963 Professional Liability Survey, 189 J.A.M.A. 859 (1964). See Hessel, Good Samaritan Laws: Bad Legislation, 2 J.Leg.Med. 40 (1974). For a proposal for a uniform statute, see Comment, Good Samaritan Statutes: Time for Uniformity, 27 Wayne L.Rev. 217 (1980).

5.   If the purpose of Good Samaritan statutes is to encourage emergency aid, should they instead impose a civil or criminal penalty on those who fail to offer such assistance? That is the case in many European countries, and—on the books—in Vermont, which imposes a $100 fine for failure to render aid under some circumstances. See 12 Vt.Stat.Ann. § 519. Should we require even more in the way of a duty to rescue? See generally Jean Elting Rowe and Theodore Silver, The Jurisprudence of Action and Inaction in the Law of Tort: Solving the Puzzle of Nonfeasance and Misfeasance from the Fifteenth Through the Twentieth Centuries, 33 Duquesne L.Rev. 807 (1995); Saul Levmore, Waiting for Rescue: An Essay on the Evolution and Incentive Structure of the Law of Affirmative Obligations, 72 Va.L.Rev. 879 (1986).

E.   CONTRIBUTORY FAULT OF THE PATIENT

Patients through their own mistakes or lifestyle often enhance, or even cause, their injuries. People don't take their doctor's advice; they fall off their diets, stop exercising, start smoking, or act in a variety of ways counterproductive to their health. Very few tort cases have raised the issue directly, by raising a patient's lifestyle choice as a defense to a malpractice claim. Consider the following case.

OSTROWSKI v. AZZARA
Supreme Court of New Jersey, 1988.
111 N.J. 429, 545 A.2d 148.

O'HERN, J.

This case primarily concerns the legal significance of a medical malpractice claimant's pre-treatment health habits. Although the parties agreed that such habits should not be regarded as evidencing comparative fault for the medical injury at issue, we find that the instructions to the jury failed to draw the line clearly between the normal mitigation of damages expected of any claimant and the concepts of comparative fault that can preclude recovery in a fault-based system of tort reparation. Accordingly, we reverse the judgment below that disallowed any recovery to the diabetic plaintiff who had bypass surgery to correct a loss of circulation in a leg. The need for this bypass was found by the jury to have been proximately caused by the physician's neglect in performing an improper surgical procedure on the already weakened plaintiff.

I

As noted, the parties do not dispute that a physician must exercise the degree of care commensurate with the needs of the patient as she presents herself. This is but another way of saying that a defendant takes the plaintiff as she finds her. The question here, however, is much more subtle and complex. The complication arose from the plaintiff's seemingly routine need for care of an irritated toe. The plaintiff had long suffered from diabetes attributable, in unfortunate part perhaps, to her smoking and to her failure to adhere closely to her diet. Diabetic patients often have circulatory problems. For purposes of this appeal, we shall accept the general version of the events that led up to the operation as they are set forth in defendant-physician's brief.

On May 17, 1983, plaintiff, a heavy smoker and an insulin-dependent diabetic for twenty years, first consulted with defendant, Lynn Azzara, a doctor of podiatric medicine, a specialist in the care of feet. Plaintiff had been referred to Dr. Azzara by her internist whom she had last seen in November 1982. Dr. Azzara's notes indicated that plaintiff presented a sore left big toe, which had troubled her for approximately one month, and calluses. She told Dr. Azzara that she often suffered leg cramps that caused a tightening of the leg muscles or burning in her feet and legs after walking and while lying in bed. She had had hypertension (abnormally high blood pressure) for three years and was taking a diuretic for this condition.

Physical examination revealed redness in the plaintiff's big toe and elongated and incurvated toenails. Incurvated toenails are not ingrown; rather, they press against the skin. Diminished pulses on her foot indicated decreased blood supply to that area, as well as decreased circulation and impaired vascular status. Dr. Azzara made a diagnosis of onychomycosis (a fungous disease of the nails) and formulated a plan of treatment to debride (trim) the incurvated nail. Since plaintiff had informed her of a high blood sugar level, Dr. Azzara ordered a fasting blood sugar test and a urinalysis; she also noted that a vascular examination should be considered for the following week if plaintiff showed no improvement.

Plaintiff next saw Dr. Azzara three days later, on May 20, 1983. The results of the fasting blood sugar test indicated plaintiff's blood sugar was high, with a reading of 306. The urinalysis results also indicated plaintiff's blood sugar was above normal. At this second visit, Dr. Azzara concluded that plaintiff had peripheral vascular disease, poor circulation, and diabetes with a very high sugar elevation. She discussed these conclusions with plaintiff and explained the importance of better sugar maintenance. She also explained that a complication of peripheral vascular disease and diabetes is an increased risk of losing a limb if the diabetes is not controlled. The lack of blood flow can lead to decaying tissue. The parties disagree on whether Dr. Azzara told plaintiff she had to return to her internist to treat her blood sugar and circulation problems, or whether, as plaintiff indicates, Dr. Azzara merely suggested to plaintiff that she see her internist.

In any event, plaintiff came back to Dr. Azzara on May 31, 1983, and, according to the doctor, reported that she had seen her internist and that the internist had increased her insulin and told her to return to Dr. Azzara for further treatment because of her continuing complaints of discomfort about her toe. However, plaintiff had not seen the internist. Dr. Azzara contends that she believed plaintiff's representations. A finger-stick glucose test administered to measure plaintiff's non-fasting blood sugar yielded a reading of 175.

A physical examination of the toe revealed redness and drainage from the distal medial (outside front) border of the nail, and the toenail was painful to the touch. Dr. Azzara's proposed course of treatment was to avulse, or remove, all or a portion of the toenail to facilitate drainage.

Dr. Azzara says that prior to performing the removal procedure she reviewed with Mrs. Ostrowski both the risks and complications of the procedure, including nonhealing and loss of limb, as well as the risks involved with not treating the toe. Plaintiff executed a consent form authorizing Dr. Azzara to perform a total removal of her left big toenail. The nail was cut out. (Defendant testified that she cut out only a portion of the nail, although her records showed a total removal.)

Two days later, plaintiff saw her internist. He saw her four additional times in order to check the progress of the toe. As of June 30, 1983, the internist felt the toe was much improved. While plaintiff was seeing the internist, she continued to see Dr. Azzara, or her associate, Dr. Bergman. During this period the toe was healing slowly, as Dr. Azzara said one would expect with a diabetic patient.

During the time plaintiff was being treated by her internist and by Dr. Azzara, she continued to smoke despite advice to the contrary. Her internist testified at the trial that smoking accelerates and aggravates peripheral vascular disease and that a diabetic patient with vascular disease can by smoking accelerate the severity of the vascular disease by as much as fifty percent. By mid-July, plaintiff's toe had become more painful and discolored.

At this point, all accord ceases. Plaintiff claims that it was the podiatrist's failure to consult with the patient's internist and defendant's failure to establish by vascular tests that the blood flow was sufficient to heal the wound, and to take less radical care, that left her with a non-healing, pre-gangrenous wound, that is, with decaying tissue. As a result, plaintiff had to undergo immediate bypass surgery to prevent the loss of the extremity. If left untreated, the pre-gangrenous toe condition resulting from the defendant's nail removal procedure would have spread, causing loss of the leg. The plaintiff's first bypass surgery did not arrest the condition, and she underwent two additional bypass surgeries which, in the opinion of her treating vascular surgeon, directly and proximately resulted from the unnecessary toenail removal procedure on May 31, 1983. In the third operation a vein from her right leg was transplanted to her left leg to increase the flow of blood to the toe.

At trial, defense counsel was permitted to show that during the pre-treatment period before May 17, 1983, the plaintiff had smoked cigarettes and had failed to maintain her weight, diet, and blood sugar at acceptable levels. The trial court allowed this evidence of the plaintiff's pre-treatment health habits to go to the jury on the issue of proximate cause. Defense counsel elicited admissions from plaintiff's internist and vascular surgeon that some doctors believe there is a relationship between poor self-care habits and increased vascular disease, perhaps by as much as fifty percent. But no medical expert for either side testified that the plaintiff's post-treatment health habits could have caused her need for bypass surgery six weeks after defendant's toenail removal. Nevertheless, plaintiff argues that defense counsel was permitted to interrogate the plaintiff extensively on her post-avulsion and post-bypass health habits, and that the court allowed such evidence of plaintiff's health habits during the six weeks after the operation to be considered as acts of comparative negligence that could bar recovery rather than reduce her damages. The jury found that the doctor had acted negligently in cutting out the plaintiff's toenail without adequate consideration of her condition, but found plaintiff's fault (fifty-one percent) to exceed that of the physician (forty-nine percent). She was therefore disallowed any recovery. On appeal the Appellate Division affirmed in an unreported decision. We granted certification to review plaintiff's claims. [ ] We are told that since the trial, the plaintiff's left leg has been amputated above the knee. This was foreseen, but not to a reasonable degree of medical probability at the time of trial.

II

Several strands of doctrine are interwoven in the resolution of this matter. The concepts of avoidable consequences, the particularly susceptible victim, aggravation of preexisting condition, comparative negligence, and proximate cause each play a part. It may be useful to unravel those strands of doctrine for separate consideration before considering them in the composite.

Comparative negligence is a legislative amelioration of the perceived harshness of the common-law doctrine of contributory negligence. [ ] In a fault-based system of tort reparation, the doctrine of contributory negligence served to bar any recovery to a plaintiff whose fault contributed to the accident. Whatever its conceptual underpinnings, its effect was to serve as a "gatekeeper." Epstein, "The Social Consequences of Common Law Rules," 95 *Harv.L.Rev.* 1717, 11736–37 (1982). Any fault kept a claimant from recovering under the system. Fault in that context meant a breach of a legal duty that was comparable to the duty of the other actors to exercise such care in the circumstances as was necessary to avoid the risk of injury incurred. Its prototype was the carriage driver who crossed the train tracks as the train was approaching the crossing. [ ] Harsh, but clear.

Comparative negligence was intended to ameliorate the harshness of contributory negligence but should not blur its clarity. It was designed only to leave the door open to those plaintiffs whose fault was not greater than the defendant's, not to create an independent gate-keeping function. Comparative negligence, then, will qualify the doctrine of contributory negligence when that doctrine would otherwise be applicable as a limitation on recovery. * * *

* * * The doctrine [of avoidable consequences] proceeds on the theory that a plaintiff who has suffered an injury as the proximate result of a tort cannot recover for any portion of the harm that by the exercise of ordinary care he could have avoided. [ ] * * * Avoidable consequences, then, normally comes into action when the injured party's carelessness occurs *after* the defendant's legal wrong has been committed. Contributory negligence, however, comes into action when the injured party's carelessness occurs *before* defendant's wrong has been committed or concurrently with it. [ ]

A counterweight to the doctrine of avoidable consequences is the doctrine of the particularly susceptible victim. This doctrine is familiarly expressed in the maxim that "defendant 'must take plaintiff as he finds him.' " [ ] * * * It is ameliorated by the doctrine of aggravation of a preexisting condition. While it is not entirely possible ot separate the doctrines of avoidable conseuence and preexisting condition, perhaps the simplest way to distinguish them is to understand that the injured person's conduct is irrelevant to the consideration of the doctrine of aggravation of a preexisting condition. Negligence law generally calls for an apportionment of damages when a plaintiff's antecedent negligence is "found not to contribute in any way to the original accident or injury, but to be a substantial contributing factor in increasing the harm which ensues." *Restatement (Second) of Torts*, § 465 at 510–11, comment c. Courts recognize that a defendant whose acts aggravate a plaintiff's preexisting condition is liable only for the amount of harm actually caused by the negligence. [ ] * * *

Finally, underpinning all of this is that most fundamental of risk allocators in the tort reparation system, the doctrine of proximate cause. * * *

We have sometimes melded proximate cause with foreseeability of unreasonable risk. * * *

We have been candid in New Jersey to see this doctrine, not so much as an expression of the mechanics of causation, but as an expression of line-drawing by courts and juries, an instrument of "overall fairness and sound public policy." [ ] * * * [ ].

III

Each of these principles, then, has some application to this case.[4] Plaintiff obviously had a preexisting condition. It is alleged that she failed to minimize the damages that she might otherwise have sustained due to mistreatment. Such mistreatment may or may not have been the proximate cause of her ultimate condition.

But we must be careful in reassembling these strands of tort doctrine that none does double duty or obscures underlying threads. In particular, we must avoid the indiscriminate application of the doctrine of comparative negligence (with its fifty percent qualifier for recovery) when the doctrines of avoidable consequences or preexisting condition apply.

The doctrine of contributory negligence bars any recovery to the claimant whose negligent action or inaction *before* the defendant's wrongdoing has been completed has contributed to cause actual invasion of plaintiff's person or property. By contrast,

> "[t]he doctrine of avoidable consequences comes into play at a later stage. Where the defendant has already committed an actionable wrong, whether tort or breach of contract, then this doctrine [avoidable consequences] limits the plaintiff's recovery by disallowing only those items of damages which could reasonably have been averted * * * [.]" "[C]ontributory negligence is to be asserted as a complete defense, whereas the doctrine of avoidable consequences is not considered a defense at all, but merely a rule of damages by which certain particular items of loss may be excluded from consideration * * *." * * *

4. Each principle, however, has limitations based on other policy considerations. For example, the doctrine of avoidable consequences, although of logical application to some instances of professional malpractice, is neutralized by countervailing policy. Thus, a physician who performed a faulty tubal litigation cannot suggest that the eventual consequences of an unwanted pregnancy could have been avoided by termination of the fetus. [ ]

Hence, it would be the bitterest irony if the rule of comparative negligence, designed to ameliorate the harshness of contributory negligence, should serve to shut out any recovery to one who would otherwise have recovered under the law of contributory negligence. Put the other way, absent a comparative negligence act, it would have never been thought that "avoidable consequences" or "mitigation of damages" attributable to post-accident conduct of any claimant would have included a shutout of apportionable damages proximately caused by another's negligence. * * *

* * *

In this context of post-injury conduct by a claimant, given the understandable complexity of concurrent causation, expressing mitigation of damages as a percentage of fault which reduces plaintiff's damages may aid juries in their just apportionment of damages, provided that the jury understands that neither mitigation of damages nor avoidable consequences will bar the plaintiff from recovery if the defendant's conduct was a substantial factor without which the ultimate condition would not have arisen.

* * * In the field of professional health care, given the difficulty of apportionment, sound public policy requires that the professional bear the burden of demonstrating the proper segregation of damages in the aggravation context. [ ] The same policy should apply to mitigation of damages. [ ] Hence, overall fairness requires that juries evaluation apportionment of damages attributable in substantial part to a faulty medical procedure be given understandable guidance about the use of evidence of post-treatment patient fault that will assist them in making a just apportionment of damages and the burden of persuasion on the issues. This is consistent with our general view that a defendant bear the burden of proving the causal link between a plaintiff's unreasonable conduct and the extent of damages. [ ] Once that is established, it should be the "defendant who also has the burden of carving out that portion of the damages which is to be attributed to the plaintiff." [ ]

IV

As noted, in this case the parties agree on certain fundamentals. The pre-treatment health habits of a patient are not to be considered as evidence of fault that would have otherwise been pled in bar to a claim of injury due to the professional misconduct of a health professional. This conclusion bespeaks the doctrine of the particularly susceptible victim or recognition that whatever the wisdom or folly of our life-styles, society, through its laws, has not yet imposed a normative life-style on its members; and, finally, it may reflect in part an aspect of that policy judgment that health care professionals have a special responsibility with respect to diseased patients. [ ]

This does not mean, however, that the patient's poor health is irrelevant to the analysis of a claim for reparation. While the doctor may well take the patient as she found her, she cannot reverse the frames to make it appear that she was presented with a robust vascular condition; likewise, the physician cannot be expected to provide a guarantee against a cardiovascular incident. All that the law expects is that she not mistreat such a patient so as to become a proximate contributing cause to the ultimate vascular injury.

However, once the patient comes under the physician's care, the law can justly expect the patient to cooperate with the health care provider in their mutual interests. Thus, it is not unfair to expect a patient to help avoid the consequences of the condition for which the physician is treating her. * * *

Hence, we approve in this context of post-treatment conduct submission to the jury of the question whether the just mitigation or apportionment of damages may be expressed in terms of the patient's fault. If used, the numerical allocation of fault should be explained to the jury as a method of achieving the just apportionment of the damages based on their relative evaluation of each actor's contribution to the end result—that the allocation is but an aspect of the doctrine of avoidable consequences or of mitigation of damages. In this context, plaintiff should not recover more than she could have reasonably avoided, but the patient's fault will not be a bar to recovery except to the extent that her fault caused the damages.

An important caveat to that statement would be the qualification that implicitly flows from the fact that health care professionals bear the burden of proving that their mistreatment did not aggravate a preexisting condition: that the health care professional bear the burden of proving the damages that were avoidable.

Finally, before submitting the issue to the jury, a court should carefully scrutinize the evidence to see if there is a sound basis in the proofs for the assertion that the post-treatment conduct of the patient was indeed a significant cause of the increased damages. Given the short onset between the contraindicated surgery and the vascular incident here, plaintiff asserts that defendant did not present proof, to a reasonable degree of medical probability, that the plaintiff's post-treatment conduct was a proximate cause of the resultant condition. Plaintiff asserts that the only evidence given to support the defense's theory of proximate cause between plaintiff's post-treatment health habits and her damages was her internist's testimony regarding generalized studies showing that smoking increases vascular disease by fifty percent, and her vascular surgeon's testimony that some physicians believe there is a relationship among diabetes, smoking, and vascular impairment. Such testimony did not address with any degree of medical probability a relationship between her smoking or not between May 17, 1983, and the plaintiff's need for bypass surgery in July 1983. Defendant points to plaintiff's failure to consult with her internist as a cause of her injury, but the instruction to the jury gave no guidance on whether this was to be considered as conduct that concurrently or subsequently caused her injuries. [ ]

V

We acknowledge that it is difficult to parse through these principles and policies in the course of an extended appeal. We can well imagine that in the ebb and flow of trial the lines are not easily drawn. There are regrettably no easy answers to these questions.

* * *

[The court noted the factual complexities of the case, and concluded that "the instructions to the jury in this case did not adequately separate or define the concepts that were relevant to the disposition of the plaintiff's case." The case was remanded for a new trial.]

Notes and Questions

1. Do you advocate applying contributory negligence, or comparative negligence (depending upon the jurisdiction), to situations such as that of *Ostrowski*? Such cases raise fundamental questions about the limits of medicine and the role of patients in their own illnesses. Can a smoker easily stop? Is it fair to bar his recovery when his smoking is not a simple, easily abandoned, choice? See Sawka v. Prokopowycz, 104 Mich.App. 829, 306 N.W.2d 354 (1981), where the plaintiff sued the defendant for his failure to diagnose lung cancer. The court rejected the claim that the plaintiff's continued smoking and failure to return for further examination as instructed were contributory negligence.

Would you treat an overzealous jogger who had cardiac arrest while running in the same way as a chain smoking or obese sedentary patient? How much of your decision is based on your desire to punish the smoker or glutton for immoral or irresponsible behavior which may be virtually impossible to control? Blaming the victim, or scapegoating, is a frequent argument used by employers, insurers and the government to reduce obligations to insure, pay benefits, or, as in *Ostrowski*, to pay damages for patient injury. See Robert Schwartz, Life Style, Health Status, and Distributive Justice, 3 Health Matrix 195, 198 (1993) ("If all of those whose life style choices have health consequences were required to bear the full burden of those consequences, there would be few of us (and few diseases or injuries) that would not be implicated.")

2. Consider the case of Smith v. Hull, 659 N.E.2d 185 (Ind.App.1995). Michael Smith was bald. He underwent hair implants over several years from Dr. Hull, who used human hair obtained from women in Indonesia. He also underwent scalp reduction to draw his scalp skin together. Becoming dissatisfied with the scarring on his scalp, he went back to wearing a hairpiece and sued Dr. Hull for malpractice. Dr. Hull raised contributory negligence as a defense. Smith had signed several consent forms and had been told to wait on scalp reduction until his hair implants fell out, but insisted on proceeding with further surgery. The court found that "Smith's desire to sport a full head of hair motivated him to pursue remedies that he knowingly undertook at his own peril." It upheld the trial court's instructions on contributory negligence.

A finding of contributory negligence was upheld in Ray v. Wagner, 286 Minn. 354, 176 N.W.2d 101, 104 (1970), where the physician performed a pap smear on the plaintiff, got back a positive test result, but was unable to reach the plaintiff by telephone for five months. The court noted:

> Ordinarily, a patient can rely on a doctor's informing her if the results of a test are positive. Here, however, plaintiff gave the doctor somewhat misleading information as to her status, she had no phone at the address where she lived, and she did not live at the address where she had a phone.

See also Harlow v. Chin, 405 Mass. 697, 545 N.E.2d 602 (1989) (plaintiff failed to return for further treatment when pain got worse; plaintiff held to be 13% comparatively negligent.)

3. The theory is typically invoked when a patient failed to follow a physician's instructions after a procedure was performed, or while in the hospital. Thus in Butler v. Berkeley, 25 N.C.App. 325, 213 S.E.2d 571 (1975), the plaintiff removed the nasogastric tube that had been inserted to prevent wounds from being contaminated by food after plastic surgery. This action might have caused

the infection that the patient then developed, and the court granted summary judgment for the surgeon on grounds of contributory negligence. In Musachia v. Rosman, 190 So.2d 47 (Fla.App.1966), the decedent left the hospital over the objections of, and contrary to the advice of, the defendants. He drank liquor and ignored instructions to eat only baby food. He then died from fecal peritonitis due to small perforations in the bowel, and his recovery was barred on the basis of contributory negligence. See also Faile v. Bycura, 297 S.C. 58, 374 S.E.2d 687 (App.1988) (patient refused to wear a medically prescribed postoperative orthotic device after foot surgery).

The failure of a patient to follow a treating physician's warnings about behavior can also be considered by the jury under contributory negligence instructions. In Cobo v. Raba, 347 N.C. 541, 495 S.E.2d 362 (N.C.1998), a physician who suffered from depression was treated by the defendant Dr. Raba. Dr. Cobo refused drug treatment for chronic depression, refused to allow the defendant to take notes, and insisted on psychoanalysis as the only mode of treatment. During this period he engaged regularly in unprotected homosexual intercourse with prostitutes, in spite of regular admonitions by the defendant as to the risks, including unprotected sex with a drug-addicted prostitute in a San Francisco bathhouse; he abused alcohol and drugs, and when he became HIV-positive, he substantially delayed his treatment. The court held that the plaintiff's conduct was "clearly active and related directly to his physical complaint," and the jury should be allowed to evaluate it through a contributory negligence instruction.

4.   Comparative fault is rarely applied against a patient. In Weil v. Seltzer, 873 F.2d 1453 (D.C.Cir.1989), the defendant argued that the patient was contributorily negligent in failing to discover that the medication given him over a twenty year period was steroids rather than antihistamines as told by the defendant; the court strongly rejected this argument, holding that while a patient must cooperate with her physician, "[i]t is a quantum leap * * * to permit a duty to be placed on a patient * * * ". The court also rejected the assumption of the risk defense, since there was no evidence that the plaintiff knew of the danger of prolonged steroid use and voluntarily accepted the risks. Physicians are expected to consider the needs and limitations of their patients. Bryant v. Calantone, 286 N.J.Super. 362, 669 A.2d 286 (N.J.Super.A.D.1996).

In Windisch v. Weiman, 161 A.D.2d 433, 555 N.Y.S.2d 731 (1990), the court held that the failure of a physician to properly follow-up a patient, resulting in a missed diagnosis of lung cancer, may provide the basis for imposing liability even when the patient is partially responsible for the delay in diagnosis. See also Jensen v. Archbishop Bergan Mercy Hospital, 236 Neb. 1, 459 N.W.2d 178 (1990) (the court held that a patient's failure to lose weight may have been causally related to his pulmonary embolism, but it was not contributory negligence with respect to a subsequent malpractice claim against the hospital for treatment of the embolism.)

A patient's lack of compliance with treatment instructions may be submitted to the jury under comparative negligence statutes for comparison with the malpractice of the treating physician. In Cox v. Lesko, 263 Kan. 805, 953 P.2d 1033 (Kan.1998), the physician performed shoulder surgery for traumatic posterior subluxation in the left shoulder. The plaintiff then missed most of her physical therapy sessions over several months, which were aimed to strengthen her muscles and increase her shoulder's range of motion. Her condition failed to improve. Plaintiff's lack of compliance with therapy instructions was properly submitted to the jury under the comparative negligence statute as fault to be compared with the malpractice of the physician who performed the surgery.

5. Almost all American jurisdictions have adopted comparative fault, simplifying the issue by eliminating the harsh all-or-nothing effect of contributory negligence. Courts in comparative fault jurisdictions are likely to be more willing to allow evidence of plaintiffs' contributions to their injuries. See generally Victor Schwartz, Comparative Negligence (2nd ed. 1986). The court in McIntyre v. Balentine, 833 S.W.2d 52 (Tenn.1992), lists only four states remaining without comparative fault: Alabama, Maryland, North Carolina, and Virginia.

6. Assumption of the risk. The doctrine of assumption of the risk is a viable defense even in many comparative fault jurisdictions. In Schneider v. Revici, 817 F.2d 987, 995 (2d Cir.1987), the Second Circuit considered whether a patient undergoing unconventional treatment for breast cancer after signing a consent form had waived all her rights to sue or assumed the risk of injury from the treatment. The court held that the consent form was not clear and unequivocal as a covenant not to sue, but that the doctrine of assumption of risk was available:

> * * * we see no reason why a patient should not be allowed to make an informed decision to go outside currently approved medical methods in search of an unconventional treatment. While a patient should be encouraged to exercise care for his own safety, we believe that an informed decision to avoid surgery and conventional chemotherapy is within the patient's right to "determine what shall be done with his own body," [ ]

The court held that the jury could consider assumption of the risk as a total bar to recovery, based on the language of the signed consent form and the patient's general awareness of the risks of treatment.

Assumption of the risk is rarely argued except in cases of obvious defects of which the patient should have been aware, such as hazards in the hospital room. See, e.g., Charrin v. Methodist Hospital, 432 S.W.2d 572 (Tex.Civ.App.1968) (plaintiff tripped over television cord in hospital room; she knew it was there, having previously pointed it out to the staff.) The problem of assumption of the risk, in the sense of a conscious explicit assumption of medical risks, blends into the issues of informed consent and waivers of liability, discussed in Chapter 5, below.

Problem: The Eyes Have It

Dr. Guerra was an ophthalmologist who specialized in corneal surgery. He used a laser procedure—photorefractive keratectomy—to correct nearsightedness in his patients. The procedure involves first peeling off the epithelium, the skin covering the cornea; then the computer-controlled laser, set and positioned by the doctor, shoots pulses of cool ultraviolet light to reshape the cornea. Finally, a contact lens is placed over the eye.

Dr. Guerra had developed his own laser device to allow him more accuracy and control than the machines commercially available (manufactured by Summit Technology and VISX Inc.) for this procedure. He had custom-built his device and used the prototype on several dozen patients with success and with few side effects. This year Dr. Guerra operated on Eva Hendrix, who was nearsighted. He had told her that his machine was built to his own design and was more accurate than the devices on the market. She agreed to go ahead with the procedure, signing all consent forms. Unfortunately, the device malfunctioned; the laser shifted slightly in its mount and improperly shaped her cornea, so that her vision was made much worse. Even with contacts she cannot now be corrected to her previous level of vision.

Does Ms. Hendrix have any recourse against Dr. Guerra for the impairment of her vision?

F. ERISA PREEMPTION

ERISA preemption, discussed in Chapter 9 infra, has been held to preempt common law malpractice actions against managed care organizations, although a variety of exceptions are emerging. Whether ERISA preempts an action against treating physicians for their malpractice is a different issue. The following case provides a first look at this issue.

NEALY v. U.S. HEALTHCARE HMO

Court of Appeals of New York, 1999.
93 N.Y.2d 209, 689 N.Y.S.2d 406, 711 N.E.2d 621.

KAYE, CHIEF JUDGE:

The novel question presented by this appeal is whether the Employee Retirement Income Security Act (ERISA) preempts plaintiff's medical malpractice, breach of contract and breach of fiduciary duty claims against a primary care physician who allegedly delayed in submitting a specialist's referral form for approval by a health maintenance organization (HMO) governed by ERISA. Concluding that ERISA does not preempt plaintiff's claims, we reverse the Appellate Division's dismissal order and reinstate the complaint against the doctor.

In January 1992, plaintiff's husband, Glenn Nealy, then 37 years old, was diagnosed with coronary arteriosclerosis and a coronary artery lesion. As a result, Mr. Nealy took disability leave from his job at Photocircuits Corporation and was treated for his condition by a cardiologist, Dr. Stephen Green. His treatment, which included an angioplasty performed by Dr. Green in March 1992, was in large part covered by Blue Cross/Massachusetts Mutual, the carrier selected by Photocircuits to provide employee medical insurance. Around the time of Mr. Nealy's angioplasty, Photocircuits replaced its carrier with a choice of three HMOs, including U.S. Healthcare, and informed its employees that coverage would become effective April 1, 1992. Mr. Nealy promptly enrolled in the U.S. Healthcare Versatile Plus HMO, which allowed its members to see non-participating physicians, and paid his first monthly premium.

On April 2, and again on April 3, Mr. Nealy visited the offices of defendant, Dr. Ralph Yung, whom he had selected as his primary care provider under the U.S. Healthcare HMO.[5] He experienced renewed chest pain and also required follow-up care as a result of the angioplasty. On his first visit, Mr. Nealy was denied an appointment because he had not yet received a U.S. Healthcare identification number. The next day, he spoke with a U.S. Healthcare representative who told him that a copy of his enrollment form could be presented in lieu of an identification number, and he made a

---

5. Dr. Yung disputes plaintiff's allegation that Mr. Nealy visited his offices on April 2 and 3, admitting only that he first saw Mr. Nealy on or about April 10.

second attempt to visit Dr. Yung. Again he was turned away—this time because his enrollment form bore the wrong primary physician number.

On April 10, 1992—having received his U.S. Healthcare identification card the previous day—Mr. Nealy was examined by Dr. Yung. During that visit, Dr. Yung took a patient history that noted a history of angina and angioplasty, performed a routine new-patient physical examination, and renewed all the medications that had been prescribed by Dr. Green. At Dr. Yung's request, Mr. Nealy returned on April 13 to provide blood and urine samples for laboratory analysis. When Dr. Yung informed him during one or both of these visits that he should see a cardiologist, Mr. Nealy requested a referral to Dr. Green, who was not a participating U.S. Healthcare provider. Dr. Yung allegedly assured his patient that he would submit a request to U.S. Healthcare to approve an out-of-plan referral and do what he could to secure approval of the request. It was not until approximately April 20, however, that Dr. Yung completed a non-participating provider request form and submitted it for approval to U.S. Healthcare.[6]

On May 4th, Mr. Nealy received a copy of a letter from U.S. Healthcare addressed to Dr. Yung denying the request for a referral to Dr. Green. The reason given was that U.S. Healthcare had a participating provider in the area. After the referral to Dr. Green was denied, Mr. Nealy decided to accept a referral to Dr. Carl Spivak, a participating U.S. Healthcare cardiologist. He obtained the referral to Dr. Spivak on May 18 and promptly made an appointment for the next day. Tragically, however, on May 18 Mr. Nealy suffered a massive myocardial infarction and died.

Seeking to recover damages for her husband's death, plaintiff commenced this action in Supreme Court asserting breach of contract, breach of fiduciary duty, wrongful death, negligence and other claims against defendants Dr. Yung, Dr. Richard H. Bernstein (Vice President and Director of U.S. Healthcare), U.S. Healthcare and two subsidiaries. Plaintiff also asserted medical malpractice claims against Dr. Yung and Dr. Bernstein. Dr. Bernstein and U.S. Healthcare successfully sought removal of the case to Federal court, where the claims were dismissed on the ground that they were preempted by ERISA (844 F.Supp. 966 [SDNY]), and no appeal was taken to determine the correctness of that decision. Because Dr. Yung—who had not yet been served with the summons and complaint—did not take part in the removal motion, the Federal court remanded the case against him, as the sole remaining defendant, to Supreme Court.

After service of process and discovery, Dr. Yung moved for summary judgment seeking dismissal of the complaint, alleging that ERISA preempted plaintiff's claims against him as well. Supreme Court denied the motion. The Appellate Division, however, reversed and dismissed the complaint, conclud-

---

6. The parties dispute whether the non-participating referral form—instead of a "Versatile" form—was submitted to U.S. Healthcare at Mr. Nealy's request or the result of Dr. Yung's error. A "Versatile" referral would have allowed treatment by a non-participating doctor but required Mr. Nealy to pay a $250 deductible. Plaintiff maintains that Mr. Nealy never expressed a desire to avoid payment of the deductible and was motivated only by a desire to see his cardiologist as soon as possible. Dr. Yung claims that Mr. Nealy did not want to pay the deductible, which is why the non-participating referral form was submitted.

ing that ERISA preempted plaintiff's claims. We disagree and now reinstate plaintiff's complaint against Dr. Yung.

DISCUSSION

Concerned with employee pension plan abuses and mismanagement, Congress in 1974 enacted ERISA, a comprehensive statute "designed to promote the interests of employees and their beneficiaries in employee benefit plans" (Aetna Life Ins. v. Borges, 869 F.2d 142, 144 [2d Cir], cert. denied 493 U.S. 811, 110 S.Ct. 57, 107 L.Ed.2d 25; see also, 29 USC §§ 1001, 1001a, 1001b). ERISA subjects employee benefit plans to participation, funding and vesting requirements as well as rules regarding reporting, disclosure and fiduciary responsibility [ ]. By imposing these requirements, Congress sought "to insure against the possibility that the employee's expectation of * * * benefit[s] would be defeated through poor management by the plan administrator" (Massachusetts v. Morash, 490 U.S. 107, 115, 109 S.Ct. 1668, 104 L.Ed.2d 98). In aid of its goal of protecting plan participants and their beneficiaries, ERISA facilitates the development of a uniform national law governing employee benefit plans, and a standard system to guide the processing of claims and disbursement of benefits (New York State Conference of Blue Cross & Blue Shield Plans v. Travelers Ins. Co., 514 U.S. 645, 656–657, 115 S.Ct. 1671, 131 L.Ed.2d 695 [Travelers]).

ERISA's preemption provision is central to achievement of its statutory purposes. The provision reads that ERISA "shall supersede any and all State laws insofar as they * * * relate to any employee benefit plan" covered by ERISA, and it applies to both State statutes and common law (§ 514[a], 29 USC § 1144[a]; id., at § 514[c][1], 29 USC § 1144[c][1]; Pilot Life Ins. Co. v. Dedeaux, 481 U.S. 41, 46, 107 S.Ct. 1549, 95 L.Ed.2d 39). Although the language of the preemption clause is "deliberately expansive," there is a presumption that Congress does not intend to supplant State law, and a claim traditionally within the domain of State law will not be superseded by Federal law "unless that was the clear and manifest purpose of Congress" (Travelers, 514 US, at 654–655).

The issue before us is whether ERISA's preemption clause bars plaintiff's medical malpractice, breach of contract and breach of fiduciary duty claims against her husband's primary care physician, Dr. Yung. All of these claims fall within the traditional domain of State regulation. Dr. Yung, therefore, bears the "considerable burden" of overcoming the presumption that Congress did not intend to preempt them [ ]. In an attempt to surmount that formidable hurdle, Dr. Yung alleges that ERISA preempts these claims because they "relate to" the administration of the U.S. Healthcare HMO. The Appellate Division agreed, holding that he was protected by ERISA preemption because he had acted in a "purely administrative" capacity, and not as an "actual provider of medical care" (___ A.D.2d ___, ___). We conclude that plaintiff's claims against Dr. Yung do not "relate to" an employee benefit plan.

The simple statutory words "relate to" have been the subject of significant scholarly comment and litigation, including considerable attention from the United States Supreme Court [ ] On the one hand, virtually any State law may be said to "relate to" an employee benefit plan, for "universally, relations stop nowhere" (Travelers, supra, 514 US, at 655). On the other hand, application of the preemption clause to "the furthest stretch of its indeterminancy" would render Congress' words of limitation a "mere sham" and nullify the presumption against preemption (id.). Plainly, there is tension between the "deliberately expansive" language of the preemption clause—which, applied literally, would operate to shield benefit plans—and ERISA's goal of protecting employees from abuses at the hands of such entities.

After many years of broadly interpreting ERISA's preemption clause, in 1995 the United States Supreme Court adopted a more pragmatic approach, noting that its prior efforts to define "relate to" did not always afford "much help drawing the line" (Travelers, 514 US, at 655–656). Whereas the Court had previously explained that a law "relates to" an employee benefit plan if it has a connection with or makes reference to such a plan, in Travelers the Court acknowledged that even that definition of the phrase failed to provide adequate guidance (id., at 656). Thus, the Court concluded, in determining whether a State law relates to an employee benefit plan, it is often necessary to "go beyond the unhelpful text and the frustrating difficulty of defining its key term, and look instead to the objectives of the ERISA statute as a guide to the scope of the state law that Congress understood would survive" (Travelers, 514 US, at 656; see also, DeBuono, supra, 117 S.Ct., at 1751 [where there is no clear "connection with or reference to" an ERISA benefit plan, consideration must be given to the objectives of ERISA to determine whether the presumption against preemption has been overcome]).

In Travelers itself, the Supreme Court concluded that a State statute imposing surcharges on hospital bills paid by certain employee benefit plans, but exempting Blue Cross/Blue Shield plans, was not preempted by ERISA. Arguing for preemption, the commercial insurers asserted that the surcharges had an indirect economic effect on choices made by insurance buyers, including ERISA plans, and as such, the State statute had a "connection with" those plans. The Supreme Court, however, held that the indirect economic influence of the surcharges did not interfere with the congressional goal of uniform standards of plan administration. The statute did not "bind plan administrators to any particular choice and thus function as a regulation of an ERISA plan itself," nor did it "preclude uniform administrative practice or the provision of a uniform interstate benefit package" (514 US, at 659–660). The effect of the law bore only on "the costs of benefits and the relative costs of competing insurance to provide them," and the law was therefore not preempted by ERISA [ ]

Here, plaintiff alleges that Dr. Yung, as a direct provider of medical services, violated the duties and standard of care owed to his patient by improperly assessing the nature and extent of his condition and by failing to take reasonable steps to provide for his timely treatment by a specialist. Viewed pragmatically, those claims are not preempted by ERISA. Plaintiff's allegations of negligent medical care do not "relate to" the administration of an ERISA plan merely because they refer to Dr. Yung's delay in submitting the U.S. Healthcare form seeking a referral to Dr. Green. Plaintiff does not allege that Dr. Yung is responsible for delay caused by U.S. Healthcare's decision-making process with respect to coverage or benefits. Her claim against Dr. Yung is that he failed to take timely action to treat her husband.

Provision of medical treatment under an HMO or other managed care plan often requires reference to that plan's administrative procedures or requirements. In this case, for example, under the terms of the U.S. Healthcare HMO plan, Mr. Nealy's primary care physician was required to complete and submit a referral form in order to obtain treatment by a specialist for his patient. That alone, however, does not transform Dr. Yung into an ERISA plan administrator, or plaintiff's State law action charging violations of a physician's duty of care into claims that "relate to" ERISA plan administration. While plaintiff's claims make reference to U.S. Healthcare's administrative framework, any effect those claims may have on an employee benefit plan is "too tenuous, remote or peripheral" to warrant a finding that they "relate to" such a plan (Shaw, supra, 463 US, at 100 n. 21).

Moreover, considering the objectives of the ERISA statute, it is clear that Congress did not intend to preempt claims such as those now before us. Plaintiff's claims do not bind an employee plan to any particular choice of benefits, do not dictate the administration of such a plan and do not interfere with a uniform administrative scheme [ ]. Indeed, plaintiff does not challenge any administrative determination relating to an employee benefit plan or the extent of rights and benefits under such a plan. In short, there is nothing about plaintiff's claims that "conflicts with the provisions of ERISA or operates to frustrate its [objectives]" (Boggs, supra, 117 S.Ct., at 1760). To the contrary, plaintiff's claims are consistent with ERISA's "principal object": the protection of plan participants and beneficiaries (id., at 1762).

Finally, the Appellate Division would have dismissed plaintiff's complaint on the independent ground that she failed to demonstrate that any deviation from professional standards was a proximate cause of Mr. Nealy's demise. At this juncture in the litigation, however, we cannot agree with that conclusion as a matter of law.

Notes and Questions

1. Can you make a case that the design of the health plan in fact narrowed the treating physicians' choice? The requirement of approval before referring a patient to a non-participating specialist constrains the treating physician, does it not? And the time delay in denying the request for the referral to a non-participating cardiologist was arguably a causal factor in the ultimate death of the plaintiff. These arguments go to a suit against the Plan, which will risk preemption by ERISA in most jurisdictions. See Chapter 9 infra. But what about the argument that these elements of the plan's operation were intended to do exactly what happened in this case–deter the treating physician from making referrals expeditiously?

2. The application of ERISA preemption to the individual physician does not make much sense from a policy perspective. ERISA was designed to govern pension plan administration, not individual medical treatment decisions. Using the "relate to" language, the Court properly rejects ERISA preemption as a defense.

V. CAUSATION PROBLEMS: DELAYED, UNCERTAIN, OR SHARED RESPONSIBILITY

A. THE DISCOVERY RULE

MASTRO v. BRODIE

Supreme Court of Colorado, 1984.
682 P.2d 1162.

NEIGHBORS, JUSTICE.

* * *

On February 5, 1977, Mastro surgically removed a small nodule from the back of Brodie's shoulder. He obtained Brodie's consent to the surgery after explaining that she would have a scar, "but it wouldn't be a bad one." Several months later, however, the scar from the surgery became "large, unsightly and uncomfortable." Brodie returned to Mastro in July 1977, but received no further treatment and no explanation of what had happened. He told her only that "there was nothing else he could do about [the scar]." Since that time, Brodie has had no contact with Mastro. She received treatment, including a series of injections into the scar, from two other physicians during the next two years. She also discussed the scar with at least two attorneys for whom she worked during this time period. Her scar, however, has remained approximately the same in size and appearance as when she first became aware of it. In August 1979, a physician at the University of Colorado Medical Center informed Brodie that she had developed a "keloid"[3] on her shoulder. Further, he told her that a surgical procedure on the shoulder of young, dark-skinned individuals frequently results in the formation of a keloid, which, while unpredictable, does occur in a percentage of such patients. He indicated to Brodie's attorney that "the risk of keloid should have been anticipated" and that Mastro should have warned Brodie of such a risk before operating on her shoulder.[4]

Three months later, in November 1979, Brodie filed a complaint against Mastro * * * alleging medical malpractice. She claimed that, when she consulted him about the nodule on her shoulder, Mastro knew or should have know of the inherent risk of keloid development in a person with her physical characteristics, and that he knew or should have known that disclosure of this risk "would be of great significance to a person in [Brodie's] position in deciding to submit to surgery." Since Mastro was "under a duty to inform [Brodie] of any substantial or special risks inherent in the procedure," his failure to mention keloid scarring before the surgery prevented her from making "an intelligent choice as to alternative treatments consonant with the

---

3. *Dorland's Illustrated Medical Dictionary* 695 (26th ed. 1981) defines "keloid" as "a sharply elevated, irregularly-shaped, progressively enlarging scar due to the formation of excessive amounts of collagen [fibrous tissue] * * * during connective tissue repair."

4. She described her racial background in her deposition as "half black and half Mexican." Brodie's father had been a patient of Mastro's before her surgery.

underlying premise of informed consent." As a result, Brodie suffered "a serious, permanent disfiguring injury" in the form of "a large, unsightly growth" that was "plainly visible on her shoulder." While admitting that she was aware of the scar by July 1977, Brodie concluded by alleging that she was not aware and could not reasonably have been aware of "[Mastro's] negligence in failing to inform her" of the high risk of keloid formation until she consulted the physician at the medical center in August 1979, at the direction of her attorney.

After depositions of the parties were taken, Mastro filed a motion for summary judgment, claiming that the two-year statute of limitations for medical malpractice actions based on lack of informed consent barred Brodie's claim. [ ] Under this provision, the two-year period begins to run when the injured person discovers or in the exercise of reasonable diligence should have discovered "the injury." Mastro claimed that there was no genuine issue of material fact since Brodie "has admitted that she knew of the injury (unsightly scar) more than two years prior to initiation of her Complaint."

* * *

We conclude that the pivotal question in this case is whether Brodie filed suit within two years after she "discovered, or in the exercise of reasonable diligence and concern should have discovered, the *injury*." Section 13–80–105(1) (emphasis added). Therefore, we must interpret the word "injury" as it appears in the statute of limitations governing medical malpractice cases.

* * *

C.

There are at least three possible interpretations of the word "injury": (1) the alleged negligent act or omission; (2) the physical damage or manifestation resulting from the act or omission; or (3) the legal injury, i.e., all the essential elements of a claim for medical malpractice.

At least two courts have adopted the first definition. [ ] We reject this interpretation of the word. * * *

Likewise, we reject the interpretation that the "injury" occurs for purposes of the statute of limitations on the date that the injury manifests itself in a physically objective and ascertainable manner. The physical damage test fails to account adequately for all relevant factors. In some cases, such as the discovery of a sponge left in the patient during surgery * * * the discovery of the physical injury may occur simultaneously with the discovery of the only possible cause, i.e., the doctor's negligence. However, where the injury is consistent with post-operative recovery and treatment is continued by the treating doctor who reassures the patient that there is no permanent damage, the patient who reasonably trusts the doctor and relies upon the physician's advice would be unfairly barred from bringing suit. In addition, the physical injury standard requires a claimant to immediately file suit against a physician, even though the plaintiff has no knowledge of any wrongful conduct on the part of the doctor. Courts should not adopt a construction of a statute which may encourage the filing of frivolous claims. * * *

* * *

We hold that the statute of limitations begins to run when the claimant has knowledge of facts which would put a reasonable person on notice of the nature and extent of an injury and that the injury was caused by the wrongful conduct of another. The overwhelming majority of state appellate courts which have addressed the issue here have adopted the "legal injury" construction of the word "injury" used in statutes of limitation governing medical malpractice actions. The focus is on the plaintiff's knowledge of facts, rather than on discovery of applicable legal theories. * * *

The judgment of the court of appeals is affirmed.

Notes and Questions

1. Has the discovery rule simplified or complicated malpractice litigation? The older cases generally held that a cause of action accrued when the right to bring an action arose, i.e. when the medical error had occurred. Shearin v. Lloyd, 246 N.C. 363, 98 S.E.2d 508 (1957). See also Goldsmith v. Howmedica, Inc., 67 N.Y.2d 120, 500 N.Y.S.2d 640, 491 N.E.2d 1097 (1986) (plaintiff received a total hip replacement in 1973; in 1981 the hip broke and plaintiff sued in 1983. Held: action accrued in 1973 and was barred by the statute of limitations.)

This older rule has the advantage of a bright line approach to the statute of limitation. The newer discovery rule like that adopted in *Brodie* was created to be fair to patients who suffered latent injuries. What does such a rule cost? Can the malpractice insurance crisis be traced in some small way to the uncertainties bred by such a rule? The discovery rule makes it actuarially difficult for a malpractice insurer to predict losses, by creating a long period of time after a medical intervention during which a claim can be "discovered." As a result, insurers must raise premiums to compensate for the uncertainty of future unknown claims not barred by a rigid statute of limitations rule. Or they might change the design of policies to a claims-made basis to eliminate this uncertainty about future claims.

2. The modern discovery rule creates difficult problems. Does the statute begin to run when the initial harm surfaces or when the injury matures or worsens? See Burns v. Hartford Hosp., 192 Conn. 451, 472 A.2d 1257 (1984) (patient had infection due to contaminated IV tube. Court held that " * * * the harm need not have reached its fullest manifestation before the statute begins to run.")

3. In suits against the federal government, the statute of limitations begins to run when the plaintiff learns of an injury's existence and cause, rather than when he learns the injury was negligently inflicted. Once the injury and its causes are known, the plaintiff can "protect himself by seeking advice in the medical and legal community." United States v. Kubrick, 444 U.S. 111, 100 S.Ct. 352, 62 L.Ed.2d 259 (1979) (suit against government under Tort Claims Act).

B. MULTIPLE DEFENDANTS

1. *Joint Tortfeasor Doctrine*

In the typical malpractice case in which the parties acted together to commit the wrong, or the parties' acts, if independent, unite to cause a single injury, multiple defendants are considered joint rather than separate tortfeasors. In determining whether to assess liability jointly, the courts have considered factors such as whether each defendant has a similar duty; whether the same evidence will support an action against each; the indivisible nature of the plaintiff's injury; and identity of the facts as to time, place or result. See Riff v. Morgan Pharmacy, 353 Pa.Super. 21, 508 A.2d 1247 (1986).

What if a doctor fails to diagnose a patient's problem, and subsequently another doctor is negligent in treating it? The first negligent treating doctor might be liable to the injured plaintiff for all foreseeable injuries resulting from the later negligent medical treatment of a second doctor. Two or more physicians who fail to make a proper diagnosis on successive occasions are co-tortfeasors under contribution statutes. Foote v. United States, 648 F.Supp. 735 (N.D.Ill.1986). See, e.g., Gilson v. Mitchell, 131 Ga.App. 321, 205 S.E.2d 421 (1974):

> " * * * if the separate and independent acts of negligence of several persons combine naturally and directly to produce a single indivisible injury, and a rational basis does not exist for an apportionment of damages, the actors are joint tortfeasors."

Where an existing injury is aggravated by malpractice, the innocent plaintiffs are not required to establish that share of expenses, pain, suffering, disability or impairment attributable solely to malpractice. The burden of proof shifts to the culpable defendant, who is responsible for all damages unless he can demonstrate that the damages for which he is responsible are capable of some reasonable apportionment.

Concurrent causation instructions are required to help the trier of fact sort out the causation complexities. In Zigman v. Cline, 664 So.2d 968 (Fla.App. 4 Dist.1995), the plaintiff was rendered a paraplegic after an complicated surgery "to correct the severe and normally fatal injuries ... suffered in an automobile accident". Without the surgery he would have died; but a possibility existed that the surgeon erred in his choice of technique in repairing the plaintiff's torn aorta. The court held that the jury should have been instructed as to concurrent causation where a defendant's negligence combines with plaintiff's physical condition.

For the physician who knows that his patients see alternative practitioners, or who offers such treatments as an option, what are his or her liabilities? Joint and several liability is likely to hook the physician firmly if injury is the end result of a continuum of care that includes alternative practitioners. For example, in Samuelson v. McMurtry, 962 S.W.2d 473 (Tenn.1998), the plaintiff was treated by physicians and a chiropractor. His problems began with a boil under his arm, treated by Dr. Holland. The next day he returned to the hospital with a fever and inflammation around the boil and was treated by Dr. McMurty. 8 days later, he went to the hospital emergency room with complaints of back pain. The next day he twice returned to the emergency room. On the first visit he was seen by Dr. Holland but on the second visit he was discouraged by hospital personnel from seeing a physician. The next day, he went to see Dr. Totty, a chiropractor, with complaints of intense back and chest pain and he was treated twice that day by Dr. Totty. The next day he died of pneumonia, "which had not been diagnosed by any of the health care providers." He could have been treated within 6–12 hours of his death. This case presents an apportionment of fault issue, since Dr. Totty was severed as a defendant. The court held that it was an error to sever the claim against him. The general rule will bind all practitioners who treat a patient for the same ailment:

There can be little doubt that the participation of all potentially responsible persons as parties in the original action would have resulted in a fuller and fairer presentation of the relevant evidence and would have enabled the jury to make a more informed and complete determination of liability.

2. *Multiple Defendants and Burden Shifting*

Where only one of several defendants could have caused the plaintiff's injuries, but the plaintiff cannot adduce evidence as to which defendant is responsible, the courts have developed special rules to protect the obviously deserving plaintiff. Cases like Ybarra v. Spangard, and Anderson v. Somberg, supra, reflect judicial attempts to use doctrines like *res ipsa loquitur* to cover multiple defendant/uncertain proof situations. An equitable doctrine of burden shifting is derived from the exception in the Restatement (Second) Torts, § 433B(3) (1965):

> Where the conduct of two or more actors is tortious, and it is proved that harm has been caused to the plaintiff by only one of them, but there is uncertainty as to which one has caused it, the burden is upon each actor to prove that he has not caused the harm.

The reason for this burden shift is " * * * the injustice of permitting proved wrongdoers, who among them have inflicted an injury upon the entirely innocent plaintiff, to escape liability merely because the nature of their conduct and the resulting harm has made it impossible to prove which of them has caused the harm." Id., comment f.

The DES cases, involving the marketing of drugs and multiple defendants, have taken burden shifting well beyond the common law precedents, with the courts developing a variety of special tests. In Hymowitz v. Eli Lilly and Co., 73 N.Y.2d 487, 541 N.Y.S.2d 941, 539 N.E.2d 1069 (1989), New York's highest court chronicled the efforts by other courts to come to grips with the difficulties inherent in identifying the manufacturer of the particular DES that injured the plaintiff. The court noted the rationale behind burden-shifting generally, to force defendants to come forward or else be held jointly and severally liable.

See Sindell v. Abbott, 26 Cal.3d 588, 163 Cal.Rptr. 132, 607 P.2d 924 (1980). The law review article that gave rise to market share liability is Naomi Sheiner, Comment, DES and a Proposed Theory of Enterprise Liability, 46 Fordham L.Rev. 963 (1978). The best articles on the subject, with full citations to other literature, are David Rosenberg, The Causal Connection in Mass Exposure Cases: A "Public Law" Vision of the Tort System, 97 Harv. L.Rev. 851 (1984), and Richard Wright, Causation in Tort Law, 73 Cal.L.Rev. 1735 (1985). For a useful analysis of the trauma experienced by DES daughters, see R. Apfel and S. Fisher, To Do No Harm: DES and the Dilemmas of Modern Medicine (1984).

The market share theories, while developed in the DES cases, have often been disallowed in vaccine cases. In Shackil v. Lederle Laboratories, 116 N.J. 155, 561 A.2d 511(N.J.1989), New Jersey rejected a risk-modified market share approach to manufacturers of the pertussis antigen component of a diphtheria, pertussis and tetanus toxoid vaccine (DPT). The court in a long and thoughtful analysis of market share approaches held that such an approach in the vaccine context might discourage a highly valuable activity.

C. ALTERNATIVE CAUSAL TESTS

Proximate cause instructions continue to be given in most states, often confusing jurors just as the doctrine has confused generations of law students. Courts worry that jurors will be misled, particularly where multiple sources of causation are involved. In Peterson v. Gray, 137 N.H. 374, 628 A.2d 244 (N.H. 1993), the plaintiff suffered from arthritis in her hand, and the defendant, a hand surgeon, performed a trapexiectomy that later required wrist fusion. The plaintiff's preexisting condition was clearly implicated in the harm that resulted. The court observed that " ... if the jury determined that the plaintiff's arthritis was '*a* proximate cause' of her wrist fusion, then the defendant's actions could not possibly have been '*the* proximate cause' ". Id. at 246. At least one state, California, has rejected instructions on proximate cause as unduly confusing to the jury, adopting instead the "substantial factor" test. In Mitchell v. Gonzales, 54 Cal.3d 1041, 1 Cal.Rptr.2d 913, 819 P.2d 872 (Cal. 1991) the California Supreme Court in effect mandated a jury instruction that asks the jury to determine where the defendant's conduct was a "substantial factor" in bringing about harm, allowing a jury to find against the defendant even if their conduct was only a contributing factor. This "substantial factor" test has been around for 25 years, but the influence of California on tort law evolution is likely to push other states to replace the confusing proximate cause instructions with the "substantial factor" test.

The "substantial factor" has come to be used in lieu of the "but for" test in jury instructions where multiple medical actors and concurrent causation are involved. See Vincent By Staton v. Fairbanks Mem. Hosp., 862 P.2d 847 (Alaska 1993).

VI. DAMAGE INNOVATIONS

A. THE "LOSS OF A CHANCE" DOCTRINE

HERSKOVITS v. GROUP HEALTH COOPERATIVE OF PUGET SOUND

Supreme Court of Washington, 1983.
99 Wash.2d 609, 664 P.2d 474.

DORE, JUSTICE.

This appeal raises the issue of whether an estate can maintain an action for professional negligence as a result of failure to timely diagnose lung cancer, where the estate can show probable reduction in statistical chance for survival but cannot show and/or prove that with timely diagnosis and treatment, decedent probably would have lived to normal life expectancy.

Both counsel advised that for the purpose of this appeal we are to *assume* that the respondent Group Health Cooperative of Puget Sound and Dr. William Spencer negligently failed to diagnose Herskovits' cancer on his first visit to the hospital and *proximately* caused a 14 percent reduction in his chances of survival. It is undisputed that Herskovits had less than a 50 percent chance of survival at all times herein.

The main issue we will address in this opinion is whether a patient, with less than a 50 percent chance of survival, has a cause of action against the hospital and its employees if they are negligent in diagnosing a lung cancer which reduces his chances of survival by 14 percent.

* * *

I

The complaint alleged that Herskovits came to Group Health Hospital in 1974 with complaints of pain and coughing. In early 1974, chest x-rays revealed infiltrate in the left lung. Rales and coughing were present. In mid-1974, there were chest pains and coughing, which became persistent and chronic by fall of 1974. A December 5, 1974 entry in the medical records confirms the cough problem. Plaintiff contends that Herskovits was treated thereafter only with cough medicine. No further effort or inquiry was made by Group Health concerning his symptoms, other than an occasional chest x-ray. In the early spring of 1975, Mr. and Mrs. Herskovits went south in the hope that the warm weather would help. Upon his return to the Seattle area with no improvement in his health, Herskovits visited Dr. Jonathan Ostrow on a private basis for another medical opinion. Within 3 weeks, Dr. Ostrow's evaluation and direction to Group Health led to the diagnosis of cancer. In July of 1975, Herskovits' lung was removed, but no radiation or chemotherapy treatments were instituted. Herskovits died 20 months later, on March 22, 1977, at the age of 60.

At hearing on the motion for summary judgment, plaintiff was unable to produce expert testimony that the delay in diagnosis "probably" or "more likely than not" caused her husband's death. The affidavit and deposition of plaintiff's expert witness, Dr. Jonathan Ostrow, construed in the most favorable light possible to plaintiff, indicated that had the diagnosis of lung cancer been made in December 1974, the patient's possibility of 5–year survival was 39 percent. At the time of initial diagnosis of cancer 6 months later, the possibility of a 5–year survival was reduced to 25 percent. Dr. Ostrow testified he felt a diagnosis perhaps could have been made as early as December 1974, or January 1975, about 6 months before the surgery to remove Mr. Herskovits' lung in June 1975.

Dr. Ostrow testified that if the tumor was a "stage 1" tumor in December 1974, Herskovits' chance of a 5–year survival would have been 39 percent. In June 1975, his chances of survival were 25 percent assuming the tumor had progressed to "stage 2". Thus, the delay in diagnosis may have reduced the chance of a 5–year survival by 14 percent.

Dr. William Spencer, the physician from Group Health Hospital who cared for the deceased Herskovits, testified that in his opinion, based upon a reasonable medical probability, earlier diagnosis of the lung cancer that afflicted Herskovits would not have prevented his death, nor would it have lengthened his life. He testified that nothing the doctors at Group Health could have done would have prevented Herskovits' death, as death within several years is a virtual certainty with this type of lung cancer regardless of how early the diagnosis is made.

Plaintiff contends that medical testimony of a reduction of chance of survival from 39 percent to 25 percent is sufficient evidence to allow the proximate cause issue to go to the jury. Defendant Group Health argues conversely that Washington law does not permit such testimony on the issue of medical causation and requires that medical testimony must be at least sufficiently definite to establish that the act complained of "probably" or "more likely than not" caused the subsequent disability. It is Group Health's contention that plaintiff must prove that Herskovits "probably" would have survived had the defendant not been allegedly negligent; that is, the plaintiff must prove there was at least a 51 percent chance of survival.

II

* * *

This court heretofore has not faced the issue of whether, under § 323(a), [of the Restatement (Second) of Torts (1965)] proof that the defendant's conduct increased the risk of death by decreasing the chances of survival is sufficient to take the issue of proximate cause to the jury. Some courts in other jurisdictions have allowed the proximate cause issue to go to the jury on this type of proof. [ ] These courts emphasized the fact that defendants' conduct deprived the decedents of a "significant" chance to survive or recover, rather than requiring proof that with absolute certainty the defendants' conduct caused the physical injury. The underlying reason is that it is not for the wrongdoer, who put the possibility of recovery beyond realization, to say afterward that the result was inevitable. [ ]

Other jurisdictions have rejected this approach, generally holding that unless the plaintiff is able to show that it was *more likely than not* that the harm was caused by the defendant's negligence, proof of a decreased chance of survival is not enough to take the proximate cause question to the jury. [ ] These courts have concluded that the defendant should not be liable where the decedent more than likely would have died anyway.

The ultimate question raised here is whether the relationship between the increased risk of harm and Herskovits' death is sufficient to hold Group Health responsible. Is a 36 percent (from 39 percent to 25 percent) reduction in the decedent's chance for survival sufficient evidence of causation to allow the jury to consider the possibility that the physician's failure to timely diagnose the illness was the proximate cause of his death? We answer in the affirmative. To decide otherwise would be a blanket release from liability for doctors and hospitals any time there was less than a 50 percent chance of survival, regardless of how flagrant the negligence.

III

[The court then discusses at length the case of *Hamil v. Bashline*, [481 Pa. 256, 392 A.2d 1280 (1978)], where the plaintiff's decedent, suffering from severe chest pains, was negligently treated in the emergency unit of the hospital. The wife, because of the lack of help, took her husband to a private physician's office, where he died. If the hospital had employed proper treatment, the decedent would have had a substantial chance of surviving the attack, stated by plaintiff's medical expert as a 75 percent chance of survival.

The defendant's expert witness testified that the patient would have died regardless of any treatment provided by the defendant hospital.]

* * *

* * * In *Hamil* and the instant case, however, the defendant's act or omission failed in a *duty* to protect against harm from *another source*. Thus, as the *Hamil* court noted, the fact finder is put in the position of having to consider not only what *did* occur, but also what *might have* occurred.

* * *

The *Hamil* court held that once a plaintiff has demonstrated that the defendant's acts or omissions have increased the risk of harm to another, such evidence furnishes a basis for the jury to make a determination as to whether such increased risk was in turn a substantial factor in bringing about the resultant harm.

* * *

Under the *Hamil* decision, once a plaintiff has demonstrated that defendant's acts or omissions in a situation to which § 323(a) applies have increased the risk of harm to another, such evidence furnishes a basis for the fact finder to go further and find that such increased risk was in turn a substantial factor in bringing about the resultant harm. The necessary proximate cause will be established if the jury finds such cause. It is not necessary for a plaintiff to introduce evidence to establish that the negligence resulted in the injury or death, but simply that the negligence increased the *risk* of injury or death. The step from the increased risk to causation is one for the jury to make.

* * *

Where percentage probabilities and decreased probabilities are submitted into evidence, there is simply no danger of speculation on the part of the jury. More speculation is involved in requiring the medical expert to testify as to what would have happened had the defendant not been negligent.

Conclusion

* * * We reject Group Health's argument that plaintiffs *must show* that Herskovits "probably" would have had a 51 percent chance of survival if the hospital had not been negligent. We hold that medical testimony of a reduction of chance of survival from 39 percent to 25 percent is sufficient evidence to allow the proximate cause issue to go to the jury.

Causing reduction of the opportunity to recover (loss of chance) by one's negligence, however, does not necessitate a total recovery against the negligent party for all damages caused by the victim's death. Damages should be awarded to the injured party or his family based only on damages caused directly by premature death, such as lost earnings and additional medical expenses, etc.

We reverse the trial court and reinstate the cause of action.

PEARSON, J., concurring.

* * *

* * * I am persuaded * * * by the thoughtful discussion of a recent commentator. King, *Causation, Valuation, and Chance in Personal Injury Torts Involving Preexisting Conditions and Future Consequences*, 90 Yale L.J. 1353 (1981).

* * *

Under the all or nothing approach, typified by *Cooper v. Sisters of Charity of Cincinnati, Inc.*, 27 Ohio St.2d 242, 272 N.E.2d 97 (1971), a plaintiff who establishes that but for the defendant's negligence the decedent had a 51 percent chance of survival may maintain an action for that death. The defendant will be liable for all damages arising from the death, even though there was a 49 percent chance it would have occurred despite his negligence. On the other hand, a plaintiff who establishes that but for the defendant's negligence the decedent had a 49 percent chance of survival recovers nothing.

This all or nothing approach to recovery is criticized by King on several grounds, 90 Yale L.J. at 1376–78. First, the all or nothing approach is arbitrary. Second, it

subverts the deterrence objectives of tort law by denying recovery for the effects of conduct that causes statistically demonstrable losses * * *. A failure to allocate the cost of these losses to their tortious sources * * * strikes at the integrity of the torts system of loss allocation.

90 Yale L.J. at 1377. Third, the all or nothing approach creates pressure to manipulate and distort other rules affecting causation and damages in an attempt to mitigate perceived injustices. [ ] Fourth, the all or nothing approach gives certain defendants the benefit of an uncertainty which, were it not for their tortious conduct, would not exist. * * * Finally, King argues that the loss of a less than even chance is a loss worthy of redress.

These reasons persuade me that the best resolution of the issue before us is to recognize the loss of a less than even chance as an actionable injury. Therefore, I would hold that plaintiff has established a prima facie issue of proximate cause by producing testimony that defendant probably caused a substantial reduction in Mr. Herskovits' chance of survival. * * *

Finally, it is necessary to consider the amount of damages recoverable in the event that a loss of a chance of recovery is established. Once again, King's discussion provides a useful illustration of the principles which should be applied.

To illustrate, consider a patient who suffers a heart attack and dies as a result. Assume that the defendant-physician negligently misdiagnosed the patient's condition, but that the patient would have had only a 40% chance of survival even with a timely diagnosis and proper care. Regardless of whether it could be said that the defendant caused the decedent's death, he caused the loss of a chance, and that chance-interest should be completely redressed in its own right. Under the proposed rule, the plaintiff's compensation for the loss of the victim's chance of surviving the heart attack would be 40% of the compensable value of the victim's life had he survived (including what his earning capacity would otherwise have been in the years following death). The value placed on the patient's life would reflect such factors as his age, health, and earning potential, including the fact that he had suffered the heart attack and the assumption that he had survived it. The 40% computation would be applied to that base figure.

(Footnote omitted.) 90 Yale L.J. at 1382.

I would remand to the trial court for proceedings consistent with this opinion.

BRACHTENBACH, JUSTICE (dissenting).

I dissent because I find plaintiff did not meet her burden of proving proximate cause. While the statistical evidence introduced by the expert was relevant and admissible, it was not alone sufficient to maintain a cause of action.

Neither the majority nor Justice Dolliver's dissent focus on the key issue. Both opinions focus on the significance of the 14 percent differentiation in the patient's chance to survive for 5 years and question whether this statistical data is sufficient to sustain a malpractice action. The issue is not so limited. The question should be framed as whether all the evidence amounts to sufficient proof, rising above speculation, that the doctor's conduct was a proximate cause of the patient's death. While the relevancy and the significance of the statistical evidence is a subissue bearing on the sufficiency of the proof, such evidence alone neither proves nor disproves plaintiff's case.

II

Furthermore, the instant case does not present evidence of proximate cause that rises above speculation and conjecture. The majority asserts that evidence of a statistical reduction of the chance to survive for 5 years is sufficient to create a jury question on whether the doctor's conduct was a proximate cause of the death. I disagree that this statistical data can be interpreted in such a manner.

Use of statistical data in judicial proceedings is a hotly debated issue. [ ] Many fear that members of the jury will place too much emphasis on statistical evidence and the statistics will be misused and manipulated by expert witnesses and attorneys. [ ]

Such fears do not support a blanket exclusion of statistical data, however. Our court system is premised on confidence in the jury to understand complex concepts and confidence in the right of cross examination as protection against the misuse of evidence. Attorneys ought to be able to explain the true significance of statistical data to keep it in its proper perspective.

Statistical data should be admissible as evidence if they are relevant, that is, if they have

> any tendency to make the existence of any fact that is of consequence to * * * the action more probable or less probable than it would be without the evidence.

ER 401. The statistics here met that test; they have some tendency to show that those diagnosed at stage one of the disease may have a greater chance to survive 5 years than those diagnosed at stage two.

The problem is, however, that while this statistical fact is relevant, it is not sufficient to prove causation. There is an enormous difference between the "any tendency to prove" standard of ER 401 and the "more likely than not" standard for proximate cause.

* * *

Thus, I would not resolve the instant case simply by focusing on the 14 percent differentiation in the chance to survive 5 years for the different stages of cancer. Instead, I would accept this as an admissible fact, but not as proof of proximate cause. To meet the proximate cause burden, the record would need to reveal other facts about the patient that tended to show that he would have been a member of the 14 percent group whose chance of 5 years' survival could be increased by early diagnosis.

Such evidence is not in the record. Instead, the record reveals that Mr. Herskovits' cancer was located such that corrective surgery "would be more formidable". This would tend to show that his chance of survival may have been less than the statistical average. Moreover, the statistics relied on did not take into consideration the location of the tumor, therefore their relevance to Mr. Herskovits' case must be questioned. Clerk's Papers, at 41.

In addition, as the tumor was relatively small in size when removed (2 to 3 centimeters), the likelihood that it would have been detected in 1974, even if the proper test were performed, was less than average. This uncertainty further reduces the probability that the doctor's failure to perform the tests was a proximate cause of a reduced chance of survival.

Other statistics admitted into evidence also tend to show the inconclusiveness of the statistics relied on by the majority. One study showed the *two*-year survival rate for this type of cancer to be 46.6 percent for stage one and 39.8 percent for stage two. Mr. Herskovits lived for 20 months after surgery, which was 26 months after defendant allegedly should have discovered the cancer. Therefore, regardless of the stage of the cancer at the time Mr. Herskovits was examined by defendant, it cannot be concluded that he survived significantly less than the average survival time. Hence, it is pure speculation to suppose that the doctor's negligence "caused" Mr. Herskovits to die sooner than he would have otherwise. Such speculation does not rise to the level of a jury question on the issue of proximate cause. Therefore, the trial court correctly dismissed the case. [ ]

The apparent harshness of this conclusion cannot be overlooked. The combination of the loss of a loved one to cancer and a doctor's negligence in diagnosis seems to compel a finding of liability. Nonetheless, justice must be dealt with an even hand. To hold a defendant liable without proof that his actions *caused* plaintiff harm would open up untold abuses of the litigation system.

Cases alleging misdiagnosis of cancer are increasing in number, perhaps because of the increased awareness of the importance of early detection. These cases, however, illustrate no more than an inconsistency among courts in their treatment of the problems of proof. *See* Annot., *Malpractice in Connection with Diagnosis of Cancer*, 79 A.L.R.3d 915 (1977). Perhaps as medical science becomes more knowledgeable about this disease and more sophisticated in its detection and treatment of it, the balance may tip in favor of imposing liability on doctors who negligently fail to promptly diagnose the disease. But, until a formula is found that will protect doctors against liability imposed through speculation as well as afford truly aggrieved plaintiffs their just compensation, I cannot favor the wholesale abandonment of the principle of proximate cause. For these reasons, I dissent.

Notes and Questions

1. How would damages be figured under the majority's approach? Under the Pearson/King theory? What is the relationship between causation and damages in these cases? The majority and Pearson opinions would effectively permit recovery but reduce damages as the causation link weakens. Is this a reasonable approach?

2. Judicial approaches to the loss of a chance can be grouped into four categories.

a. All or nothing. The traditional rule allows the plaintiff no recovery unless survival was more likely than not. A less than 51% chance of survival receives nothing. Borowski v. Von Solbrig, 60 Ill.2d 418, 328 N.E.2d 301 (1975). Plaintiff who proves a chance of survival greater than 50% can receive judgment with no discount for the chance that the loss would have occurred without negligence. This award is based on the physical injury suffered and not the lost chance to avoid it. See Cooper v. Sisters of Charity, Inc., 27 Ohio St.2d 242, 272 N.E.2d 97 (1971).

Texas rejected the loss of a chance doctrine in Kramer v. Lewisville Memorial Hospital, 858 S.W.2d 397, 405 (Tex.1993). "Below reasonable probability, however, we do not believe that a sufficient number of alternative explanations and hypotheses for the cause of the harm are eliminated to permit a judicial determination of responsibility.... The more likely than not standard is thus not some arbitrary, irrational benchmark for cutting off malpractice recoveries, but rather a fundamental prerequisite of an ordered system of justice." See also Pillsbury–Flood v. Portsmouth Hospital, 128 N.H. 299, 512 A.2d 1126 (1986) (doctrine rejected; "causation is a matter of probability, not possibility"); Gooding v. University Hosp. Bldg., Inc., 445 So.2d 1015 (Fla.1984) ("Health care providers could find themselves defending cases simply because a patient fails to improve or where serious disease processes are not arrested because another course of action could possibly bring a better result.")

b. Loss of an appreciable or substantial chance of recovery. Jeanes v. Milner, 428 F.2d 598 (8th Cir.1970). This approach does not give proportional recovery based on the percentage of harm attributable to the defendant, instead manipulating the burden of proof rather than acknowledging the lost chance as the real injury. See Hicks v. United States, 368 F.2d 626 (4th Cir.1966). Defining "substantial possibility" has troubled some courts. Borgren v. United States, 716 F.Supp. 1378 (D.Kan.1989).

c. Increased risk of harm. This approach, found in the Restatement (Second), Torts, section 323(a) and adopted by the majority in Herskovits, lowers causation requirements to allow causes of action for those who have a less than 50% chance of survival. Hamil v. Bashline, 481 Pa. 256, 392 A.2d 1280 (Pa. 1978). Compensation is for the increased risk of harm rather than loss of a chance, and damage awards are not discounted for the percentage of harm caused by the physician, death is typically the compensable injury. Any percentage is enough to get to the jury. See Thompson v. Sun City Community Hospital, Inc., 141 Ariz. 597, 688 P.2d 605 (Ariz. 1984) (linking Restatement (Second), Torts, section 323A to the interest seen as "the chance itself"); Mayhue v. Sparkman, 653 N.E.2d 1384 (Ind.1995)(rejects lost chance but lightens plaintiff's burden of proving causation.) For further discussion, see Beth Clemens Boggs, Lost Chance of

Survival Doctrine: Should Courts Ever Tinker With Chance? 16 So. Ill. Univ. L. U. 421 (1992).

d. Compensation for the loss of a chance. This looks at damages that include the value of the patient's life reduced in proportion to the lost chance. This approach was developed by Joseph King in his seminal article, Causation, Valuation and Chance in Personal Injury Torts Involving Pre-existing Conditions and Future Consequences, 90 Yale L.J. 1353 (1981). The approach requires a percentage probability test, with the value of the patient's life determined and damages decreased accordingly. This approach was considered in Pearson's concurring opinion in *Herskovits*. Iowa adopted the approach in DeBurkarte v. Louvar, 393 N.W.2d 131 (Iowa 1986). Ohio adopted it in Roberts v. Ohio Permanente Medical Group, Inc., 76 Ohio St.3d 483, 668 N.E.2d 480 (1996), and South Dakota in Jorgenson v. Vener, 616 N.W.2d 366 (S.D.2000).

Loss of a chance and increased risk are grounded in the same justifications of deterring negligent conduct and compensating for real harms that happen to fall below the fifty percent threshold of traditional tort doctrine. Increased risk allows recovery for harm that has not yet occurred, while loss of a chance requires the plaintiff to wait until the condition occurs and then sue. See generally United States v. Anderson, 669 A.2d 73 (Del.1995).

2. What problems do you foresee with the application of the "loss of a chance" doctrine to medical practice? Note that the evidence as to risk must be put in probabilistic form for the jury to consider. What about Judge Brachtenbach's concerns about the weight to be given statistical evidence? Would his concerns always prevent the use of statistics in litigation? Or can you offer some solutions to his problems?

3. Ultimate outcome instructions. Lost chance cases require calculations that assume a probability of loss and an ultimate outcome if the defendant's treatment had been faultless. One example of an "ultimate outcome" charge is found in the New Jersey Model Jury Charges (Civil)(4th ed.) § 5.36E (emphasis added):

> If you find that defendant has sustained his/her burden of proof, then you must determine based on the evidence what is the likelihood, on a percentage basis, that the plaintiff's ultimate injuries (*condition*) would have occurred even if defendant's treatment was proper. When you are determining the amount of damages to be awarded to the plaintiff, you should award the total amount of damage. Your award should not be reduced by your allocation of harm. The adjustment in damages which may be required will be performed by the Court.

See generally Fischer v. Canario, M.D., 143 N.J. 235, 670 A.2d 516, 524–526 (1996).

4. A judicial illustration of the calculation process for loss of a chance is found in McKellips v. St. Francis Hospital, Inc., 741 P.2d 467 (Okl.1987):

> "To illustrate the method in a case where the jury determines from the statistical findings combined with the specific facts relevant to the patient, the patient originally had a 40% chance of cure and the physician's negligence reduced the chance of cure to 25%, (40%–25%) 15% represents the patient's loss of survival. If the total amount of damages proved by the evidence is $500,000, the damages caused by defendant is 15% x $500,000 or $75,000 * * *."

This has come to be called the percentage apportionment of damages method. A detailed application of the percentage apportionment approach is found in Boody v. United States, 706 F.Supp. 1458 (D.Kan.1989). See also Mays v. United States, 608 F.Supp. 1476 (D.Colo.1985).

5.   Another judicial approach to these calculations is to treat the loss of a chance as a wrong separate from wrongful death, and allow the jury to set a dollar amount based on all the evidence, without mechanically applying a percentage to a total damage award. See Smith v. State of Louisiana, 676 So.2d 543 (1996), where the court held that

> * * * the method we adopt today in this decision, is for the factfinder—judge or jury—to focus on the chance of survival lost on account of malpractice as a distinct compensable injury and to value the lost chance as a lump sum award based on all the evidence in the record, as is done for any other item of general damages.

A third approach is simply to recognize the full survival or wrongful death damages, without regard to the lost chance of survival.

6.   Can a person recover for the loss of a chance if a physician negligently fails to diagnose AIDS or improperly performs the tests for the HIV virus? In Morton v. Mutchnick, 904 S.W.2d 14 (Mo.App.1995), the court held that if doctors negligently fail to diagnose AIDS, the doctrine does not apply. Their reasoning was that with AIDS, death is inevitable, so that a decedent does not suffer "loss of life, but rather, a shortening of life." Isn't death inevitable for everyone? Why would the court carve out AIDS as a special case? Given new drug therapies for AIDS, life expectancy has increased substantially.

7.   One author has described the "loss of a chance" doctrine as one of the "ethereal" torts. See Nancy Levit, Ethereal Torts, 61 Geo. Wash. L. Rev. 136 (1992), arguing that such torts should be taken seriously: "The individual expectancy, dignity, and autonomy interests that ethereal torts protect are intrinsically valuable." Other useful articles discussing the "loss of a chance" problem include: Joseph King, Causation, Valuation and Chance in Personal Injury Torts Involving Preexisting Conditions and Future Consequences, 90 Yale L.J. 1353 (1981); Darrell L. Keith, Loss of Chance: A Modern Proportional Approach to Damages in Texas, 44 Baylor L. Rev. 759 (1992); Lisa Perrochet, Sandra J. Smith and Ugo Colella, Lost Chance Recovery and the Folly of Expanding Medical Malpractice Liability, 27 Tort & Ins. L.J. 615 (1992) (50–state survey of the doctrine's acceptance or rejection in the courts; the authors attack the doctrine because it may have "an adverse impact on the cost and quality of health care.")

Problem: The Patient's Choice?

Jane Rogers was a fair complected woman in her early thirties. She had worked every summer during high school and college as a lifeguard at the beach. While she was in graduate school, one of her sisters was diagnosed as having melanoma, a deadly cancer that is often fatal if not detected and treated early. Melanoma is more prevalent in people who have fair complexions, and prolonged exposure to the sun over time, particularly severe sun burns, are a risk factor for the cancer.

Ms. Roger's sister died. The family physician, Dr. James, told the family members that they should all get a thorough physical to check for signs of skin tumors that might be precancerous. Ms. Rogers went to the University Student Clinic and requested a physical examination. She explained why she was worried. Dr. Gillespie, an older physician who had retired from active practice and now helped out part-time at the Clinic, examined her. He observed a nodule on her upper back, but incorrectly diagnosed it as a birthmark. He told her not to worry. She continued her lifeguarding and water safety instruction activities during the summer, to pay for her graduate education.

At a party one Friday night, Ms. Rogers met a young physician who was a resident at the University hospital. She was wearing a shoulderless dress, and the resident, Dr. Wunch, noted a mole on her shoulder. He recognized it as a melanoma. He pointed it out to her, and told her that she really ought to get it checked. He gave her his card, with his phone number, and said he would be glad to set her up with an appointment with a good cancer specialist at the hospital. Ms. Rogers called, made an appointment, and filled out the forms required by the University Hospital, but then missed her appointment. She never went back.

A year later, during a routine physical as part of an employment application, the examining physician found several large growths on Ms. Roger's back. She was diagnosed as having melanoma, which had spread into her blood and had metastasized into her lymph nodes. She was dead within a year.

What problems do you see with the suit by her estate against the available defendants?

B.　INCREASED RISKS AND FEAR OF THE FUTURE

PETRIELLO v. KALMAN

Supreme Court of Connecticut, 1990.
215 Conn. 377, 576 A.2d 474.

[The court considered two issues on appeal. First, plaintiff alleged that the defendant hospital had a duty to ensure that the plaintiff had given her informed consent to surgery before she was medicated. The court held no such duty existed. Second, the defendant physician contended that the plaintiff could not be rewarded damages for increased risk of future injury.]

SHEA, ASSOC. J.

* * *

The jury could reasonably have found the following facts from the evidence. On April 13, 1984, the plaintiff, who was sixteen weeks pregnant, was seen by the defendant Kalman regarding her complaints of low back pain and vaginal bleeding. Kalman, a specialist in obstetrics,[1] had been treating the plaintiff throughout her pregnancy. As a result of his examination, Kalman diagnosed a possible missed abortion or threatened abortion and, therefore, admitted the plaintiff to the Griffin Hospital later that evening. On the basis of his belief that the plaintiff's child had died, an ultrasound examination was performed the next morning. This test revealed that the child had in fact died in utero. Kalman was advised of the ultrasound results and he then telephoned the plaintiff, who remained at the hospital, informing her that the results of the test indicated fetal death and that he intended to perform, later that afternoon, a surgical procedure known as a dilatation and curettage to remove the fetus from the plaintiff's womb.

* * *

1.　The defendant was not employed by the hospital, but, rather, was an independent phy-　sician possessing privileges at the hospital.

That afternoon, during the procedure to remove the fetus, Kalman, utilizing a suction device, perforated the plaintiff's uterus and drew portions of her small intestine through the perforation, through her uterus and into her vagina. The plaintiff's expert, Phillip Sullivan, an obstetrician, testified that Kalman had used excessive force in the operation of the suction device and that the perforation had resulted from a deviation from the prevailing standard of care. Kalman, in an attempt to repair the damage to the uterine wall, made a transverse incision on the plaintiff's abdomen and requested the assistance of Jose Flores, a general surgeon. Because he could not adequately explore the plaintiff's abdomen, Flores made another incision perpendicular to the one made by the defendant. Flores repaired the injury to the plaintiff's intestine by means of a bowel resection, removing approximately one foot of the intestine and connecting the two ends of the remaining intestine.

Flores, testifying for the plaintiff, stated that, as a result of the bowel resection, adhesions had more probably than not formed in the plaintiff's abdomen. He also testified that the plaintiff faces an increased risk of future bowel obstruction as a result of these adhesions, but that he thought the risk was remote. Flores stated that, in his experience, adhesions were a prominent cause of small bowel obstruction and that he had advised the plaintiff, after the surgery, that adhesions would form in her abdomen and that they could result in a future bowel obstruction. The plaintiff testified that she was also advised of this increased risk of future bowel obstruction by Flores' partner, who was also a physician. The plaintiff's expert, Sullivan, also testified that the plaintiff was subject to an increased risk of future bowel obstruction and that, based on literature he had consulted, she had an 8 to 16 percent chance of developing such an obstruction.

The plaintiff brought her revised complaint in two counts, alleging that Kalman was negligent in that he: (1) performed the dilatation and curettage without first attempting other nonsurgical methods; (2) perforated the plaintiff's uterus during the surgical procedure; (3) suctioned out portions of the plaintiff's small intestine during the surgical procedure; and (4) made an improper incision in the plaintiff's abdomen during his attempt to repair the plaintiff's small intestine. * * *

I

* * *

II

In his appeal, the defendant claims that the trial court erred by: (1) allowing expert testimony concerning the plaintiff's increased risk of a bowel obstruction; (2) charging the jury that the plaintiff could be compensated for her fear that such an obstruction will occur; and (3) charging the jury that the plaintiff could be compensated for the increased risk that she will suffer a future bowel obstruction. We conclude that the expert testimony was admissible and that the court correctly instructed the jury.

A

The defendant claims that the plaintiff should not have been permitted to present any testimony regarding her increased susceptibility to a future bowel obstruction resulting from the defendant's actions. * * * During a hearing conducted as a result of the defendant's motion in limine, the plaintiff argued that the evidence concerning her increased risk of bowel obstruction was admissible for three reasons: (1) as evidence of her fear of future disability; (2) as evidence that her fear was rational; and (3) as evidence of a presently compensable injury. We conclude that the evidence was admissible for all three purposes.

The defendant has chosen to ignore the fact that the plaintiff, in her revised complaint, alleged that as a result of the defendant's actions she "experienced extreme emotional distress." At trial, she sought to prove that her emotional distress was caused, at least in part, by her fear of suffering an obstruction of her bowel at some later date and that she should be compensated for that fear. We have previously held that evidence concerning an increased risk of injury, although insufficient to justify an award of damages based upon the occurrence of that injury in the future, may, nevertheless, be presented to the jury as evidence of emotional distress. * * * [T]he jury was entitled, in this case, to hear testimony that the plaintiff had been informed of the increased risk of future bowel obstruction, as well as testimony regarding any anxiety this information produced in the plaintiff's mind.

The expert testimony, regarding the plaintiff's increased risk of suffering a future bowel obstruction, was also admissible on the issue of whether the plaintiff's anxiety was rationally based. Although "[s]ome courts have permitted recovery where there is not even a possibility that the feared disability will develop * * * [m]ore often there is a requirement that the plaintiff's anxiety have some reasonable basis." D. Faulkner & K. Woods, "Fear of Future Disability—An Element of Damages in a Personal Injury Action," 7 W.New Eng.L.Rev. 865, 877–78 (1985). [ ] Thus, the evidence objected to by the defendant was admissible to show that the plaintiff's anxiety regarding the possibility of a future bowel obstruction was both subjectively held and objectively reasonable.

Finally, given that we resolve the question of the compensability of an increased risk of future injury in favor of the plaintiff, the expert testimony, regarding the extent of that risk in this case, was also admissible for the purpose of showing how likely it was that the plaintiff would experience a bowel obstruction at some later date.

B

The defendant also claims that, even if the expert testimony was admissible, the court erred in allowing the jury to award the plaintiff compensation for her fear of a future bowel obstruction, since the evidence established that there was only a possibility that the plaintiff would develop a bowel obstruction and this possibility was too speculative to support the inclusion in the verdict of damages for such a fear. The defendant argues that "the Plaintiff's [chance] of incurring a bowel obstruction is 'so remote' that it is not a proper element of damages." We conclude that the evidence presented was sufficient to establish a reasonable basis for the plaintiff's fear that she will suffer from a future bowel obstruction and, therefore, was also sufficient to support compensation for that fear. Although one of the plaintiff's expert witnesses, Flores, testified that there was a "very remote" chance that such a blockage would occur, the testimony of another expert, Sullivan, presented to the jury the results of research conducted by him which indicated that, according to two studies he consulted, there was between an 8 and 16 percent chance that the plaintiff would suffer a future bowel obstruction as a result of the bowel resection necessitated by the defendant's actions. Thus, even if Flore's [sic] testimony was insufficient to establish a reasonable ground for the plaintiff's anxiety, we conclude that the jury could have found a sufficient basis in the opinion rendered by Sullivan. [ ] We conclude, therefore, that the court correctly instructed the jury that it might award the plaintiff damages for her fear of the increased risk that she will someday suffer from a bowel obstruction.

C

The defendant's principal claim on appeal is that the court erred by instructing the jury that the plaintiff could be awarded compensation for the increased risk that the defendant's negligence would cause her to experience a bowel obstruction at some future date. The defendant excepted to this instruction at trial upon the ground that the "intestinal blockage [was] purely speculation" and had not been shown to be "reasonably probable." He raises essentially the same claim on appeal.

The defendant contends that the evidence in this case established no reasonable probability that the plaintiff would suffer a bowel obstruction at some future date, and, therefore, the trial court incorrectly instructed the jury that the plaintiff should be compensated for whatever risk there was of some future injury. The jury heard expert testimony that the risk of the plaintiff suffering a future bowel obstruction was somewhere between 8 and 16 percent. There is no question that such a degree of probability of the occurrence of future injury would not support an award of damages to the same extent as if that injury had in fact occurred. In *Healy v. White,* supra, at 444, 378 A.2d 540, we reasoned that in order to be awarded full compensation for an injury that has not yet manifested itself, a plaintiff must show that there exists a reasonable probability that the injury will in fact occur. * * *

In *Healy,* we affirmed our adherence to the prevailing all or nothing standard for compensating those who have either suffered present harm and seek compensation as if the harm will be permanent, or have suffered present harm and seek compensation for possible future consequences of that harm. * * * By denying any compensation unless a plaintiff proves that a future consequence is more likely to occur than not, courts have created a system in which a significant number of persons receive compensation for future consequences that never occur and, conversely, a significant number of persons receive no compensation at all for consequences that later ensue from risks not rising to the level of probability. This system is inconsistent with the goal of compensating tort victims fairly for all the consequences of the injuries they have sustained, while avoiding, so far as possible, windfall awards for consequences that never happen.

In seeking to enforce their right to individualized compensation, plaintiffs in negligence cases are confronted by the requirements that they must claim all applicable damages in a single cause of action; [ ] and must bring their actions no "more than three years from the date of the act or omission complained of." General Statutes § 52–584. Under these circumstances, no recovery may be had for future consequences of an injury when the evidence at trial does not satisfy the more probable than not criterion approved in *Healy*, despite a substantial risk of such consequences. Conversely, a defendant cannot seek reimbursement from a plaintiff who may have recovered for a future consequence, which appeared likely at the time of trial, on the ground that subsequent events have made that consequence remote or impossible. Our legal system provides no opportunity for a second look at a damage award so that it may be revised with the benefit of hindsight. * * *

If the plaintiff in this case had claimed that she was entitled to compensation to the extent that a future bowel obstruction was a certainty, she would have been foreclosed from such compensation solely on the basis of her experts' testimony that the likelihood of the occurrence of a bowel obstruction was either very remote or only 8 to 16 percent probable. Her claim, however, was for compensation for the increased risk that she would suffer such an obstruction sometime in the future. If this increased risk was more likely than not the result of the bowel resection necessitated by the defendant's actions, we conclude that there is no legitimate reason why she should not receive present compensation based upon the likelihood of the risk becoming a reality. When viewed in this manner, the plaintiff was attempting merely to establish the extent of her present injuries. She should not be burdened with proving that the occurrence of a future event is more likely than not, when it is a present risk, rather than a future event for which she claims damages. In our judgment, it was fairer to instruct the jury to compensate the plaintiff for the increased risk of a bowel obstruction based upon the likelihood of its occurrence rather than to ignore that risk entirely. The medical evidence in this case concerning the probability of such a future consequence provided a sufficient basis for estimating that likelihood and compensating the plaintiff for it.

This view is consistent with the Second Restatement of the Law of Torts, which states, in § 912, that "[o]ne to whom another has tortiously caused harm is entitled to compensatory damages for the harm if, but only if, he establishes by proof the extent of the harm and the amount of money representing adequate compensation with as much certainty as the nature of the tort and the circumstances permit." Damages for the future consequences of an injury can never be forecast with certainty. With respect to awards for permanent injuries, actuarial tables of average life expectancy are commonly used to assist the trier in measuring the loss a plaintiff is likely to sustain from the future effects of an injury. Such statistical evidence does, of course, satisfy the more likely than not standard as to the duration of a permanent injury. Similar evidence, based upon medical statistics of the average incidence of a particular future consequence from an injury, such as that produced by the plaintiff in this case, may be said to establish with the same degree of certitude the likelihood of the occurrence of the future harm to which a tort victim is exposed as a result of a present injury. Such evidence provides an adequate basis for measuring damages for the risk to which the victim has been exposed because of a wrongful act.

The probability percentage for the occurrence of a particular harm, the risk of which has been created by the tortfeasor, can be applied to the damages that would be justified if that harm should be realized. We regard this system of compensation as preferable to our present practice of denying any recovery for substantial risks of future harm not satisfying the more likely than not standard. We also believe that such a system is fairer to a defendant, who should be required to pay damages for a future loss based upon the statistical probability that such a loss will be sustained rather than upon the assumption that the loss is a certainty because it is more likely than not. We hold, therefore, that in a tort action, a plaintiff who has established a breach of duty that was a substantial factor in causing a present injury which has resulted in an increased risk of future harm is entitled to compensation to the extent that the future harm is likely to occur. [ ]

Applying this holding to the facts of this case, we conclude that the trial court correctly instructed the jury that the plaintiff could be awarded compensation for the increased likelihood that she will suffer a bowel obstruction some time in the future. The court's instruction was fully in accord with our holding today. * * *

The judgment of the trial court is affirmed.

* * *

Notes and Questions

1. *Petriello* allows a plaintiff to recover for the risk of future harm, and for the fear that such a risk will materialize. Is this double recovery? *Herskovits* and other "loss of a chance" cases involve missed diagnoses, usually in oncology situations. *Petriello* involves a botched procedure, leaving the plaintiff at an enhanced risk of future injury. What kind of evidence may the plaintiff produce as to the fear of future harm? How do *Petriello* and *Herskovits* differ?

2. Recovery for fear of future harm, based on increased risk, is relatively rare in American case law. See Ferrara v. Galluchio, 5 N.Y.2d 16, 176 N.Y.S.2d 996, 152 N.E.2d 249 (1958); Howard v. Mt. Sinai Hospital, Inc., 63 Wis.2d 515, 217 N.W.2d 383 (1974).

C. PUNITIVE DAMAGES

In the normal malpractice case, damages typically include special damages, such as costs of treating a condition and loss of earning capacity; and general damages, primarily pain and suffering. Punitive damages are extremely rare. See Chapter 5, Section III.D. for a discussion of such punitive damages in informed consent cases. Impatience and inattention to a patient's condition can however lead to punitive damage awards in egregious cases. In Dempsey v. Phelps, 700 So.2d 1340 (Ala.1997), the parents of a two year old child sued, after the child was treated for a clubfoot condition caused by spina bifida and got an infection after surgery, ultimately losing his big toe. The central issue was whether the physician's conduct rose to the level of wantonness, meriting punitive damages. After the surgery, Dr. Dempsey told the mother to bring the boy back a month later, even though postoperative wound healing infections are a common complication that need to be monitored more frequently. The mother testified that "on the top of the foot all the toes were purple and blue and red on the side some. And the top of the foot had kind of a mushy looking place on it that it was draining. It had some drainage on it there and it was—a little black around the edges and it was red. It was just 'real inflamed looking' ". The boy also had diarrhea and fever and wouldn't eat. Dr. Dempsey's response to Mrs. Phelps was that these were common conditions, nothing to worry about, and he did nothing for the fever or anything else. She came back the next day and Dr. Dempsey wouldn't even see the boy at first, and then he said it was just cast blisters, even though, in the mother's words, "[i]t was starting to smell." She came back again the next day and he was very annoyed, and failed to take the boy's temperature, check his lungs or do anything else. The jury awarded $125,000 punitive damage award, on top of other damages, in light of Dr. Dempsey's failures to properly follow-up the child's care.

Problem: The Toxic Dentist

You have been approached by the family of a young woman, Kim Brennan, to explore the possibilities of a tort suit. Kim, a twenty-one year old college student, recently underwent oral surgery and had several wisdom teeth extracted by Dr. James, a local oral surgeon.

Kim has recently learned that Dr. James is now hospitalized with AIDS. She has been tested for the HIV virus and her last test was negative. She has been reading up on AIDS, however, and learned that a small percentage of individuals can carry the HIV virus and not seroconvert (become HIV positive) for an extended period of time, so that they will not test positive (95% of exposed individuals will seroconvert within six months after exposure). She is terrified of entering into romantic relationships now and feels constantly anxious.

Can Kim sue Dr. James? What theories of recovery are possible? Is there any merit to such a suit?

Chapter 5

THE PROFESSIONAL–PATIENT RELATIONSHIP

INTRODUCTION

Health care today is delivered within institutions, whether hospitals, ambulatory care clinics, or offices of managed care organizations, but the individual physician still sees the patient, diagnoses the problem, and prescribes the treatment. Professional liability, discussed in Chapter 4, supra, focuses upon a breach of duty of care owed by the physician to a particular patient. The threshold question is whether the doctor had a relationship with the patient sufficient to create a duty of care.

A physician-patient relationship is usually a prerequisite to a professional malpractice suit against a doctor. When for example a doctor employed by an insurance company examines an individual for the purpose of qualifying him for insurance coverage, most courts considering the issue have held that a doctor owes no duty to the individual to treat or to disclose problems discovered during the examination. See Ervin v. American Guardian Life Assur., 376 Pa.Super. 132, 545 A.2d 354 (1988) (no duty owed by doctor employed by an insurance company to the plaintiff, where doctor examined the plaintiff for purposes of insurance and failed to discover or disclose his cardiac abnormalities to him; plaintiff died a month after the examination from his heart condition); Ney v. Axelrod, 723 A.2d 719 (Pa.Super.1999). But see Ranier v. Frieman, 294 N.J.Super. 182, 682 A.2d 1220 (1996)(social security claimant sued ophthalmologist retained by the government to examine claimant, who failed to diagnose a brain tumor; the court held that the physician had a duty to make a professionally reasonable and competent diagnosis, in spite of the lack of privity of contract); Smith v. Welch, 265 Kan. 868, 967 P.2d 727 (Kan.1998)(Where a physician is retained to provide an expert medical opinion by performing a physical examination, he has a duty to use reasonable and ordinary care in the examination).

Workplace examinations of employees may give rise to a physician-patient relationship. See Green v. Walker, 910 F.2d 291 (5th Cir.1990) (physician-patient relationship should include employees examined by a company physician for employment purposes; "[t]his relationship imposes upon the examining physician a duty to conduct the requested tests and diagnose the results thereof, exercising the level of care consistent with the doctor's professional training and expertise, and to take reasonable steps to make information available timely to the examinee of any findings that pose an imminent danger to the examinee's physical or mental well-being.'')

The threshold duty continues to evolve in the setting of independent or workplace physician examinations of employees or potential insureds. In Webb v. T.D., 287 Mont. 68, 951 P.2d 1008 (Mont.1997), the court articulated a compound duty on physicians retained by third parties to do independent medical examinations:

1. to exercise ordinary care to discover those conditions which pose an imminent danger to the examinee's physical or mental well-being and take reasonable steps to communicate to the examinee the presence of any such condition;

2. to exercise ordinary care to assure that when he or she advises an examinee about her condition following an independent examination, the advice comports with the standard of care for the health care provider's profession.

I. THE CONTRACT BETWEEN PATIENT AND PHYSICIAN

A. EXPRESS AND IMPLIED CONTRACT

DINGLE v. BELIN

Court of Appeals of Maryland, 2000.
358 Md. 354, 749 A.2d 157.

The issue before us was characterized by the Court of Special Appeals in this case as one of "ghost surgery." The more precise question is whether a surgeon who is employed by a patient to perform certain surgery and who agrees, as part of that employment, to do the actual cutting, leaving to assisting residents a subordinate role, may be held liable for breach of contract, distinct from negligence in the performance of the surgery or negligence associated with the failure to obtain informed consent from the patient, if the surgeon attends and participates in the surgery but permits a resident to do that cutting.

* * *

BACKGROUND

On June 29, 1993, Ms. Belin, employed petitioner, Lenox Dingle, a general surgeon with operating privileges at Mercy Hospital in Baltimore, to perform a laparoscopic cholecystectomy—the removal of her gall bladder through a small incision in her abdomen. In brief, the surgery involves making the incision and inserting at least three ports into the abdomen. Carbon dioxide is introduced into the abdomen to expand the area and make it more visible. A camera, inserted through one of the ports, displays the interior on two high-definition television monitors. Observing the monitor, one physician, through another port, retracts the organs and tissues in order to isolate the gall bladder and the structures that connect it to other organs and tissues, and a second physician, also observing the monitor, cuts and clips those connecting structures and removes the gall bladder through a port.

The surgery occurred at Mercy on July 2. Dr. Dingle was assisted by a medical student and by a resident, Dr. Magnuson, who was just beginning her fourth year of residency training. The student was responsible for operating the camera, which was done properly. Dr. Dingle did the retractions, exposing the field. Dr. Magnuson dissected the gall bladder and removed it. She and Dr. Dingle regarded the surgery as routine, without incident. There was, however, a problem. One of the connecting structures that needed to be dissected was the cystic duct, which runs from the gall bladder to the common bile duct. The common bile duct runs from the liver to the intestines. Instead of dissecting the cystic duct, Dr. Magnuson dissected and clipped the common bile duct, which resulted in the drainage of bile into Ms. Belin's abdomen. That, in turn, led to a great deal of pain and discomfort and to the need for extensive corrective surgery at Johns Hopkins Hospital.

In November, 1996, after having waived arbitration pursuant to Maryland Code, § 3–2A–06(b) of the Courts and Judicial Proceedings Article, respondent filed suit against Dr. Dingle, Dr. Magnuson, and Mercy Hospital in the Circuit Court for Baltimore City. The amended complaint now before us contained four counts—negligence based on the lack of informed consent, battery, negligence in the performance of the surgery, and breach of contract. Aside from the negligence alleged as part of the lack of informed consent, Dr. Dingle was not charged with any separate negligence in delegating duties or responsibilities to Dr. Magnuson. The claim of general negligence focused solely on the actual conduct of the surgery.

* * *

The claims for breach of contract and lack of informed consent were both based on the assertion that, when Ms. Belin employed Dr. Dingle, she insisted, and he agreed, that, although he would be assisted in the surgery by one or more residents, he would do the actual cutting and removal of the gall bladder. In Count One—lack of informed consent—she alleged that "[b]ecause Belin was aware that Mercy was a university affiliated hospital and often used for teaching inexperienced residents in various surgical techniques, Belin requested and received assurances from Dingle that he would perform the surgical procedure in the cholecystectomy and only use a resident to assist him as was absolutely necessary." The thrust of Count One was the assertion that, without Belin's knowledge or consent, the resident Magnuson "played a very active role in the surgery" and "did the cutting, clamping and stapling that should have been performed by [Dingle]" and that, by failing to inform Belin of the scope of responsibilities that would be performed by Magnuson, Dingle and Magnuson "breached their duty to secure the fully informed consent of Belin prior to commencing operating upon her." Had she been aware of the active role to be played by Magnuson, Belin asserted, she would not have consented to having the surgery performed at Mercy or by Drs. Dingle and Magnuson. For that breach of duty, Ms. Belin sought compensation for all injuries and losses, past, present, and future, sustained by her, all of which, she claimed, were caused by the defendants' negligence in failing to obtain her informed consent.

Count Four, alleging the breach of contract, incorporated all of the allegations stated in the other counts. It added that Dingle had entered into an oral contract with Belin under which he had agreed "that he would do the identification of the anatomy and the cutting and clipping required during the [surgery] and not a resident or other assistant," and that, in consideration of that agreement, she agreed to allow Dingle to perform the surgery. Dingle breached that contract, she averred, by permitting Dr. Magnuson to perform the cutting and clipping of the gall bladder and related structures. The same measure of damages was asserted—"compensation for all injuries, damages and losses, past, present and future, which she has sustained, is sustaining and will sustain in the future, all of which were caused by the breach of contract."

It was undisputed that Drs. Dingle and Magnuson both participated in the surgery, that Dr. Dingle did the necessary retractions, and that Dr. Magnuson performed the dissections and removed the gall bladder. It was also undisputed that Ms. Belin had no contact whatever with Dr. Magnuson before the surgery, although she was aware that one or more residents would be assisting Dr. Dingle.

The evidence regarding the alleged contract and what Dr. Dingle said and agreed to do was in sharp dispute. Ms. Belin testified that she told Dingle "that I wanted him to be the one that was going to cut me and identify the gall bladder and take it out," that he advised her that he could not do the surgery by himself, and that she said she understood "but if you have a resident in there, I just want that person to maybe suture me up." She added, "I want you to be the one to do my surgery. And he agreed." Ms. Belin informed the jury that, as a surgical technician who worked at Mercy, she was aware that it was a teaching hospital and that surgeons often allowed residents to play a major role in surgery, and she did not want her surgery to be used for training purposes.

The written consent that Ms. Belin signed authorized Dr. Dingle "and/or such assistants as may be selected and supervised by him" to perform the laparoscopic cholecystectomy. The form has a place for "Special remarks or comments by patient," which was left blank. There was no indication on the written consent form, in other words, of any allocation between Dr. Dingle and the assistants selected and supervised by him as to what, precisely, each was to do during the surgery. Dr. Dingle denied that he ever had the conversation testified to by Ms. Belin and stated that he never would have agreed to the conditions she alleged. Although at one point he said that, to satisfy those conditions, the surgery would have to have been performed at another hospital, Dr. Dingle indicated that, if faced with that demand, he would have offered Ms. Belin only two options—"allow me to do what I thought was best unrestricted, or to get another surgeon."

The evidence was essentially undisputed that the particular surgery requires three medical participants—one to operate the camera, one to do the necessary retractions, and one to do the dissection and removal. It would thus not have been possible for Dr. Dingle to do both the retraction and the dissection and removal, as Ms. Belin said he agreed to do. Dr. Dingle and the defense experts opined that the retraction and exposure of the field was often the more difficult and demanding aspect of this kind of laparoscopic surgery.

One of Dr. Dingle's expert witnesses, Dr. Bailey, testified that in most instances the attending surgeon does the retracting and the resident does the dissecting and clipping. The reason, he said, was that the retraction requires a high hand-to-eye skill level, to be able to manipulate and maneuver the gall bladder and keep it properly exposed. Ms. Belin's expert witness, Dr. Goldstone, agreed that it would not breach the standard of care for the resident to do the cutting and clipping and the attending surgeon to do the retracting, "[p]rovided there isn't some previous agreement that this would not occur."

All of the experts agreed that, when one surgeon does the retraction and another does the clipping and cutting, both consult and agree on where the clips are to be put and where the cuts are to be made. They both have the benefit of the television monitors. Dr. Goldstone testified that "not one clip is applied until you both agree where it is to be put" and "not one cut is made with the scissors until you both agree that the cut is being made in the proper place." The evidence indicated that that procedure was followed in Ms. Belin's case—that Drs. Dingle and Magnuson consulted and agreed on where the cuts were to be made and the clips applied.

* * *

In its instructions to the jury, the court essentially merged the two claims of negligence on the part of Dr. Dingle—negligence in the performance of the surgery and negligence in failing to obtain an informed consent. It informed the jury that a health care provider is negligent if the provider "does not use that degree of care and skill which a reasonably competent health care provider engaged in a similar practice and acting in similar circumstances would use" or, "[p]ut another way, a health care provider is negligent if he or she breached or deviated from the applicable standard of care." The court immediately followed that instruction with the statements that "[a] surgeon must obtain consent from the patient to perform a surgery" and "[t]o obtain the required consent, the surgeon must explain the surgery to the patient and warn of all material risks or dangers in the surgery." A material risk, the court continued, "is one which a physician knows or ought to know would be significant to a reasonable person in the patient's position in deciding whether or not to submit to a particular medical treatment or procedure." The surgeon is negligent, it added, "if the surgeon fails to disclose to the patient all the material information, risks, and warnings."

* * *

We granted certiorari principally to consider whether a physician who, as part of his or her contractual undertaking with a patient, agrees to an allocation of tasks between the physician and other physicians, may be liable for breach of contract if that agreement is violated.

DISCUSSION

* * *

Sorting Out Causes of Action

Ms. Belin urges that there is a proper cause of action for breach of contract when a physician promises to fulfill a particular surgical function but fails to do so, resulting in harm, and that that action is independent of any negligence on anyone's part. Her point is that Dr. Magnuson made a mistake in cutting and clipping the common bile duct which, even if not negligent, might not have been made had the cutting and clipping been done by Dr. Dingle, a more experienced surgeon. Dr. Dingle contends that Maryland should not recognize, under any theory, "a claim for 'ghost surgery' against a physician arising out of an alleged agreement regarding the role a resident is to play during a surgical procedure." At the very least, he contends, such a claim should not be permitted as part of an action for lack of informed consent or breach of contract. Creating a duty to disclose a resident's precise role, he warns, "would permit patients to choreograph how an operation is to be performed negating all possibility of informed medical judgment occurring during the operation."

The courts, in proper cases, have recognized a number of different causes of action that might lie against a health care provider when a medical procedure or course of therapy produces unintended and harmful results or fails to produce the positive results reasonably anticipated by the patient. These actions, often bearing the common appellation of "malpractice," differ in their underlying theory, in some of the elements that must be proved, and in the kind of damages that may be recovered. Most are tort-based, sounding either in battery or in negligence of one kind or another, and, occasionally, in misrepresentation or fraud; some are contract-based. When they are pursued either alternatively or in combination, care must be taken to keep the actions separate and not to allow the theories, elements, and recoverable damages to become improperly intertwined.

We have long recognized, as have most courts, that, except in those unusual circumstances when a doctor acts gratuitously or in an emergency situation, recovery for malpractice "is allowed only where there is a relationship of doctor and patient as a result of a contract, express or implied, that the doctor will treat the patient with proper professional skill and the patient will pay for such treatment, and there has been a breach of professional duty to the patient." Hoover v. Williamson, 236 Md. 250, 253, 203 A.2d 861, 862 (1964). The relationship that spawns the malpractice claim is thus ordinarily a contractual one. Largely because of the greater facility offered by tort-based actions for recovering damages for non-economic loss—predominantly pain, suffering, and disfigurement—malpractice actions have traditionally been tort-based, the tort arising from the underlying contractual relationship. [ ]

The traditional action has been for negligence in the performance (or non-performance) of a course of therapy or a medical procedure. [ ] The negligence consists of the breach of the duty that a physician has "to use that degree of care and skill which is expected of a reasonably competent practitioner in the same class to which [the physician] belongs, acting in the same or similar circumstances." Shilkret v. Annapolis Emergency Hosp., 276 Md. 187, 200, 349 A.2d 245, 252 (1975). To recover in such an action, the plaintiff must show that the doctor's conduct—the care given or withheld by the doctor—was not in accordance with the standards of practice among members of the same health care profession with similar training and experience situated in the same or similar communities at the time of the act (or omission) giving rise to the cause of action. [ ] That action necessarily focuses on the manner in which the physician diagnosed and treated the patient's medical problem and, except as it may bear on other issues, such as contributory negligence, causation, or damages, not so much on what was told to the patient or what the patient's expectations may have been.

* * *

Unlike the traditional action of negligence, a claim for lack of informed consent focuses not on the level of skill exercised in the performance of the procedure itself but on the adequacy of the explanation given by the physician in obtaining the patient's consent. * * *

Although, as in Sard v. Hardy, claims based on lack of informed consent usually involve allegations that the physician failed to make adequate disclosure of a material risk or collateral effect of the contemplated procedure or of an available alternative not carrying that risk or effect, the duty is not so limited. Risks, benefits, collateral effects, and alternatives normally must be disclosed routinely, but other considerations, at least if raised by the patient, may also need to be discussed and resolved. See Aaron D. Twerski & Neil B. Cohen, The Second Revolution in Informed Consent: Comparing Physicians to Each Other, 94 NW. U.L.REV. 1 (1999); Johnson v. Kokemoor, 199 Wis.2d 615, 545 N.W.2d 495 (1996). One of those considerations, in an expanding era of more complex medical procedures, group practices, and collaborative efforts among health care providers, may be who, precisely, will be conducting or superintending the procedure or therapy. This may be especially important with respect to surgical procedures, which usually involve collaboration between the chosen surgeon and other medical professionals who may be unknown to the patient. The physician, as Dr. Dingle indicated was the case here, may be unwilling to accept limitations on the actual performance of the surgery, but, if the identity of the persons who will be performing aspects of the surgery is important to the patient, the matter must be discussed and resolved.

Despite Dr. Dingle's protestation to the contrary, a physician who agrees to a specific allocation of responsibility or a specific limitation on his or her discretion in order to obtain the consent of the patient to the procedure and then, absent some emergency or other good cause, proceeds in contravention of that allocation or limitation has not obtained the informed consent of the patient. We do not see this result as having the pernicious effects suggested by Dr. Dingle, of permitting patients to "choreograph" surgery and unduly restrict the flexibility that the surgeon must retain. Precisely as Dr. Dingle stated was the case here, the surgeon does not have to agree to any such limitations, and, presumably, few, if any, of them will so agree. The issue is raised only when there is a claim that such an agreement was made and, without good cause, violated.

Notwithstanding the existence of these tort-based actions, courts have universally recognized that, except in emergency or gratuitous situations, the relationship between doctor and patient is a contractual one, either expressly or by implication, and, from that premise, many have held that, as an alternative to tort-based actions, a separate action for breach of the contract may lie when the doctor acts in contravention of a contractual undertaking, at least in some settings. Those actions are often founded either on a breach of warranty theory, alleging a warranty by the physician of a particular result, or on a promise independent of a medical procedure. * * * [ ]

* * *

Actions for breach of contract have been founded on a variety of alleged promises and commitments. Most have alleged a promise to cure, or to cure within a certain period of time, or of some other particular result. [ ] Others * * * have been based on a commitment to do a certain procedure, to deliver a child by means of a Caesarean section. [ ]

We are unaware of any case precisely like this one, where the dispute is over an alleged allocation of specific functions between or among surgeons, all of whom were expressly authorized to participate and perform some role in the procedure. There have, however, been a number of cases in which a patient was informed that Dr. A would do the procedure, consented to Dr. A's performing the procedure, and later learned that the procedure was performed entirely or predominantly by Dr. B, with little or no participation by Dr. A. Liability has been found in those situations, but on different theories. * * *

* * *

[The court discusses the law of other states, and several cases that have allowed a breach of contract claim when a physician has agreed to do a procedure and then does not.]

We draw a number of conclusions from this judicial landscape. Because the doctor-patient relationship is normally a contractual one, it is permissible for the parties, if they choose to do so, to define with some precision the role that the doctor is to play. The parties may well have conflicting interests in that regard—the doctor wanting as much flexibility and discretion as possible and the patient, if choosing the physician because of some special confidence in that physician's particular abilities, desiring that the selected physician oversee and personally perform the most difficult part of the procedure. As noted in footnote 3 above, the medical community itself recognizes the interest that the patient has in the matter and the need for disclosure and agreement if there is likely to be a significant participation by other persons. The lack of a clear understanding prior to the procedure may well engender a later finding that informed consent was not obtained. A violation of an understanding so reached may constitute the lack of informed consent, negligent delegation, and a breach of the contract, not to mention the risk of a claim of misrepresentation or fraud. It would be prudent, of course, for the written consent form presented to the patient either to set forth any special understanding in this regard or note affirmatively that there is no such understanding.

The scenarios in which these claims can arise are too varied to attempt any complete analysis of how they all may relate, one to another. In the context of this case, it will suffice to say that a doctor who partially abandons his or her patient by improperly delegating to others professional tasks that the doctor was engaged personally to do and agreed personally to do may be liable for traditional professional negligence, lack of informed consent, and breach of contract, depending in part on the nature of the consequences that flow from that abandonment.

The problem for Ms. Belin in this case is that the one issue, common and central to both her claim of lack of informed consent and her claim for breach of contract was, in fact, submitted to the jury, which necessarily found against her. There was no question as to how the surgery proceeded—what Dr. Dingle did and what Dr. Magnuson did; nor was there any claim by Ms. Belin that Dr. Dingle failed to advise her of material risks, of collateral consequences, or of alternative therapies. [ ] The only issue, as to both the informed consent and breach of contract claims, was whether Dr. Dingle ever agreed to the allocation of functions claimed by Ms. Belin. As noted, plaintiff's counsel made clear to the jury, in the context of the informed consent claim, that, to render a defendants' verdict, the jury would have to disbelieve Ms. Belin's version of her conversation with Dr. Dingle. It obviously did so. The breach of contract claim asserted by Ms. Belin could not survive in the face of that finding.

JUDGMENT OF COURT OF SPECIAL APPEALS VACATING JUDGMENT OF CIRCUIT COURT ON BREACH OF CONTRACT CLAIM REVERSED; CASE REMANDED TO COURT OF SPECIAL APPEALS WITH INSTRUCTIONS TO AFFIRM JUDGMENT OF CIRCUIT COURT; COSTS IN THIS COURT AND IN COURT OF SPECIAL APPEALS TO BE PAID BY RESPONDENT.

Notes and Questions

1.   The physician-patient relationship can be considered initially as a contractual one. Physicians in private practice may contract for their services as they see fit, and retain substantial control over the extent of their contact with patients. Physicians may limit their specialty, their scope of practice, their geographic area, and the hours and conditions under which they will see patients. They have no obligation to offer services that a patient may require that are outside the physician's competence and training; or services outside the scope of the original physician-patient agreement, where the physician has limited the contract to a type of procedure, to an office visit, or to consultation only. They may transfer responsibility by referring patients to other specialists. They may refuse to enter into a contract with a patient, or to treat patients, even under emergency conditions. Hiser v. Randolph, 126 Ariz. 608, 617 P.2d 774, 776 (1980).

2.   Physicians may also expressly contract with a patient for a specific result. Stewart v. Rudner, 349 Mich. 459, 84 N.W.2d 816, 822–23 (1957) (couple contracted with physician to have wife's child delivered by Caesarian section, as she had had two stillbirths and was worried about normal vaginal delivery; the court held that "a doctor and his patient * * * have the same general liberty to contract with respect to their relationship as other parties entering into consensual relationship with one another, and a breach thereof will give rise to a cause of action."). Courts will sometimes allow parol evidence to fill in the terms of these contracts, where the patient has signed other consent forms. Murray v. University of Penn. Hospital, 340 Pa.Super. 401, 490 A.2d 839 (1985) (court allowed parol evidence to show the existence of an oral agreement to guarantee the prevention of future pregnancies by a tubal ligation).

3.   Once the physician-patient relationship has been created, however, physicians are subject to an obligation of "continuing attention." Ricks v. Budge, 91 Utah 307, 64 P.2d 208 (1937). Termination of the physician-patient relationship, once created, is subject in some jurisdictions to a "continuous treatment" rule to determine when the statute of limitations is tolled. Treatment obligations cease if

the physician can do nothing more for the patient, or ceases to attend the patient. See Jewson v. Mayo Clinic, 691 F.2d 405 (8th Cir.1982).

4. An express written contract is rarely drafted for specific physician-patient interactions. An implied contract is usually the basis of the relationship between a physician and a patient. A physician who talks with a patient by telephone may be held to have an implied contractual obligation to that patient. Bienz v. Central Suffolk Hospital, 163 A.D.2d 269, 557 N.Y.S.2d 139 (2d Dept., 1990). Likewise, a physician, such as a pathologist, who renders services to a patient but has not contracted with him, is nonetheless bound by certain implied contractual obligations. When the physician evaluates information provided by a nurse and makes a medical decision as to a patient's status, a doctor-patient relationship may be established. Wheeler v. Yettie Kersting Memorial Hospital, 866 S.W.2d 32 (Tex. App.1993).

5. When a physician treating a patient consults by telephone or otherwise with another physician, some courts are reluctant to find a doctor-patient relationship created by such a conversation. The concern is that such informal conferences will be deterred by the fear of liability. See Reynolds v. Decatur Memorial Hosp., 277 Ill.App.3d 80, 214 Ill.Dec. 44, 49, 660 N.E.2d 235, 240 (4th Dist.1996) ("It would have a chilling effect upon practice of medicine. It would stifle communication, education and professional association, all to the detriment of the patient.") Others find a duty in such a consultation. See e.g. Diggs v. Arizona Cardiologists, Ltd., 198 Ariz. 198, 8 P.3d 386 (Ariz.App. Div. 1 2000), where a cardiologist informally consulting with a physician about a patient has a duty to that patient, even though no contractual relationship exists.

6. When a patient goes to a doctor's office with a particular problem, he is offering to enter into a contract with the physician. When the physician examines the patient, she accepts the offer and an implied contract is created. The physician is free to reject the offer and send the patient away, relieving herself of any duty to that patient. See, e.g., Childs v. Weis, 440 S.W.2d 104 (Tex.Civ.App.1969). Some courts state as a starting principle that " * * * [a]s a practical matter, health professionals cannot be required to obtain express consent before each touch or test they perform on a patient. Consent may be express or implied; implied consent may be inferred from the patient's action or seeking treatment or some other act manifesting a willingness to submit to a particular course of treatment * * *." Jones v. Malloy, 226 Neb. 559, 412 N.W.2d 837, 841 (Neb. 1987). But see Tisdale v. Pruitt, infra, for judicial difficulties with contextual consent.

7. The apparent voluntariness of the physician-patient relationship and its reciprocity, i.e., a fee for a service, or consideration, make the relationship look like a traditional contract. In other ways, however, the analogy to a contract is limited. First, the terms of the contract are largely fixed in advance of any bargaining, by standard or customary practices that the physician must follow at the risk of liability for malpractice. The exact nature of the work to be done by the physician is usually left vaguely defined at best. The relationship seems closer to quasi-contract, where we impute to both the physician and the patient standard intentions and reasonable expectations. See Robert Goodin, Protecting the Vulnerable 63, 64–65 (1985).

Second, professional ethics impose fiduciary obligations on physicians in a variety of ways, as the cases in Section II reveal. Courts often look outside the parameters of contract law analysis in judging the obligations of a physician to treat a patient. The courts stress that the physician's obligation to his patient, while having its origins in contract, is governed also by fiduciary obligations and other public considerations "inseparable from the nature and exercise of his calling * * *." Norton v. Hamilton, 92 Ga.App. 727, 89 S.E.2d 809, 812 (1955) (doctor withdrew from case at time when wife was in premature labor; while husband searched for a substitute, wife delivered child). See Chatman v. Millis, 257 Ark. 451, 453 517 S.W.2d 504, 505 (1975) (malpractice action requires a doctor-patient relationship, a duty owed from doctor to patients, although "[w]e do not flatly state that a cause for malpractice must be predicated upon a contractual agreement between a doctor * * * and patient * * *."). For a history of this fiduciary duty, see Michelle Oberman, Mothers and Doctors' Orders: Unmasking the Doctor's Fiduciary Role in Maternal–Fetal Conflicts, 94 N.W.Univ. L.Rev. 451 (2000).

Third, professionals are constrained in their ability to withdraw from their contracts by judicial caselaw defining patient abandonment. A doctor who withdraws from the physician-patient relationship before a cure is achieved or the patient is transferred to the care of another may be liable for abandonment. To escape liability, the physician must give the patient time to find alternative care. See Norton v. Hamilton, 92 Ga.App. 727, 89 S.E.2d 809 (1955). Implied abandonment is a negligence-based theory judged by the overall conduct of the physician. See Meiselman v. Crown Heights Hosp., 285 N.Y. 389, 34 N.E.2d 367 (1941); Ascher v. Gutierrez, 533 F.2d 1235 (D.C.Cir.1976).

B. PHYSICIANS IN INSTITUTIONS

Physicians who practice in institutions must provide health care within the limits of the health plan coverage or their employment contracts with the institution. In this case, the contact between the physician and the patient is preceded by an express contract spelling out the details of the relationship. Physicians who are members of a health maintenance organization or a health plan have a duty to treat plan members as a result of their contractual obligation to the HMO. In these situations, the express contract is between the physician and the health plan, and the subscriber and the plan, with an implied contract between the subscriber and the treating physician.

HAND v. TAVERA

Court of Appeal of Texas, San Antonio, 1993.
864 S.W.2d 678.

Opinion

In this medical malpractice case, plaintiff Lewis Hand appeals from a take-nothing summary judgment rendered on the sole ground that defendant Dr. Robert Tavera owed him no duty because the two never had a physician-patient relationship. We conclude that Tavera did not refute the existence of a physician-patient relationship as a matter of law, and therefore we reverse and remand for further proceedings.

* * * Hand went to the Humana Hospital (Village Oaks) emergency room complaining of a three-day headache. The emergency-room physician (Dr. Boyle) was told that Hand had a personal history of high blood pressure and that his father had died of an aneurism. Boyle observed that Hand's symptoms rose and fell with his blood pressure, which Boyle was able to reduce periodically with medication. After two or three hours of observation, Boyle decided that Hand should be admitted to the hospital, a decision that required

approval from another doctor. Hand had presented a Humana Health Care Plan card, and the front desk told Boyle that defendant Tavera was the doctor responsible that evening for authorizing such admissions. Boyle briefed Tavera by telephone and recommended hospitalization, but ultimately Tavera disagreed with Boyle and concluded that Hand could be treated as an outpatient. Boyle said Tavera told him that Hand's problems "should be controlled by outpatient medication and follow-up in the office" and he also "recommended something for pain." Hand was sent home, where he suffered a stroke a few hours later. He and his wife brought this lawsuit against the hospital, Tavera, and Boyle. Eventually Hand nonsuited Boyle and settled with the hospital.

Tavera moved for summary judgment on the sole ground that he and Hand never established a physician-patient relationship and therefore he owed Hand no duty. Thus this appeal does not present the question whether Tavera's conduct constituted negligence that proximately caused Hand's damages.

Hand argues first that as a member in the Humana Health Care Plan, Tavera owed him a duty of care. There is summary judgment evidence that Hand had Humana Health Care Plan coverage and that Tavera was designated as the doctor acting for the Humana plan that night. The following clauses in the contract between Humana and Southwest Medical Group (which employed Tavera) obligated its doctors to treat Humana enrollees as they would treat their other patients:

> PHYSICIAN agrees to provide or arrange for covered health care services for ENROLLEES in accordance with Attachment B. [Attachment B specifies various physician responsibilities, including "emergency care of a covered ENROLLEE who has been assigned to PHYSICIAN."]
>
> . . . .
>
> PHYSICIAN agrees to provide ENROLLEES with medical services which are within the normal scope of PHYSICIAN's medical practice. These services shall be made available to ENROLLEES without discrimination and in the same manner as provided to PHYSICIAN's other patients. PHYSICIAN agrees to provide medical services to ENROLLEES in accordance with the prevailing practices and standards of the profession and community.

Thus the contracts in the record show that the Humana plan brought Hand and Tavera together just as surely as though they had met directly and entered the physician-patient relationship. Hand paid premiums to Humana to purchase medical care in advance of need; Humana met its obligation to Hand and its other enrollees by employing Tavera's group to treat them; and Tavera's medical group agreed to treat Humana enrollees in exchange for the fees received from Humana. In effect, Hand had paid in advance for the services of the Humana plan doctor on duty that night, who happened to be Tavera, and the physician-patient relationship existed. We hold that when the health-care plan's insured shows up at a participating hospital emergency room, and the plan's doctor on call is consulted about treatment or admission, there is a physician-patient relationship between the doctor and the insured.

* * *

Tavera also argues that Hand is a third party who cannot assert rights under the Tavera–Humana contract, which expressly provides that it creates no third-party beneficiaries. But Hand does not assert rights under the Humana–Tavera contract in isolation or seek to recover for breach of contract; instead he contends that the entire health-care plan arrangement establishes that Tavera had a physician-patient relationship with him and therefore owed him a duty of care. He argues in essence that when the Hand–Humana contract is read together with the Humana–Tavera contract, he has a right to care from the doctor on call when his medical condition falls within his coverage with Humana. We agree and hold that when a patient who has enrolled in a prepaid medical plan goes to a hospital emergency room and the plan's designated doctor is consulted, the physician-patient relationship exists and the doctor owes the patient a duty of care.

* * *

We reverse the summary judgment and remand this cause for further proceedings on Hand's negligence action based on the physician-patient relationship created by the Humana Health Care Plan.

Notes and Questions

1. A physician who has staff privileges at a hospital also agrees to abide by hospital bylaws and policies and has therefore agreed to a doctor-patient relationship with whomever comes into the hospital, according to most courts that have considered the issue. Physicians on call to treat emergency patients are under a duty to treat patients. See Noble v. Sartori, 799 S.W.2d 8 (Ky.1990); Hastings v. Baton Rouge Gen. Hosp., 498 So.2d 713 (La.1986). Texas requires some further affirmative step by the physician to establish the relationship. Merely volunteering to be "on call" at a hospital is not sufficient. Ortiz v. Shah, 905 S.W.2d 609, 611 (Tex.App.—Houston[14th Dist.] 1995). See also Anderson v. Houser, 240 Ga.App. 613, 523 S.E.2d 342 (Ga.App. 1999)(physician scheduled to be on call when patient admitted to emergency room, who never met or treated patient and was out of town during her hospitalization, owed no duty). However, the on-call physician owes a duty to foreseeable emergency room patients to provide reasonable notice to hospital personnel when he or she will not be able to respond to calls, and this duty exists independent of any physician-patient relationship. Oja v. Kin, 229 Mich.App. 184, 581 N.W.2d 739 (Mich.App.1998)(implied consent to doctor-patient relationship may be found only where the physician has done something such as participate in the patient's diagnosis and treatment).

2. Physician contract obligations bind them to treat individual subscribers. And the traditional scope of the contractual relationship may also include obligations such as completing a variety of benefit forms for a patient. If these forms are not properly and timely completed, and a patient suffers an economic detriment, courts have held that a suit for breach of contract will lie. Chew v. Meyer, M.D., P.A., 72 Md.App. 132, 527 A.2d 828 (1987).

C. SPECIFIC PROMISES AND WARRANTIES OF CURE

A contract claim may have several advantages for the plaintiff. The statute of limitations is typically longer than for a tort action. The plaintiff need not establish the medical standard of care and thus may not need to present expert testimony. A contract claim may be viable even when the doctor has made the proper risk disclosure, satisfying the requirements of the tort doctrine of informed consent. Finally, a contract claim offers a remedy to the plaintiff who underwent the procedure because of the enticements of the physician.

The contract between physician and patient can be breached in a variety of ways. The physician may promise to use a certain procedure and then use an alternative procedure. See Stewart v. Rudner, 349 Mich. 459, 84 N.W.2d 816 (1957) (breached promise by physician to perform Caesarean section); Moser v. Stallings, 387 N.W.2d 599 (Iowa 1986) (plastic surgeon did not perform chin implant as part of cosmetic surgery on plaintiff, after telling patient that implant would be a part of the procedure; court in dicta suggested that patient might have had a contract claim). Contra, see Labarre v. Duke University, 99 N.C.App. 563, 393 S.E.2d 321 (1990), where the pregnant plaintiff had been assured that if, during delivery she needed an epidural anesthetic, the Director of Obstetric Anesthesia or another fully-trained faculty anesthesiologist would administer it. Instead, a resident administered the anesthesia, causing the plaintiff to suffer injury. The court held that the promise was not supported by consideration and was therefore unenforceable.

Breach of warranty claims have been rare against health care providers. A breach may also be found where the doctor promises a particular result which fails to occur. The classic case is Guilmet v. Campbell, 385 Mich. 57, 188 N.W.2d 601 (1971), where the physician treated the patient for a bleeding ulcer. The doctor had allegedly told the patient prior to the operation:

> Once you have an operation it takes care of all your troubles. You can eat as you want to, you can drink as you want to, you can go as you please. Dr. Arena and I are specialists, there is nothing to it at all—it's a very simple operation. You'll be out of work three to four weeks at most. There is no danger at all in this operation. After the operation you can throw away your pill box. 385 Mich. 57, 68, 188 N.W.2d 601, 606 (1971).

The patient suffered serious after-effects, and the jury found for the plaintiff on a breach of contract theory. Michigan then added a provision to their Statute of Frauds that covered "[a]n agreement, promise, contract, or warranty of cure relating to medical care or treatment". MCL s.566.132(g).

One emerging area in which warranties are being offered is that of fertility treatment. Fertility clinics in Minnesota and California have begun to offer a guarantee that their patients become pregnant, or they will get their money back. See Stephen L. Cohen, Should Health Care Come With a Warranty? The New York Times 12 (November 10, 1996).

The remedial options for a breach by a physician of a warranty of good results are discussed in Sullivan v. O'Connor, 363 Mass. 579, 296 N.E.2d 183 (1973), where the surgeon promised the plaintiff, a professional entertainer, that he would improve the appearance of her nose. He failed, and her nose ended up bulbous and asymmetrical. Justice Kaplan noted the problems with the application of a contract theory to the medical enterprise:

> It is not hard to see why the courts should be unenthusiastic or skeptical about the contract theory. Considering the uncertainties of medical science and the variations in the physical and psychological conditions of individual patients, doctors can seldom in good faith promise

specific results. Therefore it is unlikely that physicians of even average integrity will in fact make such promises. Statements of opinion by the physician with some optimistic coloring are a different thing, and may indeed have therapeutic value. But patients may transform such statements into firm promises in their own minds, especially when they have been disappointed in the event, and testify in that sense to sympathetic juries. If actions for breach of promise can be readily maintained, doctors, so it is said, will be frightened into practicing "defensive medicine." On the other hand, if these actions were outlawed, leaving only the possibility of suits for malpractice, there is fear that the public might be exposed to the enticements of charlatans, and confidence in the profession might ultimately be shaken.

The measure of damages in a breach of contract suit might be "expectancy" damages, that amount sufficient to place the plaintiff in the position he would be in if the contract had been performed, or "restitution" damages, an amount equivalent to the benefit conferred by the plaintiff upon the defendant. In *Sullivan*, the Massachusetts Supreme Judicial Court considered an intermediate position, a "reliance" basis, a more lenient standard for breach of an agreement "to effect a cure, attain a stated result, or employ a given medical method: * * * the substance is that the plaintiff is to recover any expenditures made by him and for other detriment * * * following proximately and foreseeably upon the defendant's failure to carry out his promise." The Court allowed pain and suffering as an item of damages, as a foreseeable consequence of a surgical operation which fails.

See also Stewart v. Rudner, supra, where the court noted that ordinarily damages are not recoverable for mental anguish or disappointment. "Yet not all contracts are purely commercial in their nature. Some involve rights we cherish, dignities we respect, emotions recognized by all as both sacred and personal. In such cases the award of damages for mental distress and suffering is a commonplace, even in actions ex contractu."

Courts will sometimes allow contract claims, but then define the "contract" restrictively. Courts typically distinguish "therapeutic assurances" from express warranties to effect a cure. In Anglin v. Kleeman, 140 N.H. 257, 665 A.2d 747 (N.H. 1995), the court found that the statement by a physician to patient upon whom knee surgery was performed—that the operation could make the knee stronger than before—did not give rise to contract or warranty claim. See also Ferlito v. Cecola, 419 So.2d 102 (La.App.1982), where the court held that a dentist's statement that crown work would make the plaintiff's teeth "pretty" did not constitute a guarantee. Other courts have imposed evidentiary burdens, requiring proof by clear and convincing evidence. See Burns v. Wannamaker, 281 S.C. 352, 315 S.E.2d 179 (App.1984). Even if the burden of proof is not elevated from the preponderance test to clear and convincing evidence, the jury will be instructed that they must find that the physician "clearly and unmistakably [gave] a positive assurance [that he or she would] produce or * * * avoid a particular result * * *." Scarzella v. Saxon, 436 A.2d 358 (D.C.App.1981). In some states, the Statute of Frauds specifically requires that for agreements guaranteeing therapeutic results to be enforceable, they must be in writing and signed. See, e.g., West's Ann.Ind. Code 16–915–1–4. What effect might such a requirement have?

D. EXCULPATORY CLAUSES

TUNKL v. REGENTS OF UNIV. OF CALIFORNIA

Supreme Court of California, 1963.
60 Cal.2d 92, 32 Cal.Rptr. 33, 383 P.2d 441.

TOBRINER, JUSTICE.

This case concerns the validity of a release from liability for future negligence imposed as a condition for admission to a charitable research hospital. For the reasons we hereinafter specify, we have concluded that an agreement between a hospital and an entering patient affects the public interest and that, in consequence, the exculpatory provision included within it must be invalid under Civil Code section 1668.

Hugo Tunkl brought this action to recover damages for personal injuries alleged to have resulted from the negligence of two physicians in the employ of the University of California Los Angeles Medical Center, a hospital operated and maintained by the Regents of the University of California as a nonprofit charitable institution. Mr. Tunkl died after suit was brought, and his surviving wife, as executrix, was substituted as plaintiff.

The University of California at Los Angeles Medical Center admitted Tunkl as a patient on June 11, 1956. The Regents maintain the hospital for the primary purpose of aiding and developing a program of research and education in the field of medicine; patients are selected and admitted if the study and treatment of their condition would tend to achieve these purposes. Upon his entry to the hospital, Tunkl signed a document setting forth certain "Conditions of Admission." The crucial condition number six reads as follows: "RELEASE: The hospital is a nonprofit, charitable institution. In consideration of the hospital and allied services to be rendered and the rates charged therefor, the patient or his legal representative agrees to and hereby releases The Regents of the University of California, and the hospital from any and all liability for the negligent or wrongful acts or omissions of its employees, if the hospital has used due care in selecting its employees."

Plaintiff stipulated that the hospital had selected its employees with due care. The trial court ordered that the issue of the validity of the exculpatory clause be first submitted to the jury and that, if the jury found that the provision did not bind plaintiff, a second jury try the issue of alleged malpractice. When, on the preliminary issue, the jury returned a verdict sustaining the validity of the executed release, the court entered judgment in favor of the Regents.[1] Plaintiff appeals from the judgment.

We shall first set out the basis for our prime ruling that the exculpatory provision of the hospital's contract fell under the proscription of Civil Code section 1668; we then dispose of two answering arguments of defendant.

We begin with the dictate of the relevant Civil Code section 1668. The section states: "All contracts which have for their object, directly or indirectly, to exempt anyone from responsibility for his own fraud, or willful injury to

---

1. Plaintiff at the time of signing the release was in great pain, under sedation, and probably unable to read. At trial plaintiff contended that the release was invalid, asserting that a release does not bind the releasor if at the time of its execution he suffered from so weak a mental condition that he was unable to comprehend the effect of his act. [ ]

the person or property of another, or violation of law, whether willful or negligent, are against the policy of the law."

* * *

In one respect, as we have said, the decisions are uniform. The cases have consistently held that the exculpatory provision may stand only if it does not involve "the public interest."

* * *

If, then, the exculpatory clause which affects the public interest cannot stand, we must ascertain those factors or characteristics which constitute the public interest. * * *

* * * It concerns a business of a type generally thought suitable for public regulation. The party seeking exculpation is engaged in performing a service of great importance to the public, which is often a matter of practical necessity for some members of the public. The party holds himself out as willing to perform this service for any member of the public who seeks it, or at least for any member coming within certain established standards. As a result of the essential nature of the service, in the economic setting of the transaction, the party invoking exculpation possesses a decisive advantage of bargaining strength against any member of the public who seeks his services. In exercising a superior bargaining power the party confronts the public with a standardized adhesion contract of exculpation, and makes no provision whereby a purchaser may pay additional reasonable fees and obtain protection against negligence. Finally, as a result of the transaction, the person or property of the purchaser is placed under the control of the seller, subject to the risk of carelessness by the seller or his agents.

* * *

In the light of the decisions, we think that the hospital-patient contract clearly falls within the category of agreements affecting the public interest. To meet that test, the agreement need only fulfill some of the characteristics above outlined; here, the relationship fulfills all of them. Thus the contract of exculpation involves an institution suitable for, and a subject of, public regulation. [ ] That the services of the hospital to those members of the public who are in special need of the particular skill of its staff and facilities constitute a practical and crucial necessity is hafdly open to question.

The hospital, likewise, holds itself out as willing to perform its services for those members of the public who qualify for its research and training facilities. While it is true that the hospital is selective as to the patients it will accept, such selectivity does not negate its public aspect or the public interest in it. The hospital is selective only in the sense that it accepts from the public at large certain types of cases which qualify for the research and training in which it specializes. But the hospital does hold itself out to the public as an institution which performs such services for those members of the public who can qualify for them.

In insisting that the patient accept the provision of waiver in the contract, the hospital certainly exercises a decisive advantage in bargaining. The would-be patient is in no position to reject the proffered agreement, to bargain with the hospital, or in lieu of agreement to find another hospital.

The admission room of a hospital contains no bargaining table where, as in a private business transaction, the parties can debate the terms of their contract. As a result, we cannot but conclude that the instant agreement manifested the characteristics of the so-called adhesion contract. Finally, when the patient signed the contract, he completely placed himself in the control of the hospital; he subjected himself to the risk of its carelessness.

* * *

We turn to a consideration of the * * * arguments urged by defendant to save the exemptive clause. Defendant contends that while the public interest may possibly invalidate the exculpatory provision as to the paying patient, it certainly cannot do so as to the charitable one. * * *

* * *

In substance defendant here asks us to modify our decision in *Malloy*, which removed the charitable immunity; defendant urges that otherwise the funds of the research hospital may be deflected from the real objective of the extension of medical knowledge to the payment of claims for alleged negligence. Since a research hospital necessarily entails surgery and treatment in which fixed standards of care may not yet be evolved, defendant says the hospital should in this situation be excused from such care. But the answer lies in the fact that possible plaintiffs must *prove negligence;* the standards of care will themselves reflect the research nature of the treatment; the hospital will not become an insurer or guarantor of the patient's recovery. To exempt the hospital completely from any standard of due care is to grant it immunity by the side-door method of a contractual clause exacted of the patient. We cannot reconcile that technique with the teaching of *Malloy*.

* * *

The judgment is reversed.

Notes and Questions

1. Why shouldn't a patient be able to waive the right to sue in exchange for lower cost or free treatment? Is there something special about medical care in general, or Tunkl's situation in particular, that makes such a choice by a patient suspect? Do the court's arguments convince you as to the reasons for invalidating such attempts by health care institutions to limit their liability? Short of a complete waiver of a right to sue, how else might hospitals or doctors protect themselves? Can a patient be asked to waive the right to sue for punitive damages? Could the parties agree on liquidated damages? Could the parties agree that an action would be brought in the local state court? Could treatment be conditioned on the patient submitting any malpractice claim to an administrative body, or to arbitration?

Courts continue to follow *Tunkl's* analysis, rejecting exculpatory agreements signed by patients. See, e.g., Cudnik v. William Beaumont Hospital, 207 Mich.App. 378, 525 N.W.2d 891 (Mich.App. 1994)(patient receiving radiation therapy for prostate cancer signed agreement; court held it to be "invalid and unenforceable as against public policy."); Ash v. New York Univ. Dental Center, 164 A.D.2d 366, 564 N.Y.S.2d 308(1990). The only exception courts find acceptable is an exculpatory agreement for treatments involving experimental procedures as the patient's last hope for survival. See Colton v. New York Hospital, 98 Misc.2d 957, 414 N.Y.S.2d 866 (1979).

For a thoughtful analysis of *Tunkl*, and a proposal to allocate medical risks by contract, see Glen Robinson, Rethinking the Allocation of Medical Malpractice Risks Between Patients and Providers, 49 Law & Contemp.Probs. 173 (1986). See also Emory University v. Porubiansky, 248 Ga. 391, 282 S.E.2d 903 (1981) (dental clinic could not ask patients to waive right to sue for negligence; the court noted however that the clinic could enter into binding contracts with patients, asking patients for example to waive the right to insist on complete treatment.).

E. PARTIAL LIMITATIONS ON THE RIGHT TO SUE

SHORTER v. DRURY

Supreme Court of Washington, 1985.
103 Wash.2d 645, 695 P.2d 116.

DOLLIVER, JUSTICE.

This is an appeal from a wrongful death medical malpractice action arising out of the bleeding death of a hospital patient who, for religious reasons, refused a blood transfusion. Plaintiff, the deceased's husband and personal representative, appeals the trial court's judgment on the verdict in which the jury reduced plaintiff's wrongful death damages by 75 percent based on an assumption of risk by the Shorters that Mrs. Shorter would die from bleeding. The defendant doctor appeals the judgment alleging that a plaintiff-signed hospital release form completely barred the wrongful death action. Alternatively, defendant asks that we affirm the trial court's judgment on the verdict. Defendant does not appeal the special verdict in which the jury found the defendant negligent.

The deceased, Doreen Shorter, was a Jehovah's Witness, as is her surviving husband, Elmer Shorter. Jehovah's Witnesses are prohibited by their religious doctrine from receiving blood transfusions.

Doreen Shorter became pregnant late in the summer of 1979. In October of 1979, she consulted with the defendant, Dr. Robert E. Drury, a family practitioner. Dr. Drury diagnosed Mrs. Shorter as having had a "missed abortion". A missed abortion occurs when the fetus dies and the uterus fails to discharge it.

When a fetus dies, it is medically prudent to evacuate the uterus in order to guard against infection. To cleanse the uterus, Dr. Shorter recommended a "dilation and curettage" (D and C). There are three alternative ways to perform this operation. The first is with a curette, a metal instrument which has a sharp-edged hoop on the end of it. The second, commonly used in an abortion, involves the use of a suction device. The third alternative is by use of vaginal suppositories containing prostaglandin, a chemical that causes artificial labor contractions. Dr. Drury chose to use curettes.

Although the D and C is a routine medical procedure there is a risk of bleeding. Each of the three principal methods for performing the D and C presented, to a varying degree, the risk of bleeding. The record below reflects that the curette method which Dr. Drury selected posed the highest degree of puncture-caused bleeding risk due to the sharpness of the instrument. The record also reflects, however, that no matter how the D and C is performed, there is always the possibility of blood loss.

Dr. Drury described the D and C procedure to Mr. and Mrs. Shorter. He advised her there was a possibility of bleeding and perforation of the uterus. Dr. Drury did not discuss any alternate methods in which the D and C may be performed. Examination of Mr. Shorter at trial revealed he was aware that the D and C posed the possibility, albeit remote, of internal bleeding.

The day before she was scheduled to receive the D and C from Dr. Drury, Mrs. Shorter sought a second opinion from Dr. Alan Ott. Mrs. Shorter advised Dr. Ott of Dr. Drury's intention to perform the D and C. She told Dr. Ott she was a Jehovah's Witness. Although he confirmed the D and C was the appropriate treatment, Dr. Ott did not discuss with Mrs. Shorter the particular method which should be used to perform it. He did, however, advise Mrs. Shorter that "she could certainly bleed during the procedure" and at trial confirmed she was aware of that possibility. Dr. Ott testified Mrs. Shorter responded to his warning by saying "she had faith in the Lord and that things would work out. * * * "

At approximately 6 a.m. on November 30, Mrs. Shorter was accompanied by her husband to Everett General Hospital. At the hospital the Shorters signed the following form (underlining after heading indicates blanks in form which were completed in handwriting):

GENERAL HOSPITAL OF EVERETT

REFUSAL TO PERMIT BLOOD TRANSFUSION

Date *November 30, 1979* Hour *6:15 a.*m.

I request that no blood or blood derivatives be administered to

Doreen v. Shorter

during this hospitalization. I hereby release the hospital, its personnel, and the attending physician from any responsibility whatever for unfavorable reactions or any untoward results due to my refusal to permit the use of blood or its derivatives and I fully understand the possible consequences of such refusal on my part.

Patient

[/s/ Elmer Shorter]

Patient's Husband or Wife

The operation did not go smoothly. Approximately 1 hour after surgery, Mrs. Shorter began to bleed internally and go into shock. Emergency exploratory surgery conducted by other surgeons revealed Dr. Drury had severely lacerated Mrs. Shorter's uterus when he was probing with the curette.

Mrs. Shorter began to bleed profusely. She continued to refuse to authorize a transfusion despite repeated warnings by the doctors she would likely die due to blood loss. Mrs. Shorter was coherent at the time she refused to accept blood. While the surgeons repaired Mrs. Shorter's perforated uterus and abdomen, Dr. Drury and several other doctors pleaded with Mr. Shorter to permit them to transfuse blood into Mrs. Shorter. He likewise refused. Mrs. Shorter bled to death. Doctors for both parties agreed a transfusion in substantial probability would have saved Doreen Shorter's life.

Mr. Shorter thereafter brought this wrongful death action alleging Dr. Drury's negligence proximately caused Mrs. Shorter's death; the complaint did not allege a survival cause of action. The release was admitted into evidence over plaintiff's objection. Plaintiff took exception to jury instructions numbered 13 and 13A which dealt with assumption of the risk.

The jury found Dr. Drury negligent and that his negligence was "a proximate cause of the death of Doreen Shorter". Damages were found to be $412,000. The jury determined, however, that Mr. and/or Mrs. Shorter "knowingly and voluntarily" assumed the risk of bleeding to death and attributed 75 percent of the fault for her death to her and her husband's refusal to authorize or accept a blood transfusion. Plaintiff was awarded judgment of $103,000. Both parties moved for judgment notwithstanding the verdict. The trial court denied both motions. Plaintiff appealed and defendant cross-appealed to the Court of Appeals, which certified the case pursuant to RCW 2.06.030(d).

The three issues before us concern the admissibility of the "Refusal to Permit Blood Transfusion" (refusal); whether assumption of the risk is a valid defense and if so, whether there is sufficient evidence for the jury to have found the risk was assumed by the Shorters; and whether the submission of the issue of assumption of the risk to the jury violated the free exercise clause of the First Amendment. The finding of negligence by Dr. Drury is not appealed by defendant.

I

Plaintiff argues the purpose of the refusal was only to release the defendant doctor from liability for not transfusing blood into Mrs. Shorter had she required blood during the course of a nonnegligently performed operation. He further asserts the refusal as it applies to the present case violates public policy since it would release Dr. Drury from the consequences of his negligence.

Defendant concedes a survival action filed on behalf of Mrs. Shorter for her negligently inflicted injuries would not be barred by the refusal since enforcement would violate public policy. Defendant argues, however, the refusal does not release the doctor for his negligence but only for the consequences arising out of Mrs. Shorter's voluntary refusal to accept blood, which in this case was death.

While the rule announced by this court is that contracts against liability for negligence are valid except in those cases where the public interest is involved [ ], the refusal does not addrss the negligence of Dr. Drury. This being so it cannot be considered as a release from liability for negligence. * * *

Plaintiff categorizes the refusal as an all or nothing instrument. He claims that if it is a release of liability for negligence it is void as against public policy and if it is a release of liability where a transfusion is required because of nonnegligent treatment then it is irrelevant. We have already stated the document cannot be considered as a release from liability for negligence. The document is more, however, than a simple declaration that the signer would refuse blood only if there was no negligence by Dr. Drury. * * *

We find the refusal to be valid. There was sufficient evidence for the jury to find it was not signed unwittingly but rather voluntarily. * * *

We also hold the release was not against public policy. We emphasize again the release did not exculpate Dr. Drury from his negligence in performing the surgery. Rather, it was an agreement that Mrs. Shorter should receive no blood or blood derivatives. The cases cited by defendant, Tunkl v. Regents of Univ. of Cal.; Colton v. New York Hosp., 98 Misc.2d 957, 414 N.Y.S.2d 866 (1979); Olson v. Molzen, 558 S.W.2d 429 (Tenn.1977), all refer to exculpatory clauses which release a physician or hospital from all liability for negligence. The Shorters specifically accepted the risk which might flow from a refusal to accept blood. Given the particular problems faced when a patient on religious grounds refuses to permit necessary or advisable blood transfusions, we believe the use of a release such as signed here is appropriate. [ ] Requiring physicians or hospitals to obtain a court order would be cumbersome and impractical. Furthermore, it might subject the hospital or physician to an action under 42 U.S.C. § 1983. [ ] The alternative of physicians or hospitals refusing to care for Jehovah's Witnesses is repugnant in a society which attempts to make medical care available to all its members.

We believe the procedure used here, the voluntary execution of a document protecting the physician and hospital and the patient is an appropriate alternative and not contrary to the public interest.

If the refusal is held valid, defendant asserts it acts as a complete bar to plaintiff's wrongful death claim. We disagree. While Mrs. Shorter accepted the consequences resulting from a refusal to receive a blood transfusion, she did not accept the consequences of Dr. Drury's negligence which was, as the jury found, a proximate cause of Mrs. Shorter's death. Defendant was not released from his negligence. We next consider the impact of the doctrine of assumption of the risk on this negligence.

II

[In Part II the court considered assumption of the risk as a defense.]

* * * Defendant argues, and we agree, that the Shorters could be found by the jury to have assumed the risk of death from an operation which had to be performed without blood transfusions and where blood could not be administered under any circumstances including where the doctor made what would otherwise have been correctable surgical mistake. The risk of death from a failure to receive a transfusion to which the Shorters exposed themselves was created by, and must be allocated to, the Shorters themselves.

* * *

III

[The court in Part III rejected the argument that the submission of the issue of assumption of the risk to the jury violated the free exercise clause of the First Amendment, since no state action was present.]

* * *

Affirmed.

Notes and Questions

1.   Jehovah's Witnesses rarely sue physicians who respect their decisions not to receive blood. A decision to vitiate the partial release in Shorter might have discouraged surgeons from agreeing to treat Jehovah's Witnesses consistent with their religious beliefs.

The refusal by Jehovah's Witnesses to accept blood transfusions has its origins in their interpretation of the Bible. Their religious doctrine mandates that they "abstain from blood":

> A human is not to sustain his life with the blood of another creature. (Genesis 9:3, 4) When an animal's life is taken, the blood representing that life is to be 'poured out,' given back to the Life–Giver. (Leviticus 17:13, 14) And as decreed by the apostolic council, Christians are to 'abstain from blood,' which applies to human blood as well as to animal blood. (Acts 15:28, 29.)

Jehovah's Witnesses and the Question of Blood 17 (1977).

Jehovah's Witnesses make no distinction between taking blood in by mouth and into the blood vessels, and treat the issue of blood as involving "the most fundamental principles on which they as Christians base their lives. Their relationship with their Creator and God is at stake." Id. at 19. The Jehovah's Witnesses have prepared brochures for health care professionals that explain these beliefs, stating that they will sign consent forms that relieve doctors of any responsibility for possible adverse consequences of blood refusal.

2.   How does the court support its allowance of the partial release? What does the court fear might happen to patients with particular religious beliefs? Can you think of any other methods by which a hospital or doctor might protect against the risk of lawsuits by patients who refuse certain kinds of medical interventions? Is the contract an adhesion contract, as were the contracts in *Tunkl* or *Porubianksy?*

3.   *Shorter* offers a defense of a partial waiver, under a special set of circumstances. The issue is important for two reasons. First, providers would like to limit their liability exposure in order to keep malpractice premiums under control. Second, economists and other reformers of the tort system advocate the use of contracts that allocate risk by agreement.

Several states have already adopted contract approaches, such as elective arbitration contracts that allow the provider and the patient to change the forum for resolving the dispute. Similarly, living wills and durable powers of attorney allow a patient to control the extent of treatment, while protecting the treating doctor from liability for complying with the patient's refusal of treatment.

4.   The contract approach to allocating the risks of health care has been advocated by many commentators. See William Ginsburg et al., Contractual Revisions to Medical Malpractice Liability, 49 Law & Contemp.Probs. 253 (1986); Clark Havighurst, Reforming Malpractice Law Through Consumer Choice, 3 Health Affairs 63 (1984).

Reliance on provider-patient contracts has also been criticized. See Maxwell Mehlman, Fiduciary Contracting: Limitations on Bargaining Between Patients and Health Care Providers, 51 Univ.Pitt.L.Rev. 365 (1990); P.S. Atiyah, Medical Malpractice and the Contract/Tort Boundary, 49 Law & Contemp.Probs. 287, 302 (1986) ("So American reformers turn, as a last resort, to the law of contract, however unsatisfactory this may be as an instrument of legal change compared with legislation or appropriate changes in common law doctrine."); Sylvia Law, A

Consumer Perspective on Medical Malpractice, 49 Law & Contemp.Probs. 305 (1989).

Problem: Arbitrating Disaster

Rhoda Cumin went to the Gladstone Clinic in Las Vegas, Nevada to get a prescription for an oral contraceptive. Her medical history put her at a higher risk of a stroke from use of birth control pills. She did not know this, but her medical records and history would have alerted an obstetrician to the risk. She obtained a prescription for the pills, and began taking them. Six months later she suffered a cerebral incident that left her partially paralyzed.

Ms. Cumin has asked you to handle her suit against the clinic. Your investigation determines that the clinic was negligent in prescribing the contraceptive in light of Ms. Cumin's history. You file a negligence action. The clinic then moves to stay the lawsuit pending arbitration, and for a court order to compel arbitration. Its affidavit states that the clinic requires all patients to sign an arbitration agreement before receiving treatment. This agreement provides that all disputes must be submitted to binding arbitration and that the parties expressly waive their right to a trial. The clinic's standard procedure is to have the receptionist hand the patient the agreement along with two information sheets, informing her that any questions will be answered. The patient must sign the agreement before receiving treatment; the physician signs later. If the patient refuses to sign, the clinic refuses treatment. The agreement, signed by Rhoda Cumin, is attached to the affidavit.

Ms. Cumin tells you that she does not remember either signing the agreement or having it explained to her, and you file an affidavit to that effect. Prepare a memorandum of law in support of your motion in opposition to arbitration.

II. CONFIDENTIALITY AND DISCLOSURE IN THE PHYSICIAN–PATIENT RELATIONSHIP

A. BREACHES OF CONFIDENCE

One of the most important obligations owed by a professional to a patient is the protection of confidences revealed by the patient to the professional. There is also an emerging trend to impose on professionals a duty to disclose to the patient information which the professional has regarding the patient. These obligations are discussed in this section.

HUMPHERS v. FIRST INTERSTATE BANK OF OREGON

Supreme Court of Oregon, In Banc, 1985.
298 Or. 706, 696 P.2d 527.

LINDE, JUSTICE.

We are called upon to decide whether plaintiff has stated a claim for damages in alleging that her former physician revealed her identity to a daughter whom she had given up for adoption.

In 1959, according to the complaint, plaintiff, then known as Ramona Elwess or by her maiden name, Ramona Jean Peek, gave birth to a daughter in St. Charles Medical Center in Bend, Oregon. She was unmarried at the time, and her physician, Dr. Harry E. Mackey, registered her in the hospital as "Mrs. Jean Smith." The next day, Ramona consented to the child's adoption by Leslie and Shirley Swarens of Bend, who named her Leslie Dawn. The hospital's medical records concerning the birth were sealed and marked to show that they were not public. Ramona subsequently remarried and raised a family. Only Ramona's mother and husband and Dr. Mackey knew about the daughter she had given up for adoption.

Twenty-one years later the daughter, now known as Dawn Kastning, wished to establish contact with her biological mother. Unable to gain access to the confidential court file of her adoption (though apparently able to locate the attending physician), Dawn sought out Dr. Mackey, and he agreed to assist in her quest. Dr. Mackey gave Dawn a letter which stated that he had registered Ramona Jean Peek at the hospital, that although he could not locate his medical records, he remembered administering diethylstilbestrol to her, and that the possible consequences of this medication made it important for Dawn to find her biological mother. The latter statements were untrue and made only to help Dawn to breach the confidentiality of the records concerning her birth and adoption. In 1982, hospital personnel, relying on Dr. Mackey's letter, allowed Dawn to make copies of plaintiff's medical records, which enabled her to locate plaintiff, now Ramona Humphers.

Ramona Humphers was not pleased. The unexpected development upset her and caused her emotional distress, worry, sleeplessness, humiliation, embarrassment, and inability to function normally. She sought damages from the estate of Dr. Mackey, who had died, by this action against defendant as the personal representative. After alleging the facts recounted above, her complaint pleads for relief on five different theories: First, that Dr. Mackey incurred liability for "outrageous conduct";[1] second, that his disclosure of a professional secret fell short of the care, skill and diligence employed by other physicians in the community and commanded by statute; third, that his disclosure wrongfully breached a confidential or privileged relationship; fourth, that his disclosure of confidential information was an "invasion of privacy" in the form of an "unauthorized intrusion upon plaintiff's seclusion, solitude, and private affairs;" and fifth, that his disclosures to Dawn Kastning breached a contractual obligation of secrecy. The circuit court granted defendant's motion to dismiss the complaint on the grounds that the facts fell short of each theory of relief and ordered entry of judgment for defendant. On appeal, the Court of Appeals affirmed the dismissal of the first, second, and fifth counts but reversed on the third, breach of a confidential relationship, and the fourth, invasion of privacy. [ ] We allowed review. We hold that if plaintiff has a claim, it arose from a breach by Dr. Mackey of a professional duty to keep plaintiff's secret rather than from a violation of plaintiff's privacy.

A physician's liability for disclosing confidential information about a patient is not a new problem. In common law jurisdictions it has been more discussed than litigated throughout much of this century.[2] There are prece-

---

1. This court has attempted, so far unsuccessfully, to discourage the idea that there is a general tort of "outrageous conduct," partly because the phrase misleadingly suggests potential recovery of damages whenever someone's conduct could be said to deserve this epithet. [ ] Plaintiff in this case actually alleged the factual elements of intentional or reckless infliction of severe emotional distress as well as "outrageous" conduct.

2. *See, e.g.,* Hanning and Brady, *Extra-judicial Truthful Disclosure of Medical Confidences: A Physician's Civil Liability,* 44 Den. L.J. 463 (1967) (citing the earlier literature);

dents for damage actions for unauthorized disclosure of facts conveyed in confidence, although we know of none involving the disclosure of an adoption. Because such claims are made against a variety of defendants besides physicians or other professional counselors, for instance against banks [ ], and because plaintiffs understandably plead alternative theories of recovery, the decisions do not always rest on a single theory.

Sometimes, defendant may have promised confidentiality expressly or by factual implication, in this case perhaps implied by registering a patient in the hospital under an assumed name. Plaintiffs were allowed to proceed on implied contract claims in *Horne v. Patton*, 291 Ala. 701, 287 So.2d 824 (1973), in *Hammonds v. Aetna Casualty & Surety Company*, 243 F.Supp. 793 (N.D.Ohio 1965), and in *Doe v. Roe*, 93 Misc.2d 201, 400 N.Y.S.2d 668 (1977) (psychiatrist). * * * A contract claim may be adequate where the breach of confidence causes financial loss, and it may gain a longer period of limitations; but contract law may deny damages for psychic or emotional injury not within the contemplation of the contracting parties, [ ] though perhaps this is no barrier when emotional security is the very object of the promised confidentiality. A contract claim is unavailable if the defendant physician was engaged by someone other than the plaintiff [ ] and it would be an awkward fiction at best if age, mental condition, or other circumstances prevent the patient from contracting; yet such a claim might be available to someone less interested than the patient, for instance her husband, [ ].

Malpractice claims, based on negligence or statute, in contrast, may offer a plaintiff professional standards of conduct independent of the defendant's assent. * * * Finally, actions for intentional infliction of severe emotional distress, *see supra* note 1, fail when the defendant had no such intention or * * * when a defendant was not reckless or did not behave in a manner that a factfinder could find to transcend "the farthest reaches of socially tolerable behavior." [ ] Among these diverse precedents, we need only consider the counts of breach of confidential relationship and invasion of privacy on which the Court of Appeals allowed plaintiff to proceed. Plaintiff did not pursue her other theories * * * and we express no view whether the dismissal of those counts was correct.

PRIVACY

Although claims of a breach of privacy and of wrongful disclosure of confidential information may seem very similar in a case like the present, which involves the disclosure of an intimate personal secret, the two claims depend on different premises and cover different ground. Their common denominator is that both assert a right to control information, but they differ in important respects. Not every secret concerns personal or private information; commercial secrets are not personal, and governmental secrets are neither personal nor private. Secrecy involves intentional concealment. * * *

For our immediate purpose, the most important distinction is that only one who holds information in confidence can be charged with a breach of confidence. If an act qualifies as a tortious invasion of privacy, it theoretically could be committed by anyone. In the present case, Dr. Mackey's professional role is relevant to a claim that he breached a duty of confidentiality, but he

Boyle, *Medical Confidence—Civil Liability for   Breach,* 24 N.Ire.Leg.Q. 19 (1973).

could be charged with an invasion of plaintiff's privacy only if anyone else who told Dawn Kastning the facts of her birth without a special privilege to do so would be liable in tort for invading the privacy of her mother.

Whether "privacy" is a usable legal category has been much debated in other English-speaking jurisdictions as well as in this country, especially since its use in tort law, to claim the protection of government against intrusions by others, became entangled with its use in constitutional law, to claim protection against rather different intrusions by government. No concept in modern law has unleashed a comparable flood of commentary, its defenders arguing that "privacy" encompasses related interests of personality and autonomy, while its critics say that these interests are properly identified, evaluated, and protected below that exalted philosophical level. Indeed, at that level, a daughter's interest in her personal identity here confronts a mother's interest in guarding her own present identity by concealing their joint past. But recognition of an interest or value deserving protection states only half a case. Tort liability depends on the defendant's wrong as well as on the plaintiff's interest, or "right," unless some rule imposes strict liability. One's preferred seclusion or anonymity may be lost in many ways; the question remains who is legally bound to protect those interests at the risk of liability.

* * *

In this country, Dean William L. Prosser and his successors, noting that early debate was more "preoccupied with the question whether the right of privacy existed" than "what it would amount to if it did," concluded that invasion of privacy "is not one tort but a complex of four" * * * Prosser and Keeton, Torts 851, § 117 (5th ed. 1984). They identify the four kinds of claims grouped under the "privacy" tort as, first, appropriation of the plaintiff's name or likeness; second, unreasonable and offensive intrusion upon the seclusion of another; third, public disclosure of private facts; and fourth, publicity which places the plaintiff in a false light in the public eye. *Id.* at 851–66. The same classification is made in the Restatement (Second) Torts §§ 652A to 652E. * * *

This court has not adopted all forms of the tort wholesale. * * *

* * *

* * * The Court of Appeals concluded that the complaint alleges a case of tortious intrusion upon plaintiff's seclusion, not by physical means such as uninvited entry, wiretapping, photography, or the like, but in the sense of an offensive prying into personal matters that plaintiff reasonably has sought to keep private. *See* Prosser and Keeton, *supra* at 854–55, § 117.[11] We do not believe that the theory fits this case.

Doubtless plaintiff's interest qualifies as a "privacy" interest. That does not require the judgment of a court or a jury; it is established by the statutes that close adoption records to inspection without a court order. ORS 7.211,

---

11. Hospital patients have recovered on a variety of theories for what courts recognized as an injury to privacy when the patient, without knowing consent, was exposed to nonmedical personnel, beginning with *DeMay v. Roberts,* 46 Mich. 160, 9 N.W. 146 (1881) (finding the nonmedical stranger's touch to be a bat-

tery). *See* LeBlang, *Invasion of Privacy: Medical Practice and the Tort of Intrusion,* 18 Washburn L.J. 205, 219–39 (1979). This court recognized that intrusive surveillance could be a tort, though not made out on the facts, in *McLain v. Boise Cascade Corp.,* 271 Or. 549, 533 P.2d 343 (1975).

432.420. * * * But as already stated, to identify an interest deserving protection does not suffice to collect damages from anyone who causes injury to that interest. Dr. Mackey helped Dawn Kastning find her biological mother, but we are not prepared to assume that Ms. Kastning became liable for invasion of privacy in seeking her out. Nor, we think, would anyone who knew the facts without an obligation of secrecy commit a tort simply by telling them to Ms. Kastning.

Dr. Mackey himself did not approach plaintiff or pry into any personal facts that he did not know; indeed, if he had written or spoken to his former patient to tell her that her daughter was eager to find her, it would be hard to describe such a communication alone as an invasion of privacy. The point of the claim against Dr. Mackey is not that he pried into a confidence but that he failed to keep one. If Dr. Mackey incurred liability for that, it must result from an obligation of confidentiality beyond any general duty of people at large not to invade one another's privacy. We therefore turn to plaintiff's claim that Dr. Mackey was liable for a breach of confidence, the third count of the complaint.

BREACH OF CONFIDENCE

It takes less judicial innovation to recognize this claim than the Court of Appeals thought. A number of decisions have held that unauthorized and unprivileged disclosure of confidential information obtained in a confidential relationship can give rise to tort damages. *See, e.g., Horne v. Patton, supra; MacDonald v. Clinger,* 84 A.D.2d 482, 446 N.Y.S.2d 801 (1982); * * *.

* * *

In the case of the medical profession, courts in fact have found sources of a nonconsensual duty of confidentiality. Some have thought such a duty toward the patient implicit in the patient's statutory privilege to exclude the doctor's testimony in litigation, enacted in this state in OEC 504–1(2). *See, e.g., Berry v. Moench,* 8 Utah 2d 191, 331 P.2d 814 (1958); *Hammonds v. Aetna Cas. & Sur. Co., supra;* [ ] More directly in point are legal duties imposed as a condition of engaging in the professional practice of medicine or other occupations.[15]

[The court noted that medical licensing statutes and professional regulations have been used as sources of a duty.]

This strikes us as the right approach to a claim of liability outside obligations undertaken expressly or implied in fact in entering a contractual relationship. [ ] The contours of the asserted duty of confidentiality are determined by a legal source external to the tort claim itself.

* * *

Because the duty of confidentiality is determined by standards outside the tort claim for its breach, so are the defenses of privilege or justification. Physicians, like members of many ordinary confidential professions and occupations, also may be legally obliged to report medical information to

---

15. *See, e.g., In re Lasswell,* 296 Or. 121, 124–26, 673 P.2d 855 (1983) (sustaining professional constraints on disclosure if disclosure is incompatible with professional function and sanction is limited to the professional role or relationship). * * *

others for the protection of the patient, of other individuals, or of the public. *See, e.g.,* ORS 418.750 (physician's duty to report child abuse); ORS 433.003, 434.020 (duty to report certain diseases). * * * Even without such a legal obligation, there may be a privilege to disclose information for the safety of individuals or important to the public in matters of public interest. [ ] Some cases have found a physician privileged in disclosing information to a patient's spouse, *Curry v. Corn,* 52 Misc.2d 1035, 277 N.Y.S.2d 470 (1966) or perhaps an intended spouse, *Berry v. Moench, supra.* In any event, defenses to a duty of confidentiality are determined in the same manner as the existence and scope of the duty itself. They necessarily will differ from one occupation to another and from time to time. A physician or other member of a regulated occupation is not to be held to a noncontractual duty of secrecy in a tort action when disclosure would not be a breach or would be privileged in direct enforcement of the underlying duty.

A physician's duty to keep medical and related information about a patient in confidence is beyond question. It is imposed by statute. ORS 677.190(5) provides for disqualifying or otherwise disciplining a physician for "wilfully or negligently divulging a professional secret." * * *

It is less obvious whether Dr. Mackey violated ORS 677.190(5) when he told Dawn Kastning what he knew of her birth. She was not, after all, a stranger to that proceeding. * * * If Ms. Kastning needed information about her natural mother for medical reasons, as Dr. Mackey pretended, the State Board of Medical Examiners likely would find the disclosure privileged against a charge under ORS 677.190(5); but the statement is alleged to have been a pretext designed to give her access to the hospital records. If only ORS 677.190(5) were involved, we do not know how the Board would judge a physician who assists at the birth of a child and decades later reveals to that person his or her parentage. But as already noted, other statutes specifically mandate the secrecy of adoption records. * * * Given these clear legal constraints, there is no privilege to disregard the professional duty imposed by ORS 677.190(5) solely in order to satisfy the curiosity of the person who was given up for adoption.

For these reasons, we agree with the Court of Appeals that plaintiff may proceed under her claim of breach of confidentiality in a confidential relationship. The decision of the Court of Appeals is reversed with respect to plaintiff's claim of invasion of privacy and affirmed with respect to her claim of breach of confidence in a confidential relationship, and the case is remanded to the circuit court for further proceedings on that claim.

* * *

BIDDLE v. WARREN GENERAL HOSPITAL

Supreme Court of Ohio, 1999.
86 Ohio St.3d 395, 715 N.E.2d 518.

[The following facts are drawn from the court's opinion. ED. Sometime prior to 1993, appellant and cross-appellee Robert L. Heller, a shareholder in appellant and cross-appellee Elliott, Heller, Maas, Moro & Magill Co., L.P.A. ("the law firm"), attended a legal seminar, where he got the idea that the law firm could assist a hospital in determining whether unpaid medical bills could be submitted to the Social Security Administration for payment. Upon his return, Heller proposed this idea to Rush Elliott, president of the law firm and, at that time, a trustee of Warren General Hospital Foundation and president of Warren General Hospital Health Systems. Elliott asked Mark Tierney, then chief financial officer of appellant and cross-appellee Warren General Hospital ("the hospital"), to meet with Heller.]

In early 1993, a meeting was held resulting in an unwritten agreement under which, according to Tierney, "[t]he law firm would screen potential candidates for SSI [Supplemental Security Income] eligibility and contact those patients on the hospital's behalf as to their rights to apply for SSI Disability, thus having their medical claim covered under SSI and the hospital could, therefore, receive payment for services that it provided that it would otherwise have to write-off [sic] as an uncollect[i]ble account, and in return for those services, upon payment from SSI, the hospital would pay a contingency fee to Elliott, Heller & Maas."

Heller informed the hospital that in order for the law firm to perform this service, it would be necessary for the hospital to provide four pieces of information with regard to each patient to be screened: name, telephone number, age, and medical condition. Accordingly, a joint decision was made to provide the law firm with the hospital's patient registration forms.

Over the next two and one-half years, the hospital released all of its patient registration forms to the law firm without obtaining any prior consent or authorization from its patients to do so, and without prescreening or sorting them in any way. The law firm sent a courier to the hospital on a weekly basis to retrieve the forms and bring them back to its office, where they were reviewed by Heller and Sharyn Jacisin, a legal assistant employed by the law firm, and separated according to potential SSI eligibility. The forms of those patients whom the law firm determined not to be eligible for disability benefits were put in a cardboard box and eventually placed in storage, and nothing further was done on those accounts.

Those patients who were considered potential candidates for SSI were telephoned by either Jacisin or Melanie Sutton, who at that time was Heller's secretary. According to the law firm, neither Jacisin nor Sutton indicated where they worked, but instead stated that they were calling on behalf of the hospital and that "you might be entitled to Social Security benefits that might help you pay your medical bill." Those patients who showed interest were referred to Heller. Jacisin testified at deposition that she made approximately one hundred of these phone calls, the purpose of which was to make an appointment to see if those patients were eligible for Social Security benefits.

Heller testified that he met with only "[p]robably 5" individuals, that he "absolutely [did] not" tell them that he or his law firm would represent them in making application for benefits, but that these individuals did retain him, without any discussion of compensation, "to help them get their benefits so their medical bills could get paid." However, Elliott testified that it "was more or less the understood agreement * * * between the firm and the hospital" that the hospital was the initial client of the law firm, but "at some point in time" the law firm may come to represent individual patients with regard to their Social Security benefits.

One patient stated by way of affidavit that Sutton telephoned her in July 1993, indicated that she was Heller's secretary, "and stated that the law firm worked closely with Warren General Hospital and * * * was trying to help Warren General Hospital patients obtain SSI benefits." She stated that "Sutton asked me to come into the office of Attorney Heller and engage Attorney Heller to represent me regarding a potential Social Security claim." She also stated that she met with Heller, that neither he nor Sutton said anything regarding her hospital bill or whether it would be paid by SSI, and that she was a Medicaid recipient and her bill had already been paid prior to the communications from the law firm. Lastly, she stated that even though she never retained the services of Heller or the law firm, "Heller's name appears as my representative on my Social Security denial of benefits letter dated Sept. 29, 1993."

On May 12, 1994, Sutton learned that the law firm was going to terminate her employment and began photocopying the patient registration forms. It appears that Sutton later sent copies of these registration forms to WFMJ–TV in Youngstown, Ohio, and when a reporter for the station confronted the law firm in June 1995, as part of an investigation into breach of patient confidentiality, the relationship between the law firm and the hospital was terminated.

On July 10, 1995, appellees and cross-appellants, Cheryl A. Biddle, individually and as surviving spouse of Robert A. Biddle, and Gary Ball, filed a class action complaint against the hospital, the law firm, Heller, and appellant and cross-appellee Kevin Andrews, who at all pertinent times was the administrator, executive director, and chief executive officer of the hospital. The complaint seeks compensatory and punitive damages and injunctive relief on behalf of appellees and approximately twelve thousand other patients whose patient registration forms were provided by the hospital to the law firm without prior authorization. Appellees allege several causes of action, all of which are based on the premise that the arrangement between the hospital and the law firm constituted a breach of patient confidentiality. These include claims for invasion of privacy, intentional infliction of emotional distress, and negligence against the hospital and Andrews, and similar claims for inducement against the law firm and Heller. Appellees also assert claims for breach of implied contract and various statutory violations against the hospital and Andrews, and an improper solicitation claim against the law firm and Heller.[ ]

ALICE ROBIE RESNICK, J.

Aside from the procedural and evidentiary questions, these appeals present five general issues for our determination. The first issue is whether a physician or hospital can be held liable for the unauthorized, out-of-court disclosure of confidential information obtained in the course of the physician-patient relationship.

This issue is easily resolved. "In Ohio, a physician can be held liable for unauthorized disclosures of medical information...." [ ]

However, Littleton does not specify the basis or legal theory under which a physician can be held liable for unauthorized disclosures of medical information ..... [ ] The second issue, therefore, is whether this court should recognize an independent common-law tort of breach of confidence in the physician-patient setting. Since appellants raise no serious argument against the recognition of such an action, this issue need not detain us long either.

* * *

* * *[C]ourts in Ohio and elsewhere have faced common metamorphic disturbances in attempting to provide a legal identity for an actionable breach of patient confidentiality. In their efforts to devise a civil remedy "for so palpable a wrong," many of these courts have endeavored to fit a breach of confidence into a number of traditional or accepted legal theories. In much the same way as trying to fit a round peg into a square hole, courts have utilized theories of invasion of privacy, defamation, implied breach of contract, intentional and negligent infliction of emotional distress, implied private statutory cause of action, breach of trust, detrimental reliance, negligence, and medical malpractice. Invariably, these theories prove ill-suited for the purpose, and their application contrived, as they are designed to protect diverse interests that only coincidentally overlap that of preserving patient confidentiality. These courts, therefore, often find themselves forced to stretch the traditional theories beyond their reasonable bounds, or ignore or circumvent otherwise sound doctrinal limitations, in order to achieve justice within the parameters they have set for themselves. In so doing, they rely on various sources of public policy favoring the confidentiality of communications between a physician and a patient, including state licensing or testimonial privilege statutes, or the Principles of Medical Ethics of the American Medical Association (1957), Section 9, or the Oath of Hippocrates. Some note that while public policy considerations are a sound enough basis to support liability, a more appropriate basis can be found in the nature of the physician-patient relationship itself, either because of its fiduciary character or because it is customarily understood to carry an obligation of secrecy and confidence. Slowly and unevenly, through various gradations of evolution, courts have moved toward the inevitable realization that an action for breach of confidence should stand in its own right, and increasingly courts have begun to adopt it as an independent tort in their respective jurisdictions. [ ] We hold that in Ohio, an independent tort exists for the unauthorized, unprivileged disclosure to a third party of nonpublic medical information that a physician or hospital has learned within a physician-patient relationship.

The third issue, as framed by the law firm, "is whether the duty to hold this patient information confidential is absolute, as the Court of Appeals has held, or, whether, and under what circumstances the hospital may disclose the confidential information to others and for what purpose." In particular, appellants and their amici argue that a privilege should attach in this case under which a hospital may disclose confidential medical information to its attorney without obtaining prior patient authorization to do so.

We do not interpret the court of appeals' decision to provide for an absolute duty of confidentiality, but it does contain some language suggesting that a disclosure may be privileged only if mandated by statute. Disclosures of otherwise confidential medical information made pursuant to statutory mandate are certainly privileged, such as occupational diseases [ ]. diseases which are infectious, contagious, or dangerous to public health [ ] , medical conditions indicative of child abuse or neglect [ ] , and injuries indicative of criminal conduct [ ]. Otherwise, a physician would be forced into the dilemma of violating a statute for failing to report a medical condition to the appropriate state agency or incurring civil liability for disclosing it. Thus, when a physician's report "is made in the manner prescribed by law, he of course has committed no breach of duty toward his patient and has betrayed no confidence, and no liability could result." [ ]

The physician also has certain duties under the common law to disclose otherwise confidential medical information concerning the public health or safety to third persons, the breach of which can result in civil liability. [ ] If a privilege to disclose were held not to attach under these circumstances, the physician would be placed in the untenable position of incurring civil liability for breaching one of two opposing common-law duties.

More important, the privilege to disclose is not necessarily coextensive with a duty to disclose. "Even without such a legal obligation, there may be a privilege to disclose information for the safety of individuals or important to the public in matters of public interest." Humphers, supra, 298 Ore. at 720, 696 P.2d at 535. * * * Thus, special situations may exist where the interest of the public, the patient, the physician, or a third person are of sufficient importance to justify the creation of a conditional or qualified privilege to disclose in the absence of any statutory mandate or common-law duty. [ ]

We hold that in the absence of prior authorization, a physician or hospital is privileged to disclose otherwise confidential medical information in those special situations where disclosure is made in accordance with a statutory mandate or common-law duty, or where disclosure is necessary to protect or further a countervailing interest which outweighs the patient's interest in confidentiality.

[The court discusses the arguments raised by the law firm and the amicus briefs.]

* * *

The main thrust of these arguments is to focus our attention on the nature of the relationship between attorney and client, rather than between physician and patient. From this perspective, the physician's duty to keep patient confidences is irrelevant, and the action itself is viewed as an attack on the viability of the attorney-client relationship. Nevertheless, we are being asked to recognize a privilege under which a hospital can release thousands of patient registration forms without consent or authorization so that a law firm can search for potential Social Security claimants, on the sole basis that the medical bill of one or more of these patients may thereby be paid. Placed in its proper perspective, such a privilege would also protect the individual medical practitioner who releases the bulk of his or her office files without authorization so that a lawyer can search through them for potential workers' compensation or personal injury claimants.

In Neal, supra, 745 F.Supp. at 1297, the court recognized a conditional privilege under which a patient's physician can disclose medical information to another treating physician. * * *

The privilege recognized in Neal applies only to disclosures made to a third party who owes a duty of confidentiality to the patient, i.e., "a physician also bound by O.R.C. § 4731.22(B)'s mandate of confidentiality." It does not extend to disclosures made to a third party who owes a duty of confidentiality to the patient's physician, but not the patient.

* * *

Contrary to the assertions of appellants and OSBA, a refusal to recognize a privilege in this case will not sound the death knell of the attorney-client relationship. By withholding a privilege in this case, we do no more than recognize that there are some circumstances under which a hospital can be held liable for the unauthorized disclosure of confidential medical information to its attorney.

It is appropriate at this point to step back for a moment and review the facts of this case. A hospital hands over to a law firm thousands of patient registration forms containing information about the medical condition of each patient, including diagnoses of alcohol and drug abuse, mental illness, and sexually transmitted diseases. The law firm reviews these forms for the sole purpose of finding amongst them potential Social Security claimants. The firm then calls these potential claimants and gives them unsolicited advice that they should take legal action in the form of obtaining SSI. In so doing, the law firm either conceals its legal identity or, according to one account, directly asked the potential claimant to engage Attorney Heller to represent her regarding a potential Social Security claim. Those who show interest are scheduled for an appointment with Heller, which is the admitted purpose of making the calls, and the law firm ultimately accepts employment (which Elliott testified was contemplated from the outset).

We can find no interest, public or private, that would justify the recognition of a privilege under these circumstances.[ ] Thus, we agree with the court of appeals that "[i]f hospitals wish to engage in this type of procedure in the future, liability can be avoided [only] by obtaining clear patient consent for this type of informational release."

This brings us to the fourth issue presented in this case, which is whether the hospital did in fact obtain such consent. The hospital contends that its general authorization for release of information form was sufficient to permit it to disclose the patient registration forms to its attorney. The form provides:

> Authorization is hereby granted to release to my insurance company and/or third party payor such information including medical records as may be necessary for the completion of my hospitalization claims. I understand that the information released upon authority of this authorization may contain information concerning treatment for alcohol, drug abuse, a psychiatric condition, or HIV test results, an AIDS diagnosis, or AIDS-related condition.

By its express terms, this form authorizes the hospital to release medical information only "to my insurance company and/or third party payor," and then only "as may be necessary for the completion of my hospitalization claims." It does not authorize the release of medical information to the hospital's lawyer, and certainly not for the purpose of determining the patient's status as a potential Social Security claimant.

* * *

In this case, the hospital's general consent form did not provide the authority to release medical information to the law firm and, therefore, the disclosures were unauthorized.

The fifth and final substantive issue is whether a third party can be held liable for inducing the unauthorized, unprivileged disclosure of nonpublic medical information. Those courts that have considered this issue have answered in the affirmative, and, for the reasons expressed in those decisions, we now do the same. [ ]

* * *

* * *[T]here may be special situations where the interests of the patient will justify the creation of a privilege to disclose. However, the only interest that has been recognized in this regard is the patient's interest in obtaining medical care and treatment, and disclosure is limited to those who have a legitimate interest in the patient's health. [ ] Otherwise, it is for the patient— not some medical practitioner, lawyer, or court—to determine what the patient's interests are with regard to personal confidential medical information.

We hold that a third party can be held liable for inducing the unauthorized, unprivileged disclosure of nonpublic medical information that a physician or hospital has learned within a physician-patient relationship. "To establish liability the plaintiff must prove that: (1) the defendant knew or reasonably should have known of the existence of the physician-patient relationship; (2) the defendant intended to induce the physician to disclose information about the patient or the defendant reasonably should have anticipated that his actions would induce the physician to disclose such information; and (3) the defendant did not reasonably believe that the physician could disclose that information to the defendant without violating the duty of confidentiality that the physician owed the patient." [ ]

* * *

For all the foregoing reasons, the judgment of the court of appeals is affirmed, and the cause is remanded to the trial court for further proceedings consistent with this opinion.

Notes and Questions

1. What harms were the plaintiffs exposed to by the disclosure of their medical information to the law firm? Wasn't this practice one that could primarily accrue to the benefit of patients who might have claims?

2. Every time a person consults a medical professional, is admitted to a health care institution, or receives a medical test, a medical record is created or an entry is made in an existing record. Billions of such records exist in the United States, most of which will be retained from 10 to 25 years. Many of these records contain very personal information—revelations to psychotherapists or documentation of treatment for alcoholism or venereal disease, for example—the disclosure of which could prove devastating to the patient. Yet most records are available to many users for a variety of legitimate and more questionable purposes. The conflict between the need for confidentiality and various claims to access have traditionally been resolved by professional ethics and institutional management practices, but is increasingly being litigated in legal forums.

3. Who uses medical information? Professional and non-professional medical staff must have access to records of patients in medical institutions for treatment purposes. Consent to such access is commonly presumed. Third party payors are the most common requestors of medical records outside the treatment setting. Access to records also is sought routinely for a variety of medical evaluation and support purposes. For example, in-house quality assurance committees, JCAHO accreditation inspection teams, and state institutional licensure reviewers all must review medical records to assess the quality of hospital care. Medical researchers frequently use information from medical records. If researchers are affiliated with the institution holding the records, access is routinely granted; if they are external to the institution, a request to review records may be reviewed more carefully, but will often be granted. State public health laws require medical professionals and institutions to report a variety of medical conditions and incidents: venereal disease, contagious diseases, wounds inflicted by violence, poisonings, industrial accidents, abortions, and child abuse.

Access to medical records is also sought for secondary, nonmedical, purposes. Law enforcement agencies, for example, often seek access to medical information. A moderate-size Chicago hospital reported that the FBI requested information about patients as often as twice a month. Attorneys seek medical records to establish disability, personal injury, or medical malpractice claims for their clients. Though they most commonly will ask for records of their own clients, they may also want to review records of other patients to establish a pattern of knowing medical abuse by a physician or the culpability of a hospital for failing to supervise a negligent practitioner. Life, health, disability and liability insurers often seek medical information, as do employers and credit investigators. Disclosure of information from medical records may occur without a formal request. Though secondary users of medical information commonly receive information pursuant to patient record releases, they have been known to seek and compile information surreptitiously. See Privacy Protection Study Commission, Personal Privacy in an Information Society, 285, 286 (1977) [hereafter Personal Privacy]. Another study found that 51% of doctors and 70% of medical students discuss confidential information at parties. Obviously these secondary disclosures of medical information are of great import to patients, as disclosure can result in loss of employment or denial of insurance or credit, or, at least, severe embarrassment.

4. What legal devices protect the confidentiality of medical information? The physician-patient privilege comes first to mind, but in fact it plays a very limited role. First, and most important, it is only a testimonial privilege, not a general obligation to maintain confidentiality: though it may permit a doctor to refuse to disclose medical information in court, it does not require the doctor to keep information from employers or insurers. Second, it is a statutory privilege or one created through judicial rulemaking and does not exist in all jurisdictions. According to the Privacy Protection Study Commission 43 states have some form of testimonial privilege, yet some of these are only applicable to psychiatrists. Third, as a privilege created by state statute, it does not apply in non-diversity federal court proceedings, Personal Privacy, supra, at 284. Fourth, the privilege is in most states subject to many exceptions. In California, it is subject to twelve exceptions, including cases where the patient is a litigant, criminal proceedings, will contests, and physician licensure proceedings. State privilege statutes often cover physicians only, who today deliver only about 5% of health care. Finally, the privilege applies only to confidential disclosures made to a physician in the course of treatment and is easily waived.

5. Several federal and state statutes protect the confidentiality of medical information. Most notable among these are amendments to the Drug Abuse and Treatment Acts and Comprehensive Alcohol Abuse and Alcoholism Prevention, Treatment, and Rehabilitation Act, 42 U.S.C.A. §§ 290dd–3, 390ee–3 (West 1982 & Supp.1986), and implementing regulations, 42 C.F.R. Part 2 (1985), which impose rigorous requirements on the disclosure of information from alcohol and drug abuse treatment programs. Some state statutes provide civil penalties for disclosure of confidential information. See Ill.Rev.Stat. ch. 91½, § 815; West's Fla.Stat.Ann. § 395.018.

6. State courts have imposed liability on doctors for violating a duty of confidentiality expressed or implied in state licensure or privilege statutes. See Berry v. Moench, 8 Utah 2d 191, 331 P.2d 814 (1958); Felis v. Greenberg, 51 Misc.2d 441, 273 N.Y.S.2d 288 (1966). Others have rejected such a duty. See Moses v. McWilliams, 379 Pa.Super. 150, 549 A.2d 950 (1988). Several common law theories have also been advanced to impose liability on professionals who disclose medical information. Two of these, invasion of privacy and breach of confidential relationship, are discussed in Humphers. See Berger v. Sonneland, 101 Wash.App. 141, 1 P.3d 1187 (Wash.App.2000)(allowing action for unauthorized disclosure of confidential information, including emotional distress damages.)

Where the doctor breaches a confidence in reporting a plaintiff's health problem to a third party, and the plaintiff arguably had an obligation to report directly, courts have refused to allow a suit for breach of confidentiality. See Alar v. Mercy Memorial Hospital, 208 Mich.App. 518, 529 N.W.2d 318 (Mich.App.1995)(psychiatrist informed Air Force Academy about suicide attempt of high school student who had been accepted to the Academy; the court held that there was no causal link between the defendant's disclosure and the harm suffered by plaintiff, since he had an independent obligation to inform.) Absent a compelling public interest or other justification, however, an action typically will life for a physician's breach of the duty to maintain patient confidences. See McCormick v. England, 328 S.C. 627, 494 S.E.2d 431 (S.C.App.1997); Marek v. Ketyer, 733 A.2d 1268 (Pa.Super.1999).

Other theories that have been argued, some of which are mentioned in Humphers, include breach of contract, Hammonds v. Aetna Casualty and Surety Co., 3 Ohio Misc. 83, 237 F.Supp. 96 (N.D.Ohio 1965) and 7 Ohio Misc. 25, 243 F.Supp. 793 (N.D.Ohio 1965); Doe v. Roe, 93 Misc.2d 201, 400 N.Y.S.2d 668 (1977); medical malpractice, Clark v. Geraci, 29 Misc.2d 791, 208 N.Y.S.2d 564 (1960) (rejecting argument); defamation, Gilson v. Knickerbocker Hospital, 280 App.Div. 690, 116 N.Y.S.2d 745 (1952) (rejecting argument). Where an accurate disclosure of information is made in good faith for a legitimate purpose, courts are generally reluctant to impose liability. See, discussing liability theories, Joseph G. White, Physicians' Liability for Breach of Confidentiality: Beyond the Limitations of the Privacy Tort, 49 S.C.L.Rev. 1271 (1998).

7. Does a patient have a right to review his or her own records? Since access to medical information is commonly granted pursuant to patient consent, it would seem that the answer to this question would obviously be yes. Surprisingly, however, a provider may still deny a patient access to medical records in a number of jurisdictions. Medical records are the property of the institution or practitioner that creates them, McGarry v. J.A. Mercier Co., 272 Mich. 501, 262 N.W. 296 (1935), though some courts have recognized a property right of the patient in the information the records contain, Pyramid Life Insurance Co. v. Masonic Hospital

Association, 191 F.Supp. 51 (W.D.Okl.1961). Many (though certainly not all) doctors argue that patients should not have access to their records, or should have access only under tight controls. They contend that patients cannot understand the information found in the records, may become anxious and upset by what they find, and may rely on medical information to engage in harmful self-treatment. They argue that patient access to medical information may violate confidences of third parties and discourage physician frankness in recording, and will impose administrative costs on institutions. Patient advocates argue that greater access will improve patient understanding of and compliance with treatment, physician-patient relations, and continuity of care. They also contend that patients cannot give informed authorization for disclosure of records to others if they do not know the contents of their own records, and thus access is important. Most of the evidence available supports the arguments for greater access—there is little evidence that patients are harmed by disclosure, some that they are helped. See Hayley Rosenman, Patients' Right to Access Their Medical Records: An Argument for Uniform Recognition of a Right of Access in the United States and Australia, 21 Fordham Int'l L.J. 1500(1998); Paul V. Stearns, Access To and Cost of Reproduction of Patient Medical Records: A Comparison of State Laws, 21 J.Leg.Med. 79 (2000).

Several states have enacted statutes permitting patients access to their medical records, though these are often subject to exceptions. Some statutes, for example, only provide access subsequent to discharge, West's Colo.Rev.Stat.Ann. §§ 25–1–801 & 802; Conn.Gen.Stat.Ann. § 4–104; 22 Me.Rev.Stat.Ann. § 1711; others permit the institution to provide only a summary of the records; West's Ann.Cal.Health & Safety Code § 25256; Or.Rev.Stat. 192.525; Minn.Stat.Ann. § 144.335; and others require the patient to show good cause for access, Tenn. Code Ann. § 53–1322(A); Miss.Code 1981, § 41–9–65. Absent statutory authority, a number of courts have permitted patients access to records under a property theory, Wallace v. University Hospitals of Cleveland, 164 N.E.2d 917 (Ohio Com.Pl.1959), modified, 170 N.E.2d 261 (1960), appeal dismissed, 171 Ohio St. 487, 172 N.E.2d 459 (1961); or fiduciary theory, Hutchins v. Texas Rehabilitation Commission, 544 S.W.2d 802 (Tex.Civ.App.1976); Emmett v. Eastern Dispensary and Casualty Hospital, 396 F.2d 931 (D.C.Cir.1967). Some courts, however, have denied patients access to their records, Gotkin v. Miller, 379 F.Supp. 859 (E.D.N.Y.1974).

8. Medical records often play a pivotal role in medical malpractice cases. By the time a malpractice action comes to trial memories may have dimmed as to what actually occurred at the time negligence is alleged to have taken place, leaving the medical record as the most telling evidence. Medical records, if properly authenticated, will usually be admitted under the business records exception to the hearsay rule. Because either documentation of inadequate care or inadequate documentation of care may result in liability, physicians are sometimes tempted to destroy records or to alter them to reflect the care they wish in retrospect they had rendered. There is nothing wrong with correcting records, so long as corrections are made in such a way as to leave the previous entry clearly readable and the new entry clearly identified as a corrected entry. Conscious concealment, fabrication, or falsification of records may result in an inference of awareness of guilt, Pisel v. Stamford Hospital, 180 Conn. 314, 340, 430 A.2d 1, 15 (1980); Thor v. Boska, 38 Cal.App.3d 558, 113 Cal.Rptr. 296 (1974); or punitive damages. It may also toll the statute of limitations. Finally, premature disposition of records could result in negligence liability, Fox v. Cohen, 84 Ill.App.3d 744, 40 Ill.Dec. 477, 406 N.E.2d 178 (1980).

9. The duty to maintain confidentiality occasionally comes in conflict with a duty to disclose information. Such a duty to disclose may be based on a statute, such as a child abuse or venereal disease reporting act, or on the common law duty of psychotherapists to warn identifiable persons threatened by their patients. See section B, infra.

B. FEDERAL MEDICAL PRIVACY STANDARDS

Concerns about the privacy of patient medical information have intensified with the growth of both electronic recordkeeping and the Internet. The federal government studied this problem for several years before developing a highly detailed set of standards for health care providers.

Standards for Privacy of Individually Identifiable Health Information

Department of Health and Human Services
Office of the Secretary

65 FR 82462
45 CFR Parts 160 and 164
Thursday, December 28, 2000

This regulation has three major purposes: (1) To protect and enhance the rights of consumers by providing them access to their health information and controlling the inappropriate use of that information; (2) to improve the quality of health care in the U.S. by restoring trust in the health care system among consumers, health care professionals, and the multitude of organizations and individuals committed to the delivery of care; and (3) to improve the efficiency and effectiveness of health care delivery by creating a national framework for health privacy protection that builds on efforts by states, health systems, and individual organizations and individuals.

* * *

In enacting HIPAA, Congress recognized the fact that administrative simplification cannot succeed if we do not also protect the privacy and confidentiality of personal health information. The provision of high-quality health care requires the exchange of personal, often-sensitive information between an individual and a skilled practitioner. Vital to that interaction is the patient's ability to trust that the information shared will be protected and kept confidential. Yet many patients are concerned that their information is not protected. Among the factors adding to this concern are the growth of the number of organizations involved in the provision of care and the processing of claims, the growing use of electronic information technology, increased efforts to market health care and other products to consumers, and the increasing ability to collect highly sensitive information about a person's current and future health status as a result of advances in scientific research.

Rules requiring the protection of health privacy in the United States have been enacted primarily by the states. While virtually every state has enacted one or more laws to safeguard privacy, these laws vary significantly from state to state and typically apply to only part of the health care system. Many states have adopted laws that protect the health information relating to certain health conditions such as mental illness, communicable diseases, cancer,

HIV/AIDS, and other stigmatized conditions. An examination of state health privacy laws and regulations, however, found that "state laws, with a few notable exceptions, do not extend comprehensive protections to people's medical records." Many state rules fail to provide such basic protections as ensuring a patient's legal right to see a copy of his or her medical record. See Health Privacy Project, "The State of Health Privacy: An Uneven Terrain," Institute for Health Care Research and Policy, Georgetown University (July 1999) (http://www.healthprivacy.org) (the "Georgetown Study").

Until now, virtually no federal rules existed to protect the privacy of health information and guarantee patient access to such information. This final rule establishes, for the first time, a set of basic national privacy standards and fair information practices that provides all Americans with a basic level of protection and peace of mind that is essential to their full participation in their care. The rule sets a floor of ground rules for health care providers, health plans, and health care clearinghouses to follow, in order to protect patients and encourage them to seek needed care. The rule seeks to balance the needs of the individual with the needs of the society. It creates a framework of protection that can be strengthened by both the federal government and by states as health information systems continue to evolve.

Need for a National Health Privacy Framework

The Importance of Privacy

Privacy is a fundamental right. As such, it must be viewed differently than any ordinary economic good. The costs and benefits of a regulation must, of course, be considered as a means of identifying and weighing options. At the same time, it is important not to lose sight of the inherent meaning of privacy: it speaks to our individual and collective freedom.

* * *

Increasing Public Concern About Loss of Privacy

Today, it is virtually impossible for any person to be truly "let alone." The average American is inundated with requests for information from potential employers, retail shops, telephone marketing firms, electronic marketers, banks, insurance companies, hospitals, physicians, health plans, and others. In a 1998 national survey, 88 percent of consumers said they were "concerned" by the amount of information being requested, including 55 percent who said they were "very concerned." See Privacy and American Business, 1998 Privacy Concerns & Consumer Choice Survey (http://www.pandab.org). These worries are not just theoretical. Consumers who use the Internet to make purchases or request "free" information often are asked for personal and financial information. Companies making such requests routinely promise to protect the confidentiality of that information. Yet several firms have tried to sell this information to other companies even after promising not to do so.

Americans' concern about the privacy of their health information is part of a broader anxiety about their lack of privacy in an array of areas. * * *

This growing concern stems from several trends, including the growing use of interconnected electronic media for business and personal activities, our increasing ability to know an individual's genetic make-up, and, in health care, the increasing complexity of the system. Each of these trends brings the potential for tremendous benefits to individuals and society generally. At the same time, each also brings new potential for invasions of our privacy.

Increasing Use of Interconnected Electronic Information Systems

Until recently, health information was recorded and maintained on paper and stored in the offices of community-based physicians, nurses, hospitals, and other health care professionals and institutions. In some ways, this imperfect system of record keeping created a false sense of privacy among patients, providers, and others. Patients' health information has never remained completely confidential. Until recently, however, a breach of confidentiality involved a physical exchange of paper records or a verbal exchange of information. Today, however, more and more health care providers, plans, and others are utilizing electronic means of storing and transmitting health information. In 1996, the health care industry invested an estimated $10 billion to $15 billion on information technology. See National Research Council, Computer Science and Telecommunications Board, "For the Record: Protecting Electronic Health Information," (1997). The electronic information revolution is transforming the recording of health information so that the disclosure of information may require only a push of a button. In a matter of seconds, a person's most profoundly private information can be shared with hundreds, thousands, even millions of individuals and organizations at a time. While the majority of medical records still are in paper form, information from those records is often copied and transmitted through electronic means.

This ease of information collection, organization, retention, and exchange made possible by the advances in computer and other electronic technology affords many benefits to individuals and to the health care industry. Use of electronic information has helped to speed the delivery of effective care and the processing of billions of dollars worth of health care claims. Greater use of electronic data has also increased our ability to identify and treat those who are at risk for disease, conduct vital research, detect fraud and abuse, and measure and improve the quality of care delivered in the U.S. The National Research Council recently reported that "the Internet has great potential to improve Americans" health by enhancing communications and improving access to information for care providers, patients, health plan administrators, public health officials, biomedical researchers, and other health professionals. See "Networking Health: Prescriptions for the Internet," National Academy of Sciences (2000).

At the same time, these advances have reduced or eliminated many of the financial and logistical obstacles that previously served to protect the confidentiality of health information and the privacy interests of individuals. And they have made our information available to many more people. The shift from paper to electronic records, with the accompanying greater flows of sensitive health information, thus strengthens the arguments for giving legal protection to the right to privacy in health information. In an earlier period where it was far more expensive to access and use medical records, the risk of harm to individuals was relatively low. In the potential near future, when technology makes it almost free to send lifetime medical records over the Internet, the risks may grow rapidly. It may become cost-effective, for instance, for companies to offer services that allow purchasers to obtain details of a person's physical and mental treatments. In addition to legitimate possible uses for such services, malicious or inquisitive persons may download medical records for purposes ranging from identity theft to embarrassment to prurient interest in the life of a celebrity or neighbor. The comments to the proposed privacy rule indicate that many persons believe that they have a right to live in society without having these details of their lives laid open to unknown and possibly hostile eyes. These technological changes, in short, may provide a reason for institutionalizing privacy protections in situations where the risk of harm did not previously justify writing such protections into law.

The growing level of trepidation about privacy in general, noted above, has tracked the rise in electronic information technology. Americans have embraced the use of the Internet and other forms of electronic information as a way to provide greater access to information, save time, and save money. For example, 60 percent of Americans surveyed in 1999 reported that they have a computer in their home; 82 percent reported that they have used a computer; 64 percent say they have used the Internet; and 58 percent have sent an e-mail. Among those who are under the age of 60, these percentages are even higher. See "National Survey of Adults on Technology," Henry J. Kaiser Family Foundation (February, 2000). But 59 percent of Americans reported that they worry that an unauthorized person will gain access to their information. A recent survey suggests that 75 percent of consumers seeking health information on the Internet are concerned or very concerned about the health sites they visit sharing their personal health information with a third party without their permission. Ethics Survey of Consumer Attitudes about Health Web Sites, California Health Care Foundation, at 3 (January, 2000).

Unless public fears are allayed, we will be unable to obtain the full benefits of electronic technologies. The absence of national standards for the confidentiality of health information has made the health care industry and the population in general uncomfortable about this primarily financially-driven expansion in the use of electronic data. Many plans, providers, and clearinghouses have taken steps to safeguard the privacy of individually identifiable health information. Yet they must currently rely on a patchwork of State laws and regulations that are incomplete and, at times, inconsistent. States have, to varying degrees, attempted to enhance confidentiality by establishing laws governing at least some aspects of medical record privacy. This approach, though a step in the right direction, is inadequate. These laws fail to provide a consistent or comprehensive legal foundation of health information privacy. For example, there is considerable variation among the states in the type of information protected and the scope of the protections provided. See Georgetown Study, at Executive Summary; Lawrence O. Gostin, Zita Lazzarrini, Kathleen M. Flaherty, Legislative Survey of State Confidentiality Laws, with Specific Emphasis on HIV and Immunization, Report to Centers for Disease Control, Council of State and Territorial Epidemiologists, and Task Force for Child Survival and Development, Carter Presidential Center (1996) (Gostin Study).

Moreover, electronic health data is becoming increasingly "national"; as more information becomes available in electronic form, it can have value far beyond the immediate community where the patient resides. Neither private action nor state laws provide a sufficiently comprehensive and rigorous legal structure to allay public concerns, protect the right to privacy, and correct the market failures caused by the absence of privacy protections (see discussion below of market failure under section V.C). Hence, a national policy with consistent rules is necessary to encourage the increased and proper use of electronic information while also protecting the very real needs of patients to safeguard their privacy.

Advances in Genetic Sciences

Recently, scientists completed nearly a decade of work unlocking the mysteries of the human genome, creating tremendous new opportunities to identify and prevent many of the leading causes of death and disability in this country and around the world. Yet the absence of privacy protections for health information endanger these efforts by creating a barrier of distrust and suspicion among consumers. A 1995 national poll found that more than 85 percent of those surveyed were either "very concerned" or "somewhat concerned" that insurers and employers might gain access to and use genetic information. See Harris Poll, 1995 #34. Sixty-three percent of the 1,000 participants in a 1997 national survey said they would not take genetic tests if insurers and employers could gain access to the results. See "Genetic Information and the Workplace," Department of Labor, Department of Health and Human Services, Equal Employment Opportunity Commission, January 20, 1998. "In genetic testing studies at the National Institutes of Health, thirty-two percent of eligible people who were offered a test for breast cancer risk declined to take it, citing concerns about loss of privacy and the potential for discrimination in health insurance." Sen. Leahy's comments for March 10, 1999 Introduction of the Medical Information Privacy and Security Act.

The Changing Health Care System

The number of entities who are maintaining and transmitting individually identifiable health information has increased significantly over the last 10 years. In addition, the rapid growth of integrated health care delivery systems requires greater use of integrated health information systems. The health care industry has been transformed from one that relied primarily on one-on-one interactions between patients and clinicians to a system of integrated health care delivery networks and managed care providers. Such a system requires the processing and collection of information about patients and plan enrollees (for example, in claims files or enrollment records), resulting in the creation of databases that can be easily transmitted. This dramatic change in the practice of medicine brings with it important prospects for the improvement of the quality of care and reducing the cost of that care. It also, however, means that increasing numbers of people have access to health information. And, as health plan functions are increasingly outsourced, a growing number of organizations not affiliated with our physicians or health plans also have access to health information.

According to the American Health Information Management Association (AHIMA), an average of 150 people "from nursing staff to x-ray technicians, to billing clerks" have access to a patient's medical records during the course of a typical hospitalization. While many of these individuals have a legitimate need to see all or part of a patient's records, no laws govern who those people are, what information they are able to see, and what they are and are not allowed to do with that information once they have access to it. According to the National Research Council, individually identifiable health information frequently is shared with:

— Consulting physicians;

— Managed care organizations;

— Health insurance companies

— Life insurance companies;

— Self-insured employers;

— Pharmacies;

— Pharmacy benefit managers;

— Clinical laboratories;

— Accrediting organizations;

— State and Federal statistical agencies; and

— Medical information bureaus.

Much of this sharing of information is done without the knowledge of the patient involved. While many of these functions are important for smooth functioning of the health care system, there are no rules governing how that information is used by secondary and tertiary users. For example, a pharmacy benefit manager could receive information to determine whether an insurance plan or HMO should cover a prescription, but then use the information to market other products to the same patient. Similarly, many of us obtain health insurance coverage though our employer and, in some instances, the employer itself acts as the insurer. In these cases, the employer will obtain identifiable health information about its employees as part of the legitimate health insurance functions such as claims processing, quality improvement, and fraud detection activities. At the same time, there is no comprehensive protection prohibiting the employer from using that information to make decisions about promotions or job retention.

* * *

Concerns about the lack of attention to information privacy in the health care industry are not merely theoretical. In the absence of a national legal framework of health privacy protections, consumers are increasingly vulnerable to the exposure of their personal health information. Disclosure of individually identifiable information can occur deliberately or accidentally and can occur within an organization or be the result of an external breach of security. Examples of recent privacy breaches include:

— A Michigan-based health system accidentally posted the medical records of thousands of patients on the Internet (The Ann Arbor News, February 10, 1999).

— A Utah-based pharmaceutical benefits management firm used patient data to solicit business for its owner, a drug store (Kiplingers, February 2000).

— An employee of the Tampa, Florida, health department took a computer disk containing the names of 4,000 people who had tested positive for HIV, the virus that causes AIDS (USA Today, October 10, 1996).

— The health insurance claims forms of thousands of patients blew out of a truck on its way to a recycling center in East Hartford, Connecticut (The Hartford Courant, May 14, 1999).

— A patient in a Boston-area hospital discovered that her medical record had been read by more than 200 of the hospital's employees (The Boston Globe, August 1, 2000).

— A Nevada woman who purchased a used computer discovered that the computer still contained the prescription records of the customers of the pharmacy that had previously owned the computer. The pharmacy data base included names, addresses, social security numbers, and a list of all the medicines the customers had purchased. (The New York Times, April 4, 1997 and April 12, 1997).

— A speculator bid $4000 for the patient records of a family practice in South Carolina. Among the businessman's uses of the purchased records was selling them back to the former patients. (New York Times, August 14, 1991).

— In 1993, the Boston Globe reported that Johnson and Johnson marketed a list of 5 million names and addresses of elderly incontinent women. (ACLU Legislative Update, April 1998).

— A few weeks after an Orlando woman had her doctor perform some routine tests, she received a letter from a drug company promoting a treatment for her high cholesterol. (Orlando Sentinel, November 30, 1997).

No matter how or why a disclosure of personal information is made, the harm to the individual is the same. In the face of industry evolution, the potential benefits of our changing health care system, and the real risks and occurrences of harm, protection of privacy must be built into the routine operations of our health care system.

Privacy Is Necessary To Secure Effective, High Quality Health Care

While privacy is one of the key values on which our society is built, it is more than an end in itself. It is also necessary for the effective delivery of health care, both to individuals and to populations. The market failures caused by the lack of effective privacy protections for health information are discussed below (see section V.C below). Here, we discuss how privacy is a necessary foundation for delivery of high quality health care. In short, the entire health care system is built upon the willingness of individuals to share the most intimate details of their lives with their health care providers.

The need for privacy of health information, in particular, has long been recognized as critical to the delivery of needed medical care. More than anything else, the relationship between a patient and a clinician is based on trust. The clinician must trust the patient to give full and truthful information about their health, symptoms, and medical history. The patient must trust the clinician to use that information to improve his or her health and to respect the need to keep such information private. In order to receive accurate and reliable diagnosis and treatment, patients must provide health care professionals with accurate, detailed information about their personal health, behavior, and other aspects of their lives. The provision of health information assists in the diagnosis of an illness or condition, in the development of a treatment plan, and in the evaluation of the effectiveness of that treatment. In the absence of full and accurate information, there is a serious risk that the treatment plan will be inappropriate to the patient's situation.

Patients also benefit from the disclosure of such information to the health plans that pay for and can help them gain access to needed care. Health plans and health care clearinghouses rely on the provision of such information to accurately and promptly process claims for payment and for other administrative functions that directly affect a patient's ability to receive needed care, the quality of that care, and the efficiency with which it is delivered.

Accurate medical records assist communities in identifying troubling public health trends and in evaluating the effectiveness of various public health efforts. Accurate information helps public and private payers make correct payments for care received and lower costs by identifying fraud. Accurate information provides scientists with data they need to conduct research. We cannot improve the quality of health care without information about which treatments work, and which do not.

Individuals cannot be expected to share the most intimate details of their lives unless they have confidence that such information will not be used or shared inappropriately. Privacy violations reduce consumers' trust in the health care system and institutions that serve them. Such a loss of faith can impede the quality of the health care they receive, and can harm the financial health of health care institutions.

Patients who are worried about the possible misuse of their information often take steps to protect their privacy. Recent studies show that a person who does not believe his privacy will be protected is much less likely to participate fully in the diagnosis and treatment of his medical condition. A national survey conducted in January 1999 found that one in five Americans believe their health information is being used inappropriately. See California HealthCare Foundation, "National Survey: Confidentiality of Medical Records" (January, 1999) (http://www.chcf.org). More troubling is the fact that one in six Americans reported that they have taken some sort of evasive action to avoid the inappropriate use of their information by providing inaccurate information to a health care provider, changing physicians, or avoiding care altogether. Similarly, in its comments on our proposed rule, the Association of American Physicians and Surgeons reported 78 percent of its members reported withholding information from a patient's record due to privacy concerns and another 87 percent reported having had a patient request to withhold information from their records. [ ]

* * *

To protect their privacy and avoid embarrassment, stigma, and discrimination, some people withhold information from their health care providers, provide inaccurate information, doctor-hop to avoid a consolidated medical record, pay out-of-pocket for care that is covered by insurance, and—in some cases—avoid care altogether. Best Principles Study, at 9. In their comments on our proposed rule, numerous organizations representing health plans, health providers, employers, and others acknowledged the value of a set of national privacy standards to the efficient operation of their practices and businesses.

Breaches of Health Privacy Harm More Than Our Health Status

A breach of a person's health privacy can have significant implications well beyond the physical health of that person, including the loss of a job, alienation of family and friends, the loss of health insurance, and public humiliation. For example:

— A banker who also sat on a county health board gained access to patients' records and identified several people with cancer and called in their mortgages. See the National Law Journal, May 30, 1994.

— A physician was diagnosed with AIDS at the hospital in which he practiced medicine. His surgical privileges were suspended. See Estate of Behringer v. Medical Center at Princeton, 249 N.J.Super. 597.

— A candidate for Congress nearly saw her campaign derailed when newspapers published the fact that she had sought psychiatric treatment after a suicide attempt. See New York Times, October 10, 1992, Section 1, page 25.

— A 30–year FBI veteran was put on administrative leave when, without his permission, his pharmacy released information about his treatment for depression. (Los Angeles Times, September 1, 1998) Consumer Reports found that 40 percent of insurers disclose personal health information to lenders, employers, or marketers without customer permission. "Who's reading your Medical Records," Consumer Reports, October 1994, at 628, paraphrasing Sweeny, Latanya, "Weaving Technology and Policy Together to Maintain Confidentiality," The Journal Of Law Medicine and Ethics (Summer & Fall 1997) Vol. 25, Numbers 2,3.

The answer to these concerns is not for consumers to withdraw from society and the health care system, but for society to establish a clear national legal framework for privacy. By spelling out what is and what is not an allowable use of a person's identifiable health information, such standards can help to restore and preserve trust in the health care system and the individuals and institutions that comprise that system. As medical historian Paul Starr wrote: "Patients have a strong interest in preserving the privacy of their personal health information but they also have an interest in medical research and other efforts by health care organizations to improve the medical care they receive. As members of the wider community, they have an interest in public health measures that require the collection of personal data." (P. Starr, "Health and the Right to Privacy," American Journal of Law & Medicine, 25, nos. 2 & 3 (1999) 193–201). The task of society and its government is to create a balance in which the individual's needs and rights are balanced against the needs and rights of society as a whole.

National standards for medical privacy must recognize the sometimes competing goals of improving individual and public health, advancing scientific knowledge, enforcing the laws of the land, and processing and paying claims for health care services. This need for balance has been recognized by many of the experts in this field. Cavoukian and Tapscott described it this way: "An individual's right to privacy may conflict with the collective rights of the public * * *. We do not suggest that privacy is an absolute right that reigns supreme over all other rights. It does not. However, the case for privacy will depend on a number of factors that can influence the balance—the level of harm to the individual involved versus the needs of the public."

The Federal Response

There have been numerous federal initiatives aimed at protecting the privacy of especially sensitive personal information over the past several years—and several decades. While the rules below are likely the largest single federal initiative to protect privacy, they are by no means alone in the field. Rather, the rules arrive in the context of recent legislative activity to grapple with advances in technology, in addition to an already established body of law granting federal protections for personal privacy.

* * *

As described in more detail in the next section, Congress recognized the importance of protecting the privacy of health information by enacting the Health Insurance Portability and Accountability Act of 1996. The Act called on Congress to enact a medical privacy statute and asked the Secretary of Health and Human Services to provide Congress with recommendations for protecting the confidentiality of health care information. The Congress further recognized the importance of such standards by providing the Secretary with authority to promulgate regulations on health care privacy in the event that lawmakers were unable to act within the allotted three years.

Finally, it also is important for the U.S. to join the rest of the developed world in establishing basic medical privacy protections. In 1995, the European Union (EU) adopted a Data Privacy Directive requiring its 15 member states to adopt consistent privacy laws by October 1998. The EU urged all other nations to do the same or face the potential loss of access to information from EU countries.

* * *

Subpart E—Privacy of Individually Identifiable Health Information

§ 164.104 Applicability.

Except as otherwise provided, the provisions of this part apply to covered entities: health plans, health care clearinghouses, and health care providers who transmit health information in electronic form in connection with any transaction referred to in section 1173(a)(1) of the Act.

* * *

Subpart E—Privacy of Individually Identifiable Health Information

* * *

§ 164.501 Definitions.

As used in this subpart, the following terms have the following meanings:

* * *

Individually identifiable health information is information that is a subset of health information, including demographic information collected from an individual, and:

(1) Is created or received by a health care provider, health plan, employer, or health care clearinghouse; and

(2) Relates to the past, present, or future physical or mental health or condition of an individual; the provision of health care to an individual; or the past, present, or future payment for the provision of health care to an individual; and

(i) That identifies the individual; or

(ii) With respect to which there is a reasonable basis to believe the information can be used to identify the individual.

* * *

Marketing means to make a communication about a product or service a purpose of which is to encourage recipients of the communication to purchase or use the product or service.

(1) Marketing does not include communications that meet the requirements of paragraph (2) of this definition and that are made by a covered entity:

(i) For the purpose of describing the entities participating in a health care provider network or health plan network, or for the purpose of describing if and the extent to which a product or service (or payment for such product or service) is provided by a covered entity or included in a plan of benefits; or

(ii) That are tailored to the circumstances of a particular individual and the communications are:

(A) Made by a health care provider to an individual as part of the treatment of the individual, and for the purpose of furthering the treatment of that individual; or

(B) Made by a health care provider or health plan to an individual in the course of managing the treatment of that individual, or for the purpose of directing or recommending to that individual alternative treatments, therapies, health care providers, or settings of care.

(2) A communication described in paragraph (1) of this definition is not included in marketing if:

(i) The communication is made orally; or

(ii) The communication is in writing and the covered entity does not receive direct or indirect remuneration from a third party for making the communication.

* * *

Protected health information means individually identifiable health information:

(1) Except as provided in paragraph (2) of this definition, that is:

(i) Transmitted by electronic media;

(ii) Maintained in any medium described in the definition of electronic media at § 162.103 of this subchapter; or

(iii) Transmitted or maintained in any other form or medium.

* * *

Treatment means the provision, coordination, or management of health care and related services by one or more health care providers, including the coordination or management of health care by a health care provider with a third party; consultation between health care providers relating to a patient; or the referral of a patient for health care from one health care provider to another.

Use means, with respect to individually identifiable health information, the sharing, employment, application, utilization, examination, or analysis of such information within an entity that maintains such information.

§ 164.502 Uses and disclosures of protected health information: general rules.

(a) Standard. A covered entity may not use or disclose protected health information, except as permitted or required by this subpart or by subpart C of part 160 of this subchapter.

(1) Permitted uses and disclosures. A covered entity is permitted to use or disclose protected health information as follows:

(i) To the individual;

(ii) Pursuant to and in compliance with a consent that complies with § 164.506, to carry out treatment, payment, or health care operations;

(iii) Without consent, if consent is not required under § 164.506(a) and has not been sought under § 164.506(a)(4), to carry out treatment, payment, or health care operations, except with respect to psychotherapy notes;

(iv) Pursuant to and in compliance with a valid authorization under § 164.508;

(v) Pursuant to an agreement under, or as otherwise permitted by, § 164.510; and

(vi) As permitted by and in compliance with this section, § 164.512, or § 164.514(e), (f), and (g).

(2) Required disclosures. A covered entity is required to disclose protected health information:

(i) To an individual, when requested under, and required by § 164.524 or § 164.528; and

(ii) When required by the Secretary under subpart C of part 160 of this subchapter to investigate or determine the covered entity's compliance with this subpart.

(b) Standard: Minimum necessary. (1) Minimum necessary applies. When using or disclosing protected health information or when requesting protected health information from another covered entity, a covered entity must make reasonable efforts to limit protected health information to the minimum necessary to accomplish the intended purpose of the use, disclosure, or request.

(2) Minimum necessary does not apply. This requirement does not apply to:

(i) Disclosures to or requests by a health care provider for treatment;

(ii) Uses or disclosures made to the individual, as permitted under paragraph (a)(1)(i) of this section, as required by paragraph (a)(2)(i) of this section, or pursuant to an authorization under § 164.508, except for authorizations requested by the covered entity under § 164.508(d), (e), or (f);

(iii) Disclosures made to the Secretary in accordance with subpart C of part 160 of this subchapter;

(iv) Uses or disclosures that are required by law, as described by § 164.512(a); and

(v) Uses or disclosures that are required for compliance with applicable requirements of this subchapter.

(c) Standard: Uses and disclosures of protected health information subject to an agreed upon restriction. A covered entity that has agreed to a restriction pursuant to § 164.522(a)(1) may not use or disclose the protected health information covered by the restriction in violation of such restriction, except as otherwise provided in § 164.522(a).

* * *

(h) Standard: Confidential communications. A covered health care provider or health plan must comply with the applicable requirements of § 164.522(b) in communicating protected health information.

(i) Standard: Uses and disclosures consistent with notice. A covered entity that is required by § 164.520 to have a notice may not use or disclose protected health information in a manner inconsistent with such notice. A covered entity that is required by § 164.520(b)(1)(iii) to include a specific statement in its notice if it intends to engage in an activity listed in § 164.520(b)(1)(iii)(A)-(C), may not use or disclose protected health information for such activities, unless the required statement is included in the notice.

* * *

§ 164.506 Consent for uses or disclosures to carry out treatment, payment, or health care operations.

(a) Standard: Consent requirement. (1) Except as provided in paragraph (a)(2) or (a)(3) of this section, a covered health care provider must obtain the individual's consent, in accordance with this section, prior to using or disclosing protected health information to carry out treatment, payment, or health care operations.

(2) A covered health care provider may, without consent, use or disclose protected health information to carry out treatment, payment, or health care operations, if:

(i) The covered health care provider has an indirect treatment relationship with the individual; or

(ii) The covered health care provider created or received the protected health information in the course of providing health care to an individual who is an inmate.

(3)(i) A covered health care provider may, without prior consent, use or disclose protected health information created or received under paragraph (a)(3)(i)(A)-(C) of this section to carry out treatment, payment, or health care operations:

(A) In emergency treatment situations, if the covered health care provider attempts to obtain such consent as soon as reasonably practicable after the delivery of such treatment;

(B) If the covered health care provider is required by law to treat the individual, and the covered health care provider attempts to obtain such consent but is unable to obtain such consent; or

(C) If a covered health care provider attempts to obtain such consent from the individual but is unable to obtain such consent due to substantial barriers to communicating with the individual, and the covered health care provider determines, in the exercise of professional judgment, that the individual's consent to receive treatment is clearly inferred from the circumstances.

(ii) A covered health care provider that fails to obtain such consent in accordance with paragraph (a)(3)(i) of this section must document its attempt to obtain consent and the reason why consent was not obtained.

(4) If a covered entity is not required to obtain consent by paragraph (a)(1) of this section, it may obtain an individual's consent for the covered entity's own use or disclosure of protected health information to carry out treatment, payment, or health care operations, provided that such consent meets the requirements of this section.

(5) Except as provided in paragraph (f)(1) of this section, a consent obtained by a covered entity under this section is not effective to permit another covered entity to use or disclose protected health information.

(b) Implementation specifications: General requirements. (1) A covered health care provider may condition treatment on the provision by the individual of a consent under this section.

(2) A health plan may condition enrollment in the health plan on the provision by the individual of a consent under this section sought in conjunction with such enrollment.

(3) A consent under this section may not be combined in a single document with the notice required by § 164.520.

(4)(i) A consent for use or disclosure may be combined with other types of written legal permission from the individual (e.g., an informed consent for treatment or a consent to assignment of benefits), if the consent under this section:

(A) Is visually and organizationally separate from such other written legal permission; and

(B) Is separately signed by the individual and dated.

(ii) A consent for use or disclosure may be combined with a research authorization under § 164.508(f).

(5) An individual may revoke a consent under this section at any time, except to the extent that the covered entity has taken action in reliance thereon. Such revocation must be in writing.

(6) A covered entity must document and retain any signed consent under this section as required by § 164.530(j).

* * *

§ 164.508 Uses and disclosures for which an authorization is required.

(a) Standard: Authorizations for uses and disclosures. (1) Authorization required: General rule. Except as otherwise permitted or required by this subchapter, a covered entity may not use or disclose protected health information without an authorization that is valid under this section. When a covered entity obtains or receives a valid authorization for its use or disclosure of protected health information, such use or disclosure must be consistent with such authorization.

* * *

§ 164.510 Uses and disclosures requiring an opportunity for the individual to agree or to object.

A covered entity may use or disclose protected health information without the written consent or authorization of the individual as described by ss 164.506 and 164.508, respectively, provided that the individual is informed in advance of the use or disclosure and has the opportunity to agree to or prohibit or restrict the disclosure in accordance with the applicable requirements of this section. The covered entity may orally inform the individual of and obtain the individual's oral agreement or objection to a use or disclosure permitted by this section.

* * *

§ 164.512 Uses and disclosures for which consent, an authorization, or opportunity to agree or object is not required.

A covered entity may use or disclose protected health information without the written consent or authorization of the individual as described in §§ 164.506 and 164.508, respectively, or the opportunity for the individual to agree or object as described in § 164.510, in the situations covered by this section, subject to the applicable requirements of this section. When the covered entity is required by this section to inform the individual of, or when the individual may agree to, a use or disclosure permitted by this section, the covered entity's information and the individual's agreement may be given orally.

(a) Standard: Uses and disclosures required by law. (1) A covered entity may use or disclose protected health information to the extent that such use or disclosure is required by law and the use or disclosure complies with and is limited to the relevant requirements of such law.

(2) A covered entity must meet the requirements described in paragraph (c), (e), or (f) of this section for uses or disclosures required by law.

* * *

§ 164.514 Other requirements relating to uses and disclosures of protected health information.

(a) Standard: de-identification of protected health information. Health information that does not identify an individual and with respect to which there is no reasonable basis to believe that the information can be used to identify an individual is not individually identifiable health information.

(b) Implementation specifications: requirements for de-identification of protected health information. A covered entity may determine that health information is not individually identifiable health information only if:

(1) A person with appropriate knowledge of and experience with generally accepted statistical and scientific principles and methods for rendering information not individually identifiable:

(i) Applying such principles and methods, determines that the risk is very small that the information could be used, alone or in combination with other reasonably available information, by an anticipated recipient to identify an individual who is a subject of the information; and

(ii) Documents the methods and results of the analysis that justify such determination; * * *

(d)(1) Standard: minimum necessary requirements. A covered entity must reasonably ensure that the standards, requirements, and implementation specifications of s 164.502(b) and this section relating to a request for or the use and disclosure of the minimum necessary protected health information are met.

* * *

(3) Implementation specification: Minimum necessary disclosures of protected health information. (i) For any type of disclosure that it makes on a routine and recurring basis, a covered entity must implement policies and procedures (which may be standard protocols) that limit the protected health information disclosed to the amount reasonably necessary to achieve the purpose of the disclosure.

(ii) For all other disclosures, a covered entity must:

(A) Develop criteria designed to limit the protected health information disclosed to the information reasonably necessary to accomplish the purpose for which disclosure is sought; and

(B) Review requests for disclosure on an individual basis in accordance with such criteria.

* * *

(e)(1) Standard: Uses and disclosures of protected health information for marketing. A covered entity may not use or disclose protected health information for marketing without an authorization that meets the applicable requirements of s 164.508, except as provided for by paragraph (e)(2) of this section.

(2) Implementation specifications: Requirements relating to marketing. (i) A covered entity is not required to obtain an authorization under s 164.508 when it uses or discloses protected health information to make a marketing communication to an individual that:

(A) Occurs in a face-to-face encounter with the individual;

(B) Concerns products or services of nominal value; or

(C) Concerns the health-related products and services of the covered entity or of a third party and the communication meets the applicable conditions in paragraph (e)(3) of this section.

(ii) A covered entity may disclose protected health information for purposes of such communications only to a business associate that assists the covered entity with such communications.

(3) Implementation specifications: Requirements for certain marketing communications. For a marketing communication to qualify under paragraph (e)(2)(i) of this section, the following conditions must be met:

(i) The communication must:

(A) Identify the covered entity as the party making the communication;

(B) If the covered entity has received or will receive direct or indirect remuneration for making the communication, prominently state that fact; and

(C) Except when the communication is contained in a newsletter or similar type of general communication device that the covered entity distributes to a broad cross-section of patients, enrollees, or other broad groups of individuals, contain instructions describing how the individual may opt out of receiving future such communications.

(ii) If the covered entity uses or discloses protected health information to target the communication to individuals based on their health status or condition:

(A) The covered entity must make a determination prior to making the communication that the product or service being marketed may be beneficial to the health of the type or class of individual targeted; and

(B) The communication must explain why the individual has been targeted and how the product or service relates to the health of the individual.

(iii) The covered entity must make reasonable efforts to ensure that individuals who decide to opt out of receiving future marketing communications, under paragraph (e)(3)(i)(C) of this section, are not sent such communications.

* * *

§ 164.520 Notice of privacy practices for protected health information.

(a) Standard: notice of privacy practices. (1) Right to notice. Except as provided by paragraph (a)(2) or (3) of this section, an individual has a right to adequate notice of the uses and disclosures of protected health information that may be made by the covered entity, and of the individual's rights and the covered entity's legal duties with respect to protected health information.

* * *

§ 164.522 Rights to request privacy protection for protected health information.

(a)(1) Standard: Right of an individual to request restriction of uses and disclosures. (i) A covered entity must permit an individual to request that the covered entity restrict:

(A) Uses or disclosures of protected health information about the individual to carry out treatment, payment, or health care operations; and

(B) Disclosures permitted under s 164.510(b).

(ii) A covered entity is not required to agree to a restriction.

(iii) A covered entity that agrees to a restriction under paragraph (a)(1)(i) of this section may not use or disclose protected health information in violation of such restriction, except that, if the individual who requested the restriction is in need of emergency treatment and the restricted protected health information is needed to provide the emergency treatment, the covered entity may use the restricted protected health information, or may disclose such information to a health care provider, to provide such treatment to the individual.

(iv) If restricted protected health information is disclosed to a health care provider for emergency treatment under paragraph (a)(1)(iii) of this section, the covered entity must request that such health care provider not further use or disclose the information.

(v) A restriction agreed to by a covered entity under paragraph (a) of this section, is not effective under this subpart to prevent uses or disclosures permitted or required under ss 164.502(a)(2)(i), 164.510(a) or 164.512.

* * *

§ 164.524 Access of individuals to protected health information.

(a) Standard: Access to protected health information. (1) Right of access. Except as otherwise provided in paragraph (a)(2) or (a)(3) of this section, an individual has a right of access to inspect and obtain a copy of protected health information about the individual in a designated record set, for as long as the protected health information is maintained in the designated records * * *

* * *

§ 164.526 Amendment of protected health information.

(a) Standard: Right to amend. (1) Right to amend. An individual has the right to have a covered entity amend protected health information or a record about the individual in a designated record set for as long as the protected health information is maintained in the designated record set.

* * *

§ 164.528 Accounting of disclosures of protected health information.

(a) Standard: Right to an accounting of disclosures of protected health information. (1) An individual has a right to receive an accounting of disclosures of protected health information made by a covered entity in the six years prior to the date on which the accounting is requested, except for disclosures:

  (i) To carry out treatment, payment and health care operations as provided in § 164.502;

  (ii) To individuals of protected health information about them as provided in § 164.502;

* * *

§ 164.530 Administrative requirements.

(a)(1) Standard: Personnel designations. (i) A covered entity must designate a privacy official who is responsible for the development and implementation of the policies and procedures of the entity.

Notes and Questions

1. These rules step into a vacuum created by erratic state regulation and little federal regulation. Do they strike an appropriate balance between patient privacy and provider and insurer needs for information? Do they impose substantial new compliance costs on health care providers as a by-product of protecting privacy?

Are the rules open to criticism as not being protective enough in some ways? Consider the marketing sections 164.514, particularly standard (e)(1). "A covered entity is not required to obtain an authorization under § 164.508 when it uses or discloses protected health information to make a marketing communication to an individual that: (A) Occurs in a face-to-face encounter with the individual; (B) Concerns products or services of nominal value; or (C) Concerns the health-related products and services of the covered entity or of a third party and the communication meets the applicable conditions in paragraph (e)(3) of this section."

Does this mean a tremendous increase in the medical equivalent of junk mail targeted to your particular medical problems? How do you feel about having your health information available for such use? A pregnant woman, for example, could receive sales pitches about vitamins or infant health care products; a patient treated for sexually transmitted diseases could receive telemarketing calls offering condoms or new medicines; a patient treated for depression could receive pharmaceutical advertisements for the latest anti-depressants. The medical record becomes a marketing tool. Is this offensive, or is it just American-style capitalism in action, extending options to consumers as a by-product of their medical treatment. The rules provide for opt-out provisions to avoid such marketing. How easy will it be to notify hundreds of suppliers of medical products that you do not want to be bothered?

2. The portions of the Medical Privacy Standards quoted above in a highly abbreviated form give some sense of the scope and detail of the rules. They have several laudatory goals. First and foremost, they aim to give consumers control over their own health information. Health providers must inform patients about how their information is being used and to whom it is disclosed. The rules create a "disclosure history" for individuals. Most important, the release of private health information without consent is limited. Doctors treating patients, and hospitals, must obtain the patient's written consent to use their health information even for routine purposes such as treatment and payment. Other nonroutine disclosure requires specific patient authorization. Patients may access their own health files and request correction of potentially harmful errors.

Second, the rules set boundaries on medical record use and release. The amount of information to be disclosed is restricted to the "minimum necessary", in contrast to prevailing practice of releasing a patient's entire health record even if an entity needs very specific information.

Third, the rules attempt to ensure the security of personal health information. The rules are very specific in their mandates on providers and others who might access health information. They require privacy-conscious business practices, with internal procedures and privacy officers to protect the privacy of medical records. The rules create a whole new category of compliance officer within health care institutions as a result of the mandates in the rules.

Fourth, the rules create accountability for medical record use and release, with new criminal and civil penalties for improper use or disclosure. This rule applies the standards included in HIPAA to create new criminal penalties for intentional disclosure, up to $50,000 and up to a year in prison, with new civil penalties of $100 per person for unintentional disclosure and other violations, up to $25,000 per person per year. The rules do not however create a private cause of action for damages for harm that is suffered through intentional or negligent release of information.

Fifth, the rules attempt to balance public responsibility with privacy protections, requiring that information be disclosed only limited public purposes such as public health and research. They attempt to limit disclosure of information without sacrificing public safety.

See generally James G.Hodge, The Intersection of Federal Health Information Privacy and State Administrative Law: The Protection of Individual Health Data and Workers' Compensation, 51 Adm.L. Rev. 117(1999); (Health Privacy Project, The State of Health Privacy: An Uneven Terrain, Institute for Health Care Research and Policy, Georgetown University (July 1999) http://www.healthprivacy.org)

3. The urgency underlying the new federal medical privacy rules is understandable. Computer recordkeeping is increasingly common in storing and retrieving medical records. Indiana, for example, has expressly authorized retention of medical records in computer files. See West's Ann. Ind. Code §§ 34–3–15.5–1 et seq. Sensitive health care data are stored, transferred and used with the ease that only modern computers could allow. Given the sheer volume of data collected on each patient, the movement to computerize patient records is being pushed along by pressures from the federal and state governments as well as hospital desires for efficiency. As health care as blossomed into a complex industry, the organizations involved, from employers to drug companies and managed organizations, have a compelling interest in data to control their costs, increase revenues and improve performance. Information has as a result become a central aspect of the health care enterprise. Paul Starr, Health and the Right to Privacy, 25 Am.J.L. & Med. 194, 196(1999); Committee on Maintaining Privacy & Security in Health Care Applications of the National Information Infrastructure, National Research Council, For the Record: Protecting Electronic Health Information 25 (1997) (noting that more than half of hospitals were investing in electronic medical records and the market would grow into a $$1.5 billion industry by 2000); Lawrence O. Gostin, Health Information Privacy, 80 Cornell L.Rev. 451(1995); David M. Studdert, Direct Contracts, Data Sharing and Employee Risk Selection: New Stakes for Patient Privacy in Tomorrow's Health Insurance Markets, 25 Am.J.Law & Med. 233(1999).

4. Violations of health information privacy fall into three major categories. First, medical record information is abused or misappropriated. Legal protections for the alteration of the computerized medical record are less stringent than those for release of medical records generally. New computer development may add confidential information to these porous patient files. For example, the increased use of e-mail messages from patients to their physicians can lead to the storage of these messages in the file, allowed the patient's own words to be easily accessed. Patients may reveal too much in light of the casual and conversational attributes of e-mail messaging. Hackers may also gain access to hospital medical record systems. See,e.g., Ann Carrns, Hacker's Break–In at University Hospital Heats UP Debate on Security Standards, Wall St.J., December 2000. Data security measures and sanctions against misuse can reduce this problem.

Second, health information may be used by institutions for marketing and other commercial purposes, for example by selling patient prescription information to direct mail companies. Some of these uses may be valuable and the costs to patients small.

Third, organizations may abuse confidential patient health information in substantial and serious ways that result in discrimination, loss of employment, insurance or other welfare benefits. Alissa R. Spielberg, Online Without a Net: Physician–Patient Communication by Electronic Mail, 25 Am.J.Law & Med 267, 274 (1999); Latanya Sweeney, Weaving Technology and Policy Together to Maintain Confidentiality, 25 J.Law, Med & Ethics 98 (1997).

5.   The Institute of Medicine has recommended that all providers adopt a computer-based patient record as the standard. Personally identifiable health information about individuals is available in electronic form in health databases and online networks. Such computerization of records aims to improve efficiency in health care delivery. It is likely that a standardized on-line database for all patients will become the national norm. This movement toward medical record computerization creates serious computer security and confidentiality issues. A third party with a modem and a computer can in theory download confidential patient information, opening the door to even wider proliferation of sensitive information about individuals. This raises privacy concerns about individually identifiable health information and the quality and reliability of that information. A computer security system can offer substantial confidentiality protections compared to traditional medical records because fewer access points are available to a computer; each person's access can be restricted to limited information; and information can be monitored through individual access codes. Computer storage can be designed with safeguards such as passwords, access codes, and selective "need to know" requirements for certain portions of a patient's file. Unauthorized access to computer files can also be traced through audit systems more easily than can such access to paper records. Informed consent doctrine could be redefined to require both the physician and the institution to discuss some of these informational risks with patients.

Institute of Medicine, The Computer–Based Patient Record: An Essential Technology for Health Care (Richard S. Dick and Elaine B. Steen, eds. 1991); see also, General Accounting Office, Committee on Governmental Affairs, U.S. Senate, Medical ADP Systems: Automated Medical Records Hold Promise to Improve Patient Care (January 1991). See generally, Lawrence O. Gostin, Joan Turek–Brezina, Madison Powers, and Rene Kozloff, Privacy and Security of Health Information in the Emerging Health Care System, 5 Health Matrix 1 (1995); Wendy E. Parmet, Public Health Protection and the Privacy of Medical Records, 16 Harv.C.R.–C.L. L.Rev. 265 (1981); Diane B. Lawrence, Strict Liability Computer Software and Medicine: Public Policy at the Crossroads, 23 Tort & Ins.L.J. 1 (1991); Health Privacy Working Group, Principles for Health Privacy (1999)(www.healthprivacy.org).

6.   The obvious benefits of computerized record keeping have propelled medical records to a central position in health care delivery. A standardized database of patient information has the potential to promote efficiency, further competition, and allow providers to better track patient outcomes. Only a computerized record, in spite of its confidentiality dimensions, can further such goals. The new Medical Privacy Standards offer considerable protection to patients; they also require substantial expenditures by providers to achieve compliance by 2003 with the complex requirements.

See generally, James G. Hodge, National Health Information Privacy and New Federalism, 14 Notre Dame J.L.Ethics & Pub. Pol'y 791(2000); James G. Hodge, Lawrence O. Gostin, and Peter D. Jacobson, Legal Issues Concerning Electronic Health Information: Privacy, Quality, and Liability, 282 J.A.M.A. 1466(1999); Off. of Tech. Assessment, U.S. Congress, Protecting Privacy in Computerized Medical Information (1993); John D. Rootenberg, Computer–Based Patient Records: The Next Generation of Medicine?, 267 J.A.M.A. 168 (1992); Off. of Tech. Assessment, U.S. Congress, Policy Implications of Medical Information Systems 50–51 (1997). Institute of Medicine, The Computer–Based Patient Record: An Essential Technology for Health Care (1997)(www.nap.edu/readingroom/); Janlori Goldman, Protecting Privacy to Improve Health Care, 17 Health Affairs 47(1998).

C. DUTIES TO PROTECT THIRD PARTIES

The obligations of health professionals normally extend only to the patients with whom they have a legal relationship, either under an implied or an express contract. They are not under an obligation to enter into a relationship with a patient, and cannot be compelled to treat someone outside the boundaries of this contractual relationship. The Good Samaritan laws, discussed supra in Chapter 3, reflect legislative reinforcement of the absence of a duty to rescue at the common law. But what if doctors have information about a patient which if disclosed might prevent harm to others? Requirements of confidentiality of the physician-patient relationship militate against disclosure generally, and disclosure may expose the physician to potential liability, as the *Humphers* case indicates.

Physicians and other health professionals have in many jurisdictions an affirmative obligation to protect third parties against hazards created by their patients. Consider the limits on such a duty in *Pate* and *Bradshaw*, below.

PATE v. THRELKEL

Supreme Court of Florida, 1995.
661 So.2d 278.

WELLS, JUSTICE.

We have for review the following question certified to be of great public importance: DOES A PHYSICIAN OWE A DUTY OF CARE TO THE CHILDREN OF A PATIENT TO WARN THE PATIENT OF THE GENETICALLY TRANSFERABLE NATURE OF THE CONDITION FOR WHICH THE PHYSICIAN IS TREATING THE PATIENT? ... [ ]

In March 1987, Marianne New received treatment for medullary thyroid carcinoma, a genetically transferable disease. In 1990, Heidi Pate, New's adult daughter, learned that she also had medullary thyroid carcinoma. Consequently, Pate and her husband filed a complaint against the physicians who initially treated New for the disease as well as the physicians' respective employers. Pate and her husband alleged that the physicians knew or should have known of the likelihood that New's children would have inherited the condition genetically; that the physicians were under a duty to warn New that her children should be tested for the disease; that had New been warned in 1987, she would have had her children tested at that time; and if Pate had been tested in 1987, she would have taken preventative action, and her condition, more likely than not, would have been curable. Pate claimed that as a direct and proximate cause of the physicians' negligence, she suffers from advanced medullary thyroid carcinoma and its various damaging effects.

The respondent health care providers moved to dismiss the complaint for failure to state a cause of action. Specifically, the respondents alleged that Pate did not demonstrate the existence of a professional relationship between her and respondents and thus failed to establish that respondents owed her a duty of care. The trial court granted the motion and dismissed the Pates' complaint with prejudice, finding that the plaintiffs were not patients of the respondents and that they did not fit within any exception to the requirement that there be a physician-patient relationship between the parties as a condition precedent to bringing a medical malpractice action.

The district court affirmed the trial court's dismissal. The court rejected the Pates' argument that it should, based upon past decisions recognizing a doctor's duty to inform others of a patient's contagious disease, [ ] extend a physician's duty to cover the child of a patient who suffers from an inheritable disease. The court also rejected the Pates' reliance on Schroeder v. Perkel, 87 N.J. 53, 432 A.2d 834 (1981), in which the parents of a four-year-old child brought suit against the child's pediatricians for failing to diagnose the child with cystic fibrosis early enough to prevent the parents from having a second diseased child. The New Jersey court in Schroeder recognized that due to the special nature of the family relationship, a physician's duty may extend beyond a patient to members of the patient's immediate family. [ ]

In rejecting the Pates' claim, the district court focused upon the legal issue of duty. . . . [T]he district court recognized the existence of a physician's duty. The court, however, declined to extend the boundaries of that duty to include Heidi Pate. . . . [ ]

We agree with the district court's focus on duty. We conclude that to answer the certified question we must consider two questions related to duty. First, we must determine whether New's physicians had a duty to warn New of the genetically transferable nature of her disease. We find that to make this determination we must apply section 766.102, Florida Statutes (1989), which defines the legal duty owed by a health care provider in a medical malpractice case. . . . [ ] In applying this statute to the instant case, we conclude that a duty exists if the statutory standard of care requires a reasonably prudent health care provider to warn a patient of the genetically transferable nature of the condition for which the physician was treating the patient.

> In medical malpractice cases, the standard of care is determined by a consideration of expert testimony. . . . [ ] . . . [W]e must accept as true the Pates' allegations that pursuant to the prevailing standard of care, the health care providers were under a duty to warn New of the importance of testing her children for medullary thyroid carcinoma. . . . [ ]
>
> The second question we must address in answering the certified question is to whom does the alleged duty to warn New of the nature of her disease run? The duty obviously runs to the patient who is in privity with the physician. In the past, courts have held that in order to maintain a cause of action against a physician, privity must exist between the plaintiff and the physician. [ ] In other professional relationships, however, we have recognized the rights of identified third party beneficiaries to recover from a professional because that party was the intended beneficiary of the prevailing standard of care. In such cases, we have determined that an absence of privity does not necessarily foreclose liability. [ ]. . . . [ ] We conclude that this analysis recognizing that privity is not always needed to establish liability should apply to the professional relationship between a patient's child and a health care provider.

Here, the alleged prevailing standard of care was obviously developed for the benefit of the patient's children as well as the patient. We conclude that when the prevailing standard of care creates a duty that is obviously for the benefit of certain identified third parties and the physician knows of the existence of those third parties, then the physician's duty runs to those third parties. Therefore, in accord with our decision in Baskerville–Donovan Engineers, we hold that privity does not bar Heidi Pate's pursuit of a medical malpractice action. Our holding is likewise in accord with McCain because under the duty alleged in this case, a patient's children fall within the zone of foreseeable risk.

Though not encompassed by the certified question, there is another issue which should be addressed in light of our holding. If there is a duty to warn, to whom must the physician convey the warning? Our holding should not be read to require the physician to warn the patient's children of the disease. In most instances the physician is prohibited from disclosing the patient's medical condition to others except with the patient's permission. [ ] Moreover, the patient ordinarily can be expected to pass on the warning. To require the physician to seek out and warn various members of the patient's family would often be difficult or impractical and would place too heavy a burden upon the physician. Thus, we emphasize that in any circumstances in which the physician has a duty to warn of a genetically transferable disease, that duty will be satisfied by warning the patient.

Accordingly, we conclude that the trial court erred by dismissing the complaint with prejudice. . . .

Notes and Questions

1. Define the limits imposed in *Pate*. Is there any reason for the duty to disclose to be so limited? The court in *Pate* uses existing medical customary practice as a limit, but isn't that too limited a duty in cases where no custom exists or the existing custom fails to protect third parties? After all, is a medical specialty likely to willingly and broadly define a standard of care to expand their obligations to third parties not their patients? See Jeffrey W. Burnett, A Physician's Duty to Warn a Patient's Relatives of a Patient's Genetically Inheritable Disease, 36 Hous.L.Rev.559 (1999); Lawrence O. Gostin and James G. Hodge, Genetic Privacy and the Law: An End to Genetics Exceptionalism, 40 Jurimetrics J.21 (1999); Angela Liang, The Argument Against a Physician's Duty To Warn for Genetic Diseases: The Conflicts Created by Safer v. Pack, 1 J.Health Care L. & Pol'y 437 (1998).

2. In Bradshaw v. Daniel, 854 S.W.2d 865 (Tenn.1993), the court considered whether a physician had a duty to warn a non-patient, the wife of his patient, of her risk of exposure to his patient's non-contagious disease, Rocky Mountain Spotted Fever. The plaintiff's expert had testified that the ticks carrying the disease "clustered", so that people hiking together would be exposed to the disease vector, the ticks. A physician treating a patient with symptoms of Rocky Mountain Spotted Fever should advise the family of the patient as to the incubation period, the symptoms of the disease, and the need for immediate medical attention upon manifestation of the symptoms. The disease, untreated, has a 40 percent mortality rate, but only 4 percent mortality rate if treatment is given promptly.

We, therefore, conclude that the existence of the physician-patient relationship is sufficient to impose upon a physician an affirmative duty to warn identifiable third persons in the patient's immediate family against foreseeable risks emanating from a patient's illness.

In *Bradshaw*, the risk was self-limiting. What is the unifying factor in these cases, and in most of the duty to disclose cases?

3. Duties to warn patients of medical risks may arise out of medical knowledge of how diseases are communicated. In Tenuto v. Lederle Laboratories, 90 N.Y.2d 606, 665 N.Y.S.2d 17, 687 N.E.2d 1300 (N.Y.1997), aff'd 276 A.D.2d 550, 714 N.Y.S.2d 448 (N.Y.A.D. 2 Dept.2000), Dr. Schwartz gave a second dose of oral poliomyelitis vaccine manufactured by Lederle to a five month old girl. He did not ask the girl's father Mr. Tenuto whether he had previously been vaccinated against polio, nor did he advise the parents of the risk for contact polio and precautions to avoid exposure, particularly in light of surgical wound from surgery that Mr. Tenuto was about to undergo. It was a rare but predictable risk that live viruses in an infant recipient's gastrointestinal tract may grow and revert to virulent form. When these wild viruses are excreted from the infant's bowel in feces or from the mouth in saliva, contact with feces or saliva may result in infection and in vulnerable adults in paralytic polio. These risks, known since 1961, were found since 1977 in the package inserts and the Physician Desk Reference (PDR).

The court held that plaintiffs fell within a determinate and identified class of immediate family members whose relationships to the "person acted upon have traditionally been recognized as a means of extending and yet limiting the scope of liability for injuries caused by a party's negligent acts or omissions."

> Moreover, existence of a special relationship sufficient to supply the predicate for extending the duty to warn and advise plaintiffs of their peril and the need to employ precautions is especially pointed where, as here, the physician is a pediatrician engaged by the parents to provide medical services to their infant, and whose services, by necessity, require advising the patient's parents. Thus, the special relationship factor is triangulated here, involving interconnections of reliance running directly between plaintiffs and Dr. Schwartz, and indirectly from their status and responsibility as the primary caretakers of his infant patient.

> . . . it would be inferable that in administering the vaccine and advising plaintiffs, as parents of his infant patient, Dr. Schwartz knew or should have known that his comprehensive services necessarily brought into play the protection of the health of plaintiffs, who relied upon his professional expertise in providing advice and other forms of medical services.

What about a day care teacher, an au pair caring for the infant, a visiting grandmother? Is warning the parents sufficient? Is this duty, like the duty imposed on the physician in Bradshaw, supra at n. 2, self-limiting?

4. Genetically transmissible risks elevate a physician's duty to warn beyond imminent contagious diseases to latent genetic defects that may or may not materialize over a long period of time. Consider the breast cancer gene. A woman who possesses the gene might want to step up self-monitoring, mammograms and other early detection approaches. When physicians err in analyzing patients' genetic histories, the consequences can be serious.

Many of the wrongful birth/wrongful life cases involve negligence by a genetic counselor or physician in advising parents as to their risks in having genetically impaired children. See Chapter 16 infra. Courts have split in their willingness to impose duties on physicians for such errors. In Richardson v. Rohrbaugh, 857 S.W.2d 415 (Mo.App. E.D.1993) the Richardson's son Cody was a patient of Dr. Rohrbaugh, a pediatric neurologist. Cody was severely retarded and suffered from club foot. He told them that Cody's condition was not genetic and there was no reason they should not have another child. Their second child was born with the same condition as Cody, Fahr's Syndrome. The court struggled to avoid pinning responsibility on the doctor for his obvious ignorance. It held that no doctor-patient relationship existed. In a curious holding, the court wrote:

> To allow discussions between pediatricians and the parents of the child patient to spawn a factual issue of whether a physician/patient relationship exists with the parents * * * grows dangerously close to birthing an offspring of liability that would chill communications between pediatricians and parents. We are not willing to breath life into such a claim.

5. A long line of cases involve risks of contagious diseases. In Shepard v. Redford Community Hospital, 151 Mich.App. 242, 390 N.W.2d 239 (1986) the court held that the treating physicians were negligent in part for failing to warn the mother about the risk of transmission of spinal meningitis to her young son, who ultimately died from the disease; the duty created by the physician-patient relationship extended to the patient's child. Physicians have been held liable for failing to warn the daughter of a patient with scarlet fever, a wife about the danger of infection from a patient's wounds, a neighbor about the patient's smallpox. Family members are foreseeable third parties, as are neighbors. See Skillings v. Allen, 143 Minn. 323, 173 N.W. 663 (1919); Edwards v. Lamb, 69 N.H. 599, 45 A. 480 (1899); Freese v. Lemmon, 210 N.W.2d 576 (Iowa 1973).

6. The courts have moved beyond family members to include then unknown third parties, imposing on treating physicians a duty to inform patients or to warn third parties when deadly illnesses such as AIDS or highly contagious ones such as hepatitis are involved. In Reisner v. Regents of the University of California, 31 Cal.App.4th 1195, 37 Cal.Rptr.2d 518 (2d Dist. 1995), the patient of Dr. Fonklesrud, 12–year old Jennifer Lawson, received a transfusion contaminated with HIV antibodies during surgery. Dr. Fonkelsrud learned of the contamination, continued to treat Jennifer but never told her or her parents about the tainted blood. Three years later, she started to date Daniel Reisner and they had sexual relations. Two years later, the doctor finally told Jennifer she had AIDS and Jennifer told Daniel. Jennifer died a month later. Daniel then learned he was HIV positive.

The defendants argued they owed no duty to Daniel, who was an unidentified third party at the time Jennifer was infected with HIV. The court cited *Tarasoff* and other cases that had imposed a duty to warn either the patient or third parties about risks, holding that the defendants had a duty to warn a contagious patient to take steps to protect others.

> Once the physician warns the patient of the risk to others and advises the patient how to prevent the spread of the disease, the physician has fulfilled his duty—and no more (but no less) is required....

> ... We need not decide in this case what the result would be if someone infected by Daniel sued the doctor who failed to warn Jennifer, and the fact that a duty is owed to Daniel does not mean it will be extended without limitation. However, the possibility of such an extension does not offend us, legally or morally. Viewed in the abstract ... we believe that a doctor who knows he is dealing with the 20th Century version of Typhoid Mary ought to have a very strong incentive to tell his patient what she ought to do and not do and how she ought to comport herself in order to prevent the spread of her disease.

In DiMarco v. Lynch Homes—Chester County, 525 Pa. 558, 583 A.2d 422 (1990), the sexual partner of a patient sued her physicians, who had assured her that she would not contract hepatitis. The plaintiff Janet Viscichini, a blood technician, went to the Lynch Home to take a blood sample from one of the residents. During the procedure, her skin was accidentally punctured by the needle she had used to extract blood. When she learned that the patient had hepatitis, she sought treatment from Doctors Giunta and Alwine. They told her that if she remained symptom free for six weeks, she would not be infected by the hepatitis virus. She was not told to refrain from sexual relations for any period of time following her exposure to the disease, but she practiced sexual abstinence until eight weeks after the exposure. Since she had remained symptom-free during that time, she then resumed sexual relations with the plaintiff. She was later diagnosed as suffering from hepatitis B in September; in December, the plaintiff was similarly diagnosed.

The court cited Restatement (Second) Torts, s. 324A, which provided in part that one who provides services to another may be liable to a third person for harm resulting from his failure to exercise reasonable care, if the "the harm is suffered because of reliance of the other or the third person upon the undertaking." The court allowed the action, concluding that the class of persons at risk included any one who is physically intimate with the patient.

> When a physician treats a patient who has been exposed to or who has contracted a communicable and/or contagious disease, it is imperative that the physician give his or her patient the proper advice about preventing the spread of the disease. ... Physicians are the first line of defense against the spread of communicable diseases, because physicians know what measures must be taken to prevent the infection of others.

7. Medication Side–effects. Caselaw requires physicians to warn third parties about, or take steps to protect them from, patients who are taking medication. These steps might include warning the patient about the effects of medication, or even refusing to prescribe the medication if the patient might still drive. See Welke v. Kuzilla, 144 Mich.App. 245, 375 N.W.2d 403 (1985); Myers v. Quesenberry, 144 Cal.App.3d 888, 193 Cal.Rptr. 733 (1983)(physician failed to warn his patient, a diabetic, of the dangers of driving). Contra, see Mavrogenis v. Hall, 126 N.M. 404, 970 P.2d 590 (N.M. 1998)(physician exercised no direct control over patient's ingestion of medication, and owed no duty to third parties).

8. Psychiatric Dangerousness. In Tarasoff v. Regents of the Univ. of Cal., 17 Cal.3d 425, 131 Cal.Rptr. 14, 551 P.2d 334 (1976), a psychotherapist at the University of California was treating a patient, Poddar, who had uttered explicit threats toward his former girlfriend during the therapy sessions. No one, including the defendant, attempted to warn the young woman, and Poddar ultimately killed her. The parents sued, alleging negligence in the therapist's failure to warn. The California Supreme Court held that a therapist treating a mentally ill patient owes a duty of reasonable care to warn threatened persons against foreseeable danger created by the patient's condition. The relationship between the physician or therapist and the patient is sufficient to create a duty to protect others.

The *Tarasoff* duty has been accepted by most states. See e.g. O'Keefe v. Orea, 731 So.2d 680 (Fla.App.1998); Turner v. Jordan, 957 S.W.2d 815 (Tenn.1997), with only Texas and Virginia explicitly rejecting *Tarasoff*. See Nasser v. Parker, 249 Va. 172, 455 S.E.2d 502 (Va. 1995); Thapar v. Zezulka, 994 S.W.2d 635 (Tex.1999).

Cases involving epileptics or others with conditions that might impair driving occur frequently. Courts are reluctant to require a physician to notify the state as to a patient's condition. See Crosby v. Sultz, 405 Pa.Super. 527, 592 A.2d 1337 (Pa.Super.1991) (no duty to report patient to Department of Transportation, since type of diabetes did not impose duty to warn); Estate of Witthoeft v. Kiskaddon, 557 Pa. 340, 733 A.2d 623 (Pa.1999)(Physician owed no duty to third party for injuries suffered in a car accident caused by a patient; he was ophthalmologist who did not notify the Pennsylvania Department of Transportation of the patient's poor visual acuity); Praesel v. Johnson, 967 S.W.2d 391 (Tex.1998).

Problem: The Stubborn Patient

You represent Dr. Will Toma, a physician specializing in gerontology. He regularly examines and treats elderly patients, and has come to you for advice. One of his patients, Harry Glint, 86 years old, has a mild neurological disorder that causes blurred or double vision at times. Harry complains that his double vision is worst when he drives at night, when, he says, "The middle line becomes double and I have trouble staying on my side of the road." The problem is not treatable and it will worsen over time (although changes in prescriptions of eyeglasses may reduce the problem at times). Dr. Toma has admonished Mr. Glint never to drive at night, and to stop driving during the day as soon as possible. Mr. Glint is adamant about the importance of his driving, which he says keeps him young and active.

Dr. Toma is worried about his potential liability if Mr. Glint has a car accident that injures others. What are his liability risks, and what steps can he take to minimize them?

Problem: The Tour Bus

A physician, Dr. Vivian Hayes, has been treating a patient, Steven Moore, who just returned from a bus tour of Germany. Moore has a illness caused by the bite of a small tick found on deer in the Black Forest of Germany. Dr. Hayes has successfully treated the illness. Moore took a bus tour of Germany and the Black Forest with a group put together by a travel agency, Rathskeller Travel, which declared bankruptcy shortly after the trip was over. What further obligations does Dr. Hayes have? Should she notify the state division of public health? The tour members were from twenty different states. Should she call everyone on the roster of the tour?

D. CONFIDENTIALITY AND DISCLOSURE OF AIDS–RELATED INFORMATION

DOE v. MARSELLE

Supreme Court of Connecticut, 1996.
236 Conn. 845, 675 A.2d 835.

KATZ, ASSOCIATE JUDGE.

The dispositive issue on appeal is whether in order to state a cause of action under General Statutes § 19a–590[1] for a violation of General Statutes § 19a–583 (AIDS statute)[2], the confidentiality provision of chapter 368x,

---

1. General Statutes § 19a–590 provides: "Liability for violations. Any person, except as otherwise provided in this chapter, who wilfully violates any provision of this chapter shall be liable in a private cause of action for injuries suffered as a result of such violation. Upon a finding that an individual has been injured as a result of such violation, damages shall be assessed in the amount sufficient to compensate said individual for such injury."

2. General Statutes § 19a–583 provides in relevant part: "Limitations on disclosure of HIV-related information. (a) No person who obtains confidential HIV-related information may disclose or be compelled to disclose such information. . . . "

entitled "AIDS Testing and Medical Information," a plaintiff must allege that the person who violated that provision intended to engage in the prohibited conduct and intended to produce the resulting injury. We conclude that a wilful violation of § 19a–583 requires only a knowing disclosure of confidential human immunodeficiency virus (HIV) related information.

The following facts are undisputed. The plaintiff, Jane Doe, was a patient of the defendant Dionisio C. Flores, a surgeon, to whom, during the course of her treatment, she disclosed that she was infected with HIV. A surgical assistant employed by Flores, the named defendant Doris Marselle, after learning of the plaintiff's condition from her medical chart and from personal discussions with the plaintiff, consulted Flores regarding her intention to disclose the plaintiff's HIV status to Marselle's sons who were illegal drug users and who had friends in common with the plaintiff. Flores authorized Marselle to make the disclosures provided that she not identify the plaintiff by name.

When the plaintiff learned that Marselle had told at least three other individuals in the community that she was HIV positive, the plaintiff, who had never authorized the disclosures, brought a multicount complaint against Flores and Marselle alleging that they each had: (1) violated the confidentiality provisions of § 19a–583 by intentionally disclosing her HIV status (first count); (2) violated the Connecticut Unfair Trade Practices Act (CUTPA); General Statutes § 42–110b; based upon a breach of confidentiality and Flores' false representations to her that her HIV status would be kept confidential (third and fourth counts); and (3) negligently inflicted emotional distress by disclosing her HIV status (sixth count). Additionally, the plaintiff alleged that Flores had been negligent in failing to instruct his employees regarding their obligation to comply with General Statutes § 19a–581 et seq. (second count), and that Marselle had intentionally inflicted emotional distress by wilfully disclosing the confidential medical information (fifth count).

* * *

In her appeal to the Appellate Court, the plaintiff argued that the term "wilful" in § 19a–590 means "intentionally" as opposed to "accidentally" and that the trial court improperly had defined the term to mean intending to injure. [ ] The Appellate Court disagreed * * *

Thereafter, the plaintiff petitioned this court for certification. We granted certification limited to the following questions: (1) "Did the Appellate Court correctly conclude that the second amended complaint did not allege a wilful violation of General Statutes § 19a–583 (a)?"; and (2) "Did the Appellate Court properly decide that the plaintiff's negligence, negligent infliction of emotional distress and Connecticut Unfair Trade Practices Act (CUTPA) counts had been properly stricken?" Doe v. Marselle, 235 Conn. 915, 665 A.2d

General Statutes § 19a–581 (8) defines "confidential HIV-related information" as "any information pertaining to the protected individual or obtained pursuant to a release of confidential HIV-related information, concerning whether a person has been counseled regarding HIV infection, has been the subject of an HIV-related test, or has HIV infection, HIV-related illness or AIDS, or information which identifies or reasonably could identify a person as having one or more of such conditions, including information pertaining to such individual's partners.... "

606 (1995). Because we answer both certified questions in the negative, we reverse.

* * *

The AIDS statute was designed and intended to combat the AIDS epidemic, beginning with protecting confidentiality. The legislation imposes certain requirements on the testing and treatment of persons who may be HIV positive or who have AIDS. These requirements relate principally to the areas of informed consent for HIV testing and confidential treatment of HIV-related information, and are aimed at helping health care providers to identify those people with the disease, to treat them and to educate them in an attempt to put an end to the epidemic in our state, which, at the time this legislation was under consideration, had the ninth highest number of AIDS cases per capita in the nation and the highest percentage of AIDS cases in children. [ ] As one of the bill's sponsors, Representative Benjamin N. DeZinno, Jr., explained, * * * the bill was intended to "protect the confidentiality of data related to AIDS, requires informed consent for tests for the AIDS virus, and allows for notification of partners of those that are so infected." [ ] He explained that in order to "wipe out or hope to wipe [out] this horrible epidemic disease in our lifetime ... [w]e have to start with protecting the confidentiality ... [b]ecause people will not step forward for testing and treatment of AIDS unless they know that a positive result will not become public information. I think that's very important. Now unfortunately, there is widespread discrimination against the AIDS victim, and many people would rather [forgo] treatment, than risk being stigmatized."[10] [ ]

Beth Weinstein, chief of the AIDS section for the then department of health services, now the department of public health and addiction services (department), along with James Hadler, a physician and the chief of the epidemiology section of the department, testified that the department had proposed "this critical legislation ... [to] provide us with the tools to continue fighting the AIDS epidemic in Connecticut. If passed, it will protect the confidentiality of AIDS information and will require informed consent for the test for the virus which causes AIDS.... The AIDS epidemic has magnified many problems in the existing health care system. Among the most glaring is the lack of protection [in] current Connecticut statutes for informed consent and disclosure of information. Although this problem goes beyond AIDS, we feel it is most important to solve it for AIDS because of the sensitivities regarding the disease." Conn. Joint Standing Committee Hearings, Public Health, Pt. 3, 1989 Sess., p. 766. Weinstein explained how this legislation was necessary to encourage confidential testing and to allow medical providers to provide proper follow-up treatment. "In most of the sites that the department

---

10. Studies in the medical literature indicate that fear of discrimination discourages people from seeking appropriate care. See K. Siegel, M. Levine, C. Brooks & R. Kern, "The Motives of Gay Men for Taking or Not Taking the HIV Antibody Test," 36 Social Problems 368, 378–79 (1989) (people avoid HIV testing in part because they fear discrimination if their illness or sexual behavior become known); R. Weitz, "Anonymity in Testing for HIV Antibodies Desired Option," 81 Am.J.Pub. Health 1213 (1991) (fear of discrimination based on illness or on having been tested). As one recent nationwide study found, people are more likely to undergo HIV testing if they believe that their test results will remain private. K. Phillips, "The Relationship of 1988 State HIV Testing Policies to Previous and Planned Voluntary Use of HIV Testing," 7 J. Acquired Immune Deficiency Syndromes 403, 405 (1994).

funds for counseling and testing for the AIDS virus, anonymous testing is done, largely because we don't have confidentiality protection. However, anonymous testing has limitations. Counselors have no ability to follow-up with clients to provide support for behavior change, additional counseling, public health services, social services or medical assistance. Voluntary testing in which the identity of the person tested [is] known will only be widely accepted if there is specific protection in the statutes." Id., p. 767. Weinstein concluded her testimony by emphasizing that confidentiality is essential "to protect people from the discrimination that often comes with the knowledge that a person has AIDS or HIV infection" and to help eliminate the stigma that often accompanies AIDS. Id., pp. 768–69.

In order to accomplish the aforementioned goals, disclosure of confidential HIV-related information is prohibited except in very limited and discrete circumstances. [ ][11] Even health care providers or persons who engage in

11. General Statutes § 19a–583 provides in relevant part: "Limitations on disclosure of HIV-related information. (a) No person who obtains confidential HIV-related information may disclose or be compelled to disclose such information, except to the following:

"(1) The protected individual, his legal guardian or a person authorized to consent to health care for such individual;

"(2) Any person who secures a release of confidential HIV-related information;

"(3) A federal, state or local health officer when such disclosure is mandated or authorized by federal or state law;

"(4) A health care provider or health facility when knowledge of the HIV-related information is necessary to provide appropriate care or treatment to the protected individual or a child of the individual or when confidential HIV-related information is already recorded in a medical chart or record and a health care provider has access to such record for the purpose of providing medical care to the protected individual;

"(5) A medical examiner to assist in determining the cause or circumstances of death;

"(6) Health facility staff committees or accreditation or oversight review organizations which are conducting program monitoring, program evaluation or service reviews;

"(7) A health care provider or other person in cases where such provider or person in the course of his occupational duties has had a significant exposure to HIV infection, provided the following criteria are met: (A) The worker is able to document significant exposure during performance of his occupation, (B) the worker completes an incident report within forty-eight hours of exposure, identifying the parties to the exposure, witnesses, time, place and nature of the event, (C) the worker submits to a baseline HIV test within seventy-two hours of the exposure and is negative on that test for the presence of the AIDS virus, (D) the

patient's or person's physician or, if the patient or person does not have a personal physician or if the patient's or person's physician is unavailable, another physician or health care provider has approached the patient or person and sought voluntary consent to disclosure and the patient or person refuses to consent to disclosure, except in an exposure where the patient or person is deceased, (E) the worker would be able to take meaningful immediate action as defined in regulations adopted pursuant to section 19a–589 which could not otherwise be taken, (F) an exposure evaluation group determines that the criteria specified in subparagraphs (A), (B), (C), (D) and (E) of this subdivision are met and that a worker has a significant exposure to the blood of a patient or person and the patient or person or the patient's or person's legal guardian refuses to consent to release of the information. No member of the exposure evaluation group who determines that a worker has sustained a significant exposure and authorizes the disclosure of confidential HIV-related information nor the health facility, correctional facility or other institution nor any person in a health facility, correctional facility or other institution who relies in good faith on the group's determination and discloses the result shall have any liability as a result of his action carried out under this section, unless such persons acted in bad faith. If the information is not held by a health facility, correctional facility or other institution, a physician not directly involved in the exposure has certified in writing that the criteria specified in subparagraphs (A), (B), (C), (D) and (E) of this subdivision are met and that a significant exposure has occurred;

"(8) Employees of hospitals for mental illness operated by the department of mental health * * *;

"(9) Employees of facilities operated by the department of correction * * *;

"(11) Life and health insurers, government payers and health care centers and their affili-

occupational therapy who have had significant exposure to HIV infection are not entitled to this information unless they satisfy the rigid criteria listed in § 19a–583(a)(7). See footnote 11. Similarly, employees of mental health hospitals operated by the department of mental health and correctional facilities operated by the department of correction are not entitled to this information even when the patient or inmate poses a significant risk of transmission unless the infection control committee of the hospital or the medical director and chief administrator of the correctional facility first determine that such disclosure is likely to prevent or reduce the risk of transmission and that no reasonable alternatives exist that will achieve the same goal and preserve the confidentiality of the information. [ ]

A person who does not fall within these exceptions may petition the court for disclosure, however, a court order may be issued only when the moving party demonstrates a clear and imminent danger to the health of another or the public health and further demonstrates a compelling need for the test results that cannot be accommodated by other means. In assessing compelling need, the court must weigh, among other things, the need for disclosure against the privacy interest of the test subject and the public interest that may be disserved by disclosure that deters future testing or that may lead to discrimination. [ ] Finally, even when disclosure is authorized, the AIDS statute strictly limits the terms of that disclosure. See General Statutes § 19a–585. In short, the drafters of this legislation "crafted the bill very carefully to give protection while also enabling those who care for people with AIDS and HIV infection to have access to information needed for the patient's care."[14] [ ]

Keeping this legislative history in mind, coupled with the elaborate statutory safeguards imposed against disclosure of HIV-related information, it is difficult to presume a definition of wilful that would make permissible the unauthorized disclosure of a person's HIV-related information except in the extreme situation where the person disclosing the information actually intends to injure the protected individual. We have noted that as part of its attempt to foster an increase in medical treatment for people with AIDS and HIV infection, the legislature created the AIDS statute to correct the prob-

ates, reinsurers, and contractors, except agents and brokers, in connection with underwriting and claim activity for life, health, and disability benefits; and

"(12) Any health care provider specifically designated by the protected individual to receive such information received by a life or health insurer or health care center pursuant to an application for life, health or disability insurance.

"(b) No person, except the protected individual, his legal guardian or a person authorized to consent to health care for such individual, to whom confidential HIV-related information is disclosed may further disclose such information, except as provided in this section and sections 19a–584 and 19a–585."

14. The legislature's concern for discrimination against people with AIDS is well founded. In a 1993 poll, 35.7 percent of the respondents said they were "afraid" of people with AIDS, 27.7 percent were "disgusted" and 27.1 percent were "angry." G. Herek & J. Capitanio, "Public Reactions to AIDS in the United States: A Second Decade of Stigma," 83 Am. J.Pub.Health 574, 575 (1993). More than one in five Americans (20.4 percent) would avoid an office job if they had to work with a man with AIDS, and nearly one half (47.1 percent) would avoid a neighborhood grocery store if the owner had AIDS. Id. Feelings of hostility translate into acts of discrimination against people infected with HIV. In lawsuits across the country, people have alleged discrimination based on HIV status in housing, employment and access to public accommodations, as well as in education and health care. See L. Gostin, Jr., "A National Review of Court and Human Rights Commission Decisions, Part II: Discrimination," 263 J.Am.Med.Assn. 2086 (1990) (listing nearly 150 lawsuits and other complaints stemming from such alleged discrimination).

lems, such as the lack of confidentiality, that have stood in the way of this goal. A definition of wilful that would require a plaintiff to prove that confidentiality was breached with the intent to cause injury would do nothing to advance the laudable goals of the legislation's sponsors. Indeed, were we to apply the definition of wilful proposed by Flores and adopted by the Appellate Court, a patient who is HIV positive, knowing that he or she could obtain redress for a violation of the confidentiality provisions in only the most egregious circumstances, would have no confidence that his or her status or test results would be zealously protected. This lack of confidence, in turn, would create a disincentive for that person to submit to testing. Additionally, because General Statutes § 19a–582(b)(4) requires that pretest counseling include "an explanation of the confidentiality protections afforded confidential HIV-related information, including the circumstances under which and classes of persons to whom disclosure of such information may be required, authorized or permitted by law," the lack of protection resulting from a definition of wilful that requires an evil intent would be more likely to eviscerate the purpose of the statute and consequently undermine the public health strategy against AIDS that prompted the legislation. It is not our practice to construe a statute in a way to thwart its purpose or lead to absurd results; [ ] or in a way "that fails to attain a rational and sensible result that bears directly on the purpose the legislature sought to achieve." [ ] Consequently, we cannot endorse a definition of wilful that would allow virtually any disclosure of confidential HIV-related information.

Moreover, to limit the definition of wilful to the case of a medical provider who intended to cause the patient injury, as Flores argues, would be to provide a cure for which there is no disease. No one speaking on behalf of the legislation identified a problem with medical providers seeking to sabotage the ability of their AIDS patients to obtain good medical care. Nor has Flores argued that such a problem exists. Because we do not presume that the legislature enacted legislation that was devoid of purpose; [ ] we will not interpret wilful as Flores has proposed.

Rather, we interpret wilful to mean a knowing disclosure of confidential HIV-related information. Contrary to the Appellate Court's assertion, this interpretation does not render the term superfluous. Had the term wilful not been used, persons would be liable for inadvertent disclosures or nonvolitional acts. By establishing liability only for wilful violations, the legislature indicated that inadvertent violations would not be actionable.

* * *

The judgment is reversed and the case is remanded for further proceedings according to law.

Notes and Questions

1. Consider the exceptions to nondisclosure specified in the statute in footnote 11. Do you see any problems with some of these exceptions? How about exception 7? Does it provide adequate safeguards for patients, in the face of provider anxiety about exposure to the HIV/AIDS virus? In Doe v. Protective Life Ins. Co., 1998 WL 568326 (Conn.Super.1998), the court allowed disclosure under protective orders (limited to named defendants in case).

2. Special characteristics of AIDS and of the AIDS epidemic present new and unique challenges to health care workers trying to understand their general duty

to keep confidences and their specific obligations, under some circumstances, to disclose medical information. First, widespread continuing fear of AIDS and ignorance about how it is spread, combined with a history of prejudice and discrimination against gay men among whom AIDS has been most common, have made concerns of privacy and confidentiality even more urgently important. If information about a person's AIDS infection or HIV positivity reaches employers, insurers, schools, family, or acquaintances it may have disastrous consequences. It is widely believed, therefore, that maintenance of the strictest confidentiality is essential if voluntary AIDS testing programs are to succeed—that any risk of disclosure will discourage persons who may possibly be HIV infected or who have AIDS or ARC from seeking testing and counseling.

Second, the fact that the HIV virus cannot be spread through casual contact, unlike many other contagious diseases, limits the need for disclosure of information about infection. The fact that the rate of infection through heterosexual genital intercourse is very low (about .001 per exposure) may argue against a duty to warn heterosexual partners, since it is unlikely that casual heterosexual partners will be infected, or may argue in favor of a warning, since it is possible that longer term partners may have not yet been infected. The possibility of transmission to unborn children may also argue for warning potentially infected persons who may potentially bear children.

Third, the fact that AIDS is presently incurable makes prevention all the more essential. Does this argue for maintaining strict confidentiality, so that persons who may be infected will come forward to be tested and thereafter modify their behavior voluntarily to avoid infecting others? Or does it argue for limited disclosure to protect persons who may be exposed to possible infection? Does the emergence of new treatment modalities like AZT, which may slow the infection process, argue for greater confidentiality or broader disclosure?

What is the relevance to questions of confidentiality and disclosure of the fact that HIV testing results in a significant number of false positives in low-risk populations? Of what significance is the fact that HIV positivity may not show up in testing until months, perhaps years, after a person becomes HIV infected?

3. Should medical records or laboratory specimens of patients in health care institutions who are HIV positive be specially marked to permit special precautions to protect against infection? Might doing so unduly risk further disclosure of confidential information, while offering little additional protection to health care workers who should be observing universal precautions against infection in any event? Might such special identification lull health care workers into unwarranted complacency in dealing with patients and specimens not so identified, despite the fact that patients may be infected but untested or that tests may have resulted in false negatives? Should infected medical personnel be reported to licensure agencies? What action, if any, should licensure agencies take based upon this information?

4. Health care workers should certainly counsel HIV-infected patients to take special precautions to avoid infecting others and to tell their sexual or needle-sharing partners to seek testing, counseling, and treatment. If patients indicate, however, that they will not do so, does the health care worker have an obligation to warn others? Should the health care worker rather notify the state health department of the patient's infected status and of persons who may have been infected by the patient, to permit contact tracing? Even if the health care worker has no duty to warn, is the worker permitted to do so, or does the health care

worker face liability for violating confidentiality requirements if she or he proceeds to warn potentially infected persons?

Consider the AMA position on this question:

Where there is no statute that mandates or prohibits reporting of seropositive individuals to public health authorities and it is clear that the seropositive individual is endangering an identified third party, the physician should (1) attempt to persuade the infected individual to cease endangering the third party; (2) if persuasion fails, notify authorities; and (3) if authorities take no action, notify and counsel the endangered third party.

HIV Blood Test Counseling: A.M.A. Physician Guidelines (1988)

5. The states have adopted a variety of legislative and administrative approaches to confidentiality and disclosure of information regarding HIV-positivity, ARC, and AIDS status. All states now require physicians to report AIDS cases to the state health department. A number also require reporting of cases of asymptomatic HIV infection. Several states have adopted statutes mandating strict confidentiality of AIDS-related information. See Cal.Health & Safety Code, § 199.21; West's Fla.Stat.Ann. § 14A § 381.609(2)(f); Mass.Gen.L. Ch. 111 § 70F. Other states have adopted laws permitting disclosure of HIV test results to certain persons or under certain circumstances. See Vernon's Ann.Tex.Rev.Civ.Stat. art. 4419b–1, § 9.03, (disclosure to spouse permitted); Ga.Code Ann. § 38–723(g) (disclosure to spouse, sexual partner or child permitted under some circumstances); McKinney's–N.Y.Pub.Health Law § 2782(4)(a) & (b) (physician may disclose information to persons in significant risk of infection if already infected person will not do so after counseling and physician warns that person of the physician's intention to disclose.) The identity of the infected person cannot be disclosed. (The physician is protected from liability whether he discloses or chooses not to disclose the information.) For an excellent recent review of state statutes, see David P.T. Price, Between Scylla and Charybdis: Charting A Course to Reconcile The Duty of Confidentiality and the Duty to Warn in the AIDS Context, 94 Dick.L.Rev. 435 (1990). See also *www.unaids.org/hivaidsinfo/documents.html#wad* and Report on the Global HIV/AIDS Epidemic, June 2000.

6. A number of states permit public health authorities to engage in contact tracing or partner notification with respect to persons with AIDS or who are HIV infected. Five different approaches to contact tracing have been identified: 1) solicitation of the names of all sexual and needle-sharing contacts of AIDS-and HIV-infected persons with subsequent notification of all identified contacts (with offers for testing and counseling); 2) limited contact tracing focusing on high risk or especially vulnerable groups who are likely to be unaware of the risk of infection (heterosexual contacts of individuals with AIDS); 3) voluntary contact tracing: infected persons are asked to notify potentially infected persons voluntarily and assistance is offered to those who want help in notifying others; 4) notification in special circumstances, as to rescue or emergency personnel potentially infected in the line of duty; 5) notification of specific persons in specific situations, such as those exposed to infected blood. See Karen Rothenberg, et al. The AIDS Project: Creating a Public Health Policy—Rights and Obligations of Health Care Workers, 48 Md.L.Rev. 94, 181–183 (1989). Colorado has been particularly active in contact tracing, and claims that its program has resulted in the identification and treatment of a number of individuals who would not otherwise have been aware of their HIV positive status. See Partner Notification for Preventing Immunodeficiency Virus (HIV) Infection—Colorado, Idaho, South Carolina, Virginia, 260 J.A.M.A. 613 (1988). Does the fact that contact tracing

usually depends on voluntary disclosure of sexual and needle-sharing partners by the infected person render it ineffective in situations where the infected person refuses to notify others voluntarily? See generally Lawrence O. Gostin and James G. Hodge, Piercing the Veil of Secrecy in HIV/AIDS and Other Sexually Transmitted Diseases: Theories of Privacy and Disclosure in Partner Notification, 5 Duke J. Gender L. & Pol'y 9 (1998).

7.   One particular situation in which the disclosure of the identify of HIV-infected persons has been frequently sought is where a person who has become HIV infected through tainted blood seeks disclosure of the identity of the donor who donated the infected blood, either to assist in establishing negligence on the part of the blood service or to permit a suit against the donor. These cases have tended to deny discovery, relying on various privacy, physician patient privilege, or discovery protection theories and on the importance of protecting the identity of blood donors to encourage voluntary blood donations. See Krygier v. Airweld, Inc., 137 Misc.2d 306, 520 N.Y.S.2d 475 (1987); Rasmussen v. South Florida Blood Service, Inc., 500 So.2d 533 (Fla.1987); contra, see Gulf Coast Regional Blood Center v. Houston, 745 S.W.2d 557 (Tex.App.1988). See Kevin Hopkins, Blood, Sweat, and Tears: Toward a New Paradigm for Protecting Donor Privacy, 7 Va.J.Soc.Pol'y & L. 141(2000).

Problem: The HIV–Positive Physician

One of your established clients, Joel Feinberg, an internist, has consulted you concerning a problem that has arisen in his practice. Two weeks ago one of his patients, Dr. Alan Miller, a resident at Mercy hospital where Dr. Feinberg is on staff, came in for a physical. Dr. Feinberg met Dr. Miller last year when Dr. Miller did an internal medicine rotation under Dr. Feinberg's supervision, and they have seen each other socially from time to time since. After his blood had been drawn for routine blood work, Dr. Miller requested that an HIV test be done on the blood. The test results came back positive for HIV antibodies. Dr. Feinberg immediately called Dr. Miller to tell him of the results. Dr. Miller, however, told Dr. Feinberg not to worry, the test was undoubtedly a false positive, and assured him that he would follow up with further testing later when he could find the time.

Dr. Feinberg has been deeply troubled by the test and by Dr. Miller's response to it. First, Dr. Feinberg knows that Dr. Miller is scheduled for orthopedic surgery to correct an old knee injury next month. He wonders whether he should inform the surgeon who will be doing the surgery, a colleague, of the test results. He also wonders whether nurses, surgical assistants, laboratory personnel and others who may be exposed to body fluids from the surgery should be informed. Second, he knows that Dr. Miller has applied for permanent staff privileges at Mercy hospital. Should the hospital medical staff or administration be informed of the test results? Does Dr. Feinberg have any obligation under state law to inform the public health department of the results? Should he inform the state medical licensure board? Finally, he knows that Dr. Miller is planning to marry another intern, Dr. Anne Bowen, early next year. When he asked Dr. Miller whether he would inform Anne of the test results, however, Dr. Miller said he would rather not bother her with results that were probably wrong in any event. Dr. Feinberg wants to know whether he should tell Dr. Bowen himself, ask the Department of Health to contact her through its contact-tracing program, or say nothing? Dr. Feinberg is well aware of his general obligation to keep patient confidences, but wonders whether any exceptions apply in this situation or whether, in fact, he has any obligations to disclose.

III. INFORMED CONSENT: THE PHYSICIAN'S OBLIGATION

A. ORIGINS OF THE INFORMED CONSENT DOCTRINE

Informed consent has developed out of strong judicial deference toward individual autonomy, reflecting a belief that an individual has a right to be free from nonconsensual interference with his or her person, and a basic moral principle that it is wrong to force another to act against his or her will. This principle was articulated in the medical context by Justice Cardozo in Schloendorff v. Society of New York Hospital, 211 N.Y. 125, 105 N.E. 92 (1914): "Every human being of adult years and sound mind has a right to determine what shall be done with his own body * * *". Informed consent doctrine has guided medical decisionmaking by setting boundaries for the doctor-patient relationship and is one of the forces altering the attitudes of a new generation of doctors toward their patients. It has provided the starting point for federal regulations on human experimentation, and is now reflected in consent forms that health care institutions require all patients to sign upon admission and before various procedures are performed.

Professor Alexander Capron has argued that the doctrine can serve six salutory functions. It can:

1) protect individual autonomy;

2) protect the patient's status as a human being;

3) avoid fraud or duress;

4) encourage doctors to carefully consider their decisions;

5) foster rational decision-making by the patient; and

6) involve the public generally in medicine.

Alexander Capron, "Informed Consent in Catastrophic Disease Research and Treatment," 123 U.Penn.L.Rev. 340, 365–76 (1974).

This chapter will examine how the doctrine developed and how it now functions as a litigation tool in American jurisdictions.

Informed consent has been an unnatural graft onto medical practice. As Jay Katz wrote in The Silent World of Doctor and Patient 1 (1984), " * * * disclosure and consent, except in the most rudimentary fashion, are obligations alien to medical thinking and practice." The function of disclosure historically has been to get patients to agree to what the doctors wanted. In ancient Greece, patients' participation in decision-making was considered undesirable, since the doctor's primary task was to inspire confidence. Medieval medical writing likewise viewed conversations between doctors and patients as an opportunity for the former to offer comfort and hope, but emphasized the need for the doctor to be manipulative and even deceitful. Authority needed to be coupled with obedience to create a patient's faith in the cure. By the Enlightenment, the view had emerged that patients had a capacity to listen to the doctor, but that deception was still needed to facilitate patient management. By the nineteenth century, the profession was split over such issues as disclosure of a dire prognosis, although the majority of doctors still argued against disclosure. The beginnings of the twentieth century showed no progress in the evolution of the doctor-patient relationship toward collaboration.

The judicial development of informed consent into a distinct doctrine can be roughly divided into three periods, according to Katz. During the first period, up to the mid-twentieth century, courts built upon the law of battery and required little more than disclosure by doctors of their proposed treatment. The second period saw an emerging judicial feeling that doctors should disclose the alternatives to a proposed treatment and their risks, as well as of risks of the proposed treatment itself. The third period, from 1972 to the present, has seen legislative retrenchment and judicial inertia.

During the first period of doctrinal development, the doctrine of battery provided the theoretical underpinnings for a cause of action. The doctrine of battery protects a patient's physical integrity from harmful contacts and her personal dignity from unwanted bodily contact, requiring a showing only that the patient was not informed of the very nature of the medical touching, typically a surgical procedure. Physical injury is not necessary. When a surgeon, in the course of surgery, removes or operates upon an organ other than the one he and the patient discussed, a battery action lies. The most obvious medical battery cases, e.g., where a surgeon amputates the wrong leg, can be readily brought as a negligence case.

The procedural and other advantages of a battery-based action tip the scales substantially in the favor of the patient. First, the focus is on the patient's right to be free from a touching different from that to which she consented. The physician has few defenses to a battery. Second, the plaintiff need not prove through expert testimony what the standard of care was; the proof is only that the particular physician failed to explain to the patient the nature and character of the particular procedure. Third, to prove causation, the plaintiff need only show that an unconsented-to touching occurred. Under a negligence theory the plaintiff must show that he would have declined a procedure if he had known all the details and risks. See generally Kohoutek v. Hafner, 383 N.W.2d 295 (Minn.1986). In Chouinard v. Marjani, 21 Conn.App. 572, 575 A.2d 238 (1990), the plaintiff sued the defendant surgeon, claiming that the surgeon had performed bilateral breast surgery although the plaintiff had consented only to surgery on her left breast. She admitted that if the surgeon had asked, she would have consented to the surgery on her right breast. The court applied battery doctrine, holding that plaintiff did not need to present either expert testimony nor testify that she would not have consented if the surgeon had asked.

Use of a battery theory therefore reduces the need for medical testimony, restricting the scope of physicians' beliefs about what patients should know and might want as therapy. A judicial sense that medical judgment should be allowed more leeway has led to a movement from battery to negligent nondisclosure over the years. Malpractice reform in the states has often included abrogation of the battery basis of informed consent. See Rubino v. DeFretias, 638 F.Supp. 182 (D.Ariz.1986) (holding statute unconstitutional on grounds that the Arizona constitution establishes a fundamental right to bring an action against a physician based on common law theory of battery.)

As you read the cases in this section, ask how far the courts have gone toward permitting patients to control treatment decisions that affect them.

Consider also what a plaintiff must show to make out an informed consent case in various jurisdictions. Finally, ask if any other processes are likely to serve the purposes of informed consent more efficiently, and with less adverse effect on the doctor-patient relationship.

B. THE LEGAL FRAMEWORK OF INFORMED CONSENT

1. Negligence as a Basis for Recovery

CANTERBURY v. SPENCE

United States Court of Appeals, District of Columbia Circuit, 1972.
464 F.2d 772.

SPOTTSWOOD W. ROBINSON, III, CIRCUIT JUDGE:

This appeal is from a judgment entered in the District Court on verdicts directed for the two appellees at the conclusion of plaintiff-appellant Canterbury's case in chief. His action sought damages for personal injuries allegedly sustained as a result of an operation negligently performed by appellee Spence, a negligent failure by Dr. Spence to disclose a risk of serious disability inherent in the operation, and negligent post-operative care by appellee Washington Hospital Center. On close examination of the record, we find evidence which required submission of these issues to the jury. We accordingly reverse the judgment as to each appellee and remand the case to the District Court for a new trial.

I

The record we review tells a depressing tale. A youth troubled only by back pain submitted to an operation without being informed of a risk of paralysis incidental thereto. A day after the operation he fell from his hospital bed after having been left without assistance while voiding. A few hours after the fall, the lower half of his body was paralyzed, and he had to be operated on again. Despite extensive medical care, he has never been what he was before. Instead of the back pain, even years later, he hobbled about on crutches, a victim of paralysis of the bowels and urinary incontinence. In a very real sense this lawsuit is an understandable search for reasons.

At the time of the events which gave rise to this litigation, appellant was nineteen years of age, a clerk-typist employed by the Federal Bureau of Investigation. In December, 1958, he began to experience severe pain between his shoulder blades. He consulted two general practitioners, but the medications they prescribed failed to eliminate the pain. Thereafter, appellant secured an appointment with Dr. Spence, who is a neurosurgeon.

Dr. Spence examined appellant in his office at some length but found nothing amiss. On Dr. Spence's advice appellant was x-rayed, but the films did not identify any abnormality. Dr. Spence then recommended that appellant undergo a myelogram—a procedure in which dye is injected into the spinal column and traced to find evidence of disease or other disorder—at the Washington Hospital Center.

Appellant entered the hospital on February 4, 1959. The myelogram revealed a "filling defect" in the region of the fourth thoracic vertebra. Since a myelogram often does no more than pinpoint the location of an aberration, surgery may be necessary to discover the cause. Dr. Spence told appellant that he would have to undergo a laminectomy—the excision of the posterior arch of the vertebra—to correct what he suspected was a ruptured disc. Appellant did not raise any objection to the proposed operation nor did he probe into its exact nature.

Appellant explained to Dr. Spence that his mother was a widow of slender financial means living in Cyclone, West Virginia, and that she could be reached through a neighbor's telephone. Appellant called his mother the day after the myelogram was performed and, failing to contact her, left Dr. Spence's telephone number with the neighbor. When Mrs. Canterbury returned the call, Dr. Spence told her that the surgery was occasioned by a suspected ruptured disc. Mrs. Canterbury then asked if the recommended operation was serious and Dr. Spence replied "not any more than any other operation." He added that he knew Mrs. Canterbury was not well off and that her presence in Washington would not be necessary. The testimony is contradictory as to whether during the course of the conversation Mrs. Canterbury expressed her consent to the operation. Appellant himself apparently did not converse again with Dr. Spence prior to the operation.

Dr. Spence performed the laminectomy on February 11 at the Washington Hospital Center. Mrs. Canterbury traveled to Washington, arriving on that date but after the operation was over, and signed a consent form at the hospital. The laminectomy revealed several anomalies: a spinal cord that was swollen and unable to pulsate, an accumulation of large tortuous and dilated veins, and a complete absence of epidural fat which normally surrounds the spine. A thin hypodermic needle was inserted into the spinal cord to aspirate any cysts which might have been present, but no fluid emerged. In suturing the wound, Dr. Spence attempted to relieve the pressure on the spinal cord by enlarging the dura—the outer protective wall of the spinal cord—at the area of swelling.

For approximately the first day after the operation appellant recuperated normally, but then suffered a fall and an almost immediate setback. Since there is some conflict as to precisely when or why appellant fell, we reconstruct the events from the evidence most favorable to him. Dr. Spence left orders that appellant was to remain in bed during the process of voiding. These orders were changed to direct that voiding be done out of bed, and the jury could find that the change was made by hospital personnel. Just prior to the fall, appellant summoned a nurse and was given a receptacle for use in voiding, but was then left unattended. Appellant testified that during the course of the endeavor he slipped off the side of the bed, and that there was no one to assist him, or side rail to prevent the fall.

Several hours later, appellant began to complain that he could not move his legs and that he was having trouble breathing; paralysis seems to have been virtually total from the waist down. Dr. Spence was notified on the night of February 12, and he rushed to the hospital. Mrs. Canterbury signed another consent form and appellant was again taken into the operating room. The surgical wound was reopened and Dr. Spence created a gusset to allow the spinal cord greater room in which to pulsate.

Appellant's control over his muscles improved somewhat after the second operation but he was unable to void properly. As a result of this condition, he came under the care of a urologist while still in the hospital. In April, following a cystoscopic examination, appellant was operated on for removal of bladder stones, and in May was released from the hospital. He reentered the hospital the following August for a 10–day period, apparently because of his urologic problems. For several years after his discharge he was under the care of several specialists, and at all times was under the care of a urologist. At the time of the trial in April, 1968, appellant required crutches to walk, still suffered from urinal incontinence and paralysis of the bowels, and wore a penile clamp.

In November, 1959 on Dr. Spence's recommendation, appellant was transferred by the F.B.I. to Miami where he could get more swimming and exercise. Appellant worked three years for the F.B.I. in Miami, Los Angeles and Houston, resigning finally in June, 1962. From then until the time of the trial, he held a number of jobs, but had constant trouble finding work because he needed to remain seated and close to a bathroom. The damages appellant claims include extensive pain and suffering, medical expenses, and loss of earnings.

II

* * *

At the close of appellant's case in chief, each defendant moved for a directed verdict and the trial judge granted both motions. The basis of the ruling, he explained, was that appellant had failed to produce any medical evidence indicating negligence on Dr. Spence's part in diagnosing appellant's malady or in performing the laminectomy; that there was no proof that Dr. Spence's treatment was responsible for appellant's disabilities; and that notwithstanding some evidence to show negligent post-operative care, an absence of medical testimony to show causality precluded submission of the case against the hospital to the jury. The judge did not allude specifically to the alleged breach of duty by Dr. Spence to divulge the possible consequences of the laminectomy.

We reverse. The testimony of appellant and his mother that Dr. Spence did not reveal the risk of paralysis from the laminectomy made out a prima facie case of violation of the physician's duty to disclose which Dr. Spence's explanation did not negate as a matter of law. * * *

III

* * *

* * * True consent to what happens to one's self is the informed exercise of a choice, and that entails an opportunity to evaluate knowledgeably the options available and the risks attendant upon each. The average patient has little or no understanding of the medical arts, and ordinarily has only his physician to whom he can look for enlightenment with which to reach an intelligent decision. From these almost axiomatic considerations springs the need, and in turn the requirement, of a reasonable divulgence by physician to patient to make such a decision possible.[15]

15. The doctrine that a consent effective as authority to form therapy can arise only from   the patient's understanding of alternatives to and risks of the therapy is commonly denom-

A physician is under a duty to treat his patient skillfully but proficiency in diagnosis and therapy is not the full measure of his responsibility. The cases demonstrate that the physician is under an obligation to communicate specific information to the patient when the exigencies of reasonable care call for it. Due care may require a physician perceiving symptoms of bodily abnormality to alert the patient to the condition. It may call upon the physician confronting an ailment which does not respond to his ministrations to inform the patient thereof. It may command the physician to instruct the patient as to any limitations to be presently observed for his own welfare, and as to any precautionary therapy he should seek in the future. It may oblige the physician to advise the patient of the need for or desirability of any alternative treatment promising greater benefit than that being pursued. Just as plainly, due care normally demands that the physician warn the patient of any risks to his well-being which contemplated therapy may involve.

The context in which the duty of risk-disclosure arises is invariably the occasion for decision as to whether a particular treatment procedure is to be undertaken. To the physician, whose training enables a self-satisfying evaluation, the answer may seem clear, but it is the prerogative of the patient, not the physician, to determine for himself the direction in which his interests seem to lie. To enable the patient to chart his course understandably, some familiarity with the therapeutic alternatives and their hazards becomes essential.

A reasonable revelation in these respects is not only a necessity but, as we see it, is as much a matter of the physician's duty. It is a duty to warn of the dangers lurking in the proposed treatment, and that is surely a facet of due care. It is, too, a duty to impart information which the patient has every right to expect. The patient's reliance upon the physician is a trust of the kind which traditionally has exacted obligations beyond those associated with arms-length transactions. His dependence upon the physician for information affecting his well-being, in terms of contemplated treatment, is well-nigh abject. As earlier noted, long before the instant litigation arose, courts had recognized that the physician had the responsibility of satisfying the vital

---

inated "informed consent." See, *e.g.,* Waltz & Scheuneman, Informed Consent to Therapy, 64 Nw.U.L.Rev. 628, 629 (1970). The same appellation is frequently assigned to the doctrine requiring physicians, as a matter of duty to patients, to communicate information as to such alternatives and risks. See, *e.g.,* Comment, Informed Consent in Medical Malpractice, 55 Calif.L.Rev. 1396 (1967). While we recognize the general utility of shorthand phrases in literary expositions, we caution that uncritical use of the "informed consent" label can be misleading. See, *e.g.,* Plante, An Analysis of "Informed Consent," 36 Ford.L.Rev. 639, 671–72 (1968).

In duty-to-disclose cases, the focus of attention is more properly upon the nature and content of the physician's divulgence than the patient's understanding or consent. Adequate disclosure and informed consent are, of course, two sides of the same coin—the former a *sine qua non* of the latter. But the vital inquiry on duty to disclose relates to the physician's performance of an obligation, while one of the difficulties with analysis in terms of "informed consent" is its tendency to imply that what is decisive is the degree of the patient's comprehension. As we later emphasize, the physician discharges the duty when he makes a reasonable effort to convey sufficient information although the patient, without fault of the physician, may not fully grasp it. See text *infra* at notes 82–89. Even though the factfinder may have occasion to draw an inference on the state of the patient's enlightenment, the factfinding process on performance of the duty ultimately reaches back to what the physician actually said or failed to say. And while the factual conclusion on adequacy of the revelation will vary as between patients—as, for example, between a lay patient and a physician-patient—the fluctuations are attributable to the kind of divulgence which may be reasonable under the circumstances.

informational needs of the patient. More recently, we ourselves have found "in the fiducial qualities of [the physician-patient] relationship the physician's duty to reveal to the patient that which in his best interests it is important that he should know." We now find, as a part of the physician's overall obligation to the patient, a similar duty of reasonable disclosure of the choices with respect to proposed therapy and the dangers inherently and potentially involved.

* * *

IV

Duty to disclose has gained recognition in a large number of American jurisdictions, but more largely on a different rationale. The majority of courts dealing with the problem have made the duty depend on whether it was the custom of physicians practicing in the community to make the particular disclosure to the patient. If so, the physician may be held liable for an unreasonable and injurious failure to divulge, but there can be no recovery unless the omission forsakes a practice prevalent in the profession. We agree that the physician's noncompliance with a professional custom to reveal, like any other departure from prevailing medical practice, may give rise to liability to the patient. We do not agree that the patient's cause of action is dependent upon the existence and nonperformance of a relevant professional tradition.

There are, in our view, formidable obstacles to acceptance of the notion that the physician's obligation to disclose is either germinated or limited by medical practice. To begin with, the reality of any discernible custom reflecting a professional concensus [sic] on communication of option and risk information to patients is open to serious doubt. We sense the danger that what in fact is no custom at all may be taken as an affirmative custom to maintain silence, and that physician-witnesses to the so-called custom may state merely their personal opinions as to what they or others would do under given conditions. We cannot gloss over the inconsistency between reliance on a general practice respecting divulgence and, on the other hand, realization that the myriad of variables among patients makes each case so different that its omission can rationally be justified only by the effect of its individual circumstances. Nor can we ignore the fact that to bind the disclosure obligation to medical usage is to arrogate the decision on revelation to the physician alone. Respect for the patient's right of self-determination on particular therapy demands a standard set by law for physicians rather than one which physicians may or may not impose upon themselves.

* * * The caliber of the performance exacted by the reasonable-care standard varies between the professional and non-professional worlds, and so also the role of professional custom. * * *

We have admonished, however, that "[t]he special medical standards are but adaptations of the general standard to a group who are required to act as reasonable men possessing their medical talents presumably would." There is, by the same token, no basis for operation of the special medical standard where the physician's activity does not bring his medical knowledge and skills peculiarly into play. And where the challenge to the physician's conduct is not to be gauged by the special standard, it follows that medical custom cannot furnish the test of its propriety, whatever its relevance under the proper test may be. The decision to unveil the patient's condition and the chances as to remediation, as we shall see, is ofttimes a non-medical judgment and, if so, is a decision outside the ambit of the special standard. Where that is the situation, professional custom hardly furnishes the legal criterion for measuring the physician's responsibility to reasonably inform his patient of the options and the hazards as to treatment.

The majority rule, moreover, is at war with our prior holdings that a showing of medical practice, however probative, does not fix the standard governing recovery for medical malpractice. Prevailing medical practice, we have maintained, has evidentiary value in determinations as to what the specific criteria measuring challenged professional conduct are and whether they have been met, but does not itself define the standard. That has been our position in treatment cases, where the physician's performance is ordinarily to be adjudicated by the special medical standard of due care. We see no logic in a different rule for nondisclosure cases, where the governing standard is much more largely divorced from professional considerations. And surely in nondisclosure cases the factfinder is not invariably functioning in an area of such technical complexity that it must be bound to medical custom as an inexorable application of the community standard of reasonable care.

Thus we distinguished, for purposes of duty to disclose, the special-and general-standard aspects of the physician-patient relationship. When medical judgment enters the picture and for that reason the special standard controls, prevailing medical practice must be given its just due. In all other instances, however, the general standard exacting ordinary care applies, and that standard is set by law. In sum, the physician's duty to disclose is governed by the same legal principles applicable to others in comparable situations, with modifications only to the extent that medical judgment enters the picture. We hold that the standard measuring performance of that duty by physicians, as by others, is conduct which is reasonable under the circumstances.

V

Once the circumstances give rise to a duty on the physician's part to inform his patient, the next inquiry is the scope of the disclosure the physician is legally obliged to make. The courts have frequently confronted this problem but no uniform standard defining the adequacy of the divulgence emerges from the decisions. Some have said "full" disclosure, a norm we are unwilling to adopt literally. It seems obviously prohibitive and unrealistic to expect physicians to discuss with their patients every risk of proposed treatment—no matter how small or remote—and generally unnecessary from the patient's viewpoint as well. Indeed, the cases speaking in terms of "full" disclosure appear to envision something less than total disclosure, leaving unanswered the question of just how much.

The larger number of courts, as might be expected, have applied tests framed with reference to prevailing fashion within the medical profession. Some have measured the disclosure by "good medical practice," others by what a reasonable practitioner would have bared under the circumstances, and still others by what medical custom in the community would demand. We have explored this rather considerable body of law but are unprepared to follow it. The duty to disclose, we have reasoned, arises from phenomena apart from medical custom and practice. The latter, we think, should no more establish the scope of the duty than its existence. Any definition of scope in terms purely of a professional standard is at odds with the patient's prerogative to decide on projected therapy himself. That prerogative, we have said, is at the very foundation of the duty to disclose, and both the patient's right to know and the physician's correlative obligation to tell him are diluted to the extent that its compass is dictated by the medical profession.

In our view, the patient's right of self-decision shapes the boundaries of the duty to reveal. That right can be effectively exercised only if the patient possesses enough information to enable an intelligent choice. The scope of the physician's communications to the patient, then, must be measured by the patient's need, and that need is the information material to the decision. Thus the test for determining whether a particular peril must be divulged is its materiality to the patient's decision: all risks potentially affecting the decision must be unmasked. And to safeguard the patient's interest in achieving his own determination on treatment, the law must itself set the standard for adequate disclosure.

Optimally for the patient, exposure of a risk would be mandatory whenever the patient would deem it significant to his decision, either singly or in combination with other risks. Such a requirement, however, would summon the physician to second-guess the patient, whose ideas on materiality could hardly be known to the physician. That would make an undue demand upon medical practitioners, whose conduct, like that of others, is to be measured in terms of reasonableness. Consonantly with orthodox negligence doctrine, the physician's liability for nondisclosure is to be determined on the basis of foresight, not hindsight; no less than any other aspect of negligence, the issue on nondisclosure must be approached from the viewpoint of the reasonableness of the physician's divulgence in terms of what he knows or should know to be the patient's informational needs. If, but only if, the fact-finder can say that the physician's communication was unreasonably inadequate is an imposition of liability legally or morally justified.

Of necessity, the content of the disclosure rests in the first instance with the physician. Ordinarily it is only he who is in position to identify particular dangers; always he must make a judgment, in terms of materiality, as to whether and to what extent revelation to the patient is called for. He cannot know with complete exactitude what the patient would consider important to his decision, but on the basis of his medical training and experience he can sense how the average, reasonable patient expectably would react. Indeed, with knowledge of, or ability to learn, his patient's background and current condition, he is in a position superior to that of most others—attorneys, for example—who are called upon to make judgments on pain of liability in damages for unreasonable miscalculation.

From these considerations we derive the breadth of the disclosure of risks legally to be required. The scope of the standard is not subjective as to either the physician or the patient; it remains objective with due regard for the patient's informational needs and with suitable leeway for the physician's situation. In broad outline, we agree that "[a] risk is thus material when a reasonable person, in what the physician knows or should know to be the patient's position, would be likely to attach significance to the risk or cluster of risks in deciding whether or not to forego the proposed therapy."

The topics importantly demanding a communication of information are the inherent and potential hazards of the proposed treatment, the alternatives to that treatment, if any, and the results likely if the patient remains untreated. The factors contributing significance to the dangerousness of a medical technique are, of course, the incidence of injury and the degree of the harm threatened. A very small chance of death or serious disablement may well be significant; a potential disability which dramatically outweighs the potential benefit of the therapy or the detriments of the existing malady may summon discussion with the patient.

There is no bright line separating the significant from the insignificant; the answer in any case must abide a rule of reason. Some dangers—infection, for example—are inherent in any operation; there is no obligation to communicate those of which persons of average sophistication are aware. Even more clearly, the physician bears no responsibility for discussion of hazards the patient has already discovered, or those having no apparent materiality to patients' decision on therapy. The disclosure doctrine, like others marking lines between permissible and impermissible behavior in medical practice, is in essence a requirement of conduct prudent under the circumstances. Whenever nondisclosure of particular risk information is open to debate by reasonable-minded men, the issue is for the finder of the facts.

Notes and Questions

1. Although states are almost equally divided, a slight majority has adopted the professional disclosure standard, measuring the duty to disclose by the standard of the reasonable medical practitioner similarly situated. Expert testimony is required to establish the content of a reasonable disclosure. The *Canterbury* rule, using the "reasonable patient" as the measure of the scope of disclosure, has won over several states in the last few years. See Carr v. Strode, 79 Hawai'i 475, 904 P.2d 489 (1995). Georgia finally recognized the informed consent doctrine in Ketchup v. Howard, 247 Ga.App. 54 (2000)(with full appendix surveying other states' laws).

This professional standard is justified by three arguments. First, it protects good medical practice—the primary duty of physicians is to advance their patients' best interests, and they should not have to concern themselves with the risk that an uninformed lay jury will later decide they acted improperly. Woolley v. Henderson, 418 A.2d 1123 (Me.1980). Second, a patient-oriented standard would force doctors to spend unnecessary time discussing every possible risk with their patients, thereby interfering with the flexibility that they need to decide on the best form of treatment. Third, only physicians can accurately evaluate the psychological and other impact that risk would have on particular patients.

These jurisdictions ordinarily require the plaintiff to offer medical testimony to establish 1) whether a reasonable medical practitioner in the same or similar community would make this disclosure, and 2) that the defendant did not comply with this community standard. Fuller v. Starnes, 268 Ark. 476, 597 S.W.2d 88 (1980). Expert testimony is essential, since determination of what information needs to be disclosed is viewed as a medical question.

2. Judge Robinson suggests that the *Canterbury* standard is nothing more than the uniform application of the negligence principle to medical practice.

However, the negligence principle normally evaluates the conduct of a reasonable actor—not the expectations of a reasonable victim. The values served by the doctrine—patient autonomy and dignity—are unrelated to the values served by the doctrine of negligence. Informed consent really serves the values we otherwise identify with the doctrine of battery. It is ironic that a doctrine developed to foster and recognize individual choice should be measured by an objective standard.

3. The effect of a patient-oriented disclosure standard is to ease the plaintiff's burden of proof, since the trier of fact could find that a doctor acted unreasonably in failing to disclose, in spite of unrebutted expert medical testimony to the contrary. The question of whether a physician disclosed risks which a reasonable person would find material is for the trier of fact, and technical expertise is not required. Pedersen v. Vahidy, 209 Conn. 510, 552 A.2d 419 (1989). In Savold v. Johnson, 443 N.W.2d 656 (S.D.1989), the South Dakota Supreme Court held that expert testimony as to informed consent information was not needed, where a factual dispute exists as to whether any information of the material risks was given at all. Expert testimony is still needed, however, to clarify the treatments and their probabilities of risks. Thus in Cross v. Trapp,170 W.Va. 459, 294 S.E.2d 446, 455 (1982), the court held that experts were needed to establish " * * * (1) the risks involved concerning a particular method of treatment, (2) alternative methods of treatment, (3) the risks relating to such alternative methods of treatment and (4) the results likely to occur if the patient remains untreated." Accord, Festa v. Greenberg, 354 Pa.Super. 346, 511 A.2d 1371 (Pa.Super.1986); Sard v. Hardy, 281 Md. 432, 379 A.2d 1014 (Md.1977).

4. *Information to be disclosed.* The doctor must consider disclosure of a variety of factors:

a. Diagnosis. This includes the medical steps preceding diagnosis, including tests and their alternatives. The right of informed refusal, as established in Truman v. Thomas, 27 Cal.3d 285, 165 Cal.Rptr. 308, 611 P.2d 902 (1980), requires disclosure of the risks of foregoing a diagnostic procedure.

b. Nature and purpose of the proposed treatment.

c. Risks of the treatment. Risks that are remote can be omitted. The threshold of disclosure, as the *Canterbury* court suggests, varies with the product of the probability and the severity of the risk. Thus a five percent risk of lengthened recuperation might be ignored, while a one percent risk of paralysis, as in *Canterbury,* or an even smaller risk of death, should be disclosed. Cobbs v. Grant, 8 Cal.3d 229, 104 Cal.Rptr. 505, 502 P.2d 1 (1972). In Hartke v. McKelway, 707 F.2d 1544, 1549 (D.C.Cir.1983) the doctor performed a laparoscopic cauterization to prevent pregnancy of the plaintiff, who later became pregnant and had a healthy child. "In this case, the undisclosed risk was a .1% to .3% chance of subsequent pregnancy. For most people this risk would be considered very small, but this patient was in a particularly unusual position. In view of the very serious expected consequences of pregnancy for her—possibly including death—as well as the ready availability of ways to reduce the risk * * * a jury could conclude that a reasonable person in what Dr. McKelway knew to be plaintiff's position would be likely to attach significance to the risk here."

The difference between a temporary and permanent risk can be critical, and even mention in a consent form of the general risk, but characterized as temporary, will be insufficient to constitute full disclosure. See, e.g., Johnson v. Brandy, 1995 WL 29230 (Ohio App.1995)(risk of scalp numbness after scalp-reduction surgery for baldness not described as permanent risk, but only temporary; consent form held to be inadequate disclosure).

Where a drug or injectable substance is part of treatment, a patient is entitled to know whether that drug or substance has been tested or approved by Federal authorities such as the Food and Drug Administration. Gaston v. Hunter, 121 Ariz. 33, 588 P.2d 326 (Ariz.App.1978)(investigational procedure must be disclosed); Retkwa v. Orentreich, 154 Misc.2d 164, 584 N.Y.S.2d 710 (S.C., N.Y.Cty. 1992)(patient entitled to information about FDA status of liquid injectable silicone).

d.   Treatment alternatives. Doctors should disclose those alternatives that are generally acknowledged within the medical community as feasible, Martin v. Richards, 192 Wis.2d 156, 531 N.W.2d 70, 78 (Wisc. 1995), their risks and consequences, and their probability of success. Even if the alternative is more hazardous, some courts have held that it should be disclosed. Logan v. Greenwich Hospital Association, 191 Conn. 282, 465 A.2d 294 (1983). In Wenger v. Oregon Urology Clinic, P.C., 102 Or.App. 665, 796 P.2d 376 (1990), the court held that defendants failed to properly inform plaintiff of several treatment alternatives to treat Peyonie's disease, a male genital condition which can impair sexual function. The procedure used by the defendant caused an infection, ultimately leading to the amputation of the plaintiff's penis. In Stover v. Surgeons, 431 Pa.Super. 11, 635 A.2d 1047 (1993), the court upheld a duty of disclosure of alternative replacement heart valves and their merits.

A physician must disclose medical information even if the procedure is noninvasive, considering that observation rather than more aggressive treatments may entail significant risks. Martin v. Richards, 192 Wis.2d 156, 531 N.W.2d 70, 79 (Wisc. 1995)(physician failed to disclose to parents the risks of intracranial bleeding and the need for a CT scan or transfer to another facility in that case).

If the alternative is not a legitimate treatment option, it need not be disclosed to the patient. See Morris v. Ferriss, 669 So.2d 1316 (La.App. 4 Cir.1996)(physician did not have to advise patient that psychiatric treatment was an alternative treatment for epileptic partial complex seizures, since it was not accepted as feasible); Lienhard v. State, 431 N.W.2d 861 (Minn.1988) (managing pregnancy at home rather than in hospital not a choice between alternative methods of treatment; disclosure therefore not required).

e.   Doing nothing as an option. In a health care environment of managed care, conservative practice is the goal and doing nothing and "watchful waiting" are desirable clinical approaches to patient care. In Wecker v. Amend, 22 Kan.App.2d 498, 918 P.2d 658 (C.A. Kansas 1996), the plaintiff contended that Dr. Amend failed to obtain her informed consent before performing laser surgery on her cervix. She had a human papilloma virus wart on her cervix. Since this might be precancerous, Dr. Amend recommended laser surgery to remove it. She watched a video about laser surgery, which stated that "Laser surgery involves the same risks as with any surgical procedure. There is a small risk of excessive bleeding and possible infection, but those cases are not common and can be treated". Following the surgery, she suffered excessive bleeding and he had to perform a total hysterectomy to control the bleeding. She underwent further surgeries and injections to control her pain. She argue that he failed to inform her of alternatives including the option of no treatment at all.

One expert testified that it was reasonable to do nothing and see if the wart disappeared. In the court's words,

> ... how can a patient give an informed consent to treatment for a condition if the patient is not informed that the condition might resolve itself without any treatment at all? The court held that the jury must be instructed that a physician has a duty to advise a patient of the option of choosing no treatment at all. (Italics mine).

The definition of treatment has been construed broadly to include diagnostic options and choices of hospitals for performing a procedure. Physicians must disclose diagnostic procedures that might assist patients in making an informed decision about treatment. In Martin v. Richards, 176 Wis.2d 339, 500 N.W.2d 691 (Wis.App.1993), the court held that it was for the jury to decide whether the physicians' failure to inform the parents of a minor patient of the availability of a CAT scan to detect intracranial bleeding and the unavailability of a neurosurgeon at the hospital to operate caused the patient's brain damage. In Vachon v. Broadlawns Medical Foundation, 490 N.W.2d 820 (Iowa 1992), the plaintiff suffered severe multiple trauma injuries and the issue was whether his transfer to a university hospital two hours away instead of to closer trauma hospitals was reasonable. The court held that the decision to transfer was part of treatment and raised an issue of reasonable care.

5. *The patient's state of mind.* Courts do not usually consider whether the patient comprehended the risk discussion. If the patient is competent, the focus is typically on the content of the physician's disclosure and whether the risks and alternatives were discussed. However, when a patient might lack the state of mind to objectively evaluate treatment alternatives, at least one court has allowed the jury to consider factors that might cause a patient to disregard the discussion. In Macy v. Blatchford, 330 Or. 444, 8 P.3d 204, 211 (Or.2000), the court held that evidence of a sexual relationship between a physician and patient might be relevant to prove that the physician failed to obtain the patient's informed consent. " * * * [A] reasonable juror might believe that a sexual relationship between defendant and Macy would undermine Macy'[s] ability to listen objectively to and utilize information provided by the physician, in making an independent and informed decision about her health care."

2. *Disclosure of Physician–Specific Risk Information*

As medical knowledge grows and institutional tracking of physician performance becomes the norm, much more information is available in theory to patients not only about a particular disease and its treatment, but also about the particular physician's skill and track record. Consider the following case.

JOHNSON v. KOKEMOOR

Supreme Court of Wisconsin, 1996.
199 Wis.2d 615, 545 N.W.2d 495.

SHIRLEY S. ABRAHAMSON, JUSTICE.

* * *

Donna Johnson (the plaintiff) brought an action against Dr. Richard Kokemoor (the defendant) alleging his failure to obtain her informed consent to surgery as required by Wis.Stat. § 448.30 (1993–94). The jury found that the defendant failed to adequately inform the plaintiff regarding the risks associated with her surgery. The jury also found that a reasonable person in the plaintiff's position would have refused to consent to surgery by the defendant if she had been fully informed of its attendant risks and advantages.

This case presents the issue of whether the circuit court erred in admitting evidence that the defendant, in undertaking his duty to obtain the plaintiff's informed consent before operating to clip an aneurysm, failed (1) to divulge the extent of his experience in performing this type of operation; (2) to compare the morbidity and mortality rates[1] for this type of surgery among experienced surgeons and inexperienced surgeons like himself; and (3) to refer the plaintiff to a tertiary care center staffed by physicians more experienced in performing the same surgery. The admissibility of such physician-specific evidence in a case involving the doctrine of informed consent raises an issue of first impression in this court and is an issue with which appellate courts have had little experience.

* * *

We conclude that all three items of evidence were material to the issue of informed consent in this case. As we stated in Martin v. Richards, 192 Wis.2d 156, 174, 531 N.W.2d 70 (1995), "a patient cannot make an informed, intelligent decision to consent to a physician's suggested treatment unless the physician discloses what is material to the patient's decision, i.e., all of the viable alternatives and risks of the treatment proposed." In this case information regarding a physician's experience in performing a particular procedure, a physician's risk statistics as compared with those of other physicians who perform that procedure, and the availability of other centers and physicians better able to perform that procedure would have facilitated the plaintiff's awareness of "all of the viable alternatives" available to her and thereby aided her exercise of informed consent. We therefore conclude that under the circumstances of this case, the circuit court did not erroneously exercise its discretion in admitting the evidence.

I.

We first summarize the facts giving rise to this review, recognizing that the parties dispute whether several events occurred, as well as what inferences should be drawn from both the disputed and the undisputed historical facts.

On the advice of her family physician, the plaintiff underwent a CT scan to determine the cause of her headaches. Following the scan, the family physician referred the plaintiff to the defendant, a neurosurgeon in the Chippewa Falls area. The defendant diagnosed an enlarging aneurysm at the rear of the plaintiff's brain and recommended surgery to clip the aneurysm.[9] The defendant performed the surgery in October of 1990.

---

1. As used by the parties and in this opinion, morbidity and mortality rates refer to the prospect that surgery may result in serious impairment or death.

9. The defendant acknowledged at trial that the aneurysm was not the cause of the plaintiff's headaches.

The defendant clipped the aneurysm, rendering the surgery a technical success. But as a consequence of the surgery, the plaintiff, who had no neurological impairments prior to surgery, was rendered an incomplete quadriplegic. She remains unable to walk or to control her bowel and bladder movements. Furthermore, her vision, speech and upper body coordination are partially impaired.

At trial, the plaintiff introduced evidence that the defendant overstated the urgency of her need for surgery and overstated his experience with performing the particular type of aneurysm surgery which she required. According to testimony introduced during the plaintiff's case in chief, when the plaintiff questioned the defendant regarding his experience, he replied that he had performed the surgery she required "several" times; asked what he meant by "several," the defendant said "dozens" and "lots of times."

In fact, however, the defendant had relatively limited experience with aneurysm surgery. He had performed thirty aneurysm surgeries during residency, but all of them involved anterior circulation aneurysms. According to the plaintiff's experts, operations performed to clip anterior circulation aneurysms are significantly less complex than those necessary to clip posterior circulation aneurysms such as the plaintiff's.[10] Following residency, the defendant had performed aneurysm surgery on six patients with a total of nine aneurysms. He had operated on basilar bifurcation aneurysms only twice and had never operated on a large basilar bifurcation aneurysm such as the plaintiff's aneurysm.[11]

The plaintiff also presented evidence that the defendant understated the morbidity and mortality rate associated with basilar bifurcation aneurysm surgery. According to the plaintiff's witnesses, the defendant had told the plaintiff that her surgery carried a two percent risk of death or serious impairment and that it was less risky than the angiogram procedure she would have to undergo in preparation for surgery. The plaintiff's witnesses also testified that the defendant had compared the risks associated with the plaintiff's surgery to those associated with routine procedures such as tonsillectomies, appendectomies and gall bladder surgeries.[12]

The plaintiff's neurosurgical experts testified that even the physician considered to be one of the world's best aneurysm surgeons, who had performed hundreds of posterior circulation aneurysm surgeries, had reported a morbidity and mortality rate of ten-and-seven-tenths percent when operating upon basilar bifurcation aneurysms comparable in size to the plaintiff's aneurysm. Furthermore, information in treatises and articles which the defendant reviewed in preparation for the plaintiff's surgery set the morbidity and mortality rate at approximately fifteen percent for a basilar bifurcation

---

10. The plaintiff's aneurysm was located at the bifurcation of the basilar artery. According to the plaintiff's experts, surgery on basilar bifurcation aneurysms is more difficult than any other type of aneurysm surgery.

11. The defendant testified that he had failed to inform the plaintiff that he was not and never had been board certified in neurosurgery and that he was not a subspecialist in aneurysm surgery.

12. The defendant testified at trial that he had informed the plaintiff that should she decide to forego surgery, the risk that her unclipped aneurysm might rupture was two percent per annum, cumulative. Since he informed the plaintiff that the risk accompanying surgery was two percent, a reasonable person in the plaintiff's position might have concluded that proceeding with surgery was less risky than non-operative management.

aneurysm. The plaintiff also introduced expert testimony that the morbidity and mortality rate for basilar bifurcation aneurysm operations performed by one with the defendant's relatively limited experience would be between twenty and thirty percent, and "closer to the thirty percent range."[13]

Finally, the plaintiff introduced into evidence testimony and exhibits stating that a reasonable physician in the defendant's position would have advised the plaintiff of the availability of more experienced surgeons and would have referred her to them. The plaintiff also introduced evidence stating that patients with basilar aneurysms should be referred to tertiary care centers—such as the Mayo Clinic, only 90 miles away—which contain the proper neurological intensive care unit and microsurgical facilities and which are staffed by neurosurgeons with the requisite training and experience to perform basilar bifurcation aneurysm surgeries.

In his testimony at trial, the defendant denied having suggested to the plaintiff that her condition was urgent and required immediate care. He also denied having stated that her risk was comparable to that associated with an angiogram or minor surgical procedures such as a tonsillectomy or appendectomy. While he acknowledged telling the plaintiff that the risk of death or serious impairment associated with clipping an aneurysm was two percent, he also claims to have told her that because of the location of her aneurysm, the risks attending her surgery would be greater, although he was unable to tell her precisely how much greater.[14] In short, the defendant testified that his disclosure to the plaintiff adequately informed her regarding the risks that she faced.

The defendant's expert witnesses testified that the defendant's recommendation of surgery was appropriate, that this type of surgery is regularly undertaken in a community hospital setting, and that the risks attending anterior and posterior circulation aneurysm surgeries are comparable. They placed the risk accompanying the plaintiff's surgery at between five and ten percent, although one of the defendant's experts also testified that such statistics can be misleading. The defendant's expert witnesses also testified that when queried by a patient regarding their experience, they would divulge the extent of that experience and its relation to the experience of other physicians performing similar operations.[14]

13. The plaintiff introduced into evidence as exhibits articles from the medical literature stating that there are few areas in neurosurgery where the difference in results between surgeons is as evident as it is with aneurysms. One of the plaintiff's neurosurgical experts testified that experience and skill with the operator is more important when performing basilar tip aneurysm surgery than with any other neurosurgical procedure.

14. The defendant maintained that characterizing the risk as two percent was accurate because the aggregate morbidity and mortality rate for all aneurysms, anterior and posterior, is approximately two percent. At the same time, however, the defendant conceded that in operating upon aneurysms comparable to the plaintiff's aneurysm, he could not achieve morbidity and mortality rates as low as the ten-and-seven-tenths percent rate reported by a physician reputed to be one of the world's best aneurysm surgeons.

14. The defendant's expert witness Dr. Patrick R. Walsh testified: In my personal practice, I typically outline my understanding of the natural history of aneurysms, my understanding of the experience of the neurosurgical community in dealing with aneurysms and then respond to specific questions raised by the patient. If a patient asks specifically what my experience is, I believe it is mandatory that I outline that to him as carefully as possible.

Dr. Walsh also stated that "[i]t certainly is reasonable for [the defendant] to explain to [the plaintiff] that other surgeons are available."

Dr. Douglas E. Anderson, who also testified for the defense, stated that "if the patient is

II.

[In Part II The court discussed Wisconsin's approach to informed consent, essentially the Canterbury position. The court noted that significant potential risks must be disclosed, as part of all information material to a patient's decision.]

III.

[In Part III the court discussed the standard of review in informed consent cases.]

IV.

[In Part IV, the court considered whether a physician's experience with a procedure should be considered by the trier of fact. It held that information as to such experience could be important to the plaintiff's decision as to whether to proceed with a medical procedure.]

In this case, the plaintiff introduced ample evidence that had a reasonable person in her position been aware of the defendant's relative lack of experience in performing basilar bifurcation aneurysm surgery, that person would not have undergone surgery with him. According to the record the plaintiff had made inquiry of the defendant's experience with surgery like hers. In response to her direct question about his experience he said that he had operated on aneurysms comparable to her aneurysm "dozens" of times. The plaintiff also introduced evidence that surgery on basilar bifurcation aneurysms is more difficult than any other type of aneurysm surgery and among the most difficult in all of neurosurgery. We conclude that the circuit court did not erroneously exercise its discretion in admitting evidence regarding the defendant's lack of experience and the difficulty of the proposed procedure. A reasonable person in the plaintiff's position would have considered such information material in making an intelligent and informed decision about the surgery.

* * *

V.

The defendant next argues that the circuit court erred in allowing the plaintiff to introduce evidence of morbidity and mortality rates associated with the surgery at issue. The defendant particularly objects to comparative risk statistics purporting to estimate and compare the morbidity and mortality rates when the surgery at issue is performed, respectively, by a physician of limited experience such as the defendant and by the acknowledged masters in the field. Expert testimony introduced by the plaintiff indicated that the morbidity and mortality rate expected when a surgeon with the defendant's experience performed the surgery would be significantly higher than the rate expected when a more experienced physician performed the same surgery.

The defendant asserts that admission of these morbidity and mortality rates would lead the jury to find him liable for failing to perform at the level

asking issues about prior experience, it is reasonable ... to proceed with a discussion of your prior experience." Dr. Anderson also stat-ed that "if the patient asks a surgeon if there is someone who has performed more surgeries than he, it is reasonable to tell the truth."

of the masters rather than for failing to adequately inform the plaintiff regarding the risks associated with her surgery. Furthermore, contends the defendant, statistics are notoriously inaccurate and misleading.

As with evidence pertaining to the defendant's prior experience with similar surgery, the defendant requests that the court fashion a bright line rule as a matter of law that comparative risk evidence should not be admitted in an informed consent case. For many of the same reasons which led us to conclude that such a bright line rule of exclusion would be inappropriate for evidence of a physician's prior experience, we also reject a bright line rule excluding evidence of comparative risk relating to the provider.

The medical literature identifies basilar bifurcation aneurysm surgery as among the most difficult in neurosurgery. As the plaintiff's evidence indicates, however, the defendant had told her that the risks associated with her surgery were comparable to the risks attending a tonsillectomy, appendectomy or gall bladder operation. The plaintiff also introduced evidence that the defendant estimated the risk of death or serious impairment associated with her surgery at two percent. At trial, however, the defendant conceded that because of his relative lack of experience, he could not hope to match the ten-and-seven-tenths percent morbidity and mortality rate reported for large basilar bifurcation aneurysm surgery by very experienced surgeons.

The defendant also admitted at trial that he had not shared with the plaintiff information from articles he reviewed prior to surgery. These articles established that even the most accomplished posterior circulation aneurysm surgeons reported morbidity and mortality rates of fifteen percent for basilar bifurcation aneurysms. Furthermore, the plaintiff introduced expert testimony indicating that the estimated morbidity and mortality rate one might expect when a physician with the defendant's relatively limited experience performed the surgery would be close to thirty percent.

Had a reasonable person in the plaintiff's position been made aware that being operated upon by the defendant significantly increased the risk one would have faced in the hands of another surgeon performing the same operation, that person might well have elected to forego surgery with the defendant. Had a reasonable person in the plaintiff's position been made aware that the risks associated with surgery were significantly greater than the risks that an unclipped aneurysm would rupture, that person might well have elected to forego surgery altogether. In short, had a reasonable person in the plaintiff's position possessed such information before consenting to surgery, that person would have been better able to make an informed and intelligent decision.

The defendant concedes that the duty to procure a patient's informed consent requires a physician to reveal the general risks associated with a particular surgery. The defendant does not explain why the duty to inform about this general risk data should be interpreted to categorically exclude evidence relating to provider-specific risk information, even when that provider-specific data is geared to a clearly delineated surgical procedure and identifies a particular provider as an independent risk factor. When different physicians have substantially different success rates, whether surgery is performed by one rather than another represents a choice between "alternate, viable medical modes of treatment" under § 448.30.

For example, while there may be a general risk of ten percent that a particular surgical procedure will result in paralysis or death, that risk may climb to forty percent when the particular procedure is performed by a relatively inexperienced surgeon. It defies logic to interpret this statute as requiring that the first, almost meaningless statistic be divulged to a patient while the second, far more relevant statistic should not be. Under Scaria and its progeny as well as the codification of Scaria as Wis.Stat. § 448.30, the second statistic would be material to the patient's exercise of an intelligent and informed consent regarding treatment options. A circuit court may in its discretion conclude that the second statistic is admissible.

The doctrine of informed consent requires disclosure of "all of the viable alternatives and risks of the treatment proposed" which would be material to a patient's decision. [ ] We therefore conclude that when different physicians have substantially different success rates with the same procedure and a reasonable person in the patient's position would consider such information material, the circuit court may admit this statistical evidence.[32]

We caution, as did the court of appeals, that our decision will not always require physicians to give patients comparative risk evidence in statistical terms to obtain informed consent.[33] Rather, we hold that evidence of the morbidity and mortality outcomes of different physicians was admissible under the circumstances of this case.

In keeping with the fact-driven and context-specific application of informed consent doctrine, questions regarding whether statistics are sufficiently material to a patient's decision to be admissible and sufficiently reliable to be non-prejudicial are best resolved on a case-by-case basis. The fundamental issue in an informed consent case is less a question of how a physician chooses to explain the panoply of treatment options and risks necessary to a patient's informed consent than a question of assessing whether a patient has been advised that such options and risks exist.

As the court of appeals observed, in this case it was the defendant himself who elected to explain the risks confronting the plaintiff in statistical terms. He did this because, as he stated at trial, "numbers giv[e] some perspective to the framework of the very real, immediate, human threat that is involved

---

32. See Aaron D. Twerski & Neil B. Cohen, Comparing Medical Providers: A First Look at the New Era of Medical Statistics, 58 Brook. L.Rev. 5 (1992). Professors Twerski and Cohen note that the development of sophisticated data regarding risks of various procedures and statistical models comparing the success rates of medical providers signal changes in informed consent law. Specifically, they state:

The duty to provide information may require more than a simple sharing of visceral concerns about the wisdom of undertaking a given therapeutic procedure. Physicians may have a responsibility to identify and correlate risk factors and to communicate the results to patients as a predicate to fulfilling their obligation to inform. Id. at 6.

See also Douglas Sharrott, Provider–Specific Quality-of-Care Data: A Proposal for Limited Mandatory Disclosure, 58 Brook L.Rev. 85

(1992) (stating that it is difficult to refute the argument that provider-specific data, once disclosed to the public by the government, should also be disclosed to patients because the doctrine of informed consent requires a physician to inform a patient of both material risks and alternatives to a proposed course of treatment).

33. For criticisms of medical performance statistics and cautions that provider-specific outcome statistics must be carefully evaluated to insure their reliability and validity when used as evidence, see, e.g., Jesse Green, Problems in the Use of Outcome Statistics to Compare Health Care Providers, 58 Brook.L.Rev. 55 (1992); Paul D. Rheingold, The Admissibility of Evidence in Malpractice Cases: The Performance Records of Practitioners, 58 Brook. L.Rev. 75, 78–79 (1992); Sharrott, supra, at 92–94, 120; Twerski & Cohen, supra, at 8–9.

with this condition." Because the defendant elected to explain the risks confronting the plaintiff in statistical terms, it stands to reason that in her effort to demonstrate how the defendant's numbers dramatically understated the risks of her surgery, the plaintiff would seek to introduce other statistical evidence. Such evidence was integral to her claim that the defendant's nondisclosure denied her the ability to exercise informed consent.

VI.

The defendant also asserts that the circuit court erred as a matter of law in allowing the plaintiff to introduce expert testimony that because of the difficulties associated with operating on the plaintiff's aneurysm, the defendant should have referred her to a tertiary care center containing a proper neurological intensive care unit, more extensive microsurgical facilities and more experienced surgeons. While evidence that a physician should have referred a patient elsewhere may support an action alleging negligent treatment, argues the defendant, it has no place in an informed consent action.

* * *

When faced with an allegation that a physician breached a duty of informed consent, the pertinent inquiry concerns what information a reasonable person in the patient's position would have considered material to an exercise of intelligent and informed consent. [ ] Under the facts and circumstances presented by this case, the circuit court could declare, in the exercise of its discretion, that evidence of referral would have been material to the ability of a reasonable person in the plaintiff's position to render informed consent.

The plaintiff's medical experts testified that given the nature and difficulty of the surgery at issue, the plaintiff could not make an intelligent decision or give an informed consent without being made aware that surgery in a tertiary facility would have decreased the risk she faced. One of the plaintiff's experts, Dr. Haring J.W. Nauta, stated that "it's not fair not to bring up the subject of referral to another center when the problem is as difficult to treat" as the plaintiff's aneurysm was. Another of the plaintiff's experts, Dr. Robert Narotzky, testified that the defendant's "very limited" experience with aneurysm surgery rendered reasonable a referral to "someone with a lot more experience in dealing with this kind of problem." Dr. Fredric Somach, also testifying for the plaintiff, stated as follows:

> [S]he should have been told that this was an extremely difficult, formidable lesion and that there are people in the immediate geographic vicinity that are very experienced and that have had a great deal of contact with this type of aneurysm and that she should consider having at least a second opinion, if not going directly to one of these other [physicians].

Articles from the medical literature introduced by the plaintiff also stated categorically that the surgery at issue should be performed at a tertiary care center while being "excluded" from the community setting because of "the limited surgical experience" and lack of proper equipment and facilities available in such hospitals.

* * * Hence under the materiality standard announced in Scaria, we conclude that the circuit court properly exercised its discretion in admitting evidence that the defendant should have advised the plaintiff of the possibility of undergoing surgery at a tertiary care facility.

The defendant asserts that the plaintiff knew she could go elsewhere. This claim is both true and beside the point. Credible evidence in this case demonstrates that the plaintiff chose not to go elsewhere because the defendant gave her the impression that her surgery was routine and that it therefore made no difference who performed it. The pertinent inquiry, then, is not whether a reasonable person in the plaintiff's position would have known generally that she might have surgery elsewhere, but rather whether such a person would have chosen to have surgery elsewhere had the defendant adequately disclosed the comparable risks attending surgery performed by him and surgery performed at a tertiary care facility such as the Mayo Clinic, only 90 miles away.

* * *

Finally, the defendant argues that if his duty to procure the plaintiff's informed consent includes an obligation to disclose that she consider seeking treatment elsewhere, then there will be no logical stopping point to what the doctrine of informed consent might encompass. We disagree with the defendant. As the plaintiff noted in her brief to this court, "[i]t is a rare exception when the vast body of medical literature and expert opinion agree that the difference in experience of the surgeon performing the operation will impact the risk of morbidity/mortality as was the case here," thereby requiring referral. Brief for Petitioner at 40. At oral argument before this court, counsel for the plaintiff stated that under "many circumstances" and indeed "probably most circumstances," whether or not a physician referred a patient elsewhere would be "utterly irrelevant" in an informed consent case. In the vast majority of significantly less complicated cases, such a referral would be irrelevant and unnecessary.

Moreover, we have already concluded that comparative risk data distinguishing the defendant's morbidity and mortality rate from the rate of more experienced physicians was properly before the jury. A close link exists between such data and the propriety of referring a patient elsewhere. A physician who discloses that other physicians might have lower morbidity and mortality rates when performing the same procedure will presumably have access to information regarding who some of those physicians are. When the duty to share comparative risk data is material to a patient's exercise of informed consent, an ensuing referral elsewhere will often represent no more than a modest and logical next step.[37]

Given the difficulties involved in performing the surgery at issue in this case, coupled with evidence that the defendant exaggerated his own prior experience while downplaying the risks confronting the plaintiff, the circuit court properly exercised its discretion in admitting evidence that a physician of good standing would have made the plaintiff aware of the alternative of

---

37. The Canterbury court included a duty to refer among its examples of information which, under the facts and circumstances of a particular case, a physician might be required to disclose in order to procure a patient's informed consent. The court stated: "The typical situation is where a general practitioner discovers that the patient's malady calls for specialized treatment, whereupon the duty generally arises to advise the patient to consult a specialist." Canterbury, 464 F.2d at 781 n. 22.

lower risk surgery with a different, more experienced surgeon in a better-equipped facility.

For the reasons set forth, we conclude that the circuit court did not erroneously exercise its discretion in admitting the evidence at issue, and accordingly, we reverse the decision of the court of appeals and remand the cause to the circuit court for further proceedings consistent with this opinion.

The decision of the court of appeals is reversed and the cause is remanded to the circuit court with directions.

Notes and Questions

1. Do you see any problems with the duty to disclose articulated in *Johnson*? Can a surgeon manage to disguise poor results or repackage the data to confuse the patient? Or is this likely to represent the future, in which patients peruse batting averages before choosing their providers? Is there anything wrong with a consumer-driven model of medicine?

Consumer advocates have lobbied with success for disclosure of hospital and physician performance data in a variety of formats, including report cards and other rankings. Studies of the effects of disclosure of such data have not been encouraging. See for example Eric C. Schneider, Arnold M. Epstein, Use of Public Performance Reports: A Survey of Patients Undergoing Cardiac Surgery, 279 J.A.M.A. 1638, 1642(1998). The authors concluded that "... public reporting of mortality outcomes in Pennsylvania has had virtually no direct impact on patients' selection of hospitals or surgeons. Nevertheless, a substantial number of patients expressed interest in data on mortality outcomes and claimed that they would use such reports in their decision making ... [w]ithout a tailored and intensive program for dissemination and patient education, efforts to aid patient decision making with performance reports are unlikely to succeed." See also Judith H. Hibbard, Paul Slovic, and Jacquelyn J. Jewett, Informing Consumer Decisions in Health Care: Implications from Decision–Making Research, 75 Milbank Q. 395, 411–412 (1997) (finding little congruence between current report card strategies and decision-making research.); Stephen T. Mennemeyer, Michael A. Morrisey, and Leslie Z. Howard, Death and Reputation: How Consumers Acted Upon HCFA Mortality Information, 34 Inquiry 117 (1997) (quality measures aimed at the public must be very simply designed and described; complex measures are largely ignored).

2. Most courts resist requirements that specific percentages of risks be disclosed, arguing that medicine is an inexact science. In Ditto v. McCurdy, 86 Hawai'i 84, 947 P.2d 952 (1997) two patients underwent breast implant procedures and had complications, and sued the cosmetic surgeon. They argued among other claims that the surgeon's experience should have been disclosed to them, since he was not certified as a plastic surgeon, but only as an otolaryngologist, facial surgeon, and cosmetic surgeon. The court concluded that "[u]nder the circumstances of the present case, we decline to hold that a physician has a duty to affirmatively disclose his or her qualifications or the lack thereof to a patient. Id at 958. The court preferred to leave such disclosure requirements to the legislature."

See also Kennedy v. St. Charles General Hospital Auxiliary, 630 So.2d 888, 892 (La.App.1993). But see Hales v. Pittman, 118 Ariz. 305, 576 P.2d 493 (Ariz.1978) (discussing the battery count of the plaintiff's complaint; the court proposed that the doctor should disclose both the general statistical success rate for a given procedure, and his particular experience with that procedure.) See also

Hidding v. Williams, 578 So.2d 1192 (La.Ct.App.1991) (plaintiff sued on an informed consent theory, alleging in part that the physician had failed to disclose that he was a chronic alcoholic; held, such a failure to inform violated Louisiana informed consent requirements); contra, Ornelas v. Fry, 151 Ariz. 324, 727 P.2d 819 (Ariz.Ct.App.1986) (court refused to allow evidence as to alcoholism of anesthesiologist as a separate claim of negligence, absent a showing that the physician was impaired at the time of the procedure.)

3.   Suppose that a surgeon in his late fifties is aware that his skill level—his vision, his fine motor skills—is diminishing. His success rate is dropping, which means that his patient survival statistics are worsening. The odds of an iatrogenic injury with this surgeon have increased from 1 in 1,000 to 1 in 750. His record is still excellent. Should he disclose to his patients that he is beginning to suffer the inevitable results of aging? Or just that his success rate is a certain percentage? Institutional peer review is likely to restrict the surgeon's practice to those procedures he is competent to perform, with regular proctoring to guarantee good results, when he falls below a reasonable norm. We might also expect a physician with integrity to recognize his limits and begin to cut back on procedures. The role of the institution and peers in controlling these practices is central to reducing risks, backstopped by the ever present threat of a tort suit for damages. Hospital medical staff law has focused on provider competency in articulating the limits of negligent staff selection. Hospitals screen their medical staff to reduce the level of risk of injury to their patient population, refusing to credential high risk physicians, defining risk by a competency/quality definition.

For good general discussions of contemporary informed consent issues, see Robert Gatter, Informed Consent and the Forgotten Duty of Physician Inquiry, 1 Loy. U. Chi. L.J. 557 (2000); Arnold J. Rosoff, Informed Consent in the Electronic Age, 25 Am.J.L. & Med.367(1999); Frances H. Miller, Health Care Information Technology and Informed Consent: Computers and the Doctor–Patient Relationship, 31 Ind. L. Rev. 1019 (1998).

4.   The disclosure of a contagious status that exposes a patient to a risk of death is arguably different from performance-based risks. A competent physician may expose a patient to the HIV virus, while the risks discussed above are created by performance failures. The distinction is however not compelling. From the patient's perspective, the source of the risk is less important than the risk itself, whether death or impairment. From a patient's perspective, if the low risk of transmission of the HIV-virus must be disclosed, then surely so must alcoholism in a surgeon. A provider's performance can be affected by fatigue, depression, anger, and other psychological states with potentially lethal results for the patient. We don't presently require disclosure of the various forces that affect providers, and it is hard to imagine how this could be done. If a court is to avoid singling out AIDs as presenting unique risks to a patient, then vastly expanded disclosure obligations may well be next.

The courts have not often agreed with these arguments. In Behringer v. The Medical Center at Princeton, 249 N.J.Super. 597, 592 A.2d 1251 (1991), the plaintiff, a surgeon at the medical center, was diagnosed as having AIDS. The information leaked out in the hospital, and he lost most of his patients. The court held that informed consent doctrine mandated disclosure of the doctor's contagious status in spite of evidence that the risk of transmission of the HIV virus from provider to patient was extremely low. The court wrote:

If there is to be an ultimate arbiter of whether the patient is to be treated invasively by an AIDS-positive surgeon, the arbiter will be the fully-informed patient. The ultimate risk to the patient is so absolute—so devastating—that it is untenable to argue against informed consent combined with a restriction on procedures which present "any risk" to the patient.

While the theory and application of informed consent doctrine by the courts seems to justify disclosure of HIV positive status, the efficacy of the doctrine in actually inducing providers to so act is unclear at best. HIV status does not pose unique risks: the risk of either contagion or death is inherent in a range of provider-created risks. A better way to frame the risks for the courts is to think of such status risks as better regulated by both threshold screening of providers for staff privileges, by institutional policies to promote safer health care delivery, and by use of tort law to set a standard of unreasonable risk creation. A provider who fails to protect residents or medical staff may be liable for negligence. See, e.g., Doe v. Yale University, 252 Conn. 641, 748 A.2d 834 (2000)(noting that a physician employee may be limited to Workers' Compensation).

Methods of achieving such threshold screening to protect patients against high-risk providers include staff privilege limitations, the threat of a negligence suit against a provider who is truly a "typhoid surgeon", and professional self-restraint by physicians who become aware that they are high-risk providers. Informed consent doctrine seems ill-suited to carry such additional baggage—it is unfair to providers, moves doctrine into an area of risk disclosure that lacks a clear stopping point or bright line, and is simply not justified by a risk analysis.

See generally Lawrence O. Gostin, A Proposed National Policy on Health Care Workers Living With HIV/AIDS and Other Blood–Borne Pathogens, 284 JAMA 1965 (2000); Anthony L. Osterlund, The Unequal Balancing Act Between HIV–Positive Patients and Physicians, 25 Ohio N.U. L. Rev. 149 (1999); Mara E. Zazzali, HIV–Infected Health Care Workers Who Perform Invasive, Exposure–Prone Procedures: Defining the Risk and Balancing the Interests of Health Care Workers and Patients, 28 Seton Hall L. Rev. 1000 (1998); American Bar Association Aids Coordinating Committee, (Edited by Eric N. Richardson and Salvatore J. Russo), Calming AIDS Phobia: Legal Implications of the Low Risk of Transmitting HIV in the Health Care Setting, 28 U. Mich. J.L. Ref. 733 (1995); Leonard H. Glantz et al., Risky Business: Setting Public Health Policy for HIV-infected Health Care Professionals, 70 The Milbank Quart. 43, 72–73 (1992); Norman Daniels, HIV–Infected Health Care Professionals: Public Threat or Public Sacrifice?, 70 Milbank Quart. 3(1992).

5. The American Medical Association (AMA) and the American Dental Association (ADA) have taken the position that HIV infected professionals should abstain from performing risky invasive procedures, or should disclose their seropositive status to their patients. The burden is placed on the individual professional. The calculation of the professional organizations appears to be that some patients will stick with the provider because they will take on the low risks of infection, valuing their relationship with the professional, or the professional's reputation for quality. But why should the professional disclose his status, if he knows it? He may see his practice diminish or disappear as patients spread the word. If a hospital or managed care organization finds out, they may restrict his practice and cut his income. It is more likely that they will restrict his privileges, or in the case of a managed care organization, remove him from panel membership. The infected provider therefore has little incentive to disclose and substantial incentives to remain silent.

Disclosure of a provider's HIV status to a patient, particularly prior to invasive surgery, is often required. In Doe v. Noe No. 1, 293 Ill.App.3d 1099, 228

Ill.Dec. 937, 690 N.E.2d 1012 (Ill.App. 1 Dist.1997), the court followed Maryland's approach in Faya v. Almaraz, 329 Md. 435, 620 A.2d 327 (1993), finding that a physician should disclose his or her HIV-positive status to a patient who is going to submit to an invasive surgery.

6.   The studies to date have found no evidence of transmission from provider to patient, with the possible exception of the Bergalis case. See Jeffrey J. Sacks, AIDS in a Surgeon, 313 New Eng. J. Med. 1017 (1985) (study of 400 Florida patients of surgeon); Frances P. Armstrong et al, Investigation of a Health Care Worker with Symptomatic Immunodeficiency Virus Infection: An Epidemiologic Approach, 152 Military Medicine 414 (1987) (1004 patients of military surgeon); John D. Porter et al, Management of Patients Treated by Surgeon with HIV Infection, The Lancet, January 1990, at 113 (339 patients of British surgeon); Ban Mishu et al, A Surgeon with AIDS: Lack of Evidence of Transmission to Patients, 264 JAMA 467 (1990) (study of 2160 patients of Nashville surgeon).

7.   The perils of 3rd party disclosure. Disclosure of HIV-positive status to third parties, where the patients have not faced risks of exposure, can lead to liability by the party disclosing this status information. In Tolman v. Doe, 988 F.Supp. 582 (D.C.E.D.Va. 1997), the HIV-positive physician sued another physician in state court, alleging causes of action including defamation and intentional infliction of emotional distress based on a letter by defendant to plaintiff's patients informing them that plaintiff had Acquired Immune Deficiency Syndrome (AIDS) and that defendant would not want plaintiff as his cardiologist.

The plaintiff Dr.Tolman was a physician. He was also gay. He has not kept this fact secret from family, close friends, or acquaintances. In 1994, he learned that he had AIDS. Dr. Tolman was in compliance with the Center for Disease Control ("CDC") guidelines while treating patients and, specifically, performing cardiology procedures. Recommendations For Preventing Transmission Of Human Immunodeficiency Virus and Hepatitis B Virus To Patients During Exposure–Prone Invasive Procedures MMWR, Vol. 40/No. RR–8 ("CDC Rec."), at 1.

Defendant Dr. Doe was a physician who practiced with Dr. Tolman until 1996, when he left to take a position out of state. In September or October of 1995, Dr. Doe learned that Dr. Tolman had AIDS. Dr. Doe stated that his "personal opinion" is to disagree with the CDC's determination that a physician with AIDS who complies with the CDC's guidelines may safely perform the procedures that Dr. Tolman was performing. In May 1996 Dr. Doe had a conversation with a patient, during which the patient expressly asked Dr. Doe if Dr. Tolman had AIDS. The patient also asked what Dr. Doe recommended regarding the patient's continued treatment by Dr. Tolman. Dr. Doe told the patient that Dr. Tolman had AIDS and that he (Dr. Doe) would not want a physician with AIDS treating him if he were a patient.

In December 1996, Dr. Doe wrote a letter to between ten and fifteen patients. The letter stated in relevant part:

> I would like to tell you that I left the program for personal reasons and because my personal career at ... was not going anywhere, and also because I could not work any more with Dr. Tolman, especially when I learned that he had AIDS and continues to perform invasive procedres [sic] on the [cardiology] patients.
>
> (Unfortunately, he never told me any thing about it himself, maybe because he did not want me to know that he was homosexual.)

I don't realy [sic] know what to tell you regarding your heart transplant care after you learn this fact. Howevr [sic], I will leave this to your personal judgment. I personally will not want somebody with AIDS to be my physcian [sic], let alone being my [cardiologist]. You may want to think of an alternative that will beter [sic] serve you.

The court held that the plaintiff, for purposes of a motion for summary judgment, had established that a defamatory publication was false. The letter reasonably implied that Dr. Tolman was unfit to practice as a physician, specifically to perform invasive procedures, and that he was placing his patients at an inappropriate risk by continuing these procedures while having contracted AIDS. The court noted the CDC report described the procedures done by the plaintiffs as not "exposure prone" procedures. The court further found that the "CDC has determined that physicians with AIDS, such as Dr. Tolman, are fit to practice medicine and to perform the procedures at issue." He was also in compliance with CDC guidelines in treating patients.

The evidence offered by Defendant consists of the type of speculative inferences, glancing statistics, and unsupported conclusions that Abbott warns against. Indeed, Doe's effort to rebut the consensus of public health officials is much weaker than the effort that was rejected on summary judgment by the Abbott trial court and affirmed on appeal. No reasonable jury could disagree that Defendant's insinuations that Plaintiff was unfit to be a physician, and more specifically, to perform the procedures in question, were false.

Problem: Impaired Physicians

Mercy Hospital employs Dr. Frank Tehr, a surgeon who in the past has sexually assaulted female patients. Suppose that he sees a thousand patients a year, half of them women, and has only assaulted two women over five years, making the risk for the individual female patient $2/2500$, or .0008, or .08%. Should every female patient be informed of the low risk of sexual assault, in light of Behringer? What else might the hospital do?

Boosier City Memorial Hospital has a staff surgeon, Dr. Williams, who is an alcoholic. He is an excellent surgeon when he is not impaired by drinking, but because he is a chronic alcoholic it is hard to predict when he may be impaired. Should Dr. Williams be required to disclose to patients that he is an alcoholic, so they can choose whether to continue with him?

3. Disclosure of Statistical Mortality Information

Patients with diseases such as cancer usually face a reduced life expectancy even with the best medical treatment. Such patients would presumably like to know as much as possible about their life expectancy for a variety of reasons—estate planning, goodbyes to family and friends, fortifying themselves to face death for personal and religious reasons. Must the doctor inform the patient of his life expectancy based on statistical tables?

ARATO v. AVEDON

Supreme Court of California, 1993.
5 Cal.4th 1172, 23 Cal.Rptr.2d 131, 858 P.2d 598.

ARABIAN, JUSTICE.

A physician's duty to disclose to a patient information material to the decision whether to undergo treatment is the central constituent of the legal doctrine known as "informed consent." In this case, we review the ruling of a divided Court of Appeal that, in recommending a course of chemotherapy and radiation treatment to a patient suffering from a virulent form of cancer, the treating physicians breached their duty to obtain the patient's informed consent by failing to disclose his statistical life expectancy.

* * *

I

A

Miklos Arato was a successful 42–year–old electrical contractor and part-time real estate developer when, early in 1980, his internist diagnosed a failing kidney. On July 21, 1980, in the course of surgery to remove the kidney, the operating surgeon detected a tumor on the "tail" or distal portion of Mr. Arato's pancreas. After Mrs. Arato gave her consent, portions of the pancreas were resected, or removed, along with the spleen and the diseased kidney. A follow-up pathological examination of the resected pancreatic tissue confirmed a malignancy. Concerned that the cancer could recur and might have infiltrated adjacent organs, Mr. Arato's surgeon referred him to a group of oncology practitioners for follow-up treatment.

During his initial visit to the oncologists, Mr. Arato filled out a multipage questionnaire routinely given new patients. Among the some 150 questions asked was whether patients "wish[ed] to be told the truth about [their] condition" or whether they wanted the physician to "bear the burden" for them. Mr. Arato checked the box indicating that he wished to be told the truth.

The oncologists discussed with Mr. and Mrs. Arato the advisability of a course of chemotherapy known as "F.A.M.," a treatment employing a combination of drugs which, when used in conjunction with radiation therapy, had shown promise in treating pancreatic cancer in experimental trials. The nature of the discussions between Mr. and Mrs. Arato and the treating physicians, and in particular the scope of the disclosures made to the patient by his doctors, was the subject of conflicting testimony at trial. By their own admission, however, neither the operating surgeon nor the treating oncologists specifically disclosed to the patient or his wife the high statistical mortality rate associated with pancreatic cancer.

Mr. Arato's oncologists determined that a course of F.A.M. chemotherapy was indicated for several reasons. According to their testimony, the high statistical mortality of pancreatic cancer is in part a function of what is by far the most common diagnostic scenario—the discovery of the malignancy well after it has metastasized to distant sites, spreading throughout the patient's body. As noted, in Mr. Arato's case, the tumor was comparatively localized, having been discovered in the tail of the pancreas by chance in the course of surgery to remove the diseased kidney.

Related to the "silent" character of pancreatic cancer is the fact that detection in such an advanced state usually means that the tumor cannot as a practical matter be removed, contributing to the high mortality rate. In Mr. Arato's case, however, the operating surgeon determined that it was possible to excise cleanly the tumorous portion of the pancreas and to leave a margin of about one-half centimeter around the surgical site, a margin that appeared clinically to be clear of cancer cells. Third, the mortality rate is somewhat lower, according to defense testimony, for pancreatic tumors located in the distal part of the organ than for those found in the main body. Finally, then-recent experimental studies on the use of F.A.M. chemotherapy in conjunction with therapeutic radiation treatments had shown promising response rates—on the order of several months of extended life—among pancreatic cancer patients.

Mr. Arato's treating physicians justified not disclosing statistical life expectancy data to their patient on disparate grounds. According to the testimony of his surgeon, Mr. Arato had exhibited great anxiety over his condition, so much so that his surgeon determined that it would have been medically inappropriate to disclose specific mortality rates. The patient's oncologists had a somewhat different explanation. As Dr. Melvin Avedon, his chief oncologist, put it, he believed that cancer patients in Mr. Arato's position "wanted to be told the truth, but did not want a cold shower." Along with the other treating physicians, Dr. Avedon testified that in his opinion the direct and specific disclosure of extremely high mortality rates for malignancies such as pancreatic cancer might effectively deprive a patient of any hope of cure, a medically inadvisable state. Moreover, all of the treating physicians testified that statistical life expectancy data had little predictive value when applied to a particular patient with individualized symptoms, medical history, character traits and other variables.

According to the physicians' testimony, Mr. and Mrs. Arato were told at the outset of the treatment that most victims of pancreatic cancer die of the disease, that Mr. Arato was at "serious" or "great" risk of a recurrence and that, should the cancer return, his condition would be judged incurable. This information was given to the patient and his wife in the context of a series of verbal and behavioral cues designed to invite the patient or family member to follow up with more direct and difficult questions. Such follow-up questions, on the order of "how long do I have to live?," would have signaled to his doctors, according to Dr. Avedon's testimony, the patient's desire and ability to confront the fact of imminent mortality. In the judgment of his chief oncologist, Mr. Arato, although keenly interested in the clinical significance of the most minute symptom, studiously avoided confronting these ultimate issues; according to his doctors, neither Mr. Arato nor his wife ever asked for information concerning his life expectancy in more than 70 visits over a period of a year. Believing that they had disclosed information sufficient to enable him to make an informed decision whether to undergo chemotherapy, Mr. Arato's doctors concluded that their patient had as much information regarding his condition and prognosis as he wished.

Dr. Avedon also testified that he told Mr. Arato that the effectiveness of F.A.M. therapy was unproven in cases such as his, described its principal adverse side effects, and noted that one of the patient's options was not to undergo the treatment. In the event, Mr. Arato consented to the proposed course of chemotherapy and radiation, treatments that are prolonged, difficult and painful for cancer patients. Unfortunately, the treatment proved ineffective in arresting the spread of the malignancy. Although clinical tests showed him to be free of cancer in the several months following the beginning of the F.A.M. treatments, beginning in late March and into April of 1981, the clinical signs took an adverse turn.[1] By late April, the doctors were convinced by the results of additional tests that the cancer had returned and was spreading. They advised the patient of their suspicions and discontinued chemotherapy. On July 25, 1981, a year and four days following surgery, Mr. Arato succumbed to the effects of pancreatic cancer.

B

Not long after his death, Mr. Arato's wife and two children brought this suit against the physicians who had treated their husband and father in his last days, including the surgeon who performed the pancreas resection and the oncologists who had recommended and administered the chemotherapy/radiation treatment. As presented to the jury, the gist of the lawsuit was the claim that in discussing with their patient the advisability of undergoing a course of chemotherapy and radiation, Mr. Arato's doctors had failed to disclose adequately the shortcomings of the proposed treatment in light of the diagnosis, and thus had failed to obtain the patient's informed consent. Specifically, plaintiffs contended that the doctors were aware that, because early detection is difficult and rare, pancreatic cancer is an especially virulent malignancy, one in which only 5 to 10 percent of those afflicted live for as long as five years, and that given the practically incurable nature of the disease, there was little chance Mr. Arato would live more than a short while, even if the proposed treatment proved effective.

Such mortality information, the complaint alleged—especially the statistical morbidity rate of pancreatic cancer—was material to Mr. Arato's decision whether to undergo postoperative treatment; had he known the bleak truth concerning his life expectancy, he would not have undergone the rigors of an unproven therapy, but would have chosen to live out his last days at peace with his wife and children, and arranging his business affairs. Instead, the complaint asserted, in the false hope that radiation and chemotherapy treatments could effect a cure—a hope born of the negligent failure of his physicians to disclose the probability of an early death—Mr. Arato failed to order his affairs in contemplation of his death, an omission that, according to the complaint, led eventually to the failure of his contracting business and to substantial real estate and tax losses following his death.

As the trial neared its conclusion and the court prepared to charge the jury, plaintiffs requested that several special instructions be given relating to the nature and scope of the physician's duty of disclosure. Two proffered instructions in particular are pertinent to this appeal. In the first, plaintiffs asked the trial court to instruct the jury that "A physician has a fiduciary duty to a patient to make a full and fair disclosure to the patient of all facts which materially affect the patient's rights and interests." The second instruction sought by plaintiffs stated that "The scope of the physician's duty to disclose is measured by the amount of knowledge a patient needs in order to

---

1. Around this time—on March 12, 1981, according to the record—an article appeared in the Los Angeles Times stating that only 1 percent of males and 2 percent of females diagnosed as having pancreatic cancer live for five years. According to his wife's testimony, Mr. Arato read the Times article and brought it to the attention of his oncologists. One of his oncologists confirmed such a discussion but denied that he told Mr. Arato that the statistics did not apply to his case, as Mrs. Arato testified. Mr. Arato continued to undergo chemotherapy treatment after reading the article and evidently made no changes in his estate planning or business and real estate affairs.

make an informed choice. All information material to the patient's decision should be given."

The trial judge declined to give the jury either of the two instructions sought by plaintiffs. Instead, the court read to the jury a modified version of BAJI No. 6.11, the so-called "reality of consent" instruction drawn from our opinion in Cobbs v. Grant [ ]. * * *

After concluding its deliberations, the jury returned two special verdicts—on a form approved by plaintiffs' counsel—finding that none of the defendants was negligent in the "medical management" of Mr. Arato, and that defendants "disclosed to Mr. Arato all relevant information which would have enabled him to make an informed decision regarding the proposed treatment to be rendered him." Plaintiffs appealed from the judgment entered on the defense verdict, contending that the trial court erred in refusing to give the jury the special instructions requested by them. As noted, a divided Court of Appeal reversed the judgment of the trial court, and ordered a new trial. We granted defendants' ensuing petition for review and now reverse the judgment of the Court of Appeal.

C

[The court in section C discusses the Court of Appeal decision, which required that Mr. Arato's doctors disclose numerical life expectancy information so that he could reduce the risks of financial loss; and found that the trial court instructions were defective in several regards].

II

A

[The court discusses Cobbs v. Grant at length, and the duty it imposed on a treating physician "of reasonable disclosure of the available choices with respect to proposed therapy and of the dangers inherently and potentially involved in each." [ ] It also considered both Truman v. Thomas and Moore v. Board of Regents, and their refinement of California's informed consent law.]

B

* * *

Despite the critical standoff between these extremes of "patient sovereignty" and "medical paternalism," indications are that the Cobbs-era decisions helped effect a revolution in attitudes among patients and physicians alike regarding the desirability of frank and open disclosure of relevant medical information. The principal question we must address is whether our holding in Cobbs v. Grant, [ ] as embodied in BAJI No. 6.11, accurately conveys to juries the legal standard under which they assess the evidence in determining the adequacy of the disclosures made by physician to patient in a particular case or whether, as the Court of Appeal here appeared to conclude, the standard instruction should be revised to mandate specific disclosures such as patient life expectancy as revealed by mortality statistics.

In our view, one of the merits of the somewhat abstract formulation of BAJI No. 6.11 is its recognition of the importance of the overall medical context that juries ought to take into account in deciding whether a challenged disclosure was reasonably sufficient to convey to the patient information material to an informed treatment decision. The contexts and clinical settings in which physician and patient interact and exchange information material to therapeutic decisions are so multifarious, the informational needs and degree of dependency of individual patients so various, and the professional relationship itself such an intimate and irreducibly judgment-laden one, that we believe it is unwise to require as a matter of law that a particular species of information be disclosed.... [ ]

* * *

This sensitivity to context seems all the more appropriate in the case of life expectancy projections for cancer patients based on statistical samples. Without exception, the testimony of every physician-witness at trial confirmed what is evident even to a nonprofessional: statistical morbidity values derived from the experience of population groups are inherently unreliable and offer little assurance regarding the fate of the individual patient; indeed, to assume that such data are conclusive in themselves smacks of a refusal to explore treatment alternatives and the medical abdication of the patient's well-being. Certainly the jury here heard evidence of articulable grounds for the conclusion that the particular features of Mr. Arato's case distinguished it from the typical population of pancreatic cancer sufferers and their dismal statistical probabilities—a fact plaintiffs impliedly acknowledged at trial in conceding that the oncologic referral of Mr. Arato and ensuing chemotherapy were not in themselves medically negligent.

* * *

Rather than mandate the disclosure of specific information as a matter of law, the better rule is to instruct the jury that a physician is under a legal duty to disclose to the patient all material information—that is, "information which the physician knows or should know would be regarded as significant by a reasonable person in the patient's position when deciding to accept or reject a recommended medical procedure"—needed to make an informed decision regarding a proposed treatment. That, of course, is the formulation embodied in BAJI No. 6.11 and the instruction given in this case. Having been properly instructed, the jury returned a defense verdict—on a form approved by plaintiffs' counsel—specifically finding that defendants had "disclosed to Mr. Arato all relevant information which would have enabled him to make an informed decision regarding the proposed treatment to be rendered him."

We decline to intrude further, either on the subtleties of the physician-patient relationship or in the resolution of claims that the physician's duty of disclosure was breached, by requiring the disclosure of information that may or may not be indicated in a given treatment context. Instead, we leave the ultimate judgment as to the factual adequacy of a challenged disclosure to the venerable American jury, operating under legal instructions such as those given here and subject to the persuasive force of trial advocacy.

Here, the evidence was more than sufficient to support the jury's finding that defendants had reasonably disclosed to Mr. Arato information material to his decision whether to undergo the proposed chemotherapy/radiation treatment. There was testimony that Mr. and Mrs. Arato were informed that cancer of the pancreas is usually fatal; of the substantial risk of recurrence, an event that would mean his illness was incurable; of the unproven nature of the F.A.M. treatments and their principal side effects; and of the option of forgoing such treatments. Mr. Arato's doctors also testified that they could not with confidence predict how long the patient might live, notwithstanding statistical mortality tables.

In addition, the jury heard testimony regarding the patient's apparent avoidance of issues bearing upon mortality; Mrs. Arato's testimony that his physicians had assured her husband that he was "clear" of cancer; and the couple's common expectation that he had been "cured," only to learn, suddenly and unexpectedly, that the case was hopeless and life measurable in weeks. The informed consent instructions given the jury to assess this evidence were an accurate statement of the law, and the Court of Appeal in effect invaded the province of the trier of fact in overturning a fairly litigated verdict.[ ]

C

In addition to their claim that his physicians were required to disclose statistical life expectancy data to Mr. Arato to enable him to reach an informed treatment decision, plaintiffs also contend that defendants should have disclosed such data because it was material to the patient's nonmedical interests, that is, Mr. Arato's business and investment affairs and the potential adverse impact of his death upon them. In support of this proposition, plaintiffs rely on the following statement in Bowman v. McPheeters [ ]: "As fiduciaries it was the duty of defendants [physicians] to make a full and fair disclosure to plaintiff of all facts which materially affected his rights and interests." Plaintiffs contend that since Mr. Arato's contracting and real estate affairs would suffer if he failed to make timely changes in estate planning in contemplation of imminent death, and since these matters are among "his rights and interests," his physicians were under a legal duty to disclose all material facts that might affect them, including statistical life expectancy information. We reject the claim as one founded on a premise that is not recognized in California.

The short answer to plaintiffs' claim is our statement in *Moore* [ ] that a "physician is not the patient's financial adviser."[ ] From its inception, the rationale behind the disclosure requirement implementing the doctrine of informed consent has been to protect the patient's freedom to "exercise ... control over [one's] own body" by directing the course of medical treatment.[ ] We recently noted that "the principle of self-determination ... embraces all aspects of medical decisionmaking by the competent adult.... "[ ] Although an aspect of personal autonomy, the conditions for the exercise of the patient's right of self-decision presuppose a therapeutic focus, a supposition reflected in the text of BAJI No. 6.11 itself. The fact that a physician has "fiducial" obligations ... which ... prohibit misrepresenting the nature of the patient's medical condition, does not mean that he or she is under a duty, the scope of which is undefined, to disclose every contingency that might affect the patient's nonmedical "rights and interests." Because plaintiffs' open-ended proposed instruction—that the physician's duty embraces the "disclosure ... of all facts which materially affect the patient's rights and interests"—failed to reflect the therapeutic limitation inherent in the doctrine of informed consent, it would have been error for the trial judge to give it to the jury.

Finally, plaintiffs make much of the fact that in his initial visit to Dr. Avedon's office, Mr. Arato indicated in a lengthy form he was requested to complete that he "wish[ed] to be told the truth about [his] condition." In effect, they contend that as a result of Mr. Arato's affirmative answer, defendants had an absolute duty to make specific life expectancy disclosures to him. Whether the patient has filled out a questionnaire indicating that he or she wishes to be told the "truth" about his or her condition or not, however, a physician is under a legal duty to obtain the patient's informed consent to any recommended treatment. Although a patient may validly waive the right to be informed, we do not see how a request to be told the "truth" in itself heightens the duty of disclosure imposed on physicians as a matter of law.

III.

The final issue we must resolve concerns the use of expert testimony at trial. As noted, the Court of Appeal concluded that expert testimony offered on behalf of defendants went beyond what was appropriate in support of the so-called "therapeutic exception" to the physician's duty of disclosure, misleading the jury and prejudicing plaintiffs' case. Resolution of this issue requires an understanding of the proper, albeit limited, role of expert testimony in informed consent cases.

Over plaintiffs' objection, the trial court admitted the testimony of two medical experts, Drs. Plotkin and Wellisch, the former a professor of clinical medicine and the latter an expert in the psychological management of cancer patients. Both testified that the standard of medical practice cautioned against disclosing to pancreatic cancer patients specific life expectancy data unless the patient directly requested such information and that, in effect, defendants complied with that standard in not disclosing such information to Mr. Arato under the circumstances. Plaintiffs offered expert medical testimony of their own to counter this evidence; their expert testified that there are a number of indirect and compassionate ways to approach the issue of imminent mortality in dealing with patients with terminal cancer and that the standard of professional practice required that a patient in Mr. Arato's circumstances be given specific numerical life expectancy information.

Plaintiffs now complain that it was error for the trial court to admit expert defense testimony, relying on our statement in Cobbs v. Grant, supra, 8 Cal.3d at page 243, 104 Cal.Rptr. 505, 502 P.2d 1, that the weighing of the risks accompanying a given therapy "against the individual subjective fears and hopes of the patient is not an expert skill." Plaintiffs fail to distinguish between the two kinds of physician disclosure discussed in Cobbs. Our formulation of the scope of the duty of disclosure encompassed "the potential of death or serious harm" known to be inherent in a given procedure and an explanation "in lay terms [of] the complications that might possibly occur." [ ] In addition to these disclosures, which we termed the "minimal" ones required of a physician to insure the patient's informed decisionmaking, we said that the physician must also reveal to the patient "such additional information as a skilled practitioner of good standing would provide under similar circumstances." [ ]

As its verbatim presence in BAJI No. 6.11 testifies, the quoted language, including the reference to the standard of professional practice as the benchmark for measuring the scope of disclosure beyond that implicated by the risks of death or serious harm and the potential for complications, has become an integral part of the legal standard in California for measuring the adequacy of a physician's disclosure in informed consent cases. [ ]

In reckoning the scope of disclosure, the physician will for the most part be guided by the patient's decisional needs * * * [ ] A physician, however, evaluates the patient's decisional needs against a background of professional understanding that includes a knowledge of what information beyond the significant risks associated with a given treatment would be regarded by the medical community as appropriate for disclosure under the circumstances.

* * * [S]ituations will sometimes arise in which the trier of fact is unable to decide the ultimate issue of the adequacy of a particular disclosure without an understanding of the standard of practice within the relevant medical community. For that reason, in an appropriate case, the testimony of medical experts qualified to offer an opinion regarding what, if any, disclosures—in addition to those relating to the risk of death or serious injury and significant potential complications posed by consenting to or declining a proposed treatment—would be made to the patient by a skilled practitioner in the relevant medical community under the circumstances is relevant and admissible.

We underline the limited and essentially subsidiary role of expert testimony in informed consent litigation. * * * Nevertheless, as explained above, there may be a limited number of occasions in the trial of informed consent claims where the adequacy of disclosure in a given case may turn on the standard of practice within the relevant medical community. In such instances, expert testimony will usually be appropriate.

Because statistical life expectancy data is information that lies outside the significant risks associated with a given treatment * * * it falls within the scope of the "additional information ... a skilled practitioner ... would provide...." [ ] And since the question of whether a physician should disclose such information turns on the standard of practice within the medical community, the trial court did not err in permitting expert testimony directed at that issue.

* * *

CONCLUSION

The judgment of the Court of Appeal is reversed and the cause is remanded with directions to affirm the judgment of the trial court.

Notes and Questions

1. The California Supreme Court says it is simply applying the *Cobbs* analysis to the facts of the *Arato* case. It refuses to impose as a matter of law any requirement that a physician disclose to the patient his life expectancy. Why? Is it a desire to leave the lay jury some "wriggle" room, empowering it as the trier of fact? Or a desire to give physicians the flexibility to avoid difficult disclosures? Is life expectancy data so inherently untrustworthy that patients should not be told?

2.   Does *Arato* in effect expand the defense of "therapeutic privilege", giving professional standards undue weight in both the instructions and the expert testimony? If a patient has a cancer that is often lethal in a short time, how much more terrifying is specific knowledge as to life expectancy?

3.   To what extent should a health care provider's informational power expand its obligations to protect a patient's financial interests? A middle-aged patient, facing imminent death, might pursue several alternatives to protect assets for his or her family: he or she might declare personal bankruptcy to wipe out debts; might undertake estate planning to protect assets for the family; might restructure a small business to bring in new administrators. *Arato* seems to blame the plaintiff for not asking, letting the physicians off the hook. Should we let them off so easily? Physicians historically had to discuss treatment costs with patients. In the early days of fee-for-service medicine, patients had to choose between expensive treatments and their other needs, since insurance was not readily available. Today, patients seeking organ transplantation or experimental therapies need to know about their insurance coverage or the availability of Medicaid or other government sources. The health care provider clearly has some role in helping a patient sort out payment sources and costs.

4.   Courts have generally refused to find a hospital or physician negligent for failing to advise patients that they were eligible for government funding. See, e.g., Mraz v. Taft, 85 Ohio App.3d 200, 619 N.E.2d 483 (8 Dist.1993) (neither hospital nor nursing home had any duty to advise husband that he qualified for Medicaid). Nor is a physician liable for the financial consequences of a misdiagnosis, for example a patient's cancellation of a life insurance policy upon being erroneously informed that he did not have cancer. See Estate of Blacher v. Garlett, 857 P.2d 566, 568 (Colo.App.Div.III 1993). But see the discussion in Chapter 3 of the *Wickline* and *Wilson* cases.

5.   One study suggests that the defendants' approach in Arato can create problems. Physician failures to help cancer patients understand their survival odds may lead patients to overestimate their odds of survival, and may influence their preference for medical therapies that are highly toxic and unproductive, in light of the prognosis of a short life expectancy. This describes the facts of Arato. See Jane C. Weeks et al., Relationship Between Cancer Patients' Predictions of Prognosis and Their Treatment Preferences, 279 J.A.M.A. 1709 (1998).

4.   *Disclosure of Risks of NonTreatment*

TRUMAN v. THOMAS
Supreme Court of California, 1980.
27 Cal.3d 285, 165 Cal.Rptr. 308, 611 P.2d 902.

BIRD, C.J.

This court must decide whether a physician's failure to inform a patient of the material risks of not consenting to a recommended pap smear, so that the patient might make an informed choice, may have breached the physician's duty of due care to his patient, who died from cancer of the cervix.

I

Respondent, Dr. Claude R. Thomas, is a family physician engaged in a general medical practice. He was first contacted in April 1963 by appellants' mother, Rena Truman, in connection with her second pregnancy. He continued to act as the primary physician for Mrs. Truman and her two children until March 1969. During this six-year period, Mrs. Truman not only sought his medical advice, but often discussed personal matters with him.

In April 1969, Mrs. Truman consulted Dr. Casey, a urologist, about a urinary tract infection which had been treated previously by Dr. Thomas. While examining Mrs. Truman, Dr. Casey discovered that she was experiencing heavy vaginal discharges and that her cervix was extremely rough. Mrs. Truman was given a prescription for the infection and advised to see a gynecologist as soon as possible. When Mrs. Truman did not make an appointment with a gynecologist, Dr. Casey made an appointment for her with a Dr. Ritter.

In October 1969, Dr. Ritter discovered that Mrs. Truman's cervix had been largely replaced by a cancerous tumor. Too far advanced to be removed by surgery, the tumor was unsuccessfully treated by other methods. Mrs. Truman died in July 1970 at the age of 30.

Appellants are Rena Truman's two children. They brought this wrongful death action against Dr. Thomas for his failure to perform a pap smear test on their mother. At the trial, expert testimony was presented which indicated that if Mrs. Truman had undergone a pap smear at any time between 1964 and 1969, the cervical tumor probably would have been discovered in time to save her life. There was disputed expert testimony that the standard of medical practice required a physician to explain to women patients that it is important to have a pap smear each year to "pick up early lesions that are treatable rather than having to deal with [more developed] tumor[s] that very often aren't treatable. * * * "[1]

Although Dr. Thomas saw Mrs. Truman frequently between 1964 and 1969, he never performed a pap smear test on her. Dr. Thomas testified that he did not "specifically" inform Mrs. Truman of the risk involved in any failure to undergo the pap smear test. Rather, "I said, 'You should have a pap smear.' We don't say by now it can be Stage Two [in the development of cervical cancer] or go through all of the different lectures about cancer. I think it is a widely known and generally accepted manner of treatment and I think the patient has a high degree of responsibility. We are not enforcers, we are advisors." However, Dr. Thomas' medical records contain no reference to any discussion or recommendation that Mrs. Truman undergo a pap smear test.

For the most part, Dr. Thomas was unable to describe specific conversations with Mrs. Truman. For example, he testified that during certain periods he "saw Rena very frequently, approximately once a week or so, and I am sure my opening remark was, 'Rena, you need a pap smear,' ... I am sure we discussed it with her so often that she couldn't [have] fail[ed] to realize that we wanted her to have a complete examination, breast examination, ovaries and pap smear." Dr. Thomas also testified that on at least two occasions when he performed pelvic examinations of Mrs. Truman she refused him permission

---

1. Dr. Thomas conceded at the trial that it is the accepted standard of practice for physicians in his community to recommend that women of child-bearing age undergo a pap smear each year. His records indicate that during the period in which he acted as Mrs. Truman's family physician he performed between 10 and 20 pap smears per month.

to perform the test, stating she could not afford the cost. Dr. Thomas offered to defer payment, but Mrs. Truman wanted to pay cash.

Appellants argue that the failure to give a pap smear test to Mrs. Truman proximately caused her death. Two instructions requested by appellants described alternative theories under which Dr. Thomas could be held liable for this failure. First, they asked that the jury be instructed that it "is the duty of a physician to disclose to his patient all relevant information to enable the patient to make an informed decision regarding the submission to or refusal to take a diagnostic test. [¶] Failure of the physician to disclose to his patient all relevant information including the risks to the patient if the test is refused renders the physician liable for any injury legally resulting from the patient's refusal to take the test if a reasonably prudent person in the patient's position would not have refused the test if she had been adequately informed of all the significant perils." Second, they requested that the jury be informed that "as a matter of law . . . a physician who fails to perform a Pap smear test on a female patient over the age of 23 and to whom the patient has entrusted her general physical care is liable for injury or death proximately caused by the failure to perform the test." Both instructions were refused.

The jury rendered a special verdict, finding Dr. Thomas free of any negligence that proximately caused Mrs. Truman's death. This appeal followed.

II

The central issue for this court is whether Dr. Thomas breached his duty of care to Mrs. Truman when he failed to inform her of the potentially fatal consequences of allowing cervical cancer to develop undetected by a pap smear.

* * *

* * * The scope of a physician's duty to disclose is measured by the amount of knowledge a patient needs in order to make an informed choice. All information material to the patient's decision should be given. [ ]

Material information is that which the physician knows or should know would be regarded as significant by a reasonable person in the patient's position when deciding to accept or reject the recommended medical procedure. [ ] To be material, a fact must also be one which is not commonly appreciated. [ ] If the physician knows or should know of a patient's unique concerns or lack of familiarity with medical procedures, this may expand the scope of required disclosure. [ ]

Applying these principles, the court in *Cobbs* stated that a patient must be apprised not only of the "risks inherent in the procedure [prescribed, but also] the risks of a decision not to undergo the treatment, and the probability of a successful outcome of the treatment." [ ] This rule applies whether the procedure involves treatment or a diagnostic test. On the one hand, a physician recommending a risk-free procedure may safely forego discussion beyond that necessary to conform to competent medical practice and to obtain the patient's consent. [ ] If a patient indicates that he or she is going to *decline* the risk-free test or treatment, then the doctor has the additional duty of advising of all material risks of which a reasonable person would want to be informed before deciding not to undergo the procedure. On the other hand, if the recommended test or treatment is itself risky, then the physician should always explain the potential consequences of declining to follow the recommended course of action.

Nevertheless, Dr. Thomas contends that *Cobbs* does not apply to him because the duty to disclose applies only where the patient *consents* to the recommended procedure. He argues that since a physician's advice may be presumed to be founded on an expert appraisal of the patient's medical needs, no reasonable patient would fail to undertake further inquiry before rejecting such advice. Therefore, patients who reject their physician's advice should shoulder the burden of inquiry as to the possible consequences of their decision.

This argument is inconsistent with *Cobbs*. The duty to disclose was imposed in *Cobbs* so that patients might meaningfully exercise their right to make decisions about their own bodies. [ ] The importance of this right should not be diminished by the manner in which it is exercised. Further, the need for disclosure is not lessened because patients reject a recommended procedure. Such a decision does not alter "what has been termed the 'fiducial qualities' of the physician-patient relationship," since patients who reject a procedure are as unskilled in the medical sciences as those who consent. [ ] To now hold that patients who reject their physician's advice have the burden of inquiring as to the potential consequences of their decisions would be to contradict *Cobbs*. It must be remembered that Dr. Thomas was not engaged in an arms-length transaction with Mrs. Truman. Clearly, under *Cobbs,* he was obligated to provide her with all the information material to her decision.

Dr. Thomas next contends that, as a matter of law, he had no duty to disclose to Mrs. Truman the risk of failing to undergo a pap smear test because "the danger [is] remote and commonly appreciated to be remote." (*Cobbs, supra,* 8 Cal.3d at p. 245, 104 Cal.Rptr. at p. 516, 502 P.2d at p. 12.) The merit of this contention depends on whether a jury could reasonably find that knowledge of this risk was material to Mrs. Truman's decision.

The record indicates that the pap smear test is an accurate detector of cervical cancer. Although the probability that Mrs. Truman had cervical cancer was low, Dr. Thomas knew that the potential harm of failing to detect the disease at an early stage was death. This situation is not analogous to one which involves, for example, "relatively minor risks inherent in [such] common procedures" as the taking of blood samples. [ ] These procedures are not central to the decision to administer or reject the procedure. In contrast, the risk which Mrs. Truman faced from cervical cancer was not only significant, it was the principal reason why Dr. Thomas recommended that she undergo a pap smear.

Little evidence was introduced on whether this risk was commonly known. Dr. Thomas testified that the risk would be known to a reasonable person. Whether such evidence is sufficient to establish that there was no general duty to disclose this risk to patients is a question of fact for the jury. Moreover, even assuming such disclosure was not generally required, the circumstances in this case may establish that Dr. Thomas did have a duty to inform Mrs. Truman of the risks she was running by not undergoing a pap smear.

Dr. Thomas testified he never specifically informed her of the purpose of a pap smear test. There was no evidence introduced that Mrs. Truman was aware of the serious danger entailed in not undergoing the test. However, there was testimony that Mrs. Truman said she would not undergo the test on certain occasions because of its cost or because "she just didn't feel like it." Under these circumstances, a jury could reasonably conclude that Dr. Thomas had a duty to inform Mrs. Truman of the danger of refusing the test because it was not reasonable for Dr. Thomas to assume that Mrs. Truman appreciated the potentially fatal consequences of her conduct. Accordingly, this court cannot decide as a matter of law that Dr. Thomas owed absolutely no duty to Mrs. Truman to make this important disclosure that affected her life.

* * *

Refusal to give the requested instruction meant that the jury was unable to consider whether Dr. Thomas breached a duty by not disclosing the danger of failing to undergo a pap smear. Since this theory finds support in the record, it was error for the court to refuse to give the requested instruction. [ ] If the jury had been given this instruction and had found in favor of the appellants, such a finding would have had support in the record before us. Reversal is therefore required. [ ]

* * *

The judgment is reversed.

* * *

Notes and Questions

1. Is there such a thing as a "risk-free test or treatment," as the *Truman* court characterizes the choice? Think back to Helling v. Carey and the notes following the case. Why did Mrs. Truman persist in refusing the Pap smear? Was it just the cost, an aversion to the procedure, generalized anxiety over the thought of cancer, or her sense that it wasn't necessary? What if Mrs. Truman had third-party health insurance that covered the full costs of a pap smear? Do you think that Dr. Thomas would have tried harder to convince her of the necessity of the test?

2. Dr. Thomas argued that a patient who rejects her physician's advice has the burden of inquiring as to the consequences of this decision. Isn't this a reasonable position for a physician to take? The court says the 'fiducial qualities' of the physician-patient relationship mandate disclosure, given patient ignorance. How far does this fiduciary obligation extend?

Justice Clark, dissenting, worried about an "intolerable burden" of explanation about every procedure and the risks if it is foregone. He feared that the burden would extend beyond pap smears to "all diagnostic procedures allegedly designed to detect illness which could lead to death or serious complication if not timely treated." Id. at 910.

3. The dissent in *Truman* also talks about "how far a doctor should go in selling his services without alienating the patient from all medical care." Id. at 910. Must the doctor do a "hard sell" in order to avoid the application of the *Truman* rule, manipulating information in order to get the patient to do what he thinks is best therapeutically?

4. Some courts are uncomfortable with the potential scope of Truman. In Farina v. Kraus, 333 N.J.Super. 165, 754 A.2d 1215 (N.J.Sup., App. 1999), the plaintiff claimed negligent diagnosis and treatment of bladder cancer. His wife Marie Farina died as a result of a claimed failure to diagnose and treat a "transitional cell carcinoma" of the bladder. She had been diagnosed with cancer, underwent surgery that removed her bladder and uterus. Her diagnosis was metastatic cancer. She underwent chemotherapy and radiation therapy in a futile attempt to control the spread of the disease. She died of the advanced spread of cancer. The court said: "This case before us is not about options for a course of treatment or for surgery but about suitable diagnostic testing. If the doctor wrongly failed to use the cytology test and this led to a diagnostic mistake which adversely affected the outcome, the doctor can be liable. If the standard of reasonable care did not require using the cytology test to aid a diagnosis, then there is no liability here. There is either a deviation, or there is not. A malpractice defendant does not have a duty to discuss every possible non-invasive, risk-free diagnostic or laboratory test with a patient and secure a consent to or waiver thereof. The doctor must, of course, use reasonable care and skill in choosing the diagnostic tests and interpreting the results. If he does not, he is vulnerable."

5. Are physicians exposed to conflicting incentives with regard to testing patients? Consider emerging genetic diagnostic technologies. The adoption of such diagnostics by physicians will be driven by both clinical and economic motivations. Genetic testing will proliferate if third party payers reimburse such testing. Providers paid on a fee-for-service basis will adopt them if they are profitable. Malpractice fears will also cause physicians to use new tests if there is any chance of detecting a predisposition to disease. And of course some providers will want the information even if it is of marginal value. Blumenthal and Zeckhauser, Genetic Diagnosis: Implications for Medical Practice, 5 Intl.J.Tech.Assess. in Health Care 579, 585 (1989). See Hillman et al., Frequency and Costs of Diagnostic Imaging in Office Practice—A Comparison of Self–Referring and Radiologist–Referring Physicians, 323 N.Eng.J.Med. 1604 (1990) (finding that physicians who self-referred patients for diagnostic imaging performed imaging from 2½ to 11 times as often as the physician who referred patients to outside radiologists).

6. What is best for the patient therapeutically? Consider new techniques of genetic diagnosis, performed on adults to see if they might be carriers of the gene for Huntington's disease, cystic fibrosis, manic-depressive illness and other neurological disorders. The purpose of these tests is to assess whether the patient will develop a particular condition. However, the presence of particular genetic structures and the development of clinically relevant disease is not straightforward for diseases such as heart disease, hypertension, mental illness, or cancer. An abnormal gene may not result in clinical disease. In Huntington's chorea, for example, the time of onset varies from early childhood to the seventies. Thus, a patient needs to know a great deal about the likelihood of a disease developing, before it is useful to face the anxiety produced by a positive test result indicating the presence of a genetic marker for a disease.

The very existence of techniques for prenatal diagnosis also produces stress in potential parents. Negative results give relief, alleviating anxiety that the very existence of the tests created. The tests' availability "sharpens what might otherwise be low-level, diffuse concerns that surface only, as one woman put it, 'on bad days,' and turns them into real and dreaded possibilities." Kolker, Advances in Prenatal Diagnosis: Social–Psychological and Policy Issues, 5 Intl.J.Tech.Assess. in Health Care 601, 608 (1989). For further discussion of genetic counseling and screening, see Chapter 16.

See generally Joan H. Krause, Reconceptualizing Informed Consent in an Era of Health Care Cost Containment, 85 Iowa L.Rev. 261 (1999).

Problem: Information Overload

You have been asked by one of your clients, the Gladstone Womens Clinic, to draft some guidelines to help staff physicians handle disclosures to patients who are reluctant to discuss risks of tests or procedures or who are uninsured and therefore careful about medical costs. What are the safe outer limits of physician silence about diagnostic options and their risks? Consider the kinds of tests that might be available to women who come to the clinic:

1. Pap Smears and mammograms to detect cancer;

2. Amniocentesis, chorionic villus sampling (CVS) and ultrasound imaging for evaluating fetal development and health;

3. HIV tests to look for the possibility of the AIDS virus in a woman who may want to get pregnant;

4. Genetic diagnostic technologies used to assess whether a patient will develop a given condition such as breast cancer.

5. Disclosure of Physician Conflicts of Interest

Medical professionals are in a position of dominance with regard to their patients. The relationship is inherently unequal. The physician has superior knowledge produced by long years of training and practice, expertise the patient cannot have; the physician is less concerned about the patient's health than is the patient; the patient is often anxious and ill-equipped to process complex medical information; and the physician can usually get another patient more easily than the patient can obtain another doctor. Patients are thus vulnerable, and this vulnerability imposes on physicians a "trust", a fiduciary obligation justified by the physician's dominant position in the relationship.

MOORE v. REGENTS OF THE UNIVERSITY OF CALIFORNIA

Supreme Court of California, 1990.
51 Cal.3d 120, 271 Cal.Rptr. 146, 793 P.2d 479.

[The plaintiff John Moore underwent treatment for hairy-cell leukemia at the Medical Center of the University of California at Los Angeles (UCLA Medical Center). The defendants were Dr. David Golde, the attending physician; the Regents of the University of California, who own and operate the university; Shirley Quan, a researcher at the University; Genetics Institute; and Sandoz Pharmaceuticals Corporation. The Supreme Court granted review to determine whether Moore had stated a cause of action for breach of the physician's disclosure obligations and for conversion. The Court rejected the conversion cause of action.]

* * *

II. Facts
* * *

Moore first visited UCLA Medical Center on October 5, 1976, shortly after he learned that he had hairy-cell leukemia. After hospitalizing Moore and "withdr[awing] extensive amounts of blood, bone marrow aspirate, and other bodily substances," Golde confirmed that diagnosis. At this time all defendants, including Golde, were aware that "certain blood products and blood components were of great value in a number of commercial and scientific efforts" and that access to a patient whose blood contained these substances would provide "competitive, commercial, and scientific advantages."

On October 8, 1976, Golde recommended that Moore's spleen be removed. Golde informed Moore "that he had reason to fear for his life, and that the proposed splenectomy operation * * * was necessary to slow down the progress of his disease." Based upon Golde's representations, Moore signed a written consent form authorizing the splenectomy.

Before the operation, Golde and Quan "formed the intent and made arrangements to obtain portions of [Moore's] spleen following its removal" and to take them to a separate research unit. Golde gave written instructions to this effect on October 18 and 19, 1976. These research activities "were not intended to have * * * any relation to [Moore's] medical * * * care." However, neither Golde nor Quan informed Moore of their plans to conduct this research or requested his permission. Surgeons at UCLA Medical Center, whom the complaint does not name as defendants, removed Moore's spleen on October 20, 1976.

Moore returned to the UCLA Medical Center several times between November 1976 and September 1983. He did so at Golde's direction and based upon representations "that such visits were necessary and required for his health and well-being, and based upon the trust inherent in and by virtue of the physician-patient relationship. * * * "On each of these visits Golde withdrew additional samples of "blood, blood serum, skin, bone marrow aspirate, and sperm." On each occasion Moore travelled to the UCLA Medical Center from his home in Seattle because he had been told that the procedures were to be performed only there and only under Golde's direction.

"In fact, [however,] throughout the period of time that [Moore] was under [Golde's] care and treatment, * * * the defendants were actively involved in a number of activities which they concealed from [Moore]. * * * "Specifically, defendants were conducting research on Moore's cells and planned to "benefit financially and competitively * * * [by exploiting the cells] and [their] exclusive access to [the cells] by virtue of [Golde's] on-going physician-patient relationship. * * * "

Sometime before August 1979, Golde established a cell line from Moore's T-lymphocytes. On January 30, 1981, the Regents applied for a patent on the cell line, listing Golde and Quan as inventors. "[B]y virtue of an established policy * * *, [the] Regents, Golde, and Quan would share in any royalties or profits * * * arising out of [the] patent." The patent issued on March 20, 1984, naming Golde and Quan as the inventors of the cell line and the Regents as the assignee of the patent. (U.S. Patent No. 4,438,032 (Mar. 20, 1984).)

The Regent's patent also covers various methods for using the cell line to produce lymphokines. Moore admits in his complaint that "the true clinical potential of each of the lymphokines * * * [is] difficult to predict, [but] * * * competing commercial firms in these relevant fields have published reports in biotechnology industry periodicals predicting a potential market of approximately $3.01 Billion Dollars by the year 1990 for a whole range of [such lymphokines]. * * * "

With the Regents' assistance, Golde negotiated agreements for commercial development of the cell line and products to be derived from it. Under an agreement with Genetics Institute, Golde "became a paid consultant" and "acquired the rights to 75,000 shares of common stock." Genetics Institute also agreed to pay Golde and the Regents "at least $330,000 over three years, including a pro-rata share of [Golde's] salary and fringe benefits, in exchange for * * * exclusive access to the materials and research performed" on the cell line and products derived from it. On June 4, 1982, Sandoz "was added to the agreement," and compensation payable to Golde and the Regents was increased by $110,000. "[T]hroughout this period, * * * Quan spent as much as 70 [percent] of her time working for [the] Regents on research" related to the cell line.

* * *

III. DISCUSSION

A. *Breach of Fiduciary Duty and Lack of Informed Consent*

Moore repeatedly alleges that Golde failed to disclose the extent of his research and economic interests in Moore's cells before obtaining consent to the medical procedures by which the cells were extracted. These allegations, in our view, state a cause of action against Golde for invading a legally protected interest of his patient. This cause of action can properly be characterized either as the breach of a fiduciary duty to disclose facts material to the patient's consent or, alternatively, as the performance of medical procedures without first having obtained the patient's informed consent.

Our analysis begins with three well-established principles. First, "a person of adult years and in sound mind has the right, in the exercise of control over his own body, to determine whether or not to submit to lawful medical treatment." [ ] Second, "the patient's consent to treatment, to be effective, must be an informed consent." [ ] Third, in soliciting the patient's consent, a physician has a fiduciary duty to disclose all information material to the patient's decision. * * * [ ]

These principles lead to the following conclusions: (1) a physician must disclose personal interests unrelated to the patient's health, whether research or economic, that may affect the physician's professional judgment; and (2) a physician's failure to disclose such interests may give rise to a cause of action for performing medical procedures without informed consent or breach of fiduciary duty.

To be sure, questions about the validity of a patient's consent to a procedure typically arise when the patient alleges that the physician failed to disclose medical risks, as in malpractice cases, and not when the patient alleges that the physician had a personal interest, as in this case. The concept of informed consent, however, is broad enough to encompass the latter. "The scope of the physician's communication to the patient * * * must be measured by the patient's need, and that need is whatever information is material to the decision." (*Cobbs v. Grant,* supra, 8 Cal.3d at p. 245, 104 Cal.Rptr. 505, 502 P.2d 1.)

Indeed, the law already recognizes that a reasonable patient would want to know whether a physician has an economic interest that might affect the physician's professional judgment. As the Court of Appeal has said, "[c]ertainly a sick patient deserves to be free of any reasonable suspicion that his doctor's judgment is influenced by a profit motive." (*Magan Medical Clinic v. Cal. State Bd. of Medical Examiners* (1967) 249 Cal.App.2d 124, 132, 57 Cal.Rptr. 256.) The desire to protect patients from possible conflicts of interest has also motivated legislative enactments. Among these is Business and Professions Code section 654.2. Under that section, a physician may not charge a patient on behalf of, or refer a patient to, any organization in which the physician has a "significant beneficial interest, unless [the physician] first discloses in writing to the patient, that there is such an interest and advises the patient that the patient may choose any organization for the purposes of obtaining the services ordered or requested by [the physician]." (Bus. & Prof.Code, § 654.2, subd. (a). See also Bus. & Prof.Code, § 654.1 [referrals to clinical laboratories].) Similarly, under Health and Safety Code section 24173, a physician who plans to conduct a medical experiment on a patient must, among other things, inform the patient of "[t]he name of the sponsor or funding source, if any, * * * and the organization, if any, under whose general aegis the experiment is being conducted." (Health & Saf.Code, § 24173, subd. (c)(9).)

It is important to note that no law prohibits a physician from conducting research in the same area in which he practices. Progress in medicine often depends upon physicians, such as those practicing at the university hospital where Moore received treatment, who conduct research while caring for their patients.

Yet a physician who treats a patient in whom he also has a research interest has potentially conflicting loyalties. This is because medical treatment decisions are made on the basis of proportionality—weighing the *benefits* to the patient against the *risks* to the patient. As another court has said, "the determination as to whether the burdens of treatment are worth enduring for any individual patient depends upon the facts unique in each case," and "the patient's interests and desires are the key ingredients of the decision-making process." (*Barber v. Superior Court* (1983) 147 Cal.App.3d 1006, 1018–1019, 195 Cal.Rptr. 484.) A physician who adds his own research interests to this balance may be tempted to order a scientifically useful procedure or test that offers marginal, or no, benefits to the patient. The possibility that an interest extraneous to the patient's health has affected the physician's judgment is something that a reasonable patient would want to know in deciding whether to consent to a proposed course of treatment. It is material to the patient's decision and, thus, a prerequisite to informed consent. [ ]

Golde argues that the scientific use of cells that have already been removed cannot possibly affect the patient's medical interests. The argument is correct in one instance but not in another. If a physician has no plans to conduct research on a patient's cells at the time he recommends the medical procedure by which they are taken, then the patient's medical interests have not been impaired. In that instance the argument is correct. On the other hand, a physician who does have a preexisting research interest might, consciously or unconsciously, take that into consideration in recommending the procedure. In that instance the argument is incorrect: the physician's extraneous motivation may affect his judgment and is, thus, material to the patient's consent.

We acknowledge that there is a competing consideration. To require disclosure of research and economic interests may corrupt the patient's own judgment by distracting him from the requirements of his health. But California law does not grant physicians unlimited discretion to decide what to disclose. Instead, "it is the prerogative of the patient, not the physician, to determine for himself the direction in which he believes his interests lie." (*Cobbs v. Grant,* supra, 8 Cal.3d at p. 242, 104 Cal.Rptr. 505, 502 P.2d 1.) * * *

Accordingly, we hold that a physician who is seeking a patient's consent for a medical procedure must, in order to satisfy his fiduciary duty[10] and to obtain the patient's informed consent, disclose personal interests unrelated to the patient's health, whether research or economic, that may affect his medical judgment.

1. Dr. Golde

We turn now to the allegations of Moore's third amended complaint to determine whether he has stated such a cause of action. We first discuss the adequacy of Moore's allegations against Golde, based upon the physician's disclosures prior to the splenectomy.

Moore alleges that, prior to the surgical removal of his spleen, Golde "formed the intent and made arrangements to obtain portions of his spleen following its removal from [Moore] in connection with [his] desire to have regular and continuous access to, and possession of, [Moore's] unique and rare Blood and Bodily Substances." Moore was never informed prior to the splenectomy of Golde's "prior formed intent" to obtain a portion of his spleen. In our view, these allegations adequately show that Golde had an undisclosed research interest in Moore's cells at the time he sought Moore's consent to the splenectomy. Accordingly, Moore has stated a cause of action for breach of fiduciary duty, or lack of informed consent, based upon the disclosures accompanying that medical procedure.

We next discuss the adequacy of Golde's alleged disclosures regarding the postoperative takings of blood and other samples. In this context, Moore alleges that Golde "expressly, affirmatively and impliedly represented * * * that these withdrawals of his Blood and Bodily Substances were necessary and required for his health and well-being." However, Moore also alleges that Golde actively concealed his economic interest in Moore's cells during this time period. "[D]uring each of these visits * * *, and even when [Moore] inquired as to whether there was any possible or potential commercial or

---

10. In some respects the term "fiduciary" is too broad. In this context the term "fiduciary" signifies only that a physician must disclose all facts material to the patient's decision. A physician is not the patient's financial adviser. As we have already discussed, the reason why a physician must disclose possible conflicts is not because he has a duty to protect his patient's financial interests, but because certain personal interests may affect professional judgment.

financial value or significance of his Blood and Bodily Substances, or whether the defendants had discovered anything * * * which was or might be * * * related to any scientific activity resulting in commercial or financial benefits * * *, the defendants repeatedly and affirmatively represented to [Moore] that there was no commercial or financial value to his Blood and Bodily Substances * * * and in fact actively discouraged such inquiries."

Moore admits in his complaint that defendants disclosed they "were engaged in strictly academic and purely scientific medical research. * * * "However, Golde's representation that he had no financial interest in this research became false, based upon the allegations, at least by May 1979, when he "began to investigate and initiate the procedures * * * for [obtaining] a patent" on the cell line developed from Moore's cells.

In these allegations, Moore plainly asserts that Golde concealed an economic interest in the postoperative procedures. Therefore, applying the principles already discussed, the allegations state a cause of action for breach of fiduciary duty or lack of informed consent.

We thus disagree with the superior court's ruling that Moore had not stated a cause of action because essential allegations were lacking. We discuss each such allegation. First, in the superior court's view, Moore needed but failed to allege that defendants knew his cells had potential commercial value *on October 5, 1976* (the time blood tests were first performed at UCLA Medical Center) and had *at that time* already formed the intent to exploit the cells. We agree with the superior court that the absence of such allegations precludes Moore from stating a cause of action based upon the procedures undertaken on October 5, 1976. But, as already discussed, Moore clearly alleges that Golde had developed a research interest in his cells by October 20, 1976, when the splenectomy was performed. Thus, Moore can state a cause of action based upon Golde's alleged failure to disclose that interest before the splenectomy.

The superior court also held that the lack of essential allegations prevented Moore from stating a cause of action based on the splenectomy. According to the superior court, Moore failed to allege that the operation lacked a therapeutic purpose or that the procedure was totally unrelated to therapeutic purposes. In our view, however, neither allegation is essential. Even if the splenectomy had a therapeutic purpose,[11] it does not follow that Golde had no duty to disclose his additional research and economic interests. As we have already discussed, the existence of a motivation for a medical procedure unrelated to the patient's health is a potential conflict of interest and a fact material to the patient's decision.

Notes and Questions

1. In *Moore,* the court explicitly uses both fiduciary duty and informed consent doctrine in order to impose an obligation on the physicians to disclose their research and economic interests. Does a claim of breach of fiduciary duty add anything to an informed consent claim? If so, what? What worries the California Supreme Court? Is it that the patient's medical interests will somehow be

---

11. The record shows that the splenectomy did have a therapeutic purpose. The Regents' patent application, which the superior court and the Court of Appeal both accepted as part of the record, shows that Moore had a grossly enlarged spleen and that its excision improved his condition.

impaired, since the physician's judgment during treatment may be corrupted by the promise of financial gain? Or is the court concerned about the patient's economic interests?

Judge Mosk, dissenting, argues that the nondisclosure cause of action is inadequate on three grounds. First, a damage remedy will not give physician-researchers an incentive to disclose conflicts of interest prior to treatment, since it is hard to establish the causal connection between injury and the failure to inform. The patient must show he would have declined, if given full information. Even if the patient claims that he would have refused, he must prove that "no reasonably prudent" person so situated would have declined. Id. at 519. Second, " * * * it gives the patient only the right to refuse consent, i.e., the right to prohibit the commercialization of his tissue; it does not give him the right to grant consent to that commercialization on the condition that he share in its proceeds." Id. at 520. Third, the cause of action " * * * fails to reach a major class of potential defendants: all those who are outside the strict physician-patient relationship with the plaintiff." Id. at 521. This may include other researchers and corporations exploiting the tissue.

Judge Broussard, concurring and dissenting, disagrees with Judge Mosk as to the efficacy of the nondisclosure action. He argues that the breach of fiduciary duty encompasses the postoperative conduct of defendants as well as the presurgical failure to disclose, so that the plaintiff can recover by "establishing that he would not have consented to some or all of the extensive postoperative medical procedures if he had been fully aware of defendants' research and economic interests and motivations." Id. at 500. He also observes that the fiduciary duty, unlike an informed consent cause of action, requires " * * * only that the doctor's wrongful failure to disclose information proximately caused the plaintiff some type of compensable damage." Id. at 500. Punitive as well as compensatory damages will be available.

2. Does the normal treatment setting pose any comparable conflicts of interest, in which the physician's treatment decision may be affected by his financial interests in treating a particular patient? Suppose a physician examines a boy brought into the emergency room of a small community hospital after an auto accident. The boy has an injured leg and foot. The x-ray suggests a dislocated foot. The doctor can either try to reduce the dislocation in the hospital, or he can refer the boy to an orthopedic specialist in a large city a hundred miles away. If the physician chooses to treat, he gets a fee, while the referral generates no further income for him. What should the physician choose to disclose to the boy's parents? The medical risks in either approach? The economic issue that may color his judgment? See David Hilifiker, Facing Our Mistakes, 310 N.Eng.J.Med. 118, 119 (1984). Ison v. McFall, 55 Tenn.App. 326, 400 S.W.2d 243 (1964); Larsen v. Yelle, 310 Minn. 521, 246 N.W.2d 841 (1976) (physician in general practice liable for failing to refer patient with fractured wrist to orthopedic specialist). See Principles of Medical Ethics of the American Medical Association § 8 (requiring doctor to seek consultation "whenever it appears that the quality of medical services may be enhanced thereby.")

3. Physicians may at times want to try a new or innovative approach to a patient's problems. What are their obligations to disclose that they are in effect "experimenting" on the patient? In Estrada v. Jaques, 70 N.C.App. 627, 321 S.E.2d 240 (1984), the surgeons treated the plaintiff for a gunshot wound to his leg. They tried a new technique, inserting a small steel coil into his weakened artery upstream from his aneurysm to cut off the flow of blood. Plaintiff signed a

consent form prior to surgery. The surgery failed, and Estrada had to have his leg amputated. He argued that his consent was not "informed" since neither the surgeons nor the radiologists told him the procedure was experimental. The court held that the patient had a right to know that the embolization procedure was experimental.

> * * * [W]e hold that where the health care provider offers an experimental procedure or treatment to a patient, the health care provider has a duty, in exercising reasonable care under the circumstances, to inform the patient of the experimental nature of the proposed procedure. With experimental procedures the "most frequent risks and hazards" will remain unknown until the procedure becomes established. If the health care provider has a duty to inform of *known* risks for *established* procedures, common sense and the purposes of the statute equally require that the health care provider inform the patient of any *uncertainty* regarding the risks associated with *experimental* procedures. This includes the experimental nature of the procedure and the *known or projected most likely risks.* The evidence presented in this case illustrates the logic of our holding perfectly: taken in Estrada's favor, it shows that the surgeons presented a full picture of the risks of the surgical procedure and simply advised him that the embolization might not work, without informing him of its experimental nature and their consequent lack of knowledge of the risks of whether it would fail or not. Not surprisingly, Estrada chose the experimental procedure. * *

* * *

> Our decision that health care providers must inform their patients that proposed procedures are experimental accords with the majority of courts and commentators which have considered the problem. * * * [ ] The psychology of the doctor-patient relation, and the rewards, financial and professional, attendant upon recognition of experimental success, increase the potential for abuse and strengthen the rationale for uniform disclosure. We have found little authority supporting a contrary rule. Accordingly, we reaffirm our holding that reasonable standards of informed consent to an experimental procedure require disclosure to the patient that the procedure is experimental.

How does the court in *Estrada* define "experimental" for purposes of disclosure to patients? They mention the fact that the surgeons and radiologists were aware of only one previous operation and one article, and that the surgeons had no personal experience. Does the court have the same attitude toward such clinical experimentation as the court did in *Brook,* in Chapter 3, supra?

What should be disclosed to a patient about to undergo an experimental procedure? That this is the first time this team has attempted this procedure? That the literature lacks support at present for it? That the surgeons and radiologists will benefit financially or in career recognition if the procedure succeeds? Must the motivations of the team be clearly disclosed to the patient? Should the physicians' motivations even matter, so long as the patient and the physicians believe that the new procedure offers a better chance for the patient?

* * *

NEADE v. PORTES

Supreme Court of Illinois, 2000.
193 Ill.2d 433, 250 Ill.Dec. 733, 739 N.E.2d 496.

JUSTICE McMORROW delivered the opinion of the court:

Plaintiff filed a three-count complaint in the circuit court of Lake County, two counts of which were directed against defendants Steven Portes and Primary Care Family Center. In count I, plaintiff alleged that defendants were liable for medical negligence, and in count II, plaintiff charged defendants with a breach of fiduciary duty. The principle issue in this appeal is whether, in a complaint alleging medical negligence, a patient has a cause of action for breach of fiduciary duty against a physician for that physician's failure to disclose incentives that exist under the physician's arrangement with the patient's health maintenance organization (HMO). We hold that a patient may not bring a breach of fiduciary duty claim against a physician under these circumstances.

BACKGROUND

According to the allegations in plaintiff Therese Neade's complaint, plaintiff's husband, Anthony Neade, had a family history of heart disease, suffered from hypertension and a high cholesterol count, smoked heavily and was overweight. In 1990, at age 37, Mr. Neade began to exhibit symptoms of coronary artery blockage. Specifically, Mr. Neade experienced chest pain extending into his arm and shortness of breath. Mr. Neade's primary care physician, Steven Portes, M.D., hospitalized Mr. Neade from August 10 through August 13, 1990. During this hospitalization, Mr. Neade received several tests, including a thallium stress test and an electrocardiogram (EKG). Dr. Thomas Engel (not a party to this appeal) found the results of the tests to be normal and diagnosed Mr. Neade with hiatal hernia and/or esophagitis. Mr. Neade was thereafter discharged.

After his hospitalization, Mr. Neade visited Dr. Portes on August 17, August 28 and September 24, 1990, at the Primary Care Family Center (Primary Care), complaining of continued chest pain radiating to his neck and arm. Relying on the results of the thallium stress test and EKG taken during Mr. Neade's hospitalization, Dr. Portes informed Mr. Neade that his chest pain was not cardiac related. In October 1990, Mr. Neade returned to Dr. Portes, this time complaining of stabbing chest pain. At the request of Dr. Portes, his associate, Dr. Huang, examined Mr. Neade. Dr. Huang recommended that Mr. Neade undergo an angiogram-a test that is more specific for diagnosing coronary artery disease than a thallium stress test. Dr. Huang was employed on a part-time basis at Primary Care and had no hospital privileges. Dr. Portes, as Mr. Neade's primary care physician, was responsible for ordering any necessary hospitalization or additional tests. Despite Dr. Huang's recommendation, Dr. Portes did not authorize an angiogram for Mr. Neade.

Mr. Neade again returned to Primary Care in June 1991, complaining of chest pain. Dr. Portes asked Dr. Schlager, another part-time physician at Primary Care, to examine Mr. Neade. After this examination, Dr. Schlager also recommended that Mr. Neade undergo an angiogram, but Dr. Portes, relying on the thallium stress test, did not authorize the angiogram and advised Dr. Schlager that Mr. Neade's chest pain was not cardiac related. Subsequently, on September 16, 1991, Mr. Neade suffered a massive myocardial infarction caused by coronary artery blockage. Nine days later, Mr. Neade died.

Plaintiff's complaint alleges that Dr. Portes was the president of Primary Care and, as such, negotiated contracts with various organizations on behalf of himself and the clinic. Chicago HMO, of which Mr. Neade was a member, was one of the organizations with which Dr. Portes had contracted for the provision of services. According to plaintiff's complaint, Dr. Portes personally negotiated with Chicago HMO in 1990 and 1991 and agreed that Dr. Portes and his group would receive from Chicago HMO, inter alia, $75,000 annually. The $75,000 was to be used by Dr. Portes and his group to cover costs for patient referrals and outside medical tests prescribed for Chicago HMO members. This fund was termed the "Medical Incentive Fund."

Pursuant to the contract between Dr. Portes, Primary Care and Chicago HMO, any portion of the Medical Incentive Fund that was not used for referrals or outside tests would be divided at the end of each year between Primary Care's full time physicians and Chicago HMO, with the physicians receiving 60% of the remaining money and Chicago HMO receiving 40%. If the Medical Incentive Fund was exhausted prior to the end of the year, Dr. Portes and his group would be required to fund any additional consultant fees and outside tests. Plaintiff and Mr. Neade were not informed of this arrangement between Dr. Portes, Primary Care and Chicago HMO.

Count I of plaintiff's amended complaint alleges that Dr. Portes' reliance on the thallium stress test and EKG and his failure to authorize an angiogram constituted medical negligence which proximately resulted in Mr. Neade's death. In count I, plaintiff alleged facts regarding the Medical Incentive Fund. Count II of plaintiff's amended complaint alleges that Dr. Portes had a fiduciary duty to act in good faith and in the best interest of Mr. Neade, and that he breached that duty by refusing to authorize further testing, by refusing to refer Mr. Neade to a specialist and by refusing to disclose to the Neades Dr. Portes' financial relationship (including the Medical Incentive Fund) with Chicago HMO. Count II further alleges that Dr. Portes breached his fiduciary duty by entering into a contract with Chicago HMO that put his financial well-being in direct conflict with Mr. Neade's physical well-being.

The trial court agreed with defendants' argument that financial motive was not relevant to whether Dr. Portes violated the applicable standard of care in treating Mr. Neade. The trial court therefore struck the allegations relating to the Medical Incentive Fund from count I. With respect to count II, the trial court found that there existed no cause of action against a physician for breach of fiduciary duty and granted defendants' motion to dismiss. Plaintiff thereafter filed a motion to reconsider, to which she attached her own affidavit and portions of the deposition of plaintiff's expert, Dr. Jay Schapira. Plaintiff's affidavit stated that, if she had known of the Medical Incentive Fund, she would have sought a second opinion from a physician outside of Dr. Portes' group concerning the necessity of an angiogram. In his deposition, Dr. Schapira stated that both the applicable standard of care and ethical considerations obligate a doctor to disclose his financial interest in withholding care. According to Dr. Schapira, a patient can then make an informed decision concerning the quality of care he is receiving and his doctor's motivations in treating him. Defendants filed a motion to strike the affidavit and deposition excerpts from plaintiff's motion to reconsider. The trial court denied defendants' motion to strike and also denied plaintiff's motion to reconsider.

On appeal, plaintiff argued that allegations concerning the Medical Incentive Fund are relevant to count I of plaintiff's complaint, in which plaintiff alleged medical negligence, to show that Dr. Portes deviated from the standard of care. The appellate court determined that allegations relating to financial motive are not appropriate in a medical negligence claim, and affirmed the trial court's holding on this issue. However, the appellate court held that evidence relating to the Medical Incentive Fund may be relevant at trial to attack Dr. Portes' credibility if he testifies. The appellate court reversed the trial court's dismissal of count II and held that plaintiff stated a cause of action for breach of fiduciary duty against Dr. Portes for Dr. Portes' failure to disclose the Medical Incentive Fund. [ ]

On appeal to this court, defendants argue for reversal of the appellate court's finding that: (1) a cause of action for breach of fiduciary duty exists for Dr. Portes' failure to disclose the Medical Incentive Fund; and (2) evidence of the Medical Incentive Fund is relevant in plaintiff's medical negligence action if Dr. Portes testifies at trial. We allowed the Illinois Trial Lawyers Association to file an amicus curiae brief in support of plaintiff and the Illinois State Medical Society and American Medical Association to file an amicus curiae brief in support of defendant.

ANALYSIS

* * *

I. Breach of Fiduciary Duty

The primary issue in this appeal is whether plaintiff can state a cause of action for breach of fiduciary duty against Dr. Portes for Dr. Portes' failure to disclose his interest in the Medical Incentive Fund. A fiduciary relationship imposes a general duty on the fiduciary to refrain from "seeking a selfish benefit during the relationship." Kurtz v. Solomon, 275 Ill.App.3d 643, 651, 212 Ill.Dec. 31, 656 N.E.2d 184 (1995), citing Collins v. Nugent, 110 Ill.App.3d 1026, 1036, 66 Ill.Dec. 594, 443 N.E.2d 277 (1982). Illinois courts have recognized a fiduciary relationship between a physician and his patient [ ] but Illinois courts have never recognized a cause of action for breach of fiduciary duty against a physician.

Though Illinois courts have never addressed the issue of whether a plaintiff can state a cause of action for breach of fiduciary duty against a physician, courts have rejected breach of fiduciary duty claims brought against attorneys on the basis that they are duplicative of negligence or malpractice claims. For example, our appellate court has held that where a claim for legal malpractice and a claim for breach of fiduciary duty are based on the same operative facts and result in the same injury to the plaintiff, the breach of fiduciary duty claim should be dismissed as duplicative. [ ]

Courts in other jurisdictions have dismissed claims for breach of fiduciary duty when those claims are duplicative of medical negligence claims. Such claims for breach of fiduciary duty have also been dismissed where they constitute an impermissible recasting of a medical negligence claim, even though plaintiff's complaint did not include a medical negligence claim. The appellate court in the case at bar discussed decisions from Minnesota, Colorado, Arizona and New Mexico. Each of these jurisdictions held that a breach of fiduciary duty claim is duplicative of a negligence claim. [ ] * * *

In a case involving facts similar to the case at bar, the United States Supreme Court recently refused to recognize a breach of fiduciary duty under ERISA. Pegram v. Herdrich, 530 U.S. 211, 120 S.Ct. 2143, 147 L.Ed.2d 164 (2000). In Herdrich, the plaintiff, a member of the Carle Clinic Association, P.C., Health Alliance Medical Plans, Inc., and Carle Health Insurance Management Co., Inc. (collectively Carle), an HMO, visited her primary care physician complaining of groin pain. The following week, the physician found an inflamed mass in the plaintiff's abdomen. The physician required the plaintiff to wait eight days to receive an ultrasound at a Carle facility over 50 miles away. In the interim, the plaintiff's appendix ruptured, causing peritonitis. The plaintiff filed a suit for both medical malpractice against her physician and breach of fiduciary duty against Carle. The breach of fiduciary duty claim alleged that Carle's act of providing incentives for its physicians to limit medical care and procedures constituted a breach of fiduciary duty under ERISA. Herdrich, 530 U.S. at——, 120 S.Ct. at 2147, 147 L.Ed.2d at 173. The Supreme Court reversed the Seventh Circuit's determination that the plaintiff stated a cause of action for breach of fiduciary duty under ERISA. Herdrich, 530 U.S. at——, 120 S.Ct. at 2158–59, 147 L.Ed.2d at 186. The Supreme Court noted the nature of a breach of fiduciary claim against an HMO physician. The Court stated:

> [T]he defense of any HMO would be that its physician did not act out of financial interest but for good medical reasons, the plausibility of which would require reference to standards of reasonable and customary medical practice in like circumstances. That, of course, is the traditional standard of the common law. [Citation.] Thus, for all practical purposes, every claim of fiduciary breach by an HMO physician making a mixed decision [about a patient's eligibility for treatment under an HMO and the appropriate treatment for the patient] would boil down to a malpractice claim, and the fiduciary standard would be nothing but the malpractice standard traditionally applied in actions against physicians. Herdrich, 530 U.S. at——, 120 S.Ct. at 2157, 147 L.Ed.2d at 185.

See also B. Furrow, Managed Care Organizations and Patient Injury: Rethinking Liability, 31 Ga. L.Rev. 419, 484 (1997).

We find the reasoning in the foregoing cases persuasive in analysis of the case at bar and decline to uphold plaintiff's breach of fiduciary duty claim. The appellate court held that because plaintiff pled different facts in support of her breach of fiduciary duty claim from those facts pled in her medical negligence claim, she stated two separate causes of action. Though many of the facts pled in counts I and II are identical, in her breach of fiduciary duty claim, plaintiff did plead the additional fact that Dr. Portes failed to disclose the Medical Incentive Fund. However, as our appellate court in Majumdar stated, it is operative facts together with the injury that we look to in order to determine whether a cause of action is duplicative. In the case at bar, the operative fact in both counts is Dr. Portes' failure to order an angiogram for Mr. Neade. Plaintiff alleges in both counts that Mr. Neade's failure to receive an angiogram is the ultimate reason for his subsequent death. Plaintiff also alleges the same injury in both her medical negligence claim and her breach of fiduciary duty claim, namely, Mr. Neade's death and its effect on plaintiff and her family. We determine that plaintiff's breach of fiduciary duty claim is a re-presentment of her medical negligence claim.

An examination of the elements of a medical negligence claim and breach of fiduciary duty claim illustrates the way in which a breach of fiduciary duty claim would "boil down to a malpractice claim." Herdrich, 530 U.S. at——, 120 S.Ct. at 2157, 147 L.Ed.2d at 185. To sustain an action for medical negligence, plaintiff must show: (1) the standard of care in the medical community by which the physician's treatment was measured; (2) that the physician deviated from the standard of care; and (3) that a resulting injury was proximately caused by the deviation from the standard of care. [ ] Thus, the standard of care is the relevant inquiry by which we judge a physician's actions in a medical negligence case. Under a standard of care analysis, a defendant will be held to "the reasonable skill which a physician in good standing in the community would use in a similar case." Newell v. Corres, 125 Ill.App.3d 1087, 1094, 81 Ill.Dec. 283, 466 N.E.2d 1085 (1984). If a physician deviates from the standard of care and that deviation proximately causes injury to a patient, the physician is liable for damages caused by his medical negligence.

In contrast to an action for medical negligence, in order to state a claim for breach of fiduciary duty, it must be alleged that a fiduciary duty exists, that the fiduciary duty was breached, and that such breach proximately caused the injury of which the plaintiff complains. [ ] In the case at bar, plaintiff alleged in her complaint that "as a direct and proximate result of Defendant's breach of fiduciary duty * * *, Anthony Neade suffered a massive myocardial infarction." The appellate court agreed, holding that "[i]t is conceivable that a trier of fact could find * * * that Dr. Portes did breach his fiduciary duty in not disclosing his financial incentive arrangement and, as a proximate result thereof, Neade did not obtain a second opinion, suffered a massive coronary infarction, and died." 303 Ill.App.3d at 814, 237 Ill.Dec. 788, 710 N.E.2d 418.

In order to sustain a breach of fiduciary duty claim against Dr. Portes, plaintiff would have to allege, inter alia, that: (1) had she known of the Medical Incentive Fund she would have sought an opinion from another physician; (2) that the other physician would have ordered an angiogram for Mr. Neade; (3) that the angiogram would have detected Mr. Neade's heart condition; and (4) that treatment could have prevented his eventual myocardial infarction and subsequent death. [ ] In order to prove the second element, plaintiff would have been required to present expert testimony that the expert, after examining Mr. Neade and considering his history, would have ordered an angiogram. This requirement relates to the standard of care consideration-the first prong in a traditional medical negligence claim-under which a physician is held to "the reasonable skill which a physician in good standing in the community would use." Newell, 125 Ill.App.3d at 1094, 81

Ill.Dec. 283, 466 N.E.2d 1085. That is precisely what plaintiff must prove to support her breach of fiduciary duty claim. As the Supreme Court stated in Herdrich, the breach of fiduciary duty claim "would boil down to a malpractice claim, and the fiduciary standard would be nothing but the malpractice standard traditionally applied in actions against physicians." Herdrich, 530 U.S. at——, 120 S.Ct. at 2157, 147 L.Ed.2d at 185. Thus, we need not recognize a new cause of action for breach of fiduciary duty when a traditional medical negligence claim sufficiently addresses the same alleged misconduct. The breach of fiduciary duty claim in the case at bar would be duplicative of the medical negligence claim.

An examination of the damages pled in plaintiff's complaint further supports our conclusion that a medical negligence claim sufficiently addresses plaintiff's injuries. While pleading in the alternative is generally permitted [ ] duplicate claims are not permitted in the same complaint. Count I of plaintiff's amended complaint sounds in medical negligence committed by Dr. Portes. In count I, plaintiff alleges that Mr. Neade's death deprived plaintiff and her children of Mr. Neade's "companionship as well as other attributes that they would normally receive as wife and children respectively, now and in the future, as well as the support of money and valuable services which he had provided." Plaintiff requests $50,000 in addition to costs of the law suit in damages under count I. Count II of plaintiff's amended complaint attempts to state a cause of action for Dr. Portes' breach of fiduciary duty. The damages alleged in count II are identical to those alleged in count I. Here, though attempting to couch the claim in different terms, plaintiff is essentially pleading the same cause of action which caused the same damages.

Our decision to refrain from permitting the creation of this new cause of action finds additional support in statutory law. The Illinois legislature has placed the burden of disclosing HMO incentive schemes on HMOs themselves. The Illinois General Assembly recently enacted the Managed Care Reform and Patient Rights Act (hereinafter, the Managed Care Act), which states: "Upon written request, a health care plan shall provide to enrollees a description of the financial relationships between the health care plan and any health care provider * * *." 215 ILCS 134/15(b) (West Supp.1999). The Managed Care Act, effective on January 1, 2000, requires that managed care organizations disclose physician incentive plans to patients. Thus, the legislature has chosen to put the burden of disclosing any financial incentive plans on the HMO, rather than on the physician. The legislature has put the burden of disclosure on the entities that create financial incentive plans and require physicians to adhere to them. If the legislature had wished to place the burden of disclosing financial incentives on physicians, it could have done so.

Moreover, the outcome that would result if we were to allow the creation of a new cause of action for breach of fiduciary duty against a physician in these circumstances may be impractical. For example, physicians often provide services for numerous patients, many of whom may be covered by different HMOs. In order to effectively disclose HMO incentives, physicians would have to remain cognizant at all times of every patient's particular HMO and that HMO's policies and procedures. See, e.g., M. Hall, A Theory of Economic Informed Consent, 31 Ga. L.Rev. 511, 525–26 (1997) ("[A] typical primary care physician in a metropolitan city may have a dozen or more contracts with managed care networks, while specialists may have several dozen or even a hundred. It is not feasible to ask physicians to keep track of the payment incentives and treatment rules for each of these many different plans, nor is this necessarily good public policy"). If we were to recognize a breach of fiduciary duty claim in the context of the case at bar, we fear the effects of such a holding may be unworkable.

Plaintiff and the appellate court rely on Current Opinions of the Council on Ethical and Judicial Affairs of the American Medical Association (AMA) in support of the argument that plaintiff can state a cause of action for breach of fiduciary duty against Dr. Portes for his failure to disclose the Medical Incentive Fund. Specifically, they rely on Opinion 8.132 entitled "Referral of Patients: Disclosure of Limitations," which states:

> Physicians must assure disclosure of any financial inducements that may tend to limit the diagnostic and therapeutic alternatives that are offered to patients or that may tend to limit patients' overall access to care. Physicians may satisfy this obligation by assuring that the managed care plan makes adequate disclosure to patients enrolled in the plan. AMA Council on Ethical and Judicial Affairs, Current Op. 8.132 (1995–2000).

As previously noted in this opinion, the Illinois legislature determined that disclosure to patients is to be made by managed care plans.

In addition to AMA opinions, plaintiff and the appellate court also rely on Herdrich v. Pegram, 154 F.3d 362 (7th Cir.1998), Shea v. Esensten, 107 F.3d 625 (8th Cir.1997), and Moore v. Regents of the University of California, 51 Cal.3d 120, 271 Cal.Rptr. 146, 793 P.2d 479 (1990), to support the establishment of a cause of action for breach of a fiduciary duty by medical professionals. As discussed, the United States Supreme Court has reversed Herdrich and held that, under ERISA, a physician's "mixed" decisions about HMO eligibility and patient treatment is not a fiduciary decision. Herdrich, 530 U.S. at___, 120 S.Ct. at 2158, 147 L.Ed.2d at 186. Shea held that a plaintiff could state a cause of action against an HMO for breach of fiduciary duty under ERISA for the HMO's failure to disclose physician incentive schemes. Shea, 107 F.3d at 629. The Shea court, like the Illinois General Assembly, placed the burden of disclosing financial incentive plans on the entity that both creates those plans and is more equipped to make those disclosures-the HMO. However, the issue of whether an HMO breaches its fiduciary duty in failing to disclose incentive schemes is not before us today. As our appellate court pointed out, both Herdrich, before it was reversed, and Shea "recognize that patients should be informed of financial arrangements that may negatively impact their health care." 303 Ill.App.3d at 808, 237 Ill.Dec. 788, 710 N.E.2d 418. While we may agree that patients should be told of financial considerations which may negatively impact their healthcare, we will not place the burden of that disclosure on physicians.

Moreover, plaintiff's reliance on Moore is misplaced. Moore involved a plaintiff who alleged that his doctor breached his fiduciary duty when the doctor used portions of the plaintiff's spleen and other cells, which he recommended be removed, to conduct research and benefit financially without informing the plaintiff. Moore, 271 Cal.Rptr. at 148, 793 P.2d at 481. The California appellate court held that the plaintiff could state a cause of action for either breach of fiduciary duty or for the performance of medical procedures without informed consent. [ ] However, a physician's failure to disclose

HMO incentive plans is significantly unlike the egregious nature of the alleged behavior at issue in Moore. Further, in Moore, the plaintiff had no way of discovering the physician's research plans unless disclosed by his physician. In Illinois, a patient can obtain information about the relationship and payment practices between her physician and her HMO by contacting the HMO.

Plaintiff also cites numerous cases that allow breach of fiduciary duty claims against professionals other than physicians. [ ] These cases are inapposite, as the plaintiffs in those cases did not bring causes of action sounding in both breach of fiduciary duty and negligence. Thus, the courts in the cited cases did not determine whether the plaintiffs' injuries were sufficiently addressed by traditional negligence claims.

* * *

We decline to recognize a new cause of action for breach of fiduciary duty against a physician for the physician's failure to disclose HMO incentives in a suit brought against the physician for medical negligence. We hold that, under the facts in the case at bar, a breach of fiduciary duty claim is duplicative of a medical negligence claim. The injuries suffered by plaintiff as a result of Dr. Portes' medical care are sufficiently addressed by application of traditional concepts of negligence.

II. EVIDENCE OF FINANCIAL INCENTIVES AT TRIAL

The appellate court held that evidence of the Medical Incentive Fund may be relevant in the event that Dr. Portes testifies in the medical negligence trial. [ ] The appellate court noted that, in general, a witness may be cross-examined on issues relating to interest and bias, and found that "issues concerning Dr. Portes' financial gain go to his credibility." We agree. Therefore, we hold that evidence of the Medical Incentive Fund may be relevant if Dr. Portes testifies at trial. The relevance and admission of such evidence is for the discretion of the trial court.

CONCLUSION

For the foregoing reasons, we hold that plaintiff may not state a cause of action for breach of fiduciary duty against Dr. Portes. Therefore, we reverse the appellate court's reinstatement of count II. The judgment of the circuit court is affirmed, and the cause is remanded to that court for further proceedings.

[The opinion of the dissenting justice is omitted.]

Notes and Questions

1. The Illinois Supreme Court sees the fiduciary claim as adding nothing to a basic negligence claim. They argue that plaintiff would end up having to show that she would have chosen differently with knowledge of the salary incentive system, and that another physician would have offered the test, and the test would have detected the plaintiff's condition. What would a physician have to say to a patient? And how much would a patient have to know about the incentives that operate on other physicians that she might choose over Dr. Portes? Isn't it sufficient that a physician will always face the threat of a malpractice suit for breaching the standard of care, and this is a powerful counterforce to the subtle

effects of salary incentives operating on physicians? How would you go about studying these questions?

2. Can you make an argument that a right to information in such cases does add something to a plaintiff's rights? Isn't this claim similar to the underlying goals of a battery-based informed consent claim? Is it in the same category as claimed rights to know about a physician's performance record, mental status, and substance abuse?

3. Is the court right that any meaningful disclosure of how physicians are paid should be done at the level of the managed care plan itself at the time the subscriber selects the plan. They distinguish the 8th Circuit Shea case on the grounds that it required disclosure only at the plan level. See generally Chapter 8 for a discussion of managed care regulation and liability, and Chapter 9 for a discussion of disclosure obligations under ERISA.

C. CAUSATION COMPLEXITIES

CANTERBURY v. SPENCE

United States Court of Appeals, District of Columbia Circuit, 1972.
464 F.2d 772.

VII

No more than breach of any other legal duty does nonfulfillment of the physician's obligation to disclose alone establish liability to the patient. An unrevealed risk that should have been made known must materialize, for otherwise the omission, however unpardonable, is legally without consequence. Occurrence of the risk must be harmful to the patient, for negligence unrelated to injury is nonactionable. And, as in malpractice actions generally, there must be a causal relationship between the physician's failure to adequately divulge and damage to the patient.

A causal connection exists when, but only when, disclosure of significant risks incidental to treatment would have resulted in a decision against it. The patient obviously has no complaint if he would have submitted to the therapy notwithstanding awareness that the risk was one of its perils. On the other hand, the very purpose of the disclosure rule is to protect the patient against consequences which, if known, he would have avoided by foregoing the treatment. The more difficult question is whether the factual issue on causality calls for an objective or a subjective determination.

It has been assumed that the issue is to be resolved according to whether the factfinder believes the patient's testimony that he would not have agreed to the treatment if he had known of the danger which later ripened into injury. We think a technique which ties the factual conclusion on causation simply to the assessment of the patient's credibility is unsatisfactory. To be sure, the objective of risk-disclosure is preservation of the patient's interest in intelligent self-choice on proposed treatment, a matter the patient is free to decide for any reason that appeals to him. When, prior to commencement of therapy, the patient is sufficiently informed on risks and he exercises his choice, it may truly be said that he did exactly what he wanted to do. But when causality is explored at a post-injury trial with a professedly uninformed patient, the question whether he actually would have turned the treatment down if he had known the risks is purely hypothetical: "Viewed from the point at which he had to decide, would the patient have decided differently had he known something he did not know?" And the answer which the patient supplies hardly represents more than a guess, perhaps tinged by the circumstance that the uncommunicated hazard has in fact materialized.

In our view, this method of dealing with the issue on causation comes in second-best. It places the physician in jeopardy of the patient's hindsight and bitterness. It places the factfinder in the position of deciding whether a speculative answer to a hypothetical question is to be credited. It calls for a subjective determination solely on testimony of a patient-witness shadowed by the occurrence of the undisclosed risk.

Better it is, we believe, to resolve the causality issue on an objective basis: in terms of what a prudent person in the patient's position would have decided if suitably informed of all perils bearing significance. If adequate disclosure could reasonably be expected to have caused that person to decline the treatment because of the revelation of the kind of risk or danger that resulted in harm, causation is shown, but otherwise not. The patient's testimony is relevant on that score of course but it would not threaten to dominate the findings. And since that testimony would probably be appraised congruently with the factfinder's belief in its reasonableness, the case for a wholly objective standard for passing on causation is strengthened. Such a standard would in any event ease the fact-finding process and better assure the truth as its product.

* * *

Notes and Questions

1. Causation can only be established if there is a link between the failure of a doctor to disclose and the patient's injury. Two tests of causation have emerged: the objective reasonable patient test and the subjective particular patient test. The former asks what a reasonable patient would have done. The latter asks what the particular patient would have done. *Canterbury* adopted the objective test, after a good deal of vacillation. The court was concerned with patient hindsight testimony that he or she would have foregone the treatment, testimony which the court feared would be " * * * hardly * * * more than a guess, perhaps tinged by the circumstance that the uncommunicated hazard has in fact materialized." The fear is of self-serving testimony.

The risk must be "material" to a reasonable patient in the shoes of the plaintiff. Under this standard, a patient's testimony is not needed to get the issue of causation to the jury. The testimony may be admissible and relevant on causation, but not dispositive. The jury can decide without it "what a reasonable person in that position would have done." Hartke v. McKelway, 707 F.2d 1544 (D.C.Cir.1983). See also Sard v. Hardy, 281 Md. 432, 450, 379 A.2d 1014, 1025 (1977).

Even if the plaintiff can establish that a reasonable patient would not have consented if properly informed, evidence that the plaintiff would have consented if fully informed may be presented to the jury. Bourgeois v. McDonald, 622 So.2d 684 (La.App. 4 Cir.1993).

2. Is it easy for a jury to put themselves in the shoes of a particular plaintiff? To some extent, that is what the jury is always asked to do in tort cases, particularly as to pain and suffering awards. In that sense, therefore, the courts' rejection of the particular patient test seems unreasonable. Is, however, the jury's

empathetic attempt to understand the plaintiff's pain in a personal injury case the same as the jury's collective attempt to second guess the plaintiff's decision whether or not to undergo the diagnosis or treatment proposed by the doctor? Consider the following argument:

> "Interferences with self-determination occur in all situations in which a person's dignitary interests have been violated. They are not limited to those in which physical harm has occurred. Lack of informed consent is itself a violation. It is the harm. The additional presence of physical harm only adds injury to insult * * * As citizens, patients are wronged when physicians begin treatment without fulfilling their disclosure obligation. What patients might or might not have agreed to, if properly informed, is beside the point."

Jay Katz, The Silent World of Doctor and Patient 79 (1984). Adoption of an objective standard on causation takes away most of what the *Canterbury* court granted as to risk disclosure. It asks the jury to put themselves in the place of a reasonable person, rather than the particular person. Is a jury likely to find causation in these cases, unless (1) the doctor was clearly negligent, so no reasonable person would have agreed to the treatment; (2) the doctor offered an experimental procedure which a person might refuse in spite of the doctor's urging; (3) the jury ignores its instructions and applies a subjective standard?

In Cheung v. Cunningham, 214 N.J.Super. 649, 520 A.2d 832, 834 (Sup.Ct., A.D. N.J. 1987), the court held that the subjective test for causation was preferable to Canterbury's objective test. " . . . [T]he totally objective standard used in the court's charge denies the individual's right to decide what is to be done with his or her body and may deny the individual the right to base consent on proper information in light of their individual fears, apprehensions, religious beliefs and the like."

3. The majority of American jurisdictions have adopted the objective test of causality. See Fain v. Smith, 479 So.2d 1150 (Ala.1985) and cases cited.

D. DAMAGE ISSUES

1. *The "Benefits" Doctrine*

In a typical informed consent case, the plaintiff is not informed of a certain risk, undergoes treatment, and suffers a bad result. The plaintiff then argues that if the risks had been disclosed, he would not have undergone the procedure and would have avoided the risk that materialized, either by choosing another alternative or doing nothing. Damages are then measured by comparing the bad outcome with the probable result if an alternative procedure were performed, or nothing was done. What if the procedure achieves the success promised by the physician and no alternatives to the treatment were available, but an undisclosed side-effect does occur? Some states apply the benefits doctrine in such a situation. In Gracia v. Meiselman, 220 N.J.Super. 317, 531 A.2d 1373 (1987), the plaintiff who underwent jaw reconstruction contended that the surgeon did not advise him of the risk of medial nerve damage inherent in the operation. The plaintiff claimed that if he had known that there was any risk in the proposed operation, he would have withheld his consent. He suffered a loss of feeling in the area of his chin, about three centimeters in length and two centimeters in width. The plaintiff alleged that "he has had post-operative marital problems because he does not want to be kissed by his wife because of the numbness, and that he is angry in general because he is left with the numbness above described."

The condition to be compared in an informed consent case is (where the risk is the only complication of surgery) the condition that the patient would have been in without having the operation and the condition that the patient is in after having had the operation. * * * In an informed consent case, where there are no alternatives of treatment, the operation could not have been performed without the inherent risk. Therefore, the comparison is between plaintiff's condition without having the operation and plaintiff's condition after having the operation.

The Court therefore offset the complications of surgery and its benefits, holding that "if an operation is properly performed, of overall benefit to the patient, and there are no alternative options for treatment, there should be no compensable damages awarded against the physician." Isn't non-treatment always an option for any medical procedure?

2. *Punitive Damages*

TISDALE v. PRUITT, JR., M.D.

Court of Appeals of South Carolina, 1990.
302 S.C. 238, 394 S.E.2d 857.

LITTLEJOHN, J.

In this medical malpractice action, Plaintiff, Laurel S. Tisdale, Respondent (the patient) sued Defendant A. Bert Pruitt Jr., Appellant (Dr. Pruitt) seeking damages alleged to have grown out of an unauthorized dilation and curettage (D & C). The Complaint alleges assault and battery, negligence, recklessness and willfulness and charges that the D & C was performed by the doctor without the informed consent of the patient. The Answer of Dr. Pruitt amounts to a general denial, asserting a medical emergency as justification and alleging the two-year statute of limitations as a bar to the assault and battery claim.

Among the allegations of the Complaint are found the following:

The Defendant's conduct toward the Plaintiff was negligent, reckless, willful, and in conscious disregard of the Plaintiff's rights in the following particulars:

* * *

b) In failing to read the Plaintiff's chart in order to determine that the sole purpose of her visit to him was for him to render a second opinion to Dr. Murphy concerning her intended hospital stay.

* * *

d) In failing to obtain her consent prior to performing any procedures upon her other than obtaining a biopsy in order to render a second opinion to Dr. Murphy; * * *.

The trial judge granted a directed verdict by reason of the statute of limitations as to the assault and battery cause of action, and submitted the other causes of action to the jury which returned a verdict for $5,000 actual damages plus $25,000 punitive damages. The doctor appeals. We affirm.

FACTS

The patient had been seeing her own family physician, Dr. Murphy, for approximately ten years. She was having problems with a pregnancy and consulted him. He recommended a D & C and arranged for her to be admitted to St. Francis Hospital for a final diagnosis and for treatment under general anesthesia.

Before hospitalization insurance coverage would be afforded, her carrier required a second opinion, and she was referred by the insurance company to Dr. Pruitt. She went to his office and filled out an information sheet and told his receptionist that she was there for a second opinion. The receptionist initiated a patient's chart and indicated on it in two places that the patient was there for the purpose of a second opinion. Dr. Pruitt admitted that he did not read the chart and placed her on the examination table with feet in stirrups and proceeded not only to examine her so as to supply a second opinion but to perform the D & C. It was not completely satisfactory, and a supplemental D & C was required thereafter; it was performed by Dr. Murphy at the hospital under general anesthesia.

It is the testimony of the patient that she preferred not to have an abortion and if the same was to be performed, she wanted it to be performed by her own doctor rather than by the second opinion doctor whom she had never seen before.

She testified as follows:

Q. And Mrs. Tisdale, if Dr. Pruitt had fully informed you, and asked you for permission, or asked you for your consent to perform a D & C in his office that day, would you have given that consent?

A. No sir. No sir.

Q. Tell the jury why not?

A. I had known Dr. Pruitt for about fifteen minutes. I have known my doctor for over ten years, and I would never consent to have something that painful done in an office, whereas you could go to the hospital and be under general anesthesia, and be confident that everything is all right.

Dr. Pruitt does not with specificity testify as to exactly what he told the patient but says " * * * I explained everything to her * * * "He further testified relative to the patient's consent as follows:

Q. * * * [W]hat were the signals? What made you think that she agreed?

A. I don't know how you would even say. What are vibes? You know, you can sometimes sense hostility, sometimes you can sense grief. Sometimes you can sense disapproval or approval. I could well have missed—I obviously misread Mrs. Tisdale's vibes or signals, or things, but when someone is really upset, that's not hard to do.

ISSUES

While Dr. Pruitt filed thirteen exceptions as appear in the record, the gravamen of his appeal is found in his brief as follows:

* * * Accordingly, the main issue for the Court's decision is whether the evidence presented at trial was sufficient to sustain a verdict based on the doctrine of informed consent. In deciding this issue, the Court is asked to consider the essential elements of *informed consent,* whether the Plaintiff proved causation, and whether the damages awarded were proper. Additionally, the Court is also asked to decide whether consent to a medical procedure may be implied from the patient's conduct and silence, and whether the jury should have been so instructed.

ANALYSIS

* * * Under the doctrine of informed consent, it is generally held that a physician who performs a diagnostic, therapeutic, or surgical procedure has a duty to disclose to a patient of sound mind, in the absence of an emergency that warrants immediate medical treatment, (1) the diagnosis, (2) the general nature of the contemplated procedure, (3) the material risks involved in the procedure, (4) the probability of success associated with the procedure, (5) the prognosis if the procedure is not carried out, and (6) the existence of any alternatives to the procedure.

In a letter (written by Dr. Pruitt to Dr. Murphy after the D & C had been performed) we think that Dr. Pruitt effectively pleads guilty to negligence, recklessness and willfulness. From that letter we quote:

Again, let me say that I am most distressed that I did not realize Mrs. Tisdale was referred to the office by the Prudential Insurance Co. for a second opinion. Although my receptionist had put this on the chart, I did not notice it, and as I did not realize that D & C's required second opinions, the thought literally never occurred to me. I have been asked on numerous occasions to give second opinions on hysterectomies and other procedures but never for D & C's, especially for missed abortions.

* * *

I do hope that you will pardon my "goof". I only wish Mrs. Tisdale at the time I was doing the procedure, had mentioned to me more clearly why she was sent to the office. If she did, it fell on deaf ears.

An analysis of Dr. Pruitt's testimony leaves much to be desired in the way of informing a patient of facts upon which an intelligent, informed consent can be made. * * * [W]e hold that the trial judge must be affirmed because of a lack of consent on the part of the patient. The circumstance under which Dr. Pruitt would have us find that the patient consented are relevant in determining whether or not the patient should have ordered Dr. Pruitt to stop what he was doing. She was in the office of a strange doctor recommended by the insurance company. She was greatly disturbed and was crying, experiencing pain. She was on the examining table with her feet in the stirrups. The procedure lasted about five minutes.

Dr. Pruitt's own testimony relative to her acquiescence is relevant. He relies mostly on her silence. He testified as follows:

* * * I just falsely assumed, or incorrectly assumed that this was what she was there for.

* * *

* * * Dewey, just for the record—and this may sound offensive, but I obviously, looking back, misread Mrs. Tisdale's feelings, but when I talked with her during the history taking, she very, very much wanted this pregnancy.

* * * She was just absolutely docile I guess, and I just assumed that she was acquiescing, but I thought I had her consent and her inform— very informed consent * * *

The argument of counsel that the evidence does not make at least a jury issue on whether damages were sustained and proximately caused by Dr. Pruitt's wrongful conduct is without merit. There is testimony that she suffered pain from the procedure without anesthesia; she was deprived of her right to choose the doctor to perform her D & C; in addition, she sustained emotional injury. Both actual and punitive damages are supported by the evidence. We hold that the evidence is not susceptible of the inference that the patient gave an informed consent, expressed or implied. Accordingly, the trial judge properly declined to charge the law of implied consent.

Affirmed.

Notes and Questions

1. The Tisdale court refused to imply consent by the plaintiff, given the context and her passivity. Given the doctor's admissions, the court went further and allowed punitive damages, even though the battery count had been dismissed. Might this kind of award increase a doctor's enthusiasm for conversation with his more quiet patients?

2. Punitive damages are typically awarded as part of the damage claims for an intentional tort such as battery. The focus is on the reprehensible nature of defendant's conduct, which may be reckless or motivated by malice or fraud. Even gross negligence in a malpractice suit usually will not suffice. The circumstances surrounding a tortious act may however warrant an inference of a wilful or wanton attitude, or reckless disregard of the patient's wishes. In Tisdale, the physician's cavalier assumptions about the patient's consent, his lack of a conversation with her, and her obvious vulnerability, together constituted reckless behavior, justifying punitive damages. Battery theory normally applies when the surgery is completely unauthorized. Negligence covers situations where surgery was authorized but the consent was uninformed. Fraud and deceit in obtaining a patient's consent has always sounded in battery. The burden of proving fraudulent inducement is a heavy one. See Tonelli v. Khanna, 238 N.J.Super. 121, 569 A.2d 282 (1990) (plaintiff alleged that defendant surgeon rushed her into surgery for his own financial gain; no intentional tort found.) In Perna, the issue of physician deceit is explicitly discussed by the court as justification for the result. One advantage of the battery-based action in informed consent is the possibility of getting punitive damages, even where actual damages are small. Punitive damages have been criticized as unfair and out of control in tort litigation generally. In malpractice cases, courts are not willing to allow such damages except under extreme circumstances. Deceit and breach of fiduciary obligations by a physician are examples of causes of action that may justify such damages.

3. If a material fact is concealed with the intention to mislead a patient, fraud may be found, and the patient's consent to a procedure is vitiated. See Smith v. Wilfong, 218 Ga.App. 503, 462 S.E.2d 163 (1995) (plaintiff claimed that doctor misrepresented the extent of her kidney problem and alternative treat-

ments; there was sufficient evidence to deny defendant's motion for summary judgment.)

For an excellent discussion of punitive damages generally, see Daniel Dobbs, Ending Punishment in "Punitive Damages": Deterrence–Measured Remedies, 40 Ala.L.Rev. 831 (1989).

4. In Strauss v. Biggs, 525 A.2d 992 (Del.Sup.1987), defendant surgeon began to operate on the plaintiff after having worked for sixteen hours straight prior to the surgery; he proposed a procedure that would give only partial relief, when he knew that another procedure would give complete relief, but he was incapable of performing it. He then failed to perform his proposed procedure, but neglected to tell the plaintiff, and continued with surgery after the plaintiff had screamed in pain on the first incision. He finally billed the insurer for procedures both unnecessary and not done. The court found these facts "compelling" for purposes of allowing the jury to find punitive damages. The case seems to add "greed" to "fraud" or "malice" as sufficient to establish physician conduct reprehensible enough for punitive damages.

E. EXCEPTIONS TO THE DUTY TO DISCLOSE

CANTERBURY v. SPENCE

United States Court of Appeals, District of Columbia Circuit, 1972.
464 F.2d 772.

VI

Two exceptions to the general rule of disclosure have been noted by the courts. Each is in the nature of a physician's privilege not to disclose, and the reasoning underlying them is appealing. Each, indeed, is but a recognition that, as important as is the patient's right to know, it is greatly outweighed by the magnitudinous circumstances giving rise to the privilege. The first comes into play when the patient is unconscious or otherwise incapable of consenting, and harm from a failure to treat is imminent and outweighs any harm threatened by the proposed treatment. When a genuine emergency of that sort arises, it is settled that the impracticality of conferring with the patient dispenses with need for it. Even in situations of that character the physician should, as current law requires, attempt to secure a relative's consent if possible. But if time is too short to accommodate discussion, obviously the physician should proceed with the treatment.

The second exception obtains when risk-disclosure poses such a threat of detriment to the patient as to become unfeasible or contraindicated from a medical point of view. It is recognized that patients occasionally become so ill or emotionally distraught on disclosure as to foreclose a rational decision, or complicate or hinder the treatment, or perhaps even pose psychological damage to the patient. Where that is so, the cases have generally held that the physician is armed with a privilege to keep the information from the patient, and we think it clear that portents of that type may justify the physician in action he deems medically warranted. The critical inquiry is whether the physician responded to a sound medical judgment that communication of the risk information would present a threat to the patient's well-being.

The physician's privilege to withhold information for therapeutic reasons must be carefully circumscribed, however, for otherwise it might devour the disclosure rule itself. The privilege does not accept the paternalistic notion that the physician may remain silent simply because divulgence might prompt the patient to forego therapy the physician feels the patient really needs. That attitude presumes instability or perversity for even the normal patient, and runs counter to the foundation principle that the patient should and ordinarily can make the choice for himself. Nor does the privilege contemplate operation save where the patient's reaction to risk information, as reasonably foreseen by the physician, is menacing. And even in a situation of that kind, disclosure to a close relative with a view to securing consent to the proposed treatment may be the only alternative open to the physician.

VIII

In the context of trial of a suit claiming inadequate disclosure of risk information by a physician, the patient has the burden of going forward with evidence tending to establish prima facie the essential elements of the cause of action, and ultimately the burden of proof—the risk of nonpersuasion—on those elements. These are normal impositions upon moving litigants, and no reason why they should not attach in nondisclosure cases is apparent. The burden of going forward with evidence pertaining to a privilege not to disclose, however, rests properly upon the physician. This is not only because the patient has made out a prima facie case before an issue on privilege is reached, but also because any evidence bearing on the privilege is usually in the hands of the physician alone. Requiring him to open the proof on privilege is consistent with judicial policy laying such a burden on the party who seeks shelter from an exception to a general rule and who is more likely to have possession of the facts.

Notes and Questions

1. The common law has long recognized the right of a doctor in a true emergency to act without patient consent, so long as he acts in conformity with customary practice in such emergencies. Jackovach v. Yocom, 212 Iowa 914, 237 N.W. 444 (1931). Some courts hold that consent is presumed in these situations. What constitutes an emergency situation is often unclear; the courts tend to err on the side of permitting arguable emergency treatment without formal consent.

An unconscious or incompetent patient cannot consent, and the physician may turn to a substitute decisionmaker such as a spouse or sibling. Even disorientation may be enough for most courts to allow such substitution. See King v. Our Lady of the Lake Regional Medical Center, 623 So.2d 139 (La.App. 1 Cir.1993).

2. Where the patient has consented to a procedure to remedy his condition, he is presumed to have consented to all steps necessary to correct it, even though the procedure in fact used varies from that authorized specifically. Kennedy v. Parrott, 243 N.C. 355, 90 S.E.2d 754 (1956). Does this make sense? If the alternative procedure is part of the repertoire of treatment for the patient's illness, then shouldn't the doctor have advised the patient of the possibility of this procedure as well as the intended one?

3. The most controversial privilege is the therapeutic privilege. Though this privilege is often discussed in dicta, it has not formed the basis for court rulings. *Canterbury* seems to have defined the privilege narrowly: information may be withheld in some situations, since "patients occasionally become so ill or emotionally distraught on disclosure as to foreclose a rational decision." The court used

the word *menacing* to describe the patient reaction, but then it equivocated, suggesting that the privilege would be justified where disclosure would complicate or hinder treatment or pose psychological damage to the patient. Given physician unhappiness with requirements of disclosure generally, the therapeutic privilege exception threatens in theory to swallow the informed consent doctrine whole. See generally Margaret Somerville, "Therapeutic Privilege: Variation on the Theme of Informed Consent," 12 Law, Med. & Health Care 4 (1984). In analyzing risks to be disclosed, some courts talk of the need to avoid scaring a patient away from a "needed" procedure, recognizing the effect of disclosure of risks on the patient's choices. Pedersen v. Vahidy, 209 Conn. 510, 552 A.2d 419 (1989).

4. *Waiver.* Suppose a patient, trusting his doctor to do the best for him, says, "I don't want to know a thing, Doc, just do what you think is best". Should the doctor be able to use this as a defense? It appears that the patient is exercising self-determination in choosing a veil of ignorance. See, e.g., Henderson v. Milobsky, 595 F.2d 654 (D.C.Cir.1978). Alan Meisel, The "Exceptions" to the Informed Consent Doctrine: Striking a Balance Between Competing Values in Medical Decisionmaking, 1979 Wis.L.Rev. 413, 453–60. Should a patient's waiver be readily allowed, or should a duty to converse be imposed, even in the face of a waiver by the patient of his right to information? Should a patient be forced to listen to a full risk disclosure? If an informed consent form is the primary device for risk disclosure, the patient can choose not to read it as a way of avoidance. Should the patient be forced to read it? See Mark Strasser, "Mill and the Right to Remain Uninformed", 11 J.Med. & Philosophy 65 (1986); David E. Ost, The "Right" Not to Know, 9 J.Med. & Philosophy 301, 306–7 (1984).

5. *Statutory Limits.* More than half of the states have enacted legislation dealing with informed consent, largely in response to the "malpractice crisis" of 1974, or more recent perceived crises in their states. The statutes take a variety of forms, from specific to general, but they all share the common thread of moving the informed consent standard toward greater deference to medical judgment. Given the current state and national mood of legislative limitations on common law tort remedies, it may be expected that the common law of informed consent will continue to be affected by legislative action.

Problem: Whose Benefit Is It Anyway?

You represent Croziere Hospital, a small nonprofit hospital in Northeast Washington, D.C. The Chief of Surgery, Dr. Leaf, has just come into your office seeking your advice on a patient problem. A patient, Mrs. Jan Lee, was admitted to the hospital yesterday through the emergency room in the final stages of labor. She gave birth just an hour ago to a baby boy, healthy in all respects except that his right foot is a club foot. The staff surgeon can easily correct this anomaly now so that the child would be able to walk normally. Without surgery now, the risks of failure are progressively greater.

Mrs. Lee and her husband are Asian immigrants recently arrived in the United States. Dr. Leaf knows from past experience in the military in Asia that Asians from the Lee's area of Asia believe that birth defects are an expression of divine anger, punishing the parents for past misdeeds. The Lees are therefore likely to consider any attempts to correct their son's defects to be an insult to their gods. Dr. Leaf is afraid that if he talks with the Lees, they will refuse the surgery and leave the hospital immediately. They have not yet seen their son and are not aware of the club foot. Dr. Leaf would like to operate on the boy without their permission immediately, given what he sees as the clear benefits of an operation now.

What do you advise him to do, in light of informed consent doctrine and its privileges and exceptions?

IV. INFORMED CONSENT: THE INSTITUTION'S OBLIGATION

Consent forms are universally used in institutions, where most health care is provided. Hospitals use them at several points in a patient's progress through the institution—upon admission, when a generic form is signed; and before surgery or anesthesia, when more detailed forms may be offered. These forms have to operate as a legal surrogate for consent, sometimes memorializing an actual physician-patient discussion, sometimes acting simply as a fiction. The courts have had little to say about consent forms.

A consent form, or other written documentation of the patient's verbal consent, is treated in many states as presumptively valid consent to the treatment at issue, with the burden on the patient to rebut the presumption. See West's Florida Statutes Ann. § 766.103(4); Official Code Georgia Ann. § 88–2906.1(b)(2); Idaho Code § 39–4305; Iowa Code Ann. § 147.137; LSA–R.S. 24, Tit. 40, § 1299.40.A; Maine Revised Statutes Ann. § 2905.2; Nevada Revised Statutes § 41A/110; North Carolina G.S., § 90–21.13(b); Ohio Revised Code § 2317.54; Vernon's Ann.Texas Revised Civil Statutes, Art. 4590i, § 6.06; Utah Code Ann. § 78–14–5(2)(e); West's Washington Revised Code Ann. § 7.70.060.

Institutional responsibility to ensure that a patient's informed consent is obtained exists only in two limited areas: documentation of patient consent for the record, and experimental therapies. If a nurse fails to obtain a properly executed consent form and make it part of the patient record, the hospital may be liable for this failure as a violation of its own internal procedures. See, e.g., Butler v. South Fulton Medical Center, Inc., 215 Ga.App. 809, 452 S.E.2d 768, 772 (1994). If a hospital participates in a study of an experimental procedure, it must ensure that the patient is properly informed of the risks of the procedure. See Kus v. Sherman Hospital, 268 Ill.App.3d 771, 206 Ill.Dec. 161, 644 N.E.2d 1214 (1995) (hospital was part of a research study on intraocular lens implantation; the court held that " . . . a hospital, as well as a physician, may be held liable for a patient's defective consent in a case involving experimental intraocular lenses . . . ")

Does the hospital have a duty to see that a patient's informed consent to surgery by a nonemployee attending physician is properly obtained? In Petriello v. Kalman, 215 Conn. 377, 576 A.2d 474 (1990), the Connecticut Supreme Court held that a hospital had no duty to obtain a patient's consent to surgery, nor to conduct any kind of inquiry into the quality of the plaintiff's consent. The plaintiff had suffered a miscarriage, and the treating physician scheduled the plaintiff for a dilation and curettage to remove the fetus. A hospital nurse medicated the plaintiff before the procedure, without getting the plaintiff's signature on the consent form. This violated a hospital policy requiring completion of such forms.

The court held that the responsibility lay with the attending physician, rejecting the plaintiff's claims that the hospital had a duty to get her signature on the form: "This contention is unsound, however, because it equates the signing of the form with the actuality of informed consent, which it is the sole responsibility of the attending physician to obtain.'' 576 A.2d at 478. Most other jurisdictions have agreed with Petriello. See e.g. Johnson v. Sears, Roebuck and Co., 113 N.M. 736, 832 P.2d 797 (App.1992), cert. denied 113 N.M. 744, 832 P.2d 1223 (1992); Goss v. Oklahoma Blood Inst., 856 P.2d 998 (Okla.Ct.App.1990); Howell v. Spokane & Inland Empire Blood Bank, 114 Wash.2d 42, 785 P.2d 815 (1990) (rejecting appellant's "corporate negligence" claim); Kershaw v. Reichert, 445 N.W.2d 16 (N.D.1989); Krane v. St. Anthony Hosp. Systems, 738 P.2d 75 (Colo.App.1987) (hospital assumes no duty by adopting standardized consent form). But see Magana v. Elie, 108 Ill.App.3d 1028, 64 Ill.Dec. 511, 439 N.E.2d 1319 (1982) (hospital has duty to obtain patient's informed consent).

The law of informed consent is highly variable, and at the same time it lacks specificity as a guide to physicians. One commentator has proposed that explicit contracts between providers and patient groups might better serve the doctrine, allowing specific guidelines to be developed by agreement. This would allow the law to be tailor-made to the different settings in which risks arise, contextualizing consent. Contextualization would advance the aim of cost-effectiveness and would also be desirable in its own right. Each goal seeks to improve the informed consent dialogue, and the doctrine that regulates it, by tailoring the law's requirements more carefully to the different settings in which risks arise and are discussed, assessed, and acted upon. Peter H. Schuck, Rethinking Informed Consent, 103 Yale L.J. 899, 906 (1994).

What might be the effect of imposing a duty on the hospital and its staff to ensure that patient consent is properly obtained by attending physicians? Might the hospital not work harder to make sure that consent is properly obtained? Or is deference to physicians too much a part of the hospital-physician relationship? Would it make any difference to the reality of patient consent? See Catherine Jones, Autonomy and Informed Consent in Medical Decisionmaking: Toward a New Self–Fulfilling Prophecy, 47 Wash. & Lee. L.Rev. 379, 429 (1990).

A study by Charles W. Lidz et al., Informed Consent: A Study of Decisionmaking in

Psychiatry 318, 326 (1985) concluded that informed consent forms were not important in the decisionmaking process: they were presented too late, were too complex, were unread by the patients before signed, and were treated by both staff and patients as simply a ritual for confirming a decision already made. How can such forms be improved, so that they will facilitate doctor-patient conversation and risk disclosure?

Problem: Forcing Conversation

You have recently gone to work for the assistant administrator of the Health Care Financing Administration (HCFA) of the Department of Health and Human Services. HCFA is responsible for the Medicare program, which pays physicians for medical services they provide to elderly patients who are Medicare-eligible.

Your superior, Dr. Tuff, has two concerns. First, he is concerned that too many Medicare patients are being treated without much discussion by physicians of the risks of treatment or nontreatment. He reasons that this is due in part to physician attempts to impose their own treatment preferences on patients, thereby maximizing their reimbursement, wherever possible, while also spending as little time as possible with each patient. The proliferation of Medicare HMOs also concerns him, because of the risk of undertreatment by physicians to increase their bonuses. He would like to use informed consent doctrine as a way of gaining further control over the costs of health care, while also giving the elderly a better level of control over their treatments.

Second, he is worried about the salary incentives that many Medicare HMOs use to promote cost-effective practices in their physicians. He fears that such salary incentives, combined with the aversion some physicians already have to treating the demanding and complex health problems of the elderly, will promote undertreatment.

He asks that you consider the following recommendation, to be incorporated into Medicare requirements:

> No Medicare payments for treatments rendered by either individual or institutional health care providers shall be made absent proof that the claimed medical service was consented to by the patient or a suitable surrogate decision maker in a voluntary, competent, and informed manner, or that the risks of nontreatment were fully and completely explained.

> Any physician treating a Medicare patient must fully disclose to that patient in advance of treatment all details of his or her salary compensation, including the types of incentive arrangement chosen.

What problems do you foresee with this proposal? What standards for disclosure do you suggest? What modes of proof that consent was obtained? What weight should be given the proof?

Managed care organizations are currently required to provide information on the incentive arrangements affecting an MCO's physicians to any person receiving Medicare or Medicaid benefits who requests the information. Suggested language is found at the Web site of the Health Care Financing Administration, at *http://www.hcfa.gov/medicare/physincp/beneinfo.htm.*

See generally Marshall Kapp, "Enforcing Patient Preferences: Linking Payment for Medical Care to Informed Consent," 261 J.A.M.A. 1935, 1936 (1989). For a critical response to Kapp's proposal, see Ruth Faden, Editorial: Enforcing Informed Consent Requirements: Form or Substance? 261 J.A.M.A. 1948 (1989).

Chapter 6

LIABILITY OF HEALTH CARE INSTITUTIONS

INTRODUCTION

The modern hospital—with its operating theaters, stainless steel equipment, and its large staffs of nurses, doctors, and support personnel—has come to symbolize the delivery of medical care. It was not always so. For centuries, in Europe and in America, hospitals tended the sick and the insane but made no attempt to treat or cure. They were supported by the philanthropy of the wealthy and by religious groups. In the 1870's it could be said that only a small minority of doctors practiced in hospitals, and even they devoted only a small portion of their practice to such work. A person seeking medical care before 1900 did not consider hospitalization, since doctors made house calls and even operated in the home. By the late 1800's, however, developments in medical knowledge moved the hospital toward a central position in health care. The development of antiseptic and aseptic techniques reduced the previously substantial risk of infection within hospitals; the growing scientific content of medicine made hospitals a more attractive place for medical practice.

Therapeutic and diagnostic improvements became identified with hospital doctors. These doctors, the product of the modernization of medicine, discovered that the hospital was well suited to their practice needs. Control over the hospital began to shift from the trustees to the doctors during the early 1900's. As the hospital evolved, physicians became increasingly dependent upon hospital affiliation. By the 1970s, no doctor would consider practicing without the resources that a hospital offered, and 25 percent of active physicians practiced fulltime in a hospital. Today health care delivery has shifted again, from the hospital setting to outpatient settings for many kinds of surgery. The American hospital is moving from the hub of the health care delivery system to a satellite. For an excellent extended discussion of the history of the hospital, see Paul Starr, The Social Transformation of American Medicine (1982), particularly Chapter 4.

Traditionally, the relationship of doctor to hospital was one of independent contractor rather than employee. The hospital was therefore not regularly targeted as a defendant in a malpractice suit. Only if the doctor whose negligence injured a patient was an employee could the hospital be reached through the doctrine of vicarious liability. The hospital was independently liable only if it were negligent in its administrative or housekeeping functions, for example causing a patient to slip and fall on a wet floor. Otherwise, the hospital was often immune from liability.

I. FROM IMMUNITY TO VICARIOUS LIABILITY

A. CHARITABLE AND OTHER IMMUNITIES

Until recently hospitals have been considered as charitable institutions, as such exempted from the general rule that a corporation is responsible for the acts of its employees. The doctrine of charitable immunity protected hospitals from liability in any form through the 1940's. In the 1950's, however, courts began to observe the increasing importance of the hospital in providing health care and supervising their staffs.

BING v. THUNIG

Supreme Court of New York, 1957.
2 N.Y.2d 656, 163 N.Y.S.2d 3, 143 N.E.2d 3.

The doctrine declaring charitable institutions immune from liability was first declared in this country in 1876. McDonald v. Massachusetts Gen. Hosp., 120 Mass. 432. Deciding that a charity patient, negligently operated upon by a student doctor, could not hold the hospital responsible, the court reasoned that the public and private donations that supported the charitable hospital constituted a trust fund which could not be diverted. * * * The second reason which the court advanced was that the principle of *respondeat superior* was not to be applied to doctors and nurses. It was the court's thought that, even though employed by the hospital, they were to be regarded as independent contractors rather than employees because of the skill they exercised and the lack of control exerted over their work—and yet, we pause again to interpolate, the special skill of other employees (such as airplane pilots, locomotive engineers, chemists, to mention but a few) has never been the basis for denying the application of *respondeat superior* and, even more to the point, that very principle has been invoked to render a public hospital accountable for the negligence of its doctors, nurses and other skilled personnel. [ ]

Nor may the exemption be justified by the fear, the major impetus originally behind the doctrine, that the imposition of liability will do irreparable harm to the charitable hospital. At the time the rule originated, in the middle of the nineteenth century, not only was there the possibility that a substantial award in a single negligence action might destroy the hospital, but concern was felt that a ruling permitting recovery against the funds of charitable institutions might discourage generosity and "constrain * * * [them], as a measure of self-protection, to limit their activities." Schloendorff v. New York Hosp., supra, 211 N.Y. 125, 135, 105 N.E. 92, 95, 52 L.R.A.,N.S., 505. Whatever problems today beset the charitable hospital, and they are not to be minimized, the dangers just noted have become less acute. Quite apart from the availability of insurance to protect against possible claims and lawsuits, we are not informed that undue hardships or calamities have overtaken them in those jurisdictions where immunity is withheld and liability imposed. * * * In any event, today's hospital is quite different from its predecessor of long ago; it receives wide community support, employs a large number of people and necessarily operates its plant in businesslike fashion.

The conception that the hospital does not undertake to treat the patient, does not undertake to act through its doctors and nurses, but undertakes instead simply to procure them to act upon their own responsibility, no longer reflects the fact. Present-day hospitals, as their manner of operation plainly demonstrates, do far more than furnish facilities for treatment. They regularly employ on a salary basis a large staff of physicians, nurses and interns, as well as administrative and manual workers, and they charge patients for medical care and treatment, collecting for such services, if necessary, by legal action. Certainly, the person who avails himself of "hospital facilities" expects that the hospital will attempt to cure him, not that its nurses or other employees will act on their own responsibility.

Hospitals should, in short, shoulder the responsibilities borne by everyone else. There is no reason to continue their exemption from the universal rule of *respondeat superior*. The test should be, for these institutions, whether charitable or profit-making, as it is for every other employer, was the person who committed the negligent injury-producing act one of its employees and, if he was, was he acting within the scope of his employment.

The rule of nonliability is out of tune with the life about us, at variance with modern day needs and with concepts of justice and fair dealing. * * *

In sum, then, the doctrine according the hospital an immunity for the negligence of its employees is such a rule, and we abandon it. The hospital's liability must be governed by the same principles of law as apply to all other employers.

The judgment of the Appellate Division should be reversed and a new trial granted, with costs to abide the event.

* * *

Note: Elimination of Immunity

Most hospitals prior to 1940 were protected from suit either by charitable or governmental immunity. The reasons were related to hospital difficulties in obtaining liability insurance and the fiscal fragility of many hospitals in a time before extensive government financing of health care.

The trend over the past few decades in the states have been to abolish charitable immunity. The charitable immunity doctrine disappeared with remarkable speed from American law. Prior to 1942, some form of immunity was recognized by most American jurisdictions. The case of President and Directors of Georgetown College v. Hughes, 130 F.2d 810 (D.C.Cir.1942) was a watershed case eliminating immunity. Since that case, a clear majority of jurisdictions have abrogated charitable immunity, while the remainder retain immunity to the extent of statutory ceilings on recoverable damages, or only up to available insurance coverage, or as to charity care. See Etheridge v. Medical Center Hospitals, 237 Va. 87, 376 S.E.2d 525 (Va.1989)(upholding Virginia $1 million cap on recovery in a malpractice judgment for a single incident); Pulliam v. Coastal Emergency Services of Richmond, Inc., 257 Va. 1, 509 S.E.2d 307 (Va. 1999); Daniel v. Jones, 39 F.Supp.2d 635 (E.D.Va.1999); Cutts v. Fulton–DeKalb Hosp. Auth., 192 Ga.App. 517, 385 S.E.2d 436 (Ga.App.1989).

Governmental immunity has proved more resistant to elimination by the courts. State courts have split on governmental immunity, with some eliminating it, others leaving it to the legislatures, and others retaining immunity in various forms. The Federal Tort Claims Act (FTCA), 28 U.S.C.A. §§ 1346(b) and 2671–2680, defines the extent to which the Federal government can be sued. Section 2680 provides for an exception to the Federal government's waiver of immunity for claims based upon "the exercise or performance or the failure to exercise or perform a discretionary function or duty on the part of a federal agency or an employee of the Government, whether or not the discretion involved be abused." Several states have adopted acts similar to the FTCA, and "discretionary" has been narrowly construed by both the federal courts and state courts to cover primarily policy making of a broad sort. See Hyde v. University of Mich. Board of Regents, 426 Mich. 223, 393 N.W.2d 847 (1986), granting immunity to state hospitals. Municipal and county immunity has likewise seen erosion by the courts.

Judicial and legislative actions have left most hospitals responsible for the torts of their employees, including doctors. Principles of vicarious liability became applicable to health care institutions once charitable and governmental immunities were abrogated. A master-servant relationship, a partnership, or a joint venture could lead to liability. The hospital came to be viewed as an enterprise liable for the acts of its employees, and the physician became liable for the acts of her employees, a partner, or another physician working jointly with her.

B. VICARIOUS LIABILITY DOCTRINE

1. The Captain of the Ship Doctrine

The Captain of the Ship doctrine provides that a physician who exercises control and authority over nurses and other health care professionals should be held liable for their negligence. It is a harsher version of the "borrowed servant" doctrine, which provides that a surgeon borrows nurses or support personnel during surgery. In the typical case, the surgeon is held responsible for an error in a sponge count done by the nursing staff after surgery, even though the surgeon does not participate in such sponge counts. See Johnston v. Southwest Louisiana Ass'n, 693 So.2d 1195 (La.App.1997) (surgeon had nondelegable duty to remove sponges from patient's body). If the surgeon is held liable, of course, the hospital will not be, since the nurses are considered to have been "borrowed" by the physician, so that temporarily the hospital is not vicariously liable for their errors. See Restatement (Second) of Agency § 227.

The Captain of the Ship doctrine is a special application of this agency rule of borrowed servant in the medical context, on the theory that the surgeon is in complete control of the operating room. It is a strict liability theory, often predicated on the surgeon's "right to control", rather than actual control. As the court noted in Truhitte v. French Hospital, 128 Cal.App.3d 332, 348, 180 Cal.Rptr. 152, 160 (1982), " * * * the 'captain of the ship' doctrine arose from the need to assure plaintiffs a source of recovery for malpractice at a time when many hospitals enjoyed charitable immunity." See Stephen H. Price, The Sinking of the "Captain of the Ship": Reexamining the Vicarious Liability of an Operating Surgeon for the Negligence of Assisting Hospital Personnel, 10 J.Leg.Med. 323 (1989).

2. *Stretching Vicarious Liability Doctrine*

Hospitals continued through the sixties to be protected from most litigation for patient injuries by a treating physician, even though charitable immunity was abrogated, since most doctors were independent contractors. The courts then began to articulate doctrines to give the plaintiff a possible defendant, where the hospital had immunity or where vicarious liability would not work. Thus the "borrowed servant" rule and the "Captain of the Ship" doctrine placed the doctor in the position of responsibility in some specialized situations.

In the last four decades the courts have begun to grapple with the independent doctor's connection to the institution, using a number of doctrines to circumvent vicarious liability limitations.

a.   *The General Rule*

SCHLOTFELDT v. CHARTER HOSPITAL OF LAS VEGAS

Supreme Court of Nevada, 1996.
112 Nev. 42, 910 P.2d 271.

YOUNG, JUSTICE:

On Saturday, March 4, 1989, appellant/cross-respondent Debra Schlotfeldt ("Schlotfeldt") presented herself to respondent/cross-appellant Charter Hospital of Las Vegas, a Nevada corporation ("Charter") that specializes in the treatment of alcoholism and drug addiction. Charter personnel observed that Schlotfeldt was extremely depressed and displayed rapid changes in her emotions. Schlotfeldt admitted at trial that she had abused alcohol and ingested methamphetamine prior to her admission to Charter. Schlotfeldt stated during a psychiatric examination that she gambled out of control when under the influence of drugs, was depressed for over a year and a half, and had thoughts of suicide. In a statement revealing the depth of Schlotfeldt's emotional difficulties, Schlotfeldt told Charter staff that "I don't trust myself," "I feel like I'm going crazy," and "I feel like I am at the end of my rope." After this conversation, Schlotfeldt went home to retrieve personal belongings. Escorted by her husband, Schlotfeldt returned to Charter and signed documents requesting voluntary admission and authorizing such care and treatment as ordered by her attending physician.

A Charter psychiatrist prepared an admitting diagnosis of Schlotfeldt that concluded she suffered from major depression and suicidal ideation. Anil Batra, M.D., also examined Schlotfeldt and diagnosed a major depressive disorder. On Sunday morning, March 5, 1989, Gilles M.K. Desmarais, M.D. ("Desmarais") examined Schlotfeldt. According to Charter, Desmarais was an independent doctor who was not assigned by Charter to Schlotfeldt. Instead, Desmarais attended to Schlotfeldt at the request of a Charter psychiatrist who was busy with other patients. Desmarais' examination revealed that Schlotfeldt had marital problems that led to alcohol abuse, drug use and compulsive gambling. Desmarais concluded that Schlotfeldt was a suicide risk because her severe depression of one and a half years was nearing a pinnacle.

Schlotfeldt argues that she made repeated requests to return home after the morning of March 5, 1989. Charter admits that Schlotfeldt requested to return home, but claims that because she was a suicide risk and her husband was out of town, releasing her at the time was imprudent. Desmarais urged her to stay voluntarily until her husband returned. Eventually, Desmarais allowed Schlotfeldt to leave because the effects of the drugs had worn off, she was no longer a suicide risk, and her husband had returned. Schlotfeldt spent a total of sixty-six hours at Charter.

Eighteen months later, Schlotfeldt filed suit against Charter and Desmarais. Schlotfeldt's initial complaint contained numerous claims for relief. However, all claims except the false imprisonment claim were withdrawn prior to trial. Schlotfeldt claimed she was admitted to Charter against her will and that she requested to leave Charter, but Charter and Desmarais continued to hold her against her will. Charter claimed that Schlotfeldt admitted herself voluntarily and it was obligated to urge her to remain until she was no longer a danger to herself or others. The district court excluded evidence showing Schlotfeldt was hospitalized for her psychiatric condition on multiple occasions after her stay at the Charter facility. Also, the district court found, as a matter of law, that Charter was vicariously liable for the acts of Desmarais. At the conclusion of trial, a jury found Charter and Desmarais liable for false imprisonment and awarded Schlotfeldt $50,000.00 in compensatory damages. After the district court entered a second amended judgment on the jury's verdict, Schlotfeldt and Charter appealed.

DISCUSSION

* * *

Agency Relationship

The district court instructed the jury that Charter was vicariously liable, as a matter of law, for the acts of Desmarais.[2] Based on the ostensible agency theory, the district court found that Charter should be held liable for the acts of Desmarais because he was chosen by Charter to examine Schlotfeldt. Charter opposed the instruction because it claimed an issue of fact existed as to whether an agency relationship existed between Charter and Desmarais. The district court's instruction, according to Charter, was improper and materially prejudiced its position by binding its liability to the improper acts of Desmarais.

The existence of an agency relationship is generally a question of fact for the jury if the facts showing the existence of agency are disputed, or if conflicting inferences can be drawn from the facts. [ ] A question of law exists as to whether sufficient competent evidence is present to require that the agency question be forwarded to a jury. []

* * *

Medical malpractice cases also serve as a guide for establishing the presence of agency between a doctor and hospital and evoking vicarious liability. Those cases have found that absent an employment relationship, a

---

2. The district court instructed the jury as follows:

The law holds an employer responsible for the acts of his employees while acting in the course of their employment. The law also holds a principal liable for the acts of its agent. Therefore, defendant Charter Hospital is legally responsible for the acts and omissions of all its employees and the acts or omissions of defendant Dr. Desmarais.

doctor's mere affiliation with a hospital is not sufficient to hold a hospital vicariously liable for the doctor's negligent conduct. [ ] A physician or surgeon who is on a hospital's staff is not necessarily an employee of the hospital, and the hospital is not necessarily liable for his tortious acts. [] A hospital does not generally expose itself to vicarious liability for a doctor's actions by merely extending staff privileges to that doctor. [] Further, evidence that a doctor maintains a private practice may tend to dispel any claim of an agency relationship between a doctor and a hospital.

The evidence admitted in this case on the issue of agency was limited. Desmarais testified that he was not an employee of Charter but had staff privileges. Desmarais also testified that he was covering for another doctor the night Schlotfeldt was admitted to Charter. Charter's administrator stated that Desmarais only had staff privileges at Charter and was covering for another Charter doctor during the period in question. Also, evidence indicated that Desmarais may have maintained an independent practice because he billed Schlotfeldt separately for the services he rendered at Charter. Other than the fact that Desmarais went to Schlotfeldt's room to conduct a medical examination, no evidence was presented to show an employment or agency relationship existed between Charter and Desmarais.

* * *

Charter presented evidence suggesting that no employment relationship existed with Desmarais, that Desmarais merely had staff privileges, and that Desmarais operated a private practice. This evidence was sufficiently competent to raise a question of fact for the jury regarding the existence of agency. Further, the district court's use of the ostensible agency theory to find agency as a matter of law was improper because application of the theory required a determination of numerous issues of fact. Accordingly, the jury should have decided the agency issue. Because Charter was materially prejudiced by having its liability linked to the acts of Desmarais, the district court committed reversible error.

CONCLUSION

In considering this case, it is not necessary to resolve the issues raised by Schlotfeldt on appeal. The district court erred by excluding essential evidence and concluding as a matter of law that an agency relationship was present. Accordingly, the district court's judgment against Charter is reversed and this matter is remanded for a new trial.

Notes and Questions

1.   The hospital-physician relationship is an unusual one. A typical hospital may have several categories of practicing physicians, but the largest group is comprised of private physicians with staff privileges. Staff privileges include the right of the physicians to admit and discharge their private patients to the hospital and the right to use the hospital's facilities.

The organized medical staff of a hospital, private physicians with privileges, governs the hospital's provision of medical services. The typical medical staff operates under its own bylaws, elects its own officers, and appoints its own committees. It is not simply another administrative component of the hospital, and is subject to only limited authority of the governing board of the hospital.

While the hospital board must approve the staff's bylaws and can approve or disapprove particular staff actions, it cannot usually discipline individual physicians directly or appoint administrative officers to exercise direct authority. A hospital's medical staff is therefore a powerful body within the larger organization. See generally Clark C. Havighurst, Doctors and Hospitals: An Antitrust Perspective on Traditional Relationships, 1984 Duke L.J. 1071, 1084–92.

2. What explains this curious structure, where two parallel structures exist side-by-side, with nurses and other allied health professionals operating as hospital employees subject to master-servant rules, and the medical staff operating relatively autonomously as independent contractors? The professional status and power of physicians? See generally Charles E. Rosenberg, The Care of Strangers: The Rise of America's Hospital System 66–68, 262–267 (1987).

b. The Control Test

BEREL v. HCA HEALTH SERVICES OF TEXAS, INC.

Court of Appeals of Texas, 1994.
881 S.W.2d 21.

[Plaintiffs consulted Dr. Robinson in her professional capacity as a psychiatrist. Dr. Robinson recommended that Kristy and Jake Berel, and Beverly Berel and her children Kelly and Brian, be hospitalized in Houston International Hospital for treatment of alleged emotional disturbances. The plaintiffs claimed that Dr. Robinson, as an agent of the hospital, was negligent in admitting them to the hospital on the basis of insufficient observation; recommending inpatient treatment; and negligently treating them. They further alleged that the hospital was negligent because it should have known of the malpractice committed by its agent, Dr. Robinson, and because it did not properly supervise and regulate her. The trial court granted the hospital's motion for summary judgment, in part on the grounds that Dr. Robinson was an independent contractor, and that the hospital had no right to control the details of her medical practice.

The Court of Appeals noted that independent contractor physicians normally transmit no liability to the hospital, but then continued:]

If, however, a hospital retains the right to control the details of the work to be performed by a contracting party, a master-servant relationship exists that will authorize the application of the doctrine of respondeat superior.[ ] It is the right of control, not actual control, that gives rise to a duty to see that the independent contractor performs his work in a safe manner. [ ] ...

* * *

The plaintiffs rely on Dr. Robinson's deposition testimony. She testified that the hospital's staff included a "quality assurance person" who "reviewed charts to ... assure appropriate patient care." The plaintiffs' trial counsel asked Dr. Robinson additional questions regarding the quality assurance person: Q. If that quality assurance person felt like that there had been an over utilization or an under utilization, what would they do? A. As far as I can recall that person would discuss that with the doctor and also would—would write those recommendations up in a particular form as—as best of my recall and we present that to the particular doctor who's treating the patient and could also possibly—feeling that needed further information or clarification or whatever—talk with the medical director and also possibly the medical director of the—of the hospital and also possibly the utilization review committee. Q. Could the utilization review committee and the medical director of the hospital override the admitting physician's orders? A. Yes. Q. Okay. Did the utilization review committee and the medical director have authority to discharge a patient that they thought was—had been admitted or did not need the services of Houston International Hospital? A. The medical director of the utilization review committee as far as my recall, there were appropriate procedures if they felt that the patient was not being administered appropriate treatment and needed—needed to—which would be if the patient did not need to be there, they could have overruled the admitting physician's order. Q. And have the patient discharged? A. If that was what was indicated that was needed.

We agree with the plaintiffs that Dr. Robinson's own testimony raises a fact question regarding whether the hospital maintained control over Dr. Robinson's treatment to a degree that would make the hospital liable for her negligent acts. We sustain this point of error.

Notes and Questions

1.   What are the implications of the *Berel* decision? Does the court mean that a physician's independent contractor status no longer provides a shield for a hospital or a managed care organization, since such institutions now have utilization review and quality assurance activities that exercise substantial oversight over physicians? If this is so, then the more intensive the utilization review, the more control exercised under agency principles. This is a real Catch–22 for the institution.

2.   The first approach to determining an agency relationship is to test whether the doctor was an employee or subject to the control of the hospital, applying a number of standard criteria for evaluating the existence of a master-servant relationship. If the contract gave the hospital substantial control over the doctor's choice of patients or if the hospital furnished equipment, then an employee relationship might be found. The caselaw reflects divergent applications of the "control" test, because of the breadth of the factors involved. See Mduba v. Benedictine Hospital, 52 A.D.2d 450, 384 N.Y.S.2d 527 (3d Dept.1976) (doctor failed to give blood to patient, resulting in his death; hospital, in the contract with doctor, had guaranteed doctor's salary and controlled his activities. Held: doctor is an employee); Kober v. Stewart, 148 Mont. 117, 417 P.2d 476 (1966) (contract establishes the method by which hospital hired a doctor as supervisor).

c.   The "Ostensible Agency" Test

Some courts have held that in settings such as the emergency room or the radiology labs, the hospital holds itself out as offering services to the patient through a doctor, even though the doctor who renders the service is not an employee. The following case illustrates a modern application of this test to a contemporary contractual relationship between a hospital and a physician.

SWORD v. NKC HOSPITALS, INC.

Supreme Court of Indiana, 1999.
714 N.E.2d 142.

SELBY, J.

* * *

FACTS

The facts taken in the light most favorable to the non-moving party are as follows. Diana Sword lives in southern Indiana. On April 24, 1991, Diana Sword and her husband entered Norton in Louisville, Kentucky for the delivery of their first child. Prior to entering the hospital, Sword consulted with her obstetrician about whether or not to deliver with the help of an anesthetic. Her obstetrician recommended using an epidural; he told Sword that the epidural procedure would numb her from the waist down, and that he used them frequently. Sword decided to have an epidural. She, however, did not know in advance who would administer the epidural.

Sword also made arrangements to go to Norton through her obstetrician's office. Norton aggressively marketed its services to the public. It stated in brochures that its Women's Pavilion is "the most technically sophisticated birthplace in the region." (R. at 228.) Norton also advertised that it offers:

[I]nstant access to the specialized equipment and facilities, as well as to physician specialists in every area of pediatric medicine and surgery. Every maternity patient has a private room and the full availability of a special anesthesiology team, experienced and dedicated exclusively to OB patients.

Id. (emphasis added). One brochure stated that:

The Women's Pavilion medical staff includes the only physicians in the region who specialize exclusively in obstetrical anesthesiology. They are immediately available within the unit 24 hours a day and are experts in administering continuous epidural anesthesia.

(R. at 232.) (emphasis added).

At some point during her labor, an anesthesiologist came into Sword's room. He explained the epidural procedure and how it would make her feel. He told her that he would stick the tubing for the epidural in her lower back and then she would feel numbness from the waist down. As the anesthesiologist was preparing to begin the procedure, he was called out of the room.

Five to ten minutes later, a second anesthesiologist, Dr. Luna, came into Sword's room to administer the epidural. The parties do not dispute that Dr. Luna practiced medicine at Norton as an independent contractor. After verifying that the previous anesthesiologist had explained the procedure to Sword, Dr. Luna began the epidural procedure. As Sword sat on the bed and leaned forward, Dr. Luna began inserting the epidural tubing. Dr. Luna first inserted the tubing near the top of Sword's neck. Shortly thereafter, Dr. Luna removed the epidural tubing "because it did not take" and then reinserted it in Sword's lower back. (R. at 181–82.)

Soon after the delivery of her healthy baby, Sword began to have headaches which recur every four to six weeks. When the headaches occur, Sword is very sensitive to light and sound. In addition to the headaches, she also feels a numbness in her back where the second epidural was administered. Sword alleges that these symptoms are a result of Dr. Luna's negligent placement of the epidural tubing and that Norton is liable.

* * *

III. APPARENT OR OSTENSIBLE AGENCY

The principal issue in this case is whether, under Indiana law, Norton can be held liable for the alleged negligence of an independent contractor anesthesiologist. Sword is seeking to hold Norton liable for the alleged negligence which caused her injuries. There are no allegations of direct corporate negligence, that is, that the hospital itself was negligent. Because the alleged negligence was not committed by Norton, but instead by a physician working at Norton, Sword must present a theory by which a court can find the hospital vicariously liable for the actions of a physician who practices there. After reviewing the basic tort and agency concepts relevant to theories of vicarious liability, as well as the jurisprudence in Indiana and other jurisdictions, in the specific context of this case, we adopt the theory of apparent and ostensible agency formulated in the Restatement (Second) of Torts section 429 (1965). We then conclude that there are genuine issues of material fact in dispute as to the existence of an apparent or ostensible agency relationship here.

A. *Vicarious Liability*

Vicarious liability is "indirect legal responsibility." BLACK'S LAW DICTIONARY 1404 (5th ed.1979). It is a legal fiction by which a court can hold a party legally responsible for the negligence of another, not because the party did anything wrong but rather because of the party's relationship to the wrongdoer. See KEETON, TORTS § 69. Courts employ various legal doctrines to hold people vicariously liable, including respondeat superior, apparent or ostensible agency, agency by estoppel,[3] and the non-delegable duty doctrine.[4] Some doctrines are based in tort law, some are based in agency law. Courts often discuss the various doctrines as if they are interchangeable; they are not. We will address each applicable doctrine in turn.

---

3. Courts holding hospitals liable under an agency theory often interchangeably describe the theory as "apparent agency" and "agency by estoppel." See Martin C. McWilliams, Jr. & Hamilton E. Russell, III, Hospital Liability for Torts of Independent Contractor Physicians, 47 S.C.L.REV. 431, 445–46 n. 76 (1996); Diane M. Janulis & Alan D. Hornstein, Damned if You Do, Damned if You Don't: Hospitals' Liability for Physicians' Malpractice, 64 NEB. L.REV. 689, 696 (1985). The distinction, if any, is that agency by estoppel requires both reliance and a change in position. Restatement (Second) of Agency § 8 cmt. d. [ ]

4. While a master is generally not liable for the negligence of an independent contractor,

the master may be liable if the independent contractor was performing a non-delegable duty.[ ] A non-delegable duty is one that public policy holds to be so important that one party should not be permitted to transfer the duty (and its resultant liability) to another party.[ ] Sword argues that Norton had a non-delegable duty to provide anesthesiological care because such care is essential and the patient has no choice in the anesthesiologist who provides this care. Given our resolution of the apparent or ostensible agency issue, we need not address the concept of non-delegable duty in this opinion.

Respondeat superior is the applicable tort theory of vicarious liability. Under respondeat superior, an employer, who is not liable because of his own acts, can be held liable "for the wrongful acts of his employee which are committed within the scope of employment." Stropes v. Heritage House Childrens Ctr., 547 N.E.2d 244, 247 (Ind.1989); see also KEETON, TORTS §§ 69, 70; WARREN A. SEAVEY, AGENCY § 83 (1964). In this context, "employer" and "employee" are often stated in broader terms as "master" and "servant." [ ]

One important aspect in applying respondeat superior is differentiating between those who are servants and those who are independent contractors. A servant is defined in the following general manner: one who is employed by a master to perform personal services and whose physical conduct is subject to the right to control by the master. [ ] It is the employer's right to control that generally separates a servant from an independent contractor. [ ] See Keeton, Torts § 71; Seavey, Agency § 84 cmt. c; Restatement (Second) of Agency § 2 cmt. a. An independent contractor can, therefore, be defined as "a person who contracts with another to do something for him but who is not controlled by the other nor subject to the other's right to control with respect to his physical conduct in the performance of the undertaking." Restatement (Second) of Agency § 2(3).

It is important to distinguish between servants and independent contractors in the tort context because, while a master can be held liable for a servant's negligent conduct under respondeat superior, a master generally cannot be held liable for the negligence of an independent contractor. [ ] The theory behind non-liability for independent contractors is that it would be unfair to hold a master liable for the conduct of another when the master has no control over that conduct. See Restatement (Second) of Torts § 409 cmt. b.

Apparent agency is a doctrine based in agency law. It is most often associated with contracts and the ability of an agent with "apparent authority" to bind the principal to a contract with a third party. [ ] Apparent authority "is the authority that a third person reasonably believes an agent to possess because of some manifestation from his principal." [ ] The manifestation must be made by the principal to a third party and reasonably cause the third party to believe that an individual is an agent of the principal and to act upon that belief. [ ] The manifestations can originate from direct or indirect communication.[ ] They can also originate from advertisements to the community. [ ]

In certain instances, apparent or ostensible agency also can be a means by which to establish vicarious liability. One enunciation of this doctrine is set forth in the Restatement (Second) of Agency section 267, which provides that:

> One who represents that another is his servant or other agent and thereby causes a third person justifiably to rely upon the care or skill of such apparent agent is subject to liability to the third person for harm caused by the lack of care or skill of the one appearing to be a servant or other agent as if he were such.

(emphasis added) [hereinafter "Section 267"]. Under a Section 267 analysis, if, because of the principal's manifestations, a third party reasonably believes that in dealing with the apparent agent he is dealing with the principal's servant or agent and exposes himself to the negligent conduct because of the principal's manifestations, then the principal may be held liable for that negligent conduct. See Restatement (Second) of Agency § 267 cmt. a; see also Restatement (Second) of Torts § 429; Seavey, Restatement (Second) of AgencyYY §§ 8 cmt. D, 90 cmt. A, 91 cmt. B.

Another similar enunciation of this doctrine is set forth in the Restatement (Second) of Torts section 429 (1965), which is captioned "Negligence in Doing Work Which is Accepted in Reliance on the Employer's Doing the Work Himself" and which provides:

> One who employs an independent contractor to perform services for another which are accepted in the reasonable belief that the services are being rendered by the employer or by his servants, is subject to liability for physical harm caused by the negligence of the contractor in supplying such services, to the same extent as though the employer were supplying them himself or by his servants.

(emphasis added) [hereinafter "Section 429"]. Both Section 267 and Section 429 are estoppel-based. To the extent that Section 429 differs from Section 267 when applied in the hospital context, the primary difference appears to be that the reliance element is less subjective under Section 429.

B. Indiana Jurisprudence

In the hospital setting, Indiana courts have long followed the general rule that hospitals could not be held liable for the negligent actions of independent contractor physicians. * * *

* * * [C]ourts no longer allow hospitals to use their inability to practice medicine as a shield to protect themselves from liability.[ ] Moreover, although Indiana law may support a claim of vicarious liability through apparent or ostensible agency in some instances, courts in this jurisdiction rarely have considered this doctrine in a hospital setting and have never applied it to hold a hospital liable for the acts of an independent contractor physician. Rather, Indiana courts have continued to limit hospital liability under the doctrine of respondeat superior and have continued to focus on the question of whether the alleged acts of negligence were committed by an employee of the hospital or by an independent contractor. [ ] If the alleged negligence was committed by an independent contractor physician, the courts generally have held that the hospital cannot be held liable for those actions. [ ]

C. Evolving Law in Other Jurisdictions

In the area of hospital liability, there has been an ongoing movement by courts to use apparent or ostensible agency as a means by which to hold hospitals vicariously liable for the negligence of some independent contractor physicians.[ ][10] Many of these cases employ the doctrine of apparent agency

10. See also Seneris v. Haas, 45 Cal.2d 811, 291 P.2d 915 (1955); Paintsville Hosp. Co. v. Rose, 683 S.W.2d 255 (Ky.1985); Grewe v. Mt. Clemens Gen. Hosp., 404 Mich. 240, 273 N.W.2d 429 (1978); Kashishian v. Port, 167 Wis.2d 24, 481 N.W.2d 277 (1992); Pamperin v. Trinity Mem'l Hosp., 144 Wis.2d 188, 423 N.W.2d 848 (1988); Sharsmith v. Hill, 764 P.2d 667 (Wyo.1988). See generally Martin C. McWilliams, Jr. and Hamilton E. Russell, III, Hospital Liability for Torts of Independent Contractor Physicians, 47 S.C.L.REV. 431 (1996); Kenneth S. Abraham and Paul C. Weiler, Enterprise Medical Liability and the Evolution of the American Health Care System, 108 HARV.L.REV. 381, 386–89 (1994); Diane M. Janulis and Alan D. Hornstein, Damned if You Do, Damned if You Don't: Hospitals' Liability

when the plaintiff was negligently injured by a physician's actions while visiting the hospital's emergency room. [ ] Courts, however, also have employed the doctrine of apparent agency to hold a hospital liable for assertedly negligent acts committed in non-emergency room settings, including negligent acts committed by anesthesiologists. See Seneris v. Haas, 45 Cal.2d 811, 291 P.2d 915, 917, 926–27 (1955) (discussing negligence of an anesthesiologist during the delivery of a baby); see also Williams v. St. Claire Med. Ctr., 657 S.W.2d 590, 592–93 (Ky.Ct.App.1983) (discussing negligence of an independent contractor nurse anesthetist).[11]

Courts that have held hospitals liable for the negligence of independent contractor physicians under apparent agency have sometimes referred to or adopted Section 267, Section 429, or both, and sometimes have not referred to or adopted either Section 267 or Section 429. While the language employed by these courts sometimes varies, generally they have employed tests which focus primarily on two basic factors. The first factor focuses on the hospital's manifestations and is sometimes described as an inquiry whether the hospital "acted in a manner which would lead a reasonable person to conclude that the individual who was alleged to be negligent was an employee or agent of the hospital." Kashishian, 481 N.W.2d at 284–85; Gilbert, 190 Ill.Dec. 758, 622 N.E.2d at 795–96 (quoting Pamperin v. Trinity Mem'l Hosp., 144 Wis.2d 188, 423 N.W.2d 848, 855–56 (1988)); see also Seneris, 291 P.2d at 927. Courts considering this factor often ask whether the hospital "held itself out" to the public as a provider of hospital care, for example, by mounting extensive advertising campaigns. [ ] In this regard, the hospital need not make express representations to the patient that the treating physician is an employee of the hospital; rather a representation also may be general and implied. [ ]

The second factor focuses on the patient's reliance. It is sometimes characterized as an inquiry as to whether "the plaintiff acted in reliance upon the conduct of the hospital or its agent, consistent with ordinary care and prudence." Kashishian, 481 N.W.2d at 285; Gilbert, 190 Ill.Dec. 758, 622 N.E.2d at 795 (quoting Pamperin, 423 N.W.2d at 855–56); see also Seneris, 291 P.2d at 927. Courts considering this factor sometimes ask whether, because of the hospital's manifestations, the plaintiff believed that the hospital was providing the pertinent medical care as opposed to simply acting as a situs for the physician to provide health care as an independent contractor. [ ] Other courts, however, seem to employ a less subjective form of reliance or even to presume reliance absent any evidence that the patient knew or should have known that the physician was not an employee of the hospital and that it

for Physician Malpractice, 64 NEB.L.REV. 689 (1985).

11. See also Kashishian, 481 N.W.2d at 278 (discussing negligence of a cardiologist arising out of a cardiology consultation). See generally Abraham, supra note 10, at 388 (noting that patients are certainly under the impression that it is the hospital and not the individual physicians that provides such services as emergency, radiology, and anesthesiology, and that patients have maintained successful apparent agency suits against hospitals for the acts of emergency room physicians, anesthesiologists, pathologists, and radiologists); Janulis, supra note 10, at 693 (explaining that hospitals often

execute exclusive service contracts with groups of independent contractor physicians to staff areas such as radiology, pathology, and emergency room services and that consequently patients' ability to select physicians becomes limited by the restriction of clinical practice to the contracting physicians); McWilliams, supra note 10, 437 (explaining that hospitals try to utilize the doctrine of respondeat superior to insulate themselves or limit their liability by utilizing independent contractors in many high-risk specialties such as radiology, pathology, anesthesiology, and emergency room services).

is the physician and not the hospital who is responsible for his medical care. [ ] An example of a situation where a patient might be in a position to know that the physician was an independent contractor may exist if the patient establishes an independent relationship with the physician or selects a particular physician in advance of going to the hospital. [ ] Even in such circumstances, however, the courts have reasoned that the patient may not have had reason to know of the contractual arrangements between the physician and the hospital.[ ]

Central to both of these factors—that is, the hospital's manifestations and the patient's reliance—is the question of whether the hospital provided notice to the patient that the treating physician was an independent contractor and not an employee of the hospital. [ ]

D. Adoption of Restatement (Second) of Torts Section 429

In the present case, Sword argues that, under the doctrine of apparent or ostensible agency, Norton is vicariously liable for the actions of its apparent agent Dr. Luna, whom the parties agree was an independent contractor. * * * The Court of Appeals invited us to consider the appropriateness of more clearly defining a test and adopting one of the two formulations of the test set forth in the Restatements. [ ] We agree with the conclusion of the Court of Appeals and now, in the specific context of a hospital setting, expressly adopt the formulation of apparent or ostensible agency set forth in the Restatement (Second) of Tort section 429.

Under Section 429, as we read and construe it, a trier of fact must focus on the reasonableness of the patient's belief that the hospital or its employees were rendering health care. This ultimate determination is made by considering the totality of the circumstances, including the actions or inactions of the hospital, as well as any special knowledge the patient may have about the hospital's arrangements with its physicians. We conclude that a hospital will be deemed to have held itself out as the provider of care unless it gives notice to the patient that it is not the provider of care and that the care is provided by a physician who is an independent contractor and not subject to the control and supervision of the hospital. A hospital generally will be able to avoid liability by providing meaningful written notice to the patient, acknowledged at the time of admission. See Cantrell v. Northeast Georgia Med. Ctr., 235 Ga.App. 365, 508 S.E.2d 716, 719–20 (1998) (concluding that hospital did not hold physician out as its employee as evidenced by conspicuous signs posted in hospital's registration area and express language in the patient consent to treatment form); Valdez v. Pasadena Healthcare Management, Inc., 975 S.W.2d 43, 48 (Tex.App.1998) (finding written notice, signed by the patient, that physician served as an independent contractor was sufficient to release hospital from liability for physician's medical malpractice). Under some circumstances, such as in the case of a medical emergency, however, written notice may not suffice if the patient had an inadequate opportunity to make an informed choice.

As to the meaning and importance of reliance in this specific context, we agree with the cases that hold that if the hospital has failed to give meaningful notice, if the patient has no special knowledge regarding the arrangement the hospital has made with its physicians, and if there is no reason that the patient should have known of these employment relationships, then reliance is presumed. [ ]

Applying this test here, we conclude that there are genuine material issues of fact in dispute as to whether Dr. Luna was an apparent or ostensible agent of Norton and whether Norton may be held liable for any of Dr. Luna's asserted negligent acts. First, there is nothing in this record which indicates that the hospital did anything to put plaintiff on notice that it was her physician, an independent contractor, who was responsible for her medical care and not the hospital.[16] Second, this is clearly not a case where plaintiff selected her own anesthesiologist prior to admission, for she specifically testified that she did not know who would administer the epidural until just before the procedure, and if she had any special knowledge of the hospital's employment arrangement with Dr. Luna or with the hospital's general employment practices with respect to physicians, it is not apparent on this record. Finally, Norton held itself out, through an extensive advertising campaign, as a full-service hospital which specializes in obstetric care.

Based on this record and under Section 429 as we construe it today, there are clearly genuine issues of material fact as to whether Dr. Luna is an apparent agent of Norton. The trial court erred when it entered summary judgment for defendant on this issue.

Notes and Questions

1. What can a hospital do to avoid liability under the court's analysis in Sword? Will explicit notice to the plaintiff at the time of admission be sufficient? How about a large time in the admitting area of the hospital? A brochure handed to each patient? If the hospital advertises aggressively, perhaps the reliance created by such advertising overwhelms all targeted attempts to inform patients about the intricacies of the physicians' employment relationships with the hospital?

2. Some courts have put it more sharply: the patient relies on the reputation of the hospital, not any particular doctor, and for that reason selects that hospital. See e.g., White v. Methodist Hosp. South, 844 S.W.2d 642 (Tenn.App.1992). If the negligence results from emergency room care, most courts have held that a patient may justifiably rely on the physician as an agent unless the hospital explicitly disclaims an agency relationship. Ballard v. Advocate Health and Hospitals Corporations, 1999 WL 498702 (N.D.Ill. 1999). A promotional campaign or advertising can create such reliance. Clark v. Southview Hospital & Family Health Center, 68 Ohio St.3d 435, 628 N.E.2d 46 (Ohio 1994)(promotional and marketing campaign stressed the emergency departments); Gragg v. Calandra, 297 Ill.App.3d 639, 231 Ill.Dec. 711, 696 N.E.2d 1282 (A.C.Ill. 1998)(unless patient is put on notice of the independent status of the professionals in a hospital, he or see will reasonably assume they are employees).

---

16. In a deposition colloquy, counsel made a general reference to a document titled "Condition of Admission and Authorization for Treatment," which assertedly informed plaintiff that her physician is not an employee of the hospital, and that the hospital is not liable for any acts of the practicing physician. That document, however, is not in the record, and no witness testified regarding that document. Nevertheless, even assuming the accuracy of counsel's representations during this colloquy, it is far from clear that this document would constitute sufficient notice of the relationship between the hospital and the physician within the meaning of the rule we articulate today. In fact, it is likely insufficient notice if it is the sole source of notice and if plaintiff did not read or sign that form until she arrived at the hospital in active labor.

To avoid liability, a hospital can try to avoid patient misunderstanding by its billing procedures, the letterhead used, signs , and other clues of the true nature of the relationship of the physician to the institution. Cantrell v. Northeast Georgia Medical Center, 235 Ga.App. 365, 508 S.E.2d 716 (C.A.Ga. 1998)(sign over registration desk stated that the physicians in the emergency room were independent contracts; consent form repeated this.) The court is likely however to cut through these devices if the reliance on reputation by the patient is strong enough. It appears that a few states allow a clear statement in a consent form that physicians in the hospital are independent contractors and not agents has been held to be sufficient to put a patient on notice. Valdez v. Pasadena Healthcare Management, Inc., 975 S.W.2d 43 (C.A.Tex. 1998); James v. Ingalls Memorial Hospital, 299 Ill.App.3d 627, 233 Ill.Dec. 564, 701 N.E.2d 207 (App.Ct. Ill. 1998); Roberts v. Galen of Virginia, Inc., 111 F.3d 405 (6th Cir. 1997)(statement in outpatient registration and authorization for medical treatment form stated that "physicians, residents, and medical students are independent practitioners and are not employees or agents of the hospital"; even though patient had neither read nor signed this, it is the action of the hospital that governs as to ostensible agency.)

3. The second element—justifiable reliance by the patient to her detriment on the appearance of an apparent agency—has been found by many courts through the context in which health care is delivered. Hospitals are big businesses, spending millions marketing themselves through "expensive advertising campaigns." Kashishian v. Port, 167 Wis.2d 24, 481 N.W.2d 277 (Wis.1992) (noting the substantial sums of money spent by U.S. hospitals on advertising in 1989, and the fact the many people recall such advertising.) They provide a range of health services, and the public expects emergency care and other functions, as a result of hospitals' self-promotion. Hospitals do not actively inform the public about the various statuses of emergency room and other physicians. As the role and image of the hospital have evolved, judicial willingness to stretch agency exceptions has likewise followed suit.

Recent decisions have declined to limit the doctrine to just emergency room services, but rather have left it as a question of fact as to whether the patient knew the physician was an independent contractor. See, e.g., Dahan v. UHS of Bethesda, Inc., 295 Ill.App.3d 770, 230 Ill.Dec. 137, 692 N.E.2d 1303 (A.C. Ill. 1998)(physicians's contract with the hospital required him to see hospital employees free of charge; a reasonable person would conclude that he was an agent of the hospital). Even the fact that a patient had contracted with a private physician as primary surgeon may not be sufficient to block the use of apparent authority doctrine.

d. The Inherent Function Test

A third approach, the inherent function doctrine, is discussed in the following case.

BEECK v. TUCSON GENERAL HOSPITAL

Supreme Court of Arizona, 1972.
18 Ariz.App. 165, 500 P.2d 1153.

[The plaintiff contracted pneumonia as the result of the insertion of a needle into her spine during a lumbar myelogram, due to the collision by the x-ray machine screen with the needle. She brought a malpractice suit against

Tucson General and the radiologists who administered the test. The trial court granted the hospital's motion for summary judgment on the ground that Dr. Rente was an independent contractor. Plaintiff appealed.]

Having undertaken one of mankind's most critically important and delicate fields of endeavor, concomitantly therewith the hospital must assume the grave responsibility of pursuing this calling with appropriate care. The care and service dispensed through this high trust, however technical, complex and esoteric its character may be, must meet standards of responsibility commensurate with the undertaking to preserve and protect the health, and indeed, the very lives of those placed in the hospital's keeping. [ ]

* * *

The radiology department of Tucson General was operated virtually on a monopoly basis. Dr. Rente and his colleagues were the only ones authorized to perform x-ray work for the department. Any choice by Mrs. Beeck was eliminated. The hospital had chosen for her. It had placed the "hospital radiologists" in the position of exclusive radiologists for the hospital. Further, the hospital furnished everything. The equipment belonged to the hospital and the radiologist paid no rent for use of the equipment or for space at the hospital. Working hours, vacation time, billing and employment of technicians were all controlled by the hospital. The radiology services were obviously furnished under the auspices of Tucson General. Clearly the hospital could regulate operation of its x-ray department to the extent of requiring that the descent-arresting stop be in place before undertaking the type of procedure in question here. Checklists are commonly used in operating complicated equipment. Furthermore, it is well known that hospitals undertake control of the highly technical service with which they deal through overseeing boards and supervisors and peer group mechanisms of various types. [ ]

* * * Further, the hospital had the right to control the standards of performance of this chosen radiologist. The radiologist was employed by the hospital for an extended period of time (five years) to perform a service which was an inherent function of the hospital, a function without which the hospital could not properly achieve its purpose. All facilities and instrumentalities were provided by the hospital together with all administrative services for the radiology department.

* * * [W]e hold that an employee-employer relationship existed between Dr. Rente and the hospital and the doctrine of respondeat superior applies.

* * *

For the reasons given, the judgment is reversed and the case remanded for further proceedings consistent with this opinion.

Notes and Questions

1.   Do the above cases reflect the changing balance of power between health care institutions and physicians? The control test is closest to vicarious liability principles, looking to the terms of the contract and the actual relationship between the hospital and the physician. The evolution of corporate concepts of accountability and control have come to permeate health care delivery, and Berel indicates the willingness of courts to see such control mechanisms as sufficient to override agency defenses.

2. Apparent authority tests look at patient expectations and reasonable, justifiable reliance. Sword describes three different approaches to such apparent agency. See also Gilbert v. Sycamore Municipal Hospital, 156 Ill.2d 511, 190 Ill.Dec. 758, 622 N.E.2d 788 (1993); Hardy v. Brantley, 471 So.2d 358 (Miss.1985).

3. The inherent function test takes the inquiry one step further, looking at those functions of a hospital that are essential to its operation rather than stopping the inquiry at patient reliance. Radiology labs and emergency rooms are often held to be two such functions. See, e.g., Adamski v. Tacoma General Hospital, 20 Wash.App. 98, 579 P.2d 970 (1978). This notion of "inherent function" overlaps substantially with the "nondelegable duty" rule in agency law, as expressed in corporate negligence cases.

4. Hospitals have been held liable for the acts of radiologists, residents, emergency room physicians, and surgeons, even though these persons were not hospital employees. The number of courts that have adopted exceptions to vicarious liability is increasing. See James by James v. Ingalls Memorial Hospital, 299 Ill.App.3d 627, 233 Ill.Dec. 564, 701 N.E.2d 207 (Ill.App. 1 Dist., 1998); Pamperin v. Trinity Memorial Hospital, 144 Wis.2d 188, 423 N.W.2d 848 (1988) (radiologists); Thompson v. The Nason Hospital, 527 Pa. 330, 591 A.2d 703 (Pa. 1991) (surgeons); Richmond County Hospital Authority v. Brown, 257 Ga. 507, 361 S.E.2d 164 (Ga. 1987) (emergency room physicians); Strach v. St. John Hospital Corp.,160 Mich.App. 251, 408 N.W.2d 441 (Mich.App.1987) (physicians referred to surgery unit as part of hospital's team and surgery team doctors exercised direct authority over hospital employees.); Barrett v. Samaritan Health Services, Inc., 153 Ariz. 138, 735 P.2d 460 (App.1987) (emergency room physicians). Contra, see Baptist Memorial Hospital v. Sampson, 969 S.W.2d 945 (Tex.1998)(rejecting ostensible agency for emergency room physician who failed to diagnose and treat a poisonous spider bite).

Problem: Creating a Shield

You represent Bowsman Hospital, a small rural hospital in Iowa. The hospital has until now relied on Dr. Francke for radiology services. It provides him with space, equipment and personnel for the radiology department, sends and collects bills on his behalf, and provides him with an office. It also pays him $300 a day in exchange for which Dr. Francke agrees to be at the hospital one day a week. Bowsman is one of several small hospitals in this part of Iowa that use Dr. Francke's services. Bowsman advertises in the local papers of several nearby communities. Its advertisements stress its ability to handle trauma injuries, common in farming areas. The ads say in part:

"Bowsman treats patient problems with big league medical talent. Our physicians and nurses have been trained for the special demands of farming accidents and injuries."

What advice can you give as to methods of shielding Bowsman from liability for the negligent acts of Dr. Francke? Must it insist that Dr. Francke operate his own outside laboratory? Or furnish his own equipment? Pay his own bills? Should the hospital hire its own radiologist?

The Chief Executive Officer asks you to develop guidelines to protect the hospital from liability for medical errors of the radiologist. Your research has uncovered the following cases.

Estates of Milliron v. Francke, 243 Mont. 200, 793 P.2d 824 (1990). The plaintiff was referred to the hospital and the radiologist who practiced there by his family physician, for evaluation of prostatis and uropathy. The radiologist used an intravenous pyelogram, to which the plaintiff had a reaction. The patient suffered brain damage. The hospital provided space, equipment and personnel for the radiology department, sent and collected bills on his behalf, and provided him with an office. The court granted summary judgment for the defendant on the ostensible agency claim. The court noted that this was a small hospital in a rural area, and the radiologist rotated between this and several other small hospitals. This was an ordinary practice in smaller communities in Montana.

> Providing these traveling physicians with offices at the hospital simply helps ensure that these smaller and more remote communities will be provided with adequate medical care and is not a sufficient factual basis to establish an agency relationship. Id. at 827.

Gregg v. National Medical Health Care Services, Inc., 145 Ariz. 51, 699 P.2d 925 (1985). Gregg went to the hospital's emergency room at 3 a.m. after having three episodes of crushing substernal chest pain accompanied by nausea and vomiting. The court noted that the hospital's right to control the physician was critical to its liability for the physician's acts, and held that the facts raised a jury question. The physician was paid $300 per week to commute from his office to the hospital clinic to act as a consultant. He was required to be at the hospital at least once a week.

II. HOSPITAL DIRECT LIABILITY

A. NEGLIGENCE

WASHINGTON v. WASHINGTON HOSPITAL CENTER

District of Columbia Court of Appeals, 1990.
579 A.2d 177.

[The Court considered two issues: whether the testimony of the plaintiff's expert was sufficient to create a issue for the jury; and whether the hospital's failure to request a finding of liability of the settling defendants or to file a cross claim for contribution against any of the defendants defeated the hospital's claim for a pro rata reduction in the jury verdict. The discussion of the first issue follows.]

FARRELL, ASSOCIATE JUDGE:

This appeal and cross-appeal arise from a jury verdict in a medical malpractice action against the Washington Hospital Center (WHC or the hospital) in favor of LaVerne Alice Thompson, a woman who suffered permanent catastrophic brain injury from oxygen deprivation in the course of general anesthesia for elective surgery * * *

* * *

I. THE FACTS

On the morning of November 7, 1987, LaVerne Alice Thompson, a healthy 36-year-old woman, underwent elective surgery at the Washington Hospital Center for an abortion and tubal ligation, procedures requiring general anesthesia. At about 10:45 a.m., nurse-anesthetist Elizabeth Adland, under the supervision of Dr. Sheryl Walker, the physician anesthesiologist, inserted an endotracheal tube into Ms. Thompson's throat for the purpose of conveying oxygen to, and removing carbon dioxide from, the anesthetized patient. The tube, properly inserted, goes into the patient's trachea just above the lungs. Plaintiffs alleged that instead Nurse Adland inserted the tube into Thompson's esophagus, above the stomach. After inserting the tube, Nurse Adland "ventilated" or pumped air into the patient while Dr. Walker, by observing physical reactions—including watching the rise and fall of the patient's chest and listening for breath sounds equally on the patient's right and left sides—sought to determine if the tube had been properly inserted.

At about 10:50 a.m., while the surgery was underway, surgeon Nathan Bobrow noticed that Thompson's blood was abnormally dark, which indicated that her tissues were not receiving sufficient oxygen, and reported the condition to Nurse Adland, who checked Thompson's vital signs and found them stable. As Dr. Bobrow began the tubal ligation part of the operation, Thompson's heart rate dropped. She suffered a cardiac arrest and was resuscitated, but eventually the lack of oxygen caused catastrophic brain injuries. Plaintiffs' expert testified that Ms. Thompson remains in a persistent vegetative state and is totally incapacitated; her cardiac, respiratory and digestive functions are normal and she is not "brain dead," but, according to the expert, she is "essentially awake but unaware" of her surroundings. Her condition is unlikely to improve, though she is expected to live from ten to twenty years.

* * *

The plaintiffs alleged that Adland and Walker had placed the tube in Thompson's esophagus rather than her trachea, and that they and Dr. Bobrow had failed to detect the improper intubation in time to prevent the oxygen deprivation that caused Thompson's catastrophic brain injury. WHC, they alleged, was negligent in failing to provide the anesthesiologists with a device known variously as a capnograph or end-tidal carbon dioxide monitor which allows early detection of insufficient oxygen in time to prevent brain injury.

* * *

II. WASHINGTON HOSPITAL CENTER'S CLAIMS ON CROSS-APPEAL

A. Standard of Care

On its cross-appeal, WHC first asserts that the plaintiffs failed to carry their burden of establishing the standard of care and that the trial court therefore erred in refusing to grant its motion for judgment notwithstanding the verdict.

* * *

In a negligence action predicated on medical malpractice, the plaintiff must carry a tripartite burden, and establish: (1) the applicable standard of care; (2) a deviation from that standard by the defendant; and (3) a causal relationship between that deviation and the plaintiff's injury. [ ] * * *

Generally, the "standard of care" is "the course of action that a reasonably prudent [professional] with the defendant's specialty would have taken under the same or similar circumstances." [] With respect to institutions such as hospitals, this court has rejected the "locality" rule, which refers to the standard of conduct expected of other similarly situated members of the profession in the same locality or community, [] in favor of a national standard. [] Thus, the question for decision is whether the evidence as a whole, and reasonable inferences therefrom, would allow a reasonable juror to find that a reasonably prudent tertiary care hospital,[3] at the time of Ms. Thompson's injury in November 1987, and according to national standards, would have supplied a carbon dioxide monitor to a patient undergoing general anesthesia for elective surgery.

WHC argues that the plaintiffs' expert, Dr. Stephen Steen, failed to demonstrate an adequate factual basis for his opinion that WHC should have made available a carbon dioxide monitor. The purpose of expert opinion testimony is to avoid jury findings based on mere speculation or conjecture. [ ] The sufficiency of the foundation for those opinions should be measured with this purpose in mind. * * *

* * *

* * * [WHC] asserts that * * * Steen gave no testimony on the number of hospitals having end-tidal carbon dioxide monitors in place in 1987, and that he never referred to any written standards or authorities as the basis of his opinion. We conclude that Steen's opinion * * * was sufficient to create an issue for the jury.

Dr. Steen testified that by 1985, the carbon dioxide monitors were available in his hospital (Los Angeles County—University of Southern California Medical Center (USC)), and "in many other hospitals." In response to a question whether, by 1986, "standards of care" required carbon dioxide monitors in operating rooms, he replied, "I would think that by that time, they would be [required]." As plaintiffs concede, this opinion was based in part on his own personal experience at USC, which * * * cannot itself provide an adequate foundation for an expert opinion on a national standard of care. But Steen also drew support from "what I've read where [the monitors were] available in other hospitals." He referred to two such publications: The American Association of Anesthesiology (AAA) Standards for Basic Intra–Operative Monitoring, approved by the AAA House of Delegates on October 21, 1986, which "encouraged" the use of monitors, and an article entitled *Standards for Patient Monitoring During Anesthesia at Harvard Medical School*, published in August 1986 in the Journal of American Medical Association, which stated that as of July 1985 the monitors were in use at Harvard, and that "monitoring end-tidal carbon dioxide is an emerging standard and is strongly preferred."

WHC makes much of Steen's concession on cross-examination that the AAA Standards were recommendations, strongly encouraged but not mandatory, and that the Harvard publication spoke of an "emerging" standard. In its brief WHC asserts, without citation, that "[p]alpable indicia of widespread *mandated* practices are necessary to establish a standard of care" (emphasis added), and that at most the evidence spoke of "recommended" or "encouraged" practices, and "emerging" or "developing" standards as of 1986–87. A standard of due care, however, necessarily embodies what a *reasonably*

---

3. Plaintiffs' expert defined a tertiary care hospital as "a hospital which has the facilities to conduct clinical care management of pa-   tients in nearly all aspects of medicine and surgery."

prudent hospital would do, [ ] and hence care and foresight exceeding the minimum required by law or mandatory professional regulation may be necessary to meet that standard. It certainly cannot be said that the 1986 recommendations of a professional association (which had no power to issue or enforce mandatory requirements), or an article speaking of an "emerging" standard in 1986, have no bearing on an expert opinion as to what the standard of patient monitoring equipment was fully one year later when Ms. Thompson's surgery took place.

Nevertheless, we need not decide whether Dr. Steen's testimony was sufficiently grounded in fact or adequate data to establish the standard of care. The record contains other evidence from which, in combination with Dr. Steen's testimony, a reasonable juror could fairly conclude that monitors were required of prudent hospitals similar to WHC in late 1987. The evidence showed that at least four other teaching hospitals in the United States used the monitors by that time. In addition to Dr. Steen's testimony that USC supplied them and the article reflecting that Harvard University had them, plaintiffs introduced into evidence an article entitled *Anesthesia at Penn,* from a 1986 alumni newsletter of the Department of Anesthesia at the University of Pennsylvania, indicating that the monitors were then in use at that institution's hospital, and that they allowed "instant recognition of esophageal intubation and other airway problems. * * * " Moreover, WHC's expert anesthesiologist, Dr. John Tinker of the University of Iowa, testified that his hospital had installed carbon dioxide monitors in every operating room by early 1986, and that "by 1987, it is certainly true that many hospitals were in the process of converting" to carbon dioxide monitors.[5]

Perhaps most probative was the testimony of WHC's own Chairman of the Department of Anesthesiology, Dr. Dermot A. Murray, and documentary evidence associated with his procurement request for carbon dioxide monitors. In December 1986 or January 1987, Dr. Murray submitted a requisition form to the hospital for end-tidal carbon dioxide units to monitor the administration of anesthesia in each of the hospital's operating rooms, stating that if the monitors were not provided, the hospital would "fail to meet the national standard of care." The monitors were to be "fully operational" in July of 1987.[6] Attempting to meet this evidence, WHC points out that at trial

> Dr. Murray was *never asked to opine,* with a reasonable degree of medical certainty, that the applicable standard of care at the relevant time *required* the presence of CO_2 monitors. Indeed, his testimony was directly

---

5. In its reply brief, WHC argues that

the fact that four teaching hospitals used CO_2 monitors during the relevant time period is almost irrelevant. Institutions with significantly enhanced financial resources and/or government grants which accelerate their testing and implementation of new and improved technologies would naturally have available to them items which, inherently, were not yet required for the general populace of hospitals.

In fact, Dr. Steen, in voir dire examination on his qualification as an expert on the standard required of hospitals in WHC's position in regard to equipment, testified that his review of WHC's President's Report for 1986–87 led him to conclude that WHC was a teaching hospital. Counsel for the hospital could have identified and probed fully before the jury any differences between WHC and the hospitals relied on to establish the standard of care. To the extent the record was not so developed, the jury could credit Steen's testimony that WHC was required to adhere to the standard applicable to teaching hospitals.

6. As supporting documentation for the requisition, Dr. Murray attached a copy of the Journal of the American Medical Association article on standards at Harvard University. The requisitions, with attachments, were exhibits admitted in evidence.

to the contrary. Moreover, the procurement process which he had initiated envisioned obtaining the equipment * * * over time, not even beginning until fiscal year 1988, a period ending June 30, 1988. [Emphasis by WHC.]

Dr. Murray opined that in November 1987 there was *no* standard of care relating to monitoring equipment. The jury heard this testimony and Dr. Murray's explanation of the procurement process, but apparently did not credit it, perhaps because the requisition form itself indicated that the equipment ordered was to be operational in July 1987, four months before Ms. Thompson's surgery, and not at some unspecified time in fiscal year 1988 as Dr. Murray testified at trial.

On the evidence recited above, a reasonable juror could find that the standard of care required WHC to supply monitors as of November 1987. The trial judge therefore did not err in denying the motion for judgment notwithstanding the verdict.

* * *

Notes and Questions

1. Does the plaintiff present sufficient evidence that the carbon dioxide monitor is now standard equipment for tertiary care hospitals? Is the Washington Hospital Center stuck in a zone of transition between older precautions and emerging technologies that improve patient care? Why did they not purchase such monitors earlier?

A companion device to the carbon dioxide monitor is the blood-monitoring pulse oximeter, which has become a mandatory device in hospital operating rooms. In 1984 no hospital had them; by 1990 all hospitals used oximeters in their operating rooms. The device beeps when a patient's blood oxygen drops due to breathing problems or overuse of anesthesia. That warning can give a vital three or four minutes warning to physicians, allowing them to correct the problem before the patient suffers brain damage. These devices have so improved patient safety that malpractice insurers have lowered premiums for anesthesiologists. See Appleby, Pulse Oximeters Pump Up Bottom Lines and Patient Safety, Deflate Malpractice Risk, HealthWeek 17–18 (October 9, 1990).

The Joint Commission on Accreditation of Healthcare Organization (JCAHO) now requires hospitals to develop protocols for anesthesia care that mandate pulse oximetry equipment for measuring oxygen saturation. See Revisions to Anesthesia Care Standards Comprehensive Accreditation Manual for Hospitals Effective January 1, 2001 (Standards and Intents for Sedation and Anesthesia Care), *http://www.jcaho.org/standard/aneshap.html.*

2. A health care institution, whether hospital, nursing home, or clinic, is liable for negligence in maintaining its facilities, providing and maintaining medical equipment, hiring, supervising and retaining nurses and other staff, and failing to have in place procedures to protect patients. Basic negligence principles govern hospital liability for injuries caused by other sources than negligent acts of the medical staff. As *Washington* holds, hospitals are generally held to a national standard of care for hospitals in their treatment category. They must provide a safe environment for diagnosis, treatment, and recovery of patients. Bellamy v. Appellate Department, 50 Cal.App.4th 797, 57 Cal.Rptr.2d 894 (Cal.App. 5 Dist. 1996).

a. Hospitals must have minimum facility and support systems to treat the range of problems and side effects that accompany procedures they offer. In Hernandez v. Smith, 552 F.2d 142 (5th Cir.1977), for example, an obstetrical clinic that lacked surgical facilities for caesarean sections was found liable for " * * * the failure to provide proper and safe instrumentalities for the treatment of ailments it undertakes to treat * * *." See also Valdez v. Lyman–Roberts Hosp., Inc., 638 S.W.2d 111 (Tex.App.1982).

b. Staffing must be adequate. Short staffing can be negligence. See Merritt v. Karcioglu, 668 So.2d 469 (La.App. 4th Cir.1996)(hospital ward understaffed in having only three critical care nurses for six patients). If existing staff can be juggled to cover a difficult patient, short staffing is no defense. See Horton v. Niagara Falls Memorial Medical Center, 51 A.D.2d 152, 380 N.Y.S.2d 116 (1976).

c. Equipment must be adequate for the services offered, although it need not be the state of the art. See Emory University v. Porter, 103 Ga.App. 752, 120 S.E.2d 668, 670 (1961); Lauro v. Travelers Ins. Co., 261 So.2d 261 (La.App.1972). If a device such as an expensive CT scanner has come into common use, however, a smaller and less affluent hospital can argue that it should be judged by the standards of similar hospitals with similar resources. This variable standard, reflecting resource differences between hospitals, would then protect a hospital in a situation where its budget does not allow purchase of some expensive devices. If an institution lacks a piece of equipment that has come to be recognized as essential, particularly for diagnosis, it may have a duty to transfer the patient to an institution that has the equipment. In Blake v. D.C. General Hospital (discussed in Maxwell Mehlman, Rationing Expensive Lifesaving Medical Treatments, 1985 Wisc.L.Rev. 239) the trial court allowed a case to go to the jury where the plaintiff's estate claimed that she died because of the hospital's lack of a CT scanner to diagnose her condition. The court found a duty to transfer in such circumstances.

d. A hospital and its contracting physicians may be liable for damages caused by inadequate or defective systems they develop and implement, particularly where emergency care is involved. In the case of Marks v. Mandel, 477 So.2d 1036 (Fla.App.1985), the plaintiff brought a wrongful death action against the hospital, alleging negligence based on the failure of the on-call system to produce a thoracic surgeon and failure of the hospital staff to send the patient to a hospital with a trauma center. The Florida Supreme Court held that the trial court erred in excluding from evidence the hospital's emergency room policy and procedure manual. This manual set out in detail how the on-call system should operate and itemized procedures for responding to calls made from ambulances. The court held that evidence was sufficient to go to the jury on the issue of liability of the hospital and the emergency room supervisor for the failure of the on-call system to produce a thoracic surgeon in a timely fashion. See also Habuda v. Trustees of Rex Hospital, 3 N.C.App. 11, 164 S.E.2d 17 (1968), where the hospital was liable for inadequate rules for handling, storing, and administering medications; Herrington v. Hiller, 883 F.2d 411 (5th Cir.1989) (failure to provide for adequate 24–hour anesthesia service). See also Ball Memorial Hosp. v. Freeman, 245 Ind. 71, 196 N.E.2d 274 (1964).

e. A hospital's own safety rules or internal regulations serve as a source of a standard of care, as would any non-legislative safety standard. They are material and relevant on the issue of quality of care, but are usually not sufficient by themselves to establish the degree of care due. Jackson v. Oklahoma Memorial Hospital, 909 P.2d 765 (Okl.1995).

3. An institution's own internal rules and regulations for medical procedures may be offered as evidence of a standard of care for the trier of fact to consider. In Williams v. St. Claire Medical Center, 657 S.W.2d 590 (Ky.App.1983), the court held that a hospital owes a duty to all patients, including the private patients of staff physicians, to enforce its published rules and regulations pertaining to patient care. The nurse anesthetist was required under hospital rules to work under the direct supervision of a certified registered nurse anesthetist, and he was alone when he administered the anesthesia to the plaintiff. Because of problems with the administration, the plaintiff went into a coma.

The court stated:

> * * * [W]hile the patient must accept all the rules and regulations of the hospital, he should be able to expect that the hospital will follow its rules established for his care. Whether a patient enters a hospital through the emergency room or is admitted as a private patient by a staff physician, the patient is entering the hospital for only one reason * * *

> "Indeed, the sick leave their homes and enter hospitals because of the superior treatment there promised them."

There is no rational reason or public policy why a hospital's duty to properly administer its policies should be any less to one patient than another depending upon how the patient initially arrived at the hospital.

See also Adams v. Family Planning Associates Medical Group, Inc., 315 Ill.App.3d 533, 248 Ill.Dec. 91, 733 N.E.2d 766 (Ill.C.A. 2000)(internal policies and procedures of family planning clinic admissible as evidence of standard of care).

B. NEGLIGENCE PER SE

EDWARDS v. BRANDYWINE HOSPITAL

Superior Court of Pennsylvania, 1995.
438 Pa.Super. 673, 652 A.2d 1382.

OPINION BY Olszewski

In 1986, Charles Edwards was a 69–year-old retired steel worker with an artificial hip. He arrived at the Brandywine Hospital emergency room on August 25, complaining of hip pain. The hospital admitted him, and the nursing staff installed a heparin lock on his left hand. A heparin lock is a device which allows multiple intravenous fluids to be introduced at a common point.

Mr. Edwards stayed at the hospital for five days. The heparin lock was left in place for either three or four days, in apparent violation of standards promulgated by the Pennsylvania Department of Health.[10] The day after his discharge from the hospital, Mr.Edwards noticed a red spot on the back of his hand where the heparin lock had been. He returned to the hospital that day for physical therapy, and his therapist referred him to the emergency room.

---

10. 28 Pa.Code § 146.1. The regulation requires hospitals to develop written standards regarding such antiseptic practices as changing intravenous catheter sites. The regulation states that these standards should comply with those described in the American Hospital Association's publication entitled Infection Control in the Hospital (1979), which recommends that intravenous catheter sites be changed every 48 hours in order to avoid infection. The longer the catheter remains in the same site, the greater the risk of infection. [ ]

An ER physician checked Mr. Edwards' hand, took a sample of pus for analysis, and sent him home with a prescription for oral antibiotics. The lab results came back the next day showing a staphylococcus aureus (staph) infection. The ER physician placed the lab results and diagnosis in Mr. Edwards' chart, as required by hospital rules.

A few days later, Mr. Edwards returned to the hospital with leg pains. Somehow, his treating physicians did not notice the recent diagnosis of a staph infection in his chart. After a week, Mr. Edwards' treating physicians ordered a second lab test, which again showed the presence of a staph infection. Now Mr. Edwards' doctors put him on intravenous antibiotics. By the end of September Mr. Edwards' doctors believed they had wiped out the infection, and discharged him. He was back again a week later with pain and a fever. This time his doctors suspected that the obviously-not-yet-defeated staph infection had spread to Mr. Edwards' artificial hip.

Mr. Edwards stayed in the hospital for a month. He claimed he was discharged not for medical reasons, but because his Medicare hospitalization coverage was about to expire. He endured more treatment and hospitalizations over the next two years, until his doctors decided to remove his artificial hip and wipe out the staph infection with massive doses of antibiotics. Without his hip prosthesis, Mr. Edwards now needs crutches or a walker to get around.

Mr. Edwards sued the hospital and the doctors who treated him there for professional negligence. The trial court took notice of the Health Department regulation regarding catheter site changing, and ruled that the hospital's admitted failure to move the heparin lock for at least three days constituted negligence per se. After this ruling, Mr. Edwards' treating physicians settled, leaving only the hospital as a defendant.

At the close of Mr. Edwards' case, the trial court granted the hospital's motion for a directed verdict. The court held that while the negligence per se ruling established the hospital's breach of a duty of care, Mr. Edwards could not prove causation as a matter of law. * * *

* * * Because we disagree with the trial court's analysis that Mr. Edwards failed to establish causation, we must reverse and remand for a new trial.

Before launching into a discussion of causation and the other questions presented, it would be helpful to review the theory of this case, and how it unfolded at trial. Mr. Edwards claimed that his doctors and the hospital made a number of mistakes in treating him which led to his severe bacterial infection and the removal of his hip prosthesis. The big mistake was allowing him to develop a staph infection. Mr. Edwards sought to prove that the hospital was negligent for leaving the heparin lock in his hand for too long, which allowed the staph infection to develop. Mr. Edwards also sought to prove that a series of lesser mistakes exacerbated the initial infection, leading to the ultimate result of his hip loss: the ER doctor should have prescribed intravenous antibiotics, not oral antibiotics; the diagnosis of staph infection should have been noted by his treating physicians immediately upon his return to the hospital; his treating physicians should have consulted with an infectious disease expert early on; and the hospital should not have discharged him so soon, without a prescription for more antibiotics, and without adequate follow up.

The trial court took note of the Department of Health regulation which referred to a rule that intravenous catheter sites should be changed every 48 hours. The hospital was prepared to argue that this standard was never mandatory, and by 1986 was superseded by a 72–hour standard promulgated by the Centers for Disease Control. The trial court held that the Department of Health regulation, even if outdated and superseded, was still the applicable standard. It ruled that the hospital was negligent per se in leaving the heparin lock in the same place for over 48 hours. S.R.R. at 325a–29a.

The trial court then held that while duty and breach were established as a matter of law, Mr. Edwards had failed to prove causation as a matter of law, and that none of the other alleged mistakes by the hospital could constitute negligence. The court therefore directed a verdict in favor of the hospital.

I.

[The court first considered the trial court's ruling on causation. The trial court had held that even if the hospital violated a standard for leaving the heparin lock in longer than appropriate, this breach could not have caused the staph infection. The court applied the causation standard of Hamil v. Bashline, requiring only that the plaintiff introduce evidence that the defendant's negligent act increased the risk of harm, and the harm was in fact sustained, to raise a jury question.]

* * *

III.

This finally brings us to the issue which the hospital has prudently raised in its cross-appeal: did the trial court err in holding that leaving the heparin lock in the same spot for over 48 hours constituted negligence per se?

The trial court arrived at this ruling by examining a Pennsylvania Department of Health regulation: (a) A multidisciplinary committee made up of representatives of the medical staff, the administration, the microbiology laboratory, and the nursing staff shall establish effective measures for the control and prevention of infections. (b) The multidisciplinary committee described in subsection (a) shall do the following: (1) Develop written standards for hospital sanitation and medical asepsis. Copies of the standards shall be made available to all appropriate personnel. Adequate standards should comply with those described in Infection Control in the Hospital, published by the American Hospital Association, Chicago, Illinois. 28 Pa.Code s 146.1 (emphasis added); R.R. 222a. Page 166 of Infection Control states that intravenous catheter sets should be changed and moved to a different site every 48 hours. [ ]

The hospital was prepared to argue at trial that Infection Control in the Hospital (1979) was an outdated publication, and that the 48–hour standard had been superseded by a 72–hour standard promulgated by the Centers for Disease Control. The trial court ruled that even if the 48–hour standard was outdated, the Pennsylvania Department of Health expressly adopted it by reference in its regulation, so the hospital had to follow the 48–hour rule until the Department got around to changing it. [ ]

We see no need to determine whether the 48–hour standard was current or outdated, because the regulation only referenced the standard, and did not require its adoption. The regulation merely states that whatever standards a hospital's infection committee chooses to adopt should be in line with Infection Control. The regulation did not require Brandywine Hospital to follow in lock step with the 48–hour rule, so its decision to adopt a 72–hour rule is not necessarily negligent. We do not express any opinion about what the correct standard should be, or whether the hospital's actions were negligent. We merely hold that the hospital's failure to move Mr. Edwards' heparin lock after 48 hours did not constitute negligence per se.

* * *

Order reversed and remanded for a new trial.

Notes and Questions

1. What is the point of state regulations that specify hour limits, if they are not to be treated as enforceable rules? If elasticity is intended by the regulations, why not spell out the conditions under which deviation from the 48–hour rule is appropriate? If the regulation had required the adoption of the standard, would the court have been comfortable imposing negligence per se on the hospital?

2. The usual American practice in a tort case not involving health care is to treat violation of a statute as negligence per se, giving rise to a rebuttable presumption of negligence. If the defendant fails to rebut the presumption, the trier of fact must find against him on the negligence issue. The classic statement of the rule is found in Martin v. Herzog, 228 N.Y. 164, 126 N.E. 814 (1920). Negligence per se is usually applied in cases where a statute is used to show a standard of care. In malpractice cases, however, standards are typically used to create only a permissive inference of negligence, allowing the plaintiff to get the jury which can then accept or reject the inference of fault.

3. Hospitals are regulated by their states. The majority are also subject generally to the standards of the Joint Commission on Accreditation of Healthcare Organizations (JCAHO). The standard of care that the courts have applied reflects a baseline mandated by JCAHO standards, including peer review through internal committee structures. The court in the *Darling* case, infra, allowed evidence of JCAHO standards, which the trier of fact could accept or reject. The JCAHO Guidelines therefore operated to create a permissive inference of negligence.

This baseline has largely doomed the locality rule for hospitals. See Shilkret v. Annapolis Emergency Hospital Association, 276 Md. 187, 349 A.2d 245 (1975). As to the JCAHO generally, see Timothy S. Jost, The Joint Commission on Accreditation of Hospitals: Private Regulation of Health Care and the Public Interest, 24 B.C.L.Rev. 835 (1983).

4. Courts have proved resistant to the application of negligence per se to health care institutions, even to create an inference of negligence, unless the standard is specific and supported by expert testimony. In Van Iperen v. Van Bramer, 392 N.W.2d 480 (Iowa 1986), the court considered the effect of JCAHO standards on a hospital. The plaintiff had argued that the hospital should have provided drug monitoring services, based on JCAHO accreditation standards requiring that a hospital provide drug monitoring services through its pharmacy, including a medication record or drug profile and a review of the patient's drug

regimen for potential problems. The court rejected the argument, holding that the standards were not sufficiently specific to justify a negligence per se standard.

C.   DUTIES TO TREAT PATIENTS

The relationship of the medical staff to the hospital insulates the hospital from liability, while giving physicians substantial autonomy in their treating decisions. What happens when the patient's insurance or other resources are exhausted but the staff physician believes that continued hospitalization is needed?

MUSE v. CHARTER HOSPITAL OF WINSTON–SALEM, INC.

Court of Appeals of North Carolina, 1995.
117 N.C.App. 468, 452 S.E.2d 589.

LEWIS, JUDGE.

This appeal arises from a judgment in favor of plaintiffs in an action for the wrongful death of Delbert Joseph Muse, III (hereinafter "Joe"). Joe was the son of Delbert Joseph Muse, Jr. (hereinafter "Mr. Muse") and Jane K. Muse (hereinafter "Mrs. Muse"), plaintiffs. The jury found that defendant Charter Hospital of Winston–Salem, Inc. (hereinafter "Charter Hospital" or "the hospital") was negligent in that, inter alia, it had a policy or practice which required physicians to discharge patients when their insurance expired and that this policy interfered with the exercise of the medical judgment of Joe's treating physician, Dr. L. Jarrett Barnhill, Jr. The jury awarded plaintiffs compensatory damages of approximately $1,000,000. The jury found that Mr. and Mrs. Muse were contributorily negligent, but that Charter Hospital's conduct was willful or wanton, and awarded punitive damages of $2,000,000 against Charter Hospital. Further, the jury found that Charter Hospital was an instrumentality of defendant Charter Medical Corporation (hereinafter "Charter Medical") and awarded punitive damages of $4,000,000 against Charter Medical.

The facts on which this case arose may be summarized as follows. On 12 June 1986, Joe, who was sixteen years old at the time, was admitted to Charter Hospital for treatment related to his depression and suicidal thoughts. Joe's treatment team consisted of Dr. Barnhill, as treating physician, Fernando Garzon, as nursing therapist, and Betsey Willard, as social worker. During his hospitalization, Joe experienced auditory hallucinations, suicidal and homicidal thoughts, and major depression. Joe's insurance coverage was set to expire on 12 July 1986. As that date neared, Dr. Barnhill decided that a blood test was needed to determine the proper dosage of a drug he was administering to Joe. The blood test was scheduled for 13 July, the day after Joe's insurance was to expire. Dr. Barnhill requested that the hospital administrator allow Joe to stay at Charter Hospital two more days, until 14 July, with Mr. and Mrs. Muse signing a promissory note to pay for the two extra days. The test results did not come back from the lab until 15 July. Nevertheless, Joe was discharged on 14 July and was referred by Dr. Barnhill to the Guilford County Area Mental Health, Mental Retardation and Substance Abuse Authority (hereinafter "Mental Health Authority") for outpatient treatment. Plaintiffs' evidence tended to show that Joe's condition upon discharge was worse than when he entered the hospital. Defendants' evidence, however, tended to show that while his prognosis remained guarded, Joe's condition at discharge was improved. Upon his discharge, Joe went on a one-week family vacation. On 22 July he began outpatient treatment at the Mental Health Authority, where he was seen by Dr. David Slonaker, a clinical psychologist. Two days later, Joe again met with Dr. Slonaker. Joe failed to show up at his 30 July appointment, and the next day he took a fatal overdose of Desipramine, one of his prescribed drugs.

On appeal, defendants present numerous assignments of error. We find merit in one of defendants' arguments.

II.

Defendants next argue that the trial court submitted the case to the jury on an erroneous theory of hospital liability that does not exist under the law of North Carolina. As to the theory in question, the trial court instructed: "[A] hospital is under a duty not to have policies or practices which operate in a way that interferes with the ability of a physician to exercise his medical judgment. A violation of this duty would be negligence." The jury found that there existed "a policy or practice which required physicians to discharge patients when their insurance benefits expire and which interfered with the exercise of Dr. Barnhill's medical judgment." Defendants contend that this theory of liability does not fall within any theories previously accepted by our courts.

* * *

Our Supreme Court has recognized that hospitals in this state owe a duty of care to their patients. Id. In Burns v. Forsyth County Hospital Authority, Inc. [ ] this Court held that a hospital has a duty to the patient to obey the instructions of a doctor, absent the instructions being obviously negligent or dangerous. Another recognized duty is the duty to make a reasonable effort to monitor and oversee the treatment prescribed and administered by doctors practicing at the hospital. [] In light of these holdings, it seems axiomatic that the hospital has the duty not to institute policies or practices which interfere with the doctor's medical judgment. We hold that pursuant to the reasonable person standard, Charter Hospital had a duty not to institute a policy or practice which required that patients be discharged when their insurance expired and which interfered with the medical judgment of Dr. Barnhill.

III.

Defendants next argue that even if the theory of negligence submitted to the jury was proper, the jury's finding that Charter Hospital had such a practice was not supported by sufficient evidence. * * * We conclude that in the case at hand, the evidence was sufficient to go to the jury.

Plaintiffs' evidence included the testimony of Charter Hospital employees and outside experts. Fernando Garzon, Joe's nursing therapist at Charter Hospital, testified that the hospital had a policy of discharging patients when their insurance expired. Specifically, when the issue of insurance came up in treatment team meetings, plans were made to discharge the patient. When Dr. Barnhill and the other psychiatrists and therapists spoke of insurance, they seemed to lack autonomy. For example, Garzon testified, they would state, "So and so is to be discharged. We must do this." Finally, Garzon testified that when he returned from a vacation, and Joe was no longer at the hospital, he asked several employees why Joe had been discharged and they all responded that he was discharged because his insurance had expired. Jane Sims, a former staff member at the hospital, testified that several employees expressed alarm about Joe's impending discharge, and that a therapist explained that Joe could no longer stay at the hospital because his insurance had expired. Sims also testified that Dr. Barnhill had misgivings about discharging Joe, and that Dr. Barnhill's frustration was apparent to everyone. One of plaintiffs' experts testified that based on a study regarding the length of patient stays at Charter Hospital, it was his opinion that patients were discharged based on insurance, regardless of their medical condition. Other experts testified that based on Joe's serious condition on the date of discharge, the expiration of insurance coverage must have caused Dr. Barnhill to discharge Joe. The experts further testified as to the relevant standard of care, and concluded that Charter Hospital's practices were below the standard of care and caused Joe's death. We hold that this evidence was sufficient to go to the jury.

Defendants further argue that the evidence was insufficient to support the jury's finding that Charter Hospital engaged in conduct that was willful or wanton. An act is willful when it is done purposely and deliberately in violation of the law, or when it is done knowingly and of set purpose, or when the mere will has free play, without yielding to reason. [ ] * * * We conclude that the jury could have reasonably found from the above-stated evidence that Charter Hospital acted knowingly and of set purpose, and with reckless indifference to the rights of others. Therefore, we hold that the finding of willful or wanton conduct on the part of Charter Hospital was supported by sufficient evidence.

* * *

For the reasons stated, we find no error in the judgment of the trial court, except for that part of the judgment awarding punitive damages, which is reversed and remanded for proceedings consistent with this opinion.

No error in part, reversed in part and remanded.

Notes and Questions

1. Should the *Muse* duty extend to all situations in which the physician and the hospital administration are in conflict? If the physician always prevails, then how does a hospital control its costs and its bad debts? Why does the court treat health care as special in this case? Surely a grocery store does not have to give us free groceries if we are short of cash as the checkout counter, nor does our landlord have to allow us to stay for free if we cannot cover our next month's rent. Is it simply the advantage of hindsight here that impels the court's allowance of such a duty on hospitals?

2. How does this holding square with the *Wickline* and *Wilson* decisions discussed in Chapter 4, supra. What can a hospital do in such situations? Offer free care?

3. Does such a duty extend as well to managed care organizations, whose very design is premised on mechanisms for containing health care costs? What would happen to the underlying premises of cost control in managed care organizations, if the *Muse* doctrine were held to apply?

D. STRICT LIABILITY

KARIBJANIAN v. THOMAS JEFFERSON
UNIVERSITY HOSPITAL

United States District Court, Eastern District of Pennsylvania, 1989.
717 F.Supp. 1081.

LORD.

Plaintiff claims that her husband died as a result of exposure in 1956 to the substance Thorotrast, a form of thorium dioxide, with which he was injected during a diagnostic medical procedure called a cerebral arteriography.[1] She alleges Thorotrast is an inherently unsafe product and that defendants knew or should have known that it is so. Defendant Thomas Jefferson University Hospital ("Hospital") moves to dismiss several paragraphs of the complaint, pursuant to Fed.R.Civ.P. 12(b)(6). * * * [ ]

* * *

Finally, the Hospital asks me to dismiss paragraphs 80 and 81 of the complaint, which allege

80. [The Hospital] sold, supplied and/or distributed a defective and dangerous product, Thorotrast, which was administered to plaintiff's decedent substantially unchanged from the form that it was received in.

81. [The Hospital] is strictly liable to plaintiff's decedent for the injuries and resulting death sustained under §§ 402A and/or 519 and 520 of the *Restatement (Second) of Torts* as adopted in the Commonwealth of Pennsylvania.

Section 402A provides, in part, that

(1) One who sells any product in a defective condition unreasonably dangerous to the user or consumer * * * is subject to liability * * * if (a) the seller is engaged in the business of selling such a product. * * *

The Hospital cites two Superior Court decisions which hold that a hospital cannot be liable under § 402A when a defective surgical tool injures a patient during an operation. *Podrat v. Codman–Shurtleff*, 384 Pa.Super. 404, 558 A.2d 895 (1989) (forceps); *Grubb v. Albert Einstein Medical Center*, 255 Pa.Super. 381, 387 A.2d 480 (1978) (bone plug cutter).[4] The *Podrat* court reasoned that a hospital is primarily in the business of supplying services, and "supplies" surgical tools only incidentally; and that the medical service (a back operation) could not have been performed without the use of the instrument. ___ Pa.Super. at ___, 558 A.2d at 898. The Hospital contends that likewise it was not in the "business of selling" Thorotrast; rather that it was in the business of providing services.

---

1. According to *Stedman's Medical Dictionary*, 5th Ed. (1982), a cerebral arteriography, also called a cerebral angiography, is "visualization of an artery or arteries by x-rays after injection of a radiopaque contrast medium." "[I]njection may be made by percutaneous puncture or after exposure. * * * " It appears from the complaint that Thorotrast was used as the contrast medium.

4. In *Grubb*, the per curiam opinion states that a hospital can be liable under § 402A; however, four of the seven judges dissented from this statement, and the hospital was held liable only under a negligence theory.

Plaintiff seeks to limit the holding in *Podrat* to products which are approved but turn out to be defective; she argues that Thorotrast, because it is alleged to be inherently unsafe, is distinguishable. I do not find this proposed distinction persuasive.

It might be supposed that surgical tools like the forceps in *Podrat* and the bone plug cutter in *Grubb* are different from contrast media because those surgical tools may be reused on a number of patients, while a dose of Thorotrast is completely consumed by a single patient. However, in *Francioni v. Gibsonia,* 472 Pa. 362, 372 A.2d 736, 739 (1977), the court held that lessors of durable products are liable to the same degree as sellers of such products.

A decision of a state's intermediate appellate court "is a datum for ascertaining state law which is not to be disregarded by a federal court unless it is convinced by other persuasive data that the highest court of the state would decide otherwise." [] There are, I think, significant data which suggest Pennsylvania's Supreme Court would in some circumstances hold a hospital liable under § 402A as a seller of a product like Thorotrast, if it is the product itself rather than the procedure by which it was administered which is alleged to have been defective.

Comment (f) to § 402A explains what the *Restatement's* authors meant by the "business of selling."

It is not necessary that the seller be engaged solely in the business of selling such products. Thus the rule applies to the owner of a motion picture theatre who sells popcorn or ice cream, either for consumption on the premises or in packages to be taken home.

The rule does not, however, apply to the occasional seller of food or other such products who is not engaged in that activity as a part of his business. Thus it does not apply to the housewife who, on one occasion, sells to her neighbor a jar of jam. * * *

So long as a hospital *regularly* supplies contrast media to its patients, albeit as an incidental part of its service operations, it seems to fall within § 402A as explained by comment (f). The comment draws no distinction between suppliers of goods who also supply services, and those suppliers who simply supply goods.

* * *

It is not beyond doubt that plaintiff can prove no facts which would establish that the Hospital was a seller of Thorotrast for purposes of § 402A. Unlike the product auctioned in *Musser,* the Thorotrast allegedly came from the Hospital's own inventory, ¶ 33, which I take to mean the Hospital owned it until it supplied it to plaintiff's decedent, via his physician, and that the Hospital regularly supplied Thorotrast to other patients. Plaintiff must be given the opportunity to present evidence concerning the other factors identified in *Musser* and *Francioni.*

I am also influenced by the thoughtful discussion of Judge Pollak in *Villari v. Terminix,* 677 F.Supp. 330, 333–334 (E.D.Pa.1987), in which he held that a professional pesticide application firm could be liable under § 402A even though it provided services as well as the pesticides themselves.[5] Judge

5. To offer another analogy, a restaurant   patron who enjoys an exquisite souffle values

Pollak noted that the defendant was the sole "retail" supplier of the pesticide, and that it told its customers that the product was safe. On the other hand, at least one court, in California, has held that hospitals cannot be liable under § 402A for defective drugs, under reasoning similar to that in *Podrat. Carmichael v. Reitz,* 17 Cal.App.3d 958, 95 Cal.Rptr. 381 (1971). *See also Flynn v. Langfitt,* 710 F.Supp. 150, 152 (E.D.Pa.1989) (hospital not liable under § 402A for defective tissue graft).

I will deny the Hospital's motion to dismiss ¶¶ 80 and 81 of the complaint. Plaintiff will, however, have to establish the factual bases I outlined above before she can recover against the Hospital under § 402A. Neither party has briefed the question of whether the Hospital can be liable under § 519 and § 520 of the *Restatement (Second) of Torts,* dealing with abnormally dangerous activities. I will leave that imaginative theory of liability for another day.

Notes and Questions

1. The hospital in *Karibjanian* considers Pennsylvania Superior Court cases rejecting the application of Restatement (Second) Torts, section 402A, to hospitals for defective surgical tools. It then rejects these decisions as predictive of what the Pennsylvania Supreme Court might do. In Podrat v. Codman–Shurtleff, Inc., 384 Pa.Super. 404, 558 A.2d 895 (1989) (involving forceps that broke, leaving piece in patient's disc space), the court stressed the hospital's actual function of providing a service to a patient. The instrument's use was simply incidental to the provision of this medical service. In Grubb v. Albert Einstein Medical Center, 255 Pa.Super. 381, 387 A.2d 480 (1978) (defective plug cutter), the per curiam opinion stated that a hospital could be liable under § 402A; however, since four of the seven judges dissented, the hospital was liable only under a negligence theory.

What is the "persuasive data" that leads the court to reject these lower court decisions? The court does not seem impressed by the argument that providers of medical services should be treated specially. It cites as analogous activities auctioneering and pesticide application. What facts must the plaintiff now establish before she can recover against the hospital?

How about the analogy in footnote 5? Is the provision of expensive restaurant food and service an apt comparison to hospital-based care involving drugs and devices? A chef cannot, after all, make a souffle without eggs; neither can a surgeon operate on a patient without medical devices, nor a radiologist do testing without contrast media. A plurality of the Pennsylvania Superior Court in *Grubb,* supra, in dicta, stated that " * * * if a hospital supplies equipment to an operating physician the hospital must appraise themselves of the risks involved and adopt every effort to insure the safety of the equipment chosen."

2. The court also suggests, in a tantalizing last paragraph, that the hospital might be liable under sections 519 and 520 of the Restatement (Second) of Torts, Abnormally Dangerous Activities, which the plaintiffs had pleaded. Is the court kidding? Or is there a possible argument to be made against hospital-based health care? See the discussion in Chapter 1 on iatrogenic injury.

the services of the chef more than the eggs with which it is made, since the eggs could be had for less than a dollar at any store. Nonetheless, if fate has it that the eggs are bad, the restaurant would be liable under § 402A as a supplier of eggs, even though the eggs were but an incidental part of what the patron paid for. And this is not to mention the services of the maitre d' who seats her, and the waiter who serves her.

3. A medical intervention often requires the use of medical products: knee joints, bone graft material, pig heart valves. Breast implant prostheses are a common example of such a service-product intervention. Courts apply strict liability to the distributors of such products but are reluctant to extend strict liability to a health care provider using the product in a way incidental to the primary function of providing medical services. See, e.g., Cafazzo v. Central Medical Health Services, 430 Pa.Super. 480, 635 A.2d 151 (Pa.Super.1993)(mandibular prosthesis); Hoff v. Zimmer, 746 F.Supp. 872 (W.D.Wis.1990)(hip prosthesis); Hector v. Cedars–Sinai Medical Center, 180 Cal.App.3d 493, 225 Cal.Rptr. 595 (2d Dist.1986) (pacemaker). Contra, see Budding v. SSM Healthcare System, 19 S.W.3d 678 (Mo. 2000).

4. The devices that a hospital furnishes its staff and patients, as part of the provision of medical service, must be properly maintained. Strict liability arguments imported from product defects litigation have made some inroads in lawsuits against hospitals. Both implied warranty doctrine and Section 402A of the Restatement, Second, have on rare occasions been applied to devices used in hospitals. The growth of technological medicine has made physicians increasingly dependent upon diagnostic machinery, computer-assisted tests, and drugs and devices. Many of the *res ipsa loquitur* cases, for example, involve medical devices that failed during surgery. These devices are bought by a hospital's purchasing department, subject to the controls imposed by the hospital's administration. The standard use of devices such as fetal monitors and CT scanners implicate the hospital as middleman in a stream of commerce of the sort courts discuss in products liability cases.

In Skelton v. Druid City Hosp. Board, 459 So.2d 818 (Ala.1984), a suture needle broke off in the patient during ventral hernia repair. These needles were reused several times by the hospital, and there was no way to be sure exactly how many times. Section 2–315 of the Uniform Commercial Code, implied warranty of fitness for a particular purpose, was applied to this "hybrid" service-product transaction between hospital and patient. The court held:

> The gist of an action under this section is reliance. Patients are rarely in a position to judge the quality of the medical supplies and other goods sold to them and used in their care; often, those supplies are of an inherently dangerous nature. The complete dependence of patients on the staff of a hospital to choose fit products justifies the imposition of an implied warranty under s. 7–2–315, whether the hospital is a "merchant" or not. Id. at 823.

5. Hospitals often reuse medical devices, such as pulmonary catheters, hemodialyzers, biopsy needles, electrosurgical devices, and endotracheal tubes. The pressure to contain costs is one of the primary reasons for this practice. When a reused device proves defective and a patient is injured as a result, liability may fall on the manufacturer, the retailer, the hospital, and health care professionals. Strict liability and breach of warranty theories, as well as negligence, are likely to be attractive doctrines to apply, by analogy to the products liability area generally. Janice M. Hogan and Thomas E. Cdolonna, 53 Food & Drug L.J. 385 (1998).

6. Drugs are normally prescribed by the treating physician, and are purchased by the patient from third party pharmacies. In the hospital setting, however, the patient is usually administered a variety of drugs as part of treatment and these drugs come from hospital supplies. Should a duty to warn a patient of possible side-effects of the drug fall on the hospital as well as the treating physician? The court in *Karibjanian* allowed the plaintiff's cause of action claiming a hospital duty to supervise physicians, which included ensuring that

informed consent was obtained. This has not been a popular position. See, e.g., Kirk v. Michael Reese Hospital and Medical Center, 117 Ill.2d 507, 111 Ill.Dec. 944, 513 N.E.2d 387 (1987), where the Illinois Supreme Court held that a hospital which had dispensed and administered psychotropic drugs to the plaintiff as an inpatient had no duty to warn him of the drug's side effects upon discharge a few hours later.

7. Hospital administrative and mechanical services have been held to be subject potentially to strict liability, Johnson v. Sears, 355 F.Supp. 1065, 1067 (E.D.Wis.1973), as have hospital operations that are not "integrally related to its primary function of providing medical services", Silverhart v. Mount Zion Hospital, 20 Cal.App.3d 1022, 98 Cal.Rptr. 187 (1971) (gift shop as example of such a nonessential function).

Problem: The Monitor Failed

Jane Rudd has approached you as to the merits of a suit for injuries sustained by her infant during childbirth. Ms. Rudd went into labor at full term and was admitted to the Columbia Hospital. She was examined, placed in a labor room, and attached to a fetal monitor. She objected to the use of the monitor, but the Chief Resident, after a lengthy debate with the staff, strongly urged her to use it. She finally acquiesced. The monitor is manufactured by Rohm Instruments and leased to the hospital by Medex Equipment Ltd. Medex maintains the monitors it leases to hospitals on a monthly basis, or as needed.

The nurse responsible for Ms. Rudd checked the monitor printout several times an hour. The machine has a warning buzzer that sounds if abnormal fetal heart rates are detected. It did not sound at any time. Neither the doctor nor the nurses checked the fetal heart rate with a stethoscope after the first two hours. At 6 a.m. on Sunday morning, the doctor on duty delivered Ms. Rudd's baby. Its umbilical cord was wrapped tightly around its neck and it showed signs of fetal distress at delivery. The child has extensive brain damage due to oxygen deprivation.

Because of comments made by the delivery room nurse, Ms. Rudd believes that the monitor may have malfunctioned and failed to either detect or print out variations in fetal heartrate near the end of labor.

What tort doctrines can you invoke in drafting a complaint? What defendants might you pursue? What further information do you need?

E. THE EMERGENCE OF CORPORATE NEGLIGENCE

The courts' stretching of vicarious liability doctrine to sweep in doctors as conduits to hospital liability led inevitably to the direct imposition of corporate negligence liability on the hospital. The courts effectively made the medical personnel who used the hospital part of this "enterprise", whether they were staff employees or independent contractors.

1. The Duty to Protect Patients From Medical Staff Negligence

The next step was to hold the hospital directly liable for the failure of administrators and staff to properly monitor and supervise the delivery of health care within the hospital. The leading case is *Darling v. Charleston Community Memorial Hospital*.

DARLING v. CHARLESTON COMMUNITY MEMORIAL HOSPITAL

Supreme Court of Illinois, 1965.
33 Ill.2d 326, 211 N.E.2d 253.

This action was brought on behalf of Dorrence Darling II, a minor (hereafter plaintiff), by his father and next friend, to recover damages for allegedly negligent medical and hospital treatment which necessitated the amputation of his right leg below the knee. The action was commenced against the Charleston Community Memorial Hospital and Dr. John R. Alexander, but prior to trial the action was dismissed as to Dr. Alexander, pursuant to a covenant not to sue. The jury returned a verdict against the hospital in the sum of $150,000. This amount was reduced by $40,000, the amount of the settlement with the doctor. The judgment in favor of the plaintiff in the sum of $110,000 was affirmed on appeal by the Appellate Court for the Fourth District, which granted a certificate of importance. 50 Ill.App.2d 253, 200 N.E.2d 149.

On November 5, 1960, the plaintiff, who was 18 years old, broke his leg while playing in a college football game. He was taken to the emergency room at the defendant hospital where Dr. Alexander, who was on emergency call that day, treated him. Dr. Alexander, with the assistance of hospital personnel, applied traction and placed the leg in a plaster cast. A heat cradle was applied to dry the cast. Not long after the application of the cast plaintiff was in great pain and his toes, which protruded from the cast, became swollen and dark in color. They eventually became cold and insensitive. On the evening of November 6, Dr. Alexander "notched" the cast around the toes, and on the afternoon of the next day he cut the cast approximately three inches up from the foot. On November 8 he split the sides of the cast with a Stryker saw; in the course of cutting the cast the plaintiff's leg was cut on both sides. Blood and other seepage were observed by the nurses and others, and there was a stench in the room, which one witness said was the worst he had smelled since World War II. The plaintiff remained in Charleston Hospital until November 19, when he was transferred to Barnes Hospital in St. Louis and placed under the care of Dr. Fred Reynolds, head of orthopedic surgery at Washington University School of Medicine and Barnes Hospital. Dr. Reynolds found that the fractured leg contained a considerable amount of dead tissue which in his opinion resulted from interference with the circulation of blood in the limb caused by swelling or hemorrhaging of the leg against the construction of the cast. Dr. Reynolds performed several operations in a futile attempt to save the leg but ultimately it had to be amputated eight inches below the knee.

The evidence before the jury is set forth at length in the opinion of the Appellate Court and need not be stated in detail here. The plaintiff contends that it established that the defendant was negligent in permitting Dr. Alexander to do orthopedic work of the kind required in this case, and not requiring him to review his operative procedures to bring them up to date; in failing, through its medical staff, to exercise adequate supervision over the case, especially since Dr. Alexander had been placed on emergency duty by the hospital, and in not requiring consultation, particularly after complications had developed. Plaintiff contends also that in a case which developed as this one did, it was the duty of the nurses to watch the protruding toes constantly for changes of color, temperature and movement, and to check circulation every ten to twenty minutes, whereas the proof showed that these things were done only a few times a day. Plaintiff argues that it was the duty of the hospital staff to see that these procedures were followed, and that either the nurses were derelict in failing to report developments in the case to the hospital administrator, he was derelict in bringing them to the attention of the medical staff, or the staff was negligent in failing to take action. Defendant is a licensed and accredited hospital, and the plaintiff contends that the licensing regulations, accreditation standards, and its own bylaws define the hospital's duty, and that an infraction of them imposes liability for the resulting injury.

* * *

The basic dispute, as posed by the parties, centers upon the duty that rested upon the defendant hospital. That dispute involves the effect to be given to evidence concerning the community standard of care and diligence, and also the effect to be given to hospital regulations adopted by the State Department of Public Health under the Hospital Licensing Act (Ill.Rev.Stat. 1963, chap. 111½, pars. 142–157.), to the Standards for Hospital Accreditation of the American Hospital Association, and to the bylaws of the defendant.

As has been seen, the defendant argues in this court that its duty is to be determined by the care customarily offered by hospitals generally in its community. Strictly speaking, the question is not one of duty, for " * * * in negligence cases, the duty is always the same, to conform to the legal standard of reasonable conduct in the light of the apparent risk. What the defendant must do, or must not do, is a question of the standard of conduct required to satisfy the duty." (Prosser on Torts, 3rd ed. at 331.) * * * Custom is relevant in determining the standard of care because it illustrates what is feasible, it suggests a body of knowledge of which the defendant should be aware, and it warns of the possibility of far-reaching consequences if a higher standard is required. [ ] But custom should never be conclusive.

In the present case the regulations, standards, and bylaws which the plaintiff introduced into evidence, performed much the same function as did evidence of custom. This evidence aided the jury in deciding what was feasible and what the defendant knew or should have known. It did not conclusively determine the standard of care and the jury was not instructed that it did.

"The conception that the hospital does not undertake to treat the patient, does not undertake to act through its doctors and nurses, but undertakes instead simply to procure them to act upon their own responsibility, no longer reflects the fact. Present-day hospitals, as their manner of operation plainly demonstrates, do far more than furnish facilities for treatment. They regularly employ on a salary basis a large staff of physicians, nurses and interns, as well as administrative and manual workers, and they charge patients for medical care and treatment, collecting for such services, if necessary, by legal action. Certainly, the person who avails himself of 'hospital facilities' expects that the hospital will attempt to cure him, not that its nurses or other employees will act on their own responsibility." (Fuld, J., in Bing v. Thunig (1957), 2 N.Y.2d 656, 163 N.Y.S.2d 3, 11, 143 N.E.2d 3, 8.) The Standards for

Hospital Accreditation, the state licensing regulations and the defendant's bylaws demonstrate that the medical profession and other responsible authorities regard it as both desirable and feasible that a hospital assume certain responsibilities for the care of the patient.

* * * Therefore we need not analyze all of the issues submitted to the jury. Two of them were that the defendant had negligently: "5. Failed to have a sufficient number of trained nurses for bedside care of all patients at all times capable of recognizing the progressive gangrenous condition of the plaintiff's right leg, and of bringing the same to the attention of the hospital administration and to the medical staff so that adequate consultation could have been secured and such conditions rectified; * * * 7. Failed to require consultation with or examination by members of the hospital surgical staff skilled in such treatment; or to review the treatment rendered to the plaintiff and to require consultants to be called in as needed."

We believe that the jury verdict is supportable on either of these grounds. On the basis of the evidence before it the jury could reasonably have concluded that the nurses did not test for circulation in the leg as frequently as necessary, that skilled nurses would have promptly recognized the conditions that signalled a dangerous impairment of circulation in the plaintiff's leg, and would have known that the condition would become irreversible in a matter of hours. At that point it became the nurses' duty to inform the attending physician, and if he failed to act, to advise the hospital authorities so that appropriate action might be taken. As to consultation, there is no dispute that the hospital failed to review Dr. Alexander's work or require a consultation; the only issue is whether its failure to do so was negligence. On the evidence before it the jury could reasonably have found that it was.

[The remainder of the opinion, discussing expert testimony and damages, is omitted.]

Notes and Questions

1. Consider the issues submitted to the jury. It is alleged that both the nurses and the administrators were negligent in not taking steps to curtail Dr. Alexander's handling of the case. How can a nurse "blow the whistle" on a doctor without risking damage to her own career? See the section on labor law in health care institutions, infra. How can a nurse exercise medical judgment in violation of Medical Practice statutes?

In Jensen v. Archbishop Bergan Mercy Hospital, 236 Neb. 1, 459 N.W.2d 178, 183 (1990), the plaintiffs alleged that the nursing staff should have altered the attending physician's orders if they had reason to believe they were wrong. The court disagreed, holding that " * * * hospital staff members lack authority to alter or depart from an attending physician's order for a hospital patient and lack authority to determine what is a proper course of medical treatment for a hospitalized patient. The foregoing is recognition of the realities and practicalities inherent in the physician-hospital nurse relationship."

In Gafner v. Down East Community Hospital, 735 A.2d 969 (Me.1999), the plaintiff's daughter suffered a brachial plexus injury while the defendant physician was trying to deliver the baby. The plaintiff argued that the hospital's lack of written policies regarding consultation constituted corporate negligence. Maine refused to recognize corporate negligence in an action against independent physicians for failing to control their actions. "Creating a duty that would place external controls upon the medical judgments and actions of physicians should not be undertaken without a thorough and thoughtful analysis. We decline to create such a duty from whole cloth and therefore decline to recognize the cause of action . . . . "

2. *Darling* disclosed the prevailing attitude of hospital administrators toward affiliated doctors, reflecting the earlier concept of the doctor as independent contractor. The hospital administrator was subjected to a prolonged cross-examination by the plaintiff's attorney exploring his obligations to evaluate doctor training and conduct. The administrator testified:

"As the Board's representative, I did nothing to see that Dr. Alexander reviewed his operating techniques for the handling of broken bones. So far as I know, Dr. Alexander may not have reviewed his operating techniques since he was first licensed to practice in 1928. No examinations were ever given. I never asked questions of the doctor about this matter. The governing board, neither through me nor through any other designated administrative representative, ever checked up on the ability of Dr. Alexander as compared by medical text books. I had access at the hospital to some good orthopedic books. * * * Other than buying these books, I never made any effort to see that Dr. Alexander, or any other physician admitted to practice more than thirty years ago, read them." Darling v. Charleston Community Memorial Hosp., 50 Ill.App.2d 253, 295, 200 N.E.2d 149, 171 (1964).

How can a hospital administrator devise procedures to trigger an alarm when a physician is incompetent? Must the administrator himself be an M.D.? Can you think of methods that would have avoided the *Darling* tragedy? Consider the ideas developed by Leape in Chapter 1. What systems might you implement to prevent such errors?

In Albain v. Flower Hospital, 50 Ohio St.3d 251, 553 N.E.2d 1038, 1046 (1990), the Ohio Supreme Court recognized a hospital's independent duty to exercise due care in granting staff privileges and retaining competent physicians, but qualified the duty. The Court held that an act of physician malpractice does not create a presumption that the hospital negligently granted staff privileges, and that a hospital is not expected "to constantly supervise and second-guess the activities of its physicians, beyond the duty to remove a known incompetent. Most hospital administrators are laypersons with no medical training at all." They added: " * * * the hospital is not an *insurer* of the skills of physicians to whom it has granted staff privileges."

3. See, for a description of the *Darling* case by the plaintiff's lawyer, Appelman, Hospital Liability for Acts of Nonsalaried Staff Physicians, Personal Injury Annual 161 (1964); see also (describing the case), Spero, Hospital Liability, 15 Trial 22 (Sept. 1979). For an older case imposing direct liability for the failure of a hospital to control the use of its facilities, see Hendrickson v. Hodkin, 276 N.Y. 252, 11 N.E.2d 899 (1937) (hospital liable for allowing a quack to treat a patient on its premises).

* * *

THOMPSON v. NASON

Supreme Court of Pennsylvania, 1991.
527 Pa. 330, 591 A.2d 703.

ZAPPALA, JUSTICE.

Allocatur was granted to examine the novel issue of whether a theory of corporate liability with respect to hospitals should be recognized in this Commonwealth. For the reasons set forth below, we adopt today the theory of corporate liability as it relates to hospitals. * * *

* * *

Considering this predicate to our analysis, we now turn to the record which contains the facts underlying this personal injury action. At approximately 7 a.m. on March 16, 1978, Appellee, Linda A. Thompson, was involved in an automobile accident with a school bus. Mrs. Thompson was transported by ambulance from the accident scene to Nason Hospital's emergency room where she was admitted with head and leg injuries. The hospital's emergency room personnel were advised by Appellee, Donald A. Thompson, that his wife was taking the drug Coumadin, that she had a permanent pacemaker, and that she took other heart medications.

Subsequent to Mrs. Thompson's admission to Nason Hospital, Dr. Edward D. Schultz, a general practitioner who enjoyed staff privileges at Nason Hospital, entered the hospital via the emergency room to make his rounds. Although Dr. Schultz was not assigned duty in the emergency room, an on-duty hospital nurse asked him to attend Mrs. Thompson due to a prior physician-patient relationship. Dr. Schultz examined Mrs. Thompson and diagnosed her as suffering from multiple injuries including extensive lacerations over her left eye and the back of her scalp, constricted pupils, enlarged heart with a Grade III micro-systolic murmur, a brain concussion and amnesia. X-rays that were taken revealed fractures of the right tibia and right heel.

Following Dr. Schultz's examination and diagnosis, Dr. Larry Jones, an ophthalmologist, sutured the lacerations over Mrs. Thompson's left eye. It was during that time that Dr. Schultz consulted with Dr. Rao concerning orthopedic repairs. Dr. Rao advised conservative therapy until her critical medical condition improved.

Dr. Schultz knew Mrs. Thompson was suffering from rheumatic heart and mitral valve disease and was on anticoagulant therapy. Because he had no specific training in establishing dosages for such therapy, Dr. Schultz called Dr. Marvin H. Meisner, a cardiologist who was treating Mrs. Thompson with an anticoagulant therapy. Although Dr. Meisner was unavailable, Dr. Schultz did speak with Dr. Meisner's associate Dr. Steven P. Draskoczy.

Mrs. Thompson had remained in the emergency room during this time. Her condition, however, showed no sign of improvement. Due to both the multiple trauma received in the accident and her pre-existing heart disease, Dr. Schultz, as attending physician, admitted her to Nason Hospital's intensive care unit at 11:20 a.m.

The next morning at 8:30 a.m., Dr. Mark Paris, a general surgeon on staff at Nason Hospital, examined Mrs. Thompson. He found that she was unable to move her left foot and toes. It was also noted by Dr. Paris that the patient had a positive Babinski—a neurological sign of an intracerebral problem. Twelve hours later, Dr. Schultz examined Mrs. Thompson and found more bleeding in her eye. He also indicated in the progress notes that the problem with her left leg was that it was neurological.

On March 18, 1978, the third day of her hospitalization, Dr. Larry Jones, the ophthalmologist who treated her in the emergency room, examined her in the intensive care unit. He indicated in the progress notes an "increased hematuria secondary to anticoagulation. Right eye now involved". Dr. Schultz also examined Mrs. Thompson that day and noted the decreased movement of her left leg was neurologic. Dr. Paris's progress note that date approved the withholding of Coumadin and the continued use of Heparin.

The following day, Mrs. Thompson had complete paralysis of the left side. Upon examination by Dr. Schultz he questioned whether she needed to be under the care of a neurologist or needed to be watched there. At 10:30 a.m. that day, Dr. Schultz transferred her to the Hershey Medical Center because of her progressive neurological problem.

Linda Thompson underwent tests at the Hershey Medical Center. The results of the tests revealed that she had a large intracerebral hematoma in the right frontal temporal and parietal lobes of the brain. She was subsequently discharged on April 1, 1978, without regaining the motor function of her left side.

* * * The complaint alleged inter alia that Mrs. Thompson's injuries were the direct and proximate result of the negligence of Nason Hospital acting through its agents, servants and employees in failing to adequately examine and treat her, in failing to follow its rules relative to consultations and in failing to monitor her conditions during treatment. * * *

* * *

The first issue Nason Hospital raised is whether the Superior Court erred in adopting a theory of corporate liability with respect to a hospital. This issue had not heretofore been determined by the Court. Nason Hospital contends that it had no duty to observe, supervise or control the actual treatment of Linda Thompson.

Hospitals in the past enjoyed absolute immunity from tort liability. [ ] The basis of that immunity was the perception that hospitals functioned as charitable organizations. [ ] However, hospitals have evolved into highly sophisticated corporations operating primarily on a fee-for-service basis. The corporate hospital of today has assumed the role of a comprehensive health center with responsibility for arranging and coordinating the total health care of its patients. As a result of this metamorphosis, hospital immunity was eliminated. [ ]

Not surprisingly, the by-product of eliminating hospital immunity has been the filing of malpractice actions against hospitals. Courts have recognized several bases on which hospitals may be subject to liability including respondeat superior, ostensible agency and corporate negligence. [ ]

The development of hospital liability in this Commonwealth mirrored that which occurred in other jurisdictions. * * * We now turn our attention to the theory of corporate liability with respect to the hospital, which was first recognized in this Commonwealth by the court below.

Corporate negligence is a doctrine under which the hospital is liable if it fails to uphold the proper standard of care owed the patient, which is to ensure the patient's safety and well-being while at the hospital. This theory of liability creates a nondelegable duty which the hospital owes directly to a patient. Therefore, an injured party does not have to rely on and establish the negligence of a third party.

The hospital's duties have been classified into four general areas: (1) a duty to use reasonable care in the maintenance of safe and adequate facilities and equipment—Candler General Hospital Inc. v. Purvis, 123 Ga.App. 334, 181 S.E.2d 77 (1971); (2) a duty to select and retain only competent physicians—Johnson v. Misericordia Community Hospital, 99 Wis.2d 708, 301 N.W.2d 156 (1981); (3) a duty to oversee all persons who practice medicine within its walls as to patient care—Darling v. Charleston Community Memorial Hospital, supra.; and (4) a duty to formulate, adopt and enforce adequate rules and policies to ensure quality care for the patients–Wood v. Samaritan Institution, 26 Cal.2d 847, 161 P.2d 556 (Cal. Ct. App.1945). [ ]

Other jurisdictions have embraced this doctrine of corporate negligence or corporate liability such as to warrant it being called an "emerging trend". [ ]

* * *

Today, we take a step beyond the hospital's duty of care delineated in Riddle in full recognition of the corporate hospital's role in the total health care of its patients. In so doing, we adopt as a theory of hospital liability the doctrine of corporate negligence or corporate liability under which the hospital is liable if it fails to uphold the proper standard of care owed its patient. In addition, we fully embrace the aforementioned four categories of the hospital's duties. It is important to note that for a hospital to be charged with negligence, it is necessary to show that the hospital had actual or constructive knowledge of the defect or procedures which created the harm. [ ] Furthermore, the hospital's negligence must have been a substantial factor in bringing about the harm to the injured party. [ ].

The final question Nason Hospital raises is did Superior Court err in finding that there was a material issue of fact with respect to the hospital's duty to monitor and review medical services provided within its facilities. Nason Hospital contends that during Linda Thompson's hospitalization, it did not become aware of any exceptional circumstance which would require or justify its intervention into her treatment. The Hospital Association of Pennsylvania, as amicus curiae, argues that it is neither realistic nor appropriate to expect the hospital to conduct daily review and supervision of the independent medical judgment of each member of the medical staff of which it may have actual or constructive knowledge.

Conversely, Appellees argue that Nason Hospital was negligent in failing to monitor the medical services provided Mrs. Thompson. Specifically, Appellees claim that the hospital ignored its Rules and Regulations governing Medical Staff by failing to ensure the patient received adequate medical attention through physician consultations. Appellees also contend that Nason Hospital's medical staff members and personnel treating Mrs. Thompson were aware of her deteriorating condition, brought about by being over anticoagulated, yet did nothing.

It is well established that a hospital staff member or employee has a duty to recognize and report abnormalities in the treatment and condition of its patients. [ ] If the attending physician fails to act after being informed of such abnormalities, it is then incumbent upon the hospital staff member or employee to so advise the hospital authorities so that appropriate action might be taken. [ ] When there is a failure to report changes in a patient's condition and/or to question a physician's order which is not in accord with standard medical practice and the patient is injured as a result, the hospital will be liable for such negligence. [ ]

A thorough review of the record of this case convinces us that there is a sufficient question of material fact presented as to whether Nason Hospital was negligent in supervising the quality of the medical care Mrs. Thompson received, such that the trial court could not have properly granted summary judgment on the issue of corporate liability.

The order of Superior Court is affirmed. Jurisdiction is relinquished.

Notes and Questions

1. What does *Thompson* add to *Darling*'s discussion of the scope of corporate negligence? The fourth duty, "to formulate, adopt and enforce adequate rules and policies to ensure quality care for the patients", moves well beyond monitoring staff, drawing our scrutiny to how the institution operates as a system, and allowing plaintiffs to search for negligence in the very design of the operating framework of the hospital. Is this a useful advance over the caselaw thus far?

2. **Selection and retention of medical staff.** Probably the most important function of a hospital is to select high quality physicians for its medical staff. A typical hospital has several categories of practicing physicians. The largest category is comprised of private physicians with staff privileges. These privileges include the right of the physicians to admit and discharge their private patients to the hospital and the right to use the hospital's facilities. Hospitals will also have physicians in training present, including interns, residents, and externs. Hospitals will often also have full-time salaried physicians, including teaching hospital faculty, and physicians under contract with the hospital to provide services for an agreed upon price. H. Ward Classen, Hospital Liability for Independent Contractors: Where Do We Go From Here?, 40 Ark.L.Rev. 469, 478 (1987).

The organized medical staff of a hospital, private physicians with privileges, comprises the largest group of hospital-based physicians. The medical staff governs the hospital's provision of medical services. The typical medical staff operates under its own bylaws, elects its own officers, and appoints its own committees. It is not simply another administrative component of the hospital, under the authority of the governing board of the hospital. While the hospital board must approve the staff's bylaws and can approve or disapprove particular staff actions, it cannot usually discipline individual physicians directly or appoint administrative officers to exercise direct authority. A hospital's medical staff is therefore a powerful body within the larger organization. See generally Clark C. Havighurst, Doctors and Hospitals: An Antitrust Perspective on Traditional Relationships, 1984 Duke L.J. 1071, 1084–92. The requirement of staff self-governance under

JCAHO standards maintains and reinforces this physician authority within hospitals.

The process by which the medical staff is selected is of crucial importance. A hospital has an obligation to its patients to investigate the qualifications of medical staff applicants. The Wisconsin Supreme Court elaborated on this obligation in Johnson v. Misericordia Community Hospital, 99 Wis.2d 708, 301 N.W.2d 156 (Wis. 1981).

> In summary, we hold that a hospital owes a duty to its patients to exercise reasonable care in the selection of its medical staff and in granting specialized privileges. The final appointing authority resides in the hospital's governing body, although it must rely on the medical staff and in particular the credentials committee (or committee of the whole) to investigate and evaluate an applicant's qualifications for the requested privileges. However, this delegation of the responsibility to investigate and evaluate the professional competence of applicants for clinical privileges does not relieve the governing body of its duty to appoint only qualified physicians and surgeons to its medical staff and periodically monitor and review their competency. The credentials committee (or committee of the whole) must investigate the qualifications of applicants. The facts of this case demonstrate that a hospital should, at a minimum, require completion of the application and verify the accuracy of the applicant's statements, especially in regard to his medical education, training and experience. Additionally, it should: (1) solicit information from the applicant's peers, including those not referenced in his application, who are knowledgeable about his education, training, experience, health, competence and ethical character; (2) determine if the applicant is currently licensed to practice in this state and if his licensure or registration has been or is currently being challenged; and (3) inquire whether the applicant has been involved in any adverse malpractice action and whether he has experienced a loss of medical organization membership or medical privileges or membership at any other hospital. The investigating committee must also evaluate the information gained through its inquiries and make a reasonable judgment as to the approval or denial of each application for staff privileges. The hospital will be charged with gaining and evaluating the knowledge that would have been acquired had it exercised ordinary care in investigating its medical staff applicants and the hospital's failure to exercise that degree of care, skill and judgment that is exercised by the average hospital in approving an applicant's request for privileges is negligence. This is not to say that hospitals are *insurers* of the competence of their medical staff, for a hospital will not be negligent if it exercises the noted standard of care in selecting its staff. Id. 174–75.

Hospitals are expected to investigate adverse information with regard to possible appointments or reappointments of medical staff. See Elam v. College Park Hospital, 132 Cal.App.3d 332, 183 Cal.Rptr. 156 (1982); Purcell v. Zimbelman, 18 Ariz.App. 75, 500 P.2d 335 (1972); Oehler v. Humana Inc., 105 Nev. 348, 775 P.2d 1271 (Nev.1989).

3. The hospital must also have proper procedures developed to detect impostors. Insinga v. LaBella, 543 So.2d 209 (Fla.1989) (non physician fraudulently obtained an appointment to the medical staff, after having assumed the name of a deceased Italian physician; the court applied corporate negligence.)

4. A hospital should also properly restrict the clinical privileges of staff physicians who are incompetent to handle certain procedures, or detect conceal-

ment by a staff doctor of medical errors. See Cronic v. Doud, 168 Ill.App.3d 665, 119 Ill.Dec. 708, 523 N.E.2d 176 (1988); Corleto v. Shore Memorial Hospital, 138 N.J.Super. 302, 350 A.2d 534 (1975).

5. The medical staff has also been held liable in a few cases independently for its failure to supervise and regulate the activity of its members. *Corleto,* supra.

6. Under the Health Care Quality Improvement Act of 1986 (HCQIA), hospitals must check a central registry, a national database maintained by the Unisys Corporation under contract with the Department of Health and Human Services, before a new staff appointment is made. This National Practitioner Data Bank contains information on individual physicians who have been disciplined, had malpractice claims filed against them, or had privileges revoked or limited. If the hospital fails to check the registry, it is held constructively to have knowledge of any information it might have gotten from the inquiry. See discussion of staff privileges in Chapter 7, infra. The Data Bank has been criticized by the Government Accounting Office as having unreliable and incomplete data. See U.S. Government Accounting Office, National Practitioner Data Bank: Major Improvements are Needed to Enhance Data Bank's Reliability, *http://www.gao.gov.*

Equifax, a major credit reporting entity, operates a physician database to enable subscribers such as hospitals and managed care organizations to instantly verify physician credentials. The database has information on more than 600,000 U.S. physicians, including educational background, registrations for prescribing medications, board certifications and any other disciplinary actions that might have been taken by state or federal bodies. The sources for the database include the Drug Enforcement Administrations, the American Medical Association and state and federal licensing and regulatory agencies. Credentials Verifications Services are also available to hospitals and managed care organizations for a fee. See for example Medirisk at *www.medirisk.com.*

Problem: Proctoring Peers

You have been asked by Hilldale Adventist Hospital to advise them on the implications of their use of proctors for assessing candidates for medical staff privileges. The hospital has used Dr. Hook, a surgeon certified by the American Board of Orthopedic Surgery, as a proctor during two different operations on the plaintiff at two different hospitals during the process of evaluation of Dr. Frank DiBianco for staff privileges. Dr. Hook had been asked to observe ten surgeries by Dr. DiBianco and then file a report. He observed an operation on the plaintiff during one of these observations. Two months later, he was again asked to proctor Dr. DiBianco at another hospital, and he again observed a procedure on the plaintiff. Prior to each procedure, Dr. Hook had reviewed the x-rays and discussed the operative plan, but he otherwise had taken no part in the care and treatment of the plaintiff. He did not participate in the operations, did not scrub in, and always observed from outside the "sterile field". He got no payment for his proctoring efforts, and he had never met the plaintiff nor had any other contact with her.

Can Hilldale be liable for their use of Dr. Hook as a proctor? Can Dr. Hook be directly liable for failing to stop negligent work by Dr. DiBianco?

Problem: The "Love" Surgeon

You have recently been contacted by Ms. Helen Brown as to the merits of a suit against Drs. Ruth and Blue, physicians on staff at St. Helen's Medical Center (SHMC). Ms. Brown had gone to Dr. Blue, a urologist, for bladder infections and difficulties she experienced voiding urine. Blue performed surgery upon Brown but her condition failed to improve. She began to complain of constant bladder pain and of pain during sexual relations with her husband. Blue then referred her to Dr. Ruth for "exploratory pelvic laparotomy with lysis" and "vaginoplasty."

Dr. Ruth met with Brown prior to surgery. He explained to Brown that the pain she experienced during sexual relations was caused by her husband's penis striking her bladder. Ruth explained that he and Dr. Blue would perform surgery to place her bladder upon a "pedestal," and that this procedure would correct her problems voiding urine and alleviate the pain she suffered during intercourse. Ruth also indicated that he would do some "cosmetic things" to improve Brown's sex life.

Ruth and Blue had staff privileges at St. Helen's Medical Center (SHMC). The hospital required that a form letter be given by Dr. Ruth to each of his patients prior to the surgical procedures he did to Ms. Brown. The form letter, which bears the SHMC letterhead, stated:

"Dear Patient:

"The Executive Committee of the Medical Staff of St. Elizabeth Medical Center wishes to inform you that the 'female coital area reconstruction' surgery you are about to undergo is:

"1. Not documented by ordinary standards of scientific reporting and publication.

"2. Not a generally accepted procedure.

"3. As yet not duplicated by other investigators.

"4. Detailed only in non-scientific literature.

"You should be informed that the Executive Committee of the Medical Staff considers the aforementioned procedure an unproven, non-standard practice of gynecology."

Drs. Ruth and Blue performed "vaginal reconstruction surgery" upon Brown at SHMC, purportedly to correct her painful bladder condition. The surgery actually performed upon Brown consisted of an exploratory pelvic laparotomy, vaginal reconstruction, circumcision of the clitoris and insertion of a urinary catheter. The vaginal reconstruction consisted of, among other things, a redirection and elongation of her vagina.

Brown has told you that after her "love surgery," she continued to suffer from bladder infections and developed problems with urinary incontinence. Her bladder infections after the surgery were more frequent than before. Following the surgery, Brown could not engage in sexual relations without extreme pain and difficulties. At some point, she also began to develop severe kidney problems. She underwent further surgery to correct her problems, with the final surgery removing her right kidney. She continued to suffer bladder infections, difficulties voiding, problems during sexual intercourse, and periods of urinary incontinence. She also developed bowel problems sometime during her treatment with Ruth and Blue. She was told by a gynecologist two months before she came to your office that the surgery performed upon her could not be corrected, and that Dr. Ruth "had cut away everything."

Consider any theories you might develop against the hospital in a malpractice action.

2. The Duty to Protect Non-patients

Darling for the first time imposed a duty on the hospital administrators to supervise and evaluate care delivered by physicians within the hospital. The court drew on JCAHO standards, the hospital's own bylaws, and other documents in outlining the extent of the responsibility. Later cases refined and limited the concept of corporate negligence.

PEDROZA v. BRYANT

Supreme Court of Washington, 1984.
101 Wash.2d 226, 677 P.2d 166.

The issue before us is whether a hospital may be held liable under a theory of corporate negligence for its action in granting privileges to a nonemployee doctor who allegedly commits malpractice while in private practice off the hospital premises.

In December of 1978, Maria Pedroza was in her 35th week of pregnancy and under the care of Dr. Ben Bryant. During the week of December 3 through 9, Maria became ill and exhibited the classical symptoms of preeclampsia (a toxemia of pregnancy), namely, hypertension, headaches, and edema of the lower extremities. Mrs. Pedroza visited Dr. Bryant's office on December 6 and 7, and telephoned him on December 8. Dr. Bryant prescribed no medicine other than bed rest and aspirin. He did not refer Mrs. Pedroza to another health care provider.

On December 9, 1978, Maria Pedroza was admitted, comatose, to defendant Skagit Valley Hospital. She was admitted to surgery, with a diagnosis of irreversible cerebral death due to intracerebral hemorrhage resulting from eclampsia. Dr. Bryant was neither the admitting nor the treating physician for this hospitalization. Indeed, the hospital had, on April 13, 1977, limited Dr. Bryant's obstetrical and newborn privileges to Class II for the years 1977 and 1978. Dr. Bryant was thus required to consult with a Class I physician on all "seriously ill patients," including pregnancies with "major medical complications" and "[l]ate or severe toxemia of pregnancy." Thus, Dr. Bryant would not have been allowed to treat Maria Pedroza for eclampsia in the hospital.

In surgery, Mrs. Pedroza's child was successfully delivered by emergency cesarean section. After family consent was obtained, respiratory support for Mrs. Pedroza was discontinued on December 15, 1978, whereupon she died.

It should be noted at the outset that plaintiff is not claiming that defendant hospital is vicariously liable for the negligence of Dr. Bryant under the theory of respondeat superior. Dr. Bryant is an independent contractor, not an employee of defendant hospital. Plaintiff is instead relying solely on the doctrine of corporate negligence, which differs from respondeat superior in that it imposes on the hospital a nondelegable duty owed directly to the patient, regardless of the details of the doctor-hospital relationship. Plaintiff contends that defendant hospital owed a duty to Maria Pedroza of carefully selecting and reviewing the competency of its staff physicians. ("Staff physicians" are those doctors who have been given "staff privileges" at the hospital. A physician must be a member of the hospital's medical staff in order to regularly admit patients to the hospital.) Plaintiff alleges that defendant hospital breached this duty by allowing Dr. Bryant to possess staff privileges at the hospital, and that this breach was the proximate cause of Mrs. Pedroza's death.

II.

The first question we must address, then, is whether the doctrine of corporate negligence applies to hospitals in Washington. * * *

[The court adopted the doctrine of corporate negligence in Washington, citing several justifications:

(1) "the public's perception of the modern hospital as a multifaceted health care facility responsible for the quality of medical care and treatment rendered, and the public's subsequent reliance on the hospital";

(2) the hospital's "superior position to monitor and control physician performance", given its opportunities to observe professional practices on a daily basis, to adopt procedures to detect problems, and the use of its medical staff to monitor quality;

(3) incentives on hospitals, created by imposing corporate negligence, "to insure the competency of their medical staffs", thereby reducing their malpractice insurance costs.]

III.

Having adopted the doctrine of corporate negligence, we turn now to the task of defining the standard of care to which hospitals will be held. [The court noted that hospitals are members of national organizations such as the Joint Commission on Accreditation of Healthcare Organizations, subject to accreditation requirements.]

* * *

Also relevant to a hospital's standard of care are the hospital's own bylaws. [ ] Hospitals are required by statute and regulation to adopt bylaws with respect to medical staff activities. [ ] It is "recommended" that the organization and functions of the medical staff under the bylaws be in accord with the JCAH standards. [ ] Bylaws are therefore based on national standards, and their use in defining a standard of care for hospitals is appropriate. * * *

IV.

Our decision to adopt the doctrine of corporate negligence as enunciated by other jurisdictions does not necessarily entitle plaintiff in the case at bar to a reversal of the summary judgment against him. The alleged acts of malpractice committed by Dr. Bryant occurred entirely outside the hospital. Mrs. Pedroza was not a patient of the hospital at the time. For plaintiff to prevail, we must decide that the duty of care owed by hospitals under the corporate negligence doctrine extends not only to hospital patients, but also to patients treated by hospital staff members in those staff members' private office practices, where the hospital is not involved. No other jurisdiction appears to have done this; all the cases involve acts of malpractice committed at the hospital.

Defendant argues that extending a hospital's duty of care to patients outside the hospital would require a hospital to supervise and, if necessary, limit the private medical practices of its staff members outside the hospital. Such intervention could adversely affect the delicate physician-patient relationship. Substantial administrative problems would probably result as well.

This argument appears to be based upon a misconception of the doctrine of corporate negligence. The doctrine does not impose vicarious liability on a hospital for the acts of a medical staff member. The pertinent inquiry is whether the hospital exercised reasonable care in the granting, renewal, and delineation of staff privileges. This inquiry focuses on the procedures for the granting and renewal of staff privileges set forth in the hospital bylaws. In no case adopting corporate negligence premised upon a hospital's independent duty to select and maintain a competent medical staff has there been a suggestion that a hospital, in order to fulfill its duty of reasonable care, must supervise a physician's office practice. Acts of malpractice committed by a staff physician outside the hospital are relevant only if the hospital has actual or constructive notice of them, and where failure to take some action as a result of such notice is negligence. [ ]

Plaintiff argues that defendant hospital's independent duty of care should extend to Maria Pedroza because she was a foreseeable plaintiff. Foreseeability determines the extent and scope of duty. [] Plaintiff alleges that Maria Pedroza used Dr. Bryant's services only because Dr. Bryant possessed admitting and obstetrical privileges at defendant hospital (each of Maria Pedroza's seven children had been born at Skagit Valley Hospital), and that it was, therefore, foreseeable that the hospital's alleged negligence in the granting or renewal of Dr. Bryant's staff privileges might result in harm to his obstetrical patients. Plaintiff argues that it should make no difference whether the harm occurred in or out of the hospital, as long as the harm was foreseeable. The doctrine of corporate negligence focuses on the negligence of the hospital in failing to rescind Dr. Bryant's privileges.

The fact remains, however, that every jurisdiction that has adopted corporate negligence has based the hospital's liability on the duty owed by the hospital *to its patients.* * * * The hospital holds itself out to the community as a competent provider of medical care. The hospital does *not* hold itself out as an inspector or insurer of the private office practices of its staff members. The delineation of staff privileges by the hospital can only affect the procedures used by staff members while they are inside hospital walls. The public cannot reasonably expect anything more.

This court has in the past recognized a hospital's independent duty of care only in those situations where the plaintiff was a patient of the hospital. [ ] RCW 70.41, which controls the licensing and regulation of hospitals, supports the limitation of a hospital's duty of care to those who are patients in the hospital. RCW 70.41.010 provides in pertinent part: "The primary purpose of this chapter is to promote safe and adequate care of individuals in hospitals * * *."

Extending the hospital's duty of care to those who are not its patients would be undesirable in that it would likely grant those people a windfall, as any increased hospital costs resulting from such an extension of liability would be spread among hospital patients, rather than those who would benefit from the extended liability.

Accordingly, we hold that a hospital's duty of care under the doctrine of corporate negligence extends only to those who are patients within the hospital. Defendant Skagit Valley Hospital owed no duty to Maria Pedroza under the doctrine because she was not a hospital patient when the harm occurred. The fact that she had been a patient at defendant hospital in years past does not make her a patient for purposes of this case. Each of those prior hospital-patient relationships ended upon her discharge from the hospital; they did not continue indefinitely.

Since there are no allegations of negligence after Mrs. Pedroza was admitted to the hospital, we affirm the trial court's order of summary judgment.

Notes and Questions

1. Washington later applied its new corporate negligence doctrine in Schoening v. Grays Harbor Community Hospital, 40 Wash.App. 331, 698 P.2d 593 (1985). The plaintiff was treated in the emergency room for an infection. The plaintiff's expert, in his affidavit, wrote that the hospital should have been aware of "obvious negligence." The court held that where the care by the attending physician is questionable and the patient's condition is deteriorating, the hospital staff should have continuously monitored and observed the patient and sought additional evaluations. The court held that a fact question was raised by the expert's affidavit as to the hospital's duty to intervene.

See, rejecting the doctrine of corporate negligence, Albain v. Flower Hospital, 50 Ohio St.3d 251, 553 N.E.2d 1038 (1990).

2. Can you make a stronger argument that a hospital should be responsible, under some circumstances, for the negligent acts of physicians in their private practice, so long as they have staff privileges? What if the hospital is on notice of a long history of malpractice claims against one of its staff, resulting from negligence in that physician's private practice? If the physician has performed adequately while treating patients within the hospital, should the hospital have any further responsibility?

3. Some states by statute have adopted corporate negligence for institutional providers. Florida, for example, has by statute incorporated "institutional liability" or "corporate negligence" in its regulation of hospitals. Hospitals and other providers will be liable for injuries caused by inadequacies in the internal programs that are mandated by the statute. West's Fla.Stat.Ann. § 768.60.

4. Consider the case of Copithorne v. Framingham Union Hospital, 401 Mass. 860, 520 N.E.2d 139 (1988). The plaintiff, Copithorne, was a technologist at Framingham Union Hospital who was drugged and sexually assaulted by a physician with staff privileges at the hospital. The Massachusetts Supreme Judicial Court imposed liability on the hospital. The court summarized the facts as follows:

At the time of the incident, Helfant was a practicing neurosurgeon and a visiting staff member of the hospital. He was not a hospital employee, but had been affiliated with the hospital for about seventeen years, having been reappointed to the visiting staff each year since his initial appointment. Copithorne was a hospital employee. In the course of her employment, she injured her back, and, aware of Helfant's reputation within the hospital as a good neurosurgeon and a specialist in back injuries, she sought his profession-al assistance. In the course of treating her, Helfant made a house call to Copithorne's apartment, where he committed the drugging and rape for which he was convicted and which caused the injuries for which Copithorne seeks compensation.

The court assumed, as did the trial court, that the hospital was negligent in retaining Dr. Helfant on staff.

> We think that a jury reasonably could find that the hospital owed a duty of care to Copithorne, as an employee who, in deciding to enter a doctor-patient relationship with Helfant, reasonably relied on Helfant's good standing and reputation within the hospital community, and that the hospital violated this duty by failing to take sufficient action in response to previous allegations of Helfant's wrongdoing.

The hospital had received actual notice, prior to the assault on the plaintiff, of at least two prior incidents of sexual assault in which Helfant had caressed and otherwise improperly fondled female patients in the hospital. One of these patients filed a complaint with the Board of Registration in Medicine, copying the complaint to the hospital. The hospital then took action.

> * * * Dr. Byrne [Chief of Surgery] met with Helfant, who denied any wrongdoing. Dr. Byrne then instructed Helfant to have a chaperon present in the future when visiting female patients in the hospital. Based on Helfant's "excellent record" at the hospital, Dr. Bryne "felt that no further action was necessary as it was his opinion that he had no need to worry about Dr. Helfant harming a patient. In effect, Dr. Helfant was given an oral warning." Dr. Bryne also told the nurses on the floor to "keep an eye on Dr. Helfant."

The court found that the facts would support a jury finding that

> the risk of injury to Copithorne was within the range of foreseeable conse-quences of the hospital's negligence in continuing Helfant's staff privileges. Where the hospital had received actual notice of allegations that Helfant had sexually assaulted patients, both on the hospital premises and off the premis-es in his office and in a patient's home, and yet took only the limited measures indicated, it was not unforeseeable that Helfant would continue to act in a consistent, if not worse, manner.

The court also rejected the trial judge's ruling that the withdrawal of Helfant's staff privileges would not have prevented his assault on the plaintiff.

> Copithorne asserted that, by reason of her employment, she was aware of Helfant's good reputation within the hospital, and that she relied on this reputation in entering in a doctor-patient relationship with him; that as an employee, any change in Helfant's status would have become known to her; and that, if she had had any reason to know that the hospital has suspended Helfant's staff privileges or imposed any disciplinary sanctions on him, she would not have entered into a doctor-patient relationship with him. A different question would be presented if a member of the general public claimed that the hospital was liable for similar harm simply because Helfant was a staff member and should not have been.

The court reversed the summary judgment in favor of the defendant, and remanded the case for further proceedings.

How broad is the holding in *Copithorne?* Does this case contradict *Pedroza,* or is it distinguishable? Analyze the relationship of the hospital to the plaintiff and the defendant. Is the employer-employee relationship between the hospital and the nurse crucial to the holding? Or does this simply reinforce the reliance by the plaintiff on the defendant's implied representation that its staff is trustworthy? As hospitals devote more attention to staff privileges, driven by their need to avoid liability and achieve the best possible staffs, and as physicians come to restrict their privileges to fewer hospitals, or just one, does the reliance interest of the public increase?

Are your encouraged by the action of the medical disciplinary board of the state, which did nothing? See Doctors Rarely Lose Licenses: Maryland Panel Allowed Rapist to Keep Practicing, Washington Post, Part I, p. 1, January 10, 1988.

Problem: Referrals

You represent Chadds Hospital, a small nonprofit hospital that is trying to increase its patient count. One of the strategies it is contemplating is a physician referral service. The hospital plans to advertise, in local newspapers and on the radio, that individuals should call Chadds Hospital for the name of a doctor for specific problems. The referral service operator will then offer to make the appointment for the caller with the particular doctor, to be seen in his office practice. The draft of the advertising copy that the hospital marketing staff has prepared states: "You can trust the high quality of these doctors because they are members of the medical staff of Chadds Hospital, and our doctors are the best."

What is your advice to the hospital in light of the above cases? Do you foresee any legal risks in this marketing strategy?

Problem: The Birthing Center

You have been approached by Rosa Hernandez to handle a tort suit for damages for the death of her infant during delivery at the Hastings Birthing Center. Discovery reveals the following facts.

The death of the infant is attributable to the negligence of Dr. Jones, the physician who attended Ms. Hernandez at the Center during delivery. The death was caused in part by the infant's aspiration of meconium into the lungs. Although the Center is equipped to suction meconium and other material from a newborn's throat, it is not equipped to perform an intubation and attach the infant to a ventilator. To intubate the infant, it would have to be transferred to the hospital. Even if the infant had been transferred, it would probably have suffered brain damage due to oxygen deprivation before the procedure could have been undertaken.

Dr. Jones has a spotless record, but over the two weeks preceding the incident he had appeared at the hospital smelling of alcohol and evidencing other signs of intoxication. He was apparently having marital problems at the time. Nurses at the hospital had reported this behavior to their supervisor and had watched the physician's work very carefully, calling his attention to things he missed. The nurse supervisor had reported the situation to the head of OB/GYN, who said he would "look into it". Ms. Hernandez noticed the smell of liquor on Dr. Jones' breath during her labor, and was upset by his apparent intoxication. Dr. Jones has also dropped his malpractice insurance coverage, a fact of which the hospital is aware.

Further discovery has revealed that the nurse-midwife had observed that Dr. Jones' acts were questionable, but she had not intervened because she knew of his excellent reputation. She knew that doctors were resentful of the independence of nurse-midwives at the Center, and she believed she could "compensate" for his mistakes during the delivery. By the time she realized the extent of Dr. Jones' intoxication and took over the delivery, it was too late.

Your discovery reveals that there is a complicated relationship between the Birthing Center and the nearby Columbia Hospital. The hospital found that it had needed to increase its patient census, and that neonatology was one of its most profitable services. To increase its census in this area and to better serve the community, Columbia established the Hastings Birthing Center last year. The hospital receives a percentage of the profits of the Center.

The Center is located in a former convent one block from the hospital. The hospital owns the building and rents it to the Center. This particular birthing center, according to its promotional literature, offers "both a home-like setting for the delivery of your child and the security of the availability of back-up physicians and hospital care." The Center is separately incorporated and has its own Board of Directors. It is totally self-governing and is solely responsible for staff, provision of equipment, and policy.

The phone listing in the Yellow Pages describes the Hospital as a "cooperating hospital that will provide hospital care for mother and child if needed." Columbia has a contract with the Center requiring the Center to establish a screening program that will exclude high-risk patients and requiring that doctors attending patients at the Center have privileges at Columbia Hospital. The hospital allows the employees of the Center to participate in the hospital's group health and pension plans. Nurses from the hospital moonlight at the Center. When they do so, they receive a separate paycheck from the Center.

Although the Center's by-laws provide for a committee to review the qualifications of physicians who attend at the Center, it has in fact relied on the hospital's review of qualifications, since the hospital has a better opportunity to review credentials and performance. It is not clear that the hospital is aware of this; while it does notify the Center of the suspension, denial or revocation of privileges, it does not provide the Center with information used in investigations.

If you decide to litigate, should you sue both the Center and the hospital as well as Dr. Jones? Describe your theories, based on the information you have discovered to date, and consider what other facts you would like to know.

Part II

ACCESS AND COST CONTROL

Chapter 7

HEALTH CARE COST AND ACCESS: THE POLICY CONTEXT

I. THE PROBLEMS

Millions of Americans are just a pink slip away from losing their health insurance, and one serious illness away from losing all of their savings. Millions more are locked into the jobs they have now just because they or someone in their family had once been sick and they have what is called a pre-existing condition. And on any given day, over 37 million Americans—most of them working people and their little children—have no health insurance at all. And in spite of all this, our medical bills are growing at over twice the rate of inflation, and the United States spends over a third more of its income on health care than any other nation on earth. And the gap is growing, causing many of our companies in global competition severe disadvantage.

President Clinton, Address to Congress on Health Care, September 22, 1993.

Much has changed in the years since then President Clinton put forth the last major proposal to reform comprehensively the health care system of the United States, but the problems he identified still remain very much with us. On the one hand, the problem of access to health care has gotten worse—six million more persons are uninsured today than in 1993. This is true even though the American economy has enjoyed during the intervening period one of the greatest booms in history though generating record levels of employment—and though public program coverage has expanded during much of the past decade. On the other hand, health care cost inflation has moderated in recent years, though costs seem to be edging up again at the beginning of the 21st century. Accordingly, the problem of cost, which was a primary driver of health reform proposals in the early 1990s, seemed less urgent in the latter half of that decade, though it may soon be back on the agenda. Finally, new issues—the problem of underinsurance of the elderly for drug costs because of the lack of a Medicare drug benefit or access problems caused by managed care rationing—have become more pressing at the dawn of the twenty-first century.

This chapter presents the policy context for the chapters that follow. It first describes the problems that many Americans experience obtaining access to health insurance and health care. Second, it considers the issue of cost:

How big a problem is health care cost inflation? What causes it? The chapter then turns to a discussion of proposals for health care reform. This section begins by presenting proposals for public and private solutions to the problem of access. Second it analyzes market and regulatory solutions to the cost problem. With respect to both of these issues it also looks at the experience of other nations.

A. THE PROBLEM OF ACCESS

Between 1998 and 1999, the last year for which data are available as of this writing, the number of Americans not covered by health insurance fell from 44.3 million to 42.6 million, that is, from 16.3 percent of the population to 15.5 percent. This drop was the first since 1987 when the Census Bureau began keeping statistics and followed a sustained growth in the number of the uninsured by a million a year for the preceding decade. The reasons for this continuous growth in the number of uninsured, and for the recent, perhaps temporary decline, are complex.

Between 1989 and 1993 the number of uninsured grew dramatically as the proportion of the nonelderly population covered by employer-sponsored health insurance fell from 66 percent to 60 percent. This decline was partially offset by a growth in the Medicaid program, which increased its coverage from 7 to 10 percent of the nonelderly population during this period. In the latter half of the 1990s the proportion of the nonelderly population covered by employment-based coverage began again to climb, but this increase was more than offset by a drop in Medicaid coverage, a largely unintended consequence of welfare reform, and by a decline in coverage under individual insurance policies and other public programs (such as military programs). At the very end of the decade continued growth in employment-related coverage and renewed growth in Medicaid coverage, supplemented by the new State Children's Health Insurance Program, led finally to a decline in the number of the uninsured.

Who are the uninsured? Most are adults under the age of 65, live in families with incomes higher than the federal poverty level and with at least one full time worker, and are white. Those most at risk of being uninsured, however, are younger adults, particularly men; racial and ethnic minorities (particularly Hispanics from Mexico or Central and South America), members of families with only part-time workers or no workers; workers employed in low-paying jobs and/or by small businesses; individuals in families with incomes below 200 percent of the federal poverty level; and children being cared for by persons other than their own parents. Coverage also differs significantly among the various states, with the proportion of insurance coverage ranging from 50 percent in Texas to 79 percent in Minnesota for low-income adults between the age of 18 and 64.

Why are these persons uninsured? Most are uninsured because they are both ineligible for Medicaid (because they do not fit into a covered category or earn too much) and without employment-related coverage. Though the percentage of employers offering health insurance has increased dramatically in recent years, many employees are still not eligible for coverage, either because they work part-time, are seasonal employees (e.g. in agriculture or construction), or work for very small businesses, many of which still do not offer coverage. While 99 percent of businesses with 200 or more employees offer insurance coverage, 40 percent of businesses with 3–9 employees do not. A more important factor than employer offer rates, however, may be employee acceptance rates. Employees of low wage firms tend to face higher premium costs for health insurance than employees of high wage firms, and an increasing number of employees have been declining coverage rather than pay this cost. Indeed, 74 percent of uninsured adults report that they do not have health insurance because it costs too much, only 3 percent report as their most important reason for not having health insurance that they do not think they need it.

Just because a person is not insured, however, does not automatically mean that he or she cannot get access to health care. As President George W. Bush stated during the third presidential debate, the issue in the end is really not insurance coverage ("that's a Washington term"), but rather "are people getting health care?" In fact, a growing proportion of Americans (up from 43 percent in 1993 to 57 percent in 1999 according to one study) believe that the uninsured are able to get needed care from physicians and hospitals. See Robert J. Blendon, et al., (The Uninsured, The Working Uninsured, and the Public, 18 Health Aff., Nov./Dec., 1999 at 203, 207). (Bush did not argue this, of course, but rather proposed direct government provision of health care through community health centers as a response to the problem). An overwhelming and steadily growing body of evidence, however, shows a direct correlation between lack of insurance, lack of health care, and poor health. The long-term uninsured are more likely than the insured to fail to get necessary medical care for serious conditions, forego filling prescriptions or getting recommended tests, experience hospitalization for avoidable conditions like pneumonia or uncontrolled diabetes, and be diagnosed for cancer at later stages when treatment is less likely to succeed. They are less likely than the insured to have a regular doctor or to receive cancer screening, cardiovascular risk reduction assistance, or diabetes care. The uninsured are far more likely than the insured to have problems paying their medical bills, one of the leading causes of bankruptcy in the United States. Uninsured children, particularly those with special health needs like asthma or recurring ear infections, are much less likely than insured children to get regular treatment. Lack of health insurance is generally correlated with worse health status, and with premature death.

See, discussing the scope of the problem of the uninsured, John Holahan and Niall Brennan, Who Are the Uninsured (2000); Stephen Zuckerman, et al., Health Insurance, Access and Health Status of Nonelderly Adults (2000) (both available at the Urban Institute website, www.urban.org); John Gabel, et al., Job–Based Health Insurance in 2000: Premiums Rise Sharply While Coverage Grows, 19 Health Aff., Sept./Oct. 2000 at 144; and The Kaiser Commission on the Uninsured, Uninsured in America: A Chart Book (2d ed., 2000) (available at www.kff.org). See, discussing the health problems of the uninsured, American College of Physicians, No Health Insurance? It's Enough to Make You Sick (2000), (www.acponline.org/uninsured) John Z. Ayanian, et al., Unmet Medical Needs of Uninsured Adults in the United States, 284 JAMA 2061 (2000); and David W. Baker, et al., Health Insurance and Access to Care for Symptomatic Conditions, 160 Arch. Int. Med. 1269 (2000). Finally, see describing how uninsured persons get by, Kaiser Commission on Medicaid and the Uninsured, In Their Own Words: The Uninsured Talk About Living Without Health Insurance (2000)(www.kff.org).

Although the problems of the uninsured in obtaining health care are our most obvious access problems, there is a growing awareness that Americans face other access problems as well. A major issue in the 2000 election was the fact that many Medicare recipients lacked access to outpatient drugs. Medicare does not cover most outpatient drugs, and over 30 percent of Medicare recipients have no form of drug coverage. Many elderly persons with Medicare Supplement coverage, moreover face high premiums, deductibles, and cost-sharing that render this coverage of little value, while Medicare managed care plans that cover prescription drugs often impose low coverage caps that limit their usefulness for catastrophic expenditures. This issue is discussed further in chapter 10.

Many other insured persons also face low coverage maximums or high cost-sharing requirements that limit their access to care. One in ten insured persons surveyed during a recent study reported that they had postponed seeking health care they needed but could not afford, 18 percent reported that they had experienced problems paying medical bills in the past year, and 27 percent had been contacted by a collection agency about unpaid medical bills. See Uninsured in America, supra.

Finally, recipients of managed care increasingly face rationing programs that limit their access to health care, even though they are fully insured. These limitations will be discussed further in chapters 8 and 9 below.

Do you have health insurance? If not, why not? If you are uninsured, how much would it cost you to purchase insurance? If you were involved in a serious accident on your way home today, who would pay for your medical care? If you are insured, how much does your insurance cost? Do you pay for this cost yourself directly, do you pay indirectly, or does someone else bear the cost? Does this cost reflect accurately your preferences for medical care as compared to other goods and services? Do you think it accurately reflects your need for medical care? Do you have a copy of your insurance policy readily available? If so, examine it. What deductibles and coinsurance or copayments does it impose? What caps does it provide for the insurer's obligations? Is your responsibility for cost-sharing capped under the policy? What services does the policy excluded? Does it cover dental services or pharmaceuticals? Under what circumstances must care be preapproved? Who determines whether care is "necessary" or not? Does it cover "experimental" treatment? Do you have any recourse if care that you or your doctor thinks you need is denied? Why did you buy this particular policy? Did you get what you thought you bought?

B. THE PROBLEM OF COST

1. Recent Developments in Health Care Cost Inflation

By any measure, Americans spend a great deal on health care. In 1998, the most recent year for which data are available, we spent $1,149.1 billion dollars on health care, 13.5 percent of the gross national product, $4,270 for every man, woman, and child. We spend more on health care than on anything else. In 1997, Americans spent $957.3 billion on personal medical care compared to $829.8 billion on housing, $832.3 billion on food, and $636.4

billion on transportation. We also spend more than anyone else. In 1998, the United States spent 14 percent of its GDP, $4,270 per capita, on health care. By contrast, the United Kingdom spent 6.9 percent of its GDP, $1,450 per capita, and Japan spent 7.4 percent of its GDP, $1,780 per capita, on health care.

Despite these facts, for the past half decade the cost of health care has not been the burning issue that it was in the late 1980s and early 1990s. In 1990 national health care expenditures increased 11 percent from the year before, a trend consistent with much of the preceding decade. Between 1980 and 1990 health expenditures per capita had grown two and a half times, and health care costs had risen as a percentage of GNP from 8.9 percent to 12.2 percent. More importantly, perhaps, public health care program expenditures had grown from $105.3 billion to $286.5 billion.

During the mid–1990s, however, spending growth moderated significantly. From 1993 to 1997 the share of GDP spent on health care actually dropped, from 13.7 percent to 13.3 percent, while from 1995 to 1997 health care expenditure growth rates fell below 5 percent a year, less than 3 percent adjusted for inflation. In 2000, as this book is being written, health care expenditures seem to be on the rise once again, though not at the levels experienced in the 1980s. Between Spring, 1999 and Spring, 2000, premiums for employer-provided health insurance rose 8.3 percent, according to one survey, while some reports project that premiums may rise by over 10 percent in 2001.

In fact, health care costs have been rising gradually since 1996, and are likely to continue to rise in the foreseeable future. Much of the increase has been driven by dramatic growth in the cost of prescription drugs, which increased 15.6 percent in 1998. The proportion of private insurance benefits spent on prescription drugs increased from 6.6 percent to 12.7 percent between 1993 and 1998. Some of the increase is also attributable to the attempt by health insurers and managed care organizations to make up for underwriting losses in the late 1990s and to the increasing aggressiveness of providers at the bargaining table.

Despite this renewed growth, there are two reasons why health care cost increases do not have the political saliency (as of this writing) that they had a decade ago. First, the remarkable economic boom of the 1990s allowed— and the tight labor market of the same period forced—employers to absorb increased health care costs, rather than to pass them on directly to workers. Between 1996 and 2000 the average monthly employee payment for single health insurance coverage actually dropped, while the average payment for family coverage increased modestly. The percentage of firms offering health coverage also continued to grow between 1998 and 2000, particularly for firms with few employees, despite increased costs.

Second, growth in public expenditures slowed significantly in the late 1990s and with them the political importance of the cost issue. The government spent $522.7 billion on health care in 1998, 45.5 percent of health care expenditures. While this was up considerably from 40.4 percent in 1990, it was down somewhat from 46.2 percent in 1997. As stringent cost-cutting measures imposed by the Balanced Budget Act of 1997 were implemented at the end of the 1990s, annual growth in spending for Medicare, the nation's largest public health care program, slowed from 7.6 percent in 1996 to 2.5 percent in 1998, and growth was actually negative in 1999. The assets of the Part A Trust Fund were almost 12 percent higher at the end of 1999 than the previous year, and the Trust Fund is as of this writing expected to remain in the black until 2025. As recently as 1995, Medicare costs had been increasing at an annual rate of 11 percent and insolvency of the Trust Fund was expected by 2002. Medicaid cost increase also slowed in the late 1990s as a combination of cost cutting measures imposed by the 1997 BBA and enrollment declines brought about by welfare reform limited program growth. These developments eased considerably the political pressure that had existed in the early 1990s for doing something about health care costs.

There is, nonetheless, reason to be concerned about increases in health care costs. When, as is inevitable, the economy takes a down turn, or at least starts to grow more slowly (leading to a loosening of the labor market), and if, as is likely, at the same time health insurance premiums and health care costs continue to rise, some employers will drop health insurance benefits, while more will raise employee premium contributions. This will in turn contribute to (an increase in the uninsured) the access problem discussed above.

A weakened economy would also reduce tax revenues and payroll tax collections, which, coupled with increasing health care costs, would once again put the Medicare program under pressure. A recent upturn in Medicaid enrollment (up 1.1 million in 1999) will also increase the cost of that program. Health care cost control is likely, therefore to soon be back on the health policy agenda.

Recent sources discussing health care cost issues include Gerard F. Anderson, et al., Health Spending and Outcomes: Trends in OECD Countries, 1960–1998, 19 Health Aff., May/June 2000 at 150; Jon Gabel, Job–Based Insurance in 2000: Premiums Rise Sharply While Coverage Grows, 19 Health Aff., Sept./Oct. 2000 at 144; Christopher Hogan, et al., Tracking Health Care Costs: Inflation Returns, Health Aff., Nov/Dec. 2000 at 217; and Katharine Levit, Health Spending in 1998: Signals of Change, 19 Health Aff. 124, Jan./Feb. 2000. Health Affairs publishes each year reports on health care costs from the Health Care Financing Administration (the Levit article above), as well as reports on comparative OECD data (the Anderson article above), and is always an excellent source for tracking health care costs.

2. *A Primer on Health Economics*

As noted at the outset, the health reform debate at the beginning of the 1990s was based in part on the premise that we spend too much on health care, and that our expenditures on health care were at that point in time growing too rapidly. While expenditure growth has moderated, we still spend a great deal on health care. Do we spend too much? How would we know it if we did?

The fact that we spend more proportionately on health care than other developed nations is not necessarily a bad thing. Other nations spend more proportionately on food or housing than we do, but this does not necessarily mean that they spend too much. In the excerpt above President Clinton asserted that the high cost of employer-financed health insurance raises the prices of American products, decreasing their competitiveness in international markets. Economists generally agree, however, that in the long run increases in health insurance premiums are reflected in lower wages, not higher prices, and that in any event adjustments in international financial markets compensate for higher prices by diminishing the value of the dollar. In fact, between 1970 and 1991, the years in which the United States experienced the greatest growth of health care costs, real wages and salaries per employee grew only .4 percent, while employer health expenditures per employee grew 234.1 percent. If workers, however, prefer to take their compensation in health benefits rather than take home pay, is there a problem?

It is widely believed that the market for health care is distorted, and that the amount we spend on health care is not the amount we would freely choose to spend in a true competitive market. More particularly, the allocation of compensation just described is not that which would have been chosen by employees in a non-distorted market. The except that follows offers a classic explanation of the problems:

ECONOMIC IMPLICATIONS OF RISING HEALTH CARE COSTS

Congressional Budget Office (1992).

In most circumstances, the free market provides an efficient mechanism for allocating resources in the economy. To achieve such efficiencies, however, free markets must operate under certain conditions. They work best when the consumer has good information about the characteristics of products and their prices—information that is most easily obtained if products are well defined and standardized and if prices can be readily ascertained without excessive search. In addition, market efficiency requires that a large number of sellers compete with each other over prices that reflect true resource costs. With a large number of sellers, no single vendor has the power to control prices, and price competition among sellers lowers prices to the point that they reflect the marginal costs of production.

The market for health care, however, does not meet many of these conditions. * * *

Consumers lack key information about the quality and price of medical services. Their ignorance about quality has two dimensions. First, most consumers do not have the expertise they need to evaluate the qualifications of their health care providers. Second, when consumers need medical care, they may not have information (independent of what they are told by a provider) about the full range of alternative treatments and the prospective outcomes of these alternatives.

Consumers also lack rudimentary information about the prices of the medical care they buy and have difficulty assessing what that price information means. Price information, such as that concerning physicians' charges, in many cases is not available to patients in advance of treatment. In some instances, the patient can call a doctor and obtain quotes for different services, but prices of physicians' services are not advertised and it may be embarrassing to ask. Sometimes even the doctor does not know the full costs of treatment, especially if it requires hospitalization or drugs. Although a patient can acquire some price information with repeated visits to a doctor, many reasons for seeing a doctor do not occur again.

Even if the price information is available, it can be hard to interpret. If a doctor charges a low price, he or she could be offering a bargain—or inferior— service. Without information on quality, price information has no meaning. * * *

Because consumers delegate a considerable amount of decision making authority to their physicians, medical practitioners act both as agents for consumers and suppliers of medical services. With such power, physicians are in the position of being able to create a demand for their own services.

Such a delegation of authority occurs in other markets as well. For instance, when consumers take their cars in for repair, they usually have to rely heavily on the advice of their mechanics, who (like physicians) are put in the powerful position of giving advice that can determine demand. But there is an upper limit on how much it is worth to fix a car. By contrast, when they are sick, few people limit what they are willing to pay to be made well, in part because they do not expect to pay for all of it themselves. This gives physicians extraordinary power.

Physicians' training and professional standards strongly predispose them to use their power to give the best possible medical care without regard to cost. To many physicians, it is unethical to do otherwise. * * * Moreover, because physicians can earn higher incomes by providing more care, their financial self-interest may also contribute to excessive spending.

Efficient use of medical resources requires consumers and providers to weigh the costs and benefits of alternative medical treatments. Unfortunately, this is very difficult. Obviously, patients have little knowledge upon which to judge the benefits of a new technology. But even physicians cannot always be fully informed about all the new treatments and technologies, especially given the rapid pace of complex medical advances. More important, good statistical information concerning the effectiveness of many treatments—even many common treatments—is simply not available.

The lack of good information on the outcomes of many medical treatments has created an environment in which the doctors' preferences for particular procedures—rather than science—appear to determine how they are used, a situation that leads to significant variations in the patterns and costs of medical care around the country. * * *

* * *

For markets to allocate resources efficiently, sellers must actively compete. In a competitive environment, individual vendors have no control over the price of what they sell or over the number of competitors. Also, more efficient suppliers can offer lower prices than those who fail to control their costs.

Although there are obviously many providers in the health care sector, they do not always compete effectively on price. Of course, the medical market is diverse, and active competition can be found in some subsectors of that market. But too often, competition among medical care providers for consumers (and for the services of other providers) is directed toward the nonprice aspects of medical care. * * * This type of competition, however, can tend to increase costs. Moreover, once a new technology is introduced, it tends to be used regardless of cost.

The lack of price competition in the medical market reflects many factors. The presence of third-party payers dulls the incentives for consumers to pay much attention to costs at the point of service. The tax subsidy for employment-based insurance * * * also reduces some of the pressures on workers to pay attention to the costs of insurance. Difficulties in assessing information about the quality of doctors weaken the already weak incentives for consumers to seek out the lowest-cost providers. And last, many consumers have long-standing relationships with their physicians and may be reluctant to switch doctors to save money.

* * *

Moreover, consumers are legally or effectively prohibited from making many medical decisions. Although there is a vast market for over-the-counter drugs and home remedies, most advanced drugs are sold only by prescription. In many cases, a sick person can obtain treatment only if it is prescribed by a physician, who may be highly trained but perhaps more expensive than the patient can afford. Gaining access to health services—other than those supervised by the physician, or what the druggist is willing to offer—is generally difficult.

Limited entry and control over demand are the key elements that allow a provider to earn more than necessary to attract talented, well-trained people into the profession. Economists use the term "rents" to describe a situation in which the returns to labor or capital are above the returns needed to attract the appropriate supply of resources to an activity.

It seems likely that physicians earn rents in their profession, for two reasons. First, the number of qualified applicants for medical school is far greater than the number of student slots available, so the entry limits probably matter. Second, studies of the financial returns from education and training suggest that the private returns on an investment in medical school compare favorably with the returns on investments in general and exceed the returns in most other occupations.

In addition, physicians in the United States earn about five and one-half times the average annual compensation of other wage earners. The gap is smaller in other countries. * * *

* * *

The bulk of medical care is purchased through third-party payers. These payers include not only private insurance companies but federal, state, and local governments.

As new and more elaborate methods of treatment are developed, the cost of an episode of illness can become extremely high. In addition, an individual's need for major medical care occurs largely by chance and is difficult to predict. Most types of illnesses are statistically predictable, however, for groups of individuals. Health insurance enables consumers to take advantage of this group predictability by pooling their risks for serious accidents or diseases.

Insurance, however, imposes its own costs. Insurance means that the effective price that the patient faces at the time of treatment is much lower than the actual cost of treatment. Sick individuals and their doctors have every incentive to buy expensive treatments and tests as long as they do any good at all, because the patient does not bear much of the cost. * * *

* * *

The market for medical care is also different from other markets because of the large role played by government. In particular, the government subsidizes health care, which allows some consumers greater access to medical care than they would otherwise have. Although these programs provide essential—and in some cases life-saving—medical care to millions of people, the programs also dull the price signals from the health care markets, encouraging overuse of services. The major subsidies are provided in three ways: Medicare, Medicaid, and tax expenditures.

* * *

Although there is strong justification for government involvement in health care, this involvement may cause markets to work less well in conventional terms of efficiency. When the government subsidizes the purchase or becomes the insurer, the budget constraints on consumers of health care are relaxed and, as a result, lose some effectiveness in controlling less-valued spending. Likewise, federal budget constraints for health care do not operate with the same force as they do in the private sector or in much of the rest of the public-sector budget. * * *

* * *

Notes and Questions

1. This excerpt was written almost a decade ago, when our health care system looked somewhat different than it does today. To what extent does the decisive movement to managed care in the American health care system in the intervening period alter or eliminate the problems described above? What role can increased competition between managed care organizations play in bringing down costs? What new problems are created by the changed incentives found in managed care? Think about these questions as you work through the remaining sections of this chapter, and through chapters and below.

2. Most economists have placed particular emphasis on the role of tax subsidies for health insurance in driving health care cost increases. Payments for employee-related health insurance are taxable neither to employers nor employees. Federal income tax subsidies for health benefits exceeded $111 billion in 1998, making this expenditure program our largest federal health care program after Medicare and Medicaid. John Sheils and Paul Hogan, Cost of Tax–Exempt Health Benefits in 1998, Health Aff. March/April 1999, 176 at 178. Because before-tax dollars are more valuable than after-tax dollars, it is believed that workers might prefer to take compensation in the form of benefits, even though they might have preferred to take compensation in cash absent the tax subsidy. Because these tax subsidies are offered through deductions rather than credits, moreover, they are highly inequitable: A family earning $100,000 or more in income on average received $2,357 through this tax subsidy in 1998, a family earning less than $15,000, only $71. See generally, reviewing the arguments against the income tax

deduction for employee health benefits, Empowering Health Care Consumers Through Tax Reform (Grace–Marie Arnett, ed., 1999).

Are there any arguments in favor of the tax deduction, however? Is it not in fact possible that the tax deduction has served us relatively well in creating a system where the vast majority of working age Americans are covered by private insurance? Might not tax credits impose their own significant costs and inefficiencies, particularly if they were used to subsidize the purchase of individual rather than group insurance, which carries with it much higher administrative costs? See Jonathan Gruber & Larry Levitt, Tax Subsidies for Health Insurance: Costs and Benefits, 19 Health Aff., Jan./Feb. 2000, at 72. Is it not also possible that employees might opt for health benefits even without tax subsidies? Most Medicare recipients, for example, buy Medigap policies, even though these policies are purchased with after-tax dollars.

3.   Factors that Explain High American Health Care Costs

While understanding the economic mechanisms that drive health care cost growth might help us to understand better the high cost of health care, it might also be helpful for us to know more about the factors that contribute to cost growth, and in particular the respects in which the American health care system differs from those of countries where costs are much lower. A number of factors have been nominated as major drivers of health care increases. We will consider these in turn:

● Demographic changes. The population of the United States is steadily aging and older people, particularly those over 80, require a great deal of health care. This change explains, however only a small proportion of the general growth in health care costs, perhaps 7 percent over the past thirty years. Nevertheless,But aging of the population has a much greater impact on public programs, where eligibility is often age-related. As people reach the age of 65 they become eligible for Medicare (and for Medicaid if they are financially needy). Additionally, if they retire, they cease contributing to the Medicare trust fund and reduce payments of the taxes that support Medicaid. The growth in the "very old" segment of the population also disproportionately affects public programs, which bear most of the cost of the very expensive long term care consumed by this population. As Medicaid is the primary source of payment for nursing home care in the United States, demographic shifts have hit Medicaid particularly hard. Though the elderly make up only 10.1 percent of the Medicaid population, they account for 27.6 percent of the program's costs. Nevertheless, the United States has one of the youngest populations of any OECD nation, and all other countries have been able to keep their health care expenditures below ours despite their older populations.

● Waste, fraud and abuse. There is a widespread belief among the public that waste, fraud, and abuse are major factors contributing to health care costs. It is convenient to believe this, for if it were true health care costs could be controlled painlessly without limiting "necessary" care. Fraud and abuse probably account for more than a trivial share of health care costs—recent aggressive enforcement of the fraud and abuse laws has been widely credited with playing a role in decreasing Medicare costs—but combating fraud and abuse also imposes costs—both the direct costs of law enforcement and the indirect costs of more intrusive oversight of physician and patient behavior. "Waste" is both more difficult to define and to police than fraud and abuse, since the practice of medicine remains far from an exact science and tests and procedures that some regard as wasteful, others regard as necessary.

• Administrative costs. We pay more proportionately for administrative costs than does any other nation in the world, $150 per person in 1990 compared to $23 per person in Canada. Jean–Pierre Poullier, Administrative Costs in Selected Industrialized Countries, 13 Health Care Fin. Rev. 167, 170 (1992). Private insurance systems simply cost more to administer than public systems because private systems carry with them costs for marketing, underwriting, monitoring, and billing that do not exist in public systems. While Medicare spends 2 cents on the dollar on administrative costs, private health insurance companies spend 25 cents on the dollar in small group markets and 5.5 cents on the dollar in large-group markets for administrative costs. A doctor in the United States must contend with the particular billing forms and practices of dozens of insurance companies and managed care plans, while in most other countries and in public programs in the United States, there is only one form and one payer to deal with. But any health care system costs something to administer, and as long as we remain committed to a private insurance-based system of health care finance we must be content with relatively high administrative costs. On the other hand, many believe that private markets bring with them efficiencies that outweigh their higher administrative costs, and thus, in the end, cost less.

• Malpractice. Though malpractice continues to be a major source of irritation to medical professionals, it is not a major contributor to medical costs. The direct costs of malpractice premiums account for less than 1 percent of health care costs, though these costs tend to be borne disproportionately by physicians in particular specialties and geographic areas. Defensive medicine arguably is of greater concern, but most responsible research does not establish defensive medicine as a major factor driving the increase of health care costs.

• Treating "hopeless cases." Some have argued that we spend far too much in the United States prolonging the life of patients who are near death through heroic interventions. In fact, studies show that we spend relatively little on truly hopeless cases. Ezekiel Emanuel & Linda Emanuel, The Economics of Dying: The Illusion of Cost Savings at the End of Life, 330 New Eng. J. Med. 540 (1994). The problem is that it is often not clear at the outset when treatment is futile, and that a great deal is spent on persons who are expected to live but die, or expected to die but live. It should not be surprising that most health care is consumed by those who are the sickest, and even those who are clearly dying require at least comfort care. Widespread use of advanced directives could contribute to cost control, but probably not significantly.

• Labor costs. A striking feature of the American health care system is that even though we spend more on health care than any other nation, we consume no more health care than do many other nations if some measures of utilization are considered, and less than most if others are. The average American sees a doctor 6 times a year, compared to 6.5 for the average Frenchman or 15.8 for the average Japanese. The average American spends 1.1 days per year in a hospital, compared to 2.8 days for the average German and 1.7 for the average Englishman. In fact, however, we pay dramatically more per unit of health care consumed and, in many instances, per health care worker than do most other nations. (We also, incidentally, pay more for drugs than do the citizens of many other nations, even for the same drugs).

This observation has two ramifications. First, it implies that the true "cost" of medical care in the United States, in terms of productive resources allocated to health care that could be allocated elsewhere, is relatively low. Mark Pauly, U.S. Health Care Costs: The Untold True Story, Health Affairs, Fall 1993 at 100. We just pay more for the resources we use for health care. Second, it means that we could, at least in theory, cut health care costs without diminishing the volume of health care we receive if we could pay less to those who provide health care. Uwe Reinhardt, Resource Allocation in Health Care: The Allocation of Lifestyles to Providers, 65 Milbank Q. 153 (1987). Arguably, if we could put in place mechanisms to counter market failures that cause us to pay excessive prices for health care, we could reach the lower "true" market resource price.

This second observation is particularly important, because it explains one of the reasons why managed care contributes to cost control, despite its high administrative costs. Managed care companies pay high salaries to their executives and employ a host of workers who monitor and administer health care who do not themselves provide any health care services. The administrative costs of managed care organizations are far higher than the costs of Medicare or of the public health care programs of other countries. See Kip Sullivan, On the "Efficiency" of Managed Care Plans, 19 Health Aff., July/ Aug. 2000, 139. On the other hand, managed care plans are able not only to control the utilization of health care, but also to demand much deeper discounts from health care professionals or providers than do most fee-for-service plans, public or private. Physician annual income growth slowed dramatically in the mid–1990s as managed care grew. To the extent that the costs of administering managed care firms are less than the savings they achieve in driving down the use of and costs of health care labor, managed care can result in health care savings.

● Technology. An alternative (or additional) explanation of the comparative data, however, is that we are not only paying more than other nations for the same services, but rather that we are paying higher prices to purchase "better," i.e. more intensive and technical services. A consensus has emerged that the primary reason health care costs so much in the United States is because of the widespread and rapid adoption of new medical technology. See Timothy Stoltzfus Jost, The American Difference in Health Care Costs: Is There a Problem? Is Medical Necessity the Solution? 43 St. Louis U. L. J. 1 (1999). The issue is complex—the extent to which other countries engage in "rationing" of technology varies from nation to nation and from technology to technology. See Steven A. Schroeder, Rationing Medical Care: A Comparative Perspective, 331 New Eng. J. Med. 1089 (1994). In the end, however, the most significant single factor explaining the high cost of American health care is that Americans receive—and arguably demand—more technically complex tests and procedures than do the citizens of other nations, and that American expect that the equipment for providing these tests will be immediately available at all times and at all places. For us to make significant progress toward limiting health care costs we will need to accept the more limited availability and use of health care technology. Here also, managed care makes a significant contribution to cost control to the extent that managed care firms are capable of limiting the technology available to their members or the frequency with which that technology is used.

See, exploring further these issues, Victor Fuchs, No Pain, No Gain, Perspectives on Cost Containment, 269 JAMA 631 (1993); Jerry L. Mashaw & Theodore R. Marmor, Conceptualizing, Estimating, and Reforming Fraud, Waste, and Abuse in Healthcare Spending, 11 Yale J. Reg. 456 (1994) and Joseph P. Newhouse, An Iconoclastic View of Health Care Cost Containment, Health Affairs, Supp. 1993 at 152.

How much value do you place on health care? Do you think that we as a society spend too much, too little, about the right amount? Do you think that you as an individual have to spend too much, too little, or the right amount on health care? Would you be willing to tolerate diminished access to expensive, high technology, diagnostic or treatment equipment to save health care costs? Would you be willing to travel further or wait longer to access such equipment? Should public programs such as Medicare consider the cost of technologies in deciding whether or not to pay for them? What would be the consequences of compelling the reduction of the income of health care professionals? What would be the consequences of forcing drug companies to accept lower prices? Should cost considerations play a role in deciding when to terminate care for dying persons?

II. APPROACHES TO HEALTH CARE REFORM

During 1993 and 1994, it appeared possible that Congress might adopt legislation to reform comprehensively the American health care system in response to these cost and access problems. A number of the states also embraced the goal of health care reform and several—Florida, Hawaii, Minnesota, Oregon, Washington, and Massachusetts, to name only the most ambitious—adopted reform programs during these years. Health care reform, however, failed at the federal level because of complex political problems that cannot be explored here (see Jacob Hacker, The Road to Nowhere (1997); Carolyn Touhy, Accidental Logic (1999) and Symposium, The Failure of Health Care Reform, J. Health Pol. Pol'y & L., Summer 1995, for varied analyses of the political failure of the Clinton reform), and state reform programs were scaled back in many states.

As we finish this book in the fall of 2000, comprehensive health care reform seems as unlikely as ever. Nevertheless, the failure of health reform in 1994 was followed by a very modest effort at health reform in 1996 in the Health Insurance Portability and Accountability Act (discussed in chapter 9 below) and by the somewhat more ambitious Balanced Budget Act of 1997. The BBA created the State Children's Health Insurance Program (SCHIP), the first major new federal health care program in three decades, which covered 2.5 million children within three years. Access to health care was a major issue in the 2000 election, and it is likely that Congress and the President will make some attempt at addressing the issue.

Approaches to expanding access to and controlling the cost of health care can be basically divided between those that rely on direct public action and those that rely more on private initiatives and markets. All nations on Earth, including the United States, have adopted a mixed strategy for addressing cost control issues. All have public programs for providing health insurance or health care to a portion of their population. Even in the United States, the bastion of private enterprise, almost half of health care expenditures are borne by the government (more if one adds tax expenditures and the cost of insurance for government employees), even though government programs cover only about one third of the population. All nations also have private insurance markets. Even in the United Kingdom, whose National Health Service is the quintessential example of socialized medicine, about one ninth of the population has private insurance.

This section will first consider the options available for expanding access to health care, describing first the range of options for providing publicly financed health care, then examining "private", tax subsidy-financed options that are more likely to succeed politically in the United States. Next we will examine options for controlling health care costs, looking first at regulatory options, then at market-based options.

A. OPTIONS FOR EXPANDING ACCESS TO CARE

1. Approaches Relying on Public Finance

While all developed nations have private health insurance markets, the United States is very unusual in the extent to which it relies on private finance of health care, and unique in that it fails to provide some form of public coverage for those who cannot afford private insurance. The models of health care finance followed by European nations (as well as other developed nations) are described in the excerpt that follows:

EUROPEAN PARLIAMENT, DIRECTORATE GENERAL RESEARCH, WORKING PAPER: HEALTH CARE SYSTEMS IN THE EU: A COMPARATIVE STUDY 17–19, 22, 61–66, 114–17, 120–23 (1998)

* * *

Although EU countries have each developed their own funding mechanisms, similar objectives and common historical developments have resulted in systems which have much in common. All systems rely on a mixture of funding sources, but the majority of funds are state-controlled, whether directly or indirectly. * * *

State regulation in the Member States provides for universal health insurance or service coverage (Denmark, Finland, Greece, Italy, Portugal, Sweden, United Kingdom) or nearly universal coverage (99 and 99.5% of the population in Austria, Belgium, France, Luxembourg, Spain, and 92.2% of the population in Germany) for health care through compulsory schemes. In Ireland, universal coverage for primary care only applies to low income groups. In the Netherlands, compulsory health insurance covers only 60% of the population. The rest of the population are usually covered by voluntary private or public insurance (Belgium, France, Germany, Luxembourg, and the Netherlands.)

* * *

There are three predominant systems of health care finance in the European Union. The first is public finance by general taxation (often referred to as the Beveridge model). Secondly, there is public finance based on compulsory social insurance (the Bismarck model). Thirdly, there is private finance based on voluntary insurance, which covers only a small minority of

EU citizens entirely, but which also operates on top of social insurance as a supplementary form of funding health care.

* * *

Compulsory and voluntary insurance is administered by insurance funds—autonomous organisations which collect a share of work-related income and in turn provide payment for health care either at the time of use, or by repayment afterwards.

Most of the tax-based systems operate with a national health service where services are provided through a central public institution. However, it does not necessary follow that finance from government budgets leads to services owned by the government and that all staff working in the health services are salaried staff. Only in Greece and Portugal do salaried staff predominate among doctors working in ambulatory care. Alternative payment systems in office-based care are: fee-for-service (payments according to fixed service charges), and capitation (where the provider receives a fixed amount per enrolled person). More recently-developed forms of payment to the primary care provider include payments by a lump sum (budget) under which services have to be managed. Under study are payment systems based on a certain diagnosis or on achieved medical outcome. In General Practice and Specialist care out-of-hospital, fee-for-service arrangements tend to be the predominant payment type in social insurance systems in the EU (Belgium, France, Germany and Luxembourg).* * *

Allocation of hospital funds differs widely between the Member States, the main basic elements being per-diem payments, budget payments, and payments based on the clinical diagnosis ("Diagnosis Related Groups").

* * *

The question of whether to set up a National Health Service has been important in all Member States and there is a wide range of different attitudes and approaches to this issue. A fully developed NHS implies that resources and services are largely provided directly by the public sector and consumed free at the point of use.

None of the EU countries provides a wholly public sector service and, in fact, the trend has been towards a decrease in the state's role in service provision, for example in the United Kingdom and Italy. In ambulatory medical and dental care a private practitioner approach is the norm in the European Union.

The situation is somewhat different in relation to more expensive hospital based services. In some countries, such as Denmark, Italy and Ireland, state controlled hospitals are a dominant feature whereas in others, such as Germany, France and Belgium the private sector holds a large share of service provision. In a number of countries such as the UK, Portugal and Ireland there have been recent developments allowing major hospital services a greater degree of freedom from state control. The 1990 health care reform in the UK has provided for hospitals to become "Trusts" which are more operationally independent from the state than has previously been the case. * * *

* * *

GERMANY

The German health care system is a model system of compulsory social insurance. The system has experienced no fundamental structural change since its foundations were laid by Bismarck in 1883, although it has expanded significantly and there have been some fundamental reforms in health insurance structure.

The system has managed to achieve comprehensive health care coverage and provides for equal access to a high volume of advanced medical services. A majority of the German population seems to consider its health care system as either very or fairly satisfactory.

The reason for this success has been attributed to the highly decentralised decision-making and an effective negotiation system between provider parties and third-party payers at central, state, and local level.

* * *

Organisation and finance of health care in Germany is based on the traditional principles of social solidarity, decentralisation and self-regulation. The role of the central government is limited to providing the legislative framework in which health services are delivered while much of the executive responsibility lies with the administrations of the individual states (Länder). The Federal Ministry of Health is the key institution on the federal level, assisted by subordinate authorities with scientific expertise. The "Advisory Council for Concerted Action" in health care plays an advisory role in medical and broader economic matters.

The statutory social insurance system covers nearly 88% of the German population. Workers below a certain income threshold are required to take out statutory health insurance, the unemployed are entirely covered by the State. In 1997, 75% of the population were mandatory members and 13% voluntary members of the approximately 600 sickness funds* * * . Another 10% of Germans, mainly civil servants, are covered by their employers and high income earners are privately insured with one of the 45 private insurance companies. Less than 0.5% of the population is uninsured. Sickness funds are either organised by districts, occupation, or specific enterprises. Employees have been granted free choice of sickness funds since 1996.

The benefit package for social insurance is regulated by federal legislation, providing for the following benefits in kind: prevention of disease, screening for disease, diagnostic procedures, treatment of disease, rehabilitation, and transportation.

Around 60% of funding is derived from compulsory and voluntary contributions to statutory health insurance, about 21% is derived from general taxation, private insurance accounts for approximately 7% and the remaining 11% is covered by direct payments by the patient.

Contributions to sickness funds are collected from all work-related income, payroll taxes being divided equally between employer and employee.* * *

There is a strict separation of purchasers (sickness funds) and health care services in the German system. Service fees are subject to a highly decentralised process of bargaining between the major health care institutions.

Hospitals, whether public or private, * * * are financed by a dual system involving coverage of capital costs by the Länder and payment of operating costs by the sickness fends.* * *

Ambulatory care is financed throughout a complex formal negotiation process between representatives of the sickness funds and physician and dental associations. To provide services to members of statutory insurance funds, practitioners are required to join the respective associations.

The principal mechanism of reimbursement is fee-for-service for general practitioner, specialist services and dental care. There is a federal fee schedule, the Uniform Evaluation Standard. The actual monetary value is negotiated regionally, adjusted to the overall income of physicians.

* * *

UNITED KINGDOM

The National Health Service (NHS) has been regarded in the UK for decades as the "jewel in the crown of the Welfare State", pioneering universal access to medical care when introduced in 1948. The NHS is a public health care service financed mainly by taxes. With over a million employees, it is Europe's largest non-military employer.

NHS coverage for services is comprehensive and mostly free at the point of use. The organization of health care in the United Kingdom has undergone substantial changes since 1990. The main changes to the previous system are the separation of purchasers from the providers of health care and the introduction of an "internal market" within the NHS. * * *

The system's focus on primary care and the GP as the strict entry point for health care have frequently been seen as strengths in comparison with other EU health care systems. Health status indicators when considered as outcome indicators of health care perform relatively well. Expenditure growth has been remarkably slow compared with the trend in other EU Member States. However, the level of health care funding, which is under tight central government budgetary control, has been the object of an ongoing political and public debate. The level of resources devoted to secondary care is seen as being particularly critical, for it appears to be one cause of long waiting lists for inpatient hospital services. Waiting lists are one reason for only moderate satisfaction with the system among a sample UK population when surveyed in 1996. With few exceptions the system copes well with serious and urgent illness, but less well with minor (although no less distressing for the patient) conditions.

* * *

The NHS is mainly funded from the general tax system (95%) and other payments (5%) under an overall budget which is set by the Ministry and subject to approval by Parliament. Insurance-based schemes are associated with a small private sector which grew rapidly during the 80's and early 90's. In 1996 about 9% of the population took out supplementary private insurance to secure consultant inpatient services and to avoid long waiting times for non-emergency treatment, since NHS waiting-lists are perceived to be fairly long. Nonetheless, finance is predominately focused on services delivered within or for the NHS and only 3.5% of expenditure is covered by private insurance. In addition, the new Labour Government abolished tax relief on private health insurance in 1997. Direct payments have increased annually for a number of drugs, dental care and eye testing, but many patients are exempted, including children, senior citizens, pregnant mothers, the unemployed and those receiving social security payments.

In 1995 public hospitals became NHS hospital trusts * ** which are now more independent, especially in employing their own medical staff and in providing services to a wider range of providers. * * *

In 1997, 60% of staff worked under contracts agreed with local trusts. Hospital employees are salaried, and many doctors additionally work in private practice.

The remuneration system for GPs is a complex mixture of fees and allowances specified in their contracts. The major payment is a capitation fee for each patient on the doctors list. The level of payment depends on the age of the patient. A few services, such as contraception and vaccination are paid fee-for-service. There are also incentive payments for achieving, for example, an immunisation target. * * *

Notes and Questions

1. The possibility of a publicly financed health care system (often called in the 1990s a "single-payer" system, though this term does not accurately describe social insurance systems), has been debated in the United States for decades. It has always, however, faced strong opposition from some sectors of the health care industry (in the 40s, 50s and 60s from physicians, now primarily from insurers), and has rarely enjoyed broad political support. Even when some form of national health reform seemed possible in the early 1990s, a single-payer alternative received little political support. The political makeup and ideological bent of the United States is quite different from that of Canada and most European countries, and was, in particular, very different in the post-World War II era when many of these nations adopted public health insurance systems. See Theodore Marmor, The Politics of Medicare (2d ed. 2000); Carolyn Hughes Tuohy, Accidental Logics (1999).

What explains the political aversion of most Americans to a national health system? Why has the rest of the world not followed our example? What benefits does our privately financed system offer? What problems does it cause?

2. Comparative public satisfaction with health care systems is surveyed on a regular basis. In the most recently published survey as of this writing, 17 percent of surveyed Americans expressed the opinion that our system on the whole works pretty well, while 46 percent believed fundamental changes were necessary, and 33 percent believed that the system needed to be completely rebuilt. By contrast, 25 percent of those surveyed in the U.K. and 20 percent in Canada were largely satisfied, while 14 percent in the U.K. and 23 percent in Canada thought the system needed to be completely rebuilt. Fourteen percent of Americans reported an instance of not being able to get needed medical care in the past 12 months, compared to 10 percent in both Canada and the U.K., but 55 percent of respondents from Canada and 69 percent from the U.K. reported waits of a month or more for nonemergency surgery, compared to only 29 percent in the U.S. Forty-nine percent of Americans reported that the medical care received by their families in the past 12 months was very good or excellent, compared to 50 percent of respondents from the U.K. and 54 percent from Canada. Karen Donelan, et al.,

The Cost of Health System Change: Public Discontent in Five Nations, 18 Health Aff., May/June 1999 at 206.

A comparable recent comparative survey of physicians finds that American physicians are more likely to report that their hospitals are addressing medical errors, that they are able to keep up with medical developments, and that they have access to resources such as the latest medical equipment or medical specialists than their counterparts in the U.K. or Canada. American physicians, however, are also more likely to report that their patients have difficulty affording out-of-pocket costs. The Commonwealth Fund, 2000 International Health Policy Survey of Physicians.

3. Despite our attachment to private health insurance, public programs do play a very important role in the United States. The Medicare and Medicaid programs, created in the 1960s, now cover about 28 percent of the population and are growing in size. Medicaid expansions adopted in the 1980s, for example, will by 2002 extend eligibility to all children under the federal poverty level ($17,050 for a family of 4 for 2000) and under the age of 19. The SCHIP program provides federal funding for states to cover children in families with income up to twice the federal poverty level. An expansion of Medicare to cover prescription drugs seems very much on the table at this writing. A number of states also provide state funding for insuring poor adults. It is quite possible that marginal expansion of public programs for the poor will continue in the coming years.

4. Further, the state and federal governments play an important, and often unrecognized role, in direct funding or provision of health care services through "safety-net" providers. In 1998 8.1 million individuals were provided primary care in more than 600 federally financed community health centers. Many other obtained care in more than 100 public hospitals and health care systems, local health departments or inner-city teaching hospitals. See Christopher B. Forrest and Ellen–Marie Whelan, Primary Care Safety-net Delivery Sites in the United States, 284 JAMA 2077 (2000); Raymond J. Baxter and Robert E. Mechanic, The Status of Local Health Care Safety Nets, 16 Health Aff., July/Aug. 1997 at 7. These safety net providers, like their patients, have in recent years endured a precarious financial existence. See, Institute of Medicine, America's Health Care Safety Net: Intact but Endangered (Marion Ein Lewin and Stuart Altman, eds., 2000). While safety net providers do not offer an adequate substitute for health insurance for providing health care access for the poor, they do provide a means of access to health care services, and in particular primary health care services, for many who would otherwise have to do without.

5. See, for further information on access to health care in other nations, Timothy Stoltzfus Jost, Readings in Comparative Health Law and Bioethics (2000).

2. *Approaches to Insuring the Uninsured Based on Private Insurance*

If publicly-financed approaches to insuring the uninsured are not politically feasible at this time, proposals based on providing tax incentives for the purchase of private insurance might be. A broad range of analysts and interest groups, centered on the right but in fact spanning much of the political spectrum, have proposed that we build on our current system of tax subsidies for health insurance by offering tax credits to uninsured persons to purchase health insurance. Here is the proposal made by President Bush during the 2000 campaign (found at www.bush2000.com).

Governor Bush's Proposals

To help individuals and families afford quality health care, Governor Bush will:

Offer a Refundable Health Credit: Families that don't qualify for Medicaid and other government programs and who don't get insurance through their employer, will be offered a $2000 health credit ($1000 for individuals) to assist in purchasing a basic health insurance plan. Those most in need will receive the most help.

For example, if a family earning $30,000 purchases a health insurance plan costing $2,222, the government's contribute $2,000 (90 percent), and the family will pay just $18.50 per month ($222 annually, or 10 percent).

If a family earning $50,000 purchases the same $2,222 health plan, the government's contribution will be $667, and the family's contribution will be $129 amount ($1,555 annually, or 70 percent.)

Many advocates of tax credits further propose that credits replace our current tax exclusions and deductions for employee health benefits, which, as noted above, benefit wealthier persons more than poorer, and arguably lead to inefficient levels of insurance coverage. See Empowering Health Care Consumers, above. Proposals to abolish one of the most widely claimed tax subsidies offered by the federal government, however, and to replace it with a subsidy much less valuable to many taxpayers is unlikely to be politically popular. Proposals to use tax credits for expanding the purchase of private insurance by those currently uninsured, however, enjoy wide popularity at this writing. How effective, however, would this strategy be?

First, for tax credits to be of any value they would have to be fully refundable, as was the tax credit proposed by candidate Bush. It would have, that is, to be paid to taxpayers whether or not their tax liability was sufficient to cover the credit. Because many of those Americans currently uninsured do not have tax liabilities approaching the level of subsidy proposed, a standard nonrefundable tax credit (i.e. one that is simply subtracted from taxes due), would be of little help. Administering a refundable tax credit, however, is much more costly and complex administratively, as a program must be established to review applications, set payment levels, and mail out checks. It would also be important, moreover, that tax credits be refundable in advance, as a credit is of little value to an uninsured person if it arrives months after the cost of a policy is incurred. On the other hand, projecting future income initially, and reconciling projected income with actual income at the end of the year leads to further bureaucratic complexities.

A bigger problem with tax credit proposals is that to really make a difference tax credits need to be set at a high enough level that they actually make the purchase of health insurance viable. In the Spring of 2000, the average annual premium for employer-provided health insurance, according to one survey, was $2,426 for single coverage, $6,351 for family coverage. Another study projected that employers will pay on average $4,707 for employee health coverage in 2001. The cost of the individual policies that many advocates of tax credits propose because of an ideological opposition to employment-related group insurance would cost even more, because insurers face higher underwriting, marketing and administrative costs for individual policies than for group policies. Even if the rates were the same, however, a family of three at the poverty level of $14,150 would have to pay $4,351 after the $2000 tax credit to purchase insurances, over 30 percent of its before tax income on health insurance.

Tax credits are also, arguably, very inefficient as a means of insuring the uninsured, particularly if they are used to purchase individual insurance policies that include high administrative costs for marketing and underwriting. They cost much more per uninsured person covered than do public programs, though they allow such persons to enter the private market, and might give them more choice of health coverage.

In fact, tax credits are likely to be of most use to those who are already purchasing individual policies. The availability of such credits will also undoubtedly tempt many employers to drop insurance coverage as an employee benefit, urging their employees instead to avail themselves of the tax credit and purchase their own policies. There is likely to be a substantial "crowd out" effect of any such program, therefore. One simulation of the implementation of a refundable tax credit (worth up to $1000 for singles and $2000 for families) estimated that 18.4 million persons would take up such a policy, but of these 8.6 million would be persons previously insured under nongroup policies, 4.7 million persons previously covered by employment-based insurance, .4 million persons previously covered by Medicaid, and only 4.7 million persons previously uninsured. Jonathan Gruber and Larry Levitt, Tax Subsidies for Health Insurance: Costs and Benefits, 19 Health Aff., Jan./Feb. 2000 at 72, 75.

The implementation of such a program would, therefore, only expand coverage to slightly more than 10 percent of the currently uninsured. The cost of covering each uninsured person would be $3,300, and most of the benefit of the program would go to persons with incomes above the poverty level. Substantial equity arguments can be made for a program that would relieve the financial burden of firms that employ low wage workers or of individuals that currently buy individual policies without federal tax subsidies, but as a program for reaching the uninsured, tax credit programs are far more expensive and less effective than expansion of public programs.

In the end, however tax credit programs are politically popular, and some combination of such programs and marginal expansions of public programs such as Medicaid or SCHIP are the most likely programs to get adopted during the shelf-life of this edition. See Charles N. Kahn III & Ronald F. Pollack, Building a Consensus for Expanding Health Coverage, Health Aff. Jan./Feb. 2001 at 40.

Why do tax credit proposals enjoy such popularity? What benefits do they offer to the uninsured? What benefits do they offer to the insurance industry? Why might they prove more attractive to some employers than the current system of deductions? Will they prove to be more attractive to currently insured employees? If we are to use tax credits to subsidize the purchase of insurance, should they be used to subsidize individual or group insurance policies?

B. COST CONTROL

1. *Regulatory Strategies*

Both public and market-based strategies are also possible for addressing the problem of cost control. In most developed nations, costs are controlled through public program budgets. In countries like the United Kingdom, where most funds come from a single source, budgeting is a relatively straightforward process—funds are allocated by the central government to the NHS, which distributes them to the various health authorities according to an allocation formula. The health authorities in turn use the funds for purchasing health care. Health care costs are, quite simply, whatever the government decides to spend on health care in a given year, supplemented by limited private funds spent on private care. In countries like Germany, social insurance programs are administered by a number of quasi-private insurance funds which must negotiate budgets with corporately organized providers. The government only sets general guidelines for budgets, which are in turn worked out on a decentralized basis. Less control over cost, of course, is possible in this type of system. Controlling costs is also more difficult in federal systems like Canada where both the federal and provincial governments provide funds for health care. Nevertheless, countries with public systems have generally been able to limit costs with considerable success.

But cost control through budgets imposes its own costs. Countries that place relatively severe limits on cost, like the United Kingdom, tend to develop shortages and waiting lists. Access to the latest technology and to elective procedures like hip replacements, that are not life-saving, but increase comfort and functioning, is often limited. Countries with more generous budgets face fewer rationing constraints, but can experience problems from bureaucratic misallocation of funds. See Karen Donelan, et al., All Payer, Single Payer, Managed Care, No Payer: Patients' Perspectives in Three Nations, 15 Health Aff. (Summer 1996) at 254.

Within the United States public budgets have rarely been tried. Even the Medicare and Medicaid programs are entitlement programs, under which eligible providers are entitled to payment for all covered goods and services that are provided to eligible beneficiaries and recipients. Cost control efforts in Medicare and Medicaid have focused rather on limiting the prices paid for goods and services, and on managed care. These themes are explored further below in chapter 10. Because, however, it is difficult to imagine the United States adopting anything resembling a single payer system in the foreseeable future, little time needs to be spent here debating the merits or demerits of budgets as a means of controlling health care costs in the United States.

With respect to private health care cost control, public interventions in the United States have been regulatory. Historically, our most significant regulatory cost control program was the health planning, certificate of need, program, which was established at the federal level in 1974 and abolished in 1986, but which still continues in many states. Under health planning, states attempted to project their needs for various health services through a planning process, and then to require health care providers (particularly hospitals and nursing homes), to obtain a "certificate of need" before adding new beds or making major expenditures for technology. The program was based on the theory that controlling supply would control demand, but the program had only a limited effect on costs.

The other major regulatory state program for controlling costs was hospital rate setting, which was attempted by a half dozen states in the 1970s and 1980s. At this point rate setting has been abandoned, and certificate of need programs are on the wane. There is little enthusiasm currently among health policy analysts or health economists for regulatory approaches to cost control (other than through the antitrust laws, explored further in chapter 15).

If the problem of health care costs is ultimately attributable to market failure, as was contended above, then the market must be reformed to make it work. Potential markets exist, however, both at the level of health care delivery and of health care finance. Therefore, market reforms can alternatively attempt to create functioning markets for health care services or for health insurance. In general, more politically conservative reformers, who were in the ascendancy in Congress in the late 1990s, proposed the creation of markets at the point of purchase of health care by encouraging cost-sharing and medical savings accounts, primarily through changes in the tax code. Alternatively, managed competition proposals, popular earlier in the decade, would control costs by enhancing competition among health insurers and managed care plans for individual consumers. In fact, health care costs were substantially controlled in the 1990s by managed care plans operating in largely unregulated markets, thus this alternative must also be considered.

2. CONSUMER CHOICE IN PURCHASING HEALTH CARE SER-VICES: THE MEDICAL SAVINGS ACCOUNT

Proponents of the point of purchase control strategy believe that the primary factor driving health care cost inflation is insurance, which shields individuals from the consequences of their own health care purchasing decisions. The collective consequence of this irresponsible individual conduct is spiraling health care inflation. The fact that employer payments for insurance premiums are not subject to the income tax exacerbates this problem by encouraging individuals to purchase more insurance coverage than they would if it were not tax-subsidized.

If there were no insurance, these analysts argue, there would be no problem of excessive health care costs. Each individual would decide whether or to spend money for a hip replacement or a new car when confronted with the choice. Because most consumers are risk averse, however, insurance exists and is widely purchased by those who can afford it. Moreover, because medical expenses may in particular situations outstrip the resources of all but the most wealthy, some form of insurance, private or public, is probably necessary if providers are to be paid.

Advocates of the point-of-service market approach, therefore, would permit insurance, but would encourage high levels of cost-sharing (deductibles, coinsurance, and copayments) so that, to the extent possible, consumers would make trade-off choices at the point of purchase of services. Cost-sharing both encourages consumers to avoid unnecessary care and to shop for the least expensive providers when care is necessary. Advocates of this approach would tax insurance payments made by employers as income to the employee (or, at least limit the exclusion of such payments from taxation) to force health insurance to compete with other consumer goods on a level playing field. They would also encourage medical savings accounts, a form of individual self-insurance, by giving favorable tax treatment to such accounts. This approach has been advocated by conservative think tanks such as the Heritage Foundation and American Enterprise Institute and by economists such as Mark Pauly. See Mark Pauly & John Goodman, Incremental Steps Toward Health Care Reform, Health Affairs, Spring 1995 at 125; Stuart M. Butler, A Conservative Agenda for Health Reform, Health Affairs, Spring 1995 at 150; Mark V. Pauly, et al., Responsible National Health Insurance (1992).

Haavi Morreim is an articulate proponent of the point-of-service market position in the legal literature:

E.   Haavi Morreim, REDEFINING QUALITY BY REASSIGNING RESPONSIBILITY, 20 Am.J.L. & Med., 79, 99 (1994).

Broad choices among health care plans are important, but probably insufficient by themselves. If patients' sole economic involvement is to select one plan over another, even with year-end monetary savings to reward a wise choice, many patients will bring to these plans the same entitlement mentality that currently prompts people to game the system or to demand virtually limitless care on the ground that paying their premium endows them with a right to receive whatever they think they need. On a narrower level, then, patients arguably need to experience directly some economic consequences of their decisions. * * *

In one proposal a high deductible, such as $3000, might be matched by a tax exempt Medical Savings Account (MSA) from which to pay routine medical bills, with supplementary catastrophic insurance to address costs exceeding this amount. The MSA funds might be initially raised by the patient, the employer, the government, or even the insurer. Since the patient would pay directly for all the ordinary costs of care, he would have serious reason to inquire whether a proposed intervention is really necessary, and how else his medical needs might be met most efficiently. At the same time, he never lacks the money to pay for care. The MSA fund is ready and waiting, and for the relatively few patients who exceed it, the catastrophic policy takes over. Further, directly paying for care in this way could save enormous administrative costs by bypassing the need to file myriad small claims with insurers. A debit card, presented at the time of service, would obviate the need to bill the patient or insurer. Any money left in the fund from year to year becomes a cushion against potential future illness and could be used for the higher health care costs usually incurred after retirement, or could even be rolled over into that person's retirement fund.

See also, E. Haavi Morreim, Diverse and Perverse Incentives of Managed Care: Bringing Patients Into Alignment, 1 Widener Law Symposium J. 89 (1996).

A number of states, including Arizona, Colorado, Idaho, Ohio and West Virginia have adopted legislation recognizing and giving favorable state income tax treatments to MSAs. The question of whether this policy should be adopted at the federal level was hotly debated during the spring and summer of 1996 in the context of the Health Insurance Portability and Accountability

Act of 1996 (HIPAA). In the end, this legislation, Pub. L. 104–191, established an experiment to test the MSA concept.

Under the experiment set up under HIPPA, employees of small employers (who employ less than 50 employees) and self-employed persons, insured under "High Deductible Health Plans" (with annual deductibles of from $1500 to $2500 for individual coverage and from $3000 to $4500 for family coverage) were allowed to claim a tax deduction for monthly deposits in MSAs totalling up to 65 percent of the annual deductible for individual coverage and 75 percent for family coverage. 26 U.S.C.A. § 220(a). Employer tax contributions to MSAs within the same limits were also excluded from taxable income. 26 U.S.C.A. § 106(b). The MSAs were trusts generally managed by banks or insurance companies. 26 U.S.C.A. § 220(d). Expenditures from MSAs for qualified medical expenses were not taxable, but expenditures from MSAs for nonmedical expenses were taxable, and additionally subject to a 15 percent excise tax. 26 U.S.C.A. § 220(e).

The tax deduction for MSAs was to be only available on an experimental and limited basis and only during the four year period of 1997–2000. Only about 750,000 individuals were under statute allowed to participate in the experiment at any one time. Beyond the year 2000, only persons with established accounts were to be able to continue to take advantage of the deduction unless Congress took action to extend or expand the program (which it did under the 2001 budget bill). The impact of the experimental program on health care access and costs was to be carefully evaluated.

A similar experiment was established for Medicare beneficiaries under the Medicare + Choice program by the 1997 Balanced Budget Act. The BBA experiment permitted up to 390,000 participants. MSA plan beneficiaries were to be covered by a catastrophic insurance plan with a deductible of up to $6000. MSA plan beneficiaries would receive from Medicare the difference between the premium of the high deductible plan and the amount that Medicare would pay for other M + C plans to be deposited in a tax free MSA from which medical expenses could be paid, and from which money could eventually be withdrawn for other purposes. 42 U.S.C.A. §§ 1395w–21(d)(3) & (4); 1395w–23(e), 1395w–28(b)(3).

MSAs have proved intensely controversial. Extensive research conducted by the Rand Corporation in the early 1980s demonstrated that requiring consumers to bear the costs of medical care (usually referred to as cost-sharing) in fact lowers costs. See Willard G. Manning, et al., Health Insurance and the Demand for Medical Care: Evidence from a Randomized Experiment, 77 Am.Econ.Rev. 251 (1987). A Rand study based on this data predicted that MSAs could result in substantial savings of health care costs, though the amount of savings would depend on the design of the program. Emmett Keeler, et al., Can Medical Savings Accounts for the Nonelderly Reduce Health Care Costs?, 275 JAMA 1666 (1996).

Opponents of MSAs, however, argue that the savings of cost-sharing in general, and of MSAs in particular, come at a price. M. Edith Rasell, Cost Sharing in Health Insurance—A Reexamination, 332 New Eng. J. Med. 1164 (1995). High cost-sharing obligations are burdensome to those who have chronic diseases and need health care on a continual basis. Generally, persons who require little health care would be better off with higher cost-sharing, people who require a great deal of health care, worse off. This is particularly true under MSA proposals that permit persons with MSAs to withdraw money from the accounts for non-health expenditures. (The HIPAA imposes an excise tax on such withdrawals, 26 U.S.C.A. § 220(e)). On the other hand, if high deductible plans were accompanied by unlimited, first-dollar comprehensive coverage once the deductible is met, they could be more attractive to those in very poor health than insurance plans with lower deductibles but unlimited cost-sharing or with coverage capped at low levels. (Under the HIPAA, qualified high deductible policies were required to cap out-of-pocket expenses at $3000 for individual policies and $5500 for family coverage, 26 U.S.C.A. § 220(c)(2)(A)(iii).)

Perhaps the most significant problem for MSAs as a cost-saving device is the fact that the most common medical savings account proposals affect directly only a small percentage of medical costs. If the deductible on an insurance policy were set at $3000, over 84 percent of adults would not have had expenses that qualified for insurance coverage in 1995. These persons would cover their own expenses out-of-pocket or out of their MSA, and would presumably spend this money wisely. There would also, as Prof. Morreim points out, be considerable savings on administrative costs for these expenditures. These adults are only responsible, however, for less than 17 percent of all medical charges. The remaining 16 percent of the population would be responsible for the other 83 percent of medical charges. See American Academy of Actuaries, Medical Savings Accounts 6–7 (1995). These high-cost persons would quickly reach the limit of their cost-sharing obligations, and face no obvious incentives to limit their costs thereafter. In other words, cost-sharing would limit expenditures on primary care by the healthy, but would do little to limit the cost of the vast majority of medical care which is consumed by the unhealthy. It might even tend to discourage use of preventive care, necessitating the use of more expensive acute care at a later point.

If MSAs and high-deductible insurance policies were offered as an alternative to traditional low-deductible plans to employees or public program beneficiaries, what is known in the health insurance literature as "biased selection" could also take place. The relatively healthy may "take the money and run" while the sicker and older population would choose to remain with the low deductible plans. This might progressively drive up the cost of low deductible plans, resulting either in increased costs of the program as a whole or increased cost-shifting to the older and sicker population. MSAs short, it could threaten insurance as a form of cost-sharing across populations.

Finally, cost-sharing strategies disproportionately affect those who have less money and, therefore, fewer choices. This effect could be ameliorated to some extent through employer funding of MSAs or by tax credits used to subsidize this population, but subsidies would in turn diminish the effectiveness of MSAs. Also tax credits offered to encourage the use of MSAs would reduce tax revenues, a cost that must be set off against savings MSAs might produce from the perspective of government.

In fact, the HIPPA experiment failed to substantiate the problems predicted by the opponents of MSAs. On the other hand, it also failed to support the case of MSA advocate. In the end very few persons took advantage of the HIPPA MSA program. According to IRS figures, only about 45,000 persons had MSAs under the HIPAA experiment in 1998. Only about one quarter of these were previously uninsured. Although 54 insurers offered the plans when the experiment began, only 48 remained in the market at the end of 1997, and most had sold fewer than 1000 policies, with one insurer accounting for more than half of the policies. MSA plans were most often offered to highly-paid professionals, farmers and ranchers, partnership firms, and association groups. No plans stepped forward to offer MSAs to Medicare recipients under the 1997 Balanced Budget Act. However elegant the theoretical arguments may be that support MSAs, almost nobody wants to purchase insurance that leaves the insured responsible for virtually all health care costs. See GAO, Medical Savings Accounts: Results from Surveys of Insurers (GAO/HEHS–99–34, 1998). Nevertheless, the advocates of MSAs continue to argue that the HIPPA experiment failed because it imposed too many constraints, and that MSA's could thrive if these constraints were removed.

See, advocating MSAs, Gail A.Jensen, Making Room for Medical Savings Accounts inthe U.S. Health Care System, in American Health Care! Government Market Process, andthe Public Interest (Roger D.Feldman, ed. 2000).

Would you buy an MSA? How would its value to you compare with your current insurance plan? Would your parents be better off with an MSA? Your grandparents? How would an MSA affect your health care purchasing decisions? How might it simplify, or complicate, your life?

2. MANAGED COMPETITION

The second major market-based strategy for restructuring the health care industry is managed competition, the approach which formed the basis of the Clinton plan and on which some current proposals for reforming Medicare are built. Managed competition attempts to organize the market for health care financing entities—health insurers, managed care plans, and integrated delivery systems (usually designated collectively as "health plans")—to make this market for health care finance more competitive. It then relies on these financing entities to control the cost of health care services. Under managed competition proposals, consumers would be organized into purchasing alliances to give them market power in dealing with health plans. Health plans are usually, under such proposals, required to sell a uniform product or a manageable number of standardized products to permit price and quality comparisons. Explicit risk selection is a real danger under managed competition, as plans could easily compete with each other for the best risks rather than by offering the best deals. Risk selection is under most proposals, therefore, outlawed and open-enrollment and community or modified community rating required. (See chapter 8 below for an explanation of these concepts.) Payments to health plans may also be standardized based on risk so that health plans do not face incentives to try to select insureds based on risk.

The hope of managed competition is that health plans in turn intelligently purchase services, bargaining with providers for low prices and high quality. Consumers are provided with comparative quality and price information to facilitate selection of health plans. In short, the market in general, and the health care purchasing alliances more specifically, are to be organized to correct for the market failures discussed earlier.

The strategy of managed competition was originated by Alain Enthoven, a Stanford economist. See Alain Enthoven, Health Plan (1980). It was developed by the Jackson Hole group, consisting of Enthoven, Paul Ellwood, and others. See Alain C. Enthoven, The History and Principles of Managed Competition, Health Affairs, Supp. 1993 at 24. It formed the basis, not only for the Clinton plan, but also for health reform legislation adopted in a number of states, including Florida, Minnesota, and Washington, in the early 1990s. Varying forms of managed competition are in use in a range of contexts today.

Established and proposed structures for facilitating managed competition vary considerably. Proposals usually require the development of health care purchasing alliances, which create a market within which insurers compete for the business of alliance members. Health insurance purchasing alliances could include all insureds in a geographic area, all insureds except for employees of firms large enough to exercise substantial power in the market themselves, or only insureds who are not employed or are employed by firms small enough to be at a substantial disadvantage in purchasing insurance. To be effective, purchasing alliances must be large enough to achieve administrative economies of scale and to possess significant power in bargaining with health plans. As more insureds are permitted to opt out of purchasing alliances, both of these strengths are compromised. Another important structural issue is whether there will be one or several alliances in any particular area. If only one alliance is permitted it will not be subject to the discipline of a competitive market, and may become excessively regulatory and inefficient. If competing alliances are permitted, however, the advantages of economies of scale and market power may be lost, and risk selection becomes more of a problem.

The extent of regulatory power exercised by purchasing alliances must also be determined. The proposed Clinton Health Security Act would have required alliances to determine eligibility of insureds for premium or cost-sharing subsidies, investigate complaints against plans, and hear appeals from utilization review decisions. Critics of the plan were able to characterize the alliances as bureaucratic monstrosities. While the Clinton plan would have given the purchasing alliances extensive regulatory power, it gave them little authority to bargain with health plans to negotiate premiums. Alternative models could allow purchasing alliances to bargain aggressively with health plans and to only offer to their members the plans that offered the lowest prices. See, discussing these issues, Henry T. Greely, Policy Issues in Health Alliances: of Efficiency, Monopsony, and Equity, 5 Health Matrix 37–82 (1995); Frances H. Miller, Health Insurance Purchasing Alliances: Monopsony Threat or Procompetitive Rx for Health Sector Ills? 79 Cornell L. Rev. 1546–72 (1994).

Existing examples of managed competition have enjoyed some success with holding down costs. Getting a comprehensive national system of managed competition underway, however, would be a daunting task. A particular problem would be assuring the development of enough health plans to compete in each relevant market, particularly in rural markets. One study found that 42 percent of the nation's population lives in areas that would not support three competitive HMOs. Richard Kronick et al., The Marketplace in Health Care Reform—The Demographic Limitations of Managed Competition,

328 New Eng. J. Med. 148 (1993). Control over risk selection by the plans would also likely be a major problem. As noted above, if plans were allowed to compete for the most healthy and least costly insureds, they would have little reason to compete with respect to price. It is questionable, however, whether the technology exists currently to adjust payments made to health plans adequately for risk and thus to avoid risk selection. And managed competition would do little to control administrative costs, indeed, it could arguably simply add another layer of administration.

Nationwide, there are a number of purchasing cooperatives that operate more or less in conformity to the managed competition model. Among the best known examples are the Federal Employees Health Benefits Plan (FEHBP), the California Public Employees Retirement System (CalPERS) and Pacific Health Advantage (known until 1999 as the Health Insurance Plan of California See, Thomas C. Buchmueller, et al)., The Health Insurance Plan of California: The First Five Years, 19 Health Aff., Sept./Oct. 2000 at 158, and describing the FEHBP, Kenneth E. Thorpe, et al., Market Incentives, Plan Choice, and Price Increases, 18 Health Aff., Nov./Dec. 1999 at 194. Pooled purchasing arrangements, created to expand insurance coverage by small businesses, also often exhibit characteristics of managed competition models. See Stephen H. Long and M. Susan Marquis, Pooled Purchasing: Who are the Players? 18 Health Aff., July/Aug. 1999 at 105.

Arguably, the most prevalent variant of managed competition is found, however, not in formal purchasing alliances, but rather at the employer level. The vast majority of large employers (and many smaller employers) offer their employees a choice among health care plans, usually requiring greater employee contributions where employees choose more expensive plans that offer greater choice of provider or other additional benefits. Many of these employers attempt to provide their employees information with which to make an informed choice, including sometimes quality information. The employee then chooses among the options, weighing cost, provider choice, and other factors. This form of managed competition has reportedly proved successful for some employers in holding down premium costs. James Maxwell, et al., Managed Competition in Practice, "Value Purchasing" by Fourteen Employers, 17 Health Aff., May/June 1998 at 216.

Several legal scholars have suggested an alternative approach to using health financing entities for controlling health care costs. Clark Havighurst, long an advocate of market-strategies, contends that health plan contracts could be written to accurately articulate and enforce consumer preferences for levels of coverage, and thus for health care cost. See Clark Havighurst, Health Care Choices (1995). Contracts could, for example, reference practice guidelines or limit liability for practitioners who adopted economical approaches to delivering care, and thus limit health care cost to the level preferred by the purchaser. Mark Hall has similarly suggested that health insurance contracts be written to limit costs. See Mark A. Hall, Making Medical Spending Decisions (1997). This model could supplement, or perhaps serve as an alternative to, managed competition.

4. MANAGED CARE

Though managed competition did not in fact catch on during the 1990s as a widely applied strategy for reducing health care costs, managed care did. See

M. Susan Marquis and Stephen H. Long, Trends in Managed Care and Managed Competition, 1993–1997, 18 Health Aff., Nov./Dec. 1999 at 75. While managed competition involves reorganizing markets to force competition among health plans, managed care refers to the cost control functions of health plans themselves.

There is considerable support for the argument that managed care plans have had the effect of controlling health care costs in the United States. Managed care grew rapidly during the 1990s, and is the dominant approach to financing health care in the United States at the beginning of the 21st century. See Jon Gabel, et al., Job–Based Health Insurance in 2000: Premiums Rise Sharply While Coverage Grows, 19 Health Aff., Sept./Oct. 2000 at 144. It is clear that health care cost increases slowed dramatically during the mid–1990s, and, though they are accelerating again at the beginning of the 2000s, the rates of increase are lower than those experienced a decade earlier. See Christopher Hogan, et al., Tracking Health Care Costs: Inflation Returns, 19 Health Aff., Nov./Dec. 2000 at 217. There is considerable evidence that managed care organizations are able to reduce the utilization of health care services and to negotiate significant discounts with providers, both of which hold down the cost of medical care. See John F. Shiels and Randall A. Haught, Managed Care Savings for Employers and Households: 1990 through 2000 (1997); H.E. Frech III and James Langenfeld, The Impact of Antitrust Exemptions for Health Care Professionals on Health Care Costs (2000). There is also some evidence that higher market penetration by HMOs, the most restrictive form of managed care, leads to moderation of cost growth through the entire market. Laurence C. Baker, et al., HMO Market Penetration and the Costs of Employer–Sponsored Health Plans, 19 Health Aff., Sept./Oct. 2000 at 121.

Some argue, however, that the role of managed care in decreasing increases in health care costs has been oversold. The administrative costs of managed care, are higher than those of traditional health insurance, and there is far less evidence for a causal relationship between the growth of managed care and the reduction of health care cost increases in the 1990s than is commonly assumed. See Kip Sullivan, On the "Efficiency" of Managed Care Plans, 19 Health Aff., July/August 2000 at 139.

Accepting the general belief that managed care has proved an effective cost control strategy, it bears noting that the growth in managed care has been driven by and large by large purchasers, employers, unions, multi-employer associations, and government program—sophisticated purchasers that could drive a hard bargain with managed care plans. See William S. Custer, et al., Why We Should Keep the Employment–Based Health Insurance System, 18 Health Aff., Nov./Dec. 1999 at 115; Robert Kuttner, Employer–Sponsored Health Care, 340 New. Eng. J. Med. 248 (1999). It has not, by and large, been driven by government policy, except in public programs. It has, also, however, not been directly driven by consumer behavior, if consumers are defined as the individuals and families who ultimately consume health care services. Consumers, indeed, are widely perceived as resisting the excesses of managed care, contributing to a growth in less restrictive preferred provider or point of service plans at the expense of the more restrictive, but less costly, health maintenance organizations during the late 1990s. It may be, therefore, that market-based strategies for decreasing health care costs should focus on purchasers rather than consumers.

Problem: Health Reform

Imagine that you been asked by a President, who was elected as a centrist (pick the party you prefer) with a vague promise of health care reform, to craft a program that will bring down the number of the uninsured, while holding down health care cost inflation. You have the confidence of the President, who is distracted by many other issues. The public is generally supportive of health care reform, but is vague on what it wants, generally suspicious of government, and opposed to major new expenditures. Your party dominates Congress, though Congress is not necessarily responsive to presidential leadership. There is the possibility, however, of getting a reform package through, particularly if it promises to control the costs of public programs. Design a health care reform program following the following steps.

1) Clarify the values that you would think should drive and govern the health care reform effort. Which is more important if trade-offs must be made, equity or efficiency? Is universal coverage essential? How quickly must it be achieved? Is it important that markets be preserved? What level of government intervention in markets is tolerable?

2) Identify the key interest groups and what their goals will be with respect to the reform package. Obvious interest groups include health care providers (doctors, hospitals, nursing facilities, pharmaceutical companies, etc.), insurers, managed care companies, big businesses, small businesses, the states, the elderly, pro-life groups, and persons with particular diseases. Can you think of others? What divisions might occur within these groups: primary care physicians versus specialists; academic medical centers versus community hospitals; large employers versus small employers; large insurers, Blue Cross/Blue Shield plans, small insurers, and managed care plans against each other; the old versus the young, etc. What alliances do you see forming to support or oppose various approaches? What will be the wedge issues weakening these alliances?

3) Now design a reform program that is consistent with the values that you believe are important and politically feasible, given the interest groups that you believe will be active in the debate. Consider:

a) How will you go about expanding coverage: tax incentives, public programs, or some other alternative or combination of alternatives?

b) What will be your basic approach to cost control: point-of-service competition based on cost-sharing; managed competition; government regulation; or some other alternative or combination of alternatives?

c) How will you pay for the program? Will you use social insurance contributions, the income tax, mandated premium payments, some other form of tax? What level of cost-sharing is appropriate? Should cost-sharing take the form of deductibles or co-insurance? How will you get this part of the program through Congress?

d) What benefits should be offered by the program? Should long-term care be included? If so, should both nursing facility and home health care be covered? To what extent should mental health and substance abuse benefits be mandated? Should abortions be covered, and to what extent? What limits, if any, should be placed on coverage of "futile" care? Should utilization review be required, forbidden, or regulated? Should coverage be limited to traditional medicine, or should nurse practitioners, chiropractors, massage therapists, acupuncturists, and/or reflexologists be covered? What about eyeglasses and dental care? Should all persons get the same benefits? What organizing principle or principles govern your choices among these alternatives?

e) Who should administer and/or regulate the program? What should be the respective roles of government and private insurers or providers? What should be the respective roles of the federal and state governments? If you support a large role for the states, what effect will this have on large businesses that operate throughout the country? Should regulatory responsibilities be borne by government or private accreditation bodies?

4) Design a strategy for getting your program through Congress and implemented.

5) After you complete this exercise as an individual, attempt as a class to reach a consensus on each of the issues you have considered as an individual.

6) Review your response to this problem after you have completed the next four chapters dealing with current programs for private and public health care financing.

Chapter 8

PRIVATE HEALTH INSURANCE AND MANAGED CARE: STATE REGULATION AND LIABILITY

I. INSURANCE AND MANAGED CARE: SOME BASIC CONCEPTS

A. THE CONCEPT OF MANAGED CARE

The United States is unique among modern industrialized nations in the extent to which it relies on private payment for health care services. In 1999 Americans paid $186.5 billion out-of-pocket to health care providers for health care services, 15.4 percent of the $1210.7 billion national health expenditures in that year. Private health insurance, amounting to $375 billion, covered 33.1 percent of personal health care costs. The federal and state governments paid $548.5 billion, most of the rest, or 45.3 percent of the total. Government funding, however, goes primarily for financing health care for the elderly and disabled, and indigent families and children. Most working age Americans rely on private health insurance to cover the cost of their health care. Today, of course, private health insurance means managed care.

In previous editions of this book we have had separate sections discussing regulation of health insurance and of managed care. Until recently it was possible, and indeed sensible, to make a distinction between insurance (meaning indemnity or service benefit insurance) and managed care as different approaches to financing health care. In fact, regulatory programs continue even now to treat traditional commercial insurance and some forms of managed care organizations differently. But in general health insurance has become managed care, and it no longer makes sense to consider them as distinct approaches to health care finance, though it continues to be useful to distinguish between the insurance and care management function of managed care.

Health insurance in the United States is of quite recent origin. It did not become truly widespread until the Second World War. Insurance for medical costs was available on a limited basis in the early twentieth century, usually as an adjunct to disability policies. Some employers or unions also offered employee medical care programs quite early on, often through their own contracted physicians or clinics. Prior to the 1930s, however, health insurance was very unusual. Most Americans paid for health care services out of pocket.

During the 1930s, however, hospitals reacted to the extreme financial distress of the Depression by forming hospital-sponsored "service benefit" plans to ensure a more consistent flow of revenues. These "Blue Cross" plans negotiated payment rates with participating hospitals and charged the same "community-rated" premium to the whole community. The states created special incorporation statutes and regulatory programs for these plans, and often exempted them from state taxes as well. In the late 1930s and 1940s, doctors followed on the accomplishment of the Blue Cross plans by creating their own Blue Shield plans, which operated in much the same way.

Observing the success of Blue Cross and Blue Shield plans, commercial insurers began to offer health insurance themselves, providing "indemnity coverage." Commercial insurers, unlike the Blue Cross and Blue Shield plans, did not pay providers directly, but rather indemnified their insureds for services, first for hospital expenses, and later for physicians services and surgery. Commercial insurers were not limited by the community-rating requirements that constrained the Blues, however, and were often able to pick-off less expensive groups, using "experience rating".

During World War II, many employers, limited from raising wages by war time wage controls, began to offer health insurance benefits as an incentive to attract employees. The Internal Revenue Code permitted employers to claim health insurance premiums as business expenses, while not taxing the premiums to employees as income. This created a significant tax subsidy for employment-based health insurance, which encouraged its rapid spread even after the war ended.

The Employee Retirement Income Security Act of 1974 (ERISA, discussed in chapter 9), freed self-insured employee benefit plans from state regulation, thus offering a significant incentive for large employers to self-insure. Self-insured employers often purchase stop-loss insurance and administer their health insurance plans through third-party administrators. Their plans, therefore, are often almost indistinguishable from insured plans, except for their exemption from state regulation.

Throughout the twentieth century there were always prepaid health plans, such as the Kaiser Permanente group in California, the Group Health Association of Washington, D.C., and the Health Insurance Plan of Greater New York. Prepaid medical practice was vigorously opposed by organized medicine, however. Indeed the AMA was convicted of criminal antitrust violations in 1942 for its efforts to suppress it. AMA v. United States, 130 F.2d 233 (D.C.Cir.1942), affirmed, 317 U.S. 519, 63 S.Ct. 326, 87 L.Ed. 434 (1943). In the 1970s, Paul Ellwood renamed prepaid health care "Health Maintenance Organizations", and HMOs became the cornerstone of President Nixon's health reform plan. Federal legislation to encourage the growth of HMOs was adopted in 1973.

It was not federal incentives, however, but the double-digit increases in health insurance premiums in the late 1980s and early 1990s that led to the triumph of "managed care", a term that emerged to describe HMOs and other forms of health insurance that attempted not just to pay for, but also to control the cost of, health care services. At present, private health insurance is managed care—only a trivial number of classical indemnity insurance policies without care management care elements continue to be sold in the

United States. Most of the surviving Blue Cross and Blue Shield plans (and indeed most state Medicaid programs and, to a lesser extent Medicare) now predominantly offer managed care products. Private health care finance in the United States has become managed care. The history of these developments is traced in Paul Starr's Pulitzer Prize winning, The Social Transformation of American Medicine (1982); Eleanor Kinney, Protecting American Consumers of Health Care (2001); and Gail A. Jensen, et al., The New Dominance of Managed Care: Insurance Trends in the 1990s, 16 Health Aff., Jan.-Feb. 1997 at 125.

But what exactly is "managed care"?

JACOB S. HACKER AND THEODORE R. MARMOR, HOW NOT TO THINK ABOUT "MANAGED CARE"

32 U. Mich. J. L. Ref. 661 (1999).

* * * The * * * critical question that [came] to preoccupy health policy analysts [at the end of the twentieth century] was how to make sense of the "managed care revolution" and its future prospects.

The premise of our argument is that this question cannot be answered as currently formulated. The very term "managed care"—much like that ubiquitous reform phrase of the early 1990s, "managed competition"—is a confused assemblage of sloganeering, aspirational rhetoric, and business school jargon that sadly reflects the general state of discourse about American medical institutions. Because "managed care" is an incoherent subject, most claims about it will suffer from incoherence as well. Moreover, to incorporate "managed care" and other similar marketing terms into health policy research is to presuppose answers to some of the most crucial questions about the recent evolution of medical care in the United States.

* * *

Expressions like "managed care," "integrated delivery systems," and "evidence-based medicine" are in some respects all slogans—persuasively defined terms that imply success by their very use. We do not, for example, routinely speak of "unmanaged care," "disintegrated delivery systems," or "non-evidence based medicine." The relative absence of such categories suggests that the purpose of terms like "managed care" is less to clarify than to convince, less to illuminate what an organization is or does than to bolster empirical claims and normative connotations that are neither self-evident nor, in most cases, subject to critical scrutiny.

* * *

The expression "managed care" came into widespread use only in the past decade. * * * The term "managed care" does not appear once in Paul Starr's exhaustive 1982 history of American medical care, The Social Transformation of American Medicine, nor can it be found in other books on American health policy written before the early 1980s, * * *. Because "managed care" has become such a commonly used and widely recognized expression, it is difficult to recognize just how recently it entered the mainstream of American discourse.

From the beginning, "managed care" was a category with a strong ideological edge, employed to imply competence, concern, and, above all, control over a dangerously unfettered health insurance structure. "Managed care," * * * was an alternative "to the unbridled fee-for-service non-system" that sent "blank checks to hospitals, doctors, dentists, etc." and led to "referrals of dubious necessity" and "unmanaged and uncoordinated care . . . of poor or dubious quality." As these words indicate, managed care was portrayed less as a means to control patient behavior than as a way to bring doctors and hospitals in line with perceived economic realities. Moreover, managed care promised not only cost-control but also coordination and cooperation, not only better management but also better care. By imposing managerial authority on an anarchic "non-system," managed care would simultaneously restrain costs and rationalize an allegedly archaic structure of medical care finance and delivery.

What exactly constitutes "managed care," however, has never been made clear, even by its strongest proponents. To some, the crucial distinguishing feature is a shift in financing from indemnity-style fee-for-service, in which the insurer is little more than a bill-payer, to capitated payment, in which medical providers are paid a fixed amount to treat an individual patient regardless of the volume of services delivered. However, there is nothing intrinsic in fee-for-service payment that requires open-ended reimbursement or passive insurance behavior. Conversely, many, if not most, health insurance plans labeled "managed care" do not rely primarily on capitation. To other proponents, the distinctive characteristic is the creation of administrative protocols for reviewing and sometimes denying care demanded by patients or medical professionals. Such micro-level managerial controls are likewise not universal among so-called managed care health plans. In fact, such controls may be obviated by particular payment methods, like capitation or regulated fee-for-service reimbursement, that create more diffuse constraints on medical practice. Finally, to some, what distinguishes managed care is its reliance on "integrated" networks of health professionals from which patients are required to obtain care. Yet some self-styled managed care plans have no such networks, and what is called a network by many plans is little more than a list of providers willing to accept discounted fee-for-service payments—hardly the dense coordination and integration that industry insiders routinely celebrate.

Perhaps the most defensible interpretation of "managed care" is that it represents a fusion of two functions that once were regarded as largely separate: the financing of medical care and the delivery of medical services. This interpretation, at least, provides a reasonably accurate description of the most familiar organizational entity that marched under the managed care banner until the late 1980s: the health maintenance organization (HMO), a successor to the pre-paid group practice plans that began in the 1930s. When the vast majority of American health insurers used fee-for-service payment and placed few restrictions on patient or provider discretion, it was at least possible to identify a small subset of renegade health plans that existed outside this insurance mainstream, however poorly the expression "managed care" described the organization of such plans or what they did.

Today, however, that is no longer the case. In 1997, * * * between eighty and ninety-eight percent of today's private health insurers appear to fall into the broad category of managed care. "Managed care" therefore does not offer any guidance as to how to distinguish among the vast majority of contemporary health plans.

The standard response to this problem has been to subdivide the managed care universe into a collage of competing acronyms, most coined by industry executives and marketers: HMOs, Preferred Provider Organizations (PPOs), and Exclusive Provider Organizations (EPOs). This is the approach taken by Jonathan Weiner and Gregory de Lissovoy in their frequently cited 1993 article, Razing a Tower of Babel: A Taxonomy for Managed Care and Health Insurance Plans. [18 J. Health Pol. Pol'y & L. (1993).]

* * *

The central problem with Weiner and de Lissovoy's taxonomy—and, indeed, with most contemporary commentary about health insurance—is the tendency to confuse reimbursement methods, managerial techniques, and organizational forms. For example, fee-for-service, a payment method, is regularly contrasted with "managed care," presumably an organizational form. In Weiner and de Lissovey's taxonomy, MIPs [managed indemnity plans] are distinguished from traditional fee-for-service plans by their reliance on a particular managerial technique, namely utilization review. In contrast, PPOs and EPOs are distinguished from MIPs by their particular organizational form, namely their reliance on a network of participating providers. And HMOs are distinguished from all these plans by their particular payment method, namely capitation.

The practice of conflating organization, technique, and incentives leads to unnecessary confusion. It means that when we contrast health plans we are often comparing them across incommensurable dimensions. So, for instance, an HMO becomes by definition more "managed" than a fee-for-service plan with utilization review even when the latter uses much stricter controls on individual treatment decisions. By conflating distinct characteristics, we also are tempted to presume necessary relationships between particular features of health plans (such as their payment method) and specific outcomes that are claimed to follow from these features (such as the degree of integration of medical finance and delivery). Finally, the desire to describe an assortment of disparate plan features with a few broad labels encourages a wild goose chase of efforts to come up with black-and-white standards for identifying plan types. * * *

* * *

In understanding the structure of health insurance, the crucial relationship is between those who deliver medical care and those who pay for it. Even a passive indemnity insurer stands between the patient and the medical provider as a financial intermediary and an underwriter of risk. Today, with risk shifting from insurers to employers, and with financial intermediaries playing more of an administrative role than in the past, the trilateral relationship is more complex. Nonetheless, it still remains the locus of the insurance contract. To characterize this trilateral relationship, we focus on three of its essential features: first, the degree of risk-sharing between providers and the primary bearer of risk (whether an insurer or a self-insured employer); second, the degree to which administrative oversight constrains clinical decisions; and, third, the degree to which enrollees in a plan are required to receive their care from a specified roster of providers. * * *

* * * Our argument is that health plans differ across at least [these] three principal dimensions * * *. Each dimension crucially affects the trilateral connections among provider, patient, and plan. We also wish to emphasize that there is no simple relationship between plan label and the placement of a plan along these axes. Staff-model HMOs may seem like the quintessence of "managed care," yet because they place financial constraints at the group level they do not necessarily concentrate as much risk on physicians as do other network-based health plans, nor do they not necessarily entail as much clinical regulation at the micro-level. Microregulation may go hand in hand with restrictions on patient choice of provider, but it also may not. Indeed, management of individual clinical decisions and the creation of broad incentives for conservative practice patterns may very well be alternative mechanisms for lowering the cost of medical care. Finally, as recent developments in the health insurance market suggest, greater risk-sharing can co-exist with almost any set of arrangements. It does not require a closed network, much less strict utilization review. Risk sharing is a product of the payment methods and incentive structures that connect risk-bearing agents and medical providers. It does not exclusively occur in HMOs, nor does it require capitation.

Notice, too, that [we make] no mention of those popular buzzwords "integration" and "coordination." Movement toward a closed network, toward greater utilization control, or toward increased risk-sharing can create the conditions under which integration or coordination may occur. They do not imply, however, that such integrative activities actually take place. Getting the right care to the right patient at the right time is a managerial accomplishment, not a product of labels.

Finally, the conventional fee-for-service versus capitation dichotomy does not remain a useful means of distinguishing among different health plans. Instead, the crucial issue is what incentives medical providers actually face. The particular mix of payment methods that create those incentives is less important and will undoubtedly change as health plans experiment with new reimbursement modalities in the future.

Disaggregating health insurance into its constituent features not only helps to clarify what health plans do and how they are structured, but it also makes it easier to identify the specific trends in medical finance and delivery that are carelessly jumbled together when we speak of such grand events as the "managed care revolution." Although we cannot provide a comprehensive empirical survey in this context, our reading of the evidence leads us to believe that the developments of the past decade have not pushed American health insurance in a consistent direction, much less toward any single organized entity that might be labeled "managed care."

Indeed, movement along these axes has been halting and inconsistent. Through roughly the late 1980s, an increasing number of health plans moved toward closed networks. In the 1990s, by contrast, the trend has been toward intermediate levels of compulsion, with formerly closed plans offering opportunities for patients to opt out with a penalty and with new plans shying away from closed-network structures. Utilization review was also fashionable during the 1980s, yet it too has fallen somewhat into disfavor as plans have moved toward greater reliance on plan-provider risk-sharing, which in turn has become more focused at the level of the individual provider and individual service category over time. If there has been any general movement in the past two decades—and surely there has been—it has been [toward imposing all three types of controls]. Even this development, however, has been neither consistent nor evenly paced. In fact, the clearest and most unmistakable trend has been in the direction of straightforward price-discounting, as plans have used their market clout to selectively contract with physicians willing to accept negotiated rates. This is an important development, but in both international and historical perspective, it is hardly as unprecedented as grand phrases like "the managed-care revolution" imply.

* * *

Note

Following the lead of Hacker and Marmor, we will examine the regulation of managed care, not in terms of traditional distinctions between various types of managed care organizations (i.e. HMOs, PPOs, PSOs, etc.), but rather focusing on how the states regulate the various techniques described above for managing care: networks, utilization controls, and provider incentives. Before we do so, however, we must first learn a bit about the nature of insurance, and its regulation.

B. THE CONCEPT OF INSURANCE

Despite the triumph of "managed care" in the United States, it continues to make analytic sense to consider separately the insurance and the health care management functions of private health care financing. Insurance involves by definition the transfer of risk from the insured (called also variously the beneficiary, recipient, member, or enrollee) to a financing entity (the insurer, managed care organization, or self-insured benefits plan). It is invariably the case in health care that a small proportion of all insureds account for a very high proportion of health care costs. Ten percent of the population account for 72 percent of health care costs, 2 percent for 41 percent of costs. Health insurance essentially involves transferring costs from those insureds who account for most of health care costs to those who provide most of the premiums through the medium of the insurer.

Insurers transfer risk by pooling the risks of large numbers of insureds. The insurer, however, must be prudent about the risk it assumes from these insureds, and assure that it has the resources to cover the risk. Obtaining insurance, therefore, customarily involves an assessment of the risk of the insured (underwriting), and the payment of an appropriate premium.

When financing is provided through employment-related group insurance, of course, part of the premium is paid by the employer and the underwriting is of the group as a whole. When an employer self-insures its employee benefits plan, no premium exchanges hands (except insofar as the employee contributes to the cost) and there is no underwriting, except insofar as an person's health status might affect an employer's willingness to take on the person as an employee, or when the employer purchases stop-loss insurance.

Though managed care plans typically include an insurance function, managed care plans have not always been regarded as insurers. Managed care entities that themselves provide care, the classic staff-model HMO or the more recent provider-based integrated delivery system (or provider-sponsored organization), have sometimes been regarded as sellers of services on a prepaid basis (a bit like appliance service agreements) rather than insurers. But managed care organizations in fact do assume, and spread, risk, and are often, though not always, regulated much like insurers. See generally, John S. Conniff, Regulating Managed Health Care Provider Sponsored Organizations, 16 J. Ins. Reg. 377 (1998); Edward Hirshfeld., Provider Sponsored Organizations and Provider Service Networks, 22 Am.J.L. & Med. 263 (1996).

There are a number of concepts that must be mastered to understand health insurance and health insurance law. The excerpt that follows discusses these:

CONGRESSIONAL RESEARCH SERVICE, INSURING THE UNINSURED: OPTIONS AND ANALYSIS

(House Comm. on Education & Labor, Comm. Print, 1988).

II.   PRINCIPLES OF HEALTH INSURANCE

Insurance is a response to risk, to uncertainty about specific outcomes, and to the possibility that those outcomes will be unfavorable. * * * Most people * * * choose to transfer the risk of a financially costly illness to an insurer (or comparable third-party payer). In this way, insurance provides an economic device whereby a person substitutes a certain payment (a premium) for the uncertain financial loss that would occur in the event of an uninsured accident or illness.

* * *

For insurance to operate, there has to be a way to predict the likelihood or probability that a loss will occur as a result of a specific outcome. Such predictions in insurance are based upon probability theory and the law of large numbers. According to probability theory, "while some events appear to be a matter of chance, they actually occur with regularity over a large number of trials." [ ] By examining patterns of behavior over a large number of trials, it is therefore possible for the insurer to infer the likelihood of such behaviors in the future.

* * * Applied to insurance, probability allows the insurer to make predictions on the basis of historical data. In so doing, the insurer " ... implicitly says, 'if things continue to happen in the future as they happened in the past, and if our estimate of what has happened in the past is accurate, this is what we may expect.' " [ ]

Losses seldom occur exactly as expected, so insurance companies have to make predictions about the extent to which actual experience might deviate from predicted results. For a small group of insured units, there is a high probability that losses will be much greater or smaller than was predicted. For a very large group, the range of probable error diminishes, especially if the insured group is similar in composition to the group upon which the prediction is based. Thus, to predict the probability of a loss, insurers seek to aggregate persons who are at a similar risk for that loss. * * *

In theory all probabilities of loss can be insured. Insurance could cover any risk for a price. As the probability of loss increases, however, the premium will increase to the point at which it approaches the actual potential pay-out.

To keep premiums competitive, there are in practice some risks that insurers will not accept. In general, insurable risks must meet the following criteria:

- There has to be uncertainty that the loss will occur, and that the loss must be beyond the control of the insured. Insurers will not sell hospital insurance to a person who is on his way to a hospital, nor fire insurance to someone holding a lit match. * * *

- The loss produced by the risk must be measurable. The insurer has to be able to determine that a loss has occurred and that it has a specific dollar value.

- There must be a sufficiently large number of similar insured units to make the losses predictable. * * *

- Generally, the loss must be significant, but there should be a low probability that a very high loss will occur. A person does not need to insure against a trivial loss. However, it would not be prudent for an insurer to accept a risk in which there is a high probability that an expensive loss will occur to a large percentage of the insured units at the same time. * * *

* * *

III. RATEMAKING

Ratemaking is the "process of predicting future losses and future expenses and allocating those costs among the various classes of insureds." The outcome of the ratemaking process is a "premium" or price of policy. The premium is made up of expected claims against the insurer and the insurer's "administrative expenses." The term "administrative expenses" is used to mean any expense that the insurance company charges that is not for claims (including reserves for potential claims). * * * In the case of employer group coverage, a third part of the premium is set aside in a reserve held against unexpected claims. This reserve is often refundable to the employer if claims do not exceed expectations.

In the textbook descriptions of ratemaking for health insurance, insurers predict losses on the basis of predicted claims costs. This prediction involves an assessment of the likely morbidity (calculated in terms of the number of times the event insured against occurs) and severity (the average magnitude of each loss) of the policyholder or group of policyholders. * * *

* * *

There are different approaches to determining rates. In health insurance, the most frequently used approaches are "experience rating" and "community rating."

Under experience rating, the past experience of the group to be insured is used to determine the premium. For employer groups, experience rating would take into account the company's own history of claims and other expenses. * * *

* * *

The advantage of experience rating is that it adjusts the cost of insurance for a specific group in a manner more commensurate with the expected cost of that particular group than is possible through the exclusive use of manual rates. In addition, the increasingly competitive environment among insurers demands that each one "make every effort to retain groups with favorable experience. Unless an insurer can provide coverage to such groups at a reasonable cost, it runs the risk of losing such policyholders to another insurer which more closely reflects the expected costs of their programs in its rates." [ ]

Under community rating, premium rates are based on the allocation of total costs to all the individuals or groups to be insured, without regard to the past experience of any particular subgroup. * * * Community or class rating has the advantage of allowing an insurer to apply a single rate or set of rates to a large number of people, thus simplifying the process of determining premiums.

* * *

IV. ADVERSE AND FAVORABLE SELECTION

If everyone in the society purchased health insurance, and if everyone opted for an identical health insurance plan, then insurance companies could adhere strictly to the models of prediction and rate-setting described above. However, everyone does not buy insurance, nor do all the purchasers of insurance choose identical benefits. People who expect to need health services are more likely than others to purchase insurance, and are also likely to seek coverage for the specific services they expect to need. * * *

Insurers use the term "adverse selection" to describe this phenomenon. Adverse selection is defined by the health insurance industry as the "tendency of persons with poorer than average health expectations to apply for, or continue, insurance to a greater extent than do persons with average or better health expectations." [ ]

* * *

Adjusting premiums for adverse selection results in further adverse selection. As the price of insurance goes up, healthier people are less likely to want to purchase insurance. Each upward rate adjustment will leave a smaller and sicker group of potential purchasers. If there were only a single insurance company, it would serve a steadily shrinking market paying steadily increasing premiums. However, because multiple insurance companies are operating in the market, each company may strive to enroll the lower cost individuals or groups, leaving the higher cost cases for its competitors. In this market, adverse selection consists (from the insurer's point of view) of drawing the least desirable cases from within the pool of insurance purchasers. "Favorable'' selection occurs if the insurer successfully enrolls lower risk clients than its competitors.

It is thus necessary to distinguish between the more traditional use of "adverse selection," as a term to describe the differences between people who do and do not buy insurance, and the sense in which the term is often used today, to describe the differences among purchasers choosing various insurers or types of coverage. This second type of adverse selection can occur within an insured group, if the individuals in that group are permitted to select from among different insurance options.

Insurers are still concerned about the more traditional type of adverse selection. They use underwriting rules, to exclude or limit the worst risks. Some insurers may also attempt to limit adverse selection by careful selection of where they market and to whom they sell a policy. For example, a company offering a Medicare supplement (Medigap) plan might be more likely to advertise its plan in senior citizen recreation centers, where the patrons tend to be relatively young and healthy, than in nursing homes, where the residents are probably older and have chronic health conditions. Thus, from the perspective of the individual or group applying for insurance, the insurer's attempts to avoid adverse selection may result in lack of availability of coverage, denial of coverage, incomplete coverage or above-average premiums.

Notes and Questions

The text asserts that the purpose of insurance is to spread risk from individuals to all members of a group. This suggests a vision of distributive justice based on group solidarity. Can you think of other understandings of the purpose of insurance? Should insurance alternatively be based on a principle of actuarial fairness, under which every individual pays for insurance based on his own risks? Which principle best explains the market for health insurance, as it exists in the United States today? See Deborah Stone, The Struggle for the Soul of Health Insurance, 18 J. Health Pol. Pol'y & L. 287 (1993).

* * *

Having now introduced the basic concepts of insurance and managed care, we will proceed to examine relevant state law, first considering the liability of insurers and managed care organizations under state contract and tort law, and then looking at state programs that regulate health insurers and managed care organizations.

II. CONTRACT LIABILITY OF PRIVATE INSURERS AND MANAGED CARE ORGANIZATIONS

Insurance companies and insurance contracts have historically been governed primarily by state law, and states continue to have primary responsibility for regulating managed care. In the first instance, insurance and managed care contracts are contracts, and the failure of an insurer or managed care plan to perform to the expectations of the insured may result in contract litigation in state court. Our discussion begins, therefore, with an examination of state insurance contract law.

LUBEZNIK v. HEALTHCHICAGO, INC.

Appellate Court of Illinois, 1994.
268 Ill.App.3d 953, 206 Ill.Dec. 9, 644 N.E.2d 777.

JUSTICE JOHNSON delivered the opinion of the court:

Plaintiff, Bonnie Lubeznik, filed this action in the Circuit Court of Cook County seeking a permanent injunction requiring defendant, Healthchicago, Inc., to pre-certify her for certain medical treatment. Following a hearing, the trial court granted the injunction. Defendant appeals, contending the trial court improperly (1) determined that the requested treatment was a covered benefit under plaintiff's insurance policy; (2) interpreted portions of the Illinois Health Maintenance Organization Act; (3) * * *; and (4) granted the injunction.

We affirm.

The record reveals that in November 1988 plaintiff was diagnosed with Stage III ovarian cancer. At the time of her diagnosis, the cancer had spread through plaintiff's abdomen and liver and she had a 20 percent survival rate over the next five years. * * *

In June 1991, plaintiff was referred to Dr. Patrick Stiff, the director of the bone marrow treatment program at Loyola University Medical Center (hereinafter Loyola). Dr. Stiff sought to determine the prospect of treating plaintiff with high dose chemotherapy with autologous bone marrow transplant (hereinafter HDCT/ABMT). HDCT/ABMT is a procedure where bone marrow stem cells are removed from the patient's body and frozen in storage until after the patient has been treated with high dose chemotherapy. Following chemotherapy, which destroys the cancer, the marrow previously extracted is reinfused to proliferate and replace marrow destroyed by the chemotherapy. HDCT/ABMT had been a state of the art treatment for leukemia and Hodgkin's disease for many years. It began to be used in the late 1980's for women who were in the late stages of breast cancer.

* * *

On October 28, 1991, Dr. Stiff contacted defendant requesting that it pre-certify plaintiff for the HDCT/ABMT, i.e., agree in advance to pay for the treatment. Plaintiff's insurance policy required her to get pre-certified before receiving elective treatment, procedures and therapies. Dr. Wayne Mathy, defendant's medical director, received Dr. Stiff's pre-certification request and telephoned him shortly thereafter. During his conversation with Dr. Stiff, Dr. Mathy stated that the ABMT/HDCT was not a covered benefit under plaintiff's insurance policy because the treatment was considered experimental.

On October 31, 1991, plaintiff filed a two-count complaint against defendant and Loyola. In count one, plaintiff sought a mandatory injunction against defendant to pre-certify her for the HDCT/ABMT. In her second count, plaintiff sought an injunction against Loyola to admit her for medical treatment without a deposit of $100,000. Both defendant and Loyola filed motions to dismiss plaintiff's complaint. Subsequently, plaintiff took a voluntary non-suit against Loyola.

Following a hearing, the trial court denied defendant's motion to dismiss and defendant filed its answer instanter. Thereafter, a hearing on the complaint was held at which Dr. Stiff testified that the HDCT/ABMT was an effective treatment for plaintiff given that all conventional treatments for her had been exhausted. He stated that he had performed 21 HDCT/ABMT procedures on patients with Stage III ovarian cancer and as a result, 75 percent of those patients were in complete remission.

During further testimony, Dr. Stiff opined that the HDCT/ABMT was not experimental and presented documents and literature in support of his testimony. * * *

Dr. Mathy testified at the hearing that his responsibilities as defendant's medical director included determining whether a requested medical treatment is covered under an insurance policy issued by defendant. He stated that after he received plaintiff's request for pre-certification, a member of defendant's benefit analysis staff contacted the National Institute of Health, the National Cancer Institute, and Medicare seeking an assessment as to whether the requested treatment was experimental. According to Dr. Mathy, defendant determined that the HDCT/ABMT was experimental based on information received from those medical assessment bodies. * * *

During cross-examination, Dr. Mathy testified that he first learned on October 29, 1991, that Dr. Stiff was contemplating treating plaintiff with HDCT/ABMT. Dr. Mathy admitted that immediately upon learning of the proposed treatment, he decided that the HDCT/ABMT was experimental and that plaintiff's pre-certification request should be denied. Dr. Mathy stated that he did not consult with the National Institute of Health or the National Cancer Institute before making the decision to deny plaintiff's request.

At the conclusion of the testimony, the parties presented final arguments to the trial court. Subsequently, the trial court issued an injunction against defendant ruling that the ABMT/HDCT is neither an experimental therapy for ovarian cancer, nor a transplant within the meaning of Illinois Health Maintenance Organization Act (Ill.Rev.Stat.1991, ch. 111 1/2, par. 1408.5) (hereinafter the Act). Defendant then filed this appeal.

Defendant initially argues that the trial court erroneously determined that the HDCT/ABMT procedure is a covered benefit under plaintiff's insurance policy. Defendant claims it supported its determination that the procedure is experimental with similar conclusions by appropriate medical technology boards as required by plaintiff's insurance contract. Plaintiff's insurance policy provides that "[e]xperimental medical, surgical, or other procedures as determined by the [Insurance] Plan in conjunction with appropriate medical technology assessment bodies," are excluded from coverage. Defendant contends that the trial court improperly disregarded the terms of the insurance contract, which, defendant argues, were clear and unambiguous.

At the outset, we note that coverage provisions in an insurance contract are to be liberally construed in favor of the insured to provide the broadest possible coverage.[ ] In determining whether a certain provision in an insurance contract is applicable, a trial court must first determine whether the specific provision is ambiguous.[ ] A provision which is clear or unambiguous, i.e., fairly admits but of one interpretation, must be applied as written.[ ]

However, where a provision is ambiguous, its language must be construed in favor of the insured.[ ]

Moreover, where an insurer seeks to deny insurance coverage based on an exclusionary clause contained in an insurance policy, the clause must be clear and free from doubt.[ ] This is so because all doubts with respect to coverage are resolved in favor of the insured. * * *

After carefully reviewing the evidence, we cannot agree with defendant that the trial court improperly determined the HDCT/ABMT to be a covered benefit under plaintiff's insurance policy. First, we disagree with defendant that the exclusionary language was clear and unambiguous. We note that the plaintiff's insurance policy does not define the phrase "appropriate medical technology boards." The plain language of the policy does not indicate who will determine whether a certain medical board is appropriate. Further, the policy fails to outline any standards for determining how a medical board is deemed appropriate. Thus, the phrase, without more, gives rise to a genuine uncertainty about which medical boards are considered appropriate and how and by whom the determination is made.

Second, despite defendant's argument to the contrary, the exclusionary language in plaintiff's insurance contract varies significantly from the language in section 4–5 of the Act which provides as follows:

"No contract or evidence of coverage issued by a health maintenance organization which provides coverage for health care services shall deny reimbursement for an otherwise covered expense incurred for any organ transplantation procedure solely on the basis that such procedure is deemed experimental or investigational unless supported by the determination of the Office of Health Care Technology Assessment within the Agency for the Health Care Policy and Research within the federal Department of Health and Human Services that such a procedure is either experimental or investigational * * *." (Ill.Rev.Stat.1991, ch. 111 1/2, par. 1408.5.)

Unlike plaintiff's insurance contract, the Act specifically provides which agency has the authority to determine whether a procedure is experimental.

Third, we must note that even if the exclusionary language did apply, defendant failed to follow the terms of the insurance policy. Plaintiff's insurance policy excludes from coverage medical and surgical procedures that are considered experimental by defendant "in conjunction with appropriate technology assessment bodies." At the hearing, Dr. Mathy testified that upon learning of plaintiff's pre-certification request, he had already determined that the HDCT/ABMT was experimental prior to receiving or reviewing any information from the medical assessment boards. Given our careful review of the evidence, including defendant's admitted disregard for the terms of the insurance policy, we hold that the trial court did not err in ruling that the requested treatment was a covered benefit under the policy.

* * *

Lastly, defendant claims that the trial court improperly granted the mandatory injunction because plaintiff failed to meet the requirements for an injunction to issue. An injunction may be granted only after the plaintiff establishes that (1) a lawful right exists; (2) irreparable injury will result if the injunction is not granted; and (3) his or her remedy at law is inadequate.[ ] * * *

* * *

At the hearing, Dr. Stiff testified that given the steady development of plaintiff's disease, it was imperative to begin the HDCT/ABMT treatment as quickly as possible. He opined that delaying the HDCT/ABMT any further might have rendered plaintiff ineligible for such treatment due to further development of the disease. Based on our understanding of Dr. Stiff's testimony, we do not believe, as defendant now posits, that plaintiff was not eligible for the treatment.

Moreover, Dr. Stiff further testified that the HDCT/ABMT was an effective treatment for plaintiff and offered her a "very high chance of a complete disappearance of her disease." In addition, when asked during direct examination to give a prognosis of plaintiff's condition, Dr. Stiff gave the following response:

"[Plaintiff] has a fatal illness with a zero percent to one percent chance of being alive at five years, let alone alive and disease free."

Given the evidence presented at the hearing, including Dr. Stiff's testimony, we do not agree with defendant that plaintiff failed to show she would suffer irreparable harm without the treatment.[ ] Therefore, we hold that the trial court did not abuse its discretion in granting the requested injunctive relief.

* * *

Notes and Questions

1.   Courts have traditionally viewed insurance contracts as adhesion contracts and interpreted them under the doctrine of contra proferentem. This has made it difficult for insurance companies to control their exposure to risk through general clauses that refuse payment for care that is not "medically necessary" or that it "experimental". Usually when such clauses are litigated, as in the principal case, the treating physician testifies that care is standard and is urgently necessary, the insurer's medical director testifies that the care is experimental or unnecessary. What conflicts of interest does each face? Whom should the court believe? Are there more appropriate ways of resolving these disputes? What are the ramifications of these disputes for the cost of medical care? In one recent case a jury returned a verdict for $77 million in punitive damages and $12.1 million in compensatory damaged against an HMO which had denied coverage of ABMT for breast cancer. Fox v. Health Net of California, No. 219692 (Cal.Sup.Ct.1993) cited at 3 Health Law Reporter (BNA) 18, 19 (Jan. 6, 1994). What effect might such a decision have on medical necessity determinations?

On the other hand, a number of courts have upheld insurers who have denied coverage for ABMT. See Fuja v. Benefit Trust Life Insurance Co., 18 F.3d 1405 (7th Cir.1994); Holder v. Prudential Ins. Co. of America 951 F.2d 89 (5th Cir.1992), finding that the language of the policy was sufficiently clear to support denial. Paradoxically, though most insurers eventually came to cover ABMT for breast cancer, the most recent research indicates that its efficacy is highly questionable. See Karen Antman, et al., High Dose Chemotherapy for Breast Cancer, 282 JAMA 1701 (1999).

2. A fascinating empirical study of coverage disputes is reported in Mark Hall, et al., Judicial Protection of Managed Care Consumers: An Empirical Study of Insurance Coverage Disputes, 26 Seton Hall 1055 (1996). Professor Hall found that patients win coverage disputes over half of the time, and that the specificity of the language with which the insurer attempts to exclude coverage does not significantly affect its likelihood of winning. See also, analyzing medical necessity disputes, Peter D. Jacobson, et al., Defining and Implementing Medical Necessity in Washington State and Oregon, 34 Inquiry 143 (1997); and William M. Sage, Judicial Opinions Involving Health Insurance Coverage: Trompe L'Oeil or Window on the World?, 31 Ind. L. Rev. 49 (1998). The issue of how medical necessity should be defined and who should determine it has become an important and controversial issue in managed care reform proposals. See Sara Rosenbaum, David M. Frankford, Brad More & Phyllis Borzi, Who Should Determine When Health Care is Medically Necessary? 340 JAMA 229 (1999). See also, regarding experimental treatment exclusions, J. Gregory Lahr, What is the Method to Their "Madness?" Experimental Treatment Exclusions in Health Insurance Policies, 13 J. Contemp. Health L. & Pol'y 613 (1997).

See discussing the policy issues raised by cases interpreting medical necessity and experimental treatment clauses, Mark A. Hall & Gerard F. Anderson, Health Insurers' Assessment of Medical Necessity, 140 U. Pa. L. Rev. 1637 (1992); Richard S. Saver, Note: Reimbursing New Technologies: Why are the Courts Judging Experimental Medicine?, 44 Stan. L. Rev. 1095 (1992); Frank P. James, The Experimental Treatment Exclusion Clause: A Tool For Silent Rationing of Health Care?, 12 J. Legal Med. 359 (1991).

Insurance and managed care coverage disputes present not only contract interpretation issues, but also issues of tort law, to which we now turn.

III. TORT LIABILITY OF MANAGED CARE

Managed care organizations are increasingly defendants in liability suits, facing the same theories that hospitals face, as well as newer theories related to the cost-conserving functions of managed care. "Managed care" is a phrase often used to describe organizational groupings that attempt to control the utilization of health care services through a variety of techniques, including prepayment by subscribers for services on a contract basis, use of physicians as "gatekeepers" for hospital and specialty services, and others. The groups cover a wide variety of plans—from plans that require little more than preauthorization of patient hospitalization, to staff model HMOs—that focus on utilization and price of services. The goal is reduction of health care costs and maximization of value to both patient and payer. A Managed Care Organization (MCO) is a reimbursement framework combined with a health care delivery system, an approach to the delivery of health care services that contrasts with "fee-for-service" medicine. Managed care is usually distinguished from traditional indemnity plans by the existence of a single entity responsible for integrating and coordinating the financing and delivery of services that were once scattered between providers and payers.

Managed care has rapidly supplanted fee-for-service medicine. The shift from traditional indemnity plans to health maintenance organizations and other network plans has been rapid over the past decade. By 1998 only 14 percent of employees in large firms of more than 200 employees were enrolled in conventional plans, with small firms seeing a similar shift to managed care. By contrast, in 1980 only five to ten percent of the workforce was enrolled in such plans. By 1999 HMO enrollment had exceeded 81 million members, with almost 30 percent of the U.S. population enrolled in an HMO. Managed care organizations have taken over the financing of American health care primarily because they promise to control costs. And they have in fact contributed to a substantial slowing in health care inflation. Looking at the period from 1960 to 1996, expenditure growth has slowed to 4.4%—the lowest rate in thirty-seven years of measuring health care spending.

See generally Contemporary Managed Care: Readings in Structure, Operations, and Public Policy (Marsha R. Gold, ed.1998); M. Susan Marquis and Stephen H. Long, Trends in Managed Care and Managede Competition, 1993–1997, 18 Health Affairs 75(1999); Robert H. Miller and Harold S. Luft, Managed Care: Past Evidence and Potential Trends, 9 Frontiers of Health Services Management 3 (1993); Robert Shouldice, Introduction to Managed Care: Health Maintenance Organizations, Preferred Provider Organizations, and Competitive Medical Plans (1991); Jonathan P. Weiner and Gregory de Lissovoy, Razing a Tower of Babel: A Taxonomy for Managed Care and Health Insurance Plans, 18 J. Health Pol., Pol'y & Law 75 (1993). See Total HMO Enrollment and Growth Rate, January 1990 to January 1999, 4 On Managed Care 3 (Nov.1999).Katherine R. Levit et al, National Health Spending Trends in 1996, 17 Health Affairs 35(1998).

This growth of "virtual" managed care means less integration and as a result less patient satisfaction and trust. An increase in litigation has resulted, and plaintiff lawyers have borrowed heavily from hospital liability law. David Mechanic and Marsha Rosenthal, Responses of HMO Medical Directors to Trust Building in Managed Care, 77 Milb.Q. 283(1999).

A. VICARIOUS LIABILITY

Health maintenance organizations (HMOs) and Independent Practice Associations (IPAs) in theory face the same vicarious and corporate liability questions as hospitals, since they provide services through physicians, whether the physicians are salaried employees or independent contractors. These medical services can injure patients/subscribers, leading to a malpractice suit for such injuries.

Vicarious liability theories have provided the first wave of successful litigation against managed care organizations.

PETROVICH v. SHARE HEALTH PLAN OF ILLINOIS, INC.

Supreme Court of Illinois, 1999.
188 Ill.2d 17, 241 Ill.Dec. 627, 719 N.E.2d 756.

JUSTICE BILANDIC delivered the opinion of the court:

The plaintiff brought this medical malpractice action against a physician and others for their alleged negligence in failing to diagnose her oral cancer in a timely manner. The plaintiff also named her health maintenance organization (HMO) as a defendant. The central issue here is whether the plaintiff's HMO may be held vicariously liable for the negligence of its independent-contractor physicians under agency law. The plaintiff contends that the HMO is vicariously liable under both the doctrines of apparent authority and implied authority.

* * *

FACTS

In 1989, plaintiff's employer, the Chicago Federation of Musicians, provided health care coverage to all of its employees by selecting Share and enrolling its employees therein. Share is an HMO and pays only for medical care that is obtained within its network of physicians. In order to qualify for benefits, a Share member must select from the network a primary care physician who will provide that member's overall care and authorize referrals when necessary. Share gives its members a list of participating physicians from which to choose. Share has about 500 primary care physicians covering Share's service area, which includes the counties of Cook, Du Page, Lake, McHenry and Will. Plaintiff selected Dr. Marie Kowalski from Share's list, and began seeing Dr. Kowalski as her primary care physician in August of 1989. Dr. Kowalski was employed at a satellite facility of Illinois Masonic Medical Center (Illinois Masonic), which had a contract with Share to provide medical services to Share members.

In September of 1990, plaintiff saw Dr. Kowalski because she was experiencing persistent pain in the right sides of her mouth, tongue, throat and face. Plaintiff also complained of a foul mucus in her mouth. Dr. Kowalski referred plaintiff to two other physicians who had contracts with Share: Dr. Slavick, a neurologist, and Dr. Friedman, an ear, nose and throat specialist.

Plaintiff informed Dr. Friedman of her pain. Dr. Friedman observed redness or marked erythema alongside plaintiff's gums on the right side of her mouth. He recommended that plaintiff have a magnetic resonance imaging (MRI) test or a computed tomography (CT) scan performed on the base of her skull. According to plaintiff's testimony at her evidence deposition, Dr. Kowalski informed her that Share would not allow new tests as recommended by Dr. Friedman. Plaintiff did not consult with Share about the test refusals because she was not aware of Share's grievance procedure. Dr. Kowalski gave Dr. Friedman a copy of an old MRI test result at that time. The record offers no further information about this old MRI test.

Nonetheless, Dr. Kowalski later ordered an updated MRI of plaintiff's brain, which was performed on October 31, 1990. Inconsistent with Dr. Friedman's directions, however, this MRI failed to image the right base of the tongue area where redness existed. Plaintiff and Dr. Kowalski discussed the results of this MRI test on November 19, 1990, during a follow-up visit. Plaintiff testified that Dr. Kowalski told her that the MRI revealed no abnormality.

Plaintiff's pain persisted. In April or May of 1991, Dr. Kowalski again referred plaintiff to Dr. Friedman. This was plaintiff's third visit to Dr. Friedman. Dr. Friedman examined plaintiff and observed that plaintiff's tongue was tender. Also, plaintiff reported that she had a foul odor in her mouth and was experiencing discomfort. On June 7, 1991, Dr. Friedman performed multiple biopsies on the right side of the base of plaintiff's tongue and surrounding tissues. The biopsy results revealed squamous cell carcinoma, a cancer, in the base of plaintiff's tongue and the surrounding tissues of the pharynx. Later that month, Dr. Friedman operated on plaintiff to remove the cancer. He removed part of the base of plaintiff's tongue, and portions of her palate, pharynx and jaw bone. After the surgery, plaintiff underwent radiation treatments and rehabilitation.

Plaintiff subsequently brought this medical malpractice action against Share, Dr. Kowalski and others. Dr. Friedman was not named a party defendant. Plaintiff's complaint, though, alleges that both Drs. Kowalski and Friedman were negligent in failing to diagnose plaintiff's cancer in a timely manner, and that Share is vicariously liable for their negligence under agency principles. Share filed a motion for summary judgment, arguing that it cannot be held liable for the negligence of Dr. Kowalski or Friedman because they were acting as independent contractors in their treatment of plaintiff, not as Share's agents. Plaintiff countered that Share is not entitled to summary judgment because Drs. Kowalski and Friedman were Share's agents. The parties submitted various depositions, affidavits and exhibits in support of their respective positions.

Share is a for-profit corporation. At all relevant times, Share was organized as an "independent practice association-model" HMO under the Illinois Health Maintenance Organization Act (Ill.Rev.Stat.1991, ch. 111 1/2 , par. 1401 et seq.). This means that Share is a financing entity that arranges and pays for health care by contracting with independent medical groups and practitioners. [ ] Share does not employ physicians directly, nor does it own, operate, maintain or supervise the offices where medical care is provided to its members. Rather, Share contracts with independent medical groups and physicians that have the facilities, equipment and professional skills necessary to render medical care. Physicians desiring to join Share's network are required to complete an application procedure and meet with Share's approval.

Share utilizes a method of compensation called "capitation" to pay its medical groups. Share also maintains a "quality assurance program." Share's capitation method of compensation and "quality assurance program" are more fully described later in this opinion.

Share provides a member handbook to each of its members, including plaintiff. The handbook states to its members that Share will provide "all your healthcare needs" and "comprehensive high quality services." The handbook also states that the primary care physician is "your health care manager" and "makes the decisions" about the member's care. The handbook further states that Share is a "good partner in sickness and in health." Unlike the master agreements and benefits contract discussed below, the member handbook which plaintiff received does not contain any provision that identifies Share physicians as independent contractors or nonemployees of Share. Rather, the handbook describes the physicians as "your Share physician," "Share physicians" and "our staff." Furthermore, Share refers to the physicians' offices as "Your Share physician's office" and states: "All of the Share staff and Medical Offices look forward to serving you * * *."

Plaintiff confirmed that she received the member handbook. Plaintiff did not read the handbook in its entirety, but read portions of it as she needed the information. She relied on the information contained in the handbook while Drs. Kowalski and Friedman treated her.

The record also contains a "Health Care Services Master Agreement," entered into by Share and Illinois Masonic. Dr. Kowalski is a signatory of this agreement. The agreement states, "It is understood and agreed that [Illinois Masonic] and [primary care physicians] are independent contractors and not employees or agents of SHARE." A separate agreement between Share and Dr. Friedman contains similar language. Plaintiff did not receive these agreements.

Share's primary care physicians, under their agreements with Share, are required to approve patients' medical requests and make referrals to specialists. These physicians use Share's standard referral forms to indicate their approval of the referral. Dr. Kowalski testified at an evidence deposition that she did not feel constrained by Share in making medical decisions regarding her patients, including whether to order tests or make referrals to specialists.

Another document in the record is Share's benefits contract. The benefits contract contains a subscriber certificate. The subscriber certificate sets forth a member's rights and obligations with respect to Share. Additionally, the subscriber certificate states that Share's physicians are independent contractors and that "SHARE Plan Providers and Enrolling Groups are not agents or employees of SHARE nor is SHARE or any employee of SHARE an agent or employee of SHARE Plan Providers or Enrolling Groups." The certificate elaborates: "The relationship between a SHARE Plan Provider and any Member is that of provider and patient. The SHARE Plan Physician is solely responsible for the medical services provided to any Member. The SHARE Plan Hospital is solely responsible for the Hospital services provided to any Member."

Plaintiff testified that she did not recall receiving the subscriber certificate. In response, Share stated that Share customarily provides members with this information. Share does not claim to know whether Share actually provided plaintiff with this information. Plaintiff acknowledged that she received a "whole stack" of information from Share upon her enrollment.

Plaintiff was not aware of the type of relationship that her physicians had with Share. At the time she received treatment, plaintiff believed that her physicians were employees of Share.

In the circuit court, Share argued that it was entitled to summary judgment because the independent-contractor provision in the benefits contract established, as a matter of law, that Drs. Kowalski and Friedman were not acting as Share's agents in their treatment of plaintiff. The circuit court agreed and entered summary judgment for Share.

The appellate court reversed, holding that a genuine issue of material fact is presented as to whether plaintiff's treating physicians are Share's apparent agents. 296 Ill.App.3d 849, 231 Ill.Dec. 364, 696 N.E.2d 356. The appellate court stated that a number of factors support plaintiff's apparent agency claim, including plaintiff's testimony, Share's member handbook, Share's quality assessment program and Share's capitation method of compensation. The appellate court therefore remanded the cause for trial. The appellate court did not address the theory of implied authority.

ANALYSIS

This appeal comes before us amidst great changes to the relationships among physicians, patients and those entities paying for medical care. Traditionally, physicians treated patients on demand, while insurers merely paid the physicians their fee for the services provided. Today, managed care organizations (MCOs) have stepped into the insurer's shoes, and often attempt to reduce the price and quantity of health care services provided to patients through a system of health care cost containment. MCOs may, for example, use prearranged fee structures for compensating physicians. MCOs may also use utilization-review procedures, which are procedures designed to determine whether the use and volume of particular health care services are appropriate. MCOs have developed in response to rapid increases in health care costs.

HMOs, i.e., health maintenance organizations, are a type of MCO. HMOs are subject to both state and federal laws. [ ] Under Illinois law, an HMO is defined as "any organization formed under the laws of this or another state to provide or arrange for one or more health care plans under a system which causes any part of the risk of health care delivery to be borne by the organization or its providers." Ill.Rev.Stat.1991, ch. 111 1/2, par. 1402(9), now 215 ILCS 125/1–2(9) (West 1998). Because HMOs may differ in their structures and the cost-containment practices that they employ, a court must discern the nature of the organization before it, where relevant to the issues. As earlier noted, Share is organized as an independent practice association (IPA)-model HMO. IPA-model HMOs are financing entities that arrange and pay for health care by contracting with independent medical groups and practitioners. [ ]

This court has never addressed a question of whether an HMO may be held liable for medical malpractice. Share asserts that holding HMOs liable for medical malpractice will cause health care costs to increase and make health care inaccessible to large numbers of people. Share suggests that, with this consideration in mind, this court should impose only narrow, or limited, forms of liability on HMOs. We disagree with Share that the cost-containment role of HMOs entitles them to special consideration. The principle that organizations are accountable for their tortious actions and those of their agents is fundamental to our justice system. There is no exception to this principle for HMOs. Moreover, HMO accountability is essential to counterbalance the HMO goal of cost-containment. To the extent that HMOs are profit-making entities, accountability is also needed to counterbalance the inherent drive to achieve a large and ever-increasing profit margin. Market forces alone "are insufficient to cure the deleterious [e]ffects of managed care on the health care industry." Herdrich v. Pegram, 154 F.3d 362, 374–75 (7th Cir. 1998), cert. granted, 527 U.S. 1068, 120 S.Ct. 10, 144 L.Ed.2d 841 (1999). Courts, therefore, should not be hesitant to apply well-settled legal theories of liability to HMOs where the facts so warrant and where justice so requires.

Indeed, the national trend of courts is to hold HMOs accountable for medical malpractice under a variety of legal theories, including vicarious liability on the basis of apparent authority, vicarious liability on the basis of respondeat superior, direct corporate negligence, breach of contract and breach of warranty.[ ] * * * Share concedes that HMOs may be held liable for medical malpractice under these five theories.

This appeal concerns whether Share may be held vicariously liable under agency law for the negligence of its independent-contractor physicians. We must determine whether Share was properly awarded summary judgment on the ground that Drs. Kowalski and Friedman were not acting as Share's agents in their treatment of plaintiff. Plaintiff argues that Share is not entitled to summary judgment on this record. Plaintiff asserts that genuine issues of material fact exist as to whether Drs. Kowalski and Friedman were acting within Share's apparent authority, implied authority or both.

* * *

As a general rule, no vicarious liability exists for the actions of independent contractors. Vicarious liability may nevertheless be imposed for the actions of independent contractors where an agency relationship is established under either the doctrine of apparent authority [ ] or the doctrine of implied authority [ ].

I. Apparent Authority

Apparent authority, also known as ostensible authority, has been a part of Illinois jurisprudence for more than 140 years. [ ] Under the doctrine, a principal will be bound not only by the authority that it actually gives to another, but also by the authority that it appears to give. [ ]. The doctrine functions like an estoppel. [ ]. Where the principal creates the appearance of authority, a court will not hear the principal's denials of agency to the prejudice of an innocent third party, who has been led to reasonably rely upon the agency and is harmed as a result.[ ]

* * *

We now hold that the apparent authority doctrine may also be used to impose vicarious liability on HMOs. * * * [ ]

To establish apparent authority against an HMO for physician malpractice, the patient must prove (1) that the HMO held itself out as the provider of health care, without informing the patient that the care is given by independent contractors, and (2) that the patient justifiably relied upon the conduct of the HMO by looking to the HMO to provide health care services, rather than to a specific physician. Apparent agency is a question of fact. [ ]

A. Holding Out

The element of "holding out" means that the HMO, or its agent, acted in a manner that would lead a reasonable person to conclude that the physician who was alleged to be negligent was an agent or employee of the HMO. [ ] Where the acts of the agent create the appearance of authority, a plaintiff must also prove that the HMO had knowledge of and acquiesced in those acts. [ ] The holding-out element does not require the HMO to make an express representation that the physician alleged to be negligent is its agent or employee. Rather, this element is met where the HMO holds itself out as the provider of health care without informing the patient that the care is given by independent contractors. [ ] Vicarious liability under the apparent authority doctrine will not attach, however, if the patient knew or should have known that the physician providing treatment is an independent contractor. [ ]

Here, Share contends that the independent-contractor provisions in the two master agreements and the benefits contract conclusively establish, as a matter of law, that Share did not hold out Drs. Kowalski and Friedman to be Share's agents. Although all three of these contracts clearly express that the physicians are independent contractors and not agents of Share, we disagree with Share's contention for the reasons explained below.

First, the two master agreements at issue are private contractual agreements between Share and Illinois Masonic, with Dr. Kowalski as a signatory, and between Share and Dr. Friedman. The record contains no indication that plaintiff knew or should have known of these private contractual agreements between Share and its physicians. Gilbert expressly rejected the notion that such private contractual agreements can control a claim of apparent agency. [ ] * * * We hold that this same rationale applies to private contractual agreements between physicians and an HMO. [ ] Because there is no dispute that the master agreements at bar were unknown to plaintiff, they cannot be used to defeat her apparent agency claim.

Share also relies on the benefits contract. Plaintiff was not a party or a signatory to this contract. The benefits contract contains a subscriber certificate, which states that Share physicians are independent contractors. Share claims that this language alone conclusively overcomes plaintiff's apparent agency claim. We do not agree.

Whether a person has notice of a physician's status as an independent contractor, or is put on notice by the circumstances, is a question of fact. [ ] In this case, plaintiff testified at her evidence deposition that she did not recall receiving the subscriber certificate. Share responded only that it customarily provides members with this information. Share has never claimed to know whether Share actually provided plaintiff with this information. Thus, a question of fact exists as to whether Share gave this information to plaintiff. If this information was not provided to plaintiff, it cannot be used to defeat her apparent agency claim.

* * *

Evidence in the record supports plaintiff's contentions that Share held itself out to its members as the provider of health care, and that plaintiff was not aware that her physicians were independent contractors. Notably, plaintiff stated that, at the time that she received treatment, plaintiff believed that Drs. Kowalski and Friedman were Share employees. Plaintiff was not aware of the type of relationship that her physicians had with Share.

Moreover, Share's member handbook contains evidence that Share held itself out to plaintiff as the provider of her health care. The handbook stated to Share members that Share will provide "all your healthcare needs" and "comprehensive high quality services." The handbook did not contain any provision that identified Share physicians as independent contractors or nonemployees of Share. Instead, the handbook referred to the physicians as "your Share physician," "Share physicians" and "our staff." Share also referred to the physicians' offices as "Your Share physician's office." The record shows that Share provided this handbook to each of its enrolled members, including plaintiff. Representations made in the handbook are thus directly attributable to Share and were intended by Share to be communicated to its members.

* * *

We hold that the above testimony by plaintiff and Share's member handbook support the conclusion that Share held itself out to plaintiff as the provider of her health care, without informing her that the care was actually provided by independent contractors. Therefore, a triable issue of fact exists as to the holding-out element. We need not resolve whether any other evidence in the record also supports plaintiff's claim. Our task here is to review whether Share is entitled to summary judgment on this element. We hold that Share is not.

B. Justifiable Reliance

A plaintiff must also prove the element of "justifiable reliance" to establish apparent authority against an HMO for physician malpractice. This means that the plaintiff acted in reliance upon the conduct of the HMO or its agent, consistent with ordinary care and prudence. [ ]

The element of justifiable reliance is met where the plaintiff relies upon the HMO to provide health care services, and does not rely upon a specific physician. This element is not met if the plaintiff selects his or her own personal physician and merely looks to the HMO as a conduit through which the plaintiff receives medical care. [ ]

Concerning the element of justifiable reliance in the hospital context, Gilbert explained that the critical distinction is whether the plaintiff sought care from the hospital itself or from a personal physician. * * *

This rationale applies even more forcefully in the context of an HMO that restricts its members to the HMO's chosen physicians. Accordingly, unless a person seeks care from a personal physician, that person is seeking care from the HMO itself. A person who seeks care from the HMO itself accepts that care in reliance upon the HMO's holding itself out as the provider of care.

Share maintains that plaintiff cannot establish the justifiable reliance element because she did not select Share. * * *

* * *We reject Share's argument. It is true that, where a person selects the HMO and does not rely upon a specific physician, then that person is relying upon the HMO to provide health care. This principle, derived directly from Gilbert, is set forth above. Equally true, however, is that where a person has no choice but to enroll with a single HMO and does not rely upon a specific physician, then that person is likewise relying upon the HMO to provide health care.

In the present case, the record discloses that plaintiff did not select Share. Plaintiff's employer selected Share for her. Plaintiff had no choice of health plans whatsoever. Once Share became plaintiff's health plan, Share required plaintiff to obtain her primary medical care from one of its primary care physicians. If plaintiff did not do so, Share did not cover plaintiff's medical costs. In accordance with Share's requirement, plaintiff selected Dr. Kowalski from a list of physicians that Share provided to her. Plaintiff had no prior relationship with Dr. Kowalski. As to Dr. Kowalski's selection of Dr. Friedman for plaintiff, Share required Dr. Kowalski to make referrals only to physicians approved by Share. Plaintiff had no prior relationship with Dr. Friedman. We hold that these facts are sufficient to raise the reasonable inference that plaintiff relied upon Share to provide her health care services.

Were we to conclude that plaintiff was not relying upon Share for health care, we would be denying the true nature of the relationship among plaintiff, her HMO and the physicians. Share, like many HMOs, contracted with plaintiff's employer to become plaintiff's sole provider of health care, to the exclusion of all other providers. Share then restricted plaintiff to its chosen physicians. Under these facts, plaintiff's reliance on Share as the provider of her health care is shown not only to be compelling, but literally compelled. Plaintiff's reliance upon Share was inherent in Share's method of operation.

* * *

In conclusion, as set forth above, plaintiff has presented sufficient evidence to support justifiable reliance, as well as a holding out by Share. Share, therefore, is not entitled to summary judgment against plaintiff's claim of apparent authority.

* * *

II. IMPLIED AUTHORITY

Implied authority is actual authority, circumstantially proved. [ ] One context in which implied authority arises is where the facts and circumstances show that the defendant exerted sufficient control over the alleged agent so as to negate that person's status as an independent contractor, at least with respect to third parties. [ ] The cardinal consideration for determining the existence of implied authority is whether the alleged agent retains the right to control the manner of doing the work. [ ] Where a person's status as an independent contractor is negated, liability may result under the doctrine of respondeat superior.

Plaintiff contends that the facts and circumstances of this case show that Share exerted sufficient control over Drs. Kowalski and Friedman so as to negate their status as independent contractors. Share responds that the act of providing medical care is peculiarly within a physician's domain because it requires the exercise of independent medical judgment. Share thus maintains that, because it cannot control a physician's exercise of medical judgment, it cannot be subject to vicarious liability under the doctrine of implied authority.

* * *

We now address whether the implied authority doctrine may be used against HMOs to negate a physician's status as an independent contractor. Our appellate court in Raglin suggested that it can. Raglin v. HMO Illinois, Inc., 230 Ill.App.3d 642, 647, 172 Ill.Dec. 90, 595 N.E.2d 153 (1992). Case law from other jurisdictions lends support to this view as well. [ ]

* * *

We do not find the above decisions rendered in the hospital context to be dispositive of whether an HMO may exert such control over its physicians so as to negate their status as independent contractors. We can readily discern that the relationships between physicians and HMOs are often much different than the traditional relationships between physicians and hospitals. * * *

Physicians, of course, should not allow the exercise of their medical judgment to be corrupted or controlled. Physicians have professional ethical, moral and legal obligations to provide appropriate medical care to their patients. These obligations on physicians, however, will not act to relieve an HMO of its own legal responsibilities. Where an HMO effectively controls a physician's exercise of medical judgment, and that judgment is exercised negligently, the HMO cannot be allowed to claim that the physician is solely responsible for the harm that results. In such a circumstance, both the physician and the HMO are liable for the harm that results. We therefore hold that the implied authority doctrine may be used against an HMO to negate a physician's status as an independent contractor. An implied agency exists where the facts and circumstances show that an HMO exerted such sufficient control over a participating physician so as to negate that physician's status as an independent contractor, at least with respect to third parties. [ ] No precise formula exists for deciding when a person's status as an independent contractor is negated. Rather, the determination of whether a person is an agent or an independent contractor rests upon the facts and circumstances of each case. [ ] As noted, the cardinal consideration is whether that person retains the right to control the manner of doing the work. [ ] Facts bearing on the question of whether a person is an agent or an independent contractor include "the question of the hiring, the right to discharge, the manner of direction of the servant, the right to terminate the relationship, and the character of the supervision of the work done." Merlo, 381 Ill. at 319, 45 N.E.2d 665. The presence of contractual provisions subjecting the person to control over the manner of doing the work is a traditional indicia that a person's status as an independent contractor should be negated. [ ] The presence of one or more of the above facts and indicia are not necessarily conclusive of the issue. They merely serve as guides to resolving the primary question of whether the alleged agent is truly an independent contractor or is subject to control.

With these established principles in mind, we turn to the present case. Plaintiff contends that her physicians' status as independent contractors should be negated. Plaintiff asserts that Share actively interfered with her physicians' medical decisionmaking by designing and executing its capitation method of compensation and "quality assurance" programs. Plaintiff also points to Share's referral system as evidence of control.

Plaintiff submits that Share's capitation method of compensating its medical groups is a form of control because it financially punishes physicians for ordering certain medical treatment. The record discloses that Share utilizes a method of compensation called "capitation."[ ]. Under capitation, Share prepays contracting medical groups a fixed amount of money for each member who enrolls with that group. In exchange, the medical groups agree to render health care to their enrolled Share members in accordance with the Share plan. Each medical group contracting with Share has its own capitation account. Deducted from that capitation account are the costs of any services provided by the primary care physician, the costs of medical procedures and tests, and the fees of all consulting physicians. The medical group then retains the surplus left in the capitation account. The costs for hospitalizations and other services are charged against a separate account. Reinsurance is provided for the capitation account and the separate account for certain high cost claims. Share pays Illinois Masonic in accordance with its capitation method of compensation. Dr. Kowalski testified that Illinois Masonic pays her the same salary every month. Plaintiff maintains that a reasonable inference to be drawn from Share's capitation method of compensation is that Share provides financial disincentives to its primary care physicians in order to discourage them from ordering the medical care that they deem appropriate. Plaintiff argues that this is an example of Share's influence and control over the medical judgment of its physicians.

Share counters that its capitation method of compensation cannot be used as evidence of control here because Dr. Kowalski is paid the same salary every month. We disagree with Share that this fact makes Share's capitation system irrelevant to our inquiry. Whether control was actually exercised is not dispositive in this context. Rather, the right to control the alleged agent is the proper query, even where that right is not exercised. [ ]

[The court rejects Share's "quality assurance program" as evidence of control, since it is done primarily to comply with state regulations of the Department of Public Health. The court however allows as evidence of control chart review by Share; control over referral to specialists; and use of primary care physicians as gatekeepers].

We conclude that plaintiff has presented adequate evidence to entitle her to a trial on the issue of implied authority. All the facts and circumstances before us, if proven at trial, raise the reasonable inference that Share exerted such sufficient control over Drs. Kowalski and Friedman so as to negate their status as independent contractors. As discussed above, plaintiff presents relevant evidence of Share's capitation method of compensation, Share's "quality assurance review," Share's referral system and Share's requirement that its primary care physicians act as gatekeepers for Share. These facts support plaintiff's argument that Share subjected its physicians to control over the manner in which they did their work. The facts surrounding treatment also support plaintiff's argument. According to plaintiff's evidence, Dr. Kowalski referred plaintiff to Dr. Friedman. Dr. Friedman evaluated plaintiff and recommended that plaintiff have either an MRI test or a CT scan performed on the base of her skull. Dr. Friedman, however, did not order the test that he recommended for plaintiff. Rather, he reported this information back to Dr. Kowalski in her role as plaintiff's primary care physician. Dr. Kowalski initially sent Dr. Friedman a copy of an old MRI test. Dr. Kowalski later ordered that an updated MRI be taken. In doing so, she directed that the MRI be taken of plaintiff's "brain." Hence, that MRI failed to image the base of plaintiff's skull as recommended by Dr. Friedman. Dr. Kowalski then reviewed the MRI test results herself and informed plaintiff that the results revealed no abnormality. From all the above facts and circumstances, a trier of fact could reasonably infer that Share promulgated such a system of control over its physicians that Share effectively negated the exercise of their independent medical judgment, to plaintiff's detriment.

We note that Dr. Kowalski testified at an evidence deposition that she did not feel constrained by Share in making medical decisions regarding her patients, including whether to order tests or make referrals to specialists. This testimony is not controlling at the summary judgment stage. The trier of fact is entitled to weigh all the conflicting evidence above against Dr. Kowalski's testimony.

In conclusion, plaintiff has presented adequate evidence to support a finding that Share exerted such sufficient control over its participating physicians so as to negate their status as independent contractors. Share, therefore, is not entitled to summary judgment against plaintiff's claim of implied authority.

* * *

CONCLUSION

An HMO may be held vicariously liable for the negligence of its independent-contractor physicians under both the doctrines of apparent authority and implied authority. Plaintiff here is entitled to a trial on both doctrines. The circuit court therefore erred in awarding summary judgment to Share. The appellate court's judgment, which reversed the circuit court's judgment and remanded the cause to the circuit court for further proceedings, is affirmed.

Affirmed.

Notes and Questions

1.   Does a subscriber to an IPA-style managed care organization look to it for care rather than solely to the individual physicians? In an IPA, there is no central office, staffed by salaried physicians; the subscriber instead goes to the individual offices of the primary care physicians or the specialists. What justifies extending ostensible agency doctrine to this arrangement?

Managed care advertising often holds out the plan in words such as "total care program", as "an entire health care system". A reliance by the subscriber on the managed care organization for their choice of physicians, and any holding out by the MCO as a provider, is sufficient. See McClellan v. Health Maintenance Organization of Pennsylvania, 413 Pa.Super. 128, 604 A.2d 1053 (1992) (ostensible agency based on advertisements by HMO claiming that it carefully screened in primary care physicians).

In Petrovich, the court allowed both an apparent authority claim and an implied authority claim. Implied authority required a court to find sufficient elements of plan control over a physician to reject the independent contractor defense. In Petrovich, the court found that utilization review, limits on referrals to specialists and hospitals, and other financial constraints were sufficient to create implied authority.

2.   IPA-model HMOs that become "the institution", that "hold out" the independent contractor as an employee, and also restrict provider selection are vulnerable to ostensible agency arguments. Where the HMO exercises substantial control over the independent physicians by controlling the patients they must see and by paying on a per capita basis, an agency relationship has been found. See Dunn v. Praiss, 256 N.J.Super. 180, 606 A.2d 862 (N.J.Super.Ct.App.Div.1992); Boyd v. Albert Einstein Medical Center, 377 Pa.Super. 609, 547 A.2d 1229 (Sup. Pa. 1988).

3.   The court in Decker v. Saini, 14 Employee Benefits Cas. 1556, 1991 WL 277590 (Mich.Cir.Ct.1991) observed that the application of vicarious liability has a powerful incentive effect on MCOs to select better physicians:

As a matter of public policy, the Court notes that imposing vicarious liability on HMOs for the malpractice of their member physicians would strongly encourage them to select physicians with the best credentials. Otherwise, HMO's would have no such incentive and might be driven by economics to retain physicians with the least desirable credentials, for the lower prices.

4. Some courts have pushed the boundaries even further, using agency principles to reach consulting physicians chosen by physicians employed by the HMO. In *Schleier v. Kaiser Foundation Health Plan*, 876 F.2d 174 (D.C.Cir.1989), a staff model HMO was held vicariously liable for physician malpractice, not of its employee-physician, but of an independent consulting physician. The court found four grounds for holding the HMO vicariously liable: (1) the consultant physician had been engaged by an HMO-employed physician, (2) the HMO had the right to discharge the consultant, (3) services provided by the consultant were part of the regular business of the HMO, and (4) the HMO had some ability to control the consultant's behavior, since he answered to an HMO doctor, the plaintiff's primary care physician. This judicial willingness to impose respondeat superior liability for the negligence of a consulting, non-employee physician clearly applies to the IPA model HMOs and even PPOs.

5. The development of complex cost and quality controls, which strengthen the supervisory role of the MCO, together with the managed care industry's preference for the capitation method of physician compensation, are likely to lead the courts to hold the IPA model HMO-physician relationship to respondeat superior liability. Even a plan-sponsored network risks exposure to ostensible agency arguments if a court can find that the plan sponsor has created an expectation on the part of patients that the plan will provide high-quality providers of care. If the plan restricts a member's choice of providers, as will be likely in most situations, the network providers look like "agents" of the sponsor. The alternative—disclaimers in a PPO directory or other subscriber material as to quality of care, reminders to patients that they are responsible for choosing their physicians—may provide a legal shield against ostensible agency arguments. Such disclaimers are, however, not very reassuring when marketing to subscribers of a network plan. Capitation has begun to fade as an HMO tool in the face of physician resistance. Use of fee-based service claims that doctors must submit for each procedure is becoming more common. See Leigh Page, Capitation at the crossroads, 44 AMA News 17 (March 5, 2001).

6. A breach of contract suit can be brought against an MCO on the theory of a "contract" to provide quality health care. In *Williams v. HealthAmerica* 41 Ohio App.3d 245, 535 N.E.2d 717 (Ohio App.1987), a subscriber sued an IPA model HMO, and her primary care physician, for injuries resulting from a delay in referring her to a specialist. The theory was that the physician and HMO failed to deliver quality health benefits as promised, i.e. the right to be referred to a specialist. The court upheld the breach of contract action against the primary care physician but recast the action against the HMO as a tort claim for breach of the duty to handle the plaintiff's claim in good faith.

MCO contracts and literature may also contain provisions to the effect that "quality" health care will be provided or that the organization will promote or enhance subscriber health. The Share literature contained such language. Where such assurances are made in master contracts of HMO-physician agreements, subscribers may be able to bring a contract action under a third party beneficiary theory. In Williams, for example, the court suggested that the subscriber could be a third-party beneficiary of the HMO-physician contract that required the physician to "promote of the rights of enrollees as patients."

A claim for breach of an express contract or an implied contract may also be argued based on representations by an HMO as to quality of care. This would seem to overlap with a malpractice claim to the extent it is based on a contract to provide "adequate and qualified medical care in accordance with the generally accepted standards of the community". Natale v. Meia, 1998 WL 236089 (Sup.Ct. Conn., 1998)(defendant's motion to strike denied) ... But express promises, if proven, can give rise to a separate claim.

Health care providers are not held to guarantee a cure, based on general language. "Mere puffery", as the courts view it, is not the same as a warranty of a good result, and will not create a claim. Pulvers v. Kaiser Foundation Health Plan, 99 Cal.App.3d 560, 160 Cal.Rptr. 392 (1979)(breach of warranty claim rejected on grounds that a warranty of a good result was just "generalized puffing.") However, an assurance of high quality care in marketing materials and brochures might be treated by a court or jury as a promise that standards of quality will be met, leading to warranty liability. In *Boyd* the plaintiff pleaded both ostensible agency and breach of warranty. The concurring opinion argued that summary judgment on the warranty count was inappropriate because there was a factual issue as to "whether the literature in which HMO 'guaranteed' and 'assured' the quality of care to its subscribers, had been distributed to * * * [the plaintiff]."

MCOs also typically market themselves by describing the quality of the providers on the panel. An assertion of quality furnishes courts another reason to impose on the organization the duty to investigate the competency of participating physicians. Such assertions might even be viewed as a warranty that all panel members maintain a certain minimum competence.

7. Common law fraud or state consumer fraud statutes are another possible source of recovery. Representations in contracts and marketing brochures, or omissions of material information from these documents, inducing the patient to subscribe to the MCO or submit to a certain medical treatment, might be actionable. These theories are more demanding, however, often requiring proof of intentional misrepresentation and justifiable reliance.

Common law bad faith claims may be brought against non-ERISA managed car plans. Courts have held that a staff model HMO acts as an insurer when it refers a subscriber to an out-of-network provider, under the contract, and then denies reimbursement for that out-of-network care without reasonable grounds. This kind of non-medical, coverage-related decision is subject to a bad faith analysis. McEvoy v. Group Health Cooperative of Eau Claire, 213 Wis.2d 507, 570 N.W.2d 397 (Wis. 1997) (allowing bad faith action against a non-ERISA HMO for a coverage denial). The managed care organization is liable for any damages from the breach, including damages. Such actions are not intended to be duplicative of malpractice actions. They require a showing "by clear, satisfactory, and convincing evidence that an HMO acted improperly, and that financial considerations were given unreasonable weight in the decision maker's cost-benefit analysis."ID at 405. The court in McEvoy noted that HMO subscribers are "in an inferior position for enforcing their contractual health care rights" (id. at 403.) Such actions are likely to be rare in light of the higher burden of proof required and ERISA preemption,[1] but the question of what "unreasonable weight" means in considering the financial effects of treatment opens the door to more litigation.

---

1. Pilot Life Insurance Co. v. Dedeaux, 481 U.S. 41, 107 S.Ct. 1549, 95 L.Ed.2d 39 (1987)

B. DIRECT INSTITUTIONAL LIABILITY: CORPORATE NEGLIGENCE

SHANNON v. McNULTY

Superior Court of Pennsylvania, 1998.
718 A.2d 828.

ORIE MELVIN, JUDGE:

Mario L. Shannon and his wife, Sheena Evans Shannon, in their own right and as co-administrators of the Estate of Evan Jon Shannon, appeal from an order entered in the Court of Common Pleas of Allegheny County denying their motion to remove a compulsory nonsuit. This appeal concerns the Shannons' claims of vicarious and corporate liability against HealthAmerica stemming from the premature delivery and subsequent death of their son. We reverse the order refusing to remove the compulsory nonsuit and remand for trial.

This medical malpractice action arises from the pre-natal care provided by appellees, Larry P. McNulty, M.D. and HealthAmerica, to Mrs. Shannon. The Shannons claimed Dr. McNulty was negligent for failing to timely diagnose and treat signs of pre-term labor, and HealthAmerica was vicariously liable for the negligence of its nursing staff in failing to respond to Mrs. Shannon's complaints by timely referring her to an appropriate physician or hospital for diagnosis and treatment of her pre-term labor. The Shannons also alleged HealthAmerica was corporately liable for its negligent supervision of Dr. McNulty's care and its lack of appropriate procedures and protocols when dispensing telephonic medical advice to subscribers.

The case went to trial before a jury, and at the close of the plaintiffs' case HealthAmerica moved for a compulsory nonsuit. The trial court denied the motion. HealthAmerica then proceeded to put on its case by calling two of its triage nurses. At the conclusion of the testimony of the second nurse the court recessed for the day. The following morning the court, sua sponte, reconsidered HealthAmerica's motion for compulsory nonsuit, entertained argument thereon, and granted the nonsuit. The Shannons filed timely post trial motions seeking to have the nonsuit removed. After denial of such motions, this appeal followed.

On appeal the Shannons present two questions for this Court to review:

1. [DID] THE TRIAL COURT [ERR] IN GRANTING A COMPULSORY NONSUIT IN FAVOR OF [APPELLEE], HEALTHAMERICA, AND AGAINST THE [APPELLANTS] [IN THAT APPELLANTS] MADE OUT A PRIMA FACIE CASE AGAINST HEALTHAMERICA FOR BOTH COMMON LAW VICARIOUS LIABILITY REGARDING THE ACTIONS OF HEALTHAMERICA'S TRIAGE NURSES AND EMPLOYEES, AND DIRECT CORPORATE LIABILITY.

held that actions such as bad faith sufficiently "relate to" employee benefits plans to fall within ERISA preemption.

2. [DID] THE TRIAL COURT [ERR] IN GRANTING A COMPULSORY NONSUIT AFTER [APPELLEE] HEALTHAMERICA PRESENTED EVIDENCE IN ITS CASE IN CHIEF.

(Appellants' Brief at 2). Initially, we note that the scope of review in an appeal from the denial of a motion to remove a compulsory nonsuit is limited to determining whether the trial court abused its discretion or committed an error of law. [ ] * * *

Generally, in a medical malpractice case the plaintiff must establish: (1) a duty owed by the health care provider to the patient; (2) a breach of that duty; (3) the breach was the proximate cause of, or a substantial factor in, bringing about the harm suffered by the patient; and (4) damages suffered by the patient that were a direct result of that harm. [ ] Moreover, except where it is obvious, the plaintiff must present expert testimony that the health care provider's conduct deviated from an accepted standard of care and such deviation was the proximate cause of the harm suffered.

The theory of corporate liability as it relates to hospitals was first adopted in this Commonwealth in the case of Thompson v. Nason Hospital, 527 Pa. 330, 591 A.2d 703 (Pa.1991). Our supreme court upheld a direct theory of liability against the hospital, stating:

Corporate negligence is a doctrine under which the hospital is liable if it fails to uphold the proper standard of care owed the patient, which is to ensure the patient's safety and well-being while at the hospital. This theory of liability creates a nondelegable duty which the hospital owes directly to a patient. Therefore, an injured party does not have to rely on and establish the negligence of a third party. Id. at 707. (footnote omitted) The court then set forth four general areas of corporate liability:

(1) A duty to use reasonable care in the maintenance of safe and adequate facilities and equipment;

(2) A duty to select and retain only competent physicians;

(3) A duty to oversee all persons who practice medicine within its walls as to patient care;

(4) A duty to formulate, adopt and enforce adequate rules and policies to ensure quality care for patients. Id. The court further stated that "we adopt as a theory of hospital liability the doctrine of corporate negligence or corporate liability under which the hospital is liable if it fails to uphold the proper standard of care owed its patient." Id. at 708.

The evidence introduced by the Shannons may be summarized in relevant part as follows. Mrs. Shannon testified during the trial of this case that she was a subscriber of the HealthAmerica HMO when this child was conceived. It was Mrs. Shannon's first pregnancy. When she advised HealthAmerica she was pregnant in June 1992, they gave her a list of six doctors from which she could select an OB/GYN. She chose Dr. McNulty from the list. [ ] Her HealthAmerica membership card instructed her to contact either her physician or HealthAmerica in the event she had any medical questions or emergent medical conditions. The card contained the HealthAmerica emergency phone number, which was manned by registered nurses. [ ] She testified it was confusing trying to figure out when to call Dr. McNulty and when to call HealthAmerica because she was receiving treatment from both for various medical conditions related to her pregnancy, including asthma and reflux. [ ]

She saw Dr. McNulty monthly but also called the HealthAmerica phone line a number of times for advice and to schedule appointments with their in-house doctors. [ ] She called Dr. McNulty on October 2, 1992 with complaints of abdominal pain. The doctor saw her on October 5, 1992 and examined her for five minutes. He told Mrs. Shannon her abdominal pain was the result of a fibroid uterus, he prescribed rest and took her off of work for one week. He did no testing to confirm his diagnosis and did not advise her of the symptoms of pre-term labor. [ ]

She next called Dr. McNulty's office twice on October 7 and again on October 8 and October 9, 1992, because her abdominal pain was continuing, she had back pain, was constipated and she could not sleep. She asked Dr. McNulty during the October 8th call if she could be in pre-term labor because her symptoms were similar to those described in a reference book she had on labor. [ ] She told Dr. McNulty her pains were irregular and about ten minutes apart, but she had never been in labor so she did not know what it felt like. He told her he had just checked her on October 5th, and she was not in labor.[ ] The October 9th call was at least her fourth call to Dr. McNulty about her abdominal pain, and she testified that Dr. McNulty was becoming impatient with her. [ ]

On October 10th, she called HealthAmerica's emergency phone line and told them about her severe irregular abdominal pain, back pain, that her pain was worse at night, that she thought she may be in pre-term labor, and about her prior calls to Dr. McNulty. The triage nurse advised her to call Dr. McNulty again. [ ] Mrs. Shannon did not immediately call Dr. McNulty because she did not feel there was anything new she could tell him to get him to pay attention to her condition. She called the HealthAmerica triage line again on October 11, 1992, said her symptoms were getting worse and Dr. McNulty was not responding. The triage nurse again advised her to call Dr. McNulty. [ ] Mrs. Shannon called Dr. McNulty and told him about her worsening symptoms, her legs beginning to go numb, and she thought that she was in pre-term labor. He was again short with her and angry and insisted that she was not in pre-term labor.[ ]

On October 12, 1992, she again called the HealthAmerica phone service and told the nurse about her symptoms, severe back pain and back spasms, legs going numb, more regular abdominal pain, and Dr. McNulty was not responding to her complaints. One of HealthAmerica's in-house orthopedic physicians spoke with her on the phone and directed her to go to West Penn Hospital to get her back examined. [ ] She followed the doctor's advice and drove an hour from her house to West Penn, passing three hospitals on the way. At West Penn she was processed as having a back complaint because those were HealthAmerica's instructions, but she was taken to the obstetrics wing as a formality because she was over five (5) months pregnant. She delivered a one and one-half pound baby that night. He survived only two days and then died due to his severe prematurity. [ ]

The Shannons' expert, Stanley M. Warner, M.D., testified he had experience in a setting where patients would call triage nurses. Dr. Warner opined that HealthAmerica, through its triage nurses, deviated from the standard of care following the phone calls to the triage line on October 10, 11 and 12, 1992, by not immediately referring Mrs. Shannon to a physician or hospital for a cervical exam and fetal stress test. As with Dr. McNulty, these precautions would have led to her labor being detected and increased the baby's chance of survival. [ ] Dr. Warner further testified on cross examination that Mrs. Shannon turned to HealthAmerica's triage nurses for medical advice on these three occasions when she communicated her symptoms. She did not receive appropriate advice, and further, if HealthAmerica's triage nurses intended for the referrals back to Dr. McNulty to be their solution, they had a duty to follow up Mrs. Shannon's calls by calling Dr. McNulty to insure Mrs. Shannon was actually receiving the proper care from him.[ ]

CORPORATE LIABILITY

[The court concludes that the third duty of Thompson, the duty to oversee all those who deliver care, is applicable.] * * *

Similarly, in the present case Dr. Warner, on direct examination, offered the following opinion when asked whether or not HealthAmerica deviated from the standard of care:

I believe they did deviate from the standard of care. I believe on each occasion of the calls on October 10th, 11th, and October 12th, that Mrs. Shannon should have been referred to the hospital, and the hospital notified that this woman was probably in preterm labor and needed to be handled immediately. They did have the alternative of calling for a physician, if they wanted to, for him to agree with it, but basically she needed to be evaluated in a placd [sic] where there was a fetal monitor and somebody to do a pelvic examination to see what was happening with her.

[ ]. When asked whether this deviation increased the risk of harm Dr. Warner stated that "it did increase the risk of harm to the baby, and definitely decreased the chance of [the baby] being born healthy." Id., at 147.

Dr. Warner further testified in response to a series of hypothetical questions as follows:

Q. I want you to assume that on Saturday, October 10th, that Mrs. Shannon calls Health America and she talks to a triage nurse, and she relates to the triage nurse she is experiencing severe abdominal pain. I want you to assume that she is told, the triage nurse who answered the phone, that she has related these symptoms to Dr. McNulty, and she related Dr. McNulty's response, or lack of response, to her complaints of abdominal pain. I want you to assume that the triage nurse's advice is simply to call the doctor back again. Now, under those facts do you have an opinion, within a reasonable degree medical certainty, whether or not Health America deviated from the standard of care?

A. I do.

Q. What is that opinion?

A. I believe they deviated from the standard of care, the nurse.

Q. We're talking now with respect to October 10th.

A. Yes, sir. The nurse at that time would have a responsibility to know these are signs and symptoms of preterm labor, and to make sure she gets care in a facility where the ability to have fetal monitoring and cervix examination are. She should call up Dr. McNulty and ask him to make arraignments [sic] for that, or she can send the patient directly to the hospital. She should, in any event, make sure that happens in a very timely fashion. In other words, do it right away, you don't delay in doing this. You want to get her there before it's too late, before the cervix dilates too far, before it's too late to inhibit labor.

* * *

Q. I want you to assume, Dr. Warner, that on October 11, 1992, Mrs. Shannon called Health America again, and again relayed her complaints of either abdominal pain, back pain or side pain. Once again she also relayed her history of what I just told you, and she relayed what Dr. McNulty had done and what he hadn't done up to October 11th, and that the advice from Health America was the same, call Dr. McNulty back again. Now, under that factual scenario do you have an opinion, within a reasonable degree of medical certainty, whether or not Health America deviate from the standard of care on October 11, 1992?

A. I do have an opinion.

Q. And what is that?

A. That they deviated from the standard of care on October 11, 1992, as well. This woman was obviously searching for help. She was worried, and nobody was responding to her. She needed to be brought into the hospital and monitored and examined, and Dr. McNulty did not provide for it. She tlaked [sic] to Health America, who is one of her medical providers, and they at least had to get her into the hospital on an emergency condition, seen right away and monitored and examined right away, and if they called ahead to the emergency room to let them know that, then the emergency room is conditioned to respond, they know they have to respond rapidly to this preterm labor situation before they lose the chance to stop the labor.

Q. Moving down to October 12th, I want you to assume that Sheena Shannon called Health America on October 12, 1992, and relayed the same history. That is, the history now of back pain. I want you to assume that the nurse at Health America asked Sheena whether or not she had experienced any type of trauma over the course of the past year. Although she was also informed of her pregnancy and her gestational status, the nurse under this assumption was told that she had been in two automobile accidents, and the triage nurse then called an internist. The internist under this assumption called Sheena and told Sheena to go to the hospital, West Penn Hospital, for an orthopedic consult. I want you also to assume under this scenario that no provision was made by Health America to this hospital. Now, under that scenario did Health America deviate from the standard of care?

A. Yes, they did deviate from the standard of care. Again she should have been sent to the emergency room right away, and the emergency room notified there was a possibility that she was in preterm labor, regardless of the fact she had prior car accidents. Once again, you can't differentiate back pain caused by preterm labor from other sources of back pain without going through a Physical examination and measurements [sic] that you need to determine whether or not she was in labor or not. So, she had to go in and be seen right away. Her call was at 12:42, as I understand, or about 12:30, I think I saw in one place.

Q. That's right, 12:42.

A. And she was five centimeters at 4:00 a.m., approximately. Since the first part of labor moves rather slowly, especially in a first baby, an hour or two could have made a significant difference. There's a good probability that if they had seen her at 2:00 a.m. she would still be at four centimeters or less, and they could have inhibited labor even on that night if they had gotten her in quickly enough.

Id. at 158–162.

Viewing the evidence in the light most favorable to the Shannons as the non-moving party, our examination of the instant record leads us to the conclusion that the Shannons presented sufficient evidence to establish a prima facie case of corporate liability pursuant to the third duty set forth in Thompson, supra. However, due to the different entities involved, this determination does not end our inquiry. The Welsh case involved a suit against a hospital and thus Thompson was clearly applicable. Instantly, HealthAmerica, noting this Court's decision not to extend corporate liability under the facts in McClellan v. Health Maintenance Organization of Pennsylvania, 413 Pa.Super. 128, 604 A.2d 1053 (Pa.Super.1992), argues that the Thompson duties are inapplicable to a health maintenance organization. We disagree.

In adopting the doctrine of corporate liability the Thompson court recognized "the corporate hospital's role in the total health care of its patients." Thompson, at 708. Likewise, we recognize the central role played by HMOs in the total health care of its subscribers. A great deal of today's healthcare is channeled through HMOs with the subscribers being given little or no say so in the stewardship of their care. Specifically, while these providers do not practice medicine, they do involve themselves daily in decisions affecting their subscriber's medical care. These decisions may, among others, limit the length of hospital stays, restrict the use of specialists, prohibit or limit post hospital care, restrict access to therapy, or prevent rendering of emergency room care. While all of these efforts are for the laudatory purpose of containing health care costs, when decisions are made to limit a subscriber's access to treatment, that decision must pass the test of medical reasonableness. To hold otherwise would be to deny the true effect of the provider's actions, namely, dictating and directing the subscriber's medical care.

Where the HMO is providing health care services rather than merely providing money to pay for services their conduct should be subject to scrutiny. We see no reason why the duties applicable to hospitals should not be equally applied to an HMO when that HMO is performing the same or similar functions as a hospital. When a benefits provider, be it an insurer or a managed care organization, interjects itself into the rendering of medical decisions affecting a subscriber's care it must do so in a medically reasonable manner. Here, HealthAmerica provided a phone service for emergent care staffed by triage nurses. Hence, it was under a duty to oversee that the dispensing of advice by those nurses would be performed in a medically reasonable manner. Accordingly, we now make explicit that which was implicit in McClellan and find that HMOs may, under the right circumstances, be held corporately liable for a breach of any of the Thompson duties which causes harm to its subscribers.

[The court also held that HealthAmerican was vicariously liable for the negligent rendering of services by its triage nurses, under Section 323 of the Restatement (Second) of Torts.]

* * *

JONES v. CHICAGO HMO LTD. OF ILLINOIS

Supreme Court of Illinois, 2000.
191 Ill.2d 278, 246 Ill.Dec. 654, 730 N.E.2d 1119.

JUSTICE BILANDIC delivered the opinion of the court:

This appeal asks whether a health maintenance organization (HMO) may be held liable for institutional negligence. We answer in the affirmative.

The plaintiff, Sheila Jones (Jones), individually and as the mother of the minor, Shawndale Jones, brought this medical malpractice action against the defendants, Chicago HMO Ltd. of Illinois (Chicago HMO), Dr. Robert A. Jordan and another party. The Joneses were members of Chicago HMO, an HMO. Dr. Jordan was a contract physician of Chicago HMO and the primary care physician of Shawndale.

* * *

FACTS

In reviewing an award of summary judgment, we must view the facts in the light most favorable to the nonmoving party. Petrovich v. Share Health Plan of Illinois, Inc., 188 Ill.2d 17, 30–31, 241 Ill.Dec. 627, 719 N.E.2d 756 (1999). The following facts thus emerge.

On January 18, 1991, Jones' three-month-old daughter Shawndale was ill. Jones called Dr. Jordan's office, as she had been instructed to do by Chicago HMO. Jones related Shawndale's symptoms, specifically that she was sick, was constipated, was crying a lot and felt very warm. An assistant advised Jones to give Shawndale some castor oil. When Jones insisted on speaking with Dr. Jordan, the assistant stated that Dr. Jordan was not available but would return her call. Dr. Jordan returned Jones' call late that evening. After Jones described the same symptoms to Dr. Jordan, he also advised Jones to give castor oil to Shawndale.

On January 19, 1991, Jones took Shawndale to a hospital emergency room because her condition had not improved. Chicago HMO authorized Shawndale's admission. Shawndale was diagnosed with bacterial meningitis, secondary to bilateral otitis media, an ear infection. As a result of the meningitis, Shawndale is permanently disabled.

The medical expert for the plaintiff, Dr. Richard Pawl, stated in his affidavit and deposition testimony that Dr. Jordan had deviated from the standard of care. In Dr. Pawl's opinion, upon being advised of a three-month-old infant who is warm, irritable and constipated, the standard of care requires a physician to schedule an immediate appointment to see the infant or, alternatively, to instruct the parent to obtain immediate medical care for the infant through another physician. Dr. Pawl gave no opinion regarding whether Chicago HMO was negligent.

* * *

Chicago HMO is a for-profit corporation. During all pertinent times, Chicago HMO was organized as an independent practice association model HMO under the Illinois Health Maintenance Organization Act (Ill.Rev.Stat. 1991, ch. 111 1/2, par. 1401 et seq.).

In her deposition testimony, Jones described how she first enrolled in Chicago HMO while living in Park Forest. A Chicago HMO representative visited her home. According to Jones, he "was telling me what it was all about, that HMO is better than a regular medical card and everything so I am just listening to him and signing my name and stuff on the papers. * * * I asked him what kind of benefits you get out of it and stuff, and he was telling me that it is better than a regular card."

The "HMO ENROLLMENT UNDERSTANDING" form signed by Jones in 1987 stated: "I understand that all my medical care will be provided through the Health Plan once my application becomes effective." Jones remembered that, at the time she signed this form, the Chicago HMO representative told her "you have got to call your doctor and stuff before you see your doctor; and before you go to the hospital, you have got to call."

Jones testified that when she later moved to Chicago Heights another Chicago HMO representative visited her home. This meeting was not arranged in advance. It occurred because the representative was "in the building knocking from door to door." Jones informed the representative that she was already a member.

When Jones moved to Chicago Heights, she did not select Dr. Jordan as Shawndale's primary care physician. Rather, Chicago HMO assigned Dr. Jordan to her. Jones explained:

"They gave me * * * Dr. Jordan. They didn't ask me if I wanted a doctor. They gave me him.

* * *

* * * They told me that he was a good doctor * * * for the kids because I didn't know what doctor to take my kids to because I was staying in Chicago Heights so they gave me him so I started taking my kids there to him."

Dr. Mitchell J. Trubitt, Chicago HMO's medical director, testified at his deposition that Dr. Jordan was under contract with Chicago HMO for two sites, Homewood and Chicago Heights. The service agreement for the Homewood site was first entered into on May 5, 1987. The service agreement for the Chicago Heights site was first entered into on February 1, 1990. Dr. Jordan was serving both patient populations in January of 1991 when Shawndale became ill.

Dr. Trubitt stated that, before Chicago HMO and Dr. Jordan executed the Chicago Heights service agreement, another physician serviced that area. Chicago HMO terminated that physician for failing to provide covered immunizations. At the time that Chicago HMO terminated that physician, Dr. Jordan agreed "to go into the [Chicago Heights] area and serve the patients." Chicago HMO then assigned to Dr. Jordan all of the patients of that physician. Dr. Trubitt explained:

"Q. So then with the elimination of [the other physician], Dr. Jordan then-were the members notified that Dr. Jordan would be their [primary care physician] from that point on?

A. Yes.

Q. They weren't given a choice?

A. At that point in the area there was no choice.

Q. So they weren't given a choice?

A. They were directed to Dr. Jordan."

Dr. Trubitt also explained that Dr. Jordan was Chicago HMO's only physician who was willing to serve the public aid membership in Chicago Heights. Dr. Trubitt characterized this lack of physicians as "a problem" for Chicago HMO.

Dr. Jordan testified at his deposition that, in January of 1991, he was a solo practitioner. He divided his time equally between his offices in Homewood and Chicago Heights. Dr. Jordan was under contract with Chicago HMO for both sites. In addition, Dr. Jordan was under contract with 20 other HMOs, and he maintained his own private practice of non-HMO patients. Dr. Jordan estimated that he was designated the primary care physician of 3,000 Chicago HMO members and 1,500 members of other HMOs. In contrast to Dr. Jordan's estimate, Chicago HMO's own "Provider Capitation Summary Reports" listed Dr. Jordan as being the primary care provider of 4,527 Chicago HMO patients as of December 1, 1990.

Jones' legal counsel and Dr. Trubitt engaged in the following colloquy concerning patient load:

"Q. In entering into an agreement with a provider, is any consideration given to the number of patients to be designated as the primary provider for?

A. Yes, there is consideration given to that element in terms of volume of patients that he is capable of handling.

Q. And who determines the volume of patients he is capable of handling? The Chicago HMO or the provider or-

A. There is some guidelines that HCFA provides.

Q. Who provides?

A. HCFA. The Health [Care Finance Administration], the governmental health and welfare.

Q. Do you happen to know what those limits are with respect to pediatricians?

A. I am going to say I believe they are 3,500 patients to a primary care physician. The number can be expanded depending on the number of physicians in the office and the number of hours of operation.

Q. So you can't tell me whether or not if Dr. Jordan had 6,000 or 6,500 that would be an unusually large number?

A. If he himself had it.

Q. It would be unusually large?

A. It would.

Q. And that would be of some concern to the Chicago HMO, right?

A. Well, yes, if he had those."

In January of 1991, Dr. Jordan employed four part-time physicians, in addition to himself. This included an obstetrician/gynecologist, an internist, a family practitioner and a pediatrician. Dr. Jordan, however, did not explain in what capacities these physicians served. The record contains no further information regarding these physicians.

The record also contains evidence concerning Chicago HMO procedures for obtaining health care. Chicago HMO's "Member Handbook" told members in need of medical care to "Call your Chicago HMO doctor first when you experience an emergency or begin to feel sick." (Emphasis in original.) Also, Chicago HMO gave its contract physicians a "Provider Manual." The manual contains certain provisions with which the providers are expected to comply. The manual contains a section entitled, "The Appointment System/Afterhours Care," which states that all HMO sites are statutorily required to maintain an appointment system for their patients.

Dr. Trubitt testified that Chicago HMO encouraged its providers to maintain an appointment system and also "to retain open spaces on their schedules so that patients who came in as walk-ins could be seen." Retaining space on the schedule for walk-ins was recommended because it offers quicker access to care, keeping patients out of the emergency room with its increased costs, and because, historically, the Medicaid patient population often did not make or keep appointments.

Dr. Jordan related that his office worked on an appointment system and had its own written procedures and forms for handling patient calls and appointments. When a patient called and Dr. Jordan was not in the office, written forms were used by his staff or his answering service to relay the information to him. If Dr. Jordan was in the office, the procedure was as follows:

"Q. * * * [I]f it was a routine appointment for the purpose of having a routine shot or checkup, [the office staff] could make the appointment themselves?

A. Yes.

Q. But if the caller calls and says there is some problem, then they would take the temperature and find out the complaints and refer that call to you; is that correct?

A. That's correct.

Q. And you were the one who would make the determination as to whether or not to schedule an appointment, is that correct?

A. Medical decision, yes.

Q. Medical decision. And I assume there were times when people would call and after you reviewed the information and talked to them that you decided that they didn't need the appointment; is that correct?

A. Of course.

Q. In other words, you would perform some type of triage over the telephone; is that correct?

A. Yes."

Three agreements appear in the record. First, Chicago HMO and the Department of Public Aid entered into a 1990 "AGREEMENT FOR FUR-NISHING HEALTH SERVICES." This agreement was "for the delivery of medical services to Medicaid recipients on a prepaid capitation basis." Jones and her children, Medicaid recipients, fall within the agreement's definition of beneficiaries.

The preamble to the agreement stated that Chicago HMO "is organized primarily for the purpose of providing health care services." It continued: "[Chicago HMO] warrants that it is able to provide the medical care and services required under this Agreement in accordance with prevailing community standards, and is able to provide these services promptly, efficiently, and economically."

Article V of the agreement described various duties of Chicago HMO, as follows. Chicago HMO "shall provide or arrange to have provided all covered services to all Beneficiaries under this Agreement." Chicago HMO "shall provide all Beneficiaries with medical care consistent with prevailing community standards." In addition, a section entitled "Choice of Physicians" provided in relevant part:

"[Chicago HMO] shall afford to each Beneficiary a health professional who will supervise and coordinate his care, and, to the extent feasible within appropriate limits established by [Chicago HMO] and approved by the Department, shall afford the Beneficiary a choice of a physician.

There shall be at least one full-time equivalent, board eligible physician to every 1,200 enrollees, including one full-time equivalent, board certified primary care physician for each 2,000 enrollees. * * * There shall be * * * one pediatrician for each 2,000 enrollees under age 17."

Another article V duty stated that, although Chicago HMO may furnish the services required by the agreement by means of subcontractors, Chicago HMO "shall remain responsible for the performance of the subcontractors."

Regarding appointments, this agreement stated that Chicago HMO "shall encourage members to be seen by appointment, except in emergencies." The agreement also stated that "[m]embers with more serious or urgent problems not deemed emergencies shall be triaged and provided same day service, if necessary," and that "emergency treatment shall be available on an immediate basis, seven days a week, 24–hours a day." Finally, the agreement directed that Chicago HMO "shall have an established policy that scheduled patients shall not routinely wait for more than one hour to be seen by a provider and no more than six appointments shall be made for each primary care physician per hour."

The record also contains a second agreement, a 1990 "MEDICAL GROUP SERVICE AGREEMENT" between Chicago HMO and Dr. Jordan, that lists a Chicago Heights office address for Dr. Jordan. This agreement described numerous duties of Dr. Jordan. Pertinent here, Dr. Jordan would provide to Chicago HMO subscribers specified medical services "of good quality and in accordance with accepted medical and hospital standards of the community." Pursuant to a "PUBLIC AID AMENDMENT TO THE MEDICAL GROUP SERVICE AGREEMENT," Dr. Jordan agreed to "abide by any conditions imposed by [Chicago HMO] as part of [Chicago HMO's] agreement with [the Department]."

The third agreement appearing of record is a second "MEDICAL GROUP SERVICE AGREEMENT" between Chicago HMO and Dr. Jordan. This agreement was entered into in 1987 and lists a Homewood office address for Dr. Jordan.

Both agreements between Chicago HMO and Dr. Jordan provided for a capitation method of compensation. Under capitation, Chicago HMO paid Dr. Jordan a fixed amount of money for each member who selected Dr. Jordan as the member's primary care provider. In exchange, Dr. Jordan agreed to render health care to his enrolled Chicago HMO members in accordance with the Chicago HMO health plan. Dr. Jordan was paid the same monthly capitation fee per member regardless of the services he rendered. For example, for each female patient under two years old, Chicago HMO paid Dr. Jordan $34.19 per month regardless of whether he treated that patient. In addition, Chicago HMO utilized an incentive fund for Dr. Jordan. Certain costs such as inpatient hospital costs were paid from this fund. Chicago HMO would then pay Dr. Jordan 60% of any remaining, unused balance of the fund at the end of each year.

* * *

ANALYSIS

* * *

I. INSTITUTIONAL NEGLIGENCE

Institutional negligence is also known as direct corporate negligence. Since the landmark decision of Darling v. Charleston Community Memorial Hospital, 33 Ill.2d 326, 211 N.E.2d 253 (1965), Illinois has recognized that hospitals may be held liable for institutional negligence. * * *

* * *

[The court adopts the doctrine of institutional negligence for HMOs, citing to Shannon and Petrovich, supra.]

Having determined that institutional negligence is a valid claim against HMOs, we turn to the parties' arguments in this case. Jones contends that Chicago HMO is not entitled to summary judgment on her claim of institutional negligence. She asserts that genuine issues of material fact exist as to whether Chicago HMO (1) negligently assigned more enrollees to Dr. Jordan than he was capable of serving, and (2) negligently adopted procedures requiring Jones to call first for an appointment before visiting the doctor's office.

Chicago HMO argues that Jones' claim of institutional negligence cannot proceed because she failed to provide sufficient evidence delineating the standard of care required of an HMO in these circumstances. In particular, Chicago HMO contends that Jones should have presented expert testimony on the standard of care required of an HMO.

Jones responds that she has provided sufficient evidence showing the standard of care required of an HMO in these circumstances. She argues further that her claim does not require expert testimony on this point. In support, Jones relies on Darling, where a claim of institutional negligence was allowed against a hospital without expert testimony because other evidence established the hospital's standard of care. [ ]

[The court discussed the need for expert testimony as to the standard of care in light of Darling and other precedents.

* * *

Darling and its progeny have firmly established that, in an action for institutional negligence against a hospital, the standard of care applicable to a hospital may be proved via a number of evidentiary sources, and expert testimony is not always required. [ ] We likewise conclude that, in an action for institutional negligence against an HMO, the standard of care applicable to an HMO may be proved through a number of evidentiary sources, and expert testimony is not necessarily required. Accordingly, expert testimony concerning the standard of care required of an HMO is not a prerequisite to Jones' claim. Nonetheless, Jones, as the plaintiff here, still bears the burden of establishing the standard of care required of an HMO through other, proper evidentiary sources. We must therefore evaluate the evidence presented on this point to determine whether Jones' claim withstands Chicago HMO's motion for summary judgment. In deciding whether Jones' standard of care evidence is sufficient, we look to whether that evidence can equip a lay juror to determine what constitutes the standard of care required of a "reasonably careful HMO" under the circumstances of this case.

A. Patient Load

We first consider Jones' assertion that Chicago HMO negligently assigned more patients to Dr. Jordan than he was capable of serving. Parenthetically, we note that this assertion involves an administrative or managerial action by Chicago HMO, not the professional conduct of its physicians. Therefore, this claim properly falls within the purview of HMO institutional negligence. Jones argues that the standard of care evidence in the record is sufficient to support her claim. She points to Dr. Trubitt's testimony, as well as the contract between Chicago HMO and the Department of Public Aid.

Dr. Trubitt was the medical director for Chicago HMO. He testified that, when Chicago HMO entered into agreements with primary care physicians, it considered the number of patients that the physician is capable of handling. The HMO would look to federal "guidelines" in making this determination. Based on those guidelines, Dr. Trubitt expressed 3,500 as the maximum number of patients that should be assigned to any one primary care physician. He stated that, if Dr. Jordan himself had 6,000 or more patients, then that would be an unusually large number and of concern to Chicago HMO.]

We agree with Jones that Dr. Trubitt's testimony is proper and sufficient evidence of the standard of care on this issue. According to Dr. Trubitt, an HMO should not assign more than 3,500 patients to any single primary care physician. Chicago HMO even concedes in its brief that the maximum patient load to which Dr. Trubitt testified "represent[s] a 'standard of care' whose violation could affect the quality of patient care." This particular standard of care evidence, setting forth a limit of 3,500 patients per primary care physician, is adequate to equip a lay juror to determine what constitutes the standard of care required of a "reasonably careful HMO" under the circumstances of this case. Whether Dr. Trubitt relied on an unidentified federal regulation or some other source in arriving at a maximum patient load of 3,500 is of no consequence. It is enough that Chicago HMO, through its medical director, admitted that it used the 3,500 limit as a guide in assigning patient loads. [ ]

Chicago HMO, however, submits that there is no evidence in the record that Dr. Jordan's patient load exceeded 3,500. We disagree. Chicago HMO's "Provider Capitation Summary Reports" listed Dr. Jordan as being the primary care provider of 4,527 Chicago HMO members as of December 1, 1990. Thus, Chicago HMO's own records show Dr. Jordan's patient load as exceeding the 3,500 limit by more than 1,000 patients. In addition, Dr. Jordan estimated that he himself was designated the primary care physician for an additional 1,500 members of other HMOs. He also maintained his own private practice of non-HMO patients. This evidence supports Jones' theory that Dr. Jordan had more than 6,000 HMO patients.

Chicago HMO, in support of its position, points to Dr. Jordan's testimony that he employed four part-time physicians in his office. We disagree with Chicago HMO concerning the significance of this testimony. Although Dr. Jordan testified that he employed four part-time physicians, he never explained in what capacities these physicians served. In fact, the record contains no further information regarding these physicians. Notably, the agreements between Chicago HMO and Dr. Jordan do not refer to any physicians other than Dr. Jordan himself. The evidence in the record, therefore, supports Jones' theory that Chicago HMO negligently assigned more than 3,500 patients to Dr. Jordan himself. At best, the testimony regarding the four part-time physicians creates a genuine issue of material fact as to how many patients Dr. Jordan actually served himself. Consequently, this limited information in the record about part-time physicians does not entitle Chicago HMO to summary judgment. As earlier noted, it is well established that summary judgment is a drastic remedy and should be awarded only where the right of the moving party is clear and free from doubt.

Chicago HMO also submits that Jones' claim of patient overload must fail because there is no evidence of a causal connection between the number of patients that Dr. Jordan was serving and his failure to schedule an appointment to see Shawndale. We disagree. We can easily infer from this record that Dr. Jordan's failure to see Shawndale resulted from an inability to serve an overloaded patient population. A lay juror can discern that a physician who has thousands more patients than he should will not have time to service them all in an appropriate manner.

We note, moreover, that additional evidence in the record supports Jones' claim. The record indicates that Chicago HMO was actively soliciting new members door-to-door around the same time that it lacked the physicians willing to serve those members. Jones described how she first enrolled in Chicago HMO while living in Park Forest. A Chicago HMO representative visited her home and persuaded her to become a member, telling her that Chicago HMO "is better than a regular medical card." When Jones later moved to Chicago Heights, another Chicago HMO representative visited her home. Jones explained that this meeting was not arranged in advance. Rather, the representative was "in the building knocking from door to door." Jones also testified that, when she moved to Chicago Heights, Chicago HMO assigned Dr. Jordan to her and did not give her a choice of primary care physicians.

The latter aspect of Jones' testimony was supported by Dr. Trubitt. He explained that, before Chicago HMO and Dr. Jordan executed the Chicago Heights service agreement, another physician serviced that area. When Chicago HMO terminated that other physician, Dr. Jordan agreed "to go into the [Chicago Heights] area and serve the patients." Chicago HMO then assigned to Dr. Jordan all of the patients of that physician. Chicago HMO directed its members to Dr. Jordan; they had no other choice of a physician because "[a]t that point in the area there was no choice." According to Dr. Trubitt, Dr. Jordan was Chicago HMO's only physician who was willing to serve the public aid membership in Chicago Heights. Dr. Trubitt stated that this lack of physicians was "a problem" for Chicago HMO.

The record further reflects that Chicago HMO directed its Chicago Heights members to Dr. Jordan, even though it knew that Dr. Jordan worked at that location only half the time. Chicago HMO entered into two service agreements with Dr. Jordan, the first for a Homewood site in 1987, and the second for the Chicago Heights site in 1990. Dr. Trubitt indicated that Chicago HMO and Dr. Jordan executed the Chicago Heights service agreement at the time that Chicago HMO terminated the other physician. Dr. Jordan confirmed that, in January of 1991, he was dividing his time equally between his two offices. All of the foregoing evidence supports Jones' theory that Chicago HMO acted negligently in assigning more enrollees to Dr. Jordan than he was capable of handling.

Jones also relies on the contract between Chicago HMO and the Department of Public Aid as standard of care evidence. That contract stated that Chicago HMO shall have one full-time equivalent primary care physician for every 2,000 enrollees. We need not address in this appeal whether this contractual provision may serve as standard of care evidence. Our role here is to determine whether Chicago HMO is entitled to summary judgment on the patient overload aspect of the institutional negligence claim. Even if this contractual provision is removed from consideration, Chicago HMO is not entitled to summary judgment. Accordingly, we express no opinion on whether this provision may properly serve as standard of care evidence.

One final matter with respect to patient load remains to be considered. Chicago HMO contends that imposing a duty on HMOs to ascertain how many patients their doctors are serving would be unreasonably burdensome. Chicago HMO asserts that only physicians, and not HMOs, should have the duty to determine if the physician has too many patients.

To determine whether a duty exists in a certain instance, a court considers the following factors: (1) the reasonable foreseeability of injury, (2) the likelihood of injury, (3) the magnitude of the burden of guarding against the injury, and (4) the consequences of placing that burden upon the defendant. [ ] Lastly, the existence of a duty turns in large part on public policy considerations. [ ] Whether a duty exists is a question of law to be determined by the court.[ ]

Here, given the circumstances of this case, we hold that Chicago HMO had a duty to its enrollees to refrain from assigning an excessive number of patients to Dr. Jordan. HMOs contract with primary care physicians in order to provide and arrange for medical care for their enrollees. It is thus reasonably foreseeable that assigning an excessive number of patients to a primary care physician could result in injury, as that care may not be provided. For the same reason, the likelihood of injury is great. Nor would imposing this duty on HMOs be overly burdensome. Here, for example, Chicago HMO needed only to review its "Provider Capitation Summary Reports" to obtain the number of patients that it had assigned to Dr. Jordan. This information is likely to be available to all HMOs, as they must know the number of patients that a physician is serving in order to compute the physician's monthly capitation payments. The HMO may also simply ask the physician how many patients the physician is serving. Finally, the remaining factors favor placing this burden on HMOs as well. Public policy would not be well served by allowing HMOs to assign an excessive number of patients to a primary care physician and then "wash their hands" of the matter. The central consequence of placing this burden on HMOs is HMO accountability for their own actions. This court in Petrovich recognized that HMO accountability is needed to counterbalance the HMO goal of cost containment and, where applicable, the inherent drive of an HMO to achieve profits. [ ]

In conclusion, Chicago HMO is not entitled to summary judgment on Jones' claim of institutional negligence for assigning too many patients to Dr. Jordan.

* * *

CONCLUSION

An HMO may be held liable for institutional negligence. Chicago HMO is not entitled to summary judgment on Jones' claim charging Chicago HMO with institutional negligence for assigning more enrollees to Dr. Jordan than he was capable of serving. We therefore reverse the award of summary judgment to Chicago HMO on count I of Jones' second amended complaint and remand that claim to the circuit court for further proceedings. As to count III, we affirm the award of summary judgment to Chicago HMO.

* * *

JUSTICE RATHJE, also concurring in part and dissenting in part:

I agree with both the majority's affirmance of summary judgment on the breach of contract claim and its determination that plaintiff has waived the breach of warranty claim. I strongly disagree, however, with the majority's holding that Chicago HMO can be liable under a theory of institutional liability.

The majority reasons that, because an HMO is an "amalgam of many individuals" like a hospital, then Chicago HMO can be institutionally liable under the rule set forth in Darling v. Charleston Community Memorial Hospital, 33 Ill.2d 326, 211 N.E.2d 253 (1965). 191 Ill.2d at 293, 246 Ill.Dec. at 664, 730 N.E.2d at 1129. Although both a hospital and an HMO hire many different people for many different reasons, the reasons for holding hospitals liable under this theory do not hold true for Chicago HMO.

Generally, institutional liability attaches when an organization breaches a duty it owes as an organization. Under Darling, hospitals are vulnerable to institutional liability partly because, as organizations, they offer complete medical services, including nurses, doctors, orderlies, and administration. [ ] Hospital facilities include both the place and the staff, and hospitals "assume certain responsibilities for the care of the patient." Darling, 33 Ill.2d at 332, 211 N.E.2d 253. In Darling, the hospital was negligent for two reasons: it failed to properly review the work of an independent doctor, and its nurses failed to administer necessary tests. [ ] The rule set forth in Darling is that a hospital must act as a reasonably careful hospital would and is responsible for reviewing and supervising the medical care given to its patients.[ ]

[The judge notes that in Shannon v. McNulty the HMO hired nurses to work its triage service and advise members on medical decisions, rather than acting only as a vehicle through which member bills were paid.] * * *

* * * Under Chicago HMO's contract with Dr. Jordan, Chicago HMO is responsible for enrolling members, providing the doctor's group with a current list of those members, paying capitation fees, providing a list of hospitals and health care providers, providing other funding, and obtaining the appropriate regulatory licensure for the doctor's group. The doctor's group is solely responsible for providing the health services. Moreover, Chicago HMO's member's handbook specifically explains that the individual doctors are responsible for nurses and all other medical attention. Unlike the HMO in Shannon, which "provid[ed] health care services," Chicago HMO "merely provid[ed] money to pay for services." Thus, institutional liability is inappropriate in this case.

The primary flaw in the majority's analysis is that it attempts to create a rule of general application that fails to take into account not only the differences that exist between a hospital and an HMO but also those that exist among HMOs. To determine whether an HMO should have the same duty to its members that a hospital has to its patients, a court must assess not only whether hospitals are similar to HMOs but also whether the patient's relationship to the hospital is similar to the member's relationship to the HMO. [ ].

Hospitals are "institutions holding themselves out as devoted to the care and saving of human life." Johnson v. St. Bernard Hospital, 79 Ill.App.3d 709, 716, 35 Ill.Dec. 364, 399 N.E.2d 198 (1979). Institutional liability makes sense in the hospital context because a person in need of treatment must be assured that the hospital will abide by a sufficient standard of care. That patient generally does not have the time or opportunity to compare hospital bylaws or look for the hospital with the best administrative policies and the highest standard of care. A person goes to the nearest hospital in an emergency or to a hospital where his doctor has privileges in a nonemergency. In many cases, including most emergent cases, the patient has no time to make an informed choice. In his relationship with a hospital, the patient is at a severe disadvantage, which the law acknowledges by subjecting hospitals to institutional liability.

By contrast, the goal of an HMO is to provide health care in a cost-sensitive manner. B. Furrow, Managed Care Organizations and Patient Injury: Rethinking Liability, 31 Ga. L.Rev. 419, 457 (1997). HMOs offer medical services, but they do not do so in the same way that hospitals do. HMOs offer the funding and the contact with the medical professionals. In Chicago HMO, for instance, the way in which daily business is conducted, the duties of nurses and other staff, and other day-to-day decisions are made by the individual doctor or hospital with whom the HMO has contracted. This type of HMO makes no decision as to what type of care is ultimately given; they only decide whether the HMO will pay for that care.

Moreover, when a person joins an HMO, he knows beforehand what that HMO will cover and, in most cases, chooses which HMO he will join based on his assessment of the costs and benefits. To become a member, that person usually has to contract with the HMO. As a result, the HMO will be held accountable for any failure to comply with its own policies through a contract action.

In this case, the Chicago HMO representative arrived at plaintiff's door and asked her whether she would prefer to receive her public aid medical benefits through the HMO or continue receiving them directly through public aid. He reviewed the policies, and plaintiff made the decision to join, signing a statement that her participation in the HMO was voluntary and that she could disenroll at any time. Plaintiff was given the opportunity to make an informed choice and chose to receive her medical services through an HMO.

Just as hospitals can differ substantially from HMOs, substantial differences may exist among HMOs. Generally, HMOs are organized under one of four major models: (1) staff, in which the providers are all salaried employees of the HMO; (2) medical group, in which the HMO contracts with an organized group of doctors who have combined their practices; (3) independent practice association, in which the HMO contracts with individual physicians who are solo or group practitioners; and (4) network models, in which the HMO contracts with two or more physician group practices who may serve several HMOs at the same time. Both the methods of organization and the methods of reimbursement vary among the models. E. Weiner, Managed Health Care: HMO Corporate Liability, Independent Contractors, and the Ostensible Agency Doctrine, 15 J. Corp. L. 535, 540 (1990). In some cases, an HMO may behave very much like a hospital, and institutional liability might be appropriate in such cases. In most cases, however, an HMO will do everything in its power not to behave like a hospital, precisely to avoid the liability that comes with operating as one. Having a uniform standard of care for all HMOs makes little sense, given the major differences in structure.

Before concluding, I wish to stress that I by no means believe that HMOs should not be held accountable for their actions. Ordinarily, an HMO will be accountable to its members through the contract that is signed by both parties. Unfortunately, in this case, plaintiff was receiving benefits from the HMO through public aid and, therefore, did not contract with the HMO. Consequently, as the majority correctly holds, her particular situation leaves her unable to enforce the policy provisions because she was not a party to the contract. [ ] While I sympathize with plaintiff's unenviable position, the fact remains that plaintiff's theory of liability is not one permissible under our laws.

Notes and Questions

1. Consider the underlying failures of the systems in *Shannon* and *Jones*. In *Shannon*, the treating physician was impatient and inattentive to warning signs, but it was the triage nurses staffing the phone lines who failed to properly direct Shannon to a physician or hospital. How should the system have been designed to avoid such an error? What would you suggest to avoid a repetition of this kind of disaster? In *Jones*, what was the cause of the physician's failure to respond appropriately? Was it his heavy caseload of patients? Or just an erroneous judgment call on that occasion for which it is unfair to blame the MCO? What would you proposed to avoid such a problem in the future?

2. Administration of rules and policies to ensure quality care. Many of the ERISA preemption cases involve claims of negligent design of the managed care plan, including telephone call-in services staffed by nurses, such as those found defective. Other claims of negligent design and administration of the delivery of health care services have been allowed. See McDonald v. Damian, 56 F.Supp.2d 574 (E.D.Pa.1999)(claim for inadequacies in the delivery of medical services). The court in Pappas v. Asbel noted that contractual benefits provided in "such a dilatory fashion that the patient was injured are intertwined with the provision of safe care" This would give right to a negligent administration claim. 555 Pa. 342, 724 A.2d 889, 893 (Pa. 1998). In Pappas, the issue was a delay in transporting the plaintiff to a specialty trauma unit for care. The delay was arguably caused by the utilization review process of the managed care organization, which did not allow transport to the best hospital unit in the area for spinal injuries. Pappas involves a delay induced by a plan determination as to out-of-network care and a benefits question as to which hospitals were available to U.S. Healthcare providers.

2. Selection of providers. Neither *Shannon* nor *Jones* consider the other elements of corporate negligence. The managed care organization, like the hospital, has been held to owe its subscribers a duty to properly select its panel members. In *Harrell v. Total Health Care, Inc.*, 1989 WL 153066 (Mo.App.1989), affirmed 781 S.W.2d 58 (Mo.1989), the court stated that an IPA model HMO owed a duty to its participants to investigate the competence of its panel members and to exclude physicians who posed a "foreseeable risk of harm." This logic also applies to PPOs, which control entry of physicians to the provider panel. While the merits of this claim were not reached, the case suggests that courts are willing to impose upon managed care organizations the duty to determine the competency of the providers on its panel.

The logic of a direct duty imposed on MCOs to properly select providers is even stronger for an MCO than for a hospital. In the hospital setting, the patient usually has selected the physician. He is then admitted to the hospital because his physician has admitting privileges at that hospital. By contrast, in a managed care program the patient has chosen the particular program, but not the physicians who are provided. The patient must use the physicians on the panel. The patient thus explicitly relies on the MCO for its selection of health care providers. The MCO's obligations for the patient's total care are more comprehensive than in the hospital setting. A plan sponsor that establishes provider networks and channels patients to those networks is likely to be liable for negligent selection. If, however, a plan sponsor uses a PPO sponsor as an intermediary to set up PPO networks, the chance of liability is less likely, although a court may still find a duty to properly select and monitor the sponsor.

A duty of proper selection will expose a managed care organization to liability both for failing to properly screen its physicians' competence, and also for failing to evaluate physicians for other problems. If the MCO selects a panel physician or dentist who has evidenced incompetence in her practice, it may risk liability. This is comparable to negligently granting staff privileges to an impaired physician with alcohol or other substance abuse problems, or one with sexual pathologies that might affect patients. See McClellan v. Health Maintenance Organization of Pennsylvania, 413 Pa.Super. 128, 604 A.2d 1053 (1992), where the court allowed a suit against HMO to proceed for negligence in selecting, retaining and evaluating primary care physician, misrepresenting the screening process for selecting its primary care physicians, and breach of contract.

3.   The duty to supervise and control staff. Hospitals are required to supervise the medical care given to patients by staff physicians; to detect physician incompetence; and to take steps to correct problems upon learning of information raising concerns of patient risk. A hospital should also properly restrict the clinical privileges of staff physicians who are incompetent to handle certain procedures, or detect concealment by a staff doctor of medical errors.

Managed care organizations are likely to face similar duties to supervise. MCO liability for negligent control of its panel physicians derives from the same common law duty that underlies the negligent selection basis of liability as well as federal and state quality assurance regulations. As courts continue to characterize MCOs as health care providers, suits are likely to increase. Only PPOs with their reduced level of physician control might have an argument that liability should not be imposed for negligent supervision. However, statutes in some states require PPOs to implement quality assurance programs and others contemplate the use of such programs by PPOs. Iowa Code Ann. § 514.21; Ky. Rev. Stat. § 211.461; La. Stat. Ann.—Rev.Stat. § 22:2021; Me. Rev. Stat. Ann. tit. 24 § 2342 & tit. 24–A § 2771. The existence of such systems, with the PPOs having the right to remove a participating physician from the panel based on information generated by the quality assurance mechanism, imposes a duty to supervise. Managed care is likely to be forced to undertake both a duty to select with care and a duty to engage in continuous supervision.

4.   Managed care organizations are motivated by goals of both quality and efficiency—the objective of cost sensitive health care. The style of practice in MCOs is different from fee-for-service practice, assuming a more conservative, less intensive level of intervention, specialist use, and hospitalization. Commentators have therefore proposed that courts allow MCO physicians to be judged by a different standard of care than fee-for-service physicians, in recognition of the different approach to care that MCOs have adopted to control costs. Randall Bovbjerg, The Medical Malpractice Standard of Care: HMOs and Customary Practice 1975 Duke L.J. 1375.

Some courts have recognized that managed care plans should give providers leeway to practice a more conservative, cost-effective style. See, e.g., Harrell v.

Total Health Care, Inc., 781 S.W.2d 58, 61 (Mo.1989)("People are concerned both about the cost and the unpredictability of medical expenses. A plan such as Total offered would allow a person to fix the cost of physicians' services.").

C. PHYSICIAN INCENTIVE SYSTEMS

Most managed care programs have three relevant features from a liability perspective. First, such programs select a restricted group of health care professionals who provide services to the program's participants. Second, such programs accept a fixed payment per subscriber, in exchange for provision of necessary care. This pressures managed care organizations to search for ways to minimize costs. Third, following from number two, managed care organizations use a variety of strategies to ensure cost effective care. Altering physician incentives is central to managed care, since physicians influence seventy percent of total health spending, while receiving only about twenty percent of each health care dollar. Such plans use utilization review techniques, incentives systems, and gatekeepers to control costs. Managed care organizations create a new set of relationships between payers, subscribers and providers. These new relationships create new liability risks. The subscriber typically pays a fee to the MCO rather than the provider, relinquishing control over treatment and choice of treating physician. The payor in turn shifts some of its financial risk to its approved providers, who must also accept certain controls over their practice.

The argument that physician judgment might be "corrupted" by cost-conserving payment systems in managed care systems has been litigated without much success.

BUSH v. DAKE

State of Michigan, Circuit Court, County of Saginaw, 1989.
File No. 86–25767 NM–2.

PRESENT: Honorable Robert L. Kaczmarek, Circuit Judge.

Defendant Group Health Services of Michigan, Inc. (hereinafter referred to as GHS) has filed a Motion for Partial Summary Disposition pursuant to MCR 2.116(C)(10)), in which defendants Network Family Physicians, P.C., Scott, Gugino, Mulhern, and Brasseur have joined. The motion seeks dismissal of the allegations in Plaintiffs' Complaint a) that GHS's system of financial incentives, risk sharing, and utilization review is contrary to public policy and medical ethics and b) that the use of this system constituted negligence, gross negligence, fraud, a breach of trust, and a tortious breach of the relationship between plaintiff Sharon Bush and her doctors in this particular case. Defendants contend that there is no genuine issue as to any material fact regarding these allegations and that they are therefore entitled to judgment as a matter of law.

This case arises out of the alleged failure of Dr. Dake and Dr. Foltz to timely diagnose and treat plaintiff's uterine cancer. During the period in question, Mrs. Bush was insured by GHS through her husband's employer. As the GHS system requires, she had chosen a primary care physician, Dr. Dake. For any medical problem she might have, it was necessary for Mrs. Bush to first see Dr. Dake and obtain his permission to be examined by a specialist, in order for the specialist's service to be covered by her insurance.

Dr. Dake was one of five physicians comprising Network Family Physicians, P.C. (Network). * * * Network had an agreement with GHS whereby GHS would pay Network a certain amount per month per patient, called a "capitation," for primary care services. In exchange, the physicians would see the patients an unlimited number of times, whenever the patients sought medical care.

GHS set aside a certain amount of money each year for a "referral pool" and a "hospital/ancillary pool" for the Network physicians. The money in these pools would be depleted with each referral to a specialist or hospitalization of a patient during the year. At the end of the year, any money left over in these pools would be divided between GHS and the individual physicians in Network. The result was that the fewer referrals a doctor made and the fewer hospitalizations he ordered for his patients, the more money he made.

The plaintiffs contend that it was this arrangement which led in part to the deficient medical care that Sharon Bush received in this case. Mrs. Bush first consulted Dr. Dake in late August of 1985 with regard to vaginal bleeding and mucous discharge unrelated to menstruation. Dr. Dake prescribed various medications to cure what he considered to be an infection. The condition nevertheless persisted over a period of several months. In January of 1986, the plaintiff asked Dr. Dake for a referral to Dr. Foltz, a specialist in obstetrics and gynecology. Dr. Dake agreed to make the referral, and Mrs. Bush then saw Dr. Foltz on February 18, 1986. Dr. Foltz took a vaginal smear to test for chlamydia, a sexually transmitted disease. When the results of that test came back negative, Dr. Foltz's office advised Mrs. Bush to wait until after her next menstrual period, and then if the bleeding persisted to return to Dr. Foltz for a follow-up visit. When the bleeding did persist and Mrs. Bush attempted to obtain a second referral to Dr. Foltz from Dr. Dake, he refused to make the referral. Eventually, on May 13, 1986, Mrs. Bush presented herself at the emergency room of Saginaw General Hospital, a biopsy was taken, and a diagnosis of cervical cancer was made.

It turned out, in retrospect, that a pap smear, if it had been done, would have revealed the cancer at a earlier stage. In the GHS system, pap smears are to be done by the primary care physician only. However, the primary care physician is not paid anything in addition to the existing capitation for performing pap smears.

The plaintiffs contend that the system in question is wrongful, in that it provides the physicians involved with financial disincentives to properly treat, refer, and hospitalize patients. They contend that this Court should find a) that the system violates public policy and b) that there is a jury question presented as to whether the system itself contributed to the malpractice in this case.

After examining the briefs and statutory and case authority submitted by the parties, the Court agrees with the defendants that it is not for this Court to say whether the HMO system represents sound social policy. It is the Legislature, and not this Court, that determines public policy in this state. * * * In this instance, the Legislature has approved the existence of HMO's, MCLA 333.21001, et seq.; MSA 14.15(21001), et seq., and their use of health care provider incentives, MCLA 333.21023(3); MSA 14.15(21023)(3), risk sharing, MCLA 333.21075; MSA 14.15(21075), and utilization review, MCLA

333.21083(d); MSA 14.15(21083)(d) in an effort to contain health care costs. This Court will not second-guess the wisdom of this legislation.

The Court therefore grants defendants partial summary disposition with regard to the plaintiffs' allegations that GHS's system of financial incentives, risk sharing, and utilization review is contrary to public policy. MCR 2.116(C)(10).

With regard to the second portion of defendants' motion, the Court finds that there is a genuine issue of material fact presented as to whether GHS's system in and of itself proximately contributed to the malpractice in this case. * * * Documentary evidence has been presented which supports the plaintiffs' theory that the manner in which the system operated in this case contributed to the improper treatment and delay in diagnosis of Mrs. Bush's cancerous condition. See *Wickline v. California,* 228 Cal.Rptr. 661, 670 (Cal. App. 2 Dist., 1986). The question should be submitted to the jury for determination at trial.

The Court therefore denies defendants' motion for partial summary disposition with regard to plaintiffs' allegations that the use of the GHS system in this case constituted negligence, gross negligence, fraud, a breach of trust, and a tortious breach of the relationship between Sharon Bush and her doctors.

PEGRAM v. HERDRICH

Supreme Court of the United States, 2000.
530 U.S. 211, 120 S.Ct. 2143, 147 L.Ed.2d 164.

[The treating plan physician examined the plaintiff Herdrich, who had pain in the midline area of her groin. Six days later Dr. Pegram found an inflamed mass in her abdomen, but failed to order an ultrasound at a local hospital, instead making her wait eight additional days for an ultrasound to be performed at a Carle facility more than 50 miles away. Herdrich's appendix ruptured, causing peritonitis. The Seventh Circuit in Herdrich v. Pegram, 170 F.3d 683 (7th Cir.1999) had been impressed by the conflicts of interest in the "intricacies of the defendants' incentive structure." In the words of the Seventh Circuit, "[w]ith a jaundiced eye focused firmly on year-end bonuses, it is not unrealistic to assume that the doctors rendering care under the Plan were swayed to be most frugal when exercising their discretionary authority to the detriment of their membership." On motion for rehearing, Judge Esterbrook J., dissenting, noted that the panel decision looked like a blanket condemnation of managed care generally, in favor of fee-for-service medicine. Even though the panel had tried to distinguish this case by its physician ownership and control, the use of bonuses and salary holdbacks by any managed care plan could be similarly criticized.]

The full opinion can be found in Chapter Nine, discussing ERISA fiduciary duties. The U.S. Supreme Court rejected the reasoning of the Seventh Circuit. With regard to the incentive structure of managed care organizations, Justice Souter, writing for the Court, stated:

Traditionally, medical care in the United States has been provided on a "fee-for-service" basis. A physician charges so much for a general physical exam, a vaccination, a tonsillectomy, and so on. The physician bills the patient for services provided or, if there is insurance and the doctor is willing, submits the bill for the patient's care to the insurer, for payment subject to the terms of the insurance agreement. [ ] In a fee-for-service system, a physician's financial incentive is to provide more care, not less, so long as payment is forthcoming. The check on this incentive is a physician's obligation to exercise reasonable medical skill and judgment in the patient's interest.

Beginning in the late 1960's, insurers and others developed new models for health-care delivery, including HMOs. [ ] The defining feature of an HMO is receipt of a fixed fee for each patient enrolled under the terms of a contract to provide specified health care if needed. The HMO thus assumes the financial risk of providing the benefits promised: if a participant never gets sick, the HMO keeps the money regardless, and if a participant becomes expensively ill, the HMO is responsible for the treatment agreed upon even if its cost exceeds the participant's premiums.

Like other risk-bearing organizations, HMOs take steps to control costs. At the least, HMOs, like traditional insurers, will in some fashion make coverage determinations, scrutinizing requested services against the contractual provisions to make sure that a request for care falls within the scope of covered circumstances (pregnancy, for example), or that a given treatment falls within the scope of the care promised (surgery, for instance). They customarily issue general guidelines for their physicians about appropriate levels of care. See id., at 568–570. And they commonly require utilization review (in which specific treatment decisions are reviewed by a decisionmaker other than the treating physician) and approval in advance (precertification) for many types of care, keyed to standards of medical necessity or the reasonableness of the proposed treatment. [ ] These cost-controlling measures are commonly complemented by specific financial incentives to physicians, rewarding them for decreasing utilization of health-care services, and penalizing them for what may be found to be excessive treatment [ ]. Hence, in an HMO system, a physician's financial interest lies in providing less care, not more. The check on this influence (like that on the converse, fee-for-service incentive) is the professional obligation to provide covered services with a reasonable degree of skill and judgment in the patient's interest. [ ]

The adequacy of professional obligation to counter financial self-interest has been challenged no matter what the form of medical organization. HMOs became popular because fee-for-service physicians were thought to be providing unnecessary or useless services; today, many doctors and other observers argue that HMOs often ignore the individual needs of a patient in order to improve the HMOs' bottom lines. See, e.g., 154 F.3d, at 375–378 (citing various critics of HMOs). In this case, for instance, one could argue that Pegram's decision to wait before getting an ultrasound for Herdrich, and her insistence that the ultrasound be done at a distant facility owned by Carle, reflected an interest in limiting the HMO's expenses, which blinded her to the need for immediate diagnosis and treatment."

Notes and Questions

1.   Bush v. Dake, an unpublished opinion, is one of the early cases raising the issue of the effect of HMO incentives on the medical care received by beneficiaries. While on appeal it was settled. See also, Sweede v. Cigna Healthplan of Delaware, Inc., 1989 WL 12608 (Del.Super.) (claim that doctor withheld necessary care because of financial incentives rejected on facts of case) and Teti v. U.S. Health-care, Inc., 1989 WL 143274 (E.D.Pa.1989) (RICO claim against HMO for failing to disclose physician incentives to withhold medical care dismissed). What explains the paucity of such cases, which are greatly outnumbered by articles in the popular and trade press noting their potential? Is it the difficulty of proving what motivates physician decisionmaking? How would you establish that a particular HMO payment structure motivated physicians to forego needed care for their patients? What other countervailing pressures operate on physicians?

2.   Financial incentives and patient care. Every medical decision is also a spending decision. Since physicians as agents for patients control a large percentage of the health care dollar, should we trust them to have unfettered freedom to spend the money of others and use others's resources? The record of health care cost inflation suggests that unfettered physician discretion is not desirable. Managed care organizations are institutional structures developed as a response to health care inflation, to better manage the cost of health care by reducing utilization of hospitalization, specialists and testing. See E. Haavi Morreim, Playing Doctor: Corporate Medical Practice and Medical Malpractice, 32 U.Mich. J.L.Ref. 939, 972–73(1999).

The incentives that HMOs create for providers to under-utilize health care for their patients—the possibility that these incentives will "corrupt" the medical judgment of a physician—is raised frequently. The fear with managed care—and its goal of reducing expenditures by its physicians—is that some patients will be undertreated and suffer injury as a result. Bush v. Dake is a early example of these concerns. The U.S. Supreme Court in Pegram, however, acknowledged a national health care policy to use managed care to constrain the rapid health care cost inflation so evidence by the 1970s.

Little evidence exists that HMO incentives have a detrimental effect on patient care. The argument about incentives assumes that physicians' sensitivity to financial incentives is so fine-tuned that they will vary the intensity of care they give to each patient. The alternative possibility is that professional norms, risk of malpractice suits, and the daily pressures of practice will be more powerful forces on physician behavior. This would mean that a physician will treat all patients in light of his sense of best practice as adopted to a particular locality. The evidence has not yet resolved this question of physician response to incentives. Some form of incentive for cost-conservation in health care is desirable, and the ongoing debate is over the extent to which payment incentives can strike the right balance. While incentives may create conflicts of interest, they also give physicians flexibility in their clinical decision-making. The alternative–administrative rules and review mechanisms for denying benefits–is both more inefficient and arguably more constraining of physician decision-making. This debate–incentives versus rules–is an ongoing one. Plaintiffs have nonetheless argued that payment systems can cause a reduction in the quality of care delivered by physicians in managed care organizations, an argument that Pegram finally rejected. Robert H. Miller and Harold S. Luft, Does Managed Care Lead to Better or Worse Quality of Care? 16 Health Affairs 7, 18 (1997); David Orentlicher,

Paying Physicians More to Do Less: Financial Incentives to Limit Care, 30 U.Rich.L.Rev. 155 (1996); Uwe E. Reinhardt, The Economist's Model of Physician Behavior, 281 J.A.M.A. 462, 464 (1999); Lawrence C. Baker, Association of Managed Care Market Share and Health Expenditures for Fee–For–Service Medicare Patients, 281 J.A.M.A. 432(1999). See William M. Sage, Physicians As Advocates, 35 Houston L.Rev.1529, 1620 (1999)("... the use of financial incentives in managed care preserves professional autonomy and improves efficiency even if it compromises advocacy at the margin.")

The debate over the use of physician incentives to promote cost sensitive practice will continue. Some managed care companies have decided, in the face of class action litigation and bad publicity, to restrict their use of some incentives. Aetna has announced that it will end the use of financial incentives to physicians that might have the effect of restricting member access to care. Aetna will limit the use of capitated fees, as well as the use of medical guidelines created by actuarial firms and used by some insurers to restrict reimbursement for care. See Milo Geyelin and Barbara Martinez, Aetna Weighs a Managed–Care Overhaul, Wall St. J. A3–10 (January 17, 2001). The REPAIR litigation, discussed below, combined with the possibility that Congress will legislate a patients' bill of rights that expands tort suits against managed care, has undoubtedly spurred these changes in the industry.

D. REPAIR TEAM LITIGATION AND RICO

A series of class action lawsuits was filed in 1999 by a group of lawyers known as the REPAIR Team, short for RICO and ERISA Prosecutors Advocating for Insurance Industry Reform. This group, which had litigated state lawsuits against the tobacco industry, filed class actions lawsuits against several large HMOs–Aetna, Cigna, Foundation, Humana, PacifiCare, Prudential, and United–accusing them of depriving enrollees of adequate treatment and engaging in a fraudulent scheme of misrepresenting coverage and treatment decisions.

MAIO v. AETNA

Third Circuit Court of Appeals, 2000.
221 F.3d 472.

[This case, filed prior to the REPAIR team class action litigation, asserted similar claims against Aetna, Inc., Aetna–U .S. Healthcare, Inc., and Aetna U.S. Healthcare, Inc.'s 24 regional subsidiary health plans (collectively "Aetna" or "appellees") for violations of the Racketeer Influenced and Corrupt Organizations Act ("RICO"), 18 U.S.C. § 1961 et seq., and state law. The case attacked "Aetna's failure to disclose its restrictive and coercive internal policies and practices, which render its advertising, marketing and membership materials false and misleading in violation of RICO." They claimed that "Aetna has engaged in a massive nationwide fraudulent advertising campaign designed to induce people to enroll in its HMO by representing that Aetna affirmatively manages its members' health care so as to, inter alia, raise the quality of care to a 'level of health care never available under the old fee-for-service system,' 'when in fact, Aetna designed undisclosed internal policies to "improve defendants' profitability at the expense of quality of care." The relief sought was compensatory damages and an injunction enjoining appellees from pursuing the "policies, acts and practices" alleged in the complaint, together with punitive damages, treble damages, and attorney's fees under RICO.' "

The class action was brought on behalf of members of a class consisting "of all persons in the United States who are, or were, enrolled in [Aetna's] Health Maintenance Organization (the 'HMO') plans (the 'Plan') at any time during the period from July 19, 1996 to the present (the 'class period')." [FN1] JA–14. The class allegedly consists of millions of both present and former Aetna HMO members who, as a group, "were targeted by [Aetna] and induced into enrolling in Aetna's HMO by virtue of defendants' standardized and uniform misrepresentations and omissions of material facts contained in advertising, marketing and membership* materials." The charges were that (1) Aetna engaged in a fraudulent scheme designed to induce individuals to enroll in its HMO plan by representing "that its primary commitment, in connection with the healthcare services provided to its HMO members, is to maintain and improve the quality of care given to such members and that defendants' policies are designed to accomplish these goals; "(2) Aetna represented that HMO members would receive high quality health care from physicians who are solely responsible for providing all medical care and maintaining the physician-patient relationship, when in reality Aetna's internal policies restrict the physicians' ability to provide the high quality health care that appellants have been promised; (3) despite Aetna's representations that it compensated its physicians under a system that provides them with incentives based upon the quality of care provided, Aetna's provider contracts actually offer the physicians financial incentives to withhold medical services and reduce the quality of care to HMO members. These representations were made through marketing, advertising and membership materials distributed to each and every prospective enrollee including the appellants.]

* * *

The question presented in this appeal therefore is whether the facts as pleaded in the complaint are sufficient to support appellants' assertion that they have suffered a present injury to property, which, according to them, takes the form of a financial loss stemming from their overpayment for their membership in Aetna's HMO plan. To resolve this issue, we must examine the allegations in the complaint and any reasonable inferences that may be drawn from those allegations, and consider their legal significance in view of appellants' injury theory proffered in support of the damage element of their RICO claim.

* * *

For the reasons that follow, we reject appellants' theory that their complaint states valid RICO claims based on the financial losses they purportedly sustained by enrolling in Aetna's "inferior" HMO plan in the absence of allegations to the effect that each appellant suffered negative medical consequences resulting from Aetna's enactment of the policies and practices at issue. Stated another way, in the context of this case, we hold that appellants cannot establish that they suffered a tangible economic harm compensable under RICO unless they allege that health care they received under Aetna's plan actually was compromised or diminished as a result of Aetna's management decisions challenged in the complaint. It seems clear to us that unless appellants claim that Aetna failed to provide sufficient health insurance coverage to the members of their HMO plan in the sense that such individuals were denied medically necessary benefits, received inadequate, inferior or delayed medical treatment, or even worse, suffered personal injuries as a result of Aetna's systemic policies and practices, there is no factual basis for appellants' conclusory allegation that they have been injured in their "property" because the health insurance they actually received was inferior and therefore "worth less" than what they paid for it. Of course, such losses would have to be alleged and proven on an individual basis. Inasmuch as we hold that appellants have not alleged facts sufficient to establish the fact of damage, i.e., appellants' injury to property stemming from their purchase of an "inferior" product, they have no cause of action under RICO.

* * *

Because appellants' property interests in their memberships in Aetna's HMO plan take the form of contractual rights to receive a certain level (quantity and quality) of benefits from Aetna through its participating providers, see Pegram, ___ U.S. at ___, 120 S.Ct. at 2149, it inexorably follows that appellants cannot establish a RICO injury to those property rights (which in turn would cause financial loss in the form of overpayment for inferior health insurance) absent proof that Aetna failed to perform under the parties' contractual arrangement. [ ]

In this factual setting, Aetna's failure to perform (and concomitantly appellants' injury to their property) would be evidenced by appellants' receipt of inadequate, inferior delayed care, personal injuries resulting therefrom, or Aetna's denial of benefits due under the insurance arrangement. Absent allegations of such losses, which appellants specifically indicate are not involved in this case, they cannot establish that they have suffered an injury to their property rights encompassed in their HMO memberships—i.e., their right to receive necessary medical services covered under their plan, and cannot prove a consequential financial loss flowing from their property. [ ]

Apparently recognizing that the property interests at stake are in the nature of contractual rights to health care benefits rather than tangible property rights from which injury is demonstrated by events causing a diminution in value, appellants make a secondary argument that they have pleaded injury in this case by referring to Aetna's failure to implement policies and practices in accordance with its commitment to its members to "raise the quality of health care." [ ] Analogizing to the district court's analysis in Dornberger, see 961 F.Supp. at 522, see reply br. at 8, appellants claim to have suffered economic harm, i.e., lost money, by virtue of Aetna's breach of its specific promise to implement policies and practices which supposedly permitted physicians to provide Aetna's HMO enrollees with quality health care.

Invoking the legal principle that payment for services not rendered can constitute a valid injury to property under RICO, see id. at 523, appellants claim that they suffered that exact loss here-they paid a specific part of their premium dollars for the benefit of Aetna's promises to implement policies designed to foster quality health care and have been injured in their property by Aetna's "failure to perform as promised." Because the "services not rendered" aspect of their injury argument only refers to Aetna's purported promise to implement policies and practices geared towards quality health care, appellants contend that "what the doctors do or don't do is irrelevant." Tr. of Oral Arg. at 14; see also br. at 25–26 ("Plaintiffs do allege . . . that they were denied something Aetna promised it would provide its members as an inducement for, and in consideration of, the members' enrollment. . . . [P]laintiffs and other Class members paid premiums and copayments, not just to receive treatment from physicians, but also to obtain the benefit of Aetna's services in arranging and providing increased quality of care.").

We need not tarry on this argument, as it is premised on an erroneous characterization of Aetna's responsibilities to its enrollees as defined by the parties' contractual arrangement and Aetna's alleged extra-contractual promises to deliver "quality health care." Notwithstanding appellants' creative description of Aetna's obligations to its HMO members, as we have explained they undoubtedly sought from Aetna, and Aetna promised to provide its members, with a different contractual benefit—namely the right to receive covered health care benefits in the form of medically necessary supplies, health care services and treatment through Aetna's participating providers. See Pegram, ___ U.S. at ___, 120 S.Ct. at 2149. Indeed, our review of the relevant contractual provisions and purported extra-contractual promises confirms our understanding of Aetna's obligations to its HMO members as their health insurer. [ ]

Accordingly, regardless of appellants' description of Aetna's obligations to its HMO enrollees, contractual or otherwise, it is obvious that Aetna's primary commitment to its HMO plan members is to provide quality health care services through its participating provider network. Concomitantly, appellants' contractual benefit is their receipt of quality medical services from those sources. We reach this conclusion because the provision and receipt of covered medical care is at the heart of the parties' contractual arrangement and is the driving force behind the purchase of health care insurance. [ ]

It necessarily follows from this observation that appellants' hypothesis that they suffered financial losses as result of Aetna's failure to implement policies designed to increase the quality of health care is untenable. Their argument rests on the faulty proposition that Aetna's implementation of the policies and practices outlined in the complaint amounts to a failure to perform a specific promise to its members, and misconstrues the nature of Aetna's role and its ultimate duty in arranging and providing for its members' health care. [ ] Indeed, while we do not quarrel with appellants' statement that Aetna implemented the managerial policies at issue while performing its role in arranging and providing medical treatment to its members rather than its role as plan administrator, [ ] that observation does not alter the fact that Aetna's contractual duty to its members is to provide medically necessary health care benefits in the form of covered services and supplies, i.e., medication, either directly or through contracts with third party medical providers. [ ] Accordingly, we decline appellants' invitation to define Aetna's duties as narrowly as they suggest.

It is evident to us from the foregoing analysis that given the nature of the property interests at stake, appellants' RICO injury theory predicated on the concept of a "diminution in product value" simply has no application here. Rather, in the context of this RICO suit based on what appellants have deemed to be "inferior" health insurance they received under Aetna's HMO plan, it follows from the nature of their property interests in their HMO memberships that they would be injured only to the extent that they could show that they suffered medical injuries, a denial or delay of medically necessary care, or the receipt of inferior or inadequate care. We emphasize that any personal injuries resulting from Aetna's policies and practices would not constitute a compensable RICO injury, see Genty, 937 F.2d at 918–19, Oscar, 965 F.2d at 786, but instead would serve as the necessary factual predicate for their argument that they suffered an injury to their property interests—their contractual rights to receive insurance coverage and necessary medical services under Aetna's HMO plan—which in turn caused them consequential financial loss in the form of overpayment for the coverage they actually received.

B.

[The court also rejects the claim of RICO injury based on a diminution in property value, since the class members could not show they actually received something "inferior" and "worth less" absent individualized allegations concerning the quantity and quality of health care benefits Aetna provided under its HMO plan.]

* * *

C.

When we analyze appellants' argument as to why they need not plead and prove allegations concerning the level of care they received to establish the fact of damage, i.e., their RICO "injury to property," it becomes evident why their position is fundamentally flawed. Given the total absence of any particularized allegations to the effect that the medical care appellants received pursuant to Aetna's HMO plan was compromised or diminished as a consequence of Aetna's internal policies and practices, the fact of damage, according to appellants' theory of financial injury, obviously is predicated on the concept that the mere possibility that a physician might be influenced by Aetna's policies to provide substandard medical care to Aetna's enrollees as a class demonstrates that the health care insurance they actually received is inferior or "worth less" than the amount appellants expended in premium payments. As the district court described it, appellants' claim of out-of-pocket losses as articulated rests on "a vague allegation that quality of care may suffer in the future.... " [ ]

Overall, we are satisfied that if we were to permit appellants to proceed with their RICO claims based on allegations of monetary loss proved solely by reference to what they consider to be the existence of coercive internal policies and practices which inevitably will affect the quality of care they will receive in the future, we would be expanding the concept of RICO injury beyond the boundaries of reason. [ ] * * *

If there were any doubt concerning the result we reach, which there is not, with respect to the message underlying appellants' damages theory, it surely would vanish when considered against the backdrop of the Supreme Court's recent decision in Pegram v. Herdrich, 530 U.S. 211, 120 S.Ct. 2143. Given our analysis, it is evident that in the absence of allegations that the quantity or quality of benefits have been diminished, the only theoretical basis for appellants' claim that they received an "inferior health care product" is their subjective belief that Aetna's policies and practices are so unfavorable to enrollees that their very existence in Aetna's HMO scheme demonstrates that they overpaid for the coverage they received. Indeed, the concept underlying appellants' injury theory is unmistakable—the very structure of Aetna's HMO plan is poor in the sense that its policies and practices inevitably will result in physicians providing inadequate health care to Aetna's HMO enrollees, which in turn means that appellants are paying too much for inferior health care benefits.

Put differently, we believe that the not-so hidden message underlying appellants' RICO claims (and more specifically their injury theory) is as follows: while these policies might be good for Aetna's business (because that they promote increased profits and induce physicians to ration care), they certainly are not beneficial to Aetna's HMO members because they are medically unsound in that they restrict a physician's ability to make independent medical judgments and encourage physicians to withhold otherwise appropriate health care so as to increase Aetna's "bottom line" profits. [ ] Thus, we think it fair to characterize appellants' injury theory as bottomed on the notion that Aetna's policies challenged in the complaint render its HMO structure "bad" in comparison to the other types of health care insurance available in the marketplace.

The force of this position, we believe, has been undermined significantly by the Supreme Court's recent decision in Pegram in which the Court rejected the plaintiff's attempt to challenge the existing structure of an incentive scheme of one particular HMO under the rubric of a breach of fiduciary duty claim under ERISA. * * *

* * *

We read the Court's approach in Pegram as undermining the validity of appellants' RICO injury theory predicated on the notion that their health insurance was rendered "inferior" by Aetna's implementation of its managerial policies outlined in the complaint. In particular, given that the very concept underlying appellants' economic harm is the notion that the structure of Aetna's HMO plan is faulty, we cannot ignore the circumstance that appellants' injury theory in essence asks us to pass judgment on the legal validity of the policies and practices themselves. Accordingly, we find particularly compelling that aspect of Pegram which articulated clearly the myriad of practical problems which undoubtedly arise in a situation in which the federal courts are asked to determine the social utility of one particular HMO structure as compared to another. See id. at ___, 120 S.Ct. at 2150. Indeed, we believe that the Court's observations in evaluating the validity of the plaintiff's ERISA claim in that case apply with equal force where, as here, appellants' theory of economic injury is predicated on the notion that the structure of Aetna's HMO plan, with its "coercive and restrictive" internal policies and practices, renders the health insurance appellants actually received from Aetna less valuable than it otherwise would have been without those management decisions in place.

The critical point here is that if we were to accept appellants' argument that the fact of damage can be demonstrated without specific reference to the level or quality of care actually provided to them under Aetna's HMO plan, we would be making the social and medical judgment that the particular structure of Aetna's HMO plan, by its very nature, places it in the category of a "bad HMO" as opposed to a "good HMO." There is no escaping that analytical step because it is the very nature of Aetna's HMO's structure which, according to appellants' theory, demonstrates that the economic value of their health insurance is reduced, that their insurance is inferior, and that they paid too much in premium dollars for what they actually received. But it seems clear that in view of the Supreme Court's reluctance in Pegram to devise a uniform standard by which federal courts could distinguish one HMO scheme from another in terms of its social utility in the context of an ERISA breach of fiduciary duty claim, we must decline appellants' invitation to pass judgment on the social utility of Aetna's particular HMO structure, albeit in the context of evaluating whether appellants have stated an injury to property under section 1964(c) of RICO. We especially are constrained to reach our result in light of the fact that appellants ask us to make such a determination without reference to the level or quality of care that Aetna's HMO members received while enrolled in its health plan. Cf. id. at ___, 120 S.Ct. at 2157 ("[T]he Federal Judiciary would be acting contrary to the congressional policy of allowing HMO organizations if it were to entertain an ERISA fiduciary claim portending wholesale attacks on existing HMOs solely because of their structure, untethered to claims of concrete harm.").

* * *

In any event, inasmuch as we read Pegram as suggesting that federal courts are ill-equipped to make the kind of social judgment that our acceptance of appellants' injury theory would require us to make, we remain convinced that in order to demonstrate the fact of RICO injury to property in the context of this case, appellants are required to demonstrate that the benefits they received under Aetna's HMO plan were compromised or diminished as a direct consequence of the systemic practices alleged in the complaint. Appellants therefore must allege and prove, for example, that they suffered personal injuries, were denied benefits, or received delayed or inadequate treatment because of the structure of Aetna's HMO plan. In the absence of such allegations, the district court's dismissal was appropriate.

V. CONCLUSION

Based on the information pleaded in the complaint, we hold that appellants have failed to allege the facts necessary to support their assertion that they paid too much for the health insurance they received from Aetna. Specifically, appellants have not alleged, for example, that they suffered medical injuries, received inadequate or inferior care, or sought but were denied necessary care as a consequence of the structure of Aetna's HMO plan, which includes the "systemic policies and practices" challenged in the complaint. In the circumstances, appellants cannot establish that they suffered a cognizable "injury to business or property" flowing from appellees' conduct, an essential element of a civil action pursuant to section 1964(c) of RICO.

For the foregoing reasons, the district court's judgment of September 29, 1999, will be affirmed.

Notes and Questions

1. What is at the heart of these claims against managed care? That any attempt by an MCO to restrict a physician's decisionmaking is presumptively undesirable? How would you develop standards that allow physicians proper discretion to make treatment decisions while still attempting to control costs? In Chapter One we discussed the uncertainties of much of medical practice and the lack of evidence of effectiveness of much that is done. The RICO statute has been used primarily against organized crime, and RICO claims have not been successful against managed care plans historically. See Teti v. U.S. Healthcare, Inc., 1989 WL 143274 (E.D.Pa.1989)(RICO claim against HMO for failing to disclose physician incentives to withhold medical care dismissed).

2. For the last several years, the Supreme Court has been reevaluating its interpretation of the McCarran Ferguson Act's deference to state regulation of "the business of insurance." Lower courts had used the Act to void the application of RICO to insurance companies, and had used it to determine the scope of state law of preempted by ERISA. Passed in 1944, the McCarran Ferguson Act was enacted in response to a Supreme Court decision that held, for the first time, that insurance was interstate commerce subject to Congressional legislation. The Act was intended to preclude the contention that federal legislation of general applicability, such as the securities and antitrust laws, were applicable to insurance companies. Instead the McCarran Ferguson Act requires deference to state insurance laws unless federal laws specifically regulate insurance.

In Humana v. Forsyth, 525 U.S. 299, 119 S.Ct. 710, 142 L.Ed.2d 753 (1999), policyholders sued their health plan under RICO for fraudulently failing to pass along to subscribers discounted fee arrangements with providers in the form of reduced co-payment obligations. The health plan argued that application of the federal law would invalidate, supersede, or impair state insurance laws regulating fraudulent acts by insurers and was thus precluded .. The Supreme Court, construing the first clause in the McCarren Ferguson Act, held that it would not. The state law in question, Nevada's insurance fraud statute, permitted private actions against insurers for fraud, in addition to actions by the state insurance commission. The Court held that although the damages recoverable under the federal statute were much greater, the federal and state statute's were complimentary. The Court reasoned that Congress could not have intended federal laws of general applicability to be preempted when they do not impair state insurance regulation. After *Forsyth*, it was clear that the McCarran Ferguson Act does not categorically exempt the insurance industry from liability to consumers under RICO that is applied to all other industries.

2. The REPAIR Team class actions. The REPAIR Team is led by a group of plaintiffs lawyers who were successful in suits against the tobacco companies, and saw managed care as the next vulnerable and destructive institution in our culture. REPAIR's strategy, in the words of one commentator, is to "(r)aise the stakes so high that neither side can afford to lose.... " Adam Bryant, Who's Afraid of Dickie Scruggs?, Newsweek, Dec. 6, 1999, at 46.

In their complaints, MCO plaintiffs allege that the managed care organizations have operated the affairs of an enterprise in interstate commerce through a pattern of racketeering activity and have injured the business or property of the plaintiffs as a result, in violation of sections 18 U.S.C. 1964 and 1962(c) of RICO. The racketeering activity is the use of the U.S. mails and wire services to defraud consumers—both by misrepresenting coverage and operations of the health plans, so as to fraudulently induce them to enroll, and by fraudulently misrepresenting the reasons why their claims were denied.

In *Maio*, plaintiffs alleged a violation of RICO based on the alleged misrepresentation that Aetna was primarily concerned with quality of care defendants, when, in fact, Aetna was more interested in profits and cost containment. The district court found this allegation—that "quality of care" might suffer in the future—too vague and hypothetical to confer standing on the plaintiff policyholders. Unlike *Maio*, the REPAIR Team suits allege past injury resulting from a misrepresentation of coverage—not a lack of quality of care in the future or compensation for the denial of particular benefit claims. Their claim depends upon the representations made to class members in their policies and benefit materials, not public advertising.

Plaintiffs allege a pattern of racketeering activity consisting of the MCO's repeated acts of mail and wire fraud over a period of at least four years and the prospect of its continuing. The scheme involves fraudulent misrepresentation of the coverage provided by policies sold by defendants—not the puffery found by the District Court in Maio. The class action plaintiffs contend that defendant's wrongful scheme further involves the fraudulent representations made to subscribers that their claims do not meet the medical necessity conditions in their policies, when defendants have actually only determined that the claims do not meet their undisclosed restrictive criteria.

The class action complaints allege that the enterprise, whose affairs were operated through the pattern of racketeering activity, is an "association-in-fact enterprise" consisting of the national MCO and its subsidiaries, on the one hand, and its network of providers, on the other. They maintain that on-going association of these entities "for a common purpose of engaging in a course of conduct" is sufficient under RICO to allege the existence of an enterprise within the meaning of the statute citing United States v. Turkette, 452 U.S. 576, 583, 101 S.Ct. 2524, 69 L.Ed.2d 246 (1981). National MCOs centralized, national structure and their mechanisms for controlling and directing the affairs of the group support the concept that MCOs and their networks share a common purpose of providing health insurance coverage and medical services to customers and earning profits from providing those services.

In the class cases against MCOs, the injury to policyholders' property that is proximately caused by defendants violations of RICO is the loss of money—the amount of money paid for coverage lost as a result violations MCO's. Plaintiffs believe that the value of the lost coverage can be quantified as the difference between the value of the coverage as represented and the value of coverage actually provided to policyholder, an amount to be established at trial.

Class action plaintiffs contend that premiums are paid for coverage—the transfer of risk to the MCO-insurer—that exists independent of whether the risk materializes. Insureds do not get their premiums back at the end of the year if they never filed a claim. Plaintiff therefor conferred that defendant MCOs are therefore enriched unjustly by the misrepresentation as to "quality" coverage.

Problem: Wanting the "Best"

Cheryl Faber, twenty years old and newly married, joined a managed care organization, Freedom Plus [the Plan], one of several choices offered by her employer, Primerica Bank. Cheryl had examined the literature for the various plan choices during her open enrollment period. She chose the Plan because its literature talked of a "high quality" program, with the "best doctors" in the area, and "no cost-cutting where subscriber health is concerned".

The Plan sets aside a certain amount of money each year for a "referral pool" and a "hospital/ancillary pool" for Plan physicians. The money in these pools is depleted with each referral to a specialist or hospitalization of a patient during the year. At the end of the year, any money left over in these pools is divided between the Plan and the individual physicians.

Cheryl went to her primary care physician in the Plan, Dr. Hanks, for her initial physical examination. Dr. Hanks found small lumps in her breasts, which he noted in the patient record as fibroid tumors. He talked briefly with Cheryl about the lumps, but stated that she shouldn't worry.

A year later Cheryl came back for another checkup. Dr. Hanks had left the Plan. It turned out Dr. Hanks had been the defendant in several malpractice suits filed against him in the five years he had worked for another HMO and he was terminated by that HMO. The Plan could have discovered this by accessing the National Practitioners Data Bank, or by calling up the previous employer.

Cheryl was then examined by another primary care physician, Dr. Wick. Dr. Wick was concerned about the lumps, and she prepared a referral to an oncologist, Dr. Scanem, who had recently joined the panel of specialists affiliated with the Plan. Cheryl went to Dr. Scanem, who ordered a biopsy and confirmed that the lumps were malignant Stage III cancer. Stage III cancers have about a 10% five year survival rate, Stage II a 40% five year survival, and Stage I almost 100% survival with prompt treatment.

Dr. Scanem recommended a treatment regime for Cheryl that included limited radical mastectomy and chemotherapy. He planned to use a new drug for breast cancers that had recently become available through a research protocol in which he was participating. This drug appeared to offer a slightly higher cure rate with young patients such as Cheryl with advanced breast cancer.

The Plan approved Dr. Scanem's recommendations, with the exception of the new drug. The Plan rejected his proposal for use of this drug, stating that it only reimbursed for chemotherapy using the standard drugs used generally by oncologists. The new drug was extremely expensive, and would have increased the cost of Cheryl's chemotherapy by about 200%. Dr. Scanem was angry about the refusal by the Plan to reimburse Cheryl's treatment in full, and told her so. He told her that there was nothing he could do about it, and so he said he would use the standard approach that most oncologists used. Cheryl was a very nervous patient, terrified of her cancer. Dr. Scanem was worried about upsetting her too much, given the other stresses created by the surgery and the side-effects from chemotherapy. She asked him what her chances were, and he said only that she had "a reasonable shot at beating it, with luck and prayer." He did not tell her anything more about the prognosis, nor did she ask.

Cheryl underwent the radical mastectomy and chemotherapy. Optimistic about her chances, Cheryl proceeded to get pregnant. She and her husband also bought a new house, assuming that she would recover and her salary would continue.

Cheryl's cancer proved to be too far advanced to respond to treatment. She died six months after the chemotherapy regime finished. Her fetus could not be saved, in spite of efforts by Plan obstetricians to do so. Her husband lost their new house since he could no longer afford the mortgage payments.

What advice will you give Mr. Faber about the merits of litigation against the Plan?

IV. REGULATION OF PRIVATE HEALTH INSURANCE UNDER STATE LAW

A. TRADITIONAL INSURANCE REGULATION

Historically the states bore primary responsibility for regulating private health care finance, a role confirmed by Congress in the McCarran–Ferguson Act in the 1945. 15 U.S.C.A. §§ 1011–1015. In the next chapter we will consider the effect that the Employee Retirement Income Security Act of 1974 (ERISA) has had on eroding state authority. The states remain, however, primarily responsible for regulating many health plans subject to ERISA as well as insurance plans not governed by ERISA, such as individual health insurance plans, group insurance plans covering church employees or employees of state and local government, no-fault auto insurance, uninsured motorist policies, and workers' compensation.

All states tax the premiums of commercial insurers and about half of the states tax Blue Cross/Blue Shield plan premiums. States oversee the financial solvency of insurers both by imposing minimal requirements for financial reserves and for allowable investments, and through requiring annual statements and conducting periodic examinations of insurers (usually on a triennial basis).

In most states, insurers must file policy forms with the state insurance regulatory agency. Some states allow a form to be used once it has been filed with the insurance agency (if it is not disapproved), while others require explicit approval of the policy form before it can be used. States also regulate insurance marketing and claims practices, including coordination of benefits where an insured is covered by more than one policy. (This is often the case in today's society with two-income and blended families.) State insurance commissions investigate consumer complaints and place insolvent companies into receivership. The National Association of Insurance Commissioners (NAIC) has issued model codes and regulations on many of these subjects, the wide adoption of which has brought about some uniformity among the states. See, generally on state insurance regulation, Kathleen Heald Ettlinger, et al., State Insurance Regulation (1995); GAO, Private Health Insurance: Wide Variations in State Insurance Departments' Regulatory Authority, Oversight and Resources (1993).

How do these traditional concerns of insurance regulation change in a managed care environment? Should health maintenance organizations be subject to the same solvency requirements as commercial insurers? Should provider-sponsored integrated delivery systems also be required to meet these requirements? Should they be subject to any solvency requirements? Do marketing and claims practices become more or less of a concern under managed care? How might these practices change as commercial insurers become managed care plans?

B. ATTEMPTS TO INCREASE ACCESS TO INSURANCE THROUGH REGULATION

States have not historically regulated the rates of commercial health insurers. Because the market for health insurance has been relatively competitive and because most insurance is sold to employers or large groups that have some bargaining power, rate regulation was not generally thought necessary. Rates and rate information are commonly filed with the insurance commissioner, and some states permit the commissioner to disapprove these filings if benefits do not bear a reasonable relationship to premiums charged. But most states have historically not set health insurance rates as such and, have rarely intervened in insurer rate setting processes. States also have not traditionally regulated underwriting practices, other than to attempt to assure that rates were not obviously discriminatory. Regulation of Blue Cross and Blue Shield rates and underwriting, however, has been much more common because of a belief that the Blues have a greater obligation to make their services readily available to the public at a fair rate in exchange for the favorable tax and regulatory treatment they have historically received.

In recent years, however, states have increasingly regulated underwriting practices, and sometimes even premium rates, in an effort to assure equity of access to insurance. As was noted in Chapter Seven, the number of uninsured in America has grown through most of the past decade, and at this writing nearly 43 million Americans are uninsured. Most of the uninsured are either employed or the dependents of employed persons. A major reason why so many employed persons are uninsured is that persons who are self-employed or who are employed by small employers are far less likely to be insured, or even to have insurance available through their place of employment, than are employees of large businesses. Only about two thirds of employers with fewer than 200 employees offer health insurance benefits, while nearly all employers with more than 200 do. Although the increase in the number of the uninsured throughout the 1990s was attributable primarily to an increase in the number of employees declining insurance offered by their employers rather than to a decrease in the number of employers offering insurance, employees of small firms still purchase insurance at high rates when it is offered, encouraging the hope that an increase in the number of small employers offering health insurance as an option might decrease the number of the uninsured.

For purposes of regulation directed at increasing access to insurance, states usually distinguish between large groups, small groups, and individuals. While the boundaries vary from state to state (and can sometimes be manipulated by insurers), small groups are usually defined as groups with between 2 and 50 members, large groups with more than 50 members. The underwriting of insurance for large group plans is unregulated in most states. Most states, on the other hand, regulate underwriting practices with respect to individuals. Every state has, however, adopted small group reforms during the past decade, which usually go further in limiting insurer discretion than reforms in individual insurance markets. These reforms were encouraged by the 1996 federal Health Insurance Portability and Accountability Act (HIPAA), which mandated the enactment of certain small group and individual reforms, and which will be discussed in detail in the next chapter. Many of the reforms required by HIPAA, however, were already in place in numerous states before it went into effect, while many states have also adopted reforms going beyond HIPAA, thus HIPAA's incremental effects have been marginal. Why might access to affordable insurance be less of a problem for large groups? Why might states be more willing to pass laws protecting small groups than individuals? What protections do small groups need?

COLONIAL LIFE INSURANCE COMPANY
OF AMERICA v. CURIALE

Supreme Court, Appellate Division, Third Department, 1994.
205 A.D.2d 58, 617 N.Y.S.2d 377.

PETERS, JUSTICE.

* * *

Petitioner is a commercial insurance company which issues small group health insurance policies in this State. Petitioner challenged two regulations promulgated by respondent Superintendent of Insurance to implement chapter 501 of the Laws of 1992. Chapter 501 requires a commercial insurer doing business in this State to employ "community rating"[2] and to offer "open enrollment"[3] for any insurance policies issued in this State. The underpinning of the new law was to spread the risk among more people and provide greater rate stability. The Superintendent was directed to promulgate regulations designed to protect insurers writing policies from claim fluctuations and "unexpected significant shifts in the number of persons insured"[ ]. Pursuant thereto, the Superintendent promulgated 11 NYCRR parts 360 and 361 which implemented what he deemed a statutory directive that insurers be required to share the risk of high-cost claims by establishing a pool system which compares the risk of insurers in seven regions of the State [ ]. After these comparisons were made, insurers with worse than average demographic factors would get money from regional pooling funds, while insurers with better than average factors would pay money into these pooling funds.

Petitioner commenced this proceeding seeking to have 11 NYCRR part 361 and two provisions of 11 NYCRR part 360 invalidated. Supreme Court dismissed the petition to the extent that it challenged 11 NYCRR part 361, but granted the petition with respect to 11 NYCRR part 360. The parties have cross-appealed from the adverse portions of the court's judgment.

* * *

Petitioner contends that the pool system established by 11 NYCRR part 361 violates the intent of chapter 501 since the Legislature did not intend that (1) contributions to the system be mandatory, (2) contributions be based on existing policies, and (3) Empire Blue Cross and Blue Shield (hereinafter Empire) participate. We first note that it is well settled that the Superintendent's interpretation of the Insurance Law provisions is entitled to great deference because of his special competence and expertise with respect to the insurance industry unless such interpretation is irrational or contrary to the clear wording of a statutory provision [ ].

The Superintendent established the pool system pursuant to Insurance Law § 3233 which provided that "the superintendent shall promulgate regulations to assure an orderly implementation and ongoing operation of the

---

2. Community rating requires the insurer to base the policy premium on the experience of the entire pool of risks covered by that policy without regard to age, sex, health status or occupation [ ].

3. Open enrollment requires that any individual or small group applying for health insurance coverage must be accepted for any coverage offered by the insurer [ ].

open enrollment and community rating required by [Insurance Law §§ 3231 and 4317] * * *. The regulations shall apply to all insurers and health maintenance organizations subject to community rating" (Insurance Law § 3233 [a]). Based upon such language, there exists a clear expression by the Legislature that regulations shall be promulgated to further open enrollment which "shall include reinsurance or a pooling process involving insurer contributions to, or receipts from, a fund" [ ] and that those regulations "shall apply to all insurers and health maintenance organizations subject to community rating" [ ]. * * *

[The Court next held that the regulations were not improperly retroactive, and that Empire Blue Cross was properly included in the scheme].

Finally, petitioner contends that 11 NYCRR part 361 imposes an unconstitutional tax, gives State money to private organizations and takes property without just compensation. Our review indicates that the Legislature intended pool payments be mandatory and that those payments consist of the amounts necessary to permit sharing or equalization of the risk of high cost claims [ ]. Having chosen to require such payments, the Legislature could therefore delegate the responsibility to the Superintendent to collect such amounts [ ] We find that such pool contributions are a valid exercise of the Legislature's power to regulate [ ] and as the enactment intended to regulate rather than generate revenue it is not a tax [ ].

We further find that Supreme Court properly rejected the contention that the pooling contributions constituted a gift of State money to a private organization in violation of N.Y. Constitution, article VII, § 8(1). * * * [T]he State Constitution "provides authority for the legislature to protect New Yorkers against sickness, by insurance or otherwise". Since the Legislature directed the Superintendent to promulgate such regulations to implement chapter 501, we find that there is nothing in NY Constitution, article VII, § 8(1) which indicates that the delegation was invalid. We further agree with Supreme Court that there has not been an unconstitutional taking of what petitioner contends is its low-risk value of its book of business. We find, as did Supreme Court, that petitioner cannot support its contention that it has a constitutionally protected interest in maintaining a healthier than average risk pool [ ].

Supreme Court invalidated 11 NYCRR 360.4(c) and 360.3(a)(1)(ii), holding that they exceeded the scope of the authority delegated to the Superintendent by chapter 501. The Superintendent promulgated 11 NYCRR 360.4(c) in response to his understanding of the statutory directive contained in Insurance Law § 3231(b), which reads as follows:

Nothing herein shall prohibit the use of premium rate structures to establish different premium rates for individuals as opposed to family units or separate community rates for individuals as opposed to small groups. Individual proprietors and groups of two must be classified in the individual or small group rating category by the insurer.

Supreme Court held that this requirement exceeded the Superintendent's authority, determining that Insurance Law § 3231(b) applied only to the rating of policies and "does not provide authority for requiring insurers of small groups to extend coverage to individual proprietors and groups of two". Should the Superintendent's regulation be permitted to stand, Supreme Court reasoned, and we agree, that the definition of "small group" contained in Insurance Law § 3231(a) would be impermissibly expanded to now require small group insurers to cover individual proprietors and/or groups of two contrary to the clear and unambiguous language in the statute. It would also run counter to the legislative directive that the implementing regulations shall not require any insurer to enter any line of business as a condition of continuing in any other line of business [ ] Hence, as Supreme Court reasoned, since "an administrative agency may not promulgate a regulation that adds a requirement that does not exist under the statute"[ ], we affirm Supreme Court's determination to annul this provision.

As to 11 NYCRR 360.3(a)(1)(ii), we find that Supreme Court's findings should not be disturbed. Under Insurance Law § 4235(c)(1), if less than 50 percent of employees in a group do not agree to participate in a plan, the insurer does not have to offer coverage to the group. The Superintendent, however, promulgated 11 NYCRR part 360.3(a)(1)(ii) which provides as follows:

> [F]or purposes of determining said participation requirements, insurers must include as participating all eligible employees or members of the group covered under all the alternative health maintenance organization plans made available by the group.

Supreme Court properly invalidated the regulation since chapter 501 did not amend or change the minimum participation requirements set forth in Insurance Law § 4235(c)(1) and the Superintendent therefore exceeded his authority by redefining the calculation of participation levels [ ].

* * *

Notes and Questions

1. What is the purpose of laws requiring community rating and open enrollment? Why do these requirements in turn necessitate the creation of an insurance risk pool? Why would commercial insurers object to including Blue Cross in this pool? Why are individual insureds not included in the small group pooling requirements? Why are insurers permitted to exclude from coverage groups in which fewer than 50 percent of the group members elect to be insured?

2. All states currently require insurers that sell in small group markets to offer coverage and guarantee renewal to any small group that requests it, regardless of the health status or claims experience of the groups members. Thirty-eight states had guaranteed issue and forty-three guaranteed renewal requirements before HIPAA, but HIPAA made these requirements universal. HIPAA also requires restrictions on preexisting conditions clauses (clauses that exclude coverage for conditions that existed prior to the inception of the insurance contract), but forty-five states had restricted preexisting conditions clauses for small group policies before HIPAA. A number of states go beyond HIPAA in limiting preexisting conditions clauses, moreover, including three states that outlaw them altogether.

Though HIPAA does not address the level of insurance premiums, many states do. Twenty-seven states limit the variation in premiums charged to small groups to a band range of 2:1 (i.e. the highest premiums may only be twice as high as the lowest), to permit insurers to take into account to a limited extent claims experience, health status, or duration of coverage of the group, as recommended by the National Association of Insurance Commissioners. Several states impose tighter rating bands, and fifteen states require a form of community rating by prohibiting rating based on experience, health status or duration of coverage. New York, the most restrictive of the states, even limits variance of premiums based on age. Ten states have also established mandatory reinsurance pools and twenty voluntary reinsurance pools, assuring that small group plans that end up carrying high risk groups can spread some of their risks to other insurers with more favorable risk experience.

Finally, about twenty-one states have laws authorizing the formation of small group purchaser pools to facilitate small groups banding together to achieve economies in purchasing insurance. Though approximately a third of establishments with fewer than 10 employees and 28 percent of firms with 10–49 employees purchase health insurance through pooled arrangements, pools seem to have had little impact on the affordability or availability of insurance.

3. Most of the states have also attempted to reform the individual insurance market. The most common individual market reform is guaranteed renewal, required by HIPAA but adopted by twenty-one states before HIPAA. Thirty one states have adopted restrictions on preexisting conditions limitations covering persons beyond those who must be covered under HIPAA. Among other individual market reforms adopted by the states are 1) restrictions on the use of experience, health status or duration for setting premiums (8 states); 2) prohibitions against the use of experience, health status or duration of coverage in underwriting (11 states); provision for voluntary or mandatory participation in reinsurance pools (9 states); and designation of minimum loss ratios (percentage of premiums that must be paid out in claims) (9 states).

4. In the end, regulatory approaches seem to have had a limited impact for making insurance available in small group and individual markets, though the reforms have certainly helped some individuals and firms that might otherwise not have been able to secure insurance. In part their limited effect seems to be due to the endless creativity of insurers in evading regulations and limiting their risk. By manipulating coverage, imposing cost-sharing obligations, and marketing selectively, as well as by creating "association" plans or using other devices that allow small group or individual plans to masquerade as large group plans, insurers can still often control the risk to which they are exposed, allowing them on the one hand to remain prosperous, but on the other hand, to continue to exclude high-risk individuals.

On the other hand, the disastrous effects of these reforms that many in the health insurance industry had predicted have also have not materialized. Insurers have generally remained in business even in states that have adopted rigorous reforms, and markets have remained competitive, though individual reforms have had a more damaging effect on markets than small group reforms have had. To a considerable degree, however, the effects that small group reforms might have had on insurers or insureds has been masked by a dramatic growth of managed care in small group markets, which has held down increases in premiums that reforms might otherwise have caused.

Mark Hall has written an excellent series of articles on health insurance reforms as part of a project funded by the Robert Wood Johnson Foundation, including The Competitive Impact of Small Group Health Insurance Reforms, 32 Mich.J.L.Ref. 685 (1999); The Competitive Impact of Small Group Health Insurance Reform Laws, 37 Inquiry 376 (2001); The Geography of Health Insurance Regulation 19 Health Aff., March/Apr.2000 at 173; and two contributions to a symposium on the individual health insurance market, in volume 25 of the

Journal of Health Politics, Policy and Law. Other useful sources include Gail A. Jensen and Michael A. Morrisey, Small Group Reforms and Insurance Provision by Small Firms, 1989–1995, 36 Inquiry 176 (1999); and John Gabel, et al., Health Benefits of Small Employers in 1998 (1999). For a comparative perspective, see Timothy S. Jost, Private or Public Approaches to Insuring the Uninsured: Lessons from International Experience with Private Insurance, N.Y.U. L. Rev. (2001).T

Problem: Expanding Insurance Coverage

You are a state legislator and the chair of the legislative health and welfare committee. You have run on a platform calling for increased regulation to address the problem of the uninsured, which is quite serious in your state. You would like to make insurance coverage more attractive to small businesses, which often do not offer insurance to their employees in your state, and to self-employed individuals. What regulatory strategies will you consider? Whom will you invite to testify at hearings you will hold on this subject? What do you expect them to say at the hearings?

V. STATE REGULATION OF MANAGED CARE

A. *Introduction*

Managed Care Organizations (MCOs) differ from traditional health insurers, of course, insofar as they manage care. As Marmor and Hacker note above, they do this through restricting members to the use of particular providers, reviewing the utilization of services, and creating incentives for limiting the cost of care. Some MCOs also attempt to oversee the quality of care their members receive. Though managed care was generally welcomed at first as offering the potential both to restrain costs and to improve quality, there has been a decided "backlash" against managed care in the recent past. See, Symposium, The Managed Care Backlash, 24 J.Health Pol., Pol'y & L. 873 (1999). There is a general perception—often encouraged by the media—that managed care controls have become excessive, threatening access to care. Almost every state has adopted some form of legislation, nearly 1000 statutes in all, during the past half decade, and far more legislative proposals have been considered by state legislatures. While many of these statutes address fairly narrow problems, a number of states have adopted comprehensive legislation addressing a variety of problems. The following law, adopted in 2000 by Massachusetts, addresses most of the issues with which such legislation has been concerned.

H.B. NO. 4525, AN ACT RELATIVE TO MANAGED CARE PRACTICES IN THE INSURANCE INDUSTRY.

* * *

Section 217. (a) There is hereby established within the department [of Public Health] an office of patient protection. The office shall:—

(1) have the authority to administer and enforce the standards and procedures established by sections 13, 14, 15 and 16 of chapter 176O, and to promulgate regulations therefor. * * *

(2) establish a site on the internet and through other communication media in order to make managed care information collected by the office readily accessible to consumers. Said internet site shall, at a minimum, include (i) the health plan report card developed pursuant to * * *, (ii) a chart,

prepared by the office, comparing the information obtained on premium revenue expended for health care services as provided pursuant to * * *, and (iii) [HEDIS data];

(3) assist consumers with questions or concerns relating to managed care, including but not limited to exercising the grievance and appeals rights * * *;

(4) monitor quality-related health insurance plan information relating to managed care practices;

(5) regulate the establishment and functions of [external review panels];

* * *

(c) Each entity that compiles the health plan employer data and information set, [HEDIS] so-called, for the National Committee on Quality Assurance, or collects other information deemed by the entity as similar or equivalent thereto, shall * * * concurrently submit to the office of patient protection a copy thereof excluding, at the entity's option, proprietary financial data.

* * *

Section 5. (a) As used in this section, the following words shall have the following meanings:—

* * *

"Emergency medical condition", a medical condition, whether physical or mental, manifesting itself by symptoms of sufficient severity, including severe pain, that the absence of prompt medical attention could reasonably be expected by a prudent layperson who possesses an average knowledge of health and medicine, to result in placing the health of a member or another person in serious jeopardy, serious impairment to body function, or serious dysfunction of any body organ or part, or, with respect to a pregnant woman, as further defined in [EMTALA, See chapter 11].

"Stabilization for discharge", an emergency medical condition shall be deemed to be stabilized for purposes of discharging a member, * * *, when the attending physician has determined that, within reasonable clinical confidence, the member has reached the point where further care, including diagnostic work-up or treatment, or both, could be reasonably performed on an outpatient basis or a later scheduled inpatient basis if the member is given a reasonable plan for appropriate follow-up care and discharge instructions, * * *. Stabilization for discharge does not require final resolution of the emergency medical condition.

* * *

(b) A health maintenance organization shall cover emergency services provided to members for emergency medical conditions. After the member has been stabilized for discharge or transfer, the health maintenance organization or its designee may require a hospital emergency department to contact the * * * the health maintenance organization * * * for authorization of post-stabilization services to be provided. * * * Such authorization shall be deemed granted if the health maintenance organization or its designee has not responded to said call within 30 minutes. Notwithstanding the foregoing provision, in the event the attending physician and * * * on-call physician do not agree on what constitutes appropriate medical treatment, the opinion of the attending physician shall prevail and such treatment shall be considered appropriate treatment for an emergency medical condition provided that such treatment is consistent with generally accepted principles of professional medical practice and a covered benefit under the member's evidence of coverage. * * *

* * *

(e) * * * No member shall in any way be discouraged from using the local pre-hospital emergency medical service system, the 911 telephone number, or the local equivalent, or be denied coverage for medical and transportation expenses incurred as a result of an emergency medical condition.

(f) A health maintenance organization shall provide or arrange for indemnity payments to a member or provider for a reasonable amount charged for the cost of emergency medical services by a provider who is not normally affiliated with the health maintenance organization when the member requires services for an emergency medical condition. * * *

Chapter 176O: Health Insurance Consumer Protections.

Section 1. As used in this chapter, the following words shall have the following meanings:—

"Adverse determination", a determination, based upon a review of information provided by a carrier or its designated utilization review organization, to deny, reduce, modify, or terminate an admission, continued inpatient stay, or the availability of any other health care services, * * *.

* * *

"Capitation", a set payment per patient per unit of time made by a carrier to a licensed health care professional, health care provider group or organization that employs or utilizes services of health care professionals to cover a specified set of services and administrative costs without regard to the actual number of services provided.

* * *

"Grievance", any oral or written complaint submitted to the carrier which has been initiated by an insured, or on behalf of an insured with the consent of the insured, concerning any aspect or action of the carrier relative to the insured, including, but not limited to, review of adverse determinations regarding scope of coverage, denial of services, quality of care and administrative operations, * * *.

* * *

"Incentive plan", any compensation arrangement between a carrier and licensed health care professional or licensed health care provider group or organization that employs or utilizes services of one or more licensed health care professionals that may directly or indirectly have the effect of reducing or limiting services furnished to insureds of the organization.

* * *

"Medical necessity" or "medically necessary", health care services that are consistent with generally accepted principles of professional medical practice.

* * *

Section 2. (a) There is hereby established * * * a bureau of managed care. Said bureau shall by regulation establish minimum standards for the accreditation of carriers in the following areas:

(1) utilization review;

(2) quality management and improvement;

(3) credentialing;

(4) preventive health services; and

(5) compliance with sections 2 to 12, inclusive.

(b) In establishing said minimum standards, the bureau shall consult and use, where appropriate, standards established by national accreditation organizations. Notwithstanding the foregoing, the bureau shall not be bound by said standards established by such organizations, but wherever the bureau promulgates standards different from said national standards, it shall * * * (2) state the reason for such variation, and (3) take into consideration any projected compliance costs for such variation. * * *.

* * *

(e) A carrier may apply to the bureau for deemed accreditation status. A carrier may be deemed to be in compliance with the bureau's standards, and may be so accredited by the bureau, only if the carrier, or an entity with which it contracts: (1) is accredited by a national accreditation organization; (2) is in compliance with all of the requirements of this chapter; and (3) demonstrates compliance with, and has obtained the highest possible rating from said national accreditation organization for: (i) utilization review, (ii) quality management, and (iii) member rights and responsibilities, as promulgated by the bureau pursuant to this chapter. * * *

* * *

Section 3. (a) The bureau shall investigate all complaints made against a carrier or any entity with which it contracts for allegations of noncompliance with the accreditation requirements established by section 2. The bureau shall notify a carrier when, in the opinion of the bureau, the complaints made against such a carrier indicate a pattern of noncompliance with a particular accreditation requirement. The notice shall detail the alleged noncompliance and establish a hearing date for the matter * * * The hearing shall provide such a carrier with the opportunity to respond to the alleged noncompliance.

(b) The bureau may, after said hearing, suspend or revoke the accreditation of such a carrier, or reprimand, censure or impose a civil administrative penalty not to exceed $10,000 for each classification of violation.

* * *

Section 4. A carrier shall not refuse to contract with or compensate for covered services an otherwise eligible health care provider solely because such provider has in good faith communicated with or advocated on behalf of one or more of his prospective, current or former patients regarding the provisions, terms or requirements of the carrier's health benefit plans as they relate to the needs of such provider's patients, or communicated with one or more of his prospective, current or former patients with respect to the method by which such provider is compensated by the carrier for services provided to the patient. Nothing in this section shall be construed to preclude a carrier from requiring a health care provider to hold confidential specific compensation terms.

Section 5. No contract between a carrier and a health care provider for the provision of services to insureds may require the health care provider to indemnify the carrier for any expenses and liabilities, including, without limitation, judgments, settlements, attorneys' fees, court costs and any associated charges, incurred in connection with any claim or action brought against the carrier based on the carrier's management decisions, utilization review provisions or other policies, guidelines or actions.

Section 6. (a) A carrier shall issue and deliver to at least one adult insured in each household residing in the commonwealth, upon enrollment, an evidence of coverage and any amendments thereto. Said evidence of coverage shall contain a clear, concise and complete statement of:

(1) the health care services and any other benefits which the insured is entitled to on a nondiscriminatory basis;

* * *

(3) the limitations on the scope of health care services and any other benefits to be provided, including an explanation of any deductible or copayment feature and all restrictions relating to preexisting condition exclusions;

(4) the locations where, and the manner in which, health care services and other benefits may be obtained;

(5) the criteria by which an insured may be disenrolled or denied enrollment and the involuntary disenrollment rate among insureds of the carrier;

(6) a description of the carrier's method for resolving insured complaints, including a description of the formal internal grievance process * * * and the external grievance process * * * for appealing decisions pursuant to said grievances, as required by this chapter;

* * *

(8) a summary description of the procedure, if any, for out-of-network referrals and any additional charge for utilizing out-of-network providers;

(9) a summary description of the utilization review procedures and quality assurance programs used by the carrier, including the toll-free telephone number to be established by the carrier that enables consumers to determine the status or outcome of utilization review decisions;

(10) a statement detailing what translator and interpretation services are available to assist insureds; * * *

(11) a list of prescription drugs excluded from any restricted formulary available to insureds under the health benefit plan; * * * ;

(12) a summary description of the procedures followed by the carrier in making decisions about the experimental or investigational nature of individual drugs, medical devices or treatments in clinical trials;

(13) a statement on how to obtain the report regarding grievances from the office of patient protection * * *;

(14) the toll-free telephone number, facsimile number, and internet site for the office of patient protection in the department of public health; * * *

* * *

Section 7. (a) A carrier shall provide to at least one adult insured in each household upon enrollment, and to a prospective insured upon request, the following information:

(1) a list of health care providers in the carrier's network, organized by specialty and by location and summarizing for each such provider the method used to compensate or reimburse such provider; provided, however, that nothing in this clause shall be construed to require disclosure of the specific details of any financial arrangements between a carrier and a provider; * * *;

(2) a statement that physician profiling information, so-called, may be available from the board of registration in medicine;

(3) a summary description of the process by which clinical guidelines and utilization review criteria are developed;

(4) the voluntary and involuntary disenrollment rate among insureds of the carrier;

* * *

(b) A carrier shall provide all of the information required under section 6 and subsection (a) of this section to the office of patient protection in the department of public health and, in addition, shall provide to said office the following information:

(1) a list of sources of independently published information assessing insured satisfaction and evaluating the quality of health care services offered by the carrier;

(2) the percentage of physicians who voluntarily and involuntarily terminated participation contracts with the carrier during the previous calendar year * * * and the three most common reasons for voluntary and involuntary physician disenrollment;

(3) the percentage of premium revenue expended by the carrier for health care services provided to insureds for the most recent year for which information is available; and

(4) a report detailing, for the previous calendar year, the total number of: (i) filed grievances, grievances that were approved internally, grievances that were denied internally, and grievances that were withdrawn before resolution; and (ii) external appeals pursued after exhausting the internal grievance process and the resolution of all such external appeals. The report shall identify for each such category, to the extent such information is available,

the demographics of such insureds, which shall include, but need not be limited to, race, gender and age.

* * *

Section 10. (a) No contract between a carrier and a licensed health care provider group shall contain any incentive plan that includes a specific payment made to a health care professional as an inducement to reduce, delay or limit specific, medically necessary services covered by the health care contract. Health care professionals shall not profit from provision of covered services that are not medically necessary and appropriate. Carriers shall not profit from denial or withholding of covered services that are medically necessary and appropriate. Nothing in this section shall be construed to prohibit contracts that contain incentive plans that involve general payments such as capitation payments or shared risk agreements that are made with respect to physicians or physician groups or which are made with respect to groups of insureds if such contracts, which impose risk on such physicians or physician groups for the costs of medical care, services and equipment provided or authorized by another physician or health care provider, comply with subsection (b).

(b) * * * no carrier shall enter into a new contract, revise the risk arrangements in an existing contract, * * * which imposes financial risk on such physician or physician group for the costs of medical care, services or equipment provided or authorized by another physician or health care provider unless such contract includes specific provisions with respect to the following: (1) stop loss protection, (2) minimum patient population size for the physician or physician group, and (3) identification of the health care services for which the physician or physician group is at risk.

(c) A carrier or utilization review organization shall conduct an annual survey of insureds to assess satisfaction with access to specialist services, ancillary services, hospitalization services, durable medical equipment and other covered services. Said survey shall compare the actual satisfaction of insureds with projected measures of their satisfaction. Carriers that utilize incentive plans shall establish mechanisms for monitoring the satisfaction, quality of care and actual utilization compared with projected utilization of health care services of insureds.

* * *

Section 12. (a) Utilization review conducted by a carrier or a utilization review organization shall be conducted pursuant to a written plan, under the supervision of a physician and staffed by appropriately trained and qualified personnel, and shall include a documented process to (i) review and evaluate its effectiveness, (ii) ensure the consistent application of utilization review criteria, and (iii) ensure the timeliness of utilization review determinations.

A carrier or utilization review organization shall * * * conduct all utilization review activities pursuant to [written] criteria. The criteria shall be, to the maximum extent feasible, scientifically derived and evidence-based, and developed with the input of participating physicians, consistent with the development of medical necessity criteria * * *.

Adverse determinations rendered by a program of utilization review, or other denials of requests for health services, shall be made by a person licensed in the appropriate specialty related to such health service and, where applicable, by a provider in the same licensure category as the ordering provider.

(b) A carrier or utilization review organization shall make an initial determination regarding a proposed admission, procedure or service that requires such a determination within two working days of obtaining all necessary information. * * * In the case of a determination to approve an admission, procedure or service, the carrier or utilization review organization shall notify the provider rendering the service by telephone within 24 hours, * * * In the case of an adverse determination, the carrier or utilization review organization shall notify the provider rendering the service by telephone within 24 hours, * * *

(c) A carrier or utilization review organization shall make a concurrent review determination within one working day of obtaining all necessary information. * * * The service shall be continued without liability to the insured until the insured has been notified of the determination.

(d) The written notification of an adverse determination shall include a substantive clinical justification therefor that is consistent with generally accepted principles of professional medical practice, and shall, at a minimum: (1) identify the specific information upon which the adverse determination was based; (2) discuss the insured's presenting symptoms or condition, diagnosis and treatment interventions and the specific reasons such medical evidence fails to meet the relevant medical review criteria; (3) specify any alternative treatment option offered by the carrier, if any; and (4) reference and include applicable clinical practice guidelines and review criteria.

(e) A carrier or utilization review organization shall give a provider treating an insured an opportunity to seek reconsideration of an adverse determination from a clinical peer reviewer in any case involving an initial determination or a concurrent review determination. Said reconsideration process shall occur within one working day of the receipt of the request and shall be conducted between the provider rendering the service and the clinical peer reviewer * * *. If the adverse determination is not reversed by the reconsideration process, the insured, or the provider on behalf of the insured, may pursue the grievance process * * *. The reconsideration process allowed herein shall not be a prerequisite to the formal internal grievance process or an expedited appeal required by section 13.

Section 13. (a) A carrier or utilization review organization shall maintain a formal internal grievance process that provides for adequate consideration and timely resolution of grievances, which shall include but not be limited to: * * * (2) the provision of a clear, concise and complete description of the carrier's formal internal grievance process and the procedures for obtaining external review * * *; (3) the carrier's toll-free telephone number for assisting insureds in resolving such grievances and the consumer assistance toll-free telephone number maintained by the office of patient protection; (4) a written acknowledgement of the receipt of a grievance within 15 days and a written resolution of each grievance within 30 days from receipt thereof; and

(5) a procedure to accept grievances by telephone, in person, by mail, or by electronic means, * * *

(b) The formal internal grievance process maintained by a carrier or utilization review organization shall provide for an expedited resolution of a grievance concerning a carrier's coverage or provision of immediate and urgently needed services. Said expedited resolution policy shall include, but not be limited to:

(i) a resolution before an insured's discharge from a hospital if the grievance is submitted by an insured who is an inpatient in a hospital;

(ii) provisions for the automatic reversal of decisions denying coverage for services * * *, pending the outcome of the appeals process, within 48 hours, * * *, of receipt of certification by said physician that, in the [treating] physician's opinion, the service * * * at issue in a grievance or appeal is medically necessary, that a denial of coverage for such services * * * would create a substantial risk of serious harm to the patient, and that the risk of that harm is so immediate that the provision of such services * * * should not await the outcome of the normal appeal or grievance process * * *;

(iii) a resolution within five days from the receipt of such grievance if submitted by an insured with a terminal illness.

If the expedited review process affirms the denial of coverage or treatment to an insured with a terminal illness, the carrier shall provide the insured, within five business days of the decision (1) a statement setting forth the specific medical and scientific reasons for denying coverage or treatment; (2) a description of alternative treatment, services or supplies covered or provided by the carrier, if any; and (3) said procedure shall allow the insured to request a conference. The carrier or utilization review organization shall schedule such a conference within ten days of receiving such a request from an insured, at which the information provided to the insured pursuant to clauses (1) and (2) shall be reviewed by the insured and a representative of the carrier who has authority to determine the disposition of the grievance. The carrier shall permit attendance at the conference of the insured, a designee of the insured or both, * * *.

(c) A grievance not properly acted on by the carrier within the time limits required by this section shall be deemed resolved in favor of the insured.

Section 14. (a) An insured who remains aggrieved by an adverse determination and has exhausted all remedies available from the formal internal grievance process * * *, may seek further review of the grievance by a review panel established by the office of patient protection * * *. The insured shall pay the first $25 of the cost of the review to said office which may waive the fee in cases of extreme financial hardship. The commonwealth shall assess the carrier for the remainder of the cost of the review * * * * The office of patient protection shall contract with at least three unrelated and objective review agencies * * *, and refer grievances to one of the review agencies on a random selection basis. The review agencies shall develop review panels appropriate for the given grievance, which shall include qualified clinical decision-makers experienced in the determination of medical necessity, utilization management protocols and grievance resolution, and shall not have any financial relationship with the carrier making the initial determination.

The standard for review of a grievance by such a panel shall be the determination of whether the requested treatment or service is medically necessary, as defined herein, and a covered benefit under the policy or contract. The panel shall consider, but not be limited to considering: (i) written documents submitted by the insured, (ii) additional information from the involved parties or outside sources that the review panel deems necessary or relevant, and (iii) information obtained from any informal meeting held by the panel with the parties. The panel shall send final written disposition of the grievance, and the reasons therefor, to the insured and the carrier within 60 days of receipt of the request for review, * * *.

(b) If a grievance is filed concerning the termination of ongoing coverage or treatment, the disputed coverage or treatment shall remain in effect through completion of the formal internal grievance process. An insured may apply to the external review panel to seek continued provision of health care services which are the subject of the grievance during the course of said external review upon a showing of substantial harm to the insured's health absent such continuation, or other good cause as determined by the panel.

(c) The decision of the review panel shall be binding. The superior court shall have jurisdiction to enforce the decision of the review panel.

* * *

(e) The grievance procedures authorized by this section shall be in addition to any other procedures that may be available to any insured pursuant to contract or law, and failure to pursue, exhaust or engage in the procedures described in this subsection shall not preclude the use of any other remedy provided by any contract or law.

* * *

Section 15. (a) A carrier that allows or requires the designation of a primary care physician shall notify an insured at least 30 days before the disenrollment of such insured's primary care physician and shall permit such insured to continue to be covered for health services, consistent with the terms of the evidence of coverage, by such primary care physician for at least 30 days after said physician is disenrolled, other than disenrollment for quality-related reasons or for fraud. * * *

(b) A carrier shall allow any female insured who is in her second or third trimester of pregnancy and whose provider in connection with her pregnancy is involuntarily disenrolled, * * * to continue treatment with said provider, consistent with the terms of the evidence of coverage, for the period up to and including the insured's first postpartum visit.

(c) A carrier shall allow any insured who is terminally ill and whose provider in connection with said illness is involuntarily disenrolled, * * *, consistent with the terms of the evidence of coverage, until the insured's death.

(d) A carrier shall provide coverage for health services for up to 30 days from the effective date of coverage to a new insured by a physician who is not a participating provider in the carrier's network if: (1) the insured's employer only offers the insured a choice of carriers in which said physician is not a participating provider, and (2) said physician is providing the insured with an ongoing course of treatment or is the insured's primary care physician. * * * * * *

(f) A carrier that requires an insured to designate a primary care physician shall allow such a primary care physician to authorize a standing referral for specialty health care provided by a health care provider participating in such carrier's network when (1) the primary care physician determines that such referrals are appropriate, (2) the provider of specialty health care agrees to a treatment plan for the insured and provides the primary care physician with all necessary clinical and administrative information on a regular basis, and (3) the health care services to be provided are consistent with the terms of the evidence of coverage. * * *.

(g) No carrier shall require an insured to obtain a referral or prior authorization from a primary care physician for the following specialty care provided by an obstetrician, gynecologist, certified nurse-midwife or family practitioner participating in such carrier's health care provider network: (1) annual preventive gynecologic health examinations, including any subsequent obstetric or gynecological services determined by such obstetrician, gynecologist, certified nurse-midwife or family practitioner to be medically necessary as a result of such examination; (2) maternity care; and (3) medically necessary evaluations and resultant health care services for acute or emergency gynecological conditions. * * *

(h) A carrier shall provide coverage of pediatric specialty care, including mental health care, by persons with recognized expertise in specialty pediatrics to insureds requiring such services.

(i) A carrier shall provide health care providers applying to be participating providers who are denied such status with a written reason or reasons for denial of such application.

(j) No carrier shall make a contract with a health care provider which includes a provision permitting termination without cause. A carrier shall provide a written statement to a provider of the reason or reasons for such provider's involuntary disenrollment.

(k) A carrier shall provide insureds, upon request, interpreter and translation services related to administrative procedures.

Section 16. (a) The physician treating an insured, shall, consistent with generally accepted principles of professional medical practice and in consultation with the insured, make all clinical decisions regarding medical treatment to be provided to the insured, including the provision of durable medical equipment and hospital lengths of stay. Nothing in this section shall be construed as altering, affecting or modifying either the obligations of any third party or the terms and conditions of any agreement or contract between either the treating physician or the insured and any third party.

(b) A carrier shall be required to pay for health care services ordered by a treating physician if (1) the services are a covered benefit under the insured's health benefit plan; and (2) the services are medically necessary. A carrier may develop guidelines to be used in applying the standard of medical necessity, as defined herein. Any such medical necessity guidelines utilized by a carrier in making coverage determinations shall be: (i) developed with input from practicing physicians in the carrier's or utilization review organization's service area; (ii) developed in accordance with the standards adopted by national accreditation organizations; (iii) updated at least biennially or more often as new treatments, applications and technologies are adopted as generally accepted professional medical practice; and (iv) evidence-based, if practicable. In applying such guidelines, a carrier shall consider the individual health care needs of the insured.

* * *

Section 31. (a) The office of patient protection in the department of public health shall establish a pilot program in a labor market area, other than the city of Boston, which requires carriers offering health care benefits through a network also to offer such benefits through a point of service option to all insureds. For the purposes of this section, "point of service option" means a choice exercised by an insured and their dependents to obtain diagnostic and treatment services from a provider of health care services who is not under contract with or otherwise a participating provider in a carrier's network.

(b)(1) A carrier may require an insured that accepts the additional coverage under a point of service option under subsection (a) to be responsible for the payment of a reasonable additional cost over the amount of the premium for the coverage offered by the carrier for the services restricted to network providers.

(2) A carrier may impose reasonable cost sharing provisions for the point of service option based on whether the health care services are provided through the carrier's network or outside the carrier's network.

Notes and Questions

1.   What information about health plans must be provided under this legislation to consumers? Is this information that will be useful to consumers? How might they use it? What information is provided only to the regulator and not to consumers? Why? What information does the statute permit plans to conceal from consumers? Why does it permit this? Are the emergency access provisions (which also extend, under separate provisions, to commercial insurers, Blue Cross and Blue Shield plans and preferred provider organizations) adequate to assure that members will be covered for true emergency care? Who might benefit from these provisions other than plan members? How does the way in which this statute uses accreditation resemble or differ from the regulatory use of accreditation with respect to hospitals? What is the concern which motivated the statute's prohibition against "gag clauses"? What exactly do the statute's limitations on incentives prohibit? Does this provide sufficient protection to consumers? Do the restrictions go too far? How many layers of internal and external review does this statute provide? Are all of these mechanisms necessary? Useful? Are the statute's time limits reasonable? How does the statute use the term "grievance"? What limitations does the statute impose on termination of provider contracts? What effect might these limitations have on health plans? How much discretion does this statute give physicians to decide what care is medically necessary? How much control does it give to MCOs (carriers)? What explains the choice of specialists to which members are given direct access? How great an impact will these requirements have on primary care gatekeeper plans? What protections does this statute afford providers? Might these protections also be of use to consumers? How much

will this legislation cost health plans? Who will pay for these costs? How will these costs affect access to care?

2. State laws regulating private health care finance are often drafted with an eye toward model statutes and regulations drafted by the National Association of Insurance Commissioners (see http://www.naic.org). Among the NAIC's important relevant model acts are the Health Maintenance Organization Model Act (now in revised draft form), Managed Care Plan Network Adequacy Model Act, Grievance Procedures Model Act, Utilization Review Model Act, and Health Carrier External Review Model Act.

3. The Hacker and Marmor excerpt at the beginning of this chapter identified strategies through which MCOs managed care. The sections that follow examine each of these strategies and the forms of managed care legislation that address each of them. The best source for keeping up with managed care legislation is the National Association of State Legislator's Health Policy Tracking Service, from which many of the statistics below have been drawn. The Blue Cross/Blue Shield Association also publishes an annual summary of State Legislative Health Care and Insurance Issues survey. Other good recent sources on legislation include Jill A. Marsteller and Randall R. Bovbjerg, Federalism and Patient Protection: Changing Roles for the State and Federal Government, http://newfederalism.urban.org/html/occa28.html (1999), from the Urban Institute; Families U.S.A., Hit and Miss: State Managed Care Laws (1998); and Patricia A. Butler, The Current Status of State and Federal Regulation, in Regulating Managed Care: Theory, Practice and Future Options (Stuart H. Altman, Uwe E. Reinhardt, & David Shactman, eds., 1999). See also, describing the evolution of managed care regulation, Alice A. Noble and Troyen A. Brennan, The Status of Managed Care Regulation: Developing Better Rules, 24 J. Health Pol., Pol'y & L. 1275 (1999).

Problem: Advising Under State Managed Care Law

Resolve the following problems under the Massachusetts statute reproduced above:

1) Sam Rogers has been feeling severe pain on the left side of his chest for the past two hours. It is Saturday, and his primary care physician is not available. He is reluctant to go to the emergency room at the local hospital, however, because he knows that emergency room care is very expensive, and he has heard that managed care organizations sometimes refuse to pay for emergency room care when they later determine that it was not necessary. He does not know the exact terms of his own policy (and can't find it), but knows that the arrangement he is under very restrictive. What should Sam do?

2) Mary Gomez found out several months ago that she has cancer. She discovered the cancer fairly late, and it is quite advanced. Through her own research on the web, however, she has learned of a new form of treatment that is still in clinical trials. She has found a specialist in her health plan that is willing to attempt the procedure. He is concerned, however, as to whether Mary's health plan will cover it. Under what circumstances can Mary's plan refuse to cover the procedure? She needs the procedure very quickly if she is to have it at all, so she also wants to know how quickly the plan must make a decision on her request? What avenues are open to Mary to appeal the decision if her plan denies coverage? To whom can she turn for help, if she needs it?

3) The Omega Health Plan has entered into a contract with the Springdale Medical Group to provide primary care services to its members. Under the terms

of the arrangement, Springdale is fully at risk for its own services and for any specialist services or medical tests that its doctors order for patients insured by Omega. Omega provides stop-loss coverage if specialist or test procedures for any member of Omega exceed $100,000 a year. Is this arrangement legal? Dr. Johnson, a physician affiliated with Springdale, is very unhappy with this arrangement, and has sent his patients who are insured with Omega a letter informing of them of the arrangement and asking that they complain to Omega about it. Can Omega terminate Dr. Johnson's credentials as a plan provider?

4) Cindy Sparks has just changed jobs, and become insured with the Red Sword health plan. She is in her sixth month of pregnancy and is in treatment with Dr. Samuels. Dr. Samuels is not a network provider under Red Sword. Can she remain in treatment with Dr. Samuels throughout the delivery? if she changes obstetricians, and her new obstetrician is subsequently terminated from plan participation, can she remain with him through the delivery.

5) Sue Shank has just begun working for a new employer. Her employer offers her a choice of four different HMOs. She would like to learn as much as she can about each of them before she chooses among them. What information is she entitled to under the law? How would she get access to it?

B.   STATE LAW REGULATING MCO NETWORKS

Virtually all MCOs either limit their members to a particular network of providers or impose disincentives to discourage their members from "going out of network." The type of limitations on access to providers imposed by an MCO has historically been seen as a defining characteristic of some forms of MCO. The preferred provider organization (PPO), for example, has traditionally been defined as an organized system of health care providers who agree to provide services on a discounted (usually fee-for-service) basis to subscribers. PPO subscribers are not limited to plan providers, but face financial disincentives, such as deductibles or larger copayments, if they elect non-preferred providers. By contrast, health maintenance organizations (HMOs) usually limit their members to an exclusive network of providers, permitting their members to go to non-network providers only in extraordinary circumstances, like medical emergencies. Point-of-service plans (POSs) resemble HMOs but allow their members to obtain services outside the network at an additional cost, and often subject to gatekeeper controls. Finally, provider-sponsored-organizations (PSOs), also called, in their various guises, integrated delivery systems (IDSs), physician-hospital organizations (PHOs), and provider-sponsored networks (PSNs), are networks organized by providers that contract directly with employers or other purchasers of health benefits to provide their own services on a capitated basis.

Why might MCOs want to limit their members to particular providers? Of course, if the providers have agreed to deliver services to MCO members at a discount the answer is obvious, but more is at stake than this. MCOs are also interested in limiting participating professionals and providers to those who share their vision of cost and utilization control. They may also want to limit participating professionals and providers to those who offer high quality care, or at least to exclude providers who present clear quality problems. Finally, MCOs also often try to control through "gatekeeper" arrangements access to specialists for the problems that can be handled more cheaply by primary care physicians, in effect creating separate networks of primary care and specialist physicians.

The earliest response of the states to network limitations was to enact "free choice of provider" laws, which limit the ability of MCOs/insurers to build provider networks. Free choice laws prohibit MCOs from restricting their members to particular providers or, more often, limit the size of the cost-sharing obligations that MCOs can impose on their members who go out of plan. Twenty-two states currently have free-choice of provider laws, though most antedate the mid–90s, and the vast majority apply only to pharmacies.

Another regulatory response to networks has been "any willing provider" (AWP) laws, which require MCO/insurers to accept into their network any provider who is willing to accept the terms offered by the MCO. Although AWP laws continue to be proposed on a regular basis (25 states considered AWP legislation in 1999 and 11 in 2000), few have been adopted in recent years, and most of the laws on the books date from the mid–1990s or earlier. AWP legislation continues to receive strong support from provider groups, but strikes at the heart of managed care network contracting and is strongly opposed by managed care advocates. About 23 states have AWP statutes, though in most states these apply only to pharmacies. The laws of two states, Arkansas and Louisiana, have been rendered unenforceable by federal court judgments finding that they conflict with ERISA, as will be discussed in the next chapter.

Recent legislative efforts to limit the ability of MCOs to restrict access of their members to providers have been more modest in their reach. Some laws focus on network adequacy, requiring MCOs to maintain an acceptable ratio of providers to enrollees. Access to providers may be measured in terms of the time it takes members to get to providers or the distance of members from providers. Other states require MCOs to allow members to go out of network if network coverage is inadequate. Other states simply require plans to disclose their network selection criteria.

The most ambitious recent laws regulating networks require MCOs to offer point-of service-options, allowing members to go out of plan for care at their option with higher cost-sharing obligations. Nineteen states currently require insurers to offer a point-of-service option, usually with higher premiums and cost-sharing. Some of these laws, however, apply only to dental care.

Most legislation adopted recently focuses on narrower access issues, however. A number of states have adopted laws guaranteeing MCO members access to particular specialists, such as gynecologists or pediatricians. Thirty-seven states currently require MCOs to allow women direct access to obstetrical and gynecological providers, and 19 require plans to permit women to use OB/GYNs as their primary care physician. Many states also require plans to allow specialists to serve as primary care providers, especially when a patient with a chronic condition is under the regular care of a specialist. A number of states also require MCOs to offer "standing referrals" of persons with chronic conditions to specialists in lieu of requiring continual rereferrals from primary care physicians. Some states have also adopted laws requiring inclusion of alternative providers, such as acupuncturists.

Also common are "continuity of care" requirements, which assure plan members continuing access to a particular health care provider for a period of time after the plan terminates the provider. Some continuity of care statutes also permit new members to continue to see their previous, non-network, provider for a period of time if the patient has a serious condition or is pregnant. Thirty states now have continuity of care provisions, with transitional care periods lasting from 30 to 120 days.

Finally, a number of states have adopted "due process" requirements, limiting the ability of MCOs to terminate providers from their networks or to deny providers access to their networks without permitting some form of appeal. Other statutes go further, prohibiting "without cause" terminations. Plan terminations of providers are discussed in chapter 12 below.

Which of these provisions is found in the Massachusetts statute? Whom do these provisions primarily benefit? What explains the fact that some forms of legislation have lost and others have gained popularity over time? What effect do these provisions have on the cost of coverage? To the extent that they increase costs, what effect will this have on access?

C. UTILIZATION CONTROLS

Utilization review (UR) was historically the central means through which MCOs managed costs, and continues to be the approach that most irritates consumers and providers. UR refers to external case-by-case evaluation conducted by insurers, purchasers, or UR contractors to determine the necessity and appropriateness (and sometimes the quality) of medical care. It is a strategy that attempts to control costs by limiting demand. It is based fundamentally on the knowledge that there are wide variations in the use of many medical services, and the belief that considered review of medical care by payers can eliminate wasteful and unnecessary care.

UR can take several forms. The oldest form is retrospective review, under which an insurer denies payment for care already provided, normally by judging it to be medically unnecessary, experimental, or cosmetic. Retrospective review is of limited value for containing costs—since the cost of the care has already been incurred by the time the review takes place—and can lead to costly disputes between the insurer resisting payment and the provider or patient who has already incurred the cost of the care. Compare Sarchett v. Blue Shield of California, 43 Cal.3d 1, 233 Cal.Rptr. 76, 729 P.2d 267 (1987); Van Vactor v. Blue Cross Association, 50 Ill.App.3d 709, 8 Ill.Dec. 400, 365 N.E.2d 638 (1977).

In recent years, UR programs have stressed prior or concurrent review and high-cost case management. Prior and concurrent review techniques include preadmission review (before elective hospital admissions); admission review (within 24 to 72 hours of emergency or urgent admissions); continued stay review (to assess length of stay and sometimes accompanied by discharge planning); preprocedure or preservice review (to review specific proposed procedures) and voluntary or mandatory second-opinions. High-cost case management addresses the small number (1–7 percent) of very expensive cases that account for most benefit plan costs. Case managers create individualized treatment plans for high-cost beneficiaries. Compliance with the plan is usually voluntary, but may be rewarded by the plan paying for services not otherwise covered by the insurer (such as home health or nursing home care), but less costly than covered alternatives.

Traditional UR can be conducted by free-standing UR contractors, by payers (employers and insurers, with or without direct contracts with providers) or by providers. Review is usually initiated by plan beneficiaries or by physicians or hospitals who are aware that admissions or procedures must be preapproved to secure payment. Requests for approval are usually first reviewed by nurses or medical records reviewers, applying established criteria (often though computers) to determine appropriateness. Initial reviewers may approve care, but if the care does not comply with applicable criteria, the case must usually be referred to a physician adviser for denial. Physician advisers will often contact the attending physician and negotiate an appropriate care plan, though some plans deny payment without direct contact with the attending physician. Plans usually have formal or informal appeals processes or provide other opportunities for further discussion of proposed denials.

UR seems to reduce inpatient hospital use and costs. One of the best studies found that it reduced hospital admissions by 12.3 percent, inpatient days by 8 percent, and hospital expenditures by 11.9 percent. In particular, it reduced patient days by 34 percent and hospital expenditures by 30 percent for groups that had previously had high admission rates. Paul Feldstein, et al., Private Cost Containment, 318 New Eng.J.Med. 1310 (1988). It is less clear that UR reduces total health care costs, however, since it often moves care from inpatient to outpatient settings, increasing outpatient costs as it reduces inpatient costs. (the Feldstein study found that it reduced total medical expenditures by 8.3 percent). Moreover, UR is most effective in the short run and has less effect on long-term cost increases. See, on UR generally, Institute of Medicine, Controlling Costs and Changing Patient Care?: The Role of Utilization Management (1989).

At the margins, utilization control blends into other care management strategies. Some MCOs have, for example, retreated from individual case review, instead keeping track of the practice patterns of particular physicians and using the information to decide which physicians to decertify from plan participation. Primary care gatekeeper systems, on the other hand, delegate UR decisions to primary care physicians, but motivate them to control utilization through the use of incentives.

UR decisions are basically coverage determinations—under UR payment is denied for experimental and medically unnecessary care because such care is not covered under the plan contract. This was the argument made by the plan in Lubeznik above. UR decisions are also, however, medical treatment determinations, because in most instances they determine whether or not the insured will receive medical treatment. UR determinations can thus raise scope of practice issues. Is the utilization review entity or its employees engaged in the unauthorized practice of medicine when it makes coverage decisions? Is a nurse reviewer outside of her scope of practice if she challenges the diagnosis and treatment plan of an attending physician? Is a physician reviewer retained by a utilization review entity engaged in unauthorized practice of medicine if she reviews a case in a state in which she is not licensed? Might the acts of a utilization review entity violate a state's corporate practice of medicine statute or doctrine? Compare Murphy v. Board of Medical Examiners, 190 Ariz. 441, 949 P.2d 530 (Ariz.Ct.App.1997) (utilization review physician practicing medicine); with Morris v. District of Columbia Board of Medicine, 701 A.2d 364 (D.C.1997) (Blue Cross medical director not practicing medicine in particular UR situation). Twenty-six states have adopted statutes requiring HMO medical directors to be licensed physicians, while 20 of these require medical directors to be licensed in the state where they work. See also, E. Haavi Morreim, Playing Doctor: Corporate Medical Practice and Medical Malpractice, 32 U. Mich. J. L. Ref. 939 (1999); J. Scott Andresen, is Utilization Review the Practice of Medicine: Implications for Managed Care Administrators, 19 J. Legal Med. 431 (1998); John Blum, An Analysis of Legal Liability in Health Care Utilization Review and Case Management, 26 Hous.L.Rev. 191 (1989).

One approach to control of utilization is simply to rewrite contracts with greater specificity to clarify that certain services are not covered, regardless of their necessity. An insurance contract that excludes organ transplants elides the question of whether a particular organ transplant is necessary (though it may raise the question of whether a particular procedure is an organ transplant). While this approach to contract formation may avoid some forms of legislative controls, it also stimulates others, as will be discussed below.

UR has, as was noted above, become perhaps the most unpopular approach to managing care. While plans in fact rarely deny coverage, coverage denial can have disastrous consequences. Also, the hassle involved in fulfilling UR requirements (the interminably busy fax, the voicemail messages that are never returned, the endless arguing with reviewers) undoubtedly deters physicians from offering or ordering services that would otherwise been given. Enough reports of horrendous cases have been picked by the media to make utilization review a major concern of the public, and of legislators.

A variety of regulatory strategies have been adopted for addressing utilization review issues. First, many states have adopted statutes addressing the utilization review process itself. These statutes, for example, impose time limits on UR decisions, in particular requiring expedited decisions for urgent or emergency cases. Statutes oblige MCOs to involve health care professionals in establishing criteria, and some require disclosure of UR criteria, at least to the regulatory authority. Some state statutes also require MCOs to state in writing the basis for UR denial decisions.

Every state has now adopted a law requiring MCOs to offer their members internal consumer grievance and appeal procedures. These statutes often establish time frames for the appeals (again requiring expedited hearings for emergencies), specify who must decide the appeal (specifying, for example, the professional credentials of the decision maker, or requiring a decision maker not involved in the initial decision), and provide the format for the final decision (in writing, giving reasons, etc.). Statutes often require the MCO to give assistance to its members in filing appeals.

As of 2000, 38 states also require external or independent reviews. The statutes generally specify the issues subject to review, usually an adverse determination. Review statutes generally specify who may make the decision, usually an independent reviewer appointed or approved by the regulatory authority. Statutes again commonly provide time limits for proceedings. Twenty-eight states provide that the external review decision is binding on the MCO, the remainder either specify that it is non-binding or do not address the issue. See, on the resolution of grievances, appeals, and other disputes in managed care, Symposium, Conflict Resolution and Managed Health Care: The Challenge of Achieving Both Equity and Efficiency, National Institute for Dispute Resolution Forum (1997); Karen Pollitz, et al., External Review of Health Plan Decisions: An Overview of Key Program Features in the States and Medicare (1998); Eleanor D. Kinney, Procedural Protections for Patients in Capitated Health Plans, 22 Am.J.L. & Med. 301 (1996); Tracy E. Miller, Center Stage on the Patient Protection Agenda: Grievance and Appeal Rights, 26 J. L.Med. & Ethics 89 (1998).

A key issue in UR decisions is the definition of medical necessity. At least 23 states have adopted statutory definitions of medical necessity, though in some states the definition applies only to particular insurers (Medicaid, HMOs) or particular areas of care (mental health, long term care, inpatient care). Definitions vary significantly in length and specificity, though most define medical necessity in language like "necessary and appropriate for the diagnosis or treatment of an illness or injury in accord with generally accepted standards of medical practice." A number of these statutes also require some level of deference to the decision of the treating physician on medical necessity issues.

With respect to some forms of care, state statutes have simply preempted coverage decisions by imposing mandates. Providers and consumer groups have for decades lobbied successfully for state insurance "mandates" that require insurance companies to provide certain benefits (mammography, mental health and substance abuse treatment); cover the services of certain providers (chiropractors, podiatrists); or cover certain insureds or dependents (newborn infants, laid-off employees). In recent years, however, state statutes mandating particular benefits, have often also been in essence laws limiting the reach of utilization controls.

The most common examples of this are emergency care mandates, which, as of 2000, had been adopted by all but three states. These statutes commonly adopt a "prudent layperson" standard for defining "emergency." (These statutes provide that an emergency exists when a prudent layperson would expect that the absence of medical care could result in serious health consequences), require coverage without prior authorization until the patient is stabilized, and permit emergency care at the most accessible facility, regardless of its network status.

Other statutes, however, address length of stay issues, requiring at least 48 hours of hospitalization coverage for vaginal or 72 hours for Cesarean deliveries (the famous "drive through delivery" statutes of the mid–1990s) or hospitalization coverage for mastectomies. Still other statutes prohibit plans from denying access to particular benefits, such as off-formulary drugs (37 states, usually specifically for cancer or life-threatening diseases) or access to clinical trials (9 states).

While some of these mandates address typical UR limitations (non-coverage of "experimental" treatment or non-formulary drugs, for example), other mandates look much more like traditional insurance benefit mandates. Popular benefit mandates in recent years include requirements of coverage for mental health care, cancer screenings, contraceptives, infertility treatment, osteoporosis prevention, newborn hearing treatments, and reconstructive surgery following mastectomy.

Statutes that banned "gag" clauses (i.e. contract provisions that prohibit physicians from communicating with MCO plan members about particular issues), or that forbade more specifically MCO contract clauses prohibiting providers from discussing noncovered treatment options, making disparaging comments about an MCO, or disclosing confidential information about a plan's financial or UR arrangements with patients, were adopted by all but two of the states in the mid–1990s. Though a GAO analysis of 529 HMO contracts subsequently revealed that none of them in fact prohibited the discussion of treatment options, a number of the contracts prohibited disparagement or disclosure of business information. See GAO, Managed Care: Explicit Gag Clauses not Found in HMO Contracts, (But Physician Concerns Remain GAO/HEHS–97–175, 1997). These statutes do not directly limit UR requirements, but allow treating physicians to be open about the constraints these requirements impose.

A few states have adopted state-funded, independent consumer assistance programs for MCO recipients, while other states offer some sort of consumer advocacy or ombudsperson office within a regulatory authority. While the primary function of these offices is often to provide objective information, education, and counselling, they also can assist consumers in investigating and resolving complaints and help consumers to file and pursue appeals. Marc A. Rodwin has written several thoughtful articles exploring the strategy of strengthening consumer representation and advocacy in managed care. See Marc A. Rodwin, Promoting Accountable Managed Care: The Potential Role for Consumer Voice (2000); Marc A. Rodwin, The Neglected Remedy: Strengthening Consumer Voice in Managed Care, 34 The American Prospect 45 (1997); and Marc A. Rodwin, Consumer Protection and Managed Care, 22 Hous.L.Rev. 1319 (1996).

Finally, as of 2000, 7 states had adopted laws providing for liability suits against plans for failure to exercise ordinary care in the provision of medical care. To the extent that UR decisions are in fact decisions with respect to plan provision of medical care, they would seem to be covered by these liability statutes. Though the enforceability of these statutes against ERISA plans remains in doubt, such statutes will continue to be proposed and adopted by some states.

Which of the provisions in the Massachusetts statute above address UR issues? Which of these provisions is likely to gain the strongest support from plan members? Which is most likely in fact to be of use to them? Which provisions also benefit providers? Which providers benefit from these provisions? Which provisions would you most oppose most strongly if you represented a managed care trade association?

D. PROVIDER INCENTIVES

The third strategy that MCOs have used to manage care is financial incentives. The earliest form of MCO financial incentive was capitation. Under capitation the provider gets paid a fixed fee for providing care for the MCO beneficiary for a fixed period of time. If the services the beneficiary receives cost more than this payment, the provider loses money; if the services the beneficiary receives cost less, the provider makes money. In other words, the provider becomes the true insurer, i.e. risk bearer, with respect to the patient.

A provider (a primary care physician for example) may be capitated for his, her, or its own services, but can also be paid on a capitated basis for other services the patient may need, for example specialist services, laboratory tests, hospitalization, or even drugs. Some of these services, however, cost far more than primary care services, and putting a single primary care physician, or even physician group, at risk for these services might in many instances impose unreasonable risks.

Instead, MCOs usually put the primary care provider only partially at risk. This is done through the use of bonuses or withholds. A pool is established either from money withheld from payments made directly to the physician (a withhold) or from funds provided in addition to regular payments (a bonus). Specified expenses—for specialists or hospitalization, for example—are paid out of this pool. Any money left over at the end of an accounting period (a year for example), is paid over to the physician. In addition, the physician may or may not be fully capitated for his or her own services.

While incentives are an effective way to hold down costs, they can also result in underservice if the responses they elicit from providers become unreasonable. It is more difficult to regulate incentives, however, than it is to regulate network or utilization controls because it is more difficult to identify discrete unacceptable practices or to create procedures that address these practices.

Thirty states in fact currently have statutes purporting to ban the use of financial incentives, usually prohibiting incentives that "deny, reduce, limit or delay medically necessary care." The statutes, however, usually go on to say that they are not intended to prohibit MCOs from using capitation payments or other risk-sharing arrangements. As MCOs would generally insist that their incentives are intended to deter unnecessary, rather than necessary care, these statutes have little effect on MCO incentive programs.

More useful are statutes or regulations intended to limit excessive incentives, restricting, for example, the proportion of a provider's income that can be put at risk or the size of the pool of patients or providers over which the risk is spread, or requiring stop-loss insurance. Another possibility is to limit incentives with respect to certain services, such as preventive services.

A rather different approach is simply to require disclosure of financial incentives. Disclosure—by health plans, providers, or both—has long been an approach favored by market oriented reformers. Why not simply require health plans to let their members know how their incentive plan is structured? Insureds can go elsewhere if they don't like the incentives the plan offers.

Not surprisingly, there are problems with this approach as well. First, the vast majority of insured Americans receive their health coverage through their place of employment, and half of all employees are offered a choice of only one (35%) or two (15%) plans. Even employees offered a choice of two or more plans, of course, may not have much of a choice among incentive plan structures. Second, it is not at all clear how most plan members would use information about incentive plans structures, i.e. whether their understanding of health care finance and delivery is sophisticated enough to evaluate incentive structures. Finally, requiring disclosure imposes costs both on regulators, who need to devise a meaningful form of disclosure and police compliance, and on MCOs, which need to compile and disseminate the information.

Even if requiring plan disclosure to allow consumer choice is problematic, there may be other reasons for requiring disclosure. In a recent thoughtful article, William Sage identifies three other reasons for why we might want to require MCOs and providers to disclose information. First, disclosure increases the likelihood that providers and MCOs will act as honest agents for their patients and members, while it facilitates the ability of patients and members to monitor fiduciary loyalty. Second, requiring collection and disclosure of particular kinds of performance-related information might serve to incentivize performance in certain directions deemed to be socially important. Requiring disclosure of immunization rates, for example, may promote immunization programs. Finally, disclosure of more information might facilitate public deliberation and provider and MCO accountability. William M. Sage, Regulating Through Information: Disclosure Laws and American Health Care, 99 Columb. L. Rev. 1701 (1999). See also Tracy E. Miller & William M. Sage, Disclosing Physician Financial Incentives, 281 JAMA 1424 (1999).

Which of the requirements in the Massachusetts statute address plan incentive structures? How enforceable will these limitations be? How useful will they be to plan members.

E. QUALITY REGULATION

The final issue addressed by state managed care statutes is the quality of care provided by MCOs. One of the aspirations of managed care has always been to manage care to improve quality. The term "health maintenance organization" evidences a commitment to maintaining health, not simply to providing medical services, and MCO marketing materials often talk about coordination or integration of care.

In a sense, most of the statutes discussed so far at least touch on quality issues. Assuring better access to care and accuracy in plan or provider decision making, for example, presumably improves the care received by the plan member. Quality of care is addressed more directly, however, by statutes or regulations requiring MCOs to have quality assurance or improvement programs or to take quality of care into consideration in provider credentialing. Other statutes require or encourage MCOs to seek accreditation, in the hope that accreditation agencies will provide quality oversight. Finally, a number of statutes require disclosure of quality-related information through the use of report cards or other forms of disclosure. See Barry R. Furrow, Regulating the Managed Care Revolution: Private Accreditation and a new System Ethos, 43 Vill. L. Rev. 361 (1998).

VI. PERSPECTIVES ON MANAGED CARE REGULATION

The topic of managed care regulation has unleashed an avalanche of academic commentary, sharply divided along lines that have come to typify health policy debate. On the one hand are those who distrust the ability of health care markets to protect consumer's interests absent government intervention and, on the other, those who trust markets and have little faith in government. An article by George Annas, a long-time champion of patient's rights, for example, exemplifies the position of those who favor protective legislation:

> The key to understanding patients' rights in managed care is to understand managed care's attempt to transform the patient into a consumer. Persons can be considered consumers of health plans if they can choose a plan on the basis of cost, coverage, and quality. But the choice of a health plan is usually made by employers, and even when it is not, the choice is necessarily much more often based on cost than on coverage or quality. Nor is being a consumer of a health plan the same as being a consumer of health care. In virtually all settings, patients (not consumers) seek the help of physicians when they are sick and vulnerable because of illness or disability. * * * Sick people, who are in no position to bargain and who know little about medicine, must be able to trust their physicians to be on their side in dealing with pain, suffering, disease, or disability.

> Attempts to transform the physician-patient relationship into a business transaction fundamentally threaten not just physicians as professionals but people as patients. This threat is real, frightening, and intolerable, which is why the new patients' rights movement aims not simply to preserve the physician-patient relationship in general but also to eliminate the financial conflicts of interest in managed care that are most threatening to the relationship. Thus, the new patients' rights movement seeks to shift power * * * from managed-care companies, insurance companies, and health care facilities to patients and their physicians.

George J. Annas, A National Bill of Patients' Rights, 338 New Eng. J. Med. 695, 696 (1998). See also, contending that a consumer model does not adequately protect patient's rights, Wendy K. Mariner, Standards of Care and Standard Form Contracts: Distinguishing Patient Rights and Consumer Rights, 15 J. Contemp. Health L. & Pol'y 1 (1998).

Holding down the other end of the spectrum, David Hyman has written a series of articles trashing the Patient Bill of Rights movement:

David Hyman, Regulating Managed Care: What's Wrong with a Patient Bill of Rights, 73 S. Cal. L. Rev. 221 (2000).

Set aside for just a moment what everyone "knows" about the perils of managed care and the need for a patient bill of rights. Set aside as well the inconvenient fact that customer surveys show a high degree of satisfaction among managed care participants, and extensive research indicates that the quality of care is as good (or better) in managed care plans than in fee-for-service health care. Instead, consider the case for regulation from an empirical perspective. If the absence of regulation is a bad thing, one would expect the frequency of complaints and avoidable bad outcomes to be higher (and the quality of care that is rendered to be lower) in managed care plans that are subject to fewer regulations. [Because of ERISA (see next chapter)], some forms of health insurance are heavily regulated, others are subject to only modest regulation, and others effectively fall into a regulatory "free-fire" zone. If there is any evidence suggesting that complaints and avoidable bad outcomes are less frequent in plans which are more aggressively regulated, I am unaware of it. Similarly, if there is any evidence suggesting that the quality of care is better in plans which are aggressively regulated, I am unaware of it. One would have thought such evidence would be readily available (and widely trumpeted by advocates of consumer protection) if the problems with managed care are as severe as the anecdotes suggest. In the absence of empirical evidence regarding such matters, the case for a patient bill of rights is based on fear (of markets) and faith (in anecdote-driven regulation), but not on fact.

Despite its popular appeal, a patient bill of rights is a deeply flawed strategy for addressing the inadequacies of managed care. The kinds of rights which are likely to result from the legislative process (and have emerged to date) are likely to make things worse, rather than better, whether one considers cost, quality, or access. The backlash against managed care may have been sold to the public as a response to concerns about quality, but the legislation that has emerged has more to do with "provider lobbying, gut instincts, negative anecdotes, and popular appeal" than with quality. Indeed, the unfortunate reality is that quality has long been used as a stalking horse by providers wishing to disguise less public spirited objectives * * *—a point [made by] Robert Pitofsky, the chairman of the Federal Trade Commission,* * *:

> "[Q]uality-of-care" arguments ... can be invoked as a justification for even the most egregious anticompetitive conduct. They have been advanced to support, among other things, broad restraints on almost any form of price competition, policies that inhibited the development of managed care organizations, and concerted refusals to deal with providers or organizations that represented a competitive threat to physicians.

Worse still, to the extent the patient bill of rights strategy is based on the sanctity of physician discretion, it makes it much more difficult to address the real quality-based problems with American medicine, which, in fact, are attributable to the unconstrained discretion previously accorded physicians. Legislators have ignored this basic point; the patient bills of rights that have been offered demonstrate a distinct preference for safeguarding physician decisionmaking from MCO interference. However, if physicians are such good agents for patients with regard to medical spending decisions, why is there such significant geographic variation in the delivery of health care services? Why did hospital lengths-of-stay decline so precipitously after Medicare abandoned cost-based per-diem reimbursement, and moved to prospective payment based on discharge diagnosis? * * * Why did the Institute of Medicine recommend a systems-based approach to improving health care quality?

Of course, we should not indulge in the nirvana fallacy in assessing the merits of a patient bill of rights, but neither should we deploy regulations merely because managed care delivers something short of perfection. The government brings a great deal to the table, but so do private parties. Regulatory enthusiasts are prone to forget that in a world of imperfect alternatives, it is unhelpful to catalog the weaknesses of an existing market, and disregard the deficiencies of the proffered solution.

* * *

It is understandable that managed care horror stories trigger outrage and a demand for additional regulations. However, any given rule or standard for making coverage and treatment decisions will necessarily have imperfections. So long as we have created the appropriate institutional arrangements—and there certainly remains much to do with regard to that goal—leaving well enough alone with regard to the specifics of the resulting coverage is likely to be sufficient unto the day. Such a strategy lacks the moral certainty of stringing up a few managed care desperados in black hats, but it will do more to improve the status quo than any ten patient bills of rights.

* * *

See also, David A. Hyman, Drive–Through Deliveries: Is "Consumer Protection" Just What the Doctor Ordered? 85 N.C. L. Rev. 5 (1999); David A. Hyman, Assessing the Policies We Have: Scenes From a Maul, 24 J. Health Pol., Pol'y and L. 1061 (1999); David A. Hyman, Accountable Managed Care: Should we be Careful What we Wish For, 32 U. Mich. J. L. Ref. 785 (1999); and David A. Hyman, Consumer Protection in a Managed Care World: Should Consumers Call 911, 43 Vill. L. Rev. 409 (1998).

Taking a middle course, some authors accept the assumptions of the primacy of markets, but contend that market failures necessitate some forms of regulation. Russell Korobkin, for example—relying on mathematical game theory and empirical evidence that consumers have cognitive limitations that render their decisions only "boundedly rational"—argues that government regulation of managed care, even including coverage mandates, might be justifiable in some instances. Russell Korobkin, The Efficiency of Managed Care "Patient Protection" Laws: Incomplete Contracts, Bounded Rationality, and Market Failures, 85 Cornell L. Rev. 1 (1999). Marc Rodwin argues for reforms to empower consumers in their dealings with MCOs, through supporting consumer advocacy and requiring external review. See Marc A. Rodwin, Backlash as Prelude to Managing Managed Care, 24 J. Health Pol., Pol'y & L. 1115 (1999).

Finally, a number of authors have noted that the political obsession with the abuses of managed care is distracting us from a much more significant problem, the problem of those Americans who are excluded from managed care—and from all other form of health insurance—our 43 million uninsured. See, David M. Frankford, Regulating Managed Care: Pulling Tails to Wag the Dog, 24 J. Health Pol, Pol'y & L. 1191 (1999); Deborah Stone, Managed Care and the Second Great Transformation, 24 J. Health Pol, Pol'y & L. 1213 (1999). Surely their access problems are much more persistent than are the problems of those who struggle with the irrationalities of MCOs.

Chapter 9

REGULATION OF INSURANCE AND MANAGED CARE: THE FEDERAL ROLE

I. INTRODUCTION

Though regulation of health insurance has traditionally been the responsibility of the states, the federal government has taken in recent years an increasingly significant role. The most important federal law affecting health insurance is the Employee Retirement Income Security Act of 1974, ERISA, which has already been alluded to several times in previous chapters. ERISA's primary role in recent years has been deregulatory, as its preemptive provisions have repeatedly blocked state common law actions against health plans as well as state attempts at plan regulation. ERISA also provides its beneficiaries, however, with a positive right to sue to recover denied benefits, while also imposing fiduciary obligations on plan fiduciaries. ERISA regulations promulgated in the last days of the Clinton administration also afford procedural rights to plan beneficiaries.

ERISA is not the only federal statute to affect health plans, moreover. The Americans with Disabilities Act places at least minimal constraints on the ability of employers and insurers to discriminate against the disabled in the provision of health insurance. The Health Insurance Portability and Accountability Act of 1996 (which amended ERISA, as well as other federal statutes), limits the use of preexisting condition clauses while prohibiting intragroup discrimination in coverage and rates. It also offers certain protections in the small group and individual insurance markets. Earlier, the Consolidated Omnibus Budget Reconciliation Act of 1985 provided continuation coverage under certain circumstances. All of these federal initiatives will be considered in this chapter.

II. THE EMPLOYEE RETIREMENT INCOME SECURITY ACT OF 1974 (ERISA)

A. ERISA PREEMPTION OF STATE HEALTH INSURANCE REGULATION

As noted above, ERISA expressly preempts state both regulatory statutes and common law claims that "relate to" employee benefit plans, while at the

601

same time providing for exclusive federal court jurisdiction over cases that could be brought as ERISA claims. The primary ERISA preemption statute (29 U.S.C.A. § 1144), however, explicitly saves from preemption state regulation of insurance, though also prohibiting state regulation of self-insured plans. The task of sorting out ERISA's complex preemption scheme has resulted in a tremendous volume of litigation, including, to date, eighteen Supreme Court decisions.

This subsection discusses ERISA preemption of state regulation, while the next considers preemption of common law claims.

CORPORATE HEALTH INSURANCE, INC. v. TEXAS DEPARTMENT OF INSURANCE

United States Court of Appeals, Fifth Circuit, 2000.
215 F.3d 526.

PATRICK E. HIGGINBOTHAM, CIRCUIT JUDGE:

* * *

This suit is a preemption challenge to Texas's Senate Bill 386. Through that legislation, Texas asserted its police power to protect its citizens in regulating the new field of managed health care in three ways. First, it created a statutory cause of action against managed care entities that fail to meet an ordinary care standard for health care treatment decisions (the "liability" provisions). Second, it established procedures for the independent review of health care determinations to decide whether they were appropriate and medically necessary (the "independent review" provisions). Finally, it protected physicians from HMO-imposed indemnity clauses and from retaliation by HMOs for advocating medically necessary care for their patients.

* * *

Senate Bill 386 became effective on May 22, 1997. Aetna promptly filed suit in the United States District Court, claiming that the Act was preempted by ERISA's general preemption clause, section 514, which preempts "any and all state laws insofar as they ... relate to any employee benefit plan" and by the Federal Employees Health Benefit Act ("FEHBA"). * * *

The parties filed cross-motions for summary judgment, which the district court granted in part and denied in part. The district court found no FEHBA or ERISA preemption of the liability provisions of Senate Bill 386 but found that ERISA preempted the anti-retaliation, anti-indemnification, and independent review provisions of the legislation. Both Aetna and Texas appeal.

* * *

We have repeatedly struggled with the open-ended character of the preemption provisions of ERISA and FEHBA. We faithfully followed the Supreme Court's broad reading of "relate to" preemption under § 502(a) in its opinions decided during the first twenty years after ERISA's enactment. Since then, in a trilogy of cases, the Court has confronted the reality that if "relate to" is taken to the furthest stretch of its indeterminacy, preemption will never run its course, for "really, universally, relations stop nowhere."[1] Justice Souter, speaking for a unanimous court in Travelers, acknowledged that "our prior attempt to construe the phrase 'relate to' does not give us much help drawing the line here." Rather, the Court determined that it "must go beyond the unhelpful text . . . and look instead to the objectives of the ERISA statute as a guide to the scope of the state law that Congress understood would survive."

In Travelers, a New York statute required hospitals to collect surcharges from patients insured by a commercial carrier but not from certain HMOs. The plain purpose of the surcharge was to encourage the HMOs to provide open enrollment coverage. The Second Circuit found that the surcharges "related to" ERISA plans because they imposed economic burdens with an impermissible impact on plan administration and structure. In rejecting the Second Circuit's approach, and in shifting its own approach, the Court observed that such indirect economic influences "d[id] not bind plan administrators to any particular choice," but rather affected the costs of benefits and the "relative costs of competing insurance to provide them." The Court grounded the "relate to" clause in the complex realities of the market for medical services.

[The court proceeded to discuss De Buono and Dillingham, in which the Supreme Court had also narrowed § 514 preemption, ed.]

In each of these three cases, the Court was returning to a traditional analysis of preemption, asking if a state regulation frustrated the federal interest in uniformity. * * * And significantly for our case, this return has included the observation that a broader reading of "relates to" would sweep away common state action with indirect economic effects on the costs of health care plans, such as quality standards which may vary from state to state.

This brings us to the merits of the claim that Senate Bill 386 is preempted. We turn first to its liability provisions. In Section 88.002, the bill provides:

> A health insurance carrier, health maintenance organization, or other managed care entity for a health care plan has the duty to exercise ordinary care when making health care treatment decisions and is liable for damages for harm to an insured or enrollee proximately caused by its failure to exercise such ordinary care.

The statute gives "health care treatment decision" a defined meaning:

> [A] determination made when medical services are actually provided by the health care plan and a decision which affects the quality of the diagnosis, care, or treatment provided to the plan's insureds or enrollees.

The Act also defines the agents for whose health care decisions the entities can be vicariously liable. Further, the Act includes a disclaimer: it

---

1. De Buono v. NYSA–ILA Med. & Clinical Serv's Fund, 520 U.S. 806, 117 S.Ct. 1747, 138 L.Ed.2d 21 (1997); California Div. of Labor Standards Enforcement v. Dillingham Constr., N.A., Inc., 519 U.S. 316, 117 S.Ct. 832, 136 L.Ed.2d 791 (1997); New York State Conference of Blue Cross & Blue Shield Plans v. Travelers Ins. Co., 514 U.S. 645, 115 S.Ct. 1671, 131 L.Ed.2d 695 (1995).

avoids imposing any obligation on the entity "to provide to an insured or enrollee treatment which is not covered by the health care plan of the entity."

Aetna argues that the liability provisions "relate to" an ERISA plan and affect plan administration. Aetna contends that a claim that medical services were negligently provided will inevitably question the provider's determinations of coverage under an ERISA plan. Texas replies that Senate Bill 356 has avoided the difficult genre of cases complaining of medical care and services which were not provided by excluding a duty to provide treatment not covered by a plan.

We agree with Texas's interpretation of the Act. When the liability provisions are read together, they impose liability for a limited universe of events. The provisions do not encompass claims based on a managed care entity's denial of coverage for a medical service recommended by the treating physician: that dispute is one over coverage, specifically excluded by the Act. Rather, the Act would allow suit for claims that a treating physician was negligent in delivering medical services, and it imposes vicarious liability on managed care entities for that negligence.

This vicarious liability does not "relate to" the managed care provider's role as an ERISA plan administrator or affect the structure of the plans themselves so as to require preemption. Courts have observed that HMOs and MCOs typically perform two independent functions—health care insurer and medical care provider. A managed care entity can provide administrative support for an insurance plan, which may entail determining eligibility or coverage. At the same time, a managed care entity can act as an arranger and provider of medical treatment.

Although state efforts to regulate an entity in its capacity as plan administrator are preempted, managed care providers operate in a traditional sphere of state regulation when they wear their hats as medical care providers. ERISA preempts malpractice suits against doctors making coverage decisions in the administration of a plan, but it does not insulate physicians from accountability to their state licensing agency or association charged to enforce professional standards regarding medical decisions. Such accountability is necessary to ensure that plans operate within the broad compass of sound medicine. We are not persuaded that Congress intended for ERISA to supplant this state regulation of the quality of medical practice. * * *

We also are not persuaded that the liability provisions are preempted as "referring to" ERISA plans. Under this strain of preemption analysis, we examine whether the law acts immediately and exclusively upon ERISA plans or whether the existence of an ERISA plan is essential to the law's operation. A law does not "refer to" ERISA plans if it applies neutrally to ERISA plans and other types of plans. * * * The provisions are indifferent to whether the health care plan operates under ERISA and do not rely on the existence of ERISA plans for their operation.

We see nothing to take the liability provisions from the regulatory reach of states exercising their traditional police powers in regulating the quality of health care. A suit for medical malpractice against a doctor is not preempted by ERISA simply because those services were arranged by an HMO and paid for by an ERISA plan. Likewise, the vicarious liability of the entities for whom the doctor acted as an agent is rooted in general principles of state agency law. Seen in this light, the Act simply codifies Texas's already-existing standards regarding medical care. These standards of care are at the heart of Texas's regulatory power.

We turn to the anti-retaliation and anti-indemnification provisions under sections 88.002(f) and (g) of the Act. The anti-retaliation provision forbids a managed care entity from dropping or refusing to renew a doctor or health care provider for advocating medically necessary treatment. The anti-indemnification provision prohibits a managed care entity from including an indemnification clause in its contracts with doctors and other health care providers that would hold it harmless for its own acts. Aetna contends that these provisions improperly mandate the structure and administration of ERISA plan benefits because ERISA plans are forced to contract with doctors only on those terms.

We are not persuaded that these provisions mandate the structure and administration of plans. * * * The anti-indemnity and anti-retaliation rules govern the managed care entities as health care providers by regulating the terms on which the provider contracts with its agents. The rules do not compel the entities to provide any substantive level of coverage as health care insurers.

* * *

The anti-retaliation and anti-indemnity provisions complement the Act's liability provisions by realigning the interests of managed care entities and their doctors. The liability and indemnity provisions force the managed care entity to share in its doctors' risk of tort liability; the anti-retaliation provision avoids the situation in which the doctor must choose between satisfying his professional responsibilities and facing retaliatory action by the managed care entity. Together, the provisions thus better preserve the physician's independent judgment in the face of the managed care entity's incentives for cost containment. Such a scheme is again the kind of quality of care regulation that has been left to the states.[2]

We come to the statute's provisions for independent review of determinations by managed care entities. * * *

* * *

* * * The Act adds procedures through which patients may appeal "adverse determinations"—

[A] determination by [an HMO] or utilization review agent that the health care services furnished or proposed to be furnished to an enrollee are not medically necessary or are not appropriate.

The Act further requires that a utilization review agent "comply" with the independent review organization's determination of medical necessity.

It is apparent that "adverse determinations" include determinations by managed care entities as to coverage, not just negligent decisions by a

---

2. The Supreme Court's most recent discussion of ERISA confirms this analysis. In Pegram v. Herdrich, the Court held that ERISA confers no cause of action against HMOs for providing incentives to their doctors for limiting the costs of testing and treatment. Part of the Court's reasoning was that states are currently allowed to impose malpractice liability on HMOs for such action. 530 U.S. 211, 120 S.Ct. 2143, 147 L.Ed.2d 164 (2000).

physician. The provisions allow a patient who has been denied coverage to appeal to an outside organization. Such an attempt to impose a state administrative regime governing coverage determinations is squarely within the ambit of ERISA's preemptive reach.

Texas and the federal government urge that the preempted independent review provisions are saved under ERISA's saving clause for laws regulating insurance. The Supreme Court has interpreted the clause as designed to preserve Congress's reservation of the business of insurance to the states under the McCarran–Ferguson Act. In determining whether the clause applies, the Supreme Court considers whether the rule regulates insurance as a common sense matter, looking as well to the three McCarran–Ferguson factors as "guideposts:" (1) whether the practice has the effect of transferring or spreading the policyholder's risk; (2) whether it is an integral part of the policy relationship between the insured and the insurer; and (3) whether the practice is limited to entities in the insurance industry. The law need not satisfy each of these tests.

The common sense test measures whether the law is specifically directed toward the insurance industry. A law is so aimed when the state has developed a specific scheme governing insurance, as opposed to a flexible rule used in many legal contexts. Here, the independent review provisions create a regulatory scheme governing health benefit determinations. They do not rely on general legal rights used in other areas of law.

That the provisions apply to managed care entities as well as to traditional insurers does not exclude them from the saving clause. In determining whether a statute regulates the insurance industry, courts have examined whether a statute governs only entities acting as insurers. A statute may regulate insurance if it applies to insurers, health care service contractors, and HMOs. If the law sweeps more broadly, however, covering employers and others not engaged in insurance practices, it cannot be said to be regulating insurance. * * * Our own cases are consistent with this distinction. Here, the preempted provisions apply to HMOs and to utilization review agents for insurers, administrators, and non-ERISA health benefit plans. In making benefit determinations, these entities are functioning as insurers.

The common sense test also considers whether the law plays an integral part in the policy relationship between the insured and the insurer. Laws that create a mandatory contract term between the parties, including procedural requirements, go to the core insured-insurer relationship. Here, the independent review provisions create a procedural right of the insured against the entity. As the independent review provisions are aimed at insuring entities and regulate the insured-insurer relationship, they meet the common sense test of the saving clause.

For the same reasons, the provisions satisfy the second and third prongs of the McCarran–Ferguson test: they are integral to the policy relationship and regulate the insurance industry. While the provisions probably do not meet the first factor of reallocating the risk between the insured and insurer, that failure is not fatal to Texas's saving clause claim.

Our analysis does not end here, however, because even if the provisions would otherwise be saved, they may nonetheless be preempted if they conflict with a substantive provision of ERISA. In Pilot Life v. Dedeaux, the Supreme

Court held that "our understanding of the saving clause must be informed by the legislative intent concerning [ERISA's] civil enforcement provisions." The Court interpreted Congress's intent regarding the exclusivity of ERISA's enforcement scheme very broadly, concluding that the scheme preempts not only directly conflicting remedial schemes, but also supplemental state law remedies. Thus, the saving clause does not operate if the state law at issue creates an alternative remedy for obtaining benefits under an ERISA plan.

Here, the independent review provisions do not create a cause of action for the denial of benefits. They do, however, establish a quasi-administrative procedure for the review of such denial and bind the ERISA plan to the decision of the independent review organization. This scheme creates an alternative mechanism through which plan members may seek benefits due them under the terms of the plan—the identical relief offered under § 1132(a)(1)(B) of ERISA. As such, the independent review provisions conflict with ERISA's exclusive remedy and cannot be saved by the saving clause.

* * *

AFFIRMED IN PART; REVERSED IN PART.

Notes and Questions

1. ERISA only governs employee benefit plans, i.e. benefit plans established and maintained by employers to provide benefits to their employees. It does not reach health insurance purchased by individuals as individuals (including self-employed individuals) or health benefits not provided through employment-related group plans, such as uninsured motorist insurance policies or workers' compensation. Certain church and government-sponsored plans are also not covered. Finally, ERISA does not regulate group insurance offered by insurers to the employees of particular businesses without employer contributions or administrative involvement. See 29 C.F.R. § 2510.3–1(j); Taggart Corp. v. Life & Health Benefits Admin., 617 F.2d 1208 (5th Cir.1980), cert. denied, 450 U.S. 1030, 101 S.Ct. 1739, 68 L.Ed.2d 225 (1981). Nevertheless, ERISA does govern the vast majority of private health insurance provided in America, which is provided through employment-related group plans.

2. Part of the confusion inherent in ERISA preemption decisions is attributable to the fact that there are three distinct forms of ERISA preemption. One of these is express or "ordinary" preemption based on § 514(a) (29 U.S.C. § 1144(a)). Section 514(a) provides that ERISA "supersedes" any state law that "relates to" an employee benefits plan.

Another form of preemption is based on § 502(a) of ERISA (29 U.S.C. § 1132(a)) which provides for federal court jurisdiction over specified types of claims against ERISA plans. The federal courts have, on the basis of § 502(a), permitted ERISA plans to remove into federal court claims that were brought in state courts but could have been brought under § 502(a) in federal court. Removal is permitted under the "complete preemption" exception to the well-pleaded complaint rule. The well-pleaded complaint rule normally permits removal only when federal claims are explicitly raised in the plaintiff's complaint. However, under the "complete preemption" exception to this rule (sometimes called "super-preemption") federal jurisdiction is permitted when Congress has so completely preempted an area of law that any claim within it is brought under federal law, and thus removable to federal court. "Complete preemption" is in reality not a preemption doctrine, but rather a rule of federal jurisdiction.

Third, Section 502(a) also plays another role in ERISA jurisprudence, ousting state claims and remedies that would take the place of § 502 claims. The federal courts have interpreted this section as indicating a Congressional intent to preempt comprehensively the "field" of judicial oversight of employee benefits plans. Thus state tort or contract, or even statutory, claims that could have been brought as claims for benefits or for breach of fiduciary duty under § 502(a) are preempted by § 502(a). Section 502(a) preemption, like § 514(a) explicit preemption, is not comprehensive. In particular, ERISA does not necessarily preempt state court malpractice cases brought against managed care plans that provide as well as pay for health care, as we will see in the next section. Also claims brought by persons who are not proper plaintiffs under § 502(a), or against persons who are not ERISA fiduciaries, may evade ERISA § 502(a) preemption.

Section 502(a) and § 514(a) preemption are not coextensive. Just because a lawsuit invokes a law that might be preempted as relating to an employee benefits claim does not mean that the claim could be brought under § 502(a), and is thus subject to "complete preemption." Not infrequently federal courts remand actions that could not have been brought as § 502(a) claims to state court for resolution of § 514(a) preemption issues. As we see in the principle case, moreover, laws that are saved from preemption by an exception to § 514(a), may still be preempted as inconsistent with § 502(a) field preemption.

3.   Early cases interpreting § 514(a) read it very broadly. The Supreme Court's first consideration of § 514(a), Shaw v. Delta Air Lines, 463 U.S. 85, 103 S.Ct. 2890, 77 L.Ed.2d 490 (1983), adopted a very literal and liberal reading of "relates to" as including any provisions having a "connection with or reference to" a benefits plan. The Court rejected narrower readings of ERISA preemption that would have limited its reach to state laws that explicitly attempted to regulate ERISA plans or that dealt with subjects explicitly addressed by ERISA. For over a decade following Shaw, the Court applied the § 514(a) tests developed in *Shaw* expansively in a variety of contexts, almost always finding preemption when it found an ERISA plan to exist. The Court repeatedly expressed allegiance to the opinion that ERISA § 514(a) preemption had a "broad scope" (Metropolitan Life v. Massachusetts, 471 U.S. 724 at 739, 105 S.Ct. 2380, 85 L.Ed.2d 728 (1985)), and "an expansive sweep" (Pilot Life v. Dedeaux, 481 U.S. 41, 47, 107 S.Ct. 1549, 95 L.Ed.2d 39 (1987)). and that it was "conspicuous for its breadth," (FMC v. Holliday, 498 U.S. 52, 58, 111 S.Ct. 403, 112 L.Ed.2d 356 (1990)).

Attending to Supreme Court pronouncements that § 514(a) preemption was to be applied broadly, lower courts in the 1980s and 1990s held to be preempted a wide range of state regulatory programs and common law claims that arguably "related to" the administration of an ERISA plan or imposed costs upon plans. Thus state laws were struck down regulating rates charged by hospitals or pharmacies General Motors Corp. v. Caldwell, 647 F.Supp. 585 (N.D.Ga.1986) (prescription rates); United Health Servs., Inc. v. Upstate Admin. Servs., Inc., 151 Misc.2d 783, 573 N.Y.S.2d 851 (N.Y.Sup.1991) (hospital rates); mandating health insurance coverage for employees (Standard Oil Co. v. Agsalud, 442 F.Supp. 695 (N.D.Cal.1977), affirmed 633 F.2d 760 (9th Cir.1980), affirmed mem. 454 U.S. 801, 102 S.Ct. 79, 70 L.Ed.2d 75 (1981) (striking down the Hawaii Prepaid Health Care Act, subsequently saved by an amendment to ERISA specifically protecting it, 29 U.S.C.A. § 1144(b)(5)); or prohibiting discrimination against persons with AIDS (Westhoven v. Lincoln Foodservice Products, Inc., 616 N.E.2d 778 (Ind.App.1993).

The Supreme Court finally recognized limits to ERISA preemption in New York State Conference of Blue Cross and Blue Shield Plans v. Travelers Ins. Co.,

514 U.S. 645, 115 S.Ct. 1671, 131 L.Ed.2d 695 (1995). *Travelers* held that a New York law that required hospitals to charge different rates to insured, HMO, and self-insured plans was not preempted by § 514(a). Reversing earlier expansive readings of ERISA preemption, the Court expressed allegiance to the principle applied in other areas of the law that Congress is generally presumed not to intend to preempt state law. 514 U.S. at 654. The Court proceeded to note that in cases involving traditional areas of state regulation, such as health care, Congressional intent to preempt state law should not to be presumed unless it was "clear and manifest." Id. at 655. Recognizing that the term "relate to" was not self-limiting, the Court turned for assistance in defining the term to the purpose of ERISA, which it determined to be freeing benefit plans from conflicting state and local regulation. Id. at 656–57. Preemption was intended, the Court held, to affect state laws that operated directly on the structure or administration of ERISA plans, Id. at 657–58, not on laws that only indirectly raised the cost of various benefit options, Id. at 658–64. Accordingly, the court held that the challenged rate setting law was not "related to" an ERISA plan, and thus not preempted.

The Court's post-*Travelers* preemption cases suggest that the Court in fact turned a corner in *Travelers*. It has rejected preemption in the majority of these cases, though it had almost never done so before *Travelers*. Post *Traveler*'s lower court cases have on the whole continued to apply ERISA preemption broadly, generally finding that state programs aimed at regulating insurance and managed care "relate to" ERISA plan, and are therefore preempted. In Prudential Insurance Company of America v. National Park Medical Center, 154 F.3d. 812 (8th Cir.1998), for example, the Eighth Circuit concluded that the Arkansas "Patient Protection Act" related to ERISA plans because it explicitly and implicitly made reference to them. The most recent cases, however, evidence a greater reluctance to find preemption, and a greater willingness to recognize the states' rights to regulate managed care, as the principal case illustrates.

4. As *Corporate Health* notes, state law that is otherwise preempted under § 514(a) is saved from preemption if it regulates insurance under § 514(b)(2)(A) (29 U.S.C.A. § 1144(b)(2)(A)). In its early cases interpreting this clause, the Court read it conservatively, applying both a "common sense" test as well as the three part test developed in antitrust cases applying the McCarran Ferguson Act for determining whether a law regulated "the business of insurance," (i.e. 1) whether the regulation affected the transferring and spreading of policy-holder risk, 2) whether it affected the relationship between the insurer and insured, and 3) whether it affected only entities within the insurance industry). Metropolitan Life Insurance Company v. Massachusetts, 471 U.S. 724, 740–44, 105 S.Ct. 2380, 85 L.Ed.2d 728 (1985). The Court applied this test two years later in Pilot Life Insurance Co. v. Dedeaux, 481 U.S. 41, 107 S.Ct. 1549, 95 L.Ed.2d 39 (1987), a case involving a Mississippi common law bad faith breach of contract claim, which held that the state law in that case was not saved from preemption because it was not specifically "directed at" the insurance industry and thus did not meet the McCarran Ferguson criteria. Pilot Life, 481 U.S. at 50–51.

In recent years, however, the Supreme Court has begun to back off the mechanical approach it set forth in *Metropolitan Life* and *Pilot Life* for determining the application of the savings clause. In UNUM Life Insurance Company of America v. Ward, 526 U.S. 358, 119 S.Ct. 1380, 143 L.Ed.2d 462 (1999), the Court specifically held that the three McCarran–Ferguson criteria were merely relevant criteria to a determination of whether the savings clause should be applied, and not conclusive. The Court proceeded to read two of the criteria expansively and withhold judgment on a third in upholding California's notice-prejudice rule against an ERISA challenge. Id. at 1389–90. Perhaps most importantly, Justice Ginsberg, stated in footnote 7:

> In the instant case, the Solicitor General, for the United States as amicus curiae, has endeavored to qualify the argument advanced in Pilot Life [that all state causes of action against ERISA insurers were preempted]. * * * the Solicitor General now maintains that the discussion of § 502(a) in Pilot Life "does not in itself require that a state law that 'regulates insurance,' and so comes within the terms of the savings clause, is nevertheless preempted if it provides a state-law cause of action or remedy." [ ] ("[T]he insurance savings clause, on its face, saves state law conferring causes of action or affecting remedies that regulate insurance, just as it does state mandated-benefits laws."). We need not address the Solicitor General's current argument, for Ward has sued under § 502(a)(1)(B) for benefits due, and seeks only the application of saved state insurance law as a relevant rule of decision in his § 502(a) action.

The Supreme Court in *UNUM* seems to be continuing its trend towards broadening the space left for state regulation of health insurance plans. The decision offers encouragement to states that are eager to move forward with managed care regulation.

5. *Corporate Health* holds that even though a statute (the Texas external appeal statute in this case) is saved from § 514(a) preemption by the savings clause, it may nevertheless be preempted by § 502(a) if it provides a state remedy that takes the place of § 502(a). The Seventh Circuit, however, in Moran v. Rush Prudential HMO, Inc., 230 F.3d 959 (7th Cir.2000), upheld the Illinois external appeals statute, holding that the statute did not displace the civil remedy provided by § 502, but rather modified the insurance contract to include an additional contract term requiring the plan administrator to abide by the decision of the external reviewer and an additional dispute resolution mechanism that needed to be pursued before a § 502 action could be brought. As of this writing, the state of Texas has requested the Supreme Court to resolve the conflict among the circuits.

6. ERISA's § 514(b)(2)(A) savings clause is subject to its own exception, the § 514(b)(2)(B) "deemer" clause. This subsection provides that "neither an employee benefit * * * nor any trust established under such a plan, shall be deemed to be an insurance company or other insurer, * * * or to be engaged in the business of insurance * * * for purposes of any law of any State purporting to regulate insurance companies, [or] insurance contracts, * * *." 29 U.S.C.A. § 1144(b)(2)(B). In FMC Corporation v. Holliday, 498 U.S. 52, 111 S.Ct. 403, 112 L.Ed.2d 356 (1990), the Supreme Court interpreted this clause broadly to except self-funded ERISA plans entirely from state regulation and state law claims.

The deemer clause offers a significant incentive for employers to become self-insured. Self-insurance, however, also has disadvantages—it imposes upon the employer the burden of administering the plan as well as open-ended exposure for claims made to the plan. To avoid these problems, self-insured employers often contract with third-party administrators to administer claims and with stop-loss insurers to limit their claims exposure. The courts overwhelmingly hold that employer plans remain self-insured, even though they are reinsured through stop-loss plans, and prohibit state regulation of stop loss coverage for self-insured plans. See, e.g., Tri–State Machine v. Nationwide Life Ins. Co., 33 F.3d 309 (4th Cir.1994); Lincoln Mutual Casualty v. Lectron Products, Inc. 970 F.2d 206 (6th Cir.1992). Third-party administrators that administer self-insured plans are also protected from state insurance regulation. NGS American, Inc. v. Barnes, 805

F.Supp. 462 (W.D. Texas 1992). Thus an employer who is willing to bear some risk can escape state regulation under the "deemer" clause, even though most of the risk of insuring the plan is borne by a stop-loss insurer and the burden of administering the plan is assumed by a third-party administrator.

7.   State statutes requiring external reviews are not the only regulatory statutes to be challenged under ERISA preemption. Perhaps the most litigated regulatory issue has been whether state "any willing provider" legislation is preempted by ERISA. The Eighth Circuit in Prudential Insurance Co. of America v. National Park Medical Center, Inc., 154 F.3d 812 (8th Cir., 1998) and Fifth Circuit in Texas Pharmacy Ass'n v. Prudential Insurance Co., 105 F.3d 1035 (5th Cir.1997) and CIGNA Healthplan of La., Inc. v. Louisiana, 82 F.3d 642 (5th Cir.1996), invalidated the AWP provisions of Arkansas, Texas, and Louisiana respectively, finding that they "related to" ERISA plans, and were not saved from preemption. These holdings were based, in part, on the fact that these statutes were not limited in their reach to traditional insurance plans, since the statutes covered entities such as HMOs, PPOs, and third party administrators.

On the other hand, the Sixth Circuit recently in Kentucky Association of Health Plans, Inc. v. Nichols, 227 F.3d 352 (6th Cir., 2000); and Community Health Partners, Inc. v. Kentucky, 230 F.3d 1357 (6th Cir.2000), applying the more liberal interpretation of the savings clause suggested by Ward, found that the Kentucky AWP statute was saved from preemption. In an earlier case, Stuart Circle Hosp. Corp. v. Aetna Health Management, 995 F.2d 500 (4th Cir.1993), the Fourth Circuit had also upheld a Virginia AWP statute, also finding that the statute properly regulated insurance. The 9th Circuit, in a related case, recently upheld Washington state's alternative provider statute, requiring HMOs and health care service contractors to cover alternative medical treatments, such as acupuncture, massage therapy, naturopathy, and chiropractic services, Washington Physicians Service Ass'n v. Gregoire, 147 F.3d 1039 (9th Cir. 1998), finding that the statute did not relate to ERISA plans, and but also that it would be saved from preemption as regulating insurance.

8.   Another issue that has arisen occasionally in savings clause litigation is whether health maintenance organizations are in the business of insurance and thus subject to state regulation. Early cases tended to say no, often on very formalistic grounds, see, e.g. O'Reilly v. Ceuleers, 912 F.2d 1383 (11th Cir.1990), as did some of the any willing provider cases, see Texas Pharmacy Ass'n v. Prudential, 105 F.3d 1035 (5th Cir.1997). Recent cases, however, have recognized quite sensibly that:

> In the end, HMOs function the same way as a traditional health insurer: The policyholder pays a fee for a promise of medical services in the event that he should need them. It follows that HMOs * * * are in the business of insurance.

Washington Physicians Service Ass'n v. Gregoire, 147 F.3d 1039, 1046 (9th Cir.1998), See also Kentucky Ass'n of Health Plans v. Nichols, 227 F.3d 352, 364–65, 371 (6th Cir.2000).

9.   The topic of ERISA preemption has unleashed a torrent of scholarship. Among the most recent articles discussing ERISA's effect on health insurance regulation are, Karen A. Jordan, Coverage Denials in ERISA Plans' Assessing the Federal Legislative Solution, 65 Mo. L. Rev. 405 (2000); Donald T. Brogan, Protecting Patient Rights Despite ERISA: Will the Supreme Court Allow the States to Regulate Managed Care? 74 Tul. L. Rev. 951 (2000); Jana K. Strain and Eleanor D. Kinney, The Road Paved With Good Intentions: Problems and Poten-

tial for Employer–Sponsored Health Insurance Under ERISA, 31 Loy.U.Chi.L.J. 29 (1999); Edward A. Zelinsky, Travelers, Reasoned Textualism, and the New Jurisprudence of ERISA Preemption, 21 Cardozo L. Rev. 807 (1999); Peter D Jacobson & Scott D. Pomfret, Form, Function, and Managed Care Torts: Achieving Fairness and Equity in ERISA Jurisprudence, 35 Hous. L. Rev. 985 (1998); Scott D. Pomfret, Emerging Theories of Liability for Utilization Review under ERISA Health Plans, 35 Hous. L. Rev. 985 (1998); Karen A. Jordan, The Shifting Preemption Paradigm: Conceptual and Interpretive Issues, 51 Vand. L. Rev. 1149 (1998); Howard Shapiro, Rene E. Thorne, Edward F. Harold, ERISA Preemption: To Infinity and Beyond and Back Again? 58 La. L. Rev. 997 (1998); E. Haavi Morreim, Benefits Decisions in ERISA Plans: Diminishing Deference to Fiduciaries and an Emerging Problem for Provider–Sponsored Organizations, 65 Tenn. L. Rev. 511 (1998); Curtis D. Rooney, The States, Congress, or the Courts: Who Will be First to Reform ERISA Remedies, 7 Annals Health L. 73 (1998); and Karen A. Jordan, Travelers Insurance: New Support for the Argument to Restrain ERISA Preemption, 13 Yale J. Reg. 255 (1996).

B.   ERISA PREEMPTION OF STATE TORT LITIGATION

The Employee Retirement Income Security Act of 1974 (ERISA), establishing uniform national standards for employee benefit plans, has broadly preempted state regulation of these plans, as discussed in the previous section. 29 U.S.C.A. § 1144(a) states that ERISA supersedes state laws to the extent that they "relate to any employee benefit plan" covered by ERISA. The interaction of ERISA with state laws that attempt to regulate employee health insurance has caused a great deal of controversy and litigation in malpractice cases. The following cases and notes illustrate judicial struggles to limit ERISA and its "relate to" language.

ESTATE OF FRAPPIER v. WISHNOV

District Court of Appeal of Florida, Fourth District, 1996.
678 So.2d 884.

SPEISER, MARK A., ASSOCIATE JUDGE.

* * * Appellant, the estate of Robert Frappier Jr., appeals a trial court order dismissing its complaint with prejudice. The estate sued Health Options, Inc., a health maintenance organization (HMO), and two physicians, Drs. Wishnov and Patel, who were assigned by Health Options to attend to the medical needs of Frappier. The estate contended that Frappier died as a result of the medical malpractice of the two doctors.

Health Options, the only party defendant to this appeal, was the subject of counts III through VI of the estate's six count complaint. Count III charged Health Options with direct negligence in selecting the two doctors whom the estate claims were incompetent. Count IV alleged Health Options was vicariously liable for the actions of its agents or apparent agents namely Drs. Wishnov and Patel. Count V was premised upon a corporate liability theory based upon Health Options' breach of a common law and statutory duty to assure the competence of its physicians. Finally, Count VI of the complaint asserted that Health Options breached an implied contractual non-delegable duty to provide appropriate medical care. The trial court dismissed these counts based upon Health Options' contention that the estate's claims "relate to" an ERISA (Employee Retirement Income Security Act) plan and therefore federal question jurisdiction required Frappier's cause of action to be preempted to federal court. [ ]

The estate's motion for rehearing, ultimately denied, alleged that Health Options failed to prove and the trial court failed to determine that an ERISA plan ever existed. The estate now argues that this threshold question must be resolved prior to addressing the issue of whether the dismissed counts are preemptable. We agree and reverse.

Before a state court can conclude that the applicable ERISA federal preemption statute divests it of subject matter jurisdiction, it must be proven that the HMO was an ERISA plan. [ ]

On appeal, the second district concluded that the trial judge failed to make an adequate evidentiary finding as to the propriety of the defendant's assertion that the court lacked subject matter jurisdiction because of federal preemption. Id. at 35. We approve the following quote from the opinion of the second district:

> Thus, the party claiming preemption bears the burden of proof and must establish that Congress has clearly and unmistakably manifested its intent to supersede state law.

* * * On this issue we are compelled to reverse and remand for an evidentiary hearing to determine if Health Options is an ERISA subject to federal preemption.

Nevertheless, presented with the opportunity, we feel compelled to address the merits of the trial court's determination that the estate's claims against Health Options are preempted by the federal ERISA statute. Generally, actions that "relate to" an ERISA are preempted by federal law. Several Florida state decisions have already resolved various ERISA preemption issues. [ ] However, no state case has addressed whether direct negligence or vicarious liability claims against an ERISA are preempted and we therefore seek guidance from federal courts.

The ERISA regulatory scheme was promulgated to entrench as exclusively a federal matter pension plan legislation. Pilot Life Ins. Co. v. Dedeaux, 481 U.S. 41, 107 S.Ct. 1549, 95 L.Ed.2d 39 (1987). The governing provision of ERISA relevant to this discussion is section 514(a) which provides that "this Chapter shall supersede any and all state laws insofar as they may now or hereafter 'relate to' any employee benefit plan." 29 U.S.C.A. § 1144(a).

Properly phrased, the issue becomes whether Frappier's claims against Health Options as delineated in counts III–VI of the complaint are to recover plan benefits due, or to enforce rights, or to clarify rights to benefits under the terms of the plan, as those concepts are detailed in section 502(a)(1)(B) of ERISA, 29 U.S.C.A. § 1132(a)(1)(B). Although Pilot Life suggested an expansive interpretation of the triggering jurisdictional clause of the ERISA federal regulatory scheme, the United States Supreme Court in New York Blue Cross v. Travelers Inc., 514 U.S. 645, 115 S.Ct. 1671, 131 L.Ed.2d 695 (1995), and several more recent lower federal court decisions caution against a literal reading of section 514(a) in determining whether preemption is appropriate. New York Blue Cross directs that in construing the "relate to" phrase of section 514(a), trial courts must analyze the objectives of the ERISA statute to resolve which state laws Congress contemplated would continue to survive the ambit of federal regulation. Id. at ___, 115 S.Ct. at 1677. In other words, statutory or common law claims actionable in state court that are periphery or remotely related to competing laws affecting ERISA should not be preempted to federal court. [ ]

Frappier's claims are grounded on various theories of negligence, breach of an implied contract and vicarious liability (Count IV). * * *

* * *

Thus where, as here, an ERISA is implicated by a complaint for failing to provide, arrange for, or supervise qualified doctors to provide the actual medical treatment for plan participants, federal preemption is inappropriate. [ ] Therefore, even if Health Options is an ERISA subject to federal preemption, we must conclude that the trial court erred in dismissing the vicarious liability count of the instant complaint.

Concerning the direct negligence, corporate liability and implied contract claims, we concur with the lower court's decision that these allegations would be completely preempted because they present issues unequivocally related to the administration of the plan and are within the scope of section 502(a)(1)(B); [ ].

Accordingly, this case is remanded with directions to the trial court to hold an evidentiary hearing to determine whether Health Options is an ERISA plan subject to federal preemption. Upon an appropriate finding, the trial court may dismiss the estate's direct negligence, corporate liability and implied contract claims for a lack of subject matter jurisdiction. However, in no event may the vicarious liability count be dismissed as the same does not "relate to" an employee benefit plan.

PAPPAS v. ASBEL

Supreme Court of Pennsylvania, 2001.
___ Pa. ___, 768 A.2d 1089.

OPINION

MR. JUSTICE CAPPY

[The Pennsylvania Supreme Court, in their earlier decision in *Pappas*, had decided, based on *Travelers*, that medical malpractice claims against U.S. Healthcare were not preempted by ERISA. Their decision was appealed to the U.S. Supreme court, which remanded the case for further consideration in light of their decision in Pegram v. Herdrich.] For all the reasons that follow, we adhere to our original opinion and order.

The facts and procedural history, as set forth in *Pappas I*, bear repeating.

At 11:00 a.m. on May 21, 1991, Basile Pappas ("Pappas") was admitted to Haverford Community Hospital ("Haverford") through its emergency room complaining of paralysis and numbness in his extremities. At the time of his admission, Pappas was an insured of HMO–PA, a health maintenance organization operated by U.S. Healthcare.

Dr. Stephen Dickter, the emergency room physician, concluded that Pappas was suffering from an epidural abscess which was pressing on

Pappas' spinal column. Dr. Dickter consulted with a neurologist and a neurosurgeon; the physicians concurred that Pappas' condition constituted a neurological emergency. Given the circumstances, Dr. Dickter felt that it was in Pappas' best interests to receive treatment at a university hospital.

Dr. Dickter made arrangements to transfer Pappas to Jefferson University Hospital ("Jefferson") for further treatment. At approximately 12:40 p.m. when the ambulance arrived, Dr. Dickter was alerted to the fact that U.S. Healthcare was denying authorization for treatment at Jefferson. Ten minutes later, Dr. Dickter contacted U.S. Healthcare to obtain authorization for the transfer to Jefferson. At 1:[05]p.m., U.S. Healthcare responded to Dr. Dickter's inquiry and advised him that authorization for treatment at Jefferson was still being denied, but that Pappas could be transferred to either Hahnemann University ("Hahnemann"), Temple University or Medical College of Pennsylvania ("MCP").

Dr. Dickter immediately contacted Hahnemann. That facility advised Haverford at approximately 2:20 p.m. that it would not have information on its ability to receive Pappas for at least another half hour. MCP was then reached and within minutes it agreed to accept Pappas; Pappas was ultimately transported there at 3:30 p.m. Pappas now suffers from permanent quadriplegia resulting from compression of his spine by the abscess.

Pappas and his wife filed suit against Dr. David Asbel, his primary care physician, and Haverford. They claimed that Dr. Asbel had committed medical malpractice and that Haverford was negligent in causing an inordinate delay in transferring him to a facility equipped and immediately available to handle his neurological emergency.

Haverford then filed a third party complaint against U.S. Healthcare, joining it as a party defendant for its refusal to authorize the transfer of Pappas to a hospital selected by the Haverford physicians. Dr. Asbel also filed a cross-claim against U.S. Healthcare seeking contribution and indemnity. * * *

* * *

[The Court restated its earlier conclusion that the U.S. Supreme Court in *Travelers* had recognized "fairly significant bounds on preemption" and had "cautioned that 'nothing in the language of [ERISA] or in the context of its passage indicates that Congress chose to displace general health care regulation, which historically has been a matter of local concern.' *Id.* at 892 (*quoting Travelers*, 514 U.S. at 706, 708–709). Applying Travelers, the Court concluded that the negligence claims were not preempted; in their words, "* * * we held it would have been inappropriate to conclude that Haverford's claims, in which the issue of U.S. Healthcare's allegedly dilatory delivery of contractually-guaranteed medical benefits were intertwined with the question of safe medical care, are preempted by ERISA."]

[The court then recited the facts of *Pegram*.]

The Supreme Court granted certiorari to determine whether treatment decisions made by an HMO, acting through its physicians, are fiduciary acts within the meaning of ERISA. The Court held that they are not. []

In the course of doing so, the Court set forth two guiding principles. First, HMO physicians occupy dual roles. They act like plan administrators when they determine, for example, whether a participant's condition is covered, and as health care providers, when they decide upon the medical treatment a participant will receive. *Id.* at 2153–54.

Second, HMO physicians make three types of decisions. "[P]ure 'eligibility decisions' turn on the plan's coverage of a particular condition or medical procedure for its treatment," *id.* at 2154, such as "whether a plan covers an undisputed case of appendicitis." *Id.* at 2155. " 'Treatment decisions,' by contrast, are choices about how to go about diagnosing and treating a patient's condition: given a patient's constellation of symptoms, what is the appropriate medical response?" *Id.* at 2154. "Mixed eligibility and treatment decisions" are just what their name implies-decisions in which coverage and medical judgment are intertwined. *Id.* at 2154–55. * * *

* * *

While *Travelers* and *Pegram* deal with different aspects of ERISA, for our present purposes, they share common ground. *Travelers* instructs that ERISA does not preempt state law that regulates the provision of adequate medical treatment. *Pegram* instructs that an HMO's mixed eligibility and treatment decision implicates a state law claim for medical malpractice, not an ERISA cause of action for fiduciary breach. Thus, if Haverford's third party claim against U.S. Healthcare arose out of a mixed decision, it is, according to *Pegram*, subject to state medical malpractice law, which is what Haverford asserted. Moreover, under *Travelers,* it is not preempted by ERISA.

* * *

Having looked again at the record, there are facts that are not disputed, in addition to those set forth in *Pappas I,* that are important to our analysis. Dr. Dickter, the physician who first saw Pappas in the emergency room of Haverford on May 21, 1991, at about 11:00 a.m., received permission from Jefferson to admit Pappas to its spinal cord trauma center. Dr. Dickter chose Jefferson because it, unlike other hospitals, had designated space for spinal trauma cases and was able to determine immediately whether it was in a position to receive a new patient. When Dr. Dickter learned at 12:40 p.m. from ambulance personnel that Pappas' transfer to Jefferson was not HMO approved, he telephoned U.S. Healthcare at 12:50 p.m. and asked that it reconsider its decision. Dr. Dickter spoke to Elaine Norman, a U.S. Healthcare representative, and told her that Pappas' condition constituted a neurological emergency that needed immediate attention, and for which he had made arrangements with Jefferson. Ms. Norman advised Dr. Dickter that she was not authorized to take action one way or the other, but that she would consult with someone who was. At 1:05 p.m., Dr. Dickter spoke with Carol DeLark, another U.S. Healthcare representative. She told him that Dr. Liebowitz, one of U.S. Healthcare's physicians who had the authority to decide such matters, reviewed Pappas' case; that the referral to Jefferson, a non-HMO hospital, continued to be denied; and that a referral to the facilities affiliated with Hahnemann, Temple University or MCP was approved. At about 3:30 p.m., through Dr. Dickter's efforts, Pappas was admitted to MCP.

Not surprisingly, U.S. Healthcare argues that its decision about Pappas' referral "constituted a quintessential 'coverage' determination". We, however, disagree. In our view, the undisputed facts in this case, and the inferences drawn from them, establish the sort of mixed eligibility and treatment decision that *Pegram* discussed. Dr. Leibowitz, U.S. Healthcare's physician, reviewed Pappas' case, and rejected another medical doctor's opinion based on his clinical judgment that Pappas needed to be referred to Jefferson for treatment of a medical emergency. Instead of referring Pappas to Jefferson, a non-HMO hospital, as Dr. Dickter recommended, Dr. Leibowitz referred Pappas to one of three other facilities for medical care. He did not, in the Supreme Court's words, only make a "simple yes or no" decision as to whether Pappas' condition was covered; it clearly was. Rather, Dr Leibowitz also determined where and, under the circumstances, when Pappas' epidural abscess would be treated. His was a mixed eligibility and treatment decision, the adverse consequences of which, if any, are properly redressed, as *Pegram* teaches, through state medical malpractice law. This law as *Travelers* teaches, is not preempted by ERISA.

We conclude, therefore, that our reasoning and result in *Pappas I* are consistent with the Supreme Court's decision in *Pegram*. Accordingly, we confirm our original disposition; the order of the Superior Court, reversing the grant of summary judgment to U.S. Healthcare is affirmed. This matter is remanded to the trial court for further proceedings consistent with this opinion.

[Justice Saylor, in dissent, criticizes the majority for oversimplifying Pegram, in terms of conflict preemption and the extent to which ERISA still preempts many health plan decisions. He writes: "First, in my view, *Pegram II* gives cause for the exercise of a degree of caution on the part of state courts and legislators in terms of defining the duties of managed care organizations (or at least those that are deemed to perform administrative functions under ERISA) for purposes of tort jurisprudence. Second, I question whether a full, fair, and final resolution of the conflict preemption inquiry can be effected unless and until some more precise definition is afforded to any duties being ascribed to U.S. Healthcare under state tort law."]

Notes and Questions

1. *Frappier* illustrates the threshold question: is the health plan named as defendant in a tort suit an ERISA-qualified plan? If so, defendant can then remove the case to federal court and argue that the plaintiff's claims are preempted.

Most managed care plans are now ERISA-qualified. If a plan is ERISA-qualified, then state law claims are preempted and the plaintiff is relegated to s. 502(a)(1)(B) of ERISA, 29 U.S.C.A. § 1132(a)(1)(B). § 502(a)(1)(B) states that a civil action may be brought—

(1) by a participant or beneficiary—

(B) to recover benefits due to him under the terms of his plan, to enforce his rights under the terms of the plan, or to clarify his rights to future benefits under the terms of the plan....

In Massachusetts Mutual Life Insurance Co. v. Russell, 473 U.S. 134, 105 S.Ct. 3085, 87 L.Ed.2d 96 (1985), the Court held that an employee covered under her employer's welfare benefit plan could not recover compensatory and punitive damages for financial losses that allegedly occurred when the benefit plan mishandled the processing of the employee's claim for disability benefits. Section 409(a)'s statement that the fiduciary "shall be subject to such other equitable or remedial relief as the court may deem appropriate" precludes compensatory and punitive damages to compensate beneficiaries for personal injuries. Although a beneficiary can sue a benefit plan, a benefit plan manager, or other fiduciary, she cannot collect any personal compensatory or punitive damages under section 409(a).

See generally Karen A. Jordan, Travelers Insurance: New Support for the Argument to Restrain ERISA Pre-emption, 13 Yale J. on Reg. 255 (1996); Wendy K. Mariner, Liability for Managed Care Decisions: The Employee Retirement Income Security Act (ERISA) and the Uneven Playing Field, 86 Am.J. Pub.Health 863 (1996).

2.   The *Pappas* decision interprets Pegram as narrowing the scope of ERISA preemption even further—holding that mixed eligibility and treatment decisions are properly redressed through state medical malpractice law. The U.S. Supreme Court's lengthy discussion of ERISA preemption does suggest, however, that mixed eligibility/treatment decisions are not acts of plan administration and therefore, these potentially "unrelated-to-ERISA" claims can be pursued in state courts.

Do you see problems with this distinction? Does Pappas treat virtually all health plan coverage decisions as "mixed" and therefore not preempted? Can you develop a more helpful set of distinctions for determining when ERISA properly preempts a state malpractice claim?

3.   ERISA was interpreted by the federal courts in the first wave of litigation as totally preempting common law tort claims. See, e.g., Ricci v. Gooberman, 840 F.Supp. 316 (D.N.J.1993); Butler v. Wu, 853 F.Supp. 125, 129–30 (D.N.J.1994); Nealy v. U.S. Healthcare HMO, 844 F.Supp. 966, 973 (S.D.N.Y.1994) (plaintiff's attempts to hold an HMO liable under several common law theories held preempted); Altieri v. Cigna Dental Health, Inc., 753 F.Supp. 61, 63–65 (D.Conn.1990) (ERISA preempts plaintiff's negligent supervision claim against an HMO). It appeared from this caselaw that any managed care plan that was ERISA-qualified would receive virtually complete tort immunity.

The federal courts began to split, however, as to the limits of such preemption. Recent decisions have limited the preemption clause of ERISA, holding that many tort theories have little or nothing to do with the administration of pension plan or other benefits. The result has been a litigation explosion against managed care as theories are imported from hospital liability caselaw, fiduciary law, and contract law to use against managed care organizations. Prihoda v. Shpritz, 914 F.Supp. 113 (D.Md.1996) (ERISA does not preempt an action against physicians and an HMO for physicians' failure to diagnose a cancerous tumor, allowing a vicarious liability action to proceed). See also Independence HMO, Inc. v. Smith, 733 F.Supp. 983 (E.D.Pa.1990) (ERISA does not preempt medical malpractice-type claims brought against HMOs under a vicarious liability theory); Elsesser v. Hospital of the Philadelphia College of Osteopathic Medicine, 802 F.Supp. 1286 (E.D.Pa.1992) (same for a claim against an HMO for the HMO's negligence in selecting, retaining, and evaluating plaintiff's primary-care physician); Kearney v. U.S. Healthcare, Inc., 859 F.Supp. 182 (E.D.Pa.1994) (ERISA preempts plaintiff's direct negligence claim, but not its vicarious liability claim). See generally Peter D. Jacobson, Legal Challenges to Managed Care Cost Containment Programs: An Initial Assessment, 18 Health Affairs 69 (1999); Karen A. Jordan, Tort Liability for Managed Care: The Weakening of ERISA's Protective Shield, 25 J. Law, Med. & Ethics 160 (1997).

4. Dukes and the quality–quantity distinction. The watershed decision, opening up a substantial crack in preemption doctrine, was Dukes v. U.S. Healthcare, Inc., 57 F.3d 350 (3d Cir. 1995). In *Dukes*, the court found that Congress intended in passing ERISA to insure that promised benefits would be available to plan participants, and that section 502 was "intended to provide each individual participant with a remedy in the event that promises made by the plan were not kept." The court was unwilling, however, to stretch the remedies of 502 to "control the quality of the benefits received by plan participants." The court concluded that ... [q]uality control of benefits, such as the health care benefits provided here, is a field traditionally occupied by state regulation and we interpret the silence of Congress as reflecting an intent that it remain such. The court developed the distinction between benefits to care under a plan and a right to good quality care:

> The plaintiffs are not attempting to define new "rights under the terms of the plan"; instead, they are attempting to assert their already-existing rights under the generally-applicable state law of agency and tort. Inherent in the phrases "rights under the terms of the plan" and "benefits due ... under the terms of [the] plan" is the notion that the plan participants and beneficiaries will receive something to which they would not be otherwise entitled. But patients enjoy the right to be free from medical malpractice regardless of whether or not their medical care is provided through an ERISA plan.

The court distinguished between the quantity of benefits due under a welfare plan and the quality of those benefits. Quality of care could be so poor that it is essentially a denial of benefits. Or the plan could describe a benefit in terms that are quality-based, such as a commitment that all x-rays will be analyzed by radiologists with a certain level of training. But absent either of these extremes, poor medical care—malpractice—is not a benefits issue under ERISA.

5. Chinks in the preemption armor. Theories of liability can be grouped into several categories, depending on the activity engaged in by the managed care organization. This functional organization helps determine what is preempted and what allowed under ERISA

a. Contract claims. The managed care organization as insurer must recruit subscribers to its plan, typically through employment-based plans offered to employees. It must properly enroll these subscribers to ensure they are covered in exchange for their premiums. It must clearly describe any exclusions that operate under its coverage, including exclusions of coverage of certain diseases and "experimental" treatments. Policies also typically impose a requirement of "medical necessity" as a prerequisite to payment for treatment. Policies may impose coverage limitations for certain treatments, such as psychiatric hospitalization. Such coverage restrictions may create a subscriber right to sue under section 502 of ERISA, but the courts have held that malpractice claims for damages for violation of this provision are preempted. See, e.g., Brandon v. Aetna Services, Inc., 46 F.Supp.2d 110 (D.C.Conn.1999)(claim against plan administrator for refusing to pay for in-patient and out-patient care for substance-abuse and anxiety disorder problems; held a benefits issue, preempted under ERISA); Parrino v. FHP, Inc., 146 F.3d 699 (9th Cir.1998)(patient had brain tumor removed and FHP initially refused to authorize payment for proton beam therapy prescribed by physicians as experimental and unnecessary; held that claim is completely preempted); Huss v. Green Spring Health Services, Inc., 1999 WL 225885

(E.D.Pa.1999)(failure of defendant to correctly inform plaintiff of coverage under plan goes to quantity of benefits, and is preempted); Garcia v. Kaiser Foundation Hospitals, 90 Hawai'i 425, 978 P.2d 863 (1999)(plaintiff's claims that plan failed to provide him with reasonable and necessary medical treatment to which he was entitled, preempted; claims included breach of contract, tortious breach of contract, infliction of emotional distress, fraud, unfair and deceptive trade practice, loss of consortium, and punitive damages).

Common law bad faith claims are excluded under ERISA. Pilot Life Insurance Co. v. Dedeaux, 481 U.S. 41, 107 S.Ct. 1549, 95 L.Ed.2d 39 (1987), held that actions such as bad faith sufficiently "relate to" employee benefits plans to fall within ERISA preemption.

    b.   Operational restrictions on subscriber choices.

Many managed care organizations offer a restricted set of choices for subscribers. Their drug formularies limit the choices of drugs available to plan physicians. Hospital choices are restricted to those which whom the MCO has a contract, as is access to specialists. Use of physician gatekeepers restricts access to hospitals and specialists on the MCO's acceptable list.

The courts have generally held that ERISA preempts claims based on plan strategies to discourage referrals to specialists. Pell v. Shmokler, 1997 WL 83743 (E.D.Pa.1997)(refusal of treating physician to refer plaintiff to pulmonologist is a withholding of benefits, subject to complete preemption); see also Kohn v. Delaware Valley HMO, Inc., 1991 WL 275609 (E.D.Pa.1991).

Pre-certification and other forms of utilization review are designed to filter out demands for "unnecessary" treatments. Such forms of review of physician medical decisions to determine their necessity and cost-effectiveness prior to treatment or hospitalization are either completely preempted under § 502(a)(1)(B) or subject to an ERISA preemption defense under § 514(a). See Jass v. Prudential Health Care Plan Inc., 88 F.3d 1482 (7th Cir. 1996)(claim against pre-certification review administrator who denied patient's request of physical therapy to rehabilitate knee after surgery held completely preempted); Kuhl v. Lincoln Nat'l Health Plan of Kansas City, Inc., 999 F.2d 298, 302 (8th Cir. 1993)(decision to delay pre-certification of heart surgery preempted); Corcoran v. United HealthCare, Inc., 965 F.2d 1321, 1332 (5th Cir. 1992).

Such forms of review may affect the quantity of benefits received directly, but they have attendant effects on quality as well. Thus a failure to provide in-home visits for a subscriber, when the plan allegedly offered such a service, is a benefit issue subject to preemption under § 502. See Kuhl v. Lincoln Nat'l Health Plan of Kansas City, Inc., 999 F.2d 298, 302 (8th Cir. 1993)(decision to delay pre-certification of heart surgery preempted); Corcoran v. United HealthCare, Inc., 965 F.2d 1321, 1332 (5th Cir. 1992).

Claims that fall within the administrator's core functions–determining eligibility for benefits, disbursing them to the participant, monitoring available funds and recordkeeping—are completely preempted.

Denials based on "medical necessity" determinations are more complicated than the courts have generally acknowledged. They entail two determinations: first, a medical judgment that the patient's condition can be treated by available treatments of varying efficacy and cost; second, an administrative decision of whether to pay for the care, considering the cost-benefit trade-off of the treatment alternatives. The HMO decision can be characterized as a medical determination, although most courts have held that refusals to pay for care that the treating physician recommends are preempted. See Danca v. Private Health Care Sys., Inc., 185 F.3d 1 (1st Cir.1999); Brandon v. Aetna Servs., Inc., 46 F.Supp. 2d 110 (D.Conn.1999); Person v. Physicians Health Plan, Inc., 20 F.Supp.2d 918 (E.D.Va. 1998); Tolton v. American Biodyne, Inc., 48 F.3d 937 (6th Cir. 1995); Spain v. Aetna Life Ins. Co., 11 F.3d 129 (9th Cir.1993); Toledo v. Kaiser Permanente Med. Group, 987 F.Supp. 1174 (N.D.Cal.1997); Schmid v. Kaiser Found. Health Plan of the Northwest, 963 F.Supp. 942 (D.Or.1997). Attacks on utilization review necessarily also attack the methods by which benefits are administered or denied.

   c.   Plan design and delivery of health care services.

   MCOs are businesses. They market their care to potential employers and subscribers in a competitive marketplace for health care. They recruit and organize their physicians through their networks. They design a corporate system in which health care is delivered. And they must administer this system in a safe fashion that avoids injury to subscribers caused by the negligence of plan physicians and other providers. Malpractice claims based on vicarious liability, corporate negligence, negligence per se and intentional inflection of mental distress may be allowed under current law as quality of care issues not involving ERISA claims for benefits. Herrera v. Lovelace Health Systems, Inc., 35 F.Supp.2d 1327 (D.C.N.M.1999); Hoose v. Jefferson Home Health Care, Inc., 1998 WL 114492 (E.D.Pa.1998) (claims of negligence in selection of therapists, providing postoperative care, vicarious liability, and negligence in overall supervision of care; the court noted that "this case is noting more than a medical malpractice case", and refused to uphold ERISA preemption).

   ● Agency doctrine. Under theories of agency, physicians and other professionals may be held liable and that liability imputed to the managed care organization. Such vicarious liability has been held by the majority of courts considering the question not to be preempted by ERISA. Harris v. Deaconess Health Services Corp., et al., 61 F.Supp.2d 889 (E.D.Mo.1999); Herrera v. Lovelace Health Sys., Inc., 35 F.Supp.2d 1327 (D.N.M. 1999); Visconti v. U.S. Healthcare, 1998 WL 968473 (E.D.Pa.1998); Petrovich v. Share Health Plan of Illinois, Inc., 188 Ill.2d 17, 241 Ill.Dec. 627, 719 N.E.2d 756 (Ill.1999); Dykema v. King, 959 F.Supp. 736 (D.S.C.1997); Prihoda v. Shpritz, 914 F.Supp. 113 (D.C.Maryland 1996); Pacificare of Oklahoma, Inc. v. Burrage, 59 F.3d 151 (10th Cir.1995); Lupo v. Human Affairs Int'l, Inc., 28 F.3d 269 (2d Cir.1994); Dearmas v. Av–Med, Inc., 865 F.Supp. 816 (S.D.Fla.1994); Gilbert v. Sycamore Municipal Hospital, 156 Ill.2d 511, 190 Ill.Dec. 758, 622 N.E.2d 788 (Ill. 1993).

   The plan is irrelevant to the claim, since the claim of agency does not rise and fall with the plan, but is established by reference to reliance and representations, a question of fact not involving the interpretation of an ERISA plan. See Rice v. Panchal, 65 F.3d 637 (7th Cir.1995). If the underlying claim against the treating physician is a failure to treat—a denial of benefits—then it relates to the benefits plan; a vicarious liability claim would also be grounded in this benefits denial claim. The negligence claim then could not be resolved without reference to the benefits determination. In such a situation, one circuit court has held that ERISA completely preempts the agency claim. Jass v. Prudential Health Care Plan, Inc., 88 F.3d 1482 (7th Cir.1996)

   The law of vicarious liability varies substantially from state to state, and plans have argued that allowing vicarious liability claims would create a patchwork of regulations affecting ERISA plans, interfering with the administration of benefits and the need for uniformity. However, as the court noted in *Prihoda*, while liability might vary from state to state, "[t]he liability of HMOs ... would not be subject to inconsistent administrative obligations of the type that occur when inconsistent local laws and court decisions cause benefit levels to vary from state to state."

● Treatment recommendations. When a plan or its non-physician employees get involved in treatment orders, they may be liable. In Roessert v. Health Net, 929 F.Supp. 343, 351 (N.D.Cal.1996), the patient sued her HMO, medical group and treating physicians in part for seeking her commitment to a psychiatric facility. The court found that an action for intentional or negligent infliction of mental distress against the HMO and the medical group was not preempted by ERISA. The plan's recommendation to commit could be decided apart from the terms of the plan. If a plan used under-qualified employees to treat a patient and they fail to recognize the seriousness of the condition, the plan is acting as a provider, not in its administrative capacity, and the claim could proceed in state court. Blaine v. Community Health Plan, 179 Misc.2d 331, 687 N.Y.S.2d 854 (S.C. N.Y. 1998)(claim that patient's injuries were caused by the plan's failure to provide her with a physician rather than physician's assistant, failing to provide tests, and failing to adequately supervise the physician's assistant and have written policies governing required supervision.)

If a plan requires that a subscriber first telephone an advisory nurse prior to seeking medical attention, this has been construed as a misdiagnosis and the giving of negligent medical advice rather than as utilization review pre-certification. Crum v. Health Alliance–Midwest, Inc., 47 F.Supp.2d 1013 (D.C.Ill.1999)(advisory nurse told plaintiff with chest pains that he just had gas pains, and he died that evening of acute myocardial infarction); Phommyvong v. Muniz, 1999 WL 155714 (N.D.Tex.1999). But see Jass v. Prudential Health Care Plan, Inc., 88 F.3d 1482 (7th Cir.1996)(nurse's denial of physical therapy held to be a claim for denial of benefits).

● Substandard plan design and administration. Claims of negligent design and administration of the delivery of health care services have been allowed in recent cases. See McDonald v. Damian, 56 F.Supp.2d 574 (E.D.Pa.1999)(claim for inadequacies in the delivery of medical services). In the Pappas case, the court held that a negligence claim against a plan for providing contractual benefits in "such a dilatory fashion that the patient was injured are intertwined with the provision of safe care". The issue was a delay in transporting the plaintiff to a specialty trauma unit for care. The delay was arguably caused by the utilization review process of the managed care organization, which did not allow transport to the best hospital unit in the area for spinal injuries. The case appears to involve both a system-induced delay and also a benefits question as to which hospitals were available to U.S. Healthcare providers and when a proper emergency allowed sending a subscriber outside the hospital network. Under the *Dukes* analysis, it is not clear in such a case where the quality-quantity distinction can be clearly drawn.

● Adoption of policies that discourage physicians from offering needed care. Explicit rules that discourage physicians from giving patients necessary care or hospitalization, such as discharging at-risk patients from hospitals, can be the basis for negligence claims. In Bauman v. U.S. Healthcare, 1 F.Supp.2d 420 (D.C.N.J.1998), plan participants whose newborn infant died on the day following discharge from the hospital sued. They argued that the plan policy that pressured or required that physicians discharge newborn infants and mothers within 24 hours of birth was negligent, and that a policy that discouraged readmission when health problems were identified after the original discharge was negligent. The

Third Circuit held that "when the HMO acts under the ERISA plan as a health care provider, it arranges and provides medical treatment, directly or through contracts with hospitals, doctors, or nurses." 193 F.3d 151. A 24–hour discharge policy fits within a quality of care claim, as does a hospital utilization review policy that discourages readmission.

A challenge to the appropriateness of medical decisions by a plan and its agents, as to quality and level of care and treatment, have been held to fall outside § 502(a) and may be tried in state court. In Moscovitch v. Danbury Hospital, 25 F.Supp.2d 74 (D.C.Conn.1998), the plaintiffs sued the plan and providers for the suicide of their son, on grounds that the plan failed to properly diagnose and assess the decedent's psychiatric condition, failed to monitor, care and treat him and oversee his treatment and failed to prescribe and administer the proper medications. The court held that this was a quality of care issue and the plaintiff can show on remand that the plan crossed the line from making a benefits determination to a treatment decision. See also Cyr v. Kaiser Found. Health Plan of Texas, 12 F.Supp.2d 556 (N.D.Tex.1998)(claims for negligence, fraudulent concealment, and tortious interference with the doctor/patient relationship held not preempted.)

The financial arrangement generally between the managed care organization and a hospital may arguably cause a hospital to commit malpractice, and this does not require courts to review a plan's utilization review or otherwise construe a plan's benefits. Preemption may therefore be avoided. Ouellette v. Christ Hospital, 942 F.Supp. 1160 (S.D.Ohio 1996).

● Substandard plans. A claim that a managed care plan is "substandard", leading to patient injury as a result, would seem to go directly to the administration of a plan and therefore be preempted. However, in Moreno v. Health Partners Health Plan, 4 F.Supp.2d 888 (D.C.Ariz.1998), the District Court held that there is "no relation between an action for medical malpractice and the recovery of benefits or the clarification of rights to future benefits under an ERISA plan". A plan decision to discharge a patient from the hospital to her home rather than a skilled nursing facility is considered a "quality" issue, not suitable for preemption. Miller v. Riddle Memorial Hospital, 1998 WL 272167 (E.D.Pa.1998). Where a plan is responsible for the continuum of care and it proves to be inadequate, even if that means they refuse to cover a benefit at a rehabilitation hospital or other facility, courts have found this to be nothing more a complaint of substandard care, not preempted by ERISA. Snow v. Burden, 1999 WL 387196 (E.D.Pa.1999). If a plan is negligent in failing to provide appropriate screening tests and studies, this can be viewed, not as a benefits denial, but a negligent provision of benefits, not subject to ERISA. Newton v. Tavani, 962 F.Supp. 45 (D.C.N.J.1997).

d. Physician selection and retention.

MCOs must select physicians who have appropriate credentials and training. They must then have procedures in place for reviewing these physicians' conduct and deciding whether or not to retain physicians at the end of their contract periods. Negligence in hiring, employment and supervision of medical personnel involved in treatment is a classic example of corporate negligence, defined in the hospital setting and imported into the managed care environment. As such, it is not subject to preemption, based on the Dukes rationale that such selection relates to the quality of care offered. See, e.g., Giles v. NYLCare Health Plans, Inc., 172 F.3d 332 (5th Cir.1999)(claim for negligence in selecting plan providers remanded); Visconti v. U.S. Healthcare, 1998 WL 968473 (E.D.Pa.1998); Hoyt v. Edge, 1997 WL 356324 (E.D.Pa.1997)(negligent supervision of Plan physicians).

    e.   Physician payment mechanisms.

One of the primary goals of managed care is conservative, cost-efficient practice. Physician behavior in prescribing, hospitalizing and referring may be altered by designing payment systems that promote cost-sensitive practice through bonuses and penalties. Claims regarding design of and concealment of financial incentives continue to be disallowed under complete preemption doctrine. The claim is that such incentives to undertreat cause a physician to deny benefits to a subscriber, resulting in injury. A plaintiff may claim that a physician negligently diagnosed or failed to treat, and the mere reference to the effect of an incentive system on his or her motivations will not lead to preemption. Lancaster v. Kaiser Foundation Health Plan of Mid–Atlantic States, Inc., 958 F.Supp. 1137, 1145 (E.D.Va.1997)(it may be appropriate for plaintiff to show that an incentive program induced physicians to refrain from ordering tests, to rebut their claim that their decision was based on "sound medical consideration.").

When, however, the claim is that the plan is negligent in the very design of the payment system, the courts have noted that this is an attack on administrative systems designed to curb rising health care costs by rewarding physicians for not ordering tests or treatment. As an attack on the administration of benefits, a denial of benefits as a result triggers section 502(a)(1)(B) and complete preemption. Lancaster v. Kaiser Foundation Health Plan of Mid–Atlantic States, Inc., 958 F.Supp. 1137 (E.D.Va.1997). If the effect of a payment incentive system is recast as having the effect, not of denying benefits, but of discouraging physicians from providing proper care, then it is viewed by some courts as a quality of care issue following the *Dukes* analysis and held not to be preempted. DeLucia v. St. Luke's Hospital, 1999 WL 387211 (E.D.Pa.1999); Ouellette v. Christ Hospital, 942 F.Supp. 1160 (S.D.Ohio 1996). After the Supreme Court decision in *Pegram*, however, where a unanimous court acknowledged the validity of the use by HMOs of various incentives to curb health care costs, it is unlikely that such attacks on the physician incentive systems will prevail.

Courts are steadily eroding ERISA categorical preemption in favor of subscriber rights to sue the organization for injuries. The recasting of malpractice claims as "quality" complaints, rather than benefit denials, has been accepted by several recent federal court decisions. The courts seem inclined to narrow ERISA preemption whenever possible and are likely to continue to do so. The Supreme Court in *Pegram*, acknowledging the role of state malpractice litigation and by using the Dukes "quantity-quality" distinction, has left this door wide open for continued common law litigation that circumvents ERISA preemption.

C. BENEFICIARY REMEDIES PROVIDED BY ERISA

1. *Judicial Claims Under ERISA*

ERISA takes away, but ERISA also gives. ERISA obligates employee benefit plans to fulfill their commitments to their beneficiaries, and provides a federal cause of action when they fail to do so. But the vision of health insurance that undergirds ERISA is very different from that found in state law.

State insurance regulation has generally been driven by a concern for access rights: e.g., the right of employees to have continued access to insurance coverage when they lose their jobs; the right of insureds to obtain mental health or mammography screening coverage; the right of chiropractors to have their services paid for by insurance; the right of "any willing provider" to participate in a PPO; the right of small businesses to purchase insurance at community rates; the right of beneficiaries to insurer compliance with the insurance contract; and right of beneficiaries to fair procedure. This body of law looks to public utility regulation, and, more recently, civil rights laws, for its models.

The bodies of law that define ERISA, on the other hand, are trust law and classical contract law. ERISA does not compel employers to provide health insurance and prohibits the states from imposing such a requirement. If, however, employers choose voluntarily (or under collective bargaining agreements) to establish health benefit plans, any contributions made by employers (or employees) to such plans are held in trust for all of the participants (employee plan members) and beneficiaries (dependents and others covered under a participant's policy) of the plan and must be paid out according to the contract that defines its terms. If the plan fiduciary or administrator wrongfully withholds benefits, a participant or beneficiary is entitled to sue in federal or state court. If a fiduciary or administrator exercises its properly delegated discretion to withhold benefits that are not expressly granted or denied by the plan, the court must defer to the judgment of the administrator or fiduciary. When the fiduciary or administrator wrongfully withholds benefits, moreover, no matter how egregious its conduct in doing so, the court will merely order the plan to pay the beneficiary the amount due. The statute does not, as interpreted by the Supreme Court, authorize tort relief or punitive damages.

While the limited rights that beneficiaries enjoy under ERISA trouble courts and commentators, they are consistent with ERISA's underlying theory. State insurance law—be it the common law of contra proferentem or statutory mandates enacted by the legislature—focus on the absolute claims of beneficiaries whose life or health is in jeopardy to the assets held by the insurer: your money or my life. They also honor the political claims of providers who demand their turn at the insurance trough. The insurance pot is, apparently, infinitely elastic and must be expanded to fulfil the demands of many claimants, each of whom, considered individually, makes a compelling case.

ERISA, by contrast, sees a zero sum game. The pot is only so big, and when it is empty it is empty. To fudge the rules in favor of one beneficiary may result in the plan not being able to honor the legitimate claims of other beneficiaries. If one claimant who has been treated egregiously by the plan is permitted to recover extracontractual damages from its administrator, these damages will ultimately come out of the pockets of the other beneficiaries, who have themselves done nothing wrong. In a world of scarce resources, not everyone can be taken care of. But the administrator, nevertheless, is also a fiduciary, and there are some limits to its discretion.

DOE v. GROUP HOSPITALIZATION
& MEDICAL SERVICES

United States Court of Appeals, Fourth Circuit, 1993.
3 F.3d 80.

NIEMEYER, CIRCUIT JUDGE:

John Doe, a 59–year-old law partner of Firm Doe in Washington, D.C., was diagnosed in late 1991 with multiple myeloma, a rare and typically fatal form of blood cancer. His physician, Dr. Kenneth C. Anderson of the Dana–Farber Cancer Institute, affiliated with Harvard Medical School, prescribed a treatment that involved an initial course of chemotherapy to reduce the percentage of tumor cells. Provided Doe responded to the therapy and achieved a "minimal disease status," Dr. Anderson recommended that Doe then undergo high-dose chemotherapy and radiation therapy combined with an autologous bone marrow transplant. * * * The cost of the entire treatment was estimated at $100,000. Dr. Anderson stated that the prescribed treatment "offers this gentleman his only chance of long-term survival."

John Doe and Firm Doe sought health insurance benefits for the prescribed treatment from Group Hospitalization and Medical Services, Inc., doing business as Blue Cross and Blue Shield of the National Capital Area (Blue Cross). Blue Cross insured and administered Firm Doe's employee welfare benefit plan pursuant to a group insurance contract entered into effective January 1, 1989. Relying on language in the contract that excludes benefits for bone marrow transplants undergone in treating multiple myeloma, as well as for "related" services and supplies, Blue Cross denied benefits. John Doe and Firm Doe promptly filed suit against Blue Cross under § 502 of the Employee Retirement Insurance Security Act (ERISA), 29 U.S.C. § 1132, claiming that Blue Cross denied benefits based solely upon improperly adopted amendments to the group insurance contract and that, in any event, the contract's language as amended did not exclude coverage for the treatment. On cross-motions for summary judgment, the district court entered judgment for Blue Cross, holding that "Blue Cross may properly deny coverage to John Doe and his physicians based on the Group Contract and amendments thereto." This appeal followed

* * *

The group insurance contract to which we must look to resolve the issues in this case was purportedly amended by a letter sent to Firm Doe dated November 30, 1990. The amendment is important because it supplied the language on which Blue Cross relied to deny coverage and gave Blue Cross discretion in deciding eligibility and contract interpretation issues.

* * *

In December 1991 John Doe was evaluated and diagnosed with multiple myeloma, * * *. By letter dated January 30, 1992, John Doe's physician, Dr. Anderson, prescribed a treatment of chemotherapy and radiation that included an autologous bone marrow transplant. On March 30, 1992, Dr. Gregory K. Morris, vice president and medical director of Blue Cross, wrote Dr. Anderson denying the request for coverage of the proposed treatment. Specifically referring to the language of the November 30, 1990, amendment that excludes from coverage treatment of myeloma by means of bone marrow transplant and services and supplies related thereto, Dr. Morris stated that Blue Cross will be "unable to provide benefits for Mr. [Doe]." * * *[4]

---

4. After denying coverage and rejecting John Doe's appeal, Blue Cross amended the group insurance contract on May 28, 1992, effective August 1, 1992, to confirm its interpretation of the contract and to exclude the treatment for which John Doe had requested precertification. Because ERISA requires that specific reasons for denial of a claim be given, see 29 U.S.C. § 1133, our review in this case is limited to only those reasons which Blue Cross

The November 30 letter was a form letter apparently sent to all administrators of Blue Cross group insurance contracts. It opens by stating that its purpose is to "inform you of updates" to the group contract. It then addresses changes to no less than eight separate aspects of coverage in four single-spaced pages, including one headed "Organ Transplants" that includes the language in question. * * *

John Doe and Firm Doe contend that the amendment was ineffective for two reasons: It was not adopted in accordance with the contract's specified time periods for making amendments, and, even if it was timely, the language of the amendment misled the contract holder, Firm Doe, and its employees about the nature of the changes.

[The court found that the amendment was effective because Blue Cross had provided 30 days notice of the change in accordance with the contract. ed.]

In connection with their second point, John Doe and Firm Doe argue that while the language contained in the section headed "Organ Transplants" purports to "clarify" the types of transplants covered ("In order to clarify which types of transplants are covered, a list of the covered procedures [is] being added to your Contract as follows" (emphasis added)), coverage was in fact narrowed by the amendment because before the amendment transplants were simply not addressed and were therefore presumptively covered so long as they were not excluded under some other provision. They argue, therefore, that Blue Cross failed to disclose the intended effect of the limitation for organ transplants, downplaying the significance of the letter. * * * In short, they maintain that Blue Cross failed to put Firm Doe on notice of an amendment. From our review of the letter and the parties' conduct in response to it, we find this argument unpersuasive.

Health care benefits provided in an employee benefit plan are not vested benefits; the employer may modify or withdraw these benefits at any time, provided the changes are made in compliance with ERISA and the terms of the plan. * * * Firm Doe established its benefit plan through a contract with Blue Cross, and as part of this contract, Firm Doe accepted the provision that "benefits, provisions, terms, or conditions" could be changed by Blue Cross upon timely written notice. We believe that the November 30 letter provided sufficient notice that benefits under the contract were being changed. It states at the outset that the letter is an "update" of the terms of the contract. The body of the letter refers to specific coverages, outlining the changes in the language for each. * * *

Evidence was also presented that Firm Doe in fact relied on the changes made by the November 30 letter in connection with other coverages and it continued to pay premiums under the contract without objection. Moreover, the amendment was circulated well before John Doe evidenced any symptoms of or was diagnosed with cancer. More than 15 months after the amendment was sent, Blue Cross relied on its language in reviewing the coverage, and we believe that it was correct in doing so.

gave for denying coverage. [ ] However, any attempt by Blue Cross to rely on a post-precertification pre-therapy amendment to deny benefits to John Doe, which would be inappropriate to anticipate now, might raise serious questions concerning Blue Cross' duties, both as a fiduciary and under the insurance contract with Firm Doe, and its good faith.

John Doe and Firm Doe contend that even the amended language of their group insurance contract with Blue Cross does not provide a basis for the insurance company's decision to deny John Doe benefits. Before turning to the validly amended contract to review this decision, we must address the appropriate standard of review to apply.

Court actions challenging the denial of benefits under 29 U.S.C. § 1132(a)(1)(B) are subject to the standard of review announced in Firestone Tire and Rubber Co. v. Bruch, 489 U.S. 101, 109 S.Ct. 948, 103 L.Ed.2d 80 (1989). The Court observed there, deriving guidance from principles of trust law, that in reviewing actions of a fiduciary who has been given discretionary powers to determine eligibility for benefits and to construe the language of an ERISA plan deference must be shown, and the fiduciary's actions will be reviewed only for abuse. [ ] If discretionary authority is not provided, denials of claims are to be reviewed de novo. [ ] Thus, where a fiduciary with authorized discretion construes a disputed or doubtful term, we will not disturb the interpretation if it is reasonable, even if we come to a different conclusion independently. [ ] In Firestone, however, the Supreme Court went on to recognize that a conflict of interest could lower the level of deference to be applied to a discretionary decision by a fiduciary:

> Of course, if a benefit plan gives discretion to an administrator or fiduciary who is operating under a conflict of interest, that conflict must be weighed as a "facto[r] in determining whether there is an abuse of discretion."

489 U.S. at 115, 109 S.Ct. at 957

Under the group insurance contract with Firm Doe, the employer, Blue Cross both insures and administers the payment of health care benefits for Firm Doe's employee welfare benefit plan. In its role as plan administrator, Blue Cross clearly exercises discretionary authority or discretionary control with respect to the management of the plan and therefore qualifies as a fiduciary under ERISA. 29 U.S.C. § 1002(21)(A). Only if Blue Cross has also been given discretionary authority with regard to decisions about eligibility for benefits and construction of the plan, however, will those decisions be entitled to deferential review. [ ]

Blue Cross asserts that it has been given discretionary authority to review claims, determine eligibility, and construe contract terms and that our review of its decision to deny Doe benefits is therefore only for abuse of discretion. We agree that the express terms of the group insurance contract give Blue Cross discretion to the extent it claims. The terms were stated in the November 30, 1990, letter of amendment as follows:

> [Blue Cross] shall have the full power and discretionary authority to control and manage the operation and administration of the Contract, subject only to the Participant's rights of review and appeal under the Contract. [Blue Cross] shall have all powers necessary to accomplish these purposes in accordance with the terms of the contract including, but not limited to:
>
> a. Determining all questions relating to Employee and Family Member eligibility and coverage;

b. Determining the benefits and amounts payable therefor to any Participant or provider of health care services;

c. Establishing and administering a claims review and appeal process; and

d. Interpreting, applying, and administering the provisions of the Contract.

John Doe and Firm Doe contend, however, that in denying benefits to John Doe, Blue Cross operated under a conflict of interest, and that therefore no deference to its discretion is warranted. They note that ERISA imposes on fiduciaries a duty of loyalty to act "with respect to a plan solely in the interest of the participants and beneficiaries and for the exclusive purpose of providing benefits ... and defraying reasonable expenses." 29 U.S.C. § 1104(a)(1)(A) [ ] Blue Cross apparently is compensated by a fixed premium, and when it pays a claim it funds the payment from the premiums collected. No evidence has been presented to suggest it has a mechanism to collect from the employer retrospectively for unexpected liabilities. It therefore bears the financial risk for claims made beyond the actuarial norm. John Doe and Firm Doe point out that "each time [Blue Cross] approves a payment of benefits, the money comes out of its own pocket" and argue that Blue Cross' fiduciary role as decisionmaker in approving benefits under the plan therefore "lies in perpetual conflict with its profitmaking role as a business." [ ] They urge that, because of this conflict, when we review Blue Cross' decision to deny Doe benefits, no deference to its judgment is due.* * *

We were first presented with the question of what effect a fiduciary's conflict of interest might have in De Nobel [v. Vitro Corp., 885 F.2d 1180 (4th Cir.1989)]. There, the employee-claimants, who were beneficiaries of an employee retirement plan, contended that decisions of the administrators of the plan were not entitled to deferential review because the administrators operated under a conflict of interest arising from their dual role as plan administrators and employees of the sponsoring company. The beneficiaries argued that decisions by the administrator favorable to the employer would save the plan "substantial sums."[ ] In deciding the case, however, we never reached the effect that a conflict of interest might have on the applicable standard of review because we concluded that no substantial conflict existed when the plan was fully funded and any savings would inure to the direct benefit of the plan, and therefore to the benefit of all beneficiaries and participants. * * *

In this case, Blue Cross insured the plan in exchange for the payment of a fixed premium, presumably based on actuarial data. Undoubtedly, its profit from the insurance contract depends on whether the claims allowed exceed the assumed risks. To the extent that Blue Cross has discretion to avoid paying claims, it thereby promotes the potential for its own profit. That type of conflict flows inherently from the nature of the relationship entered into by the parties and is common where employers contract with insurance companies to provide and administer health care benefits to employees through group insurance contracts.* * *

* * *

Because of the presence of a substantial conflict of interest, we therefore must alter our standard of review. We hold that when a fiduciary exercises discretion in interpreting a disputed term of the contract where one interpretation will further the financial interests of the fiduciary, we will not act as deferentially as would otherwise be appropriate. Rather, we will review the merits of the interpretation to determine whether it is consistent with an exercise of discretion by a fiduciary acting free of the interests that conflict with those of the beneficiaries. In short, the fiduciary decision will be entitled to some deference, but this deference will be lessened to the degree necessary to neutralize any untoward influence resulting from the conflict. [ ] With that lessened degree of deference to Blue Cross' discretionary interpretation of the group insurance contract, we turn to review Blue Cross' decision to deny benefits.

[The court then described the high dose chemotherapy, autologous bone marrow transplantation procedure, ed.]

* * *

Without consideration of a potential bone marrow transplant, treatment of blood cancer by chemotherapy and radiation is accordingly clearly covered by the contract.

* * *

* * * [T]he contract as amended November 30, 1990, provides that an autologous bone marrow transplant for multiple myeloma and "services or supplies for or related to" the transplant are excluded from the plan's coverage.

Blue Cross argues that the language excluding "services or supplies for or related to" the autologous bone marrow transplant reaches to exclude high-dose chemotherapy and radiation treatments because without the autologous bone marrow transplant, the high-dose chemotherapy could not be performed. * * * We believe that such an argument misdirects the analysis required for determining the scope of coverage and fails to accommodate harmoniously all provisions of the contract.

The bone marrow transplant, while necessary to avoid a disastrous side effect, is not the procedure designed to treat the cancer. The first question to be asked, therefore, is whether the cancer treating procedure is covered by the contract, and, as already noted, we have found it is. While Blue Cross is well within its rights to exclude from coverage the ancillary bone marrow transplant procedure, the exclusion should not, in the absence of clear language, be construed to withdraw coverage explicitly granted elsewhere in the contract.

* * *

We additionally note that in determining whether a decision has been made solely for the benefit of the participants, we may take account of the principle that in making a reasonable decision, ambiguity which remains in the scope of the "related to" language must be construed against the drafting party, particularly when, as here, the contract is a form provided by the insurer rather than one negotiated between the parties. [ ]

Because Blue Cross' discretionary interpretation to the contrary is not entitled to the deference we might otherwise accord, * * * we will construe the contract for the benefit of its beneficiaries and enforce the coverage provided by Part 3 of the group insurance contract and not otherwise explicitly excluded.

* * *

AFFIRMED IN PART, REVERSED IN PART, AND REMANDED FOR FURTHER PROCEEDINGS.

Notes and Questions

1. Section 502(a) of ERISA permits a plan participant or beneficiary to sue to "recover benefits due to him under the terms of the plan * * * " in federal or state court. 29 U.S.C.A. § 1132(a)(1). Though on its face this provision permits a suit against a plan for benefits denied, the courts have treated it instead as authorizing a review of the decision of the ERISA plan, i.e. the ERISA administrator is treated as an independent decisionmaker whose decision is subject to judicial review, much like an administrative agency, rather than as a defendant who has allegedly wronged the claimant. See Jay Conison, Suits for Benefits Under ERISA, 54 Univ. Pitt. L. Rev. 1 (1992).

As the principal case notes, Firestone Tire & Rubber Co. v. Bruch, 489 U.S. 101, 109 S.Ct. 948, 103 L.Ed.2d 80 (1989), held that the courts should apply de novo review in reviewing ERISA plan decisions. In doing so the Court rejected the "arbitrary and capricious" standard of review generally applied in earlier lower federal court ERISA review cases. The Court went on to observe, however, that arbitrary and capricious review, rather than de novo review, would apply if "the benefit plan gives the administrator or fiduciary discretionary authority to determine eligibility for benefits or to construe the terms of the plan." 489 U.S. at 115, 109 S.Ct. at 957.

In doing so, the Court created an exception that swallowed the rule, since post-*Firestone* plans are generally drafted to give the plan administrator discretionary authority. Even where de novo review is available, moreover, some appellate courts have cabined it by limiting judicial review to consideration of the evidence considered by the plan administrator, Perry v. Simplicity Engineering, 900 F.2d 963 (6th Cir.1990); or by retaining deferential review for factual determinations of plan administrators and limiting de novo review to plan interpretations. Pierre v. Connecticut General Life Insurance Company, 932 F.2d 1552 (5th Cir.1991), cert. denied, 502 U.S. 973, 112 S.Ct. 453, 116 L.Ed.2d 470 (1991).

Although *Firestone* authorized arbitrary and capricious review where a plan fiduciary is granted decisionmaking discretion, it also observed that if "an administrator or fiduciary * * * is operating under a conflict of interest, that conflict must be weighed as a 'facto[r] in determining whether there is an abuse of discretion.' " 489 U.S. at 114.

The lower courts are sharply divided in their approaches to determining whether an administrator faces a conflict of interest in making the benefit determination, and what effect a conflict should have on the level of review if one is found. See Judith C. Brostron, The Conflict of Interest Standard in ERISA cases: Can it be Avoided in the Denial of High Dose Chemotherapy Treatment for Breast Cancer, 3 DePaul J. Health Care L. 1 (1999); Haavi Morreim, Benefits

Decisions in ERISA Plans: Diminishing Deference to Fiduciaries and an Emerging Problem for Provider Sponsored Organizations, 65 Tenn L Rev. 511 (1998).

At one end of the spectrum, courts hold that if the plaintiff demonstrates that the fiduciary is operating under a substantial conflict of interest, the fiduciary's decision is afforded little deference. See Killian v. Healthsource, 152 F.3d 514 (6th Cir.1998); McGraw v. Prudential Ins. Co. 137 F.3d 1253 (10th Cir.1998). Indeed, some go so far as to hold the decision to be "presumptively void". See Armstrong v. Aetna Life Ins. Co., 128 F.3d 1263 (8th Cir.1997); Brown v. Blue Cross & Blue Shield, 898 F.2d 1556, 1566–67 (11th Cir.1990). Courts applying this test tend to assume that an insurer or self-insured company faces a conflict almost by definition, since approval of any particular claim reduces its profits. See Killian v. Healthsource Provident Administrators, 152 F.3d 514, 521 (6th Cir.1998); Peruzzi v. Summa Med. Plan, 137 F.3d 431, 433 (6th Cir.1998); Edmonds v. Hughes Aircraft Co., 145 F.3d 1324 (4th Cir.1998). Under this "presumptively void" test, a decision rendered by a plan fiduciary operating under a substantial conflict of interest is presumed to be arbitrary and capricious unless the administrator can demonstrate that either (1) the result reached would nevertheless be found to be "right" if subjected to de novo review, or (2) the decision was not made to serve the administrator's conflicting interest.

Courts at the other end of the spectrum insist that conflicts of interest are rarely a problem because of market competition. The denial of any one claim by a benefit plan, they contend, has a negligible effect on the profit margins of a plan, but routine denial of claims will give a plan a bad reputation and make it less competitive. See Mers v. Marriott International Group Accidental Death & Dismemberment Plan, 144 F.3d 1014 (7th Cir.1998); Farley v. Arkansas Blue Cross and Blue Shield, 147 F.3d 774 (8th Cir.1998). Under this interpretation, arbitrary and capricious review, untempered by consideration of conflicting interests, is almost always appropriate.

Courts in the middle take interest conflicts into account only if the plaintiff can show both that a substantial conflict of interest exists and that the conflict in fact caused a breach of the fiduciary's duty and motivated an improper decision See Friedrich v. Intel Corp., 181 F.3d 1105 (9th Cir.1999); Barnhart v. UNUM Life Ins. Co., 179 F.3d 583, 588 (8th Cir.1999); Atwood v. Newmont Gold, Inc. 45 F.3d 1317, 1322 (9th Cir.1995); Elsroth v. Consolidated Edison Co., 10 F.Supp.2d 427 (S.D.N.Y.1998); Sullivan v. LTV Aerospace and Defense Co., 82 F.3d 1251 (2d Cir.1996). For example, the failure of a plan to consult independent reviewers in processing a claim, Woo v. Deluxe Corp., 144 F.3d 1157 (8th Cir.1998); McGraw v. Prudential Ins. Co. of America, 137 F.3d 1253 (10th Cir.1998), or to follow internal plan procedures, Friedrich v. Intel Corp., 181 F.3d 1105 (9th Cir.1999), are evidence of improper decisionmaking. On the other hand, decisions made through the use of independent consultants or by salaried employees who do not face direct incentives to approve or deny claims, or through the application of fair procedures, will generally be accepted. See Hendrix v. Standard Ins. Co., 182 F.3d 925 (9th Cir.1999); Jones v. Kodak Medical Assistance Plan, 169 F.3d 1287 (10th Cir.1999); Hightshue v. AIG Life Ins. Co., 135 F.3d 1144 (7th Cir.1998). Other courts apply a "sliding scale" approach, using an abuse of discretion review standard, but exercising greater scrutiny where a greater conflict is found. See Chambers v. Family Health Plan Corp., 100 F.3d 818, 825 (10th Cir.1996); Sullivan v. LTV Aerospace & Defense Co., 82 F.3d 1251, 1255 (2d Cir.1996); Taft v. Equitable Life Assurance Soc'y, 9 F.3d 1469, 1474 (9th Cir.1993); Van Boxel v. Journal Co. Employees' Pension Trust, 836 F.2d 1048, 1052–53 (7th Cir.1987). Most courts have held that the finding of a conflict of interest does not result in the abandonment of the arbitrary and capricious standard, but rather in giving it "more bite." A few courts, however, apply de novo review when a conflict is found.

What deference, if any, should federal courts afford plan administrators in reviewing ERISA benefit decisions? Should plan drafters be permitted to evade de novo review simply by drafting plan documents to give discretion to plan administrators? Do the interests of plan administrators inevitably conflict with the interests of plan participants and beneficiaries? Does the degree of conflict vary depending on whether the administrator is a self-insured employer, a third-party administrator for a self-insured employer, a risk-bearing insurer, a trust affiliated with a labor union, or a multiple employer trust that administers health benefits for a number of small employers? Should the court in Doe have considered the fact that Blue Cross plans are non-profit? Does the market for insurance in fact correct the conflict-of-interest problem? Should courts be permitted to consider evidence not presented initially to plan administrators when they review plan decisions, or should they be limited to reviewing the plan administrator's decision on the record? Might concern on the part of federal courts about being swamped by insurance claims affect the eagerness of the courts to review these claims? Should it?

2. Whether or not extracontractual damages can ever be available under ERISA is a question that has provoked considerable controversy. At this point the answer seems to be no, though a good argument can be made that this is not the result Congress intended. See George Flint, ERISA: Extracontractual Damages Mandated for Benefit Claims Actions, 36 Ariz. L. Rev. 611 (1994); Note, Available Remedies Under ERISA Section 502(a), 45 Ala. L. Rev. 631 (1994). In Massachusetts Mutual Life Insurance Co. v. Russell, 473 U.S. 134, 105 S.Ct. 3085, 87 L.E.2d 96 (1985), the Supreme Court held that ERISA does not authorize recovery of extracontractual damages by plan participants for breach of fiduciary duty. In Mertens v. Hewitt Associates, 508 U.S. 248, 113 S.Ct. 2063, 124 L.Ed.2d 161 (1993), the Court read provisions of ERISA permitting plan participants and beneficiaries "to obtain other appropriate equitable relief(i) to redress such violations ... " (29 U.S.C.A. § 1132(a)(3)) to not authorize damage actions, as damages are not equitable in nature.

The Supreme Court, however, in its most recent ERISA case to address this issue, held that 29 U.S.C.A. § 1132(a)(3) does authorize individual beneficiaries the right to sue for equitable relief for breaches of fiduciary duty. Varity Corp. v. Howe, 516 U.S. 489, 116 S.Ct. 1065, 134 L.Ed.2d 130 (1996). This case breaks from a long line of cases limiting ERISA relief, and might signal openness on the part of the court to entertaining claims for broader relief for plan participants and beneficiaries.

The effect of these cases is that an ERISA participant or beneficiary denied benefits can only recover the value of the claim itself and cannot recover damages caused by the claim denial. Punitive damages are also unavailable against plan administrators and fiduciaries under even the most egregious circumstances. What effect might the lack of this relief have on ERISA fiduciaries and administrators? To what extent might the fact that ERISA permits courts to award attorneys fees ameliorate this effect? 29 U.S.C.A. § 1132(g).

3. While ERISA preempts state common law, federal courts have, with some hesitancy, developed federal common law in ERISA cases. See Jayne Zanglein, Closing the Gap: Safeguarding Participants' Rights by Expanding the Federal Common Law of ERISA, 72 Wash. U.L Q. 671 (1994); William Carr & Robert Liebross, Wrongs Without Rights: The Need for A Strong Federal Common Law of

ERISA, 4 Stanford L & Pol'y Rev. 221 (1993). Under what circumstances might federal common law or equitable doctrine apply? See Kane v. Aetna Life Insurance, 893 F.2d 1283 (11th Cir.1990), cert. denied, 498 U.S. 890, 111 S.Ct. 232, 112 L.Ed.2d 192 (1990) (court can apply equitable estoppel to interpret but not to change the terms of an ERISA plan); Nash v. Trustees of Boston University, 946 F.2d 960 (1st Cir.1991) (fraud in the inducement can be raised as an affirmative defense in ERISA case); but see Watkins v. Westinghouse Hanford Co., 12 F.3d 1517 (9th Cir.1993) (equitable doctrines may not be relied on to provide remedies not available under ERISA). Should the federal courts adopt state common law of insurance in interpreting ERISA policies, or do different considerations govern in ERISA cases? In particular, could a court apply the contract interpretation principles applied in *HealthChicago* in an ERISA case?

4. ERISA does not by its terms permit providers to sue plans. Courts have generally rejected the argument that providers are "beneficiaries" under ERISA plans. Pritt v. Blue Cross & Blue Shield, Inc., 699 F.Supp. 81 (S.D.W.Va.1988). Providers have been more successful in asserting their rights as assignees of participants and beneficiaries, City of Hope National Medical Center v. Healthplus, Inc., 156 F.3d 223 (1st Cir.1998); Hermann Hosp. v. MEBA Medical & Benefits Plan, 845 F.2d 1286 (5th Cir.1988), though a few courts have held that assignees have no standing to sue as they are not mentioned as protected parties within the statute. Other courts have upheld anti-assignment clauses in plan contracts.

Courts have split on whether providers can recover from insurers when the insurer leads the provider to believe that the insured or the service is covered, and then subsequently refuses payment and claims ERISA protection. Several courts have held that ERISA is intended to control relationships between employers and employees and should not preempt common law or statutory misrepresentation claims brought by providers. Transitional Hospitals Corp. v. Blue Cross & Blue Shield of Texas, 164 F.3d 952 (5th Cir.1999); Hospice of Metro Denver, Inc. v. Group Health Ins. of Okla., Inc., 944 F.2d 752 (10th Cir.1991). Other courts have held that misrepresentation claims are claims for benefits that are preempted by ERISA. Cromwell v. Equicor–Equitable HCA Corp., 944 F.2d 1272 (6th Cir.1991), cert. denied, 505 U.S. 1233, 113 S.Ct. 2, 120 L.Ed.2d 931 (1992). Finally, several courts have allowed a provider to sue an ERISA plan on a contract claim, stating that the claim was not preempted by ERISA because the provider had no standing to sue under ERISA. See, generally, Jeffrey A. Brauch, Health Care Providers Meet ERISA: Are Provider Claims for Misrepresentation of Coverage Preempted: 20 Pepperdine L. Rev. 497 (1993); David P. Kallus, ERISA: Do Health Care Providers Have Standing to Bring a Civil Enforcement Action Under Section 1132(a)? 30 Santa Clara L. Rev. 173 (1990)

5. ERISA also requires health benefit plans to acknowledge and effectuate "qualified medical child support orders." These are state court orders that require a group health plan that covers dependents to extend group medical coverage to the children of a plan participant, even though the participant does not have legal custody of the children. 29 U.S.C.A. § 1169. Under this law, adopted in 1993, a plan participant can be required under court order to pay for family coverage to cover a dependent child not in the parent's custody, even though the parent might have otherwise chosen not to purchase coverage. Who benefits from this law, other than the children it protects?

Problem: ERISA Litigation

John Mendez is in the advanced stages of a condition that results in degeneration of his nervous system. His doctor believes that he would be helped by a new gene therapy. John receives coverage under his employer's self-insured employee benefits plan. The plan has denied coverage for the therapy, claiming that it is experimental. The terms of the plan give the administrator discretion to decide whether or not to cover experimental procedures, but does not define "experimental." John's doctor claims that the procedure is still quite new, but has advanced beyond the experimental stage. What standard will a court apply in reviewing the administrator's decision if John sues under § 502? How does this standard differ from that a court would have applied had John sued an insurer under an individual health insurance policy under standard state insurance contract law?

2. *ADMINISTRATIVE CLAIMS AND APPEALS PROCEDURES UNDER ERISA*

29 U.S.C.A. § 1133 provides:

In accordance with regulations of the Secretary, every employee benefit plan shall—

> (1) provide adequate notice in writing to any participant or beneficiary whose claim for benefits under the plan has been denied, setting forth the specific reasons for such denial, written in a manner calculated to be understood by the participant, and

> (2) afford a reasonable opportunity to any participant whose claim for benefits has been denied for a full and fair review by the appropriate named fiduciary of the decision denying the claim.

The Department of Labor promulgated regulations in 1977 permitting an aggrieved ERISA participant to request a review of a decision, review pertinent documents, submit issues and comments in writing, and receive a written decision, including specific reasons for the decision and reference to specific plan provisions on which it is based, usually within 60 days. As indemnification insurance faded into history, and managed care came to the fore, these regulations seemed increasingly archaic. In 1998 then President Clinton directed the Department of Labor to promulgate new ERISA claims procedure regulations to implement recommendations of the President's Advisory Commission on Consumer Protection and Quality in the Health Care Industry, which had issued its final report early that year. Proposed regulations were issued in the fall of 1998, and then sat for two years as the Department mulled over more than 700 letters of comment and heard more than sixty speakers at public hearings. Finally late in November, 2000, again under orders from President Clinton, now in the last few days of his administration, DOL finally issued the final rules.

20 C.F.R. § 2560.503-1 CLAIMS PROCEDURE.

* * *

(b) Every employee benefit plan shall establish and maintain reasonable procedures governing the filing of benefit claims, notification of benefit determinations, and appeal of adverse benefit determinations * * *. The claims procedures for a plan will be deemed to be reasonable only if—

(1) The claims procedures comply with the [procedural requirements of this regulation] * * *;

(2) A description of all claims procedures (including, in the case of a group health plan * * *, any procedures for obtaining prior approval as a prerequisite for obtaining a benefit, such as preauthorization procedures or utilization review procedures) and the applicable time frames is included as part of a summary plan description * * * [a document each plan member must get; describing the plan];

(3) The claims procedures do not contain any provision, and are not administered in a way, that unduly inhibits or hampers the initiation or processing of claims for benefits. For example, a provision or practice that requires payment of a fee or costs as a condition to making a claim or to appealing an adverse benefit determination would be considered to unduly inhibit the initiation and processing of claims for benefits. Also, the denial of a claim for failure to obtain a prior approval under circumstances that would make obtaining such prior approval impossible or where application of the prior approval process could seriously jeopardize the life or health of the claimant (e.g., in the case of a group health plan, the claimant is unconscious and in need of immediate care at the time medical treatment is required) would constitute a practice that unduly inhibits the initiation and processing of a claim;

(4) The claims procedures do not preclude an authorized representative of a claimant from acting on behalf of such claimant in pursuing a benefit claim or appeal of an adverse benefit determination. * * * [I]n the case of a claim involving urgent care, * * *, a health care professional, * * * with knowledge of a claimant's medical condition shall be permitted to act as the authorized representative of the claimant; and

(5) The claims procedures contain administrative processes and safeguards designed to ensure and to verify that benefit claim determinations are made in accordance with governing plan documents and that, where appropriate, the plan provisions have been applied consistently with respect to similarly situated claimants.

(6) In the case of a plan established and maintained pursuant to a collective bargaining agreement * * *—

(i) Such plan will be deemed to comply with the [claims determination and appeal] provisions of * * * this section if the collective bargaining agreement * * * sets forth or incorporates by specific reference—

(A) Provisions concerning the filing of benefit claims and the initial disposition of benefit claims, and

(B) A grievance and arbitration procedure to which adverse benefit determinations are subject.

(ii) Such plan will be deemed to comply with the [appeal] provisions of * * * this section (but will not be deemed to comply with [the claims determination] paragraphs * * *) if the collective bargaining agreement pursuant to which the plan is established or maintained sets forth or incorporates by specific reference a grievance and arbitration procedure to which adverse benefit determinations are subject (but not provisions concerning the filing and initial disposition of benefit claims).

(c) Group health plans. The claims procedures of a group health plan will be deemed to be reasonable only if, in addition to complying with the requirements of paragraph (b) of this section—

(1)(i) The claims procedures provide that, in the case of a failure by a claimant or an authorized representative of a claimant to follow the plan's procedures for filing a pre-service claim, * * * the claimant or representative shall be notified of the failure and the proper procedures to be followed in filing a claim for benefits. This notification shall be provided to the claimant or authorized representative, as appropriate, as soon as possible, but not later than 5 days (24 hours in the case of a failure to file a claim involving urgent care) following the failure. * * *

* * *

(ii) Paragraph (c)(1)(i) of this section shall apply only in the case of a failure that—

(A) Is a communication by a claimant or an authorized representative of a claimant that is received by a person or organizational unit customarily responsible for handling benefit matters; and

(B) Is a communication that names a specific claimant; a specific medical condition or symptom; and a specific treatment, service, or product for which approval is requested.

(2) The claims procedures do not contain any provision, and are not administered in a way, that requires a claimant to file more than two appeals of an adverse benefit determination prior to bringing a civil action under section 502(a) of the Act;

(3) To the extent that a plan offers voluntary levels of appeal (except to the extent that the plan is required to do so by State law), including voluntary arbitration or any other form of dispute resolution, in addition to those permitted by paragraph (c)(2) of this section, the claims procedures provide that:

(i) The plan waives any right to assert that a claimant has failed to exhaust administrative remedies because the claimant did not elect to submit a benefit dispute to any such voluntary level of appeal provided by the plan;

(ii) The plan agrees that any statute of limitations or other defense based on timeliness is tolled during the time that any such voluntary appeal is pending;

(iii) The claims procedures provide that a claimant may elect to submit a benefit dispute to such voluntary level of appeal only after exhaustion of the appeals permitted by paragraph (c)(2) of this section;

(iv) The plan provides to any claimant, upon request, sufficient information relating to the voluntary level of appeal to enable the claimant to make an informed judgment about whether to submit a benefit dispute to the voluntary level of appeal, including a statement that the decision of a claimant as to whether or not to submit a benefit dispute to the voluntary level of appeal will have no effect on the claimant's rights to any other benefits under the plan and information about the applicable rules, the claimant's right to representation, the process for selecting the decisionmaker, and the circumstances, if any, that may affect the impartiality of the decisionmaker, such as any financial or personal interests in the result or any past or present relationship with any party to the review process; and

(v) No fees or costs are imposed on the claimant as part of the voluntary level of appeal.

(4) The claims procedures do not contain any provision for the mandatory arbitration of adverse benefit determinations, except to the extent that the plan or procedures provide that:

(i) The arbitration is conducted as one of the two appeals described in paragraph (c)(2) of this section and in accordance with the requirements applicable to such appeals; and

(ii) The claimant is not precluded from challenging the decision under section 502(a) of the Act or other applicable law.

* * *

(f) Timing of notification of benefit determination.

* * *

(2) Group health plans.

* * *

(i) Urgent care claims. In the case of a claim involving urgent care, the plan administrator shall notify the claimant of the plan's benefit determination (whether adverse or not) as soon as possible, taking into account the medical exigencies, but not later than 72 hours after receipt of the claim by the plan, unless the claimant fails to provide sufficient information to determine whether, or to what extent, benefits are covered or payable under the plan. In the case of such a failure, the plan administrator shall notify the claimant as soon as possible, but not later than 24 hours after receipt of the claim by the plan, of the specific information necessary to complete the claim. * * * The plan administrator shall notify the claimant of the plan's benefit determination as soon as possible, but in no case later than 48 hours after the earlier of—

(A) The plan's receipt of the specified information, or

(B) The end of the period afforded the claimant to provide the specified additional information.

(ii) Concurrent care decisions. If a group health plan has approved an ongoing course of treatment to be provided over a period of time or number of treatments—

(A) Any reduction or termination by the plan of such course of treatment (other than by plan amendment or termination) before the end of such period of time or number of treatments shall constitute an adverse benefit determination. The plan administrator shall notify the claimant, * * * of the adverse benefit determination at a time sufficiently in advance of the reduction or termination to allow the claimant to appeal and obtain a determination on review of that adverse benefit determination before the benefit is reduced or terminated.

(B) Any request by a claimant to extend the course of treatment beyond the period of time or number of treatments that is a claim involving urgent care shall be decided as soon as possible, taking into account the medical exigencies, and the plan administrator shall notify the claimant of the benefit determination, whether adverse or not, within 24 hours after receipt of the claim by the plan, provided that any such claim is made to the plan at least 24 hours prior to the expiration of the prescribed period of time or number of treatments. * * *

(iii) Other claims.

(A) Pre-service claims. In the case of a pre-service claim, the plan administrator shall notify the claimant of the plan's benefit determination (whether adverse or not) within a reasonable period of time appropriate to the medical circumstances, but not later than 15 days after receipt of the claim by the plan. This period may be extended one time by the plan for up to 15 days, provided that the plan administrator both determines that such an extension is necessary due to matters beyond the control of the plan and notifies the claimant, prior to the expiration of the initial 15–day period, of the circumstances requiring the extension of time and the date by which the plan expects to render a decision. * * *

(B) Post-service claims. In the case of a post-service claim, the plan administrator shall notify the claimant, in accordance with paragraph (g) of this section, of the plan's adverse benefit determination within a reasonable period of time, but not later than 30 days after receipt of the claim [subject to one 15 day extension if necessary due to matters beyond the plan's control].* * *

* * *

(g) Manner and content of notification of benefit determination. (1) Except as provided in paragraph (g)(2) of this section, the plan administrator shall provide a claimant with written or electronic notification of any adverse benefit determination. * * * The notification shall set forth, in a manner calculated to be understood by the claimant—

(i) The specific reason or reasons for the adverse determination;

(ii) Reference to the specific plan provisions on which the determination is based;

(iii) A description of any additional material or information necessary for the claimant to perfect the claim and an explanation of why such material or information is necessary;

(iv) A description of the plan's review procedures and the time limits applicable to such procedures, including a statement of the claimant's right to bring a civil action under section 502(a) of the Act following an adverse benefit determination on review;

(v) In the case of an adverse benefit determination by a group health plan or a plan providing disability benefits,

(A) If an internal rule, guideline, protocol, or other similar criterion was relied upon in making the adverse determination, either the specific rule, guideline, protocol, or other similar criterion; or a statement that such a rule, guideline, protocol, or other similar criterion was relied upon in making the adverse determination and that a copy of such rule, guideline, protocol, or other criterion will be provided free of charge to the claimant upon request; or

(B) If the adverse benefit determination is based on a medical necessity or experimental treatment or similar exclusion or limit, either an explanation of the scientific or clinical judgment for the determination, applying the terms of the plan to the claimant's medical circumstances, or a statement that such explanation will be provided free of charge upon request.

(vi) In the case of an adverse benefit determination by a group health plan concerning a claim involving urgent care, a description of the expedited review process applicable to such claims.

* * *

(h) Appeal of adverse benefit determinations.

* * *

(3) Group health plans. The claims procedures of a group health plan will not be deemed to provide a claimant with a reasonable opportunity for a full and fair review of a claim and adverse benefit determination unless * * * the claims procedures—

(i) Provide claimants at least 180 days * * * within which to appeal the determination;

(ii) Provide for a review that does not afford deference to the initial adverse benefit determination and that is conducted by an appropriate named fiduciary of the plan who is neither the individual who made the adverse benefit determination that is the subject of the appeal, nor the subordinate of such individual;

(iii) Provide that, in deciding an appeal of any adverse benefit determination that is based in whole or in part on a medical judgment, including determinations with regard to whether a particular treatment, drug, or other item is experimental, investigational, or not medically necessary or appropriate, the appropriate named fiduciary shall consult with a health care professional who has appropriate training and experience in the field of medicine involved in the medical judgment;

(iv) Provide for the identification of medical or vocational experts whose advice was obtained on behalf of the plan in connection with a claimant's adverse benefit determination, * * *;

(v) Provide that the health care professional engaged for purposes of a consultation * * * shall be an individual who is neither an individual who was consulted in connection with the adverse benefit determination that is the subject of the appeal, nor the subordinate of any such individual; and

(vi) Provide, in the case of a claim involving urgent care, for an expedited review process * * *

* * *

(k) Preemption of State law. (1) Nothing in this section shall be construed to supersede any provision of State law that regulates insurance, except to the extent that such law prevents the application of a requirement of this section.

(2) (i) For purposes of paragraph (k)(1) of this section, a State law regulating insurance shall not be considered to prevent the application of a requirement of this section merely because such State law establishes a review procedure to evaluate and resolve disputes involving adverse benefit determinations under group health plans so long as the review procedure is conducted by a person or entity other than the insurer, the plan, plan fiduciaries, the employer, or any employee or agent of any of the foregoing.

(ii) The State law procedures described in paragraph (k)(2)(i) of this section are not part of the full and fair review required by section 503 of the Act. Claimants therefore need not exhaust such State law procedures prior to bringing suit under section 502(a) of the Act.

(*l*) Failure to establish and follow reasonable claims procedures. In the case of the failure of a plan to establish or follow claims procedures consistent with the requirements of this section, a claimant shall be deemed to have exhausted the administrative remedies available under the plan and shall be entitled to pursue any available remedies under section 502(a) of the Act on the basis that the plan has failed to provide a reasonable claims procedure that would yield a decision on the merits of the claim.

(m) Definitions. The following terms shall have the meaning ascribed to such terms in this paragraph (m) whenever such term is used in this section:

(1)(i) A "claim involving urgent care" is any claim for medical care or treatment with respect to which the application of the time periods for making non-urgent care determinations—

(A) Could seriously jeopardize the life or health of the claimant or the ability of the claimant to regain maximum function, or,

(B) In the opinion of a physician with knowledge of the claimant's medical condition, would subject the claimant to severe pain that cannot be adequately managed without the care or treatment that is the subject of the claim.

(ii) Except as provided in paragraph (m)(1)(iii) of this section, whether a claim is a "claim involving urgent care" within the meaning of paragraph (m)(1)(i)(A) of this section is to be determined by an individual acting on behalf of the plan applying the judgment of a prudent layperson who possesses an average knowledge of health and medicine.

(iii) Any claim that a physician with knowledge of the claimant's medical condition determines is a "claim involving urgent care" within the meaning of paragraph (m)(1)(i) of this section shall be treated as a "claim involving urgent care" for purposes of this section.

* * *

[The rules also provide time frames for appeals, 72 hours for urgent care claims, 30 days for pre-service claims (or 15 days for each stage if two stage appeals are provided), and 60 days for post-service plans. The information that the plan must provide in an adverse appeal decision is similar to that which must be provided under an initial adverse decision.]

Notes and Questions

1. As is discussed in the next chapter, all states have adopted laws prescribing internal review procedures for health plans, and many require external reviews as well. Are these state law provisions enforceable under this regulation? In what respects does this regulation supplement state law?

2. Under what circumstances does the regulation permit arbitration of health care claims? Why does it limit plans to two stage appeals? The 1998 proposed regulations prohibited plan provisions that required claimants to submit claims to arbitration or to file more than one appeal. Can you see why these provisions proved quite controversial?

3. A number of other provisions of the proposed rule proved controversial. Representatives of employers, plans, and plan administrators opposed the provisions of the proposed rule requiring plans to disclose the internal rules, protocols and guidelines on which their decisions were based. Why would they have objected to this requirement? To what extent did they win this battle? Employer and plan representatives did convince the Department not to include a rule it had considered that would have required plans to disclose "after an adverse benefit determination on review, documents and records relating to previous claims involving the same diagnosis and treatment decided by the plan within the five years prior to the adverse benefit determination (up to a maximum of 50 such claims)." 65 Fed. Reg. 70246, 70251. What purpose would such a requirement have served? Why was it abandoned?

4. The Department did not require external reviews, which it considered beyond its authority under the statute set out above.

Problem: Beneficiary Protection Under State Law and ERISA

Review the problems following the Massachusetts managed care regulation statute in the preceding chapter. Which of these problems are addressed by the new ERISA rules, and which are not? How, if at all, do the ERISA rules change the rights that members of insured employment-related managed care plans would be entitled to under the state statute? How does it change the rights to which members of self-insured ERISA plans would be entitled? In particular, how do the rules affect the external review scheme created by the Massachusetts statute? Are the state or federal rules more protective of plan members?

D. PROVIDER FIDUCIARY OBLIGATIONS UNDER ERISA

Subscribers have claimed that managed care's cost-conserving strategies are a breach of ERISA fiduciary obligations. The Supreme Court laid this claim to rest.

PEGRAM v. HERDRICH

Supreme Court of the United States, 2000.
530 U.S. 211, 120 S.Ct. 2143, 147 L.Ed.2d 164.

Justice Souter delivered the opinion of the Court.

The question in this case is whether treatment decisions made by a health maintenance organization, acting through its physician employees, are fiduciary acts within the meaning of the Employee Retirement Income Security Act of 1974 (ERISA) [ ]. We hold that they are not.

I

Petitioners, Carle Clinic Association, P. C., Health Alliance Medical Plans, Inc., and Carle Health Insurance Management Co., Inc. (collectively Carle) function as a health maintenance organization (HMO) organized for profit. Its owners are physicians providing prepaid medical services to participants whose employers contract with Carle to provide such coverage. Respondent, Cynthia Herdrich, was covered by Carle through her husband's employer, State Farm Insurance Company.

The events in question began when a Carle physician, petitioner Lori Pegram, examined Herdrich, who was experiencing pain in the midline area of her groin. Six days later, Dr. Pegram discovered a six by eight centimeter inflamed mass in Herdrich's abdomen. Despite the noticeable inflammation, Dr. Pegram did not order an ultrasound diagnostic procedure at a local hospital, but decided that Herdrich would have to wait eight more days for an ultrasound, to be performed at a facility staffed by Carle more than 50 miles away. Before the eight days were over, Herdrich's appendix ruptured, causing peritonitis. [ ]

Herdrich sued Pegram and Carle in state court for medical malpractice, and she later added two counts charging state-law fraud. Carle and Pegram responded that ERISA preempted the new counts, and removed the case to federal court, where they then sought summary judgment on the state-law fraud counts. The District Court granted their motion as to the second fraud count but granted Herdrich leave to amend the one remaining. This she did by alleging that provision of medical services under the terms of the Carle HMO organization, rewarding its physician owners for limiting medical care, entailed an inherent or anticipatory breach of an ERISA fiduciary duty, since these terms created an incentive to make decisions in the physicians' self-interest, rather than the exclusive interests of plan participants.[5]

5. The specific allegations were these:

"11. Defendants are fiduciaries with respect to the Plan and under 29 [U.S.C. §]1109(a) are obligated to discharge their duties with respect to the Plan solely in the interest of the participants and beneficiaries and "a. for the exclusive purpose of:

"i. providing benefits to participants and their beneficiaries; and

"ii. defraying reasonable expenses of administering the Plan;

"b. with the care, skill, prudence, and diligence under the circumstances then prevailing that a prudent man acting in a like capacity and familiar with such matters would use in the conduct of an enterprise of a like character and like aims.

"12. In breach of that duty:

"a. CARLE owner/physicians are the officers and directors of HAMP and CHIMCO and receive a year-end distribution, based in large part upon, supplemental medical expense payments made to CARLE by HAMP and CHIMCO;

"b. Both HAMP and CHIMCO are directed and controlled by CARLE owner/physicians and seek to fund their supplemental medical expense payments to CARLE:

"i. by contracting with CARLE owner/physicians to provide the medical services contemplated in the Plan and then having those contracted owner/physicians:

"(1) minimize the use of diagnostic tests;

"(2) minimize the use of facilities not owned by CARLE; and

"(3) minimize the use of emergency and non-emergency consultation and/or referrals to non-contracted physicians.

"ii. by administering disputed and non-routine health insurance claims and determining:

"(1) which claims are covered under the Plan and to what extent;

"(2) what the applicable standard of care is;

Herdrich sought relief under 29 U.S.C. § 1109(a), which provides that

[a]ny person who is a fiduciary with respect to a plan who breaches any of the responsibilities, obligations, or duties imposed upon fiduciaries by this subchapter shall be personally liable to make good to such plan any losses to the plan resulting from each such breach, and to restore to such plan any profits of such fiduciary which have been made through use of assets of the plan by the fiduciary, and shall be subject to such other equitable or remedial relief as the court may deem appropriate, including removal of such fiduciary.

When Carle moved to dismiss the ERISA count for failure to state a claim upon which relief could be granted, the District Court granted the motion, accepting the Magistrate Judge's determination that Carle was not "involved [in these events] as" an ERISA fiduciary. App. to Pet. for Cert. 63a. The original malpractice counts were then tried to a jury, and Herdrich prevailed on both, receiving $35,000 in compensation for her injury. 154 F.3d, at 367. She then appealed the dismissal of the ERISA claim to the Court of Appeals for the Seventh Circuit, which reversed. The court held that Carle was acting as a fiduciary when its physicians made the challenged decisions and that Herdrich's allegations were sufficient to state a claim:

"Our decision does not stand for the proposition that the existence of incentives automatically gives rise to a breach of fiduciary duty. Rather, we hold that incentives can rise to the level of a breach where, as pleaded here, the fiduciary trust between plan participants and plan fiduciaries no longer exists (i.e., where physicians delay providing necessary treatment to, or withhold administering proper care to, plan beneficiaries for the sole purpose of increasing their bonuses)." Id., at 373.

We granted certiorari [ ] and now reverse the Court of Appeals.

II

Whether Carle is a fiduciary when it acts through its physician owners as pleaded in the ERISA count depends on some background of fact and law about HMO organizations, medical benefit plans, fiduciary obligation, and the meaning of Herdrich's allegations.

A

Traditionally, medical care in the United States has been provided on a "fee-for-service" basis. A physician charges so much for a general physical exam, a vaccination, a tonsillectomy, and so on. The physician bills the patient for services provided or, if there is insurance and the doctor is willing, submits the bill for the patient's care to the insurer, for payment subject to the terms of the insurance agreement. [ ] In a fee-for-service system, a physician's financial incentive is to provide more care, not less, so long as payment is forthcoming. The check on this incentive is a physician's obligation to exercise reasonable medical skill and judgment in the patient's interest.

"(3) whether a course of treatment is experimental;

"(4) whether a course of treatment is reasonable and customary; and

"(5) whether a medical condition is an emergency." App. to Pet. for Cert. 85a–86a.

Beginning in the late 1960's, insurers and others developed new models for health-care delivery, including HMOs. [ ] The defining feature of an HMO is receipt of a fixed fee for each patient enrolled under the terms of a contract to provide specified health care if needed. The HMO thus assumes the financial risk of providing the benefits promised: if a participant never gets sick, the HMO keeps the money regardless, and if a participant becomes expensively ill, the HMO is responsible for the treatment agreed upon even if its cost exceeds the participant's premiums.

Like other risk-bearing organizations, HMOs take steps to control costs. At the least, HMOs, like traditional insurers, will in some fashion make coverage determinations, scrutinizing requested services against the contractual provisions to make sure that a request for care falls within the scope of covered circumstances (pregnancy, for example), or that a given treatment falls within the scope of the care promised (surgery, for instance). They customarily issue general guidelines for their physicians about appropriate levels of care. See id., at 568–570. And they commonly require utilization review (in which specific treatment decisions are reviewed by a decisionmaker other than the treating physician) and approval in advance (precertification) for many types of care, keyed to standards of medical necessity or the reasonableness of the proposed treatment. [ ] These cost-controlling measures are commonly complemented by specific financial incentives to physicians, rewarding them for decreasing utilization of health-care services, and penalizing them for what may be found to be excessive treatment [ ]. Hence, in an HMO system, a physician's financial interest lies in providing less care, not more. The check on this influence (like that on the converse, fee-for-service incentive) is the professional obligation to provide covered services with a reasonable degree of skill and judgment in the patient's interest. [ ]

The adequacy of professional obligation to counter financial self-interest has been challenged no matter what the form of medical organization. HMOs became popular because fee-for-service physicians were thought to be providing unnecessary or useless services; today, many doctors and other observers argue that HMOs often ignore the individual needs of a patient in order to improve the HMOs' bottom lines. See, e.g., 154 F.3d, at 375–378 (citing various critics of HMOs).[6] In this case, for instance, one could argue that Pegram's decision to wait before getting an ultrasound for Herdrich, and her insistence that the ultrasound be done at a distant facility owned by Carle, reflected an interest in limiting the HMO's expenses, which blinded her to the need for immediate diagnosis and treatment.

B

Herdrich focuses on the Carle scheme's provision for a "year-end distribution," n. 3, supra, to the HMO's physician owners. She argues that this particular incentive device of annually paying physician owners the profit resulting from their own decisions rationing care can distinguish Carle's organization from HMOs generally, so that reviewing Carle's decisions under a fiduciary standard as pleaded in Herdrich's complaint would not open the door to like claims about other HMO structures.

---

6. There are, of course, contrary perspectives, and we endorse neither side of the debate today.

While the Court of Appeals agreed, we think otherwise, under the law as now written.

Although it is true that the relationship between sparing medical treatment and physician reward is not a subtle one under the Carle scheme, no HMO organization could survive without some incentive connecting physician reward with treatment rationing. The essence of an HMO is that salaries and profits are limited by the HMO's fixed membership fees. [ ] This is not to suggest that the Carle provisions are as socially desirable as some other HMO organizational schemes; they may not be. [ ] But whatever the HMO, there must be rationing and inducement to ration.

Since inducement to ration care goes to the very point of any HMO scheme, and rationing necessarily raises some risks while reducing others (ruptured appendixes are more likely; unnecessary appendectomies are less so), any legal principle purporting to draw a line between good and bad HMOs would embody, in effect, a judgment about socially acceptable medical risk. A valid conclusion of this sort would, however, necessarily turn on facts to which courts would probably not have ready access: correlations between malpractice rates and various HMO models, similar correlations involving fee-for-service models, and so on. And, of course, assuming such material could be obtained by courts in litigation like this, any standard defining the unacceptably risky HMO structure (and consequent vulnerability to claims like Herdrich's) would depend on a judgment about the appropriate level of expenditure for health care in light of the associated malpractice risk. But such complicated factfinding and such a debatable social judgment are not wisely required of courts unless for some reason resort cannot be had to the legislative process, with its preferable forum for comprehensive investigations and judgments of social value, such as optimum treatment levels and health care expenditure. [ ]

We think, then, that courts are not in a position to derive a sound legal principle to differentiate an HMO like Carle from other HMOs. For that reason, we proceed on the assumption that the decisions listed in Herdrich's complaint cannot be subject to a claim that they violate fiduciary standards unless all such decisions by all HMOs acting through their owner or employee physicians are to be judged by the same standards and subject to the same claims.

C

We turn now from the structure of HMOs to the requirements of ERISA. A fiduciary within the meaning of ERISA must be someone acting in the capacity of manager, administrator, or financial adviser to a "plan," see 29 U.S.C. §§ 1002(21)(A)(i)-(iii), and Herdich's ERISA count accordingly charged Carle with a breach of fiduciary duty in discharging its obligations under State Farm's medical plan. App. to Pet. for Cert. 85a–86a. ERISA's definition of an employee welfare benefit plan is ultimately circular: "any plan, fund, or program ... to the extent that such plan, fund, or program was established ... for the purpose of providing ... through the purchase of insurance or otherwise ... medical, surgical, or hospital care or benefits." § 1002(1)(A). One is thus left to the common understanding of the word "plan" as referring to a scheme decided upon in advance, see Webster's New International

Dictionary 1879 (2d ed.1957); Jacobson & Pomfret, Form, Function, and Managed Care Torts: Achieving Fairness and Equity in ERISA Jurisprudence, 35 Houston L.Rev. 985, 1050 (1998). Here the scheme comprises a set of rules that define the rights of a beneficiary and provide for their enforcement. Rules governing collection of premiums, definition of benefits, submission of claims, and resolution of disagreements over entitlement to services are the sorts of provisions that constitute a plan. [ ] Thus, when employers contract with an HMO to provide benefits to employees subject to ERISA, the provisions of documents that set up the HMO are not, as such, an ERISA plan, but the agreement between an HMO and an employer who pays the premiums may, as here, provide elements of a plan by setting out rules under which beneficiaries will be entitled to care.

D

As just noted, fiduciary obligations can apply to managing, advising, and administering an ERISA plan, the fiduciary function addressed by Herdrich's ERISA count being the exercise of "discretionary authority or discretionary responsibility in the administration of [an ERISA] plan," 29 U.S.C. § 1002(21)(A)(iii). And as we have already suggested, although Carle is not an ERISA fiduciary merely because it administers or exercises discretionary authority over its own HMO business, it may still be a fiduciary if it administers the plan.

In general terms, fiduciary responsibility under ERISA is simply stated. The statute provides that fiduciaries shall discharge their duties with respect to a plan "solely in the interest of the participants and beneficiaries," § 1104(a)(1), that is, "for the exclusive purpose of (i) providing benefits to participants and their beneficiaries; and (ii) defraying reasonable expenses of administering the plan," § 1104(a)(1)(A).[7] These responsibilities imposed by ERISA have the familiar ring of their source in the common law of trusts. [ ] Thus, the common law (understood as including what were once the distinct rules of equity) charges fiduciaries with a duty of loyalty to guarantee beneficiaries' interests: "The most fundamental duty owed by the trustee to the beneficiaries of the trust is the duty of loyalty.... It is the duty of a trustee to administer the trust solely in the interest of the beneficiaries." 2A A. Scott & W. Fratcher, Trusts § 170, 311 (4th ed.1987) (hereinafter Scott); see also G. Bogert & G. Bogert, Law of Trusts and Trustees § 543 (rev.2d ed. 1980) ("Perhaps the most fundamental duty of a trustee is that he must display throughout the administration of the trust complete loyalty to the interests of the beneficiary and must exclude all selfish interest and all consideration of the interests of third persons"); Central States, supra, at 570–571, 105 S.Ct. 2833; Meinhard v. Salmon, 249 N.Y. 458, 464, 164 N.E.

---

7. In addition, fiduciaries must discharge their duties

"(B) with the care, skill, prudence, and diligence under the circumstances then prevailing that a prudent man acting in a like capacity and familiar with such matters would use in the conduct of an enterprise of a like character and with like aims;

"(C) by diversifying the investments of the plan so as to minimize the risk of large losses, unless under the circumstances it is clearly prudent not to do so; and

"(D) in accordance with the documents and instruments governing the plan insofar as such documents and instruments are consistent with the provisions of this subchapter and subchapter III of this chapter." 29 U.S.C. § 1104(a)(1).

545, 546 (1928) (Cardozo, J.) ("Many forms of conduct permissible in a workaday world for those acting at arm's length, are forbidden to those bound by fiduciary ties. A trustee is held to something stricter than the morals of the market place. Not honesty alone, but the punctilio of an honor the most sensitive, is then the standard of behavior").

Beyond the threshold statement of responsibility, however, the analogy between ERISA fiduciary and common law trustee becomes problematic. This is so because the trustee at common law characteristically wears only his fiduciary hat when he takes action to affect a beneficiary, whereas the trustee under ERISA may wear different hats.

Speaking of the traditional trustee, Professor Scott's treatise admonishes that the trustee "is not permitted to place himself in a position where it would be for his own benefit to violate his duty to the beneficiaries." 2A Scott, § 170, at 311. Under ERISA, however, a fiduciary may have financial interests adverse to beneficiaries. Employers, for example, can be ERISA fiduciaries and still take actions to the disadvantage of employee beneficiaries, when they act as employers (e.g., firing a beneficiary for reasons unrelated to the ERISA plan), or even as plan sponsors (e.g., modifying the terms of a plan as allowed by ERISA to provide less generous benefits). Nor is there any apparent reason in the ERISA provisions to conclude, as Herdrich argues, that this tension is permissible only for the employer or plan sponsor, to the exclusion of persons who provide services to an ERISA plan.

ERISA does require, however, that the fiduciary with two hats wear only one at a time, and wear the fiduciary hat when making fiduciary decisions. [ ] Thus, the statute does not describe fiduciaries simply as administrators of the plan, or managers or advisers. Instead it defines an administrator, for example, as a fiduciary only "to the extent" that he acts in such a capacity in relation to a plan. 29 U.S.C. § 1002(21)(A). In every case charging breach of ERISA fiduciary duty, then, the threshold question is not whether the actions of some person employed to provide services under a plan adversely affected a plan beneficiary's interest, but whether that person was acting as a fiduciary (that is, was performing a fiduciary function) when taking the action subject to complaint.

E

The allegations of Herdrich's ERISA count that identify the claimed fiduciary breach are difficult to understand. In this count, Herdrich does not point to a particular act by any Carle physician owner as a breach. She does not complain about Pegram's actions, and at oral argument her counsel confirmed that the ERISA count could have been brought, and would have been no different, if Herdrich had never had a sick day in her life. Tr. of Oral Arg. 53–54.

What she does claim is that Carle, acting through its physician owners, breached its duty to act solely in the interest of beneficiaries by making decisions affecting medical treatment while influenced by the terms of the Carle HMO scheme, under which the physician owners ultimately profit from their own choices to minimize the medical services provided. She emphasizes the threat to fiduciary responsibility in the Carle scheme's feature of a year-end distribution to the physicians of profit derived from the spread between subscription income and expenses of care and administration. App. to Pet. for Cert. 86a.

The specific payout detail of the plan was, of course, a feature that the employer as plan sponsor was free to adopt without breach of any fiduciary duty under ERISA, since an employer's decisions about the content of a plan are not themselves fiduciary acts. Lockheed Corp. v. Spink, 517 U.S. 882, 887, 116 S.Ct. 1783, 135 L.Ed.2d 153 (1996) ("Nothing in ERISA requires employers to establish employee benefit plans. Nor does ERISA mandate what kind of benefit employers must provide if they choose to have such a plan").[8] Likewise it is clear that there was no violation of ERISA when the incorporators of the Carle HMO provided for the year-end payout. The HMO is not the ERISA plan, and the incorporation of the HMO preceded its contract with the State Farm plan. See 29 U.S.C. § 1109(b) (no fiduciary liability for acts preceding fiduciary status).

The nub of the claim, then, is that when State Farm contracted with Carle, Carle became a fiduciary under the plan, acting through its physicians. At once, Carle as fiduciary administrator was subject to such influence from the year-end payout provision that its fiduciary capacity was necessarily compromised, and its readiness to act amounted to anticipatory breach of fiduciary obligation.

F

The pleadings must also be parsed very carefully to understand what acts by physician owners acting on Carle's behalf are alleged to be fiduciary in nature. It will help to keep two sorts of arguably administrative acts in mind. Cf. Dukes v. U.S. Healthcare, Inc., 57 F.3d 350, 361 (C.A.3 1995) (discussing dual medical/administrative roles of HMOs). What we will call pure "eligibility decisions" turn on the plan's coverage of a particular condition or medical procedure for its treatment. "Treatment decisions," by contrast, are choices about how to go about diagnosing and treating a patent's condition: given a patient's constellation of symptoms, what is the appropriate medical response?

These decisions are often practically inextricable from one another, as amici on both sides agree. [ ] This is so not merely because, under a scheme like Carle's, treatment and eligibility decisions are made by the same person, the treating physician. It is so because a great many and possibly most coverage questions are not simple yes-or-no questions, like whether appendicitis is a covered condition (when there is no dispute that a patient has appendicitis), or whether acupuncture is a covered procedure for pain relief (when the claim of pain is unchallenged). The more common coverage question is a when-and-how question. Although coverage for many conditions will be clear and various treatment options will be indisputably compensable, physicians still must decide what to do in particular cases. The issue may be,

---

8. It does not follow that those who administer a particular plan design may not have difficulty in following fiduciary standards if the design is awkward enough. A plan might lawfully provide for a bonus for administrators who denied benefits to every 10th beneficiary, but it would be difficult for an administrator who received the bonus to defend against the claim that he had not been solely attentive to the beneficiaries' interests in carrying out his administrative duties. The important point is that Herdrich is not suing the employer, State Farm, and her claim cannot be analyzed as if she were.

say, whether one treatment option is so superior to another under the circumstances, and needed so promptly, that a decision to proceed with it would meet the medical necessity requirement that conditions the HMO's obligation to provide or pay for that particular procedure at that time in that case. The Government in its brief alludes to a similar example when it discusses an HMO's refusal to pay for emergency care on the ground that the situation giving rise to the need for care was not an emergency, Brief for United States as Amicus Curiae 20–21. In practical terms, these eligibility decisions cannot be untangled from physicians' judgments about reasonable medical treatment, and in the case before us, Dr. Pegram's decision was one of that sort. She decided (wrongly, as it turned out) that Herdrich's condition did not warrant immediate action; the consequence of that medical determination was that Carle would not cover immediate care, whereas it would have done so if Dr. Pegram had made the proper diagnosis and judgment to treat. The eligibility decision and the treatment decision were inextricably mixed, as they are in countless medical administrative decisions every day.

The kinds of decisions mentioned in Herdrich's ERISA count and claimed to be fiduciary in character are just such mixed eligibility and treatment decisions: physicians' conclusions about when to use diagnostic tests; about seeking consultations and making referrals to physicians and facilities other than Carle's; about proper standards of care, the experimental character of a proposed course of treatment, the reasonableness of a certain treatment, and the emergency character of a medical condition.

We do not read the ERISA count, however, as alleging fiduciary breach with reference to a different variety of administrative decisions, those we have called pure eligibility determinations, such as whether a plan covers an undisputed case of appendicitis. Nor do we read it as claiming breach by reference to discrete administrative decisions separate from medical judgments; say, rejecting a claim for no other reason than the HMO's financial condition. The closest Herdrich's ERISA count comes to stating a claim for a pure, unmixed eligibility decision is her general allegation that Carle determines "which claims are covered under the Plan and to what extent," App. to Pet. for Cert. 86a. But this vague statement, difficult to interpret in isolation, is given content by the other elements of the complaint, all of which refer to decisions thoroughly mixed with medical judgment. [ ] Any lingering uncertainty about what Herdrich has in mind is dispelled by her brief, which explains that this allegation, like the others, targets medical necessity determinations. [ ]

III

A

Based on our understanding of the matters just discussed, we think Congress did not intend Carle or any other HMO to be treated as a fiduciary to the extent that it makes mixed eligibility decisions acting through its physicians. We begin with doubt that Congress would ever have thought of a mixed eligibility decision as fiduciary in nature. At common law, fiduciary duties characteristically attach to decisions about managing assets and distributing property to beneficiaries. [ ] Trustees buy, sell, and lease investment property, lend and borrow, and do other things to conserve and nurture assets. They pay out income, choose beneficiaries, and distribute remainders at termination. Thus, the common law trustee's most defining concern historically has been the payment of money in the interest of the beneficiary.

Mixed eligibility decisions by an HMO acting through its physicians have, however, only a limited resemblance to the usual business of traditional trustees. To be sure, the physicians (like regular trustees) draw on resources held for others and make decisions to distribute them in accordance with entitlements expressed in a written instrument (embodying the terms of an ERISA plan). It is also true that the objects of many traditional private and public trusts are ultimately the same as the ERISA plans that contract with HMOs. Private trusts provide medical care to the poor; thousands of independent hospitals are privately held and publicly accountable trusts, and charitable foundations make grants to stimulate the provision of health services. But beyond this point the resemblance rapidly wanes. Traditional trustees administer a medical trust by paying out money to buy medical care, whereas physicians making mixed eligibility decisions consume the money as well. Private trustees do not make treatment judgments, whereas treatment judgments are what physicians reaching mixed decisions do make, by definition. Indeed, the physicians through whom HMOs act make just the sorts of decisions made by licensed medical practitioners millions of times every day, in every possible medical setting: HMOs, fee-for-service proprietorships, public and private hospitals, military field hospitals, and so on. The settings bear no more resemblance to trust departments than a decision to operate turns on the factors controlling the amount of a quarterly income distribution. Thus, it is at least questionable whether Congress would have had mixed eligibility decisions in mind when it provided that decisions administering a plan were fiduciary in nature. Indeed, when Congress took up the subject of fiduciary responsibility under ERISA, it concentrated on fiduciaries' financial decisions, focusing on pension plans, the difficulty many retirees faced in getting the payments they expected, and the financial mismanagement that had too often deprived employees of their benefits. [ ] Its focus was far from the subject of Herdrich's claim.

Our doubt that Congress intended the category of fiduciary administrative functions to encompass the mixed determinations at issue here hardens into conviction when we consider the consequences that would follow from Herdrich's contrary view.

B

First, we need to ask how this fiduciary standard would affect HMOs if it applied as Herdrich claims it should be applied, not directed against any particular mixed decision that injured a patient, but against HMOs that make mixed decisions in the course of providing medical care for profit. Recovery would be warranted simply upon showing that the profit incentive to ration care would generally affect mixed decisions, in derogation of the fiduciary standard to act solely in the interest of the patient without possibility of conflict. Although Herdrich is vague about the mechanics of relief, the one point that seems clear is that she seeks the return of profit from the pockets of the Carle HMO's owners, with the money to be given to the plan for the benefit of the participants. See 29 U.S.C. § 1109(a) (return of all profits is an appropriate ERISA remedy). Since the provision for profit is what makes the

HMO a proprietary organization, her remedy in effect would be nothing less than elimination of the for-profit HMO. Her remedy might entail even more than that, although we are in no position to tell whether and to what extent nonprofit HMO schemes would ultimately survive the recognition of Herdrich's theory.[11] It is enough to recognize that the Judiciary has no warrant to precipitate the upheaval that would follow a refusal to dismiss Herdrich's ERISA claim. The fact is that for over 27 years the Congress of the United States has promoted the formation of HMO practices. The Health Maintenance Organization Act of 1973, 87 Stat. 914, 42 U.S.C. § 300e et seq., allowed the formation of HMOs that assume financial risks for the provision of health care services, and Congress has amended the Act several times, most recently in 1996. See 110 Stat.1976, codified at 42 U.S.C. § 300e (1994 ed., Supp. III). If Congress wishes to restrict its approval of HMO practice to certain preferred forms, it may choose to do so. But the Federal Judiciary would be acting contrary to the congressional policy of allowing HMO organizations if it were to entertain an ERISA fiduciary claim portending wholesale attacks on existing HMOs solely because of their structure, untethered to claims of concrete harm.

C

The Court of Appeals did not purport to entertain quite the broadside attack that Herdrich's ERISA claim thus entails, see 154 F.3d, at 373, and the second possible consequence of applying the fiduciary standard that requires our attention would flow from the difficulty of extending it to particular mixed decisions that on Herdrich's theory are fiduciary in nature.

The fiduciary is, of course, obliged to act exclusively in the interest of the beneficiary, but this translates into no rule readily applicable to HMO decisions or those of any other variety of medical practice. While the incentive of the HMO physician is to give treatment sparingly, imposing a fiduciary obligation upon him would not lead to a simple default rule, say, that whenever it is reasonably possible to disagree about treatment options, the physician should treat aggressively. After all, HMOs came into being because some groups of physicians consistently provided more aggressive treatment than others in similar circumstances, with results not perceived as justified by the marginal expense and risk associated with intervention; excessive surgery is not in the patient's best interest, whether provided by fee-for-service surgeons or HMO surgeons subject to a default rule urging them to operate. Nor would it be possible to translate fiduciary duty into a standard that would allow recovery from an HMO whenever a mixed decision influenced by the HMO's financial incentive resulted in a bad outcome for the patient. It would be so easy to allege, and to find, an economic influence when sparing care did not lead to a well patient, that any such standard in practice would allow a factfinder to convert an HMO into a guarantor of recovery.

---

11. Herdrich's theory might well portend the end of nonprofit HMOs as well, since those HMOs can set doctors' salaries. A claim against a nonprofit HMO could easily allege that salaries were excessively high because they were funded by limiting care, and some nonprofits actually use incentive schemes similar to that challenged here, see Pulvers v. Kaiser Foundation Health Plan, 99 Cal.App.3d 560, 565, 160 Cal.Rptr. 392, 393–394 (1979) (rejecting claim against nonprofit HMO based on physician incentives). See Brody, Agents Without Principals: The Economic Convergence of the Nonprofit and For–Profit Organizational Forms, 40 N.Y.L.S.L.Rev. 457, 493, and n. 152 (1996) (discussing ways in which nonprofit health providers may reward physician employees).

These difficulties may have led the Court of Appeals to try to confine the fiduciary breach to cases where "the sole purpose" of delaying or withholding treatment was to increase the physician's financial reward, ibid. But this attempt to confine mixed decision claims to their most egregious examples entails erroneous corruption of fiduciary obligation and would simply lead to further difficulties that we think fatal. While a mixed decision made solely to benefit the HMO or its physician would violate a fiduciary duty, the fiduciary standard condemns far more than that, in its requirement of "an eye single" toward beneficiaries' interests [ ]. But whether under the Court of Appeals's rule or a straight standard of undivided loyalty, the defense of any HMO would be that its physician did not act out of financial interest but for good medical reasons, the plausibility of which would require reference to standards of reasonable and customary medical practice in like circumstances. That, of course, is the traditional standard of the common law. [ ]. Thus, for all practical purposes, every claim of fiduciary breach by an HMO physician making a mixed decision would boil down to a malpractice claim, and the fiduciary standard would be nothing but the malpractice standard traditionally applied in actions against physicians.

What would be the value to the plan participant of having this kind of ERISA fiduciary action? It would simply apply the law already available in state courts and federal diversity actions today, and the formulaic addition of an allegation of financial incentive would do nothing but bring the same claim into a federal court under federal-question jurisdiction. It is true that in States that do not allow malpractice actions against HMOs the fiduciary claim would offer a plaintiff a further defendant to be sued for direct liability, and in some cases the HMO might have a deeper pocket than the physician. But we have seen enough to know that ERISA was not enacted out of concern that physicians were too poor to be sued, or in order to federalize malpractice litigation in the name of fiduciary duty for any other reason. It is difficult, in fact, to find any advantage to participants across the board, except that allowing them to bring malpractice actions in the guise of federal fiduciary breach claims against HMOs would make them eligible for awards of attorney's fees if they won. [ ] But, again, we can be fairly sure that Congress did not create fiduciary obligations out of concern that state plaintiffs were not suing often enough, or were paying too much in legal fees.

The mischief of Herdrich's position would, indeed, go further than mere replication of state malpractice actions with HMO defendants. For not only would an HMO be liable as a fiduciary in the first instance for its own breach of fiduciary duty committed through the acts of its physician employee, but the physician employee would also be subject to liability as a fiduciary on the same basic analysis that would charge the HMO. The physician who made the mixed administrative decision would be exercising authority in the way described by ERISA and would therefore be deemed to be a fiduciary. [ ]. Hence the physician, too, would be subject to suit in federal court applying an ERISA standard of reasonable medical skill. This result, in turn, would raise a puzzling issue of preemption. On its face, federal fiduciary law applying a malpractice standard would seem to be a prescription for preemption of state malpractice law, since the new ERISA cause of action would cover the subject of a state-law malpractice claim. See 29 U.S.C. § 1144 (preempting state laws that "relate to [an] employee benefit plan"). To be sure, New York State

Conference of Blue Cross & Blue Shield Plans v. Travelers Ins. Co., 514 U.S. 645, 654–655, 115 S.Ct. 1671, 131 L.Ed.2d 695 (1995), throws some cold water on the preemption theory; there, we held that, in the field of health care, a subject of traditional state regulation, there is no ERISA preemption without clear manifestation of congressional purpose. But in that case the convergence of state and federal law was not so clear as in the situation we are positing; the state-law standard had not been subsumed by the standard to be applied under ERISA. We could struggle with this problem, but first it is well to ask, again, what would be gained by opening the federal courthouse doors for a fiduciary malpractice claim, save for possibly random fortuities such as more favorable scheduling, or the ancillary opportunity to seek attorney's fees. And again, we know that Congress had no such haphazard boons in prospect when it defined the ERISA fiduciary, nor such a risk to the efficiency of federal courts as a new fiduciary-malpractice jurisdiction would pose in welcoming such unheard-of fiduciary litigation.

IV

We hold that mixed eligibility decisions by HMO physicians are not fiduciary decisions under ERISA. Herdrich's ERISA count fails to state an ERISA claim, and the judgment of the Court of Appeals is reversed.

Notes and Questions

1. What exactly does *Pegram* mean for ERISA preemption and for future claims against managed care plans? Speaking for a unanimous Supreme Court, Souter was emphatic: "[t]he eligibility decision and the treatment decision were inextricably mixed, as they are in countless medical administrative decisions every day." He enumerates examples of such mixed decisions: "... physicians' conclusions about when to use diagnostic tests; about seeking consultations and making referrals to physicians and facilities other than Carle's; about proper standards of care, the experimental character of a proposed course of treatment, the reasonableness of a certain treatment, and the emergency character of a medical condition."

Pegram does not directly address the complex preemption issues raised by ERISA caselaw in the federal courts. However, the decision does not suggest expansion of ERISA preemption. To the contrary, the Court objected to extending the reach of federal fiduciary law to medical malpractice on the grounds that it would duplicate state law and and risk preempting state law. Citing to its own caselaw holding that ERISA does not preempt state health law regulation without clear congressional intent to the contrary, the Court concluded that Congress did not consider that ERISA would open federal court doors to fiduciary malpractice claims. The implication is that state courts are a natural forum for such claims.

The Court also suggests that mixed eligibility/treatment decisions are not acts of plan administration, and can therefore be considered as "unrelated-to-ERISA" malpractice claims. So long as medical judgment is involved, a claim may not "relate to" ERISA. State courts would appear to be available for a range of malpractice arguments against managed care plans for a variety of errors, with the risk of ERISA preemption. Many courts have already found ways around ERISA preemption, and the trend is likely to continue.

E. PROVIDER DISCLOSURE REQUIREMENTS

Managed care organizations typically use various financial incentives, such as salary-holdback pools, to affect physician behavior and thereby reduce system costs. This has troubled critics, who fear cost-cutting that might endanger patient care. Critics have therefore advocated disclosure to subscribers of the existence of such incentives that might impact physician decision-making. Federal law requires such disclosure to Medicare beneficiaries under some circumstances.

HEALTH MAINTENANCE ORGANIZATIONS, COMPETITIVE MEDICAL PLANS, AND HEALTH CARE PREPAYMENT PLANS

42 C.F.R. Part 417, S. 417.479.
(Effective April 26, 1996).

(h) Disclosure requirements for organizations with physician incentive plans—

(1) Disclosure to HCFA. Each organization must provide to HCFA information concerning its physician incentive plans as required or requested. The disclosure must contain the following information in detail sufficient to enable HCFA to determine whether the incentive plan complies with the requirements specified in this section:

(i) Whether services not furnished by the physician or physician group are covered by the incentive plan. If only the services furnished by the physician or physician group are covered by the incentive plan, disclosure of other aspects of the plan need not be made.

(ii) The type of incentive arrangement; for example, withhold, bonus, capitation.

(iii) If the incentive plan involves a withhold or bonus, the percent of the withhold or bonus.

(iv) The amount and type of stop-loss protection.

(v) The panel size and , if the patients are pooled according to one of the following permitted methods, the method used * * *;

(vi) In the case of capitated physicians or physician groups, capitation payments paid to primary care physicians for the most recent year broken down by percent for primary care services, referral services to specialists, and hospital and other types of provider * * *

(3) Disclosure to Medicare beneficiaries. An organization must provide the following information to any Medicare beneficiary who requests it:

(i) Whether the prepaid plan uses a physician incentive plan that affects the use of referral services.

(ii) The type of incentive arrangement.

(iii) Whether stop-loss protection is provided.

(iv) If the prepaid plan was required to conduct a survey, a summary of the survey results.

Notes and Questions

1. The Medicare disclosure requirements are a compromise between those who believed that disclosure of incentive plans should be mandatory at the time of

enrollment, and those who maintained that incentive plans are proprietary information exempt from disclosure under the Freedom of Information Act. The Comments to the rules state:

> We agree that disclosure of the incentive plans to patients can aid them in ensuring that they receive needed services. This information in the hands of Medicare beneficiaries and Medicaid recipients will also help physicians to counter pressure from the prepaid plans to reduce services. At the same time, we want to protect the proprietary aspects of the information. * * * We have not asked that more information be provided for the following reasons:
>
> — We do not want to put an undue burden on the prepaid plans.
>
> — We do not require fee-for-service physicians to provide a notice that they have incentives to provide excessive services.
>
> — Certain information in the incentive plans is proprietary information and is exempt from disclosure under the FOIA.

2. Early critics of managed care had called for such disclosures, proposing that

> [A]ll health insurance plans should be required to provide formal disclosure statements to prospective subscribers concerning restrictions on the choice of service and capitation payments and financial incentives for reduced use. These statements should be simple and concise, and supplemented by a more complete description of the arrangement, including fees, out-of-pocket costs, and allowable benefits.

Donald F. Levinson, Toward Full Disclosure of Referral Restrictions and Financial Incentives by Prepaid Health Plans, 317 New Eng. J. Med. 1729 (1987). For a comprehensive legal discussion, see Deven C. McGraw, Financial Incentives to Limit Services: Should Physicians be Required to Disclose These To Patients? 83 Geo. L.J. 1821 (1995).

The critics assumed that patients are not aware of the cost-sensitive nature of incentives operating on physicians in MCOs, such as salary-holdback provisions in some HMO plans. Such plans held back a small percentage of physician salaries in HMOs in a pool, and at the end of the budget year physicians who have too many referrals may "lose" this percentage of their salary, typically 20 percent. Such a pool is intended to create a financial incentive for primary physicians to minimize referrals of members. Under most HMO arrangements, subscribers are not informed of such arrangements, and primary physicians are prohibited from disclosing to subscribers the existence and nature of these incentive arrangements. See, e.g., Alan L. Hillman, et al., How Do Financial Incentives Affect Physicians' Clinical Decisions and the Financial Performance of Health Maintenance Organizations?, 321 New Eng. J. Med. 86 (1989); Alan L. Hillman, Financial Incentives for Physicians in HMOs: Is There a Conflict of Interest?, 317 New Eng. J. Med. 1743 (1987).

The idea is that patients are not aware of the cost-sensitive nature of incentives operating on physicians in MCOs, and should be made aware of them prior to joining, since physicians have a conflict of interest in such MCOs. See e.g., Steven Z. Pantilat, Margaret Chesney and Bernard Lo, Effect of Incentives on the Use of Indicated Services in Managed Care, 170 West. J. Med. 137 (1999); Alan L.

Hillman, et al., How Do Financial Incentives Affect Physicians' Clinical Decisions and the Financial Performance of Health Maintenance Organizations?, 321 New Eng. J. Med. 86 (1989); Alan L. Hillman, Financial Incentives for Physicians in HMOs: Is There a Conflict of Interest?, 317 New Eng. J. Med. 1743 (1987).

Disclosure is a remedy that coincides with developments in informed consent, fiduciary law, and Fraud and Abuse legislation. The Stark Amendment, for example, specifically prohibits HMOs with Medicaid contracts from "knowingly making a payment, directly or indirectly, to a physician as an inducement to reduce or limit services provided with respect to Medicare and Medicaid beneficiaries". Omnibus Budget Reconciliation Act of 1986, Pub. L. No. 99–509, § 9313(c), 100 Stat. 2003, as amended by Pub. L. No. 100–203, § 4016, 101 Stat. 1330–64 and H.R. 3299, § 6207. It appears to give the patient options that she or he did not previously have. Such disclosure presents several problems. First, patients may lack a choice of alternative providers, even if disclosure is made. Given the increased prevalence of managed care organizations as employee options, employees face diminishing choices between fee-for-service and managed care physicians. Second, patients already in such MCOs or closed panel plans lack ready flexibility to consult physicians outside the panel who are not themselves subject to financial constraints. Recent writing on the subject includes Stephen R. Latham, Regulation of Managed Care Incentive Payments to Physicians, 22 Am.J.L. & Med. 399 (1996); Henry T. Greely, Direct Financial Incentives in Managed Care: Unanswered Questions, 6 Health Matrix 53 (1996); R.Adams Dudley et al., The Impact of Financial Incentives on Quality of Health Care, 76 The Milbank Quarterly 649 (1998); Marc A. Rodwin, Medicine, Money & Morals: Physicians' Conflicts of Interest 214–217 (1993).

Third, disclosure assumes that cost-sensitive care is less high quality care, when in fact fee-for-service medicine may often result in overtreatment, with its own iatrogenic costs. P. Franks, et al., Sounding Board: Gatekeeping Revisited— Protecting Patients from Overtreatment, 327 New Eng. J. Med. 424, 426 (1992).

The earlier caselaw that discussed the disclosure issue generally rejected such claims. In Teti v. U.S. Healthcare, 1989 WL 143274 (E.D.Pa.1989), affirmed 904 F.2d 696 (3d Cir.1990), the plaintiffs claimed that the HMO's failure to disclose the disincentives for physicians to make specialist or hospital referrals was fraud, breach of contract and RICO violations. The case was dismissed for lack of federal court jurisdiction.

Some courts have been receptive to such claims. In Shea v. Esensten, 107 F.3d 625 (8th Cir.1997), the court considered a claim that the HMO's failure to disclose its practice of giving primary-care physicians financial incentives to minimize referrals to specialists caused employee's death from heart failure. Mr. Shea's physician failed to give him a referral to a cardiologist in spite of warning signs of a cardiac condition. Mr. Shea's widow contended that if her husband had know that his doctor could earn a bonus for treating less, he would have sought out his own cardiologist. The Seventh Circuit agreed that a financial incentive system aimed at influencing a physician's referral patterns is "a material piece of information,"Id at 628, and that a subscriber has a right to know that his physician's judgment could be "colored" by such incentives. The court rested its conclusion on the obligation of an ERISA fiduciary to speak out if it "knows that silence might be harmful." The court held that information about a plan's financial incentives must be disclosed when they might lead a treating physician to deny necessary referrals for conditions covered by the plan. Such a requirement of disclosure, while problematic in some aspects, is consistent with federal policy in HMO regulation and with a trend to use disclosure of information to counteract provider power in health care. For an excellent discussion of these issues, see Tracy E. Miller and William M. Sage, Disclosing Physician Financial Incentives, 281 JAMA 1424 (1999); William M. Sage, Physicians as Advocates, 35 Houston L.Rev. 1529 (1999); Kim Johnston, Patient Advocates or Patient Adversaries? Using Fiduciary Law to Compel Disclosure of Managed Care Financial Incentives, 35 San Diego L.Rev. 951 (1998); Bethany J. Spielman, Managed Care Regulation and the Physician–Advocate, 47 Drake L.Rev. 713 (1999).

The related disclosure theory is that of informed consent: a physician in an MCO should always discuss with a patient all alternative approaches, even those that are more expensive and therefore are not generally recommended by the cost-sensitive physician. Such an obligation is based upon the line of "informed refusal" cases, such as Truman v. Thomas. Truman imposes on the physician a duty to disclose to a patient the risks of omitting a useful risk-free test, arguably expanding the duty to discuss more expensive diagnostic and treatment procedures that might be useful and helpful to the patient. This could expand the obligations of HMO physicians in situations where some treatments were preferred because of the cost-benefit tradeoff, but exposed patients to slightly higher risks at the same time.

The use of financial incentives in managed care, and the possible effect of these incentives in "corrupting" physician judgment, has led some critics to raise ethical objections to managed care: it creates conflicts of interest of physicians, impairing their judgment; patient trust will suffer as a result. See Council on Ethical and Judicial Affairs, American Medical Association, Ethical Issues in Managed Care, 273 JAMA 330, 330–31 (1995). The Council expressed concern that managed care incentives that make physicians more costs conscious can compromise patient care. "First, physicians have an incentive to cut corners in their patient care, by temporizing too long, eschewing extra diagnostic tests, or refraining from an expensive referral.... Second, even in the absence of actual patient harm, the incentives may erode patient trust as patients wonder whether they are receiving all necessary care or are being denied care because of the physicians' pecuniary concerns.... Financial incentives to limit care exploit the financial motive of physicians" and are less likely to coincide with patients' interests, "because patients generally prefer the risk of too much care to the risk of too little care" Id. at 333. Third, patients are less likely to notice the effects of incentives, such as the withholding of a treatment option. See generally Ezekiel Emanuel, Managed Competition and the Patient–Physician Relationship, 329 N.E.J.M. 879 (1993).

"Bedside rationing" is often raised as a threat to medical professionalism and ethical behavior. These critics have contended that neither rationing nor the use of incentives is ethical. While the critics are correct that inappropriate incentives can be damaging, they often fail to acknowledge that physicians have always responded to incentives: fee-for-service may push toward overtreatment, while salaried physicians receive no signals at all about appropriate uses of resources. An ethical model is needed that recognizes the value of physician autonomy and also the need to provide signals as to appropriate use of health care services. Physicians need to think about what they do, and they must also be able to advocate for patients in particular cases. Hall and Berenson propose an approach that recognizes the value of cost-effective medicine in managed care while trying to create an ethical model:

... financial incentives should influence physicians to maximize the health of the group of patients under their care; physicians should not enter into incentive arrangements that they would be embarrassed to describe accurately to their patients or that are not in common use in the market; physicians should treat each patient impartially, without regard to source of payment, and in a manner consistent with the physician's own treatment style; if physicians depart from this ideal, they must tell their patients honestly; and it is desirable, although not mandatory, to differentiate medical treatment recommendations from insurance coverage decisions by clearly assigning authority over these different roles and by having physicians to advocate for recommended treatment that is not covered.

Mark A. Hall and Robert A. Berenson, The Ethics of Managed Care: A Dose of Realism, 28 Cumb.L.Rev. 287, 288–89 (1999). A properly designed managed care system does not violate professional medical ethics. The purpose of incentive systems are to provide a counterbalance to the inflationary pressures of the American health care system. Such incentives can be provided within a framework that allows sound clinical judgment to be exercised, giving physicians substantial bedside autonomy while also providing incentives for sensitivity to both cost and appropriate care. Hall and Berenson, id. at 304, note that "[t]he strength of various payment methods vary according to at least six dimensions, each with multiple components:" (1) the type of service covered; (2) the practice setting and base reimbursement method; (3) the size of the incentive; (4) the incentive's immediacy; (5) the presence of various counterbalancing monitoring mechanisms; and (6) the relative generosity of the base reimbursement. Such an approach can be found in recent Medicare HMO rules, 61 Fed. Reg. 13430 (to be codified at 42 C.F.R. § 417.479(e)-(f)).

III. FEDERAL INITIATIVES TO EXPAND PRIVATE INSURANCE COVERAGE: THE HEALTH INSURANCE PORTABILITY AND ACCOUNTABILITY ACT OF 1996, THE CONSOLIDATED OMNIBUS RECONCILIATION ACT OF 1995 AND THE AMERICANS WITH DISABILITIES ACT

Though the ERISA has done much to limit the rights that participants in employee benefit plans might otherwise have had under state law and ERISA's own remedial provisions do little to fill the void left by preemption, federal law does in fact provide privately insured individuals some rights that they might not have had under state law. The most important of these are the rights to insurance portability provided by the Health Insurance Portability and Accountability Act of 1996 (HIPAA); the continuation of coverage benefits available under the Consolidated Omnibus Budget Reconciliation Act of 1985, commonly called "COBRA coverage"; rights under recently adopted federal statutes mandating minimum maternity benefits and parity for mental health coverage, and the right to freedom from discrimination on the basis of disability found in the Americans with Disabilities Act (ADA).

A. THE HEALTH INSURANCE PORTABILITY AND ACCOUNTABILITY ACT OF 1996 AND COBRA COVERAGE REQUIREMENTS

HIPAA began as an attempt to enact the least controversial elements of the much more ambitious health insurance reform proposals of 1993 and 1994. In the end it became a lengthy "Christmas tree" bill addressing a hodge-podge of topics. HIPAA included, for example, major changes in the fraud and abuse laws and provisions for medical savings accounts, discussed elsewhere in this book. It also provided tax incentives intended to encourage the purchase of long term care insurance and the availability of accelerated death benefits for the terminally and chronically ill, and the creation of insurance pools to benefit high-risk individuals by states that may increase access to health care.

The most important provisions of the legislation, however, are those amending ERISA, the Public Health Services Act, and the Internal Revenue Code, which follow:

HEALTH INSURANCE PORTABILITY AND ACCOUNTABILITY ACT OF 1996

Pub.L. 104–191.

Sec. 701. Increased Portability Through Limitation on Preexisting Condition Exclusions.

(a) Subject to subsection (d), a group health plan, and a health insurance issuer offering group health insurance coverage, may, with respect to a participant or beneficiary, impose a preexisting condition exclusion only if—

(1) such exclusion relates to a condition (whether physical or mental), regardless of the cause of the condition, for which medical advice, diagnosis, care, or treatment was recommended or received within the 6–month period ending on the enrollment date;

(2) such exclusion extends for a period of not more than 12 months (or 18 months in the case of a late enrollee) after the enrollment date; and

(3) the period of any such preexisting condition exclusion is reduced by the aggregate of the periods of creditable coverage (* * *) applicable to the participant or beneficiary as of the enrollment date.

(b) DEFINITIONS. * * *

(1)(A) The term "preexisting condition exclusion" means, with respect to coverage, a limitation or exclusion of benefits relating to a condition based on the fact that the condition was present before the date of enrollment for such coverage, whether or not any medical advice, diagnosis, care, or treatment was recommended or received before such date.

(B) Genetic information shall not be treated as a condition described in subsection (a)(1) in the absence of a diagnosis of the condition related to such information. * * *

* * *

(3) The term "late enrollee" means, with respect to coverage under a group health plan, a participant or beneficiary who enrolls under the plan other than during—

(A) the first period in which the individual is eligible to enroll under the plan, or

(B) a special enrollment period under subsection (f) [which permits individuals who had earlier declined coverage to apply for coverage if they lose coverage they had under another policy or gain dependents].

* * *

(c) RULES RELATING TO CREDITING PREVIOUS COVERAGE.—

(1) For purposes of this part, the term "creditable coverage" means, with respect to an individual, coverage of the individual under any of the following:

(A) A group health plan.

(B) Health insurance coverage.

(C)–(J) [Enumerated federal and state insurance programs].

(2) NOT COUNTING PERIODS BEFORE SIGNIFICANT BREAKS IN COVERAGE.—

(A) A period of creditable coverage shall not be counted, with respect to enrollment of an individual under a group health plan, if, after such period and before the enrollment date, there was a 63–day period during all of which the individual was not covered under any creditable coverage.

* * *

(d) EXCEPTIONS.

(1) Subject to paragraph (4), a group health plan, and a health insurance issuer offering group health insurance coverage, may not impose any preexisting condition exclusion in the case of an individual who, as of the last day of the 30–day period beginning with the date of birth, is covered under creditable coverage.

(2) Subject to paragraph (4), a group health plan, and a health insurance issuer offering group health insurance coverage, may not impose any preexisting condition exclusion in the case of a child who is adopted or placed for adoption before attaining 18 years of age and who, as of the last day of the 30–day period beginning on the date of the adoption or placement for adoption, is covered under creditable coverage. * * *

(3) A group health plan, and health insurance issuer offering group health insurance coverage, may not impose any preexisting condition exclusion relating to pregnancy as a preexisting condition.

(4) Paragraphs (1) and (2) shall no longer apply to an individual after the end of the first 63–day period during all of which the individual was not covered under any creditable coverage.

* * *

Sec. 702. Prohibiting Discrimination Against Individual Participants and Beneficiaries Based on Health Status.

(a) IN ELIGIBILITY TO ENROLL.—

(1) Subject to paragraph (2), a group health plan, and a health insurance issuer offering group health insurance coverage in connection with a group health plan, may not establish rules for eligibility (including continued eligibility) of any individual to enroll under the terms of the plan based on any of the following health status-related factors in relation to the individual or a dependent of the individual:

(A) Health status.

(B) Medical condition (including both physical and mental illnesses).

(C) Claims experience.

(D) Receipt of health care.

(E) Medical history.

(F) Genetic information.

(G) Evidence of insurability (including conditions arising out of acts of domestic violence).

(H) Disability.

* * *

(2) To the extent consistent with section 701, paragraph (1) shall not be construed—

(A) to require a group health plan, or group health insurance coverage, to provide particular benefits other than those provided under the terms of such plan or coverage, or

(B) to prevent such a plan or coverage from establishing limitations or restrictions on the amount, level, extent, or nature of the benefits or coverage for similarly situated individuals enrolled in the plan or coverage.

* * *

(b) IN PREMIUM CONTRIBUTIONS.—

(1) A group health plan, and a health insurance issuer offering health insurance coverage in connection with a group health plan, may not require any individual (as a condition of enrollment or continued enrollment under the plan) to pay a premium or contribution which is greater than such premium or contribution for a similarly situated individual enrolled in the plan on the basis of any health status-related factor in relation to the individual or to an individual enrolled under the plan as a dependent of the individual.

(2) Nothing in paragraph (1) shall be construed—

(A) to restrict the amount that an employer may be charged for coverage under a group health plan; or

(B) to prevent a group health plan, and a health insurance issuer offering group health insurance coverage, from establishing premium discounts or rebates or modifying otherwise applicable copayments or deductibles in return for adherence to programs of health promotion and disease prevention.

* * *

Sec. 2711. Guaranteed Availability of Coverage for Employers in the Group Market.

(a) ISSUANCE OF COVERAGE IN THE SMALL GROUP MARKET.—

(1) Subject to subsections (c) through (f), each health insurance issuer that offers health insurance coverage in the small group market in a State—

(A) must accept every small employer [defined as an employer with 2–50 employees] in the State that applies for such coverage; and

(B) must accept for enrollment under such coverage every eligible individual * * * who applies for enrollment during the period in which the individual first becomes eligible to enroll under the terms of the group health plan and may not place any [discriminatory] restriction * * * on an eligible individual being a participant or beneficiary.

* * *

[Special rules follow permitting network plans to deny coverage for persons outside of their coverage area. Network plans and insurers are also permitted under the Act to deny coverage in a non-discriminatory fashion where necessary because of limited financial capacity. Finally, HIPAA also permits insurers to require employers to meet a minimum level of contributions for benefit costs, and to impose minimum levels of beneficiary participation in group plans. ed.]

Sec. 2712. Guaranteed Renewability of Coverage for Employers in the Group Market.

(a) Except as provided in this section, if a health insurance issuer offers health insurance coverage in the small or large group market in connection with a health plan, the issuer must renew or continue in force coverage at the option of the plan sponsor of the plan.

(b) [Nonrenewal is permitted for nonpayment of premiums; fraud; violation of participation or contribution rules, as defined above; or if the issuer ceases to offer coverage in the market.]

* * *

Sec. 2741. Guaranteed Availability of Individual Health Insurance Coverage to Certain Individuals With Prior Group Coverage.

(a)(1) Subject the succeeding subsections of this section and section 2744 [which permits states flexibility to create other options to cover individuals], each health insurance issuer that offers health insurance coverage * * * in the individual market in a State may not, with respect to an eligible individual (as defined in subsection (b)) desiring to enroll in individual health insurance coverage—

> (A) decline to offer such coverage to, or deny enrollment of, such individual; or

> (B) impose any preexisting condition exclusion (* * *)

(2) The requirement of paragraph (1) shall not apply to health insurance coverage offered in the individual market in a State in which the State is implementing an acceptable alternative mechanism [as permitted by the statute]

(b) In this part, the term "eligible individual" means an individual—

(1)(A) for whom, as of the date on which the individual seeks coverage under this section, the aggregate of the periods of creditable coverage (* * *) is 18 or more months and

> (B) whose most recent prior creditable coverage was under a group health plan, governmental plan, or church plan (or health insurance coverage offered in connection with any such plan);

(2) who is not eligible for coverage under (A) a group health plan, (B) [Medicare], or (C) [Medicaid], and does not have other health insurance coverage;

(3) with respect to whom the most recent coverage within the coverage period described in paragraph (1)(A) was not terminated based on [nonpayment of premiums or fraud];

(4) if the individual had been offered the option of continuation coverage under a COBRA continuation provision or under a similar State program, who elected such coverage; and

(5) who, if the individual elected such continuation coverage, has exhausted such continuation coverage under such provision or program.

(c)(1) In the case of health insurance coverage offered in the individual market * * * the health insurance issuer may elect to limit the coverage offered under subsection (a) so long as it offers at least two different [widely held or representative] policy forms of health insurance coverage * * *

* * *

[Network plans may also limit coverage to individuals in their service area and plans generally may limit coverage to their financial capacity]

* * *

Sec. 2742. Guaranteed Renewability of Individual Health Insurance Coverage.

(a) Except [in cases of fraud, nonpayment of premium, general termination of the plan, the insured's moving from the service area, or the insured's loss of association membership where the plan is an association plan] a health insurance issuer that provides individual health insurance coverage to an individual shall renew or continue in force such coverage at the option of the individual.

* * *

Notes and Questions

1. Perhaps the most popular provision of HIPAA was its limitation on pre-existing condition exclusions. Why had preexisting conditions clauses been relatively common in insurance policies? What are the distributional effects of preexisting conditions clauses? Why might they be less important to insurers (or employer-financed health plans) in situations where insurance applicants are merely changing insurers (usually incident to a change of jobs) rather than applying for insurance for the first time? Why might insurers and employers prefer a longer preexisting condition exclusion where employees who have previously declined offered insurance change their minds and request it? Why should coverage of pregnancy or of newborn or adopted children be specially excluded from preexisting condition exclusions? Preexisting conditions clauses were, prior to HIPAA, believed to have resulted in "job-lock" because employees could not change employers without losing coverage for "preexisting conditions." See GAO, Employer–Based Health Insurance, High Costs, Wide Variation Threaten System (1992). Does HIPAA adequately address this issue?

Prior to the adoption of the HIPAA, many states limited the use of preexisting conditions clauses, often to a greater extent that does HIPAA. The statute defers to more restrictive state requirements. Does the statute serve a useful purpose, nevertheless, in states with such requirements?

2. Does HIPAA's requirement of guaranteed issue and renewability for small groups adequately assure the availability of insurance for these groups? What obvious problem is not addressed by this statute? How does it interact with the state small group reforms discussed in the previous chapter?

3. What problems do HIPAA's provisions for individual coverage fail to address? Thirty-eight of the states chose to adopt alternative mechanisms for extending coverage to individuals, thus the federal rules apply in only twelve states. Twenty-two of the alternative states are using a high-risk pool to provide coverage. Even in the states following the federal rule, there is evidence of widespread ignorance of HIPAA protections, and some indication that HIPAA is being circumvented by insurers by refusing to pay brokers commissions for selling it, delaying processing of applications to cause a break in coverage in excess of the sixty-three days permitted by the statute, or suspending issuance of individual policies during the HIPAA implementation period. Even complying insurers are charging very high rates for HIPAA policies, often exceeding 200% of the rates charged for non-HIPAA policies. See U.S.General Accounting Office, Health Insurance Standards: New Federal Law Creates Challenges for Consumers, Insurers, Regulators, GAO/HEHS–98–67 (Feb. 1998); U.S. General Accounting Office, Private Health Insurance: Progress and Challenges in Implementing 1996 Federal Standards, GAO/HEHS–99–100 (1999).

4. The HIPAA requirement of guaranteed issue to individuals supplements the earlier requirements of COBRA, the Consolidated Omnibus Budget Act of 1985. COBRA applies to private employers and state and local government entities that employ twenty or more employees on a typical business day and that sponsor a group health plan. 29 U.S.C.A. § 1161. COBRA protects "qualified beneficiaries" whose group insurance is terminated because of a "qualifying event." Qualified beneficiaries include covered employees and their spouses and dependent children who were plan beneficiaries on the day before the qualifying event. 29 U.S.C.A. § 1167(3). Formerly insured employees become qualified beneficiaries if they lose coverage because of termination from employment (other than

termination because of the employee's gross misconduct) or through a reduction of hours. 29 U.S.C.A. § 1163(2). Qualifying events entitling the spouses and dependent children of an employee to continuation coverage include loss of coverage due to the death of the covered employee; termination of the employee's employment or reduction in hours (not caused by the employee's "gross misconduct"); divorce or legal separation of the covered employee from the employee's spouse; eligibility of the employee for Medicare; or the cessation of dependent child status under the health plan. 29 U.S.C.A. § 1163. Filing of bankruptcy proceedings by an employer is a qualifying event with respect to a retired employee who retired before the elimination of coverage and the employee's spouse, dependent child, or surviving spouse, where the employer substantially eliminates coverage within one year of the bankruptcy filing. 29 U.S.C.A. § 1163(6).

Qualified beneficiaries are entitled upon the occurrence of a qualifying event to purchase continuation coverage for 18 months where the qualifying event is termination of work or reduction in hours or for 36 months for most other qualifying events. 29 U.S.C.A. § 1162(2). The right to continuation coverage terminates before the end of the coverage period if the employer ceases to provide group health insurance to any employee; the qualified beneficiary fails to make a timely payment of the plan premium; the qualified beneficiary becomes covered under another group health plan which does not exclude or limit coverage for a preexisting condition; or the qualified beneficiary becomes eligible for Medicare. 29 U.S.C.A. § 1162(2)(B),(C),(D).

COBRA offers a significant advantage over the individual insurance guarantees of the HIPAA: beneficiaries need only pay a premium which may not exceed 102% of the total cost of the plan for similarly situated beneficiaries who continued to be covered. 29 U.S.C.A. §§ 1162(3), 1164. Where the employer is self-insured, the employer may either make a reasonable estimate of plan cost for similarly situated beneficiaries on an actuarial basis or base the premium on the costs of the preceding determination period adjusted for inflation. 29 U.S.C.A. § 1164(2). Who pays for COBRA coverage: employers, insurers, employees or health insurance consumers? See generally on COBRA, Vicki Gottlich & Esther Koblenz, COBRA Continuation Coverage: It's Not Just for Health Lawyers Anymore, 24 Clearinghouse Rev. 538 (1990); Somers, COBRA: An Incremental Approach to National Health Insurance, 5 J. Contemp. Health L. & Pol'y 141 (1989); Jane Perkins & Judith Waxman, The COBRA Continuation Option: Questions and Answers, 21 Clearinghouse Rev. 1315 (1988).

5. Congress for the first time in 1996 adopted limited coverage mandates, including a "drive through delivery" bill requiring health plans to offer at least 48 hours of hospital coverage for vaginal deliveries, 96 hours for C–Sections; and a mental health parity law forbidding health plans from placing lifetime or annual limits on mental health coverage less generous than those placed on medical or surgical benefits. The mental health parity law does not apply to small employers or in situations where it would increase the cost of health coverage more than 1%. In 1998 Congress adopted the Women's Health and Cancer Rights Act, imposing a third mandate requiring health plans that cover mastectomies to also cover breast reconstruction surgery.

Does the maternity bill address a real or imagined problem? If you were a lobbyist representing health plans, how strenuously would you argue against it? What would be your arguments? What are the likely effects of the mental health parity bill? Why is Congress beginning to impose coverage requirements on health plans? Why were these particular coverage requirements chosen?

Problem: Advising under HIPAA and COBRA

Martha Phillips has recently lost her job at naturalway.com, a short-lived attempt to sell alternative medicines on the web. She was only with the company for ten months, most of its brief existence. She was covered during the ten month period by naturalway group health plan. Martha is experienced with web-based technology, and thinks she will soon be again employed. She is quite concerned, however, because she has chronic diabetes and needs to have health insurance coverage. She asks:

1) Does any federal law give her the right to insurance coverage? If so, what would be the terms of the coverage?

2) If she is able to find employment with health insurance coverage, as she hopes, can she be subjected to a preexisting conditions clause that will exclude coverage for her diabetes?

3) If she is able to find employment with health insurance coverage, can she be charged higher rates than other employees because of her diabetes?

B. FEDERAL PROHIBITIONS AGAINST DISCRIMINATION ON THE BASIS OF DISABILITY AND OTHER FEDERAL ANTI-DISCRIMINATION STATUTES

Among the most important provisions of the HIPAA are those protecting individuals insured under group policies from discrimination on the basis of health status in terms of health insurance availability or premiums. Persons with chronic or costly diseases, such has AIDS, have faced a particularly difficult time finding health insurance in the individual insurance market, and increasingly in the group insurance market as well. Much has been written on the problem of AIDS and health insurance. Among the many good articles are Michael T. Isbell, AIDS and Access to Care: Lessons for Health Care Reformers, 3 Cornell J. L. & Pub. Pol'y 7 (1993); Randall Bovbjerg, AIDS and Insurance: How Private Health Coverage Relates to HIV/AIDS Infection and to Public Programs, 77 Iowa L. Rev. 1561 (1992); Alan Widiss, To Insure or Not to Insure Persons Infected with the Virus that Causes AIDS, 77 Iowa L. Rev. 1617 (1992); Henry Greeley, AIDS and the American Health Care Financing System, 51 U.Pitt.L.Rev. 73, 96–97 (1989); and Daniel Fox, Financing Health Care for Persons with HIV Infection: Guidelines for State Action, 16 Am.J.L. & Med. 223 (1990).

Does the HIPAA completely solve the problems faced by persons with AIDS who seek private insurance coverage for medical care? Consider the following quote from the conference committee report that accompanied the bill:

It is the intent of the conferees that a plan cannot knowingly be designed to exclude individuals and their dependents on the basis of health status. However, generally applicable terms of the plan may have a disparate impact on individual enrollees. For example, a plan may exclude all coverage of a specific condition, or may include a lifetime cap on all benefits, or a lifetime cap on specific benefits. * * * [S]uch plan characteristics would be permitted as long as they are not directed at individual sick employees or dependents. 142 Cong. Rec. H9473, H9519.

Are other legal strategies available for defending persons with disabilities against limitations on access to insurance that are legal under the HIPAA? Are such access limitations, when imposed by insurance companies or self-insured employers defensible? Are they necessary?

Prior to the adoption of the HIPAA, the clearest prohibition against discrimination on the basis of health status was found in the Americans with Disabilities Act, which forbids discrimination in the terms, conditions and privileges of employment on the basis of disability. 42 U.S.C.A. § 12112. The EEOC has in fact obtained settlements in several ADA enforcement actions brought against employers who limited insurance benefits for persons with AIDS. See, discussing the ADA, Michael Zablocki, et al., Americans With Disabilities Act Update, 15 Whittier L. Rev. 177, 181–82 (1994); Note, The Future of Self–Funded Health Plans, 79 Iowa L.Rev. 413, 421–425 (1994); and Lawrence Gostin & Alan Widiss, What's Wrong With the ERISA Vacuum? 269 JAMA 2527 (1993).

When the Americans with Disabilities Act (ADA) (42 U.S.C.A. §§ 12101–12113) was adopted in 1990, it was widely believed that the Act would limit the ability of employers and insurers to vary the terms and conditions of insurance coverage on the basis of medical condition. A spate of recent cases, however, indicate that the impact of the ADA on health care financing will be very limited. The following case concerns a long-term disability rather than a health insurance policy, but the issues raised are identical to those at stake in the health insurance setting. As the notes following the case indicate, it is unusually sympathetic to the claimant.

WINSLOW v. IDS LIFE INSURANCE CO.

United States District Court, Minnesota, 1998.
29 F.Supp.2d 557.

DAVIS, DISTRICT JUDGE.

Susan M. Winslow filed this action for declaratory and injunctive relief and for damages under the Americans with Disabilities Act ("ADA"), 42 U.S.C. § 12101 et seq., and the Minnesota Human Rights Act ("MHRA"), Minn.Stat. § 363.01 et seq. when she applied for and was denied long-term disability insurance by IDS Life Insurance Co. due to her current history of treatment for a mental health condition. The matter is before the Court on Defendant's motion for summary judgment which, for the foregoing reasons, is denied in part and granted in part.

BACKGROUND

On approximately October 27, 1994, Plaintiff Susan Winslow applied to IDS Life Insurance Co. for standard long-term disability insurance or, in the alternative, long-term disability insurance with a rider excluding coverage for periods of disability due to her mental health condition. Plaintiff indicated on her application that she had been treated for mental illness—dysthymia or mild depression—within the past year and was currently taking Zoloft, an anti-depressant. IDS refused both requests for insurance based on its policy of automatically denying long-term disability insurance to applicants who report having received treatment for a mental or nervous condition, regardless of seriousness, within the twelve months prior to application. The IDS policy allows such applicants to be reconsidered for long-term disability insurance after a year has passed since their last treatment for a mental or nervous condition. IDS asserts that its above-stated policy is based on industry-wide claims experience and actuarial data that indicates that the highest number of payments are made for depression-related claims. Plaintiff notes, however, that the IDS policy differs from that in the Paul Revere Underwriting Manual—a manual used by IDS in making other underwriting decisions—which does not require automatic rejection of applicants with current histories of mental or nervous conditions, such as Plaintiff's dysthymia, but instead provides for a long-term disability insurance policy with a longer exclusion period.[ ]

Plaintiff received notice of the denial of her long-term disability insurance application in November 1994 and requested reconsideration. In her request for reconsideration Plaintiff asserted to IDS that she had never been hospitalized or missed work due to her mental health condition and provided corroborative letters from two psychiatrists from whom she had received treatment, affirming that Plaintiff suffered only mild symptoms, which did not manifest themselves in work situations. * * * IDS received Plaintiff's additional documents, and after internal discussions, agreed that denial of Plaintiff's application was appropriate.

* * *

II. Disability Under the ADA

In order to defeat summary judgment plaintiff Winslow must demonstrate that she is a person with a disability as defined by the ADA and therefore a plaintiff covered by the ADA. The ADA defines "disability" as "(A) a physical or mental impairment that substantially limits one or more of the major life activities of such individual; (B) a record of such an impairment; or (C) being regarded as having such an impairment." 42 U.S.C. § 12102(2)(A)-(C). Winslow does not argue that she meets criteria (A) or (B) of the ADA definition. Instead, Plaintiff asserts that IDS regarded her as disabled and treated her as having "a physical or mental impairment that substantially limits one or more of the major life activities," in this case, her future ability to work.[ ]

* * * Both the ADA and EEOC regulations establish that a plaintiff, such as Winslow, whose claim asserts only that she was regarded by a defendant as having a substantially limiting impairment, need not prove that she in fact suffered such impairment. * * *

Plaintiff claims that the "major life activity" that Defendant perceives as "substantially limited" by her dysthymia is her future ability to work. It is undisputed that work is a "major life activity," which if substantially limited or regarded as substantially limited by a significant impairment qualifies a person as disabled under the ADA.[ ] 29 C.F.R. § 1630.2(i)[ ]

This Court finds, as a matter of law, that when IDS denied Plaintiff Winslow's application for long-term disability insurance based on her depression and anxiety, diagnosed as dysthymia, IDS implicitly considered her to be "impaired" and likely unable to perform "either a class of jobs or a broad range of jobs in various classes" in the future. * * *

Defendant asserts that even if Plaintiff can show that IDS regarded her as likely to suffer a substantially limiting impairment in the future, she has failed to show that IDS regarded her as disabled at the time it denied her application for long-term disability insurance as required by the statutory language of the ADA, which contains no future tense. See 42 U.S.C. § 12102(2)(C) ("regarded as having such an impairment") * * *

In Doukas v. Metropolitan Life Insurance Company, 1997 WL 833134 (D.N.H.), the court held that "the distinction between present and future limitations [in the ADA] is not dispositive."[ ] In Doukas, Plaintiff Susan Doukas applied for and was denied mortgage disability insurance by MetLife. MetLife based its denial on information in Doukas' application indicating that she had been diagnosed with and was being treated for bipolar disorder and was therefore likely to become totally disabled from work in the future. MetLife moved for summary judgment on the grounds that Doukas did not fall within the ADA definition of disabled because she was not regarded as currently disabled and incapable of working but rather as presenting a future risk of disability. The court denied MetLife's motion, finding that "the 'regarded as' definition of disability seeks to eradicate discrimination based on prejudice or irrational fear. Fear, almost by definition, refers not to actual present conditions, but to anticipated future consequences."[ ] Courts have noted that the perception of impairment is included by Congress within the definition of disabled to combat the effects of " 'archaic attitudes,' erroneous perceptions, and myths that work to the disadvantage of persons with or regarded as having disabilities." * * *

* * * This Court finds the reasoning set forth in Doukas persuasive and holds that the purpose of the ADA requires that ADA protection extend to cover perception of possible future disability.

III. APPLICABILITY OF THE ADA TO INSURANCE POLICIES

Title III of the ADA provides:

No individual shall be discriminated against on the basis of disability in the full and equal enjoyment of the goods, services, facilities, privileges, advantages, or accommodations of any place of public accommodation by any person who owns, leases (or leases to), or operates a place of public accommodation.

42 U.S.C. § 12182(a). Section 12181(7) provides an illustrative list of entities considered public accommodations for the purposes of Title III. See Parker v. Metropolitan Life Ins. Co., 121 F.3d 1006, 1010 (6th Cir.1997); Carparts Distribution Center, Inc. v. Automotive Wholesaler's Association of New England, Inc., 37 F.3d 12, 19 (1st Cir.1994). The issue before this Court is whether "public accommodations" are limited to actual physical structures or whether Title III of the ADA prohibits more than physical impediments to public accommodations for the disabled.

This issue is one of first impression for the Eighth Circuit and has been decided only by the First and Sixth Circuits, which split on the matter, and a smattering of district courts, some of which have followed the First Circuit in

Carparts and others of which have adopted the reasoning of the Sixth Circuit in Parker.

In Parker, the Sixth Circuit reviewed the regulations applicable to Title III of the ADA to interpret "places" of public accommodation and found that a "place," as defined by 28 C.F.R. § 36.104, is "a facility, operated by a private entity, whose operations affect commerce and fall within at least one of the twelve 'public accommodation' categories."[ ] A "facility," in turn, is defined by 28 C.F.R. § 36.104 as "all or any portion of buildings, structures, sites, complexes, equipment, rolling stock or other conveyances, roads, walks, passageways, parking lots, or other real or personal property, including the site where the building, property, structure, or equipment is located." Parker, 121 F.3d at 1011. The court concluded that the plain meaning of the statutory language and the applicable regulations is that places of public accommodation are limited to physical places open to public access.[ ]

In Carparts, the First Circuit reached the opposite conclusion, determining that "public accommodations" are not limited to actual physical structures. Kotev v. First Colony Life Insurance Company, 927 F.Supp. 1316 (C.D.Cal.1996) followed the Carparts holding and addressed the issue at greater length. Kotev noted that the limited interpretation of "public accommodation" adopted by the Parker court would contravene the broadly stated purpose of the ADA to "provide a clear and comprehensive national mandate for the elimination of discrimination against individuals with disabilities ... and invoke the sweep of congressional authority ... in order to address the major areas of discrimination faced day-to-day by people with disabilities."[ ]

"Disability" under the ADA includes both physical and mental impairments as well as those with records of or regarded as having such impairments. See 42 U.S.C. § 12102(2)(A)-(C). By restricting "public accommodations" to include only physical structures, the protection under the ADA for individuals with mental disabilities would be virtually negated, absent circumstances in which a physical structure denied access to the mentally impaired.[ ]

Especially relevant to the present case is ADA statutory language that would be rendered irrelevant if Title III were held to apply only to physical access to public accommodations:

(i) the imposition or application of eligibility criteria that screen out * * * an individual with a disability * * * from fully and equally enjoying any goods, services, facilities, privileges, advantages, or accommodations, unless such criteria can be shown to be necessary ...

(ii) a failure to make reasonable modifications in policies, practices, or procedures, when such modifications are necessary to afford such goods, services, facilities, privileges, advantages, or accommodations to individuals with disabilities ...

* * *

42 U.S.C. § 12182(b)(2)(A)(i-iii)[ ] Also rendered superfluous by such a narrow interpretation would be the Title III provision for injunctive relief set forth in 42 U.S.C. § 12188(a)(2) that "shall also include requiring the ... modification of policy."

Further supporting the conclusion reached by Kotev and a growing number of district courts—that ADA Title III applies to the provision of insurance policies—is the "Safe Harbor" provision of Title III, specifically addressing insurance. * * * The Safe Harbor provision states, in relevant part:

Subchapters I through III of this chapter and Title IV of this Act shall not be construed to prohibit or restrict-

(1) an insurer, hospital or medical service company, health maintenance organization, or any agent, or entity that administers benefit plans, or similar organizations from underwriting risks, classifying risks, or administering such risks that are based on or not inconsistent with State law;

. . .

Paragraphs (1), (2), and (3) shall not be used as a subterfuge to evade the purposes of subchapter[s] I and III of this chapter. 42 U.S.C. § 12201(c).

Courts have concluded, and this Court agrees, that the Safe Harbor provision would be superfluous if "insurers could never be liable under Title III for conduct such as discriminatory denial of insurance coverage."[ ]

* * * The DOJ [in its legislative history of the ADA also] interprets Title III as prohibiting "differential treatment of individuals with disabilities in insurance offered by public accommodations unless the differences are justified."

* * *

Based on the legislative history, the DOJ interpretation of Title III of the ADA, and the reasoning adopted by a growing number of district courts, this Court finds that Title III of the ADA is applicable to insurance policies and not limited to access to actual physical structures.

A. The McCarran–Ferguson Act

Defendant argues that the McCarran–Ferguson Act, 15 U.S.C. § 1012 et seq., precludes application of the ADA to insurance policies because Title III is not intended to regulate the business of private insurance carriers. The McCarran–Ferguson Act provides, in relevant part:

No Act of Congress shall be construed to invalidate, impair or supersede any law enacted by any State for the purpose of regulating the business of insurance ... unless such Act specifically related to the business of insurance.

15 U.S.C. § 1012(b)[ ]. The McCarran–Ferguson Act bars the application of a federal statute if:

(1) the statute does not specifically relate to the business of insurance; (2) a state statute has been enacted for the purpose of regulating the business of insurance; and (3) the federal statute would invalidate, impair, or supersede the state statute.

* * *

This Court identifies two fundamental provisions of the ADA that specifically relate to the business of insurance. The Court finds that the "subterfuge" provision of the ADA, see supra, 42 U.S.C. § 12201(c), which prohibits the use of the Safe Harbor provision to evade the purpose of Title III of the ADA is a statutory provision specifically related to the business of insurance. * * * The Court also interprets the inclusion of an "insurance office" as an entity considered a public accommodation for the purposes of Title III of the ADA, see 42 U.S.C. § 12181(7)(F), as an explicit indication that the ADA is intended to specifically relate to the business of insurance.

* * *

The McCarran–Ferguson Act is a form of inverse preemption, so principles defining when state remedies conflict with . . . federal law are pertinent in deciding when federal rules " 'invalidate, impair, or supersede' state rules."[ ] * * * "[D]uplication is not conflict '[however] and * * * as a general rule,' state and federal rules that are substantively identical but differ in penalty do not conflict with or displace each other," * * * This court * * * holds that the McCarran–Ferguson Act does not "invalidate, impair, or supersede" the relevant Minnesota statutes and does not bar plaintiff's ADA claims.

IV. THE SAFE HARBOR PROVISION

As indicated above, the ADA provides a Safe Harbor provision for insurance providers under the ADA. See supra, 42 U.S.C. § 12201(c). Under the Safe Harbor provision, the risk underwriting engaged in by insurance companies must be based on or not inconsistent with state law.[ ] The subterfuge provision, see supra 42 U.S.C. § 12201(c), provides, however, that even if an insurer's practices are consistent with applicable state law, they can still violate the ADA if plaintiff demonstrates that the insurance policies are a subterfuge to evade the purpose of the ADA.[ ] Thus, the Court must perform a two-part analysis to determine whether the IDS policies in question violate the Safe Harbor provision of the ADA: (1) is the eligibility criteria employed by IDS based on and consistent with state law; and (2) is the eligibility criteria a subterfuge to evade the purposes of the ADA.

Minn.Stat. § 72A.20 provides in relevant part:

Subd. 9. Making or permitting any unfair discrimination between individuals of the same class and of essentially the same hazard in the amount of premium, policy fees, or rates charged for any policy or contract of accident or health insurance or in the benefits payable thereunder, or in any terms or conditions of such contract, or in any other manner whatever, or in making or permitting the rejection of an individual's application for accident or health insurance coverage, as well as the determination of the rate class for such individual, on the basis of a disability, shall constitute an unfair method of competition and an unfair and deceptive act or practice, unless the claims experience and actuarial projections and other data establish significant and substantial differences in class rates because of the disability.

Subd. 19. No life or health insurance company doing business in this state shall engage in any selection or underwriting process unless the insurance company establishes beforehand substantial data, actuarial projections, or claims experience which support the underwriting standards used by the insurance company. * * *

Minn.Stat. § 72A.20, subd. 9, 19.

IDS categorically denies long-term disability insurance to any applicant who has been treated for a mental health condition within the past year, allowing the applicant to be reconsidered after one year has passed since the last treatment. To comply with Minnesota law, IDS must justify such eligibility criteria with claims experience, actuarial projections, or other data to "establish significant and substantial differences in class rates because of the disability."[ ]

IDS asserts that it has presented such justification for its eligibility criteria and therefore does not violate state law. The Court acknowledges that IDS presents specific industry data based on claims experience and actuarial projections that show a dramatic increase in payments on long-term disability insurance claims due to mental health and nervous disorders. Plaintiff counters that while Defendant establishes that claims for disability due to mental or nervous conditions have increased since 1989, Defendant fails to demonstrate that individuals receiving treatment for mental or nervous conditions at or near the time of application for insurance are more likely to file claims under their long-term disability insurance. Furthermore, Plaintiff notes that the Paul Revere Underwriting Manual includes various impairments, such as dysthymia, and establishes procedures for processing applications from individuals with such impairments without recommending total denial of insurance for such applicants. * * * Thus, Plaintiff claims that a genuine issue of material fact exists as to whether IDS' long-term disability insurance eligibility criteria conforms to sound actuarial principles, claims experience, or substantial data as required by Minnesota state law. The Court agrees and denies summary judgment on the matter.

Defendant also asserts that it is entitled to Safe Harbor protection under Title III of the ADA because its eligibility criteria are not a subterfuge. See supra, 42 U.S.C. § 12201(c). * * * As this Court has determined that a genuine issue of material fact exists as to whether IDS eligibility criteria violates Minnesota law, the Court need not pass on the issue as to whether the criteria is a subterfuge of the ADA.

V. DISABILITY-BASED DISTINCTION UNDER THE ADA

Plaintiff asserts that the IDS policy of denying long-term disability insurance to all applicants having received mental health treatment within the past year is founded on a disability-based distinction violative of the ADA. Courts have found that broad-based distinctions that distinguish between mental and physical health conditions do not qualify as illicit disability-based distinctions under the ADA because the ADA is only applicable to discrimination against disabled persons compared to non-disabled persons, not discrimination among the disabled.[ ] [EEOC Interim Enforcement Guidelines also permit broad-based distinctions between mental and physical conditions for health care benefits, ed.]

The aforementioned cases and the EEOC Interim Guidance, however, address disability-based discrimination among the disabled that affects the quality and extent of coverage offered to one class of disabled as compared to another and do not address the categorical denial of access to insurance coverage to a class of disabled individuals. When courts have addressed the exclusion of a class of disabled from an insurance plan, they have found such exclusions violative of the ADA.[ ]

Legislative history of Title III of the ADA further supports the proposition that while disability-based distinctions in an insurance policy's terms are permissible under the ADA, a policy to deny insurance coverage categorically to mentally disabled is unacceptable:

* * * This Court finds that as Defendant's policy of denying long-term disability insurance to those treated for mental conditions within the past year denies said individuals access to insurance coverage, the policy is founded on a disability-based discrimination violative of the ADA.

VI. Minnesota Human Rights Act

[The court also found that IDS denial violated the Minnesota Human Rights Act, which is similar to the ADA, but concluded that punitive damages were not available under that Act, because the defendant's conduct did not demonstrate "willful indifference" to the plaintiff's rights.]

Notes and Questions

Title I of the ADA prohibits discrimination "against a qualified individual with a disability because of the disability of such individual in regard to * * * [the] terms, conditions, and privileges of employment." 42 U.S.C.A. § 12112. Discrimination prohibited by the statute extends to "fringe benefits." 42 U.S.C.A. § 12112(b)(4); 29 C.F.R. § 1630.4(f). Title II similarly prohibits discrimination by public entities. 42 U.S.C.A. § 12132. Title III proscribes discrimination "on the basis of disability in the full and equal enjoyment of the goods, services, facilities, privileges, advantages, or accommodations of any place of public accommodation * * *." 42 U.S.C.A. § 12182. "Public accommodation" is specifically defined to include an "insurance office." 42 U.S.C.A. § 12181(7)(F). Finally, Title V of the Act contains a specific "safe harbor" providing that the ADA is not to be construed to restrict insurers, HMOs, employers, plan or administrators from "underwriting risks, classifying risks, or administering such risks that are based on or not inconsistent with State law," as long as the entity does not use this provision "as a subterfuge to evade the purposes" of the ADA. 42 U.S.C.A. § 12201(c).

The ADA would seem to prohibit insurers and employers administering benefit plans from imposing coverage terms and conditions that discriminate against persons with particular disabilities. Cases have been brought under the ADA, therefore, challenging policies that provided less coverage for treatment of mental than for treatment of physical conditions, Rogers v. Department of Health and Environmental Control, 174 F.3d 431 (4th Cir.1999); Ford v. Schering–Plough Corp., 145 F.3d 601 (3d Cir. 1998); that capped coverage for AIDS but not for other conditions, Doe v. Mutual of Omaha, 179 F.3d 557 (7th Cir.1999); or that excluded coverage for particular services, like heart transplants, Lenox v. Healthwise of Ky., Ltd., 149 F.3d 453 (6th Cir.1998); or infertility, Krauel v. Iowa Methodist Medical Center, 95 F.3d 674 (8th Cir.1996). See D'Andra Millsap, Sex, Lies and Health Insurance: Employer–Provided Health Insurance Coverage of Abortion and Infertility Services and the ADA, 22 Am.J. Law & Med. 51 (1996).

Though some of these cases have succeeded, they have encountered increasingly serious obstacles. First, several courts have held that the ADA does not require employers or insurers to offer any particular form of coverage, but merely prohibits them from offering different terms and conditions of coverage to disabled persons than those offered to nondisabled persons. Doe v. Mutual of Omaha Ins. Co., 179 F.3d 557 (7th Cir.1999); Ford v. Schering–Plough Corp., 145 F.3d 601 (3d Cir. 1998). These courts hold that the ADA does not demand that all disabilities be treated similarly, but only that disabled persons be not disfavored in comparison to nondisabled persons. Providing different coverage for different conditions, moreover, is not even necessarily discrimination against persons with a disability unless the condition itself is a disability or unless discrimination in coverage of a particular condition disproportionately affects disabled persons. By this reasoning, an employer or insurer who offers limited coverage for mental illness and unlimited coverage for physical conditions is in ADA compliance, as long as it offers the same terms and conditions of coverage to all of its employees, regardless of disability. Rogers v. Department of Health and Environmental Control, 174 F.3d 431 (4th Cir.1999). In the specific context of differential coverage of mental and physical conditions, courts have relied further on the limited scope of the Mental Health Parity Act of 1997 (mentioned above) to support their position that Congress did not intend in the ADA to achieve sweeping parity in treatment for all conditions. Lewis v. Kmart Corp., 180 F.3d 166 (4th Cir.1999); Parker v. Metropolitan Life Ins. Co., 121 F.3d 1006, 1017–18 (6th Cir.1997) (en banc).

Second, there is considerable debate as to when and whether the ADA applies to insurance policies. Though Title III clearly covers insurance offices, several courts that have addressed the issue have held that Title III only applies to physical places, and does not extend to the terms and conditions of the products the insurers offer independent of these places. Weyer v. Twentieth Century Fox Film Corp., 198 F.3d 1104 (9th Cir.2000); Ford v. Schering–Plough Corp., 145 F.3d 601 (3d Cir. 1998); Lenox v. Healthwise of Ky., Ltd., 149 F.3d 453 (6th Cir.1998); Parker v. Metropolitan Life Ins. Co., 121 F.3d 1006 (6th Cir. 1997) (en banc). The EEOC Guidelines and a number of other courts, on the other hand, have held that Title III might extend to the contents of insurance policies as well. Pallozzi v. Allstate Life Ins. Co., 198 F.3d 28 (2d Cir.1999); Carparts Distribution Ctr., Inc. v. Automotive Wholesaler's Ass'n of New England, 37 F.3d 12 (1st Cir.1994). See Jill L. Schultz, Note: The Impact of Title III of the Americans with Disabilities Act on Employer–Provided Insurance Plans: Is the Insurance Company Subject to Liability? 56 Wash. & Lee L. Rev 343 (1999). Of course, if insurance is offered through an employer, discrimination is prohibited under Title I even if the insurer's practices are not covered by Title III.

Third, several courts have read Title V's insurance "safe harbor" broadly to protect insurer practices that are not intentional stratagems to effectuate discrimination beyond the particular benefit at issue, following Supreme Court precedent in interpreting the term "subterfuge" in other areas. Ford v. Schering–Plough Corp., 145 F.3d 601 (3d Cir. 1998) and Krauel v. Iowa Methodist Medical Center, 95 F.3d 674, 678–9 (8th Cir.1996); relying on Public Employees Retirement System of Ohio v. Betts, 492 U.S. 158, 175, 109 S.Ct. 2854, 106 L.Ed.2d 134 (1989). Other courts, however, have required actuarial support for treating different conditions differently, particularly when the insurance practice is also suspect under state law. Morgenthal v. American Telephone and Telegraph Co., 1999 WL 187055 (S.D.N.Y.1999); Chabner v. United of Omaha Life Ins. Co., 994 F.Supp. 1185 (N.D.Cal.1998).

Finally, the McCarran–Ferguson Act, discussed earlier, is emerging as a brooding presence in ADA insurance litigation. Some courts are reluctant to find that Congress meant to turn over the job of regulating insurance underwriting practices from the states to the federal courts in the absence of excruciating clear Congressional intent to accomplish this result—intent that is lacking in the ADA setting. Doe v. Mutual of Omaha Ins. Co., 179 F.3d 557 (7th Cir.1999). Again, however, other courts, like the principal case, reject this position. Pallozzi v. Allstate Life Ins. Co., 198 F.3d 28 (2d Cir.1999).

The ADA is far from dead as a means of challenging egregious insurance practices. The absolute refusal of an employer or insurer to provide health insurance on the basis of disability, for example, would violate the Act. But the Act is increasingly proving a disappointment for advocates who had hoped that it would lead to more equitable and rational insurance coverage.

C. OTHER ANTIDISCRIMINATION LAWS

A number of other federal laws prohibit discrimination in health insurance on other bases, though their impact is relatively modest. First, an employer covered by Title VII of the Civil Rights Act cannot treat medical costs associated with pregnancy or childbirth different than other medical costs covered by its health insurance plan. Title VII prohibits sex discrimination, and the Pregnancy Discrimination Act of 1978 (PDA) defines sex discrimination to include treatment of pregnancy, childbirth, or related medical conditions differently from other medical conditions under fringe benefit programs. 42 U.S.C.A. § 2000e(k). Maternity-related medical conditions must, therefore, be treated the same as other medical conditions under group health insurance with respect to terms of reimbursement (including payment maximums); deductibles, copayments, coinsurance, and out-of-pocket maximums; preexisting condition limitations; extension of benefits following termination of employment; and limitations on freedom of choice. See 29 C.F.R. App. to Pt. 1604, Questions 25–29. The PDA does not, however, extend to coverage of fertility services. Krauel v. Iowa Methodist Medical Ctr., 95 F.3d 674 (8th Cir.1996).

Second, the Age Discrimination in Employment Act (ADEA) 29 U.S.C.A. §§ 621–630, limits the ability of covered employers to discriminate among employees with respect to the provision of health insurance benefits. The Older Workers Benefit Protection Act of 1990 amended the ADEA to clarify that discrimination in the provision of benefits, including health insurance benefits is prohibited.29 U.S.C.A. § 630(*l*). The Act and implementing regulations, however, do permit employers offering bona fide benefit plans to offer older workers fewer benefits or to charge older workers more for benefits in voluntary contributory plans (as long as the proportion of total premium charged the employee does not change with age), if the distinctions are justified by cost data and the employer does not pay less than it does for benefit plans for younger workers. 29 U.S.C.A. § 623(f)(2)(B)(1); 29 C.F.R. § 1625.10.

Third, Section 105 of the Internal Revenue Code limits the ability of self-insured employer health plans to discriminate in favor of highly-compensated individuals. 26 U.S.C.A. § 105(h), 26 C.F.R. §§ 1–105–5–1–105–11(c).

Problem: Private Cost Containment

You are an attorney representing Amtech Inc., which employs about 1500 employees. Since its founding in 1985, Amtech's business has grown rapidly and profits have been high. Amtech has traditionally offered generous salaries and an extensive benefits plan to attract the well-trained and educated employees it needs. In the last two years, however, growth and profits have flagged. Moreover, Amtech has recently been purchased on a highly-leveraged basis and must cut costs to service its high debt. Finally, last year the premiums of Amtech's group health plan, which it has always purchased from a conventional insurer, increased dramatically. The new management has decided, therefore, that action is necessary to control corporate costs generally and health care costs in particular.

The group health plan that Amtech has offered its employees for since its inception was a traditional conventional insurance plan. Individual coverage has been free to employees. Family coverage has been offered subject to payment of a small premium, which has risen slowly to its present level of about $100.00 a month. The health plan covered basic hospitalization on a first dollar basis. It paid hospitals directly on a reasonable charge basis. Physician services were covered on an indemnity basis, subject to a $250.00 deductible for family coverage and a 10% copayment for which the employee was responsible. There was no maximum for plan benefits, nor was there a maximum out-of-pocket expenditure limit. Prescription drugs were also covered subject to a 20% copayment. Claims were subject to utilization review, but rarely denied.

Amtech's benefits manager has devised the following plan for controlling benefit's costs. Amtech will offer its employees a triple option. Employees may opt for coverage through an HMO, provider-sponsored PPO, or conventional indemnity plan with utilization review. They must make their choice of plans within two months of the introduction of the new benefits scheme, and will only be able to change plans once a year during a one month open enrollment period.

Amtech will enter into a competitive bidding process with the five HMOs currently operating in the area, and will select the one that offers it the lowest price for coverage similar in breadth to the existing conventional plan. Employees who choose the HMO option will have to pay no more for coverage than they do currently, but will be strictly limited to the HMO for medical care and receive no payment for care provided outside of the HMO, even in emergencies.

Amtech will also offer to contract directly with Community Memorial, a large hospital located near Amtech's plant to provide care to its employees. Initial contacts with Community Memorial, which has recently experienced a sharp drop in occupancy, indicate that it is very interested in such a contract and would be willing to offer a substantial discount from its normal charges. Community Memorial will identify primary care physicians and specialists with privileges at Community Memorial to participate in the plan on a contract basis, and negotiate discounts with them. Primary care physicians will operate as "gatekeepers," i.e. access to specialists will only be available upon referral from one of the plan's primary care physicians.

The Community Memorial plan will provide for care with cost-sharing terms similar to those now in place under the current conventional plan. Plan enrollees can receive care out-of-plan (that is, they can choose care from a specialist or hospital not affiliated with the plan), but will be responsible for a $500 deductible and 30% copayments for out-of-plan care.

Third, Amtech will also continue to offer a plan identical to its current conventional contract, raising the deductible to $500 per individual and raising the coinsurance amount to 20% for physician's services and 5% for hospitalization. Amtech will offer this coverage on a self-funded basis, renegotiating its contract with the current insurer as an administrative services only contract. Amtech will purchase a $1,000,000 deductible reinsurance policy for coverage for which it is at risk.

Coverage for prescription drugs under all three options will be provided through a plan administered by a pharmacy benefits management company and subject to a $10 copayment for generic drugs and $20 for name-brand. Only drugs on a formulary maintained by the pharmacy benefits manager will be covered. Mental health and substance abuse benefits will also be covered separately under all three plans through a managed behavioral care plan. Mental health and substance abuse benefits will be capped at $10,000 a year.

Amtech will contract with a utilization management firm to provide preadmission and length of stay review for hospitalization and preprocedure review for surgery under the PPO and conventional plans. Unapproved care will not be covered. The utilization management contract will establish performance goals, including denial of about 5% of claims per year, given estimates from the literature that the incidence of unnecessary care is much higher than this. All three plan contracts also provide that "experimental treatment" is not covered (the term is not defined) and that the plan administrator may deny payment for unnecessary care at its own discretion. Decisions of the plan administrator in either event are reviewable only through binding arbitration.

All plans will be subject to a pre-existing conditions exclusion for new employees, or for existing employees who have not previously enrolled in a plan but do so for the first time. Under this exclusion, the plan will not cover any expenditures attributable to medical conditions for which the employee received treatment or for which treatment was recommended during the six month period preceding the employee's request for coverage. The exclusion will last for the first year of coverage.

Regardless of the employee's choice of plan, Amtech will only pay an employer contribution equal to that it must make for the HMO plan. (It will separately cover the mental health and pharmacy benefits without required employee contributions). Any additional premium costs required for coverage under the PPO or conventional plan have to be paid for by employees. Employees whose medical costs exceed 500% of the average medical expenditures incurred per employee in any particular year will have their premiums increased by 100% the following year. Employees who are non-smokers and who sign-in at Amtech's health club at least once a week will receive a 10% premium discount.

Amtech asks you to review the proposal and identify any potential legal problems under federal law, or under the Massachusetts law found in the previous chapter. Comment on any potential problems you see with the plan and make suggestions as to how it could be improved.

Chapter 10

PUBLIC HEALTH CARE PROGRAMS: MEDICARE AND MEDICAID

I. INTRODUCTION

Government provision or financing of health care has a long history in the United States. The first federal medical program was established in 1798 to provide care for sick seamen in the coastal trade. State hospitals for the mentally ill and local public hospitals were well established by the mid-nineteenth century.

Today, government at all levels finances a plethora of health care institutions and programs. In 1999, government accounted for $548.5 billion, 45.3 percent, of total national expenditures on personal health care. The federal government provides health care to veterans in 150 veterans' health care facilities and in the community; to the military and their dependents in 115 military hospitals and through the Civilian Health and Medical Program of the Uniformed Services (CHAMPUS) (which in turn provides care through the TRICARE managed care program); to 1.5 million Native Americans in almost 200 hospitals, health centers, and clinics run by the Indian Health Service; to disabled coal miners through the Black Lung program; and to a variety of special groups through block grants to the states for maternal and child health, alcohol and drug abuse treatment, mental health, preventive health, and primary care. States provide health care both through traditional programs like mental and tuberculosis hospitals, state university hospitals, and worker's compensation, but also increasingly through a variety of newer programs intended to shore up the tattered safety net, including insurance pools for the high-risk uninsured, drug benefit programs for the elderly, and programs to provide health insurance for the poor uninsured. County and local governments operate local hospitals. Federal, state, and local governments provide comparatively generous health insurance programs for their own employees and less generous health care programs for their prisoners (the only Americans constitutionally entitled to health care).

By far the largest public health care programs, however, are the federal Medicare program and the state and federal Medicaid program, which respectively spent about $213.6 billion and about $187.7 billion in 1999. This chapter focuses on these two programs, though it also briefly discusses the State Children's Health Insurance Program, established in 1997 to provide health insurance for poor children.

With the waning of interest in comprehensive health care reform in the mid–1990s, the health care debate at the federal level has focused primarily on the future of Medicare and Medicaid. There are several reasons why this debate has been focused on these programs and why it has been so passionate and contentious. First, Medicare and Medicaid policy have been driven by federal budget policy. Together the two programs consume 19 percent of the federal budget. Moreover, if one excludes from consideration the costs of defense, Social Security, and the national debt—all of which are more or less protected from cuts at this time—the two programs consume 38 percent of what remains of the federal budget. Medicaid is also one of the largest items in state budgets. Further, the cost of Medicare and Medicaid through much of the 1990s grew much faster than the cost of other federal programs and state programs. While slowed program growth following the Balanced Budget Act of 1997, and budget surpluses at the end of the decade, have taken some of the pressure off of these programs, Congress is very aware of their cost.

Second, growth in the Medicare program threatens not only to continue to claim a large slice of the federal budget, but also ultimately to overwhelm the financing mechanisms that currently support it. In 1995 and 1996, the Republican Congressional majority made much of the imminent insolvency of the Part A Trust Fund, though the Trust Fund has never been far from insolvency and has always been kept solvent through incremental increases in the payroll tax. The 1997 Balanced Budget Act (BBA) and a very strong economy at the end of the 1990s put off projected insolvency until 2029, indeed Trust Fund assets grew by 11.7 percent during 1999. The long-term viability of the Medicare program remains in doubt, however, as a huge group of baby-boomers becomes eligible for Medicare in the first half the 21st century. By 2030, Medicare will be responsible for the health care of 22 percent of the American population, compared to 14 percent today. By the middle of the 21st century, moreover, there will be two workers for every Medicare beneficiary compared to today's four to one ratio.

Third, debates about how to reform the programs touch repeatedly upon issues that divide policy makers sharply along ideological lines. Can costs be most effectively controlled through regulatory or market strategies? Should the financing of health care services for the poor be a federal or state responsibility? Should poor persons have an entitlement to health care coverage, or should access be discretionary?

Finally, Medicare and Medicaid together insure about a quarter of the American population, including one of the most politically active segments of the American populace (the elderly). They also affect immediately the fortunes of most health care providers, who are invariably contributors to political campaigns. Politicians are acutely aware, therefore, of the existence and the exigencies of these programs.

To understand the debates raging around these programs, we must first understand how the programs work. Anyone designing or seeking to understand a health care financing program must begin by considering several basic questions.

First, who receives the program's benefits? Are the targeted recipients characterized by economic need, a particular disease, advanced age, disability, residence in a particular geographic jurisdiction, employment in a certain

industry, or status as an enrollee and contributor to a social insurance fund?
From these questions others follow: Who in fact receives most of the program's benefits? Who does the program leave out? Why are some groups
included and others excluded? Also, should beneficiaries receive an entitlement or should eligibility be at the government's discretion?

Second, what benefits will be provided? For example, should the program
stress institutional services such as hospitalization or nursing home care, or
non-institutional alternatives such as home health care? Should the program
be limited to services commonly covered by private insurance like hospital and
physician care, or should it also cover services such as dental care and
eyeglasses that private insurance often does not cover because middle class
insureds can afford to pay for them? These services may be inaccessible to the
poor unless the program covers them. Should the program cover medically
controversial services, such as care provided by chiropractors or midwives?
Should a public program cover socially controversial services such as abortions? Should it cover services that provide relatively small marginal benefits
at a very high cost, such as some organ transplants or cancer therapies?
Finally, how can the benefits package be kept up to date? For example, when
Medicare was created in 1965 it did not cover pharmaceuticals, in part,
because most private insurance programs did not cover them. Today, however,
most private insurance programs have a pharmacy benefit, and drug costs
have become a major problem for senior citizens. It is argued, therefore, that
Medicare is out of date.

Third, how should the program provide benefits? Should it pay private
professionals and institutions to deliver the services, as do Medicare and
Medicaid, or should it deliver services itself directly, as does the Veterans'
Administration through its hospitals? Should it pay "vendor payments" on a
fee-for-service basis to providers at the same rate that they charge their
private customers, or should it cover their costs, or pay an average charge, or
pay for the "value" of the services or of the resources that are required to
produce them, or be based on negotiations? Alternatively, should the program
purchase care on a capitated basis from managed care plans? Should beneficiaries simply be given vouchers and be expected to purchase their own
insurance in the private market? Should public programs, that is, be defined-
contribution or defined-benefit programs? Should recipients be expected to
share in the costs through coinsurance or deductibles?

Finally, who should play what role in administering the program? Should
the program be run by the federal, state, or local government? Should policy
be set by the legislature or by an administrative agency? Should payments to
providers be administered by the government or by private contractors?
Should program beneficiaries (or providers) have rights enforceable in court,
or should the government retain unreviewable discretion in running the
program? If rights are recognized, should these rights be enforceable in state
or federal court, or perhaps only through administrative proceedings? This
chapter will explore each of these issues with respect first to the Medicare and
then to the Medicaid and SCHIP programs.

As you consider these major questions, keep in mind several other
themes. First, notice the fragmentation and fragmentariness of our public
health care programs. Unlike other nations, we do not have a single public

system creating a safety net for all of society, but rather a patchwork of programs, creating a host of safety nets, some higher and some lower, many fairly tattered, and none catching everyone. Whom do the safety nets miss? What problems does this fragmented system create? What opportunities does it offer?

Second, notice who, other than covered populations of patients, benefits from federal and state programs. Consider which providers benefit most from public programs. Note the role Medicare and Medicaid have played in financing medical education, for example, or in subsidizing care for safety net providers, such as inner city hospitals. Consider how providers position their operations to maximize their benefits from public programs, and how the mix of health care services in this country reflects the policies of these programs.

II. MEDICARE

A. ELIGIBILITY

Medicare covers about 40 million elderly and disabled beneficiaries, one in seven Americans. Medicare eligibility is generally linked to that of the Social Security program, the other major social insurance program of the United States. Persons who are eligible for retirement benefits under Social Security are automatically eligible for Medicare upon reaching age 65. (this will remain true even though the full Social Security retirement age increases to 67 by 2007). If a person eligible for Social Security decides to continue working beyond age 65, he or she may still begin receiving Medicare at 65. Spouses or former spouses who qualify for Social Security as dependents may also begin receiving Medicare at 65, as may former federal employees eligible for Civil Service Retirement and Railroad Retirement beneficiaries, 42 U.S.C.A. § 426(a).

Disabled persons who are eligible for Social Security or Railroad Retirement benefits may also receive Medicare, but only after they have been eligible for cash benefits for at least two years, 42 U.S.C.A. § 426(b). (Under the 2001 budget bill, persons suffering from Lou Gehrig's disease are eligible immediately and do not have to wait for the two years.) About five million disabled persons are currently covered by Medicare, and this group is growing rapidly. Benefits are also available to two groups of persons who need not be Social Security beneficiaries. First, any person over 65 who is a United States citizen or has legally resided in the United States for at least five years may voluntarily enroll in Medicare if he or she is willing and able to pay a premium for the insurance, 42 U.S.C.A. § 1395i–2(a). Second, persons eligible for Social Security, though not necessarily receiving it, who have end-stage renal (kidney) disease may receive Medicare benefits after a three-month waiting period, 42 U.S.C.A. § 426–1. About 300,000 Medicare beneficiaries are eligible for this reason.

Why is Medicare, a social insurance program, only available to the elderly and disabled? Why is it available to all members of these groups, regardless of their income or wealth? What effect has Medicare had on the workers who support it through their payroll taxes? What effect does it have on the children of Medicare recipients? What effect might it have on the children of Medicare recipients at the death of the recipient? During the health care reform debate of 1994 the idea surfaced briefly of extending Medicare to cover all of the uninsured. Why did this idea attract little support?

Medicare has been generally successful in assuring broad and equitable access to health care for many who would probably otherwise be uninsured. 74 percent of Medicare expenditures go for beneficiaries with incomes of less than $25,000 a year, and 60 percent of elderly Medicare beneficiaries receive at least half of their income from Social Security. When the program began only 56 percent of the elderly had hospital insurance and the poor and nonwhite elderly received substantially less medical care than did the wealthier or white elderly. While these disparities have been substantially reduced, some disparities still remain, notably between southern blacks and whites, and between the urban and rural elderly. Even greater disparities exist in the actual benefits received by recipients. In particular, the very old and those who are near death receive a much greater proportion of benefits than do younger recipients. Nearly 70 percent of program payments are made for 10 percent of Medicare beneficiaries, while 22 percent have no program expenditures made on their behalf, and an additional 30 percent are responsible for only 2 percent of total program spending. Health Care Financing Administration, Medicare 2000 (2000); Nancy De Lew, The First 30 Years of Medicare and Medicaid, 274 JAMA 262 (1995); Margaret Davis & Sally T. Burner, Three Decades of Medicare: What the Numbers Tell Us, 14 Health Aff. Win. 1995 at 231. Are these disparities troublesome? Why or why not?

B. BENEFITS

1. *Coverage*

The Medicare Hospital Insurance (HI) program, Part A, pays for hospital, nursing home, home health and hospice services. The Medicare Supplemental Medical Insurance (SMI) program, Part B, covers physicians' services and a variety of other items and services including outpatient hospital services, home health care, physical and occupational therapy, prosthetic devices, durable medical equipment, and ambulance services. Medicare covers only 150 days of hospital services in a single benefit period ("spell of illness"[1]). A one time deductible, set at $792 in 2001, must be paid before hospital coverage begins, and a daily copayment of $198 (in 2001) must be paid after the sixtieth day of hospital care, 42 U.S.C.A. § 1395e. Though the Medicare statute provides for coverage of up to 100 days of skilled nursing care, 42 U.S.C.A. § 1395d(a)(2), the nursing home benefit is basically available only to those recovering from an acute illness or injury, and is of little value to those who require long term care. Hospice benefits are provided on a very limited basis, 42 U.S.C.A. § 1395d(a)(4). Physicians' services are provided subject to an annual deductible of $100 and a 20 percent coinsurance amount. In recent years, Medicare has added some preventive services, including prostate cancer screening; bone mass density measurement; diabetes self-management; mammography screening; glaucoma screening; pap smears; and hepatitis B, pneumococcal, and flu shots.

---

1. A spell of illness begins when a patient is hospitalized, and continues until the patient has been out of a hospital or nursing home for at least 60 days. 42 U.S.C.A. § 1345x(a). Thus, a chronically ill person could remain indefinitely in a single spell of illness.

The Medicare benefits package resembles very closely the standard Blue Cross/Blue Shield package available in the mid–1960s when Medicare was established. It varies significantly, therefore, from standard benefit packages available today, which are likely to be managed care rather than fee-for-service based, have copayment rather than coinsurance requirements, require lower deductibles for in-plan providers, have higher catastrophic coverage limits, and cover prescription drugs. Medicare also has historically been weak in covering preventive services, though some of these have been picked up under recent budget acts. The absence of a prescription drug benefit is increasingly perceived as the most significant gap in the Medicare program. The problem of providing drug coverage is discussed further below.

Medicare pays for about 55 percent of the health care received by the elderly in this country, while private sources (including both private insurance and out-of-pocket expenditures) pay for 28 percent, Medicaid for 12 percent, and other sources for 5 percent. The majority of Medicare recipients purchase, or receive as a retirement benefit, Medicare Supplement (Medigap) insurance, which covers their cost-sharing obligations and some services not covered by Medicare. The average Medicare beneficiary spends 19 percent of household income on medical expenses not covered by Medicare, but the average beneficiary below the poverty level pays 35 percent of household income for medical expenses. Medicare accounts for 33 percent of the nation's expenditures for hospital care and 21 percent of physician expenditures. It also pays for the preponderance of hospice, home health, and renal dialysis services.

Beyond the broad political decisions of what categories of medical care Medicare will finance are the infinitely more numerous decisions as to whether a particular item or service will be covered by Medicare at all or for a particular beneficiary. Decisions as to whether Medicare will finance new technologies are made at different levels. Decisions regarding coverage of major new technologies are made at the national level. In late 1998 the Health Care Financing Administration (HCFA), which administers Medicare, created a Medicare Coverage Advisory Committee (MCAC), consisting of 120 health care experts to assist it in developing Medicare coverage policy. In 1999 HCFA issued procedures for using this panel, and in 2000 it published a notice, at 65 Fed. Reg. 31124, describing standards it proposes to follow in making these determinations. HCFA uses the MCAC, together with its own staff and independent research and extramural assessment, to develop coverage policy. It reviews technologies either at its own instance or in response to formal requests. It uses its web page to air coverage issues. It proposes reviewing technologies considering whether a new item or service demonstrates medical benefit and provides added value to the program. It will not consider the cost of the service unless the item or service is more expensive than existing alternatives and offers no added value.

Most coverage decisions are made less formally, however, by Medicare's carriers and intermediaries. Ultimately, whether any particular service is provided to any particular Medicare beneficiary will depend on the decision of a private carrier or intermediary (or perhaps of a Peer Review Organization) interpreting federal policy as mediated by Medicare regulations, manuals and manual transmittals, regional office instructions, rumor and innuendo. This process is attended by a fair bit of inconsistency.

Professor Eleanor Kinney has written series of articles that examine Medicare coverage policy, Eleanor Kinney, The Role of Judicial Review Regarding Medicare and Medicaid Program Policy, Past Experience and Future Expectations, 35 St. Louis U.L.J. 759 (1991); Eleanor Kinney, Setting Limits: A Realistic Assignment for the Medicare Program, 33 St. Louis U.L.J. 631 (1989); Eleanor Kinney, National Coverage Policy Under the Medicare Program: Problems and Proposals for Change, 32 St. Louis U.L.J. 869 (1988); Eleanor Kinney, The Medicare Appeals System for Coverage and Payment Disputes: Achieving Fairness in a Time of Constraint, 1 Admin.L.J. 1 (1987). She has also written a book that looks at public and private coverage policy, Protecting American Consumers of Health Care (2001).

Sizeable sectors of the health care industry have emerged or developed in particular ways largely because of the availability of Medicare coverage. The home health care industry, for example, burgeoned and then withered in response to Medicare policy. In 1967, when Medicare began, there were 1,850 Medicare-certified home health agencies in the United States, by 1981 there were 3,110. In the three years following 1981, when Medicare home health benefits were dramatically expanded, about 1,600 new home health agencies were certified. Also in 1981 the Medicare law, which previously had paid only for home health care provided by non-profit agencies, was amended to permit coverage of proprietary home health. Between 1980 and 1984 the proportion of proprietary home health agencies increased almost three-fold, from 7.1 percent to 20.5 percent, Wayne Callahan, Medicare Use of Home Health Services, 7 Health Care Financing Review 89 (Winter 1985).

Home health expenditures grew rapidly in the early 90s from $3.7 billion in 1990 (3.2 percent of total Medicare expenditures) to $17.8 billion (9 percent) in 1997, a growth rate of 25.2 percent per annum, compared to 8 percent for the program generally. During the same period the number of Medicare home health users grew from 57 to 109 per 1000 beneficiaries, and the average number of visits per user went from 36 to 73. The 1997 Balanced Budget Act put the brakes on home health expenditures, imposing limits on payments for visits and a per beneficiary cap, and mandating the creation of a prospective payment system. Between 1997 and 1999 Medicare home health spending dropped 45 percent, and the number of home health agencies dropped from 10,500 to fewer than 8000. See GAO, Medicare Home Health Agencies: Closures Continue with Little Evidence Beneficiary Access is Impaired (1999).

In 1972, the Medicare law was amended to extend end-stage renal dialysis (ESRD) to all persons who were fully or currently insured or entitled to monthly insurance benefits under Social Security as well as to their spouses or dependent children, even if they had not reached the age of 65. Medicare now pays for virtually all renal dialysis in the United States. In large part because of this program, more dialysis is performed in the United States than almost anywhere else in the world. In 1992 the United States had a rate of 802 ESRD per million, compared to 518 in Canada, 387 in Germany and 382 in the U.K. Only Japan had a higher rate. Eli Friedman, End–State Renal Disease Therapy: An American Success Story, 275 JAMA 1118 (1996). Though ESRD recipients account for less than 1 percent of the total Medicare population, they account for 5.5 percent of Medicare expenditures.

What categories of services should Medicare cover? Should its coverage be identical to employment-related benefit packages, or should it vary in some respects? What items might be more, or less, important to its beneficiary population? Why do you think Medicare does not cover nursing home care—a benefit of obvious interest to the elderly—to a greater extent? With respect to coverage of new technologies, should Medicare take cost into account in setting coverage policy? If so, what role should cost play in coverage determinations? Should Medicare cover clinical trials for experimental drugs or technology? (In June of 2000 President Clinton directed Medicare to pay for routine patient costs associated with clinical trials.)

2. *Prescription Drugs*

As this book goes to press in late 2000, one of the most pressing issues affecting Medicare is whether the program should be expanded to cover prescription drugs. Drug coverage is a major issue for the elderly. Drug expenditures per Medicare beneficiary were $848 in 1998, 4.1 percent of average income. About a third of Medicare beneficiaries currently do not have drug coverage, and many others have limited coverage. Typical Medigap policies, for example, impose a $250 annual deductible, 50 percent copayment, and $1250 maximum annual benefit. Medicare was amended in 1988 to include a drug benefit, but the method of financing this benefit (raising Part B premiums for middle and high income beneficiaries), proved intensely unpopular, and the program was abolished a year later. Proposals currently on the table, therefore, are more modest, voluntary, and subsidized by public revenues. The major controversies at this point surround the extent of coverage and subsidies for coverage, the benefit design, the relationship of the program to fee-for-service Medicare, and the role of private entities in program administration. Some of these issues are discussed in the excerpt that follows:

MEDICARE PAYMENT ADVISORY COMMISSION REPORT TO CONGRESS, SELECTED MEDICARE ISSUES, JUNE 2000

Medicare Beneficiaries and Prescription Drug Coverage.
Benefit Design

Plan sponsors-entities offering a drug benefit-have at their disposal many techniques for influencing the behavior of beneficiaries, physicians, and pharmacists. When deciding how to structure a drug benefit, plan sponsors must carefully define the goals of the plan. For example, is the goal to target certain beneficiary segments (such as high users), or is the goal to provide a broad-based benefit to all?

* * *

Deductibles, out-of-pocket maximums, and benefit limits. A deductible is the amount of money that beneficiaries must spend in a year before the plan begins to pay for expenses. An out-of-pocket maximum caps beneficiaries' annual cost sharing at a certain amount, after which the plan pays all expenses for the remainder of the plan year. An annual benefit limit is the amount above which beneficiaries must pay the full amount for additional services. * * *

* * * To steer beneficiaries to cost-effective providers and drugs, drug-specific deductibles can apply only to non-network pharmacies or non-formulary claims. In contrast, out-of-pocket maximums and benefit limits are typically imposed not to encourage particular behaviors, but to limit the exposure of the beneficiary or the insurer.

* * *

If enrollment in the drug benefit is voluntary, then the plan sponsor faces other considerations in structuring the benefit. If the benefit encourages sicker beneficiaries to enroll, then risk will not be evenly spread and the cost of the benefit will increase. A plan with a high deductible and an out-of-pocket maximum might increase the likelihood of attracting sicker enrollees. Beneficiaries who anticipate that they will meet the deductible and may need the out-of-pocket maximum are most likely to enroll. On the other hand, a benefit with a low deductible and no out-of-pocket maximum will be more appealing to healthier beneficiaries, whose inclusion in the purchasing pool will keep the average cost per beneficiary of the benefit lower. This is important if beneficiaries are paying all or part of the premium. To the extent that a low deductible is financed by higher copayments or coinsurance, beneficiaries who use many services will pay more.

* * *

[Coinsurance and copayments] influence beneficiary behavior. For example, copayments may vary depending on whether the drug is generic, brand on-formulary, or brand off-formulary. In specifying a lower copayment for preferred brand drugs and generics, patients are steered toward these preferred or less expensive alternatives. Currently, a common copayment structure is a "three-tier" system, under which the copayments might be $5 for a generic drug, $10 for an on-formulary or preferred name-brand drug, and $25 for other branded drugs.

A variation on the three-tiered approach would make cost-sharing dependent on the price of designated "reference" drugs—those drugs deemed most cost efficient in each class. * * * [T]his copayment arrangement is designed to encourage the use of those drugs deemed the most cost efficient; therefore, a beneficiary selecting a drug priced higher than the reference drug in a given class would pay the difference in price, in addition to the copayment.

Reference pricing would make drug manufacturers more likely to price their products competitively than would a three-tier copayment model. Under a three-tier copayment, manufacturers that believe their drugs will not be on the formulary have little incentive to price their products competitively, because beneficiaries pay a flat copayment for all off-formulary brand drugs regardless of price. In contrast, under a reference price approach, beneficiaries pay all of the additional cost above the reference drug price, which can be quite substantial. This difference in price sensitivity may induce manufacturers to bid more competitively, even for off-formulary drugs.

* * *

BENEFIT MANAGEMENT

To control the use and cost of prescription drugs, plan sponsors have techniques, other than benefit parameters, that address provider and pharmacy behavior. Many of these tools have been developed and used by PBMs [pharmaceutical benefit management companies] or other organizations that handle large volumes of claims and have relationships with pharmacy networks. Therefore, private third-party payers often contract with PBMs to manage their drug benefits. * * *

For years, PBMs have negotiated discounts with pharmacies and rebates from pharmaceutical manufacturers. More recently, PBMs have taken more active roles in encouraging the substitution of lower-cost or more appropriate medications. This may involve communication with plan enrollees, phone calls to prescribing physicians, and dispensing through mail service vendors who supply maintenance medications for patients with chronic conditions. [Tools for benefit management include:]

* * *

Generic substitution: Generic drugs contain the same active ingredients as their counterparts and are judged by the FDA to be bioequivalent. Generic drugs cost less than their brand-name counterparts and have played a significant role in constraining total prescription drug spending. * * *

The most direct way to encourage use of generic drugs is to require higher beneficiary cost sharing for brand drugs. * * *

Through their pharmacy networks, PBMs can also encourage pharmacies to dispense generics when available by paying a higher dispensing fee for generics. * * *

Formularies and rebates: A formulary is a list of drugs promoted for therapeutic and cost reasons. Within a group of therapeutically equivalent drugs, a subset of the group might be placed on the formulary because it is priced favorably by the manufacturer. Negotiations between PBMs (or provider groups) and manufacturers are common for the placement of drugs on formularies. * * *

* * * Formularies differ in their degree of rigor. Open formularies, the most common type, are structured such that doctors are merely encouraged to prescribe from the formulary. Managed formularies provide coverage for a broad range of drugs, but typically involve more intervention with physicians and higher copayments when a non-formulary prescription is filled. Closed formularies often require beneficiaries to pay the fall cost of drugs not on the formulary.

Discount arrangements with pharmacies: Almost all pharmacies accept discounted payment arrangements. The dispensing fee may also be negotiated. Under certain circumstances, "restricted" networks of preferred providers— sometimes "high-performance" pharmacies that are effective in promoting formulary compliance-accept deeper discounts than average in return for the promise of greater market share.

Therapeutic interchange: Therapeutic interchange occurs when doctors permit one drug to be substituted for a different one (not generically equivalent) in the same therapeutic class. PBMs and beneficiaries may be motivated to contact the physician for permission to make the switch if the drug originally prescribed is not on the formulary. * * *

* * *

[Other interventions such as prior authorization, disease management, drug utilization review, and mail order pharmacy are also discussed. ed.]

* * *

Benefit Administrator and Pricing Issues

Policymakers must decide how a new drug benefit should be administered, who should bear the insurance risk, and how the prices for drugs would be determined. There is a continuum of approaches on these issues that ranges from a centralized, regulatory approach to a decentralized approach that delegates authority to multiple private-sector entities. * * *

HCFA administers the benefit. Under this model, HCFA would bear the insurance risk and might set a fee schedule, as it does currently with physicians. * * *

Federal agency contracts with PBMs to administer a defined drug benefit to FFS beneficiaries. The PBMs would be responsible for negotiating prices with drug manufacturers, managing the benefit, contracting with pharmacies, and processing claims for beneficiaries. Because HCFA would pay the PBMs on primarily a FFS basis, HCFA would bear the risk of the cost of the benefit.

Beneficiaries contract with drugs-only insurance plans. These plans would offer a defined drug benefit. This proposal would allow beneficiaries to receive drug coverage from other currently available sources as well. The insurance plans would bear the risk.

Federal agency contracts with private insurance plans to offer a comprehensive array of Medicare benefits, including prescription drugs, as proposed under a premium support model. Although this approach is similar to Medicare + Choice, beneficiaries would likely have an increased financial incentive to join these plans. Beneficiaries who choose to remain in the traditional FFS program could also purchase a prescription drug benefit. * * *

A more centralized approach would take advantage of Medicare's market power in purchasing drugs on behalf of beneficiaries. This approach may also be considered inevitable, if not initially desirable, to restrain costs if private-sector entities are not permitted the same flexibility they have in the private sector to manage a cost-effective benefit. * * *

In contrast, the intended advantages of delegating management to private entities or insurance plans are to achieve cost savings similar to that achieved in the private sector and retain a more pluralistic marketplace for prescription drugs, rather than creating a monolithic purchaser that could distort the marketplace.

* * *

Ideally, policymakers should balance achieving fair prices for drugs for beneficiaries with retaining investment incentives for drug research and development. However, many controversial issues would need to be addressed. How much profit do manufacturers need to continue to invest in R & D? How should that be determined? Is it possible for government to judge and direct where manufacturers should spend money (for example, on marketing versus R & D)?

The impact on R & D could be adverse if prices were set such that manufacturers did not perceive sufficient returns on future investments. However, several factors may limit the threat to R & D for the foreseeable future. First, price reductions may be, at least in part, offset by a potentially higher volume of sales resulting from greater access of Medicare beneficiaries to prescription drugs.

Second, discounts for Medicare beneficiaries will likely encourage manufacturers to increase private-sector prices. This has been the previous experience with the Medicaid program. * * *

* * *

If multiple purchasers were to negotiate with drug manufacturers on behalf of a subset of beneficiaries, there may be less pressure on R & D investments. However, to the extent that multiple purchasers lacked market power to negotiate reasonable discounts or were restricted from managing the benefit effectively, beneficiaries and taxpayers (depending on how the benefit was financed) would pay a higher price for this benefit.

Reducing Adverse Selection

Any proposal that requires beneficiaries to pay a portion of premiums and choose between insurers or PBMs for drug coverage creates a concern about adverse selection. To avoid adverse selection, there first must be enrollment rules that limit beneficiaries' abilities to opt for coverage only when high drug costs are expected. Otherwise, beneficiaries have no incentive to participate when they expect low costs, limiting the program's ability to spread risk across high and low users.

One way to help avoid adverse selection in a voluntary benefit is to subsidize the cost of the benefit. Subsidies can help attract a more even distribution of beneficiaries because they may make it cost effective for the vast majority of beneficiaries to participate, regardless of health status. The effect of the subsidy is illustrated in Medicare program experience. Part A is subsidized at 100 percent, requiring no beneficiary contribution. Part B is subsidized at 75 percent, and 97 percent of eligible elderly participate.

* * *

Selection of Contractors

How should drug administrators be selected to contract with Medicare? Should they receive the sole contract in a region or compete with other regional drug administrators for beneficiaries in the region?

Selecting one administrator per region through a competitive contracting process mitigates the adverse selection that can occur when plans compete for beneficiaries. * * * Further, a single administrator per area has an enhanced ability to negotiate discounts because it has a guaranteed market share. Presumably, the contracting criteria would value cost and service.

On the other hand, if more than one administrator were selected per region, competition would be present for both contract awards and market share, which might further improve the quality of service. Multiple administrators may also reduce barriers to market entry, as new administrators would not have to prove they could serve the whole market overnight or be at a competitive disadvantage due to transition confusion that beneficiaries might experience with wholesale change.

Having multiple administrators in a region could also reduce the need for federal regulation on formularies or other management tools related to beneficiary satisfaction, because beneficiaries could "vote with their feet" by selecting the administrator that best met their needs. Also, a single administrator might not have sufficient capacity to meet the needs of all the beneficiaries in a given geographic area.

PAYMENTS FOR THE ADMINISTRATORS

PBMs do not appear to be eager to become risk-bearing entities, largely because they have no direct control over physician prescribing practices. Nevertheless, pharmacy administrators can influence some costs and have negotiated performance guarantees in the private sector. They typically keep about 20 percent of the negotiated rebates and often have contractual incentives to meet certain service or generic substitution targets. * * *

This model could be adopted and expanded by Medicare. Administrators could be placed at limited financial risk within a "corridor" around a claims target. For example, administrators might assume 50 percent of the risk for savings or losses within 10 percent of the target, making the total risk for a pharmacy administrator 5 percent of the target. Another approach would be to establish bonus payments for meeting performance standards, including enrollee satisfaction, speed in processing and paying claims, and access to pharmacies. To the extent that such arrangements were possible, administrators would add value and efficiency to the system and function less like claims processors.

Notes and Questions

1. Who should fund a prescription drug benefit, beneficiaries, the taxpayers, or workers who pay Medicare payroll taxes? Should the benefit be structured to assist the maximum number of beneficiaries, or those with the highest drug bills? What effect will the prescription drug benefit have on drug companies? In particular, is it likely to dampen pharmaceutical research? Should this be a concern of the Medicare program? Why might private insurers be reluctant to issue drug only policies to the elderly? What are the advantages and disadvantages of having a single PBM or competing PBMs in each region? What are the advantages and disadvantages of putting a PBM at risk for the drug benefit cost?

2. An excellent source of information regarding the Medicare prescription drug benefit debate is the symposium found in the March/April 2000 issue of Health Affairs, Prescription Drugs: What Next? See also GAO, Prescription Drugs, Increasing Medicare Beneficiary Access and Related Implications (GAO/T–HEHS/AIMD–00–99)(2000); Joshua P. Cohen, PBMs and a Medicare Prescription Drug Benefit, 55 Food & Drug L.J. 311 (2000).

C. PAYMENT FOR SERVICES

1. Introduction

Though one issue in the current Medicare reform debate is updating the Medicare benefits package, the main focus of the debate has been on how Medicare should pay for health care items and services. Over Medicare's history, the program has relied primarily on two payment strategies. At the outset, it followed health insurance practice existing at the time by paying institutions on the basis of their reported costs and professionals on the basis of their charges. This proved, not surprisingly, to be wildly inflationary, and over time Medicare increasingly imposed restrictions on cost- and charge-based payment. In the end Medicare abandoned cost and charge-based payment in favor of administered payment systems, under which Medicare sets the price it will pay for services. It did this with respect to inpatient hospital services in the early 1980s by implementing prospective payment, and with respect to physicians through its resource-based relative value scale implemented in the early 1990s. Medicare is continuing to create new administered price systems under the Balanced Budget Act of 1997 for home health, nursing facility, outpatient hospital, and inpatient rehabilitation hospital services. Paying for one third of the nation's hospital care and one fifth of physician care, Medicare has been able to offer payment rates on a take it or leave it basis, and to hold rates to levels that are below those paid generally in the private market. It has been less successful, however, at controlling the volume of services it pays for, leading to continuing increases in overall costs.

Between 1993 and 1997, Medicare experienced cost increases in excess of those experienced by the private insurance market (7.5 percent as compared to 3.5 percent). The private insurance market had by the mid–1990s turned to managed care, and conservative critics, who had always distrusted Medicare's administered price approach, argued that this disparity proved that the use of administered prices is inferior to managed care as a strategy for controlling costs. Some went further, contending that Medicare should merely provide vouchers to its recipients, who would then purchase insurance in the private insurance and managed care market. The Republican Balanced Budget Act of 1995 would have turned Medicare into a voucher-based managed competition program, but it was vetoed by President Clinton. The more moderate Balanced Budget Act of 1997, created a new Medicare Part C, the Medicare + Choice managed care program, and attempted to woo rather than drive Medicare patients into managed care. After 1997, paradoxically, the tables turned and Medicare expendituress rose much less quickly than private insurance expenditures (1.2 percent for Medicare compared to 7.2 percent for private insurance between 1997 and 1998). But, despite this reality, calls for making Medicare function more like the private sector have continued unabated.

The following subsections review the major administered price programs under Medicare, the diagnosis-related group prospective payment system for hospitals and the resource-based relative value scale for physicians. A third subsection examines the issue of whether doctors and beneficiaries should be allowed to opt out of Medicare and enter into private contracts. The final subsection examines the Medicare + Choice program. At the end of our consideration of Medicare, we will return to the issue of Medicare payment reform.

It is important to have some understanding as to how Medicare's administered payment systems work, not just because they provide a contrast to managed care alternatives, but also because they are used for dispensing tens of billions of dollars of Medicare payments and have a predictably significant effect on the behavior of health care providers. In particular, lawyers are often called upon to help health care providers structure themselves to maximize access to these Medicare payments.

2. Medicare Prospective Payment Under Diagnosis–Related Groups

When Medicare was established in the mid 1960s, it borrowed from the Blue Cross programs a cost-based system of reimbursement. This program proved predictably inflationary: between 1967 and 1983 Medicare hospital expenditures (which then constituted two-thirds of program expenditures) increased elevenfold from $3 billion to $33 billion. In 1982, Congress mandated the implementation of a prospective payment system. The model that it looked to was that of New Jersey, where diagnosis-related groups (DRG) prospective payment, implemented through an all-payer reimbursement system, had dramatically reduced hospital costs.

A DRG is a means of categorizing patients to reflect relative intensity of use of services. DRG-based payment treats hospitals as coordinating services to produce particular products, such as the diagnosis and treatment of heart attacks, ulcers, or tumors. The DRG system groups patients primarily by principal (admitting) diagnoses, which are categorized by body system into 23 systems or major diagnostic categories (MDCs). These groupings are then broken down into 511 separate DRGs by considering principal and secondary diagnoses and whether a surgical procedure was performed, and, where relevant, by further considering age, gender and discharge status. Cases are sorted into the correct DRG by the GROUPER computer program. The purpose of this analysis is to yield groups of hospital patients, each covered by a distinct DRG, that more or less require the same quantity of medical resources. Once DRGs were defined, HHS, arrayed DRGs by relative intensity of resource consumption, with the average resource used defined as a single unit. Thus, for 2001, DRG 75, surgery, major chest procedures, is weighted at 3.1331 (or over three times the average admission cost); DRG 59, tonsillectomy and/or adenoidectomy only on a patient over 17 years of age, at .6943 (about 7/10 the average cost). DRG weights are recalibrated annually to recognize changes in treatment patterns, technology, or other changes that might affect relative use of resources for providing hospital care.

To determine a hospital's actual payment for caring for a Medicare patient, the relative DRG weight assigned to that patient is first multiplied by standardized amounts for labor, non-labor, and capital costs. The standardized amounts in theory represent the cost to an efficient hospital of an average case. There are currently two categories of standardized amounts, one for large urban areas (with populations in excess of one million) and one for the remainder of the country, though the distinction is being phased out. (There are also separate amounts for Puerto Rico.) For FY 2001, the standardized amounts for large urban areas are $2864.19 for labor costs and $1164.21 for non-labor costs. For other areas the rates are slightly lower. The capital cost rate for all areas other than Puerto Rico is $381.03. These amount are multiplied by the DRG weight (e.g. 6943 for tonsillectomy) to achieve the basic DRG reimbursement amount.

This basic amount is only the starting point for determining PPS hospital reimbursement, however. The sum of the product of the DRG weight and standardized amounts (or rather the sum of the products of the total DRG weights of all Medicare cases treated in the hospital during the payment period and the standardized amounts) is adjusted in several respects to determine a hospital's actual PPS payment. Because labor costs vary greatly throughout the country, the labor-related portion of the PPS payment is adjusted by an area wage index factor. The result of this adjustment is that hospitals in high-cost labor markets receive significantly higher Medicare payments than those in low-cost labor markets.

PPS payments are further adjusted to recognize the cost of extraordinarily expensive cases. Cases in which the cost of care greatly exceeds the norm for the DRG assigned to the case can qualify as "outliers" for which Medicare will pay part of the additional costs the hospital incurs. PPS payments are also enhanced to compensate teaching hospitals for the indirect costs of operating educational programs. Finally, PPS payments are increased or otherwise adjusted to benefit special categories of hospitals: disproportionate share hospitals (which serve large numbers of low income patients, who presumably cost more to treat); sole community hospitals (which serve communities distant from other hospitals, and are protected by federal policy); rural referral centers (hospitals located in rural areas that resemble larger urban hospitals in the complexity of cases that they handle); and Medicare-dependent small rural hospitals (small rural hospitals 60 percent or more of whose patients are covered by Medicare).

These adjustments can be very important for hospitals in particular situations. Whereas straight unadjusted PPS payment accounts for 91 percent of Medicare payment for non-teaching hospitals, major urban teaching hospitals receive about 32 percent of their PPS payments from disproportionate share and indirect medical education cost adjustments. Most of the litigation concerning PPS reimbursement deals with the issue of whether a particular hospital was correctly classified within these categories.

A few categories of hospital costs continue to be reimbursed on a cost basis. The direct costs of medical education programs are reimbursed on a pass-through cost basis, as are hospital bad debts related to uncollectible Medicare deductible and co-insurance amounts and a few other miscellaneous expenses. A variety of special hospitals, including psychiatric and long-term, and continue to be reimbursed on a cost basis outside of the PPS program.

Good descriptions of PPS reimbursement are found in Terry Coleman, Legal Aspects of Medicare and Medicaid Reimbursement, 21–56 (1990) and J. Timothy Philips and Don Wineberg, Medicare Prospective Payment: A Quiet Revolution, 87 W.Va.L.Rev. 13, 30–9 (1984).

Any evaluation of DRG–PPS must certainly be mixed. PPS has succeeded at its principal goal, limiting the escalation of Medicare expenditures for inpatient care: during the six years preceding PPS, Medicare inpatient hospital payments grew at a real rate of 9.1 percent per year. During the six years following the implementation of PPS they grew at a real rate of 2.5 percent per year. It has also succeeded in doing this without a substantial decline in the quality of care received by Medicare beneficiaries. See William Rogers, et al., Quality of Care Before and After Implementation of the DRG–Based Prospective Payment System, 264 JAMA 1989 (1990). DRG–PPS did not succeed immediately, however, in stemming the growth of hospital costs generally, which continued to grow until the mid–1990s, when spending constraints in private programs began to have an effect. This growth in hospital costs resulted in the late 1980s and early 1990s in a disparity between the actual costs of hospital care and what Medicare paid, requiring increasing shifting of the cost of caring for Medicare patients to the private sector. Private managed care initiatives in the 1990s forced hospitals to cut, rather than merely shift, costs, resulting in growing profits from Medicare. These were, in turn, slashed by the cuts of the BBA 1997.

PPS has also resulted in (or at least been accompanied by) a massive shift of care within hospitals from inpatient to outpatient settings or to long-term care units, often within or owned by the same hospitals that had previously provided inpatient care. A great deal of surgery that used to be done on an inpatient basis, such as cataract surgery, is now done outpatient. Patients who in 1980 would have remained in the hospital, were by the mid–1990s often discharged to hospital-owned nursing or rehabilitation facilities or to home health care, where Medicare paid for their care on a cost-related basis until recently. From 1990 to 1995, Medicare payments for nursing home care increased at a rate of 33 percent per year, while Medicare home health payments increased fourfold. In 1994, 70 percent of hospitals owned a home health agency, skilled nursing beds, or a rehabilitation unit, and about a quarter of patients discharged from PPS hospitals received post-acute care. See PPRC, Medicare and the American Health Care System: Report to Congress, 91–113 (1996). By 2000, hospital inpatient PPS Medicare revenues made up only one third of total hospital Medicare revenues. In 1997 Congress attempted to put an end to growth in cost-reimbursed provider payments by imposing prospective payment on outpatient, skilled nursing facility, home health, and rehabilitation hospital services. What lessons can we learn from this experience about administrated payment systems?

DRG–PPS does not seem to have brought about a hoped for rationalization of the health care industry: hospitals do not seem have tailored their production to specialize in delivering services they can produce most efficiently to maximize profits under DRG reimbursement. Why might this be so? DRG–PPS has also grown increasingly complex over time as, straying ever further from its goal of simplifying hospital reimbursement. What might explain the ever increasing number of add-ons and adjustments?

For good summaries of the literature on the effects of PPS, see the annual Medicare Payment Advisory Commission's Report to Congress on Medicare Payment Policy, filed every March. Other good sources critiquing PPS and describing its effects include Louise Russell, Medicare's New Hospital Payment System: Is it Working? (1989); David Frankford, Efficiency and Organizational Rationality, 10 Yale J. Reg. 273 (1993); David Frankford, The Complexity of Medicare's Hospital Reimbursement System: The Complexity of Averaging, 78 Iowa L. Rev. 517 (1993); Bruce Vladeck, Medicare's Prospective Payment System at Age Eight: Mature Success or Midlife Crisis, 14 U. Pug. Sound L. Rev. 453 (1991); and Judith Lave, The Impact of the Medicare

Prospective Payment System and Recommendations for Change, 7 Yale J. Reg. 499 (1990).

PPS does not seem to be making much business for lawyers. This is in marked contrast to Medicare cost reimbursement which preceded PPS. If cost-based reimbursement was a gold mine for hospitals, it also made lawyers rich. Cost-based reimbursement continually raised questions of the sort that lawyers (and accountants) love to argue about. Should a loss incurred in advance refunding of bonds be claimed in the year in which it is incurred, as it would normally be under generally accepted accounting principles (GAAP), or should it be amortized over the term of the original loan, as the HHS Provider Reimbursement Manual requires? See Shalala v. Guernsey Memorial Hospital, 514 U.S. 87, 115 S.Ct. 1232, 131 L.Ed.2d 106 (1995) (believe it or not the Supreme Court spends its time on such issues, with the Court often dividing along lines that defy the normal center-to-right arrays we are used to seeing in other areas). Should the fact that Medicare patients benefit from a relatively small proportion of malpractice recoveries be taken into account in determining the share of a hospital's malpractice costs that should be borne by the Medicare program? See Tallahassee Memorial Regional Medical Center v. Bowen, 815 F.2d 1435 (11th Cir.1987); St. Marys Hospital Medical Center v. Heckler, 753 F.2d 1362 (7th Cir.1985). Should a woman in a labor or delivery room bed at a hospital's census hour be counted as an inpatient (increasing the hospital's occupancy and decreasing Medicare's proportionate share of its costs, since few women on Medicare have babies)? See Central DuPage Hospital v. Heckler, 761 F.2d 354 (7th Cir.1985); Saint Mary of Nazareth Hosp. Center v. Schweiker, 718 F.2d 459 (D.C.Cir.1983). Litigation about such cost-finding and apportionment questions, and about the timing and procedures for review of cost-reimbursement issues, the appropriateness of HHS rulemaking on cost-reimbursement issues, and interest rates on eventual judgments against HHS, continue to occupy the courts with respect to facilities that are still paid on a cost-related basis.

In contrast to cost-reimbursement, PPS raises remarkably few justiciable issues. Issues raised by PPS are either political questions, such as the standardized amount update level for any particular year, or technical questions, such as how a particular DRG should be weighted or which DRG should be assigned by a hospital to a particular admission. Congress has made it clear that it does not want the courts getting involved in these determinations:

42 U.S.C.A. § 1395ww(d)(7)

There shall be no administrative or judicial review under Section 1395oo of this title or otherwise of

> (A) the determination of the requirement, or the proportional amount of any adjustment effected pursuant to subsection (e)(1) of this section [providing for updates in the standardized amount], and

> (B) the establishment of diagnosis-related-groups, of the methodology for the classification of discharges under within groups, and of the appropriate weighing of factors thereof * * *

Congress has established a tri-partite dialogue among itself, HCFA, and an independent body called until 1997 the Prospective Payment Assessment Commission and then replaced by the Medicare Payment Advisory Commission, to determine these questions and has left no place for the courts. See Timothy Stoltzfus Jost, Governing Medicare, 51 Admin. L. Rev. 39 (1999); Eleanor Kinney, Making Hard Choices Under the Medicare Prospective Payment System: One Administrative Model for Allocating Resources under a Government Health Insurance Program, 19 Ind. L. Rev. 1151 (1986).

Such Medicare provider payment litigation as continues under DRG–PPS consists primarily of fact-intensive disputes entailing particular providers, such as whether a hospital qualifies for special treatment under PPS as a disproportionate share hospital, see North Broward Hosp. Dist. v. Shalala, 172 F.3d 90 (D.C.Cir. 1999); sole community hospital, Community Hosp. v. Sullivan, 986 F.2d 357 (10th Cir.1993); or rural referral center, Board of Trustees of Knox Co. Hosp. v. Shalala, 135 F.3d 493 (7th Cir.1998). Perhaps the biggest source of disputes has been whether or not hospitals should be reclassified from the geographical area in which they are physically found to other, nearby, areas from which they draw their patients or employees and which are favored by more bountiful Medicare rates. Such reclassifications can be granted by the Medicare Geographic Classification Review Board, 42 U.S.C.A. § 1395ww(d)(10), and occasionally denials of reclassification applications result in litigation.

To the extent that some costs, most notably graduate medical education costs, are still passed through under PPS, the opportunity exists for raising traditional accounting-type questions. See Regions Hospital v. Shalala, 522 U.S. 448, 118 S.Ct. 909, 139 L.Ed.2d 895 (1998); Thomas Jefferson University v. Shalala, 512 U.S. 504, 114 S.Ct. 2381, 129 L.Ed.2d 405 (1994). Case-specific decisions are also subject to administrative review: a hospital may request an intermediary to reconsider a DRG assignment or the provider reimbursement review board to review reimbursement issues not precluded from review by statute.

Insofar as PPS makes work for lawyers, it is primarily in the area of advising clients how to live with PPS. Consider the following problem:

Problem: DRGs

You are the in-house counsel for a large urban hospital that has a high percentage of Medicare patients. In recent years your hospital has either lost money or barely broken even. In particular, since program cuts imposed by the 1997 BBA, your payments from inpatient services from Medicare have not met your costs. At the request of the hospital's CEO, you are serving on a committee considering how to improve the financial situation of the hospital, focusing particularly on your situation with respect to Medicare.

What strategies might be available for increasing your hospital's DRG revenues? Would changing your case-mix help? How might you achieve that? What opportunities might be available in terms of how discharges are coded? (Reconsider this question after you study Medicare fraud and abuse in chapter 14). What possibilities are available under Medicare prospective payment for increasing your Medicare payments that are not strictly tied to your case-mix? How does the teaching mission of your hospital affect your Medicare reimbursement? How might you go about increasing your Medicare reimbursement for non-inpatient services?

Alternatively, how might you go about lowering the cost of treating Medicare patients? Will cost-reductions be accompanied by Medicare payment reductions?

3. *Medicare Payment of Physicians*

Medicare Part B payment for most services (including physician services) was based traditionally, at least in theory, on reimbursement of actual charges (minus deductibles and co-insurance). Over time, however, actual charges became subject to increasingly numerous and restrictive screens that rendered the relationship between actual charges and actual payments ever more tenuous.

The restrictions imposed on charge reimbursement in the 1980s ultimately failed to stem the tide of increases in physician payments under Part B, which grew nearly three times faster than expenditures for Part A between 1985 and 1989, nearly doubling between 1983 and 1988. Even during years in which physician fees were frozen, expenditures for physician services continued to grow rapidly because of increases in the volume and intensity of the services physicians provided.

Concern about beneficiary access to affordable services also increased during the late 1980s. Unlike hospitals, physicians are not required to bill Medicare directly or to accept Medicare payment rates as payment in full. Part B was initially conceived as a government run indemnity insurance program, and continues to resemble such a program in its fundamentals. A physician can agree to accept assignment of a beneficiary's claim and bill directly the Medicare carrier (the insurance and data-processing companies that handle Medicare Part B claims), accepting the Medicare payment (plus copayments and deductibles for which the beneficiary is responsible) as payment in full. Alternatively, the physician can bill the beneficiary directly, who then must turn to the carrier for indemnification. In the early 1980s there was concern that many physicians were not providing services to Medicare beneficiaries on an assignment basis. A participating physician incentive program, instituted in 1984, had some effect—by 1989, 41 percent of physicians billing Medicare were participating physicians (i.e. physicians who agreed to bill only on an assignment basis) and over 80 percent of claims were billed on an assigned basis. Several states also enacted laws prohibiting physicians from "balance-billing" (billing beneficiaries for charges above the Medicare payment amount), thus effectively requiring physicians to take assignment, for all or for low-income Medicare beneficiaries. See Massachusetts Medical Soc'y v. Dukakis, 815 F.2d 790 (1st Cir.1987), cert. denied, 484 U.S. 896, 108 S.Ct. 229, 98 L.Ed.2d 188 (1987) (upholding legislation prohibiting balance-billing in Massachusetts). Yet participation rates remained low in some specialties, and balance billing continued to stretch the resources of some Medicare beneficiaries.

Awareness also increased in the late 1980s of the inequities inherent in reasonable charge reimbursement. Reasonable charge reimbursement had merely accepted the charge structure existing in the market for physician services without questioning the rationality of that structure. Given the severe distortions found in the market for physician services, however, this structure had become increasingly irrational and politically unacceptable. In particular, the disparity between the generous reimbursement offered by Medicare for technical procedures and its parsimonious payments for cognitive services had become impossible to rationalize.

Finally, policy-makers also became increasingly concerned that Medicare physician reimbursement did not do enough to encourage the quality and appropriateness of care provided beneficiaries. In 1989 a political consensus came together around a package of reforms designed to address these problems. These reforms were enacted by the Omnibus Budget Reconciliation Act of 1989 and codified at 42 U.S.C.A. 1395w–4(a) to (j).

At the heart of the payment reform was the creation of a physician fee schedule. As with Part A prospective payment, fees are determined by multiplying a weighted value (in this case representing a medical procedure times a conversion factor, which is adjusted to consider geographic variations in cost. Relative value units (RVUs) are assigned to procedures based on the HCFA Common Procedure Coding System (HCPCS) and AMA Common Procedural Terminology (CPT) codes. These codes do not vary by specialty. The Relative Value Scale consists of three components: a physician work component, a practice expense component, and a malpractice component. Thus, for example, for CPT 66983, "remove cataract, insert lens" for 2001, the work RVU is 8.99, the fully-implemented practice expense RVU for facility-based practice is 5.17, the malpractice RVU is .49, and the total RVU is 14.65.

The physician work component is based on estimates prepared by William Hsiao and his colleagues at Harvard of the relative time and intensity of physician work involved in delivering specified services. With respect to major surgeries, physician work is defined globally to include pre-operative evaluation and consultation (inpatient or outpatient), beginning with the day before surgery, and post-operative care for a normal recovery from surgery for the ninety days following the surgery. The physician work component accounts for slightly more than half of the total relative value scale.

The practice expense component accounts for physician overhead, including, for example, rent and office expenses. The practice expense component is currently moving from a historical charge-based to a resource use-based measure. Different practice expense RVUs are applied depending on whether the services are furnished in a facility (hospital, SNF or ASC) or in a physicians office. Malpractice expenses for particular services are separated out from other practice expenses, and as of the year 2000 are based on the malpractice expense resources required to furnish the service.

A RVU is adjusted by a geographic adjustment factor (GAF) before it is multiplied by the conversion factor to reach a final fee payment amount (of which Medicare pays 80 percent, the other 20 percent representing the beneficiary coinsurance obligation). The GAF recognizes that the various costs included in the RVUs differ in different parts of the country. GAFs are multiplied by the components of the RVU before the conversion factor is applied.

While the resource-based prices set by RBRVS addressed the problem of price inflation in physician payment, previous attempts to control prices through fee freezes had been defeated by increases in volume of services. To address this problem, the 1989 legislation established the Medicare Volume Performance Standard (MVPS). The MVPS represented Congresses attempt to create a global budget for physician expenditures. It set a target rate for increases in intensity and volume of services. If this rate was exceeded in a year, the conversion factor of the second following year was to be adjusted downward, so that total expenditures continued to grow at a target rate. In effect, increases in the intensity and volume of services would simply lead to a lower price per service.

The volume performance adjustment in RBRVS failed to achieve its goal, and Congress repeatedly intervened directly to change the conversion factor. In particular, the use of three separate volume performance standards for surgical, primary, and other nonsurgical care, led in some years to the perverse and paradoxical result that payment rates increased more rapidly for surgical than non-surgical services, contrary to federal policy of encouraging primary care. Finally in the 1997 Balanced Budget Act, Congress abandoned the MVPS in favor of a "sustainable growth rate," applicable to all specialties and based on growth in the real gross domestic product and increases in Medicare population and coverage. 42 U.S.C. § 1395w–4(f). This rate will allow physician payment growth in line with growth in the larger economy, but is unlikely to keep pace with growth in physician income outside of Medicare.

While Medicare fees have lagged behind fees paid by private insurance under the RBRVS system, deep discounts demanded by private managed care companies have narrowed the difference. In fact, Medicare rates as a proportion of private insurer payments increased from 66 percent in 1994 to 71 percent in 1996. Access to physicians has not been a problem for most Medicare recipients. Ninety-five percent of physicians accepting new patients reported accepting new Medicare fee-for-service patients in 1995. While only half of doctors accepted assignment of Medicare claims in the early 1980s, by 1996, 97 percent of doctors accepted Medicare assignment, effectively accepting Medicare prices as payment in full. Nevertheless, almost half of the doctors queried in a recent survey reported that Medicare reimbursement levels are a serious problem, (though almost two thirds also claimed that HMO reimbursement rates are a serious problem). See Marilyn Moon, Freedom to Pay or Freedom to Choose? Private Contracting and Medicare Beneficiaries, 10 Health Matrix 21 (2000); Medicare Payment Advisory Commission, Medicare Payment Policy, Report to Congress (March 2000).

See explaining RBRVS, James Dechene, Reform of Medicare Physician Reimbursement for Physician Services, 23 J. Health & Hosp. L. 33 (Feb.1990); and symposium, Medicare Physician Payment Reform, 34 S. Louis L.J. 759ff (1990).

Problem: Physician Fees

Sometime in the early 2000s it becomes apparent to Congress that the high cost of legal services is having a substantial negative effect on the American economy and on our international competitive position. Congress also becomes concerned that there are gross and irrational disparities among the payments lawyers receive for legal services. Congress, therefore, adopts a resource-based relative value schedule, limiting lawyers to the charges allowed by such a schedule (plus 15 percent where the client agrees). Adherence to the charges is enforced by criminal laws plus civil penalties ($5000 per infraction).

Legal services for representing corporations in corporate takeovers and tax and securities work and for representing individuals in estate planning, domestic relations, real estate transactions or criminal defense matters, are all evaluated considering the (1) time, (2) mental effort and judgment, and (3) psychological stress involved in delivering each service.[2] Geographic variations in practice overhead are also recognized in fee-setting, though historic geographical variations in payments for the work of lawyers are recognized only to a very limited extent (i.e. a lawyer will be paid for his or her own work—as opposed to overhead—the same payment for similar work whether it is performed in Manhattan or in Peoria). No explicit recognition is given in the fee schedule for experience, skill, or law school class standing of individual practitioners.

How might such a fee schedule affect access to legal services? The volume of legal services provided? The geographic and specialty distribution of lawyers? The quality of legal services? Innovation in developing new legal theories? Your plans after law school? How hard you study for the final in this class?

Where does the analogy between this problem and RBRVS break down? How, that is, does the market for physician services differ from the market for legal services?

4. Private Contracting—The Kyl Amendment

Though physicians could historically refuse to accept Medicare assignment and balance bill, from the outset of the Medicare program they could not bar a beneficiary from claiming the benefit of Medicare payment. As controls on balance-billing became stricter and doctors fees were increasingly dictated by Medicare, this became more of a sore point with doctors. In response to physician complaints, the Balanced Budget Act of 1997 made provision for private contracting for services for which no Medicare claim was submitted or payment received. 42 U.S.C.A. § 1395a(b)(1). This provision was named the Kyl Amendment after its sponsor, Senator Jon Kyl (R. Ariz). Kyl's bill was amended in the legislative process, however, to impose beneficiary protections, described below. These provisions set off a storm of controversy provoked by those who saw it as a tightening, rather than a loosening, of private contract rights, resulting in litigation:

UNITED SENIORS ASSOCIATION, INC. v. SHALALA

United States Court of Appeals, District of Columbia Circuit, 1999.
182 F.3d 965.

GARLAND, CIRCUIT JUDGE:

Section 4507 of the Balanced Budget Act of 1997 provides that, for certain medical services, a doctor may not contract with a Medicare beneficiary outside of Medicare unless the doctor agrees to abstain from participating in the Medicare program for two years. Plaintiffs, a senior citizens' organization and four individual Medicare beneficiaries, contend that section 4507 is unconstitutional on a number of grounds. The district court found the statute constitutional and granted summary judgment for the Secretary of Health and Human Services. We affirm the grant of summary judgment without

---

2. These factors plus technical skill and physical effort are all being considered in setting the physician RBRVS, see William Hsaio, et. al., Estimating Physicians' Work for A Resource–Based Relative–Value Scale, 319 New Eng. J. Med. 835 (1988). Unless the additional physical exertion on the golf course consumed in soliciting corporate clients is considered, this latter factor does not seem relevant to legal services.

reaching the constitutional questions because the Secretary's recently-clarified interpretation of section 4507, to which we must defer, eliminates the injury that is the basis of plaintiffs' constitutional attack.

Medicare is a comprehensive insurance program designed to provide health insurance benefits for individuals 65 and over, as well as for certain others who come within its terms.[ ] * * * Medicare Part B, which is the focus here, covers medical services including those provided by physicians. * * * Doctors who provide medical services to Part B beneficiaries must submit claim forms identifying the services provided.[ ] They receive compensation in accordance with fee schedules that limit the amount they may charge and be paid.[ ][3]

Certain kinds of medical services, such as routine physical checkups, are categorically excluded from Medicare coverage.[ ] Those that are not categorically excluded may only be reimbursed when medically "reasonable and necessary."[ ] If a service is deemed not to have been reasonable and necessary, Medicare will not make payment and the doctor generally is prohibited from charging the patient. [ ]

Because at the time a physician provides a service it may not be certain whether Medicare will regard it as reasonable and necessary, the Medicare program includes a provision for an "Advance Beneficiary Notice" ("ABN"). Under this provision, in advance of providing a service the doctor may give the patient an ABN, which advises that Medicare may not pay for the service. [ ] If the patient agrees to pay from his or her own funds if Medicare does not, and if Medicare subsequently denies payment, the doctor may bill the patient directly. [ ]

In August 1997, Congress enacted section 4507 of the Balanced Budget Act of 1997 (codified at 42 U.S.C. § 1395a). The section establishes rules for what it describes as "the use of private contracts by medicare beneficiaries."[ ] Section 4507(b)(1) permits doctors and patients to contract for certain services outside of Medicare and without its fee limitations* * *

Section 4507(b)(2), entitled "[b]eneficiary protections," lists certain provisions that private contracts authorized by (b)(1) must include:

Any contract to provide items and services to which paragraph (1) applies shall clearly indicate ... that by signing such contract the beneficiary—

(i) agrees not to submit a claim (or to request that the physician or practitioner submit a claim) under this title for such items or services even if such items or services are otherwise covered by this subchapter;

(ii) agrees to be responsible, whether through insurance or otherwise, for payment of such items or services and understands that no reimbursement will be provided under this title for such items or services;

(iii) acknowledges that no limits under this title ... apply to amounts that may be charged for such items or services;

---

3. Under Medicare, "participating physicians" generally do not bill their patients, but instead take an assignment of their patients' rights and receive payment directly from Medicare. "Nonparticipating physicians" may accept assignments on a case-by-case basis or bill their patients directly. In the latter circumstance, it is the patient who obtains reimbursement from Medicare. In all cases, however, the fee schedules effectively limit the doctor's compensation. [ ]

. . .; and

(v) acknowledges that the Medicare beneficiary has the right to have such items or services provided by other physicians or practitioners for whom payment would be made under this title.

* * * [Under further provisions of § 4507, a] doctor who enters into a section 4507 private contract with even a single patient is barred from submitting a claim to Medicare on behalf of any patient for a two-year period.

Plaintiffs contend that section 4507 effectively makes it impossible for them to contract for medical services outside of the Medicare system—particularly for services Medicare will not cover, either because they are categorically excluded or because Medicare deems them unreasonable or unnecessary in a particular case. As plaintiffs read the section, it governs almost any agreement between a doctor and patient to provide medical services outside of Medicare, without regard to whether Medicare would pay for the service if a claim were submitted. Plaintiffs argue that it will be virtually impossible to find a doctor willing to enter into such an agreement, given the importance of Medicare to doctors' practices and the two-year bar the statute imposes for entering into even a single private contract.[4] The Secretary concedes that very few doctors will be willing to opt out of Medicare, [ ] and generally agrees that the two-year restriction "represents a substantial barrier to the receipt of contracted services." [ ]

Plaintiffs also reject the suggestion that the ABN procedure provides a way to relieve the constraints imposed by section 4507. They recognize that an agreement under an ABN is not a "private contract" under section 4507, and hence is not subject to its two-year bar.[ ] In theory this should mean that patients can obtain services they and their doctors consider reasonable or necessary, even if Medicare ultimately does not, by executing ABNs. But plaintiffs regard the ABN option as unworkable. First, it does not apply to services categorically excluded from Medicare. Second, plaintiffs contend that under HCFA rules, doctors who routinely use ABNs to obtain reimbursement for services Medicare deems unreasonable or unnecessary are subject to penalties and sanctions. * * *

Nor, plaintiffs contend, is it realistic to suggest that senior citizens can avoid the restrictions of section 4507 by simply opting out of Medicare Part B altogether. Notwithstanding the government's repeated suggestion that "plaintiffs may disenroll at any time" from Part B, [ ] at oral argument it conceded there is no "meaningful equivalent to Medicare" in the private market.[ ][5] Accordingly, opting out is hardly a viable way for patients to bypass section 4507.

Plaintiffs' complaint charges that the restrictions imposed by section 4507 violate the First, Fourth, Fifth, Ninth, Tenth and Fourteenth Amendments to the Constitution, as well as the Spending Clause of Article I, section 8. Plaintiffs contend those restrictions violate their liberty to contract private-

---

4. Plaintiffs note that over 96% of practicing physicians receive Medicare Part B reimbursement.[ ] They also note that to date, only 300 doctors nationwide have filed section 4507 contracts with the Secretary of Health and Human Services.

5. "Medicare is, in effect, the only primary health insurance available to people over 65. No private health insurance companies offer 'first dollar' insurance to this group; they offer only supplemental insurance."

ly for health care services, violate their ability to maintain the privacy of their medical information by requiring them to file claims for all medical services, and violate their equal protection and due process rights by denying them the same liberty to contract enjoyed by other citizens. They also contend that section 4507 exceeds Congress' powers under the Spending Clause, and invades the reserved powers of the States and the people under the Tenth Amendment, by regulating health care for which the federal government does not pay.

Critical to our analysis is that the injury plaintiffs assert is to their ability to purchase services for which Medicare will not itself pay, thus rendering them unable to obtain those services on any terms. [ ] The right they assert is to contract for services they and their doctors regard as necessary or even merely salutary, regardless whether Medicare agrees. Section 4507 abridges this right, they contend, by making it virtually impossible to find a doctor willing to enter into a private contract with a Medicare beneficiary. Plaintiffs made clear at oral argument, however, that they disavow any claim to a constitutional right to pay their doctors more than the Medicare fee limits for services they can obtain through Medicare. [ ]

The district court examined plaintiffs' constitutional claims, rejected them on the merits, and granted summary judgment for the Secretary.[ ] We review the grant of summary judgment de novo.[ ] When we do so, we find we have no need to reach the merits of plaintiffs' constitutional claims. After careful examination and clarification of the Secretary's interpretation of section 4507, we find that interpretation effectively eliminates the injury— whether of constitutional magnitude or not—that plaintiffs fear, and provides them with all the relief they seek.

The Secretary contends that plaintiffs have simply misunderstood section 4507. The purpose of the section, she argues, is to prevent doctors from coercing elderly patients into paying more for Medicare-covered services than Medicare's fee schedules permit.[ ] Consistent with that purpose, the section—including its two-year bar—applies only to services that Medicare would reimburse but for the private contract.[ ] * * *

The Secretary stresses, however, that section 4507 does not do what plaintiffs assert—that is, it does not impose restrictions on agreements to provide services for which Medicare would not pay. Hence, if a doctor and patient agree with respect to a service that would not be reimbursed by Medicare—either because it is categorically excluded or because it is deemed unreasonable or unnecessary in the particular case—then the agreement does not fall within section 4507 and the doctor is not subject to the two-year bar.[ ] The Secretary also contends that plaintiffs have misunderstood the ABN procedure which, she says, provides a workable way to handle those charges as to which Medicare payment is uncertain.[ ]

At oral argument, plaintiffs made clear that if section 4507 really says what the Secretary says it says, then their case is at an end.[ ] Plaintiffs have no interest, they aver, in obtaining the right to enter into agreements to pay more for services they can obtain for less under Medicare.[ ] Rather, their interest—and the constitutional right they assert—is in obtaining services they cannot get under Medicare at any price.[ ] The plaintiffs are skeptical, however, that section 4507 really means what the Secretary says it means—and equally skeptical that the Secretary actually reads and applies it that way.

Plaintiffs' skepticism is not unjustified. The meaning of section 4507 is hardly plain on its face. Moreover, because HCFA did not promulgate formal regulations regarding the section until ten days after the oral argument in this case, its own interpretation could only be gleaned from memoranda issued to Medicare carriers and testimony delivered to Congress, of which Medicare beneficiaries may well have been unaware. Nonetheless, as we discuss below, the Secretary's interpretation is a reasonable interpretation of the less-than-plain language of section 4507. In addition, the Secretary's current interpretation, as foreshadowed in the briefs filed in this case and expressed in the subsequent regulations, is consistent with the position HCFA has taken since the section was enacted. Under Chevron U.S.A. Inc. v. Natural Resources Defense Council, Inc., if a statute is ambiguous we must defer to an agency's reasonable interpretation of its terms. 467 U.S. 837, 842–45, 104 S.Ct. 2778, 81 L.Ed.2d 694 (1984)* * * [The Court then reviewed the history of the legislation and the Secretary's interpretation of it, and found the interpretation to be reasonable and consistent.]

* * *

Finally, we briefly address plaintiffs' contention that the ABN procedure is not a realistic way to ensure patients' access to services they or their doctors regard as necessary but Medicare does not. Under the ABN procedure, before providing a service the physician informs the patient that Medicare may not pay, and obtains the patient's agreement to pay on his or her own if Medicare denies the claim. See 42 U.S.C. § 1395u(l)(1)(C)(ii). As noted above, because an ABN is not considered a private contract under section 4507, if Medicare does not pay the doctor may receive payment from the patient without being subject to the opt-out rule.[ ]

Plaintiffs contend that the ABN option is illusory because HCFA has a policy of sanctioning doctors who repeatedly use ABNs for services they believe warranted but Medicare regards as unnecessary and will not reimburse.[ ] The Secretary vehemently denies having such a policy.[ ]

The preamble to HCFA's new regulations should also give plaintiffs some comfort.* * * [I]t closes with an effort to assuage precisely the concern plaintiff expresses here: "[P]hysicians and practitioners should not hesitate to furnish services to Medicare beneficiaries when the physician or practitioner believes that those services are in accordance with accepted standards of medical care, even when those services do not meet Medicare's particular and often unique coverage requirements."[ ]

It should not be missed, of course, that HCFA exempts from this note of encouragement those services not "in accordance with accepted standards of medical care."[ ] This qualifier may well explain some of the confusion. Although a HCFA regulation does state that ABNs are not acceptable if the "physician routinely gives this notice to all beneficiaries for whom he or she furnishes services," 42 C.F.R. § 411.408(f)(2)(i), the Secretary makes clear that this rule is aimed at a doctor who "require[s] all his patients to sign ABNs on a blanket basis in order to bill them for unwarranted procedures."[ ]

Needless to say, billing patients for unwarranted procedures may well be subject to sanction,[ ] and plaintiffs do not urge otherwise.

* * *

Because the Secretary's reading of section 4507 eliminates the constitutional injury plaintiffs allege, and because we are bound under Chevron to defer to that interpretation, the order of the district court is affirmed.

Notes and Questions

Should doctors be able to charge beneficiaries rates in excess of those allowed by Medicare for Medicare financed services? Under what circumstances might they do so? Could some beneficiaries benefit from being able to pay higher rates? Might others suffer if some could do so? What problems are encountered when private arrangements are permitted to contract out of the terms of public programs? See Marilyn Moon, Freedom to Pay or Freedom to Choose? Private Contracting and Medicare Beneficiaries, 10 Health Matrix 21 (2000); Thomas W. Greeson & Heather L. Gunas, Section 4507 and the Importance of Private Contracts, 10 Health Matrix 35 (2000).

5. Medicare Managed Care

Though Medicare began as a fee-for-service program, it has offered managed care options for nearly two decades. Managed care enrollment grew slowly at first, but growth was rapid in the mid 1990s: between 1995 and 1997 enrollment doubled from 3 to 6 million. Prior to the Balanced Budget Act of 1997, Medicare health maintenance organizations (HMOs) were paid 95 percent of the cost of Medicare fee-for-service costs in the same county (with crude risk adjustment). Because of biased selection (i.e. HMOs got healthier beneficiaries), HMOs did quite well, particularly in high cost counties. Because they were required to share their excess income with beneficiaries, they generally offered attractive benefit packages, in particular prescription drug coverage, which in turn led to rapid growth. The Balanced Budget Act of 1997 attempted to encourage growth in Medicare managed care, while at the same time dealing with some of the problems of the prior program. A description of its effects follows:

MEDICARE PAYMENT ADVISORY COMMISSION REPORT TO CONGRESS: MEDICARE PAYMENT POLICY (2000)

Medicare + Choice: Trends Since the Balanced Budget Act.

The Congress had two explicit goals when it created the Medicare + Choice program as part of the Balanced Budget Act: (1) to provide beneficiaries with more choice of plan options, similar to that available in the private sector and the Federal Employees Health Benefits Program, and (2) to help control the growth in Medicare spending. Balanced Budget Act proponents had other implicit goals. Some members of the Congress wanted to see the Medicare + Choice plans provide beneficiaries with benefit packages richer than the traditional Medicare fee-for-service package, particularly with respect to outpatient prescription drugs. Other policymakers wanted to see continual, rapid enrollment increases in Medicare + Choice plans to help set the stage for possible future changes in the structure of Medicare.

Since the passage of the Balanced Budget Act (BBA), progress toward these goals has been halting. The availability of plan options has not increased; most beneficiaries in rural areas still cannot enroll in Medicare + Choice (M + C) plans; benefit packages have become less generous; and enrollment growth in M + C plans has slowed. However, the rate of increase in program payments per beneficiary has decreased.

* * *

The BBA has been successful in controlling the growth in Medicare spending; per capita spending actually has decreased since its enactment. The majority of savings has come from provider payment reductions in the traditional Medicare fee-for-service (FFS) program, but some BBA provisions also restricted the payment rate growth for M + C plans. * * *

* * *

The M + C program can increase plan options for beneficiaries in two ways. It can extend operations of Medicare HMOs to new areas of the country and increase the number of active plans in existing markets. It also can introduce new types of plans to the program. Neither has occurred.

A substantial number of health plans have withdrawn from the M + C program over the past two years. In January 1999, there were 45 terminated contracts and 54 service area reductions. Of 310 M + C contacts in existence in July 1999, 41 were terminated effective January 2000. Another 58 contractors reduced their service areas by withdrawing from at least one county. These changes meant that in 1999 about 405,000 beneficiaries could not stay in the M + C plans in which they were enrolled in July 1998. At the beginning of 2000, about 327,000 M + C enrollees were in the same circumstance.* * *

Counties in which all available plans withdraw are a particular concern in view of the Congress's goal to provide more choice to beneficiaries. All available plans withdrew from 105 counties for 2000, leaving more than 79,000 M + C enrollees with no M + C alternative. * * *

When BBA was enacted in 1997, plans were still joining the program and 74 percent of beneficiaries had access to at least one M + C plan in 1998. Access dropped to 71 percent of beneficiaries in 1999 and to 69 percent in 2000. Approximately one million fewer beneficiaries have access to an M + C plan in 2000 than had access in 1999, and two million fewer than had access in 1998.

The BBA expanded plan options to allow four new types of plans: provider sponsored organizations (PSOs), preferred provider organizations (PPOs), private fee-for-service plans, and plans attached to medical savings accounts (MSAs). Almost no progress has been made toward the availability of these new types of M + C plans. The BBA set up a waiver process to encourage the development of PSO plans, but potential PSO plans said the process did not eliminate enough of the regulatory burden faced by HMOs. Instead, PSOs in the M + C program operate under HMO licenses. At this time, there is only one PSO operating under a waiver. * * *

The BBA also allows PPOs to become M + C plans. However, PPOs have complained that they are not structured to meet the quality requirements developed by the Health Care Financing Administration (HCFA) under the authority of the BBA. Although other factors also may be in play, no PPOs have become M + C plans.

The BBA introduced the possibility that private fee-for-service plans could become M + C plans. To date, no private FFS plans have joined, but one application for a plan awaiting HCFA approval would cover parts of 30 states. [It has subsequently been approved, and the plan has expanded, ed.] The BBA also provided for the creation of M + C plans attached to MSAs. As yet, there have been no MSA plan applications.

* * *

While overall M + C enrollment is higher than ever—accounting for 16 percent of the Medicare population—it is clear that the BBA has not yet produced the rapid increase in enrollment that policymakers expected. Instead, the growth in M + C enrollment slowed to 5 percent in 1999, from a high of more than 35 percent in 1995.

Plan availability and the richness of benefits in the plans affect enrollment. Coupled with the decrease in overall plan availability, plans continuing in the M + C program have reduced average benefit packages and increased premiums. * * * Further, both the availability of zero-premium plans and of zero-premium plans that provide any outpatient drug coverage have fallen.

Achieving all of the Congress's goals simultaneously has been difficult because they are partially at odds. For example, there is a basic conflict between the goals of controlling Medicare spending and of providing richer benefits for beneficiaries. If Medicare spending is controlled by bringing payments to M + C plans closer to the cost of providing the basic benefit, it becomes difficult to maintain generous benefit packages and zero premiums for the fortunate beneficiaries who have them, much less to extend those benefits to others. Without generous benefits, encouraging enrollment in M + C plans is more difficult; many people do not want to give up their choice of providers without a financial reward. * * *

* * *

How would we know the Medicare + Choice program is helping to control spending in the Medicare program? By one definition, M + C controls spending if Medicare payments for beneficiaries enrolled in M + C plans are less than or equal to what payments would have been for those same beneficiaries under traditional FFS coverage.

Under this definition, before the BBA, the predecessor to the M + C program (the risk-HMO program) was not controlling spending. Plans enjoyed favorable selection—they enrolled beneficiaries with lower-than-average health care costs—and the program lost from 5 to 7 percent for each beneficiary enrolled in a risk-HMO. The plans may have been delivering health care more efficiently than the traditional program (by negotiating lower rates, avoiding fraudulent or high-cost providers, and curtailing use), but administrative and marketing costs and plan profits offset some of the efficiency savings. Any remaining efficiency savings either were retained by the plan or passed on to beneficiaries in the form of more benefits, due to competition for enrollees in local markets. The plans almost never chose to return money to the Medicare program.

These findings prompted Congress to (1) include risk adjustment in the BBA to counteract favorable selection, so payments for plans would approximate more closely the cost of care, and (2) try to decrease what was deemed to be excessive variability in county payments, * * * However, the Congress also mandated a 2 percent minimum increase in county rates. As a result, annual growth in counties in which more than 90 percent of M+C plan members lived was 2 percent in 1998 and 1999.

Did the Congress's actions control Medicare spending? Not relative to growth in Medicare program payments per beneficiary in the traditional program. Average Medicare spending per beneficiary in the FFS program increased by 0.2 percent in 1998 and actually fell by 2.5 percent in 1999. At the same time, average Medicare spending per M+C enrollee increased 2.5 percent in 1998 and 2.7 percent in 1999. In addition, these larger increases were applied to 1997 base payment rates that themselves were too high, due to favorable selection and because they incorporated an overestimate of future spending.* * *

Achieving other goals, such as expanding the population in M+C plans or expanding benefits, will not help control spending unless payments to plans reflect the health status of the beneficiaries and base payment rates are appropriate.* * *

The BBA permitted new kinds of plans to participate in the Medicare+Choice program. To date, few have joined the program. Why hasn't there been more participation? * * *

Provider sponsored organizations were encouraged to enter the program by receiving waivers to certain technical HMO requirements. * * * Two other reasons make it difficult to attract PSOs into Medicare+Choice. First, PSOs must be large enough to achieve economies of scale, make an up-front investment to establish and market themselves, and meet solvency requirements. Second, there is a basic contradiction between the way managed care plans achieve savings and the interests of providers. For example, a key technique used by managed care plans is the substitution of outpatient services for hospital inpatient admissions and longer lengths of stay. For a hospital-based PSO, the substitution of outpatient services for hospital admissions and longer lengths of stay decreases its hospital revenues. Similarly, limiting provider payments to achieve savings decreases provider revenues. * * *

* * *

Medicare+Choice plans attached to medical savings accounts also have not entered the market, perhaps because of perceived risk aversion in the beneficiary population or unfamiliarity with the concept.

Notes and Questions

1. In 1999 and 2000 M+C plans lobbied hard for more money and for regulatory relief, claims to which "pro-market" forces in Congress were quite responsive. The 1999 Balanced Budget Refinement Act offered plans $4.9 billion in new money over five years, a slow-down in the phase-in of risk adjustment, a roll-back of some regulatory requirements, and special incentives for plans in rural areas, which were hit hard by plan withdrawals. The 2001 budget bill put off

risk adjustment even further, and offered financial incentives to plans that accepted two year rather than one year contracts.

2. Does the disappointing showing of the M+C program demonstrate that managed care is less effective than administered prices as a means of paying for Medicare services? Or was there something wrong with the experiment? If managed care plans cannot survive without being paid more than fee-for-service providers for the same services, how can they save money for the Medicare program? Why have the alternative plans permitted by the 1997 BBA not materialized? Why might the elderly and disabled prove an unattractive market for managed care, unless cream-skimming is rewarded?

3. Medicare beneficiaries receiving care from managed care organizations are potentially subject to all of the abuses discussed in chapter 8 above, which may be potentially greater because of the greater needs and lesser capacity of some beneficiaries. M+C organizations are, therefore, subject to a host of regulatory requirements. M+C organizations are responsible for providing their members with detailed descriptions of plan provisions, including disclosure of any coverage limitations or regulations. 42 U.S.C.A. § 1395w–22(c). M+C coordinated care plans must provide access to providers 24 hours a day, 7 days a week; must ensure services are "culturally competent" and that hours of operation of providers are convenient and non-discriminatory; provide adequate and coordinated specialist treatment for persons with complex or serious medical conditions; and allow women enrollees direct access to women's health specialists. 42 U.S.C.A. § 1395w–22(d). M+C plans must have an ongoing quality assurance and performance improvement program. 42 U.S.C.A. § 1395w–22(e). They must have mechanisms in place to detect both under and over utilization. Most types of plans must make provision for independent quality review. Organizations accredited by approved national accreditation agencies can be deemed to meet quality requirements. 42 U.S.C.A. § 1395w–22(e)(4).

M+C organizations may not discriminate against professionals on the basis of their licensure or certification, and must provide notice and hearing to physicians whose participation rights are terminated. 42 C.F.R. § 422.204(b) & (c). Organizations may not interfere with provider advice to enrollees regarding care and treatment. 42 U.S.C.A. § 1395w–22(j)(3). Physician incentives to reduce care are regulated and must be disclosed.42 U.S.C.A. § 1395w–22(j)(4). Plans that fail substantially to provide medically necessary services where the failure adversely affects (or is substantially likely adversely to affect) health; impose unpermitted premiums; wrongly expel or refuse to reenroll a beneficiary; provide false information; interfere with practitioner's advice to enrollees; or commit other specified wrongful acts, may be subject to civil money penalties of not more than $25,000. Plans that deny or discourage enrollment of persons on the basis of medical condition or provide false information to HCFA are subject to fines of up to $100,000. 42 U.S.C.A. 1395w–27(g)(2). HCFA may also impose civil penalties of $25,000 for deficiencies that directly affect or have a substantial likelihood of adversely affecting enrollees, plus $10,000 a week if the deficiency remains uncorrected. 42 U.S.C.A. § 1395w–27(g)(2).

One of the primary criticisms that the managed care industry has leveled at the M+C program is that it has imposed excessive regulations. Which of the regulations just described would you abolish? Why?

D.　ADMINISTRATION AND APPEALS

The major decisions about federal Medicare and Medicaid policy are ultimately made by the United States Congress, which is constantly tinkering with the program. Congressional decisions are in turn fleshed-out by the Health Care Financing Administration (HCFA) of the Department of Health and Human Services (HHS) and implemented by the carriers and intermediaries that make individual claims determinations. Though some of the provisions of the Medicare Act are overly detailed, it has often been in the interest of Congress to enact very general provisions and to leave the hard and politically dangerous work of hammering out the details of the program to HHS. In the early years of Medicare, HHS frequently deferred to the health care industry and attempted to make program decisions by consensus. Since the late 1970s, however, HHS has exercised its authority more aggressively, as is illustrated by the DRG hospital reimbursement and RBRVS physician payment programs discussed above. See Timothy Stoltzfus Jost, Governing Medicare, 51 Admin. L. Rev. 39 (1999); Lawrence Brown, Technocratic Corporatism and Administrative Reform in Medicare, 10 J. Health Pol. Pol'y and L. 579 (1985).

The courts have had only a minor role in making major policy decisions about Medicare, but have been active at the fringes, trying to correct some of the program's worst bureaucratic excesses. Their role has been circumscribed by the strict limits placed on judicial review by the Supreme Court's interpretation of the Social Security Act. 42 U.S.C.A. § 1395ii provides that 42 U.S.C.A. § 405(h) applies to the Medicare program. Section 405(h) provides, in part, that

> No findings of fact or decision of the Secretary shall be reviewed by any person, tribunal, or governmental agency except as herein provided. No action against the United States, the Secretary, or any officer or employee thereof shall be brought under section 1331 or 1346 of title 28 to recover on any claim arising under this subchapter.

The Supreme Court's most recent interpretations of these statutes are discussed in the following case:

SHALALA v. ILLINOIS COUNCIL ON LONG TERM CARE, INC.

Supreme Court of the United States, 2000.
529 U.S. 1, 120 S.Ct. 1084, 146 L.Ed.2d 1.

JUSTICE BREYER.

The question before us is one of jurisdiction. An association of nursing homes sued, inter alios, the Secretary of Health and Human Services (HHS) * * * (hereinafter Secretary) in Federal District Court claiming that certain Medicare-related regulations violated various statutes and the Constitution. The association invoked the court's federal-question jurisdiction, 28 U.S.C. § 1331. The District Court dismissed the suit on the ground that it lacked jurisdiction. It believed that a set of special statutory provisions creates a separate, virtually exclusive, system of administrative and judicial review for denials of Medicare claims; and it held that one of those provisions explicitly barred a § 1331 suit. See 42 U.S.C. § 1395ii (incorporating to the Medicare Act 42 U.S.C. § 405(h), which provides that "[n]o action ... to recover on any claim" arising under the Medicare laws shall be "brought under section 1331 ... of title 28"). The Court of Appeals, however, reversed.

We conclude that the statutory provision at issue, § 405(h), as incorporated by § 1395ii, bars federal-question jurisdiction here. The association or its members must proceed instead through the special review channel that the Medicare statutes create.[ ]

* * * Medicare Act Part A provides payment to nursing homes which provide care to Medicare beneficiaries after a stay in hospital. To receive payment, a home must enter into a provider agreement with the Secretary of HHS, and it must comply with numerous statutory and regulatory requirements. State and federal agencies enforce those requirements through inspections. Inspectors report violations, called "deficiencies." And "deficiencies" lead to the imposition of sanctions or "remedies."[ ]

The regulations at issue focus on the imposition of sanctions or remedies. [The sanctions imposed under these regulations are described in chapter 3 above. ed.] * * *

* * *

The association's complaint filed in Federal District Court attacked the regulations as unlawful in four basic ways. In its view: (1) certain terms, e.g., "substantial compliance" and "minimal harm," are unconstitutionally vague; (2) the regulations and manual, particularly as implemented, violate statutory requirements seeking enforcement consistency,[ ] and exceed the legislative mandate of the Medicare Act; (3) the regulations create administrative procedures inconsistent with the Federal Constitution's Due Process Clause; and (4) the manual and other agency publications create legislative rules that were not promulgated consistent with the Administrative Procedure Act's demands for "notice and comment" and a statement of "basis and purpose," 5 U.S.C. § 553.[ ]

* * *

The case before us began when the Illinois Council on Long Term Care, Inc. (Council), an association of about 200 Illinois nursing homes participating in the Medicare (or Medicaid) program, filed the complaint * * * in Federal District Court. * * * The District Court, as we have said, dismissed the complaint for lack of federal-question jurisdiction.[ ] In doing so, the court relied upon § 405(h) as interpreted by this Court in Weinberger v. Salfi, 422 U.S. 749, 95 S.Ct. 2457, 45 L.Ed.2d 522 (1975), and Heckler v. Ringer, 466 U.S. 602, 104 S.Ct. 2013, 80 L.Ed.2d 622 (1984).[ ]

The Court of Appeals reversed the dismissal.[ ] In its view, a later case, Bowen v. Michigan Academy of Family Physicians, 476 U.S. 667, 106 S.Ct. 2133, 90 L.Ed.2d 623 (1986), had significantly modified this Court's earlier case law. * * *

Section 405(h) purports to make exclusive the judicial review method set forth in § 405(g). Its second sentence says that "[n]o findings of fact or decision of the [Secretary] shall be reviewed by any person, tribunal, or governmental agency except as herein provided." § 405(h). Its third sentence, directly at issue here, says that "[n]o action against the United States, the [Secretary], or any officer or employee thereof shall be brought under section 1331 or 1346 of title 28 to recover on any claim arising under this subchapter."

The scope of the * * * language "to recover on any claim arising under" the Social Security (or, as incorporated through § 1395ii, the Medicare) Act is, if read alone, uncertain. Those words clearly apply in a typical Social Security or Medicare benefits case, where an individual seeks a monetary benefit from the agency (say a disability payment, or payment for some medical procedure), the agency denies the benefit and the individual challenges the lawfulness of that denial. The statute plainly bars § 1331 review in such a case, irrespective of whether the individual challenges the agency's denial on evidentiary, rule-related, statutory, constitutional, or other legal grounds. But does the statute's bar apply when one who might later seek money or some other benefit from (or contest the imposition of a penalty by) the agency challenges in advance (in a § 1331 action) the lawfulness of a policy, regulation, or statute that might later bar recovery of that benefit (or authorize the imposition of the penalty)? * * *

In answering the question, we temporarily put the case on which the Court of Appeals relied, Michigan Academy, supra, to the side. Were we not to take account of that case, § 405(h) as interpreted by the Court's earlier cases of Weinberger v. Salfi, supra, and Heckler v. Ringer, supra, would clearly bar this § 1331 lawsuit.

In Salfi, a mother and a daughter, filing on behalf of themselves and a class of individuals, brought a § 1331 action challenging the constitutionality of a statutory provision that, if valid, would deny them Social Security benefits. * * * This Court held that § 405(h) barred § 1331 jurisdiction for all members of the class because "it is the Social Security Act which provides both the standing and the substantive basis for the presentation of th[e] constitutional contentions." * * *

* * *

In Ringer, four individuals brought a § 1331 action challenging the lawfulness (under statutes and the Constitution) of the agency's determination not to provide Medicare Part A reimbursement to those who had undergone a particular medical operation. The Court held that § 405(h) barred § 1331 jurisdiction over the action, even though the challenge was in part to the agency's procedures, the relief requested amounted simply to a declaration of invalidity (not an order requiring payment), and one plaintiff had as yet no valid claim for reimbursement because he had not even undergone the operation and would likely never do so unless a court set aside as unlawful the challenged agency "no reimbursement" determination. * * *

As so interpreted, the bar of § 405(h) reaches beyond ordinary administrative law principles of "ripeness" and "exhaustion of administrative remedies," [ ] doctrines that in any event normally require channeling a legal challenge through the agency. * * * Doctrines of "ripeness" and "exhaustion" contain exceptions, however, which exceptions permit early review when, for example, the legal question is "fit" for resolution and delay means hardship,[ ] or when exhaustion would prove "futile," [ ]

Insofar as § 405(h) prevents application of the "ripeness" and "exhaustion" exceptions, i.e., insofar as it demands the "channeling" of virtually all legal attacks through the agency, it assures the agency greater opportunity to apply, interpret, or revise policies, regulations, or statutes without possibly premature interference by different individual courts applying "ripeness" and "exhaustion" exceptions case by case. But this assurance comes at a price, namely, occasional individual, delay-related hardship. In the context of a massive, complex health and safety program such as Medicare, embodied in hundreds of pages of statutes and thousands of pages of often interrelated regulations, any of which may become the subject of a legal challenge in any of several different courts, paying this price may seem justified. In any event, such was the judgment of Congress as understood in Salfi and Ringer. [ ]

* * *

The Court of Appeals held that Michigan Academy modified the Court's earlier holdings by limiting the scope of "1395ii and therefore § 405(h)" to "amount determinations."[ ] But we do not agree. Michigan Academy involved a § 1331 suit challenging the lawfulness of HHS regulations that governed procedures used to calculate benefits under Medicare Part B—which Part provides voluntary supplementary medical insurance, e.g., for doctors' fees. [ ] The Medicare statute, as it then existed, provided for only limited review of Part B decisions. It allowed the equivalent of § 405(g) review for "eligibility" determinations.[ ] It required private insurance carriers (administering the Part B program) to provide a "fair hearing" for disputes about Part B "amount determinations."[ ] But that was all.

Michigan Academy first discussed the statute's total silence about review of "challenges mounted against the method by which ... amounts are to be determined."[ ] It held that this silence meant that, although review was not available under § 405(g), the silence did not itself foreclose other forms of review, say review in a court action brought under § 1331.[ ]

The Court then asked whether § 405(h) barred 28 U.S.C. § 1331 review of challenges to methodology. Noting the Secretary's Salfi/Ringer-based argument that § 405(h) barred § 1331 review of all challenges arising under the Medicare Act and the respondents' counter-argument that § 405(h) barred challenges to "methods" only where § 405(g) review was available, [ ] the Court wrote:

> "Whichever may be the better reading of Salfi and Ringer, we need not pass on the meaning of § 405(h) in the abstract to resolve this case. Section 405(h) does not apply on its own terms to Part B of the Medicare program, but is instead incorporated mutatis mutandis by § 1395ii. The legislative history of both the statute establishing the Medicare program and the 1972 amendments thereto provides specific evidence of Congress' intent to foreclose review only of 'amount determinations'—i.e., those [matters] ... remitted finally and exclusively to adjudication by private insurance carriers in a 'fair hearing.' By the same token, matters which Congress did not delegate to private carriers, such as challenges to the validity of the Secretary's instructions and regulations, are cognizable in courts of law." [ ].

The Court's words do not limit the scope of § 405(h) itself to instances where a plaintiff, invoking § 1331, seeks review of an "amount determination." Rather, the Court said that it would "not pass on the meaning of § 405(h) in the abstract."[ ] Instead it focused upon the Medicare Act's cross-referencing provision, § 1395ii, which makes § 405(h) applicable "to the same extent as "it is "applicable" to the Social Security Act.[ ] It interpreted that phrase as applying § 405(h) "mutatis mutandis," i.e., "[a]ll necessary changes having been made."[ ] And it applied § 1395ii with one important change of detail—a change produced by not applying § 405(h) where its application to a particular category of cases, such as Medicare Part B "methodology" challenges, would not lead to a channeling of review through the agency, but would mean no review at all. The Court added that a " 'serious constitutional question' . . . would arise if we construed § 1395ii to deny a judicial forum for constitutional claims arising under Part B."[ ]

More than that: Were the Court of Appeals correct in believing that Michigan Academy limited the scope of § 405(h) itself to "amount determinations," that case would have significantly affected not only Medicare Part B cases but cases arising under the Social Security Act and Medicare Part A as well. It accordingly would have overturned or dramatically limited this Court's earlier precedents, such as Salfi and Ringer, which involved, respectively, those programs. It would, moreover, have created a hardly justifiable distinction between "amount determinations" and many other similar HHS determinations.* * * This Court does not normally overturn, or so dramatically limit, earlier authority sub silentio. And we agree with those Circuits that have held the Court did not do so in this instance. [ ]

Justice THOMAS [in dissent] maintains that Michigan Academy "must have established," by way of a new interpretation of § 1395ii, the critical distinction between a dispute about an agency determination in a particular case and a more general dispute about, for example, the agency's authority to promulgate a set of regulations, i.e., the very distinction that this Court's earlier cases deny. * * *

* * *

* * * [I]t is more plausible to read Michigan Academy as holding that § 1395ii does not apply § 405(h) where application of § 405(h) would not simply channel review through the agency, but would mean no review at all. * * * This latter holding, as we have said, has the virtues of consistency with Michigan Academy's actual language; consistency with the holdings of earlier cases such as Ringer; and consistency with the distinction that this Court has often drawn between a total preclusion of review and postponement of review. * * * As we have said, * * * Congress may well have concluded that a universal obligation to present a legal claim first to HHS, though postponing review in some cases, would produce speedier, as well as better, review overall. And this Court crossed the relevant bridge long ago when it held that Congress, in both the Social Security Act and the Medicare Act, insisted upon an initial presentation of the matter to the agency. * * *

The Council argues that in any event it falls within the exception that Michigan Academy creates, for here as there, it can obtain no review at all unless it can obtain judicial review in a § 1331 action. In other words, the Council contends that application of § 1395ii's channeling provision to the portion of the Medicare statute and the Medicare regulations at issue in this case will amount to the "practical equivalent of a total denial of judicial review." [ ] The Council, however, has not convinced us that is so.

The Council says that the special review channel that the Medicare statutes create applies only where the Secretary terminates a home's provider agreement; it is not available in the more usual case involving imposition of a lesser remedy, say the transfer of patients, the withholding of payments, or the imposition of a civil monetary penalty.

* * *

The Secretary states in her brief that the relevant "determination" that entitles a "dissatisfied" home to review is any determination that a provider has failed to comply substantially with the statute, agreements, or regulations, whether termination or "some other remedy is imposed." * * * The statute's language, though not free of ambiguity, bears that interpretation. And we are aware of no convincing countervailing argument. We conclude that the Secretary's interpretation is legally permissible. See Chevron U.S.A. Inc. v. Natural Resources Defense Council, Inc., 467 U.S. 837, 843 (1984); [ ].

* * *

Proceeding through the agency * * * provides the agency the opportunity to reconsider its policies, interpretations, and regulations in light of those challenges. Nor need it waste time, for the agency can waive many of the procedural steps set forth in § 405(g),[ ] and a court can deem them waived in certain circumstances,[ ] even though the agency technically holds no "hearing" on the claim.[ ] At a minimum, however, the matter must be presented to the agency prior to review in a federal court. This the Council has not done.

* * *

For these reasons, this case cannot fit within Michigan Academy's exception. The bar of § 405(h) applies. The judgment of the Court of Appeals is Reversed.

Notes and Questions

1. *Illinois Council* was decided by a five to four vote, with Justices Stevens, Scalia, Thomas and Kennedy dissenting in three separate opinions. The dissenters would have expanded on *Michigan Academy* to allow federal question jurisdiction over cases involving "challenges to the validity of the Secretary's instructions and regulations" as opposed to individualized benefit determinations, which would still have to first be presented to HHS through administrative channels.

2. Though *Illinois Council* involved an attempt to challenge Medicare regulations pursuant to federal question jurisdiction, other earlier cases have rejected challenges under the Administrative Procedures Act, Califano v. Sanders, 430 U.S. 99, 97 S.Ct. 980, 51 L.Ed.2d 192 (1977); or in the Court of Claims, United States v. Erika, 456 U.S. 201, 102 S.Ct. 1650, 72 L.Ed.2d 12 (1982).

3. In the same year as *Michigan Academy*, Congress 42 U.S.C.A. § 1395ff to permit judicial review of Part B decisions where the amount in controversy was $1000 or more. Part B procedures were further amended by the Omnibus Budget Reconciliation Act of 1987 to permit administrative law judges to certify legal issues to the federal district court when they determine, on motion of an appellant, that no factual issues exist in a case.

Though these provisions extended judicial review over Medicare cases, serious questions still remain as to whether judicial review is available for several classes of cases. There is still, for example, no judicial review for Part A and B claims involving less than $1000. Situations can also still arise, as in *Heckler v. Ringer*, where providers will not provide services that HCFA refuses to cover, making it impossible for a recipient to file a claim and thus to begin to exhaust administrative remedies. Review of national coverage determinations deciding whether a particular class of items or services are covered under Medicare is further subject to specific statutory limitations. Such determinations may not be reviewed by any administrative law judge and they may not be held unlawful or set aside on the ground that a requirement of the APA relating to publication in the Federal Register or opportunity for public comment was not satisfied. If a court determines that the rulemaking record for a national coverage determination was incomplete or finds that the determination was otherwise not based of adequate information, the court must remand the matter to the Secretary for additional proceedings to supplement the record and may not determine that an item or service is covered except upon review of the supplemented record. 42 U.S.C.A. § 1395ff(b)(3). Collectively, these exceptions cover a large proportion of the Medicare issues worth litigating.

4. Not only do the courts defer to HHS procedurally by refusing to take jurisdiction over direct challenges to HHS regulations, they also defer substantively by generally upholding HHS's interpretation of the Medicare statutes and its own regulations (as we see in *Illinois Council* and saw earlier in *United Seniors*). This deference is stronger in the appellate courts than at the district court level, and has grown over time. The Supreme Court has ruled in favor of HHS in all five Medicare cases it has decided since 1990, and a recent study found that the courts of appeals and district courts in two one year periods during the 1990s had ruled for HHS 88 percent and 70 percent of the time respectively. In particular, the courts have applied the *Chevron* rule of agency deference much more faithfully with respect to Medicare than in other areas. See Jost, Governing Medicare, supra.

Should Medicare decisions and policies be immediately reviewable by the courts? Should the courts be able to review all Medicare claims, or just those involving more than a certain amount of money? Is it more important that providers or beneficiaries have access to the courts? (Justice Stevens in dissent in *Illinois Council* argued that the statute only precluded direct review of beneficiaries claims to benefits, not claims of providers to reimbursement, 120 S.Ct. at 1102). Why might the courts defer to HHS in its interpretation of the statute? What might be the effect of such deference on beneficiaries? On providers?

Notes: Medicare Administrative Appeals

1. An administrative appeal is available for Medicare Part A claims of $100 or more and Part B claims involving $500 or more. The only administrative review available to Medicare recipients denied Part B claims between $100 and $500 is a review on the written record or an oral hearing before a hearing officer appointed by the private insurance carrier that administers the program in the recipient's area. Even in cases involving more than $500, HCFA has insisted that the claim first be reviewed on the record and then submitted to a carrier fair hearing before the case can be submitted to an administrative law judge, a procedure upheld in Isaacs v. Bowen, 865 F.2d 468 (2d Cir.1989). Does this procedure satisfy due process? Will hearing officers selected by a private insurance company be biased towards upholding the decisions of that carrier? Does it make any difference that the carrier is paying claims from federal funds and the hearing officers' salaries

are paid by the federal government? Is due process violated because the hearing officers are often not attorneys? See Schweiker v. McClure, 456 U.S. 188, 102 S.Ct. 1665, 72 L.Ed.2d 1 (1982). Is due process violated because an oral hearing is not available for Part B denials involving less than $100? See Gray Panthers v. Schweiker, 652 F.2d 146 (D.C.Cir.1980), appeal after remand, 716 F.2d 23 (D.C.Cir.1983).

2. The Medicare statute and regulations provide a variety of other procedures for administrative appeals and judicial review. First, eligibility for Medicare is determined by the Social Security Administration and is subject to administrative review through SSA's three level reconsideration, administrative hearing, and Appeals Council procedures. The initial decision as to payment of an Part A claim is made by the private intermediary processing the claim. A beneficiary can ask the intermediary to reconsider this decision, 42 C.F.R. § 405.710. This consideration is a paper review performed by an employee of the intermediary other than the initial decisionmaker. Though Part A beneficiaries seek review of very few (.05 percent) claims, 25 percent of the reviewed decisions are reversed at the reconsideration stage. A beneficiary dissatisfied with the reconsideration decision may obtain an oral, evidentiary hearing before an administrative law judge (ALJ) of the Social Security Administration, 42 C.F.R. § 405.720. Claimants enjoy a 50–60 percent reversal rate at this stage of review. If the ALJ decision is not satisfactory, the beneficiary may appeal to the Social Security Appeals Council, 42 C.F.R. § 405.724.

A provider denied or terminated from participation in Medicare is entitled to review by a Social Security ALJ and by the Appeals Council, and, in most cases, to judicial review, 42 C.F.R. §§ 405.1501–405.1595. A Part A provider dissatisfied with the amount of reimbursement may receive a hearing before an intermediary hearing officer if the amount at issue is between $1,000 and $10,000. 42 C.F.R. §§ 405.1803–405.1813. If the amount is $10,000 or more (or if smaller claims involving a common controversy can be aggregated in an amount of $50,000 or more), the provider can receive a hearing before the Medicare Provider Reimbursement Review Board (PRRB), 42 U.S.C.A. § 1395oo(a)(2), (b).

3. Medicare + Choice organizations must provide their beneficiaries with a meaningful grievance resolution mechanisms. 42 U.S.C.A. § 1395w–22(f). They must explain their adverse coverage determinations in writing and must make initial determinations within 30 days for payment decisions, 14 days for health care services requests, and 72 hours for requests for services where lack of the service could seriously jeopardize life or health. If a reconsideration is requested, it must be completed within 30 days if a health service is requested, and within 72 hours in emergencies. Coverage reconsiderations may be appealed to an independent review organization under contract with HCFA, and may ultimately be appealed to an administrative law judge if $100 or more is at stake, and to court if the amount in controversy is $1000 or more. 42 U.S.C.A. § 1395w–22(g)(4) & (5).

In Grijalva v. Shalala, 152 F.3d 1115 (9th Cir.1998), certiorari granted and judgment vacated and case remanded, 526 U.S. 1096, 119 S.Ct. 1573, 143 L.Ed.2d 669 (1999), the Ninth Circuit held that notice and appeal provisions then in effect for Medicare managed care organizations violated the requirements of the Due Process Clause. The court held that the HMOs were making decisions for the Medicare program, and were thus "government actors" rather than private entities and thus covered by the Constitution. The Supreme Court vacated and remanded the Ninth Circuit appeal for further consideration in light of the new managed care appeal procedures imposed by the BBA and implementing regulations. Significantly, however, the Court also required further consideration in light of its decision in American Manufacturers Mutual Insurance Co. v. Sullivan, 526 U.S. 40, 119 S.Ct. 977, 143 L.Ed.2d 130 (1999), which had held that the decisions of private insurers participating in a workers' compensation program were not state actors when they made medical necessity determinations, and thus not subject to the due process clause.

If the Supreme Court were ultimately to hold that Medicare managed care organizations are private actors not subject to constitutional constraints, the federal government would be effectively permitted to contract out its responsibilities under the Medicare program beyond constitutional control, though it would probably still have to provide some government means of review for managed care decisions. But is Medicare sufficiently different from state workers' compensation programs that the holding of Sullivan might not apply to managed care organizations to which Medicare contracts out its statutory responsibilities? See Healey v. Shalala, 2000 WL 303439 (D.Conn.2000) (Sullivan does not support the argument that home health agencies providing Medicare benefits are not state actors). See also, Jennifer E. Gladieux, Medicare + Choice Appeal Procedures: Reconciling Due Process Rights and Cost Containment, 25 Am.J.L. & Med. 61 (1999); Jody Freeman, The Private Role in Public Governance, 75 N.Y.U. Law Rev. 543 (2000).

4. For a review of Medicare appeal procedures, see Terry Coleman, Legal Aspects of Medicare and Medicaid Reimbursement, 135–146 (1990); National Senior Citizens Law Center, Representing Older Persons, An Advocates Manual, 42–44 (1985); Judith Stein and Alfred J. Chiplin, Jr., A Practical Guide to Medicare Hearings and Appeals, 34 Real Prop. Prob. & Tr. J., 403 (1999); Eleanor D. Kinney, Consumer Grievance and Appeal Procedures in Managed Care Plans, 10 Health Lawyer (3), 17 (1998); Phyllis Bernard, Social Security and Medicare Adjudications at HHS, 3 Health Matrix 339 (1993); Bess Brewer, Risky Business: Five Years of Navigating the Medicare Part B Appeals Process, 26 Clearinghouse Rev. 537 (1992).

E. MEDICARE REFORM

The 1997 Balanced Budget Act created the National Bipartisan Commission on the Future of Medicare to craft a bipartisan proposal for Medicare reform. The chair of the Commission, Senator John Breaux, presented the following proposal, which received the support of ten of the seventeen members of the Commission. Because the Commission's rules permitted it to make a recommendation only with the support of eleven members, the Commission was unable to make a final recommendation to Congress. Senator Breaux subsequently introduced versions of this plan in the Senate in 1999 and 2000, together with Senator William Frist, one of the few physicians in Congress. President George W. Bush also expressed support for the proposal during the 2000 campaign. A response to the proposal from an eminent group of health policy scholars follows:

NATIONAL BIPARTISAN COMMISSION ON THE FUTURE OF MEDICARE

BUILDING A BETTER MEDICARE FOR TODAY AND TOMORROW

* * *

We believe a premium support system is necessary to enable Medicare beneficiaries to obtain secure, dependable, comprehensive high quality health care coverage comparable to what most workers have today. * * * Our proposal would allow beneficiaries to choose from among competing comprehensive health plans in a system based on a blend of existing government protections and market-based competition. Unlike today's Medicare program, our proposal ensures that low income seniors would have comprehensive health care coverage.

* * *

In reviewing * * * this proposal, it is important to keep in mind the different government roles in the premium support system and in current law. We believe the guarantee our society makes to every senior is to ensure that they can obtain the highest quality health care, and that their health care coverage not be allowed to fall behind that available to people in their working years. We believe that our society's commitment to seniors, the Medicare entitlement, can be made more secure only by focusing the government's powers on ensuring comprehensive coverage at an affordable price rather than continuing the inefficiency, inequity, and inadequacy of the current Medicare program.

The Medicare Board

A Medicare Board should be established to oversee and negotiate with private plans and the government-run fee-for-service plan. Some examples of the Board's role are: direct and oversee periodic open enrollment periods; provide comparative information to beneficiaries regarding the plans in their areas; transmit information about beneficiaries' plan selections and corresponding premium obligations to the Social Security Administration to permit premium collection as occurs today with Medicare Part B premiums; enforce financial and quality standards; review and approve benefit packages and service areas to ensure against the adverse selection that could be created through benefit design, delineation of service areas or other techniques; negotiate premiums with all health plans; and compute payments to plans (including risk and geographic adjustment).

* * *

Ensuring Plan Performance and Dependability

All plans (private plans and the government-run FFS plan) would compete in the premium support system; all plans would have Board-approved benefit designs and premiums. The Board would ensure that the benefits provided under all plans are self-funded and self-sustaining, determining whether plan premium submissions meet strict tests for actuarial soundness, assessing the adequacy of reserves, and monitoring their performance capacity.

Management of Government-run Fee-for-service in Premium Support

The government plan would have to be self-funded and self-sustaining and meet the same requirements applied to all private plans, including whether its premium submissions meet strict tests for actuarial soundness, the adequacy of reserves, and performance capacity.

Cost containment measures would be necessary. The provisions of the Balanced Budget Act of 1997 should be extended, or comparable savings achieved. In any region where the price control structure of the government run plan is not competitive, the government-run fee-for-service plan could operate on the basis of contracts negotiated with local providers on price and performance, just as is the case with private plans. * * *

Benefits Package

A standard benefits package would be specified in law. This benefits package would consist of all services covered under the existing Medicare statute. Plans would be able to offer additional benefits beyond the core package and plans would be able to vary cost sharing, including copay and deductible levels, subject to Board approval. Benefits would be updated through the annual negotiations process between plans and the Board, although the Board would not have the power to expand the standard benefit package without Congressional approval. Health plans would establish rules and procedures to assure delivery of benefits in a manner consistent with prevailing private standards and procedures offered to employer groups and other major purchasers.

The Medicare Board would approve benefit offerings and could allow variation within a limited range, for example not more than 10% of the actuarial value of the standard package, provided the Board was satisfied that the overall valuation of the package would be consistent with statutory objectives and would not lead to adverse or unfavorable risk selection problems in the Medicare market.

Outpatient prescription drug coverage and stop-loss protection

Private plans would be required to offer a high option that includes at least Medicare covered services plus coverage for outpatient prescription drugs and stop-loss protection. Plans would be able to vary copay and deductible structures. Minimum drug benefits for high option plans would be based on an actuarial valuation. High option and standard option plans each would be required to be self-funded and self-sustaining.

The government-run fee-for-service plan would be required to offer high option (including outpatient prescription drugs and stop-loss) in addition to standard option plans. The Medicare Board approval process would be the same as for private plans. High option and standard option plans would be required to be separately self-funded and self-sustaining. Government contracts would be based on prices commonly available in the market, without recourse to price controls or rebates.

Coverage would be provided through high option plans [for low-income beneficiaries]. The federal government would pay 100% of the premiums of the high option plans at or below 85% of the national weighted average premium of all high option plans for all eligible individuals up to 135% of poverty * * * on a fully federally funded basis. In areas where all high option plans cost more than this 85% threshold, the percentage will be determined locally to ensure that all low-income beneficiaries have access to high option plans. This financial support does not limit these beneficiaries' choice of plans nor restrict plans' design with regard to cost-sharing or other flexibility authorized by the Board. States would maintain their current level of effort, but the federal government would pay 100% of additional costs for these individuals.

* * *

On average, beneficiaries would be expected to pay 12 percent of the total cost of standard option plans. For plans that cost at or less than 85 percent of the national weighted average plan price, there would be no beneficiary premium. For plans with prices above the national weighted average, beneficiaries' premiums would include all costs above the national weighted average.

Only the cost of the standard package would count toward the computation of the national weighted average premium. Plans with a high option, whether private plans or government-run would separately identify the incremental costs of benefits beyond the standard package in their submissions to the Board, and the government contribution would be calculated without regard to the costs of these additional benefits.

The government-run fee-for-service plan would be treated the same as private plans.

* * *

Guaranteed premium levels where competition develops more slowly

In areas where no competition to the government-run fee-for-service plan exists, beneficiaries' obligations would be no greater than 12 percent of the FFS premium or the national weighted average, whichever is lower. * * *

Medicare's Special Payments in a Premium Support System

Congress should examine all non-insurance functions, special payments and subsidies to determine whether they should be funded through the Trust fund or from another source. For example, payments for Direct Medical Education (DME) would be financed and distributed independent of a Medicare premium support system. Since the Part A and Part B trust funds would be combined and the traditionally separate funding sources of payroll taxes and general revenues would be blurred, Congress should provide a separate mechanism for continued funding through either a mandatory entitlement or multi-year discretionary appropriation program. On the other hand, Indirect Medical Education (IME) presents a unique problem since it is difficult to identify the actual statistical difference in costs between teaching and non-teaching hospitals. Therefore, for now Congress should continue to fund IME from the Trust Fund as an adjustment to hospital payments.

* * *

[Senator Breaux's proposal also recommended immediately providing outpatient prescription drug coverage under Medicare for beneficiaries with incomes up to 135% of poverty, improving access to outpatient prescription drugs through Medigap policies, combining Parts A and B, combining and lowering the A & B deductible, extending copayment requirements, and conforming the Medicare eligibility age to that of Social Security. Finally, the proposal recommended that the artificiality of the notion of a Medicare Trust fund be recognized, and that the financial stability of the Medicare be evaluated in terms of its demand on general revenue funds rather than in terms of the Part A trust fund.]

THE BREAUX PLAN: WHY IT'S THE WRONG MEDICINE FOR MEDICARE

Jonathan Oberlander, Jacob Hacker, Mark Goldberg, Theodore Marmor.

* * * Although Social Security currently tops the domestic policy agenda, Medicare actually faces a more uncertain budgetary outlook, because its costs are driven by medical inflation as well as demographic change. * * * A national discussion of how to improve and strengthen Medicare is therefore necessary, unavoidable, and even welcome. What is not welcome is the reform proposal that Senator Breaux and a majority of the Medicare Commission endorsed: a radical transformation of Medicare that would sacrifice the inclusive character of the program in pursuit of chimerical cost savings through private health plan competition.

The centerpiece of the Breaux plan is a proposal to transform Medicare into a "premium support" or voucher program. The federal government would replace current Medicare insurance with a fixed financial contribution that beneficiaries would use toward the purchase of insurance from a dizzying array of private plans, including Preferred Provider Organizations (PPOs), fee-for-service insurers, and HMOs. The traditional Medicare program would also remain an option. If beneficiaries chose a health plan that cost more than the amount of the federal voucher, they would have to pay the difference out of pocket. The theory here is that health plans would compete for enrollees by improving their efficiency and lowering their costs. Advocates expect, and hope, that introducing vouchers would encourage many beneficiaries to leave traditional Medicare for lower-cost managed care plans.

If the Commission's Medicare "premium support" plan sounds familiar, it should. The Breaux proposal bears a striking resemblance to the "managed competition" plan proposed by President Clinton in 1993. Ironically, the same coalition of Republicans and conservative Democrats that helped defeat the Clinton plan are now promoting managed competition for Medicare. And while this coalition strongly objected to the Clinton plan, they have voiced few qualms about pushing elderly and disabled Medicare enrollees into a competitive insurance market, despite evidence that these groups have nothing like the disposable income necessary to shop around in a competitive market and that chronically-ill seniors are at risk for inadequate medical care in HMOs.

What was recently wrong for the entire population has strangely been deemed appropriate for the most vulnerable groups in society.

Senator Breaux's voucher solution for Medicare rests on four flawed assumptions: that Medicare faces a demographic crisis that requires immediate enactment of a radical solution; that vouchers will save substantial amounts of money for Medicare; that a competitive health market will enhance the choices and improve the medical care of Medicare beneficiaries; and that social insurance is no longer the appropriate means of ensuring health security for America's elderly and disabled.

Myth 1: Demographic Realities Demand Radical Reform

Perhaps the most fundamental flaw in the Breaux plan is its misdiagnosis of the problem. Put simply, the Bipartisan Commission's starting point is that there is demographic imperative to restructure Medicare. * * *

This definition of the problem in Medicare suffers from two basic difficulties. The first is the odd assumption that having more of the nation's population in Medicare is somehow a sign of program failure. Medicare's enrollment will undoubtedly grow in the coming decades, and with that growth will surely come higher levels of program spending. Yet this is hardly an indictment of Medicare. * * *

The second problem is that long-term forecasts of health spending—which in the case of Medicare stretch 75 years into the future—are notoriously unreliable and provide a poor basis for public policy. No public program can, or should be, fully funded now for 2075. And while increased enrollment due to population aging will raise Medicare costs, how much those costs rise depends not simply on demography but crucially, on health costs per Medicare beneficiary. Incremental policy measures to raise revenues and slow down those costs can generate substantial savings over time and thereby moderate the fiscal expense of an aging population.

* * * Many European nations have older populations than the United States and have an age structure that this country will not reach for another two decades. Yet of all these "older" countries spend substantially less on medical care than the United States. That is possible because all of these nations have universal health systems that control costs through budgeting and regulation of payments to medical care providers. Not one of the countries that have been successful in moderating the health care costs associated with an aging population has done so through vouchers. Vouchers are not the only solution to controlling the medical care costs of an aging population. In fact, they are the only unproven policy course.

Myth 2: Managed Competition Guarantees Big Savings

The Breaux plan projects substantial savings from competition among private insurance plans. The question is, with what justification? After all, during the past year, health care inflation in the private sector has surged, and the managed care industry has been beset by financial losses. * * * The Bipartisan Commission is jumping on a bandwagon that already shows signs of breaking down.

Meanwhile, Medicare costs rose by only 1.5% in 1998, slowed by regulatory controls on payments to medical providers. And program costs are now projected to grow less rapidly in coming years than health spending in the private sector, which was precisely the dominant pattern of the 1980s. It simply makes no sense for the federal government to imitate the faltering cost control strategies of the private sector, when its own Medicare regulatory policies are proving more effective.

The claim that managed competition would produce substantial savings in Medicare is no more than a leap of faith. And if that faith is not rewarded, and private plans do not hold their costs down as much as projected, the premium support scheme can save money only by shifting costs to Medicare beneficiaries, most of whom could ill afford the new expense. * * * Placing the main burden of rising Medicare costs on the elderly and disabled is hardly a reasonable solution to the program's financial troubles.

Myth 3: Vouchers Mean Choice

Voucher advocates claim that the Breaux plan will enhance choice for Medicare beneficiaries by broadening their access to the private insurance market. This is nonsense. The Commission plan would actually lead to a substantial loss of choice, because the "premium support" plan is essentially a Trojan Horse for moving Medicare beneficiaries out of traditional Medicare and into managed care plans. Under a voucher system, private insurers will compete aggressively to avoid enrolling the most expensive and sickest Medicare patients. Traditional Medicare would thus be left with a sicker population, and the costs of the program would inevitably rise. As it did, the vulnerable beneficiaries remaining in Medicare would be left with a true Hobson's choice: pay more or leave traditional Medicare.

Moreover, the "enhanced choices" promised by voucher advocates are, in reality, likely to result in widespread confusion among elderly beneficiaries. Medicare enrollees reportedly are already having trouble deciphering the market changes introduced by the 1997 Balanced Budget Act. A voucher plan would only increase that confusion while making the consequences of choosing the wrong health plan even greater.

The reality is that voucher advocates are not really interested in expanding meaningful choice. Their priority is creating financial pressures for enrollees to leave traditional Medicare. * * * The Breaux plan, then, would cause many Medicare beneficiaries to lose access to the one insurance program——traditional Medicare——that guarantees them free choice of physician.

Myth 4: Social Insurance is Outdated

* * * Since its enactment in 1965, the aspiration of Medicare has been that all elderly, regardless of their income before or after retirement, would participate in the same insurance program. * * * In a voucher system, beneficiaries are likely to segment into different health insurance plans on the basis of their wealth and health status. Inequality in health care among the elderly would worsen. And the political constituency for Medicare would be divided as enrollment in private insurance advances. And with that, the program's philosophical commitment to collective responsibility for financing medical care and social insurance would be substantially replaced by an ethos of individualism.

Notes and Questions

1.   See, supporting the concept of premium support, Matthew Miller, Premium Idea, 220 New Republic, Apr. 12, 1999, at 24; Gail R. Wilensky and Joseph P. Newhouse, Medicare: What's Right? What's Wrong? What's Next?, 18 Health Aff., Jan./Feb. 1999 at 92; and examining managed competition proposals for Medicare reform, Barbara Markham Smith and Sara Rosenbaum, Potential Effects of the "Premium Support" Proposal on the Security of Medicare, 282 JAMA 1760 (1999); Urban Institute, Can Competition Improve Medicare? A Look at Premium Support (www.urban.org/Medicare.comp.html); and National Academy of Social Insurance, Medicare and the American Social Contract (www.nasi.org/Medicare/Reports/what'snext/steerpt.htm).

2.   One of the changes Senator Breaux has made in Medicare reform bills he has subsequently introduced is to drop the idea of an independent Medicare Board. The Department of Justice had taken the position that the creation of an independent board which was responsible for 11 percent of the federal budget but reported to Congress rather than the President would pose "a serious threat to the core constitutional values of political accountability and coordinated Executive Branch policy-making," and could be unconstitutional.

3.   In an attempt to test out the feasibility of allowing market forces to control health care costs, the Health Care Financing Administration has tried on several occasions, most recently on the basis of authority granted by the 1997 Balanced Budget Act, to let contracts to health plans by way of competitive bidding. On each occasion HCFA has met fierce opposition from local health plans, supported by the congressional delegations from their districts (including, in some instances, members of Congress who are strong supporters of competition in theory). A former HCFA administrator, reviewing this experience concluded that providers see Medicare as an entitlement program for them, that "everyone wants market competition until they don't like the results," and that fee-for-service Medicare, based on administered prices, does a better job at saving money than does managed care. Barbara S. Cooper and Bruce C. Vladeck, Bringing Competitive Pricing to Medicare, 19 Health Aff., Sept./Oct. 2000 at 49. (This article was one of several in a symposium on Medicare competitive pricing.)

Problem: Lobbying Medicare Reform

You are a Washington lobbyist retained to lobby Congress with respect to the Breaux Medicare reform plan. What would your position be if retained to represent each of the following constituencies: 1) Community hospitals? 2) Large academic medical centers? 3) Primary care physicians? 3) Ophthalmologists? 4) Large insurance companies? 5) Small local managed care organizations? 6) Pharmaceutical companies? 7) Pharmacies? 8) Beneficiaries with incomes exceeding $100,000 a year? 9) Beneficiaries largely dependent on Social Security for their income? 10) Beneficiaries who are also eligible for Medicaid? 11) Blue Cross plans that are currently Part A intermediaries? 12) Thirty year old workers? 13) Sixty year old workers?

III.   MEDICAID

Medicare is a social insurance program whose benefits are available to the elderly and disabled without regard for their means. It is popular and enjoys broad-based support. The debate surrounding Medicare has focused on its enormous cost and on how the mechanisms used to pay for items and services under Medicare might be altered to lower that cost. There has been little discussion about cutting eligibility or benefits, nor about devolving responsibility for Medicare from the federal to the state governments. Medicaid, on the other hand, is a welfare program for the poor. It was created almost as an afterthought during the Medicare debate in the 1960s and has always been controversial, always vulnerable. All aspects of the program, eligibility, benefits, payment mechanisms, federal and state responsibility for the program—even whether Medicaid should continue to exist as an entitlement program—have been hotly contested over the past decade.

This section will examine Medicaid as it has developed over the past three decades and as it exists in the winter of 2000. When you read this book, Medicaid may have continued to evolve slowly and incrementally from the state in which it existed when this material was written or it may have radically changed. It is indeed possible that it will no longer exist. The poor, however, will always be with us, and they will always need health care. Any governmental program intended to help them obtain health care will need to consider the issues of eligibility, benefits, payment structure, and administration addressed in this section.

A. ELIGIBILITY

Medicaid eligibility is very complex. Medicaid is a state-administered program, and each state establishes its own eligibility requirements, although the discretion of the states in doing so is constrained by federal laws and regulations. Because Medicaid is a welfare program, eligibility is always related to economic need and every Medicaid applicant must show that his or her income and resources fall below certain levels set by the states pursuant to broad federal guidelines. Not every poor person is eligible for Medicaid, however. Rather Medicaid is intended to assist certain favored groups of the needy who are considered to be the "deserving" poor, though in recent years utilitarian considerations have arguably become as important as moral judgments in determining who should receive Medicaid. See Sandra Tanenbaum, Medicaid Eligibility Policy in the 1980s: Medical Utilitarianism and the "Deserving" Poor, 20 J. Health Pol., Pol'y & L. 933 (1995). The CCH Medicare and Medicaid Guide (an excellent source of legal information respecting these programs) identifies over thirty discrete categories of the poor that must be covered by state Medicaid programs under current federal law, and twenty-two groups that may, but need not, be covered, 4 Medicare & Medicaid Guide (CCH), ¶ ¶ 14,231, 14,251.

Who are the "deserving" poor? Historically they were the aged, blind, and permanently and totally disabled, who were either eligible for assistance under the Federal Supplemental Security Income Program (SSI) or, if a state elected the "209(b)" option, persons who would have been eligible for state assistance under the eligibility requirements in effect in 1972.[6] They were also

---

6. Section 209(b) was adopted in 1972 when the federal SSI program replaced preexisting state Aid to the Aged, Blind and Disabled (AABD) programs as the primary welfare program for adults. Prior to that time states had tied Medicaid eligibility for adults to

AABD financial eligibility levels. In many states these eligibility levels were much lower than the new federal SSI eligibility levels. These states, therefore, faced the possibility of a sudden dramatic increase in the number of adults eligible for Medicaid, and thus of Medic-

dependent children and their caretaker relatives who were eligible for assistance under the former federal/state Aid to Families with Dependent Children Program (AFDC). These groups have been known as the "categorically needy" because they are eligible for Medicaid by virtue of their membership in categories of persons eligible for financial assistance, and states that participate in the Medicaid program have generally been required to cover these groups.

The deserving poor also included the "optional categorically needy," a variety of small groups that states may choose to cover, but who then must be provided the full scope of benefits offered the categorically needy. Such groups include, for example, persons who would be eligible for Medicaid if institutionalized, but who are rather receiving services in the community. 42 C.F.R. § 436.217.

States have also long been permitted to elect to cover a third group, the "medically needy". The medically needy are categorically related (aged, disabled, blind, or families with dependent children) persons whose income exceeds the financial eligibility levels established by the state programs but who incur regular medical expenses that, when deducted from their income, bring their net disposable income below the eligibility level for financial assistance. Thirty-four Medicaid programs currently cover the medically needy. The medically needy are generally persons in need of expensive nursing home or hospital care. The medically needy program is effectively a catastrophic health insurance program for those who fall into the categories favored by the welfare system.

In recent years, these traditional categories have ceased to define Medicaid eligibility. Beginning with gradual Medicaid expansions in the mid–1980s, eligibility became over time decoupled from welfare recipient status. This decoupling became complete for families with dependent children with the abolition of the AFDC program and creation of the Temporary Assistance for Needy Families (TANF) program by the Personal Responsibility and Work Opportunities Reconciliation Act (PRWORA) of 1996 (though for some groups Medicaid eligibility continues to be tied awkwardly to former AFDC eligibility). By 1998, only 43 percent of Medicaid enrollees also received cash assistance.

Medicaid expansion has taken place primarily among four groups. First, coverage of pregnant women has been extended, so that now all pregnant women in families with incomes of up to 133 percent of the poverty level must be covered by state Medicaid programs, and pregnant women in families with incomes of up to 185 percent of the poverty level may be covered. (The federal poverty level is $8,350 for an individual, $17,050 for a family of four for the year 2000). Thirty states have opted to extend coverage to the 185 percent level. This expansion is eminently pragmatic—expenditures on prenatal care are widely considered to be highly cost-effective in avoiding future health care costs. In 1995, Medicaid paid for 39 percent of the 3.1 million births in the United States, and in some states it paid for more than half.

aid expenditures, upon the implementation of SSI. To avoid this problem, Section 209(b) permits states to use any Medicaid financial eligibility level between what they used in 1972 and current SSI levels. About a dozen states currently choose the § 209(b) option.

Second, Medicaid coverage has expanded to cover children. States must now cover all children under age six with family incomes below 133 percent of the poverty level and children under age 19 born after 1983 in families with incomes up to 100 percent of the poverty level. They may also cover infants in families with incomes up to 185 percent of the poverty level. Medicaid currently covers about one fifth of the children in the United States, and by the year 2002, all children in poverty will be eligible for Medicaid. Most Medicaid recipients (51.8 percent) are children, but children are very cheap to cover, accounting for only 15.1 percent of Medicaid expenditures.

Third, Medicaid has become a Medicare supplement policy for low-income Medicare recipients. Under amendments adopted in the late 1980s and early 1990s, Medicaid must cover the Medicare premiums and cost-sharing obligations for "Qualified Medicare Beneficiaries", Medicare eligible individuals whose income does not exceed 100 percent of the poverty level. It must also cover Medicare Part B premiums for "Specified Low–Income Medicare Beneficiaries," persons who would otherwise qualify as QMBs except that their income is between 100 percent and 120 percent of the federal poverty level. Medicaid is also the nation's primary payor for nursing facility care (a service only marginally covered by Medicare) and provides outpatient prescription drug coverage for one tenth of Medicare beneficiaries. It thus covers, for its recipients, the two most problematic gaps in Medicare coverage.

Fourth, Medicaid has become our most important program for providing medical care to the disabled. The Supreme Court's decision in Sullivan v. Zebley, 493 U.S. 521, 110 S.Ct. 885, 107 L.Ed.2d 967 (1990), expanded SSI coverage of children, leading in turn to dramatic growth in Medicaid coverage of disabled children, since SSI recipients are generally eligible for Medicaid. Though the 1996 PRWORA cut back on SSI eligibility for children, it also provided that children formerly eligible for SSI could continue to receive Medicaid. Medicaid continues to cover, therefore, many disabled children. Further, many states provide home and community based care services to disabled persons under federal Medicaid waiver programs, which permit the use of more liberal eligibility standards than those that normally govern Medicaid eligibility under certain circumstances. Finally, 1997 Balanced Budget Act and the Ticket to Work and Work Incentives Improvement Act of 1999 have permitted states to cover working disabled persons whose income would otherwise have rendered them ineligible for Medicaid, or who would otherwise have lost eligibility coverage due to "medical improvement". The disabled are a very expensive group of Medicaid enrollees. Though they constitute 16.8 percent of enrollees, they account for 37.5 percent of expenditures.

In the end, therefore, it is useful to think of there being not one but several Medicaid programs. First, Medicaid is our national program for providing prenatal and postnatal care for poor mothers and infants. Second (Medicaid, supplemented by the SCHIP program described below) is our national health insurance program for children, covering about one fifth of all children in the United States. Only about half of these children are on welfare, over one third live in two parent families, and more than half have at least one working parent. Third, Medicaid is our federal Medicare supplement policy and catastrophic care program for the poor elderly. This is one of Medicaid's most expensive functions. Though the elderly make up only about 10 percent of Medicaid recipients, they account for almost 28 percent of

Medicaid expenditures. Over one quarter of Medicaid expenditures are for nursing home care, and another 9 percent for home health care. Fourth, Medicaid is our national health insurance program for the disabled, including severely disabled children of middle-class families. It pays, for example, for 40 percent of the care provided to persons with AIDS and for much of the institutional care required by the severely mentally disabled. Finally, in addition, Medicaid finances the core of programs in a number of states that have attempted to use Medicaid waivers and state funds to insure poor persons not otherwise eligible for Medicaid. See Sharon Silow–Carroll, et al., State and Local Initiatives to Enhance Health Coverage for the Working Uninsured (Commonwealth Fund, 2000).

Medicaid is, however, far from a comprehensive health insurance program for the poor. About 10 million children in the United States remain uninsured, despite recent expansions in Medicaid. Medicaid does not cover non-disabled childless couples or single individuals, no matter how poor they are. Coverage also still varies significantly from state to state, both because states differ in their cash assistance eligibility levels and because states make more or less generous choices with respect to coverage of optional categories or participation in waiver programs.

Medicaid also fails to cover many persons who in fact are in eligible categories. PRWORA specifically provided, for example, that families who lost cash assistance because of the end of the AFDC program should continue to be eligible for Medicaid. 42 U.S.C.A. §§ 1396a(a)(10)(A)(i)(I), 1396u–1(a). Nevertheless, following the implementation of TANF, Medicaid coverage of families dropped significantly. Much of this decline seems to have been due to states improperly terminating Medicaid coverage or discouraging Medicaid applications as their enthusiasm for ending "welfare as we know it" spilled over onto the Medicaid program. See Sara Rosenbaum and Kathleen A. Maloy, The Law of Unintended Consequences: The 1996 Personal Responsibility and Work Opportunity Reconciliation Act and Its Impact on Medicaid for Families with Children, 60 Ohio St. L.J. 1443 (1999).

The best source of information on Medicaid eligibility and coverage is the Kaiser Family Foundation website, www.kff.org, which offers online a wide variety of studies addressing Medicaid issues. Also useful is the Health Care Financing Administration's Medicaid Chartbook, available at www.hcfa.gov/stats/2Tchartbk.pdf. Another excellent source that came out just as this book was going to press is the winter 2001 Symposium issue of the Saint Louis University Law Journal on Reconceptualizing Medicaid.

Note: The Policy Context of Medicaid Eligibility

Determining who should be covered by welfare programs such as Medicaid poses intractable public policy problems. First, limiting Medicaid eligibility to individuals and families with very low incomes creates significant disincentive for poor persons to become employed. Part-time jobs and jobs that pay at or near minimum wage levels often come without health insurance. If a family has any significant medical needs, it can be worse off if its wage earners work at low paying jobs without health benefits than it would be with less income but Medicaid. 42 U.S.C. § 13964–6(a), which permits families of persons who lose TANF eligibility because of increased income from employment to continue to receive Medicaid for up to six months thereafter, is a partial response to this problem. The 1999 Ticket to Work legislation for the disabled is another.

The role of assets in determining eligibility is as important as the role of income. Sooner or later most persons who require long-term nursing facility care become impoverished, regardless of their financial status at the time they entered a nursing facility. Medicaid eligibility requirements mandate that such persons "spend down" their assets until they reach Medicaid asset eligibility levels, and thereafter spend all of their income except a very small personal needs allowance on their medical care, with Medicaid paying the difference between the amount the recipient can pay and the allowed nursing facility reimbursement level. A temptation exists, therefore, for persons who anticipate the need for nursing home care to transfer their assets to their children or to others in order to establish premature Medicaid eligibility. They may also be tempted (or advised by lawyers who specialize in Medicaid planning) to put their assets into a trust so that they can continue to enjoy the benefit of the assets until such time as nursing home care is required. Finally, if the institutionalized individual leaves behind a spouse in the community, it is necessary to provide for the needs of the community spouse at some decent level before directing the income of the institutionalized spouse toward the cost of care.

Beginning in 1980, Congress (encouraged by the states and the long term care insurance industry) adopted a series of laws attempting to deter asset transfers intended to create eligibility. In response, attorneys who specialize in Medicaid planning became increasingly creative in devising strategies for circumventing these restrictions. In a series of budget reconciliation acts, Congress became increasingly restrictive. Finally, in a fit of pique, Congress adopted as part of the 1996 Health Insurance Portability and Accountability Act a provision stipulating that a person who "knowingly and willfully disposes of assets (including by any transfer in trust) in order for an individual to become eligible for medical assistance under [Medicaid], if disposing of the assets results in the imposition of a period of ineligibility for [Medicaid]" is guilty of a federal crime. Pub.L. 104–191, § 217. This "granny goes to jail" provision provoked a public outcry, and the following year Congress revoked the rule, putting in its place a statute providing that a person who "knowingly and willfully counsels or assists an individual to dispose of assets" to become eligible for Medicaid could be fined $10,000 and imprisoned for a year. 42 U.S.C.A. § 1320a–7b(a)(6). Attorney General Reno refused to defend the constitutionality of this provision, and its enforcement was enjoined. New York State Bar Association v. Reno, 999 F.Supp. 710 (N.D.N.Y. 1998). See Note, John M. Broderick, To Transfer or Not to Transfer: Congress Failed to Stiff Penalties for Medicaid Estate Planning, But Should the Practice Continue? 6 Elder L. J. 257 (1999).

For all of the passion that Medicaid estate planning unleashes among law makers, it does not appear to be a major cause of expenditures to state Medicaid programs. See Joshua M. Wiender, Can Medicaid Long–Term Care Expenditures for the Elderly be Reduced? 36 Gerontologist 800 (1996). It is one of the few areas of Medicaid representation of interest to the private bar, however, and results in a steady trickle of articles in practitioner bar journals.

Significant public policy issues are also encountered if Medicaid eligibility is considered in the context of the potential support networks in which Medicaid recipients are found. Most poor persons have families, which may or may not themselves be impoverished. One of the pervasive tensions in welfare programs is the conflict between familial and social responsibility. Should adult children be responsible for the medical expenses of their indigent elderly parents? Is it fair for elderly persons to expect the taxpayers to finance their medical care through Medicaid rather than look to their children for help? On the other hand, is it fair to require children of indigent parents to contribute to their support, when our society does not otherwise expect adult children to support their parents? What effect would such a requirement have on parent-child relationships? Would it perpetuate a cycle of poverty? Might the cost of collecting exceed the funds collected? Should children be responsible for the cost of care of parents who did not support them when they were young or who abused them? See Norman Daniels, Just Health Care (1985); Charles Brecher & James Knickman, A Reconsideration of Long–Term–Care Policy, 10 J.Health Pol. Pol'y and L. 245, 264–6 (1985); Daniel Callahan, What Kind of Life: The Limits of Medical Progress (1990); James Callahan, et al., Responsibility of Families for their Severely Disabled Adults, 1 Health Care Fin.Rev. 29 (Winter, 1980); Norman Daniels, Family Responsibility Initiatives and Justice Between Age Groups, 13 Law, Medicine & Health Care 153 (1985).

The Medicaid act expressly forbids holding adult children responsible for the care of their parents, 42 U.S.C.A. § 1986a(a)(17)(D). In 1982, the Health Care Financing Administration (HCFA) suggested that the states could compel filial support through their family responsibility laws, see Toby Edelman, Family Supplementation in Nursing Homes, 18 Clearinghouse Rev. 504 (1984). Many states have such laws on the books (which date back to the Elizabethan poor laws), but they are seldom enforced, and the states declined HCFA's suggestion. The idea may not be dead, however. The budget bill adopted by the Republican Congress in 1995, but vetoed by President Clinton, would have permitted states to require adult children of Medicaid recipients to contribute to the cost of nursing facility or other long term care services if the adult child's income was at or above the median income of the state.

Should parents bear the full burden of the very expensive care required by severely disabled children in nursing facilities? Institutionalized disabled children are currently eligible regardless of the wealth of their families because SSI eligibility rules do not attribute the income or resources of parents to a child who has been institutionalized for more than 30 days. States electing the "Katie Beckett" Medicaid option can also provide Medicaid coverage to noninstitutionalized disabled children who are being cared for in their homes, but who would be eligible for SSI if institutionalized. In states not electing this option, middle class parents may need to institutionalize their children to get Medicaid coverage.

Should the federal government mandate state coverage of particular groups? What explains the current law's choice of some groups for mandated eligibility, others for optional coverage? Would removal of a federal mandate in fact result in other groups being dropped from coverage? Which groups would most likely be dropped in your state? Why?

B. BENEFITS

As is true with eligibility, the benefits provided by state Medicaid programs vary from state to state. The Medicaid statute lists twenty-six categories of services that states may cover, but also permits under a twenty-seventy category coverage of "any other medical care, and any other type of remedial care recognized under State law, specified by the Secretary"; 42 U.S.C.A. § 1396d(a)(27). At least one state has covered acupuncture under this category. The original Medicaid law required the states to provide comprehensive services by 1975, Public Law No. 89–97, § 1903(e), but this deadline was first delayed and then abandoned. Currently states must provide the categorically needy with inpatient hospital services; outpatient hospital services and rural health clinic services; other laboratory and X-ray services; nursing facility services; rural and federally-qualified health center services; early and period-ic screening, diagnostic and treatment (EPSDT) services for children; family planning services and supplies; physicians' services; and nurse-midwife and other certified nurse practitioner services. 42 U.S.C.A. § 1396a(a)(10)(A).

States have considerably more discretion in covering the medically needy. There are some limits to this discretion, however. States that elect to offer coverage to the medically needy must provide ambulatory care for children and prenatal and delivery services for pregnant women, 42 U.S.C.A. § 1396a(a)(10)(C)(iii)(II) and states that provide institutional services for any group must also cover ambulatory services, 42 U.S.C.A. § 1396a(a)(10)(C)(iii). Moreover, if a state covers institutional care for the mentally ill or retarded, it must also provide them either the services it provides to the categorically needy or any seven services offered generally to Medicaid recipients, and if a state covers nursing facility services, it must also pay for home health services 42 U.S.C.A. § 1396a(a)(10)(C)(iv). What policy considerations explain these requirements?

A striking feature of the benefit packages provided by Medicaid is its emphasis on institutional care. In 1998, 50 percent of Medicaid payments went to hospitals and nursing homes (compared to about 41 percent of personal health care expenditures generally). Medicaid pays for almost half of the nursing home care provided in the United States, almost ten times the amount paid for by private insurance. About 4/5 of Medicaid nursing facility expenditures are for the elderly, and about 3/4 of these funds are for persons not otherwise eligible for cash assistance. Medicaid also pays for much of the care provided by intermediate care facilities for the mentally disabled. Most of the residents of nursing facilities and ICF–MRs are very debilitated, physically and mentally. Many of these people would not have survived in other periods in history or in other cultures. Medicaid is, in a very real sense, the cost that we pay as a society for valuing the lives of these persons.

While all state Medicaid programs cover hospital, skilled nursing care, and intermediate care services, some states do not cover optional services such as podiatry, dental care, eyeglasses, or dentures. Further, when economic conditions or federal cutbacks have resulted in state Medicaid cutbacks, as they did in the early 1980s, the optional services are the first to go.

What explains the choice of services covered under Medicaid or dropped in lean times? Does Medicaid cover services that are most vital to health or that are most cost-effective? Are covered services those that poor persons or elderly persons would themselves choose to have covered if they were purchas-ing insurance? Why does Medicaid cover some services for which private insurance is not generally purchased, such as nursing home care? What role might provider associations, their lawyers and lobbyists play in determining benefit coverage? Might services currently available under Medicaid mirror those covered by health programs previously financed by the states with their own money before federal matching funds became available (many of the residents of ICF–MRs were formerly in state mental institutions)?

In considering these questions, it is important to realize that Medicaid, like Medicare, does not just purchase services for its beneficiaries, but also plays a vital role in supporting the nation's health care infrastructure. Medicaid disproportionate share payments to hospitals that provide a disproportionate amount of care to Medicaid and uninsured patients, and thus cannot rely on private pay patients to cross-subsidize the burden of caring for these patients, constitute almost 10 percent of Medicaid expenditures. Medicaid pays for much of the obstetric and pediatric care delivered in the United States, and plays a vital role in supporting teaching hospitals. Medicaid is largely responsible, therefore, for there being a safety net in the United States even for those not eligible for Medicaid itself.

States must also determine coverage of particular items and services, and of particular persons, under their Medicaid programs. The following case considers the constraints they face in doing so.

HERN v. BEYE

United States Court of Appeals, Tenth Circuit, 1995.
57 F.3d 906.

TACHA, CIRCUIT JUDGE.

Plaintiffs are a physician and three women's health care facilities that provide abortion services to women in Colorado. They brought this action * * * to enjoin the defendant Karen Beye, the executive director of Colorado's Department of Social Services, from enforcing Colo. Const. art. V, § 50, Colo.Rev.Stat. §§ 26–4–105.5, 26–4–512, and 26–15–104.5, and 10 Colo.Code Regs. § 2505–10 (8.733). * * *

I

By initiative, the voters of Colorado amended the state's constitution in 1984 to add the following section:

No public funds shall be used by the State of Colorado, its agencies or political subdivisions to pay or otherwise reimburse, either directly or indirectly, any person, agency or facility for the performance of any induced abortion, PROVIDED HOWEVER, that the General Assembly, by specific bill, may authorize and appropriate funds to be used for those medical services necessary to prevent the death of either a pregnant woman or her unborn child under circumstances where every reasonable effort is made to preserve the life of each.

Colo. Const. art. V, § 50. Colorado has incorporated the mandate of section 50 into its statutes, * * *

In 1976, eleven years after the creation of the Medicaid program, Congress passed the Hyde Amendment, * * * Congress has subsequently altered the Hyde Amendment several times. The version in force from 1981 until 1993 prohibited the use of federal funds for abortions "except where the life of the mother would be endangered if the fetus were carried to term." [ ]

On October 22, 1993, President Clinton signed into law * * * a new version of the Hyde Amendment that expanded the category of abortions for which federal funds are available under Medicaid. [ ]

None of the funds appropriated under this Act shall be expended for any abortion except when it is made known to the Federal entity or official to which funds are appropriated under this Act that such procedure is necessary to save the life of the mother or that the pregnancy is the result of an act of rape or incest.

On November 8, 1993, plaintiffs brought this action seeking injunctive relief. They claimed that, because Colorado's funding restriction denies coverage for abortions for which federal funds are available under the 1994 Hyde Amendment—namely, abortions to terminate pregnancies resulting from rape or incest—Colorado's Medicaid program violates mandatory federal requirements. * * * The district court granted plaintiffs injunctive relief, enjoining defendant from enforcing Colorado's abortion funding restriction to the extent that it conflicts with federal law. Defendant now appeals.

II

Title XIX of the Social Security Act of 1965, 42 U.S.C.A. §§ 1396–1396v, establishes Medicaid, a jointly funded federal-state program designed to finance medical care for indigent Americans. Its stated purpose is to "enabl[e] each State, as far as practicable under the conditions in such State, to furnish ... medical assistance [to those persons] whose income and resources are insufficient to meet the costs of necessary medical services." 42 U.S.C.A. § 1396. Each state's participation in Medicaid is purely optional. [ ] But "[o]nce a State voluntarily chooses to participate in Medicaid, the State must comply with the requirements of Title XIX and applicable regulations." [ ]* * *

The Hyde Amendment circumscribes participating states' obligations to fund abortions under Medicaid. On its face, the Hyde Amendment appears to be only an appropriations measure; it merely prohibits the use of federal funds for certain services. But in Harris v. McRae, 448 U.S. at 297, 100 S.Ct. at 2677–78, the Supreme Court construed the Hyde Amendment as indirectly modifying states' obligations under Title XIX. The plaintiffs in McRae contended that, despite the Hyde Amendment, Title XIX required states to fund all medically necessary abortions, including those for which federal funds were unavailable. [ ] The Court, however, reasoned that "Title XIX was designed as a cooperative program of shared financial responsibility, not as a device for the Federal Government to compel a State to provide services that Congress itself is unwilling to fund." [ ] As a result, by the normal operation of Title XIX, even if a State were otherwise required to include medically necessary abortions in its Medicaid plan, the withdrawal of federal funding under the Hyde Amendment would operate to relieve the State of that obligation for those abortions for which federal reimbursement is unavailable. [ ]

* * *

Importantly, however, the Hyde Amendment does not affect states' underlying obligations imposed by Title XIX and federal Medicaid regulations. That is, although the Hyde Amendment relieves states of having to fund abortions for which federal funding is unavailable, it does not alter states' obligations with respect to abortions for which federal funding is available. Because the 1994 Hyde Amendment permits federal funding for abortions to end pregnancies resulting from rape or incest, the only issue here is whether Colorado's funding restriction contravenes the requirements of Title XIX and accompanying regulations.

III

Title XIX requires participating states to provide medical assistance to the "categorically needy"—individuals who qualify for Medicaid because they receive some form of federal cash assistance (e.g., Aid to Families with Dependent Children or Supplemental Security Income). 42 U.S.C.A. § 1396a(a)(10)(A)(i); 42 C.F.R. § 436.100–.128. States may also, at their option, cover "medically needy" individuals—persons who do not qualify as categorically needy but nevertheless cannot afford adequate medical care. 42 U.S.C.A. § 1396a(a)(10)(A)(ii); 42 C.F.R. § 436.300–.330.

While states have considerable flexibility in determining the scope of their Medicaid coverage, * * * Title XIX requires states to cover at least seven general categories of medical services for categorically needy individuals, 42 U.S.C.A. § 1396a(a); id. § 1396d(a)(1)–(5), (17), (21); 42 C.F.R. § 440.210. Abortion falls under several of these "mandatory coverage" categories, including "inpatient hospital services," 42 U.S.C.A. § 1396d(a)(1), "outpatient hospital services," id. § 1396d(a)(2)(A), "family planning services," id. § 1396d(a)(4)(C), and "physicians' services furnished by a physician," id. § 1396d(a)(5)(A).

Participating states are not required, however, to fund all medical services falling under one of the mandatory coverage categories.[ ] Rather, Title XIX "confers broad discretion on the States to adopt standards for determining the extent of medical assistance" offered in their Medicaid programs.[ ] In addition, federal Medicaid regulations expressly permit participating states to "place appropriate limits on a service based on such criteria as medical necessity or on utilization control procedures." 42 C.F.R. § 440.230(d).

Nonetheless, there are important restrictions on states in their exercise of this discretion. * * * First, Title XIX requires participating states to establish "reasonable standards ... for determining ... the extent of medical assistance under [their Medicaid] plan which ... are consistent with the objectives of [Title XIX]." 42 U.S.C.A. § 1396a(a)(17). Second, state Medicaid plans "may not arbitrarily deny or reduce the amount, duration, or scope of [such] service[s] ... to an otherwise eligible recipient solely because of the diagnosis, type of illness, or condition." 42 C.F.R. § 440.230(c).

IV

Colorado's restriction on abortion funding is essentially a limit based on the patient's degree of medical necessity pursuant to 42 C.F.R. § 440.230(d): It restricts Medicaid funding for abortions to those instances when the expectant mother's life is at stake. We conclude that this restriction violates the requirements of federal law—requirements that Colorado is compelled to follow as a condition of its participation in Medicaid.

First, Colorado's Medicaid program as amended by the abortion funding restriction impermissibly discriminates in its coverage of abortions on the basis of a patient's diagnosis and condition. While 42 C.F.R. § 440.230(c) allows states to use medical need as a criterion for placing appropriate limits on coverage, a state may not single out a particular, medically necessary service and restrict coverage to those instances where the patient's life is at risk.[ ] Such a "policy denies service solely on the basis of diagnosis or condition, and does so arbitrarily because the denial is not in accordance with a uniform standard of medical need."[ ] Indeed, "[w]hen a state singles out one particular medical condition . . . and restricts treatment for that condition to life and death situations it has . . . crossed the line between permissible discrimination based on degree of need and entered into forbidden discrimination based on medical condition."[ ]

Second, Colorado's restriction violates 42 U.S.C.A. § 1396a(a)(17) because it is inconsistent with the basic objective of Title XIX—to provide qualified individuals with medically necessary care. The purpose of Medicaid as stated in the Act is to enable states to provide medical treatment to needy persons "whose income and resources are insufficient to meet the cost of necessary medical services." Id. § 1396 This circuit, as well as several other courts, has interpreted Title XIX and its accompanying regulations as imposing a general obligation on states to fund those mandatory coverage services that are medically necessary.[ ]

It may be that, pursuant to a generally applicable funding restriction or utilization control procedure, a participating state could deny coverage for a service deemed medically necessary in a particular case.[ ] But a state law that categorically denies coverage for a specific, medically necessary procedure except in those rare instances when the patient's life is at stake is not a "reasonable standard[ ] . . . consistent with the objectives of [the Act]," 42 U.S.C.A. § 1396a(a)(17), but instead contravenes the purposes of Title XIX.[ ]

* * *

Finally, our interpretation of Title XIX and the Medicaid regulations plainly comports with Congress' understanding of the effect of passing the 1994 Hyde Amendment. The floor debates in the Senate and the House of Representatives reveal Congress's understanding that participating states must fund those abortions for which federal funds are available. For instance, Senator Hatch stated that if the Hyde Amendment were repealed, "every State will be required to provide matching funds for abortion on demand." * * *

We acknowledge that Colorado "has legitimate interests from the outset of the pregnancy in protecting . . . the life of the fetus that may become a child."[ ] We also recognize that Colorado "has a valid and important interest in encouraging childbirth."[ ] If Colorado chose not to participate in Medicaid, it would not be required to fund any abortions whatsoever.[ ] But because Colorado has decided to participate and accept federal Medicaid funds, it must do so on the terms established by Congress. So long as Colorado continues to participate in Medicaid, it cannot deny Medicaid funding for abortions to qualified women who are the victims of rape or incest.

* * *

[Judgment affirmed]

Notes and Questions

1.   Who should make coverage decisions under the Medicaid program: the personal physicians of beneficiaries, low level bureaucrats, national professional consensus groups, grass roots consensus panels? What should be the relationship between the federal and state governments in making coverage decisions? In particular, what role should the federal courts play?

2.   A state's Medicaid plan must specify the amount, duration, and scope of each service that it provides for the categorically needy and each group of the medically needy. 42 C.F.R. § 440.230(a). Each service must be of sufficient amount, duration, and scope to achieve its purpose reasonably. 42 C.F.R. § 440.230(b). The Medicaid agency may not arbitrarily deny or reduce the amount, duration, or scope of a required service solely because of the diagnosis, type of illness, or condition. 42 C.F.R. § 440.230(c). Thus a state provision covering eyeglasses for individuals suffering from eye disease, but not for individuals with refractive error, was invalidated, White v. Beal, 555 F.2d 1146 (3d Cir.1977), as was a $50,000 cap on payment for hospital services which precluded coverage of $200,000 liver transplants, Montoya v. Johnston, 654 F.Supp. 511 (W.D.Tex.1987), and a state's refusal to cover sex reassignment surgery, Smith v. Rasmussen, 57 F.Supp.2d 736 (N.D.Iowa 1999).

In 1998 HCFA issued an instruction directing the states to cover payment for Viagra under similar provisions found in 42 U.S.C.A. 1396r–8 dealing with drug coverage. This direction unleashed a storm of protest from the states, and almost led to new legislation, though HCFA in a subsequent instruction pointed out that only 10 percent of Medicaid recipients are adult males, thus the burden on the states should not be extraordinary.

Why is Medicaid coverage so comprehensive, indeed in some instances more comprehensive than private insurance, and certainly more comprehensive than Medicare coverage? Why are the courts (at least sometimes), open to recipient complaints when coverage of services is denied? Early in 2001, a committee of the National Governors' Association proposed changing Medicaid into a program that would cover more of the population, but with less generous benefits. Is this a good idea?

3.   One of the most innovative, and controversial, approaches to determining coverage has been that of Oregon. In the early 1990s, Oregon proposed to expand its Medicaid program to cover all persons under the poverty line, increasing by 120,000 the 243,000 persons then covered by Medicaid. It proposed to do this by ranking 688 health services and denying coverage for low ranked procedures. It asked for a waiver from a number of the requirements of the Medicaid program to implement this proposal. The Bush (the elder) Administration denied the Oregon waiver request in 1992 because of concerns that the proposed Oregon program would violate the Americans with Disabilities Act by denying coverage for some services to persons with certain disabilities. For example, the rationing program originally proposed by Oregon would have denied liver transplants for alcoholic cirrhosis or for extremely low-birth-weight babies under twenty-three weeks gestation. The Clinton Administration approved a revised waiver request in 1993. The waiver was approved conditional upon Oregon meeting certain requirements that would lessen the impact of considerations of disability on prioritizing treatments.

Oregon's program seems to have been largely successful—It has expanded a fairly generous package of coverage to 130,000 persons not previously covered. It has done so, on the other hand, primarily by increasing funding from general revenues and a tobacco tax, and by holding the line on expenses through managed care. The "rationing" has proved an important political tool to refocus political debate on what should be covered rather than who. See Howard M. Leichter, Oregon's Bold Experiment: Whatever Happened to Rationing? 24 J. Health Pol., Pol'y & L 147 (1999); Lawrence Jacobs, et al., The Oregon Health Plan and the Political Paradox of Rationing, 24 J. Health Pol., Pol'y & L 161 (1999).

4. Does the Constitution have any relevance to the question of whether certain items or services should be covered by public benefits programs? Harris v. McRae, 448 U.S. 297, 100 S.Ct. 2671, 65 L.Ed.2d 784 (1980) addressed the constitutionality of the original Hyde Amendment. In upholding the Hyde amendment against due process and equal protection challenges, Justice Stewart wrote for the court

> * * * [R]egardless of whether the freedom of a woman to choose to terminate her pregnancy for health reasons lies at the core or the periphery of the due process liberty recognized in Roe v. Wade, 410 U.S. 113, 93 S.Ct. 705, 35 L.Ed.2d 147 (1973), it simply does not follow that a woman's freedom of choice carries with it a constitutional entitlement to the financial resources to avail herself of the full range of protected choices. * * * Although the liberty protected by the Due Process Clause affords protection against unwarranted government interference with freedom of choice in the context of certain personal decisions, it does not confer an entitlement to such funds as may be necessary to realize all the advantages of that freedom * * *

Harris v. McRae, 448 U.S. 297, 100 S.Ct. 2671, 65 L.Ed.2d 784 (1980).

Since Harris v. McRae, several state supreme courts have recognized a state constitutional right to have Medicaid pay for abortions as it does other medical procedures. See Right to Choose v. Byrne, 91 N.J. 287, 450 A.2d 925 (1982); Moe v. Secretary of Administration and Finance, 382 Mass. 629, 417 N.E.2d 387 (1981); Committee to Defend Reproductive Rights v. Myers, 29 Cal.3d 252, 172 Cal.Rptr. 866, 625 P.2d 779 (1981). In these states, the state pays 100 percent of these costs, as federal financial participation is not available for the costs of abortions except where necessary to save the mother's life or in cases of rape or incest.

5. Various civil rights acts might also limit state discretion in determining what benefits to provide under the Medicaid program. In Olmstead v. L.C., 527 U.S. 581, 119 S.Ct. 2176, 144 L.Ed.2d 540 (1999), Justice Ginsburg, writing for a majority of the Court concluded that, under Title II of the Americans with Disabilities Act of 1990 (ADA), and implementing regulations requiring public entities to administer "programs in the most integrated setting appropriate to the needs of qualified individuals with disabilities." 28 CFR § 35.130(d), the state of Georgia was obligated to care for persons with mental disabilities in community-based programs rather than state institutions, when the state's treatment professionals had concluded that community placement was appropriate, the transfer from institutional care to a less restrictive setting was not opposed by the affected individual, and the placement could reasonably be accommodated, taking into account the resources available to the State and the needs of others with mental disabilities. The Court noted specifically that since 1981, the federal Medicaid program had provided funding for state-run home and community-based care through a waiver program, and did not as a matter of policy favor institutional over community-based treatment.

Justice Ginsburg, joined by Justice O'Connor, Justice Souter, and Justice Breyer, concluded in Part III—B of the opinion that the State's responsibility to provide community-based treatment to qualified persons with disabilities was not unlimited. The State, they contended, should be allowed to show that, in allocating available resources, immediate relief for the plaintiffs would be inequitable given the State's responsibility to care for a large and diverse population of persons with mental disabilities. The opinion further stated that the ADA did not obligate the state to eliminate institutions for the mentally disabled, which might be appropriate for some patients. The opinion approved a rationing approach to allocation of places in community-based facilities. Ginsburg stated that, if the State were to demonstrate that it had a comprehensive, effectively working plan for placing qualified persons with mental disabilities in less restrictive settings, and a waiting list that moved at a reasonable pace not controlled by the State's endeavors to keep its institutions fully populated, persons at the top of the community-based treatment waiting list should not be displaced by individuals lower down simply because they had sued under the ADA.

The continued possibility of ADA actions against the states is to some extent limited by the Supreme Court's recent decision of Board of Trustees v. Garrett, ___ U.S. ___, 121 S.Ct. 955, 148 L.Ed.2d 866 (2001), which upheld the sovereign immunity of the states against ADA Title I actions. The Court expressly, however, declined to rule in *Garrett* on the continued vitality of Title II actions against the states, and *Olmstead* is a Title II action. See *Garrett*, supra, at note 1.

6. Title VI addressing racial disparities also applies, at least in theory, to Medicaid. Very few successful cases have been brought against Medicaid programs, however, based on race discrimination. One such case held a state's policy of letting nursing homes put a limit on their number of nursing home beds to violate Title VI because of its disparate impact on minorities, see, Linton v. Carney, 779 F.Supp. 925 (M.D.Tenn.1990).

C. PAYMENT FOR SERVICES

1. *Fee-for-Service Medicaid*

The original vision of the Medicaid program was that it would provide mainstream care for its recipients. The Medicaid statute guaranteed recipients free choice of participating providers. 42 U.S.C.A. § 1396a(a)(23). With respect to access to physician services, however, this goal has always been more a dream than a reality. Physicians also have freedom of choice as to whether or not to participate in Medicaid. Medicaid physician fee schedules have been largely driven by state budget constraints, and low Medicaid fees have discouraged physician participation in the program. One recent study found that on average Medicaid only pays physicians about 64 percent of Medicare rates, which are themselves well below private rates. The situation is also getting worse: as recently as 1993, Medicaid fees had been 75 percent of Medicare fees. Stephen Norton and Stephen Zuckerman, Trends in Medicaid Physician Fees, 1993–1998, 19 Health Aff., July/Aug. 2000, 222. Low fee levels, along with paperwork and billing hassles, have contributed to low physician participation in Medicaid. A 1992 study found that only 65 percent of physicians who were accepting new patients were accepting Medicaid patients, and primary care physicians were less likely to accept Medicaid than other physicians. Physician Payment Assessment Commission, Annual Report to Congress, 349–366 (1994).

Fee-for-service Medicaid recipients have also received a very distinctive sort of physician care. One study of pediatricians who treated a high volume of Medicaid patients in New York City, for example, found that 91 percent had attended Medical schools outside the United States, only 42 percent were board certified (compared to 89 percent statewide), and only 49 percent had hospital admitting privileges. Gerry Fairbrother, et al., New York City Physicians Serving High Volumes of Medicaid Children, 32 Inquiry 345 (Fall 1995). When physicians are not readily available, Medicaid recipients have often had to often rely on hospital outpatient clinics and emergency rooms for primary care.

Hospitals and nursing homes are more limited in their ability to refuse Medicaid patients. Many hospitals are obligated to serve Medicaid patients because of their tax exempt status or because of lingering obligations under the Hill–Burton program (see chapter 11). Few nursing homes can count on enough private pay business to permit them to decline Medicaid participation.

Until 1997, hospitals and nursing facilities enjoyed some protection under the Boren Amendment, enacted in 1980, which required States to pay these institutions rates "reasonable and adequate to meet the costs which must be incurred by efficiently and economically operated facilities" former 42 U.S.C.A. § 1396a(a)(13)(A). In Wilder v. Virginia Hosp. Ass'n, 496 U.S. 498, 110 S.Ct. 2510, 110 L.Ed.2d 455 (1990) the Supreme Court permitted providers to enforce the terms of the Boren Amendment under 42 U.S.C.A. § 1983. This unleased a flood of litigation brought by providers seeking increased rates.

The 1997 Balanced Budget Act repealed the Boren Amendment, putting in its place a much less burdensome process that requires the states to publish proposed rates, including the methodologies underlying them and the justifications supporting them; afford providers, beneficiaries, and others a reasonable opportunity to comment on them; and publish final rates, their methodologies and justifications. 42 U.S.C.A. § 1396a(a)(13)(A). Subsequent court decisions have held that the new provision does not create rights enforceable by providers. Children's Seashore House v. Waldman, 197 F.3d 654 (3d Cir. 1999); HCMF Corp. v. Gilmore, 26 F.Supp.2d 873 (W.D.Va.1998).

The 1997 Balanced Budget Act did not necessarily end litigation over Medicaid rates, however. Federal Medicaid law also requires payment rates to be "consistent with efficiency, economy, and quality of care and * * * sufficient to enlist enough providers so that care and services are available under the plan at least to the extent that such care and services are available to the general population in the geographic area." 42 U.S.C.A. § 1396a(a)(30). Several courts have held that this statute gives providers enforceable rights, Orthopaedic Hospital v. Belshe, 103 F.3d 1491 (9th Cir.1997); Arkansas Medical Soc'y v. Reynolds, 6 F.3d 519 (8th Cir.1993); Visiting Nurse Ass'n of N. Shore, Inc. v. Bullen, 93 F.3d 997 (1st Cir.1996). But see Evergreen

Presbyterian Ministries v. Hood, 235 F.3d 908 (5th Cir.2000) (beneficiaries have right to sue under equal access provision, but not providers). Florida Pharmacy Ass'n v. Cook, 17 F.Supp.2d 1293 (N.D.Fla., 1998), rejected this position, however, while Minnesota HomeCare Ass'n, Inc. v. Gomez, 108 F.3d 917 (8th Cir.1997), and Rite Aid of Pennsylvania v. Houstoun, 171 F.3d 842 (3d Cir. 1999), have held that the provision does not compel the state to follow any particular methodology in rate-setting.

Should providers be able to sue in federal court to challenge state Medicaid rates? Are courts in fact competent to evaluate the complex issues involved in Medicaid rate setting? Are they more or less likely than state legislatures and agencies to discern and effectuate congressional intent? Compare, offering contrasting answers to these questions, Rand Rosenblatt, Statutory Interpretation and Distributive Justice: Medicaid Hospital Reimbursement and the Debate Over Public Choice, 35 St. Louis U. L. J. 793 (1991) with Gerard Anderson and Mark Hall, The Adequacy of Hospital Reimbursement Under Medicaid's Boren Amendment, 13 J. Leg. Med. 205 (1992).

2. *Medicaid Managed Care*

Though the original vision of Medicaid was that recipients would have the same free access to providers enjoyed by the general population, Medicaid has in recent years moved dramatically in the direction of managed care. By 1999, 17.8 million Medicaid beneficiaries (almost 56 percent) were enrolled in managed care, compared to 2.7 million in 1991. In twenty states, over 70 percent of Medicaid recipients were enrolled in managed care, and in three 100 percent were enrolled.

This move to managed care has been driven by several motivations. The most important, perhaps, has been the hope of saving money. Managed care seems to have cut costs in the private sector, and it was hoped that it would work for Medicaid as well. It was hoped, moreover, that managed care might not only reduce the price of services, but that it would also reduce inappropriate use of expensive services, like emergency room care. The move to managed care was also driven by the hope, however, that it would increase access by Medicaid recipients to providers, and improve quality and coordination of care. A number of states, including Tennessee and Oregon, also hoped that savings from managed care might enable them to expand coverage of low income uninsureds not otherwise eligible for Medicaid.

Attempts to move Medicaid recipients to managed care was thwarted for a time by federal requirements that guaranteed Medicaid recipients free choice of providers. In the late 1980s and 1990s, however, It became increasingly common for states to seek waivers under § 1915(b) of the Social Security Act (42 U.S.C.A. § 1396n(b)) which permits HCFA to waive the freedom of choice requirement, or under § 1115 (42 U.S.C.A. § 1315), which permits HCFA to waive virtually all statutory requirements in the context of approved research and demonstration projects.

Arizona, which had previously refused to establish a Medicaid program, set up a statewide Medicaid managed care program under an 1115 waiver in 1992. Arizona's program has matured over the years, and is now widely regarded as one of the most successful Medicaid managed care programs.

Tennessee launched its Tenncare program under an 1115 waiver in 1994, seeking both to control rapidly growing Medicaid costs and to expand dramatically coverage to the uninsured. Tennessee's program got off to a rocky start, both because the program was implemented very quickly and because Tennessee had had minimal experience with managed care before the program began. As the program matured, it has enjoyed some success, though it also has experienced difficulties, including most recently the withdrawal of from the program of Blue Cross/Blue Shield, which was by far its largest participant. See, analyzing the Tenncare program and the legal issues raised by managed care in great depth, James F. Blumstein and Frank A. Sloan, Health Care Reform Through Medicaid Managed Care: Tennessee (Tenncare) as a Case Study and a Paradigm, 53 Vand. L. Rev. 125 (2000). See, also reporting on the early Tenncare experience, Sidney Watson, Medicaid Physician Participation: Patients, Poverty, and Physician Self–Interest, 21 Am. J. L. & Med. 191 (1995).

The 1997 Balanced Budget Act amended the Medicaid statute to permit states to require recipients to enroll with a Medicaid Managed Care (MMC) organizations or primary care case manager. 42 U.S.C. § 1396u–2. States are not permitted, however, to require dual-eligible Medicare beneficiaries, Native Americans, or special need children to enroll in managed care plans without federal permission. States must generally permit recipients a choice of two or more MMC plans, but this requirement is loosened in rural areas. 42 U.S.C.A. § 1396u–2(a)(3). Medicaid recipients who do not exercise their choice may be assigned by the State through a default enrollment process, and states may establish enrollment priorities for plans that are oversubscribed. 42 U.S.C.A. § 1396u–2(a)(4)(C) & (D). Recipients may terminate (or change) enrollment in a MMC organization for cause at any time, but may only do so without cause during the 90 day period following enrollment and once a year thereafter. 42 U.S.C.A. § 1396u–2(a)(4)(A). MMC plans are not permitted to discriminate on the basis of health status or need for health service in enrollment, reenrollment, or disenrollment of recipients. 42 U.S.C.A. § 1396b(m)(2)(A)(v).

The federal law establishes a number of protections for MMC recipients. Recipients must be afforded access to services to evaluate and stabilize emergency medical conditions (as identified by a prudent lay person) without prior authorization requirements or provider participation limitations. 42 U.S.C.A. §§ 1396b(m)(2)(A)(vii); 1396u–2(b)(2). The statute prohibits MMC organizations from interfering with communications from health care professionals to beneficiaries, and requires plans to have in place grievance procedures. 42 U.S.C.A. § 1396u–2(b)(3) & (4).

States that operate MMC plans are required to develop and implement a quality improvement strategy that complies with standards developed by HCFA and addresses concerns of timely access to care, continuity of care, quality and appropriateness of care and services. 42 U.S.C.A. § 1396u–2(c)(1).

States must have available "intermediate sanctions" for dealing with MMC organizations that fail substantially to provide medically necessary items; impose unpermitted premiums or cost-sharing; discriminate among enrollees on the basis of health status or need for health services; misrepresent or present false information to HCFA or to enrollees, potential enrollees, or providers; or operate prohibited physician incentive plans. 42 U.S.C.A.

§ 1396u–2(3)(1). Intermediate sanctions include, among other possible actions, civil penalties of up to $25,000 ($100,000 for discrimination and false statements) 42 U.S.C.A. § 1396u–2(e)(2), (3), and (4); 1396b(m)(5). Regulations issued on the last day of the Clinton administration to implement these protections met with a storm of protest from managed care organizations and the states, and were put on hold by the administration of Bush the younger.

Medicaid managed care has, not surprisingly, a mixed record. Because Medicaid payment rates, particularly for physicians, had historically been very low, there has been little room for managed care to save money by forcing discounts from providers, as managed care does in the private sector. Safety net providers, which had been able to subsidize care for the uninsured through relatively generous Medicaid disproportionate share hospital payments and special cost reimbursement provisions for community health centers, were forced in a number of states to compete for managed care business with commercial MCOs, and often suffered financially. See, Bradford H. Gray and Catherine Rowe, Safety–Net Health Plans: A Status Report, 19 Health Aff., Jan./Feb. 2000 at 185. While commercial plans initially competed for Medicaid business, many of them lost money on Medicaid and withdrew from state programs by the late 1990s. See Sidney D. Watson, Commercialization of Medicaid, 45 St.Louis U.L.J. 53 (2001).

The states generally found it relatively easy to move children and their families to MMC. This population is relatively healthy and their care inexpensive and predictable. It has proved much more difficult to provide managed care for the disabled and elderly. These groups are, as was noted above, responsible for a much greater share of Medicaid costs. Discovering how to provide adequate behavioral health (mental health) services through managed care organizations has proved a particularly intractable problem. See, e.g., Mary Crossley, Medicaid Managed Care and Disability Discrimination Issues, 54 Tenn. L. Rev. 419 (1998); Cyril Chang, et al., TennCare Partners: Tennessee's Failed Managed Care Program for Mental Health and Substance Abuse, 11 JAMA 864 (1998); S.A. Somers, et al, The Coverage of Chronic Populations under Medicaid Managed Care: An Essay on Emerging Challenges, 65 Tenn. L. Rev. 649 (1998); Robert N., Swidler, Special Needs Plans: Adapting Medicaid Managed Care for Persons with Serious Mental Illness or HIV/AIDS, 61 Alb.L.Rev. 1113 (1998).

The success of Medicaid managed care, moreover, whether measured by savings in money or improvements in access or quality, has varied significantly from state to state. It has also changed within states over time, as political forces have fluctuated. In both Tennessee and Oregon administrations that had supported relatively generous MMC programs were followed by administrations more interested in saving money and less interested in expanding coverage.

An excellent overview of MMC is found in Remaking Medicaid: Managed Care for the Public Good (Stephen M. Davidson and Stephen A. Somers, eds. 1998). A good description of state oversight of MMC is found in James W. Fossett, Managing Medicaid Managed Care: Are States Becoming Prudent Purchasers? 19 Health Aff., July/Aug. 2000 at 36. The 2001 Symposium issue of the St. Louis Law Journal (Vol 45, Winter 2001) includes articles discussing a range of Medicaid and MMC issues. The Kaiser Family Foundation website (www.kff.org), also provides a continuous stream of useful information on MMC.

D. PROGRAM ADMINISTRATION: FEDERAL/STATE RELATION-SHIPS

Perhaps the most contentious of all of the controversial issues surrounding the Medicaid program is how the relationship between the federal and state governments in setting policy and administering the program should be structured. Particularly problematic has been the role of the federal courts in enforcing the rights that the program affords recipients and providers.

As of this writing in late 2000, Medicaid is a federal entitlement program administered and partially funded by the states. It is an entitlement program in the sense that the federal Medicaid statute and regulations create rights under federal law enforceable against the states. The federal government also contributes a share of the Medicaid program's cost, known as Federal Financial Participation or FFP, which currently ranges from 50 percent to 83 percent depending on the wealth of the recipient state.

The Medicaid programs are also in a very real sense state programs. As should be clear by now, state legislatures and Medicaid agencies have significant discretion in deciding what groups to cover, which benefits to provide, and how much to pay for benefits, and have had even more after the 1997 BBA than they had before. Nevertheless, states consider the federal role in the Medicaid program as intrusive and oppressive. The program is subject to federal oversight at several levels. States must submit a Medicaid state plan to HCFA demonstrating that its program conforms with the federal statutes and regulations. If a state Medicaid program ceases to be in substantial compliance with federal requirements, HCFA may, after a hearing, terminate its federal funding. Because this remedy is so drastic, HCFA has rarely convened a hearing and has never terminated a state program. See Patricia Butler, Legal Problems in Medicaid, in Ruth Roemer and George McCray, Legal Aspects of Health Policy: Issues and Trends, 214, 225 (1980). Additional statutory provisions permit HHS to disallow reimbursement claimed by the state where the services covered by the state (such as elective abortions) are not eligible for reimbursement, 42 U.S.C.A. § 1316d. These provisions are used more frequently, and occasionally result in litigation between the federal government and the states. For an excellent review of the range of administrative law issues involved in the governance of the Medicaid Program, see Eleanor Kinney, Rule and Policy Making for the Medicaid Program: A Challenge to Federalism, 51 Ohio St.L.J. 855 (1990).

The substantial federal contribution to state-operated programs has also permitted the federal government to force the states to toe the federal line on other issues of health policy, such as initiating certificate of need programs. This use of the federal spending power has generally been upheld by the courts. See North Carolina ex rel. Morrow v. Califano, 445 F.Supp. 532 (E.D.N.C.1977), affirmed mem., 435 U.S. 962, 98 S.Ct. 1597, 56 L.Ed.2d 54 (1978), Kenneth Wing and Andrew Silton, Constitutional Authority For Extending Federal Control over the Delivery of Health Care, 57 N.C. L. Rev. 1423 (1979).

Perhaps most objectionable to the states, however, is the fact that the courts have interpreted the federal Medicaid statute to permit both recipients and providers a federal cause of action under 42 U.S.C.A. § 1983 to sue for violations of rights guaranteed by the Medicaid statute. See, e.g. Wilder v. Virginia Hosp. Ass'n, 496 U.S. 498, 110 S.Ct. 2510, 110 L.Ed.2d 455 (1990); Boulet v. Cellucci, 107 F.Supp.2d 61 (D.Mass. 2000); Doe v. Chiles, 136 F.3d 709 (11th Cir.1998). Though the issue is far from settled, a number of federal courts also permit recipients to sue the states in federal court to enforce federal regulations, at least under some circumstances. Compare Boatman v. Hammons, 164 F.3d 286 (6th Cir.1998) and West Virginia Univ. Hosps., Inc. v. Casey, 885 F.2d 11, 18 (3d Cir. 1989) (recognizing right to sue under federal regulation having the force of law) with Harris v. James, 127 F.3d 993 (11th Cir.1997) (holding 1983 does not permit suits under federal regulations). See also Concourse Rehabilitation & Nursing Ctr. Inc. v. Wing, 150 F.3d 185 (2d Cir.1998) (failure of state to follow state plan not a violation of federal law justifying suit in federal court).

Medicaid litigation in federal court can lead to prospective declaratory or injunctive relief, but can a recipient denied benefits or a provider denied payment recover damages or restitution against the state? Is such relief barred by the 11th Amendment? Edelman v. Jordan, 415 U.S. 651, 94 S.Ct. 1347, 39 L.Ed.2d 662 (1974) (yes). Does the state consent to damage suits in federal court by agreeing to abide by the terms of the federal Medicaid act in paying providers? See Florida Department of Health and Rehabilitative Services v. Florida Nursing Home Association, 450 U.S. 147, 101 S.Ct. 1032, 67 L.Ed.2d 132 (1981) (no); Jane Perkins, et al., That Was Then, This is Now: Reviewing the Supreme Court's Eleventh Amendment Activities, 23 Clearinghouse Rev. 966 (1989). A recent district court case, moreover, has gone much further and held that the 11th Amendment bars all medicaid litigation, Mothers v. Haveman, 133 F.Supp.2d 549 (E.D.Mich. 2001)

Federal law also provides administrative as well as judicial relief to recipients. The states must provide recipients with a notice and fair hearing before denying or terminating medical assistance, 42 U.S.C.A. § 1396a(a)(3), 42 C.F.R. § 431.220, unless the action is dictated by a federal or state law requiring an automatic change, 42 C.F.R. § 431.220(b). The procedures afforded must provide due process, 42 C.F.R. § 431.205(d).

While the states complain about federal oversight, the states have also proved quite adept at manipulating the program to serve their own ends. It has always been true that states that spend more on Medicaid can attract more federal matching funds and that federal funds flow disproportionately to a few states with generous programs. Recently, however, states have become more creative in extracting FFP. One means to this end has been provider donations or provider-specific taxes. The idea behind these exactions (first tried in West Virginia in 1986 and adopted by thirty-seven states by October of 1990) was that money could be taken from providers, passed through the Medicaid program where it would be matched by FFP, and paid back to the providers to enhance their payments, without any additional state money entering the system. By 1992, it is estimated that this practice resulted in additional federal expenditures of $5.5 billion being collected by the states without the expenditure of any additional state funds. This practice was accompanied by expanded state definitions of disproportionate share hospitals, which permitted the states to target reimbursement at certain hospitals from which it had extracted funds.

Attempts by HHS to limit state use of provider taxes and donations resulted in an outcry from the states. A "compromise" amendment adopted by Congress in the fall of 1991 significantly limited reliance on such donations and taxes. The leeway given states to obtain additional federal funds through manipulation of program requirements remains, however, a very sensitive one under current budget debates. The latest "scam" has involved states overpaying state and municipal facilities with matched funds, then reclaiming the state contribution, but not the federal match. This issue was partially addressed by the 2001 budget act.

IV. THE STATE CHILDREN'S HEALTH INSURANCE PROGRAM (SCHIP)

Though one of the primary functions of Medicaid in recent years has been to provide health insurance for children, many children have remained uninsured. Even after Medicaid eligibility expansions in the late 1980s and early 1990s, over 10 million children, many of them in low-income families, were still without health insurance. In response to this continuing problem, Congress created, as part of the 1997 BBA the State Children's Health Insurance Program (SCHIP), title XXI of the Social Security Act. 42 U.S.C.A. §§ 1397aa—1397jj.

The SCHIP program, however, was created in a very different political climate than that which saw the birth of the Medicaid program. It was thus not established as an entitlement for recipients, but rather as a grant-in-aid program to the states, established for ten years with a budget of $20.3 between the fiscal years of 1998 and 2002 and affording the states considerable flexibility in program administration within broad federal guidelines. The SCHIP program now covers 2.5 million children.

States that wish to participate in the SCHIP program may use SCHIP funds either to expand Medicaid coverage for children or to establish a new SCHIP program to cover children who are neither eligible for Medicaid nor covered by private health insurance or use a combination of these approaches. Nineteen states have used SCHIP funds to expand Medicaid coverage, sixteen have created or expanded a separate program, and fifteen have used a combined approach.

SCHIP programs are to target children in families with incomes of at or below 200 percent of the federal poverty level or 150 percent of the state's Medicaid income level, whichever is greater. 42 U.S.C.A. §§ 1397bb(b)(1); 1397jj(b), (c)(4). States may set eligibility standards that take into account geographic location, age, income and resources, residency, disability status, access to other health coverage, and duration of eligibility. They cannot discriminate on the basis of diagnosis or exclude children on the basis of preexisting condition.

SCHIP explicitly does not create an entitlement for any particular child to receive coverage. 42 U.S.C.A. § 1396bb(b)(4). Children who are eligible for Medicaid coverage, however, must be enrolled under Medicaid, and SCHIP coverage is not to substitute for coverage under group health plans. States are also not supposed to cover children with higher family incomes unless children from poorer families are covered nor may they cover children in state institutions or children eligible for insurance as dependents of state employees. States are to establish outreach programs to identify children eligible for SCHIP coverage or other public programs, including Medicaid.

States that choose to establish separately administered SCHIP programs must provide health care benefit packages equivalent to coverage provided by one of several benchmark benefit plans; or that include certain basic services and have an aggregate actuarial value equal to a benchmark plan, or that are approved by HHS.42 U.S.C.A. § 1397cc(a)-(c).

States may impose cost-sharing obligations on SCHIP beneficiaries, including premiums and copayments. About half the states require either premium payments or copayments for services, in part to reduce program costs, but also to make the program look less like a welfare program and to discourage "crowd out", i.e. families dropping employment-related insurance for SCHIP coverage. Though cost-sharing might achieve these results, it also discourages participation and increases administrative complexity. See Mary Jo O'Brien, et al., State Experiences with Cost–Sharing Mechanisms in Children's Health Insurance Expansions (Commonwealth Fund, 2000).

States that participate in SCHIP must match federal funds in accordance with a formula that provides more generous federal participation than is afforded under Medicaid. This invites gaming on the part of the states to move children from Medicaid to SCHIP, even though this is prohibited under the statute. Federal funds are allotted according to a formula that takes into account the number of low income children in the states and geographic variations in health care costs.

In summary, SCHIP is a remarkably different program than Medicaid, evidencing a very different philosophy of federal responsibility for health care financing. SCHIP affords maximum flexibility to the states in the apparent hope that they will generously and responsibly provide for poor children if given an incentive to do so. On the other hand, it provides minimal protection to beneficiaries, who are wholly dependent on state generosity and responsibility.

What explains the differences between the SCHIP program and Medicaid? Why was a separate program created instead of Medicaid expanded? Why was Medicaid coverage of indigent children continued when SCHIP was created? What barriers does SCHIP erect to participation that are not present with Medicaid? Why might SCHIP reach some children who whose families might refuse Medicaid coverage? An excellent analysis of the SCHIP program is found in Sara Rosenbaum, et al., The Children's Hour: The State Health Insurance Program, 17 Health Aff., Jan./Feb. 1998 at 75.

Problem: Health Care Coverage for the Poor

Imagine that you are a member of the staff of a recently elected member of the House of Representatives who is very concerned about reforming the Medicaid program. You are working for this congresswoman because her ideological commitments mirror your own. She asks you to review the current Medicaid program and to come up with a proposal that would substantially improve the current program. Consider your response to her request in light of the following questions:

Whom should the program cover? What financial eligibility requirements should be imposed? What provisions should be made for relative responsibility?

Spousal impoverishment? Should eligibility be defined in terms of some definition of the worthy poor? How would you decide who is worthy and who is not?

What benefits should be afforded by the program? What mix of preventive, acute, and long-term care benefits should be covered? How should providers be paid? What role should managed care organizations play in providing care? What kind of oversight should providers be subject to? Are there some providers who might require closer oversight than others?

What should be the respective roles of the federal and state governments in administering the plan? What should be the respective roles of the legislative, executive, and judicial branches? Should recipients have any federally defined rights? Should providers have any rights? Should these rights be enforceable in federal or state court?

What interest groups do you expect to be most supportive of or opposed to your proposal? Would you expect that the members of any of these groups might be major contributors to your congresswoman? Do the members of these groups represent voting blocks important to your congresswoman?

Chapter 11

ACCESS TO HEALTH CARE: THE OBLIGATION TO PROVIDE CARE

A number of factors can impede an individual's access to adequate health care. Ability to pay is a key determinant of access to health care in the U.S. Persons unable to pay, whether out-of-pocket or through insurance or through government programs, must rely largely on voluntary charity or public institutions where available. Medicaid is severely limited in terms of eligibility; between 1975 and 1986 the proportion of poor persons eligible for Medicaid fell from 63% to under 40%, a proportion that persisted for many years. U.S. House of Representatives, Committee on Ways and Means: 1996 Green Book: Overview of Entitlement Programs. Washington, D.C. U.S. Government Printing Office, 1996. Public hospitals have closed in droves. Powerful non-financial obstacles exist as well, including discrimination based on race, gender or medical condition of the patient. See generally, Altman, Stuart H. et al., The Future U.S. Health Care System: Who Will Care For The Poor and Uninsured (1999); Symposium on Nonfinancial Barriers to Health Care, 32 Houston L. Rev. 1187 (1996). See also Sidney D. Watson, Health Care in The Inner City: Asking The Right Question, 71 N.C.L. Rev. 1647 (1993), detailing problems in public hospitals and clinics including waiting time of several weeks to several months for treatment; and Barry Furrow, Forcing Rescue: The Landscape of Health Care Provider Obligations to Treat Patients, 3 Health Matrix 31 (1993), providing statistical information on access to care.

As a general legal principle, private health care providers do not have a duty to provide uncompensated care, and the traditional legal principle of the physician-patient relationship has been that it is a voluntary and personal relationship which the physician may choose to enter or not for a variety of reasons. Legal obligations on the part of providers to furnish care operate as exceptions to this general rule.

Most of the expansion of duties to provide care has been legislative, with state and federal statutes prohibiting discrimination on the basis of certain characteristics of the patient, or mandating treatment for all patients in exchange for the receipt of government funds for the treatment of some patients. Some current legal obligations to provide care have emerged from limited common law doctrines, as you will see in the first set of cases below.

I. PHYSICIANS' DUTY TO TREAT

A. COMMON LAW

RICKS v. BUDGE

Supreme Court of Utah, 1937.
91 Utah 307, 64 P.2d 208.

EPHRAIM HANSON, JUSTICE.

This is an action for malpractice against the defendants who are physicians and surgeons at Logan, Utah, and are copartners doing business under the name and style of the "Budge Clinic." ... [P]laintiff alleges that he was suffering from an infected right hand and was in immediate need of medical and surgical care and treatment, and there was danger of his dying unless he received such treatment; that defendants for the purpose of treating plaintiff sent him to the Budge Memorial Hospital at Logan, Utah; that while at the hospital and while he was in need of medical and surgical treatment, defendants refused to treat or care for plaintiff and abandoned his case ...

* * *

[T]he evidence shows that when plaintiff left the hospital on March 15th, Dr. Budge advised him to continue the same treatment that had been given him at the hospital, and that if the finger showed any signs of getting worse at any time, plaintiff was to return at once to Dr. Budge for further treatment; that on the morning of March 17th, plaintiff telephoned Dr. Budge, and explained the condition of his hand; that he was told by the doctor to come to his office, and in pursuance of the doctor's request, plaintiff reported to the doctor's office at 2 p.m. of that day. Dr. Budge again examined the hand, and told plaintiff the hand was worse; he called in Dr. D.C. Budge, another of the defendants, who examined the hand, scraped it some, and indicated thereon where the hand should be opened. Dr. S.M. Budge said to plaintiff: "You have got to go back to the hospital." ... Within a short time after the arrival of plaintiff, Dr. S.M. Budge arrived at the hospital. Plaintiff testified: "He [meaning Dr. S.M. Budge] came into my room and said, 'You are owing us. I am not going to touch you until that account is taken care of.' " (The account referred to was, according to plaintiff, of some years' standing and did not relate to any charge for services being then rendered.) Plaintiff testified that he did not know what to say to the doctor, but that he finally asked the doctor if he was going to take care of him, and the doctor replied: "No, I am not going to take care of you. I would not take you to the operating table and operate on you and keep you here thirty days, and then there is another $30.00 at the office, until your account is taken care of." Plaintiff replied: "If that is the idea, if you will furnish me a little help, I will try to move."

Plaintiff testified that this help was furnished, and that after being dressed, he left the Budge Memorial Hospital to seek other treatment. At that time it was raining. He walked to the Cache Valley Hospital, a few blocks away, and there met Dr. Randall, who examined the hand. Dr. Randall testified that when the plaintiff arrived at the Cache Valley Hospital, the hand was swollen with considerable fluid oozing from it; that the lower two-thirds of the forearm was red and swollen from the infection which extended up in the arm, and that there was some fluid also oozing from the back of the hand, and that plaintiff required immediate surgical attention; that immediately after the arrival of plaintiff at the hospital he made an incision through the fingers and through the palm of the hand along the tendons that led from the palm, followed those tendons as far as there was any bulging, opened it up thoroughly all the way to the base of the hand, and put drain tubes in. Plaintiff remained under the care of Dr. Randall for approximately a month. About two weeks after the plaintiff entered the Cache Valley Hospital, it became necessary to amputate the middle finger and remove about an inch of the metacarpal bone.

* * *

Defendants contend: (1) That there was no contract of employment between plaintiff and defendants and that defendants in the absence of a valid contract were not obligated to proceed with any treatment; and (2) that if there was such a contract, there was no evidence that the refusal of Dr. S.M. Budge to operate or take care of plaintiff resulted in any damage to plaintiff.

* * *

Under this evidence, it cannot be said that the relation of physician and patient did not exist on March 17th. It had not been terminated after its commencement on March 11th. When the plaintiff left the hospital on March 15th, he understood that he was to report to Dr. S.M. Budge if the occasion required and was so requested by the doctor. Plaintiff's return to the doctor's office was on the advice of the doctor. While at the doctor's office, both Dr. S.M. Budge and Dr. D.C. Budge examined plaintiff's hand and they ordered that he go at once to the hospital for further medical attention. That plaintiff was told by the doctor to come to the doctor's office and was there examined by him and directed to go to the hospital for further treatment would create the relationship of physician and patient. That the relationship existed at the time the plaintiff was sent to the hospital on March 17th cannot be seriously questioned.

We believe the law is well settled that a physician or surgeon, upon undertaking an operation or other case, is under the duty, in the absence of an agreement limiting the service, of continuing his attention, after the first operation or first treatment, so long as the case requires attention. The obligation of continuing attention can be terminated only by the cessation of the necessity which gave rise to the relationship, or by the discharge of the physician by the patient, or by the withdrawal from the case by the physician after giving the patient reasonable notice so as to enable the patient to secure other medical attention. A physician has the right to withdraw from a case, but if the case is such as to still require further medical or surgical attention, he must, before withdrawing from the case, give the patient sufficient notice so the patient can procure other medical attention if he desires. [ ]

* * *

We cannot say as a matter of law that plaintiff suffered no damages by reason of the refusal of Dr. S.M. Budge to further treat him. The evidence shows that from the time plaintiff left the office of the defendants up until the time that he arrived at the Cache Valley Hospital his hand continued to swell; that it was very painful; that when he left the Budge Memorial Hospital he was in such condition that he did not know whether he was going to live or die. That both his mental and physical suffering must have been most acute cannot be questioned. While the law cannot measure with exactness such suffering and cannot determine with absolute certainty what damages, if any, plaintiff may be entitled to, still those are questions which a jury under proper instructions from the court must determine.

* * *

FOLLAND, JUSTICE (concurring in part, dissenting in part).

* * *

. . . The theory of plaintiff as evidenced in his complaint is that there was no continued relationship from the first employment but that a new relationship was entered into. He visited the clinic on March 17th; the Doctors Budge examined his hand and told him an immediate operation was necessary and for him to go to the hospital. I do not think a new contract was entered into at that time. There was no consideration for any implied promise that Dr. Budge or the Budge Clinic would assume the responsibility of another operation and the costs and expenses incident thereto. As soon as Dr. Budge reached the hospital he opened negotiations with the plaintiff which might have resulted in a contract, but before any contract arrangement was made the plaintiff decided to leave the hospital and seek attention elsewhere. As soon as he could dress himself he walked away. There is conflict in the evidence as to the conversation. Plaintiff testified in effect that Dr. Budge asked for something to be done about an old account. The doctor's testimony in effect was that he asked that some arrangement be made to take care of the doctor's bill and expenses for the ensuing operation and treatment at the hospital. The result, however, was negative. No arrangement was made. The plaintiff made no attempt whatsoever to suggest to the doctor any way by which either the old account might be taken care of or the expenses of the ensuing operation provided for. . . . Dr. Budge had a right to refuse to incur the obligation and responsibility incident to one or more operations and the treatment and attention which would be necessary. If it be assumed that the contract relationship of physician and patient existed prior to this conversation, either as resulting from the first employment or that there was an implied contract entered into at the clinic, yet Dr. Budge had the right with proper notice to discontinue the relationship. While plaintiff's condition was acute and needed immediate attention, he received such immediate attention at the Cache Valley Hospital. There was only a delay of an hour or two, and part of that delay is accounted for by reason of the fact that the doctor at the Cache Valley Hospital would not operate until some paper, which plaintiff says he did not read, was signed. Plaintiff said he could not sign it but that it was signed by his brother before the operation was performed. We are justified in believing that by means of this written obligation, provision was made for the expenses and fees about to be incurred. I am satisfied from my reading of the record that no injury or damage resulted from the delay occasioned by plaintiff leaving the Budge Hospital and going to the Cache Valley Hospital. He was not in such desperate condition but that he was able to walk the three or four blocks between the two hospitals. ...

CHILDS v. WEIS

Court of Civil Appeals of Texas, 1969.
440 S.W.2d 104.

WILLIAMS, J.

On or about November 27, 1966 Daisy Childs, wife of J.C. Childs, a resident of Dallas County, was approximately seven months pregnant. On that date she was visiting in Lone Oak, Texas, and about two o'clock A.M. she presented herself to the Greenville Hospital emergency room. At that time she stated she was bleeding and had labor pains. She was examined by a nurse who identified herself as H. Beckham. According to Mrs. Childs, Nurse Beckham stated that she would call the doctor. She said the nurse returned and stated "that the Dr. said that I would have to go to my doctor in Dallas. I stated to Beckham that I'm not going to make it to Dallas. Beckham replied that yes, I would make it. She stated that I was just starting into labor and that I would make it. The weather was cold that night. About an hour after leaving the Greenville Hospital Authority I had the baby while in a car on the way to medical facilities in Sulphur Springs. The baby lived about 12 hours."

[Dr. Weis] said that he had never examined or treated Daisy Childs and in fact had never seen or spoken to either Daisy Childs or her husband, J.C. Childs, at any time in his life. He further stated that he had never at any time agreed or consented to the examination or treatment of either Daisy Childs or her husband. He said that on a day in November 1966 he recalled a telephone call received by him from a nurse in the emergency room at the Greenville Surgical Hospital; that the nurse told him that there was a negro girl in the emergency room having a "bloody show" and some "labor pains." He said the nurse advised him that this woman had been visiting in Lone Oak, and that her OB doctor lived in Garland, Texas, and that she also resided in Garland. The doctor said, "I told the nurse over the telephone to have the girl call her doctor in Garland and see what he wanted her to do. I knew nothing more about this incident until I was served with the citation and a copy of the petition in this lawsuit."

* * *

Since it is unquestionably the law that the relationship of physician and patient is dependent upon contract, either express or implied, a physician is not to be held liable for arbitrarily refusing to respond to a call of a person even urgently in need of medical or surgical assistance provided that the relation of physician and patient does not exist at the time the call is made or at the time the person presents himself for treatment.

* * *

Applying these principles of law to the factual situation here presented we find an entire absence of evidence of a contract, either express or implied, which would create the relationship of patient and physician as between Dr. Weis and Mrs. Childs. Dr. Weis, under these circumstances, was under no duty whatsoever to examine or treat Mrs. Childs. When advised by telephone that the lady was in the emergency room he did what seems to be a reasonable thing and inquired as to the identity of her doctor who had been treating her. Upon being told that the doctor was in Garland he stated that the patient should call the doctor and find out what should be done. This action on the part of Dr. Weis seems to be not only reasonable but within the bounds of professional ethics.

We cannot agree with appellant that Dr. Weis' statement to the nurse over the telephone amounted to an acceptance of the case and affirmative instructions which she was bound to follow. Rather than give instructions which could be construed to be in the nature of treatment, Dr. Weis told the nurse to have the woman call her physician in Garland and secure instructions from him.

The affidavit of Mrs. Childs would indicate that Nurse Beckham may not have relayed the exact words of Dr. Weis to Mrs. Childs. Instead, it would seem that Nurse Beckham told Mrs. Childs that the doctor said that she would "have to go" to her doctor in Dallas. Assuming this statement was made by Nurse Beckham, and further assuming that it contained the meaning as placed upon it by appellant, yet it is undisputed that such words were uttered by Nurse Beckham, and not by Dr. Weis. * * *

[The court affirmed summary judgment in favor of the defendant.]

HISER v. RANDOLPH

Court of Appeals of Arizona, 1980.
126 Ariz. 608, 617 P.2d 774.

JACOBSON, JUDGE.

* * *

[The trial court entered] summary judgment in favor of the defendant physician, Dr. W. Alan Randolph, and the decedent's spouse has appealed.

* * *

Mohave County General Hospital is the only hospital serving the community of Kingman, Arizona. It maintains an emergency room for the treatment of people in need of immediate medical service. Dr. Randolph and seven other doctors, comprising the medical profession in the Kingman area with admitting privileges at the hospital, established a program with the hospital by which each would take turns in manning the emergency room as the "on call physician" for a 12 hour period.

* * *

From the record it appears that plaintiff's wife, Bonita Hiser, went with her husband to the emergency room at the hospital at approximately 11:45 p.m. on June 12, 1973. She was in a semi-comatose condition and the nurse in charge of the emergency room evaluated her as appearing to be very ill. Mrs. Hiser had an acute diabetic condition described as juvenile onset diabetes of the "brittle" variety. She had been treated in the emergency room at the hospital on the preceding day by Dr. Arnold of Kingman, her regular physician.

The emergency room nurse, after viewing Mrs. Hiser, immediately contacted Dr. Randolph, the "on call physician" at that time. Upon being advised as to who the patient was, Dr. Randolph stated to the nurse, at 11:50 p.m., that he would not attend or treat Mrs. Hiser, and that the nurse should call Dr. Arnold. When the nurse called Dr. Arnold he responded by stating that he would not come to the hospital at that time and that the on call physician should attend Mrs. Hiser. The nurse relayed this information to Dr. Randolph who again refused to attend to or see Mrs. Hiser. The nurse then called Dr. Lingenfelter, Chief of Staff of the hospital. After a subsequent telephone conversation between Dr. Lingenfelter and Dr. Randolph in which Dr. Randolph reiterated that he would not treat Mrs. Hiser, Dr. Lingenfelter came to the hospital and attended Mrs. Hiser, arriving at approximately 12:30 a.m. Dr. Lingenfelter immediately commenced tests and treatment for Mrs. Hiser, whom he regarded as being very ill at the time. Dr. Lingenfelter stayed at the hospital throughout the night until Dr. Arnold arrived in the morning. Mrs. Hiser died at 11:00 a.m. on June 13.

As to the reason for Dr. Randolph's refusal to attend to Mrs. Hiser, a factual dispute exists. Dr. Randolph testified by deposition that the refusal was based upon his inability to adequately treat diabetes. From the evidence presented, however, a trier of fact could conclude that the refusal was based upon a personal animosity between Dr. Randolph and Mrs. Hiser or the fact that Mrs. Hiser's husband was a lawyer. Because the fact that Dr. Randolph refused to treat is undisputed and because of the posture in which this matter reaches us, we assume the refusal was medically unjustified.

* * *

In examining this issue we start with the general rule, with which we agree, that a medical practitioner is free to contract for his services as he sees fit and in the absence of prior contractual obligations, he can refuse to treat a patient, even under emergency situations. [ ]

The question remains whether Dr. Randolph has contracted away this right, while being the doctor "on call" in charge of the emergency room at Mohave General Hospital and being paid the sum of $100 a day to perform those services.

* * *

In our opinion, Dr. Randolph, by assenting to these bylaws [describing the duties of the on-call physician] and rules and regulations, and accepting payment from the hospital to act as the emergency room doctor "on call," personally became bound "to insure that all patients * * * treated in the Emergency Room receive the best possible care," and agreed to insure "in the case of emergency the provisional diagnosis shall be started as soon after admission as possible." Moreover, these services were to be performed for all persons whom the "hospital shall admit ... suffering from all types of disease."

* * *

Reversed and remanded.

Notes and Questions

1.   Why did the doctor refuse to treat Mr. Ricks? Ms. Childs? Ms. Hiser? How did the courts approach the claims of the plaintiffs? On what foundation did they place the doctor's duty to treat? Did they examine the reason for the doctor's refusal to treat the patient in these cases? Should the courts distinguish among such cases on the basis of the reason for the physician's refusal?

2.   In a footnote in *Hiser*, the court referred to the ethical duty of a doctor to render emergency treatment and noted the distinction between legal obligation and ethical obligation. When should ethical obligations be enforced by law, if ever? Would you support a statute that required physicians to render a certain amount of charity care as a condition of licensure? Would you support such a rule established by a local medical society as a condition of membership?

3.   Note that the doctor's duty in *Hiser* is based on his contract with the hospital. Hospital-physician contracting has increased substantially since 1980, as have physician contracts with managed care plans. These latter contracts usually require physicians to treat any subscriber to the plan. How might such a contract apply to discrimination claims? How might such a contractual obligation arise in an abandonment claim? Under *Ricks* or *Childs,* may the doctor be liable to the patient for nontreatment if a current patient's health care plan has refused authorization for the proposed treatment? See discussion of liability in managed care in Chapter 8.

4.   Once the court in *Hiser* decided that Dr. Randolph had a duty to treat Ms. Hiser, it went on to discuss whether Dr. Randolph's breach of this duty, and thus the 40–minute delay in treatment, was the proximate cause of Ms. Hiser's death. The court held that the plaintiff must prove that Ms. Hiser "probably died as a result of the 40 minutes delay in treatment." At 778. It stated that "the mere loss of an unspecified increment of the chance for survival is, of itself, insufficient to meet the standard of probability." At 779. Should the law recognize damages for increased stress, anxiety or pain in the absence of proof of any physical injury? See discussion of the problem of causation and damages in Chapter 5.

5.   The physician may not have a duty to continue treatment for a variety of reasons, including: 1) termination by mutual consent; 2) explicit dismissal by the patient; 3) services required by the patient that are outside the physician's competence and training; 4) services outside the scope of the original doctor-patient agreement, where the physician has limited the contract to a type of procedure, to an office visit, or to consultation only; 5) failure of the patient to cooperate with the physician. The "lack of cooperation" cases require actions by the patient that suggest an implied unilateral termination of the relationship by the patient. This may occur, for example when the patient refuses to comply with the prescribed course of treatment or fails to return for further treatment. See, e.g., Payton v. Weaver, 131 Cal.App.3d 38, 182 Cal.Rptr. 225 (1982). Of course, all of these defenses are very fact-sensitive.

Problem: Cheryl Hanachek

Cheryl Hanachek, a resident of Boston, discovered she was pregnant during an "action" called by the city's obstetricians in protest against declining insurance payments for physician childbirth services. Ms. Hanachek first called Dr. Cunetto, who had been her obstetrician for the birth of her first child two years earlier. Dr. Cunetto's receptionist informed Ms. Hanachek that Dr. Cunetto was not able to take any new patients because her practice was "full." In fact, Dr. Cunetto had limited her practice due to her patient load.

About two weeks later, Ms. Hanachek called Dr. Simms, who had been recommended by her friends. Dr. Simms' receptionist told Ms. Hanachek that Dr. Simms was not taking any new patients as the fees paid by insurance plans were so low that he was even considering discontinuing his obstetrical practice. Ms. Hanachek reported to the receptionist that she was having infrequent minor cramping, and the receptionist told her that this was "nothing to worry about at this stage." Later that night Ms. Hanachek was admitted to the hospital on an emergency basis. Ms. Hanachek was in shock from blood loss due to a ruptured ectopic pregnancy. As a result of the rupture and other complications, Ms. Hanachek underwent a hysterectomy.

She has brought suit against Dr. Cunetto and Dr. Simms. If you were representing Ms. Hanachek, how would you proceed in arguing and proving your case?

B.   THE AMERICANS WITH DISABILITIES ACT

Although the common law does not impose a duty to treat upon a physician in the absence of an established physician-patient relationship, legislatures sometimes, though rarely, have established duties upon the physician.

BRAGDON v. ABBOTT

Supreme Court of the United States, 1998.
524 U.S. 624, 118 S.Ct. 2196, 141 L.Ed.2d 540.

KENNEDY, J., delivered the opinion of the Court, in which STEVENS, SOUTER, GINSBERG, and BREYER, JJ., joined. STEVENS, J., filed a concurring opinion. REHNQUIST, C.J., filed an opinion concurring in the judgment in part and dissenting in part , in which SCALIA and THOMAS, JJ., joined, and in Part II of which O'CONNOR, J., joined. O'CONNOR, J., filed an opinion concurring in the judgment in part and dissenting in part.

We address in this case the application of the Americans with Disabilities Act of 1990 (ADA), 104 Stat. 327, 42 U.S.C. § 12101 *et seq.,* to persons infected with the human immunodeficiency virus (HIV). We granted certiorari to review, first, whether HIV infection is a disability under the ADA when the infection has not yet progressed to the so-called symptomatic phase; and, second, whether the Court of Appeals, in affirming a grant of summary judgment, cited sufficient material in the record to determine, as a matter of law, that respondent's infection with HIV posed no direct threat to the health and safety of her treating dentist.

I

Respondent Sidney Abbott has been infected with HIV since 1986. When the incidents we recite occurred, her infection had not manifested its most serious symptoms. On September 16, 1994, she went to the office of petitioner Randon Bragdon in Bangor, Maine, for a dental appointment. She disclosed her HIV infection on the patient registration form. Petitioner completed a dental examination, discovered a cavity, and informed respondent of his policy against filling cavities of HIV-infected patients. He offered to perform the work at a hospital with no added fee for his services, though respondent would be responsible for the cost of using the hospital's facilities. Respondent declined.

Respondent sued petitioner under § 302 of the ADA, [ ] alleging discrimination on the basis of her disability. Section 302 of the ADA provides:

"No individual shall be discriminated against on the basis of disability in the full and equal enjoyment of the goods, services, facilities, privileges, advantages, or accommodations of any place of public accommodation by any person who ... operates a place of public accommodation." [ ]

The term "public accommodation" is defined to include the "professional office of a health care provider." [ ]

A later subsection qualifies the mandate not to discriminate. It provides:

"Nothing in this subchapter shall require an entity to permit an individual to participate in or benefit from the goods, services, facilities, privileges, advantages and accommodations of such entity where such individual poses a direct threat to the health or safety of others." [ ]

... The District Court ruled in favor of the plaintiffs, holding that respondent's HIV infection satisfied the ADA's definition of disability. [ ] ...

The Court of Appeals affirmed. It held respondent's HIV infection was a disability under the ADA, even though her infection had not yet progressed to the symptomatic stage. [ ] The Court of Appeals also agreed that treating the respondent in petitioner's office would not have posed a direct threat to the health and safety of others. [ ] ...

II

We first review the ruling that respondent's HIV infection constituted a disability under the ADA. The statute defines disability as:

"(A) a physical or mental impairment that substantially limits one or more of the major life activities of such individual; (B) a record of such an impairment; or (C) being regarded as having such impairment."[ ]

* * *

Our consideration of subsection (A) of the definition proceeds in three steps. First, we consider whether respondent's HIV infection was a physical impairment. Second, we identify the life activity upon which respondent relies (reproduction and child bearing) and determine whether it constitutes a major life activity under the ADA. Third, tying the two statutory phrases together, we ask whether the impairment substantially limited the major life activity.

A

[Ed. note: The Court states that the definition of disability in the ADA is drawn from and intended to provide at least as much protection as the definition of handicap in the Rehabilitation Act of 1973.]

1

The first step in the inquiry under subsection (A) requires us to determine whether respondent's condition constituted a physical impairment. The

Department of Health, Education and Welfare (HEW) issued the first regulations interpreting the Rehabilitation Act in 1977. ... The HEW regulations, which appear without change in the current regulations issued by the Department of Health and Human Services, define "physical or mental impairment" to mean:

> "(A) any physiological disorder or condition, cosmetic disfigurement, or anatomical loss affecting one or more of the following body systems: neurological; musculoskeletal; special sense organs; respiratory, including speech organs; cardiovascular; reproductive, digestive, genito-urinary; hemic and lymphatic; skin; and endocrine; or

> "(B) any mental or psychological disorder, such as mental retardation, organic brain syndrome, emotional or mental illness, and specific learning disabilities." [ ]

In issuing these regulations, HEW decided against including a list of disorders constituting physical or mental impairments, out of concern that any specific enumeration might not be comprehensive. [ ] ...

* * *

HIV infection is not included in the list of specific disorders constituting physical impairments, in part because HIV was not identified as the cause of AIDS until 1983. [ ] HIV infection does fall well within the general definition set forth by the regulations, however.

* * *

The initial stage of HIV infection is known as acute or primary HIV infection.... The assault on the immune system is immediate. The victim suffers from a sudden and serious decline in the number of white blood cells.... Mononucleosis-like symptoms often emerge between six days and six weeks after infection, at times accompanied by fever, headache, enlargement of the lymph nodes (lymphadenopathy), muscle pain (myalgia), rash, lethargy, gastrointestinal disorders, and neurological disorders. Usually these symptoms abate within 14 to 21 days. HIV antibodies appear in the bloodstream within 3 weeks; circulating HIV can be detected within 10 weeks. [ ]

After the symptoms associated with the initial stage subside, the disease enters what is referred to sometimes as its asymptomatic phase. The term is a misnomer, in some respects, for clinical features persist throughout, including lymphadenopathy, dermatological disorders, oral lesions, and bacterial infections. Although it varies with each individual, in most instances this stage lasts from 7 to 11 years....

* * *

In light of the immediacy with which the virus begins to damage the infected person's white blood cells and the severity of the disease, we hold it is an impairment from the moment of infection.... HIV infection satisfies the statutory and regulatory definition of a physical impairment during every stage of the disease.

2

The statute is not operative, and the definition not satisfied, unless the impairment affects a major life activity. Respondent's claim throughout this case has been that the HIV infection placed a substantial limitation on her ability to reproduce and to bear children. [ ] We ask, then, whether reproduction is a major life activity.

We have little difficulty concluding that it is. As the Court of Appeals held, "[t]he plain meaning of the word 'major' denotes comparative importance" and "suggest[s] that the touchstone for determining an activity's inclusion under the statutory rubric is its significance." [ ] Reproduction falls well within the phrase "major life activity." Reproduction and the sexual dynamics surrounding it are central to the life process itself.

While petitioner concedes the importance of reproduction, he claims that Congress intended the ADA only to cover those aspects of a person's life which have a public, economic, or daily character. [ ] The argument founders on the statutory language. Nothing in the definition suggests that activities without a public, economic, or daily dimension may somehow be regarded as so unimportant or insignificant as to fall outside the meaning of the word "major." . . .

As we have noted, the ADA must be construed to be consistent with regulations issued to implement the Rehabilitation Act. [ ] Rather than enunciating a general principle for determining what is and is not a major life activity the Rehabilitation Act regulations instead provide a representative list, defining term to include "functions such as caring for one's self, performing manual tasks, walking, seeing, hearing, speaking, breathing, learning, and working." [ ] As the use of the term "such as" confirms, the list is illustrative, not exhaustive.

3

The final element of the disability definition in subsection (A) is whether respondent's physical impairment was a substantial limit on the major life activity she asserts. The Rehabilitation Act regulations provide no additional guidance. [ ]

Our evaluation of the medical evidence leads us to conclude that respondent's infection substantially limited her ability to reproduce in two independent ways. First, a woman infected with HIV who tries to conceive a child imposes on the man a significant risk of becoming infected. . . .

Second, an infected woman risks infecting her child during gestation and childbirth . . .

* * *

The Act addresses substantial limitations on major life activities, not utter inabilities. Conception and childbirth are not impossible for an HIV victim but, without doubt, are dangerous to the public health. This meets the definition of a substantial limitation. The decision to reproduce carries economic and legal consequences as well. There are added costs for antiretroviral therapy, supplemental insurance, and long-term health care for the child who must be examined and, tragic to think, treated for the infection. The laws of some States, moreover, forbid persons infected with HIV from having sex with others, regardless of consent. [ ]

In the end, the disability definition does not turn on personal choice. When significant limitations result from the impairment, the definition is met even if the difficulties are not insurmountable. . . . [ ] We agree with the District Court and the Court of Appeals that no triable issue of fact impedes a ruling on the question of statutory coverage. Respondent's HIV infection is a physical impairment which substantially limits a major life activity, as the ADA defines it. In view of our holding, we need not address the second question presented, *i.e.,* whether HIV infection is a *per se* disability under the ADA.

B

Our holding is confirmed by a consistent course of agency interpretation before and after enactment of the ADA. Every agency to consider the issue under the Rehabilitation Act found statutory coverage for persons with asymptomatic HIV. . . .

* * *

Every court which addressed the issue before the ADA was enacted in July 1990, moreover, concluded that asymptomatic HIV infection satisfied the Rehabilitation Act's definition of a handicap. [ ] We are aware of no instance prior to the enactment of the ADA in which a court or agency ruled that HIV infection was not a handicap under the Rehabilitation Act.

* * *

C
* * *

We also draw guidance from the views of the agencies authorized to administer other sections of the ADA. [ ] . . . Most categorical of all is EEOC's conclusion that "an individual who has HIV infection (including asymptomatic HIV infection) is an individual with a disability." [ ] In the EEOC's view, "impairments . . . such as HIV infection, are inherently substantially limiting." [ ]

III

[We granted certiorari on the following question:]

When deciding under title III of the ADA whether a private health care provider must perform invasive procedures on an infectious patient in his office, should courts defer to the health care provider's professional judgment, as long as it is reasonable in light of then-current medical knowledge?

* * *

. . . The question is phrased in an awkward way, for it conflates two separate inquiries. In asking whether it is appropriate to defer to petitioner's judgment, it assumes that petitioner's assessment of the objective facts was reasonable. The central premise of the question and the assumption on which it is based merit separate consideration.

. . . Notwithstanding the protection given respondent by the ADA's definition of disability, petitioner could have refused to treat her if her infectious condition "posed a direct threat to the health or safety of others." [ ] The ADA defines a direct threat to be "a significant risk to the health or safety of others that cannot be eliminated by a modification of policies, practices, procedures, or by the provision of auxiliary aids or services." [ ] ...

The ADA's direct threat provision stems from the recognition in School Bd. of Nassau Cty. v. Arline [ ] of the importance of prohibiting discrimination against individuals with disabilities while protecting others from significant health and safety risks, resulting, for instance, from a contagious disease. In *Arline,* the Court reconciled these objectives by construing the Rehabilitation Act not to require the hiring of a person who posed "a significant risk of communicating an infectious disease to others." [ ] ... [A]DA's direct threat provision codifies *Arline.* Because few, if any, activities in life are risk free, *Arline* and the ADA do not ask whether a risk exists, but whether it is significant. [ ]

The existence, or nonexistence, of a significant risk must be determined from the standpoint of the person who refuses the treatment or accommodation, and the risk assessment must be based on medical or other objective evidence. [ ] As a health care professional, petitioner had the duty to assess the risk of infection based on the objective, scientific information available to him and others in his profession. His belief that a significant risk existed, even if maintained in good faith, would not relieve him from liability. To use the words of the question presented, petitioner receives no special deference simply because he is a health care professional. It is true that *Arline* reserved "the question whether courts should also defer to the reasonable medical judgments of private physicians on which an employer has relied." [ ] At most, this statement reserved the possibility that employers could consult with individual physicians as objective third-party experts. It did not suggest that an individual physician's state of mind could excuse discrimination without regard to the objective reasonableness of his actions.

... In assessing the reasonableness of petitioner's actions, the views of public health authorities, such as the U.S. Public Health Service, CDC, and the National Institutes of Health, are of special weight and authority. [ ] The views of these organizations are not conclusive, however. A health care professional who disagrees with the prevailing medical consensus may refute it by citing a credible scientific basis for deviating from the accepted norm. [ ]

[An] illustration of a correct application of the objective standard is the Court of Appeals' refusal to give weight to the petitioner's offer to treat respondent in a hospital. [ ] Petitioner testified that he believed hospitals had safety measures, such as air filtration, ultraviolet lights, and respirators, which would reduce the risk of HIV transmission. [ ] Petitioner made no showing, however, that any area hospital had these safeguards or even that he had hospital privileges. [ ] His expert also admitted the lack of any scientific basis for the conclusion that these measures would lower the risk of transmission. [ ] Petitioner failed to present any objective, medical evidence showing that treating respondent in a hospital would be safer or more efficient in preventing HIV transmission than treatment in a well-equipped dental office.

We are concerned, however, that the Court of Appeals might have placed mistaken reliance upon two other sources. In ruling no triable issue of fact existed on this point, the Court of Appeals relied on the CDC Dentistry

Guidelines and the 1991 American Dental Association Policy on HIV. [ ] This evidence is not definitive.... [T]he CDC Guidelines recommended certain universal precautions which, in CDC's view, "should reduce the risk of disease transmission in the dental environment." [ ] The Court of Appeals determined that, "[w]hile the guidelines do not state explicitly that no further risk-reduction measures are desirable or that routine dental care for HIV-positive individuals is safe, those two conclusions seem to be implicit in the guidelines' detailed delineation of procedures for office treatment of HIV-positive patients." [ ] In our view, the Guidelines do not necessarily contain implicit assumptions conclusive of the point to be decided. The Guidelines set out CDC's recommendation that the universal precautions are the best way to combat the risk of HIV transmission. They do not assess the level of risk.

Nor can we be certain, on this record, whether the 1991 American Dental Association Policy on HIV carries the weight the Court of Appeals attributed to it. The Policy does provide some evidence of the medical community's objective assessment of the risks posed by treating people infected with HIV in dental offices. It indicates:

"Current scientific and epidemiologic evidence indicates that there is little risk of transmission of infectious diseases through dental treatment if recommended infection control procedures are routinely followed. Patients with HIV infection may be safely treated in private dental offices when appropriate infection control procedures are employed. Such infection control procedures provide protection both for patients and dental personnel." [ ]

We note, however, that the Association is a professional organization, which, although a respected source of information on the dental profession, is not a public health authority. It is not clear the extent to which the Policy was based on the Association's assessment of dentists' ethical and professional duties in addition to its scientific assessment of the risk to which the ADA refers. Efforts to clarify dentists' ethical obligations and to encourage dentists to treat patients with HIV infection with compassion may be commendable, but the question under the statute is one of statistical likelihood, not professional responsibility. Without more information on the manner in which the American Dental Association formulated this Policy, we are unable to determine the Policy's value in evaluating whether petitioner's assessment of the risks was reasonable as a matter of law.

* * *

We acknowledge the presence of other evidence in the record before the Court of Appeals which, subject to further arguments and examination, might support affirmance of the trial court's ruling. For instance, the record contains substantial testimony from numerous health experts indicating that it is safe to treat patients infected with HIV in dental offices. [ ] We are unable to determine the import of this evidence, however. The record does not disclose whether the expert testimony submitted by respondent turned on evidence available in September 1994. [ ]

There are reasons to doubt whether petitioner advanced evidence sufficient to raise a triable issue of fact on the significance of the risk. Petitioner relied on two principal points: First, he asserted that the use of high-speed drills and surface cooling with water created a risk of airborne HIV transmission. The study on which petitioner relied was inconclusive, however, determining only that "further work is required to determine whether such a risk exists." [ ] Petitioner's expert witness conceded, moreover, that no evidence suggested the spray could transmit HIV. His opinion on airborne risk was based on the absence of contrary evidence, not on positive data. Scientific evidence and expert testimony must have a traceable, analytical basis in objective fact before it may be considered on summary judgment. [ ]

[P]etitioner argues that, as of September 1994, CDC had identified seven dental workers with possible occupational transmission of HIV. [ ] These dental workers were exposed to HIV in the course of their employment, but CDC could not determine whether HIV infection had resulted. [ ] It is now known that CDC could not ascertain whether the seven dental workers contracted the disease because they did not present themselves for HIV testing at an appropriate time after their initial exposure. [ ] It is not clear on this record, however, whether this information was available to petitioner in September 1994. If not, the seven cases might have provided some, albeit not necessarily sufficient, support for petitioner's position. Standing alone, we doubt it would meet the objective, scientific basis for finding a significant risk to the petitioner.

* * *

We conclude the proper course is to give the Court of Appeals the opportunity to determine whether our analysis of some of the studies cited by the parties would change its conclusion that petitioner presented neither objective evidence nor a triable issue of fact on the question of risk.

JUSTICE STEVENS, with whom JUSTICE BREYER joins, concurring.

... I do not believe petitioner has sustained his burden of adducing evidence sufficient to raise a triable issue of fact on the significance of the risk posed by treating respondent in his office.... I join the opinion even though I would prefer an outright affirmance. [ ]

JUSTICE GINSBURG, concurring.

... No rational legislator, it seems to me apparent, would require nondiscrimination once symptoms become visible but permit discrimination when the disease, though present, is not yet visible. I am therefore satisfied that the statutory and regulatory definitions are well met.... [ ]

I further agree, in view of the "importance [of the issue] to health care workers," that it is wise to remand, erring, if at all, on the side of caution. By taking this course, the Court ensures a fully informed determination whether respondent Abbott's disease posed "a significant risk to the health, or safety of [petitioner Bragdon] that [could not] be eliminated by a modification of policies, practices, or procedures...." [ ]

CHIEF JUSTICE REHNQUIST, with whom JUSTICE SCALIA and JUSTICE THOMAS join, and with whom JUSTICE O'CONNOR joins as to Part II, concurring in the judgment in part and dissenting in part.

* * *

[T]he ADA's definition of a "disability" requires that the major life activity at issue be one "of such individual." [ ] The Court truncates the question, perhaps because there is not a shred of record evidence indicating that, prior to becoming infected with HIV, respondent's major life activities included reproduction [ ] (assuming for the moment that reproduction is a major life activity at all). At most, the record indicates that after learning of her HIV status, respondent, whatever her previous inclination, conclusively decided that she would not have children. [ ] There is absolutely no evidence that, absent the HIV, respondent would have had or was even considering having children. Indeed, when asked during her deposition whether her HIV infection had in any way impaired her ability to carry out any of *her* life functions, respondent answered "No." [ ] It is further telling that in the course of her entire brief to this Court, respondent studiously avoids asserting even once that reproduction is a major life activity *to her*. To the contrary, she argues that the "major life activity" inquiry should not turn on a particularized assessment of the circumstances of this or any other case. [ ]

But even aside from the facts of this particular case, the Court is simply wrong in concluding as a general matter that reproduction is a "major life activity." ...

* * *

No one can deny that reproductive decisions are important in a person's life. But so are decisions as to who to marry, where to live, and how to earn one's living. Fundamental importance of this sort is not the common thread linking the statute's listed activities. The common thread is rather that the activities are repetitively performed and essential in the day-to-day existence of a normally functioning individual. They are thus quite different from the series of activities leading to the birth of a child.

* * *

But even if I were to assume that reproduction *is* a major life activity of respondent, I do not agree that an asymptomatic HIV infection "substantially limits" that activity. The record before us leaves no doubt that those so infected are still entirely able to engage in sexual intercourse, give birth to a child if they become pregnant, and perform the manual tasks necessary to rear a child to maturity. [ ] While individuals infected with HIV may choose not to engage in these activities, there is no support in language, logic, or our case law for the proposition that such voluntary choices constitute a "limit" on one's own life activities.

* * *

Respondent contends that her ability to reproduce is limited because "the fatal nature of HIV infection means that a parent is unlikely to live long enough to raise and nurture the child to adulthood." [ ] ... Respondent's argument, taken to its logical extreme, would render every individual with a genetic marker for some debilitating disease "disabled" here and now because of some possible future effects.

* * *

II

I agree with the Court that "the existence, or nonexistence, of a significant risk must be determined from the standpoint of the person who refuses the treatment or accommodation," as of the time that the decision refusing treatment is made. [ ] I disagree with the Court, however, that "in assessing the reasonableness of petitioner's actions, the views of public health authorities ... are of special weight and authority." [ ] Those views are, of course, entitled to a presumption of validity when the actions of those authorities themselves are challenged in court, and even in disputes between private parties where Congress has committed that dispute to adjudication by a public health authority. But in litigation between private parties originating in the federal courts, I am aware of no provision of law or judicial practice that would require or permit courts to give some scientific views more credence than others simply because they have been endorsed by a politically appointed public health authority (such as the Surgeon General). In litigation of this latter sort, which is what we face here, the credentials of the scientists employed by the public health authority, and the soundness of their studies, must stand on their own. The Court cites no authority for its limitation upon the courts' truth-finding function, except the statement in School Bd. of Nassau Cty. v. Arline, [ ] that in making findings regarding the risk of contagion under the Rehabilitation Act, "courts normally should defer to the reasonable medical judgments of public health officials." But there is appended to that dictum the following footnote, which makes it very clear that the Court was urging respect for *medical* judgment, and not necessarily respect for "official" medical judgment over "private" medical judgment: "This case does not present, and we do not address, the question whether courts should also defer to the reasonable medical judgments of private physicians on which an employer has relied." [ ]

Applying these principles here, it is clear to me that petitioner has presented more than enough evidence to avoid summary judgment on the "direct threat" question.... Given the "severity of the risk" involved here, *i.e.*, near certain death, and the fact that no public health authority had outlined a protocol for *eliminating* this risk in the context of routine dental treatment, it seems likely that petitioner can establish that it was objectively reasonable for him to conclude that treating respondent in his office posed a "direct threat" to his safety.

* * *

JUSTICE O'CONNOR, concurring in the judgment in part and dissenting in part.

I agree with The Chief Justice that respondent's claim of disability should be evaluated on an individualized basis and that she has not proven that her asymptomatic HIV status substantially limited one or more of her major life activities. In my view, the act of giving birth to a child, while a very important part of the lives of many women, is not generally the same as the representative major life activities of all persons—"caring for one's self, performing manual tasks, walking, seeing, hearing, speaking, breathing, learning, and working"—listed in regulations relevant to the Americans with Disabilities Act of 1990....

I join in Part II of The Chief Justice's opinion concurring in the judgment in part and dissenting in part, which concludes that the Court of Appeals failed to properly determine whether respondent's condition posed a direct threat. Accordingly, I agree that a remand is necessary on that issue.

Notes and Questions

1. On remand, the Ninth Circuit upheld the District Court's grant of summary judgment in favor of the plaintiff:

The CDC did not write the 1993 Guidelines in a vacuum, but, rather, updated earlier versions issued in 1986 and 1987, respectively. The 1986 text calls the universal precautions "effective for preventing hepatitis B, acquired immunodeficiency syndrome, and other infectious diseases caused by bloodborne viruses." The 1987 edition explains that use of the universal precautions eliminates the need for additional precautions that the CDC formerly had advocated for handling blood and other bodily fluids known or suspected to be infected with bloodborne pathogens. Neither the parties nor any of the amici have suggested that the 1993 rewrite was intended to retreat from these earlier risk assessments, and we find no support for such a position in the Guidelines' text . . .

The [American Dental] Association formulates scientific and ethical policies by separate procedures, drawing on different member groups and different staff complements. The Association's Council on Scientific Affairs, comprised of 17 dentists (most of whom hold advanced dentistry degrees), together with a staff of over 20 professional experts and consultants, drafted the Policy at issue here. By contrast, ethical policies are drafted by the Council on Ethics, a wholly separate body. Although the Association's House of Delegates must approve policies drafted by either council, we think that the origins of the Policy satisfy any doubts regarding its scientific foundation.

For these reasons, we are confident that we appropriately relied on the Guidelines and the Policy. . . . Thus, we again conclude, after due reevaluation, that Ms. Abbott served a properly documented motion for summary judgment.

We next reconsider whether Dr. Bragdon offered sufficient proof of direct threat to create a genuine issue of material fact and thus avoid the entry of summary judgment. . . . The Supreme Court suggested that one such piece of evidence—the seven cases that the CDC considered "possible" HIV patient-to-dental worker transmissions—should be reexamined. Since an objective standard pertains here, the existence of the list of seven "possible" cases does not create a genuine issue of material fact as to direct threat. . . . Each piece of evidence to which [defendant directs] us is still "too speculative or too tangential (or, in some instances, both) to create a genuine issue of material fact."

. . . Upon reflection, we again find that Dr. Bragdon did not submit evidence to the district court demonstrating a genuine issue of material fact on the direct threat issue.

Abbott v. Bragdon, 163 F.3d 87 (1st Cir.1998), cert. denied 526 U.S. 1131, 119 S.Ct. 1805, 143 L.Ed.2d 1009 (1999). What impact does this decision have on the importance of the Supreme Court's decision as to the issue of "direct threat?"

2. How far can the Court's determination that asymptomatic HIV is a disability under the ADA be taken? See e.g., Quick v. Tripp, Scott, Conklin & Smith, P.A., 43 F.Supp.2d 1357 (S.D.Fla.1999) (hepatitis C is a disability); McGraw v. Sears, Roebuck & Co., 21 F.Supp.2d 1017 (D.Minn.1998) (menopause

is not a disability); Gutwaks v. American Airlines, Inc., 1999 WL 1611328 (N.D.Tex.1999) (HIV is not a disability because the specific plaintiff had no intention to procreate). In 1999, the Supreme Court decided two more ADA cases concerning the application of the definition of disability. In Sutton v. United Airlines, 527 U.S. 471, 119 S.Ct. 2139, 144 L.Ed.2d 450 (1999), Murphy v. United Parcel Service, 527 U.S. 516, 119 S.Ct. 2133, 144 L.Ed.2d 484(1999), the Supreme Court held that disabilities that were correctable with devices such as eyeglasses were not disabilities under the Act.

3.   Access to dental care has been a particular concern in litigation over refusals to treat persons with HIV. See Scott Burris, Dental Discrimination Against the HIV–Infected: Empirical Data, Law and Public Policy, 13 Yale J. on Reg. 1 (1996), for data on the incidence of refusals to treat, factors that depress lawsuits for discriminatory practices, and an analysis of the impact of legal and other forces on professional behavior. For a discussion of other access issues, see Linda C. Fentiman, AIDS as a Chronic Illness: a Cautionary Tale for the End of the Twentieth Century, 61 Alb. L. Rev. 989, (1998), part of a Symposium on Health Care Policy: What Lessons Have We Learned from the AIDS Pandemic.

4.   Although some persons with HIV/AIDS require very specialized treatment, most need the same medical services as other generally healthy individuals and as other chronically or intermittently disabled persons. In 1988, the AMA Council on Ethical and Judicial Affairs announced that "a physician may not ethically refuse to treat a patient whose condition is within the physician's current realm of competence solely because the patient is (HIV) seropositive." Council Report on Ethical Issues, 259 JAMA 1360 (1988). What is the significance of the AMA's use of the word "solely?" Does the AMA's statement address the risk of transmission in medical situations? Does it intend to address unsupported fears of transmission? Does it reach homophobia? Racism? Again, should the reason for refusing the patient make a difference? Many state legislatures have amended their medical practice acts to provide that discrimination against persons with HIV is ground for disciplinary action, and usually this is the only antidiscrimination provision in the medical practice act. See e.g., Wisc. Stat. S 252.14.

5.   Chief Justice Rehnquist implies that no risk of transmission is tolerable if the disease is fatal. For a discussion of risk assessment and the ADA, see discussion in Chapter 12.

6.   The Americans with Disabilities Act also applies to insurance (see Chapter 9); to governmental health care decisions (see Chapter 10); and to employment (see Chapter 12).

II. HOSPITALS' DUTY TO PROVIDE TREATMENT

A hospital may have a common law duty to provide emergency care. In Wilmington Gen. Hospital v. Manlove, 54 Del. 15, 174 A.2d 135 (1961), the court held that even though a hospital might not have an obligation to have an emergency room, if it did it, must provide emergency care to a person who relies on the presence of an emergency room in coming to the hospital. In New Biloxi Hospital, Inc. v. Frazier, 245 Miss. 185, 146 So.2d 882 (1962), the Mississippi Supreme Court held a hospital liable for the death of a patient who had been taken to the hospital's emergency room by ambulance after suffering a gunshot wound. The patient remained untreated in the emergency room for two hours, despite heavy blood loss and shock, and died twenty-five minutes after transfer to a Veterans Administration hospital. The Mississippi Supreme Court based their holding on the hospital's breach of the duty to exercise reasonable care once treatment was "undertaken." The Court found that the hospital had undertaken treatment of the patient by virtue of the patient's presence in the emergency room for two hours and his being recorded as an emergency room patient. In Thompson v. Sun City Community Hospital, 141 Ariz. 597, 688 P.2d 605 (1984), the court relied on state hospital regulations and standards of the Joint Commission on Accreditation of Healthcare Organizations to find a duty enforceable through private litigation. Do the varying theories of these cases make a difference in litigating a duty to provide emergency care? The scope of that duty?

The common-law duty of the hospital toward the emergency patient was captured traditionally in the phrase "stabilize and transfer" indicating that once the patient's emergency condition was stabilized, the patient could be transferred. Some few states established broader duties, while in some states there was no statute or case law on the point. Whether the patient was stable at transfer was often a key issue in the legal dispute. For an excellent analysis of the history and scope of this legal doctrine see, Karen Rothenberg, Who Cares? The Evolution of the Legal Duty to Provide Emergency Care, 26 Hous.L.Rev. 21 (1989).

The federal Emergency Medical Treatment and Labor Act. 42 U.S.C.A. § 1395dd (EMTALA) was enacted in response to widespread "patient dumping," a practice in which patients would be transferred from one hospital's emergency room to another's for admission. Several empirical studies of hospital transfers documented this problem. A study in Chicago, for example, reported that transfers from private hospitals to public hospitals increased from 1295 in 1980 to 6769 in 1983, with 24% being unstable at time of transfer. Lack of insurance was the reason given for 87% of the transfers. The cost to the public hospital was $3.35 million, of which $2.81 million would not be reimbursed by insurance, Medicaid or Medicare. Robert L. Schiff *et al.*, Transfers to a Public Hospital, 314 New Eng. J. Med. 552 (1986), one of several studies documenting such transfers. What might explain the substantial increase from 1980 to 1983?

EMTALA applies *only* to hospitals that accept payment from Medicare *and* operate an emergency department. (EMTALA does not require a hospital to offer emergency room services, though some state statutes may). There are two major requirements under the statute. The first requirement is that the hospital give the patient an "appropriate medical screening" upon presentation at the hospital's emergency department and the determination that the patient has an emergency medical condition. The second major requirement is that the hospital stabilize the patient prior to transfer, if transfer is necessary. Violations of these requirements are treated differently when the violations are reported against hospitals or physicians. The statute allows a patient to bring a civil suit for damages for an EMTALA violation against a participating hospital, 42 U.S.C.A. § 1395dd(d)(2)(A); however, no section permits an individual to bring a similar action against a treating physician. Instead, the enforcement sections of EMTALA allow an action against a physician only by the Department of Health and Human Services to bar his participation in Medicare programs and/or to seek administrative sanctions in the form of civil monetary penalties. 42 U.S.C.A.§§ 1395dd(d)(1) & (2)(B). Thus, nothing in the language of the statute permits a private individual to recover personal injury damages from a physician for an EMTALA violation.

BABER v. HOSPITAL CORPORATION OF AMERICA

United States Court of Appeals, Fourth Circuit, 1992.
977 F.2d 872.

WILLIAMS, CIRCUIT JUDGE:

Barry Baber, Administrator of the Estate of Brenda Baber, instituted this suit against Dr. Richard Kline, Dr. Joseph Whelan, Raleigh General Hospital (RGH), Beckley Appalachian Regional Hospital (BARH), and the parent corporations of both hospitals. Mr. Baber alleged that the Defendants violated the Emergency Medical Treatment and Active Labor Act (EMTALA) [ ]. The Defendants moved to dismiss the EMTALA claim under Rule 12(b)(6) of the Federal Rules of Civil Procedure. Because the parties submitted affidavits and depositions, the district court treated the motion as one for summary judgment. See Fed.R.Civ.P. 12(b).

* * *

Mr. Baber's complaint charged the various defendants with violating EMTALA in several ways. Specifically, Mr. Baber contends that Dr. Kline, RGH, and its parent corporation violated EMTALA by:

(a) failing to provide his sister with an "appropriate medical screening examination;"

(b) failing to stabilize his sister's "emergency medical condition;" and

(c) transferring his sister to BARH without first providing stabilizing treatment.

* * *

After reviewing the parties' submissions, the district court granted summary judgment for the Defendants. . . . Finding no error, we affirm.

* * *

. . . Brenda Baber, accompanied by her brother, Barry, sought treatment at RGH's emergency department at 10:40 p.m. on August 5, 1987. When she entered the hospital, Ms. Baber was nauseated, agitated, and thought she might be pregnant. She was also tremulous and did not appear to have orderly thought patterns. She had stopped taking her anti-psychosis medications, . . . and had been drinking heavily. Dr. Kline, the attending physician, described her behavior and condition in the RGH Encounter Record as follows: Patient refuses to remain on stretcher and cannot be restrained verbally despite repeated requests by staff and by me. Brother has not assisted either verbally or physically in keeping patient from pacing throughout the Emergency Room. Restraints would place patient and staff at risk by increasing her agitation.

In response to Ms. Baber's initial complaints, Dr. Kline examined her central nervous system, lungs, cardiovascular system, and abdomen. He also ordered several laboratory tests, including a pregnancy test.

While awaiting the results of her laboratory tests, Ms. Baber began pacing about the emergency department. In an effort to calm Ms. Baber, Dr. Kline gave her [several medications]. The medication did not immediately control her agitation. Mr. Baber described his sister as becoming restless, "worse and more disoriented after she was given the medication," and wandering around the emergency department.

While roaming in the emergency department around midnight, Ms. Baber ... convulsed and fell, striking her head upon a table and lacerating her scalp. [S]he quickly regained consciousness and emergency department personnel carried her by stretcher to the suturing room, [where] Dr. Kline examined her again. He obtained a blood gas study, which did not reveal any oxygen deprivation or acidosis. Ms. Baber was verbal and could move her head, eyes, and limbs without discomfort. ... Dr. Kline closed the one-inch laceration with a couple of sutures. Although she became calmer and drowsy after the wound was sutured, Ms. Baber was easily arousable and easily disturbed. Ms. Baber experienced some anxiety, disorientation, restlessness, and some speech problems, which Dr. Kline concluded were caused by her pre-existing psychiatric problems of psychosis with paranoia and alcohol withdrawal.

Dr. Kline discussed Ms. Baber's condition with Dr. Whelan, the psychiatrist who had treated Ms. Baber for two years ... Dr. Whelan concluded that Ms. Baber's hyperactive and uncontrollable behavior during her evening at RGH was compatible with her behavior during a relapse of her serious psychotic and chronic mental illness. Both Dr. Whelan and Dr. Kline were concerned about the seizure she had while at RGH's emergency department because it was the first one she had experienced ... They also agreed Ms. Baber needed further treatment ... and decided to transfer her to the psychiatric unit at BARH because RGH did not have a psychiatric ward, and both doctors believed it would be beneficial for her to be treated in a familiar setting. The decision to transfer Ms. Baber was further supported by the doctors' belief that any tests to diagnose the cause of her initial seizure, such as a computerized tomography scan (CT scan), could be performed at BARH once her psychiatric condition was under control. The transfer to BARH was discussed with Mr. Baber who neither expressly consented nor objected. His only request was that his sister be x-rayed because of the blow to her head when she fell.

* * *

Because Dr. Kline did not conclude Ms. Baber had a serious head injury, he believed that she could be transferred safely to BARH where she would be under the observation of the BARH psychiatric staff personnel. At 1:35 a.m. on August 6, Ms. Baber was admitted directly to the psychiatric department of BARH upon Dr. Whelan's orders. She was not processed through BARH's emergency department. Although Ms. Baber was restrained and regularly checked every fifteen minutes by the nursing staff while at BARH, no physician gave her an extensive neurological examination upon her arrival. Mr. Baber unsuccessfully repeated his request for an x-ray.

At the 3:45 a.m. check, the nurse found Ms. Baber having a grand mal seizure. At Dr. Whelan's direction, the psychiatric unit staff transported her to BARH's emergency department. Upon arrival in the emergency department, her pupils were unresponsive, and hospital personnel began CPR. The emergency department physician ordered a CT scan, which was performed around 6:30 a.m. The CT report revealed a fractured skull and a right subdural hematoma. BARH personnel immediately transferred Ms. Baber back to RGH because that hospital had a neurosurgeon on staff, and BARH did not have the facility or staff to treat serious neurological problems. When RGH received Ms. Baber for treatment around 7 a.m., she was comatose. She died later that day, apparently as a result of an intracerebrovascular rupture.

The district court granted summary judgment for Dr. Kline and Dr. Whelan because it found that EMTALA does not give patients a private cause of action against their doctors. We review this finding de novo because the interpretation of a statute is a question of law. [ ] Because we hold EMTALA does not permit private suits for damages against the attending physicians, we affirm the district court's grant of summary judgment for Dr. Whelan and Dr. Kline.

* * *

Mr. Baber ... alleges that RGH, acting through its agent, Dr. Kline, violated several provisions of EMTALA. These allegations can be summarized into two general complaints: (1) RGH failed to provide an appropriate medical screening to discover that Ms. Baber had an emergency medical condition as required by 42 U.S.C.A. § 1395dd(a); and (2) RGH transferred Ms. Baber before her emergency medical condition had been stabilized, and the appropriate paperwork was not completed to transfer a non-stable patient as required by 42 U.S.C.A. §§ 1395dd(b) & (c). Because we find that RGH did not violate any of these EMTALA provisions, we affirm the district court's grant of summary judgment to RGH.

Mr. Baber first claims that RGH failed to provide his sister with an "appropriate medical screening". He makes two arguments. First, he contends that a medical screening is only "appropriate" if it satisfies a national standard of care. In other words, Mr. Baber urges that we construe EMTALA as a national medical malpractice statute, albeit limited to whether the medical screening was appropriate to identify an emergency medical condition. We conclude instead that EMTALA only requires hospitals to apply their standard screening procedure for identification of an emergency medical condition uniformly to all patients and that Mr. Baber has failed to proffer sufficient evidence showing that RGH did not do so. Second, Mr. Baber contends that EMTALA requires hospitals to provide some medical screening. We agree, but conclude that he has failed to show no screening was provided to his sister.

* * *

While [the Act] requires a hospital's emergency department to provide an "appropriate medical screening examination," it does not define that term other than to state its purpose is to identify an "emergency medical condition."

* * *

[T]he goal of "an appropriate medical screening examination" is to determine whether a patient with acute or severe symptoms has a life threatening or serious medical condition. The plain language of the statute requires a hospital to develop a screening procedure designed to identify such critical conditions that exist in symptomatic patients and to apply that screening procedure uniformly to all patients with similar complaints.

[W]hile EMTALA requires a hospital emergency department to apply its standard screening examination uniformly, it does not guarantee that the emergency personnel will correctly diagnose a patient's condition as a result of this screening.* The statutory language clearly indicates that EMTALA does not impose on hospitals a national standard of care in screening patients. The screening requirement only requires a hospital to provide a screening examination that is "appropriate" and "within the capability of the hospital's emergency department," including "routinely available" ancillary services. 42 U.S.C.A. § 1395dd(a). This section establishes a standard, which will of necessity be individualized for each hospital, since hospital emergency departments have varying capabilities. Had Congress intended to require hospitals to provide a screening examination which comported with generally-accepted medical standards, it could have clearly specified a national standard. Nor do we believe Congress intended to create a negligence standard based on each hospital's capability ... EMTALA is no substitute for state law medical malpractice actions.

* * *

The Sixth Circuit has also held that an appropriate medical screening means "a screening that the hospital would have offered to any paying patient" or at least "not known by the provider to be insufficient or below their own standards."**

* * *

Applying our interpretation of section (a) of EMTALA, we must next determine whether there is any genuine issue of material fact regarding whether RGH gave Ms. Baber a medical screening examination that differed from its standard screening procedure. Because Mr. Baber has offered no evidence of disparate treatment, we find that the district court did not err in granting summary judgment.

* * *

Mr. Baber does not allege that RGH's emergency department personnel treated Ms. Baber differently from its other patients. Instead, he merely claims Dr. Kline did not do enough accurately to diagnose her condition or

---

* Some commentators have criticized defining "appropriate" in terms of the hospital's medical screening standard because hospitals could theoretically avoid liability by providing very cursory and substandard screenings to all patients, which might enable the doctor to ignore a medical condition. See, e.g., Karen I. Treiger, Note, Preventing Patient Dumping: Sharpening COBRA's Fangs, 61 N.Y.U.L.Rev. 1186 (1986). Even though we do not believe it is likely that a hospital would endanger all of its patients by establishing such a cursory standard, theoretically it is possible. Our holding, however, does not foreclose the possibility that a future court faced with such a situation may decide that the hospital's standard was so low that it amounted to no "appropriate medical screening." We do not decide that question in this case because Ms. Baber's screening was not so substandard as to amount to no screening at all.

** While a hospital emergency room may develop one general procedure for screening all patients, it may also tailor its screening procedure to the patient's complaints or exhibited symptoms. For example, it may have one screening procedure for a patient with a heart attack and another for women in labor. Under our interpretation of EMTALA, such varying screening procedures would not pose liability under EMTALA as long as all patients complaining of the same problem or exhibiting the same symptoms receive identical screening procedures. We also recognize that the hospital's screening procedure is not limited to personal observation and assessment but may include available ancillary services through departments such as radiology and laboratory.

treat her injury. [ ] The critical element of an EMTALA cause of action is not
the adequacy of the screening examination but whether the screening examination that was performed deviated from the hospital's evaluation procedures
that would have been performed on any patient in a similar condition.

* * *

Dr. Kline testified that he performed a medical screening on Ms. Baber in
accordance with standard procedures for examining patients with head injuries. He explained that generally, a patient is not scheduled for advanced tests
such as a CT scan or x-rays unless the patient's signs and symptoms so
warrant. While Ms. Baber did exhibit some of the signs and symptoms of
patients who have severe head injuries, in Dr. Kline's medical judgment these
signs were the result of her pre-existing psychiatric condition, not the result
of her fall. He, therefore, determined that Ms. Baber's head injury was not
serious and did not indicate the need at that time for a CT scan or x-rays. In
his medical judgment, Ms. Baber's condition would be monitored adequately
by the usual nursing checks performed every fifteen minutes by the psychiatric unit staff at BARH. Although Dr. Kline's assessment and judgment may
have been erroneous and not within acceptable standards of medical care in
West Virginia, he did perform a screening examination that was not so
substandard as to amount to no examination. No testimony indicated that his
procedure deviated from that which RGH would have provided to any other
patient in Ms. Baber's condition.

* * *

The essence of Mr. Baber's argument is that the extent of the examination and treatment his sister received while at RGH was deficient. While Mr.
Baber's testimony might be sufficient to survive a summary judgment motion
in a medical malpractice case, it is clearly insufficient to survive a motion for
summary judgment in an EMTALA case because at no point does Mr. Baber
present any evidence that RGH deviated from its standard screening procedure in evaluating Ms. Baber's head injury. Therefore, the district court
properly granted RGH summary judgment on the medical screening issue.

Mr. Baber also asserts that RGH inappropriately transferred his sister to
BARH. EMTALA's transfer requirements do not apply unless the hospital
actually determines that the patient suffers from an emergency medical
condition. Accordingly, to recover for violations of EMTALA's transfer provisions, the plaintiff must present evidence that (1) the patient had an emergency medical condition; (2) the hospital actually knew of that condition; (3) the
patient was not stabilized before being transferred; and (4) prior to transfer of
an unstable patient, the transferring hospital did not obtain the proper
consent or follow the appropriate certification and transfer procedures.

* * *

Mr. Baber argues that requiring a plaintiff to prove the hospital had
actual knowledge of the patient's emergency medical condition would allow
hospitals to circumvent the purpose of EMTALA by simply requiring their
personnel to state in all hospital records that the patient did not suffer from
an emergency medical condition. Because of this concern, Mr. Baber urges us
to adopt a standard that would impose liability upon a hospital if it failed to

provide stabilizing treatment prior to a transfer when the hospital knew or should have known that the patient suffered from an emergency medical condition.

The statute itself implicitly rejects this proposed standard. Section 1395dd(b)(1) states the stabilization requirement exists if "any individual ... comes to a hospital and the hospital determines that the individual has an emergency medical condition." Thus, the plain language of the statute dictates a standard requiring actual knowledge of the emergency medical condition by the hospital staff.

Mr. Baber failed to present any evidence that RGH had actual knowledge that Ms. Baber suffered from an emergency medical condition. Dr. Kline stated in his affidavit that Ms. Baber's condition was stable prior to transfer and that he did not believe she was suffering from an emergency medical condition. While Mr. Baber testified that he believed his sister suffered from an emergency medical condition at transfer, he did not present any evidence beyond his own belief that she actually had an emergency medical condition or that anyone at RGH knew that she suffered from an emergency medical condition. In addition, we note that Mr. Baber's testimony is not competent to prove his sister actually had an emergency medical condition since he is not qualified to diagnose a serious internal brain injury.

... [W]e hold that the district court correctly granted RGH summary judgment on Mr. Baber's claim that it transferred Ms. Baber in violation of EMTALA.

* * *

Therefore, the district court's judgment is affirmed.

AFFIRMED

Notes and Questions

1. Under what authority does the federal government require hospitals to provide emergency medical screening and treatment to people who are not covered by Medicare? Is this an appropriate use of that authority? Why did Congress not appropriate Medicare or other funds to reimburse hospitals for EMTALA care? Why did Congress link EMTALA to participation in Medicare rather than Medicaid? How far, if at all, should legal obligations of uncompensated care extend? The cost of the EMTALA obligation has been significant. In December 2000, Congress directed the GAO to study EMTALA. The House Conference Report delineates the following questions:

> (1) the extent to which hospitals, emergency physicians, and physicians covering emergency department call provide uncompensated services in relation to the requirements of EMTALA; (2) the extent to which the regulatory requirements and enforcement of EMTALA have expanded beyond the legislation's original intent; (3) estimates for the total dollar amount of EMTALA-related care uncompensated costs to emergency physicians, physicians covering emergency department call, hospital emergency departments, and other hospital services; (4) the extent to which different portions of the United States may be experiencing different levels of uncompensated EMTALA-related care; (5) the extent to which EMTALA would be classified as an unfunded mandate if it were enacted today; (6) the extent to which States

have programs to provide financial support for such uncompensated care; (7) possible sources of funds, including Medicare hospital bad debt accounts, that are available to hospitals to assist with the cost of such uncompensated care; and (8) the financial strain that illegal immigration populations, the uninsured, and the underinsured place on hospital emergency departments, other hospital services, emergency physicians, and physicians covering emergency department call. H.R. CONF. REP. 106–1004.

Where did the costs now borne by the hospitals fall before the enactment of EMTALA?

See, Lynn Healey Scaduto, The Emergency Medical Treatment and Active Labor Act Gone Astray: A Proposal to Reclaim EMTALA for Its Intended Beneficiaries, 46 UCLA L. Rev. 943 (1999); Michael J. Frank, Tailoring EMTALA to Better Protect the Indigent: The Supreme Court Precludes One Method of Salvaging a Statute Gone Awry, 3 DePaul J. Health Care L. 195 (2000). But see, Lawrence E. Singer, Look What They've Done to My Law, Ma: COBRA's Implosion, 33 Hous. L. Rev. 113 (1996); Erik J. Olson, No Room at the Inn: A Snapshot of an American Emergency Room, 46 Stan. L. Rev. 449 (1994); Maria O'Brien Hylton, The Economics and Politics of Emergency Health Care for the Poor: The Patient Dumping Dilemma, 1992 B.Y.U.L. Rev. 971; Kristine Marie Meece, The Future of Emergency Department Liability after the Ravenswood Hospital Incident: Redefining the Duty the Duty to Treat?, 3 De Paul J. Health Care L. 101 (1999), each examining the impact of EMTALA.

2. The Sixth Circuit, in considering EMTALA, declared the word "appropriate" to be "one of the most wonderful weasel words in the dictionary, and a great aid to the resolution of disputed issues in the drafting of legislation." Cleland v. Bronson Health Care Group, 917 F.2d 266 (6th Cir.1990). Why would Congress choose to leave such a critical term undefined? Leaving this term undefined has generated many court opinions that try to give meaning to the term. *Baber* is typical of the majority of these cases in the standard it uses to decide whether the medical screening provided by the hospital was appropriate. How does this standard differ from that which would be used in a medical malpractice case? In contrast to the standard the courts have applied in relation to the adequacy of medical screening, the standard generally applied to the question of whether the patient was discharged or transferred in an unstable condition is an objective professional standard, as in *Howe* (see below). How should plaintiff structure discovery to meet these two standards? What would be the role for expert testimony, if any? May the plaintiff simply choose to pursue an "unstable transfer or discharge" claim instead of an "inappropriate screening" claim?

3. The Supreme Court, in Roberts v. Galen of Virginia, Inc., 525 U.S. 249, 119 S.Ct. 685, 142 L.Ed.2d 648 (1999), addressed the question of whether improper motive is required under EMTALA for violation of the requirement that the patient be stabilized. In doing so, the Court overturned the decision of the Sixth Circuit. Earlier, the Sixth Circuit in *Cleland* had held that improper motive was required for a violation of the Act in regard to the requirement that the hospital provide an appropriate medical screening. The Supreme Court expressed no opinion on the correctness of the *Cleland* decision. Is it possible to distinguish the two provisions at issue. How are they different? See e.g., Newsome v. Mann, 105 F.Supp.2d 610 (E.D.Ky.2000). The Circuits have almost uniformly held that EMTALA reaches beyond economically motivated decisions and that proof of motive is not required. Could proof of improper motive be useful to the plaintiff in

distinguishing negligent misdiagnosis from an EMTALA claim? How might such proof assist plaintiff in making his or her case? See *Howe*, infra.

4. Another persistent issue in the interpretation of EMTALA is whether the patient is required to have come "to the emergency department" to trigger the obligations of the Act. In Lopez–Soto v. Hawayek, 175 F.3d 170 (1st Cir. 1999), the court considered a district court opinion that had held that the Act should be read to require that the patient have come to the hospital's emergency department in order to raise the obligation to provide an appropriate medical screening and that the appropriate medical screening provided must reveal the emergency condition and, thus, trigger the obligation to stabilize the patient. The Court of Appeals reversed and remanded in considering the case of an infant born in the hospital's maternity ward and transferred in distress and without stabilizing treatment.

Federal regulations under EMTALA deal with other questions regarding whether the patient has come to the emergency department. For instance, 49 CFR 489.24(b) states:

> An individual "coming to the emergency department" means ... that the individual is on the hospital property (property includes ambulances owned and operated by the hospital, even if the ambulance is not on hospital grounds). An individual in a nonhospital-owned ambulance off hospital property is not considered to have come to the hospital's emergency department, even if a member of the ambulance staff contacts the hospital by telephone or telemetry communications and informs the hospital that they want to transport the individual to the hospital for examination and treatment. In such situations, the hospital may deny access if it is in "diversionary status," that is, it does not have the staff or facilities to accept any additional emergency patients. If, however, the ambulance staff disregards the hospital's instructions and transports the individual on to hospital property, the individual is considered to have come to the emergency department.

5. Many EMTALA claims are resolved through summary judgment, perhaps reflecting judicial concerns that the Act is too broad. See e.g., Summers v. Baptist Medical Center Arkadelphia, 91 F.3d 1132 (8th Cir.1996). Judge Heaney, who had written the majority opinion in favor of the plaintiff for the Eighth Circuit panel that originally heard the appeal of *Summers* (at 69 F.3d 902 (8th Cir.1995)), dissented from the majority opinion following the court's *en banc* hearing of the case. Judge Heaney writes in his dissent:

> The majority ... accepts as true that Summers complained to the doctor about his chest pains and throbbing chest. Baptist even concedes this point. The Majority assumes, however, that the physician: "through inadvertence or inattention, did not perceive Summers to have cracking or popping noises in his chest, or pain in the front of his chest. This is why no chest x-rays were taken. In the medical judgement of the physician, Summers did not need a chest x-ray. Summers did receive substantial medical treatment. It was not perfect, perhaps negligent, but he was treated no differently from any other patient perceived to have the same condition." ... It was for the jury, not the district court or this court , to determine the relative credibility of the parties and what occurred in the emergency room that day. We should not assume that the doctor did not hear Summers or forgot about his complaints. Nor should we assume that it was the physician's medical judgment that prompted his failure to give Summers a chest x-ray. It is possible that the doctor heard Summers' complaints and, for no legitimate reason, failed to do anything

about them. That alternative would establish the essentials of an EMTALA cause of action.

What is at stake for plaintiffs and defendants when federal courts resolve most EMTALA screening claims on summary judgment rather than submitting the case to the jury?

6. For a guide to the requirements of EMTALA in litigation see, Barry R. Furrow, An Overview and Analysis of the Impact of the Emergency Medical Treatment and Active Labor Act, 16 J. Legal Med. 325 (1995); Wendy W. Berra "Preventing Patient–Dumping: The Supreme Court Turns Away the Sixth Circuit's Interpretation of EMTALA," 36 Hous. L. Rev. 615 (1999); Alicia K. Dowdy et al., The Anatomy of EMTALA: A Litigator's Guide, 27 St. Mary's L. J.463 (1996).

7. Substantial conflicts have occurred between hospitals and managed care plans, which typically require pre-treatment authorization by the plan for services provided by a hospital to an individual subscriber. Hospitals claim that managed care plans take advantage of the hospitals' obligations under EMTALA, counting on the hospital to provide necessary care and allowing the plan more latitude in refusing to authorize or pay for care. Managed care organizations claim that hospitals are facing financial difficulties that require them to overtreat in their emergency departments and to overadmit from the emergency room to generate more revenue, especially from privately insured patients. See e.g., Loren A. Johnson and Robert W. Derlet, Conflicts between Managed Care Organizations and Emergency Departments in California, 164 Western Journal of Medicine 137 (1996); Anna–Katrina S. Christakis (Comment), Emergency Room Gatekeeping: A New Twist on Patient Dumping, 1997 Wis.L.Rev. 295 (1997).

What should an emergency room physician do if the patient's insurance plan denies authorization for tests or treatment? If you were asked to advise a hospital on its emergency department policies manual, what would you advise them to do in this scenario? Does the insurer's refusal to authorize payment provide a defense under EMTALA? Maryland has required payment from managed care organizations participating in the state's medical assistance program to hospitals that have provided emergency care in defined circumstances, including where the care would be required to meet the hospital's obligations under EMTALA. Md. Code Health § 15–103(b)(11).

IN THE MATTER OF BABY "K"

United States Court of Appeals, Fourth Circuit, 1994.
16 F.3d 590.

WILKINS, J.:

The Hospital instituted this action against Ms. H, Mr. K, and Baby"K", seeking a declaratory judgment that it is not required under the Emergency Medical Treatment and Active Labor Act (EMTALA), [ ], to provide treatment other than warmth, nutrition, and hydration to Baby "K", an anencephalic infant. Because we agree with the district court that EMTALA gives rise to a duty on the part of the Hospital to provide respiratory support to Baby "K" when she is presented at the Hospital in respiratory distress and treatment is requested for her, we affirm.

Baby "K" was born at the Hospital in October of 1992 with Anencephaly . . .

When Baby "K" had difficulty breathing on her own at birth, Hospital physicians placed her on a mechanical ventilator. This respiratory support allowed the doctors to confirm the diagnosis and gave Ms. H, the mother, an opportunity to fully understand the diagnosis and prognosis of Baby "K"'s condition. The physicians explained to Ms. H that most anencephalic infants die within a few days of birth due to breathing difficulties and other complications. Because aggressive treatment would serve no therapeutic or palliative purpose, they recommended that Baby "K" only be provided with supportive care in the form of nutrition, hydration, and warmth. Physicians at the Hospital also discussed with Ms. H the possibility of a "Do Not Resuscitate Order" that would provide for the withholding of lifesaving measures in the future.

The treating physicians and Ms. H failed to reach an agreement as to the appropriate care. Ms. H insisted that Baby "K" be provided with mechanical breathing assistance whenever the infant developed difficulty breathing on her own, while the physicians maintained that such care was inappropriate. As a result of this impasse, the Hospital sought to transfer Baby "K" to another hospital. This attempt failed when all of the hospitals in the area with pediatric intensive care units declined to accept the infant. In November of 1992, when Baby "K" no longer needed the services of an acute-care hospital, she was transferred to a nearby nursing home.

Since being transferred to the nursing home, Baby "K" has been readmitted to the Hospital three times due to breathing difficulties. Each time she has been provided with breathing assistance and, after stabilization, has been discharged to the nursing home. Following Baby "K's" second admission, the Hospital filed this action to resolve the issue of whether it is obligated to provide emergency medical treatment to Baby "K" that it deems medically and ethically inappropriate. Baby "K's" guardian ad litem and her father, Mr. K, joined in the Hospital's request for a declaration that the Hospital is not required to provide respiratory support or other aggressive treatments. Ms. H contested the Hospital's request for declaratory relief. . . . [The district court denied the hospital the requested relief and the petitioners appealed to the Court of Appeals.]

* * *

In the application of these provisions to Baby "K", the Hospital concedes that when Baby "K" is presented in respiratory distress a failure to provide "immediate medical attention" would reasonably be expected to cause serious impairment of her bodily functions. [ ] Thus, her breathing difficulty qualifies as an emergency medical condition, and the diagnosis of this emergency medical condition triggers the duty of the hospital to provide Baby "K" with stabilizing treatment or to transfer her in accordance with the provisions of EMTALA. Since transfer is not an option available to the Hospital at this juncture, the Hospital must stabilize Baby "K's" condition.

The Hospital acknowledged in its complaint that aggressive treatment, including mechanical ventilation, is necessary to "assure within a reasonable medical probability, that no material deterioration of Baby "K"'s condition is likely to occur." Thus, stabilization of her condition requires the Hospital to provide respiratory support through the use of a respirator or other means necessary to ensure adequate ventilation. In sum, a straightforward application of the statute obligates the Hospital to provide respiratory support to Baby "K" when she arrives at the emergency department of the Hospital in respiratory distress and treatment is requested on her behalf.

In an effort to avoid the result that follows from the plain language of EMTALA, the Hospital offers four arguments. The Hospital claims: (1) that this court has previously interpreted EMTALA as only requiring uniform treatment of all patients exhibiting the same condition; (2) that in prohibiting disparate emergency medical treatment Congress did not intend to require physicians to provide treatment outside the prevailing standard of medical care; (3) that an interpretation of EMTALA that requires a hospital or physician to provide respiratory support to an anencephalic infant fails to recognize a physician's ability, under Virginia law, to refuse to provide medical treatment that the physician considers medically or ethically inappropriate; and (4) that EMTALA only applies to patients who are transferred from a hospital in an unstable condition. We find these arguments unavailing.

* * *

If, as the Hospital suggests, it were only required to provide uniform treatment, it could provide any level of treatment to Baby "K", including a level of treatment that would allow her condition to materially deteriorate, so long as the care she was provided was consistent with the care provided to other individuals. [ ] The definition of stabilizing treatment advocated by the Hospital directly conflicts with the plain language of EMTALA.

. . . The terms of EMTALA as written do not allow the Hospital to fulfill its duty to provide stabilizing treatment by simply dispensing uniform treatment. Rather, the Hospital must provide that treatment necessary to prevent the material deterioration of each patient's emergency medical condition. In the case of Baby "K", the treatment necessary to prevent the material deterioration of her condition when she is in respiratory distress includes respiratory support.

* * *

The second argument of the Hospital is that, in redressing the problem of disparate emergency medical treatment, Congress did not intend to require physicians to provide medical treatment outside the prevailing standard of medical care. The Hospital asserts that, because of their extremely limited life expectancy and because any treatment of their condition is futile, the prevailing standard of medical care for infants with anencephaly is to provide only warmth, nutrition, and hydration. Thus, it maintains that a requirement to provide respiratory assistance would exceed the prevailing standard of medical care. However, the plain language of EMTALA requires stabilizing treatment for any individual who comes to a participating hospital, is diagnosed as having an emergency medical condition, and cannot be transferred . . . We recognize the dilemma facing physicians who are requested to provide treatment they consider morally and ethically inappropriate, but we cannot ignore the plain language of the statute . . .

The Hospital further argues that EMTALA cannot be construed to require it to provide respiratory support to anencephalics when its physicians deem such care inappropriate, because Virginia law permits physicians to refuse to provide such care.

* * *

It is well settled that state action must give way to federal legislation where a valid "act of Congress, fairly interpreted, is in actual conflict with the law of the state," [ ] and EMTALA provides that state and local laws that directly conflict with the requirements of EMTALA are preempted.

* * *

It is beyond the limits of our judicial function to address the moral or ethical propriety of providing emergency stabilizing medical treatment to anencephalic infants. We are bound to interpret federal statutes in accordance with their plain language and any expressed congressional intent. EMTALA does not carve out an exception for anencephalic infants in respiratory distress any more than it carves out an exception for comatose patients, those with lung cancer, or those with muscular dystrophy-all of whom may repeatedly seek emergency stabilizing treatment for respiratory distress and also possess an underlying medical condition that severely affects their quality of life and ultimately may result in their death . . .

SPROUSE, J., dissenting:

. . . I simply do not believe, that Congress, in enacting EMTALA, meant for the judiciary to superintend the sensitive decision-making process between family and physicians at the bedside of a helpless and terminally ill patient under the circumstances of this case. Tragic end-of-life hospital dramas such as this one do not represent phenomena susceptible of uniform legal control. In my view, Congress, even in its weakest moments, would not have attempted to impose federal control in this sensitive, private area.

I also submit that EMTALA's language concerning the type and extent of emergency treatment to be extended to all patients was not intended to cover the continued emergencies that typically attend patients like Baby "K" . . . . The hospital argues that anencephaly, not the subsidiary respiratory failure, is the condition that should be reviewed in order to judge the applicability vel non of EMTALA. I agree. I would consider anencephaly as the relevant condition and the respiratory difficulty as one of many subsidiary conditions found in a patient with the disease. EMTALA was not designed to reach such circumstances.

The tragic phenomenon Baby "K" represents exemplifies the need to take a case-by-case approach to determine if an emergency episode is governed by EMTALA. Baby "K"'s condition presents her parents and doctors with decision-making choices that are different even from the difficult choices presented by other terminal diseases . . . Given this unique medical condition, whatever treatment is appropriate for her unspeakably tragic illness should be regarded as a continuum, not as a series of discrete emergency medical conditions to be considered in isolation.

Humanitarian concerns dictate appropriate care. However, if resort must be had to our courts to test the appropriateness of the care, the legal vehicle should be state malpractice law.

Notes and Questions

1. Should Congress amend EMTALA to avoid the result in *Baby K*? Is the interpretation of stabilization in *Baby K* appropriate? Was refusal to treat Baby K discriminatory? Did the court simply apply the requirements of the Act equally to her?

2. If Baby K had never left the hospital, would resuscitation have been required under EMTALA? In Bryan v. Rectors and Visitors of the University of Virginia, 95 F.3d 349 (4th Cir.1996), the Court of Appeals held that the plaintiff did not have an EMTALA claim where the patient had been admitted to the hospital in an emergency condition but where the hospital had entered a "do not resuscitate" (DNR) order some twelve days after admission. The order was entered over the protests of the patient's family. A week after the order was entered, the patient died, according to the plaintiff due to the DNR order. Is this case distinguishable from the Circuit's earlier decision in *Baby K*? See also, Thornton v. Southwest Detroit Hospital, 895 F.2d 1131 (6th Cir.1990). In that case, Elease Thornton suffered a stroke and was admitted to the hospital's intensive care unit through its emergency room. Her doctor wanted her admitted to the Detroit Rehabilitation Institute for post-stroke therapy, but the Institute refused to admit her because her insurance did not cover their services. The doctor then discharged her from the hospital and her condition deteriorated further. Thornton sued the hospital for violation of the Act claiming that the hospital had discharged her before her condition was stabilized. The trial court granted summary judgment in favor of the hospital and the Court of Appeals affirmed. A concurring opinion stated that that release by Thornton's personal physician was "enough evidence" that her condition had stabilized. Was the court's reliance on the attending physician's release appropriate under the Act? Should the duty under EMTALA dissipate over time? Do we need a similar statute that would require continuing treatment?

3. The claims by the hospital and physicians in *Baby K*, that physicians ought to be able to refuse treatment that they consider futile, are considered in the discussion of "medical futility" in Chapter 19.

4. Baby "K" was shuffled back and forth between the nursing home and the hospital six times until she died, shortly after her second birthday, on April 15, 1995. Upon her death her mother, who had fought so hard to keep her alive, said, "She's in heaven. She's in peace. Knowing that she's with God is a comfort." See M. Tousignant, Death of Baby "K" Leaves a Legacy of Legal Precedents, Washington Post, April 7, 1985, p. 8. Baby "K", who was known by her real name, Stephanie, when she died, amassed medical bills of $500,000 during her short life. The hospital bill, which itself ran $250,000, was fully paid by Stephanie's mother's insurance and by Medicaid. Is the cost of her care relevant in determining what care is proper? How would you use that information in making a general policy decision about the treatment that ought to be afforded anencephalic infants? About the treatment that ought to be afforded Stephanie herself?

5. Doctors may disagree over the appropriate emergency treatment. Consider Cherukuri v. Shalala, 175 F.3d 446 (6th Cir.1999):

> Dr. Cherukuri determined by 4:00 A.M. that it would be best to operate on both [accident victims] to stop the internal bleeding.... But he was unable to

do so for the next three hours because Dr. Thambi, the anesthesiologist on call, advised strongly against operating and did not come to the hospital. [H]e advised Dr. Cherukuri that the patients should be immediately transferred.... He advised repeatedly and adamantly that administering anesthesia for the abdominal surgery was too risky because they had no equipment to monitor its effect on the pressure in the brain.

Dr. Cherukuri testified that over the next two hours [he and a nurse] requested Dr. Thambi by phone several times to come to the hospital but he maintained that anesthesia was out of the question and did not come. They tried to locate other anesthesiologists during this period but were unsuccessful.

* * *

While recognizing that Dr. Thambi had made his position very clear that he did not intend to provide anesthesiology because it might kill the brain injured patients, the ALJ concluded that EMTALA required the surgeon to force Dr. Thambi to perform by expressly ordering him to administer anesthesia. The ALJ states ... that the law "necessarily required" Dr. Cherukuri to stop the bleeding for the patients to be considered "stabilized" under the statute and that this required Dr. Cherukuri to force Dr. Thambi against his will to administer anesthesia. Nothing in EMTALA demands such a confrontation, and for good reasons.

In this case, the action had been brought by the federal government against Dr. Cherukuri, and a fine of $100,000 was overturned by the court. (As discussed earlier, EMTALA does not permit private actions against physicians but does provide for government enforcement of the Act against both physicians and hospitals.) Would a private plaintiff suing the hospital in this case have been successful? How would the plaintiff structure his claim?

HOWE v. HULL

United States District Court, Northern District of Ohio, 1994.
874 F.Supp. 779.

POTTER, SENIOR JUDGE.

Plaintiff brought suit in the current action alleging that on April 17, 1992, defendants refused to provide Charon medical treatment because he was infected with HIV. Plaintiff claims that defendants' actions violate the Americans with Disabilities Act (ADA), the Federal Rehabilitation Act of 1973 (FRA) [and] the Emergency Transfer and Active Labor Act (EMTALA). The defendants vehemently dispute these claims and allegations and have moved for summary judgment on all of plaintiff's claims.

* * *

On April 17, 1992, Charon and plaintiff Howe were traveling through Ohio, on their way to vacation in Wisconsin. Charon was HIV positive. That morning Charon took a floxin tablet for the first time. Floxin is a prescription antibiotic drug. Within two hours of taking the drug, Charon began experiencing fever, headache, nausea, joint pain, and redness of the skin.

Due to Charon's condition, Charon and plaintiff ... sought medical care at the emergency room of Fremont Memorial Hospital. Charon was examined by the emergency room physician on duty, Dr. Mark Reardon.

Dr. Reardon testified that Charon suffered from a severe drug reaction, and that it was his diagnosis that this reaction was probably Toxic Epidermal Necrolysis (TEN). This diagnosis was also recorded in Charon's medical records. Dr. Reardon also testified regarding Charon's condition that "possibly it was an early stage of toxic epidermal necrolysis, although I had never seen one . . . ."

* * *

Dr. Reardon determined that Charon "definitely needed to be admitted" to Memorial Hospital. Since Charon was from out of town, procedure required that Charon be admitted to the on-call physician, Dr. Hull. Dr. Reardon spoke with Dr. Hull on the telephone and informed Dr. Hull that he wanted to admit Charon, who was HIV-positive and suffering from a non-AIDS related severe drug reaction.

. . . Dr. Hull inquired neither into Charon's physical condition nor vital signs, nor did he ask Dr. Reardon about the possibility of TEN. During this conversation, it is undisputed that Dr. Hull told Dr. Reardon that "if you get an AIDS patient in the hospital, you will never get him out," and directed that plaintiff be sent to the "AIDS program" at MCO. When Dr. Hull arrived at the hospital after Dr. Reardon's shift but prior to Charon's transfer, he did not attempt to examine or meet with Charon.

It is undisputed that Charon was never admitted to Memorial Hospital . . . .

Charon was transferred to the Medical College of Ohio some time after 8:45 P.M. on April 17. After his conversation with Dr. Hull and prior to the transfer, Dr. Reardon told Charon and plaintiff that "I'm sure you've dealt with this before . . ." Howe asked, "What's that, discrimination?" Dr. Reardon replied, "You have to understand, this is a small community, and the admitting doctor does not feel comfortable admitting [Charon]."

Plaintiff and defendants dispute whether Charon's physical condition was stable at the time of transfer and whether Charon's physical condition deteriorated during the transfer.

Charon was admitted and treated at the Medical College of Ohio (MCO). Despite the TEN diagnosis, Charon was not diagnosed by MCO personnel as having TEN and, in fact, was never examined by a dermatologist. After several days, Charon recovered from the allergic drug reaction and was released from MCO.

* * *

It is important to note that, even if Memorial Hospital did transfer Charon solely because of his HIV status, there will be no liability under the EMTALA if he was stabilized prior to the transfer. If Charon's condition was not stable, however, defendant could be liable if it provided Charon with substandard care due to his HIV status. [ ] The initial inquiry then, focuses on whether the defendants stabilized Charon before the transfer.

[A medical expert] testified that he did not agree that there was no material deterioration of Charon's condition during the transfer, and that there was a "50/50 chance" that a material deterioration in Charon's condition would occur at the time of transfer. [He] further testified that Charon's vital signs were dangerous, that he would have been uncomfortable transferring Charon, and that Charon was in near shock condition. From this testimony, a reasonable jury could find that defendant had not stabilized Charon prior to transfer.

* * *

Much of this case turns on what in fact Dr. Reardon's initial diagnosis of Charon's condition was. Dr. Reardon testified that the diagnosis was TEN, and this is supported by the entry Dr. Reardon made in the medical records.... Plaintiff's expert, however, testified that TEN was not the "likely or even probable" diagnosis. Dr. Reardon also never told Dr. Lynn, the admitting physician at MCO, about the TEN diagnosis. Given [these factors], a jury could reasonably conclude that the TEN diagnosis was a fabrication or ad hoc justification for Charon's transfer.... Dr. Hull's statement about AIDS patients could cause a reasonable jury to believe that the sole reason for transfer was Charon's HIV status. Plaintiff also presented evidence that Charon was not given the appropriate medical treatment by defendant. Further, if the jury found that Charon's actual diagnosis was simply a non-AIDS-related severe allergic drug reaction, that jury could reasonably conclude that Memorial Hospital transferred Charon, while he was unstable, without providing him with necessary medical care that was within their capability to provide.

* * *

[The Court denies defendants' motion for summary judgment.]

* * *

Defendant Memorial Hospital and defendant Hull also move for summary judgment on plaintiff's ADA claim as well as plaintiff's FRA [Rehabilitation Act] claim, on the basis that the evidence does not establish that Charon was denied treatment solely on the basis of his HIV status, and that plaintiff was not "otherwise qualified" for treatment due to the TEN diagnosis.

* * *

[D]iscrimination can take the form of the denial of the opportunity to receive medical treatment, segregation unnecessary for the provision of effective medical treatment, unnecessary screening or eligibility requirements for treatment, or provision of unequal medical benefits based upon the disability [ ]. A defendant can avoid liability by establishing that it was unable to provide the medical care that a patient required. [ ]

Similarly, to establish a prima facie case under the FRA the plaintiff must show

a) the plaintiff has a disability; b) plaintiff was otherwise qualified to participate in the program; c) defendants discriminated against plaintiff solely on the basis of the disability; and d) the program received federal funding. 29 U.S.C. § 794(a).

As this Court has already stated, a reasonable jury could conclude that the TEN diagnosis was a pretext and that Charon was denied treatment solely because of his disability. Further, there is no evidence to support the conclusion that Memorial Hospital was unable to treat a severe allergic drug reaction. In fact, the evidence indicates that Dr. Reardon initially planned to admit Charon for treatment. Therefore, Charon was "otherwise qualified" for treatment within the meaning of the FRA. Defendants' arguments in this regard are not persuasive.

The Court notes that defendant Memorial hospital argues that the "solely on the basis of ..." standard that appears in the FRA should be imported into the ADA as well. This argument is without merit.

The FRA states that "no otherwise qualified individual with a disability ... shall, solely by reason of his or her disability ... be subjected to discrimination...." [ ]. The equivalent portion of the ADA reads "No individual shall be discriminated against on the basis of disability...."[ ]. It is abundantly clear that the exclusion of the "solely by reason of ... disability" language was a purposeful act by Congress and not a drafting error or oversight.... [ ]

The inquiry under the ADA, then, is whether the defendant, despite the articulated reasons for the transfer, improperly considered Charon's HIV status.... [T]he Court finds plaintiff has presented sufficient evidence to preclude a grant of summary judgment on these claims.

Notes and Questions

1. In the trial after the court's denial of defendants' summary judgment motions in *Howe*, the jury returned a verdict in favor of the plaintiff on the Rehabilitation Act claim, awarding plaintiff's estate $62,000 in compensatory damages and punitive damages of $150,000 against Dr. Hull and $300,000 against the hospital. The jury found in favor of the defendants on the plaintiff's EMTALA claim and on his state claim of emotional distress. The ADA claim was tried to the bench, and the judge found that defendants' actions violated the Act and awarded injunctive relief.

2. The trial court noted in its findings that Dr. Reardon had recorded Dr. Hull's statements about AIDS patients in the official emergency room record and also recorded that Charon's allergic reaction was not related to AIDS or HIV infection in any way. Was it appropriate for Dr. Reardon to document this? Would it have been ethical for him to have omitted this from the patient's record?

3. Would the hospital in *Baby K* have been obligated to provide resuscitation under the ADA or Rehabilitation Act? In its findings, the District Court in *Howe* stated:

Clearly, where the disability and the medical condition for which treatment is sought are unrelated, the health care provider may not properly consider the disability in referring the patient elsewhere. The more complicated question, however, concerns a medical condition that is complicated by the disability. Given the disposition of this case, the Court need not reach, and specifically declines to address, whether a health care provider may properly consider an individual's disability when that disability complicates the medical condition for which the individual is seeking treatment.

In Baby "K", the Court of Appeals did not reach the question of the application of the disability acts. The District Court, however, held that the Rehabilitation Act and the ADA required a hospital to provide resuscitation and ventilator support. 832 F.Supp. 1022 (E.D.Va.1993).

4. Haavi Mooreim offers the following as indicators of "discriminatory" decisions to withhold treatment: where the medical judgment is based on "inaccurate facts" resulting from presumptions or prejudices against person's with the patient's medical condition; where the reasoning underlying the treatment decision is "irrational" as for example where a surgeon would decide not to perform surgery only because of the high risk of mortality even though the surgery would provide the patient's only hope of survival; or where the decision is based on "inappropriate values" such as a conclusion that certain persons are by race or gender inherently inferior. E. Haavi Morreim, Futilitarianism, Exoticare, and Coerced Altruism: The ADA Meets Its Limits, 25 Seton Hall L. Rev. 883 (1995). How would this framework apply to *Howe*? To *Baby K*? See also, Mary A. Crosley, Of Diagnoses and Discrimination: Discriminatory Nontreatment of Infants with HIV Infection, 93 Colum. L. Rev. 1581 (1993) and Medical Futility and Disability Discrimination, 81 Iowa L. Rev. 179 (1995); David Orentlicher, Destructuring Disability: Rationing of Health Care and Unfair Discrimination Against the Sick, 31 Harv. C.R.–C.L. Rev. 49 (1996).

5. In Johnson v. Thompson, 971 F.2d 1487 (10th Cir.1992), parents of infants born with spina bifida claimed that their children were selected for nontreatment in an experiment, without their knowledgeable consent and in a discriminatory fashion based on the infants' physical handicap *and* on the families' socio-economic status. The parents lost their § 504 claim. How might the result have differed under the ADA?

6. Other federal statutes create a duty to furnish care upon hospitals. For example, the federal Hill–Burton Act, enacted in 1946, provided federal financing for the construction and expansion of private health care facilities through the early 1960's. (42 U.S.C.A. § 291) Facilities receiving funding under the Act were required to assure that they would make the federally financed facility "available to all persons residing in the territorial area of the applicant" (the "community service obligation") and would provide in the financed facility a reasonable volume of services to people unable to pay therefore. This latter free care requirement was interpreted to extend for twenty years after the federal financing, and so most Hill–Burton financed facilities are no longer required to provide free care under the statute. The community service obligation continues indefinitely. For commentary on the Hill–Burton litigation, see Kenneth Wing, The Community Service Obligation of Hill–Burton Health Facilities, 23 B.C.L.Rev. 577 (1982); James Blumstein, Court Action, Agency Reaction: The Hill–Burton Act as a Case Study, 69 Iowa L.Rev. 1227 (1984); and Sylvia A. Law, A Right to Health Care That Cannot be Taken Away: The Lessons of Twenty–Five Years of Health Care Advocacy, 61 Tenn. L.Rev 771 (1994). See the discussion of tax exempt status in Chapter 13.

Note: Title VI and Racial Discrimination In Health Care

Class theory maintains that the primary factor affecting differences in health care status between racial groups is socioeconomic.... The class theory, however, oversimplifies the issue and completely ignores the independent role of race in American society. Race influences not only life-style, personal behavior, psycho-social behavior, physical environment, and biology, but also socioeconomic status. Thus race has a double influence.

Racism in America establishes separate and independent barriers to health care institutions and to medical care. Those who advocate for the class theory ignore the fact that removing economic barriers does not remove racial barriers.

Vernellia R. Randall, Racist Health Care: Reforming an Unjust Health Care System to Meet the Needs of African–Americans, 3 Health Matrix 127 (1993). See also, David R. Williams and Chiquita Collins, US Socioeconomic and Racial Differences in Health: Patterns and Explanations, 21 Annual Review of Sociology 349 (1995). The literature on race inequality in health care is substantial and empirically based. In addition to Professor Randall's article, see Sidney Dean Watson, Minority Access and Health Reform: A Civil Right to Health Care, 22 J. of Law, Med. & Ethics 127 (1994); Council on Ethical and Judicial Affairs, Black–White Disparities in Health Care, 263 JAMA 2344 (1990); and Barbara A. Noah, Racial Disparities in the Delivery of Health Care, 35 San Diego L.Rev. 135 (1998); Evidence of Race–Based Discrimination Triggers New Legal and Ethical Scrutiny, BNA Health Law Reporter, Dec. 16, 1999. Under legislation enacted in 2000, the National Institutes of Health will be establishing a National Center on Minority Health and Health Disparities. AMA, HHS Announce Pact to Eliminate Racial, Ethnic Disparities in Health Care, BNA Health Law Reporter, Dec. 7, 2000.

If poverty and race intersect with diminished health, in terms of increased risk of heart disease, diabetes, low birth weight and other illnesses and injuries, how should equality in health care be defined? Are institutional decisions such as the decision to move from urban to suburban locations; to require pre-admission deposits or admission only by a physician with staff privileges; to require that the nursing-home resident or family have resources adequate to support a year or two years of care upon admission in order to be eligible for a Medicaid bed in the facility when it is needed; to place childbirth services at a suburban rather than urban hospital within an integrated delivery system; to acquire physician practices only in high income areas; or to limit the home-care agency's services to a particular geographic area discriminatory on the basis of race? Does discrimination depend on the intent or motive of the decision maker? If a hospital transferred all patients (after stabilizing treatment) who could not provide proof of ability to pay, is that hospital acting in a racially discriminatory manner if 89% of those transferred were African–American or Hispanic? See Robert L. Shiff, et al., Transfers to a Public Hospital: A Prospective Study of 467 Patients. 314 NEJM 552 (1986), reporting data concerning pre-EMTALA hospital transfers.

Title VI of the Civil Rights Act of 1964 (42 U.S.C.A. § 2000d et seq.) prohibits discrimination on the basis of race, color or national origin by any program receiving federal financial assistance and provides for both federal enforcement and private actions. Private activity under Title VI has recently increased but with limited success thus far. The most successful of these is a challenge to Tennessee's Medicaid plan in Linton v. Tennessee Commissioner of Health and Environment, 65 F.3d 508 (6th Cir.1995). In this litigation, the district court judge found that the state Medicaid plan allowing nursing homes to limit the number of "beds" certified for Medicaid reimbursement within the facility violated Title VI. The Sixth Circuit affirmed the district court's acceptance of the remedial plan submitted by the state over the objections of nursing home providers. See also, Latimore v. County of Contra Costa, 77 F.3d 489 (9th Cir.1996) (table), opinion at 1996 WL 68196, in which the Court of Appeals affirmed dissolution of a preliminary injunction against use of county financing in reconstruction of a hospital in one area of the county while residents in poorer sections of the county received inadequate health care. The district court dissolved the injunction after the county had expanded hospital, clinic and transportation services to residents in areas represented by the plaintiffs. But see, Madison–Hughes v. Shalala, 80 F.3d 1121 (6th Cir.1996) challenging HHS' failure to collect racial data concerning the delivery of covered health services that would allow examination of minority access to federally funded health care. The Court of Appeals held that the court had no jurisdiction since the collection of data was not mandated by Title VI.

Scholars reviewing the implementation of Title VI by the government or in private litigation generally have concluded that its effectiveness has been limited by ineffective federal enforcement and by other barriers to private litigation. A leading expert and litigator in Title VI cases proposes new civil rights legislation for health care. See Sidney Dean Watson, *supra*. For a description of current federal enforcement activity under TitleVI, see Donna E. Shalala, Federal Efforts to Remove Nonfinancial Barriers to Health Care, 32 Houston L. Rev. 1195 (1996).

Problem: Emmaus House I

You are a volunteer attorney for a nonprofit organization that provides services to the homeless through a community center called Emmaus House. You and several other attorneys come to Emmaus House to offer legal services a couple of hours each week as part of a program organized by the local bar association. While you are there, the director of the center comes rushing into the cubicle where you are conducting interviews and tells you there is an emergency.

Mr. Jack Larkin, a homeless man who comes frequently to the center, is complaining of chest pains and shortness of breath. He has had these episodes before and, in fact, went to the public hospital very early this morning because of them. The doctor at the public hospital examined Mr. Larkin and concluded that he was not having a heart attack but rather was suffering from influenza. You and the director get Mr. Larkin into your car and take him to the nearest hospital which happens to be Eastbrook Memorial, a private hospital. Mr. Larkin is guided to a cubicle where the emergency room physician examines him. The doctor then tells you that they are going to transfer Mr. Larkin to the public hospital, twenty minutes away. What do you do?

Assume that Mr. Larkin is admitted to the public hospital but dies within the week. If you brought suit against Eastbrook, what would you have to prove? How would you structure discovery? Do you have a claim against the doctor?

Problem: Emmaus House II

Elaine Osborne lives in Springfield. There is no public hospital. The state contracts with private hospitals for care of the indigent although it is approximately a year in arrears in reimbursing these hospitals for indigent care they have already provided. Ms. Osborne works in a minimum-wage job that provides no health insurance. As a woman with no dependent children, she would not qualify for Medicaid even if she meets the income standards for eligibility.

Ms. Osborne discovered a lump in her breast, and a mammogram provided at a free public health fair has revealed suspicious tissue in the breast. The doctor who reviewed the results recommended a biopsy which must be performed by a surgeon. Ms. Osborne went to the emergency department of each of the local hospitals but was told that she was not in need of emergency care. The hospitals each required a cash deposit prior to admitting Ms. Osborne for the biopsy because she has no insurance, does not qualify for Medicaid, and may not qualify for state assistance due to her income. Does Ms. Osborne have a claim against the hospitals or the doctors?

Six months later, Ms. Osborne goes to Westhaven Hospital complaining of pain and shortness of breath. She was admitted to Westhaven because it was suspected that she had had a heart attack or was suffering from arterial blockage. The physicians eventually concluded, however, that her pain and shortness of breath was due to the spread of the breast cancer. Ms. Osborne was discharged from the hospital with a prescription for pain medication. Where should Ms. Osborne go for treatment of these symptoms of the breast cancer? Does she have a claim against Westhaven?

Part III

ORGANIZING THE HEALTH CARE ENTERPRISE

Chapter 12

PROFESSIONAL RELATIONSHIPS IN HEALTH CARE ENTERPRISES

INTRODUCTION

Access to hospital facilities for the treatment of their patients is essential to the practice of most physicians and many other health care professionals. But a relationship with one or more hospitals is no longer the only affiliation required for successful medical practice. Increasingly, the professional's relationships with third-party payers, especially with managed care organizations, and with primary care, specialist or diversified group practices, have become critical as well.

Along with a shift in the location or source of important practice affiliations has come a change in the relative power of the professional and the health care organization. In the context of the customary staff privileges system, with which this chapter begins, physicians exercised considerable control over the conditions under which they practiced; the resources that the hospital would provide them; the selection of other physicians who would be able to practice in the hospital; and the oversight exercised by the institution over physician decisionmaking. Doctors generally have witnessed a loss of this degree of control. Changes in the financing of health care and particularly the emergence of managed care and other cost containment measures have allowed organizations to exert more control over physician decisionmaking. Increasing insecurity for physicians—from termination of hospital contracts, layoffs from employment with physician partnerships and group practices, and "deselection" from managed care provider lists—has been a by-product, or goal, of change in health care delivery and finance systems (depending on your point of view).

In most instances, the law governing professional relationships has borrowed from very familiar legal tools to structure professional relationships that respond to the health care environment of the twenty-first century. This chapter examines how different legal relationships—whether staff privileges, contract or employment—can be used to allocate power, control and financial risk in the health care system.

I. STAFF PRIVILEGES AND HOSPITAL–PHYSICIAN CONTRACTS

A physician or other health care professional may treat patients in a particular hospital only if the practitioner has "privileges" at that hospital. The hospital does not pay a fee or salary to a health care professional who only holds privileges and who has no other relationship (such as employment, a contract for services, or a joint business venture) with the hospital. Hospital privileges, or staff privileges as they are commonly called, include several distinct parts. Privileges may include admitting privileges for the authority to admit patients to the hospital and clinical privileges for the authority to use hospital facilities to treat patients, among other subsets of authority. The scope of an individual provider's clinical privileges must be delineated specifically by the hospital in each case. A provider who is awarded clinical privileges becomes a member of the hospital's medical staff and so is said to hold staff privileges.

The hospital medical staff historically has functioned as a relatively independent association within the hospital organization, operating within the hospital's by-laws but under its own medical staff by-laws as well. The medical staff traditionally has held substantial authority over the hospital's internal quality assurance system and its credentialing process, which is the process through which physicians receive and maintain privileges. Only the hospital's governing board has legal authority to grant, deny, limit or revoke privileges; but it is the hospital's medical staff that generally controls the credentialing process to that ultimate point. The medical staff structure has allowed substantial physician control over access to hospital privileges, for the purpose of assuring the quality of patient care through the staff's medical expertise and devotion to professional values. Most observers of the exercise of this control conclude that its purpose is not always fulfilled, however. If you study the materials on antitrust in this text, for example, you will see that doctors sometimes have controlled access to the medical staff to achieve an advantage over competing physicians rather than solely for the benefit of the quality of health care provided to patients.

When hospitals depended entirely on doctors for a stream of patients and when the hospital's interests and doctors' interests coalesced around the principle that more is better (i.e., longer stays, more tests, more interventions, more staff and more equipment), hospitals were more likely to allow their medical staffs great latitude in the governance of privileges. Many developments have pushed hospitals toward greater administrative control of physician decisionmaking in general and staff privileges in particular. These include the hospital's potential corporate liability for failure to adequately monitor the quality of its medical staff and the effectiveness of its credentialing process. Cost containment mechanisms that place hospitals at financial risk for length of stay and utilization of resources per patient—decisions traditionally directed by the patient's doctor—prodded hospitals to exert more control over physician practices. Since the positive and negative financial consequences of physician practices are experienced by the hospital, many facilities explicitly consider the financial impact of a doctor's treatment patterns in their privileges decisions.

The staff privileges system has changed in several ways that reflect these pressures. Many of these changes are discussed in this section. For example, hospitals have shifted their medical staff structures in some areas toward contract or employment relationships and away from the more independent traditional staff privileges relationships. Contracts for medical services are especially prevalent among the hospital-based practice areas such as radiology, anesthesiology, pathology and emergency medicine.

Hospitals still depend on doctors, however, to provide patients and increasingly as an essential component of what a provider must supply to employers, state governments and insurers shopping for integrated, managed health care. Hospitals and physicians in the 1980s increasingly entered into mutually beneficial enterprises which involve the exchange of services, compensation, joint ownership of resources, and other financial and business relationships. These relationships, including the acquisition of physician practices by hospitals or other practice groups, typically use the structures discussed in this chapter as building blocks. In the late 1990s, however, a trend toward "disintegration" was clearly observable. See discussion in Chapter 13.

Generalizations about the relative power of hospitals and physicians are likely to be inaccurate descriptions of any particular circumstance. Each geographic market is different—including the extent of managed care coverage; the supply of physicians; and the degree of integration among facilities or among physicians. And each hospital is different in terms of its own relationships with managed care plans; its own dependence on physicians as the direct source of patients; and its own competitive position in the market for hospital and related services.

SOKOL v. AKRON GENERAL MEDICAL CENTER

United States Court of Appeals for the Sixth Circuit, 1999.
173 F.3d 1026.

NORRIS, CIRCUIT JUDGE.

Plaintiff is a cardiac surgeon on staff at Akron General. The Medical Council at Akron General received information in the mid–1990's indicating that plaintiff's patients had an excessively high mortality rate. Concerned about plaintiff's performance of coronary artery bypass surgery ("CABG"), the Medical Council created the CABG Surgery Quality Task Force in 1994 to conduct a review of the entire cardiac surgery program at Akron General. The Task Force hired Michael Pine, M.D., a former practicing cardiologist who performs statistical risk assessments for evaluating the performance of hospitals. At a presentation in 1994 attended by plaintiff, Dr. Pine identified plaintiff as having a mortality rate of 12.09%, a "high risk-adjusted rate." Risk adjustment analyzes the likelihood that a particular patient or group of patients will die, as compared to another patient or group of patients. Dr. Pine stated in a summary of his findings that the predicted mortality rate for plaintiff's CABG patients was 3.65%, and plaintiff's "high mortality rate was of great concern and warrants immediate action."

James Hodsden, M.D., Chief of Staff at Akron General, requested that the Medical Council consider plaintiff for possible corrective action. Pursuant to the Medical Staff Bylaws, the Medical Council forwarded the complaint to the chairman of plaintiff's department, who appointed an Ad Hoc Investigatory Committee to review plaintiff's CABG surgery performance. The Medical Staff Bylaws require the Investigatory Committee to interview the staff member being reviewed and provide the Medical Council with a record of the interview and a report. The Investigatory Committee met with plaintiff three times. At the first meeting, the Investigatory Committee identified the issues before it to include addressing questions raised by plaintiff about the Pine study and determining the cause of plaintiff's excessive mortality rate. At the second meeting, the Investigatory Committee examined the mortality rate of plaintiff's patients using the Society of Thoracic Surgeons ("STS") methodology. Under STS methodology, the Investigatory Committee, like Dr. Pine, determined that plaintiff's CABG risk-adjusted mortality rate was roughly three times higher than the predicted mortality rate. The Investigatory Committee discussed the results of this analysis with plaintiff at the meeting.

At the third meeting, the Investigatory Committee reviewed with plaintiff various records of his twenty-six CABG patients who died either during or around the time of surgery. The Investigatory Committee determined that one factor leading to the deaths of these patients was poor case selection, meaning plaintiff did not adequately screen out those patients for whom CABG surgery was too risky. The Investigatory Committee also found that the excessive number of deaths may have been due to insufficient myocardial protection, which led to heart attacks.

The Investigatory Committee ultimately reported to the Medical Council that plaintiff's mortality rate was excessively high and that the two principal causes for this high mortality rate were poor case selection and "improper myocardial protection." The Investigatory Committee recommended that all cases referred to plaintiff for CABG surgery undergo a separate evaluation by another cardiologist who could cancel surgery felt to be too risky. It also recommended that plaintiff not be permitted to do emergency surgery or serve on "cathlab standby" and that there be an ongoing review of his CABG patients by a committee reporting to the Medical Council. Finally, it recommended that a standardized myocardial protection protocol be developed, and that all cardiac surgeons should be required to comply with the protocol.

Plaintiff appeared before the Medical Council on November 21, 1996, and the Medical Council voted to implement the recommendations. Under the Akron General Medical Staff Bylaws, when the Medical Council makes a decision adverse to the clinical privileges of a staff member, the staff member must be given notice of the decision of the Medical Council, and the notice shall specify "what action was taken or proposed to be taken and the reasons for it." This notice allows the staff member to prepare for a hearing to review the Medical Council's decision. . . .

Plaintiff and representatives from the Medical Council appeared before an Ad Hoc Hearing Committee on March 27, 1997. Plaintiff was represented by legal counsel, submitted exhibits, and testified on his own behalf. Dr. Gardner, a member of the Investigatory Committee, testified that although the Pine study and the STS methodology tended to underestimate the actual risk in some of plaintiff's cases, the Investigatory Committee concluded that the STS risk stratification tended to corroborate the Pine analysis. When asked about the Medical Council's determination that plaintiff engaged in poor case selection, Dr. Gardner had difficulty identifying specific cases that should not have had CABG surgery, yet he stated that "in the aggregate" there was poor case selection.

The Hearing Committee recommended that the Medical Council restore all plaintiff's CABG privileges. The Medical Council rejected the recommendation of the Hearing Committee and reaffirmed its original decision. In accordance with the Bylaws, plaintiff appealed the Medical Council's determination to the Executive Committee of the Board of Trustees of Akron General. This Committee affirmed the Medical Council's decision. Plaintiff then asked the district court for injunctive relief against Akron General.

* * *

Under Ohio law, private hospitals are accorded broad discretion in determining who will enjoy medical staff privileges at their facilities, and courts should not interfere with this discretion "unless the hospital has acted in an arbitrary, capricious or unreasonable manner or, in other words, has abused its discretion." [ ] However, hospitals must provide "procedural due process . . . in adopting and applying" "reasonable, nondiscriminatory criteria for the privilege of practicing" surgery in the hospital. [ ]

A.   INSUFFICIENT NOTICE

This appeal requires us to examine the extent of the procedural protections afforded plaintiff under Ohio law. In addition to an appeals process, "[f]air procedure requires meaningful notice of adverse actions and the grounds or reasons for such actions" when a hospital makes an adverse decision regarding medical staff privileges. [ ] Akron General's Medical Staff Bylaws require that notice of an adverse decision by the Medical Council state "what action was taken or proposed to be taken and the reasons for it" and thus do not contractually provide for a quality of notice exceeding that required by Ohio law.

The President of Akron General sent plaintiff a letter notifying him of the Medical Council's initial decision. The letter refers plaintiff to the minutes of the Medical Council's meeting which set out the reasons for the Council's decision. These minutes, provided to plaintiff, indicate that the findings and recommendations of the Investigatory Committee were presented. The Investigatory Committee found that "[t]he number and percentage of deaths in Dr. Sokol's population was excessively high compared to the published national statistics and other local surgeons." Two reasons for this high percentage were offered—poor case selection and problems with protecting against myocardial infarctions. . . .

According to the magistrate judge, the notice provided plaintiff was insufficient because [it failed] to provide Dr. Sokol with specific cases where he engaged in poor case selection and where he failed to provide appropriate myocardial protection.

The sort of notice demanded by the magistrate judge was not required by the circumstances of this case. Had Akron General restricted plaintiff's rights because the Medical Council determined that he had poor case selection or provided insufficient protections against myocardial infarctions, then perhaps specific patient charts should have been indicated, along with specific problems with each of those charts. However, Akron General had a more fundamental concern with plaintiff's performance: too many of his patients, in the aggregate, were dying, even after accounting for risk adjustment. Poor case selection and problems in preventing myocardial infarction were just two reasons suggested by the Investigatory Committee for the high mortality rate.

Plaintiff takes issue with the Pine study and the STS algorithm, claiming that they do not present an accurate picture of his performance as a surgeon because he is the "surgeon of last resort." In other words, so many of his patients die because so many of his patients are already at death's door. Perhaps plaintiff is correct about that. However, it is not for us to decide whether he has been inaccurately judged by the Investigatory Committee and the Medical Council. Instead, we are to determine whether plaintiff had sufficient notice of the charges against him to adequately present a defense before the Hearing Committee. He knew that the Medical Council's decision was based upon the results of the Pine study and the STS analysis, knew the identity of his patients and which ones had died, and had access to the autopsy reports and medical records of these patients. . . . Manifestly, he had notice and materials sufficient to demonstrate to the Hearing Committee's satisfaction that limiting his privileges was inappropriate.

It was well within Akron General's broad discretion to base its decision upon a statistical overview of a surgeon's cases. We are in no position to say that one sort of evidence of a surgeon's performance—a statistical overview—is medically or scientifically less accurate than another sort of evidence—the case-by-case study plaintiff suggests we require of Akron General.

B. ARBITRARY DECISION

The magistrate judge also ruled that the Medical Council's decision was arbitrary. She reasoned that because Akron General did not have a fixed mortality rate by which to judge its surgeons before it limited plaintiff's privileges, it was arbitrary to take action against him based upon his mortality rate. We cannot agree. Surely, if plaintiff's mortality rate were 100%, the Medical Council would not be arbitrary in limiting his medical staff privileges, despite not having an established mortality rate. The magistrate judge's reasoning would prevent the Medical Council from instituting corrective action unless there were a preexisting standard by which to judge its staff. It is true that surgeons must be judged by "nondiscriminatory criteria." [ ]. However, in this context, that means, for example, that if it came to the attention of the Medical Council that another surgeon had a mortality rate as high as plaintiff's, the latter surgeon's medical privileges would be similarly limited. . . .

On appeal, plaintiff argues that the Medical Council's decision was so wrong that it was arbitrary, capricious, or unreasonable. He points to evidence tending to show that the Medical Council's case against him was assailable. Indeed, the Hearing Committee recommended that plaintiff's full privileges be restored. But as the Ohio Supreme Court has recognized, "[t]he board of trustees of a private hospital has broad discretion in determining who shall be permitted to have staff privileges." [ ] The board of trustees will not have abused its discretion so long as its decision is supported by any evidence. Here, the Medical Council had both the Pine Study and the STS analysis. While it is conceivable that these are inaccurate measurements of plaintiff's performance, they are evidence that the hospital was entitled to rely upon, and accordingly, we are unable to say that Akron General abused its discretion in limiting plaintiff's privileges.

MERRITT, CIRCUIT JUDGE, dissenting.

* * *

The heart surgeon has been treated unfairly by his hospital. The Hearing Committee was the only group composed of experts independent of the hospital administration. It included a distinguished heart surgeon from Boston. The Committee completely exonerated Dr. Sokol. No one has cited a single operation or a single instance in which Dr. Sokol has made a mistake, not one.

* * *

Notes and Questions

1. *Sokol* is unusual in that the hospital used outcomes measures as a basis for the action against the staff privileges of a physician. The use of mortality rates as an indicator of the quality of hospitals, and the disclosure of those rates to the public by state governments, is relatively new and somewhat controversial, although release of such data is gaining broader acceptance. Such data is often included in a hospital "report card." See e.g., Pa. Stat. Ann. Tit.35, § 449.7 Data on mortality in coronary artery bypass surgery was among the first to be disclosed to the public. See, Mark R. Chassin, et al., Benefits and Hazards of Reporting Medical Outcomes Publicly, 334 New Eng. J. Med. 394 (1996) and William M. Sage, Regulating Through Information Disclosure Laws and American Health Care, 99 Colum. L. Rev. 1701 (1999).

2. The dissenting judge in *Sokol* noted that the only group of experts independent from hospital administration involved in Dr. Sokol's case concluded that his privileges should not be limited in any way. On what basis might that committee have reached that conclusion? Since the mortality rates for CABG are commonly used in hospital report cards, could the decision of the hospital have been a business decision rather than a quality decision? Does it matter?

3. The court in *Sokol* examines the fairness of the procedures used by the hospital. The basis for this requirement of fair process is not the constitutional doctrine of due process which is applicable to public hospitals. See Scheiner v. New York City Health and Hospitals Corp., 1999 WL 771383 (S.D.N.Y. 1999). Rather, it is the common law doctrine of "fundamental fairness" applied to private associations. The exact requirements of fundamental fairness have been established on a case-by-case basis, and so its minimum requirements are not always clear. See the discussion in *Potvin* in the next section. Some courts have held that hospital by-laws create a contract with the physician at least in relation to the procedures to be afforded the physician. See e.g., East Texas Medical Center Cancer Institute v. Anderson, 991 S.W.2d 55 (Tex.App.1998). The hospital accreditation standards of the Joint Commission on Healthcare Organizations establish substantial required procedures. Some states impose additional procedural requirements by statute. See e.g., N.Y. Public Health Law § 2801–b, which requires that the hospital provide a written statement of reasons and provides for review by the state's Public Health Council of any denial or diminution of privileges.

Are the public's interests well-served by statutory or common law requirements of minimum procedures, or do these efforts create an obstacle to the removal of incompetent physicians?

4.   The Sixth Circuit, applying Ohio law, limits its scope of review over the privileges decision of the hospital, testing only whether the hospital's decision was "arbitrary." A few other states also allow judicial review of the merits of staff privileges decisions. For example, California law allows the courts to review privileges decisions under a substantial evidence standard. Mir v. Charter Suburban Hospital, 27 Cal.App.4th 1471, 33 Cal.Rptr.2d 243 (Cal.App. 1994). Would this broader standard have changed the result in *Sokol*? In fact, the law in the great majority of states does not allow the courts to review the merits of privileges decisions at all. Instead, in most states judicial review is restricted to the question of whether the hospital followed its own by-laws, and for most of these states, the question is limited to compliance with by-laws' procedural requirements only. See e.g., Samuel v. Herrick Memorial Hospital, 201 F.3d 830 (6th Cir.2000), applying Michigan law. See, also, Rao v. St. Elizabeth's Hospital, 140 Ill.App.3d 442, 94 Ill.Dec. 686, 488 N.E.2d 685 (Ill.App. 1986), in which the court refused to consider whether the immediate suspension of privileges conformed to the standards of the hospital's by-laws' provision which allowed immediate suspension where "action must be taken immediately in the best interest of patient care . . .". The court in *Rao* expressed the generally accepted rationale for the very restrictive scope of judicial review stating that the requirements of the best interest of the patients fell "within the ambit of judgment best exercised by hospital authorities" and was "properly a medical one." What policy and practical considerations support broader and narrower judicial review? Why is the staff privileges system generally considered protective of physicians if judicial review is so limited in the majority of states? Do the procedures and timeline described in *Sokol* provide any insight here?

5.   The federal Health Care Quality Improvement Act grants hospitals limited immunity for staff privileges decisions if the hospital meets the procedural standards established in the Act. 42 U.S.C.A. § 11101 et seq. See further discussion of the Act in Chapter 15. The Act also establishes a National Practitioner Data Bank. In order to earn the immunity available under the Act, hospitals must report certain adverse credentialing decisions to the Data Bank and must check the Data Bank records on the individual physician, when considering an application for privileges and every two years for physicians who hold privileges at the hospital.

MATEO–WOODBURN v. FRESNO COMMUNITY HOSPITAL

Court of Appeal, Fifth District, 1990.
221 Cal.App.3d 1169, 270 Cal.Rptr. 894.

BROWN, J.

* * *

Prior to August 1, 1985, and as early as 1970, the FCH department of anesthesiology operated as an open staff. The department was composed of anesthesiologists who were independently competing entrepreneurs with medical staff privileges in anesthesiology. Collectively, the anesthesiologists were responsible for scheduling themselves for the coverage of regularly scheduled, urgent and emergency surgeries.

[E]ach anesthesiologist was rotated, on a daily basis, through a first-pick, second-pick, etc., sequence whereby each anesthesiologist chose a particular operating room for that particular date. Usually no work was available for one or more anesthesiologists at the end of the rotation schedule. Once an anesthesiologist rotated through first-pick, he or she went to the end of the line. In scheduling themselves, the anesthesiologists established a system that permitted each anesthesiologist on a rotating basis to have the "pick" of the cases. This usually resulted in the "first-pick" physician taking what appeared to be the most lucrative cases available for that day.

The rotation system encouraged many inherent and chronic vices. For example, even though members of the department varied in their individual abilities, interests, skills, qualifications and experience, often "first-picks" were more consistent with economic advantage than with the individual abilities of the physician exercising his or her "first-pick" option. At times, anesthesiologists refused to provide care for government subsidized patients, allegedly due to economic motivations.

The department chairman had the authority to suggest to fellow physicians that they only take cases for which they were well qualified. However, the chairman was powerless to override the rotation system in order to enforce these recommendations.

Under the open-staff rotation system, anesthesiologists rotated into an "on call" position and handled emergencies arising during off hours. This led to situations where the "on-call" anesthesiologist was not qualified to handle a particular emergency and no formal mechanism was in place to ensure that alternative qualified anesthesiologists would become promptly available when needed. . . .

* * *

These chronic defects in the system led to delays in scheduling urgent cases because the first call anesthesiologists in charge of such scheduling at times refused to speak to each other. Often, anesthesiologists, without informing the nursing staff, left the hospital or made rounds while one or more of their patients were in post-anesthesia recovery. This situation caused delays as the nurses searched for the missing anesthesiologist.

The trial court found these conditions resulted in breaches of professional efficiency, severely affected the morale of the department and support staff, and impaired the safety and health of the patients. As a result of these conditions, the medical staff (not the board of trustees) initiated action resulting ultimately in the change from an "open" to a "closed" system. We recite the highlights of the processes through which this change took place.

* * *

[Mr.] Helzer, President and Chief Executive Officer of FCH, established an "Anesthesia Task Force" to study the proposed closure. In a subsequent memo to Helzer, dated April 6, 1984, the task force indicated it had considered four alternative methods of dealing with problems in the department of anesthesiology: (1) continuation of the status quo, i.e., independent practitioners with elected department chairman, (2) competitive groups of anesthesiologists with an elected department chairman, (3) an appointed director of anesthesia with independent practitioners and (4) an appointed director with subcontracted anesthesiologists, i.e., a closed staff.

The memo noted that under the third alternative—a director with independent practitioners—the director would have no power to determine who would work in the department of anesthesiology. "Any restriction or disciplinary action recommended by the director would need to go through the usual hospital staff procedure, which can be protracted." It was also noted in the memo that a director with subcontracted practitioners "would have the ability to direct their activities without following usual hospital staff procedures." The committee recommended a director with subcontracted practitioners.

[The board accepted the committee's recommendation and formed a search committee to recruit a director for the department.]

* * *

Mateo–Woodburn was offered the position of interim director on June 13, 1984, which position she accepted. Mateo–Woodburn was interviewed for the position of director on September 25, 1984. Hass was interviewed for the position on March 7, 1985.

At a special meeting of the board of trustees held on April 10, 1985, the anesthesia search committee recommended to the board that Hass be hired as director of the department of anesthesiology, and the recommendation was accepted by the board.

At the same April 10 meeting, the board authorized its executive committee to close the department of anesthesiology. On the same day, the executive committee met and ordered the department closed.

* * *

An agreement between FCH and the Hass corporation was entered into on June 7, 1985. On June 18, 1985, Helzer sent a letter to all members of the department of anesthesiology which states in relevant part:

* * *

"The Board of Trustees has now entered into an agreement with William H. Hass, M.D., a professional corporation, to provide anesthesiology services for all hospital patients effective July 1, 1985. The corporation will operate the Department of Anesthesia under the direction of a Medical Director who will schedule and assign all medical personnel. The corporation has appointed Dr. Hass as Medical Director, and the hospital has concurred with the appointment. The agreement grants to the corporation the exclusive right to provide anesthesia services to all hospital patients at all times."

"To provide the services called for by the agreement, it is contemplated that the Hass Corporation will enter into contractual arrangements with individual physician associates who must obtain Medical Staff membership and privileges as required by the staff bylaws. The negotiations with such associates are presently ongoing, and the hospital does not participate in them."

"Effective August 1, 1985, if you have not entered into an approved contractual agreement, with the Hass Corporation, you will not be permitted to engage in direct patient anesthesia care in this hospital. However, at your option, you may retain your staff membership and may render professional evaluation and assessment of a patient's medical condition at the express request of the attending physician."

The contract between the Hass corporation and FCH provided that the corporation was the exclusive provider of clinical anesthesiology services at the hospital; the corporation was required to provide an adequate number of qualified physicians for this purpose; physicians were to meet specific qualifications of licensure, medical staff membership and clinical privileges at FCH, and to have obtained at least board eligibility in anesthesiology; and the hospital had the right to review and approve the form of any contract between the corporation and any physician-associate prior to its execution.

Subject to the terms of the master contract between the Hass corporation and FCH, the corporation had the authority to select physicians with whom it would contract on terms chosen by the corporation subject to the approval of FCH. The contract offered to the anesthesiologists, among many other details, required that a contracting physician be a member of the hospital staff and be board certified or board eligible. The Hass corporation was contractually responsible for all scheduling, billing and collections. Under the contract, the corporation was to pay the contracting physician in accordance with a standard fee arrangement. The contracting physician was required to limit his or her professional practice to FCH except as otherwise approved by the FCH board of trustees.

[The contract also provided:] "... Provider shall not be entitled to any of the hearing rights provided in the Medical Staff Bylaws of the Hospital and Provider hereby waives any such hearing rights that Provider may have. However, the termination of this Agreement shall not affect Provider's Medical Staff membership or clinical privileges at the Hospital other than the privilege to provide anesthesiology services at the Hospital."

Seven of the thirteen anesthesiologists on rotation during July 1985 signed the contract. Of the six plaintiffs in this case, five refused to sign the contract offered to them. The sixth plaintiff, Dr. Woodburn, was not offered a contract but testified that he would not have signed it, had one been offered.

* * *

Some of the reasons given for refusal to sign the contract were: (1) the contract required the plaintiffs to give up their vested and fundamental rights to practice at FCH; (2) the 60–day termination clause contained no provisions for due process review; (3) the contract failed to specify amounts to be taken out of pooled income for administrative costs; (4) the contract required plaintiffs to change medical malpractice carriers; (5) the contract required plaintiffs to obtain permission to practice any place other than FCH; (6) the contract imposed an unreasonable control over plaintiffs' financial and professional lives; (7) the contract failed to provide tenure of employment. The Hass corporation refused to negotiate any of the terms of the contract with plaintiffs.

* * *

... Numerous cases recognize that the governing body of a hospital, private or public, may make a rational policy decision or adopt a rule of general application to the effect that a department under its jurisdiction shall be operated by the hospital itself through a contractual arrangement with one or more doctors to the exclusion of all other members of the medical staff except those who may be hired by the contracting doctor or doctors. ...

* * *

[The position] of a staff doctor in an adjudicatory one-on-one setting, wherein the doctor's professional or ethical qualifications for staff privileges is in question, take[s] on a different quality and character when considered in light of a rational, justified policy decision by a hospital to reorganize the method of delivery of certain medical services, even though the structural change results in the exclusion of certain doctors from the operating rooms. If the justification is sufficient, the doctor's vested rights must give way to public and patient interest in improving the quality of medical services.

It is also noted, where a doctor loses or does not attain staff privileges because of professional inadequacy or misconduct, the professional reputation of that doctor is at stake. In that circumstance, his or her ability to become a member of the staff at other hospitals is severely impaired. On the other hand, a doctor's elimination by reason of a departmental reorganization and his failure to sign a contract does not reflect upon the doctor's professional qualifications and should not affect his opportunities to obtain other employment. The trial court correctly found the decision to close the department of anesthesiology and contract with Hass did not reflect upon the character, competency or qualifications of any particular anesthesiologist.

* * *

[I]f the hospital's policy decision to make the change is lawful, and we hold it is, then the terms of the contracts offered to the doctors was part of the administrative decision and will not be interfered with by this court unless those terms bear no rational relationship to the objects to be accomplished, i.e., if they are substantially irrational or they illegally discriminate among the various doctors.

Given the conditions existing under the open rotation method of delivering anesthesia services, including among others the lack of control of scheduling and the absence of proper discipline, we cannot say the terms of the contract were irrational, unreasonable or failed to bear a proper relationship to the object of correcting those conditions. Considered in this light, the terms are not arbitrary, capricious or irrational.

* * *

As to the contract provision which required waiver of hearing rights set forth in the staff bylaws, ... those rights do not exist under the circumstances of a quasi-legislative reorganization of a department by the board of trustees. This quasi-legislative situation is to be distinguished from a quasi-judicial proceeding against an individual doctor grounded on unethical or unprofessional conduct or incompetency. Accordingly, the waiver did not further detract from or diminish plaintiffs' rights.

* * *

Plaintiffs contend the department of anesthesiology could not be reorganized without amending the bylaws of the medical staff in accordance with the procedure for amendment set forth therein. Closely allied to this argument is the assertion the hospital unlawfully delegated to Hass the medical staff's authority to make staff appointments.

... The hospital's action did not change the manner or procedure by which the medical staff passes upon the qualifications, competency or skills of particular doctors in accordance with medical staff bylaws. ... In fact, plaintiffs remain members of the staff and the contract requires contracting anesthesiologists to be members of the staff. Moreover, it is clear the medical staff does not appoint medical staff members—it makes recommendations to the board of trustees who then makes the final medical staff membership decision. Hass was never given authority to appoint physicians to medical staff and never did so. Hass was merely hired to provide anesthesiology services to the hospital. His decision to contract with various anesthesiologists in order to provide those services was irrelevant to medical staff appointments except that all persons contracting with Hass were required to qualify as members of the medical staff.

We conclude the trial court's determination that the defendants' "actions were proper under the circumstance and that plaintiffs' Medical Staff privileges were not unlawfully terminated, modified or curtailed" is fully supported by the evidence and is legally correct.

Notes and Questions

1. The court in *Mateo-Woodburn* issued its opinion more than ten years ago, and it now represents the majority of cases considering a hospital's authority to restructure its medical staff without recourse to the hearings provisions of the medical staff by-laws. See, for example, Tenet Health Ltd. v. Zamora, 13 S.W.3d 464 (Tex.App.2000); Bloom v. Hennepin County, 783 F.Supp. 418 (D.Minn.1992); Van Valkenburg v. Paracelsus Healthcare Corp., 606 N.W.2d 908 (N.D.2000). But see, Volcjak v. Washington County Hospital Association, 124 Md.App. 481, 723 A.2d 463 (Md.App. 1999), stating that the court "had no doubt that the hospital ... had the right to make a business decision to enter into an exclusive contract ... and not to reappoint Volcjak to the medical staff," but that the hospital had to follow its by-laws' procedures in doing so.

2. In *Mateo-Woodburn* there was no implication of any performance or quality problems in any single physician's practice. If there had been, would the doctors have been entitled to a hearing as you read the court's opinion? In Major v. Memorial Hospitals Assn., 71 Cal.App.4th 1380, 84 Cal.Rptr.2d 510 (Cal.App. 1999), the court considered a case in which a hospital made the decision to enter into an exclusive contract for anesthesiology after repeated scheduling problems, altercations among the doctors, and quality problems attributed specifically to the plaintiff doctors. The plaintiffs claimed that they were entitled to a hearing under *Mateo-Woodburn* because the revocation of their privileges required by the closing of the anesthesiology staff reflected on their personal character and competency and so required the by-laws' procedures. The court rejected this argument, and further held that "to the extent the decision [in *Mateo-Woodburn*] could be read to require that subcontracts be offered to incumbent physicians as a precondition to finding the decision to close a department is quasi-legislative, we expressly reject that interpretation."

3. In *Mateo-Woodburn*, the medical staff supported the hospital's decision. What do you think the result would be if the medical staff as a whole had not supported the decision? What would you advise a hospital as to what role its medical staff should have in decisions to engage in exclusive contracts or otherwise limit access to privileges? What strategies would you suggest in the face of entrenched resistance? See, Bartley v. Eastern Maine Medical Center, 617 A.2d 1020 (Me.1992) (holding that a clause in the hospital's corporate by-laws specifying that the board had the "necessary authority and responsibility" to engage in "general management" gave the board authority to enter into an exclusive contract for services and that the medical staff by-laws were subject to the corporate by-laws); but see, Austin v. Mercy Health System, 541 N.W.2d 838 (Wis.App.1995) (holding that hospital must consult with medical staff on change in credentials required for physicians treating patients in the intensive care and special care units where hospital followed advice of medical director alone and terminated privileges of several doctors who did not meet the new criteria).

4. In *Mateo-Woodburn*, the hospital defendant cited quality concerns as the motivation for its decision to move to an exclusive contract for anesthesiology services. If Fresno Community Hospital had chosen Hass over Mateo–Woodburn simply because Hass had made the lower bid, would the court have rejected the hospital's decision? "Economic credentialing," at least as defined by the AMA, occurs when a hospital makes privileges decisions based on factors unrelated to quality. Of course, a single factor may relate both to cost and to quality. Thus far, the courts generally have accepted bare financial benefit as a legitimate ground for structuring of the medical staff. See e.g., Bartley v. Eastern Maine Medical Center, 617 A.2d 1020 (Me.1992); St. Mary's Hospital of Athens v. Radiology Professional Corporation, 205 Ga.App. 121, 421 S.E.2d 731 (Ga.App.1992). But see, Ray v. St. John's Health Care Corp., 582 N.E.2d 464 (Ind.App.1991). On economic credentialing, see John Blum, Economic Credentialing: A New Twist in Hospital Appraisal Process, 12 J.Leg.Med. 427 (1991); June D. Zellers and Michael R. Poulin, Termination of Hospital Privileges for Economic Reasons: An Appeal for Consistency, 46 Maine L.Rev. 67 (1994).

5. *Mateo-Woodburn* considers two issues related to exclusive contracting. In addition to resolving the question of the procedural rights of the physician who held privileges prior to the institution of the exclusive contract, it reviews the termination provision in the exclusive contract itself. What contractual provision is made for termination of the contract and termination of staff privileges between Hass, P.C., and the anesthesiologists at Fresno Community Hospital? Would a contract clause that provides that termination of the contract will result automatically in the termination of staff privileges without benefit of the by-laws' procedures (a "clean sweep" clause) be enforceable? Contracts such as those in *Mateo-Woodburn* allocate power and control differently. Which situation is more compatible with a goal of cost containment? With a goal of quality?

Problem: General Hospital, Dr. Casey and
The Physicians' Practice Group

General Hospital is a 300–bed hospital in Metropolis, a major city with six other hospitals. Several health insurance plans and major employers have begun to negotiate substantial discounts with Metropolis hospitals for hospital services provided to their insureds or to their employees. The hospitals have actually been quite interested in such negotiations because the insurers and employers asking for the discounts control the choice of hospital for thousands of insured individuals in Metropolis. What the hospital might lose in the "discount," it will gain in having a relatively stable stream of patients.

General Hospital has been constrained in its negotiations for a number of reasons. For example, it has exclusive contracts for physician services in anesthesiology and radiology that are comparatively costly. The contracts are near the end of their terms, and General Hospital wants to renegotiate the terms of the contracts or replace the current physician groups with others more compatible with a cost-conscious and outcomes-oriented style of practice. The anesthesiology group, Physicians' Practice Group (PPG), has been responsive to the needs of the hospital relating to coverage and quality of anesthesia services, but a new group, General Anesthesiology Services (GAS), has approached General with much more favorable terms. Although the surgeons have been very happy with PPG, General believes that they will become equally satisfied with GAS. General has agreed to enter into an exclusive contract with GAS and has given PPG notice that their exclusive contract will not be renewed. General has the right to terminate the PPG contract without cause.

Two of the three PPG anesthesiologists have already joined GAS, though at lower salaries than they enjoyed with PPG; but GAS has refused to consider hiring Dr. Casey.

Dr. Casey is considered somewhat difficult. He does not work well with the nurse anesthetists, and sometimes has conflicts with the surgeons. He has had two malpractice suits filed against him in the last few years, but both were dropped by the plaintiffs, one after the payment of a settlement and one without any payment. Other than these problems, his patient care has been of very good quality.

Casey's contract with PPG provides that PPG may terminate him "without cause with 60 days' notice," but is silent on the question of his privileges at General. The PPG contract with General states that the contract is exclusive and "only physician members of PPG may provide anesthesiology services at General." The original letter from General awarding Dr. Casey staff privileges, including clinical privileges in anesthesiology, states: "Because you will be providing services at General under an exclusive contract, your clinical privileges will be automatically terminated upon termination of that contract." Each of the subsequent renewal letters contained the same statement. The medical staff had been quite concerned a few years ago about automatic termination of privileges of physicians who had taken on administrative functions within the hospital and amended its by-laws to provide: "A physician member of the medical staff providing services to the hospital under contract will retain privileges even if that contract is terminated." The Board of Directors never approved of this amendment to the by-laws and has essentially ignored it.

What should General do? Should it simply terminate Casey's privileges without procedural review and for no cause? Or, should it follow the procedures in the by-laws? Should General proceed against Casey on the basis of the quality of his work? If the medical staff by-laws provided that the hospital may revoke privileges of "any physician whose inability to work well with others jeopardizes patient care," would you recommend that they proceed under that clause? Are there any other alternatives? How might a court handle the case under each of these alternatives should Casey sue? How would you redraft the termination provisions of the contracts for use with GAS?

II. MANAGED CARE CONTRACTS FOR PROFESSIONAL SERVICES

POTVIN v. METROPOLITAN LIFE INS. CO.

California Supreme Court, 2000.
22 Cal.4th 1060, 95 Cal.Rptr.2d 496, 997 P.2d 1153.

KENNARD, J.

* * *

On September 10, 1990, Metropolitan Life Insurance (MetLife) entered into an agreement with Dr. Louis E. Potvin, an obstetrician and gynecologist, to include him as one of 16,000 participants on two of its preferred provider lists. Potvin had practiced medicine for more than 35 years; he was a past president of the Orange County Medical Association; and he held full staff privileges at Mission Regional Hospital, where he had served as Chairman of the Obstetrics and Gynecology Department for nine years. Under the contract, Potvin was to provide medical services to MetLife's insureds in return for agreed-upon payment by MetLife. The agreement created no employment or agency relationship, and it allowed Potvin to also "contract with other preferred provider organizations, health maintenance organizations or other participating provider arrangements." It provided for termination by either party "at any time, with or without cause, by giving thirty (30) days prior written notice to the other party."

On July 22, 1992, MetLife notified Potvin in writing that effective August 31, 1992, it was terminating his preferred provider status. Potvin asked for clarification; MetLife replied that the termination, which the parties here also refer to as "delistment," was consistent with the contract, which allowed termination "without cause." When Potvin insisted on a further explanation, MetLife reiterated its right to terminate without cause. MetLife then stated that even though it did not have to give a reason, Potvin's "delistment from the provider network was related to the fact that [he] did not meet [MetLife's] current selection and retention standard for malpractice history." At the time, MetLife would not include or retain on its preferred provider lists any physician who had more than two malpractice lawsuits, or who had paid an aggregate sum of $50,000 in judgment or settlement of such actions. Potvin's patients had sued him for malpractice on four separate occasions, all predating his 1990 agreement with MetLife. In three of these actions, the plaintiffs had abandoned their claims, while the fourth case had settled for $713,000.

After MetLife failed to respond to Potvin's request for a hearing, Potvin filed this lawsuit. . . . Potvin alleged that MetLife's termination of his preferred provider status devastated his practice, reducing it to "a small fraction" of his former patients. He asserted that he was required to reveal his termination to other insurers and managed care entities, which then removed him from their preferred provider lists, and that he suffered rejection by "physician groups . . . dependent upon credentialing by MetLife" and by current MetLife preferred provider physicians, who ceased referring patients to him.

The trial court granted MetLife's motion for summary judgment. . . .

The Court of Appeal reversed. It disagreed with the trial court that Potvin's complaint failed to allege a claim for violation of the common law right to fair procedure. It also held that, before removing Potvin from its preferred provider lists, MetLife should have given him notice of the grounds for its action and a reasonable opportunity to be heard. With respect to Potvin's assertion that the removal violated [the California statute] setting forth procedures for physician peer review, the Court of Appeal agreed with the trial court that those provisions did not apply to the preferred provider contract involved here.

We granted MetLife's petition for review. We affirm the Court of Appeal's reversal of the trial court's grant of summary judgment for MetLife, but we disagree with the Court of Appeal that MetLife necessarily must comply with the common law doctrine of fair procedure before removing physicians from its preferred provider lists. In this case, that issue needs to be resolved by further proceedings in the trial court under the standards set forth below.

[Ed. Note: The court details the history of the application of "fundamental fairness" by the California courts over the past 100 years.]

Plaintiff here points out that when an insurance company with fiduciary obligations to its insureds maintains a list of preferred provider physicians to render medical services to the insureds, a significant public interest is affected. One practical effect of the health care revolution, which has made quality care more widely available and affordable through health maintenance organizations and other managed care entities, is that patients are less free to choose their own doctors for they must obtain medical services from providers approved by their health plan. The Managed Care Health Improvement Task Force stressed in its 1997 report to the California Legislature that the provision of health care "has a special moral status and therefore a particular public interest." [ ] But an even greater public interest is at stake when those medical services are provided through the unique tripartite relationship among an insurance company, its insureds, and the physicians who participate in the preferred provider network. . . .

Our conclusion that the relationship between insurers and their preferred provider physicians significantly affects the public interest does not necessarily mean that every insurer wishing to remove a doctor from one of its preferred provider lists must comply with the common law right to fair procedure. The obligation to do so arises only when the insurer possesses power so substantial that the removal significantly impairs the ability of an ordinary, competent physician to practice medicine or a medical specialty in a particular geographic area, thereby affecting an important, substantial economic interest.*

* * *

Here, plaintiff's amici curiae, the American Medical Association and the California Medical Association, assert in their joint brief that "the managed

---

* Our decision here does not apply to employer-employee contractual relations. Rather, it applies only to an insurer's decision to remove individual physicians from its preferred providers lists. We express no view on whether the factors giving rise to the common law right of fair procedure would be present when an insurer, acting to limit its service in a geographic area or medical field, reduces the total number of physicians on its preferred provider lists.

care organizations operating in California hold substantial economic power over physicians and their patients." They also contend that "the control exercised by managed care organizations makes access to provider panels a 'practical prerequisite' to any effective practice as a health care provider." ... If participation in managed care arrangements is a practical necessity for physicians generally and if only a handful of health care entities have a virtual monopoly on managed care, removing individual physicians from preferred provider networks controlled by these entities could significantly impair those physicians' practice of medicine.

Potvin alleged that among the adverse effects of removal from MetLife's preferred provider lists were rejection by "physician groups which were dependent upon credentialing by MetLife" and devastation of his practice, which was reduced to "a small fraction" of his former patients. Proof of these allegations might establish that, in terminating a physician's preferred provider status, MetLife wields power so substantial as to significantly impair an ordinary, competent physician's ability to practice medicine or a medical specialty in a particular geographic area, thereby affecting an important, substantial economic interest.

* * *

Our holding does not prevent an insurer subject to obligations of common law fair procedure from exercising its sound business judgment when establishing standards for removal of physicians from its preferred provider lists. We simply hold that, under principles recognized by the common law of this state for over a century, such removal must be "both substantively rational and procedurally fair."

* * *

MetLife contends that even if removal of a physician from its preferred provider lists is subject to the common law right to fair procedure, here Potvin waived that right by agreeing that MetLife could terminate the provider arrangement without cause. Potvin responds that the public policy considerations supporting the common law right to fair procedure render the "without cause" clause in the MetLife preferred provider agreement unenforceable. Faced with similar arguments, the New Hampshire Supreme Court declined to enforce a "without cause" provision in a contract between a health maintenance organization and one of its preferred provider physicians, allowing the case to go to trial on the physician's claim that the summary termination of his provider status violated the contractual obligations of good faith and fair dealing. Harper v. Healthsource New Hampshire, 674 A.2d 962 (1996). California courts, too, are loathe to enforce contract provisions offensive to public policy. [ ] We therefore agree with Potvin that the "without cause" termination clause is unenforceable to the extent it purports to limit an otherwise existing right to fair procedure under the common law.

The judgment of the Court of Appeal is affirmed.

GEORGE, C.J., MOSK, J., and WERDEGAR, J., concur.

Dissenting Opinion by BROWN, J.

... With its decision today, the majority, in effect, declares that it is the public policy of this state that physicians are entitled to a minimum income and, therefore, if removal of a physician from an insurer's preferred provider list would reduce the physician's income below that guaranteed minimum, the physician is entitled to a hearing and to the judicial review that would inevitably follow upon an adverse decision. . . .

* * *

. . . According to Dr. Potvin, the average physician who practices his specialty, obstetrics/gynecology, has been sued for malpractice 2.3 times. MetLife wishes to restrict its preferred provider lists to physicians with a slightly better than average malpractice history, to those who have not been sued more than twice. Potvin, by contrast, has been sued 4 times—nearly twice the average. Now the majority's public policy antennae may be more sensitive than mine, but I suspect the jury is still out on the question of whether an insurer should be able to control its costs by restricting its preferred provider lists to physicians with slightly better than average malpractice histories. That, surely, is a business judgment, and if the insurer makes the wrong judgment by depriving itself of doctors that patients insist upon, then the market will punish the insurer and force it to retreat from the impracticable standard.

* * *

My initial objection to the majority's standard is that it simply makes no sense. There is no necessary relationship between a physician's income and a physician's ability to practice medicine. Did Albert Schweitzer's ability to practice medicine diminish along with his income when he became a medical missionary in Africa?

Moreover, despite the majority's effort to cloak it in the public interest, this case has never been about Dr. Potvin's ability to practice medicine. It has been about money . . . As far as we can tell from this record, during the three and a half years that passed between his initial correspondence with MetLife and the filing of his motion for summary adjudication, Potvin's ability to practice medicine and his medical specialty was unaffected. He just wasn't making as much money at it.

Now I am not saying that it is somehow unbecoming for physicians to be concerned about loss of income. What I am saying is that this court has made doctors a protected class. Until the economy turned around recently, one could hardly open a newspaper without reading of yet another company that had laid off thousands of its employees. However, no one suggested that textile workers or bank employees, for example, had a right to a hearing before losing their jobs. The layoffs certainly affected "important, substantial economic interest[s]" of theirs. Indeed, they may well have exhausted their savings and lost their homes. And yet textile workers and bank employees must fend for themselves, while doctors are treated by the majority as if they are entitled to a minimum income.

The standard announced by the majority is unworkable, too, in the sense that decisions under it will be unpredictable. . . . The majority's standard purports to draw distinctions based on an insurer's share of the market in a particular geographic area. . . . In theory, a physician in Riverside might be entitled to a hearing before being terminated by a given insurer, while a physician in Fremont might not be, but as a practical matter, denying the

Fremont physician a hearing would only result in expensive litigation with an uncertain outcome, so the insurer will be forced to give them both hearings. Or, more likely, the insurer will simply give up on its cost-cutting efforts as not worth the candle.... That such an outcome, the abandonment of cost-control measures, would be in the public interest is certainly debatable, as inflation of health care costs is one of the greatest public policy challenges of our day....

* * *

... Upon examination, *Harper* provides little support for the majority's refusal to enforce the "without cause" termination clause of Potvin's contract with MetLife. *Harper* is distinguishable because California law differs from New Hampshire's in three respects that are critical to the decision in that case. First, the New Hampshire Supreme Court has "carved out exceptions to the common law employment-at-will doctrine, noting that in some cases 'the employer's interest in running his business as he sees fit must be balanced against the interest of the employee in maintaining his employment, and the public's interest in maintaining a proper balance between the two.' [ ]" In California, on the other hand, the common law employment-at-will doctrine has been reinforced by statute, and this court has not "carved out" the exception upon which the *Harper* court relied. Second, in New Hampshire "[t]he public policy to which a court may refer [in refusing to enforce a contract] may be statutory or nonstatutory in origin." By contrast, this court, as I have just explained, is generally "reluctant to declare contractual provisions void or unenforceable on public policy grounds without firm legislative guidance" and we have specifically held that exceptions to the employment-at-will doctrine must be "tethered to fundamental policies that are delineated in constitutional or statutory provisions." Third, *Harper* relied upon an expression of policy by the New Hampshire Legislature "that preferred provider agreements must be 'fair and in the public interest.'" No similar expression of policy by the California Legislature has been brought to our attention.

Finally, the *Harper* court emphasized that the rule it was declaring "does not eliminate a health maintenance organization's contractual right to terminate its relationship with a physician without cause." Rather, under the *Harper* rule, a physician terminated pursuant to a "without cause" provision is entitled to review only if "the physician believes that the decision to terminate was, in truth, made in bad faith or based upon some factor that would render the decision contrary to public policy." Indeed, under the *Harper* rule, the "without cause" termination provision of MetLife's contract with Dr. Potvin should be enforced because there is no showing that MetLife's decision was "made in bad faith or based upon some other factor that would render the decision contrary to public policy."

* * *

In conclusion, the judgment of the trial court granting MetLife's motion for summary judgment should have been affirmed.

BAXTER, J., and CHIN, J., concur.

Notes and Questions

1. Is Dr. Potvin entitled to a hearing prior to being delisted by MetLife? If he is entitled to a hearing, the California Supreme Court indicates that he is also

entitled to have MetLife's decision reviewed on the basis of whether it is "rational." Was MetLife's decision to exclude Dr. Potvin because of his malpractice history irrational? How would MetLife and Dr. Potvin go about proving whether the decision was irrational? The *Harper* case, cited by the court in *Potvin*, allowed no-cause terminations, but allowed the physician the opportunity to prove that the delisting was done in bad faith or for a reason that would violate public policy. How does this differ from the California standard for review? How would each of the following fair under *Potvin* and *Harper*: de-capitation for a Caesarean section rate in excess of the norm for plan physicians or in excess of the plan's target rate; disenrollment for specialist referrals or hospital stays in excess of the average of all plan physicians; termination for disclosure of the plan's physician financial incentive systems to patients or to a competing plan?

2.   As is apparent in *Potvin*, case law on hospital privileges and hospital physician contracts as well as the employment-at-will doctrine discussed in the next section forms the current doctrinal framework for common law claims in disputes arising from selection and deselection in managed care programs. Should the employment, staff privileges, contracting and payer relationships all be treated the same, or are there significant differences?

3.   Is *Potvin* consistent with *Mateo-Woodburn* in its treatment of no-cause termination clauses?

4.   *Potvin* was an eagerly awaited decision (taking nearly three years for the California Supreme Court to issue its decision), but its actual impact on a national level remains to be seen. Do you think it will have a substantial effect outside of California? Several state courts have addressed the issues in *Potvin* with varying results. See, for example, Mayer v. Pierce County Medical Bureau, 80 Wash.App. 416, 909 P.2d 1323 (1995), holding that a no-cause termination clause was enforceable; Grossman v. Columbine Medical Group, Inc., 12 P.3d 269 (1999, as modified Jan. 14, 2000), holding that state statute established public policy supporting no-cause terminations. Several states have enacted legislation addressing health plan terminations, and these also vary. See, for example, Colo.Stat. 10–16–705, providing that no-cause terminations simply require 60 days' notice, but that physicians cannot be delisted for reporting quality concerns to federal or state agencies, for disclosing financial incentives to patients, or for giving patients "standing referrals" to specialists. See also, Tex.Ins.Code Ann. Art. 20A.18A which provides that HMOs must provide physicians with a written explanation of the reasons for termination and that, with specific exceptions, physicians are entitled to review by a panel composed of physicians and providers, although the opinion of the panel is advisory only. There has been a particular concern over physician claims that they are subject to termination if they advocate on behalf of their patients or disclose the financial incentives offered by the insurer to the physician. A California statute addresses that concern:

(b) It is public policy of the State of California that a physician and surgeon be encouraged to advocate for medically appropriate health care for his or her patients. For purposes of this section, "to advocate for medically appropriate health care" means to appeal a payor's decision to deny payment for a service pursuant to the reasonable grievance or appeal procedure established by a medical group, independent practice association, preferred provider organization, foundation, hospital medical staff and governing body, or payer, or to protest a decision, policy, or practice that the physician, consistent with that degree of learning and skill ordinarily possessed by reputable physicians practicing according to the applicable legal standard of care, reasonably believes impairs the physician's ability to provide medically appropriate health care to his or her patients.

(c) The application and rendering by any person of a decision to terminate an employment or other contractual relationship with or otherwise penalize a physician and surgeon principally for advocating for medically appropriate health care consistent with that degree of learning and skill ordinarily possessed by reputable physicians practicing according to the applicable legal standard of care violates the public policy of this state. No person shall terminate, retaliate against, or otherwise penalize a physician and surgeon for that advocacy, nor shall any person prohibit, restrict, or in any way discourage a physician and surgeon from communicating to a patient information in furtherance of medically appropriate health care.

(d) This section shall not be construed to prohibit a payer from making a determination not to pay for a particular medical treatment or service, or to prohibit a medical group, independent practice association, preferred provider organization, foundation, hospital medical staff, hospital governing body acting pursuant to the [state statute on peer review which provides that peer review shall not be exercised arbitrarily] or payer from enforcing reasonable peer review or utilization review protocols or determining whether a physician has complied with those protocols. Cal. Bus & Prof. Code § 2056.

Although this statute was intended to apply to managed care organizations, the California Court of Appeal held that it applied to a situation in which a physician employed by a physician group practice was terminated after disagreeing with another physician in the practice over whether it was advisable to perform surgery on a particular patient. Khajavi v. Feather River Anesthesia Medical Group, 84 Cal.App.4th 32, 100 Cal.Rptr.2d 627 (Cal.App. 2000).

For an excellent collection of articles on these issues, see Symposium on Managed Care and the Physician–Patient Relationship, 35 Hous.L.Rev. 1529 et seq. (1999), and in particular, William M. Sage, Physicians as Advocates, 35 Hous.L.Rev. 1529 (1999). See also, Bethany J. Speilman, Managed Care Regulation and the Physician–Advocate, 47 Drake L. Rev. 713 (1999); Mark A. Kadzielski, et al., Managed Care Contracting: Pitfalls and Promises, 20 Whittier L. Rev. 385 (1998).

5. Courts differ in deciding whether ERISA preempts state law regarding physician contracting in managed care. See discussion of ERISA in Chapter 9.

III. LABOR AND EMPLOYMENT

A. EMPLOYMENT–AT–WILL

Doctors, nurses, administrators, and in-house counsel working without any employment contract or under a contract that does not provide for a specific term of employment are subject to the doctrine of employment-at-will. Employees working under a collective bargaining agreement or under a contract with express provisions concerning length of employment or termination for just cause only are not employees-at-will.

The common law at-will doctrine varies widely among the states, but generally provides that the employment relationship can be terminated without cause at the will of either the employer or the employee. The at-will doctrine allows a few exceptions, which in most states are relatively narrow.

The majority of nurses have long practiced as at-will employees. In contrast, doctors traditionally have practiced as owners of their own practices and have had the further protection of the staff privileges system for their economically necessary relationship with a hospital. Increasingly, however, doctors have become employees (often at-will employees) of health care organizations, including group practices, health maintenance organizations or hospitals that have purchased the physician's private practice. Some courts have borrowed from at-will doctrine in deciding cases of physician termination or delisting from insurance plans as well.

WRIGHT v. SHRINERS HOSPITAL FOR CRIPPLED CHILDREN

Supreme Court of Massachusetts, 1992.
412 Mass. 469, 589 N.E.2d 1241.

O'CONNOR, JUSTICE.

In this case, which is here on direct appellate review, we consider the sufficiency of the evidence to warrant a jury's verdict of $100,000 in favor of the plaintiff, Anita Wright against her employer, the defendant Shriners Hospital for Crippled Children (Shriners Hospital), on Wright's claim that Shriners Hospital wrongfully terminated her at-will employment in violation of public policy. ...We hold that the evidence was insufficient to warrant [the] verdict and that the trial judge should have allowed the defendants' motion for judgment notwithstanding the verdict....

We summarize the evidence in the light most favorable to the plaintiff. [ ] Shriners Hospital hired Wright, a registered nurse, in 1976. Subsequently, she became assistant director of nursing, and she held that position until she was discharged in late February of 1987. At all times, she was an employee at will. Wright received excellent evaluations throughout her employment, including an evaluation in December, 1986, two months before her discharge. In June, 1986, a former assistant head nurse wrote a letter to the director of clinical affairs for the Shriners national headquarters detailing her concerns about the medical staff and administration at Shriners Hospital. Shriners Hospital is a separate corporation, but it is one of many Shriners facilities that are affiliated with the national headquarters. As a result of the letter, the national headquarters notified the defendant hospital administrator, Russo, that a survey team would visit Shriners Hospital in November, 1986. Russo was visibly upset. He spoke to the director of nursing about the letter and asked her: "Are you behind this? Is Anita Wright behind this?" The director of nursing denied that she was responsible for the letter. She did not address the question whether Wright was "behind" the letter.

The survey team visited the hospital in November and interviewed Wright and other employees. Wright told the survey team that there were communication problems between the medical and nursing staffs. She detailed problems with the assistant chief of staff and gave specific examples of patient care problems. The survey team reported Wright's comments to the assistant chief of staff.

Two members of the survey team prepared reports. In his report issued on December 22, 1986, Dr. Newton C. McCollough, director of medical affairs for the national organization, wrote: "The relationships between nursing administration, hospital administration, and chief of staff are much less than satisfactory, and significant friction exists both as regard nursing/administration relationships and nursing/medical staff relationships. Communication and problem solving efforts in this relationship are poor to nonexistent." A report issued on January 5, 1987, by Jack D. Hoard, executive administrator for the national Shriners organization, also documented the problematic relationship between the nursing and medical staff. Both reports recommended a follow-up site survey to determine the impact of this conflict on patient care. McCollough's report stated that during her interview, Wright had made severe criticisms of the medical staff and had expressed concern over a lack of consistent procedures and standards for patient care. Hoard's report stated that Wright discussed the breakdown in communication between the nursing staff and the attending medical staff, which she said was leading to deteriorating morale among nurses.

* * *

Upon reading the survey team's reports, Russo again became upset and told the director of nursing that it was the nursing department's fault that the team was making another visit. The survey team returned on February 18 and 19, 1987, specifically to review the problems between the medical and nursing staffs. On February 26, after consulting with the chairman and several officers of the board of governors of Shriners Hospital and with national corporate counsel, Russo ordered that Wright's employment be terminated for "patient care issues that had arisen as a result of the surveys."

Wright contends, and the defendants dispute, that the jury would have been warranted in finding that Shriners Hospital fired her from her employment at will in retaliation for her having criticized the hospital, specifically in regard to the quality of care rendered to patients, to the Shriners national headquarters survey team. Wright further asserts that such a retaliatory firing violates public policy and is therefore actionable. We hold that a termination of Wright's employment at will in reprisal for her critical remarks to the survey team would not have violated public policy. . . .

We begin with the general rule that "[e]mployment at will is terminable by either the employee or the employer without notice, for almost any reason or for no reason at all." [ ] We have recognized exceptions to that general rule, however, when employment is terminated contrary to a well-defined public policy. Thus, "[r]edress is available for employees who are terminated for asserting a legally guaranteed right (e.g., filing workers' compensation claim), for doing what the law requires (e.g., serving on a jury), or for refusing to do that which the law forbids (e.g., committing perjury)." [ ] . . .

The trial judge's view of the law was that public policy was violated if Shriners Hospital fired Wright in reprisal for her having criticized the hospital in interviews with the survey team. As is clear from his instructions to the jury, the judge's view was based in part on "the duty of doctors and nurses, found in their own code of ethics, to report on substantial patient care issues." We would hesitate to declare that the ethical code of a private professional organization can be a source of recognized public policy. . . .

It is also clear from his instructions that the judge's view was based in part on "various state laws of the commonwealth, requiring reports on patient abuse." The judge did not identify the State laws he had in mind. General Laws c. 119, § 51A (1990 ed.), requires nurses and others to make a report to the Department of Social Services concerning any child under eighteen years of age who they have reason to believe is suffering from physical or sexual abuse or neglect. Similarly, G.L. c. 19A, § 15(a) (1990 ed.), requires nurses and others who have reasonable cause to believe that an elderly person is suffering from abuse to report it to the Department of Elder Affairs. Subsection (d) of that provision provides that no employer or supervisor may discharge an employee for filing a report. Finally, G.L. c. 111, § 72G (1990 ed.), requires nurses and others to report to the Department of Public Health (department) when they have reason to believe that any patient or resident of a facility licensed by the department is being abused, mistreated, or neglected and provides a remedy of treble damages, costs, and attorney's fees for any employee who is discharged in retaliation for having made such a report. None of these statutes applies to Wright's situation, however, and we are unaware of any statute that does. Also, we are unaware of any statute that clearly expresses a legislative policy to encourage nurses to make the type of internal report involved in this case. In fact, Wright testified that she did not consider the patient care that caused her concern to be abuse, neglect, or mistreatment warranting a report to the department, nor did she feel that there was an issue of physician incompetence warranting a report to the board of registration in medicine as required by G.L. c. 112, § 5F (1990 ed.).

Wright urges us to recognize a regulation promulgated by the Board of Registration in Nursing as a source of public policy sufficient to create an exception to the general rule regarding termination of at-will employment. Title 244 Code Mass.Regs. § 3.02(3)(f) (1986) describes the responsibilities and functions of a registered nurse, including the responsibility to "collaborate, communicate and cooperate as appropriate with other health care providers to ensure quality and continuity of care." Even if that regulation called for Wright to report perceived problems or inadequacies to the survey team, a doubtful proposition, we have never held that a regulation governing a particular profession is a source of well-defined public policy sufficient to modify the general at-will employment rule, and we decline to do so now. Furthermore, as we have noted above, Wright's report was an internal matter, and "[i]nternal matters," we have previously said, "could not be the basis of a public policy exception to the at-will rule."

* * *

We reverse the judgments for the plaintiff and remand to the Superior Court for the entry of judgments for the defendants.

LIACOS, CHIEF JUSTICE (dissenting).

I disagree with the court's conclusion that a hospital employer violates no public policy when it fires an employee for alerting supervisors to matters detracting from good patient care. The court has construed far too narrowly the public policy exception to the doctrine of employment at will. Moreover, in demanding a statutory basis for public policy, the court has relinquished to the Legislature its role in shaping the common law. I dissent.

* * *

Given the public interest in good patient care, it must be the public policy of the Commonwealth to protect, if not encourage, hospital employees who perceive and report detriments to patient care. Only when problems are identified can they be adequately addressed; an employee's failure to report perceived detriments to patient care may allow the problems to persist. A hospital employer therefore violates public policy when it fires an employee for trying to improve the quality of patient care. That an employer may deter other employees from reporting problems (for fear of losing their jobs) inhibits the provision of good patient care and offends the public interest.

... The plaintiff was not terminated for contributing to the hospital's problems, nor for refusing to accept her supervisor's method of addressing the problems; she was fired for reporting the problems to appropriate accreditation authorities. Such a termination offends the public interest and is actionable. I dissent.

Notes and Questions

1. *Wright* represents the majority view concerning the scope of the public policy exception to employment-at-will. See e.g., Lampe v. Presbyterian Medical Center, 41 Colo.App. 465, 590 P.2d 513 (Colo.App.1978). But see, Winkelman v. Beloit Memorial Hosp., 168 Wis.2d 12, 483 N.W.2d 211 (Wis.1992), allowing wrongful discharge claim to nurse who refused to "float" to another unit in the hospital, arguing that it would require her to perform services for which she was unqualified. Should doctors and nurses working under at-will arrangements receive broader legal protection for complaints and actions concerning quality of patient care? Should they be treated differently than other workers?

2. Wrongful discharge cases may also involve specific medical treatment decisions. For example, in Warthen v. Toms River Community Memorial Hospital, 199 N.J.Super. 18, 488 A.2d 229 (1985), the court rejected the nurse's claim of wrongful discharge under the public policy exception where a nurse refused to dialyze a patient who had twice suffered heart attacks and severe internal hemorrhaging during dialysis. Warthen based her legal claim on a provision of the American Nurses Association Code for Nurses allowing nurses to refuse to provide treatment that was contrary to the nurse's personal beliefs so long as the patient would not be abandoned. The court held as a matter of law that the Code did not state public policy, but rather was beneficial only to the nursing profession and the individual nurse. See also, Farnam v. CRISTA Ministries, 116 Wash.2d 659, 807 P.2d 830 (1991). But see Kirk v. Mercy Hospital Tri–County, 851 S.W.2d 617 (Mo.App.1993), in which the court allowed a wrongful discharge claim by a nurse who was fired after a dispute over a particular patient's care. In *Kirk*, the nurse had asked her supervisor repeatedly about a patient admitted with life-threatening toxic shock syndrome for whom no antibiotics had been ordered. The nurse alleged that she had been told to document the situation and "stay out of it." The patient died, and the nurse suggested that the family obtain the patient's medical record. See also, Deerman v. Beverly California Corp., 135 N.C.App. 1, 518 S.E.2d 804 (N.C.App. 1999), holding that a nurse would have a claim of wrongful discharge if she could prove she was terminated because she advised a patient's family to replace the patient's doctor.

3. Most states accept a theory of "implied contract" to take a relationship out of the at-will category. Personnel manuals may be a source of an implied contract, but employers ordinarily can avoid this effect by inserting a clear, unambiguous and prominently displayed disclaimer stating that the manual does not constitute a contract and that employees are terminable at will. Furthermore, medical staff by-laws may be viewed by the courts as contracts for other purposes, but they have not generally been viewed as implied contracts in the context of at-will employment. See e.g., Hrehorovich v. Harbor Hospital Center, 93 Md.App. 772, 614 A.2d 1021 (Md.App.1992).

4. The federal government and many states have "whistleblower" statutes that specifically protect employees who report wrongdoing to government agencies. These statutes typically are drafted narrowly and have been interpreted by the courts quite strictly. See e.g., Hays v. Beverly Enterprises, Inc., 766 F.Supp. 350 (W.D.Pa.1991); Radice v. Elderplan, Inc., 217 A.D.2d 690, 630 N.Y.S.2d 326 (1995); Minnesota Association of Nurse Anesthetists v. Unity Hospital, 59 F.3d 80 (8th Cir.1995). As detailed in *Wright*, some state abuse reporting statutes may provide some protection to reporters. The Federal False Claims Act prohibits retaliation against employees for actions, reports or suits under the Act. See e.g. Neal v. Honeywell, Inc., 33 F.3d 860 (7th Cir.1994); University of Texas Medical Branch v. Hohman, 6 S.W.3d 767 (Tex.App.1999).

5. The Supreme Court in Waters v. Churchill, 511 U.S. 661, 114 S.Ct. 1878, 128 L.Ed.2d 686 (1994) considered the case of a nurse-employee of a public hospital who claimed that her termination violated her right to free speech under the First Amendment because she was terminated for opposing the hospitals' use of cross-training. "Cross-training" is a staffing pattern that requires that nurses shift among the various units of the facility depending on the volume of work available. Churchill had criticized the policy as causing inadequately trained nurses to staff particular units at particular times. The employer claimed that Churchill's discharge was not due to her complaints about cross-training but rather due to her disruptive behavior. The Supreme Court recognized that public employees retained First Amendment rights, but that the government as employer had wider latitude in this context than it had in others because of its needs to achieve the goals for which the enterprise had been established. The Court held that even if the plaintiff's criticism of the hospital were protected by the First Amendment, the disruptiveness of the plaintiff's behavior may outweigh the free speech protections. The Court remanded the case for trial because the plaintiff had produced "enough evidence that her criticisms of the hospital, rather than her disruptive behavior, formed the basis for her termination."

B. NATIONAL LABOR RELATIONS ACT

The beginning of the 21st century has seen a terrific surge in interest in unionization in the health care field, especially unionization of doctors and nurses. In the mid–1990s, unionization of nurses formed a platform for concerns over staffing patterns in hospitals and other working conditions in nursing homes. See e.g., Lacy McCrary, Nurses Protest in D.C., Saying Job Cuts Erode Care, Philadelphia Inquirer (March 31, 1995), covering a demonstration of 30,000 nurses; Efforts by Hospitals to Reduce Costs Have Cut Patient Care Quality, Union Says, Daily Labor Report News, May 11, 1995; AFSCME Nurses Reject Final Offer from Kaiser in Southern California, Daily Labor Report News, July 5, 1995; CAN Members Ratify Contract with Kaiser in Northern California, Daily Labor Report, April 27, 1998 (reporting on agreement, after six strikes, in which Kaiser agreed to establish nurse committees as "quality liaisons"). Union organizing among hospital nurses continues to see increasing success.

In the late 1990s, doctors began to organize unions in hospitals and in private practice, especially in connection with managed care relationships. In 1999, the American Medical Association created a union that would seek to represent doctors. Physicians for Responsible Negotiation, the AMA union, currently represents doctors at several sites.

With these developments, the scope of the National Labor Relations Act has become quite important to health care lawyers. This section presents materials on three particular issues: the distinction between employee and independent contractor (important because the NLRA does not reach independent contractors); the determination of whether an employee is a supervisor, as supervisors are not protected by the Act; and the prohibition against retaliation against employees who engage in "concerted action" over terms and conditions of employment.

1. *Employee or Independent Contractor?*

AMERIHEALTH AND UNITED FOOD AND COMMERCIAL WORKERS UNION

329 NLRB No. 76 (1999).

By Chairman Truesdale and Members Fox and Brame:

* * *

[T]he legal issue presented in the instant case is not whether collective bargaining by the unit physicians would benefit them or their patients, or whether "inequality in bargaining power," if it exists, between the physicians and AmeriHealth [a managed care plan] could be remedied by the Act's protections. Nor is the issue whether the physicians have become agents of AmeriHealth in its efforts to control health care costs. Rather, the issue is whether the physicians, in their work for AmeriHealth, are so integrated with and controlled by AmeriHealth that they meet the statutory definition of employees which, in turn, is based on the common law definition of "servants."

* * *

The definition of servants [in the Restatement] is based on the theory that they are a particular kind of agent; . . . that persons who are doing things for others are servants if there is the very close economic relation and control described in this Section; and, that this is true whether or not the persons are primarily engaged to do manual work or to make contracts. Indeed, fully employed but highly placed employees of a corporation, such as presidents and general managers, are not less servants because they are not controlled in their day-to-day work by other human beings. Their physical activities are controlled by their sense of obligation to devote their time and energies to the interests of the enterprise. [ ]

* * *

The record establishes that AmeriHealth controls, or has the right to control, many details of the services the physicians deliver to AmeriHealth members pursuant to the physicians' contractual relationships with Ameri-Health. To begin with, the physicians must accept and treat AmeriHealth members who select the physicians or are referred to them. Though PCPs [primary care physicians] can opt to limit their panel size after it reaches a minimum of 150, they must continue treating the AmeriHealth patients they have. As the Physicians Managed Care Agreement automatically renews each year, a physician's obligation to treat AmeriHealth patients continues indefi-nitely, until either party terminates the Agreement. AmeriHealth has only rarely terminated Agreements. The record does not indicate how often physi-cians terminate Agreements, but suggests that they are generally unwilling to do so for fear of losing their AmeriHealth patients.

In providing services to AmeriHealth members, the physicians are re-quired to adhere to detailed Standards of Service and Site Standards for their office facilities, equipment, accessibility, safety practices and record keeping. Some of these standards appear to be State-mandated minimums or generally-followed professional standards. Others are AmeriHealth's own standards, such as the maximum number of patients a physician may see each hour, the size of the patient waiting room and the maximum length of time a patient may be kept waiting there. AmeriHealth also expects physicians to adhere to its Wellness Guidelines for preventive care and Clinical Practice Guidelines for treating certain medical conditions. AmeriHealth monitors adherence to its Standards and Guidelines through recredentialing site visits and record reviews for PCPs and high-volume specialty physicians, and annual perfor-mance reviews and appraisals of PCPs. AmeriHealth attempts to enforce compliance through performance improvement plans and the threat of termi-nation. Indeed, the physicians' Agreements with AmeriHealth give Ameri-Health the unilateral right to terminate the contract for "contract breach" if the physician fails to adhere to AmeriHealth's rules, standards or guidelines. To date, AmeriHealth has not exercised such a right of termination, and does not regularly monitor adherence to its quality assurance standards and guidelines by most specialty physicians. However, the common law agency test examines a master's right to control, and not just his exercise of control.

[T]he record does not support the Petitioner's assertion that "what goes on" in the physicians' offices is "closely monitored and regulated by Ameri-Health." At most, AmeriHealth representatives visit physician offices for a few hours once every year or two, and even then they only conduct random spot checks of patient records. Many physicians never receive any site visits. AmeriHealth requires that it be notified of services rendered and have access to the physicians' records of such services, but AmeriHealth's standards and guidelines do not attempt to control or supervise the manner in which the physicians or their staffs actually perform the medical procedures and tests for which AmeriHealth pays them. AmeriHealth does not observe the physi-cians or their staffs providing medical care, and, as a practical matter, has no way of doing so. The Agreements require that the physicians provide services to members "with the same standard of care, skill and diligence customarily used by similar physicians in the community," but AmeriHealth does not define that standard or, as far as the record indicates, attempt to enforce it. For the most part, the medical procedures involved in this case are not performed "under the direction" of AmeriHealth, but "by a specialist without supervision."

AmeriHealth controls, through its Patient Care Management program, a wide variety of decisions about what services physicians may provide pursuant to their contracts with AmeriHealth (i.e., services for which AmeriHealth will pay them). AmeriHealth determines the sites where certain services must be performed in order to be covered. Through precertification, concurrent review and other case management procedures, AmeriHealth reviews the "medical appropriateness" or "necessity" of procedures recommended by physicians. AmeriHealth also requests and monitors compliance with its Drug Formulary. Notwithstanding this evidence of control, the record does not support the Petitioner's assertion that physicians "must get the approval from Ameri-Health for every significant step in the process of treating a patient." Many, if not most procedures performed by the physicians currently require no precer-tification. In particular, many routine referrals to specialty physicians are controlled by PCPs, not AmeriHealth. However, AmeriHealth unilaterally sets the scope of its precertification requirements. The set of procedures it reviews is neither mandated nor controlled by State law, and AmeriHealth is free to expand the requirements to encompass other services. Although AmeriHealth ultimately approves most precertification requests, it retains the right to deny them.

[T]he record fails to support the Petitioner's assertion that AmeriHealth and other HMOs control the physicians' access to patients. AmeriHealth's market share of insured patients in Atlantic and Cape May Counties is less than 10 percent. HMOs have enrolled about 35 percent of the insured population nationwide, though no figures on Atlantic and Cape May Counties were offered into evidence. Given current trends, these market shares may increase, but at the present time there are many insured patients who are not enrolled with AmeriHealth or any other HMO. Not all physicians in Cape May and Atlantic Counties have signed contracts with AmeriHealth. Some who signed, including one of the six physician witnesses at the hearing, have terminated their relationships. It may be true that, in the short-term, an HMO controls access to the HMO's own members because members are unlikely to use out-of-network providers, but there appears to be considerable movement of patients between plans, and physicians appear to have some, albeit limited, influence on where they move. At any rate, the petitioned-for physicians do not exclusively rely on AmeriHealth's marketing to obtain patients, but instead advertise and promote themselves on their own, and add new lines of services to attract patients and increase revenues.

In addition, the physicians maintain their separateness from Ameri-Health. AmeriHealth has no direct financial interest in the physicians' prac-tices. The physicians are free to contract with other insurance companies, including competing HMOs, and all or nearly all have done so. In fact, AmeriHealth patients account for only a small portion of the medical services the physicians provide. Physicians are also free to provide non-covered ser-vices to AmeriHealth members, if the members are willing to pay for them. The physicians advertise and do business in their own names or the names of their practices, and not in AmeriHealth's name. They compete for patients against other physicians within AmeriHealth's network. The physicians are highly skilled professionals engaged in a distinct occupation who receive no training from AmeriHealth. As members of their profession they must abide by standards and ethical rules apart from any requirements that AmeriHealth may impose. They do not work at AmeriHealth's facilities, but instead supply "the instrumentalities, tools and the place of work." Thus, the physicians lack the "close economic relation" and integration with AmeriHealth that would support a finding of employee status.

The physicians also make important business decisions that affect the profitability of their practices. AmeriHealth pays physicians not "by the time" but "by the job." The physicians receive a flat rate either per member/per month under capitation or per service under fee for service, while they are responsible for all the expenses of their practices. Thus, physicians have the opportunity to use their professional and business judgment to operate efficiently to maximize their profits or compensation. They decide whether they will associate with other physicians, and how their practices will be organized and owned....

Finally, the record does not support the Petitioner's assertion that "the physicians do not have a meaningful opportunity to negotiate over the terms, or the fees provided by AmeriHealth for their services." Clearly, AmeriHealth attempts to maintain a standard fee structure and discourages individual negotiations. Nonetheless, it has negotiated "special prices" with 10 percent or more of the physicians. For many physicians, AmeriHealth can impose its own price schedules, as evidenced by AmeriHealth's unilateral imposition of fee for service reductions in July 1998. However, in response to those new fees a number of physicians sought and obtained revised offers from AmeriHealth. . . .

* * *

. . . I . . . conclude that the physicians are not employees of AmeriHealth but are independent contractors within the meaning of the Act.

Notes and Questions

1. This decision does not resolve entirely the question of whether physicians contracting with HMOs can unionize. In fact, in its introduction to its decision in *AmeriHealth*, the Board states: "In denying review, we are not necessarily precluding a finding that physicians under contract to health maintenance organizations may, in other circumstances, be found to be statutory employees." What facts might lead the board to a different result? Unions have been certified by the Board in HMOs that employ, rather than contract with, physicians. See e.g., Physicians at Detroit HMO Vote for Union After NLRB Rejects Health Plan Appeal, Daily Labor Report, March 13, 2000.

2. The Board's complete decision contains an extraordinarily detailed analysis of the contract between AmeriHealth and its physicians and is an excellent source for background on HMO-physician contracting.

3. At the end of 1999, the Board reversed a 23–year-old precedent and held that residents and interns, who are also students, were employees and, therefore, were covered by the NLRA. Boston Medical Center Corporation and House Officers' Association/Committee of Interns and Residents, 330 N.L.R.B. No. 30.

4. Staff privileges decisions in hospitals in which the doctors are represented by a union may be subject to arbitration under the collective bargaining agree-

ment. See, for example, Scheiner v. New York City Health and Hospitals Corp., 1999 WL 771383 (S.D.N.Y.1999), in which a physician's privileges were revoked after full recourse to the by-laws' procedures and where, under a New York statutory provision, the revocation was affirmed by the New York State Public Health Council but where the revocation was rejected in arbitration. The hospital contested the arbitration result in state court, but the court refused to overturn the decision. Under the Federal Arbitration Act, a court is to overturn an arbitration award only in unusual circumstances. (The federal district court considered only the plaintiff's constitutional claims.)

5. See the discussion of the antitrust implications of physician unions in Chapter 15.

2. *Supervisor?*

KENTUCKY RIVER COMMUNITY CARE, INC. v. N.L.R.B.

United States Court of Appeals for the Sixth Circuit, 1999.
193 F.3d 444.

* * *

KRCC maintains that ... the registered nurses ... it employs are supervisors and therefore exempt from the collective bargaining unit [ ].... Individuals employed as supervisors are specifically excluded from the definition of employee and from the protection of the NLRA.

The NLRA defines "supervisor" as:

any individual having authority, in the interest of the employer, to hire, transfer, suspend, lay off, recall, promote, discharge, assign, reward, or discipline other employees, or responsibly to direct them, or to adjust their grievances, or effectively to recommend such action, if in connection with the foregoing the exercise of such authority is not of a merely routine or clerical nature, but requires the use of independent judgment.

Thus, an employee is a supervisor if he (1) has the authority to engage in one of the activities enumerated [above], (2) uses independent judgment in that activity, and (3) does so in the interest of the employer....

* * *

Although we have issued a number of opinions in the last year finding that nurses are supervisors, and rejecting the NLRB's stubborn insistence that they are not, we acknowledge that whether an employee is a supervisor is a highly fact-intensive inquiry, and therefore, each case must be scrutinized carefully.

During some of the second and all of the third shift at Caney Creek—almost two thirds of the day—the registered nurses act as building supervisors. Although a registered nurse is the highest ranking employee in the building throughout these periods, an administrator is always "on call." According to Caney Creek's procedures, the registered nurses acting as building supervisors are "in charge of the facility and all rehabilitation staff." The building supervisor is responsible for patient care and must ensure adequate staffing. According to an internal memorandum in the record, the nurses acting as building supervisors at Caney Creek are authorized to shift staff between units and must "write up anyone who does not comply with the request immediately." In addition, the nurses have authority to call employees into work early or ask employees to remain on duty beyond the normal end of shift in the event of staff shortages, although the nurses do not have authority to force an employee to work in these situations. The registered nurses do not retain keys to the facility, although they have access to a set of keys that they must give to the security guard when he comes on duty.

The registered nurses are responsible for medical services, particularly when there are no doctors in the building, which is frequently the case. The registered nurses are also responsible for ensuring that the licensed practical nurses properly dispense patient medications. The registered nurses do not make the initial work schedules, but they are expected to deal with situations in which the facility might become shorthanded for any reason. A nurse, acting as building supervisor, could send an employee home, but the nurse would then need to inform that employee's immediate supervisor.

Our task is to decide whether these responsibilities call for the exercise of "independent judgment." Unfortunately, the NLRB has continuously interpreted "independent judgment" in a manner that is inconsistent with this circuit's precedent. According to NLRB interpretations, the practice of a nurse supervising a nurse's aide in administering patient care, for example, does not involve "independent judgment." The NLRB classifies these activities as "routine" because the nurses have the ability to direct patient care by virtue of their training and expertise, not because of their connection with "management." This court, however, has repeatedly rejected this interpretation, and found that nurses are supervisors when they direct assistants with respect to patient care, rectify staffing shortages, fill out evaluation forms, and serve as the highest ranking employee in the building during off-peak shifts. [ ].

The registered nurses at KRCC direct the LPNs in the proper dispensing of medication, regularly serve as the highest ranking employees in the building, seek additional employees in the event of a staffing shortage, move employees between units as needed, and have the authority to write up employees who do not cooperate with staffing assignments. These duties involve independent judgment which is not limited to, or inherent in, the professional training of nurses. These duties are supervisory in nature, and there can be no doubt that these activities are conducted in the interest of the employer. See NLRB v. Health Care & Retirement Corp. of Am., 511 U.S. 571, 577, 114 S.Ct. 1778, 128 L.Ed.2d 586 (1994). After a careful examination of the record, we conclude that the evidence readily establishes that Caney Creek's registered nurses are supervisors, and does not support the NLRB's decision to include them in the bargaining unit.

* * *

JONES, CIRCUIT JUDGE, dissenting.

* * *

Having conducted the "highly fact-intensive inquiry" required by the majority, I would find the NLRB's determination—that the six registered nurses employed at KRCC are not supervisors—supported by substantial evidence. The NLRB found, in relevant part, as follows:

The RNs do not receive any extra compensation for serving as "building supervisors" and do not have keys to the facility.

* * *

[T]he only extra responsibility assumed by the RNs when serving as "building supervisors" is to obtain needed help if for some reason a shift is not fully staffed. In the event a shift is understaffed, the RNs on duty will first attempt to find a volunteer to stay over from among the employees on the proceeding shift. If a volunteer cannot be obtained from the employees on the preceding shift, the "building supervisor," using a list containing the names, telephone numbers and addresses of the employees, will attempt to reach an off-duty employee who lives nearby to come in and cover the shift. The "building supervisors" do not have any authority, however, to compel an employee to stay over or come in to fill a vacancy under threat of discipline.

It appears that the RNs may occasionally request other employees to perform routine tasks, but they apparently have no authority to take any action if the employee refuses their directives. The RNs may also complete incident reports, but so can any other employee. All incident reports are independently investigated by the nursing or unit coordinators to determine if any disciplinary action is warranted and it does not appear that these management officials seek any input from the RNs involved. Although [KRCC] asserts ... that RNs can "write-up" employees, there is no evidence in the record that they have ever done so....

* * *

The RNs in their normal capacity or as "building supervisors" do not have the authority to hire, fire, reward, promote or independently discipline employees or to effectively recommend such action. They do not evaluate employees or take any action which would affect their employment status. Indeed, the RNs, including when they are serving as "building supervisors," for the most part, work independently and by themselves without any subordinates.

Notes and Questions

1. The Sixth Circuit chastises the National Labor Relations Board for not following its directions as to the applications of the standards for supervisory employees. The circuits have been in serious conflict, however, over the application of these standards ever since the Supreme Court's opinion in *Health Care & Retirement Corp.*, which had rejected the Board's earlier policy on the matter. See e.g., Schnurmacher Nursing Home v. N.L.R.B., 214 F.3d 260 (2d Cir.2000), holding that charge nurses were supervisors; Northern Montana Health Care Center v. N.L.R.B., 178 F.3d 1089 (9th Cir.1999) and N.L.R.B. v. Hilliard Development Corp., 187 F.3d 133 (1st Cir.1999), enforcing Board's decision that charge nurses were not supervisors; N.L.R.B. v. Attleboro Associates, Ltd., 176 F.3d 154 (3d Cir.1999) and Beverly Enterprises, Virginia, Inc. v. N.L.R.B., 165 F.3d 290 (4th Cir.1999), rejecting Board's decision that LPN's were not supervisors; N.L.R.B. v. GranCare, Inc., 170 F.3d 662 (7th Cir.1999), enforcing Board's decision that LPN's were not supervisors. As this is written, there is a petition for certiorari before the Supreme Court in *Kentucky River*.

2.   As discussed earlier, the NLRB has certified a union representing doctors employed by an HMO. What facts would the HMO have to marshall in order to prove that all or some of the doctors are supervisors, and, therefore, cannot be represented by the union?

3. *Concerted Action*

NEW YORK UNIVERSITY MEDICAL CENTER AND ASSOCIATION OF STAFF PSYCHIATRISTS, BELLEVUE PSYCHIATRIC HOSPITAL
324 NLRB No. 139 (1997).

* * *

[T]he evidence shows that the Association [of Staff Psychiatrists is a labor organization under the Act even though it is not a union because it] has an already defined unit, that of staff psychiatrists at Bellevue Psychiatric Hospital, was formed in 1973 for the purpose of dealing with the Respondent regarding such matters as salaries, working hours and conditions, and grievances of its members, has elected officials (executive board) by elections held every 2 years, has dues paying membership, holds membership meetings, and has actually dealt with the Respondent, mainly through the director of psychiatry, Dr. Manual Trujillo, concerning issues such as wages (equalizing or improving the salary structure of the psychiatrists at Bellevue), the hours and working conditions of the psychiatrists, and grievances. . . .

* * *

The complaint alleges in substance, that the Respondent violated Section 8(a)(1) of the Act by threatening employees with cutbacks, layoffs, and other consequences if they continued to protest a change in employee work hours, and violated Section 8(a)(1) and (3) of the Act by discharging Drs. John Graham, Ebrahim Kermani, Martin Geller, Jerome Steiner, Stanley Portnow, and Meave Mahon [all members of the executive committee of the Association] because they engaged in protected concerted activities.

* * *

Under an affiliated contract with HHC, the Respondent provides psychiatrists and other health care professionals to Bellevue Hospital Center for the purpose of delivering medical and psychiatrist patient care and services. . . . HHC is a quasi public corporation responsible for operating the municipal hospital system of New York City, including Bellevue Hospital. . . .

* * *

For a number of years, HHC had expressed dissatisfaction with a practice under which certain psychiatrists employed by the Respondent at Bellevue Hospital worked from 9 a.m. to 3 p.m., HHC maintained that . . . the affiliation contract required physicians to provide at least 40 hours of service per week, inclusive of unpaid meal hours. By memorandum dated September 30, 1994, HHC Executive Director Pam Brier advised Dr. Trujillo that because of an extremely serious fiscal situation, "Effective November 1, 1994, all full-time staff must fulfill the obligation explicitly delineated in the affiliate contract to work at least 35 hours per week. As we've discussed, there really can be no exception to this policy regardless of any informal agreements."

On September 30, 1994, the Respondent conducted the first of several staff meetings to discuss the "9 to 3" issue. About 30–40 psychiatrists attended, including association executive board members Drs. Graham, Kermani, Mahon, Geller, and Portnow, among others. Dr. Trujillo announced that because of budget problems there would no longer be any "9 to 3" hours, that everybody had to increase productivity and work 9 a.m. to 4:30 p.m. or take a decrease in salary, as the only solution. Dr. Maeve Mahon testified that she suggested that clinical work be assigned to [the physician] administrators. Dr. Mahon related that it was chiefly the members of the executive board [of the Association], particularly Drs. Graham and Kermani, who spoke out against the Respondent's announced changes in working hours ...

* * *

Dr. Mahon also testified that she attended another meeting in which Dr. Trujillo mentioned that the "9–3" psychiatrists were going to have to work more hours, and she asked why [the physician administrators] couldn't "come downstairs from their offices and do some clinical care?" Dr. Mahon testified that she perceived animosity from Dr. Trujillo at every meeting she attended as an elected member of the Association. Dr. Trujillo appeared angry, difficult, and stated that the Association wasn't a union or labor group and represented no one.

Dr. Portnow's testimony which substantially supported that of Dr. Mahon as to what occurred at these meetings testified that after [a] meeting had ended, and while he was waiting for an elevator, Dr. Trujillo told him that "Dr. Mahon's behavior was disgraceful, disloyal, undesirable and that it would lead to trouble for the attendings." Portnow also recalled that within the same day or the next Dr. Trujillo said to him that "the Association would be punished" for its position on the "9 to 3" issue; that it was a political issue and that "we should have taken the offer of renegotiating our time to eight-tenths time."

* * *

[I]n the fall of 1994 HHC notified the Respondent that the mental health portion of the affiliation contract budget at Bellevue had to be reduced by approximately $2 million. According to the testimony of several of the Respondent's witnesses they "tried to protect the psychiatrists working at Bellevue" by arguing against the reduction and offering an alternate proposal. After prolonged negotiations, however, HHC insisted on the budget cut and determined it could only be achieved by a reduction in the staff of 10 psychiatrists.

... Dr. Trujillo and his senior administrators implemented plans to reorganize the psychiatric department.... [T]hey first determined that the reduction should be made in the in-patient rather than the out-patient units. They then decided that a unit would have to be closed and other medical units combined or reorganized. Because the new system would require the implementation of a treatment plan to rapidly stabilize and dispose of patients, the Respondent began to review the productivity and performance, especially the management and leadership skills of psychiatrists and of the unit chiefs, to determine which would be most effective in the new structure and "enable the department to fulfill its mission with ten less psychiatrists."

[Ed. Note: Six members of the executive committee of the Association were among the ten psychiatrists terminated. The Board details the reorganization plan developed to comply with the $2 million cut required by HHC. One illustration is reproduced below as an example.]

* * *

The plan identifies 12 South as a general unit which "will continue to function as previously." The Respondent terminated Drs. Kermani and Steiner and replaced them with Dr. Buckingham and, on a part-time basis, Dr. Sageman. The Respondent did not terminate or otherwise remove Drs. Brodie, Ravelo, or Hazzi from the unit.

At the time he was terminated, Dr. Kermani had been employed by Bellevue for approximately 25 years, was a full clinical professor at NYU's School of Medicine, and had earned certification by the American Boards of Psychiatry and Neurology, Child Psychiatry, and Forensic Psychiatry. In addition, Dr. Kermani had authored approximately 25 academic articles, including articles on AIDS, as well as a book on forensic psychiatry. For the past 15 years of his employment by the Respondent, Dr. Kermani served as the unit chief of Bellevue's medical-psychiatric unit.

[A senior administrator] testified that the administrators felt the internists were providing the primary "leadership" in the unit and that they needed someone who could better coordinate and/or integrate the medical and psychiatric care of the patients on the unit. [He] stated that he did not put such concerns in writing but that he had spoken to Dr. Kermani about his "goals" for the unit. [He also] stated that ... Dr. Buckingham had demonstrated expertise in treating medical as well as psychiatric patients, and was board-certified in family medicine. [He] further noted that Dr. Sagemen had run the consultation-liaison unit at Bellevue for 16 years and that Dr. Ravelo was bilingual and had fellowship training in geriatric psychiatry.

With respect to Dr. Kermani's termination, [a senior administrator] testified that the most important factor for him was that Dr. Kermani had difficulty implementing policies intended to upgrade the unit. However, while [he] admitted that Dr. Kermani was a competent scholar he maintained that Dr. Kermani had difficulty "mobilizing" the team and providing an efficient treatment program on the unit.

Dr. Trujillo stated that he recalled that [senior] administrators said that Dr. Kermani did not have the updated clinical skills to run a hyper-acute unit, that he lacked the "leadership" skills to motivate the staff on the unit, and that he did not have the capacity to ensure that the documentation and quality assurance programs would be implemented.

* * *

[T]he evidence clearly establishes that the Association and its member psychiatrists engaged in a series of concerted actions in protest against the

Respondent's announced changes in their working hours and that the Respondent was aware of such activities.

* * *

... Dr. Trujillo [admitted] that he often told [a group of psychiatrists] that if they did not do something "constructive" to deal with the 9 a.m. to 3 p.m. issue, there would be further budgetary problems, that the problem would just get worse and effect everybody. Dr. Trujillo admitted that he may have [said] ... that "it was not a good idea, in a budgeting shortness to have an open issue like the 9:00 to 3:00. It makes you very visible for the chopping block."

The record is replete with evidence of statements of animus by Dr. Trujillo toward the Association and the Association's executive board and would lend credence to the view that Dr. Trujillo would not hesitate to tell the Association that it would be "punished" for opposing a change in the 9 a.m. to 3 p.m. work schedules. The Respondent's contentions that Dr. Trujillo was simply trying to warn the psychiatrists that a failure to resolve the 9 a.m. to 3 p.m. issue would cause more budgeting problems and possibly layoffs is irrelevant. However, given Dr. Trujillo's demonstrated history of animus toward the Association and its officers, no reasonable person would have believed that Dr. Trujillo's pronouncements were anything but a threat. This remains true even if one credits Dr. Trujillo's statement that a failure to resolve the 9 to 3 issue makes the psychiatrists "very visible for the chopping block." ...

* * *

... I am persuaded that ... a motivating factor in the discharge of the six alleged discriminatees was their protected concerted activities based on the abundant evidence of animus toward the Association and its various executive board members on the part of the Respondent, their open opposition to the change in the 9 to 3 work schedule and other activities on behalf of the psychiatrists and the Respondent's knowledge thereof, the unlawful implicit threats of cutbacks, layoffs and other consequences if they continued to protest such change, and the timing of the discharges relative to their protected activity. Accordingly, the burden shifts to the Respondent to establish that it would have terminated Drs. Graham, Kermani, Geller, Steiner, Portnow and Mahon even in the absence of their protected concerted activities. [ ] The Respondent asserts that the layoff of the six alleged discriminatees was not in violation of Section 8(a)(1) and (3) of the Act because it was motivated by a reduction in budget mandated by the Health and Hospital Corporation of New York City and based on the Respondent's judgment concerning the best personnel to operate the reorganized department and not by their activity on behalf of the Association.

I do not agree.

* * *

Note and Questions

1. The NYU case involved a statutory labor organization; but this is not required in order for an employee to be engaged in concerted action protected by

the NLRA. For example, in N.L.R.B. v. Main Street Terrace Care Center, 218 F.3d 531 (6th Cir.2000), the court held that a dietary aide who had helped other employees review their paychecks and report errors and who had made a statement about needing a union at the facility had engaged in concerted action and that her discharge was in retaliation for that activity rather than for the reason stated by the employer. See also, Misericordia Hospital Medical Center v. N.L.R.B., 623 F.2d 808 (2d Cir.1980), holding that a nurse engaged in concerted action when she participated in preparing a report critical of the hospital.

2.   The Board rejected the University's defense because of statements made by the administrator. Once those statements were made, was there anything the University could have done to reduce the risk of an adverse decision by the Board, other than retaining the six psychiatrists? The concerns identified by NYU revolved around Kermani's leadership skills. What kind of evidence should NYU produce to prove that this was the reason for the termination?

Problem: Changing Things

St. Margaret's Hospital is experiencing financial difficulties because of the decrease in federal reimbursement, the increase in indigent care, changes in the payment policies of private insurers, and problems in its own billing and collection operations. It has undertaken an initiative, called "Take Charge!", which is intended to increase volume, decrease costs, and improve quality.

As part of this initiative, St. Margaret's decided to enter into exclusive contracts for anesthesiology and radiology. Current medical staff were not happy about the situation. The physicians who provide services in each of these departments hold staff privileges, and are not paid a salary by the hospital, although the hospital provides all of their equipment and supplies. The hospital does the billing for services the doctors provide in the hospital, but the charges are payable directly to the doctors.

Each of these departments holds regular medical staff meetings each quarter to review events at the hospital, to discuss concerns about nurse staffing and equipment, and to air any problems that might be developing. The medical staff in the departments elect their own chairperson to handle these meetings. The chair has no appointment with the hospital itself. At a meeting last spring, the medical staff in the department of radiology decided to send a joint letter to hospital administration opposing the move to exclusive contracting. Dr. Stitch and Dr. Morales agreed to draft the letter and to meet with administration to discuss the physicians' concerns. They did so. Although reports of the meeting vary, it was pleasant enough even though the hospital CEO said that he thought Dr. Stitch and Dr. Morales should focus on more constructive responses to the situation. Later, when the hospital announced that it was seeking a physician group to provide exclusive radiology services, Dr. Stitch and Dr. Morales bid for the contract. St. Margaret's granted the contract to another group. Physicians who did not have a contract with that group, including Doctors Stitch and Morales, were told that they could retain privileges, but could not provide radiology services unless by specific request of a physician.

Also, as part of the Take Charge! initiative, St. Margaret's changed its nurse staffing in surgery to require nurses to work on a prn basis. If no surgeries were scheduled, the nurses would be assigned to other units or would be released for the day without pay. Nurse Jones was particularly vocal in her concern over this change. She was concerned that nurses would be sent to work in units where they were not qualified and that emergency surgeries would not be adequately covered.

Nurse Jones felt a particular accountability for the nurses as she was the head nurse in the intensive care unit. As head nurse, she monitored the performance of the nurses in that unit and dealt with conflicts as they arose. She didn't have authority to hire or discipline the nurses who worked in her unit, but the Director of Nursing and the Personnel Office usually followed her suggestions. Roberta Farr, the Director of Nursing, met privately with Nurse Jones and subtly indicated that she shared Nurse Jones' concerns, but said that the system should be tried first. The DON's comments were quickly circulated along the hospital's grapevine. Ms. Farr demoted Nurse Jones because of her lack of discretion in this matter; and one week later, the hospital discharged Ms. Farr.

Do Doctors Stitch and Morales have an action against St. Margaret's? Does Ms. Farr? Nurse Jones?

IV. DISCRIMINATION LAW

ESTATE OF MAURO v. BORGESS MEDICAL CENTER

United States Court of Appeals for the Sixth Circuit, 1998.
137 F.3d 398.

GIBSON, CIRCUIT JUDGE.

William C. Mauro brought an action against his former employer, Borgess Medical Center, alleging violations of the Americans with Disabilities Act, 42 U.S.C. §§ 12101–12213 (1994), and the Rehabilitation Act, 29 U.S.C. §§ 701–796 (1994). The district court granted Borgess's motion for summary judgment, determining that Mauro, who was infected with human immunodeficiency virus, or HIV, the virus that causes AIDS, was a direct threat to the health and safety of others that could not be eliminated by reasonable accommodation and thus concluded that Borgess took no illegal action in removing Mauro from his position as surgical technician. [ ]. Mauro appeals, arguing that as a surgical technician at Borgess he did not pose a direct threat to the health and safety of others and that therefore the district court erred in granting summary judgment to Borgess. We affirm.

Borgess employed Mauro from May 1990 through August 24, 1992 as an operating room technician. In June of 1992, an undisclosed source telephoned Robert Lambert, Vice President of Human Resources for Borgess Medical Center and Borgess Health Alliance, and informed Lambert that Mauro had "full blown" AIDS. Because of Borgess's concern that Mauro might expose a patient to HIV, Georgiann Ellis, Vice President of Surgical, Orthopedic and Clinical Services at Borgess, and Sharon Hickman, Mauro's supervisor and Operating Room Department Director, created a new full-time position of case cart/instrument coordinator, a position that eliminated all risks of transmission of the HIV virus. In July of 1992, Borgess officials offered Mauro this position, which he refused.

After Mauro's refusal of the case cart/instrument coordinator position, Borgess created a task force to determine whether an HIV-positive employee could safely perform the job responsibilities of a surgical technician. Lambert and Ellis informed Mauro by a letter dated August 10, 1992, that the task force had determined that a job requiring an HIV-infected worker to place his or her hands into a patient's body cavity in the presence of sharp instrumentation represented a direct threat to patient care and safety. Because the task force had concluded that an essential function of a surgical technician was to enter a patient's wound during surgery, the task force concluded that Mauro could no longer serve as a surgical technician. Lambert and Ellis concluded by offering Mauro two choices: to accept the case cart/instrument coordinator position, or be laid off. Mauro did not respond by the deadline stated in the letter, and Borgess laid him off effective August 24, 1992. Mauro filed this suit in January 1994.

* * *

Mauro's first claim alleges that Borgess discriminated against him in violation of section 504 of the Rehabilitation Act, which provides that no otherwise qualified individual with handicaps shall, solely by reason of his or her handicap, be excluded from participation in, or be denied benefits of any program receiving federal financial assistance. Through the passage of the Rehabilitation Act, Congress intended to protect disabled individuals "from deprivations based on prejudice, stereotypes, or unfounded fear, while giving appropriate weight to such legitimate concerns ... as avoiding exposing others to significant health and safety risks." School Board of Nassau County v. Arline, 480 U.S. 273, 107 S.Ct. 1123, 94 L.Ed.2d 307 (1987). Arline specifically noted:

"Few aspects of a handicap give rise to the same level of public fear and misapprehension as contagiousness.... The Act is carefully structured to replace such reflexive reactions to actual or perceived handicaps with actions based on reasoned and medically sound judgments.... The fact that some persons who have contagious diseases may pose a serious health threat to others under certain circumstances does not justify excluding from the coverage of the Act all persons with actual or perceived contagious diseases. Such exclusion would mean that those accused of being contagious would never have the opportunity to have their condition evaluated in light of medical evidence.... Rather, they would be vulnerable to discrimination on the basis of mythology—precisely the type of injury Congress sought to prevent.

In order to recover under the Rehabilitation Act, a plaintiff must establish that he or she is "otherwise qualified" to do the job within the meaning of the Act. An "otherwise qualified" person is one who can perform the "essential functions" of the job at issue. [ ] In a situation regarding the employment of a person with a contagious disease, the inquiry should also include a determination of whether the individual poses "a significant risk of communicating the disease to others in the workplace." [ ]

Mauro's second claim alleges that Borgess discriminated against him in violation of the Americans with Disabilities Act, which provides that no qualified individual with a disability shall, by reason of such disability, be excluded from participation in or denied the benefits of the services of public entities . .

To prevail under his Americans with Disabilities Act claim, Mauro must show that he is "otherwise qualified" for the job at issue. [ ] A person is "otherwise qualified" if he or she can perform the essential functions of the job in question. [ ] A disabled individual, however, is not "qualified" for a specific employment position if he or she poses a "direct threat" to the health or safety of others which cannot be eliminated by a reasonable accommodation. [ ]

The "direct threat" standard applied in the Americans with Disabilities Act is based on the same standard as "significant risk" applied by the Rehabilitation Act. [ ]. Our analysis under both Acts thus merges into one question: Did Mauro's activities as a surgical technician at Borgess pose a direct threat or significant risk to the health or safety of others?

Arline laid down four factors to consider in this analysis: (a) the nature of the risk (how the disease is transmitted), (b) the duration of the risk (how long is the carrier infectious), (c) the severity of the risk (what is the potential harm to third parties) and (d) the probabilities the disease will be transmitted and will cause varying degrees of harm. [ ]

To show that one is "otherwise qualified", neither Act requires the elimination of all risk posed by a person with a contagious disease. In Arline the Supreme Court determined that a person with an infectious disease "who poses a significant risk of communicating an infectious disease to others in the workplace," is not otherwise qualified to perform his or her job. [ ] If the risk is not significant, however, the person is qualified to perform the job. The EEOC guidelines provide further insight:

> An employer, however, is not permitted to deny an employment opportunity to an individual with a disability merely because of a slightly increased risk. The risk can only be considered when it poses a significant risk, i.e. high probability, of substantial harm; a speculative or remote risk is insufficient. [ ]

... Thus, our analysis in the instant case must not consider the possibility of HIV transmission, but rather focus on the probability of transmission weighed with the other three factors of the Arline test.

The parties agree that the first three factors of the Arline test: the nature, duration, and severity of the risk, all indicate that Mauro posed a significant risk to others. Mauro argues, however, that because the probability of transmission, the fourth factor of Arline, was so slight, it overwhelmed the first three factors and created a genuine issue of material fact.

In determining whether Mauro posed a significant risk or a direct threat in the performance of the essential functions of his job as a surgical technician, Arline, instructs that courts should defer to the "reasonable medical judgments of public health officials." [ ] The Centers for Disease Control is such a body of public health officials. [ ] The Centers for Disease Control has released a report discussing its recommendations regarding HIV-positive health care workers. See Centers for Disease Control, U.S. Dep't of Health & Human Servs., Recommendations for Preventing Transmission of Human Immunodeficiency Virus and Hepatitis B Virus to Patients During Exposure–Prone Invasive Procedures, 40 Morbidity & Mortality Weekly Report, 1, 3–4 (July 12, 1991).

The Report states that the risk of transmission of HIV from an infected health care worker to a patient is very small, and therefore recommends allowing most HIV-positive health care workers to continue performing most surgical procedures, provided that the workers follow safety precautions outlined in the Report. [ ] The Report, however, differentiates a limited category of invasive procedures, which it labels exposure-prone procedures, from general invasive procedures. [ ] General invasive procedures cover a wide range of procedures from insertion of an intravenous line to most types of surgery. [ ] Exposure-prone procedures, however, involve those that pose a greater risk of percutaneous (skin-piercing) injury. Though the Centers for Disease Control did not specifically identify which types of procedures were to be labeled exposure-prone, it supplies a general definition: "Characteristics of exposure-prone procedures include digital palpation of a needle tip in a body cavity or the simultaneous presence of the [health care worker's] fingers and a needle or other sharp instrument or object in a poorly visualized or highly confined anatomic site." [ ] The Report advises that individual health care institutions take measures to identify which procedures performed in their hospital should be labeled exposure-prone and recommends that HIV- infected health care workers should not perform exposure-prone procedures unless they have sought counsel from an expert review panel and have been advised under what circumstances they may continue to perform these procedures. The Report further recommends that those health care workers who engage in exposure-prone procedures notify prospective patients of their condition.

We must defer to the medical judgment expressed in the Report of the Centers for Disease Control in evaluating the district court's ruling on whether Mauro posed a direct threat in the essential functions of his job.

Mauro stated in his deposition that during surgery his work did not include assisting in surgery, but instead handing instruments to the surgeon and helping the surgeon with whatever else he or she needed. During surgery, Mauro would at times hold a retractor with one hand in the wound area, and pass instruments as needed with his other hand. When asked if he would be actually inside a wound holding a retractor, Mauro answered "Me personally, no." But when questioned further about his hands in the wound area, he stated: "Usually if I have my hands near the wound, it would be to like, on an abdominal incision, to kind of put your finger in and hold—kind of pull down on the muscle tissue and that—where the two met in like a V shape at the bottom and the top, and pull that back. But it happened very, very rarely because they had retractors to do that." The purpose of this action was to give the surgeon more room and more visibility.

The continued questioning led to a distinction between the wound and the body cavity. Mauro was asked if he ever had his hands in a body cavity, described as being past the wound area, and Mauro stated that he personally never had his hand in a body cavity because the small size of the surgical incision prevented too many hands from being placed inside the body cavity.

* * *

Mauro explained that during his training, discussion had occurred indicating that nicks and cuts were always a possibility for a surgical technician. In fact, the record included two incident reports involving Mauro. One report indicated that Mauro had sliced his right index finger while removing a knife blade from a handle on June 25, 1991, and another report indicated that he had scratched his hand with the sharp end of a dirty needle while threading it on June 8, 1990.

* * *

Sharon Hickman, a registered nurse, was the interim director of operating rooms at Borgess in June and July of 1992. While serving as interim director Hickman supervised the surgical technicians at Borgess, including Mauro. In her affidavit Hickman described a meeting of the Ad Hoc HIV Task Force for the hospital on July 23, 1992 and the statements she made at that meeting. Hickman stated that she told the task force that the duties of a surgical technician include preparing and maintaining the equipment used during surgery, but that: on an infrequent basis, the Surgical Technician is required to assist in the performance of surgery by holding back body tissue, with the use of either retractors or the Technician's hands, to assist the surgeon in visualizing the operative site. The Surgical Technician also may assist the surgeon with suturing and other duties related to the performance of the operation.

She also advised the task force that, although the need for a surgical technician's assistance in the performance of a surgical procedure arises infrequently, it is not possible to restructure the job to eliminate the surgical technician from performing such functions because this need arises on an emergency basis and cannot be planned in advance. In some cases, particularly on off-shifts, Hickman stated that the surgical technician is required to assist at the surgery because a registered nurse or surgical assistant is not available. In other surgical proceedings a nurse or surgical assistant may be present, but due to the complexity or other unexpected requirements of the procedure, another pair of hands may be needed in the operative site, and the surgical technician is then required to assist. Most often, the surgical technician is required to assist in the operative site because more hands are needed to visualize the surgical area.

* * *

We conclude that the district court did not err in determining that Mauro's continued employment as a surgical technician posed a direct threat to the health and safety of others.

* * *

BOGGS, CIRCUIT JUDGE, dissenting.

The concept of "significant risk" that emerges from the [statutes] directly mandates that patients be exposed to, and employers be required to expose their patients to, some amount of risk that is deemed "insignificant" to some determining body. As with other questions of fact and degree in a civil case, a district judge may find that the relevant risk is so small as to be insignificant as a matter of law; so large as to be significant as a matter of law (in each case because no reasonable person could differ with the court's judgment, even though the contrary is staunchly asserted by the opposing attorneys); or, somewhere in between, so that reasonable minds could differ on the degree of risk, and so a jury must be permitted to determine the question.

* * *

Mauro poses some risk. It is not ontologically impossible for him to transmit a disease of very great lethality. However, the chance that he will do so to any given patient is "small." Whether we call the risk "extremely small," "vanishingly small," "negligible," or whatever, assessing the risk remains a judgment that must be made by considering both the actual probability of harm and the degree of the consequences, just as the Supreme Court instructed us.

That is what the District Court did not do, and that is why I would reverse its decision and remand for reconsideration under the correct standard—a full assessment of both the risk and the consequence. . . . [T]he exact nature of Mauro's duties [is] a matter of considerable dispute, especially when the record is read, as we must read it, in a light most favorable to him. Whether the procedures he may perform cross the line from the merely "invasive" to the actionable "exposure-prone" is a genuine and material issue, on which reasonable minds can differ.

* * *

The CDC "has estimated that the risk to a single patient from an HIV-positive surgeon ranges from .0024% (1 in 42,000) to .00024% (1 in 417,000)." [ ] This estimate, of course, is for surgeons, who by the very nature of their work enter surgical wounds with sharp instruments during virtually every procedure they perform. Common sense—and, of course, the court's obligation to interpret the evidence in the light most favorable to the nonmovant—requires us to suppose, in the absence of contrary information, that the activities of a surgical technician such as Mauro who touched only the margin of the wound, and that only very rarely, would pose an even smaller risk. So may the resulting coefficients of risk—numbers somewhat smaller than .0024% to .00024%—still be deemed "significant?"

. . . To assess whether Mauro posed a significant risk, the decision-maker should know more about any particular hazards (physical or moral) that might have affected the likelihood that this individual would transmit HIV to others. If surgeons whom the surgical technician assisted were to testify, for instance, that the assistant had a record of impeccable reliability, technical skills, and professionalism, and that they themselves were not concerned about risks they incurred by performing surgery with him, then a fact-finder could easily conclude that an employee with a contagious blood-borne disease did not pose a significant risk. On the other hand, if the testimony showed that the employee's co-workers found him to be inattentive, careless, and physically clumsy, then the jury might well conclude that, however small the theoretical risk of transmission, it would not be a safe bet for this particular person to continue working in surgery, and that he was not, therefore, "otherwise qualified."

It is perhaps to this end that the court notes that "the record included two incident reports involving Mauro [one of which] indicated that Mauro had sliced his right index finger while removing a knife blade from a handle on June 25, 1991, and another [of which] indicated that he had scratched his hand with the sharp end of a dirty needle while threading it on June 8, 1990." However, there is absolutely no indication in the record, other than Nurse Hickman's wholly vague assertion that one of these incidents "might have resulted in patient exposure," that either of these events occurred during surgery, in proximity to a patient or another worker, or threatened anyone other than Mauro in any way . . . . . One can imagine many other important facts that could be developed at trial and influence a jury's conclusions—for instance, the employees' viral load (and therefore his degree of contagiousness) at the time of his termination, and whether the person reliably took prescribed antiviral medications, and the effectiveness thereof.

* * *

The court apparently has concluded, though without an explicit statement, that Mauro sometimes participated, or might be expected to participate, in "exposure-prone" procedures. This conclusion seems to flow from the belief that any time a health-care worker enters or touches the surgical wound with his fingers or hands, then it is an "exposure-prone" procedure. The court appears to have misunderstood the Guidelines, which clearly contemplate that, in the ordinary case, "surgical entry into tissues, cavities, or organs or repair of major traumatic injuries" should be regarded only as "invasive" procedures, not "exposure-prone" ones.

* * *

Notes and Questions

1. *Mauro* is typical of cases that have considered claims by health care workers performing surgical functions. See e.g., Bradley v. University of Texas M.D. Anderson Cancer Center, 3 F.3d 922 (5th Cir.1993); Doe v. University of Maryland Medical System Corp., 50 F.3d 1261 (4th Cir. 1995). Still, there are decisions in other health care contexts in which the courts reject claims of unacceptable risk, viewing those risks as more speculative or hypothetical. In Doe v. Attorney General, 62 F.3d 1424 (9th Cir.1995), for example, the appellate court held that an HIV-infected physician performing medical exams was "otherwise qualified" as defined under § 504 of the Rehabilitation Act. Risk assessment is a critical function in the development of institutional policies relating to health care workers with HIV infection. See e.g., Leonard Glantz, Wendy Mariner & George Annas, Risky Business: Setting Public Health Policy for HIV-infected Health Care Professionals, 70 Milbank Q. 43 (1992); Sidney D. Watson, Eliminating Fear Through Comparative Risk: Docs, AIDS and the Anti–Discrimination Ideal, 40 Buffalo L. Rev. 739 (1992).

2. Some have criticized the CDC guidelines essentially for leaving open the kind of decision represented by *Mauro*; i.e., for failing to identify more precisely which activities are "exposure-prone" and from which HIV-infected health care workers can be excluded in particular circumstances and for deferring the evaluation of specific circumstances to expert review panels. See e.g., Mary Anne Bobinski, Risk and Rationality: The Centers for Disease Control and the Regulation of HIV–Infected Workers, 36 St. Louis U.L.J. 213 (1991); Donald H. Hermann, A Call for Authoritative CDC Guidelines for HIV-infected Health Care Workers, 22 J.L. Med. & Ethics 176 (1994). Should the CDC issue more specific guidelines? What level of risk of transmission should the CDC set as tolerable?

3. The plaintiff in an ADA or Rehabilitation Act case must prove that he or she is disabled as defined by the Act. In Bragdon v. Abbott, 524 U.S. 624, 118 S.Ct. 2196, 141 L.Ed.2d 540 (1998), the Supreme Court held that asymptomatic HIV is an "impairment from the moment of infection" because it substantially limited one of plaintiff's major life functions; i.e., reproduction. See *Bragdon* in Chapter 11.

4. There is a greater risk of transmission from HIV-positive patients to health care workers than from HIV-positive health care workers to patients. The health care employer has a duty to provide a safe workplace for its employees. The

Occupational Safety and Health Administration, in collaboration with the Centers for Disease Control and the Department of Health and Human Services, has issued standards for controlling exposure to bloodborne pathogens. These standards rely primarily on risk assessment, post-exposure surveillance, training and education, work practices, engineering controls, labeling and waste disposal methods. 29 C.F.R. § 1910.1030. The CDC has recommended prophylactic treatment of health care workers who have been exposed to HIV-infected blood. The recommendation distinguishes among types of exposures based on the risk of transmission of the virus. 7/1/96 AIDS Alert 73. Health care employees who become HIV infected due to a workplace exposure may be limited to workers' compensation in actions against the employer. But see, Goins v. Mercy Center for Health Care Services, 281 Ill.App.3d 480, 217 Ill.Dec. 563, 667 N.E.2d 652 (1996); Juneau v. Humana, Inc., 657 So.2d 457 (La.App.1995). Tort actions are difficult due to problems in proving causation and negligence. See e.g., Artiste v. Kingsbrook Jewish Medical Center, 221 A.D.2d 81, 645 N.Y.S.2d 593 (1996); Madrid v. Lincoln County Medical Center, 121 N.M. 133, 909 P.2d 14 (N.M.App.1995) cert. granted by New Mexico Supreme Court; Casarez v. NME Hospitals, Inc., 883 S.W.2d 360 (Tex.App. 1994).

5. Health care workers with a wide variety of disabilities, including mental disorders and past substance abuse, have brought claims under § 504 and the ADA. These cases raise similar issues of accommodation and patient risk as do the HIV cases. See e.g., Bekker v. Humana Health Plan, Inc., 229 F.3d 662 (7th Cir.2000) (alcoholism); Zenor v. El Paso Healthcare System, Ltd., 176 F.3d 847 (5th Cir.1999) (drug addiction); Webb v. Clyde L. Choate Mental Health and Development Center, 230 F.3d 991 (7th Cir.2000) (mental illness). For an overview of how courts have applied statutory requirements related to nondiscrimination on the basis of disability in cases involving health care professionals, see Laura F. Rothstein, Health Care Professionals With Mental and Physical Impairments: Developments in Disability Discrimination Law, 41 St.L.U.L.J. 973 (1997).

6. The ADA, Title VII (42 U.S.C.A. § 2000e prohibiting gender and race discrimination) and the ADEA (29 U.S.C.A. § 621 prohibiting age discrimination) each prohibit discrimination in "employment;" however, these statutes do not use the term in its limited, commonly understood sense. Relationships in which the defendant exercises a sufficient degree of control over the plaintiff's activities and has certain economic relationships with plaintiff will meet the statutory definition of employment. Alternatively, if the plaintiff can prove that he or she is dependent upon the defendant for opportunities to practice, the plaintiff generally will meet the requirement of an employment relationship. See, e.g., Sibley Memorial Hospital v. Wilson, 488 F.2d 1338 (D.C.Cir.1973). Health care professionals whose only relationship with a hospital is traditional staff privileges may not meet the statutory standard for employment. See e.g., Bender v. Suburban Hospital, Inc., 159 F.3d 186 (4th Cir.1998); and Alexander v. Rush North Shore Medical Center, 101 F.3d 487 (7th Cir.1996).

Chapter 13

THE STRUCTURE OF THE HEALTH CARE ENTERPRISE

I. INTRODUCTION: WHERE'S WALDO?—PART I

In 1978, Waldo, a 35 year old graphic artist, visited his family physician, Doctor Goodscalpel, complaining of gas, bloating and irregularity. Doctor Goodscalpel, a solo practitioner, took a brief history and ordered blood tests, urinalysis and various chemistry tests, all of which were performed at Llama Labs. Llama Labs was an outpatient facility organized as a corporation, the shares of which were owned by Dr. Goodscalpel and two other physicians. On a subsequent office visit several weeks later, Dr. Goodscalpel performed a rigid sigmoidoscopy and ordered x-rays for an upper GI which were done at the Midstate Hospital. Midstate was a small community hospital from which Dr. Goodscalpel leased his office and at which he maintained staff privileges.

The results of these tests led Dr. Goodscalpel to recommend that Waldo consult a specialist, Dr. Jones, a gastroenterologist, who was a member of Practice Group, a professional corporation located in an adjacent town. Dr. Jones admitted Waldo as an inpatient and performed a colonoscopy at Mt. St. Hilda Hospital, a not-for-profit teaching hospital controlled by the Order of Caramel Fellowship, a religious denomination that operates 20 hospitals nationwide. Unfortunately, during this procedure Waldo suffered a perforated colon and required additional surgery which was performed by Dr. Smith, whom Waldo met the night before the surgery and Dr. Mack, a resident studying at Mt. St. Hilda.

The bill for these services ran four pages and included over 150 separate services, items and supplies. Waldo's not-for-profit health insurance company, Red Flag, paid each provider separately for their services, although Waldo was responsible for nominal co-payments and in some cases, for the "balance billing" where the billed charges of the provider exceeded Red Flag's "maximum allowable charges."

Waldo's encounter with the health care system brought him into contact with a number of different kinds of health care providers doing business in a variety of organizational structures. Arrangements of this kind were not unusual a few years ago and persist even today in many communities. What kinds of problems and inefficiencies do you see arising from this "system" of delivery of services? What are its advantages? As a "consumer" of health services, was Waldo well-served in this episode? For example, how were choices made and on what basis?

This chapter will explore the legal issues posed by many of these business and institutional arrangements. It will also analyze the trend toward integration that has created many new organizational structures designed to unite the various providers of care. These new arrangements, it will be seen, are still in their formative stages and entail a host of legal issues for the modern health law practitioner.

II.   FORMS OF BUSINESS ENTERPRISES AND THEIR LEGAL CONSEQUENCES

Like other businesspersons, health care providers may choose among a variety of organizational forms for conducting their businesses. Lawyers advising clients in the health care industry are increasingly called upon to devise arrangements that satisfy a number of distinct (and sometimes conflicting) objectives. These include: complying with various legal constraints; promoting the client's business or strategic goals; allocating risk and power among the parties in accordance with their desires; minimizing tax liabilities; and numerous others. Usually there is no single "correct" choice of business form and the process is best described as more of an art than a science. Plainly, effective counseling in this area requires a firm grasp of the numerous legal and strategic issues that will be involved.

A.   CHOICE OF ENTITY

The following section briefly reviews the alternative legal entities and their principal advantages and disadvantages. For the most part, state law governs the principal legal relationships among participants in these organizational forms. In many important respects, legal relationships may be altered by carefully drafted agreements or by modifications of the statutory norm through the organizational documents. See Alson R. Martin, et al., Choice of Entity for Professional and Other Organizations, SD 53 ALI–ABA 489 (1999).

For-Profit Corporations. This form of business organization offers the important advantages of limited liability for its owners (shareholders), centralized management through a board of directors and its officers, continuity of existence, and easy transferability of ownership. Of great practical importance is the capacity of the for-profit corporation form to raise capital for business enterprises. A significant downside is the possibility of double taxation, as both the entity and its shareholders may be taxed on the same income. (One method of avoiding double taxation is choosing the S Corporation form; however, this option is in practice limited to small corporations because of requirements that it have 35 or fewer shareholders, ownership only by individuals and not business entities, and that it offer only one class of stock.)

Control of the corporation is shared by its shareholders, board of directors and officers. Shareholders elect the board and have voting rights on certain matters such as amending the articles of incorporation or bylaws, selling a major portion of corporate assets or merging with another business. However, shareholders have no control over routine business decisions. These powers are vested in the board of directors, which may delegate substantial authority to the corporate officers. The power to control the corporation flows from the power to elect the board of directors. Voting shares in "plain vanilla" corporate structures are distributed according to the shareholders' contributions of capital, property or services. However, it is possible to allocate control by a variety of devices, such as issuance of debt, preferred or other stock with limited voting rights, classified shares, and other means.

In large, publicly traded corporations, it is common for the board to perform at most an advisory or counseling role: in practice, the officers run the corporation. Members of the board of directors and officers are bound by common law and statutory fiduciary duties to exercise care and avoid self-dealing when overseeing the business affairs of the corporation. Publicly traded corporations, i.e. those whose shares are exchanged on national securities or over-the-counter exchanges, offer the ability to raise large amounts of capital more easily than other forms. However, state and federal securities laws may impose substantial costs on corporations that are not exempt from regulation.

Not-for-profit Corporations. Not-for-profit corporations do not have owners who share in the entity's profits. However, this form may have members who elect the board of directors and reserve certain powers such as amending the entity's articles of incorporation or bylaws. The defining characteristic of not-for-profit corporations is the so-called "nondistribution constraint." That is, although these entities may earn substantial profits (or "surpluses," as they are euphemistically called), those funds must be devoted to the entities' charitable, religious or other public purposes. Moreover, to avoid taxation, it must comply with the requirements for exemption under section 501 (c)(3) of the Internal Revenue Code. Although unable to sell stock, not-for-profits may obtain tax-exempt financing as a source of capital.

Professional Corporations. All states permit professionals to conduct business under the corporate form. For the most part these statutes adopt the same legal rules that apply to other business corporations. However, several important differences typically exist. First, shareholders are not shielded from personal liability for their own acts of professional negligence or for the acts of others working under their direct supervision. However, the statutes typically provide limited liability for the negligence of other professionals and for the corporation's liabilities for nonprofessional activities. Second, most statutes stipulate that only licensed professionals may be shareholders of professional corporations and that the board of directors must be comprised entirely or by a majority of professionals.

Partnerships. General partnerships are associations of two or more persons who act as co-owners of a business. Important features include unlimited personal liability of all partners for partnership debts and the ability of all partners to participate in the management of the partnership and to bind the partnership. A significant advantage of this business form is the absence of double taxation: While each partner is liable for his or her share of partnership income, the partnership is not taxed on its business income. A second attractive feature is the informal means by which business can be conducted.

Limited Partnerships. Limited partnerships differ from general partnerships in that the former include limited partners who enjoy limited liability similar to that of corporate shareholders. The limited partner is restricted in the extent to which he may participate in the management and control of the business. Limited partnerships must have at least one general partner who bears the same unlimited liability as a partner in a general partnership and who assumes responsibility for management of the business. Hence the limited partnership affords many of the corporate advantages of raising capital through passive investment. However, limited partnership interests are also treated as securities and are subject to regulation under federal and state securities laws.

Limited Liability Companies and Limited Liability Partnerships. Almost all states have adopted statutes authorizing limited liability companies and limited liability partnerships. These business forms combine some of the most attractive features of partnerships and corporations: limited liability for all owners; pass-through tax treatment; free transferability of ownership; and centralized management. The statutes generally place no ceiling on the permissible number of owners, permit different classes of ownership, and allow for ownership by entities such as corporations.

Questions

What are the advantages and disadvantages of each business form for two small-town family practitioners joining together to form a medical group? For a big city hospital establishing a jointly-owned MRI facility with its specialists? What factors would be relevant in making your recommendation? What information would you need to elicit from each client?

B. GOVERNANCE AND FIDUCIARY DUTIES IN BUSINESS ASSOCIATIONS

The governance of corporations is shared by three groups: shareholders (or members in the case of some not-for-profits), the board of directors, and officers. In practice, particularly in large corporations, the officers have almost complete control over the business affairs of the corporation. This separation of ownership and control in the for-profit corporate setting may give rise to the exploitation of shareholders. It also poses problems in not-for-profit corporations as boards may not faithfully or diligently pursue the entity's charitable purposes. To deal with this problem, the common law imposes fiduciary duties on those who govern the corporation, essentially obligating directors and officers to act in its best interests.

STERN v. LUCY WEBB HAYES NATIONAL TRAINING SCHOOL FOR DEACONESSES AND MISSIONARIES

United States District Court, District of Columbia, 1974.
381 F.Supp. 1003.

GESELL, DISTRICT JUDGE.

This is a class action which was tried to the Court without a jury. Plaintiffs were certified as a class under Rule 23(b)(2) of the Federal Rules of Civil Procedure and represent patients of Sibley Memorial Hospital, a District of Columbia non-profit charitable corporation organized under D.C.Code s 29–1001 et seq. They challenge various aspects of the Hospital's fiscal management. The amended complaint named as defendants nine members of the Hospital's Board of Trustees, six financial institutions, and the Hospital itself. Four trustees and one financial institution were dropped by plaintiffs prior to trial, and the Court dismissed the complaint as to the remaining financial institutions at the close of plaintiffs' case.

* * *

The two principal contentions in the complaint are that the defendant trustees conspired to enrich themselves and certain financial institutions with which they were affiliated by favoring those institutions in financial dealings with the Hospital, and that they breached their fiduciary duties of care and loyalty in the management of Sibley's funds. The defendant financial institutions are said to have joined in the alleged conspiracy and to have knowingly benefitted from the alleged breaches of duty. The Hospital is named as a nominal defendant for the purpose of facilitating relief.

I. CORPORATE HISTORY.

The Lucy Webb Hayes National Training School for Deaconesses and Missionaries was established in 1891 by the Methodist Women's Home Missionary Society for the purpose, in part, of providing health care services to the poor of the Washington area. The School was incorporated under the laws of the District of Columbia as a charitable, benevolent and educational institution by instrument dated August 8, 1894. During the following year, the School built the Sibley Memorial Hospital on North Capitol Street to facilitate its charitable work. Over the years, operation of the Hospital has become the School's principal concern, so that the two institutions have been referred to synonymously by all parties and will be so treated in this Opinion.

* * *

Under the ... by-laws, the Board was to consist of from 25 to 35 trustees, who were to meet at least twice each year. Between such meetings, an Executive Committee was to represent the Board, and was authorized, inter alia, to open checking and savings accounts, approve the Hospital budget, renew mortgages, and enter into contracts. A Finance Committee was created to review the budget and to report regularly on the amount of cash available for investment. Management of those investments was to be supervised by an Investment Committee, which was to work closely with the Finance Committee in such matters.

In fact, management of the Hospital from the early 1950's until 1968 was handled almost exclusively by two trustee officers: Dr. Orem, the Hospital Administrator, and Mr. Ernst, the Treasurer. Unlike most of their fellow trustees, to whom membership on the Sibley Board was a charitable service incidental to their principal vocations, Orem and Ernst were continuously involved on almost a daily basis in the affairs of Sibley. They dominated the Board and its Executive Committee, which routinely accepted their recommendations and ratified their actions. Even more significantly, neither the Finance Committee nor the Investment Committee ever met or conducted business from the date of their creation until 1971, three years after the death of Dr. Orem. As a result, budgetary and investment decisions during this period, like most other management decisions affecting the Hospital's finances, were handled by Orem and Ernst, receiving only cursory supervision from the Executive Committee and the full Board.

Dr. Orem's death on April 5, 1968, obliged some of the other trustees to play a more active role in running the Hospital. The Executive Committee, and particularly defendant Stacy Reed (as Chairman of the Board, President of the Hospital, and ex officio member of the Executive Committee), became more deeply involved in the day-to-day management of the Hospital while efforts were made to find a new Administrator. The man who was eventually selected for that office, Dr. Jarvis, had little managerial experience and his performance was not entirely satisfactory. Mr. Ernst still made most of the financial and investment decisions for Sibley, but his actions and failures to act came slowly under increasing scrutiny by several of the other trustees, particularly after a series of disagreements between Ernst and the Hospital Comptroller which led to the discharge of the latter early in 1971.

Prompted by these difficulties, Mr. Reed decided to activate the Finance and Investment Committee in the Fall of 1971. However, as Chairman of the Finance Committee and member of the Investment Committee as well as Treasurer, Mr. Ernst continued to exercise dominant control over investment decisions and, on several occasions, discouraged and flatly refused to respond to inquiries by other trustees into such matters. It has only been since the death of Mr. Ernst on October 30, 1972, that the other trustees appear to have assumed an identifiable supervisory role over investment policy and Hospital fiscal management in general.

Against this background, the basic claims will be examined.

II. CONSPIRACY

Plaintiffs first contend that the five defendant trustees and the five defendant financial institutions were involved in a conspiracy to enrich themselves at the expense of the Hospital. They point to the fact that each named trustee held positions of responsibility with one or more of the defendant institutions as evidence that the trustees had both motive and opportunity to carry out such a conspiracy.

* * *

Plaintiffs further contend that the defendants accomplished the alleged conspiracy by arranging to have Sibley maintain unnecessarily large amounts of money on deposit with the defendant banks and savings and loan associations, drawing inadequate or no interest. [T]he Hospital in fact maintained much of its liquid assets in savings and checking accounts rather than in Treasury bonds or investment securities, at least until the investment review instituted by Mr. Reed late in 1971. In that year, for example, more than one-third of the nearly four million dollars available for investment was deposited in checking accounts, as compared to only about $135,000 in securities and $311,000 in Treasury bills.

* * *

It is also undisputed that most of these funds were deposited in the defendant financial institutions. A single checking account, drawing no interest whatever and maintained alternately at Riggs National Bank and Security National Bank, usually contained more than $250,000 and on one occasion grew to nearly $1,000,000.

Defendants were able to offer no adequate justification for this utilization of the Hospital's liquid assets. By the same token, however, plaintiffs failed to establish that it was [the] result of a conscious direction on the part of the named defendants.

* * *

[The court concluded that plaintiffs failed to establish a conspiracy between the trustees and the financial institutions or among the members of each group.]

III. BREACH OF DUTY

Plaintiffs' second contention is that, even if the facts do not establish a conspiracy, they do reveal serious breaches of duty on the part of the defendant trustees and the knowing acceptance of benefits from those breaches by the defendant banks and savings and loan associations.

A. *The Trustees*

Basically, the trustees are charged with mismanagement, nonmanagement and self-dealing. * * * [T]he modern trend is to apply corporate rather than trust principles in determining the liability of the directors of charitable corporations, because their functions are virtually indistinguishable from those of their "pure" corporate counterparts.

1. *Mismanagement*

Both trustees and corporate directors are liable for losses occasioned by their negligent mismanagement of investments. However, the degree of care required appears to differ in many jurisdictions. A trustee is uniformly held to a high standard of care and will be held liable for simple negligence, while a director must often have committed "gross negligence" or otherwise be guilty of more than mere mistakes of judgment.

This distinction may amount to little more than a recognition of the fact that corporate directors have many areas of responsibility, while the traditional trustee is often charged only with the management of the trust funds and can therefore be expected to devote more time and expertise to that task. Since the board members of most large charitable corporations fall within the corporate rather than the trust model, being charged with the operation of ongoing businesses, it has been said that they should only be held to the less stringent corporate standard of care. Beard v. Achenbach Mem. Hospital Ass'n, 170 F.2d 859, 862 (10th Cir.1948). More specifically, directors of charitable corporations are required to exercise ordinary and reasonable care in the performance of their duties, exhibiting honesty and good faith. Beard v. Achenbach Mem. Hospital Ass'n, supra, at 862.

2. Nonmanagement

Plaintiffs allege that the individual defendants failed to supervise the management of Hospital investments or even to attend meetings of the committees charged with such supervision. Trustees are particularly vulnerable to such a charge, because they not only have an affirmative duty to "maximize the trust income by prudent investment," Blankenship v. Boyle, 329 F.Supp. 1089, 1096 (D.D.C.1971), but they may not delegate that duty, even to a committee of their fellow trustees. Restatement (Second) of Trusts s 171, at 375 (1959). A corporate director, on the other hand, may delegate his investment responsibility to fellow directors, corporate officers, or even outsiders, but he must continue to exercise general supervision over the activities of his delegates. Once again, the rule for charitable corporations is closer to the traditional corporate rule: directors should at least be permitted to delegate investment decisions to a committee of board members, so long as all directors assume the responsibility for supervising such committees by periodically scrutinizing their work.

Total abdication of the supervisory role, however, is improper even under traditional corporate principles. A director who fails to acquire the information necessary to supervise investment policy or consistently fails even to attend the meetings at which such policies are considered has violated his fiduciary duty to the corporation. While a director is, of course, permitted to rely upon the expertise of those to whom he has delegated investment responsibility, such reliance is a tool for interpreting the delegate's reports, not an excuse for dispensing with or ignoring such reports. A director whose failure to supervise permits negligent mismanagement by others to go unchecked has committed an independent wrong against the corporation; he is not merely an accessory under an attenuated theory of respondent [sic] superior or constructive notice.

3. Self-dealing

Under District of Columbia Law, neither trustees nor corporate directors are absolutely barred from placing funds under their control into a bank having an interlocking directorship with their own institution. In both cases, however, such transactions will be subjected to the closest scrutiny to determine whether or not the duty of loyalty has been violated. A deliberate conspiracy among trustees or Board members to enrich the interlocking bank at the expense of the trust or corporation would, for example, constitute such a breach and render the conspirators liable for any losses. In the absence of clear evidence of wrongdoing, however, the courts appear to have used different standards to determine whether or not relief is appropriate, depending again on the legal relationship involved. Trustees may be found guilty of a breach of trust even for mere negligence in the maintenance of accounts in banks with which they are associated, while corporate directors are generally only required to show "entire fairness" to the corporation and "full disclosure" of the potential conflict of interest to the Board.

Most courts apply the less stringent corporate rule to charitable corporations in this area as well. It is, however, occasionally added that a director should not only disclose his interlocking responsibilities but also refrain from voting on or otherwise influencing a corporate decision to transact business with a company in which he has a significant interest or control.

Although defendants have argued against the imposition of even these limitations on self-dealing by the Sibley trustees, the Hospital Board recently adopted a new by-law, based upon guidelines issued by the American Hospital Association, which essentially imposes the modified corporate rule. * * *

* * *

Having surveyed the authorities as outlined above and weighed the briefs, arguments and evidence submitted by counsel, the Court holds that a director or so-called trustee of a charitable hospital organized under the Non–Profit Corporation Act of the District of Columbia [ ] is in default of his fiduciary duty to manage the fiscal and investment affairs of the hospital if it has been shown by a preponderance of the evidence that:

(1) while assigned to a particular committee of the Board having general financial or investment responsibility under the by-laws of the corporation, he has failed to use due diligence in supervising the actions of those officers, employees or outside experts to whom the responsibility for making day-to-day financial or investment decisions has been delegated; or

(2) he knowingly permitted the hospital to enter into a business transaction with himself or with any corporation, partnership or association in which he then had a substantial interest or held a position as trustee, director, general manager or principal officer without having previously informed the persons charged with approving that transaction of his interest or position and of any significant reasons, unknown to or not fully appreciated by such persons, why the transaction might not be in the best interests of the hospital; or

(3) except as required by the preceding paragraph, he actively participated in or voted in favor of a decision by the Board or any committee or subcommittee thereof to transact business with himself or with any corporation, partnership or association in which he then had a substantial interest or held a position as trustee, director, general manager or principal officer; or

(4) he otherwise failed to perform his duties honestly, in good faith, and with a reasonable amount of diligence and care.

Applying these standards to the facts in the record, the Court finds that each of the defendant trustees has breached his fiduciary duty to supervise the management of Sibley's investments. All except Mr. Jones were duly and repeatedly elected to the Investment Committee without ever bothering to object when no meetings were called for more than ten years. Mr. Jones was a member of the equally inactive Finance Committee, the failure of which to report on the existence of investable funds was cited by several other defendants as a reason for not convening the Investment Committee. In addition, Reed, Jones and Smith were, for varying periods of time, also members of the Executive Committee, which was charged with acquiring at least enough information to vote intelligently on the opening of new bank accounts. By their own testimony, it is clear that they failed to do so. And all of the individual defendants ignored the investment sections of the yearly audits which were made available to them as members of the Board. In short, these men have in the past failed to exercise even the most cursory supervision over the handling of Hospital funds and failed to establish and carry out a defined policy.

The record is unclear on the degree to which full disclosure preceded the frequent self-dealing which occurred during the period under consideration. It is reasonable to assume that the Board was generally aware of the various bank affiliations of the defendant trustees, but there is no indication that these conflicting interests were brought home to the relevant committees when they voted to approve particular transactions. Similarly, while plaintiffs have shown no active misrepresentation on defendants' part, they have established instances in which an interested trustee failed to alert the responsible officials to better terms known to be available elsewhere.

It is clear that all of the defendant trustees have, at one time or another, affirmatively approved self-dealing transactions. Most of these incidents were of relatively minor significance.

* * *

That the Hospital has suffered no measurable injury from many of these transactions—including the mortgage and the investment contract—and that the excessive deposits which were the real source of harm were caused primarily by the uniform failure to supervise rather than the occasional self-dealing vote are both facts that the Court must take into account in fashioning relief, but they do not alter the principle that the trustee of a charitable hospital should always avoid active participation in a transaction in which he or a corporation with which he is associated has a significant interest.

* * *

IV. RELIEF
* * *

[The Court ordered by injunction (1) that the appropriate committees and officers of the Hospital present to the full Board a written policy statement governing investments and the use of idle cash in the Hospital's bank accounts and other funds, (2) the establishment of a procedure for the periodic reexamination of existing investments and other financial arrangements to insure compliance with Board policies, and (3) that each trustee fully disclose his affiliation with financial institutions doing business with the Hospital. Declining to remove defendant trustees from the Board or to impose personal liability on directors, Judge Gesell offered the following guidance.]

The management of a non-profit charitable hospital imposes a severe obligation upon its trustees. A hospital such as Sibley is not closely regulated by any public authority, it has no responsibility to file financial reports, and its Board is self-perpetuating. The interests of its patients are funneled primarily through large group insurers who pay the patients' bills, and the patients lack meaningful participation in the Hospital's affairs. It is obvious that, in due course, new trustees must come to the Board of this Hospital, some of whom will be affiliated with banks, savings and loan associations and other financial institutions. The tendency of representatives of such institutions is often to seek business in return for advice and assistance rendered as trustees. It must be made absolutely clear that Board membership carries no right to preferential treatment in the placement or handling of the Hospital's investments and business accounts. The Hospital would be well advised to restrict membership on its Board to the representatives of financial institutions which have no substantial business relationship with the Hospital. The best way to avoid potential conflicts of interest and to be assured of objective advice is to avoid the possibility of such conflicts at the time new trustees are selected.

As an additional safeguard, the Court will require that each newly-elected trustee read this Opinion and the attached Order. [The Court also required public disclosure of all business dealings between the hospital and any financial institution with which any officer or trustee of the hospital is affiliated and that the hospital make summaries of all such dealings available on request to all patients.]

IN RE CAREMARK INTERNATIONAL INC. DERIVATIVE LITIGATION

Court of Chancery of Delaware, 1996.
698 A.2d 959.

ALLEN, CHANCELLOR.

Pending is a motion ... to approve as fair and reasonable a proposed settlement of a consolidated derivative action on behalf of Caremark International, Inc. ("Caremark"). The suit involves claims that the members of Caremark's board of directors (the "Board") breached their fiduciary duty of care to Caremark in connection with alleged violations by Caremark employees of federal and state laws and regulations applicable to health care providers. As a result of the alleged violations, Caremark was subject to an extensive four year investigation by the United States Department of Health and Human Services and the Department of Justice. In 1994 Caremark was charged in an indictment with multiple felonies. It thereafter entered into a number of agreements with the Department of Justice and others. Those agreements included a plea agreement in which Caremark pleaded guilty to a single felony of mail fraud and agreed to pay civil and criminal fines. Subsequently, Caremark agreed to make reimbursements to various private and public parties. In all, the payments that Caremark has been required to make total approximately $250 million.

This suit was filed in 1994, purporting to seek on behalf of the company recovery of these losses from the individual defendants who constitute the board of directors of Caremark. The parties now propose that it be settled.

* * *

The ultimate issue then is whether the proposed settlement appears to be fair to the corporation and its absent shareholders.

* * *

Legally, evaluation of the central claim made entails consideration of the legal standard governing a board of directors' obligation to supervise or monitor corporate performance. For the reasons set forth below I conclude, in light of the discovery record, that there is a very low probability that it would be determined that the directors of Caremark breached any duty to appropriately monitor and supervise the enterprise. Indeed the record tends to show an active consideration by Caremark management and its Board of the Caremark structures and programs that ultimately led to the company's indictment and to the large financial losses incurred in the settlement of those claims. It does not tend to show knowing or intentional violation of law. Neither the fact that the Board, although advised by lawyers and accountants, did not accurately predict the severe consequences to the company that would ultimately follow from the deployment by the company of the strategies and practices that ultimately led to this liability, nor the scale of the liability, gives rise to an inference of breach of any duty imposed by corporation law upon the directors of Caremark.

[As part of its patient care business, which accounted for the majority of its revenues, Caremark provided alternative site health care services, including infusion therapy, growth hormone therapy, HIV/AIDS-related treatments and hemophilia therapy. Caremark's managed care services included prescription drug programs and the operation of multi-specialty group practices and it employed over 7,000 employees in ninety branch operations. It had a decentralized management structure but began to centralize operations in 1991 to increase supervision over branch operations. Caremark had taken a number of steps to assure compliance with the antikickback provisions of the Medicare fraud and abuse law discussed in Chapter 14. As early as 1989, Caremark's predecessor issued an internal "Guide to Contractual Relationships" ("Guide"), which was reviewed and updated, annually, to govern its employees in entering into contracts with physicians and hospitals. Caremark claimed there was uncertainty concerning the interpretation of federal antikickback laws because of the scarcity of court decisions and the "limited guidance" afforded by HHS "safe harbor" regulations. After the federal government had commenced its investigation, Caremark announced that it would no longer pay management fees to physicians for services to Medicare and Medicaid patients and required its regional officers to approve each contractual relationship it entered into with a physician. Caremark established an internal audit plan designed to assure compliance with business and ethics policies. Although a report by Price Waterhouse, its outside auditor, concluded that there were no material weaknesses in Caremark's control structure, the Board's ethics committee adopted a new internal audit charter and took various other steps throughout to assure compliance with its policies.

In August and September, 1994, two federal grand juries indicted Caremark and individuals for violations of the anti-kickback laws, charging among other things that Caremark had made payments to a physician under "the guise of research grants ... and consulting agreements" so he would prescribe Protropin, a Caremark-manufactured drug. Plaintiff shareholders filed this derivative suit claiming Caremark directors breached their duty of care by failing adequately to supervise Caremark employees or institute corrective measures thereby exposing the company to liability. In September, 1994, Caremark publicly announced that as of January 1, 1995, it would terminate all remaining financial relationships with physicians in its home infusion, hemophilia, and growth hormone lines of business.]

B.   DIRECTORS' DUTIES TO MONITOR CORPORATE OPERATIONS

The complaint charges the director defendants with breach of their duty of attention or care in connection with the on-going operation of the corporation's business. The claim is that the directors allowed a situation to develop and continue which exposed the corporation to enormous legal liability and that in so doing they violated a duty to be active monitors of corporate performance. The complaint thus does not charge either director self-dealing or the more difficult loyalty-type problems arising from cases of suspect director motivation, such as entrenchment or sale of control contexts. The theory here advanced is possibly the most difficult theory in corporation law upon which a plaintiff might hope to win a judgment. * * * The good policy reasons why it is so difficult to charge directors with responsibility for corporate losses for an alleged breach of care, where there is no conflict of interest or no facts suggesting suspect motivation involved, were recently described in Gagliardi v. TriFoods Int'l, Inc., Del.Ch., 683 A.2d 1049, 1051 (1996).

1. Potential liability for directoral decisions: Director liability for a breach of the duty to exercise appropriate attention may, in theory, arise in two distinct contexts. First, such liability may be said to follow from a board decision that results in a loss because that decision was ill advised or "negligent". Second, liability to the corporation for a loss may be said to arise from an unconsidered failure of the board to act in circumstances in which due attention would, arguably, have prevented the loss. The first class of cases will typically be subject to review under the director-protective business judgment rule, assuming the decision made was the product of a process that was either deliberately considered in good faith or was otherwise rational. What should be understood, but may not widely be understood by courts or commentators who are not often required to face such questions, is that compliance with a director's duty of care can never appropriately be judicially determined by reference to the content of the board decision that leads to a corporate loss, apart from consideration of the good faith or rationality of the process employed. That is, whether a judge or jury considering the matter after the fact, believes a decision substantively wrong, or degrees of wrong extending through "stupid" to "egregious" or "irrational", provides no ground for director liability, so long as the court determines that the process employed was either rational or employed in a good faith effort to advance corporate interests. To employ a different rule—one that permitted an "objective" evaluation of the decision—would expose directors to substantive second guessing by ill-equipped judges or juries, which would, in the long-run, be injurious to investor interests.[1] Thus, the business judgment rule is process oriented and informed by a deep respect for all good faith board decisions.

2. Liability for failure to monitor: The second class of cases in which director liability for inattention is theoretically possible entail circumstances in which a loss eventuates not from a decision but, from unconsidered

---

[1]. The vocabulary of negligence while often employed, is not well-suited to judicial review of board attentiveness, especially if one attempts to look to the substance of the decision as any evidence of possible "negligence." * * * It is doubtful that we want business men and women to be encouraged to make decisions as hypothetical persons of ordinary judgment and prudence might. The corporate form gets its utility in large part from its ability to allow diversified investors to accept greater investment risk. If those in charge of the corporation are to be adjudged personally liable for losses on the basis of a substantive judgment based upon what persons of ordinary or average judgment and average risk assessment talent regard as "prudent," "sensible" or even "rational", such persons will have a strong incentive at the margin to authorize less risky investment projects.

inaction. Most of the decisions that a corporation, acting through its human agents, makes are, of course, not the subject of director attention. Legally, the board itself will be required only to authorize the most significant corporate acts or transactions: mergers, changes in capital structure, fundamental changes in business, appointment and compensation of the CEO, etc. As the facts of this case graphically demonstrate, ordinary business decisions that are made by officers and employees deeper in the interior of the organization can, however, vitally affect the welfare of the corporation and its ability to achieve its various strategic and financial goals.

Modernly this question has been given special importance by an increasing tendency, especially under federal law, to employ the criminal law to assure corporate compliance with external legal requirements, including environmental, financial, employee and product safety as well as assorted other health and safety regulations. In 1991, pursuant to the Sentencing Reform Act of 1984, the United States Sentencing Commission adopted Organizational Sentencing Guidelines which impact importantly on the prospective effect these criminal sanctions might have on business corporations. The Guidelines set forth a uniform sentencing structure for organizations to be sentenced for violation of federal criminal statutes and provide for penalties that equal or often massively exceed those previously imposed on corporations. The Guidelines offer powerful incentives for corporations today to have in place compliance programs to detect violations of law, promptly to report violations to appropriate public officials when discovered, and to take prompt, voluntary remedial efforts.

* * *

[I]t would, in my opinion, be a mistake to conclude that our Supreme Court's [prior statements regarding directors' duty to monitor] means that corporate boards may satisfy their obligation to be reasonably informed concerning the corporation, without assuring themselves that information and reporting systems exist in the organization that are reasonably designed to provide to senior management and to the board itself timely, accurate information sufficient to allow management and the board, each within its scope, to reach informed judgments concerning both the corporation's compliance with law and its business performance.

Obviously the level of detail that is appropriate for such an information system is a question of business judgment. And obviously too, no rationally designed information and reporting system will remove the possibility that the corporation will violate laws or regulations, or that senior officers or directors may nevertheless sometimes be misled or otherwise fail reasonably to detect acts material to the corporation's compliance with the law. But it is important that the board exercise a good faith judgment that the corporation's information and reporting system is in concept and design adequate to assure the board that appropriate information will come to its attention in a timely manner as a matter of ordinary operations, so that it may satisfy its responsibility.

Thus, I am of the view that a director's obligation includes a duty to attempt in good faith to assure that a corporate information and reporting system, which the board concludes is adequate, exists, and that failure to do so under some circumstances may, in theory at least, render a director liable for losses caused by non-compliance with applicable legal standards. [The Court went on to find that the Caremark directors had not breached their duty of care because, first, there was no evidence they knew of the violations of the law and they reasonably relied on expert reports that their company's practices, although "contestable," were lawful. Second, applying a test of whether there was a "sustained or systematic failure ... to exercise reasonable oversight," it found no actionable failure to monitor. The court concluded that the corporate oversight systems described above constituted a "good faith effort to be informed of relevant facts."]

Notes and Questions

1. Section 8.30 of The Revised Model Nonprofit Corporation Act adopts the corporate standard for the members of the board ("trustees") of not-for-profits, as do many state statutes. What arguments support a stricter standard for not-for-profit corporations? For one case applying a trust standard, see Lynch v. John M. Redfield Foundation, 9 Cal.App.3d 293, 88 Cal.Rptr. 86 (Cal.Ct.App.1970). See generally Daniel L. Kurtz, Board Liability: Guide for Nonprofit Directors 22 (1988). Might a shifting standard of care apply, depending on the nature of the decision and how important that decision is to the organization's core functions or the community benefits it was designed to supply? See James J. Fishman & Stephen Schwarz, Nonprofit Organizations (2d. ed. 2000); 1 Furrow, et al., Health Law § 5–15—5–16 (2d ed. 2000). See also discussion of IRC § 501(c)(3) requirements infra this chapter.

2. In the case of for-profit corporations, the business judgment rule has come to pose an almost impermeable shield protecting directors and officers charged with breaches of the duty of care in connection with business decisions that prove to be unwise or imprudent. As long as the director has made a business judgment that is informed, in good faith and without conflicts of interest, that judgment will not be subject to attack, even if the decision would not meet the simple negligence standard applicable to the "ordinarily prudent person." See Charles Hansen, The ALI Governance Project: Of the Duty of Care and the Business Judgment Rule, 41 Bus. Law. 1237 (1986); Robert W. Hamilton, Corporations Including Partnerships and Limited Partnerships 748–58 (5th ed. 1994). Should the business judgment rule apply with equal force to not-for-profit corporations? See Beard v. Achenbach Memorial Hospital Association, 170 F.2d 859, 862 (10th Cir.1948) (business judgment rationale used to uphold hospital's payment of questionable retroactive "incentive bonuses"). Does the absence of shareholders or a public market for the stock make a difference? Are directors of not-for-profit boards more or less likely to be vigilant and savvy businesspersons than their for-profit counterparts? See 1 Furrow et al., Health Law § 5–15a (2d ed. 2000).

Does the standard established by the Chancellor in approving the settlement of the Caremark litigation give directors and senior officers of large, far-flung corporate enterprises sufficient incentives to ensure that their employees comply with the law? What factors mitigate against imposing a simple negligence standard with regard to the duty to monitor? Are the interests of the Caremark shareholders advanced by this holding? What role, if any, should the public interest in compliance with the anti-kickback laws play?

For the view that the decision in the Sibley Hospital case typified the tendency of courts to be more receptive to duty of care complaints where the transaction is tainted by duty-of-loyalty implications, see Evelyn Brody, The

Limits of Charity Fiduciary Law, 57 Md. L. Rev. 1401, 1442–43, (1998)("One wonders whether Judge Gesell would have found any duty-of-care breach—or, more important, even granted standing to the plaintiff patients—had the funds been deposited at banks where the hospitals' directors were not also directors."). On the fiduciary duties of boards in health care institutions generally, see Naomi Ono, Boards of Directors Under Fire: An Examination of Nonprofit Board Duties in the Health Care Environment, 7 Annals Health L. 107 (1998).

3.   The duty of loyalty applies to a variety of transactions in which directors or officers acting in their corporate capacity serve their own interests at the expense of those of the corporation. Self-dealing, taking of corporate opportunities, and acting in competition with the corporation may violate this duty. See, e.g. Gilbert v. McLeod Infirmary, 219 S.C. 174, 64 S.E.2d 524 (S.C. 1951) (sale of property by hospital to trustees void where board members participated in the approval of the transaction and the hospital did not seek other buyers). However, directors owe fiduciary duties only to their corporations, not to individual shareholders. Hence a professional corporation's termination of the contract of a physician shareholder-employee will not implicate the duty of loyalty. Berman v. Physical Medicine Associates, 225 F.3d 429 (4th Cir.2000). State attorneys general have frequently advanced claims based on breaches of the duty of loyalty in cases involving conflicts of interest such as a hospital entering into an emergency room contract with a physician group owned by the chairman of its board; loans from a hospital to a physician serving on the board; and the hiring of architectural firms and employment agencies in which trustees have an interest. See Michael W. Peregrine, The Nonprofit Board's Duty of Loyalty in an "Integrated" World, 29 J. Health L. 211 (1996).

Most state statutes governing nonprofit and for-profit corporations make it relatively easy to resolve such conflicts of interest. (Can you explain the policy underlying this?) For example, most allow a majority of disinterested directors, shareholders or members in the case of not-for-profit corporations to validate in advance interested transactions provided there is full disclosure of all material facts about the transaction, and the approving directors reasonably believe the transaction is fair to the corporation. See, e.g., Revised Model Business Corp. Act. §§ 8.60 et seq.; Revised Model Nonprofit Corporations Act (RMNCA) § 8.30. Suppose a medical group was planning to sell its lithotripter to a hospital. What disclosures would a physician who was both a member of the group and of the hospital board have to make to the hospital? What complications might arise if the physician was also on the board of his medical group's professional corporation? Conflicting interests involving not-for-profit corporations may also be resolved if the transaction was "fair" at the time it was entered into (i.e. it "carries the earmarks of an arms-length transaction"). RMNCA § 8.30(a), § 8.30 cmt. 2(a). Otherwise they may be approved before or after the transaction by the state attorney general, § 8.30(b)(2)(i), or a court of proper jurisdiction § 8.30(b)(2)(ii). Under what circumstances might each method of sanitizing conflicting interest arrangements be used? As counsel for a not-for-profit hospital, what practical steps would you advise it to take to ensure compliance with the law in this area? See Peregrine, supra, at 219.

The obligation of fiduciaries to make full disclosures in self-dealing transactions is illustrated by Boston Children's Heart Foundation, Inc. v. Nadal–Ginard, 73 F.3d 429 (1st Cir.1996). The case involved the activities of a physician, Dr. Nadal–Ginard, who was president and a member of the board of Boston Children's Heart Foundation ("BCHF"), a non-profit corporation established to conduct the clinical and research activities of the cardiology department at Boston Children's

Hospital. The defendant was also chairman of the cardiology department at the hospital and a member of the faculty of Harvard Medical School. Conflicting interest problems arose in connection with Dr. Nadal–Ginard's activities on behalf of the Howard Hughes Medical Institute ("Institute"), which provided him substantial compensation for directing the activities of the Institute's Laboratory of Cellular and Molecular Cardiology at Boston Children's Hospital. In his capacity as president of BCHF, Dr. Nadal–Ginard was empowered to set his own salary and determine other compensation-related matters. In so doing, however, Dr. Nadal–Ginard failed to disclose that BCHF was paying him for much of the same work for which he was receiving substantial compensation from the Institute. The First Circuit concluded that Dr. Nadal–Girard's actions setting his own compensation at BCHF constituted self-dealing and required full disclosure of all material information regarding his salary and compensation determinations. Despite the fact that the BCHF by-laws granted Dr. Nadal–Ginard exclusive authority to set his own salary, the Court found that he had not acted in good faith in failing to make full disclosure. 73 F.3d at 434. It further held the information regarding his compensation arrangements with the Institute was material because, had BCHF been armed with the information, it may have found he was over-compensated. In so holding, the First Circuit rejected the defendant's claim that no breach occurred because the salary was fair and reasonable, as the failure to act in good faith was sufficient to establish the breach regardless of the reasonableness of the salary. Id.

For an analysis of the implications of fiduciary duties and other legal obligations for physicians serving on hospital boards, see Michael Peregrine, Structuring Physician Membership on the Hospital Governing Board, 31 J. Health L. 133 (1998).

4. Should there simply be a flat prohibition against all self-dealing by insiders of not-for-profit corporations? See Henry B. Hansmann, Reforming Nonprofit Corporation Law, 129 U. Pa. L. Rev. 497 (1981)(arguing for strict prohibition for self dealing by directors of "commercial" nonprofits such as hospitals). Most states prohibit not-for-profit corporations from making loans to their directors though no similar law inhibits similar loans involving for-profit corporations. See, e.g., RMNCA § 8.32; Haw. Rev. Stat. § 415B–70 (1993).

5. Controlling shareholders may also have fiduciary obligations. In closely held corporations, minority shareholders are at risk of being financially injured by a variety of "oppressive" tactics by the majority. For example, the majority may use its control over the corporation to attempt to "freeze out" minority shareholders by refusing to pay dividends or to give them corporate offices and salaries. With no public market for their shares and no access to the corporation's funds, minority shareholders are faced with the Hobson's choice of selling their interest in the corporation for a pittance or having their capital tied up in an enterprise from which they can expect no returns. Although most courts invoke the business judgment rule and refuse to interfere with corporate affairs involving dividends or salaries, a few jurisdictions have recognized a special duty to minority shareholders in the close corporation setting. For example, in Wilkes v. Springside Nursing Home, 370 Mass. 842, 353 N.E.2d 657, 663–64 (1976), the Massachusetts Supreme Court found that the majority shareholders had violated their fiduciary duties to a minority owner of a nursing home when they removed him from his salaried position in an apparent attempt to freeze him out. The court's approach allowed defendants to defend their actions by demonstrating a legitimate business purpose. The burden then shifted to plaintiff to show the availability of alternative means to accomplish this purpose that were less burdensome to his interests.

6. *The Duty of Obedience and the Charitable Trust Doctrine.* Directors of not-for-profit organizations are subject to another fiduciary duty, sometimes referred to as the duty of obedience. This duty, which is similar to the duty of trustees to administer trusts in a manner faithful to the wishes of the creator of the trust, obligates directors to adhere to the dictates of the corporation's "mission" or other statement of charitable or public interest purpose. Any substantial deviation from such purpose may subject directors to personal liability. See Michael W. Peregrine, Charitable Trust Laws and the Evolving Nature of the Nonprofit Hospital Corporation, 30 J. Health L. 11 (1997). Courts generally allow directors considerable leeway in interpreting broadly-stated corporate purposes (which are usually found in the corporation's charter or bylaws). However, directors must follow clearly-stated charitable objectives even if other alternatives exist that are more profitable, efficient, or needed by the community.

Under the so-called charitable trust doctrine, nonprofit corporations cannot legally divert their donated assets to any purposes other than charitable ones and their assets are treated as "irrevocably dedicated" to such purposes. Thus, in Queen of Angels Hospital v. Younger, 66 Cal.App.3d 359, 136 Cal.Rptr. 36 (1977), a not-for-profit corporation sponsored by the Franciscan Sisters leased a hospital it had operated for 44 years to a proprietary organization, with the intention of using the proceeds to operate medical clinics providing free medical care in the community. The court found that the corporation's articles of incorporation, which described Queen of Angels as a "hospital," and its history of functioning as a hospital established that its assets were held in trust for the purposes of operating a hospital. See also Attorney General v. Hahnemann Hospital, 397 Mass. 820, 494 N.E.2d 1011 (Mass. 1986); see generally, Health Care Corporate Law: Facilities and Transactions § 6.3.3 (Mark A. Hall & William S. Brewbaker III, eds. 1996); Daniel W. Coyne & Kathleen Russell Kas, The Not–For–Profit Hospital as a Charitable Trust: To Whom does Its Value Belong?, 24 J. Health & Hosp. L. 48 (1991). Should the parties convince the court that maintaining the original purpose has become "impossible, impractical or illegal," the equitable doctrine of *cy pres* may be available to clear the way for the alternative use of the assets. Where the court so finds, *cy pres* principles mandate that the trustees dedicate the charitable assets to a purpose that resembles the original intent of the settlor as closely as possible. See Evelyn Brody, The Limits of Charity Fiduciary Law, 57 Md. L.Rev. 1400 (1998); M. Gregg Bloche, Corporate Takeovers of Teaching Hospitals, 65 S. Cal. L. Rev. 1035, 1143–96 (1992).

Note on Conversions of Not-for-Profit Corporations

In recent years, a large number of not-for-profit health insurance companies, HMOs and hospitals have chosen to convert to for-profit status or to merge with, be acquired by, or joint venture with for-profit entities. Most Blue Cross organizations have undertaken steps to do so, and hundreds of hospitals have been acquired by or entered into some form of joint venture with proprietary entities. See Sandy Lutz, Not-for-Profits up for Grabs by the Giants, Modern Healthcare, May 30, 1994 at 24; Greg Jaffe & Monica Langley, Generous to a Fault? Fledgling Charities Get Billions From Sale of Nonprofit Hospitals, Wall St. J. (Nov. 6, 1996) at A1; Judith Bell, et al., the Preservation of Charitable Health Care Assets, Health Aff. March 1, 1997, at 125 (describing restructuring of Blue Cross in California resulting in charitable foundations with $3.2 billion in assets; calculating number of conversions of acute care hospitals at 59 in 1995). Lee A. Sheppard, HMO Conversions and Self–Dealing, 93 Tax Notes Today 206–5 (Oct. 6, 1993). In the typical conversion, the assets of the not-for-profit organization are sold to a for-profit entity (often controlled by management of the not-for-profit). The proceeds must be distributed, to organizations eligible under § 501(c)(3) of the Internal Revenue Code or pursuant to applicable state law. Once the assets are distributed, the not-for-profit entity dissolves. Often the for-profit entity later makes a public sale of its stock which may occur at a substantial premium over the price paid by the investors. See John D. Colombo, A Proposal for An Exit Tax on Nonprofit Conversion Transactions, 23 J. Corp. L. 779 (1998) (estimating actual value of assets of California's Healthnet HMO to be approximately 500% higher than originally estimated and describing funding of charitable foundations on conversion of PacifiCare Health Systems at less than 1% of actual value of the enterprise). In a number of HMO conversions, insiders grossly undervalued the value of their corporations by persuading regulators to ignore goodwill and the value of the HMO trademark or to ignore competing bids for the entity. For a detailed account of the numerous instances of undervaluation in such conversions and the successful efforts of Consumers Union to have hundreds of millions of dollars turned over to independent foundations, see Eleanor Hamburger et al., The Pot of Gold: Monitoring Health Care Conversions Can Yield Billions of Dollars for Health Care, 29 Clearinghouse Rev. 473 (1995). James J. Fishman, Checkpoints on the Conversion Highway: Some Trouble Spots in the Conversion of Nonprofit Health Care Organizations to For-profit Status, 23 J. Corp. L. 701 (1998). On the complex and controversial issues surrounding valuation of not-for-profit HMOs, see Theresa McMahon, Fair *Value*? The Conversion of Nonprofit HMOs, 30 U.S.F.L. Rev. 355 (1996); Stephen J. Weiser, Sale of a Tax Exempt Hospital to a For–Profit Corporation: Federal Tax Issues, 25 J. Health & Hosp. L. 129 (1992); see also Robert Kuttner, Columbia/HCA and the Resurgence of the For Profit Hospital Business (Pt. 1), 335 New Eng. J. Med. 362 (1996) (describing the difficulty in ascertaining whether purchase price will establish a foundation adequate to perpetuate a hospital's historic commitment to community services); Kenneth Thorpe, et al., Hospital Conversions, Margins, And The Provision Of Uncompensated Care, 19 Health Affs. 187 (Nov./Dec. 2000)(empirical study showing that uncompensated care declines after hospitals convert from not-for-profit to for profit form).

This phenomenon has focused considerable attention on the fiduciary duties of not-for-profit directors, the application of the charitable trust doctrine and other legal issues surrounding this type of sale. First, not-for-profit directors risk breaching their duty of obedience should the use of the sale's proceeds not comport with the not-for-profit hospital's charitable purpose or should the revenue received not reflect the true value of the assets conveyed. Moreover, at least one Attorney General has suggested that board members approving a not-for-profit hospital's joint venture with Columbia/HCA Healthcare Corporation may have breached their fiduciary duties by failing to consider the hospital's potential Medicare and Medicaid recapture liabilities and by not exploring alternatives to the joint venture, such as an outright sale. California AG Action Underscores New Aggressiveness by State Officials, 5 Health L. Rep.(BNA)(November 21, 1996). The Attorney General of Tennessee intervened in a sale of a nonprofit hospital to a for-profit chain where it found the nonprofit hospital's board had failed to adequately inform itself about the value of the hospital when it voted to enter into a letter of intent. Burson v. Nashville Memorial Hospital Inc., No. 94–744–1 (Tenn. Ch. Ct. 1994) (consent decree mandating creation of new charitable trust and establishing conflict of interest rules for directors of the new foundation).

In other states, attorneys general have relied upon the charitable trust doctrine or other features of their state's not-for-profit laws to challenge conversions and joint ventures. In Kelley v. Michigan Affiliated Healthcare System Inc., No. 96–83848–CZ (Mich. Cir. Ct. 1996), a court held that a hospital system was barred from donating its system to Columbia/HCA as part of a joint venture based on a Michigan statute prohibiting commingling of assets with a for-profit corporation. In Blue Cross and Blue Shield of Missouri v. Angoff, 1998 WL 435697 (Mo. Ct. App. 1998), the court confronted a "reorganization" by Blue Cross and Blue Shield of Missouri (BCBSMO) pursuant to which it had transferred over 80 percent of its most valuable, managed care assets to a for-profit subsidiary. The court found that BCBSMO had thereby abandoned its nonprofit purposes of offering nonprofit health plans and hence exceeded its legal authority. The court's holding appears to rest on a conclusion that the magnitude of the change amounted to such a radical departure as to constitute an abandonment of defendant's purposes, despite the fact that it continued to hold substantial assets and conduct significant business in furtherance of its nonprofit purposes. In a number of other situations involving claims of abandonment of nonprofit purposes, parties have reached settlements after legislative interventions clarified the legal responsibilities of the converting entity. However, not all nonprofit corporations are charitable and their conversion may not give rise to obligations to fund a charitable trust. For example, a Texas court concluded that Blue Cross and Blue Shield of Texas (BCBST) was not a charitable corporation and therefore found it did not fall within the Texas Attorney General's charitable trust jurisdiction. Morales v. Blue Cross and Blue Shield of Texas, No. 96–13907 (D. Ct. Travis City, TX 1998). Consequently, the court held that the company could merge with a mutual insurance company without dedicating any of its assets to charitable purposes. In reaching its decision, the Texas court relied on several operational factors, including that BCBST: was regulated as an insurance company; provided no charity care or other traditionally charitable services; did not receive charitable gifts or contributions; charged competitive market prices for its product; and operated for the benefit of its policy holders, not the public at large.

Where the not-for-profit corporation sells a substantial part of its assets but remains in existence, it may be the case that, unlike the conversion situation, there is nothing owed to the public. One particularly notorious example involved the establishment by Blue Cross of California of a for-profit subsidiary, Wellpoint Health Networks, which acquired the parent HMO, PPO and other insurance assets. After legislation was introduced to force contributions to the public, Blue Cross agreed to establish a multi-billion charitable foundation. The subsequent proposed merger of Wellpoint with Health Systems International, a combination that would have created the largest for-profit health plan in the country, gave rise to a host of new questions regarding the complex relationships among Blue Cross, Wellpoint, the foundations and the new merged companies. Hamburger, supra; Thomas Gilroy, California Department of Corporations Raises Concerns With Blue Cross Merger, 4 Health L. Rep. (BNA) 1209 (Aug. 10, 1995). After the proposed Wellpoint–Health Systems International merger was abandoned, Blue Cross agreed to a recapitalization plan for Wellpoint that would transfer all its assets, valued at approximately $3 billion, to charitable foundations, a development that consumer advocates heralded as precedent for insisting that charitable foundations receive 100 percent of the assets of conversions underway in other states. Non Profit Conversions: Blue Cross of California Unveils Details of Charitable Foundation, 5 Health L. Rep. (BNA) (February 29, 1996).

State Statutes Regulating Conversions. A majority of states have enacted statutes governing the process and setting standards for regulatory approvals of conversions of not-for-profit entities. E.g., Cal. Corp. Code §§ 5913–5919 (West

1999); Colo. Rev. Stat. § 10–16–324 (1998); 1997 Conn. Acts 188 (Reg. Sess.); 1998 Conn. Acts. 36 (Reg. Sess.); D.C. Code Ann. §§ 32–551 to 32–560 (1998); Neb. Rev. Stat. §§ 71–20,102 to 71–20,114 (1998). See generally 1 Furrow et al, Health Law (2d ed. 2000) § 5–22; Kevin F. Donahue, Crossroads in Hospital Conversions: A Survey of Nonprofit Hospital Conversion Legislation, 8 Annals Health L. 39 (1999). Most place a variety of procedural requirements upon converting entities, such as mandating prior notification of conversion transactions and requiring information concerning the details of the transaction be provided to the reviewing authority and, in some cases, to the public. Some go further, specifying substantive standards that must be considered by the reviewer. To the extent that the statutes lack such specificity, traditional concepts of fiduciary duties, charitable trust law and nonprofit corporation law presumably apply to the regulators' review. For alternative approaches, see John D. Colombo, A Proposal for An Exit Tax on Nonprofit Conversion Transactions, 23 J. Corp. L. 779 (1998) (proposing an "exit tax" which would require nonprofit entities to surrender the value of appreciation of the economic assets of the entity where the converted enterprise has not needed the tax exemption to operate or where partnership principles would so dictate); Nat'l Ass'n of Attorneys General, Model Act for Nonprofit Healthcare Conversions. See also, Donahue, supra; Mark Krause, Comment, "First, Do No Harm": An Analysis of the Nonprofit Hospital Sale Acts, 45 UCLA L. Rev. 503 (1997).

C. LIMITED LIABILITY FOR INVESTORS

An important objective for many investors is limited liability, i.e., the guarantee that they will not be liable for the acts or debts of the business except to the extent of their investment. This characteristic of corporations, limited partnerships, limited liability companies and limited liability partnerships, is subject to some limitations under the case law. However, as the following case indicates, courts have been willing to disregard the corporate form, or "pierce the corporate veil," and hold shareholders personally liable in a number of circumstances.

UNITED STATES v. PISANI

United States Court of Appeals, Third Circuit, 1981.
646 F.2d 83.

VAN DUSEN, SENIOR CIRCUIT JUDGE.

Defendant Dr. Anthony J. Pisani appeals from a judgment for $151,413 which the district court entered against him after a trial without a jury. The judgment held Pisani personally liable for Medicare overpayments which the former Department of Health, Education and Welfare ("HEW") made to his solely-owned corporation, Eaton Park Associates, Inc. ("corporation"). This court has jurisdiction under 28 U.S.C.A. § 1291 (1976). We affirm.

I. FACTS

From January 18, 1967, to February 28, 1970, the corporation, doing business as Eaton Park Nursing Home ("Provider"), participated in the Medicare program. During this time, Prudential Insurance Company was the fiscal intermediary between the Provider and HEW, and it supervised the nursing home's financial participation in the Medicare program and advanced interim reimbursements to the home for Medicare services.

* * *

[Prudential made interim payments that exceeded by $151,413 the amount later deemed to be due to corporation.] The corporation never repaid the $151,413 since it had no assets. On March 27, 1972, "the corporate entity became void" for failure to pay state taxes.

Pisani was president, registered agent, and sole stockholder of the corporation during the Provider's participation in the Medicare program. He used personal funds, often obtained through personal bank loans, to finance the corporation. He also loaned money to the corporation. It always operated at a loss, was undercapitalized, and never paid dividends. Pisani kept no corporate minute books and observed no corporate formalities. He testified that all the corporate records were in a briefcase which was stolen from the trunk of his car, but the district court did not believe this testimony.

* * *

[In 1967, Dr. Pisani loaned the corporation $184,922.] Although Pisani repeatedly denied that the loans were repaid, he later admitted that he signed documents showing that the corporation repaid $116,000 to him. He knew during the time the corporation repaid his loans that it was on the verge of financial collapse. The nursing home was sold at a foreclosure sale in January 1970 after it defaulted on its mortgage payments.

The district court held Pisani liable for the $151,413 of overpayments as the alter ego of the corporation.

* * *

II.   Discussion of Law
* * *

B.   Piercing the Corporate Veil

[W]e turn to cases which articulate the alter ego theory.[3] DeWitt Truck Brokers v. W. Ray Flemming Fruit Co., 540 F.2d 681 (4th Cir.1976), sets out in detail the relevant factors. First is whether the corporation is grossly undercapitalized for its purposes. Other factors are

"failure to observe corporate formalities, non-payment of dividends, the insolvency of the debtor corporation at the time, siphoning of funds of the corporation by the dominant stockholder, non-functioning of other officers or directors, absence of corporate records, and the fact that the corporation is merely a facade for the operations of the dominant stockholder or stockholders."

Also, the situation "must present an element of injustice or fundamental unfairness," but a number of these factors can be sufficient to show such

---

3. Zubik v. Zubik, 384 F.2d 267 (3d Cir. 1967), cert. denied, 390 U.S. 988, 88 S.Ct. 1183, 19 L.Ed.2d 1291 (1968), stated that the corporate existence could be disregarded to "prevent fraud, illegality, or injustice, or when recognition of the corporate entity would defeat public policy" Id. at 272. It did not explicitly adopt the alter ego theory, and it apparently relied at least partially on federal rather than state law. Zubik, however, involved a corporate tort and the court recognized that business transactions often involve much stronger cases for piercing the veil of an undercapitalized corporation. Id. A party to a contract may have relied on conduct by the defendant shareholder, while tort plaintiffs like those in Zubik usually never knew the shareholder, much less relied on his conduct or representations.

unfairness. The district court opinion considered these factors carefully. It stated:

> "The corporation was undercapitalized and, in my view, the corporate formalities were not observed notwithstanding Dr. Pisani's testimony that corporate records had been maintained but stolen. The corporation did not pay dividends and eventually became insolvent. The reduction of the corporation's indebtedness to Dr. Pisani from approximately $184,000 in 1967 to $0 in 1969 indicates that Dr. Pisani siphoned corporate funds."

United States v. Normandy House Nursing Home, Inc., 428 F.Supp. 421 (D.Mass.1977), is the case most nearly on point here. There, the district court denied a motion to dismiss because it held that an issue of fact existed as to whether the defendant doctor was the alter ego of the nursing home corporation. He was the sole shareholder. The provider corporation had sold all its assets and ceased operating as a nursing home at the time the audits were beginning. The court held that, despite the lack of allegations of fraud, the doctor could be liable if the sale of assets was carried out to avoid returning overpayments to HEW. It also held, alternatively, that it could pierce the corporate veil to prevent circumvention of a statute or avoidance of a clear legislative purpose. The legislative purpose, the court found, was paying only the reasonable cost of Medicare services, and the corporate form could circumvent this goal under the alleged facts of the case.

Pisani's situation is remarkably similar to that of the doctor in Normandy House Nursing Home. Also, additional factors not present there, but present here, favor piercing the corporate veil in this case. Pisani followed no corporate formalities, operated the corporation with his personal funds, loaned large sums to the corporation and then repaid the loans to himself with corporate funds while the corporation was failing, and kept the corporation undercapitalized by loaning it money instead of investing equity in it. These facts are relevant under DeWitt Truck Brokers.

Pisani also falls under the alternative holding of Normandy House, since the Medicare statute can be circumvented if he is not personally liable. Owners of nursing homes would be able to operate them with all the financing in the form of loans, with little or no equity, and then submit inflated cost reports. After receiving the overpayments, an owner could have the corporation repay his loans and then put the corporation through bankruptcy. By keeping few or no records, the owner would make it difficult for HEW to prove fraud. Without fear of individual liability, such an owner would have an incentive to encourage overpayments and then delay audits and collection efforts until after bankruptcy. If HEW had to prove fraud where such a defendant kept no corporate records and inadequate books, such schemes would be difficult to prevent. Thus, we hold that this case is appropriate for applying the alter ego doctrine as set forth in DeWitt Truck Brokers, to pierce the corporate veil.

* * *

Notes and Questions

1. Was Dr. Pisani engaged in fraud? Would the court have pierced the corporate veil if this was a contract suit against Dr. Pisani brought by a supplier

of medical equipment? By a victim of Dr. Pisani's negligence? What explains the result in this case? Do health care corporations run special risks that courts will disregard the corporate form? In cases involving hospital systems with multiple corporate entities, courts are usually reluctant to pierce the corporate veil even where the parent exercises extensive control over the subsidiary and its name is prominently displayed in the advertising, signs and literature of the subsidiary hospital. See, e.g., Humana, Inc. v. Kissun, 221 Ga.App. 64, 471 S.E.2d 514 (1996); see also, Ritter v. BJC Barnes Jewish Christian Health Systems, 987 S.W.2d 377 (Mo. Ct. App.1999) (refusing to hold parent entity liable on agency, veil-piercing, vicarious liability or apparent authority theories despite extensive control over subsidiary hospital's operations).

2. Courts are remarkably prone to rely on labels or characterizations of relationships (like "alter ego," "instrumentality" or "sham") or mechanically recite piercing factors (such as the failure to follow corporate formalities, the absence of adequate capitalization, or the commingling of personal and corporate assets) without explaining why it is appropriate to upset the parties' expectation of limited liability. Although the basis for piercing is usually justified in broad generalities such as "avoiding fraud or injustice," a coherent piercing jurisprudence has yet to emerge. For a useful attempt to reconcile the hodge-podge of factors relied upon by the courts and to rationalize the cases by reference to the body of law protecting creditors from sham transactions designed to shield assets, see Robert Charles Clark, Corporate Law 91 (1986).

3. Many professional corporations statutes provide for: (1) limited liability for shareholders as to the ordinary business obligations of the corporation (e.g., business debts, negligence unassociated with professional services, bankruptcy); (2) unlimited liability as to the shareholder's own professional negligence and the negligence of those under her direct supervision and control; and (3) limited liability (or capped joint and several liability) for the negligent acts of other shareholders or other employees not under their supervision or control. See, e.g., Kan. Stat. Ann. § 17–2715 (Supp. 1994); 1995 Me. Legis. Serv. H. P. 231 (West). What policies justify these differences? Are they still valid in an era of greater integration among practitioners operating in business entities? What arrangements might you advise for a professional corporation that anticipates purchasing expensive assets like an MRI or valuable interests in real estate? Are there arrangements that might also help allocate capital expenditures in a multi-specialty practice where not every physician will be using the MRI?

4. As not-for-profit and for-profit hospitals diversified and expanded in the 1970s and 1980s many "restructured" their corporate organizations. This process often entailed creating numerous corporate entities to provide distinct services or serve certain functions on behalf of the enterprise. Such restructurings are motivated by a variety of impulses: separating assets from operational units that may incur liabilities; maximizing cost-based reimbursement; avoiding regulatory constraints; facilitating financing arrangements; and achieving management efficiencies. After reimbursement methodologies changed to eliminate some advantages of multi-corporate arrangements, many hospitals found themselves left with a cumbersome, labyrinthine structure that itself had to be "restructured."

Corporate structures vary considerably, but three principle models may be identified. First, hospitals may establish wholly-owned subsidiaries. Second, they may create sibling corporations which are separate from the hospital but whose board of directors are selected by the hospital (for example, the hospital might be the sole member of a nonprofit entity or the sole shareholder of a for-profit entity). Finally, hospitals may create a parent holding company which owns all the shares or is the sole member of the hospital corporation and the other corporations providing hospital functions, providing health care services, or engaging in unrelated businesses. Where the objective of the multi-corporate structure is to insulate a hospital's assets from potential liabilities, care must obviously be taken to observe the requirements imposed by the "veil piercing" cases. What steps would you counsel that a hospital take to assure that a court would not disregard the corporate entity?

D. PROFESSIONALISM AND THE CORPORATE PRACTICE OF MEDICINE DOCTRINE

BERLIN v. SARAH BUSH LINCOLN HEALTH CENTER

Supreme Court of Illinois, 1997.
179 Ill.2d 1, 227 Ill.Dec. 769, 688 N.E.2d 106.

JUSTICE NICKELS delivered the opinion of the court:

Plaintiff, Richard Berlin, Jr., M.D., filed a complaint for declaratory judgment and a motion for summary judgment seeking to have a restrictive covenant contained in an employment agreement with defendant, Sara Bush Lincoln Health Center (the Health Center), declared unenforceable. The circuit court of Coles County, finding the entire employment agreement unenforceable, granted summary judgment in favor of Dr. Berlin. The circuit court reasoned that the Health Center, as a nonprofit corporation employing a physician, was practicing medicine in violation of the prohibition on the corporate practice of medicine. A divided appellate court affirmed, and this court granted the Health Center's petition for leave to appeal.

The central issue involved in this appeal is whether the "corporate practice doctrine" prohibits corporations which are licensed hospitals from employing physicians to provide medical services. We find the doctrine inapplicable to licensed hospitals and accordingly reverse.

BACKGROUND

The facts are not in dispute. The Health Center is a nonprofit corporation duly licensed under the Hospital Licensing Act to operate a hospital. In December 1992, Dr. Berlin and the Health Center entered into a written agreement whereby the Health Center employed Dr. Berlin to practice medicine for the hospital for five years. The agreement provided that Dr. Berlin could terminate the employment relationship for any reason prior to the end of the five-year term by furnishing the Health Center with 180 days advance written notice of such termination. The agreement also contained a restrictive covenant which prohibited Dr. Berlin from competing with the hospital by providing health services within a 50–mile radius of the Health Center for two years after the end of the employment agreement.

On February 4, 1994, Dr. Berlin informed the Health Center by letter that he was resigning effective February 7, 1994, and accepting employment with the Carle Clinic Association. After his resignation, Dr. Berlin immediately began working at a Carle Clinic facility located approximately one mile from the Health Center. Shortly thereafter, the Health Center sought a preliminary injunction to prohibit Dr. Berlin from practicing at the Carle

Clinic based on the restrictive covenant contained in the aforesaid employment agreement.

* * *

HOSPITAL EMPLOYMENT OF PHYSICIANS

The Health Center and its supporting amici curiae contend that no judicial determination exists which prohibits hospitals from employing physicians. In support of this contention, the Health Center argues that this court has acknowledged the legitimacy of such employment practices in past decisions. See, e.g., Gilbert v. Sycamore Municipal Hospital, 156 Ill.2d 511, 190 Ill.Dec. 758, 622 N.E.2d 788 (1993); Darling v. Charleston Community Memorial Hospital, 33 Ill.2d 326, 211 N.E.2d 253 (1965). In the alternative, the Health Center contends that if a judicial prohibition on hospital employment of physicians does exist, it should be overruled. In support of this contention, the Health Center argues that the public policies behind such a prohibition are inapplicable to licensed hospitals, particularly nonprofit hospitals.

The Health Center also contends that there is no statutory prohibition on the corporate employment of physicians. The Health Center notes that no statute has ever expressly stated that physicians cannot be employed by corporations. To the contrary, the Health Center argues that other legislative actions recognize that hospitals can indeed employ physicians. Citing Illinois' Emergency Medical Treatment Act and Osteopathic and Allopathic Healthcare Discrimination Act.

Dr. Berlin and supporting amici curiae contend that this court, in People ex rel. Kerner v. United Medical Service, Inc. adopted the corporate practice of medicine doctrine, which prohibits corporations from employing physicians. Dr. Berlin concludes that the Health Center, as a nonprofit corporation, is prohibited by the Kerner rule from entering into employment agreements with physicians.

Dr. Berlin also disputes the Health Center's contention that public policy supports creating an exception to the Kerner rule for hospitals. He argues that, because no legislative enactment subsequent to the Kerner case expressly grants hospitals the authority to employ physicians, the legislature has ratified the corporate practice of medicine doctrine as the public policy of Illinois. At this point, a review of the corporate practice of medicine doctrine is appropriate.

CORPORATE PRACTICE OF MEDICINE DOCTRINE

The corporate practice of medicine doctrine prohibits corporations from providing professional medical services. Although a few states have codified the doctrine, the prohibition is primarily inferred from state medical licensure acts, which regulate the profession of medicine and forbid its practice by unlicensed individuals. See A. Rosoff, The Business of Medicine: Problems with the Corporate Practice Doctrine, 17 Cumb. L.Rev. 485, 490 (1987). The rationale behind the doctrine is that a corporation cannot be licensed to practice medicine because only a human being can sustain the education, training, and character-screening which are prerequisites to receiving a professional license. Since a corporation cannot receive a medical license, it follows that a corporation cannot legally practice the profession.

The rationale of the doctrine concludes that the employment of physicians by corporations is illegal because the acts of the physicians are attributable to the corporate employer, which cannot obtain a medical license. The prohibition on the corporate employment of physicians is invariably supported by several public policy arguments which espouse the dangers of lay control over professional judgment, the division of the physician's loyalty between his patient and his profitmaking employer, and the commercialization of the profession.

APPLICATION OF DOCTRINE IN ILLINOIS

This court first encountered the corporate practice doctrine in Dr. Allison, Dentist, Inc. v. Allison, 360 Ill. 638, 196 N.E. 799 (1935). In Allison, the plaintiff corporation owned and operated a dental practice. When defendant, a dentist formerly employed by plaintiff, opened a dental office across the street from plaintiff's location, plaintiff brought an action to enforce a restrictive covenant contained in defendant's employment contract. Defendant's motion to dismiss the action was granted on the grounds that plaintiff was practicing dentistry in violation of the Dental Practice Act. In affirming the judgment of the lower court, this court stated:

> "To practice a profession requires something more than the financial ability to hire competent persons to do the actual work. It can be done only by a duly qualified human being, and to qualify something more than mere knowledge or skill is essential. The qualifications include personal characteristics, such as honesty, guided by an upright conscience and a sense of loyalty to clients or patients, even to the extent of sacrificing pecuniary profit, if necessary. These requirements are spoken of generically as that good moral character which is a pre-requisite to the licensing of any professional man. No corporation can qualify." [The Court next discussed cases finding the corporate practice doctrine barred corporations from operating dental clinics employing dentists and prevented a medical clinic providing medical services through licensed physicians.]

* * *

Prior to the instant action, apparently no Illinois court has applied the corporate practice of medicine rule set out in People ex rel. Kerner v. United Medical Service, Inc., or specifically addressed the issue of whether licensed hospitals are prohibited from employing physicians. We therefore look to other jurisdictions with reference to the application of the corporate practice of medicine doctrine to hospitals.

APPLICABILITY OF DOCTRINE TO HOSPITALS IN OTHER JURISDICTIONS

Although the corporate practice of medicine doctrine has long been recognized by a number of jurisdictions, the important role hospitals serve in the health care field has also been increasingly recognized. Accordingly, numerous jurisdictions have recognized either judicial or statutory exceptions to the corporate practice of medicine doctrine which allow hospitals to employ physicians and other health care professionals. See, e.g., Cal. Bus. & Prof.Code § 2400 (West 1990) (exception for charitable hospitals). . . . A review of this authority reveals that there are primarily three approaches utilized in determining that the corporate practice of medicine doctrine is inapplicable to hospitals.

First, some states refused to adopt the corporate practice of medicine doctrine altogether when initially interpreting their respective medical practice act. These states generally determined that a hospital corporation which employs a physician is not practicing medicine, but rather is merely making medical treatment available. See, e.g., State ex rel. Sager v. Lewin, 128 Mo.App. 149, 155, 106 S.W. 581, 583 (1907) ("[H]ospitals are maintained by private corporations, incorporated for the purpose of furnishing medical and surgical treatment to the sick and wounded. These corporations do not practice medicine but they receive patients and employ physicians and surgeons to give them treatment") . . . .

Under the second approach, the courts of some jurisdictions determined that the corporate practice doctrine is inapplicable to nonprofit hospitals and health associations. These courts reasoned that the public policy arguments supporting the corporate practice doctrine do not apply to physicians employed by charitable institutions. See, e.g., Group Health Ass'n v. Moor, 24 F.Supp. 445, 446 (D.D.C.1938) (actions of nonprofit association which contracts with licensed physicians to provide medical treatment to its members in no way commercializes medicine and is not the practice of medicine), aff'd, 107 F.2d 239 (D.C.Cir.1939) . . . .

In the third approach, the courts of several states have determined that the corporate practice doctrine is not applicable to hospitals which employ physicians because hospitals are authorized by other laws to provide medical treatment to patients . . . .

We find the rationale of the latter two approaches persuasive. We decline to apply the corporate practice of medicine doctrine to licensed hospitals. The instant cause is distinguishable from Kerner, Allison, and Winberry. None of those cases specifically involved the employment of physicians by a hospital. More important, none of those cases involved a corporation licensed to provide health care services to the general public.

The corporate practice of medicine doctrine set forth in Kerner was not an interpretation of the plain language of the Medical Practice Act. The Medical Practice Act contains no express prohibition on the corporate employment of physicians.[4] Rather, the corporate practice of medicine doctrine was inferred from the general policies behind the Medical Practice Act. Such a prohibition is entirely appropriate to a general corporation possessing no licensed authority to offer medical services to the public, such as the appellant in Kerner. However, when a corporation has been sanctioned by the laws of this state to operate a hospital, such a prohibition is inapplicable.

The legislative enactments pertaining to hospitals provide ample support for this conclusion. For example, the Hospital Licensing Act defines "hospital" as:

> "any institution, place, building, or agency, public or private, whether organized for profit or

---

4. In contrast, the Dental Practice Act, applied by this court in [the dental clinic and Allison cases], expressly prohibited a corpora-tion from furnishing dentists and owning and operating a dental office.

not, devoted primarily to the maintenance and operation of facilities for the diagnosis and treatment or care of * * * persons admitted for overnight stay or longer in order to obtain medical, including obstetric, psychiatric and nursing, care of illness, disease, injury, infirmity, or deformity." (Emphasis added.) 210 ILCS 85/3 (West Supp.1995).

In addition, the Hospital Lien Act provides "[e]very hospital rendering service in the treatment, care and maintenance, of such injured person" a lien upon a patient's personal injury cause of action. (Emphasis added.) Pub. Act 89–280, eff. January 1, 1996 (amending 770 ILCS 35/1 (West 1994)). Moreover, the Hospital Emergency Service Act (210 ILCS 80/0.01 et seq. (West 1994)) requires "[e]very hospital * * * which provides general medical and surgical hospital services" to also provide emergency services. (Emphasis added.) 210 ILCS 80/1 (West 1994). . . .

The foregoing statutes clearly authorize, and at times mandate, licensed hospital corporations to provide medical services. We believe that the authority to employ duly-licensed physicians for that purpose is reasonably implied from these legislative enactments. We further see no justification for distinguishing between nonprofit and for-profit hospitals in this regard. The authorities and duties of licensed hospitals are conferred equally upon both entities.

In addition, we find the public policy concerns which support the corporate practice doctrine inapplicable to a licensed hospital in the modern health care industry. The concern for lay control over professional judgment is alleviated in a licensed hospital, where generally a separate professional medical staff is responsible for the quality of medical services rendered in the facility.[5]

Furthermore, we believe that extensive changes in the health care industry since the time of the Kerner decision, including the emergence of corporate health maintenance organizations, have greatly altered the concern over the commercialization of health care. In addition, such concerns are relieved when a licensed hospital is the physician's employer. Hospitals have an independent duty to provide for the patient's health and welfare. [Citations to Darling and other cases omitted].

We find particularly appropriate the statement of the Kansas Supreme Court that "[i]t would be incongruous to conclude that the legislature intended a hospital to accomplish what it is licensed to do without utilizing physicians as independent contractors or employees. * * * To conclude that a hospital must do so without employing physicians is not only illogical but ignores reality." St. Francis Regional Med. Center v. Weiss, 254 Kan. 728, 745, 869 P.2d 606, 618 (1994). Accordingly, we conclude that a duly-licensed hospital possesses legislative authority to practice medicine by means of its staff of licensed physicians and is excepted from the operation of the corporate practice of medicine doctrine.

---

5. Moreover, in the instant case, the employment agreement expressly provided that the Health Center had no control or direction over Dr. Berlin's medical judgment and practice, other than that control exercised by the professional medical staff. Dr. Berlin has never contended that the Health Center's lay management attempted to control his practice of medicine.

Consequently, the employment agreement between the Health Center and Dr. Berlin is not unenforceable merely because the Health Center is a corporate entity.

* * *

JUSTICE HARRISON, dissenting:

In People ex rel. Kerner v. United Medical Service, Inc., this court held that a corporation cannot employ physicians and collect fees for their services because such conduct constitutes the practice of medicine and the practice of medicine by corporations is prohibited. The court based its conclusion on the Medical Practice Act, reasoning that under the statute, a license is required to practice medicine and

> "[t]he legislative intent manifest from a view of the entire law is that only individuals may obtain a license thereunder. No corporation can meet the requirements of the statute essential to the issuance of a license." Kerner, 362 Ill. at 454, 200 N.E. 157.

More than 60 years have passed since Kerner was decided. If the legislature believed that our construction of the Act was erroneous or that the rule announced in Kerner should be changed, it could have amended the law to authorize the practice of medicine by entities other than individuals. With limited exceptions not applicable here, it has not done so. To the contrary, it has continued to adhere to the requirements that medicine can only be practiced by those who hold valid licenses from the state and that only individuals can obtain such licenses.... When it amends a statute but does not alter a previous interpretation by this court, we assume that the legislature intended for the amendment to have the same interpretation previously given ...

That the legislature has acquiesced in the judiciary's construction of the Medical Practice Act is especially clear given recent developments in the law. Under ... the Regulatory Agency Sunset Act, the Medical Practice Act was scheduled for repeal on December 31, 1997, unless the General Assembly enacted legislation providing for its continuation. On April 12, 1996, the appellate court filed its opinion in this case, holding under Kerner that the Medical Practice Act bars the corporate practice of medicine by hospitals. Subsequent to that decision, the General Assembly passed and the Governor signed new legislation extending the Medical Practice Act until January 1 of the year 2007. The new legislation made no substantive changes to the licensing requirements and included no provisions contrary to the appellate court's holding. Because the legislature is presumed to know the construction the statute has been given by the courts, its reenactment of the law can only be understood as an endorsement of the construction followed by the appellate court here. The corporate practice of medicine by hospitals is prohibited.

* * *

Hospitals do not fall within any of [the exceptions contained in the Medical Practice Act]. The majority argues that additional exceptions can be implied based on other statutes enacted by the General Assembly. It is a fundamental rule of statutory construction, however, that the enumeration of certain things in a statute implies the exclusion of all other things ...

Wholly aside from this problem, none of the other statutes invoked by my colleagues supports their position. The most that can be said of those statutes is that they authorize hospitals to operate facilities for the diagnosis and care of patients and to make emergency service available regardless of ability to pay. Hospitals may also employ physician's assistants, provided such assistants function under the supervision of a licensed physician. None of those endeavors, however, requires that hospitals have the power to employ physicians directly or to charge patients for the physicians' services. All may be accomplished by granting staff privileges to duly licensed private physicians, and the Hospital Licensing Act presumes that hospitals will staff their facilities in precisely that way....

In addition to creating special rules for HMOs, the General Assembly has also decided to allow physicians to employ various forms of business organizations in practicing their profession. Physicians may incorporate [as professional corporations or in other forms permitted under Illinois law and may operate limited liability companies]. ...Again, however, none of these provisions pertains to hospitals, and no inference can be drawn from any of them that the General Assembly intended to alter the prohibition against the corporate practice of medicine by hospitals.

For the foregoing reasons, I agree with the appellate court that the corporate practice doctrine prohibited defendant, Sarah Bush Lincoln Health Center, from entering into an employment agreement with Dr. Berlin. That agreement, including its restrictive covenant, was void and unenforceable....

Notes and Questions

1.   Consider the following rationale for the corporate practice of medicine doctrine offered by the Illinois Supreme Court:

[T]he practice of a profession is subject to licensing and regulation and is not subject to commercialization or exploitation. To practice a profession ... requires something more than the financial ability to hire competent persons to do the actual work. It can be done only by a duly qualified human being, and to qualify something more than mere knowledge or skill is essential ... No corporation can qualify.

People v. United Medical Service, 362 Ill. 442, 200 N.E. 157, 163 (1936). Can you articulate the specific concerns that underlie the court's statement? Are the sources of the doctrine statutory or do they emanate from general public policy principles? If the latter, what are those principles and are they still valid today? For a decidedly negative assessment of the doctrine, see Mark A. Hall, Institutional Control of Physician Behavior: Legal Barriers to Health Care Cost Containment, 137 U.Pa. L. Rev. 431, 509–518 (1988)("puzzling doctrine ... clouded with confused reasoning and ... founded on an astounding series of logical fallacies"); Arnold J. Rosoff, The Business of Medicine: Problems with the Corporate Practice Doctrine, 17 Cumb. L. Rev. 485 (1986–87). See also, American Health Lawyers Association, Patient Care and Professional Responsibility: The Impact of the Corporate Practice of Medicine Doctrine and Related Laws and Regulations (1998).

2.   Does the Court's analysis in Berlin provide any grounds for upsetting the corporate practice of medicine doctrine outside of the context of employment of physicians by hospitals? What arguments can be used to allow MSOs or other integrating entities to employ physicians? Are the majority's arguments based on

legislative intent persuasive, or are they simply a way to rationalize overturning long-established precedent? Do changes in the nature of the practice of medicine justify courts amending the common law where the legislature has failed to act? How should corporate practice concepts apply in the context of a general partnership? Recall that a lay partner has the right to participate in control of and bind the partnership. See Morelli v. Ehsan, 48 Wash. App. 14, 737 P.2d 1030 (Wash. Ct. App.1987), rev'd on other grounds, 110 Wash. 2d 555, 756 P.2d 129 (Wash. 1998).

3.   As noted above, commentators have been highly critical of the corporate practice of medicine doctrine. Can it be argued that the doctrine can help rectify the problems associated with risk sharing and managed care? Does it help restore the fiduciary ties between patient and physician that have been eroded by managed care? For an affirmative answer, see Andre Hampton, Resurrection of the Prohibition on the Corporate Practice of Medicine: Teaching Old Dogma New Tricks, 66 U. Cin. L. Rev. 489 (1998).

4.   In 1974, a Federal court in Texas upheld the Texas prohibition of "layman corporations" that "practice medicine" by hiring physicians to treat patients. The court found the prohibition to be a rational exercise of the police power: "Without licensed, professional doctors on Boards of Directors, who and what criteria govern the selection of medical and paramedical staff members? To whom does the doctor owe his first duty—the patient or the corporation?" Garcia v. Texas State Board of Medical Examiners, 384 F.Supp. 434, 440 (W.D.Tex.1974), aff'd mem., 421 U.S. 995, 95 S.Ct. 2391, 44 L.Ed.2d 663 (1975).

5.   Early "corporate medical practice" involved corporations contracting with physicians to provide medical care for their employees for a fixed salary or corporations that marketed physicians' services to the public. The AMA considered the corporate practice of medicine the "commercialization" of medicine, and believed that it would increase physician workload, decrease the quality of patient care, and would introduce lay control over the practice of medicine that would interfere with the physician-patient relationship. The AMA promulgated ethical guidelines that restricted or prohibited the corporate practice of medicine. The prohibition against corporate medical practice was enforced by the courts, using statutory prohibitions against the practice of medicine by unlicensed individuals. See Jeffrey F. Chase–Lubitz, The Corporate Practice of Medicine Doctrine: An Anachronism in the Modern Health Care Industry, 40 Vand. L. Rev. 445 (1987). What does it matter that a doctor is employed by a partnership of doctors or a professional corporation rather than by a lay person or business entity controlled by non-physicians? Should the state eliminate corporate practice prohibitions and pursue quality concerns directly through quality-control regulation or malpractice litigation? What quality controls respond to the financial incentives presented in fee-for-service practice?

6.   In most states the corporate practice of medicine doctrine is the product of antiquated, rarely enforced case law. See Department of Health and Human Services, Office of Inspector General, State Prohibitions on Hospital Employment of Physicians, No. OEI–0109100770 (1991) (concluding that only five states, California, Colorado, Iowa, Ohio and Texas currently prohibit hospitals from employing physicians, although others have old precedents not yet expressly rejected). How should an attorney counsel a client as to the legal risks and propriety of undertaking actions that violate old precedent which is likely to be overturned if ever challenged? See Norman P. Jeddeloh, Physician Contract Audits: A Hospital Management Tool, 21 J. Health & Hosp. L. 105 (1988)("Obviously, in modern practice the rule against physician employment is honored

mainly in the breach. That does not mean that these traditional prohibitions cannot again serve as a basis for hospital liability.... Therefore, it is usually best, whenever possible, to establish true independent contractor arrangements or retain physicians through a separate corporation."). For an insightful analysis of the dangers of ignoring this latent doctrine, see Rosoff, supra.

III. INTEGRATION AND NEW ORGANIZATIONAL STRUCTURES: WHERE'S WALDO—PART II

The year is 1996 and Waldo, now 53 years old, visits Dr. Goodscalpel for a routine check-up. Doctor Goodscalpel, who has joined a 10–doctor partnership called Medical Associates, recommends a PSA screening test. He sends Waldo down the hall to MedServices, an outpatient for-profit corporation owned by a subsidiary of the Llama Hilda Foundation. Llama Hilda is a not-for-profit corporation that now controls Mt. St. Hilda Hospital and numerous other entities providing health and administrative services. Unfortunately, the lab tests come back positive and Dr. Goodscalpel refers Waldo to a surgeon, Dr. Mack, who has joined Doctors Inc., a large (50 doctor) multi-specialist group organized as a professional corporation. Doctors Inc. and Medical Associates both are co-owners, along with Mt. St. Hilda Hospital, of a physician-hospital organization (PHO), an entity that negotiates contracts with insurance companies and supplies billing and other services to the medical groups.

After receiving prior approval from the PHO utilization manager, Dr. Mack sends Waldo to the Radiology Center for an MRI. The Radiology Center, an outpatient facility on Mt. St. Hilda's campus, is a joint venture organized as a corporation. Fifty percent of its stock is owned by Llama Hilda Foundation, and the other 50 percent is owned by a partnership comprised of 5 radiologists. After getting the MRI report back from the consulting radiologists, Dr. Mack recommends surgery to be performed at Mt. St. Hilda.

Waldo has joined BlueStaff's new managed care plan, CarePlan, which provides coverage only if he visits participating providers. Although Waldo had wanted Dr. Immel, an internationally known anesthesiologist who teaches at a local medical school, to assist in the operation, Dr. Immel was not a CarePlan participating provider and did not have staff privileges at Mt. St. Hilda hospital. Instead, Mt. St. Hilda has an exclusive contract with GasAssociates, a professional group organized as a limited liability company controlled by its anesthesiologist-owners. The anesthesia was furnished by a CRNA under the supervision of an anesthesiologist.

Most of the providers furnishing services to Waldo were paid on a prepaid capitated basis. Waldo was responsible for a small co-payment on certain services.

Comparing Waldo's recent episode of care to his experience in 1978 (set forth at the beginning of this chapter), what changes have occurred in terms of provider coordination and control of their activities? How do the organizational structures to which the physicians and hospitals belong accommodate the changed environment? How have the economic incentives facing the providers changed? Is Waldo, the "consumer," better off under the modern arrangements?

A. THE CHANGING STRUCTURE OF THE MODERN HEALTH CARE ENTERPRISE

Not very long ago health care services were delivered primarily by doctors working in solo practice or as members of small groups usually practicing the same specialty, and by non-profit hospitals operating independently or as part of relatively simple systems that shared a few administrative or operational services. This began to change in the 1980's as hospitals adopted more complex organizational structures and entered into joint ventures and alliances with other hospitals. In the last several years, however, we have witnessed an unprecedented wave of innovation and change in the way health care providers conduct business. Prompted by developments in health care financing and the possibility of health care reform, physicians, hospitals and other providers have begun to reorganize their business enterprises and contractual relationships. In particular, they have developed so-called "integrated delivery systems" and other methods of increasing inter-provider linkages in order to meet the needs of managed care purchasers, such as HMOs, PPOs and self-insured employers.

The rapid growth of managed care has provided the principal impetus for the tremendous surge in integrative activity. Employers, government and other entities that pay for health care are increasingly demanding cost containment in the delivery of health services. They frequently do this by requiring competitive bidding among providers and/or insisting that providers accept financial risk for the cost and volume of the services provided. Consequently, health care providers found it necessary to realign themselves and devise organizational structures in order to meet the demands of this new environment. Among the important goals in forming such organizations are: providing broad geographic coverage; giving patients a "seamless" system that provides a comprehensive continuum of care; offering payers the advantages of "one-stop shopping"; enabling providers to assume financial risk; facilitating the pooling of capital; and aligning the interests of physicians and hospitals. Moreover, providers, especially physicians, need to acquire the management and administrative support necessary to effectively adjust their practice patterns and bid effectively for prepaid contracts. Needless to say, it takes money to reorganize delivery systems in this way. An important role of the emerging structures is to provide the means for pooling capital and management expertise toward accomplishing these ends.

Integration among providers occurs at both "horizontal" and "vertical" levels. That is, physicians may combine horizontally with other physicians to form group practices, IPAs and other networks. Likewise, hospitals may merge or establish joint ventures and alliances with other hospitals. Hospitals and physicians have also integrated vertically by creating various kinds of integrated delivery systems which bring together complementary provider services at several levels. Some of these organizations only loosely link hospitals and physicians and are primarily devices to facilitate joint contracting with payers. Other forms of vertical integration more fully bind hospitals and physicians by having them share both financial risk and control. In these forms, physicians and hospitals may co-own and co-manage services or enterprises; the hospital may undertake administrative or management services for physicians; the hospital may purchase the physician practices, with the physicians becoming employees of or independent contractors for the organization; or the physicians may control the enterprise with hospitals assuming a contracting relationship. Vertical integration may also include the insurance component, as provider systems may integrate into insurance or insurers may integrate into delivery through HMOs or joint ventures with providers.

As the following excerpt from the Physician Payment Review Commission suggests, providers have a wide variety of organizational models to choose among for promoting greater integration. The selection of any given arrangement seems to depend on a number of diverse and market-specific factors such as the degree of managed care penetration in the area; the nature and extent of rivalry among providers; the "politics" and "culture" of the provider community; and the business judgments of those in leadership positions.

PHYSICIAN PAYMENT REVIEW COMMISSION, ANNUAL REPORT TO CONGRESS

(1995).

PROVIDER–DRIVEN INTEGRATION

The U.S. Health Care System has been moving steadily away from delivery of health care through independent practitioners and toward more integrated approaches. As late as 1987, more than half of U.S. physicians were self-employed in solo or two-partner practice. By 1993, this figure had fallen to 37 percent.

While some of this reorganization of health care had been done directly by insurers, for example, through ownership of facilities and exclusive contracting with physicians, in other cases providers developed integrated arrangements on their own. Multispecialty group practices have long served to bring physicians together under common medical and financial management. More recently, physicians, hospitals, and other providers have begun to form new types of organizations at a fairly rapid pace. These new organizations range from relatively loose associations of physicians, through physician-hospital joint ventures, up to fully integrated insurer-provider HMOs.

* * *

INTEGRATING ORGANIZATIONS

Defining the new integrating organizations is not an easy task. Health care organizations are in flux as markets move toward more intensive management of care. A definition that describes the typical organization today might be obsolete two years from now as the typical style of practice changes. Consequently there are no agreed-upon standard definitions, and these definitions should be taken as approximate only.

* * *

Independent Practice Association

The independent practice association (IPA) is typically a physician-organized entity that contracts with payers on behalf of its member physicians. The typical IPA negotiates contracts with insurers and pays physicians on a fee-for-service basis with a withhold. Physicians may maintain significant business outside the IPA, join multiple IPAs, retain ownership of their own practices, and typically continue in their traditional style of practice. Physicians usually invest a modest fee (a few thousand dollars) to join the IPA. IPAs may also undertake a variety of additional roles, including utilization review, and practice management functions such as billing and group purchasing, resulting in greater centralization and standardization of medical practice.

* * *

Physician-Hospital Organization

The physician-hospital organization [PHO] contracts with payers on behalf of the hospital and its affiliated physicians. The organization is responsible for negotiating health plan contracts, and in some cases, conducting utilization review, credentialing, and quality assurance. The PHO may centralize some aspects of administrative services or encourage use of shared facilities for coordination of clinical care.

The typical PHO is a hospital-sponsored organization that centers around a single hospital and its medical staff. PHOs may also form as joint ventures between hospitals and existing physician organizations such as a large multi-specialty medical group or an IPA. PHOs are further divided into open PHOs, which are open to all members of the hospital's staff, and closed PHOs, where the PHO chooses some physicians and excludes others.

As with the IPA, the typical PHO accounts for only a modest share of the physician's (or the hospital's) business. Physicians retain their own practices, and their relationship to payers other than those with whom the PHO negotiates is unchanged. As with IPAs, the PHO can move toward greater centralized control over practice management and medical practice.

* * *

Group Practice

A medical group practice is defined as "the provision of health care services by three or more physicians who are formally organized as a legal entity in which business and clinical facilities, records, and personnel are shared. Income from medical services provided by the group are treated as receipts of the group and are distributed according to some prearranged plan."

The group practice is a well-established form of organization and one of the few organizational types for which good data are available. In 1991, physicians were split almost equally among three practice settings: group practice, solo or two-physician practice, or other patient care such as hospital-based practice.

* * *

Group Practice Without Walls

A group practice without walls (GPWW) refers to physicians in physically independent facilities who form a single legal entity to centralize the business aspects of their organization. In the typical case, the GPWW is organized by a strong, centralized clinic that adds individual physicians or small groups in satellite offices. In some cases, the GPWW is financially identical to a traditional group practice: It owns the assets of the individual practices and physicians share ownership of the GPWW, making it a unified business organization for the decentralized delivery of care. In other cases, physicians retain ownership of their own practices but enter into agreements for administrative and marketing functions. The GPWW may itself own certain ancillary services such as laboratory services.

Management Services Organization

The management services organization provides administrative and practice management services to physicians. An MSO may typically be owned by a hospital, hospitals, or investors. Large group practices may also establish MSOs as a way of capitalizing on their organizational skill by selling management services to otherwise unorganized physician groups.

MSOs can provide a very wide variety of services. Smaller and not-for-profit MSOs may limit operations to selling to physicians various administrative support services, such as billing, group purchasing, and various aspects of office administration. In other cases, hospital-owned MSOs are the vehicle through which hospitals purchase physician practices outright, leaving the physician either as an employee of the hospital or as an independent contractor with the physical assets of the practice owned by the hospital. Large, for-profit MSOs typically purchase the assets of physician practices outright, install office managers and other personnel, hire the physician through a professional services contract, and negotiate contracts with managed-care plans, all in exchange for a share of gross receipts typically based on the physicians' current practice expenses.

* * *

Hospital-Owned Medical Practice

In addition to the purchase of a medical practice through an MSO, hospitals can directly purchase medical practices, typically as part of their outpatient department.

* * *

Integrated Delivery System

Finally, a number of functionally similar organizations are built around hospitals and physicians linked in exclusive arrangements. In these integrated delivery systems (IDSs), a hospital or hospitals and large multispecialty group practices form an organization for the delivery of care, with all physician revenues coming through the organization.[6] These include foundation model, staff model, and equity model IDSs.

The main difference among these organizations is in the legal formalities of who works for whom and in the professional autonomy of the affiliated physicians. In a typical foundation model system, the hospital establishes a

---

6. While some researchers would call these integrated delivery systems a form of PHO, most reserve the term PHO for those organizations where only a small fraction of the physicians' revenues come through the organization.

not-for-profit foundation that purchases the assets of an existing physician group, signing an exclusive professional services contract with the physician corporation. Payers pay the foundation, which then pays the physicians' professional corporation.[7] In a staff model system, physicians work directly for the system without the intervening not-for-profit foundation and professional corporation. In an equity model system, physicians own a part of the system and share significantly in its financial success or failure.

In some markets, large group practices appear to be a significant alternative to these types of physician-hospital systems. In testimony before the Commission, [one witness] identified the capitated multispecialty group practice as the "center of gravity" of integrating activities in Southern California. In that marketplace, some large multispecialty groups are accepting capitation contracts from payers, then purchasing hospital services and coordinating the delivery of care, achieving system-type organization without a formal alliance with the hospital.

Notes

1. Through most of the 1990's, integration between hospitals and physicians grew rapidly, with most large hospital systems developing PHOs and acquiring physician practices. Many health industry experts confidently predicted that the new integrating organizations such as PHOs and MSOs were really transitional vehicles that would serve to "acclimatize" hospitals and physicians to the new environment created by managed care. By this account, after becoming accustomed to cooperating with each other, most providers would ultimately wind up in more fully integrated organizations that entail employment relationships and asset purchases. Some analysts disagreed, contending that much of the consolidation would be undone and that providers would revert to more flexible contractual arrangements. See Jeff Goldsmith, The Illusive Logic of Integration, Healthcare Forum 26 (Sept./Oct. 1994). The experience at the end of the decade suggests that skeptics of the integration movement were closer to the mark. Some large for-profit health systems that aggressively acquired or networked with physicians were spectacularly unsuccessful; in the notorious case of Columbia/HCA, the largest multi-hospital system in the nation was dismantled after settling public and private lawsuits charging rampant illegal practices. Several publicly traded physician practice management companies, once the darlings of Wall Street, also went into bankruptcy. The picture was no brighter in the nonprofit sector. Many systems that expanded rapidly did not fare well, as most dramatically evidenced by the $1.3 billion bankruptcy of the Allegheny Health, Education and Research Foundation. Acquisitions of physician practices have posed a monumental drain on the budgets of nonprofit hospitals; 80 percent of all physician practices acquired by hospitals are losing money, by some estimates at a rate of nearly $50,000–100,000 per year per physician. Finally, countless large IPAs and group practices have been forced to disband for financial reasons. For accounts and analyses of these developments, see James Robinson, The Future of Managed Care, 18 Health Aff. 7 (March/April 1999); Thomas Bodenheimer, The American Health Care System—Physicians and the Changing Medical Marketplace, 340 New Eng. J. Med. (Feb. 18, 1999); Lawton R. Burns & James Joo–Jinn, The Fall of the House of AHERF: The Allegheny Bankruptcy, 19 Health Aff. 7 (Jan/Feb

---

7. The presence of the foundation model system is due in part to state laws prohibiting the corporate practice of medicine, and the need for arms-length financial agreements between for-profit and not-for-profit entities.

2000); Mary Chris Jaklevic, Dealing With Docs: Dropping Money–Losing Practices Can Be A Costly Decision, Modern Healthcare 42, March 1, 1999; Bob Cook, Thinking Fast: Many Doctors are Avoiding the Risks of Repurchasing Their Assets, Modern Physician, Apr. 1, 1999. Whether the problems experienced to date are attributable to flaws in the concept of vertical integration among providers or to changes in the healthcare financing and market environment is not yet certain. Nor is it clear whether integration will give way to greater reliance on less rigid, "virtual" networks. At present, integration, "dis-integration," and new forms of networking are all in evidence.

2. What changes for health insurance and delivery systems might be in store as a result of the internet and improved computing capacity? Increasing use of the internet holds the promise of reducing employer and consumer reliance on fixed networks of providers. Further, Professor Nicolas Terry has suggested that by expanding information flows and opening access to the system, internet and new technology may vastly change provider and payer relationships:

> Web and attendant e-Commerce phenomena are irretrievably at odds with the traditional structure and hence legal regulation of health delivery. e-Health delivers information, diagnosis, treatment, care and prescribing in a non-linear, non-hierachical manner that encourages patients to "enter" the system at an infinite number of points. With the declining influence of proximity or geography, patients and others in (e-Health space) will have more choice, a phenomenon that will accelerate the decline in traditional professional relationships . . .

Nicolas P. Terry, Structural and Legal Implications of e-Health, 33 J. Health L. 605 (1999). The possibilities include growing "disintermediation," i.e., elimination of third party insurers and other middlemen; use of web technology to enable individuals to tailor their own provider networks using on-line auctions; integration of claims management and medical management and development of more sophisticated and accurate captitation and other forms of reimbursement. See Jeff Goldsmith, Internet and Managed Care: A New Wave of Innovation, 19 Health Affs. 42 (Nov/Dec. 2000). For a less sanguine view, see J.D. Kleinke, Vaporware.com: The Failed Promise of the Health Care Internet, 19 Health Aff. 57 (Nov/Dec 2000).

3. There is a sizeable literature discussing the various organizational models for integration and analyzing the legal issues posed by each form. See, e.g., Andrew J. Demitriou & Thomas E. Dutton, Health Care Integration: Structural and Legal Issues (1996); Gerald R. Peters, Healthcare Integration: A Legal Manual for Constructing Integrated Organizations (1995); Carl H. Hitchner, et al., Integrated Delivery Systems: A Survey of Organizational Models, 29 Wake Forest L. Rev. 273 (1994); Integrated Delivery Systems Manual (Allan Fine, ed. 1993); Health Law Center, Managed Care Law Manual (1994); 1 Furrow, et al., Health Law § 5–49 (2d ed. 2000). See also Integrated Delivery Systems: Creation, Management and Governance (Douglas Conrad, ed. 1997); Steven M. Shortell et al., The New World of Managed Care: Creating Organized Delivery Systems, 13 Health Aff. 46 (Winter, 1994); Douglas G. Cave, Vertical Integration Models to Prepare Health Systems for Capitation, 20 Health Care Mgmt. Rev. 26 (1995).

B. THE MECHANICS OF INTEGRATION AND DISINTEGRATION

Strategy and Objectives. Much of the integrative activity involves bringing together physicians, hospitals and other providers that have heretofore operated independently. In counseling in this area, it is obviously critical to have a firm understanding of the different objectives of the various parties. For example, physicians typically are looking for a structure that will assist them in the contracting process by providing capital, administrative and management support for their practices, and a competitively strong network that will be attractive to third party payers. At the same time, physicians want some assurance that their incomes will not erode and that they will have a substantial voice in the governance of the new organization. Hospitals are eager to assure themselves of an adequate flow of patients to fill their beds and outpatient facilities and a cadre of physicians committed to their organization. At the same time, hospitals are reluctant to give up control of the organizational structure of the enterprise (after all, they usually supply the lion's share of the financial investment), although shared control is sometimes attempted.

Joint Ventures and Mergers. There are two basic ways in which integration can be achieved: by contract or by ownership. When firms combine by contract, they often establish what is commonly referred to as a joint venture. A joint venture may take a variety of forms: the two parents may create a new legal entity (e.g., a corporation, LLC, or partnership) which they jointly own; or the parents may simply undertake a series of contractual commitments which bind them to operate as a common enterprise. For example, physicians form PPOs and IPAs, which are joint ventures that enable them to bid for managed care contracts. A change in ownership, on the other hand, entails one party surrendering its independent existence. One hospital may acquire another and merge it into its organizational structure in one of several ways. In such circumstances, although management of the acquired hospital may or may not change, ultimate control passes to the acquiring entity. Hospitals also are increasingly acquiring physician practices, which often entails physicians selling their practice assets, both physical (e.g., equipment, real estate and buildings) and intangible (e.g., patient files, goodwill). The physicians may then enter into employment contracts with the hospital.

1. *Organizational Structures for Physician Integration*

Physicians may organize themselves to contract with managed care purchasers in several ways. The least complete form of integration is the Preferred Provider Organization, a joint venture which usually entails contractual agreements to deliver care to a defined group of patients at discounted fee-for-service rates and to submit to certain controls on utilization or membership restrictions based on quality and utilization criteria. Similarly, physicians may join Independent Practice Associations (IPAs), which also involve only limited operational integration of physician practices through billing services and utilization review. An important difference from PPOs is that IPA members agree to accept distributions of capitated revenues, which create incentives to alter practice styles. However, IPAs lack controls over physician behavior and the percentage of each physician's revenues from the IPA is often not sufficient to cause significant changes in the way he or she provides care. See generally, Peters, supra at 25 ("All too often an IPA represents a grudging compromise by physicians who want capitated business, but do not want to otherwise change the nature of their practice").

Another form of integration available to physicians is to form group practices. Group practices vary significantly in the extent to which they entail organizational integration. For example, Partially Integrated Medical Groups (PIMGs) or Group Practices Without Walls (GPWWs) entail physicians operating as a single legal entity (e.g. a professional corporation) with common management, staff and administrative services. However, physicians in PIMGs may maintain their practice locations and employment relationships with certain staff; they also retain autonomy in many respects such as participation in managed care contracts and purchasing and other business decisions. Costs and profits are frequently allocated on an individualized or "cost center" basis. In contrast, Fully Integrated Medical Groups (FIMGs) entail far greater operational integration, most notably in the form of: centralized governance that controls all aspects of the group's business; formal quality control and utilization management programs; FIMG responsibility for entering into managed care contracts; and income allocation systems that rely on achievement of group rather than individual performance. See Peters, supra at 27.

The following table illustrates the degree of integration involved in these various organizational arrangements.

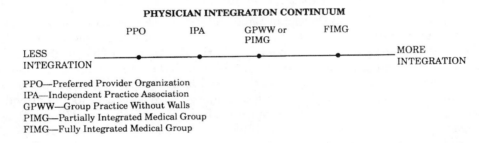

PHYSICIAN INTEGRATION CONTINUUM

	PPO	IPA	GPWW or PIMG	FIMG	
LESS INTEGRATION					MORE INTEGRATION

PPO—Preferred Provider Organization
IPA—Independent Practice Association
GPWW—Group Practice Without Walls
PIMG—Partially Integrated Medical Group
FIMG—Fully Integrated Medical Group

How would these forms rank along a continuum ranging from less to more physician autonomy?

Physician Management Companies. Physicians may also achieve the benefits of integration by selling their practices to a third party that will supply the services and capital necessary for integration. Physician Management Companies (PMCs) offer a rapidly growing alternative means of integration for physicians. PMCs are for-profit companies that acquire tangible and certain intangible assets of physician practices, usually paying cash or stock in the company. Physicians remain in formally independent professional corporations, partnerships or other entities and deliver services pursuant to long-term management services agreements with the PMC for which the latter receives a management fee. Most PMCs initiate public offerings of 20% to 40% of their equity and thereby provide access to capital markets for further expansion and development while also enabling retiring physicians (and promoters of the PMC) to cash out their interests. A host of important issues are subject to negotiation in these arrangements such as: control and governance of the physician entity; valuation of the acquired practice assets; valuation of the PMC stock exchanged for assets; non-compete agreements; the management fee; termination terms; and many more. See Theodore N. McDowell, Jr. and Martin D. Brown, *Physician Management Companies: Just*

What the Doctor Ordered, in Health Law Handbook, (1996 Edition) (Alice Gosfield, ed. 1996).

PPMCs initially proved very popular on Wall Street as many firms experienced meteoric rises in their stock values. See Hayes & Rudnitsky, M.D. Inc., Forbes, Sept. 11, 1995. Recently, however, the PPMC industry has come on hard times, losing 64 percent of its market value on Wall Street between 1997 and 1998. Leading firms like FPA Management entered bankruptcy and other firms like Phycor and Medpartners downsized or exited the industry entirely. Uwe Reihardt concludes that the PPMC industry "tried to grow mindlessly fast, in a fatal pas de deux with a financial market that egged the industry on with unrealistic expectations about future earnings." Uwe Reinhardt, The Rise and Fall of the Physician Practice Management Industry, 19 Health Aff. (2000). Rather than create value through cost savings, many came to resemble "pyramid schemes" whose success depended upon rapid acquisition of practices and mistaken valuations by securities analysts who did not accurately appraise their capacity to influence medical practice patterns. Id.

2. *Organizational Structures for Physician–Hospital Integration*

As described by the Physician Payment Review Commission supra, physicians and hospitals desiring to achieve some degree of integration can choose from several organizational models: e.g., the MSO, the PHO or the staff, equity or foundation model (fully integrated) IDS. The PHO is in most respects the least structurally integrated and least complex form. Its primary purpose is to negotiate and administer managed care contracts for its providers, and may even do so on a capitated basis, in which case the PHO is regarded as a provider of care. However, PHOs typically provide fewer services for physician practices than do the other forms and do not significantly alter the clinical practice patterns of providers. MSOs also provide contracting services as well as many of the "back-room" functions necessary to operate physician offices including billing, claims processing, ancillary services and many of the credentialing and utilization control services needed for contracting. In the more comprehensive form, MSOs may acquire physician practices outright or supply "turnkey" operations by purchasing and leasing equipment and office space and hiring staff for physicians. Finally, fully integrated systems, including the foundation model IDS, are entities that bring together ownership of an organization that supplies all types of health services and coordinates case management and the flow of information. This may be done through foundations or clinics that acquire physician practices or through "equity models" that enable physicians to acquire an ownership interest in the system.

The following graph illustrates the relative degree of integration of the various forms of physician-hospital organizations.

PHYSICIAN-HOSPITAL INTEGRATION CONTINUUM

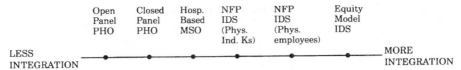

Open Panel PHO	Closed Panel PHO	Hosp. Based MSO	NFP IDS (Phys. Ind. Ks)	NFP IDS (Phys. employees)	Equity Model IDS

LESS INTEGRATION ●———————●———————●———————●———————●———————● MORE INTEGRATION

Open Panel PHO—Physician hospital organization, membership open to all hospital staff physicians
Closed Panel PHO—Physician hospital organization, membership limited to selected staff physicians
Hosp. Based MSO—Management services organization controlled by hospital
NFP IDS (Phys. Ind. K)—Not-for-profit integrated delivery system in which physicians are independent contractors
NFP IDS (Phys. Employees)—Not-for-profit integrated delivery system in which physicians are employees.

Each of these integrating organizations may be formed using a variety of legal and ownership structures. For example, the PHO may be controlled by the hospital, by physicians or by a commonly-controlled joint venture. It may take the LLC, for-profit corporation or not-for-profit corporate form. The selection and design of any health care organization depends on the preferences and bargaining position of the parties, the competitive conditions of the market and the legal constraints they face.

3. *Dis–Integration and Bankruptcy.* As discussed above, the assumption made by many policymakers and health care analysts that market forces would propel providers inexorably toward more complete integration has proved inaccurate. The pace of integration has slowed with many IDSs proving unprofitable as they have failed to realize cost savings, improve quality, or increase volume or revenues as originally promised. Edric B. Engert & Douglas W. Emery, Integrated Delivery Systems: Non Fait Accompli, 7 Managed Care Q. 29 (1999). Among the many factors contributing to these financial difficulties is that IDSs vastly overpaid for physician practices they purchased, and were unprepared to take on the insurance role and failed to develop information and case management systems capable of dealing with the complexities of providing quality care, reducing unnecessary services and avoiding adverse selection. Engert & Emery at 34–36. At the same time, payors have not adopted capitation as a form of payment as readily as anticipated as discounted fee-for-service remains the dominant form of payment used by managed care systems. See C. J. Simon & David Emmons, Physician Earnings at Risk: an Examination of Capitated Contracts, 16 Health Aff. 120 (Spring,1997). Finally, greater demand for access and choice has led to less global capitation than anticipated and reliance on other payment methods that are less well-suited to IDS structures. See Engert & Emery at 33.

Integrated systems face a number of problems and choices as they undergo the "unwinding" process. Many are attempting to sell unprofitable physician practices. This process is fraught with legal perils, including sorting out contractual issues with their physicians and managed care companies; avoiding liability under Stark and anti-kickback laws for making payments in return for future referrals; and in the case of tax exempt entities, risks of private inurement or private benefit. These issues are discussed later in this chapter and Chapter 14. For many systems facing mounting losses, the question is whether to declare bankruptcy under Chapter 7 or Chapter 11 of the Bankruptcy Code or to attempt to negotiate the disposition and sale of assets and allocation of liabilities. Where multiple (and often antagonistic) parties own the IDS, there is a risk that at least one may attempt to block the unwinding or hold out so as to lessen the enterprise value of the IDS and impair returns to creditors. See Robert A. Klyman, Bankruptcy Opportunities and Pitfalls: Strategies for Restructuring and Unwinding Integrated Delivery Systems, 31 J. Health L. 163 (1998). See generally David C. Hillman, Sales And Mergers Of Healthcare Entities Through The Bankruptcy Process: Key Issues, Risks, And Benefits (2000). In addition, IDS owners run the legal risks of fraudulent transfers, contract breaches and contingent liabilities. In these circumstances, the Bankruptcy Code may provide an effective tool for unwinding the entity in a manner that will preserve the going concern value of the IDS's assets and avoid various legal entanglements. For a thoughtful review of the legal and strategic issues presented by a Chapter 11 filing in the health care context, see Klyman, supra.

Health care industry bankruptcies pose a number of special problems. For example, one controversial issue under the Bankruptcy Code is whether HMOs or similar organizations in integrated systems are eligible for bankruptcy relief, or whether they are "domestic insurance companies" and subject to state insurance regulation. See Patrick Collins, HMO Eligibility for Bankruptcy: The Case for Federal Definitions of 109(b)(2) Entities, 2 Am. Bankr. Inst. L. Rev. 425 (1994). Other issues concern the role of Medicare as a creditor of the bankrupt entity, see, e.g., United States v. Consumer Health Services of America, 108 F.3d 390 (D.C. Cir. 1997)(assessing applicability of automatic stay in context of Medicare statute), and whether the automatic stay involving a bankrupt HMO may be extended to providers that did not contract with the HMO. See Family Health Services, Inc. v. Centinela Mammoth Hospital, 105 B.R. 937 (Bankr.C.D.Cal.1989)(applying the stay because allowing creditors to directly bill patients would interfere with the ability of bankrupt HMOs to reorganize).

Concerns about bankruptcies in the health care sector have given rise to Congressional action. Legislation passed by the Senate in 2000 would require appointment of an ombudsman to act as a patient advocate when any "health care business" files for bankruptcy. The Bankruptcy Reform Act of 2000, S. 3186, 106th Cong. §§ 1101–06 (1999). The ombudsman would act on behalf of the patient to assist the court in balancing the interests of the creditors and the patients of a facility to be closed. Additionally, the bill would impose a duty on the bankruptcy trustee to use reasonable and best efforts to ensure transfer of patients to a nearby facility with substantially the same services as the bankrupt entity. The impetus for the legislation was concern over nursing home closings due to bankruptcy and the possible adverse effects, such as "transfer trauma," that such closings might have on residents. See 145 Cong. Rec. S4,789–02 (daily ed. May 5, 1999) (statement of Sen. Grassley). The bill would also curtail the practice under current bankruptcy law by which doctors and other individual health care providers declared bankruptcy under Chapter 13 in order to shield themselves from paying civil damages awarded in personal injury cases, by requiring payment of judgments on claims for acts resulting in "willful or malicious injury," including death. The bill was vetoed by President Clinton on December 19, 2000, based on other aspects of the legislation. See Nursing Homes: Clinton Vetoes Bankruptcy Bill with SNF Patient Protection, 10 Health L. Rep. (BNA) 36 (January 4, 2001).

Problem: Organizing All Saints Health Care

All Saints Health Care Enterprise, a not-for-profit religiously affiliated corporation, operates two hospitals, St. Timothy's and St. Patrick's, in River City. River City and the surrounding metropolitan area are served by 20 acute care hospitals and 3000 physicians. Like most markets, managed care has begun to make serious inroads in River City. As a result of the growth of managed care contracting, employers and insurers are insisting that hospitals and physicians assume financial risk through capitation or other means. A notable byproduct of these changes has been a sharp increase in the demand for primary care physicians and a surplus of specialists.

Two rivals have begun to form integrated systems. Madison Hospital, a large teaching hospital, has recently acquired five other hospitals and has developed a PHO, signing up as co-owners some 300 physicians who have staff privileges at these hospitals. Jefferson Medical Enterprises, a for-profit entity, owns three hospitals in the market and has formed an IPA-style HMO.

St. Timothy's Hospital, located in downtown River City, has 250 physicians with staff privileges, including 150 family practitioners and a large proportion of specialists practicing obstetrics and pediatric health specialties. A core group of 100 doctors, mostly in solo practice, concentrate their admissions at St. Timothy's. A relatively large proportion of these physicians are over 45 years old and many of the older doctors are amenable to selling their practices. Most of the remaining doctors, however, are fiercely independent and highly suspicious of managed care contract proposals being offered by insurance companies. There is a widespread consensus that St. Timothy's needs to recruit additional doctors to maintain its viability.

St. Patrick's, located in an affluent suburb adjacent to River City, has a much heavier proportion of specialists on its staff and offers a wide range of sophisticated services. Five group practices, including two large multispecialty groups, supply a large percentage of St. Patrick's inpatient and outpatient business.

Assuming you represent All Saints, what model or models of integrating organizations would you recommend that it consider forming? What form of business organization should each adopt and how should control be allocated between the hospital and physicians? What governance arrangements would you recommend to avoid conflicts and deadlocks in the future?

What advice would you give if you represented one of the multispecialty physician groups practicing at St. Patrick's? Suppose some of the independent All Saints physicians not currently in a group practice wanted to organize some form of entity before affiliating with the All Saints system. Explain the advantages and disadvantages of the organizational forms they might adopt.

IV. TAX–EXEMPT HEALTH CARE ORGANIZATIONS

INTRODUCTION

For most nonprofit organizations, even more important than nonprofit status under state corporation law is obtaining tax exemption under federal and state tax laws. Section 501(c)(3) of the Internal Revenue Code exempts from federal income tax entities "organized and operated exclusively for religious, charitable, scientific, testing for public safety, literary, or educational purposes, or to foster . . . amateur sports competition. . .or for the prevention of cruelty to animals." An organization must meet three important requirements to qualify for for tax exempt status:

(1) no part of its net earnings may inure to the benefit of any private shareholder or individual;

(2) no substantial part of its activities may consist of certain activities aimed at influencing legislation; and

(3) it may not participate or intervene in any political campaign on behalf of any candidate for public office.

26 U.S.C.A. § 501(c)(3). Is there an internal logic to these requirements? Does the view that foregoing taxes on charitable and other organizations amounts to a "subsidy" help explain these provisions?

Exemption under § 501(c)(3) entails a wide range of tax benefits besides exemption from federal income tax: eligibility to receive tax-deductible contributions; ability to issue tax-exempt bonds; exemption from federal unemployment taxes; preferred postal rates; and various other benefits respecting pensions and special treatment under antitrust, securities, labor, bankruptcy and other regulatory laws. See James J. Fishman & Stephen Schwarz, Nonprofit Organizations: Cases and Materials 329–330 (2000). Finally, organizations exempt under 501(c)(3) are likely to qualify for exemption from state and local income, property, sales and other taxes. As discussed in the next section, most healthcare organizations qualifying for exemption do so as entities organized for a "charitable purpose."

A. CHARITABLE PURPOSES: HOSPITALS

Eighteenth and nineteenth century hospitals were supported primarily by charitable contributions and provided care to poor, sick people who had some chance of recovery. Wealthy persons received medical care in their own homes. In the early twentieth century, the development of aseptic practices, the increasing successes in surgery, and the professionalization of hospital nursing eventually made the hospital the preferred location for medical treatment. Medical goals and objectives replaced the earlier religious goals as the primary focus of the hospital. See generally, R. Stevens, In Sickness and In Wealth: American Hospitals in the Twentieth Century, (Basic Books 1989); Paul Starr, The Social Transformation of American Medicine (Basic Books 1982) and Elliot Friedson, The Hospital in Modern Society (Free Press 1963).

The active treatment of acute illness, which emerged in full force after World War II, costs far more than the simple room, board and care provided in hospitals of previous centuries. Revenue from government and private insurers eventually displaced philanthropy as the primary source of hospital income. Still, most private U.S. hospitals are not-for-profit while only a small minority of nursing homes are nonprofit.

Intermountain Health Care, below, discusses the standards of "charitable purpose" in the context of modern tax-exempt hospitals. *Intermountain Health Care* is decided under Utah law. It is representative, not only of similar activity in many other states but also of a consistent concern in federal tax exemption. Federal tax-exempt status requires that tax-exempt hospitals satisfy a "charitable purpose;" and *Intermountain's* analysis of the policies underlying this requirement is applicable to the federal debate as well.

UTAH COUNTY v. INTERMOUNTAIN HEALTH CARE, INC.

Supreme Court of Utah, 1985.
709 P.2d 265.

DURHAM, JUSTICE:

Utah County seeks review of a decision of the Utah State Tax Commission reversing a ruling of the Utah County Board of Equalization. The Tax Commission exempted Utah Valley Hospital, owned and operated by Intermountain Health Care (IHC), and American Fork Hospital, leased and operated by IHC, from *ad valorem* property taxes. At issue is whether such a tax exemption is constitutionally permissible. We hold that, on the facts in this record, it is not, and we reverse.

IHC is a nonprofit corporation that owns and operates or leases and operates twenty-one hospitals throughout the intermountain area, including Utah Valley Hospital and American Fork Hospital. IHC also owns other subsidiaries, including at least one for-profit entity. It is supervised by a board of trustees who serve without pay. It has no stock, and no dividends or pecuniary profits are paid to its trustees or incorporators. Upon dissolution of the corporation, no part of its assets can inure to the benefit of any private person.

* * *

* * * These [tax] exemptions confer an indirect subsidy and are usually justified as the *quid pro quo* for charitable entities undertaking functions and services that the state would otherwise be required to perform. A concurrent rationale, used by some courts, is the assertion that the exemptions are granted not only because charitable entities relieve government of a burden, but also because their activities enhance beneficial community values or goals. Under this theory, the benefits received by the community are believed to offset the revenue lost by reason of the exemption.

* * *

An entity may be granted a charitable tax exemption for its property under the Utah Constitution only if it meets the definition of a "charity" or if its property is used exclusively for "charitable" purposes. Essential to this definition is the element of gift to the community.

* * * A gift to the community can be identified either by a substantial imbalance in the exchange between the charity and the recipient of its services or in the lessening of a government burden through the charity's operation.

* * *

Given the complexities of institutional organization, financing, and impact on modern community life, there are a number of factors which must be weighed in determining whether a particular institution is in fact using its property "exclusively for * * * charitable purposes." Utah Const. art. XIII, § 2 (1895, amended 1982). These factors are: (1) whether the stated purpose of the entity is to provide a significant service to others without immediate expectation of material reward; (2) whether the entity is supported, and to what extent, by donations and gifts; (3) whether the recipients of the "charity" are required to pay for the assistance received, in whole or in part; (4) whether the income received from all sources (gifts, donations, and payment from recipients) produces a "profit" to the entity in the sense that the income exceeds operating and long-term maintenance expenses; (5) whether the beneficiaries of the "charity" are restricted or unrestricted and, if restricted, whether the restriction bears a reasonable relationship to the entity's charitable objectives; and (6) whether dividends or some other form of financial benefit, or assets upon dissolution, are available to private interests, and whether the entity is organized and operated so that any commercial activities are subordinate or incidental to charitable ones. * * *

Because the "care of the sick" has traditionally been an activity regarded as charitable in American law, and because the dissenting opinions rely upon decisions from other jurisdictions that in turn incorporate unexamined assumptions about the fundamental nature of hospital-based medical care, we deem it important to scrutinize the contemporary social and economic context of such care. We are convinced that traditional assumptions bear little relationship to the economics of the medical-industrial complex of the 1980's. Nonprofit hospitals were traditionally treated as tax-exempt charitable institutions because, until late in the 19th century, they were true charities providing custodial care for those who were both sick and poor. The hospitals' income was derived largely or entirely from voluntary charitable donations, not government subsidies, taxes, or patient fees.[8] The function and status of hospitals began to change in the late 19th century; the transformation was substantially completed by the 1920's. "From charities, dependent on voluntary gifts, [hospitals] developed into market institutions financed increasingly out of payments from patients." The transformation was multidimensional: hospitals were redefined from social welfare to medical treatment institutions; their charitable foundation was replaced by a business basis; and their

---

8. Paul Starr, *The Social Transformation of American Medicine* at 150 (1982). "Voluntary" hospitals, like public hospitals (which evolved from almshouses for the dependent poor), performed a "welfare" function rather than a medical or curing function: the poor were housed in large wards, largely cared for themselves, and often were not expected to recover. *See id.* at 145, 149, 160. Early volun-

tary hospitals had paternalistic, communal social structures in which patients entered at the sufferance of their benefactors, "had the moral status of children," and received more moralistic and religious help than medical treatment. *Id.* at 149, 158. * * *

[Ed. note: The opinion relies on Starr's book extensively. Further citations have been omitted.]

orientation shifted to "professionals and their patients," away from "patrons and the poor."

* * *

Also of considerable significance to our review is the increasing irrelevance of the distinction between nonprofit and for-profit hospitals for purposes of discovering the element of charity in their operations. The literature indicates that two models, described below, appear to describe a large number of nonprofit hospitals as they function today.

(1) The "physicians' cooperative" model describes nonprofit hospitals that operate primarily for the benefit of the participating physicians. Physicians, pursuant to this model, enjoy power and high income through their direct or indirect control over the nonprofit hospitals to which they bring their patients. * * * A minor variation of the above theory is the argument that many nonprofit hospitals operate as "shelters" within which physicians operate profitable businesses, such as laboratories. [ ]

(2) The "polycorporate enterprise" model describes the increasing number of nonprofit hospital chains. Here, power is largely in the hands of administrators, not physicians. Through the creation of holding companies, nonprofit hospitals have grown into large groups of medical enterprises, containing both for-profit and nonprofit corporate entities. Nonprofit corporations can own for-profit corporations without losing their federal nonprofit tax status as long as the profits of the for-profit corporations are used to further the nonprofit purposes of the parent organization.

* * *

* * * Dramatic advances in medical knowledge and technology have resulted in an equally dramatic rise in the cost of medical services. At the same time, elaborate and comprehensive organizations of third-party payers have evolved. Most recently, perhaps as a further evolutionary response to the unceasing rise in the cost of medical services, the provision of such services has become a highly competitive business.

* * *

The stated purpose of IHC regarding the operation of both hospitals clearly meets at least part of the first criterion we have articulated for determining the existence of a charitable use. Its articles of incorporation identify as "corporate purposes," among other things, the provision of "care and treatment of the sick, afflicted, infirm, aged or injured within and/or without the State of Utah." The same section prevents any "part of the net earnings of this Corporation" to inure to the private benefit of any individual. Furthermore, under another section, the assets of the corporation upon dissolution likewise may not be distributed to benefit any private interest.

The second factor we examine is whether the hospitals are supported, and to what extent, by donations and gifts. * * * [W]e have examined the testimony and exhibits in evidence on this question. The latter demonstrate that current operating expenses for both hospitals are covered almost entirely by revenue from patient charges. * * * The evidence was that both hospitals charge rates for their services comparable to rates being charged by other similar entities, and no showing was made that the donations identified resulted in charges to patients below prevailing market rates.

* * *

One of the most significant of the factors to be considered in review of a claimed exemption is the third we identified: whether the recipients of the services of an entity are required to pay for that assistance, in whole or in part. The Tax Commission in this case found as follows:

The policy of [IHC's hospitals] is to collect hospital charges from patients whenever it is reasonable and possible to do so; however, no person in need of medical attention is denied care solely on the basis of a lack of funds.

The record also shows that neither of the hospitals in this case demonstrated any substantial imbalance between the value of the services it provides and the payments it receives apart from any gifts, donations, or endowments. The record shows that the vast majority of the services provided by these two hospitals are paid for by government programs, private insurance companies, or the individuals receiving care.

* * *

Between 1978 and 1980, the value of the services given away as charity by these two hospitals constituted less than one percent of their gross revenues. Furthermore, the record also shows that such free service as did exist was deliberately not advertised out of fear of a "deluge of people" trying to take advantage of it. Instead, every effort was made to recover payment for services rendered. * * *

The defendants argue that the great expense of modern hospital care and the universal availability of insurance and government health care subsidies make the idea of a hospital solely supported by philanthropy an anachronism. We believe this argument itself exposes the weakness in the defendants' position. It is precisely because such a vast system of third-party payers has developed to meet the expense of modern hospital care that the historical distinction between for-profit and nonprofit hospitals has eroded. * * *

The fourth question we consider is whether the income received from all sources by these IHC hospitals is in excess of their operating and maintenance expenses. Because the vast majority of their services are paid for, the nonprofit hospitals in this case accumulate capital as do their profit-seeking counterparts.

* * *

A large portion of the profits of most for-profit entities is used for capital improvements and new, updated equipment, and the defendant hospitals here similarly expend their revenues in excess of operational expenses. There can be no doubt, in reviewing the references in the record by members of IHC's administrative staff, that the IHC system, as well as the two hospitals in question, has consistently generated sufficient funds in excess of operating costs to contribute to rapid and extensive growth, building, competitive employee and professional salaries and benefits, and a very sophisticated management structure. While it is true that no financial benefits or profits are available to private interests in the form of stockholder distributions or ownership advantages, the user *entity* in this case clearly generates substantial "profits" in the sense of income that exceeds expenses.

* * *

On the question of benefits to private interests, certainly it appears that no individuals who are employed by or administer the defendants receive any distribution of assets or income, and some, such as IHC's board of trustees members, volunteer their services. We have noted, however, that IHC owns a for-profit entity, as well as nonprofit subsidiaries, and there is in addition the consideration that numerous forms of private commercial enterprise, such as pharmacies, laboratories, and contracts for medical services, are conducted as a necessary part of the defendants' hospital operations. The burden being on the taxpayer to demonstrate eligibility for the exemption, the inadequacies in the record on these questions cannot be remedied by speculation in the defendants' favor. * * *

Neither can we find on this record that the burdens of government are substantially lessened as a result of the defendants' provision of services. The record indicates that Utah County budgets approximately $50,000 annually for the payment of hospital care for indigents. Furthermore, the evidence described two instances within a three-month period where, after a Utah County official had declined to authorize payment for a person in the emergency room, Utah Valley Hospital refused to admit the injured person on the basis of that person's inability to pay. The county official was told in these instances to either authorize payment or to "come and get" the person. Such behavior on the hospital's part is inconsistent with its argument that it functions to relieve government of a burden. Likewise, as we have pointed out, there has been no showing that the tax exemption is a significant factor in permitting these defendants to operate, thereby arguably relieving government of the burden of establishing its own medical care providers. In fact, government is already carrying a substantial share of the operating expenses of defendants, in the form of third-party payments pursuant to "entitlement" programs such as Medicare and Medicaid.

* * *

We reverse the Tax Commission's grant of an *ad valorem* property tax exemption to defendants as being unconstitutional.

* * *

STEWART, JUSTICE (dissenting):

* * *

III. DEFINITION OF CHARITY
* * *

The legal concept of charity does not require, as the majority apparently requires, that a hospital incur a deficit to qualify as a charitable institution. Charitable hospitals need not be self-liquidating.

* * *

It is true that the hospitals in this case receive substantial revenues from third-party payors and patients, but there is not a shred of evidence in this record, much less a finding by the Tax Commission, that one cent of the revenues is used for any purpose other than furthering the charitable purposes of providing hospital services to the sick and infirm. On the contrary, the Tax Commission's findings affirmatively establish that no person has profited from the revenues produced at either Utah Valley or American Fork Hospitals other than patients. Under time-honored legal principles, both hospitals qualify as charitable institutions.

IV.   UTAH VALLEY HOSPITAL'S AND AMERICAN FORK
HOSPITAL'S GIFTS TO THE COMMUNITY

* * *

A.   Direct Patient Subsidies

* * *

During the years 1978–80, Utah Valley Hospital rendered wholly free services to indigents in the amount of $200,000, and in each of those years the amount increased substantially over the preceding year. During the same period, the hospital subsidized services rendered to Medicare, Medicaid, and worker's compensation patients in the amount of $3,174,024. The corresponding figures for American Fork Hospital were $39,906 in indigent care and $421,306 for subsidization of Medicare, Medicaid, and worker's compensation benefits.

However, the value of the charity extended to indigents is in fact greater than the amounts stated. The cost of the charity extended to patients who are first identified as charity patients *after* admission rather than *at* admission is charged to the "bad debts" account, along with traditional uncollectible accounts or bad debts, instead of being charged to charity.

* * *

In sum, the *direct* cost of patient charity given away by Utah Valley Hospital for the period in question is in excess of $3,374,024, but less than $4,942,779 (which includes bad debts). The *direct* cost of the charity given away by American Fork Hospital is in excess of $461,212, but less than $639,024 (which includes bad debts). * * * Unlike for-profit hospitals, Utah Valley and American Fork have a policy against turning away indigent patients. Therefore, that portion of the hospitals' bad debts which is attributable to indigency is bona fide charity since the charges would have been initially made to the charity account had the patient's indigency been discovered at admission. Those charges are not just ordinary business bad debts experienced by all commercial enterprises, as the majority would have it.

* * *

B.   Capital Subsidies and Gifts

The most glaring lapse in the majority opinion, in my view, is its flat-out refusal to recognize that there would be no Utah Valley Hospital—at all—if it had not been given lock, stock, and barrel to IHC by the Church of Jesus

Christ of Latter–Day Saints, which initially built the hospital. American Fork Hospital apparently was initially erected by taxpayers' money. At the City's request, IHC took over the operation of the hospital as a lessee of American Fork City to relieve the City of a governmental burden. It follows that all patients at both hospitals, whether indigent, part-paying, or fully paying patients, are direct beneficiaries of large monetary investments in land, buildings, and medical equipment. * * *

In addition to the "gift to the community" of the actual physical facilities, each and every patient benefits from the fact that IHC is a nonprofit corporation whose hospitals make no profit on the value of the assets dedicated to hospital care. The majority's effort to portray IHC hospitals as if they were operated as for-profit entities has no substance in the record whatsoever. A for-profit hospital, unlike a nonprofit hospital, must necessarily price its services to make a profit on its investment if it is to stay in business. The surplus that Utah Valley and American Fork budget for is not by any means the equivalent of profit, as the majority wrongly suggests. * * *

Furthermore, the majority inaccurately asserts that Utah Valley charges rates comparable to other similar entities. The evidence is to the contrary. Utah Valley Hospital, with its 385 beds and expensive, sophisticated acute care equipment, charges rates comparable to the rates charged by Payson Hospital, a small for-profit hospital that renders inexpensive types of services. * * * In addition, there are no "prevailing market rates" for tertiary care hospitals, if by that term the majority means prevailing rates of competitive for-profit hospitals. There is no for-profit tertiary care hospital in the entire state of Utah; all tertiary care hospitals are non-profit institutions. In fact, there is no

other tertiary care hospital, whether nonprofit or for-profit, in the immense, sparsely populated area served by the Utah Valley Hospital, which extends from Utah County to the Nevada–Arizona border. Indeed, the facts strongly suggest that a for-profit tertiary care hospital could not survive in the geographical market area served by Utah Valley. * * *

V. TAX EXEMPT STATUS OF NON-PROFIT HOSPITALS UNDER THE MAJORITY OPINION

The record also demonstrates that the primary care hospital and the tertiary care hospital involved in this case relieve a significant governmental burden, one of the two alternative tests for determining whether a nonprofit hospital qualifies to be treated as a charitable institution. * * * In the wide-open spaces of the West, where small communities are widely separated, the profit motive has not been sufficient to provide the needed impetus for the building of community hospitals (except in rare instances). Nor has it resulted in the construction of tertiary care hospitals in the more populous parts of the state.

The majority's argument is that no government burden is relieved by providing hospital service to those who can pay for it on a for-profit basis. The argument misses the mark for two reasons. First, the alternatives are not for-profit or nonprofit hospitals. The alternatives are nonprofit hospital care or no hospital care at all, at least within the relevant geographical markets. Second, the charitable status of a hospital does not turn on whether it provides care for patients who can pay. The basic policy is not to tax the sick and infirm irrespective of ability to pay. A county provides many services to rich and poor alike without charging the rich for those services. Parks and playgrounds are but examples. Providing medical services may not be mandatory for counties or cities, but if they do, they most certainly promote the public health, safety, morals, and welfare in a most fundamental way. Surely cities and counties would, as a practical matter, be compelled to provide hospital services if the nonprofit hospitals in this state did not exist.

* * *

VI. DIFFERENCES BETWEEN FOR-PROFIT AND NONPROFIT HOSPITALS
* * *

[A] for-profit hospital's investment decisions as to what markets or communities to enter and what kinds of equipment to invest in are made from a basically different motive than a nonprofit hospital's. The decisions of a for-profit hospital corporation must be based upon careful calculations as to the rate of return that may be expected on invested capital. If the rate of return is not sufficient, the investment is not made. Whether the surplus is reinvested in part or paid out to investors in dividends in whole or in part, the investor receives personal monetary benefit either in the increased value of his stock or in dividends.

Nonprofit hospitals must, of course, be concerned with generating sufficient revenue to maintain themselves, but they are not concerned with earning a return on their investment for the benefit of stockholders. Their purposes are altruistic. Any surplus must be used in a manner that aggrandizes no one, such as for the lowering of rates, the acquisition of new equipment, or the improvement of facilities.

* * *

. . . IHC's Board of Trustees considers itself a trustee of the health care facilities for the public. "[W]e see ourselves as owned by the community since the corporation owns itself and in effect the church gave the hospitals to the communities, and we're entrusted with the running of the hospitals. We see them as in effect owned by the communities. . . . ".

* * *

Notes and Questions

1. The states have continued to scrutinize the provision of charity care by hospitals exempt from state tax. For example, Pennsylvania has been particularly aggressive in policing its exemption for hospitals. See City of Washington v. Board of Assessment, 550 Pa. 175, 704 A.2d 120 (1997)(applying five-part test governing hospitals' purposes and sufficiency of efforts to serve charitable ends). Several states have enacted legislation requiring nonprofit hospitals to account for and report their community benefits. For example, California established a presumption that hospitals earning less than a ten percent surplus or making an appropriate showing concerning their use of profits are entitled to the welfare property tax exemption. Cal. Rev. & Tax'n Code § 214 (a)(1). See also Ind. Code Ann. § 16–21–6–6 et seq. (1997)(reporting and assessment requirements); N.Y. Public Health Law § 2803–1 (same); Tex. Health & Safety Code Ann. § 311.031 (reporting

requirements with prescribed levels of charity care). See also, Margaret A. Potter and Beaufort B. Longest, Jr., The Divergence of Federal and State Policies on the Charitable Tax Exemption of Nonprofit Hospitals, 19 J. Health Pol. Pol'y & L 393 (1994); G.J. Simon, Jr., Non–Profit Hospital Tax Exemptions: Where Did They Come From and Where Are They Going?, 31 Duq. L. Rev. 343 (1993); Developments in the Law—Non-profit Corporations, 105 Harv. L. Rev. 1612 (1992). In contrast to *Intermountain* and the Pennsylvania actions, see Callaway Community Hospital Association v. Craighead, 759 S.W.2d 253 (Mo.App.1988) (granting state tax exemption for a hospital that transferred indigent patients and viewing transfers as within individual physicians' and not hospital's control); Rideout Hospital Foundation, Inc. v. County of Yuba, 8 Cal.App.4th 214, 10 Cal.Rptr.2d 141 (Cal.App.1992) (upholding tax exemption to hospital with surplus revenue in excess of 10%). Utah voters rejected a constitutional amendment to bar state taxation of hospitals in 1986 after *Intermountain*. See NHLA, Health Lawyers News Report, May 1988. However, subsequent to the *Intermountain* decision, the Utah Tax Commission issued guidelines governing the standards for tax exemption of hospitals. See Howell v. County Bd. of Cache County, 881 P.2d 880 (Utah 1994).

2. To qualify for § 501(c)(3) status, a health care facility must meet both an "organizational test," which requires that the hospital's constitutive documents, such as the corporate articles of incorporation, limit its activities to exempt purposes, and an "operational test," which requires that the hospital be operated primarily for exempt purposes, including "charitable," "educational," or "religious" purposes. Most hospitals must qualify as charities. The definition of charitable purposes under the Code has been quite controversial, with the Internal Revenue Service attempting to adjust the definition to meet changes in the modern health care sector while the statute remained unchanged. For example, a 1956 Revenue Ruling required a tax-exempt hospital to be operated "to the extent of its financial ability for those not able to pay for the services rendered." Rev. Ruling 56–185. In 1958, the Tax Court upheld the denial of exempt status for a hospital that devoted between 2% and 5% of its revenue to care for the indigent (Lorain Avenue Clinic v. Commissioner, 31 T.C. 141). A later Revenue Ruling stated instead that "the promotion of health * * * is one of the purposes in the general law of charity," Rev.Ruling 69–545. The 1969 Revenue Ruling illustrated its position by describing a hospital that operated an emergency room that was open to all regardless of ability to pay and whose care for the indigent was not otherwise described, as meeting the Revenue Ruling's standards for exemption. In a 1983 Revenue Ruling, a hospital that did not even operate an emergency room and usually referred indigent patients to another hospital was described as qualifying for tax-exempt status. The illustrative hospital did not operate an ER because the state health planning agency had concluded that the emergency room was not needed in the area, as other nearby hospitals had adequate emergency services. The Revenue Ruling stated that, although this hospital could not offer the ER as evidence that it was operated for the benefit of the community, "[o]ther significant factors * * * including a board of directors drawn from the community" supported exempt status. Rev.Ruling 83–157.

The current IRS position on whether "charitable purpose" requires charity care is somewhat ambiguous. According to the Service, promotion of health by a hospital is a charitable purpose; the hospital must provide a community benefit by providing health care broadly to the community; and, although a specific amount of charity care is not required, it remains an important indication of community benefit. See IRS Coursebook on Introduction to the Health Care Industry, 95 Tax

Notes Today 112–35 (June 9, 1995). The IRS Examination Guidelines, used by revenue agents to determine whether a hospital qualifies for tax exempt status, list the following factors: whether the hospital has a governing board composed of prominent civic leaders; if the hospital is part of a multi-entity system, whether its records reflect separateness and are board members understand the purposes of the various entities; whether the medical staff membership is open to all qualified physicians in the area; whether the hospital operates a full time emergency room open to all, regardless of ability to pay; and whether the hospital provides non-emergency care to everyone able to pay either privately or through third parties including Medicare and Medicaid. Ann. 92–83, 1992–22 I.R.B.59 § 333.1. What factors might have prompted the changes that have occurred over time in the standard for tax exempt status applicable to hospitals? Do the standards in effect today continue to make sense? How should the IRS evaluate "carve-out" or specialty hospitals that do not offer emergency room services and serve populations that have low levels of utilization by indigent citizens? See also Nina J. Crimm, Evolutionary Forces: Changes in For–Profit and Not-for-Profit Health Care Delivery Structures: A Regeneration of Tax Exemption Standards, 37 B.C. L. Rev. 1 (1995), for a historical analysis and critique.

3. Whether the amount of charity care provided by tax-exempt hospitals justifies the benefit of the tax exemption is hotly disputed. A major report on for-profit health care produced by the Institute of Medicine of the National Academy of Sciences examining the impact of for-profit health care on access to care by patients who are unable to pay. The Report found that nonprofit hospitals provided somewhat higher levels of uncompensated care than did for-profit hospitals. Institute of Medicine, National Academy of Sciences, For–Profit Enterprise in Health Care (1986). A 1990 General Accounting Office report found that, on average, nonprofit hospitals provided uncompensated care at levels that exceeded their tax subsidy. The GAO report recommended that tax exemption be linked to care provided to Medicaid patients; free care provided to the poor; and efforts to improve health status in underserved communities. General Accounting Office Report, Nonprofit Hospitals: Better Standards Needed for Exemption, GAO/HRD–90–84 (May 1990). A more recent study of California hospitals found that, on average, the levels of uncompensated care provided by nonprofit hospitals exceeded their tax subsidies and that the sector failing to provide adequate levels of uncompensated care was a small subset of all hospitals. Michael Morrissey, et al., Do Nonprofit Hospitals Pay Their Way?, 15 Health Aff. 132 (1996).

An important question is whether charity care should be provided through the tax system or in the form of direct outlays. Critics of exemption point to the lack of oversight and control that occurs when care is financed publicly through foregone revenue, and that benefits awarded through the tax system are not subject to budgetary discipline as they are not reported as budget outlays. See Harry G. Gourevitch, Congressional Research Service, Tax Aspects of Health Care Reform: The Tax Treatment of Health Care Providers, 94 Tax Notes Today 94–90 (May 16, 1994). Should Congress require tax-exempt hospitals to provide a certain amount of charity care? See M. Gregg Bloche, Health Policy Below the Waterline: Medical Care and the Charitable Exemption, 80 Minn. L. Rev. 299 (1995). For an economic and financial analysis of the tax advantages of nonprofit hospitals, concluding that nonprofit hospitals consequently owe society more uncompensated community benefits than do for profit counterparts, see Uwe E. Reinhardt, The Economics of For–Profit and Not–For–Profit Hospitals, 19 Health Aff. 178 (Nov./Dec. 2000). Some empirical studies claim that nonprofit hospitals provide lower levels of community benefits than they should. See e.g., Sean Nicholson, et al., Measuring Community Benefits Provided by For–Profit and Nonprofit Hospitals, 19 Health Aff. 168 (Nov./Dec. 2000). What problems does *Intermountain Health Care* raise in relation to defining, evaluating and measuring charity care?

4. What accounts for society's reliance on nonprofits to supply health services in the first place? A number of theories have been set forth to explain and justify the law's encouragement of the tax-exempt sector. In The Rationale for Exempting Nonprofit Organizations from Corporate Income Taxation, 91 Yale L.J. 54 (1981), Henry Hansman justifies the tax exemption as a means to compensate for constraints on capitalization of nonprofits that operate in transactions characterized by market failure. Other scholars also maintain that not-for-profits share unique characteristics that justify their continued state and federal tax advantages despite arguments that the current business endeavors of not-for-profits makes them indistinguishable from their for-profit counterparts. See e.g., Seay and Vladeck, Mission Matters, in In Sickness and In Health, The Mission of Voluntary Health Care Institutions (J. Seay and B. Vladeck, eds. 1988). Mark A. Hall and John D. Colombo offer another rationale: subsidization is appropriate for those organizations capable of attracting a substantial level of donative support in the face of market imperfections. The Charitable Status of Nonprofit Hospitals: Toward a Donative Theory of Tax Exemption, 66 Wash. L. Rev. 307 (1991). Finally, it has been argued that not-for-profit hospitals preserve valuable diversity of mission and method in the hospital industry. Falcone and Warren, The Shadow Price of Pluralism: The Use of Tax Expenditures to Subsidize Hospital Care in the United States, 13 J. Health Pol. Pol'y & L. 735 (1988). For a contrasting view, see M. Gregg Bloche, supra.

Problem: St. Andrew's Medical Center

St. Andrew's Medical Center is a 750–bed not-for-profit hospital in a metropolitan area. It offers residency programs in internal medicine, obstetrics, surgery and several other areas. St. Andrew's is facing an uncertain financial future, and its Board of Directors is concerned about serious cutbacks in federal funds for graduate medical education, further reductions in health care reimbursement and its own inability to raise enough capital for modernization through retained earnings and donations. The Board is hesitant to increase the facility's substantial debt to make capital improvements in its 40–year–old physical plant. It also finds that it provides a significant amount of charity care each year in part because of its self-identified institutional mission and in part because it is one of only three hospitals in the area. The other two hospitals are a for-profit, 250–bed hospital operated by Americare, Inc., which is an investor-owned multi-facility system, and a municipal hospital, which regularly operates at 98% capacity and is often unable to receive transfers from St. Andrew's.

St. Andrew's has been approached by Health Care Enterprises (HCE), a for-profit corporation that owns eighty-five hospitals in thirty states and is interested in acquiring St. Andrew's. HCE has made an initial offer of $100 million for St. Andrew's, which would include the acquisition of all assets of St. Andrew's, including the name itself. The Board is very interested in the offer but is concerned that the provision of charity care continue at St. Andrew's and that HCE conform with the mission of St. Andrew's as a religiously affiliated hospital. For the Board, this latter concern relates, in part, to their interest in having St.

Andrew's not offer abortion or assisted suicide services and in assuring an adequate pastoral care program.

HCE has suggested to St. Andrew's that St. Andrew's place $75 million (the amount of purchase money remaining after St. Andrew's pays off outstanding debts) into an endowment for a new St. Andrew's Foundation. The income from this endowment would then be paid to HCE for charity care and the medical education program at St. Andrew's. HCE has also suggested that it is itself also willing to provide "appropriate" charity care and adhere to the "traditional mission of St. Andrew's." HCE has suggested that it would agree to a buy-back provision in the sales agreement through which St. Andrew's could repurchase the hospital at a price to be agreed upon at the time of purchase should HCE fail to perform on either item.

The community is generally quite upset about the proposal. Many have charged that St. Andrew's is abandoning the community and that HCE is simply seeking to build a reputation by owning a teaching hospital and to "corner the market" by eliminating the only not-for-profit hospital in the metropolitan area. Others see HCE as the only realistic option if St. Andrew's is to continue operating at all.

The Board meeting to decide whether St. Andrew's will be sold to HCE is tomorrow morning. You are a member of the Board. What will you recommend? If the transfer is approved, how would you draft the agreement between St. Andrew's and HCE? For example, how would you draft a contract with enforceable standards for conformance with the religious mission? For "appropriate charity care"? How should the buy-back provision be structured? Will the hospital still be called "St Andrew's"?

For excellent analyses of issues relating to religious affiliation see, Kathleen M. Boozang, Deciding The Fate of Religious Hospitals in The Emerging Health Care Market, 31 Hous. L. Rev. 1429 (1995); Lawrence E. Singer & Elizabeth Johnson Lantz, The Coming Millennium: Enduring Issues Confronting Catholic Health Care, 8 Annals Health L. 299 (1999).

As discussed earlier, sales of not-for-profit, tax-exempt entities to for-profit providers have been quite controversial. The Internal Revenue Service's authority in these situations is limited and the rules have not been interpreted to restrict conversions as long an entity remains properly organized as a nonprofit entity and continues to pursue an exempt purpose. However, the Internal Revenue Service has the authority to prevent private inurement which may contribute to ensuring an adequate purchase price. With the enactment of intermediate sanctions authority, discussed infra, the IRS now has greater flexibility and capacity to monitor conflicts of interest; however, it still lacks legal authority to require advance approval except for joint ventures between for-profit and nonprofit organizations. Consequently, regulation of conversions has been governed principally by state common law and statutes. See generally, IRS Should Oversee Sales of Nonprofit Hospitals, Organization Asserts, 95 Tax Notes Today 111–46 (June 8, 1995); Private Letter Ruling 9643036 (July 31, 1996). For further discussions of conversion and sales of not-for-profit organizations, especially with regard to the role of the states see the previous sections of this chapter. See also, M. Gregg Bloche, Corporate Takeover of Teaching Hospitals, 65 So. Cal. L.Rev. 1035 (1992) and Charles F. Kaiser and T.J. Sullivan, Integrated Delivery Systems and Health Care Update in the IRS Exempt Organizations CPE Technical Instruction Program Textbook, 95 Tax Notes Today, 168–68 (Aug. 28, 1995).

B. CHARITABLE PURPOSES: HEALTH MAINTENANCE ORGANI-ZATIONS

Health maintenance organizations typically deliver both office-based primary care and hospital-based acute care to their subscribers who prepay a premium to the HMO to cover needed services regardless of the amount or cost of medical services actually used. In this way, HMOs combine the functions of insurance and health care delivery. In their provision of office-based primary care, HMOs resemble doctors' medical practices, which traditionally have not been organized on a not-for-profit basis and have not received tax exemption.

As described earlier in this chapter, HMOs organize their provision of services in a variety of ways. Staff model HMOs employ physicians and operate primary care offices. Group model HMOs contract with physician partnerships or corporations to provide services to subscribers on a capitation basis. Typically, the group model HMO operates in a site owned or leased by the HMO. In the IPA model HMO, an independent practice association acts as agent for its physician members in negotiating and contracting with the HMO for medical services to be provided by its physician members in their own offices. Network HMOs typically contract with a number of physician group practices and other providers. Some HMOs use several of these methods.

The structure through which the HMO provides its physician services has been an important factor in whether it will qualify for § 501(c)(3) tax exempt status.

GEISINGER HEALTH PLAN v. COMMISSIONER OF INTERNAL REVENUE

United States Court of Appeals, Third Circuit, 1993.
985 F.2d 1210.

Lewis, Circuit Judge.

... This case requires us to decide whether a health maintenance organization (an "HMO") which serves a predominantly rural population, enrolls some Medicare subscribers, and which intends to subsidize some needy subscribers but, at present, serves only its paying subscribers, qualifies for exemption from federal income taxation under 26 U.S.C.A. § 501(c)(3). We hold that it does not.

* * *

... GHP was formed as a nonprofit corporation in 1984 and, by March 31, 1988, had enrolled 4,396 individuals and 448 groups (accounting for another 66,441 individual subscribers).

The Geisinger System consists of GHP and eight other nonprofit entities. All are involved in some way in promoting health care in 27 counties in northeastern and north central Pennsylvania. They include: the Geisinger Foundation (the "Foundation"); Geisinger Medical Center ("GMC"); the Geisinger Clinic (the "Clinic"); Geisinger Wyoming Valley Medical Center ("GWV"); Marworth; Geisinger System Services ("GSS") and two professional liability trusts. Each of these entities is exempt from federal income taxation under one or more sections of the Internal Revenue Code (the "Code").

In order to provide cost-effective delivery of health care to areas it had identified as medically underserved, GMC experimented with a pilot prepaid health plan between 1972 and 1985. The results were sufficiently favorable that the Geisinger System formed GHP to provide its own prepaid health plan. GHP's service area encompasses 17 predominantly rural counties within the area served by the Geisinger System. As of November 30, 1987, according to a finding of a bureau of the federal Department of Health and Human Services, 23 percent of GHP's subscribers resided in medically underserved areas while 65 percent resided in counties containing medically underserved areas.

GHP has two types of subscribers. First, it is open to all adult individuals who reside in its service area and satisfactorily complete a routine questionnaire regarding their medical history. From its inception through June 30, 1987, GHP accepted all but 11 percent of its individual applicants. Second, it enrolls group subscribers. Any individual who resides in GHP's service area and belongs to a group of at least 100 eligible enrollees may enroll as a group subscriber without completing a health questionnaire.

* * *

GHP describes itself as "providing health services." In reality, it contracts with other entities in the Geisinger System (at least one of which will contract with physicians from outside the Geisinger System) to provide services to GHP's subscribers. It also contracts with entities such as pharmacies to provide medical and hospital services to its subscribers in exchange for compensation. Under the terms of these contracts, GHP reimburses the hospitals and clinics by paying a negotiated per diem charge for inpatient services and a discounted percentage of billed charges for outpatient services. For the fiscal year ended June 30, 1987, the Clinic and GWV provided 80 percent of all hospital services to GHP subscribers. The remaining 20 percent were provided by other hospitals.

All physician services are provided to GHP subscribers pursuant to a contract between GHP and the Clinic. The contract requires the Clinic to open its emergency rooms to all GHP subscribers, regardless of ability to pay, just as the Clinic's emergency rooms are open to all members of the public, regardless of ability to pay. The Clinic will contract with unaffiliated physicians to provide required services, but for the year ended June 30, 1987, more than 84 percent of the physician services which the Clinic provided to GHP's subscribers were performed by physicians who were employees of the Clinic. GHP compensates the Clinic for the physicians' services by paying a fixed amount per subscriber.

* * *

GHP has adopted a subsidized dues program which has not yet been implemented. The program would establish a fund comprised of charitable donations and operating funds to subsidize GHP subscribers who are unable to pay their premiums. The fund would, in GHP's view, "add to the security of [subscribers], any of whom may at some time suffer financial misfortune due to loss of employment, physical or mental disability or other causes beyond their control and which impute no dishonor to the [subscriber]." Although the program makes reference to subsidizing people who are already subscribers, GHP's submissions indicate that it also intends to admit people who require subsidization at the time they apply.

Despite GHP's initial projection that it would fund the program by raising $125,000 in contributions over its first three years of operation, it has been unable to do so, it claims, because potential donors cannot be assured that contributions will be deductible on their federal income tax returns until GHP receives recognition of tax-exempt status under section 501(c)(3). GHP has likewise been unable to support the program with operating funds because it operated at a loss from its inception through the time the record in this case closed.

GHP enrolls some subscribers who are covered by Medicare and Medicaid. As of March 31, 1988, it had enrolled 1,064 Medicare recipients at a reduced rate on a wraparound basis, meaning that it will cover what Medicare does not. It also has enrolled a small number of Medicaid recipients in a few exceptional situations. Generally, however, GHP cannot offer coverage to Medicaid recipients until and unless it contracts with the Pennsylvania Department of Welfare, which administers Pennsylvania's Medicaid program. GHP has negotiated with the Department to obtain such a contract, but efforts to reach agreement have thus far been unsuccessful.

Shortly after its incorporation, GHP applied to the IRS for recognition of exemption. The Commissioner ruled that GHP was not exempt because (1) it was not operated exclusively for exempt purposes under section 501(c)(3); and (2) it could not vicariously qualify for exemption as an "integral part" of the Geisinger System. [GHP filed suit in Tax Court, which reversed the IRS denial of tax-exempt status.]

* * *

GHP argues that it qualifies for exemption because it serves the charitable purpose of promoting health in the communities it serves. There are no published revenue rulings and only one previously litigated case addressing whether an HMO may qualify for exemption under section 501(c)(3). The sole case on this issue is a Tax Court case, Sound Health Association v. Commissioner, 71 T.C. 158 (1978), acq. 1981–2 C.B. 2.

* * *

In Sound Health, the Tax Court applied the law pertaining to nonprofit hospitals as charitable entities in measuring an HMO's claim for exemption. Although this case does not involve a hospital, neither the IRS nor GHP argue that this distinction rendered inappropriate the Tax Court's reliance upon Sound Health in examining GHP's request for exemption. To the contrary, in fact, the IRS concedes that GHP's stated purpose, like a hospital's stated purpose, is to promote health; it simply argues that Sound Health and the hospital precedents require more than mere promotion of health in order to qualify for tax exemption. The IRS argues that the relevant precedents require at least some "indicia of charity" in the form of serving the public and providing some services free of charge.

While we are not bound by any approach taken by the Tax Court, we find no reason to conclude that the Tax Court erred in applying hospital precedent to its analysis of GHP's exempt status. Accordingly, in light of the parties' and the Tax Court's reliance on the law regarding the tax-exempt status of nonprofit hospitals in formulating the test to be applied to HMOs seeking exemption under section 501(c)(3), we will measure GHP's tax-exempt status against that standard. In doing so, we recognize that courts are to give weight to IRS revenue rulings but may disregard them if they conflict with the statute they purport to interpret or its legislative history, or if they are otherwise unreasonable. [ ]

* * *

[N]o clear test has emerged to apply to nonprofit hospitals seeking tax exemptions. Instead, a nonprofit hospital will qualify for tax-exempt status if it primarily benefits the community. One way to qualify is to provide emergency room services without regard to patients' ability to pay; another is to provide free care to indigents. A hospital may also benefit the community by serving those who pay their bills through public programs such as Medicaid or Medicare. For the most part, however, hospitals must meet a flexible "community benefit" test based upon a variety of indicia.

* * *

The Sound Health HMO resembled GHP in many ways. Its articles of incorporation listed a number of charitable purposes relating to the promotion of health. Like GHP's subscribers, its subscribers paid for services based upon a community rating system, and a subsidized dues program assisted those who could not afford subscribership. Subscribers also had to satisfy eligibility requirements similar to GHP's.

Unlike GHP, however, the Sound Health HMO provided health care services itself rather than simply arranging for others to provide them to its subscribers. It also employed doctors, health care providers and medical personnel who were not affiliated with the HMO to provide health care to its subscribers. Significantly, the Sound Health HMO provided services to both subscribers and members of the general public through an outpatient clinic which it operated and at which it treated all emergency patients, subscribers or not, and regardless of ability to pay. It also adjusted rates for and provided some free care to patients who were not subscribers. It offered public educational programs regarding health.

* * *

The Sound Health court went to great lengths to find a benefit to the community rather than simply a benefit to the HMO's subscribers. It rejected the argument that the HMO at issue benefitted only its subscribers, finding:

The most important feature of the Association's [subscribership] form of organization is that the class of persons eligible for [subscribership], and hence eligible to benefit from the Association's activities, is practically unlimited. The class of possible [subscribers] of the Association is, for all practical purposes, the class of members of the community itself. The major barrier to [subscribership] is lack of money, but a subsidized dues program demonstrates that even this barrier is not intended to be absolute.... It is safe to say that the class of persons potentially benefitted by the Association is not so small that its relief is of no benefit to the community.

As we have observed, however, the court listed several factors in addition to open subscribership as indications that the Sound Health HMO was operated for charitable purposes. Chief among these were the HMO's operation of an emergency room open to all persons, subscribers or not, and regardless of ability to pay; rendering some free care to both subscribers and those who did not subscribe; conducting research; and offering an educational program. GHP refers to these as "marketing techniques," but, as the Sound Health court noted, the HMO benefitted the community by engaging in these activities.

* * *

... GHP cannot say that it provides any health care services itself. Nor does it ensure that people who are not GHP subscribers have access to health care or information about health care. According to the record, it neither conducts research nor offers educational programs, much less educational programs open to the public. It benefits no one but its subscribers.

GHP argues that the Sound Health requirement that an HMO seeking exemption must provide an emergency room open to all is rendered obsolete by Rev.Rul. 83–157. This may indeed be the case. Under the logic of Rev.Rul. 83–157, GHP need not provide an emergency room if doing so would unnecessarily duplicate services offered elsewhere in the area. Because the Clinic and other Geisinger System facilities provide emergency care to GHP's subscribers, requiring GHP to operate an emergency room may be unnecessarily duplicative and wasteful.

This conclusion would not, however, automatically bestow upon GHP an entitlement to tax-exempt status. The test remains one of community benefit, and GHP cannot demonstrate that it benefits anyone but its subscribers.

It is true that GHP is open to anyone who can afford to pay and that, like the HMO in Sound Health, GHP apparently intends to lower, or even to remove, this potential economic barrier to subscribing through its subsidized dues program. As we explain below, however, the mere presence of the subsidized dues program does not necessarily invite a conclusion that GHP benefits the community.

First, the Sound Health court ventured too far when it reasoned that the presence of a subsidized dues program meant that the HMO in question served a large enough class that it benefitted the community.

* * *

The mere fact that a person need not pay to belong does not necessarily mean that GHP, which provides services only to those who do belong, serves a public purpose which primarily benefits the community. The community benefitted is, in fact, limited to those who belong to GHP since the requirement of subscribership remains a condition precedent to any service. Absent any additional indicia of a charitable purpose, this self-imposed precondition suggests that GHP is primarily benefitting itself (and, perhaps, secondarily benefitting the community) by promoting subscribership throughout the areas it serves.

* * *

Second, the Sound Health court need not have gone as far as it did. The presence of a subsidized dues program was not the only factor it considered when deciding that the HMO in question qualified for tax-exempt status. For example, the HMO in Sound Health "in effect, [ran] a substantial outpatient clinic as an important ingredient of its medical care services." It also provided free care even to persons who did not subscribe and offered educational programs to the public.

Finally, even considering the subsidized dues program, the amount of benefit GHP intends to confer on people other than paying subscribers is minuscule. GHP anticipates subsidizing approximately 35 people. We cannot say that GHP operates primarily to benefit the community at large rather than its subscribers by arranging for health care for only 35 people, who would not otherwise belong, as compared to more than 70,000 paying subscribers. GHP argues that the HMO in Sound Health had provided only $158.50 in subsidies when it was granted tax-exempt status. This is true, but, as previously noted, the HMO in that case also benefitted the community in other ways, most notably by providing free or reduced-cost care to people who were not subscribers. An HMO must primarily benefit the community, not its subscribers plus a few people, in order to qualify for tax-exempt status under section 501(c)(3).

Notes and Questions

1.   How did GHP organize its provision of health care services? Where and from whom would its members receive primary-care services? Hospital services? What interest did the Geisinger Health System have in organizing GHP?

2.   What does GHP need to do to gain § 501(c)(3) status under this case? Must it reorganize itself as a staff model HMO? Must it establish an emergency room? Could it simply expand its subsidy program? Does the Service or the Third Circuit in this case accept "promotion of health," standing alone, as a charitable purpose adequate to support § 501(c)(3) tax-exempt status?

3.   How do the requirements for § 501(c)(3) status for HMOs compare to those for hospitals? Should subsidized memberships, which satisfy an unmet need for primary care, be considered the equivalent of charity care? Should the provision of primary care in medically underserved areas be counted favorably as a charitable purpose? Or, does the fact that the subsidized or free enrollees become "members" of the HMO simply make it definitionally impossible for the subsidization to be counted as a "community" benefit? On the other hand, is it appropriate to carry over standards used to evaluate the tax exempt status of hospitals to HMOs? In today's managed care market, for example, what purpose does the requirement of maintaining an open medical staff serve? Is it realistic to insist on the maintenance of emergency room or similar services? Note the Third Circuit's reliance on the fact that, unlike the Sound Health HMO, GHP did not directly provide care, but instead contracted with physicians who provided services. In a series of cases, the IRS has denied or revoked tax exempt status to network model HMOs that contract directly with primary care physicians for services including one case in which the HMO paid capitated reimbursement to its

primary care physicians. See IHC Care, Inc. v. Commissioner, U.S. Tax Court Docket No. 14601–99X (1999). If promotion of health is a legitimate charitable purpose within the meaning of section 501(c)(3), why should the IRS attach significance to whether the HMO directly provides care? See John D. Columbo, Health Care Reform and Federal Tax Exemption: Rethinking the Issues, 29 Wake Forest L.Rev. 215 (1994). On HMO tax-exempt status, see Kenneth L. Levine, Geisinger Health Plan Likely to Adversely Affect HMOs and Other Health Organizations, 79 J. Tax'n 90 (1993).

4. A final hurdle for HMOs seeking exempt status is Section 501(m)(1) of the Internal Revenue Code which provides that an organization described in § 501(c)(3) or § 501(c)(4) shall be exempt "only if no substantial part of its activities consists of providing commercial-type insurance." Although the legislative history indicates that this provision was intended to bar continued § 501(c)(4) exemption for Blue Cross/Blue Shield organizations, which had enjoyed such status for many years, the IRS has applied the provision to deny exempt status to HMOs whose activities resemble those of commercial insurers. See H.R. Rep. No. 99–426, at 662–66 (1986). In the following technical advice memorandum, the IRS revoked the § 501(c)(3) status of a health maintenance organization, finding that it essentially provided insurance under § 501(m)(1). Using the "risk of economic loss" analysis used in the Memorandum below, how might the IRS rule if (a) the HMO pays its contracted physicians "capitated fees," paying the physicians the same fees regardless of the amount of health care services the HMO's enrollees require?; (b) the HMO pays its contracted physicians almost exclusively under a fee schedule that represents a meaningful discount from the physicians' usual and customary charges ("discounted fee-for-service") and also withholds from these payments a significant percent of the fees otherwise payable, pending compliance with periodic budget or utilization standards?; (c) the HMO pays its contracted physicians on a discounted fee-for-service basis and does not withhold from these payments a significant portion of the fees otherwise payable pending compliance with periodic budget or utilization standards, but the physicians are eligible to receive a bonus based on the achievement of a budget surplus? See generally, General Counsel Memorandum 39829 (Aug. 24, 1990). The IRS Examination Guidelines provide detailed instructions regarding: the interpretation of § 501(m), including a safe harbor if less than 15% of an HMO's activities consist of commercial-type insurance; the implications of stop-loss insurance and deficit sharing arrangements; and the scope of "incidental health insurance" customarily provided by an HMO under § 501(m)(3)(B). IRS Manual, § 7.8.1.27.10.

INTERNAL REVENUE SERVICE NATIONAL OFFICE TECHNICAL ADVICE MEMORANDUM

Dec. 14, 1998.

* * *

FACTS

[L, a § 501(c)(3) corporation, is a member of a nonprofit, multicorporate health care system ("M") and has been licensed as a qualified health maintenance organization ("HMO"). Under this HMO offered by L, enrollees are permitted to utilize physicians other than network physicians by paying a higher premium. L provides primary care and specialty care physician services through contracts with various physicians ("Participating Physician Services Agreement"). Under the Participating Physician Services Agreement, L compensates physicians on a fee-for-service basis by paying the greater of a capitated fee or 85 percent of the physician's usual and customary billed charges. The Agreement does not provide for L to withhold any portion of these fees. In some cases, in the event of budget surpluses, the physicians may be eligible to receive additional payments ("Participating Physician Settlement Payments"). However, in the event of budget deficit, the physicians have no financial obligations.]

SECTION 501(c)(3)

[The IRS finds that L does not satisfy the requirements for exemption under section 501(c)(3) of the Code because it (1) does not satisfy the "community benefit standard" and (2) does not satisfy the integral part doctrine.]

SECTION 501(m)

When individuals enroll in an HMO and pay the HMO fixed premiums, the HMO agrees that it will arrange for the provision of health care services to treat the enrollees' injuries and illnesses. Under this arrangement, enrollees protect themselves against the risk that they would suffer economic loss from having to pay for health care services that are necessary because of injuries or illnesses. By enrolling in an HMO, individuals shift the risk of this economic loss to the HMO. When the HMO enrolls a large number of such individuals, the HMO distributes this risk of loss among all of its enrollees. For HMOs that operate on a staff model basis, this risk is predominantly a normal business risk of an organization engaged in furnishing medical services on a fixed-price basis, rather than an insurance risk.... On the other hand, for HMOs that operate on other than a staff model basis, this arrangement constitutes a contract of insurance.

However, if a non-staff model HMO shifts a substantial portion of its risk of economic loss to its health care providers, it would no longer bear a substantial portion of the risk of economic loss that would result from having to provide health care services to its enrollees.

* * *

L is not a staff model HMO. Instead, L contracts with hospitals ... and with primary care and specialty physicians ... to provide medical services for its enrollees.... [T]he arrangement with L's enrollees to provide health care services in return for a fixed fee constitutes a contract of insurance[.]

* * *

As a result of this fee-for-service compensation arrangement with its participating physicians, L has shifted to these physicians only an incidental portion of its total economic risk of loss associated with its obligation to provide health care services to its enrollees.

* * *

Since the compensation L pays to its physician providers represents 52.4 percent of its total medical expenses, these services are substantial. Thus, by retaining a substantial portion of the risk of loss, L remains substantially engaged in providing health insurance to its enrollees.

Since this health insurance is the same type of health insurance as that which is offered by commercial insurance companies, it is "commercial-type" insurance under § 501(m)(1) of the Code.

* * *

[Therefore, L does not qualify for exemption either under § 501(c)(3) or § 501(c)(4).]

C. CHARITABLE PURPOSES: INTEGRATED DELIVERY SYSTEMS (IDSS)

The Geisinger System, described in the previous case and in the case below, is an example of an integrated system, discussed earlier in this chapter, which combines physician, hospital and other provider services with management and support services and HMOs.

The structures chosen for integration will have implications for the tax status of individual organizations within the system and of the integrated system itself. In *"Geisinger II"*, below, the Third Circuit considers whether the relationship between the Geisinger System and the Geisinger HMO aids the HMO, which had earlier been denied exempt status on its own, in satisfying the threshold requirements for tax-exempt status. In the Friendly Hills exemption letter, also reproduced below, the Service reviews the application of Friendly Hills Healthcare Network, which sought tax-exempt status for the entire system as an entity rather than for its individual pieces.

GEISINGER HEALTH PLAN v. COMMISSIONER OF INTERNAL REVENUE

United States Court of Appeals, Third Circuit, 1994.
30 F.3d 494.

Lewis, Circuit Judge.

* * *

The Geisinger System consists of GHP and eight other entities, all involved in some way in promoting health care in 27 counties in northeastern and north central Pennsylvania. They are: the Geisinger Foundation (the "Foundation"), Geisinger Medical Center ("GMC"), Geisinger Clinic (the "Clinic"), Geisinger Wyoming Valley Medical Center ("GWV"), Marworth, Geisinger System Services ("GSS") and two professional liability trusts. All of these other entities are recognized as exempt from federal income taxation under one or more sections of the Internal Revenue Code.

The Foundation controls all these entities, as well as three for-profit corporations. It has the power to appoint the corporate members of GHP, GMC, GWV, GSS, the Clinic, and Marworth, and those members elect the boards of directors of those entities. The Foundation also raises funds for the Geisinger System. . . .

GMC operates a 569–bed regional medical center. . . . It accepts patients without regard to ability to pay, including Medicare, Medicaid and charity patients. It operates a full-time emergency room open to all, regardless of ability to pay. It also serves as a teaching hospital.

GWV is a 230–bed hospital located in Wilkes–Barre, Pennsylvania. It accepts patients regardless of ability to pay, and it operates a full-time emergency room open to all, regardless of ability to pay.

The Clinic provides medical services to patients at 43 locations throughout the System's service area. It also conducts extensive medical research in conjunction with GMC and physicians who perform medical services for GMC, GWV and other entities in the Geisinger System. . . . It accepts patients without regard to their ability to pay.

Marworth operates two alcohol detoxification and rehabilitation centers and offers educational programs to prevent alcohol and substance abuse.

GSS employs management and other personnel who provide services to entities in the Geisinger System.

* * *

[The Geisinger System] organized GHP as a separate entity within the System (as opposed to operating it from within the Clinic, GMC or GWV) for three reasons. First, HMOs in Pennsylvania are subject to extensive regulation by the Commonwealth's Departments of Health and Insurance. [ ] Operating GHP separately enables other entities in the System to avoid having to comply with the burdensome requirements associated with that regulation. Second, those administering the System believe it preferable for GHP's organization and management to remain separate from those of the System's other entities because it serves a wider geographic area than any of those other entities. Finally, under Pennsylvania law at least one-third of GHP's directors must be subscribers. [ ] Establishing GHP as a separate entity avoids disrupting the governance of the other Geisinger System entities to comply with this requirement. For example, establishing an HMO within GMC would have required GMC to canvass its board of directors to ensure that one-third of them subscribed to the HMO. If they did not, GMC would have had to amend its by-laws or other governing documents to add directorships so that one-third of the directors were subscribers. Incorporating GHP separately eliminates the need for such reorganization.

* * *

GHP's interaction with other Geisinger System entities is varied. Its most significant contact is with the Clinic, from which it purchases the physician services its subscribers require by paying a fixed amount per member per month, as set forth in a Medical Services Agreement. Eighty-four percent of physician services are provided by doctors who are employees of the Clinic; the remaining 16 percent are provided by doctors who are not affiliated with the Clinic but who have contracted with the Clinic to provide services to GHP subscribers. GHP has similarly entered into contracts with GMC and GWV, as well as 20 non-related hospitals. When GHP subscribers require hospital care, these hospitals provide it pursuant to the terms of their contracts, for either a negotiated per diem charge or a discounted percentage of billed charges. GHP has also contracted with GSS to purchase office space, supplies and administrative services.

* * *

GHP argues that [the "integral part" doctrine requires the court] to examine whether the Clinic or GMC could retain tax-exempt status if it were to absorb GHP. It thus compares the attributes of a hypothetically merged Clinic/GHP or GMC/GHP entity to the attributes of the HMO held to be exempt in [Sound Health]. Concluding that the merged entity would display more indicia of entitlement to exemption than the Sound Health HMO, GHP urges that it is exempt because of the characteristics of the hypothetical merged entity. Despite its superficial appeal, we reject this argument and hold that the integral part doctrine does not mean that GHP would be exempt solely because either GMC or the Clinic could absorb it while retaining its tax-exempt status. While this is a necessary condition to applying the doctrine, it is not the only condition. GHP is separately incorporated for reasons it found administratively and politically advantageous. While it may certainly benefit from that separate incorporation, it must also cope with the consequences flowing from it. [ ]

* * *

Distilling [regulations and case law] into a general rule leads us to conclude that a subsidiary which is not entitled to exempt status on its own may only receive such status as an integral part of its § 501(c)(3) qualified parent [ ] if (i) it is not carrying on a trade or business which would be an unrelated trade or business (that is, unrelated to exempt activities) if regularly carried on by the parent, and (ii) its relationship to its parent somehow enhances the subsidiary's own exempt character to the point that, when the boost provided by the parent is added to the contribution made by the subsidiary itself, the subsidiary would be entitled to § 501(c)(3) status.* * *

Here, we do not think that GHP receives any "boost" from its association with the Geisinger System. In Geisinger I, we determined that while GHP helps to promote health, it does not do so for a significant enough portion of the community to qualify for tax-exempt status on its own. [] And * * * the contribution that GHP makes to community health is not increased at all by the fact that GHP is a subsidiary of the System rather than being an independent organization which sends its subscribers to a variety of hospitals and clinics.

As our examination of the manner in which GHP interacts with other entities in the System makes clear, its association with those entities does nothing to increase the portion of the community for which GHP promotes health—it serves no more people as a part of the System than it would serve otherwise. It may contribute to the System by providing more patients than the System might otherwise have served, thus arguably allowing the System to promote health among a broader segment of the community than could be served without it, but its provision of patients to the System does not enhance its own promotion of health; the patients it provides—its subscribers—are the same patients it serves without its association with the System. To the extent it promotes health among non-GHP-subscriber patients of the System, it does so only because GHP subscribers' payments to the System help finance the provision of health care to others. An entity's mere financing of the exempt purposes of a related organization does not constitute furtherance of that organization's purpose so as to justify exemption....

* * *

Notes and Questions

1.   Structuring complex health care delivery systems often requires trade-offs between the advantages and disadvantages of particular organizational forms. What were the trade-offs faced by the Geisinger System in its choice of organizational form for GHP? Why did it separately incorporate GHP rather than simply offering pre-paid care contracts through one of the clinics or the foundation?

2.   The court states that GHP "serves no more people as a part of the System than it would serve otherwise" and concludes that GHP receives no "boost" from its operation within the Geisinger System. Should the court have attributed the charity care of the System's hospitals to GHP? Should the court have viewed managed care contracting as an essential component of the tax-exempt activities of the not-for-profit entities in the System? The "boost" concept has been widely criticized:

> The "boost" requirement in Giesinger II is incomprehensible and cannot be distilled from prior decisions or Treasury Regulations. No other circuit nor the Tax Court has followed the "boost" requirement iterated by the Third Circuit....[In the IHC Health Plan Technical Advice Memorandum], the Service implicitly reflects its discomfort with the Third Circuit's interpretation of the integral part doctrine. It suggests the boost requirement would only apply where the enrollees of an HMO that is a member of an exempt hospital system and the patients of the hospital are not essentially the same.... The Service also suggests that the "boost" requirement would not apply where almost all of the HMO's enrollees are patients of the hospital.

Douglas M. Mancino, Tax Exemption Issues Facing Managed Care Organizations, in American Health Lawyers, Tax Issues for Healthcare Organizations (2000). See also Elizabeth M. Mills, New Geisinger II Health Care Organizations Tax–Exemption Test Is No Improvement on Prior Model, 11 No. 10 Health Span 3 (1994).

3.   The court states that the mere fact that an entity produces dollars that the exempt organization may then use for exempt purposes is not sufficient justification for tax exemption. This is a well-accepted principle and applies to all exempt organizations. For example, should a tax-exempt law school happen to own a pasta company, the fact that the pasta company's profits are devoted entirely to the law school's exempt activities does not of itself qualify the pasta company for tax-exempt status. See discussion of unrelated business income in section on joint ventures, below. Is the court correct however in viewing GHP's role as primarily providing funds for GHS?

4.   As you study the Friendly Hills Healthcare Network exemption ruling below, consider whether the Geisinger System as a whole, including GHP, could qualify for tax-exempt status as an integrated delivery system as did Friendly Hills.

FRIENDLY HILLS HEALTHCARE NETWORK INTERNAL REVENUE SERVICE EXEMPTION RULING
January 29, 1993.

You are a nonprofit corporation formed under the laws of the State of California. Your sole corporate member is Loma Linda University Medical Center ("LLUMC"), a California nonprofit religious corporation. You have deleted all provisions from your bylaws that would have allowed for withdrawal or termination of the sole corporate member. You have stated that you intend for LLUMC to be your permanent member.

You have represented that you will operate a vertically integrated, primary care-driven, regional health care delivery system in a managed care environment. You describe yourself as a medical foundation-type of integrated delivery system. You represent that you will enhance the accessibility, quality and cost-efficiency of services rendered to the communities you serve.

You have stated that you will enter an Asset Purchase and Donation Agreement ("Purchase Agreement") under which you will acquire the assets of four California partnerships and one corporation commonly owned by various subgroups of the partners of Friendly Hills Medical Group ("Medical Group"). These assets include the real estate and facilities of a 274–bed general acute care hospital, Friendly Hills Regional Medical Center ("Medical Center"), and 10 clinic facilities that currently provide the services of 155 full-time health care professionals. Other assets include improvements, fixtures, furnishings, equipment, inventories, medical records, intangible assets (including covenants not to compete, health maintenance organization contracts, other contracts, an assembled work force, warranty rights, prepaid assets and deposits, utility rights, trademarks, and trade names).

You have represented that you will pay not more than $110 million for the above-referenced assets and the Medical Group physicians will make charitable donations in an aggregate amount, and deduct from their income proportionate amounts of that aggregate, which, when combined with the cash purchase price, will not total more than $125 million. You will pay the cash purchase price with a combination of the proceeds of a tax-exempt bond issue and a 10–year installment note. You represent that the assets are being acquired at or below fair market value. However, this letter does not make a determination regarding whether the purchase or lease of this property is at fair market value.

You will have a ten member board. No more than two of the ten members will represent the Medical Group. You have stated that you intend to ensure the independence of your board as a body controlled by members of the community.

Following the asset acquisition, you will operate a general acute care hospital and the 10 clinic facilities. You will provide all assets, personal property, management services, and non-physician support personnel. You will contract with the former Medical Group, which has reorganized into a new Medical Group that no longer owns any of the assets used by the integrated health delivery system, to provide all professional medical services for your enrollees. Substantially all the compensation from you to the Medical Group will be established on a capitated basis. . . .

* * *

You have represented that, after the acquisition, the Medical Center will maintain an open medical staff in order to make its services as readily accessible to the community as possible.

You stated in your original application that the Medical Center will continue to operate an emergency room that is open to the public and accept paramedic runs, providing emergency care to everyone without regard to ability to pay. In addition, anyone in immediate need of care will be treated at any of your clinic locations without regard to ability to pay. You stated that indigent emergency room patients requiring hospitalization will be admitted to the hospital for inpatient care and will receive all necessary follow-up care free or at discounted rates, depending on the patient's means, including outpatient care through your clinics and use of your affiliated magnetic resonance imaging unit.

You represented in your December 17, 1992, and your January 6, 1993, submissions that you already participate in, or have made good faith efforts to participate in, the three existing managed care initiatives of the federal-state Medicaid program in California, "Medi–Cal." In your January 22, 1993, submission you stated that you will participate in both the Medicare and Medi–Cal programs in a nondiscriminatory manner. You will make available to Medicare and Medi–Cal beneficiaries all primary, specialty, and diagnostic care made available to other patients. You will participate in the fee-for-service programs of both Medicare and Medi–Cal at all of your clinic locations. The Medical Center will serve Medicare patients. You have entered into and will pursue good faith negotiations with the California Medical Assistance Commission in an effort to obtain an inpatient Medi–Cal contract for the Medical Center, and you will arrange for adequate physician participation in your clinics to ensure access to Medicare and Medi–Cal beneficiaries.

You have additionally represented that you will conduct significant programs of medical research and health education and that you will offer extensive medical and record keeping advantages.

Based on information supplied, and assuming your operations will be as stated in your application for recognition of exemption, we have determined you are exempt from federal income tax under section 501(a) of the Code as an organization described in section 501(c)(3).

* * *

Notes and Questions

1. Is the Third Circuit's holding (and the Service's litigation position) in *Geisinger* consistent with the Service's grant of § 501(c)(3) status to Friendly Hills Healthcare Network? The facts represented by Friendly Hills stated that it would participate in the Medi–Cal managed care programs. It is also stated that the Network would pay the Medical Group on a capitated basis. Would the presence of a Geisinger-type health maintenance organization in the Friendly Hills IDS have caused the IRS to deny tax-exempt status to the IDS? Could Geisinger Health System have applied successfully for exemption as an IDS? What might have led it not to apply for that status as an entity?

2. What standards for IDS tax-exempt status can you identify from this exemption letter? Why might an IDS choose tax-exempt over for-profit status and vice versa? (How did Friendly Hills get some of the capital to purchase the physician practice, for example?). In Friendly Hills and subsequent approvals of IDSs, the IRS seemed to look with favor upon the fact that physician membership on the board was only 20 percent. However, the Service has subsequently indicated that it had a flexible policy on the matter of board composition and that a board with a disinterested majority of board members that adopted a conflict of interest policy and routinely monitored compliance with the entity's charitable

mission would satisfy its requirements. Model Conflicts of Interest Policy, 1997 CPE Text reprinted in 97 Tax Notes Today 198–80; see also Marlis L. Carson, IRS Eases Stance on Physician Board Representation, 96 Tax Notes Today 132–1 (July 8, 1996).

Why is the IRS concerned with the composition of the governance body in the first place? Would a PHO choose tax-exempt status in the face of the restriction on governance participation by physicians? Would the hospital participant in the PHO be more interested in limiting physician influence in governance than would the physician participants?

3. What is the community benefit to be realized through Friendly Hills Healthcare Network? The Congressional Research Service, in a report on health care reform, stated about the Friendly Hills Network:

> What is immediately striking about this transaction is that the physicians stand to receive $110 million to be financed in part with tax-exempt bonds, while there is no evidence that the foundation will provide any new community benefits that are not already supposed to be provided by LLUMC. It is not clear from the ruling whether LLUMC and the acquired facilities serve the same or different communities and geographic areas. The ruling letter does recite that the acquired facilities will maintain an open medical staff and an open emergency room, that indigent emergency patients requiring hospitalization will be admitted for inpatient care free of charge or at reduced rates, and that the facilities will be open to Medicare and Medi–Cal patients. But it is not clear whether these community benefits would duplicate community benefits that under its tax-exemption LLUMC is already required to provide.

Congressional Research Service, Tax Aspects of Health Care Reform: The Tax Treatment of Health Care Providers, April 25, 1994. Is increased efficiency sufficient justification for extending exempt status to an IDS? Improved competitive capacity? Since Friendly Hills, the Service has granted exempt status to many IDSs organized in a variety of ways. See e.g., Facey Medical Foundation Exemption Ruling, 93 Tax Notes Today 83–116 (Apr. 15, 1993); Northwestern Healthcare Network Exemption Ruling, 93 Tax Notes Today 187–169 (Sept. 9, 1993); Rockford Memorial Health Services Corporation Exemption Ruling, 1994 WL 510148 (April 4, 1994); Private Letter Ruling 9636026 (Sept. 6, 1996); Private Letter Ruling 9635029 (Aug. 30, 1996). See also JOA [Joint Operating Agreement] Exemption Rulings Provide Needed Guidance for Healthcare Arrangements, 96 Tax Notes Today 218–4 (Nov. 7, 1996).

If you were asked to develop standards to rationalize the Service's approach to integrated delivery systems, what would you recommend? Should the Service treat Geisinger Health System and Friendly Hills Healthcare Network the same or differently? Should the Service resist or require an approach that separately examines each constitutive entity within a system? On IDSs, see Amy L. Woodhall, Integrated Delivery Systems: Reforming the Conflicts Among Federal Referral, Tax Exemption, and Antitrust Laws, 5 Health Matrix 181 (1995); John D. Colombo, Health Care Reform and Federal Tax Exemption: Rethinking the Issues, 29 Wake Forest L. Rev. 215 (1994).

4. Physician–hospital organizations (PHOs), described in detail earlier in this chapter, are often used as structures to more closely bind hospitals and physicians. PHOs generally negotiate health plan contracts to cover both physician and hospital services. Some also take on utilization review, credentialing and quality management activities, and some may foster shared administrative services. Many of the functions of the typical PHO will be provided within a fully

integrated tax-exempt IDS. Outside of a fully integrated system, however, PHOs standing alone face difficult issues in gaining tax-exempt status (including issues relating to control by physicians and charitable purpose) and typically do not qualify as tax-exempt. Because most PHOs do not themselves provide care and merely negotiate contracts on behalf of providers, it is difficult to make a case that a charitable purpose is served; even more difficult is compliance with the requirement that no more than incidental private benefits are provided. See Thomas K. Hyatt and Bruce R. Hopkins, The Law of Tax Exempt Health–Care Organizations § 23.2(b) (1995 & 1998 Supp.); Charles Kaiser and T.J. Sullivan, IRS Exempt Organizations CPE Technical Instruction Program Textbook: Part II, Chapter P: Integrated Delivery Systems; Tax–Exempt Physician Hospital Organization Not your Typical PHO, Says IRS, 95 Tax Notes Today 81–7 (Apr. 26, 1995). However, at least one PHO has run the gauntlet, although its approval may be attributable to its base in an academic medical center and other unique factors. See Hyatt & Hopkins, supra, § 23.2(b) (1998 Supp.). Of course, a tax-exempt entity may establish or participate in a for-profit PHO if the tax-exempt abides by the restrictions of its tax-exempt status.

5.   The IRS's treatment of physician organizations within integrated systems is still blurred. For example, the Service granted exempt status to Marietta Health Care Physicians, Inc. an entity incorporated as a for-profit professional corporation established to "recruit and employ physicians" and to act as "the physician's services component of [a tax-exempt hospital's] integrated delivery system." Exemption Ruling, 1995 WL 594915 (Oct. 3, 1995). The Service recited MHCP's representation that state law required physician service groups to be organized as a professional corporation and looked behind the organizational form to see that MHCP's board was an entity controlled by the tax-exempt hospital; its articles of incorporation included only exempt purposes; and it had a charity care budget. In C.H. Wilkenson Physician Network Exemption Ruling, 1996 WL 343384 (June 19, 1996), the Service granted exempt status to an organization whose board was entirely made up of physicians, with the Service again repeating the state law justification offered by the organization. In each of these, the prohibition on the corporate practice of medicine was the state law presented as driving the structure of the entity.

D.   JOINT VENTURES BETWEEN TAX–EXEMPT AND FOR–PROFIT ORGANIZATIONS

Tax-exempt organizations may engage in business activities jointly with for-profit organizations; may own for-profit organizations; and may themselves directly engage in non-tax-exempt activities. An exempt organization's participation in a joint venture with a for-profit entity will not affect its tax exempt status provided the purpose of its involvement in the ventures is in furtherance of its exempt purpose. Section 501(c)(3) requires that the exempt entity be organized and operated "exclusively" for exempt purposes, but the regulations interpret that standard as requiring that exempt organizations engage "primarily in activities that accomplish one or more ... exempt purposes" and further state that the exempt organization violates this standard if "more than an insubstantial" amount of its activities are not in furtherance of exempt purposes. 26 C.F.R. § 1.501(c)(3)–1(c)(1). Thus, § 501(c)(3) organizations may engage in trade or business unrelated to their exempt purposes, though income from such unrelated business is taxable and not tax-exempt.

GENERAL COUNSEL MEMORANDUM
39862.
(Dec. 2, 1991).

[The Service reviews a physician-hospital agreement in which the hospital sold its future net income from certain departments to entities that were owned by physicians who admitted and treated patients at the hospital. So, for example, obstetricians who treated patients at the hospital could invest in the hospital's OB department with the return on investment being a proportionate share of the net income of that department. Thus, the physician practicing in the department would experience financial gain or loss depending on the department's financial performance.]

The [net income stream] joint venture arrangements ... are just one variety of an increasingly common type of competitive behavior engaged in by hospitals in response to significant changes in their operating environment. Many medical and surgical procedures once requiring inpatient care, still the exclusive province of hospitals, now are performed on an outpatient basis, where every private physician is a potential competitor. The marked shift in governmental policy from regulatory cost controls to competition has fundamentally changed the way all hospitals, for-profit and not, do business.

A driving force behind the new hospital operating environment was the federal Medicare Program's 1983 shift from cost-based reimbursement for covered inpatient hospital services to fixed, per-case, prospective payments. This change to a diagnosis-related prospective payment system ("PPS") dramatically altered hospital financial incentives. PPS severed the link between longer hospital stays with more services provided each patient and higher reimbursement. It substituted strong incentives to control the costs of each individual inpatient's care while attracting a greater number of admissions. Medicare policies are highly influential; the program accounts for nearly 40% of the average hospital's revenues.

The need to increase admission volume was accompanied by a perceived need to influence physician treatment decisions which, by and large, were unaffected by the change to PPS. Hospitals realized that, in addition to attracting more patients, they needed to control utilization of ancillary hospital services, discharge Medicare beneficiaries as quickly as is medically appropriate, and operate more efficiently. Traditionally, physicians treating their private patients at a hospital had enjoyed nearly complete independence of professional judgement. Since they are paid separately by Medicare and other third party payers on the basis of billed charges, they still have an incentive to render more services to each patient over a longer period in order to enhance their own earnings. Once hospital and physician economic incentives diverged, hospitals began seeking ways to stimulate loyalty among members of their medical staffs and to encourage or reward physician behaviors deemed desirable.

* * *

... Here, there appears to be little accomplished that directly furthers the hospitals' charitable purposes of promoting health. No expansion of health care resources results; no new provider is created. No improvement in treatment modalities or reduction in cost is foreseeable. We have to look very carefully for any reason why a hospital would want to engage in this sort of arrangement.

* * *

Assuming, arguendo, that [a hospital engaged in the transaction because it] did have a pressing need for an advance of cash, we could examine this type of transaction strictly as a financing mechanism.... [W]e do not believe it would be proper under most circumstances for a charitable organization to borrow funds under an agreement, even with an outside commercial lender, where the organization would pay as interest a stated percentage of its earnings.... In any event, we do not believe these transactions were undertaken to raise needed cash.

Whether admitted or not, we believe the hospitals engaged in these ventures largely as a means to retain and reward members of their medical staffs; to attract their admissions and referrals; and to pre-empt the physicians from investing in or creating a competing provider [of outpatient services].

* * *

... In our view, there are a fixed number of individuals in a community legitimately needing hospital services at any one time. Paying doctors to steer patients to one particular hospital merely to improve its efficiency seems distant from a mission of providing needed care. We question whether the Service should ever recognize enhancing a hospital's market share vis-a-vis other providers, in and of itself, as furthering a charitable purpose. In many cases, doing so might hamper another charitable hospital's ability to promote the health of the same community.

* * *

Notes and Questions

1. Evaluate the economic incentives created by the proposed arrangement. How would a physician gain by making such an investment? Why would a hospital sell a share of its income? Isn't the potential improvement in the hospital's competitive position in the community or enhancement of its efficiency a community benefit?

2. The IRS has approved a "gainsharing" arrangement between a tax-exempt hospital and group of cardiologists on the hospital's staff. Under the gainsharing program agreement, the cardiologists design and implement cost-effective "process improvement initiatives" (such as care pathways) and any cost savings garnered under the improvement plans fund a "process improvement award pool." The cardiologists' performance with respect to the process improvement initiatives are evaluated annually under predetermined evaluation criteria. If the cardiologists satisfy the criteria, they are eligible to receive an award from the pool. What distinguishes gainsharing arrangements from the sale of revenue stream at issue in GCM 39862? See Stacey L. Murphy & Edward J. Buchholz, Internal Revenue Service Approval of Two Gainsharing Programs—The Rulings and Their Implications, 32 J. Health L. 381 (1999). Although passing IRS scrutiny, the arrangement did not receive the OIG's approval based on § 1128A(b)(1) which prohibits payments to physicians to reduce or limit services. See Chapter 14 infra.

3. Unrelated trade or business is that which is regularly carried on "the conduct of which is not substantially related (aside from the need of such organization for income or funds or the use it makes of the profits derived)" to its exempt purpose. 26 CFR § 1.513–1(a). Services that contribute to patient recovery and convenience are related to the exempt purposes of the health care organization. Income from these activities is not taxable. Those provided to non-hospital patients would be taxable unless they fall within certain narrow exceptions relating to 1) whether the services to non-patients are otherwise available in the community or 2) whether the services to non-patients contribute to the achievement of other exempt purposes, such as medical education. See Private Letter Ruling 8125007 (undated), in which the Service decided that sophisticated lab services, not otherwise available, provided by an exempt hospital to industry for employee examinations, did not produce unrelated business taxable income (UBTI). The PLR concluded, however, that the provision of ordinary lab services performed for non-hospital patients of private physicians may do so. This may lead to rather confusing results. A hospital's revenues from providing MRI services to patients of another hospital or to outpatients served by its staff physicians might well be UBTI, though the revenues from the same services to admitted patients would not. If the hospital owned the doctors' practices, as in an integrated system, would all of the doctors' patients be the hospital's patients? Income from management or administrative services sold by a tax-exempt hospital to physicians in private practices could certainly be considered UBTI. If the hospital purchased the physician practices (as in the Friendly Hills Network), would the provision of these services to the hospital-owned practices produce taxable income? In the first situation, the hospital (usually through a Management Services Organization) charges a physician for these services, requiring the physician to in effect transfer some of his revenue to the hospital in the amount of that charge, and perhaps requiring the hospital to pay UBTI on that amount. How are the services "paid for" if the practice is part of a tax-exempt IDS?

REVENUE RULING 98–15

1998–12 I.R.B. 6.

[In this Revenue Ruling, the IRS provides the following examples to illustrate whether an organization that operates an acute care hospital constitutes an organization whose principal purpose is providing charitable hospital care when it forms a limited liability company (LLC) with a for-profit corporation and then contributes its hospital and all of its related operating assets to the LLC, which then operates the hospital.]

Situation 1

A is a nonprofit corporation that owns and operates an acute care hospital. A has been recognized as exempt from federal income tax under § 501(a) as an organization described in § 501(c)(3) and as other than a private foundation as defined in § 509(a) because it is described in § 170(b)(1)(A)(iii). B is a for-profit corporation that owns and operates a number of hospitals.

A concludes that it could better serve its community if it obtained additional funding. B is interested in providing financing for A's hospital, provided it earns a reasonable rate of return. A and B form a limited liability company, C. A contributes all of its operating assets, including its hospital to C. B also contributes assets to C. In return, A and B receive ownership interests in C proportional and equal in value to their respective contributions.

C's Articles of Organization and Operating Agreement ("governing documents") provide that C is to be managed by a governing board consisting of three individuals chosen by A and two individuals chosen by B. A intends to appoint community leaders who have experience with hospital matters, but who are not on the hospital staff and do not otherwise engage in business transactions with the hospital.

The governing documents further provide that they may only be amended with the approval of both owners and that a majority of three board members must approve certain major decisions relating to C's operation including decisions relating to any of the following topics:

    A.   C's annual capital and operating budgets;

    B.   Distributions of C's earnings;

    C.   Selection of key executives;

    D.   Acquisition or disposition of health care facilities;

    E.   Contracts in excess of $x per year;

    F.   Changes to the types of services offered by the hospital; and

    G.   Renewal or termination of management agreements.

The governing documents require that C operate any hospital it owns in a manner that furthers charitable purposes by promoting health for a broad cross section of its community. The governing documents explicitly provide that the duty of the members of the governing board to operate C in a manner that furthers charitable purposes by promoting health for a broad cross section of the community overrides any duty they may have to operate C for the financial benefit of its owners. Accordingly, in the event of a conflict between operation in accordance with the community benefit standard and any duty to maximize profits, the members of the governing board are to satisfy the community benefit standard without regard to the consequences for maximizing profitability.

The governing documents further provide that all returns of capital and distributions of earnings made to owners of C shall be proportional to their ownership interests in C. The terms of the governing documents are legal, binding, and enforceable under applicable state law.

C enters into a management agreement with a management company that is unrelated to A or B to provide day-to-day management services to C. The management agreement is for a five-year period, and the agreement is renewable for additional five-year periods by mutual consent. The management company will be paid a management fee for its services based on C's gross revenues. The terms and conditions of the management agreement, including the fee structure and the contract term, are reasonable and comparable to what other management firms receive for similar services at similarly situated hospitals. C may terminate the agreement for cause.

None of the officers, directors, or key employees of A who were involved in making the decision to form C were promised employment or any other inducement by C or B and their related entities if the transaction were approved. None of A's officers, directors, or key employees have any interest, including any interest through attribution determined in accordance with the principles of § 318, in B or any of its related entities.

Pursuant to § 301.7701–3(b) of the Procedure and Administrative Regulations, C will be treated as a partnership for federal income tax purposes.

A intends to use any distributions it receives from C to fund grants to support activities that promote the health of A's community and to help the indigent obtain health care. Substantially all of A's grantmaking will be funded by distributions from C. A's projected grantmaking program and its participation as an owner of C will constitute A's only activities.

Situation 2

D is a nonprofit corporation that owns and operates an acute care hospital. D has been recognized as exempt from federal income tax under § 501(a) as an organization described in § 501(c)(3) and as other than a private foundation as defined in § 509(a) because it is described in § 170(b)(1)(iii). E is a for-profit hospital corporation that owns and operates a number of hospitals and provides management services to several hospitals that it does not own.

D concludes that it could better serve its community if it obtained additional funding. E is interested in providing financing for D's hospital, provided it earns a reasonable rate of return. D and E form a limited liability company, F. D contributes all of its operating assets, including its hospital to F. E also contributes assets to F. In return, D and E receive ownership interests proportional and equal in value to their respective contributions.

F's Articles of Organization and Operating Agreement ("governing documents") provide that F is to be managed by a governing board consisting of three individuals chosen by D and three individuals chosen by E. D intends to appoint community leaders who have experience with hospital matters, but who are not on the hospital staff and do not otherwise engage in business transactions with the hospital.

The governing documents further provide that they may only be amended with the approval of both owners and that a majority of board members must approve certain major decisions relating to F's operation, including decisions relating to any of the following topics:

A.   F's annual capital and operating budgets;

B.   Distributions of F's earnings over a required minimum level of distributions set forth in the Operating Agreement;

C.   Unusually large contracts; and

D.   Selection of key executives.

F's governing documents provide that F's purpose is to construct, develop, own, manage, operate, and take other action in connection with operating the health care facilities it owns and engage in other health care-related activities. The governing documents further provide that all returns of capital and distributions of earnings made to owners of F shall be proportional to their ownership interests in F.

F enters into a management agreement with a wholly-owned subsidiary of E to provide day-to-day management services to F. The management agreement is for a five-year period, and the agreement is renewable for additional five-year periods at the discretion of E's subsidiary. F may terminate the agreement only for cause. E's subsidiary will be paid a management fee for its services based on gross revenues. The terms and conditions of the management agreement, including the fee structure and the contract term other than the renewal terms, are reasonable and comparable to what other management firms receive for similar services at similarly situated hospitals.

As part of the agreement to form F, D agrees to approve the selection of two individuals to serve as F's chief executive officer and chief financial officer. These individuals have previously worked for E in hospital management and have business expertise. They will work with the management company to oversee F's day-to-day management. Their compensation is comparable to what comparable executives are paid at similarly situated hospitals.

Pursuant to § 301.7701–3(b). F will be treated as a partnership for federal tax income purposes.

D intends to use any distributions it receives from F to fund grants to support activities that promote the health of D's community and to help the indigent obtain health care. Substantially all of D's grantmaking will be funded by distributions from F. D's projected grantmaking program and its participation as an owner of F will constitute D's only activities.

ANALYSIS

For federal income tax purposes, the activities of a partnership are often considered to be the activities of the partners. Aggregate treatment is also consistent with the treatment of partnerships for purpose of the unrelated business income tax under § 512(c). In light of the aggregate principle discussed in Butler and reflected in § 512(c), the aggregate approach also applies for purposes of the operational test set forth in § 1.501(c)(3)–1(c). Thus, the activities of an LLC treated as a partnership for federal income tax purposes are considered to be the activities of a nonprofit organization that is an owner of the LLC when evaluating whether the nonprofit organization is operated exclusively for exempt purposes within the meaning of § 501(c)(3).

A § 501(c)(3) organization may form and participate in a partnership, including an LLC treated as a partnership for federal income tax purposes, and meet the operational test if participation in the partnership furthers a charitable purpose, and the partnership arrangement permits the exempt organization to act exclusively in furtherance of its exempt purpose and only incidentally for the benefit of the for-profit partners. Similarly, a § 501(c)(3) organization may enter into a management contract with a private party giving that party authority to conduct activities on behalf of the organization and direct the use of the organization's assets provided that the organization retains ultimate authority over the assets and activities being managed and the terms and conditions of the contract are reasonable, including reasonable compensation and a reasonable term. However, if a private party is allowed to control or use the non-profit organization's activities or assets for the benefit of the private party, and the benefit is not incidental to the accomplishment of exempt purposes, the organization will fail to be organized and operated exclusively for exempt purposes.

Situation 1

After A and B form C, and A contributes all of its operating assets to C, A's activities will consist of the health care services it provides through C and any grantmaking activities it can conduct using income distributed to C. A will receive an interest in C equal in value to the assets it contributes to C, and A's and B's returns from C will be proportional to their respective investments in C. The governing documents of C commit C to providing health care services for the benefit of the community as a whole and to give charitable purposes priority over maximizing profits for C's owners. Furthermore, through A's appointment of members of the community familiar with the hospital to C's board, the board's structure, which gives A's appointees voting control, and the specifically enumerated powers of the board over changes in activities, disposition of assets, and renewal of the management agreement. A can ensure that the assets it owns through C and the activities it conducts through C are used primarily to further exempt purposes. Thus, A can ensure that the benefit to B and other private parties, like the management company, will be incidental to the accomplishment of charitable purposes. Additionally, the terms and conditions of the management contract, including the terms for renewal and termination are reasonable. Finally, A's grants are intended to support education and research and give resources to help provide health care to the indigent. All of these facts and circumstances establish that, when A participates in forming C and contributes all of its operating assets to C, and C operates in accordance with its governing documents, A will be furthering charitable purposes and continue to be operated exclusively for exempt purposes.

Because A's grantmaking activity will be contingent upon receiving distributions from C, A's principal activity will continue to be the provision of hospital care. As long as A's principal activity remains the provision of hospital care. A will not be classified as a private foundation in accordance with § 509(a)(1) as an organization described in § 170(b)(1)(A)(iii).

Situation 2

When D and E form F, and D contributes its assets to F, D will be engaged in activities that consist of the health care services it provides through F and any grantmaking activities it can conduct using income distributed by F. However, unlike A, D will not be engaging primarily in activities that further an exempt purpose. "While the diagnosis and cure of disease are indeed purposes that may furnish the foundation for characterizing the activity as 'charitable,' something more is required." See Sound Health and Geisinger. In the absence of a binding obligation in F's governing documents for F to serve charitable purposes or otherwise provide its services to the community as a whole, F will be able to deny care to segments of the community, such as the indigent. Because D will share control of F with E, D will not be able to initiate programs within F to serve new health needs within the community without the agreement of at least one governing board member appointed by E. As a business enterprise, E will not necessarily give priority to the health needs of the community over the consequences for F's profits. The primary source of information for board members appointed by D will be the chief executives, who have a prior relationship with E and the management company, which is a subsidiary of E. The management company itself will have broad discretion over F's activities and assets that may not always be under the board's supervision. For example, the management company is permitted to enter into all but "unusually large" contracts without board approval. The management company may also unilaterally renew the management agreement. Based on all these facts and circumstances, D cannot establish that the activities it conducts through F further exempt purposes. "[I]n order for an organization to qualify for exemption under § 501(c)(3) the organization must "establish" that it is neither organized nor operated for the 'benefit of private interests.' " Consequently, the benefit to E resulting from the activities D conducts through F will not be incidental to the furtherance of an exempt purpose. Thus, D will fail the operational test when it forms F, contributes its operating assets to F, and then serves as an owner to F.

HOLDING

A will continue to qualify as an organization described in § 501(c)(3) when it forms C and contributes all of its operating assets to C because A has established that A will be operating exclusively for a charitable purpose and only incidentally for the purpose of benefitting the private interests of B. Furthermore, A's principal activity will continue to be the provision of hospital care when C begins operations. Thus, A will be an organization described in § 170(b)(1)(A)(iii) and thus, will not be classified as a private foundation in accordance with § 509(a)(1), as long as hospital care remains its principal activity.

D will violate the requirements to be an organization described in § 501(c)(3) when it forms F and contributes all of its operating assets to F because D has failed to establish that it will be operated exclusively for exempt purposes.

Notes

1. Some recommended changes for the hospital in Situation 2 to retain its § 501(c)(3) status include shortening the management term to five years, requiring a 24–hour emergency room at one or more of the LLC hospitals, and adopting a list of reserved powers similar to those in Situation 1. See Gerald M. Griffith, Revenue Ruling 98–15: Dimming the Future of All Nonprofit Joint Ventures?, 31 J. Health L. 71, 88 (1998). How do these relate to the criteria for tax exemption discussed earlier? What other changes would you recommend? Why?

2. Although eagerly awaited, the guidance offered by Revenue Ruling 98–15 has met with criticism for what it does not address. See Robert C. Louthian, III, IRS Provides Whole Hospital Joint Venture Guidance in Revenue Ruling 98–15, 7 Health L. Rep. 477 (BNA) (March 19, 1998). Many feel that the ruling's "polar opposite" situations do not help to clarify the many gray areas experienced in joint ventures. What situations would still be left unanswered by the ruling? Perhaps in response to such criticism, the IRS recently released a professional education text containing articles highlighting various tax issues. See Exempt Organizations: Hospitals To Receive Scrutiny This Year in IRS Text Spotlighting Areas of Interest, 7 Health L. Rep. 1307 (BNA) (Aug. 13, 1998). Included in the IRS text is an article on Revenue Ruling 98–15, described as "required reading"

and being an "important piece to complement the analysis of [98–15]." Id. The article lists questions that IRS agents should review when determining if a hospital joint venture furthers the exempt purpose of the not-for-profit entity while scrutinizing any nonincidental private benefit to the for-profit managers, and concludes that a hospital joint venture will pass scrutiny if the "charitable purposes supersede profit maximization purposes." If you were the IRS employee drafting questions for the list, what questions would you include? Why?

3. Why are management control issues important to the analysis of whole hospital joint ventures? See Gregory A. Petroff, Whole Hospital Joint Ventures: The IRS Position On Control, 98 Tax Notes Today 138–89 (July 20, 1998). Consider how the Tax Court defines and weighs control in the following case.

REDLANDS SURGICAL SERVICES v. COMMISSIONER OF INTERNAL REVENUE

United States Tax Court, 1999.
113 T.C. 47.

THORNTON, J.

[Petitioner Redlands Surgical Services is a nonprofit member corporation whose sole member is RHS Corp. (RHS), a nonprofit public benefit corporation that is also parent of tax-exempt Redlands Community Hospital. Surgical Care Affiliates Inc. (SCA), a for-profit, publicly held corporation that owns and manages 40 ambulatory surgical centers, owns two for-profit subsidiaries: Redlands–Centers and Redlands Management.

Petitioner entered into two partnerships relevant to this proceeding: (1) the Redlands Ambulatory Surgery Center Partnership (the General Partnership) with Redlands Centers as co-partner; and (2) the Inland Surgery Center Limited Partnership (Inland or the Operating Partnership) of which the General Partnership is the general partner and 32 physicians from Redlands Hospital's medical staff are limited partners. The Operating Partnership owned the Surgery Center, an ambulatory surgical center located two blocks away from Redlands Hospital. The IRS denied Petitioner's Application for Recognition of Exemption stating, "Basically all you have done is invest in a for-profit entity, Inland, and transfer the profits from this investment to your parent."]

OPINION

I. The Parties' Positions

Respondent contends that petitioner is not operated exclusively for charitable purposes because it operates for the benefit of private parties and fails to benefit a broad cross-section of the community. In support of its position, respondent contends that the partnership agreements and related management contract are structured to give for-profit interests control over the Surgery Center. Respondent contends that both before and after the General Partnership acquired an ownership interest in it, the Surgery Center was a successful profit-making business that never held itself out as a charity and never operated as a charitable health-care provider.

Petitioner argues that it meets the operational test under section 501(c)(3) because its activities with regard to the Surgery Center further its purpose of promoting health for the benefit of the Redlands community, by providing access to an ambulatory surgery center for all members of the community based upon medical need rather than ability to pay, and by integrating the outpatient services of Redlands Hospital and the Surgery Center. Petitioner argues that its dealings with the for-profit partners have been at arm's length, and that its influence over the activities of the Surgery Center has been sufficient to further its charitable goals. Petitioner further contends that it qualifies for exemption because it is organized and operated to perform services that are integral to the exempt purposes of RHS, its tax-exempt parent, and Redlands Hospital, its tax-exempt affiliate.

II.   Applicable Legal Principles

* * *

B.   Promotion of Health as a Charitable Purpose

Section 501(c)(3) specifies various qualifying exempt purposes, including "charitable" purposes. The term "charitable" is not defined in section 501(c)(3), but is used in its generally accepted legal sense. See Nationalist Movement v. Commissioner, 102 T.C. 558 (1994), affd. per curiam 37 F.3d 216 (5th Cir.1994); sec. 1.501(c)(3)–1(d)(2), Income Tax Regs. In applying this standard, courts have looked to the law of charitable trusts. See Sound Health Association v. Commissioner, 71 T.C. 158, 177 (1978); see also Bob Jones Univ. v. United States, 461 U.S. 574, 588 n. 12 (1983).

The promotion of health for the benefit of the community is a charitable purpose* * *As applied to determinations of qualification for tax exemption, the definition of the term "charitable" has not been static.[ ]Suffice it to say that, in recognition of changes in the health-care industry, the standard no longer requires that "the care of indigent patients be the primary concern of the charitable hospital, as distinguished from the care of paying patients". Sound Health Association v. Commissioner, supra at 180. Rather, the standard reflects "a policy of insuring that adequate health care services are actually delivered to those in the community who need them." [ ] Under this standard, health-care providers must meet a flexible community benefit test based upon a variety of indicia, one of which may be whether the organization provides free care to indigents. * * *To benefit the community, a charity must serve a sufficiently large and indefinite class; as a corollary to this rule, private interests must not benefit to any substantial degree.

[Discussion of the proscription against private benefit omitted.]

* * *

III.   Petitioner's Claim to Exemption on a "Stand–Alone" Basis

Applying the principles described above, we next consider whether petitioner has established that respondent improperly denied it tax-exempt status as a section 501(c)(3) organization.

A.   The Relevance of Control—The Parties' Positions

Respondent asserts that petitioner has ceded effective control over its sole activity—participating as a co-general partner with for-profit parties in the partnerships that own and operate the Surgery Center—to the for-profit partners and the for-profit management company that is an affiliate of petitioner's co-general partner. Respondent asserts that this arrangement is indicative of a substantial nonexempt purpose, whereby petitioner impermissibly benefits private interests.

Without conceding that private parties control its activities, petitioner challenges the premise that the ability to control its activities determines its purposes. Petitioner argues that under the operational test, "the critical issue in determining whether an organization's purposes are noncharitable is not whether a for profit or not for profit entity has control. Rather, the critical issue is the sort of conduct in which the organization is actually engaged." * * *

We disagree with petitioner's thesis. It is patently clear that the Operating Partnership, whatever charitable benefits it may produce, is not operated "in an exclusively charitable manner". As stated by Justice Cardozo (then Justice of the New York Court of Appeals), in describing one of the "ancient principles" of charitable trusts, "It is only when income may be applied to the profit of the founders that business has a beginning and charity an end." Butterworth v. Keeler, 219 N.Y. 446, 449–450, 114 N.E. 803, 804 (1916). The Operating Partnership's income is, of course, applied to the profit of petitioner's co-general partner and the numerous limited partners.* * * It is no answer to say that none of petitioner's income from this activity was applied to private interests, for the activity is indivisible, and no discrete part of the Operating Partnership's income-producing activities is severable from those activities that produce income to be applied to the other partners' profit.

Taken to its logical conclusion, petitioner's thesis would suggest that an organization whose main activity is passive participation in a for-profit health-service enterprise could thereby be deemed to be operating exclusively for charitable purposes. Such a conclusion, however, would be contrary to well-established principles of charitable trust law. * * *

Clearly, there is something in common between the structure of petitioner's sole activity and the nature of petitioner's purposes in engaging in it. An organization's purposes may be inferred from its manner of operations; its "activities provide a useful indicia of the organization's purpose or purposes." Living Faith, Inc. v. Commissioner, 950 F.2d 365, 372 (7th Cir.1991), affg. T.C. Memo.1990–484. The binding commitments that petitioner has entered into and that govern its participation in the partnerships are indicative of petitioner's purposes. To the extent that petitioner cedes control over its sole activity to for-profit parties having an independent economic interest in the same activity and having no obligation to put charitable purposes ahead of profit-making objectives, petitioner cannot be assured that the partnerships will in fact be operated in furtherance of charitable purposes. In such a circumstance, we are led to the conclusion that petitioner is not operated exclusively for charitable purposes.

Based on the totality of factors described below, we conclude that petitioner has in fact ceded effective control of the partnerships' and the Surgery Center's activities to for-profit parties, conferring on them significant private benefits, and therefore is not operated exclusively for charitable purposes within the meaning of section 501(c)(3).

B. Indicia of For–Profit Control Over the Partnerships' Activities

1. No Charitable Obligation

Nothing in the General Partnership agreement, or in any of the other binding commitments relating to the operation of the Surgery Center, establishes any obligation that charitable purposes be put ahead of economic objectives in the Surgery Center's operations. * * *

After the General Partnership acquired its 61–percent interest, the Operating Partnership—which had long operated as a successful for-profit enterprise and never held itself out as a charity—never changed its organizing documents to acknowledge a charitable purpose. * * *

2. Petitioner's Lack of Formal Control

a. Managing Directors

Under the General Partnership agreement, control over all matters other than medical standards and policies is nominally divided equally between petitioner and SCA Centers, each appointing two representatives to serve as managing directors. (As discussed infra, matters of medical standards and policies are determined by the Medical Advisory Group, half of whom are chosen by the General Partnership's managing directors.) Consequently, petitioner may exert influence by blocking actions proposed to be taken by the managing directors, but it cannot initiate action without the consent of at least one of SCA Center's appointees to the managing directors.* * *

The administrative record shows that petitioner has successfully blocked various proposals to expand the scope of activities performed at the Surgery Center. Petitioner's ability to veto expansion of the scope of the Surgery Center's activities, however, does not establish that petitioner has effective control over the manner in which the Surgery Center conducts activities within its predesignated sphere of operations. Nor does it tend to indicate that the Surgery Center is not operated to maximize profits with regard to those activities. * * *

In sum, the composition of the managing directorship evidences a lack of majority control by petitioner whereby it might assure that the Surgery Center is operated for charitable purposes.[ ]Consequently, we look to the binding commitments made between petitioner and the other parties to ascertain whether other specific powers or rights conferred upon petitioner might mitigate or compensate for its lack of majority control.

b. Arbitration Process

[The court notes that although the General Partnership agreement provides for an arbitration process in the event that the managing directors of the General Partnership deadlock, the ground rules for the arbitration process are minimal and provide petitioner no assurance that charitable objectives will govern the outcome and the arbitrators are not required to take into account any charitable or community benefit objective. It concludes that the arbitration process does not significantly mitigate petitioner's lack of majority control.]

c. The Management Contract

[The court observes that the management contract between the Operating Partnership and SCA Management confers broad powers on SCA Management to enter into contracts, to negotiate with third-party payers and state and federal agencies, and to set patient charges. The court also notes that, as a practical matter, the Operating Partnership is locked into the management agreement with SCA Management for at least 15 years.]

[N]either the General Partnership agreement, the Operating Partnership agreement, nor the management contract itself requires that SCA Management be guided by any charitable or community benefit, goal, policy, or objective. Rather, the management contract simply requires SCA Management to render services as necessary and in the best interest of the Operating Partnership, "subject to the policies established by [the Operating Partnership], which policies shall be consistent with applicable state and Federal law."

* * *

Respondent asserts, and we agree, that this long-term management contract with an affiliate of SCA Centers is a salient indicator of petitioner's surrender of effective control over the Surgery Center's operations to SCA affiliates, whereby the affiliates were given the ability and incentive to operate the Surgery Center so as to maximize profits. This surrender of effective control reflects adversely on petitioner's own charitable purposes in contracting to have its sole activity managed in this fashion

d.   Medical Advisory Group

The Operating Partnership agreement delegates authority for making decisions about care and treatment of patients and other medical matters to the Operating Partnership's Medical Advisory Group. This group was inactive before the General Partnership became involved with the Operating Partnership, but there is no evidence to show that role, if any, petitioner played in reconstituting the Medical Advisory Group. * * *

e.   Termination of Quality Assurance Activities

As required by the General Partnership agreement, on April 30, 1990, SCA Management entered into a quality assurance agreement with RHS. The term of the quality assurance agreement was conditioned on maintenance of a specified level of surgery activity in the Surgery Center. Petitioner concedes that the quality assurance agreement terminated after the first year. Although the agreement required the parties to negotiate a new quality assurance agreement in the event of such a termination, there is no evidence in the record that such negotiations ever occurred.

The termination of the quality assurance agreement vividly evidences petitioner's lack of effective control over vital aspects of the Surgery Center's operations. * * * The record does not reflect that petitioner performed any quality assurance work. Likewise, the record is silent as to how petitioner, in the absence of any operable quality assurance agreement, purports to assure itself that these vital functions will be discharged consistently with charitable objectives.

3.   Lack of Informal Control

The administrative record provides no basis for concluding that, in the absence of formal control, petitioner possesses significant informal control by which it exercises its influence with regard to the Surgery Center's activities.

Nothing in the administrative record suggests that petitioner commands allegiance or loyalty of the SCA affiliates or of the limited partners to cause them to put charitable objectives ahead of their own economic objectives. Indeed, until April 1992, petitioner was in a debtor relationship to SCA.

* * *

b. Provision for Indigent Patients

Petitioner concedes that as of December 31, 1993, Medi–Cal patients accounted for only 0.8 percent of total procedures performed at the Surgery Center. Petitioner argues that the type of services which the Service Center offers is not the type of services typically sought by low-income individuals. Petitioner notes that Redlands Hospital has negotiated certain provider agreements that designate the Surgery Center as a subcontractor to provide outpatient services for Medi–Cal patients, and that Redlands Hospital has caused the Surgery Center to increase its number of managed care contracts. Petitioner suggests that these efforts demonstrate petitioner's influence over the operations of the Surgery Center and evidence petitioner's charitable purposes.

We do not find petitioner's arguments convincing. The facts remain that the Surgery Center provides no free care to indigents and only negligible coverage for Medi–Cal patients. * * *

c. Coordination of Activities of Redlands Hospital and the Surgery Center

* * *

Although there may be cooperation between the Surgery Center and Redlands Hospital, nothing in the record suggests that these various cooperative activities are more than incidental to the for-profit orientation of the Surgery Center's activities. Cf. Harding Hosp., Inc. v. United States, supra at 1075–1076 (educational, training and community-oriented programs conducted at a hospital and funded by a third party were not sufficient to merit the hospital's tax exemption where other disqualifying factors were present).

C. Competitive Restrictions and Market Advantages

By entering into the General Partnership agreement, RHS (petitioner's parent corporation and predecessor in interest in the General Partnership) not only acquired an interest in the Surgery Center, but also restricted its future ability to provide outpatient services at Redlands Hospital or elsewhere without the approval of its for-profit partner. Paragraph 16 of the General Partnership agreement, supra, prohibits the co-general partners and their affiliates from owning, managing, or developing another freestanding outpatient surgery center within 20 miles of the Surgery Center, without the other partner's consent. Moreover, Redlands Hospital may not "expand or promote its present outpatient surgery program within the Hospital." In fact, outpatient surgeries performed at Redlands Hospital decreased about 17 percent from 1990 to 1995, while those performed at the Surgery Center increased.

* * * Consequently, RHS effectively restricted its own ability to assess and service community needs for outpatient services until the year 2020. It is

difficult to conceive of a significant charitable purpose that would be furthered by such a restriction.

* * *

Viewed in its totality, the administrative record is clear that SCA and
petitioner derive mutual economic benefits from the General Partnership
agreement. By borrowing necessary up-front capital from SCA, RHS (petitioner's predecessor in interest in the General Partnership), overcame a capital
barrier to gain entry into a profitable and growing market niche. By forming a
partnership with RHS, SCA Centers was able to benefit from the established
relationship between Redlands Hospital and the limited partner physicians to
acquire its interest in the Surgery Center at a bargain price.

By virtue of this arrangement, petitioner and SCA Centers realized
further mutual benefits by eliminating sources of potential competition for
patients, as is evidenced by the restrictions on either party's providing future
outpatient services outside the Surgery Center, and by Redlands Hospital's
agreeing not to expand or promote its existing outpatient surgery facility at
the hospital. In light of the statement in the record that it is typical for
national chains such as SCA to "shadow-price" hospitals in charging for
services at outpatient surgery centers, it seems most likely that one purpose
and effect of the containment and contraction of Redlands Hospital's outpatient surgery activities is to eliminate a competitive constraint for setting
Surgery Center fees (a matter delegated to SCA Management under the
management contract, excluding charges for physicians' services).

* * *

There is no per se proscription against a nonprofit organization's entering
into contracts with private parties to further its charitable purposes on
mutually beneficial terms, so long as the nonprofit organization does not
thereby impermissibly serve private interests. Cf. Plumstead Theatre Socy. v.
Commissioner, 675 F.2d 244 (9th Cir.1982); Broadway Theatre League v.
United States, 293 F.Supp. 346 (W.D.Va.1968). In the instant case, however,
RHS relied on the established relationship between Redlands Hospital and
Redlands physicians to enable RHS and SCA affiliates jointly to gain foothold,
on favorable terms, in the Redlands ambulatory surgery market. Then, by
virtue of their effective control over the Surgery Center, the SCA affiliates
have been enabled to operate it as a profit-making business, with significantly
reduced competitive pressures from Redlands Hospital, and largely unfettered
by charitable objectives that might conflict with purely commercial objectives.
[ ]

D.   Conclusion

Based on all the facts and circumstances, we hold that petitioner has not
established that it operates exclusively for exempt purposes within the meaning of section 501(c)(3). In reaching this holding, we do not view any one
factor as crucial, but we have considered these factors in their totality: The
lack of any express or implied obligation of the for-profit interests involved in
petitioner's sole activity to put charitable objectives ahead of noncharitable
objectives; petitioner's lack of voting control over the General Partnership;
petitioner's lack of other formal or informal control sufficient to ensure
furtherance of charitable purposes; the long-term contract giving SCA Man-

agement control over day-to-day operations as well as a profit-maximizing incentive; and the market advantages and competitive benefits secured by the SCA affiliates as the result of this arrangement with petitioner. Taken in their totality, these factors compel the conclusion that by ceding effective control over its operations to for-profit parties, petitioner impermissibly serves private interests.

IV. PETITIONER'S CLAIM TO EXEMPTION UNDER THE INTEGRAL PART DOCTRINE

Petitioner argues that even if it does not qualify for tax exemption on a "stand alone" basis, it qualifies for exemption under the integral part doctrine.

* * *

Similarly [to Geisinger], in the instant case, petitioner has failed to establish that the Surgery Center's patient population overlaps substantially with that of Redlands Hospital. The record does not reveal what percentage of persons served at the Surgery Center are patients of Redlands Hospital. Clearly, however, the Surgery Center was performing ambulatory surgery on a for-profit basis for its own patients before petitioner was ever involved and presumably continued to do so afterward.

Even if we were to assume, arguendo, that the patient populations of the Surgery Center and Redlands Hospital overlap substantially, this circumstance would not suffice to confer exemption on petitioner under the integral part doctrine. In all the precedents cited above in which courts have applied the integral part doctrine to recognize a derivative exemption, the organization has been under the supervision or control of the exempt affiliate (or a group of exempt affiliates with common exempt purposes) or otherwise expressly limited in its purposes to advancing the interests of the affiliated exempt entity or entities, and serving no private interest* * *

By contrast, as previously discussed, petitioner's sole activity (the Surgery Center) is effectively controlled by for-profit parties. The operations of the Surgery Center plainly are not dedicated to advancing the interests of petitioner's exempt affiliates other than as those interests might happen to coincide with the commercial interests of petitioner's for-profit partners. Moreover, as previously discussed, petitioner impermissibly serves private interests. Petitioner's activity is not so substantially and closely related to the exempt purposes of its affiliates that these private interests may be disregarded. To reflect the foregoing,

Decision will be entered for respondent.

Notes and Questions

1. In a per curiam decision, the Ninth Circuit denied review of the Tax Court's decision. Redlands Surgical Services v. Commissioner, 242 F.3d 904 (2001). The succinct verdict of the commentators after Revenue Ruling 98–15 and the Tax Court's decision in Redlands is that "control is king." Why should that be so? Can you make an argument based on the language and history of the tax code that control should not be the ultimate touchstone for exemption? Can you imagine a compelling set of circumstances in which exemption is warranted even

though the exempt organization lacked control over a partnership with a for-profit entity?

2. What distinguishes the standard that can be gleaned from Rev. Ruling 98–15 and Redlands? Did the IRS win a complete victory or is the standard somewhat looser than it would have liked? See David M. Flynn, Tax Court's Decision in Redlands Provides Limited Endorsement for IRS Position on Joint Ventures, 91 J. Tax'n 241 (1999). How would you characterize the Tax Court's treatment of the "integral part" test? What kind of structural relationships and usage statistics would satisfy the Tax Court in the future? How would you advise a tax-exempt organization to structure an "ancillary joint venture," i.e. one which involves the exempt organization contributing assets to a venture with a for profit firm to provide services and revenue needed to serve its patients? Note that the issues of private inurement and private benefit discussed by the Tax Court in Redlands are analyzed in the next section of this chapter.

E.   RELATIONSHIPS BETWEEN PHYSICIANS AND TAX–EXEMPT HEALTH CARE ORGANIZATIONS

As you have seen in the previous sections, hospitals may structure the acquisition of a particular resource as a joint venture with physicians to ensure the efficient use of the resource and to cement their relationships with the physicians on other fronts. Or, an integrated delivery system may buy physician practices (as described in the Friendly Hills exemption letter). Less fully integrated systems, including stand-alone hospitals, commonly purchase physician practices. Or, hospitals and other health care entities may need to recruit a physician to establish a private practice in their geographic area; and although this physician may not be an employee of the hospital, there is likely to be some form of financial support provided to entice the doctor to relocate or open a practice.

Each of these relationships between physicians and tax-exempt organizations raises issues for the tax-exempt provider. Several of these have been explored in the earlier sections of this chapter. As described earlier, the exempt organization will be concerned with complying with IRS limitations on control in joint ventures; standards for unrelated trade or business income; and the achievement and protection of its charitable purposes.

In addition, the exempt organization must comply with two other major legal constraints on relationships between non-exempt (which includes physicians) and tax-exempt health care organizations. These are the proscriptions against private benefit and against private inurement. Private benefit and private inurement apply in relationships between the tax-exempt entity and any non-exempt entity or individual. However, as the following sections illustrate, the issues for health care providers have arisen most pointedly in the business relationships between doctors and tax-exempt hospitals.

1.   *Joint Ventures with Physicians*

GENERAL COUNSEL MEMORANDUM
39862 (Dec. 2, 1991).

[The Service reviews a physician-hospital agreement in which the hospital sold its future net income from certain departments to entities owned by physicians who admitted and treated patients at the hospital. Other excerpts are included in the previous section on Joint Ventures.]

I. SALE OF THE REVENUE STREAM FROM A HOSPITAL ACTIVITY ALLOWS
NET PROFITS TO INURE TO THE BENEFIT OF PHYSICIAN-INVESTORS

* * *

[The Service's] position [that physician members of the hospital's medical staff have a close working relationship with and a private interest in the exempt hospital and so are subject to the prohibition against inurement] clearly fits the facts in the present cases. While most physicians on the medical staffs of the subject hospitals presumably are not employees and do not provide any compensable services directly to the hospitals, they do have a close professional working relationship with the hospitals. The physicians have applied for and been granted privileges to admit and treat their private patients at the hospital. They are bound by the medical staff bylaws, which may be viewed as a constructive contract between them and the hospital. Individually, and as a group, they largely control the flow of patients to and from the hospital and patients' utilization of hospital services while there. Some may serve other roles at the hospital, such as that of part-time employee, department head, Board member, etc. Moreover, once the arrangements at issue commenced, each physician-investor became a joint venture partner of the hospital or an affiliate.

Even though medical staff physicians are subject to the inurement proscription, that does not mean there can be no economic dealings between them and the hospitals. The inurement proscription does not prevent the payment of reasonable compensation for goods or services. It is aimed at preventing dividend-like distributions of charitable assets or expenditures to benefit a private interest. This Office has stated "inurement is likely to arise where the financial benefit represents a transfer of the organization's financial resources to an individual solely by virtue of the individual's relationship with the organization, and without regard to the accomplishment of exempt purposes." ... GCM 38459, EE–68–79 (July 31, 1980).

* * *

Whether admitted or not, we believe the hospitals engaged in these ventures largely as a means to retain and reward members of their medical staffs; to attract their admissions and referrals; and to pre-empt the physicians from investing in or creating a competing provider.... Giving (or selling) medical staff physicians a proprietary interest in the net profits of a hospital under these circumstances creates a result that is indistinguishable from paying dividends on stock. Profit distributions are made to persons having a personal and private interest in the activities of the organization and are made out of the net earnings of the organization. Thus, the arrangements confer a benefit which violates the inurement proscription of section 501(c)(3).

* * *

II. SALE OF THE REVENUE STREAM FROM A HOSPITAL ACTIVITY
BENEFITS PRIVATE INTERESTS MORE THAN INCIDENTALLY

Another key principle in the law of tax exempt organizations is that an entity is not organized and operated exclusively for exempt purposes unless it serves a public rather than a private interest. Thus, in order to be exempt, an organization must establish that it is not organized or operated for the benefit of private interests such as designated individuals, the creator or his family, shareholders of the organization, or persons controlled, directly or indirectly, by such private interests. Treas. Reg. section 1.501(c)(3)–1(d)(1). However, this private benefit prohibition applies to all kinds of persons and groups, not just to those "insiders" subject to the more strict inurement proscription.

* * *

In our view, some private benefit is present in all typical hospital-physician relationships. Physicians generally use hospital facilities at no cost to themselves to provide services to private patients for which they earn a fee. The private benefit accruing to the physicians generally can be considered incidental to the overwhelming public benefit resulting from having the combined resources of the hospital and its professional staff available to serve the public. Though the private benefit is compounded in the case of certain specialists, such as heart transplant surgeons, who depend heavily on highly specialized hospital facilities, that fact alone will not make the private benefit more than incidental.

In contrast, the private benefits conferred on the physician-investors by the instant revenue stream joint ventures are direct and substantial, not incidental. If for any reason these benefits should be found not to constitute inurement, they nonetheless exceed the bounds of prohibited private benefit. Whether viewed as giving the physicians a substantial share in the profits of the hospital or simply as allowing them an extremely profitable investment, the arrangements confer a significant benefit on them. Against this, we must balance the public benefit achieved by the hospitals in entering into the arrangements. The public benefit expected to result from these transactions— enhanced hospital financial health or greater efficiency achieved through improved utilization of their facilities—bears only the most tenuous relationship to the hospitals' charitable purposes of promoting the health of their communities. Obtaining referrals or avoiding new competition may improve the competitive position of an individual hospital, but that is not necessarily the same as benefitting its community.

* * *

2. *Physician Recruitment*

REVENUE RULING 97–21

1997–18 I.R.B. 8.

* * *

Situation 1

Hospital A is located in County V, a rural area, and is the only hospital within a 100 mile radius. County V has been designated by the U.S. Public Health Service as a Health Professional Shortage Area for primary medical care professionals (a category that includes obstetricians and gynecologists). Physician M recently completed an ob/gyn residency and is not on Hospital A's medical staff. Hospital A recruits Physician M to establish and maintain a full-time private ob/gyn practice in its service area and become a member of its medical staff. Hospital A provides Physician M a recruitment incentive package pursuant to a written agreement negotiated at arm's-length. The agreement is in accordance with guidelines for physician recruitment that Hospital A's Board of Directors establishes, monitors, and reviews regularly to ensure that recruiting practices are consistent with Hospital A's exempt purposes. The agreement was approved by the committee appointed by Hospital A's Board of Directors to approve contracts with hospital medical staff. Hospital A does not provide any recruiting incentives to Physician M other than those set forth in the written agreement.

In accordance with the agreement, Hospital A pays Physician M a signing bonus, Physician M's professional liability insurance premium for a limited period, provides office space in a building owned by Hospital A for a limited number of years at a below market rent (after which the rental will be at fair market value), and guarantees Physician M's mortgage on a residence in County V. Hospital A also lends Physician M practice start-up financial assistance pursuant to an agreement that is properly documented and bears reasonable terms.

Situation 2

Hospital B is located in an economically depressed inner-city area of City W. Hospital B has conducted a community needs assessment that indicates both a shortage of pediatricians in Hospital B's service area and difficulties Medicaid patients are having obtaining pediatric services. Physician N is a pediatrician currently practicing outside of Hospital B's service area and is not on Hospital B's medical staff. Hospital B recruits Physician N to relocate to City W, establish and maintain a full-time pediatric practice in Hospital B's service area, become a member of Hospital B's medical staff, and treat a reasonable number of Medicaid patients. Hospital B offers Physician N a recruitment incentive package pursuant to a written agreement negotiated at arm's-length and approved by Hospital B's Board of Directors. Hospital B does not provide any recruiting incentives to Physician N other than those set forth in the written agreement.

Under the agreement, Hospital B reimburses Physician N for moving expenses as defined in § 217(b), reimburses Physician N for professional liability "tail" coverage for Physician N's former practice, and guarantees Physician N's private practice income for a limited number of years. The private practice income guarantee, which is properly documented, provides that Hospital B will make up the difference to the extent Physician N practices full-time in its service area and the private practice does not generate a certain level of net income (after reasonable expenses of the practice). The amount guaranteed falls within the range reflected in regional or national surveys regarding income earned by physicians in the same specialty.

Situation 3

Hospital C is located in an economically depressed inner city area of City X. Hospital C has conducted a community needs assessment that indicates indigent patients are having difficulty getting access to care because of a shortage of obstetricians in Hospital C's service area willing to treat Medicaid and charity care patients. Hospital C recruits Physician O, an obstetrician who is currently a member of Hospital C's medical staff, to provide these services and enters into a written agreement with Physician O. The agreement is in accordance with guidelines for physician recruitment that Hospital C's Board of Directors establishes, monitors, and reviews regularly to ensure that recruiting practices are consistent with Hospital C's exempt purpose. The agreement was approved by the officer designated by Hospital C's Board of Directors to enter into contracts with hospital medical staff. Hospital C does not provide any recruiting incentives to Physician O other than those set forth in the written agreement. Pursuant to the agreement, Hospital C agrees to reimburse Physician O for the cost of one year's professional liability insurance in return for an agreement by Physician O to treat a reasonable number of Medicaid and charity care patients for that year.

Situation 4

Hospital D is located in City Y, a medium to large size metropolitan area. Hospital D requires a minimum of four diagnostic radiologists to ensure adequate coverage and a high quality of care for its radiology department. Two of the four diagnostic radiologists currently providing coverage for Hospital D are relocating to other areas. Hospital D initiates a search for diagnostic radiologists and determines that one of the two most qualified candidates is Physician P.

Physician P currently is practicing in City Y as a member of the medical staff of Hospital E (which is also located in City Y). As a diagnostic radiologist, Physician P provides services for patients receiving care at Hospital E, but does not refer patients to Hospital E or any other hospital in City Y. Physician P is not on Hospital D's medical staff. Hospital D recruits Physician P to join its medical staff and to provide coverage for its radiology department. Hospital D offers Physician P a recruitment incentive package pursuant to a written agreement, negotiated at arm's-length and approved by Hospital D's Board of Directors. Hospital D does not provide any recruiting incentives to Physician P other than those set forth in the written agreement.

Pursuant to the agreement, Hospital D guarantees Physician P's private practice income for the first few years that Physician P is a member of its medical staff and provides coverage for its radiology department. The private practice income guarantee, which is properly documented, provides that Hospital D will make up the difference to Physician P to the extent the private practice does not generate a certain level of net income (after reasonable expenses of the practice). The net income amount guaranteed falls within the range reflected in regional or national surveys regarding income earned by physicians in the same specialty.

3. Acquisition of Physician Practices by Exempt Organizations

TECHNICAL ADVICE MEMORANDUM
9451001
(Dec. 23, 1994).

From June 6, 1986 through December 11, 1987, M [the hospital] purchased seven practices from private physician groups at a total cost of approximately $17.4 million. M entered into service agreements with the physician(s) who previously owned the practices.

On June 6, 1986, M entered into a Purchase and Sale Agreement (the "Sale Agreement") with a professional association owned, directly or indirectly, by five physicians (the "Physicians") regarding the purchase of a particular medical practice (the "Practice"). Under the terms of the Sale Agreement, M agreed to purchase all patient records, including but not limited to, patient medical charts, accompanying x-rays, and patient lists; goodwill; and the going concern value of the Practice for the sum of $6 million.

M retained the services of an appraiser (the "Appraiser") to assess the value of the Practice. The appraiser estimated the fair market value of the Practice to be $6,800,000.

Documents accompanying the Sale Agreement indicate that the total tangible assets of the Seller were $170,093 for the period ended April 30, 1986. The Practice incurred losses in its 1984 and 1985 tax years.

An industry economist employed by the Internal Revenue Service appraised the value of the Practice and found it to be worth $2 million at the time of the sale. Reviewing the appraisal commissioned by M, the economist states that the Appraiser's selection of the Capitalized Income Method to value the Practice is appropriate, but the application of that method to the Practice is seriously flawed by the use of an incorrect capitalization rate and the elimination of normal expenses inappropriately determined by the Appraiser to be discretionary.

In response to our letter dated May 27, 1993, regarding the price paid for the Practice, B [an officer of M] states that with regard to the purchase of the Practice, the Appraiser may have been "too optimistic."

In a letter to the Service dated August 31, 1993, B discusses the purchase of the Practice. He states that while there may be a difference of opinion as to the correct application of valuation methodology, "there is no evidence of intentional overpayment . . . ".

The minutes of the December 1, 1987, meeting of M's board of trustees, establish that A [an officer of M] states that there was a conscious overpayment to the Physicians for the Practice in order to gain their patients and credibility. [In addition to the purchase price, the physician-sellers received a salary as employees of M. The salary amounted, on average, to more than a 50% increase over their previous income from the practice.]

* * *

On October 19, 1992, M sold the Medical Assets—the medical practices it purchased during 1986 and 1987 as well as its interest in six other health care centers—to O in exchange for a promissory note in the amount of $4.5 million. Thirteen physicians ("Purchasing Physicians") who were employed by M prior to the sale of the Medical Assets hold, indirectly, 70% of the ownership interest in O. [In 1994, the value of the promissory note was reduced in the book value of the hospital due to its "doubtful collectibility."]

[M's exemption was revoked for violation of inurement.]

Notes and Questions

1. The core of the analysis of private benefit and private inurement is the relationship between what the exempt organization pays and the value, to its

achievement of its exempt purposes, of what it receives. Might not-for-profit entities behave differently than for-profits in acquiring physician practices, recruiting physicians or in physician compensation and investment? Who might be concerned with the payments made to and value received from physicians by for-profit hospitals or investor-owned physician management companies? In the Service's CPE Technical Instruction Program Textbook, the authors explain that arms-length negotiation would ordinarily produce a purchase price that equates to fair market value in other transactions, but that in the purchase of practices by hospitals from physicians, especially those currently on the staff of the hospital, this assumption may not be valid. Charles F. Kaiser and Amy Henchey, Valuation of Medical Practices, CPE Technical Instruction Program Textbook, 95 Tax Notes Today 168–69 (Aug. 28, 1995). Why might this be so? How do the prohibitions on private inurement and private benefit respond to this problem? Is the IRS placing § 501(c)(3) hospitals at a significant disadvantage in competing with for-profits for physicians? The fact that the standards for private inurement were not altogether clean and that a finding of inurement led automatically to revocation of exempt status promoted Congress to adopt the Intermediate Sanctions legislation described in the note at the end of this section.

2. What is the difference between private inurement and private benefit? What are the goals of the proscriptions against private inurement and private benefit? Are you persuaded that a tax-exempt hospital's relationships with physicians require more careful scrutiny than with others? Compare the prohibition on private inurement to the new legislative approach to insider transactions contained in the discussion of Intermediate Sanctions on Excess Benefits in the next section of this chapter. Who is considered an insider for inurement purposes? Might a prominent donor and fundraiser for a tax exempt hospital qualify even if she holds no formal office with the hospital? An influential consultant under contract to give management advice? For Judge Posner's ascerbic rejection of the IRS's attempt to reach the activities of a professional fundraiser for a charity, see United Cancer Council v. Commissioner, 165 F.3d 1173 (7th Cir.1999).

3. The IRS has not issued Revenue Rulings in the area of tax-exempt health care very frequently. The Service's action in issuing the proposed Revenue Ruling on physician recruitment responded to repeated calls for more guidance once there were indications of serious enforcement intentions on the part of the Service. For example, much reliance was put on the highly proscriptive terms of a closing agreement between the IRS and a hospital. See Closing Agreement with Hermann Hospital (September 16, 1994), reprinted in 94 Tax Notes Today 203 (Oct. 17, 1994). See Gerald M. Griffith, IRS Guidance on Physician Recruitment: From the Seeds of Herman Hospital to the Proposed and Final Rulings and Beyond, 30 J. Health & Hosp. L., 75 (1997); Carolyn D. Wright, EO Experts Give Physician Recruitment Ruling High Marks, 97 Tax Notes Today 78–3 (Apr. 23, 1998).

4. The requirement that the § 501(c)(3) organization pay no more than fair market value for the physician practice or for physician compensation or for services received in a joint venture is a clear and understandable goal. It is hard to monitor, however, in the absence of functioning markets. The valuation of physician practices in particular presents substantial problems. Appraisal of the future income potential of the practice itself is particularly difficult and subject to differences among professional appraisers. Furthermore, although the IRS wants to assure that the § 501(c)(3) organization pays for no more than it receives in value, the Medicare and Medicaid programs prohibit payment for the value of future referrals by the doctors to the hospital. Thus, the parties might lean toward inflating the value of certain intangibles or certain allowable items (such as copy

expenses for patient records) to bear the value of the referrals to the hospital. Does GCM 39862 indicate that the Service does not consider future referrals a value received? What issues arise when a system decides to divest itself of unprofitable physician practices and decides to sell the practices back to the physicians at a much lower price than it originally paid?

5.   Many other issues raised in the purchase of physician practices, physician recruitment and hospital-physician joint ventures are covered elsewhere in this text. For example, issues of self-referral and fraud and abuse are discussed in Chapter 14; antitrust concerns are covered in Chapter 15; and physician contracts are discussed in Chapter 12.

Note on Intermediate Sanctions for Excess Benefit Transactions

Responding to needs for an alternative to the sanction of revocation and for greater clarity in the substantive standards applicable to private inurement transactions, Congress adopted the Taxpayer Bill of Rights II (26 U.S.C.A. § 4958) in 1996. The legislation imposes "intermediate sanctions," consisting of an excise tax, on persons engaged in "excess benefit transactions." The new law will undoubtedly become an important part of the tax-exempt organization landscape, as the Internal Revenue Service has indicated that it will shift enforcement resources to vigorously implement its prohibitions. The Department of the Treasury has issued proposed regulations which supply guidance concerning the numerous new concepts contained in § 4958 63 Fed. Reg. 41,486 (1998). Following receipt of numerous comments, it released temporary regulations on January 10, 2001, 66 Fed. Reg. 2144 (Jan. 10, 2001).

Applicability and Scope. The sanctions apply with respect to both 501(c)(3) public charities and 501(c)(4) social welfare organizations. Congress intended § 4958 to be the exclusive sanction unless the conduct arises to such an extreme level (evidenced by the size and scope of the excess benefit and the organization's efforts to prevent the conduct) that the tax exempt organization can no longer be regarded as "charitable" and hence revocation is the appropriate sanction. See 63 Fed. Reg. 41486 (1998)(listing factors to be considered in determining whether revocation of exemption is appropriate).

Excess Benefit Transactions. The statute defines an "excess benefit transaction" as any transaction in which an economic benefit is provided by a tax exempt organization directly or indirectly to or for the use of a "disqualified person" where the value of the economic benefit provided by the organization exceeds the value of the consideration (including the performance of services) received for providing the benefit. 26 U.S.C.A. § 4958(c)(1). Prohibited transactions include those in which the disqualified person engages in a non-fair market transaction, such as a bargain sale or loan; unreasonable compensation arrangements; and proscribed revenue sharing arrangements (payments based on the revenue of the exempt organization that violate the inurement provisions of current law).

Disqualified Persons. "Disqualified persons" include "any person who was, at any time during the 5–year period ending on the date of such transaction, in a position to exercise substantial influence over the affairs of the organization, a member of the family of [such] an individual and, a 35–percent controlled entity [an entity in which such persons own more than 35% of the combined voting power if a corporation or of the profits interest if a partnership or of the beneficial interest of a trust or estate]."

Below are two examples in the proposed regulations that provide guidance on who would and who would not be considered a "disqualified person" under the statute.

[1.]   A, an applicable tax-exempt organization for purposes of section 4958, owns and operates one acute care hospital. B is a for-profit corporation that owns and operates a number of hospitals. A and B form C, a limited liability company. In exchange for proportional ownership interests, A contributes its hospital, and B contributes other financial assets, to C. All of A's assets then consist of its membership interest in C. A continues to be operated for exempt purposes based almost exclusively on the activities it conducts through C. C enters into a management agreement with a management company, M, to provide day-to-day management services to C. M is generally subject to supervision by C's board, but M is given broad discretion to manage C's day-to-day operation. Under these facts and circumstances, M is in a position to exercise substantial influence over the affairs of A because it has day to day control over the hospital operated by C, A's ownership interest in C is its primary asset, and C's activities form the basis for A's continued exemption as an organization described in section 501(c)(3). Therefore, M is a disqualified person with respect to any transaction involving A, including any transaction that A conducts through C, that provides economic benefits to M directly or indirectly.

[2.]   X is a radiologist employed by U, a large acute-care hospital that is an applicable tax-exempt organization for purposes of section 4958. X has no managerial authority over any part of U or its operations. X gives instructions to staff with respect to the radiology work X conducts, but X does not serve as supervisor to other U employees. X's total compensation package includes nontaxable retirement and welfare benefits and a specified amount of salary. X's compensation is greater than the amount of compensation referenced for a highly compensated employee ... in the year benefits are provided. X is not related to any other disqualified person of U. X does not serve on U's governing body or as an officer of U. Although U participates in a provider-sponsored organization ... X does not have a material financial interest in that organization. Whether X is a disqualified person is determined by all relevant facts and circumstances. X did not found U, and although X makes a modest annual financial contribution to U, the amount of the contribution does not make X a substantial contributor.... X does not receive compensation based on revenues derived from activities of U that X controls, and has no authority to control or determine a significant portion of U's capital expenditures, operating budget, or compensation for employees. Under these facts and circumstances, X does not have substantial influence over the affairs of U, and therefore X is not a disqualified person with respect to any transaction involving U that provides economic benefits to X directly or indirectly.

63 Fed. Reg. 41,486, 41,499 (1998).

Organization managers. The act also imposes excise taxes on "organization managers," whose participation in the transaction was knowing, willful and not excepted due to reasonable cause. The regulations define organization managers to include directors, trustees or officers and administrators with delegated or regularly exercised administrative powers, but not independent contractors such as lawyers and accountants.

Rebuttable Presumption of Reasonableness. A key element of the intermediate sanctions statutory scheme is a rebuttable presumption of reasonableness applicable to compensation arrangements with a disqualified person where certain procedural steps are followed. To qualify for the presumption, the terms of the transaction must be approved by a board of directors or committee thereof composed entirely of individuals who have no conflicts of interest with respect to the transaction and who have obtained and relied upon appropriate comparability data prior to making their determination and have adequately documented the basis for the determination. The presumption may be rebutted by information showing that the compensation was not reasonable or the transfer was not at fair market value.

Penalties. Sanctions, in the form of an initial tax of 25 per cent of the excess benefit, are imposed on individuals who benefited from the transaction; the excess benefit is calculated as the amount by which a transaction differs from fair market value. Disqualified persons are subject to an additional tax of 200 per cent of the excess benefit unless the transaction is "corrected" promptly (generally meaning that the disqualified person must undo the transaction and compensate the exempt organization for any losses caused by the transaction). While no sanctions are imposed on the exempt organization, organizational managers who knowingly and wilfully participate are subject to a 10 per cent tax unless their participation is due to reasonable cause. In one of the first uses of § 4958, The IRS imposed sanctions against the trustees of an estate in Hawaii who paid themselves exorbitant salaries for its management. See Carolyn D. Wright, IRS Assesses Intermediate Sanctions Against Bishop Estate Incumbent Trustees, 2001 Tax Notes Today 405 (January 5, 2001).

Safe Harbor. The temporary regulations establish a reliance-on-counsel safe harbor, that provide that an organization manager's participation in an excess benefit transaction will ordinarily not be deemed "knowing" if the manager can demonstrate several facts. First, there must be full disclosure of the factual situation to an appropriate professional. Appropriate professionals include legal counsel, certified public accountants or accounting firms with relevant expertise, and qualified independent valuation experts. The manager must further show that he or she relied upon on a reasoned written opinion of that professional regarding the elements of the transaction within the professional's expertise.

Problem: St. Andrew's Medical Center, Part Two

The Board of tax-exempt St. Andrew's voted against selling the hospital to for-profit Health Care Enterprises. Instead, it has chosen to follow an aggressive strategic plan to achieve the following objectives:

To develop closer working relationships with compatible health care institutions in our region in order to create a comprehensive system of health care delivery that will allow St. Andrew's to better respond to the needs of the purchasers of health care and the patients themselves;

To establish more effective collaborative and mutually beneficial relationships with the physicians who currently hold privileges at St. Andrew's and to develop new alliances with physicians who do not currently admit patients to St. Andrew's;

To develop new, more efficient and more accessible forms of delivery for our services.

St. Andrew's has served primarily an urban and suburban population, but its home city is actually located in a rural state. There is a very small for-profit, free-standing hospital called Parkdale Hospital, located about 50 miles southwest of St. Andrew's. It was originally established by the lead mining company located in that town, but is now owned by a group of three physicians. The physicians are finding the hospital management business terribly trying these days as they do not have the capital that is needed to renovate and improve Parkdale; and St. Anthony's sees Parkdale as a very low-cost facility that has a strong patient census for its size and that, most importantly, can "feed" St. Andrew's patients who need a higher level of care. St. Andrew's has proposed a number of arrangements that might serve the interests of both Parkdale and St. Andrew's. St. Andrew's has asked you to advise them on the tax implications in light of St. Andrew's § 501(c)(3) status. If you see problems in the transactions, describe how you would remedy them to allow the transaction to go forward and achieve its essential purposes.

1. St. Andrew's has offered Parkdale a Management Services Agreement, in which St. Andrew's agrees to manage and administer Parkdale, providing it with all administrative services, including personnel management, financial planning, quality assurance and so on. The agreement would include a base price of approximately $150,000 per year plus 1% of Parkdale's net revenues. In coming to the price, St. Andrew's did consider its hope that the relationship with Parkdale will develop over time.

2. Alternatively, St. Andrew's has proposed that Parkdale and St. Andrew's establish a new entity called Rural Healthcare Partners. Partners would be structured as a limited partnership, with Parkdale and St. Andrew's as general partners and the three physician-owners of Parkdale as limited partners. St. Andrew's will provide 80% of the capital for the entity. Parkdale and St. Andrew's will share equally in decisionmaking through a management committee. Profits will be distributed in proportion to the contribution to capital, although it is understood that any excess of revenue over expenses will be re-invested in Partners during its first years. Much of it will be passed through to Parkdale for essential improvements. It is not clear exactly what Partners will do eventually. It is being established now as a vehicle for the development of future joint ventures between St. Andrew's and Parkdale. It will begin by doing physician recruitment for Parkdale, and perhaps later for rural hospitals outside of the area, and providing public relations for the Parkdale–St. Andrew's affiliation.

3. Dr. Simpson is a member of St. Andrew's board with strong professional and personal contacts in the medical community in and around Parksdale Hospital. He was instrumental in originating the contacts which gave rise to the discussions resulting in the preceding proposals. St. Andrew plans to reward Dr. Simpson with a one year consulting contract for a sum of $100,000 for his past and future liaison efforts with Parksdale.

4. Recently, twenty obstetricians/gynecologists in the suburban area near St. Andrew's have formed an organization through which they operate as an entity even though they still practice in their own offices. Although these doctors currently admit patients both to St. Andrew's and to the other private hospital in town, they have been approached with an offer by the other hospital, Memorial, which is owned by a for-profit organization. Memorial Hospital has offered the entity below-market-value space in the doctor's office building attached to the hospital; free administrative services in the management of their practices including free use of the hospital's management information system; and the opportunity to become limited partners in the "Birthing Center," a special area which will be developed on the OB floor at the hospital and which will be the subject of an intense media campaign. The doctors will receive a proportionate share of the net revenue of the Center. In exchange, the doctors would agree to take any patient who wishes to receive OB/GYN services at Memorial as long as they have the

requisite skills to care for the patient and as long as the patient has the ability to pay. Memorial has several contracts with health maintenance organizations for hospital services to their enrollees, and this arrangement between the OBs and Memorial would require the physicians to contract with and take patients covered by those HMOs. The physicians will not become employees of the HMO. A large number of the physicians' patients are located near the suburban Memorial Hospital, and fewer are located in the more urban area in which St. Andrew's is located, so the attraction to Memorial is strong despite the doctors' distrust of its for-profit structure.

Although obstetrics is not a very "profitable" service for St. Andrew's, OB patients are highly desirable to a hospital because they represent a potential stream of patients from the family. St. Andrew's wants to maintain active OB and neonatal services and requires a minimum number of patients to do so. There are a few OBs who are not members of this new entity, but they tend to be older and tend to practice in less desirable geographic areas, though no one spot in town is more than twenty minutes away from any other spot.

St. Andrew's plans to match Memorial's offer. In addition, it intends to further strengthen its ties to Parkdale by offering the physicians a generous income guarantee if they will establish an office near Parkdale where there is only one OB practicing part time. St. Andrew's will also require that the physicians agree to provide back-up services and consultation for high-risk pregnancies referred to it by Parkdale. The doctors will also be paid for any services they actually provide under this arrangement.

Chapter 14

FRAUD AND ABUSE

Health care providers are subject to a large body of law governing their financial arrangements with each other and with payors. These state and federal laws cover many practices that amount to fraud, bribery or stealing. In addition, they prohibit many contractual relationships, investments, and marketing and recruitment practices that are perfectly legal in other businesses. As will be seen, these laws are well-intentioned: they seek to rectify a number of serious flaws in the health care financing system, save the government money, and prevent conflicts of interest that taint the physician-patient relationship. Indeed, they have been used to bring to justice a large number of providers, including some major corporate entities, that have engaged in systematic fraud. Unfortunately, the particular statutes (and the regulations, cases and interpretative rulings and guidelines they have spawned) are also bewilderingly complicated and have generated confusion and cynicism in the health care industry. Further, some aspects of these laws may prove anachronistic in the new competitive environment. Nevertheless, they continue to have a profound impact on the health care industry and generate an enormous amount of work for health care lawyers designing organizational structures that must comply with their strictures.

I. FALSE CLAIMS

According to some estimates, Medicare and Medicaid fraud and abuse costs federal and state governments tens of billions of dollars per year. See Jerry L. Mashaw and Theodore R. Marmor, Conceptualizing, Estimating, and Reforming Fraud, Waste, and Abuse in Healthcare Spending, 11 Yale J. on Reg. 455 (1994) (citing studies estimating that fraud and abuse adds 10% to total health care spending). The Office of Inspector General of the Department of Health and Human Services estimated that in 1999 Medicare paid $13.5 billion in improper payments, a sum that amounts to almost eight per cent of its fee-for-service reimbursement. Department of Health and Human Services, Office of Inspector General, Improper Fiscal Year 1999 Medicare Fee-for-Service Payments. Much of this problem undoubtedly can be traced to the structure and complexities of Medicare and Medicaid payment systems which give incentives and opportunities to engage in fraud or to "game" the system to maximize reimbursement. See Timothy Stoltzfus Jost & Sharon

Davies, Medicare and Medicaid Fraud and Abuse § 1–5 (2000). The term "fraud and abuse" is a broad one, covering a large number of activities ranging from negligent or careless practices that result in overbilling, to "self-referral arrangements" that are seen as improperly enriching providers and encouraging overutilization, to outright fraudulent schemes to bill for services never rendered. Indeed, the "fraud" aspects of "fraud and abuse" prosecutions have involved overtly criminal schemes, sometimes with elements of racketeering and the involvement of organized crime. This section deals with the law of false claims, which is designed to protect the government from paying for goods or services that have not been provided or were not provided in accordance with government regulations. Specific problems addressed by the law include: provider charges or claims for unreasonable costs, services not rendered, services provided by unlicensed or unapproved personnel, excessive or unnecessary care, and services not in compliance with Medicare and Medicaid regulations, cost reports or other requirements. See Alice G. Gosfield, Unintentional Part B False Claims: Pitfalls for the Unwary, in 1993 Health Law Handbook 205, 212–16 (Alice G. Gosfield, ed., 1993).

There are a number of civil and criminal statutes that deal with false claims. In addition to the Medicare and Medicaid fraud and abuse law (discussed in the next section), the following criminal penalties may attach to false claims: federal and state false claim statutes, which make it a felony to knowingly and willfully make or cause to be made a false claim or statement under the Medicare program or a state health program including Medicaid, 42 U.S.C.A. § 1320a–7b(a); the mail fraud statute, 18 U.S.C.A. § 1341; laws prohibiting persons from knowingly making or presenting false or fraudulent claims to the United States government, 18 U.S.C.A. § 287; statutes prohibiting the making of false or fraudulent statements or representations, 18 U.S.C.A. § 1001; and wire fraud, 18 U.S.C.A. § 1343. Secondary offenses such as aiding and abetting, 18 U.S.C.A. § 2, conspiracy, 18 U.S.C.A. § 371, and theft of government property, 18 U.S.C.A. § 1961–68 are also sometimes included in government charges. In addition, the submission of multiple false claims by an "enterprise" engaged in interstate commerce may constitute a violation of the Racketeer Influenced and Corrupt Organizations statute, 18 U.S.C.A. § 1961. Among the most important civil claims statutes are the Civil False Claims Act, 31 U.S.C.A. §§ 3729–33, which permits the federal government to recover from individuals who knowingly submit false claims civil penalties of $5,500 to $11,000 per claim plus three times the amount of damages sustained by the federal government, 31 U.S.C.A. § 3729, and private "qui tam" actions which enable private individuals to bring actions to enforce the False Claims Act, 31 U.S.C.A. § 3730(b).

A. GOVERNMENTAL ENFORCEMENT

UNITED STATES v. KRIZEK

United States District Court, District of Columbia, 1994.
859 F.Supp. 5.

Sporkin, District Judge.

Memorandum Opinion and Order

On January 11, 1993, the United States filed this civil suit against George O. Krizek, M.D. and Blanka H. Krizek under the False Claims Act, 31

U.S.C.A. §§ 3729–3731, and at common law. The government brought the action against the Krizeks alleging false billing for Medicare and Medicaid patients. The five counts include claims for (1) "Knowingly Presenting a False or Fraudulent Claim", 31 U.S.C.A. § 3729(a)(1); (2) "Knowingly Presenting a False or Fraudulent Record", 31 U.S.C.A. § 3729(a)(2); (3) "Conspiracy to Defraud the Government"; (4) "Payment under Mistake of Fact"; and (5) "Unjust Enrichment". In its claim for relief, the government asks for triple the alleged actual damages of $245,392 and civil penalties of $10,000 for each of the 8,002 allegedly false reimbursement claims pursuant to 31 U.S.C.A. § 3729.

The government alleges two types of misconduct related to the submission of bills to Medicare and Medicaid. The first category of misconduct relates to the use of billing codes found in the American Medical Association's "Current Procedural Terminology" ("CPT"), a manual that lists terms and codes for reporting procedures performed by physicians. The government alleges that Dr. Krizek "up-coded" the bills for a large percentage of his patients by submitting bills coded for a service with a higher level of reimbursement than that which Dr. Krizek provided. As a second type of misconduct, the government alleges Dr. Krizek "performed services that should not have been performed at all in that they were not medically necessary." []

Given the large number of claims, and the acknowledged difficulty of determining the "medical necessity" of 8,002 reimbursement claims, it was decided that this case should initially be tried on the basis of seven patients and two hundred claims that the government believed to be representative of Dr. Krizek's improper coding and treatment practices. [] It was agreed by the parties that a determination of liability on Dr. Krizek's coding practices would be equally applicable to all 8,002 claims in the complaint. A three week bench trial ensued.

Findings of Fact

Dr. Krizek is a psychiatrist. Dr. Krizek's wife, Blanka Krizek was responsible for overseeing Dr. Krizek's billing operation for a part of the period in question. Dr. Krizek's Washington, D.C. psychiatric practice consists in large part in the treatment of Medicare and Medicaid patients. Much of Doctor Krizek's work involves the provision of psychotherapy and other psychiatric care to patients at the Washington Hospital Center.

Under the Medicare and Medicaid systems, claims for reimbursement are submitted on documents known as Health Care Financing Administration ("HCFA") 1500 Forms. These forms are supposed to contain the patient's identifying information, the provider's Medicaid or Medicare identification number, and a description of the provided procedures for which reimbursement is sought. These procedures are identified by a standard, uniform code number as set out in the American Medical Association's "Current Procedural Terminology" ("CPT") manual, a book that lists the terms and codes for reporting procedures performed by physicians.

* * *

The government in its complaint alleges both improper billing for services provided and the provision of medically unnecessary services. The latter of these two claims will be addressed first.

Medical Necessity

The record discloses that Dr. Krizek is a capable and competent physician. * * * The trial testimony of Dr. Krizek, his colleagues at the Washington Hospital Center, as well as the testimony of a former patient, established that Dr. Krizek was providing valuable medical and psychiatric care during the period covered by the complaint. The testimony was undisputed that Dr. Krizek worked long hours on behalf of his patients, most of whom were elderly and poor.

Many of Dr. Krizek's patients were afflicted with horribly severe psychiatric disorders and often suffered simultaneously from other serious medical conditions.* * *

The government takes issue with Dr. Krizek's method of treatment of his patients, arguing that some patients should have been discharged from the hospital sooner, and that others suffered from conditions which could not be ameliorated through psychotherapy sessions, or that the length of the psychotherapy sessions should have been abbreviated. The government's expert witness's opinions on this subject came from a cold review of Dr. Krizek's notes for each patient. The government witness did not examine or interview any of the patients, or speak with any other doctors or nurses who had actually served these patients to learn whether the course of treatment prescribed by Dr. Krizek exceeded that which was medically necessary.

Dr. Krizek testified credibly and persuasively as to the basis for the course of treatment for each of the representative patients. The medical necessity of treating Dr. Krizek's patients through psychotherapy and hospitalization was confirmed via the testimony of other defense witnesses. The Court credits Dr. Krizek's testimony on this question as well as his interpretation of his own notes regarding the seriousness of each patients' condition and the medical necessity for the procedures and length of hospital stay required. The Court finds that the government was unable to prove that Dr. Krizek rendered services that were medically unnecessary.

Improper Billing

On the question of improper billing or "up-coding", the government contends that for approximately 24 percent of the bills submitted, Dr. Krizek used the CPT Code for a 45–50 minute psychotherapy session (CPT Code 90844) when he should have billed for a 20–30 minute session (CPT Code 90843). The government also contends that for at least 33 percent of his patients, Dr. Krizek billed for a full 45–50 minute psychotherapy session, again by using CPT code 90844, when he should have billed for a "minimal psychotherapy" session (CPT 90862). These two latter procedures are reimbursed at a lower level than 90844, the 45–50 minute psychotherapy session, which the government has referred to as "the Cadillac" of psychiatric reimbursement codes.

The primary thrust of the government's case revolves around the question whether Dr. Krizek's use of the 90844 CPT code was appropriate. For the most part, the government does not allege that Dr. Krizek did not see the patients for whom he submitted bills. Instead, the government posits that the services provided during his visits either did not fall within the accepted definition of "individual medical psychotherapy" *or*, if the services provided *did* fit within this definition, the reimbursable service provided was not as extensive as that which was billed for. In sum, the government claims that whenever Dr. Krizek would see a patient, regardless of whether he simply checked a chart, spoke with nurses, or merely prescribed additional medication, his wife or his employee, a Mrs. Anderson, would, on the vast majority of occasions, submit a bill for CPT code 90844—45–50 minutes of individual psychotherapy.

[Documents sent to providers by Pennsylvania Blue Shield, the Medicare carrier for Dr. Krizek's area, explained the services in the 90800 series of codes as involving "[i]ndividual medical psychotherapy by a physician, with continuing medical diagnostic evaluation, and drug management when indicated, including insight oriented, behavior modifying or supportive psychotherapy" for specified periods of time.]

* * *

The government's witnesses [] testified that as initially conceived, the definition of the CPT codes is designed to incorporate the extra time spent in its level of reimbursement. It was expected by the authors of the codes that for a 45–50 minute 90844 session a doctor would spend additional time away from the patient reviewing or dictating records, speaking with nurses, or prescribing medication. The government's witnesses testified that the reimbursement rate for 90844 took into account the fact that on a 45–50 minute session the doctor would likely spend twenty additional minutes away from the patient. As such, the doctor is limited to billing for time actually spent "face-to-face" with the patient.

Dr. and Mrs. Krizek freely admit that when a 90844 code bill was submitted on the doctor's behalf, it did not always reflect 45–50 minutes of face-to-face psychotherapy with the patient. Instead, the 45–50 minutes billed captured generally the total amount of time spent on the patient's case, including the "face-to-face" psychotherapy session, discussions with medical staff about the patient's treatment/progress, medication management, and other related services. Dr. Krizek referred to this as "bundling" of services, all of which, Dr. and Mrs. Krizek testified, they reasonably believed were reimbursable under the 90844 "individual medical psychotherapy" code.

Defendant's witnesses testified that it was a common and proper practice among psychiatrists nationally, and in the Washington, D.C. area, to "bundle" a variety of services, including prescription management, review of the patient file, consultations with nurses or the patients' relatives into a bill for individual psychotherapy, whether or not these services took place literally in view of the patient. Under the defense theory, if a doctor spent 20 minutes in a session with a patient and ten minutes before that in a different room discussing the patient's symptoms with a nurse, and fifteen minutes afterwards outlining a course of treatment to the medical staff, it would be entirely appropriate, under their reading and interpretation of the CPT, to bill the 45 minutes spent on that patients' care by using CPT code 90844.

The testimony of the defense witnesses on this point was credible and persuasive. * * * The CPT codes which the government insists require face-to-face rendition of services never used the term "face-to-face" in its code description during the time period covered by this litigation. The relevant language describing the code is ambiguous.

The Court finds that the government's position on this issue is not rational and has been applied in an unfair manner to the medical community, which for the most part is made up of honorable and dedicated professionals. One government witness testified that a 15 minute telephone call made to a consulting physician in the patient's presence would be reimbursable, while if the doctor needed to go outside the patient's room to use the telephone—in order to make the *same* telephone call—the time would not be reimbursable. * * *

* * *

The Court will not impose False Claims Act liability based on such a strained interpretation of the CPT codes. The government's theory of liability is plainly unfair and unjustified. Medical doctors should be appropriately reimbursed for services legitimately provided. They should be given clear guidance as to what services are reimbursable. The system should be fair. The system cannot be so arbitrary, so perverse, as to subject a doctor whose annual income during the relevant period averaged between $100,000 and $120,000, to potential liability in excess of 80 million dollars[1] because telephone calls were made in one room rather than another.

The Court finds that Doctor Krizek did not submit false claims when he submitted a bill under CPT Code 90844 after spending 45–50 minutes working on a patient's case, even though not all of that time was spent in direct face-to-face contact with the patient. * * * The Court finds that the defendants' "bundled" services interpretation of the CPT code 90844 is not inconsistent with the plain, common-sense reading of the "description of services" listed by Pennsylvania Blue Shield in its published Procedure Terminology Manual.

Billing Irregularities

While Dr. Krizek was a dedicated and competent doctor and cannot be faulted for his interpretation of the 90844 code, his billing practices, or at a minimum his oversight of his wife's and Mrs. Anderson's billing system, was seriously deficient. Dr. Krizek knew little or nothing of the details of how the bills were submitted by his wife and Mrs. Anderson. * * *

The basic method of billing by Mrs. Krizek and Mrs. Anderson was to determine which patients Dr. Krizek had seen, and then to assume what had

---

1. The government alleges in the complaint that overbills amounted to $245,392 during the six-year period covered by the lawsuit. Trebling this damage amount, and adding the $10,000 statutory maximum penalty requested by the government for each of the 8,002 alleged false claims, results in a total potential liability under the complaint of more than $80,750,000. Dr. Krizek is not public enemy number one. He is at worst, a psychiatrist with a small practice who keeps poor records. For the government to sue for more than eighty million dollars in damages against an elderly doctor and his wife is unseemly and not justified. During this period, a psychiatrist in most instances would be reimbursed between $48 and $60 for a 45–50 minute session and $40 or less for a 20–30 minute session. This is hardly enough for any professional to get rich.

taken place was a 50–minute psychotherapy session, unless told specifically by Dr. Krizek that the visit was for a shorter duration. Mrs. Krizek frequently made this assumption without any input from her husband. Mrs. Krizek acknowledged at trial that she never made any specific effort to determine exactly how much time was spent with each patient. Mrs. Krizek felt it was fair and appropriate to use the 90844 code as a rough approximation of the time spent, because on some days, an examination would last up to two hours and Mrs. Krizek would still bill 90844.

Mrs. Anderson also would prepare and submit claims to Medicare/Medicaid with no input from Dr. Krizek. Routinely, Mrs. Anderson would simply contact the hospital to determine what patients were admitted to various psychiatrists' services, and would then prepare and submit claims to Medicare/Medicaid without communicating with Dr. or Mrs. Krizek about the claims she was submitting and certifying on Dr. Krizek's behalf. * * *

The net result of this system, or more accurately "nonsystem," of billing was that on a number of occasions, Mrs. Krizek and Mrs. Anderson submitted bills for 45–50 minute psychotherapy sessions on Dr. Krizek's behalf when Dr. Krizek could not have spent the requisite time providing services, face-to-face, or otherwise. * * * The defendants do not deny that these unsubstantiated reimbursement claims occurred or that billing practices which led to such inaccurate billings continued through March of 1992.

While the Court does not find that Dr. Krizek submitted bills for patients he did not see, the Court does find that because of Mrs. Krizek's and Mrs. Anderson's presumption that whenever Dr. Krizek saw a patient he worked at least 45 minutes on the matter, bills were improperly submitted for time that was not spent providing patient services. Again, the defendants admit this occurred. []

At the conclusion of the trial, both parties agreed that an appropriate bench-mark for excessive billing would be the equivalent of twelve 90844 submissions (or nine patient-service hours) in a single service day. [] Considering the difficulty of reviewing all Dr. Krizek's patient records over a seven-year period, Dr. Wilson's testimony as to having submitted as many as twelve 90844 submissions in a single day, and giving full credence to unrefuted testimony that Dr. Krizek worked very long hours, the Court believes this to be a fair and reasonably accurate assessment of the time Dr. Krizek actually spent providing patient services. *See Bigelow v. RKO Radio Pictures, Inc.*, 327 U.S. 251, 264, 66 S.Ct. 574, 579, 90 L.Ed. 652 (1946) (permitting factfinder to make "just and reasonable estimate of damage based on relevant data" where more precise computation is not possible). Dr. and Mrs. Krizek will therefore be presumed liable for bills submitted in excess of the equivalent of twelve 90844 submissions in a single day.

Nature of Liability

While the parties have agreed as to the presumptive number of excess submissions for which Dr. and Mrs. Krizek may be found liable, they do not agree on the character of the liability. The government submits that the Krizeks should be held liable under the False Claims Act, 31 U.S.C.A. § 3729, *et seq.* By contrast, defendants posit that while the United States may be entitled to reimbursement for any unjust enrichment attributable to the excess billings, the Krizeks' conduct with regard to submission of excess bills to Medicare/Medicaid was at most negligent, and not "knowing" within the definition of the statute. In their defense, defendants emphasize the "Ma and Pa" nature of Dr. Krizek's medical practice, the fact that Mrs. Krizek did attend some Medicare billing seminars in an effort to educate herself, and the fact that Mrs. Krizek consulted hospital records and relied on information provided by her husband in preparing bills.

By its terms, the False Claims Act provides, *inter alia*, that: Any person who—

> (1) knowingly presents, or causes to be presented, to [the Government] ... a false or fraudulent claim for payment or approval;

> (2) knowingly makes, uses, or causes to be made or used, a false record or statement to get a false or fraudulent claim paid or approved by the Government;

> (3) conspires to defraud the Government by getting a false or fraudulent claim allowed or paid;

> * * *

> is liable to the United States Government for a civil penalty of not less than $5,000.00 and not more than $10,000.00, plus three times the amount of damages which the Government sustains because of the act of that person. . . .

31 U.S.C.A. § 3729(a). The mental state required to find liability under the False Claims Act is also defined by the statute:

> For the purposes of this section, the terms "knowing" and "knowingly" mean that a person, with respect to information—

> (1) has actual knowledge of the information;

> (2) acts in deliberate ignorance of the truth or falsity of the information; or

> (3) acts in reckless disregard of the truth or falsity of the information, and no proof of specific intent is required.

31 U.S.C.A. § 3729(b). The provision allowing for a finding of liability without proof of specific intent to defraud was a feature of the 1986 amendments to the Act.

> * * *

The Court finds that, at times, Dr. Krizek was submitting claims for 90844 when he did not provide patient services for the requisite 45 minutes. The testimony makes clear that these submissions were made by Mrs. Krizek or Mrs. Anderson with little, if any, factual basis. Mrs. Krizek made no effort to establish how much time Dr. Krizek spent on a particular matter. Mrs. Krizek and Mrs. Anderson simply presumed that 45–50 minutes had been spent. There was no justification for making that assumption. In addition, Dr. Krizek failed utterly in supervising these agents in their submissions of claims on his behalf. As a result of his failure to supervise, Dr. Krizek received reimbursement for services which he did not provide.

These were not "mistakes" nor merely negligent conduct. Under the statutory definition of "knowing" conduct, the Court is compelled to conclude that the defendants acted with reckless disregard as to the truth or falsity of the submissions. As such, they will be deemed to have violated the False Claims Act.

Conclusion

Dr. Krizek must be held accountable for his billing system along with those who carried it out. Dr. Krizek was not justified in seeing patients and later not verifying the claims submitted for the services provided to these patients. Doctors must be held strictly accountable for requests filed for insurance reimbursement.

The Court believes that the Krizeks' billing practices must be corrected before they are permitted to further participate in the Medicare or Medicaid programs. Therefore an injunction will issue, enjoining the defendants from participating in these systems until such time as they can show the Court that they can abide by the relevant rules.

The Court also will hold the defendants liable under the False Claims Act on those days where claims were submitted in excess of the equivalent of twelve (12) 90844 claims (nine patient-treatment hours) in a single day and where the defendants cannot establish that Dr. Krizek legitimately devoted the claimed amount of time to patient care on the day in question. The government also will be entitled to introduce proof that the defendants submitted incorrect bills when Dr. Krizek submitted bills for less than nine (9) hours in a single day. The assessment of the amount of overpayment and penalty will await these future proceedings.

Other Observations

While the Court does not discount the seriousness of the Krizeks' conduct here, this case demonstrates several flaws in this country's government health insurance program. The government was right in bringing this action, because it could not countenance the reckless nature of the reimbursement systems in this case. While we are in an age of computers, this does not mean that we can blindly allow coding systems to determine the amount of reimbursement without the physician being accountable for honestly and correctly submitting proper information, whether by code or otherwise.

Nonetheless, the Court found rather troubling some of the government's procedures that control reimbursements paid to providers of services. Here are some of these practices:

1) The government makes no distinction in reimbursement as to the status or professional attainment or education of the provider. Thus, a non-technical person rendering a coded service will be reimbursed the same amount as a board-certified physician.

2) The sums that the Medicare and Medicaid systems reimburse physicians for services rendered seem to be so far below the norm for charges reimbursed by non-governmental insurance carriers. Indeed, the amount could hardly support a medical practice. As the evidence shows in this case, Board certified physicians in most instances were paid at a rate less than $60 per hour and less than $35 per ½ hour. The government must certainly review

these charges because if providers are not adequately compensated, they may not provide the level of care that our elderly and underprivileged citizens require. What is more, the best physicians will simply not come into the system or will refuse to take on senior citizens or the poor as patients.

3) The unrealistic billing concept of requiring doctors to bill only for face-to-face time is not consistent with effective use of a doctor's time or with the provision of good medical services. Doctors must be able to study, research, and discuss a patient's case and be reimbursed for such time.

4) When Medicare dictates that a physician must report each service rendered as a separate code item, the physician is entitled to believe that he will be reimbursed for each of the services rendered. In actuality, the system pays for only one of the multitude of services provided. If this were done by a private sector entity, it would be considered deceitful. Because the government engages in such a deceitful practice does not make it right.

These are the lessons learned by this Court during this case. Hopefully, HCFA will reexamine its reimbursement practices to see what, if any, changes should be made.

UNITED STATES v. KRIZEK

United States Court of Appeals, District of Columbia Circuit, 1997.
111 F.3d 934.

Sentelle, Circuit Judge.

This appeal arises from a civil suit brought by the government against a psychiatrist and his wife under the civil False Claims Act ("FCA"), and under the common law. The District Court found defendants liable for knowingly submitting false claims and entered judgment against defendants for $168,105.39. The government appealed, and the defendants filed a cross-appeal. We hold that the District Court erred and remand for further proceedings.

[The Court held that the district court erred in changing its benchmark for a presumptively false claim from 9 hours billed in any given day to 24 hours because it did not afford the government the opportunity to introduce additional evidence.]

* * *

The Krizeks cross-appeal on the grounds that the District Court erroneously treated each CPT code as a separate "claim" for purposes of computing civil penalties. The Krizeks assert that the claim, in this context, is the HCFA 1500 [form] even when the form contains a number of CPT codes.

The FCA defines "claim" to include any request or demand, whether under a contract or

> otherwise, for money or property which is made to a contractor, grantee, or other recipient if the United States Government provides any portion of the money or property which is requested or demanded, or if the Government will reimburse such contractor, grantee, or other recipient for any portion of the money or property which is requested or demanded.

31 U.S.C. § 3729(c). Whether a defendant has made one false claim or many is a fact-bound inquiry that focuses on the specific conduct of the defendant. . . .

The gravamen of these cases is that the focus is on the conduct of the defendant. The Courts asks, "With what act did the defendant submit his demand or request and how many such acts were there?" In this case, the Special Master adopted a position that is inconsistent with this approach. He stated,

> The CPT code, not the HCFA 1500 form, is the source used to permit federal authorities to verify and account for discrete units of medical service provided, billed and paid for. In sum, the government has demanded a specific accounting unit to identify and verify the services provided, payments requested and amounts paid under the Medicare/Medicaid program. The CPT code, not the HCFA 1500 form, is that basic accounting unit.

The Special Master concluded that because the government used the CPT code in processing the claims, the CPT code, and not the HCFA 1500 in its entirety, must be the claim. This conclusion, which was later adopted by the District Court, misses the point. The question turns, not on how the government chooses to process the claim, but on how many times the defendants made a "request or demand." 31 U.S.C. § 3729(c). In this case, the Krizeks made a request or demand every time they submitted an HCFA 1500.

Our conclusion that the claim in this context is the HCFA 1500 form is supported by the structure of the form itself. The medical provider is asked to supply, along with the CPT codes, the date and place of service, a description of the procedures, a diagnosis code, and the charges. The charges are then totaled to produce one request or demand—line 27 asks for total charges, line 28 for amount paid, and line 29 for balance due. The CPT codes function in this context as a type of invoice used to explain how the defendant computed his request or demand.

The government contends that fairness or uniformity concerns support treating each CPT code as a separate claim, arguing that "[t]o count woodenly the number of HCFA 1500 forms submitted by the Krizeks would cede to medical practitioners full authority to control exposure to [FCA] simply by structuring their billings in a particular manner." Precisely so. It is conduct of the medical practitioner, not the disposition of the claims by the government, that creates FCA liability. Moreover, even if we considered fairness to be a relevant consideration in statutory construction, we would note that the government's definition of claim permitted it to seek an astronomical $81 million worth of damages for alleged actual damages of $245,392. We therefore remand for recalculation of the civil penalty.

* * *

[W]e turn now to the question whether, in considering the sample, the District Court applied the appropriate level of scienter. The FCA imposes liability on an individual who "knowingly presents" a "false or fraudulent claim." 31 U.S.C. § 3729(a). A person acts "knowingly" if he:

(1) has actual knowledge of the information;

(2) acts in deliberate ignorance of the truth or falsity of the information; or

(3) acts in reckless disregard of the truth or falsity of the information,

and no proof of specific intent to defraud is required.

31 U.S.C. § 3729(b). The Krizeks assert that the District Court impermissibly applied the FCA by permitting an aggravated form of gross negligence, "gross negligence-plus," to satisfy the Act's scienter requirement.

In Saba v. Compagnie Nationale Air France, 78 F.3d 664 (D.C.Cir.1996), we considered whether reckless disregard was the equivalent of willful misconduct for purposes of the Warsaw Convention. We noted that reckless disregard lies on a continuum between gross negligence and intentional harm. In some cases, recklessness serves as a proxy for forbidden intent. Such cases require a showing that the defendant engaged in an act known to cause or likely to cause the injury. Use of reckless disregard as a substitute for the forbidden intent prevents the defendant from "deliberately blind[ing] himself to the consequences of his tortuous action." Id. at 668. In another category of cases, we noted, reckless disregard is "simply a linear extension of gross negligence, a palpable failure to meet the appropriate standard of care." Id. In Saba, we determined that in the context of the Warsaw Convention, a showing of willful misconduct might be made by establishing reckless disregard such that the subjective intent of the defendant could be inferred.

The question, therefore, is whether "reckless disregard" in this context is properly equated with willful misconduct or with aggravated gross negligence. In determining that gross negligence-plus was sufficient, the District Court cited legislative history equating reckless disregard with gross negligence. A sponsor of the 1986 amendments to the FCA stated,

Subsection 3 of Section 3729(c) uses the term "reckless disregard of the truth or falsity of the information" which is no different than and has the same meaning as a gross negligence standard that has been applied in other cases. While the Act was not intended to apply to mere negligence, it is intended to apply in situations that could be considered gross negligence where the submitted claims to the Government are prepared in such a sloppy or unsupervised fashion that resulted in overcharges to the Government. The Act is also intended not to permit artful defense counsel to require some form of intent as an essential ingredient of proof. This section is intended to reach the "ostrich-with-his-head-in-the-sand" problem where government contractors hide behind the fact they were not personally aware that such overcharges may have occurred. This is not a new standard but clarifies what has always been the standard of knowledge required.

132 Cong. Rec. H9382–03 (daily ed. Oct. 7, 1986) (statement of Rep. Berman).

While we are not inclined to view isolated statements in the legislative history as dispositive, we agree with the thrust of this statement that the best reading of the Act defines reckless disregard as an extension of gross negligence. Section 3729(b)(2) of the Act provides liability for false statements made with deliberate ignorance. If the reckless disregard standard of section 3729(b)(3) served merely as a substitute for willful misconduct—to prevent the defendant from "deliberately blind[ing] himself to the consequences of his tortuous action"—section (b)(3) would be redundant since section (b)(2) already covers such struthious conduct. Moreover, as the statute explicitly states that specific intent is not required, it is logical to conclude that reckless disregard in this context is not a "lesser form of intent," [ ] but an extreme version of ordinary negligence.

We are unpersuaded by the Krizeks' citation to the rule of lenity to support their reading of the Act. Even assuming that the FCA is penal, the rule of lenity is invoked only when the statutory language is ambiguous. Because we find no ambiguity in the statute's scienter requirement, we hold that the rule of lenity is inapplicable.

We are also unpersuaded by the Krizeks' argument that their conduct did not rise to the level of reckless disregard. The District Court cited a number of factors supporting its conclusion: Mrs. Krizek completed the submissions with little or no factual basis; she made no effort to establish how much time Dr. Krizek spent with any particular patient; and Dr. Krizek "failed utterly" to review bills submitted on his behalf. Most tellingly, there were a number of days within the seven-patient sample when even the shoddiest record keeping would have revealed that false submissions were being made—those days on which the Krizeks' billing approached twenty-four hours in a single day. On August 31, 1985, for instance, the Krizeks requested reimbursement for patient treatment using the 90844 code thirty times and the 90843 code once, indicating patient treatment of over 22 hours. Outside the seven-patient sample the Krizeks billed for more than twenty-four hours in a single day on three separate occasions. These factors amply support the District Court's determination that the Krizeks acted with reckless disregard.

Finally, we note that Dr. Krizek is no less liable than his wife for these false submissions. As noted, an FCA violation may be established without reference to the subjective intent of the defendant. Dr. Krizek delegated to his wife authority to submit claims on his behalf. In failing "utterly" to review the false submissions, he acted with reckless disregard.

* * *

Notes and Questions

1. Exactly what conduct by Dr. Krizek did the government charge violated the False Claims Act? For what conduct and on what basis was he exonerated by the district court? Did the court's liability finding rest on the actions of Dr. Krizek or those of his subordinates?

2. The United States introduced expert evidence that the CPT codes 90843 and 90844 (individual psychotherapy) envisioned face-to-face therapy with the patient for the entire time for which the service was billed (either 25 or 50 minutes). The Krizeks admitted they received reimbursement for time spent other than in face-to-face therapy, and introduced evidence from other physicians that "bundling" was common practice in obtaining reimbursement for private payors. What was the legal basis for absolving Dr. Krizek of liability for "upcoding"?

3. What hurdles does the government face in proving that services provided by a physician were not "medically necessary?" Do the patient's medical records and the physician's notes supply persuasive evidence on this issue? What reform efforts would assist the government in proving a knowing violation of the law?

Should the provider be required to sign a certification for each claim attesting that he has reviewed the claim and certifies it to be true? How does the growing practice of electronic claims submission affect the proof problem?

4. Does the opinion of the Court of Appeals in Krizek clarify the boundary between "reckless disregard" and willful misconduct? Between "reckless disregard" and gross negligence? What evidence did it rely upon to reach its conclusion that the Krizeks had run afoul of that standard? Can you explain at what point evidence of shoddy record keeping and submission of implausible claims would constitute "reckless disregard" under the False Claims Act?

5. Following the Court of Appeals' determination that each 1500 Form constituted a "claim," the district court faced on remand the question of how many of the multiple forms, which taken together exceeded 24 hours in a single day, constituted separate "claims." Absent proof as to which specific claims were submitted beyond the 24–hour limit, the district court chose to count only the number of days (three) exceeding the 24–hour benchmark rather than the total number of claims exceeding that benchmark (eleven). United States v. Krizek, 7 F. Supp.2d 56 (D.D.C.1998). Judge Sporken voiced continued frustration with the government's case: "The Government's pursuit of Dr. Krizek is reminiscent of Inspector Javert's quest to capture Jean Valjean in Victor Hugo's Les Miserables ... [T]here comes a point when a civilized society must say enough is enough." 5 F.2d at 60. Evaluate this and Judge Sporkin's "other observations." Do they betray a judicial sympathy toward medical professionals that is not customarily afforded to other defendants charged with violating statutory directives? Are they persuasive? Has the government brought this criticism on itself by "piling on," i.e., using all the weapons in its arsenal?

6. How should the "reckless disregard" standard be applied in practice? Consider the following situations:

> A defendant continues to submit claims despite having had similar claims rejected in the past by the Medicare carrier and receiving explicit warnings that such claims would not be reimbursed in the future. The defendant is able to point to advice by a consultant that, notwithstanding the above, his billing was proper. See United States v. Lorenzo, 768 F.Supp. 1127 (E.D. Pa. 1991).

> A defendant who is charged with improperly billing Medicare for services asserts that the HCFA Provider Handbook (which sets forth general billing guidelines for physician services) contains no specific instructions concerning the services that the government claims were improperly billed. In addition, the defendant sought to clarify his obligations by making inquiries through the Freedom of Information Act to HCFA. However, language in HCFA's Carrier Manual suggests that the billing may be improper. Expert testimony establishes that physicians are generally familiar with the provisions of the Carrier Manual, but it dictates whether carriers should pay claims and is not intended to guide the physician's decision to submit a claim for reimbursement. Finally, in internal discussions with other defendants, the doctor stated his concern that the billings were "on uncertain ground." See United States ex rel. Swafford v. Borgess Medical Center, 98 F.Supp. 2d 822 (W.D. Mich. 2000).

7. What steps would you advise a provider client to take to guard against false billing? What internal safeguards, billing practices or supervision should the provider implement?

8. Although specific statutes cover false statements or representations made in connection with federal health programs such as Medicare and Medicaid claims

(see next section), federal prosecutors tend to prefer to use 18 U.S.C.A. § 287, which prohibits "false, fictitious, or fraudulent" claims; 18 U.S.C.A. § 1001, which prohibits false statements; and 18 U.S.C.A. § 1341, which prohibits mail fraud. These criminal charges are more familiar to prosecutors and carry the additional advantage of enabling them to move under 18 U.S.C.A. § 1345 for injunctions to freeze the bank accounts of persons or entities that have violated these statutes.

9. The combined effect of the Health Insurance Portability and Accountability Act of 1996 (HIPAA) and the Balanced Budget Act of 1997 (BBA) has been to vastly increase federal and state resources devoted to prosecuting false claims against the government. These acts provided increased funding for federal government prosecutions, enhanced fraud and abuse data collection programs and added new prosecutorial tools to pursue claims against providers. They have resulted in major new investigative initiatives and litigation and have produced significant governmental recoveries. In fiscal year 1998, the federal government secured 300 convictions under various claims for fraud and abuse and false claims, prosecuted over 1,000 civil suits resulting in paybacks to the government, and secured 3000 exclusions from the Medicare and Medicaid programs. Remarks of D. McCarty Thornton, Chief Counsel to the Inspector General, Department of Health and Human Services at the American Health Lawyers Association Institute on Medicare and Medicaid Payment Issues, Mar. 24–26, 1999. Government officials claim that these prosecutions are having an important "sentinel effect." That is, based on Medicare audits showing decreases in improper claims and declines in the average Medicare case mix, they assert that their efforts in prosecuting fraud and abuse are contributing to improved compliance and lower costs for federal programs. D. McCarty Thornton, Perspectives on Current Enforcement: "Sentinel Effect" Shows Fraud Control Works, 32 J. Health L. 493 (1999).

The Department of Justice and HCFA have undertaken a number of investigative initiatives targeting specific areas of concern. For example, the Physicians at Teaching Hospitals Audit Program (PATH) focused on Medicare and Medicaid requirements that attending physicians must be present and directly supervise the provision of services by residents in teaching hospitals. The program resulted in a number of important settlements against major teaching hospitals (the University of Pennsylvania settled for $30 million and Thomas Jefferson University for $12 million). It has also engendered litigation challenging whether the PATH audits reflect appropriate standards for teaching physician services and claiming coercion by the OIG in threatening to seek potentially devastating penalties to compel teaching hospitals into large settlements. See Association of American Medical Colleges v. United States, 34 F.Supp.2d 1187 (C.D.Cal.1998). See also General Accounting Office, Medicare: Concerns With Physicians at Teaching Hospitals (PATH) Audits (July 23, 1998) (finding the government has legal cause to pursue these claims but questioning whether the hospitals' errors were as serious as publicly portrayed). Other major initiatives include the "Lab Scam" project investigating fraudulent laboratory test schemes which has resulted in $642 million in settlements and OIG's investigation of improper billing for non-physician out-patient services under prospective payment (the "DRG Payment Window" investigation.) See Federal Resources Are Stacking up to Tackle Health Care Fraud, Mod. Health Care, March 9, 1998 at 32; OIG Report No. A–03–94–0021, Medicare & Medicaid Guide (CCH) ¶ 43, 631 (Aug. 29, 1995). The government has also focused its attention on certain providers whose practices have raised red flags. See, e.g., Office of Inspector General, Special Fraud Alert: Fraud and Abuse in Nursing Home Arrangements With Hospices, 63 Fed. Reg. 10, 415 (1998); Special Fraud Alert on Physician Liability for Certifications in the Provision of Medical Equipment and Supplies and Home Health Services, 64 Fed. Reg. 1813 (1999); Fraud Alert: Providers Target Medicare Patients in Nursing Facilities, 61 Fed. Reg. 30, 623 (1996). Recently, the OIG has raised the possibility of applying the False Claims Act to abuses in the managed care area, targeting such practices as HMOs illegally enrolling Medicare beneficiaries, knowingly submitting incorrect enrollment data, illegally delaying referrals of patients for care, and improperly denying care. See Laurie McGinley & David S. Cloud, U.S. Takes Aim at HMO Fraud in Medicare and Medicaid, Wall St. J., Oct. 19, 1998, at A28. For a sharp criticism of the government's enforcement record, especially its use of enforcement initiatives in lieu of formal rulemaking, and its failure to give adequate guidance to the industry, see Gary Eiland, A Call for Balancing of Agency Sentinel Priorities, 32 J. Health L. 503 (1999). See generally, Timothy S. Jost and Sharon L. Davies, The Empire Strikes Back: A Critique of the Backlash Against Fraud and Abuse Enforcement, 51 Ala. L. Rev. 239 (1999); Lewis Morris and Gary W. Thompson, Reflections on the Government's Stick and Carrot Approach to Fighting Health Care Fraud, 51 Ala. L. Rev. 319 (1999); Gordon E. Rountree, Jr., Health Care Providers and Fraud Investigations: What Can You Do When the Government Changes the Rules in the Middle of the Game?, 8 Ann. Health L. 97 (1999).

LUCKEY v. BAXTER HEALTHCARE CORPORATION

United States Court of Appeals, Seventh Circuit, 2000.
183 F.3d 730.

EASTERBROOK, CIRCUIT JUDGE.

Among the products of Baxter Healthcare Corp. are blood plasma derivatives, useful to promote blood clotting and provide antibodies against disease. Federal regulations require that incoming units of plasma be tested for hepatitis and human immunodeficiency virus before it is commingled with a larger pool from which commercial blood plasma products are prepared. 21 C.F.R. §§ 610.40, 610.45, 640.67. Joan P. Luckey, a former employee of Baxter Screening Laboratory (the division of Baxter Healthcare that tests plasma), filed this qui tam action in the name of the United States under the False Claims Act,[]² Luckey also sought relief in her own right, claiming that she had been dismissed in violation of § 3730(h) for exposing Baxter's false claims. The district court granted summary judgment in Baxter's favor. []

Blood plasma is clear. This tempts outside vendors to cheat—to palm off saline solution as plasma, or to dilute plasma with saline to sell a larger volume. On some occasions saline contamination is accidental, for saline solution is used to clean the machinery used to extract plasma from whole blood. Normal tests for hepatitis virus and HIV give meaningless results when applied to pure saline solution, and the presence of saline contamination in blood plasma leads to false negatives in some cases. Luckey believes that Baxter should use a total protein test to determine whether each incoming plasma unit contains saline solution. Managers at Baxter Screening Laboratory disagreed with Luckey's proposal. Testing is costly, and the managers thought that saline dilution is not a sufficiently common problem that a separate test always is justified. Blood plasma is pooled before being packaged for sale, and a total protein test is administered to the pool. Thus there is no

---

2. [Ed. Note] Qui Tam litigation is discussed in the following section of this chapter.

risk that saline will cause any shipping product to defeat the tests for hepatitis virus or HIV (tests that are performed on the pool at the end of processing, just as they are performed on each unit of plasma at the outset). Baxter also applies viral inactivation processes to each pool, reducing risks to a negligible level for the final product.

None of the federal regulations requires a supplier to administer a total protein test to each incoming unit. Nonetheless, the regulations do demand testing for hepatitis and HIV; to administer ineffective tests is the same as to administer no tests, Luckey contends. A representation that blood plasma has been tested, when no (proper) tests have been performed, is fraud on the federal government, Luckey submits, and therefore is actionable in a qui tam suit. Baxter denies that it makes any representation to the United States about its testing; when it sells plasma products to federal agencies, its only relevant statements are that it holds a license from the Food and Drug Administration and that the products are free of hepatitis and HIV. But we shall assume for current purposes that Luckey could show that a representation about testing is made indirectly. The assumption does not assist her.

The principal difficulty with Luckey's position is its equation of ineffective testing with no testing, followed by the proposition that a battle of experts in litigation determines whether testing is "effective." Only in Humpty Dumpty's world of word games would anyone apply the label "fraud" to the kind of representations Baxter made. Perhaps Luckey could persuade the Food and Drug Administration to require more or different testing; but when a supplier complies with the existing regulations, it is entitled to represent to the government (and the world) that it has done so, without facing a claim of deception.

What tests to perform, and when, are difficult questions. No one doubts that, when saline contamination is a possibility, a total protein test reduces the numbers of false negatives from other tests. Similarly, however, no one believes (at least, no one should believe) that every possible test, no matter how expensive, should be administered to avoid every conceivable risk, no matter how small. Some form of cost-benefit inquiry must be carried out. See Stephen Breyer, Breaking the Vicious Circle: Toward Effective Risk Regulation (1993). Are the extra costs worth the extra expense? That depends not only on the volume of saline-contaminated plasma received, and the probability that saline will lead to false negative results from standard tests, but also on the effectiveness of the tests that are applied to the plasma after pooling. Tests performed on the pool have few if any false negatives. Thus the real cost of not using a total protein test earlier is that some plasma with hepatitis or HIV will get into a larger pool and cause the rejection of the whole pool, wasting quantities of plasma that were sound when received. Waste is regrettable, but the cost of thrown-out plasma may be measured in dollars; and if Baxter is willing to bear the expense (thinking the cost of rejected pools to be less than the cost of more comprehensive testing earlier), it is hard to see why the federal government should force it to use the total protein test on each unit—and absolutely impossible to see why Baxter's resolution of the testing issue should be called "false" or "fraudulent." Most companies in Baxter's position will have scientists who argue for additional precautions, and others who think that the existing precautions are enough (if not excessive). Luckey, a lab technician, was in the more-precautions camp. As written, the regulations do not resolve this debate. Baxter had to make a decision for itself. Since 1995 Baxter has subjected some incoming units of plasma to total protein tests, but this change in its testing protocol does not imply that representations about the former protocol were false.

Equating "imperfect tests" with "no tests" would strain language past the breaking point. True enough, a claim can be false or fraudulent if the speaker offers a misleading half-truth. Thus the assertion "we performed all appropriate tests" could be called false if Baxter meant by "appropriate" only "required by regulation," while knowing that the test results were worthless and the product defective. What keeps this approach from swallowing the norm that literal truth is enough is the requirement that the plaintiff show not only that the omitted facts were material to the listener's decision, see Neder v. United States, 527 U.S. 1, 119 S.Ct. 1827, 144 L.Ed.2d 35 (1999), but also that the speaker intend the statement or omission to deceive, Ernst & Ernst v. Hochfelder, 425 U.S. 185, 96 S.Ct. 1375, 47 L.Ed.2d 668 (1976). See 31 U.S.C. § 3729(b). Luckey has not offered any evidence tending to show that the omission of a total protein test at the plasma intake stage (before pooling) was material to the United States' buying decision; the Department of Justice has conspicuously declined to adopt Luckey's position or to prosecute this claim on its own behalf. As far as this record reveals, the federal government is 100% satisfied with the blood products it receives from Baxter and with the representations made in connection with the sales. Moreover, there is no evidence that Baxter intended to deceive anyone about what it was doing, or the validity of the test results. All this record reveals is a dispute about whether Baxter's testing protocols could be improved. An affirmative answer to that question would not suggest that Baxter's representations to the United States in years past were false or fraudulent. United States ex rel. Lamers v. Green Bay, 168 F.3d 1013, 1019 (7th Cir.1999), holds that technical violations of a federal regulation on which a claim is based do not make the claim "false"; in this case we do not even have an established violation.

AFFIRMED

Notes and Questions

1. The False Claims Act makes illegal "false or fraudulent" claims, but does not define those terms. Use of the disjunctive "or" indicates that claims that are false, but not fraudulent, are prohibited; does that suggest that mistakes or errors fall within the statute's reach? The cases hold, consistent with Luckey, that "falsity" implies an attempt to deceive. Hence, scientific errors, good faith mistakes in filling out forms, and misunderstandings of complex coding requirements for payment are not false claims. See Wang v. FMC Corp., 975 F.2d 1412, 1420–21 (9th Cir. 1992)("Bad math is no fraud.... The phrase known to be false does not mean scientifically untrue; it means 'a lie.' The Act is concerned with ferreting out wrongdoing, not scientific errors. What is false as a matter of science is not, by that very fact, wrong as a matter of morals. The Act would not put either Ptolemy or Copernicus on trial."). At some point, however, the choice of bad methodologies or highly dubious scientific methods may cross the boundary and render the providers' claim false. What factual showing would have sufficed to change the court's conclusion in Luckey?

2. Falsity may arise from the defendant's certification to the payor of acts or procedures performed or standards applied in connection with rendering care or

services. As one moves away from the straightforward case in which a provider certifies that he has provided services when he has not done so, see e.g., Peterson v. Weinberger, 508 F.2d 45 (5th Cir. 1975), one encounters circumstances in which the link between the regulatory requirement invoking the false statement and the services for which the government is billed are attenuated. A growing number of cases have examined whether a provider *impliedly* certified certain facts or compliance with governmental regulations. Where the government has conditioned payment of a claim upon certification of compliance with a statute or regulation, a claimant submits a false or fraudulent claim when he or she falsely certifies compliance with that statute or regulation. United States ex rel. Thompson v. Columbia/HCA Healthcare Corp., 125 F.3d 899, 902 (5th Cir. 1997); Ab–Tech Constr., Inc. v. United States, 31 Fed. Cl. 429 (1994); but cf. Hindo v. University of Health Sciences/Chicago Med. School, 65 F.3d 608, 613–14 (7th Cir. 1995) (rejecting allegation that medical center impliedly certified in each invoice that it had obtained funding for residents). See Pamela H. Bucy, Growing Pains: Using the False Claims Act to Combat Health Care Fraud, 51 Ala. L. Rev. 57, 78–79 (1999); John R. Munich & Elizabeth W. Lane, When Neglect Becomes Fraud: Quality of Care and False Claims, 43 St. Louis U. L.J. 27, 42–46 (1999).

3.   Especially controversial has been the use of the implied certification theory to support False Claims Act challenges to quality deficiencies in rendering care. In United States v. NHC Healthcare Corp., 115 F. Supp.2d 1149, 1153 (W.D. Mo. 2000), the court allowed the government's case to proceed where it contended that the defendants' nursing home "was so severely understaffed that it could not possibly have administered all of the care it was obligated to perform" under Medicare and Medicaid program standards. The court reasoned that the failure to provide the level of quality of care which "promotes the maintenance and the enhancement of the quality of life," as required under federal regulations, could amount to claims for services not actually performed. See also United States ex rel. Aranda v. Community Psychiatric Centers, 945 F. Supp. 1485, 1487 (W.D. Okla. 1996) (denying motion to dismiss False Claims Act case involving a psychiatric hospital that allegedly failed to comply with Medicaid regulations requiring that facilities afford patients a "reasonably safe environment"). What problems do you anticipate might be associated with extending the False Claims Act to reach quality of care concerns? Are there potential benefits from allowing federal prosecutors to bring these cases that regulation and malpractice law cannot achieve? See Munich & Lane, supra; John T. Boese, When Angry Patients Become Angry Prosecutors: Medical Necessity Determinations, Quality of Care and the Qui Tam Law, 43 St. Louis U. L.J. 53, 56–57 (1999) (explaining why managed care is likely to generate suits based on deficiencies in quality of care); Pamela H. Bucy, Fraud By Fright: White Collar Crime By Health Care Providers, 67 N.C. L. Rev. 855, 920–24 (1989).

Is the next step to use the False Claims Act as a weapon to deal with the problem of medical error? Given the Institute of Medicine's attribution of cause for persistently high rates of error to systemic failures in health care institutions, an argument could be made that the Act would be an effective and efficient tool for challenging providers' systemic and long-term failures to meet the community's standard of care. For a thoughtful analysis of this issue, ultimately concluding that the balance tips against using the Act to challenge medical error, see Joan H. Krause, Medical Error as False Claim, ___ Am. J. L. & Med. ___ (2000).

4.   How does the Seventh Circuit's opinion in Luckey confine the potential reach of the implied certification theory? What role should materiality and harm to the government play in the analysis? See United States v. White, 27 F.3d 1531

(11th Cir. 1994); see generally Jost & Davies, supra. § 2–2; John T. Boese & Beth C. McClain, Why Thompson is Wrong: Misuse of the False Claims Act to Enforce the Anti–Kickback Act, 51 Ala. L. Rev. 1 (1999).

5. Under the so-called "reverse false claims" provision of the Act, § 3729(a)(7), anyone who "knowingly makes, uses, or cause to be made or used, a false record or statement to conceal, avoid or decrease an obligation to pay or transmit money or property to the government" may be subject to liability under the Civil False Claims. Act. Plaintiffs invoked this subsection to claim that Columbia/HCA had concealed potential obligations to the government arising from its violation of the fraud and abuse laws when it filed annual cost reports that did not mention these abuses. See United States ex re. Thompson v. Columbia/HCA, 20 F. Supp.2d 1017, 1049 (S.D. Tex. 1998). For a critical assessment of the theory and its application in this case, see Boese & McClain, supra, 51 Ala. L. Rev. at 50–55; see also U.S. v. Oakwood Downriver Medical Center, 687 F. Supp. 302 (E.D. Mich. 1988).

Note on Corporate Fraud and Abuse

Recent efforts on the part of the Departments of Justice and Health and Human Services and other federal and state agencies to enforce more vigorously Medicare and Medicaid fraud and abuse laws have uncovered a number of serious violations by large corporate entities. For example, Caremark, an Illinois-based home health care company, settled charges that it had paid for patient referrals from physicians and other providers. According to the government's allegations, providers who referred patients to the company's home infusion unit received kickbacks in the form of payments for patient monitoring or for the provision of research data. The company then used the referrals as a source of Medicare claims. Caremark's settlement agreement with the Justice Department provided that it will pay $85.3 million in civil penalties and restitution, $29 million in criminal fines, $44.6 million to affected states, and $2 million to an AIDS grant program. Barnaby J. Feder, Caremark to Pay $161 Million in Accord, N.Y. Times, June 16, 1995, at D2. The fiduciary duties of corporate officers and directors to uncover wrongdoing in this matter were the subject of a shareholder's derivative suit, set forth at page 851 of this book.

Two of the most egregious and costly examples to date of corporate health care corruption health care law have involved the nation's largest for-profit health systems. In 1993, National Medical Enterprises, Inc. ("NME") pled guilty to a seven-count information charging numerous violations of the fraud and abuse statute and other laws for conduct that included paying for referrals, multiple billing of services to Medicare, billing for services that never took place, and actually billing Medicare for kickback payments it made to doctors for patient referrals. The government alleged that as part of its scheme, NME had administered unnecessary treatments and extended the hospital stays of patients in the company's chain of psychiatric hospitals. In June, 1994, NME paid $379 million in combined civil and criminal penalties to federal and state governments and also agreed to sell its psychiatric hospitals and substance abuse services. Its chief executive, Kirk Wascom, was sentenced to seven-and-a-half years in federal prison. NME To Pay $379 Million in Penalties Under Settlement with Federal Agencies, 3 Health L. Rep. (BNA) (July 7, 1994). In perhaps the most notorious episode of corporate corruption, Columbia/HCA was charged with engaging in a wide variety of illegal conduct including paying physicians kickbacks for referrals to its hospitals, upcoding, and furnishing fraudulent Medicare billing and cost reports. In 2000, it agreed to pay $745 million to resolve civil claims (in part triggered by whistleblower qui tam relators) and two Columbia/HCA subsidiaries pleaded guilty to several counts of criminal conduct, agreed to pay the government $95 million in penalties and fines and signed a corporate integrity agreement with the OIG. Lucette Lagnade, HCA Units' Guilty Pleas Resolve Largest Medicare Criminal Probe, Wall Street J., Dec. 15, 2000 at B10.

The government's allegations in these cases reveal a shocking disregard for the law and a pattern of systematic abuse that permeated these large corporations. Indeed, NME company manuals directed employees to pay for referrals, hospital officials discussed these practices at marketing meetings, and illicit referrals were formally tracked in internal documents. What do these cases suggest about the need for criminal sanctions and specifically about the advisability of seeking jail terms for responsible individuals? What remedies are needed to assure that higher-ups in corporations do not simply adopt a "hear no evil" approach and neglect to monitor the activities of those under their supervision? See generally Alice G. Gosfield, Unintentional Part B False Claims: Pitfalls for the Unwary, 1993 Health Law Handbook 205 (Alice G. Gosfield ed., 1993). Note also the increasing importance of corporate compliance plans for both mitigating potential penalties and preventing violations. See Thornton, supra; Kim Roeder & Sara Kay Sledge, Concentrated Government Efforts to Prosecute Fraud, and Corporate Sentencing Guidelines Make Compliance Programs Necessary for Health Care Organizations, Nat'l L.J., Oct. 14, 1996, at B5. What kinds of compliance programs would be most effective? See Health Attorneys See Rapid Growth in Adoption of Compliance Plans, 5 Health L. Rep. (BNA) (Aug. 15, 1996) (citing survey results viewing codes of conduct, though widely used, as ineffective compared to employee training and hot-lines). Consider as you read the following sections whether the need for both detection and prevention of abuse justifies the multiplicity of legal remedies.

B. QUI TAM ACTIONS

31 U.S.C.A. § 3730. Civil actions for false claims

* * *

(b) Actions by private persons.—(1) A person may bring a civil action for a violation of [the False Claims Act] for the person and for the United States Government. The action shall be brought in the name of the Government. The action may be dismissed only if the court and the Attorney General give written consent to the dismissal and their reasons for consenting.

(2) A copy of the complaint and written disclosure of substantially all material evidence and information the person possesses shall be served on the Government ... The complaint shall be filed in camera, shall remain under seal for at least 60 days, and shall not be served on the defendant until the court so orders. The Government may elect to intervene and proceed with the action within 60 days after it receives both the complaint and the material evidence and information.

* * *

(4) Before the expiration of the 60–day period or any extensions obtained under paragraph (3), the Government shall—(A) proceed with the action, in which case the action shall be conducted by the Government; or

(B) notify the court that it declines to take over the action, in which case the person bringing the action shall have the right to conduct the action.

* * *

(c) Rights of the parties to Qui Tam actions.—(1) If the Government proceeds with the action, it shall have the primary responsibility for prosecuting the action, and shall not be bound by an act of the person bringing the action. Such person shall have the right to continue as a party to the action, subject to the limitations set forth in paragraph (2).

* * *

(d) Award to Qui Tam plaintiff. If the Government proceeds with an action brought by a person under subsection (b), such person [shall receive between 15 and 25 percent of the proceeds of the action or settlement of the claim, depending on the extent to which the person contributed to the prosecution, plus attorneys' fees and costs. If the government does not proceed the person may receive between 25 and 30 percent plus attorneys' fees and costs. If the action was brought by a person who planned and initiated the violation of the statutes, the court may reduce the person's share of proceeds and if the person is convicted of a crime for his or her role that person may not share any proceeds.]

(e) Certain actions barred.

* * *

(3) In no event may a person bring an action under subsection (b) which is based upon allegations or transactions which are the subject of a civil suit or an administrative civil money penalty proceeding in which the Government is already a party.

(4)(A) No court shall have jurisdiction over an action under this section based upon the public disclosure of allegations or transactions in a criminal, civil, or administrative hearing, in a congressional, administrative, or Government Accounting Office report, hearing, audit, or investigation, or from the news media, unless the action is brought by the Attorney General or the person bringing the action is an original source of the information.

(B) For purposes of this paragraph, "original source" means an individual who has direct and independent knowledge of the information on which the allegations are based and has voluntarily provided the information to the Government before filing an action under this section which is based on the information.

* * *

(h) Any employee who is discharged, demoted, suspended, threatened, harassed, or in any other manner discriminated against in the terms and conditions of employment by his or her employer because of lawful acts done by the employee on behalf of the employee or others in furtherance of an action under this section, including investigation for, initiation of, testimony for, or assistance in an action filed or to be filed under this section, shall be entitled to all relief necessary to make the employee whole. Such relief shall include reinstatement with the same seniority status such employee would have had but for the discrimination, two times the amount of back pay, interest on the back pay, and compensation for any special damages sustained as a result of the discrimination, including litigation costs and reasonable attorneys' fees. An employee may bring an action in the appropriate district court of the United States for the relief provided in this subsection.

Notes and Questions

1. What advice would you have given to Mrs. Anderson, Dr. Krizek's assistant in United States v. Krizek, supra, if she had approached you for legal advice before any investigation had begun of her employer? How would you have handled discussions with the U.S. Attorney's Office concerning her involvement in the matter? Could she continue to perform her job responsibilities for Dr. Krizek if she became a whistleblower or would it be necessary for her to quit? Before advising her, you may want to consult Luckey v. Baxter Healthcare Corp., 183 F.3d 730, discussed in the preceding section of this chapter. In a portion of the opinion not reprinted above, Judge Easterbrook rejected the relator's claim for whistleblower protection under § 3730(h). Baxter had fired Ms. Luckey before her qui tam suit was unsealed and the court concluded that Baxter was not aware of the pending action. The court rejected the claim that because the employer knew of her strongly-held feelings about its testing practices, it should have been on notice of the possibility of her "assistance in" a suit. Likewise, despite Luckey's statements to co-workers that she planned to "shut down" the lab and "get rid" of her supervisors, the court concluded that Baxter was not prohibited from firing her: "Sabre-rattling is not protected conduct. Only investigation, testimony, and litigation are protected, and none of these led to Luckey's firing." 183 F.3d at 733.

2. If you represented Dr. Krizek and the matter went to trial, how would you seek to impeach the testimony of Mrs. Anderson? As a lawyer for the Department of Justice (assuming it has entered and taken over the lawsuit), how would you insulate against this cross-examination or mitigate it? Suppose instead that it is Mrs. Krizek who decided to become the qui tam "relator." Would your advice change? What information would you need to elicit before advising her?

3. The constitutionality of the qui tam statute has come under attack on several grounds. In Vermont Agency of Natural Resources v. United States ex rel. Stevens, 529 U.S. 765, 120 S.Ct. 1858, 146 L.Ed.2d 836 (2000), the Supreme Court laid one question to rest, holding that, as partial assignees of the claim of the United States, qui tam relators satisfy the "case or controversy" requirements of Article III. Not decided by the Court, however, was the issue of whether the statute was unconstitutional because it violated the Take Care Clause or the separation of powers doctrine. Id. at 1865 n.8. One circuit has held the act unconstitutional based on its grant of executive power to relators who are not controlled by the executive branch. Riley v. St. Luke's Episcopal Hosp., 196 F.3d 514 (5th Cir. 1999). In Vermont Agency the Supreme Court also held that states and state entities could not be subject to qui tam liability. However, case law establishing that state employees and states may be qui tam relators remains undisturbed. See United States ex rel. Wisconsin v. Dean, 729 F.2d 1100 (7th Cir.1984); United States ex rel. Fine v. Chevron, U.S.A., Inc., 72 F.3d 740 (9th Cir.1995). See also Dorthea Beane, Are Government Employees Proper Qui Tam Plaintiffs?, 14 J. Leg. Med. 279 (1993); Jost & Davies, supra, § 6–3. Should a discharged employee who has signed an agreement with her employer releasing the employer of all claims and agreeing not to sue be able to pursue a qui tam action? What public policy arguments can be raised in favor of and against allowing such an action to proceed? See United States ex rel. Pogue v. American Healthcorp, Inc., 1995 WL 626514 (M.D.Tenn.1995).

4. There has been an explosive growth in both false claims and qui tam actions involving health care providers in recent years. The number of qui tam actions has grown from 33 in 1987 to 482 in 1999 and 361 in 2000. See Taxpayers Against Fraud, Qui Tam Statistics, available at *www.taf.org/taf/docs/ qtstats99.html*. In recent years over sixty percent of all qui tam actions involved the health care industry. Plaintiffs' attorneys increasingly use web sites and other promotional devices to find qui tam relators, typically aiming their information at employees of hospitals, physician practices and laboratories. What is the justification for qui tam actions? Do they appropriately advance legitimate law enforcement objectives or do they create undesirable incentives that poison the employer-employee relationship? In evaluating the effectiveness of the qui tam law in improving deterrence, consider the need to assure that damages are set at levels that take into account the likelihood of detection and the total social costs imposed by the violator. See Gary Becker, Crime and Punishment: An Economic Approach, 76 J.Pol.Econ. 169 (1968); Robert Lande, Optimal Sanctions for Antitrust Violations, 50 U.Chi.L.Rev. 652 (1983). For a discussion of the use of qui tam actions in the health care context, see David J. Ryan, The False Claims Act: An Old Weapon With New Firepower Is Aimed at Health Care Fraud, 4 Annals Health L. 127 (1995).

II. MEDICARE AND MEDICAID FRAUD AND ABUSE

A. THE STATUTE: 42 U.S.C.A. § 1320A–7B

(a) Making or causing to be made false statements or representations.

Whoever—

(1) knowingly and willfully makes or causes to be made any false statement or representation of a material fact in any application for any benefit or payment under a Federal health care program (as defined in subsection (f) of this section)

(2) at any time knowingly and willfully makes or causes to be made any false statement or representation of a material fact for use in determining rights to such benefit or payment,

* * *

shall (i) in the case of such a statement, representation, concealment, failure, or conversion by any person in connection with the furnishing (by that person) of items or services for which payment is or may be made under the program, be guilty of a felony and upon conviction thereof fined not more than $25,000 or imprisoned for not more than five years or both, or (ii) in the case of such a statement, representation, concealment, failure, conversion, or provision of counsel or assistance by any other person, be guilty of a misdemeanor and upon conviction thereof fined not more than $10,000 or imprisoned for not more than one year, or both. * * *

(b) Illegal remunerations

(1) Whoever knowingly and willfully solicits or receives any remuneration (including any kickback, bribe, or rebate) directly or indirectly, overtly or covertly, in cash or in kind—

(A) in return for referring an individual to a person for the furnishing or arranging for the furnishing of any item or service for which payment may be made in whole or in part under a Federal health care program, or

(B) in return for purchasing, leasing, ordering, or arranging for or recommending purchasing, leasing, or ordering any good, facility, service, or item for which payment may be made in whole or in part under a Federal health care program,

shall be guilty of a felony and upon conviction thereof, shall be fined not more than $25,000 or imprisoned for not more than five years, or both.

(2) Whoever knowingly and willfully offers or pays any remuneration (including any kickback, bribe or rebate) directly or indirectly, overtly or covertly, in cash or in kind to any person to induce such person—

(A) to refer an individual to a person for the furnishing or arranging for the furnishing of any item or service for which payment may be made in whole or in part under a Federal health care program, or

(B) to purchase, lease, order, or arrange for or recommend purchasing, leasing, or ordering any good, facility, service, or item for which payment may be made in whole or in part under a Federal health care program,

shall be guilty of a felony and upon conviction thereof shall be fined not more than $25,000 or imprisoned for not more than five years, or both.

* * *

[Subsection (c) prohibits knowing and willful false statements or representations of material facts with respect to the conditions or operation of any entity in order to qualify such an entity for Medicare or Medicaid certification. Subsection (d) prohibits knowingly and willfully charging patients for Medicaid services where such charges are not otherwise permitted.]

(f) For purposes of this section, the term "Federal health care program" means—

(1) any plan or program that provides health benefits, whether directly, through insurance, or otherwise, which is funded directly, in whole or in part, by the United States Government [other than the federal employees health benefit program];

(2) any State health care program, as defined in section 1320a–7(h).

B. PROBLEMS: ADVISING UNDER THE FRAUD AND ABUSE LAWS

Do any of the following transactions violate the fraud and abuse laws? Is there anything else wrong with them from a legal, ethical, or public policy perspective?

1. Starkville Community Hospital is located in a rural area in a distant corner of a large mid-western state. Recently, Dr. McPherson, the hospital's only obstetrician, announced his retirement. Few new physicians have settled in Starkville in recent years, and the community and hospital are very

concerned about the loss of obstetric services. The hospital has decided, therefore, to implement a plan to attract a new obstetrician. It is offering to provide any board-certified obstetrician who will settle in Starkville and obtain privileges at Starkville Memorial the following for the first two years the physician is on staff at the hospital: (1) a guaranteed annual income of $110,000, (2) free malpractice insurance through the hospital's self-insurance plan, and (3) free rent in the hospital's medical practice building. The new obstetrician would not be required to refer patients to Starkville Community, though the closest alternative hospital is 60 miles away. The obstetrician would also be expected to assume some administrative duties in exchange for the compensation package Starkville is offering. Starkville Community is currently engaged in negotiations with a young doctor who has just finished her residency and appears likely to accept this offer. There is a potential problem, however. Dr. Waxman, who came to Starkville two years ago and is the hospital's only cardiologist, has threatened that he will leave unless he gets the same terms.

2.   Dr. Ness, a successful ophthalmologist, advertises in the weekly suburban shopping newspaper, offering free cataract examinations for senior citizens. He in fact does not charge those who respond to the offer for the Medicare deductible or co-insurance amounts, but bills Medicare for the maximum charge allowable for the service.

3.   Managed care organizations are insisting that Samaritan Hospital offer wider geographic coverage in order to bid on contracts. A market study reveals that Samaritan is receiving few admissions from Arlington, a rapidly growing affluent suburb eight miles to the northwest. To remedy this problem, Samaritan has formed an MSO and has entered into negotiations to purchase the Arlington Family Practice Center, a successful group practice containing five board-certified family practitioners. The MSO has offered a generous price for the practice, which would be renamed Samaritan–Arlington Family Practice Center and its doctors would become salaried employees of the MSO entity. They would thereafter be required to admit patients only at Samaritan and to refer only to specialists who have privileges at Samaritan. The five doctors, who are weary of the administrative hassles of private practice, are eager to sell.

4.   A consultant to Community Memorial Hospital has suggested a strategy to deal with the rapid growth in managed care contracting in its market. Many of Community Memorial's doctors rent space in Community Memorial's Medical Office building, but have admitting privileges at one of the other two hospitals in town, and often admit patients to one of those hospitals. The consultant has recommended that Community Memorial establish an MSO to handle leases of the hospital's properties. Staff physicians would be offered a minority ownership interest in the MSO and MSO physicians would receive a reduction of monthly rental payments by .5% for each patient that the doctor admits to Community Memorial during that month.

5.   Twenty-three small rural hospitals in a mid-western state have entered into a contract with a group-purchasing agent to purchase medical equipment and supplies for them. The agent will take advantage of volume discounts and of careful market research to significantly lower the cost of

supplies and equipment purchased for the hospitals. The agent obtains, on average, a 5% rebate from suppliers for all goods it purchases.

6. Intermodal Health System, an integrated delivery system, has suffered losses averaging $100,000 per year per doctor on the physician practices it acquired five years ago. It has developed a plan to terminate the contracts of half of the physicians it now employs. Pursuant to their employment contract, each physician will receive a severance fee of $50,000. Intermodal will also waive covenants not to compete contained in contracts with terminated physicians. In addition, Intermodal plans to offer to its "most valued" terminated physicians lease agreements to continue to occupy the medical office space owned by an Intermodal subsidiary.

C. PENALTIES FOR FRAUD AND ABUSE

As we have seen, false billing, illegal remuneration (bribes and kickbacks), misrepresentation of compliance with conditions of participation, and a variety of other abuses involving federal health care plans are federal crimes and in most instances felonies. Of equal concern to providers, however, are the civil penalty and exclusion powers of the Office of Inspector General (OIG) of the Department of Health and Human Services (HHS). For providers dependent on Medicare and Medicaid for a large share of their business, exclusion from these programs can be effectively a death warrant, at least as serious as a felony conviction. Civil sanction proceedings are administrative in nature, criminal intent need not be shown, and the standard of proof is a preponderance of the evidence rather than beyond a reasonable doubt.

The list of behaviors for which HHS can assess civil money penalties is long and grows with every annual budget reconciliation act. For example, civil penalties of up to $10,000 per item or service plus twice the amount claimed can be assessed for an item or service that a person "knows or should know" was "not provided as claimed." 42 U.S.C.A. § 1320a–7a(a)(1)(A). The long list of additional sanctions includes: civil money penalties against any person who provides false or misleading information that could reasonably be expected to influence the decision of when to discharge a Medicare beneficiary from a hospital, 42 U.S.C.A. § 1320a–7a(3); penalties against Medicare or Medicaid HMOs that fail substantially to provide medically necessary services with a substantial likelihood of adversely affecting beneficiaries, or that impose premiums in excess of permitted amounts, 42 U.S.C.A. § 1395mm(i)(6)(A)(i)-(iii); penalties against hospitals that make direct or indirect payments to physicians as incentives for reducing or limiting services provided to beneficiaries or against physicians who accept such payments, 42 U.S.C.A. § 1320a–7a(b); and penalties of up to $2000 per violation may be imposed on doctors who fail to provide diagnosis codes on non-assigned Medicare claims, 42 U.S.C.A. § 1395u(p)(3). Finally the government may seek an injunction to enjoin any person from "concealing, removing, encumbering or disposing" of its assets when seeking a civil monetary penalty. 42 U.S.C.A. § 1320a–7a(m).

Exclusion from participation in Federal health care programs is a potent and widely used weapon in the arsenal of those combating fraud. Nearly 3000 providers were excluded from the Medicare program in fiscal year 1999; 550 of those exclusions resulted from criminal convictions for program-related crimes, 323 for patient abuse and neglect, and 1416 were based on license revocations. Department of Health and Human Services and Department of Justice, Health Care Fraud and Abuse Control Program Annual Report (1999). The OIG must exclude individuals or entities for at least five years in four circumstances: conviction of a criminal offense related to the delivery of Medicare or state health care program services; conviction of a crime relating to neglect or abuse of patients; any federal or state felony conviction with respect to any act or omission in any health care program financed by any Federal, state or local government agency or involving fraud, theft, embezzlement, breach of fiduciary responsibility or other financial misconduct; or felony conviction of unlawful manufacture, distribution, prescription or dispensing of controlled substances. 42 U.S.C.A. § 1320a–7(a)(1)—(a)(4) & (2). See also Travers v. Sullivan, 791 F.Supp. 1471 (E.D. Wash. 1992) (no contest plea constitutes conviction of program-related crime and requires mandatory exclusion).

The OIG also has discretion to exclude providers for numerous other categories of offenses, including loss of professional license, submission of bills substantially in excess of usual charges or costs, substantial failure of an HMO to provide medically necessary services, substantial failure of a hospital to comply with a corrective plan for unnecessary admissions or other inappropriate practices to circumvent PPS, or default by health professionals on student loans. 42 U.S.C.A. § 1320a–7(b). An important recent amendment to the law allows for permissive exclusions of (1) persons who have direct or indirect ownership or control interests in a sanctioned entity and have acted in deliberate ignorance of the information; and (2) officers or managing employees, even if the individual did not participate in the wrongdoing. 42 U.S.C.A. § 1320a–7(b)(8). The law also fixes minimum periods of exclusion ranging from 1 to 3 years depending on the basis for exclusion. However, in determining the length of permissive exclusions, the agency may consider other factors such as the availability of alternative sources of health care in the community. Exclusion or criminal conviction frequently results in disciplinary action by state professional licensure boards, and can thus end the professional career of even a professional who sees few Medicaid and Medicare patients. For a comprehensive review of the law governing exclusions, see Timothy Stoltfus Jost & Sharon Davies, Medicare and Medicaid Fraud and Abuse (2000), §§ 5–2—5–3. See also Pamela H. Bucy, The Poor Fit of Tradition Evidentiary Doctrine and Sophisticated Crime: Empirical Analysis of Health Care Fraud Prosecutions, 63 Fordham L. Rev. 383 (1994).

D. TREATMENT OF REFERRAL FEES UNDER FRAUD AND ABUSE LAWS

Sharing the profits of collective economic activity is common throughout the economy generally. Landlords rent commercial properties under percentage leases, agents sell goods and services produced by others on commission, merchants grant discounts to those who use their services or encourage others to do so. Such activity has, however, long been frowned upon as it relates to health care. It is widely believed that patients lack the knowledge and information (or even the legal right, in the case of prescription drugs) to make health care decisions for themselves (choosing appropriate drugs or specialists, for example). Therefore, providers have a fiduciary obligation to recommend goods and services for patients considering only the patient's medical needs and not the provider's own economic interest. With the advent of government financing of health care, this concern has been supplemented by another: that financial rewards to providers for patient referrals might drive up program costs by encouraging the provision of unnecessary or inordinately expensive medical care.

For these reasons, the fraud and abuse statutes reproduced above prohibit paying or receiving any remuneration (directly or indirectly, overtly or covertly) for referring, purchasing, or ordering goods, facilities, items or services paid for by Medicare or Medicaid. Interpreted broadly, however, these provisions seem to proscribe a wide variety of transactions that might encourage competition or efficient production of health care. Indeed, many of the arrangements undertaken in connection with forming or operating PHOs, MSOs or integrated delivery systems discussed in Chapter 13 might, under a literal reading of the fraud and abuse statute, be felonies under the federal law. Considerable attention has been focused recently on the question of whether the statute and the judicial and administrative interpretations thereof successfully distinguish beneficial and detrimental conduct in the current market environment.

UNITED STATES v. GREBER

United States Court of Appeals, Third Circuit, 1985.
760 F.2d 68, cert. denied, 474 U.S. 988, 106 S.Ct. 396, 88 L.Ed.2d 348.

WEIS, CIRCUIT JUDGE.

In this appeal, defendant argues that payments made to a physician for professional services in connection with tests performed by a laboratory cannot be the basis of Medicare fraud. We do not agree and hold that if one purpose of the payment was to induce future referrals, the Medicare statute has been violated. * * *

After a jury trial, defendant was convicted on 20 of 23 counts in an indictment charging violations of the mail fraud, Medicare fraud, and false statement statutes. Post-trial motions were denied, and defendant has appealed.

Defendant is an osteopathic physician who is board certified in cardiology. In addition to hospital staff and teaching positions, he was the president of Cardio–Med, Inc., an organization which he formed. The company provides physicians with diagnostic services, one of which uses a Holter-monitor. This device, worn for approximately 24 hours, records the patient's cardiac activity on a tape. A computer operated by a cardiac technician scans the tape, and the data is later correlated with an activity diary the patient maintains while wearing the monitor.

Cardio–Med billed Medicare for the monitor service and, when payment was received, forwarded a portion to the referring physician. The government charged that the referral fee was 40 percent of the Medicare payment, not to exceed $65 per patient.

Based on Cardio–Med's billing practices, counts 18–23 of the indictment charged defendant with having tendered remuneration or kickbacks to the referring physicians in violation of 42 U.S.C.A. § 1395nn(b)(2)(B) (1982).

* * *

The proof as to the Medicare fraud counts (18–23) was that defendant had paid a Dr. Avallone and other physicians "interpretation fees" for the doctors' initial consultation services, as well as for explaining the test results to the patients. There was evidence that physicians received "interpretation fees" even though defendant had actually evaluated the monitoring data. Moreover, the fixed percentage paid to the referring physician was more than Medicare allowed for such services.

The government also introduced testimony defendant had given in an earlier civil proceeding. In that case, he had testified that " ... if the doctor didn't get his consulting fee, he wouldn't be using our service. So the doctor got a consulting fee." In addition, defendant told physicians at a hospital that the Board of Censors of the Philadelphia County Medical Society had said the referral fee was legitimate if the physician shared the responsibility for the report. Actually, the Society had stated that there should be separate bills because "for the monitor company to offer payment for the physicians ... is not considered to be the method of choice."

The evidence as to mail fraud was that defendant repeatedly ordered monitors for his own patients even though use of the device was not medically indicated. As a prerequisite for payment, Medicare requires that the service be medically indicated.

The Department of Health and Human Services had promulgated a rule providing that it would pay for Holter-monitoring only if it was in operation for eight hours or more. Defendant routinely certified that the temporal condition had been met, although in fact it had not.

* * *

I.   MEDICARE FRAUD

The Medicare fraud statute was amended by P. L. 95–142, 91 Stat. 1183 (1977). Congress, concerned with the growing problem of fraud and abuse in the system, wished to strengthen the penalties to enhance the deterrent effect of the statute. To achieve this purpose, the crime was upgraded from a misdemeanor to a felony.

Another aim of the amendments was to address the complaints of the United States Attorneys who were responsible for prosecuting fraud cases. They informed Congress that the language of the predecessor statute was "unclear and needed clarification." H. Rep. No. 393, Part II, 95th Cong., 1st Sess. 53, *reprinted in* 1977 U.S. CODE CONG. & AD. NEWS 3039, 3055.

A particular concern was the practice of giving "kickbacks" to encourage the referral of work. Testimony before the Congressional committee was that "physicians often determine which laboratories would do the test work for their medicaid patients by the amount of the kickbacks and rebates offered by the laboratory.... Kickbacks take a number of forms including cash, long-term credit arrangements, gifts, supplies and equipment, and the furnishing of business machines." *Id.* at 3048–3049.

To remedy the deficiencies in the statute and achieve more certainty, the present version of 42 U.S.C.A. § 1395nn(b)(2) was enacted. It provides:

"whoever knowingly and willfully offers or pays any remuneration (including any kickback, bribe or rebate) directly or indirectly, overtly or covertly in cash or in kind to induce such person—

* * *

(B) to purchase, lease, order, or arrange for or recommend purchasing . . . or ordering any . . . service or item for which payment may be made . . . under this title, shall be guilty of a felony."

The district judge instructed the jury that the government was required to prove that Cardio–Med paid to Dr. Avallone some part of the amount received from Medicare; that defendant caused Cardio–Med to make the payment; and did so knowingly and willfully as well as with the intent to induce Dr. Avallone to use Cardio–Med's services for patients covered by Medicare. The judge further charged that even if the physician interpreting the test did so as a consultant to Cardio–Med, that fact was immaterial if a purpose of the fee was to induce the ordering of services from Cardio–Med.

Defendant contends that the charge was erroneous. He insists that absent a showing that the only purpose behind the fee was to improperly induce future services, compensating a physician for services actually rendered could not be a violation of the statute.

The government argues that Congress intended to combat financial incentives to physicians for ordering particular services patients did not require.

The language and purpose of the statute support the government's view. Even if the physician performs some service for the money received, the potential for unnecessary drain on the Medicare system remains. The statute is aimed at the inducement factor.

The text refers to "any remuneration." That includes not only sums for which no actual service was performed but also those amounts for which some professional time was expended. "Remunerates" is defined as "to pay an equivalent for service." Webster Third New International Dictionary (1966). By including such items as kickbacks and bribes, the statute expands "remuneration" to cover situations where no service is performed. That a particular payment was a remuneration (which implies that a service was rendered) rather than a kickback, does not foreclose the possibility that a violation nevertheless could exist.

In United States v. Hancock, 604 F.2d 999 (7th Cir.1979), the court applied the term "kickback" found in the predecessor statute to payments made to chiropractors by laboratories which performed blood tests. The chiropractors contended that the amounts they received were legitimate handling fees for their services in obtaining, packaging, and delivering the specimens to the laboratories and then interpreting the results. The court rejected that contention and noted, "The potential for increased costs to the Medicare–Medicaid system and misapplication of federal funds is plain, where payments for the exercise of such judgments are added to the legitimate cost of the transaction. . . . [T]hese are among the evils Congress sought to prevent by enacting the kickback statutes. . . ." *Id.* at 1001.

Hancock strongly supports the government's position here, because the statute in that case did not contain the word "remuneration." The court nevertheless held that "kickback" sufficiently described the defendants' criminal activity. By adding "remuneration" to the statute in the 1977 amendment, Congress sought to make it clear that even if the transaction was not considered to be a "kickback" for which no service had been rendered, payment nevertheless violated the Act.

We are aware that in United States v. Porter, 591 F.2d 1048 (5th Cir.1979), the Court of Appeals for the Fifth Circuit took a more narrow view of "kickback" than did the court in *Hancock*. *Porter's* interpretation of the predecessor statute which did not include "remuneration" is neither binding nor persuasive. We agree with the Court of Appeals for the Sixth Circuit, which adopted the interpretation of "kickback" used in *Hancock* and rejected that of the *Porter* case. *United States v. Tapert*, 625 F.2d 111 (6th Cir.1980) [].

We conclude that the more expansive reading is consistent with the impetus for the 1977 amendments and therefore hold that the district court correctly instructed the jury. If the payments were intended to induce the physician to use Cardio–Med's services, the statute was violated, even if the payments were also intended to compensate for professional services.

A review of the record also convinces us that there was sufficient evidence to sustain the jury's verdict.

* * *

Having carefully reviewed all of the defendant's allegations, we find no reversible error. Accordingly, the judgment of the district court will be affirmed.

Notes and Questions

1. What is controversial about the *Greber* decision? What kinds of salutary or benign practices might be affected?

2. Other courts dealing with arrangements that have multiple purposes have generally followed *Greber's* holding that the purpose to induce referrals need not be the dominant or sole purpose of the scheme in order to fall within the anti-kickback law's prohibition. See, e.g., United States v. McClatchey, 217 F.3d 823, 834–35 (10th Cir. 2000). However, several decisions have introduced variations on that theme. For example, one court has required proof of a "material purpose" to obtain money for the referral of services to support a conviction under the statute. United States v. Kats, 871 F.2d at 105 (9th Cir. 1989). Another, more demanding, approach holds that proof that a "primary purpose" of the payment was to induce future referrals is required. United States v. Bay State Ambulance and Hospital Rental Service, 874 F.2d 20, 22 (1st Cir. 1989). Not surprisingly, the OIG has chosen to follow the *Greber* standard. 42 C.F.R. § 1001.951(a)(2)(i) (exclusion applies "regardless of whether the individual or entity may be able to prove that the remuneration was also intended for some other purpose . . ."). For criticism of *Greber*, see Eugene E. Elder, The Hypocrisy of the One Purpose Test in the Anti–Kickback Enforcement Law, 11 Medicare Rep. (BNA) 802 (Jul 28, 2000).

3. What purposes does the anti-kickback legislation serve? Does it advance or impede the provision of quality medical services? What economic or efficiency

arguments might be made in support of the law? On the other hand, can it be argued that the law sweeps too broadly given the dynamics of today's market? At the time the legislation was passed, providers were almost uniformly paid on a cost-based, fee-for-service basis. With most of the private sector switching to managed care or capitated provider payments, should a less restrictive rule be devised? See James Blumstein, The Fraud and Abuse Statute in an Evolving Health Care Marketplace: Life in the Health Care Speakeasy, 22 Am.J.L. & Med. 205 (1996). For the regulatory response to this problem, see the new statutory exception applicable to risk-sharing arrangements, discussed infra.

4.   With defendant's intent to obtain referrals in exchange for remuneration as the central issue in most criminal prosecutions under the anti-kickback statute, courts often must evaluate circumstantial evidence regarding defendant's mental state. A widely noted case, United States v. McClatchey, 217 F.3d 823 (10th Cir. 2000), involved the appeal from conviction under the act by Dennis McClatchey, Chief Operating Officer of Baptist Medical Center. McClatchey oversaw negotiations with doctors Robert and Ronald LaHue who were principals in Blue Valley Medical Group, a medical practice providing care to nursing home patients. Prior contracts between Baptist and the LaHues had provided for payment of $75,000 per year to the doctors for serving as co-directors of gerontology services at Baptist; however, the LaHues performed almost no services and circumstances strongly suggested that the payments were made in return for their providing patient referrals to Baptist. Id. at 828–29. The evidence at trial showed that McClatchy directed negotiations which resulted in a revised contract that was legal and that McClatchy sought and received legal advice throughout the process. Weighing competing inferences regarding defendant's intent, the Tenth Circuit upheld a jury verdict convicting McClatchy. The court found that his knowledge that the LaHues had not performed substantial services under prior contracts, that the hospital staff did not want the LaHues' services, and that McClatchey stressed the importance of maximizing admissions from BVMG patients constituted sufficient evidence to sustain the jury's findings. Id. at 830. Concerning McClatchey's reliance on counsel, the court held as follows:

> McClatchey also argues that his actions throughout the negotiation process cannot give rise to an inference of his criminal intent because they were entirely directed and controlled by legal counsel. McGrath [a subordinate directly involved in the negotiations with the LaHues] testified however, that he and McClatchey told the lawyers what services to include in the contracts, not visa versa. Thus, the jury could reasonably attribute to McClatchey and McGrath both the decision to remove a minimum hour provision from the contract after the LaHues objected to such a requirement and the inculpatory inference of intent that can be drawn therefrom. Moreover, it was not the attorneys but McClatchey, Anderson, and McGrath who made the important decision to negotiate a new contract rather than ending Baptist's relationship with BVMG. Finally, McClatchey did not always heed the attorneys' advice.... The evidence, therefore, permitted the jury to reasonably reject McClatchey's good faith reliance on counsel defense and instead find he harbored the specific intent to violate the Act.

Id. at 830–31. The advice of counsel "defense" in this context really amounts to a claim that the government did not establish that the defendant "knowingly and willfully" engaged in unlawful kickback activities. To avail oneself of this defense, however, defendant must establish that he disclosed all relevant facts to his attorneys and that he relied in good faith on that advice and acted in strict accordance with it. See Jost & Davies, supra § 3–16. What problems do you foresee for a defendant wanting to invoke this defense at trial? The government also named several prominent attorneys as unindicted co-conspirators. A court subsequently held that the government had violated the due process rights of these individuals by identifying them in a pre-trial motion. See Fraud and Abuse: Court Finds Government Violated Attorneys' Due Process Rights in Pre–Trial Naming, Health Care Daily (BNA) June 9, 1999.

5. *Greber* dealt with the issue of whether defendant's purpose satisfied the statutory standard that remuneration be given or received "in return for" an item or service reimbursable under Medicare or Medicaid. A second and distinct *mens rea* requirement concerns whether defendant knew that the transaction was unlawful. In Hanlester Network v. Shalala, 51 F. 3d 1390 (9th Cir. 1995), the Ninth Circuit held that the statute's "knowing and willful" language requires the government to prove not only that the defendant intentionally engaged in conduct prohibited by the statute, but that the defendant did so with the knowledge that his conduct violated the law. Under this standard, the government must show not only that the defendant intentionally entered into a referral arrangement later determined to violate the statute, but also that when the defendant entered into the arrangement, or while the defendant benefited from it, he or she knew the arrangement violated the dictates of the anti-kickback law.

The Supreme Court's decision in Bryan v. United States, 524 U.S. 184, 118 S.Ct. 1939, 141 L.Ed.2d 197 (1998), went a long way toward clarifying the general principles of intent applicable in criminal cases, but did not fully resolve the issue with respect to the Medicare and Medicaid Fraud and Abuse Statute. First, the Court made it clear that "willfully" will be construed in the criminal context to require proof of knowledge of some law or legal standard: "As a general matter, when used in the criminal context, a 'willful' act is one undertaken with a 'bad purpose.'" 118 S.Ct. at 1945. This standard, however, may be satisfied by showing that the defendant "acted with an evil-meaning mind," which the Court defined as acting "with knowledge that his conduct was unlawful." Id. At the same time, *Bryan* lowered the standard of proof necessary to satisfy its test by accepting an accused's knowledge of general illegality unless the relevant statute is "highly technical." See Sharon L. Davies, Willfulness Under the Anti–Kickback Rules— Lessons from Bryan v. United States, 10 Health Lawyer 14 (July 1998). In a vigorous dissent, Justice Scalia argued that the majority's approach in *Bryan* might allow convictions where the defendant's knowledge of the illegality of his conduct went to issues peripheral to the conduct with which he was charged. For example, the dissenters posited that the defendant in *Bryan* might be guilty of the offense of selling firearms without a license even if he did not know of the license requirement but was aware that some other aspect of his conduct, such as filing serial numbers off the guns, was prohibited. 118 S.Ct. at 1950. The following case applies *Bryan* to the anti-kickback law.

UNITED STATES v. STARKS

United States Court of Appeals, Eleventh Circuit, 1998.
157 F.3d 833.

BIRCH, CIRCUIT JUDGE:

Defendants Angela Starks and Andrew Siegel seek to overturn their convictions under the anti-kickback provision of the Social Security Act, 42 U.S.C. § 1320a–7b ("the Anti–Kickback statute"). Specifically, Starks and Siegel argue that the district court erred by refusing to instruct the jury concerning the relevant mens rea. In addition, Starks and Siegel contend that the Anti–Kickback statute is unconstitutionally vague. We AFFIRM IN PART, REVERSE IN PART, and REMAND.

BACKGROUND

In 1992, Andrew Siegel was both the president and the sole shareholder of Future Steps, Inc., a corporation that developed and operated treatment programs for drug addiction. On April 22, 1992, Future Steps contracted with Florida CHS, Inc. to run a chemical dependency unit for pregnant women at Florida CHS's Metropolitan General Hospital ("the Hospital"). In return, Florida CHS promised to pay Future Steps a share of the Hospital's profits from the program. As a Medicaid provider, the Hospital performed medical services for indigent and disabled persons and received payment for these activities through Consultec, the fiscal intermediary for the Florida Medicaid program. Before executing the Future Steps–Florida CHS contract, Siegel initialed each page of the agreement, which included a provision explicitly forbidding Future Steps from making any payment for patient referrals in violation of the Anti–Kickback statute.

At the time Siegel signed this contract, Angela Starks and Barbara Henry had just become community health aides in the employ of the State of Florida Department of Health and Rehabilitative Services ("HRS"). Although Starks and Henry were employees of HRS, they actually worked in a federally-funded research project in Tampa, Florida known as "Project Support." As part of their duties, Starks and Henry advised pregnant women about possible treatment for drug abuse. Upon beginning their work at HRS, Starks and Henry learned from their supervisor both that they could not accept any outside employment that might pose a conflict of interest with their work at HRS and that they were obligated to report any outside employment to HRS.

During the spring of 1992, Future Steps had difficulty attracting patients. One of Future Steps's salaried "liaison workers," Robin Doud–Lacher, however, identified Project Support as a potential source of referrals because of its relationship with high-risk pregnant women. When Doud–Lacher's initial efforts to establish a referral relationship between Future Steps and Project Support failed, Siegel suggested to Doud–Lacher that she spend more time at Project Support, give diapers to Project Support, take Project Support workers to lunch, and otherwise build a relationship with Project Support's employees.

During one of her subsequent visits to Project Support, Doud–Lacher learned from Starks and Henry that cuts in federal spending threatened to reduce their work hours. When Starks and Henry asked if Doud–Loucher knew of other available work, she promised to inquire for them about opportunities at Future Steps.

After discussing Starks and Henry's interest with her immediate supervisor, Doud–Lacher spoke directly with Siegel about hiring the two women. Despite Starks and Henry's extant employment with HRS, Siegel told Doud–Loucher that he would pay Starks and Henry $250 for each patient they referred: $125 when a referred woman began inpatient drug treatment with Future Steps and $125 after each such woman had stayed in Future Steps's program for two weeks.[3] After accepting Siegel's terms, Starks and Henry did not report their referral arrangement to anyone at Project Support or HRS.

At the outset of their work for Future Steps, Starks and Henry received checks written on Future Steps's account and signed by Siegel. Before issuing these checks, Siegel verified that the referred patients had actually entered the Future Steps program; he did not, though, verify that the referrals were legal. Although the checks Siegel signed were coded variously as payments for aftercare, counseling, and marketing expenses, Siegel was actually only paying Starks and Henry for their referrals. In fact, Siegel did not at any time pay Starks and Henry for any of their time, effort, or business expenses, or for any covered Medicare service.

When Doud–Lacher left Future Steps, Siegel had Michael Ix, another liaison worker, assume responsibility for the Starks and Henry referral arrangement. Generally, either Starks or Henry would call Ix and ask him to pick up a referral directly from the Project Support clinic. When Ix arrived at Future Steps with the referred patient, Siegel would give Ix a check for Starks and Henry. Later, after Henry told Ix that she did not want anyone at Project Support to see her receiving checks from Future Steps, Ix agreed to deliver the checks to Starks and Henry either in the Project Support parking lot or at a restaurant. Between June 1992 and January 1993, Future Steps wrote checks payable to Starks totaling $2750 and to Henry totaling $1975.

At the end of 1992, Future Steps began paying Starks and Henry in cash. To make these payments, Ix would withdraw cash from his personal bank account and meet Starks and Henry either at a restaurant or at a twelve-step program; Siegel and Future Steps would then reimburse Ix. On one occasion, Siegel accomplished this reimbursement by meeting Ix in a restaurant restroom and giving him $600. In total, Ix paid Starks and Henry approximately $1000 to $1200 in cash.

Beyond the impropriety of Starks and Henry's acceptance of referral payments from Siegel, the referral arrangement directly affected Starks and Henry's counseling of the pregnant women who relied on them and Project Support for help. At trial, several of Future Steps's clients testified that Starks and Henry threatened that HRS would take away their babies if they did not receive treatment for their drug addictions; in some instances, Starks and Henry threatened women with the loss of their babies if they did not go specifically to Future Steps. According to these women's testimony, Starks and Henry informed them only about Future Steps's program (eschewing discussion of alternative treatments), and most waited with Starks and Henry at the Project Support clinic until someone from Future Steps arrived to take them to the Hospital. Starks and Henry's physician supervisor also testified that she told the two HRS employees to be more evenhanded in their advice to Project Support's patients, after the number of women going to Future Steps from Project Support increased substantially.

---

3. Although Starks and Henry had suggested limiting their referrals to patients living outside the area surrounding Project Support and/or restricting their recruiting for Future Steps to their non-HRS hours, Siegel imposed no bounds on the nature of their referral efforts.

In total, Starks and Henry referred eighteen women from Project Support to Future Steps. From these referrals, the Hospital received $323,023.04 in Medicaid payments.

On July 29, 1994, a federal grand jury indicted Siegel, Starks, Henry, and Doud–Lacher on five counts related to the referrals. Count One charged all four defendants with conspiring against the United States, in violation of 18 U.S.C. § 371, by offering to pay remuneration for referral of Medicare patients, in violation of 42 U.S.C. § 1320a–7b(b)(2)(A), and by soliciting and receiving such referral payments, in violation of 42 U.S.C. § 1320a–7b(b)(1)(A). Counts Two and Three charged Siegel and Doud–Loucher with paying remuneration to Starks and Henry to induce referrals of Medicaid patients, in violation of 42 U.S.C. § 1320a–7b(b)(2)(A). Finally, Count Four charged Starks and Count Five charged Henry with soliciting and receiving referral payments, in violation of 42 U.S.C. § 1320a–7b(b)(1)(A).

DISCUSSION

On appeal, defendants Starks and Siegel renew two contentions from their trial. First, they claim that the district court committed reversible error when it refused to instruct the jury that, because of the Anti–Kickback statute's mens rea requirement, Starks and Siegel had to have known that their referral arrangement violated the Anti–Kickback statute in order to be convicted. Second, Starks and Siegel argue that the Social Security Act's prohibition on paid referrals, when considered together with the Act's safe harbor provision, 42 U.S.C. § 1320a–7b(b)(3) ("the Safe Harbor provision"), is unconstitutionally vague. We address each of these arguments before turning to the government's cross-appeals concerning Siegel's sentence.

I. Starks and Siegel's Appeals

A. The "Willfully" Instruction

Starks and Siegel argue that the district court erred in its instruction concerning the mens rea required under the Anti–Kickback statute. According to 42 U.S.C. § 1320a–7b(b), it is illegal for a person to "knowingly and willfully solicit[ ] or receive[ ] any remuneration" for referrals for services covered by the federal government. At trial, the district court gave our circuit's pattern instruction regarding the term "willfully":

> The word willfully, as that term is used from time to time in these instructions, means the act was committed voluntarily and purposely, with the specific intent to do something the law forbids, that is with a bad purpose, either to disobey or disregard the law.

In reviewing the district court's charge, we determine whether the court's instructions as a whole sufficiently informed the jurors so that they understood the issues and were not misled. [ ]

In support of their claim, Starks and Siegel rely heavily on United States v. Sanchez-Corcino, 85 F.3d 549 (11th Cir.1996), and Ratzlaf v. United States, 510 U.S. 135, 114 S.Ct. 655, 126 L.Ed.2d 615 (1994). Since we heard oral argument on this case, however, the Supreme Court has issued an opinion in Bryan v. United States, 524 U.S. 184, 118 S.Ct. 1939, 141 L.Ed.2d 197 (1998), that clearly refutes Starks and Siegel's position.

In Sanchez–Corcino, a panel of this court held that the term "willfully" in 18 U.S.C. § 922(a)(1)(D) (requiring license for firearms), meant that the government had to prove that a defendant "acted with knowledge of the [§ 922(a)(1)(D)] licensing requirement." Id. at 553, 554 ("[k]nowledge of the general illegality of one's conduct is not the same as knowledge that one is violating a specific rule"). In Bryan, though, the Supreme Court explicitly rejected our decision in Sanchez–Corcino. See Bryan, 524 U.S. at 193 S.Ct. at 1946. According to the Bryan Court, a jury may find a defendant guilty of violating a statute employing the word "willfully" if it believes "that the defendant acted with an evil-meaning mind, that is to say, that he acted with knowledge that his conduct was unlawful." Id. at 193, 118 S.Ct. at 1946. Further, the Supreme Court distinguished tax or financial cases, such as Ratzlaf, that "involved highly technical statutes that presented the danger of ensnaring individuals engaged in apparently innocent conduct." Id.[4] Because "the jury found that [the defendant] knew that his conduct was unlawful," the Bryan Court wrote, "[t]he danger of convicting individuals engaged in apparently innocent activity that motivated our decisions in the tax cases and Ratzlaf is not present here." Id. (footnote omitted). Thus, the Court held that "the willfulness requirement of [the firearms statute] does not carve out an exemption to the traditional rule that ignorance of the law is no excuse; knowledge that conduct is unlawful is all that is required." Id.[5]

Analogously, the Anti–Kickback statute does not constitute a special exception. Section 1320a–7b is not a highly technical tax or financial regulation that poses a danger of ensnaring persons engaged in apparently innocent conduct. Indeed, the giving or taking of kickbacks for medical referrals is hardly the sort of activity a person might expect to be legal; compared to the licensing provisions that the Bryan Court considered, such kickbacks are more clearly malum in se, rather than malum prohibitum. Thus, we see no error in the district court's refusal to give Starks and Siegel's requested instruction.[6]

B. Vagueness

Starks and Siegel also argue that the Anti–Kickback statute is unconstitutionally vague because people of ordinary intelligence in either of their positions could not have ascertained from a reading of its Safe Harbor provision that their conduct was illegal.[7] Under the Safe Harbor provision, the

---

4. In Ratzlaf, the Court reviewed a gambler's conviction for illegally structuring his banking transactions so as to avoid technical reporting requirements.

5. The Bryan Court thus upheld a jury instruction strikingly similar to the district court's "willfully" charge in this case:

A person acts willfully if he acts intentionally and purposely and with the intent to do something the law forbids, that is, with the bad purpose to disobey or to disregard the law. Now, the person need not be aware of the specific law or rule that his conduct may be violating. But he must act with the intent to do something that the law forbids. [ ]

6. Starks and Siegel also claim that the evidence was not sufficient to prove that they acted "willfully." Given that the government only had to show that they knew that they

were acting unlawfully, however, this claim is unpersuasive. The government produced ample evidence, including the furtive methods by which Siegel remunerated Starks and Henry, from which the jury could reasonably have inferred that Starks and Siegel knew that they were breaking the law—even if they may not have known that they were specifically violating the Anti–Kickback statute.

7. Starks and Siegel offer a variety of arguments to the effect that persons working in the medical field cannot anticipate what is prohibited under the Anti–Kickback statute and what is protected by that statute's Safe Harbor provision. They do not, and cannot, challenge, however, the government's contention that, since this is not a First Amendment case, we must evaluate their claim of vagueness only on an as-applied basis. [ ] Thus, we consider

Anti–Kickback statute's prohibition on referral payments shall not apply to ... any amount paid by an employer to an employee (who has a bona fide employment relationship with such employer) for employment in the provision of covered items and services.... According to Starks and Siegel, this provision is vague because ordinary people in their position might reasonably have thought that Starks and Henry were "bona fide employees" who were exempt from the Anti–Kickback statute's prohibition on remuneration for referrals.

Starks and Siegel are correct that a criminal statute must define an offense with sufficient clarity to enable ordinary people to understand what conduct is prohibited. Both the particular facts of this case and the nature of the Anti–Kickback statute, however, undercut Starks and Siegel's vagueness argument. First, even if Starks and Siegel believed that they were bona fide employees, they were not providing "covered items or services." As the government has shown, Starks received payment from Siegel and Future Steps only for referrals and not for any legitimate service for which the Hospital received any Medicare reimbursement. At the same time, persons in either Siegel's or Starks's position could hardly have thought that either Starks or Henry was a bona fide employee; unlike all of Future Steps's other workers, Starks and Henry did not receive regular salary checks at the Hospital. Instead, they clandestinely received their checks (often bearing false category codes) or cash in parking lots and other places outside the Project Support clinic so as to avoid detection by other Project Support workers.

Furthermore, beyond these particular facts, we see no reason to view the Anti–Kickback statute as vague. In Village of Hoffman Estates v. The Flipside, 455 U.S. 489, 498–499, 102 S.Ct. 1186, 1193, 71 L.Ed.2d 362 (1982), the Supreme Court set out several factors for a court to consider in determining whether a statute is impermissibly vague, including whether the statute (1) involves only economic regulation, (2) provides only civil, rather than criminal, penalties, (3) contains a scienter requirement mitigating vagueness, and (4) threatens any constitutionally protected rights. As two of our sister circuits have already concluded, these factors militate against finding the Anti–Kickback statute unconstitutional. [ ] Indeed, the statute regulates only economic conduct,[8] and it does not chill any constitutional rights. Moreover, although the statute does provide for criminal penalties, it requires "knowing and willful" conduct, a mens rea standard that mitigates any otherwise inherent vagueness in the Anti–Kickback statutes's provisions. [ ] In sum, we agree with the district court that the Anti–Kickback statute gave Starks and Siegel fair warning that their conduct was illegal and that the statute therefore is not unconstitutionally vague.

* * *

Starks and Siegel's claim in light of the facts of this individual case, looking only to the constitutionality of the Anti–Kickback statute as the government has applied it to Starks and Siegel. [ ]

8. In Hoffman Estates, the Court explained that "economic regulation is subject to a less strict vagueness test because its subject is often more narrow, and because businesses, which face economic demands to plan behavior carefully, can be expected to consult relevant legislation in advance of action." 455 U.S. at 498, 102 S.Ct. at 1193 (footnote omitted).

CONCLUSION

... With regard to Starks and Siegel's appeal, we hold that the district court did not err when it refused to give their requested instruction, and that the Anti–Kickback statute is not unconstitutionally vague as applied to Starks and Siegel. Therefore, we AFFIRM these parts of the district court's judgment. ...

Notes and Questions

1. What aspects of the anti-kickback law does the 11th Circuit rely upon in *Starks* in holding that specific knowledge of that statute is not required? Are you satisfied that this approach does not run a risk of "ensnaring persons engaged in apparently innocent conduct" under the test set out in *Bryan*? What evidence going to the defendant's intent was available to satisfy the government's burden of showing that the defendants knew they were acting unlawfully? Were the inferences drawn from the defendants' conduct sufficient in this case? See generally Sharon L. Davies, The Jurisprudence of Willfullness: An Evolving Theory of Excusable Ignorance, 48 Duke L. J. 341 (1998).

2. Defendants claimed that they qualified as bona fide employees under the statutory exception, 42 U.S.C. § 1320a–7b(b)(3), and safe harbor regulations, 42 C.F.R. § 1001.952, governing the anti-kickback law. The latter regulations, which are discussed in the next section of this chapter, shelter certain arrangements from legal challenge. The employment exception excepts remuneration paid to "bona fide" employees which are defined in accordance with Internal Revenue Code, 36 U.S.C.A. 3121(d)(2), and excludes independent contractor relationships. Why did Starks and Siegel not qualify for the exception? As a general matter, what policy or rationale supports allowing an entity to hire a person who may solicit Medicare-related business to that entity? Don't such arrangements pose the same risks as other forms of remuneration in exchange for referrals?

3. An area of continuing controversy is whether violation of the anti-kickback provisions can be prosecuted as a false claim under the False Claims Act. The Fifth Circuit has rejected the argument that an illegal kickback taints the provider's claim for reimbursement so as to bring it within the FCA. Thompson v. Columbia/HCA Healthcare Corporation, 125 F.3d 899 (5th Cir. 1997). At the same time, that court held that a hospital could be liable for submitting false claims and false statements if it explicitly certified compliance with program regulations and payment was conditioned on such certification. Id. Recurring issues include whether an implicit certification of compliance with administrative regulations will trigger liability and whether the government must prove that compliance with the regulations was material to its decision to pay the claim. See John T. Boese & Beth C. McCain, Why Thompson is Wrong: Misuses of the False Claims Act to Enforce the Anti–Kickback Act, 51 Ala.L.Rev. 1 (1999); Pamela H. Bucy, Growing Pains: Using the False Claims Act to Combat Health Care Fraud, 51 Ala. L. Rev. 57, 78–79 (1999). Finally, an issue arises as to whether the government has suffered any injury where no overcharge, upcoding or false billing occurred. On remand the district court in *Thompson* noted that it was not necessary for the government to prove that it had sustained damages, but also found that the government had incurred administrative and costs as a result of the false claim. United States ex rel. Thompson v. Columbia/HCA Healthcare Corporation, 20 F. Supp. 1017, 1047 (S.D. Tex. 1998). Is the use of the False Claims Act to enforce violations of the anti-kickback statute and regulations an example of government overreaching? Should qui tam relators be permitted to use the statute in this way

as well, even when the government has elected not to pursue technical violations of the anti-kickback law? See Boese & McCain supra; Robert Salcido, Mixing Oil and Water: The Government's Mistaken Use of the Medicare Anti–Kickback Statute in False Claims Act Prosecutions, 6 Annals Health L. 105 (1997).

4. When might the actions of attorneys advising clients and preparing documents that result in violations of the anti-kickback laws result in criminal liability? In the *McClatchey* case, discussed earlier in this chapter, for the first time in Medicare fraud litigation, two attorneys were charged with participating in a conspiracy. The district court dismissed all charges against the lawyers, holding that no reasonable jury could find beyond a reasonable doubt that they willfully committed any of the criminal acts charged in the indictment. United States v. Anderson, No. 98–20030 (D. Kan., transcript filed Mar. 9, 1999). The judge stressed that the record revealed that the lawyers held a good faith belief that it was possible to structure the deal between the hospitals and the medical group legally and that they had advised their clients that if fair market value were paid for legitimate consulting services, the relationship would pass legal muster. It also observed that the record showed that the lawyers relied on their clients for information and were not engaged to monitor the activities of consultants. Furthermore, when potential compliance problems were brought to their attention, the attorneys urged their clients to make sure that they were insisting upon paying fair market value for real services. Id. The court went on to observe that:

> [E]ven if patient referrals were devoutly hoped for and anticipated; even if the volume of patients could be large; even if the parties might never have come together but for [one hospital] having embarked on a long-range plan that depended on attracting nursing home patients, there is nothing in the evidence of the law that would have a priori precluded a legal relationship from being entered into under these circumstances. The state of the law was in flux and the lawyers adapted their advice to it as it changed.... The problem here is that a very simple concept, "payment for patients is illegal," became far from simple as Congress, the Executive Branch, and the Courts got more deeply involved.

Do these comments suggest a different view of the anti-kickback statute than that expressed by the 11th Circuit in *Starks*? The result for the providers charged in the conspiracy was quite different, however. The jury convicted two hospital executives and both doctors who received the kickbacks for violations of the Medicare fraud statute and for participating in a conspiracy to defraud the federal government. Relying heavily on incriminating documents and statements, the government was apparently able to persuade the jury, which was instructed under the Greber "one purpose" standard, that payments to the doctors were designed at least in part to induce referrals, notwithstanding evidence of legitimate patient care and improved continuity of care purposes surrounding the arrangement. See United States v. Anderson, 85 F. Supp. 2d 1047 (D. Kan. 1999), aff'd United States v. McClatchey, 217 F.3d 823 (10th Cir. 2000). For criticism of the decision to indict lawyers for their role in advising clients on fraud and abuse matters, see Gerson & Gladieux, Advice of Counsel: Eroding Confidentiality, 51 Ala. L. Rev 163 (1999); Michal M. Schmidt, Neither an Aider nor Abettor Be; Attorneys Become Prosecutorial Targets for Federal Healthcare Crimes, 32 J. Health L. 251 (1999).

Problem: Enforcement of the Fraud and Abuse Law by Private Parties

Several years ago, Drs. Vaughn, Canseco and Clemens leased space from Yawkey Community Hospital. The hospital gave each doctor discounts from prevailing market rates in the rent it charged them. Although the leases allowed for periodic increases based on the Consumer Price Index, the hospital did not enforce this provision on a regular basis. The doctors' testimony reveals a lack of awareness that the rents were below market rates and all deny having any understanding that referrals would be expected of them. Testimony of members of the hospital's board indicates that they believed that physicians located in nearby offices were more likely to refer to Yawkey Hospital; that the hospital's decision not to raise rents was based on a desire to increase physician "loyalty"; and that below-market rental rates were established in order to encourage patient referrals.

Accepting as true the testimony of all parties, has the hospital violated the fraud and abuse laws? Assume now that Fenway Health System has acquired Yawkey Community Hospital. Can Fenway Health Systems walk away from the leases arguing they are invalid because they violate federal and state anti-kickback laws?

E. STATUTORY EXCEPTIONS, SAFE HARBORS AND FRAUD ALERTS

The fraud and abuse statute contains several common sense exceptions. For example, discounts or reductions in price obtained by providers of services, literally proscribed by the language of the statute, are permitted if properly disclosed and reflected in the claimed costs or charges of the provider. Likewise, amounts paid by employers to employees and rebates obtained by group purchasing organizations are exempted under specified circumstances. (The employment exception is discussed in Note 2 following U.S. v. Starks, supra.) The Health Insurance Portability and Accountability Act of 1996 added an important new exception for "risk-sharing" arrangements. As described below, this exception is designed to answer criticisms that the law unreasonably deters arrangements such as capitated payments that foster delivery of cost-effective care and pose no substantial risk of overutilization, the key concern of the anti-kickback rules.

In addition to these statutory exceptions, the Secretary of HHS, acting pursuant to Congressional directive, has promulgated so called "Safe Harbor" regulations to describe conduct that is not criminal under the fraud and abuse laws. This is a somewhat unusual provision in that it permits an administrative agency to designate conduct otherwise illegal under federal law as not subject to prosecution by the Justice Department. 42 C.F.R. § 101.952. With the final adoption of new safe harbors in November, 1999, the total number of safe harbors, including the interim final rules for risk sharing arrangements, now stands at twenty-three. Among the more important of the safe harbors are the following:

Rental, Personal Services, and Management Contracts

Three safe harbors for space and equipment rentals and for personal services and management contracts have very similar standards. Leases for space or equipment must be in writing and signed by the parties; must identify the space or equipment covered; must specify when and for how long space or equipment will be used and the precise rental charge for each use if the lease is not for full time use; and must be for at least one year. The amount of rent must be set in advance, must not take into account the volume and value of any referrals or business generated, and, most importantly, must reflect the fair market value of the space or equipment. Fair market value is defined as the value of the property for "general commercial purposes," or "the value of the equipment when obtained from a manufacturer or professional distributor," and cannot take into account the proximity or convenience of the equipment or space to the referral course. The requirements for personal services or management contracts are nearly identical to the rental provisions.

Sale of Practice and Physician Recruitment

A limited safe harbor exists to protect sales of practices by retiring physicians. The sale must be completed within one year from the date of the agreement, after which the selling practitioner must no longer be in a professional position to refer Medicare or Medicaid patients or otherwise generate business for the purchasing practitioner. Sale options are not permitted unless they are completely performed within a year. The increasingly common practice of hospitals and MSOs purchasing the practices of physicians who thereafter are retained on staff is explicitly not protected by this rule, though a separate safe harbor for physician recruitment currently under consideration may protect some of these activities, and buying out a physician for a flat payment and then later employing the physician may be permissible.

A practitioner recruitment safe harbor protects recruitment efforts by hospitals and entities located in government-specified health professional shortage areas (HPSAs). It permits payments or other exchanges to induce practitioners relocating from a different geographic area or new practitioners (in practice within their current specialty for less than one year) provided seven conditions are met. Among those conditions are that the agreement be in writing; that at least 75 per cent of the new practice revenue be generated from the HPSA; that the practitioner not be barred from establishing staff privileges with or referring to other entities; and that benefits and amendments to the contract may not be based on the value or volume of practitioners' referrals.

Safe Harbor for Price Reductions Offered to Eligible Managed Care Organizations

After a lengthy negotiated rulemaking process, the OIG announced two interim final rules to implement the statutory exception governing certain Eligible Managed Care Organizations (EMCOs). The two new safe harbors apply to (1) financial arrangements between managed care entities paid by a federal health care program on a capitated basis and individuals or entities agreeing to provide to the manage care entity items or services under a written agreement and (2) financial agreements that, through a risk sharing arrangement, place individuals or entities at "substantial financial risk" for the cost or utilization of the items or services which they are obligated to provide. Recognizing that EMCOs having risk contracts which operate on a capitated rather than fee-for-service basis present little risk of overutilization and increased health program costs, the safe harbor protects price reductions (and other exchanges or remunerations) between eligible MCOs and individuals and entities. The second part of the price reduction safe harbor regulation addresses financial arrangements (subcontracts) between first tier contractors and other individuals or entities, known as downstream contractors.

Referral Agreements for Specialty Services.

This new safe harbor is designed to reduce any untoward effects that the anti-kickback laws may have on continuity of care and patient access to specialists. It protects any exchange of value among individuals and entities if one provider agrees to refer a patient to another provider for the rendering of a specialty service in exchange for an agreement by the other party to refer that patient back at a later time, as long as neither party may pay the other for the referral, although members of the same group practice may share revenues of the group practice.

Ambulatory Surgery Centers.

This new safe harbor provides a detailed regulatory scheme that protects returns on an investment interest, such as a dividend or interest income, in four kinds of Ambulatory Surgery Centers (ASCs): surgeon-owned ASCs, single-specialty ASCs, multi-specialty ASCs, and hospital/physician ASCs. It does not apply to an ASC located on a hospital's premises that shares operating or recovery room space with the hospital for treatment of the hospital's inpatients or outpatients.

Investment Interests

This complex safe harbor provides that there is no violation for returns on "investment interests" including both equity and debt interests in corporations, partnerships and other entities held directly or indirectly through family members or other indirect ownership vehicles. It covers, first, investments in large, publicly-traded entities registered with the SEC and having $50 million in net tangible assets. The investment must also be obtained on terms equally available to the public, the entity must market items and services in the same way to investors and noninvestors, and must comply with other requirements. Second, certain investments in small entities are permitted provided no more than 40 percent of the value of the investment interests in each class of investment is held by persons who are in a position to make or influence referrals to, furnish items or services to, or otherwise generate business for the entity. Moreover, no more than 40 percent of the gross revenue of the entity may come from referrals, items or services from investors. A number of other requirements apply including several that are different for active investors and passive investors. The 1999 amendments to this safe harbor allow for higher investment percentages in medically underserved areas. The importance of this safe harbor is limited by the fact that it does not shelter arrangements covered by the Stark Law (discussed in the next section of this chapter) which applies different standards to investments. However, for services not covered by Stark, the safe harbor has continuing importance.

A wide variety of other arrangements are covered by safe harbors, including investment interests in group practices, subsidies for obstetrical malpractice insurance subsidies, and waivers of copayments and deductibles for inpatient hospital care and group purchasing organizations. Many of these safe harbors are narrowly drawn and afford only limited protection despite sometimes broader coverage sometimes implied by their titles. Moreover, safe harbor protection requires compliance with every requirement of all applicable safe harbors and the OIG has refused to adopt a standard of "substantial compliance" or to declaim intention to pursue "technical" or de minimis violations. See 56 Fed. Reg. 35,953, 35,957 (1991). At the same time, however, the safe harbors are not standards; conduct falling outside their boundaries may still pass muster under the intent-based statutory standard. Useful sources on the safe harbors include: Jost & Davies, supra, Sections 3–11—3–13; Linda A. Baumann, Navigating the New Safe Harbors to the Anti-Kickback Statute, 12 Health Lawyer 1 (Feb. 2000).

Another important source of guidance in this area is the fraud alerts issued by the Office of Inspector General of HHS. These alerts set forth the OIG's interpretation of the statute as applied in certain situations and are intended to encourage individuals to report suspected violations to the government. Most notable among these is the Special Fraud Alert on Joint Venture Arrangements issued in 1989. The alert identified "questionable features" of certain joint ventures such as where: investors chosen are potential referral sources; the investment shares of physician investors are proportionate to the volume of referrals; physicians are encouraged to refer to the entity or to divest their interest if referrals fall below an acceptable level or if physicians become unable to refer; the joint venture is structured as a "shell"; or the amounts of the investment are disproportionately small and returns disproportionately large. A special Fraud Alert on Hospital Incentives to Physicians issued on May 7, 1992, addressed physician-to-hospital referrals, identifying as "suspect incentive arrangements" the payment of incentives for each referral; free or discounted office space, equipment or office staff training; minimum income guarantees; low interest loans or loans subject to forgiveness based on referrals; payment of physicians' travel expenses to conferences; payment of physicians' continuing education; disproportionately low health insurance rates for physicians; and payment for services at above-market rates. Other areas targeted by fraud alerts have included health care; nursing facilities reimbursement for care; prescription drug marketing schemes; the provision of clinical lab services; nursing home arrangements with hospices; physician certification for medical equipment supplies and home health services; rental of space in physician offices; and routine waivers of copayments or deductibles under Medicare Part B; nursing home arrangements with hospices; and physician certifications in the provision of medical equipment and supplies and home services and rental of space in physician offices. A source of fact-specific guidance is the advisory opinion process illustrated by the following response letter from the OIG.

DEPARTMENT OF HEALTH AND HUMAN SERVICES
OFFICE OF THE INSPECTOR GENERAL
ADVISORY OPINION NO. 98–4

April 15, 1998.

Dear [Name Redacted]:

We are writing in response to your request for an advisory opinion, in which you ask whether a proposed management services contract between a medical practice management company and a physician practice, which provides that the management company will be reimbursed for its costs and paid a percentage of net practice revenues (the "Proposed Arrangement"), would constitute illegal remuneration as defined in the anti-kickback statute, § 1128B(b) of the Social Security Act (the "Act").

You have certified that all of the information you provided in your request, including all supplementary letters, is true and correct, and constitutes a complete description of the material facts regarding the Proposed Arrangement. In issuing this opinion, we have relied solely on the facts and information you presented to us. We have not undertaken any independent investigation of such information.

Based on the information provided, we conclude that the Proposed Arrangement may constitute prohibited remuneration under § 1128B(b) of the Act.

I. FACTUAL BACKGROUND

A. The Parties

Dr. X is a family practice physician who has incorporated as, and practices under the name of, Company A ("Company A"). Company A is proposing to enter into an agreement to establish a family practice and walk-in clinic with a corporation, Company B ("Company B"). Dr. X is the sole Requestor of this advisory opinion.

B. The Arrangement

Under the Proposed Arrangement, Company A will provide all physician services at the clinic. Company A may hire additional physicians and other medical personnel with the mutual agreement of Company B. Company A will pay all physician compensation and fringe benefits, including but not limited to, licensing fees, continuing education, and malpractice premiums.

Company B will find a suitable location for the clinic and furnish the initial capital for the office, furniture, and operating expenses. Once operational, Company B will provide or arrange for all operating services for the clinic, including accounting, billing, purchasing, direct marketing, and hiring of non-medical personnel and outside vendors.

Company B will also provide Company A with management and marketing services for the clinic, including the negotiation and oversight of health care contracts with various payors, including indemnity plans, managed care plans, and Federal health care programs.

In addition to Company B's activities on behalf of Company A, Company B will set up provider networks. These networks may include Company A and, if required by Company B, Company A has agreed that it will refer its patients to the providers in such networks.

In return for its services, Company B's payment will have three components. Company A will be required to make a capital payment equal to a percentage of the initial cost of each capital asset purchased for Company A per year for six years. Company B will also receive a fair market value payment for the operating services it provides and an at-cost payment for any operating services for which it contracts. Company B will receive a percentage of Company A's monthly net revenues for its management services.

If the percentage payment described above is not permitted by law, then the parties will establish a management fee reflecting the contemplated financial results of the arrangement or, if the parties cannot agree to a fixed amount, the parties will hire an accounting firm to determine an appropriate fixed fee (the "Alternative Proposed Arrangement").

II. Legal Analysis

A. Anti–Kickback Statute

[The Advisory Opinion summarizes the provisions of the anti-kickback statute, § 1128(B)(b), and notes the holding in Greber that liability may be ascribed to both sides of an illegal arrangement where "one purpose" of the remuneration was to obtain money for referrals or induce further referrals.]

B. Safe Harbor Regulations

In 1991, the Department of Health and Human Services (the "Department") published safe harbor regulations that define practices that are not subject to the anti-kickback statute because such practices would be unlikely to result in fraud or abuse. Failure to comply with a safe harbor provision does not make an arrangement per se illegal. For this Proposed Arrangement, the only safe harbor regulation potentially available is the personal services and management contracts safe harbor. See 42 C.F.R. § 1001.952(d).

The personal services and management contracts safe harbor provides protection for personal services contracts if all of the following six standards are met: (i) the agreement is set out in writing and signed by the parties; (ii) the agreement specifies the services to be performed; (iii) if the services are to be performed on a part-time basis, the schedule for performance is specified in the contract; (iv) the agreement is for not less than one year; (v) the aggregate amount of compensation is fixed in advance, based on fair market value in an arms-length transaction, and not determined in a manner that takes into account the volume or value of any referrals or business otherwise generated between the parties for which payment may be made by Medicare or a State health care program; and (vi) the services performed under the agreement do not involve the promotion of business that violates any Federal or State law.

We conclude that the Proposed Arrangement does not qualify for this safe harbor. In order for an agreement to be protected by this safe harbor, strict compliance with all six standards is necessary. In this case, the compensation is not an aggregate amount, fixed in advance, as the safe harbor requires. Accordingly, the safe harbor standards are not satisfied.

C. Percentage Compensation Arrangement

Because compliance with a safe harbor is not mandatory, the fact that the Proposed Arrangement does not fit within a safe harbor does not mean that the Proposed Arrangement is necessarily unlawful. Rather, we must analyze this Proposed Arrangement on a case-by-case basis.

Percentage compensation arrangements for marketing services may implicate the anti-kickback statute. In our preamble to the 1991 final safe harbor rules, 56 Fed. Reg. 35952 (July 29, 1991), we explained that the anti-kickback statute "on its face prohibits offering or acceptance of remuneration, inter alia, for the purposes of 'arranging for or recommending purchasing, leasing, or ordering any . . . service or item' payable under Medicare or Medicaid. Thus, we believe that many marketing and advertising activities may involve at least technical violations of the statute." 56 Fed. Reg. at 35974.

This Proposed Arrangement is problematic for the following reasons.

• The Proposed Arrangement may include financial incentives to increase patient referrals. The compensation that Company B receives for its management services is a percentage of Company A's net revenue, including revenue from business derived from managed care contracts arranged by Company B. Such activities may potentially implicate the anti-kickback statute, because the compensation Company B will receive will be in part for marketing services. Where such compensation is based on a percentage, there is at least a potential technical violation of the anti-kickback statute. In addition, Company B will be establishing networks of specialist physicians to whom Company A may be required to refer in some circumstances. Further, Company B will presumably receive some compensation for its efforts in connection with the development and operation of these specialist networks. In these circumstances, any evaluation of the Proposed Arrangement requires information about the relevant financial relationships. However, Company B is not a requestor for this advisory opinion, and Company A does not have information regarding Company B's related business arrangements.

Accordingly, we have insufficient information to ascertain the level of risk of fraud or abuse presented by the Proposed Arrangement.[9]

• The Proposed Arrangement contains no safeguards against overutilization. In light of the proposed establishment of provider networks with required referral arrangements, there is a risk of potential overutilization. Under the Proposed Arrangement, we are unable to determine what, if any, controls will be implemented under managed care contracts negotiated for Company A by Company B. Without such controls, we can not be assured that items and services paid for by Federal health care programs will not be overutilized.

• The Proposed Arrangement may include financial incentives that increase the risk of abusive billing practices. Since Company B receives a percentage of Company A's revenue and will arrange for Company A's billing, Company B has an incentive to maximize Company A's revenue. This Office has a longstanding concern that percentage billing arrangements may increase the risk of upcoding and similar abusive billing practices.

9. We are also precluded from reaching a conclusion about the Alternative proposed Arrangement. Such a determination would require us to evaluate whether the agreed upon fee is fixed at fair market value. We are prevented from making that determination by § 1128D(b)(3)(A) of the Act, which prohibits our opining on fair market value in an advisory opinion.

III. CONCLUSION

The advisory opinion process permits the OIG to protect specific arrangements that "contain[ ] limitations, requirements, or controls, that give adequate assurances that Federal health care programs cannot be abused." See 62 Fed. Reg. 7350, 7351 (February 19, 1997). Based on the facts we have been presented, the Proposed Arrangement appears to contain no limitations, requirements, or controls that would minimize any fraud or abuse.

Therefore, since we cannot be confident that there is no more than a minimal risk of fraud or abuse, we must conclude that the Proposed Arrangement may involve prohibited remuneration under the anti-kickback statute and thus potentially be subject to sanction under the anti-kickback statute, § 1128B(b) of the Act. Any definitive conclusion regarding the existence of an anti-kickback violation requires a determination of the parties' intent, which determination is beyond the scope of the advisory opinion process.[10]

IV. LIMITATIONS

The limitations applicable to this opinion include the following:

● This advisory opinion is issued only to Dr. X, who is the Requestor of this opinion. This advisory opinion has no application, and cannot be relied upon, by any other individual or entity.

● This advisory opinion is applicable only to the statutory provision specifically noted above. No opinion is herein expressed or implied with respect to the application of any other Federal, state, or local statute, rule, regulation, ordinance, or other law that may be applicable to the Proposed Arrangement.

● This advisory opinion will not bind or obligate any agency other than the U.S. Department of Health and Human Services.

This opinion is also subject to any additional limitations set forth at 42 C.F.R. Part 1008.

Sincerely,
/s/
D. McCarty Thornton
Chief Counsel to the Inspector General

Notes

1. Trace the remunerations in the transaction described in Advisory Opinion 98–4. How does each run a risk of inducing referrals? Does the compensation for management services received by Company B create financial incentives to increase referrals? Would "safeguards against overutilization" mentioned in the Opinion have assuaged the Inspector's General's concerns? What risk does Company B's involvement in setting up networks pose? Are there steps which could be taken to avoid anti-kickback concerns?

---

10. Our conclusion regarding the risk of fraud or abuse in relation to the anti-kickback statute should not be construed to mean that a finding of fraud or abuse is an implied element necessary to establish a violation of the statute.

2. Can a meaningful determination on the riskiness of a proposed venture be made without information regarding the parties' intent? What specific questions should be posed to those requesting an advisory opinion to clarify the intent underlying a proposed transaction? Is it even possible to undertake such a proceeding in the context of the advisory opinion process? See generally Scott J. Kelly, The Health Insurance Portability and Accountability Act of 1996: A Medicare Fraud Advisory Opinion Mandates Sends the Inspector "Shopping for Hats," 59 Ohio St. L. J. 303 (1998). For an important recent advisory opinion allowing a hospital-physician "gainsharing" arrangement see Dept. of Health & Human Servs., Office of Inspector General Advisory Op. No. 01–1 (Jan. 11, 2001), available at www.dhhs.gov/oig/advopn/2001.

3. An important outgrowth of the government's close attention to the fraud and abuse problem has been widespread adoption of corporate compliance programs by health care entities. Here, too, the government has offered guidance. In 1999, the OIG released several sector-specific model compliance plans. Through these compliance plans, the OIG "provides its views on the fundamental elements of . . . compliance programs, as well as the principles that each . . . facility should consider when developing and implementing an effective compliance program." See http://www.hhs.gov/oig/modcomp/index.htm (providing links to OIG's model compliance plans). The guidelines are intended for use not as an actual compliance plan, but rather for procedural and structural guidance in setting up a facility specific plan. See e.g., Durable Medical Equipment Compliance Plan, 64 Fed. Reg. 36,368 (July 9, 1999).

Problem: Sorting It Out

When you have completed your analysis of the problems at the beginning of this section, reconstruct the arrangements there presented to accomplish as substantially as possible the legitimate goals of the parties to the transaction without offending the fraud and abuse laws.

Next, consider the following problems affecting the formation of integrating organizations discussed in Chapter 13. For each of the scenarios below, explain how the anti-kickback law and any relevant safe harbor might apply and what steps should be taken to reduce legal risks.

- A hospital-controlled MSO provides staff, administrative services and equipment rentals to member physicians at "cost" or at levels below the fees it charges to non-members.

- An Integrated Delivery System purchases the tangible assets and patient records of a physician practice and pays on a five-year installment arrangement. The physicians work as employees at the hospital.

- A hospital-controlled MSO leases office space to its member physicians pursuant to a signed, written agreement for a five-year term. The lease terms reflect the fair market value of the leased space. In each of the first three years, the MSO has lost money.

- A PHO is jointly owned (50–50 equity split) by a hospital and its physicians. The hospital contributes 80% of the PHO's capital.

III. STARK I & II: A TRANSACTIONAL APPROACH TO SELF–REFERRALS

An alternative approach to dealing with fraud and abuse is to list and describe exhaustively transactions that are alternatively legitimate or illegitimate under the law. The Ethics in Patient Referrals Act (commonly referred to as Stark I in recognition of the legislation's principal sponsor, Rep. Fortney "Pete" Stark) did just that with respect to physician referrals for Medicare-financed services to clinical laboratories in which the physician (or immediate family member) has a financial interest. Besides making it illegal for physicians to make such referrals, Stark I also prohibits any billings by the laboratory to charge for services provided pursuant to illegal referrals. The coverage of the Stark self-referral legislation was significantly expanded by Stark II, a bill enacted as part of the 1993 Omnibus Budget Reconciliation Act. The Stark legislation now applies to services paid for by Medicaid as well as by Medicare and covers eleven "designated health services": clinical laboratory services; physical therapy services; occupational therapy services; radiology, including MRI, CAT and ultrasound services; radiation therapy services and supplies; durable medical equipment and supplies; parenteral and enteral nutrients, equipment, and supplies; prosthetics, orthotics, and prosthetic devices; home health services and supplies; outpatient prescription drugs; and inpatient and outpatient hospital services. No payment can be made by Medicare or Medicaid for referrals for such services where the referring physician or member of his family has a financial interest. Any amounts billed in violation of the section must be refunded. Any person knowingly billing or failing to make a refund in violation of the prohibition is subject to a civil fine of $15,000 per item billed and to exclusion.

The Stark legislation responded to increasing evidence that "self-referrals" had become quite common, and quite costly. An OIG study issued in 1989 found that of 2690 physicians who responded to its study, 12% had ownership interests and 8% had compensation arrangements with businesses to which they referred patients. Office of Inspector General, Financial Arrangements Between Physicians and Health Care Businesses: Report to Congress (1989). It further determined that nationally 25% of independent clinical laboratories (ICLs), 27% of independent laboratories, and 8% of durable medical equipment suppliers were owned at least in part by referring physicians. Beneficiaries treated by physicians who owned or invested in ICLs received 45% more clinical laboratory services and 34% more services directly from ICLs than beneficiaries in general, resulting in $28 million in additional costs to the Medicare program. Do studies finding high rates of self-referral patterns establish that the additional services provided were unnecessary? Is strong and consistent empirical evidence of higher utilization among self-referring physicians sufficient to justify legislative decisions to broadly proscribe the practice?

Note that, subject to the exceptions discussed below, Stark adopts a "bright line" test. Unlike Medicare fraud and abuse laws, there is no requirement that the conduct involve the knowing and willful receipt of a kickback: if no exception applies, the law has been violated. On January 3, 2001, the Department of Health and Human Services released the first part of its final regulations concerning Stark II. 66 Fed. Reg. 905 (Jan. 4, 2001). The regulations provide detailed interpretations, guidance and new exceptions and take up 109 pages in the Federal Register. Seventy pages of Regulations governing Stark I were adopted in final form in 1995. 60 Fed. Reg. 41,914 (1995). As you read the following materials, consider whether the development of "bright line" rules in this area is a realistic objective.

A. SCOPE OF THE PROHIBITION

Stark I and II prohibit physicians who have (or whose immediate family member has) a "financial relationship" with a provider of designated health care services from making "referrals" of Medicare or Medicaid patients to such providers for purposes of receiving any of the eleven "designated health services." The key terms are defined in 42 U.S.C.A. § 1395nn as follows:

(a) Prohibitions of certain referrals

* * *

(2) Financial relationship specified

For purposes of this section, a financial relationship of a physician (or an immediate family member of such physician) with an entity specified in this paragraph is—

(A) except as provided in subsections (c) and (d) of this section, an ownership or investment interest in the entity, or

(B) except as provided in subsection (e) of this section, a compensation arrangement (as defined in subsection (h)(1) of this section) between the physician (or an immediate family member of such physician) and the entity.

An ownership or investment interest described in subparagraph (A) may be through equity, debt, or other means and includes an interest in an entity that holds an ownership or investment interest in any entity providing the designated health service.

* * *

(h) Definitions and special rules

For purposes of this section:

(1) Compensation arrangement; remuneration

(A) The term "compensation arrangement" means any arrangement involving any remuneration between a physician (or an immediate family member of such physician) and an entity other than an arrangement involving only remuneration described in subparagraph (C).

(B) The term "remuneration" includes any remuneration, directly or indirectly, overtly or covertly, in cash or in kind.

(C) Remuneration described in this subparagraph is any remuneration consisting of any of the following:

(i) The forgiveness of amounts owed for inaccurate tests or procedures, mistakenly performed tests or procedures, or the correction of minor billing errors.

(ii) The provision of items, devices, or supplies that are used solely to—

(I) collect, transport, process, or store specimens for the entity providing the item, device, or supply, or

(II) order or communicate the results of tests or procedures for such entity.

(iii) A payment made by an insurer or a self-insured plan to a physician to satisfy a claim, submitted on a fee for service basis, for the furnishing of health services by that physician to an individual who is covered by a policy with the insurer or by the self-insured plan, if—

(I) the health services are not furnished, and the payment is not made, pursuant to a contract or other arrangement between the insurer or the plan and the physician,

(II) the payment is made to the physician on behalf of the covered individual and would otherwise be made directly to such individual,

(III) the amount of the payment is set in advance, does not exceed fair market value, and is not determined in a manner that takes into account directly or indirectly the volume or value of any referrals, and

(IV) the payment meets such other requirements as the Secretary may impose by regulation as needed to protect against program or patient abuse.

* * *

(5) Referral; referring physician

(A) Physicians' services

Except as provided in subparagraph (C), in the case of an item or service for which payment may be made under part B, the request by a physician for the item or service, including the request by a physician for a consultation with another physician (and any test or procedure ordered by, or to be performed by (or under the supervision of) that other physician), constitutes a "referral" by a "referring physician".

* * *

(6) Designated health services

The term "designated health services" means any of the following items or services:

(A) Clinical laboratory services.

(B) Physical therapy services.

(C) Occupational therapy services.

(D) Radiology services, including magnetic resonance imaging, computerized axial tomography scans, and ultrasound services.

(E) Radiation therapy services and supplies.

(F) Durable medical equipment and supplies.

(G) Parenteral and enteral nutrients, equipment, and supplies.

(H) Prosthetics, orthotics, and prosthetic devices and supplies.

(I) Home health services.

(J) Outpatient prescription drugs.

(K) Inpatient and outpatient hospital services.

Notes

Note several things about these provisions. First, recall that the principal problem identified by academic studies that led to the enactment of Stark I was excessive and perhaps inappropriate referrals by physicians to entities in which they had an ownership interest. Why did Congress extend the law's reach beyond "ownership and investment interests"? Was this a necessary or wise policy choice? Second, Stark II reaches arrangements in which the flow of money is reversed from the normal self-referral pattern, i.e., the physician pays the entity for services provided. Why should such arrangements be outlawed? Third, consider the broad sweep of the term "referral" as used in the Act. Suppose Dr. Gillespe requests a consultation from Dr. Demento who in turn orders a lab test and physical therapy for the patient. For what referrals is Dr. Gillespe responsible?

Complying with the Stark law may pose problems for integrated organizations. Consider a joint venture PHO entity which is owned by staff physicians and a hospital in which the PHO will negotiate and administer managed care contracts for the physicians and the hospital. Assume the physicians have been given 50 percent ownership in the entity even though the bulk of the start-up costs were paid by the hospital. Do the physicians have an ownership or investment interest in the hospital? Is there a compensation arrangement? The answer is that no ownership or investment interest is present because the participating physicians have an ownership interest in the PHO, not the hospital to which they refer, and the PHO has no ownership interest in the hospital. A compensation arrangement may well exist because physicians may receive an indirect form of remuneration when, after an HMO contract is secured by the PHO, they begin to refer patients to the hospital. While conceivably certain exceptions might apply, the arrangement is obviously risky. See Leonard C. Homer, How New Federal Laws Prohibiting Physician Self–Referrals Affect Integrated Delivery Systems, 11 HealthSpan 21 (April, 1994).

MSO arrangements may also face close scrutiny under Stark. Recall that MSOs typically provide an array of administrative and other support services to physicians such as billing, space rental and equipment. Where the hospital to which the physicians refer owns (or co-owns) the MSO, there may be an indirect compensation arrangement if any of these services are provided at rates not consistent with fair market value. Essentially, each service must be separately scrutinized. See Homer, supra.

Strong criticisms have been lodged against Stark and strenuous efforts to repeal or substantially modify the law are expected under the Bush administration. Organized medicine argues that the law is too complex and needlessly duplicative of other laws affecting self-referrals. Moreover, opponents assert that the law goes far beyond prohibiting physician ownership of facilities and invites governmental "micromanagement" of evolving network structures. Even Representative Stark has asked the Institute of Medicine to study ways to improve and simplify the statute. Medicare: Stark Asks Institute of Medicine to Form Working Group on Self–Referral Laws, Health Care Daily (BNA) (July 28, 1998). On the other side, the law has been defended as a pragmatic legislative choice that avoids the pitfalls of case-by-case litigation over issues of intent or reasonableness while unambiguously barring the most risk-prone referrals and permitting the most efficiency-enhancing arrangements. Representative William M. Thomas, chairman of the House Ways and Means Health Subcommittee and a vocal critic of the Stark II law has proposed eliminating the "compensation arrangement" ban under Stark II, asserting that it is unenforceable, burdensome and ineffective, and precludes essential business activities. See Fraud and Abuse: Thomas, Stark Introduce Competing Bills to Revamp, Simplify Self–Referral Statute, Health Care Daily (BNA) (July 29, 1999). Representative Stark has opined that total elimination of the compensation provision would be a "loophole you can drive an Armored Division through." Id. What are the pros and cons of amending the Stark law so that it applies only to investment and ownership interests?

B. EXCEPTIONS

The Stark anti-referral law is an example of what is sometimes called an "exceptions bill." It sweepingly prohibits self-referrals but then legitimizes a large number of specific arrangements. Stark's exceptions are of three kinds: (1) those applicable to ownership or investment financial relationships; (2) those applicable to compensation arrangements; and (3) generic exceptions that apply to all financial arrangements.

Many of the exceptions cover self-referral arrangements that pose little risk of abuse. For example, the statute rules out liability where referring physicians' incentives are controlled in some way, as with prepaid health plans; or where other circumstances reduce the risk of excess utilization, such as where the physician is an employee of the entity to which the referral is made, has a personal services contract or a space or equipment rental that meets commercial reasonableness tests or engages in isolated, one-time transactions with the entity. Perhaps the most important category, however, involves situations in which the physician is part of a group practice that is directly involved in providing the service. These latter provisos, the ancillary services and group practice exceptions, which do not necessarily involve circumstances that reduce the threat of overutilization, seem primarily designed to encourage the integration of practice among physicians.

Problem: Space and Equipment Rentals, Physician Recruitment

Stark I and II cover much of the same conduct as the bribe and kickback prohibition, but the legislation has its own exceptions that are worded somewhat differently. How does your analysis of problems 1, 4 and 6 at pages 967–969 change under the self-referral provisions reproduced below?

42 U.S.C.A. § 1395nn (Supp. 1995).

(e) Exceptions relating to other compensation arrangements

The following shall not be considered to be a compensation arrangement described in subsection (a)(2)(B) of this section:

(1) Rental of office space; rental of equipment

(A) Office space

Payments made by a lessee to a lessor for the use of premises if—

(i) the lease is set out in writing, signed by the parties, and specifies the premises covered by the lease,

(ii) the space rented or leased does not exceed that which is reasonable and necessary for the legitimate business purposes of the lease or rental and is used exclusively by the lessee when being used by the lessee, * * *

(iii) the lease provides for a term of rental or lease for at least 1 year,

(iv) the rental charges over the term of the lease are set in advance, are consistent with fair market value, and are not determined in a manner that takes into account the volume or value of any referrals or other business generated between the parties,

(v) the lease would be commercially reasonable even if no referrals were made between the parties, and

(vi) the lease meets such other requirements as the Secretary may impose by regulation as needed to protect against program or patient abuse.

* * *

(3) Personal service arrangements

[Certain personal service contracts are permitted if they meet certain conditions, including the condition that compensation not be related to the volume or value of referrals.]

* * *

(B) Physician incentive plan exception

(i) In general

In the case of a physician incentive plan (as defined in clause (ii)) between a physician and an entity, the compensation may be determined in a manner (through a withhold, capitation, bonus, or otherwise) that takes into account directly or indirectly the volume or value of any referrals or other business generated between the parties, if the plan meets the following requirements:

(I) No specific payment is made directly or indirectly under the plan to a physician or a physician group as an inducement to reduce or limit medically necessary services provided with respect to a specific individual enrolled with the entity.

(II) In the case of a plan that places a physician or a physician group at substantial financial risk as determined by the Secretary pursuant to section 42 U.S.C.A. § 1395mm(i)(8)(A)(ii) of this title, [which establishes the requirements for Medicare HMOs], the plan complies with any requirements the Secretary may impose pursuant to such section.

(III) Upon request by the Secretary, the entity provides the Secretary with access to descriptive information regarding the plan, in order to permit the Secretary to determine whether the plan is in compliance with the requirements of this clause.

(ii) Physician incentive plan defined

For purposes of this subparagraph, the term "physician incentive plan" means any compensation arrangement between an entity and a physician or physician group that may directly or indirectly have the effect of reducing or limiting services provided with respect to individuals enrolled with the entity.

* * *

(5) Physician recruitment

In the case of remuneration which is provided by a hospital to a physician to induce the physician to relocate to the geographic area served by the hospital in order to be a member of the medical staff of the hospital, if—

(A) the physician is not required to refer patients to the hospital,

(B) the amount of the remuneration under the arrangement is not determined in a manner that takes into account (directly or indirectly) the volume or value of any referrals by the referring physician, and

(C) the arrangement meets such other requirements as the Secretary may impose by regulation as needed to protect against program or patient abuse.

Note on Stark I and II Regulations

In 1995, some six years after the passage of Stark I, HCFA issued its final rule governing physician self-referrals under that Act. 60 Fed. Reg. 41,914 (codified at 42 C.F.R. § 411.350). One of the most important clarifications concerns the requirement in the "group practices" exception that "substantially all" of the services of the physicians in the group be provided through the group and that these services be billed under a billing number assigned to the group so that amounts so received are treated as receipts of the group. 42 U.S.C.A. § 1395nn(h)(A)(ii). The Stark I regulations fix the "substantially all" requirement at 75 percent of all patient care services, as measured by time spent (rather than the dollar value of physician services provided) and as an average for all of the group members during a specific 12–month period. Notably, time spent on physician care services includes time devoted to consultation, diagnosis or "any tasks performed ... that address the medical needs of specific patients." The regulations also define group members as "physicians, partners and full-time and part-time physician contractors and employees during the time they furnish services to patients of the group practice...." 42 C.F.R. § 411.351 (1996). Why might these provisions be important to physicians?

In January, 1998, HCFA published its long-awaited proposed Stark II rules and on January 3, 2001 it issued Part I of the final regulations dealing with paragraphs (a), (b), and (h) of the statute. 66 Fed. Reg. 905 (Jan. 4, 1001) These rules, which generated a large number of comments, provide detailed explanations and guidance on some of the minutiae of the Stark II statute and offer HCFA's interpretation of the intent of some of its provisions. See Albert Shay & Gary

Francesconi, Proposed Stark II Rules: Clarification or More Confusion?, 312 J. Health & Hosp. L. 95 (1998) (analyzing the proposed Stark II Rules).

The rules fashion several substantial changes including new exceptions and definitional clarifications that should grant additional breathing room to physicians engaged in self-referral joint ventures. The final regulations specify the boundaries of a number of the "designated health services," making it clear, for example, that the in-hospital use of lithotripsy is a DHS while cardiac catherdization laboratory services are not. It also does some fine line drawing, concluding that certain "invasive" radiology procedures such as those used to guide a needle, catheter or probe are not within the meaning of the DHS covering radiology and other imaging services. Another important definitional change states that the term "referral" no longer includes services personally performed by the referring physician.

Among the most noteworthy developments contained in the final Stark II regulations is the announcement of several significant new general exceptions to otherwise prohibited compensation arrangements between physicians and health care entities. First, the rules announce a new "fair market value" exception which exempts arrangements between physicians or groups of physicians (even if they do not qualify as a group practice) and an entity, where the compensation or payment is based on fair market value and is not reflective of the volume or value of referrals. However, several conditions must be met. The agreement must: be in writing and cover only identifiable specified items or services; cover all the items or services provided between the parties; be effective for a specified time period (the period may be less than one year); provide for compensation that is set in advance; and be commercially reasonable to further the legitimate business purposes of the parties. This exception is notable because of its potential sweep. It may, for example, provide a catch-all that protects transactions that fail to meet the detailed specifics of many other exceptions contained in the statute. A second proposed exception allows physicians to receive incidental compensation or benefits such as free samples of drugs or note pads which are small in value (up to $300 per year) and are not based on the volume or value of referrals and not in the form of cash or cash equivalents. Third, the Stark II regulations establish a new exception, not found in the proposed rules, for the compensation of faculty who work in academic medical centers. This exception accommodates special problems arising from medical school faculty practice plans which often involve multiple sources of compensation in complex organizational arrangements involving universities, hospitals and other entities. Finally, the regulations add a compensation exception for *bona fide* risk sharing arrangements between a physician and a health plan for the provision of items or services to enrollees of the health plan. This exception would encompass those risk-sharing arrangements in which a physician assumes the risk for the costs of the services, either through capitation, or through a withhold, bonus, or risk-corridor approach.

The regulations interpret a number of the existing exceptions more expansively so as to permit greater flexibility in joint arrangements among physicians. The following problem concerns referrals for physician services in the same group practice and for in-office ancillary services. The Stark II regulations provide extensive analyses of the meanings of certain key words in these exceptions, such as "direct supervision"; "same building"; and "furnish." As you work through the problem, consider how alternative interpretations of those terms might affect the advice you give.

Problem: Group Practices

Drs. Chung, Snyder, Williams, Mendez, Patel, and Jones have heretofore each operated independent solo practices. All have offices within a three square mile area, but none share offices with each other. Several years ago, they formed a joint venture to provide a variety of laboratory services to their patients. Their attorney has now informed them that their joint venture violates the prohibitions of the Stark legislation. He has suggested that they consider forming a group practice to operate the laboratory. What steps must they take to form a group practice that will permit them to operate a laboratory together under the relevant language of revised 42 U.S.C.A. § 1395nn?

42 U.S.C.A. § 1395nn:

(b) General exceptions to both ownership and compensation arrangement prohibitions

[The self-referral prohibitions] of this section shall not apply in the following cases:

(1) Physicians' services

In the case of physicians' services * * * provided personally by (or under the personal supervision of) another physician in the same group practice (as defined in subsection (h)(4) of this section) as the referring physician.

(2) In-office ancillary services

In the case of services (other than durable medical equipment (excluding infusion pumps) and parenteral and enteral nutrients, equipment, and supplies)—

    (A) that are furnished—

        (i) personally by the referring physician, personally by a physician who is a member of the same group practice as the referring physician, or personally by individuals who are directly supervised by the physician or by another physician in the group practice, and

        (ii)(I) in a building in which the referring physician (or another physician who is a member of the same group practice) furnishes physicians' services unrelated to the furnishing of designated health services, or

            (II) in the case of a referring physician who is a member of a group practice, in another building which is used by the group practice—

                (aa) for the provision of some or all of the group's clinical laboratory services, or

                (bb) for the centralized provision of the group's designated health services (other than clinical laboratory services), unless the Secretary determines other terms and conditions under which the provision of such services does not present a risk of program or patient abuse, and

(B) that are billed by the physician performing or supervising the services, by a group practice of which such physician is a member under a billing number assigned to the group practice, or by an entity that is wholly owned by such physician or such group practice, * * *

* * *

(h)(4)

    (A) Definition of group practice

The term "group practice" means a group of 2 or more physicians legally organized as a partnership, professional corporation, foundation, not-for-profit corporation, faculty practice plan, or similar association—

    (i) in which each physician who is a member of the group provides substantially the full range of services which the physician routinely provides, including medical care, consultation, diagnosis, or treatment, through the joint use of shared office space, facilities, equipment and personnel,

    (ii) for which substantially all of the services of the physicians who are members of the group are provided through the group and are billed under a billing number assigned to the group and amounts so received are treated as receipts of the group,

    (iii) in which the overhead expenses of and the income from the practice are distributed in accordance with methods previously determined,

    (iv) except as provided in subparagraph (B)(i), in which no physician who is a member of the group directly or indirectly receives compensation based on the volume or value of referrals by the physician,

    (v) in which members of the group personally conduct no less than 75 percent of the physician-patient encounters of the group practice, and

    (vi) which meets such other standards as the Secretary may impose by regulation.

    (B) Special rules

        (i) Profits and productivity bonuses

A physician in a group practice may be paid a share of overall profits of the group, or a productivity bonus based on services personally performed or services incident to such personally performed services, so long as the share or bonus is not determined in any manner which is directly related to the volume or value of referrals by such physician.

* * *

IV. STATE STATUTES AND ALTERNATIVE APPROACHES TO REFERRALS AND FEE SPLITTING

Most states have enacted laws that prohibit kickbacks or deal in some way with the specific problem of referrals. These laws vary considerably in scope and detail. For example, most states prohibit Medicaid fraud, though some rely on more general statutes outlawing fraud or theft by deception or false statements to public officials. See, e.g., Me. Rev. Stat. Ann. tit. 17–A § 354 (West 1994). Some state laws impose both criminal and civil penalties for kickbacks and many apply regardless of whether government or private payment plans were involved. See, e.g., Cal. Bus. & Prof. Code § 650 (Deering 1995) (prohibiting the "offer, delivery, receipt, or acceptance by any [physician] of any rebate, refund, commission, preference, patronage dividend, discount, or other consideration, whether in the form of money or otherwise, as compensation or inducement for referring patients . . . ."). A few states have broadened federal anti-kickback laws, e.g., by prohibiting the provision of unnecessary care, see Conn. Gen. Stat. § 17b–99(a) (1995) or care of inadequate quality, see Ill. Ann. Stat. ch. 305, para. 5/12–4.25(A)(e) (Smith–Hurd 1995).

A. SELF–REFERRALS

Over thirty states have enacted self-referral legislation which applies to all health care providers and patients. With significant variations in the types of medical professionals, goods and services covered, these state initiatives can be classified into two broad categories: (1) the "federal model" approach, i.e., free-standing statutes tracking with some variation either the Medicare fraud and abuse or Stark legislation; and (2) disclosure statutes that do not prohibit physician ownership interests in facilities to which they refer, but require that the referring provider reveal such interests to her patients. Though many of the prohibitions in these statutes are broader than those contained in Stark, several of them include "community need" statutes that permit self-referrals in special circumstances, such as where the community lacks a facility of reasonable quality and approval is received from a state agency. Others prohibit only ownership and investment interests, and do not reach compensation arrangements; in these states, however, laws prohibiting "bribes" and "kickbacks" may reach such activities. For excellent discussions of the variations among state self-referral initiatives, see Thomas William Mayo, State Illegal–Remuneration and Self–Referral Laws (Health Lawyers 1996); Joan H. Krause, The Role of the States in Combating Managed Care Fraud and Abuse, 8 Ann. Health L. 179 (1999); see generally, Jennifer H. Puryear, Note, The Physician As Entrepreneur: State and Federal Restrictions on Physician Joint Ventures, 73 N.C. L. Rev. 293 (1994); James C. Dechene & Karen P. O'Neil, "Stark II" and State Self–Referral Restrictions, 29 J. Health & Hosp. L. 65 (1996). See generally Jost & Davies, Medicare and Medicaid Fraud and Abuse, supra, § 4–9.

What advantages and disadvantages do you see with each approach? For example, do "federal model" statutes supplement enforcement by adding an additional watchdog, perhaps one better able to detect violations or do they just add to the noise and confusion facing providers? See David Burda, States Lag in Regulating Self Referrals, Mod. Healthcare, Dec. 23, 1991, at 40 (citing HHS study finding that due to insufficient staffing and funding, few if any states are able to effectively monitor compliance with their self-referral laws). The recently enacted amendments to the federal anti-kickback law include increased funding for joint federal-state enforcement efforts.

Is mandating disclosure of providers' financial conflicts of interest a realistic solution? Are patients capable of evaluating the risks they face in accepting referrals from a doctor with a financial interest in the referred product or service? What kind of verbal disclosure can be expected from an interested physician? What effect would such disclosures have on the physician-patient relationship? What predictions would you make about the operation of a disclosure requirement based on your knowledge of informed consent? See Puryear, supra; E. Haavi Morreim, Conflicts of Interest: Profits and Problems in Physician Referrals, 262 JAMA 390 (1989); Marc A. Rodwin,

Physicians' Conflicts of Interest, The Limitations of Disclosure, 321 New Eng.J.Med. 1405 (1989).

Finally, how valid are the premises of state community need laws? Are physicians likely to invest in facilities in areas where private investors are lacking? If so, why? Do these statutes create regulatory processes that may themselves be subject to abuse? This approach may be contrasted with Stark II, which includes an exception for self-referrals of designated health services if provided in a rural area (using metropolitan statistical areas for delineating regions) and if substantially all the services are furnished to persons who reside in the rural area. 42 U.S.C.A. § 1395nn(d)(2) (Supp. 1995). What are the pros and cons of the demonstrated community need approach as compared to the Stark II exemption?

B. STATE MEDICAL PRACTICE ACTS AND FEE–SPLITTING PROHIBITIONS

Another source of law governing physician referral practices are the state medical practice acts. Such laws commonly provide that paying referral fees or "fee-splitting" constitutes grounds for revocation or suspension of a physician's license. See, e.g., Mass. Gen. L. ch. 112 §§ 12AA, 23P½ (1991). These statutes have sometimes been construed to prohibit arrangements that go beyond simple sharing of fees in connection with referral arrangements. For example, in Lieberman & Kraff v. Desnick, 244 Ill. App. 3d 341, 185 Ill.Dec. 245, 614 N.E.2d 379 (1993), the court considered plaintiffs' sale of their medical practice where payment was based on a percentage of defendant's gross revenue for a twenty year period. After making payments for four years, defendant stopped, claiming the purchase agreement was void as an illegal fee-splitting agreement under the Illinois Medical Practice Act. That law prohibited physicians from: "[d]irectly or indirectly giving to or receiving from any physician, person, firm or corporation any fee, commission, rebate or other form of compensation for any professional services not actually and personally rendered." (Ill. Rev. Stat. ch. 111, para. 4433(14) (1985)). Noting that Illinois' broadly-worded statute went beyond prohibiting fee-splitting over patient referrals, the court found the practice barred and the contract void. Rejecting plaintiffs' public policy arguments, the court observed that the arrangement created, in effect, a silent partnership pursuant to which the plaintiffs would share in the patient fees generated by the practice while insulating themselves from any correlative responsibilities to patients.

Florida's fee-splitting statute has called into question the legality of many physician practice management arrangements whereby a physician pays a large organization a percentage of profits in exchange for management, marketing, and networking services. In Phymatrix Management Co. v. Bakarania, 737 So.2d 588 (Fla. Dist. Ct. App. 1999), an appellate court upheld a state board ruling that a contract between a management company and a physician group constituted illegal fee splitting. The board had found that paying a specified percentage of net income without regard to the cost of services was effectively a fee split, and that the provision marketing and networking services was a referral within the meaning of Florida law. The *Bakarania* decision has been interpreted to suggest that any agreement in Florida which imposes upon a management company an obligation to bring more patients into the physician's practice is probably invalid, and possibly illegal. On the other hand, the Board has upheld arrangements where no such direct obligation is imposed and a cap is placed on the amount of profits paid to the management company. See Florida: State Board Approved Management Contract that Splits Income Without Ties to Referrals, 8 Health L. Rep. 1313 (Aug. 12, 1999). Thus, a central issue in the analysis has been the nexus between the amount of profits that could be paid and the services to be rendered, as well as between the fee and the contractual provision encouraging referrals. For analyses of the Florida fee-splitting law, see Richard O. Jacobs & Elizabeth Goodman, Splitting Hairs? Fee Splitting and Health Care—The Florida Experience, 8 Annals Health L. 239 (1999); 1 Furrow et al., Health Law § 5–10(d).

In other states, conduct such as fee-splitting may constitute a breach of general standards prohibiting unprofessional conduct, with courts frequently relying on the interpretations of the American Medical Association's Code of Ethics for guidance. The AMA has vacillated in its interpretations of whether self-referrals constitute unprofessional conduct. In a series of extremely contentious and divisive debates, the AMA has reversed itself on this issue. See Brian McCormick, AMA Reverses Self–Referral Stance, Am. Med. News, Dec. 21, 1992 at 1. The AMA now takes the position that physicians should, in general, not refer patients to facilities outside their office practices when they have an investment interest in that facility, unless there is a demonstrated community need for such services and other requirements are met. See AMA Report on the Council on Ethical and Judicial Affairs (Dec. 19, 1991). See also American Medical Association Council on Ethical and Judicial Affairs, Conflicts of Interest: Physician Ownership of Medical Facilities, 267 JAMA 2366 (1992).

C. OTHER APPROACHES TO PHYSICIAN REFERRALS

In addition to the federal and state laws discussed in this chapter there are a number of alternative approaches to dealing with the problem of referrals. One potential solution to the problem is to distinguish between "earned" and "unearned" referral fees. If the doctors who cooperated with Dr. Greber were only compensated for the market value of their services in interpreting the tests, they did no wrong, and should not be punished. To the extent, however, that the payment was only for the referral itself and not otherwise earned, a sanction would be appropriate. See Mark Hall, Institutional Control of Physician Behavior: Legal Barriers to Health Care Cost Containment, 137 U. Pa. L. Rev. 431 (1988). Will it always be possible to distinguish between the earned and unearned portion of referral fees? Moreover, if the test for measuring the fairness of earned compensation for services is market value, how is market value determined in the health care market where prices are often administrative constructs created by financing programs? Is it possible to determine the market value of legitimate conduct in markets that do not discriminate between that portion of the value of a transaction attributable to legitimate conduct and that portion attributable to illegitimate conduct? See Frankford, Creating and Dividing the Fruits of Collective Economic Activity: Referrals Among Health Care Providers, 89 Col.L.Rev. 1862, 1889–1900 (1989).

It also has been suggested that the entire attempt to solve the problem through statutory or regulatory approaches is misguided. Perhaps the problem is already adequately addressed by the common law. Patients already have a right to information affecting their care (including cost information) and doctors have an obligation to disclose such information as they possess relevant to such care (including information about the cost and quality of goods and services which they advise the patient to purchase for health care purposes.) Doctors already have a fiduciary obligation to put their patients' welfare above their own financial gain when the two come in conflict. Patients who are harmed by incompetent medical services provided pursuant to a referral from their physician, based on their physician's financial interest, might well be able to recover against the physician for medical negligence. What more is needed? See E. Haavi Morreim, Physician Investment and Self–Referral: Philosophical Analysis of a Contentious Debate, 15 J.Med.Phil. 425 (1990). Do you agree that common law solutions are adequate?

Chapter 15

ANTITRUST

INTRODUCTION

Antitrust law has played a pivotal role in the development of institutional and professional arrangements in health care. Following the Supreme Court's decision in Goldfarb v. Virginia State Bar, 421 U.S. 773, 95 S.Ct. 2004, 44 L.Ed.2d 572 (1975), which held that "learned professions" were not implicitly exempt from the antitrust laws and found the Sherman Act's interstate commerce requirement satisfied with regard to legal services, extensive antitrust litigation spurred significant changes in the health care industry. Most importantly, cases following *Goldfarb* helped remove a series of private restraints of trade that had long inhibited competition. Antitrust enforcement has come to assume a somewhat different, albeit equally important, focus in today's market. The law has emerged as a powerful overseer of institutional and professional arrangements and ideally helps assure the evolution of market structures that will preserve the benefits of a competitive marketplace.

At the same time, however, applying antitrust law to the health care industry has not been without controversy. Some in the provider community have argued that the complex and uncertain nature of antitrust law will thwart efforts by providers to efficiently reorganize their business affairs through mergers and joint ventures. See, e.g., James S. Todd, Physicians As Professionals, Not Pawns, 12 Health Aff. 145 (Fall 1993); Frederic J. Entin, et al., Hospital Collaboration: The Need For An Appropriate Antitrust Policy, 29 Wake Forest L. Rev. 107 (1994). This view has been sharply disputed by those who contend that competitive market forces are critical to any public policy relying on competitive markets, see, e.g., James F. Blumstein, Health Care Reform and Competing Visions of Medical Care: Antitrust and State Provider Cooperation Legislation, 79 Cornell L. Rev. 1459 (1994) and Thomas L. Greaney, When Politics and Law Collide: Why Health Care Reform Does Not Need Antitrust "Reform," 39 St. Louis U. L.J. 135 (1994). Nevertheless, calls for limited antitrust immunity for collaborative activities among providers are a recurring feature in the nation's ongoing policy debates about the future of the health care industry.

It should be noted that applying antitrust law to the health care industry entails some special problems. In particular, the peculiarities and distortions of health care markets often necessitate a sophisticated analysis in order to reach economically sound results. A host of questions arise: What place is there for defenses related to the quality of health care in a statutory regime designed to leave such issues to the market? Does the behavior of not-for-profit health care providers conform to traditional economic assumptions about competitors? If not, should they somehow be treated differently? What impact do the widespread interventions by state and federal government have on the application of federal antitrust law? Do "market failures" in health care, particularly imperfect information, suggest special approaches to applying antitrust law? See Peter J. Hammer, Questioning Traditional Antitrust Presumptions: Price and Non–Price Competition in Hospital Markets, 32 U. Mich. J.L. Ref. 727 (1999); William M. Sage & Pater Hammer, Competing on Quality of Health Care: The Need to Develop a Competition Policy for Health Care Markets, 32 U. Mich. J. L. Reform 1069 (1999).

The Statutory Framework

The principal antitrust statutes are notable for their highly generalized proscriptions. Rather than specifying activities that it deemed harmful to competition, Congress vested the federal courts with the power to create a common law of antitrust. This chapter will not deal with all of the antitrust laws applicable to the health care industry. The following introduction summarizes portions of the three principal federal statutes: the Sherman Act, the Federal Trade Commission Act and the Clayton Act. It should be noted that most states have enacted antitrust statutes that are identical to or closely track these federal laws.

Sherman Act § 1: Restraints of Trade

Section One of the Sherman Act prohibits "every contract, combination . . . or conspiracy in restraint of trade." 15 U.S.C.A. § 1. This broad proscription establishes two substantive elements for finding a violation: an agreement and conduct that restrains trade. The concept of an agreement—the conventional shorthand for Section One's "contract, combination or conspiracy" language—limits the law's reach to concerted activities, i.e., those that are a result of a "meeting of the minds" of two or more independent persons or entities. The second requirement of Section One, that the agreement restrain trade, has generated extensive analysis by the courts. Recognizing that all agreements restrain trade, the Supreme Court has narrowed the inquiry to condemn only "unreasonable restraints" and has developed presumptive ("per se") rules to simplify judicial inquiries in particular circumstances. Among the restraints of trade that are reached by Section One are: price fixing (the setting of prices or terms of sale cooperatively by two or more businesses that do not involve sharing substantial risk in a common business enterprise); market division (allocating product lines, customers or territories between competitors); exclusive dealing (requiring that a person deal exclusively with an enterprise so that competitors are foreclosed or otherwise disadvantaged in the marketplace); group boycotts (competitors collectively refusing to deal, usually taking the form of denying a rival an input or something it needs to compete in the marketplace); and tying arrangements (a firm with market power selling one product on the condition that the buyer buy a second product from it).

Sherman Act § 2: Monopolization and Attempted Monopolization

Section Two of the Sherman Act prohibits monopolization, attempted monopolization, and conspiracies to monopolize. 15 U.S.C.A. § 2. Unlike Section One, it is primarily directed at unilateral conduct. Monopolization entails two elements: the possession of monopoly power, defined as the power to control market prices or exclude competition, and the willful acquisition or maintenance of that power as distinguished from growth or development as a consequence of a superior product, business acumen, or historic accident.

Clayton Act § 7: Mergers and Acquisitions

Section Seven of the Clayton Act prohibits mergers and acquisitions where the effect may be "substantially to lessen competition" or "to tend to create a monopoly." 15 U.S.C.A. § 18 (1994). To test the legality of a proposed merger or acquisition, courts emphasize market share and concentration data but also take other factors into consideration to determine whether a merger makes it more likely than not that the merged firm will exercise market power.

Federal Trade Commission Act § 5: Unfair Methods of Competition

Section Five of the Federal Trade Commission Act prohibits "unfair methods of competition" (which the courts have interpreted to include all violations of the Sherman Act and Clayton Act), and "unfair or deceptive acts or practices." 15 U.S.C.A. § 45(a)(1). The Act empowers the FTC to enforce the provisions of the Sherman Act in civil suits, as well as by administrative procedures. The FTC has no jurisdiction over not-for-profit organizations.

Defenses and Exemptions

There are numerous statutory and judicially-crafted defenses to antitrust liability, several of which are of particular importance to health care antitrust litigation. The state action doctrine exempts from antitrust liability actions taken pursuant to a clearly expressed state policy to restrict free competition, where the challenged conduct is under the active control and supervision of the state. The high degree of state regulation of health care has spawned state action defenses in staff privileges cases, for example, when state law authorizes public hospitals to undertake mergers that lessen competition and supervises their conduct. The McCarran–Ferguson Act, 15 U.S.C.A. § 1012(b) (1994), generally exempts the "business of insurance" from antitrust enforcement to the extent that the particular insurance activities are regulated by state law. 15 U.S.C.A. § 1011. (This should not be taken to mean, however, that "insurance companies" are exempt from antitrust scrutiny.) The Noerr–Pennington doctrine protects the exercise of the First Amendment right to petition the government, so long as the "petitioning" is not merely a "sham" to cover anti-competitive behavior. This defense is relevant to lobbying efforts on health care issues and to participation in administrative proceedings, such as certificate-of-need applications, each of which may lead to an outcome that lessens competition. The most recent statutory defense relevant to health care is the Health Care Quality Improvement Act, 42 U.S.C.A. §§ 11101–11152, enacted by Congress in 1986, which grants limited immunity for peer review activities.

Interpretive Principles

The Law's Exclusive Focus on Competitive Concerns

There has long been widespread agreement in the case law that antitrust inquiries should focus exclusively on competitive effects and should not take into account purported non-economic benefits of collective activities such as advancing social policies or even protecting public safety. See National Society of Professional Engineers v. United States, 435 U.S. 679, 98 S.Ct. 1355, 55 L.Ed.2d 637 (1978) (rejecting as a matter of law a professional society's safety justifications for its ban on competitive bidding). This self-imposed boundary is based on the judiciary's skepticism about its competence to balance disparate social policies and the judgment that such concerns are more appropriately addressed to the legislature. Importantly, then, under Section One of the Sherman Act, courts will not consider justifications other than those asserting that a practice, on balance, promotes competition. As discussed *infra* in Section IA2, this constraint is in obvious tension with justifications by professionals that their collective activities have the purpose of advancing the quality of patient care.

An important corollary to the foregoing is the often-repeated maxim that antitrust law seeks to "protect competition, not competitors." Brown Shoe Co. v. United States, 370 U.S. 294, 344, 82 S.Ct. 1502, 1534, 8 L.Ed.2d 510 (1962). This tenet serves to emphasize the distinction between harm to competitors who lose out in the competitive struggle due to chance or their own inadequacies and harm resulting from the impermissible conduct of rivals. Only the latter are cognizable under the federal antitrust laws. Courts have fashioned rules regarding standing and antitrust injury for private plaintiffs as well as substantive doctrines that serve to preserve this distinction. See e.g., Todorov v. DCH Healthcare Authority, 921 F.2d 1438 (11th Cir.1991); see generally, 2 Barry R. Furrow, et al., Health Law § 14–3 (2d ed. 2000).

Per Se Rules and The Rule of Reason

Traditionally, judicial analyses of conduct under Section One of the Sherman Act have employed two approaches to testing the "reasonableness" of restraints. Some activities, such as price fixing, market allocations, and certain group boycotts have been considered so likely to harm competition that they are deemed illegal "per se." That is, if a plaintiff can prove that the defendant's conduct fits within one of these categories, the inquiry ends; the agreement itself constitutes a violation of the statute. In effect, then, the per se categorization establishes a conclusive presumption of illegality.

Activities not falling within the per se rubric are subject to broader examination under the rule of reason. Under this form of analysis, defendants escape liability if they prove that the pro-competitive benefits of the challenged activity outweigh any anticompetitive effects so that competition, the singular policy concern of the statute, is strengthened rather than restrained. In theory, courts undertaking a full-blown rule of reason analysis will balance competitive harms against competitive benefits. For example, if a large number of hospitals collectively assembled and shared information about the utilization practices of physicians on their staffs, a court might balance the potential collusive harm resulting from lessened inter-hospital competition against the market-wide competitive benefits of dispensing such information—assuming the information was shared with payors.

In practice, however, such balancing is rarely done. Courts usually truncate the process in one of several ways. For example, they may find that an alleged restraint has no possibility of harming competition where the colluding parties lack "market power." As a proxy for market power, which is defined as the ability profitably to raise price (or reduce quality or output), courts estimate the market shares of the colluding parties and examine other market conditions. (A firm's market share is the ratio of its volume of business in a market to that of all of its competitors.) Doing this, of course, requires that the factfinder define the dimensions of the geographic and product markets—determinations that require the exercise of considerable judgment. Even where a party has a high market share and there are relatively few competitors, however, market power still may be lacking. For example, the colluding parties may be unable to raise price because entry by others is easy or because buyers would quickly detect such an increase and cease dealing with the parties.

Indeed, in recent years, a series of Supreme Court decisions have shifted antitrust analyses away from a rigid per se/rule of reason dichotomy, treating the approaches instead as "complementary" and essentially establishing a continuum of levels of scrutiny. See, e.g., National Collegiate Athletic Ass'n v. Board of Regents of the University of Oklahoma, 468 U.S. 85, 104 S.Ct. 2948, 82 L.Ed.2d 70 (1984). Thus, the modern approach allows courts to undertake threshold examinations of purported justifications and competitive effect before characterizing the conduct as governed by the per se rule. By the same token, courts may need only a "quick look" to condemn conduct under the rule of reason; they may dispense with prolonged factual inquiries when the truncated review reveals that purported efficiency benefits are lacking or an anticompetitive effect is obvious.

Joint Ventures and Ancillary Restraints

Among the most difficult and most important issues facing antitrust courts and enforcers today is the treatment to be accorded joint ventures. As a general matter, the rather elastic concept of the joint venture embraces agreements between separate business firms to jointly provide a service or produce a new product. When two or more competing entities are members of a joint venture, the arrangement may raise antitrust concerns because of the prospect that the venture may enable the parties together to exercise market power. At the same time, however, joint ventures have the propensity to improve the efficiency (i.e., lower the costs) of the participants.

True joint ventures are evaluated under the rule of reason. In contrast, "sham" arrangements—e.g., cartels that produce no integrative efficiencies but adopt the joint venture label—are treated under the per se rule. Legitimate joint ventures are characterized by some meaningful level of economic integration that allows the ventures to offer a new or improved product or significant efficiencies. See BMI v. CBS, 441 U.S. 1, 99 S.Ct. 1551, 60 L.Ed.2d 1 (1979). But because such legitimate joint ventures entail restraints of trade among participants (e.g., price agreements or market allocations), they do not escape scrutiny entirely. For the joint venture with valid efficiency justifications, further examination of its competitive effect is required under the rule of reason.

The methodology for evaluating joint ventures derives from a seminal opinion by Judge Taft in United States v. Addyston Pipe & Steel Co., 85 F. 271 (6th Cir.1898), *aff'd as modified*, 175 U.S. 211, 20 S.Ct. 96, 44 L.Ed. 136 (1899). The so-called "ancillary restraints doctrine" first inquires into the purpose of the arrangement to determine whether it is a "naked" restraint, i.e., one having no objective other than suppressing competition; if so, summary condemnation is usually appropriate. Where the joint venture possesses sufficient integration or efficiency justifications to escape per se classification, the analysis turns on three questions:

(1) are possible restraints of trade subordinate and collateral to a legitimate joint undertaking?

(2) are they necessary to the success of that joint undertaking? and

(3) are they no more restrictive of competition than necessary to accomplish the pro-competitive ends?

An important source of guidance for health law attorneys in applying these principles to joint activities is the Statements of Antitrust Enforcement Policy in Health Care, 4 Trade Reg. Rep. (CCH) para. 13, 153 (August 18, 1996) ("Policy Statements"), released jointly by the Department of Justice and the Federal Trade Commission. These statements, which are discussed throughout this chapter, apply the joint venture analysis set forth above in a variety of health industry contexts. Other important sources of information include the numerous "advisory opinions" of the Federal Trade Commission and "business review letters" of the Department of Justice, which are prospective statements of each agency's enforcement intentions regarding proposed conduct.

The growing literature on antitrust and its application to the health care industry includes: 2 Furrow, et al., Health Law, ch. 14 (2d ed. 2000); John J. Miles, Health Care and Antitrust Law: Principles and Practices (1996); American Bar Association, Section of Antitrust Law, Antitrust Health Care Handbook (1993); Antitrust Immunity Legislation for Health Care Providers (2000). Good, basic introductions to antitrust are available in a number of antitrust hornbooks. A brief and useful introduction is presented in William E. Kovacic & Ernest Gellhorn, Antitrust Law and Economics in a Nutshell (4th ed. 1994). Other useful sources include: E. Thomas Sullivan & Jeffrey L. Harrison, Understanding Antitrust and Its Economic Implications (2d ed. 1994); Stephen F. Ross, Principles of Antitrust Law (1993); and Herbert Hovenkamp, Federal Antitrust Policy: The Law of Competition and Its Practice (1994).

I. CARTELS AND PROFESSIONALISM

A. CLASSIC CARTELS

IN RE MICHIGAN STATE MEDICAL SOCIETY

101 F.T.C. 191 (1983).
Opinion of the Commission

BY CLANTON, COMMISSIONER:

I. INTRODUCTION

This case involves allegations that direct competitors, acting through a professional association, conspired to restrain trade by organizing boycotts and tampering with the fees received from third party insurers of their services. Of particular antitrust significance is the fact that the competitors are medical doctors practicing in Michigan, the association is the Michigan State Medical Society, and the insurers are Blue Cross and Blue Shield of Michigan ("BCBSM") and Michigan Medicaid.

More specifically, the complaint in this matter charges, and the administrative law judge found, that the medical society unlawfully conspired with its members to influence third-party reimbursement policies in the following ways: by seeking to negotiate collective agreements with insurers; by agreeing to use coercive measures like proxy solicitation and group boycotts; and by actually making coercive threats to third party payers. * * *

* * *

Becoming frustrated in its negotiations with BCBSM on (issues regarding reimbursement), MSMS authorized its first proxy solicitation. Reacting to what it perceived to be the recalcitrant attitude of Blue Shield on the subjects of regionalization of fees and physician profiles, coupled with what appears to be a total lack of willingness to cooperate with MSMS in the development of a uniform claim form or even consider the use of the CPT procedural code, the Negotiating Committee recommended that the House of Delegates urge MSMS members to write letters to BCBSM withdrawing from participation but mail them to the Negotiating Committee to be held as "proxies." The House of Delegates authorized the committee to collect the proxies, but to use them only at the discretion of the Council, with prior notice to the members who submitted them, "if a negotiating impasse develops with Michigan Blue Cross/Blue Shield."

* * *

Each member of MSMS was urged by letter to resist "so-called cost-containment programs that in effect reduce reimbursement to physicians or place the responsibility for the reduction of costs solely on the practicing physician." The letter, from the Council chairman, referred pointedly to the fact that a threshold percentage of physicians must formally participate in order for BCBSM to operate under its enabling legislation. It enclosed two blank "powers of attorney," one for BCBSM and one for Medicaid, empowering the Negotiating Committee to cancel the signer's participation in either program if such action was deemed warranted by the Council. These powers of attorney were revocable at any time. * * *

As a result of this response, [a] dispute over radiologists' and pathologists' reimbursement was resolved in MSMS' favor with the status quo being preserved and BCBSM withdrawing its proposal. [ ] As explained below, these proxies also played a role in MSMS' dealings with Medicaid.

[In response to additional efforts by BCBSM to reduce utilization, the leadership of MSMS advised members to react to new reimbursement policies by writing letters threatening departicipation or actually withdrawing from participation. In addition MSMS representatives protested cuts of approximately 11% in physician reimbursement under the Medicaid program by "waving" the departicipation proxies in meetings with the Governor and Medicaid officials. Although evidence suggested that physician participants in the Medicaid program fell off markedly after the MSMS collective action, it did not find that state officials had been coerced by these actions.]

* * *

Conspiracy Allegations

The threshold issue here is whether MSMS' importunings with BCBSM and the Medicaid program amounted to conspiratorial conduct of the kind alleged in the complaint or simply represented nonbinding expressions of views and policy, as argued by respondent. * * * As discussed previously, the evidence quite clearly reveals that MSMS members, acting through their House of Delegates, agreed in 1976 to establish a Division of Negotiations for the purpose of working out differences with third party payers. The Division was specifically empowered, inter alia, to coordinate all negotiating activities of MSMS, collect "non-participation" proxies and obtain a negotiated participation agreement with third party payers that would obviate the need for physician non-participation. It also was specifically contemplated by MSMS that the Division of Negotiations would obtain authorization of all members to serve as their "exclusive bargaining agent." The debate in the House of Delegates clearly indicated that, although the Division would not negotiate specific fees, it would have authority to negotiate the manner by which fees or reimbursement levels would be established. [ ]

Thus, at the outset we find that the very creation of the Division of Negotiations reveals a collective purpose on the part of MSMS and its members to go beyond the point of giving advice to third party payers; in fact, it reveals a purpose to organize and empower a full-fledged representative to negotiate and resolve controversies surrounding physician profiles, screens and other similar matters. [ ] There is, in fact, considerable additional evidence that the Negotiating Division not only had the authority to reach understandings with third party payers but also utilized that authority (acting as agent for its members) in soliciting, collecting and threatening to exercise physician departicipation proxies, as well as in other negotiations with third party payers.

* * *

Turning to the boycott issue, the law is clear that the definition of that term is not limited to situations where the target of the concerted refusal to deal is another competitor or potential competitor. As the Supreme Court indicated, * * * a concerted refusal to deal may be characterized as an unlawful group boycott where the target is a customer or supplier of the combining parties. * * * In the instant case, the alleged boycott involves concerted threats by MSMS and its members to refrain from participating in BCBSM and Medicaid unless the latter modified their reimbursement policies. Although BCBSM and Medicaid—the targets of the boycott—are not in competitive relationships with MSMS, that fact alone does not preclude a finding of a boycott.

Respondent, however, argues that the proxies were not exercised and, in the case of the departicipation letter campaign, that there was no adverse effect on BCBSM. As to the latter contention, MSMS points out that more physicians signed up to participate in BCBSM during the relevant period than withdrew from the program as a result of the campaign. The success [or] failure of a group boycott or price-fixing agreement, however, is irrelevant to the question of either its existence or its legality. Whether or not the action succeeds, "[i]t is the concerted activity for a common purpose that constitutes the violation." * * * Furthermore, an agreement among competitors affecting price does not have to be successful in order to be condemned.

It is the "contract, combination . . . or conspiracy in restraint of trade or commerce" which § 1 of the [Sherman] Act strikes down, whether the concerted activity be wholly nascent or abortive on the one hand, or successful on the other. United States v. Socony–Vacuum Oil Co., 310 U.S. 150, 224 n. 59 (1940). Moreover, even if less than all members of an organization or association agree to participate, that fact does not negate the presence of a conspiracy or combination as to those who do participate. [ ]

As for the collection of proxies that were never exercised, the law does not require that a competitor actually refuse to deal before a boycott can be found or liability established. Rather, the threat to refuse to deal may suffice to constitute the offense. Fashion Originators' Guild of America v. Federal Trade Commission, 312 U.S. 457, 462 (1941); Eastern States Retail Lumber Dealers' Association v. United States, 234 U.S. 600 (1914). The evidence indicates that the threat implicit in the collection of departicipation proxies and the attendant publicity can be as effective as the actual execution of the threatened action. Indeed, it may be assumed that parties to a concerted refusal to deal hope that the announcement of the intended action will be sufficient to produce the desired response. That appears to be precisely what happened here, and there are contemporaneous testimonials by MSMS officials confirming the success of that strategy. For example, Dr. Crandall suggested that MSMS' "waving the proxies in the face of the legislature" persuaded the state attorney general that if he sued MSMS the state would have "orchestrated the demise of the entire Michigan Medicaid program." Also, as noted above, the Negotiations Division credited the members' response to the proxy solicitation with the favorable outcome of the dispute between the radiologists and BCBSM. And, as further evidence, there is the fact that MSMS reached a formal agreement with BCBSM which included the implementation of a statewide screen.

* * *

B. *Legality of the Concerted Action*

* * *

[I]t would appear that respondent's conduct approaches the kind of behavior that previously has been classified as per se illegal. Nevertheless, since this conduct does not involve direct fee setting, we are not prepared to declare it per se illegal at this juncture and close the door on all asserted pro-competitive justifications.

To briefly recap, respondent has offered the following justifications for its behavior: (1) the practices had no effect on fee levels and, in any event, BCBSM and Medicaid took independent action to correct the perceived problems; (2) MSMS simply sought to insure that physicians were treated fairly especially in view of BCBSM's bargaining power; (3) the actions were, in part, an effort to counter BCBSM's violations of its charter and Michigan law in connection with its modified participation program; and (4) MSMS was striving to correct abuses of the Medicaid system and the poor perpetrated by "Medicaid mills."

With respect to respondent's first contention, MSMS claims that the conduct never led to uniform fees or prevented individual physicians from deciding whether to participate in BCBSM or Medicaid. We believe that these arguments miss the point with respect to the likely competitive effects of the restrictive practices. Where horizontal arrangements so closely relate to prices or fees as they do here, a less elaborate analysis of competitive effects is required. [ ] The collective actions under scrutiny clearly interfere with the rights of physicians to compete independently on the terms of insurance coverage offered by BCBSM and Medicaid. Moreover, the joint arrangements directly hamper the ability of third party payers to compete freely for the patronage of individual physicians and other physician business entities. * * *

* * *

On the question of whether the proposed policies of BCBSM and Medicaid were fair to physicians, respondent would apparently have us become enmeshed in weighing the comparative equities of the different parties to these transactions. In fact, considerable portions of the record are devoted to an assessment of the relative merits of MSMS' bargaining position. For us to consider whether the terms offered by the third party payers were fair or reasonable would lead us into the kind of regulatory posture that the courts have long rejected. * * * It would be analogous to the Commission serving as a quasi-public utility agency concerned with balancing interests unrelated to antitrust concerns. We believe that it is undesirable and inappropriate for us to step in and attempt to determine which party had the better case in these dealings. [Citing Fashion Originators' Guild v. FTC, 312 U.S. 668, 61 S.Ct. 703, 85 L.Ed. 949 (1941), the Commission found that the objective of correcting violations of law cannot justify a group boycott because alternative means of seeking redress were available.]

* * *

Respondent also suggests that its activities were motivated by concern for the welfare of its members' patients, especially in the case of Medicaid where, it is alleged, reductions in reimbursement levels might lead to lower physician participation rates and force low-income patients to seek less reputable providers (the so-called Medicaid mills). We concluded there that the relationship between such reimbursement mechanisms and health care quality was simply too tenuous, from a competitive perspective, to justify the broad restrictions imposed. * * * While we are not addressing ethical standards in this case, many of the quality and patient welfare arguments asserted here have a ring similar to those advanced in AMA. [In re AMA, discussed infra, in which the FTC rejected a ban on advertising justified by defendants as protecting informed consumer choice and a prohibition on contract based reimbursement which defendants claimed resulted in harm to the public and inferior quality of medical service]. Even in the case of Medicaid reductions, where an argument might be made that arbitrary cuts could be counter-productive by impairing physicians' economic incentives to treat the poor, it is difficult to see how concerted agreements and refusals to deal can be sanctioned as a means of fighting proposed payment cutbacks. While granting MSMS' laudable concerns about the effects of physician withdrawal from Medicaid, we observe that respondent clearly had public forums available to it to correct perceived mistakes made by the state legislature or the administrators of Medicaid; it could have expressed its views in ways that fell well short of organized boycott threats.

Finally, we find no suggestion among MSMS' justifications that the concerted behavior here enhanced competition in any market by injecting new elements or forms of competition, reducing entry barriers, or facilitating or broadening consumer choice. The price-related practices in question here are not ancillary to some broader pro-competitive purpose, such as a joint venture, an integration of activities, or an offer of a new product or service. * * *

* * *

In fact, we believe there are less anti-competitive ways of providing such information to insurers. The order that we would impose upon respondent allows it to provide information and views to insurers on behalf of its members, so long as the Society does not attempt to extract agreements, through coercion or otherwise, from third party payers on reimbursement issues. In allowing respondent to engage in non-binding, non-coercive discussions with health insurers, we have attempted to strike a proper balance between the need for insurers to have efficient access to the views of large groups of providers and the need to prevent competitors from banding together in ways that involve the unreasonable exercise of collective market power.

Notes and Questions

1. Does a decision by competing physicians to deal collectively in their negotiations with third party payers constitute price fixing? If so, why didn't the FTC treat this as a per se offense?

2. Consider the justifications offered by the Michigan State Medical Society physicians for their actions. Do any meet the requirement discussed in the introduction to this chapter that justifications must concern pro-competitive benefits arising from the restraint? Could collective negotiations be viewed as a market-improving step if they corrected market imperfections? Did they here? See Thomas E. Kauper, The Role of Quality of Health Care Considerations in Antitrust Analysis, 51 L. & Contemp. Probs. 273 (Spring, 1988); Thomas L. Greaney, Quality of Care and Market Failure Defenses in Antitrust Health Care Litigation, 21 Conn. L. Rev. 605, 650–52 (1989).

3. Note that the conduct at issue can also be characterized as a "boycott." Boycotts have also traditionally been subject to per se analysis, although the Supreme Court has cautioned in recent years that only certain collective refusals to deal will be summarily condemned. In Northwest Wholesale Stationers, Inc. v. Pacific Stationery, 472 U.S. 284, 105 S.Ct. 2613, 86 L.Ed.2d 202 (1985), the Court

noted somewhat elliptically that, in order to merit per se treatment, some of the following factors must be present: (1) cutting off access to a supply, facility or market necessary to enable the boycotted firms to compete; (2) market power in the boycotting firms; and (3) no plausible efficiency justifications. Only a few years later, however, the Court applied the per se rule to a boycott by lawyers serving as court-appointed counsel for indigent defendants and strongly defended presumptive treatment as administratively efficient and as a means of discouraging individuals from attempting inherently dangerous conduct. FTC v. Superior Court Trial Lawyers Ass'n, 493 U.S. 411, 110 S.Ct. 768, 107 L.Ed.2d 851 (1990). While the exact boundaries of the doctrine remain murky, plausible pro-competitive justifications for collective refusals to deal will remove conduct from per se classification. Lower courts have readily applied rule of reason analysis to alleged boycotts where, for example, providers were excluded from an IPA based on valid cost containment objectives. Hassan v. Independent Practice Associates, 698 F.Supp. 679 (E.D. Mich.1988); see also Hahn v. Oregon Physicians' Service, 868 F.2d 1022 (9th Cir. 1988), cert. denied, 493 U.S. 846, 110 S.Ct. 140, 107 L.Ed.2d 99 (1989).

4. In a few instances, criminal charges have been filed against providers who have engaged in price fixing or price-affecting boycotts. In United States v. Alston, 974 F.2d 1206 (9th Cir.1992), the Justice Department had indicted a group of dentists who allegedly conspired to fix co-payment fees received from insurers. The Ninth Circuit affirmed a jury verdict based on circumstantial evidence of meetings, discussions of mutual dissatisfaction and parallel conduct that the dentist entered into a price fixing conspiracy; however, the court upheld a motion for a new trial based on the contention that defendants lacked the necessary *mens rea* because they believed the payor had proposed the revised fee schedule. *Alston* was the first federal criminal prosecution involving health care providers since AMA v. United States, 130 F.2d 233 (D.C.Cir.1942), aff'd, 317 U.S. 519, 63 S.Ct. 326, 87 L.Ed. 434 (1943), in which the AMA and an affiliated society were convicted of violating the Sherman Act by engaging in a variety of efforts to suppress HMOs. These efforts included expulsion from the medical society and the circulation of "white lists" to encourage boycotts of those doctors cooperating with HMOs. More recently, the government charged that a trade association of optometrists discussed and agreed upon prices they would charge for eye exams and monitored and enforced that agreement. United States v. Lake Country Optometric Society, Crim. No. W–95–CR–114 (W.D.Tex. 1995).

FEDERAL TRADE COMMISSION v. INDIANA FEDERATION OF DENTISTS

Supreme Court of the United States, 1986.
476 U.S. 447, 106 S.Ct. 2009, 90 L.Ed.2d 445.

JUSTICE WHITE delivered the opinion of the Court.

This case concerns commercial relations among certain Indiana dentists, their patients, and the patients' dental health care insurers. The question presented is whether the Federal Trade Commission correctly concluded that a conspiracy among dentists to refuse to submit x-rays to dental insurers for use in benefits determinations constituted an "unfair method of competition" in violation of § 5 of the Federal Trade Commission Act. * * *

I

Since the 1970's, dental health insurers, responding to the demands of their policyholders, have attempted to contain the cost of dental treatment by, among other devices, limiting payment of benefits to the cost of the "least expensive yet adequate treatment" suitable to the needs of individual patients. Implementation of such cost-containment measures, known as "alternative benefits" plans, requires evaluation by the insurer of the diagnosis and recommendation of the treating dentist, either in advance of or following the provision of care. In order to carry out such evaluation, insurers frequently request dentists to submit, along with insurance claim forms requesting payment of benefits, any dental x-rays that have been used by the dentist in examining the patient as well as other information concerning their diagnoses and treatment recommendations. Typically, claim forms and accompanying x-rays are reviewed by lay claims examiners, who either approve payment of claims or, if the materials submitted raise a question whether the recommended course of treatment is in fact necessary, refer claims to dental consultants, who are licensed dentists, for further review. On the basis of the materials available, supplemented where appropriate by further diagnostic aids, the dental consultant may recommend that the insurer approve a claim, deny it, or pay only for a less expensive course of treatment.

Such review of diagnostic and treatment decisions has been viewed by some dentists as a threat to their professional independence and economic well-being. * * *

* * *

The relevant factual findings are that the members of the Federation conspired among themselves to withhold x-rays requested by dental insurers for use in evaluating claims for benefits, and that this conspiracy had the effect of suppressing competition among dentists with respect to cooperation with the requests of the insurance companies.

* * *

IV

The question remains whether these findings are legally sufficient to establish a violation of § 1 of the Sherman Act—that is, whether the Federation's collective refusal to cooperate with insurers' requests for x-rays constitutes an "unreasonable" restraint of trade. * * *

* * *

The policy of the Federation with respect to its members' dealings with third-party insurers resembles practices that have been labeled "group boycotts": the policy constitutes a concerted refusal to deal on particular terms with patients covered by group dental insurance. * * * Although this Court has in the past stated that group boycotts are unlawful per se, * * * we decline to resolve this case by forcing the Federation's policy into the "boycott" pigeonhole and invoking the per se rule. As we observed last Term in Northwest Wholesale Stationers, Inc. v. Pacific Stationery & Printing Co., the category of restraints classed as group boycotts is not to be expanded indiscriminately, and the per se approach has generally been limited to cases in which firms with market power boycott suppliers or customers in order to discourage them from doing business with a competitor—a situation obviously not present here. Moreover, we have been slow to condemn rules adopted by professional associations as unreasonable per se, * * * and, in general, to extend per se analysis to restraints imposed in the context of business relationships where the economic impact of certain practices is not immediately obvious. * * * Thus, as did the FTC, we evaluate the restraint at issue in this case under the Rule of Reason rather than a rule of per se illegality.

Application of the Rule of Reason to these facts is not a matter of any great difficulty. The Federation's policy takes the form of a horizontal agreement among the participating dentists to withhold from their customers a particular service that they desire—the forwarding of x-rays to insurance companies along with claim forms. "While this is not price fixing as such, no elaborate industry analysis is required to demonstrate the anti-competitive character of such an agreement." * * * A refusal to compete with respect to the package of services offered to customers, no less than a refusal to compete with respect to the price term of an agreement, impairs the ability of the market to advance social welfare by ensuring the provision of desired goods and services to consumers at a price approximating the marginal cost of providing them. Absent some countervailing pro-competitive virtue—such as, for example, the creation of efficiencies in the operation of a market or the provision of goods and services,—such an agreement limiting consumer choice by impeding the "ordinary give and take of the market place," [ ] cannot be sustained under the Rule of Reason. No credible argument has been advanced for the proposition that making it more costly for the insurers and patients who are the dentists' customers to obtain information needed for evaluating the dentists' diagnoses has any such pro-competitive effect.

The Federation advances three principal arguments for the proposition that, notwithstanding its lack of competitive virtue, the Federation's policy of withholding x-rays should not be deemed an unreasonable restraint of trade. First, as did the Court of Appeals, the Federation suggests that in the absence of specific findings by the Commission concerning the definition of the market in which the Federation allegedly restrained trade and the power of the Federation's members in that market, the conclusion that the Federation unreasonably restrained trade is erroneous as a matter of law, regardless of whether the challenged practices might be impermissibly anti-competitive if engaged in by persons who together possessed power in a specifically defined market. This contention, however, runs counter to the Court's holding in National Collegiate Athletic Assn. v. Board of Regents of Univ. of Okla., supra, that "[a]s a matter of law, the absence of proof of market power does not justify a naked restriction on price or output," and that such a restriction "requires some competitive justification even in the absence of a detailed market analysis." [ ] Moreover, even if the restriction imposed by the Federation is not sufficiently "naked" to call this principle into play, the Commission's failure to engage in detailed market analysis is not fatal to its finding of a violation of the Rule of Reason. The Commission found that in two localities in the State of Indiana (the Anderson and Lafayette areas), Federation dentists constituted heavy majorities of the practicing dentists and that as a result of the efforts of the Federation, insurers in those areas were, over a period of years, actually unable to obtain compliance with their requests for submission of x-rays. Since the purpose of the inquiries into market definition and market power is to determine whether an arrangement has the potential for genuine adverse effects on competition, "proof of actual detrimental effects, such as a reduction of output," can obviate the need for an inquiry into market power, which is but a "surrogate for detrimental effects." 7 P. Areeda, Antitrust Law ¶ 1511, p. 429 (1986). In this case, we conclude that the finding of actual, sustained adverse effects on competition in those areas where IFD dentists predominated, viewed in light of the reality that markets for dental services tend to be relatively localized, is legally sufficient to support a finding that the challenged restraint was unreasonable even in the absence of elaborate market analysis. [ ]

Second, the Federation, again following the lead of the Court of Appeals, argues that a holding that its policy of withholding x-rays constituted an unreasonable restraint of trade is precluded by the Commission's failure to make any finding that the policy resulted in the provision of dental services that were more costly than those that the patients and their insurers would have chosen were they able to evaluate x-rays in conjunction with claim forms. This argument, too, is unpersuasive. Although it is true that the goal of the insurers in seeking submission of x-rays for use in their review of benefits claims was to minimize costs by choosing the least expensive adequate course of dental treatment, a showing that this goal was actually achieved through the means chosen is not an essential step in establishing that the dentists' attempt to thwart its achievement by collectively refusing to supply the requested information was an unreasonable restraint of trade. A concerted and effective effort to withhold (or make more costly) information desired by consumers for the purpose of determining whether a particular purchase is cost justified is likely enough to disrupt the proper functioning of the price-setting mechanism of the market that it may be condemned even absent proof that it resulted in higher prices or, as here, the purchase of higher priced services, than would occur in its absence. [ ] Moreover, even if the desired information were in fact completely useless to the insurers and their patients in making an informed choice regarding the least costly adequate course of treatment—or, to put it another way, if the costs of evaluating the information were far greater than the cost savings resulting from its use—the Federation would still not be justified in deciding on behalf of its members' customers that they did not need the information: presumably, if that were the case, the discipline of the market would itself soon result in the insurers' abandoning their requests for x-rays. The Federation is not entitled to pre-empt the working of the market by deciding for itself that its customers do not need that which they demand.

[The Court next rejected defendants' "quality of care justifications." This issue is discussed in Section IA2 infra.]

Notes and Questions

1. Was the dentists' conduct price fixing or a boycott? Does it matter in which antitrust pigeonhole the conduct is placed?

2. What was the purpose of the insurers' requirement that the dentists submit x-rays to them? What effect would this requirement have on the total cost of dental services to the consumer? What purposes did defendants advance to justify their conduct? Do these concerns constitute legitimate justifications under the *National Society of Professional Engineers* paradigm? Note the Court's willingness to truncate its inquiry under the rule of reason. That is, it examined

defendants' justifications but did not require elaborate proof of effect, market power, or other factors once those justifications were found wanting.

3. The federal agencies have successfully challenged scores of provider cartels that engaged in a wide variety of practices designed to raise prices, thwart competition from other providers, or stymie cost containment efforts of managed care organizations. For example, the FTC entered into a consent decree with Montana Associated Physicians, Inc. (MAPI), an organization of 115 physicians practicing in over 30 independent physician practices and constituting 43% of all the physicians in Billings, Montana. In re Montana Associated Physicians, Inc. and Billings Physician Hospital Alliance, Inc., FTC Docket No. C–3704, 62 Fed. Reg. 11,201 (1997). According to the FTC's complaint, physicians formed MAPI to present a "united front" when dealing with managed care plans in an attempt to "resist competitive pressures to discount fees" and forestall entry of HMOs and PPOs into the area. Individual members of MAPI told HMOs that they would negotiate only through their organization and no individual MAPI member contracted with HMOs. See also United States v. North Dakota Hospital Associa-tion, 640 F.Supp. 1028 (D.N.D.1986) (hospitals' joint refusal to extend discounts in bidding for contracts); American Medical Association, 94 F.T.C. 701 (1979) (final order and opinion), aff'd 638 F.2d 443 (2d Cir.1980), aff'd by an equally divided court, 455 U.S. 676, 102 S.Ct. 1744, 71 L.Ed.2d 546 (1982) (ethical rules barring salaried employment, working for "inadequate compensation" and affiliat-ing with non-physicians); Medical Staff of Holy Cross Hospital, 114 F.T.C. 555 (1991) (consent order) (conspiracy by medical staff to obstruct development of Cleveland Clinic's multi-specialty group practice by denying staff privileges to clinic doctors); Medical Staff of Doctor's Hospital of Prince George's County, 110 F.T.C. 476 (1988) (consent order) (threats of boycott by medical staff designed to coerce hospital to abandon plans to open HMO facility); United States v. Massa-chusetts Allergy Society, Inc., 1992–1 Trade Cas. (CCH) ¶ 69,846 (D. Mass. 1992) (consent decree) (collectively-set fee schedule by physicians engaged in joint negotiations with HMOs); see generally 2 Furrow, et al., Health Law §§ 14–27— 14–30; 2 John J. Miles, Health Care and Antitrust Law §§ 15–4—15–5. Collective bargaining undertaken by "sham" networks or purported physician unions are discussed infra.

B.   COLLECTIVE ACTIVITIES WITH JUSTIFICATIONS

1.   *Restrictions on Advertising and Dissemination of Information*

CALIFORNIA DENTAL ASSOCIATION v. FEDERAL TRADE COMMISSION

Supreme Court of the United States, 1999.
526 U.S. 756, 119 S.Ct. 1604, 143 L.Ed.2d 935.

JUSTICE SOUTER delivered the opinion of the Court.

There are two issues in this case: whether the jurisdiction of the Federal Trade Commission extends to the California Dental Association (CDA), a nonprofit professional association, and whether a "quick look" sufficed to justify finding that certain advertising restrictions adopted by the CDA violated the antitrust laws. We hold that the Commission's jurisdiction under the Federal Trade Commission Act (FTC Act) extends to an association that, like the CDA, provides substantial economic benefit to its for-profit members, but that where, as here, any anticompetitive effects of given restraints are far from intuitively obvious, the rule of reason demands a more thorough enquiry into the consequences of those restraints than the Court of Appeals performed.

I

[Petitioner CDA, a nonprofit association of local dental societies to which about three-quarters of the State's dentists belong, provides desirable insurance and preferential financing arrangements for its members and engages in lobbying, litigation, marketing, and public relations for members' benefit. Members agree to abide by the CDA's Code of Ethics, which, inter alia, prohibits false or misleading advertising. The CDA has issued interpretive advisory opinions and guidelines relating to advertising. The FTC claimed that in applying its guidelines so as to restrict two types of truthful, nondeceptive advertising (price advertising, particularly discounted fees, and advertising relating to the quality of dental services), the CDA violated § 5 of the FTC Act. In its administrative proceedings, the Commission held that the advertising restrictions violated the Act under an abbreviated rule-of-reason analysis. In affirming, the Ninth Circuit sustained the Commission's jurisdiction and concluded that an abbreviated or "quick look" rule of reason analysis was proper in this case.]

The dentists who belong to the CDA ... agree to abide by a Code of Ethics (Code) including the following § 10:

> "Although any dentist may advertise, no dentist shall advertise or solicit patients in any form of communication in a manner that is false or misleading in any material respect. In order to properly serve the public, dentists should represent themselves in a manner that contributes to the esteem of the public. Dentists should not misrepresent their training and competence in any way that would be false or misleading in any material respect."

The CDA has issued a number of advisory opinions interpreting this section, and through separate advertising guidelines intended to help members comply with the Code and with state law the CDA has advised its dentists of disclosures they must make under state law when engaging in discount advertising.[1]

Responsibility for enforcing the Code rests in the first instance with the local dental societies, to which applicants for CDA membership must submit copies of their own advertisements and those of their employers or referral services to assure compliance with the Code. The local societies also actively seek information about potential Code violations by applicants or CDA members. Applicants who refuse to withdraw or revise objectionable advertisements may be denied membership; and members who, after a hearing, remain

---

1. The disclosures include:

"1. The dollar amount of the nondiscounted fee for the service[.]

"2. Either the dollar amount of the discount fee or the percentage of the discount for the specific service[.]

"3. The length of time that the discount will be offered[.]

"4. Verifiable fees[.]

"5. [The identity of] [s]pecific groups who qualify for the discount or any other terms and conditions or restrictions for qualifying for the discount." Id., at 724.

similarly recalcitrant are subject to censure, suspension, or expulsion from the CDA. [ ]

* * *

II

[The Court held that the Commission's jurisdiction extends to associations that, like the CDA, provide substantial economic benefit to their for-profit members. It interpreted the FTC Act, which gives the Commission authority over a "corporatio[n]" that is "organized to carry on business for its own profit or that of its members," 15 U.S.C. §§ 44, 45(a)(2), as conferring jurisdiction over nonprofit associations whose activities provide substantial economic benefits to their for-profit members. The Court declined to predicate FTC jurisdiction on a showing that a supporting organization devoted itself entirely to its members' profits or that its activities focused on raising members' bottom lines. While the Act does not cover all membership organizations of profit-making corporations, the Court concluded that the economic benefits conferred upon CDA's profit-seeking professionals plainly fell within the object of enhancing its members' "profit," which is the Act's jurisdictional touchstone.]

III

The Court of Appeals treated as distinct questions the sufficiency of the analysis of anticompetitive effects and the substantiality of the evidence supporting the Commission's conclusions. Because we decide that the Court of Appeals erred when it held as a matter of law that quick-look analysis was appropriate (with the consequence that the Commission's abbreviated analysis and conclusion were sustainable), we do not reach the question of the substantiality of the evidence supporting the Commission's conclusion.[2]

In National Collegiate Athletic Assn. v. Board of Regents of Univ. of Okla.[ ] we held that a "naked restraint on price and output requires some competitive justification even in the absence of a detailed market analysis." [ ]. Elsewhere, we held that "no elaborate industry analysis is required to demonstrate the anticompetitive character of" horizontal agreements among competitors to refuse to discuss prices, National Soc. of Professional Engineers v. United States, [ ] or to withhold a particular desired service, FTC v. Indiana Federation of Dentists [ ]. In each of these cases, which have formed the basis for what has come to be called abbreviated or "quick-look" analysis under the rule of reason, an observer with even a rudimentary understanding of economics could conclude that the arrangements in question would have an anticompetitive effect on customers and markets. . . . As in such cases, quick-look analysis carries the day when the great likelihood of anticompetitive effects can easily be ascertained. . . .

The case before us, however, fails to present a situation in which the likelihood of anticompetitive effects is comparably obvious. Even on Justice BREYER's view that bars on truthful and verifiable price and quality adver-

---

2. We leave to the Court of Appeals the question whether on remand it can effectively assess the Commission's decision for substantial evidence on the record, or whether it must remand to the Commission for a more extensive rule-of-reason analysis on the basis of an enhanced record.

tising are prima facie anticompetitive, and place the burden of procompetitive justification on those who agree to adopt them, the very issue at the threshold of this case is whether professional price and quality advertising is sufficiently verifiable in theory and in fact to fall within such a general rule. Ultimately our disagreement with Justice BREYER turns on our different responses to this issue. Whereas he accepts, as the Ninth Circuit seems to have done, that the restrictions here were like restrictions on advertisement of price and quality generally, it seems to us that the CDA's advertising restrictions might plausibly be thought to have a net procompetitive effect, or possibly no effect at all on competition. The restrictions on both discount and nondiscount advertising are, at least on their face, designed to avoid false or deceptive[3] in a market characterized by striking disparities between the information available to the professional and the patient.[4] Cf. Carr & Mathewson, The Economics of Law Firms: A Study in the Legal Organization of the Firm, 33 J. Law & Econ. 307, 309 (1990) (explaining that in a market for complex professional services, "inherent asymmetry of knowledge about the product" arises because "professionals supplying the good are knowledgeable [whereas] consumers demanding the good are uninformed"); Akerlof, The Market for "Lemons": Quality Uncertainty and the Market Mechanism, 84 Q.J. Econ. 488 (1970) (pointing out quality problems in market characterized by asymmetrical information). In a market for professional services, in which advertising is relatively rare and the comparability of service packages not easily established, the difficulty for customers or potential competitors to get and verify information about the price and availability of services magnifies the dangers to competition associated with misleading advertising. What is more, the quality of professional services tends to resist either calibration or monitoring by individual patients or clients, partly because of the specialized knowledge required to evaluate the services, and partly because of the difficulty in determining whether, and the degree to which, an outcome is attributable to the quality of services (like a poor job of tooth-filling) or to something else (like a very tough walnut). See Leland, Quacks, Lemons, and Licensing: A Theory of Minimum Quality Standards, 87 J. Pol. Econ. 1328, 1330 (1979); 1 B. Furrow, T. Greaney, S. Johnson, T. Jost, & R. Schwartz, Health Law § 3–1, p. 86 (1995) (describing the common view that "the lay public is incapable of adequately evaluating the quality of medical services"). Patients' attachments to particular professionals, the rationality of which is difficult to assess, complicate the picture even further. Cf. Evans, Professionals and the Production Function: Can Competition Policy Improve Efficiency in the Licensed Professions?, in Occupational Licensure and Regulation 235–236 (S. Rottenberg ed.1980) (describing long-term relationship between professional and client not as "a series of spot contracts" but rather as "a long-

---

3. That false or misleading advertising has an anticompetitive effect, as that term is customarily used, has been long established. Cf. FTC v. Algoma Lumber Co., 291 U.S. 67, 79–80, 54 S.Ct. 315, 78 L.Ed. 655 (1934) (finding a false advertisement to be unfair competition).

4. "The fact that a restraint operates upon a profession as distinguished from a business is, of course, relevant in determining whether that particular restraint violates the Sherman Act. It would be unrealistic to view the practice of professions as interchangeable with other business activities, and automatically to apply to the professions antitrust concepts which originated in other areas. The public service aspect, and other features of the professions, may require that a particular practice, which could properly be viewed as a violation of the Sherman Act in another context, be treated differently." Goldfarb v. Virginia State Bar, 421 U.S. 773, 788–789, n. 17, 95 S.Ct. 2004, 44 L.Ed.2d 572 (1975).

term agreement, often implicit, to deal with each other in a set of future unspecified or incompletely specified circumstances according to certain rules," and adding that "[i]t is not clear how or if these [implicit contracts] can be reconciled with the promotion of effective price competition in individual spot markets for particular services"). The existence of such significant challenges to informed decisionmaking by the customer for professional services immediately suggests that advertising restrictions arguably protecting patients from misleading or irrelevant advertising call for more than cursory treatment as obviously comparable to classic horizontal agreements to limit output or price competition.

[The Court of Appeals] brushe[d] over the professional context and describe[d] no anticompetitive effects. Assuming that the record in fact supports the conclusion that the CDA disclosure rules essentially bar advertisement of across-the-board discounts, it does not obviously follow that such a ban would have a net anticompetitive effect here. Whether advertisements that announced discounts for, say, first-time customers, would be less effective at conveying information relevant to competition if they listed the original and discounted prices for checkups, X-rays, and fillings, than they would be if they simply specified a percentage discount across the board, seems to us a question susceptible to empirical but not a priori analysis. . . . Put another way, the CDA's rule appears to reflect the prediction that any costs to competition associated with the elimination of across-the-board advertising will be outweighed by gains to consumer information (and hence competition) created by discount advertising that is exact, accurate, and more easily verifiable (at least by regulators). As a matter of economics this view may or may not be correct, but it is not implausible, and neither a court nor the Commission may initially dismiss it as presumptively wrong.[5]

* * *

The Court of Appeals was comparably tolerant in accepting the sufficiency of abbreviated rule-of-reason analysis as to the nonprice advertising restrictions. The court began with the argument that "[t]hese restrictions are in effect a form of output limitation, as they restrict the supply of information about individual dentists' services." Although this sentence does indeed appear as cited, it is puzzling, given that the relevant output for antitrust purposes here is presumably not information or advertising, but dental services themselves. The question is not whether the universe of possible advertisements has been limited (as assuredly it has), but whether the limitation on advertisements obviously tends to limit the total delivery of dental services. The court came closest to addressing this latter question

---

5. Justice Breyer suggests that our analysis is "of limited relevance," because "the basic question is whether this . . . theoretically redeeming virtue in fact offsets the restrictions' anticompetitive effects in this case." He thinks that the Commission and the Court of Appeals "adequately answered that question," but the absence of any empirical evidence on this point indicates that the question was not answered, merely avoided by implicit burden-shifting of the kind accepted by Justice Breyer. The point is that before a theoretical claim of anticompetitive effects can justify shifting to a defendant the burden to show empirical evidence of procompetitive effects, as quick-look analysis in effect requires, there must be some indication that the court making the decision has properly identified the theoretical basis for the anticompetitive effects and considered whether the effects actually are anticompetitive. Where, as here, the circumstances of the restriction are somewhat complex, assumption alone will not do.

when it went on to assert that limiting advertisements regarding quality and safety "prevents dentists from fully describing the package of services they offer," adding that "[t]he restrictions may also affect output more directly, as quality and comfort advertising may induce some customers to obtain non-emergency care when they might not otherwise do so," ibid. This suggestion about output is also puzzling. If quality advertising actually induces some patients to obtain more care than they would in its absence, then restricting such advertising would reduce the demand for dental services, not the supply; and it is of course the producers' supply of a good in relation to demand that is normally relevant in determining whether a producer-imposed output limitation has the anticompetitive effect of artificially raising prices.[6] ...

Although the Court of Appeals acknowledged the CDA's view that "claims about quality are inherently unverifiable and therefore misleading," it responded that this concern "does not justify banning all quality claims without regard to whether they are, in fact, false or misleading." As a result, the court said, "the restriction is a sufficiently naked restraint on output to justify quick look analysis." The court assumed, in these words, that some dental quality claims may escape justifiable censure, because they are both verifiable and true. But its implicit assumption fails to explain why it gave no weight to the countervailing, and at least equally plausible, suggestion that restricting difficult-to-verify claims about quality or patient comfort would have a procompetitive effect by preventing misleading or false claims that distort the market. It is, indeed, entirely possible to understand the CDA's restrictions on unverifiable quality and comfort advertising as nothing more than a procompetitive ban on puffery. . . .

The point is not that the CDA's restrictions necessarily have the procompetitive effect claimed by the CDA; it is possible that banning quality claims might have no effect at all on competitiveness if, for example, many dentists made very much the same sort of claims. And it is also of course possible that the restrictions might in the final analysis be anticompetitive. The point, rather, is that the plausibility of competing claims about the effects of the professional advertising restrictions rules out the indulgently abbreviated review to which the Commission's order was treated. The obvious anticompetitive effect that triggers abbreviated analysis has not been shown.

In light of our focus on the adequacy of the Court of Appeals's analysis, Justice Breyer's thorough-going, de novo antitrust analysis contains much to impress on its own merits but little to demonstrate the sufficiency of the Court of Appeals's review. The obligation to give a more deliberate look than a quick one does not arise at the door of this Court and should not be satisfied here in the first instance. Had the Court of Appeals engaged in a painstaking discussion in a league with Justice Breyer's (compare his 14 pages with the Ninth Circuit's 8), and had it confronted the comparability of these restric-

---

6. Justice Breyer wonders if we "mea[n] this statement as an argument against the anticompetitive tendencies that flow from an agreement not to advertise service quality." But as the preceding sentence shows, we intend simply to question the logic of the Court of Appeals's suggestion that the restrictions are anticompetitive because they somehow "affect output," presumably with the intent to raise prices by limiting supply while demand remains constant. We do not mean to deny that an agreement not to advertise service quality might have anticompetitive effects. We merely mean that, absent further analysis of the kind Justice Breyer undertakes, it is not possible to conclude that the net effect of this particular restriction is anticompetitive.

tions to bars on clearly verifiable advertising, its reasoning might have sufficed to justify its conclusion. Certainly Justice Breyer's treatment of the antitrust issues here is no "quick look." Lingering is more like it, and indeed Justice BREYER, not surprisingly, stops short of endorsing the Court of Appeals's discussion as adequate to the task at hand.

Saying here that the Court of Appeals's conclusion at least required a more extended examination of the possible factual underpinnings than it received is not, of course, necessarily to call for the fullest market analysis. Although we have said that a challenge to a "naked restraint on price and output" need not be supported by "a detailed market analysis" in order to "requir[e] some competitive justification," ... The truth is that our categories of analysis of anticompetitive effect are less fixed than terms like "per se," "quick look," and "rule of reason" tend to make them appear. We have recognized, for example, that "there is often no bright line separating per se from Rule of Reason analysis," since "considerable inquiry into market conditions" may be required before the application of any so-called "per se" condemnation is justified. As the circumstances here demonstrate, there is generally no categorical line to be drawn between restraints that give rise to an intuitively obvious inference of anticompetitive effect and those that call for more detailed treatment. What is required, rather, is an enquiry meet for the case, looking to the circumstances, details, and logic of a restraint. The object is to see whether the experience of the market has been so clear, or necessarily will be, that a confident conclusion about the principal tendency of a restriction will follow from a quick (or at least quicker) look, in place of a more sedulous one. And of course what we see may vary over time, if rule-of-reason analyses in case after case reach identical conclusions. For now, at least, a less quick look was required for the initial assessment of the tendency of these professional advertising restrictions. Because the Court of Appeals did not scrutinize the assumption of relative anticompetitive tendencies, we vacate the judgment and remand the case for a fuller consideration of the issue.

It is so ordered.

JUSTICE BREYER, with whom JUSTICE STEVENS, JUSTICE KENNEDY, and JUSTICE GINSBURG join, concurring in part and dissenting in part.

I agree with the Court that the Federal Trade Commission has jurisdiction over petitioner, and I join Parts I and II of its opinion. I also agree that in a "rule of reason" antitrust case "the quality of proof required should vary with the circumstances," that "[w]hat is required ... is an enquiry meet for the case," and that the object is a "confident conclusion about the principal tendency of a restriction." But I do not agree that the Court has properly applied those unobjectionable principles here. In my view, a traditional application of the rule of reason to the facts as found by the Commission requires affirming the Commission—just as the Court of Appeals did below.

I

The Commission's conclusion is lawful if its "factual findings," insofar as they are supported by "substantial evidence," "make out a violation of Sherman Act § 1." [ ] To determine whether that is so, I would not simply ask whether the restraints at issue are anticompetitive overall. Rather, like the Court of Appeals (and the Commission), I would break that question down into four classical, subsidiary antitrust questions: (1) What is the specific restraint at issue? (2) What are its likely anticompetitive effects? (3) Are there offsetting procompetitive justifications? (4) Do the parties have sufficient market power to make a difference?

A

The most important question is the first: What are the specific restraints at issue? [ ] Those restraints do not include merely the agreement to which the California Dental Association's (Dental Association or Association) ethical rule literally refers, namely, a promise to refrain from advertising that is " 'false or misleading in any material respect.' [ ] Instead, the Commission found a set of restraints arising out of the way the Dental Association implemented this innocent-sounding ethical rule in practice, through advisory opinions, guidelines, enforcement policies, and review of membership applications. As implemented, the ethical rule reached beyond its nominal target, to prevent truthful and nondeceptive advertising. In particular, the Commission determined that the rule, in practice:"

(1) "precluded advertising that characterized a dentist's fees as being low, reasonable, or affordable,"

(2) "precluded advertising . . . of across the board discounts," and

(3) "prohibit[ed] all quality claims."

Whether the Dental Association's basic rule as implemented actually restrained the truthful and nondeceptive advertising of low prices, across-the-board discounts, and quality service are questions of fact. The Administrative Law Judge (ALJ) and the Commission may have found those questions difficult ones. But both the ALJ and the Commission ultimately found against the Dental Association in respect to these facts. And the question for us—whether those agency findings are supported by substantial evidence, is not difficult.

The Court of Appeals referred explicitly to some of the evidence that it found adequate to support the Commission's conclusions. It pointed out, for example, that the Dental Association's "advisory opinions and guidelines indicate that . . . descriptions of prices as 'reasonable' or 'low' do not comply" with the Association's rule; that in "numerous cases" the Association "advised members of objections to special offers, senior citizen discounts, and new patient discounts, apparently without regard to their truth"; and that one advisory opinion "expressly states that claims as to the quality of services are inherently likely to be false or misleading," all "without any particular consideration of whether" such statements were "true or false." [ ]

The Commission itself had before it far more evidence. It referred to instances in which the Association, without regard for the truthfulness of the statements at issue, recommended denial of membership to dentists wishing to advertise, for example, "reasonable fees quoted in advance," "major savings," or "making teeth cleaning . . . inexpensive." It referred to testimony that "across-the-board discount advertising in literal compliance with the requirements 'would probably take two pages in the telephone book' and '[n]obody is going to really advertise in that fashion.' " And it pointed to many instances in which the Dental Association suppressed such advertising claims as "we guarantee all dental work for 1 year," "latest in cosmetic dentistry," and "gentle dentistry in a caring environment."

* * *

B

Do each of the three restrictions mentioned have "the potential for genuine adverse effects on competition"? I should have thought that the anticompetitive tendencies of the three restrictions were obvious. An agreement not to advertise that a fee is reasonable, that service is inexpensive, or that a customer will receive a discount makes it more difficult for a dentist to inform customers that he charges a lower price. If the customer does not know about a lower price, he will find it more difficult to buy lower price service. That fact, in turn, makes it less likely that a dentist will obtain more customers by offering lower prices. And that likelihood means that dentists will prove less likely to offer lower prices. But why should I have to spell out the obvious? To restrain truthful advertising about lower prices is likely to restrict competition in respect to price—"the central nervous system of the economy." For present purposes, I need not decide whether the Commission was right in applying a per se rule. I need only assume a rule of reason applies, and note the serious anticompetitive tendencies of the price advertising restraints.

The restrictions on the advertising of service quality also have serious anticompetitive tendencies. This is not a case of "mere puffing," as the FTC recognized. The days of my youth, when the billboards near Emeryville, California, home of AAA baseball's Oakland Oaks, displayed the name of "Painless" Parker, Dentist, are long gone—along with the Oakland Oaks. But some parents may still want to know that a particular dentist makes a point of "gentle care." Others may want to know about 1–year dental work guarantees. To restrict that kind of service quality advertisement is to restrict competition over the quality of service itself, for, unless consumers know, they may not purchase, and dentists may not compete to supply that which will make little difference to the demand for their services. That, at any rate, is the theory of the Sherman Act. And it is rather late in the day for anyone to deny the significant anticompetitive tendencies of an agreement that restricts competition in any legitimate respect, let alone one that inhibits customers from learning about the quality of a dentist's service.

Nor did the Commission rely solely on the unobjectionable proposition that a restriction on the ability of dentists to advertise on quality is likely to limit their incentive to compete on quality. Rather, the Commission pointed to record evidence affirmatively establishing that quality-based competition is important to dental consumers in California. [The dissent goes on to summarize evidence that advertising concerning quality will bring in more patients and that restrictions adversely affected dentists who advertise.]

C

We must also ask whether, despite their anticompetitive tendencies, these restrictions might be justified by other procompetitive tendencies or redeeming virtues. [ ] This is a closer question—at least in theory. The Dental Association argues that the three relevant restrictions are inextricably tied to a legitimate Association effort to restrict false or misleading advertising. The Association, the argument goes, had to prevent dentists from engaging in the kind of truthful, nondeceptive advertising that it banned in order effectively to stop dentists from making unverifiable claims about price or service quality, which claims would mislead the consumer.

The problem with this or any similar argument is an empirical one. Notwithstanding its theoretical plausibility, the record does not bear out such a claim. The Commission, which is expert in the area of false and misleading advertising, was uncertain whether petitioner had even made the claim. It characterized petitioner's efficiencies argument as rooted in the (unproved) factual assertion that its ethical rule "challenges only advertising that is false or misleading." Regardless, the Court of Appeals wrote, in respect to the price restrictions, that "the record provides no evidence that the rule has in fact led to increased disclosure and transparency of dental pricing." With respect to quality advertising, the Commission stressed that the Association "offered no convincing argument, let alone evidence, that consumers of dental services have been, or are likely to be, harmed by the broad categories of advertising it restricts." Nor did the Court of Appeals think that the Association's unsubstantiated contention that "claims about quality are inherently unverifiable and therefore misleading" could "justify banning all quality claims without regard to whether they are, in fact, false or misleading."

With one exception, my own review of the record reveals no significant evidentiary support for the proposition that the Association's members must agree to ban truthful price and quality advertising in order to stop untruthful claims. The one exception is the obvious fact that one can stop untruthful advertising if one prohibits all advertising. But since the Association made virtually no effort to sift the false from the true, [ ] that fact does not make out a valid antitrust defense. [ ]

In the usual Sherman Act § 1 case, the defendant bears the burden of establishing a procompetitive justification. [ ] And the Court of Appeals was correct when it concluded that no such justification had been established here.

D

I shall assume that the Commission must prove one additional circumstance, namely, that the Association's restraints would likely have made a real difference in the marketplace. The Commission, disagreeing with the ALJ on this single point, found that the Association did possess enough market power to make a difference. In at least one region of California, the mid-Peninsula, its members accounted for more than 90% of the marketplace; on average they accounted for 75%. In addition, entry by new dentists into the market place is fairly difficult. Dental education is expensive (leaving graduates of dental school with $50,000–$100,000 of debt), as is opening a new dentistry office (which costs $75,000–$100,000). And Dental Association members believe membership in the Association is important, valuable, and recognized as such by the public.

These facts, in the Court of Appeals' view, were sufficient to show "enough market power to harm competition through [the Association's] standard setting in the area of advertising." 128 F.3d, at 730. And that conclusion is correct. . . .

II

In the Court's view, the legal analysis conducted by the Court of Appeals was insufficient, and the Court remands the case for a more thorough application of the rule of reason. But in what way did the Court of Appeals fail? I find the Court's answers to this question unsatisfactory—when one divides the overall Sherman Act question into its traditional component parts and adheres to traditional judicial practice for allocating the burdens of persuasion in an antitrust case.

Did the Court of Appeals misconceive the anticompetitive tendencies of the restrictions?

[The majority] criticizes the Court of Appeals for failing to recognize that "the restrictions at issue here are very far from a total ban on price or discount advertising" and that "the particular restrictions on professional advertising could have different effects from those 'normally' found in the commercial world, even to the point of promoting competition...."

The problem with these statements is that the Court of Appeals did consider the relevant differences. It rejected the legal "treatment" customarily applied "to classic horizontal agreements to limit output or price competition"—i.e., the FTC's (alternative) per se approach. It did so because the Association's "policies do not, on their face, ban truthful nondeceptive ads"; instead, they "have been enforced in a way that restricts truthful advertising." [ ] ...

Did the Court of Appeals misunderstand the nature of an anticompetitive effect? The Court says:

"If quality advertising actually induces some patients to obtain more care than they would in its absence, then restricting such advertising would reduce the demand for dental services, not the supply; and ... the producers' supply ... is normally relevant in determining whether a ... limitation has the anticompetitive effect of artificially raising prices."

But if the Court means this statement as an argument against the anticompetitive tendencies that flow from an agreement not to advertise service quality, I believe it is the majority, and not the Court of Appeals, that is mistaken. An agreement not to advertise, say, "gentle care" is anticompetitive because it imposes an artificial barrier against each dentist's independent decision to advertise gentle care. That barrier, in turn, tends to inhibit those dentists who want to supply gentle care from getting together with those customers who want to buy gentle care. There is adequate reason to believe that tendency present in this case.

Did the Court of Appeals inadequately consider possible procompetitive justifications? The Court seems to think so ... The basic question is whether this, or some other, theoretically redeeming virtue in fact offsets the restrictions' anticompetitive effects in this case. Both court and Commission adequately answered that question.

The Commission found that the defendant did not make the necessary showing that a redeeming virtue existed in practice. ...

With respect to the restraint on advertising across-the-board discounts, the majority summarizes its concerns as follows: "Assuming that the record in fact supports the conclusion that the [Association's] disclosure rules essentially bar advertisement of [such] discounts, it does not obviously follow that such a ban would have a net anticompetitive effect here." I accept, rather than assume, the premise: The FTC found that the disclosure rules did bar advertisement of across-the-board discounts, and that finding is supported by substantial evidence. And I accept as literally true the conclusion that the Court says follows from that premise, namely, that "net anticompetitive effects" do not "obviously" follow from that premise. But obviousness is not the point. With respect to any of the three restraints found by the Commission, whether "net anticompetitive effects" follow is a matter of how the Commission, and, here, the Court of Appeals, have answered the questions I laid out at the beginning. Has the Commission shown that the restriction has anticompetitive tendencies? It has. Has the Association nonetheless shown offsetting virtues? It has not. Has the Commission shown market power sufficient for it to believe that the restrictions will likely make a real world difference? It has.

The upshot, in my view, is that the Court of Appeals, applying ordinary antitrust principles, reached an unexceptional conclusion. It is the same legal conclusion that this Court itself reached in Indiana Federation—a much closer case than this one. There the Court found that an agreement by dentists not to submit dental X rays to insurers violated the rule of reason. The anticompetitive tendency of that agreement was to reduce competition among dentists in respect to their willingness to submit X rays to insurers, [ ]—a matter in respect to which consumers are relatively indifferent, as compared to advertising of price discounts and service quality, the matters at issue here. The redeeming virtue in Indiana Federation was the alleged undesirability of having insurers consider a range of matters when deciding whether treatment was justified—a virtue no less plausible, and no less proved, than the virtue offered here. The "power" of the dentists to enforce their agreement was no greater than that at issue here (control of 75% to 90% of the relevant markets). It is difficult to see how the two cases can be reconciled.

* * *

I would note that the form of analysis I have followed is not rigid; it admits of some variation according to the circumstances. The important point, however, is that its allocation of the burdens of persuasion reflects a gradual evolution within the courts over a period of many years. That evolution represents an effort carefully to blend the procompetitive objectives of the law of antitrust with administrative necessity. I hope that this case does not represent an abandonment of that basic, and important, form of analysis.

For these reasons, I respectfully dissent from Part III of the Court's opinion.

Notes and Questions

1. Is there a significant difference between the facts before the Court in *California Dental* and *Indiana Federation of Dentists*? Didn't both cases involve actions by a sizable majority of dentists to withhold information from purchasers on the grounds that they could not adequately evaluate it? Was there direct proof of the restraint's effect on consumers in either case? Has the Court shifted the

requirement for "quick look" evaluations? See Thomas C. Arthur, A Workable Rule of Reason: A Less Ambitious Role for the Federal Courts, 68 Antitrust L.J. 337 (2000). What does *California Dental* suggest about the way courts should evaluate restrictions involving professionals in the future? Are the problems associated with asymmetry of information so pronounced in health care markets that professionals should be free from antitrust scrutiny? See Marina Lao, Comment, The Rule of Reason and Horizontal Restraints Involving Professionals, 68 Antitrust L.J. 499 (2000). For an insightful analysis of how antitrust might evaluate restraints of trade that improve overall welfare by overcoming market imperfections, see Peter J. Hammer, Antitrust Beyond Competition: Market Failures, Total Welfare, and the Challenge of Intramarket Second Best Tradeoffs, 98 Mich. L. Rev. 849 (2000).

2. On remand, the Ninth Circuit ordered dismissal finding the FTC had failed to show that the CDA's restrictions had a net anticompetitive effect and that the evidence of anticompetitive intent was ambiguous. 224 F.3d 942 (9th Cir.2000). While acknowledging that the Supreme Court had not mandated a full blown rule of reason inquiry, the Ninth Circuit "opt[ed] for a particularly searching rule-of-reason inquiry in light of the plausibility and strength of the procompetitive justifications" supplied by expert testimony that advertising restrictions tend to protect the public from false or misleading information or unscrupulous providers. Id. at 947 n.3. In view of the Supreme Court's decision and the Ninth Circuit's prior findings, do you find this approach surprising? If you do, you are in good company; see Stephen Calkins, California Dental Association: Not a Quick Look but Not the Full Monty, 67 Antitrust L.J. 495 (2000); William J. Kolasky, California Dental Association v. FTC: The New Antitrust Empiricism, 14 Antitrust 68 (Fall 1999). Equally controversial was the Ninth Circuit's decision not to remand to the FTC for further proceedings. The Court concluded that the FTC had ample opportunity to present evidence under a rule of reason theory but had failed to do so. 224 F.3d at 958–59.

In finding the FTC's proof of net anticompetitive effect wanting, the Ninth Circuit parsed a number of economic studies advanced by the Commission in support of the proposition that restrictions on advertising tend to raise prices and do not materially improve quality of services. See, e.g., Carolyn Cox & Susan Foster, The Costs and Benefits of Occupational Regulation (1990); Lee Benham, The Effect of Advertising on the Price of Eyeglasses, 15 J.L. & Econ. 337 (1972); James A. Langenfeld & John R. Morris, Analyzing Agreements Among Competitors: What Does the Future Hold?, 36 Antitrust Bull. 651 (1991). Ultimately it declined to rely on empirical studies which dealt with complete bans on advertising (in contrast to the partial restrictions imposed by the CDA) or with professions other than dentistry, such as optometry or law. 224 F.3d at 950–56. How exacting should a court's proof requirements be when dealing with empirical economic evidence? Does the expertise of the FTC as an administrative agency charged with combating misleading advertising supply a basis for decreasing the role of the court as arbiters of competing economic studies? For a useful survey of the evidence concerning the effects of advertising, concluding that evidence not in the record before the Supreme Court "overwhelmingly demonstrates that the fears of the CDA majority [were] unjustified," see Timothy J. Muris, The Rule of Reason After California Dental, 68 Antitrust L.J. 527 (2000).

3. Under what circumstances would competing providers sharing information on fees or other competitively sensitive topics pose a significant threat? Should it ever be deemed per se illegal? See United States v. Burgstiner, 1991–1 Trade Cas. (CCH) ¶ 69,422 (S.D. Ga. 1991) (consent decree) (exchange of informa-

tion about fees among twenty-two OB/GYNs after local businesses announced their intention to form a PPO; fees for normal deliveries and caesarean sections increased by $500 after the exchange). However, in some circumstances, joint provision and dissemination of data may improve competitive conditions and should be evaluated under the rule of reason. The federal enforcement agencies' enforcement guidelines allow providers to collectively provide factual information concerning fees provided that they adopt "reasonable safeguards" against anti-competitive activities. See U.S. Dept. of Justice & Federal Trade Commission, Statement of Antitrust Enforcement Policy in Health Care, Stmt. 5 (1996).

4. How should antitrust law treat price surveys by business coalitions or other buyers of health services? When might buyer power (monopsony) pose competitive problems? See Clark C. Havighurst, Antitrust Issues in the Joint Purchasing of Health Care, 1995 Utah L. Rev. 409 (1995); Frances H. Miller, Health Insurance Purchasing Alliances: Monopsony Threat or Procompetitive Rx for Health Sectors Ills, 79 Cornell L. Rev. 1546 (1994). The FTC and DOJ have issued numerous advisory opinions and business review letters approving such arrangements. See, e.g., Business Review Letter from Charles F. Rule, Assistant Attorney General, Antitrust Division, U.S. Department of Justice, to James Stutz, Executive Director, St. Louis Area Business Health Coalition (Mar. 24, 1988). Can an information exchange constitute a Section One violation or must there be an implicit agreement to fix prices? See United States v. Utah Society for Healthcare Human Resources, 1994–2 Trade Cas. (CCH) ¶ 70,795 (D. Utah 1994) (consent decree) (defendant hospital associations and eight individual hospitals charged with conspiring to restrain wage competition among themselves through a series of telephone calls and wage surveys that resulted in smaller wage increases than defendants would otherwise have paid). Under what circumstances might professional societies be allowed to operate "peer review" programs that advise payors about the reasonableness of fees charged by physicians? What if the societies reserve the right to punish "fee-gougers"? See American Medical Ass'n, 1994 Trade Cas. (CCH) ¶ 23602 (1994) (FTC advisory opinion); See also, 2 Furrow, et al., Health Law § 14–32.

2. *Private Accreditation and Professional Standard–Setting*

One of the most challenging problems posed by the application of anti-trust law to health care concerns the activities of private organizations of health professionals designed to promote high standards of professionalism and advance scientific learning through the promulgation of standards, guide-lines, and ethical norms. Although antitrust analysis explicitly considers only the competitive effects of an association's challenged activities, evidence of quality goals frequently enters the picture, sometimes appropriately and sometimes not.

WILK v. AMERICAN MEDICAL ASSOCIATION

United States Court of Appeals, Seventh Circuit, 1990.
895 F.2d 352, cert. denied, 498 U.S. 982, 111 S.Ct. 513, 112 L.Ed.2d 524 (1990).

MANION, CIRCUIT JUDGE.

The district court held that the American Medical Association ("AMA") violated § 1 of the Sherman Act, 15 U.S.C.A. § 1, by conducting an illegal boycott in restraint of trade directed at chiropractors generally, and the four plaintiffs in particular. The court granted an injunction * * * requiring, among other things, wide publication of its order. * * * Wilk v. American Medical Association, 671 F.Supp. 1465 (N.D.Ill.1987). The AMA appeals the finding of liability, and contends that, in any event, injunctive relief is unnecessary. * * * We affirm.

I.

* * * Plaintiffs Chester A. Wilk, James W. Bryden, Patricia B. Arthur, and Michael D. Pedigo, are licensed chiropractors. Their complaint, originally filed in 1976, charged several defendants with violating §§ 1 and 2 of the Sherman Act, 15 U.S.C.A. §§ 1 and 2. It sought both damages and an injunction. * * * At the first trial, plaintiffs' primary claim was that the defendants engaged in a conspiracy to eliminate the chiropractic profession by refusing to deal with plaintiffs and other chiropractors. * * *

A jury returned a verdict for the defendants. An earlier panel of this court, however, reversed that judgment. Wilk v. American Medical Association, 719 F.2d 207 (7th Cir.1983) (Wilk I). In reversing and ordering a new trial, we held that, in applying the rule of reason, the jury had been allowed to consider factors beyond the effect of the AMA's conduct on competition. The district court had improperly failed to confine the jury's consideration to the "patient care motive as contrasted with [the] generalized public interest motive." Id. at 229.

[The court recounts the history of the AMA's opposition to and actions against chiropractic.]

At trial, the AMA raised the so-called "patient care defense" which this court had formulated in its earlier opinion in this case. * * * That defense required the AMA generally to show that it acted because of a genuine, and reasonable, concern for scientific method in patient care and that it could not adequately satisfy this concern in a way that was less restrictive of competition. The district court rejected the defense. The court found the AMA failed to establish that throughout the relevant period (1966–1980) their concern for scientific methods in patient care had been objectively reasonable. The court also found the AMA similarly failed to show it could not adequately have satisfied its concern for scientific method in patient care in a manner less restrictive of competition than a nationwide conspiracy to eliminate a licensed profession. * * *

The AMA's present position regarding chiropractic is that it is ethical for a medical physician to professionally associate with chiropractors, if the physician believes that the association is in his patient's best interests. The district court found that the AMA had not previously communicated this position to its membership.

Based on these findings, the court held that the AMA and its members violated § 1 of the Sherman Act by unlawfully conspiring to restrain trade. According to the court, the AMA's boycott's purpose had been to eliminate chiropractic; the boycott had substantial anti-competitive effects; the boycott had no counterbalancing pro-competitive effects; and the AMA's unlawful conduct injured the plaintiffs.

Despite the fact that the district court found the conspiracy ended in 1980, it concluded that the illegal boycott's "lingering effects" still threatened plaintiffs with current injury and ordered injunctive relief. * * * [The district court required the AMA to mail the court's order to all AMA members; to publish the order in JAMA; and to revise other publications.]

B. *Unreasonable Restraint of Trade*

The central question in this case is whether the AMA's boycott constituted an unreasonable restraint of trade under § 1 of the Sherman Act. * * *

* * *

The threshold issue in any rule of reason case is market power. * * * Market power is the ability to raise prices above the competitive level by restricting output. * * * Whether market power exists in an appropriately defined market is a fact-bound question, and appellate courts normally defer to district court findings on that issue. * * * Several facts demonstrated the AMA's market power within the health care services market. AMA members constituted a substantial force in the provision of health care services in the United States and they constituted a majority of medical physicians. AMA members received a much greater portion of fees paid to medical physicians in the United States than non-AMA members. The evidence showed that AMA members received approximately 50% of all fees paid to health care providers. Finally, according to plaintiffs' expert, the AMA enjoyed substantial market power. The district court also found there was substantial evidence that the boycott adversely affected competition, and that a showing of such adverse effects negated the need to prove in any elaborate fashion market definition and market power[.] * * *

The AMA first contests the district court's finding of market power. It challenges the court's reliance on market share evidence as a basis to find market power and the district court's lumping together all AMA members as a group in assessing market share as a basis for its market power finding. We are not convinced the trial court erred. The district court properly relied on the AMA membership's substantial market share in finding market power. While we cautioned against relying solely on market share as a basis for inferring market power * * *, we did not rule out that approach. * * * This is especially so where there are barriers to entry and no substitutes from the consumer's perspective. * * *

The district court also relied on substantial evidence of adverse effects on competition caused by the boycott to establish the AMA's market power. In Indiana Federation of Dentists, the Supreme Court explained that since "the purpose of the inquiries into market definition and market power is to determine whether an arrangement has the potential for genuine adverse effects on competition, 'proof of actual detrimental effects, such as reduction of out-put' can obviate the need for an inquiry into market power, which is but a 'surrogate for detrimental effects.'" 476 U.S. at 460–61, 106 S.Ct. at 2018–19, quoting 7 P. Areeda, *Antitrust Law* ¶ 1511, p. 429 (1986). * * * Thus, the district court recited the boycott's anti-competitive effects:

> It is anti-competitive and it raises costs to interfere with the consumer's free choice to take the product of his liking; it is anti-competitive to prevent medical physicians from referring patients to a chiropractor; it is anti-competitive to impose higher costs on chiropractors by forcing them

to pay for their own x-ray equipment rather than obtaining x-rays from hospital radiology departments or radiologists in private practice; and it is anti-competitive to prevent chiropractors from improving their education in a professional setting by preventing medical physicians from teaching or lecturing to chiropractors. * * *

These findings eliminated the need for an inquiry into market power.

* * * Moving on, the AMA argues that even if market power existed, it escapes liability under the rule of reason because [the AMA rule against associating with chiropractors] had overriding pro-competitive effects. The AMA's argument is not unpersuasive in the abstract; but unfortunately it relies on evidence which the district court rejected as "speculative." * * * Essentially, the AMA argues that the market for medical services is one where there is "information asymmetry." In other words, health care consumers almost invariably lack sufficient information needed to evaluate the quality of medical services. This increases the risk of fraud and deception on consumers by unscrupulous health care providers possibly causing what the AMA terms "market failure": consumers avoiding necessary treatment (for fear of fraud), and accepting treatment with no expectation of assured quality. The AMA's conduct, the theory goes, ensured that physicians acquired reputations for quality (in part, by not associating with unscientific cultists), and thus allowed consumers to be assured that physicians would use only scientifically valid treatments. This in effect simultaneously provided consumers with essential information and protected competition.

Getting needed information to the market is a fine goal, but the district court found that the AMA was not motivated solely by such altruistic concerns. Indeed, the court found that the AMA intended to "destroy a competitor," namely, chiropractors. It is not enough to carry the day to argue that competition should be eliminated in the name of public safety. * * *

* * *

In sum, we agree with the district court that the AMA's boycott constituted an unreasonable restraint of trade under § 1 of the Sherman Act under the rule of reason. Therefore, the district court's findings that the AMA's boycott was anti-competitive, and was not counter-balanced by any pro-competitive effects were not erroneous. * * *

C. Patient Care Defense

In the AMA's first appeal, we modified the rule of reason to allow the AMA to justify its boycott of chiropractors if it could show that it was motivated by a concern for "patient care." * * * We were persuaded that measuring former Principle 3's reasonableness required a more flexible approach than the traditional rule of reason inquiry provided. Thus, we explained that if plaintiffs met their burden of persuasion on remand by showing that [the rule against chiropractic] and the implementing conduct had restricted competition rather than promoting it, the burden of persuasion would shift to the defendants to show:

> (1) that they genuinely entertained a concern for what they perceive as scientific method in the care of each person with whom they have entered into a doctor-patient relationship; (2) that this concern is objec-

tively reasonable; (3) that this concern has been the dominant motivating factor in defendants' promulgation of [the rule] and in the conduct intended to implement it; and (4) that this concern for scientific method in patient care could not have been adequately satisfied in a manner less restrictive of competition.

* * *

The district court held that the AMA failed to meet the defense's second and fourth elements: that its concern for scientific method in patient care was objectively reasonable, and that the concern for scientific method in patient care could not have been satisfied adequately in a manner less restrictive of competition, respectively. While only those two rulings are at issue, it is useful to summarize the district court's treatment of the entire defense.

Although doubting the AMA's genuineness regarding its concern for scientific method in patient care, the district court concluded that the AMA established that element. While it was attacking chiropractic as unscientific, the AMA simultaneously was attacking other unscientific methods of disease treatment (e.g., the Krebiozen treatment of cancer), and, as the district court noted, the existence of medical standards or guidelines against unscientific practice was relatively common. * * * The court, however, found that the AMA failed to carry its burden of persuasion as to whether its concern for scientific method in patient care was objectively reasonable.

The court acknowledged that during the period that the Committee on Quackery was operating, there was plenty of material supporting the belief that all chiropractic was unscientific. But, according to the court (and this is unchallenged), at the same time, there was evidence before the Committee that chiropractic was effective, indeed more effective than the medical profession, in treating certain kinds of problems, such as back injuries. The Committee was also aware, the court found, that some medical physicians believed chiropractic could be effective and that chiropractors were better trained to deal with musculoskeletal problems than most medical physicians. Moreover, the AMA's own evidence suggested that at some point during its lengthy boycott, there was no longer an objectively reasonable concern that would support a boycott of the entire chiropractic profession. Also important was the fact that "it was very clear" that the Committee's members did not have open minds to pro-chiropractic arguments or evidence. * * *

Next, the court found that the AMA met its burden in establishing that its concern about scientific method was the dominant motivating factor for promulgating [the rule] and in the conduct undertaken and intended to implement it. * * * But even so, the court acknowledged there was evidence showing that the AMA was motivated by economic concerns, as well.

Finally, the court concluded that the AMA failed to meet its burden in demonstrating that its concern for scientific method in patient care could not have been satisfied adequately in a manner less restrictive of competition. The court stated that the AMA had presented no evidence of other methods of achieving their objectives such as public education or any other less restrictive approach. * * *

* * *

Notes and Questions

1. The Supreme Court addressed the defendants' quality of care justifications in *Indiana Federation of Dentists*, supra:

> The gist of [defendant's] claim is that x-rays, standing alone, are not adequate bases for diagnosis of dental problems or for the formulation of an acceptable course of treatment. Accordingly, if insurance companies are permitted to determine whether they will pay a claim for dental treatment on the basis of x-rays as opposed to a full examination of all the diagnostic aids available to the examining dentist, there is a danger that they will erroneously decline to pay for treatment that is in fact in the interest of the patient, and that the patient will as a result be deprived of fully adequate care.

> The Federation's argument is flawed both legally and factually. The premise of the argument is that, far from having no effect on the cost of dental services chosen by patients and their insurers, the provision of x-rays will have too great an impact: it will lead to the reduction of costs through the selection of inadequate treatment. Precisely such a justification for withholding information from customers was rejected as illegitimate in *National Society of Professional Engineers*. The argument is, in essence, that an unrestrained market in which consumers are given access to the information they believe to be relevant to their choices will lead them to make unwise and even dangerous choices. Such an argument amounts to "nothing less than a frontal assault on the basic policy of the Sherman Act." *National Society of Professional Engineers*, supra.

> Moreover, there is no particular reason to believe that the provision of information will be more harmful to consumers in the market for dental services than in other markets. Insurers deciding what level of care to pay for are not themselves the recipients of those services, but it is by no means clear that they lack incentives to consider the welfare of the patient as well as the minimization of costs. They are themselves in competition for the patronage of the patients—or, in most cases, the unions or businesses that contract on their behalf for group insurance coverage—and must satisfy their potential customers that they will not only provide coverage at a reasonable cost, but also that the coverage will be adequate to meet their customers' dental needs. There is thus no more reason to expect dental insurance companies to sacrifice quality in return for cost savings than to believe this of consumers in, say, the market for engineering services. Accordingly, if noncompetitive quality-of-service justifications are inadmissible to justify the denial of information to consumers in the latter market, there is little reason to credit such justifications here.

Does the Supreme Court's holding in *Indiana Federation of Dentists* overrule the Seventh Circuit's "patient care defense"? Can the defense be easily asserted? The *Wilk* "patient care defense" requires that a court evaluate whether the defendant's "concern" was "objectively reasonable." How is the court to do this? Do you agree with the opinion's assumptions about the insurers' capacity and incentive to monitor quality?

2. Koefoot v. American College of Surgeons, 652 F.Supp. 882 (N.D.Ill.1986) involved a challenge to a bylaw of the American College of Surgeons (ACS) that proscribed "itinerant surgery." Under this rule, ACS surgeons were prohibited from delegating post-operative care for their patients to physicians other than surgeons. Plaintiffs contended that the promulgation and enforcement of the

bylaw by ACS constituted an illegal market allocation by ACS surgeons enabling them to block entry into their markets; a boycott of Dr. Koefoot and other visiting surgeons and a boycott of general physicians providing post-operative care; and an illegal tie-in of two separate services. The District Court refused to allow defendant ACS to invoke the *Wilk* patient care defense: "[T]he dispute in this case between licensed medical doctors, all of whom share common training and beliefs concerning human pathology, is fundamentally different from the dispute * * * between rival professions whose fundamental concepts of the treatment of disease are radically at odds." 652 F.Supp. 882, 891 (N.D.Ill.1986). The court found arguments premised on a "patient care motive" defense to be inconsistent with *Indiana Federation* and other recent Supreme Court decisions. It did hold, however, that evidence of motive would be admissible not as a defense, but for its relevance to the proof of anti-competitive or pro-competitive effect. The court strongly cautioned defendant on the use of evidence of the patient care rationale for the itinerant surgery rule because of its highly prejudicial nature. Why would such a defense be "prejudicial"? Why should the courts be willing to admit evidence of motive at all?

The *Koefoot* court rejected plaintiffs' attempt to brand the rule a per se violation observing that the "rule of reason analysis is appropriate when facially legitimate ethical canons are challenged under the Sherman Act. [This] Court defines facially legitimate ethical canons as being rules of professional practice which, on their face, establish professional standards of care without reference to the economic interests of the professionals." The *Koefoot* case went to trial in early 1987. Defendant ACS prevailed, and plaintiffs' motion for a new trial was denied. 1987–1 (CCH) Trade Cases ¶ 67,511 (N.D.Ill. 1987). Is this result surprising?

> ACS also claimed that designation as a Fellow of the American College of Surgery (FACS) was a "seal of approval." Its informational value to consumers, according to ACS, could be judged pro-competitive only if itinerant surgery is actually harmful, and therefore, evidence of harm must be admissible. The court rejected defendant's argument stating:

> The ACS cannot claim to be an independent standard-making organization similar to [Underwriters Laboratory] for the simple reason that the ACS is not truly an independent third party setting standards of general applicability. The defendants admit that ACS members are in competition with itinerant surgeons. Additionally, the ACS appears to perform no true testing function. The ACS has never claimed that it routinely "tests" whether its members comply with the ACS rules of professional conduct. * * *

> * * *

> The defendants fervently desire to argue to the jury that the FACS label is pro-competitive because it enables consumers to choose better surgeons. Once the smoke surrounding this argument has been cleared away, the true desire of the defendants is found. The defendants, again, are attempting to convince the jury that the itinerant surgery rule is pro-competitive because it results in better patient care. As the Court has taken great pains to explain, that is not a proper antitrust argument.

> There is a possible pro-competitive effect provided by the FACS label that is independent of a value judgment on the merits of itinerant surgery. If a label enables consumers to more quickly find a product or service that they desire, then the label increases efficiency by reducing needless delay. A way

for the ACS to prove that the FACS label has pro-competitive value is not for it to prove that itinerant surgery is harmful, but rather for it to prove that the FACS label provides consumers with a shorthand method of locating something they already desire, which in this case would be post-operative care rendered by a surgeon. The ACS can argue that by finding an ACS surgeon, the consumer has found a surgeon who does not delegate post-operative care to non-surgeons. Whether the ACS is correct in an abstract sense that the itinerant surgery rule enhances patient care, is irrelevant to the advantage to consumers that follows from having a reliable labeling mechanism.

The Court has never hindered the defendants from making the argument outlined above. All the Court has done is to limit the parties to relevant evidence. If the defendants can prove that consumers desire post-operative care to be rendered by surgeons, then the defendants are free to argue that the FACS label has a pro-competitive use.

652 F.Supp. at 903–4.

3. Although *Wilk* and *Koefoot* allow some limited role for quality-of-care justifications, they express hostility toward such evidence and strive to limit its influence. What is the basis for this position? In applying the patient care defense, the District Court in *Wilk*, affirmed by the Court of Appeals, held that the AMA failed to prove that its quality-of-care concern could not be achieved in a "manner less restrictive of competition." What other possible strategies exist for private accreditation or professional associations to achieve their quality-of-care goals?

4. Is it possible to present evidence of patient care and quality-improving benefits under the rationale that such proof demonstrated that a professional restraint counteracts market imperfections? Under a "market failure defense," in balancing the anticompetitive and procompetitive effects of a restraint, courts would analyze the functioning of the market in which the restraint operates. Defendant would be allowed to prove that the challenged restraint improved competition by offsetting a market failure. See Thomas L. Greaney, Quality of Care and Market Failure Defenses in Antitrust Health Care Litigation, 21 Conn. L. Rev. 605 (1989). The health care market is generally observed to suffer from market imperfections, such as problems with information, and from market failures, such as a comparatively higher incidence of natural monopolies. Jonathan E. Fielding and Thomas Rice, Can Managed Competition Solve the Problem of Market Failure, 12 Health Aff. 216 (Supp. 1993).

5. Can denial of accreditation or membership in a prestigious professional society constitute a valid antitrust claim? Marrese v. American Academy of Orthopaedic Surgeons, 1991–1 Trade Cas. (CCH) ¶ 69,398 (N.D.Ill. 1991), aff'd, 977 F.2d 585 (7th Cir. 1992) (unpublished opinion), is instructive in this regard. Dr. Marrese claimed that his rejection by the AAO amounted to an illegal boycott that harmed his reputation and denied him important professional benefits including patient referrals and access to the AAO's continuing medical education services. The Seventh Circuit's basis for upholding the trial court's decision rested on plaintiff's failure to prove that denial of membership caused a restraint of trade. Noting that membership was not necessary to practice medicine, obtain a staff appointment or receive referrals, the court found no restriction of output in any market. Moreover, it rejected the claim that withholding membership, which plaintiff analogized to a "seal of approval," stigmatized Dr. Marrese. Besides questioning whether such a stigma was significant (because plaintiff continued to receive referrals), the court of appeals stated that the loss of referrals would not

be sufficient absent evidence that the Academy had prevented others from dealing with the doctor.

6. Several scholars have proposed approaches to the application of antitrust laws and other government regulation to the activities of private credentialing organizations in a manner that will preserve the organizations' beneficial activities but that will discourage undesirable anticompetitive activities. See, e.g., Clark C. Havighurst, Accrediting and the Sherman Act, 57 Law & Contemp. Probs. 1 (1994); Havighurst and Nancy M.P. King, Private Credentialing of Health Care Personnel: An Antitrust Perspective (pts. 1 & 2), 9 Am. J.L. & Med. 131, 263 (1983); Timothy S. Jost, The Joint Commission on Accreditation of Hospitals: Private Regulation of Health Care and the Public Interest, 24 B.C. L. Rev. 835 (1983); and Philip C. Kissam, Government Policy Toward Medical Accreditation and Certification: The Antitrust Laws and Other Pro-competitive Strategies, 1983 Wis. L. Rev. 1.

3. *Staff Privileges*

OKSANEN v. PAGE MEMORIAL HOSPITAL

United States Court of Appeals, Fourth Circuit, 1991.
945 F.2d 696.

WILKINSON, CIRCUIT JUDGE:

Appellant Dr. Owen D. Oksanen contends that the Sherman Antitrust Act was violated when the medical staff of Page Memorial Hospital allegedly conspired amongst itself and with the hospital's Board of Trustees to revoke Oksanen's staff privileges. Whether such conspiracies are cognizable under federal antitrust law has significant implications for the nation's health care system because the peer review process that Oksanen challenges has become an important element of hospital governance.

In our view, the Board of Trustees and the medical staff of Page Memorial comprised a single entity during the peer review process. Because an entity cannot conspire with itself, the Board and the staff lacked the capacity to conspire. [ ] While the members of a medical staff may have the capacity to conspire among themselves, such a conspiracy did not occur in this case. We likewise affirm the district court's dismissal of Oksanen's other claims and its refusal to cloak in federal antitrust law what is in essence a workplace dispute.

I.

Upon completing a residency program in 1978, Dr. Owen D. Oksanen began practicing family medicine in Luray, Virginia. Luray is located in Page County, a county of approximately 18,000 residents. In 1979, Oksanen received full medical staff privileges at the sole hospital in Page County, the fifty-four bed Page Memorial Hospital.

* * *

Almost immediately after the medical staff granted privileges to Oksanen the complaints about his conduct began. For example, in October 1979, administrator Berry wrote to Oksanen questioning his attitude toward the use of laboratory facilities and the treatment of laboratory personnel. The chronicle of complaints pertaining to Oksanen's abusive attitude mounted over time. Oksanen reportedly addressed or referred to hospital employees and third party professional reviewers with profanity. In another incident, this time in the emergency room, he termed the mother of a young patient a "red neck from Stanley." Many of Oksanen's outbursts were made publicly and disrupted hospital operations. One nurse who worked with him commented that he "has a volatile personality and you just don't know when it's going to erupt."

Oksanen contends that the friction which developed at the hospital could not be attributed to him alone. He responds that his actions simply reflected his concern with the quality of patient care at the hospital. For instance, he states that he questioned whether Drs. Horng and Ancheta recognized the appropriate limitations on their surgical abilities. As a result, he began referring his patients to other hospitals where he contended they would receive a better quality of care. Oksanen also claims that his poor relationship with Dr. Holsinger stemmed from his earlier refusal to accept a position in Dr. Holsinger's office.

* * *

II.

To prove a violation of section one of the Sherman Act, 15 U.S.C.A. s 1, a plaintiff must show the existence of an agreement in the form of a contract, combination, or conspiracy that imposes an unreasonable restraint on trade. E.g., White & White, Inc. v. American Hosp. Supply Corp., 723 F.2d 495, 504 (6th Cir.1983).[7] Oksanen advances two different but related theories on whether an impermissible contract, combination, or conspiracy existed in this case. He first contends that during the peer review process, the medical staff conspired with the hospital to exclude him from practicing medicine at Page Memorial. Oksanen also argues that the members of the medical staff, during the peer review process and on other occasions, conspired among themselves to exclude him from the market. We shall address these arguments in this section and in Section III address the restraint of trade issues.

A.

Section one of the Sherman Act applies only to concerted action; unilateral conduct is excluded from its purview. [ ] Proof of concerted action requires evidence of a relationship between at least two legally distinct persons or entities. Oksanen contends that this plurality requirement is met in this case because the medical staff and the hospital are legally discrete entities. We think, to the contrary, that the staff is acting as an agent of Page Memorial

---

7. Demonstrating that an alleged agreement would affect interstate commerce has been treated as a jurisdictional prerequisite to bringing a section one claim that must be satisfied before the other two elements of such a claim are addressed. See Summit Health, Ltd. v. Pinhas, 500 U.S. 322, 111 S.Ct. 1842, 114 L.Ed.2d 366 (1991). Oksanen notes that the hospital and its staff purchase supplies and receive insurance payments from out-of-state sources and that they treat non-Virginia residents. Oksanen further alleges that the peer review process was used as a vehicle to punish him for sending patients to other area hospitals, which were engaged in interstate commerce. Finally, Oksanen argues that the peer review process serves a gatekeeping function so that an unfavorable review from Page Memorial could affect his ability to obtain staff privileges at other hospitals. Based on the similarity between Oksanen's allegations and those allegations considered by the Pinhas Court to affect interstate commerce, we believe that the jurisdictional requirement for an antitrust action is met in this case.

Hospital during the peer review process and as such is indistinct from the hospital.

Our view is premised upon the principle of intracorporate immunity announced in Copperweld Corp. v. Independence Tube Corp., 467 U.S. 752, 104 S.Ct. 2731, 81 L.Ed.2d 628 (1984). Copperweld established that the unilateral actions of a single enterprise are immune from the coverage of section one despite any corresponding restraint on trade. As an example of unilateral conduct, the Court pointed to agreements among corporate officers. "The officers of a single firm are not separate economic actors pursuing separate economic interests, so agreements among them do not suddenly bring together economic power that was previously pursuing divergent goals." Id. at 769, 104 S.Ct. at 2740–41. Applying that reasoning, the Court held that agreements between a parent corporation and its wholly owned subsidiary are not concerted actions for purposes of section one. The Court noted that a parent and its subsidiary always have a unity of interest so the law's concern with a sudden joining of independent interests is not present in such a case. Id. at 771, 104 S.Ct. at 2741.

We think a similar unity of interest is present in the relationship between the hospital and its staff, both of which seek to upgrade the quality of patient care. Oksanen contends, however, that intracorporate immunity should not shield the participants in the peer review process for the simple reason that the medical staff and the hospital, unlike a corporation and its officers, are legally separate entities. Bolt v. Halifax Hosp. Med. Ctr., 891 F.2d 810, 819 (11th Cir.1990). This argument, however, ignores the functional approach to the question of intracorporate characterization which we believe is mandated by the Copperweld decision. * * *

Like a corporation delegating authority to its officers, the Board of Trustees at Page Memorial delegated peer review decisionmaking in the first instance to the medical staff. "As such, with regard to these decisions, the medical staff operated as an officer of a corporation would in relation to the corporation." Weiss v. York Hosp., 745 F.2d 786, 817 (3d Cir.1984). * * *

This type of delegation of authority does not implicate the concerns of section one of the Sherman Act. The decision to conduct the peer review process does not represent the sudden joining of independent economic forces that section one is designed to deter and penalize. * * *

* * *

As an additional aspect of our functional inquiry into the relationship between the hospital and the medical staff, we must assess the degree of control the hospital exercised over the staff during the peer review process. * * * [A]lthough the Board of Trustees sought advice from the medical staff, the Board could modify the staff's recommendations at any time and it retained ultimate responsibility for all of the hospital's credentialing decisions. In this regard, the by-laws of Page Memorial Hospital provide that "[n]o assignment, referral, or delegation of authority by the Board of Trustees to ... the Medical Staff ... shall preclude the Board of Trustees from exercising the Authority required to meet its responsibility for the conduct of the hospital." The Board's ultimate control over peer review decisions enables it to employ peer review to pursue its interests.

Moreover, a hospital's interests generally would not be furthered by engaging in a conspiracy to restrain competition among doctors. Given that hospitals compete for the admission of patients, they have an incentive to maximize the number of physicians to whom they grant admitting and staff privileges. If a physician is qualified and does not disrupt the hospital's operations, it is in the hospital's interest to include, not exclude, that physician. * * *

Oksanen seems to suggest that Page Memorial's incentives were different because it wanted to exclude him from the staff in retaliation for referring patients to other hospitals. Appellant's argument ignores the realities of the marketplace. If the hospital dismissed him for illegitimate reasons, he could presumably continue to treat at least some of his patients at Shenandoah Memorial Hospital where he remained on staff. Moreover, Page Memorial had to anticipate that Oksanen might obtain admitting privileges at another competitor hospital eager to accord privileges to a physician with his self-proclaimed large patient base. In sum, a hospital "makes its decisions to serve its own interests, not those of the staff, and thus should not be seen as a possible co-conspirator with them." P. Areeda and H. Hovenkamp, Antitrust Law, P 1471b (1990 Supp.).

B.

Oksanen argues that even if the hospital and the medical staff are part of the same enterprise, intraenterprise immunity is inapplicable because individual doctors on the medical staff had personal stakes in the outcome of the peer review process. According to Oksanen, the physicians' personal stakes are their medical practices that would benefit if he were eliminated as a competitor. * * *

* * * Here, only one member of the medical staff, Dr. Dale, could be said to have been in competition with Oksanen when any of the disputed peer review decisions occurred. Dr. Dale's areas of practice apparently overlapped somewhat with Oksanen's, but Dale did not begin practice at Page Memorial until August, 1983—well after much of the basis for disciplining Oksanen was established—and he did not take part in the proceedings leading to Oksanen's suspension. * * *

In any event, the more important aspect of [the case law] for the purposes of peer review is the degree of control the officer or agent with the independent interest exercised over the defendant firm's decisionmaking process. If the officer cannot cause a restraint to be imposed and his firm would have taken the action anyway, then any independent interest is largely irrelevant to antitrust analysis. * * *

Because the challenged decision was subject to review by the hospital and because decisionmaking authority in Dr. Oksanen's case was dispersed among a number of individuals, the personal stake exception is inapplicable.

We thus conclude that under the principle of intracorporate immunity, Page Memorial and its medical staff lacked the capacity to conspire during the peer review process.

C.

The question remains whether the medical staff has the capacity to conspire among itself either during peer review or at other times. We recognize that a medical staff can be comprised of physicians with independent and at times competing economic interests. As a result, when these actors join together to take action among themselves, they are unlike a single entity and therefore they have the capacity to conspire as a matter of law. To conclude that members of the medical staff have the capacity to conspire among themselves does not mean, however, that every action taken by the staff satisfies the contract, combination, or conspiracy requirement of section one. * * *

* * * Simply making a peer review recommendation does not prove the existence of a conspiracy; there must be something more such as a conscious commitment by the medical staff to coerce the hospital into accepting its recommendation. To speak of a conspiracy among a medical staff during the peer review process is not very meaningful in antitrust terms if the staff lacks the final authority to implement any agreement that it does reach. In this case, there is no evidence that the staff attempted to usurp the Board's power to make the final decision on Oksanen's status. Nor is there any evidence that the staff illicitly agreed to exclude Oksanen from the market or engaged in anti-competitive activity outside the official meeting and hearing process. * * *

* * * The litany of complaints from a variety of sources concerning Dr. Oksanen provides ample evidence that the doctors on the staff were justified in disciplining a fellow physician who was perceived to be both unprofessional and uncooperative. Where, as here, the peer review process has been operating in accordance with proper procedures, under the aegis of the hospital, and with a substantial basis in the evidence, the likelihood of an antitrust conspiracy is also substantially diminished.

Oksanen, however, points to evidence of actions taken outside of the peer review context that he claims demonstrate that the medical staff engaged in a group boycott of him. For instance, he contends that the medical staff acted in a concerted refusal to provide on-call coverage for him. Dr. Holsinger, however, apparently had no obligation to provide such coverage because of his seniority. Dr. Dale continued to provide on-call coverage for Oksanen through June 1984, while Drs. Ancheta and Horng apparently declined to provide such coverage. The choice of these two doctors not to provide on-call coverage can readily be explained, however, as a result of their earlier alienation from the quarrelsome Oksanen. * * *

* * *

* * * Within this framework, Oksanen has simply failed to meet his summary judgment burden of establishing that "the inference of conspiracy is reasonable in light of the competing inferences of independent action." Matsushita, 475 U.S. at 588, 106 S.Ct. at 1356.

III.

Oksanen also bears the burden of proving under section one of the Sherman Act that any concerted action that did take place caused an "antitrust injury'' by imposing an unreasonable restraint on trade. * * * As a result, a plaintiff cannot demonstrate the unreasonableness of a restraint merely by showing that it caused him an economic injury. For example, the fact that a hospital's decision caused a disappointed physician to practice medicine elsewhere does not of itself constitute an antitrust injury. * * * If the law were otherwise, many a physician's workplace grievance with a hospital would be elevated to the status of an antitrust action. To keep the antitrust laws from becoming so trivialized, the reasonableness of a restraint is evaluated based on its impact on competition as a whole within the relevant market. * * *

* * *

* * * Oksanen seems to contend that the combined actions of the hospital and the medical staff amounted to a group boycott and should be classified as per se violations of the Act. The Court has cautioned, however, that the category of restraints classed as group boycotts should not be expanded indiscriminately, particularly where, as here, the economic effects of the restraint are far from clear. FTC v. Indiana Fed. of Dentists, 476 U.S. 447, 458–59, 106 S.Ct. 2009, 2017–18, 90 L.Ed.2d 445 (1986).

We believe that the second approach to analyzing restraints, the rule of reason, is applicable to this case. Under the rule of reason, Oksanen bears the burden of proving that the actions of the defendants have unreasonably restrained trade. * * * To meet this burden, Oksanen must prove what market he contends was restrained and that the defendants played a significant role in the relevant market. Absent this market power, any restraint on trade created by the defendants' actions is unlikely to implicate section one.

Oksanen asserts, with little proof, that Page County is the relevant market and that Page Memorial and its medical staff exert complete control over the market. Although Page Memorial may be where Oksanen prefers to practice, this preference alone does not justify excluding other hospitals and other doctors from the relevant market definition. * * * Oksanen's narrow market definition violates a fundamental tenet of antitrust law that the relevant market definition must encompass the realities of competition. * * * The defendants note that they compete with hospitals and doctors in surrounding counties. For example, four hospitals, aside from Page Memorial, are situated within twenty-five miles of Page County. Based on statistics derived from a 1979 study, Page Memorial's share of the market served by these five hospitals is 5.2%. Moreover, 53.8% of Page County's residents went to hospitals other than Page Memorial, including Rockingham Memorial which attracted 30% of all Page County residents in 1979. Under these circumstances, we doubt whether the defendants possess the market power necessary to significantly restrain trade.

Of course, a detailed inquiry into a firm's market power is not essential when the anti-competitive effects of its practices are obvious. * * * If any anti-competitive effects exist in this case, however, they are far from clear. For instance, Oksanen has neither demonstrated a rise in the price of medical services above a competitive level nor a decrease in the supply of doctors in the relevant market. [ ] In fact, from August 1983 to 1987 seven additional doctors began practicing at Page Memorial. The aphorism that "the antitrust laws were enacted for 'the protection of competition, not competitors' " rings true in this case. * * * This case is not one in which a representative of a class of competitors is being excluded from the market. Cf. Oltz (attempt to exclude nurse anesthetist); Cooper (attempt to exclude podiatrists); Weiss (attempt to exclude osteopath). Oksanen, as an individual competitor, may have been hurt by the hospital's decision to revoke his privileges, but there is no evidence that competition as a whole in the relevant market has been harmed.

Moreover, the peer review process, by policing the competence and conduct of doctors, can enhance competition. "By restricting staff privileges to doctors who have achieved a predetermined level of medical competence, a hospital will enhance its reputation and the quality of care that it delivers." Weiss, 745 F.2d at 821 n. 60. Similarly, the friction created between a hospital and a doctor with a legacy of trouble in interpersonal relationships can decrease efficiency, discourage other qualified doctors from joining the staff, and detract from a hospital's ability to provide quality patient service. Id.

In sum, the anti-competitive effects are by no means so clear and one-sided as Oksanen would have them, and the revocation of Oksanen's staff privileges, while undoubtedly impacting adversely on his practice, has not been shown to have had any adverse impact on competition in the relevant market. Consequently, his section one claim fails.

* * *

IV.

[The court found no violation of Section Two of the Sherman Act because of the absence of proof of market power and because the hospital had valid business reasons for revoking Dr. Oksanen's privileges].

V.

This case illustrates well the dilemma that hospitals face when they consider disciplining a physician by altering his admitting privileges. On the one hand, if the hospital failed to discipline a physician against whom documented complaints were legion, the efficiency of the entire institution could be affected and the hospital could even be exposing itself to malpractice liability. Yet, if the hospital takes corrective action, it and its medical staff face the prospect of a disgruntled physician bringing an antitrust suit against them.

In our view, the antitrust laws were not intended to inhibit hospitals from promoting quality patient care through peer review nor were the laws intended as a vehicle for converting business tort claims into antitrust causes of action. While we cannot say that no peer review decision would ever implicate the Sherman Act's concern for competition, this assuredly is not such a case. Page Memorial simply took measured steps to discipline an imperious physician. In taking these actions, Page Memorial and its medical staff have violated neither federal nor state law. The judgment of the district court is therefore

AFFIRMED.

Notes and Questions

1. In 1986 Congress enacted the Health Care Quality Improvement Act, 42 U.S.C.A. §§ 11101–11152 (1995), in response to claims that effective professional peer review activity was being chilled by antitrust challenges. The Act provides limited antitrust immunity to peer review participants who act in good faith and meet certain due process and reporting requirements in their professional review activities. HCQIA also authorizes the award of costs and attorneys' fees to peer review defendants who meet the Act's good faith and due process criteria and prevail in litigation against a frivolous or bad faith claim. The Act provides protection only from actions for monetary damages and does not preclude criminal prosecutions, suits for injunctive or declaratory relief or litigation by governmental entities. In addition, the Act does not reach peer review of non-physicians. Finally, the Act applies to "professional review actions" but only when such actions concern "conduct of a professional review activity, which is based on the competence or professional conduct of an individual physician (which conduct affects or could affect adversely the health and welfare of patient or patients)." 42 U.S.C.A. at § 11151(9) (1995). Note also that the Act requires that peer review decisions be based on "the reasonable belief that ... [they were made] ... in furtherance of quality health care." What effect might this requirement have on the Act's avowed purpose of limiting litigation? How would it affect the Act's applicability in situations involving "economic credentialing?" Although the Act provides only modest litigation disincentives and may not significantly deter the filing of frivolous suits, a growing line of cases has found the conduct of peer reviews immune under the HCQIA and has been willing to apply the fee-shifting provisions of the act. See Mathews v. Lancaster General Hospital, 87 F.3d 624 (3d Cir. 1996); Addis v. Holy Cross Health System, 88 F.3d 482 (7th Cir. 1996); Austin v. McNamara, 979 F.2d 728 (9th Cir. 1992). For a thorough review of HCQIA and its effect on staff privileges litigation, see Charity Scott, Medical Peer Review, Antitrust, and the Effect of Statutory Reform, 50 Md. L. Rev. 316 (1991).

2. Courts are divided over whether a hospital is legally capable of conspiracy with its staff. The Third, Fourth, Sixth and Seventh Circuits have held that the intra-corporate immunity doctrine bars such a finding of conspiracy. Weiss v. York Hospital, 745 F.2d 786 (3d Cir. 1984), cert. denied, 470 U.S. 1060, 105 S.Ct. 1777, 84 L.Ed.2d 836 (1985); Nurse Midwifery Associates v. Hibbett, 918 F.2d 605 (6th Cir. 1990); Pudlo v. Adamski, 2 F.3d 1153 (7th Cir.1993), cert. denied, 510 U.S. 1072, 114 S.Ct. 879, 127 L.Ed.2d 75 (1994). Several circuits, however, have concluded that a conspiracy between a hospital and its medical staff is not impossible as a matter of law. See, for example, Bolt v. Halifax Hosp. Medical Center, 891 F.2d 810 (11th Cir. 1990), cert. denied, 495 U.S. 924, 110 S.Ct. 1960, 109 L.Ed.2d 322 (1990); Oltz v. St. Peter's Community Hospital, 861 F.2d 1440 (9th Cir. 1988). See also Pinhas v. Summit Health, Ltd., 880 F.2d 1108, amended and superseded, 894 F.2d 1024 (9th Cir. 1989), cert. denied, 498 U.S. 817, 111 S.Ct. 61, 112 L.Ed.2d 36 (1990), in which the Ninth Circuit did not explicitly resolve the question of a hospital-medical staff conspiracy, but did find that plaintiff "sufficiently alleges that [the hospital attorneys] exerted their influence over [defendants] so as to direct them to engage in the complained of acts for an anticompetitive purpose."

What is at stake in this issue? Are the purposes of antitrust law better served by a rule that a hospital and medical staff either can or cannot conspire or by a case-by-case, fact-specific approach? In contrast to hospital staff conspiracies, it is well-settled that members of the medical staff can conspire. How can this be so?

What factual requirements does *Oksanen* establish for such a finding of fact? For an excellent analysis of these issues concluding that the principles underlying intra-corporate immunity do not justify barring hospital-staff conspiracies, see James F. Blumstein & Frank A. Sloan, Antitrust and Hospital Peer Review, 51 L. & Contemp. Probs. 7 (1988). See also, William S. Brewbaker III, Antitrust Conspiracy Doctrine and the Hospital Enterprise, 74 B.U.L. Rev. 67 (1994) (hospital privilege determinations involving staff participation should escape scrutiny only if staff acts in purely advisory role). Consider the many other contexts in which the intra-enterprise conspiracy doctrine may arise. May a hospital be found to conspire with a subsidiary that is partially owned by its physicians? With another hospital with which it jointly controls a third entity that in turn has control over the business affairs of the hospitals? See also the discussion of this issue in the IPA context in *Capital Imaging v. Mohawk Valley Medical Associates*, infra.

3. Following the Supreme Court's decision in Northwest Wholesale Stationers, Inc. v. Pacific Stationery and Printing Co., 472 U.S. 284, 105 S.Ct. 2613, 86 L.Ed.2d 202 (1985), discussed supra, courts have refused to apply per se analysis to boycott claims involving staff privileges decisions. See, e.g., Goss v. Memorial Hospital System, 789 F.2d 353 (5th Cir. 1986). What factors militate in favor of applying the rule of reason to staff privilege determinations? Should denials ever be treated as naked restraints, for example in the case of a wholesale exclusion of a class of practitioners? Compare Weiss v. York Hospital, 745 F.2d 786 (3d Cir. 1984), cert. denied, 470 U.S. 1060, 105 S.Ct. 1777, 84 L.Ed.2d 836 (1985) with Flegel v. Christian Hosp., 4 F.3d 682 (8th Cir. 1993). While conceding that per se analysis is generally inappropriate for credentialing decisions, Blumstein and Sloan argue that certain credentialing actions that pose the "most significant potential for anticompetitive effects" ought to trigger a "rebuttable presumption of invalidity" under a rule of reason analysis. If the plaintiff is able to show that the credentialing policies or decisions excluded a particular class of practitioners (e.g., osteopaths), excluded practitioners who engaged in particular practices (e.g., working with HMOs or advertising), or excluded practitioners who were not members of favored physician groups or partnerships, the burden would shift to the credentialing body to rebut the presumption of illegality. Blumstein & Sloan, supra. See also Clark C. Havighurst, Doctors and Hospitals: An Antitrust Perspective on Traditional Relationships, 1984 Duke L.J. 1071 (analogizing hospital-staff relationships to joint ventures and urging judicial deference under a "quick look approach").

4. Under the rule of reason, plaintiffs face the daunting task of proving that defendant possesses market power and that the anticompetitive effects of the restraint outweigh any procompetitive effects. Under what market conditions is this likely to be the case? For a seminal decision providing a useful road map to these issues, see Robinson v. Magovern, 521 F.Supp. 842 (W.D.Pa.1981), aff'd 688 F.2d 824 (3d Cir.1982), cert. denied, 459 U.S. 971, 103 S.Ct. 302, 74 L.Ed.2d 283 (1982). See generally, 1 Furrow, Health Law § 10–22.

5. Many challenges to staff privileges determinations involve exclusive contracts, pursuant to which certain medical services such as radiology, pathology and anesthesiology are provided in a hospital by a single group of physicians. Plaintiffs challenging these contracts on antitrust grounds have attempted to characterize the contracts as "tying" arrangements which are per se illegal. This claim requires the plaintiff to prove that a seller with market power in one product (the tying product) has forced a buyer to purchase another product (the tied product) that the buyer ordinarily would prefer to purchase separately. In

Jefferson Parish Hospital Dist. No. 2 v. Hyde, 466 U.S. 2, 104 S.Ct. 1551, 80 L.Ed.2d 2, (1984), the Supreme Court considered an antitrust challenge to an exclusive contract for anesthesia services in which plaintiff claimed that the arrangement illegally tied hospital services and anesthesiology. The plurality opinion held that, although there were two products involved, the hospital (which had a 30% share of the hospital services market) did not have market power in the tying product. Plaintiff doctors have been uniformly unsuccessful in challenging exclusive contracts as illegal tying arrangements. See, for example, Collins v. Associated Pathologists, Ltd., 844 F.2d 473 (7th Cir.1988), cert. denied, 488 U.S. 852, 109 S.Ct. 137, 102 L.Ed.2d 110 (1988), and White v. Rockingham Radiologists, Ltd., 820 F.2d 98 (4th Cir.1987).

Exclusive contracts may also be challenged as "exclusive dealing arrangements" under Section One of the Sherman Act. Exclusive dealing, which is examined under the rule of reason, also requires a showing of market power in some relevant market. A concurring opinion in the *Hyde* case rejected plaintiff's claim on this theory: "Exclusive dealing is an unreasonable restraint of trade only when a significant fraction of buyers or sellers are frozen out of a market by the exclusive deal. * * * There is no suggestion that East Jefferson Hospital is likely to create a 'bottleneck' in the availability of anesthesiological services that might deprive other hospitals of access to needed anesthesiological services, or that the [contracting anesthesiology group's associates] have unreasonably narrowed the range of choices available to other anesthesiologists in search of a hospital or patients that will buy their services. A firm of four anesthesiologists represents only a very small fraction of the total number of anesthesiologists whose services are available for hire by other hospitals, and East Jefferson is one among numerous hospitals buying such services." 466 U.S. at 46, 104 S.Ct. at 1576. See also *Collins,* supra, in which the court rejected the plaintiff pathologist's exclusive dealing claim finding the appropriate market to be the job market for pathologists and concluding that this market was national in scope and clearly one that the contracting hospital did not dominate.

For a case in which an exclusive contract was challenged as an illegal boycott, see Oltz v. St. Peter's Community Hospital, 861 F.2d 1440 (9th Cir.1988). The court relied on evidence that a group of anesthesiologists had acquired an exclusive contract with a hospital by coercing it to terminate the staff privileges of Tafford Oltz, a popular nurse anesthetist. After Oltz left St. Peter's, each of the anesthesiologists experienced a forty to fifty percent increase in earnings. Citing *Indiana Federation of Dentists*, the court found that extended market analysis was unnecessary because plaintiff had demonstrated actual detrimental effects in the form of higher prices and profits in the market after Dr. Oltz's termination. Is plaintiff's success in *Oltz* attributable to the characterization of the conduct as a boycott? What facts made this a particularly compelling case?

6.   Staff privileges cases have been aptly termed the "junk food of antitrust health care litigation." Despite the fact that only a handful of plaintiffs have succeeded in the hundreds of antitrust cases filed challenging staff privileges determinations, and despite the large arsenal of doctrinal weapons available to defend against such claims, cases continue to be brought. What explains the continued flow of this seemingly futile litigation? For a rare example of a successful challenge to a staff privileges action, see Boczar v. Manatee Hospitals & Health Systems, Inc., 993 F.2d 1514 (11th Cir.1993). The appellate court in *Boczar* found ample evidence to support a jury finding of anticompetitive intent and effect in the hospital's use of pretextual explanations to defend its actions, the plaintiff doctor's involvement in bringing to light deficiencies of other physicians and the

hospital's economic concerns about threatened loss of admissions from competing physicians who were opposed to plaintiff's membership on the staff. See also Brown v. Presbyterian Healthcare Servs., 101 F.3d 1324 (10th Cir.1996).

II.   HEALTH CARE ENTERPRISES, INTEGRATION AND FINANCING

As discussed in Chapter 13, supra, the burgeoning integration and consolidation of the health care industry has spawned countless new networks, health plans, alliances and other business enterprises. These entities and contractual relationships often entail cooperation or outright merger between previously competing providers or health plans. As such, they also raise the full spectrum of antitrust issues. For health care attorneys counselling clients forming new integrated organizations, these issues are often the subject of close attention because many entities are quite openly seeking to acquire the maximum leverage they can in the competitive fray.

A.   PROVIDER–CONTROLLED NETWORKS AND HEALTH PLANS

ARIZONA v. MARICOPA COUNTY MEDICAL SOCIETY

Supreme Court of the United States, 1982.
457 U.S. 332, 102 S.Ct. 2466, 73 L.Ed.2d 48.

JUSTICE STEVENS delivered the opinion of the Court.

The question presented is whether § 1 of the Sherman Act [ ] has been violated by agreements among competing physicians setting, by majority vote, the maximum fees that they may claim in full payment for health services provided to policyholders of specified insurance plans. The United States Court of Appeals for the Ninth Circuit held that the question could not be answered without evaluating the actual purpose and effect of the agreements at a full trial. [ ] Because the undisputed facts disclose a violation of the statute, we granted certiorari, and now reverse.

* * *

II

The Maricopa Foundation for Medical Care is a nonprofit Arizona corporation composed of licensed doctors of medicine, osteopathy, and podiatry engaged in private practice. Approximately 1,750 doctors, representing about 70% of the practitioners in Maricopa County, are members.

The Maricopa Foundation was organized in 1969 for the purpose of promoting fee-for-service medicine and to provide the community with a competitive alternative to existing health insurance plans. [ ] The foundation performs three primary activities. It establishes the schedule of maximum fees that participating doctors agree to accept as payment in full for services performed for patients insured under plans approved by the foundation. It reviews the medical necessity and appropriateness of treatment provided by its members to such insured persons. It is authorized to draw checks on insurance company accounts to pay doctors for services performed for covered patients. In performing these functions, the foundation is considered an "insurance administrator" by the Director of the Arizona Department of Insurance. Its participating doctors, however, have no financial interest in the operation of the foundation.

The Pima Foundation for Medical Care, which includes about 400 member doctors, [ ] performs similar functions. For the purposes of this litigation, the parties seem to regard the activities of the two foundations as essentially the same. No challenge is made to their peer review or claim administration functions. Nor do the foundations allege that these two activities make it necessary for them to engage in the practice of establishing maximum-fee schedules.

At the time this lawsuit was filed, [ ] each foundation made use of "relative values" and "conversion factors" in compiling its fee schedule. The conversion factor is the dollar amount used to determine fees for a particular medical specialty. * * * The fee schedule has been revised periodically. The foundation board of trustees would solicit advice from various medical societies about the need for change in either relative values or conversion factors in their respective specialties. The board would then formulate the new fee schedule and submit it to the vote of the entire membership.[8]

The fee schedules limit the amount that the member doctors may recover for services performed for patients insured under plans approved by the foundations. To obtain this approval the insurers—including self-insured employers as well as insurance companies[9]—agree to pay the doctors' charges up to the scheduled amounts, and in exchange the doctors agree to accept those amounts as payment in full for their services. The doctors are free to charge higher fees to uninsured patients, and they also may charge any patient less than the scheduled maxima. A patient who is insured by a foundation-endorsed plan is guaranteed complete coverage for the full amount of his medical bills only if he is treated by a foundation member. He is free to go to a nonmember physician and is still covered for charges that do not exceed the maximum-fee schedule, but he must pay any excess that the nonmember physician may charge.

The impact of the foundation fee schedules on medical fees and on insurance premiums is a matter of dispute. The State of Arizona contends that the periodic upward revisions of the maximum-fee schedules have the effect of stabilizing and enhancing the level of actual charges by physicians, and that the increasing level of their fees in turn increases insurance premiums. The foundations, on the other hand, argue that the schedules impose a meaningful limit on physicians' charges, and that the advance agreement by the doctors to accept the maxima enables the insurance carriers to limit and to calculate more efficiently the risks they underwrite and

8. The parties disagree over whether the increases in the fee schedules are the cause or the result of the increases in the prevailing rate for medical services in the relevant markets. There appears to be agreement, however, that 85–95% of physicians in Maricopa County bill at or above the maximum reimbursement levels set by the Maricopa Foundation.

9. Seven different insurance companies underwrite health insurance plans that have been approved by the Maricopa Foundation, and three companies underwrite the plans approved by the Pima Foundation. The record contains no firm data on the portion of the health care market that is covered by these plans. The State relies upon a 1974 analysis indicating that insurance plans endorsed by the Maricopa Foundation had about 63% of the prepaid health care market, but the respondents contest the accuracy of this analysis.

therefore serves as an effective cost-containment mechanism that has saved patients and insurers millions of dollars. * * *

III

The respondents recognize that our decisions establish that price-fixing agreements are unlawful on their face. But they argue that the *per se* rule does not govern this case because the agreements at issue are horizontal and fix maximum prices, are among members of a profession, are in an industry with which the judiciary has little antitrust experience, and are alleged to have pro-competitive justifications. Before we examine each of these arguments, we pause to consider the history and the meaning of the *per se* rule against price-fixing agreements.

A

* * *

The elaborate inquiry into the reasonableness of a challenged business practice entails significant costs. Litigation of the effect or purpose of a practice often is extensive and complex. * * * Judges often lack the expert understanding of industrial market structures and behavior to determine with any confidence a practice's effect on competition. * * * And the result of the process in any given case may provide little certainty or guidance about the legality of a practice in another context. * * *

* * *

B

Our decisions foreclose the argument that the agreements at issue escape *per se* condemnation because they are horizontal and fix maximum prices. [The cases] place horizontal agreements to fix maximum prices on the same legal—even if not economic—footing as agreements to fix minimum or uniform prices. [ ] The per se rule "is grounded on faith in price competition as a market force [and not] on a policy of low selling prices at the price of eliminating competition." * * * In this case the rule is violated by a price restraint that tends to provide the same economic rewards to all practitioners regardless of their skill, their experience, their training, or their willingness to employ innovative and difficult procedures in individual cases. Such a restraint also may discourage entry into the market and may deter experimentation and new developments by individual entrepreneurs. It may be a masquerade for an agreement to fix uniform prices, or it may in the future take on that character.

* * *

We are equally unpersuaded by the argument that we should not apply the *per se* rule in this case because the judiciary has little antitrust experience in the health care industry. [ ] The argument quite obviously is inconsistent with U.S. v. Socony–Vacuum Oil Co., 310 U.S. 150 (1940). * * * [Y]et the Court of Appeals refused to apply the *per se* rule in this case in part because the health care industry was so far removed from the competitive model.[10]

10. "The health care industry, moreover,   presents a particularly difficult area. The first

Consistent with our prediction in Socony–Vacuum [ ] the result of this reasoning was the adoption by the Court of Appeals of a legal standard based on the reasonableness of the fixed prices, [ ] an inquiry we have so often condemned. [ ] Finally, the argument that the *per se* rule must be rejustified for every industry that has not been subject to significant antitrust litigation ignores the rationale for per se rules, which in part is to avoid "the necessity for an incredibly complicated and prolonged economic investigation into the entire history of the industry involved, as well as related industries, in an effort to determine at large whether a particular restraint has been unreasonable—an inquiry so often wholly fruitless when undertaken." * * *

The respondents' principal argument is that the *per se* rule is inapplicable because their agreements are alleged to have pro-competitive justifications. The argument indicates a misunderstanding of the *per se* concept. The anticompetitive potential inherent in all price-fixing agreements justifies their facial invalidation even if pro-competitive justifications are offered for some. [ ] Those claims of enhanced competition are so unlikely to prove significant in any particular case that we adhere to the rule of law that is justified in its general application. Even when the respondents are given every benefit of the doubt, the limited record in this case is not inconsistent with the presumption that the respondents' agreements will not significantly enhance competition.

The respondents contend that their fee schedules are pro-competitive because they make it possible to provide consumers of health care with a uniquely desirable form of insurance coverage that could not otherwise exist. The features of the foundation-endorsed insurance plans that they stress are a choice of doctors, complete insurance coverage, and lower premiums. The first two characteristics, however, are hardly unique to these plans. Since only about 70% of the doctors in the relevant market are members of either foundation, the guarantee of complete coverage only applies when an insured chooses a physician in that 70%. If he elects to go to a nonfoundation doctor, he may be required to pay a portion of the doctor's fee. It is fair to presume, however, that at least 70% of the doctors in other markets charge no more than the "usual, customary, and reasonable" fee that typical insurers are willing to reimburse in full. [ ] Thus, in Maricopa and Pima Counties as well as in most parts of the country, if an insured asks his doctor if the insurance coverage is complete, presumably in about 70% of the cases the doctor will say "Yes" and in about 30% of the cases he will say "No."

It is true that a binding assurance of complete insurance coverage—as well as most of the respondents' potential for lower insurance premiums[11]—

step to understanding is to recognize that not only is access to the medical profession very time consuming and expensive both for the applicant and society generally, but also that numerous government subventions of the costs of medical care have created both a demand and supply function for medical services that is artificially high. The present supply and demand functions of medical services in no way approximate those which would exist in a purely private competitive order. An accurate description of those functions moreover is not available. Thus, we lack baselines by which could be measured the distance between the

present supply and demand functions and those which would exist under ideal competitive conditions." 643 F.2d, at 556.

11. We do not perceive the respondents' claim of procompetitive justification for their fee schedules to rest on the premise that the fee schedules actually reduce medical fees and accordingly reduce insurance premiums, thereby enhancing competition in the health insurance industry. Such an argument would merely restate the long-rejected position that fixed prices are reasonable if they are lower than free competition would yield. It is arguable,

can be obtained only if the insurer and the doctor agree in advance on the maximum fee that the doctor will accept as full payment for a particular service. Even if a fee schedule is therefore desirable, it is not necessary that the doctors do the price fixing. The record indicates that the Arizona Comprehensive Medical/Dental Program for Foster Children is administered by the Maricopa Foundation pursuant to a contract under which the maximum-fee schedule is prescribed by a state agency rather than by the doctors. [ ] This program and the Blue Shield plan challenged in Group Life & Health Insurance Co. v. Royal Drug Co., 440 U.S. 205, 99 S.Ct. 1067, 59 L.Ed.2d 261 (1979), indicate that insurers are capable not only of fixing maximum reimbursable prices but also of obtaining binding agreements with providers guaranteeing the insured full reimbursement of a participating provider's fee. In light of these examples, it is not surprising that nothing in the record even arguably supports the conclusion that this type of insurance program could not function if the fee schedules were set in a different way.

The most that can be said for having doctors fix the maximum prices is that doctors may be able to do it more efficiently than insurers. The validity of that assumption is far from obvious,[12] but in any event there is no reason to believe that any savings that might accrue from this arrangement would be sufficiently great to affect the competitiveness of these kinds of insurance plans. It is entirely possible that the potential or actual power of the foundations to dictate the terms of such insurance plans may more than offset the theoretical efficiencies upon which the respondents' defense ultimately rests.[13]

* * *

IV

Having declined the respondents' invitation to cut back on the per se rule against price fixing, we are left with the respondents' argument that their fee schedules involve price fixing in only a literal sense. For this argument, the respondents rely upon Broadcast Music, Inc. v. Columbia Broadcasting System, Inc., 441 U.S. 1, 99 S.Ct. 1551, 60 L.Ed.2d 1 (1979).

however, that the existence of a fee schedule, whether fixed by the doctors or by the insurers, makes it easier—and to that extent less expensive—for insurers to calculate the risks that they underwrite and to arrive at the appropriate reimbursement on insured claims.

12. In order to create an insurance plan under which the doctor would agree to accept as full payment a fee prescribed in a fixed schedule, someone must canvass the doctors to determine what maximum prices would be high enough to attract sufficient numbers of individual doctors to sign up but low enough to make the insurance plan competitive. In this case that canvassing function is performed by the foundation; the foundation then deals with the insurer. It would seem that an insurer could simply bypass the foundation by performing the canvassing function and dealing

with the doctors itself. Under the foundation plan, each doctor must look at the maximum-fee schedule fixed by his competitors and vote for or against approval of the plan (and, if the plan is approved by majority vote, he must continue or revoke his foundation membership). A similar, if to some extent more protracted, process would occur if it were each insurer that offered the maximum-fee schedule to each doctor.

13. In this case it appears that the fees are set by a group with substantial power in the market for medical services, and that there is competition among insurance companies in the sale of medical insurance. Under these circumstances the insurance companies are not likely to have significantly greater bargaining power against a monopoly or doctors than would individual consumers of medical services.

In *Broadcast Music* we were confronted with an antitrust challenge to the marketing of the right to use copyrighted compositions derived from the entire membership of the American Society of Composers, Authors and Publishers (ASCAP). The so-called "blanket license" was entirely different from the product that any one composer was able to sell by himself. [ ] Although there was little competition among individual composers for their separate compositions, the blanket-license arrangement did not place any restraint on the right of any individual copyright owner to sell his own compositions separately to any buyer at any price. [ ] But a "necessary consequence" of the creation of the blanket license was that its price had to be established. [ ] We held that the delegation by the composers to ASCAP of the power to fix the price for the blanket license was not a species of the price-fixing agreements categorically forbidden by the Sherman Act. The record disclosed price fixing only in a "literal sense." [ ]

This case is fundamentally different. Each of the foundations is composed of individual practitioners who compete with one another for patients. Neither the foundations nor the doctors sell insurance, and they derive no profits from the sale of health insurance policies. The members of the foundations sell medical services. Their combination in the form of the foundation does not permit them to sell any different product. [ ] Their combination has merely permitted them to sell their services to certain customers at fixed prices and arguably to affect the prevailing market price of medical care.

The foundations are not analogous to partnerships or other joint arrangements in which persons who would otherwise be competitors pool their capital and share the risks of loss as well as the opportunities for profit. In such joint ventures, the partnership is regarded as a single firm competing with other sellers in the market. The agreement under attack is an agreement among hundreds of competing doctors concerning the price at which each will offer his own services to a substantial number of consumers. It is true that some are surgeons, some anesthesiologists, and some psychiatrists, but the doctors do not sell a package of three kinds of services. If a clinic offered complete medical coverage for a flat fee, the cooperating doctors would have the type of partnership arrangement in which a price-fixing agreement among the doctors would be perfectly proper. But the fee agreements disclosed by the record in this case are among independent competing entrepreneurs. They fit squarely into the horizontal price-fixing mold.

The judgment of the Court of Appeals is reversed.

It is so ordered.

JUSTICE BLACKMUN and JUSTICE O'CONNOR took no part in the consideration or decision of this case.

JUSTICE POWELL, with whom THE CHIEF JUSTICE and JUSTICE REHNQUIST join, dissenting.

The medical care plan condemned by the Court today is a comparatively new method of providing insured medical services at predetermined maximum costs. It involves no coercion. Medical insurance companies, physicians, and patients alike are free to participate or not as they choose. On its face, the plan seems to be in the public interest.

* * * I do not think today's decision on an incomplete record is consistent with proper judicial resolution of an issue of this complexity, novelty, and importance to the public. I therefore dissent.

* * *

II

This case comes to us on a plaintiff's motion for summary judgment after only limited discovery. Therefore, as noted above, the inferences to be drawn from the record must be viewed in the light most favorable to the respondents. * * * This requires, as the Court acknowledges, that we consider the foundation arrangement as one that "impose[s] a meaningful limit on physicians' charges," that "enables the insurance carriers to limit and to calculate more efficiently the risks they underwrite," and that "therefore serves as an effective cost-containment mechanism that has saved patients and insurers millions of dollars." The question is whether we should condemn this arrangement forthwith under the Sherman Act, a law designed to benefit consumers.

Several other aspects of the record are of key significance but are not stressed by the Court. First, the foundation arrangement forecloses *no* competition. Unlike the classic cartel agreement, the foundation plan does not instruct potential competitors: "Deal with consumers on the following terms and no others." Rather, physicians who participate in the foundation plan are free both to associate with other medical insurance plans—at any fee level, high or low—and directly to serve uninsured patients—at any fee level, high or low. Similarly, insurers that participate in the foundation plan also remain at liberty to do business outside the plan with any physician—foundation member or not—at any fee level. Nor are physicians locked into a plan for more than one year's membership. Thus freedom to compete, as well as freedom to withdraw, is preserved. The Court cites no case in which a remotely comparable plan or agreement is condemned on a per se basis.

Second, on this record we must find that insurers represent consumer interests. Normally consumers search for high quality at low prices. But once a consumer is insured [ ]—i.e., has chosen a medical insurance plan—he is largely indifferent to the amount that his physician charges if the coverage is full, as under the foundation-sponsored plan.

The insurer, however, is not indifferent. To keep insurance premiums at a competitive level and to remain profitable, insurers—including those who have contracts with the foundations—step into the consumer's shoes with his incentive to contain medical costs. Indeed, insurers may be the only parties who have the effective power to restrain medical costs, given the difficulty that patients experience in comparing price and quality for a professional service such as medical care.

On the record before us, there is no evidence of opposition to the foundation plan by insurance companies—or, for that matter, by members of the public. Rather seven insurers willingly have chosen to contract out to the foundations the task of developing maximum-fee schedules. [ ] Again, on the record before us, we must infer that the foundation plan—open as it is to insurers, physicians, and the public—has in fact benefitted consumers by "enabl[ing] the insurance carriers to limit and to calculate more efficiently the risks they underwrite." Nevertheless, even though the case is here on an incomplete summary judgment record, the Court conclusively draws contrary inferences to support its per se judgment.

III

It is settled law that once an arrangement has been labeled as "price fixing" it is to be condemned per se. But it is equally well settled that this characterization is not to be applied as a talisman to every arrangement that involves a literal fixing of prices. Many lawful contracts, mergers, and partnerships fix prices. But our cases require a more discerning approach. * * *

* * *

* * * [T]he fact that a foundation-sponsored health insurance plan literally involves the setting of ceiling prices among competing physicians does not, of itself, justify condemning the plan as *per se* illegal. Only if it is clear from the record that the agreement among physicians is "so plainly anticompetitive that no elaborate study of [its effects] is needed to establish [its] illegality" may a court properly make a per se judgment. * * * And, as our cases demonstrate, the per se label should not be assigned without carefully considering substantial benefits and pro-competitive justifications. This is especially true when the agreement under attack is novel, as in this case. * * *

IV

The Court acknowledges that the *per se* ban against price fixing is not to be invoked every time potential competitors literally fix prices. One also would have expected it to acknowledge that *per se* characterization is inappropriate if the challenged agreement or plan achieves for the public pro-competitive benefits that otherwise are not attainable. The Court does not do this. And neither does it provide alternative criteria by which the *per se* characterization is to be determined. It is content simply to brand this type of plan as "price fixing" and describe the agreement in *Broadcast Music*—which also literally involved the fixing of prices—as "fundamentally different."

In fact, however, the two agreements are similar in important respects. Each involved competitors and resulted in cooperative pricing. [ ] Each arrangement also was prompted by the need for better service to the consumers. [ ] And each arrangement apparently makes possible a new product by reaping otherwise unattainable efficiencies. [ ] The Court's effort to distinguish *Broadcast Music* thus is unconvincing.[14]

14. The Court states that in Broadcast Music "there was little competition among individual composers for their separate compositions." This is an irrational ground for distinction. Competition *could* have existed, [ ], but did not because of the cooperative agreement. That competition yet persists among physicians is not a sensible reason to invalidate their agreement while refusing, similarly to condemn the Broadcast Music agreements that were *completely* effective in eliminating competition.

The Court also offers as a distinction that the foundations do not permit the creation of "any different product." But the foundations provide a "different product" to precisely the same extent as did Broadcast Music's clearinghouses. The clearinghouses provided only what copyright holders offered as individual sellers—the rights to use individual compositions. The clearinghouses were able to obtain these same rights more efficiently, however, because they eliminated the need to engage in individual bargaining with each individual copyright owner.

Notes and Questions

1. *Maricopa* has been criticized for its wooden application of the per se rule. See, e.g., Peter M. Gerhart, The Supreme Court and the (Near) Triumph of the Chicago School, 1982 Sup. Ct. Rev. 319 (1984). Can you detect, notwithstanding the opinion's more sweeping pronouncements, an attempt to evaluate the nature and necessity of the price agreements and the justifications offered? Consider how the ancillary restraints doctrine would apply in this case: what, for example, is the plurality's assessment of the "reasonable necessity" of the price agreement? See 1 Furrow, et al., Health Law § 10–27.

2. Should the fact that the foundations adopted maximum, rather than minimum, fee schedules have affected the Court's willingness to apply per se analysis? What are the inherent dangers of maximum price fixing? Are these risks sufficiently probable to justify per se treatment? For a negative answer, see Frank H. Easterbrook, Maximum Price Fixing, 48 U. Chi. L.Rev. 886 (1981). Is it possible that the foundation may have adopted its pricing policies with an eye to limiting the risk of entry by HMOs? In that case wouldn't the arrangement be objectionable for its propensity to preserve supracompetitive prices, albeit at a lower level than existed before the foundations were formed? See Keith B. Leffler, Arizona v. Maricopa County Medical Society: Maximum–Price Agreements in Markets with Insured Buyers, 2 Sup.Ct. Econ. Rev. 187 (1983).

3. An important consequence of *Maricopa* was to foster the notion that financial risk sharing was necessary in order for physician-controlled networks to avoid per se condemnation. Does the opinion compel this conclusion? PPOs and IPAs contracting with managed care organizations or employers on a fee-for-service basis ran the risk of being declared per se price-fixing agreements, even though they might undertake substantial utilization review, risk management and other integrative activities. The initial version of the Department of Justice/FTC Policy Statements seemed to adopt this position and subsequent advisory opinions issued by both agencies suggested that all non-financially integrated networks would be challenged. See e.g., FTC Staff Advisory Letter to Paul W. McVay, (July 5, 1994).

Consider the approach to risk sharing contained in the revised version of Statement 8 of the Department of Justice/FTC Policy Statements reproduced below. What kinds of shared nonfinancial risk will be sufficient to avoid per se treatment? Is this approach consistent with *Maricopa*? What practical steps should a physician network take to meet the Policy Statements' standards on financial risk sharing? On nonfinancial risk sharing? With the ancillary restraints doctrine? Note that the Statement applies to "physician network joint ventures," defined as "physician-controlled ventures in which the network's physician participants collectively agree on prices or price-related terms and jointly market their services." The agencies' requirement of meaningful integration, financial or clinical, to avoid per se categorization finds support in a close economic analysis of

In the same manner, the foundations set up an innovative means to deliver a basic service—insured medical care from a wide range of physicians of one's choice—in a more economical manner. The foundations' maximum-fee schedules replace the weak cost containment incentives in typical "usual, customary, and reasonable" insurance agreements with a stronger cost control mechanism: an absolute ceiling on maximum fees that can be charged.

The conduct of the insurers in this case indicates that they believe that the foundation plan as it presently exists is the most efficient means of developing and administering such schedules. At this stage in the litigation, therefore, we must agree that the foundation plan permits the more economical delivery of the basic insurance service—"to some extent, a different product." Broadcast Music, 441 U.S., at 22, 99 S.Ct., at 1563.

the agency costs and other imperfections of the physician market. Antitrust rules that promote organizational structures that counteract these problems can be justified where their net effect is to improve market performance. See Peter J. Hammer, Medical Antitrust Reform: Arrow, Coase and the Changing Structure of the Firm, in The Privatization of Health Care Reform (Gregg Bloche ed., 2000).

U.S. DEPARTMENT OF JUSTICE AND FEDERAL TRADE COMMISSION, STATEMENTS OF ANTITRUST ENFORCEMENT POLICY IN HEALTH CARE

4 Trade Reg. Rep. (CCH) para. 13,153.
(August 18, 1996).

8. STATEMENT OF DEPARTMENT OF JUSTICE AND FEDERAL TRADE COMMISSION ENFORCEMENT POLICY ON PHYSICIAN NETWORK JOINT VENTURES

* * *

A. *Antitrust Safety Zones*

This section describes those physician network joint ventures that will fall within the antitrust safety zones designated by the Agencies. The antitrust safety zones differ for "exclusive" and "non-exclusive" physician network joint ventures. In an "exclusive" venture, the network's physician participants are restricted in their ability to, or do not in practice, individually contract or affiliate with other network joint ventures or health plans. In a "non-exclusive" venture, on the other hand, the physician participants in fact do, or are available to, affiliate with other networks or contract individually with health plans. * * *

1. Exclusive Physician Network Joint Ventures That The Agencies Will Not Challenge, Absent Extraordinary Circumstances

The Agencies will not challenge, absent extraordinary circumstances, an exclusive physician network joint venture whose physician participants share substantial financial risk and constitute 20 percent or less of the physicians [ ] in each physician specialty with active hospital staff privileges who practice in the relevant geographic market. [ ] In relevant markets with fewer than five physicians in a particular specialty, an exclusive physician network joint venture otherwise qualifying for the antitrust safety zone may include one physician from that specialty, on a non-exclusive basis, even though the inclusion of that physician results in the venture consisting of more than 20 percent of the physicians in that specialty.

2. Non–Exclusive Physician Network Joint Ventures That The Agencies Will Not Challenge, Absent Extraordinary Circumstances

The Agencies will not challenge, absent extraordinary circumstances, a non-exclusive physician network joint venture whose physician participants share substantial financial risk and constitute 30 percent or less of the physicians in each physician specialty with active hospital staff privileges who practice in the relevant geographic market. In relevant markets with fewer than four physicians in a particular specialty, a non-exclusive physician network joint venture otherwise qualifying for the antitrust safety zone may include one physician from that specialty, even though the inclusion of that physician results in the venture consisting of more than 30 percent of the physicians in that specialty.

3. *Indicia Of Non–Exclusivity*

* * * [T]he Agencies caution physician participants in a non-exclusive physician network joint venture to be sure that the network is non-exclusive in fact and not just in name. The Agencies will determine whether a physician network joint venture is exclusive or non-exclusive by its physician participants' activities, and not simply by the terms of the contractual relationship. * * *

4. *Sharing Of Substantial Financial Risk By Physicians In A Physician Network Joint Venture*

To qualify for either antitrust safety zone, the participants in a physician network joint venture must share substantial financial risk in providing all the services that are jointly priced through the network. [ ] The safety zones are limited to networks involving substantial financial risk sharing not because such risk sharing is a desired end in itself, but because it normally is a clear and reliable indicator that a physician network involves sufficient integration by its physician participants to achieve significant efficiencies. [ ] Risk sharing provides incentives for the physicians to cooperate in controlling costs and improving quality by managing the provision of services by network physicians.

The following are examples of some types of arrangements through which participants in a physician network joint venture can share substantial financial risk: [ ]

(1) agreement by the venture to provide services to a health plan at a "capitated" rate; [ ]

(2) agreement by the venture to provide designated services or classes of services to a health plan for a predetermined percentage of premium or revenue from the plan;

(3) use by the venture of significant financial incentives for its physician participants, as a group, to achieve specified cost-containment goals. Two methods by which the venture can accomplish this are:

(a) withholding from all physician participants in the network a substantial amount of the compensation due to them, with distribution of that amount to the physician participants based on group performance in meeting the cost-containment goals of the network as a whole; or

(b) establishing overall cost or utilization targets for the network as a whole, with the network's physician participants subject to subsequent substantial financial rewards or penalties based on group performance in meeting the targets; and

(4) agreement by the venture to provide a complex or extended course of treatment that requires the substantial coordination of care by physicians in different specialties offering a complementary mix of services, for a fixed, predetermined payment, where the costs of that course of treatment for any individual patient can vary greatly due to the individual patient's condition, the choice, complexity, or length of treatment, or other factors. * * *

1064 ANTITRUST Ch. 15

B. The Agencies' Analysis Of Physician Network Joint Ventures That Fall Outside The Antitrust Safety Zones

Physician network joint ventures that fall outside the antitrust safety zones also may have the potential to create significant efficiencies, and do not necessarily raise substantial antitrust concerns.

* * *

1. Determining When Agreements Among Physicians In A Physician Network Joint Venture Are Analyzed Under The Rule Of Reason

Antitrust law treats naked agreements among competitors that fix prices or allocate markets as per se illegal. Where competitors economically integrate in a joint venture, however, such agreements, if reasonably necessary to accomplish the pro-competitive benefits of the integration, are analyzed under the rule of reason. [ ] In accord with general antitrust principles, physician network joint ventures will be analyzed under the rule of reason, and will not be viewed as per se illegal, if the physicians' integration through the network is likely to produce significant efficiencies that benefit consumers, and any price agreements (or other agreements that would otherwise be per se illegal) by the network physicians are reasonably necessary to realize those efficiencies. [ ]

Where the participants in a physician network joint venture have agreed to share substantial financial risk as defined in Section A.4. of this policy statement, their risk-sharing arrangement generally establishes both an overall efficiency goal for the venture and the incentives for the physicians to meet that goal. The setting of price is integral to the venture's use of such an arrangement and therefore warrants evaluation under the rule of reason.

Physician network joint ventures that do not involve the sharing of substantial financial risk may also involve sufficient integration to demonstrate that the venture is likely to produce significant efficiencies. Such integration can be evidenced by the network implementing an active and ongoing program to evaluate and modify practice patterns by the network's physician participants and create a high degree of interdependence and cooperation among the physicians to control costs and ensure quality. This program may include: (1) establishing mechanisms to monitor and control utilization of health care services that are designed to control costs and assure quality of care; (2) selectively choosing network physicians who are likely to further these efficiency objectives; and (3) the significant investment of capital, both monetary and human, in the necessary infrastructure and capability to realize the claimed efficiencies.

* * *

Determining that an arrangement is merely a vehicle to fix prices or engage in naked anti-competitive conduct is a factual inquiry that must be done on a case-by-case basis to determine the arrangement's true nature and likely competitive effects. However, a variety of factors may tend to corroborate a network's anti-competitive nature, including: statements evidencing anti-competitive purpose; a recent history of anti-competitive behavior or collusion in the market, including efforts to obstruct or undermine the development of managed care; obvious anti-competitive structure of the network (e.g., a network comprising a very high percentage of local area physicians, whose participation in the network is exclusive, without any plausible business or efficiency justification); the absence of any mechanisms with the potential for generating significant efficiencies or otherwise increasing competition through the network; the presence of anti-competitive collateral agreements; and the absence of mechanisms to prevent the network's operation from having anti-competitive spillover effects outside the network.

2. Applying The Rule Of Reason

A rule of reason analysis determines whether the formation and operation of the joint venture may have a substantial anti-competitive effect and, if so, whether that potential effect is outweighed by any pro-competitive efficiencies resulting from the joint venture. The rule of reason analysis takes into account characteristics of the particular physician network joint venture, and the competitive environment in which it operates, that bear on the venture's likely effect on competition.

* * *

The steps ordinarily involved in a rule of reason analysis of physician network joint ventures are set forth below.

Step one: Define the relevant market. The Agencies evaluate the competitive effects of a physician network joint venture in each relevant market in which it operates or has substantial impact. In defining the relevant product and geographic markets, the Agencies look to what substitutes, as a practical matter, are reasonably available to consumers for the services in question. [ ] The Agencies will first identify the relevant services that the physician network joint venture provides. Although all services provided by each physician specialty might be a separate relevant service market, there may be instances in which significant overlap of services provided by different physician specialties, or in some circumstances, certain nonphysician health care providers, justifies including services from more than one physician specialty or category of providers in the same market. For each relevant service market, the relevant geographic market will include all physicians (or other providers) who are good substitutes for the physician participants in the joint venture.

Step two: Evaluate the competitive effects of the physician joint venture. The Agencies examine the structure and activities of the physician network joint venture and the nature of competition in the relevant market to determine whether the formation or operation of the venture is likely to have an anti-competitive effect. Two key areas of competitive concern are whether a physician network joint venture could raise the prices for physician services charged to health plans above competitive levels, or could prevent or impede the formation or operation of other networks or plans.

In assessing whether a particular network arrangement could raise prices or exclude competition, the Agencies will examine whether the network physicians collectively have the ability and incentive to engage in such conduct. The Agencies will consider not only the proportion of the physicians in any relevant market who are in the network, but also the incentives faced by physicians in the network, and whether different groups of physicians in a network may have significantly different incentives that would reduce the likelihood of anti-competitive conduct. The Department of Justice has entered into final judgments that permit a network to include a relatively large proportion of physicians in a relevant market where the percentage of physicians with an ownership interest in the network is strictly limited, and the network subcontracts with additional physicians under terms that create a sufficient divergence of economic interest between the subcontracting physicians and the owner physicians so that the owner physicians have an incentive to control the costs to the network of the subcontracting physicians.[15] * * *

If, in the relevant market, there are many other networks or many physicians who would be available to form competing networks or to contract directly with health plans, it is unlikely that the joint venture would raise significant competitive concerns. The Agencies will analyze the availability of suitable physicians to form competing networks, including the exclusive or non-exclusive nature of the physician network joint venture.

The Agencies recognize that the competitive impact of exclusive arrangements or other limitations on the ability of a network's physician participants to contract outside the network can vary greatly. For example, in some circumstances exclusivity may help a network serve its subscribers and increase its physician participants' incentives to further the interests of the network. In other situations, however, the anti-competitive risks posed by such exclusivity may outweigh its pro-competitive benefits. Accordingly, the Agencies will evaluate the actual or likely effects of particular limitations on contracting in the market situation in which they occur.

An additional area of possible anti-competitive concern involves the risk of "spillover" effects from the venture. For example, a joint venture may involve the exchange of competitively sensitive information among competing physicians and thereby become a vehicle for the network's physician participants to coordinate their activities outside the venture. * * *

Step three: Evaluate the impact of pro-competitive efficiencies. [ ] This step requires an examination of the joint venture's likely pro-competitive efficiencies, and the balancing of these efficiencies against any likely anti-competitive effects. The greater the venture's likely anti-competitive effects, the greater must be the venture's likely efficiencies. In assessing efficiency claims, the Agencies focus on net efficiencies that will be derived from the operation of the network and that result in lower prices or higher quality to consumers. The Agencies will not accept claims of efficiencies if the parties reasonably can achieve equivalent or comparable savings through significantly less anti-competitive means. In making this assessment, however, the Agencies will not search for a theoretically least restrictive alternative that is not practical given business realities.

Experience indicates that, in general, more significant efficiencies are likely to result from a physician network joint venture's substantial financial risk sharing or substantial clinical integration. However, the Agencies will

---

15. See, e.g. Competitive Impact Statements in United States v. Health Choice of Northwest Missouri, Inc., Case No. 95–6171–CV SJ–6 (W.D.Mo.; filed Sept. 13, 1995), 60 Fed.Reg. 51808 (Oct. 3, 1995); United States and State of Connecticut v. HealthCare Partners, Inc., Case No. 395–CV–01946–RNC (D.Conn.; filed Sept. 13, 1995), 60 Fed. Reg. 52018, 52020 (Oct. 4, 1995).

consider a broad range of possible cost savings, including improved cost controls, case management and quality assurance, economies of scale, and reduced administrative or transaction costs.

Step four: Evaluation of collateral agreements. This step examines whether the physician network joint venture includes collateral agreements or conditions that unreasonably restrict competition and are unlikely to contribute significantly to the legitimate purposes of the physician network joint venture. The Agencies will examine whether the collateral agreements are reasonably necessary to achieve the efficiencies sought by the joint venture. For example, if the physician participants in a physician network joint venture agree on the prices they will charge patients who are not covered by the health plans with which their network contracts, such an agreement plainly is not reasonably necessary to the success of the joint venture and is an antitrust violation. * * *

U.S. DEPARTMENT OF JUSTICE, BUSINESS REVIEW LETTER RE: SANTA FE MANAGED CARE ORGANIZATION

February 12, 1997

* * *

This letter responds to your request on behalf of Santa Fe, New Mexico Managed Care Organization ("SFMCO") . . . seeking the issuance of a business review letter under the Department of Justice's Business Review Procedure. SFMCO will be a provider-controlled network organization that will offer hospital and physician services to health insurance plans and other third-party payers using capitation and global fee contracts as well as other types of contract arrangements. Based on the information you have provided and our interviews with a number of payers and providers knowledgeable about the market, the Department has no present intention to challenge under the antitrust laws the formation of SFMCO's proposed network.

[SFMCO will be organized as a nonprofit corporation; its members will be (1) St. Vincent's Hospital ("St. Vincent's"), a nonprofit hospital which is the only acute care hospital open to the general public within approximately 60 miles of Santa Fe, and (2) approximately 70–75 physician members. Both St Vincent's and the physician members will share substantial financial risk for SFMCO's operations].

* * *

SFMCO will also subcontract individually with non-member physicians to provide services as part of SFMCO's physician panel. The non-member participating physicians will not share financial risk with SFMCO's members. Any Santa Fe physician who is not a SFMCO member will be eligible to subcontract as a non-member participating physician.

Both SFMCO's members and its non-member participating physicians will participate in the network on a non-exclusive basis. There will be no restriction on their ability to compete with the SFMCO venture, and they will not be discouraged from joining other networks or contracting directly with health benefit plans. You state that SFMCO is intended to be a de jure and de facto non-exclusive network.

SFMCO's primary interest is in negotiating risk contracts with payers. SFMCO's By–Laws define "risk contracts" as agreements between SFMCO and third-party payers that include a 20 percent or greater payment withhold or capitated or percentage of premium payment arrangements or other risk payment methodology. In further describing these provisions, you cite and quote language from the Statements of Antitrust Enforcement Policy in Health Care, issued by the Department and the Federal Trade Commission in August 1996 (the "Policy Statements"). From this description, we understand, and assume for purposes of this business review, that in all SFMCO's risk contracts SFMCO's member physicians will share "substantial financial risk" as that term is described in the Policy Statements.

For contracts that do not involve substantial financial risk sharing, SFMCO will act as a "messenger" to facilitate contracting between third-party payers and SFMCO's individual member and non-member participating physicians. We understand from your letters and your telephone conversations with staff, and we assume for purposes of this letter, that all such messenger arrangements will carefully avoid agreements among competing network providers on prices and price-related terms, will not facilitate collective decision-making by network providers, and will satisfy the description of such messenger arrangements found in Statement 9 of the Policy Statements.

With three exceptions, SFMCO's member physicians together with any physician employees of St. Vincent's will not exceed 30 percent of the physicians with offices in the City of Santa Fe in any physician specialty. The exceptions, which are discussed below, are for (1) physician specialties in which all the SFMCO member physicians in the specialty are in a preexisting integrated practice group that has not been formed or expanded to avoid the 30 percent limitation, (2) family practitioners and internists who, you have told us, are good substitutes for each other in the Santa Fe area, and (3) pediatricians.

The non-member participating physicians will subcontract individually with SFMCO to provide physician services as part of SFMCO's provider panel. The subcontract will establish a capitated payment as compensation for non-member participating primary care physicians and a discounted fee-for-service schedule for all other non-member participating physicians. Unlike SFMCO's member physicians (whose compensation will be linked to SFMCO's overall financial performance through a formula that will make them liable for a share of SFMCO's deficits and eligible for a share of SFMCO's surplus), the non-member participating physicians' compensation will not depend on the overall economic performance of SFMCO.

SFMCO will bear, and not pass through to payers, the risk that its non-member participating physicians might deliver services inefficiently. No increases in fee schedules or capitation payments for non-member participating physicians will be automatically passed on to any payer; SFMCO, through its members, will absorb any such increases. In addition, no contract between SFMCO and a payer will be structured so that changes in SFMCO's payments to non-member participating physicians will automatically affect payments to SFMCO from the payer. Similarly, payments to non-member participating physicians will not depend on, or automatically vary in response to, the provisions of SFMCO's contracts with payers. You represent that SFMCO will be structured so that it will have the incentive to bargain down the compensation to be paid to non-member participating physicians.

No third-party payer will directly compensate a non-member participating physician for that physician's services pursuant to a contract with SFMCO. However, on behalf of SFMCO, a payer may administer payments to all physicians on SFMCO's provider panel, including non-member participating physicians. In all cases, the ultimate payment risk will remain with SFMCO.

We understand that non-member participating physicians will not participate in any discussion, negotiation, decision or agreement concerning fees or fee-related contract provisions for member physicians or each other....

ANTITRUST ANALYSIS

As proposed, SFMCO appears to be an economically integrated joint venture designed with the stated purpose of producing significant efficiencies that should benefit third-party payers and their subscribers. To the extent that competitors will be participating in price or price-related agreements, they will share substantial financial risk in a manner that will create incentives to achieve efficiencies. In all situations not involving substantial financial risk sharing, SFMCO will utilize "messenger" arrangements that should avoid agreements on price and price-related terms if implemented carefully. Consequently, we have analyzed SFMCO's proposal under the rule of reason.

* * *

SFMCO will, with three exceptions, limit the sum of its members and the physician employees of St. Vincent's in any physician specialty to 30 percent of the physicians in that specialty with offices in the City of Santa Fe ... The first exception to the 30 percent limitation is for a preexisting integrated physician group not formed or expanded to avoid the 30 percent limitation. Where all SFMCO members in a specialty belong to such a preexisting group, the group's inclusion in SFMCO would not increase market concentration or power in that physician specialty.

The second exception is for family practitioners and internists. (We have assumed for purposes of this business review that you are correct in asserting that these physicians are good substitutes for each other in the Santa Fe area.) We understand that of the 50 internists and family practitioners in the Santa Fe area, 14 are expected to become SFMCO members and an additional four are employed by St. Vincent's. Thus, 36 percent of the internists and family practitioners will be SFMCO members or employees of the hospital. Nevertheless, we have concluded that the percentage is not so large that it is likely to cause anticompetitive effects under the circumstances and assumptions described in this letter.

The third exception to the 30 percent limitation is for pediatricians. There are a total of only 11 pediatricians in the area. Of these, two will become SFMCO members and an additional six are employed by St. Vincent's (some on a part-time basis). The two pediatricians that will become SFMCO members constitute a fully integrated group practice.

The two member pediatricians plus the six pediatrician employees of St. Vincent's are more than 70 percent of the pediatricians in the area. Although SFMCO points out that the six hospital-employed pediatricians (as well as the hospital-employed internists and family practitioners) will not be SFMCO members, the hospital will be a member and its interest in SFMCO could affect how and the extent to which it will make those physicians available either to payers contracting outside SFMCO or as SFMCO non-member participating physicians. However, you have pointed out that the SFMCO member pediatricians will be a small minority among the primary care physicians whose compensation will be paid out of a single fixed revenue pool. Since paying the pediatricians supra competitive amounts would reduce the revenues available to compensate the other physicians participating in the pool, those other physicians will have strong incentives to keep the pediatricians' compensation at competitive levels. This is more likely to be the case here since neither the six St. Vincent's pediatricians nor St. Vincent's itself will be involved in any of SFMCO's physician pricing discussions or decisions.

Nevertheless, we are concerned that managed care plans desiring to enter the market in Santa Fe could have difficulty obtaining sufficient pediatric care for their enrollees without SFMCO. Despite the presence in the market of family practitioners who do provide care to children, the availability of pediatrician services is important to the marketability of managed care plans. Thus, it is particularly important that both the member and non-member participating pediatricians in SFMCO will in fact participate non-exclusively as you have represented. The conclusion reached in this letter is based in significant part on this representation, and we caution that particular care must be taken to ensure that competition is not injured because of the concentration of pediatricians in SFMCO's provider panel.

Another matter of considerable concern is SFMCO's proposal to supplement its panel of physician members by subcontracting with additional physicians to offer payers a panel that could include virtually all of the physicians in Santa Fe. The Department has entered into final judgments that permitted such subcontracting arrangements where there appeared to be a demand for multi-specialty physician panels with high percentages of the physicians in the market, where the subcontract arrangements created divergence of economic interest between the subcontracting physicians and the member physicians so that the members had an incentive to control the network's costs from the physician subcontracts, and where market conditions otherwise indicated that the subcontract arrangements creating divergence of interest were sufficient to make exclusive behavior unlikely.[16]

SFMCO asserts that payers in the Santa Fe area desire physician panels that are as broad as possible and certainly more inclusive than 30 percent of the physicians in each physician specialty. SFMCO believes that managed care plans in the Santa Fe area need to offer as large a physician panel as possible in order to be attractive to payers. The information we have obtained from payers in the Santa Fe area is generally consistent with these representations,

---

16. See, e.g., Competitive Impact Statements in United States v. Health Choice of Northwest Missouri, Inc., Case No. 95–6171–CV–SJ–6 (W.D. Mo.; filed Sept. 13, 1995), 60 Fed. Reg. 51808, 51815 (October 3, 1995); United States and State of Connecticut v. Health Care Partners, Inc., Case No. 395–CV–01946–RNC (D. Conn.; filed Sept. 13, 1995), 60 Fed. Reg. 52018, 52020 (Oct. 4, 1995).

and we have assumed these representations to be correct for purposes of this business review letter.

SFMCO's proposed subcontracting arrangements also appear to be structured in a manner to create a divergence of economic interest between SFMCO's members and the subcontracting participating physicians that will reduce the likelihood of anticompetitive conduct. SFMCO will bear the ultimate responsibility for payment of compensation to the non-member participating physicians. Unlike the subcontracting physicians whose compensation will not depend on the overall economic performance of SFMCO, the compensation of SFMCO's members will be directly and substantially linked to how well SFMCO performs financially. Member physicians will be both liable for a share of SFMCO's deficits and eligible for a share of the venture's surplus. SFMCO members will have the incentive to bargain down the compensation to be paid to non-member participating physicians.

We have spoken to payers, employers, physicians, and others, and reviewed documents and other information provided by SFMCO. While our investigation indicates the existence of significant actual and potential competition to SFMCO, clearly SFMCO's proposal creates the potential for anticompetitive conduct with harmful effects on consumers. In some physician specialities, more than 30 percent of the physicians in the area will be joining SFMCO as members who will set fees and decide other competitively sensitive matters for the venture. In addition, the members will be subcontracting with most, if not all, of the remaining physicians in the area. If the members and non-member physicians in fact view their interests as congruent, they could easily assert market power with serious anticompetitive consequences.

However, SFMCO's provider-controlled network also has the potential for creating significant efficiencies by offering payers capitation and global fee arrangements that are not now generally available in the Santa Fe area. These benefits must be weighed against the potential for competitive harm. Taking this into account and under all the circumstances here, we are unable to say that SFMCO's plan will likely cause anticompetitive harm if it is implemented carefully as proposed.

We have also considered the possible effects of including St. Vincent's in the network, since it is the only acute care inpatient hospital in the area. The inclusion of St. Vincent's will not reduce competition among hospitals, and we have found no reason to conclude that its inclusion in the network is likely to cause anticompetitive vertical effects.

For these reasons, and based on the facts you have represented, the Department of Justice has no present intention of challenging the formation of SFMCO's proposed network. However, we strongly emphasize that if in practice its formation and operation causes anticompetitive harm, the Department remains free to bring whatever action or proceeding it subsequently comes to believe is required by the public interest. . . .

Sincerely,

Joel I. Klein

Assistant Attorney General

Notes and Questions

1.   The Statements repeatedly emphasize that merely because a physician network joint venture does not fall within a safety zone does not mean that it is unlawful under the antitrust laws. Many such arrangements have received favorable business review letters or advisory opinions from the agencies. See, e.g., Letter from Anne K. Bingaman, Assistant Attorney General, to John F. Fischer (Oklahoma Physicians Network, Inc.)(Jan. 17, 1996)(approving non-exclusive network with "substantially more" than 30% of several specialties, including more than 50% in one specialty). What facts might be particularly persuasive in mitigating the agencies' concerns about a network whose size exceeded safety zone thresholds? Consider the Department of Justice's Business Review Letter in the Sante Fe Managed Care Organization matter. Specifically, which factors justified approval where safety zone thresholds were exceeded in certain specialties? Are you satisfied with the Department's explanation concerning its decision to permit SFMCO to include 70% of all pediatricians in the relevant market? Finally, note that the organization has the potential to include 100% of all physicians, as non-members may subcontract with the organization in the future. What assurances satisfied the Department of Justice that this arrangement would not enable SFMCO to push prices to anticompetitive levels? The FTC and Department of Justice have issued over 100 advisory opinions concerning the health care industry, a large proportion of which concern provider-controlled networks. DOJ business review letters and FTC advisory opinions may be found on the Internet at http://www.usdoj.gov and http://www.ftc.gov. Additional helpful guidance is found in the several hypothetical scenarios and analysis contained in the Policy Statements.

2.   How would you compare the potential harm to competition from exclusive networks as opposed to nonexclusive networks? Under what circumstances might exclusivity foster greater competitiveness? Do the guidelines adequately recognize this potential? See Thomas L. Greaney, Managed Competition, Integrated Delivery Systems and Antitrust, 79 Cornell L. Rev. 1507, 1535–7 (1994).

3.   Do recognized areas of specialization constitute a distinct market for analysis under the Policy Statements? Compare Letter from Anne K. Bingaman, Assistant Attorney General, Antitrust Division, to Steven J. Kern and Robert J. Conroy (March 1, 1996) (concluding that family practitioners and other primary care physicians who treat children were not widely accepted substitutes for pediatricians) with Letter from Anne K. Bingaman, Assistant Attorney General, Antitrust Division to James M. Parker (Oct. 27, 1994) (board-certified pulmonologists are not exclusive providers of pulmonology-type services; merger of two pulmonology groups allowed to proceed because of significant competition from surgeons, family practitioners and other primary care physicians). What facts would you gather and what witnesses would you interview to decide whether a given specialty constitutes a relevant market?

4.   *Multiprovider networks.* Statement 9 of the Policy Statements analyzes the competitive implications of "multiprovider networks," i.e., ventures such as PHOs, whereby providers who offer both competing and complementary services may jointly market their services. Because many such networks are controlled by competing providers, much of the analysis about horizontal restraints of trade contained in Statement 8 is directly applicable and is repeated and elaborated upon in Statement 9. A PHO, it should be noted, might raise competitive concerns in any of a number of markets: the various services markets in which its

physicians compete; inpatient and outpatient hospital services markets; and the market for multiprovider networks themselves. Statement 9 also attempts to clarify the circumstances in which a network may escape the charge of price fixing altogether by employing a neutral "messenger" to communicate contractual offers, counteroffers and acceptances between payors and individual providers without divulging the responses of providers to each other or in any way serving as a negotiator. What limits do you think should be placed on the messenger? Is this a practical alternative?

Multiprovider networks may raise vertical issues as well. Where a network establishes vertical exclusive arrangements that restrict providers from dealing with other networks or other providers, the effect may be to exclude those providers or networks (or impair their ability to compete). For example, a network may enlist such a large proportion of the market's general surgeons that competition from rival networks or hospitals may be inhibited. These concerns arise only where the other networks have few alternatives to which they may turn and they are unable to recruit needed providers from outside the market. For a discussion of the circumstances under which exclusive contracting may constitute an anticompetitive clog on the market, see Section C infra. For cases settling charges that dominant hospitals established PHOs with large percentages of area physicians in order to retard the growth of managed care by foreclosing the development of new networks, see United States and State of Connecticut v. Healthcare Partners, 60 Fed.Reg. 52014 (Oct. 4, 1995)(notice of proposed final judgment) and U.S. v. Health Choice of Northwest Missouri, 60 Fed. Reg. 51808 (Oct. 3, 1995)(notice of proposed final judgment).

Note on Physician Unions and Legislative Proposals to Legalize Collective Bargaining by Physicians

Of the roughly 750,000 practicing doctors in the United States, only about 42,000 are members of labor unions, some 6,000 to 9,000 of whom are residents employed at hospitals. Recently, however, there has been a strong upsurge in interest in joining unions. Physicians have been attracted by promises that unions will enable them to "level the playing field" in contractual bargaining with managed care entities and may improve their ability to assure quality of care for their patients. See Robert L. Lowes, Strength in Numbers: Could Doctor Unions Really Be the Answer? 75 Med. Econ. 114 (1998); Steven Greenhouse, Angered by H.M.O.'s Treatment, More Doctors Are Joining Unions, N.Y. Times, Feb. 4, 1999.

Because many activities of unions, most notably collective bargaining over salaries or compensation, involve collective agreements by competitors, physician unions raise obvious antitrust problems. The critical issue facing these unions is whether they qualify for the labor exemption under the antitrust laws. This exemption has two parts: (1) a statutory exemption, found in Sections 6 and 20 of the Clayton Act and Section 4 of the Norris LaGuardia Act, which together combine to protect unions and their members carrying out their legitimate objectives and permits strikes and boycotts in the course of disputes "concerning terms and conditions of employment;" and (2) a non-statutory exemption that harmonizes antitrust policy with the National Labor Relations Act of 1935 and extends antitrust immunity to certain concerted actions involving unions and employers. Both the statutory and non-statutory exemptions require that the activity arise out of a "labor dispute," which must involve a labor organization comprised only of employees, not independent contractors, and the promotion of legitimate labor interests, as opposed to entrepreneurial or nonlabor interests unrelated to the employer-employee relationship. For an excellent analysis of the law and policies governing physician unions and a discussion of the possibility that independent contractor physicians may be able to engage in collective bargaining in some circumstances, see William S. Brewbaker III, Physician Unions and the Future of Competition in the Health Care Sector, 33 U.C. Davis L. Rev. 545 (2000). An additional qualification is that employees holding managerial or supervisory positions are not authorized under the NRLA to bargain collectively through labor organizations. NLRB v. Yeshiva University, 444 U.S. 672, 100 S.Ct. 856, 63 L.Ed.2d 115 (1980). Labor issues affecting health care providers are discussed in Chapter 12.

The upshot of this is that the antitrust labor exemption enables only physicians who are employees and occupy non-supervisory positions to collectively bargain through labor unions. Unions consequently have organized doctors who are employees of hospitals, HMOs and employer organizations. Courts have interpreted the labor exemption not to apply to physicians in independent practice. American Med. Ass'n v. United States, 317 U.S. 519, 63 S.Ct. 326, 87 L.Ed. 434 (1943); FTC v. Indiana Federation of Dentists, 101 F.T.C. 57 (1983), rev'd on other grounds, 745 F.2d 1124 (7th Cir.1984). Recently, however, independent doctors participating in managed care plans have sought to unionize claiming that they are in effect "employees" of such organizations because the latter exercise extensive control over their practices and have strong economic leverage over them. See Edward B. Hirshfeld, Physicians, Union and Antitrust, 32 J. Health L. 39 (1999). To improve their prospects of being treated as employees for antitrust exemption purposes, some physicians in independent practice have sought certification by the National Labor Relations Board. In an important decision, the Board rejected such a petition, affirming a regional director's finding that the managed care company with which the physicians contracted did not have substantial control "with respect to the physical conduct in the performance of the services" the doctors provide and that the doctors had "wide entrepreneurial discretion that affects the profitability of their practices." See AmeriHealth, Inc./ AmeriHealth HMO, 329 N.L.R.B. No. 76, slip op. at 1, n.1 (1999). Although the NLRB denied review of the matter on remand, it stated that its ruling did not "preclude a finding that physicians under contract to health maintenance organizations may, in other circumstances, be found to be statutory employees" and that, contrary to the regional director, it "accord[s] little weight to the fact that AmeriHealth does not exercise substantial control with respect to the physicians' physical conduct in the performance of services . . . since it is not customary in the medical profession for fully trained staff physicians. . . to be subject to substantial controls over the manner in which they perform their professional duties." Id.

The government has challenged several attempts to organize physician unions that did not meet the prevailing standard for an exemption under the antitrust laws. In FTC and the Commonwealth of Puerto Rico v. College of Physicians–Surgeons of Puerto Rico, 5 Trade Reg. Rep. (CCH) § 335 (D.P.R.1997), the FTC alleged that the College, a quasi-public organization consisting of all physicians in Puerto Rico, engaged in an illegal boycott when it held a 72–hour action in which members refused to provide services except on an emergency basis to protest health reform legislation that had a capitation rate that was too low in the view of members. The College agreed to a Consent Order with the FTC barring future boycotts and paid a $300,000 fine. See also United States v. Federation of Physicians and Dentists, Inc., 63 F.Supp.2d 475 (D.Del.1999) (civil action charging a physician union consisting of nearly all orthopedic surgeons in Delaware with organizing a boycott and jointly terminating contracts with Blue Cross of Delaware in order to resist fee reductions).

Legislative Proposals. In 2000, the U.S. House of Representatives passed, by a vote of 276–136, a bill that would grant health care professionals the same treatment afforded to bargaining unions under the NLRA; see Brewbaker, supra; Richard M. Scheffler, Physician Collective Bargaining: A Turning Point in U.S. Medicine, 24 J. Health Pol. Pol'y & l. 1071, 1073–74 (1999). If enacted, the bill would legalize per se conduct such as collective negotiations by physicians on both price and non-price issues when undertaken in compliance with the legislation. Quality Health–Care Coalition Act of 1999, H.R. 1304, 106th Cong. (1999). The principal sponsor of the bill, Representative Thomas Campbell, observed that it would allow health care professionals to form their own associations to bargain with HMOs and other insurers on an even playing field. This, he asserted, would inure to the benefit of consumers: "It's the best way I can see to let the market deal with the complaints so many health care professionals have raised with HMOs." Physicians: Judiciary Committee to Consider Bill Allowing Doctors to Bargain Collectively, Health Care Daily (BNA), July 24, 1998. FTC Chairman Robert Pitofsky criticized the Campbell Bill in testimony to Congress, describing it as unnecessary to protect consumer interests in quality of care and as likely to discourage vigorous price and quality competition among managed care organizations. See Statement of Robert Pitofsky, Chairman, Federal Trade Commission, before the Committee of Judiciary, U.S. House of Representatives, concerning H.R. 4277 (July 29, 1998). How effective do you think the proposed exemption will be in assuring quality of care for consumers? At lessening managed care "abuses"? Do physicians have other means at their disposal to effectively advocate for patients' rights and high quality care? Is it likely in your view that physicians will use the exemption to negotiate in their self-interests, e.g. for higher fees and less restrictive managed care controls?

Several states have considered adopting statutes that would permit collective negotiations. For example, Texas has enacted legislation that gives physicians a limited exemption to state antitrust laws by allowing collective bargaining with health plans over fee-related issues where (1) the health plan has "substantial market power and those terms and conditions have already affected or threatened to adversely affect the quality and availability of patient care" and (2) the physicians represent not more than ten percent of the physicians in the plan's geographic service area. Tex. Ins. Code §§ 29.06 (a) & 29.09 (b). The Texas statute requires that physicians seeking this exemption must first file a report with and obtain the approval of the state Attorney General. The significance of the Texas law will hinge on two issues: whether it is too administratively complex and limited in scope to provide the kind of relief physicians desire and whether it ultimately has an impact on federal antitrust enforcement. The key question on the latter issue will be whether the statute provides for sufficient oversight and control by the state so as to afford the conduct state action immunity from federal antitrust laws. See American Bar Association Section of Antitrust Law, Antitrust Immunity Legislation for Health Care Providers 53–70 (2000).

Note on Exclusion of Providers by Managed Care

In contrast to the extensive attention paid to provider-controlled networks that are overinclusive or engage in price fixing, discussed supra, little antitrust concern has been raised about the exclusion of physicians or hospitals from such plans or networks. Indeed, government agencies and commentators have generally extolled the benefits of "selective contracting." See, e.g., Department of Justice/FTC Policy Statement 9 ("selective contracting may be a method through which networks limit their provider panels in an effort to achieve quality and cost containment goals and enhance their ability to compete against other networks"). Courts have uniformly applied the rule of reason where the rationale for exclusion from a provider-controlled IPA or PPO has been the providers' incompetence or overutilization of services. See, e.g., Levine v. Central Florida Medical Affiliates, Inc., 72 F.3d 1538 (11th Cir.1996); Hassan v. Independent Practice Associates, 698 F.Supp. 679 (E.D.Mich.1988). Where members are at risk for each others' utilization practices in such plans, should economic credentialing be treated as a presumptively reasonable ancillary restraint? On the other hand, defendants bear the burden of coming forward with a plausible rationale for excluding an entire class of providers. See Hahn v. Oregon Physicians' Service, 868 F.2d 1022 (9th Cir. 1989), (denying defendants' motion for summary judgment where excluded podiatrists rebutted justifications based on overutilization of services); see also, Summit Health v. Pinhas, 500 U.S. 322, 337, 111 S.Ct. 1842, 114 L.Ed.2d 366 (1991) (Scalia, J., dissenting)(citing Robert Bork, The Antitrust Paradox 331–332 (1978) ("group boycotts are per se violations ... not because they necessarily affect competition in the relevant market, but because they deprive at least some consumers of a preferred supplier."))

Once the rule of reason is applied to provider deselection or exclusion, the often dispositive threshold question is whether the plan had market power. An illustrative case is Capital Imaging Associates v. Mohawk Valley Medical Associates, Inc., 996 F.2d 537 (2d Cir. 1993), in which the plan had less than three per cent of the market's HMO subscribers and contracted with only seven per cent of the area's physicians. At what level of concentration would a problem arise? Should one look only to the market share of the defendant plan or should it consider the overall concentration of plans in the market? Is the percentage of total physicians participating in the plan a better surrogate for the plan's market power? These difficult questions have not been definitively answered by the courts, but the Department of Justice/FTC Policy Statements offer the following guidance:

> Where a geographic market can support several multiprovider networks, there are not likely to be significant competitive problems associated with the exclusion of particular providers by particular networks. ...[E]xclusion may present competitive concerns if providers are unable to compete effectively without access to the networks, and competition is thereby harmed.

Policy Statements, supra, Statement No. 9.

Plaintiffs need not prove market power, however, if they can demonstrate that their exclusion has had actual detrimental effects on competition, such as higher prices to consumers. Establishing such effects is usually not possible. In Levine v. Central Florida Medical Affiliates, Inc., 72 F.3d 1538 (11th Cir.1996) (for example, the court found "actual detrimental effect" because plaintiff was able to establish a profitable solo practice and defendants' conduct did not raise the price of service in the market). It likewise found no "potential adverse effect on competition" because insureds had several choices for health care coverage and were free to change coverage choices at any time. See also Capital Imaging, 996 F.2d at 547–8 (finding no effects where deselected providers would charge the same price whether or not admitted into the defendant's plan). See generally, Neil P. Motenko, Provider Exclusion Issues Raised by Integrated Delivery Systems in Antitrust Developments in Evolving Health Care Markets (H. Feller, ed. 1996). Finally, provider selection decisions by payors or networks that are not controlled by providers are vertical in nature and have been viewed as posing little threat to competition. Exclusion, deselection, and exclusive panel arrangements have been regarded as legitimate marketplace decisions and any adverse consequences to excluded physicians are thus a normal consequence of competition. Glen Eden Hospital v. Blue Cross & Blue Shield, 740 F.2d 423 (6th Cir.1984); Barry v. Blue Cross, 805 F.2d 866 (9th Cir.1986).

B. EXCLUSIVE CONTRACTING

U.S. HEALTHCARE, INC. v. HEALTHSOURCE, INC.

United States Court of Appeals, First Circuit, 1993.
986 F.2d 589.

BOUDIN, CIRCUIT JUDGE.

U.S. Healthcare and two related companies (collectively "U.S. Healthcare") brought this antitrust case in the district court against Healthsource, Inc., its founder and one of its subsidiaries. Both sides are engaged in providing medical services through health maintenance organizations ("HMOs") in New Hampshire. In its suit U.S. Healthcare challenged an exclusive dealing clause in the contracts between the Healthsource HMO and doctors who provide primary care for it in New Hampshire. After a trial in district court, the magistrate judge found no violation, and U.S. Healthcare appealed. We affirm.

I. BACKGROUND

Healthsource New Hampshire is an HMO founded in 1985 by Dr. Norman Payson and a group of doctors in Concord, N.H. Its parent company, Healthsource, Inc., is headed by Dr. Payson and it manages or has interests in HMOs in a number of states. We refer to both the parent company and its New Hampshire HMO as "Healthsource."

* * *

Healthsource's HMO operations in New Hampshire were a success. At the time of suit, Healthsource was the only non-staff HMO in the state with 47,000 patients (some in nearby areas of Massachusetts), representing about 5 percent of New Hampshire's population. Stringent controls gave it low costs, including a low hospital utilization rate; and it sought and obtained favorable rates from hospitals and specialists. Giving doctors a further stake in Healthsource's success and incentive to contain costs, Dr. Payson apparently encouraged doctors to become stockholders as well, and at least 400 did so. By 1989 Dr. Payson was proposing to make Healthsource a publicly traded company, in part to permit greater liquidity for its doctor shareholders. U.S. Healthcare is also in the business of operating HMOs.

U.S. Healthcare, Inc., the parent of the other two plaintiff companies—U.S. Healthcare, Inc. (Massachusetts) and U.S. Healthcare of New Hampshire, Inc.—may be the largest publicly held provider of HMO services in the country, serving over one million patients and having total 1990 revenues of well over a billion dollars. Prior to 1990, its Massachusetts subsidiary had done some recruiting of New Hampshire doctors to act as primary care providers for border-area residents served by its Massachusetts HMO. In 1989, U.S. Healthcare had a substantial interest in expanding into New Hampshire.

Dr. Payson was aware in the fall of 1989 that HMOs operating in other states were thinking about offering their services in New Hampshire. He was also concerned that, when Healthsource went public, many of its doctor-shareholders would sell their stock, decreasing their interest in Healthsource and their incentive to control its costs. After considering alternative incentives, Dr. Payson and the HMO's chief operating officer conceived the exclusivity clause that has prompted this litigation. Shortly after the Healthsource public offering in November 1989, Healthsource notified its panel doctors that they would receive greater compensation if they agreed not to serve any other HMO.

The new contract term, effective January 26, 1990, provided for an increase in the standard monthly capitation paid to each primary care physician, for each Healthsource HMO patient cared for by that doctor, if the doctor agreed to the following optional paragraph in the basic doctor-Healthsource agreement:

11.01 Exclusive Services of Physicians. Physician agrees during the term of this Agreement not to serve as a participating physician for any other HMO plan; this shall not, however, preclude Physician from providing professional courtesy coverage arrangements for brief periods of time or emergency services to members of other HMO plans.

A doctor who adopted the option remained free to serve non-HMO patients under ordinary indemnity insurance policies, under Blue Cross/Blue Shield plans, or under preferred provider arrangements. A doctor who accepted the option could also return to non-exclusive status by giving notice.[17]

Although Healthsource capitation amounts varied, a doctor who accepted the exclusivity option generally increased his or her capitation payments by a little more than $1 per patient per month; the magistrate judge put the amount at $1.16 and said that it represented an average increase of about 14 percent as compared with non-exclusive status. The dollar benefit of exclusivity for an individual doctor obviously varies with the number of HMO patients handled by the doctor. Many of the doctors had less than 100 Healthsource patients while about 50 of them had 200 or more. About 250 doctors, or 87 percent of Healthsource's primary care physicians, opted for exclusivity.

* * *

In this court, U.S. Healthcare attacks the exclusivity clause primarily as a per se or near per se violation of section 1; accordingly we begin by examining the case through the per se or "quick look" lenses urged by U.S. Healthcare. We then consider the claim recast in the more conventional framework of Tampa Electric Co. v. Nashville Coal Co., 365 U.S. 320, 81 S.Ct. 623, 5 L.Ed.2d 580 (1961), the Supreme Court's latest word on exclusivity contracts, appraising them under section 1's rule of reason. Finally, we address U.S. Healthcare's claims of section 2 violation and its attacks on the market-definition findings of the magistrate judge.

---

17. The original notice period was 180 days. This was reduced to 30 days in March or April 1991. It appears, at least in practice, that a doctor could switch to non-exclusive status more rapidly by returning some of the extra compensation previously paid.

The Per Se and "Quick Look" Claims

U.S. Healthcare's challenge to the exclusivity clause, calling it first a per se violation and later a monopolization offense, invokes a signal aspect of antitrust analysis: the same competitive practice may be reviewed under several different rubrics and a plaintiff may prevail by establishing a claim under any one of them. Thus, while an exclusivity arrangement is often considered under section 1's rule of reason, it might in theory play a role in a per se violation of section 1. But each rubric has its own conditions and requirements of proof.

* * *

U.S. Healthcare's main argument for per se treatment is to describe the exclusivity clause as a group boycott. To understand why the claim ultimately fails one must begin by recognizing that per se condemnation is not visited on every arrangement that might, as a matter of language, be called a group boycott or concerted refusal to deal. Rather, today that designation is principally reserved for cases in which competitors agree with each other not to deal with a supplier or distributor if it continues to serve a competitor whom they seek to injure.

We doubt that the modern Supreme Court would use the boycott label to describe, or the rubric to condemn, a joint venture among competitors in which participation was allowed to some but not all, although such a restriction might well fall after a more complete analysis under the rule of reason. What is even more clear is that a purely vertical arrangement, by which (for example) a supplier or dealer makes an agreement exclusively to supply or serve a manufacturer, is not a group boycott. Were the law otherwise, every distributor or retailer who agreed with a manufacturer to handle only one brand of television or bicycle would be engaged in a group boycott of other manufacturers.

There are multiple reasons why the law permits (or, more accurately, does not condemn per se) vertical exclusivity; it is enough to say here that the incentives for and effects of such arrangements are usually more benign than a horizontal arrangement among competitors that none of them will supply a company that deals with one of their competitors. No one would think twice about a doctor agreeing to work full time for a staff HMO, an extreme case of vertical exclusivity. Imagine, by contrast, the motives and effects of a horizontal agreement by all of the doctors in a town not to work at a hospital that serves a staff HMO which competes with the doctors.

In this case, the exclusivity arrangements challenged by U.S. Healthcare are vertical in form, that is, they comprise individual promises to Healthsource made by each doctor selecting the option not to offer his or her services to another HMO. The closest that U.S. Healthcare gets to a possible horizontal case is this: it suggests that the exclusivity clause in question, although vertical in form, is in substance an implicit horizontal agreement by the doctors involved. U.S. Healthcare appears to argue that stockholder-doctors dominate Healthsource and, in order to protect their individual interests (as stockholders in Healthsource), they agreed (in their capacity as doctors) not to deal with any other HMO that might compete with Healthsource. We agree that such a horizontal arrangement, if devoid of joint venture efficiencies, might warrant per se condemnation.

The difficulty is that there is no evidence of such a horizontal agreement in this case. Although U.S. Healthcare notes that doctor-stockholders predominate on the Healthsource board that adopted the option, there is nothing to show that the clause was devised or encouraged by the panel doctors. On the contrary, the record indicates that Dr. Payson and Healthsource's chief operating officer developed the option to serve Healthsource's own interests. Formally vertical arrangements used to disguise horizontal ones are not unknown, but U.S. Healthcare has supplied us with no evidence of such a masquerade in this case.

* * *

Rule of Reason

Exclusive dealing arrangements, like information exchanges or standard settings, come in a variety of forms and serve a range of objectives. Many of the purposes are benign, such as assurance of supply or outlets, enhanced ability to plan, reduced transaction costs, creation of dealer loyalty, and the like. But there is one common danger for competition: an exclusive arrangement may "foreclose" so much of the available supply or outlet capacity that existing competitors or new entrants may be limited or excluded and, under certain circumstances, this may reinforce market power and raise prices for consumers.

Although the Supreme Court once said that a "substantial" percentage foreclosure of suppliers or outlets would violate section 1, the Court's *Tampa* decision effectively replaced any such quantitative test by an open-ended inquiry into competitive impact. What is required under *Tampa* is to determine "the probable effect of the [exclusive] contract on the relevant area of effective competition, taking into account. . . . [various factors including] the probable immediate and future effects which pre-emption of that share of the market might have on effective competition therein." 365 U.S. at 329, 81 S.Ct. 623, 5 L.Ed.2d 580.

* * *

U.S. Healthcare simply asserts that competitive impact has already been discussed and that the exclusivity clause has completely foreclosed U.S. Healthcare and any other non-staff HMO from operation in New Hampshire.

This is not a persuasive treatment of a difficult issue or, rather, a host of issues. First, the extent to which the clause operated economically to restrict doctors is a serious question. True, most doctors signed up for it; but who would not take the extra compensation when no competing non-staff HMO was yet operating? The extent of the financial incentive to remain in an exclusive status is unclear, since it varies with patient load, and the least loaded (and thus least constrained by the clause) doctors would normally be the best candidates for a competing HMO. Healthsource suggests that by relatively modest amounts, U.S. Healthcare could offset the exclusivity bonus for a substantial number of Healthsource doctors. U.S. Healthcare's reply brief offers no response.

Second, along with the economic inducement is the issue of duration. Normally an exclusivity clause terminable on 30 days' notice would be close to a de minimus constraint (*Tampa* involved a 20–year contract, and one year is sometimes taken as the trigger for close scrutiny). On the other hand, it may be that the original 180–day clause did frustrate U.S. Healthcare's initial efforts to enlist panel doctors, without whom it would be hard to sign up employers. Perhaps even a 30–day clause would have this effect, especially if a reimbursement penalty were visited on doctors switching back to non-exclusive status. Once again, U.S. Healthcare's brief offers conclusions and a few record references, but neither the precise operation of the clause nor its effects on individual doctors are clearly settled.

Third, even assuming that the financial incentive and duration of the exclusivity clause did remove many of the Healthsource doctors from the reach of new HMOs, it is unclear how much this foreclosure impairs the ability of new HMOs to operate. Certainly the number of primary care physicians tied to Healthsource was significant—one figure suggested is 25 percent or more of all such primary care physicians in New Hampshire—but this still leaves a much larger number not tied to Healthsource. It may be, as U.S. Healthcare urges, that many of the remaining "available" doctors cannot fairly be counted (e.g., those employed full time elsewhere, or reaching retirement, or unwilling to serve HMOs at all). But the dimensions of this limitation were disputed and, by the same token, new doctors are constantly entering the market with an immediate need for patients.

U.S. Healthcare lays great stress upon claims, supported by some meeting notes of Healthsource staff members, that the latter was aware of new HMO entry and conscious that new HMOs like U.S. Healthcare could be adversely affected by the exclusivity clause.[93] Healthsource in turn says that these were notes made in the absence of policy-making officers and that its real motivation for the clause was to bolster loyalty and cost-cutting incentives. Motive can, of course, be a guide to expected effects, but effects are still the central concern of the antitrust laws, and motive is mainly a clue. This case itself suggests how far motives in business arrangement may be mixed, ambiguous, and subject to dispute. In any event, under *Tampa* the ultimate issue in exclusivity cases remains the issue of foreclosure and its consequences.

Absent a compelling showing of foreclosure of substantial dimensions, we think there is no need for us to pursue any inquiry into Healthsource's precise motives for the clause, the existence and measure of any claimed benefits from exclusivity, the balance between harms and benefits, or the possible existence and relevance of any less restrictive means of achieving the benefits. We are similarly spared the difficulty of assessing the fact that the clause is limited to HMOs, a fact from which more than one inference may be drawn. The point is that proof of substantial foreclosure and of "probable immediate and future effects" is the essential basis under Tampa for an attack on an exclusivity clause. U.S. Healthcare has not supplied that basis.

* * *

93. Two examples of these staff notes give their flavor: "Looking at '90 rates—and a deterrent [sic] to joining other HMOs (like Healthcare)"; and "amend contract (sending this or next week) based on exclusivity. HMOs only (careful about restraint of trade) will be sent to even those in Healthcare already. . . ."

Whether the law requires such a further showing of likely impact on consumers is open to debate. Our own case law is not crystal clear on this issue. Ultimately the issue turns upon antitrust policy, where a permanent tension prevails between the "no sparrow shall fall" concept of antitrust, [ ] (violation "not to be tolerated merely because the victim is just one merchant whose business is so small that his destruction makes little difference to the economy"), and the ascendant view that antitrust protects "competition, not competitors." See Brunswick Corp. v. Pueblo Bowl–O–Mat, Inc., 429 U.S. 477, 488 (1977). We need not confront this issue in a case where the cardinal requirement of a valid claim—significant foreclosure unreasonably restricting competitors—has not been demonstrated.

Section 2

Exclusive contracts might in some situations constitute the wrongful act that is an ingredient in monopolization claims under section 2. The magistrate judge resolved these section 2 claims in favor of Healthsource primarily by defining the market broadly to include all health care financing in New Hampshire. So defined, Healthsource had a share of that market too small to support an attempt charge, let alone one of actual monopolization. U.S. Healthcare argues, however, that the market was misdefined.

It may be unnecessary to consider this claim since, as we have already held, U.S. Healthcare has failed to show a substantial foreclosure effect from the exclusivity clause. After all, an act can be wrongful in the context of section 2 only where it has or threatens to have a significant exclusionary impact. But a lesser showing of likely effect might be required if the actor were a monopolist or one within striking distance. More important, the magistrate judge dismissed the section 2 claims based on market definition and, if his definition were shown to be wrong, a remand might be required unless we were certain that U.S. Healthcare could never prevail.

There is no subject in antitrust law more confusing than market definition. One reason is that the concept, even in the pristine formulation of economists, is deliberately an attempt to oversimplify—for working purposes—the very complex economic interactions between a number of differently situated buyers and sellers, each of whom in reality has different costs, needs, and substitutes. Further, when lawyers and judges take hold of the concept, they impose on it nuances and formulas that reflect administrative and antitrust policy goals. This adaption is legitimate (economists have no patent on the concept), but it means that normative and descriptive ideas become intertwined in the process of market definition.

Nevertheless, rational treatment is assisted by remembering to ask, in defining the market, why we are doing so: that is, what is the antitrust question in this case that market definition aims to answer? This threshold inquiry helps resolve U.S. Healthcare's claim that the magistrate judge erred at the outset by directing his analysis to the issue whether HMOs or health care financing was the relevant product market. This approach, says U.S. Healthcare, mistakenly focuses on the sale of health care to buyers whereas its concern is Healthsource's buying power in tying up doctors needed by other HMOs in order to compete.

The magistrate judge's approach was correct. One can monopolize a product as either a seller or a buyer; but as a buyer of doctor services,

Healthsource could never achieve a monopoly (monopsony is the technical term), because doctors have too many alternative buyers for their services.[94] Rather, the only way to cast Healthsource as a monopolist is to argue, as U.S. Healthcare apparently did, that HMO services (or even IPA HMOs) are a separate health care product sold to consumers such as employers and employees. If so, it might become possible (depending on market share and other factors) to describe Healthsource as a monopolist or potential monopolist in the sale of HMO (or IPA HMO) services in New Hampshire, using the exclusionary clause to foster or reinforce the monopoly.

Thus, the magistrate judge asked the right question. Even so U.S. Healthcare argues that he gave the wrong answer in finding that HMOs were not a separate market (it uses the phrase "submarket" but this does not alter the issue). This is a legitimate contention and U.S. Healthcare has at least some basis for it: HMOs are often cheaper than other care methods because they emphasize illness prevention and severe cost control. U.S. Healthcare also seeks to distinguish cases defining a broader "health care financing market"—cases heavily relied on by the magistrate judge—as involving quite different types of antitrust claims. See, e.g., Ball Memorial Hosp., Inc. v. Mutual Hosp. Ins., Inc., 784 F.2d 1325 (7th Cir.1986). Once again, we agree that the nature of the claim can affect the proper market definition.

The problem with U.S. Healthcare's argument is that differences in cost and quality between products create the possibility of separate markets, not the certainty. A car with more features and a higher price is, within some range, in the same market as one with less features and a lower price. In practice, the frustrating but routine question how to define the product market is answered in antitrust cases by asking expert economists to testify. Here, the issue for an economist would be whether a sole supplier of HMO services (or IPA HMOs if that is U.S. Healthcare's proposed market) could raise price far enough over cost, and for a long enough period, to enjoy monopoly profits. Usage patterns, customer surveys, actual profit levels, comparison of features, ease of entry, and many other facts are pertinent in answering the question.

Once again, U.S. Healthcare has not made its case in this court. The (unquantified) cost advantage of HMOs is the only important fact supplied; consumers might, or might not, regard this benefit as just about offset by the limits placed on the patient's choice of doctors. To be sure, there was some expert testimony in the district court on both sides of the market definition issue. But if there is any case in which counsel has the obligation to cull the record, organize the facts, and present them in the framework of a persuasive legal argument, it is a sophisticated antitrust case like this one. Without such a showing on appeal, we have limited ability to reconstruct so complex a record ourselves and no basis for overturning the magistrate judge.

---

94. U.S. Healthcare, of course, is not concerned with Healthsource's ability as a monopsonist to exploit doctors; it is concerned with its own ability to find doctors to serve it. The latter question—one of foreclosure—depends on the available supply of doctors, the constraint imposed by the exclusivity clause, the prospect for entry of new doctors into the market, and similar issues. Whether U.S. Healthcare is foreclosed, however, does not depend on whether consumers treat HMOs as a part of health care financing or as a unique and separate product.

Absent the showing of a properly defined product market in which Healthsource could approach monopoly size, we have no reason to consider the geographic dimension of the market. If health care financing is the product market, as the magistrate judge determined, plainly Healthsource has no monopoly or anything close to it, given the number of other providers in New Hampshire, such as insurers, staff HMOs, Blue Cross/Blue Shield and individual doctors. This is equally so whether the geographic market is southern New Hampshire (as U.S. Healthcare claims) or the whole state (as the magistrate judge found).

Notes and Questions

1.   What factors did the court suggest would be determinative in proving that an exclusive contract violated the Sherman Act? For example, would significant foreclosure for a substantial period of time be sufficient or must the plaintiff prove that actual anticompetitive effects would result from the clause? See Barr Labs. v. Abbott Labs., 978 F.2d 98 (3d Cir.1992); Jefferson Parish Hosp. District No. 2 v. Hyde, 466 U.S. 2, 104 S.Ct. 1551, 80 L.Ed.2d 2 (1984). If the latter, how might a plaintiff meet its burden?

2.   On what basis did the court discount the importance of evidence of defendant's motive and intent in imposing the exclusivity clause? Do you agree that such evidence is "mainly a clue"? Is such proof less reliable than an economist's (or court's) analysis as a guide to the likely effects of the challenged restraint?

3.   The Court did not rule out the possibility that the relevant market might consist of HMO services. What evidence would be most probative in demonstrating that such a market existed? For an opinion dismissing the possibility of an HMO services market because of the ease with which physicians can switch from one plan to another, see Blue Cross & Blue Shield v. Marshfield Clinic, 65 F.3d 1406 (7th Cir.1995).

C.   PAYORS WITH MARKET POWER

KARTELL v. BLUE SHIELD OF MASSACHUSETTS, INC.

United States Court of Appeals, First Circuit, 1984.
749 F.2d 922, cert. denied, 471 U.S. 1029, 105 S.Ct. 2040, 85 L.Ed.2d 322 (1985).

BREYER, CIRCUIT JUDGE.

Blue Shield pays doctors for treating patients who are Blue Shield health insurance subscribers, but only if each doctor promises not to make any additional charge to the subscriber. The basic issue in this case is whether this Blue Shield practice—called a "ban on balance billing"—violates either Sherman Act § 1 forbidding agreements "in restraint of trade," 15 U.S.C.A. § 1, or Sherman Act § 2 forbidding "monopolization" and "attempts to monopolize," [ ]. The district court, 582 F.Supp. 734 (D.Mass.1984) held that the practice constituted an unreasonable restraint of trade in violation of section 1. We conclude that the practice does not violate either section of the Sherman Act; and we reverse the district court.

As the district court noted, the relevant facts are "not ... generally ... disputed." Blue Shield provides health insurance for physician services while its sister, Blue Cross, insures against hospital costs. The consumers of Blue

Shield insurance, at least those who buy "full service" prepaid medical benefits, can see any "participating doctor," *i.e.*, a doctor who has entered into a standard Participating Physician's Agreement with Blue Shield. (If a doctor has not signed the Agreement, Blue Shield will reimburse him only if he provides emergency or out-of-state services.) Under the standard agreement, a participating doctor promises to accept as payment in full an amount determined by Blue Shield's "usual and customary charge" method of compensation. * * * Blue Shield pays this amount directly to the doctor; the patient pays nothing out of his own pocket and therefore receives no reimbursement.

The district court also found that Blue Shield provides some form of health insurance to about 56 percent of the Massachusetts population ... [or] about 74 percent of those Massachusetts residents who *privately* insure against health costs. * * * Virtually all practicing doctors agree to take Blue Shield subscribers as patients and to participate in its fee plan.

The district court found that, because of the large number of subscribers, doctors are under "heavy economic pressure" to take them as patients and to agree to Blue Shield's system for charging the cost of their care. The court believed that the effect of this payment system, when combined with Blue Shield's size and buying power, was to produce an unreasonably rigid and unjustifiably low set of prices. In the court's view, the fact that doctors cannot charge Blue Shield subscribers more than the Blue Shield payment-schedule amounts interferes with the doctors' freedom to set higher prices for more expensive services and discourages them from developing and offering patients more expensive (and perhaps qualitatively better) services. For these and related reasons, the district court held that Blue Shield's ban on "balance billing" unreasonably restrains trade, and thereby violates Sherman Act § 1. Blue Shield appeals from this holding. The plaintiff doctors cross-appeal from other rulings of the district court in Blue Shield's favor.

* * *

I

We disagree with the district court because we do not believe that the facts that it found show an unreasonable restraint of trade. We can best explain our reasons by first discussing the basic antitrust issue in general terms, then turning to the specific, detailed arguments advanced by the parties, and finally noting several special reasons here that militate against a finding of liability.

A

We disagree with the district court's finding of "restraint." To find an unlawful restraint, one would have to look at Blue Shield as if it were a "third force," intervening in the marketplace in a manner that prevents willing buyers and sellers from independently coming together to strike price/quality bargains. Antitrust law typically frowns upon behavior that impedes the striking of such independent bargains. The persuasive power of the district court's analysis disappears, however, once one looks at Blue Shield, not as an inhibitory "third force," but as itself the purchaser of the doctors' services. * * * Antitrust law rarely stops the buyer of a service from trying to determine the price or characteristics of the product that will be sold. Thus, the more closely Blue Shield's activities resemble, in essence, those of a purchaser, the less likely that they are unlawful.

Several circuits have held in antitrust cases that insurer activity closely analogous to that present here amounts to purchasing, albeit for the account of others. And, they have held that an insurer may lawfully engage in such buying of goods and services needed to make the insured whole. The Second Circuit has held lawful a Blue Shield plan requiring pharmacies to accept Blue Shield reimbursement as full payment for drugs they supply to Blue Shield subscribers. Medical Arts Pharmacy of Stamford, Inc. v. Blue Cross & Blue Shield of Connecticut, Inc., 675 F.2d 502 (2d Cir.1982). The Third Circuit has allowed a hospital cost insurer (Blue Cross) to reimburse hospitals directly (and apparently completely) for services to subscribers. Travelers Insurance Co. v. Blue Cross of Western Pennsylvania, 481 F.2d 80 (3d Cir.), *cert. denied,* 414 U.S. 1093, 94 S.Ct. 724, 38 L.Ed.2d 550 (1973). * * *

At the same time, the facts before us are unlike those in cases where courts have forbidden an "organization" to buy a good or service—cases in which the buyer was typically a "sham" organization seeking only to combine otherwise independent buyers in order to suppress their otherwise competitive instinct to bid up price. Mandeville Island Farms, Inc. v. American Crystal Sugar Co., 334 U.S. 219, 235, 68 S.Ct. 996, 1005, 92 L.Ed. 1328 (1948) (horizontal price-fixing by purchasers held *per se* illegal); * * *. No one here claims that Blue Shield is such a "sham" organization or anything other than a legitimate, independent medical cost insurer. But cf. Virginia Academy of Clinical Psychologists v. Blue Shield of Virginia, 624 F.2d 476 (4th Cir.1980) (Blue Shield found to be a combination, not of policyholders, but of physicians), *cert. denied,* 450 U.S. 916, 101 S.Ct. 1360, 67 L.Ed.2d 342 (1981).

Once one accepts the fact that, from a commercial perspective, Blue Shield in essence "buys" medical services for the account of others, the reasoning underlying the Second, Third, and Seventh Circuit views indicates that the ban on balance billing is permissible. To understand that reasoning, consider some highly simplified examples. Suppose a father buys toys for his son—toys the son picks out. Or suppose a landlord hires a painter to paint his tenant's apartment, to the tenant's specifications. Is it not obviously lawful for the father (the landlord) to make clear to the seller that the father (the landlord) is in charge and will pay the bill? Why can he not then forbid the seller to charge the child (the tenant) anything over and above what the father (the landlord) pays—at least if the seller wants the buyer's business? To bring the example closer to home, suppose that a large manufacturing company hires doctors to treat its employees. Can it not insist that its doctors not charge those employees an additional sum over and above what the company agrees to pay them to do the job? In each of these instances, to refuse to allow the condition would disable the buyer from holding the seller to the price of the contract. Yet, if it is lawful for the buyer to buy for the third party in the first place, how can it be unlawful to bargain for a price term that will stick? Given this argument, it is not surprising the courts have unanimously upheld contracts analogous in various degrees to the one at issue here—contracts in which those who directly provide goods or services to insureds have agreed to cap or forego completely additional charges to those insureds in return for direct payment by the insurer. * * *

* * *

[T]he doctors seek to distinguish these precedents by pointing to an important district court finding either not present or not discussed in depth in these other cases. The district court here found that Blue Shield is a buyer with significant "market power"—*i.e.*, the power to force prices below the level that a freely competitive market would otherwise set. They argue that Blue Shield's "market power" makes a significant difference. We do not agree.

At the outset, we note that Blue Shield disputes the existence of significant "market power." It points out that the district court relied heavily upon participation by 99 percent of all Massachusetts doctors in Blue Shield's program, as "prov[ing] * * * Blue Shield's economic power." But, Blue Shield says, this by itself proves little. Participating in Blue Shield's program does not stop doctors from taking other patients or from charging those other patients what they like. As long as Blue Shield's rates are even marginally remunerative, 99 percent of all doctors might sign up with Blue Shield if it had only ten policyholders or ten thousand instead of several million.

Blue Shield adds that the record does not prove the existence of the single harm most likely to accompany the existence of market power on the buying side of the market, namely lower seller output. [ ] Indeed, here the district court found that the supply of doctors in Massachusetts has "increased steadily during the past decade." Blue Shield also claims that whatever power it possesses arises from its ability as an "expert" to prevent doctors from charging unknowledgeable patients *more* than a free (and informed) market price. See generally Comment, 75 Nw.U.L.Rev. [506 (1980)].

On the other hand, several doctors testified that low prices discouraged them from introducing new highly desirable medical techniques. And, they argue that fully informed patients would have wanted to pay more for those techniques had they been allowed to do so.

To resolve this argument about the existence of market power—an issue hotly debated by the expert economists who testified at trial—would force us to evaluate a record that the district court described as "two competing mountains of mostly meaningless papers." Rather than do so, we shall assume that Blue Shield possesses significant market power. We shall also assume, but purely for the sake of argument, that Blue Shield uses that power to obtain "lower than competitive" prices.

We next ask whether Blue Shield's assumed market power makes a significant legal difference. As a matter of pure logic, to distinguish the examples previously mentioned one must accept at least one of the following three propositions: One must believe either (1) that the law forbids a buyer with market power to bargain for "uncompetitive" or "unreasonable" prices, or (2) that such a buyer cannot buy for the account of others, or (3) that there is some relevant difference between obtaining such price for oneself and obtaining that price for others for whom one can lawfully buy. In our view, each of these propositions is false, as a matter either of law or of logic.

First, the antitrust laws interfere with a firm's freedom to set even uncompetitive prices only in special circumstances, where, for example, a price is below incremental cost. Such a "predatory" price harms competitors, cannot be maintained, and is unlikely to provide consumer benefits. [ ] Ordinarily, however, even a monopolist is free to exploit whatever market power it may possess when that exploitation takes the form of charging uncompetitive prices. As Professor Areeda puts it, "Mere monopoly pricing is not a violation of the Sherman Act." [ ] * * *

The district court did not suggest here that the prices subject to the "balance billing" ban were "predatory." Nor (with one possible exception, see [infra]) do the parties point to evidence of any price below anyone's "incremental cost." [ ] Rather, the district court suggested that Blue Shield's prices were "uncompetitively low," "unreasonably low," lower than the doctors might have charged to individual patients lacking market power. That is to say, Blue Shield obtained prices that reflected its market power. For the reasons just mentioned then, if Blue Shield had simply purchased those services for itself, the prices paid, in and of themselves, would not have amounted to a violation of the antitrust laws. [ ]

Second, as we previously mentioned, there is no law forbidding a legitimate insurance company from itself buying the goods or services needed to make its customer whole. The cases that we have cited are unanimous in allowing such arrangements. The rising costs of medical care, the possibility that patients cannot readily evaluate (as competitive buyers) competing offers of medical service, the desirability of lowering insurance costs and premiums, the availability of state regulation to prevent abuse—all convince us that we ought not create new potentially far-reaching law on the subject. And, the parties have not seriously argued to the contrary.

Third, to reject the first two propositions is, as a matter of logic, to reject the third. If it is lawful for a monopoly buyer to buy for the account of another, how can it be unlawful for him to insist that no additional charge be made to that other? To hold to the contrary is, in practice, to deny the buyer the right to buy for others, for the seller would then be free to obtain a different price from those others by threatening to withhold the service. This reasoning seems sound whether or not the buyer has "market power."

In essence, then, the lawfulness of the term in question stems from the fact that it is an essential part of the price bargain between buyer and seller. Whether or not that price bargain is, in fact, reasonable is, legally speaking, beside the point, even in the case of a monopolist. As Blue Shield stresses in its brief, health maintenance organizations, independent practice associations, and preferred provider organizations all routinely agree with doctors that the doctors will accept payment from the plan as payment in full for services rendered to subscribers. We can find no relevant analytical distinction between this type of purchasing decision and the practice before us—even on the assumption that Blue Shield possesses market power.

B

We now consider more closely the specific arguments raised by the district court and the parties to show that Blue Shield's "balance billing ban" is anti-competitive in practice. The [plaintiffs'] brief sets forth in summary form the following allegedly harmful effects of the ban:

(1) Price competition among physicians for services covered by Blue Shield's service benefit policies is "virtually eliminated."

(2) Doctor's prices have tended to cluster around Blue Shield's "maximum price levels."

(3) Doctors wanting to compete by offering innovative or "premium" services are inhibited from doing so because Blue Shield's pricing structure assumes that physicians' services are fungible and mandates the same price ceilings for virtually all physicians.

(4) Doctors just entering practice are discouraged from doing so by particularly low levels of Blue Shield reimbursement.

(5) Blue Shield's low prices lead doctors to charge higher prices to others.

(6) Blue Shield discourages doctors from charging others low prices by insisting that its subscribers be given the benefit of any such low prices.

(7) Blue Shield's pricing system discourages doctors from trying out more expensive services that could bring about lower total medical costs, *e.g.*, a "colonoscopy with polypectomy," an expensive service that is nonetheless cheaper than the surgery that would otherwise be needed to cure the patient.

(8) Blue Shield, by reason of its pricing practices, has been able to attract more subscribers, extending its "competitive edge" over other health insurers, and increasing its dominance in the health insurance business.

The first seven of these arguments attack the price term in the agreement between Blue Shield and the doctors. To argue that Blue Shield's pricing system is insufficiently sensitive to service differences, or that it encourages high costs, or does not give the patients what they really need, or to claim that the buyer is making a bad decision is like arguing that the buyer of a fleet of taxicabs ought to buy several different models, or allow the seller to vary color or horsepower or gearshift because doing so either will better satisfy those passengers who use the fleet's services, or will in the long run encourage quality and innovation in automobile manufacture. The short—and conclusive—answer to these arguments is that normally the choice of what to seek to buy and what to offer to pay is the buyer's. And, even if the buyer has monopoly power, an antitrust court (which might, in appropriate circumstances, restructure the market) will not interfere with a buyer's (nonpredatory) determination of price.

* * * A legitimate buyer is entitled to use its market power to keep prices down. The claim that Blue Shield's price scheme is "too rigid" because it ignores qualitative differences among physicians is properly addressed to Blue Shield or to a regulator, not to a court. There is no suggestion that Blue Shield's fee schedule reflects, for example, an effort by, say, one group of doctors to stop other doctors from competing with them. [ ] Here, Blue Shield and the doctors "sit on opposite sides of the bargaining table" [ ]. And Blue Shield seems simply to be acting "as every rational enterprise does, *i.e.*, [to] get the best deal possible" [ ]. The first seven adverse consequences to which appellees point are the result of this unilateral behavior.

Plaintiffs' eighth argument focuses on the health insurance business: Blue Shield's "ban on balance billing," by attracting more subscribers, augments its share of the health insurance business, thereby enabling it to secure still lower doctor charges. This argument, however, comes down to saying that Blue Shield can attract more subscribers because it can charge them less. If Blue Shield is free to insist upon a lower doctor charge, it should be free to pass those savings along to its subscribers in the form of lower prices. * * *

Finally, the district court rested its decision in large part upon the Supreme Court's recent case, Arizona v. Maricopa County Medical Society, 457 U.S. 332, 102 S.Ct. 2466, 73 L.Ed.2d 48 (1982). *Maricopa,* however, involved a *horizontal* agreement among competing doctors about what to charge. A horizontal agreement among competitors is typically unlawful because the competitors prevent themselves from making *independent* decisions about the terms as to which they will bargain. * * * [T]he antitrust problems at issue when a single firm sets a price—whether, when, and how courts can identify and control an individual exercise of alleged market power—are very different from those associated with agreements by competitors to limit independent decision-making. A decision about the latter is not strong precedent for a case involving only the former. *Maricopa* is simply not on point. * * *

C

Three additional circumstances militate strongly here against any effort by an antitrust court to supervise the Blue Shield/physician price bargain. * * *

First, the prices at issue here are low prices, not high prices. [ ] Of course, a buyer, as well as a seller, can possess significant market power; and courts have held that *agreements* to fix prices—whether maximum or minimum—are unlawful. [ ] Nonetheless, the Congress that enacted the Sherman Act saw it as a way of protecting consumers against prices that were too *high,* not too low. * * *

Second, the subject matter of the present agreement—medical costs—is an area of great complexity where more than solely economic values are at stake. * * * This fact, too, warrants judicial hesitancy to interfere.

Third, the price system here at issue is one supervised by state regulators. [ ] While that fact does not automatically carry with it antitrust immunity, [ ] it suggests that strict antitrust scrutiny is less likely to be necessary to prevent the unwarranted exercise of monopoly power. * * *

These general considerations do not dictate our result in this case. They do, however, counsel us against departing from present law or extending it to authorize increased judicial supervision of the buyer/seller price bargain. * * *

* * *

Notes and Questions

1. Is the Court's skepticism about Blue Shield's market power warranted? After all, it did control 74 percent of the private insurance market in Massachu-

setts and had provider contracts with 99 percent of the state's physicians. On the other hand, is market share data alone a reliable indicator of market power? See Ball Memorial Hospital, Inc. v. Mutual Hospital Insurance Co., 784 F.2d 1325 (7th Cir.1986)(absence of entry barriers in health insurance refuted possibility that insurer with large market share possessed market power); see also Frank H. Easterbrook, Maximum Price Fixing, 48 U. Chi. L. Rev. 886, 904 (1981)("[health insurer] monopsony power is inconceivable in most instances"). For a telling refutation of Easterbrook's position, see Mark V. Pauly, Competition in Health Insurance Markets, 51 Law & Contemp. Probs. 237 (1988). Pauly argues that brand loyalty and switching costs undermine the assumption that ease of entry always obviates concerns about insurer market power. He also demonstrates that monopsony insurers may well profit from pushing provider prices "too low" so that consumers do not receive an adequate level of service and quality.

2. The essence of the doctors' complaint in *Kartell* was that Blue Shield was exercising monopoly power (or more accurately, because it is a buyer of physician services, monopsony power) in violation of Section 2 of the Sherman Act. In addition, the same conduct was alleged to constitute an illegal restraint of trade under Section 1. Section 2 does not make illegal the possession of monopoly power or even the charging of monopoly prices. Rather, plaintiff must prove willful acts that helped defendant obtain or preserve market power "as distinguished from growth or development as a consequence of a superior product, business acumen or historic accident." United States v. Grinnell Corp., 384 U.S. 563, 570–71, 86 S.Ct. 1698, 1703–04, 16 L.Ed.2d 778 (1966). Did the Court adequately analyze whether the balance billing ban contributed to preserving Blue Shield's market power, such as by excluding rivals? Were the long-run effects of driving price below market levels explored? See Frances H. Miller, Vertical Restraints and Powerful Health Insurers: Exclusionary Conduct Masquerading as Managed Care? 51 Law & Contemp. Probs., 195, 220–24 (1988). How satisfactory is the court's analysis of the effects of the ban on the physician market? Does the fact that physicians were not leaving Massachusetts in droves prove the absence of monopsonistic effects? Aren't there a host of other variables affecting the total supply of physicians over time? See Herbert Hovenkamp, Antitrust Policy After Chicago, 84 Mich. L. Rev. 213 (1985) (faulting the reasoning of the court in *Kartell* for its "static market fallacy").

Some courts may have been too quick to dismiss the possibility that a dominant insurer might exercise market power. In Travelers Insurance Company v. Blue Cross of Western Pennsylvania, 481 F.2d 80 (3d Cir.1973), cert. denied, 414 U.S. 1093, 94 S.Ct. 724, 38 L.Ed.2d 550 (1973), a commercial insurer charged that a Blue Cross plan's favorable contracts with hospitals (enabling it to pay 15 percent less for hospital services than other insurers) assured it of lower premium rates and market dominance. Applying reasoning later echoed by the *Kartell* court, the Third Circuit observed that the defendant was doing "no more than conduct[ing] its business as every rational enterprise does, i.e., to get the best deal possible." 481 F.2d at 84. A close examination of the facts, however, suggests that Blue Cross was engaged in strategic behavior that rings a strikingly anticompetitive note. The most plausible explanation for the discounts lies in the appreciation by the hospitals and Blue Cross of their mutual, anticompetitive interest in the arrangement. By granting the largest insurer a standard discount, the hospitals could reduce pressures to grant other discounts because there would be no other formidable buyers in the market. At the same time, the absence of competition at the payer level was assured because no rival could match the low hospital costs incurred by Blue Cross. See Clark C. Havighurst, The Questionable Cost–Containment Record of Commercial Health Insurers in Health Care in America: The Political Economy of Hospitals and Health Insurance, 221 (H.E. Frech III ed., 1988). The foregoing analysis is a good example of the impact on antitrust of new economic models demonstrating the possibility of exclusion through vertical contracting and "raising rivals' costs." In cases such as this, "Post–Chicago" economic analysis demands closer investigation of arrangements that would easily pass muster under conventional "Chicago School" principles. See Thomas G. Krattenmaker and Steven C. Salop, Anti-competitive Exclusion: Raising Rivals' Costs to Achieve Power Over Price, 96 Yale L.J. 209 (1986).

3. Government antitrust enforcers have devoted considerable attention in recent years to "most favored nations" (MFN) clauses in provider contracts with health plans. These clauses typically stipulate that the health plan will not pay the provider any more than the lowest discounted price the provider gives to any other payor. The limited case law on the subject is mixed.

Ocean State Physicians Health Plan, Inc. v. Blue Cross & Blue Shield of Rhode Island, 883 F.2d 1101 (1st Cir.1989) involved an MFN imposed by a Blue Cross/Blue Shield plan that controlled 80% of the Rhode Island private health insurance market. When Ocean State, a new HMO, began to make significant inroads into its market, the Blue plan insisted that participating physicians grant them the same discount they granted Ocean State. Thereafter about 350 of Ocean State's 1200 participating physicians left the plan. A jury found the Blue plan guilty of violating Section 2 and of tortious interference with Ocean State's contractual relationships and awarded Ocean State $3.2 million. Citing *Kartell*, the First Circuit affirmed a judgment notwithstanding the verdict, finding that the "most favored nations" clause was a legitimate competitive strategy to assure that the Blue plan could get the lowest price for services rather than an attempt to monopolize the health insurance market. See also Blue Cross & Blue Shield of Michigan v. Michigan Association of Psychotherapy Clinics, 1980 WL 1848 (E.D.Mich.1980) (rejecting per se price fixing claim against insurer's "non-discrimination clause"); but cf., Willamette Dental Group, P.C. v. Oregon Dental Service Corp., 130 Ore. App. 487, 882 P.2d 637 (1994) (criticizing *Ocean State* and rejecting defendants' argument that an MFN can never constitute predatory pricing); Reazin v. Blue Cross and Blue Shield of Kansas, Inc., 899 F.2d 951 (10th Cir.), cert. denied, 497 U.S. 1005, 110 S.Ct. 3241, 111 L.Ed.2d 752 (1990) (MFN is evidence that insurer possessed monopoly power and MFN contributed to that power). The FTC and Department of Justice have obtained consent decrees in several recent challenges to MFN clauses. See e.g., United States v. Vision Service Plan, 1996–1 Trade Cas. (CCH) ¶ 71,404 (D.D.C. 1996) (consent decree); In re Rx Care of Tennessee, 121 F.T.C. 762 (1996) (consent order).

Most of the MFN cases have involved insurers with substantial market shares. However, in United States v. Delta Dental of Rhode Island, 943 F.Supp. 172 (D.R.I.1996), 1997–2 Trade Cas. ¶ 71,860 (1997) (consent decree), the government alleged that the defendant's MFN amounted to an illegal agreement under § 1 of the Sherman Act even though it insured only 35–45% of all persons with dental insurance in the market while having provider contracts with over 90% of all dentists. How can an MFN harm competition in such circumstances? If a health plan is not dominant in its market, what conditions are necessary before it can have an exclusionary effect on other plans by using an MFN? Note that, in addition to "raising rivals' costs," MFNs can cause several other kinds of anticompetitive harm. For example, they can facilitate collusion by eliminating the dynamic mechanisms whereby prices are effectively ratcheted down and they can "dampen competition" by reducing the aggressiveness of competitors. See Jonathan B. Baker, Vertical Restraints with Horizontal Consequences: Competitive Effects of "Most–Favored–Nations" Clauses, 64 Antitrust L.J. 517 (1996); Arnold Celnicker, A Competitive Analysis of Most Favored Nations Clauses in Contracts Between Health Care Providers and Insurers, 69 N.C. L.Rev. 863 (1991).

4. The McCarran–Ferguson Act provides a limited exemption for the "business of insurance" if the state regulates those activities and they do not constitute "boycott, coercion or intimidation." 15 U.S.C.A. §§ 1011–15. Two cases, Group Life and Health Insurance v. Royal Drug Co., 440 U.S. 205, 99 S.Ct. 1067, 59 L.Ed.2d 261 (1979) rehearing denied, 441 U.S. 917, 99 S.Ct. 2017, 60 L.Ed.2d 389 (1979) and Union Labor Life Insurance Co. v. Pireno, 458 U.S. 119, 102 S.Ct. 3002, 73 L.Ed.2d 647 (1982), have interpreted the term "business of insurance" very restrictively, limiting the meaning of that term to activities involving risk-spreading and transferring the policyholders' risk; relationships between insurers; and insureds and usually only parties in the insurance industry. This leaves many cost-containment activities of insurers subject to antitrust oversight. The Insurance Antitrust Handbook (M. Horning & R. Langsdorf, eds. 1995). At the same time, the McCarran–Ferguson Act shields a wide range of obviously anticompetitive conduct. Agreements among insurers to fix subscriber premiums or actions of a dominant insurer regarding the types of policies it will sell or the conditions attached thereto are exempt. See Royal Drug, supra; Klamath–Lake Pharmaceutical Ass'n v. Klamath Medical Service Bureau, 701 F.2d 1276 (9th Cir.1983). In Ocean State Physicians Health Plan v. Blue Cross, 883 F.2d 1101 (1st Cir.1989) the court found that the McCarran–Ferguson Act immunized defendants' marketing and pricing policies in its HMO coverage and the imposition of higher rates on employers that offered a competing HMO option. The statute has been strongly criticized and market-based health reform proposals have included provisions repealing the law. See Edward Correia, How to Reform the McCarran–Ferguson Act, 22 Mem. St. L. Rev. 43 (1991). Insurers have also enjoyed some success in arguing that certain activities mandated by state law are exempt from antitrust scrutiny under the state action doctrine. Llewellyn v. Crothers, 765 F.2d 769 (9th Cir.1985).

5. May "unfair" business practices be challenged as business torts even though they may not constitute violations of the antitrust laws? In Brokerage Concepts, Inc. v. U.S. Healthcare, Inc., 140 F.3d 494 (3d Cir.1998), the Court of Appeals overturned a jury verdict that found an antitrust violation in a case in which a prominent HMO allegedly coerced a self-insured pharmacy chain to switch third-party administrators (TPAs) which serviced the chain's employee health plan. The plaintiff claimed that the requirement that it use the defendant HMO's subsidiary as its TPA in order to remain a part of the HMO's pharmacy network constituted an illegal tying agreement or coerced reciprocal dealing under § 1 of the Sherman Act. The Third Circuit found no antitrust offense, questioning whether a sale transaction actually existed. Applying the Rule of Reason, it went on to hold that the HMO's lack of market power precluded a claim under the Sherman Act. Id. At the same time, however, the court allowed the plaintiff's claim for intentional interference with contractual or prospective contractual relations under state law to go to trial. A jury subsequently awarded the plaintiffs $105,000 on the tortuous interference charge and rejected the defense that the conduct was justified by a "business competitor's privilege." Under the charge to the jury, the latter defense would not apply where a defendant used "wrongful means" to advance its interest in competing for business (which the court defined as "taking away a competitor's business by applying economic pressure in an area that is unrelated to the field in which the parties compete"). See Contract

Disputes: U.S. Healthcare's Competitor's Privilege Defense Fails to Sway Pennsylvania Jury, 8 Health L. Rptr. (BNA), Feb. 4, 1999. On the question of whether tort law should apply a different standard than antitrust law, see Marina Lao, Tortious Interference and the Federal Antitrust Law of Vertical Restraints, 83 Iowa L. Rev. 35 (1997).

D. MERGERS AND ACQUISITIONS

1. *Hospital Mergers*

HOSPITAL CORPORATION OF AMERICA

106 F.T.C. 361 (1985).

CALVANI, COMM'R.

I. INTRODUCTION TO THE CASE

A. *The Acquisitions*

In August 1981, Respondent Hospital Corporation of America ("HCA"), the largest proprietary hospital chain in the United States, acquired Hospital Affiliates International ("HAI") in a stock transaction valued at approximately $650 million. [ ] At the time of the acquisition, HAI owned or leased 57 hospitals and managed 78 hospitals nationwide. Prior to its acquisition by HCA, HAI owned or managed five acute care hospitals in the general area of Chattanooga, Tennessee, and HCA acquired ownership or management of these hospitals through the transaction. Some four months later HCA acquired yet another hospital corporation, Health Care Corporation ("HCC"), in a stock transaction valued at approximately $30 million. At the time of the acquisition, HCC owned a single acute care hospital in Chattanooga. These two transactions provide the genesis for the instant case.

As a result of the HCA–HAI acquisition, Respondent increased its hospital operations in Chattanooga and its suburbs from ownership of one acute care hospital to ownership or management of four of the area's eleven acute care hospitals. Within the six-county Chattanooga Metropolitan Statistical Area ("Chattanooga MSA"), HCA changed its position from owner of one hospital to owner or manager of six of fourteen acute care hospitals. With the acquisition of HCC, HCA obtained yet another acute care hospital in Chattanooga. Thus, HCA became owner or manager of five of the eleven acute care hospitals within the Chattanooga urban area and seven of the fourteen in the Chattanooga MSA.

* * * Administrative Law Judge Parker found that the acquisitions violated Section 7 of the Clayton Act and Section 5 of the Federal Trade Commission Act, and ordered HCA to divest two of the hospitals of which it had acquired ownership. Judge Parker also ordered that HCA provide prior notification to the Commission of certain of its future hospital acquisitions. HCA appeals the Initial Decision on several grounds; Complaint Counsel appeal certain of Judge Parker's findings as well.

* * * We affirm Judge Parker's finding of liability and modify his opinion only as stated below.

* * *

III. THE PRODUCT MARKET

An acquisition violates Section 7 of the Clayton Act "where in any line of commerce in any section of the country, the effect of such acquisition may be substantially to lessen competition, or to tend to create a monopoly." 15 U.S.C.A. Sec. 18 (1982). Accordingly, we now turn to the definition of the relevant "line of commerce" or "product market" in which to measure the likely competitive effects of these acquisitions. In measuring likely competitive effects, we seek to define a product or group of products sufficiently distinct that buyers could not defeat an attempted exercise of market power on the part of sellers of those products by shifting purchases to still different products. Sellers might exercise market power by raising prices, limiting output or lowering quality. * * *

Complaint Counsel argued below that the product market [ ] was properly defined as the provision of acute inpatient hospital services and emergency hospital services provided to the critically ill. [ ] This definition would exclude non-hospital providers of outpatient services, e.g., free standing emergency centers, as well as non-hospital providers of inpatient services, e.g., nursing homes, from the product market. It would also exclude the outpatient business of hospitals, except for that provided to the critically ill in the emergency room. The rationale for excluding outpatient care is that inpatient services are the reason for being of acute care hospitals; inpatient services are needed by and consumed by patients in combination and therefore can be offered only by acute care hospitals. Inpatients in almost all cases will purchase a range of services and not just one test or procedure; they will typically consume a "cluster" of services involving 24–hour nursing, the services of specialized laboratory and X-ray equipment, the services of equipment needed to monitor vital functions or intervene in crises, and so forth. An acutely ill patient must be in a setting in which all of these various services can be provided together. * * * According to this reasoning, outpatient services are not an integral part of this "cluster of services" offered by acute care hospitals, and therefore must be excluded.

Respondent, on the other hand, urged that the market be defined to include outpatient care as well as inpatient care. Respondent's expert witness, Dr. Jeffrey E. Harris, testified that outpatient care is growing rapidly for hospitals, as well as for free-standing facilities such as emergency care and one-day surgery centers, which compete with hospitals for outpatients. Moreover, because of substantial changes in medical technology, there are a growing number of procedures that can be provided on an outpatient basis that previously could have been done on only an inpatient basis.

Judge Parker agreed that the market should include outpatient services provided by hospitals but excluded outpatient services provided by non-hospital providers, holding that only hospitals can provide the "unique combination" of services which the acute care patient needs. He defined the relevant product market to be the cluster of services offered by acute care hospitals, including outpatient as well as inpatient care, "since acute care hospitals compete with each other in offering both kinds of care and since ... acute care outpatient facilities feed patients to the inpatient facilities."

Neither HCA nor Complaint Counsel appeal Judge Parker's product market definition. See Commission Rule of Practice 3.52(b). Accordingly, for purposes of this proceeding only we accept Judge Parker's finding on this issue. [ ]

However, we do note that Judge Parker's definition does not necessarily provide a very happy medium between the two competing positions; the evidence in this case tended to show *both* that free-standing outpatient facilities compete with hospitals for many outpatients and that hospitals offer and inpatients consume a cluster of services that bears little relation to outpatient care. If so, it may be that defining the cluster of hospital inpatient services as a separate market better reflects competitive reality in this case. * * * Certainly, it is clear that anti-competitive behavior by hospital firms could significantly lessen competition for hospital inpatients that could not be defeated by competition from non-hospital outpatient providers. Our analysis will hence proceed with primary reference to the cluster of services provided to inpatients.

IV.   THE GEOGRAPHIC MARKET

* * * Because we are concerned only with an area in which competition could be harmed, the relevant geographic market must be broad enough that buyers would be unable to switch to alternative sellers in sufficient numbers to defeat an exercise of market power by firms in the area. Again, sellers may exercise market power by raising prices, reducing output or reducing quality. * * * If an exercise of market power could be defeated by the entry of products produced in another area, both areas should be considered part of the same geographic market for Section 7 purposes, since competition could not be harmed in the smaller area. That is, the geographic market should determine not only the firms that constrain competitors' actions by currently selling to the same customers, but also those that would be a constraint because of their ability to sell to those customers should price or quality in the area change. * * *

* * *

HCA would have us adopt Hamilton County, Tennessee, together with Walker, Dade and Catoosa counties in Georgia, the "Chattanooga urban area," as the relevant geographic market. HCA predicates its conclusion largely on an analysis of evidence concerning physician admitting patterns.

* * * With few exceptions, every physician who admitted to Chattanooga urban area hospitals admitted exclusively to other hospitals in the Chattanooga urban area. Conversely, physicians admitting and treating patients at hospitals outside the Chattanooga urban area rarely admitted and treated patients at hospitals in the Chattanooga urban area.

* * *

Additionally, the weight of the evidence concerning patient origin suggests that patients admitted to Chattanooga urban area hospitals who live outside of the Chattanooga urban area are, with few exceptions, in need of specialized care and treatment unavailable in their own communities. * * * Hospitals in outlying communities do not always provide quite the same product that the urban area hospitals provide such patients, and therefore patient inflows are not necessarily indicative of the willingness of patients to leave their home areas for services that are available in those areas. Judge

Parker agreed with HCA that the Chattanooga urban area is the relevant geographic market in this case. [ ]

On appeal, Complaint Counsel agree that the Chattanooga urban area is an appropriate geographic area in which to assess the competitive effects of these acquisitions. However, they claim that a much more appropriate geographic market is the federally designated Metropolitan Statistical Area that includes Chattanooga. In effect, Complaint Counsel would have us add the Tennessee counties of Marion and Sequatchie to the market proffered by HCA and adopted by Judge Parker. By adding this area, three additional hospitals—South Pittsburgh Municipal Hospital, Sequatchie General Hospital, and Whitwell Community Hospital—would be included in the relevant market. Both South Pittsburgh and Sequatchie were acquired by HCA from HAI, and Complaint Counsel seek divestiture by HCA of its long-term lease arrangement with South Pittsburgh. [ ]

* * *

* * * Geopolitical designations such as "MSA" may reflect a host of considerations that do not concern the issue of competition between hospitals. * * * Nor do we find any evidence that MSA designations were ever intended to reflect an economic market for purposes of Section 7. We do not here conclude that an MSA will never accurately reflect the relevant geographic market in a hospital merger case. But where, as here, the MSA designation excludes important sources of potential competition, it must be rejected. * * *

* * *

V. THE EFFECT ON COMPETITION

A. *The Effect of HCA–Managed Hospitals*

One of the major dimensions of HCA's purchase of HAI was the acquisition of some 75 to 80 hospital management contracts. * * * Two of these were management contracts HAI had with two hospitals in the Chattanooga urban area——Downtown General Hospital and Red Bank Community Hospital. * * * HCA argues, and Judge Parker agreed, that Downtown General and Red Bank hospitals should be treated as entities completely separate from HCA, incapable of being significantly influenced by HCA in its role as administrator. * * *

We conclude that treating the two managed hospitals as entities completely independent of HCA is contrary to the overwhelming weight of the evidence in this case. As manager, HCA controls the competitive variables needed for successful coordination with the activities of HCA-owned hospitals in Chattanooga. Moreover, as manager it knows the competitive posture of managed hospitals so well that the likelihood of any anti-competitive behavior HCA wished to engage in is greatly increased.

* * *

Indeed, the very reason that a management firm is hired, as reflected in the management contracts, is to direct the competitive operations of the managed hospital. The evidence shows clearly that management recommendations, including proposed rate increases, are almost invariably followed by the boards of directors of Downtown General and Red Bank. * * *

* * *

* * * The evidence compels us to consider the market shares of Downtown General and Red Bank as part of HCA's market share in considering the effect on competition in this case. [ ] Even were the evidence not as compelling, we would consider HCA's management of the two hospitals to greatly enhance the likelihood of collusion in this market. [ ]

* * *

B. The Nature of Competition Among Chattanooga Hospitals

Traditionally, hospitals have competed for patients in three general ways: first, by competing for physicians to admit their patients; second, by competing directly for patients on the basis of amenities and comfort of surroundings; and third, by competing to a limited degree on the basis of price. The first two constitute "non-price" or "quality" competition, and by far have been in the past the most important of the three.

Non-price competition for physicians includes the provision of up-to-date equipment, a qualified and reliable nursing staff and other technically trained personnel, convenient office space to make it easier for the physician to concentrate both his ambulatory and inpatient work within the same location, a nice doctors' lounge with a good selection of journals—everything that will convince physicians that their patients are receiving the best care possible and make physicians' lives more comfortable. Competition directed at patients themselves has traditionally been through the provision of amenities, such as pleasant surroundings, attractive rooms, televisions and telephones, high nurse-to-patient ratios, convenient parking—everything that will make patients more comfortable.

* * *

Over the last decade, two major trends increasing competition among hospitals beyond its traditional limits have developed. First, both non-price and price competition are now being directed much more toward patients themselves than in the past. Second, beginning in the late 1970s the hospital industry has seen the clear emergence of direct price competition. At the same time, traditional non-price competition for patients on the basis of amenities has intensified somewhat, through the provision of such amenities as private rooms. Non-price competition for physicians remains pervasive, since physicians still largely determine the disposition and treatment of their patients.

* * *

* * * [The] increasing concern of employers and employees with the costs of insurance means that differences in prices between hospitals matter to them and their third-party payors, since insurance will cost less when hospital care costs less. The result is that hospitals are now far more likely to present themselves to insurers, employers and employee groups as less costly than their competitors as one method of attracting more business. Price competi-

tion, fostered by these new insurance mechanisms, is therefore growing in the hospital industry.

* * *

Thus, it is obvious that price has been a competitively sensitive matter among Chattanooga hospitals. We do not here conclude that price has been the prime arena in which hospitals in Chattanooga compete. However, we do think it clear that even though rates are not constantly adjusted due to a changing price structure, they have been periodically set with some reference to what the market will bear in face of the prices of other hospitals.

It is clear that Section 7 protects whatever price competition exists in a market, however limited. * * *

* * *

C. Respondent's Market Share and Concentration in the Chattanooga Urban Area

Three ways to measure a hospital's share of the acute care hospital services market are by using: (1) bed capacity; (2) inpatient days; and (3) net revenues. Bed capacity and inpatient days measure a hospital's position with regard to the cluster of inpatient services, the heart of hospital care. Net revenues, on the other hand, account for both inpatient and outpatient services.

Naturally, because of their proposed market definitions, Complaint Counsel advocate use of inpatient measures, while HCA urges net revenues as the preferable measure since it accounts for outpatient services. We conclude, however, that the three measures are so similar in this case that they yield the same result whatever measure is used.

* * *

The Herfindahl–Hirschman Index ("HHI") of market concentration is calculated by summing the squares of the individual market shares of all the firms in the market. The HHI reflects the distribution of market shares between firms and gives proportionately greater weight to the market shares of the larger firms, which likely accords with their relative importance in any anti-competitive interaction. * * * [U]sing any measure of market power the Herfindahl index was above 1900 before the acquisitions. Thus, the acquisitions occurred in a market already highly concentrated. * * * Following HCA's acquisition of HAI, the HHI increased some 295 points using net patient revenues and over 300 using beds or patient days. With the acquisition of HCC, the HHI additionally increased well over 100 points using any measure. Again using any measure, the HHI at the very least rests at 2416 after the acquisitions. We consider such an increase in concentration in an already concentrated market to be of serious competitive concern, all other things being equal. * * * [ ]

More traditional measures of market share also support this conclusion. For example, using patient days HCA's market share increased from 13.8% to 25.8% in the Chattanooga urban area, while four-firm concentration increased to almost 92% and two-firm concentration to 61%. The figures for approved beds and net patient revenues are almost identical. These figures support an inference of harm to competition, all other things equal. * * * [ ]

Moreover, all other things being equal, an increase in market concentration through a reduction in the absolute number of competitive actors makes interdependent behavior more likely. * * * These acquisitions decreased the number of independent firms in the market from 9 to 7. [ ] The costs of coordination or of policing any collusive agreement are less with fewer participants, and the elimination of competitive forces in this market facilitates joint anti-competitive behavior.

In sum, evidence of the increased concentration caused by these acquisitions points toward a finding of likely harm to competition, all other things being equal. [ ] HCA's acquisitions have made an already highly concentrated market more conducive to collusion by eliminating two of the healthiest sources of competition in the market and increasing concentration substantially. But all other things are not equal in this market, and statistical evidence is not the end of our inquiry. In the absence of barriers to entry, an exercise of market power can be defeated or deterred by the entry or potential entry of new firms regardless of the structure of the existing market.* * * We now turn to the issue of entry barriers and conclude that they confirm and even magnify the inference to be drawn from the concentration evidence in this case.

D. Barriers to Entry

* * *

* * * [T]here is hardly free entry into the acute care hospital industry in either Tennessee or Georgia. Indeed, the CON [certificate of need] laws at issue here create a classic "barrier to entry" under every definition of that term. In *Echlin Manufacturing Co.*, we defined a "barrier to entry" to include "additional long-run costs that must be incurred by an entrant relative to the long-run costs faced by incumbent firms." * * * We explained that "[t]he rationale underlying this definition is that low-cost incumbent firms can keep prices above the competitive level as long as those prices remain below the level that would provide an incentive to higher-cost potential entrants."

If a potential entrant desires to build a new hospital in Chattanooga, he must incur all the costs in time and money associated with obtaining a CON. The cost of starting a new hospital includes not only the start-up costs that any firm would incur to enter the market but also the costs of surviving the administrative process. Incumbents in this market, however, did not incur such costs during initial construction. They have only had to incur those costs for additions made to bed capacity since the enactment of the CON laws a decade ago. [ ] Incumbents thus have a long run cost advantage over potential entrants. The result is that market power could be exercised by incumbents without attracting attempts at entry as long as supracompetitive profits are not high enough for a potential entrant to justify incurring all the ordinary costs of starting a hospital *plus* the significant costs of obtaining a CON.

The evidence is clear that those costs are significant in this market. We agree with Judge Parker that because incumbent hospitals can oppose new entry, even an unsuccessful opposition to a CON application may delay its disposition by several years. * * *

Thus the CON process provides existing hospitals in the Chattanooga urban area ample opportunity to significantly forestall the entry of a new hospital or the expansion of an existing hospital within the area. Indeed, the evidence shows that existing hospitals frequently oppose CON applications when they feel competitively threatened. * * *

* * *

In sum, it is not merely the costs of obtaining a CON that a potential entrant faces, but the significant risk of being denied entry once those costs have been incurred. This risk, which incumbents did not have to face when building their hospitals, in effect raises the costs of entry a significantly greater amount. As a result, many potential entrants may decide not to even attempt entry. Indeed, the evidence shows that CON regulation has had a deterrent effect in the Chattanooga market.

* * *

E. The Nature and Likelihood of Anti-competitive Behavior in the Chattanooga Hospital Market

1. The Nature of Anti-competitive Behavior

* * *

Some of the most likely forms of collusion between hospitals would involve collective resistance to emerging cost containment pressures from third-party payors and alternative providers. For example, joint refusals to deal with HMOs or PPOs may occur, or perhaps joint refusals to deal on the most favorable terms. Conspiracies to boycott certain insurance companies that are generating price competition may occur. Utilization review programs may also be resisted. Hospitals could concertedly refuse to provide the information desired by third-party payors—information that would otherwise be provided as hospitals vie to attract the business of those payors and their subscribers. The result of any such boycott would be to raise prices, reduce quality of services or both. [ ]

* * *

Quality competition itself might also be restricted. For example, the group of hospitals in a relevant market might agree to staff their wards with fewer nurses yet continue to maintain current rates for inpatient services. Patients would be harmed by the resulting drop in quality of services without any compensating reduction in price of services. Colluding hospitals in the market, however, would profit from their agreement by cutting costs without cutting revenues. Again, hospitals could accomplish anti-competitive ends not only by fixing staff-patient ratios but by agreeing on wages or benefits to be paid certain personnel—for example, laboratory technicians. Indeed, wage and salary surveys are common in this market. The result would be the same—to hold the cost of inputs down with probable harm to the quality of output of health care services. [ ] Hospitals could also agree not to compete for each other's personnel or medical staff. Indeed, some Chattanooga urban area hospital firms have already engaged in such behavior.

Moreover, under certificate of need legislation, the addition of new services and purchases of certain kinds of new equipment require a demonstration of need for the expenditure, and the existence of need is determined in part by the facilities already provided in the community. It would thus be to the advantage of competing hospitals to enter into agreements among themselves as to which competitor will apply for which service or for which piece of equipment. * * * Such market division by private agreement would save hospitals the expense of applying for numerous CONs but may harm the quality of care that would be available to patients were CON approval sought independently by each hospital with reference to its own merits and expertise.

Concerted opposition to the CON application of a potential new entrant is yet another manner in which Chattanooga hospitals could successfully collude. * * *

Anti-competitive pricing behavior could also take several forms. For example, hospitals could work out agreements with respect to pricing formulas. * * * Hospitals could also successfully collude with respect to price by agreeing not to give discounts to businesses, insurers and other group purchasers such as HMOs and PPOs. * * *

In sum, we conclude that hospitals compete in a myriad of ways that could be restricted anti-competitively through collusion. [ ] Thus, it appears that a merger analysis in this case need be no different than in any other case; market share and concentration figures, evidence of entry barriers and other market evidence taken together appear to yield as accurate a picture of competitive conditions as they do in other settings. Nevertheless, although HCA concedes that many of the above described forms of collusion *could* occur, the heart of HCA's case is that collusion in this market is inherently unlikely, and to that contention we now turn.

2. The Likelihood of Anti-competitive Behavior

Section 7 of the Clayton Act prohibits acquisitions that may have the effect of substantially lessening competition or tending to create a monopoly. Because Section 7 applies to "incipient" violations, actual anti-competitive effects need not be shown; an acquisition is unlawful if such an effect is reasonably probable. * * *

The small absolute number of competitors in this market, the high concentration and the extremely high entry barriers indicate a market in which anti-competitive behavior is reasonably probable after the acquisitions. The fact that industry members recognize the enormity of entry barriers makes collusion even more probable. In addition, hospital markets have certain features that evidence a likelihood of collusion or other anti-competitive behavior when they become highly concentrated.

First, price elasticity of demand for hospital services is very low, which makes anti-competitive behavior extremely profitable and hence attractive. * * * Second, because consumers of hospital services cannot arbitrage or resell them as is often possible with goods, discrimination among different groups of consumers is possible. That is, collusion may be directed at a certain group or certain groups of consumers, such as a particular insurance company, without the necessity of anti-competitive behavior toward other groups. Third, the traditions of limited price competition and disapproval of advertising provide an incentive for future anti-competitive restrictions of those activities. Fourth, and in the same vein, the advent of incentives to resist new cost containment pressures may create a substantial danger of hospital collusion to meet pressures. Fifth, the hospital industry has a tradition of cooperative problem solving which makes collusive conduct in the future more likely. Hospitals have historically participated in voluntary health planning in a coordinated manner, and along with other professional organizations, such as medical societies, have participated in developing joint solutions to industry problems.

* * * The most convincing evidence of the facility with which such collusion could occur is a blatant market allocation agreement executed in 1981 between Red Bank Community Hospital and HCC. The parties actually *signed a contract* under which Red Bank agreed that for a period of three years it would not "file any application for a Certificate of Need for psychiatric facilities or nursing home facilities." Moreover, the parties agreed that they would not compete for each other's personnel and medical staff during that time period, and that they would not oppose each other's CON applications in certain areas. Such an overt agreement to refrain from competition at the very least demonstrates the predisposition of some firms in the market to collude when it is in their interest; at worst it shows a callous disregard for the antitrust laws. [ ]

* * *

Furthermore, a basis for collusion is provided by the exchanges of rate, salary and other competitively sensitive information that occur in this market. * * *

* * *

* * * It is true that the undisputed evidence shows that more vigorous competition, including more direct price competition, is emerging in the health care industry, but it is a fallacy to conclude that growing competition in health care markets means that these acquisitions pose no threat to that competition. In fact, it is just that emerging competition that must be protected from mergers that facilitate the suppression of such competition. * * *

a. Non-profit Hospitals and the Likelihood of Collusion

HCA contends that the most fundamental difference between hospitals in Chattanooga is that several of the hospitals are "non-profit" institutions. Economic theory presumes that businesses in an industry are profit-maximizers and that output will be restricted in pursuit of profits. Non-profit hospitals, the argument goes, have no incentive to maximize profits, rather, they seek to maximize "output" or the number of patients treated. HCA contends that non-profit hospitals may have other goals as well, such as providing the most sophisticated and highest quality care possible, or pursuing religious or governmental goals. In short, HCA argues that collusion would not occur because the "for-profit" and "non-profit" competitors have no common goal.

We disagree that non-profit hospitals have no incentive to collude with each other or with proprietary hospitals to achieve anti-competitive ends.

First, we note that non-profit status of market participants is no guarantee of competitive behavior. * * *

* * *

In addition, administrators of non-profit hospitals may seek to maximize their personal benefits and comfort through what would otherwise be known as profit-seeking activity. * * *

* * *

[T]wo major non-profit hospitals, Erlanger and Tri–County, have a tremendous incentive to participate in price collusion. Erlanger has sole responsibility for unreimbursed indigent care in Hamilton County. * * * Because it must subsidize unreimbursed care out of the rates charged to paying customers, Erlanger cannot compete effectively through price cutting. Erlanger's rates are 50 dollars per day *or 10%* higher than they would be if such cross-subsidization between paying and non-paying patients were not necessary. Because it cannot price below a level that covers the direct costs it incurs for indigent care, Erlanger would in fact benefit from a decrease in price competition through interdependent behavior. The same analysis applies to Tri–County, which must provide care for indigent residents of Walker, Dade and Catoosa counties in Georgia, and shift costs from non-paying to paying patients. * * *

* * *

b. *Purported Obstacles to Successful Coordination*

Relying entirely upon the testimony of its expert, Dr. Harris, HCA argues that even if hospitals in Chattanooga were inclined to collude, the administrators of those hospitals would find it difficult to reach anti-competitive agreements or understandings, or to sustain them if they ever were reached. This is so because the ideal market circumstances for collusion are not present, i.e. where manufacturers are selling "some simple, relatively homogeneous good, well characterized by a single price." HCA contends that hospital services are heterogeneous and influenced by a variety of complicating factors. Hospitals provide a large number of varied medical tests and treatments and each patient receives unpredictable personalized service the extent of which is determined by physicians. Moreover, HCA claims costs and demand vary between hospitals. And because the dominant avenues of competition relate to the quality of medical care and patient amenities, hospitals would have to agree on a whole host of things to eliminate competition in a manner sufficient to earn monopoly returns, it is alleged.

* * *

HCA's analysis of the likelihood of collusion distorts competitive reality. HCA would have us believe that the world of possible collusion is limited to complicated formulae concerning every aspect of hospital competition——that market power can only be exercised with respect to the entire cluster of services that constitutes the acute care hospital market through a conspiracy fixing the overall quantity or quality of treatment running to each patient in the market. Rather than focus on the likely avenues of collusion among hospitals, HCA assumes into existence a world in which collusion is infeasible.

* * *

HCA offers an additional reason why the acquisitions allegedly create no risk that Chattanooga hospitals will collude to eliminate price competition, arguing that price collusion is unlikely because of the role of Blue Cross in this market. * * *

We cannot accept HCA's claims that Blue Cross has both the omniscience and market power to halt successful collusion by Chattanooga hospitals. First, under the current Blue Cross charge approval system, collusion could be difficult to detect. If all the hospital firms in Chattanooga attempt to raise prices a similar amount in the review process, coordinated pricing could be overlooked; there is no *a priori* reason why Blue Cross would consider this to be the result of collusion rather than a rise in costs. * * *

Furthermore, even if detected, we do not think such collusion could be easily deterred by Blue Cross. HCA ignores the fact that Blue Cross has a contract not only with participating hospitals but also with its subscribers. Blue Cross must serve its subscribers in the Chattanooga area, and HCA does not explain how Blue Cross could reject a concerted effort by the hospitals there even if it wanted to; certainly, Blue Cross could not ask its subscribers to all go to Knoxville for hospital care if Chattanooga urban area hospitals colluded. * * *

* * *

VII. CONCLUSION

We hold that HCA's acquisitions of HAI and HCC may substantially lessen competition in the Chattanooga urban area acute care hospital market in violation of Section 7 of the Clayton Act and Section 5 of the Federal Trade Commission Act.

Notes and Questions

1. The Seventh Circuit reviewed and upheld the decision of the Federal Trade Commission in Hospital Corporation of America v. FTC, 807 F.2d 1381 (7th Cir.1986). Calling the FTC's decision a "model of lucidity," Judge Posner reviewed the Commission's analysis of the merger:

> When an economic approach is taken in a section 7 case, the ultimate issue is whether the challenged acquisition is likely to facilitate collusion. In this perspective the acquisition of a competitor has no economic significance in itself; the worry is that it may enable the acquiring firm to cooperate (or cooperate better) with other leading competitors on reducing or limiting output, thereby pushing up the market price. *Hospital Corporation* calls the issue whether an acquisition is likely to have such an effect "economic," which of course it is. But for purposes of judicial review, as we have said, it is a factual issue subject to the substantial evidence rule. * * *

* * *

Considering the concentration of the market, the absence of competitive alternatives, the regulatory barrier to entry (the certificate of need law), the low elasticity of demand, the exceptionally severe cost pressures under which American hospitals labor today, the history of collusion in the industry, and the sharp reduction in the number of substantial competitors in this market brought about by the acquisition of four hospitals in a city with only eleven (one already owned by *Hospital Corporation*), we cannot say that the Commission's prediction [of a danger to competition] is not supported by substantial evidence.

Judge Posner discussed HCA's arguments that collusion is unlikely because of the heterogeneity of hospital markets, the rapid technological and economic change experienced by the hospital industry, and the size of third party payers. Judge Posner concluded: "Most of these facts do detract from a conclusion that collusion in this market is a serious danger, but it was for the Commission—it is not for us—to determine their weight." For an explication of the overall methodology followed by the federal enforcement agencies in evaluating mergers see U.S. Department of Justice and Federal Trade Commission, Merger Guidelines (1992), 57 Fed. Reg. 41552 (Sept. 10, 1992).

2. Following *Hospital Corporation*, the Department of Justice and the FTC won almost all of their litigated cases and obtained a large number of consent decrees barring other attempted hospital mergers. See, e.g., United States v. Rockford Memorial Corp., 898 F.2d 1278 (7th Cir.1990), cert. denied, 498 U.S. 920, 111 S.Ct. 295, 112 L.Ed.2d 249 (1990); FTC v. University Health, Inc., 938 F.2d 1206 (11th Cir.1991); Health Trust Inc., FTC No. 941–0020 (June 14, 1994) (consent order requiring divestiture of hospital and other assets); but see United States v. Carilion Health System, 707 F.Supp. 840, aff'd without opinion 892 F.2d 1042 (4th Cir.1989). Virtually all of these cases involved relatively small communities in which only a handful of hospitals competed in relatively isolated markets. As discussed below, however, defendants have prevailed in a series of hospital merger cases and have raised important questions regarding the nature and quantity of proof required to establish a violation of Section 7 of the Clayton Act.

3. *Geographic Markets.* An essential first step in merger analysis is to identify economically meaningful markets. The dimensions of the product and geographic markets define the universe within which merging parties compete and thus determine the parties' market shares. Hence, these issues are of central importance to the outcome of most cases and, needless to say, are usually hotly contested. The geographic market determination turns on the question of where customers could practicably turn in the event that competitors attempted to raise prices. See generally, United States v. Philadelphia National Bank, 374 U.S. 321, 83 S.Ct. 1715, 10 L.Ed.2d 915 (1963); Merger Guidelines § 1.2. In the context of hospital mergers, patient origin data (usually compiled using the zip code of the residence of each patient) provides a useful starting point by identifying the inflow and outflow of patients to hospitals within a geographic region. This data, however, cannot supply a final answer to the geographic market definition question. Courts must ask where buyers (patients) or their health plans or employers would turn in the event of a price increase resulting from the merger. Given the prevalence of managed care contracting, what evidence would you put forward to satisfy the government's burden of proving the boundaries of the geographic market? Specifically, what witnesses would you call and what data or other proof would you offer to establish the potential responses of buyers in a market to potential price increases?

In four recent cases, defendants have successfully asserted that the government's "static" proof has fallen short given the "dynamic" issue involved and the changing nature of the health care market. In Federal Trade Commission v. Freeman Hospital, 69 F.3d 260 (8th Cir.1995), the Eighth Circuit upheld the district court's denial of a preliminary injunction sought by the FTC to stop the merger of two of three hospitals located in Joplin, Missouri. The Court held that the FTC had not adequately proved its geographic market (alleged to extend to a 26–mile radius from Joplin) because its patient origin data did not address the "decisive question of where consumers could practically go for alternative [hospital] services . . . [and] provided no insight into the future effects of the allegedly anti-competitive merger of the hospitals." Id. at 270–71. Of particular concern to the court was the in-migration of patients from distant rural areas. Although the FTC sought to explain this phenomenon by claiming that the patients willing to travel considerable distances were seeking more sophisticated, specialized services, the court found the government's proof on this point inadequate. At the same time, the court downplayed the testimony of employers and health plans that few of the hospitals' in-migrating patients would travel to hospitals located outside of the FTC's proposed market even if the merged hospitals were to institute a price increase. In FTC and State of Missouri v. Tenet Health Care Corp., 186 F.3d 1045 (8th Cir.1999), the Eighth Circuit reversed the district court's finding that competition between the merging hospitals was limited to a geographic area extending approximately thirty miles from the location of the merging hospitals. The court again discounted the almost unanimous view of payers and employers that a price increase would not induce them to steer patients to more distant hospitals, a fact supported by evidence that hospital prices in the next most plausible market were considerably higher. It concluded that the government had failed to negate the possibility that a small "critical loss" of patients from towns at the fringe of the government's market would make price increases impossible and that it had failed to account for quality differences that would offset higher prices in adjacent markets. In United States v. Mercy Health Services, 902 F.Supp. 968 (N.D.Iowa, 1995), the district court accepted defendants' contention that the geographic market for inpatient acute care services extended as far as 70–100 miles. Again, despite considerable evidence of managed care organizations' unwillingness to negotiate contracts with distant hospitals, the court found the government had failed to incorporate a sufficiently "dynamic" approach because it had not adequately addressed how patients might respond to financial incentives to travel greater distances than they do under current market conditions. Finally, in California v. Sutter Health System, 84 F. Supp. 2d 1057 (N.D.Cal.2000), the district court rejected the state's proposed geographic market for a merger of hospitals located in Berkeley and Oakland, California. The court declined to confine the relevant market to the East Bay area, placing heavy emphasis on proof of patients' mobility to San Francisco and other areas for acute care service (noting that one in seven patients residing in the inner East Bay already leave the area for hospital care) and discounting testimony of managed care administrators and demographic evidence.

In the face of these decisions, can you envision the government successfully bringing suit to enjoin a hospital merger? What combination of hospitals in your own community would test the limits of these holdings: that is, at what point would residents not agree to contract with managed care organizations that "steered" them to more distant hospitals? Would sizeable discounts in co-payments for hospital care induce such switching? For a thoughtful economic analysis suggesting that courts have failed to recognize that distinct geographic markets exist for enlisting hospitals into managed care networks and for attracting patients whether in network or not, see Gregory S. Vistnes, Hospitals, Mergers and Two–Stage Competition, 67 Antitrust L.J. 671 (2000). Given the courts' propensity to conclude that managed care companies will effectively steer patients to more distant hospitals if a merger results in the exercise of market power, the economic evidence regarding such behavior may prove critical in future cases.

4. *Product Markets.* Note that the enforcement agencies, affirmed by the courts, have identified as the relevant product market in hospital merger cases a "cluster market" consisting of most inpatient services and some outpatient services for which there are no practical alternatives. See *Rockford,* supra. Again, however, given the dynamic nature of health care marketplace, the core cluster of inpatient services is rapidly shrinking, as many services formerly performed in a hospital are now routinely performed in outpatient surgery centers, physicians offices, and other facilities. How might this affect product market definition in the future? Can an argument be made that hospital's pricing of inpatient services is "linked" to their pricing of outpatient care in which they face competition from physicians, stand-alone facilities and other providers? If so, what are the implications for the dimensions of the geographic market? See Santa Cruz Medical Clinic v. Dominican Santa Cruz Hospital, 1995–2 Trade Cas. (CCH) ¶ 71,254 (N.D. Cal. 1995). Note also, that in some circumstances there might be a separate market for outpatient services that includes *both* hospital and non-hospital outpatient surgical facilities. See, e.g., Columbia/HCA Healthcare Corporation, Prohibited Trade Practices, and Affirmative Corrective Actions, 60 Fed Reg. 464 (January 4, 1995) (consent order).

Another factor complicating product market definition is the fact that the numerous services in the "cluster" have widely differing geographic market dimensions. For some sophisticated tertiary care services like organ transplants, the geographic market is certainly regional or perhaps national, while the markets for emergency care and many routine acute care services are obviously very local. Might it, therefore, be necessary to refine the analysis further by delineating those portions of the product market which are predominantly local and not subject to substitution by distant hospitals? Should each DRG be a separate product market? See, *Freeman Hospital* supra; FTC v. Butterworth Health Corp., 946 F.Supp. 1285 (W.D.Mich.1996). See also FTC v. Cardinal Health, Inc., 12 F. Supp. 2d 34 (D.D.C.1998) in which a district court enjoined two mergers involving wholesale drug distributors. The court rejected defendants' argument that the relevant market should include self-distribution by large pharmaceutical chains that purchased and warehoused their own pharmaceuticals directly from manufacturers.

Antitrust enforcement has reached mergers involving numerous other segments of the health care industry besides hospitals. For example, state and federal enforcers have challenged mergers of physician groups (Maine v. Cardiovascular & Thoracic Assocs., P.A., 1992–2 Trade Cas. (CCH) ¶ 69,985 (Maine Sup. Ct., Kennebec Cnty., 1992) (consent decree)); Maine v. Mid Coast Anesthesia, P.A., 1991–2) Trade Cas. (CCH) ¶ 69,683 (Maine Sup. Ct., Kennebec Cty., 1992) (consent decree)), and Letter from Charles F. Rule, Assistant Attorney General, Antitrust Division, to William L. Trombetta (Aug. 28, 1987) (Business Review Letter to Danbury Surgical Associates)); rehabilitation hospitals (Healthsouth Rehabilitation Corp., 60 Fed. Reg. 5,401–01 (Dept. of Justice, 1994) (consent order); hospitals providing inpatient psychiatric care (Charter Medical and National Medical Enterprises, 59 Fed. Reg. 60,804–01 (Dept. of Justice, 1994)); skilled nursing facilities (United States v. Beverly Enterprises, 1984–1 Trade Cas. (CCH) ¶ 66,052 (M.D. Ga. 1984) (consent decree)); retail pharmacy services (THC Corp., 59 Fed. Reg. 46,438 (Dept. of Justice, 1994); and HMOs, (In the Matter of Harvard Community Health Plan, Inc. and Pilgrim Health Care, Inc., No. 95–0331 (Suffolk

Superior Ct. Mass. 1995)); and an "innovation market" in gene therapy techniques (Ciba–Geigy Ltd., 62 Fed. Reg. 409 (1997) (consent decree). Market definition poses difficult questions in these cases. For example, how would you go about determining the geographic market for skilled nursing home services? Who is the "buyer" of these services? What would be the relevant product market in a merger involving two specialty groups composed of board-certified cardiologists? Should chain pharmacies constitute a separate product market (i.e., excluding small individually-owned pharmacies)? Do HMOs constitute a separate product market? Managed care plans? (See discussion of managed care mergers and physician mergers at the end of this chapter).

5. *Overcoming the Presumption of Illegality: Nonprofit Status and Other Factors.* If the government establishes a prima facie case of illegality based on market share and market concentration date, defendants may overcome that presumption by showing that the merger is not likely to have anticompetitive effects. They may do this by proving that market conditions or special characteristics of the merging firms make it unlikely that they will exercise market power after the merger is consummated. See Merger Guidelines, § 2; 2 Furrow, et al., Health Law § 14–58. Although a number of courts have refused to find that the not-for-profit status of the merging hospitals constitutes sufficient grounds to rebut the government's prima facie case, see, e.g., U.S. v. Rockford Memorial, 898 F.2d at 1286, a district court recently closely examined the issue with novel results. In FTC v. Butterworth Health Corporation and Blodgett Memorial Medical Center, 946 F.Supp. 1285 (W.D.Mich.1996), aff'd 121 F.3d 708 (6th Cir.1997) the court found that not-for-profit hospitals do not operate in the same manner as profit maximizing businesses, especially when their boards of directors are comprised of community business leaders who have a direct stake in maintaining high quality, low cost hospitals. Do you agree that such hospitals are, as the court suggested, more likely to behave as "consumer cooperatives" rather than as profit maximizers? What assumptions does this finding make about the role of board members in directing the affairs of a hospital? What limits are placed on them by their fiduciary duties as board members? In this connection, the district court also relied on a number of voluntary "community commitments" made by the merging hospitals, including a freeze on prices or charges, commitments to limit profit margins, and promises to serve the medically needy. Do such assurances provide a sufficient guarantee that the parties will not exercise market power? See 2 Furrow, et al., Health Law § 14–58c; Amanda J. Vaughn, The Use of the Nonprofit "Defense" Under Section of the Clayton Act, 52 Vand. L. Rev. 557 (1999). For an attempt to look back at whether the merger in the Butterworth case actually caused competitive harms despite the restrictions imposed by the court, see David Baltos and Maleah Geertsma, Hospital Merger Retrospective: Blodgett-Butterworth, Grand Rapids, Michigan, 34 J. Health L. 129 (2001).

Other factors sometimes advanced to rebut the presumption of illegality include the financial weakness of one of the merging firms and the relative strength of buyers in the market. Entities claiming protection under the "failing firm" defense face high proof burdens, see Merger Guidelines § 5.1, but the defense was successfully asserted in California v. Sutter Health System, 84 F. Supp. 2d 1057 (N.D.Cal.2000). Courts have been even more reluctant to consider as a mitigating factor situations in which a hospital is not actually failing, but is in financial distress (the so-called "flailing firm defense"). See, e.g., FTC and State of Missouri v. Tenet Healthcare Corp., 17 F. Supp. 2d 937 (E.D.Mo.1998), rev'd on other grounds, 186 F.3d 1085 (8th Cir.1999). In FTC v. Cardinal Health, Inc., supra, the court carefully analyzed the defendants' rebuttal claims that ease of entry into the wholesale drug distribution market should obviate competitive concerns. The court found that, despite a few examples of successful entry by new drug wholesalers, the defendants had failed to demonstrate that significant and effective entry was likely given various barriers that had impeded or slowed new competitors' effectiveness in the market. 12 F. Supp. 2d at 56–59. The court also rejected the defendants' claim that powerful buyers would likely offset the defendants' market power. Id. at 59–60.

6. *Efficiencies.* The law on efficiencies as a defense to an otherwise anticompetitive merger is somewhat unclear. Although Supreme Court case law and the legislative history of the Clayton Act does not seem to support an efficiencies defense, see Alan A. Fisher & Robert Lande, Efficiency Considerations in Merger Enforcement, 71 Cal. L.Rev. 1580 (1983), a number of lower courts have explicitly considered potential cost-savings and other efficiencies associated with mergers both as an absolute defense and as a factor to be considered in evaluating the merger's likely competitive effects. See, e.g., FTC v. University Health, Inc., 938 F.2d 1206 (11th Cir.1991). The federal enforcement agencies also recognize the efficiencies defense as a factor they consider in deciding whether to challenge a merger, but require that the parties show that the efficiencies cannot be realized by means short of a merger. Merger Guidelines, § 4. Defendants in hospital merger cases have for the most part been unable to demonstrate that the claimed efficiencies were of sufficient magnitude to offset anticompetitive harms and were not attainable through other means (such as through less anticompetitive mergers or joint ventures with other hospitals). FTC v. University Health, 938 F.2d at 1222–3; United States v. Rockford Mem. Hospital, 717 F.Supp. at 1289; but see FTC v. Butterworth Health Corporation, supra (approving merger based in part on savings from capital expenditure avoidance and operating efficiencies; pass-on of savings to consumers assured by community commitment entered into by hospitals).

7. *Safety Zone.* The Department of Justice/FTC Policy Statements provide a "safety zone" for mergers of general acute care hospitals where one of the merging hospitals has fewer than 100 beds, has an inpatient census of fewer than 40 patients per day, and is more than five years old. Given that the minimum efficient scale of an acute care hospital is 200 or more beds, how effectively does this provision address concerns about the ability of small hospitals to cope with the reorganization of the health care industry? On the other hand, might the safety zone be criticized as being too permissive, i.e., permitting anticompetitive transactions without regard to their impact on consumers? See Policy Statements, Dissenting Statement of Commissioner Mary L. Azcuenaga, 4 Antitrust Trade Reg. Rep. ¶ 12,104. Further, don't many rural hospitals and specialized hospital services markets have the characteristics of a natural monopoly? If so is public utility rate regulation preferable to antitrust scrutiny? See Dayna B. Matthew, Doing What Comes Naturally: Antitrust Law and Hospital Mergers, 31 Hou. L. Rev. 813 (1994).

8. *Relief and Settlement.* A joint venture with a rival hospital may in some cases constitute a less anticompetitive alternative than an outright merger. Can you see why? In United States and State of Florida v. Morton Plant Health Systems, Inc., 59 Fed. Reg. 49,996–02 (Dept. of Justice 1994), a consent decree settling a challenge to a hospital merger permitted two hospitals to form a joint venture to provide certain tertiary care services such as open-heart surgery; outpatient services capable of being provided outside general acute care hospitals; certain high-tech procedures; and administrative and information services. The consent decree prohibited the hospitals from combining their operations in the

provision of other acute care services and from bidding jointly for managed care contracts. Can you justify this settlement in terms of the relevant product and geographic markets and the potential efficiencies that may be realized by the hospitals? How might a joint venture for administrative and information services differ from the long-term management contracts discussed in *HCA*?

A number of state attorneys general have settled antitrust challenges to hospital mergers and other affiliations by allowing the merger to go forward subject to various commitments and payments by the hospitals. For example, in Commonwealth of Pennsylvania v. Capital Health System Services, 1995–2 Trade Cas. (CCH) ¶ 71,205 (M.D. Pa. 1995)(consent decree), the Pennsylvania Attorney General entered into a consent decree approving the merger of two Harrisburg, Pennsylvania hospitals subject to the condition that they pass on to the community $56 million (of a projected $70 million in cost savings attributable to the merger) in the form of various free or low cost services such as child immunization, mammograms and substance abuse programs. In addition, the merged hospitals agreed to hold price increases for five years to changes in the Consumer Price Index plus two percent. What are the advantages and disadvantages of entering into "regulatory" consent decrees of this kind? Is the public better served than by employing the conventional relief afforded in antitrust merger cases, namely an injunction prohibiting the merger?

2. *Managed Care Mergers*

The health insurance industry has witnessed a rapid succession of major mergers. In the years 1993 to 1998, a dozen health insurers were acquired by the six principal remaining companies: Aetna, Cigna, United Healthcare, Foundation Health Systems, Pacificare and Wellpoint Health Networks. The most recent and largest acquisition is Aetna's buyout of Prudential Health Care, which was the subject of a proposed consent decree filed jointly by the U.S. Department of Justice and the Texas Attorney General's Office. U.S. and State of Texas v. Aetna Inc., No. 3–99 CV 1398–H (N.D.Tex.), 64 Fed. Reg. 44946–01 (1999). As a condition of obtaining approval of the merger, the decree requires that Aetna divest certain HMOs operated by a subsidiary in Texas. The government's complaint contended that the proposed merger would have made Aetna the dominant provider of health maintenance organization and HMO-point of service plans in Houston and Dallas, with 63 percent and 42 percent of enrollees in those areas. Is a product market consisting only of HMO and HMO–POS plans defensible? What factual issues might have been raised by defendants had this case gone to trial? What evidence and testimony would the government have relied upon? Review the First Circuit's decision in U.S. Healthcare v. Healthsource, Inc. (page 1077 of the casebook) in formulating your responses to these questions.

As an alternative theory of harm, the government alleged that the market would reduce competition in the market for physician services. The complaint states, "the proposed acquisition will give Aetna the ability to depress physicians' reimbursement rates in Houston and Dallas, likely leading to a reduction in quantity or degradation in quality of physicians' services." Assuming that physicians in the relevant markets are reimbursed by non-HMO and HMO POS plans (including Medicare and Medicaid) and that such reimbursement constitutes, say, three-quarters of total reimbursements in the markets, how might the government prove its theory of competitive harm? For a critical analyses of the government's theory in this case, see Robert E. Bloch, Scott P. Perlman & Lawrence Wu,

A New And Uncertain Future For Managed Care Mergers: an Antitrust Analysis of The Aetna/Prudental Merger, Antitrust Rep. 37 (Dec. 1999); Thomas L. Greaney, Antitrust and the Healthcare Industry: The View from the Three Branches, 32 J.Health L. 391 (1999). The government's economic analysis is set forth in Marius Schwartz, Buyer Power Concentration and the Aetna–Prudential Merger (Oct. 20, 1999) (available at http://www.usdoj.gov/atr/public/speeches.)

3. *Physician Mergers*

Rapid consolidation among providers has focused antitrust attention on physician mergers. In the only case thus far decided by the courts, HTI Health Services v. Quorum Health Group, 960 F.Supp. 1104 (S.D.Miss.1997), the district court refused to enjoin a merger of the two largest physician clinics in Vicksburg, Mississippi with one of two hospitals in town. Notably, the court held that plaintiff had properly alleged four distinct physician service markets: primary care, general surgery, urology, and otolaryngology; in addition, it accepted a primary care sub-market for pediatrics. However, the court rejected plaintiff's argument that a distinct market for managed care purchasers could be established based on discounting practices. The case is notable for its treatment of the competitive implications of the merger in these markets notwithstanding the extremely high market shares held by the parties. For example, with respect to urology, the court noted there were only two urologists in the market and concluded that it was inconceivable that Congress had intended for the Clayton Act to prohibit the two physicians from practicing together under the same roof and characterized the market as a "natural monopoly." 960 F. Supp. at 1128. With respect to primary care services in which the merged entity would control between 58% and 70% of the market (which it defined to include general practitioners, family practitioners and internists, but not ob/gyns), the court emphasized that the absence of barriers to entry effectively obviated concerns about the defendant's potential exercise of market power. Id. at 1133. In this connection, the court relied upon the fact that the plaintiff hospital (Columbia/HCA) had a highly successful record in recruiting new physicians into the market to serve its facility.

The antitrust enforcement agencies have also reviewed several physician mergers. Because these investigations involved acquisitions of groups practicing in certain specialty areas, analyses of market definition and entry were critical. For example, in examining a proposed merger between a group of cardiovascular thoracic surgeons and a group of vascular surgeons, the Justice Department analyzed the specific vascular procedures that the two groups performed and defined the relevant product markets based on sixty or more overlapping procedures performed by these specialists. In clearing the merger, the Department emphasized the fact that payers needed to include only a very few peripheral vascular surgeons (the relevant market) in a managed care network and that there were sufficient independent providers of such services who were not a part of the merging groups to obviate competitive concerns raised by the high market shares of the merging parties. In addition, it noted that sponsored entry or expansion by existing competing groups would defeat attempts to raise prices. Letter from Joel I. Klein, Assistant Attorney General, Antitrust Division, U.S. Department of Justice to Bob D. Tucker (Re: CVT Surgical Center and Vascular Surgery Associates) (Apr. 16, 1997). By contrast, in another business review letter, the Department indicated that there was a substantial likelihood that it would challenge a proposed merger of two physician groups of board certified gastroenterologists in Allentown, Pennsylvania. Letter from Joel I. Klein, Assistant Attorney General, Antitrust Division, U.S. Department of Justice to Donald H. Lipson (Gastroenterology Associates Limited, et al.) (July 7, 1997). The Department concluded that although there was some overlap in the procedures performed by gastroenterologists and other physician specialties, gastroenterologists could probably collectively raise prices because managed care organizations required gastroenterologists on their panels as a "critical selling point." The Department also concluded that the service market was highly localized because of patients' "psychological barriers" to traveling even a small distance for treatment.

4. *Vertical Mergers*

Mergers between firms that are not direct competitors may also substantially lessen competition. Vertical mergers cause concern where they raise barriers to entry (such as by requiring new entrants to compete in two, rather than one market) or foreclose competition in the sense that they inhibit the ability of firms to compete because of the lack of outlets or sources of business resulting from the merger. Case law suggests that vertical mergers foreclosing 20–25% of the market will be questioned where entry barriers and other factors suggest that competition will lessened. See Herbert Hovenkamp, Federal Antitrust Policy: The Law of Competition and its Practice § 9.4 (2d ed. 1999). For example, a hospital's acquisition of physician practices may be anticompetitive if other hospitals' ability to compete in the market is impaired because utilization or referrals from such physicians is necessary. Consent decrees in several cases have limited physician acquisitions to anywhere from 20 to 40 percent of the relevant market. See Missouri v. Sisters of Mercy Health System (settling challenge to physician acquisition and exclusive contracting by the dominant hospital in the market; hospital agreed to employ no more than 40% of physicians in various specialties); Pennsylvania v. Capital Health Systems, supra (settling challenge to hospital merger; hospital prohibited from employing more than 20% of physicians in family medicine, pediatrics, OB/GYN); but cf. Reazin v. Blue Cross & Blue Shield, 663 F.Supp. 1360, 1489 (D.Kan.1987), aff'd 899 F.2d 951 (10th Cir.1990)(approving hospital chain's acquisition of HMO, stating vertical mergers are not a "suspect category").

The FTC has challenged the acquisition by pharmaceutical corporations of pharmaceutical benefit management firms ("PBMs"). See, e.g., Eli Lilly and Company, 61 Fed. Reg. 31117 (June 19, 1996) (consent order). PBMs act as intermediaries for managed care organizations and others, negotiating discounts for the MCO with manufacturers and pharmacists. The FTC's concern focused on the risk that these acquisitions might foreclose the products of other pharmaceutical manufacturers from the PBM's formulary (a list of preferred drugs) and that the acquisition might facilitate coordination or collusion among vertically integrated pharmaceutical manufacturers. In addition, the acquisition could raise entry barriers by effectively requiring a competitor to enter at more than one level. Ultimately, these cases were settled by consent decrees that allowed the merger to go forward subject to certain constraints, such as requiring that the PBM maintain an open formulary (although closed formularies were not prohibited); and also by creating a "firewall" to preclude communication between the manufacturer and its PBM concerning the bids, proposals, prices, and other information regarding other drug manufacturers' products. The results of these cases has been criticized by Congress and the GAO, as three large pharmaceutical companies now control 80% of the PBMs. See Pharmacy Benefits Management: Wyden Questions

FTC's Pitofsky on Impact of Vertical Integration, 5 Health Law Reporter (June 27, 1996).

5. *Virtual Mergers*

In recent years, many hospitals have entered into agreements with other hospitals to substantially integrate their operations and governance without undertaking a full-blown acquisition or merger. They do this through various contractual arrangements, including strategic alliances and joint operating agreements, pursuant to which control of the hospitals is typically ceded to a single board or other entity. These affiliations often involve at least one nonprofit or religiously affiliated hospital that is reluctant to give up its own identity or autonomy in a merger. A critical issue in these arrangements is whether the hospitals will be treated as a single entity for antitrust purposes. If it is not, the affiliated hospitals are viewed as separate firms and their joint actions on pricing and other competitive variables may constitute per se violations of Section 1 of the Sherman Act. If, on the other hand, the affiliation is deemed to create a single entity, traditional merger analysis under Section 7 of the Clayton Act is applied. The most pertinent case law involves arrangements between parent and subsidiary corporations in which the courts have questioned whether single entity status is appropriate. In Copperweld Corp. v. Independence Tube Corp., 467 U.S. 752, 104 S.Ct. 2731, 81 L.Ed.2d 628 (1984), the Supreme Court held that a parent corporation and its wholly-owned subsidiary constituted a single entity. Therefore the parent and subsidiary were incapable as a matter of law of conspiring under the Sherman Act. The Court emphasized that the parent-subsidiary relationship is distinguished by a complete unity of the entity's purposes and interests and also by the ability of the parent corporation to exercise its control to assure that the aligned interests are pursued. Application of these principles in the case of virtual mergers between hospitals entails a close factual examination of the specific control arrangements among the affiliated hospitals. The relevant questions would include whether one hospital retains veto power over significant transactions, the role of each hospital's board in choosing or replacing board members, the entity's individual control over strategic decisionmaking, budgets and contracting, and the parties' rights of termination. See generally Roxanne C. Busey, Antitrust Aspects of "Virtual Mergers" and Affiliations, Remarks before the American Health Lawyers Association Annual Meeting, July 1, 1998. In a recent case, two hospitals undertook a joint venture arrangement which involved joint negotiations with health plans and agreements not to compete with each other for the provision of the same or similar services. New York v. Saint Francis Hospital, 94 F. Supp. 2d 399 (S.D.N.Y.2000). Finding no meaningful integration between the firms and rejecting justifications based on state CON approvals, the nonprofit status of the hospitals and improved quality of services, the district court applied per se analysis to strike down the arrangement.

Chapter 16

HUMAN REPRODUCTION AND BIRTH

The rights, obligations, privileges, and relationships previously described in this book are generally rights, obligations, privileges, and relationships of people. But who ought to be recognized as a person, subject to the principles that apply to persons, and not to human limbs, individual cells, hair pieces, animals, disembodied souls, hospitals, state legislatures or other entities? While a fertilized ovum is life in some form, so is a single still-functioning liver cell taken from the body of a person who died yesterday. Is there a difference in these two entities? When does a person, entitled to formal legal respect as such, come into existence? When does one who is so defined go out of existence? The obvious answers—at the point of life and at the point of death—are fraught with ambiguities that can be resolved only through an analysis of medicine, ethics, law, social history, anthropology, theology and other disciplines which seek to answer the basic questions of human existence. Physicians and lawyers have been deeply involved in determining when life begins and when it ends, and it is therefore appropriate to consider these issues in this text. The first portion of this chapter deals with the definition of human life; the definition of death is taken up in the next chapter.

Physicians and lawyers have also been deeply involved in developing and defining new forms of procreation, and in determining the role that the society ought to play in limiting and facilitating reproduction. Issues surrounding contraception, genetic screening (and control and protection of those involved in this process), sterilization, abortion, the social allocation of the cost of failed reproductive, potential fetal-maternal conflicts, and government intervention to preserve sexuality (in outlawing practices that result in genital mutilation, for example) have all been addressed by law-makers, in either a judicial or legislative forum. In addition, such forms of facilitating reproduction as artificial insemination, *in vitro* fertilization, ovum transfer and surrogacy have also been addressed in legal fora. The second portion of this chapter examines the interdisciplinary debate that has given rise to legal intervention that may result in limiting or facilitating reproduction.

Problem: Death During Pregnancy

Ms. Baggins was carrying a fetus in the twenty-fifth week of gestation when the automobile she was driving was struck by a truck racing away from a convenience store and pursued by a city police car. The driver of the truck, who was unlicensed and highly intoxicated, was attempting to escape after committing an armed robbery at the convenience store when the collision occurred. The truck struck the driver's door of Ms. Baggins's car and flung her through the passenger window onto the ground about thirty feet from the car. The chasing police officer arrested the intoxicated driver, who was subsequently charged with armed robbery, driving while intoxicated, and driving without a license. The police officer did not call for medical help for Ms. Baggins, and no ambulance came for her until a passing motorist called the fire department. The ambulance arrived to find her unconscious.

When Ms. Baggins arrived at the hospital, physicians immediately provided her cardiopulmonary support. An examination revealed that the fetus she was carrying had suffered serious cranial injuries which could result in severe brain dysfunction if the child were born alive. Tests done about 24 hours after Ms. Baggins's admission to the hospital indicated no spontaneous activity in any part of her brain. Physicians have determined that maintaining Ms. Baggins on the cardiopulmonary support systems would provide the only chance for the fetus to be born alive.

Ms. Baggins was widowed in the fifth month of her pregnancy, two months ago. Her only living relatives are her two sisters, whom she despises. In fact, to avoid the possibility that they might inherit some of her wealth, last month she executed a will leaving all of her property to "my children, and, if I have none at the time of my death, to the National Abortion Rights League and the American Eugenics Society."

What actions should the hospital staff take in this case? Should Ms. Baggins be maintained on cardiopulmonary support, or should she be removed?

Consider the medical, social, political and legal (both civil and criminal) consequences of your actions as you read this chapter.

I. WHEN DOES HUMAN LIFE BECOME A "PERSON"?

This society has had difficulty defining who is a "person." In part, this arises out of the different and inconsistent purposes for which we seek a definition. The "person" from whom we wish to harvest a kidney for transplantation is likely to be different from the "person" who is protected by the Fourteenth Amendment, federal civil rights laws, and various other federal and state laws. Even when the purpose of the definition is settled—as when we seek to know who is a person able to bring an action under state tort law—there is no consensus on when the status of "personhood" first attaches. The most obvious definition of personhood is a recursive one: a human being (and, thus, a "person") is the reproductive product of other human beings. Even if we accept this "human stock" definition of person, however, the inquiry remains open. Does that human stock become a person, for tort law or other purposes, upon conception? Upon quickening? Upon viability? Upon birth? A year after birth? Upon physical maturity?

The definition of "person" is not limited to various stages in the development of human stock. "Personhood" could commence upon ensoulment, upon the development of self concept, upon the development of a sense of personal history, or upon the ability to communicate through language. The resolution of the question appears to require a resort to first principles.

In the vast majority of cases, it is not difficult to distinguish a person from something else. You are easily distinguishable from your arms, your dog, your insurance company and your gold bust of Elvis, as close as you may feel to each of them. The most difficult questions tend to arise at the very beginning and at the very end of human life. Just as you may be able to identify the fact that you were in love, but not be able to identify exactly when it began, or the moment when it ended, the beginnings and the endings of "personhood" are the fuzzy portions.

There are limits to what may reasonably be considered a "person," even when we limit our consideration to human stock. No one suggests that anything independent of the unified sperm and ovum, or its consequences, ought to be considered a person. A great many religious groups consider "personhood" to attach at conception. Aristotle viewed the development of the person as a three stage process, going from vegetable (at conception), to animal (in utero), to rational (sometime after birth). For many centuries, Christian theology fixed the point of "immediate animation" when the fetus was "ensouled" as forty days after conception for males and eighty days after conception for females. St. Thomas Aquinas determined that the ensoulment took place at the time of quickening, usually fourteen to eighteen weeks after conception, and his determination had a very substantial effect on the development of the common law in England and in this country. Recently some philosophers have suggested that "personhood," at least to the extent that it includes a right to life, depends on attributes that are not likely to be developed until sometime after birth. For example, Michael Tooley, a philosopher, defends infanticide on the grounds that it is indistinguishable from abortion and that neither constitutes the improper killing of a human being because there can be no human being until the being possesses a concept of itself as a continuing subject of experiences and other mental states, and recognizes that it is such a continuing entity. Professor Tooley suggests that this occurs sometime after birth, perhaps many weeks after birth. M. Tooley, *Abortion and Infanticide* (1983).

The most comprehensive set of attributes of personhood has been developed by Joseph Fletcher, a bioethicist. Consider his fifteen criteria, described below, and determine whether some or all of them can be used to properly define who is your colleague in personhood and who is not. Consider whether the fact that many of these criteria disqualify fetuses, newborns, and the seriously developmentally disabled affects their acceptability as standards. Further, does the fact that some animal or some man-made machine might eventually fulfill all of these criteria cause you to doubt their validity? What are the consequences of our failure to define a cloned person, a highly intelligent and communicative ape, or a robot as a "person" in terms of our conceptions of "democracy" and "slavery," for example?

A. THE ATTRIBUTES OF PERSONHOOD

JOSEPH FLETCHER, "HUMANNESS," IN HUMANHOOD: ESSAYS IN BIOMEDICAL ETHICS

12–16 (1979).

Synthetic concepts such as human and man and person require operational terms, spelling out the which and what and when. Only in that way can we get down to cases—to normative decisions. There are always some people who prefer to be visceral and affective in their moral choices, with no desire to have any rationale for what they do. But ethics is precisely the business of rational, critical reflection (encephalic and not merely visceral) about the problems of the moral agent—in biology and medicine as much as in law, government, education, or anything else.

To that end, then, for the purposes of biomedical ethics, I now turn to a *profile of man* in concrete and discrete terms.* * * There is time only to itemize the inventory, not to enlarge upon it, but I have fifteen positive propositions. Let me set them out, in no rank order at all, and as hardly more than a list of criteria or indicators, by simple title.

1. Minimum Intelligence

Mere biological life, before minimal intelligence is achieved or after it is lost irretrievably, is without personal status.

2. Self-awareness

* * *

3. Self–control

If an individual is not only not controllable by others (unless by force) but not controllable by the individual himself or herself, a low level of life is reached about on a par with that of a paramecium. * * *

4. A Sense of Time

* * *

5. A Sense of Futurity

How "truly human" is any man who cannot realize there is a time yet to come as well as the present? Subhuman animals do not look forward in time; they live only on what we might call visceral strivings, appetites. Philosophical anthropologies (one recalls that of William Temple, the Archbishop of Canterbury, for instance) commonly emphasize purposiveness as a key to humanness. Chesterton once remarked that we would never ask a puppy what manner of dog it wanted to be when it grows up. * * *

6. A Sense of the Past

* * *

7. The Capability to Relate to Others

Interpersonal relationships, of the sexual-romantic and friendship kind, are of the greatest importance for the fullness of what we idealize as being truly personal. * * *

8.   Concern for Others

Some people may be skeptical about our capacity to care about others (what in Christian ethics is often distinguished from romance and friendship as "neighbor love" or "neighbor concern"). * * * But whether concern for others is disinterested or inspired by enlightened self-interest, it seems plain that a conscious extra-ego orientation is a trait of the species * * *.

9.   Communication

Utter alienation or disconnection from others, if it is irreparable, is dehumanization. * * *

10.   Control of Existence

It is of the nature of man that he is not helplessly subject to the blind workings of physical or physiological nature. He has only finite knowledge, freedom, and initiative, but what he has of it is real and effective. * * *

11.   Curiosity

To be without affect, sunk in *anomie,* is to be not a person. Indifference is inhuman. Man is a learner and a knower as well as a tool maker and user. * * *

12.   Change and Changeability

To the extent that an individual is unchangeable or opposed to change, he denies the creativity of personal beings. It means not only the fact of biological and physiological change, which goes on as a condition of life, but the capacity and disposition for changing one's mind and conduct as well. Biologically, human beings are developmental: birth, life, health, and death are processes, not events, and are to be understood progressively, not episodically. All human existence is on a continuum, a matter of becoming. * * *

13.   Balance of Rationality and Feeling

* * * As human beings we are not coldly rational or cerebral, nor are we merely creatures of feeling and intuition. It is a matter of being both, in different combinations from one individual to another. * * *

14.   Idiosyncrasy

The human being is idiomorphous, a distinctive individual. * * * To be a person is to have an identity, to be recognizable and callable by name.

15.   Neocortical Function

In a way, this is the cardinal indicator, the one all the others are hinged upon. Before cerebration is in play, or with its end, in the absence of the synthesizing function of the cerebral cortex, the person is nonexistent. Such individuals are objects but not subjects. This is so no matter how many other spontaneous or artificially supported functions persist in the heart, lungs, neurologic and vascular systems. Such noncerebral processes are not personal. * * * But what is definitive in determining death is the loss of cerebration, not just of any or all brain function. Personal reality depends on cerebration and to be dead "humanly" speaking is to be excerebral, no matter how long the body remains alive.

Notes and Questions

1. Which attributes does Fletcher consider to be necessary for personhood? Are any sufficient? Would you add any others to his list? Is there any underlying principle that describes the fifteen attributes selected by Fletcher? Are they all really a subset of the first?

2. Which attributes of personhood, if any, does Ms. Baggins or her fetus possess?

3. Dr. Fletcher commenced a serious debate over whether the persons protected by law ought to be defined in terms of attributes we wish to protect or in terms of the human stock from which the person is created. Both forms of definition may be valuable for different purposes. We provide some rights to people because they possess many or all of the attributes that distinguish human beings. The right to make medical decisions, based on the autonomy of individuals, is not accorded to those without some "minimum intelligence." On the other hand, we provide minimally adequate housing, food, medical care, and other necessities for those of human stock, even when they do not meet some of Dr. Fletcher's criteria, and even when we do not provide those same benefits to others, (e.g., animals) who fail the same criteria. In the end, the Fletcher propositions may be useful in determining some of the rights of persons and the "human stock" definition may be helpful in determining others. Just as property is often described as a bundle of rights, it may turn out that "personhood" is a bundle of rights that need to be separated out and individually analyzed.

4. As we saw earlier, even the adoption of a "human stock" definition does not answer the question of when that human stock becomes a person. What is the attribute of the human stock that makes it a person—genetic uniqueness? Responsiveness? The potential to be born? The appearance of a human being? Consider the following list of the alternative medical points of personhood.

C.R. AUSTIN, HUMAN EMBRYOS: THE DEBATE ON ASSISTED REPRODUCTION 22–31 (1989):

When does a person's life really begin?

* * * Probably most people who were asked this question would answer "at fertilization" (or "conception"). Certainly, several interesting and unusual things happen then—it is really the most *obvious* event to pick—but for biologists the preceding and succeeding cellular processes are *equally* important. Nevertheless, "fertilization" continues to be the cry of many religious bodies and indeed also of the august World Medical Association, who, in 1949, adopted the Geneva Convention Code of Medical Ethics, which contains the clause: "I will maintain the utmost respect for human life from the time of conception." So we do need to look more closely at this choice, for a generally acceptable "beginning" for human life would be a great help in reaching ethical and legal consensus.

In the first place human *life,* as such, obviously begins before fertilization, since the egg or oocyte is alive before sperm entry, as were innumerable antecedent cells, back through the origin of species into the mists of time. A more practical starting point would be that of the life of the human *individual,* so it is individuality that we should be looking for, at least as one of the essential criteria. Now the earliest antecedents of the eggs, as of sperm, are the primordial germ cells, which can be seen as a group of distinctive little entities migrating through the tissues of the early embryo. When they first become recognizable, they number only about a dozen or two, but they multiply fast and soon achieve large numbers, reaching a peak of 7–10 million about 6 months after conception. Then, despite continued active cell division, there is a dramatic decline in the cell population, which has tempted people to suggest that some sort of "selection of the fittest" occurs, but there is no good evidence in support of this idea; nor is there any good reason to look for individuality in that mercurial population. In due course, the primordial germ cells, while still undergoing cell divisions, settle down in the tissues of the future ovary, change subtly in their characteristics, and thus become oogonia; and then, soon after birth, *cell division ceases,* the cells develop large nuclei and are now recognizable as primary oocytes. From now on, there are steady cell losses but no further cell divisions * * *; it is the same entity that was a primary oocyte, becomes a fertilized egg, and then develops as an embryo. The primary oocytes are very unusual cells, for they have the capacity to live for much longer than most other body cells; the *same* oocytes can be seen in the ovaries of women approaching the menopause—cells that have lived for about 40 years or longer. And it is with the emergence of the primary oocytes that we can hail the start of *individuality.* Then, in those oocytes that are about to be ovulated, the first meiotic division takes place—another important step, for the "shuffling" of genes that occurs at that point bestows *genetic uniqueness* on the oocyte. So both individuality and genetic uniqueness are established before sperm penetration and fertilization; these processes have distinctly different actions—providing the stimulus that initiates cleavage and contributing to biparental inheritance. Thus, the preferred choice for the start of the human individual should surely be the formation of the primary oocyte, but there is certainly no unanimity on this score.

Passing over now the popularity of fertilization, for many people it is instead the emergence of the embryonic disc and primitive streak that most appeals as the stage in which to identify the start of "personhood" (one or more persons, in view of the imminent possibility of twinning), and there is much to support this opinion. Here, for the first time, are structures that are designed to have a different destiny than *all the rest of the embryo*—they represent the primordium of the fetus, and the developmental patterns of embryo and fetus progressively diverge from this stage onwards. An additional point is that this new emergence is not inevitable, for in around one in two-thousand pregnancies the embryo grows, often to quite a large size, but there is no fetus; the clinical conditions are known as blighted ovum, dropsical ovum, hydatidiform mole, etc. Evidence suggests that hydatidiform mole is attributable to fertilization of a faulty egg, the embryo developing only under the influence of the sperm chromosomes.

At the time of appearance of the embryonic disc, and shortly beforehand, the process of implantation is occurring, and this is considered by many to have special significance in relation to embryonic potential—so far as we know, implantation cannot occur once the development of the embryo has passed the stage when interaction with * * * the uterus normally takes place.

But despite all that has been said, there are still many folk who remain unconvinced—is the being at this stage sufficiently "human" to qualify as the start of a person? After all, the disc is just a collection of similar cells, virtually undifferentiated, poorly delineated from its surroundings, about a fifth of a millimetre long, non-sentient, and without the power of movement. It is in no way a "body" and it does not bear the faintest resemblance to a human being—*and* the soul cannot enter yet, for the disc may yet divide in the process of twinning, and the soul being unique is indivisible. Also, it is argued that we should be looking for some spark of personality, and a moral philosopher has proposed that some sort of responsiveness is an essential feature.

One of the earliest succeeding changes in the direction of humanness could be the development of the heart primordium, and soon after that the beginnings of a circulatory system; the first contractions of the heart muscle occur possibly as early as day 21, with a simple tubular heart at that stage, and in the fourth week a functional circulation begins. With the heart beats we have the first movements initiated within the embryo (?fetus) and thus in a way the first real "sign of life." The conceptus is now about 6 mm long. During the fifth and sixth weeks, nerve fibres grow out from the spinal cord and make contact with muscles, so that at this time or soon afterwards, a mechanical or electrical stimulus might elicit a muscle twitch; this is important for it would be the first indication of sentient existence—of "responsiveness." At this stage, too, the embryo could possibly feel pain. But, still, some would find cause to demur: only an expert could tell that this embryo/fetus, now 12–13 mm in length, with branchial arches (corresponding to the "gill-slits" in non-mammalian embryos), stubby limbs, and a prominent tail, is human. A marginally more acceptable applicant is the fetus at 7½ weeks, when the hands and feet can be seen to have fingers and toes, and thereafter physical resemblance steadily improves; also at this time, a special gene on the Y-chromosome (the "testis-determining factor" or TDF) is switched on, and the fetuses that have this chromosome, the males, proceed thenceforward to develop *as* males, distinguishable from females.

At about 12 weeks, electrical activity can be detected in the brain of the fetus, which could signal the dawn of consciousness. Here, we would seem to have a very logical stage marking the *start* of a person, for the cessation of electrical activity in the brain ("brain death") is accepted in both medical and legal circles as marking the *termination* of a person—as an indication that life no longer exists in victims of accidents or in patients with terminal illnesses. Around the fourth or fifth month of pregnancy, the mother first experiences movements of the fetus ('quickening'), which were regarded by St. Thomas Aquinas as the first indication of life, for he believed that life was distinguished by two features, knowledge and movement; moreover, it would seem logical that the fetus would move when the *animus* (life or soul) took up residence.[1] * * *

At about 24 weeks, the fetus reaches a state in which it can commonly survive outside the maternal body, with assistance. * * * Just which stage marks the start of a person's life is a matter of personal opinion. Much of the foregoing argumentation may seem to some people difficult to comprehend, especially if they have not had formal training in biology, and to others may even seem irrelevant, in view of the firm line taken by many church authorities. But it really is important that we should try to reach a consensus on just when a person's life should be held to begin, for the decision does have important practical consequences—it directly affects the rights of other embryos, of fetuses, and of people.

B. LEGAL RECOGNITION OF THE BEGINNING OF HUMAN LIFE

The law is increasingly forced to confront the question of when rights and privileges of persons attach to fetuses and young children. While children have always been treated differently from adults in the law, those fundamental common law and constitutional rights that uniformly extend to both

1. The modern equivalent would be at about day 21, when the heart begins to beat.

competent and incompetent adults also have been extended to children from the time of birth. Courts have had greater difficulty determining which rights, if any, attach to a fetus.

The trend over the past twenty years has been for states to expand the common law rights of the fetus and to recognize that the fetus can be an independent victim for purposes of the criminal law. For example, most states now permit a tort action to be filed by an estate of a stillborn child. Just fifteen years ago, the vast majority of states required that the child be born alive before any right to sue would attach. Similarly, many states now extend the protection of their homicide law to fetuses; several years ago that extension was very unusual. The extent of any constitutional protection of fetuses is far less certain.

1. Constitutional Recognition

While the Supreme Court has never formally determined when a fetus becomes a "person" for constitutional purposes, it has not been able to completely avoid that question despite its several attempts to finesse it. Indeed, some commentators thought that the matter was finally resolved in the watershed case of Roe v. Wade, 410 U.S. 113, 93 S.Ct. 705, 35 L.Ed.2d 147 (1973), in which the Supreme Court was called upon to determine whether a fetus was a person for purposes of the protections of the Fourteenth Amendment. While *Roe v. Wade* will be considered in some greater detail below, it is significant to know that the Court held that the term "person," at least as that term appears in the Fourteenth Amendment, was not intended to encompass the fetus. After reviewing over 2,000 years of the history of abortion the Court addressed the question directly:

> The appellee and certain amici argue that the fetus is a "person" within the language and meaning of the Fourteenth Amendment. In support of this, they outline at length and in detail the well-known facts of fetal development. If this suggestion of personhood is established, the appellant's case, of course, collapses, for the fetus' right to life is then guaranteed specifically by the Amendment. The appellant conceded as much on reargument. On the other hand, the appellee conceded on reargument that no case could be cited that holds that a fetus is a person within the meaning of the Fourteenth Amendment.

> The Constitution does not define "person" in so many words. Section 1 of the Fourteenth Amendment contains three references to "person." The first, in defining "citizens," speaks of "persons born or naturalized in the United States." The word also appears both in the Due Process Clause and in the Equal Protection Clause. "Person" is used in other places in the Constitution: in the listing of qualifications for Representatives and Senators, Art I, § 2, cl 2, and § 3, cl 3; in the Apportionment Clause, Art I, § 2, cl 3;[2] in the Migration and Importation provision, Art I, § 9, cl 1; in the Emolument Clause, Art I, § 9, cl 8; in the Electors provisions, Art II, § 1, cl 2, and the superseded cl 3; in the provision outlining qualifications for the office of President, Art II, § 1, cl 5; in the

2. We are not aware that in the taking of any census under this clause, a fetus has ever   been counted.

Extradition provisions, Art IV, § 2, cl 2, and the superseded Fugitive Slave Clause 3; and in the Fifth, Twelfth, and Twenty-second Amendments, as well as in §§ 2 and 3 of the Fourteenth Amendment. But in nearly all these instances, the use of the word is such that it has application only postnatally. None indicates, with any assurance, that it has any possible prenatal application.[3]

* * *

All this, together with our observation * * * that throughout the major portion of the 19th century prevailing legal abortion practices were far freer than they are today, persuades us that the word "person," as used in the Fourteenth Amendment, does not include the unborn. * * * 410 U.S. at 156–157, 93 S.Ct. at 728–729.

The Supreme Court recognized that there were protectable interests beyond those specified in the Constitution and determined:

[W]e do not agree that, by adopting one theory of life, Texas may override the rights of the pregnant woman that are at stake. We repeat, however, that the state does have an important and legitimate interest in preserving and protecting the health of the pregnant woman * * *, and that it has still *another* important and legitimate interest in protecting the potentiality of human life. 410 U.S. at 162, 93 S.Ct. at 731.

Thus, a state may be able to define and protect rights in the fetus, but these are not the Fourteenth Amendment rights of "persons."

Of course, the continued viability of *Roe v. Wade* itself has been called into question continually since 1973. See section II, below. In Webster v. Reproductive Health Services, 492 U.S. 490, 109 S.Ct. 3040, 106 L.Ed.2d 410 (1989), the Supreme Court reviewed a Missouri statute that restricted the availability of abortions in several ways. In addition, that statute included a preamble that defined personhood:

1. The general assembly of this state finds that:

(1) the life of each human being begins at conception;

(2) unborn children have protectable interests in life, health, and well being; * * *

2. * * * the laws of this state shall be interpreted and construed to acknowledge on behalf of the unborn child at every stage of development, all the rights, privileges, and immunities available to other persons,

---

3. When Texas urges that a fetus is entitled to Fourteenth Amendment protection as a person, it faces a dilemma. Neither in Texas nor in any other State are all abortions prohibited. Despite broad proscription, an exception always exists. The exception contained in Art 1196, for an abortion procured or attempted by medical advice for the purpose of saving the life of the mother, is typical. But if the fetus is a person who is not to be deprived of life without due process of law, and if the mother's condition is the sole determinant, does not the Texas exception appear to be out of line with the Amendment's command?

There are other inconsistencies between Fourteenth Amendment status and the typical abortion statute. It has already been pointed out [ ] that in Texas the woman is not a principal or an accomplice with respect to an abortion upon her. If the fetus is a person, why is the woman not a principal or an accomplice? Further, the penalty for criminal abortion specified by Art 1195 is significantly less than the maximum penalty for murder prescribed by Art 1257 of the Texas Penal Code. If the fetus is a person, may the penalties be different?

citizens, and residents of this state, subject only to the Constitution of the United States, and decisional interpretations thereof. * * *

3. As used in this section, the term "unborn children" or "unborn child" shall include all unborn child or children or the offspring of human beings from the moment of conception until birth at every stage of biological development. * * *

Vernon's Ann.Mo.Stat. § 1.205. This preamble was attacked on the grounds that it was beyond the constitutional authority of the state legislature to define personhood, at least to the extent that the definition extended personhood to pre-viable fetuses. The Supreme Court sidestepped that question by concluding that the preamble was nothing more than a state value judgment favoring childbirth over abortion, and that such a value judgment was clearly within the authority of the legislature.

There are two separate constitutional issues that surround the definition of person. First, is there a definition of "person" for purposes of the Constitution? Second, do the substantive provisions of the Constitution put any limit on the way that *states* may define "person" for any other purpose? Could each state define "person" differently for constitutional purposes? States effectively did so before the Thirteenth Amendment, of course. Could the definition of "person" for constitutional purposes be different from that definition for other purposes?

2. *Statutory Recognition*

As Justice Blackmun pointed out in *Roe v. Wade,* courts have generally considered killing a fetus to be substantially different from killing a person who was born alive. This is reflected in the different penalties that usually attach to feticide and other forms of homicide and the fact that feticide itself has been distinguished from murder or manslaughter in most jurisdictions. Over the past several years, however, some states have made the penalties for feticide commensurate with the penalties for homicide, and several have promulgated new homicide statutes that explicitly include fetuses as those whose death may give rise to homicide prosecutions. Most commonly, these statutes seek to impose the homicide penalty on one who kills an "unborn child," although the California statute provides:

Murder is the unlawful killing of a human being, *or a fetus,* with malice aforethought.

Cal. Penal Code Sec. 187(a). The words "or a fetus" were added to the statute in 1970 in reaction to a California Supreme Court decision, Keeler v. Superior Court, 2 Cal.3d 619, 87 Cal.Rptr. 481, 470 P.2d 617 (1970), which defined "human being" as a person born alive.

The statutes which do not distinguish between viable and nonviable fetal victims of a homicide have been unsuccessfully attacked on due process and equal protection grounds in at least three states—Minnesota, Illinois and California. The due process attack is two pronged. First, criminal defendants argue that the statutes violate their due process rights because they apply even when the perpetrator (and, for that matter, the pregnant woman) do not know of the existence of the pregnancy. As the Minnesota court said in rejecting such an argument, though, "[t]he fair warning rule has never been understood to excuse criminal liability simply because the defendant's victim proves not to be the victim the defendant had in mind." State v. Merrill, 450

N.W.2d 318, 323 (Minn.1990). Second, defendants argue that terms like "unborn child" are unconstitutionally vague because it is uncertain when a conceptus, embryo or fetus becomes an "unborn child." As an Illinois appellate court pointed out, the statute "only requires proof that whatever the entity within the mother's womb is called, it had life, and, because of the acts of the defendant, it no longer does." People v. Ford, 221 Ill.App.3d 354, 163 Ill.Dec. 766, 777, 581 N.E.2d 1189, 1200 (1991).

The defendant's equal protection argument is based in the failure of the statutes to distinguish between viable and nonviable fetuses. Defendants have argued that the state makes an improper distinction when it treats some who end the life of a nonviable fetus as murderers, while others, including the pregnant woman herself and her doctor, who are protected by the Constitutionally recognized right to an abortion, are not treated as murderers. This argument has also failed to garner a majority in any state. See State v. Merrill, supra, and People v. Ford, supra.

The California statute was upheld and applied to both nonviable and viable fetuses by a divided court in People v. Davis, 7 Cal.4th 797, 30 Cal.Rptr.2d 50, 872 P.2d 591 (1994), where the Court found that the history of applying the statute only when the victim was a viable fetus required that it be applied to cases where the victims were nonviable fetuses only prospectively, and not to the case before it. The dissent argued that the majority's application of the statute to nonviable fetuses "will make our murder law unique in the nation in its severity: it appears that in no other state is it a capital offense to cause the death of a nonviable and invisible fetus that the actor neither knew nor had reason to know existed." 30 Cal.Rptr.2d at 79, 872 P.2d at 620. For an excellent survey of the way state laws now deal with feticide, an account of those that criminalize only the killing of a viable fetus and those that also criminalize the killing of a nonviable fetus, and a survey of punishments imposed on those whose acts result in the death of a fetus, see People v. Davis, 30 Cal.Rptr.2d at 79–83, 872 P.2d at 621–623 (Mosk, J. dissenting).

In State v. Merrill, supra, the majority distinguished human life from "personhood," and determined that the feticide statute was designed to protect human life, not persons. Could the legislature also protect other forms of human life—human blood cells, for example—in the same way that it has decided to protect "nonperson" human life in this case, or is the potential personhood of the embryo fundamental to the majority's decision that the statute's protection of human life is constitutional?

Do you agree with the decisions in Merrill, Ford and Davis? Whose interests were really at stake in those cases? To what extent should these courts depend upon the interests of the pregnant woman, and to what extent should the courts depend on the interests of the embryo or fetus in deciding these cases?

In her dissent in the Merrill case, Justice Wahl argues that Roe v. Wade forbids a state from treating a nonviable fetus like a person, at least for purposes of the criminal law. How strong is that argument? For purposes of the homicide law, is there any reason to draw a line between a viable and a nonviable fetus if the mother of each intends to carry the fetus in utero to term? If not, why have so many states decided to criminalize only the killing of a viable fetus? Might it be that at the point of viability the fact of pregnancy is likely to be obvious to the assailant? Are any purposes of the criminal law served by application of a feticide statute to a case (like the Merrill case) in which neither the pregnant woman nor the assailant knew of the pregnancy?

3. Common Law Recognition

The debate over the common law recognition of the personhood of the fetus has been waged primarily over whether a fetus may recover under state wrongful death and survival statutes. Until recently courts were divided over whether such actions would be permitted only if the decedent were born alive, or whether such actions would be permitted if the decedent had reached the point of viability, even though the decedent was not born alive. In Amadio v. Levin, 509 Pa. 199, 501 A.2d 1085 (1985), the court listed the five reasons courts had traditionally articulated for limiting such actions to children born alive:

> First, the Court surmised that the real objective of such a lawsuit was to compensate the parents of the deceased child for their emotional distress, and that since parents already had the ability in their own right to institute such an action, it would only be duplication to permit parents to file a second action on behalf of the estate of the child.

> Second, because wrongful death actions are derivative, and since the Court refused to acknowledge that a stillborn child was an individual under the wrongful death or survival statutes, it was concluded that the Acts were not intended to provide for recovery by the estate of a stillborn child.

> Third, extending causes of actions to the estates of stillborn children was felt to increase problems of causation and damages.

> Fourth, the prior cases arose out of an era when most jurisdictions did not permit the filing of such actions. * * *

> Fifth, it was reasoned that since only children born alive may take property by descent under our Intestate Laws, the Court assumed that the Legislature had already limited the creation of causes of actions to those instances where the existence or estate of a child was recognized by the laws of intestacy.

That court rejected those five arguments and determined that the live birth requirement was an arbitrary line that served no purpose of the wrongful death and and survival statute:

> Today's holding merely makes it clear that the recovery afforded the estate of a stillborn is no different than the recovery afforded the estate of a child that dies within seconds of its release from its mother's womb. In view of the current attitude throughout our sister states to let the representatives of the stillborn's estate prove their losses, it would be illogical to continue to deny that such claims could be established, when we permit them for the child that survives birth for an instant.

Others more influenced by the arguments over abortion urged that such actions should be recognized for another reason: the fetus is, they argued, a full human being entitled to all protections accorded to all other human beings. Those who opposed recovery on behalf of fetuses who were not born alive argued that there was no genuine loss that was being compensated in such cases, and that the real reason for permitting the recovery was to allow plaintiffs a greater chance at a larger recovery—i.e., a pro-plaintiff bias.

Many courts now distinguish between a viable and a pre-viable fetus for purposes of recovery under wrongful death and survival statutes. Is such a distinction justifiable? If a fetus becomes a "person" for purposes of commencing a tort action only upon viability, the court must address several questions when it hears a tort action commenced on behalf of a fetus. First, what is the legally relevant moment when the fetus must be viable for that fetus to possess a cause of action—is it the time of the injury or the time of the tortious action? Second, when is a fetus viable as a general matter? Is this a matter of law or fact? Third, was the plaintiff-fetus viable at the legally relevant time in the instant case?

All of these questions were before the court upon a motion for summary judgment in In re Air Crash Disaster at Detroit Metropolitan Airport on August 16, 1987, Rademacher v. McDonnell Douglas Corporation, 737 F.Supp. 427 (E.D.Mich.1989), an action brought on behalf of the fetus of a flight attendant killed in an air crash. The District Court determined that Michigan law would permit recovery on behalf of the fetus only if the fetus were "viable at the time of the injury." Further, the court rejected evidence that fetuses could be viable as early as twenty weeks, and adopted the "generally accepted Roe [v. Wade] proposition that viability occurs at twenty-four weeks." Finally, the court concluded:

> [The plaintiff] submits a sonogram report from July 13, 1987, which concludes that the "[e]stimated gestational age is 15.8 + /_ 2 weeks." The fatal accident involving Northwest Flight 255 occurred five weeks later. Therefore, on the date of the accident the * * * fetus was 20.8 weeks old + / − 2 weeks. Therefore, the fetus was, at most, 22.8 weeks old. * * *
>
> Thus, the subject fetus in this case was nonviable as a matter of law [and has no cause of action under Michigan law].

The Rademacher case also discusses the irony in allowing the estate of a fetus to recover damages even if the tortious act was committed at a time when the mother could have chosen to abort the fetus. The court suggests that while a mother's interest in terminating a pregnancy may outweigh a state's interest in maintaining the life of a pre-viable fetus, a third party's interest does not overcome both the state's and the mother's interest in continuing the pregnancy. Is this distinction sound? Is there any place for abortion jurisprudence in analyzing the propriety of tort liability for the death of a fetus?

In fact, is there any reason to draw the line for recovery at viability? Why not just permit a wrongful death recovery on behalf of a fetus of any gestational age, from the moment of conception? While this was generally uncharted territory before 1995, since then three states which have considered the issue have recognized such a cause of action. In Wiersma v. Maple Leaf Farms, 543 N.W.2d 787 (S.D.1996), the South Dakota court, in response to a certified question, announced that the wrongful death statute permitted an action on behalf of a first trimester fetus who was alleged to have been miscarried as a result of salmonella in a frozen dinner consumed by the decedent-fetus's mother. The court treated the case as a simple one of statutory construction: the statute allowed actions on behalf of an "unborn child," and that term was unqualified. The dissent argued that such a term was necessarily ambiguous, and thus it needed to be interpreted. As the dissenting justice pointed out, "The heart of the issue, in my opinion, is whether an action for wrongful death can stand where no sustainable life exists at the time of the negligent act." 543 N.W.2d at 794. Shortly before the South Dakota court rendered its opinion, courts in West Virginia and Missouri had allowed similar actions on behalf of nonviable fetuses. See Connor v. Monkem Co., 898 S.W.2d 89 (Mo.1995) and Farley v. Sartin, 195 W.Va. 671, 466 S.E.2d 522 (W.Va.1995). Such actions also appear to be allowed in Illinois, see Smith v. Mercy Hosp. and Medical Center, 203 Ill.App.3d 465, 148 Ill.Dec. 567, 560 N.E.2d 1164 (Ill.App.1990) and in Georgia, Porter v. Lassiter, 91 Ga.App. 712, 87 S.E.2d 100 (1955)(permitting such actions only after quickening).

Consider the Baggins problem on pages 1115–1116. Would the estate of Ms. Baggins or the estate of her fetus have a tort action against a police department that negligently failed to seek medical assistance for her? Suppose Ms. Baggins is declared dead and then gives birth to a child who lives for two days. Should Ms. Baggins's estate be distributed to the beneficiaries listed in her will, or might her sisters be able to argue successfully that her child inherited her estate, and that they were the heirs of that child? Would your answer be different if Ms. Baggins were declared dead and the fetus were subsequently stillborn? What if Ms. Baggins died before the fetus were even viable? Should any of these distinctions make a legal difference?

A host of cases have considered the issue of whether a wrongful death action may be brought on behalf of a fetus who dies in utero. Among those that have allowed such actions for *viable* fetuses are DiDonato v. Wortman, 320 N.C. 423, 358 S.E.2d 489 (1987), Luff v. Hawkins, 551 A.2d 437 (Del.Super.1988); Summerfield v. Superior Court, 144 Ariz. 467, 698 P.2d 712 (1985); O'Grady v. Brown, 654 S.W.2d 904 (Mo.1983); See also Johnson v. Ruark Obstetrics, 327 N.C. 283, 395 S.E.2d 85 (1990) (permitting recovery for physician's failure to treat maternal diabetes which resulted in the death of a viable fetus) and Terrell v. Rankin, 511 So.2d 126 (Miss.1987) (also permitting a wrongful death action on behalf of a viable fetus for whose mother the physician prescribed medicine for symptoms typical of pregnancy up to the eighth month without ever diagnosing the pregnancy itself). In addition, consider Johnson v. Verrilli, 134 Misc.2d 582, 511 N.Y.S.2d 1008 (1987), modified, 139 A.D.2d 497, 526 N.Y.S.2d 600 (1988) (since a fetus is not a person under New York law, it must be a part of the mother. Thus, its death in utero constitutes a physical injury to the mother).

For cases which have not permitted wrongful death recovery for the death of a fetus in utero, see Smith v. Columbus Community Hospital, Inc., 222 Neb. 776, 387 N.W.2d 490 (1986) (excellent dissent suggests that the live birth requirement is inconsistent with the developing theories of causation), Witty v. American General Capital Distributors, Inc., 727 S.W.2d 503 (Tex. 1987) (while not a person, a fetus is not a chattel either; thus, mother cannot recover for negligent destruction of a chattel), Milton v. Cary Medical Center, 538 A.2d 252 (Me.1988) (majority depends upon legislative history to show that wrongful death statute intended to include only children born alive; dissent would find power in the courts to interpret the statute in matters unanticipated by the legislature when it first promulgated it).

Among the courts that have rejected wrongful death actions on behalf of nonviable fetuses are Gentry v. Gilmore, 613 So.2d 1241 (Ala.1993), Ferguson v. District of Columbia, 629 A.2d 15 (D.C.App.1993), and Coveleski v. Bubnis, 535 Pa. 166, 634 A.2d 608 (1993). For a complete account of the cases that have considered this issue, see Sheldon R. Shapiro, Annotation, Right to Maintain Action or to Recover Damages for Death of Unborn Child, 84 ALR3d 411 (1978, and supplements)

II. MEDICAL INTERVENTION IN REPRODUCTION

The law has been invoked regularly to order the relationships of private individuals and to constrain government to its appropriate role with regard to the limitation of reproduction. The law has also been engaged to regulate medical interventions designed to facilitate reproduction, such as artificial insemination, ovum and embryo transfer, in vitro fertilization, and surrogacy. While the propriety of legal intervention in these matters will undoubtedly remain a matter of dispute, the sexual nature of the issues, as well as their novelty and moral complexity, is likely to cause society to maintain a high interest in regulating them. This section of this chapter is not intended to be a comprehensive analysis of all of these questions; many related issues are discussed elsewhere in this text or in other courses. It is the purpose of this section of this chapter to provide structure to those issues surrounding procreation and reproduction that are likely to be of special concern to attorneys representing health care professionals, institutions and their patients.

A. LIMITING REPRODUCTION

1. *Government Prohibitions on Reproduction*

Is there a role for the government in prohibiting reproduction, at least in some circumstances? To control population growth, as China has attempted to do? To serve political, economic, or environmental goals? For eugenic purposes? Dr. Joseph Fletcher has argued that there is a moral obligation to prevent the birth of genetically diseased or defective children, and a failure to carry out that obligation to those children "who would suffer grievously if conceived or born * * * would be tantamount to rejecting the whole notion of preventive medicine, sanitation, environmental protection law, and all the other ways in which we express our obligation to the unborn." Consider the following argument and determine whether it is strong enough to overcome the potential abuses inherent in allowing the government to determine who can reproduce, and under what circumstances.

> My fundamental commitment is that survival of the human species is a good and that it is a good of such importance and value that it can be accredited as a right. From this I deduce that individuals and social units have the concomitant obligation to pursue courses of actions that will foster and protect the right of the species' survival. Among these acknowledged and traditional courses of action is general health care. One

segment of that health care involves the protection of the population from the transmission of identifiable, seriously deleterious genes and from debilitating and costly (in terms of natural, economic and human resources) genetic disease which can neither be cured nor treated with any preservation of the quality of life and relative independence of the afflicted. Because individual human rights are negotiable according to their historical context, and because there is legal precedent for restricting the exercise of reproductive rights, those who are at high risk for passing on clearly identifiable and severely deleterious genes and debilitating genetic disease should not be allowed to exercise their reproductive prerogative.

E. Ulrich, Reproductive Rights and Genetic Disease, in J. Humber and R. Almender, Biomedical Ethics and the Law, 351, 360 (1976).

Of course, manipulation of the gene pool is not the only reason governments seek to regulate procreation. Because of the theological, ethical, and social values related to sexual conduct and its consequences, governments have often regulated techniques designed to limit reproduction. In the United States, legislatures and courts have often considered the propriety of contraception, sterilization, and abortion. Because these issues are considered in detail in constitutional law courses, they are only briefly addressed here.

2. Contraception

Historical and religious reasons explain why some states made the use of contraceptives a crime. The question of the propriety of those statutes reached the Supreme Court in Griswold v. Connecticut, 381 U.S. 479, 85 S.Ct. 1678, 14 L.Ed.2d 510 (1965). An official of the Planned Parenthood League of Connecticut and a Yale physician were charged with aiding and abetting "the use of a drug, medicinal article, or instrument for the purpose of preventing conception," a crime under Connecticut law, by providing contraceptives to a married couple. The Supreme Court reversed their conviction. Justice Douglas, writing for the Court, concluded:

> [s]pecific guarantees in the Bill of Rights have penumbras, formed by emanations from those guarantees that helped give them life and substance. Various guarantees create zones of privacy. The rights of association contained in the penumbra of the first amendment is one * * * the third amendment in its prohibition against the quartering of soldiers "in any house" in time of peace without the consent of the owner is another facet of that privacy. The fourth amendment explicitly affirms the right of the people to be secure in their persons, houses, papers, and effects against unreasonable searches and seizures. The fifth amendment in its self-incrimination clause enables the citizen to create a zone of privacy which government may not force him to surrender to his detriment. The ninth amendment provides "the enumeration in the constitution of certain rights will not be construed to deny or disparage others retained by the people."

> The present case * * * concerns a relationship lying within the zone of privacy created by several fundamental constitutional guarantees * * *.

We deal with a right of privacy older than the Bill of Rights—older than our political parties, older than our school system. Marriage is a coming together for better or worse, hopefully enduring, and intimate to the degree of being sacred. It is an association that promotes a way of life, not causes; a harmony in living, not political faith; a bilateral loyalty, not commercial or social projects. Yet it is an association for as noble a purpose as any involved in our prior decisions.

381 U.S. at 484, 85 S.Ct. at 1681. Although a majority concurred in Justice Douglas's opinion, Chief Justice Warren and Justices Brennan and Goldberg based their determination on the Ninth Amendment. Justice Harlan based his concurrence entirely on the due process clause of the Fourteenth Amendment. Separately, Justice White concurred in the judgment and based his determination on the fourteenth amendment. Justices Black and Stewart dissented. Justice Black wrote:

There is no single one of the graphic and eloquent strictures and criticisms fired at the policy of this Connecticut law either by the court's opinion or by those of my concurring brethren to which I cannot subscribe—except their conclusion that the evil qualities they see in the law make it unconstitutional * * *

I like my privacy as well as the next one, but I am nevertheless compelled to admit the government has a right to invade it unless prohibited by some specific constitutional provision. For these reasons, I cannot agree with the court's judgment and the reasons it gives for holding this Connecticut law unconstitutional.

381 U.S. at 510, 85 S.Ct. at 1696. The *Griswold* case left open the question of whether this new right of privacy extended only to married couples or to single people as well. It also left open the question of whether it extended only to decisions related to procreation or whether it extended to all health care decisions. The first of these questions was answered in 1972 when the Court determined that a law that allowed married people, but not unmarried people, to have access to contraceptives violated the equal protection clause of the Fourteenth Amendment because there could be no rational basis for distinguishing between married and unmarried people in permitting access to contraceptives. The Court suggested that "if the right of privacy means anything, it is the right of the individual, married or single, to be free from unwarranted government intrusion into matters so fundamentally affecting a person as a decision whether to bear a child." Eisenstadt v. Baird, 405 U.S. 438, 453, 92 S.Ct. 1029, 1038, 31 L.Ed.2d 349 (1972). In Carey v. Population Services International, 431 U.S. 678, 97 S.Ct. 2010, 52 L.Ed.2d 675 (1977), the Supreme Court confirmed that since *Griswold* declared it unconstitutional for a state to deny contraceptives to married couples, and *Eisenstadt* declared it unconstitutional for a state to distinguish between married couples and unmarried people in controlling access to contraceptives, a state was without authority to ban the distribution of contraceptives to any adult.

More recently governments have been faced with the prospect of whether some "contraceptives" that work by making implantation difficult (like the "morning after pill") are really contraceptives, subject to very limited government regulation, or agents of abortion, subject to far greater restriction and regulation (and, perhaps, prohibition). For a further discussion of this issue, see Note: The Blurry Distinction Between Contraception and Abortion and the Advent of Mifepristone (RU–486), pages 1163–1165.

3. *Abortion*

The right to privacy discussed (and perhaps invented) in *Griswold* found its most significant articulation in Roe v. Wade, 410 U.S. 113, 93 S.Ct. 705, 35 L.Ed.2d 147 (1973), the abortion case. Imagine Justice Blackmun writing this opinion, going through medicine and history texts hoping to find out just when a person protected by the Fourteenth Amendment really did come into existence. Justice Blackmun, who had been counsel to the Mayo Clinic earlier in his legal career, was keenly aware of the medical consequences of his determination. A comparison of Justice Blackmun's approach to this problem and Justice Douglas's approach, which appears in his concurring opinion, suggests that Justice Blackmun viewed abortion as a medical problem, while Justice Douglas viewed it as a personal issue. In any case, *Roe v. Wade* clearly recognized a constitutionally based right of privacy which extended to personal procreative decisions. Further, this right was based on the due process clause of the Fourteenth Amendment, not the penumbras and emanations that formed the unstable foundation for *Griswold*. While *Roe* was increasingly narrowed during the 1980s, and while its death was often predicted, in 1992 the Court concluded that "the essential holding of *Roe v. Wade* should be retained and once again reaffirmed." *Planned Parenthood of Southeastern Pennsylvania v. Casey*, 505 U.S. 833, 112 S.Ct. 2791, 120 L.Ed.2d 674 (1992). In 2000 the Supreme Court narrowly decided "not [to] revisit those legal principles" and to reaffirm *Roe* and *Casey* yet one more time. *Stenberg v. Carhart*, 530 U.S. 914, 120 S.Ct. 2597, 147 L.Ed.2d 743 (2000). But what is the "essential holding" of *Roe* that was retained in *Casey* and applied in *Stenberg*?

ROE v. WADE

Supreme Court of the United States, 1973.
410 U.S. 113, 93 S.Ct. 705, 35 L.Ed.2d 147.

Mr. Justice Blackmun delivered the opinion of the Court.

* * *

We forthwith acknowledge our awareness of the sensitive and emotional nature of the abortion controversy, of the vigorous opposing views, even among physicians, and of the deep and seemingly absolute convictions that the subject inspires. One's philosophy, one's experiences, one's exposure to the raw edges of human existence, one's religious training, one's attitudes toward life and family and their values, and the moral standards one establishes and seeks to observe, are all likely to influence and to color one's thinking and conclusions about abortion.

In addition, population growth, pollution, poverty, and racial overtones tend to complicate and not to simplify the problem.

Our task, of course, is to resolve the issue by constitutional measurement, free of emotion and of predilection. We seek earnestly to do this, and, because we do, we have inquired into, and in this opinion place some emphasis upon, medical and medical-legal history and what that history reveals about man's attitudes toward the abortion procedure over the centuries. We bear in mind, too, Mr. Justice Holmes' admonition in his now-vindicated dissent in Lochner v. New York, 198 U.S. 45, 76, 49 L.Ed. 937, 25 S.Ct. 539 (1905):

"[The Constitution] is made for people of fundamentally differing views, and the accident of our finding certain opinions natural and familiar or novel and even shocking ought not to conclude our judgment upon the question whether statutes embodying them conflict with the Constitution of the United States."

* * *

The principal thrust of appellant's attack on the Texas statutes is that they improperly invade a right, said to be possessed by the pregnant woman, to choose to terminate her pregnancy. Appellant would discover this right in the concept of personal "liberty" embodied in the Fourteenth Amendment's Due Process Clause; or in personal, marital, familial, and sexual privacy said to be protected by the Bill of Rights or its penumbras, [ ]; or among those rights reserved to the people by the Ninth Amendment [ ]. Before addressing this claim, we feel it desirable briefly to survey, in several aspects, the history of abortion, for such insight as that history may afford us, and then to examine the state purposes and interests behind the criminal abortion laws.

VI

It perhaps is not generally appreciated that the restrictive criminal abortion laws in effect in a majority of States today are of relatively recent vintage. Those laws, generally proscribing abortion or its attempt at any time during pregnancy except when necessary to preserve the pregnant woman's life, are not of ancient or even of common-law origin. Instead, they derive from statutory changes effected, for the most part, in the latter half of the 19th century.

[The Court then reviewed, in great detail, ancient attitudes, the Hippocratic Oath, the common law, English statutory law, American Law, the position of the American Medical Association, the position of the American Public Health Association, and the position of the American Bar Association.]

VII

Three reasons have been advanced to explain historically the enactment of criminal abortion laws in the 19th century and to justify their continued existence.

[The first, Victorian sexual morality, is dismissed as an anachronism.]

A second reason is concerned with abortion as a medical procedure. When most criminal abortion laws were first enacted, the procedure was a hazardous one for the woman.* * * Thus, it has been argued that a State's real concern in enacting a criminal abortion law was to protect the pregnant woman, that is, to restrain her from submitting to a procedure that placed her life in serious jeopardy.

Modern medical techniques have altered this situation. Appellants and various amici refer to medical data indicating that abortion in early pregnancy, this is, prior to the end of the first trimester, although not without its risk, is now relatively safe. Mortality rates for women undergoing early abortions, where the procedure is legal, appear to be as low as or lower than the rates for normal childbirth. Consequently, any interest of the State in protecting the woman from an inherently hazardous procedure, except when it would be equally dangerous for her to forgo it, has largely disappeared. Of course, important state interests in the area of health and medical standards do remain. The State has a legitimate interest in seeing to it that abortion, like any other medical procedure, is performed under circumstances that assure maximum safety for the patient. * * *

The third reason is the State's interest—some phrase it in terms of duty—in protecting prenatal life.

* * *

It is with these interests, and the weight to be attached to them, that this case is concerned.

VIII

The Constitution does not explicitly mention any right of privacy. In a line of decisions, however, going back perhaps as far as [ ] 1891 the Court has recognized that a right of personal privacy, or a guarantee of certain areas or zones of privacy, does exist under the Constitution. In varying contexts, the Court or individual Justices have, indeed, found at least the roots of that right in the First Amendment, [ ] in the Fourth and Fifth Amendments, Terry v. Ohio, [ ] in the penumbras of the Bill of Rights, Griswold v. Connecticut, [ ] the Ninth Amendment, [ ] or in the concept of liberty guaranteed by the first section of the Fourteenth Amendment. [ ] These decisions make it clear that only personal rights that can be deemed "fundamental" or "implicit in the concept of ordered liberty," [ ] are included in this guarantee of personal privacy. They also make it clear that the right has some extension to activities relating to marriage, [ ] family relationships, [ ] and child rearing and education [ ].

This right of privacy, whether it be founded in the Fourteenth Amendment's concept of personal liberty and restrictions upon state action, as we feel it is, or, as the District Court determined, in the Ninth Amendment's reservation of rights to the people, is broad enough to encompass a woman's decision whether or not to terminate her pregnancy. The detriment that the State would impose upon the pregnant woman by denying this choice altogether is apparent. Specific and direct harm medically diagnosable even in early pregnancy may be involved. Maternity, or additional offspring, may force upon the woman a distressful life and future. Psychological harm may be imminent. Mental and physical health may be taxed by child care. There is also the distress, for all concerned, associated with the unwanted child, and there is the problem of bringing a child into a family already unable, psychologically and otherwise, to care for it. In other cases, as in this one, the additional difficulties and continuing stigma of unwed motherhood may be involved. All these are factors the woman and her responsible physician necessarily will consider in consultation.

On the basis of elements such as these, appellant and some amici argue that the woman's right is absolute and that she is entitled to terminate her pregnancy at whatever time, in whatever way, and for whatever reason she alone chooses. With this we do not agree.* * * [A] State may properly assert important interests in safeguarding health, in maintaining medical standards, and in protecting potential life. At some point in pregnancy, these respective interests become sufficiently compelling to sustain regulation of the factors that govern the abortion decision.

* * *

X
* * *

With respect to the State's important and legitimate interest in the health of the mother, the "compelling" point, in the light of present medical knowledge, is at approximately the end of the first trimester. This is so because of the now-established medical fact * * * that until the end of the first trimester mortality in abortion may be less than mortality in normal childbirth. It follows that, from and after this point, a State may regulate the abortion procedure to the extent that the regulation reasonably relates to the preservation and protection of maternal health. * * *

This means, on the other hand, that, for the period of pregnancy prior to this "compelling" point, the attending physician, in consultation with his patient, is free to determine, without regulation by the State, that, in his medical judgment, the patient's pregnancy should be terminated. If that decision is reached, the judgment may be effectuated by an abortion free of interference by the State.

With respect to the State's important and legitimate interest in potential life, the "compelling" point is at viability. This is so because the fetus then presumably has the capability of meaningful life outside the mother's womb. State regulation protective of fetal life after viability thus has both logical and biological justifications. If the State is interested in protecting fetal life after viability, it may go so far as to proscribe abortion during that period, except when it is necessary to preserve the life or health of the mother.

* * *

XI

To summarize and to repeat:

1. A state criminal abortion statute of the current Texas type, that excepts from criminality only a *lifesaving* procedure on behalf of the mother, without regard to pregnancy stage and without recognition of the other interests involved, is violative of the Due Process Clause of the Fourteenth Amendment.

(a) For the stage prior to approximately the end of the first trimester, the abortion decision and its effectuation must be left to the medical judgment of the pregnant woman's attending physician.

(b) For the stage subsequent to approximately the end of the first trimester, the State, in promoting its interest in the health of the mother, may, if it chooses, regulate the abortion procedure in ways that are reasonably related to maternal health.

(c) For the stage subsequent to viability, the State in promoting its interest in the potentiality of human life may, if it chooses, regulate, and even proscribe, abortion except where it is necessary, in appropriate medical judgment, for the preservation of the life or health of the mother.

* * *

Notes and Questions

1. Justice Blackmun's Fourteenth Amendment analysis is not the only way that the Court could have reached this result. Justice Douglas, concurring, would have depended on the Ninth Amendment, as did the District Court. His approach would have recognized a far broader right of privacy:

> The Ninth Amendment obviously does not create federally enforceable rights. It merely says, "The enumeration in the Constitution, of certain rights, shall not be construed to deny or disparage others retained by the people." But a catalogue of these rights includes customary, traditional, and time-honored rights, amenities, privileges, and immunities that come within the sweep of "the Blessings of Liberty" mentioned in the preamble to the Constitution. Many of them, in my view, come within the meaning of the term "liberty" as used in the Fourteenth Amendment.

> *First is the autonomous control over the development and expression of one's intellect, interests, tastes, and personality.*

> *Second is freedom of choice in the basic decisions of one's life respecting marriage, divorce, procreation, contraception, and the education and upbringing of children.*

> *Third is the freedom to care for one's health and person, freedom from bodily restraint or compulsion, freedom to walk, stroll, or loaf.*

Consider how the subsequent history of abortion legislation and litigation might have been different had this less medical, much broader, definition of the right been accepted by the Court in 1973.

2. The Court's opinion stirred into action political forces opposed to abortion. They have encouraged state legislatures to seek creative ways to discourage abortions without running afoul of the requirements of *Roe v. Wade.* The Supreme Court at first resisted attempts to limit the underlying rights recognized in 1973, although the number of justices supporting that decision declined over time. *Roe* was reaffirmed more than a dozen times in its first decade, but by 1986 the 7–2 majority was down to 5–4, Thornburgh v. American College of Obstetricians and Gynecologists, 476 U.S. 747, 106 S.Ct. 2169, 90 L.Ed.2d 779 (1986), and by 1989 the Court appeared to be evenly divided, with Justice O'Connor unwilling to confront the issue. Webster v. Reproductive Health Services, 492 U.S. 490, 109 S.Ct. 3040, 106 L.Ed.2d 410 (1989). *Roe* was revived in Planned Parenthood of Southeastern Pennsylvania v. Casey, 505 U.S. 833, 112 S.Ct. 2791, 120 L.Ed.2d 674 (1992), and in this revived form, by the narrowest of majorities, it remained the governing law in 2001. Stenberg v. Carhart, 530 U.S. 914, 120 S.Ct. 2597, 147 L.Ed.2d 743 (2000).

3. *Roe v. Wade* has been vigorously criticized, both as a matter of policy and a matter of law. While Congress has not taken action to promulgate a constitutional amendment allowing states to prohibit abortions, government funding for abortions has been limited and the restrictions on the use of government funds for abortions have generally been upheld by the courts. In 1977, the Supreme Court upheld state statutes and Medicaid plans that refused to fund nontherapeutic

abortions as well as a city's determination that its hospitals would not provide nontherapeutic abortions. Beal v. Doe, 432 U.S. 438, 97 S.Ct. 2366, 53 L.Ed.2d 464 (1977); Maher v. Roe, 432 U.S. 464, 97 S.Ct. 2376, 53 L.Ed.2d 484 (1977); Poelker v. Doe, 432 U.S. 519, 97 S.Ct. 2391, 53 L.Ed.2d 528 (1977). Three years later in Harris v. McRae, 448 U.S. 297, 100 S.Ct. 2671, 65 L.Ed.2d 784 (1980), the Supreme Court upheld the Hyde amendment, which provided that federal funds could not be used for virtually any abortion.

4.   There were two legal lines of attack on the Supreme Court's decision in *Roe v. Wade*. The first argued that the Supreme Court had returned to the unhappy Lochnerian days of substantive due process, during which the Court acted as if it were free to make social policy without regard to legal or constitutional restrictions. Of course, the authors of the Fourteenth Amendment were not confronted with abortion as a political and social issue, and the intent of the framers with regard to this particular question is not likely to be helpful in resolving this issue. While the Fourteenth Amendment has been broadly interpreted, *Roe v. Wade* and the subsequent abortion cases are among the very few examples of the application of a "right to privacy" that arise out of that amendment. It is a difficult jurisprudential feat to support the creation and application of that right. The Supreme Court has refused to extend this right of privacy to other areas, even within the health care system. See United States v. Rutherford, 442 U.S. 544, 99 S.Ct. 2470, 61 L.Ed.2d 68 (1979) (no privacy right to use an unproven cancer drug.) The Supreme Court also explicitly rejected the application of the right of privacy to protect those engaging in homosexual conduct. Bowers v. Hardwick, 478 U.S. 186, 106 S.Ct. 2841, 92 L.Ed.2d 140 (1986). In the first right to die case considered by the Court, none of the Justices even used the word "privacy" to describe the underlying constitutional right; instead they depended upon the apparently more limited "liberty interest" explicitly mentioned in the Fourteenth Amendment. Cruzan v. Director, Missouri Dept. of Health, 497 U.S. 261, 110 S.Ct. 2841, 111 L.Ed.2d 224 (1990). See Chapter 19. In a strictly legal, conceptual sense, *Roe v. Wade* remains a derelict on the waters of the law.

The second line of attack focused on the opinion's scientific foundation. *Roe v. Wade* made two kinds of distinctions. First, it identified that point at which it became more dangerous to abort than to bear the child; second, it identified that point at which the fetus was viable. The court identified those points as occurring at the end of the first and second trimesters. As the science of obstetrics improves and safer techniques of abortion are developed, the first point is being moved back, closer to the time of delivery, and the second point is being moved forward, closer to the time of conception. It is now quite safe to have an abortion long after the end of the first trimester, and a fetus may be viable before the end of the second trimester. Should the Supreme Court stick to its scientifically justifiable points (the point of increased danger and the point of viability), which would create an ambiguity because it changes with the latest medical developments, or should it stick with the arbitrary first and second trimester timelines, which are easy to apply, even though they are no longer supported by science? The Court attempted to answer this question in City of Akron v. Akron Center for Reproductive Health, Inc., 462 U.S. 416, 103 S.Ct. 2481, 76 L.Ed.2d 687 (1983), and finally reconsidered the trimester division altogether in 1992.

PLANNED PARENTHOOD OF SOUTHEASTERN PENNSYLVANIA v. CASEY

Supreme Court of the United States, 1992.
505 U.S. 833, 112 S.Ct. 2791, 120 L.Ed.2d 674.

JUSTICE O'CONNOR, JUSTICE KENNEDY, and JUSTICE SOUTER announced the judgment of the Court and delivered the opinion of the Court with respect to Parts I, II, III, V–A, V–C, and VI, an opinion with respect to Part V–E, in which JUSTICE STEVENS joins, and an opinion with respect to Parts IV, V–B, and V–D.

I.

Liberty finds no refuge in a jurisprudence of doubt. Yet 19 years after our holding that the Constitution protects a woman's right to terminate her pregnancy in its early stages, [ ] that definition of liberty is still questioned. * * *

At issue in these cases are five provisions of the Pennsylvania Abortion Control Act of 1982. * * * The Act requires that a woman seeking an abortion give her informed consent prior to the abortion procedure, and specifies that she be provided with certain information at least 24 hours before the abortion is performed. [ ] For a minor to obtain an abortion, the Act requires the informed consent of one of her parents, but provides for a judicial bypass option if the minor does not wish to or cannot obtain a parent's consent. [ ] Another provision of the Act requires that, unless certain exceptions apply, a married woman seeking an abortion must sign a statement indicating that she has notified her husband of her intended abortion. [ ] The Act exempts compliance with these three requirements in the event of a "medical emergency," which is defined in the Act. [ ] In addition to the above provisions regulating the performance of abortions, the Act imposes certain reporting requirements on facilities that provide abortion services. [ ]

* * *

After considering the fundamental constitutional questions resolved by *Roe*, principles of institutional integrity, and the rule of stare decisis, we are led to conclude this: the essential holding of *Roe v. Wade* should be retained and once again reaffirmed.

It must be stated at the outset and with clarity that *Roe's* essential holding, the holding we reaffirm, has three parts. First is a recognition of the right of the woman to choose to have an abortion before viability and to obtain it without undue interference from the State. Before viability, the State's interests are not strong enough to support a prohibition of abortion or the imposition of a substantial obstacle to the woman's effective right to elect the procedure. Second is a confirmation of the State's power to restrict abortions after fetal viability, if the law contains exceptions for pregnancies which endanger a woman's life or health. And third is the principle that the State has legitimate interests from the outset of the pregnancy in protecting the health of the woman and the life of the fetus that may become a child. These principles do not contradict one another; and we adhere to each.

II.

* * *

Men and women of good conscience can disagree, and we suppose some always shall disagree, about the profound moral and spiritual implications of terminating a pregnancy, even in its earliest stage. Some of us as individuals find abortion offensive to our most basic principles of morality, but that cannot control our decision. Our obligation is to define the liberty of all, not to mandate our own moral code. The underlying constitutional issue is whether the State can resolve these philosophic questions in such a definitive way that a woman lacks all choice in the matter, except perhaps in those rare circumstances in which the pregnancy is itself a danger to her own life or health, or is the result of rape or incest. * * * Abortion is a unique act. It is an act fraught with consequences for others: for the woman who must live with the implications of her decision; for the persons who perform and assist in the procedure; for the spouse, family, and society which must confront the knowledge that these procedures exist, procedures some deem nothing short of an act of violence against innocent human life; and, depending on one's beliefs, for the life or potential life that is aborted. Though abortion is conduct, it does not follow that the State is entitled to proscribe it in all instances. That is because the liberty of the woman is at stake in a sense unique to the human condition and so unique to the law. The mother who carries a child to full term is subject to anxieties, to physical constraints, to pain that only she must bear. That these sacrifices have from the beginning of the human race been endured by woman with a pride that ennobles her in the eyes of others and gives to the infant a bond of love cannot alone be grounds for the State to insist she make the sacrifice. Her suffering is too intimate and personal for the State to insist, without more, upon its own vision of the woman's role, however dominant that vision has been in the course of our history and our culture. The destiny of the woman must be shaped to a large extent on her own conception of her spiritual imperatives and her place in society.

* * *

While we appreciate the weight of the arguments made on behalf of the State in the case before us, arguments which in their ultimate formulation conclude that *Roe* should be overruled, the reservations any of us may have in reaffirming the central holding of *Roe* are outweighed by the explication of individual liberty we have given combined with the force of stare decisis. We turn now to that doctrine.

III.

A.

[In this section, the court discussed the conditions under which it is appropriate for the Court to reverse its own precedent.]

So in this case we may inquire whether *Roe's* central rule has been found unworkable; whether the rule's limitation on state power could be removed without serious inequity to those who have relied upon it or significant damage to the stability of the society governed by the rule in question; whether the law's growth in the intervening years has left *Roe's* central rule a doctrinal anachronism discounted by society; and whether *Roe's* premises of fact have so far changed in the ensuing two decades as to render its central holding somehow irrelevant or unjustifiable in dealing with the issue it addressed.

* * *

The sum of the precedential inquiry to this point shows *Roe's* underpinnings unweakened in any way affecting its central holding. While it has engendered disapproval, it has not been unworkable. An entire generation has come of age free to assume *Roe's* concept of liberty in defining the capacity of women to act in society, and to make reproductive decisions; no erosion of principle going to liberty or personal autonomy has left *Roe's* central holding a doctrinal remnant; *Roe* portends no developments at odds with other precedent for the analysis of personal liberty; and no changes of fact have rendered viability more or less appropriate as the point at which the balance of interests tips. Within the bounds of normal stare decisis analysis, then, and subject to the considerations on which it customarily turns, the stronger argument is for affirming *Roe's* central holding, with whatever degree of personal reluctance any of us may have, not for overruling it.

B.

[The Court next distinguished the rule in the abortion cases from the rules in *Lochner* and the "separate but equal" cases, two areas in which the Supreme Court did reverse its well settled precedents this century. The Court also explained that it should not expend its political capital and put the public respect for the Court and its processes at risk by reversing *Roe*.]

IV.

From what we have said so far it follows that it is a constitutional liberty of the woman to have some freedom to terminate her pregnancy. We conclude that the basic decision in *Roe* was based on a constitutional analysis which we cannot now repudiate. The woman's liberty is not so unlimited, however, that from the outset the State cannot show its concern for the life of the unborn, and at a later point in fetal development the State's interest in life has sufficient force so that the right of the woman to terminate the pregnancy can be restricted.

* * *

We conclude the line should be drawn at viability, so that before that time the woman has a right to choose to terminate her pregnancy. We adhere to this principle for two reasons. First, as we have said, is the doctrine of stare decisis. * * *

The second reason is that the concept of viability, as we noted in *Roe,* is the time at which there is a realistic possibility of maintaining and nourishing a life outside the womb, so that the independent existence of the second life can in reason and all fairness be the object of state protection that now overrides the rights of the woman. * * *

The woman's right to terminate her pregnancy before viability is the most central principle of *Roe v. Wade*. It is a rule of law and a component of liberty we cannot renounce.

* * *

Yet it must be remembered that *Roe v. Wade* speaks with clarity in establishing not only the woman's liberty but also the State's "important and legitimate interest in potential life." [ ] That portion of the decision in *Roe* has been given too little acknowledgment and implementation by the Court in its subsequent cases. Those cases decided that any regulation touching upon the abortion decision must survive strict scrutiny, to be sustained only if drawn in narrow terms to further a compelling state interest. [ ] Not all of the cases decided under that formulation can be reconciled with the holding in *Roe* itself that the State has legitimate interests in the health of the woman and in protecting the potential life within her. In resolving this tension, we choose to rely upon *Roe,* as against the later cases.

* * *

We reject the trimester framework, which we do not consider to be part of the essential holding of *Roe*. [ ] Measures aimed at ensuring that a woman's choice contemplates the consequences for the fetus do not necessarily interfere with the right recognized in *Roe*, although those measures have been found to be inconsistent with the rigid trimester framework announced in that case. A logical reading of the central holding in *Roe* itself, and a necessary reconciliation of the liberty of the woman and the interest of the State in promoting prenatal life, require, in our view, that we abandon the trimester framework as a rigid prohibition on all previability regulation aimed at the protection of fetal life.

* * *

The fact that a law which serves a valid purpose, one not designed to strike at the right itself, has the incidental effect of making it more difficult or more expensive to procure an abortion cannot be enough to invalidate it. Only where state regulation imposes an undue burden on a woman's ability to make this decision does the power of the State reach into the heart of the liberty protected by the Due Process Clause.

* * *

Roe v. Wade was express in its recognition of the State's "important and legitimate interests in preserving and protecting the health of the pregnant woman [and] in protecting the potentiality of human life." [ ] The trimester framework, however, does not fulfill *Roe's* own promise that the State has an interest in protecting fetal life or potential life. *Roe* began the contradiction by using the trimester framework to forbid any regulation of abortion designed to advance that interest before viability. [ ] Before viability, *Roe* and subsequent cases treat all governmental attempts to influence a woman's decision on behalf of the potential life within her as unwarranted. This treatment is, in our judgment, incompatible with the recognition that there is a substantial state interest in potential life throughout pregnancy. [ ]

The very notion that the State has a substantial interest in potential life leads to the conclusion that not all regulations must be deemed unwarranted. Not all burdens on the right to decide whether to terminate a pregnancy will be undue. In our view, the undue burden standard is the appropriate means of reconciling the State's interest with the woman's constitutionally protected liberty.

* * *

A finding of an undue burden is a shorthand for the conclusion that a state regulation has the purpose or effect of placing a substantial obstacle in the path of a woman seeking an abortion of a nonviable fetus. A statute with this purpose is invalid because the means chosen by the State to further the interest in potential life must be calculated to inform the woman's free choice, not hinder it. And a statute which, while furthering the interest in potential life or some other valid state interest, has the effect of placing a substantial obstacle in the path of a woman's choice cannot be considered a permissible means of serving its legitimate ends. * * *

Some guiding principles should emerge. What is at stake is the woman's right to make the ultimate decision, not a right to be insulated from all others in doing so. Regulations which do no more than create a structural mechanism by which the State, or the parent or guardian of a minor, may express profound respect for the life of the unborn are permitted, if they are not a substantial obstacle to the woman's exercise of the right to choose. [ ]

[The Justices then summarized their new undue burden test:]

(a) To protect the central right recognized by *Roe v. Wade* while at the same time accommodating the State's profound interest in potential life, we will employ the undue burden analysis as explained in this opinion. An undue burden exists, and therefore a provision of law is invalid, if its purpose or effect is to place a substantial obstacle in the path of a woman seeking an abortion before the fetus attains viability.

(b) We reject the rigid trimester framework of *Roe v. Wade*. To promote the State's profound interest in potential life, throughout pregnancy the State may take measures to ensure that the woman's choice is informed, and measures designed to advance this interest will not be invalidated as long as their purpose is to persuade the woman to choose childbirth over abortion. These measures must not be an undue burden on the right.

(c) As with any medical procedure, the State may enact regulations to further the health or safety of a woman seeking an abortion. Unnecessary health regulations that have the purpose or effect of presenting a substantial obstacle to a woman seeking an abortion impose an undue burden on the right.

(d) Our adoption of the undue burden analysis does not disturb the central holding of *Roe v. Wade,* and we reaffirm that holding. Regardless of whether exceptions are made for particular circumstances, a State may not prohibit any woman from making the ultimate decision to terminate her pregnancy before viability.

(e) We also reaffirm *Roe's* holding that "subsequent to viability, the State in promoting its interest in the potentiality of human life may, if it chooses, regulate, and even proscribe, abortion except where it is necessary, in appropriate medical judgment, for the preservation of the life or health of the mother." [ ]

* * *

V.

* * *

A.

Because it is central to the operation of various other requirements, we begin with the statute's definition of medical emergency. Under the statute, a medical emergency is "that condition which, on the basis of the physician's good faith clinical judgment, so complicates the medical condition of a pregnant woman as to necessitate the immediate abortion of her pregnancy to avert her death or for which a delay will create serious risk of substantial and irreversible impairment of a major bodily function." [ ]

Petitioners argue that the definition is too narrow, contending that it forecloses the possibility of an immediate abortion despite some significant health risks.

[The Justices accepted the Court of Appeals interpretation of the statute, which assured that "abortion regulation would not in any way pose a significant threat to the life or health of a woman," and determined that the definition imposed no undue burden on a woman's right to an abortion.]

B.

We next consider the informed consent requirement. [ ] Except in a medical emergency, the statute requires that at least 24 hours before performing an abortion a physician inform the woman of the nature of the procedure, the health risks of the abortion and of childbirth, and the "probable gestational age of the unborn child." The physician or a qualified nonphysician must inform the woman of the availability of printed materials published by the State describing the fetus and providing information about medical assistance for childbirth, information about child support from the father, and a list of agencies which provide adoption and other services as alternatives to abortion. An abortion may not be performed unless the woman certifies in writing that she has been informed of the availability of these printed materials and has been provided them if she chooses to view them.

* * *

To the extent [our prior cases] find a constitutional violation when the government requires, as it does here, the giving of truthful, nonmisleading information about the nature of the procedure, the attendant health risks and those of childbirth, and the "probable gestational age" of the fetus, those cases go too far, are inconsistent with *Roe's* acknowledgment of an important interest in potential life, and are overruled. * * * If the information the State requires to be made available to the woman is truthful and not misleading, the requirement may be permissible.

We also see no reason why the State may not require doctors to inform a woman seeking an abortion of the availability of materials relating to the consequences to the fetus, even when those consequences have no direct relation to her health. * * * As we have made clear, * * * we permit a State to further its legitimate goal of protecting the life of the unborn by enacting legislation aimed at ensuring a decision that is mature and informed, even when in so doing the State expresses a preference for childbirth over abortion. In short, requiring that the woman be informed of the availability of information relating to fetal development and the assistance available should she decide to carry the pregnancy to full term is a reasonable measure to insure an informed choice, one which might cause the woman to choose childbirth over abortion. This requirement cannot be considered a substantial obstacle to obtaining an abortion, and, it follows, there is no undue burden.

* * *

All that is left of petitioners' argument is an asserted First Amendment right of a physician not to provide information about the risks of abortion, and childbirth, in a manner mandated by the State. To be sure, the physician's First Amendment rights not to speak are implicated, [ ] but only as part of the practice of medicine, subject to reasonable licensing and regulation by the State. We see no constitutional infirmity in the requirement that the physician provide the information mandated by the State here.

The Pennsylvania statute also requires us to reconsider the holding [ ] that the State may not require that a physician, as opposed to a qualified assistant, provide information relevant to a woman's informed consent. [ ] Since there is no evidence on this record that requiring a doctor to give the information as provided by the statute would amount in practical terms to a substantial obstacle to a woman seeking an abortion, we conclude that it is not an undue burden. Our cases reflect the fact that the Constitution gives the States broad latitude to decide that particular functions may be performed only by licensed professionals, even if an objective assessment might suggest that those same tasks could be performed by others. [ ] Thus, we uphold the provision as a reasonable means to insure that the woman's consent is informed.

Our analysis of Pennsylvania's 24–hour waiting period between the provision of the information deemed necessary to informed consent and the performance of an abortion under the undue burden standard requires us to reconsider the premise behind the decision in *Akron I* invalidating a parallel requirement. In *Akron I* we said: "Nor are we convinced that the State's legitimate concern that the woman's decision be informed is reasonably served by requiring a 24–hour delay as a matter of course." [ ] We consider that conclusion to be wrong. The idea that important decisions will be more informed and deliberate if they follow some period of reflection does not strike us as unreasonable, particularly where the statute directs that important information become part of the background of the decision. * * *

Whether the mandatory 24–hour waiting period is nonetheless invalid because in practice it is a substantial obstacle to a woman's choice to terminate her pregnancy is a closer question. The findings of fact by the District Court indicate that because of the distances many women must travel to reach an abortion provider, the practical effect will often be a delay of much more than a day because the waiting period requires that a woman seeking an abortion make at least two visits to the doctor. * * *

These findings are troubling in some respects, but they do not demonstrate that the waiting period constitutes an undue burden. We do not doubt that, as the District Court held, the waiting period has the effect of "increasing the cost and risk of delay of abortions," [ ] but the District Court did not conclude that the increased costs and potential delays amount to substantial obstacles.* * *

We are left with the argument that the various aspects of the informed consent requirement are unconstitutional because they place barriers in the way of abortion on demand. Even the broadest reading of *Roe,* however, has not suggested that there is a constitutional right to abortion on demand. [ ] Rather, the right protected by *Roe* is a right to decide to terminate a pregnancy free of undue interference by the State. Because the informed consent requirement facilitates the wise exercise of that right it cannot be classified as an interference with the right *Roe* protects. The informed consent requirement is not an undue burden on that right.

C.

Pennsylvania's abortion law provides, except in cases of medical emergency, that no physician shall perform an abortion on a married woman without receiving a signed statement from the woman that she has notified her spouse that she is about to undergo an abortion.

* * *

This information and the District Court's findings reinforce what common sense would suggest. In well-functioning marriages, spouses discuss important intimate decisions such as whether to bear a child. But there are millions of women in this country who are the victims of regular physical and psychological abuse at the hands of their husbands. Should these women become pregnant, they may have very good reasons for not wishing to inform their husbands of their decision to obtain an abortion. Many may have justifiable fears of physical abuse, but may be no less fearful of the consequences of reporting prior abuse to the Commonwealth of Pennsylvania. Many may have a reasonable fear that notifying their husbands will provoke further instances of child abuse; these women are not exempt from [the] notification requirement. Many may fear devastating forms of psychological abuse from their husbands, including verbal harassment, threats of future violence, the destruction of possessions, physical confinement to the home, the withdrawal of financial support, or the disclosure of the abortion to family and friends. * * *

The spousal notification requirement is thus likely to prevent a significant number of women from obtaining an abortion. It does not merely make abortions a little more difficult or expensive to obtain; for many women, it will impose a substantial obstacle. We must not blind ourselves to the fact that the significant number of women who fear for their safety and the safety of their children are likely to be deterred from procuring an abortion as surely as if the Commonwealth had outlawed abortion in all cases.

Respondents attempt to avoid the conclusion that [the spousal notification provision] is invalid by pointing out that it imposes almost no burden at all for the vast majority of women seeking abortions. * * * Respondents argue that since some of [the 20% of women who seek abortions who are married] will be able to notify their husbands without adverse consequences or will qualify for one of the exceptions, the statute affects fewer than one percent of women seeking abortions. For this reason, it is asserted, the statute cannot be invalid on its face. [ ] We disagree with respondents' basic method of analysis.

The analysis does not end with the one percent of women upon whom the statute operates; it begins there. Legislation is measured for consistency with the Constitution by its impact on those whose conduct it affects. * * * [A]s we have said, [the Act's] real target is narrower even than the class of women seeking abortions * * *: it is married women seeking abortions who do not wish to notify their husbands of their intentions and who do not qualify for one of the statutory exceptions to the notice requirement. The unfortunate yet persisting conditions * * * will mean that in a large fraction of the cases * * *, [the statute] will operate as a substantial obstacle to a woman's choice to undergo an abortion. It is an undue burden, and therefore invalid.

* * *

[The spousal notification provision] embodies a view of marriage consonant with the common-law status of married women but repugnant to our present understanding of marriage and of the nature of the rights secured by the Constitution. Women do not lose their constitutionally protected liberty when they marry. * * *

D.

* * *

Our cases establish, and we reaffirm today, that a State may require a minor seeking an abortion to obtain the consent of a parent or guardian, provided that there is an adequate judicial bypass procedure. [ ] Under these precedents, in our view, the [Pennsylvania] one-parent consent requirement and judicial bypass procedure are constitutional.

The only argument made by petitioners respecting this provision and to which our prior decisions do not speak is the contention that the parental consent requirement is invalid because it requires informed parental consent. For the most part, petitioners' argument is a reprise of their argument with respect to the informed consent requirement in general, and we reject it for the reasons given above. Indeed, some of the provisions regarding informed consent have particular force with respect to minors: the waiting period, for example, may provide the parent or parents of a pregnant young woman the opportunity to consult with her in private, and to discuss the consequences of her decision in the context of the values and moral or religious principles of their family. [ ]

E.

[The Justices upheld all of the record keeping and reporting requirements of the statute, except for that provision requiring the reporting of a married woman's reason for failure to give notice to her husband.]

VI.

Our Constitution is a covenant running from the first generation of Americans to us and then to future generations. It is a coherent succession. Each generation must learn anew that the Constitution's written terms embody ideas and aspirations that must survive more ages than one. We accept our responsibility not to retreat from interpreting the full meaning of the covenant in light of all of our precedents. We invoke it once again to define the freedom guaranteed by the Constitution's own promise, the promise of liberty.

* * *

[In addition to those parts of the statute found unconstitutional in the three-justice opinion, Justice Stevens would find unconstitutional the requirement that the doctor deliver state-produced materials to a woman seeking an abortion, the counseling requirements, and the 24-hour-waiting requirement. His concurring and dissenting opinion is omitted. Justice Blackman's opinion, concurring in the judgment in part and dissenting in part, is also omitted.]

CHIEF JUSTICE REHNQUIST, with whom JUSTICE WHITE, JUSTICE SCALIA, and JUSTICE THOMAS join, concurring in the judgment in part and dissenting in part.

The joint opinion, following its newly-minted variation on stare decisis, retains the outer shell of *Roe v. Wade*, [ ] but beats a wholesale retreat from the substance of that case. We believe that *Roe* was wrongly decided, and that it can and should be overruled consistently with our traditional approach to stare decisis in constitutional cases.

* * *

The end result of the joint opinion's paeans of praise for legitimacy is the enunciation of a brand new standard for evaluating state regulation of a woman's right to abortion—the "undue burden" standard. As indicated above, *Roe v. Wade* adopted a "fundamental right" standard under which state regulations could survive only if they met the requirement of "strict scrutiny." While we disagree with that standard, it at least had a recognized basis in constitutional law at the time *Roe* was decided. The same cannot be said for the "undue burden" standard, which is created largely out of whole cloth by the authors of the joint opinion. It is a standard which even today does not command the support of a majority of this Court. And it will not, we believe, result in the sort of "simple limitation," easily applied, which the joint opinion anticipates. [ ] In sum, it is a standard which is not built to last.

In evaluating abortion regulations under that standard, judges will have to decide whether they place a "substantial obstacle" in the path of a woman seeking an abortion. [ ] In that this standard is based even more on a judge's subjective determinations than was the trimester framework, the standard will do nothing to prevent "judges from roaming at large in the constitutional field" guided only by their personal views. [ ]

* * *

The sum of the joint opinion's labors in the name of stare decisis and "legitimacy" is this: *Roe v. Wade* stands as a sort of judicial Potemkin Village, which may be pointed out to passers by as a monument to the importance of adhering to precedent. But behind the facade, an entirely new method of analysis, without any roots in constitutional law, is imported to decide the constitutionality of state laws regulating abortion. Neither stare decisis nor "legitimacy" are truly served by such an effort.

* * *

JUSTICE SCALIA, with whom the CHIEF JUSTICE, JUSTICE WHITE, and JUSTICE THOMAS join, concurring in the judgment in part and dissenting in part.

* * *

The States may, if they wish, permit abortion-on-demand, but the Constitution does not require them to do so. The permissibility of abortion, and the limitations upon it, are to be resolved like most important questions in our democracy: by citizens trying to persuade one another and then voting. As the Court acknowledges, "where reasonable people disagree the government can adopt one position or the other." [ ] The Court is correct in adding the qualification that this "assumes a state of affairs in which the choice does not intrude upon a protected liberty," [ ]—but the crucial part of that qualification is the penultimate word. A State's choice between two positions on which reasonable people can disagree is constitutional even when (as is often the case) it intrudes upon a "liberty" in the absolute sense. Laws against bigamy, for example—which entire societies of reasonable people disagree with— intrude upon men and women's liberty to marry and live with one another. But bigamy happens not to be a liberty specially "protected" by the Constitution.

That is, quite simply, the issue in this case: not whether the power of a woman to abort her unborn child is a "liberty" in the absolute sense; or even whether it is a liberty of great importance to many women. Of course it is both. The issue is whether it is a liberty protected by the Constitution of the United States. I am sure it is not. I reach that conclusion not because of anything so exalted as my views concerning the "concept of existence, of meaning, of the universe, and of the mystery of human life." [ ] I reach it for the same reason I reach the conclusion that bigamy is not constitutionally protected—because of two simple facts: (1) the Constitution says absolutely nothing about it, and (2) the longstanding traditions of American society have permitted it to be legally proscribed.

* * *

I am certainly not in a good position to dispute that the Court has saved the "central holding" of *Roe*, since to do that effectively I would have to know what the Court has saved, which in turn would require me to understand (as I do not) what the "undue burden" test means. * * * I thought I might note, however, that the following portions of *Roe* have not been saved:

• Under *Roe*, requiring that a woman seeking an abortion be provided truthful information about abortion before giving informed written consent is unconstitutional, if the information is designed to influence her choice [ ]. Under the joint opinion's "undue burden" regime (as applied today, at least) such a requirement is constitutional [ ].

• Under *Roe*, requiring that information be provided by a doctor, rather than by nonphysician counselors, is unconstitutional [ ]. Under the "undue burden" regime (as applied today, at least) it is not [ ].

• Under *Roe*, requiring a 24–hour waiting period between the time the woman gives her informed consent and the time of the abortion is unconstitutional. Under the "undue burden" regime (as applied today, at least) it is not [ ].

• Under *Roe*, requiring detailed reports that include demographic data about each woman who seeks an abortion and various information about each abortion is unconstitutional [ ]. Under the "undue burden" regime (as applied today, at least) it generally is not [ ].

* * *

STENBERG v. CARHART

Supreme Court of the United States, 2000.
530 U.S. 914, 120 S.Ct. 2597, 147 L.Ed.2d 743.

JUSTICE BREYER delivered the opinion of the Court.

We again consider the right to an abortion. We understand the controversial nature of the problem. Millions of Americans believe that life begins at conception and consequently that an abortion is akin to causing the death of an innocent child; they recoil at the thought of a law that would permit it. Other millions fear that a law that forbids abortion would condemn many American women to lives that lack dignity, depriving them of equal liberty and leaving those with least resources to undergo illegal abortions with the attendant risks of death and suffering. Taking account of these virtually irreconcilable points of view, aware that constitutional law must govern a society whose different members sincerely hold directly opposing views, and considering the matter in light of the Constitution's guarantees of fundamental individual liberty, this Court, in the course of a generation, has determined and then redetermined that the Constitution offers basic protection to the woman's right to choose. *Roe v. Wade*; *Planned Parenthood of Southeastern Pa. v. Casey*.[ ] We shall not revisit those legal principles. Rather, we apply them to the circumstances of this case.

Three established principles determine the issue before us. We shall set them forth in the language of the joint opinion in Casey. First, before "viability * * * the woman has a right to choose to terminate her pregnancy."

Second, "a law designed to further the State's interest in fetal life which imposes an undue burden on the woman's decision before fetal viability" is unconstitutional. An "undue burden is * * * shorthand for the conclusion that a state regulation has the purpose or effect of placing a substantial obstacle in the path of a woman seeking an abortion of a nonviable fetus."

Third, " 'subsequent to viability, the State in promoting its interest in the potentiality of human life, may, if it choose, regulate, and even proscribe, abortion except where it is necessary, in appropriate medical judgment, for the preservation of the life or health of the mother.' "

We apply these principles to a Nebraska law banning "partial birth abortion." The statute reads as follows:

"No partial birth abortion shall be performed in this state, unless such procedure is necessary to save the life of the mother whose life is endangered by a physical disorder, physical illness, or physical injury, including a life-endangering physical condition caused by or arising from the pregnancy itself."

The statute defines "partial birth abortions" as:

"an abortion procedure in which the person performing the abortion partially delivers vaginally a living unborn child before killing the unborn child and completing the delivery."

It further defines "partially delivers vaginally a living unborn child before killing the unborn child" to mean

"deliberately and intentionally delivering into the vagina a living unborn child, or a substantial portion thereof, for the purpose of performing a procedure that the person performing such procedure know will kill the unborn child and does kill the unborn child."

The law classifies violation of the statute as a "Class III felony" carrying a prison term of up to 20 years, and a fine of up to $25,000. It also provides for the automatic revocation of a doctor's license to practice medicine in Nebraska.

We Hold that this statute violates the Constitution.

* * *

[The Court next described two kinds of medical procedures used to perform abortions, the dilation and evacuation ("D & E") and dilation and extraction ("D & X") procedures. The D & E is the most common previability second trimester abortion procedure, and sometimes the safest procedure available for the mother. The D & X procedure is the one commonly referred to as "partial birth abortion." The D & E procedure includes] (1) dilation of the cervix; (2) removal of at least some fetal tissue using nonvacuum instruments; and (3) (after the 15th week) the potential need for instrumental disarticulation or dismemberment of the fetus or the collapse of fetal parts to facilitate evacuation from the uterus.

* * *

[The D & X procedure, on the other hand, includes:]

1. deliberate dilatation of the cervix, usually over a sequence of days;

2. instrumental conversion of the fetus to a footling breech;

3. breech extraction of the body excepting the head; and

4. partial evacuation of the intracranial contents of a living fetus to effect vaginal delivery of a dead but otherwise intact fetus[ ]

* * *

The question before us is whether Nebraska's statute, making criminal the performance of a "partial birth abortion," violates the Federal Constitution, as interpreted in *Planned Parenthood of Southeastern Pa. v. Casey* * * * and *Roe v. Wade* * * *. We conclude that it does for at least two independent reasons. First, the law lacks any exception " 'for the preservation of the * * *

health of the mother.' " *Casey*. Second, it "imposes an undue burden on a woman's ability" to choose a D & E abortion, thereby unduly burdening the right to choose abortion itself.

* * *

In sum, using this law some present prosecutors and future Attorneys General may choose to pursue physicians who use D & E procedures, the most commonly used method for performing previability second trimester abortions. All those who perform abortion procedures using that method must fear prosecution, conviction, and imprisonment. The result is an undue burden upon a woman's right to make an abortion decision. We must consequently find the statute unconstitutional.

JUSTICE STEVENS, with whom JUSTICE GINSBURG joins, concurring.

Although much ink is spilled today describing the gruesome nature of late-term abortion procedures, that rhetoric does not provide me a reason to believe that the procedure Nebraska here claims it seeks to ban is more brutal, more gruesome, or less respectful of "potential life" than the equally gruesome procedure Nebraska claims it still allows. Justice Ginsburg and Judge Posner have, I believe, correctly diagnosed the underlying reason for the enactment of this legislation—a reason that also explains much of the Court's rhetoric directed at an objective that extends well beyond the narrow issue that this case presents. The rhetoric is almost, but not quite, loud enough to obscure the quiet fact that during the past 27 years, the central holding of *Roe v. Wade*, has been endorsed by all but 4 of the 17 justices who have addressed the issue. That holding—that the word "liberty" in the Fourteenth Amendment includes a woman's right to make this difficult and extremely personal decision—makes it impossible for me to understand how a State has any legitimate interest in requiring a doctor to follow any procedure other than the one that he or she reasonably believes will best protect the woman in her exercise of this constitutional liberty * * *.

JUSTICE O'CONNOR, concurring.

* * *

First, the Nebraska statute is inconsistent with *Casey* because it lacks an exception for those instances when the banned procedure is necessary to preserve the health of the mother.

* * *

The statute at issue here * * * only excepts those procedures "necessary to save the life of the mother whose life is endangered by a physical disorder, physical illness or physical injury." * * * This lack of a health exception necessarily renders the statute unconstitutional.

* * *

Second, Nebraska's statute is unconstitutional on the alternative and independent ground that it imposes an undue burden on a woman's rights to choose to terminate her pregnancy before viability. Nebraska's ban covers not just the dilation and extraction (D & X) procedure, but also the dilation and evacuation (D & E) procedure, "the most commonly used method for performing previability second trimester abortions."

* * *

It is important to note that, unlike Nebraska, some other States have enacted statutes more narrowly tailored to proscribing the D & X procedure alone. Some of those statutes have done so by specifically excluding from their coverage the most common methods of abortion, such as the D & E and vacuum aspiration procedures.

* * *

[A] ban on partial birth abortion that only proscribed the D & X method of abortion and that included an exception to preserve the life and health of the mother would be constitutional in my view.

* * *

JUSTICE GINSBURG, with whom JUSTICE STEVENS joins, concurring.

* * *

[As] Chief Judge Posner commented, the law prohibits the [partial birth abortion] procedure because the State legislators seek to chip away at the private choice shielded by *Roe v. Wade*, even as modified by *Casey*.

* * *

Again, as stated by Chief Judge Posner, "if a statute burdens constitutional rights and all that can be said on its behalf is that it is the vehicle that legislators have chosen for expressing their hostility to those rights, the burden is undue."[ ]

* * *

CHIEF JUSTICE REHNQUIST, dissenting.

I did not join the joint opinion in *Casey*, and continue to believe that case is wrongly decided. Despite my disagreement with the opinion, the *Casey* joint opinion represents the holding of the Court in that case. I believe Justice Kennedy and Justice Thomas have correctly applied Casey's principles and join their dissenting opinions.

JUSTICE SCALIA, dissenting.

I am optimistic enough to believe that, one day, *Stenberg v. Carhart* will be assigned its rightful place in the history of this Court's jurisprudence beside *Korematsu* and *Dred Scott*. The method of killing a human child—one cannot even accurately say an entirely unborn human child—proscribed by this statute is so horrible that the most clinical description of it evokes a shudder of revulsion.... The notion that the Constitution of the United States, designed, among other things, "to establish Justice, insure domestic Tranquility, ... and secure the Blessings of Liberty to ourselves and our Posterity," prohibits the States from simply banning this visibly brutal means of eliminating our half-born posterity is quite simply absurd.

* * *

In my dissent in *Casey*, I wrote that the "undue burden" test made law by the joint opinion created a standard that was "as doubtful in application as it is unprincipled in origin," * * * "hopelessly unworkable in practice," * * * "ultimately standardless," * * * .Today's decision is the proof.* * *

While I am in an I-told-you-so mood, I must recall my bemusement, in *Casey*, at the joint opinion's expressed belief that *Roe v. Wade* had "call[ed] the contending sides of a national controversy to end their nation division by accepting a common mandate rooted in the Constitution," and that the decision is *Casey* would ratify that happy truce. It seemed to me, quite to the contrary, that "Roe fanned into life an issue that has inflamed our national politics in general, and has obscured with its smoke the selection of Justices to this Court in particular, ever since"; and that, "by keeping us in the abortion-umpiring business, it is the perpetuation of that disruption, rather than of any Pax Roeana, that the Court's new majority decrees." * * *

Justice Kennedy, with whom The Chief Justice joins, dissenting.

For close to two decades after *Roe v. Wade*, the Court gave but slight weight to the interests of the separate States when their legislatures sought to address persisting concerns raised by the existence of a woman's right to elect an abortion in defined circumstances. When the Court reaffirmed the essential holding of *Roe*, the central premise was that the States retain a critical and legitimate role in legislating on the subject of abortion, as limited by the woman's right the Court restated and again guaranteed. *Planned Parenthood of Southeastern Pa. v. Casey* [ ] . The political processes of the State are not to be foreclosed from enacting laws to promote the life of the unborn and to ensure respect for all human life and its potential. * * *

The Court's decision today, in my submission, repudiates this understanding by invalidating a statute advancing critical state interests, even though the law denies no woman the right to choose an abortion and places no undo burden upon the right. The legislation is well within the State's competence to enact. Having concluded Nebraska's law survives the scrutiny dictated by a proper understanding of *Casey*, I dissent from the judgment invalidating it.

* * *

Casey is premised on the States having an important constitutional role in defining their interests in the abortion debate. It is only with this principle in mind that Nebraska's interests can be given proper weight. The state's brief describes its interests as including concern for the life of the unborn and "for the partially-born," in preserving the integrity of the medical profession, and in "erecting a barrier to infanticide."

* * *

Courts are ill-equipped to evaluate the relative worth of particular surgical procedures. The legislatures of the several States have superior factfinding capabilities in this regard. In an earlier case, Justice O'CONNOR had explained that the general rule extends to abortion cases, writing that the Court is not suited to be "the Nation's ex officio medical board with powers to approve or disapprove medical and operative practices and standards throughout the United States." * * * "Irrespective of the difficulty of the task, legislatures, with their superior factfinding capabilities, are certainly better able to make the necessary judgments than are courts.'' Nebraska's judgment here must stand.

* * *

The Court fails to acknowledge substantial authority allowing the State to take sides in a medical debate, even when fundamental liberty interests are at stake and even when leading members of the profession disagree with the conclusions drawn by the legislature.

* * *

JUSTICE THOMAS, with whom THE CHIEF JUSTICE and JUSTICE SCALIA join, DISSENTING.

In 1973, this Court struck down an Act of the Texas Legislature that had been in effect since 1857, thereby rendering unconstitutional abortion statutes in dozens of states. *Roe v. Wade.* As some of my colleagues on the Court, past and present, ably demonstrated, that decision was grievously wrong.... Abortion is a unique act, in which a woman's exercise of control over her own body ends, depending on one's view, human life or potential human life. Nothing in our Federal Constitution deprives the people of this country of the right to determine whether the consequences of abortion to the fetus and to society outweigh the burden of an unwanted pregnancy on the mother. Although a State may permit abortion, nothing in the Constitution dictates that a State must do so.

* * *

The majority assiduously avoids addressing the actual standard articulated in *Casey*—whether prohibiting partial birth abortion without a health exception poses a substantial obstacle to obtaining an abortion. And for good reason: Such an obstacle does not exist. There are two essential reasons why the Court cannot identify a substantial obstacle. First, the Court cannot identify any real, much less substantial, barrier to any woman's ability to obtain an abortion. And second, the Court cannot demonstrate that any such obstacle would affect a sufficient number of women to justify invalidating the statute on its face.

* * *

We were reassured repeatedly in *Casey* that not all regulations of abortions are unwarranted and that the States may express profound respect for fetal life. Under *Casey*, the regulation before us today should easily pass constitutional muster. But the Court's abortion jurisprudence is a particularly virulent strain of constitutional exegesis. And so today we are told that 30 States are prohibited from banning one rarely used form of abortion that they believe to border on infanticide. It is clear that the Constitution does not compel this result.

Notes and Questions

1. How, exactly, is a court to apply the Supreme Court's ''undue burden'' test of *Casey*? In finding whether a state law ''has the purpose or effect of placing a substantial obstacle in the path of a woman seeking an abortion of a nonviable

fetus," is the Court really proposing a two-part (purpose and effect) analysis? How is the court expected to divine the purpose of such an act? From the terms of the law? From formal legislative statements of the purpose? Are many state legislatures likely to promulgate enacting clauses declaring that their purpose is to unduly burden those who seek to abort nonviable fetuses? It may be even more difficult for a court to evaluate the effect of a statute which limits or conditions access to abortions. Of course, we know that a state law has the effect of establishing an "undue burden" when it puts a "substantial obstacle" in the path of a woman seeking to abort a nonviable fetus, but how much does that advance the inquiry? Is an obstacle substantial because it imposes a serious limitation on any identifiable woman, or because it affects a large number of women, or because it affects a large percentage of the cases in which women would seek abortions?

Unlike in Roe v. Wade, though, in which the Court dealt with virtually absolute bans on abortion, in Casey the Court faced several narrow regulations on abortion that had been promulgated by the Pennsylvania legislature, and it thus was required to apply its test to a series of articulated restrictions. These included the requirement that particular state-mandated information be provided to the pregnant woman before the abortion is performed, the requirement that the information be provided by a physician, a 24 hour waiting period between the receipt of the information and the pregnant woman's formal consent to the abortion (and thus a "two-step" procedure), the requirement that a minor get parental consent (with a judicial bypass procedure to avoid that requirement in some cases), and various state reporting requirements, none of which were found to constitute "undue burdens," at least in Pennsylvania on the evidence presented to the Court in 1992. On the other hand, the Court did find that a spousal notification requirement did constitute an undue burden (as did any reporting requirement related to that notification requirement), and the Court struck that down.

Thus, in Casey the Supreme Court provided a template that could be used by lower courts in evaluating the constitutional sufficiency of abortion legislation. It also provided a template that could be used by state legislatures in determining what kinds of legislation would be likely to withstand constitutional attack. Between 1973 and 1992 many state legislatures had attempted to impose the most restrictive abortion laws arguably permitted. Since 1992 few have gone beyond what is clearly permitted in Casey, although legislatures have tested the limits of Casey by promulgating partial birth abortion bans and other comparatively insignificant restrictions. Why have the state legislatures become so restrained? Is it because the standard of Casey really is clearer than the standard of Roe? Is it because the pro-life forces in these states have grown weary of further judicial battles? Is it because the pro-choice forces have decided to focus on making those abortions that are legal actually available to those who seek them? Is it because those provisions found to be constitutional in Casey are, in fact, the very provisions that have the strongest political support anyway? Is it because both sides in this battle have moved on to other issues of the day (including physician assisted death)? While the abortion debate remains a lively one in this country, state legislatures have not shown the same creativity in seeking to restrict abortions since 1992 that they did for the two decades before that.

In those few cases where state legislatures have insisted on going far beyond what Pennsylvania did in Casey, the courts have had no trouble striking down the statutes by applying the "undue burden" test. See, e.g. Sojourner T. v. Edwards, 974 F.2d 27 (5th Cir.1992), cert. denied 507 U.S. 972, 113 S.Ct. 1414, 122 L.Ed.2d 785 (1993)(statute would have outlawed all abortions except to save the life or health of the fetus, to remove a dead fetus, to save the life of the pregnant woman, or, if performed in the first trimester only, if the pregnancy was a result of rape or incest); Women's Medical Professional Corporation v. Voinovich, 911 F.Supp. 1051 (S.D.Ohio 1995) (preliminary injunction against statute that would, inter alia, ban all postviability abortions, even if the mother's life were at stake).

2. If you live in one of the thirty states that had statutes restricting partial birth abortions at the time Stenberg was decided in 2000, review your state statute. Is it constitutional under the principle supplied by Casey and applied in Stenberg? As majority or minority counsel to a legislative committee considering a new statute limiting partial birth abortions, what would you advise? If you supported restricting partial birth abortions, how would you draft a statute that would be acceptable to the Supreme Court? If you opposed any legislative restrictions on partial birth abortions, what would you want to include to increase the likelihood that the statute would be found unconstitutional? In her opinion in Stenberg, Justice O'Connor does provide a description of the form of partial birth abortion ban that would meet constitutional muster; a statute that made an exception to preserve the life and health of the mother and included a ban only on the D & X procedure (and permitted the D & E procedure) would be acceptable in constitutional terms. Is there any other justice who shares this view? If this view is held only by Justice O'Connor (and announced by her in a concurring opinion), is it appropriate to call it a part of the holding of Stenberg?

3. *Consent and Notification Requirements.* There remain, of course, other kinds of regulation with uncertain constitutional status, too. It is now clear that it does not violate the United States Constitution for minors to be required to obtain the consent of a parent to an abortion, as long as the state permits a court (or, perhaps, an appropriate administrative agency) to dispense with that requirement under some circumstances. The Supreme Court has never determined if a two-parent consent requirement (with a proper judicial bypass provision) would pass constitutional muster, however. See Barnes v. Mississippi, 992 F.2d 1335 (5th Cir.1993), cert. denied, 510 U.S. 976, 114 S.Ct. 468, 126 L.Ed.2d 419 (1993)(upholding two-parent consent requirement because involvement of both parents will increase "reflection and deliberation" on the process, and if one parent denies consent the other will be able to go to court in support of the child). The Supreme Court has suggested that a state requirement of mere parental notification (rather than consent) requires a judicial bypass, and lower courts have generally assumed that it does. Ohio v. Akron Center for Reproductive Health, 497 U.S. 502, 110 S.Ct. 2972, 111 L.Ed.2d 405 (1990). One state supreme court has found that a parental notification requirement violates the state constitution's equal protection clause when it is imposed only on those who seek abortions, not on pregnant children making other, equally medically risky, reproductive decisions. Planned Parenthood of Central New Jersey v. Farmer, 165 N.J. 609, 762 A.2d 620 (N.J. 2000).

It is not entirely clear what constitutional standard a court must apply in a "bypass" case. Is the court required to waive consent or notification (1) if it finds that the minor is sufficiently mature that she should be able to make the decision herself, or (2) if it finds that if she seeks consent from (or notifies) her parents she will be subject to abuse, or (3) if it finds that it is in her best interest to have the abortion, or (4) if it finds that it is in her best interest not to be required to notify, or get consent from, her parent, or some combination of all of these? The Supreme Court has determined that a statute that provides for the waiver of parental consent or notification when a court determines that an abortion is in the best interest of the minor is constitutionally sufficient. Further, the Court has announced that "a judicial bypass procedure requiring a minor to show that *parental notification is not* in her best interests is equivalent to a judicial bypass procedure requiring a minor to show that *abortion without notification* is in her best interests * * *." Lambert v. Wicklund, 520 U.S. 292, 297, 117 S.Ct. 1169, 137 L.Ed.2d 464 (1997)(per curiam).

If the statute does include a substantively constitutional bypass provision, what kind of procedural conditions may be placed on a bypass case? May the petitioner be required to prove her case by clear and convincing evidence? Is she entitled to counsel? Is she required to have a special guardian appointed for purposes of the litigation? Can the state require an expedited hearing? Can it allow the court to refuse an expedited hearing? Can it require the petition be filed within a very short time after the commencement of the pregnancy? Can it limit appeals by those who unsuccessfully seek judicial bypass?

The debate for and against consent and notification requirements reveals an even deeper debate about the current role of the family in contemporary life. While most agree that a teenager's abortion should be a decision made in consultation with her parents, that belief rests upon several assumptions. First, it assumes that the family dynamics are such that the daughter's disclosure will not trigger domestic violence or other forms of family abuse. Second, it assumes that the daughter lives within a traditional nuclear family, or can readily reach her biological parents. Finally, and most critically, it assumes that parents will act in the daughter's best interest. Some of these assumptions may, sadly, be based upon an idealized view of contemporary family life. While many children are brought up in healthy families, as Justice Kennard of the California Supreme Court has pointed out, "[n]ot every pregnant adolescent has parents out of the comforting and idyllic world of Norman Rockwell." American Academy of Pediatrics v. Lungren, 51 Cal.Rptr.2d 201, 224, 912 P.2d 1148, 1153 (1996)(Kennard, J., dissenting).

Those who support these consent and notification statutes offer many stories of girls who had abortions secretly and now regret not discussing it with their parents. Those who oppose these statutes offer stories about girls who committed suicide rather than go through the notification procedures. Is this anecdotal evidence offered by both sides of much value? Could respectable research data on these issues be developed? Why do you think it has not been developed in any reliable way? Does it seem ironic that under a consent or notification statute a court could declare a pregnant minor to be too immature to proceed without parental consultation, and thus order her to become a mother?

Whatever may be the uncertain status of the details surrounding parental consent and notification, it is now well established that spousal consent and spousal notification requirements are unconstitutional, even if the notification is done by the physician or someone else rather the pregnant woman. See Jane L. v. Bangerter, 61 F.3d 1493 (10th Cir.1995). One state legislature attempted to get around constitutional limitations on spousal consent by permitting the abortion without such consent but providing for the civil liability of those physicians who perform these abortions without that consent. This approach was found to be indistinguishable from requiring spousal consent, and thus unconstitutional, in Planned Parenthood of Southern Arizona v. Woods, 982 F.Supp. 1369, 1380 (D.Ariz.1997).

4. *Regulation of Medical Procedures.* As a general matter, courts have been reluctant to uphold statutory limitations on abortion procedures against arguments that those limitations—usually designed to increase the chance that an

abortion procedure will result in a live birth—impose additional health risks on the pregnant woman. This reluctance, of course, is demonstrated in Stenberg v. Carhart, and it is the reason that President Clinton vetoed those partial birth abortion bans that were rountinely passed by Congress in the late 1990s. One state supreme court has determined that a requirement that second trimester abortions be performed in a hospital violated the state constitution, which was read to be more protective of abortion rights than the United States constitution. See Planned Parenthood of Middle Tennessee v. Sundquist, 38 S.W.3d 1 (Tenn.2000)(applying Tennessee's right to privacy described in Davis v. Davis, below at 1196) But see Greenville Women's Clinic v. Bryant, 222 F.3d 157 (4th Cir. 2000)(upholding rigid South Carolina licensing requirements for facilities where abortions are performed).

Courts have had little trouble with a requirement that only physicians, not physicians' assistants or others, perform abortions, because the authority granted with professional licenses is a matter state law. See Armstrong v. Mazurek, 906 F.Supp. 561 (D.Mont.1995). Such licensing requirements are seen as ways of protecting the pregnant woman, not imposing an undue burden on her decision to have an abortion.

5. *Two-trip Requirements.* When a state imposes a waiting period between the time the pregnant woman is provided the information that is to be the basis of her informed consent to an abortion and the medical procedure itself, it may, de facto, be requiring that the pregnant woman make two trips to the medical facility where the abortion is to be performed. In Casey the Court announced that a 24-hour waiting period did not constitute an unconstitutional undue burden. Could the state require a longer waiting period? Could it impose a "three-trip" requirement or a more drawn out process? The Tennessee Supreme Court determined that imposing what amounts to a three day waiting period violated the state constitution's protected right of privacy. See Planned Parenthood of Middle Tennessee v. Sundquist, 1 S.W.3d 38 (Tenn.2000)

6. *Other Informed Consent Requirements.* In Casey the Court upheld a statute that requires that a state-approved packet of material be given to the pregnant woman as a part of the informed consent process, and that the consent process be obtained by the physician, not by anyone else. The only requirement Casey appears to put on the distributed material is that it contain information that is true. In early 1996 a couple of epidemiological studies arguably suggested a very weak relationship between having an abortion and the subsequent risk of developing breast cancer and the severity of that cancer. Subsequent reports cast doubt on this relationship. See P.A. Newcomb, B. E. Storer, M. P. Longnecker et al., Pregnancy Termination in Relation to Risk of Breast Cancer, 275 JAMA 283 (1996). May states require that physicians inform potential abortion patients that "there is a correlation between abortion and the risk of breast cancer?" May states require that patients be provided the information about this correlation even if they do not require that patients be told of the different, but significantly higher, risks of ordinary pregnancy? Could the state require that a woman attend a short course on fetal development as a condition of having an abortion? See a graphic movie dealing with that same subject? Talk to other women who have had abortions? Speak with adoptive couples?

The in-person, fully informed, two-visit consent process can also be required of a pregnant girl's parents who are required to give consent under a state law requiring such consent.

7.   Could a state ban abortions for certain purposes? Pennsylvania considered outlawing abortion for gender selection (i.e., because the parents thought that the fetus was the "wrong" sex); could they legally do so? Could the state outlaw abortion if it is used as a primary method of birth control? As a method for controlling the genetic makeup of a child? If it could do so legally, how would it do so as a practical matter?

8.   Under Casey, the "undue burden" test appears to require a factual inquiry; the question is whether a state law, as a matter of fact, imposes a substantial obstacle on the path of a woman seeking to abort a previable fetus. Is it possible to attack a state abortion statute on its face under Casey, or must the plaintiff meet some evidentiary burden by proving the fact of the substantial obstacle? Might the same statutory provisions that were constitutional in Casey be found unconstitutional in some other state? Might a "two-trip" requirement be unconstitutional in a state where patients of the state's only clinic are harassed after they make a visit to the clinic? Is each statutory restriction in each state subject to litigation that depends upon the environment surrounding abortion in that state?

In United States v. Salerno, 481 U.S. 739, 107 S.Ct. 2095, 95 L.Ed.2d 697 (1987), the United States Supreme Court found that a statute would survive a facial constitutional attack unless it could be shown that it would operate unconstitutionally under any conceivable set of circumstances. Is that test relevant in evaluating state statutory regulation of abortion? Is that test inconsistent with the "undue burden" test of Casey? Which standard should courts apply in evaluating that legislation? The circuits continue to be split on whether the restrictive Salerno test applies in this area (a position taken by two circuits) or whether Casey provides an alternative and less strict test (a position taken by five circuits). See Greenville Women's Clinic v. Bryant, 222 F.3d 157 (4th Cir.2000)(applying the Salerno standard). See also Ruth Burdick, The Casey Undue Burden Standard: Problems Predicted and Encountered, and the Split Over the Salerno Test, 23 Hastings Const. L. Q. 825 (1996).

9.   Some believe that the ultimate disappearance of abortion practice will be the result of the fact that medical schools and residency programs are discontinuing training in abortion techniques because offering that training is not worth the political cost. Should all Obstetrics and Gynecology training programs include, at the very least, some exposure to the abortion process, or may a medical school decide that it will not provide that training because it finds the practice of abortion morally unacceptable? Should students who find such practice abhorrent be able to opt out of that training? Are there constitutional implications to the removal of abortion from the medical school curriculum at a state university, or from the list of procedures done at a teaching hospital? See Barbara Gottlieb, Sounding Board, 332 JAMA 532 (1995).

10.   Neighboring states often have very different laws regulating abortion, and women from one state may go to another state to take advantage of what they consider a favorable law. May a state prohibit a woman from crossing a state line to obtain an abortion that would be illegal in the first state? In 1996 a New York jury convicted a woman of "interfering with the custody of a minor," a felony, for taking a 13 year old pregnant girl from Pennsylvania (which requires parental consent) to New York (which does not) to obtain an abortion. See David Stout, Guilty Verdict for Enabling Girl to Have An Abortion, *New York Times*, Oct. 31, 1996, A–8.

11.   There may be some basic value issues upon which the pro-choice and pro-life partisans agree. While pro-choice supporters argue that an abortion should be among the choices of a pregnant woman, no one views an abortion as a happy event. Both sides would be pleased if society reached a point where there were no need for abortions. Similarly, while some pro-life supporters believe that every fetus is entitled to be born alive, many recognize that there are some times when the mother's interest does trump that of the fetus—when the mother's life is at stake, for example, and, perhaps, when the pregnancy is a result of rape or incest—and many recognize that the quality of life of the fetus is a relevant consideration. Very few people oppose early abortions of anencephalic fetuses, for example, or early abortions of other fetuses who are virtually certain to be stillborn or to die within the first few minutes of birth. Both sides may also support expanded state funding for prenatal care and post-natal care, each of which may make abortion a less attractive alternative to pregnant women. Is there a common ground that could give rise to some kind of generally acceptable state policy on abortion, at least in some states? If pro-choice partisans and pro-life partisans were to sit with you and enumerate their common concerns, would there be some basic issues and basic principles upon which they would agree?

12.   There has been a great deal of writing about abortion law. Some of the most recent and provocative articles include Martin Belsky, Privacy: The Rehnquist Court's Unmentionable "Right," 36 Tulsa L.J. 43 (2000), David Cruz, The Sexual Freedom Cases: Contraception, Abortion, Abstinence and the Constitution, 35 Harv. Civ. Rts.-Civ. Lib. L. Rev. 299 (2000), and Melanie Price, The Privacy Paradox: The Divergent Paths of the United States Supreme Court and State Courts on Issues of Sexuality, 33 Ind. L. Rev. 863 (2000).

Note: The Freedom of Access to Clinic Entrances Act of 1994

In the 1990s the focus of the challenge to abortion practices was moving from the courts and the legislatures to medical clinics that provided abortion services. Often those clinics were the subject of protests, prayer vigils, or other demonstrations, and in a few cases violence resulted. Some employees of the clinics feared for their safety, and some were also concerned that patients coming to the clinics were being harassed and intimidated by those outside. Those participating in the demonstrations argued that they were doing nothing more than exercising their first amendment rights, and that they were doing their best to make the exercise of those rights effective by dissuading patients from having abortions. In response to some particularly egregious incidents of violence perpetrated against a few abortion clinics, Congress passed the Freedom of Access to Clinic Entrances Act of 1994 ("FACE"), which provides:

Whoever—

(1) by force or threat of force or by physical obstruction, intentionally injures, intimidates or interferes with or attempts to injure, intimidate or interfere with any person because that person is or has been, or in order to intimidate such person or any other person or any class of persons from, obtaining or providing reproductive health services; * * * (3) intentionally damages or destroys the property of a facility, or attempts to do so, because such facility provides reproductive health services * * * shall be guilty of a crime and fined or imprisoned.

18 U.S.C.A. section 248 (a). The statute provides longer prison terms and larger fines for repeat offenders and shorter prison terms and smaller fines for

offenses "involving exclusively a nonviolent physical intrusion." 18 U.S.C.A. section 248(b). The term "reproductive health services" is expansively defined to include "medical, surgical, counseling or referral services * * * including services relating to * * * the termination of a pregnancy" whether those services are provided "in a hospital, clinic, physician's office, or other facility." 18 U.S.C.A. section 248(e)(5). In addition to its criminal sanctions, the Act provides for civil enforcement by the United States Attorney General and the attorneys general of the states, and for civil damages of $5,000 per violation in lieu of actual damages, at the election of the plaintiff. 18 U.S.C.A. section 248(c)(1)(B).

The Act also extends the same protection that is accorded to those seeking access to clinics to those "seeking to exercise the First Amendment right of religious freedom at a place of religious worship." This additional protection was originally added by an amendment offered by Senator Hatch, who opposed the bill and thought (incorrectly) that this addition might kill it. The Act explicitly provides that it is not to be construed to prohibit any "expressive conduct" protected by the First Amendment, 18 U.S.C.A. section 248(d)(1). Eight circuits have found that Congress had authority to promulgate FACE against arguments that the statute exceeded the Congress's commerce clause powers; and one, United States v. Gregg, 226 F.3d 253 (3d Cir. 2000) (2–1 on the commerce clause issue), made that finding after considering the Supreme Court's restrictive reading of the commerce clause power in United States v. Morrison, 529 U.S. 598, 120 S.Ct. 1740, 146 L.Ed.2d 658 (2000), which found that Congress had no authority under the commerce clause to promulgate the civil liability provisions of the Violence Against Women Act ("VAWA") because the regulated acts were not commercial in nature. The majority in Gregg argued that Congress reasonably could have concluded that the statute was necessary to address the burden protesters were placing on the business operations of the abortion clinics, which were engaged in interstate commerce, and that FACE was thus distinguishable from VAWA. The dissent in the Gregg case argued that FACE applied to the non-economic acts of protesting abortion, not the business aspects of the operation of abortion clinics, and that FACE was indistinguishable from VAWA in this respect. The Supreme Court has not yet addressed the issue of the constitutionality of FACE.

This Act is not the only weapon provided to those who are concerned about the effects of demonstrations around clinics that perform abortions. Earlier in 1994 the United States Supreme Court declared that RICO could be applied against those who violate laws to blockade the clinics, and that created the possibility of substantial civil damage awards against organizations and individuals that encourage or participate in illegal conduct to limit the access of women to the clinics. National Organization for Women v. Scheidler, 510 U.S. 249, 114 S.Ct. 798, 127 L.Ed.2d 99 (1994). Both the Freedom of Access to Clinic Entrances Act and RICO were implicated in early 1999 when an Oregon federal court jury returned a verdict in excess of $107 million against twelve individuals, the American Coalition of Life Activists and the Advocates for Life Ministries, for maintaining a web site that threatened those who performed abortions. The site, called "The Nuremberg Files," listed physicians who performed abortions, drew lines through those who had been murdered, and listed those who had been wounded by would-be assassins in gray. The defendants also published Old West style "wanted" posters with the names and pictures of physicians who performed abortions. The defendants claimed a first amendment right to publish the web site and the wanted posters, and some first amendment analysts were concerned about the potentially chilling effect of such a large judgment on the publication of unpopular political views. The defendants also claimed that they had transferred their assets to be able to avoid paying any part of the judgment, although their unsubtle approach to the transfer is likely to hinder its legal success. See Sam Howe Verhook, Creators of Anti–Abortion Web Site Told to Pay Millions, New York Times, February 3, 1999.

Trial courts have also issued injunctions limiting abortion protesters where judges thought that was necessary to protect the rights of clinic patients. In Schenck v. Pro–Choice Network, 519 U.S. 357, 117 S.Ct. 855, 137 L.Ed.2d 1 (1997) the Supreme Court upheld an injunction which created a 15–foot protected "bubble zone" around the doorways and driveways of a clinic offering abortion services, and it also upheld a limit on the number of people who could "counsel" a woman entering the clinic. The Court determined, further, that those trying to dissuade a patient from having an abortion could be required to desist when the patient asked them to do so, although the Court found that a moveable bubble zone that followed the patient as she entered the clinic would violate the free speech rights of pro-life protesters.

Three years later, in Hill v. Colorado, 530 U.S. 703, 120 S.Ct. 2480, 147 L.Ed.2d 597 (2000), decided the same day as Stenberg v. Carhart, the Supreme Court upheld a Colorado statute that prohibited any person within 100 feet of a health care facility's entrance door from knowingly coming within 8 feet of another person, without the consent of that person, to pass a "leaflet [or] handbill, to displa[y] a sign to, or [e]ngage in oral protest, education or counseling with that person * * *." The Court distinguished the larger moveable bubble zone in Schenck, and rejected the first amendment attack on the Colorado law. In dissent, Justice Scalia complained that the Colorado statute "enjoy[ed] the benefit of the 'ad hoc nullification machine' that the Court has set in motion to push aside whatever doctrines of constitutional law stand in the way of th[e] highly favored practice [of abortion]. * * * [T]oday's decision is not an isolated distortion of our traditional constitutional principles, but is one of many aggressively proabortion novelties announced by the Court in recent years." Justice Kennedy dissented separately, suggesting that the judgment of the Court "strikes at the heart of the reasoned, careful balance I had believed was the basis for the joint opinion in Casey."

Note: The Blurry Distinction Between Contraception and Abortion, and the Advent of Mifepristone (RU–486)

If contraception refers to any process designed to prevent a pregnancy, and abortion refers to any process designed to end an established pregnancy, then the point at which the process of contraception becomes the process of abortion is at the commencement of the pregnancy. There is some ambiguity, however, about when the pregnancy begins, just as there is some ambiguity about when "conception" takes place.

> The Missouri statute defines "conception" as "the fertilization of the ovum of a female by a sperm of a male," even though standard medical texts equate "conception" with implantation in the uterus occurring about six days after fertilization.

Webster v. Reproductive Health Services, 492 U.S. at 561, 109 S.Ct. at 3080 (Stevens, J., concurring in part and dissenting in part). When does the pregnancy begin? Does the fact that a large number of fertilized eggs—perhaps 50%—never implant, suggest that pregnancy does not begin until implantation? Is the fact that cells of the fertilized ovum are identical for about three days, and then begin to separate into differentiated cells that will become the placenta, on one hand, and cells that will become the embryo and fetus, on the other, relevant?

If there is to be a legal difference between contraception and abortion, the courts will have to determine when "conception" takes place and when a pregnancy begins. As Justice Stevens points out, some forms of what we now consider contraception are really devices designed to stop the fertilized egg from implanting in the uterus, not devices designed for avoiding fertilization of the egg in the first place.

> An intrauterine device, commonly called an IUD "works primarily by preventing a fertilized egg from implanting"; other contraceptive methods that may prevent implantation include "morning-after pills," high-dose estrogen pills taken after intercourse, particularly in cases of rape, and mifepristone (also known as RU 486), a pill that works "during the indeterminate period between contraception and abortion," low level estrogen "combined" pills—a version of the ordinary, daily ingested birth control pill—also may prevent the fertilized egg from reaching the uterine wall and implanting [ ].

492 U.S. at 563, 109 S.Ct. at 3081 (Stevens, J., concurring in part and dissenting in part). If the law recognizes a distinction between contraception and abortion, should the law also be required to define that point at which contraception becomes abortion? Justice Stevens suggests that we must depend upon a medical definition of pregnancy, because any alternative would constitute the legal adoption of a theological position and thus be a violation of the establishment clause of the First Amendment. Do you agree? Can you develop a coherent legal argument that the state may regulate abortion in any way it sees fit, but *may not* prohibit a woman's choice to stop a fertilized ovum from reaching her uterus and implanting?

There are several reasons that contraception might be distinguished from abortion as a matter of law. Historically, one significant factor has been that the highly invasive and comparatively risky surgical nature of abortion has contrasted so substantially with the medical nature of contraception, which depends on the use of pills or relatively simple devices. This distinction may prove evanescent as RU–486, the "abortion pill" also known as mifepristone and distributed in the United States as Mifeprex, becomes available. This drug is now chosen by about half of the eligible women who have abortions in Europe, where it has been available since the early 1990s. This method of abortion is available only for the first seven weeks following the pregnant woman's last menstrual period; about one-third of American abortions are performed during this time window. While its costs may not be lower and its side effects may not be much better than those for surgical abortions, the availability of mifepristone may make pregnancy terminations easier to obtain in rural (and other) areas where patients have less access to surgical interventions.

Although the FDA found the drug to be safe in 1996, it was not approved for distribution until late in 2000. Its distribution in the United States has been held up by a number of problems, some stemming from the vitality of its political opposition. The Population Council, which ended up with the rights to distribute the drug in the United States, ran into more controversy when distribution was set to begin and some alleged that the Chinese firm that was manufacturing the drug for the American market had produced other medications that were found to be mislabeled. When mifepristone is available under federal law, physicians may be discouraged from its use by state laws that impose special restrictions on the performance of abortions. Still, it is expected to be fairly widely distributed in early 2001, barring any unforeseen legal restriction. See G. Kolata, F.D.A. Approves Abortion Pill, New York Times, September 28, 2000, at 1, and A. Zitner, RU–486 Firm Linked to Drug Impurities, Los Angeles Times, October 20, 2000, at A–29.

Problem: Drafting Abortion Legislation

As the legislative counsel responsible for drafting proposed legislation in your state, consider the requests of two groups of state legislators. The first asks you to draft the most restrictive abortion statute that would be constitutional under current law. The second group asks you to draft a consensus statute that would regulate abortion, but do so in such a way that it is likely to be supported by both pro-choice and pro-life constituents. Draft the two statutes and be prepared to defend each one—the first on the basis of its constitutionality, and the second on the basis of its political acceptability and good policy.

4. Sterilization

The sterilization of the mentally retarded has given rise to considerable discussion beginning with the development of the eugenics movement in the late 19th century. While there is no significant evidence that most forms of mental retardation are genetic and inheritable, there remains a residue of social support for the notion that this society can purify its gene pool by sterilizing those who would pollute it, such as the mentally retarded and criminals. The aim of the eugenics movement was confirmed by Justice Holmes in Buck v. Bell, 274 U.S. 200, 47 S.Ct. 584, 71 L.Ed. 1000 (1927), which dealt with an attempt by the State of Virginia to sterilize Carrie Buck, who had been committed to the State Colony for Epileptics and the Feeble Minded. The State was opposed on the grounds that the statute authorizing sterilization violated the Fourteenth Amendment by denying Ms. Buck due process of law and the equal protection of the law. Justice Holmes responded:

> Carrie Buck is a feeble minded white woman who was committed to the State Colony above mentioned in due form. She is the daughter of a feeble minded mother in the same institution and the mother of an illegitimate feeble minded child * * *.

> [The lower court found] "that Carrie Buck is the probable potential parent of socially inadequate offspring, likewise afflicted, that she may be sterilized without detriment to her general health and that her welfare and that of society will be promoted by her sterilization." * * * We have seen more than once that the public welfare may call upon the best citizens for their lives. It would be strange if it could not call upon those who already sapped the strength of the state for these lesser sacrifices, often not felt to be such by those concerned, in order to prevent our being swamped with incompetence. It is better for all the world if instead of waiting to execute degenerate offspring for crime, or to let them starve for their imbecility, society can prevent those who are manifestly unfit from continuing their kind. The principle that sustains compulsory vaccination is broad enough to cover cutting the fallopian tubes. [ ] Three generations of imbeciles are enough.

* * *

The Supreme Court has never overturned the decision in *Buck v. Bell*, although it is of questionable precedential value today. Society's perception of the mentally incompetent has changed and, especially after the Nazi experience, arguments based upon eugenics are held in low regard. In fact, when Carrie Buck was discovered in the Appalachian hills in 1980, she was found to be mentally competent and extremely disappointed that throughout her life she was unable to bear another child.

The Supreme Court addressed eugenic sterilizations once more, in Skinner v. Oklahoma, 316 U.S. 535, 62 S.Ct. 1110, 86 L.Ed. 1655 (1942). The Court determined that the equal protection clause prohibited Oklahoma from enforcing its statute which required sterilizing persons convicted of repeated criminal acts, but only if the crimes were within special categories. White collar crimes were exempted from these categories, and the Supreme Court's determination was based on the state's irrational distinction between blue collar (sterilizable) and white collar (unsterilizable) crimes. The Court was asked to, but did not, overrule *Buck v. Bell*.

Recent programs to sterilize individual mentally retarded people have been based on the convenience of sterilization for the patient and his (or, virtually always, her) family. Some who have sought sterilization for the mentally retarded have been worried about the consequences of sexual exposure upon people who can barely cope with the minimal requirements of daily life; some have suggested that it would be much easier to care for patients, especially menstruating women, if they were sterilized; and others have suggested that sterilization might make it practical for mentally retarded people who would otherwise be institutionalized to live at home. Generally, courts have acted to protect the mentally retarded from sterilization if there is any less restrictive alternative that would serve the same interests.

Not all of the protection has come out of the judiciary, however. In California, for example, the Probate Code was amended to prohibit the sterilization of mentally retarded persons. This statute was challenged by the conservator of an incompetent mentally retarded woman who argued that the legislature had denied her a procreative choice that was extended to all other women in the community. She argued that to deny her the opportunity for a sterilization when there would be no other safe and effective method of contraception available to her would be to deny her important constitutionally protected rights. While a mentally retarded person may have a right not to be unfairly sterilized, she argued, she has a correlative right not to be unfairly and arbitrarily denied a sterilization (and thus an opportunity to satisfy her sexuality).

In Conservatorship of Valerie N., 40 Cal.3d 143, 219 Cal.Rptr. 387, 707 P.2d 760 (1985), the California Supreme Court upheld the challenge and threw out the statute:

> True protection of procreative choice can be accomplished only if the state permits the court supervised substituted judgment of the conservator to be exercised on behalf of the conservatee who is unable to personally exercise this right. Limiting the exercise of that judgment by denying the right to effective contraception through sterilization to this class of conservatees denies them a right held not only by conservatees who are competent to consent but by all other women. Respondent has

demonstrated neither a compelling state interest in restricting this right nor a basis upon which to conclude that the prohibition contained [in the statute] is necessary to achieve the identified purpose of furthering the incompetent's right not to be sterilized.

One justice wrote a particularly strong dissent:

Today's holding will permit the state, through the legal fiction of substituted consent, to deprive many women permanently of the right to conceive and bear children. The majority run roughshod over this fundamental constitutional right in a misguided attempt to guarantee a procreative choice for one they assume has never been capable of choice and never will be. * * *

The majority opinion opens the door to abusive sterilization practices which will serve the convenience of conservators, parents, and service providers rather than incompetent conservatees. The ugly history of sterilization abuse against developmentally disabled persons in the name of seemingly enlightened social policies counsels a different choice.

Rather than place an absolute prohibition upon the sterilization of the developmentally disabled as the California legislature attempted to do, most courts attempt to safeguard those who may be subject to sterilization by applying very strict procedural requirements to any proposed sterilization. For example, the standard that has been most often emulated is that provided in In re Guardianship of Hayes, 93 Wash.2d 228, 608 P.2d 635 (1980), where the court set out the procedural requirements simply and explicitly:

The decision can only be made in a superior court proceeding in which (1) the incompetent individual is represented by a disinterested guardian ad litem, (2) the court has received independent advice based upon a comprehensive medical, psychological, and social evaluation of the individual, and (3) to the greatest extent possible, the court has elicited and taken into account the view of the incompetent individual.

Within this framework, the judge must first find by clear, cogent and convincing evidence that the individual is (1) incapable of making his or her own decision about sterilization, and (2) unlikely to develop sufficiently to make an informed judgment about sterilization in the foreseeable future.

Next it must be proved by clear, cogent and convincing evidence that there is a need for contraception. The judge must find that the individual is (1) physically capable of procreation, and (2) likely to engage in sexual activity at the present or in the near future under circumstances likely to result in pregnancy, and must find in addition that (3) the nature and extent of the individual's disability, as determined by empirical evidence and not solely on the basis of standardized tests, renders him or her permanently incapable of caring for a child, even with reasonable assistance.

Finally, there must be no alternatives to sterilization. The judge must find that by clear, cogent and convincing evidence (1) all less drastic contraceptive methods, including supervision, education and training, have been proved unworkable or inapplicable, and (2) the proposed method of sterilization entails the least invasion of the body of the individual. In addition, it must be shown by clear, cogent and convincing evidence that (3) the current state of scientific and medical knowledge does not suggest either (a) that a reversible sterilization procedure or other less drastic contraceptive method will shortly be available or (b) that science is on the threshold of an advance in the treatment of the individual's disability.

The court recognized that there was "a heavy presumption against sterilization of an individual incapable of informed consent" and that the burden "will be even harder to overcome in the case of a minor incompetent * * *." Some have read the procedural requirements of *Hayes* as effectively removing the possibility of the sterilization of the developmentally disabled. Can you imagine a case that would meet the stiff "procedural" requirements of *Hayes?*

Recently courts and legislatures have considered interventions that are designed to provide sterilization or some form of castration as criminal punishments (or "treatment" for those disposed to criminal conduct). In State v. Kline, 155 Or.App. 96, 963 P.2d 697 (Or.App.1998) the Oregon Court of Appeals found that a criminal defendant's right to procreate was not unconstitutionally abridged when he was ordered not to have children upon his conviction for mistreatment of children.

For a history of sterilization of the developmentally disabled in this country, see Richard K. Sherlock and Robert D. Sherlock, Sterilizing the Retarded: Constitutional, Statutory and Policy Alternatives, 60 N.C.L.Rev. 943 (1982). For thoughtful discussion of sexuality in the developmentally disabled, see S.F. Haavik and K. Menninger, Sexuality, Law and the Developmentally Disabled Person (1981). For a more recent analysis of the various interest at stake in such cases, see R. Adler, Estate of C.W.: A Pragmatic Approach to the Involuntary Sterilization of the Mentally Disabled, 20 Nova L.Rev. 1323 (1996). For a discussion of "chemical castration" provisions that apply to convicted sex offenders, see William Winslade et al., Castrating Pedophiles Convicted of Sex Offenses Against Children: New Treatment or Old Punishment?, 51 SMU L.Rev. 349 (1998), and Karen Rebish, Nipping the Problem in the Bud: The Constitutionality of California's Castration Law, 14 N.Y.L. Sch. J. Hum. Rts. 507 (1998). For another review of the California statute—the first to actually require "chemical castration" in some cases—see Recent Legislation: Constitutional Law, 110 Harv. L. Rev. 799 (1997).

5. Tort Remedies for Failed Reproductive Control: Wrongful Birth, Wrongful Life and Wrongful Conception

SMITH v. COTE

Supreme Court of New Hampshire, 1986.
128 N.H. 231, 513 A.2d 341.

BATCHELDER, JUSTICE.

* * *

* * * Plaintiff Linda J. Smith became pregnant early in 1979. During the course of her pregnancy Linda was under the care of the defendants, physicians who specialize in obstetrics and gynecology. Linda consulted the defendants on April 8, 1979, complaining of nausea, abdominal pain and a late menstrual period. * * *

On August 3, 1979, nearly four months after the April visits, Linda underwent a rubella titre test at the direction of the defendants. The test indicated that Linda had been exposed to rubella. At the time the test was performed, Linda was in the second trimester of pregnancy.

Linda brought her pregnancy to full term. On January 1, 1980, she gave birth to a daughter, Heather B. Smith, who is also a plaintiff in this action. Heather was born a victim of congenital rubella syndrome. Today, at age six, Heather suffers from bilateral cataracts, multiple congenital heart defects, motor retardation, and a significant hearing impairment. She is legally blind, and has undergone surgery for her cataracts and heart condition.

In March 1984 the plaintiffs began this negligence action. They allege that Linda contracted rubella early in her pregnancy and that, while she was under the defendants' care, the defendants negligently failed to test for and discover in a timely manner her exposure to the disease. The plaintiffs further contend that the defendants negligently failed to advise Linda of the potential for birth defects in a fetus exposed to rubella, thereby depriving her of the knowledge necessary to an informed decision as to whether to give birth to a potentially impaired child. * * *

The plaintiffs do not allege that the defendants caused Linda to conceive her child or to contract rubella, or that the defendants could have prevented the effects of the disease on the fetus. Rather, the plaintiffs contend that if Linda had known of the risks involved she would have obtained a eugenic abortion.

The action comprises three counts, only two of which are relevant here. In Count I, Linda seeks damages for her emotional distress, for the extraordinary maternal care that she must provide Heather because of Heather's birth defects, and for the extraordinary medical and educational costs she has sustained and will sustain in rearing her daughter.

* * *

In Count III, Heather seeks damages for her birth with defects, for the extraordinary medical and educational costs she will sustain, and for the impairment of her childhood attributable to her mother's diminished capacity to nurture her and cope with her problems.

* * * [T]he Superior Court transferred to us the following questions of law:

"A. Will New Hampshire Law recognize a wrongful birth cause of action by the mother of a wilfully conceived baby suffering from birth defects[?]"

B.   If the answer to question A is in the affirmative, will New Hampshire law allow recovery in such a cause of action for damages for emotional distress, extraordinary maternal child care, and the extraordinary medical, institutional and other special rearing expenses necessary to treat the child's impairments?

C.   Will New Hampshire law recognize a cause of action for wrongful life brought by a minor child suffering from birth defects[?]

D. If the answer to question C is in the affirmative, what general and specific damages may the child recover in such an action?"

* * *

We recognize that the termination of pregnancy involves controversial and divisive social issues. Nonetheless, the Supreme Court of the United States has held that a woman has a constitutionally secured right to terminate a pregnancy. *Roe v. Wade* [ ]. It follows from *Roe* that the plaintiff Linda Smith may seek, and the defendants may provide, information and advice that may affect the exercise of that right. The basic social and constitutional issue underlying this case thus has been resolved; we need not cover ground already traveled by a court whose interpretation of the National Constitution binds us. Today we decide only whether, given the existence of the right of choice recognized in *Roe,* our common law should allow the development of a duty to exercise care in providing information that bears on that choice.

For the sake of terminological clarity, we make some preliminary distinctions. A wrongful birth claim is a claim brought by the parents of a child born with severe defects against a physician who negligently fails to inform them, in a timely fashion, of an increased possibility that the mother will give birth to such a child, thereby precluding an informed decision as to whether to have the child. * * *

A wrongful life claim, on the other hand, is brought not by the parents of a child born with birth defects, but by or on behalf of the child. The child contends that the defendant physician negligently failed to inform the child's parents of the risk of bearing a defective infant, and hence prevented the parents from choosing to avoid the child's birth.

I. WRONGFUL BIRTH: CAUSE OF ACTION

We first must decide whether New Hampshire law recognizes a cause of action for wrongful birth. Although we have never expressly recognized this cause of action, we have considered a similar claim, one for "wrongful conception." In *Kingsbury v. Smith,* 122 N.H. 237, 442 A.2d 1003 (1982), the plaintiffs, a married couple, had had three children and wanted no more. In an attempt to prevent the conception of additional offspring, Mrs. Kingsbury underwent a tubal ligation. The operation failed, however, and Mrs. Kingsbury later gave birth to a fourth child, a normal, healthy infant. The plaintiffs sued the physicians who had performed the operation, alleging that in giving birth to an unwanted child they had sustained an injury caused by the defendants' negligence.

We held that the common law of New Hampshire permitted a claim for wrongful conception, an action "for damages arising from the birth of a child to which a negligently performed sterilization procedure or a negligently filled birth control prescription which fails to prevent conception was a contributing factor." We reasoned that failure to recognize a cause of action for wrongful conception would leave "a void in the area of recovery for medical malpractice" that would dilute the standard of professional conduct in the area of family planning. [ ]

In this case, the mother contends that her wrongful birth claim fits comfortably within the framework established in *Kingsbury* and is consistent with well established tort principles. The defendants argue that tort principles cannot be extended so as to accommodate wrongful birth, asserting that they did not cause the injury alleged here, and that in any case damages cannot be fairly and accurately ascertained.

* * *

* * * In general, at common law, one who suffers an injury to his person or property because of the negligent act of another has a right of action in tort. [ ] In order to sustain an action for negligence, the plaintiff must establish the existence of a duty, the breach of which proximately causes injury to the plaintiff. [ ]

The first two elements of a negligence action, duty and breach, present no conceptual difficulties here. If the plaintiff establishes that a physician-patient relationship with respect to the pregnancy existed between the defendants and her, it follows that the defendants assumed a duty to use reasonable care in attending and treating her. [ ] Given the decision in *Roe v. Wade,* we recognize that the "due care" standard, may have required the defendants to ensure that Linda had an opportunity to make an informed decision regarding the procreative options available to her. [ ] It is a question of fact whether this standard required the defendants, at an appropriate stage of Linda's pregnancy, to test for, diagnose, and disclose her exposure to rubella. The standard is defined by reference to the standards and recommended practices and procedures of the medical profession, the training, experience and professed degree of skill of the average medical practitioner, and all other relevant circumstances.

We note that this standard does not require a physician to identify and disclose every chance, no matter how remote, of the occurrence of every possible birth "defect," no matter how insignificant. [ ] If (1) the applicable standard of care required the defendants to test for and diagnose Linda's rubella infection in a timely manner, and to inform her of the possible effects of the virus on her child's health; and (2) the defendants failed to fulfill this obligation; then the defendants breached their duty of due care.

The third element, causation, is only slightly more troublesome. The defendants point out that proof that they caused the alleged injury depends on a finding that Linda would have chosen to terminate her pregnancy if she had been fully apprised of the risks of birth defects. The defendants argue that this hypothetical chain of events is too remote to provide the basis for a finding of causation.

We do not agree. No logical obstacle precludes proof of causation in the instant case. Such proof is furnished if the plaintiff can show that, but for the defendants' negligent failure to inform her of the risks of bearing a child with birth defects, she would have obtained an abortion. * * *

We turn to the final element of a negligence action, injury. Linda contends that, in bearing a defective child after being deprived of the opportunity to make an informed procreative decision, she sustained an injury. The defendants argue that, because both benefits (the joys of parenthood) and harms (the alleged emotional and pecuniary damages) have resulted from Heather's birth, damages cannot accurately be measured, and no injury to Linda can be proved. The defendants in effect assert that the birth of a child can never constitute an injury to its parents; hence, when an actor's negligence causes a child to be born, that actor cannot be held liable in tort.

We do not agree. We recognize * * * that in some circumstances parents may be injured by the imposition on them of extraordinary liabilities following the birth of a child. Under *Roe,* prospective parents may have constitutionally cognizable reasons for avoiding the emotional and pecuniary burdens that may attend the birth of a child suffering from birth defects. Scientific advances in prenatal health care provide the basis upon which parents may make the informed decisions that *Roe* protects. We see no reason to hold that as a matter of law those who act negligently in providing such care cannot cause harm * * *.

The defendants' emphasis on the inherent difficulty of measuring damages is misplaced. An allegation of "injury," an instance of actionable harm, is distinct from a claim for "damages," a sum of money awarded to one who has suffered an injury. We have long held that difficulty in calculating damages is not a sufficient reason to deny recovery to an injured party. [ ] Other courts have recognized that the complexity of the damages calculation in a wrongful birth case is not directly relevant to the validity of the asserted cause of action. [ ]

We hold that New Hampshire recognizes a cause of action for wrongful birth. Notwithstanding the disparate views within society on the controversial practice of abortion, we are bound by the law that protects a woman's right to choose to terminate her pregnancy. Our holding today neither encourages nor discourages this practice, [ ] nor does it rest upon a judgment that, in some absolute sense, Heather Smith should never have been born. We cannot (and need not, for purposes of this action) make such a judgment. We must, however, do our best to effectuate the first principles of our law of negligence: to deter negligent conduct, and to compensate the victims of those who act unreasonably.

II. WRONGFUL BIRTH: DAMAGES

We next must decide what elements of damages may be recovered in a wrongful birth action. The wrongful birth cause of action is unique. Although it involves an allegation of medical malpractice, it is not (as are most medical malpractice cases) a claim arising from physical injury. It is instead based on a negligent invasion of the parental right to decide whether to avoid the birth of a child with congenital defects. When parents are denied the opportunity to make this decision, important personal interests may be impaired, including an interest in avoiding the special expenses necessitated by the condition of a child born with defects, an interest in preventing the sorrow and anguish that may befall the parents of such a child, and an interest in preserving personal autonomy, which may include the making of informed reproductive choices. [ ] The task of assessing and quantifying the tangible and intangible harms that result when these interests are impaired presents a formidable challenge.

Linda seeks compensation for the extraordinary medical and educational costs that she will sustain in raising Heather, as well as for the extraordinary maternal care that she must provide her child. In addition, she asks for damages for her "emotional distress, anxiety and trauma," which she claims is a natural and foreseeable consequence of the injury she has sustained, and hence should be included as an essential element in the calculation of general damages. We consider these claims for tangible and intangible losses in turn.

A. Tangible Losses

The usual rule of compensatory damages in tort cases requires that the person wronged receive a sum of money that will restore him as nearly as possible to the position he would have been in if the wrong had not been committed. [ ] In the present case, if the defendants' failure to advise Linda of the risks of birth defects amounted to negligence, then the reasonably foreseeable result of that negligence was that Linda would incur the expenses involved in raising her daughter. According to the usual rule of damages, then, Linda should recover the entire cost of raising Heather, including both ordinary child-rearing costs and the extraordinary costs attributable to Heather's condition.

However, "few if any jurisdictions appear ready to apply this traditional rule of damages with full vigor in wrongful birth cases." [ ] Although at least one court has ruled that all child-rearing costs should be recoverable, most courts are reluctant to impose liability to this extent. A special rule of damages has emerged; in most jurisdictions the parents may recover only the extraordinary medical and educational costs attributable to the birth defects. In the present case, in accordance with the rule prevailing elsewhere, Linda seeks to recover, as tangible losses, only her extraordinary costs.

The logic of the "extraordinary costs" rule has been criticized. * * * The rule in effect divides a plaintiff's pecuniary losses into two categories, ordinary costs and extraordinary costs, and treats the latter category as compensable while ignoring the former category. At first glance, this bifurcation seems difficult to justify.

The disparity is explained, however, by reference to the rule requiring mitigation of tort damages. The "avoidable consequences" rule specifies that a plaintiff may not recover damages for "any harm that he could have avoided by the use of reasonable effort or expenditure" after the occurrence of the tort. Rigidly applied, this rule would appear to require wrongful birth plaintiffs to place their children for adoption. [ ] Because of our profound respect for the sanctity of the family, [ ] we are loathe to sanction the application of the rule in these circumstances. If the rule is not applied, however, wrongful birth plaintiffs may receive windfalls. Hence, a special rule limiting recovery of damages is warranted.

Although the extraordinary costs rule departs from traditional principles of tort damages, it is neither illogical nor unprecedented. The rule represents an application in a tort context of the expectancy rule of damages employed in breach of contracts cases. Wrongful birth plaintiffs typically desire a child (and plan to support it) from the outset. [ ] It is the defendants' duty to help them achieve this goal. When the plaintiffs' expectations are frustrated by the defendants' negligence, the extraordinary costs rule "merely attempts to put plaintiffs in the position they expected to be in with defendant's help." [ ]

Under this view of the problem, ordinary child-rearing costs are analogous to a price the plaintiffs were willing to pay in order to achieve an expected result. According to contract principles, plaintiffs "may not have a return in damages of the price and also receive what was to be obtained for the price." [ ] We note that expectancy damages are recoverable in other kinds of tort cases, [ ] and that contract principles are hardly unknown in medical malpractice litigation, which has roots in contract as well as in tort. [ ] In light of the difficulty posed by tort damages principles in these circumstances, we see no obstacle—logical or otherwise—to use of the extraordinary costs rule. [ ]

The extraordinary costs rule ensures that the parents of a deformed child will recover the medical and educational costs attributable to the child's impairment. At the same time it establishes a necessary and clearly defined boundary to liability in this area. [ ] Accordingly, we hold that a plaintiff in a wrongful birth case may recover the extraordinary medical and educational costs attributable to the child's deformities, but may not recover ordinary child-raising costs.

Three points stand in need of clarification. First, parents may recover extraordinary costs incurred both before and after their child attains majority. Some courts do not permit recovery of post-majority expenses, on the theory that the parents' obligation of support terminates when the child reaches twenty-one. [ ] In New Hampshire, however, parents are required to support their disabled adult offspring. [ ]

Second, recovery should include compensation for the extraordinary maternal care that has been and will be provided to the child. Linda alleges that her parental obligations and duties, which include feeding, bathing, and exercising Heather, substantially exceed those of parents of a normal child. One court has ruled that parents "cannot recover for services that they have rendered or will render personally to their own child without incurring financial expense." [ ] We see no reason, however, to treat as noncompensable the burdens imposed on a parent who must devote extraordinary time and effort to caring for a child with birth defects. * * * Avoiding these burdens is often among the primary motivations of one who chooses not to bear a child likely to suffer from birth defects. We hold that a parent may recover for his or her ministrations to his or her child to the extent that such ministrations:

(1) are made necessary by the child's condition;

(2) clearly exceed those ordinarily rendered by parents of a normal child; and

(3) are reasonably susceptible of valuation.

* * *

Third, to the extent that the parent's alleged emotional distress results in tangible pecuniary losses, such as medical expenses or counseling fees, such losses are recoverable. [ ]

B. Intangible Losses

Existing damages principles do not resolve the issue whether recovery for emotional distress should be permitted in wrongful birth cases. Emotional distress damages are not uniformly recoverable once a protected interest is shown to have been invaded. [The court discussed New Hampshire precedent which denied parents damages for emotional distress resulting from the death of their children.]

This case arises from a child's birth, not a child's injury or death. Nonetheless, we are struck by the parallels between the claims for emotional distress in [cases involving the death of children] and the claim before us. Moreover, we are mindful of the anomaly that would result were we to treat parental emotional distress as compensable. The negligent conduct at issue in [those cases] was the direct cause of injuries to or the death of otherwise healthy children. By contrast, in wrongful birth cases the defendant's conduct results, not in injuries or death, but in the birth of an unavoidably impaired child. It would be curious, to say the least, to impose liability for parental distress in the latter but not the former cases.

We also harbor concerns of proportionality. "[T]he unfairness of denying recovery to a plaintiff on grounds that are arbitrary in terms of principle may be outweighed by the perceived unfairness of imposing a burden on defendant that seems much greater than his fault would justify."

We hold that damages for emotional distress are not recoverable in wrongful birth actions. [ ]

III. WRONGFUL LIFE

The theory of Heather's wrongful life action is as follows: during Linda's pregnancy the defendants owed a duty of care to both Linda and Heather. The defendants breached this duty when they failed to discover Linda's exposure to rubella and failed to advise her of the possible effects of that exposure on her child's health. Had Linda been properly informed, she would have undergone an abortion, and Heather would not have been born. Because Linda was not so informed, Heather must bear the burden of her afflictions for the rest of her life. The defendant's conduct is thus the proximate cause of injury to Heather.

This theory presents a crucial problem, however: the question of injury. * * *

In order to recognize Heather's wrongful life action, then, we must determine that the fetal Heather had an interest in avoiding her own birth, that it would have been best *for Heather* if she had not been born.

This premise of the wrongful life action—that the plaintiff's own birth and suffering constitute legal injury—has caused many courts to decline to recognize the claim. * * * As one court has written,

"[w]hether it is better never to have been born at all than to have been born with even gross deficiencies is a mystery more properly to be left to the philosophers and the theologians. Surely the law can assert no competence to resolve the issue, particularly in view of the very nearly uniform high value which the law and mankind has placed on human life, rather than its absence."

Becker v. Schwartz, 46 N.Y.2d 401, 411, 386 N.E.2d 807, 812, 413 N.Y.S.2d 895, 900 (1978).

Moreover, compelling policy reasons militate against recognition of wrongful life claims. The first such reason is our conviction that the courts of this State should not become involved in deciding whether a given person's life is or is not worthwhile. * * *

* * *

The second policy reason militating against recognition of Heather's claim is related to the first.

"[L]egal recognition that a disabled life is an injury would harm the interests of those most directly concerned, the handicapped. * * * Furthermore, society often views disabled persons as burdensome misfits. Recent legislation concerning employment, education, and building access reflects a slow change in these attitudes. This change evidences a growing public awareness that the handicapped can be valuable and productive members of society. To characterize the life of a disabled person as an injury would denigrate both this new awareness and the handicapped themselves." [ ]

The third reason stems from an acknowledgment of the limitations of tort law and the adjudicative process. Wrongful life actions are premised on the ability of judges and juries accurately to apply the traditional tort concept of injury to situations involving complex medical and bioethical issues. Yet this concept applies only roughly. In the ordinary tort case the *existence* of injury is readily and objectively ascertainable. In wrongful life cases, however, the finding of injury necessarily hinges upon subjective and intensely personal notions as to the intangible value of life. * * * The danger of markedly disparate and, hence, unpredictable outcomes is manifest.

In deciding whether to recognize a new tort cause of action, we must consider the "defendant's interest in avoiding an incorrect judgment of liability because of the court's incompetence to determine certain questions raised by application of the announced standard." [ ] Wrongful life claims present problems that cannot be resolved in a "reasonably sensible, even-handed, and fair" manner from case to case. [ ] As Chief Justice Weintraub of the Supreme Court of New Jersey recognized nearly twenty years ago, "[t]o recognize a right not to be born is to enter an area in which no one could find his way." *Gleitman v. Cosgrove*, 49 N.J. 22, 63, 227 A.2d 689, 711 (1967) (Weintraub, C.J., dissenting in part).

* * *

We recognize that our rejection of the [wrongful life action] is not without cost. In the future recovery of an impaired child's necessary medical expenses may well depend on whether the child's parents are available to assert a claim for wrongful birth. * * * But this cost is the price of our paramount regard for the value of human life, and of our adherence to fundamental principles of justice. We will not recognize a right not to be born, and we will not permit a person to recover damages from one who has done him no harm.

* * *

IV. Conclusion

We answer the transferred questions as follows:

A. New Hampshire recognizes a cause of action for wrongful birth.

B. The damages that may be recovered are the extraordinary medical and educational costs of raising the impaired child. Such damages should reflect costs that will be incurred both before and after the child attains majority, and should include compensation for extraordinary parental care. In addition, the mother may recover her tangible losses attributable to her emotional distress.

C. New Hampshire does not recognize a cause of action for wrongful life.

* * *

Notes and Questions

1. Although courts have used the terms in different ways over the past two decades, "wrongful birth", "wrongful life", and "wrongful conception" have come to describe identifiably different kinds of actions. An action for wrongful birth is one commenced by parents against a defendant whose negligence led to the birth of a child with birth defects. An action for wrongful life is one commenced by a child born with birth defects against a defendant whose negligence resulted in the birth of the child. An action for wrongful conception (or wrongful pregnancy) is an action brought by a healthy child or that child's parents against a defendant whose negligence (in performing a tubal ligation, for example) resulted in the birth of the child. Is there any justification for distinguishing between "wrongful life," "wrongful birth," and "wrongful conception"? Are these distinctions based upon any real legal difference? An economic difference? A philosophical analysis? Social policy consequences?

Some courts have concluded that these labels "add nothing to the analysis, inspire[ ] confusion, and impl[y] that the court has adopted a new tort," when, in fact, the only relevant question is whether there has been medical malpractice. Bader v. Johnson, 732 N.E.2d 1212 (Ind.2000); see also Greco v. United States, 111 Nev. 405, 893 P.2d 345 (Nev. 1995). Does it make any difference that these actions are denominated as "wrongful birth," wrongful life" or "wrongful conception" cases rather than ordinary malpractice cases? Does it change the standard of care to be applied, the nature of the proof that must be offered by the parties, the application of the causation requirement, or the assessment of damages? See Mark Strasser, Misconceptions and Wrongful Births: A Call for a Principled Jurisprudence, 31 Ariz. St. L. J. 161 (1999).

2. While wrongful birth cases were not initially well received by the judiciary, see Gleitman v. Cosgrove, 49 N.J. 22, 227 A.2d 689 (1967) (first "modern" wrongful birth action; recovery denied), it has been rare for a court to refuse to entertain such an action since *Roe v. Wade* was decided in 1973. As the *Smith* court pointed out,

> Two developments help explain the trend toward judicial acceptance of wrongful birth actions. The first is the increased ability of health care professionals to predict and detect the presence of fetal defects.

> *Roe v. Wade* and its progeny constitute the second development explaining the acceptance of wrongful birth actions.

513 A.2d at 345–346. Obviously, medicine's ability to do prenatal diagnosis will only improve. Is the Court's retreat in *Casey* from some of the implications of *Roe* relevant to the state recognition of wrongful birth actions? Ultimately, are such cases really founded on abortion law or tort law?

Among those decisions that have recognized wrongful birth actions are Siemieniec v. Lutheran Gen. Hosp., 117 Ill.2d 230, 111 Ill.Dec. 302, 512 N.E.2d 691 (1987), Berman v. Allan, 80 N.J. 421, 404 A.2d 8 (1979) (overruling *Gleitman*), James G. v. Caserta, 175 W.Va. 406, 332 S.E.2d 872 (W.Va.1985), and Becker v. Schwartz, 46 N.Y.2d 401, 413 N.Y.S.2d 895, 386 N.E.2d 807 (1978). See also Robak v. United States, 658 F.2d 471 (7th Cir.1981).

3. Wrongful life actions have been far less successful than wrongful birth actions, although the California, New Jersey and Washington courts have recognized wrongful life actions. See Turpin v. Sortini, 31 Cal.3d 220, 182 Cal.Rptr. 337, 643 P.2d 954 (1982), Procanik v. Cillo, 97 N.J. 339, 478 A.2d 755 (1984) and Harbeson v. Parke–Davis, Inc., 98 Wash.2d 460, 656 P.2d 483 (1983). To the extent that a wrongful life action seeks the same damages that could be recovered in a wrongful birth action, it hardly makes sense to allow one and not the other. In fact, in such cases permitting the wrongful life action simply has the effect of extending the statute of limitations, which is usually longer for an injured newborn than for an injured adult in medical malpractice cases. See Procanik v. Cillo, 97 N.J. 339, 478 A.2d 755 (1984) (justice requires allowing the wrongful life action because the wrongful birth action is barred by the statute of limitations). Despite this, most of the courts that have considered the issue have reached the same result that was reached in New Hampshire; they permit wrongful birth actions but not wrongful life actions. See, e.g., Lininger v. Eisenbaum, 764 P.2d 1202 (Colo.1988), and Gildiner v. Thomas Jefferson Univ. Hosp., 451 F.Supp. 692 (E.D.Pa.1978).

There are several reasons that courts are reluctant to accept wrongful life actions. The first argument against such actions is that a defendant cannot have a duty to a putative plaintiff who did not exist at the time that the tortious action took place. Of course, the law does recognize such a duty under other circumstances. As John Robertson has pointed out, one would be liable to an injured party for a bomb planted in a newborn nursery and set to go off a year later; the fact that the injured party was not even conceived at the time the bomb was planted would not be dispositive. See also Renslow v. Mennonite Hosp., 67 Ill.2d 348, 10 Ill.Dec. 484, 367 N.E.2d 1250 (1977) (doctor liable to child born to a woman several years after the doctor negligently transfused the woman).

The second argument against permitting a child to sue the party whose negligence caused his birth is the presumption that being born is always better than not being born; one cannot have suffered damages because one was born alive. Do you agree? Is the general acceptance of "right to die" cases, discussed below in Chapter 19, a refutation of this "life is always better than the alternative" argument? The *Smith* court distinguished the "right to die" cases from the wrongful life cases quite directly:

> Simply put, the judiciary has an important role to play in protecting the privacy rights of the dying. It has no business declaring that among the living are people who never should have been born.

513 A.2d at 353.

Another argument raised against permitting wrongful life actions is that legal recognition of these lawsuits would constitute a social judgment that handicapped lives are worth less than other lives. Is the legal decision not to recognize wrongful life actions an appropriate way to indicate society's desire to respect the handicapped?

4. Those wrongful conception cases brought by parents to recover the costs of a pregnancy have fared well in the courts. See, e.g., O'Toole v. Greenberg, 64 N.Y.2d 427, 488 N.Y.S.2d 143, 477 N.E.2d 445 (1985) (failed tubal ligation), Hartke v. McKelway, 707 F.2d 1544 (D.C.Cir.1983) (tubal cauterization). Only one state, Nevada, refuses to recognize such an action. See Szekeres v. Robinson, 102 Nev. 93, 715 P.2d 1076 (1986). On the other hand, wrongful conception cases seeking damages that include the cost of raising the healthy child have run into the same barriers that have faced wrongful life actions.

5. The measure of damages is a significant legal issue in most wrongful birth, wrongful life, and wrongful conception cases. As a matter of general course, the courts have allowed special damages for the pregnancy itself in wrongful birth and wrongful conception cases, and they have permitted recovery of some child rearing costs, where those costs exceed the costs of raising a normal healthy child, in wrongful birth actions. Some courts deny any recovery of the cost of raising a healthy child on the rationale that a healthy child can never be an injury, as a matter of public policy. See O'Toole v. Greenberg, supra, and Hartke v. McKelway, supra. Other courts have fashioned a curious hybrid, allowing child-rearing costs but deducting a quantified estimate of the "benefit" of parenthood. A minority of courts allow child-rearing costs without any offset. See, e.g., Zehr v. Haugen, 318 Or. 647, 871 P.2d 1006 (1994) (allowing damages extending beyond the minority of the child).

In Marciniak v. Lundborg, 153 Wis.2d 59, 450 N.W.2d 243 (1990), an action to recover damages for a negligent sterilization that resulted in a normal healthy child, the public policy arguments for limiting recovery in such cases were enumerated and rejected:

Defendants first argue that child rearing costs are too speculative and that it is impossible to establish with reasonable certainty the damages to the parents. We do not agree that the damages are too speculative. * * * [S]imilar calculations are routinely performed in countless other malpractice situations. Juries are frequently called on to make far more complex damage assessments in other tort cases. * * *

Defendants next argue that because the costs of raising a child are so significant, allowing these costs would be wholly out of proportion to the culpability of the negligent physician. We find no merit in that contention. Admittedly, the cost of raising a child is substantial. However, the public policy of this state does not categorically immunize defendants from liability for foreseeable damages merely because the damages may be substantial.

Defendants next argue that "awarding damages to the parents may cause psychological harm to the child when, at a later date, it learns of its parents' action for its wrongful birth thereby creating an 'emotional bastard.'" "Again, we do not agree." The parents' suit for recovery of child rearing costs is in no reasonable sense a signal to the child that the parents consider the child an unwanted burden. The suit is for costs of raising the child, not to rid themselves of an unwanted child. They obviously want to keep the child. The love, affection, and emotional support any child needs they are prepared to give. But the love, affection, and emotional support they are prepared to give do not bring with them the economic means that are also necessary to feed, clothe, educate and otherwise raise the child. That is what this suit is about and we trust the child in the future will be well able to distinguish the two.

Defendants also argue that allowing these costs would in some way debase the sanctity of human life, stating that "[T]he courts have been loath to adopt a rule, the primary effect of which is to encourage or reward the parents' disparagement of the value of their child's life." We do not perceive that the Marciniaks in bringing this suit are in any way disparaging the value of their child's life. They are, to the contrary, attempting to enhance it.

Defendants further argue that allowing these costs would shift the entire cost of raising the child to the physician, thereby creating a new category of surrogate parent. This suit is not an attempt to shift the responsibility of parenting from the Marciniaks to the physician. The Marciniaks are assuming that responsibility. To equate the responsibility of parenting with the responsibility of paying for the costs of child raising is illogical.

We do not agree that the refusal of the Marciniaks to abort the unplanned child or give it up for adoption should be considered as a failure of the parents to mitigate their damages. The rules requiring mitigation of damages require only that reasonable measures be taken. We do not consider it reasonable to expect parents to essentially choose between the child and the cause of action.

450 N.W.2d at 245–247.

Finally, the court decided not to apply the "benefit rule" that would allow an offset for the joy of having the child against the damages awarded:

We conclude that it is not equitable to apply the benefit rule in the context of the tort of negligent sterilization. The parents made a decision not to have a child. It was precisely to avoid that "benefit" that the parents went to the physician in the first place. Any "benefits" that were conferred upon them as a result of having a new child in their lives were not asked for and were sought to be avoided. With respect to emotional benefits, potential parents in this situation are presumably well aware of the emotional benefits that might accrue to them as the result of a new child in their lives. When parents make the decision to forego this opportunity for emotional enrichment, it hardly seems equitable to not only force this benefit upon them but to tell them they must pay for it as well by offsetting it against their proven emotional damages.

450 N.W.2d at 450. The cost of raising a healthy child is, in fact, less than the special damages sought in many other kinds of medical malpractice cases, and it is far less than those damages related to the medical care of a seriously ill newborn. See Comment, Wrongful Pregnancy: Child Rearing Damages Deserve Full Judicial Consideration, 8 Pace L.Rev. 313, 333–34 (1988).

6. Because wrongful birth, wrongful life and wrongful conception actions may expand the areas in which physicians are liable for malpractice, and because they implicate abortion, about half of the state legislatures have considered legislative resolutions of these issues. While one state has promulgated a statute allowing for wrongful birth and wrongful life actions, 24 Me.Rev.Stat.Ann. § 2931, several others have promulgated legislation forbidding both wrongful birth and wrongful life actions. Most have language similar to that adopted in Minnesota, which provides that "no person shall maintain a cause of action or receive an award of damages on the claim that but for the negligent conduct of another, a child would have been aborted." Minn.Stat.Ann. § 145.424(2). The Minnesota Supreme Court upheld that statute in an action brought by a thirty-four year old mother of a child born with Down's syndrome. The mother alleged that the physician defendant negligently discouraged her from undergoing a test which would have revealed the Down's syndrome and resulted in the abortion of the

fetus. The court rejected the argument that the statute violated interests protected by *Roe v. Wade,* and that it violated the equal protection of the Fourteenth Amendment. First, the court decided that there was no state action alleged, and thus no constitutionally protected right at stake. Even if there were state action, the court concluded, the statute did not constitute a legally impermissible burden on the mother's right to seek an abortion. Three justices dissented, finding the statute to be an improper state interference with the mother's right to an abortion, Hickman v. Group Health Plan, Inc., 396 N.W.2d 10 (Minn.1986). For examples of other state legislation prohibiting wrongful birth and wrongful life actions, see Idaho Code Sec. 5–334, West's Ann. Ind. Code Sec. 34–1–1–11, Vernon's Ann. Mo. State. § 188.30.

7. There are a number of articles on the propriety of wrongful birth, wrongful life and wrongful conception actions. The seminal article in the field, and one that the court depended upon very heavily in *Smith v. Cote,* is Patrick Kelley, Wrongful Life, Wrongful Birth and Justice in Tort Law, 1979 Wash. U.L.Q. 919; See also Mark Strasser, Misconceptions and Wrongful Births: A Call for a Principled Jurisprudence, 31 Ariz. St. L. J. 161 (1999), Michael Kelly, The Rightful Position in "Wrongful Life" Actions, 42 Hast. L.J. 505 (1991); John Robertson, Toward Rational Boundaries for Tort Liability to the Unborn: Prenatal Injuries, Preconception Injuries, and Wrongful Life, 1978 Duke L.J. 1401; Alexander Capron, Tort Liability in Genetic Counselling, 79 Colum.L.Rev. 618 (1979); Thomas Rogers, Wrongful Life and Wrongful Birth: Medical Malpractice in Genetic Counselling and Prenatal Testing, 33 S.C.L.Rev. 713 (1982). The question of whether life can ever be "wrongful" is nicely discussed in Melinda A. Roberts, Distinguishing Wrongful from "Rightful" Life, 6 J. Contemporary Health L. & Policy 59 (1990). For a vigorous response to the new trend allowing full damages in wrongful conception cases, see Brett Simmons, Zehr v. Haugen and the Oregon Approach to Wrongful Conception; An Occasion for Celebration or Litigation? 31 Willamette L.R. 121 (1995). A good response to some specific legislation is found in Note, Wrongful Birth Actions: The Case Against Legislative Curtailment, 100 Harv.L.Rev. 2017 (1987) (arguing that statutory limitations infringe on parents' right to make informed procreative decisions). An interesting comparative law analysis of this issue is found in Anthony Jackson, Actions for Wrongful Life, Wrongful Pregnancy and Wrongful Birth in the United States and England, 17 Loy. L.A. Int'l & Comp. L.J. 535 (1995).

B. ASSISTING REPRODUCTION

Problem: Reproductive Arrangements Go Awry

Avery and Bertha Carp wanted a child for years, but Avery proved infertile. Artificial insemination of Bertha also proved unsuccessful because her uterus is unable to maintain a fertilized ovum. A year ago they consulted Dr. Dominguez, a specialist in the treatment of infertility. He suggested *in vitro* insemination of Bertha's ovum, which could then be implanted in the womb of a surrogate. The Carps agreed, and Dr. Dominguez arranged to have fertile sperm delivered from Nobel Labs Incorporated for impregnation of one of Bertha's ova, which he surgically removed from her. He then implanted the fertilized ovum in the uterus of Ellen Featherstone, a healthy 25–year old single woman who was referred to Dr. Dominguez by Motherhood Incorporated, a surrogate mother brokering company. The Carps agreed to the selection of Ms. Featherstone, whom they had never met, and they agreed to pay Dr. Dominguez his fee of $15,000, and Motherhood Incorporated their administrative fee of $40,000, which included "all legal and medical expenses of carrying the child to term." Motherhood Incorporated agreed to pay the legal and medical fees incurred by Ms. Featherstone, and they agreed to pay her $15,000 to carry the child to term and then place the child for adoption with the Carps. The Carps agreed to adopt the child at birth, and Motherhood Incorporated agreed to hold the $40,000 in escrow until the adoption was complete.

One month ago the child, Gerald, was born with some serious problems. He is likely to be mildly developmentally disabled as a consequence of an automobile accident Ms. Featherstone suffered during the eighth month of the pregnancy, in which Gerald's skull was partially crushed *in utero*. The automobile accident was the result of Ms. Featherstone's negligence in going through a red light. In addition, the child is likely to develop mottled, discolored teeth as a consequence of the administration to Ms. Featherstone of tetracycline in the emergency room after the automobile accident. Discolored teeth is a well known consequence of the use of that antibiotic in pregnant women. Finally, the infant suffers from Von Willebrand disease, which is a form of hemophilia that is apparently the result of a genetic defect in the biological father. The defect could have been discovered before impregnation, but only through a genetic analysis of the father. That analysis was not undertaken because the sperm, according to Nobel Incorporated, "came from a very healthy, very smart man, highly prolific with several healthy children; there was no indication that any further inquiry was necessary."

The Carps have refused to adopt the infant, and they have demanded a refund of the $40,000 from Motherhood's escrow agent. Motherhood Incorporated demands the $40,000. Ms. Featherstone is willing to keep the baby, as long as the Carps pay support, which they refuse. She is threatening a maternity action against Bertha and a contract action against Avery. The state child protection agency is threatening to take the child into state custody.

Who are Gerald's parents? Who has what rights against whom? What kind of a contract would you have drawn as counsel to the Carps? Nobel Incorporated? Motherhood Incorporated? Ms. Featherstone? Dr. Dominguez? Which of those contracts, if any, would be enforceable?

1. *Introduction*

a. *The Process of Human Reproduction*

Those seeking medical help in facilitating reproduction do so because they want a child. The birth of a child requires the growth of a fetus in a woman's uterus. This, in turn, requires the implantation of a fertilized ovum (also called an egg or an oocyte) in the uterine wall. At least until the cloning of human beings is perfected, the ovum can implant in the uterine wall only if it has been fertilized by a sperm, a process which generally takes place in the fallopian tube.

Despite the development of a variety of techniques to accomplish this, most people still use coitus as the preferred process for initiating pregnancy. Typically, an ovum leaves a woman's ovary when the wall of follicular cells in which it has been residing breaks and it is carried upon a wave of escaping follicular fluid into the upper end of the fallopian tube; this process is called ovulation and it occurs once each menstrual cycle, usually between the ninth and fourteenth day. During this stage, if a man ejaculates semen which contains motile spermatozoa (sperm) into the woman's vagina, the sperm move (at a rate of a little less than five inches per hour) through her uterus and into her fallopian tubes. Although one ejaculation may contain a billion sperm pursuing the ovum, only a much smaller number reach the upper portion of the one fallopian tube that contains the freshly released ovum. An even smaller number of sperm actually reach the ovum. Of these, the first sperm head to embed in the outer wall of the ovum releases a substance that changes the ovum's outer wall, making it impermeable to other sperm. Sperm remain alive and capable of fertilization in the uterine environment for only about 48 hours after ejaculation. Because the ovum is estimated to have a fertilizable life of less than 24 hours after it is released from the ovary, the timing of fertilization is important.

Within a day, the fertilized ovum has divided twice, into a two-and then a four-celled "embryo," and it is here that we must pause to consider the impact that our language has on our conceptualization and therefore our law. The terminology of early pregnancy is rife with alternative phraseology. For example, a fertilized ovum/egg/oocyte is also called a "zygote," or a cluster of dividing "blastomeres" which eventually divide into a "blastocyst" or hollow cellular ball. Some will argue that because there is no differentiated living matter generated in forming the blastocyst (i.e., there are no fetal or placental cells yet), this division of cell material is not a constructive development of living substance. It is a process which does nothing to distribute particular developmental qualities to particular parts of a resulting fetus. On the other hand, it is the preliminary stage which makes it possible for the blastocyst cell ball to implant and use materials from the uterine wall to grow and develop into a fetus. Obviously, the fertilization of the ovum by the sperm begins the embryonic process, although some use the term "embryo" only to apply to later stages of development.

At any rate, whether it is called an embryo, a preembryo or something else, the fertilized ovum continues its migration through the fallopian tube toward the uterus. The fertilized and subdividing ovum arrives at the lower end of the fallopian tube, hesitating for about two days before being expelled into the uterus. This delay allows the uterine lining to build up for successful implantation. The implantation of this cell cluster is a complicated biological process that takes several days. Where the fertilized ovum cell cluster adheres to the uterine lining is variable, although there is less risk of some subsequent complications if implantation occurs in the upper half of the uterus.

Even when all other conditions are met, not all fertilized ova actually do implant and not all implanted ova survive until birth. About 50% of fertilized ova are expelled from the body before the woman has any reason to know that she is pregnant. Some of these spontaneous expulsions occur before implantation, and some occur during the first few days after the commencement of the implantation process.

There are several reasons that those who wish to raise children may not conceive them through this natural process. First, some are unable to participate in coital sexual relations, or choose not to participate in such relations. Others are infertile—that is, normal coitus does not result in a fertilized ovum that implants in the uterine wall and grows into a fetus and then a child. Although estimates vary, at least 10% of American couples are infertile. There are a variety of reasons for infertility. Some men do not produce sperm that is capable of fertilizing the ovum. Some women are unable to produce ova, for example, and others have fallopian tubes that cannot adequately accept ova to be fertilized, or do not permit the travel of fertilized ova to the uterus. In some cases, the "shell" around the ovum may not admit any sperm at all. In other cases, the ovum is successfully fertilized but the uterus is incapable of allowing for implantation of the fertilized ovum or of maintaining the implanted embryo through the pregnancy. In all of these cases, some form of intervention may allow those who could not become parents through unassisted coitus to achieve parenthood nonetheless.

The variety of problems that results in the need to assist reproduction give rise to a wide variety of alternative interventions. These interventions, in turn, require the involvement of a host of other people. A sperm source (who is not necessarily a sperm donor—he is usually a sperm vendor) is necessary where the problem is the lack of a man or a man's inability to produce physiologically adequate sperm; an ovum source is necessary where the problem is a woman's inability to provide a potentially fertile ovum; a uterus source (originally called a "surrogate mother," now more generally described as a "gestational mother") is necessary where a woman is unable or unwilling to carry the fertilized ovum through the pregnancy in her own uterus. Medical treatment of an ovum may allow it to be fertilized, and treatment of a fertilized ovum may allow it to be implanted. Sometimes a combination of these needs requires that there be a series of interventions to produce a pregnancy and a child. A woman may be unable to produce ova and unable to carry a fertilized ovum in her uterus, for example. There may be several options available to allow her to obtain both an ovum that can be fertilized (from an ovum source) and a uterus for the gestation of that fertilized ovum (from a surrogate).

b. The Role of the Law

The law's involvement in human reproduction has not been limited to evaluating the propriety of techniques used to avoid bearing children: the law is also involved in regulating processes designed to facilitate reproduction. These processes include AIH (artificial insemination-homologous: artificial insemination of a woman with the sperm of the person who is intended to be the biological and nurturing father, usually the husband), AID (artificial insemination-donor: artificial insemination of the woman with the sperm of someone who is presumed to have no continuing relationship with the child), IVF (*in vitro* fertilization: fertilizing an ovum outside of the uterus and then implanting it), embryo transfer, egg transfer, and gestational surrogacy (carrying a fetus expected to be raised by an identifiable person other than the pregnant woman). There are other techniques that may be applied to aid fertilization problems—such as full IVP (*in vitro* pregnancy) and cloning—but these are unlikely to be of much practical concern over the next few years. There are hundreds of thousands of children now alive in the United States who were conceived by AID; there are tens of thousands who are the result of *in vitro* fertilization, and (probably) thousands carried by surrogate mothers. Questions surrounding their legal status are real, substantial, and immediate.

It is not hard to imagine the variety of unusual legal relationships which can develop as a consequence of medical and non-medical reproductive techniques. It is possible to have a child who is the product of sperm from one source (whose sperm may be mixed with sperm from several sources), an ovum extracted from one woman, implanted in another, and carried for the benefit of yet another set of parents who intend to nurture the child from the time of its birth. Such a child would have two genetic parents, a gestational mother, and two contractual (or intended or nurturing) parents. Who ought to be treated as the legal parents? Should the others involved in the process have any rights whatsoever? For example, if the nurturing parents have the rights normally associated with parenthood, should any rights—visitation, for example—be extended to the gestational mother, or the genetic parents? Should we consider parenthood to be a bundle of rights, much as we have come to view property, and should these rights be separated out and split among several people, each of whom would share in the privileges and responsibilities of parental status? Is there a good reason to limit a child to two legal parents?

For the original descriptions of the taxonomies of relationships resulting from reproductive technology, see Alexander Capron, Alternative Birth Technologies: Legal Challenges, 20 U.Cal. Davis L.Rev. 679, 682 (1987) and Bernard Dickens, Reproduction Law and Medical Consent, 35 Toronto L.J. 255, 280 (1985).

c. *Facilitating Reproduction and the Definition of the Family*

We are so concerned about the use of new technology to facilitate reproduction in part because of its potential effect on family structure, and because any consequent change in family structure may also have an impact on social structure. Courts and legislatures have been tentative at best in actually defining what constitutes a "family" of the kind which we wish to preserve and protect. Perhaps this should not come as a surprise; others who have attempted to define "family" have not been any more successful. As R.D. Laing explained,

> [w]e speak of families as though we all knew what families are. We identify, as families, networks of people who live together over periods of time, who have ties of marriage and kinship to one another. The more one studies family dynamics, the more *un*clear one becomes as to the ways *family* dynamics compare and contrast with the dynamics of other groups not called families, let alone the ways families differ themselves. As with dynamics, so with structure (patterns, more stable and enduring than others): Again, comparisons and generalizations must be very tentative.

R.D. Laing, The Politics of the Family and Other Essays, 3 (1971). Since 1971 American social living arrangements, and the consequent notions of the family, have become even more uncertain. Early this century a society of extended families (which were extended both horizontally, to include near relatives, and vertically, to include near generations) was transformed through increased mobility, increased urbanization, and increased industrialization into a society of nuclear families, each family possessing an identifiable head of a household (generally the father) a mother, and children; the dog was optional.

This model of the family has been tested by many forces, including those that come from women's reassessment of their roles. Even greater changes have driven us from a society of nuclear families to a society of "constructed" families—designer families, really—where relationships between adults, and between adults and children, are arranged on an *ad hoc* basis or by agreement. Of course, these *ad hoc* arrangements may provide for a different relationship between children and their parents, and between these new social units and the state, than those which traditionally have been recognized in law. Further, while many of these new "constructed" families look very much like the families of a few decades ago, many do not. Many are one parent families, some include more than two parents and some include two parents of the same gender.

The law has struggled to deal with the social and medical developments that made these families possible with only limited success. While courts have been able to develop processes to accommodate the breakup of nuclear families—custody and support arrangements, primarily—neither the courts nor legislatures have done very well in developing institutions that are capable of dealing with these previously legally unrecognized families. Ultimately this society will call upon the law to define families, declare family relationships, and allocate power within families. The solutions to the problems thus raised will depend upon the answer to the question the law has not yet asked: why does this society recognize families? Why do we strive to protect families? Why are the institutions of government so interested in preserving and restoring the authority of families? These questions have been unanswered—indeed, unasked—by the law until now because the law has not been called to address them. However, social and medical changes over the last several years have forced these questions into the legal spotlight. This society must determine first, descriptively, the role families do play in society, and, second, prescriptively, the role they ought to play in this society.

As you read the rest of this section of this chapter, ask yourself whether the law reflects forethought and purpose behind its definitional conclusions (be they explicit or implicit). Is the law consistent in this area? Is it just? For the classic academic structure of these issues, see A. Skolnick and J. Skolnick, Family in Transition: Rethinking Marriage, Sexuality, Childbearing, and Family Organization (1971).

2. *Artificial Insemination*

THE PROCESS OF ARTIFICIAL INSEMINATION

Artificial insemination is the placement of the semen in the vagina (or in the cervical canal) by means other than the penis. The sperm source produces semen through masturbation and ejaculation. The ejaculate is then put into a syringe and injected directly into the woman who intends to become pregnant. This process, using "fresh" semen, need not be a medical procedure; it can be done successfully at home by anyone who understands the underlying biological principles. Ideally, the insemination is done at about the time of ovulation, a time that can be determined with increasing accuracy through home ovulation prediction tests.

Medically performed artificial insemination now generally employs frozen semen rather than fresh semen. Although freezing semen permits subsequent tests upon the donor to determine the presence of any latent contaminant (HIV, for example, or, perhaps, a genetic defect), the freezing process is comparatively difficult and expensive. The semen is mixed with a preservative before it is frozen, and it must be carefully thawed before it is used. Once the semen is frozen, however, it is unlikely to undergo substantial deterioration; one estimate is that the risk of genetic mutation will double if the semen is kept frozen for 5,000 years. In 1990 one Seattle man successfully inseminated his wife with sperm he deposited in a New York sperm bank fourteen years earlier. The man, who became sterile after his deposit, had paid a fee each year to keep his deposit on ice. There is no reason to believe that the semen could not be kept in the freezer for hundreds of years; whether it should be is another question. One leading sperm bank now charges about $1000 to prepare a specimen for cryopreservation and to save it for five years. A five year extension is available for another $620.

There are hundreds of thousands of women artificially inseminated medically each year in the United States. The service is provided by thousands of doctors throughout the country. Frozen sperm costs between $200 and $500 per vial; preparation of fresh sperm costs about half of that. The total cost of artificial insemination, per cycle, will generally be less than $1,000.

a. Artificial Insemination—Homologous (AIH)

Virtually no legal questions have arisen surrounding the use of the sperm of a husband to inseminate his wife, even if the sperm is artificially injected into the vagina or cervical canal. Such a process may be used within a marriage to allow for processing of the semen to overcome low sperm count. In these cases, there is no question about the identity of the mother and the father of the child. While there are some religious objections to masturbation (which, obviously, is required) and to any process that alters the "natural" arrangement, AIH has now become well accepted as a social and medical matter, and it is not a matter of substantial legal concern.

b. Artificial Insemination—Donor (AID)

When the sperm is not that of the husband of the woman whose pregnancy results, the question of who ought to be considered the father of the resulting child may arise. For the most part this matter has been resolved by the adoption of the 1973 Uniform Parentage Act (adopted, at least in part, in one form or another; in most states), the Uniform Status of Children of Assisted Conception Act (adopted in two states) or another statute that serves the same purposes. In 2000 the original (1973) Uniform Parentage Act and the Uniform Status of Children of Assisted Conception Act were combined and rewritten in the form of a new (2000) Uniform Parentage Act. The portions of this new statute that deal with assisted reproduction have proven highly controversial, and it is unclear whether there will be a serious attempt to have them introduced in state legislatures.

UNIFORM PARENTAGE ACT
(1973).

* * *

§ 5. [Artificial Insemination.]

(a) If, under the supervision of a licensed physician and with the consent of her husband, a wife is inseminated artificially with semen donated by a man not her husband, the husband is treated in law as if he were the natural father of a child thereby conceived. The husband's consent must be in writing and signed by him and his wife. The physician shall certify their signatures and the date of the insemination, and file the husband's consent with the [State Department of Health], where it shall be kept confidential and in a sealed file. However, the physician's failure to do so does not affect the father and child relationship. All papers and records pertaining to the insemination, whether part of the permanent record of a court or of a file held by the supervising physician or elsewhere, are subject to inspection only upon an order of the court for good cause shown.

(b) The donor of semen provided to a licensed physician for use in artificial insemination of a married woman other than the donor's wife is treated in law as if he were not the natural father of a child thereby conceived.

* * *

§ 23.   [Birth Records.]

(a) Upon order of a court of this State or upon request of a court of another state, the [registrar of births] shall prepare [an amended birth registration] [a new certificate of birth] consistent with the findings of the court [and shall substitute the new certificate for the original certificate of birth].

(b) The fact that the father and child relationship was declared after the child's birth shall not be ascertainable from the [amended birth registration] [new certificate] but the actual place and date of birth shall be shown.

(c) The evidence upon which the [amended birth registration] [new certificate] was made and the original birth certificate shall be kept in a sealed and confidential file and be subject to inspection only upon consent of the court and all interested persons, or in exceptional cases only upon an order of the court for good cause shown.

UNIFORM PARENTAGE ACT

(2000).

§ 101. DEFINITIONS.

(4) "Assisted reproduction" means a method of causing pregnancy other than sexual intercourse. The term includes:

   (A) intrauterine insemination;

   (B) donation of eggs;

   (C) donation of embryos;

   (D) in-vitro fertilization and transfer of embryos; and

   (E) intracytoplasmic sperm injection.

§ 103. SCOPE OF [ACT]; CHOICE OF LAW.

(a) This [Act] governs every determination of parentage in this State.

(b) The court shall apply the law of this State to adjudicate the parent-child relationship. The applicable law does not depend on:

(1) the place of birth of the child; or

(2) the past or present residence of the child.

(c) This [Act] does not create, enlarge, or diminish parental rights or duties under other law of this State.

* * *

§ 201. ESTABLISHMENT OF PARENT–CHILD RELATIONSHIP.

(a) The mother-child relationship is established between a woman and a child by:

    (1) the woman's having given birth to the child [, except as otherwise provided in [Article] 8, concerning gestational surrogacy];

    (2) an adjudication of the woman's maternity; [or]

    (3) adoption of the child by the woman * * *

(b) The father-child relationship is established between a man and a child by:

    (1) an unrebutted presumption of the man's paternity of the child * * *;

    (2) an effective acknowledgment of paternity by the man * * *;

    (3) an adjudication of the man's paternity;

    (4) adoption of the child by the man; [or]

    (5) the man's having consented to assisted reproduction by his wife under [this Act] which resulted in the birth of the child * * *

ARTICLE 7—CHILD OF ASSISTED REPRODUCTION

§ 701. SCOPE OF ARTICLE.

This [article] does not apply to the birth of a child conceived by means of sexual intercourse [, or as the result of a gestational agreement as provided in [Article] 8].[For a discussion of section 8, see below]

§ 702. PARENTAL STATUS OF DONOR.

A donor is not a parent of a child conceived by means of assisted reproduction.

§ 703. HUSBAND'S PATERNITY OF CHILD OF ASSISTED REPRODUCTION.

If a husband provides sperm for, or consents to, assisted reproduction by his wife as provided in Section 704, he is the father of a resulting child.

§ 704. CONSENT TO ASSISTED REPRODUCTION.

(a) Consent by a married woman to assisted reproduction must be in a record signed by the woman and her husband. This requirement does not apply to the donation of eggs by a married woman for assisted reproduction by another woman.

(b) Failure of the husband to sign a consent required by subsection (a), before or after birth of the child, does not preclude a finding that the husband is the father of a child born to his wife if the wife and husband openly treated the child as their own.

* * *

§ 706. EFFECT OF DISSOLUTION OF MARRIAGE.

(a) If a marriage is dissolved before placement of eggs, sperm, or embryos, the former spouse is not a parent of the resulting child unless the former spouse consented in a record that if assisted reproduction were to occur after a divorce, the former spouse would be a parent of the child.

(b) The consent of a former spouse to assisted reproduction may be withdrawn by that individual in a record at any time before placement of eggs, sperm, or embryos.

§ 707. PARENTAL STATUS OF DECEASED SPOUSE.

If a spouse dies before placement of eggs, sperm, or embryos, the deceased spouse is not a parent of the resulting child unless the deceased spouse consented in a record that if assisted reproduction were to occur after death, the deceased spouse would be a parent of the child.

Notes and Questions

1.   What is the difference between the approach taken by the 1973 Uniform Parentage Act and the approach taken by the 2000 Act? In what kinds of cases would the application of the different Acts yield different parents?

Under the 2000 version of the Uniform Parentage Act, would a child born of donor semen to an unmarried woman (or to a woman whose husband did not consent to the procedure) have no father? Does it seem appropriate to create such a class of legally fatherless children? Why shouldn't the sperm source be considered the father, at least as a default position in the law?

2.   While the 2000 version of the Uniform Parentage Act applies in every case of assisted conception, it has not been widely adopted. On the other hand, the 1973 version, parts of which have been adopted in the majority of states, applies only if the woman who is inseminated is a wife (i.e., is married), if she proceeds with the consent of her husband and the procedure is carried out under the supervision of a licensed physician. If any of these conditions is not met, the statute is inapplicable and the common law will define the rights and interests of all of the parties. See Marriage of Witbeck–Wildhagen, 281 Ill.App.3d 502, 217 Ill.Dec. 329, 667 N.E.2d 122 (1996) (husband did not consent to wife's insemination; statute did not apply). Some common law cases have treated the source of the sperm to be the father, with all of the rights (including visitation) and obligations (including child support) that come with such a designation; others have not. Compare Gursky v. Gursky, 39 Misc.2d 1083, 242 N.Y.S.2d 406 (Sup.Ct. 1963) (child born of AID is illegitimate) with In re Adoption of Anonymous, 74 Misc.2d 99, 345 N.Y.S.2d 430 (Sup.Ct.1973). See also In re Baby Doe, 291 S.C. 389, 353 S.E.2d 877 (1987) (one who assists his wife's efforts to conceive by artificial insemination must be treated as the legal father of the resulting child); Strnad v. Strnad, 190 Misc. 786, 78 N.Y.S.2d 390 (Sup.Ct.1948) (husband of woman who receives AID with his consent has rights and obligations of father); People v. Sorensen, 68 Cal.2d 280, 66 Cal.Rptr. 7, 437 P.2d 495 (1968) (husband of wife impregnated by AID with his consent is liable for support of child) and C.M. v. C.C., 152 N.J.Super. 160, 377 A.2d 821 (1977) (natural father by AID liable for support). For an analysis of the sperm donor's constitutional rights to maintain a relationship with the child when the woman promised she would permit such a

relationship, see McIntyre v. Crouch, 98 Or.App. 462, 780 P.2d 239 (1989), aff'd 308 Or. 593, 784 P.2d 1100 (1989).

3. In addition to the moral arguments that are made against AIH, there are four additional arguments against the moral and social propriety of AID. First, some believe that it constitutes adultery. Second, the uncertainty of the screening of the sperm source in AID can provide for uncertainty in the health of the child, and the anonymity of the sperm source can impose upon the woman or her child unforeseen emotional consequences. Third, there is a worry that the availability of AID will reshape and dilute family structure, replacing the nuclear family with unusual and inappropriate combinations of adults and children. Finally, there is an argument that AID is inappropriate because if there is no limit on the number of times one man may donate sperm there may be a genetically unacceptably large number of "test tube" children who unknowingly have the same genetic father. This may lead to the dilution of the genetic pool of some communities. Do any of these arguments provide a good reason to prohibit the practice, or to regulate it?

4. Should a woman being inseminated be able to choose the man who will be the source of the sperm? At the least, should she be able to designate some of the attributes that she wishes the source of the sperm to possess? Alternatively, should the source of the sperm remain unknown to the child, the inseminated woman, and, perhaps, even the inseminating physician? Sperm banks do provide profiles of their various donors, and some issue catalogs of these profiles allowing their consumers to choose the profile that seems most appropriate. One "donor catalog" provides information on ethnicity, hair color and texture, eye color, height, weight, blood type, skin tone, years of education, and occupation (or major in college). Short (2 page) profiles, and longer (10 page) descriptions are available on all donors, and audio tapes are available for some. In addition to relevant health information, what kind of information, if any, about the sperm source ought to be provided to the woman who is going to be inseminated? In considering the appropriate policy for Britain, a government commission considered the American practice:

> It is the practice of some clinics in the U.S.A. to provide detailed descriptions of donors, and to permit couples to exercise choice as to the donor they would prefer. In the evidence there was some support for the use of such descriptions. It is argued that they would provide information and reassurance for the parents and, at a later date, for the child. They might also be of benefit to the donor, as an indication that he is valued for his own sake. A detailed description also offers some choice to the woman who is to have the child, and lack of such choice can be said to diminish the importance of the woman's right to choose the father of her child.

> The contrary view, also expressed in the evidence, is that detailed donor profiles would introduce the donor as a person in his own right. It is also argued that the use of profiles devalues the child who may seem to be wanted only if certain specifications are met, and this may become a source of disappointment to the parents if their expectations are unfulfilled.

Report to the Committee of Inquiry into "Human Fertilization and Embryology" (Cmnd 9314) (the "Warnock Commission") Paragraphs 4.19–20 (1984). The committee went on to recommend "that on reaching the age of 18 the child should have access to the basic information about the donor's ethnic origin and genetic health and that legislation be enacted to provide the right of access to this." Id. ¶ 4.21.

5.   Should a determination of who will be inseminated be left to physicians who perform this procedure? A 1987 study found that over half of the physicians doing artificial insemination had rejected, or would be likely to reject, a request for artificial insemination from a potential recipient with any one of the following attributes: unmarried (and with no partner), psychologically immature, homosexual, welfare dependent, evidence of child abuse, evidence of drug abuse, evidence of alcohol abuse, history of serious genetic disorder, HIV positive, under 18 years old or criminal record. Office of Technology Assessment, Artificial Insemination Practice in the United States (1988). Does the determination by these physicians not to inseminate the poor or those with criminal records harken back to the era of *Buck v. Bell* and *Skinner v. Oklahoma,* when there was a presumption that wealth and criminal proclivity were inheritable, or do such screening processes merely suggest that the physicians, who can choose whom they will make parents, are determining which of the proposed patients are likely to be the best parents? Should a physician ever be required to perform artificial insemination in a case where she believes that the woman being inseminated is not capable of the physical, mental, financial or emotional obligations of motherhood?

Might there be additional problems if a state institution were to limit those who could be provided with assisted conception? What kinds of equal protection claims would you expect to be successful? Does the Americans with Disabilities Act require medical institutions to provide treatment for infertility if they provide other necessary medical treatment? Is infertility a disability? See Erickson v. Board of Governors of State Colleges and Universities, 1997 WL 548030 (N.D.Ill. 1997) and Bielicki v. Chicago, 1997 WL 260595 (N.D.Ill.1997)

6.   The ability to freeze and preserve sperm gives rise to the possibility that the father of a child conceived through artificial insemination could have died years before that child's birth. The Social Security Administration faced this issue when Nancy Hart applied for social security survivor's benefits on behalf of her daughter, Judith. After Nancy's husband, Edward Hart, was diagnosed with cancer, he arranged to preserve some of his sperm because of his fear that the necessary chemotherapy would render him sterile. In fact, the chemotherapy was unsuccessful, and he died. Shortly thereafter Judith was conceived, using the sperm left by Edward. The Social Security Administration originally refused to recognize Judith's claim to be Edward's survivor because under the law of Louisiana, where she lived, a child could not be recognized as an heir of a person who died before that child was conceived. In fact, the Social Security Administration had previously paid a similar claim that originated in Arizona, which imposes no restriction on recognizing a child as an heir. While Judith's case was pending in the district court, the Social Security Administration changed its approach and decided to pay this claim because, in the words of the Social Security Commissioner, "[r]ecent advances ... particularly in the field of reproductive medicine, necessitate a careful review of current laws ... to ensure that they are equitable in awarding social security payments in cases such as this." Girl Conceived After Dad Dies Gets Benefits, Chicago Tribune, March 12, 1996, at 12. For a more thorough discussion of this case see Ellen Garside, Posthumous Progeny: A Proposed Resolution to the Dilemma of the Posthumously Conceived Child, 41 Loy. L. Rev. 713 (1996).

Is sperm simply property that can be passed on like any other property upon death? Ought there be any limitation on the people to whom sperm can be willed or sold? Is a child born of sperm from a "father" who died years before an heir of that man? Is the only limitation upon that heir's opportunity to partake in the estate the statute of limitations? For the few of you who remember your first year property course very well, does this problem implicate the rule against perpetuities?

The Uniform Status of Children of Assisted Conception Act explicitly provided that one who died before implantation of his or her genetic contribution was not a parent of the "resulting child." The 2000 version of the Uniform Parentage Act, on the other hand, provides that an insemination of the mother by her husband's sperm after his death does not render him a parent unless he "consented" to this in writing. Why did the drafters of Uniform Status of Children of Assisted Conception Act make such a policy choice? Why was it rejected—at least for fathers who provided consent in writing—by the drafters of the new Uniform Parentage Act? Why didn't the drafters of the 2000 act extend their exception to those other than spouses? Are you satisfied with section 707 of the Uniform Parentage Act (2000)? How would you redraft it?

7.   What is the tort liability that arises out of the provision of inadequate sperm for purposes of artificial insemination? Might the physician or the sperm bank be liable in negligence for inadequately screening the count, health and motility of the sperm? What is the standard of care for screening sperm? How would you find out? In any case, might the doctor or the sperm bank be strictly liable without negligence (on a products liability theory) for the provision of defective sperm?

Of course, the physician and the physician's staff could also be liable in negligence for failing to carry out properly the procedure or failing to adequately inform and counsel the woman to be inseminated about the risks, benefits and alternatives of the procedure.

Might there be a contract action against the physician or the sperm bank who deals commercially in the sale of sperm? If the sperm is sold to the woman who is to be inseminated, is it sold with any implied warranty—perhaps a warranty of fitness for a particular purpose—under the Uniform Commercial Code?

Could the sperm source himself be liable for providing defective sperm? What if the sperm source knew that his semen carried some venereal disease or that he had some unmanifested or secretly manifested genetic defect? Would he be liable as a manufacturer of a product? In negligence? For fraud? On some other theory?

3.   *In Vitro Fertilization, Egg Transfer and Embryo Transfer*

THE PROCESS OF *IN VITRO* FERTILIZATION AND RELATED TECHNIQUES

In vitro (literally, "in glass") fertilization is a highly technical medical intervention. Unlike artificial insemination, it cannot be performed with instruments that one finds in a kitchen. In the normal *in vitro* case, an ovum that is ready to be released from the ovary is identified through laparoscopy or ultrasound and removed from the ovary by surgery or aspiration through a hollow needle. The ovum (or ova—there usually is an attempt to get more than one) is placed in a container with the appropriate amount of semen containing fertile sperm. Most medical programs in the United States will mix between 50,000 and several hundred thousand sperm with each ovum. The fertilized ovum is then placed in the woman's uterus, where it is permitted to implant and develop.

In the United States clinics conducting *in vitro* fertilization programs try to remove several eggs so that at least a few will be fertilized *in vitro* and can be replaced in the uterus. In some cases there is no fertilization or inadequate fertilization *in vitro,* and, thus, no return to the uterus, although fertilization occurs in most of the ova in which it is attempted. Where the ova comes from a younger woman, the fertilization rate generally will be particularly high. In a normal *in vitro* fertilization effort, there is between a 10% and 60% chance that a clinical pregnancy (i.e., implantation) will result. The rate of miscarriage for *in vitro* fertilization pregnancies is higher than the rate of spontaneous miscarriages in other pregnancies. The perinatal (i.e., birth) and neonatal (i.e., newborn) mortality rates for *in vitro* fertilization babies are also higher than for others. Thus the fertilization and pregnancy rates are higher than the "take home baby" rate when these techniques are used.

Because the chances of success are substantially increased if several fertilized ova are returned to the uterus, and because of the high cost and physical burden of repeating the procedure, women undergoing *in vitro* fertilization are generally given drugs to increase the number of ova that become ripe and ready for release and fertilization in one cycle. While this "superovulation" increases the chances of successful fertilization and implantation, inducing ovulation itself may have adverse side effects. In addition, the simultaneous placement of multiple fertilized ova results in a higher rate of multiple births than in the rest of the population.

The medical cost of the ovum retrieval, fertilization and implantation process can exceed $10,000 per ovulation cycle. The drugs the prospective mother must take add another few thousand dollars each cycle. While many infertile couples are thus priced out of *in vitro* fertilization, it is the only process available to women whose fallopian tubes cannot accommodate the fertilization process, and thousands of happy and healthy children (and parents) have resulted from this process.

The development and common use of *in vitro* fertilization has given rise to several other related procedures and some variations on the original process. In gamete intra-fallopian transfer (GIFT) the ova are collected just as they would be for *in vitro* fertilization, but both the ova and the semen containing fertile sperm are then injected into the fallopian tubes, where fertilization takes place. In zygote intra-fallopian transfer (ZIFT), it is the zygote that is transferred. If the problem appears to be in the sperm penetration of the wall of the ovum, physicians may try Intracytoplasmic Sperm Injection (ICSI), in which a single sperm is injected into an ovum (at an additional cost of about $2,000). If the problem arises because the fertilized ovum cannot break free of its "shell" and implant in the uterus, physicians can use an "assisted hatching" (AZH) technique and cut into the "shell" (by the use of a hard object, a laser, or an acid solution) and render it more likely to implant (at an additional cost of over $1000).

In addition, it is possible to freeze an embryo, permitting evaluation of the genetic structure of the embryo before it is thawed and implanted. While the insertion of the fertilized ovum may be the most difficult portion of the procedure from a medical point of view, the removal of the ovum is often the most difficult process from the point of view of the woman. Thus, removing extra ova, fertilizing and freezing them, may save an additional retrieval process if the first insertion is unsuccessful.

When the ovum transferred to a woman comes from a source other than her own uterus, the process will cost her about $1,500 more. The ovum source generally is paid a few thousand dollars per retrieval; each retrieval usually results in several ova.

The legal issues that arise out of *in vitro* fertilization multiply when the fertilized ova are placed in a woman other than the one who produced them. In such a case, the pregnant woman is not the genetic mother of the child that she is carrying. Of course, the man expecting to raise the child may not be the genetic father either. Such a case may be a variant on gestational surrogacy, which is discussed below.

Notes and Questions: The Status of the Parents

1. *In vitro* fertilization using the ova of a woman into whom they are replaced and the sperm of that woman's husband should raise no more moral or legal questions, at least as to the status of the parents, than AIH. Is the essentially religious argument—that procreation should be a natural process and that the consequences of intervening are too serious and unknown for us to permit it—stronger in the case of the more highly medicalized *in vitro* fertilization than in the case of artificial insemination?

2. Analogously, *in vitro* fertilization using the ova supplied by the woman into whom it is replaced and the sperm of a man not her husband ought to be treated very much like AID, at least as regards the status of the parents. Is there any reason to give the sperm source greater (or lesser) rights as against the mother just because the fertilization process has been *in vitro* rather than *in vivo?*

3. The most difficult questions arise when the ova of one woman are placed in the uterus of another, whatever the source of the sperm. Under such circumstances, who is the mother? Perhaps the simplest case is where the ova of one woman is placed in the uterus of a second after it has been fertilized by the sperm of that second woman's husband, with the expectation of all parties that the pregnant woman and her husband will raise the child. In some respects, this is simply a gender reversed version of AID. Under what circumstances do any of the uniform acts apply to such cases?

Of course, providing an egg is not the same as providing sperm; retrieving the egg is far more invasive than retrieving the sperm. On the other hand, there is no male activity that is analogous, in time commitment, physical commitment, and emotional consequences, to carrying the pregnancy. Should that commitment and the fact that the fetus is nurtured by the pregnant woman's body make the pregnant woman the legal mother, whatever the source of the ovum? While there is a presumption that the woman from whose womb the baby emerges is that baby's mother, that presumption arose before there was any possibility that the source of the ovum and the source of the womb could be different women. Are there any circumstances in which you would want to treat the ovum source, rather than the pregnant woman, as the mother? Should a woman with fertile ova but no uterus who wishes to bear a child with her husband (or someone else) be able to enter a binding contract with another woman to have that second woman carry and give birth to her child for her? See the discussion of gestational surrogacy, below.

4. One consequence of the implantation of several embryos that were *fertilized in vitro* is that many of the embryos may continue to develop *in vivo.*

While most multiple births pose no substantial problems to the mother or the neonatal siblings, sometimes the life or health of the mother (or some of the developing fetuses) can be preserved only if the number of fetuses that the mother is carrying is reduced. Under what circumstances is it appropriate to selectively reduce the number of fetuses being carried? Is the case of such selective reduction governed by the more general law applying to abortion, described above? Are there any ethical or legal concerns present in cases of selective reduction that are not present in other situations that might give rise to abortion? Are there any legal or ethical limitations on how the mother (or the family, or the doctor, or the court) should choose which of two or more fetuses should be aborted to save the life or health of that fetus's mother or potential siblings?

5.   The legal issues raised by embryo transfer are roughly the same as those raised by ovum transfer. The hardest questions do not relate to the status of the parents but, rather, to the status of the embryos themselves. The question of the status of frozen embryos first came to a state's highest court in 1992 in the context of a divorce of a couple undergoing *in vitro* fertilization.

DAVIS v. DAVIS

Supreme Court of Tennessee, 1992.
842 S.W.2d 588.

DAUGHTREY, J.:

This appeal presents a question of first impression, involving the disposition of the cryogenically-preserved product of in vitro fertilization (IVF), commonly referred to in the popular press and the legal journals as "frozen embryos." The case began as a divorce action, filed by the appellee, Junior Lewis Davis, against his then wife, appellant Mary Sue Davis. The parties were able to agree upon all terms of dissolution, except one: who was to have "custody" of the seven "frozen embryos" stored in a Knoxville fertility clinic that had attempted to assist the Davises in achieving a much-wanted pregnancy during a happier period in their relationship.

I.   INTRODUCTION

Mary Sue Davis originally asked for control of the "frozen embryos" with the intent to have them transferred to her own uterus, in a post-divorce effort to become pregnant. Junior Davis objected, saying that he preferred to leave the embryos in their frozen state until he decided whether or not he wanted to become a parent outside the bounds of marriage.

Based on its determination that the embryos were "human beings" from the moment of fertilization, the trial court awarded "custody" to Mary Sue Davis and directed that she "be permitted the opportunity to bring these children to term through implantation." The Court of Appeals reversed, finding that Junior Davis has a "constitutionally protected right not to beget a child where no pregnancy has taken place" and holding that "there is no compelling state interest to justify [ ] ordering implantation against the will of either party." The Court of Appeals further held that "the parties share an interest in the seven fertilized ova" and remanded the case to the trial court for entry of an order vesting them with "joint control ... and equal voice over their disposition."

Mary Sue Davis then sought review in this Court, contesting the validity of the constitutional basis for the Court of Appeals decision. We granted review, not because we disagree with the basic legal analysis utilized by the intermediate court, but because of the obvious importance of the case in terms of the development of law regarding the new reproductive technologies, and because the decision of the Court of Appeals does not give adequate guidance to the trial court in the event the parties cannot agree.

We note, in this latter regard, that their positions have already shifted: both have remarried and Mary Sue Davis (now Mary Sue Stowe) has moved out of state. She no longer wishes to utilize the "frozen embryos" herself, but wants authority to donate them to a childless couple. Junior Davis is adamantly opposed to such donation and would prefer to see the "frozen embryos" discarded. The result is, once again, an impasse, but the parties' current legal position does have an effect on the probable outcome of the case, as discussed below.

If we have no statutory authority or common law precedents to guide us [in this case], we do have the benefit of extensive comment and analysis in the legal journals. In those articles, medical-legal scholars and ethicists have proposed various models for the disposition of "frozen embryos" when unanticipated contingencies arise, such as divorce, death of one or both of the parties, financial reversals, or simple disenchantment with the IVF process. Those models range from a rule requiring, at one extreme, that all embryos be used by the gamete-providers or donated for uterine transfer, and, at the other extreme, that any unused embryos be automatically discarded. Other formulations would vest control in the female gamete-provider—in every case, because of her greater physical and emotional contribution to the IVF process, or perhaps only in the event that she wishes to use them herself. There are also two "implied contract" models: one would infer from enrollment in an IVF program that the IVF clinic has authority to decide in the event of an impasse whether to donate, discard, or use the "frozen embryos" for research; the other would infer from the parties' participation in the creation of the embryos that they had made an irrevocable commitment to reproduction and would require transfer either to the female provider or to a donee. There are also the so-called "equity models": one would avoid the conflict altogether by dividing the "frozen embryos" equally between the parties, to do with as they wish; the other would award veto power to the party wishing to avoid parenthood, whether it be the female or the male progenitor.

Each of these possible models has the virtue of ease of application. Adoption of any of them would establish a bright-line test that would dispose of disputes like the one we have before us in a clear and predictable manner. As appealing as that possibility might seem, we conclude that given the relevant principles of constitutional law, the existing public policy of Tennessee with regard to unborn life, the current state of scientific knowledge giving rise to the emerging reproductive technologies, and the ethical considerations that have developed in response to that scientific knowledge, there can be no easy answer to the question we now face. We conclude, instead, that we must weigh the interests of each party to the dispute, in terms of the facts and analysis set out below, in order to resolve that dispute in a fair and responsible manner.

* * *

IV. The "Person" vs. "Property" Dichotomy

One of the fundamental issues the inquiry poses is whether the preembryos in this case should be considered "persons" or "property" in the contemplation of the law. The Court of Appeals held, correctly, that they cannot be considered "persons" under Tennessee law * * *.

Nor do preembryos enjoy protection as "persons" under federal law. * * *

Left undisturbed, the trial court's ruling would have afforded preembryos the legal status of "persons" and vested them with legally cognizable interests separate from those of their progenitors. Such a decision would doubtless have had the effect of outlawing IVF programs in the state of Tennessee. But in setting aside the trial court's judgment, the Court of Appeals, at least by implication, may have swung too far in the opposite direction.

To our way of thinking, the most helpful discussion on this point is found not in the minuscule number of legal opinions that have involved "frozen embryos," but in the ethical standards set by The American Fertility Society, as follows:

> Three major ethical positions have been articulated in the debate over preembryo status. At one extreme is the view of the preembryo as a human subject after fertilization, which requires that it be accorded the rights of a person. This position entails an obligation to provide an opportunity for implantation to occur and tends to ban any action before transfer that might harm the preembryo or that is not immediately therapeutic, such as freezing and some preembryo research.

> At the opposite extreme is the view that the preembryo has a status no different from any other human tissue. With the consent of those who have decision-making authority over the preembryo, no limits should be imposed on actions taken with preembryos.

> A third view—one that is most widely held—takes an intermediate position between the other two. It holds that the preembryo deserves respect greater than that accorded to human tissue but not the respect accorded to actual persons. The preembryo is due greater respect than other human tissue because of its potential to become a person and because of its symbolic meaning for many people. Yet, it should not be treated as a person, because it has not yet developed the features of personhood, is not yet established as developmentally individual, and may never realize its biologic potential.

* * *

In its report, the Ethics Committee then calls upon those in charge of IVF programs to establish policies in keeping with the "special respect" due preembryos and suggests:

Within the limits set by institutional policies, decision-making authority regarding preembryos should reside with the persons who have provided the gametes.... As a matter of law, it is reasonable to assume that the gamete providers have primary decision-making authority regarding preembryos in the absence of specific legislation on the subject. A person's liberty to procreate or to avoid procreation is directly involved in most decisions involving preembryos.[ ]

We conclude that preembryos are not, strictly speaking, either "persons" or "property," but occupy an interim category that entitles them to special respect because of their potential for human life. It follows that any interest that Mary Sue Davis and Junior Davis have in the preembryos in this case is not a true property interest. However, they do have an interest in the nature of ownership, to the extent that they have decision-making authority concerning disposition of the preembryos, within the scope of policy set by law.

V.   THE ENFORCEABILITY OF CONTRACT

* * *

We believe, as a starting point, that an agreement regarding disposition of any untransferred preembryos in the event of contingencies (such as the death of one or more of the parties, divorce, financial reversals, or abandonment of the program) should be presumed valid and should be enforced as between the progenitors. This conclusion is in keeping with the proposition that the progenitors, having provided the gametic material giving rise to the preembryos, retain decision-making authority as to their disposition.

At the same time, we recognize that life is not static, and that human emotions run particularly high when a married couple is attempting to overcome infertility problems. It follows that the parties' initial "informed consent" to IVF procedures will often not be truly informed because of the near impossibility of anticipating, emotionally and psychologically, all the turns that events may take as the IVF process unfolds. Providing that the initial agreements may later be modified by agreement will, we think, protect the parties against some of the risks they face in this regard. But, in the absence of such agreed modification, we conclude that their prior agreements should be considered binding.

* * *

[In this case,] we are * * * left with this situation: there was initially no agreement between the parties concerning disposition of the preembryos under the circumstances of this case; there has been no agreement since; and there is no formula in the Court of Appeals opinion for determining the outcome if the parties cannot reach an agreement in the future.

* * *

VI.   THE RIGHT OF PROCREATIONAL AUTONOMY

Although an understanding of the legal status of preembryos is necessary in order to determine the enforceability of agreements about their disposition, asking whether or not they constitute "property" is not an altogether helpful question. As the appellee points out in his brief, "[as] two or eight cell tiny lumps of complex protein, the embryos have no [intrinsic] value to either party." Their value lies in the "potential to become, after implantation, growth and birth, children." Thus, the essential dispute here is not where or how or how long to store the preembryos, but whether the parties will become parents. The Court of Appeals held in effect that they will become parents if they both agree to become parents. The Court did not say what will happen if they fail to agree. We conclude that the answer to this dilemma turns on the parties' exercise of their constitutional right to privacy.

* * *

[The Court found there was a right to individual privacy in both Federal and Tennessee State law, and that this right to individual privacy encompassed the right of procreational autonomy.]

For the purposes of this litigation it is sufficient to note that, whatever its ultimate constitutional boundaries, the right of procreational autonomy is composed of two rights of equal significance—the right to procreate and the right to avoid procreation. Undoubtedly, both are subject to protections and limitations.

The equivalence of and inherent tension between these two interests are nowhere more evident than in the context of in vitro fertilization. None of the concerns about a woman's bodily integrity that have previously precluded men from controlling abortion decisions is applicable here. We are not unmindful of the fact that the trauma (including both emotional stress and physical discomfort) to which women are subjected in the IVF process is more severe than is the impact of the procedure on men. In this sense, it is fair to say that women contribute more to the IVF process than men. Their experience, however, must be viewed in light of the joys of parenthood that is desired or the relative anguish of a lifetime of unwanted parenthood. As they stand on the brink of potential parenthood, Mary Sue Davis and Junior Lewis Davis must be seen as entirely equivalent gamete-providers.

It is further evident that, however far the protection of procreational autonomy extends, the existence of the right itself dictates that decisional authority rests in the gamete-providers alone, at least to the extent that their decisions have an impact upon their individual reproductive status. * * * [N]o other person or entity has an interest sufficient to permit interference with the gamete-providers' decision to continue or terminate the IVF process, because no one else bears the consequences of these decisions in the way that the gamete-providers do.

Further, at least with respect to Tennessee's public policy and its constitutional right of privacy, the state's interest in potential human life is insufficient to justify an infringement on the gamete-providers' procreational autonomy.

Certainly, if the state's interests do not become sufficiently compelling in the abortion context until the end of the first trimester, after very significant developmental stages have passed, then surely there is no state interest in these preembryos which could suffice to overcome the interests of the gamete-providers. The [Tennessee] abortion statute reveals that the increase in the state's interest is marked by each successive developmental stage such that, toward the end of a pregnancy, this interest is so compelling that abortion is almost strictly forbidden. This scheme supports the conclusion that the state's interest in the potential life embodied by these four-to eight-cell preembryos (which may or may not be able to achieve implantation in a uterine wall and which, if implanted, may or may not begin to develop into fetuses, subject to possible miscarriage) is at best slight. When weighed against the interests of the individuals and the burdens inherent in parenthood, the state's interest in the potential life of these preembryos is not sufficient to justify any infringement upon the freedom of these individuals to make their own decisions as to whether to allow a process to continue that may result in such a dramatic change in their lives as becoming parents. The unique nature of this case requires us to note that the interests of these parties in parenthood are different in scope than the parental interests considered in other cases. Previously, courts have dealt with the childbearing and child-rearing aspects of parenthood. Abortion cases have dealt with gestational parenthood. In this case, the Court must deal with the question of genetic parenthood. We conclude, moreover, that an interest in avoiding genetic parenthood can be significant enough to trigger the protections afforded to all other aspects of parenthood. The technological fact that someone unknown to these parties could gestate these preembryos does not alter the fact that these parties, the gamete-providers, would become parents in that event, at least in the genetic sense. The profound impact this would have on them supports their right to sole decisional authority as to whether the process of attempting to gestate these preembryos should continue. This brings us directly to the question of how to resolve the dispute that arises when one party wishes to continue the IVF process and the other does not.

VII. BALANCING THE PARTIES' INTERESTS

Resolving disputes over conflicting interests of constitutional import is a task familiar to the courts. One way of resolving these disputes is to consider the positions of the parties, the significance of their interests, and the relative burdens that will be imposed by differing resolutions. In this case, the issue centers on the two aspects of procreational autonomy—the right to procreate and the right to avoid procreation. We start by considering the burdens imposed on the parties by solutions that would have the effect of disallowing the exercise of individual procreational autonomy with respect to these particular preembryos.

Beginning with the burden imposed on Junior Davis, we note that the consequences are obvious. Any disposition which results in the gestation of the preembryos would impose unwanted parenthood on him, with all of its possible financial and psychological consequences. The impact that this unwanted parenthood would have on Junior Davis can only be understood by considering his particular circumstances, as revealed in the record.

Junior Davis testified that he was the fifth youngest of six children. When he was five years old, his parents divorced, his mother had a nervous breakdown, and he and three of his brothers went to live at a home for boys run by the Lutheran Church. Another brother was taken in by an aunt, and his sister stayed with their mother. From that day forward, he had monthly visits with his mother but saw his father only three more times before he died in 1976. Junior Davis testified that, as a boy, he had severe problems caused by separation from his parents. He said that it was especially hard to leave his mother after each monthly visit. He clearly feels that he has suffered because of his lack of opportunity to establish a relationship with his parents and particularly because of the absence of his father.

In light of his boyhood experiences, Junior Davis is vehemently opposed to fathering a child that would not live with both parents. Regardless of whether he or Mary Sue had custody, he feels that the child's bond with the non-custodial parent would not be satisfactory. He testified very clearly that his concern was for the psychological obstacles a child in such a situation would face, as well as the burdens it would impose on him. Likewise, he is opposed to donation because the recipient couple might divorce, leaving the child (which he definitely would consider his own) in a single-parent setting.

Balanced against Junior Davis's interest in avoiding parenthood is Mary Sue Davis's interest in donating the preembryos to another couple for implantation. Refusal to permit donation of the preembryos would impose on her the burden of knowing that the lengthy IVF procedures she underwent were futile, and that the preembryos to which she contributed genetic material would never become children. While this is not an insubstantial emotional burden, we can only conclude that Mary Sue Davis's interest in donation is not as significant as the interest Junior Davis has in avoiding parenthood. If she were allowed to donate these preembryos, he would face a lifetime of either wondering about his parental status or knowing about his parental status but having no control over it. He testified quite clearly that if these preembryos were brought to term he would fight for custody of his child or children. Donation, if a child came of it, would rob him twice—his procreational autonomy would be defeated and his relationship with his offspring would be prohibited.

The case would be closer if Mary Sue Davis were seeking to use the preembryos herself, but only if she could not achieve parenthood by any other reasonable means. We recognize the trauma that Mary Sue has already experienced and the additional discomfort to which she would be subjected if she opts to attempt IVF again. Still, she would have a reasonable opportunity, through IVF, to try once again to achieve parenthood in all its aspects—genetic, gestational, bearing, and rearing.

Further, we note that if Mary Sue Davis were unable to undergo another round of IVF, or opted not to try, she could still achieve the child-rearing aspects of parenthood through adoption. The fact that she and Junior Davis pursued adoption indicates that, at least at one time, she was willing to forego genetic parenthood and would have been satisfied by the child-rearing aspects of parenthood alone.

VIII. CONCLUSION

In summary, we hold that disputes involving the disposition of preembryos produced by in vitro fertilization should be resolved, first, by looking to the preferences of the progenitors. If their wishes cannot be ascertained, or if there is dispute, then their prior agreement concerning disposition should be carried out. If no prior agreement exists, then the relative interests of the parties in using or not using the preembryos must be weighed. Ordinarily, the party wishing to avoid procreation should prevail, assuming that the other party has a reasonable possibility of achieving parenthood by means other than use of the preembryos in question. If no other reasonable alternatives exist, then the argument in favor of using the preembryos to achieve pregnancy should be considered. However, if the party seeking control of the preembryos intends merely to donate them to another couple, the objecting party obviously has the greater interest and should prevail.

But the rule does not contemplate the creation of an automatic veto, and in affirming the judgment of the Court of Appeals, we would not wish to be interpreted as so holding.

For the reasons set out above, the judgment of the Court of Appeals is affirmed, in the appellee's favor. This ruling means that the Knoxville Fertility Clinic is free to follow its normal procedure in dealing with unused preembryos, as long as that procedure is not in conflict with this opinion.

Notes and Questions: The Status of the Embryo

1. In fact, the Knoxville Fertility Clinic could not "follow its normal procedure in dealing with unused preembryos" because its normal procedure was to provide those preembryos to infertile couples—a procedure that would have been in conflict with the opinion. On rehearing directed to this issue, the Tennessee court looked to the report of the American Fertility Society's Ethics Committee, which authorizes the preembryos to be donated for research purposes (which would require the consent of both of the Davises) or to be discarded. See Davis v. Davis, Order on Petitions to Rehear (Sup. Ct. Tenn., Nov. 23, 1992).

2. The court suggests that the state interest in assuring that the embryo is implanted and allowed to develop cannot be sufficiently compelling to overcome a gamete-provider's right to avoid parenthood because, by analogy, "the state's interest does not become sufficiently compelling in the abortion context until the end of the first trimester, after very significant developmental stages have passed...." Is the analogy to the abortion context a persuasive one? In the same year in which this case was decided, the United States Supreme Court reconsidered the value of drawing trimester lines in Planned Parenthood of Southeastern Pennsylvania v. Casey, supra page 1139. As a Constitutional matter, could a state now have an interest in protecting fertilized ova that would be sufficiently compelling to overcome the interests of one or both of the gamete providers?

3. The court describes several different rules that could be applied in these disputes over the status and control of extracorporeal fertilized ova or pre-embryos. One of the alternatives is to treat the pre-embryos as personal property and apply the common law of property to them; another would be to treat those pre-embryos as if they were children entitled to protection of the state law. Each view has some legal support. In York v. Jones, 717 F.Supp. 421 (E.D.Va. 1989), a federal district court treated frozen embryos prepared in the course of infertility treatment as property that would be subject to the ordinary law of bailment; thus, the court required the infertility program where they were developed (the bailee) to transfer them to a new program selected by the progenitors. In Hecht v. Superior Court, 16 Cal.App.4th 836, 20 Cal.Rptr.2d 275 (Cal.App.1993), the California Court of Appeal found that the probate court could distribute a decedent's frozen sperm, concluding that it was property subject to disposition upon death. In Louisiana, on the other hand, disputes between those who want to control the disposition of pre-embryos are resolved by applying the "best interest of the pre-embryo" standard. See La. Stat. Ann.-Rev. section 14:87:2.

4. The New York Court of Appeals followed a path close to that taken in Davis v. Davis when it concluded that the parties to assisted reproduction are bound by an unambiguous agreement which states the parties mutual intent as to the disposition of cryogenically preserved pre-embryos. In Kass v. Kass, 91 N.Y.2d 554, 673 N.Y.S.2d 350, 696 N.E.2d 174 (N.Y. 1998), the Court of Appeals applied the provisions of the informed consent document signed by both progenitors when their infertility treatment commenced. This document declared that the clinic would use any frozen pre-embryos for research in the event that the progenitors could not agree on their disposition. The court thus affirmed the Appellate Division, which had reversed the trial court's determination that after fertilization the disposition of genetic material was exclusively in the hands of the mother, who possessed all of the rights over the frozen embryo that she would possess over a fetus developing in her body.

At least one court has expressly rejected the notion that the prior agreement of the progenitors should govern the disposition of frozen embryos. In A.Z. v. B.Z., 431 Mass. 150, 725 N.E.2d 1051 (2000), the Massachusetts Supreme Judicial Court was faced with an agreement that provided that if the intended parents were to become separated, the frozen embryos then available would be given to one of the parents for implantation. In that case, though, the application of that agreement would have forced the former husband to become a parent against his will, and this, the court concluded, would be contrary to public policy. The court explained that, "forced procreation is not an area amenable to judicial enforcement."

In Davis and Kass, the enforceable prior agreements provided for the destruction of frozen embryos rather than their implantation; in A.Z., the agreement would have resulted in the creation of a child (and, of course, parents). Is that distinction sufficient to explain the difference in the outcomes of these cases? Could there be other bases for distinguishing the decisions of the courts in Tennessee and New York, on one hand, and Massachusetts on the other?

5. What is the warden of the freezer to do with frozen embryos whose contributors cannot agree upon their disposition? Can they be destroyed, or sold to the highest bidder when the storage fee remains unpaid? If one of the parties who contributed to the embryos dies, does that party's interest pass to the other?

Only a few states have dealt with this issue legislatively, and they have done so idiosyncratically; in Louisiana a pre-zygote must be implanted while in Florida there must be a written document describing the parties' dispositional intent. In 1990 the United Kingdom enacted the Human Fertilization and Embryology Act, which provides that unused pre-embryos are to be destroyed five years after they are created unless there are contrary instructions from the progenitors. Australia has employed similar rules since 1984, and Germany has outlawed freezing of embryos altogether. The American Medical Association Council on Ethical and Judicial Affairs has proposed that intended parents be encouraged to express their intent with regard to the disposition of frozen embryos, but that such an expression not be mandatory of physicians. The intended parents would be able to implant them, thaw (and thus destroy) them, permit research upon them, or donate them to another woman. They would be prohibited from selling them, however.

6. If you were employed by a clinic to draft a form contract that would provide for the disposition of excess or unneeded frozen pre-embryos, how would you write it? If you were a patient seeking treatment at a clinic, how would you

want it written? What provisions would a contract written by counsel for the patients and the counsel for the providers, negotiating at arms length, include?

7. The new reproductive technologies of *in vitro* fertilization and embryo cryopreservation can give rise to a host of different kinds of liability. Of course, the physician and medical institution could be liable in an ordinary medical malpractice case for negligently performing the procedure. Would the duty of due care extend to the fetus as well as the parents? Would it extend to a fetus not born alive? To an aborted fetus? Negligently freezing an ovum or embryo, or negligently thawing it and thus destroying or damaging it, would also subject the appropriate professionals to malpractice liability.

Presumably, an ovum source would also be liable in contract to the same extent as would a sperm source. Any warranty that would come with an ovum would be analogous to that which would come with sperm, and the nature of any such warranty under the U.C.C. could depend upon whether the ovum is a good or a service.

The value of cryogenically preserved fertilized pre-embryos (or ova) may also make them targets for theft; clinic employees (or others) may be tempted to provide excess genetic material to those who need it without seeking consent from the original progenitors. Indeed, during the late 1990s that kind of redirection of ova apparently became fairly common at the University of California–Irvine's fertility clinic, where at least fifteen children were born as a result of the use of ova from women who had not consented to their transfer. For a wonderful account of the problems created by this misconduct, see Alice Noble–Allgire, Switched at the Fertility Clinic: Determining Maternal Rights When a Child is Born from Stolen or Misdelivered Genetic Material, 64 Mo. L. Rev. 517 (1999). What kinds of civil, criminal and administrative liability could arise out of these occurrences? As clinic counsel, what could you do to limit the chance of this happening?

4. Surrogacy

THE PROCESS OF SURROGACY

Surrogacy may be the least technological of reproductive technologies. It is also the oldest; Genesis tells of Abraham's servant Hagar bearing a child to be raised by the genetic father, Abraham, and his wife Sarah. Genesis 16:1–16. Surrogacy is that arrangement in which a woman carries a child to term intending at the initiation of the pregnancy for another woman to raise the child as the social mother. As was the case with Hagar, fertilization may take place through normal coitus. It also may be a consequence of artificial insemination, *in vitro* fertilization or embryo transfer. While the genetic father is often the husband of the woman who expects to raise the child as its mother, that need not be the case. While the genetic mother is often the pregnant woman, that is not required either; an arrangement in which the pregnant woman is not the source of the ovum is called gestational surrogacy. It is possible to take the sperm from one source, the ovum from another and place the subsequently developed embryo in the uterus of a third person.

Although there is some debate about whether surrogacy ought to be considered a "medical treatment" for infertility, it provides the only way for a woman without a uterus to be the genetic mother of a child (through embryo transfer, for example), or to be the mother of a child whose genetic father is her husband (through artificial insemination of the surrogate with the husband's sperm). In addition, some women may choose to avoid pregnancy because it poses grave physical or emotional risk to them, or because it would be difficult for them to continue to work (or play) while pregnant.

It is hard to estimate the cost of the "average" surrogacy arrangement. In some cases the carrying mother is a friend or relative of the woman who expects to raise the child and seeks no compensation for her efforts. Other unrelated women may also be willing to act as surrogates for entirely altruistic reasons. Yet others engage in surrogacy for entirely economic reasons. A couple wishing to contract for a surrogate through a commercial service may pay in excess of $50,000 for the medical and legal fees and the expenses of the surrogate herself. A surrogate is likely to be paid at least $15,000 for her labor. Potential surrogates (like ova and sperm vendors, surrogacy brokers, fertility clinics, and law offices providing infertility-related legal services) can be easily discovered, and their fees can be estimated, through a web search

Commercial surrogacy arrangements have given rise to a great deal of controversy. In some states the process itself has been challenged before any particular case has arisen on the grounds that commercial surrogacy constitutes baby selling *per se*. See, e.g., Surrogate Parenting Associates, Inc. v. Commonwealth ex rel. Armstrong, 704 S.W.2d 209 (Ky.1986). While the Uniform Parentage Act (2000) now includes an article recognizing surrogacy contracts and regulating them, no state has yet adopted that provision. On the other hand, as the Reporter's Note to the "gestational agreement" portion of that uniform act points out, "eleven states allow such agreements by statutes or caselaw; six states void such agreements by statute; eight states statutorily ban compensation to the gestational mother; and two states have judicially refused to recognize them." For a more detailed accounting, see the Appendix, Article 8, Uniform Parentage Act (2000). When there is no governing statute, a dispute between the parties will require the courts to determine the rights and responsibilities of all of those involved, and the propriety and enforceability of any contractual arrangements of the parties.

IN THE MATTER OF BABY M

Supreme Court of New Jersey, 1988.
109 N.J. 396, 537 A.2d 1227.

WILENTZ, C.J.:

In this matter the Court is asked to determine the validity of a contract that purports to provide a new way of bringing children into a family. For a fee of $10,000, a woman agrees to be artificially inseminated with the semen of another woman's husband; she is to conceive a child, carry it to term, and after its birth surrender it to the natural father and his wife. The intent of the contract is that the child's natural mother will thereafter be forever separated from her child. The wife is to adopt the child, and she and the natural father are to be regarded as its parents for all purposes. The contract providing for this is called a "surrogacy contract," the natural mother inappropriately called the "surrogate mother."

We invalidate the surrogacy contract because it conflicts with the law and public policy of this State. While we recognize the depth of the yearning of infertile couples to have their own children, we find the payment of money to a "surrogate" mother illegal, perhaps criminal, and potentially degrading to women. Although in this case we grant custody to the natural father, the evidence having clearly proved such custody to be in the best interests of the infant, we void both the termination of the surrogate mother's parental rights and the adoption of the child by the wife/stepparent. We thus restore the "surrogate" as the mother of the child. We remand the issue of the natural mother's visitation rights to the trial court, since that issue was not reached below and the record before us is not sufficient to permit us to decide it *de novo*.

We find no offense to our present laws where a woman voluntarily and without payment agrees to act as a "surrogate" mother, provided that she is not subject to a binding agreement to surrender her child. Moreover, our holding today does not preclude the Legislature from altering the current law, however, the surrogacy agreement before us is illegal and invalid.

I.

Facts

In February 1985, William Stern and Mary Beth Whitehead entered into a surrogacy contract. It recited that Stern's wife, Elizabeth, was infertile, that they wanted a child, and that Mrs. Whitehead was willing to provide that child as the mother with Mr. Stern as the father.

[The Court reviewed the facts of the case with excruciating detail, and then reviewed the lower court's holding that the contract was valid, but that placement of the child—called Melissa by the Sterns and Sara by Mary Beth Whitehead—should depend upon the best interest of the child.]

* * *

II.

Invalidity and Unenforceability of Surrogacy Contract

We have concluded that this surrogacy contract is invalid. Our conclusion has two bases: direct conflict with existing statutes and conflict with the public policies of this State, as expressed in its statutory and decisional law.

One of the surrogacy contract's basic purposes, to achieve the adoption of a child through private placement, though permitted in New Jersey "is very much disfavored." [ ] Its use of money for this purpose—and we have no doubt whatsoever that the money is being paid to obtain an adoption and not, as the Sterns argue, for the personal services of Mary Beth Whitehead—is illegal and perhaps criminal. * * * In addition to the inducement of money, there is the coercion of contract: the [natural mother's] irrevocable agreement, prior to birth, even prior to conception, to surrender the child to the adoptive couple. Such an agreement is totally unenforceable in private placement adoption. [ ] Even where the adoption is through an approved agency, the formal agreement to surrender occurs only *after* birth * * *, and then, by regulation, only after the birth mother has been counseled. * * * Integral to these invalid provisions of the surrogacy contract is the related agreement, equally invalid, on the part of the natural mother to cooperate with, and not to contest, proceedings to terminate her parental rights, as well as her contractual concession, in aid of the adoption, that the child's best interests would be served by awarding custody to the natural father and his wife—all of this before she has even conceived, and, in some cases, before she has the slightest idea of what the natural father and adoptive mother are like.

The foregoing provisions not only directly conflict with New Jersey statutes, but also offend long-established State policies. These critical terms, which are at the heart of the contract, are invalid and unenforceable; the conclusion therefore follows, without more, that the entire contract is unenforceable.

A. Conflict with Statutory Provisions

The surrogacy contract conflicts with: (1) laws prohibiting the use of money in connection with adoptions; (2) laws requiring proof of parental unfitness or abandonment before termination of parental rights is ordered or an adoption is granted; and (3) laws that make surrender of custody and consent to adoption revocable in private placement adoptions.

[The court discusses the terms of the New Jersey statutes in each of these areas.]

B. Public Policy Considerations

The surrogacy contract's invalidity, resulting from its direct conflict with the above statutory provisions, is further underlined when its goals and means are measured against New Jersey's public policy. The contract's basic premise, that the natural parents can decide in advance of birth which one is to have custody of the child, bears no relationship to the settled law that the child's best interests shall determine custody.

* * *

This is the sale of a child, or, at the very least, the sale of a mother's right to her child, the only mitigating factor being that one of the purchasers is the father. Almost every evil that prompted the prohibition of the payment of money in connection with adoptions exists here.

* * *

In the scheme contemplated by the surrogacy contract in this case, a middleman, propelled by profit, promotes the sale. Whatever idealism may have motivated any of the participants, the profit motive predominates, permeates, and ultimately governs the transaction. The demand for children is great and the supply small. The availability of contraception, abortion, and the greater willingness of single mothers to bring up their children has led to a shortage of babies offered for adoption. [ ] The situation is ripe for the entry of the middleman who will bring some equilibrium into the market by increasing the supply through the use of money.

Intimated, but disputed, is the assertion that surrogacy will be used for the benefit of the rich at the expense of the poor. [ ] In response it is noted that the Sterns are not rich and the Whiteheads not poor. Nevertheless, it is clear to us that it is unlikely that surrogate mothers will be as proportionately numerous among those women in the top twenty percent income bracket as among these in the bottom twenty percent. [ ] Put differently, we doubt that infertile couples in the low-income bracket will find upper income surrogates.

* * *

The point is made that Mrs. Whitehead *agreed* to the surrogacy arrangement, supposedly fully understanding the consequences. Putting aside the issue of how compelling her need for money may have been, and how significant her understanding of the consequences, we suggest that her consent is irrelevant. There are, in a civilized society, some things that money cannot buy. * * *

The long-term effects of surrogacy contracts are not known, but feared—the impact on the child who learns her life was bought, that she is the offspring of someone who gave birth to her only to obtain money; the impact on the natural mother as the full weight of her isolation is felt along with the full reality of the sale of her body and her child; the impact on the natural father and the adoptive mother once they realize the consequences of their conduct. Literature in related areas suggests these are substantial considerations, although, given the newness of surrogacy, there is little information. [ ]

* * *

In sum, the harmful consequences of this surrogacy arrangement appear to us all too palpable. In New Jersey the surrogate mother's agreement to sell her child is void. Its irrevocability infects the entire contract, as does the money that purports to buy it.

III.

Termination

We have already noted that under our laws termination of parental rights cannot be based on contract, but may be granted only on proof of the statutory requirements. * * *

* * *

There is simply no [statutory] basis * * * to warrant termination of Mrs. Whitehead's parental rights. We therefore conclude that the natural mother is entitled to retain her rights as a mother.

IV.

Constitutional Issues

Both parties argue that the Constitutions—state and federal—mandate approval of their basic claims. The source of their constitutional arguments is essentially the same: the right of privacy, the right to procreate, the right to the companionship of one's child, those rights flowing either directly from the fourteenth amendment or by its incorporation of the Bill of Rights, or from the ninth amendment, or through the penumbra surrounding all of the Bill of Rights. They are the rights of personal intimacy, of marriage, of sex, or family, or procreation. Whatever their source, it is clear that they are fundamental rights protected by both the federal and state Constitutions. * * * The right asserted by the Sterns is the right of procreation; that asserted by Mary Beth Whitehead is the right to the companionship of her child. We find that the right of procreation does not extend as far as claimed by the Sterns. As for the right asserted by Mrs. Whitehead,[4] since we uphold it on other grounds (*i.e.,* we have restored her as mother and recognized her right, limited by the child's best interests, to her companionship), we need not decide that constitutional issue, and for reasons set forth below we should not.

* * * The right to procreate very simply is the right to have natural children, whether through sexual intercourse or artificial insemination. It is no more than that. Mr. Stern has not been deprived of that right. Through artificial insemination of Mrs. Whitehead, Baby M is his child. The custody, care, companionship, and nurturing that follow birth are not parts of the right to procreation; they are rights that may also be constitutionally protected, but that involve many considerations other than the right of procreation.

* * *

V.

Custody

[The court determined that it would be in the best interest of the child for custody to be awarded to the father, Mr. Stern.]

VI.

Visitation

The trial court's decision to terminate Mrs. Whitehead's parental rights precluded it from making any determination on visitation. [ ] Our reversal of the trial court's order, however, requires delineation of Mrs. Whitehead's rights to visitation.

[The court pointed out that Mrs. Whitehead was the legal and natural mother, and that she was entitled to be treated as such.]

* * *

* * * [T]he trial court should recall the touchstones of visitation: that it is desirable for the child to have contact with both parents; that besides the child's interests, the parents' interests also must be considered; but that when all is said and done, the best interest of the child is paramount.

We have decided that Mrs. Whitehead is entitled to visitation at some point, and that question is not open to the trial court on this remand. The trial court will determine what kind of visitation shall be granted to her, with or without conditions, and when and under what circumstances it should commence. * * *

* * *

---

4. Opponents of surrogacy have also put forth arguments based on the thirteenth amendment, as well as the Peonage Act, 42 U.S.C.A. Section 1993 (1982). We need not address these arguments because we have already held the contract unenforceable on the basis of state law.

Conclusion

This case affords some insight into a new reproductive arrangement: the artificial insemination of a surrogate mother. The unfortunate events that have unfolded illustrate that its unregulated use can bring suffering to all involved. Potential victims include the surrogate mother and her family, the natural father and his wife, and most importantly, the child. Although surrogacy has apparently provided positive results for some infertile couples, it can also, as this case demonstrates, cause suffering to participants, here essentially innocent and well-intended.

* * *

Notes and Questions

1. Upon remand, the superior court determined that Mary Beth Whitehead Gould should have "unsupervised uninterrupted liberal visitation" with Baby M. Under the court's schedule, the visitations would be increased until they included a two-day (and one overnight) visit every other week, and an annual two-week visit. See 14 Fam.L.Rep. 1276 (1988).

2. Most of the arguments against surrogacy are outlined in the opinion of the court in *Baby M.* Generally, these objections fall into three categories—those related to the contracting parties; those related to the child; and those related to the effect of the process on society as a whole.

The first argument generally advanced against surrogacy is that it exploits women who are willing to give or rent their bodies as vessels to carry other people's children. Could the inducement of payment for pregnancy cause a woman to consent to something that otherwise would be an unthinkable intrusion upon her body? Will the development of commercial surrogacy lead to a class of poor women who will become child bearers for wealthy women who do not want to spend the time or energy on pregnancy? Is it likely that the fact that there is a relationship between ethnicity and the distribution of wealth in this society mean that we will develop separate childbearing races and child-raising races?

Feminists are divided on this issue. Some are deeply offended by the overt use of the woman's body that is the whole goal of a surrogacy arrangement; others believe it is merely misguided paternalism that leads courts (and others) to conclude that women are incapable of deciding for themselves whether they should enter surrogacy contracts. Some economists argue that making surrogacy contracts unenforceable will merely lower the amount that is paid to surrogates. Thus, they suggest, making surrogacy contracts unenforceable is just another in a long history of allegedly protectionist regulations that restrict what a woman may choose to do with her body.

Some argue that surrogacy contracts ought to be prohibited or discouraged because they advance only the best interests of the contracting parties, not the best interest of the child. Normally in a custody dispute between those with claims as parents, the court will look to the best interest of the child in determining the appropriate placement. Enforcing a surrogacy contract is necessarily inconsistent with this principle. In addition, some believe that children who find out that they were carried by a surrogate will be injured by that discovery, and others argue that surrogacy contracts render children instruments for the use of parents, not ends in themselves, and that this is necessarily harmful for children.

Finally, some believe that the fabric of society as a whole is weakened by surrogacy arrangements, at least commercial ones. As Justice Wilentz points out in *Baby M,* there are some things that money cannot buy. How, exactly, does he define this class of things? Why does he conclude that surrogacy is one of them?

Perhaps a surrogacy contract, which is a contract to put one's body to work for the benefit of another, is nothing more than a form of slavery. Since the Thirteenth Amendment we have prohibited contracts for slavery, even if the contracting parties are all competent adults who are acting voluntarily. One argument for the Thirteenth Amendment is that in addition to whatever it offers those who might be or become slaves, society as a whole is better off if the status of "slave" is impossible for everyone. Are all people in this society—including those who would never participate in a surrogacy contract in any way—better off if the society simply eliminates surrogacy?

3. Why would the analysis in *Baby M* be different if the arrangement were not one that involved the exchange of money? Which ethical and legal arguments depend upon the commercial nature of the arrangement, and which remain just as strong whether or not any money changes hands?

4. In addressing one constitutional issue, Judge Wilentz announces that the "right to procreate very simply is the right to have natural children, whether through sexual intercourse or artificial insemination. It is no more than that." Why does he limit the right in this way? Why does he include artificial insemination, but not *in vitro* fertilization (even between husband and wife) among those actions protected by the constitutional "right to procreate"? How far do you think the "right to procreate" should go? Should it include *in vitro* fertilization? Egg transfer? Embryo transfer? Surrogacy? Cloning? In which of these circumstances might one person's "right to procreate" conflict with another's?

5. Surrogacy contracts are often condemned on the ground that they constitute baby selling, which is illegal in every state. There is confusion over the purpose of statutes that prohibit baby selling, though: they may be intended to protect parents from financial inducements to give up their children, or they may be intended to protect children from being reduced to the status of an ordinary commodity. Are baby selling statutes merely anachronisms left over from the 19th century practice of selling children into effective slavery? Should baby selling be prohibited? Why? Should surrogacy arrangements be governed by baby selling statutes?

6. There is no doubt that the remedy of specific performance is not available to those who offer some consideration in return for the surrogate's labor. For this reason, surrogacy contracts drafted by careful lawyers do not provide for any substantial payment to the surrogate until the baby is delivered to the commissioning party and the surrogate mother (and her husband, if necessary) relinquish their parental rights. There remains the risk that the surrogate mother will not relinquish her parental rights, and that it will be impossible to have a court order termination of those rights. Indeed, this was the case in *Baby M.* In such a case a sperm source who has commissioned the surrogate may find himself liable for child support (and eligible for visitation rights) for a child who bears no legal or physical relationship to his own wife. After *Baby M,* is there any way to draft a contract to avoid these consequences? *Should* there be a way to do so? The *Baby M* court appended to their opinion a copy of the surrogacy contract and the contract between Mr. Stern and the surrogacy agency. To see exactly what the court determined to be unenforceable, see 537 A.2d at 1265–1273.

7.   One argument against the use of surrogacy arrangements is the legal uncertainty they cause. Is this a good argument when those uncertainties could be resolved by judicial or legislative action? While many have called for legislative action to prohibit surrogacy arrangements, others have called for legislative action to regulate such arrangements so that the legal uncertainties can be avoided. See the Uniform Parentage Act (2000), below, choosing the path of regulation over the path of prohibition.

Several state legislatures have taken up the invitation to legislate in this area. Some clearly permit the practice; some formally outlaw it; some even make participating in the process a felony. For a full description of the laws of all of the states pertaining to this issue, see Uniform Parentage Act (2000), Appendix to Article 8.

8.   The technology for facilitating reproduction is not only of interest to married couples. Single men and women, and single sex couples, have a special need for this technology. The use of a surrogate is the only way that a single man could expect to have a child to whom he would be genetically related. Similarly, the use of artificial insemination may be an especially attractive way for a single woman, or a lesbian couple, to have a child. While the law has put no formal restriction on the availability of reproductive techniques, some physicians and hospitals are reluctant to provide the full range of infertility services to single people or non-traditional families. Local and state statutes restricting discrimination on the basis of sexual preference may provide avenues of relief for those gay and lesbian potential parents who are denied reproductive services. *Eisenstadt v. Baird,* which threw out a statute forbidding single people access to contraceptives under some circumstances in which they were available to married people, might suggest that the equal protection clause of the Fourteenth Amendment would also protect single people who are denied access to infertility treatment provided to married people by state hospitals and other state facilities. On the other hand, the Supreme Court's opinion in Bowers v. Hardwick, 478 U.S. 186, 106 S.Ct. 2841, 92 L.Ed.2d 140 (1986), which upheld the Georgia sodomy law, undermined the equal protection argument, at least for gays and lesbians. Justice White, for the Court, specifically reserved ruling on whether such sodomy statutes might be enforceable against married couples. There is a strong suggestion, if not a holding, that the law may treat the sexual (and presumably, procreative) relationship of gays and lesbians differently than it treats such relationships between married couples. Whether unmarried heterosexual couples may be treated differently remains uncertain:

> We first register our disagreement with the Court of Appeals and with respondent that the Court's prior cases have construed the Constitution to confer a right of privacy that extends to homosexual sodomy and for all intents and purposes have decided this case. The reach of this line of cases was sketched in Carey v. Population Services International, [ ] and deals with child rearing and education; with family relationships; with procreation; with marriage; with contraception; and with abortion. The latter three [issues were discussed in] cases [which] were interpreted as construing the Due Process Clause of the Fourteenth Amendment to confer a fundamental individual right to decide whether or not to beget or bear a child. [ ]

> Accepting the decisions in these cases and the above description of them, we think it evident that none of the rights announced in these cases bears any

resemblance to the claimed constitutional right of homosexuals to engage in acts of sodomy that is asserted in this case. No connection between family, marriage, or procreation on the one hand and homosexual activity on the other has been demonstrated either by the Court of Appeals or by respondent. Moreover, any claim that these cases nevertheless stand for the proposition that any kind of private sexual conduct between consenting adults is constitutionally insulated from state proscription is unsupportable. * * * [T]he Due Process Clause did not reach so far.

Bowers v. Hardwick, 478 U.S. at 189–92, 106 S.Ct. at 2843–44.

9. Did the Baby M court depend upon the fact that Mary Beth Whitehead Gould was the genetic mother of the child, or the fact that she was the gestational mother of the child? Would the result be different if she were not the genetic mother? Consider the following case, where the gestational mother and the genetic mother are, in fact, different women.

JOHNSON v. CALVERT

Supreme Court of California, 1993.
5 Cal.4th 84, 19 Cal.Rptr.2d 494, 851 P.2d 776.

PANELLI, J:

* * *

Mark and Crispina Calvert are a married couple who desired to have a child. Crispina was forced to undergo a hysterectomy in 1984. Her ovaries remained capable of producing eggs, however, and the couple eventually considered surrogacy. In 1989 Anna Johnson heard about Crispina's plight from a coworker and offered to serve as a surrogate for the Calverts.

On January 15, 1990, Mark, Crispina, and Anna signed a contract providing that an embryo created by the sperm of Mark and the egg of Crispina would be implanted in Anna and the child born would be taken into Mark and Crispina's home "as their child." Anna agreed she would relinquish "all parental rights" to the child in favor of Mark and Crispina. In return, Mark and Crispina would pay Anna $10,000 in a series of installments, the last to be paid six weeks after the child's birth. Mark and Crispina were also to pay for a $200,000 life insurance policy on Anna's life.

The zygote was implanted on January 19, 1990. Less than a month later, an ultrasound test confirmed Anna was pregnant.

Unfortunately, relations deteriorated between the two sides. Mark learned that Anna had not disclosed she had suffered several stillbirths and miscarriages. Anna felt Mark and Crispina did not do enough to obtain the required insurance policy. She also felt abandoned during an onset of premature labor in June.

In July 1990, Anna sent Mark and Crispina a letter demanding the balance of the payments due her or else she would refuse to give up the child. The following month, Mark and Crispina responded with a lawsuit, seeking a declaration they were the legal parents of the unborn child. Anna filed her own action to be declared the mother of the child, and the two cases were eventually consolidated. The parties agreed to an independent guardian ad litem for the purposes of the suit.

The child was born on September 19, 1990, and blood samples were obtained from both Anna and the child for analysis. The blood test results excluded Anna as the genetic mother. The parties agreed to a court order providing that the child would remain with Mark and Crispina on a temporary basis with visits by Anna.

DISCUSSION

Determining Maternity Under the Uniform Parentage Act [of 1973]

* * * [W]e are left with the undisputed evidence that Anna, not Crispina, gave birth to the child and that Crispina, not Anna, is genetically related to him. Both women thus have adduced evidence of a mother and child relationship as contemplated by the [Uniform Parentage] Act [1973]. [ ] Yet for any child California law recognizes only one natural mother, despite advances in reproductive technology rendering a different outcome biologically possible.

We decline to accept the contention of amicus curiae * * * that we should find the child has two mothers. Even though rising divorce rates have made multiple parent arrangements common in our society, we see no compelling reason to recognize such a situation here. The Calverts are the genetic and intending parents of their son and have provided him, by all accounts, with a stable, intact, and nurturing home. To recognize parental rights in a third party with whom the Calvert family has had little contact since shortly after the child's birth would diminish Crispina's role as mother.

We see no clear legislative preference in [the statutory law] as between blood testing evidence and proof of having given birth.

* * *

Because two women each have presented acceptable proof of maternity, we do not believe this case can be decided without enquiring into the parties' intentions as manifested in the surrogacy agreement. Mark and Crispina are a couple who desired to have a child of their own genes but are physically unable to do so without the help of reproductive technology. They affirmatively intended the birth of the child, and took the steps necessary to effect in vitro fertilization. But for their acted-on intention, the child would not exist. Anna agreed to facilitate the procreation of Mark's and Crispina's child. The parties' aim was to bring Mark's and Crispina's child into the world, not for Mark and Crispina to donate a zygote to Anna. Crispina from the outset intended to be the child's mother. Although the gestative function Anna performed was necessary to bring about the child's birth, it is safe to say that Anna would not have been given the opportunity to gestate or deliver the child had she, prior to implantation of the zygote, manifested her own intent to be the child's mother. No reason appears why Anna's later change of heart should vitiate the determination that Crispina is the child's natural mother.

We conclude that although the Act recognizes both genetic consanguinity and giving birth as means of establishing a mother and child relationship, when the two means do not coincide in one woman, she who intended to procreate the child—that is, she who intended to bring about the birth of a child that she intended to raise as her own—is the natural mother under

California law.[5]

* * *

Anna urges that surrogacy contracts violate several social policies. Relying on her contention that she is the child's legal, natural mother, she cites the public policy embodied in [the] Penal Code [ ], prohibiting the payment for consent to adoption of a child. She argues further that the policies underlying the adoption laws of this state are violated by the surrogacy contract because it in effect constitutes a prebirth waiver of her parental rights.

We disagree. Gestational surrogacy differs in crucial respects from adoption and so is not subject to the adoption statutes. The parties voluntarily agreed to participate in in vitro fertilization and related medical procedures before the child was conceived; at the time when Anna entered into the contract, therefore, she was not vulnerable to financial inducements to part with her own expected offspring. As discussed above, Anna was not the genetic mother of the child. The payments to Anna under the contract were meant to compensate her for her services in gestating the fetus and undergoing labor, rather than for giving up "parental" rights to the child. Payments were due both during the pregnancy and after the child's birth.

* * *

Finally, Anna and some commentators have expressed concern that surrogacy contracts tend to exploit or dehumanize women, especially women of lower economic status. Anna's objections center around the psychological harm she asserts may result from the gestator's relinquishing the child to whom she has given birth. Some have also cautioned that the practice of surrogacy may encourage society to view children as commodities, subject to trade at their parents' will.

We are unpersuaded that gestational surrogacy arrangements are so likely to cause the untoward results Anna cites as to demand their invalidation on public policy grounds. Although common sense suggests that women of lesser means serve as surrogate mothers more often than do wealthy women, there has been no proof that surrogacy contracts exploit poor women to any greater degree than economic necessity in general exploits them by inducing them to accept lower-paid or otherwise undesirable employment. We are likewise unpersuaded by the claim that surrogacy will foster the attitude that children are mere commodities; no evidence is offered to support it.

---

5. Thus, under our analysis, in a true "egg donation" situation, where a woman gestates and gives birth to a child formed from the egg of another woman with the intent to raise the child as her own, the birth mother is the natural mother under California law.

The dissent would decide parentage based on the best interests of the child. Such an approach raises the repugnant specter of governmental interference in matters implicating our most fundamental notions of privacy, and confuses concepts of parentage and custody. Logically, the determination of parentage must precede, and should not be dictated by, eventual custody decisions. The implicit assumption of the dissent is that a recognition of the genetic intending mother as the natural mother may sometimes harm the child. This assumption overlooks California's dependency laws, which are designed to protect all children irrespective of the manner of birth or conception. Moreover, the best interests standard poorly serves the child in the present situation: it fosters instability during litigation and, if applied to recognize the gestator as the natural mother, results in a split of custody between the natural father and the gestator, an outcome not likely to benefit the child. Further, it may be argued that, by voluntarily contracting away any rights to the child, the gestator has, in effect, conceded the best interests of the child are not with her.

The argument that a woman cannot knowingly and intelligently agree to gestate and deliver a baby for intending parents carries overtones of the reasoning that for centuries prevented women from attaining equal economic rights and professional status under the law. To resurrect this view is both to foreclose a personal and economic choice on the part of the surrogate mother, and to deny intending parents what may be their only means of procreating a child of their own genes.

* * *

Constitutionality of the Determination That Anna Johnson Is Not the Natural Mother

Anna argues at length that her right to the continued companionship of the child is protected under the federal Constitution.

* * *

Anna relies mainly on theories of substantive due process, privacy, and procreative freedom, citing a number of decisions recognizing the fundamental liberty interest of natural parents in the custody and care of their children. [ ] These cases do not support recognition of parental rights for a gestational surrogate.

Anna's argument depends on a prior determination that she is indeed the child's mother. Since Crispina is the child's mother under California law because she, not Anna, provided the ovum for the in vitro fertilization procedure, intending to raise the child as her own, it follows that any constitutional interests Anna possesses in this situation are something less than those of a mother. * * *

* * *

The judgment of the Court of Appeal is affirmed.

[ARABIAN, J., concurred with the majority's Uniform Parentage Act analysis, but would leave the issue of whether surrogacy contracts could be consistent with public policy to the legislature.]

KENNARD, J., dissenting.

When a woman who wants to have a child provides her fertilized ovum to another woman who carries it through pregnancy and gives birth to a child, who is the child's legal mother? Unlike the majority, I do not agree that the determinative consideration should be the intent to have the child that originated with the woman who contributed the ovum. In my view, the woman who provided the fertilized ovum and the woman who gave birth to the child both have substantial claims to legal motherhood. Pregnancy entails a unique commitment, both psychological and emotional, to an unborn child. No less substantial, however, is the contribution of the woman from whose egg the child developed and without whose desire the child would not exist.

For each child, California law accords the legal rights and responsibilities of parenthood to only one "natural mother." When, as here, the female reproductive role is divided between two women, California law requires courts to make a decision as to which woman is the child's natural mother, but provides no standards by which to make that decision. The majority's resort to "intent" to break the "tie" between the genetic and gestational mothers is unsupported by statute, and, in the absence of appropriate protections in the law to guard against abuse of surrogacy arrangements, it is ill-advised. To determine who is the legal mother of a child born of a gestational surrogacy arrangement, I would apply the standard most protective of child welfare—the best interests of the child.

* * *

POLICY CONSIDERATIONS

* * *

Surrogacy proponents generally contend that gestational surrogacy, like the other reproductive technologies that extend the ability to procreate to persons who might not otherwise be able to have children, enhances "individual freedom, fulfillment and responsibility." [ ] Under this view, women capable of bearing children should be allowed to freely agree to be paid to do so by infertile couples desiring to form a family. [ ] The "surrogate mother" is expected "to weigh the prospective investment in her birthing labor" before entering into the arrangement, and, if her "autonomous reproductive decision" is "voluntary," she should be held responsible for it so as "to fulfill the expectations of the other parties. . . . " [ ]

* * *

Surrogacy critics, however, maintain that the payment of money for the gestation and relinquishment of a child threatens the economic exploitation of poor women who may be induced to engage in commercial surrogacy arrangements out of financial need. [ ] Some fear the development of a "breeder" class of poor women who will be regularly employed to bear children for the economically advantaged. [ ] Others suggest that women who enter into surrogacy arrangements may underestimate the psychological impact of relinquishing a child they have nurtured in their bodies for nine months. [ ]

Gestational surrogacy is also said to be "dehumanizing" [ ] and to "commodify" women and children by treating the female reproductive capacity and the children born of gestational surrogacy arrangements as products that can be bought and sold. [ ]. The commodification of women and children, it is feared, will reinforce oppressive gender stereotypes and threaten the well-being of all children.

* * *

Proponents and critics of gestational surrogacy propose widely differing approaches for deciding who should be the legal mother of a child born of a gestational surrogacy arrangement. Surrogacy advocates propose to enforce pre-conception contracts in which gestational mothers have agreed to relinquish parental rights, and, thus, would make "bargained-for intentions determinative of legal parenthood." [ ] Professor Robertson, for instance, contends that "The right to noncoital, collaborative reproduction also includes the right of the parties to agree how they should allocate their obligations and entitlements with respect to the child. Legal presumptions of paternity and maternity would be overridden by this agreement of the parties." [ ]

Surrogacy critics, on the other hand, consider the unique female role in human reproduction as the determinative factor in questions of legal parentage. They reason that although males and females both contribute genetic material for the child, the act of gestating the fetus falls only on the female. [ ]

Accordingly, in their view, a woman who, as the result of gestational surrogacy, is not genetically related to the child she bears is like any other woman who gives birth to a child. In either situation the woman giving birth is the child's mother. Under this approach, the laws governing adoption should govern the parental rights to a child born of gestational surrogacy. Upon the birth of the child, the gestational mother can decide whether or not to relinquish her parental rights in favor of the genetic mother.

[The dissent's discussion of the Uniform Status of Children of Assisted Conception Act and the 1973 version of the Uniform Parentage Act is omitted.]

ANALYSIS OF THE MAJORITY'S "INTENT" TEST

Faced with the failure of current statutory law to adequately address the issue of who is a child's natural mother when two women qualify under the UPA, the majority breaks the "tie" by resort to a criterion not found in the UPA—the "intent" of the genetic mother to be the child's mother.

* * *

The majority offers four arguments in support of its conclusion to rely on the intent of the genetic mother as the exclusive determinant for deciding who is the natural mother of a child born of gestational surrogacy. Careful examination, however, demonstrates that none of the arguments mandates the majority's conclusion.

The first argument that the majority uses in support of its conclusion that the intent of the genetic mother to bear a child should be dispositive of the question of motherhood is "but-for" causation. Specifically, the majority relies on a commentator who writes that in a gestational surrogacy arrangement, " 'the child would not have been born but for the efforts of the intended parents.' " [ ] [But the resort to the "but-for" test derived from tort law is unprecedented and unjustified here.]

* * *

Behind the majority's reliance on "but-for" causation as justification for its intent test is a second, closely related argument. The majority draws its second rationale from a student note: " 'The mental concept of the child is a controlling factor of its creation, and the originators of that concept merit full credit as conceivers.' " [ ]

* * *

[This concept is taken from the law of intellectual property.] The problem with this argument, of course, is that children are not property. Unlike songs or inventions, rights in children cannot be sold for consideration, or made freely available to the general public.

Next, the majority offers as its third rationale the notion that bargained-for expectations support its conclusion regarding the dispositive significance of the genetic mother's intent. Specifically, the majority states that " 'intentions that are voluntarily chosen, deliberate, express and bargained-for ought presumptively to determine legal parenthood.' "

* * * But the courts will not compel performance of all contract obligations. [ ] The unsuitability of applying the notion that, because contract intentions are "voluntarily chosen, deliberate, express and bargained-for," their performance ought to be compelled by the courts is even more clear when the concept of specific performance is used to determine the course of the life of a child. Just as children are not the intellectual property of their parents, neither are they the personal property of anyone, and their delivery cannot be ordered as a contract remedy on the same terms that a court would, for example, order a breaching party to deliver a truckload of nuts and bolts.

* * *

The majority's final argument in support of using the intent of the genetic mother as the exclusive determinant of the outcome in gestational surrogacy cases is that preferring the intending mother serves the child's interests, which are " '[u]nlikely to run contrary to those of adults who choose to bring [the child] into being.' "[ ]

I agree with the majority that the best interests of the child is an important goal * * *. The problem with the majority's rule of intent is that application of this inflexible rule will not serve the child's best interests in every case.

* * *

THE BEST INTERESTS OF THE CHILD

* * *

In the absence of legislation that is designed to address the unique problems of gestational surrogacy, this court should look not to tort, property or contract law, but to family law, as the governing paradigm and source of a rule of decision. The allocation of parental rights and responsibilities necessarily impacts the welfare of a minor child. And in issues of child welfare, the standard that courts frequently apply is the best interests of the child. [ ] This "best interests" standard serves to assure that in the judicial resolution of disputes affecting a child's well-being, protection of the minor child is the foremost consideration. Consequently, I would apply "the best interests of the child" standard to determine who can best assume the social and legal responsibilities of motherhood for a child born of a gestational surrogacy arrangement.

* * *

Factors that are pertinent to good parenting, and thus that are in a child's best interests, include the ability to nurture the child physically and psychologically [ ] and to provide ethical and intellectual guidance. [ ] Also crucial to a child's best interests is the "well recognized right" of every child "to stability and continuity." [ ] The intent of the genetic mother to procreate a child is certainly relevant to the question of the child's best interests; alone, however, it should not be dispositive.

* * *

In this opinion, I do not purport to offer a perfect solution to the difficult questions posed by gestational surrogacy; perhaps there can be no perfect solution. But in the absence of legislation specifically designed to address the complex issues of gestational surrogacy and to protect against potential abuses, I cannot join the majority's uncritical validation of gestational surrogacy.

I would reverse the judgment of the Court of Appeal, and remand the case to the trial court for a determination of disputed parentage on the basis of the best interests of the child.

Notes and Questions

1. As was the case in *Baby M*, the gestating mother and the commissioning parents developed palpable animosity for each other in *Johnson v. Calvert*. In this case, Johnson argued that the Calverts failed to pay her adequately or treat her with respect. On the other hand, the Calverts argued that Johnson, who admitted to welfare fraud during the course of the pregnancy, was trying to extort money from them. To add a bit of complexity to this baffling case, Johnson also claimed that she was, in part, Native American, and thus subject to provisions of the Indian Child Welfare Act, which preempts state law.

Is the fact that the commissioning parents and gestating woman may develop such a deep–seated mutual hatred a reason to forbid these contracts absolutely, or a reason to regulate them?

2. Are there identifiable principles upon which the majority in *Baby M* and the majority in *Johnson v. Calvert* disagree? Why is the California court so much less concerned than the New Jersey court about the pernicious social effects of surrogacy contracts? Which court do you think better predicts the consequences of such actions? Is the fact that *Johnson* involves gestational surrogacy relevant in the California court's evaluation of the pressure surrogacy contracts will have upon our social fabric?

3. All of the justices agreed that the child could not have two mothers. Is this conclusion a good one? From the perspective of law? From the perspective of public policy? In these days of blended families, is the two parent (one father; one mother) family an anachronism? How could the court have dealt with the ultimate disposition of this case if it had decided that both Ms. Johnson and Ms. Calvert had maternal rights?

4. In her dissenting opinion in Johnson v. Calvert, Justice Kennard depended very heavily upon the surrogacy provisions of the Uniform Status of Children of Assisted Conception Act, which allows states to choose between two options with regard to surrogacy: alternative A (which permits but heavily regulates surrogacy contracts, and which has been adopted by one state) and alternative B (which prohibits those contracts, and which has also been adopted in one state). Although this uniform act provided the starting point for discussions on the propriety of state recognition and regulation of surrogacy contracts, the paucity of states that adopted it suggests that it was not very well received.

5. In McDonald v. McDonald, 196 A.D.2d 7, 608 N.Y.S.2d 477 (1994), another "true 'egg donation' "case, the New York Supreme Court, Appellate

Division, determined that a woman who gestated a child produced through the fertilization of another woman's ovum with her husband's sperm was to be considered the mother of the child that resulted. The New York court depended heavily on the reasoning of *Johnson v. Calvert*. On the other hand, the Court of Common Pleas of Ohio rejected the *Johnson* reasoning in an uncontested case initiated to determine who was to be listed as the mother on the birth certificate in the case of gestational surrogacy. In Belsito v. Clark, 67 Ohio Misc.2d 54, 644 N.E.2d 760 (Ohio Comm.Pl.1994), the court determined that parentage was to be determined by genetic contribution, not by the intent-to-procreate of the parties to the original surrogacy agreement. The court found *Johnson* unpersuasive "for the following three important reasons: (1) the difficulty in applying the *Johnson* intent test; (2) public policy; and (3) *Johnson's* failure to recognize and emphasize the genetic provider's right to consent to procreation and to surrender potential parental rights."

This issue has also arisen in the context of the child custody portion of a divorce case in which the child was born as a result of artificial insemination of a surrogate mother with the sperm of the husband. The child (fourteen at the time of the divorce) was raised by husband and wife, but the child bore no genetic relationship to the wife. Should the wife be entitled to parental rights upon divorce? Is her position weakened by the fact that she had never attempted to adopt the child? Should the court consider the case like any other custody dispute between biological parents, or should the court treat the case like one between the father and a legal stranger to the child? Should the court apply the best interest test in either case? See Doe v. Doe, 244 Conn. 403, 710 A.2d 1297 (Conn.1998).

While legal pundits were creating ultimate assisted conception hypotheticals in which the sperm from one person was joined with the ovum of a second and implanted in the womb of a third to be raised by a fourth and fifth, the real case arose in California:

BUZZANCA v. BUZZANCA

California Court of Appeal, 1998.
61 Cal.App.4th 1410, 72 Cal.Rptr.2d 280.

SILLS, P.J.,

INTRODUCTION

Jaycee was born because Luanne and John Buzzanca agreed to have an embryo genetically unrelated to either of them implanted in a woman—a surrogate—who would carry and give birth to the child for them. After the fertilization, implantation and pregnancy, Luanne and John split up, and the question of who are Jaycee's lawful parents came before the trial court.

Luanne claimed that she and her erstwhile husband were the lawful parents, but John disclaimed any responsibility, financial or otherwise. The woman who gave birth also appeared in the case to make it clear that she made no claim to the child.

The trial court then reached an extraordinary conclusion: Jaycee had no lawful parents. First, the woman who gave birth to Jaycee was not the mother; the court had—astonishingly—already accepted a stipulation that neither she nor her husband were the "biological" parents. Second, Luanne was not the mother. According to the trial court, she could not be the mother because she had neither contributed the egg nor given birth. And John could not be the father, because, not having contributed the sperm, he had no biological relationship with the child. We disagree. Let us get right to the point: Jaycee never would have been born had not Luanne and John both agreed to have a fertilized egg implanted in a surrogate.

The trial judge erred because he assumed that legal motherhood, under the relevant California statutes, could only be established in one of two ways, either by giving birth or by contributing an egg. He failed to consider the substantial and well-settled body of law holding that there are times when fatherhood can be established by conduct apart from giving birth or being genetically related to a child. The typical example is when an infertile husband consents to allowing his wife to be artificially inseminated. * * *

The same rule which makes a husband the lawful father of a child born because of his consent to artificial insemination should be applied here—by the same parity of reasoning that guided our Supreme Court in the first surrogacy case, Johnson v. Calvert [ ]—to both husband and wife. Just as a husband is deemed to be the lawful father of a child unrelated to him when his wife gives birth after artificial insemination, so should a husband and wife be deemed the lawful parents of a child after a surrogate bears a biologically unrelated child on their behalf. In each instance, a child is procreated because a medical procedure was initiated and consented to by intended parents. The only difference is that in this case—unlike artificial insemination—there is no reason to distinguish between husband and wife. We therefore must reverse the trial court's judgment and direct that a new judgment be entered, declaring that both Luanne and John are the lawful parents of Jaycee.

* * *

DISCUSSION

The Statute Governing Artificial Insemination Which Makes a Husband the Lawful Father of a Child Unrelated to Him Applies to Both Intended Parents in This Case

* * *

If a husband who consents to artificial insemination [ ] is "treated in law" as the father of the child by virtue of his consent, there is no reason the result should be any different in the case of a married couple who consent to in vitro fertilization by unknown donors and subsequent implantation into a woman who is, as a surrogate, willing to carry the embryo to term for them. The statute is, after all, the clearest expression of past legislative intent when the Legislature did contemplate a situation where a person who caused a child to come into being had no biological relationship to the child.

Indeed, the establishment of fatherhood and the consequent duty to support when a husband consents to the artificial insemination of his wife is one of the well-established rules in family law. * * *

One New York family court even went so far as to hold the lesbian partner of a woman who was artificially inseminated responsible for the support of two children where the partner had dressed as a man and the couple had obtained a marriage license and a wedding ceremony had been performed prior to the inseminations. [ ] Echoing the themes of causation and estoppel which underlie the cases, the court noted that the lesbian partner had "by her course of conduct in this case ... brought into the world two innocent children" and should not "be allowed to benefit" from her acts to the detriment of the children and public generally. [ ]

It must also be noted that in applying the artificial insemination statute to a case where a party has caused a child to be brought into the world, the statutory policy is really echoing a more fundamental idea * * * already established in the case law. That idea is often summed up in the legal term "estoppel." Estoppel is an ungainly word from the Middle French (from the word meaning "bung" or "stopper") expressing the law's distaste for inconsistent actions and positions—like consenting to an act which brings a child into existence and then turning around and disclaiming any responsibility.

* * *

Luanne is the Lawful Mother of Jaycee, Not the Surrogate, and Not the Unknown Donor of the Egg

In the present case Luanne is situated like a husband in an artificial insemination case whose consent triggers a medical procedure which results in a pregnancy and eventual birth of a child. Her motherhood may therefore be established "under this part [of the 1973 version of the Uniform Parentage Act]," by virtue of that consent. In light of our conclusion, John's argument that the surrogate should be declared the lawful mother disintegrates. The case is now postured like the Johnson v. Calvert case, where motherhood could have been "established" in either of two women under the Act, and the tie broken by noting the intent to parent as expressed in the surrogacy contract. [ ]

* * *

In the case before us, we are not concerned, as John would have us believe, with a question of the enforceability of the oral and written surrogacy contracts into which he entered with Luanne. This case is not about "transferring" parenthood pursuant to those agreements. We are, rather, concerned with the consequences of those agreements as acts which caused the birth of a child.

The legal paradigm adopted by the trial court, and now urged upon us by John, is one where all forms of artificial reproduction in which intended parents have no biological relationship with the child result in legal parentlessness. It means that, absent adoption, such children will be dependents of the state. One might describe this paradigm as the "adoption default" model: The idea is that by not specifically addressing some permutation of artificial reproduction, the Legislature has, in effect, set the default switch on adoption. * * *

The "adoption default" model is, however, inconsistent with both statutory law and the Supreme Court's Johnson decision. As to the statutory law, the Legislature has already made it perfectly clear that public policy (and, we might add, common sense) favors, whenever possible, the establishment of legal parenthood with the concomitant responsibility.

* * *

[I]n addition to its contravention of statutorily enunciated public policy and the pronouncement of our high court in Johnson, the adoption default model ignores the role of our dependency statutes in protecting children. Parents are not screened for the procreation of their own children; they are screened for the adoption of other people's children. It is the role of the dependency laws to protect children from neglect and abuse from their own parents. The adoption default model is essentially an exercise in circular reasoning, because it assumes the idea that it seeks to prove; namely, that a child who is born as the result of artificial reproduction is somebody else's child from the beginning.

* * *

CONCLUSION

* * *

Again we must call on the Legislature to sort out the parental rights and responsibilities of those involved in artificial reproduction. No matter what one thinks of artificial insemination, traditional and gestational surrogacy (in all its permutations), and—as now appears in the not-too-distant future, cloning and even gene splicing—courts are still going to be faced with the problem of determining lawful parentage. A child cannot be ignored. Even if all means of artificial reproduction were outlawed with draconian criminal penalties visited on the doctors and parties involved, courts will still be called upon to decide who the lawful parents really are and who—other than the taxpayers—is obligated to provide maintenance and support for the child. These cases will not go away.

Courts can continue to make decisions on an ad hoc basis without necessarily imposing some grand scheme, looking to the imperfectly designed Uniform Parentage Act and a growing body of case law for guidance in the light of applicable family law principles. Or the Legislature can act to impose a broader order which, even though it might not be perfect on a case-by-case basis, would bring some predictability to those who seek to make use of artificial reproductive techniques. As jurists, we recognize the traditional role of the common (i.e., judge-formulated) law in applying old legal principles to new technology. [ ] However, we still believe it is the Legislature, with its ability to formulate general rules based on input from all its constituencies, which is the more desirable forum for lawmaking.

That said, we must now conclude the business at hand.

(1) The portion of the judgment which declares that Luanne Buzzanca is not the lawful mother of Jaycee is reversed. The matter is remanded with directions to enter a new judgment declaring her the lawful mother. * * *

(2) The judgment is reversed to the extent that it provides that John Buzzanca is not the lawful father of Jaycee. The matter is remanded with directions to enter a new judgment declaring him the lawful father. Consonant with this determination, today's ruling is without prejudice to John in

future proceedings as regards child custody and visitation as his relationship with Jaycee may develop. The judgment shall also reflect that the birth certificate shall be amended to reflect John Buzzanca as the lawful father.

(3) To the degree that the judgment makes no provision for child support it is reversed. * * *

Notes and Questions

1. The California Supreme Court denied review in the Buzzanca case. Why do you think the court did so? Is it because the Buzzanca case traversed no new legal territory? Because its result is compelled by a broad reading of Johnson v. Calvert? Because the issue arises so infrequently? What other reason might there be to deny review in a case like this?

2. What theory of statutory interpretation is being applied by the California Court of Appeal to the 1973 version of the Uniform Parentage Act in this case? What would happen if the California Court of Appeal were to apply the "plain meaning" rule? How does the Court of Appeal deal with the issue that the precisely drafted 1973 Uniform Parentage Act, by its terms, applies only to sperm sources, not to sources of ova?

3. The result reached by the Court of Appeal seems compelling; as a matter of policy it is hard to accept the trial court's conclusion that the legal arrangements made in this case would leave Jaycee a legal orphan at birth. On the other hand, the reasoning requires quite an expansion of the principles announced in Johnson v. Calvert and other precedents upon which the court relied. Was there any other way for the court to reach this same result?

4. Is there any legal theory that could be applied to conclude that someone other than Luanne and John should be treated as Jaycee's parents? What legal theories would lead to the conclusion that the surrogate (i.e., birth) mother should be treated as Jaycee's mother (and her husband should be treated as Jaycee's father)? What legal theories would lead to the conclusion that the genetic sources (i.e., the sperm and ovum sources) should be treated as Jaycee's parents?

5. As a result of the decision in Buzzanca, will John be entitled to all of the rights of Jaycee's father? Will he be entitled to custody? To visitation? To participate in all important decisionmaking regarding Jaycee during the period of her minority? Is there any way to limit his right to act as a father to Jaycee while requiring that he provide child support? Should the lower court, on remand, encourage the development of a father-daughter relationship between John and Jaycee? Should Luanne foster this relationship, too?

6. Some day, years from now, Jaycee will read the California Supreme Court opinion in this case. How do you think that she will react? Should the case have been published, along with the real names of all of the parties? How would you react as a child (or a teenager, or a law student) if you were to discover that you were the subject of litigation like this?

7. Consider once again: might Jaycee be better off with more than two parents? Could the various potential claimants (sperm and ovum sources, gestating mother and the Buzzancas, who commissioned the whole process) all be found to have parental obligations? If so, must they all be given parental rights? Do you feel any differently about this now than you did after reading Johnson v. Calvert?

UNIFORM PARENTAGE ACT

(2000)

ARTICLE 8—GESTATIONAL AGREEMENT

§ 801. GESTATIONAL AGREEMENT AUTHORIZED.

(a) A prospective gestational mother, her husband if she is married, a donor or the donors, and the intended parents may enter into a written agreement providing that:

(1) the prospective gestational mother agrees to pregnancy by means of assisted reproduction;

(2) the prospective gestational mother, her husband if she is married, and the donors relinquish all rights and duties as the parents of a child conceived through assisted reproduction; and

(3) the intended parents become the parents of the child.

(b) The intended parents must be married, and both spouses must be parties to the gestational agreement.

(c) A gestational agreement is enforceable only if validated as provided in Section 803.

(d) A gestational agreement does not apply to the birth of a child conceived by means of sexual intercourse.

(e) A gestational agreement may provide for payment of consideration.

(f) A gestational agreement may not limit the right of the gestational mother to make decisions to safeguard her health or that of the embryos or fetus.

§ 802. REQUIREMENTS OF PETITION.

(a) The intended parents and the prospective gestational mother may commence a proceeding in the [appropriate court] to validate a gestational agreement.

(b) A proceeding to validate a gestational agreement may not be maintained unless:

(1) the mother or the intended parents have been residents of this State for at least 90 days;

(2) the prospective gestational mother's husband, if she is married, is joined in the proceeding; and

(3) a copy of the gestational agreement is attached to the [petition].

§ 803. HEARING TO VALIDATE GESTATIONAL AGREEMENT.

(a) If the requirements of subsection (b) are satisfied, a court may issue an order validating the gestational agreement and declaring that the intended parents will be the parents of a child born during the term of the of the agreement.

(b) The court may issue an order under subsection (a) only on finding that:

(1) the residence requirements of Section 802 have been satisfied and the parties have submitted to the jurisdiction of the court under the jurisdictional standards of this [Act];

(2) medical evidence shows that the intended mother is unable to bear a child or is unable to do so without unreasonable risk to her physical or mental health or to the unborn child;

(3) unless waived by the court, the [relevant child-welfare agency] has made a home study of the intended parents and the intended parents meet the standards of fitness applicable to adoptive parents;

(4) all parties have voluntarily entered into the agreement and understand its terms;

(5) the prospective gestational mother has had at least one pregnancy and delivery and her bearing another child will not pose an unreasonable health risk to the unborn child or to the physical or mental health of the prospective gestational mother;

(6) adequate provision has been made for all reasonable health-care expense associated with the gestational agreement until the birth of the child, including responsibility for those expenses if the agreement is terminated; and

(7) the consideration, if any, paid to the prospective gestational mother is reasonable.

(c) Whether to validate a gestational agreement is within the discretion of the court, subject to review only for abuse of discretion.

§ 804. INSPECTION OF RECORDS.

The proceedings, records, and identities of the individual parties to a gestational agreement under this [article] are subject to inspection under the standards of confidentiality applicable to adoptions as provided under other law of this State.

§ 805. EXCLUSIVE, CONTINUING JURISDICTION.

Subject to the jurisdictional standards of [Section 201 of the Uniform Child Custody Jurisdiction and Enforcement Act], the court conducting a proceeding under this [article] has exclusive, continuing jurisdiction of all matters arising out of the gestational agreement until a child born to the gestational mother during the period governed by the agreement attains the age of 180 days.

§ 806. TERMINATION OF GESTATIONAL AGREEMENT.

(a) After issuance of an order under this [article], but before the prospective gestational mother becomes pregnant by means of assisted reproduction, the prospective gestational mother, her husband, or either of the intended parents may terminate the gestational agreement by giving written notice of termination to all other parties.

(b) The court for good cause shown may terminate the gestational agreement.

(c) An individual who terminates a gestational agreement shall file notice of the termination with the court. On receipt of the notice, the court shall vacate the order issued under this [article]. An individual who does not notify the court of the termination of the agreement is subject to appropriate sanctions.

(d) Neither a prospective gestational mother nor her husband, if any, is liable to the intended parents for terminating a gestational agreement pursuant to this section.

§ 807. PARENTAGE UNDER VALIDATED GESTATIONAL AGREEMENT.

(a) Upon birth of a child to a gestational mother, the intended parents shall file notice with the court that a child has been born to the gestational mother within 300 days after assisted reproduction. Thereupon, the court shall issue an order:

> (1) confirming that the intended parents are the parents of the child ;

> (2) if necessary, ordering that the child be surrendered to the intended parents; and

> (3) directing the [agency maintaining birth records] to issue a birth certificate naming the intended parents as parents of the child.

(b) If the parentage of a child born to a gestational mother is alleged not to be the result of assisted reproduction, the court shall order genetic testing to determine the parentage of the child.

§ 808. GESTATIONAL AGREEMENT: EFFECT OF SUBSEQUENT MARRIAGE.

After the issuance of an order under this [article], subsequent marriage of the gestational mother does not affect the validity of a gestational agreement, her husband's consent to the agreement is not required, and her husband is not a presumed father of the resulting child.

§ 809. EFFECT OF NONVALIDATED GESTATIONAL AGREEMENT.

(a) A gestational agreement, whether in a record or not, that is not judicially validated is not enforceable.

(b) If a birth results under a gestational agreement that is not judicially validated as provided in this [article], the parent-child relationship is determined as provided in [Article] 2 [of the Uniform Parentage Act of 2000, which would denominate the gestational mother as the mother for all legal purposes].

(c) Individuals who are parties to a nonvalidated gestational agreement as intended parents may be held liable for support of the resulting child, even if the agreement is otherwise unenforceable. The liability under this subsection includes assessing all expenses and fees * * *

Notes and Questions

1. The drafters of the uniform act referred to the plea in *Buzzanca* for state legislative solutions to the legal problems that arise as a result of new assisted reproductive techniques. As a consequence of that—and other—judicial invitations to action, the drafters determined that the new Uniform Parentage Act should

include a provision that permits and regulates surrogacy contracts despite the "strongly held differences on this subject." Unlike the Uniform Status of Children of Assisted Conception Act promulgated twelve years earlier, the 2000 Uniform Parentage Act does not include an option A (permitting gestational agreements) and an option B (prohibiting them). In recognizing the comparatively frail support for statutes of this nature, however, the National Conference made the gestational agreement provisions of the Uniform Parentage Act optional because, it concluded, the other changes to the Uniform Parentage Act were "too * * * important * * * to jeopardize its passage because of opposition to this article."

2. The Reporter's Notes to article 8 of the 2000 Uniform Parentage Act also express concern that "voiding or criminalizing gestational agreements will force individuals to find friendly legal forums for the process," and that this forum shopping will make the legal status of their children uncertain. Must states give full faith and credit to birth certificate notations made in other states? Could one state refuse to recognize the parent-child relationships that arise out of assisted reproduction performed in other states?

3. What would have happened if the Article 8 of the Uniform Parentage Act (2000) had been adopted in the relevant states before *Baby M*, *Johnson v. Calvert* and *Buzzanca* had been decided? Would those cases have been decided differently? Could the parties have obtained judicial approval of the gestational agreements in those cases? What would have happened in those cases if Article 8 were in place, but the contracts had not been judicially approved?

4. The new Uniform Parentage Act takes strong positions on a number of controversial issues: the drafters declare that surrogacy contracts are acceptable, that the intending parents must be married, that the surrogate may be compensated for her labor, that judicial approval is necessary before such an agreement can be enforced (and that non-approved contracts are not enforceable, but not illegal, either), that the intending mother must be unable to carry a child without risk to her (or the child's) health, and that the intending parents must undergo a home study that shows them competent to be an adopting family. Is that the way those questions should be resolved? Would you redraft any particular portions of Article 8 of the Uniform Parentage Act [2000]?

5. The legal approach to the regulation of gestational agreements (and to assisted reproduction more generally) depends on the legal perspective one brings to the enterprise. Family lawyers tend to view the process as analogous to adoption, and they ask how any proposed regulation ought to be different from the regulation that governs adoption. Health lawyers are more likely to see the process as the provision of a form of health care, and they ask how regulation designed to assure the quality of our health care system can best be applied to help "patients" in this area. Criminal lawyers are more likely to ask whether there is any aspect of assisted reproductive techniques that should be prohibited. In the end, is the creation of a child through the use of assisted reproduction techniques, including surrogacy, more like ordinary procreation (for which we do not require marriage, a home study, or advance judicial approval), adoption, or a regulated medical treatment?

5. Cloning

In early 1997 the world was stunned by the revelation that a Scottish laboratory had cloned a mammal—to be precise, a Finn Dorset sheep. Scientists achieved this by removing the nucleus from a sheep ovum, replacing it with the genetic material from the sheep to be cloned, and then reimplanting the genetically changed ovum back into the surrogate mother sheep. In fact, the one cloned sheep was the only success in almost 300 attempts at this "somatic cell nuclear transfer cloning," and scientists warned that the likelihood that this technology would be available for human beings remained, for the present, a few years away. Despite this, the bioethics community began a world wide discussion on the consequences of cloning human beings.

Is it possible to talk about the creation of human beings through cloning as we talk about the creation of human beings through other processes of assisted reproduction? How are the questions raised by the existence of cloned human beings truly different from the questions raised by human beings created by other technically driven medical processes? Cloning requires in vitro manipulation (like in vitro fertilization) and then implantation in a womb (like surrogacy). Is it different from either of those two forms of assisted reproduction? Is cloning really a form of reproduction at all, or is it something different—perhaps, merely replication? Who counts as the parents of the cloned individual? Does it make sense to speak of a "mother" or "father," or must we limit ourselves to speaking of the cloned person's "antecedent" or "precursor"?

For generations, science fiction has raised fears of totalitarian regimes that can clone human beings for slave-like work for the benefit of the regime. Should this present a genuine worry to this society? Could cloning be appropriated by the state in support of a Nazi-like eugenics policy? A related worry is that a society could treat a newly cloned person as nothing more than the continuation of the source of its genetic material—or as a body parts source for the person who provided the genetic material. But wouldn't a cloned person have all of the rights of any other person? As some bioethicists argue, if our society were to treat cloned human beings as slaves or spare parts warehouses, the existence of cloning would be the least of our problems.

Would cloned people have the same relationship to each other that identical twins maintain? Identical twins have a common genetic make-up, as a clone and his source would, yet we treat those twins as separate human beings with separate lives and we have identified no social dislocation that arises out of their existence. Why should we be more worried about cloned human beings than about identical twins? In fact, because a cloned person and his source would be different ages, they would be likely to be raised in different environments, and thus to be less similar than identical twins. On the other hand, the number of identical twins is naturally limited, and there are very few identical triplets. We could, through cloning, create a much larger number of identical "siblings."

In any case, is there any justifiable reason for cloning a human being? A few have been suggested. Suppose a child were dying of a disease that could be treated with a bone marrow transplant from a genetically identical donor, but such a donor could not be found. Might it be acceptable to clone the patient, and then, independently, to determine if the newly replicated person ought to be a donor for his brother/sister/source? Alternatively, suppose a couple has an infertility problem which makes it impossible for either of them to become a parent in the ordinary course of events. Should they be able to opt for cloning so that their child will be related to one of them? What if only one of the parents is infertile, and they want a child that does not require the potentially interfering involvement of a third party?

Upon the disclosure that a mammal had successfully been cloned, President Clinton put a temporary ban on federally funded cloning research, and he asked the National Bioethics Advisory Committee to take up the matter. While scientists agreed that we should move slowly (if at all) to permit human cloning, they also agreed that we should move slowly to put any limit on genetic research because of the tremendous potential of that research. Members of the United States Senate also weighed in on the issue, and the Senate Labor and Human Resources subcommittee on public health and safety held hearings on cloning. Senator Harkin, concerned that the government would rush to limit what it did not understand, said that "I don't think there are any appropriate limits to human knowledge—none whatsoever." Senator Bond disagreed, explaining, "There are aspects of life that should be off-limits to science." See Curt Suplee, "Top Scientists Warn Against Cloning Panic," Washington Post, March 13, 1997, A–3. Which senator is right? Are their positions consistent? Ought you have a right to clone yourself? Should the right be limited in any way? Whether or not you have a right to clone oneself, do you also have a right to forbid others from cloning you? Do you have a right to protect your unique genetic identity?

The National Bioethics Advisory Commission published a comprehensive and thoughtful report on the cloning of human beings within months of the revelation that it had been successfully performed on sheep. The report includes a useful description of the relevant scientific procedures as well as a fully annotated analysis of the ethical, theological, legal and policy issues. The Recommendations are reprinted here:

Recommendations of the National Bioethics Advisory Commission (NBAC) With Regard to Cloning (1997)

With the announcement that an apparently quite normal sheep had been born in Scotland as a result of somatic cell nuclear transfer cloning came the realization that, as a society, we must yet again collectively decide whether and how to use what appeared to be a dramatic new technological power. The promise and the peril of this scientific advance was noted immediately around the world, but the prospects of creating human beings through this technique mainly elicited widespread resistance and/or concern. Despite this reaction, the scientific significance of the accomplishment, in terms of improved understanding of cell development and cell differentiation, should not be lost. The challenge to public policy is to support the myriad beneficial applications of this new technology, while simultaneously guarding against its more questionable uses.

Much of the negative reaction to the potential application of such cloning in humans can be attributed to fears about harms to the children who may result, particularly psychological harms associated with a possibly diminished sense of individuality and personal autonomy. Others express concern about a degradation in the quality of parenting and family life. And virtually all people agree that the current risks of physical harm to children associated with somatic cell nuclear transplantation cloning justify a prohibition at this time on such experimentation.

In addition to concerns about specific harms to children, people have frequently expressed fears that a widespread practice of somatic cell nuclear transfer cloning would undermine important social values by opening the door to a form of eugenics or by tempting some to manipulate others as if they were objects instead of persons. Arrayed against these concerns are other important social values, such as protecting personal choice, particularly in matters pertaining to procreation and child rearing, maintaining privacy and the freedom of scientific inquiry, and encouraging the possible development of new biomedical breakthroughs.

As somatic cell nuclear transfer cloning could represent a means of human reproduction for some people, limitations on that choice must be made only when the societal benefits of prohibition clearly outweigh the value of maintaining the private nature of such highly personal decisions. Especially in light of some arguably compelling cases for attempting to clone a human being using somatic cell nuclear transfer, the ethics of policy making must strike a balance between the values society wishes to reflect and issues of privacy and the freedom of individual choice.

To arrive at its recommendations concerning the use of somatic cell nuclear transfer techniques, NBAC also examined long-standing religious traditions that often influence and guide citizens' responses to new technologies. Religious positions on human cloning are pluralistic in their premises, modes of argument, and conclusions. Nevertheless, several major themes are prominent in Jewish, Roman Catholic, Protestant, and Islamic positions, including responsible human dominion over nature, human dignity and destiny, procreation, and family life. Some religious thinkers argue that the use of somatic cell nuclear transfer cloning to create a child would be intrinsically immoral and thus could never be morally justified; they usually propose a ban on such human cloning. Other religious thinkers contend that human cloning to create a child could be morally justified under some circumstances but hold that it should be strictly regulated in order to prevent abuses.

The public policies recommended with respect to the creation of a child using somatic cell nuclear transfer reflect the Commission's best judgments about both the ethics of attempting such an experiment and our view of traditions regarding limitations on individual actions in the name of the common good. At present, the use of this technique to create a child would be a premature experiment that exposes the developing child to unacceptable risks. This in itself is sufficient to justify a prohibition on cloning human beings at this time, even if such efforts were to be characterized as the exercise of a fundamental right to attempt to procreate. More speculative psychological harms to the child, and effects on the moral, religious, and cultural values of society may be enough to justify continued prohibitions in the future, but more time is needed for discussion and evaluation of these concerns.

Beyond the issue of the safety of the procedure, however, NBAC found that concerns relating to the potential psychological harms to children and effects on the moral, religious, and cultural values of society merited further reflection and deliberation. Whether upon such further deliberation our nation will conclude that the use of cloning techniques to create children should be allowed or permanently banned is, for the moment, an open question. Time is an ally in this regard, allowing for the accrual of further data from animal experimentation, enabling an assessment of the prospective safety and efficacy of the procedure in humans, as well as granting a period of fuller national debate on ethical and social concerns. The Commission therefore concluded that there should be imposed a period of time in which no attempt is made to create a child using somatic cell nuclear transfer.

Within this overall framework the Commission came to the following conclusions and recommendations:

I.   The Commission concludes that at this time it is morally unacceptable for anyone in the public or private sector, whether in a research or clinical setting, to attempt to create a child using somatic cell nuclear transfer cloning. We have reached a consensus on this point because current scientific information indicates that this technique is not safe to use in humans at this time. Indeed, we believe it would violate important ethical obligations were clinicians or researchers to attempt to create a child using these particular technologies, which are likely to involve unacceptable risks to the fetus and/or potential child. Moreover, in addition to safety concerns, many other serious ethical concerns have been identified, which require much more widespread and careful public deliberation before this technology may be used.

The Commission, therefore, recommends the following for immediate action:

A continuation of the current moratorium on the use of federal funding in support of any attempt to create a child by somatic cell nuclear transfer.

An immediate request to all firms, clinicians, investigators, and professional societies in the private and non-federally funded sectors to comply voluntarily with the intent of the federal moratorium. Professional and scientific societies should make clear that any attempt to create a child by somatic cell nuclear transfer and implantation into a woman's body would at this time be an irresponsible, unethical, and unprofessional act.

II.   The Commission further recommends that:

Federal legislation should be enacted to prohibit anyone from attempting, whether in a research or clinical setting, to create a child through somatic cell nuclear transfer cloning. It is critical, however, that such legislation include a sunset clause to ensure that Congress will review the issue after a specified time period (three to five years) in order to decide whether the prohibition continues to be needed. If state legislation is enacted, it should also contain such a sunset provision. Any such legislation or associated regulation also ought to require that at some point prior to the expiration of the sunset period, an appropriate oversight body will evaluate and report on the current status of somatic cell nuclear transfer technology and on the ethical and social issues that its potential use to create human beings would raise in light of public understandings at that time.

III.   The Commission also concludes that:

Any regulatory or legislative actions undertaken to effect the foregoing prohibition on creating a child by somatic cell nuclear transfer should be carefully written so as not to interfere with other important areas of scientific research. In particular, no new regulations are required regarding the cloning of human DNA sequences and cell lines, since neither activity raises the scientific and ethical issues that arise from the attempt to create children through somatic cell nuclear transfer, and these fields of research have already provided important scientific and biomedical advances. Likewise, research on cloning animals by somatic cell nuclear transfer does not raise the issues implicated in attempting to use this technique for human cloning, and its continuation should only be subject to existing regulations regarding the humane use of animals and review by institution-based animal protection committees.

If a legislative ban is not enacted, or if a legislative ban is ever lifted, clinical use of somatic cell nuclear transfer techniques to create a child should be preceded by research trials that are governed by the twin protections of independent review and informed consent, consistent with existing norms of human subjects protection.

The United States Government should cooperate with other nations and international organizations to enforce any common aspects of their respective policies on the cloning of human beings.

IV. The Commission also concludes that different ethical and religious perspectives and traditions are divided on many of the important moral issues that surround any attempt to create a child using somatic cell nuclear transfer techniques. Therefore, we recommend that:

The federal government, and all interested and concerned parties, encourage widespread and continuing deliberation on these issues in order to further our understanding of the ethical and social implications of this technology and to enable society to produce appropriate long-term policies regarding this technology should the time come when present concerns about safety have been addressed.

V. Finally, because scientific knowledge is essential for all citizens to participate in a full and informed fashion in the governance of our complex society, the Commission recommends that:

Federal departments and agencies concerned with science should cooperate in seeking out and supporting opportunities to provide information and education to the public in the area of genetics, and on other developments in the biomedical sciences, especially where these affect important cultural practices, values, and beliefs.

Bibliographical Note: Facilitating Reproduction

There has been a great deal of useful writing on the techniques available for facilitating reproduction, and on the analyses of the ethical and legal issues that they create. The best place to begin research on these issues may be in the thoughtful, creative and well annotated account of legal issues in parentage prepared by a leading family law scholar, Marsha Garrison, Law Making and Baby Making: An Interpretive Approach to the Determination of Legal Parentage, 113 Harv. L. Rev. 835 (2000). See also Janet Dolgin, The Family in Transition: From Griswold to Eisenstadt and Beyond, 82 Geo. L.J. 1519 (1994). Many of the parameters of this discussion were established in John Robertson, Embryos, Families and Procreative Liberty: The Legal Structure of the New Reproduction, 59 S.Cal. L. Rev. 939 (1986) .. For a particularly compelling account of the hopeless task of the Human Embryo Research Panel in determining the ethical status of the embryo, written by a member of that panel, see Alta Charo, The Hunting of the Snark: The Moral Status of Embryos, Right-to-Lifers, and Third World Women, 6 (2) Stan. L. & Pol. Rev. 11 (1995).

The Summer, 1999 issue of the Loyola Law Review contains an interesting symposium on interdisciplinary examinations of the new reproductive technology. The November, 1995 issue of the Virginia Law Review features a symposium on new directions in family law, which includes Richard Epstein, Surrogacy: The Case for Full Contractual Enforcement, 81 Va. L. Rev. 2305 (1995) and a response, Margaret F. Brinig, A Maternalistic Approach to Surrogacy: Comment on Richard Epstein's "Surrogacy," 81 Va. L. Rev. 2377 (1995). For a good debate on baby selling and its logical consequences, see E. Landes and R. Posner, The Economics of the Baby Shortage, 7 J. Legal. Stud. 323 (1978) and J.R.S. Prichard, A Market for Babies?, 34 U. Toronto L. J. 341 (1984). For a discussion on issues that arise out of cloning, see John Robertson, Two Models of Human Cloning, 27 Hofstra L. Rev. 609 (1999). For a helpful analysis of the problems that could arise when genetic material is accidentally (or intentionally) implanted in the wrong womb, and for an interesting solution to those problems, see Alice Noble–Allgire, Switched at the Fertility Clinic: Determining Maternal Rights When a Child is Born from Stolen or Misdelivered Genetic Material, 64 Mo. L. Rev. 517 (1999).

III.   FETAL MATERNAL DECISIONMAKING

Problem: Children Bearing Children

Elsie McIntosh is a fifteen year-old high school dropout in the fourth month of her first pregnancy. She lives at home with her mother, whose primary source of income is general assistance (i.e., state welfare) and food stamps. Elsie and her mother, who has been a desperate alcoholic for the past eight years, have spoken barely ten words in the past year. They live more like roommates than a mother-daughter family, and Elsie lives on her share of her mother's state aid, supplemented by a modest income from her own prostitution. Her prostitution has led to her arrest twice, and each of the arrests resulted in a night in juvenile detention, a morning in court, and a deferred finding of delinquency that was subsequently dismissed. Elsie has been a heavy drinker and a heavy user of crack cocaine for the past three or four years, and her drinking and cocaine use have continued during her pregnancy. She also occasionally uses heroin, and she smokes three packs of cigarettes a day. Elsie has received some health care (for an injury received in a knife fight with a customer) at the Big City HMO, the managed care organization to which she was assigned by the state Medicaid program. She felt that the health care professionals there treated her with disdain and she has not sought any prenatal care.

Knowing all of this, what should her state-assigned welfare worker do? If she were being seen by an obstetrician who knew all of this about Elsie, what should the obstetrician do? If this information about a patient were to come to the attention of a medical clinic legal counsel, what should that legal counsel do? If this information were to come to the attention of the district attorney, what should the district attorney do?

IN RE A.C.

District of Columbia Court of Appeals, 1990.
573 A.2d 1235.

TERRY, ASSOCIATE JUDGE:

* * *

We are confronted here with two profoundly difficult and complex issues. First, we must determine who has the right to decide the course of medical treatment for a patient who, although near death, is pregnant with a viable fetus. Second, we must establish how that decision should be made if the patient cannot make it for herself—more specifically, how a court should proceed when faced with a pregnant patient, *in extremis,* who is apparently incapable of making an informed decision regarding medical care for herself and her fetus. We hold that in virtually all cases the question of what is to be done is to be decided by the patient—the pregnant woman—on behalf of herself and the fetus. If the patient is incompetent or otherwise unable to give an informed consent to a proposed course of medical treatment, then her decision must be ascertained through the procedure known as substituted judgment. * * *

I

This case came before the trial court when George Washington University Hospital petitioned the emergency judge in chambers for declaratory relief as to how it should treat its patient, A.C., who was close to death from cancer and was twenty-six and one-half weeks pregnant with a viable fetus. After a hearing lasting approximately three hours, which was held at the hospital (though not in A.C.'s room), the court ordered that a caesarean section be performed on A.C. to deliver the fetus. * * * The caesarean was performed, and a baby girl, L.M.C., was delivered. Tragically, the child died within two and one-half hours, and the mother died two days later.

* * *

II

A.C. was first diagnosed as suffering from cancer at the age of thirteen. In the ensuing years she underwent major surgery several times, together with multiple radiation treatments and chemotherapy. A.C. married when she was twenty-seven, during a period of remission, and soon thereafter she became pregnant. She was excited about her pregnancy and very much wanted the child. Because of her medical history, she was referred in her fifteenth week of pregnancy to the high-risk pregnancy clinic at George Washington University Hospital.

On Tuesday, June 9, 1987, when A.C. was approximately twenty-five weeks pregnant, she went to the hospital for a scheduled check-up. Because she was experiencing pain in her back and shortness of breath, an x-ray was taken, revealing an apparently inoperable tumor which nearly filled her right lung. On Thursday, June 11, A.C. was admitted to the hospital as a patient.

By Friday her condition had temporarily improved, and when asked if she really wanted to have her baby, she replied that she did.

Over the weekend, A.C.'s condition worsened considerably. Accordingly, on Monday, June 15, members of the medical staff treating A.C. assembled, along with her family, in A.C.'s room. The doctors then informed her that her illness was terminal, and A.C. agreed to palliative treatment designed to extend her life until at least her twenty-eighth week of pregnancy. The "potential outcome [for] the fetus," according to the doctors, would be much better at twenty-eight weeks than at twenty-six weeks if it were necessary to "intervene." A.C. knew that the palliative treatment she had chosen presented some increased risk to the fetus, but she opted for this course both to prolong her life for at least another two weeks and to maintain her own comfort. When asked if she still wanted to have the baby, A.C. was somewhat equivocal, saying "something to the effect of 'I don't know, I think so.'" As the day moved toward evening, A.C.'s condition grew still worse, and at about 7:00 or 8:00 p.m. she consented to intubation to facilitate her breathing.

The next morning, June 16, the trial court convened a hearing at the hospital in response to the hospital's request for a declaratory judgment. The court appointed counsel for both A.C. and the fetus, and the District of Columbia was permitted to intervene for the fetus as *parens patriae.* * * *

* * *

There was no evidence before the court showing that A.C. consented to, or even contemplated, a caesarean section before her twenty-eighth week of pregnancy. There was, in fact, considerable dispute as to whether she would have consented to an immediate caesarean delivery at the time the hearing was held. A.C.'s mother opposed surgical intervention, testifying that A.C. wanted "to live long enough to hold that baby" and that she expected to do so, "even though she knew she was terminal." Dr. Hamner [a treating obstetrician] testified that, given A.C.'s medical problems, he did not think she would have chosen to deliver a child with a substantial degree of impairment. * * *

After hearing this testimony and the arguments of counsel, the trial court made oral findings of fact. It found, first, that A.C. would probably die, according to uncontroverted medical testimony, "within the next twenty-four to forty-eight hours;" second, that A.C. was "pregnant with a twenty-six and a half week viable fetus who, based upon uncontroverted medical testimony, has approximately a fifty to sixty percent chance to survive if a caesarean section is performed as soon as possible;" third, that because the fetus was viable, "the state has [an] important and legitimate interest in protecting the potentiality of human life;" and fourth, that there had been some testimony that the operation "may very well hasten the death of [A.C.]," but that there had also been testimony that delay would greatly increase the risk to the fetus and that "the prognosis is not great for the fetus to be delivered post-mortem * * *." Most significantly, the court found:

> The court is of the view that it does not clearly know what [A.C.'s] present views are with respect to the issue of whether or not the child should live or die. She's presently unconscious. As late as Friday of last

week, she wanted the baby to live. As late as yesterday, she did not know for sure.

Having made these findings of fact and conclusions of law, * * * the court ordered that a caesarean section be performed to deliver A.C.'s child.

The court's decision was then relayed to A.C., who had regained consciousness. [When the court reconvened later in the day, Dr. Hamner testified that A.C. then consented to the procedure.] When the court suggested moving the hearing to A.C.'s bedside, Dr. Hamner discouraged the court from doing so, but he and Dr. Weingold, together with A.C.'s mother and husband, went to A.C.'s room to confirm her consent to the procedure. What happened then was recounted to the court a few minutes later:

* * *

Dr. Weingold: She does not make sounds because of the tube in her windpipe. She nods and she mouths words. One can see what she's saying rather readily. She asked whether she would survive the operation. She asked [Dr.] Hamner if he would perform the operation. He told her he would only perform it if she authorized it but it would be done in any case. She understood that. She then seemed to pause for a few moments and then very clearly mouthed words several times, *I don't want it done, I don't want it done.* Quite clear to me.

I would obviously state the obvious and that is this is an environment in which, from my perspective as a physician, this would not be an informed consent one way or the other. She's under tremendous stress with the family on both sides, but I'm satisfied that I heard clearly what she said. * * *

Dr. Weingold later qualified his opinion as to A.C.'s ability to give an informed consent, stating that he thought the environment for an informed consent was non-existent because A.C. was in intensive care, flanked by a weeping husband and mother. He added:

I think she's in contact with reality, clearly understood who Dr. Hamner was. Because of her attachment to him [she] wanted him to perform the surgery. Understood he would not unless she consented and did not consent.

That is, in my mind, very clear evidence that she is responding, understanding, and is capable of making such decisions. * * *

After hearing this new evidence, the court found that it was "still not clear what her intent is" and again ordered that a caesarean section be performed. * * * The operation took place, but the baby lived for only a few hours, and A.C. succumbed to cancer two days later.

* * *

IV

* * *

A. Informed Consent and Bodily Integrity

* * *

* * * [O]ur analysis of this case begins with the tenet common to all medical treatment cases: that any person has the right to make an informed choice, if competent to do so, to accept or forgo medical treatment. * * *

In the same vein, courts do not compel one person to permit a significant intrusion upon his or her bodily integrity for the benefit of another person's health. See, e.g., *McFall v. Shimp,* 10 Pa.D. & C.3d 90 (Allegheny County Ct.1978). In *McFall* the court refused to order Shimp to donate bone marrow which was necessary to save the life of his cousin, McFall:

> The common law has consistently held to a rule which provides that one human being is under no legal compulsion to give aid or to take action to save another human being or to rescue. * * *

Even though Shimp's refusal would mean death for McFall, the court would not order Shimp to allow his body to be invaded. It has been suggested that fetal cases are different because a woman who "has chosen to lend her body to bring [a] child into the world" has an enhanced duty to assure the welfare of the fetus, sufficient even to require her to undergo caesarean surgery. [ ] Surely, however, a fetus cannot have rights in this respect superior to those of a person who has already been born.[6]

* * *

There are two additional arguments against overriding A.C.'s objections to caesarean surgery. First, as the American Public Health Association cogently states in its *amicus curiae* brief:

> Rather than protecting the health of women and children, court-ordered caesareans erode the element of trust that permits a pregnant woman to communicate to her physician—without fear of reprisal—all information relevant to her proper diagnosis and treatment. An even more serious consequence of court-ordered intervention is that it drives women at high risk of complications during pregnancy and childbirth out of the health care system to avoid coerced treatment.

Second, and even more compellingly, any judicial proceeding in a case such as this will ordinarily take place—like the one before us here—under time constraints so pressing that it is difficult or impossible for the mother to communicate adequately with counsel, or for counsel to organize an effective factual and legal presentation in defense of her liberty and privacy interests and bodily integrity. * * *

* * *

B. Substituted Judgment

* * * Sometimes, however, as our analysis presupposes here, a once competent patient will be unable to render an informed decision. In such a case, we hold that the court must make a substituted judgment on behalf of the patient, based on all the evidence. This means that the duty of the court,

---

6. There are also practical consequences to consider. What if A.C. had refused to comply with a court order that she submit to a caesarean? Enforcement could be accomplished only through physical force or its equivalent. A.C. would have to be fastened with restraints to the operating table, or perhaps involuntarily rendered unconscious by forcibly injecting her with an anesthetic, and then subjected to unwanted major surgery. Such actions would surely give one pause in a civilized society, especially when A.C. had done no wrong.

"as surrogate for the incompetent, is to determine as best it can what choice that individual, if competent, would make with respect to medical procedures." [ ]

* * *

We have found no reported opinion applying the substituted judgment procedure to the case of an incompetent pregnant patient whose own life may be shortened by a caesarean section, and whose unborn child's chances of survival may hang on the court's decision. Despite this precedential void, we conclude that substituted judgment is the best procedure to follow in such a case because it most clearly respects the right of the patient to bodily integrity. * * *

* * *

Because it is the patient's decisional rights which the substituted judgment inquiry seeks to protect, courts are in accord that the greatest weight should be given to the previously expressed wishes of the patient. This includes prior statements, either written or oral, even though the treatment alternatives at hand may not have been addressed. * * *

Courts in substituted judgment cases have also acknowledged the importance of probing the patient's value system as an aid in discerning what the patient would choose. We agree with this approach. [The court then discussed the ways in which it could determine the substituted judgment of the patient. For a fuller discussion of this issue, see chapter 19.]

C. The Trial Court's Ruling

* * * The [trial] court did not * * * make a finding as to what A.C. would have chosen to do if she were competent. Instead, the court undertook to balance the state's and [the fetus's] interests in surgical intervention against A.C.'s perceived interest in not having the caesarean performed.

* * *

What a trial court must do in a case such as this is to determine, if possible, whether the patient is capable of making an informed decision about the course of her medical treatment. If she is, and if she makes such a decision, her wishes will control in virtually all cases. If the court finds that the patient is incapable of making an informed consent (and thus incompetent), then the court must make a substituted judgment. * * *

Having said that, we go no further. We need not decide whether, or in what circumstances, the state's interests can ever prevail over the interests of a pregnant patient. * * * Indeed, some may doubt that there could ever be a situation extraordinary or compelling enough to justify a massive intrusion into a person's body, such as a caesarean section, against that person's will. Whether such a situation may someday present itself is a question that we need not strive to answer here. * * *

* * *

BELSON, ASSOCIATE JUDGE, concurring in part and dissenting in part:

* * *

I think it appropriate * * * to state my disagreement with the very limited view the majority opinion takes of the circumstances in which the interests of a viable unborn child can afford such compelling reasons. The state's interest in preserving human life and the viable unborn child's interest in survival are entitled, I think, to more weight than I find them assigned by the majority when it states that "in virtually all cases the decision of the patient * * * will control." I would hold that in those instances, fortunately rare, in which the viable unborn child's interest in living and the state's parallel interest in protecting human life come into conflict with the mother's decision to forgo a procedure such as a caesarean section, a balancing should be struck in which the unborn child's and the state's interest are entitled to substantial weight.

* * *

The balancing test should be applied in instances in which women become pregnant and carry an unborn child to the point of viability. This is not an unreasonable classification because, I submit, a woman who carries a child to viability is in fact a member of a unique category of persons. Her circumstances differ fundamentally from those of other potential patients for medical procedures that will aid another person, for example, a potential donor of bone marrow for transplant. This is so because she has undertaken to bear another human being, and has carried an unborn child to viability. Another unique feature of the situation we address arises from the singular nature of the dependency of the unborn child upon the mother. A woman carrying a viable unborn child is not in the same category as a relative, friend, or stranger called upon to donate bone marrow or an organ for transplant. Rather, the expectant mother has placed herself in a special class of persons who are bringing another person into existence, and upon whom that other person's life is totally dependent. Also, uniquely, the viable unborn child is literally captive within the mother's body. No other potential beneficiary of a surgical procedure on another is in that position.

* * *

I next address the sensitive question of how to balance the competing rights and interests of the viable unborn child and the state against those of the rare expectant mother who elects not to have a caesarean section necessary to save the life of her child. The indisputable view that a woman carrying a viable child has an extremely strong interest in her own life, health, bodily integrity, privacy, and religious beliefs necessarily requires that her election be given correspondingly great weight in the balancing process. In a case, however, where the court in an exercise of a substituted judgment has concluded that the patient would probably opt against a caesarean section, the court should vary the weight to be given this factor in proportion to the confidence the court has in the accuracy of its conclusion. Thus, in a case where the indicia of the incompetent patient's judgment are equivocal, the court should accord this factor correspondingly less weight. The appropriate weight to be given other factors will have to be worked out by the development of law in this area, and cannot be prescribed in a single court opinion. Some considerations obviously merit special attention in the balancing process. One such consideration is any danger to the mother's life or health, physical or mental, including the relatively small but still significant danger that necessarily inheres in any caesarean delivery, and including especially any danger that exceeds that level. The mother's religious beliefs as they relate to the operation would appear to deserve inclusion in the balancing process.

On the other side of the analysis, it is appropriate to look to the relative likelihood of the unborn child's survival. * * * The child's interest in being born with as little impairment as possible should also be considered. This may weigh in favor of a delivery sooner rather than later. The most important factor on this side of the scale, however, is life itself, because the viable unborn child that dies because of the mother's refusal to have a caesarean delivery is deprived, entirely and irrevocably, of the life on which the child was about to embark.

* * *

Notes and Questions

1. As the opinions in *A.C.* suggest, potential fetal-maternal conflicts force courts to answer two questions. First, should the court balance the interests of the fetus (or the interests of the state in protecting the fetus) with the interests of the mother? If the answer to that question is "no," as it was for the majority in *A.C.*, the issue becomes the comparatively simple one of determining the wishes of the mother. See In re Baby Boy Doe, 260 Ill.App.3d 392, 198 Ill.Dec. 267, 632 N.E.2d 326 (Ill.App.1994), where the court refused to balance the interests of a fetus (or the interests of the state in protecting a fetus) against the interests of a competent pregnant woman who refused a caesarean section, even though her decision put the life of her fetus at stake.

If there is a decision to balance the interests, however, as the dissenting opinion in *A.C.* suggests, the court must also face the question of what standards to apply. Are the interests of the fetus or the state as strong as the interests of the mother? Can the relative strengths of these different interests vary from case to case, depending upon the stage of development of the fetus, the consequences of the decision to be made, or other factors?

2. *In re A.C.* was not the first case in which a court was asked to order a pregnant woman to undergo medical treatment for the benefit of her fetus. In Raleigh–Fitkin–Paul Morgan Memorial Hospital v. Anderson, 42 N.J. 421, 201 A.2d 537 (1964), the New Jersey Supreme Court ordered blood transfusions to save an "unborn child" over the objections of the Jehovah's Witness mother. See also In re Application of Jamaica Hospital, 128 Misc.2d 1006, 491 N.Y.S.2d 898 (Sup.Ct.1985) (blood transfusion to save fetus who was not yet viable). In Jefferson v. Griffin Spalding County Hospital Authority, 247 Ga. 86, 274 S.E.2d 457 (1981), the Georgia Supreme Court ordered a caesarean section against the religiously motivated wishes of the mother when physicians argued that failure to do so would result in the death of both the mother and the fetus. The court acted because of the "duty of the state to protect a living, unborn human being from meeting * * * death before being given the opportunity to live." 274 S.E.2d at 460. More recently, the issue arose in Pemberton v. Tallahassee Memorial Regional Medical Center, 66 F. Supp. 2d 1247 (N.D.Fl.1999), in which a fully competent pregnant woman was legally (and physically) required to undergo a caesarian section to preserve the life of her full term fetus. The Pemberton court explicitly addressed the A.C. case, and determined that "A.C. left open the possibility that a

non-consenting patient's interest would yield to a more compelling countervailing interest in an 'extremely rare and truly exceptional' case.[ ] This is such a case." 66 F. Supp. 2d 1254. The court agreed that "[I]n anything other than an extraordinary and overwhelming case, the right to decide would surely rest with the mother, not with the state. * * * [T]his was an extraordinary and overwhelming case; no reasonable or even unreasonable argument could be made in favor of vaginal delivery at home with the attendant risk of death to the baby (and concomitant grave risk to the mother)." Id.

3. One reason that many commentators have opposed judicial intervention to require pregnant women to undergo medical care for the benefit of their fetuses is the fact that medical diagnosis in this area is often wrong. Doctors seem willing to testify that intervention is necessary to save the fetus even when the prognosis following nonintervention is quite uncertain. There is a series of cases that suggests that when doctors testify that a caesarean is necessary for the health of the fetus, but the mother "escapes" and attempts a normal vaginal birth, there is a good chance the child will be born without complication. J. Fletcher, Drawing Moral Lines in Fetal Therapy, 29 Clin. Obstetrics & Gynecology 595 (1986). Fletcher summarizes his review of six cases:

> First, inaccuracies and possible misdiagnosis appear to be involved in half of the cases * * * since babies were born healthy after vaginal delivery. If precedents flow from examples flawed by faulty assumptions or mistaken evaluations, errors may be replicated. These outcomes also should remind all concerned of the possibility of misdiagnosis before fetal therapy. Forced fetal therapy on the basis of misdiagnosis would constitute an ethical megadisaster.

29 Clin. Obstetrics and Gynecology at 599. See In re Baby Boy Doe, 260 Ill.App.3d 392, 198 Ill.Dec. 267, 270, 632 N.E.2d 326, 329 (1994) (mother delivered a "normal and healthy" baby despite predictions of disaster).

4. Not all moral obligations are enforceable through the use of the legal process. First, we must ask if a pregnant woman has a *moral* obligation to act to preserve the health of her fetus. Only if we find such a moral obligation must we address the second question: Should this obligation be enforceable in law? Some (including the majority in *A.C.*) argue that the wishes of the mother (who is unquestionably a person) always trump the presumed interests of the fetus (whose "personhood" status is uncertain). Some argue that the interests of the fetus (who has yet to experience life) always trump the wishes of the mother.

If you adopt neither absolute, you must address the balancing issue raised above in note 1. How do you weigh the wishes of the pregnant woman against the interests of the fetus (or the interest of the state in protecting fetal life)? What are the relevant factors? Is the viability status of the fetus relevant? Is the likely outcome of the proposed medical procedure relevant? Is the burden this procedure places on the mother relevant? Is the determination by the mother that she will bear the child—that she definitely will not have an abortion, even if that is legally permitted—relevant? Some have argued that this last factor is especially important because where the mother has decided to carry her fetus to term and give birth to a child, the mother's interest must be weighed against the greater interest of this yet-to-be-born person, not the lesser interest of a fetus who may yet be aborted. See J. Robertson and J. Schulman, Pregnancy and Prenatal Harm to Offspring: The Case of Mothers with PKU, 17 Hastings Center Rep. (4) 23 (Aug./Sept.1987).

5. If society were to enforce the moral obligation of a mother to care for the health of her fetus by law, it could do so in many ways.

a. Civil Remedies

Civil remedies could include mandatory injunctions (or their equivalents) like those sought in *A.C.* and granted in *Jefferson* or findings of abuse, neglect or dependency. Some states define children born dependent on drugs or alcohol as deprived or abused. See, e.g., Okl. Stat. Ann. Tit. 10 § 1101(4)(c) ("deprived child" includes one born dependent on a controlled substance); Ind. Code Ann. § 31–6–4–3.1(a)(1) ("children in need of services" includes fetal alcohol syndrome babies and those born with any amount of a controlled substance in their bodies). Compare In re Noah M., 212 Cal.App.3d 30, 260 Cal.Rptr. 309 (1989) (infant a deprived child because of prenatal amphetamine exposure) with In re Fletcher, 141 Misc.2d 333, 533 N.Y.S.2d 241 (Fam.Ct.1988) (prenatal cocaine use alone insufficient basis for a finding of neglect). Can a court permit a state child protective services agency to take custody of a *fetus* under civil abuse and neglect law? Can taking custody of a fetus be distinguished from taking custody of the pregnant woman whose body contains the fetus? Do you think that the fact that a pregnant woman exposed her baby to illegal drugs prenatally is sufficient to show neglect?

In a large number of high risk pregnancies the pregnant woman is herself a child, and there seems to be some relationship between drug and alcohol use and teenage pregnancy. If the pregnant woman is herself a minor, is *her* parents' inability to control her conduct to assure the safety of the fetus itself evidence that the pregnant woman is a neglected child who can be taken into custody to protect her (and, indirectly, her fetus)?

Should civil damages be available to a child born alive who is injured by the pre-birth conduct of her mother? Compare Grodin v. Grodin, 102 Mich.App. 396, 301 N.W.2d 869 (1980) (suit by child against mother who took tetracycline during pregnancy, resulting in discoloration of child's teeth; potential liability in insurance company that issued mother a homeowner's policy) with Chenault v. Huie, 989 S.W.2d 474 (Tex. Civ. App. 1999)(no tort action permitted against mother by child allegedly injured by mother's illegal drug use during pregnancy). If we allow children born alive to seek tort damages against others who injure them prenatally, is there a reason to treat their tortfeasing parents differently and more favorably?

b. Criminal Remedies

The law could also apply criminal penalties to those who put their fetuses at risk. States could apply the criminal law of child abuse and neglect to a mother's care for her fetus. Since these criminal statutes generally make failing to provide adequate medical care to a child a form of neglect, they could be interpreted to mean that failing to provide adequate medical care to a fetus would constitute neglect. Such an interpretation of the criminal law might turn any pregnant woman who fails to follow her doctor's advice into a criminal, and this might discourage women at risk from seeking prenatal care.

Other criminal laws also could be used to protect fetuses. Some lifestyle choices that put a fetus at risk (like use of cocaine or heroin) are illegal and can result independently in criminal sanctions against the pregnant woman. There have been several prosecutions for prenatal delivery of illegal drugs by a pregnant woman to her fetus. Should the fact that a subsequently born child is neither addicted nor disabled in any other way be relevant to such a prosecution against that child's mother? Should the fact that the mother is an addict be relevant? To the extent that some criminal sanctions (such as imprisonment) might protect the fetus, are they particularly appropriate for pregnant women who would continue their risky behavior unless they were confined? If a mother is imprisoned for the term of her pregnancy *in order to protect her fetus,* is she being punished for the crime she committed, or for her pregnancy? Is there any deterrence value in imprisoning a pregnant woman who violates the criminal law in a way that adversely affects her fetus?

Might the criminal law be available as a lever to encourage women to get treatment for their addiction during the "teachable moment" provided by a pregnancy? In 1989 the Medical University of South Carolina, along with other state and local law enforcement and social service agencies, hatched a plan to deal with what they saw as the pernicious effects of drug use by pregnant women. Women who met certain guidelines (e.g. those with little or incomplete prenatal care) were tested for cocaine use when they arrived at the hospital to deliver their babies. Those who tested positive were given a choice between enrolling in a substance abuse program and being arrested for their drug use. Those who chose the treatment option were not prosecuted unless they failed to adhere to the treatment plan or failed a subsequent drug test; the others were reported to, and subsequently arrested by, the police. No other hospital in Charleston chose to participate in the program. The majority of the women covered by the program were poor, and most were African American. The generally wealthier White mothers who delivered their babies at other hospitals were not given an opportunity (or forced, against their will, depending on your perspective) to participate in this program.

Ten of the arrested mothers brought suit against the hospital and others. In 2001 the Supreme Court, 6–3, determined that the Charleston process constituted an illegal warrantless search and seizure prohibited by the Fourth Amendment. Ferguson v. City of Charleston, 528 U.S. ___, 121 S.Ct. 1281, ___ L.Ed.2d ___ (2001). Justice Stevens, for the Court, pointed out that the "direct and primary purpose" of the test was to aid the police in enforcing a criminal law, and that the Fourth Amendment was implicated even if the ultimate goal of the hospital was to encourage women to get treatment. Justice Kennedy, concurring, pointed out that the case did not prohibit a state from punishing women who put their fetuses at risk, and Justice Scalia, dissenting, said that the majority "proves once again that no good deed goes unpunished."

Public health groups had filed amicus briefs opposing the policy, employing the A.C. argument that such a policy would have the effect of deterring women from seeking prenatal care. Is that a good argument? Was this policy an appropriate way of encouraging pregnant women to act in a way that did not compromise their babies? For the Fourth Circuit opinion upholding the hospital's policy, see Ferguson v. City of Charleston, 186 F.3d 469 (4th Cir.1999).

Generally, criminal prosecution for maternal drug use has been ultimately unsuccessful. See Reinesto v. Superior Court, 182 Ariz. 190, 894 P.2d 733 (Ariz.App.1995); Johnson v. State, 602 So.2d 1288 (Fla.1992) (reversing a conviction for delivery of a controlled substance from a mother to her child after birth, but before the umbilical cord was severed); State v. Gray, 62 Ohio St.3d 514, 584 N.E.2d 710 (1992); Commonwealth v. Welch, 864 S.W.2d 280 (Ky.1993); People v. Morabito, 151 Misc.2d 259, 580 N.Y.S.2d 843 (City Ct.1992). Compare Louise M. Chan, S.O.S. From the Womb: A Call For New York Legislation Criminalizing Drug Use During Pregnancy, 21 Fordham Urban L.J. 199 (1993) (advocating use of the criminal law) with Patricia Sexton, Imposing Criminal Sanctions on

Pregnant Drug Users: Throwing the Baby Out with the Bath Water, 32 Washburn L.J. 410 (1993) (opposing the use of the criminal law).

c. Civil Commitment and Court Ordered Protective Custody

Finally, the remedy of civil commitment or court ordered protective custody may be available to protect fetuses from abuse by mentally ill, drug abusing, or alcoholic mothers under some state laws that permit commitment to treat these conditions, or that provide for custody of the mother to protect the fetus under some circumstances. Some states have promulgated statutes that provide explicitly that women who put their fetuses at risk may be restrained from doing so by the court. In 1998, for example, following a judicial decision that suggested that there was no legal authority for confining a pregnant woman, State ex. rel. Angela M.W. v. Kruzicki,, 209 Wis.2d 112, 561 N.W.2d 729 (Wis. 1997), the Wisconsin legislature provided that a pregnant woman could be held in custody to protect the fetus:

> An adult expectant mother of an unborn child may be held under [this statute] if the intake worker determines that there is probable cause to believe that the adult expectant mother is within the jurisdiction of the court, to believe that if the adult expectant mother is not held, there is a substantial risk that the physical health of the unborn child, and of the child when born, will be seriously affected or endangered by the adult expectant mothers habitual lack of self-control in the use of alcohol beverages, controlled substances or controlled substance analogs, exhibited to a severe degree, and to believe that the adult expectant mother is refusing or has refused to accept any alcohol or other drug abuse services offered to her or is not making or has not made a good faith effort to participate in any alcohol or other drug abuse services offered to her.

Wis. Stat. Section 48.205. Where do you think pregnant women are held under this statute? Where should they be held—a jail? A hospital? A mental health clinic? At home? South Dakota has promulgated a statute allowing for the brief (2–day) commitment of pregnant women by family members, and court ordered commitment of those same women for up to nine months. S.D. Codified Laws section 34–20A–63 to 70. Are fetuses (and mothers) better protected because of the existence of these laws? What would make them effective? What problems are the most likely to render these laws ineffective? Is the use of the civil commitment or protective custody remedy any less troublesome than the use of the criminal sanction against the mother to protect the fetus? For a fine account of the use of commitment and custody statutes to protect fetuses from their mothers, see Kristen Burgess, Protective Custody: Will it Eradicate Fetal Abuse and Lead to the Perfect Womb?, 35 Houston L. Rev. 227 (1998).

6. What should be done if the generally appropriate commitment and treatment of a drug abusing pregnant woman is inconsistent with the best interest of the fetus? For example, heroin addicts are often "treated" by replacing their heroin addiction with a methadone addiction. Methadone is a safer addiction because its use does not result in the ups and downs brought on by heroin, and its supply and purity can be regulated by medical authorities. On the other hand, it is harder to withdraw from methadone than from heroin, and a fetus may be put at great risk if the pregnant woman switches addictions during the pregnancy. A fetus may also be put at great risk if the pregnant woman withdraws from heroin "cold turkey" during pregnancy.

Should a pregnant heroin addict who wishes to start methadone (or stop taking drugs altogether) be allowed to do so? Should she be encouraged to do so?

How should a doctor legally and ethically treat a pregnant heroin addict? May she tell her patient that she should continue using heroin throughout her pregnancy? Must she tell her that?

Some have suggested that a substantial number of places in drug rehabilitation programs be put aside for pregnant women. With the very long waiting lines for admission to these programs, would this be a good idea? Might it encourage women who are desperate for treatment to get pregnant so they will qualify for expedited assistance?

7. Of course, not all behavior that is unhealthy for the fetus is also illegal for the mother. Consumption of any amount of alcohol during pregnancy may result in fetal alcohol syndrome, which is now the most common known cause of mental retardation at birth in the United States. Is there any reason to distinguish a woman who puts her child at risk of fetal alcohol syndrome from a woman who puts her child at risk through the use of another proscribed drug? For an informative and moving account of fetal alcohol syndrome and its consequences on families and communities, see M. Dorris, The Broken Cord (1989). Author Michael Dorris raised an adopted fetal alcohol syndrome child, and it made him sensitive to the need to protect children who face a lifetime of deprivation due to the addiction of their alcoholic mothers. See In re Smith, 128 Misc.2d 976, 492 N.Y.S.2d 331 (Fam.Ct.1985) (prenatal alcohol use contributed to the birth of a neglected child). See also Claire Dineen, Fetal Alcohol Syndrome: The Legal and Social Responses to its Impact on Native Americans, 70 N. Dak. L.Rev. 1 (1994).

8. In *A.C.* the court appointed a guardian ad litem to represent the fetus. Should courts appoint guardians ad litem in cases that implicate the interests of a fetus? Is there any disadvantage in appointing a guardian ad litem under such circumstances? Does the appointment of such a guardian ad litem (or the failure to appoint one) effectively prejudge the issue of the fetus's standing to participate in the litigation, and, thus, the fetus's interest?

What, exactly, is the role of the guardian ad litem in these cases. Is the guardian ad litem always required to advocate that her client be born alive, even if that means that the client will be born with serious anomalies? Could the guardian ad litem ever argue that the decision ought to rest with the mother?

9. There is another area in which a pregnant woman's decisions have the potential to put the health of her fetus at risk, and that is the workplace. Some employment environments that are safe for workers may not be safe for workers' fetuses. Employers may seek to exclude pregnant women (or even women who may become pregnant) from jobs that could put the fetuses at risk—either because the employers wish to protect the fetuses, or because the employers wish to protect themselves from adverse publicity, increased health insurance costs and potential tort liability. The employee and her fetus may have interests in conflict: the financial advantage and emotional fulfillment of the employee may come at an increased risk of damage to her yet-to-be-born (or even yet-to-be-conceived) child. Should an employer be able to force women in the workplace to choose between ineligibility to work in certain jobs and ineligibility (through sterilization, for example) to conceive children? This issue has received attention almost exclusively where the employee is a woman (i.e., a potential mother) rather than a man (i.e., a potential father) even though occupational hazards to men may affect the health of the fetus as well. Why do you think this is the case?

The United States Supreme Court considered this issue under Title VII of the Civil Rights Act of 1964 in International Union, United Automobile Workers v. Johnson Controls, 499 U.S. 187, 111 S.Ct. 1196, 113 L.Ed.2d 158 (1991). Johnson

Controls had excluded women of child bearing age from its battery manufacturing operation unless they had been sterilized because workers in that process sometimes developed very high levels of lead in their blood. The United States Supreme Court determined that this policy constituted disparate treatment by sex, which could be justified under Title VII only if sex was a bona fide occupational qualification (BFOQ). The court's conclusion was supported by the Pregnancy Discrimination Act of 1978, which defined discrimination "because of or on the basis of pregnancy, childbirth or related medical conditions" as discrimination on the basis of sex. The Court concluded:

> It is no more appropriate for the courts than it is for individual employers to decide whether a woman's reproductive role is more important to herself and her family than her economic role. Congress has left this choice to the woman as hers to make.

10. For a good short summary of the legal issues implicated in cases of fetal-maternal decisionmaking, see J. Robertson, Legal Issues in Prenatal Therapy, 29 Clin. Obstetrics & Gynecology 603 (1986). For particularly clear descriptions of the underlying issues, see Kristen Burgess, Protective Custody: Will it Eradicate Fetal Abuse and Lead to the Perfect Womb?, 35 Houston L. Rev. 227 (1998), and Alice Noble–Allgire, Court–Ordered Caesarian Sections, 10 J. Legal Med. 211 (1989); Also see Alicia Ouellette, New Medical Technology: A Chance to Reexamine Court Ordered Medical Procedures During Pregnancy, 57 Alb. L. Rev. 927 (1994), Dawn Johnsen, Shared Interests: Promoting Healthy Births Without Sacrificing Women's Liberty, 43 Hastings L. J. 569 (1992), Lisa Ikemoto, The Code of Perfect Pregnancy: At the Intersection of the Ideology of Motherhood, the Practice of Defaulting to Science and the Interventionist Mindset of the Law, 53 Ohio State L. J. 1205 (1992), and Dawn Johnsen, The Creation of Fetal Rights: Conflicts with Women's Constitutional Rights to Liberty, Privacy, and Equal Protection, 95 Yale L.J. 599 (1986). For a Canadian perspective on this issue, see Sheilah Martin and Murray Coleman, Judicial Intervention in Pregnancy, 40 McGill L. J. 947 (1995). For a particularly helpful more general perspective, see Bonnie Steinbock, Life Before Birth: The Moral and Legal Status of Embryos and Fetuses (1992) and Nancy Rhoden, The Judge in the Delivery Room: The Emergence of Court–Ordered Cesareans, 74 Calif.L.Rev. 1951 (1986).

For a discussion on the limits of requiring fetal therapy, see Krista Newkirk, State—Compelled Fetal Surgery: The Viability Test is not so Viable, 4 Wm. & Mary J. Women & L. 467 (1998), David Blickenstaff, Defining the Boundaries of Personal Privacy: Is There a Paternal Interest in Compelling Therapeutic Fetal Surgery?, 88 Nw. U. L.Rev. 1157 (1994) and Bonnie Steinbock, Maternal—Fetal Conflict and In Utero Fetal Therapy, 57 Alb.L.Rev. 781 (1994).

Part IV

BIOETHICS

Chapter 17

LEGAL, SOCIAL AND ETHICAL ISSUES IN HUMAN GENETICS

I. INTRODUCTION

To anyone who has even a passing acquaintance with the news, it appears that each week's events have included the discovery of a "new gene" which promises an explanation of any one of a seemingly limitless range of human characteristics. Genes for cystic fibrosis, breast cancer, colon cancer, obesity, homosexuality, and many other conditions, characteristics, behaviors, and personal identities were identified in the 1990s. One magazine seemed to capture it all with a headline on its front cover: "Infidelity—Is It In Your Genes?"

The basic foundations of genetic research arose centuries ago as farmers bred domestic animals and crops to achieve the desired characteristics for productivity and durability. Observation of this manipulation around phenotype (physical characteristic) led to the work of Gregor Mendel, an Austrian monk, who came to be known as the "Father of Genetics" for his work on genetics in the nineteenth century. The first half of the twentieth century carried forward this work by linking genetics to DNA. James Watson and Francis Crick revolutionized genetics when they determined the double helix structure of DNA, with its repeated four bases (adenine, guanine, cytosine and thymine, *aka* A, G, C, and T) in 1953.

Within the past two decades, the field of genetics has "gone molecular." No longer are genes detected and identifiable only through their shadows— the phenotypes or physical expressions of the gene. Scientists are now sequencing or mapping the genome and are able to manipulate this basic material.

The specific cause for the more recent explosion in information is the Human Genome Project (HGP). The HGP is a multi-national project involving sixteen nations. The United States has worked most closely with Great Britain, France and Japan. In the U.S., the project is funded by the National Institutes of Health (through the National Center for Human Genome Research) and the Department of Energy (through the Human Genome Project). The effort was expected to cost approximately $3 billion and to take about 15 years, but is being completed ahead of schedule. The primary goal of the project is to discover and map all 30,000 to 40,000 human genes, which together make up the human genome, and to make the genome itself accessible for biological study.

From the beginning, the new genetics has created hopes and fears. The hope is that the development of knowledge concerning the genetic basis of disease will lead to therapies or other interventions that will relieve human suffering.

Despite the promise, there is a fear that history will repeat itself, for eugenics does not have a happy history. There is a concern that the Supreme Court's tragic misuse (and misunderstanding) of genetics in Buck v. Bell, 274 U.S. 200, 47 S.Ct. 584, 71 L.Ed. 1000 (1927), will be reproduced, especially in light of our often moralistic attitudes toward sickness and the continuing human history of exclusion and discrimination against minorities and the disabled. Even more terrifying is the fear that the pseudo-genetic genocidal campaign in Nazi Germany can occur once again.

What legal issues do you see arising from increased genetic information? Many of the central principles underlying legal issues studied in this course are involved in the social and ethical issues raised by the new genetics. Privacy and confidentiality; informed consent; discrimination; and fairness in risk assessment are all challenged. Even the basic notions of illness and health require re-examination.

Assume that you have been told that you, or your spouse or your child or your siblings or parents have the gene for Huntington's Disease or for breast cancer or for colon cancer or for obesity or for homosexuality or for sickle-cell anemia. What does it mean to have the gene for any of these conditions? Does it predict the future?

Some genetically-related diseases are monogenic; that is they appear to be associated with a single gene. But even with monogenic conditions, which would appear to present the most simple connection between gene and disease, the presence of the gene may not provide a clue as to whether the individual will be severely or moderately affected or will experience no symptoms of the disease at all.

Most of the genes "for" cancer are not monogenic or polygenic (requiring the interaction of more than one gene), but rather are multifactorial. Multifactorial conditions are those in which there is a genetic predisposition, but in which environmental or nongenetic factors are also essential or determinative. Nor are genes necessarily single-effect. Rather, the same gene that is associated with a particular disease may also increase resistance to another. Many diseases involve mutated genes, but not all mutated genes are associated with or cause disease. A mutated gene may not have any health consequences at all. Also, mutations do not occur only prior to birth. Gene mutation may be caused at any time of life, for example, from radiation or virus or by age.

Furthermore, it has been known for decades that someone (a carrier) may have the gene for a particular condition, such as cystic fibrosis or sickle-cell anemia, but not have the disease itself. Carriers bear the burden of the risk of having children affected by the disease itself, often depending on the genetic traits of his or her mate.

The method used to identify a genetic connection to particular conditions may also affect the meaning of a genetic association with a disease or condition. Most of the genetic connections established prior to the advances of the latter part of the last century were based on epidemiological studies of the occurrence of particular characteristics or conditions, rather than by direct identification of the gene itself. An association between genetic trait and disease established by epidemiological studies alone typically cannot predict the presence of the trait in any single individual.

Discoveries of genetic associations with what might be termed nonmedical or nondisease characteristics, including homosexuality or brilliance for example, have been particularly unstable. Such associations are regularly announced and often just as regularly disclaimed.

Because knowledge concerning the nature of the genetic basis for particular human traits evolves so rapidly, often producing conflicting information within a period of months, it is not wise to provide particular examples here. But you might find it useful to do some research on your own. What is the most recent information available concerning the genetic basis for one of the following: Alzheimer's disease; breast cancer (BRCA1 and BRCA2); cystic fibrosis; homosexuality; obesity; colon cancer, for example? By what method was the association established? Is the condition monogenic, polygenic, or multifactorial? Is there a genetic test available? Does detection require testing the family as well as the individual himself or herself? Is the condition more often associated with a particular ethnic group? Does it affect both genders in the same way? Is there a therapy available? See Catherine Baker, Your Genes, Your Choices, (1999), published by the American Association for the Advancement of Science, and available online at http://ehrweb.aaas.org/ her/books/index.html (visited January 6, 2001) for a very basic, understandable description of genetic testing. There are hundreds of sites with educational materials on genetics. A good portal is http://www.nhgri.nih.gov (visited January 6, 2001).

We still operate with an inadequate linguistics for genetics. Does it make a difference if something is called a genetic "trait" as compared to a genetic "condition" or a genetic "disease," "defect," or "anomaly"? Are these medical terms? What judgments enter the decision to view a characteristic as any of these and what impact might the chosen categorization have? Recall the material on sickness and health in the first chapter of this text, especially the case of Katskee v. Blue Cross/Blue Shield of Nebraska, 245 Neb. 808, 515 N.W.2d 645 (Neb.1994). In that case, Sindie Katskee was diagnosed with breast-ovarian carcinoma syndrome, a genetically-based condition. Her health insurance refused to pay for prophylactic surgery on the sole ground that Ms. Katskee was not being treated for an "illness." The court held that Ms. Katskee was ill, even though she experienced no symptoms or limitations and did not have cancer.

What implications might this broad definition of illness have? If Katskee were merely a carrier of a genetically-related disorder, would that also qualify her as being ill? What is the "normal" human genotype? Is it freedom from all genetically-related disorders or deficiencies? Which genetic traits should be fixed, or cured, or removed, if possible? Who decides whether a genetic trait should be remedied? Is a variable definition of illness, one that depends on the reason for the label, useful in genetics or public policy?

II. LEGAL RESPONSES TO PRIVACY, CONFIDENTIALITY, CONSENT AND DISCRIMINATION

From the beginning of the Human Genome Project, government funding was dedicated to the Ethical, Legal, and Social Implications (ELSI) project that would fund studies to explore these issues. Perhaps because of the availability of that substantial funding source, there has been a terrific explosion in the literature addressing the implications of the new genetics as well as a relatively rapid response to identified concerns on the part of state legislatures and the federal government.

As you work with the material in this section, at least one question will certainly appear repeatedly: Is there anything special about genetic information, as compared to other health information, that leads to this level of attention? That requires special treatment in law? Opinions on this question differ.

George Annas refers to human DNA as a "coded future diary" and argues that "the information contained in an individual's genome ... [provides] a basis not only for counseling, but also for stigmatization and discrimination." He argues that genetic information has "unique privacy implications" because the "genetic information is immutable ... and will also provide information about the individual's parents, siblings and children." In regard to DNA databases in particular, Annas cites the power of computer technology and the fear of "large, bureaucratic record-keeping systems." George J. Annas, Privacy Rules for DNA Databanks Protecting Coded Future Diaries, 270 JAMA 2346 (1993). In contrast, Larry Gostin and James Hodge take exception to "genetic exceptionalism" and argue that special rules for genetic information "are often unfair because they treat people facing the same social risks differently based on the biological cause of their otherwise identical health conditions," using breast cancer as an example. Lawrence O. Gostin and James G. Hodge, Jr., Genetic Privacy and the Law: An End to Genetics Exceptionalism, 40 Jurimetrics 21 (1999), part of a Symposium issue on Respecting Genetic Privacy. Mark Rothstein observes that, even if genetic information were unique, it is simply impossible to develop a "working definition" for genetic information as any definition is either too narrow or too broad. Mark A. Rothstein, Why Treating Genetic Information Separately is a Bad Idea, 4 Texas Review of Law and Politics 33 (1998). Still, Dr. Francis Collins, director of the National Human Genome Research Institute at the National Institutes of Health, has asked Congress to take action to prevent discrimination based on the information that genomics will produce. Genetic Discrimination: Leaders in Genetic Code Discoveries Underscore Need for Anti–Discrimination Law, BNA Health Law Reporter, March 2000.

Claims of special treatment for genetic information often reference the history of the social use of genetics, citing the early twentieth century eugenics movement in the United States, the Nazi's pseudo-genetic extermination of Jews, and the seemingly persistent belief in the U.S. in "genetic determinism," in which genetics is viewed as determinative of the course of human development and health. Frequently, this history has had a specific and negative impact on particular groups.

Because of the Mandelian character of genetics, genetic information is likely to have implications for groups. A very recent example of this dynamic among the more recent genetic discoveries is the case of mutations of BRCA1 and 2, tumor-suppressor genes in which particular mutations appear to create a susceptibility to breast and ovarian cancer. When the association between BRCA1 and breast cancer was first identified in 1994, popular reports of the discovery made it appear that the BRCA1 gene itself was the "culprit" and that it was "bad" to have this cancer gene, when actually it is a mutation that is associated with cancer. These reports also created the impression that the presence of the cancer gene accounted for most breast cancer. In fact, most breast cancer is not a hereditary form of cancer–only 5% to 10% of breast cancer is due to a genetic factor. In addition, most women (and men) with mutations of BRCA 1 or 2 never develop cancer. Finally, even now, the actual cancer risks for people with mutations of BRCA1 and 2 are not yet established, although it appears that women with certain mutations who are in high risk families carry a 60% to 85% lifetime risk of breast cancer and a 15% to 40% lifetime risk of ovarian cancer. (Lifetime risks for breast cancer decrease rather than increase with age. In the general population, a female at birth has a 12% lifetime risk for breast cancer, and a woman at age 70 who has not had breast cancer has a lifetime risk of 7%) Katrina Armstrong, et al., Assessing the Risk of Breast Cancer (Review Article), 342 NEJM 564 (Feb. 24, 2000). For one group, however, the association between particular mutations of BRCA1 and 2 and cancer is very powerful. For individuals of Ashkenazi (Eastern European) Jewish descent, the incidence of the identified mutations is approximately 1% (perhaps five to eight times higher than the general population), and almost 90% of hereditary breast cancer (90% of the 5–10%) seem to be associated with certain mutations of the BRCA1 and 2 genes. See Karen H. Rothenberg, Breast Cancer, The Genetic "Quick Fix," and the Jewish Community, 7 Health Matrix 97 (1997), for a description of the response of the Jewish community in the D.C. area where most of the population based research was conducted. Does the differential impact of certain genetic information on particular groups support a claim of special treatment for conditions associated with genetics or with genetic information itself?

The legal and policy issues generated by the potential of the Human Genome Project range from privacy and discrimination through criminal justice through patents and so on. This section examines only selected issues, beginning with the privacy and discrimination concerns, focusing on discrimination in insurance, using examples of state statutes as vehicles for the analysis. Privacy/confidentiality is a primary concern as genetic information becomes more available, and claims for protection for genetic information are often based on concerns about discrimination. These two questions are also the ones that have seen the most statutory activity. The section then considers two particular privacy concerns: the creation of genetic databases that may be used for public health initiatives, research, or criminal investigations, and the claims family members might make on each other in regard to genetic information. Finally, the section concludes with a brief consideration of the ethical and social implications of voluntary genetic testing.

The state statutes below will be used as reference materials for several of the subsections that follow.

CODE OF GEORGIA: GENETIC TESTING

33–54–1 Legislative findings and determinations; intent of chapter.

The General Assembly finds and determines that recent advances in genetic science have led to improvements in the diagnosis, treatment, and understanding of a significant number of human diseases. The General Assembly further finds and declares that:

(1) Genetic information is the unique property of the individual tested;

(2) The use and availability of information concerning an individual obtained through the use of genetic testing techniques may be subject to abuses if disclosed to unauthorized third parties without the willing consent of the individual tested;

(3) To protect individual privacy and to preserve individual autonomy with regard to an individual's genetic information, it is appropriate to limit the use and availability of genetic information; and

(4) The intent of this chapter is to prevent accident and sickness insurance companies, health maintenance organizations, managed care organizations, and other payors from using information derived from genetic testing to deny access to accident and sickness insurance.

33–54–2 Definitions.

As used in this chapter, the term:

(1) "Genetic testing" means laboratory tests of human DNA or chromosomes for the purpose of identifying the presence or absence of inherited alterations in genetic material or genes which are associated with a disease or illness that is asymptomatic at the time of testing and that arises solely as a result of such abnormality in genes or genetic material. For purposes of this chapter, genetic testing shall not include routine physical measurements; chemical, blood, and urine analysis; tests for abuse of drugs; and tests for the presence of the human immunodeficiency virus.

(2) "Insurer" means an insurer, a fraternal benefit society, a nonprofit medical service corporation, a health care corporation, a health maintenance corporation, or a self-insured health plan not subject to the exclusive jurisdiction of the Employee Retirement Income Security Act of 1974, 29 U.S.C. Section 1001, et seq.

33–54–3 Purpose of testing; consent required; confidential and privileged information.

(a) Except as otherwise provided in this chapter, genetic testing may only be conducted to obtain information for therapeutic or diagnostic purposes. Genetic testing may not be conducted without the prior written consent of the person to be tested.

(b) Information derived from genetic testing shall be confidential and privileged and may be released only to the individual tested and to persons specifically authorized by such individual to receive the information. Any insurer that possesses information derived from genetic testing may not release the information to any third party without the explicit written consent of the individual tested. Information derived from genetic testing may not be sought by any insurer as defined in Code Section 33–54–2.

33–54–4 Prohibited use of information.

Any insurer that receives information derived from genetic testing may not use the information for any nontherapeutic purpose.

33–54–6 Use of information for scientific research purposes authorized.

Notwithstanding the provisions of Code Sections 33–54–3 and 33–54–4, any research facility may conduct genetic testing and may use the information derived from genetic testing for scientific research purposes so long as the identity of any individual tested is not disclosed to any third party, except that the individual's identity may be disclosed to the individual's physician with the consent of the individual.

33–54–7 Applicability of chapters.

This chapter shall not apply to a life insurance policy, disability income policy, accidental death or dismemberment policy, medicare supplement policy, long-term care insurance policy, credit insurance policy, specified disease policy, hospital indemnity policy, blanket accident and sickness policy, franchise policy issued on an individual basis to members of an association, limited accident policy, health insurance policy written as a part of workers' compensation equivalent coverage, or other similar limited accident and sickness policy.

CALIFORNIA CIVIL CODE: CONFIDENTIALITY OF MEDICAL INFORMATION

56.17. Genetic test results; unlawful disclosure; written authorization; penalties

(a) This section shall apply to the disclosure of genetic test results contained in an applicant or enrollee's medical records by a health care service plan.

[Sections (b), (c), and (d) provide for civil fines and payment of damages for the disclosure of "results of a test for a genetic characteristic to any third party, in a manner that identifies or provides identifying characteristics, of the person to whom the test results apply, except pursuant to a written authorization, as described in subdivision (g)."]

(g) The applicant's "written authorization," as used in this section, shall satisfy the following requirements:

(1) Is written in plain language.

(2) Is dated and signed by the individual or a person authorized to act on behalf of the individual.

(3) Specifies the types of persons authorized to disclose information about the individual.

(4) Specifies the nature of the information authorized to be disclosed.

(5) States the name or functions of the persons or entities authorized to receive the information.

(6) Specifies the purposes for which the information is collected.

(7) Specifies the length of time the authorization shall remain valid.

(8) Advises the person signing the authorization of the right to receive a copy of the authorization. Written authorization is required for each separate disclosure of the test results.

* * *

(i) For purposes of this section, "genetic characteristic" has the same meaning as that set forth in subdivision (d) of Section 1374.7 of the Health and Safety Code.

CALIFORNIA HEALTH AND SAFETY CODE: INSURANCE

1374.7. Genetic disability characteristics; discrimination in enrollment terms, conditions, benefits, rates or commissions.

(a) No [health care service or self-insured employee welfare] plan shall refuse to enroll any person or accept any person as a subscriber after appropriate application on the basis of a person's genetic characteristics that may, under some circumstances, be associated with disability in that person or that person's offspring. No plan shall require a higher rate or charge, or offer or provide different terms, conditions, or benefits, on the basis of a person's genetic characteristics that may, under some circumstances, be associated with disability in that person or that person's offspring.

(b) No plan shall seek information about a person's genetic characteristics for any nontherapeutic purpose.

(c) No discrimination shall be made in the fees or commissions of a solicitor or solicitor firm for an enrollment or a subscription or the renewal of an enrollment or subscription of any person on the basis of a person's genetic characteristics that may, under some circumstances, be associated with disability in that person or that person's offspring.

(d) "Genetic characteristics" as used in this section means any of the following:

(1) Any scientifically or medically identifiable gene or chromosome, or combination or alteration thereof, that is known to be a cause of a disease or disorder in a person or his or her offspring, or that is determined to be associated with a statistically increased risk of development of a disease or disorder, and that is presently not associated with any symptoms of any disease or disorder.

(2) Inherited characteristics that may derive from the individual or family member, that are known to be a cause of a disease or disorder in a person or his or her offspring, or that are determined to be associated with a

statistically increased risk of development of a disease or disorder, and that are presently not associated with any symptoms of any disease or disorder.

CALIFORNIA INSURANCE CODE

10148. Test for presence of genetic characteristic for determination of insurability.

No [life or disability insurance plan] shall require a test for the presence of a genetic characteristic for the purpose of determining insurability other than for those policies that are contingent on review or testing for other diseases or medical conditions. In those cases, the test shall be done in accordance with the informed consent and privacy protection provisions [of California law].

A. Focus on Privacy

Executive Order 13145

February 8, 2000

* * *

1–201.

(d) Genetic test means the analysis of human DNA, RNA, chromosomes, proteins, or certain metabolites in order to detect disease-related genotypes or mutations. Tests for metabolites fall within the definition of "genetic tests" when an excess or deficiency of the metabolites indicates the presence of a mutation or mutations. The conducting of metabolic tests by a department or agency that are not intended to reveal the presence of a mutation shall not be considered a violation of this order, regardless of the results of the tests. Test results revealing a mutation shall, however, be subject to the provisions of this order.

(e) Protected genetic information.

(1) In general, protected genetic information means:

(A) information about an individual's genetic tests;

(B) information about the genetic tests of an individual's family members; or

(C) information about the occurrence of a disease, or medical condition or disorder in family members of the individual.

(2) Information about an individual's current health status (including information about sex, age, physical exams, and chemical, blood, or urine analyses) is not protected genetic information unless it is described in subparagraph (1).

1–202.

(c) The employing department or agency shall not request, require, collect, or purchase protected genetic information with respect to an employee, or information about a request for or the receipt of genetic services by such employee.

(d) The employing department or agency shall not disclose protected genetic information with respect to an employee, or information about a request for or the receipt of genetic services by an employee except:

(1) to the employee who is the subject of the information, at his or her request;

(2) to an occupational or other health researcher, if the research conducted complies with [federal regulations on research];

(3) if required by a Federal statute, congressional subpoena, or an order issued by a court of competent jurisdiction, except that if the subpoena or court order was secured without the knowledge of the individual to whom the information refers, the employer shall provide the individual with adequate notice to challenge the subpoena or court order, unless the subpoena or court order also imposes confidentiality requirements; or

(4) to executive branch officials investigating compliance with this order, if the information is relevant to the investigation.

(e) The employing department or agency shall not maintain protected genetic information or information about a request for or the receipt of genetic services in general personnel files; such information shall be treated as confidential medical records and kept separate from personnel files.

1–301.   The following exceptions shall apply . . . .

(a) The employing department or agency may request or require [genetic information] with respect to an applicant who has been given a conditional offer of employment or to an employee if:

(1) the request or requirement is consistent with the Rehabilitation Act and other applicable law;

(2) the information obtained is to be used exclusively to assess whether further medical evaluation is needed to diagnose a current disease, or medical condition or disorder, or under the terms of section 1–301(b) of this order;

(3) such current disease, or medical condition or disorder could prevent the applicant or employee from performing the essential functions of the position held or desired; and

(4) [genetic information] will not be disclosed to persons other than medical personnel involved in or responsible for assessing whether further medical evaluation is needed to diagnose a current disease, or medical condition or disorder, or under the terms of section 1–301(b) of this order.

(b) The employing department or agency may request, collect, or purchase protected genetic information with respect to an employee, or any information about a request for or receipt of genetic services by such employee if:

(1) the employee uses genetic or health care services provided by the employer (other than use pursuant to section 1–301(a) of this order);

(2) the employee who uses the genetic or health care services has provided prior knowing, voluntary, and written authorization to the employer to collect protected genetic information;

(3) the person who performs the genetic or health care services does not disclose protected genetic information to anyone except to the employee who uses the services for treatment of the individual; for program evaluation or assessment; for compiling and analyzing information in anticipation of or for use in a civil or criminal legal proceeding; or, for payment or accounting

purposes, to verify that the service was performed (but in such cases the genetic information itself cannot be disclosed);

(4) such information is not used in violation of . . . this order.

Notes and Questions

1. Executive Order 13145 is directed at prohibiting employment discrimination against federal employees. Why does it focus so much on restricting access to genetic information? Why not allow the employer broad access to the information, but require that it not be used to discriminate?

2. State legislatures have taken the lead in enacting legislation concerning genetic privacy. The U.S. Congress has considered legislation at each of its sessions in recent years, but has not yet enacted a statute specifically governing privacy concerns in genetics. On December 28, 2000, however, the Department of Health and Human Services, under a default provision of the Health Insurance Portability and Accountability Act, issued final regulations governing the confidentiality and privacy of medical records. 65 Fed. Reg. 82462 (Dec. 28, 2000). See discussion in Chapter 5. U.S. Congress may consider action in response to this regulation because of the projected cost of compliance and the opposition of provider groups. At this point, it seems that the regulations will not pre-empt state medical privacy statutes, and it is the position of HHS that "stronger" state laws will continue to apply.

3. Assuming that there is a reason to provide heightened protections to genetic information, do the Georgia and California statutes and the Executive Order use the correct definitions? Are they broad enough to reach all information that might reveal genetically-based medical conditions? Is it practical to segregate genetic information from other health information in a medical record? See Mark A. Rothstein, Why Treating Genetic Information Separately Is a Bad Idea, *supra*. The final rule under HIPAA, cited *supra*, specifically rejects approaches that would treat some types of medical information, and specifically genetic information, differently. See also, Mark A. Rothstein (ed.), Genetic Secrets: Protecting Privacy and Confidentiality in the Genetic Era (1997).

4. Medical records are widely viewed as private and confidential though they are usually neither. With increased computerization of medical records and increased linkages among hospitals, physicians and insurers, access to individualized health information is quite broad. In addition, payment systems for health care services have long required that individual and identifiable medical information be submitted for payment for services and have collected and used this information for a variety of purposes. On privacy of medical records generally, see Lawrence O. Gostin, Health Information Privacy, 80 Cornell L.J. 451 (1995). See the Department's prologue to the final rule on privacy of medical records for an extensive description of access to medical information. 65 Fed. Reg. 82462 (Dec. 28, 2000).

5. Both the Georgia and California statutes prohibit payer disclosure of the information without consent. Is consent an adequate protection of privacy interests? Have you signed a form to release information to your insurer for payment recently? See, Lori B. Andrews, Confidentiality of Genetic Information in the Workplace, 17 Am. J. of Law & Med. 75 (1991). Can you think of a better way to protect the information?

SAFER v. PACK

Superior Court of New Jersey, Appellate Division, 1996.
291 N.J.Super. 619, 677 A.2d 1188.

KESTIN, J.A.D.

Plaintiffs appeal from the trial court's order dismissing their complaint and denying their cross-motion for partial summary judgment as to liability only. We reverse that portion of the order dismissing the complaint and affirm the denial of plaintiffs' motion.

Donna Safer's claim arises from the patient-physician relationship in the 1950s and 1960s between her father, Robert Batkin, a resident of New Jersey, and Dr. George T. Pack, also a resident of New Jersey, who practiced medicine and surgery in New York City and treated Mr. Batkin there. It is alleged that Dr. Pack specialized in the treatment and removal of cancerous tumors and growths.

In November 1956, Mr. Batkin was admitted to the hospital with a pre-operative diagnosis of retroperitoneal cancer. A week later, Dr. Pack performed a total colectomy and an ileosigmoidectomy for multiple polyposis of the colon with malignant degeneration in one area. The discharge summary noted the finding in a pathology report of the existence of adenocarcinoma developing in an intestinal polyp, and diffuse intestinal polyposis "from one end of the colon to the other." Dr. Pack continued to treat Mr. Batkin postoperatively.

In October 1961, Mr. Batkin was again hospitalized. Dr. Pack performed an ileoabdominal perineal resection with an ileostomy. The discharge summary reported pathology findings of "ulcerative adenocarcinoma of colon Grade II with metastases to Levels II and III" and "adenomatous polyps." Dr. Pack again continued to treat Mr. Batkin postoperatively. He also developed a physician-patient relationship with Mrs. Batkin relative to the diagnosis and treatment of a vaginal ulcer.

In December 1963, Mr. Batkin was hospitalized once again at Dr. Pack's direction. The carcinoma of the colon had metastasized to the liver with secondary jaundice and probable retroperitoneal disease causing pressure on the sciatic nerve plexus. After some treatment, Mr. Batkin died on January 3, 1964, at forty-five years of age. Donna was ten years old at the time of her father's death. Her sister was seventeen.

In February 1990, Donna Safer, then thirty-six years of age and newly married, residing in Connecticut, began to experience lower abdominal pain. Examinations and tests revealed a cancerous blockage of the colon and multiple polyposis. In March, Ms. Safer underwent a total abdominal colectomy with ileorectal anastomosis. A primary carcinoma in the sigmoid colon was found to extend through the serosa of the bowel and multiple polyps were seen throughout the entire bowel. Because of the detection of additional metastatic adenocarcinoma and carcinoma, plaintiff's left ovary was also removed. Between April 1990 and mid–1991, Ms. Safer underwent chemotherapy treatment.

In September 1991, plaintiffs obtained Robert Batkin's medical records, from which they learned that he had suffered from polyposis. Their complaint was filed in March 1992, alleging a violation of duty (professional negligence) on the part of Dr. Pack in his failure to warn of the risk to Donna Safer's health.

Plaintiffs contend that multiple polyposis is a hereditary condition that, if undiscovered and untreated, invariably leads to metastatic colorectal cancer. They contend, further, that the hereditary nature of the disease was known at the time Dr. Pack was treating Mr. Batkin and that the physician was required, by medical standards then prevailing, to warn those at risk so that they might have the benefits of early examination, monitoring, detection and treatment, that would provide opportunity to avoid the most baneful consequences of the condition.

The summary judgment proceeding in the trial court was based upon a scanty record, largely comprised of hospital records. Dr. Pack himself had died in 1969; none of his individual records were before the court. The reports of the parties' medical experts and a deposition of plaintiffs' expert were submitted. Ida Batkin, Donna Safer's mother, had also given a deposition in which she testified, among other details, that neither her husband nor Dr. Pack had ever told her that Mr. Batkin suffered from cancer; and that, throughout the courses of surgery and treatment, Dr. Pack advised her that he was treating a "blockage" or an unspecified "infection". On the one or two occasions when Mrs. Batkin inquired of Dr. Pack whether the "infection" would affect her children, she was told not to worry.

In dismissing, the trial court held that a physician had no "legal duty to warn a child of a patient of a genetic risk.[ ]" In the absence of any evidence whether Dr. Pack had warned Mr. Batkin to provide information concerning his disease for the benefit of his children, the motion judge "assume[d] that Dr. Pack did not tell Robert Batkin of the genetic disease."

The motion judge's reasoning proceeded from the following legal premise: "[i]n order for a doctor to have a duty to warn, there must be a patient/physician relationship or circumstances requiring the protection of the public health or the community [at] large." Finding no physician-patient relationship between Dr. Pack and his patient's daughter Donna, the court then held genetically transmissible diseases to differ from contagious or infectious diseases or threats of harm in respect of the duty to warn, because "the harm is already present within the non-patient child, as opposed to being introduced, by a patient who was not warned to stay away. The patient is taking no action in which to cause the child harm."

* * *

The Florida Supreme Court has since dealt with the issue [in] Pate v. Threlkel, 661 So.2d 278 (1995). Because the case had initially been decided on defendants' motions to dismiss the complaint for failure to state a cause of action, the Supreme Court was required to accept as true the [plaintiffs'] allegations that pursuant to the prevailing standard of care, the health care providers were under a duty to warn [the patient] of the importance of testing her children for [the genetically transmissible] carcinoma. [ ]

The court held:

* * *

... Our holding should not be read to require the physician to warn the patient's children of the disease. In most instances the physician is prohibited from disclosing the patient's medical condition to others except with the patient's permission. See § 455.241(2), Fla.Stat. (1989). Moreover, the patient ordinarily can be expected to pass on the warning. To require the physician to seek out and warn various members of the patient's family would often be difficult or impractical and would place too heavy a burden upon the physician. Thus, we emphasize that in any circumstances in which the physician has a duty to warn of a genetically transferable disease, that duty will be satisfied by warning the patient. [Pate v. Threlkel, supra, 661 So.2d at 282.]

Because the issue before us arose on a motion for summary judgment, we, too, are obliged to accept plaintiffs' proffer through their medical expert that the prevailing standard of care at the time Dr. Pack treated Mr. Batkin required the physician to warn of the known genetic threat. The legal standard of care, knowledge and skill is that which is "ordinarily possessed and exercised in similar situations by the average member of the profession practicing in the field." [ ] Whether the conduct of a practitioner in established circumstances at a particular time comported with prevailing standards of care is preeminently a question to be determined by the finder of fact, not an issue of law to be resolved by the court. [ ] Where, as here, a genuine issue of fact in this regard is presented, the matter is not amenable to resolution on summary judgment. [ ]

Whether a legal duty exists is, however, a matter of law. [ ] We see no impediment, legal or otherwise, to recognizing a physician's duty to warn those known to be at risk of avoidable harm from a genetically transmissible condition. In terms of foreseeability especially, there is no essential difference between the type of genetic threat at issue here and the menace of infection, contagion or a threat of physical harm. [ ] The individual or group at risk is easily identified, and substantial future harm may be averted or minimized by a timely and effective warning.

The motion judge's view of this case as one involving an unavoidable genetic condition gave too little significance to the proffered expert view that early monitoring of those at risk can effectively avert some of the more serious consequences a person with multiple polyposis might otherwise experience. We cannot conclude either, as the trial court did, that Dr. Pack breached no duty because avoidable harm to Donna was not foreseeable, i.e., "that Dr. Pack's conduct did not create a 'foreseeable zone of risk.'" Such a determination would ignore the presumed state of medical knowledge at the time....

Although an overly broad and general application of the physician's duty to warn might lead to confusion, conflict or unfairness in many types of circumstances, we are confident that the duty to warn of avertible risk from genetic causes, by definition a matter of familial concern, is sufficiently narrow to serve the interests of justice. Further, it is appropriate, for reasons already expressed by our Supreme Court, [ ] that the duty be seen as owed not only to the patient himself but that it also "extend[s] beyond the interests of a patient to members of the immediate family of the patient who may be adversely affected by a breach of that duty." [ ] We need not decide, in the present posture of this case, how, precisely, that duty is to be discharged, especially with respect to young children who may be at risk, except to require that reasonable steps be taken to assure that the information reaches those likely to be affected or is made available for their benefit. We are aware of no direct evidence that has been developed concerning the nature of the communications between physician and patient regarding Mr. Batkin's disease: what Dr. Pack did or did not disclose; the advice he gave to Mr. Batkin, if any, concerning genetic factors and what ought to have been done in respect of those at risk; and the conduct or expressed preferences of Mr. Batkin in response thereto. There may be enough from Mrs. Batkin's testimony and other evidence for inferences to be drawn, however.

We decline to hold as the Florida Supreme Court did in Pate v. Threlkel, [ ] that, in all circumstances, the duty to warn will be satisfied by informing the patient. It may be necessary, at some stage, to resolve a conflict between the physician's broader duty to warn and his fidelity to an expressed preference of the patient that nothing be said to family members about the details of the disease. We cannot know presently, however, whether there is any likelihood that such a conflict may be shown to have existed in this matter or, if it did, what its qualities might have been. As the matter is currently constituted, it is as likely as not that no such conflict will be shown to have existed and that the only evidence on the issue will be Mrs. Batkin's testimony, including that she received no information, despite specific inquiry, that her children were at risk. We note, in addition, the possible existence of some offsetting evidence that Donna was rectally examined as a young child, suggesting that the risk to her had been disclosed.

This case implicates serious and conflicting medical, social and legal policies, many aptly identified in Sonia M. Suter, Whose Genes Are These Anyway? Familial Conflicts Over Access to Genetic Information, 91 Mich. L.Rev. 1854 (1993) and in other sources ... Some such policy considerations may need to be addressed in ultimately resolving this case. For example, if evidence is produced that will permit the jury to find that Dr. Pack received instructions from his patient not to disclose details of the illness or the fact of genetic risk, the court will be required to determine whether, as a matter of law, there are or ought to be any limits on physician-patient confidentiality, especially after the patient's death where a risk of harm survives the patient, as in the case of genetic consequences. See generally Janet A. Kobrin, Confidentiality of Genetic Information, 30 UCLA L.Rev. 1283 (1983).

Issues of fact remain to be resolved, as well. What was the extent of Donna's risk, for instance? We are led to understand from the experts' reports that the risk of multiple polyposis was significant and that, upon detection, an early full colectomy, i.e., an excision of her entire colon, may well have been the treatment of choice to avoid resultant cancer—including metastasis, the loss of other organs and the rigors of chemotherapy. Full factual development may, however, cast a different light on these issues of fact and others.

Difficult damage issues portend also. Not the least of these will involve distinguishing between the costs of the medical surveillance that would have followed a timely and effective warning, and the costs of medical care attributable to any breach of duty that may be found to have occurred. [ ]

Because of the necessarily limited scope of our consideration, we have highlighted only a few of the potentially troublesome issues presented by this case. Such questions are best conceived and considered in the light of a fully developed record rather than in the abstract.

* * *

Notes and Questions

1. What is the scope of the duty in *Safer* as compared to *Pate*? Is the duty established in *Safer* or in *Pate* consistent with the Georgia or California statute? How would you advise an individual physician, a health plan or a hospital in satisfying this legal duty in a practical manner? Should the prohibition on disclosure of genetic information without the patient's consent in the California and Georgia statutes apply to disclosure to family members as well? Should physicians be prohibited from informing family members? Should they be required to do so? See, Ellen Wright Clayton, What Should the Law Say About Disclosure of Genetic Information to Relatives?, 1 Journal of Health Care Law and Policy 373 (1998), part of a Symposium on Testing and Telling?: Implications for Genetic Privacy, Family Disclosure and the Law.

2. Ms. Safer was a young child at the time of her father's death. Is it appropriate to inform a child of his or her genetic characteristics, especially those that might predict disease or an increased susceptibility to disease or developmental limitations or capacities? Lainie Friedman Ross and Margaret R. Moon, Ethical Issues in Genetic Testing of Children, Am. J. of Diseases of Children (Sep. 2000). See also, Janet L. Dolgin, Choice, Tradition, and the New Genetics: The Fragmentation of the Ideology of Family, 32 Conn.L.Rev. 521 (2000), arguing that the cases depart from traditional concepts of family and privacy; Diane E. Hoffmann and Eric A. Wufsberg, Testing Children for Genetic Predispositions: Is It in Their Best Interest?, 23 J. of L., Med. & Ethics 331 (1995).

3. Was the Florida court more right than the New Jersey court in holding that the duty is satisfied by informing the patient only? Are there any circumstances in which the patient may not want his or her parents, siblings, spouse or children to know of a genetically-based condition?

4. Would the duty established in New Jersey extend to other situations or is it limited to situations in which there is avoidable physical harm? If a physician, in the course of testing parents and child for a genetically-based medical condition, discovers that the one who believes he is the father cannot possibly be so, should he or she tell the man? Must the doctor tell him? Should the doctor tell the mother? If the "child" is an adult who is making reproductive decisions himself or herself, does that child have a right to know? Consider the following problem.

Problem: The Family

Ibrahim Abdul Salaam decided to seek genetic testing to determine whether he was a carrier of the sickle cell trait when he and his wife, Sarai, who are both African American, decided to have children. Several of his and Mrs. Salaam's relatives have been afflicted with sickle-cell disease. Mr. Salaam was assured by the testing physician that the testing was simple and painless, and that the results would be confidential. The genetic screen for sickle-cell trait came back positive—i.e., Mr. Salaam is a carrier of the recessive trait for sickle cell anemia.

While Mr. Salaam was discussing the results of the test with his physician, he mentioned that his sister was recently married, and that her husband knows that he is a carrier for sickle-cell trait. The physician suggested that she be told of her brother's test result because of the increased chance that she, too, could be a carrier. Mr. Salaam decided against telling his sister because he did not want others in his family to know about his carrier status. As he pointed out to his physician, he did not intend to tell even his wife because his family is Islamic and neither his wife nor his sister would ever consider amniocentesis or abortion; he was merely seeking some personal reassurance (which he did not get, of course) through his own test.

Is Mr. Salaam or his physician obliged to provide information about his sickle cell carrier status to his wife? To his sister? Is the physician permitted to provide this information to Mr. Salaam's wife or sister without his permission?

B. Focus On Discrimination

Problem: Insurance Decisions

In each of the following cases, evaluate the insurer's decision under the Georgia and California statutes.

a.   Arlo has applied for health insurance. His father Woody died in his mid–50s from Huntington's Disease, a genetically-based disease which is usually characterized by onset in the individual's 40's or 50's and which is invariably fatal. Based only on his father having had Huntington's, Arlo has a 50% chance of developing the disease, although a genetic test is available which would confirm whether Arlo will in fact develop the disease. Arlo is 39 and has not been tested for the gene because he does not want to know. The insurer knows of Arlo's family history from insurance claims filed by Arlo's father for care during his illness. The claims had been placed in the Medical Information Bureau by Woody's insurer, and as a member of the MIB, Arlo's insurer has access to these claims. May the insurer legally deny Arlo coverage due to his risk of Huntington's?

b.   May the insurer deny coverage, but inform Arlo that it will reconsider if Arlo can produce evidence that he does not have the gene for Huntington's?

c.   Assume that Arlo has decided to be tested, and that the test has revealed that he does not have the gene for Huntington's and so will not develop that disease. May Arlo have the advantage of that result, and may the insurer reverse its earlier decision?

d.   If Arlo has been tested and the test has revealed that he does have the gene for Huntington's, how should he answer the insurance application questions concerning whether he has any known illness or disease at the time of the application?

e.   Judith's grandmother, mother and sister all died of breast cancer at an early age. At the time of their deaths, Judith was only a young teenager, but her aunt told her that she should make sure that she had very frequent physical examinations to catch the condition earlier than did her relatives. Although she followed her aunt's advice, Judith now has breast cancer herself, and her treatment for the cancer has disabled her. She has applied for payments under the partial and total disability insurance policy she purchased some years ago. The insurer has denied her claim relying on the following clause: "The policy does not cover disabilities caused by medical conditions for which medical advice, diagnosis, care, or treatment had been recommended or received prior to the purchase of the policy." Is the insurer's denial illegal under either state's statute?

f. Mark's and Mary's first child died of cystic fibrosis at the age of 16. Because of the child's CF, it is clear that Mary and Mark both carry the cystic fibrosis gene (assuming that they are the genetic parents of the child). There is a 25% risk that any one of their children will have cystic fibrosis, although Mark and Mary will never develop the disease themselves. May the insurer deny health coverage to Mark and Mary? Could the insurer condition coverage on Mark's and Mary's consent to prenatal genetic screening?

Notes and Questions

1. Are there differences among health insurance, life insurance, and disability insurance that might justify different legal standards? In each scenario, would it make a difference as a matter of policy or law if the insurer did not deny coverage but charged higher rates?

2. Insurance practices in the United States generally base the price and availability of coverage on the health status of the insured individual or group. (See Chapter 8 for a complete discussion of insurance regulation, pricing and availability.) Why would genetics raise special issues? Or does it? Is a prohibition against denial of coverage based on genetic information unfair to persons with other medical conditions? Does the scope of the definition of genetic information matter? (The federal Health Insurance Portability and Accountability Act, discussed in Chapter 9 prohibits group health plans, narrowly defined, from basing eligibility on an individual's health status, including genetic information, and does not treat genetic conditions differently from other medical conditions. The Americans with Disabilities Act, discussed in Chapter 9, also prohibits discrimination in insurance.) There have been many projects looking specifically at the issue of genetics and insurance. One of the most prominent groups recommended that the entire structure of the health insurance system in the U.S. be changed rather than providing for special treatment for genetically related conditions. See, NIH–DOE Working Group on Ethical, Legal, and Social Implications of Human Genome Research, Genetic Information and Health Insurance: Report of the Task Force on Genetic Information and Insurance (NIH Pub. No. 93–3686, May 10, 1993).

3. Although fears of uninsurability have driven much of the concern over genetic discrimination, there is some evidence that insurers do not yet, and perhaps will not, use genetic information in insurance decisions. See Mark A. Hall, Legal Rules and Industry Norms: The Impact of Laws Restricting Health Insurers' Use of Genetic Information, 40 Jurimetrics 93 (1999). But see, Governor Signs Legislation Barring Insurers From Using Genetic Tests, BNA Health Law Reporter, May 8, 1997, describing insurers' statements that they would refuse to issue long-term care and disability coverage under the new statute. As of August 1999, at least 38 states had enacted legislation prohibiting some health insurers from using genetic information in insurance decisions. See chart available at http://www.nhgri.nih.gov/Policy_and_public_affairs/Legislation/insure.htm (visited January 8, 2001).

4. Genetic discrimination in employment is frequently identified as a substantial risk of increased genetic information. See, Mark A. Rothstein, Genetic Discrimination in Employment, 29 Hous. L. Rev. 23 (1992). The Executive Order excerpted above regulates the use of genetic information in federal employment. Several states have enacted statutes regulating the use of genetic information by other employers. See, e.g., Mo. Rev. Stat. S 375.1306. The Americans with Disabilities Act is believed to cover decisions based on genetic conditions. See,

Equal Employment Opportunity Commission Compliance Manual, § 902.8, classifying asymptomatic genetic conditions as disabilities because persons with such traits may be regarded as having a disability. The EEOC's guidance uses the illustration of a genetic trait associated with susceptibility to colon cancer as an illustration. But see, Laura F. Rothstein, Genetic Discrimination: Why Bragdon Does Not Ensure Protection, 3 J. Health Care L. and Pol. 330 (2000). See also, Chapter 12.

C. Creating DNA Databases

MAYFIELD, III v. DALTON

United States District Court, District of Hawai'i, 1995.
901 F.Supp. 300.

Samuel P. King, Senior District Judge.

* * *

Beginning with Operation Desert Storm in 1991, the United States military has used DNA analysis to help with identification of soldiers' remains. Such analysis provides a means of identifying remains too badly damaged for identification through dental records or fingerprints. Identification is made by comparing DNA taken from the remains with a DNA sample previously taken from the decedent or his or her biological relatives.

Because of problems with obtaining reliable DNA samples during the Gulf War, the Department of Defense ("DOD") began a program to collect and store reference specimens of DNA from members of the active duty and reserve armed forces. That way, the reference samples would be available for use in identifying remains in future conflicts. The DOD DNA Registry, a program within the Armed Forces Institute of Pathology, was established pursuant to a December 16, 1991 memorandum of the deputy secretary of defense. Under this program, DNA specimens are collected from active duty and reserve military personnel upon their enlistment, reenlistment, or preparation for operational deployment. The military's goal is to obtain specimens from all active and reserve personnel by the year 2001.

The specimens consist of two small samples of dried blood stored on cards and a sample of epithelial cells taken from the inside of the subject's cheek using a cotton swab. One bloodstain card is sealed and stored in the service member's military health record, while the other bloodstain card and the swab sample are sent to the DOD DNA Repository. Once received by the repository, the bloodstain card is vacuum sealed, assigned a number and bar code, and stored in a refrigerated chamber. The swab sample is assigned an identical code and stored in alcohol. The specimens are to be stored in the repository for 75 years and then destroyed.

According to the military, except for a limited number of "quality assurance" tests in which the DNA is typed to ensure that the repository's storage and analytical mechanisms are working properly, DNA is not extracted from the samples unless and until there is a need for it to assist in the identification of human remains.

Also according to the military, access to the repository facility, computer system and the samples themselves is strictly limited. Specimens stored in the repository are not to be used for a purpose other than remains identification unless a request, routed through the civilian secretary of the appropriate military service, is approved by the assistant secretary of defense for health affairs. The Government notes that no such request from this program has ever been approved, though it is unclear how many, if any, such requests have been made.

Plaintiffs are members of the United States Marine Corps assigned to Company B, 1st Radio Battalion, Marine Forces Pacific. Scheduled to deploy in January 1995, the two were ordered to provide specimens for the DNA repository. Plaintiffs refused to do so, and each was charged with violation of an order from a superior commissioned officer. On May 23, 1995, the military judge in Plaintiffs' Court Martial dismissed the charges, holding that the regulations underlying the DNA Repository program were not punitive and thus no disciplinary action could be taken for refusal to provide the specimens. The Marine Corps has appealed the military judge's decision.

DISCUSSION

A. Plaintiffs' Constitutional Claims

Plaintiffs first allege that the collection, storage and use of DNA samples taken without their consent violates their "rights to freedom of expression, privacy, and due process under the First, Ninth, and Fifth Amendments to the United States Constitution, inter alia." In their moving papers and argument, however, Plaintiffs rely primarily on the Fourth Amendment to make their case for a constitutional violation.

The law is well-established that the Government's compulsory taking of blood and other bodily fluid or tissue samples constitutes a "seizure" subject to scrutiny under the Fourth Amendment. See Schmerber v. California, 384 U.S. 757, 86 S.Ct. 1826, 16 L.Ed.2d 908 (1966). However, the Fourth Amendment prohibits only "unreasonable" seizures. The Court in Schmerber upheld a conviction for driving under the influence based in part on test results from a blood sample taken without the petitioner's consent. The court found the taking of the blood sample "reasonable" where there was probable cause that the petitioner was intoxicated and a delay to obtain a warrant might have resulted in a loss of evidence.

Plaintiffs herein suggest that Schmerber established a rule that the Government may not compel a subject to give a blood sample in the absence of a judicial warrant issued upon a showing of probable cause. The court made no such holding, however. What it did say was that it found nothing inherently unreasonable in the test chosen to measure the petitioner's blood alcohol level, noting that blood tests "are a commonplace in these days of periodic physical examination ... and ... for most people the procedure involves virtually no risk, trauma or pain." Schmerber, 384 U.S. at 771, 86 S.Ct. at 1836.

* * *

The taking of blood samples and oral swabs for the purpose of remains identification presents, on its face, a far less intrusive infringement of Plaintiffs' Fourth Amendment privacy rights than the blood testing in either Schmerber [or Skinner v. Railway Labor Executives' Ass'n, 489 U.S. 602, 109

S.Ct. 1402, 103 L.Ed.2d 639 (1989) (upholding federally mandated drug and alcohol testing for railway workers) or National Treasury Employees Union v. Von Raab, 489 U.S. 656, 109 S.Ct. 1384, 103 L.Ed.2d 685 (1989) (upholding drug tests for Customs Service employees)]. The blood test at issue in Schmerber involved a seizure of evidence to be used in a possible criminal prosecution. In Skinner and Von Raab, blood, urine and breath tests were used to detect the illegal or illicit use of drugs or alcohol, the confirmation of which could be grounds for disciplinary action or criminal sanctions.

In the instant case, the blood and tissue samples at issue are not to be used as evidence against Plaintiffs, but only as a means of identifying their remains should they be killed in action with the Marine Corps. Although the military itself undoubtedly has a significant interest in being able to confirm which of its members have fallen in battle, and which ones may have been taken prisoner or are otherwise unaccounted for, it is the next of kin of service members who will derive the greatest benefit, and solace, from the speedy and definite identification of the remains of their loved ones.

Plaintiffs concede that the military's stated purpose for the DNA registry—remains identification—is a benign one. But they argue that the military could, at some point in the future, use the DNA samples for some less innocuous purpose, such as the diagnosis of hereditary diseases or disorders and the use or dissemination of such diagnoses to potential employers, insurers and others with a possible interest in such information. Plaintiffs have presented no evidence that the military has used or disclosed, or has any plans to use or disclose, information gleaned from the DNA samples for any purpose other than remains identification. A challenge to such hypothetical future use, or misuse, as the case may be, of the samples in the DNA repository does not present a justifiable case or controversy.[ ]

The court finds that the military has demonstrated a compelling interest in both its need to account internally for the fate of its service members and in ensuring the peace of mind of their next of kin and dependents in time of war. The court further finds that when measured against this interest, the minimal intrusion presented by the taking of blood samples and oral swabs for the military's DNA registry, though undoubtedly a "seizure," is not an unreasonable seizure and is thus not prohibited by the Constitution.

B. Breach of Contract

Plaintiffs also contend that the DNA sampling program constitutes a breach of their enlistment contracts with the Marine Corps. They note that the enlistment contracts they signed do not specifically warn recruits that blood and tissue samples will be taken for the DNA registry. Plaintiffs also argue that because they enlisted before the registry was begun, they cannot be deemed to have given their implied consent to the blood and tissue sampling.

In fact, the enlistment documents that Plaintiffs concede they signed make amply clear that military enlistees may be subjected to a plethora of laws, regulations, and requirements that would not normally apply to civilian employees of the Government. The documents also indicate that such laws, regulations and requirements can change at any time: Laws and regulations that govern military personnel may change without notice to me. Such changes may affect my status, pay, allowances, benefits and responsibilities as a member of the Armed Forces REGARDLESS of the provisions of this enlistment/reenlistment document. [ ]

The enlistment documents promise no limits on the military's ability to take blood or tissue samples or perform other medical tests on enlistees, whether for purposes of assessing physical fitness, detecting the use of illegal drugs, or otherwise. Indeed, Plaintiffs were undoubtedly subjected to such tests in connection with their enlistment. The sampling performed in connection with the DNA registry is not so qualitatively different so as to require a separate, more specific form of consent than that required for other testing.

The court finds that the military's taking of blood samples and oral swabs for purposes of obtaining DNA samples for the DOD DNA Registry is not a violation of any enlistment contract between Plaintiffs and the military.

Notes and Questions

1. After the decision in *Mayfield*, the Department of Defense issued a Memorandum altering its policies. In that Memorandum, the Department agreed to destroy the specimens upon the request of the donor after completion of military service and limits the use of the specimens beyond identification of remains and quality control to instances where the donor or surviving next-of-kin give consent or where compelled by law (under the following circumstances only: proper judicial order, investigation or prosecution of a crime punishable by one year or more in prison, no reasonable alternative available, and use approved by the Assistant Secretary of Defense for Health Affairs). (The 1996 Memorandum is reprinted in Mayfield v. Dalton, 109 F.3d 1423 (9th Cir.1997), holding that the case was mooted by the plaintiffs' discharge from the service and vacating the judgment of the District Court.) How significant are these changes?

2. The DOD is not the only entity that has a "DNA database." All of the states, except for Maryland and Wyoming, have mandated newborn screening for genetic or other medical conditions. The states usually have stored these blood samples (typically a small sample on a card) for many years. A specially appointed state panel in Michigan considered what the state should do with the 2 million blood (DNA) samples in its possession. The panel recommended that the state retain the samples indefinitely because of their value to future public health screenings, medical research and forensic identification. State Should Keep Blood Samples as Research, Police Resource, Panel Suggests, BNA Health Law Reporter (Feb. 11, 1999). For commentary on the use by law enforcement, see Paul E. Tracy and Vincent Morgan, Big Brother and His Science Kit: DNA Databases for 21st Century Crime Control?, 90 J. of Crim. L. and Criminology 635 (2000); Michelle Hibbert, DNA Databanks: Law Enforcement's Greatest Surveillance Tool?, 34 Wake Forest L. Rev. 767 (1999).

3. Would the DOD be prohibited under *Mayfield* from using the stored DNA samples to identify genetic sensitivities to particular environmental factors among those veterans who have complained of the post-Gulf War syndrome as compared to veterans who have reported no symptoms? Should the court order the military to undergo the expense and effort to collect DNA samples or secure consent for this purpose when they already have samples in storage, or should the court allow the research on susceptibility to chemical agents because it will benefit soldiers in the future?

4. The explosion of techniques for analyzing biological material using techniques developed by the Human Genome Project has made the value of stored human tissue and blood increase dramatically to researchers as well as to product developers. This has drawn increased attention to the use of stored tissue in medical research. The typical scenario is that the tissue was collected and stored for a purpose other than the specific research project now contemplated and that the original source/donor of the tissue may or may not be identifiable. What privacy concerns arise in the use of human tissue once separated from the source/donor? Do privacy concerns arise only when the individual is identifiable, or can totally anonymous situations also raise issues? Even if the tissue is identifiable, are the privacy concerns resolved if the researchers use the data in such a manner (through a coding system, for example) that the source cannot be identified? Does it matter whether the research will result in a commercial product? Does it matter whether the research focuses on conditions affecting some groups more than others? Should the social benefit of the use of the tissue outweigh any of these concerns? These questions have been argued passionately by many governmental groups and scholars.

The starting point for these legal issues is the federal regulations on human experimentation, discussed in Chapter _____. The NIH and the Centers for Disease Control had convened a group to consider the use of previously collected human tissue for research. The groups could not reach consensus, but an article published after that meeting issued a call for strict protections for such materials. Ellen W. Clayton, et al., Informed Consent for Genetic Research on Stored Tissue Samples, 274 JAMA 1786 (1995). The authors argued that using tissue that could be linked to identifiable sources could be harmful to those individuals even if their identity would not be revealed. They argued, therefore, that consent should be sought unless the waiver requirements of the federal human experimentation regulations could be met. A great number of scholars and professional associations responded to the article. In 1999, the National Bioethics Advisory Commission, a standing commission appointed by President Clinton, issued a report on the same issue. The NBAC report recommends that research on previously collected but unidentified tissue does not constitute human research and that research with identifiable samples may fall within an exemption to the rules provided the samples are unlinked or anonymized. The NBAC report does state, however, that general consents for the disposition of tissue does not constitute consent for research. National Bioethics Advisory Commission, Research Involving Human Biological Materials: Issues and Policy Guidance (Aug. 1999). For discussion, see Henry T. Greely, Breaking the Stalemate: A Prospective Regulatory Framework for Unforeseen Research Uses of Human Tissue Samples and Health Information, 34 Wake Forest L. Rev. 737 (1999).

5. Iceland has taken a different approach to DNA databases and has established a national DNA database that is aimed at covering the entire population of the country through the linking of data available within the health care system in Iceland. The goal of the database is medical research and improvement of the health care system. The government has contracted with a private corporation to organize existing data and has given the corporation rights to develop commercial products using the database. The project uses the concept of "presumed consent" rather than individual consent. It bases that presumption on national debate, parliamentary vote, and a poll that showed that 75% of Icelanders supported the statute, and of those who had an opinion on the act, 90% supported it. Jeffrey R. Gulcher and Kari Stefansson, The Icelandic Healthcare Database and Informed

Consent, 342 N.E.J.M. 1827 (June 15, 2000). Is the United States missing an opportunity here?

III. GENETIC SCREENING

Problem: The Genetic Screen

Mrs. J is pregnant and is offered three options for genetic screening of the fetus. The first option is a "triple screen," which can be performed at about 15 weeks of the pregnancy, with results available within one week. The triple screen tests for Down syndrome and other disorders through a sample of the woman's blood. There is no risk of loss of pregnancy from the test itself. The limitation of the triple screen is that a negative result does not necessarily mean that the child will not have the genetic disorders, nor does a positive result necessarily mean that the child will have the genetic disorders. The second option is amniocentesis, which is currently performed at about 16 weeks of pregnancy, with results following about 2 weeks thereafter. Amniocentesis screens for Down syndrome, for which Mrs. J is at high risk (1 in 365) because of her age, and neural tube defects, among other conditions. The risk of loss of the pregnancy is approximately 1 in 200 or .5%, in addition to the ordinary risk of loss at this stage of pregnancy of 2% to 3%. The limitations of amniocentesis include the increased risk of loss of the fetus (and perhaps injury to the fetus) and the fact that the results will not be known until well into the second trimester of the pregnancy. It would be possible for Mrs. J to undergo the triple screen with the follow-up amniocentesis if the triple screen is positive. The third option is CVS (chorionic villus sampling), which has a higher risk of loss of pregnancy than either of the other two options (1% to 1.5% over the expected rate of 4% to 5% for pregnancies of ten weeks duration when CVS is performed). CVS more reliably detects several genetic conditions.

Mrs. J is ambivalent about whether she should undergo testing. She believes that it is quite unlikely that she will terminate the pregnancy if the results of either screen are positive, but she is not absolutely sure as the possibility of taking care of a child who is more dependent than her first two children is quite daunting.

Mrs. J's physician counsels Mrs. J that unless she is likely to terminate the pregnancy if there is a positive result, he ordinarily would not recommend the test and would in fact discourage its use. Mrs. J is inclined toward taking the triple screen, but the doctor cautions her about the indeterminacy of the results. In the meantime, her pregnancy is progressing.

Is Mrs. J's physician providing appropriate genetic counseling? How should Mrs. J decide?

Mrs. J's insurer has a policy concerning prenatal genetic screening. It will pay for the triple screen, which costs approximately $150, for any patient, but will pay for amniocentesis, which costs approximately $800, only if the triple screen has been positive and only if the insured indicates that she is willing to consider terminating the pregnancy if the results are positive. They do not ordinarily pay for CVS, which costs approximately $1000. Are these reasonable payment policies? For discussion, see Michael Mennuti, A 35–year-old Pregnant Woman Considering Maternal Serum Screening and Amniocentesis, 275 JAMA 1440 (1996). For a discussion of the ethics of "nondirective" genetic counseling, see Mary Terrell White, Making Responsible Decisions: An Interpretive Ethic for Genetic Decisionmaking, 29 Hastings Center Rept. 14 (1999), arguing that nondirective counseling fails to recognize the community's interests.

Notes and Questions

1.   Genetic screens are available for use at several stages in the reproductive process. The potential parents may be screened for the presence of genetic disorders that may be inherited by their children, and may on that basis decide to use alternative methods of reproduction, to adopt, or to forego reproducing. In addition, however, genetic tests are commonly available for use prenatally (to test the genetic composition of the fetus) or for use preimplantation (to test the genetic composition of the pre-embryo in the case of in vitro fertilization). For discussion of one of the more controversial techniques for genetic selection in procreation, see Richard J. Tasca and Michael E. McClure, The Emerging Technology and Application of Preimplantation Genetic Diagnosis, 26 J.L., Med. & Ethics 7 (1998) and Jeffrey R. Botkin, Ethical Issues and Practical Problems in Preimplantation Genetic Diagnosis, 26 J. Law, Med. & Ethics 17 (1998).

2.   Prenatal genetic screening is often hailed as a boon to prospective parents and to public health. Some have lauded its potential for controlling health care costs: "At [the Genetics & IVF Institute], we have observed, anecdotally, ... that insurance companies and employers are beginning to realize the substantial short-and long-term savings that accrue when they accede to patient requests for reimbursement for early diagnosis, treatment, and prevention of serious genetic disorders. Perhaps at last, economic values will become a driving force towards preventive medicine...." Gene Levinson, et al., Recent Advances in Reproductive Genetic Technologies, Biotechnology (1995). Others have decried its negative impact on persons with disabilities.

Are the positive and negative impacts of prenatal genetic screening primarily social and ethical issues, or are they legal issues? Can the courts and legislatures make a contribution toward resolving these concerns? What legal principles may have a role in conflicts over prenatal genetic screening and therapy?

3.   What effect does increased emphasis on reproductive genetic testing and genetic technology have on women? Does it increase reproductive freedom and autonomy, or does it increase social expectations of duty to the pregnancy? Does increased diagnostic capacity provide the comfort of knowing, or does it increase anxiety and alienation? Should the impact on women's health and well-being be assessed and incorporated into public policy, or should the issue be left to the individuals involved? For a very complete treatment of such questions, see Women and Prenatal Testing: Facing the Challenges of Genetic Technology (Karen Rothenberg and Elizabeth Thomson, eds.) (1994). See also, Joan C. Callahan and Dorothy E. Roberts, A Feminist Social Justice Approach to Reproduction–Assisting Technologies: A Case Study of the Limits of Liberal Theory, 84 Kentucky L.J. 1197 (1995–1996); Mary B. Mahowold and Christine Cassel, The New Genetics and Women, 74 The Milbank Quarterly 239 (1996); Julia Walsh, Reproductive Rights and the Human Genome Project, 4 S. Cal. Rev. L. and Women's Studies 145 (1994).

4.   Some few genetically-based conditions are treatable with curative or preventive therapy. For example, a newborn with phenylketonuria (PKU) may avoid the serious mental retardation associated with this genetic condition if his or her diet is controlled from the earliest possible point. The promise of gene therapies has lagged enormously behind the development of genetic screening

techniques, however. (On the rapidity in development and marketing of diagnostic tests, see Paul H. Silverman, Commerce and Genetic Diagnostics, 25 Hastings Center Rep. 515 (1995).) So, in all but the rarest case, the current available treatment for conditions revealed through a prenatal or preimplantation genetic test is abortion of the fetus (often in the second trimester) or nonimplantation of the pre-embryo. How should the states regulate, if at all, selection of genetic characteristics of one's children? Does the selection method make a difference? Is there a difference between preimplantation selection and prenatal selection? Is there a difference between selection achieved by genetic alteration of the fetal genetic material (called genetic engineering or genetic therapy) or selection achieved by the selection of a mate or of donor semen? Can there be any distinction between one's position on abortion generally and one's position on abortion for genetic selection or avoidance of genetic disease?

5. Genetic screening with a view toward procreation is not limited to desires to avoid what might be considered diseases or disabilities; prospective parents might also be choosing favorable characteristics that will give their children certain advantages. See, for example, Roberta M. Berry, Genetic Enhancement in the Twenty–First Century: Three Problems in Legal Imagining, 34 Wake Forest L. Rev. 715 (1999); Michael H. Shapiro, The Impact of Genetic Enhancement on Equality, 34 Wake Forest L. Rev. 561 (1999); Maxwell J. Mehlman, The Law of Above Averages: Leveling the New Genetic Enhancement Playing Field, 85 Iowa L.Rev. 517 (2000). The prospects for human cloning raise similar issues. See, for example, Mary B. Mahowald, Genes, Clones, and Gender Equality, 3 DePaul J. Health Care L. 495 (2000).

6. John Robertson identifies all of the following as falling within the pro-creative liberty he argues protects decisions relating to human reproduction: avoidance of severe genetic disease, such as Tay Sachs, sickle cell anemia or Duchenne's muscular dystrophy; of treatable genetically-based illnesses, such as PKU; of genetic conditions with variable expressivity, such as cystic fibrosis where median age of death is mid–40s and severity of symptoms varies; of late-onset genetic diseases, such as Huntington's Disease or Alzheimer's disease where the individual has a normal life until the disease emerges in his or her later years; or of genetic susceptibilities, for example to cancer. Robertson also argues that selection for gender is protected and that selection for nonmedical traits, such as heterosexuality, "might also qualify" for presumptive protection under procrea-tive liberty because of the "widespread existence of homophobic prejudice." The protection of the procreative liberty interest, according to Robertson, shifts the burden of proof or persuasion to those who argue that choice should be restricted and prohibits reliance on "purely symbolic harms" as a basis for restriction. John A. Robertson, Genetic Selection of Offspring Characteristics, 76 B.U. L. Rev. 421 (1996).

Are each of these genetic conditions similar? Is there any basis for distin-guishing among them? For a case study of the assessment of the "seriousness" of genetic conditions revealed in prenatal testing, see Diana Punales Morejon & Marsha Saxton, Society's Diseases, 26 Hastings Center Rept. 21 (1996). If you are inclined to restrict the provision of genetic information or genetic selection services, how would you go about doing so? What lines would you draw? Is it better or worse to allow private physicians and fertility clinics to decide which tests or information to provide? Instead of restricting access to genetic selection, may a state claim a public health interest and require prenatal screening and selection? See, Lois Shepherd, Protecting Parents' Freedom to Have Children with Genetic Differences, 1995 U. Ill. L. Rev. 761 (1995).

7. Although this section has focused on prenatal genetic screening, genetic screening is broader. As noted earlier, almost every state has programs that require genetic screening of newborns. The states vary in the scope of these programs, with most including at least those conditions, such as PKU, where early intervention can avoid serious injury or death. Other states go farther, requiring screening for a number of conditions. One of the earliest public health genetic screening programs was for sickle cell, a genetic condition that occurs most frequently in African–Americans. In regard to screening for sickle cell, one scholar has noted:

> In the 1970s, large scale screening [for sickle cell] was undertaken with the goal of changing African American mating behavior. Unfortunately, the initiative promoted confusion regarding the difference between carriers and those with the disease. This confusion resulted in widespread discrimination against African Americans. Some states passed legislation requiring all African American children entering school to be screened for the sickle-cell trait, even though there was no treatment or cure for the sickle-cell disease. Some states required prisoners to be tested, even though there would be no opportunity for them to pass on the trait. Job and insurance discrimination were both real and attempted. The military considered banning all African Americans from the armed services. African American airline stewardesses were fired. Insurance rates went up for carriers. Some companies refused to insure carriers. During that period, many African Americans came to believe that the sickle-cell screening initiative was merely a disguised genocide attempt, since often the only advice given to African Americans with the trait was, "Don't have kids." Vernellia R. Randall, Trusting the Health Care System Ain't Always Easy! An African American Perspective on Bioethics, 15 St. Louis U. Public L. Rev. 191 (1996).

What criteria should a state use in deciding whether or not to test newborns for genetic traits? Should consent always be required, or are there circumstances where the state should presume consent or forego consent entirely?

Problem: Screening for Cystic Fibrosis

Cystic fibrosis is associated with a very large number of mutations of the CFTR gene. It is a recessive autosomal disorder; i.e., both parents must carry the mutation responsible for CF, and the child must have inherited the mutation from both parents. Testing for the many mutations associated with CF is quite complex. Cystic fibrosis is one of the most common genetic diseases (affecting approximately 25,000 Americans), and is most prominent in white populations, affecting 1 in 3300.

Cystic fibrosis is highly variable. Some persons are only minimally affected, but the disease will cause an early death in others. There is no cure for CF, but disease management has increased longevity. Average lifespan for persons with CF is now over 30 years. Recent data indicate that 35% of young adults with the disease work full time and over 90% have graduated from high school. There is currently no evidence that early diagnosis and intervention improves outcomes. There is research underway for genetic therapy, but it is not expected to reach success in the near future. Medical and ancillary care is estimated to average approximately $50,000 yearly per individual with CF. The cost of the genetic testing itself is between $50 and $150 per test (for 6 to 72 of the mutations associated with CF), but that figure does not include medical services and genetic counseling directly associated with testing.

Should states mandate newborn screening for CF as almost all do for PKU? Should states mandate screening for CF for all couples who are marrying? Should genetic screening for CF be offered to the general population? Should it be recommended to those with a family history of CF? Should the genetic tests be offered to all pregnant women? For a discussion of these issues, see National Institutes of Health Consensus Statement, Genetic Testing for Cystic Fibrosis, 159 Archives of Int. Med. 1529 (1999).

Chapter 18

DEFINING DEATH

Problem: When Does Death Occur?

Alberto Arcturus was face down by the side of the road, apparently after being run down by a hit-and-run driver, when a passing motorist saw him and called the local emergency medical services. An ambulance with two paramedics arrived on the scene about fifteen minutes after the call, and they found that Mr. Arcturus was not breathing and that he had no pulse. They also discovered that a substantial portion of his head (including his forehead and forebrain) was crushed. One paramedic looked at the other and said, "He's dead; let's call the morgue." The second, less experienced paramedic insisted on trying to resuscitate Mr. Arcturus, as was required by the emergency medical services manual for paramedics. They placed him in the ambulance and administered cardiopulmonary resuscitation throughout the fifteen minute ride to the nearest hospital emergency room.

At the emergency room physicians confirmed that Mr. Arcturus did not breathe spontaneously and had no spontaneous cardiac activity. One doctor told the charge nurse that he was dead, and that "dead on arrival" should be marked on his chart. A young intern balked at this, however, because the hospital emergency room protocol required more before a brain injured patient could be declared dead. The physicians then administered drugs and used paddles that sent an electric current through Mr. Arcturus's chest in an effort to start his heart. After some time they managed to get a weak pulse, and they placed Mr. Arcturus on a ventilator and moved him to the intensive care unit. A neurology consult revealed that Mr. Arcturus's neocortex was completely and irreversibly destroyed—most of it was literally gone, left on the highway—although his brain stem remained intact. Another consult revealed that Mr. Arcturus had two healthy kidneys and a healthy liver, heart and pancreas, each of which could be transplanted to save the life of another patient in the hospital. With the help of a ventilator (necessary because of the head and chest injuries to the patient), Mr. Arcturus's body could continue functioning indefinitely. If the ventilator were to be removed, Mr. Arcturus's heart and lung function would cease in the next few minutes.

After considerable investigation, police have captured a person who, they believe, was the hit-and-run driver who ran into Mr. Arcturus. They wish to know whether to charge him with vehicular homicide (a felony), or something else (all other potential offenses would be misdemeanors). The doctors and Mr. Arcturus's family want to know whether he is dead or alive. Further, if he is dead, they want to know when he died—at the roadside, in the hospital emergency room, in the intensive care unit, or somewhere else. Mr. Arcturus's health insurer is denying coverage because, they say, "we only pay for necessary medical services, and no services are necessary when the patient is dead." Finally, the transplant team at the hospital wants to know if Mr. Arcturus's organs are available for transplantation.

Would your answers to any of these questions be different if Mr. Arcturus himself had said, just two months before the accident, while delivering a sermon at his Unitarian church, that "for religious reasons and other reasons of conscience, I wish to be considered dead when my cognitive abilities are gone?"

I. INTRODUCTION

As we saw in Chapter 16, defining "personhood" has vexed commentators for centuries. Determining when a "person" died, however, was simple until the last few decades. Death occurred when several simultaneous physical changes occurred. These changes included the cessation of all cardiopulmonary (heart and lung) function, the cessation of all cognitive activity, the cessation of all responsive activity, and with only slight delay, the onset of rigormortis, livormortis, and, eventually, putrefaction. There could be no question about whether death would occur if all cognitive and responsive activity ceased but cardiopulmonary function continued because those functions were so closely related that the existence of one without the other would be impossible for more than a few hours. Because the cessation of cardiopulmonary functions was so much easier to observe than the cessation of cognitive ability, responsive activity, and other delayed attributes of death, the cessation of cardiopulmonary functions became, informally and practically, the definition of death. This test was never really anything more significant than the most convenient *evidence* of death; there is no suggestion that there was any basis for making cardiopulmonary functions definitional.

The development of mechanical substitutes for hearts and lungs has forced reconsideration of the definition of death. It is now possible for a person to be without cognitive or responsive activity (i.e., without any brain activity), and yet maintain cardiopulmonary functions with the assistance of technological devices. Logically, this temporal division of these formerly contemporaneous attributes requires a determination of what death is. Is it the cessation of cardiopulmonary functions or is it the cessation of some, or all, brain functions?

The definition of death, like any other definition in law, ought to be functional. It is impossible to determine what ought to constitute death before the purpose of the definition is articulated. It should not be surprising that the legal function of defining death might be very different from the psychological function, which might be very different from the historical, sociological, anthropological, and medical functions. For example, the law must establish a time to distribute property from the estate, to require the payment of death contracts (i.e., life insurance), and to purge voting lists. Psychologists, however, may determine that death is a period of settling relationships, mourning, and healing. Physicians may view it as a time when their obligation to act in the interest of the patient ceases. There are many definitions of death, and, ultimately, attempts to develop an interdisciplinary consensus on the definition of death may be futile.

This chapter will review the distinction between the cardiopulmonary death and brain death models, and seek to evaluate whether they are inconsistent in any way. Next, this chapter will review the development of a legal definition of death over the last several years and consider the legal consequences of the general acceptance of a brain death or combined brain death-cardiopulmonary death definition. This chapter will then review the arguably unique case of the anencephalic infant and ask whether our current definitions of death fail in that case. Finally, it will ask whether each of us ought to be able to choose our own definition of death.

Note: Religious Perspective on Death

There are a variety of social conceptions of death; many of the most pervasive of those considerations are theological. For many people, death is significant not just because it ends life, but because it begins something else.

> For Christians, death is not seen as the destruction or annihilation of the person. Although dissolution of the spirit-body bond that exists during our life is painful, death, viewed as transformation of the person to a new state of existence, is not. Furthermore, the Christian belief is that he will be resurrected, that the body in some way will share in the new life promised by Jesus Christ. Thus, the Christian is able to view the determination of death from a wider perspective than purely medical. This understanding provides the proper perspective for approaching the legal aspects of the determination of death.

J. Stuart Showalter, Determining Death: The Legal and Theological Aspects of Brain–Related Criteria, 27 Catholic Lawyer 112, 116 (1982). Many commentators have noted the importance of religious beliefs in establishing the legal definition of death. See, e.g., Michael Grodin, Religious Exemptions: Brain Death and Jewish Law, 36 J. Church & St. 357 (1994) and Scott Idleman, The Role of Religious Values in Judicial Decision Making, 68 Ind. L.J. 433 (1993). For a discussion of laws accommodating religious preferences for particular definitions of death, see Section IV, below.

II. THE DEVELOPMENT OF THE "BRAIN DEATH" DEFINITION

A. HISTORY

The first well-accepted definition of death to include brain death came from the Harvard Medical School and was published in the Journal of the American Medical Association. The Ad Hoc Committee of the Harvard Medical School used the term "irreversible coma" to define what is now generally called brain death and suggested that "no statutory change in the law should be necessary since the law treats this question essentially as one of fact to be determined by physicians."

The Ad Hoc Committee was explicit in describing its purpose in promulgating its new definition of death:

> Our primary purpose is to define irreversible coma as a new criterion for death. There are two reasons why there is need for a definition: (1) Improvements in resuscitative and supportive measures have led to increased efforts to save those who are desperately injured. Sometimes

these efforts have only partial success so that the result is an individual whose heart continues to beat but whose brain is irreversibly damaged. The burden is great on patients who suffer permanent loss of intellect, on their families, on the hospitals, and on those in need of hospital beds already occupied by these comatose patients. (2) Obsolete criteria for the definition of death can lead to controversy in obtaining organs for transplantation.

Report of the Ad Hoc Committee of the Harvard Medical School to Examine the Definition of Brain Death, 205 J.A.M.A. 85 (Aug.1968). In addition to listing the characteristics of irreversible coma—unreceptivity and unresponsitivity, no movements or breathing, no reflexes, and flat electro-encephalogram—the Ad Hoc Committee recommended that death be declared before the respirator is turned off ("in our judgment it will provide a greater degree of legal protection to those involved"), that the physician in charge consult with others before the declaration of death is made, that the physician (rather than the family) make the decision, and that the decision to declare death be made by physicians who are not involved "in any later effort to transplant organs or tissue from the deceased individual." Id.

The Ad Hoc Committee's determination that brain death ought to constitute death met surprisingly little medical opposition. There has been debate over the precise nature of the characteristics of "irreversible coma" that can give rise to brain death and over whether the issue should be left to physicians or be brought into the domain of public debate and converted into a formal legal standard. The Ad Hoc Committee contributed substantially to this debate by the publication of its report. They also contributed to the confusion that subsequently has surrounded the issue by using such terms as "irreversible coma," which is now generally used to refer to something less than brain death, and "hopelessly damaged," as synonyms for brain death. The Ad Hoc Committee Report (through the language it used) may have perpetuated the misunderstanding that "brain death" is a medical diagnosis that constitutes something very close to death, but that it does not constitute "real" death. Brain death, of course, is just as "real" a death as heart-lung death. The consensus that brain death is, in fact, death of the human being confirms that the cessation of heart-lung activity may never have been more than evidence of death. The real defining characteristic is that there be, in the words of the Ad Hoc Committee, "no discernible central nervous system activity."

The Ad Hoc Committee concluded:

From ancient times down to the recent past it was clear that, when the respiration and heart stopped, the brain would die in a few minutes; so the obvious criterion of no heart beat as synonymous with death was sufficiently accurate. In those times the heart was considered to be the central organ of the body; it is not surprising that its failure marked the onset of death. This is no longer valid when modern resuscitative and supportive measures are used. These improved activities can now restore "life" as judged by the ancient standards of persistent respiration and continuing heart beat. This can be the case even when there is not the remotest possibility of an individual recovering consciousness following massive brain damage. In other situations "life" can be maintained only by means of artificial respiration and electrical stimulation of the heart beat, or in temporarily by-passing the heart, or, in conjunction with these things, reducing with cold the body's oxygen requirement.

Id. As the leading legal and medical experts point out, the Ad Hoc Committee marked the beginning of the public debate over brain death; closure was not to come until some time later.

Not surprisingly, disquiet over the change in medical attitude and practice arose in lay as well as medical circles. The prospect of physicians agreeing amongst themselves to change the rules by which life is measured in order to salvage a larger number of transplantable organs met with something short of universal approval. Especially with increasing disenchantment over heart transplantation (the procedure in which the traditional criteria for determining death posed the most difficulties), some doubt arose whether it was wise to adopt measures which encouraged a medical "advance" that seemed to have gotten ahead of its own basic technology. Furthermore, many people—doctors included—found themselves with nagging if often unarticulated doubts about how to proceed in the situation, far more common than transplantation, in which a long-comatose patient shows every prospect of "living" indefinitely with artificial means of support. As a result of this growing public and professional concern, elected officials, with the encouragement of the medical community, have urged public discussion and action to dispel the apprehension created by the new medical knowledge and to clarify and reformulate the law. Some commentators, however, have argued that public bodies and laymen in general have no role to play in this process of change. Issue is therefore joined on at least two points: (1) ought the public to be involved in "defining" death? and (2) if so, how ought it to be involved—specifically, ought governmental action, in the form of legislation, be taken?

A. Capron and L. Kass, A Statutory Definition of the Standards for Determining Human Death: An Appraisal and a Proposal, 121 U.Pa.L.Rev. 87, 91–92 (1972).

The first state to promulgate a statute adopting brain death was Kansas. The 1970 Kansas statute provided alternatively for both brain death and traditional cardiopulmonary death:

A person will be considered medically and legally dead if, in the opinion of a physician, based on ordinary standards of medical practice, there is the absence of spontaneous respiratory and cardiac function and, because of the disease or condition which caused, directly or indirectly, these functions to cease, or because of the passage of time since these functions ceased, attempts at resuscitation are considered hopeless; and, in this event, death will have occurred at the time these functions ceased; or

A person will be considered medically and legally dead if, in the opinion of a physician, based on ordinary standards of medical practice, there is the absence of spontaneous brain function; and if based on ordinary standards of medical practice, during reasonable attempts to either maintain or restore spontaneous circulatory or respiratory function in the absence of aforesaid brain function, it appears that further attempts at resuscitation or supportive maintenance will not succeed, death will have occurred at the time when these conditions first coincide. Death is to be pronounced before artificial means of supporting respiratory and circulatory function are terminated and before any vital organ is removed for purposes of transplantation.

These alternative definitions of death are to be utilized for all purposes in this state, including the trials of civil and criminal cases, any laws to the contrary notwithstanding.

Kan.Stat.Ann. § 77–202.

The statute was quickly copied and just as quickly criticized. The primary criticism was directed to the alternative definitions of death, which some believed might lead to the conclusion that a person could be either dead or alive depending on which paragraph of the definition the determining physician invoked. It is hard to believe, however, that these alternative definitions would result in any confusion in fact, and there has been no case that has engendered such confusion in Kansas or any other state with a similar statute. Professor Capron and Dr. Kass proposed an alternative to the Kansas statute. Their proposal grew out of the Research Group on Death and Dying at the Hastings Center and sought to eliminate the notion that there were two independent definitions of death, and that physicians (and others) thus had discretion to determine whether a patient was truly dead.

The Capron and Kass analysis and recommendation had a very substantial effect on the development of the law. Combined with the ABA's Definition of Death Act proposed in 1975 and the ABA's pressure on the National Conference of Commissioners on Uniform State Laws, it led to the Uniform Brain Death Act, which was adopted by the Commissioners in 1978. This uniform act was adopted by only a couple of states before it was superseded by the Uniform Determination of Death Act (UDDA) in 1980. That act was promulgated as a political compromise that could be supported by those who had been supporting the Uniform Brain Death Act, the Definition of Death Act, another AMA model act, and other versions of statutes that recognized brain death as conclusive evidence of death. The 1980 Uniform Act, which gives explicit credit to Capron and Kass in its prefatory note, returns to the alternative definitions of death. This is not because the Commissioners determined that there were two independent definitions of death. Rather, it treated death as a phenomenon that could be *tested* by two alternative criteria.

Uniform Determination of Death Act (1980)

§ 1. [Determination of Death]

An individual who has sustained either (1) irreversible cessation of circulatory and respiratory functions, or (2) irreversible cessation of all functions of the entire brain, including the brain stem, is dead. A determination of death must be made in accordance with accepted medical standards.

* * *

Since 1980 there have been some suggested modifications to the Uniform Determination of Death Act. In 1982 three Dartmouth Medical School professors argued:

The UDDA statute is not desirable, we believe, because it too is ambiguous and it elevates the irreversible cessation of cardiopulmonary functioning to the level of a standard of death, when it is really only a test, although a test that may be used in most circumstances. Permanent cessation of spontaneous cardiopulmonary functioning works as a test of death only in the absence of artificial cardiopulmonary support because only there does it produce the true standard of death-the irreversible cessation of all brain functions. A conceptually satisfactory statute would not need to mention cessation of cardiopulmonary function at all. It would be sufficient to include only irreversible cessation of whole brain functioning and allow physicians to select validated and agreed-upon tests (prolonged absence of spontaneous cardiopulmonary function would be one) to measure irreversible cessation of whole brain function.

J. Bernat, C. Culver and B. Gert, Defining Death in Theory and Practice, 12 Hastings Center Report 5 (Feb. 1982). They proposed their own statute, which begins, "An individual who has sustained irreversible cessation of all functions of the entire brain, including the brain stem, is dead." Id. The proposed statute then lists two ways to determine whether there has been irreversible cessation of all functions of the entire brain—the prolonged absence of spontaneous circulatory and respiratory functions, or, as an alternative in the presence of artificial means of cardiopulmonary support, direct tests of brain function. Id. In part because the difference between the Uniform Determination of Death Act and the Dartmouth professors' alternative amounts to little more than a legal quibble with insubstantial practical, legal or medical consequences, there has been little interest in formally changing the language of the Uniform Act, even among those who find the unitary brain death definition (with alternative *criteria* for determining whether the entire brain is dead) intellectually preferable to the alternative-definitions form employed by the Uniform Act.

The Uniform Determination of Death Act has now been adopted, more or less as proposed by the Commission, in most states. For an excellent judicial history of the adoption of the brain death standard, see People v. Mitchell, 132 Cal.App.3d 389, 183 Cal.Rptr. 166 (1982). Bernat and his colleagues were not completely unsuccessful; there is now nearly a consensus among philosophers that it is really the irreversible cessation of all brain function that constitutes death, whether it be measured through tests of the brain function itself or tests for cardiopulmonary activity. Even those few dissenters who would return to the heart-lung criteria as the sole legal criteria agree that those who meet the whole brain death definition should be allowed to die (or even be candidates for euthanasia). See James Humber, Statutory Criteria for Determining Human Death, 42 Mercer L. Rev. 1069 (1991).

Note: Brain Death and Homicide Statutes

Brain death has not been adopted into the law wholly through statutes. In some states courts have been willing to adopt the brain death definition. This issue necessarily comes before the court in criminal cases where the defendant argues that he cannot be charged with homicide because the victim, although without any brain activity because of the criminal conduct, could have been kept "alive" with mechanically assisted heart and lungs indefinitely (or at least for a year and a day, which is all that is usually required for the defendant to avoid the homicide charge). Some homicide defendants have argued that the victims were not dead until brain death was declared by the physicians, and that the physicians really made the declaration so that organs could be removed for transplantation. They have argued that the harvesting of the organs, not their underlying criminal acts, was the proximate cause of death. Several states which have faced various manifestations of this very clever and obviously desperate argument have denied this defense; in no case has it been successful.

A representative set of facts comes from People v. Eulo, 63 N.Y.2d 341, 482 N.Y.S.2d 436, 472 N.E.2d 286 (1984), where the New York Court of Appeals dealt explicitly with the New York Legislature's failure to define death. The facts of that case provide a useful background:

On the evening of July 19, 1981, defendant and his girlfriend attended a volunteer firemen's fair in Kings Park, Suffolk County. Not long after they arrived, the two began to argue, reportedly because defendant was jealous over one of her former suitors, whom they had seen at the fair. The argument continued through the evening; it became particularly heated as the two sat in defendant's pick-up truck, parked in front of the home of the girlfriend's parents. Around midnight, defendant shot her in the head with his unregistered handgun.

The victim was rushed by ambulance to the emergency room of St. John's Hospital. A gunshot wound to the left temple causing extreme hemorrhaging was apparent. A tube was placed in her windpipe to enable artificial respiration and intravenous medication was applied to stabilize her blood pressure.

Shortly before 2:00 a.m., the victim was examined by a neurosurgeon, who undertook various tests to evaluate damage done to the brain. Painful stimuli were applied and yielded no reaction. Various reflexes were tested and, again, there was no response. A further test determined that the victim was incapable of spontaneously maintaining respiration. An electroencephalogram (EEG) resulted in "flat," or "isoelectric", readings indicating no activity in the part of the brain tested.

Over the next two days, the victim's breathing was maintained solely by a mechanical respirator. Her heartbeat was sustained and regulated through medication. Faced with what was believed to be an imminent cessation of these two bodily functions notwithstanding the artificial maintenance, the victim's parents consented to the use of certain of her organs for transplantation.

On the afternoon of July 23, a second neurosurgeon was called in to evaluate whether the victim's brain continued to function in any manner. A repetition of all of the previously conducted tests led to the same diagnosis: the victim's entire brain had irreversibly ceased to function. This diagnosis was reviewed and confirmed by the Deputy Medical Examiner for Suffolk County and another physician.

The victim was pronounced dead at 2:20 p.m. on July 23, although at that time she was still attached to a respirator and her heart was still beating. Her body was taken to a surgical room where her kidneys, spleen, and lymph nodes were removed. The mechanical respirator was then disconnected, and her breathing immediately stopped, followed shortly be a cessation of the heartbeat.

Defendant was indicted for second degree murder. After a jury trial, he was convicted of manslaughter. * * *

482 N.Y.S.2d at 439, 472 N.E.2d at 289.

The court held that "a recognition of brain-based criteria for determining death is not unfaithful to prior judicial definitions of 'death', as presumptively adopted in the many statutes using that term. Close examination of the common-law conception of death and the traditional criteria used to determine when death has occurred leads inexorably to this conclusion." Id. at 444, 472 N.E.2d at 294. The court determined that "[d]eath remains the single phenomenon identified at common law," and that the courts could appropriately adapt criteria "to account for the 'changed conditions' that a dead body may be attached to a machine so as to exhibit demonstrably false indicia of life." Id. The *Eulo* court went on:

> This court searches in vain for evidence that, apart from the concept of death, the legislature intended to render immutable the criteria used to determine death. By extension, to hold to the contrary would be to say that the law could not recognize diagnostic equipment such as the stethoscope or more sensitive equipment even when it became clear that these instruments more accurately measured the presence of signs of life.

Id. Thus, the court concluded,

> when a determination has been made according to accepted medical standards that person has suffered an irreversible cessation of heartbeat and respiration, or, when these functions are maintained solely by extraordinary mechanical means, an irreversible cessation of all functions of the entire brain, including the brain stem, no life traditionally recognized by the law is present in that body.

Id. The Court of Appeals described with some precision just when medical intervention could constitute a superseding cause that would relieve a defendant from criminal homicide liability:

> If the victims were properly diagnosed as dead, of course, no subsequent medical procedure such as organ removal would be deemed a cause of death. If victims' deaths were prematurely announced due to a doctor's negligence, the subsequent procedures may have been a cause of death, but that negligence would not constitute a superseding cause of death relieving defendants of liability [ ]. If, however, the pronouncements of death were premature due to the gross negligence or the intentional wrongdoing of doctors, as determined by a grave deviation from accepted medical practices or disregard for legally cognizable criteria for determining death, the intervening medical procedure would interrupt the chain of causation and become the legal cause of death [ ].

Id. at 447, 472 N.E.2d at 297. Surprisingly, the *Eulo* defense has come up in more subtle ways since 1984. In People v. Hall, 134 Misc.2d 515, 511 N.Y.S.2d 532 (1987), the court held that a defendant could be convicted of the murder of a viable fetus which had to be delivered prematurely after the shooting of its mother. The court concluded that the fact that the infant was maintained on a ventilator after the C-section birth did not alter its status as one who was "born alive," and thus a "person" under the murder statute. In People v. Lai, 131 A.D.2d 592, 516 N.Y.S.2d 300 (1987), the court announced that *Eulo* would allow the jury to determine whether the brain death standard or the heart-lung standard ought to be applied in a homicide case to determine the time of death. Does this seem like an issue of fact properly within the province of the jury?

Should the judicially created definition of death in *Eulo* extend to criminal actions only, or should it also apply in civil actions (in tort actions, for example)? See Strachan v. John F. Kennedy Memorial Hosp., 109 N.J. 523, 538 A.2d 346 (1988).

B. HIGHER BRAIN DEATH

Why is there such a consensus that it is brain death, not cardiopulmonary death, that is the true defining characteristic of the death of a person? The President's Commission reached that conclusion from its premise that death was "the permanent cessation of functioning of the organism as a whole." How should we deal with a person with no cerebral function, but with continued brain stem function? Such a person would be incapable of any cognitive activity—incapable of any communication, self concept, pleasure or pain—yet still be capable of breathing, maintaining heart activity and responding reflexively. Can that person be said to be functioning as a whole organism? Is the absence of higher brain function, rather than merely *any* brain function, the real evidence of the disintegration of any functioning of the organism as a whole, and thus the real definition of death? The Dartmouth professors support the conclusion of the President's Commission that whole brain death, not merely death of those portions of the brain that are responsible for higher brain function, must occur before brain death can be declared. There are two primary objections to "higher brain death" proposal. As they point out:

> An important weakness of the higher brain formulation of death is the "slippery slope" problem. Just how much neocortical damage is necessary for death? By this definition, would not severely demented patients also be considered dead? Then what about those somewhat less severely brain damaged? Because personhood is inherently a vague concept, strict criteria for its loss are difficult to identify.

J. Bernat, C. Culver and B. Gert, Defining Death in Theory and Practice, Hastings Center Report (Feb. 1982) at 6. Robert Veatch, a leading proponent of the "higher brain death" definition, disagrees:

> It does not follow that advocates of higher-brain formulations are more vulnerable to the slippery-slope problem than defenders of whole brain grounds for pronouncing a person dead. Advocates of what brain pronouncement of death must, as Harry Beecher quickly discovered, rule out spinal cord reflexes. They must rule out isolated cellular activity that continues to produce micro-volt electron potentials on an electroencephalogram. Their own question could be forced back on them: "Just how much brain tissue damage is necessary for death?" Would they consider someone alive who had a few brain stem cells functioning? What about one or two intact brain stem reflexes? The advocates of higher-brain concepts of death are in no better, but no worse a position. They think it is as easy to draw a hard and fast line between higher-brain (cortical) functions and other brain functions as between the brain stem and the high spinal cord. They can say *any cortical* function signals protectable life, just as the whole-brainers can say *any brain* function does. One is not on any slippier slope than the other. If there is a slippery slope, anyone

who leaves the comfortable confines of the pericardium and begins ascending the spinal cord toward the cerebral cortex is already on it.

Those of us who favor some version of the higher-brain formulations do so precisely because we believe that a person does not function as a whole unless some higher brain function is present. The argument goes back to old Judeo–Christian notions of what it means to be whole. While the Greeks gave priority to the soul, the Judeo–Christian tradition consistently affirms that the human is a necessarily integrated unity of body and mind. Yet [some] hold that a person can function as a whole even when all mental function is totally and irreversibly gone. What a vitalistic, animalistic, biological view of the nature of the human! It confuses the person with the body as badly as the old heart/lung formulations did.

It is all right if some people want to hold that view. If we cannot accurately measure the irreversible loss of all mental capacity today anyway, it may be better to have a conceptually inadequate formulation of what it means to be dead in order to prevent some muddled clinician from pronouncing someone dead prematurely. The problem of false positive diagnoses of life is worth thinking about, however. It protects us from confusing the person as a whole from his or her flesh and blood. If we were not worried about false positive diagnoses of life, we might as well retreat to the safe and sure heart/lung based formulations and be done with it.

Robert Veatch, Correspondence, 12 Hastings Center Report (5) at 45 (Oct. 1982). See also Francis Bennion, Legal Death of Brain–Damaged Persons, 44 N. Ireland Legal. Q. 269 (1993), advocating a definition of death that would encompass the permanently unconscious.

The primary objection to the "higher brain death" proposal is a practical one. Remember, any legal definition of death ought to serve the function of such a definition. While the "higher brain function" definition may allow for the distribution of a decedent's property and his purge from voting lists, many people would feel uncomfortable burying a person who is still breathing. Is this discomfort simply irrational and anachronistic or is it supported by some principle that ought to be recognized in law?

For a complete account of the argument supporting cardiopulmonary definition of death, whole brain death, and neocortical death, see President's Commission for the Study of Ethical Problems in Medicine and Biomedical and Behavioral Research, Defining Death: A Report on the Medical, Legal, and Ethical Issues In the Determination of Death (1981).

The best account of arguments in support of (and in opposition to) neocortical death are found in David Randall Smith, Legal Recognition of Neocortical Death, 71 Cornell L.Rev. 850 (1986) which includes a proposed neocortical death statute. See also Robert Veatch, The Definition of Death: Ethical, Philosophical and Policy Confusion, 315 Annals N.Y.Acad. of Sci. 307 (1978); R. Dworkin, Death in Context, 48 Ind.L.J. 623 (1973).

III. THE "DEAD DONOR" RULE AND EXPANDING CLASSES OF ORGAN DONORS—ANENCEPHALIC INFANTS AND "NON–HEART BEATING" DONORS

IN RE T.A.C.P.

Supreme Court of Florida, 1992.
609 So.2d 588.

KOGAN, JUSTICE.

We have for review an order of the trial court certified by the Fourth District Court of Appeal as touching on a matter of great public importance requiring immediate resolution by this Court. We frame the issue as follows:

Is an anencephalic newborn considered "dead" for purposes of organ donation solely by reason of its congenital deformity?

* * *

I. FACTS

At or about the eight month of pregnancy, the parents of the child T.A.C.P. were informed that she would be born with anencephaly. * * *

In this case, T.A.C.P. actually survived only a few days after birth. The medical evidence in the record shows that the child T.A.C.P. was incapable of developing any sort of cognitive process, may have been unable to feel pain or experience sensation due to the absence of the upper brain, and at least for part of the time was placed on a mechanical ventilator to assist her breathing. * * *

On the advice of physicians, the parents continued the pregnancy to term and agreed that the mother would undergo caesarean section during birth. The parents agreed to the caesarean procedure with the express hope that the infant's organs would be less damaged and could be used for transplant in other sick children. Although T.A.C.P. had no hope of life herself, the parents both testified in court that they wanted to use this opportunity to give life to others. However, when the parents requested that T.A.C.P. be declared legally dead for this purpose, her health care providers refused out of concern that they thereby might incur civil or criminal liability. * * *

II. THE MEDICAL NATURE OF ANENCEPHALY

Although appellate courts appear never to have confronted the issue, there already is an impressive body of published medical scholarship on anencephaly. From our review of this material, we find that anencephaly is a variable but fairly well defined medical condition. Experts in the field have written that anencephaly is the most common severe birth defect of the central nervous system seen in the United States, although it apparently has existed throughout human history.

A statement by the Medical Task Force on Anencephaly ("Task Force") printed in the New England Journal of Medicine generally described "anencephaly" as "a congenital absence of major portions of the brain, skull, and scalp, with its genesis in the first month of gestation." David A. Stumpf et al., *The Infant with Anencephaly*, 322 New Eng.J.Med. 669, 669 (1990). The large opening in the skull accompanied by the absence or severe congenital disruption of the cerebral hemispheres is the characteristic feature of the condition. *Id.*

The Task Force defined anencephaly as diagnosable only when all of the following four criteria are present:

> (1) A large portion of the skull is absent. (2) The scalp, which extends to the margin of the bone, is absent over the skull defect. (3) Hemorrhagic, fibrotic tissue is exposed because of defects in the skull and scalp. (4) Recognizable cerebral hemispheres are absent.

* * *

Thus, it is clear that anencephaly is distinguishable from some other congenital conditions because its extremity renders it uniformly lethal. * * *

The Task Force stated that most reported anencephalic children die within the first few days after birth, with survival any longer being rare. * * * The Task Force reported, however, that these survival rates are confounded somewhat by the variable degrees of medical care afforded to anencephalics. Some such infants may be given considerable life support while others may be given much less care.

The Task Force reported that the medical consequences of anencephaly can be established with some certainty. All anencephalics by definition are permanently unconscious because they lack the cerebral cortex necessary for conscious thought. Their condition thus is quite similar to that of persons in a persistent vegetative state. Where the brain stem is functioning, as it was here, spontaneous breathing and heartbeat can occur. In addition, such infants may show spontaneous movements of the extremities, "startle" reflexes, and pupils that respond to light. Some may show feeding reflexes, may cough, hiccup, or exhibit eye movements, and may produce facial expressions.

* * *

After the advent of new transplant methods in the past few decades, anencephalic infants have successfully been used as a source of organs for donation. * * *

There appears to be general agreement that anencephalics usually have ceased to be suitable organ donors by the time they meet all the criteria for "whole brain death," i.e., the complete absence of brainstem function. * * * There also is no doubt that a need exists for infant organs for transplantation. Nationally, between thirty and fifty percent of children under two years of age who need transplants die while waiting for organs to become available.* * *

III. LEGAL DEFINITIONS OF "DEATH" & "LIFE"

[The Florida Court described the legal developments that lead to the Uniform Determination of Death Act, but pointed out that Florida "struck out on its own," adopting no comprehensive statutory definition of death. Instead, the Florida statute merely permits the use of "irreversible cessation of the functioning of the entire brain" as the standard for determining death when a person's respiratory and circulatory systems are maintained "artificially;" the Florida statute does not expressly recognize cardiopulmonary death. Under this Florida definition, an anencephalic infant would be considered alive until there were irreversible cessation of the functioning of the entire brainstem.]

IV.   COMMON LAW & POLICY

* * *

The question remaining is whether there is good reason in public policy for this Court to create an additional common law standard applicable [only] to anencephalics. Alterations of the common law, while rarely entertained or allowed, are within this Court's prerogative.* * * We believe, for example, that our adoption of the cardiopulmonary definition of death today is required by public necessity and, in any event, merely formalizes what has been the common practice in this state for well over a century.

Such is not the case with petitioners' request. Our review of the medical, ethical, and legal literature on anencephaly discloses absolutely no consensus that public necessity or fundamental rights will be better served by granting this request.

We are not persuaded that a public necessity exists to justify this action, in light of the other factors in this case—although we acknowledge much ambivalence about this particular question. We have been deeply touched by the altruism and unquestioned motives of the parents of T.A.C.P. The parents have shown great humanity, compassion, and concern for others. The problem we as a Court must face, however, is that the medical literature shows unresolved controversy over the extent to which anencephalic organs can or should be used in transplants.

* * *

We express no opinion today about who is right and who is wrong on these issues—if any "right" or "wrong" can be found here. The salient point is that no consensus exists as to: (a) the utility of organ transplants of the type at issue here; (b) the ethical issues involved; or (c) the legal and constitutional problems implicated.

V.   CONCLUSIONS

Accordingly, we find no basis to expand the common law to equate anencephaly with death. We acknowledge the possibility that some infants' lives might be saved by using organs from anencephalics who do not meet the traditional definition of "death" we reaffirm today. But weighed against this is the utter lack of consensus, and the questions about the overall utility of such organ donations. The scales clearly tip in favor of not extending the common law in this instance.

To summarize: We hold that Florida common law recognizes the cardiopulmonary definition of death as stated above; and Florida statutes create a "whole-brain death" exception applicable whenever cardiopulmonary function is being maintained artificially. There are no other legal standards for determining death under present Florida law.

Because no Florida statute applies to the present case, the determination of death in this instance must be judged against the common law cardiopulmonary standard. The evidence shows that T.A.C.P.'s heart was beating and she was breathing at the times in question. Accordingly, she was not dead under Florida law, and no donation of her organs would have been legal.

COUNCIL ON ETHICAL AND JUDICIAL AFFAIRS, AMERICAN MEDICAL ASSOCIATION, THE USE OF ANENCEPHALIC NEONATES AS ORGAN DONORS

273 JAMA 1614 (1995)(subsequently withdrawn).

Hundreds of children die each year of cardiac, hepatic, or renal failure because there are not enough hearts, livers, or kidneys available for transplantation from other children. Consequently, various measures have been considered over the years to increase the organ supply for pediatric transplantation. One approach that has received particular attention is the possibility of using organs from anencephalic neonates.

* * *

In 1988, this Council examined the ethical issues surrounding the use of organs from anencephalic neonates and concluded that it is ethically acceptable to remove organs from anencephalic neonates only after they have died, whether the death occurs by cessation of cardiac function or brain function.* * * The new opinion states that it is ethically acceptable to transplant the organs of anencephalic neonates even before the neonates die, as long as there is parental consent and certain other safeguards are followed.

* * *

SHORTAGE OF ORGANS FOR TRANSPLANTING IN INFANTS AND YOUNG CHILDREN

* * *

With the scarcity of hearts, livers, and kidneys available for transplantation, 30% to 50% of children younger than 2 years die while waiting for transplants. Overall, 40% to 70% of children on the transplant waiting list die while waiting for a suitable organ. * * * Some commentators have therefore proposed that parents be allowed to donate organs from anencephalic neonates for transplantation.

ANENCEPHALY

Anencephaly is a developmental abnormality of the central nervous system that results in the "congenital absence of major portion of the brain, skull, and scalp." Because anencephalic neonates lack functioning cerebral hemispheres, they never experience any degree of consciousness. They never have thoughts, feelings, sensations, desires, or emotions. There is no purposeful action, social interaction, memory, pain, or suffering. Anencephalic neonates have fully or partially functioning brain stem tissue. Accordingly, they are able to maintain at least some of the body's autonomic function (ie, unconscious activity), including the functions of the heart, lungs, kidneys, and intestinal tract, as well as certain reflex actions. They may be able to breathe, suck, engage in spontaneous movements of their eyes, arms, and legs, respond to noxious stimuli with crying or avoidance maneuvers, and exhibit facial expressions typical of healthy infants. While all of this activity gives the appearance that the anencephalic neonate has some degree of consciousness, there is none. Anencephalic neonates are totally unaware of their existence and the environment in which they live.

* * *

Benefits of Permitting Parental Donation of Organs From Anencephalic Neonates

The argument in favor of parental donation of organs from anencephalic neonates is compelling: many children will be saved from death, and many other children will realize a substantial improvement in their quality of life. * * *

Organ transplantation from anencephalic neonates can bring profound benefit not only to the recipients of the organs but also to the parents of the anencephalic neonate. When confronted with the tragedy of bearing a child who can never experience consciousness and who will die in a matter of days, parents may find much of their psychological distress alleviated by the good that results from donating their child's organs and thereby providing lifesaving benefits to other children.* * *

Objections to Parental Donation of Organs From Anencephalic Neonates

Several objections are commonly raised against proposals for parental donation of organs from anencephalic neonates: (1) donation violates the prohibition against removal of life-necessary organs from living persons, (2) false diagnosis of anencephaly may result in the death of neonates who could achieve consciousness, (3) permitting donation from anencephalic neonates may open the door to organ removal from patients who are in a persistent vegetative state or in other severely disabling conditions, (4) anencephalic neonates would rarely be a source of organs for transplantation, and (5) allowing donation of organs from anencephalic neonates will undermine public confidence in the organ transplantation system. As discussed herein, however, these concerns do not justify a prohibition on parental donation of organs from anencephalic infants.

1. Prohibition Against Removal from Living Persons

Both law and ethics require that persons be dead before their life-necessary, nonrenewable organs are taken (the "dead donor" rule). This critical principle ensures that one person's life will not be sacrificed for the benefit of another person, even to preserve the life of that other person. While this principle must be vigorously maintained, it must not be applied without regard to whether its application serves its purposes. After consideration of the purposes of the general prohibition against removal of life-necessary organs before death, it is clear that those purposes would not be compromised by permitting parental donation of organs from anencephalic neonates.

Protecting the Interests of Persons From Whom Organs are Taken

Ordinarily, the dead donor rule protects the fundamental interest in life of persons from whom organs are taken. However, it does not make sense to speak of an interest of anencephalic neonates in staying alive. Because they have never experienced consciousness and will never experience consciousness, anencephalic neonates cannot have interests of any kind.* * *

Providing Reassurance to Other Individuals. By protecting the interests of persons from whom organs are taken, the dead donor rule provides reassurance to other individuals that, if they choose to become organ donors, their lives will not be shortened by the removal of their organs for the benefit of someone in need of an organ transplant. While this is a critical purpose of the dead donor rule, parental donation of organs from anencephalic neonates will not undermine the rule's reassuring role.* * *

Preserving the Value of Respect for Life. * * *

First it is important to emphasize that respect for the essential worth of life is an absolute value in the sense that it exists irrespective of a person's quality of life. However, it is not an absolute value in the sense of overriding all other values. Rather, it must be balanced with other important social values, including, as in this case, the fundamental social value of saving lives. * * *

Indeed, the primary argument in favor of permitting parental donation is an argument based on the value of respect for life. The whole point of allowing such donation is to ensure that many lives that would otherwise be lost are saved.

2. Accuracy of Diagnosis

There has been concern that allowing parental donation of organs from anencephalic neonates could lead to parental donation of organs from infants with similar, severe conditions but who are not anencephalic. Indeed, when researchers at Loma Linda University Medical Center conducted a protocol involving anencephalic neonates, some physicians referred infants to the protocol who were not in fact anencephalic.* * *

Nevertheless, while the possibility of misdiagnoses cannot be entirely eliminated, it can readily be reduced to an insignificant level with the adoption of appropriate safeguards.* * * To ensure that the diagnosis of anencephaly is as accurate as possible, the diagnosis should be confirmed by two physicians with special expertise in diagnosing anencephaly who are not part of the organ transplant team.* * *

3. Slippery Slope Concerns

* * *

There is an important reason why the slippery slope risk is not a serious one if society decides to permit parental donation of organs from anencephalic neonates. Anencephalic neonates are unique among persons because they have no history of consciousness and no possibility of ever being conscious.* * *

4. Number of Children Who Would Benefit

* * * The number of children who could benefit from the organs of anencephalic neonates may be considerably smaller than 1000; indeed, according to one estimate, no more than about 20 infants a year would gain a

longterm survival from a heart or liver transplant, and no more than another 25 infants would receive a long-term benefit from kidney transplantation.

This concern about the number of children who would benefit should not be a barrier to parental donation of organs from anencephalic neonates. First, the estimates are probably much too low.* * * More importantly, even assuming that there would be only 20 long-term survivals gained each year and that only long-term survivals matter, it is not clear why that should be an objection to parental donation of organs from anencephalic neonates. Among the different goals that health care can achieve, saving lives is of fundamental importance; indeed, it is never insignificant to save 20 lives.

* * *

5. *Public Trust in the Organ Procurement System*

Some commentators suggest that creating an exception to the dead donor rule may undermine society's confidence in the organ procurement system and cause a chilling effect on overall organ donations.* * * Inasmuch as the change in the definition of death has not compromised the effectiveness of the organ procurement system but has led to greater numbers of lives saved by organ transplantation, it is likely that permitting parental donation of organs from anencephalic neonates will also lead to greater numbers of lives saved rather than to compromise of the organ procurement system. In addition, while it is true that existing organ procurement practices should not be changed without due deliberation, change should be possible in response to important, unmet social needs and evolving understanding of the ethical and scientific issues surrounding anencephaly.

Accordingly, rather than prohibit parental donation of organs from anencephalic neonates, certain safeguards should be used to preserve public trust in the organ procurement system. First, parental donation of organs from anencephalic neonates should occur only if the discussion of donation is initiated by the parents of the neonates, not if it is initiated by members of the health care team. Second, parental donation should not occur without the fully informed consent of the parents of the anencephalic neonate. Third, a pilot program for parental donation of organs from anencephalic neonates should be undertaken to assess its impact before the practice becomes widespread. * * *

CONCLUSION

For the reasons described herein, the Council has developed the following opinion,

[Current Opinion] 2.162 Anencephalic Neonates as Organ Donors.

* * *

It is ethically permissible to consider the anencephalic neonate as a potential organ donor, although still alive under the current definition of death, only if: (1) the diagnosis of anencephaly is certain and is confirmed by two physicians *with special expertise* who are not part of the organ transplant team; (2) the parents of the neonate *initiate any discussions about organ retrieval and* indicate their desire for retrieval in writing, and (3) there is

compliance with the Council's Guidelines for the Transplantation of Organs
[ ].

In the alternative, a family wishing to donate the organs of their anencephalic neonate may choose to provide the neonate with ventilator assistance
and other medical therapies that might sustain organ perfusion and viability
until such time as a determination of death can be made in accordance with
current medical standards and relevant law. In this situation, the family
should be informed of the possibility that the organs might deteriorate in the
process, rendering them unsuitable for transplantation.

It is normally required that a person be legally dead before removal of
their life-necessary organs (the "dead donor rule"). The use of the anencephalic neonate as a live donor is a limited exception to the general standard
because of the fact that the infant has never experienced, and will never
experience, consciousness.

Notes on the Use of Anencephalic Infants as Organ Donors

1. The Council's opinion proved far more controversial among AMA members than was expected, and it was withdrawn shortly after it was released. The
issue is now under study——as it is expected to be for several years, until a social
consensus is reached on this issue.

2. If you were representing the parents of an anencephalic infant seeking to
have the court allow the child to be an organ donor, what arguments would you
make? Would you argue that the child is dead, and thus can provide organs
consistently with the "dead donor" rule, or would you argue that the child should
be permitted to be a donor even though he is alive? What jurisprudential concerns
are likely to motivate the court when it considers either of these arguments? Do
you think that it would be easier for a court to change the state law's definition of
death to encompass anencephalics, or to change the state law's acceptance of the
"dead donor" rule to encompass this class of living donors?

3. Did the Florida court properly decide the issue in *In re T.A.C.P.*? Would
the court have been influenced by the 1995 statement of the Council? The Council
was moved to adopt this position, in part, because of *T.A.C.P.* case, which it
discusses in the introduction to its report.

4. The AMA Council would require several procedures to safeguard the
integrity of any anencephalic who is to become an organ donor before death. First,
it would require that two physicians with special expertise who are not members
of the transplant team confirm the diagnosis of anencephaly. Given the fact that
few states require a second physician to confirm even a diagnosis of brain death,
and given the fact that anencephaly is more obvious and easier to diagnose than
brain death, is it appropriate to have this confirmation requirement?

Second, it would permit donation of live anencephalic organs only if the
discussion were initiated by the family of the anencephalic, not if it were initiated
by members of the health care team. If the choice of organ donation is a
reasonable and ethically sound one, though, shouldn't the family be informed of
possibility of donation in any case? If organ donation is psychologically important
to many parents of anencephalic infants, shouldn't the medically ignorant have
the same opportunity to donate their children's organs as the medically sophisticated who know that anencephalic neonates' organs can be made available for

transplant under some circumstances? Does the doctrine of informed consent require that the parents be told of this option?

Third, the AMA Council would begin with a pilot program for anencephalic organ donation at a "major medical center." Is there value in running such a pilot? Given the few organs likely to be transplanted from anencephalic donors, would a single-center pilot be likely to generate much generalizable knowledge on how successful this program would be? In any case, what criteria would you use to determine if such a pilot were successful?

Are there other safeguards you would add to assure the integrity of anencephalic infants who are potential donors?

5. The American Academy of Pediatrics recommends that the brain death standard not be applied to children under seven days old. Because most anencephalics do not live those seven days, the brain death analysis is unlikely ever to be applied to anencephalic infants who are potential donors. Does this help explain why the AMA Council recommended that anencephalics be treated as potential donors *even though they are alive* rather than that they be treated as dead, and, for that reason, eligible to be organ donors? Others, too, have suggested that anencephalics be treated as "brain absent" rather than "brain dead." For some purposes, the "brain absent" could be treated like dead people (e.g., they could be allowed to donate organs), while for other purposes they could be treated as living children (e.g., in a hospital they could be accorded all appropriate treatment).

6. There is some debate about whether anencephalics can feel pain or suffer. As the AMA Council points out, they may exhibit common reflexes to painful stimuli, but they cannot suffer the pain because they cannot be aware of it.

7. One reason there has been relatively little interest in the use of anencephalic infants as organ donors over the past few years is that there appear to be a relatively small (and decreasing) number of such potential donors. This is, in part, a consequence of physicians' expertise in diagnosing this condition in utero, and the subsequent availability of abortion. If the availability of abortions were to be more severely limited, there might be more anencephalic births, and thus, more potential anencephalic organ donors. Thus, any weakening of the Constitutional right to an abortion would make the resolution of the question of whether live anencephalic infants can be organ donors far more important.

8. While most studies show that anencephalic infants live for only a very short period of time—a few days—these studies do not suggest just how long anencephalics can live. Without aggressive treatment, anencephalic infants will die very quickly, and they rarely are provided any life-prolonging treatment. With very aggressive treatment, however, they may live much longer. The *Baby K* case, which follows, is a good example of a case in which an anencephalic was provided the extremely aggressive treatment her mother demanded; she lived more than two years.

9. An excellent brief bibliography on the use of anencephalic infants as organ donors is found in the "references" section of the AMA Council report, at 273 JAMA 1618 (1995). For a discussion of some of the medical issues, see Medical Task Force on Anencephaly, The Infant with Anencephaly, 322 N.Eng.J.Med. 669 (1990). See also D. Shewmon, Anencephaly: Selected Medical Aspects, 18(5) Hastings Cen. Rep. 11 (1988). For a good general account of the area, see J. Botkin, Anencephalic Infants as organ Donors, 82 Pediatrics 250 (1988). The first medical center to attempt a transplant from an anencephalic in the United States is Loma Linda Medical Center. An account of its most famous case—the "Baby

Gabrielle" case—is found in George Annas, From Canada with Love: Anencephalic Newborns as Organ Donors, 17 Hastings Cen. Rep. 36 (December 1987). For a comment on *In re T.A.C.P.*, see J.S. Justice, Personhood and Death—The Proper Treatment of Anencephalic Organ Donors Under the Law, 62 U. Cin. L. Rev. 1227 (1994). For a detailed account of the disadvantages of using anencephalics as organ donors, see David McDowell, Death of an Idea: The Anencephalic as an Organ Donor, 72 Tex. L. Rev. 893 (1994) and Paul Byrne et al., Anencephaly—Organ Transplantation?, 9 Issues L. & Med. 23 (1993).

10.   The question of whether anencephalic infants should be maintained or "allowed to die" arises in contexts other than the availability of transplantation of organs. For a discussion of whether they must be provided all available life-sustaining treatment under the Emergency Medical Treatment and Active Labor Act ("EMTALA"),"see chapter 11, above, and reconsider the following case and the accompanying notes:"

IN RE BABY K

[This case and the accompanying notes appears at pp. 780–785, above]

Problem: Non–Heart–Beating Donors

Holy Central Hospital (HCH) is a large teaching hospital associated with a medical school, and it faces a rather bleak economic future. In an effort to develop those programs that produce a substantial net revenue stream, the hospital decided to increase the size and activity of its transplant program. It hired a new transplant medical director, Dr. Joshua Niblet, who had been directing a financially very successful program at a competing hospital, and it authorized him to do "whatever is necessary" to develop HCH's transplant program. As a newly minted health lawyer and newly appointed assistant hospital counsel, you have been assigned to work with Dr. Niblet to help him institute the new program.

Dr. Niblet has reminded you that there is a substantial waiting list for all transplantable organs at HCH, and that the only real limit on the growth of transplant services is the availability of transplantable organs. To increase the supply of available organs, Dr. Niblet has already assured that an appropriate inquiry will be made of patients and their families whenever a potential donor may be available. Until now, all organs donated at HCH have come from patients who have been declared brain dead while they are on mechanical heart or lung support. The organs from these bodies tend to be the healthiest (and thus make the most successful transplants) because they remain warm and well oxygenated until the moment of removal.

Dr. Niblet would now like to obtain organs from those whose death has been declared as a result of the cessation of their heart and lung functions as well as those who are brain dead. These non-heart-beating donors (also called "asystolic donors") include those who are dead on arrival at the hospital, those who do not respond to resuscitation, and those from whom life sustaining medical treatment (e.g., a ventilator) have been withdrawn. See Yves Vanrenterghem, Cautious Approach to Use of Non–Heart–Beating–Donors, 356 Lancet 528 (2000). See also Y.W. Cho et al., Transplantation of Kidneys From Donors Whose Hearts Have Stopped Beating, 338 N. Eng. L. Med. 221 (1998). Although only about one percent of transplantable organs are retrieved from non-heart-beating donors in the United States now, some have estimated that the use of this class of donors could increase the number of organ sources by 1,000 a year. See Institute of

Medicine, Non–Heart–Beating Organ Transplantation: Medical and Ethical Issues in Procurement, 1997.

There are some practical problems with the use of organs from non-heart-beating donors. First, they don't seem to work quite as well as organs from the traditional class of brain dead donors. There seems to be a delay in graft function and a higher percentage of never-functioning organs from these sources, although the evidence is inconsistent and, Dr. Niblet insists, inconclusive. Second, very few hospitals are set up to identify potential non-heart-beating donors, even if they have developed procedures (mainly directed at the emergency room and the intensive care units) that assure that the traditional classes of potential organ donors will be identified. Dr. Niblet has assured you that these minor problems, as he describes them, will be overcome by the medical staff.

More significantly, though, there are three potential legal and ethical impediments to the development of such a plan. First, HCH must confront the unspoken uncertainty inherent in the declaration of death based on heart-lung criteria. Death is marked by the irreversible cessation of heart and lung functions, but when can a physician be certain that the cessation of those functions is truly irreversible? The longer that doctors wait after heart and lung functions have ceased before declaring the patient dead, the more the potentially transplantable organs will deteriorate. Transplant physicians (and potential recipients) generally hope that there will be little lag between the cessation of these functions and the declaration of death; others are concerned about this rush to judgment about death when a patient who could be revived might be declared dead prematurely. A number of time-lag standards have been adopted, and they differ from place to place. For example, European medical institutions seem to have settled on a ten minute delay between cessation of function and the declaration of death, while the Institute of Medicine in the United States recommends five minutes, and one of the nation's most active transplant centers, the University of Pittsburgh Medical Center, recommended only a two minute delay. See Varenterghem, supra.

Second, a non-heart-beating donor's body is often treated to preserve organs for transplant before the donor is declared dead. The donor may be given heparin and phentolamine (or other medications) in an effort to thin the blood, expand the blood vessels, cool down the body and thus preserve the organs. While a potential donor's death is always imminent when these medications are administered, these medications themselves may hasten the death of some patients–primarily, those with bleeding in the brain. Further, it is very rarely appropriate to impose a medical treatment on one person for the benefit of another; that would constitute the ethically unacceptable use of the first person for the benefit of the second. When the law does permit it (in the cases of blood donation and, rarely, live organ donation), the law is particularly skeptical of surrogate consent on behalf of incompetent donors. In the cases of non-heart-beating organ donors, however, any consent that would be obtained would, as a general matter, come from the patient's family, because the patient is likely to be incompetent. In fact, Dr. Niblet would like to be able to begin administering the medications while the HCH staff seeks out the family to obtain consent for the organ donations.

Third, and derivative of the first two, the local district attorney has declared that an attempt to obtain organs from non-heart-beating donors would appear to constitute murder. Further, the district attorney has announced that she would consider a prosecution for aggravated murder "in an appropriate case" where the murder was committed by those who would benefit financially as a result of the death, i.e., the transplant team. For an example of such a threat (and its result), see Joan Mazzolini, Guidelines Sought for Taking Organs from Patients Not Declared Brain–Dead, Cleveland Plain Dealer, December 20, 1997, pg. 1A.

What advice would you give to Dr. Niblet? Would you encourage him to begin seeking organ donations from non-heart-beating donors at the hospital? Would you discourage him? What advice would you give to him with regard to how he should operate any program he decides to undertake? What would you tell him with regard to (1) how long a delay there should be between the cessation of heart and lung functions and and the declaration of death, (2) who should make the declaration of death (i.e., can Dr. Niblet make that declaration just before he removes the organs for transplant?), (3) how consent should be obtained from the donor or the donor's surrogate, (4) whether medications can be administered to the donor (and other "treatment" provided) to preserve the organs for transplant before the donor is declared dead, (5) the potential interest of the district attorney, and (6) the public relations consequences of the decision.? Would you seek out the district attorney and talk with her about this issue? What would you tell her? Could you work out an understanding with her that would define those cases when the use of non-heart-beating donors would not subject your medical team to prosecution? With all of these factors in mind, draft the "HCH Policy on Non–Heart–Beating Donors."

IV. RELIGIOUS AND OTHER OBJECTIONS TO DEFINITIONS OF DEATH: LETTING THE PATIENT DECIDE WHICH DEFINITION TO USE

For a host of religious or moral reasons, or because one mistrusts those charged with determining death, or for some other reason, one may wish to choose a definition of death that is different from the one that has been adopted by law. Some religious groups—Orthodox Jews, some sects of Muslims and some Buddhists, for example—do not accept the notion of brain death. Should states impose their "brain death" statutes on those who oppose them on such religious grounds? To what extent, if any, should states recognize or accommodate differing religious notions of death? At least two states have promulgated laws that take into account the fact that people with some religious beliefs may not accept the state's definition of death, and in those states those people are permitted to opt out of the general state definition of death under some circumstances. The New Jersey "exemption to accommodate personal religious beliefs" provides:

> The death of an individual shall not be declared upon the basis of neurological criteria pursuant to [other] sections of this act when the licensed physician authorized to declare death, has reason to believe, on the basis of information in the individual's available medical records, or information provided by a member of the individual's family or any other person knowledgeable about the individual's personal religious beliefs that such a declaration would violate the personal religious beliefs of the individual. In these cases, death shall be declared, and the time of death fixed, solely upon the basis of cardio-respiratory criteria....

N.J. Stat. Ann. Sec. 26:6A–5. For a review of this statute, see Paul Armstrong and Robert Olick, Innovative Legislature Initiatives: The New Jersey Declaration of Death and Advance Directives for Health Care Acts, 16 Seton Hall

Legis. J. 177 (1992). New York has done much the same thing by regulation. See N.Y. Codes, Rules and Regs., Title 10, Sec. 400–16.

How should the New Jersey statute be applied? Should physicians understand the basic principles of all religious faiths concerning brain death, and also seek to know all of their patients' religious beliefs? Should physicians presume that Orthodox Jews, for example, do not want to be pronounced dead based on neurological criteria? Should they presume that Presbyterians all accept brain death (or, at least, do not reject it on religious grounds)? Is a brain dead (but not heart-lung dead) patient at the mercy of the religious whims of his family? What if some family members disagree with others over whether the patient would accept the application of brain death criteria? What if a family member disagrees with an "other person knowledgeable about the individual's personal religious beliefs"? On the other hand, doesn't it make sense for the state to honor its citizens religious beliefs over such an important and fundamental, literally life and death, matter, even if there might be an occasional uncertainty?

The "brain death" criteria may not be the only criteria for death that creates problems for individuals. Is there any reason to allow a patient to opt out of the brain death criteria but not the heart-lung criteria? What if a New Age religionist argues that his deeply held religious views require that he be treated as dead when he loses higher brain function? Must the state honor his request if it honors the Orthodox Jew's request to apply the heart-lung criteria? What if a patient claims that his personal religious beliefs require that he be treated as dead as soon as he is diagnosed as being terminally ill? Whenever he loses more than $200 at the slots? For a general discussion of these issues (except for the issue of casino gambling), see Kathleen Boozang, Deciding the Fate of Religious Hospitals in the Emerging Health Care Market, 31 Hous. L. Rev. 1429 (1995).

Not all deeply held beliefs are religious, of course. Would it be a violation of the establishment clause to allow individuals or families to opt out of the state mandated definition of death for religious reasons, but not for other moral, political or personal reasons? Law aside, is there any policy reason to treat decisions in this area based on religious views in a different way than the identical decisions based on other views? Is the solution to allow all individuals to choose their own definition of death? Perhaps the state could adopt a default position on the definition of death—perhaps the Uniform Determination of Death Act—and then maintain a central registry of all of those who would prefer to have some other standard applied. Are there any practical problems with this approach? Could they be overcome?

Chapter 19

LIFE AND DEATH DECISIONS

I. PRINCIPLES OF AUTONOMY
AND BENEFICENCE

Over the last several years the law has been invoked regularly by physicians and other health care providers concerned about the ethical, legal, and medical propriety of discontinuing what is now generally referred to as "life sustaining treatment." A number of questions taken to the courts and legislatures arguably are outside the competence of the law. For example, consider what might constitute a "terminal illness," a concept that some have considered relevant in bioethical decision making. While there surely is a medical element to a determination that a patient is "terminally ill," reflection upon the suggestion that there could be a lab test for this condition indicates that it is more than that. Classifying a patient as "terminally ill" depends on a combination of the patient's medical condition and the social, ethical, and legal consequences of the classification. If such a classification triggers a provision in a living will or a durable power of attorney, or if it allows a physician to participate in an assisted suicide, for example, it might be treated differently than if it triggers the patient's relocation from one room to another within a hospital.

If a determination of terminal illness is not solely a medical decision, but rather a hybrid medical, ethical, social, political, and legal determination, where is the locus of appropriate decision making? Should the decision be made by health care professionals alone? By a patient and his family? By a hospital committee? By some external committee? By a court appointed guardian? By the court itself? By the state legislature? By Congress? Should the decision be based upon principles and rules that emerge from medicine, ethics, religion, litigation, or legislative social policy making? Finally, what substantive principles ought to govern the decision-maker?

The difficulties in allocating decision-making authority and developing appropriate substantive principles are not limited to the "terminal illness" classification. They extend to such defining terms as "irreversible coma," "life-sustaining treatment," "death prolonging," "maintenance medical care," "extraordinary means," "heroic efforts," "intractable pain," "suffering," and even breathing and feeding. For almost every question that arises within the bioethics sphere, we must make two determinations: (1) where should the problem be resolved, and (2) what substantive principles should apply. Thus, the questions become ones of process (who will decide and how) and substance (what principles must form the basis of a recognized decision). As one might expect, the substantive questions are often hidden in apparently procedural inquiries.

Substantive Principles. Three substantive principles form the basis of many bioethics debates: autonomy, beneficence, and social justice. Autonomy and beneficence are the principles most directly implicated in the questions considered in this chapter, although questions of cost allocation and rationing generally implicate social justice.

The principle of autonomy declares that each person is in control of his own person, including his body and mind. This principle, in its purest form, presumes that no other person or social institution ought to intervene to overcome a person's desires, whether or not those desires are "right" from any external perspective. If Mr. Smith wants to die, then Mr. Smith is entitled to die as he sees fit, at least as long as he chooses a method that does not substantially affect anyone else.

The principle of beneficence declares that what is best for each person should be accomplished. The principle incorporates both the negative obligation of nonmaleficence ("primum non nocere"—"first of all, do no harm"— the foundation of the Hippocratic oath) and the positive obligation to do that which is good. Thus, a physician is obliged, under the principle of beneficence, to provide the highest quality medical care for each of his patients. Similarly, a physician ought to treat a seriously ill newborn in a way that is most medically beneficial for that infant, whatever he may think the infant "wants" and whatever the baby's parents may desire.

When a person does not desire what others determine to be in his interest, the principles of autonomy and beneficence conflict. For example, if we treat the continued life of a healthy person to be in that person's interest, the values of autonomy and beneficence become inconsistent when a healthy competent adult decides to take his own life. As a general matter, most courts now appear to recognize the principle of autonomy as the first principle of medical ethics. The principle of beneficence is generally applied by courts and bioethics scholars when autonomy is impossible to apply, as where the patient is a newborn infant who has not developed any values, wishes or desires. As we will soon see, though, the primacy of the principles can be changed by legislative enactments, and they may also change in accord with prevailing judicial philosophies.

Because issues of bioethics have started to come before the courts only over the past few decades, the courts have looked elsewhere to find principles upon which to base their judgments. Courts have regularly looked both to the traditions of the common law and the traditions of ethics and medicine. Analogously, judicial decisions have often formed the basis for new ethical and medical approaches. In fact, the debate over appropriate ethical policy in determining when life support systems should be initiated or discontinued, and over whether physicians should be permitted to aid in the death of a patient, now involve lawyers as much as bioethics scholars, and the public debates on these issues have centered on the judicial resolution of cases as much as on any other source of formal principles. The law is not merely looking to ethics for potential methods of analysis, it is usurping ethics in debate on these issues.

The law is not developed only through rationally justified and formally articulated judicial opinions. The law also comes out of political compromises, consequent legislative action, and public perceptions of well-publicized bioethical cases. Congress's decision to fund kidney dialysis through an expansion of the Medicare program for all those who need it, for example, has had a substantial effect on determining who shall live and who shall die. Although it is hard to find a scholar of bioethics who supports Dr. Kevorkian's euthanasia procedures, he is largely responsible for starting the current active public debate on physician assisted death. Infants have names, and cry, and can be cuddled, while fetuses do none of these things; not surprisingly, we are willing to spend a great deal more to treat seriously ill newborns than we are to provide prenatal care.

Finally, the increasingly overtly political nature of some questions—such as whether physicians may assist in their patients' deaths—has brought formerly nonpolitical, personal questions into the political sphere. As a matter of social policy, is this society spending too much to extend the life of the very ill? In 1985, Governor Lamm of Colorado was considered outrageous when he suggested that the elderly may have an obligation to die; today the social consequences of health care decisions have become a matter of real concern to those who realize that all of their family assets easily could be consumed by a final illness. Additionally, there is real controversy over whether there is any truth to the public perception that medical resources are being used (much less, wasted) to prolong the dying process.

While courts formally look to general rules of health care decision making to determine when a patient or a patient's family may terminate life sustaining medical treatment, those general rules are not often defined with precision. Of course, the starting point is generally the law of informed consent, which is discussed above in chapter 5. The law of informed consent is bolstered by state administrative regulations (often from the state health department or its equivalent), state statutes (for example, patients' rights provisions in some states), state constitutional provisions (including the sometimes state-protected right of privacy), federal regulations (like those governing research involving human subjects), federal statutes, and the United States Constitution. Because of the significance of medical decisions that will result in death, those decisions are more likely than other medical decisions to be litigated. As a result, general health care decision making principles frequently have been developed in these end-of-life cases, and then generalized to other, arguably easier, cases. Thus, this chapter will address "life and death decisions," but the principles that arise out of it are principles that apply to other health care decisions, too. In the Cruzan and Glucksberg cases, which you are about to read, the United States Supreme Court was called upon to apply the Constitution to end-of-life care, but the principles it established in those cases have ramifications throughout the health care system.

In reading this chapter, consider what role individuals, families, hospitals, health care professionals, courts, legislatures, and others ought to play in dealing with the ethical, medical, legal, social and political questions that often arise out of our new found technical ability to maintain life. As you review the way courts and others have considered individual cases, attempt to distill reasoned principles from their judgments and apply them to the following problem. What issues arise at each point in the course of the problem? Do the issues change? Is your analysis a procedural or substantive one? Who ought to be involved in the decision making at each point? Are the principles of autonomy and beneficence equally relevant at each point?

Problem: Right to Die

Mr. Karl, an otherwise healthy 62 year–old man, arrived at the Pleasant City General Hospital emergency room by ambulance. He had serious stab wounds to his chest and back, and he was losing blood quickly. The emergency technician on the ambulance explained to the emergency room physicians that he was called to the Howdy Podner Bar by its owner, who telephoned to report a fight and request an ambulance. He said that Mr. Karl complained that he had been knifed by his son and that Mr. Karl was generally uncooperative, but was too weak to success-fully oppose the ambulance attendants on the four block drive to the hospital. Mr. Karl's wife, who was called by another patron at the bar, arrived at the emergency room at the same time as Mr. Karl.

When an emergency room physician explained to Mr. Karl that he required several units of blood, Mr. Karl absolutely refused to accept that form of treatment. He said that he understood the consequences of not receiving blood under the circumstances—that death would be likely, if not inevitable. However, he explained that his Jehovah's Witness faith did not allow him to consent to a blood transfusion. In any case, he explained, religion or not, he "had his own reasons" for not wanting to survive this stabbing, and he did not want any blood. His wife, who is also a Jehovah's Witness, begged the doctor to provide the blood and save her husband's life. She explained that her husband was misinterpreting Jehovah's Witness doctrine, which permitted a blood transfusion in certain circumstances. In fact, she argued, their faith does not require that he not be given blood, it merely requires that he not actively give his consent to receiving blood. She pointed out that they had been married for 35 years and that she knew he wanted the transfusion, but that he felt obliged by his religion to appear to oppose it. Physicians treated his wounds but did not provide any blood. They did begin intravenous fluid support, which ameliorated the effect of lost blood.

Mr. Karl was maintained in the emergency room. He continued to object to any form of blood transfusion, but after several hours of blood loss he became less coherent. He began to cry about the guilt he suffered from stabbing his son, and he began talking about the Lord's revenge upon evil men. When he was ap-proached by physicians, he demanded that they kill him—or allow him to kill himself—or, at least, allow him to die. At one point he screamed "can't you morphine me to death like the other patients? Please, help me die; I want to die but I cannot face the pain."

About 10 hours after he arrived at the emergency room, he was afflicted with an apparent stroke and slipped into unconsciousness. He then was moved to the intensive care unit. He lost breathing capacity and the intensive care physician placed him on a ventilator. Shortly after his move, his three daughters arrived, confirmed what their mother had said earlier, and begged that their father be given all available treatment, including blood. His only son, with whom he had been fighting earlier in the evening, was arrested and remained in jail.

Within the next several hours all bleeding ceased, and Mr. Karl remained in stable condition. Given the consequences of the stroke, his physicians concluded that there was virtually no hope that Mr. Karl would regain any cognitive abilities. Although a special surgical procedure for dealing with cases like Mr. Karl's was undergoing clinical trials at a major medical center a thousand miles away, that technique (the "Watson Shunt") had never been successful, and Mr. Karl's family was not told about it. Intravenous nutritional supplementation was commenced, then replaced by a nasogastric tube (i.e., a tube inserted through the nose into the stomach) through which nutrition was passed directly to his stomach.

After her father had spent two weeks in intensive care, one of the daughters requested that her father's ventilator be removed. The doctors explained that they had several options. The ventilator could be removed at once, which would surely lead to her father's death. He could be "weaned" from the ventilator, with ventilator support slowly removed (and reinstated when necessary), a process which would not result in his immediate death but would be likely to shorten his life substantially. He could be "terminally weaned," which would be the same as the weaning process except that the support would not be reinstated, even if it were necessary; in this case he would be given enough medication to assure that he would suffer no distress although the medication would likely depress his ability to breath on his own, if he had that capacity. Finally, he could be maintained on the ventilator.

Mr. Karl's wife and daughters determined that he should be removed from the ventilator in whatever manner the physician thought proper, and he was successfully "weaned" from it. A week later Mr. Karl's wife asked that his feeding tube be removed. She said, "He always said that the worst thing that could ever happen to him was to be a vegetable like that Cruzan girl. He wouldn't want to live if he could not go hunting and watch football." In addition, his family physician reported that he had once talked to Mr. Karl about advance directives and that Mr. Karl had asked for a form, although he had not filled it out. Two of the three daughters agreed with their mother that the feeding tube should be removed, but one strongly objected, saying that she believed it would be wrong, from a moral and religious point of view, to do so. In fact, she had thoroughly researched the issue and learned about the "Watson shunt" trials. She insisted that her father be given the Watson shunt, or transferred to a hospital where he could receive it, because, "who knows, there is a 1 in a million chance it will work, and it is his best hope."

Mr. Karl's wife and children are his only heirs. He has always been particularly close to the daughter who does not want his feeding tube removed. His family physician reports that during a previous hospitalization for an ulcer, Mr. Karl depended heavily upon his wife, and left every treatment decision to her. The current medical and hospital charges of about $6500 per day are paid by Mr. Karl's insurance (80%), and by his family (through their 20% coinsurance obligation). Mr. & Mrs. Karl's savings will be exhausted in another few weeks when the maximum annual payout on the insurance policy will also have been met. Mrs. Karl has not been able to work at her full time hourly-wage job since her husband's hospitalization; although she has not been fired, she is paid only for the hours she works. Mr. Karl's employer has fired him, though regretfully. Mrs. Karl is considering a second mortgage for their modest home. It is likely that Mr. Karl's care will be covered by Medicaid, through which the State will pay medical and hospital expenses of about $2400 per day to provide for his treatment.

What treatment would have been appropriate at each point in Mr. Karl's hospitalization? How should that have been decided? What judicial consequences could (and should) each medical decision have? Would your answer be different if you were Mr. Karl? A member of Mr. Karl's family? One of his creditors? His lawyer? A member of the hospital board of directors? The hospital administrator? The doctor? A nurse? The hospital ethics committee? The hospital lawyer? The doctor's (or hospital's) insurance company? A judge? Is there other information you would need to answer these questions? What information? How, exactly, would it affect your answers?

II.   THE UNITED STATES CONSTITUTION AND THE "RIGHT TO DIE"

CRUZAN v. DIRECTOR, MISSOURI DEPARTMENT OF HEALTH

Supreme Court of the United States, 1990.
497 U.S. 261, 110 S.Ct. 2841, 111 L.Ed.2d 224.

CHIEF JUSTICE REHNQUIST delivered the opinion of the Court.

Petitioner Nancy Beth Cruzan was rendered incompetent as a result of severe injuries sustained during an automobile accident. Co-petitioners Lester and Joyce Cruzan, Nancy's parents and co-guardians, sought a court order directing the withdrawal of their daughter's artificial feeding and hydration equipment after it became apparent that she had virtually no chance of recovering her cognitive faculties. The Supreme Court of Missouri held that because there was no clear and convincing evidence of Nancy's desire to have life-sustaining treatment withdrawn under such circumstances, her parents lacked authority to effectuate such a request. We granted certiorari and now affirm.

On the night of January 11, 1983, Nancy Cruzan lost control of her car as she traveled down Elm Road in Jasper County, Missouri. The vehicle overturned, and Cruzan was discovered lying face down in a ditch without detectable respiratory or cardiac function. Paramedics were able to restore her breathing and heartbeat at the accident site, and she was transported to a hospital in an unconscious state. An attending neurosurgeon diagnosed her as having sustained probable cerebral contusions compounded by significant anoxia (lack of oxygen). The Missouri trial court in this case found that permanent brain damage generally results after 6 minutes in an anoxic state; it was estimated that Cruzan was deprived of oxygen from 12 to 14 minutes. She remained in a coma for approximately three weeks and then progressed to an unconscious state in which she was able to orally ingest some nutrition. In order to ease feeding and further the recovery, surgeons implanted a gastrostomy feeding and hydration tube in Cruzan with the consent of her then husband. Subsequent rehabilitative efforts proved unavailing. She now lies in a Missouri state hospital in what is commonly referred to as a persistent vegetative state: generally, a condition in which a person exhibits motor reflexes but evinces no indications of significant cognitive function. The State of Missouri is bearing the cost of her care.

After it had become apparent that Nancy Cruzan had virtually no chance of regaining her mental faculties her parents asked hospital employees to terminate the artificial nutrition and hydration procedures. All agree that such a removal would cause her death. The employees refused to honor the request without court approval. The parents then sought and received authorization from the state trial court for termination. The court found that a person in Nancy's condition had a fundamental right under the State and Federal Constitutions to refuse or direct the withdrawal of "death prolonging procedures." The court also found that Nancy's "expressed thoughts at age twenty-five in somewhat serious conversation with a housemate friend that if sick or injured she would not wish to continue her life unless she could live at least halfway normally suggests that given her present condition she would not wish to continue on with her nutrition and hydration."

The Supreme Court of Missouri reversed by a divided vote. * * *

We granted certiorari to consider the question of whether Cruzan has a right under the United States Constitution which would require the hospital to withdraw life-sustaining treatment from her under these circumstances.

* * *

State courts have available to them for decision a number of sources—state constitutions, statutes, and common law—which are not available to us. In this Court, the question is simply and starkly whether the United States Constitution prohibits Missouri from choosing the rule of decision which it did. This is the first case in which we have been squarely presented with the issue of whether the United States Constitution grants what is in common parlance referred to as a "right to die."

* * *

The Fourteenth Amendment provides that no State shall "deprive any person of life, liberty, or property, without due process of law." The principle that a competent person has a constitutionally protected liberty interest in refusing unwanted medical treatment may be inferred from our prior decisions. * * *

But determining that a person has a "liberty interest" under the Due Process Clause does not end the inquiry;[1] "whether respondent's constitutional rights have been violated must be determined by balancing his liberty interests against the relevant state interests." [ ]

Petitioners insist that under the general holdings of our cases, the forced administration of life-sustaining medical treatment, and even of artificially-delivered food and water essential to life, would implicate a competent person's liberty interest. Although we think the logic of the cases discussed above would embrace such a liberty interest, the dramatic consequences involved in refusal of such treatment would inform the inquiry as to whether the deprivation of that interest is constitutionally permissible. But for purposes of this case, we assume that the United States Constitution would grant a competent person a constitutionally protected right to refuse lifesaving hydration and nutrition.

---

1. Although many state courts have held that a right to refuse treatment is encompassed by a generalized constitutional right of privacy, we have never so held. We believe this issue is more properly analyzed in terms of a Fourteenth Amendment liberty interest. See *Bowers v. Hardwick,* 478 U.S. 186, 194–195 (1986).

Petitioners go on to assert that an incompetent person should possess the same right in this respect as is possessed by a competent person. * * *

The difficulty with petitioners' claim is that in a sense it begs the question: an incompetent person is not able to make an informed and voluntary choice to exercise a hypothetical right to refuse treatment or any other right. Such a "right" must be exercised for her, if at all, by some sort of surrogate. Here, Missouri has in effect recognized that under certain circumstances a surrogate may act for the patient in electing to have hydration and nutrition withdrawn in such a way as to cause death, but it has established a procedural safeguard to assure that the action of the surrogate conforms as best it may to the wishes expressed by the patient while competent. Missouri requires that evidence of the incompetent's wishes as to the withdrawal of treatment be proved by clear and convincing evidence. The question, then, is whether the United States Constitution forbids the establishment of this procedural requirement by the State. We hold that it does not.

Whether or not Missouri's clear and convincing evidence requirement comports with the United States Constitution depends in part on what interests the State may properly seek to protect in this situation. Missouri relies on its interest in the protection and preservation of human life, and there can be no gainsaying this interest. As a general matter, the States—indeed, all civilized nations—demonstrate their commitment to life by treating homicide as serious crime. Moreover, the majority of States in this country have laws imposing criminal penalties on one who assists another to commit suicide. We do not think a State is required to remain neutral in the face of an informed and voluntary decision by a physically-able adult to starve to death.

But in the context presented here, a State has more particular interests at stake. The choice between life and death is a deeply personal decision of obvious and overwhelming finality. We believe Missouri may legitimately seek to safeguard the personal element of this choice through the imposition of heightened evidentiary requirements. It cannot be disputed that the Due Process Clause protects an interest in life as well as an interest in refusing life-sustaining medical treatment. Not all incompetent patients will have loved ones available to serve as surrogate decisionmakers. * * * A State is entitled to guard against potential abuses in such situations. Similarly, a State is entitled to consider that a judicial proceeding to make a determination regarding an incompetent's wishes may very well not be an adversarial one, with the added guarantee of accurate factfinding that the adversary process brings with it. [ ] Finally, we think a State may properly decline to make judgments about the "quality" of life that a particular individual may enjoy, and simply assert an unqualified interest in the preservation of human life to be weighed against the constitutionally protected interests of the individual.

In our view, Missouri has permissibly sought to advance these interests through the adoption of a "clear and convincing" standard of proof to govern such proceedings.

* * *

We think it self-evident that the interests at stake in the instant proceedings are more substantial, both on an individual and societal level, than those involved in a run-of-the-mine civil dispute. But not only does the standard of proof reflect the importance of a particular adjudication, it also serves as "a societal judgment about how the risk of error should be distributed between the litigants." [ ] The more stringent the burden of proof a party must bear, the more that party bears the risk of an erroneous decision. We believe that Missouri may permissibly place an increased risk of an erroneous decision on those seeking to terminate an incompetent individual's life-sustaining treatment. An erroneous decision not to terminate results in a maintenance of the status quo; the possibility of subsequent developments such as advancements in medical science, the discovery of new evidence regarding the patient's intent, changes in the law, or simply the unexpected death of the patient despite the administration of life-sustaining treatment, at least create the potential that a wrong decision will eventually be corrected or its impact mitigated. An erroneous decision to withdraw life-sustaining treatment, however, is not susceptible of correction.

* * *

In sum, we conclude that a State may apply a clear and convincing evidence standard in proceedings where a guardian seeks to discontinue nutrition and hydration of a person diagnosed to be in a persistent vegetative state. * * *

The Supreme Court of Missouri held that in this case the testimony adduced at trial did not amount to clear and convincing proof of the patient's desire to have hydration and nutrition withdrawn. * * * The testimony adduced at trial consisted primarily of Nancy Cruzan's statements made to a housemate about a year before her accident that she would not want to live should she face life as a "vegetable," and other observations to the same effect. The observations did not deal in terms with withdrawal of medical treatment or of hydration and nutrition. We cannot say that the Supreme Court of Missouri committed constitutional error in reaching the conclusion that it did.

* * *

JUSTICE O'CONNOR, concurring.

I agree that a protected liberty interest in refusing unwanted medical treatment may be inferred from our prior decisions, and that the refusal of artificially delivered food and water is encompassed within that liberty interest. I write separately to clarify why I believe this to be so.

As the Court notes, the liberty interest in refusing medical treatment flows from decisions involving the State's invasions into the body. Because our notions of liberty are inextricably entwined with our idea of physical freedom and self-determination, the Court has often deemed state incursions into the body repugnant to the interests protected by the Due Process Clause. [ ] The State's imposition of medical treatment on an unwilling competent adult necessarily involves some form of restraint and intrusion. A seriously ill or dying patient whose wishes are not honored may feel a captive of the machinery required for life-sustaining measures or other medical interventions. Such forced treatment may burden that individual's liberty interests as much as any state coercion. [ ]

The State's artificial provision of nutrition and hydration implicates identical concerns. Artificial feeding cannot readily be distinguished from other forms of medical treatment. * * * Whether or not the techniques used to pass food and water into the patient's alimentary tract are termed "medical treatment," it is clear they all involve some degree of intrusion and restraint. Feeding a patient by means of a nasogastric tube requires a physician to pass a long flexible tube through the patient's nose, throat and esophagus and into the stomach. Because of the discomfort such a tube causes, "[m]any patients need to be restrained forcibly and their hands put into large mittens to prevent them from removing the tube." * * * A gastrostomy tube (as was used to provide food and water to Nancy Cruzan), or jejunostomy tube must be surgically implanted into the stomach or small intestine. * * * Requiring a competent adult to endure such procedures against her will burdens the patient's liberty, dignity, and freedom to determine the course of her own treatment. Accordingly, the liberty guaranteed by the Due Process Clause must protect, if it protects anything, an individual's deeply personal decision to reject medical treatment, including the artificial delivery of food and water.

I also write separately to emphasize that the Court does not today decide the issue whether a State must also give effect to the decisions of a surrogate decisionmaker. In my view, such a duty may well be constitutionally required to protect the patient's liberty interest in refusing medical treatment. Few individuals provide explicit oral or written instructions regarding their intent to refuse medical treatment should they become incompetent. States which decline to consider any evidence other than such instructions may frequently fail to honor a patient's intent. Such failures might be avoided if the State considered an equally probative source of evidence: the patient's appointment of a proxy to make health care decisions on her behalf.

* * *

Today's decision, holding only that the Constitution permits a State to require clear and convincing evidence of Nancy Cruzan's desire to have artificial hydration and nutrition withdrawn, does not preclude a future determination that the Constitution requires the States to implement the decisions of a patient's duly appointed surrogate. Nor does it prevent States from developing other approaches for protecting an incompetent individual's liberty interest in refusing medical treatment. * * * Today we decide only that one State's practice does not violate the Constitution; the more challenging task of crafting appropriate procedures for safeguarding incompetents' liberty interests is entrusted to the "laboratory" of the States, in the first instance.

Justice Scalia, concurring.

* * *

While I agree with the Court's analysis today, and therefore join in its opinion, I would have preferred that we announce, clearly and promptly, that the federal courts have no business in this field; that American law has always accorded the State the power to prevent, by force if necessary, suicide—including suicide by refusing to take appropriate measures necessary to preserve one's life; that the point at which life becomes "worthless," and the point at which the means necessary to preserve it become "extraordinary" or "inappropriate," are neither set forth in the Constitution nor known to the nine Justices of this Court any better than they are known to nine people picked at random from the Kansas City telephone directory; and hence, that even when it *is* demonstrated by clear and convincing evidence that a patient no longer wishes certain measures to be taken to preserve her life, it is up to the citizens of Missouri to decide, through their elected representatives, whether that wish will be honored. It is quite impossible (because the Constitution says nothing about the matter) that those citizens will decide upon a line less lawful than the one we would choose; and it is unlikely (because we know no more about "life-and-death" than they do) that they will decide upon a line less reasonable.

The text of the Due Process Clause does not protect individuals against deprivations of liberty *simpliciter*. It protects them against deprivations of liberty "without due process of law." To determine that such a deprivation would not occur if Nancy Cruzan were forced to take nourishment against her will, it is unnecessary to reopen the historically recurrent debate over whether "due process" includes substantive restrictions. [ ] It is at least true that no "substantive due process" claim can be maintained unless the claimant demonstrates that the State has deprived him of a right historically and traditionally protected against State interference. [ ] That cannot possibly be established here.

* * * "[T]here is no significant support for the claim that a right to suicide is so rooted in our tradition that it may be deemed 'fundamental' or 'implicit in the concept of ordered liberty.' "[ ]

Petitioners rely on three distinctions to separate Nancy Cruzan's case from ordinary suicide: (1) that she is permanently incapacitated and in pain; (2) that she would bring on her death not by any affirmative act but by merely declining treatment that provides nourishment; and (3) that preventing her from effectuating her presumed wish to die requires violation of her bodily integrity. None of these suffices.

[Scalia points out (1) that pain and incapacity have never constituted legal defenses to a charge of suicide, (2) that the distinction between "action" and "inaction" is logically and legally meaningless, and (3) that preventing suicide often (or always) requires the violation of bodily integrity, and it begs the question of whether the refusal of treatment is itself suicide.]

* * *

To raise up a constitutional right here we would have to create out of nothing (for it exists neither in text nor tradition) some constitutional principle whereby, although the State may insist that an individual come in out of the cold and eat food, it may not insist that he take medicine; and although it may pump his stomach empty of poison he has ingested, it may not fill his stomach with food he has failed to ingest. Are there, then, no reasonable and humane limits that ought not to be exceeded in requiring an individual to preserve his own life? There obviously are, but they are not set forth in the Due Process Clause. What assures us that those limits will not be exceeded is the same constitutional guarantee that is the source of most of our protection—what protects us, for example, from being assessed a tax of 100% of our income above the subsistence level, from being forbidden to drive cars, or from being required to send our children to school for 10 hours a day, none of which horribles is categorically prohibited by the Constitution. Our salvation is the Equal Protection Clause, which requires the democratic majority to accept for themselves and their loved ones what they impose on you and me. This Court need not, and has no authority to, inject itself into every field of human activity where irrationality and oppression may theoretically occur, and if it tries to do so it will destroy itself.

JUSTICE BRENNAN, with whom JUSTICE MARSHALL and JUSTICE BLACKMUN join, dissenting.

* * *

Today the Court, while tentatively accepting that there is some degree of constitutionally protected liberty interest in avoiding unwanted medical treatment, including life-sustaining medical treatment such as artificial nutrition and hydration, affirms the decision of the Missouri Supreme Court. The majority opinion, as I read it, would affirm that decision on the ground that a State may require "clear and convincing" evidence of Nancy Cruzan's prior decision to forgo life-sustaining treatment under circumstances such as hers in order to ensure that her actual wishes are honored. Because I believe that Nancy Cruzan has a fundamental right to be free of unwanted artificial nutrition and hydration, which right is not outweighed by any interests of the State, and because I find that the improperly biased procedural obstacles imposed by the Missouri Supreme Court impermissibly burden that right, I respectfully dissent. Nancy Cruzan is entitled to choose to die with dignity.

* * *

The right to be free from unwanted medical attention is a right to evaluate the potential benefit of treatment and its possible consequences according to one's own values and to make a personal decision whether to subject oneself to the intrusion. For a patient like Nancy Cruzan, the sole benefit of medical treatment is being kept metabolically alive. Neither artificial nutrition nor any other form of medical treatment available today can cure or in any way ameliorate her condition. Irreversibly vegetative patients are devoid of thought, emotion and sensation; they are permanently and completely unconscious. As the President's Commission concluded in approving the withdrawal of life support equipment from irreversibly vegetative patients:

> "[T]reatment ordinarily aims to benefit a patient through preserving life, relieving pain and suffering, protecting against disability, and returning maximally effective functioning. If a prognosis of permanent unconsciousness is correct, however, continued treatment cannot confer such benefits. Pain and suffering are absent, as are joy, satisfaction, and pleasure. Disability is total and no return to an even minimal level of social or human functioning is possible." [ ]

There are also affirmative reasons why someone like Nancy might choose to forgo artificial nutrition and hydration under these circumstances. Dying is personal. And it is profound. For many, the thought of an ignoble end, steeped in decay, is abhorrent. A quiet, proud death, bodily integrity intact, is a matter of extreme consequence. "In certain, thankfully rare, circumstances the burden of maintaining the corporeal existence degrades the very humanity it was meant to serve." * * *

Such conditions are, for many, humiliating to contemplate, as is visiting a prolonged and anguished vigil on one's parents, spouse, and children. A long, drawn-out death can have a debilitating effect on family members. [ ] For some, the idea of being remembered in their persistent vegetative states rather than as they were before their illness or accident may be very disturbing.

* * *

The only state interest asserted here is a general interest in the preservation of life. But the State has no legitimate general interest in someone's life, completely abstracted from the interest of the person living that life, that could outweigh the person's choice to avoid medical treatment. * * * [T]he State's general interest in life must accede to Nancy Cruzan's particularized and intense interest in self-determination in her choice of medical treatment. There is simply nothing legitimately within the State's purview to be gained by superseding her decision.

* * *

This is not to say that the State has no legitimate interests to assert here. As the majority recognizes Missouri has a *parens patriae* interest in providing Nancy Cruzan, now incompetent, with as accurate as possible a determination of how she would exercise her rights under these circumstances. Second, if and when it is determined that Nancy Cruzan would want to continue treatment, the State may legitimately assert an interest in providing that treatment. But *until* Nancy's wishes have been determined, the only state interest that may be asserted is an interest in safeguarding the accuracy of that determination.

Accuracy, therefore, must be our touchstone. Missouri may constitutionally impose only those procedural requirements that serve to enhance the accuracy of a determination of Nancy Cruzan's wishes or are at least consistent with an accurate determination. The Missouri "safeguard" that the Court upholds today does not meet that standard. The determination needed in this context is whether the incompetent person would choose to live in a persistent vegetative state on life-support or to avoid this medical treatment. Missouri's rule of decision imposes a markedly asymmetrical evidentiary burden. Only evidence of specific statements of treatment choice made by the patient when competent is admissible to support a finding that the patient, now in a persistent vegetative state, would wish to avoid further medical treatment. Moreover, this evidence must be clear and convincing. No proof is required to support a finding that the incompetent person would wish to continue treatment.

Even more than its heightened evidentiary standard, the Missouri court's categorical exclusion of relevant evidence dispenses with any semblance of accurate factfinding. The court adverted to no evidence supporting its decision, but held that no clear and convincing, inherently reliable evidence had been presented to show that Nancy would want to avoid further treatment. * * * The court did not specifically define what kind of evidence it would consider clear and convincing, but its general discussion suggests that only a living will or equivalently formal directive from the patient when competent would meet this standard.

* * *

The testimony of close friends and family members, on the other hand, may often be the best evidence available of what the patient's choice would be. It is they with whom the patient most likely will have discussed such questions and they who know the patient best. "Family members have a unique knowledge of the patient which is vital to any decision on his or her behalf." [ ] The Missouri court's decision to ignore this whole category of testimony is also at odds with the practices of other States. [ ]

* * *

Finally, I cannot agree with the majority that where it is not possible to determine what choice an incompetent patient would make, a State's role as *parens patriae* permits the State automatically to make that choice itself. [ ] Under fair rules of evidence, it is improbable that a court could not determine what the patient's choice would be. Under the rule of decision adopted by Missouri and upheld today by this Court, such occasions might be numerous. But in neither case does it follow that it is constitutionally acceptable for the State invariably to assume the role of deciding for the patient. A State's legitimate interest in safeguarding a patient's choice cannot be furthered by simply appropriating it.

* * *

JUSTICE STEVENS, dissenting.

* * *

Choices about death touch the core of liberty. Our duty, and the concomitant freedom, to come to terms with the conditions of our own mortality are undoubtedly "so rooted in the traditions and conscience of our people as to be ranked as fundamental," [ ] and indeed are essential incidents of the unalienable rights to life and liberty endowed us by our Creator. [ ]

The more precise constitutional significance of death is difficult to describe; not much may be said with confidence about death unless it is said from faith, and that alone is reason enough to protect the freedom to conform choices about death to individual conscience. We may also, however, justly assume that death is not life's simple opposite, or its necessary terminus, but rather its completion. Our ethical tradition has long regarded an appreciation of mortality as essential to understanding life's significance. It may, in fact, be impossible to live for anything without being prepared to die for something.
* * *

These considerations cast into stark relief the injustice, and unconstitutionality, of Missouri's treatment of Nancy Beth Cruzan. Nancy Cruzan's death, when it comes, cannot be an historic act of heroism; it will inevitably be the consequence of her tragic accident. But Nancy Cruzan's interest in life, no less than that of any other person, includes an interest in how she will be thought of after her death by those whose opinions mattered to her. There can be no doubt that her life made her dear to her family, and to others. How she dies will affect how that life is remembered. The trial court's order authorizing Nancy's parents to cease their daughter's treatment would have permitted the family that cares for Nancy to bring to a close her tragedy and her death. Missouri's objection to that order subordinates Nancy's body, her family, and the lasting significance of her life to the State's own interests. The decision we review thereby interferes with constitutional interests of the highest order.

To be constitutionally permissible, Missouri's intrusion upon these fundamental liberties must, at a minimum, bear a reasonable relationship to a legitimate state end. [ ] Missouri asserts that its policy is related to a state interest in the protection of life. In my view, however, it is an effort to define life, rather than to protect it, that is the heart of Missouri's policy.

* * *

Life, particularly human life, is not commonly thought of as a merely physiological condition or function. Its sanctity is often thought to derive from the impossibility of any such reduction. When people speak of life, they often mean to describe the experiences that comprise a person's history, as when it is said that somebody "led a good life."[2] They may also mean to refer to the practical manifestation of the human spirit, a meaning captured by the familiar observation that somebody "added life" to an assembly. If there is a shared thread among the various opinions on this subject, it may be that life is an activity which is at once the matrix for and an integration of a person's interests. In any event, absent some theological abstraction, the idea of life is not conceived separately from the idea of a living person. Yet, it is by precisely such a separation that Missouri asserts an interest in Nancy Cruzan's life in opposition to Nancy Cruzan's own interests.

* * *

Only because Missouri has arrogated to itself the power to define life, and only because the Court permits this usurpation, are Nancy Cruzan's life and liberty put into disquieting conflict. If Nancy Cruzan's life were defined by reference to her own interests, so that her life expired when her biological existence ceased serving *any* of her own interests, then her constitutionally protected interest in freedom from unwanted treatment would not come into conflict with her constitutionally protected interest in life. Conversely, if there were *any* evidence that Nancy Cruzan herself defined life to encompass every form of biological persistence by a human being, so that the continuation of treatment would serve Nancy's own liberty, then once again there would be no conflict between life and liberty. The opposition of life and liberty in this case are thus not the result of Nancy Cruzan's tragic accident, but are instead the artificial consequence of Missouri's effort, and this Court's willingness, to abstract Nancy Cruzan's life from Nancy Cruzan's person.

* * *

The Cruzan family's continuing concern provides a concrete reminder that Nancy Cruzan's interests did not disappear with her vitality or her consciousness. However commendable may be the State's interest in human

---

2. It is this sense of the word that explains its use to describe a biography: for example, Boswell's Life of Johnson or Beveridge's The Life of John Marshall. The reader of a book so titled would be surprised to find that it contained a compilation of biological data.

life, it cannot pursue that interest by appropriating Nancy Cruzan's life as a symbol for its own purposes. Lives do not exist in abstraction from persons, and to pretend otherwise is not to honor but to desecrate the State's responsibility for protecting life. A State that seeks to demonstrate its commitment to life may do so by aiding those who are actively struggling for life and health. In this endeavor, unfortunately, no State can lack for opportunities: there can be no need to make an example of tragic cases like that of Nancy Cruzan.

Notes and Questions

1.　Subsequent to this judgment the Missouri trial court heard additional evidence, provided by Nancy Cruzan's friends and colleagues, that she had made explicit and unambiguous statements that demonstrated, clearly and convincingly, that she would not want continued the treatment that she was receiving. Without opposition from the Attorney General of Missouri, the trial court authorized Ms. Cruzan's guardians to terminate her nutrition and hydration.

2.　Does the Opinion of the Court recognize a constitutional right to die? Many authoritative sources presumed that the opinion did recognize a constitutionally protected liberty interest in a competent person to refuse unwanted medical treatment. Indeed, the syllabus prepared for the Court says just that, and the case was hailed by the New York Times as the first to recognize a right to die. On the other hand, the Chief Justice's language does not support such a conclusion. While the majority agrees that "[t]he principle that a competent person has a constitutionally protected liberty interest in refusing unwanted medical treatment *may* be inferred from our prior decisions," (emphasis added) the Court never makes the inference itself. In fact, the opinion says explicitly that *"for purposes of this case,* we assume that the United States Constitution would grant a competent person a constitutionally protected right to refuse life saving nutrition and hydration." (emphasis added)

Why is this assumption limited to the "purposes of this case"? Does the Court question (1) whether there is a constitutionally protected liberty interest in refusing unwanted medical treatment, (2) whether the right extends to life sustaining treatment, or (3) whether it covers hydration and nutrition?

It must have been difficult for the Chief Justice to craft an opinion that would be joined by a majority of the court. Justice Scalia clearly does not believe that there is any constitutional right implicated. If the Chief Justice were to formally recognize a constitutional right, he might have lost Justice Scalia's signature—and thus lost an opportunity for there to be any majority opinion.

The dissents filed in this case are long and obviously heartfelt. Do the dissenters, all of whom would recognize a constitutionally protected right to die, and Justice O'Connor, who would also do so, create a majority in support of this constitutional position?

3.　The majority opinion permits a state to limit its consideration to those wishes previously expressed by the patient and to ignore the decisions of another person acting on behalf of the patient. In fact, the Court explicitly does not address the question of whether a state must defer to an appropriately nominated surrogate acting on behalf of the patient. See 497 U.S. at 287 n. 12, 110 S.Ct. at 2856 n. 12. On the other hand, the dissenting justices would recognize the decisions of a surrogate under appropriate circumstances, and Justice O'Connor suggests that the duty to give effect to those decisions "may well be constitutionally required." 497 U.S. at 289, 110 S.Ct. at 2857. What is the constitutional status of surrogate decision-making after *Cruzan?*

4. Note that none of the opinions refers to the "right of privacy," a term which has caused the Court such tremendous grief in the abortion context. The Chief Justice analyzes this issue in the more general terms of a fourteenth amendment liberty interest, and none of the counsel argued the case in terms of the right to privacy. Apparently the Court just did not wish to entangle itself any further with the "P" word.

5. Seven years after Cruzan was decided, the Supreme Court again considered end-of-life medical decision making in Washington v. Glucksberg, below at page 1424, which addressed the Constitutional status of physician assisted death. Chief Justice Rehnquist, writing for the Court, announced that "We have * * * assumed, and strongly suggested, that the Due Process Clause protects the traditional right to refuse unwanted lifesaving medical treatment." Is that an accurate description of the holding in Cruzan? A few pages later, in the same opinion, Chief Justice Rehnquist describes the Cruzan case slightly differently: "[A]lthough Cruzan is often described as a 'right to die' case [ ], we were, in fact, more precise: we assumed that the Constitution granted competent persons a 'constitutionally protected right to refuse lifesaving hydration and nutrition.'" Is that a more accurate account of what the Court decided in Cruzan?

Justice O'Connor, concurring in Glucksberg, says that "there is no need to address the question whether suffering patients have a constitutionally cognizable interest in obtaining relief from the suffering that they may experience in the last days of their lives." This issue, according to Justice O'Connor, was decided by Cruzan. Is she right? Justice Stevens also commented on the Cruzan case in the course of his concurring opinion in Glucksberg. He explained that "Cruzan did give recognition * * * to the more specific interest in making decisions about how to confront an imminent death. * * * Cruzan makes it clear that some individuals who no longer have the option of deciding whether to live or to die because they are already on the threshold of death have a constitutionally protected interest [in deciding how they will die] that may outweigh the State's interest in preserving life at all costs." Is this an accurate description of Cruzan? If the Justices who participated in both the Cruzan and Glucksberg cases can't agree on just what the case really means, how can your health law teacher expect you to do so?

6. Except for a glancing reference by Justice Stevens in his dissent, the opinions do not consider the cost of providing care to Nancy Cruzan. Should the cost be relevant? Should the constitutional right (to liberty or to life) vary depending on who bears the cost? See Harris v. McRae, 448 U.S. 297, 100 S.Ct. 2671, 65 L.Ed.2d 784 (1980). Would your analysis of this case be any different if the costs were being paid by an insurance company, by the health maintenance organization to which you belong, by Ms. Cruzan's parents, or by community fund raising in Nancy Cruzan's neighborhood, rather than by the state of Missouri? Should the one who pays the bills get to participate in the health care decision making?

At the oral argument of this case one Justice asked the counsel for Missouri several questions about the cost. If the cost were borne by the Cruzan family, and if the state could require the continued treatment of Nancy Cruzan, could the state also impose a duty on the family to pay for that treatment? Counsel for Missouri never argued that the state could require the family to pay for treatment that members of the family believed the patient would not want. Instead, he simply argued that the cost question was not before the Court because the entire cost was being borne by the state of Missouri. But what if the family were paying? Would it seem especially cruel to require a family to spend all its resources on treatment it believes is terribly burdensome to the patient and that it is certain the patient would not want? Should this be a matter of constitutional law?

Judge Blackmar's dissent to the Missouri Supreme Court's opinion in *Cruzan* addresses the disutility of requiring some patients to be kept alive, at great expense, while the state is unable (or unwilling) to provide adequate care to others. He points out:

> The absolutist position is also infirm because the state does not stand prepared to finance the preservation of life, without regard to the cost, in very many cases. In this particular case the state has Nancy in its possession, and is litigating its right to keep her. Yet, several years ago, a respected judge needed extraordinary treatment which the hospital in which he was a patient was not willing to furnish without a huge advance deposit and the state apparently had no desire to help out. Many people die because of the unavailability of heroic medical treatment. It simply cannot be said that the state's interest in preserving and prolonging life is absolute.

760 S.W.2d at 429. Judge Blackmar also points out, in a footnote, that "an absolutist would undoubtedly be offended by an inquiry as to whether the state, by prolonging Nancy's life at its own expense, is disabling itself from [providing] needed treatment to others who do not have such dire prognosis." 760 S.W.2d at 429 n. 4.

7. The result of the *Cruzan* case is that most law regarding health care decision making has continued to be established on a state by state basis; there seems to be very little, if any, United States constitutional limit on what states may do. The *Cruzan* case thus may have deflected the "right to die" debate to the political decision making process in the way that several recent ambivalent abortion decisions have done the same with the abortion question. See Chapter 16, above.

8. The decision of the United States Supreme Court to opt out of providing much constitutional guidance to the states may allow a crazy quilt of state laws to persist such that a patient who would have a "right to die" that could be exercised by his family in California or New Jersey would not have that right (or would not have a right that could be exercised by his family) in Missouri, Michigan or New York. Indeed, the conditions and extent of, and the restrictions and exceptions to, any "right to die" might be different in each state. State policies will thus require different results in factually identical cases. Is there anything wrong with this?

What would happen if Nancy Cruzan's family had decided to move her to the Yale Medical Center "because of the more favorable medical facilities" there? Could they have moved her from Missouri to Connecticut, where removal of the gastrostomy clearly would be legally permitted, just for the purpose of removing the gastrostomy? If they could not, then Nancy Cruzan could have become a prisoner of a state that rejects her family's values—values that have been incorporated into official state policies in other jurisdictions. If they could move her, however, Missouri would have allowed the family to undercut the important policy objectives of the state law and imperil the very life the law was designed to protect. Would it violate any criminal statute to move someone across state lines for the purpose of avoiding the laws governing termination of life support in the first state? Could a state make such an action a crime?

In early 1991 the father and guardian of Christine Busalacchi sought to have his daughter moved from Missouri to Minnesota for medical consultation with a nationally known neurologist. Ms. Busalacchi, who had been living in the same nursing home that had housed Nancy Cruzan, was arguably in a persistent vegetative state. The state of Missouri sought (and obtained) an order forbidding the move because of the fear that her father wanted only to find some place where his daughter could die. A divided Missouri Court of Appeals determined that the trial court was required to commence a new hearing on whether the move could be justified by other medical objectives. In deciding the case, the majority made it clear that " * * * we will not permit [the] guardian to forum shop in an effort to control whether Christine lives or dies." The dissent argued that " * * * Minnesota is not a medical or ethical wasteland * * *. There is a parochial arrogance in suggesting, as the state does, that only in Missouri can Christine's medical, physical, and legal well being be protected and only here will her best interests be considered." Matter of Busalacchi, 1991 WL 26851 (Mo.App.1991), transferred to Mo. Sup. Ct. Ultimately, the State decided not to pursue the case and Busalacchi died at the nursing home in Missouri. See also Mack v. Mack, 329 Md. 188, 618 A.2d 744 (Md.App.1993) (Maryland Court denies full faith and credit to Florida judgment appointing the Florida-resident wife of a Maryland patient in persistent vegetative state as guardian so that patient could be removed to Florida, where life sustaining treatment could be withdrawn.)

Might the *Cruzan* and *Busalacchi* cases give rise to medic alert bracelets that say, "If I am in a persistent vegetative state, keep me out of Missouri?"

9. Missouri is not the only state to adopt the strict standard approved by the majority and decried by the dissenters. At the least, that standard has also been adopted in New York and Michigan. See In re Westchester County Medical Center on Behalf of O'Connor, 72 N.Y.2d 517, 534 N.Y.S.2d 886, 531 N.E.2d 607 (1988) and In re Martin, 450 Mich. 204, 538 N.W.2d 399 (1995). The September/October 1990 Hastings Center Report includes an excellent symposium on all aspects of the *Cruzan* case. The symposium includes an article written by counsel for the Cruzans, one by Christine Busalacchi's father, and several by leading bioethics scholars.

III. THE "RIGHT TO DIE"—PATIENTS WITH DECISIONAL CAPACITY

Problem: The Christian Scientist in the Emergency Room

Shortly after Ms. Elizabeth Boroff was hit by a drunk driver who went through a red light and directly into her Volkswagen bus, she found herself being attended by paramedics and loaded into an ambulance for a trip to the Big County General Hospital emergency room. Although she was briefly unconscious at the scene of the accident, and although she suffered a very substantial blood loss, several broken bones and a partially crushed skull, she had regained consciousness by her arrival at the hospital. The doctors explained to her that her life was at risk and that she needed a blood transfusion and brain surgery immediately. She explained that she was a Christian Scientist, that she believed in the healing power of prayer, that she rejected medical care, and that she wished to be discharged immediately so that she could consult a Christian Science healer.

A quick conference of emergency room staff revealed a consensus that failure to relieve the pressure caused by her intracranial bleed would result in loss of consciousness within a few hours, and, possibly, her death. When this information was provided to her she remained unmoved. The hospital staff asked her to identify her next of kin, and she explained that she was a widow with no living relatives except for her seven minor children, ages 1 through 9. Further inquiries revealed that she was the sole support for these children, that she had no life insurance, that she had an elementary school education and that she had been employed as a clerk since her husband, a self employed maintenance man, was himself killed in an automobile accident a year ago. Uncertain of what to do, the emergency room staff called you, the hospital legal counsel, for advice. What advice should you give? Should they discharge Ms. Boroff, as she requests? Should you commence a legal action to keep her in the hospital and institute treatment? If you were to file a legal action, what relief would you seek, and what would be the substantive basis of your claim?

A.　THE GENERAL RULE

For years, commentators have concluded that competent adult patients (i.e. patients with the decisional capacity to make life and death decisions—a concept discussed below) have the right to refuse any form of medical treatment, even if the refusal is certain to cause death. It was not until 1984, however, that an appellate court directly confronted a situation in which a clearly competent patient refused treatment without which he would surely die. Bartling v. Superior Court, 163 Cal.App.3d 186, 209 Cal.Rptr. 220 (1984). Any tentativeness in the *Bartling* opinion was overcome by the case of Elizabeth Bouvia, in which the California Court of Appeal went so far as to require the hospital to provide adequate support to Ms. Bouvia during her dying process. The court confirmed that hospitals are obliged to serve the autonomous interests of patients, as defined by those patients. This view— that the function of the hospital is to be defined by patients, not physicians or other health care providers—is considered by some to be the single most outrageous judicial intrusion upon the medical profession in the history of the judiciary. The California hospital was not only required to refrain from providing life-sustaining treatment for Ms. Bouvia, the hospital was required to provide the medical assistance that would allow her to die without avoidable pain, i.e., that would allow her to die the way she wanted to die.

BOUVIA v. SUPERIOR COURT

California Court of Appeal, Second District, 1986.
179 Cal.App.3d 1127, 225 Cal.Rptr. 297.

BEACH, ASSOCIATE JUSTICE.

Petitioner, Elizabeth Bouvia, a patient in a public hospital, seeks the removal from her body of a nasogastric tube inserted and maintained against her will and without her consent by physicians who so placed it for the purpose of keeping her alive through involuntary forced feeding.

* * *

Petitioner is a 28–year–old woman. Since birth she has been afflicted with and suffered from severe cerebral palsy. She is quadriplegic. She is now a patient at a public hospital maintained by one of the real parties in interest, the County of Los Angeles. Other parties are physicians, nurses and the medical and support staff employed by the County of Los Angeles. Petitioner's physical handicaps of palsy and quadriplegia have progressed to the point where she is completely bedridden. Except for a few fingers of one hand and some slight head and facial movements, she is immobile. She is physically helpless and wholly unable to care for herself. * * * She suffers also from degenerative and severely crippling arthritis. She is in continual pain. * * *

She is intelligent, very mentally competent. She earned a college degree. She was married but her husband has left her. She suffered a miscarriage. She lived with her parents until her father told her that they could no longer care for her. She has stayed intermittently with friends and at public facilities. A search for a permanent place to live where she might receive the constant care which she needs has been unsuccessful. She is without financial means to support herself and, therefore, must accept public assistance for medical and other care.

She has on several occasions expressed the desire to die. In 1983 she sought the right to be cared for in a public hospital in Riverside County while she intentionally "starved herself to death." A court in that county denied her judicial assistance to accomplish that goal. * * * Thereafter, friends took her to several different facilities, both public and private, arriving finally at her present location. Efforts by * * * social workers to find her an apartment of her own with publicly paid live-in help or regular visiting nurses to care for her, or some other suitable facility have proved fruitless.

Petitioner must be spoon fed in order to eat. Her present medical and dietary staff have determined that she is not consuming a sufficient amount of nutrients. Petitioner stops eating when she feels she cannot orally swallow more, without nausea and vomiting. As she cannot now retain solids, she is fed soft liquid-like food. Because of her previously announced resolve to starve herself, the medical staff feared her weight loss might reach a life-threatening level. Her weight since admission to real parties' facility seems to hover between 65 and 70 pounds. Accordingly, they inserted the subject tube against her will and contrary to her express written instructions.[3]

Petitioner's counsel argue that her weight loss was not such as to be life threatening and therefore the tube is unnecessary. However, the trial court found to the contrary as a matter of fact, a finding which we must accept. Nonetheless, the point is immaterial, for, as we will explain, a patient has the right to refuse any medical treatment or medical service, even when such treatment is labeled "furnishing nourishment and hydration." This right exists even if its exercise creates a "life threatening condition."

THE RIGHT TO REFUSE MEDICAL TREATMENT

"[A] person of adult years and in sound mind has the right, in the exercise of control over his own body, to determine whether or not to submit to lawful medical treatment." [ ] It follows that such a patient has the right to refuse *any* medical treatment, even that which may save or prolong her life. [ ]

* * *

---

3. Her instructions were dictated to her lawyers, written by them and signed by her by means of her making a feeble "x" on the paper with a pen which she held in her mouth.

A recent Presidential Commission for the Study of Ethical Problems in Medicine and Biomedical and Behavioral Research concluded in part: "The voluntary choice of a competent and informed patient should determine whether or not life-sustaining therapy will be undertaken, just as such choices provide the basis for other decisions about medical treatment. Health care institutions and professionals should try to enhance patients' abilities to make decisions on their own behalf and to promote understanding of the available treatment options * * *. Health care professionals serve patients best by maintaining a presumption in favor of sustaining life, while recognizing that competent patients are entitled to choose to forgo any treatments, including those that sustain life."

* * *

The American Hospital Association Policy and Statement of Patients' Choices of Treatment Options, approved by the American Hospital Association in February of 1985 discusses the value of a collaborative relationship between the patient and the physician and states in pertinent part: "Whenever possible, however, the authority to determine the course of treatment, if any, should rest with the patient" and "the right to choose treatment includes the right to refuse a specific treatment *or all treatment* * * *."

* * *

Significant also is the statement adopted on March 15, 1986, by the Council on Ethical and Judicial Affairs of the American Medical Association. It is entitled "Withholding or Withdrawing Life Prolonging Medical Treatment." In pertinent part, it declares: "The social commitment of the physician is to sustain life and relieve suffering. Where the performance of one duty conflicts with the other, the choice of the patient, or his family or legal representative if the patient is incompetent to act in his own behalf, should prevail."

* * *

It is indisputable that petitioner is mentally competent. She is not comatose. She is quite intelligent, alert and understands the risks involved.

THE CLAIMED EXCEPTIONS TO THE PATIENT'S RIGHT TO CHOOSE ARE INAPPLICABLE

* * * The real parties in interest, a county hospital, its physicians and administrators, urge that the interests of the State should prevail over the rights of Elizabeth Bouvia to refuse treatment. Advanced by real parties under this argument are the State's interests in (1) preserving life, (2) preventing suicide, (3) protecting innocent third parties, and (4) maintaining the ethical standards of the medical profession, including the right of physicians to effectively render necessary and appropriate medical service and to refuse treatment to an uncooperative and disruptive patient. Included, whether as part of the above or as separate and additional arguments, are what real parties assert as distinctive facts not present in other cases, i.e., (1) petitioner is a patient in a public facility, thereby making the State a party to the result of her conduct, (2) she is not comatose, nor incurably, nor terminally ill, nor in a vegetative state, all conditions which have justified the termination of life-support system in other instances, (3) she has asked for medical treat-

ment, therefore, she cannot accept a part of it while cutting off the part that would be effective, and (4) she is, in truth, trying to starve herself to death and the State will not be a party to a suicide.

* * *

At bench the trial court concluded that with sufficient feeding petitioner could live an additional 15 to 20 years; therefore, the preservation of petitioner's life for that period outweighed her right to decide. In so holding the trial court mistakenly attached undue importance to the *amount of time* possibly available to petitioner, and failed to give equal weight and consideration for the *quality* of that life; an equal, if not more significant, consideration.

All decisions permitting cessation of medical treatment or life-support procedures to some degree hastened the arrival of death. In part, at least, this was permitted because the quality of life during the time remaining in those cases had been terribly diminished. In Elizabeth Bouvia's view, the quality of her life has been diminished to the point of hopelessness, uselessness, unenjoyability and frustration. She, as the patient, lying helplessly in bed, unable to care for herself, may consider her existence meaningless. She cannot be faulted for so concluding. If her right to choose may not be exercised because there remains to her, in the opinion of a court, a physician or some committee, a certain arbitrary number of years, months, or days, her right will have lost its value and meaning.

Who shall say what the minimum amount of available life must be? Does it matter if it be 15 to 20 years, 15 to 20 months, or 15 to 20 days, if such life has been physically destroyed and its quality, dignity and purpose gone? As in all matters lines must be drawn at some point, somewhere, but that decision must ultimately belong to the one whose life is in issue.

Here Elizabeth Bouvia's decision to forgo medical treatment or life-support through a mechanical means belongs to her. It is not a medical decision for her physicians to make. Neither is it a legal question whose soundness is to be resolved by lawyers or judges. It is not a conditional right subject to approval by ethics committees or courts of law. It is a moral and philosophical decision that, being a competent adult, is hers alone.

* * *

Here, if force fed, petitioner faces 15 to 20 years of a painful existence, endurable only by the constant administrations of morphine. Her condition is irreversible. There is no cure for her palsy or arthritis. Petitioner would have to be fed, cleaned, turned, bedded, toileted by others for 15 to 20 years! Although alert, bright, sensitive, perhaps even brave and feisty, she must lie immobile, unable to exist except through physical acts of others. Her mind and spirit may be free to take great flights but she herself is imprisoned and must lie physically helpless subject to the ignominy, embarrassment, humiliation and dehumanizing aspects created by her helplessness. We do not believe it is the policy of this State that all and every life must be preserved against the will of the sufferer. It is incongruous, if not monstrous, for medical practitioners to assert their right to preserve a life that someone else must live, or, more accurately, endure, for "15 to 20 years." We cannot conceive it to be the policy of this State to inflict such an ordeal upon anyone.

* * * Being competent she has the right to live out the remainder of her natural life in dignity and peace. It is precisely the aim and purpose of the many decisions upholding the withdrawal of life-support systems to accord and provide as large a measure of dignity, respect and comfort as possible to every patient for the remainder of his days, whatever be their number. This goal is not to hasten death, though its earlier arrival may be an expected and understood likelihood.

* * *

Moreover, the trial court seriously erred by basing its decision on the "motives" behind Elizabeth Bouvia's decision to exercise her rights. If a right exists, it matters not what "motivates" its exercise. We find nothing in the law to suggest the right to refuse medical treatment may be exercised only if the patient's *motives* meet someone else's approval. It certainly is not illegal or immoral to prefer a natural, albeit sooner, death than a drugged life attached to a mechanical device.

* * *

We do not purport to establish what will constitute proper medical practice in all other cases or even other aspects of the care to be provided petitioner. We hold only that her right to refuse medical treatment even of the life-sustaining variety, entitles her to the immediate removal of the nasogastric tube that has been involuntarily inserted into her body. The hospital and medical staff are still free to perform a substantial, if not the greater part of their duty, i.e., that of trying to alleviate Bouvia's pain and suffering.

Petitioner is without means to go to a private hospital and, apparently, real parties' hospital as a public facility was required to accept her. Having done so it may not deny her relief from pain and suffering merely because she has chosen to exercise her fundamental right to protect what little privacy remains to her.

Personal dignity is a part of one's right of privacy. * * *

Notes and Questions

1. Various attempts to get a rehearing at the Court of Appeal or certiorari from the California Supreme Court in the *Bouvia* case failed. The wide-spread support for the decision of the Court of Appeal may demonstrate a social consensus that no physician, no government agency and no social committee can overrule a competent adult's determination that death is preferable to life—at least when the death will be the consequence of forgoing medical treatment.

2. The *Bouvia* court depended, in large part, upon Bartling v. Superior Court, 163 Cal.App.3d 186, 209 Cal.Rptr. 220 (1984), the first case to confirm a competent patient's right to make decisions to forgo life sustaining treatment. Mr. Bartling was a competent adult suffering from depression (the original reason for his hospitalization), a tumor on his lung, and emphysema. He had a living will, a separate declaration asking that treatment be discontinued, and a durable power of attorney appointing his wife to make his health care decisions. He and his wife continuously asked that the ventilator that was preserving his life be removed, and he, his wife and his daughter all executed documents releasing the hospital

from any liability claims arising out of honoring Mr. Bartling's request. Still, the hospital, which was a Christian hospital established and operated on pro-life principles, opposed allowing Mr. Bartling to die on ethical grounds. The California Court of Appeal found that the trial court should have granted Mr. Bartling's request for an injunction against the hospital, concluding that, "if the right to patient self-determination as to his own medical treatment means anything at all, it must be paramount to the interests of the patient's hospital and doctors. The right of a competent adult to refuse medical treatment is a constitutionally guaranteed right which must not be abridged."

3.   Do you agree that the hospital had an obligation to accept Ms. Bouvia and provide her with medical relief from her pain and suffering, even though the physicians and hospital found her conduct immoral and her request an abuse of the medical profession? Is the obligation anything more than to provide adequate end-of-life care, even when the patient refuses a particular course of treatment? Cf. Brophy v. New England Sinai Hospital, Inc., 398 Mass. 417, 497 N.E.2d 626 (1986), where the Massachusetts Supreme Judicial Court found that a patient in a persistent vegetative state could, through his family, deny consent to feeding through a gastric tube, but that the hospital need not remove or clamp the tube if it found it to be contrary to the ethical dictates of the medical profession. The *Brophy* decision required that the family move the patient to another medical institution more receptive to his apparent desires for his feeding tube to be removed. The New Jersey Supreme Court took a middle ground In re Jobes, 108 N.J. 394, 529 A.2d 434, 450 (1987):

> The trial court held that the nursing home could refuse to participate in the withdrawal of the j-tube by keeping Mrs. Jobes connected to it until she is transferred out of that facility. Under the circumstances of this case, we disagree, and we reverse that portion of the trial court's order.

> Mrs. Jobes' family had no reason to believe that they were surrendering the right to choose among medical alternatives when they placed her in the nursing home. [ ] The nursing home apparently did not inform Mrs. Jobes' family about its policy toward artificial feeding until May of 1985 when they requested that the j-tube be withdrawn. In fact there is no indication that this policy has ever been formalized. Under these circumstances Mrs. Jobes and her family were entitled to rely on the nursing home's willingness to defer to their choice among courses of medical treatment. * * *

> We do not decide the case in which a nursing home gave notice of its policy not to participate in the withdrawal or withholding of artificial feeding at the time of a patient's admission. Thus, we do not hold that such a policy is never enforceable. But we are confident in this case that it would be wrong to allow the nursing home to discharge Mrs. Jobes. The evidence indicates that at this point it would be extremely difficult, perhaps impossible, to find another facility that would accept Mrs. Jobes as a patient. Therefore, to allow the nursing home to discharge Mrs. Jobes if her family does not consent to continued artificial feeding would essentially frustrate Mrs. Jobes' right of self-determination. See generally George Annas, "Transferring the Ethical Hot Potato," 17 Hastings Center Report 20–21 (Feb.1987) (explaining how patients' rights are threatened by legal decisions that allow medical institutions to discharge "patients who do not accept everything they offer").

Is the fact that Bouvia could not afford any other hospital care relevant? Do only private, not public, hospitals have the luxury of living up to what they view to be ethical mandates?

4. If we take seriously the *Bouvia* suggestion that hospitals have an obligation to provide comfort to patients who choose to forgo treatment and thus die, do physicians have an obligation to inform patients of the various ways of dying that are available to them, and the consequences of choosing any one of them?

Consider M. Pabst Battin, The Least Worst Death, 13 Hastings Center Rep. 13–16 (April 1983):

In the face of irreversible, terminal illness, a patient may wish to die sooner but "naturally," without artificial prolongation of any kind. By doing so, the patient may believe he is choosing a death that is, as a contributor to the *New England Journal of Medicine* has put it, "comfortable, decent, and peaceful". "[N]atural death," the patient may assume, means a death that is easier than a medically prolonged one.

[H]e may assume that it will allow time for reviewing life and saying farewell to family and loved ones, for last rites or final words, for passing on hopes, wisdom, confessions, and blessings to the next generation. These ideas are of course heavily stereotyped * * * : Even the very term "natural" may have stereotyped connotations for the patient: something close to nature, uncontrived, and appropriate. As a result of these notions, the patient often takes "natural death" to be a painless, conscious, dignified, culminative slipping-away.

Now consider what sorts of death actually occur under the rubric of "natural death." A patient suffers a cardiac arrest and is not resuscitated. Result: sudden unconsciousness, without pain, and death within a number of seconds. Or a patient has an infection that is not treated. Result: * * * fever, delirium, rigor or shaking, and lightheadedness; death usually takes one or two days, depending on the organism involved.

* * *

But active killing aside, the physician can do much to grant the dying patient the humane death he has chosen by using the sole legally protected mechanism that safeguards the right to die: refusal of treatment. This mechanism need not always backfire. For in almost any terminal condition, death can occur in various ways, and there are many possible outcomes of the patient's present condition. * * * What the patient who rejects active euthanasia or assisted suicide may realistically hope for is this: the least worst death among those that could naturally occur. Not all unavoidable surrenders need involve rout: in the face of inevitable death, the physician becomes strategist, the deviser of plans for how to meet death most favorably.

* * *

To recognize the patient's right to autonomous choice in matters concerning the treatment of his own body, the physician must provide information about all the legal options open to him, not just information sufficient to choose between accepting or rejecting a single proposed procedure.

* * *

In the current enthusiasm for "natural death" it is not patient autonomy that dismays physicians. What does dismay them is the way in which respect for patient autonomy can lead to cruel results. The cure for that dismay lies in the realization that the physician can contribute to the *genuine* honoring of the patient's autonomy and rights, assuring him of "natural death" in the way in which the patient understands it, and still remain within the confines of good medical practice and the law.

5. After the California Supreme Court confirmed Ms. Bouvia's right to choose to die, she changed her mind and decided to accept the medical care necessary to keep her alive. As of June, 2000 she was still alive. In many cases, it seems that those who seek a judicially confirmed "right to die" are really seeking control over their destiny, not death. Once they have that control—and once they know that they can choose death if life becomes truly unbearable—their lives become more valuable to them, and they become far more reluctant to give life up.

6. Is it surprising that the fundamental principle that competent adults can make all of their own health care decisions has made it into the statutes of only a very few states? For an exception to this general rule, see N.M. Stat. Ann. Section 24–7A–2. Especially after the concern shown for this issue in the Bouvia case, one might expect more legislatures to have confirmed this right. Have they failed to do so because the law is so clear that legislative confirmation is unnecessary, or because there is a real dispute about the substance of the principle?

Note: Countervailing State Interests

The right to choose to forgo life-sustaining treatment is not absolute, even for competent adults. In Superintendent of Belchertown State School v. Saikewicz, 373 Mass. 728, 370 N.E.2d 417 (1977), the Massachusetts Supreme Judicial Court first identified the four "countervailing State interests" that could overcome a patient's choice:

(1) preservation of life;

(2) protection of the interests of innocent third parties;

(3) prevention of suicide; and

(4) maintenance of the ethical integrity of the medical profession.

Saikewicz involved an incompetent, mentally retarded patient. Those four interests have also been reiterated in subsequent cases involving competent patients—including *Bouvia*—but they have never been found to be sufficient to overcome the choice of a *competent* patient.

In *Saikewicz* the Massachusetts Supreme Judicial Court explored the significance of these four state interests and their limitations:

It is clear that the most significant of the asserted State interests is that of the preservation of human life. Recognition of such an interest, however, does not necessarily resolve the problem where the affliction or disease clearly indicates that life will end soon, and inevitably be extinguished. The interest of the State in prolonging a life must be reconciled with the interest of an individual to reject the traumatic cost of that prolongation. There is a substantial distinction in the State's insistence that human life be saved where the affliction is curable, as opposed to the State interest where, as here, the issue is not whether but when, for how long, and at what cost to the individual that life may be briefly extended. Even if we assume that the State has an additional interest in seeing to it that individual decisions on the prolongation of life do not in any way tend to "cheapen" the value which is placed on the concept of living, we believe it is not inconsistent to recognize a right to decline medical treatment in a situation of incurable illness. The constitutional right to privacy, as we conceive it, is an expression of the sanctity of individual free choice and self-determination as fundamental constituents of life. The value of life as so perceived is lessened not by a decision to refuse treatment, but by the failure to allow a competent human being the right of a choice.

A second interest of considerable magnitude, which the State may have some interest in asserting, is that of protecting third parties, particularly minor children, from the emotional and financial damage which may occur as a result of the decision of a competent adult to refuse life-saving or life-prolonging treatment. Thus, even when the State's interest in preserving an individual's life was not sufficient, by itself, to outweigh the individual's interest in the exercise of free choice, the possible impact on minor children would be a factor which might have a critical effect on the outcome of the balancing process.

* * *

The last State interest requiring discussion[4] is that of the maintenance of the ethical integrity of the medical profession as well as allowing hospitals the full opportunity to care for people under their control. The force and impact of this interest is lessened by the prevailing medical ethical standards. Prevailing medical ethical practice does not, without exception, demand that all efforts toward life prolongation be made in all circumstances. Rather, the prevailing ethical practice seems to be to recognize that the dying are more often in need of comfort than treatment. Recognition of the right to refuse necessary treatment in appropriate circumstances is consistent with existing medical mores; such a doctrine does not threaten either the integrity of the medical profession, the proper role of hospitals in caring for such patients or the State's interest in protecting the same. It is not necessary to deny a right of self-determination to a patient in order to recognize the interest of doctors, hospitals, and medical personnel in attendance on the patient. Also, if the doctrines of informed consent and right of privacy have as their foundations in the right to bodily integrity, and control of one's own fate, then those rights are superior to the institutional considerations. 370 N.E.2d at 425–427.

In fact, the recitation of these four interests raises issues beyond those discussed in Saikewicz:

(1) If the value of the preservation of life is the very question faced by the court in right-to-die cases, does it make sense to define it, *a priori,* as a value that is countervailing to the patient's desire to discontinue treatment?

The nature of the state's interest in the preservation of life was discussed in the *Cruzan* case, in which it was the only interest advanced by the state of Missouri. The Chief Justice said that "a state may properly decline to make judgments about the 'quality' of life that a particular individual may enjoy, and simply assert an unqualified interest in the preservation of human life to be weighed against the constitutionally protected interests of the individual."

---

4. The interest in protecting against suicide seems to require little if any discussion. In the case of the competent adult's refusing medical treatment such an act does not necessarily constitute suicide since (1) in refusing treatment the patient may not have the specific intent to die, and (2) even if he did, to the extent that the cause of death was from natural causes, the patient did not set the death producing agent in motion with the intent of causing his own death. Furthermore, the underlying State interest in this area lies in the prevention of irrational self-destruction. What we consider here is a competent, rational decision to refuse treatment when death is inevitable, and the treatment offers no hope of cure or preservation of life. There is no connection between the conduct here in issue and any State concern to prevent suicide.

Not surprisingly, the dissenters viewed the state's interest in the preservation of life very differently. Justice Stevens objected to Missouri's policy of "equating [Cruzan's] life with the biological persistence of her bodily functions." He pointed out that, "[l]ife, particularly human life, is not commonly thought of as a merely physiological condition or function. Its sanctity is often thought to derive from the impossibility of any such reduction. When people speak of life, they often mean to describe the experiences that comprise a person's history. * * * " Justice Brennan was especially offended by the notion that the generalized state interest in life could overcome the liberty interest to forgo life-sustaining treatment. One's rights, he argued, may not be sacrificed just to make society feel good:

> If Missouri were correct that its interests outweigh Nancy's interests in avoiding medical procedures as long as she is free of pain and physical discomfort, [ ] it is not apparent why a state could not choose to remove one of her kidneys without consent on the ground that society would be better off if the recipient of that kidney were saved from renal poisoning * * *, patches of her skin could also be removed to provide grafts for burn victims, and scrapings of bone marrow to provide grafts for someone with leukemia. * * * Indeed, why could the state not perform medical experiments on her body, experiments that might save countless lives, and would cause her no greater burden than she already bears by being fed through her gastrostomy tube? This would be too brave a new world for me and, I submit, for our constitution.

497 U.S. 261, 312–14 n. 13, 110 S.Ct. 2841, 2869–70 n. 13, 111 L.Ed.2d 224. Of course, Chief Justice Rehnquist reminded us in Glucksberg that Cruzan had decided that states may choose to act to protect the sanctity of all life, independent of any inquiry into quality of life, and independent of the value of that life to the one living it.

(2) Does the protection of the interests of innocent third parties have any meaning if courts are not willing to force people to stop pursuing their own interests and to serve some undefined communal goal? Is it merely a make-weight argument in a society as individualistic as ours?

(3) Although Glucksberg confirmed that a state could make assisting suicide a crime, committing suicide is no longer a crime in any state. Is there still a consensus behind Justice Nolan's position, dissenting in Brophy, 398 Mass. 417, 497 N.E.2d 626, 640 (1986), that "suicide is direct self-destruction and is intrinsically evil. No set of circumstances can make it moral * * *." See also Section VII, below, discussing suicide.

(4) Finally, there is no longer any reason to believe that the ethics of the medical profession do not permit discontinuation of medical treatment to a competent patient who refuses it. See AMA Ethical Opinion 2.20, Withholding or Withdrawing a Life–Prolonging Medical Treatment. Even if there were, though, should the protection of the "ethical integrity of the medical profession" overcome an otherwise proper decision to forgo some form of treatment? Is there any reason for the judiciary to uphold the ethical integrity of the medical profession where it is inconsistent with good law and good social policy? If all other analyses point to allowing a patient to deny consent to some form of treatment, why should the medical profession be able to require the treatment in the interest of its own self-defined integrity?

Are there special circumstances in which the interest of the patient ought not to be recognized or the interest of the state is especially important? Does the national interest allow the military to require its soldiers to undergo life saving (or other) medical care so that they can be returned to the front? Can a prisoner refuse kidney dialysis that is necessary to save his life unless the prison administration moves him from a medium to minimum security prison? See Commissioner of Correction v. Myers, 379 Mass. 255, 399 N.E.2d 452 (1979) (interest in "orderly prison administration" outweighs any privacy right of the prisoner). For a general discussion of several court's approaches to balancing a patient's right to die with these countervailing state interests, see Alan Meisel, The Right to Die §§ 8.14–8.19 (2d ed. 1995).

Note: State Law Bases for a "Right to Die"

The strength of any of these countervailing interests depends upon the strength of the patient's right to choose to forgo treatment. That, in turn, may depend upon the source of that right. Although some courts have found that right in the United States Constitution, *Cruzan's* interpretation of the Fourteenth Amendment has forced state courts to look for other bases for this right, too; it may be found in state common law, state statutes, or state constitutions.

The vast majority of state courts that have found a "right to die" have found that right in state common law, usually in the law of informed consent. As the Chief Justice recognized in *Cruzan,* "the informed consent doctrine has become firmly entrenched in American tort law * * * the logical corollary of the doctrine of informed consent is that the patient generally possesses the right not to consent, that is, to refuse treatment. * * * "Once a court finds a common law right, it is not necessary to determine whether the right is also conferred by statute or by the constitution. See, e.g., In re Storar, 52 N.Y.2d 363, 438 N.Y.S.2d 266, 420 N.E.2d 64 (1981).Some courts, on the other hand, find that their common law basis for a "right to die" can be bolstered by references to the state and federal constitutions. See In the Matter of Tavel, 661 A.2d 1061 (Del.1995). While the New Jersey court initially recognized a constitutional "right to die" in In re Quinlan, 70 N.J. 10, 355 A.2d 647, 664 (1976), it later recognized that the constitutional determination was unnecessary and retrenched: "While the right of privacy might apply in a case such as this, we need not decide that since the right to decline medical treatment is, in any event, embraced within the common law right to self determination." In re Conroy, 98 N.J. 321, 486 A.2d 1209, 1223 (1985).

Some states have gone beyond their common law and found the right in state statutes. Generally, courts that find a statutory "right to die" also find a consistent common law right. See, e.g., McConnell v. Beverly Enterprises–Connecticut, Inc., 209 Conn. 692, 553 A.2d 596, 601–602 (1989). The Illinois Supreme Court explicitly rejected state and federal constitutional justifications for a "right to die" because of the existence of both state common law and state statutory remedies:

> Lacking guidance from the Supreme Court, we decline to address whether federal privacy guarantees the right to refuse life-sustaining medical treatment. Lacking clear expression of intent from the drafters of our 1970 state constitution, we similarly abstain from expanding the privacy provision of our state constitution to embrace this right. * * * Instead, we follow the wisdom of the Supreme Court in avoiding constitutional questions when the issue at hand may be decided upon other grounds. * * * In the present case, we find the right to refuse life-sustaining medical treatment in our state's common law and in provisions of the Illinois Probate Act.

In re Estate of Longeway, 133 Ill.2d 33, 139 Ill.Dec. 780, 785, 549 N.E.2d 292, 297 (1989).

In addition, several state courts have found the "right to die" in their state constitutions. A decision based on the state constitution may be the strongest kind of support such a right can ever find, because it is not subject to review by the United States Supreme Court (absent an improbable argument that a state created right would itself violate the United States Constitution) and it is not subject to review by the state legislature (except through the generally cumbersome state constitutional amendment process).

Relevant state constitutional provisions take different forms. For example, the Florida Constitution provides that "[e]very natural person has the right to be let alone and free from governmental intrusion into his private life except as otherwise provided herein. * * *" Fla. Const., art. 1, section 23. The Arizona Constitution provides that "[n]o person shall be disturbed in his private affairs or his home invaded, without authority of law." Arizona Const., art. 2, section 8. Both of these constitutional provisions have given rise to state court recognized rights to forgo life-sustaining treatment. See In re Guardianship of Barry, 445 So.2d 365 (Fla.App.1984) and Rasmussen v. Fleming, 154 Ariz. 207, 741 P.2d 674 (1987). See also DeGrella v. Elston, 858 S.W.2d 698 (Ky.1993) and Lenz v. L.E. Phillips Career Dev. Ctr., 167 Wis.2d 53, 482 N.W.2d 60 (1992). The California Court of Appeal also found that such a right for competent patients could be found in the California Constitution. See *Bouvia,* supra.

B. THE RIGHT TO REFUSE MEDICAL TREATMENT FOR RELIGIOUS REASONS

The right to choose to die is usually based upon the premise that a person rationally may decide that death is preferable to the pain, expense, and inconvenience of life. Given that the process of weighing the value of life and death is necessarily based in personal history, religious and moral values, and individual sensitivity to a number of different factors, and given that it finds its philosophical basis in the principle of autonomy, is there any justification for independent second-party evaluation of whether the balancing was properly, or even rationally, performed by the patient? In fact, the most difficult cases have arisen over decisions based upon the dictates of religious principles. For example, Christian Scientists generally accept the healing power of prayer to the exclusion of medical assistance—most Christian Scientists refuse almost all traditional medical care. Jehovah's Witnesses, on the other hand, accept most medical care, but they do not accept blood transfusions, which they perceive to be a violation of the biblical prohibition on the ingestion of blood. Should a court treat a Christian Scientist or Jehovah's Witness who chooses for religious reasons to forgo necessary care any differently than it treats Elizabeth Bouvia? Is it relevant that others consider the religious ban on the ingestion of blood or the rejection of all medical treatment to be irrational?

Because courts were less able to empathize with patients who had unusual religious beliefs than with others, for many years courts were less willing to entertain the right to forgo life-sustaining treatment on religious grounds than on other grounds. Are the arguments used to justify judicial intervention to require blood transfusions for Jehovah's Witnesses when such transfusions are necessary to preserve life persuasive examples of the social value of law and medicine, or are they unconvincing examples of the paternalistic heritage of both professions? Consider a venerable old case ordering a transfusion for a Jehovah's Witness adult:

APPLICATION OF THE PRESIDENT AND DIRECTORS OF GEORGETOWN COLLEGE, INC.

United States Court of Appeals, District of Columbia Circuit, 1964.
331 F.2d 1000, 9 A.L.R.3d 1367.

J. SKELLY WRIGHT, CIRCUIT JUDGE.

Mrs. Jones was brought to the hospital by her husband for emergency care, having lost two thirds of her body's blood supply from a ruptured ulcer. She had no personal physician, and relied solely on the hospital staff. She was a total hospital responsibility. It appeared that the patient, age 25, mother of a seven-month-old child, and her husband were both Jehovah's Witnesses, the teachings of which sect, according to their interpretation, prohibited the injection of blood into the body. When death without blood became imminent, the hospital sought the advice of counsel, who applied to the District Court in the name of the hospital for permission to administer blood. Judge Tamm of the District Court denied the application, and counsel immediately applied to me, as a member of the Court of Appeals, for an appropriate writ.

* * *

Mr. Jones, the husband of the patient * * * [s]aid, that if the court ordered the transfusion, the responsibility was not his.

* * *

I tried to communicate with her, advising her again as to what the doctors had said. The only audible reply I could hear was "Against my will." It was obvious that the woman was not in a mental condition to make a decision. I was reluctant [t]o press her because of the seriousness of her condition and because I felt that to suggest repeatedly the imminence of death without blood might place a strain on her religious convictions. I asked her whether she would oppose the blood transfusion if the court allowed it. She indicated, as best I could make out, that it would not then be her responsibility.

* * *

I thereupon signed the order allowing the hospital to administer such transfusions as the doctors should determine were necessary to save her life.

It has been firmly established that the courts can order compulsory medical treatment of children for any serious illness or injury, and that adults, sick or well, can be required to submit to compulsory treatment or prophylaxis, at least for contagious diseases, *e.g.*, Jacobson v. Massachusetts. [ ] And there are no religious exemptions from these orders * * *.

The right to practice religion freely does not include liberty to expose the community or the child to communicable disease or the latter to ill health or death. [ ]

Of course, there is here no sick child or contagious disease. However, the sick child cases may provide persuasive analogies because she was as little able competently to decide for herself as any child would be. Under the circumstances, it may well be the duty of a court of general jurisdiction, such as the United States District Court for the District of Columbia, to assume the responsibility of guardianship for her, as for a child, at least to the extent of authorizing treatment to save her life. And if, as shown above, a parent has no power to forbid the saving of his child's life, *a fortiori* the husband of the patient here had no right to order the doctors to treat his wife in a way so that she would die. * * *

[Another] set of considerations involved the position of the doctors and the hospital. Mrs. Jones was their responsibility to treat. The hospital doctors had the choice of administering the proper treatment or letting Mrs. Jones die in the hospital bed, thus exposing themselves, and the hospital, to the risk of civil and criminal liability in either case. * * *

[N]either the principle that life and liberty are inalienable rights, nor the principle of liberty of religion, provides an easy answer to the question whether the state can prevent martyrdom. Moreover, Mrs. Jones had no wish to be a martyr. And her religion merely prevented her consent to a transfusion. If the law undertook the responsibility of authorizing the transfusion without her consent, no problem would be raised with respect to her religious practice. Thus, the effect of the order was to preserve for Mrs. Jones the life she wanted without sacrifice of her religious beliefs.

The final, and compelling, reason for granting the emergency writ was that a life hung in the balance. There was no time for research and reflection. Death could have mooted the cause in a matter of minutes, if action were not taken to preserve the *status quo*. To refuse to act, only to find later that the law required action, was a risk I was unwilling to accept. I determined to act on the side of life.

Notes

1. The Jehovah's Witness belief that the ingestion of blood is prohibited finds its source in a number of Biblical passages. See Leviticus 17:10 ("As for any man * * * who eats any sort of blood, I hall certainly set my face against the soul that is eating the blood * * * "), Leviticus 17:14 ("You must not eat the blood of any sort of flesh * * * "), Acts 15:10 and Genesis 9:4. These passages cause Witnesses to believe that receiving blood products will render them unable to obtain resurrection and eternal life. Is the fact that Biblical and religious scholars of other faiths reject the Witness reading of these passages significant? Should the courts ever engage in Biblical exegesis? Should the courts ever attempt to decide whether an interpretation of the Bible is reasonable?

Christian Scientists may be less likely than Jehovah's Witnesses to find themselves in litigation over their refusal of medical treatment because they are less likely to be at the hospital seeking medical care. Jehovah's Witnesses do believe in medicine, remember–outside of the use of blood; many Christian Scientists reject it outright. For an account of the Christian Science position, see Mary Baker Eddy, Manual of the Mother Church, 17–19 (1935). Given the ability of eighteenth century medicine, it was likely that in its early days the Christian Science faith saved more lives than it cost by discouraging its adherents from seeing doctors. More recent literature suggests that Christian Scientists do not live quite as long as others. See W. Simpson, Comparative Longevity in a College Cohort of Christian Scientists, 262 JAMA 1657 (1989).

Many other sects also believe that God will provide any cure that is appropriate for each sick person, and their actions pose the same legal and ethical problems as do those of the Christian Scientists and the Jehovah's Witnesses. In England the "Peculiar People" presented the British courts with this issue long before the first case arose on this side of the Atlantic. See R v. Senior, All ER 511 (1895–9).

2. In *Georgetown College* Judge Wright concluded that Jehovah's Witnesses were not required by their religious code to forgo blood transfusions; they were merely required to refuse consent to those transfusions. Thus, a weak denial was taken as a plea for medical intervention against the patient's stated, but misleading, request to be left without adequate care. Would the decision, based on this reasoning, vindicate the principle of autonomy? Is it appropriate for Judge Wright, in his role as a federal judge, to determine that the Jehovah's Witness faith requires only that an adherent deny consent to a transfusion, not that she avoid actually having one? Is it relevant that Jehovah's Witness religious authorities generally reject this position?

The other reasons for the court's decision in *Georgetown College* seem equally fragile. The hospital could hardly claim that the risk of civil or criminal liability would require the transfusion after the hospital went to court to determine its legal responsibility. Finally, the presumption that anyone so ill as to need a blood transfusion to save her life is likely to be incompetent is simply unsupported by fact. These bases for the decision demonstrate why this opinion by one of the great Federal judges of the last century has come to be seen as one of the most painful examples of judicial rationalization.

3. Most of the more recent cases that have considered this issue have concluded that competent adult Jehovah's Witnesses may choose to forgo medical treatment, whatever the results of those decisions may be, because the patient bears the consequences of choosing to forgo life-sustaining treatment. See, for example, Norwood Hospital v. Munoz, 409 Mass. 116, 564 N.E.2d 1017 (1991), In re Brooks' Estate, 32 Ill.2d 361, 205 N.E.2d 435 (1965), In re Osborne, 294 A.2d 372 (D.C.App.1972), Mercy Hospital, Inc. v. Jackson, 62 Md.App. 409, 489 A.2d 1130 (1985), vacated on other grounds, 306 Md. 556, 510 A.2d 562 (1986) (affirming denial of petition to appoint a guardian to consent to Jehovah's witness blood transfusion during C–Section). Compare Fosmire v. Nicoleau, 75 N.Y.2d 218, 551 N.Y.S.2d 876, 551 N.E.2d 77 (1990) (Jehovah's witness mother permitted to forgo a blood transfusion during child birth even though her life was thus put at risk) and Raleigh Fitkin–Paul Morgan Memorial Hospital v. Anderson, 42 N.J. 421, 201 A.2d 537 (1964), cert. denied, 377 U.S. 985, 84 S.Ct. 1894, 12 L.Ed.2d 1032 (1964) (pregnant Jehovah's Witness not permitted to refuse a necessary transfusion).

Even when others (such as children) are indirectly affected, the courts now tend to recognize the competent adult's right to forgo treatment:

PUBLIC HEALTH TRUST OF DADE COUNTY v. WONS

Supreme Court of Florida, 1989.
541 So.2d 96.

* * *

The Court of Appeal has certified the following question as one of great public importance:

WHETHER A COMPETENT ADULT HAS A LAWFUL RIGHT TO REFUSE
A BLOOD TRANSFUSION WITHOUT WHICH SHE MAY WELL DIE.

* * *

The issues presented by this difficult case challenge us to balance the
right of an individual to practice her religion and protect her right of privacy
against the state's interest in maintaining life and protecting innocent third
parties.

Norma Wons entered * * * a medical facility operated by the Public
Health Trust of Dade County, with a condition known as dysfunctional
uterine bleeding. Doctors informed Mrs. Wons that she would require treatment in the form of a blood transfusion or she would, in all probability, die.
Mrs. Wons, a practicing Jehovah's Witness and mother of two minor children,
declined the treatment on ground that it violated her religious principles to
receive blood from outside her own body. At the time she refused consent Mrs.
Wons was conscious and able to reach an informed decision concerning her
treatment.

The Health Trust petitioned the Circuit Court to force Mrs. Wons to
undergo a blood transfusion. * * * [T]he court granted the petition, ordering
the hospital doctors to administer the blood transfusion, which was done
while Mrs. Wons was unconscious. The trial judge reasoned that minor
children have a right to be reared by two loving parents, a right which
overrides the mother's rights of free religious exercise and privacy. Upon
regaining consciousness, Mrs. Wons appealed to the Third District which
reversed the order. After holding that the case was not moot due to the
recurring nature of Mrs. Wons condition * * *, the district court held that
Mrs. Wons' constitutional rights of religion and privacy could not be overridden by the state's purported interests.

* * *

The Health Trust asserts that the children's right to be reared by two
loving parents is sufficient to trigger the compelling state interest [in protection of innocent third parties]. While we agree that the nurturing and support
by two parents is important in the development of any child, it is not
sufficient to override fundamental constitutional rights. * * * As the district
court noted in its highly articulate opinion below:

Surely nothing, in the last analysis, is more private or more sacred than
one's religion or view of life, and here the courts, quite properly, have given
great deference to the individual's right to make decisions vitally affecting his
private life according to his own conscience. It is difficult to overstate this
right because it is, without exaggeration, the very bedrock upon which this
country was founded.

Notes

1. A concurring opinion in *Wons* depends in part upon the fact that the
children would be cared for by relatives even if Mrs. Wons were to die. In that
opinion the Chief Justice points out:

The medical profession may consider a blood transfusion a rather ordinary or
routine procedure, but, given Mrs. Wons' religious beliefs, that procedure for

her is extraordinary. * * * [W]e must not assume from her choice that Mrs. Wons was not considering the best interests of her children. She knows they will be well cared for by her family. As a parent, however, she also must consider the example she sets for her children, how to teach them to follow what she believes is God's law if she herself does not. The choice for her can not be an easy one, but it is hers to make. It is not for this court to judge the reasonableness or validity of her beliefs. Absent a truly compelling state interest to the contrary, the law must protect her right to make that choice.

2. The dissent in *Wons* depended in part upon another portion of *Application of the President and Directors of Georgetown College, Inc.,* supra, where Judge Wright concluded that "[t]he state, as parens patriae, will not allow a parent to abandon a child, and so it should not allow this most ultimate of voluntary abandonments. The patient had a responsibility to the community to care for her infant. Thus the people had an interest in preserving the life of this mother." Would this rationale support state intervention and an injunction to stop a mother who had decided to take up hang-gliding, bronco-riding, working as a firefighter, or some other dangerous occupation? Why do you think it is applied in the case of a Jehovah's Witness, and not in any of these other cases?

3. The rule allowing patients to adhere to their religious faiths, even if that means that they choose to forgo life-sustaining treatment, is different for children. The Supreme Court has always held that children are not permitted to become martyrs to their parents' (or their own) religious beliefs. Where the refused treatment is not highly invasive, and where it is likely to return the child to full health—as in the case of a blood transfusion for a Jehovah's witnesses child— courts universally will order the treatment. On the other hand, where the chance of success is lower—as in the case of certain kinds of chemotherapy for some childhood cancers—the courts are less likely to overrule the parents and the child. See section V, below. For a general discussion of this issue, see Alan Meisel, The Right to Die § 15.6 (2d ed. 1995).

4. A patient who refuses a blood transfusion during an operation may thereby exacerbate damage caused by medical negligence. Should the refusal of a blood transfusion be considered contributory or comparative negligence for purposes of a malpractice action against a negligent physician whose negligence would have had inconsequential results if blood could have been provided to the patient? We rarely consider acting on religious principle to be negligence of any sort, even when the religious principle is unusual and dangerous. On the other hand, it seems unfair that a physician, even a negligent physician, should be liable for greatly increased damages because he decided to respect his patient's religious views and thus avoid a blood transfusion that under other circumstances would have been considered a medical necessity. See Shorter v. Drury, 103 Wash.2d 645, 695 P.2d 116 (1985) (Jehovah's Witness died as a result of medical negligence and because she demanded there be no blood transfusion; court found comparative negligence). In that case, the court pointed out that the First Amendment was not implicated because the case was a dispute between private parties. Since there was no state action, there could be no First Amendment limitation. 695 P.2d at 124. Would there be a First Amendment issue if the action were filed against a state hospital? For an excellent discussion of the role religion might play in the operation of a religious health care institution, see Kathleen Boozang, Deciding the Fate of Religious Hospitals in the Emerging Healthcare Market, 31 Hous. L. Rev. 1429 (1995).

IV. THE "RIGHT TO DIE"—PATIENTS WITHOUT DECISIONAL CAPACITY

A. DETERMINING DECISIONAL CAPACITY

Problem: Determining the Decisional Capacity of a Dying Patient

Theodore Flores is a 27 year old who has suffered from quadriplegia since a serious auto accident (in which he was driving while intoxicated) about a year ago. His spinal injury was so high and so substantial that he requires intermittent ventilator support, and he is fed through a gastrostomy tube that has been inserted directly into his stomach. Although he has not worked since his accident, he was employed as a pharmacist until the accident. He now communicates with others by winking his eyes or blowing through a straw connected to an alphabet board. The accident appears to have had no affect on his intellectual abilities, although he is now unable to concentrate for more than a few minutes at a time, and he sometimes refuses to communicate to outsiders for days at a time.

Mr. Flores has now informed his physician that he wishes to have the ventilator disconnected and the feeding tube removed. His physician has informed him of the certainty that death will follow from either of these acts. Mr. Flores refuses to respond to such information, except to repeat his request. Mr. Flores has read most of the important recent medical journal articles about his condition, and his physician believes that Mr. Flores understands the risks, benefits, and alternatives more thoroughly than most similarly situated patients. Despite this, though, the physician is concerned about whether Mr. Flores has the capacity to decide to forgo ventilator support and nutrition and hydration. His concern grows out of several circumstances, including Mr. Flores's limited concentration span, his occasional unwillingness to communicate with anyone, and the following three factors:

(1) A psychiatrist who has been seeing Mr. Flores regularly has informed his physician that Mr. Flores became seriously depressed about three weeks ago, when he began to realize that there would never be any improvement in his physical conditions. As the psychiatrist pointed out, of course, most reasonable people would become depressed upon such a realization. The psychiatrist has recommended antidepressants for Mr. Flores, but he refuses to take them.

(2) Since the accident, Mr. Flores has become a devoted follower of August Marsh, a religious leader who preaches that self abnegation (and, particularly, self abnegation leading to death) is the only way to gain salvation. In particular, Rev. Marsh believes that the self discipline of starvation (he usually recommends a period of a week) can bring eternal joy.

(3) Mr. Flores desperately wants to father a child—an event not precluded by his current condition. While the doctors have explained to Mr. Flores that his reproductive system is intact and unaffected by the accident, he simply refuses to believe that and he insists that he will not be able to have children. No matter what the medical staff does, and despite Mr. Flores's generally sophisticated understanding of his medical condition, he simply refuses to understand this fact.

Does Mr. Flores possess sufficient decisional capacity to make the choice to forgo nutrition and hydration and ventilator support? What other information would you want to have before you make this determination? Remember, you are looking only for information relevant to a determination of decisional capacity, you are not looking for information that is relevant to the substantive decision. What process should be employed to make this determination? Is a court order required to confirm Mr. Flores's capacity? Incapacity? What kind of evidence should be introduced in the hearing that would lead to an appropriate court order?

An adult with decisional capacity may choose to forgo medical care, even if that choice results in death. This necessarily follows from the principle of autonomy which underlies the physician-patient relationship. Of course, that principle is not served by allowing a patient to make a decision he does not have capacity to make. In order to determine whether a patient can choose to undergo (or forgo) medical care, someone must determine whether the patient has the capacity to make that choice. Because the theory behind decisional capacity is thus employed to serve the social principle of autonomy, capacity determinations should not be entirely medical; social, philosophical, and political factors should also be considered.

Until recently, most courts that addressed this issue referred to the "competency" of the patient. In other areas of law, such as those concerned with guardianships and conservatorships, "competency" was often employed as a term with all-or-nothing consequences. A person was either competent for all purposes and at all times, or incompetent for all purposes and at all times. When we evaluate the ability of a patient to make a health care decision, though, we are dealing with something far more subtle. A patient may have the capacity to make some, simple health care decisions, and not to make other, more complex, decisions. Similarly, a patient may be able to make certain decisions at some times but not at others. To recognize these potential variabilities in competency, some courts (and many legislatures) have begun to use the term "decisional capacity"— a term which focuses on the actual decision to be made—rather than "competency"—a term which focuses on the status of the patient. In this text, the terms are used interchangeably.

Courts have been reluctant to articulate a standard for capacity. There are few reported opinions in which courts state and apply any formal principle. Courts have been much more likely to finesse the issue out of the law and back into medicine by inviting physicians, especially psychiatrists, to testify about the mental state and, thus, capacity of a patient.

For many years, physicians were likely to find that a patient had decisional capacity to make a serious medical decision whenever that patient agreed with the physician. When the patient disagreed with the physician—especially if that disagreement would lead to the death of the patient—the physician, and subsequently the court, would be likely to find that the patient lacked capacity and then seek out some surrogate decision-maker more likely to agree with the physician. In reaction to this, and as a consequence of the frustration of attempting to develop any consistent and practical definition of competence, consumerist attorneys and physicians in the 1970s suggested that any patient who could indicate an affirmative or negative ought to be considered to have decisional capacity. Of course, this reactionary view is no more satisfactory than the previously prevailing view. Neither serves the purpose of protecting the individual personality of the patient and the authority of the patient to control his own life in a way that is consistent with his own values.

Despite the extremes described above, some scholars have attempted to categorize the possible tests for decisional capacity (or competency) that could be applied to patients of questionable capacity. Five different kinds of tests are outlined in the following article prepared by a psychiatrist, a lawyer, and a sociologist with extensive expertise in psychiatry. Compare these approaches with the President's Commission suggestion, which follows it.

LOREN H. ROTH, ALAN MEISEL, AND CHARLES W. LIDZ, TESTS OF COMPETENCY TO CONSENT TO TREATMENT

134 Am.J.Psychiatry 279 (1977).

* * *

TESTS FOR COMPETENCY

Several tests for competency have been proposed in the literature; others are readily inferable from judicial commentary. Although there is some overlap, they basically fall into five categories: 1) evidencing a choice, 2) "reasonable" outcome of choice, 3) choice based on "rational" reasons, 4) ability to understand, and 5) actual understanding.

Evidencing a Choice

This test for competency is set at a very low level and is the most respectful of the autonomy of patient decision making. Under this test the competent patient is one who evidences a preference for or against treatment. This test focuses not on the quality of the patient's decision but on the presence or absence of a decision. * * * This test of competency encompasses at a minimum the unconscious patient: in psychiatry it encompasses the mute patient who cannot or will not express an opinion.

* * *

"Reasonable" Outcome of Choice

This test of competency entails evaluating the patient's capacity to reach the "reasonable," the "right," or the "responsible" decision. The emphasis in this test is on outcome rather than on the mere fact of decision or how it has been reached. The patient who fails to make a decision that is roughly congruent with the decision that a "reasonable" person in like circumstances would make is viewed as incompetent.

This test is probably used more often than might be admitted by both physicians and courts. Judicial decisions to override the desire of patients with certain religious beliefs not to receive blood transfusions may rest in part on the court's view that the patient's decision is not reasonable. When life is at stake and a court believes that the patient's decision is unreasonable, the court may focus on even the smallest ambiguity in the patient's thinking to cast doubt on the patient's competency so that it may issue an order that will preserve life or health. * * *

Mental health laws that allow for involuntary treatment on the basis of "need for care and treatment" without requiring a formal adjudication of incompetency in effect use an unstated reasonable outcome test in abridging the patient's common-law right not to be treated without giving his or her consent. These laws are premised on the following syllogism: the patient needs treatment; the patient has not obtained treatment on his or her own initiative; therefore, the patient's decision is incorrect, which means that he or she is incompetent, thus justifying the involuntary imposition of treatment.

* * * Ultimately, because the test rests on the congruence between the patient's decision and that of a reasonable person or that of the physician, it is biased in favor of decisions to accept treatment, even when such decisions are made by people who are incapable of weighing the risks and benefits of treatment. In other words, if patients do not decide the "wrong" way, the issue of competency will probably not arise.

Choice Based on "Rational" Reasons

Another test is whether the reasons for the patient's decision are "rational," that is, whether the patient's decision is due to or is a product of mental illness. As in the reasonable outcome test, if the patient decides in favor of treatment the issue of the patient's competency (in this case, whether the decision is the product of mental illness) seldom if ever arises because of the medical profession's bias toward consent to treatment and against refusal of treatment.

In this test the quality of the patient's thinking is what counts.

* * *

The test of rational reasons, although it has clinical appeal and is probably much in clinical use, poses considerable conceptual problems; as a legal test it is probably defective. The problems include the difficulty of distinguishing rational from irrational reasons and drawing inferences of causation between any irrationality believed present and the valence (yes or no) of the patient's decision. Even if the patient's reasons seem irrational, it is not possible to prove that the patient's actual decision making has been the product of such irrationality. * * * The emphasis on rational reasons can too easily become a global indictment of the competency of mentally disordered individuals, justifying widespread substitute decision making for this group.

The Ability to Understand

This test—the ability of the patient to understand the risks, benefits, and alternatives to treatment (including no treatment)—is probably the most consistent with the law of informed consent. Decision making need not be rational in either process or outcome; unwise choices are permitted. Nevertheless, at a minimum the patient must manifest sufficient ability to understand information about treatment, even if in fact he or she weighs this information differently from the attending physician. What matters in this test is that the patient is able to comprehend the elements that are presumed by law to be a part of treatment decision making. How the patient weighs these elements, values them, or puts them together to reach a decision is not important.

The patient's capacity for understanding may be tested by asking the patient a series of questions concerning risks, benefits, and alternatives to treatment. By providing further information or explanation to the patient, the physician may find deficiencies in understanding to be remediable or not.

* * *

Furthermore, how potentially sophisticated must understanding be in order that the patient be viewed as competent? There are considerable barriers, conscious and unconscious and intellectual and emotional, to understanding proposed treatments. Presumably the potential understanding required is only that which would be manifested by a reasonable person provided a similar amount of information. A few attempts to rank degrees of understanding have been made. However, this matter is highly complex and beyond the scope of the present inquiry. Certainly, at least with respect to nonexperimental treatment, the patient's potential understanding does not have to be perfect or near perfect for him or her to be considered competent, although one court seemed to imply this with respect to experimental psychosurgery. A final problem with this test is that its application depends on unobservable and inferential mental processes rather than on concrete and observable elements of behavior.

Actual Understanding

Rather than focusing on competency as a construct or intervening variable in the decision-making process, the test of actual understanding reduces competency to an epiphenomenon of this process. The competent patient is by definition one who has provided a knowledgeable consent to treatment. Under this test the physician has an obligation to educate the patient and directly ascertain whether he or she has in fact understood. If not, according to this test the patient may not have provided informed consent. Depending on how sophisticated a level of understanding is to be required, this test delineates a potentially high level of competency, one that may be difficult to achieve.

* * *

The practical and conceptual limitations of this test are similar to those of the ability-to-understand test. What constitutes adequate understanding is vague, and deficient understanding may be attributable in whole or in part to physician behavior as well as to the patient's behavior or character. An advantage that this test has over the ability-to-understand test, assuming the necessary level of understanding can be specified *a priori,* is its greater reliability. Unlike the ability-to-understand test, in which the patient's comprehension of material of a certain complexity is used as the basis for an assumption of comprehension of other material of equivalent complexity (even if this other material is not actually tested), the actual understanding test makes no such assumption. It tests the very issues central to patient decision making about treatment.

* * *

PRESIDENT'S COMMISSION FOR THE STUDY OF ETHI-CAL PROBLEMS IN MEDICINE AND BIOMEDICAL AND BEHAVIORAL RESEARCH, DECISIONMAKING CAPACITY

1 Making Health Care Decisions 57–60 (1980).

Elements of Capacity. In the view of the Commission, any determination of the capacity to decide on a course of treatment must relate to the individual abilities of a patient, the requirements of the task at hand, and the consequences likely to flow from the decision. Decision-making capacity requires, to greater or lesser degree: (1) possession of a set of values and goals; (2) the ability to communicate and to understand information; and (3) the ability to reason and to deliberate about one's choices.

The first, a framework for comparing options, is needed if the person is to evaluate possible outcomes as good or bad. * * * The patient must be able to make reasonably consistent choices. Reliance on a patient's decision would be difficult or impossible if the patient's values were so unstable that the patient could not reach or adhere to a choice at least long enough for a course of therapy to be initiated with some prospect of being completed.

The second element includes the ability to give and receive information, as well as the possession of various linguistic and conceptual skills needed for at least a basic understanding of the relevant information. These abilities can be evaluated only as they relate to the task at hand and are not solely cognitive, as they ordinarily include emotive elements. To use them, a person also needs sufficient life experience to appreciate the meaning of potential alternatives: what it would probably be like to undergo various medical procedures, for example, or to live in a new way required by a medical condition or intervention.

Some critics of the doctrine of informed consent have argued that patients simply lack the ability to understand medical information relevant to decisions about their care. Indeed, some empirical studies purport to have demonstrated this by showing that the lay public often does not know the meaning of common medical terms, or by showing that, following an encounter with a physician, patients are unable to report what the physician said about their illness and treatment. Neither type of study establishes the fact that patients cannot understand. The first merely finds that they do not currently know the right definitions of some terms; the second, which usually fails to discover what the physician actually did say, rests its conclusions on an assumption that information was provided that was subsequently not understood.

* * *

The third element of decisionmaking capacity—reasoning and deliberation—includes the ability to compare the impact of alternative outcomes on personal goals and life plans. Some ability to employ probabilistic reasoning about uncertain outcomes is usually necessary, as well as the ability to give appropriate weight in a present decision to various future outcomes.

Notes and Questions

1. Roth, Meisel, and Lidz suggest that each of these tests is biased by the evaluator's analysis of whether the treatment would succeed—that is, whether the evaluator would consent or not. The authors conclude that where the benefit of treatment is likely to far outweigh the risk (i.e., the evaluator would choose to undergo it), there is likely to be a low standard for competency when the patient consents and a high standard for competency when the patient refuses. Analogously, where the risk greatly outweighs the benefit (again, of course, in the evaluator's mind), a low standard for competency will be applied if the patient refuses treatment, but a high standard will be applied when the patient consents. The authors point out:

> Of course, some grossly impaired patients cannot be determined to be competent under any conceivable test, nor can most normally functioning people be found incompetent merely by selective application of the test of competency. However, within limits and when the patient's competency is not absolutely clear cut, a test of competency that will achieve the desired medical or social end despite the actual condition of the patient may be selected. We do not imply that this is done maliciously either by physicians or by the court; rather we believe that it occurs as a consequence of the strong societal bias in favor of treating treatable patients so long as it does not expose them to serious risks. 134 Am.J.Psych. at 283.

The authors do not hold out much hope for the development of a clear test for competence that can be easily applied because no such test could be consistent with the different reasons that we seek to determine competence:

> The search for a single test of competency is a search for a Holy Grail. Unless it is recognized that there is no magical definition of competency to make decisions about treatment, the search for an acceptable test will never end. "Getting the words just right" is only part of the problem. In practice, judgments of competency go beyond semantics or straightforward applications of legal rules; such judgments reflect social considerations and societal biases as much as they reflect matters of law and medicine. Id.

2. What are the advantages and disadvantages of the five Roth, Meisel, and Lidz criteria, as compared to the President's Commission's criteria? Which defines decisional capacity better?

3. The issue of whether a patient of questionable capacity is competent to forgo life-sustaining treatment has arisen on many occasions. One case that squarely faced the question involved Robert Quakenbush, a seventy-two-year-old recluse whose gangrenous leg would have to be amputated to avoid a certain, quick death. He was rambunctious, belligerent, and "a conscientious objector to medical therapy" who had shunned medical care for 40 years. In deciding that the patient was competent, the court depended on the testimony of two psychiatrists, both of whom treated the issue of competency as entirely medical, and the judge's own visit with Mr. Quackenbush.

> The testimony concerning Quackenbush's mental condition was elicited from two psychiatrists. The first, appearing for the hospital, was Dr. Michael Giuliano. Dr. Giuliano * * * saw Quackenbush once on January 6. The doctor's conclusions are that Quackenbush is suffering from an organic brain syndrome with psychotic elements. He asserts that the organic brain syndrome is acute—i.e., subject to change—and could be induced by the septice-

mia * * *. [Dr. Giuliano] concluded that Quackenbush's mental condition was not sufficient to make an informed decision concerning the operation.

Dr. Abraham S. Lenzner, a Board-certified psychiatrist for 25 years and specialist in geriatric psychiatry, testified as an independent witness at the request of the court. Dr. Lenzner is Chief of Psychiatry at the Memorial Hospital and a professor at the New Jersey College of Medicine and Dentistry.

Dr. Lenzner is of the opinion, based upon reasonable medical certainty, that Quackenbush has the mental capacity to make decisions, to understand the nature and extent of his physical condition, to understand the nature and extent of the operations, to understand the risks involved if he consents to the operation, and to understand the risks involved if he refuses the operation * * *.

I visited with Quackenbush for about ten minutes on January 12. During that period he did not hallucinate, his answers to my questions were responsive and he seemed reasonably alert. His conversation did wander occasionally but to no greater extent than would be expected of a 72–year–old man in his circumstances. He spoke somewhat philosophically about his circumstances and desires. He hopes for a miracle but realizes there is no great likelihood of its occurrence. He indicates a desire—plebeian, as he described it—to return to his trailer and live out his life. He is not experiencing any pain and indicates that if he does, he could change his mind about having the operation.

* * *

The matter may be tried before a judge without a jury. My findings pursuant to this authority are that Robert Quackenbush is competent and capable of exercising informed consent on whether or not to have the operation. I do not question the events and conditions described by Dr. Giuliano but find they were of a temporary, curative, fluctuating nature, and whatever their cause the patient's lucidity is sufficient for him to make an informed choice.

* * *

In re Quackenbush, 156 N.J.Super. 282, 383 A.2d 785, 788 (1978).

Ultimately, it is difficult to determine whether the court merely chose the more credible of the two psychiatrists, or whether the court depended upon some intuitive conclusions that followed the judge's ten minute visit with the patient. Which would be the more satisfying basis for the court's determination of competency?

Whatever one may think of the process the court employed for determining competency in *Quackenbush,* the case stands for two principles that have been repeated constantly since. The first is that a patient who fluctuates between capacity and incapacity cannot be denied an opportunity to make decisions concerning medical care, even life-sustaining medical care, just because of the temporary absence of capacity. The desires of that patient, articulated during a period of competence, must be respected by the physician, the hospital, and the courts. See Lane v. Candura, 6 Mass.App.Ct. 377, 376 N.E.2d 1232 (1978). The second principle assumed in *Quackenbush* is that a patient may have capacity for some purposes and not for others. Some state statutes explicitly recognize and protect the variably competent person.

4. To what extent do value judgments and prejudices enter into decisions regarding competency? Would the Quackenbush case have been a simpler one if Mr. Quackenbush were a retired lawyer leading a middle class life rather than a belligerent hermit? One fascinating review of "right to die" cases suggests that gender may be an important factor, and that the legal system takes the expressed wishes of men more seriously than those of women. Steven Miles and Allison August, Courts, Gender, and "The Right to Die," 18 Law, Med. & Health Care 85 (1990).

5. How significant is it that terminally ill patients who seek a right to die are often perceived as depressed? Isn't it natural for someone dying of an incurable disease to be depressed? Does it make any sense to extend our social perception of suicide among the medically well to the decision of the terminally ill to forgo life sustaining treatment? Two psychiatrists have recently suggested that physicians should attempt to treat depression in the seriously ill, but that psychiatrists also should recognize that some depression in terminally ill patients is not treatable, and that "[g]ravely ill medical patients should not lose their right to refuse medical treatment simply because they have been transferred to a medical-psychiatric unit. Just as internists must at some point decide 'enough is enough,' so might psychiatrists at some point appropriately stop trying to intervene and let the dying process proceed." Mark Sullivan and Stuart Youngner, Depression, Competence, and the Right to Refuse Lifesaving Medical Treatment, 151 Am.J. Psychiatry 971, 977 (1994). The authors conclude that "[p]sychiatrists need to recognize that some treatment refusals that result in death are legitimate, even if they are accompanied by suicidal intent. * * * It is often valuable to diagnose and treat depression in the seriously ill patient, but sometimes it is valuable to accept the patient's decision to die." Id.

6. For a more comprehensive account of judicial attempts to determine competency, see Kevin R. Wolff, Determining Patient Competency in Treatment Refusal Cases, 24 Ga.L.Rev. 733 (1990). For a useful attempt at reconciling the theory and practice of judicial determinations of incapacity, see Wendy Margolis, The Doctor Knows Best?: Patient Capacity for Health Care Decisionmaking, 71 Or.L.Rev. 909 (1992).

B. DETERMINING THE PATIENT'S CHOICE

It is very difficult to serve the underlying goal of autonomy, if that goal is defined as personal choice, in patients without decisional capacity. One way to serve this principle is through the application of the doctrine of substituted judgment. Under this doctrine, a person, committee, or institution attempts to determine what the patient would do if the patient had decisional capacity. It may be possible to review the values of a formerly competent patient to determine whether that patient would choose to undergo or forgo proposed medical care. This can be done through a thoughtful analysis of the patient's values during life or, more precisely, through review of formal statements made by the patient when the patient had capacity. The most relevant considerations may be statements made by the patient about the proposed treatment itself. Indeed, such statements may provide the only *constitutionally* relevant information about an incompetent patient's wishes after *Cruzan*.

Of course, there is no way to know with certainty what the patient would do under those circumstances. Some have argued that the doctrine of substituted judgment is too speculative to be applied reliably and that there is simply no way to protect the autonomy of a patient without decisional capacity. Where there is no possible method for establishing what the autonomous patient would do, bioethicists (and increasingly, courts) move to the second principle of bioethical decision-making, beneficence. In these circumstances, the alternative to serving autonomy is serving beneficence, and the alternative to the doctrine of substituted judgment is the doctrine of the "best interest" of the patient. As we shall see, the more difficult it becomes to decide what the patient would do if that patient had decisional capacity, the more likely it is that the court will apply the principle of beneficence rather than the principle of autonomy.

1. A Statutory Framework for Health Care Decision Making: Advance Directives and Surrogate Decisionmakers

UNIFORM HEALTH–CARE DECISIONS ACT

1994.

SECTION 1. DEFINITIONS. In this [Act]:

(1) "Advance health-care directive" means an individual instruction or a power of attorney for health care.

(2) "Agent" means an individual designated in a power of attorney for health care to make a health-care decision for the individual granting the power.

(3) "Capacity" means an individual's ability to understand the significant benefits, risks, and alternatives to proposed health care and to make and communicate a health-care decision.

(4) "Guardian" means a judicially appointed guardian or conservator having authority to make a health-care decision for an individual.

(5) "Health care" means any care, treatment, service, or procedure to maintain, diagnose, or otherwise affect an individual's physical or mental condition.

(6) "Health-care decision" means a decision made by an individual or the individual's agent, guardian, or surrogate, regarding the individual's health care, including:

　(i) selection and discharge of health-care providers and institutions;

　(ii) approval or disapproval of diagnostic tests, surgical procedures, programs of medication, and orders not to resuscitate; and

　(iii) directions to provide, withhold, or withdraw artificial nutrition and hydration and all other forms of health care.

* * *

(9) "Individual instruction" means an individual's direction concerning a health-care decision for the individual.

* * *

(12) "Power of attorney for health care" means the designation of an agent to make health-care decisions for the individual granting the power.

* * *

(16) "Supervising health-care provider" means the primary physician or, if there is no primary physician or the primary physician is not reasonably available, the health-care provider who has undertaken primary responsibility for an individual's health care.

(17) "Surrogate" means an individual, other than a patient's agent or guardian, authorized under this [Act] to make a health-care decision for the patient.

SECTION 2. ADVANCE HEALTH–CARE DIRECTIVES.

(a) An adult or emancipated minor may give an individual instruction. The instruction may be oral or written. The instruction may be limited to take effect only if a specified condition arises.

(b) An adult or emancipated minor may execute a power of attorney for health care, which may authorize the agent to make any health-care decision the principal could have made while having capacity. The power must be in writing and signed by the principal. The power remains in effect notwithstanding the principal's later incapacity and may include individual instructions. * * *

(c) Unless otherwise specified in a power of attorney for health care, the authority of an agent becomes effective only upon a determination that the principal lacks capacity, and ceases to be effective upon a determination that the principal has recovered capacity.

(d) Unless otherwise specified in a written advance health-care directive, a determination that an individual lacks or has recovered capacity, or that another condition exists that affects an individual instruction or the authority of an agent, must be made by the primary physician.

(e) An agent shall make a health-care decision in accordance with the principal's individual instructions, if any, and other wishes to the extent known to the agent. Otherwise, the agent shall make the decision in accordance with the agent's determination of the principal's best interest. In determining the principal's best interest, the agent shall consider the principal's personal values to the extent known to the agent.

(f) A health-care decision made by an agent for a principal is effective without judicial approval.

(g) A written advance health-care directive may include the individual's nomination of a guardian of the person.

(h) An advance health-care directive is valid for purposes of this [Act] if it complies with this [Act], regardless of when or where executed or communicated.

SECTION 3. REVOCATION OF ADVANCE HEALTH–CARE DIRECTIVE.

(a) An individual may revoke the designation of an agent only by a signed writing or by personally informing the supervising health-care provider.

(b) An individual may revoke all or part of an advance health-care directive, other than the designation of an agent, at any time and in any manner that communicates an intent to revoke.

(c) A health-care provider, agent, guardian, or surrogate who is informed of a revocation shall promptly communicate the fact of the revocation to the supervising health-care provider and to any health-care institution at which the patient is receiving care.

(d) A decree of annulment, divorce, dissolution of marriage, or legal separation revokes a previous designation of a spouse as agent unless otherwise specified in the decree or in a power of attorney for health care.

(e) An advance health-care directive that conflicts with an earlier advance health-care directive revokes the earlier directive to the extent of the conflict.

SECTION 4. OPTIONAL FORM. The following form may, but need not, be used to create an advance health-care directive. The other sections of this [Act] govern the effect of this or any other writing used to create an advance health-care directive. An individual may complete or modify all or any part of the following form:

ADVANCE HEALTH–CARE DIRECTIVE
Explanation

You have the right to give instructions about your own health care. You also have the right to name someone else to make health-care decisions for you. This form lets you do either or both of these things. It also lets you express your wishes regarding donation of organs and the designation of your primary physician. If you use this form, you may complete or modify all or any part of it. You are free to use a different form.

Part 1 of this form is a power of attorney for health care. Part 1 lets you name another individual as agent to make health-care decisions for you if you become incapable of making your own decisions or if you want someone else to make those decisions for you now even though you are still capable. You may also name an alternate agent to act for you if your first choice is not willing, able, or reasonably available to make decisions for you. Unless related to you, your agent may not be an owner, operator, or employee of [a residential long-term health-care institution] at which you are receiving care.

Unless the form you sign limits the authority of your agent, your agent may make all health-care decisions for you. This form has a place for you to limit the authority of your agent. You need not limit the authority of your agent if you wish to rely on your agent for all health-care decisions that may have to be made. If you choose not to limit the authority of your agent, your agent will have the right to:

> (a) consent or refuse consent to any care, treatment, service, or procedure to maintain, diagnose, or otherwise affect a physical or mental condition;

> (b) select or discharge health-care providers and institutions;

> (c) approve or disapprove diagnostic tests, surgical procedures, programs of medication, and orders not to resuscitate; and

> (d) direct the provision, withholding, or withdrawal of artificial nutrition and hydration and all other forms of health care.

Part 2 of this form lets you give specific instructions about any aspect of your health care. Choices are provided for you to express your wishes regarding the provision, withholding, or withdrawal of treatment to keep you alive, including the provision of artificial nutrition and hydration, as well as the provision of pain relief. Space is also provided for you to add to the choices you have made or for you to write out any additional wishes.

Part 3 of this form lets you express an intention to donate your bodily organs and tissues following your death.

Part 4 of this form lets you designate a physician to have primary responsibility for your health care.

After completing this form, sign and date the form at the end. It is recommended but not required that you request two other individuals to sign as witnesses. Give a copy of the signed and completed form to your physician, to any other health-care providers you may have, to any health-care institution at which you are receiving care, and to any health-care agents you have named. You should talk to the person you have named as agent to make sure that he or she understands your wishes and is willing to take the responsibility.

You have the right to revoke this advance health-care directive or replace this form at any time.

PART 1

POWER OF ATTORNEY FOR HEALTH CARE

(1) DESIGNATION OF AGENT: I designate the following individual as my agent to make health-care decisions for me:

(name of individual you choose as agent)

(address) (city) (state) (zip code)

(home phone) (work phone)

OPTIONAL: If I revoke my agent's authority or if my agent is not willing, able, or reasonably available to make a health-care decision for me, I designate as my first alternate agent:

(name of individual you choose as first alternate agent)

(address) (city) (state) (zip code)

(home phone) (work phone)

* * *

(2) AGENT'S AUTHORITY: My agent is authorized to make all health-care decisions for me, including decisions to provide, withhold, or withdraw artificial nutrition and hydration and all other forms of health care to keep me alive, except as I state here:

_____

_____

_____

(Add additional sheets if needed.)

(3) WHEN AGENT'S AUTHORITY BECOMES EFFECTIVE: My agent's authority becomes effective when my primary physician determines that I am unable to make my own health-care decisions unless I mark the following box. If I mark this box [___], my agent's authority to make health-care decisions for me takes effect immediately.

(4) AGENT'S OBLIGATION: My agent shall make health-care decisions for me in accordance with this power of attorney for health care, any instructions I give in Part 2 of this form, and my other wishes to the extent known to my agent. To the extent my wishes are unknown, my agent shall make health-care decisions for me in accordance with what my agent determines to be in my best interest. In determining my best interest, my agent shall consider my personal values to the extent known to my agent.

(5) NOMINATION OF GUARDIAN: If a guardian of my person needs to be appointed for me by a court, I nominate the agent designated in this form. If that agent is not willing, able, or reasonably available to act as guardian, I nominate the alternate agents whom I have named, in the order designated.

PART 2

INSTRUCTIONS FOR HEALTH CARE

If you are satisfied to allow your agent to determine what is best for you in making end-of-life decisions, you need not fill out this part of the form. If you do fill out this part of the form, you may strike any wording you do not want.

(6) END–OF–LIFE DECISIONS: I direct that my health-care providers and others involved in my care provide, withhold, or withdraw treatment in accordance with the choice I have marked below:

[___] (a) Choice Not To Prolong Life

I do not want my life to be prolonged if (i) I have an incurable and irreversible condition that will result in my death within a relatively short time, (ii) I become unconscious and, to a reasonable degree of medical certainty, I will not regain consciousness, or (iii) the likely risks and burdens of treatment would outweigh the expected benefits, OR

[___] (b) Choice To Prolong Life

I want my life to be prolonged as long as possible within the limits of generally accepted health-care standards.

(7) ARTIFICIAL NUTRITION AND HYDRATION: Artificial nutrition and hydration must be provided, withheld, or withdrawn in accordance with the choice I have made in paragraph (6) unless I mark the following box. If I mark this box [___], artificial nutrition and hydration must be provided regardless of my condition and regardless of the choice I have made in paragraph (6).

(8) RELIEF FROM PAIN: Except as I state in the following space, I direct that treatment for alleviation of pain or discomfort be provided at all times, even if it hastens my death:

(9) OTHER WISHES: (If you do not agree with any of the optional choices above and wish to write your own, or if you wish to add to the instructions you have given above, you may do so here.) I direct that:

(Add additional sheets if needed.)

PART 3

DONATION OF ORGANS AT DEATH

(OPTIONAL)

(10) Upon my death (mark applicable box)

[___] (a) I give any needed organs, tissues, or parts, OR

[___] (b) I give the following organs, tissues, or parts only

(c) My gift is for the following purposes (strike any of the following you do not want)

(i) Transplant

(ii) Therapy

(iii) Research

(iv) Education

PART 4

PRIMARY PHYSICIAN

(OPTIONAL)

(11) I designate the following physician as my primary physician:

(name of physician)

(address) (city) (state) (zip code)(phone)

OPTIONAL: If the physician I have designated above is not willing, able, or reasonably available to act as my primary physician, I designate the following physician as my primary physician:* * *

(12) EFFECT OF COPY: A copy of this form has the same effect as the original.

(13) SIGNATURES: Sign and date the form here:

(date) (sign your name)

(address) (print your name)

(city) (state)

(Optional) SIGNATURES OF WITNESSES:

* * *

SECTION 5. DECISIONS BY SURROGATE.

(a) A surrogate may make a health-care decision for a patient who is an adult or emancipated minor if the patient has been determined by the primary physician to lack capacity and no agent or guardian has been appointed or the agent or guardian is not reasonably available.

(b) An adult or emancipated minor may designate any individual to act as surrogate by personally informing the supervising health-care provider. In the absence of a designation, or if the designee is not reasonably available, any member of the following classes of the patient's family who is reasonably available, in descending order of priority, may act as surrogate:

   (1) the spouse, unless legally separated;

   (2) an adult child;

   (3) a parent; or

   (4) an adult brother or sister.

(c) If none of the individuals eligible to act as surrogate under subsection (b) is reasonably available, an adult who has exhibited special care and concern for the patient, who is familiar with the patient's personal values, and who is reasonably available may act as surrogate.

(d) A surrogate shall communicate his or her assumption of authority as promptly as practicable to the members of the patient's family specified in subsection (b) who can be readily contacted.

(e) If more than one member of a class assumes authority to act as surrogate, and they do not agree on a health-care decision and the supervising health-care provider is so informed, the supervising health-care provider shall comply with the decision of a majority of the members of that class who have communicated their views to the provider. If the class is evenly divided concerning the health-care decision and the supervising health-care provider is so informed, that class and all individuals having lower priority are disqualified from making the decision.

(f) A surrogate shall make a health-care decision in accordance with the patient's individual instructions, if any, and other wishes to the extent known to the surrogate. Otherwise, the surrogate shall make the decision in accordance with the surrogate's determination of the patient's best interest. In determining the patient's best interest, the surrogate shall consider the patient's personal values to the extent known to the surrogate.

(g) A health-care decision made by a surrogate for a patient is effective without judicial approval.

(h) An individual at any time may disqualify another, including a member of the individual's family, from acting as the individual's surrogate by a signed writing or by personally informing the supervising health-care provider of the disqualification.

(i) Unless related to the patient by blood, marriage, or adoption, a surrogate may not be an owner, operator, or employee of [a residential long-term health-care institution] at which the patient is receiving care.

(j) A supervising health-care provider may require an individual claiming the right to act as surrogate for a patient to provide a written declaration under penalty of perjury stating facts and circumstances reasonably sufficient to establish the claimed authority.

SECTION 6. DECISIONS BY GUARDIAN.

(a) A guardian shall comply with the ward's individual instructions and may not revoke the ward's advance health-care directive unless the appointing court expressly so authorizes.

(b) Absent a court order to the contrary, a health-care decision of an agent takes precedence over that of a guardian.

(c) A health-care decision made by a guardian for the ward is effective without judicial approval.

SECTION 7. OBLIGATIONS OF HEALTH–CARE PROVIDER.

(a) Before implementing a health-care decision made for a patient, a supervising health-care provider, if possible, shall promptly communicate to the patient the decision made and the identity of the person making the decision.

(b) A supervising health-care provider who knows of the existence of an advance health-care directive, a revocation of an advance health-care directive, or a designation or disqualification of a surrogate, shall promptly record its existence in the patient's health-care record and, if it is in writing, shall request a copy and if one is furnished shall arrange for its maintenance in the health-care record.

(c) A primary physician who makes or is informed of a determination that a patient lacks or has recovered capacity, or that another condition exists which affects an individual instruction or the authority of an agent, guardian, or surrogate, shall promptly record the determination in the patient's health-care record and communicate the determination to the patient, if possible, and to any person then authorized to make health-care decisions for the patient.

(d) Except as provided in subsections (e) and (f), a health-care provider or institution providing care to a patient shall:

    (1) comply with an individual instruction of the patient and with a reasonable interpretation of that instruction made by a person then authorized to make health-care decisions for the patient; and

    (2) comply with a health-care decision for the patient made by a person then authorized to make health-care decisions for the patient to the same extent as if the decision had been made by the patient while having capacity.

(e) A health-care provider may decline to comply with an individual instruction or health-care decision for reasons of conscience. A health-care institution may decline to comply with an individual instruction or health-care decision if the instruction or decision is contrary to a policy of the institution which is expressly based on reasons of conscience and if the policy was timely communicated to the patient or to a person then authorized to make health-care decisions for the patient.

(f) A health-care provider or institution may decline to comply with an individual instruction or health-care decision that requires medically ineffective health care or health care contrary to generally accepted health-care standards applicable to the health-care provider or institution.

(g) A health-care provider or institution that declines to comply with an individual instruction or health-care decision shall:

> (1) promptly so inform the patient, if possible, and any person then authorized to make health-care decisions for the patient;

> (2) provide continuing care to the patient until a transfer can be effected; and

> (3) unless the patient or person then authorized to make health-care decisions for the patient refuses assistance, immediately make all reasonable efforts to assist in the transfer of the patient to another health-care provider or institution that is willing to comply with the instruction or decision.

(h) A health-care provider or institution may not require or prohibit the execution or revocation of an advance health-care directive as a condition for providing health care.

SECTION 8. HEALTH–CARE INFORMATION. Unless otherwise specified in an advance health-care directive, a person then authorized to make health-care decisions for a patient has the same rights as the patient to request, receive, examine, copy, and consent to the disclosure of medical or any other health-care information.

SECTION 9. IMMUNITIES.

(a) A health-care provider or institution acting in good faith and in accordance with generally accepted health-care standards applicable to the health-care provider or institution is not subject to civil or criminal liability or to discipline for unprofessional conduct for:

> (1) complying with a health-care decision of a person apparently having authority to make a health-care decision for a patient, including a decision to withhold or withdraw health care;

> (2) declining to comply with a health-care decision of a person based on a belief that the person then lacked authority; or

> (3) complying with an advance health-care directive and assuming that the directive was valid when made and has not been revoked or terminated.

(b) An individual acting as agent or surrogate under this [Act] is not subject to civil or criminal liability or to discipline for unprofessional conduct for health-care decisions made in good faith.

* * *

SECTION 11. CAPACITY.

(a) This [Act] does not affect the right of an individual to make health-care decisions while having capacity to do so.

(b) An individual is presumed to have capacity to make a health-care decision, to give or revoke an advance health-care directive, and to designate or disqualify a surrogate.

* * *

SECTION 13. EFFECT OF [ACT].

(a) This [Act] does not create a presumption concerning the intention of an individual who has not made or who has revoked an advance health-care directive.

(b) Death resulting from the withholding or withdrawal of health care in accordance with this [Act] does not for any purpose constitute a suicide or homicide or legally impair or invalidate a policy of insurance or an annuity providing a death benefit, notwithstanding any term of the policy or annuity to the contrary.

(c) This [Act] does not authorize mercy killing, assisted suicide, euthanasia, or the provision, withholding, or withdrawal of health care, to the extent prohibited by other statutes of this State.

(d) This [Act] does not authorize or require a health-care provider or institution to provide health care contrary to generally accepted health-care standards applicable to the health-care provider or institution.

[(e) This [Act] does not authorize an agent or surrogate to consent to the admission of an individual to a mental health-care institution unless the individual's written advance health-care directive expressly so provides.]

[(f) This [Act] does not affect other statutes of this State governing treatment for mental illness of an individual involuntarily committed to a [mental health-care institution under appropriate statute].]

SECTION 14. JUDICIAL RELIEF. On petition of a patient, the patient's agent, guardian, or surrogate, a health-care provider or institution involved with the patient's care, or an individual described in Section 5(b) or (c), the [appropriate] court may enjoin or direct a health-care decision or order other equitable relief. A proceeding under this section is governed by [here insert appropriate reference to the rules of procedure or statutory provisions governing expedited proceedings and proceedings affecting incapacitated persons].

* * *

Notes and Comments—Advance Directives

1. *The History of Advance Directives: The Rise of Living Living Wills.* Nearly two decades before the Uniform Health Care Decisions Act was proposed, many people first became concerned about the potential abuses of powerful new forms of life-sustaining medical treatment. Frightened by the indignity of the life of Karen Quinlan, they began to search for a way to avoid a similar fate. Within two years of the first press reports of the *Quinlan* case several states had adopted statutes that formally recognized certain forms of written statements requesting that some kinds of medical care be discontinued. These statutes, generally referred to as "living will" statutes, "right to die" legislation, or "natural death" acts, provided a political outlet for the frustration that accompanied the empathy for Ms. Quinlan.

The statutes, which still provide the governing law in most jurisdictions, differ in several respects. In some states living wills may be executed by any person, at any time (and in some states they may be executed on behalf of minors), while in other states they require a waiting period, and may not be executed during a terminal illness. In most states they are of indefinite duration, although in some states they expire after a determined number of years. Some statutes address only the terminally ill, others include those in "irreversible coma" or persistent vegetative state, and still others provide for different conditions to trigger the substantive provisions of the document. Some states require the formalities of a will for the living will to be recognized by statute, while other states require different formalities. The statutes generally relieve physicians and other health care providers of any civil or criminal liability if they properly follow the requirements of the statute and implement the desires expressed in a legally executed living will. Some of the statutes also require that any physician who cannot, in good conscience, carry out those provisions, transfer the patient to a physician who can. The statutes also provide that carrying out the provisions of a properly executed living will does not constitute suicide for insurance purposes. It is hard to know whether the absence of litigation over the terms of living wills means that these documents are working well or not at all.

Many living will statutes do not apply to those in persistent vegetative state, irreversible coma, or any other medical condition that is not terminal. Thus, these statutes would be of no assistance to people in the position of Nancy Cruzan. Is there a reason to limit legislation to terminal conditions, or should such statutes be extended to other conditions, like persistent vegetative state, where there is broad social consensus that patients should have the right to forgo life-sustaining treatment?

Many living will statutes specifically exclude "the performance of any procedure to provide nutrition or hydration" from the definition of death-prolonging procedures, and thus do not extend any statutory protection to those who remove nutrition or hydration from a patient. For the most famous example, see Vernon's Ann.Mo.Stat. § 459.010(3). After the United States Supreme Court decision in *Cruzan,* are such exceptions legally meaningful? Are they constitutional? In *Cruzan,* The Chief Justice reviewed those state cases that have treated nutrition and hydration just like any other form of medical care, apparently with approval. In her concurring opinion, Justice O'Connor cited AMA Ethical Opinion 2.20, Withholding or Withdrawing a Life–Prolonging Medical Treatment, to support her proposition that "artificial feeding cannot readily be distinguished from other forms of medical treatment." In his dissent, Justice Brennan states without reservation: "No material distinction can be drawn between the treatment to which Nancy Cruzan continues to be subject—artificial nutrition and hydration—and any other medical treatment." For a fuller discussion on the legal position of the withdrawal of nutrition and hydration, see pages 1376–1378, below. For an example of judicial avoidance of the apparent consequences of a nutrition and hydration exception to a living will statute, see McConnell v. Beverly Enterprises–Connecticut, Inc., 209 Conn. 692, 553 A.2d 596 (1989). See also In re Guardianship of Browning, 568 So.2d 4 (Fla.1990).

2. *The Next Step: Durable Powers of Attorney for Health Care.* Another means of identifying who should speak for the patient when the patient is incompetent is to allow the patient to designate a spokesperson during the

patient's period of competence. This may be accomplished through the patient's execution of a durable power of attorney.

Powers of attorney have been available over the past several centuries to allow for financial transactions to be consummated by agents of a principal. A power of attorney may be executed, under oath, by any competent person. It provides that the agent designated shall have the right to act on behalf of the principal for purposes that are described and limited in the document itself. Thus, a principal may give an agent a power of attorney to enter into a particular contract, a particular kind of contract, or all contracts. The power may be limited by time, by geographic area, or in any other way. It may be granted to any person, who, upon appointment, becomes the agent and "attorney-in-fact" for the principal. At common law a power of attorney expired upon the "incapacity" of the principal. This was necessary to assure that the principal could maintain adequate authority over his agent. As long as a power of attorney expired upon the incapacity of the principal, the power of attorney had no value in making medical decisions. After all, a competent patient could decide for himself; there was no reason for him to delegate authority to an agent.

In the mid 1970s it became clear that the value of the power of attorney could be increased if it could extend beyond the incapacity of the principal. For example, as an increasing number of very elderly people depended upon their children and others to handle their financial affairs, it became important that there be some device by which they could delegate their authority to these agents. For such principals it was most important that the authority remain with their agents when they did become incapacitated. The Uniform Probate Code was amended to provide for a durable power of attorney; that is, a power of attorney that would remain in effect (or even become effective) upon the incapacity of the principal. That statute explicitly provides:

> A durable power of attorney is a power of attorney by which a principal designates another his attorney in fact in writing and the writing contains the words "this power of attorney shall not be affected by subsequent disability or incapacity of the principal, or lapse of time," or "this power of attorney shall become effective upon the disability or incapacity of the principal," or similar words showing the intent of the principal that the authority conferred shall be exercisable notwithstanding the principal's subsequent disability or incapacity, and, unless it states a time of determination, notwithstanding the lapse of time since the execution of the instrument.

Uniform Probate Code § 35–501.

The question of whether general durable powers of attorney may be used for nonfinancial determinations, such as health care decisionmaking, was never conclusively answered by the courts. There is no reported opinion formally holding that the authority of a durable power of attorney executed under the Uniform Probate Code extends to health care decision-making. For two suggesting that there would be such authority, see In re Peter, 108 N.J. 365, 378–379, 529 A.2d 419, 426 (1987) ("Although the statute does not specifically authorize conveyance of durable authority to make medical decisions, it should be interpreted that way.") and In re Westchester County Medical Center (O'Connor), 72 N.Y.2d 517, 534 N.Y.S.2d 886, 531 N.E.2d 607,

612 fn. 2 (1988). The President's Commission assumed, without any discussion, that it could be used for this purpose. See President's Commission, Deciding to Forego Life–Sustaining Treatment, 145–149 (1983). On the other hand, two statutory sources of these acts—the Uniform Probate Code and the Model Special Power of Attorney for Small Interests Act—were conceived originally as ways of controlling property, not health care decisions. Is there any intellectual problem in extending this simple statute to health care decision-making?

The vast majority of states have now adopted statutes that formally authorize the execution of durable powers of attorney for health care decisions. There is an extremely wide variety among these statutes. One of the first, in California, turned into a nightmare of political compromise. It is long, complex, and highly technical. For example, it prescribes that a "warning to person executing this document" be included in 10–point boldface type. The California warning itself is longer than the entire durable power prescribed by statutes of other states. West's Ann.Cal.Civ.Code § 2433. The Illinois statute, which is generally far more permissive than the California alternative, contains a non-mandatory "Illinois statutory short form power of attorney for health care" which is several typed pages long. See Ill.—S.H.A. ch. 110½ para. 804–10 (Smith–Hurd Supp.1990). While the Illinois statute at least provides that "the form of health care agency in this article is not intended to be exclusive * * * ", the Rhode Island statute explicitly provides:

> "[t]he statutory form of durable power of attorney as set forth in [this act] shall be used and shall be the only form by which a person may execute a durable power of attorney for health care. * * * It shall not be altered in any manner and shall preclude the use of any other form to exercise the durable power of attorney for health care."

R.I.Gen.Laws §§ 23–410–1.

The New Mexico legislature dealt with the issue very simply by listing health care decisions among other kinds of decisions that principals may wish to delegate to attorneys-in-fact in more general durable powers of attorney. Among the boxes that can be checked off on the New Mexico statutory durable power form are real estate transactions, bond, share and commodity transactions, chattel and goods transactions, a host of other business transactions—and "decisions regarding life-saving and life-prolonging medical treatment," "decisions relating to medical treatment, surgical treatment, nursing care, medication, hospitalization, institutionalization in a nursing home or other facility and home health care," and, most remarkably, "transfer of property or income as a gift to the principal spouse for the purpose of qualifying the principal for governmental medical assistance." N.M.Stat.Ann., § 45–5–502.

Some state laws now permit durable powers of attorney to arrange not only for decisionmaking after the principal's incapacity, but also for decision-making after the principal's death. These statutes allow the principal to provide for the disposition of his body through a durable power. See, e.g., Ill.—S.H.A. ch. 110½, para. 802–10 and Kan.Stat.Ann. § 58–625.

Further, at least one state allows an agent authorized by a durable power of attorney to make health care decisions for a principal even if the principal has capacity—as long as that is the explicit desire of the principal. N.M. Stat.

Ann. § 24–7A–2 et seq. Does the grant of such authority make any sense? Why should an agent make a decision for a principal *with* capacity? Doesn't that undermine the principle of autonomy? The drafters of that statute argue that it is convenient for health care providers to have a surrogate decision-maker to turn to in the case of a patient with capacity that is highly variable. That is, some argue, in such cases health care providers ought to be able to depend upon the articulated consent of some surrogate without doing a full competency analysis each time a health care decision is to be made. Of course, the decision of the surrogate can always be overruled by the patient herself if she has capacity.

The legal significance of a durable power of attorney for health care is defined by each state's durable power statute. In her concurring opinion in the *Cruzan* case, Justice O'Connor suggests that there may also be constitutional significance to a properly executed durable power of attorney:

> I also write separately to emphasize that the Court does not today decide the issue whether a state must also give effect to the decisions of a surrogate decision-maker. In my view, such a duty may well be Constitutionally required to protect the patient's liberty interest in refusing medical treatment.

497 U.S. at 289, 110 S.Ct. at 2857. She commends those several states that have recognized "the practical wisdom of such a procedure by enacting durable power of attorney statutes" and she suggests that a written appointment of a proxy "may be a valuable additional safeguard of the patient's interest in directing his medical care." In the final paragraph of her opinion she points out that "[t]oday's decision * * * does not preclude a future determination that the Constitution requires the states to implement the decisions of a patient's duly appointed surrogate."

3. *The Development of The Uniform Health Care Decisions Act.* The Uniform Health Care Decisions Act (UHCDA), which you have just read, was designed to replace the Uniform Rights of the Terminally Ill Act, state durable powers acts and parts of the Uniform Anatomical Gifts Act. It was approved by the National Conference of Commissioners on Uniform State Laws in 1993 and by the American Bar Association House of Delegates in 1994. As you can see, the UHCDA substantially alters the form and utility of living wills and durable powers, and it provides a method of making health care decisions for incompetent patients who do not have advance directives. As of early 2001, some version of the uniform act was adopted in Alabama, Delaware, Hawaii, Maine, Mississippi and New Mexico. A new California statute governing health care decisions that became effective in 2000 is also largely based on the UHCDA. Several more states were set to consider adoption of the act in 2001.

The proposed act takes a comprehensive approach by placing the living will (which is retitled the "individual instruction"), the durable power of attorney (now called the "power of attorney for health care"), a family consent law, and some provisions concerning organ donation together in one statute. Further, the statute integrates the current living will and durable power (and statement of desire to donate organs) into a single document. The UHCDA provides a statutory form, but it also explicitly declares that the form is not a mandatory one, and that individuals may draft their own form that includes only some of the kinds of instructions permitted in the unified form.

Can you see how the UHCDA very substantially broadens the role of the living will? The new "individual instruction" can apply to virtually any health care decision, not just the end of life decisions to which living wills are typically applicable. Further, "health care decision" is defined very broadly.

The uniform act also makes the execution of the unified document very easy. It has no witness requirement, and it does not require that the document be notarized. The drafters of the proposed act concluded that the formalities often associated with living wills and durable powers served to discourage their execution more than to deter fraud.

The residual decisionmaking portion of the act is very much like the family consent statutes that have now been adopted in a majority of states, and which are discussed in note 5, below, and this section of the act applies only if there is no applicable individual instruction or appointed agent. While it provides for a common family hierarchy of decisionmakers for decisionally incapacitated patients, it also provides that the family can be trumped by an "orally designated surrogate," who may be appointed by a patient informing her "supervising physician" that the surrogate is entitled to make health care decisions on her behalf. Thus, patients can effectively orally appoint decision-making agents who previously could only be appointed in a writing signed pursuant to a rigorous process. In the same manner a patient may orally *disqualify* someone who otherwise would be entitled to make decisions on her behalf. If you do not want your brother making health care decisions for you, you need only tell your supervising physician. Thus, in essence, any health care decision will be made by the first available in this hierarchy:

(1) the patient, if competent,

(2) the patient, through an individual instruction,

(3) an agent appointed by the patient in a written power of attorney for health care, unless a court has given this authority explicitly to a guardian,

(4) a guardian appointed by the court,

(5) a surrogate appointed orally by the patient,

(6) a surrogate selected from the list of family members and others who can make health care decisions on behalf of the patient.

The drafters of the UHCDA make it clear in their comments that one purpose of the statute is to assure that these intimate health care decisions remain within the realm of the patient, the patient's family and close friends, and the health care providers, and that others not be permitted to disrupt that process. The court would very rarely have a role in any decision making under this statute, and outsiders (including outside organizations) who do not think a patient is adequately protected have no standing to seek judicial intervention. See Protection and Advocacy System, Inc. v. Presbyterian Healthcare Systems, 128 N.M. 73, 989 P.2d 890 (N.M. App. 1999).

The UHCDA has explicitly determined that the decisionmaker (whether an agent, guardian or surrogate) should make a decision based on the principle of substituted judgment (i.e., on the basis of what the patient would choose, if that patient were competent) rather than the best interest principle.

If it is impossible to apply the substituted judgment principle, the statute would apply the best interests principle.

The UHCDA includes the normal raft of recordkeeping provisions, limitations on the reach of the criminal law, assurances regarding the insurance rights of those who execute the documents, and restrictions on the liability of those who act under the statute in good faith. A provision for $500 in liquidated damages in actions for breach of the act may not encourage litigation when the statute is ignored, but the provision for attorney's fees in those cases might provide an incentive for lawyers to bring those cases. The act applies only to adults.

While there does not appear to be any strong opposition to the general intent or structure of the UHCDA, some advocates for the elderly and the disabled are worried by some parts of this proposed statute. They are worried that the streamlined procedures for execution of a document allow a greater opportunity for fraud to be perpetrated against those who wish to sign, and they are concerned about the virtually unrestrained authority the proposed act gives to physicians to make determinations that a patient lacks decisional capacity. In addition, there is some concern that any change in the law will undercut the significant amount of community education that has been directed to the current law over the past few years. Are these concerns justified? Is there a way to address these concerns that would be consistent with the values expressed in the rest of the statute?

Should your state adopt the UHCDA? If you were advising your state legislature on this issue, what portions of the uniform act would you suggest be changed? How would you change those portions?

4. *Family Consent Laws.* Over the past century it became standard medical practice to seek consent to any medical procedure from close family members of an incompetent patient. There is no common law authority for this practice; it is an example of medical practice (and good common sense) being subtly absorbed by the law. The President's Commission suggests five reasons for this deference to family members:

(1) The family is generally most concerned about the good of the patient.

(2) The family will also usually be most knowledgeable about the patient's goals, preferences, and values.

(3) The family deserves recognition as an important social unit that ought to be treated, within limits, as a responsible decisionmaker in matters that intimately affect its members.

(4) Especially in a society in which many other traditional forms of community have eroded, participation in a family is often an important dimension of personal fulfillment.

(5) Since a protected sphere of privacy and autonomy is required for the flourishing of this interpersonal union, institutions and the state should be reluctant to intrude, particularly regarding matters that are personal and on which there is a wide range of opinion in society.

President's Commission, Deciding to Forego Life–Sustaining Treatment, 127 (1983). It is difficult to determine whether the resort to close relatives to give consent is merely a procedural device to discover what the patient, if competent, would choose, or whether it is based in an independent substantive doctrine. Although it seems essentially procedural—the family is most likely to know what the patient would choose—many courts are willing to accept the decisions of family members even when there is little support for the position that these family members are actually choosing what the patient would choose. Of course, consulting with family members also neutralizes potential malpractice plaintiffs; this factor probably accounts for part of the current popularity of this decisionmaking process.

Over the past decade most states have enacted "family consent laws" that authorize statutorily designated family members to make health care decisions for their relatives in circumscribed situations. These statutes often apply to a wide range of health care decisions (including, in most cases, decisions to forgo life sustaining treatment), although sometimes they apply only when there has been a physician's certification of the patient's inability to make the health care decision and sometimes they are limited to particular kinds of treatment (e.g., cardiopulmonary resuscitation). In addition, "family consent laws" often provide immunity from liability for family members and physicians acting in good faith, and judicial authority to resolve disputes about the authority of the family members under the statutes. The definition of "family member" and the position of each family member in the hierarchy varies from state to state. In some states those in a long term spouse-like relationship with the patient are included in the list of family members who can make decisions for the incompetent patient; in some states they are not. Some lists include a residuary class of anyone who knows the values, interest and wishes of the patient; some states list the physician as the residuary decisionmaker; some provide for no residuary decisionmaker. Some states give a general guardian top priority; some states do not. Some states allow the statutory surrogate to make any health care decisions, some states put some kinds of decisions (like discontinuing nutrition and hydration) off limits. Section 5 of the UHCDA provides a good example of a family consent law. Are there other classes of decisionmakers you would add to that hierarchy?

5. Why do you think that no two state health care decisionmaking statutes are identical? What relevant political groups are likely to be stronger in some states and weaker in others? In some states the political nature of the right to die has driven the legislature to enact virtually meaningless statutes to avoid political fallout from all sides. Of course, the existence of these impotent statutes might do more harm than good. Justice Welliver, dissenting from the Missouri Supreme Court decision in *Cruzan*, points this out with regard to that state's living will statute:

> We Missourians can sign an instrument directing the withholding or withdrawing of death-prolonging procedures, but, after the Missouri amendments, "death-prolonging procedure" does not include: (1) "the administration of medication," * * * (3) "the performance of any procedure to provide nutrition," [or] (4) "the performance of any procedure to provide * * * hydration." If we cannot authorize withdrawing or withholding "medication," "nutrition" or "hydration," then what can we authorize to be withheld in Missouri? The Missouri Living Will Act is a fraud on Missourians who believe we have been given a right to execute a living will, and to die naturally, respectably, and in peace.

Cruzan v. Harmon, 760 S.W.2d 408, 422 (Mo.1988).

6.   The statutory language need not limit a clever attorney in drafting an advance directive for a client. While an attorney ought to draft a document that is consistent with the formalities of state law, most state laws allow an attorney to be expansive and directive in providing for the needs of the person who will execute the document—the formal legal applicability of the uncertain language can be determined later. For example, some attorneys use living will forms that explicitly define nutrition and hydration as kinds of treatment that may be withheld or withdrawn even when the governing statutes are silent on that point. Would such a clarification of the explicit wishes of the patients affect the validity of an otherwise legal document? After *Cruzan*, might such inclusions take on constitutional significance?

In drafting durable powers of attorney under state statutes which permit deviation from the statutory form, it makes sense to tailor the language to the principal's desires. The principal can designate any person or persons he wishes as his attorney-in-fact, and may authorize that person to make any designated group of health care decisions or to make all health care decisions on his behalf. In some states a corporation or organization may be named as an agent. The principal may require that the agent consult with named others before making certain kinds of decisions, or he may require the agent to consider certain deeply held personal values before proceeding. In determining how you would draft a durable power of attorney, consider the effect it would have on the principal's family, the physician and health-care workers, and the person who is designated as agent. What would happen if that person refused to honor the durable power of attorney, or refused to abide by some of its provisions? Some state statutes require that the agent accept the appointment before the durable power is effective. Does such a requirement make sense?

7. *The Patient Self–Determination Act and Advance Directives.* The Patient Self–Determination Act became law as a part of the Omnibus Budget Reconciliation Act of 1990, and it increases the role that advance directives—both living wills and durable powers of attorney—play in medical decisionmaking. The statute applies to hospitals, skilled nursing facilities, home health agencies, hospice programs, and HMOs that receive Medicaid or Medicare funding. It requires each of those covered by the Act to provide each patient with written information concerning:

> (i) an individual's rights under State law (whether statutory or as recognized by the courts of the State) to make decisions concerning * * * medical care, including the right to accept or refuse medical or surgical treatment and the right to formulate advance directives * * * and

> (ii) the written policies of the provider or organization respecting the implementation of such rights.

42 U.S.C.A. § 1395cc(a)(1)(f)(1)(A). In addition, those covered must document in each patient's record whether that patient has signed an advance directive, assure that the state law is followed in the institution, and provide for education of both the staff and the public concerning living wills and durable powers of attorney. A covered institution or organization that does not assure the Secretary of Health and Human Services that it is complying with all relevant portions of the Act must lose all of its Medicaid and Medicare funding; this sanction is mandatory and the Secretary has no discretion to

grant exceptions or extensions. Despite this requirement, the financial death penalty—the cutoff of Medicare and Medicaid funding—has yet to be imposed in any case.

The statute also requires states to develop written descriptions of their own state law, and it requires the Department of Health and Human Services to conduct nationwide public education on advance directives. The Act requires Social Security recipients to receive information about living wills and durable powers, and a new section on these issues was added to the Medicare handbook.

The American Medical Association, the American Hospital Association and the Health Care Financing Administration opposed the Act when it was pending in Congress; the American Bar Association opposed it also. Why do you think they took this position? Does it surprise you? Do you think their complaints about the burdens the Act would impose on health care institutions is one reason that the Department of Health and Human Services has shown so little interest in enforcing the law? Although the Department issued an interim final rule enforcing the statute early in 1992, it did not get around to issuing the final rule until June of 1995, just short of five years after the statute was passed

Although the Patient Self Determination Act showed great promise, and while it has changed the practice of some health care institutions, "[a]necdotal evidence suggests that the statute has not had the effect of encouraging physicians to initiate end-of-life discussions with patients." Alan Meisel, The Right to Die § 10.21 (2d ed. 1995) (citing Diane M. Gianelli, Many Say Doctors Aren't Living Up to Expectations of Living Will Law, Am.Med. News, May 17, 1993, at 1).

8. A few states have also taken action to increase the utility of advance directives. For example, a couple of states have central registries of advance directives, and a handful of states provide for drivers' licenses to show if a patient has an advance directive. Hawaii is implementing a new statute that requires managed health care providers to discuss advance directives with their patients/enrollees.

2. *Decisionmaking in the Absence of a Governing Statute*

a. *Discovering the Patient's Wishes*

IN RE EICHNER

New York Court of Appeals, 1981.
52 N.Y.2d 363, 438 N.Y.S.2d 266, 420 N.E.2d 64.

WACHTLER, JUDGE.

For over 66 years Brother Joseph Fox was a member of the Society of Mary, a Catholic religious order which, among other things, operates Chaminade High School in Mineola. * * *

While [an] operation was being performed * * * he suffered cardiac arrest, with resulting loss of oxygen to the brain and substantial brain damage. He lost the ability to breathe spontaneously and was placed on a respirator which maintained him in a vegetative state. The attending physicians informed Father Philip Eichner, who was the president of Chaminade and the director of the society at the school, that there was no reasonable chance of recovery and that Brother Fox would die in that state.

After retaining two neurosurgeons who confirmed the diagnosis, Father Eichner requested the hospital to remove the respirator. The hospital, however, refused to do so without court authorization. Father Eichner then applied * * * to be appointed committee of the person and property of Brother Fox, with authority to direct removal of the respirator. The application was supported by the patient's 10 nieces and nephews, his only surviving relatives. The court appointed a guardian ad litem and directed that notice be served on various parties, including the District Attorney.

At the hearing the District Attorney opposed the application and called medical experts to show that there might be some improvement in the patient's condition. All the experts agreed, however, that there was no reasonable likelihood that Brother Fox would ever emerge from the vegetative coma or recover his cognitive powers.

There was also evidence, submitted by the petitioner, that before the operation rendered him incompetent the patient had made it known that under these circumstances he would want a respirator removed. Brother Fox had first expressed this view in 1976 when the Chaminade community discussed the moral implications of the celebrated *Karen Ann Quinlan* case, in which the parents of a 19–year–old New Jersey girl who was in a vegetative coma requested the hospital to remove the respirator [ ]. These were formal discussions prompted by Chaminade's mission to teach and promulgate Catholic moral principles. At that time it was noted that the Pope had stated that Catholic principles permitted the termination of extraordinary life support systems when there is no reasonable hope for the patient's recovery and that church officials in New Jersey had concluded that use of the respirator in the *Quinlan* case constituted an extraordinary measure under the circumstances. Brother Fox expressed agreement with those views and stated that he would not want any of this "extraordinary business" done for him under those circumstances. Several years later, and only a couple of months before his final hospitalization, Brother Fox again stated that he would not want his life prolonged by such measures if his condition were hopeless.

* * *

In this case the proof was compelling. There was no suggestion that the witnesses who testified for the petitioner had any motive other than to see that Brother Fox' stated wishes were respected. The finding that he carefully reflected on the subject, expressed his views and concluded not to have his life prolonged by medical means if there were no hope of recovery is supported by his religious beliefs and is not inconsistent with his life of unselfish religious devotion. These were obviously solemn pronouncements and not casual remarks made at some social gathering, nor can it be said that he was too young to realize or feel the consequences of his statements [ ]. That this was a persistent commitment is evidenced by the fact that he reiterated the decision but two months before his final hospitalization. There was, of course, no need to speculate as to whether he would want this particular medical procedure to be discontinued under these circumstances. What occurred to him was identical to what happened in the *Karen Ann Quinlan* case, which had originally prompted his decision. In sum, the evidence clearly and convincingly shows that Brother Fox did not want to be maintained in a vegetative coma by use of a respirator.

* * *

Note: Applying the Principle of Substituted Judgment

Three states, Michigan, Missouri and New York, have, at one time or another, rejected substituted judgment except where it is based on the formally articulated desires of the patient. See *Cruzan,* above at, 1064, In re Westchester Medical Center (O'Connor), below at 1132, In re Martin, 450 Mich. 204, 538 N.W.2d 399 (1995). In these states it is almost impossible to remove life sustaining treatment from incompetent patients because it is rare indeed to have a patient foresee and describe his condition and the treatment he would wish with the specificity with which Brother Fox spoke. More often, patients have not addressed the questions and others must decide on their behalf exercising substituted judgment for the patient.

The Illinois court expressed this principle clearly and simply:

> Under substituted judgment, a surrogate decisionmaker attempts to establish, with as much accuracy as possible, what decision the patient would make if he were competent to do so. Employing this theory, the surrogate first tries to determine if the patient had expressed explicit intent regarding this type of medical treatment prior to becoming incompetent. [ ] Where no clear intent exists, the patient's personal value system must guide the surrogate. * * *

In re Estate of Longeway, 133 Ill.2d 33, 139 Ill.Dec. 780, 787, 549 N.E.2d 292, 299 (1989).

In such cases, courts (except in Michigan, Missouri and New York, as noted) look wherever they can to determine the patient's wishes. In Brophy v. New England Sinai Hospital, Inc., 398 Mass. 417, 497 N.E.2d 626 (1986), the Massachusetts Supreme Court based its conclusion that food and hydration could be withheld from a comatose adult on the substituted judgment analysis done by the lower court.

> [After full hearing] the judge found on the basis of ample evidence which no one disputes, that Brophy's judgment would be to decline the provision of food and water and to terminate his life. In reaching that conclusion, the judge considered various factors including the following: (1) Brophy's expressed preferences; (2) his religious convictions and their relation to refusal of treatment; (3) the impact on his family; (4) the probability of adverse side effects; and (5) the prognosis, both with and without treatment. The judge also considered present and future incompetency as an element which Brophy would consider in his decision-making process. The judge relied on several statements made by Brophy prior to the onset of his illness. Although he never had discussed specifically whether a G-tube or feeding tube should be withdrawn in the event that he was diagnosed as being in a persistent vegetative state following his surgery, the judge inferred that, if presently competent, Brophy would choose to forgo artificial nutrition and hydration by means of a G-tube. The judge

found that Brophy would not likely view his own religion as a barrier to that choice.

Other factors that have been considered include the patient's diagnosis, life history, ability to knowingly participate in treatment, potential quality of life, and, more generally, the patient's values and attitude toward health care. See, e.g., *Mack v. Mack*, 329 Md. 188, 618 A.2d 744 (1993) (focusing on the "moral views, life goals, and values" of the patient, and her "attitudes toward sickness, medical procedures, suffering and death"), and *DeGrella v. Elston*, 858 S.W.2d 698 (Ky.1993). For a thorough and well annotated list of twenty-two relevant factors that have been considered by the courts see Alan Meisel, The Right to Die § 7.9 (2d ed. 1995).

From time to time courts have struggled to distinguish the "substituted judgment" and "best interest" principles, and even those who appear to adopt the "best interest" approach may qualify it by requiring that the best interest of the patient be defined in terms of the wishes, values and desires of the patient. Two state courts appear to adopt the best interest test while they actually take the "substituted judgment" approach. See Conservatorship of Drabick, 245 Cal. Rptr. 840 (Cal. App. 1988), discussed in Wendland v. Wendland, 78 Cal.App.4th 517, 93 Cal.Rptr.2d 550 (Cal. App. 2000), review granted, 97 Cal.Rptr.2d 511, 2 P.3d 1065 (2000), and In re Gordy, 658 A.2d 613 (Del.Ch.1994).

The *Conroy* court also addressed the question of whether life-support systems could be removed from patients who have never clearly expressed their desires about such treatment. The court developed three tests, depending upon the existence (vel non) of any trustworthy evidence that the patient would forgo the life-sustaining treatment.

IN RE CONROY

Supreme Court of New Jersey, 1985.
98 N.J. 321, 486 A.2d 1209.

SCHREIBER, JUSTICE.

* * * [W]e hold that life-sustaining treatment may be withheld or withdrawn from an incompetent patient when it is clear that the particular patient would have refused the treatment under the circumstances involved. The standard we are enunciating is a subjective one, consistent with the notion that the right that we are seeking to effectuate is a very personal right to control one's own life. The question is not what a reasonable or average person would have chosen to do under the circumstances but what the particular patient would have done if able to choose for himself.

* * *

We * * * hold that life-sustaining treatment may also be withheld or withdrawn from a patient in Claire Conroy's situation [i.e., a patient who was competent but is now incompetent] if either of two "best interests" tests—a limited-objective or a pure-objective test—is satisfied.

Under the limited-objective test, life-sustaining treatment may be withheld or withdrawn from a patient in Claire Conroy's situation when there is some trustworthy evidence that the patient would have refused the treatment, and the decision-maker is satisfied that it is clear that the burdens of the patient's continued life with the treatment outweigh the benefits of that life for him. By this we mean that the patient is suffering, and will continue to suffer throughout the expected duration of his life, unavoidable pain, and that the net burdens of his prolonged life (the pain and suffering of his life with the treatment less the amount and duration of pain that the patient would likely experience if the treatment were withdrawn) markedly outweigh any physical pleasure, emotional enjoyment, or intellectual satisfaction that the patient may still be able to derive from life. This limited-objective standard permits the termination of treatment for a patient who had not unequivocally expressed his desires before becoming incompetent, when it is clear that the treatment in question would merely prolong the patient's suffering.

* * *

This limited-objective test also requires some trustworthy evidence that the patient would have wanted the treatment terminated. This evidence could take any one or more of the various forms appropriate to prove the patient's intent under the subjective test. Evidence that, taken as a whole, would be too vague, casual, or remote to constitute the clear proof of the patient's subjective intent that is necessary to satisfy the subjective test—for example, informally expressed reactions to other people's medical conditions and treatment—might be sufficient to satisfy this prong of the limited-objective test.

In the absence of trustworthy evidence, or indeed any evidence at all, that the patient would have declined the treatment, life-sustaining treatment may still be withheld or withdrawn from a formerly competent person like Claire Conroy if a third, pure-objective test is satisfied. Under that test, as under the limited-objective test, the net burdens of the patient's life with the treatment should clearly and markedly outweigh the benefits that the patient derives from life. Further, the recurring, unavoidable and severe pain of the patient's life with the treatment should be such that the effect of administering life-sustaining treatment would be inhumane. Subjective evidence that the patient would not have wanted the treatment is not necessary under this pure-objective standard. Nevertheless, even in the context of severe pain, life-sustaining treatment should not be withdrawn from an incompetent patient who had previously expressed a wish to be kept alive in spite of any pain that he might experience.

* * * [W]e expressly decline to authorize decision-making based on assessments of the personal worth or social utility of another's life, or the value of that life to others.

* * *

We are aware that it will frequently be difficult to conclude that the evidence is sufficient to justify termination of treatment under either of the "best interests" tests that we have described. Often, it is unclear whether and to what extent a patient such as Claire Conroy is capable of, or is in fact, experiencing pain. Similarly, medical experts are often unable to determine with any degree of certainty the extent of a nonverbal person's intellectual functioning or the depth of his emotional life. When the evidence is insufficient to satisfy either the limited-objective or pure-objective standard, however, we cannot justify the termination of life-sustaining treatment as clearly furthering the best interests of a patient like Ms. Conroy.

* * * When evidence of a person's wishes or physical or mental condition is equivocal, it is best to err, if at all, in favor of preserving life. * * *

Notes and Comments

1. *The Martin Case, the Conroy Classifications, and the Principle of Autonomy.* The most substantial criticism of the "subjective", "limited-objective" and "pure objective" classifications is provided in In re Martin, 450 Mich. 204, 538 N.W.2d 399 (1995):

> Rather than choose between the best interest standard and the substituted judgment standard, the New Jersey Supreme Court attempted to synthesize these two standards by creating an hierarchical decision-making continuum. [ ]. The starting point on the continuum is anchored by a purely subjective analysis, an approach that requires more definitive evidence of what the patient would choose than the substituted judgment standard. The other end of the continuum is anchored by a purely objective analysis, which is, in essence, a best interest standard.

> We find that a purely subjective analysis is the most appropriate standard to apply under the circumstances of this case. The pure subjective standard allows the surrogate to withhold life-sustaining treatment from an incompetent patient "when it is clear that the particular patient would have refused the treatment under the circumstances involved." [ ]. Given that the right the surrogate is seeking to effectuate is the incompetent patient's right to control his own life, "the question is not what a reasonable or average person would have chosen to do under the circumstances but what the particular patient would have done if able to chose for himself."

> The subjective and objective standards involve conceptually different bases for allowing the surrogate to make treatment decisions. The subjective standard is based on a patient's right to self-determination, while the objective standard is grounded in the state's parens patriae power. [ ]. An objective, best interest, standard cannot be grounded in the common-law right of informed consent because the right and the decision-making standard inherently conflict.

* * *

> Any move from a purely subjective standard to an analysis that encompasses objective criteria is grounded in the state's parens patriae power, not in the common-law right of informed consent or self-determination. Thus, while the clearly expressed wishes of a patient, while competent, should be honored regardless of the patient's condition, we find nothing that prevents the state from grounding any objective analysis on a threshold requirement of pain, terminal illness, foreseeable death, a persistent vegetative state, or affliction of a similar genre.

Martin, 538 N.W.2d at 407–408. Do you agree that only the decision to apply the subjective standard (and not the decision to apply the two objective standards) can be justified by the principles behind the doctrine of informed consent? Is the application of any form of objective test (whether it be termed "substituted judgment" or "best interest") a *per se* violation of the principle of autonomy, as

Martin suggests? If this is true, what is the justification for the application of the theory of substituted judgment? See Rebecca Dresser and John Robertson, Quality of Life and Non–Treatment Decisions for Incompetent Patients, a Critique of the Orthodox Approach, 17 L.Med. & Health Care 234 (1989). See also Rebecca Dresser, Life, Death and Incompetent Patients: Conceptual Infirmities and Hidden Values in the Law, 28 Ariz.L.Rev. 378 (1986).

Is the Michigan Court correct that a pure subjective analysis does not constitute a true "substituted judgment" because when we make such an analysis we are not, in fact, substituting any person's judgment for a patient's judgment; we are, instead, simply implementing the patient's decision, which we (subjectively) know? Can we ever truly know with certainty just what another person wants? Are we certain that even a competent patient truly wants what she is requesting? Do we know for sure whether the patient is accurately communicating what she wants? Is it really possible for a second (or third) party to carry out the subjective analysis, or does any decision by one person on behalf of another inevitably involve at least some element of substituted judgment?

2.   *The Conroy Standard and Patients in Persistent Vegetative State.* Despite its rejection in the *Martin* case, the *Conroy* case has been extremely influential; it is cited by most courts that have dealt with decisionmaking for incompetent patients since 1985 and its three-tiered set of tests—the subjective, limited-objective, and pure-objective tests—are generally well regarded. In 1987 the New Jersey Supreme Court decided a trilogy of cases that called into question whether every case of the discontinuation of life-sustaining treatment in an incompetent patient could be resolved by reference to one of these three Conroy tests. In re Farrell, 108 N.J. 335, 529 A.2d 404 (1987); In re Jobes, 108 N.J. 394, 529 A.2d 434 (1987); In re Peter, 108 N.J. 365, 529 A.2d 419 (1987).

In *Farrell* the court affirmed the right of a competent patient to discontinue life-sustaining treatment and, in dicta, approved the "subjective" test that had been adopted in *Conroy*. In *Jobes* and *Peter,* however, the court side-stepped the *Conroy* test because of the condition of the patients. Each of those cases involved a patient in persistent vegetative state. In an explanation subsequently adopted by the United States Supreme Court in *Cruzan,* 497 U.S. 261 n. 1, 110 S.Ct. 2841 n. 1, 111 L.Ed.2d 224 (1990), the *Jobes* court defined "persistent vegetative state" by quoting the trial testimony of Dr. Fred Plum, who created the term:

> [Persistent]   vegetative state describes a body which is functioning entirely in terms of its internal controls. It maintains temperature. It maintains heartbeat and pulmonary ventilation. It maintains digestive activity. It maintains reflex activity of muscles and nerves for low level conditioned responses. But there is no behavioral evidence of either self-awareness or awareness of the surroundings in a learned manner.

529 A.2d at 438.

The New Jersey Supreme Court held that "the balancing tests set forth in *Conroy* are [not] appropriate in the case of a persistently vegetative patient." As the court pointed out,

> Even in the case of a patient like Claire Conroy—the type of patient for whom the balancing tests were created—it can be difficult or impossible to measure the burdens of embarrassment, frustration, helplessness, rage and other emotional pain, or the benefits of enjoyable feelings like contentment, joy, satisfaction, gratitude, and well being that the patient experiences as a result of life-sustaining treatment. "[M]edical experts are often unable to determine

with any degree of medical certainty the extent of a nonverbal person's intellectual functioning or the depth of his emotional life." [citing *Conroy*]

While a benefits-burdens analysis is difficult with marginally cognitive patients like Claire Conroy, it is essentially impossible with patients in a persistent vegetative state. By definition such patients, like Ms. Peter, do not experience any of the benefits or burdens that the *Conroy* balancing tests are intended or able to appraise. Therefore, we hold that these tests should not be applied to patients in the persistent vegetative state.

In re Peter, 529 A.2d at 424–425.

In *Peter* the court was able to depend upon the subjective prong of the *Conroy* test, and thus it did not have to address the alternative test to be applied when an incompetent patient did not leave clear and convincing evidence of that patient's desires. In *Jobes,* however, the court was required to look for an alternative test. The court determined that the appropriate test in the case of a patient in persistent vegetative state who had not left clear and convincing evidence of the patient's desires was the test that had been applied in *Quinlan* almost a decade before. Although there was some ambiguity in the early *Quinlan* decision, the *Jobes* court made it clear that "the right of a patient in an irreversibly vegetative state to determine whether to refuse life-sustaining medical treatment may be exercised by the patient's family or close friend. If there are close and caring family members who are willing to make this decision there is no need to have a guardian appointed." 529 A.2d at 447. In effect, in *Peter* and *Jobes* the New Jersey Supreme Court said that the limited-objective and pure-objective tests of Conroy make it too difficult to terminate the treatment of patients in persistent vegetative states, even if those standards could reasonably be applied to other incompetent patients.

Does it make any sense to treat a patient in a persistent vegetative state any differently from another incompetent patient? Is there any reason to permit the termination of life-sustaining treatment in a patient in persistent vegetative state when it would not be permitted in an otherwise identically situated patient with a scintilla of higher brain function? Is the New Jersey retreat from *Conroy* in the case of patients in persistent vegetative state a narrowing or a broadening of the *Conroy* rule? What position does the Uniform Health Care Decisions Act take with respect to patients in a persistent vegetative state? Are they treated any differently from patients who are not in that condition?

For a description of every case in which state and federal courts have permitted the discontinuation of life support treatments in patients in persistent vegetative state, see Justice Stevens's dissent in Cruzan, 497 U.S. 261, 349 n. 21, 110 S.Ct. 2841, 2888 n. 21, 111 L.Ed.2d 224. Justice Stevens points out that the *Cruzan* case itself is unique in not permitting the termination of treatment in a patient in persistent vegetative state

3. *Distinguishing Active and Passive Conduct.* Courts have been called upon to determine the legal significance of the difference between active and passive conduct, and ordinary and extraordinary forms of medical intervention. These anachronistic distinctions have not found a safe harbor in the law, just as they have been increasingly recognized as meaningless in ethics. The Conroy opinion specifically and carefully considered each of these distinctions, and summarized the ethical and legal literature and the reasons for rejecting the distinctions. As to the distinction between active and passive conduct, the *Conroy* court announced:

We emphasize that in making decisions whether to administer life-sustaining treatment to patients such as Claire Conroy, the primary focus should be the patient's desires and experience of pain and enjoyment—not the type of treatment involved. Thus, we reject the distinction that some have made between actively hastening death by terminating treatment and passively allowing a person to die of a disease as one of limited use in a legal analysis of such a decision-making situation.

Characterizing conduct as active or passive is often an elusive notion, even outside the context of medical decision-making * * *. The distinction is particularly nebulous, however, in the context of decisions whether to withhold or withdraw life-sustaining treatment. In a case like that of Claire Conroy, for example, would a physician who discontinued nasogastric feeding be actively causing her death by removing her primary source of nutrients; or would he merely be omitting to continue the artificial form of treatment, thus passively allowing her medical condition, which includes her inability to swallow, to take its natural course? [ ] The ambiguity inherent in this distinction is further heightened when one performs an act within an over-all plan of non-intervention, such as when a doctor writes an order not to resuscitate a patient. * * *

For a similar reason, we also reject any distinction between withholding and withdrawing life-sustaining treatment. Some commentators have suggested that discontinuing life-sustaining treatment once it has been commenced is morally more problematic than merely failing to begin the treatment. Discontinuing life-sustaining treatment, to some, is an "active" taking of life, as opposed to the more "passive" act of omitting the treatment in the first instance.

This distinction is more psychologically compelling than logically sound. As mentioned above, the line between active and passive conduct in the context of medical decisions is far too nebulous to constitute a principled basis for decisionmaking. Whether necessary treatment is withheld at the outset or withdrawn later on, the consequence—the patient's death—is the same. Moreover, from a policy standpoint, it might well be unwise to forbid persons from discontinuing a treatment under circumstances in which the treatment could permissibly be withheld. Such a rule could discourage families and doctors from even attempting certain types of care and could thereby force them into hasty and premature decisions to allow a patient to die. [ ]

486 A.2d at 1233–1234.

This policy interest was recognized by Justice Brennan in his *Cruzan* dissent:

Moreover, there may be considerable danger that Missouri's rule of decision would impair rather than serve any interest the state does have in sustaining life. Current medical practice recommends use of heroic measures if there is a scintilla of a chance that the patient will recover, on the assumption that the measures will be discontinued should the patient improve. When the President's Commission in 1982 approved the withdrawal of life support equipment from irreversibly vegetative patients, it explained that "[a]n even more troubling wrong occurs when a treatment that might save life or improve health is not started because the health care personnel are afraid that they will find it very difficult to stop the treatment if, as is fairly likely, it proves to be of little benefit and greatly burdens the patient."

497 U.S. at 314, 110 S.Ct. at 2870.

4. *Distinguishing Ordinary and Extraordinary Treatment.* As to the distinction between ordinary and extraordinary treatment, *Conroy* pointed out:

> We also find unpersuasive the distinction relied upon by some courts, commentators, and theologians between "ordinary" treatment, which they would always require, and "extraordinary" treatment, which they deem optional. * * * The terms "ordinary" and "extraordinary" have assumed too many conflicting meanings to remain useful. To draw a line on this basis for determining whether treatment should be given leads to a semantical milieu that does not advance the analysis.
>
> The distinction between ordinary and extraordinary treatment is frequently phrased as one between common and unusual, or simple and complex, treatment [ ]; "extraordinary" treatment also has been equated with elaborate, artificial, heroic, aggressive, expensive, or highly involved or invasive forms of medical intervention [ ]. Depending on the definitions applied, a particular treatment for a given patient may be considered both ordinary and extraordinary. [ ] Further, since the common/unusual and simple/complex distinctions among medical treatments "exist on continuums with no precise dividing line," [ ] and the continuum is constantly shifting due to progress in medical care, disagreement will often exist about whether a particular treatment is ordinary or extraordinary. In addition, the competent patient generally could refuse even ordinary treatment; therefore, an incompetent patient theoretically should also be able to make such a choice when the surrogate decision-making is effectuating the patient's subjective intent. In such cases, the ordinary/extraordinary distinction is irrelevant except insofar as the particular patient would have made the distinction.
>
> The ordinary/extraordinary distinction has also been discussed in terms of the benefits and burdens of treatment for the patient. If the benefits of the treatment outweigh the burdens it imposes on the patient, it is characterized as ordinary and therefore ethically required; if not, it is characterized as extraordinary and therefore optional. [ ] This formulation is extremely fact-sensitive and would lead to different classifications of the same treatment in different situations.
>
> * * * Moreover, while the analysis may be useful in weighing the implications of the specific treatment for the patient, essentially it merely restates the question: whether the burdens of a treatment so clearly outweigh its benefits to the patient that continued treatment would be inhumane.

468 A.2d at 1234–1235. See also Brophy v. New England Sinai Hospital, Inc., 398 Mass. 417, 497 N.E.2d 626 (1986) ("while we believe that the distinction between extraordinary and ordinary care is a factor to be considered, the use of such a distinction as the sole, or major, factor of decision tends * * * to create a distinction without meaning.")

5. *The Special Status of Nutrition and Hydration.* The issue of withdrawing nutrition and hydration has become an especially contentious one since it found its place on some political agendas. Generally, courts have concluded that the termination of nutrition and hydration is no different from the termination of other forms of mechanical support. For example, *Conroy* suggested:

> Some commentators, * * * have made yet [another] distinction, between the termination of artificial feedings and the termination of other forms of life-sustaining medical treatment. * * * According to the Appellate Division:

If, as here, the patient is not comatose and does not face imminent and inevitable death, nourishment accomplishes the substantial benefit of sustaining life until the illness takes its natural course. Under such circumstances nourishment always will be an essential element of ordinary care which physicians are ethically obligated to provide. [ ]

Certainly, feeding has an emotional significance. As infants we could breathe without assistance, but we were dependent on others for our lifeline of nourishment. Even more, feeding is an expression of nurturing and caring, certainly for infants and children, and in many cases for adults as well.

Once one enters the realm of complex, high-technology medical care, it is hard to shed the "emotional symbolism" of food. * * * Analytically, artificial feeding by means of a nasogastric tube or intravenous infusion can be seen as equivalent to artificial breathing by means of a respirator. Both prolong life through mechanical means when the body is no longer able to perform a vital bodily function on its own.

Furthermore, while nasogastric feeding and other medical procedures to ensure nutrition and hydration are usually well tolerated, they are not free from risks or burdens; they have complications that are sometimes serious and distressing to the patient.

* * *

Finally, dehydration may well not be distressing or painful to a dying patient. For patients who are unable to sense hunger and thirst, withholding of feeding devices such as nasogastric tubes may not result in more pain than the termination of any other medical treatment. * * * Thus, it cannot be assumed that it will always be beneficial for an incompetent patient to receive artificial feeding or harmful for him not to receive it. * * *

Under the analysis articulated above, withdrawal or withholding of artificial feeding, like any other medical treatment, would be permissible if there is sufficient proof to satisfy the subjective, limited-objective, or pure-objective test. A competent patient has the right to decline any medical treatment, including artificial feeding, and should retain that right when and if he becomes incompetent. In addition, in the case of an incompetent patient who has given little or no trustworthy indication of an intent to decline treatment and for whom it becomes necessary to engage in balancing under the limited-objective or pure-objective test, the pain and invasiveness of an artificial feeding device, and the pain of withdrawing that device, should be treated just like the results of administering or withholding any other medical treatment.

98 N.J. 321, 486 A.2d 1209, 1235–1237.

See also, In re Jobes, 108 N.J. 394, 529 A.2d 434 (1987); In re Peter, 108 N.J. 365, 529 A.2d 419 (1987); Gray v. Romeo, 697 F.Supp. 580 (D.R.I.1988) ("Although an emotional symbolism attaches itself to artificial feeding, there is no legal difference between a mechanical device that allows a person to breathe artificially and a mechanical device that allows a person nourishment. If a person has right to decline a respirator, then a person has the equal right to decline a gastrostomy tube."); Brophy v. New England Sinai Hospital, Inc., 398 Mass. 417, 497 N.E.2d 626 (1986); Corbett v. D'Alessandro, 487 So.2d 368 (Fla.App.1986) ("we see no reason to differentiate between the multitude of artificial devices that may be available to prolong the moment of death."); Bouvia v. Superior Court, 179 Cal.App.3d 1127, 225 Cal.Rptr. 297 (1986).

In McConnell v. Beverly Enterprises–Connecticut, Inc., 209 Conn. 692, 553 A.2d 596 (1989), the court authorized the withdrawal of feeding by a gastrostomy tube despite a statute that appeared to say that under such circumstances "nutrition and hydration must be provided." The court reasoned that the nutrition and hydration that was implicated in the statute was that provided by "a spoon or a straw," and that feeding by gastrostomy tube was no different than any other mechanical or electronic medical intervention.

In 1990, at least, a majority of the Supreme Court (the four dissenters and concurring Justice O'Connor in *Cruzan*) viewed nutrition and hydration as another form of medical care. As Justice O'Connor pointed out, "artificial feeding cannot readily be distinguished from other forms of medical treatment. Whether or not the techniques used to pass food and water into the patient's alimentary tract are termed 'medical treatment,' it is clear they all involve some degree of intrusion and restraint." She concluded that "the liberty guaranteed by the due process clause must protect, if it protects anything, an individual's deeply personal decision to reject medical treatment, including the artificial delivery of food and water."

In his dissent, Justice Brennan reached the same conclusion, vividly describing the medical processes involved:

> The artificial delivery of nutrition and hydration is undoubtedly medical treatment. The technique to which Nancy Cruzan is subject—artificial feeding through a gastrostomy tube—involves a tube implanted surgically into her stomach through incisions in her abdominal wall. It may obstruct the intestinal tract, erode and pierce the stomach wall, or cause leakage of the stomach's contents into the abdominal cavity. [ ] The tube can cause pneumonia from reflux of the stomach's contents into the lung. [ ] Typically, and in this case, commercially prepared formulas are used, rather than fresh food. [ ] The type of formula and method of administration must be experimented with to avoid gastrointestinal problems. [ ] The patient must be monitored daily by medical personnel as to weight, fluid intake and fluid output; blood tests must be done weekly.
>
> Artificial delivery of food and water is regarded as medical treatment by the medical profession and the federal government. * * * The federal government permits the cost of the medical devices and formulas used in enteral feeding to be reimbursed under Medicare. [ ] The formulas are regulated by the Federal Drug Administration as "medical foods," [ ] and the feeding tubes are regulated as medical devices [ ].

497 U.S. at 306–308, 110 S.Ct. at 2866–67.

Medical sources generally recognize the irrelevancy of distinguishing between nutrition and hydration and other forms of medical treatment. The Council on Ethical and Judicial Affairs of the American Medical Association has determined that "[l]ife-prolonging medical treatment may include but is not limited to artificial nutrition or hydration." Opinion 2.20 (1996). Today only the Missouri courts appear to be sticking to the conclusion that nutrition and hydration are not medical treatments. In re Warren, 858 S.W.2d 263 (Mo.App.1993).

Note: Choosing Futile Medical Care

The Wanglie Case

In December 1989, Helen Wanglie, an 87–year-old retired school teacher in Minneapolis, tripped on a rug in her home and fractured her hip. One month later, after surgery in one hospital, she was transferred to Hennepin County Medical Center, where her doctors determined she needed assistance in breathing and placed her on a ventilator. Three months later, in May 1990, she was transferred to yet another hospital to see if she could be weaned from her ventilator. While there, she suffered cardiac arrest and was resuscitated, but only after she suffered severe and irreversible brain damage that put her in a persistent vegetative state. She was moved back to Hennepin County Medical Center, where she was maintained on a ventilator and fed through a gastrostomy tube. Mrs. Wanglie remained in a persistent vegetative state for several months before her physicians determined that the continuation of high-tech medical intervention was inappropriate. In essence, the doctors determined that the care Mrs. Wanglie was receiving was no longer among the reasonable medical alternatives for a person in her condition.

Mrs. Wanglie's husband and her two children disagreed. As Mrs. Wanglie's husband pointed out, "Only He who gave life has the right to take life." He also pointed out, "I am a prolifer. I take the position that human life is sacred." He and the children agreed that Mrs. Wanglie would want treatment continued, even if the doctors believed that there were no chance of recovery. This was, as the family pointed out, a determination based on the patient's values, and there was no reason to defer to the doctors' collective ethical judgment.

The physicians and the hospital searched in vain for some healthcare facility in Minnesota that would be willing to take Mrs. Wanglie and continue to provide her care. None came forward. Frustrated by what they considered the continued inappropriate use of medicine, the hospital sought a court order appointing a conservator to replace Mr. Wanglie to make healthcare decisions for Mrs. Wanglie so that her treatment could be discontinued.

The July–August 1991 issue of the Hastings Center Report contains several good articles on the *Wanglie* case, including a summary of the medical facts prepared by her neurologist. This description of the Wanglie case is reprinted from R. Schwartz, Autonomy, Futility and the Limits of Medicine, 2 Camb. Q. Healthcare Ethics 159, 160–61 (1992). The case, *Conservatorship of Wanglie*, No. PX–91–283 (Minn., Hennepin County Dist.Ct., 1993), was never appealed and is unreported.

Futility

How should a physician (or a court) deal with a request for futile medical care? When is requested care truly "futile"? Was the request for treatment of Ms. Wanglie a request for futile care? Treatment is *scientifically futile* when it cannot achieve the medical result that is expected by the patient (or by the family) making the request. Scientifically futile treatment need not be offered or provided to a patient. A seriously ill cancer patient need not be provided with laetrile, a useless drug that has been popularized by those who would prey upon desperate patients and their families, even if that treatment is requested. A child with a viral illness need not be prescribed an antibiotic, even if the child's parents request one, because, as a matter of science, the antibiotic will not be effective in treating that illness. Doctors need not do a CAT scan on a patient with a cold, even if that is what the patient wants, because there is no reason to believe that there will be any connection between what can be discovered on the scan and the appropriate treatment of the cold. As a general matter healthcare providers, who are trained in the science of medicine, are entitled to determine which treatments are scientifically futile.

A harder question arises when a patient requests treatment that is not scientifically futile, but that is, in the opinion of the health care provider, *ethically futile*. Treatment is ethically futile if it will not serve the underlying interests of the patient. For example, some providers believe that it is ethically futile to keep a patient's body aerated and nourished when that patient is in persistent vegetative state. These healthcare providers believe that it is beyond the scope of medicine to sustain mere corporeal existence if there can never be anything beyond that. Some healthcare providers believe that it would be ethically futile to engage in CPR under circumstances in which the most that can be accomplished through that intervention would be to prolong the patient's life by a few hours. Of course, families may disagree with physicians over what constitutes ethically futile treatment, and there is no reason to adopt the provider's perspective, rather than the family's, as the ethically "correct" one. In the *Wanglie* case, for example, the family viewed the continued treatment as effective (in keeping the patient alive) while the healthcare providers viewed the treatment as ineffective (in serving any of the real goals of medicine). The Council on Ethical and Judicial Affairs of the American Medical Association has determined that:

> [p]hysicians are not ethically obliged to deliver care that, in their best professional judgment, will not have a reasonable chance of benefiting their patients. Patients should not be given treatments simply because they demand them. Denials of treatment should be justified by reliance on openly stated ethical principles and acceptable standards of care, * * * not on the concept of "futility," which cannot be meaningfully defined.

Council on Ethical and Judicial Affairs, American Medical Association, Current Opinion 2.035 ("Futility"), Code of Medical Ethics (1998–99 ed.)

Is the Council's position a convincing one, or is it merely a device to transfer the authority to make ethically charged decisions from patients to physicians? Can futility be meaningfully defined? How *should* the providers deal with the arguably ethically futile treatment provided to Wanglie? Should it be continued if the family wishes it to be? Are health care providers required to tell patients and their families about treatment alternatives which they consider to be ethically futile, but which the family might wish anyway?

There is a great deal of good writing on the proper legal approach to arguably futile treatment. For a good account of the fundamental issues at stake, see L. Schneiderman and N. Jecker, Wrong Medicine (1995) and S. Rubin, When Doctors Say No: The Battleground of Medical Futility (1998). See. also Judith Daar, Medical Futility and Implications for Physician Autonomy, 21 Am. J. L. & Med. 221 (1995), Paul Sorum, Limiting Cardiopulmonary Resuscitation, 57 Alb. L. Rev. 617 (1994), Erich Loewy and Richard Carlson, Futility and Its Wider Implications: A Concept in Need of Further Examination, 153 Arch. Internal Md. 429 (1993), Daniel Callahan, Medical Futility, Medical Necessity: The Problem–Without–A–Name, Hastings Center Rep. 30 (July–August 1991).

Problem

Emile Nighthorse is a 77 year old man who has been hospitalized on and off over the past year. He suffers from serious kidney disease, congestive heart failure, severe headaches and increasingly severe dementia. His current hospitalization, which commenced two weeks ago, has resulted in him being supplied with kidney dialysis, which will, it appears, have to continue indefinitely, and a ventilator, which probably will be removed in a few weeks. He does not really understand his condition (or where he is), and he is cranky and abusive with the nurses, whom he believes to be torturing him. A psychiatrist does not believe there is any way to treat his mental condition without extremely heavy sedation. His prognosis is poor; his dementia will surely get worse, and his multi-system failure makes it likely that he will not live more than a few months. It is unlikely he will ever be discharged from the hospital.

Mr. Nighthorse never talked about his condition with anyone, and he has had a strained relationship with his wife of 50 years, who lives with him but rarely comes to the hospital to see him. He has two children who live in another city, and they both claim to have a relatively distant relationship with their father. Until his dementia became too severe, he spent most of his time at the Order of Eagles Aerie playing whist, and his long time whist partner, Ben Bitts, has been with Emile constantly from the moment he entered the hospital. Whenever Mr. Nighthorse is asked a question about his care, he turns to Ben and asks him what "they" should do.

Ben has asked the physician responsible for Emile's care to discontinue the dialysis and the ventilator, and to begin antibiotics. There is no medical reason to use antibiotics, but Ben argues that he is absolutely sure that Emile would want them anyway—he always wanted antibiotics when he was sick, even when his doctors told him that such drugs would be worthless. Ben says that he never really talked with Emile about what should be done under these circumstances, but that they had played whist together so long (almost 20 years) that he figures that he knows what Emile would want. Mrs. Nighthorse has told the doctor to do whatever Ben wants to do; she doesn't care. The two children have not returned to town. When contacted by phone, they both insist that everything should be done to save their father, but neither is willing to come to the hospital.

Mr. Nighthorse's primary physician has asked you—the hospital legal counsel—what he should do. What should you tell him? Would your answer be different if the Uniform Health Care Decisions Act had been adopted in your jurisdiction? If no statute regarding health care decision making had been adopted? What additional facts would help you render a reliable legal opinion?

b. The Role of the Courts and the Burden of Proof in Cases Involving the Decision to Forego Lifesustaining Treatment

There is a near consensus that where a patient has not left a formal prior directive, the goal of medicine should be to do what that patient, if competent, would want done. When, if ever, is it necessary for a court to be involved in making that decision—and when should the decision be left to the family, health care providers, or others? If the court is involved, what procedures should it employ? The procedural issues which have caused the greatest difficulty for state courts are the nature of evidence that would be relevant in determining a patient's wishes and the burden of proof to be applied to decisions to authorize the removal of life-sustaining treatment. As you read the next two cases, which formally address these issues, ask what kind of evidence would be (1) relevant and (2) sufficient for each of the judges.

IN RE WESTCHESTER COUNTY MEDICAL CENTER (O'CONNOR)

Court of Appeals of New York, 1988.
72 N.Y.2d 517, 534 N.Y.S.2d 886, 531 N.E.2d 607.

WACHTLER, CHIEF JUDGE.

Mary O'Connor is an elderly hospital patient who, as a result of several strokes, is mentally incompetent and unable to obtain food or drink without medical assistance. In this dispute between her daughters and the hospital the question is whether the hospital should be permitted to insert a nasogastric tube to provide her with sustenance or whether, instead, such medical intervention should be precluded and she should be allowed to die because, prior to becoming incompetent, she made several statements to the effect that she did not want to be a burden to anyone and would not want to live or be kept alive by artificial means if she were unable to care for herself.

The hospital has applied for court authorization to insert the nasogastric tube. The patient's daughters object claiming that it is contrary to her "expressed wishes", although they conceded at the hearing that they do not know whether their mother would want to decline this procedure under these circumstances, particularly if it would produce a painful death. The trial court denied the hospital's application, concluding that it was contrary to the patient's wishes. The Appellate Division affirmed. * * *

We have concluded that the order of the Appellate Division should be reversed and the hospital's petition granted. On this record there is not clear and convincing proof that the patient had made a firm and settled commitment, while competent, to decline this type of medical assistance under circumstances such as these.

I.

* * *

The treating physician, Dr. Sivak, testified that Mrs. O'Connor was suffering from multiinfarct dementia as a result of [several] strokes. This condition substantially impaired her cognitive ability but she was not in a coma or vegetative state. She was conscious, and capable of responding to simple questions or requests sometimes by squeezing the questioner's hand and sometimes verbally. She was also able to respond to noxious stimuli, such as a needle prick, and in fact was sensitive to "even minimal discomfort," although she was not experiencing pain in her present condition. When asked how she felt she usually responded "fine," "all right" or "ok." The treating physician also testified that her mental awareness had improved at the hospital and that she might become more alert in the future. * * *

The doctor stated that Mrs. O'Connor was presently receiving nourishment exclusively through intravenous feeding. * * * He testified that intravenous feeding is used as a temporary measure which generally must be discontinued within several weeks. He noted that these difficulties could be overcome with a gastric tube connected to the patient's digestive tract through her nose or abdomen. * * * If the procedure were not employed and the intravenous methods could no longer be used or were otherwise discontinued, she would die of thirst and starvation within 7 to 10 days. The doctor stated that death from starvation and especially thirst, was a painful way to die and that Mrs. O'Connor would, therefore, experience extreme, intense discomfort since she is conscious, alert, capable of feeling pain, and sensitive to even mild discomfort.

The respondents' expert * * * agreed essentially with Dr. Sivak's evaluation and prognosis. In his opinion, however, Mrs. O'Connor would not experience pain if permitted to die of thirst and starvation. * * *

* * *

Neither of the doctors had known Mrs. O'Connor before she became incompetent and thus knew nothing of her attitudes toward the use of life-sustaining measures. The respondents' first witness on this point was * * * a former co-worker and longtime friend of Mrs. O'Connor. * * * He testified that his first discussion with Mrs. O'Connor concerning artificial means of prolonging life occurred about 1969. At that time his father, who was dying of cancer, informed him that he would not want to continue life by any artificial method if he had lost his dignity because he could no longer control his normal bodily functions. The witness said that when he told Mrs. O'Connor of this she agreed wholeheartedly and said: "I would never want to be a burden on anyone and I would never want to lose my dignity before I passed away." He noted that she was a "very religious woman" who "felt that nature should take its course and not use further artificial means." They had similar conversations on two or three occasions between 1969 and 1973. During these discussions Mrs. O'Connor variously stated that it is "monstrous" to keep someone alive by using "machinery, things like that" when they are "not going to get better"; that she would never want to be in the same situation as her husband * * * and that people who are "suffering very badly" should be allowed to die.

Mrs. O'Connor's daughter Helen testified that her mother informed her on several occasions that if she became ill and was unable to care for herself she would not want her life to be sustained artificially. * * * Mrs. O'Connor's other daughter, Joan, essentially adopted her sister's testimony. She described her mother's statements on this subject as less solemn pronouncements: "it was brought up when we were together, at times when in conversations you start something, you know, maybe the news was on and maybe that was the topic that was brought up and that's how it came about."

However, all three of these witnesses also agreed that Mrs. O'Connor had never discussed providing food or water with medical assistance, nor had she ever said that she would adhere to her view and decline medical treatment "by artificial means" if that would produce a painful death. When Helen was asked what choice her mother would make under those circumstances she admitted that she did not know. Her sister Joan agreed, noting that this had never been discussed, "unfortunately, no."

* * *

II.

It has long been the common-law rule in this State that a person has the right to decline medical treatment, even life-saving treatment, absent an overriding State interest [ ]. In 1981, we held, in two companion cases, that a hospital or medical facility must respect this right even when a patient becomes incompetent, if while competent, the patient stated that he or she did not want certain procedures to be employed under specified circumstances. [*Eichner*]

* * * *Eichner* had been competent and capable of expressing his will before he was silenced by illness. In those circumstances, we concluded that it would be appropriate for the court to intervene and direct the termination of artificial life supports, in accordance with the patient's wishes, because it was established by "clear and convincing evidence" that the patient would have so

directed if he were competent and able to communicate. We selected the "clear and convincing evidence" standard in *Eichner* because it " 'impress[es] the factfinder with the importance of the decision' * * * and it 'forbids relief whenever the evidence is loose, equivocal or contradictory' "[ ] Nothing less than unequivocal proof will suffice when the decision to terminate life supports is at issue.

* * *

* * * The number and variety of situations in which the problem of terminating artificial life supports arises preclude any attempt to anticipate all of the possible permutations. However, this case, as well as our prior decisions, suggest some basic principles which may be used in determining whether the proof "clearly and convincingly" evinces an intention by the patient to reject life prolonged artificially by medical means.

III.

* * *

Every person has a right to life, and no one should be denied essential medical care unless the evidence clearly and convincingly shows that the patient intended to decline the treatment under some particular circumstances. This is a demanding standard, the most rigorous burden of proof in civil cases. It is appropriate here because if an error occurs it should be made on the side of life.

Viewed in that light, the "clear and convincing" evidence standard requires proof sufficient to persuade the trier of fact that the patient held a firm and settled commitment to the termination of life supports under the circumstances like those presented. As a threshold matter, the trier of fact must be convinced, as far as is humanly possible, that the strength of the individual's beliefs and the durability of the individual's commitment to those beliefs [ ] makes a recent change of heart unlikely. The persistence of the individual's statements, the seriousness with which those statements were made and the inferences, if any, that may be drawn from the surrounding circumstances are among the factors which should be considered.

The ideal situation is one in which the patient's wishes were expressed in some form of a writing, perhaps a "living will," while he or she was still competent. The existence of a writing suggests the author's seriousness of purpose and ensures that the court is not being asked to make a life-or-death decision based upon casual remarks. Further, a person who has troubled to set forth his or her wishes in a writing is more likely than one who has not to make sure that any subsequent changes of heart are adequately expressed, either in a new writing or through clear statements to relatives and friends. In contrast, a person whose expressions of intention were limited to oral statements may not as fully appreciate the need to "rescind" those statements after a change of heart.

Of course, a requirement of a written expression in every case would be unrealistic. Further, it would unfairly penalize those who lack the skills to place their feelings in writing. For that reason, we must always remain open to applications such as this, which are based upon the repeated oral expressions of the patient. In this case, however, the application must ultimately fail, because it does not meet the foregoing criteria.

Although Mrs. O'Connor's statements about her desire to decline life-saving treatments were repeated over a number of years, there is nothing, other than speculation, to persuade the fact finder that her expressions were more than immediate reactions to the unsettling experience of seeing or hearing of another's unnecessarily prolonged death. * * * If such statements were routinely held to be clear and convincing proof of a general intent to decline all medical treatment once incompetency sets in, few nursing home patients would ever receive life-sustaining medical treatment in the future. * * *

* * *

In sum, on this record it cannot be said that Mrs. O'Connor elected to die under circumstances such as these. Even her daughters, who undoubtedly know her wishes better than anyone, are earnestly trying to carry them out, and whose motives we believe to be of the highest and most loving kind, candidly admit that they do not know what she would do, or what she would want done under these circumstances.

* * *

HANCOCK, JUDGE (concurring).

* * *

[T]here are, I believe, several reasons why the present New York rule—requiring a factual finding of the patient's actual intent and precluding the exercise of judgment, in her best interests and on her behalf, by her physician and family, a court or guardian—is unrealistic, often unfair or inhumane and, if applied literally, totally unworkable.

The rule posits, as the only basis for judicial relief, the court's finding by clear and convincing proof of a fact which is inherently unknowable: what the incompetent patient would actually have intended at the time of the impending life-support decision. What is required here is not a finding of intent as the term is used in its fictional sense as, for example, to express the legal conclusion of what the Legislature intended when it enacted a statute or what parties intended when they signed a contract. What the rule literally demands is an impossibility: a factual determination of the incompetent patient's actual desire at the time of the decision [ ].

* * *

SIMONS, JUDGE (dissenting).

Respondents have established that Mary O'Connor did not wish any "artificial or mechanical support systems" used to sustain her life; if she were unable to function on her own, she wanted "nature to take its course." That being so, and inasmuch as no countervailing State interest has been asserted, she is entitled to have the court respect and implement her choice. The majority refuses to do so because it holds her statements were too indefinite. Its holding substantially rewrites the law of self-determination, at least for cases such as this, and has for all practical purposes foreclosed any realistic possibility that a patient, once rendered incompetent, will have his or her wishes to forego life-sustaining treatment enforced. * * *

I

Courts have resolved the question of when medical treatment of the gravely ill may be terminated by using two legal theories. The first is based on the common-law right of self-determination, which gives an individual essentially unrestricted authority to limit others' contact with his or her body. [ ] This fundamental right, similar to other privacy rights recognized at common law and by the Constitution, guarantees individuals the freedom to behave as they deem fit so long as their wishes do not conflict with the precepts of society. It encompasses a patient's freedom to refuse medical treatment even when such refusal is life threatening [ ], and it particularly includes the right of a dying patient to refuse medical care or treatment that cannot restore health. [ ] Before a patient's right of self-determination can be enforced, however, his or her wishes must be ascertained. If the patient is incompetent and cannot presently express those wishes, they will be enforced if established by clear and convincing evidence. The right to reject treatment is not absolute but, absent some overriding State interest, the courts are bound to recognize and enforce it. The test for granting relief is entirely subjective: what does the patient desire done. The court's role is limited to ensuring that effectuating the patient's wishes does not violate the State's interest; it may not intrude into this area of personal autonomy and impose its paternalistic view of the patient's best interests.[ ]

The second theory is the substituted judgment approach. Although courts apply this theory differently, generally the obligation of the court when implementing substituted judgment is to ensure that a surrogate of the patient, usually a family member or a guardian, effectuates as nearly as possible the decision the incompetent would make if he or she were able to state it [ ]. The subjective views of the patient remain important, but the absence of a clearly expressed intent is not determinative; objective factors are also considered in deciding what is best for the patient in the circumstances presented. Thus, the surrogate's decision should take into account the patient's personal values and religious beliefs, prior statements on the subject, attitudes about the impact his or her condition will have on others, and any other factors bearing on the issue. Inasmuch as the patient's wishes cannot be known with certainty, objective factors indicating that the burdens of continued life outweigh the benefits of that life for the patient are significant.

* * *

* * * Mary O'Connor clearly expressed her wishes in the only realistic way she could and, inasmuch as none of the litigants claims the State has any interest in prolonging her life, her wishes should be recognized and the order of the Appellate Division should be affirmed. The order will not be affirmed, however, because the majority, by its decision today, narrowly restricts the only available avenue of relief. Mary O'Connor's wishes will not be recognized because her daughters cannot prove she anticipated her present condition and specifically stated that under such circumstances she chose to die rather than be nourished by artificial means. The court has confined the *Eichner* holding to the singular facts of that case and inasmuch as few persons will be able to

satisfy the new test, the right of self-determination is reduced to a hollow promise.

* * *

IV

The majority refuses to recognize Mrs. O'Connor's expressed wishes because they were not solemn pronouncements made after reflection and because they were too indefinite.

Respondents have established the reliability of the statements under any standard. * * * These were not "casual remarks," but rather expressions evidencing the long-held beliefs of a mature woman who had been exposed to sickness and death in her employment and her personal life. Mrs. O'Connor had spent 20 years working in the emergency room and pathology laboratory of Jacobi Hospital, confronting the problems of life and death daily. She suffered through long illnesses of her husband, stepmother, father and two brothers who had died before her. She herself has been hospitalized for congestive heart failure and she understood the consequences of serious illnesses.

Because of these experiences, Mrs. O'Connor expressed her wishes in conversations with her daughters, both trained nurses, and a coemployee from the hospital who shared her hospital experience. There can be no doubt she was aware of the gravity of the problem she was addressing and the significance of her statements, or that those hearing her understood her intentions. She clearly stated the values important to her, a life that does not burden others and its termination with dignity, and what she believed her best interests required in the case of severe, debilitating illness. * * *

Notwithstanding this, the majority finds the statements entitled to little weight because Mrs. O'Connor's exposure was mostly to terminally ill cancer patients, or because her desire to remain independent and avoid burdening her children constituted little more than statements of self-pity by an elderly woman. There is no evidence to support those inferences and no justification for trivializing Mrs. O'Connor's statements. She is entitled to have them accepted without reservation. * * *

* * *

V
* * *

The [majority's] rule is unworkable because it requires humans to exercise foresight they do not possess. It requires that before life-sustaining treatment may be withdrawn, there must be proof that the patient anticipated his or her present condition, the means available to sustain life under the circumstances, and then decided that the alternative of death without mechanical assistance, by starvation in this case, is preferable to continued life [ ].

* * *

Even if a patient possessed the remarkable foresight to anticipate some future illness or condition, however, it is unrealistic to expect or require a lay person to be familiar with the support systems available for treatment—to say nothing of requiring a determination of which is preferable or the consequences that may result from using or foregoing them. Indeed, the conditions and consequences may change from day to day. * * *

In short, Mary O'Connor expressed her wishes in the only terms familiar to her, and she expressed them as clearly as a lay person should be asked to express them. To require more is unrealistic, and for all practical purposes, it precludes the right of patients to forego life-sustaining treatment.

* * *

WENDLAND v. WENDLAND

Court of Appeal of California, Third District, 2000.
78 Cal.App.4th 517, 93 Cal.Rptr.2d 550, review granted by the California
Supreme Court, 97 Cal.Rptr.2d 511, 2 P.3d 1065 (2000).

Sims, J.: This is the hardest case.

A 1993 motor vehicle accident left 42–year-old Robert Wendland severely brain damaged and cognitively impaired. He is conscious and sometimes able to respond to simple commands, but he is totally dependent on others for his care and is unable to speak or otherwise communicate consistently. He receives life-sustaining nutrition and hydration through a feeding tube.

The probate court appointed Robert's wife, Rose, as conservator of his person under the Probate Code and determined Robert lacks capacity to make his own health care decisions. However, the court expressly withheld from Rose the authority to remove Robert's feeding tube.

After presentation of Rose's and Robert's cases in chief, the probate court granted [Robert's mother's] motion for judgment, concluding that although Robert had a right to refuse the feeding tube, a right which survives his incompetence, Rose had failed to show by clear and convincing evidence that Robert, if competent, would want the feeding tube removed, or that withdrawal of the tube was in his best interests.

Rose and Robert appeal, arguing the probate court failed to apply or erroneously construed the controlling statute and imposed too high a burden on Rose. We shall conclude the probate court erred in requiring Rose to prove that Robert, while competent, expressed a desire to die in these circumstances and in substituting its own judgment concerning Robert's best interests, rather than limiting itself to a determination of whether the conservator considered Robert's best interests and met the other statutory requirements of the statute. We shall therefore reverse the judgment and remand for further proceedings in the probate court.

FACTUAL AND PROCEDURAL BACKGROUND

Rose and Robert were married in 1978 and have three children. _On September 29, 1993, Robert, then age 42, was involved in a single-vehicle accident. He was in a coma for 16 months, during which Rose visited him in the hospital every day.

In January 1995, Robert came out of the coma, but he remains severely cognitively impaired. He is paralyzed on the right side and is unable to communicate consistently, feed himself, or control his bowels or bladder. He wears diapers. He receives food and fluids through a feeding tube. By late spring of 1995, he was interacting with his environment, but minimally and inconsistently. At his highest level of functioning, he has been able to do (with repeated prompting and cuing [pointing] by therapists) such activities as grasp and release a ball, operate an electric wheelchair with a "joystick," move himself in a manual wheelchair with his left hand or foot, balance himself momentarily in a "standing frame" while grabbing and pulling "thera-putty," draw the letter "R," and choose and replace requested color blocks out of several color choices. Each activity is performed only after excruciatingly repetitive prompting and cuing by the therapists. Robert never smiles. What little emotion he does show is negative and combative. Since he has cognitive function, he is *not* considered to be in a "persistent vegetative state" (hereafter PVS).

Between January and July 1995, Robert's feeding tube (which at the time was a "jejunostomy" tube surgically inserted through the abdomen wall and stapled or sewn to the inside of the small intestine) became dislodged several times. The first three times, Rose agreed to surgical reinsertion of the tube (a procedure requiring general anesthesia). The fourth time—in July 1995—Rose refused to consent to reinsertion of the tube, stating she believed Robert would not want to go through it again. The attending physician, Dr. Ronald Kass, nevertheless inserted a nasogastric feeding tube * * * in order to maintain the status quo pending review by the hospital ethics committee.

The 20–member ethics committee determined it had no objection to Rose ordering withdrawal of the nutrition/hydration tubes. Dr. Kass agreed. The San Joaquin County patient ombudsman (whose job it is to look after the rights of patients in long-term care facilities) supported Rose's decision, though she (the ombudsman) had not spoken to respondents.

* * *

Robert could survive many years in his current condition, but he is susceptible to dental problems and respiratory or bladder infections, some of which he has already experienced.

Rose testified she believes Robert would have refused life-sustaining treatment in his current circumstances if he were competent, based on the following:

Three months before Robert's accident, Rose's father died after his life support machine was turned off at the family's request. Robert assured Rose she made the right choice. Rose testified, "And he [Robert] told me at that point I would never want to live like that, and I wouldn't want my children to see me like that and look at the hurt you're going through as an adult seeing your father like that." [Rose also described a few other similar conversations].

* * *

DISCUSSION

* * *

Does The Statute Authorize A Conservator To Withhold Life Sustaining
Nutrition/Hydration From A Non–PVS Conservatee?

* * *

We conclude the appropriate substantive standard in this case is that set forth in *Drabick [200 Cal. App. 3d 185 (1988)]*: The court's role is limited to determining whether the conservator's decision complies with the statute, i.e., that the conservator has acted in "good faith" and decided "based upon medical advice," that treatment is "necessary," after consideration of the conservatee's prior wishes and best interests. Thus, the conservator is not required to prove that the conservatee, while competent, expressed a desire to die in these circumstances. Moreover, it is not for the court to decide independently whether the conservator's decision is in the conservatee's best interests; the court is merely to satisfy itself that the conservator has considered the conservatee's best interests in good faith and has met the other requirements of the statute.

* * *

Constitutional Considerations
* * *

The crux of the dispute in this case revolves around the parties' different perspectives concerning what rights are at issue. Appellants appear to see this case as a matter of balancing the conservatee's right to refuse treatment against the state's abstract interest in preserving life, with the result that the individual's right outweighs the state's abstract interest. * * *[Robert's mother], on the other hand, appears to see this case as a matter of the state (through the court) protecting the conservatee's right to life. Thus, appellants' arguments assume Robert, if competent, would want to die; respondents' arguments assume he would want to live.

* * *

Generally, the state's interest in preserving life does not outweigh the individual's right to choose. * * * As a general proposition, "the notion that the individual exists for the good of the state is, of course, quite antithetical to our fundamental thesis that the role of the state is to ensure a maximum of individual freedom of choice and conduct."

* * *

Thus, the constitutional right to life—under either the California Constitution or the Fourteenth Amendment to the United States Constitution—is not infringed by allowing a surrogate to exercise a person's right to refuse medical treatment. * * *

Standard of Proof
* * *

The statute does not expressly specify any particular standard of proof for a conservator's decision to withhold life-sustaining treatment from a conservatee. Since the statute does not specify a standard, the "preponderance of evidence" standard applies by default, unless the courts find some constitutional compulsion for a higher standard.

* * *

We believe due process dictates that clear and convincing is the appropriate standard for review of a conservator's decision to withhold life-sustaining treatment because, even though the statute gives the conservator exclusive authority, the conservator's exercise of decisionmaking power for the conservatee concerning life-sustaining treatment creates a tension between the conservatee's fundamental right to life and the conservatee's right to refuse medical treatment, and the consequences of error are grave and irrevocable.
* * *

Confusion has resulted in the case law, due to a failure to distinguish between (1) the substantive standard of proof (what facts must be proven), and (2) what evidentiary burden of proof governs (clear and convincing evidence or preponderance of the evidence). As one commentator observed: "Discussions of the appropriate standard of proof have been thrown into a state of considerable confusion by the habit of courts and commentators of failing to distinguish between the standard of proof and the substantive standard for forgoing life-sustaining treatment. Discussions of these two standards are generally intermingled so that it is not always easy to discern the difference between them."

* * *

We do not base our conclusion concerning the standard of proof on Cruzan which held a state did not violate due process by requiring clear and convincing evidence of an incompetent's wishes to withdraw treatment, because Cruzan did not hold due process *required* this or any other particular standard.

* * *

We conclude the proper standard to be applied in this case is clear and convincing evidence. We emphasize our decision to apply the clear and convincing evidence standard of proof applies *only* where it is expected that withdrawal of medical treatment will certainly lead to death. We do not decide or suggest what standard should apply to other, less final decisions.

Burden of Producing Evidence/Abuse Of Discretion

The probate court imposed on Rose the burden of producing evidence to support her decision to withhold Robert's feeding tube. Appellants argue the court erred because, since the statute gives the conservator "exclusive authority," the conservator's decision is presumptively valid, and the burden must be on the person challenging the conservator's decision, to show an abuse of discretion by the conservator. Respondents, in turn, believe the burden should be on the person seeking to terminate life-sustaining treatment, which will lead to the loss of life for the conservatee. We agree with respondents.

* * *

[W]e consider it appropriate to place the burden on the conservator, at least under the circumstances of this case, where the conservator proposes to terminate life-sustaining treatment of a conservatee who appears incapable of expressing an objection. * * *

Moreover, as a practical matter, facts material to judicial resolution of the case, e.g., whether the conservator is acting in good faith and based upon medical advice, are peculiarly within the knowledge of the conservator, and it is not unfair to impose the initial burden on the conservator to produce evidence on these matters. * * *

Appellants complain the probate court improperly imposed a presumption in favor of continued existence, at the expense of the liberty interest to decide—or have a surrogate decide—to end such existence. [Robert's mother] suggests the presumption should be in favor of continued life for the conservatee to prevent abuse and because where a conservator is exercising the decisionmaking power, the state's interests—in protecting the incompetent person from potential conflicts of interest, protecting due process rights, and fulfilling its parens patriae duty to safeguard incompetent persons—and the patient's interests are no longer in opposition. However, we are mindful that excessive judicial control of a surrogate's decisionmaking power may interfere with the exercise of the individual's right to refuse treatment, condemning the patient to prolonged suffering.

We thus conclude there should be no presumption in favor of continued existence. "The state has an interest in protecting [the incompetent's] right to have appropriate medical treatment decisions made on his behalf. The problem is not to preserve life under all circumstances but to make the right decisions. A conclusive presumption in favor of continuing treatment impermissibly burdens a person's right to make the other choice. However, there should also be no presumption in favor of death, because the conservatee has a right to life."

We conclude the probate court properly placed the burden of producing evidence on Rose.

* * *

CONCLUSIONS

The trial court properly placed the burden of producing evidence on Rose and properly applied a clear and convincing evidence standard. However, the court erred in requiring Rose to prove that Robert, while competent, expressed a desire to die in the circumstances and in substituting its own judgment concerning Robert's best interests rather than merely determining whether Rose had taken Robert's best interests into consideration and had satisfied the other substantive standards we describe *ante*. * * *

Notes and Questions

1. The "clear and convincing evidence" standard applied in O'Connor is considerably different from the "clear and convincing evidence" standard applied in Wendland. The O'Connor court applies this evidentiary standard as a substantive rule of decision, announcing that, as a matter of substantive law, terminating life sustaining treatment on Ms. O'Connor would be permitted only if she had made her wishes known by clear and convincing evidence. The "clear and

convincing evidence" standard is applied to her statements in the past, not to any evidence now brought before the court. The Wendland case applies "clear and convincing" as a true evidentiary standard; it asks whether the evidence presented in court showed that the conservator met her statutory duties.

2.   The propriety of the "clear and convincing evidence" standard applied by the Missouri Supreme Court in the *Cruzan* case was the primary issue before the United States Supreme Court in that case. The Court concluded that "a state may apply a clear and convincing evidence standard in proceedings where a guardian seeks to discontinue nutrition and hydration of a person diagnosed to be in a persistent vegetative state." This holding, which, the Chief Justice assures us, describes only the outer limit of what the Constitution permits, is supported by a lengthy description of civil cases in which the "clear and convincing evidence" standard is applied. See *Cruzan*, supra at 1309. In his dissent, which cites Judge Simons's dissenting opinion in *O'Connor*, Justice Brennan discusses the New York law developed in the *O'Connor* case:

> New York is the only state besides Missouri to deny a request to terminate life support on the ground that clear and convincing evidence of prior, expressed intent was absent, although New York did so in the context of very different situations. Mrs. O'Connor, the subject of *In re O'Connor*, had several times expressed her desire not to be placed on life support if she were not going to be able to care for herself. However, both of her daughters testified that they did not know whether their mother would want to decline artificial nutrition and hydration under her present circumstances. Moreover, despite damage from several strokes, Mrs. O'Connor was conscious and capable of responding to simple questions and requests and the medical testimony suggested she might improve to some extent. [ ]

497 U.S. 261, 323, n. 22, 110 S.Ct. 2841, 2875, n. 22, 111 L.Ed.2d 224.

In fact, most states have adopted a "clear and convincing evidence" standard in "right to die" cases, although what that evidentiary standard means, and whether it is a substantive standard or a true evidentiary standard, varies from state to state—and, as the *O'Connor* case suggests, from judge to judge within a state. See, e.g., McConnell v. Beverly Enterprises–Connecticut, Inc., 209 Conn. 692, 553 A.2d 596 (1989); In re Conroy, 98 N.J. 321, 486 A.2d 1209 (1985); In re Jobes, 108 N.J. 394, 529 A.2d 434 (1987) (In New Jersey "evidence is 'clear and convincing' when it produce[s] in the mind of the trier of fact a firm belief or conviction as to the truth of the allegations sought to be established, evidence so clear, direct and weighty and convincing as to enable [the fact finder] to come to a clear conviction, without hesitancy, of the truth of the precise facts at issue.") While disputed evidence may still be "clear and convincing," it is also true that uncontroverted evidence may not rise to that level. In re Jobes, 529 A.2d at 441, citing In re Welfare of Colyer, 99 Wash.2d 114, 143–45, 660 P.2d 738, 754–55 (1983) (Dore, J. dissenting).

The choice of the appropriate burden of proof is not always between "clear and convincing evidence" and the normal civil "preponderance" standard. In *Eichner,* in which this issue was first raised before the New York Court of Appeals, the district attorney seeking the continuation of treatment for Brother Fox argued that "proof beyond a reasonable doubt" was the appropriate burden. The Court of Appeals explained why it chose the clear and convincing evidence standard:

> The Supreme Court and the Appellate Division found that the evidence on [Brother Fox's decision] as well as proof of the patient's subsequent

incompetency and chances of recovery was "clear and convincing." We agree that this is the appropriate burden of proof and that the evidence in the record satisfies this standard.

Although this is a civil case in which a preponderance of the evidence is generally deemed sufficient, the District Attorney urges that the highest burden of proof beyond a reasonable doubt should be required when granting the relief may result in the patient's death. But that burden, traditionally reserved for criminal cases where involuntary loss of liberty and possible stigmatization are at issue [ ] is inappropriate in cases where the purpose of granting the relief is to give effect to an individual's right by carrying out his stated intentions. However, we agree with the courts below that the highest standard applicable to civil cases should be required. There is more involved here than a typical dispute between private litigants over a sum of money. Where particularly important personal interests are at stake, clear and convincing evidence should be required. It is constitutionally required in cases of involuntary civil commitments and we have recognized the need for the higher standard in exceptional civil matters. Clear and convincing proof should also be required in cases where it is claimed that a person, now incompetent, left instructions to terminate life sustaining procedures when there is no hope of recovery. This standard serves to "impress the factfinder with the importance of the decision" and it " 'forbids relief whenever the evidence is loose, equivocal or contradictory' "[ ].

In re Eichner, 420 N.E.2d at 72.

3. Of course, the "clear and convincing evidence" standard is not a symmetrical one; it applies to one seeking to *terminate* life sustaining treatment, but not to one seeking to *maintain* it. Really, the application of the "clear and convincing evidence" standard to these cases serves only to recognize a policy that it is better to err on the side of maintaining life than on the side of terminating it. Many courts have repeated this principle of direction-of-error almost as a mantra, but does it make sense to establish the maintenance of life sustaining treatment as the default position in all cases? As the *Martin* court points out,

> To err either way has incalculable ramifications. To end the life of a patient who still derives meaning and enjoyment from life or to condemn persons to lives from which they cry out for release is nothing short of barbaric.

Martin at 401. Despite this, the Court goes on to say that "[i]f we are to err, however, we must err in preserving life." Id. But should the default position—the presumed desire of the patient—be the *continuation* of treatment for every subgroup of cases? Should it be the default position where the patient is in excruciating and intractable pain, or where the patient is in persistent vegetative state? How many people do you know who wish to be kept alive under those circumstances? Why should the default position be one shared by so few?

The Wendland court rejected the default position of maintaining life in this class of case, but it also would apply a "clear and convincing evidence" standard to any decision to terminate (but not any decision to continue) life sustaining medical treatment. Is this position consistent? Once the court views the issue asymmetrically (and requires less evidence to continue treatment than to discontinue it), is it making the continuation of that treatment its default position?

4. The question of what burden of proof is appropriate is different from the issue of what kinds of evidence ought to be admissible to meet the burden. While

most courts agree on the appropriate burden of proof in these cases, there is little agreement about the admissibility or weight to be given to different kinds of potential evidence.

Of course, what evidence is relevant will depend upon what facts are material to the resolution of the case under state substantive law. Assume that the wishes of the patient are material to the outcome of the case. How should the court consider previous statements of a currently incompetent patient? Should it make any difference that the statements were in writing? Made to relatives? In response to news events (like the *Cruzan* case)? In response to a family emergency or a death in the family? Would your prior statements about this issue be considered serious or off-hand by a court if tomorrow you were in a persistent vegetative state? Obviously, the characterization a court puts upon the nature of the evidence will determine the weight it is to be accorded. That, in turn, is likely to determine whether a petitioner can meet the generally accepted "clear and convincing evidence" standard.

The *Martin* majority provides one assessment of what kinds of evidence can meet the clear and convincing standard:

> Among the factors identified as important in defining clear and convincing evidence, [ ] the predominant factor is "a prior directive in which the patient addresses the situations in which the patient would prefer that medical intervention cease." Optimally, the prior directive would be expressed in a living will, patient advocate designation, or durable power of attorney. While a written directive would provide the most accurate evidence of the patient's decisions, and we strongly urge all persons to create such a directive, we do not preclude consideration of oral statements, made under the proper circumstances.

> The amount of weight accorded prior oral statements depends on the remoteness, consistency, specificity, and solemnity of the prior statement. The decisionmaker should examine the statement to determine whether it was a well thought out, deliberate pronouncement or a casual remark made in reaction to the plight of another. Statements made in response to seeing or hearing about another's prolonged death do not fulfill the clear and convincing standard.

> If such statements were routinely held to be clear and convincing proof of a general intent to decline all medical treatment once incompetency sets in, few nursing home patients would ever receive life-sustaining medical treatment in the future. The aged and infirm would be placed at grave risk if the law uniformly but unrealistically treated the expression of such sentiments as a calm and deliberative resolve to decline all life-sustaining medical assistance once the speaker is silenced by mental disability.

> While the degree of similarity between the physical conditions contemplated in the patient's prior statement and the patient's current physical situation also partakes of the fiction of substituted judgment, we do not exclude it as a factor to be considered in assessing the probative value of the prior statement. Only when the patient's prior statements clearly illustrate a serious, well thought out, consistent decision to refuse treatment under these exact circumstances, or circumstances highly similar to the current situation, should treatment be refused or withdrawn.

Martin, *supra* at 410–411.

Do you agree that "[s]tatements made in response to seeing or hearing about another's prolonged death do not fulfill the clear and convincing standard?" The dissenting judge in Martin argued that "[t]his bright line rule ignores that many persons only consider their own mortality seriously upon hearing about the end of other people's lives. Admittedly the emotional content of such statements must be carefully considered in weighing their probative value. But the majority's categorical exclusion of [this] relevant evidence dispenses with any semblance of accurate factfinding." Martin, at 399 (Levin, J., dissenting).

5. Because it is almost impossible to predict exactly what kinds of medical care one might need and what kind of medical condition one will suffer, some courts and scholars have suggested that the most helpful kind of advance directive would be one that deals generally with the medical interests and values of the patient. One form of such an advance directive would have patients anticipate the nature and extent of intervention they would want in a host of clearly described alternative medical scenarios. See Linda L. Emmanuel and Ezekiel J. Emmanuel, The Medical Directive: A New Comprehensive Advance Care Document, 261, 3288 (1989). Another possibility would be to encourage every competent person to articulate values that are likely to be significant in subsequent decisionmaking.

Perhaps the best device for encouraging such discussion (and for recording the results) is the "Values History Form," which asks prospective patients about their general values, their medical values, their relationships with family members, friends, and health care providers, their wishes in particular cases and a host of other issues likely to become relevant if they become incompetent and health care decisions must be made on their behalf. While such a values history has no formal legal significance, and while some may be put off by such questions as "What makes you laugh?" and "What makes you cry?," there is no doubt that the existence of such a document would be of great value to a substitute decisionmaker, and to any court called upon to confirm that substitute's decision. See Joan McIver Gibson, Reflecting on Values, 51 Ohio St.L.J. 451 (1990).

6. Whether the courts have any role at all in these matters has been the subject of some debate. On the one hand, there is a fear that the absence of judicial oversight will lead to arbitrary decisions and, thus, arbitrary deaths. On the other hand, any attempt to bring all of these cases to the courts would yield an intolerable caseload and delay the deaths of many patients who desperately seek that relief. In addition, as the Wendland case suggested, there is little reason to believe that courts have any wisdom that will make them better than a patient's family at making these decisions. The Massachusetts Supreme Judicial Court changed its view of the necessity of judicial confirmation of a guardian's decision that a patient should forgo life-sustaining treatment. See In re Spring, 380 Mass. 629, 405 N.E.2d 115 (1980) (no review required in most circumstances; reversing prior position). Should judicial review of all decisions to terminate life-sustaining treatment be required? Should such judicial review be required in some cases? In cases in which there is no written advance directive? In which there is no agreement among family members? In which the patients disagree with the health care providers? In which the health care providers disagree among themselves? In which the decisionmaker is self interested? In which there is an ambiguity in the previous statements of the patient? Is there any way to adequately categorize those cases in which judicial review ought to be required? If judicial review is not required, should some other form of review—by an ethics committee, for example—be required in its stead? Is the choice of the Uniform Health Care Decisions Act, which would rarely countenance judicial involvement in any health care decision, the best choice? Why?

7. When resort to a court is required, what procedure ought to be employed by the court? Should the court's involvement be limited to the appointment of a decisionmaker, should the court make the decision itself, or should the court review every decision (or some decisions) made by an appointed decisionmaker? Should the action be a special statutory action, an injunction action, a guardianship, or does the form of the action really make much difference? Should the court always appoint a guardian *ad litem* for the patient? If so, is the role of the guardian ad litem to represent what that person believes the patient would want, or what that person believes is in the best interest of the patient? Alternatively, should the guardian ad litem always oppose the petitioner (who is usually seeking the termination of the treatment)? Every state has a nursing home ombudsman. Should the ombudsman be notified whenever discontinuation of treatment of a nursing home patient is requested? Should the ombudsman participate in every such case? See In re Conroy, 486 A.2d at 1237–1242.

In In re Guardianship of Hamlin, 102 Wash.2d 810, 689 P.2d 1372 (1984), the Washington Supreme Court announced two entirely separate processes—one to be followed where there is "total agreement among the patient's family, treating physicians and prognosis committee as to the course of medical treatment," and one to be followed where there is "an incompetent with no known family, who has never made his wishes known." No judicial process and no formal guardianship is required in the first case where "the incompetent patient is in * * * a persistent vegetative state with no reasonable chance of recovery and * * * the patient's life is being maintained by life support systems." In the second situation a guardian must be appointed by the court, but that guardian need not obtain judicial confirmation of any particular decision "if the treating physicians and prognosis committee are unanimous that life-sustaining efforts should be withheld or withdrawn and the guardian concurs." Of course, most cases fall between the two extremes discussed in *Hamlin*.

Is the Uniform Health Care Decisions Act approach to this issue–that there will be no judicial hearing unless a relative or health care provider is willing to file an action–the best way of dealing with this? See Protection and Advocacy System, Inc. v. Presbyterian Healthcare Services, 128 N.M. 73, 989 P.2d 890 (N.M.App. 1999)(no standing in advocacy group to challenge unanimous decision of family members and health care providers).

8. If there is to be a judicial process, should it be an adversary process? While the Chief Justice appears to think that the adversary process is helpful in these cases, Cruzan, 497 U.S. 261 n. 9, 110 S.Ct. 2841, 2853 n. 9, 111 L.Ed.2d 224, that part of the opinion gave Justice Stevens pause:

> The Court recognizes that "the state has been involved as an adversary from the beginning" in this case only because Nancy Cruzan "was a patient at a state hospital when this litigation commenced." * * * It seems to me, however, that the Court draws precisely the wrong conclusion from this insight. The Court apparently believes that the absence of the state from the litigation would have created a problem, because agreement among the family and the independent guardian *ad litem* as to Nancy Cruzan's best interests might have prevented her treatment from becoming the focus of a "truly adversarial" proceeding. [ ] It may reasonably be debated whether some judicial process should be required before life-sustaining treatment is discontinued; this issue has divided the state courts. Compare *In re Estate of Longeway*, (requiring judicial approval of guardian's decision) with *In re Hamlin* (discussing circumstances in which judicial approval is unnecessary). * * * I tend,

however, to agree * * * that the intervention of the state in these proceedings as an *adversary* is not so much a cure as it is part of the disease.

Cruzan, 497 U.S. 261, 341, n. 13, 110 S.Ct. 2841, 2884, n. 13, 111 L.Ed.2d 224 (1990) (Stevens, J., dissenting). A decade earlier the Florida Supreme Court had expressed the same reservations: "Because the issue with its ramifications is fraught with complexity and encompasses the interests of the law, both civil and criminal, medical ethics and social morality, it is not one which is well suited for a solution in an adversary judicial proceeding." Satz v. Perlmutter, 379 So.2d 359, 360 (Fla.1980); Protection and Avocacy System, Inc. v. Presbyterian Healthcare Services, 128 N.M. 73, 989 P.2d 890 (N.M. App. 1999). Are the "advantages" of an adversary proceeding truly advantageous in these agonizing cases?

9. Several courts (including the Florida Supreme Court in *Satz*) have suggested that the issue is more appropriate for the legislature than for the judiciary. Is the legislature any better equipped than the courts to address general questions surrounding the termination of life support systems?

10. "Right to die" cases brought to vindicate the federal privacy rights of patients against state entities (like state hospitals) may be based on 42 U.S.C.A. § 1983. When one successfully raises a federal civil rights claim under that statute, the prevailing party is entitled to attorney's fees under 42 U.S.C.A. § 1988. While most such attempts to collect attorneys fees have failed, some have been successful. In Gray v. Romeo, 697 F.Supp. 580 (D.R.I.1988), the successful attorney was awarded $38,495.95. Gray v. Romeo, Order of March 8, 1989. In addition, the petitioner's legal counsel in the *Bouvia* case was awarded attorneys' fees under the state's statutory "private attorney general" provision because the case vindicated important public rights. Bouvia v. County of L.A., 195 Cal.App.3d 1075, 241 Cal.Rptr. 239 (1987). See also M. Rose Gasner, Financial Penalties for Failing to Honor Patient Wishes to Refuse Treatment, 11 St. Louis U.Pub.L.Rev. 499 (1992). The Uniform Health Care Decisions Act explicitly provides for attorneys fees in cases where there has been an "intentional" violation of the Act. Is this an appropriate standard?

11. The Wendland case explicitly provides that the "clear and convincing evidence" standard applies only to cases where the proposed termination of treatment would result in the death of the patient; the court would not apply it in other judicial actions reviewing health care decision making. The Uniform Health Care Decision Act, on the other hand, applies the standard to all health care decisions. Does it make sense to have one standard for decision that will result in death, and one standard for other cases? What are the advantages (and disadvantages) of a uniform standard, consistent across all kinds of health care decisions?

12. The California Supreme Court granted review in Wendland, and, as this casebook went to press in early 2001, the case was pending in that court. How would you argue this case to the California Supreme Court if you represented Rose? If you represented Robert's mother, the petitioner? If you were appointed guardian ad litem to represent Robert? Several organizations filed amicus briefs in the Court of Appeal in the Wendland case, including the California Medical Association and the Los Angeles County Medical Association/Bar Association Joint Committee on Biomedical Ethics (supporting Rose's attempt to discontinue treatment), and the Ethics and Advocacy Task Force of the Nursing Home Action Group, and Not Dead Yet, a disability advocacy group (supporting efforts to continue treatment). What other groups would you expect to participate as amici in the California Supreme Court? What position would you expect religious groups to take on this case? Why?

Problem: Not Quite Persistent Vegetative State

When unhelmeted 57 year old Tad Bifsteak ran his motorcycle into a bridge support post on an interstate highway, he was revived at the scene and rushed to Big Central Hospital. There he underwent several hours of emergency surgery designed to preserve his life and repair the very substantial head injuries he sustained. A few days after the surgery he began to regain consciousness, and a week later he was able to be removed from the ventilator which was supporting his breathing, although he still needs ventilator assistance from time to time. During his first two weeks in the hospital, Tad showed little improvement. He was not in a coma, but he was only occasionally responsive, and he demonstrated no awareness of Ralph, his partner of twenty-two years, or his two brothers and his parents, even though Tad had always shared a close relationship with all of them.

After two weeks, Big City Hospital transferred Tad to Commercial Affiliated Nursing Home, where he began receiving physical and occupational therapy. After a year of care there, he has shown little improvement. He still does not seem to recognize Ralph, who visits daily, or anyone else. He is able to sit up and his eyes sometimes seem to be following images on a screen. He grunts when he is hungry or uncomfortable. He cannot eat or drink, and he is fed through a feeding tube in his abdomen. He cannot control his bowels or bladder. He has regularly suffered from urinary tract infections and asthma during his nursing home stay, although his need for the ventilator is becoming more and more rare. On a few, increasingly rare, occasions, his heart stopped beating, but he was resuscitated immediately. Doctors believe that there is little chance of substantial improvement in his condition (although, in the words of one doctor, "Who knows? Anything can happen"). Tad's doctors estimate that his life expectancy could be another twenty years or more.

Tad's doctor and Ralph have developed a good working relationship, and the doctor has called upon Ralph to approve any change in Tad's treatment regimen; Tad never signed any kind of advance directive. Ralph has now informed the doctor that he believes that Tad would want the use of the feeding tube (and the occasional use of the ventilator) discontinued, and that he would want to be DNR. When the doctor challenged him on this, Ralph respectfully ordered the doctor to terminate feeding, and to note that Tad was not to be mechanically ventilated or resuscitated. Ralph explained that he had spoken with Tad often about "this kind of thing," and that Tad had said that the indignity of being fed, or wearing diapers, or being bed-bound, was not worth the value of life to him. In particular, Ralph remembers Tad describing one of their friends, another motorcyclist who became a quadriplegic and suffered some intellectual impairment after an accident, as a "big time loser who would be better off dead." Tad and Ralph promised each other that neither would ever let that happen to the other. Tad's parents and one of his brothers agree that there is no doubt that Tad would want all treatment terminated under these circumstances. Tad's other brother disagrees. As he has articulated it, "How can we know what he would want? He could never have imagined himself in this situation, and we shouldn't read anything in to what he said about other people. Maybe he thought those other people could feel more pain than he can."

Tad's doctor has approached you, the hospital counsel, to ask you what she should do. Should she discontinue feeding? The use of the ventilator? Should Tad become "DNR"? Should an action be pursued in court? How would that action be resolved?

Note: Do Not Resuscitate Orders

There may be some reason to treat cardiopulmonary resuscitation (CPR) differently from the way we treat other forms of life-sustaining therapy. CPR is the only form of life-sustaining treatment that is provided routinely without consent of the patient, and it may be the only medical treatment of any sort that is generally initiated without an order of a physician. CPR generally is provided unless a formal "Do Not Resuscitate" (DNR) order is entered in the patient's chart. Even patients in hospitals are infrequently asked to make their own decisions on cardiopulmonary resuscitation. One startling study of over 9000 patients, conducted over several years, revealed that fewer than half of the physicians with seriously ill patients in the hospital knew whether their patients wanted CPR, and almost half of those patients with DNR orders had them entered within two days of their deaths. That study also showed that intensive intervention to explain the likely outcome of CPR to physicians and improve the communication between the health care providers and the patients had virtually no effect on the treatment the patients were provided. A Controlled Trial to Improve Care for Seriously Ill Hospitalized Patients—The Study to Understand Prognoses and Preferences for Outcome and Risks of Treatment (SUPPORT), 274 JAMA 1591 (1995). For an account of the underlying medical-legal issues in general, see Tracy E. Miller, Do Not Resuscitate Orders: Public Policy and Patient Autonomy, 17 Law, Medicine and Health Care 252 (1989); and Carol A. Mooney, Deciding Not to Resuscitate Hospital Patients: Medical and Legal Perspectives, 1986 Ill.L.Rev. 1025.

Why don't doctors talk to patients about DNR orders? The medical tradition of not discussing CPR was exacerbated by the mid–1980s fear among physicians that they would be liable for damages if they did not resuscitate whenever it was possible to do so—even when attempts at resuscitation were futile or inconsistent with the desires of the patient. These factors gave rise to "slow codes" or "pencil DNRs" in which the hospital staff was instructed to provide certain patients with resuscitation under circumstances that would guarantee that the resuscitation would fail (by delaying the commencement of the treatment, for example). Sometimes the hospital staff was instructed in a more straightforward way to avoid resuscitation—but the instruction was provided in some form that would leave no record—it was written in the chart in pencil or, in New York, indicated by the placement of a removable purple dot on the patient's file.

The reaction to this transparently dishonest process was the development of formal hospital policies that provided for honest and open decision making on DNR. See, e.g., Committee on Policy for DNR Decisions, Yale–New Haven Hospital, Report on Do Not Resuscitate Decisions, 47 Conn.Med. 478 (1983); R. Levine and K. Nolan, Editorial, Do Not Resuscitate Decisions, A Policy, 47 Conn.Med. 511 (1983). These developments were accompanied by a more formal legal analysis of the problems of hospital decision making in this area, and in 1986 the New York State Task Force on Life and the Law proposed legislation on Do Not Resuscitate orders. A statute similar to that recommended by the Task Force became effective in New York in 1988, and over twenty states adopted some form of legislation to address CPR over the next few years.

The New York statute is remarkable for its precision and for the bureaucracy it has brought to making one kind of treatment decision. First, the statute sets the default position on DNR orders: "every person admitted to a hospital shall be presumed to consent to the administration of cardiopulmonary resuscitation in the event of cardiac or respiratory arrest, unless there is consent to the issuance of an order not to resuscitate as provided in this article." N.Y.Pub.Health Law § 2962. This default position is coupled with the requirement that patients or their surrogates be given appropriate information before they are allowed to choose to forgo resuscitation, and that any appropriately entered order "shall be included in writing in the patient's chart." Id. While the statute permits adults with decision-making capacity to consent to the entry of a DNR order either orally or in writing, an oral determination must be made during hospitalization in the presence of two adult witnesses, one of whom must be a doctor affiliated with the hospital. Even the written decision must be made in the presence of two adult witnesses who themselves must sign off on the determination. Id. § 2964. While the statute permits a limited therapeutic privilege, the requirements it establishes discourage decision making without participation of the patient. Id.

If a patient does not have the capacity to consent to a DNR order, a surrogate may do so under some circumstances. The process for determining capacity is included in the statute. Id. § 2963. It is notable that the statute requires that notice of the determination of incapacity be given to the patient "where there is any indication of the patient's ability to comprehend such notice." Id. When a surrogate is properly identified, that person:

> may consent to an order not to resuscitate on behalf of an adult patient only if there has been a determination by an attending physician with a concurrence of another physician selected by a person authorized by the hospital to make such a selection, given after personal examination of the patient that, to a reasonable degree of medical certainty:

> [i] the patient has a terminal condition; or [ii] the patient is terminally unconscious; or [iii] resuscitation would be medically futile or [iv] resuscitation would impose an extraordinary burden on the patient in light of the patient's medical condition and the expected outcome of resuscitation for the patient.

Id. § 2965. If no surrogate is available, the entry of a DNR order effectively is limited to those cases in which "to a reasonable degree of medical certainty, resuscitation would be medically futile." Id. § 2966.

The statute requires that DNR policies be reviewed by the attending physician every three days (for patients in a hospital) or every 60 days or whenever the patient is required to be seen by a physician (for patients in residential health facilities). Id. § 2970.

The statute requires the establishment of dispute mediation systems at hospitals to mediate decisions to consent (or refuse to consent) to DNR orders. The medical determinations are subject to judicial review, although "the person or entity challenging the decision must show, by clear and convincing evidence, that the decision is contrary to the patient's wishes including consideration of the patient's religious and moral beliefs, or, in the absence of evidence of the patient's wishes, that the decision is contrary to the patient's best interests." Id. § 2973. Those involved (physician, health care professional, nurse's aide, hospital or person employed by or under contract with the hospital) are immune from civil and criminal liability, and may not be deemed to have engaged in unprofessional conduct, for making a determination in accord with the statute. Finally, if no surrogate "is reasonably available, willing * * * and competent" to act under the statute, a court may render a judgment:

directing the physician to issue an order not to resuscitate where the patient has a terminal condition, is permanently unconscious, or resuscitation would impose an extraordinary burden on the patient in light of the patient's medical condition and the expected outcome of the resuscitation for the patient, and issuance of an order is not inconsistent with the patient's wishes including a consideration of the patient's religious and moral beliefs or, in the absence of evidence of the patient's wishes, the patient's best interests.

Id. § 2976.

Ironically the statute, which was promulgated because of the worry of overuse of CPR, has been criticized primarily because it may continue to require CPR in cases where it is inappropriate. First, the statute would seem to permit (or even require) cardiopulmonary resuscitation even when that treatment is scientifically futile unless a DNR order has been entered. See Fred Rosner, Must We Always Offer the Option of CPR: The Law in New York, 260 J.A.M.A. 3129 (1988); Donald J. Murphy, Do Not Resuscitate Orders: Time for Reappraisal in Long Term Care Institutions, 260 J.A.M.A. 2098 (1988); Leslie J. Blackhall, Must We Always Use CPR?, 317 N.Eng.J.Med. 1281 (1987).

The statute has also been criticized for its very narrow application of the therapeutic privilege—a result the drafters of the statute intended so that there would be more doctor-patient discussion about DNR orders. Those who object to the limited applicability of the therapeutic privilege may also be disappointed by the statutory requirement that the physician tell the patient when the patient has been found incapacitated to consent to a DNR order. Once again, the drafters of the statute believed that requiring this communication would encourage doctor-patient communication generally and would thus improve medical decisionmaking.

Other objections to the statute focus on its rather cumbersome process, although it has been defended as "parallel[ing] existing clinical practice." Of course, to the extent that the statute does parallel the current practice it institutionalizes and strengthens the current default position that CPR should be applied in every case unless a prior formal and bureaucratically correct determination has been made to enter a DNR order.

Other states promulgating DNR statutes generally have avoided the bureaucratic thicket created in New York. Some of the subsequent statutes permit the patient to sign an advance directive that CPR not be provided, while others provide a process by which the physician can enter a DNR order. A few states require witnesses on DNR advance directives or orders, some include DNR forms, and some provide for virtually no formalities. Some state statutes apply only in designated institutions (hospitals and nursing homes, for example), some apply specifically to prehospital treatment by paramedics, and some apply under all circumstances. Frequently statutory DNR provisions are found in advance directive statutes, although sometimes they are combined with other statutes, or they are independent of all other statutes.

Should the processes for entering DNR orders be determined by statute? Should New York (or any other state) promulgate another statute to deal with ventilators, and a third to deal with nasogastric tubes? Is there something truly unique about DNR orders that requires a statute? The New York statute was promulgated at a time when most hospitals were developing policies on DNR orders anyway. These policies, although often similar to the substantive provisions of the New York statute, varied with the local culture of the hospital in which they were adopted. Should these policies be established on a patient-by-patient basis, an attending physician-by-attending physician basis, a hospital-by-hospital basis, or by the state legislature through statute? Should religious hospitals be bound by DNR statutes offensive to their mission?

What should the effect of an outstanding DNR order be upon the patient who consents to surgery? Should a general DNR order be presumed to apply in the operating room? Should it be presumed not to apply in the operating room, unless its application there is explicitly provided? Should a DNR order entered in a hospital continue to apply when the patient is moved to a nursing home? Should it stop a paramedic responding to a 911 call from applying CPR to that patient after the patient has returned to her home?

This last class of cases has been addressed in most states which, either by statute or regulation, have provided for the durability of DNR orders that might be confronted by emergency medical providers. In most states there are approved forms that authorize emergency medical workers to avoid resuscitating patients who have signed them. Some systems provide for a state or local registry of these "EMS–DNR" patients (so that ambulance employees can find out whether they should resuscitate a particular patient), and some provide for DNR bracelets. The problem in dealing with the "EMS–DNR" decision is one of characterizing it. Is an "EMS–DNR" document a form of an advance directive, or is it a form of a doctor's order in a particular case? Which should be sufficient to make such a document effective–a patient's signature or a doctor's signature?

As usual, a thorough and well annotated discussion of all of the relevant issues and a review of the relevant literature can be found in Alan Meisel, The Right to Die §§ 9.4–9.41 (2d ed. 1995).

3. *Making Health Care Decisions for Patients Who Have Never Been Competent*

Where the patient has never been competent—where the patient has been severely retarded from birth, for example—the courts still make an attempt to determine what the patient's choice would be. Of course, it is exceptionally difficult to imagine what an incompetent person, who has never been competent, would want to do if that person were suddenly competent. Compare the next two cases, one of which confirms the principle of substituted judgment and one of which abandons that approach to apply the principle of beneficence and seeks to do what is in the best interest of such a patient. *Superintendent of Belchertown State School v. Saikewicz,* involves a 67–year–old profoundly retarded adult suffering from leukemia without any family willing to aid in decisionmaking. The court addresses the question of whether the chemotherapy that would be likely to be provided to others in his condition should be withheld. *Matter of Storar,* the companion case to *Matter of Eichner,* concerns a profoundly retarded 52–year–old cancer patient and the propriety of blood transfusions.

SUPERINTENDENT OF BELCHERTOWN STATE SCHOOL v. SAIKEWICZ

Supreme Judicial Court of Massachusetts, 1977.
373 Mass. 728, 370 N.E.2d 417.

LIACOS, JUSTICE.

* * *

The question what legal standards govern the decision whether to administer potentially life-prolonging treatment to an incompetent person encompasses two distinct and important subissues. First, does a choice exist? That is, is it the unvarying responsibility of the State to order medical treatment in all circumstances involving the care of an incompetent person? Second, if a choice does exist under certain conditions, what considerations enter into the decision-making process?

We think that principles of equality and respect for all individuals require the conclusion that a choice exists * * *. We recognize a general right in all persons to refuse medical treatment in appropriate circumstances. The recognition of that right must extend to the case of an incompetent, as well as a competent, patient because the value of human dignity extends to both.

This is not to deny that the State has a traditional power and responsibility, under the doctrine of *parens patriae,* to care for and protect the *"best interests"* of the incompetent person.

The "best interests" of an incompetent person are not necessarily served by imposing on such persons results not mandated as to competent persons similarly situated. It does not advance the interest of the State or the ward to treat the ward as a person of lesser status or dignity than others. To protect the incompetent person within its power, the State must recognize the dignity and worth of such a person and afford to that person the same panoply of rights and choices it recognizes in competent persons. If a competent person faced with death may choose to decline treatment which not only will not cure the person but which substantially may increase suffering in exchange for a possible yet brief prolongation of life, then it cannot be said that it is always in the "best interests" of the ward to require submission to such treatment. Nor do statistical factors indicating that a majority of competent persons similarly situated choose treatment resolve the issue. The significant decisions of life are more complex than statistical determinations. Individual choice is determined not by the vote of the majority but by the complexities of the singular situation viewed from the unique perspective of the person called on to make the decision. To presume that the incompetent person must always be subjected to what many rational and intelligent persons may decline is to downgrade the status of the incompetent person by placing a lesser value on his intrinsic human worth and vitality.

* * * This leads us to the question of how the right of an incompetent person to decline treatment might best be exercised so as to give the fullest possible expression to the character and circumstances of that individual.

* * *

To put the above discussion in proper perspective, we realize that an inquiry into what a majority of people would do in circumstances that truly were similar assumes an objective viewpoint not far removed from a "reasonable person" inquiry. While we recognize the value of this kind of indirect evidence, we should make it plain that the primary test is subjective in nature—that is, the goal is to determine with as much accuracy as possible the wants and needs of the individual involved. This may or may not conform to what is thought wise or prudent by most people. The problems of arriving at an accurate substituted judgment in matters of life and death vary greatly in degree, if not in kind, in different circumstances. * * * Joseph Saikewicz was profoundly retarded and noncommunicative his entire life, which was spent largely in the highly restrictive atmosphere of an institution. While it may thus be necessary to rely to a greater degree on objective criteria, such as the supposed inability of profoundly retarded persons to conceptualize or fear death, the effort to bring the substituted judgment into step with the values and desires of the affected individual must not, and need not, be abandoned.

The "substituted judgment" standard which we have described commends itself simply because of its straightforward respect for the integrity and autonomy of the individual. * * *

* * * [W]e now reiterate the substituted judgment doctrine as we apply it in the instant case. We believe that both the guardian *ad litem* in his recommendation and the judge in his decision should have attempted (as they did) to ascertain the incompetent person's actual interests and preferences. In short, the decision in cases such as this should be that which would be made by the incompetent person, if that person were competent, but taking into account the present and future incompetency of the individual as one of the factors which would necessarily enter into the decision-making process of the competent person. Having recognized the right of a competent person to make for himself the same decision as the court made in this case, the question is, do the facts on the record support the proposition that Saikewicz himself would have [declined treatment]. We believe they do.

* * *

IN RE STORAR

New York Court of Appeals, 1981.
52 N.Y.2d 363, 438 N.Y.S.2d 266, 420 N.E.2d 64.

WACHTLER, JUDGE.

* * *

John Storar was profoundly retarded with a mental age of about 18 months. At the time of this proceeding he was 52 years old and a resident of the Newark Development Center, a State facility, which had been his home since the age of 5. His closest relative was his mother * * *.

In 1979 physicians at the center noticed blood in his urine and asked his mother for permission to conduct diagnostic tests. She * * * gave her consent. The tests, completed in July, 1979, revealed that he had cancer of the bladder. It was recommended that he receive radiation therapy at a hospital in Rochester. When the hospital refused to administer the treatment without the consent of a legal guardian, Mrs. Storar applied to the court and was appointed guardian of her son's person and property in August, 1979. With her consent he received radiation therapy for six weeks after which the disease was found to be in remission.

However in March, 1980, blood was again observed in his urine. The lesions in his bladder were cauterized in an unsuccessful effort to stop the bleeding. At that point his physician diagnosed the cancer as terminal, concluding that after using all medical and surgical means then available, the patient would nevertheless die from the disease.

In May the physicians at the center asked his mother for permission to administer blood transfusions. She initially refused but the following day withdrew her objection. For several weeks John Storar received blood transfusions when needed. However, on June 19 his mother requested that the transfusions be discontinued.

The director of the center then brought this proceeding, pursuant to [ ] the Mental Hygiene Law, seeking authorization to continue the transfusions, claiming that without them "death would occur within weeks." Mrs. Storar cross-petitioned for an order prohibiting the transfusions, and named the District Attorney as a party. The court appointed a guardian ad litem and signed an order temporarily permitting the transfusions to continue, pending the determination of the proceeding.

At the hearing in September the court heard testimony from various witnesses including Mrs. Storar, several employees at the center, and seven medical experts. All the experts concurred that John Storar had irreversible cancer of the bladder, * * * with a very limited life span, generally estimated to be between 3 and 6 months. They also agreed that he had an infant's mentality and was unable to comprehend his predicament or to make a reasoned choice of treatment. In addition, there was no dispute over the fact that he was continuously losing blood.

* * *

It was conceded that John Storar found the transfusions disagreeable. He was also distressed by the blood and blood clots in his urine which apparently increased immediately after a transfusion. He could not comprehend the purpose of the transfusions and on one or two occasions had displayed some initial resistance. To eliminate his apprehension he was given a sedative approximately one hour before a transfusion. He also received regular doses of narcotics to alleviate the pain associated with the disease.

On the other hand several experts testified that there was support in the medical community for the view that, at this stage, transfusions may only prolong suffering and that treatment could properly be limited to administering pain killers. Mrs. Storar testified that she wanted the transfusions discontinued because she only wanted her son to be comfortable. She admitted that no one had ever explained to her what might happen to him if the transfusions were stopped. She also stated that she was not "sure" whether he might die sooner if the blood was not replaced and was unable to determine whether he wanted to live. However, in view of the fact that he obviously disliked the transfusions and tried to avoid them, she believed that he would want them discontinued.

* * *

John Storar was never competent at any time in his life. * * * Thus it is unrealistic to attempt to determine whether he would want to continue potentially life prolonging treatment if he were competent. * * * Mentally, John Storar was an infant and that is the only realistic way to assess his rights in this litigation. Thus this case bears only superficial similarities to *Eichner* and the determination must proceed from different principles.

A parent or guardian has a right to consent to medical treatment on behalf of an infant. [ ] The parent, however, may not deprive a child of life saving treatment, however well intentioned. * * *

In the *Storar* case there is the additional complication of two threats to his life. There was cancer of the bladder which was incurable and would in all probability claim his life. There was also the related loss of blood which posed the risk of an earlier death, but which, at least at the time of the hearing, could be replaced by transfusions. Thus, as one of the experts noted, the transfusions were analogous to food—they would not cure the cancer, but they could eliminate the risk of death from another treatable cause. Of course, John Storar did not like them, as might be expected of one with an infant's mentality. But the evidence convincingly shows that the transfusions did not involve excessive pain and that without them his mental and physical abilities would not be maintained at the usual level. With the transfusions on the other hand, he was essentially the same as he was before except of course he had a fatal illness which would ultimately claim his life. Thus, on the record, we have concluded that the application for permission to continue the transfusions should have been granted. Although we understand and respect his mother's despair, as we respect the beliefs of those who oppose transfusions on religious grounds, a court should not in the circumstances of this case allow an incompetent patient to bleed to death because someone, even someone as close as a parent or sibling, feels that this is best for one with an incurable disease.

* * *

Notes and Questions

How would the Supreme Judicial Court of Massachusetts have decided *Storar?* How would the New York Court of Appeals have decided *Saikewicz?* Might there be cases for which the principles of *Storar* and the principles of *Saikewicz* would lead to different results? Which principle is preferable? Why?

The approach of the Massachusetts court in Saikewicz has been criticized on the grounds that it makes no sense to apply the doctrine of substituted judgment to the case of a patient who has never been competent. Do you agree with this criticism? Despite it, Massachusetts has retained the Saikewicz rule. See Guardianship of Doe, 411 Mass. 512, 583 N.E.2d 1263 (1992) and In re R.H., 35 Mass.App.Ct. 478, 622 N.E.2d 1071 (1993). Not all justices on the Massachusetts court agree with the approach of the court, however. One justice strongly disagrees for reasons he expressed briefly in dissent from an opinion in which the court applied the doctrine of substituted judgment to allow for the removal of life sustaining treatment for an infant who had been in an irreversible comma since an auto accident in her first year of life:

> [T]he court again has approved application of the doctrine of substituted judgment where there is not a soupcon of evidence to support it. The trial judge did not have a smidgen of evidence on which to conclude that if this child who is now about five and one half years old were competent to decide, she would elect certain death to a life with no cognitive ability. The route by which the court arrived at its conclusion is a cruel charade which is being perpetuated whenever we are faced with a life and death decision of an incompetent person.

Care and Protection of Beth, 412 Mass. 188, 587 N.E.2d 1377, 1383 (1992) (Nolan, J., dissenting.)

How would the Uniform Health Care Decisions Act address the issue of a patient who had never been competent to make health care decisions? Many people believe that our society undervalues the lives of the disabled. Does this suggest that the courts should review decisions to remove life sustaining medical treatment from patients in this class, even if the courts need not be involved in similar cases with previously-competent patients? See Protection and Advocacy System, Inc. v. Presbyterian Healthcare Services, 128 N.M. 73, 989 P.2d 890 (N.M.App.1999).

V. THE "RIGHT TO DIE"—CHILDREN AND NEWBORNS

A. CHILDREN

Problem: Choosing to Forgo Cancer Treatment

Bob Anderson was a healthy, socially well adjusted intelligent fourteen year old when he discovered that he had testicular cancer which had also produced a mass in his liver. The prognosis was not terribly optimistic: with intensive intervention he would have about a 50% chance of surviving for 2 years, and a 25% chance of a "cure" (i.e., of surviving five years). "Intensive intervention" would include six to eight months of extremely unpleasant chemotherapy, surgery to remove part of his liver and his testes, and a substantial amount of radiation therapy. Without treatment, Bob would probably die within six months.

Bob has informed his oncologist that he has decided to forgo the proposed surgery, even though he recognizes that this will result in his death. He explained that he reached this conclusion after reading everything accessible to him about his cancer and the proposed treatment, after praying with his religious advisor and mentor (a Presbyterian minister), and after discussing the issue with his family, friends, and two patients (names provided by the oncologist) who had previously undergone the same surgery and chemotherapy. He also admits that the playground razzing he has taken over the primary location of his disease, and his consequent extreme embarrassment, were not irrelevant factors in his decision.

Bob's parents, who are divorced and have joint legal and physical custody, are split on this issue. His father believes that it is Bob's decision to make, and he supports Bob's decision. His mother insists that the oncologist and the hospital provide the proposed treatment. In addition, a social worker in the local child protective services office (which was informed about the case by one of Bob's teachers) has informed all of the parties that, in her opinion, Bob would be a neglected child if the treatment were not administered.

Bob's parents have now filed cross petitions seeking to vindicate their positions. Bob has filed a petition as well. The oncologist and the hospital have filed a declaratory judgment action seeking an order of the court before taking any action, and the child protective services agency has file a neglect petition against the father. How should the judge proceed? What kind of hearing, if any, should the judge hold? How should she rule?

NEWMARK v. WILLIAMS

Supreme Court of Delaware, 1991.
588 A.2d 1108.

MOORE, JUSTICE.

Colin Newmark, a three year old child, faced death from a deadly aggressive and advanced form of pediatric cancer known as Burkitt's Lymphoma. We were presented with a clash of interests between medical science, Colin's tragic plight, the unquestioned sincerity of his parents' religious beliefs as Christian Scientists, and the legal right of the State to protect dependent children from perceived neglect when medical treatment is withheld on religious grounds. The Delaware Division of Child Protective Services ("DCPS") petitioned the Family Court for temporary custody of Colin to authorize the Alfred I. DuPont Institute ("DuPont Institute"), a nationally recognized children's hospital, to treat Colin's condition with chemotherapy. His parents, Morris and Kara Newmark, are well educated and economically prosperous. As members of the First Church of Christ, Scientist ("Christian Science") they rejected medical treatment proposed for Colin, preferring instead a course of spiritual aid and prayer. The parents rely upon provisions of Delaware law, which exempt those who treat their children's illnesses "solely by spiritual means" from the abuse and neglect statutes. Thus, they opposed the State's petition. [ ] The Newmarks also claimed that removing Colin from their custody would violate their First Amendment right, guaranteed under the United States Constitution, to freely exercise their religion.

* * *

[The Court explained how the Newmarks discovered that Colin suffered from Burkitt's Lymphoma, an extremely fast growing and dangerous form of pediatric cancer, when they took him to the doctor "out of concern for their potential criminal liability . . . ."]

We have concluded that Colin was not an abused or neglected child under Delaware law. Parents enjoy a well established legal right to make important decisions for their children. Although this right is not absolute, the State has the burden of proving by clear and convincing evidence that intervening in the parent-child relationship is necessary to ensure the safety or health of the child, or to protect the public at large. DCPS did not meet this heavy burden. This is especially true where the purpose of the custody petition was to administer, over the objections of Colin's parents, an extremely risky, toxic and dangerously life threatening medical treatment offering less than a 40% chance for "success".

* * *

Dr. Meek [an attending physician and board certified pediatric hematologist—oncologist] opined that chemotherapy offered a 40% chance of "curing" Colin's illness. She concluded that he would die within six to eight months without treatment. The Newmarks * * * advised Dr. Meek that they would place him under the care of a Christian Science practitioner and reject all medical treatment for their son. Accordingly, they refused to authorize the chemotherapy. There was no doubt that the Newmarks sincerely believed, as part of their religious beliefs, that the tenets of their faith provided an effective treatment.

II.

We start with an overview of the relevant Delaware statutory provisions. Delaware law defines a neglected child as:

[A] child whose physical, mental or emotional health and well-being is threatened or impaired because of inadequate care and protection by the child's custodian, who has the ability and financial means to provide for the care but does not or will not provide adequate care; or a child who has been abused or neglected * * *

[The statute] further defines abuse and neglect as:

Physical injury by other than accidental means, injury resulting in a mental or emotional condition which is a result of abuse or neglect, negligent treatment, sexual abuse, maltreatment, mistreatment, nontreatment, exploitation or abandonment, of a child under the age of 18. (Emphasis added).

Sections of the Delaware Code, however, contain spiritual treatment exemptions which directly affect Christian Scientists. Specifically, the exemptions state:

No child who in good faith is under treatment solely by spiritual means through prayer in accordance with the tenets and practices of a recognized church or religious denomination by a duly accredited practitioner thereof shall for that reason alone be considered a neglected child for purposes of this chapter.

[ ] These exceptions reflect the intention of the Delaware General Assembly to provide a "safe harbor" for parents, like the Newmarks, to pursue their own religious beliefs. [We recognize] that the spiritual treatment exemptions reflect, in part, "the policy of this State with respect to the quality of life" a desperately ill child might have in the caring and loving atmosphere of his or her family, versus the sterile hospital environment demanded by physicians seeking to prescribe excruciating, and life threatening, treatments of doubtful efficacy.

* * * [W]e recognize the possibility that the spiritual treatment exemptions may violate the ban against the establishment of an official State religion guaranteed under both the Federal and Delaware Constitutions. Clearly, in both reality and practical effect, the language providing an exemption only to those individuals practicing "in accordance" with the "practices of a recognized church or religious denomination by a duly accredited practitioner thereof" is intended for the principal benefit of Christian Scientists. Our concern is that it possibly forces us to impermissibly determine the validity of an individual's own religious beliefs.

Neither party challenged the constitutionality of the spiritual treatment exemptions in either the Family Court or on appeal. Thus, except to recognize that the issue is far more complicated than was originally presented to us, we must leave such questions for another day.

III.

Addressing the facts of this case, we turn to the novel legal question whether, under any circumstances, Colin was a neglected child when his parents refused to accede to medical demands that he receive a radical form of chemotherapy having only a forty percent chance of success. [The court then explained that it would apply a balancing test to answer this question.]

* * *

A.

Any balancing test must begin with the parental interest. The primacy of the familial unit is a bedrock principle of law. [ ]. We have repeatedly emphasized that the parental right is sacred which can be invaded for only the most compelling reasons.

* * *

Courts have also recognized that the essential element of preserving the integrity of the family is maintaining the autonomy of the parent-child relationship. [ ] In Prince v. Commonwealth of Massachusetts, [ ] the United States Supreme Court announced:

It is cardinal with us that the custody, care and nurture of the child reside first in the parents, whose primary function and freedom include preparation for obligations the state can neither supply nor hinder. [ ]

Parental autonomy to care for children free from government interference therefore satisfies a child's need for continuity and thus ensures his or her psychological and physical well-being. [ ]

Parental authority to make fundamental decisions for minor children is also a recognized common law principle. A doctor commits the tort of battery if he or she performs an operation under normal circumstances without the informed consent of the patient. [ ] Tort law also assumes that a child does not have the capacity to consent to an operation in most situations. [ ] Thus, the common law recognizes that the only party capable of authorizing medical treatment for a minor in "normal" circumstances is usually his parent or guardian. [ ]

Courts, therefore, give great deference to parental decisions involving minor children. In many circumstances the State simply is not an adequate surrogate for the judgment of a loving, nurturing parent. [ ] As one commentator aptly recognized, the "law does not have the capacity to supervise the delicately complex interpersonal bonds between parent and child." [ ]

B.

We also recognize that parental autonomy over minor children is not an absolute right. Clearly, the State can intervene in the parent-child relationship where the health and safety of the child and the public at large are in jeopardy. [ ] Accordingly, the State, under the doctrine of parens patriae, has a special duty to protect its youngest and most helpless citizens.

The parens patriae doctrine is a derivation of the common law giving the State the right to act on behalf of minor children in certain property and marital disputes. [ ] More recently, courts have accepted the doctrine of parens patriae to justify State intervention in cases of parental religious objections to medical treatment of minor children's life threatening conditions. [ ] The Supreme Court of the United States [pointed out] that parental autonomy, under the guise of the parents' religious freedom, was not unlimited. [ ] Rather, the Court held:

> Parents may be free to become martyrs themselves. But it does not follow they are free, in identical circumstances, to make martyrs of their children before they have reached the age of full and legal discretion when they can make that choice for themselves. [ ]

The basic principle underlying the parens patriae doctrine is the State's interest in preserving human life. [ ] Yet this interest and the parens patriae doctrine are not unlimited. In its recent Cruzan opinion, the Supreme Court of the United States announced that the state's interest in preserving life must "be weighed against the constitutionally protected interests of the individual." [ ]

The individual interests at stake here include both the Newmarks' right to decide what is best for Colin and Colin's own right to life. We have already considered the Newmarks' stake in this case and its relationship to the parens patriae doctrine. The resolution of the issues here, however, is incomplete without a discussion of Colin's interests.

C.

All children indisputably have the right to enjoy a full and healthy life. Colin, a three year old boy, unfortunately lacked the ability to reach a detached, informed decision regarding his own medical care. This Court must therefore substitute its own objective judgment to determine what is in Colin's "best interests." [ ]

There are two basic inquiries when a dispute involves chemotherapy treatment over parents' religious objections. The court must first consider the effectiveness of the treatment and determine the child's chances of survival with and without medical care. [ ] The court must then consider the nature of the treatments and their effect on the child. [ ]

The "best interests" analysis is hardly unique or novel. Federal and State courts have unhesitatingly authorized medical treatment over a parent's religious objection when the treatment is relatively innocuous in comparison to the dangers of withholding medical care. [ ] Accordingly, courts are reluctant to authorize medical care over parental objection when the child is not suffering a life threatening or potential life threatening illness. [ ]

The linchpin in all cases discussing the "best interests of a child," when a parent refuses to authorize medical care, is an evaluation of the risk of the procedure compared to its potential success. This analysis is consistent with the principle that State intervention in the parent-child relationship is only justifiable under compelling conditions. [ ] The State's interest in forcing a minor to undergo medical care diminishes as the risks of treatment increase and its benefits decrease.

* * *

Applying the foregoing considerations to the "best interests standard" here, the State's petition must be denied. The egregious facts of this case indicate that Colin's proposed medical treatment was highly invasive, painful, involved terrible temporary and potentially permanent side effects, posed an unacceptably low chance of success, and a high risk that the treatment itself would cause his death. The State's authority to intervene in this case, therefore, cannot outweigh the Newmarks' parental prerogative and Colin's inherent right to enjoy at least a modicum of human dignity in the short time that was left to him.

IV.

Dr. Meek originally diagnosed Colin's condition as Burkitt's Lymphoma. She testified that the cancer was "a very bad tumor" in an advanced disseminated state and not localized to only one section of the body. She accordingly recommended that the hospital begin an "extremely intensive" chemotherapy program scheduled to extend for at least six months.

[The court then explained how intensive such a chemotherapy program would be, and how such a treatment program would itself threaten Colin's life.]

Dr. Meek prescribed "maximum" doses of at least six different types of cancer-fighting drugs during Colin's chemotherapy. This proposed "maximum" treatment represented the most aggressive form of cancer therapy short of a bone marrow transplant. The side effects would include hair loss, reduced immunological function creating a high risk of infection in the patient, and certain neurological problems. The drugs also are toxic to bone marrow.

The record demonstrates that this form of chemotherapy also would adversely affect other parts of Colin's body.

* * *

The physicians planned to administer the chemotherapy in cycles, each of which would bring Colin near death. Then they would wait until Colin's body recovered sufficiently before introducing more drugs.

* * *

Dr. Meek also wanted the State to place Colin in a foster home after the initial phases of hospital treatment. Children require intensive home monitoring during chemotherapy. For example, Dr. Meek testified that a usually low grade fever for a healthy child could indicate the presence of a potentially deadly infection in a child cancer patient. She believed that the Newmarks, although well educated and financially responsible, were incapable of providing this intensive care because of their firm religious objections to medical treatment.

Dr. Meek ultimately admitted that there was a real possibility that the chemotherapy could kill Colin. In fact, assuming the treatment did not itself prove fatal, she offered Colin at "best" a 40% chance that he would "survive."[5] Dr. Meek additionally could not accurately predict whether, if Colin completed the therapy, he would subsequently suffer additional tumors.

---

5. Dr. Meek testified that there was no   available medical data to conclude that Colin

A.

No American court, even in the most egregious case, has ever authorized the State to remove a child from the loving, nurturing care of his parents and subject him, over parental objection, to an invasive regimen of treatment which offered, as Dr. Meek defined the term, only a forty percent chance of "survival."

* * *

B.

The aggressive form of chemotherapy that Dr. Meek prescribed for Colin was more likely to fail than succeed. The proposed treatment was also highly invasive and could have independently caused Colin's death. Dr. Meek also wanted to take Colin away from his parents and family during the treatment phase and place the boy in a foster home. This certainly would have caused Colin severe emotional difficulties given his medical condition, tender age, and the unquestioned close bond between Colin and his family.

In sum, Colin's best interests were served by permitting the Newmarks to retain custody of their child. Parents must have the right at some point to reject medical treatment for their child. Under all of the circumstances here, this clearly is such a case. The State's important and legitimate role in safeguarding the interests of minor children diminishes in the face of this egregious record.

Parents undertake an awesome responsibility in raising and caring for their children. No doubt a parent's decision to withhold medical care is both deeply personal and soul wrenching. It need not be made worse by the invasions which both the State and medical profession sought on this record. Colin's ultimate fate therefore rested with his parents and their faith.

Notes and Questions

1. Most judicial encounters with parents' rights to refuse medical treatment for their children follow the pattern established in *Newmark*. The court first announces the legal presumption that parents can make important decisions, including health care decisions, for their children. This is a common law right in every state, and it is protected by the United States Constitution as well. See Parham v. J.R., 442 U.S. 584, 99 S.Ct. 2493, 61 L.Ed.2d 101 (1979). However, this presumption can be overcome if the conditions of the state's child protective services statute are met. Most state child abuse and neglect statutes are similar to the Delaware statute discussed in *Newmark*, and they provide—with greater or lesser specificity—that the parents' failure to provide adequate health care for their children constitutes neglect. If parents neglect their children, the state may commence a legal process (as the state did in *Newmark*) to obtain legal custody of the child to assure that the child is no longer medically neglected. The state need not take physical custody of the child, and the child can (as a technical legal matter) remain in the physical custody of the parents even while receiving the medical care to which the parents object.

could survive to adulthood. Rather, she stated that the term "survival", as applied to victims of leukemia or lymphoma, refers only to the probability that the patient will live two years after chemotherapy without a recurrence of cancer.

2.   Ultimately, what is the legal test that the court applied to determine that Colin Newmark should not be ordered to undergo the proposed chemotherapy? Did the court apply a straight "best interests" test and determine that it was in Colin's best interests not to undergo this treatment, or did the court apply a balancing test and determine that the parents' interest in maintaining custody of their child (and in making health care decisions for their child) outweighed the state's interest in providing Colin with potentially life saving treatment? The choice between these two alternative forms of analysis may make no difference in this particular case, but can you think of a case in which the choice between these two legal positions would be dispositive?

3.   As a general matter, courts reviewing young children's decisions to forgo life sustaining treatment apply the "best interests" test (with a substantial bow to the articulated desires of the parents, who are deemed to have the best interests of their children in mind when they act). While the application of the "substituted judgment" standard seems appropriate as the children approach majority, a few states attempt to apply the "substituted judgment" theory to very young children, too. Compare, e.g., Care and Protection of Beth, 412 Mass. 188, 587 N.E.2d 1377 (1992) and Custody of a Minor, 385 Mass. 697, 434 N.E.2d 601 (1982), In re L.H.R., 253 Ga. 439, 321 S.E.2d 716 (1984)(applying the substituted judgment test) with In re K.I., B.I. and D.M., 735 A.2d 448 (D.C.1999)(applying the best interests test). Does the "substituted judgment" standard make any sense when it is applied to infants or very young children? Although it may be absurd to search for the values, interests, desires, and expectancies of a newborn or a 3–month old, or even a four year old, might not a seven or eight year old child's parents be able to talk about all of those attributes? Of course, it is hard to imagine anyone other than the parents (or their legal substitutes) being able to evaluate such factors. Does that mean that a court's decision to apply a substituted judgment standard to small children amounts to a *de facto* decision to defer to the parent's wishes?

4.   Parental rights to make health care decisions for their children are terminated when the child reaches majority. Those rights may be terminated earlier if the child is a "mature minor," a condition governed by statute (in some states) or the common law (in other states) or both. At the very least, a child is a mature minor when he can "present clear and convincing evidence that he [is] mature enough to exercise an adult's judgment and [understand] the consequences of his decision." *Newmark*, at 1116 n. 9. See In re E.G., 133 Ill.2d 98, 139 Ill.Dec. 810, 549 N.E.2d 322 (1989), where a Jehovah's Witness child "just months shy of her eighteenth birthday" was found to be sufficiently mature to choose to forgo a blood transfusion in a case with a rather dim chance of long term survival. See also Belcher v. Charleston Area Medical Center, 188 W.Va. 105, 422 S.E.2d 827 (1992) (17 year old should have had the right to demand a DNR order). But see In re Application of Long Island Jewish Med. Ctr., 147 Misc.2d 724, 557 N.Y.S.2d 239 (Sup.1990). In Commonwealth v. Nixon, 761 A.2d 1151 (Pa. 2000), this issue arose in the context of a defense in a criminal action. The Pennsylvania Supreme Court unanimously rejected the parents' appeal of their involuntary manslaughter and child endangerment convictions (and their consequent 2 ½ to 5 year sentences) after their sixteen year old daughter died at home as a result of the religiously-based decision not to seek diabetes treatment. The parents had argued that their daughter had decided, on her own, against seeking treatment, and that she was a "mature minor" under Pennsylvania law and thus entitled to make that decision, but the court concluded that she didn't meet the narrow definition of a "mature minor" under Pennsylvania law.

Courts may give some weight to the statements of older children, even if those courts are reluctant to declare those children "emancipated" or "mature minors." Although it is impossible to find a case where a patient under 16 has been found to be a sufficiently mature minor to independently choose to forgo life sustaining treatment, many courts have given considerable weight to the statements made by children considerably younger than that. See, e.g., In re Guardianship of Crum, 61 Ohio Misc.2d 596, 580 N.E.2d 876 (Prob.Ct., Franklin Co.1991). For a discussion of the ways in which children could be included in advance directive legislation, see Lisa Hawkins, Living Will Statutes: A Minor Oversight, 78 Va. L. Rev. 1581 (1992).

5. As the *Newmark* court explained, courts have "unhesitatingly authorized medical treatment over a parent's religious objection when the treatment is relatively innocuous in comparison with the dangers of withholding medical care." Of course, what constitutes an innocuous treatment for most of us might constitute a very serious intrusion for others. Most people are not terribly concerned by the prospect of a blood transfusion; for others, it may eliminate a possibility of eternal salvation. Despite this, courts have not flinched when they have been presented with requests for treatment that is "medically necessary"—i.e., when the child will surely die if the treatment is not provided, and just as surely will live if the treatment is provided. Courts routinely and consistently order blood transfusions for children of objecting Jehovah's Witness parents, at least when they meet this requirement of medical necessity; in this sense the courts treat Jehovah's Witness children very differently from Jehovah's Witness adults. On the other hand, courts generally do not order treatment for children who do not face life threatening conditions. The hardest cases, like the *Newmark* case, are those cases in which the proposed treatment is highly invasive, but the child faces a life threatening condition. The *Newmark* case reviews five other such cases—all involving childhood cancer. See *Newmark*, at 1119–1120. As the chance of temporary remission and long term cure increases, the courts are more likely to order the treatment.

6. While courts regularly face parental decisions that their children not receive treatment, they are sometimes confronted with the reverse situation, too. In In re K.I., B.I. and D.M., 735 A.2d 448 (D.C.1999) the District of Columbia Court of Appeals approved a DNR order for a neglected, comatose two year old child who was born "neurologically devastated." The child was taken from his drunken mother after he had been left alone for days without his necessary heart and lung medication. The mother opposed the hospital's request that the child be given DNR status. Applying the best interest (rather than the substituted judgment) standard, the court recognized that the mother might be criminally liable for homicide if the child were to die, and it thus disregarded her request that there be aggressive attempts at resuscitation. Can you imagine other circumstances in which a parent might inappropriately demand treatment for her child? Should these cases be treated any differently from those in which the parent denies consent for (rather than demands) the recommended care?

7. Like Delaware, most states have promulgated statutes that provide that "spiritual healing" *per se* cannot constitute child abuse or neglect for purposes of the state's criminal or child protective services statutes. In fact, for some time the existence of such protections were required as a condition of receiving some forms of federal funding. These spiritual healing statutes were the consequence of lobbying by the Christian Science church, and they were written using terms (e.g., "accredited practitioner") that have well defined meanings within that church. Are such statutes Constitutional? Might they violate the establishment clause of

the first amendment because they give a preference to Christian Scientists, and protect them in ways that they do not protect others? Is it relevant that the statute only protects members of "recognized" religions, and that the state is called upon to determine which religions it will "recognize"? Might they violate the establishment clause because they disfavor children within certain religious communities? After all, Presbyterian children are protected from death at the hands of their irrational parents by the state's abuse and neglect process, while Christian Science children are not. Most commentators who have considered the issue have determined that these statutes are not Constitutional (at least as they are applied to civil abuse and neglect proceedings) because they violate either the establishment clause or the equal protection clause of the fourteenth amendment. For a good account of the best arguments on this issue, see Ann MacLean Massie, The Religion Clauses and Parental Health Care Decisionmaking for Children: Suggestions for a New Approach, 21 Hastings Const. L. Q. 725 (1994). Also see State v. Miskimens, 22 Ohio Misc.2d 43, 490 N.E.2d 931 (Com.Pl.1984) and Walker v. Superior Court, 222 Cal.Rptr. 87 (Cal.App.1986) aff'd 47 Cal.3d 112, 253 Cal.Rptr. 1, 763 P.2d 852 (1988)(especially the concurring opinion of Justice Mosk).

B. NEWBORNS

Problem: Newborn With Spina Bifida

Baby Roe's parents decided their child would be born at Pleasant City Birthing Center despite medical advice that the advanced age of the mother made a hospital delivery advisable. At birth, the baby appeared to have spina bifida and hydrocephalus, serious congenital heart problems, and several other less serious medical problems.

Spina bifida is a midline defect of the osseous spine. In this case there is an external saccular protrusion high on the spine, and the protruding sac, which is filled with spinal fluid, includes a portion of the spinal cord. This medical condition is known as myelomeningocele. Hydrocephalus, which is often associated with spina bifida, consists of a cranial capacity engorged by fluids. The pressure of this fluid on the brain can have substantial adverse consequences. None of those problems are related to advanced maternal age.

The physician on call for the birthing center was telephoned immediately, and he ordered the baby to be moved to the Pleasant City General Hospital Neonatal Intensive Care Unit, which he called to inform of the baby's imminent arrival. Physicians at the Neonatal Intensive Care Unit concluded that the child would die of infection within a few months if the opening in the spine were not closed. To give Baby Roe any chance of long term survival, dozens of operations and virtually full time hospitalization would be required over a two year period. With maximum intervention, he might live 60 or 70 years. During this existence, he might be able to feel pain and experience pleasure; the physicians simply could not be sure. If he had any cognitive ability whatsoever, he would be likely to be severely mentally and physically disabled.

The parents, who are extremely distraught, are very angry that their child was moved to the Neonatal Intensive Care Unit. They believe that he should not have been removed without their consent, which they would have denied. The parents have also denied consent for the placement of a shunt necessary to minimize the effect of the hydrocephalus by relieving pressure on the brain. In addition, they refuse consent to the heart wall repair which is necessary to keep their son alive. The family physician and all other physicians working in the Neonatal Intensive Care Unit agree that it would be medically appropriate either to provide all treatment or not to provide any treatment in this case.

One of the nurses, however, disagrees. She explains that she recognizes the awful dilemma faced by the parents, but she believes that their needs can be attained in ways that do not result in the death of their child. As she points out, the state child protective services agency has a list of members of the local Citizens for Life organization who are willing to adopt immediately any child born with any serious birth defect. People on the list are willing to provide the full cost of any treatment required by such children. The nurse believes the case should be referred to the state child protective service agency, which can then arrange for the termination of current parental rights and the adoption of the child by someone who will provide adequate medical care.

What actions ought the parents, physicians, nurses, and others take? What judicial consequences could (and should) each medical decision have?

Note: Treating Seriously Ill Newborns

If it is difficult to apply the principle of autonomy to an incompetent adult who has been competent, and nearly impossible to apply that principle to serve an incompetent adult who has never been competent (but who has expressed likes and dislikes), it is simply impossible to apply that principle to a seriously ill newborn. The principle of beneficence, then, must become primary. The obligation of health care professionals and institutions is to do what is in the best interest of the child. As a matter of general course, because parents are presumed to be acting in the best interest of their children, parents of seriously ill newborns traditionally have been permitted to determine whether their infants would receive treatment, and what kind of treatment that should be. Thus, if a parent of a newborn with some severe anomaly determined that it would be best for that child not to receive life-sustaining treatment, that determination traditionally was honored even though it would result in the certain death of a child whose life otherwise might be saved.

The question of what treatment must be provided to a seriously ill newborn, however, has proved to be not quite so simple. Philosophically, the difficulties arise out of the fact that parents of newborn infants with serious defects may not always act entirely in the best interest of those infants. While parents undoubtedly feel responsibility for all of their children, a seriously ill newborn is likely to be a particularly great financial and emotional drain on the parents and the rest of the family. With some, however minor, risk that the parents' interest will be in conflict with the newborn's best interest, should we still allow the parents to make health care decisions for their newborn child? In addition, questions surrounding seriously ill newborns often require a determination of whether life-sustaining treatment should be forgone. Is it philosophically sensible to declare that death is in the "best interest" of a newborn who may be capable of so little brain activity that he will be without pain? What can "best interest" mean under such circumstances? Is it any easier to apply the principle of beneficence than the principle of autonomy under these conditions?

These are precisely the kinds of questions that are generally answered at the local institutional level within our health care system. Indeed, that is exactly what had been happening throughout the country; the ultimate determination generally was left to the parents, who were heavily influenced by the hospital medical staff.

Without much public attention, and with discussion limited primarily to medical and ethical professional organizations, somewhat different standards were applied in somewhat different institutions. Then came Baby Doe.

THE BABY DOE CASES

Baby Doe was born on April 9, 1982, in Bloomington, Indiana. He was born with Down's Syndrome and a tracheoesophageal fistula which would require repair to allow the baby to consume nutrition orally. The parents decided not to authorize the necessary surgery, and the baby was given phenobarbital and morphine until he died, six days after birth. During Baby Doe's short life he was the subject of a suit commenced by the hospital in the local children's court, which refused to order that the surgery be done. The Indiana Supreme Court denied an extraordinary writ that would have had the same effect, and the attorneys for the hospital were on their way to Washington to seek a stay from the United States Supreme Court when the issue was rendered moot by Baby Doe's death. Baby Doe presents a very clean case for philosophical and jurisprudential analysis. The physicians refused to do the operation because the parents refused to consent. The parents refused to consent because their child had Down's Syndrome. If the child had not been born with Down's Syndrome, he would have been provided the surgery.

Several political groups, including right to life groups and advocacy groups for the developmentally disabled, were outraged by the circumstances of Baby Doe's death. Looking for some way to redress this issue, the Health and Human Services Department hit upon Section 504 of the Rehabilitation Act of 1974, 29 U.S.C.A. § 794, which forbids any agency receiving federal funds from discriminating on the basis of handicap. In March of 1983 the Secretary of Health and Human Services issued emergency regulations to assure that no hospital would avoid providing necessary treatment for seriously ill newborns. These regulations, purportedly authorized by Section 504 of the Rehabilitation Act, provided for federal "Baby Doe squads" to swoop down upon any hospital that put at risk the life or health of a handicapped infant by denying that infant life-sustaining treatment. The regulations also required large signs describing federal policy in all maternity and pediatric wards and newborn nurseries, and they established a toll free number to report violations of the regulation.

The regulations were challenged by the American Academy of Pediatrics, which successfully argued that they were defective because they had not been issued after the notice and comment period required by the Administrative Procedures Act. American Academy of Pediatrics v. Heckler, 561 F.Supp. 395 (D.D.C.1983). The Department of Health and Human Services then proposed slightly revised regulations ("Baby Doe II") and invited comments. In early 1984 the new final regulations ("Baby Doe III") were issued. These regulations were based on the articulated substantive principle that "nourishment and medically beneficial treatment (as determined with respect to reasonable medical judgments) should not be withheld from handicapped infants solely on the basis of their present or anticipated mental or physical impairments."

Under the final regulations the federal government maintained its investigatory and enforcement roles, state child protective services agencies were required to develop processes to investigate cases of non-treatment of seriously ill newborns, and individual institutions were encouraged to establish "Infant Care Review Committees" to review appropriate cases. The American Medical Association and the American Hospital Association challenged "Baby Doe III" and the Supreme Court, without any majority opinion, ultimately determined that the regulation had been improperly promulgated. Bowen v. American Hospital Association, 476 U.S. 610, 106 S.Ct. 2101, 90 L.Ed.2d 584 (1986).

While the challenge to Baby Doe III was wending its way through the courts, principals on both sides of the issue agreed to a compromise that was turned into the Child Abuse Amendments of 1984, 42 U.S.C.A. § 5102 (1986). This statute is considerably weaker than the regulation that preceded it, but it does condition each state's receipt of some federal child abuse prevention funding on the maintenance of procedures for dealing with reports of the medical neglect of newborns. Regulations issued under the Child Abuse Amendments interpret "medical neglect" to include "the withholding of medically indicated treatment from a disabled infant with a life threatening condition." 45 C.F.R. § 1340.15(b)(1). Further, the regulations provide that the

> "withholding of medically indicated treatment" means the failure to respond to the infant's life threatening conditions by providing treatment (including appropriate nutrition, hydration, and medication) which in the treating physicians' * * * reasonable medical judgment will be most likely to be effective in ameliorating or correcting all such conditions.

45 C.F.R. § 1340.15(b)(2). There is no obligation to provide care to an infant who is "chronically and irreversibly comatose," when the treatment would "merely prolong the dying process" of the infant and not ameliorate or correct the underlying medical problem (and thus be futile), or when the treatment would be "virtually futile" and "inhumane." *Id.* Are these substantively appropriate standards? How could you redraft them, if you could? Is the process for enforcing them (through the potential cut-off of federal funding for state child abuse programs) appropriate? What kind of enforcement mechanism do you think would be better?

Although the issue increasingly rarely arises in the judicial setting, courts are loathe to allow infants who can be "saved" to die. Compare, e.g., Iafelice v. Zarafu, 221 N.J.Super. 278, 534 A.2d 417 (App.Div.1987) (parents may not withhold consent to a shunt to be placed in a spina bifida infant, even when substantial mental retardation is extremely likely) with In re K.I, B.I. and D.M., 735 A.2d 448 (D.C.1999), discussed above. In the United Kingdom, on the other hand, there is far more toleration of a family decision to discontinue treatment of an infant with a "brain incapable of even limited intellectual function. * * * " The British courts are willing to explicitly consider the quality of life of a seriously ill newborn, as was demonstrated in one case in which treatment was not required for a newborn because "[c]oupled with her total physical handicap, the quality of her life will be demonstrably awful and intolerable." In re C (Minor) [1989] 2 All E.R. 782 (C.A.). See also In re J (Minor), [1990] 3 All E.R. 930 (C.A.) (court applies principle of substituted judgment to determine that a severely mentally and physically handicapped baby would not choose to live, and thus certain treatments could be withheld from him). Treatment decisions made for seriously ill newborns depend heavily on the values of the physicians involved in the decision making, and upon the country in which the decision is made. One recent study of attitudes in European neonatal intensive care units showed that newborns were more likely to be kept alive under all circumstances in Hungary, Estonia, Latvia and Italy than they were in the United Kingdom, the Netherlands and Sweden. See M. Rebagliato, Physicians' Attitudes and Relationships With Self-reported Practices in Ten European Countries, 284 JAMA 2451 (2000).

While public interest in this issue started to recede by the mid–1990s, it was revived in 1998 when Dr. Eugene Turner of Port Angeles, Washington was charged with the murder of three day old Conor McInnerney. Conor had been taken to the emergency room when he stopped breathing and the emergency room staff tried to resuscitate him. Under usual circumstances the baby would have been transported to the University Hospital in Seattle, but weather conditions did not permit that. Dr. Turner, who was a respected pediatrician who had practiced in the community for thirty years, arrived at the hospital an hour after the baby arrived, and he, too, tried to resuscitate him. When all of the attempts at resuscitation failed, Dr. Turner declared Conor dead. Later the baby appeared to breathe spontaneously, and Dr. Turner attempted resuscitation again. Again he failed, and, after this attempt, according to some nurses, he put his hand over the baby's mouth and nose until the sporadic breathing stopped. Prosecutors said it was murder, while Dr. Turner says he was just trying to stop the agonal response of a baby already dead. Should Dr. Turner be tried for murder? Should the Medical Quality Assurance Commission in Washington impose a sanction for unprofessional conduct? For abuse of a vulnerable patient? For conduct that lowers the esteem of his profession? Should Dr. Turner be liable to Conor's family in a civil action? What evidence would be significant to you in determining whether he acted appropriately, or committed murder? For a summary of the case (and its resolution), see C. Ostrom, Doctor Censured in Death of 3–Day–Old, Seattle Times, July 22, 1999, B–1.

The structure of the legal analysis regularly applied to these issues was first described in John A. Robertson, Involuntary Euthanasia of Defective Newborns: A Legal Analysis, 27 Stan.L.Rev. 213 (1975). See also Carl E. Schneider, Rights Discourse and Neonatal Euthanasia, 76 Cal. L. Rev. 151 (1988) and Robert F. Weir, Selective Nontreatment of Handicapped Newborns (1984). For an argument for not treating some impaired newborns, see Robert F. Weir and J.F. Bale, Selective Treatment of Neurologically Impaired Neonates, 7 Neurol. Clinics 807 (1989).

Problem: Conjoined Twins

In 2000, after a woman was diagnosed as carrying conjoined (i.e., "Siamese") twins, she left her home village of Xaghra on the Mediterranean island of Gozo to seek medical care at a hospital in the United Kingdom well known for its care of such birth anomalies. At the birth it was clear that one baby's heart and lungs were providing for the circulation in both babies. That baby, Jodie, was generally healthy, while her conjoined sibling, Mary, suffered from severe brain damage as well as other substantial disabilities. The doctors concluded that Jodie could lead a fairly normal life if she were separated from her mother and provided a series of other reconstructive surgeries. Of course, the separation would result in Mary's immediate death. Alternatively, the failure to separate the twins would result in both of their deaths within the next several months.

The devout Catholic parents denied consent for the surgery, saying "[w]e cannot begin to accept or contemplate that one of our children should die to enable the other one to survive." Others also pointed out that the decision to allow Mary to die during the separation surgery could be met with horror in Xaghra, and make it very difficult for the family to return home. The physicians, however, were distressed that both children would be allowed to die when one could be saved, and they sought an order from the court to authorize the separation surgery.

Would it be homicide to do the surgery with the certain knowledge that it would result in Mary's death? Is it medical neglect to deny consent to surgery which will save one child but result in the death of the second? Should the decision be left to the parents, or should the state intervene and exercise its *parens patriae* authority? What would you do if you were (1) a parent of these children? (2) the primary care physician for these children? (3) the judge before whom the case was presented? The court was well briefed in this case. In addition to counsel retained by the parents and the public health service, a guardian ad litem was appointed for each child. What position should each of those GALs take? If the same issue were to arise in the United States, would the Baby Doe regulations apply? Would the surgery be required, permitted (but not required), or forbidden by those regulations?

For a description of this case (and how it came out), see Marjorie Miller, Agonizing Over Who Lives, Dies, Los Angeles Times, September 11, 2000, page A–1, and Alexander MacLeod, Medical, Religious Values Clash Over Conjoined Twins, Christian Science Monitor, September 29, 2000, page 7.

VI.   CRIMINAL & CIVIL LIABILITY IN "RIGHT TO DIE" CASES

A.   CRIMINAL LIABILITY—HOMICIDE

Homicide statutes in the United States take many forms, but most provide for two degrees of murder, some lower degree of intentional homicide and a form of grossly negligent homicide. Murder is generally a killing that is accompanied with "malice aforethought," for which the intent to kill is sufficient. Malice aforethought does not require "malice" in the normal English sense of that word. The lower degree of intentional homicide, traditionally called voluntary manslaughter, was historically described as an intentional killing in the heat of passion and upon adequate provocation. The lowest degree of homicide, traditionally called involuntary manslaughter, is unintentional homicide and includes killings that are a result of grossly or criminally negligent conduct.

When a physician removes a ventilator or feeding tube from a patient whose death is intentionally hastened by that act, his act is unlikely to be described as one committed in the heat of passion upon adequate provocation, or as one that is grossly negligent. It constitutes murder if the health-care professional who discontinues the support acts with "malice aforethought" which, as we have seen, encompasses the intent to kill. Performing an act that is known to result in the death of another is treated as an act done with the intent to cause the death of another. When a physician discontinues a ventilator or removes a feeding tube knowing that his act will cause the death of the patient he acts with "malice aforethought" for purposes of the homicide statute. Thus, if the removal of life-support systems is to constitute homicide at all, it is likely to constitute murder, and not some lesser degree of homicide.

Further, one of the characteristics that distinguishes first degree murder from second degree in many jurisdictions is the presence of "premeditation." A murder is premeditated if the perpetrator has contemplated his act, even for a moment, before performing that act. Those health care professionals who discontinue life-support systems properly have given the matter a great deal of thought and consideration. They must admit to having reflected upon the nature and consequences of their act to avoid allegations of malpractice.

Thus, if their act constitutes homicide it must constitute murder, and if their act constitutes murder, it is likely to constitute first degree murder.

There are two defenses regularly raised in "mercy killing" cases, each doomed to be unsuccessful when it is raised in the context of the termination of life-support systems. First, it is tempting to argue that a physician terminating life-support systems is merely shortening the life of the patient, not ending it. This is an inadequate defense to a homicide charge because the most a murderer ever can do is shorten the life of his victim; no one lives forever. Second, it is argued that the health-care professional who discontinues life-support systems, or who fails to initiate them, has committed no "act," and the commission of an act is required before there can be any criminal prosecution. There are times, however, when an omission (rather than an act) can constitute the actus reus of a crime. Where there is a duty to act, a breach of that duty through inaction fulfills the requirement of an act under the criminal statute. The physician has a duty to provide adequate care to his patient; if he fails to do so his omission is treated as an act for purposes of the criminal law.

If all the elements for a homicide crime are present, a defendant may be found not guilty only if the homicide can be shown not to be unlawful. Normally, a killing is unlawful unless it is justifiable or excusable. The definitions of justifiable and excusable homicide are rather narrow and, once again, historically well defined. Excusable homicide includes accidental homicide and homicide committed by a person who is insane or, under some circumstances, by a person who acts under duress. Justifiable homicide includes killing in self-defense. Might there be other lawful homicides that are neither excusable or justifiable? *See Barber v. Superior Court*, 147 Cal.App.3d 1006, 195 Cal.Rptr. 484 (1983).

The American law of homicide, heir to 500 years of English common law development, is simply not adequate to deal with the proper termination of life-support systems. Applying the criminal law in this area seems wholly misdirected and utterly foolish. Nonetheless, the criminal law is generally strictly construed, and unless it is modified by the legislature its strict terms, however apparently irrelevant or anachronistic, may continue to be applied by the courts.

As noted above, the issue of whether the discontinuation of treatment constitutes homicide very rarely arises in the course of actual criminal prosecutions; it arises more regularly where a physician, a hospital, or the family of a patient seeks a court order allowing the discontinuation of life-support systems and a declaratory judgment that such discontinuation will not constitute criminal conduct. Virtually every court that has been faced with this issue and that has determined that it would be appropriate that life-support systems be discontinued has also found that no criminal liability would result. This result is as obvious to the courts as it is to outside observers; it would be inconsistent for a court to declare conduct to be proper and then determine that the same conduct is criminal. See Matter of Welfare of Colyer, 99 Wash.2d 114, 660 P.2d 738, 751 (1983). See also In re Guardianship of Myers, 62 Ohio Misc.2d 763, 610 N.E.2d 663 (Prob.Ct.1993).

B. CIVIL LIABILITY

Despite the fact that hospital counsel regularly inform their employees that they should minimize their risk of liability by erring on the side of keeping patients alive, physicians and medical institutions are at a greater risk of being sued for maintaining a patient against that patient's will than for allowing that patient to die. There are a host of causes of action that could be filed against a health care provider who improperly fails to discontinue life sustaining treatment: ordinary medical malpractice (negligence), informed consent, battery, negligent or intentional infliction of emotional distress and civil rights actions have all been attempted under these circumstances. While these actions seem unlikely to generate very substantial actual damages, no actual damages are necessary to commence an action for the intentional tort of battery, and it is easy to imagine a jury awarding punitive damages against a health care facility that keeps a patient on life sustaining treatment against that patients will—especially if it appears to have done so to maximize its own profit or to protect itself from liability. For an example of a case which recognized the potential civil liability arising from providing life sustaining treatment against the will of a patient, see *Estate of Leach v. Shapiro*, 13 Ohio App.3d 393, 469 N.E.2d 1047 (Ohio App.1984), (refusal to remove ventilator and nasogastric tube without a court order). But see Anderson v. St. Francis—St.George Hospital, 77 Ohio St.3d 82, 671 N.E.2d 225 (1996) (finding there is no cause of action for "wrongful living").

VII. PHYSICIAN ASSISTED DEATH

A. THE CONSTITUTIONAL FRAMEWORK

WASHINGTON v. GLUCKSBERG

Supreme Court of the United States, 1997.
521 U.S. 702, 117 S.Ct. 2258, 138 L.Ed.2d 772.

REHNQUIST, C. J., delivered the opinion of the Court, in which O'CONNOR, SCALIA, KENNEDY, and THOMAS, JJ., joined. O'CONNOR, J., filed a concurring opinion, in which GINSBURG and BREYER, JJ., joined in part. STEVENS, J., SOUTER, J., GINSBURG, J., and BREYER, J., filed opinions concurring in the judgment.

CHIEF JUSTICE REHNQUIST delivered the opinion of the Court.

The question presented in this case is whether Washington's prohibition against "causing" or "aiding" a suicide offends the Fourteenth Amendment to the United States Constitution. We hold that it does not.

* * *

The plaintiffs assert[ ] "the existence of a liberty interest protected by the Fourteenth Amendment which extends to a personal choice by a mentally competent, terminally ill adult to commit physician-assisted suicide." [ ] Relying primarily on Planned Parenthood v. Casey, [ ] and Cruzan v. Director, Missouri Dept. of Health, [ ] the District Court agreed, [ ] and concluded that Washington's assisted-suicide ban is unconstitutional because it "places an undue burden on the exercise of [that] constitutionally protected liberty interest." [ ] The District Court also decided that the Washington statute violated the Equal Protection Clause's requirement that " 'all persons similarly situated . . . be treated alike.' "[ ]

A panel of the Court of Appeals for the Ninth Circuit reversed, emphasizing that "in the two hundred and five years of our existence no constitutional right to aid in killing oneself has ever been asserted and upheld by a court of final jurisdiction." [ ] The Ninth Circuit reheard the case en banc, reversed the panel's decision, and affirmed the District Court. [ ] Like the District Court, the en banc Court of Appeals emphasized our Casey and Cruzan decisions. [ ] The court also discussed what it described as "historical" and "current societal attitudes" toward suicide and assisted suicide, [ ] and concluded that "the Constitution encompasses a due process liberty interest in controlling the time and manner of one's death—that there is, in short, a constitutionally-recognized 'right to die.' "[ ] After "weighing and then balancing" this interest against Washington's various interests, the court held that the State's assisted-suicide ban was unconstitutional "as applied to terminally ill competent [ ] adults who wish to hasten their deaths with medication prescribed by their physicians." [ ] We granted certiorari [ ] and now reverse.

I

We begin, as we do in all due-process cases, by examining our Nation's history, legal traditions, and practices. [ ] In almost every State—indeed, in almost every western democracy—it is a crime to assist a suicide. The States' assisted-suicide bans are not innovations. Rather, they are longstanding expressions of the States' commitment to the protection and preservation of all human life. [ ] Indeed, opposition to and condemnation of suicide—and, therefore, of assisting suicide—are consistent and enduring themes of our philosophical, legal, and cultural heritages. [ ]

More specifically, for over 700 years, the Anglo—American common-law tradition has punished or otherwise disapproved of both suicide and assisting suicide. * * * [The Chief Justice then reviews the common law of England and the American colonies and states with regards to suicide, from the 13th century to the present.]

* * *

Attitudes toward suicide itself have changed since [the 13th Century prohibitions on suicide] * * * but our laws have consistently condemned, and continue to prohibit, assisting suicide. Despite changes in medical technology and notwithstanding an increased emphasis on the importance of end-of-life decisionmaking, we have not retreated from this prohibition. Against this backdrop of history, tradition, and practice, we now turn to respondents' constitutional claim.

II

The Due Process Clause guarantees more than fair process, and the "liberty" it protects includes more than the absence of physical restraint. [ ] The Clause also provides heightened protection against government interference with certain fundamental rights and liberty interests. [ ] In a long line of cases, we have held that, in addition to the specific freedoms protected by the Bill of Rights, the "liberty" specially protected by the Due Process Clause includes the rights to marry, [ ]; to have children, [ ]; to direct the education and upbringing of one's children, [ ]; to marital privacy, [ ]; to use contraception, [ ]; to bodily integrity, [ ] and to abortion, [ ]. We have also assumed, and strongly suggested, that the Due Process Clause protects the traditional right to refuse unwanted lifesaving medical treatment. [ ]

But we "have always been reluctant to expand the concept of substantive due process because guideposts for responsible decisionmaking in this unchartered area are scarce and open-ended." [ ] By extending constitutional protection to an asserted right or liberty interest, we, to a great extent, place the matter outside the arena of public debate and legislative action. We must therefore "exercise the utmost care whenever we are asked to break new ground in this field" [ ] lest the liberty protected by the Due Process Clause be subtly transformed into the policy preferences of the members of this Court [ ].

Our established method of substantive-due-process analysis has two primary features: First, we have regularly observed that the Due Process Clause specially protects those fundamental rights and liberties which are, objectively, "deeply rooted in this Nation's history and tradition" [ ] and "implicit in the concept of ordered liberty," such that "neither liberty nor justice would exist if they were sacrificed" [ ]. Second, we have required in substantive-due-process cases a "careful description" of the asserted fundamental liberty interest. [ ] Cruzan, supra, at 277–278. Our Nation's history, legal traditions, and practices thus provide the crucial "guideposts for responsible decision-making" [ ] that direct and restrain our exposition of the Due Process Clause. As we stated recently in Flores, the Fourteenth Amendment "forbids the government to infringe ... 'fundamental' liberty interests at all, no matter what process is provided, unless the infringement is narrowly tailored to serve a compelling state interest." [ ]

* * *

Turning to the claim at issue here, the Court of Appeals stated that "properly analyzed, the first issue to be resolved is whether there is a liberty interest in determining the time and manner of one's death" [ ] or, in other words, "is there a right to die?" [ ]. Similarly, respondents assert a "liberty to choose how to die" and a right to "control of one's final days," [ ] and describe the asserted liberty as "the right to choose a humane, dignified death" [ ] and "the liberty to shape death" [ ]. As noted above, we have a tradition of carefully formulating the interest at stake in substantive-due-process cases. For example, although Cruzan is often described as a "right to die" case [ ] we were, in fact, more precise: we assumed that the Constitution granted competent persons a "constitutionally protected right to refuse life-saving hydration and nutrition." [ ] The Washington statute at issue in this case prohibits "aiding another person to attempt suicide," [ ] and, thus, the question before us is whether the "liberty" specially protected by the Due Process Clause includes a right to commit suicide which itself includes a right to assistance in doing so.

* * * With this "careful description" of respondents' claim in mind, we turn to Casey and Cruzan.

[The Chief Justice next discusses the Cruzan case, where, he says,] "we assumed that the United States Constitution would grant a competent person a constitutionally protected right to refuse lifesaving hydration and nutrition."

* * *

The right assumed in Cruzan, however, was not simply deduced from abstract concepts of personal autonomy. Given the common-law rule that forced medication was a battery, and the long legal tradition protecting the decision to refuse unwanted medical treatment, our assumption was entirely consistent with this Nation's history and constitutional traditions. The decision to commit suicide with the assistance of another may be just as personal and profound as the decision to refuse unwanted medical treatment, but it has never enjoyed similar legal protection. Indeed, the two acts are widely and reasonably regarded as quite distinct. [ ] In Cruzan itself, we recognized that most States outlawed assisted suicide?and even more do today—and we certainly gave no intimation that the right to refuse unwanted medical treatment could be somehow transmuted into a right to assistance in committing suicide. [ ]

Respondents also rely on Casey. There, the Court's opinion concluded that "the essential holding of Roe v. Wade should be retained and once again reaffirmed." [ ] We held, first, that a woman has a right, before her fetus is viable, to an abortion "without undue interference from the State"; second, that States may restrict post-viability abortions, so long as exceptions are made to protect a woman's life and health; and third, that the State has legitimate interests throughout a pregnancy in protecting the health of the woman and the life of the unborn child. [ ] In reaching this conclusion, the opinion discussed in some detail this Court's substantive-due-process tradition of interpreting the Due Process Clause to protect certain fundamental rights and "personal decisions relating to marriage, procreation, contraception, family relationships, child rearing, and education," and noted that many of those rights and liberties "involve the most intimate and personal choices a person may make in a lifetime." [ ]

* * *

That many of the rights and liberties protected by the Due Process Clause sound in personal autonomy does not warrant the sweeping conclusion that any and all important, intimate, and personal decisions are so protected, [ ] and Casey did not suggest otherwise.

The history of the law's treatment of assisted suicide in this country has been and continues to be one of the rejection of nearly all efforts to permit it. That being the case, our decisions lead us to conclude that the asserted "right" to assistance in committing suicide is not a fundamental liberty interest protected by the Due Process Clause. The Constitution also requires, however, that Washington's assisted-suicide ban be rationally related to legitimate government interests. [ ] This requirement is unquestionably met here. As the court below recognized, [ ] Washington's assisted-suicide ban implicates a number of state interests. [ ]

First, Washington has an "unqualified interest in the preservation of human life."

* * *

Relatedly, all admit that suicide is a serious public-health problem, especially among persons in otherwise vulnerable groups. [ ] The State has an interest in preventing suicide, and in studying, identifying, and treating its causes. [ ]

* * *

The State also has an interest in protecting the integrity and ethics of the medical profession. * * * [T]he American Medical Association, like many other medical and physicians' groups, has concluded that "physician-assisted suicide is fundamentally incompatible with the physician's role as healer." [ ] And physician-assisted suicide could, it is argued, undermine the trust that is essential to the doctor-patient relationship by blurring the time-honored line between healing and harming. [ ]

Next, the State has an interest in protecting vulnerable groups—including the poor, the elderly, and disabled persons—from abuse, neglect, and mistakes. * * * [One respected state task force] warned that "legalizing physician-assisted suicide would pose profound risks to many individuals who are ill and vulnerable.... The risk of harm is greatest for the many individuals in our society whose autonomy and well-being are already compromised by poverty, lack of access to good medical care, advanced age, or membership in a stigmatized social group." [ ] If physician-assisted suicide were permitted, many might resort to it to spare their families the substantial financial burden of end-of-life health-care costs.

* * * The State's assisted-suicide ban reflects and reinforces its policy that the lives of terminally ill, disabled, and elderly people must be no less valued than the lives of the young and healthy, and that a seriously disabled person's suicidal impulses should be interpreted and treated the same way as anyone else's. [ ]

Finally, the State may fear that permitting assisted suicide will start it down the path to voluntary and perhaps even involuntary euthanasia. * * * [Justice Rehnquist then discussed how this fear could arise out of the practice in the Nertherlands.]

We need not weigh exactingly the relative strengths of these various interests. They are unquestionably important and legitimate, and Washington's ban on assisted suicide is at least reasonably related to their promotion and protection. We therefore hold that [ ] [the Washington ban on assisting suicide] does not violate the Fourteenth Amendment, either on its face or "as applied to competent, terminally ill adults who wish to hasten their deaths by obtaining medication prescribed by their doctors."[6] [ ]

* * *

6. Justice Stevens states that "the Court does conceive of respondents' claim as a facial challenge—addressing not the application of the statute to a particular set of plaintiffs before it, but the constitutionality of the statute's categorical prohibition...." [ ] We emphasize that we today reject the Court of Appeals' specific holding that the statute is

Throughout the Nation, Americans are engaged in an earnest and profound debate about the morality, legality, and practicality of physician-assisted suicide. Our holding permits this debate to continue, as it should in a democratic society. The decision of the en banc Court of Appeals is reversed, and the case is remanded for further proceedings consistent with this opinion.

It is so ordered.

JUSTICE O'CONNOR, concurring [in both Glucksberg and Vacco].*

Death will be different for each of us. For many, the last days will be spent in physical pain and perhaps the despair that accompanies physical deterioration and a loss of control of basic bodily and mental functions. Some will seek medication to alleviate that pain and other symptoms.

The Court frames the issue in this case as whether the Due Process Clause of the Constitution protects a "right to commit suicide which itself includes a right to assistance in doing so," [ ] and concludes that our Nation's history, legal traditions, and practices do not support the existence of such a right. I join the Court's opinions because I agree that there is no generalized right to "commit suicide." But respondents urge us to address the narrower question whether a mentally competent person who is experiencing great suffering has a constitutionally cognizable interest in controlling the circumstances of his or her imminent death. I see no need to reach that question in the context of the facial challenges to the New York and Washington laws at issue here. [ ] The parties and amici agree that in these States a patient who is suffering from a terminal illness and who is experiencing great pain has no legal barriers to obtaining medication, from qualified physicians, to alleviate that suffering, even to the point of causing unconsciousness and hastening death. [ ] In this light, even assuming that we would recognize such an interest, I agree that the State's interests in protecting those who are not truly competent or facing imminent death, or those whose decisions to hasten death would not truly be voluntary, are sufficiently weighty to justify a prohibition against physician-assisted suicide. [ ]

Every one of us at some point may be affected by our own or a family member's terminal illness. There is no reason to think the democratic process will not strike the proper balance between the interests of terminally ill, mentally competent individuals who would seek to end their suffering and the State's interests in protecting those who might seek to end life mistakenly or under pressure. As the Court recognizes, States are presently undertaking extensive and serious evaluation of physician-assisted suicide and other related issues. [ ] In such circumstances, "the ... challenging task of crafting appropriate procedures for safeguarding ... liberty interests is entrusted to the 'laboratory' of the States ... in the first instance." [ ]

unconstitutional "as applied" to a particular class. [ ] Justice Stevens agrees with this holding, [ ] but would not "foreclose the possibility that an individual plaintiff seeking to hasten her death, or a doctor whose assistance was sought, could prevail in a more particularized challenge," ibid. Our opinion does not absolutely foreclose such a claim. However, given our holding that the Due Process Clause of the Fourteenth Amendment does not provide heightened protection to the asserted liberty interest in ending one's life with a physician's assistance, such a claim would have to be quite different from the ones advanced by respondents here.

* Justice Ginsburg concurs in the Court's judgments substantially for the reasons stated in this opinion. Justice Breyer joins this opinion except insofar as it joins the opinions of the Court.

In sum, there is no need to address the question whether suffering patients have a constitutionally cognizable interest in obtaining relief from the suffering that they may experience in the last days of their lives. There is no dispute that dying patients in Washington and New York can obtain palliative care, even when doing so would hasten their deaths. The difficulty in defining terminal illness and the risk that a dying patient's request for assistance in ending his or her life might not be truly voluntary justifies the prohibitions on assisted suicide we uphold here.

JUSTICE STEVENS, concurring in the judgments [in both Glucksberg and Vacco].

The Court ends its opinion with the important observation that our holding today is fully consistent with a continuation of the vigorous debate about the "morality, legality, and practicality of physician-assisted suicide" in a democratic society. [ ] I write separately to make it clear that there is also room for further debate about the limits that the Constitution places on the power of the States to punish the practice.

I

The morality, legality, and practicality of capital punishment have been the subject of debate for many years. In 1976, this Court upheld the constitutionality of the practice in cases coming to us from Georgia, Florida, and Texas. In those cases we concluded that a State does have the power to place a lesser value on some lives than on others; there is no absolute requirement that a State treat all human life as having an equal right to preservation. Because the state legislatures had sufficiently narrowed the category of lives that the State could terminate, and had enacted special procedures to ensure that the defendant belonged in that limited category, we concluded that the statutes were not unconstitutional on their face. In later cases coming to us from each of those States, however, we found that some applications of the statutes were unconstitutional.

Today, the Court decides that Washington's statute prohibiting assisted suicide is not invalid "on its face," that is to say, in all or most cases in which it might be applied. That holding, however, does not foreclose the possibility that some applications of the statute might well be invalid.

* * *

History and tradition provide ample support for refusing to recognize an open-ended constitutional right to commit suicide. Much more than the State's paternalistic interest in protecting the individual from the irrevocable consequences of an ill-advised decision motivated by temporary concerns is at stake. There is truth in John Donne's observation that "No man is an island." The State has an interest in preserving and fostering the benefits that every human being may provide to the community—a community that thrives on the exchange of ideas, expressions of affection, shared memories and humorous incidents as well as on the material contributions that its members create and support. The value to others of a person's life is far too precious to allow the individual to claim a constitutional entitlement to complete autonomy in making a decision to end that life. Thus, I fully agree with the Court that the "liberty" protected by the Due Process Clause does not include a categorical "right to commit suicide which itself includes a right to assistance in doing so." [ ]

But just as our conclusion that capital punishment is not always unconstitutional did not preclude later decisions holding that it is sometimes impermissibly cruel, so is it equally clear that a decision upholding a general statutory prohibition of assisted suicide does not mean that every possible application of the statute would be valid. A State, like Washington, that has authorized the death penalty and thereby has concluded that the sanctity of human life does not require that it always be preserved, must acknowledge that there are situations in which an interest in hastening death is legitimate. Indeed, not only is that interest sometimes legitimate, I am also convinced that there are times when it is entitled to constitutional protection.

II

In Cruzan [ ] the Court assumed that the interest in liberty protected by the Fourteenth Amendment encompassed the right of a terminally ill patient to direct the withdrawal of life-sustaining treatment. As the Court correctly observes today, that assumption "was not simply deduced from abstract concepts of personal autonomy." [ ] Instead, it was supported by the common-law tradition protecting the individual's general right to refuse unwanted medical treatment. [ ] We have recognized, however, that this common-law right to refuse treatment is neither absolute nor always sufficiently weighty to overcome valid countervailing state interests. * * *

Cruzan, however, was not the normal case. Given the irreversible nature of her illness and the progressive character of her suffering, Nancy Cruzan's interest in refusing medical care was incidental to her more basic interest in controlling the manner and timing of her death. In finding that her best interests would be served by cutting off the nourishment that kept her alive, the trial court did more than simply vindicate Cruzan's interest in refusing medical treatment; the court, in essence, authorized affirmative conduct that would hasten her death. When this Court reviewed the case and upheld Missouri's requirement that there be clear and convincing evidence establishing Nancy Cruzan's intent to have life-sustaining nourishment withdrawn, it made two important assumptions: (1) that there was a "liberty interest" in refusing unwanted treatment protected by the Due Process Clause; and (2) that this liberty interest did not "end the inquiry" because it might be outweighed by relevant state interests. [ ] I agree with both of those assumptions, but I insist that the source of Nancy Cruzan's right to refuse treatment was not just a common-law rule. Rather, this right is an aspect of a far broader and more basic concept of freedom that is even older than the common law. This freedom embraces, not merely a person's right to refuse a particular kind of unwanted treatment, but also her interest in dignity, and in determining the character of the memories that will survive long after her death. In recognizing that the State's interests did not outweigh Nancy Cruzan's liberty interest in refusing medical treatment, Cruzan rested not simply on the common-law right to refuse medical treatment, but—at least implicitly—on the even more fundamental right to make this "deeply personal decision," [ ].

* * *

While I agree with the Court that Cruzan does not decide the issue presented by these cases, Cruzan did give recognition, not just to vague, unbridled notions of autonomy, but to the more specific interest in making decisions about how to confront an imminent death. Although there is no absolute right to physician-assisted suicide, Cruzan makes it clear that some individuals who no longer have the option of deciding whether to live or to die because they are already on the threshold of death have a constitutionally protected interest that may outweigh the State's interest in preserving life at all costs. The liberty interest at stake in a case like this differs from, and is stronger than, both the common-law right to refuse medical treatment and the unbridled interest in deciding whether to live or die. It is an interest in deciding how, rather than whether, a critical threshold shall be crossed.

III

The state interests supporting a general rule banning the practice of physician-assisted suicide do not have the same force in all cases. First and foremost of these interests is the " 'unqualified interest in the preservation of human life' "[ ].

* * *. Although as a general matter the State's interest in the contributions each person may make to society outweighs the person's interest in ending her life, this interest does not have the same force for a terminally ill patient faced not with the choice of whether to live, only of how to die. * * *

Similarly, the State's legitimate interests in preventing suicide, protecting the vulnerable from coercion and abuse, and preventing euthanasia are less significant in this context. I agree that the State has a compelling interest in preventing persons from committing suicide because of depression, or coercion by third parties. But the State's legitimate interest in preventing abuse does not apply to an individual who is not victimized by abuse, who is not suffering from depression, and who makes a rational and voluntary decision to seek assistance in dying.

* * *

The final major interest asserted by the State is its interest in preserving the traditional integrity of the medical profession. The fear is that a rule permitting physicians to assist in suicide is inconsistent with the perception that they serve their patients solely as healers. But for some patients, it would be a physician's refusal to dispense medication to ease their suffering and make their death tolerable and dignified that would be inconsistent with the healing role * * * .

* * * I do not * * * foreclose the possibility that an individual plaintiff seeking to hasten her death, or a doctor whose assistance was sought, could prevail in a more particularized challenge. Future cases will determine whether such a challenge may succeed.

IV

* * *

There may be little distinction between the intent of a terminally-ill patient who decides to remove her life-support and one who seeks the assistance of a doctor in ending her life; in both situations, the patient is seeking to hasten a certain, impending death. The doctor's intent might also be the same in prescribing lethal medication as it is in terminating life support. * * *

Thus, although the differences the majority notes in causation and intent between terminating life-support and assisting in suicide support the Court's rejection of the respondents' facial challenge, these distinctions may be inapplicable to particular terminally ill patients and their doctors. Our holding today in Vacco v. Quill that the Equal Protection Clause is not violated by New York's classification, just like our holding in Washington v. Glucksberg that the Washington statute is not invalid on its face, does not foreclose the possibility that some applications of the New York statute may impose an intolerable intrusion on the patient's freedom.

There remains room for vigorous debate about the outcome of particular cases that are not necessarily resolved by the opinions announced today. How such cases may be decided will depend on their specific facts. In my judgment, however, it is clear that the so-called "unqualified interest in the preservation of human life," [ ] is not itself sufficient to outweigh the interest in liberty that may justify the only possible means of preserving a dying patient's dignity and alleviating her intolerable suffering.

JUSTICE SOUTER, concurring in the judgment.

* * *

When the physicians claim that the Washington law deprives them of a right falling within the scope of liberty that the Fourteenth Amendment guarantees against denial without due process of law, they are not claiming some sort of procedural defect in the process through which the statute has been enacted or is administered. Their claim, rather, is that the State has no substantively adequate justification for barring the assistance sought by the patient and sought to be offered by the physician. Thus, we are dealing with a claim to one of those rights sometimes described as rights of substantive due process and sometimes as unenumerated rights, in view of the breadth and indeterminacy of the "due process" serving as the claim's textual basis. The doctors accordingly arouse the skepticism of those who find the Due Process Clause an unduly vague or oxymoronic warrant for judicial review of substantive state law, just as they also invoke two centuries of American constitutional practice in recognizing unenumerated, substantive limits on governmental action. * * *

* * *

[Justice Souter explained that he was adopting Justice Harlan's approach to the Constitutional evaluation and protection of unenumerated rights under the Due Process Clause, as articulated in his dissent in Poe v. Ullman.] My understanding of unenumerated rights in the wake of the Poe dissent and subsequent cases avoids the absolutist failing of many older cases without embracing the opposite pole of equating reasonableness with past practice described at a very specific level. [ ] That understanding begins with a concept of "ordered liberty," [ ] comprising a continuum of rights to be free from "arbitrary impositions and purposeless restraints" [ ].

* * *

This approach calls for a court to assess the relative "weights" or dignities of the contending interests, and to this extent the judicial method is familiar to the common law. Common law method is subject, however, to two important constraints in the hands of a court engaged in substantive due process review. First, such a court is bound to confine the values that it recognizes to those truly deserving constitutional stature, either to those expressed in constitutional text, or those exemplified by "the traditions from which [the Nation] developed," or revealed by contrast with "the traditions from which it broke." [ ]

The second constraint, again, simply reflects the fact that constitutional review, not judicial lawmaking, is a court's business here. The weighing or valuing of contending interests in this sphere is only the first step, forming the basis for determining whether the statute in question falls inside or outside the zone of what is reasonable in the way it resolves the conflict between the interests of state and individual.

* * *

The State has put forward several interests to justify the Washington law as applied to physicians treating terminally ill patients, even those competent to make responsible choices: protecting life generally [ ] discouraging suicide even if knowing and voluntary [ ] and protecting terminally ill patients from involuntary suicide and euthanasia, both voluntary and nonvoluntary [ ].

It is not necessary to discuss the exact strengths of the first two claims of justification in the present circumstances, for the third is dispositive for me. * * * [Justice Souter then explained why the Washington state legislature, on the basis of information now available, could have reasonably decided that a statute forbidding assisting suicide might protect terminally ill patients.]

* * *

The Court should accordingly stay its hand to allow reasonable legislative consideration. While I do not decide for all time that respondents' claim should not be recognized, I acknowledge the legislative institutional competence as the better one to deal with that claim at this time.

JUSTICE BREYER, concurring in the judgments [in both Glucksberg and Vacco].

I believe that Justice O'Connor's views, which I share, have greater legal significance than the Court's opinion suggests. I join her separate opinion, except insofar as it joins the majority. * * *

I agree with the Court in Vacco v. Quill [ ] that the articulated state interests justify the distinction drawn between physician assisted suicide and withdrawal of life-support. I also agree with the Court that the critical question in both of the cases before us is whether "the 'liberty' specially protected by the Due Process Clause includes a right" of the sort that the respondents assert. [ ] I do not agree, however, with the Court's formulation of that claimed "liberty" interest. The Court describes it as a "right to commit suicide with another's assistance." [ ] But I would not reject the respondents' claim without considering a different formulation, for which our legal tradition may provide greater support. That formulation would use words roughly like a "right to die with dignity." But irrespective of the exact words used, at its core would lie personal control over the manner of death, professional medical assistance, and the avoidance of unnecessary and severe physical suffering—combined.

* * *

I do not believe, however, that this Court need or now should decide whether or a not * * * [a right to die with dignity] is "fundamental." That is because, in my view, the avoidance of severe physical pain (connected with death) would have to comprise an essential part of any successful claim and because * * * the laws before us do not force a dying person to undergo that kind of pain. [ ] Rather, the laws of New York and of Washington do not prohibit doctors from providing patients with drugs sufficient to control pain despite the risk that those drugs themselves will kill. [ ] And under these circumstances the laws of New York and Washington would overcome any remaining significant interests and would be justified, regardless.

* * *

Were the legal circumstances different?—for example, were state law to prevent the provision of palliative care, including the administration of drugs as needed to avoid pain at the end of life?—then the law's impact upon serious and otherwise unavoidable physical pain (and accompanying death) would be more directly at issue. And as JUSTICE O'CONNOR suggests, the Court might have to revisit its conclusions in these cases.

* * *

VACCO v. QUILL

Supreme Court of the United States, 1997.
521 U.S. 793, 117 S.Ct. 2293, 138 L.Ed.2d 834.

CHIEF JUSTICE REHNQUIST delivered the opinion of the Court.

In New York, as in most States, it is a crime to aid another to commit or attempt suicide, but patients may refuse even lifesaving medical treatment. The question presented by this case is whether New York's prohibition on assisting suicide therefore violates the Equal Protection Clause of the Fourteenth Amendment. We hold that it does not.

* * * Respondents, and three gravely ill patients who have since died, sued the State's Attorney General in the United States District Court. They urged that because New York permits a competent person to refuse life-sustaining medical treatment, and because the refusal of such treatment is "essentially the same thing" as physician-assisted suicide, New York's assisted-suicide ban violates the Equal Protection Clause. [ ]

The District Court disagreed * * *.

The Court of Appeals for the Second Circuit reversed. [ ] The court determined that, despite the assisted-suicide ban's apparent general applicability, "New York law does not treat equally all competent persons who are in the final stages of fatal illness and wish to hasten their deaths," because "those in the final stages of terminal illness who are on life-support systems are allowed to hasten their deaths by directing the removal of such systems; but those who are similarly situated, except for the previous attachment of life-sustaining equipment, are not allowed to hasten death by self-administering prescribed drugs." [ ] The Court of Appeals then examined whether this supposed unequal treatment was rationally related to any legitimate state interests, and concluded that "to the extent that [New York's statutes] prohibit a physician from prescribing medications to be self-administered by a mentally competent, terminally-ill person in the final stages of his terminal illness, they are not rationally related to any legitimate state interest." [ ] We granted certiorari [ ] and now reverse.

The Equal Protection Clause commands that no State shall "deny to any person within its jurisdiction the equal protection of the laws." This provision creates no substantive rights. [ ] Instead, it embodies a general rule that States must treat like cases alike but may treat unlike cases accordingly. [ ] If a legislative classification or distinction "neither burdens a fundamental right nor targets a suspect class, we will uphold [it] so long as it bears a rational relation to some legitimate end." [ ]

New York's statutes outlawing assisting suicide affect and address matters of profound significance to all New Yorkers alike. They neither infringe fundamental rights nor involve suspect classifications. [ ] These laws are therefore entitled to a "strong presumption of validity." [ ]

On their faces, neither New York's ban on assisting suicide nor its statutes permitting patients to refuse medical treatment treat anyone differently than anyone else or draw any distinctions between persons. Everyone, regardless of physical condition, is entitled, if competent, to refuse unwanted lifesaving medical treatment; no one is permitted to assist a suicide. Generally speaking, laws that apply evenhandedly to all "unquestionably comply" with the Equal Protection Clause. [ ]

The Court of Appeals, however, concluded that some terminally ill people—those who are on life-support systems—are treated differently than those who are not, in that the former may "hasten death" by ending treatment, but the latter may not "hasten death" through physician-assisted suicide. [ ] This conclusion depends on the submission that ending or refusing lifesaving medical treatment "is nothing more nor less than assisted suicide." [ ] Unlike the Court of Appeals, we think the distinction between assisting suicide and withdrawing life-sustaining treatment, a distinction widely recognized and endorsed in the medical profession and in our legal traditions, is both important and logical; it is certainly rational. [ ]

The distinction comports with fundamental legal principles of causation and intent. First, when a patient refuses life-sustaining medical treatment, he dies from an underlying fatal disease or pathology; but if a patient ingests lethal medication prescribed by a physician, he is killed by that medication. [ ]

Furthermore, a physician who withdraws, or honors a patient's refusal to begin, life-sustaining medical treatment purposefully intends, or may so intend, only to respect his patient's wishes and "to cease doing useless and futile or degrading things to the patient when [the patient] no longer stands to benefit from them." [ ] The same is true when a doctor provides aggressive palliative care; in some cases, painkilling drugs may hasten a patient's death, but the physician's purpose and intent is, or may be, only to ease his patient's pain. A doctor who assists a suicide, however, "must, necessarily and indubitably, intend primarily that the patient be made dead." [ ] Similarly, a patient who commits suicide with a doctor's aid necessarily has the specific intent to end his or her own life, while a patient who refuses or discontinues treatment might not. [ ]

The law has long used actors' intent or purpose to distinguish between two acts that may have the same result. [ ] Put differently, the law distinguishes actions taken "because of" a given end from actions taken "in spite of" their unintended but foreseen consequences. [ ]

Given these general principles, it is not surprising that many courts, including New York courts, have carefully distinguished refusing life-sustaining treatment from suicide. * * *

Similarly, the overwhelming majority of state legislatures have drawn a clear line between assisting suicide and withdrawing or permitting the refusal of unwanted lifesaving medical treatment by prohibiting the former and permitting the latter. [ ] And "nearly all states expressly disapprove of suicide and assisted suicide either in statutes dealing with durable powers of attorney in health-care situations, or in 'living will' statutes." [ ] Thus, even as the States move to protect and promote patients' dignity at the end of life, they remain opposed to physician-assisted suicide.

* * *

This Court has also recognized, at least implicitly, the distinction between letting a patient die and making that patient die. In Cruzan [ ] we concluded that "the principle that a competent person has a constitutionally protected liberty interest in refusing unwanted medical treatment may be inferred from our prior decisions," and we assumed the existence of such a right for purposes of that case [ ]. But our assumption of a right to refuse treatment was grounded not, as the Court of Appeals supposed, on the proposition that patients have a general and abstract "right to hasten death," [ ] but on well established, traditional rights to bodily integrity and freedom from unwanted touching [ ]. In fact, we observed that "the majority of States in this country have laws imposing criminal penalties on one who assists another to commit suicide." [ ] Cruzan therefore provides no support for the notion that refusing life-sustaining medical treatment is "nothing more nor less than suicide."

For all these reasons, we disagree with respondents' claim that the distinction between refusing lifesaving medical treatment and assisted suicide is "arbitrary" and "irrational."[7] Granted, in some cases, the line between the two may not be clear, but certainty is not required, even were it possible. Logic and contemporary practice support New York's judgment that the two acts are different, and New York may therefore, consistent with the Constitution, treat them differently. By permitting everyone to refuse unwanted medical treatment while prohibiting anyone from assisting a suicide, New York law follows a longstanding and rational distinction.

---

7. Respondents also argue that the State irrationally distinguishes between physician-assisted suicide and "terminal sedation," a process respondents characterize as "inducing barbiturate coma and then starving the person to death." [ ] Petitioners insist, however, that " 'although proponents of physician-assisted suicide and euthanasia contend that terminal sedation is covert physician-assisted suicide or euthanasia, the concept of sedating pharmacotherapy is based on informed consent and the principle of double effect.' "[ ] Just as a State may prohibit assisting suicide while permitting patients to refuse unwanted lifesaving treatment, it may permit palliative care related to that refusal, which may have the foreseen but unintended "double effect" of hastening the patient's death. [ ]

New York's reasons for recognizing and acting on this distinction—including prohibiting intentional killing and preserving life; preventing suicide; maintaining physicians' role as their patients' healers; protecting vulnerable people from indifference, prejudice, and psychological and financial pressure to end their lives; and avoiding a possible slide towards euthanasia—are discussed in greater detail in our opinion in Glucksberg, ante. These valid and important public interests easily satisfy the constitutional requirement that a legislative classification bear a rational relation to some legitimate end.

The judgment of the Court of Appeals is reversed.

* * *

JUSTICE SOUTER, concurring in the judgment.

Even though I do not conclude that assisted suicide is a fundamental right entitled to recognition at this time, I accord the claims raised by the patients and physicians in this case and Washington v. Glucksberg a high degree of importance, requiring a commensurate justification. [ ] The reasons that lead me to conclude in Glucksberg that the prohibition on assisted suicide is not arbitrary under the due process standard also support the distinction between assistance to suicide, which is banned, and practices such as termination of artificial life support and death-hastening pain medication, which are permitted. I accordingly concur in the judgment of the Court.

* * *

Notes and Questions

1. The Ninth Circuit's *en banc* decision and an extraordinarily diverse and thoughtful set of opinions in Glucksberg can be found at Compassion in Dying v. Washington, 79 F.3d 790 (9th Cir.1996). The en banc court reversed a 2–1 decision of the original panel, which also included an impassioned opinion on each side of the issue. See 49 F.3d 586 (9th Cir.1995). The meticulously organized district court opinion in the Compassion in Dying case is reported at 850 F.Supp. 1454 (W.D.Wash.1994). The Second Circuit's opinion in Quill v. Vacco can be found at 80 F.3d 716 (2nd Cir.1996).

2. These cases generated many highly emotional responses. Although the Supreme Court's unanimous decision brought a semblance of propriety back to the discussion of these issues, supporters and opponents of physician assisted death continue to attack the arguments of their opponents–and, as in the case of the abortion debate–they continue to attack their opponents, too. Some of the commentary on the Ninth Circuit opinions was especially personal. Judge Reinhardt (who wrote the primary decision finding the Washington law to be unconstitutional) was roundly criticized for his ACLU connections, which, some said, made it impossible for him to fairly decide the case. On the other hand, Judge Noonan (who would have upheld the statute for the first panel) had been criticized for his right-to-life connections which, others argued, made it impossible for *him* to be impartial. Should judges recuse themselves from cases involving these difficult and controversial bioethics issues if they have deeply held personal beliefs about the underlying practice—here physician assisted suicide? Does it make a difference if they were members (or officers, or high ranking employees) of organizations which have taken explicit positions on the underlying issues? On the particular case in litigation? Should they recuse themselves if the issue is one on which the religion to which they subscribe has taken a formal position? Should Catholic

judges recuse themselves from abortion and physician assisted death cases? Should judges who belong to the United Church of Christ (which has been strongly pro-choice for over 25 years) recuse themselves from abortion cases? Should the member of a congregation whose rabbi helped organize a voting rights march recuse himself from all voting rights cases? Is their obligation any different from the obligation of a judge who is a dedicated ACLU (or American Family Association, or Republican Party) member and who confronts a case upon which the ACLU (or the American Family Association, or the Republican Party) has taken a firm position? The issue of whether a judge should recuse himself because of his religious affiliation is raised almost exclusively with regard to Catholic judges. Why do you think that is the case?

3. Judge Calabresi concurred in the Second Circuit decision in the Quill case, but on entirely different grounds. Depending on the theory of statutory construction that he had explained fifteen years earlier in his text, A Common Law for the Age of Statutes (1982), he concluded that the history of the New York manslaughter statute suggested that there was no reason to believe that its framers ever intended it to apply to cases of competent terminally ill patients seeking aid in dying from physicians. Still, as he pointed out, "neither Cruzan, nor Casey, nor the language of our Constitution, nor our constitutional tradition clearly makes these laws invalid."

So, what should the court do with a "highly suspect" but "not clearly invalid" statute that may no longer serves the purposes for which it was originally promulgated? The answer, according to Judge Calabresi, is the "constitutional remand."

> I contend that when a law is neither plainly unconstitutional ... nor plainly constitutional, the courts ought not to decide the ultimate validity of that law without current and clearly expressed statements by the people or their elected officials of the state involved. It is my further contention, that, absent such statements, the courts have frequently struck down such laws, while leaving open the possibility of reconsideration if appropriate statements were subsequently made.

Thus, Judge Calabresi finds the New York statute unconstitutional, but he "takes no position" on whether verbatim identical statutes would be constitutional "were New York to reenact them while articulating the reasons for the distinctions it makes* * *." Is this a reasonable way to deal with ancient statutes effectively criminalizing physician assisted death? Is this argument still available to those challenging state statutes that forbid assisting suicide?

4. Why has physician assisted death become such a subject of interest over the last two decades? Daniel Callahan has a suggestion:

> The power of medicine to extend life under poor circumstances is now widely and increasingly feared. The combined powers of a quasi-religious tradition of respect for individual life and a secular tradition of relentless medical progress creates a bias toward aggressive, often unremitting treatment that appears unstoppable.

> How is control to be gained? For many the answer seems obvious and unavoidable: active euthanasia and assisted suicide.

19 Hastings Center Rep., Special Supplement, 4 (Jan./Feb. 1989). Dr. Callahan goes on to suggest that those who strongly oppose active euthanasia, as he does, ought to focus on "dampening * * * the push for medical progress, a return to older traditions of caring as an alternative to curing, and a willingness to accept

decline and death as part of the human conditions (not a notable feature of American medicine)." Id. Is he right? It used to be that people would fear that if they went to the hospital they would die there. Now people fear that if they go to the hospital they will be kept alive there. Is it this fear that gives rise to our current interest in euthanasia?

5. Nothing has done more to keep the spotlight on physician assisted death issues than the actions of Dr. Jack Kevorkian. Dr. Kevorkian employed a "suicide machine" that allowed patients—sometimes young and still relatively healthy patients—to end their lives. Dr. Kevorkian chose Michigan for his practice because assisted suicide *per se* was not a crime in Michigan. On the other hand, an early Michigan case, People v. Roberts, 211 Mich. 187, 178 N.W. 690 (1920), had determined that assisting suicide could constitute murder. In that case a husband pleaded guilty to murder after he placed a poisonous mixture next to his wife, who was suffering from multiple sclerosis, was in excruciating pain, and had begged her husband to help her end her misery. The Michigan court determined that murder by poison, a form of first degree murder, was the proper charge.

In 1990 prosecutors in Michigan indicted Dr. Kevorkian on homicide charges, which were subsequently dismissed. As a direct result of Kevorkian's activities, in 1992 the Michigan legislature created the crime of assistance to suicide, which rendered one criminally liable if one "provide[d] the physical means by which the other person attempt[ed] or commit[ted] suicide" or participated in the physical act of the suicide. Mich. Comp. Laws Ann. section 752–1027. The legislature created this crime with an expiration date to give the state the opportunity to work out this issue without the sense of thoughtless urgency that prevailed in 1992. The statute has since expired.

Just before Michigan's new assisted suicide statute became law, Dr. Kevorkian was again indicted—this time for murder and for the delivery of drugs for an unauthorized purpose. Dr. Kevorkian was bound over for trial on the murder charge, which was subsequently dismissed by the circuit court. As soon as the new assisted suicide statute was passed several terminally ill patients and some health care providers brought a declaratory judgment action seeking to have the new statute declared void because it violated due process, because it passed the legislature in a bill that did not have "a single object," because the purpose of the bill changed during the course of its consideration in the Michigan legislature, and because it was inadequately titled, all in violation of the Michigan constitution. Ultimately the circuit court found the statute unconstitutional in the declaratory judgment action. It was not long before Dr. Kevorkian was charged under the new assisted suicide statute—twice, in fact, once in Wayne County and once in Oakland County. In each case the circuit court dismissed the action because the court found the new assisted suicide statute to be unconstitutional.

All four cases (the second murder case, the two assisted suicide cases and the declaratory judgment case) were appealed to the Michigan Supreme Court, which consolidated them. In December of 1994 a divided Michigan Supreme Court issued a brief *per curiam* memorandum opinion and a series of separate opinions dealing with the various issues raised by the four appeals. The court decided that (1) there was no technical problem in the form of the bill passed by the legislature (by unanimous vote), (2) a criminal statute penalizing assisted suicide does not violate the United States Constitution (5–2 vote), (3) *People v. Roberts* should be overruled; merely intentionally providing the means for another to commit suicide does not, as a general matter, constitute murder (5–2 vote) and (4) whether there was sufficient evidence to prosecute Dr. Kevorkian for murder should be reconsidered by the circuit court (4–3 vote). See People v. Kevorkian, 447 Mich. 436, 527 N.W.2d 714 (1994) for the lengthy, thoughtful and heartfelt opinions on all sides of all of these issues.

Another prosecution for murder ended in a jury verdict of acquittal for Dr. Kevorkian, as did a 1996 prosecution for violation of the Michigan common law crime of assisting suicide (by 1996 he had to be charged under the common law because the Michigan statute had expired).

Finally, on March 26, 1999 Dr. Kevorkian was convicted of second-degree murder after a very short trial in which he represented himself. While past cases had involved Dr. Kevorkian's use of a suicide machine which was actually operated by his client (patient? victim?), in this case he injected a lethal drug directly into Thomas Youk, a 52 year old man suffering from amyotrophic lateral sclerosis (Lou Gehrig's disease). What is more, he filmed the entire process, which was then shown to a national audience on "60 Minutes," the CBS news show, in November, 1998.

Dr. Keviorkian was originally charged with first-degree murder and assisted suicide. The trial judge ruled that evidence of Mr. Youk's suffering, which would be provided by the testimony of his family members, would be relevant and admissible on the assisted suicide charge, but not on the murder charge. The prosecutor decided to drop the assisted suicide charge to keep out that kind of evidence, which had played so well in Dr. Kevorkian's earlier trials. The jury apparently found no premeditation, making the second degree murder conviction the most serious available. Dr. Kevorkian was also found guilty of delivery of a controlled substance.

Leading supporters of euthanasia were concerned by the conviction. The executive director of the Hemlock Society said, "To call it murder is barbaric. It highlights the necessity to change the law over the country * * * so that a compassionate physician can help a suffering patient die." One leader of a disability group expressed satisfaction that this "serial killer" of the disabled had finally been brought to justice. For an account of the trial, see Pam Belluck, Dr. Kevorkian is a Murderer, The Jury Finds, New York Times, March 27, 1999, at A–1.

6.   Physician assisted death may constitute murder, manslaughter, some other form of homicide, or no crime at all, depending on the state statute and the nature of the physician's act. While most states criminalize assisting suicide, it is not always easy to determine which acts are prohibited by those statutes. Consider one representative statute, the California statute criminalizing aiding, advising or encouraging suicide.

> Every person who deliberately aids, or advises, or encourages another to commit suicide, is guilty of a felony.

Cal. Pen. Code § 401.

Would this statute apply to a physician who clamps a feeding tube? To a physician who withholds antibiotics? To a physician who prescribes morphine to a patient in persistent pain, and provides enough tablets to take a lethal dose? To a physician who prescribes that same morphine and tells the patient what would constitute a lethal dose? To those who publish instructions on how to commit suicide for the use of those who are terminally ill or in excruciating pain? To those who make generally available information about how to commit suicide at home? For an interesting application of the statute to those who play rock music with lyrics that suggest that suicide is acceptable, see McCollum v. CBS, Inc., 202 Cal.App.3d 989, 249 Cal.Rptr. 187 (1988).

7.   Much of the American discussion on the propriety of allowing physician assisted death focuses upon the Netherlands, where euthanasia is legally tolerated. As of late 2000, the Dutch were moving towards formal legalization of the process (rather than mere legal toleration) under some circumstances. The Dutch experience is often unfairly distilled into the polemics of those who approve—or disapprove—of the process, and who thus believe that the United States should follow the successful Dutch example—or be dissuaded by its failure. An honest account of the state of euthanasia in the Netherlands is provided by a long time scholar of that issue:

MARGARET PABST BATTIN, A Dozen Caveats Concerning the Discussion of Euthanasia in the Netherlands*

in M.P. Battin, the Least Worst Death 130 (1994).

As the discussion of voluntary active euthanasia heats up in the United States, increasing attention is being given to its practice in the Netherlands. There, euthanasia (and with it, physician-assisted suicide) is more and more openly discussed and practiced; it is performed with the knowledge of the legal authorities; physicians who follow the guidelines are protected from prosecution; and, as a result of broad public discussions of the issue in the media, euthanasia is familiar to virtually all Dutch residents as an option in end-of-life medical care.

In the United States, those who think euthanasia should be legalized often cite the Netherlands as a model of conscientious practice; those who think it should not be legalized, on the other hand, often claim that Dutch practice already involves abuse and will inevitably lead to more. For the most part, these generalizations invite misunderstanding, and they often reflect only the antecedent biases of those who make them. I would like to offer a few caveats for those about to become embroiled in the discussion of euthanasia, as the United States debates whether it, too, will permit this practice—caveats offered in the hope of contributing in better mutual understanding rather than greater polarization over this extremely volatile issue.

LEGAL CLAIMS ARE MISLEADING, EITHER WAY

Many American observers of the Dutch practice of euthanasia are tempted to claim that euthanasia is legal in Holland; others insist that it is not. Both are

---

* Professor Battin's thoughtful account of the Dutch process was written in 1994, when the country was engaged in debate over whether the practice of physician assisted death should be decriminalized rather than simply legally tolerated (but, still, technically criminal). In 1998 the Dutch law was changed to provide for reporting of assisted deaths to a public registrar rather than to a prosecutor in order to separate the medical process from the formal criminal process. In late 2000 the lower house of the Dutch parliament overwhelmingly approved a measure submitted by both the Minister of Health and the Minister of Justice that would make the practice of physician assisted death legal. The new statute restates the Royal Dutch Medical Association's standards, and it provides that an election of physician assisted death be made voluntarily, by a fully informed patient, without suggestion by the

physician, when that patient is confronting unbearable suffering, and after physician consultation with one other physician. The new statute would not require that the patient be terminally ill. A provision in an earlier draft that would have permitted children as young as 12 to elect a physician assisted death was omitted in the final version; the unencumbered choice is available only to those over 16. The new law became effective in the Netherlands in 2001. See Marlise Simons, Dutch Becoming First Nation to Legalize Assisted Suicide, New York Times, November 29, 2000, at A–3, and John–Thor Dahlburg, Dutch Take Step to Make Assisted Suicide Legal, Los Angeles Times, November 29, 2000, at A–4.

You should read Professor Battin's description of this process as an historical one, describing the law and practice during the debate that gave rise to the new legislation in 2001.

right—but only partly so. Killing at the request of the person killed as well as assistance in suicide remain crimes under Dutch penal code, punishable by imprisonment; however, lower and supreme court decisions, reflected in the policies of the regional attorneys-general, further promulgated by the Royal Dutch Medical Association, have held that when euthanasia is performed in accord with a set of guidelines it may be defended under a plea of *force majeure* and so is reasonably sure of not being prosecuted. Recent legal changes have revised the earlier requirement that a physician report euthanasia he or she performs directly to the police; now, under a policy intended to encourage far more self-reporting, the physician is expected to describe the circumstances surrounding and the reasons for euthanasia to the coroner, who is to confer with the local prosecutor and if satisfied that the case meets the guidelines, will issue a certificate of no objection to burial or cremation of the body; the case is not further prosecuted.

* * *

The guidelines, incorporated into [the] statute [of] June 1, 1994, are called "rules of due care." * * * The guidelines, roughly divided into two groups, can be stated as follows:

SUBSTANTIVE GUIDELINES

(a) Euthanasia must be voluntary; the patient's request must be seriously considered and enduring.

(b) The patient must have adequate information about his or her medical condition, the prognosis, and alternative methods of treatment.

(c) The patient's suffering must be intolerable, in the patient's view, and irreversible (though it is not required that the patient be terminally ill).

(d) It must be the case that there are no reasonable alternatives for relieving the patient's suffering that are acceptable to the patient.

PROCEDURAL GUIDELINES

(e) Euthanasia may be performed only by a physician (though a nurse may assist the physician).

(f) The physician must consult with a second physician whose judgment can be expected to be independent.

(g) The physician must exercise due care in reviewing and verifying the patient's condition as well as in performing the euthanasia procedure itself.

(h) The relatives must be informed unless the patient does not wish this.

(i) There should be a written record of the case.

(j) The case may not be reported as a natural death.

Is euthanasia legal or illegal? It is a violation of the statute but is *gedoogd* or "tolerated" if it meets these guidelines, and will not be prosecuted. Yet it is not excused in advance, and the plea of *force majeure*, although often compelling in single cases, does not easily serve as a basis for policy. Until 1990, it was required that any case of euthanasia be reported to the police and investigated after the fact, further prosecution being set aside if the case met the guidelines; in fact, comparatively few cases were reported, and physicians complained that they—and patients' families—were being treated as criminal suspects even when they had met all the guidelines. Policy changes in 1990 avoided the step of initial reporting to and investigation by the police; instead, the physician provides a written account of the case to the medical examiner, who then forwards it to the public prosecutor. If the criteria are satisfied, a certificate of "no objection to burial or cremation" is issued and there is no further investigation. These policy changes, however, have not altered the delicate legal status of euthanasia in the Netherlands—prohibited by law but tolerated under guidelines developed in the courts, and now recognized though not stated in the law—a delicate balance often misunderstood by outside commentators. This delicate legal status has been seen by many observers as a deterrent to abuse; it is also seen by some as accounting for a great deal of the underreporting. In any case, it is clear why the legal status of euthanasia in the Netherlands is so frequently misinterpreted by American commentators; its delicate balance between legality and illegality—the Dutch posture of "tolerance"—would be difficult to replicate in the American legal system.

Exaggerations are Frequent

It is also sometimes supposed that euthanasia is a routine, frequent, everyday practice in the Netherlands, a commonplace that happens all the time. On the contrary, euthanasia is comparatively rare. There are about 2,300 cases of euthanasia per year; these represent just 1.8 percent of the total annual mortality * * *. In addition, there are about 400 cases of physician-assisted suicide, just 0.3 percent of the total annual mortality. Although a substantial proportion of patients, about 25,000 a year, seek their doctors' reassurance of assistance if their suffering becomes unbearable, only 9,000 explicit requests for euthanasia are made annually, and of these, fewer than one third are honored. Thus, the contention sometimes heard that there is widespread euthanasia on demand is seriously exaggerated. The actual frequency of euthanasia is about 1 in 25 deaths that occur at home, about 1 in 75 in hospital deaths, and about 1 in 800 deaths in nursing homes.

The Institutional Circumstances of Euthanasia in the Netherlands are Easily Misunderstood

Although many American observers of Dutch euthanasia risk misinterpreting many features of this practice, a particularly frequent error arises from failing to appreciate differences between health-care delivery systems and other social institutions in the Netherlands and those in the United States. In the United States virtually all physician care is provided in a professional or institutional setting: an office, clinic, care facility, or hospital. By contrast, most primary care in the Netherlands is provided in the patient's home or in the physician's home office by the *huisarts*, the general practitioner or family physician. The family physician, who typically serves a practice of about 2,300 people and is salaried on a capitation basis rather than paid on a fee-for-service basis, typically lives in the neighborhood and makes frequent house calls when a patient is ill. This provides not only closer, more personal contact between physician and patient but also an unparalleled opportunity for the physician to observe features of the patient's domestic circumstances, including any family support or pressures that might be relevant in a request for euthanasia.

Furthermore, all Dutch have a personal physician: this is a basic feature of how primary care is provided within the Netherlands' national health system. While euthanasia is sometimes performed in hospitals (about 700 of the 2,300 cases), usually when the family physician has been unable to control the patient's pain and it has been necessary to readmit the patient to the hospital, or when the patient has had extensive hospital care and feels most "at home" there, and while most hospitals now have protocols for doing so, the large majority of cases take place in the patient's home, typically after hospitalization and treatment have proved ineffective in arresting a terminal condition and the patient has come home to die. In these settings, euthanasia is most often performed by the physician who has been the long-term primary care provider for the family, and it is performed in the presence of the patient's family and others whom the patient may request, such as the visiting nurse or the pastor, but outside public view. Yet the (non) institutional circumstances of euthanasia in the Netherlands (about 40 percent of Dutch deaths occur at home, and 48 percent of cancer deaths), in the United States as many as 85 percent of deaths occur in a hospital or other health-care institution, where attendance by a long-term family physician is far less frequently the case.

* * *

THE DUTCH DON'T WANT TO DEFEND EVERYTHING

The Dutch are sometimes accused of being self-serving or, alternatively, of being self-deceived in their efforts to defend the practice of euthanasia. To be sure, not all Dutch accept the practice. There is a vocal group of about a thousand physicians adamantly opposed to it, and there is some opposition among the public and within specific political parties (in particular, the Christian Democratic Party, which has for years controlled the Netherlands coalition government) and religious groups (especially the Catholic church). Yet the practice is supported by a majority of the Dutch populace * * * as well as a majority of Dutch physicians. Of physicians interviewed for the Remmelink study [the leading neutral report on the practice in the Netherlands], 54 percent said they had practiced euthanasia at the explicit and persistent request of the patient or had assisted in suicide at least once (62 percent of the general practitioners, 44 percent of specialists, and 12 percent of nursing home physicians), and only 4 percent said they would neither perform euthanasia nor refer a patient to a physician who would. In the words of the Remmelink Commission's comment on the report, "a large majority of physicians in the Netherlands see euthanasia as an accepted element of medical practice under certain circumstances."

But this is not to say that the Dutch to seek to whitewash the practice. They are disturbed by reports of cases that do not fit the guidelines and are not explained by other moral considerations although these may be quite infrequent. Of the approximately 1,000 cases of active termination in which there was no explicit, current request * * * 36 percent of patients were competent, the physician knew the patient for an extended period (on average, 2.4 years for a specialist physician, or 7.2 years for a *huisarts* or general practitioner), and in 84 percent life was shortened somewhere between a few hours and a week. Because there was no current, explicit request, these cases are sometimes described in the United States as coldblooded murder, yet most are explained by other moral considerations. Of these 1,000 cases, * * *, about 600 did involve some form of antecedent discussion of euthanasia with the patient. These ranged from a rather vague earlier expression of a wish for euthanasia, as in comments like "If I cannot be saved anymore, you must give me something," or "Doctor, please don't let me suffer for too long," to much more extensive discussions, yet still short of an explicit request. (Thus, these cases are best understood in a way that approximates them to advance-directive cases in other situations.) In all other cases, discussion with the patient was no longer possible. In almost all of the remaining 400 cases, there was neither an antecedent nor current request from the patient, but at the time of euthanasia—possibly with a few exceptions—the patient was very close to death, incapable of communication, and suffering grievously. For the most part, this occurred when the patient underwent unexpectedly rapid deterioration in the final stages of a terminal illness. (These cases are best understood as cases of mercy killing, with emphasis on the motivation of mercy.) In these cases, * * *, "the decision to hasten death was then nearly always taken after consultation with the family, nurses, or one or more colleagues." Most Dutch also defend these cases, though as critics point out, the danger here is that the determination of what counts as intolerable suffering in these cases is essentially up to the doctor.

Direct termination of life is also performed in a handful of pediatric cases, about ten a year, usually involving newborns with extremely severe deficits who are not in the ICU and from whom, therefore, life-prolonging treatment cannot be withdrawn. These cases are regarded as difficult and controversial. Equally controversial—and as rare or rarer—are cases concerning patients in permanent coma or persistent vegetative state; patients whose suffering, though intolerable and incurable, is mental rather than physical; and patients who have made explicit requests for euthanasia by means of advance directives, but after becoming incompetent no longer appear to be suffering.

[There is also some] suggestion, though no clear evidence, that there may be a small fraction of cases in which there is no apparent choice by the patient and in which a merciful end of suffering for a patient *in extremis* is not the issue. These cases do disturb the Dutch: they are regarded as highly problematic, and it is clearly intended that if they occur, they should be stopped. * * *, [I]nterviews with physicians revealed only two instances, both from the early 1980s, in which a fully competent patient was suffering severely. * * *, [T]he physician in one of these cases indicated that under present-day circumstances, with increased openness about these issues, he probably would have initiated more extensive consultations. There is no evidence of any patient being put to death *against* his or her expressed or implied wish.

* * *

The Dutch See the Role of Law Rather Differently

Not only is Dutch law a civil law system rather than a common law one; not only does it contain the distinctive Dutch doctrine involving practices that are statutorily illegal but *gedogen*, or tolerated, by the public prosecutor, the courts, or both; and not only does it involve very little medical malpractice activity, but the Dutch also tend to see law as appropriately formulated at a different point in the evolution of a social practice. Americans, it is sometimes said, *begin* to address a social issue by first making laws and then challenging them in court to fine-tune and adjust them; the Dutch, on the other hand, allow a practice to evolve by "tolerating" but not legalizing it, and only when the practice is adequately controlled—when they've got it right, so to speak—is a law made to regulate the practice as it has evolved. That the Dutch do not yet have a law fully shaped to accommodate their open practice of euthanasia may not show, as some have claimed, that they are ambivalent about the practice, but perhaps rather that they are waiting for the practice to evolve to a point where it is under adequate, acceptable control, at which time it will be appropriate to finally revise the law.

* * *

The Economic Circumstances of Euthanasia in the Netherlands are also Easily Misunderstood

The Netherlands' national system of mixed public and private health insurance provides extensive care to all patients—including all hospitalization, nursing home care, home care, and the services of physicians, nurses, physical therapists, nutritionists, counselors, and other care providers, both in institutional settings and in the home. Virtually all residents of the Netherlands, 99.4 percent, are comprehensively insured for all medical expenses (those who are not are those who, with incomes above a stipulated level, are wealthy enough to self-insure), and 100 percent are insured for the costs of long-term illness. All insurance, both public and private, has a mandated minimum level that is very ample. Americans who raise the issue of whether some patients' requests for euthanasia are motivated by financial pressures or by fear of the effect of immense medical costs to their families are committing perhaps the most frequent mistake made by American observers: to assume that the choices of patients in the Netherlands are subject to the same pressures that the choices of patients in the United States would be. While there may be some administrative changes to the national health insurance system in the Netherlands in the near future, cost pressures on the system as a whole are met by rationing and queuing (neither currently severe), not by exclusion of individuals from coverage or by increased costs to patients. The costs to oneself or one's family of an extended illness, something that might make euthanasia attractive to a patient in the United States, are something the Dutch patient need not consider.

Differences in Social Circumstances Often Go Unnoticed

In American discussions of euthanasia, considerable emphasis is placed on slippery slope arguments, pointing out risks of abuse, particularly with reference to the handicapped, the poor, racial minorities, and other who might seem to be ready targets for involuntary euthanasia. The Netherlands, however, exhibits much less disparity between rich and poor, has much less racial prejudice, virtually no uninsured people, and very little homelessness. These differences underscore the difficulty both of treating the Netherlands as a model for the United States in advocating the legalization of euthanasia and also of assessing the plausibility of slippery slope arguments opposing legalization in the United States.

---

8. Might women, specifically, be put at risk in a society that permits physician assisted death? That is the argument that is made by Susan Wolf, who regularly has argued that women's requests should be respected by the health care system and that requests to remove life sustaining treatment should be heeded.

As I have argued, there is a strong right to be free of unwanted bodily invasion. Indeed, for women, a long history of being harmed specifically through unwanted bodily invasion such as rape presents particularly compelling reasons for honoring a woman's refusal of invasion and effort to maintain bodily intactness. When it comes to the question of whether women's suicides should be aided, however, or whether women should be actively killed, there is no right to command physician assistance, the dangers of permitting assistance are immense, and the history of women's subordination cuts the other way. Women have historically been seen as fit objects for bodily invasion, self-sacrifice, and death at the hands of others. The task before us is to challenge all three.

Certainly some women, including some feminists, will see this problem differently. That may be especially true of women who feel in control of their lives, are less subject to subordination by age or race or wealth, and seek yet another option to add to their many. I am not arguing that women should lose control of their lives and selves. Instead, I am arguing that when women request to be put to death or ask help in taking their own lives, they become part of a broader social dynamic of which we have properly learned to be extremely wary. These are fatal practices. We can no longer ignore questions of gender or insights of feminist argument.

Susan Wolf, Gender, Feminism and Death: Physician Assisted Suicide and Euthanasia, in S. Wolf, Feminism and Bioethics: Beyond Reproduction 308 (1996).

9. Organized medical groups generally oppose any medical participation in euthanasia or assisted death. See AMA Council on Ethical and Judicial Affairs, Code of Medical Ethics, Current Opinion 2.21, Euthanasia, and Opinion 2.211, Physician–Assisted Death (1998–99 ed.). Is this because it is morally reprehensible, or because it is too morally complicated? Drs. Cassel and Meier suggest that it could be, at least in part, the second:

A strict proscription against aiding in death may betray a limited conceptual framework that seeks the safety of ironclad rules and principles to protect the physician from the true complexity of individual cases. Patients seeking comfort in their dying should not be held hostage to our inability or unwillingness to be responsible for knowing right from wrong in each specific situation.

C. Cassel and D. Meier, Morals and Moralism in the Debate Over Euthanasia and Assisted Suicide, 323 N.Eng.J.Med. 750, 751 (1990).

10. Litigation seeking a right to physician assisted death need not be based only on the United States Constitution, it may have a basis in state law as well, especially in states with particularly strong constitutional privacy provisions. In Krischer v. McIver, 697 So.2d 97 (Fla.1997), a terminally ill AIDS patient and his physician sought an injunction against the prosecution of the physician for assisting in his patient's suicide. The Florida Supreme Court rejected a claim that the privacy provision of Article I, section 23 of the Florida Constitution included the right to have a physician assist in one's suicide. The Court announced that a properly drawn statute authorizing physician-assisted suicide would be constitutionally permissible, but that principles of separation of powers left the decision about whether it should be made legal to the legislature. The Chief Justice filed a vigorous dissent, arguing that, " * * *the right of privacy attaches with unusual force at the death bed. * * * What possible interest does society have in saving life when there is nothing of life to save but a final convulsion of agony? The state has no business in this arena." 697 So.2d at 111.

B. LEGISLATION TO SUPPORT PHYSICIAN ASSISTED DEATH— "DEATH WITH DIGNITY" INITIATIVES

The debate over the proper role of physicians in assisting their patients in death has been carried on through the legislative and citizen initiative processes also. "Death with Dignity" initiatives were narrowly defeated in California in 1991 and in Washington in 1992. However, Measure 16, the

Oregon "Death with Dignity" initiative, was approved by voters in the November 1994 election, and it thus became part of the statute law of Oregon.

THE OREGON DEATH WITH DIGNITY ACT

Or.Rev.Stat. §§ 127.800–.897.

127.800. Definitions.

The following words and phrases, whenever used in ORS 127.800 to 127.897, have the following meanings:

(1) "Adult" means an individual who is 18 years of age or older.

(2) "Attending physician" means the physician who has primary responsibility for the care of the patient and treatment of the patient's terminal disease.

(3) "Capable" means that in the opinion of a court or in the opinion of the patient's attending physician or consulting physician, psychiatrist or psychologist, a patient has the ability to make and communicate health care decisions to health care providers, including communication through persons familiar with the patient's manner of communicating if those persons are available.

(4) "Consulting physician" means a physician who is qualified by specialty or experience to make a professional diagnosis and prognosis regarding the patient's disease.

(5) "Counseling" means one or more consultations as necessary between a state licensed psychiatrist or psychologist and a patient for the purpose of determining that the patient is capable and not suffering from a psychiatric or psychological disorder or depression causing impaired judgment.

(6) "Health care provider" means a person licensed, certified or otherwise authorized or permitted by the law of this state to administer health care or dispense medication in the ordinary course of business or practice of a profession, and includes a health care facility.

(7) "Informed decision" means a decision by a qualified patient, to request and obtain a prescription to end his or her life in a humane and dignified manner, that is based on an appreciation of the relevant facts and after being fully informed by the attending physician of:

(a) His or her medical diagnosis;

(b) His or her prognosis;

(c) The potential risks associated with taking the medication to be prescribed;

(d) The probable result of taking the medication to be prescribed; and

(e) The feasible alternatives, including, but not limited to, comfort care, hospice care and pain control.

(8) "Medically confirmed" means the medical opinion of the attending physician has been confirmed by a consulting physician who has examined the patient and the patient's relevant medical records.

(9) "Patient" means a person who is under the care of a physician.

(10) "Physician" means a doctor of medicine or osteopathy licensed to practice medicine by the Board of Medical Examiners for the State of Oregon.

(11) "Qualified patient" means a capable adult who is a resident of Oregon and has satisfied the requirements of ORS 127.800 to 127.897 in order to obtain a prescription for medication to end his or her life in a humane and dignified manner.

(12) "Terminal disease" means an incurable and irreversible disease that has been medically confirmed and will, within reasonable medical judgment, produce death within six months.

127.805. Who may initiate a written request for medication.

(1) An adult who is capable, is a resident of Oregon, and has been determined by the attending physician and consulting physician to be suffering from a terminal disease, and who has voluntarily expressed his or her wish to die, may make a written request for medication for the purpose of ending his or her life in a humane and dignified manner in accordance with ORS 127.800 to 127.897.

(2) No person shall qualify under the provisions of ORS 127.800 to 127.897 solely because of age or disability.

127.810. Form of the written request.

(1) A valid request for medication under ORS 127.800 to 127.897 shall be in substantially the form described in ORS 127.897, signed and dated by the patient and witnessed by at least two individuals who, in the presence of the patient, attest that to the best of their knowledge and belief the patient is capable, acting voluntarily, and is not being coerced to sign the request.

(2) One of the witnesses shall be a person who is not:

(a) A relative of the patient by blood, marriage or adoption;

(b) A person who at the time the request is signed would be entitled to any portion of the estate of the qualified patient upon death under any will or by operation of law; or

(c) An owner, operator or employee of a health care facility where the qualified patient is receiving medical treatment or is a resident.

(3) The patient's attending physician at the time the request is signed shall not be a witness.

(4) If the patient is a patient in a long term care facility at the time the written request is made, one of the witnesses shall be an individual designated by the facility and having the qualifications specified by the Department of Human Services by rule.

127.815. Attending physician responsibilities.

(1) The attending physician shall:

(a) Make the initial determination of whether a patient has a terminal disease, is capable, and has made the request voluntarily;

(b) Request that the patient demonstrate Oregon residency pursuant to ORS 127.860;

(c) To ensure that the patient is making an informed decision, inform the patient of:

(A) His or her medical diagnosis;

(B) His or her prognosis;

(C) The potential risks associated with taking the medication to be prescribed;

(D) The probable result of taking the medication to be prescribed; and

(E) The feasible alternatives, including, but not limited to, comfort care, hospice care and pain control;

(d) Refer the patient to a consulting physician for medical confirmation of the diagnosis, and for a determination that the patient is capable and acting voluntarily;

(e) Refer the patient for counseling if appropriate pursuant to ORS 127.825;

(f) Recommend that the patient notify next of kin;

(g) Counsel the patient about the importance of having another person present when the patient takes the medication prescribed pursuant to ORS 127.800 to 127.897 and of not taking the medication in a public place;

(h) Inform the patient that he or she has an opportunity to rescind the request at any time and in any manner, and offer the patient an opportunity to rescind at the end of the 15 day waiting period pursuant to ORS 127.840;

(i) Verify, immediately prior to writing the prescription for medication under ORS 127.800 to 127.897, that the patient is making an informed decision;

(j) Fulfill the medical record documentation requirements of ORS 127.855;

(k) Ensure that all appropriate steps are carried out in accordance with ORS 127.800 to 127.897 prior to writing a prescription for medication to enable a qualified patient to end his or her life in a humane and dignified manner; and

(l) (A) Dispense medications directly* * *or [(B) through a pharmacist].

(2) Notwithstanding any other provision of law, the attending physician may sign the patient's death certificate.

127.820. Consulting physician confirmation.

Before a patient is qualified under ORS 127.800 to 127.897, a consulting physician shall examine the patient and his or her relevant medical records and confirm, in writing, the attending physician's diagnosis that the patient is suffering from a terminal disease, and verify that the patient is capable, is acting voluntarily and has made an informed decision.

127.825. Counseling referral.

If in the opinion of the attending physician or the consulting physician a patient may be suffering from a psychiatric or psychological disorder or depression causing impaired judgment, either physician shall refer the patient for counseling. No medication to end a patient's life in a humane and dignified manner shall be prescribed until the person performing the counseling determines that the patient is not suffering from a psychiatric or psychological disorder or depression causing impaired judgment.

127.830. Informed decision.

No person shall receive a prescription for medication to end his or her life in a humane and dignified manner unless he or she has made an informed decision as defined in ORS 127.800 (7). Immediately prior to writing a prescription for medication under ORS 127.800 to 127.897, the attending physician shall verify that the patient is making an informed decision.

127.835. Family notification.

The attending physician shall recommend that the patient notify the next of kin of his or her request for medication pursuant to ORS 127.800 to 127.897. A patient who declines or is unable to notify next of kin shall not have his or her request denied for that reason.

127.840. Written and oral requests.

In order to receive a prescription for medication to end his or her life in a humane and dignified manner, a qualified patient shall have made an oral request and a written request, and reiterate the oral request to his or her attending physician no less than fifteen (15) days after making the initial oral request. At the time the qualified patient makes his or her second oral request, the attending physician shall offer the patient an opportunity to rescind the request.

127.845. Right to rescind request.

A patient may rescind his or her request at any time and in any manner without regard to his or her mental state. No prescription for medication under ORS 127.800 to 127.897 may be written without the attending physician offering the qualified patient an opportunity to rescind the request.

127.850. Waiting periods.

No less than fifteen (15) days shall elapse between the patient's initial oral request and the writing of a prescription under ORS 127.800 to 127.897. No less than 48 hours shall elapse between the patient's written request and the writing of a prescription under ORS 127.800 to 127.897.

127.855. Medical record documentation requirements.

The following shall be documented or filed in the patient's medical record:

(1) All oral requests by a patient for medication to end his or her life in a humane and dignified manner;

(2) All written requests by a patient for medication to end his or her life in a humane and dignified manner;

(3) The attending physician's diagnosis and prognosis, determination that the patient is capable, acting voluntarily and has made an informed decision;

(4) The consulting physician's diagnosis and prognosis, and verification that the patient is capable, acting voluntarily and has made an informed decision;

(5) A report of the outcome and determinations made during counseling, if performed;

(6) The attending physician's offer to the patient to rescind his or her request at the time of the patient's second oral request pursuant to ORS 127.840; and

(7) A note by the attending physician indicating that all requirements under ORS 127.800 to 127.897 have been met and indicating the steps taken to carry out the request, including a notation of the medication prescribed.

127.860.   Residency requirement.

Only requests made by Oregon residents under ORS 127.800 to 127.897 shall be granted. Factors demonstrating Oregon residency include but are not limited to [being licensed to drive, registering to vote, owning property, and paying taxes in Oregon.]

* * *

127.880.   Construction of Act.

Nothing in ORS 127.800 to 127.897 shall be construed to authorize a physician or any other person to end a patient's life by lethal injection, mercy killing or active euthanasia. Actions taken in accordance with ORS 127.800 to 127.897 shall not, for any purpose, constitute suicide, assisted suicide, mercy killing or homicide, under the law.

* * *

127.897.   Form of the request.

A request for a medication as authorized by ORS 127.800 to 127.897 shall be in substantially the following form:

REQUEST FOR MEDICATION TO END MY LIFE
IN A HUMANE AND DIGNIFIED MANNER

I, _____, am an adult of sound mind.

I am suffering from _____, which my attending physician has determined is a terminal disease and which has been medically confirmed by a consulting physician.

I have been fully informed of my diagnosis, prognosis, the nature of medication to be prescribed and potential associated risks, the expected result, and the feasible alternatives, including comfort care, hospice care and pain control.

I request that my attending physician prescribe medication that will end my life in a humane and dignified manner.

INITIAL ONE:

_____ I have informed my family of my decision and taken their opinions into consideration.

_____ I have decided not to inform my family of my decision.

_____ I have no family to inform of my decision.

I understand that I have the right to rescind this request at any time.

I understand the full import of this request and I expect to die when I take the medication to be prescribed. I further understand that although most deaths occur within three hours, my death may take longer and my physician has counseled me about this possibility.

I make this request voluntarily and without reservation, and I accept full moral responsibility for my actions.

Signed: _____
Dated: _____

DECLARATION OF WITNESSES

We declare that the person signing this request:

(a) Is personally known to us or has provided proof of identity;

(b) Signed this request in our presence;

(c) Appears to be of sound mind and not under duress, fraud or undue influence;

(d) Is not a patient for whom either of us is attending physician.

_____ Witness 1/Date
_____ Witness 2/Date

NOTE: One witness shall not be a relative (by blood, marriage or adoption) of the person signing this request, shall not be entitled to any portion of the person's estate upon death and shall not own, operate or be employed at a health care facility where the person is a patient or resident. If the patient is an inpatient at a health care facility, one of the witnesses shall be an individual designated by the facility.

* * *

Early in 1999 the Oregon Department of Health issued its first annual report, which collected data on those who received lethal prescriptions under the Act during its first year of operation. A year later it issued its second report, which provides a helpful picture of the use of this statute. The full text of the Oregon Department of Health annual reports on the Death With Dignity Act are available on-line at *http://www.ohd.hr.state.or.us/chs/pas/pas.htm.*

Oregon's Death with Dignity Act: The Second Year's Experience Oregon Department of Health, 2000

Discussion / Conclusions:

In 1999, the second year of legal physician-assisted suicide in Oregon, the number of patients choosing this option increased compared to 1998, but remained small compared to the overall number of deaths in Oregon. Although concern about possible abuses persists, information on participating patients indicates that poverty, lack of education or insurance, or poor end-of-life care are not important factors influencing patient decisions to use the

Death with Dignity Act. Physician and family interviews suggest that the concerns contributing to patient requests for prescriptions relate to losing autonomy, losing control of bodily functions, decreasing ability to participate in activities that make life enjoyable, physical suffering, and a determination to control the timing and manner of death.

Compared with Oregonians dying from similar diseases, participating patients were better educated but otherwise alike with respect to age, race, and other demographic factors. The relative under-representation of married persons in 1998 was not seen in 1999. Although most patients spent out-of-pocket money on medical expenses (for example, on prescription drugs) all participants were insured for most other major medical expenses, often through a combination of Medicare and private supplemental policies.

The family members we interviewed reported that the majority of participating patients did not have difficulty identifying a physician willing to write the prescription for lethal medication. However, half of these patients asked more than one physician, indicating that not all Oregon physicians are willing to participate in physician-assisted suicide. This finding is consistent with reports on the attitudes of Oregon physicians and medical students toward physician-assisted suicide. Some physicians who refused to prescribe lethal medication acted as consulting physicians.

As best we could determine, all participating physicians complied with the provisions of the Act. Although the Health Division is not a regulatory agency for physicians, it does report to Oregon's Board of Medical Examiners any cases of non-compliance. Under reporting and non-compliance is thus difficult to assess because of possible repercussions for noncompliant physicians reporting to the division. In an independent anonymous survey, Oregon physicians reported writing 29 legal prescriptions for lethal doses of medication from December 1997 through August 1999. All but one physician had reported to the Health Division by the time they completed the survey (the status of one report was undetermined).

Responses from both physician and family interviews indicate that patient's decisions to request PAS were motivated by multiple interrelated concerns. Physical suffering was discussed by several families as a cause of loss of autonomy, inability to participate in activities that made life enjoyable, or a "non-existent" quality of life. For example, "She would have stuck it out through the pain if she thought she'd get better...[but she believed that] when quality of life has no meaning, it's no use hanging around." For another participant, a feeling of being trapped because of ALS contributed to concern about loss of autonomy. Family members frequently commented on loss of control of bodily functions when discussing loss of autonomy. Those reporting patient concern about being a burden on friends and family also reported concern about loss of autonomy and control of bodily functions. Reasons for requesting a prescription were sometimes so interrelated they were difficult to categorize. According to one family member being asked to distinguish reasons for the patient's decision, "It was everything; it was nothing; [he was suffering terribly]."

Difficulty categorizing and differences in interpreting the nature of the concerns made physician and family member responses hard to compare quantitatively. Nonetheless, family interviews corroborate physician reports from both years that patients are greatly concerned about issues of autonomy and control. In addition, responses of both physicians and family consistently pointed to patient concerns about quality of life and the wish to have a means of controlling the end of life should it become unbearable. As one family member said, "She always thought that if something was terminal, she would [want to] control the end...It was not the dying that she dreaded, it was getting to that death."

* * *

When family members of the patients who used PAS discussed patient's concerns about physical suffering, they included concerns about difficulty breathing and difficulty swallowing, as well as pain. Some patients were concerned that to adequately control pain, the side effects of the medication would render quality of life meaningless. A previous study found that physical factors, especially difficulty breathing, became important predictors of decreasing will to live as death drew near. However, it is important to note that among patients here, concern about physical suffering was not always equivalent to experiencing it. End-of-life care was available to participating patients, and three quarters of them were in hospice before dying. Family members noted improved pain management for the patients after entering hospice. Physician reports did note a slight increase in the number of patients concerned about pain, but this is consistent with hospital-based reports from Oregon wherein an overall increase in pain has been reported among terminally ill patients.

Oregonians choosing physician-assisted suicide appeared to want control over how they died. One woman had purchased poison over a decade before her participation, when her cancer was first diagnosed, so that she would never be without the means of controlling the end of her life should it become unbearable. Like many others who participated, she was described as "determined" to have this control. Another woman was described as a "gutsy woman" who was "...determined in her lifetime, and determined about [physician-assisted suicide]." Family members expressed profound grief at losing a loved one. However, mixed with this grief was great respect for the patient's determination and choice to use physician-assisted suicide. As one husband said about his wife of almost 50 years, "She was my only girl; I didn't want to lose her ... but she wanted to do this."

Notes and Questions

1. The Oregon Death with Dignity Act also provides that no contract or statute can affect a person's request for physician assisted suicide, and that no insurance policy can be conditioned upon, or affected by, a patient's decision to choose (or reject) physician assisted suicide. The measure includes a section providing immunity for those who follow the requirements of the statute, and imposing liability on those who violate it.

2. The United States District Court in Oregon issued a preliminary injunction against enforcing the initiative shortly after the initiative passed. The court permanently enjoined enforcement of the statute several months later. Ultimately the Ninth Circuit reversed the District Court, finding that those challenging the Oregon initiative had no standing to raise the issue in federal court. Lee v. Oregon, 107 F.3d 1382 (9th Cir.1997).

3. The Act was amended in 1999, but the changes that were made were not substantial. The legislature added the definition of "capable," added some new language designed to encourage patients to discuss the matter with their families, and provided some factors to be considered in determining residency. The amendments also made clear the broad extent of the institutional conscience exception to the statute, which permits health care institutions to limit physicians from engaging in assisted death on their premises or in their organizations, and it changed the written consent form to assure that patients recognize that death will probably, but not always, take place about three hours after taking the medication.

If you could rewrite the Oregon Death with Dignity Act how would you do it? Would you narrow its coverage to avoid abuse? Would you broaden its coverage (and, perhaps, extend it to euthanasia as well as assisted suicide)?

4. Emboldened by the success in Oregon, many "Death With Dignity" groups have sought state statutes that would accomplish what Oregon's Measure 16 sought to do. A measure similar to the Oregon statute was very narrowly defeated at the polls in Maine in 2000. On the other hand, several states have passed new statutes that outlaw (or increase the penalty for) assisting suicide. On balance, since 1997 more states have acted to outlaw or limit assisted suicide than to permit it.

5. *Intractable Pain Relief Statutes*. Is there some common ground available to those, on the one hand, who believe that permitting physician assisted death is necessary for patients to be properly treated at the end of life, and those, on the other hand, who believe that physician assisted death must be outlawed for patients to be properly treated? Both groups agree that pain is often inadequately treated at the end of life, in part because physicians fear legal action for homicide (if pain relief results in the death of the patient) or distribution of drugs (if the condition of a patient requires a larger dose of narcotic medication than is standard). In some states advocates on both sides of the physician assisted death issue have joined together to support intractable pain relief statutes, which are designed to protect health care providers who deliver adequate pain relief from adverse licensing and criminal actions. These statutes generally provide that a health care provider will not be liable in a state disciplinary proceeding or a criminal action for the aggressive prescription of pain medication as long as the use of that medication is in accord with accepted guidelines for pain management. Several states have promulgated intractable pain relief acts, and several more are considering them. For a model "Pain Relief Act," see 24 J.L., Med. & Ethics 317(1996).

6. The federal government has not ignored this issue, either. Even before the Oregon statute became effective, Congress passed the Assisted Suicide Prevention Restriction Act of 1997, which outlaws the use of federal money to aid physician assisted death, directly or indirectly.

Shortly after the Oregon Death with Dignity Act became effective, some suggested that any physician who prescribed a lethal drug under that statute would be prescribing that drug without a "legitimate medical purpose," and thus would be acting inconsistently with the federal Controlled Substances Act. A physician's violation of the Act could lead to both the loss of prescribing authority and criminal indictment. In June of 1998, after the matter had been pending for some time, the United States Department of Justice published its report concluding that use of controlled substances under the Oregon statute would satisfy the "legitimate medical purpose" requirement of the federal Act.

Immediately, members of the House and Senate introduced the Lethal Drug Abuse Prevention Act of 1998, which would have expanded the authority of the Drug Enforcement Agency to investigate lethal use of controlled substances, which could not be used with the *intent* of causing death. Supporters of physician assisted death joined many of their staunchest opponents and mainstream medical organizations (including the AMA) to oppose the bill because, they said, it would be likely to chill physicians from providing adequate pain relief at the end of life. Although the bill failed, it was resurrected in slightly milder form in 2000 as the Pain Relief Promotion Act ("PRPA"), which included a well publicized section announcing that the provision of medication with the intent to manage pain (and not the intent to cause death) was protected. The 2000 version of the bill also provided for the education of health care professionals on issues related to pain management, and it was supported by the AMA (but opposed by the ABA and the American Cancer Society). Although the stated purpose of PRPA was to promote adequate pain relief practices, its effect would be (and, some say, its real purpose was) to render it impossible for physicians in Oregon to carry out the provisions of the Death With Dignity Act. PRPA sailed through the House but was held up in the Senate, and it died when Congress adjourned in late 2000

Another version of PRPA was expected to be introduced in 2001. Supporters of PRPA also hope that the new Bush administration will reconsider the Clinton administration's decision that the use of medications to cause death under the Death With Dignity Act constitutes the use of those drugs for a "legitimate medical purpose."

7. Despite the high level of publicity given to the Oregon statute, Oregonians (like the rest of us) remain confused about what options are actually available at the end of life. M. Silveira et al., Patient's Knowledge of Options at the End of Life: Ignorance in the Face of Death, 284 JAMA 2483 (2000). What is more, terminally ill patients and their families remain highly ambivalent about physician assisted death. One recent study showed that while 60% of terminally ill patients would support the use of physician assisted death under some circumstances, only 10% had seriously considered it in their own cases. E. Emanuel et al, Attitudes and Desires Related to Euthanasia and Physician–Assisted Suicide Among Terminally Ill Patients and Their Caregivers, 284 JAMA 2460 (2000).

8. The public interest in this issue is not limited to the United States. For a discussion of the law in the Netherlands, see pages 1442–1447. In addition, Australia's Northern Territory's parliament passed The Rights of the Terminally Ill Act (1995), which permitted what some have called "voluntary euthanasia" under some limited circumstances until the national parliament effectively overturned that territorial statute.

Problem: Drafting Legislation

You are the nonpolitical legislative counsel to a state legislature. Currently that state has a statute prohibiting assisting suicide. You have been asked by several members of the legislature to draft bills designed to regulate physician assisted death for introduction at a legislative session that will soon be convened. One member has asked you to draft a bill that would outlaw all physician assisted death, under all circumstances. A second member wants you to draft a bill that would put as few limitations on physician assisted death as is possible; this libertarian member believes that the decision should be left to individual doctors and patients. Another member has asked you to draft a statute that would protect health care providers from potential liability for participating in physician assisted deaths, and would give providers an option to avoid participating in physician assisted deaths if they chose not to do so. Yet another member has asked you to draft a statute that would prohibit managed care organizations from directly or indirectly giving any incentives to their members to choose physician assisted deaths. Finally, one long time incumbent has asked you to draft a consensus statute—one with enough political support across the spectrum that it has a reasonable chance of passing.

How would you go about drafting these statutes? How would they be different? What facts (about the legal landscape in this state, about the politics of the current officeholders, about the religious backgrounds of those within the state, about other issues) would you want to have before you started drafting these statutes?

Chapter 20

INTERDISCIPLINARY DECISIONMAK-ING IN HEALTH CARE: REGULA-TION OF RESEARCH INVOLVING HUMAN SUBJECTS, ETHICS COM-MITTEES, AND ADVISORY COM-MITTEES

INTRODUCTION

If the previous eighteen chapters have made anything clear, it is that there are a great number of health care decisions that can not neatly be classified as "medical," "legal," "ethical," "social" or "economic." These issues, which range from broad social matters, such as who should have access to medical resources, to particular questions dealing with individual cases, such as whether Baby Jane Doe should receive surgery, have made obvious the value of interdisciplinary decisionmaking at the societal, institutional, and individual levels.

Within the last three decades several forms of medical decisionmaking by interdisciplinary committees have arisen. These committees include institutional review boards (IRBs) established by federal regulation and appointed by local institutions to review research involving human subjects; institutional ethics committees (IECs) established without any legal obligation by most hospitals, many nursing homes, and many other health care organizations (including HMOs) to help review ethics policies and practices; infant care review committees (ICRCs) established pursuant to the "Baby Doe" regulations to review the quality of care given to seriously ill newborns under some circumstances; diagnosis committees established to determine whether a diagnosis (like "terminal illness") that triggers an ethical and legal consequence has been properly confirmed; medical-legal malpractice review panels established by state law in some states and by medical and legal societies in others to provide screening of potential malpractice actions; the Recombinant DNA Advisory Committee (RAC) established by federal law to review research involving DNA; presidential commissions like the National Bioethics Advisory Committee (NBAC) appointed by the President to investigate and help establish national policy on matters of interdisciplinary concern and parallel state commissions to establish state policy in similar matters.

While health care professionals have sometimes viewed the development of these committees, panels, and commissions as inappropriate intrusions upon their decisionmaking authority, these institutions have brought new ideas and perspectives to the debates concerning what are ultimately social issues. The function of this chapter is to provide an introduction to such interdisciplinary agencies and their organization and operation, and to examine the value of their existence.

Problem: Making Health Care Policy

As the commissioner and chief administrative officer of a state health department that sets state policy and also operates a large general hospital, you are confronted with the need to resolve several issues:

1. What definition of brain death, if any, ought to be applied within the state? Should it allow for religious objections, or should it be uniform?

2. What level of care, if any, should the state insist that local hospitals provide to seriously ill newborns? Should the state child abuse and neglect processes be available to unrelated third parties who wish to challenge hospital actions in providing care to seriously ill newborns?

3. What ought to be done about the quality deficiencies within private nursing homes within the state?

4. Should the state's distribution of Medicaid resources be altered in such a way that health care will be more equitably distributed to those who need it most?

5. What kind of policy regarding life sustaining treatment should the state's hospital adopt? What should the hospital do if health care providers and the family do not reach a consensus on the whether life sustaining medical treatment may be withdrawn in a particular case?

6. Should the state hospital allow unlicensed traditional healers to perform their healing techniques in the institution?

7. Should the hospital sign contracts with managed care organizations? Are there any particular provisions the hospital should demand in these contracts? Are there any particular provisions the hospital should reject in these contracts?

8. Should every person admitted to a particular hospital be asked whether he or she is willing to be an organ donor?

9. Should patients be permitted to participate as research subjects in an experiment to test the safety and efficacy of a new sleeping pill, even though there is substantial evidence that sleeping medications are responsible for as much social harm as good?

10. Should the state hospital limit the practice of physicians or other health care providers who are HIV positive? Should it tell patients which providers are HIV positive? Should it test all providers for HIV?

11. Should the hospital tell health care providers which patients are HIV positive?

Some of these questions must be answered in a way that develops a policy for the entire state; some of these questions are directed to particular cases at a single hospital. Would it be helpful to appoint committees to recommend answers to these questions?

1. If so, what is it about the decisionmaking that would make committees helpful under each of these circumstances?

2. What kind of people ought to be appointed to each of these committees?

3. What procedures ought to be applied to the committees, and how ought they go about their work?

4. Should any substantive limitations be put on the work of any of these committees?

5. Is the purpose of each committee to resolve a particular case, to develop an institution-wide or state-wide policy, or to educate other principals who will be working on the underlying question?

6. To whom should these committees report? To the physician and family? To a hospital administrator? To the commissioner of health? To the legislature? To someone else?

This first section of this chapter discusses IRBs, the earliest interdisciplinary committees to be widespread and accepted, and briefly reviews the regulation of human subjects research. The next section considers other kinds of individual case-oriented interdisciplinary decisionmakers. The concluding section reviews the work of government policy commissions established to consider bioethics questions.

I. REGULATION OF RESEARCH UPON HUMAN SUBJECTS

A. THE DEVELOPMENT OF THE NUREMBERG CODE AND THE DECLARATION OF HELSINKI

The shocking horrors that could be perpetrated by medical experimentation performed by superbly qualified scientists became apparent to the world through the Nazi war crimes trials that resulted in the prosecution of several leading German physicians. These trials unveiled conduct ignominious under any circumstances. For example, they brought to light medical research in which "volunteers," usually concentration camp inmates, were exposed to extremely low atmospheric pressure until they died in order to help the German Air Force prepare for high altitude military operations. They revealed subjects who were forced to drink seawater or breathe mustard gas, were exposed to such epidemics as malaria, jaundice, and typhus, or were placed in ice water until they froze. Several of the experiments were "open" to a wide range of concentration camp inmates, while others were limited to Jews, Gypsies, Polish priests, or other "special" groups.

This experimentation was not perceived as an abuse of medicine by its perpetrators. Rather, it was justified as appropriate conduct, done in the name of healing, and carried out consistently with the Hippocratic Oath. For an account of the professional role of physicians in the Nazi policy of extermination, see R.J. Lifton, The Nazi Doctors (1986). Most of the twenty physicians accused of participating in or directing this experimentation were convicted, and some were hanged. A few were acquitted and one (Dr. Mengele) escaped. In one of the tribunal's most significant and ultimately most important judgments, the court sitting in Nuremberg promulgated a set of principles to be applied to determine when medical experimentation is appropriate. These principles provide the basis for all subsequent discussions of the substantive limitations that ought to be put upon research involving human subjects.

NUREMBERG CODE: PERMISSIBLE MEDICAL EXPERIMENTS

The great weight of the evidence before us is to the effect that certain types of medical experiments on human beings, when kept within reasonably well-defined bounds, conform to the ethics of the medical profession generally. The protagonists of the practice of human experimentation justify their views on the basis that such experiments yield results for the good of society that are unprocurable by other methods or means of study. All agree, however, that certain basic principles must be observed in order to satisfy moral, ethical and legal concepts:

1.   The voluntary consent of the human subject is absolutely essential.

This means that the person involved should have legal capacity to give consent; should be so situated as to be able to exercise free power of choice, without the intervention of any element of force, fraud, deceit, duress, over-reaching, or other ulterior form of constraint or coercion; and should have sufficient knowledge and comprehension of the elements of the subject matter involved as to enable him to make an understanding and enlightened decision. This latter element requires that before the acceptance of an affirmative decision by the experimental subject there should be made known to him the nature, duration, and purpose of the experiment; the method and means by which it is to be conducted; all inconveniences and hazards reasonably to be expected; and the effects upon his health or person which may possibly come from his participation in the experiment.

The duty and responsibility for ascertaining the quality of the consent rests upon each individual who initiates, directs or engages in the experiment. It is a personal duty and responsibility which may not be delegated to another with impunity.

2.   The experiment should be such as to yield fruitful results for the good of society, unprocurable by other methods or means of study, and not random and unnecessary in nature.

3.   The experiment should be so designed and based on the results of animal experimentation and a knowledge of the natural history of the disease or other problem under study that the anticipated results will justify the performance of the experiment.

4.   The experiment should be so conducted as to avoid all unnecessary physical and mental suffering and injury.

5.   No experiment should be conducted where there is an *a priori* reason to believe that death or disabling injury will occur; except, perhaps, in those experiments where the experimental physicians also serve as subjects.

6.   The degree of risk to be taken should never exceed that determined by the humanitarian importance of the problem to be solved by the experiment.

7.   Proper preparations should be made and adequate facilities provided to protect the experimental subject against even remote possibilities of injury, disability, or death.

8.   The experiment should be conducted only by scientifically qualified persons. The highest degree of skill and care should be required through all stages of the experiment of those who conduct or engage in the experiment.

9.   During the course of the experiment the human subject should be at liberty to bring the experiment to an end if he has reached the physical or mental state where continuation of the experiment seems to him to be impossible.

10.   During the course of the experiment the scientist in charge must be prepared to terminate the experiment at any stage, if he has probable cause to believe, in the exercise of the good faith, superior skill and careful judgment required of him, that a continuation of the experiment is likely to result in injury, disability, or death to the experimental subject.

* * *

The Nuremberg Code has been restated and expanded several times since that judgment was rendered. The most significant elaboration on the Nuremberg Code is the Declaration of Helsinki, first promulgated by the World Medical Association in 1964 and periodically updated and amended. The World Medical Association consists of representatives from most of the world's organized national medical associations; the American Medical Association is the representative from the United States. Amidst considerable controversy over the increasing use of third world populations as subjects in research conducted and funded by first world institutions, the World Medical Association adopted the most recent version of the Declaration in late 2000.

WORLD MEDICAL ASSOCIATION, DECLARATION OF HELSINKI

Ethical Principles for Medical Research Involving Human Subjects
(2000)

A.   INTRODUCTION

1.   The World Medical Association has developed the Declaration of Helsinki as a statement of ethical principles to provide guidance to physicians and other participants in medical research involving human subjects. Medical research involving human subjects includes research on identifiable human material or identifiable data.

2.   It is the duty of the physician to promote and safeguard the health of the people. The physician's knowledge and conscience are dedicated to the fulfillment of this duty.

3.   The Declaration of Geneva of the World Medical Association binds the physician with the words, "The health of my patient will be my first consideration," and the International Code of Medical Ethics declares that, "A physician shall act only in the patient's interest when providing medical care which might have the effect of weakening the physical and mental condition of the patient."

4. Medical progress is based on research which ultimately must rest in part on experimentation involving human subjects.

5. In medical research on human subjects, considerations related to the well-being of the human subject should take precedence over the interests of science and society.

6. The primary purpose of medical research involving human subjects is to improve prophylactic, diagnostic and therapeutic procedures and the understanding of the aetiology and pathogenesis of disease. Even the best proven prophylactic, diagnostic, and therapeutic methods must continuously be challenged through research for their effectiveness, efficiency, accessibility and quality.

7. In current medical practice and in medical research, most prophylactic, diagnostic and therapeutic procedures involve risks and burdens.

8. Medical research is subject to ethical standards that promote respect for all human beings and protect their health and rights. Some research populations are vulnerable and need special protection. The particular needs of the economically and medically disadvantaged must be recognized. Special attention is also required for those who cannot give or refuse consent for themselves, for those who may be subject to giving consent under duress, for those who will not benefit personally from the research and for those for whom the research is combined with care.

9. Research Investigators should be aware of the ethical, legal and regulatory requirements for research on human subjects in their own countries as well as applicable international requirements. No national ethical, legal or regulatory requirement should be allowed to reduce or eliminate any of the protections for human subjects set forth in this Declaration.

B. BASIC PRINCIPLES FOR ALL MEDICAL RESEARCH

10. It is the duty of the physician in medical research to protect the life, health, privacy, and dignity of the human subject.

11. Medical research involving human subjects must conform to generally accepted scientific principles, be based on a thorough knowledge of the scientific literature, other relevant sources of information, and on adequate laboratory and, where appropriate, animal experimentation.

12. Appropriate caution must be exercised in the conduct of research which may affect the environment, and the welfare of animals used for research must be respected.

13. The design and performance of each experimental procedure involving human subjects should be clearly formulated in an experimental protocol. This protocol should be submitted for consideration, comment, guidance, and where appropriate, approval to a specially appointed ethical review committee, which must be independent of the investigator, the sponsor or any other kind of undue influence. This independent committee should be in conformity with the laws and regulations of the country in which the research experiment is performed. The committee has the right to monitor ongoing trials. The researcher has the obligation to provide monitoring information to the committee, especially any serious adverse events. The researcher should also submit to the committee, for review, information regarding funding, sponsors,

institutional affiliations, other potential conflicts of interest and incentives for subjects.

14. The research protocol should always contain a statement of the ethical considerations involved and should indicate that there is compliance with the principles enunciated in this Declaration.

15. Medical research involving human subjects should be conducted only by scientifically qualified persons and under the supervision of a clinically competent medical person. The responsibility for the human subject must always rest with a medically qualified person and never rest on the subject of the research, even though the subject has given consent.

16. Every medical research project involving human subjects should be preceded by careful assessment of predictable risks and burdens in comparison with foreseeable benefits to the subject or to others. This does not preclude the participation of healthy volunteers in medical research. The design of all studies should be publicly available.

17. Physicians should abstain from engaging in research projects involving human subjects unless they are confident that the risks involved have been adequately assessed and can be satisfactorily managed. Physicians should cease any investigation if the risks are found to outweigh the potential benefits or if there is conclusive proof of positive and beneficial results.

18. Medical research involving human subjects should only be conducted if the importance of the objective outweighs the inherent risks and burdens to the subject. This is especially important when the human subjects are healthy volunteers.

19. Medical research is only justified if there is a reasonable likelihood that the populations in which the research is carried out stand to benefit from the results of the research.

20. The subjects must be volunteers and informed participants in the research project.

21. The right of research subjects to safeguard their integrity must always be respected. Every precaution should be taken to respect the privacy of the subject, the confidentiality of the patient's information and to minimize the impact of the study on the subject's physical and mental integrity and on the personality of the subject.

22. In any research on human beings, each potential subject must be adequately informed of the aims, methods, sources of funding, any possible conflicts of interest, institutional affiliations of the researcher, the anticipated benefits and potential risks of the study and the discomfort it may entail. The subject should be informed of the right to abstain from participation in the study or to withdraw consent to participate at any time without reprisal. After ensuring that the subject has understood the information, the physician should then obtain the subject's freely-given informed consent, preferably in writing. If the consent cannot be obtained in writing, the non-written consent must be formally documented and witnessed.

23. When obtaining informed consent for the research project the physician should be particularly cautious if the subject is in a dependent relationship with the physician or may consent under duress. In that case the

informed consent should be obtained by a well-informed physician who is not engaged in the investigation and who is completely independent of this relationship.

24. For a research subject who is legally incompetent, physically or mentally incapable of giving consent or is a legally incompetent minor, the investigator must obtain informed consent from the legally authorized representative in accordance with applicable law. These groups should not be included in research unless the research is necessary to promote the health of the population represented and this research cannot instead be performed on legally competent persons.

25. When a subject deemed legally incompetent, such as a minor child, is able to give assent to decisions about participation in research, the investigator must obtain that assent in addition to the consent of the legally authorized representative.

26. Research on individuals from whom it is not possible to obtain consent, including proxy or advance consent, should be done only if the physical/mental condition that prevents obtaining informed consent is a necessary characteristic of the research population. The specific reasons for involving research subjects with a condition that renders them unable to give informed consent should be stated in the experimental protocol for consideration and approval of the review committee. The protocol should state that consent to remain in the research should be obtained as soon as possible from the individual or a legally authorized surrogate.

27. Both authors and publishers have ethical obligations. In publication of the results of research, the investigators are obliged to preserve the accuracy of the results. Negative as well as positive results should be published or otherwise publicly available. Sources of funding, institutional affiliations and any possible conflicts of interest should be declared in the publication. Reports of experimentation not in accordance with the principles laid down in this Declaration should not be accepted for publication.

C. ADDITIONAL PRINCIPLES FOR MEDICAL RESEARCH COMBINED WITH MEDICAL CARE

28. The physician may combine medical research with medical care, only to the extent that the research is justified by its potential prophylactic, diagnostic or therapeutic value. When medical research is combined with medical care, additional standards apply to protect the patients who are research subjects.

29. The benefits, risks, burdens and effectiveness of a new method should be tested against those of the best current prophylactic, diagnostic, and therapeutic methods. This does not exclude the use of placebo, or no treatment, in studies where no proven prophylactic, diagnostic or therapeutic method exists.

30. At the conclusion of the study, every patient entered into the study should be assured of access to the best proven prophylactic, diagnostic and therapeutic methods identified by the study.

31. The physician should fully inform the patient which aspects of the care are related to the research. The refusal of a patient to participate in a study must never interfere with the patient-physician relationship.

32. In the treatment of a patient, where proven prophylactic, diagnostic and therapeutic methods do not exist or have been ineffective, the physician, with informed consent from the patient, must be free to use unproven or new prophylactic, diagnostic and therapeutic measures, if in the physician's judgement it offers hope of saving life, re-establishing health or alleviating suffering. Where possible, these measures should be made the object of research, designed to evaluate their safety and efficacy. In all cases, new information should be recorded and, where appropriate, published. The other relevant guidelines of this Declaration should be followed.

Problem: The African and Asian AIDS Trials

The roles of international research organizations, and American researchers doing research abroad, were called into question as a consequence of a series of perinatal HIV transmission studies done in Africa and Asia in the mid–1990s. There is a particular need for treatment for HIV-positive pregnant women in some African and Asian countries, where the HIV infection rate is far higher than it is in most of the developed world. There are more than a half million HIV infected babies born each year, most in the developing world. The United Nations has put a high priority on finding some genuinely feasible way of dealing with this increasingly pervasive problem.

As a general matter, without treatment between 17% and 25% of pregnant women who are infected with HIV will give birth to an HIV-positive baby, although that figure may be even higher in the developing world. In the United States, an HIV-positive mother will be offered therapy with a combination of drugs, including AZT, during her last six months of pregnancy and intravenous medication during delivery. A Caesarian section is often recommended if the mother has been taking AZT. The baby then will be treated for six weeks after birth. This protocol, which decreases the transmission rate to about 8%, is too expensive (at more than $500) for use in developing countries, where any use of a needle may also be too risky. As a consequence, the United Nations AIDS program, along with the United States National Institutes of Health, the Centers for Disease Control and others, sponsored research in which mostly impoverished HIV-positive women in poor countries were randomized to a few different relatively inexpensive courses of treatment. Some women were also randomized to a placebo. While the consent of those who participated in the study was sought by the investigators, it was not always provided in writing, and, given the alternative—no treatment at all—some believe that it was inherently coerced consent. The purpose of the research was to find some less expensive and safer way of treating HIV-positive pregnant women in very poor countries; of course, the beneficiaries of the research could include the HIV-positive pregnant women (and third party health care payers) in the United States and the rest of the developed world, too.

Do you think that the research was properly done? Was it done consistently with the Declaration of Helsinki? Was this appropriate research likely to save hundreds of thousands of lives, or was it another example of the developed world imposing a burden (here, of medical research) on the poor and on people of color?

Does it make any difference to your analysis that the research ultimately found that some (but not all) of the shorter, cheaper, less invasive protocols were almost as good (but not quite as good) as the current protocol used in the United States? For one summary account of the studies, see L. Altman, Spare AIDS Regime Is Found To Reduce Risks To Newborns, New York Times, February 2, 1999, at A–1.

Notes

1. Is the Declaration of Helsinki consistent with the Nuremberg Code? How do they vary? Which is likely to be more effective as a practical guide to those engaged in research involving human subjects?

2. Some proposals to change the Declaration in 1999 proved too controversial, and were ultimately rejected by the Association at their 2000 meeting. Probably the most vigorously discussed proposal was one that would have permitted scientists to test new treatments against "the best diagnostic, prophylactic or therapeutic method *that would otherwise be available* [to the subject]." If this language had been adopted, impoverished subjects without any access to medical care could have been given ineffective treatment (or a placebo); without it, arguably, those subjects would have to be afforded the best alternative treatment available to anyone, anywhere in the world. As one advocate for the change pointed out, a "plain meaning" approach to the current regulation would prohibit Indian drug companies carrying out drug research in India. He cited the research that led to the development of Oral Rehydration Therapy (ORT). This treatment, which has saved millions of lives, could never have been developed in Bangladesh if the researchers had been required to compare ORT to intravenous treatment.

See S. Eckstein, Ethical Issues in International Health Research Programme, 10 Dispatches (2) 2,14 (2000). Should this proposed change have been adopted? What effect would it have had on the propriety of the Asian and African AIDS trials?

3. Another 1999 proposed change would have allowed for oral, rather than written, informed consent, when the risk to the subject is "slight" and when the medical procedure to be used is "customarily used in the practice of medicine without documentation of consent." Would this attempt at streamlining research bureaucracy be worth the additional risk to research subjects?

4. Yet another proposal would have permitted the increased use of placebos when there was no risk of disability or death and the placebo control would have increased research efficiency. Like the others, the proposal was ultimately rejected.

5. What changes, if any, would you make to the Declaration? Is it too strict, thus limiting research too severely, or is it too liberal, allowing research that is inappropriate? For an account of some of the issues raised in the vigorous debate over the 1999 amendments and the 2000 redraft, see R. Levine, The Need to Revise the Declaration of Helsinki, 341 N.Eng.J.Med. 531 (1999), T. Brennan, Proposed Revisions to the Declaration of Helsinki–Will They Weaken the Ethical Principles Underlying Human Research, 341 N.Eng.J.Med.527 (1999), and B. Loff and J. Black, The Declaration of Helsinki and Research in Vulnerable Populations, 172 Med.J.Aust. 292 (2000).

B. HISTORY OF RESEARCH UPON HUMAN SUBJECTS IN THE UNITED STATES

In the United States research has also been tainted by racially and politically motivated choices of subjects for medical investigation. Indeed, one of the defenses raised at the Nazi war trials was that there was no relevant distinction between what the Nazi physicians did and the contemporaneous American practice of using conscientious objectors, the institutionalized mentally ill, and prisoners (including "political" prisoners, such as those convicted of treason) as subjects in research designed to improve America's military strength. The argument that the United States applied a double standard that condemned only Nazi research is bolstered by the fact that there was no effort to seek retribution against Japanese experimenters who were doing work with serious implications for biological warfare, but who cooperated with the United States after their capture. In addition, recent revelations show that as the United States was prosecuting the Nazi doctors, the United States government was conducting research on human radiation by injecting subjects (many of whom were inaccurately described as terminally ill) with plutonium or uranium to see what their reaction would be. These subjects were never informed of the nature of the experimentation, and their exploitation was clearly inconsistent with the code promulgated at Nuremberg. For an account of the experimentation, see Advisory Committee on Human Radiation Experiments, The Human Radiation Experiments (1996). For an account of the federal commission that investigated these experiments almost half a century after they were done, see Ruth Faden, The Advisory Committee on Human Radiation Experiments: Reflections on a Presidential Commission, 26 Hastings Center Rep. (Sept.-Oct.) 22 (1996). See also Robert Burt, The Suppressed Legacy of Nuremberg, 26 Hastings Center Rep. (Sept.-Oct.) 30 (1996).

The most famous twentieth century American breach of research ethics was the Tuskegee Syphilis Study. In this study, hundreds of poor African American men in the South were studied so that the research agency, the United States Public Health Service, could develop an understanding of the natural history of syphilis. Poor rural African Americans were chosen as subjects because of the difficulty they might have in seeking treatment for syphilis and because it was thought that African Americans, who were stereotyped as more sexually active and physically and mentally weaker than whites, would be more likely to benefit from the outcome of the study. The natural history of the disease could be discovered only if any treatment provided to the subjects were ineffective. The United States Public Health Service continued this research for some forty years. Even when penicillin, the first truly effective treatment for syphilis, became available, the Public Health Service physicians failed to offer that treatment to most of their subjects, and many were expressly and regularly discouraged from seeking effective treatment. The study came to public light in 1972 and was the topic of federal administrative and Congressional hearings in 1973. While participants in the study successfully sued the Public Health Service for compensation, no criminal actions arose out of the case. For a complete account of this tawdry episode in American medical history, see J. Jones, Bad Blood (1981).

The Tuskegee Syphilis study and the human radiation studies do not stand alone as examples of American medical research failing to respect individual subjects. Other publicized cases include the Jewish Chronic Disease Hospital case, in which live cancer cells were injected into patients without their knowledge, and the Willowbrook State Hospital hepatitis study, in which children admitted to a state hospital rife with hepatitis were given the disease as a condition of admission. In each of these cases, as in the Nazi experiments, the only authorities determining whether the subjects were properly selected were the medical investigators themselves. For an excellent history of experimentation on human subjects in the United States and its influence on bioethics, see David Rothman, Strangers at the Bedside (1991).

The first formal federal policy requiring outside review of research involving human subjects was imposed in 1966 by the Public Health Service upon those seeking grants from it. The 1966 policy required prior consideration of "the risks and potential medical benefits of the investigation" before a protocol could be submitted to the Public Health Service.

In 1974, one year after the public disclosure of the Tuskegee Syphilis Study, Congress enacted the National Research Act establishing the National Commission for Protection of Human Subjects of Biomedical and Behavioral Research, which was to "conduct a comprehensive investigation and study to identify basic ethical principles" that should underlie the conduct of human subjects research. That Commission was also to develop procedures to assure that the research would be consistent with those ethical principles and to recommend guidelines that could apply to human subjects research supported by the Department of Health, Education and Welfare. In recognition of the interdisciplinary nature of the issue, the Act also required the establishment of institutional review boards (IRBs) at institutions under contract with the Department of Health, Education and Welfare.

By 1975, when the Department of Health, Education and Welfare issued its "Policy for the Protection of Human Research Subjects," virtually every university, medical school, and research hospital had established IRBs which operated within the requirements of both federal and state regulations. The federal regulations were revised by what had become the Department of Health and Human Services (DHHS) in 1981 to remove the necessity of IRB reviews from some low-risk research and to provide for informal consent procedures in some cases. They were revised again in 1991. A host of other federal agencies, including the Food and Drug Administration, have promulgated rules that are parallel to those issued by the DHHS. This year in the United States, over three thousand IRBs will review tens of thousands of research protocols. No federally funded research will be carried out at an institution without that institution's IRB approval.

C. CURRENT REGULATION OF RESEARCH UPON HUMAN-SUBJECTS IN THE UNITED STATES

Consider the currently applicable regulations. Determine how they reflect the Nuremberg Code, the Declaration of Helsinki and the principle that health care policies ought not be determined at the national level, but, rather, should be delegated to local agencies that reflect local community values.

Problem: Research in the Emergency Room

As counsel to a small community hospital that previously has not engaged in any research, you have been asked how the hospital trustees should react to the request of one of the emergency room physicians to engage in two separate research projects. In the first, she wishes to evaluate the effectiveness of the emergency room staff in dealing with victims of rape. She wishes to ask all such patients, some of whom are likely to be minors, to answer a series of questions on their religious, cultural, and educational background and on their knowledge of social resources for rape victims. She also intends to review those patients' medical and psychological histories. Finally, she wishes to contact them by mail several weeks after their hospital admission with a follow up questionnaire. All information will be coded so that only the investigator will be able to determine the identity of any patient. The physician believes that the research will help the hospital determine what kinds of immediate care are most helpful to rape victims (e.g., what kind of psychological counseling is most important?), what kinds of physicians are best qualified to help those patients (e.g., are women physicians more likely to provide satisfactory treatment?), and what kinds of hospital policies are most likely to encourage victims to seek medical attention (e.g., should the hospital call the police if the alleged victim has not?). She expects to publish the results of her research, which will cost about $10,000 to perform. About $1500 of the costs will be underwritten by a grant from DHHS.

In the second project, she wishes to join a group from several other emergency rooms around the country in evaluating the use of two different treatment modalities for those who are admitted to the emergency room unconscious and apparently the victim of myocardial infarction. The first is the immediate administration of the drug MILINASE; the second is the delayed administration of another drug, CORAPRINE. There is some evidence that each of these two alternatives is more effective than any currently approved treatment, but neither has been the subject of adequate studies, and neither has received final approval from the FDA for this (or any other) use. This study will test each against the other, and against a placebo. None of the cost of this research will be paid by DHHS (except through Medicare or Medicaid, to the extent that such patients arrive in the emergency room and need treatment).

Is the hospital obliged to establish an institutional review board to review either of these two research proposals? If so, how is one established? Who should be on it? To whom should it report? What, precisely, should it review? What standards should it apply to the review? Is there any way that this research can be done without the establishment of such a board?

Problem: Research on Capitated Payment Plans

Gargantuan Health Maintenance Organization wishes to do research on the effect of withholds on the behavior of its primary care physicians. Each of its primary care physicians, who work exclusively for Gargantuan and serve only patients who are members of its HMO, is paid a monthly fee of $22 per capita (i.e., per patient on that physician's primary care list). The Gargantuan administration wants to involve 20 primary care physicians in the study, and to randomize half of the patients on each of those physicians' lists to "withhold" status and maintain half on pure capitation status. While the physicians would continue to receive $22 per capita for the pure capitation patients, they would receive $55 per capita for the "withhold" patients. However, $40 of this $55 would be withheld in a special suspense account, and any costs borne by the HMO as a result of any order of the primary care physician (i.e., the cost of all lab tests, referrals, prescriptions, hospitalizations, and the like) for those patients in the "withhold" group would be subtracted from the suspense account before the balance is paid to the physician at the end of the year. The payment status of each patient would be clearly identified to the primary care physician. The economists who would administer this research hypothesize that primary care physicians will order fewer additional services and less additional treatment for their "withhold" patients than for their pure capitation patients. Gargantuan intends to keep the results for their own use alone. They consider the design of their payment system to be a trade secret, although they would reveal the results, if required, in their defense of a malpractice law suit.

Does this proposal constitute research involving human subjects? Must it be approved by an IRB? Must Gargantuan establish its own IRB, or can it depend upon the approval of an IRB at a local hospital? Who are the subjects? What information should "subjects" have in order to assure that their consent is informed? If you were on the IRB reviewing this research protocol, would you vote unconditionally to approve it? If you would impose conditions, what would they be?

45 C.F.R. PART 46—BASIC HHS POLICY FOR PROTECTION OF HUMAN RESEARCH SUBJECTS

§ 46.101 To what does this policy apply?

(a) Except as provided in paragraph (b) of this section, this policy applies to all research involving human subjects conducted, supported or otherwise subject to regulation by any federal department or agency which takes appropriate administrative action to make the policy applicable to such research. This includes research conducted by federal civilian employees or military personnel, except that each department or agency head may adopt such procedural modifications as may be appropriate from an administrative standpoint. It also includes research conducted, supported, or otherwise subject to regulation by the federal government outside the United States.

(1) Research that is conducted or supported by a federal department or agency, whether or not it is regulated as defined in § 46.102(e) must comply with all sections of this policy.

(2) Research that is neither conducted nor supported by a federal department or agency but is subject to regulation as defined in § 46.102(e) must be reviewed and approved, in compliance with § 46.101 & § 46.102 and § 46.107 through § 46.117 of this policy, by an institutional review board (IRB) that operates in accordance with the pertinent requirements of this policy.

(b) Unless otherwise required by department or agency heads, research activities in which the only involvement of human subjects will be in one or more of the following categories are exempt from this policy:

(1) Research conducted in established or commonly accepted educational settings, involving normal educational practices, such as (i) research on regular and special education instructional strategies, or (ii) research on the effectiveness of or the comparison among instructional techniques, curricula, or classroom management methods.

(2) Research involving the use of educational tests (cognitive, diagnostic, aptitude, achievement), survey procedures, interview procedures or observation of public behavior, unless:

(i) Information obtained is recorded in such a manner that human subjects can be identified, directly or through identifiers linked to the subjects; and (ii) any disclosure of the human subjects' responses outside the research could reasonably place the subjects at risk of criminal or civil liability or be damaging to the subjects' financial standing, employability, or reputation.

(3) Research involving the use of educational tests (cognitive, diagnostic, aptitude, achievement), survey procedures, interview procedures, or observation of public behavior that is not exempt under paragraph (b)(2) of this section, if:

    (i) The human subjects are elected or appointed public officials or candidates for public office; or (ii) federal statute(s) require(s) without exception that the confidentiality of the personally identifiable information will be maintained throughout the research and thereafter.

(4) Research, involving the collection or study of existing data, documents, records, pathological specimens, or diagnostic specimens, if these sources are publicly available or if the information is recorded by the investigator in such a manner that subjects cannot be identified, directly or through identifiers linked to the subjects.

(5) Research and demonstration projects which are conducted by or subject to the approval of department or agency heads, and which are designed to study, evaluate, or otherwise examine:

    (i) Public benefit or service program; (ii) procedures for obtaining benefits or services under those programs; (iii) possible changes in or alternatives to those programs or procedures; or (iv) possible changes in methods or levels of payment for benefits or services under those programs.

(6) Taste and food quality evaluation and consumer acceptance studies.

* * *

(c) Department or agency heads retain final judgment as to whether a particular activity is covered by this policy.

(d) Department or agency heads may require that specific research activities or classes of research activities conducted, supported, or otherwise subject to regulation by the department or agency but not otherwise covered by this policy, comply with some or all of the requirements of this policy.

* * *

(f) This policy does not affect any state or local laws or regulations which may otherwise be applicable and which provide additional protections for human subjects.

(g) This policy does not affect any foreign laws or regulations which may otherwise be applicable and which provide additional protections to human subjects of research.

(h) When research covered by this policy takes place in foreign countries, procedures normally followed in the foreign countries to protect human subjects may differ from those set forth in this policy. [An example is a foreign institution which complies with guidelines consistent with the World Medical Assembly Declaration (Declaration of Helsinki amended 1989) issued either by sovereign states or by an organization whose function for the protection of human research subjects is internationally recognized.] In these circumstances, if a department or agency head determines that the procedures prescribed by the institution afford protections that are at least equivalent to those provided in this policy, the department or agency head may approve the substitution of the foreign procedures in lieu of the procedural requirements provided in this policy.

* * *

(i) Unless otherwise required by law, department or agency heads may waive the applicability of some or all of the provisions of this policy to specific research activities or classes of research activities otherwise covered by this policy.

* * *

§ 46.102 Definitions.

(a) Department or agency head means the head of any federal department or agency and any other office or employee of any department or agency to whom authority has been delegated.

(b) Institution means any public or private entity or agency (including federal, state, and other agencies).

(c) Legally authorized representative means an individual or judicial or other body authorized under applicable law to consent on behalf of a prospective subject to the subject's participation in the procedure(s) involved in the research.

(d) Research means a systematic investigation, including research development, testing and evaluation, designed to develop or contribute to generalizable knowledge. Activities which meet this definition constitute research for purposes of this policy, whether or not they are conducted or supported under a program which is considered research for other purposes. For example, some demonstration and service programs may include research activities.

(e) Research subject to regulation and similar terms are intended to encompass those research activities for which a federal department or agency has specific responsibility for regulating as a research activity, (for example, Investigational New Drug requirements administered by the Food and Drug Administration).

* * *

(f) Human subject means a living individual about whom an investigator (whether professional or student) conducting research obtains

(1) Data through intervention or interaction with the individual, or

(2) Identifiable private information. Intervention includes both physical procedures by which data are gathered (for example, venipuncture) or manipulations of the subject or the subject's environment that are performed for research purposes. Interaction includes communication or interpersonal contact between investigator and subject. Private information includes information about behavior that occurs in a context in which an individual can reasonably expect that no observation or record-

ing is taking place, and information which has been provided for specific purposes by an individual and which the individual can reasonably expect will not be made public (for example, a medical record). Private information must be individually identifiable (i.e., the identity of the subject is or may readily be ascertained by the investigator or associated with the information) in order for obtaining the information to constitute research involving human subjects.

(g) IRB means an institutional review board established in accord with and for the purposes expressed in this policy.

(h) IRB approval means the determination of the IRB that the research has been reviewed and may be conducted at an institution within the constraints set forth by the IRB and by other institutional and federal requirements.

(i) Minimal risk means that the probability and magnitude of harm or discomfort anticipated in the research are not greater in and of themselves than those ordinarily encountered in daily life or during the performance of routine physical or psychological examinations or tests.

* * *

§ 46.107 IRB membership.

(a) Each IRB shall have at least five members, with varying backgrounds to promote complete and adequate review of research activities commonly conducted by the institution. The IRB shall be sufficiently qualified through the experience and expertise of its members, and the diversity of the members, including consideration of race, gender, and cultural backgrounds and sensitivity to such issues as community attitudes, to promote respect for its advice and counsel in safeguarding the rights and welfare of human subjects. In addition to possessing the professional competence necessary to review specific research activities, the IRB shall be able to ascertain the acceptability of proposed research in terms of institutional commitments and regulations, applicable law, and standards of professional conduct and practice. The IRB shall therefore include persons knowledgeable in these areas. If an IRB regularly reviews research that involves a vulnerable category of subjects, such as children, prisoners, pregnant women, or handicapped or mentally disabled persons, consideration shall be given to the inclusion of one or more individuals who are knowledgeable about and experienced in working with these subjects.

(b) Every nondiscriminatory effort will be made to ensure that no IRB consists entirely of men or entirely of women, including the institution's consideration of qualified persons of both sexes, so long as no selection is made to the IRB on the basis of gender. No IRB may consist entirely of members of one profession.

(c) Each IRB shall include at least one member whose primary concerns are in scientific areas and at least one member whose primary concerns are in nonscientific areas.

(d) Each IRB shall include at least one member who is not otherwise affiliated with the institution and who is not part of the immediate family of a person who is affiliated with the institution.

(e) No IRB may have a member participate in the IRB's initial or continuing review of any project in which the member has a conflicting interest, except to provide information requested by the IRB.

(f) An IRB may, in its discretion, invite individuals with competence in special areas to assist in the review of issues which require expertise beyond or in addition to that available on the IRB. These individuals may not vote with the IRB.

§ 46.108   IRB functions and operations.

In order to fulfill the requirements of this policy each IRB shall:

* * *

(b) Except when an expedited review procedure is used (see § 46.110), review proposed research at convened meetings at which a majority of the members of the IRB are present, including at least one member whose primary concerns are in nonscientific areas. In order for the research to be approved, it shall receive the approval of a majority of those members present at the meeting.

§ 46.109   IRB review of research.

(a) An IRB shall review and have authority to approve, require modification in (to secure approval), or disapprove all research activities covered by this policy.

(b) An IRB shall require that information given to subjects as part of informed consent is in accordance with § 46.116. The IRB may require that information, in addition to that specifically mentioned in § 46.116, be given to the subjects when the IRB's judgment the information would meaningfully add to the protection of the rights and welfare of subjects.

(c) An IRB shall require documentation of informed consent or may waive documentation in accordance with § 46.117.

(d) An IRB shall notify investigators and the institution in writing of its decision to approve or disapprove the proposed research activity, or of modifications required to secure IRB approval of the research activity. If the IRB decides to disapprove a research activity, it shall include in its written notification a statement of the reasons for its decision and give the investigator an opportunity to respond in person or in writing.

(e) An IRB shall conduct continuing review of research covered by this policy at intervals appropriate to the degree of risk, but not less than one per year, and shall have authority to observe or have a third party observe the consent process and the research.

§ 46.110   Expedited review procedures for certain kinds of research involving no more than minimal risk, and for minor changes in approved research.

* * *

(b) An IRB may use the expedited review procedure to review either or both of the following:

(1) Some or all of the research appearing on the list [published by the DHHS in the Federal Register] and found by the reviewer(s) to involve no more than minimal risk.

(2) Minor changes in previously approved research during the period (of one year or less) for which approval is authorized.

Under an expedited review procedure, the review may be carried out by the IRB chairperson or by one or more experienced reviewers designated by the chairperson from among members of the IRB. In reviewing the research, the reviewers may exercise all of the authorities of the IRB except that the reviewers may not disapprove the research. A research activity may de disapproved only after review in accordance with the non-expedited procedure set forth in § 46.108(b).

(c) Each IRB which uses an expedited review procedure shall adopt a method for keeping all members advised of research proposals which have been approved under the procedure.

(d) The department or agency head may restrict, suspend, terminate, or choose not to authorize an institution's or IRB's use of the expedited review procedure.

§ 46.111   Criteria for IRB approval of research.

(a) In order to approve research covered by this policy the IRB shall determine that all of the following requirements are satisfied:

(1) Risks to subjects are minimized: (i) By using procedures which are consistent with sound research design and which do not unnecessarily expose subjects to risk, and (ii) whenever appropriate, by using procedures already being performed on the subjects for diagnostic or treatment purposes.

(2) Risks to subjects are reasonable in relation to anticipated benefits, if any, to subjects, and the importance of the knowledge that may reasonable be expected to result. In evaluating risks and benefits, the IRB should consider only those risks and benefits that may result from the research (as distinguished from risks and benefits of therapies subjects would receive even if not participating in the research). The IRB should not consider possible long-range effects of applying knowledge gained in the research (for example, the possible effects of the research on public policy) as among those research risks that fall within the purview of its responsibility.

(3) Selection of subjects is equitable. In making this assessment the IRB should take into account the purposes of the research and the setting in which the research will be conducted and should be particularly cognizant of the special problems or research involving vulnerable populations, such as children, prisoners, pregnant women, mentally disabled persons, or economically or educationally disadvantaged persons.

(4) Informed consent will be sought from each prospective subject or the subject's legally authorized representative, in accordance with, and to the extent required by § 46.116.

(5) Informed consent will be appropriately documented, in accordance with, and to the extent required by § 46.117.

(6) When appropriate, the research plan makes adequate provision for monitoring the data collected to ensure the safety of subjects.

(7) When appropriate, there are adequate provisions to protect the privacy of subjects and to maintain the confidentiality of data.

(b) When some or all of the subjects are likely to be vulnerable to coercion or undue influence, such as children, prisoners, pregnant women, mentally disabled persons, or economically or educationally disadvantaged persons, additional safeguards have been included in the study to protect the rights and welfare of these subjects.

§ 46.112   Review by institution.

Research covered by this policy that has been approved by the IRB may be subject to further appropriate review and approval or disapproval by officials of the institution. However, those officials may not approve the research if it has not been approved by an IRB.

§ 46.113   Suspension or termination of IRB approval of research.

An IRB shall have authority to suspend or terminate approval of research that is not being conducted in accordance with the IRB's requirements or that has been associated with unexpected serious harm to subjects. Any suspension or termination of approval shall include a statement of the reasons for the IRB's action and shall be reported promptly to the investigator.

§ 46.114   Cooperative research.

Cooperative research projects are those projects covered by this policy which involve more than one institution. In the conduct of cooperative research projects, each institution is responsible for safeguarding the rights and welfare of human subjects and for complying with this policy. With the approval of the department or agency head, an institution participating in a cooperative project may enter into a joint review arrangement, rely upon the review of another qualified IRB, or make similar arrangements for avoiding duplication of effort.

§ 46.116   General requirements for informed consent.

Except as provided elsewhere in this policy, no investigator may involve a human being as a subject in research covered by this policy unless the investigator has obtained the legally effective informed consent of the subject or the subject's legally authorized representative. An investigator shall seek such consent only under circumstances that provide the prospective subject or the representative sufficient opportunity to consider whether or not to participate and that minimize the possibility of coercion or undue influence. The information that is given to the subject or the representative shall be in language understandable to the subject or the representative. No informed consent, whether oral or written, may include any exculpatory language through which the subject or the representative is made to waive or appear to waive any of the subject's legal rights, or releases or appears to release the investigator, the sponsor, the institution or its agents from liability for negligence.

(a) Basic elements of informed consent. Except as provided in paragraph (c) or (d) of this section, in seeking informed consent the following information shall be provided to each subject:

(1) A statement that the study involves research, an explanation of the purposes of the research and the expected duration of the subject's participation, a description of the procedures to be followed, and identification of any procedures which are experimental;

(2) A description of any reasonably foreseeable risks or discomforts to the subject;

(3) A description of any benefits to the subject or to others which may reasonably be expected from the research;

(4) A disclosure of appropriate alternative procedures or courses of treatment, if any, that might be advantageous to the subject;

(5) a statement describing the extent, if any, to which confidentiality of records identifying the subject will be maintained;

(6) For research involving more than minimal risk, an explanation as to whether any compensation and an explanation as to whether any medical treatments are available if injury occurs and, if so, what they consist of, or where further information may be obtained;

(7) An explanation of whom to contact for answers to pertinent questions about the research and research subjects' rights, to whom to contact in the event of a research-related injury to the subject; and

(8) A statement that participation is voluntary, refusal to participate will involve no penalty or loss of benefits to which the subject is otherwise entitled, and the subject may discontinue participation at any time without penalty or loss of benefits to which the subject is otherwise entitled.

(b) Additional elements of informed consent. When appropriate, one or more of the following elements of information shall also be provided to each subject;

(1) A statement that the particular treatment or procedure may involve risks to the subject (or to the embryo or fetus, if the subject is or may become pregnant) which are currently unforeseeable;

(2) Anticipated circumstances under which the subject's participation may be terminated by the investigator without regard to the subject's consent;

(3) Any additional costs to the subject that may result from participation in the research;

(4) The consequences of a subject's decision to withdraw from the research and procedures for orderly termination of participation by the subject;

(5) A statement that significant new findings developed during the course of the research which may relate to the subject's willingness to continue participation will be provided to the subject; and

(6) The approximate number of subjects involved in the study.

(c) An IRB may approve a consent procedure which does not include, or which alters, some or all of the elements of informed consent set forth above, or waive the requirements to obtain information consent provided the IRB finds and documents that:

(1) The research or demonstration project is to be conducted by or subject to the approval of state or local government officials and is designed to study, evaluate, or otherwise examine:

(i) Public benefit of service programs; (ii) procedures for obtaining benefits or services under those programs; (iii) possible changes in or alternatives to those programs or procedures; or (iv) possible changes in methods or levels of payment for benefits or services under those programs; and

(2) The research could not practicably be carried out without the waiver or alteration.

(d) An IRB may approve a consent procedure which does not include, or which alters, some or all of the elements of informed consent set forth in this actions, or waive the requirements to obtain informed consent provided the IRB finds and documents that:

(1) The research involves no more than minimal risks to the subjects;

(2) The waiver or alteration will not adversely affect the rights and welfare of the subjects;

(3) The research could not practicably be carried out without the waiver or alteration; and

(4) Whenever appropriate, the subjects will be provided with additional pertinent information after participation.

(e) The informed consent requirements in this policy are not intended to preempt any applicable federal, state, or local laws which require additional information to be disclosed in order for informed consent to be legally effective.

(f) Nothing in this policy is intended to limit the authority of a physician to provide emergency medical care, to the extent the physician is permitted to do so under applicable federal, state, or local law.

§ 46.117 Documentation of informed consent.

(a) Except as provided in paragraph (c) of this section, informed consent shall be documented by the use of a written consent form approved by the IRB and signed by the subject or the subject's legally authorized representative. A copy shall be given to the person signing the form.

(b) Except as provided in paragraph (c) of this section, the consent form may be either of the following:

(1) A written consent document that embodies the elements of informed consent required by § 46.116. This form may be read to the subject or the subject's legally authorized representative, but in any event, the investigator shall give either the subject or the representative adequate opportunity to read it before it is signed; or

(2) A short form written consent document stating that the elements of informed consent required by § 46.116 have been presented orally to the subject or the subject's legally authorized representative. When this method is used, there shall be a witness to the oral presentation. Also, the IRB shall approve a written summary or the representative. Only the

short form itself is to be signed by the subject or the representative. However, the witness shall sign both the short form and a copy of the summary, and the person actually obtaining consent shall sign a copy of the summary. A copy of the summary shall be given to the subject or the representative, in addition to a copy of the short form.

(c) An IRB may waive the requirement for the investigator to obtain a signed consent form for some or all subjects if it finds either:

(1) That the only record linking the subject and the research would be the consent document and the principal risk would be potential harm resulting from a breach of confidentiality. Each subject will be asked whether the subject wants documentation linking the subject with the research, and the subject's wishes will govern; or

(2) That the research presents no more than minimal risk of harm to subjects and involves no procedures for which consent is normally required outside of the research context.

In cases in which the documentation requirement is waived, the IRB may require the investigator to provide subjects with a written statement regarding the research.

* * *

§ 46.122   Use of Federal funds.

Federal funds administered by a department or agency may not be expended for research involving human subjects unless the requirements of this policy have been satisfied.

* * *

§ 46.124   Conditions.

With respect to any research project or any class of research projects the department or agency head may impose additional conditions prior to or at the time of approval when in the judgment of the department or agency head additional conditions are necessary for the protection of human subjects.

Notes and Questions

1.   IRB procedures set out in the regulations are required only for research performed or funded by the United States government, or subject to "regulation by any federal department or agency," as defined in § 46.102. The regulations do not apply to other research, even when conducted at the same institutions. This distinction may not have much practical effect, however, because Food and Drug Administration (and other federal agency) regulations apply the same principles to a wide range of research. In addition, each institution that receives DHHS funding must provide the Secretary with an assurance that the institution will protect the rights of human subjects in all research conducted at the institution, without regard to research funding source. Most institutions meet this "assurance" requirement by agreeing to apply DHHS regulations to all research, even that not funded by DHHS and thus not technically otherwise governed by those regulations.

2.   IRBs are intended to reflect local conditions and local values. They may have as few as five members or as many as the institution wishes to place on the

board; some have dozens of members. IRBs are expected to reflect the racial and cultural diversity of the community and to be sensitive to community attitudes. Section 46.107(b), which requires professional diversity and a good-faith effort at gender diversity, assures that an IRB will not consist of only male physicians. There must be one non-scientist on each IRB (previous regulations suggested a lawyer, ethicist, or member of the clergy), and there must be one member who is not affiliated with the institution.

Do the regulations effectively guarantee that the IRB will represent the values that ought to be considered in making research determinations? Most IRBs include several researchers from the institution, a clinical nurse, a local clergyman, perhaps an administrator and a lawyer. What purpose does the presence of the lawyer serve? Is there anything in the background of the lawyer that makes his or her presence on the board significant? What role should the lawyer assume in serving on the IRB? Does it matter whether the lawyer is institutional counsel? If you were to rewrite § 46.107, which deals with IRB membership, what kind of interdisciplinary mix would you require on the IRB? Why?

3. While § 46.111 establishes seven substantive criteria for approval of a research protocol, most IRB time is spent discussing (1) whether the "risks to subjects are reasonable in relationship to anticipated benefits," and (2) whether the informed consent form is adequate. Should these be the primary substantive bases for community review of medical research? Consent forms can always be rewritten: thus, in the rare instance that a research protocol is turned down by an IRB the reason is usually that the IRB has determined that the risk to benefit ratio is not acceptable. The power to reach this determination gives a substantial amount of authority to the committee.

4. The IRB must determine that risks to the subjects are reasonable in relationship to (1) benefits to the subjects and (2) the importance of the knowledge that may reasonably be expected to result. The IRB must consider the long-range effects of the knowledge in evaluating *benefits,* but it may *not* consider the long range effects on evaluating *risks.* § 46.111(a)(2). Thus, an IRB could not refuse approval of a military study just because the results could be used only to promote offensive weaponry. Similarly, IRBs have been required to approve studies of sleeping pills that have a minimal benefit (and no risk) to patients under clinical conditions, even though the IRB members agreed that ultimate FDA approval of the sleeping pills and their consequent public availability would have a serious adverse effect on public health.

5. When an IRB is established at a private institution under the direction of federal regulations, is the IRB a federal agency or merely a private committee? Is it the subject of federal statutory and regulatory constraints? Must an IRB respond to a Freedom of Information Act request? If a state institution—for instance, a state hospital—establishes an IRB under federal law, is the IRB a federal agency, a state agency, some hybrid of the two, or something else entirely? If there is a conflict between the Freedom of Information Act and a state public records act, which is the appropriate vehicle for obtaining information from a state hospital IRB? Can an IRB be a federal agency and a state agency at the same time?

6. There has been some interest in obtaining records of IRBs for use elsewhere—for example, in malpractice cases. Are the IRB documents or records of their deliberations public information, entirely confidential, or something between the two? Are the IRBs medical review committees whose processes and documents are confidential and not discoverable? Would it affect the deliberations

of the IRB if those deliberations could later be made public and the participants cross-examined? Some IRBs meet privately and admit no outsiders, some admit outsiders with advance approval of the chair or the IRB, and some IRBs meet in public arenas and allow some public participation. See Bernard R. Adams, Medical Research and Personal Privacy, 30 Villanova L.Rev. 1077 (1985). For an account of a successful attempt by one United States Attorney to get information concerning the administration of federally funded medical research, see United States v. Najarian, 915 F.Supp. 1441 (D.Minn.1995) and 915 F.Supp. 1460 (D.Minn.1996).

7. In 1983 the Department of Health and Human Services promulgated regulations which provide supplementary protection to children who are research subjects. These regulations divide research upon children into three categories: "research not involving greater than the minimal risk," "research involving greater than minimal risk but presenting the prospect of direct benefit to the individual subjects," and "research involving greater than minimal risk and no prospect of direct benefit to individual subjects, but likely to yield generalizable knowledge about the subject's disorder or condition." 45 C.F.R. §§ 46.401–46.409. In all cases IRB approval must assure that "adequate provisions are made for soliciting the assent of the children and permission of their parents or guardians."

Where there is more than minimal risk but the research will also benefit the child, the risk must be justified "by the anticipated benefit to the subjects" (unleavened by any benefit that society may derive), and "[t]he relation of the anticipated benefit to the risk [must be] at least as favorable to the subjects as that presented by available alternative approaches." 45 C.F.R. § 46.405. Non-therapeutic research involving more than minimal risk may be approved only if there is a "minor" increase over minimal risk, the "experiences" that accompany the research are those that the child-subjects are likely to undergo anyway, and the research is aimed at a disorder or condition actually suffered by the subject. 45 C.F.R. § 46.406. The regulations require the consent (called "permission" in the regulations) of one parent before a child may participate in research, although the permission of both parents (if they are reasonably available) is required before a child becomes a subject in non-therapeutic research involving greater than minimal risk.

The regulations also require that "the IRB shall determine that adequate provisions are made for soliciting the assent of the children, when in the judgment of the IRB the children are capable of providing assent." 45 C.F.R. § 46.408. The IRB is required to consider the age, maturity, and psychological state of the subjects when determining whether the children are capable of assenting, and the IRB is entitled to make a determination of the propriety of requiring subject assent on either a protocol-by-protocol or child-by-child basis. Id.

Finally, the regulations put additional limitations on research involving "[c]hildren who are wards of the state or any other agency, institution, or entity. * * *" 45 C.F.R. § 46.409. The regulations attempt to discourage researchers from using these easy marks as subjects, and their use as subjects is prohibited unless the research is "related to their status as wards" or is conducted in such a way that most of the children who are subjects are not wards. Id.

8. Perhaps the most controversial federal regulations governing research are those that severely limit fetal research and research involving pregnant women as subjects. As a general matter, such research cannot be conducted unless all appropriate studies on animals and "nonpregnant individuals" is completed, the purpose of the research is to meet the health needs of the subject (either the pregnant woman or the fetus), the risk is minimized, those who are engaged in the

research "will have no part in ... any decisions as to the timing, method, and procedures used to terminate the pregnancy [or] determining the viability of the fetus ..." and there will be no change in the abortion procedure "solely in the interest" of the research. In addition, "[n]o inducements may be offered to terminate pregnancy ..." for the purpose of doing research upon the fetus. 45 C.F.R. § 46.206.

The regulation also divides research into that done on a fetus *in utero* and that done on a fetus *ex utero*. Research cannot be done upon a fetus *in utero* unless the purpose of the medical intervention is therapeutic and the risk to the fetus is minimized, or, alternatively, the risk to the fetus is minimal (as defined by the regulations) and "the purpose of the activity is the development of important biomedical knowledge which cannot be obtained by other means." 45 C.F.R. § 46.208.

A viable *ex utero* fetus is a child, of course. An *ex utero* fetus which may be viable cannot be employed as a research subject unless "[t]here will be no added risk to the fetus ... and the purpose ... is the development of important biomedical knowledge which cannot be obtained by other means," or the purpose of the research is to "enhance the possibility of the particular fetus to the point of viability." A nonviable *ex utero* fetus cannot be a research subject unless there is no attempt to artificially maintain the vital functions of the fetus, the research itself will not stop the heartbeat or respiration of the fetus, and, once again, "[t]he purpose of the activity is the development of important biomedical knowledge which cannot be obtained by other means." 45 C.F.R. § 46.209.

Pregnant women may be employed as subjects only if the research is therapeutic and the risk to the fetus is minimized, or the risk to the fetus is minimal, as defined by the regulation. 45 C.F.R. § 46.207. In any case, whether the research is done on a pregnant woman, a fetus *in utero* or a fetus *ex utero*, before the research is conducted the researcher must obtain the consent of both the mother and the father of the fetus unless the treatment is therapeutic for the mother, the father's whereabouts cannot be reasonably ascertained or he is not reasonably available, or the pregnancy is the result of rape. 45 C.F.R. § 46.208. Is this requirement of consent from the father permitted by the Constitution? Could a father block a pregnant woman from engaging in nontherapeutic research when she wishes to participate as a research subject?

The regulation governing research on fetuses and pregnant women has been in effect for almost twenty years, and some view it as an effective prohibition on research upon human fetuses. Some scientists argue that the government should be encouraging, not discouraging, research upon human fetuses because more research in this area would help many nonviable fetuses reach the point of viability, and it would help many viable fetuses live longer and happier lives. On the other hand, some argue that the special vulnerability of the fetus requires special protection by government regulation. Of course, the debate over the appropriate limitations on research involving fetuses and fetal tissue is not unrelated to the debate over the propriety of abortion. Some fear that giving physicians the authority to do research upon fetal tissue will inevitably result in the acquisition of that tissue through encouraged or solicited abortions.

9. Since 1978, the federal regulations have severely limited research using prisoners as human subjects. Such research is permitted only to study incarceration and its consequences or problems (like hepatitis, alcoholism or sexual assault) particularly affecting prisoners as a class. In a wide range of cases, even that research is permitted only after the Secretary of DHHS has consulted with

appropriate experts and the field and given notice of the intent to carry out the research in the *Federal Register*.

When prisoners are to be used as subjects, the research must be approved by an IRB that is independent of the prison, and which includes at least one prisoner or prisoner representative. That IRB can then approve the research only if prisoners are given no advantages because of their participation in the study, if the risks are the kind that unincarcerated subjects would be willing to undertake, if the subjects are equitably selected, if participation will have no effect on parole decisions (and the prisoner knows this), and if there is adequate provision for follow up. 45 C.F.R. §§ 46.301 through 46.306.

Are there good reasons for providing prisoners with so much regulatory protection from research? Some say the regulations go too far, and that we should permit prisoners to discharge their debt to society by becoming research subjects if they wish to do so. Is that a sound argument? See Sharona Hoffman, Beneficial and Unusual Punishment: An Argument in Support of Prisoner Participation in Clinical Trials, 33 Ind.L.Rev. 475 (2000). See also Allen Hornblum, Acres of Skin: Human Experiments at Holmesburg Prison (1998). For judicial consideration of these issues, see Bailey v. Lally, 481 F.Supp. 203 (D.Md.1979)(claim that prison conditions were so bad and inducements to participate in research so great that consent could not be voluntary, and thus violated prisoners' constitutional rights) and People v. Gauntlett, 134 Mich.App. 737, 352 N.W.2d 310 (1984)(sex offender could not be forced to undergo experimental "chemical castration" as a condition of probation).

10. Among others for whom additional research protections have been proposed but not adopted are those institutionalized as mentally disabled. See National Bioethics Advisory Commission, Research Involving Persons With Mental Disorders That May Affect Decisionmaking Capacity (1998)(addressing the need for protection of mentally disabled research subjects, whether institutionalized or not); for a set of proposed regulations providing protection to the institutionalized mentally disabled, see 43 Fed.Reg. 53950 (1978). While the unadopted regulations have no legal effect, the discussion that followed the proposal of regulations aimed at institutionalized mentally disabled subjects has had a real effect on the research community; there is now an attempt to avoid this class of subjects if others are available. Do you think that the institutionalized mentally disabled need additional protection from research? How would you draft regulations to protect that class of potential subjects?

11. Occasionally researchers complain that the federal regulations effectively eliminate the possibility that they can carry out important research. For example, emergency room physicians were faced with several alternative but unproven medications that could be of use to unconscious patients who arrive after suffering a heart attack or a stroke. Further, there was no generally accepted and effective treatment for these patients. Emergency room physicians had a choice with these patients—provide the ineffective traditional treatment, or try the new, possibly effective, experimental treatment. Because these patients were not competent to consent, though, they could not be employed as subjects in research to prove the efficacy of the newly developed treatment. As a result of this conundrum, it was impossible for there ever to be any clinically sound research on the promising new treatments for these emergency conditions. Faced with this problem, and with the necessity for meaningful research within the emergency room, the Food and Drug Administration in 1995 amended its regulations governing research involving

human subjects, which are parallel to (but not exactly the same as) the DHHS regulations, by adding the following provision:

§ 50.24 Exception from informed consent requirements for emergency research.

(a) The IRB responsible for the review, approval, and continuing review of the clinical investigation described in this section may approve that investigation without requiring that informed consent be obtained if the IRB (with a concurring licensed physician member or consultant) finds and documents each of the following:

(1) The human subjects are in a life-threatening situation, available treatments are unproven or unsatisfactory, and the collection of valid scientific evidence, which may include evidence obtained through randomized placebo controlled trials, is necessary to determine what particular intervention is most beneficial.

(2) Obtaining informed consent is not feasible because:

(i) The subjects will not be able to give consent as a result of their medical condition; and

(ii) The intervention under study must be administered before consent from legally authorized representatives is feasible; and

(iii) There is no reasonable way to identify prospectively the individuals likely to become eligible for the research because the emergency of the condition to be studied cannot be predicted reliably in particular individuals.

(3) The opportunity for the subjects to participate in the research is in the interest of the subjects because:

(i) A life-threatening situation necessitates intervention, and

(ii) The risk of the investigation is reasonable in light of what is known about the medical condition and the risks and benefits of current therapy, if any, and what is known about the risks and benefits of the proposed intervention or activity.

(4) The research could not practicably be carried out without the waiver.

(5) Additional protections of the rights and welfare of the subjects will be provided, including, at least:

(i) Consultation (which may include consultation carried out by the IRB itself) with representatives of the communities from which the subjects will be drawn;

(ii) Public disclosure prior to the commencement of the study sufficient to describe the study and its risks and benefits;

(iii) Public disclosure of sufficient information following completion of the study to apprise the community and researchers of the study and its results; and

(iv) The establishment of an independent data and safety monitoring board.

(6) The IRB has reviewed and approved an informed consent document for use with subjects or legal representatives in situations in which obtaining such consent may be feasible for some subjects.

(b) When possible and at the earliest possible opportunity, each subject (or, if the subject remains incapacitated, a legally authorized representative of the subject, or if such a representative is not reasonably available, a family member), will be informed of the subject's inclusion in the research study, the details of the research study, and that the subject (or, if the subject remains incapacitated, a legally authorized representative of the subject, or, if such a representative is not reasonably available, a family member) may discontinue the subject's participation at any time without penalty or loss of benefits to which the subject is otherwise entitled.

Would you support this change in the federal regulations? Does it leave any possibility of abuse of emergency room patients? Can you think of any alternative regulatory change that would allow emergency room research on unconscious patients, but would better protect those subjects? How would you feel if you found out that one of your relatives was brought into a study under this regulation, and that she was randomized to a placebo rather than to a promising new drug?

12.   Human beings are not fungible as research subjects. Medications, devices and procedures that are effective in treating men may not be as effective (or may be more effective) in treating women. Similarly, what works for patients of European extraction may not be so effective in treating Native Americans, Asians, African Americans, or others. Still, for many years most medical research appears to have been conducted using primarily (or, in some cases, only) White male subjects. There were two adverse consequences on the women and the minorities who were thus excluded from these studies—first, individuals were denied the therapeutic promise of the treatments that were the subject of the research, and, second, these groups were denied the knowledge of whether the treatment under research would be effective for them. Congress required the National Institutes of Health to address these concerns in the NIH Revitalization Act of 1993, and the NIH responded with a new policy in 1994. That policy provides:

Research Involving Human Subjects

It is the policy of NIH that women and members of minority groups and their subpopulations must be included in all NIH-supported biomedical and behavioral research projects involving human subjects, unless a clear and compelling rationale and justification establishes to the satisfaction of the relevant Institute/Center Director that inclusion is inappropriate with respect to the health of the subjects or the purpose of the research. Exclusion under other circumstances may be made by the Director, NIH, upon the recommendation of a Institute/Center Director based on a compelling rationale and justification. Cost is not an acceptable reason for exclusion except when the study would duplicate data from other sources. Women of childbearing potential should not be routinely excluded from participation in clinical research. All NIH-supported biomedical and behavioral research involving human subjects is defined as clinical research. This policy applies to research subjects of all ages.

The inclusion of women and members of minority groups and their subpopulations must be addressed in developing a research design appropriate to the scientific objectives of the study. The research plan should describe the composition of the proposed study population in terms of gender and racial/ethnic group, and provide a rationale for selection of such subjects. Such a plan should contain a description of the proposed outreach programs for recruiting women and minorities as participants.

The 1994 guideline specifically requires the investigator to review the data to determine if there is likely to be a difference in the way alternative treatments affect different gender and racial or ethnic subgroups. If the data "strongly indicate" a significant difference of clinical or public health importance, the "design of the study must specifically accommodate this." If the data "strongly indicate" no such difference, then gender and race or ethnicity need not be considered (although inclusion of all subgroups "is still strongly encouraged.") If there is no strong indication of any difference or similarity by subgroup, the research must include all relevant subgroups, although the research need not "provide high statistical power for each subgroup."

Suddenly in 1994 the almost universal practice of disqualifying all women of child bearing age from participating as research subjects virtually disappeared, and researchers were required to think seriously about how they could recruit a diverse research population. There has also been progress in including a more racially and ethnically diverse group of subjects in research, despite some uncertainty about what is considered a cognizable "minority group." The guideline defines such a group as "a readily identifiable subset of the U.S. population which is distinguished by either racial, ethnic and/or cultural heritage."

The guideline also instructs local institutions, IRBs, the NIH and its various agencies, and the Secretary, to open up research to women and minority subjects. For a good account of the issue that gave rise to this guideline, see Vanessa Merton, Ethical Obstacles to the Participation of Women in Biomedical Research, in Susan Wolf, ed., Feminism and Bioethics: Beyond Reproduction 216 (1996).

Do you think that this issue is properly handled by guidelines issued under the authority of a particular statute? Why do you think that they were issued as guidelines rather than as new or amended regulations?

13. Who ought to profit when medical researchers take unique human tissue from a subject and develop a commercial product from it? In Moore v. Regents of the University of California, 51 Cal.3d 120, 271 Cal.Rptr. 146, 793 P.2d 479 (1990) [reprinted in chapter 5, above] the plaintiff was a cancer patient at the U.C.L.A. Medical Center. Upon the physicians' recommendation that his spleen be removed to save his life, Moore consented to the surgery. For the next seven years he regularly returned to the U.C.L.A. Medical Center from his home in Seattle when asked to do so by his physicians. He was told that his treatment required his return to U.C.L.A. and that the procedures, which routinely included taking samples of blood, blood serum, skin, bone marrow aspirate and sperm, could only be performed there. Moore alleged that the defendants concealed from him the fact that they were engaged in several activities by which they would "benefit financially and competitively * * * by virtue of [their] ongoing physician-patient relationship * * *" 793 P.2d at 481. In fact, physicians at U.C.L.A. developed (and patented) a commercially valuable cell line from Moore's tissue. The California Supreme Court found that Moore stated a cause of action for breach of fiduciary duty and lack of informed consent, but that the physicians' use of his body substances did not provide the patient with a cause of action for conversion.

Moore's U.C.L.A. doctors are not the only prestigious medical researchers to be caught inappropriately profiting from their medical research. Drs. Condie and Najarian of the University of Minnesota were accused of making substantial profit from the sales of Antilymphocyte Globulin (ALG), which they developed as an antirejection drug extremely useful in organ transplant cases. Dr. Condie pled guilty in federal court to charges that grew out of his failure to seek proper licensing of ALG from the Food and Drug Administration, and to fraud charges that arose out of his failure to report adverse reactions to the drug in research subjects, as required by the regulation. The court upheld the requirements of the federal regulations against claims that they were unconstitutionally vague. U.S. v. Najarian, 915 F.Supp. 1460 (D.Minn.1996). Ultimately Dr. Condie, was sentenced to a $50,000 fine, various forms of restitution, and 200 hours of community service. See D. Peterson, Judge Rules Out Time in Prison for Key Witness in Najarian Trial, Star Tribune, May 19, 1996, at 1B. Dr. Najarian was acquitted at trial, but the University of Minnesota refused to reinstate him to its surgery faculty (of which he had been chair), even when pressed to do so by the Governor, because it found him unfit for such a position. See G. Slovut and M. Lerner, Carlson wants Najarian Reinstated, "U" Refuses, Star Tribune, July 11, 1996, at 1A.

Note that the Declaration of Helsinki requires researchers to divulge the sources of their funding and possible conflicts of interest to both subjects (as part of the informed consent process) and to the public (when the research is published), while there is no such requirement in the federal regulations. Is the requirement of the Declaration of Helsinki appropriate, or is it an invasion of the researcher's privacy and the research sponsor's proprietary rights? Should the federal regulations be amended to incorporate this requirement? Some have also argued that the current federal regulations should be amended to prohibit doctors from getting fees for referring their patients to research projects, and that investigators should not be able to participate in research in which they have a financial interest. Do you agree?

14.   The federal regulations do not directly address the question that arises when an investigator believes that one arm of a therapeutic investigation is really superior to the other. Can that investigator allow his patients to be randomized to one arm or another? One thoughtful commentator suggests that such randomization is ethical when there is "present or imminent controversy in the clinical community over the preferred treatment," whatever the individual investigator may believe. Benjamin Freedman, Equipoise and the Ethics of Clinical Research, 317 N.Eng.J.Med. 141 (1987). See also K. McPherson, The Best and the Enemy of the Good: Randomized Controlled Trials, Uncertainty, and Assessing the Role of Patient Choice in Medical Decision Making, 48 J. Epidemiology & Community Health (1994) and A. Feinstein, Clinical Judgment Revisited: The Distinction of Quantitative Models, 120 Annals Internal Med. 799 (1994) (both comparing randomized clinical trials with other ways of judging the value of treatment modalities).

II. INSTITUTIONAL ETHICS COMMITTEES

While interdisciplinary medical decisionmaking is particularly well established in the area of research involving human subjects, other substantive issues could also benefit from interdisciplinary committee discussion. Only a couple of decades ago there were a mere handful of institutional ethics committees (IECs) in this country; now there are probably over 10,000— virtually all hospitals have them, as do most nursing homes, home health organizations, and managed care organizations, where they have been slower to catch on but where patients and staff frequently face difficult ethical decisions. Unlike IRBs, which have a structure and role defined by federal regulation and operate similarly throughout the country, the function and process of an IEC at one institution may bear virtually no relationship to the function and process of an IEC at another.

There are three general functions that an IEC can serve. First, the committee may educate itself, the institution's administration, and the staff about medical-ethical issues. For example, the staff's fear of legal intervention when life support systems are removed from a terminally ill (or even brain-dead) patient can be alleviated by institutional education conducted by a thoughtful IEC. Second, an IEC may participate in policy development within an institution. For example, an IEC may draft a "Do Not Resuscitate" policy, a futility policy, a hospital-wide policy on non-traditional healers, or a policy on providing uncompensated care. Third, an IEC may be involved in the resolution of particular cases. A physician and family who are uncertain about whether it would be appropriate to discontinue therapy on a patient might consult an IEC, which could consider the issue, provide information to the physician and family, confirm the physician's and the family's previous decision, or simply decide the case itself.

In fact, ethics committees have found that they are best able to serve the educational functions and that these educational functions generally lead to policy development within the institution. It is only a committee with a good reputation for education and policy development within the institution that is likely to be consulted on individual cases. IECs generally have found that they are more likely to be accepted within the institution if they are an advisory group, not a formal and binding court of appeal on pending substantive bioethics questions. The compositions of IECs vary, as do their roles.

COUNCIL ON ETHICAL AND JUDICIAL AFFAIRS OF THE AMERICAN MEDICAL ASSOCIATION,

CURRENT OPINION 9.11: ETHICS COMMITTEES IN HEALTH CARE INSTITUTIONS

(1994).

The following guidelines have been developed to aid in the establishment and functioning of ethics committees in hospitals and other health care institutions that may chose to form such committees.

(1) Ethics committees in health care institutions should be educational and advisory in purpose. Generally, the function of the ethics committee should be to consider and assist in resolving unusual, complicated ethical problems involving issues that affect the care and treatment of patients within the health care institution. Recommendations of the ethics committee should impose no obligation for acceptance on the part of the institution, its governing board, medical staff, attending physician, or other persons. However, it should be expected that the recommendations of a dedicated ethics committee will receive serious consideration by decisionmakers.

(2) The size of the committee should be consistent with the needs of the institution but not so large as to be unwieldy. Committee members should be selected on the basis of their concern for the welfare of the sick and infirm, their interest in ethical matters, and their reputation in the community and among their peers for integrity and mature judgment. Experience as a

member of hospital or medical society committees concerned with ethical conduct or quality assurance should be considered in selecting ethics committee members. Committee members should not have other responsibilities that are likely to prove incompatible with their duties as members of the ethics committee. Preferably, a majority of the committee should consist of physicians, nurses, and other health care providers. In hospitals, medical staff bylaws should delineate the functions of the committee, general qualifications for membership, and manner of selection of members, in accordance with these guidelines.

(3) The functions of the ethics committee should be confined exclusively to ethical matters. The Code of Medical Ethics of the American Medical Association is recommended for the guidance of ethics committees in making their own recommendations. The matters to be considered by the committee should consist of ethical subjects that a majority of its members may choose to discuss on its own initiative, matters referred to it by the executive committee of the organized medical staff or by the governing board of the institution, or appropriate requests from patients, families, or health care providers.

(4) In the denominational health care institutions or those operated by religious orders, the recommendations of the ethics committee may be anticipated to be consistent with published religious tenets and principles. Where particular religious beliefs are to be taken into consideration in the committee's recommendations, this fact should be publicized to physicians, patients, and other concerned with the committee's recommendations.

(5) In its deliberations and communication of recommendations, the procedures followed by the ethics committee should comply with institutional and ethical policies for preserving the confidentiality of information regarding patients.

(6) Committee members should be prepared to meet on short notice and to render their recommendations in a timely and prompt fashion in accordance with the demands of the situation and the issues involved.

Notes and Questions

1. It is difficult to characterize the thousands of institutional ethics committees now active in the United States (and, increasingly, in other countries as well); they vary substantially from institution to institution, and they rarely fit any stereotype. The membership varies, with most committees having more than ten but fewer than fifty members. They occasionally meet together (sometimes weekly, sometimes monthly, sometimes quarterly, sometimes only when some pressing need is demonstrated), although they are more likely to meet in subcommittees. Most ethics committees include members of the institution's medical staff, other health care workers, pastoral care workers, and community representatives. Some also include representatives of the institutional administration or the institution's legal counsel, other specifically have decided not to invite the administration or the institution's attorney.

2. Dr. Mark Siegler argues that the development of ethics committees "symbolizes the dreary, depressed, and disorganized state to which American medicine has fallen." M. Siegler, Ethics Committees: Decisions by Bureaucracy, 16 Hastings Center Rep. (3) 22 (June 1986). While Dr. Siegler finds a host of

problems arising from the movement of health care institutions to create ethics committees, his primary argument is that ethics committees inevitably limit the decisionmaking authority of physicians, and this, in turn, limits physicians' ability to provide adequate care. In essence, he argues that committees cannot "care" the way doctors do. Is he right when he asserts that the interposition of a committee inevitably weakens the doctor-patient relationship?

3. Dr. Siegler recommends the development of "small advisory groups possessing great clinical expertise in their own particular specialty" in place of ethics committees. Id. One current debate over the appropriate forum for ethical consultation is between those who believe that committees make the best consultants on issues of medical ethics, and those who believe that individual clinical consultants—individual expert medical ethicists—are likely to yield the most helpful information. See J. La Puma and S. Toulmin, Ethics Consultants and Ethics Committees, 249 Arch.Internal Med. 1109 (1989). Those who support individual consultants argue that ethics, like nephrology or oncology, requires analysis by those who are truly expert in the area, not some pick-up group of uncertain academic lineage, however diverse they may be. Judith Ross disagrees. She argues that appointing an expert to deal with ethical issues sends a message that others, including the patient and the physician, ought to defer to the ethicist who knows best. As she points out,

> I would suggest that, no matter how non-directive, how non-judgmental an ethics consultant attempts to be (assuming he/she does make such an attempt), no matter how committed to being a resource, to opening up questions, to stimulating thought rather than to providing answers, such a role in this culture says that the individual who occupies this role has expertise and authority * * * and that others don't.

J. Ross, Case Consultation: The Committee or the Clinical Consultant? 2 Hosp.Ethics Comm.Forum 289, 293 (1990). She contrasts this with an ethics committee consultation:

> When it is the ethics committee that takes on individual casework as well as education and policy recommendation, the hospital communicates, in a very direct and visible manner, its commitment to the creation of an *ethical community* in which all actions, all decisions, and all lives are a part of its moral vision because all actors, all decision makers, and all participants are the creators of its moral community.

Id. at 297–8. Do you agree with Ms. Ross that the very existence and process of the ethics committee contains a message that cannot be communicated through individual expert consultants?

4. Are there any legal risks or advantages that derive from consultation with an institutional ethics committee? Should a court consider relevant the fact that a physician consulted an ethics committee, and that his actions are consistent with its recommendations, in determining whether life support can be removed? In determining whether the physician committed malpractice? In determining whether the physician committed a crime? If a physician decides to ignore the recommendation of the ethics committee, should that be relevant in any of the same ways? Finally, if the physician decides not to consult an available ethics committee, might that fact be used against him?

Increasingly, judges have come to expect that litigants will seek an ethics committee consultation before they bring their disputes to court. See, e.g., Wendland v. Wendland, 78 Cal.App.4th 517, 93 Cal.Rptr.2d 550 (Cal. App. 2000), rev. granted 97 Cal.Rptr.2d 511, 2 P.3d 1065 (Cal. 2000), reprinted above in chapter 19. Some courts have recognized that consulting with an ethics committee may even relieve patients, physicians and health care institutions from the obligation of seeking judicial approval for their actions. See, e.g., In re Guardianship of Browning, 543 So.2d 258, 269 n. 16 (Fla.App.2d Dist.1989); In re Conservatorship of Torres, 357 N.W.2d 332 (Minn.1984). Severns v. Wilmington Medical Center, 421 A.2d 1334 (Del.1980).

5.   As ethics committees become more widespread and more formally established, some commentators have suggested that they owe patients in their institution (and, perhaps, those who work there, also) due process. The difficult question, however, is what process is due. One state, Maryland, which requires all institutions to establish ethics committees, provides by statute a minimum process that ethics committees must accord those who come before them. See Md. Health Gen. Code Am. §§ 19–371 to 374.

> The most detailed process provisions in the [Maryland] statute concern the committee's process when it is advising on treatment options for patients with life-threatening conditions. In such cases the committee is obligated to notify the patient of her right to trigger the committee process as "petitioner", to meet with the committee, and "[t]o receive an explanation of the * * * committee's advice." In addition, there are others who must be notified that they hold the same rights: the patient's immediate family, her guardians, and anyone with power of attorney to make medical decisions for her. * * * Finally, the statute also suggests that the committee must render its advice in writing, by stating that the "advice * * * shall become part of the patient's medical record."
>
> A separate section covers process generally, presumably when the question is not treatment options for a patient with a life-threatening condition. Here the procedural protections are more limited. There is no mandated notice to the patient and the others. Nor is there a right to receive an explanation of the committee's advice. * * * This section does provide one safeguard with greater bite: the person triggering the committee process, who may be the patient, is entitled to "be accompanied by any persons the petitioner desires." Presumably this means the patient, if she is the petitioner, could bring her lawyer and anyone else.

* * *

> What protections are missing from this statute? One protection that is a fundamental element of anything resembling due process is notice to the patient and her representatives that the committee intends to consider her case. Strikingly, the wisdom of according even this very basic protection is debated in the literature. Yet arguments against notice are untenable. Without notice, patients and their representatives have no way of challenging, correcting, participating in, or simply monitoring ethics committee consideration of the patient's case. The ethics committee can then simply shut the patient out of its process altogether. However, this would violate the committee's legal, ethical, and transformative obligations * * *. Omitting the fundamental requirement of notice is especially indefensible when one considers the great influence ethics committees often want and wield over treatment decisions, up to and including actual decisionmaking power.
>
> It is important to recognize that notice, however, must mean more than simply notice to the patient that the committee intends to take up her case. It

must also mean that the patient is notified of the procedures the committee will follow, and the procedural options she can exercise. Without that, the patient will be at the committee's mercy, unable to anticipate what will happen, to participate actively, and to mount challenges. Finally, before a case ever gets to this point, patients or their representatives should be routinely notified of the ethics committee's existence and functions. Absent such notice, patients may not even realize that such a forum exists.

* * *

Susan Wolf, Ethics Committees and Due Process: Nesting Rights in a Community of Caring, 50 Md. L.Rev. 798, 844–849 (1991). As Professor Wolf concludes,

Ethics committees have come of age. Many of these committees have been striving for recognition and influence within their health care institutions, and they have succeeded. Many proponents of ethics committees have worked hard to gain influence for these committees even beyond the institution, in courts of law. They too have succeeded. The result of all of this success is that ethics committees wield real power over the fate of real patients.

Yet committees have thus far avoided taking responsibility for this power. Committees simultaneously seek power but offer assurances that they are merely advisory. They may exert a decisive influence over patients' legal and moral rights, yet routinely offer no protection for those rights. They claim to benefit patients while serving health care professionals.

* * *

Ethics committees were born of the movement for patients' rights. But they have grown up in the clinic. Those who have always held sway in the clinic, health care professionals and pre-eminently physicians, have controlled ethics committees too. Their ambivalence about patients' rights has fundamentally shaped these committees.

Id. at 857–858. For a response to Professor Wolf, see John Fletcher, The Bioethics Movement and Hospital Ethics Committees, 50 Md.L.Rev. 859 (1991).

If you were legal counsel to an institutional ethics committee that was engaged in drafting a written policy describing its procedure, how would you advise the committee? What procedure is required by law? What procedure ought to be provided, even if it is not required by law?

6. As is true with IRBs, the question of access to IEC deliberations, documents, and related information has arisen over the past few years, primarily in the context of malpractice cases, but also in medical licensing, defamation, civil rights, and other cases. Should patients, other physicians, plaintiffs' lawyers, courts, state medical licensing boards and others have access to IEC proceedings and records? Should those proceedings and records be confidential? If so, what is the legal basis of that confidentiality? See Andrew L. Merritt, The Tort Liability of Hospital Ethics Committees, 60 S.Cal.L.Rev. 1239 (1987). A few states, including Maryland, explicitly provide by statute for the protection of the confidentiality of the ethics committee proceedings. Should other states do the same?

7. Do IECs have an ethical or legal obligation to report wrongdoing or potential danger that they discover in the course of their activities? What should an IEC (or a member of an IEC) do upon discovering that a particularly inept physician is practicing at the hospital? Is there a duty to warn the hospital or the patients? Is there a duty to report discovery of inadequate care to the state

licensing board? What should an IEC (or a member of an IEC) do upon discovering some evidence of child abuse or neglect?

8. Might members of IECs be personally liable for their conduct on such committees? If a committee unanimously reaches a conclusion supporting the propriety of an act which a court later finds to be wrong, might IEC members be personally liable in negligence, under civil rights laws, or on some other theory? In other words, do IECs or IEC members owe a duty enforceable in tort law to the patients whose cases come before them? Even if they do, might the IEC or its members partake of the statutory immunity provided to medical peer review committees?

Professor Merritt suggests that committees could be liable for aiding and abetting tortious conduct. See Merritt, supra, Note 6 at 1274–1281. He argues that "ethics committees may best avoid any liability to patients if they establish a role as the physician's 'risk management' counselor and disclaim any interest in benefitting the patient," although he recognizes that such a role would be "a sad retreat from the idealism" that gave rise to the ethics committee movement. Id. at 1297. It is very rare for an ethics committee to be named as a defendant in an action for damages. It is not unheard of, though; after Elizabeth Bouvia had her right to refuse a nasogastric tube confirmed by a judicial order, she commenced an action against all of the members of the ethics committee that had gone along with the decision to place the tube against her wishes. The California Court of Appeal decision authorizing the removal of the nasogastric tube is reprinted in Chapter 19, above. The civil action is described in Merritt, supra at 1250–1251. For a discussion of a more recent case in which an individual philosopher-bioethicist was named as a defendant as a result of his ethical advice, see D. Nelson and R. Weiss, Penn Researchers Sued in Gene Therapy Death; Teen's Parents Also Name Ethicist as Defendant, Washington Post, Sept. 19, 2000, at A–3.

A few states have promulgated legislation that explicitly protects IECs and their members from liability, at least under some circumstances. As a general matter, these statutes provide that a committee is not liable for giving advice unless it acts maliciously or fails to make reasonable efforts to learn the facts necessary to issue a recommendation. See, e.g., Mass. Ann. Laws Ch. 112, sec. 5G, and Mont. Code Ann. sec. 37–2–201. See also Haw. Rev. Stat. sec. 663–1.7 and Md. Health–Gen. Code Ann. sec. 19–372.

Is there any way that the institution itself can act to limit liability of IEC members or provide them with indemnity? Will IECs operate better with or without the possibility of legal liability? Should IECs take on a risk management role? How should IECs treat legal risks in considering actions in particular cases?

9. As issues of cost and access become more important, should IECs play some role in determining what a hospital's policy on distribution of resources ought to be? Should an IEC always be supportive of the policies ultimately adopted by its institution, or should it be a critic (internally or externally) willing to be an advocate on ethical issues that have not been formally presented to it by the hospital administration or individual hospital employees? Should the IEC comment on the ethical propriety of managed care contracts the institution is offering to physicians? Should it comment on the ethical consequences of proposed mergers and acquisitions?

10. The Joint Committee on the Accreditation of Healthcare Organizations has a standard requiring institutions to have an appropriate method for considering ethical questions and resolving ethical disputes–a standard normally met by

the existence of an ethics committee. Should health care institutions also be required by law to have ethics committees? See Md. Health–Gen. Code Ann. §§ 19–370 to 374 for an example of such a statutory requirement

III. NATIONAL AND STATE COMMISSIONS

The need for interdisciplinary decisionmaking applies to broad issues of social policy as well as to individual cases. To the extent that society wishes to develop a national policy on the definition of death, genetic engineering, access to health care, and similar issues, a full national debate on those issues is necessary. Of course, one authority ultimately responsible for the development of social policy—the legislative branch—is a sort of multidisciplinary committee. It may be wise, however, to have those issues fully argued and debated in some other forum before the power of the Congress and the state legislatures institutionalizes any apparent consensus.

The federal government has advanced debates concerning a wide range of bioethics questions by establishing national commissions, interdisciplinary in nature, to marshal the facts and arguments that relate to each of the issues and, often, to make recommendations. The first truly significant national commission was the National Commission for the Protection of Human Subjects of Biomedical and Behavioral Research, which was statutorily created in 1974, completed its work in 1978, and is responsible for the greatest part of the current federal regulations governing research involving human subjects. At least as important is the President's Commission for the Study of Ethical Problems in Medicine and Biomedical and Behavioral Research, which was created by statute in 1978, completed its work in 1983, and has had a very substantial effect on legislative and judicial decisions in this country. Both the National Commission and the President's Commission were so important because, like most IECs, neither had any actual power to implement their recommendations. Both viewed their roles as primarily educational, and each became a vehicle for developing a national consensus on policies that would inevitably be incorporated into law. The National Commission and the President's Commission remain the most constantly cited sources on almost every issue they studied.

The President's Commission has not been free of criticism, however, even from those who influenced it (and were influenced by it). The conclusions of the President's Commission were based primarily on the principle of autonomy. That principle is an essentially procedural one; it tells us who has the authority to make a decision rather than what decision ought to be made. Daniel Callahan, a thoughtful philosopher and careful critic of commonly accepted presumptions, suggests that it is time to turn to the substance of these issues. As he points out:

> The debate over the right of the terminally ill to withdraw from treatment provides as good an example as any of our present predicament. On the surface, the most important part of the debate turns on whether the dying have a legal and moral right to have their treatment discontinued. The general answer to both questions is yes; that is, both morality and the law grant them such a right. * * *

But all the while, the most important moral questions are neglected: under what circumstances, and by what principles, may I decide that I no longer must continue struggling against death? How should I make use of my freedom to declare that I no longer want to be treated? What do I owe to myself? What do I owe to my family or those who love me? Who am I that I may declare my life no longer worth living?

* * *

We have gone through an important era that has established many new rights and privileges in the face of the power and potency of biomedicine. We have been told that we are autonomous and can make free choices— that autonomy is a key ingredient in the thread of consensus that runs through the reports of the President's Commission. In the next stage, we must begin work on the content of that freedom. For it is here that consensus will most desperately be needed; otherwise, the newly gained freedoms will turn out to be either empty or dangerous.

D. Callahan, Morality and Contemporary Culture: The President's Commission and Beyond, 6 Cardozo L.Rev. 347 (1984).

In fact, one attempt to move a government sponsored national commission into the realm of substantive bioethics proved an utter failure. The Health Research Extension Act of 1985 created the Biomedical Ethics Board (composed of six senators and six members of the House of Representatives) and the Biomedical Ethics Advisory Committee, to be appointed by the Biomedical Ethics Board. The Advisory Committee would have been a continuing agency to carry out substantive analyses of issues within the scope of the Board, which was instructed to "study and report to the Congress on a continuing basis on the ethical issues arising from the delivery of health care and biomedical and behavioral research, including the protection of human subjects of such research and developments in genetic engineering (including activities in recombinant DNA technology) which have implications for human genetic engineering." Ultimately both the Board and the Committee were paralyzed by the issue of abortion. Partisans on both sides of that issue viewed the Committee as a potentially subversive political agency. Although Senator Gore was named vice chairman of the Board, a chair was never appointed. In fact, the membership of the Advisory Committee was not fully established until the middle of 1988, and funding was cut off by the fall of 1989. As the acting staff director of the Advisory Committee said, "Politicians have been extremely reluctant to take on not only the abortion issue, but anything that may be seen as related. And there is no area of ethical analysis that isn't somehow seen as part of this issue by activists." Philip J. Hilts, Abortion Debate Clouds Research on Fetal Tissue, The New York Times, October 16, 1989, at page 19.

More recently, the federal government has done better in creating an environment in which such a commission can be established. In July of 1996 President Clinton appointed the first members of his newly created National Bioethics Advisory Commission, which met for the first time a few months later. Most members appointed have academic (not political) connections, and most have expertise in philosophy, theology, law, medicine, biology, or the social and behavioral sciences, although there are some "community members" as well. In order to avoid being drawn into the thicket surrounding the abortion issue, the Commission was asked to address two specific areas in its first meetings: (1) research involving human subjects, and (2) management of genetic information. Subsequently the President also asked the Commission to address ethical concerns relating to cloning. The Commission will set its own agenda, which it will determine with attention to four factors: (1) the importance and immediacy of the public health or public policy implications of the issue, (2) the goals of Federal investment in science, (3) the ability of the Commission to contribute to debate on the issue (as compared with the ability of other institutions), and (4) the interest in the issue in government. The Commission's reports have been well received, and it may live up to the high standard set by the President's Commission. What issues do you think ought to be addressed by this Commission? How should it proceed? Should it hold public meetings? Should it commission experts to do studies? What kinds of reports should it issue?

Perhaps more significant work towards consensus on bioethical issues could be done at the state and local level. Indeed, states also have established interdisciplinary commissions to assist in the development of bioethics policy. New York's Task Force on Law and Life was established in late 1984, about a year after the termination of the President's Commission's work. This task force has released several comprehensive reports and it has had a substantial effect, both inside and outside of New York. See, e.g., the use of the New York Task Force report in *In re Martin*, 450 Mich. 204, 538 N.W.2d 399 (1995). Most other states have established some variety of commissions, committees, panels and task forces to prepare reports and recommendations on subjects that range from malpractice reform to surrogacy to access to health care. In addition, many local communities have set up task forces to consider bioethics issues, including the availability of health care within those communities. Is there any reason to believe that these interdisciplinary committees, whether called presidential commissions, state task forces, or community blue ribbon committees, operate best at any particular level of government? Would you expect a South Dakota task force on surrogacy to come to a different conclusion than a New York City committee?

Several states have instituted "Health Decisions" programs that are modeled on one that began in Oregon in the early 1980s. These programs aim to educate the community about questions relating to health care by scheduling small discussion groups and then convening town hall meetings in an attempt to develop consensus recommendations that will influence lawmakers. The educational value of this program is immense; the political value has also proven itself in Oregon, where it has seen its recommendations taken seriously by the legislature.

Index

0–314–25192–8

90000

9 780314 251923